WHITAKER'S CONCISE
2012

CW00631792

AN

Almanack

For the Year of Our Lord

2012

ESTABLISHED 1868

BY

JOSEPH WHITAKER, FSA

CONTAINING AN ACCOUNT OF THE

ASTRONOMICAL AND OTHER PHENOMENA

AND

A vast Amount of INFORMATION respecting the
GOVERNMENT, FINANCES, POPULATION,
COMMERCE, and GENERAL STATISTICS of
the various Nations of the WORLD
with an INDEX containing
nearly 7,500
References

LONDON

OFFICE: 50 BEDFORD SQUARE
LONDON WC1B 3DP

The traditional design of the title page for Whitaker's Almanack which has appeared in each edition since 1868

WHITAKER'S CONCISE ALMANACK
2012

B L O O M S B U R Y

LONDON • BERLIN • NEW YORK • SYDNEY

Bloomsbury Publishing Plc.
50 Bedford Square, London WC1B 3DP

Whitaker's Almanack published annually since 1868
144th edition © 2011 Bloomsbury Publishing Plc.

www.bloomsbury.com

STANDARD EDITION
Cloth covers
978–1–4081–3012–4

CONCISE EDITION
Paperback
978–1–4081–4230–1

JACKET PHOTOGRAPHS
Main image: Riot police stand in line as fire rages
through a building in Tottenham, north London on
7 August 2011. © Lewis Whyld/PA Wire/Press
Association Images
Spine: Thousands of Egyptian demonstrators take part
in anti-government protests in February 2011. ©
KeystoneUSA-ZUMA/Rex Features
Top, from left to right:
1. A reader enjoys the final edition of the *News of the
World* newspaper, published on 10 July 2011. © Yui
Mok/PA Wire/Press Association Images
2. The Duke and Duchess of Cambridge arrive for a
reception with the British Consul General in Hancock
Park, Los Angeles, during the Royal Tour of the USA in
July 2011. © Stewart Cook/Rex Features
3. USA president Barack Obama gives a press
conference on the breakdown of the Debt Limit Talks in
Washington DC on 22 July 2011 © Rex Features
4. The waxwork figure of British singer Amy
Winehouse is unveiled at Madame Tussauds in central
London. © Joel Ryan/AP/Press Association Images

Typeset in the UK by RefineCatch Ltd, Bungay, Suffolk
NR35 1EF

Printed and bound in Italy by L.E.G.O. S.p.A.

FSC
www.fsc.org
MIX
Paper from
responsible sources
FSC® C023419

Whitaker's is a registered trade mark of J. Whitaker and
Sons Ltd, Registered Trade Mark Nos. (UK) 1322125/
09; 13422126/16 and 1322127/41; (EU)
19960401/09, 16, 41, licensed for use by A & C Black
(Publishers) Ltd, a subsidiary of Bloomsbury Publishing
Plc.

Whitaker's Almanack was compiled with the assistance
of: Amnesty International; Euromonitor International;
Keesing's Worldwide; Oxford Cartographers; Press
Association; Transparency International: the global
coalition against corruption; UK Hydrographic Office;
the UNESCO Institute for Statistics (UIS); WM/
Reuters; and the World Gazetteer/Stefan Helders
(W www.world-gazetteer.com).

The publishers make no representation, express or
implied, with regard to the accuracy of the information
contained in this book and cannot accept legal
responsibility for any errors or omissions that take
place.

A CIP catalogue record for this book is available from
the British Library.

EDITORIAL STAFF
Executive Editor: Ruth Northey
Project Editors: Nathan Joyce (UK); Matt Munday, Joel
Simons (International)
Editorial Assistant: Oli Lurie
Head of Yearbooks: Katy McAdam

Thanks to Omer Ali, Clare Bryant, Nicola Cutts, Rob
Hardy, Matt Rose

CONTRIBUTORS (where not listed)
Gordon Taylor (Astronomy); Anthea Lipsett, Caroline
Macready (Education); Karen Harries-Rees
(Environment); V. P. Kanitkar (Hindu Calendar); Clive
Longhurst (Insurance); Felix Coxwell (Intellectual
Property); Duncan Murray, Chris Priestley (Legal
Notes); Jill Papworth (Taxation)

CONTENTS

6

PREFACE

Turbulent is the word that springs to mind when summing up the past year's events. In November 2010, against a backdrop of civil service job cuts and pay freezes, the UK government chose to announce proposals to raise the cap on university tuition fees to £9,000 a year. Student demonstrations and university sit-ins followed across the country, with the protests in London turning violent as an angry mob burst into the Conservative Party headquarters, vandalising the premises and hurling missiles from the roof of the building. Then in August 2011 came four days of unprecedented civil disorder – violent riots and looting across the capital and in other major cities around the country – forcing the prime minister to break off his holiday and recall parliament.

In the turmoil of such headline events it is easy to forget the detail. The media became part of the 'news' itself when allegations of widespread 'phone-hacking' at the *News of the World* led to arrests, resignations and the closure of the country's best-selling Sunday newspaper. The 2012 edition of *Whitaker's Almanack* has all the facts, distilled into easily digestible chunks: a chapter on the UK education system; the infrastructure of the UK in minute detail, including extensive coverage of the regional elections which took place in May; and information on the media.

It was also a busy year for the royal family – first the wedding of Prince William to Kate Middleton in April and then, in July, that of Zara Phillips, daughter of the Princess Royal, to England rugby player Mike Tindall. As always the royal family chapter has been fully updated to include, not just the latest newcomers, but also information on the royal finances, military ranks and titles currently held by members of the royal family, plus an up-to-date list of the order of succession.

Whatever your interests, you can be sure that *Whitaker's Almanack 2012* gives the complete picture.

It has also been a year of changes for *Whitaker's Almanack,* and we are now settled comfortably into our new offices in Bedford Square, with our parent company Bloomsbury Publishing. As usual I would like to thank the dedicated team of in-house editors and expert contributors for their efforts in compiling this year's edition. I hope you enjoy the new edition and please feel free to contact us with feedback and suggestions.

Ruth Northey
Executive Editor

THE YEAR 2012

CHRONOLOGICAL CYCLES AND ERAS

Dominical Letter	AG
Epact	6
Golden Number (Lunar Cycle)	XVIII
Julian Period	6725
Roman Indiction	5
Solar Cycle	5

	Beginning
Muslim year AH 1433*	26 Nov 2011
Japanese year Heisei 24	1 Jan
Roman year 2765 AUC	14 Jan
Regnal year 61	6 Feb
Chinese year of the Dragon	23 Jan
Sikh new year	14 Mar
Hindu new year (Chaitra)	23 Mar
Indian (Saka) year 1934	21 Mar
Jewish year AM 5773*	17 Sep

* Year begins at sunset on the previous day

RELIGIOUS CALENDARS

CHRISTIAN

Epiphany	6 Jan
Presentation of Christ in the Temple	2 Feb
Ash Wednesday	22 Feb
The Annunciation	25 Mar
Palm Sunday	1 Apr
Maundy Thursday	5 Apr
Good Friday	6 Apr
Easter Day (western churches)	8 Apr
Easter Day (Eastern Orthodox)	15 Apr
Rogation Sunday	13 May
Ascension Day	17 May
Pentecost (Whit Sunday)	27 May
Trinity Sunday	3 Jun
Corpus Christi	7 Jun
All Saints' Day	1 Nov
Advent Sunday	2 Dec
Christmas Day	25 Dec

HINDU

Makara Sankranti	14 Jan
Vasant Panchami (Sarasvati Puja)	28 Jan
Mahashivaratri	20 Feb
Holi	8 Mar
Chaitra (Spring new year)	23 Mar
Ramanavami	1 Apr
Raksha Bandhan	2 Aug
Janmashtami	10 Aug
Ganesh Chaturthi, first day	19 Sep
Navaratri festival (Durga Puja), first day	16 Oct
Dasara	24 Oct
Diwali (New Year festival of lights), first day	13 Nov

JEWISH

Purim	8 Mar
Pesach (Passover), first day	7 Apr
Shavuoth (Feast of Weeks), first day	27 May
Rosh Hashanah (Jewish new year)	17 Sep
Yom Kippur (Day of Atonement)	26 Sep
Succoth (Feast of Tabernacles), first day	1 Oct
Hanukkah, first day	9 Dec

MUSLIM

Al-Hijra (Muslim new year)	26 Nov 2011
Ashura	5 Dec 2011
Ramadan, first day	20 Jul
Eid-ul-Fitr	19 Aug
Hajj	24 Oct
Eid-ul-Adha	26 Oct

SIKH

Birthday of Guru Gobind Singh Ji	5 Jan
Hola Mohalla Mela	9 Mar†
1 Chet (Sikh new year)	14 Mar
Baisakhi Mela	13 Apr
Birthday of Guru Nanak Dev Ji	14 Apr†
Martyrdom of Guru Arjan Dev Ji	16 Jun
Martyrdom of Guru Tegh Bahadur Ji	24 Nov

† This festival is also currently celebrated according to the lunar calendar

CIVIL CALENDAR

Countess of Wessex's birthday	20 Jan
Accession of the Queen	6 Feb
Duke of York's birthday	19 Feb
St David's Day	1 Mar
Earl of Wessex's birthday	10 Mar
Commonwealth Day	12 Mar
St Patrick's Day	17 Mar
Birthday of the Queen	21 Apr
St George's Day	23 Apr
Europe Day	9 May
Coronation Day	2 Jun
Duke of Edinburgh's birthday	10 Jun
The Queen's Official Birthday	16 Jun
Duchess of Cornwall's birthday	17 Jul
Princess Royal's birthday	15 Aug
Lord Mayor's Day	10 Nov
Remembrance Sunday	11 Nov
Prince of Wales' birthday	14 Nov
Wedding Day of the Queen	20 Nov
St Andrew's Day	30 Nov

LEGAL CALENDAR

LAW TERMS

Hilary Term	11 Jan to 4 Apr
Easter Term	17 Apr to 1 Jun
Trinity Term	12 Jun to 31 Jul
Michaelmas Term	1 Oct to 21 Dec

QUARTER DAYS	TERM DAYS
England, Wales and Northern Ireland	*Scotland*
Lady – 25 Mar	Candlemas – 28 Feb
Midsummer – 24 Jun	Whitsunday – 28 May
Michaelmas – 29 Sep	Lammas – 28 Aug
Christmas – 25 Dec	Martinmas – 28 Nov

2012

JANUARY

Sunday	1	8	15	22	29
Monday	2	9	16	23	30
Tuesday	3	10	17	24	31
Wednesday	4	11	18	25	
Thursday	5	12	19	26	
Friday	6	13	20	27	
Saturday	7	14	21	28	

FEBRUARY

Sunday		5	12	19	26
Monday		6	13	20	27
Tuesday		7	14	21	28
Wednesday	1	8	15	22	29
Thursday	2	9	16	23	
Friday	3	10	17	24	
Saturday	4	11	18	25	

MARCH

Sunday		4	11	18	25
Monday		5	12	19	26
Tuesday		6	13	20	27
Wednesday		7	14	21	28
Thursday	1	8	15	22	29
Friday	2	9	16	23	30
Saturday	3	10	17	24	31

APRIL

Sunday	1	8	15	22	29
Monday	2	9	16	23	30
Tuesday	3	10	17	24	
Wednesday	4	11	18	25	
Thursday	5	12	19	26	
Friday	6	13	20	27	
Saturday	7	14	21	28	

MAY

Sunday		6	13	20	27
Monday		7	14	21	28
Tuesday	1	8	15	22	29
Wednesday	2	9	16	23	30
Thursday	3	10	17	24	31
Friday	4	11	18	25	
Saturday	5	12	19	26	

JUNE

Sunday		3	10	17	24
Monday		4	11	18	25
Tuesday		5	12	19	26
Wednesday		6	13	20	27
Thursday		7	14	21	28
Friday	1	8	15	22	29
Saturday	2	9	16	23	30

JULY

Sunday	1	8	15	22	29
Monday	2	9	16	23	30
Tuesday	3	10	17	24	31
Wednesday	4	11	18	25	
Thursday	5	12	19	26	
Friday	6	13	20	27	
Saturday	7	14	21	28	

AUGUST

Sunday		5	12	19	26
Monday		6	13	20	27
Tuesday		7	14	21	28
Wednesday	1	8	15	22	29
Thursday	2	9	16	23	30
Friday	3	10	17	24	31
Saturday	4	11	18	25	

SEPTEMBER

Sunday		2	9	16	23	30
Monday		3	10	17	24	
Tuesday		4	11	18	25	
Wednesday		5	12	19	26	
Thursday		6	13	20	27	
Friday		7	14	21	28	
Saturday	1	8	15	22	29	

OCTOBER

Sunday		7	14	21	28
Monday	1	8	15	22	29
Tuesday	2	9	16	23	30
Wednesday	3	10	17	24	31
Thursday	4	11	18	25	
Friday	5	12	19	26	
Saturday	6	13	20	27	

NOVEMBER

Sunday		4	11	18	25
Monday		5	12	19	26
Tuesday		6	13	20	27
Wednesday		7	14	21	28
Thursday	1	8	15	22	29
Friday	2	9	16	23	30
Saturday	3	10	17	24	

DECEMBER

Sunday		2	9	16	23	30
Monday		3	10	17	24	31
Tuesday		4	11	18	25	
Wednesday		5	12	19	26	
Thursday		6	13	20	27	
Friday		7	14	21	28	
Saturday	1	8	15	22	29	

PUBLIC HOLIDAYS	England and Wales	Scotland	Northern Ireland
New Year	2 January†	2, 3† January	2 January†
St Patrick's Day	—	—	17 March
*Good Friday	6 April	6 April	6 April
Easter Monday	9 April	—	9 April
Early May	7 May†	7 May	7 May†
Spring	4 June	28 May†	4 June
Queen's Diamond Jubilee	5 June	5 June	5 June
Battle of the Boyne	—	—	12 July‡
Summer	27 August	6 August	27 August
St Andrew's Day	—	30 Nov§	—
*Christmas	25, 26 December	25†, 26 December	25, 26 December

* In England, Wales and Northern Ireland, Christmas Day and Good Friday are common law holidays

† Subject to royal proclamation

‡ Subject to proclamation by the Secretary of State for Northern Ireland

§ The St Andrew's Day Holiday (Scotland) Bill was approved by parliament on 29 November 2006; it does not oblige employers to change their existing pattern of holidays but provides the legal framework in which the St Andrew's Day bank holiday could be substituted for an existing local holiday from another date in the year

Note: In the Channel Islands, Liberation Day is a bank and public holiday

2013

JANUARY					
Sunday		6	13	20	27
Monday		7	14	21	28
Tuesday	1	8	15	22	29
Wednesday	2	9	16	23	30
Thursday	3	10	17	24	31
Friday	4	11	18	25	
Saturday	5	12	19	26	

FEBRUARY					
Sunday		3	10	17	24
Monday		4	11	18	25
Tuesday		5	12	19	26
Wednesday		6	13	20	27
Thursday		7	14	21	28
Friday	1	8	15	22	
Saturday	2	9	16	23	

MARCH						
Sunday		3	10	17	24	31
Monday		4	11	18	25	
Tuesday		5	12	19	26	
Wednesday		6	13	20	27	
Thursday		7	14	21	28	
Friday	1	8	15	22	29	
Saturday	2	9	16	23	30	

APRIL					
Sunday		7	14	21	28
Monday	1	8	15	22	29
Tuesday	2	9	16	23	30
Wednesday	3	10	17	24	
Thursday	4	11	18	25	
Friday	5	12	19	26	
Saturday	6	13	20	27	

MAY					
Sunday		5	12	19	26
Monday		6	13	20	27
Tuesday		7	14	21	28
Wednesday	1	8	15	22	29
Thursday	2	9	16	23	30
Friday	3	10	17	24	31
Saturday	4	11	18	25	

JUNE					
Sunday		2	9	16	23	30
Monday		3	10	17	24	
Tuesday		4	11	18	25	
Wednesday		5	12	19	26	
Thursday		6	13	20	27	
Friday		7	14	21	28	
Saturday	1	8	15	22	29	

JULY					
Sunday		7	14	21	28
Monday	1	8	15	22	29
Tuesday	2	9	16	23	30
Wednesday	3	10	17	24	31
Thursday	4	11	18	25	
Friday	5	12	19	26	
Saturday	6	13	20	27	

AUGUST					
Sunday		4	11	18	25
Monday		5	12	19	26
Tuesday		6	13	20	27
Wednesday		7	14	21	28
Thursday	1	8	15	22	29
Friday	2	9	16	23	30
Saturday	3	10	17	24	31

SEPTEMBER					
Sunday	1	8	15	22	29
Monday	2	9	16	23	30
Tuesday	3	10	17	24	
Wednesday	4	11	18	25	
Thursday	5	12	19	26	
Friday	6	13	20	27	
Saturday	7	14	21	28	

OCTOBER					
Sunday		6	13	20	27
Monday		7	14	21	28
Tuesday	1	8	15	22	29
Wednesday	2	9	16	23	30
Thursday	3	10	17	24	31
Friday	4	11	18	25	
Saturday	5	12	19	26	

NOVEMBER					
Sunday		3	10	17	24
Monday		4	11	18	25
Tuesday		5	12	19	26
Wednesday		6	13	20	27
Thursday		7	14	21	28
Friday	1	8	15	22	29
Saturday	2	9	16	23	30

DECEMBER					
Sunday	1	8	15	22	29
Monday	2	9	16	23	30
Tuesday	3	10	17	24	31
Wednesday	4	11	18	25	
Thursday	5	12	19	26	
Friday	6	13	20	27	
Saturday	7	14	21	28	

PUBLIC HOLIDAYS	*England and Wales*	*Scotland*	*Northern Ireland*
New Year	1 January†	1, 2† January	1 January†
St Patrick's Day	—	—	17 March
*Good Friday	29 March	29 March	29 March
Easter Monday	1 April	—	1 April
Early May	6 May†	6 May	6 May†
Spring	27 May	27 May†	27 May
Battle of the Boyne	—	—	12 July‡
Summer	26 August	5 August	26 August
St Andrew's Day	—	30 Nov§	—
*Christmas	25, 26 December	25†, 26 December	25, 26 December

* In England, Wales and Northern Ireland, Christmas Day and Good Friday are common law holidays

† Subject to royal proclamation

‡ Subject to proclamation by the Secretary of State for Northern Ireland

§ The St Andrew's Day Holiday (Scotland) Bill was approved by parliament on 29 November 2006; it does not oblige employers to change their existing pattern of holidays but provides the legal framework in which the St Andrew's Day bank holiday could be substituted for an existing local holiday from another date in the year

Note: In the Channel Islands, Liberation Day is a bank and public holiday

FORTHCOMING EVENTS

* Provisional dates
† Venue not confirmed

JANUARY 2012

6–15	London Boat Show, Excel, London Docklands
11–29	London International Mime Festival
17–19	UK Open Dance Championships, Bournemouth International Centre
18–22	London Art Fair, Business Design Centre
19–5 Feb	Celtic Connections Music Festival, Glasgow
28–29	RSPB Big Garden Birdwatch

FEBRUARY

2–5	London Motorcycle Show, Excel, London Docklands
3–19	Leicester Comedy Festival
12	British Academy Film Awards, Royal Opera House, London
11–18	Jorvik Viking Festival, Jorvik Viking Centre, York
24–26	Ceramic Art London, Royal College of Art

MARCH

1	World Book Day
2–11	Bath Literature Festival
8	International Women's Day
8–11	Crufts Dog Show, NEC, Birmingham
9–18	National Science and Engineering Week
10–13	Affordable Art Fair, Battersea Park, London
16–1 Apr	Ideal Home Show, Earls Court, London
21–27	BADA Antiques and Fine Art Fair, Duke of York's Square, London

APRIL

2–10	Oxford Literary Festival
16–18	London Book Fair, Earls Court, London
22	Earth Day

MAY

20–26 Aug	Glyndebourne Festival
22–26	RHS Chelsea Flower Show, Royal Hospital, Chelsea
31 May–10 June	Hay Festival, Hay-on-Wye, Hereford

JUNE

4–12 Aug	Royal Academy of Arts Summer Exhibition, Burlington House, London
10–26	Aldeburgh Festival of Music and the Arts, Snape, Suffolk
16	Trooping the Colour, Horse Guards Parade, London
27–7 July	New Designers Exhibition, Business Design Centre, London

JULY

3–8	RHS Hampton Court Palace Flower Show, Surrey
4–15	Cheltenham Music Festival
6–14	York Early Music Festival
7	Pride Parade, London
7–25	Buxton Festival, Derbyshire
Mid-Jul–Mid-Sep	BBC Promenade Concerts, Royal Albert Hall, London
18–22	RHS Flower Show, Tatton Park, Cheshire
*21–30	The Welsh Proms, St David's Hall, Cardiff
26–29	Cambridge Folk Festival
27–29	WOMAD Festival, Charlton Park, Wiltshire
29–7 Aug	Edinburgh Jazz and Blues Festival

AUGUST

4–11	National Eisteddfod of Wales, Wrexham
5–27	Edinburgh Military Tattoo, Edinburgh Castle
*10–2 Sep	Edinburgh International Festival
21–28	Three Choirs Festival, Worcester
*28–29	Notting Hill Carnival, London
31–4 Nov	Blackpool Illuminations, Blackpool Promenade

SEPTEMBER

1	Braemar Royal Highland Gathering, Aberdeenshire
8	International Literacy Day
6–9	Heritage Open Days, England (nationwide)
6–9	RHS Wisley Flower Show, RHS Garden, Wisley
10–13	TUC Annual Congress, Brighton
*11	Mercury Music Prize
22–26	Liberal Democrat Party Conference, Brighton
30–4 Oct	Labour Party Conference, Manchester

OCTOBER

8–11	Conservative Party Conference, Birmingham
11–14	Frieze Art Fair, Regent's Park, London
Mid-Oct	Booker Prize
Mid-Oct	London Film Festival
Mid-Oct–Jan	Turner Prize Exhibition, Tate Britain, London

NOVEMBER

Mid-Nov   Classic Motor Show, NEC,
           Birmingham
Mid-Nov   Lord Mayor's Procession and Show,
           City of London
Mid-Nov   CBI Annual Conference

SPORTS EVENTS

JANUARY 2012
13–22   Winter Youth Olympics, Innsbruck,
           Austria
15–22   Snooker: Masters, Alexandra Palace,
           London
16–29   Tennis: Australian Open, Melbourne,
           Australia
21–12 Feb Football: African Cup of Nations,
           Gabon and Equatorial Guinea

FEBRUARY
4–17 Mar   Rugby Union: Six Nations
           Championship
7–12   Squash: British National
           Championships, Manchester
12–13   Rugby League: Super League,
           Millennium Stadium, Cardiff
26   Football: League Cup Final,
           Wembley Stadium, London

MARCH
6–11   Badminton: English National
           Championships, Birmingham

APRIL
7   Rowing: Oxford and Cambridge
           Boat Race, Putney to Mortlake,
           London
14   Horse racing: Grand National,
           Aintree, Liverpool
21–7 May   Snooker: World Championship,
           Crucible Theatre, Sheffield
22   Athletics: London Marathon

MAY
3–7   Equestrian: Badminton Horse Trials,
           Badminton
Early May Horse racing: Guineas Festival,
           Newmarket
5   Football: FA Cup Final, Wembley
           Stadium, London
9–13   Royal Windsor Horse Show, Home
           Park, Windsor
19   Football: Scottish FA Cup Final,
           Hampden Park, Glasgow
19–20   Rugby Union: Heineken Cup Final,
           Twickenham, London
19   Football: UEFA Champions League
           Final, Allianz Arena, Munich
†26   Football: FA Women's Cup Final

27–11 Jun Tennis: French Open, Paris
*28–8 Jun Motorcycling: TT Races, Isle of
           Man

JUNE
2   Horse racing: The Derby, Epsom
           Downs
8–1 July   Football: UEFA European
           Championships, Poland and
           Ukraine
18–23   Golf: British Amateur Golf
           Championship, Royal Troon,
           South Ayrshire
19–23   Horse racing: Royal Ascot
25–8 Jul   Tennis: Wimbledon Championship,
           All England Lawn Tennis Club,
           London
27–1 Jul   Rowing: Henley Royal Regatta,
           Henley-on-Thames
30–22 Jul Cycling: Tour de France

JULY
7–21   Shooting: NRA Imperial Meeting,
           Bisley Camp, Surrey
15–22   Golf: Open Championship, Lytham,
           Lancashire
Late Jul   Horse racing: King George VI and
           Queen Elizabeth Diamond Stakes,
           Ascot
27–12 Aug Olympic Games, London

AUGUST
11–18   Sailing: Cowes Week, Isle of Wight
25   Rugby League: Challenge Cup Final,
           Wembley Stadium, London
29–9 Sep   Paralympic Games, London
29–12 Sep Tennis: US Open, New York

SEPTEMBER
Early Sep Equestrian: Burghley Horse Trials,
           Stamford, Lincolnshire
Early Sep Horse racing: St Leger, Doncaster
13–16   Golf: Women's British Open, Royal
           Liverpool, Hoylake
Mid-Sep   Cricket: Twenty20 World Cup,
           Sri Lanka
Late Sep– Horse racing: Cambridgeshire
Early Oct Meeting, Newmarket
Late Sep– Athletics: Great North Run,
Early Oct Newcastle

OCTOBER
Early Oct Equestrian: Horse of the Year Show,
           NEC, Birmingham
Mid-Oct   Horse racing: Champions Meeting,
           Newmarket
Early–Mid-Oct Rugby League: Super League Final,
           Old Trafford, Manchester

CENTENARIES

2012

1512
5 Mar   Gerardus Mercator, Flemish-German cartographer, born
10 Apr   King James V of Scotland, born

1612
17 Jan   Sir Thomas Fairfax, commander of the New Model Army, born

1712
28 Jun   Jean-Jacques Rousseau, French philosopher, born
12 Jul   Richard Cromwell, Lord Protector 1658–9, died
14 Oct   William Grenville, First Lord of the Treasury 1763–5, born

1812
7 Feb   Charles Dickens, novelist and essayist, born
1 Mar   Augustus Pugin, architect, born
6 Apr   Alexander Herzen, Russian political theorist and writer, born
7 May   Robert Browning, poet, born
11 May   Spencer Perceval, prime minister 1809–12, died
12 May   Edward Lear, poet and illustrator, born
19 Sep   Mayer Amschel Rothschild, German banker, died
16 Nov   John Walter, founder of *The Times,* died

1912
28 Jan   Jackson Pollock, painter, born
10 Feb   Sir Joseph Lister, surgeon, died
27 Feb   Lawrence Durrell, novelist and poet, born
14 Mar   Cliff Bastin, football player, born
27 Mar   James Callaghan, prime minister 1976–9, born
20 Apr   Bram Stoker, Irish novelist, died
28 May   Patrick White, Australian novelist, born
30 May   Wilbur Wright, American aviation pioneer, died
13 Jun   Sir Georg Solti, conductor, born
14 Jul   Woody Guthrie, American musician, born
17 Jul   Jules Henri Poincaré, French mathematician, died
13 Aug   Ben Hogan, American golfer, born
20 Aug   Gen. William Booth, founder of the Salvation Army, died
23 Aug   Gene Kelly, actor and choreographer, born

2013

1413
20 Mar   Henry IV, King of England 1399–1413, died

1513
9 Sep   James IV, King of Scotland 1488–1513, died

1813
26 Feb   Robert Livingston, American diplomat, died
19 Mar   David Livingstone, explorer, born
5 May   Soren Kierkegaard, Danish philospher, born
22 May   Richard Wagner, German composer, born

1913
4 Jan   Alfred von Schlieffen, German field marshal, died
6 Jan   Loretta Young, American actor, born
9 Jan   Richard Nixon, 37th president of USA, born
4 Feb   Rosa Parks, American civil rights activist, born
25 Feb   Gert Fröbe, German actor, born
13 Mar   William J. Casey, American director of the CIA, born
31 Mar   John Pierpont Morgan, American financier, died
25 May   Richard Dimbleby, journalist and broadcaster, born
8 Jun   Emily Davison, women's suffrage activist, died
11 Jun   Vince Lombardi, American football coach, born
14 Jul   Gerald Ford, 38th president of USA, born
23 Jul   Michael Foot, politician, born
16 Aug   Menachem Begin, Israeli prime minister, born
12 Sep   Jesse Owens, American athlete, born
29 Sep   Rudolf Diesel, inventor of the diesel engine, died
2 Nov   Burt Lancaster, American actor, born
5 Nov   Vivien Leigh, actor, born
7 Nov   Albert Camus, French novelist and essayist, born
22 Nov   Benjamin Britten, composer and conductor, born
18 Dec   Willy Brandt, German chancellor, born

THE UNITED KINGDOM

THE UK IN FIGURES

The United Kingdom comprises Great Britain (England, Wales and Scotland) and Northern Ireland. The Isle of Man and the Channel Islands are Crown dependencies with their own legislative systems and are not part of the UK.

ABBREVIATIONS

| ONS | Office for National Statistics |
| NISRA | Northern Ireland Statistics and Research Agency |

All data is for the UK unless otherwise stated.

AREA OF THE UNITED KINGDOM

	Sq. km	Sq. miles
United Kingdom	243,122	93,870
England	130,280	50,301
Wales	20,733	8,005
Scotland	77,958	30,100
Northern Ireland	14,150	5,463

Source: ONS (Crown copyright)

POPULATION

The first official census of population in England, Wales and Scotland was taken in 1801 and a census has been taken every ten years since, except in 1941 when there was no census because of Second World War. The last official census in the UK was taken on 29 April 2001 and the next is due in April 2011.

The first official census of population in Ireland was taken in 1841. However, all figures given below refer only to the area which is now Northern Ireland. Figures for Northern Ireland in 1921 and 1931 are estimates based on the censuses taken in 1926 and 1937 respectively.

Estimates of the population of England before 1801, calculated from the number of baptisms, burials and marriages, are:

1570	4,160,221	1670	5,773,646
1600	4,811,718	1700	6,045,008
1630	5,600,517	1750	6,517,035

Further details are available on the Office for National Statistics (ONS) website (W www.statistics.gov.uk).

CENSUS RESULTS *Thousands*

	United Kingdom			England and Wales			Scotland			Northern Ireland		
	Total	Male	Female	Total	Male	Female	Total	Male	Female	Total	Male	Female
1801	—	—	—	8,893	4,255	4,638	1,608	739	869	—	—	—
1811	13,368	6,368	7,000	10,165	4,874	5,291	1,806	826	980	—	—	—
1821	15,472	7,498	7,974	12,000	5,850	6,150	2,092	983	1,109	—	—	—
1831	17,835	8,647	9,188	13,897	6,771	7,126	2,364	1,114	1,250	—	—	—
1841	20,183	9,819	10,364	15,914	7,778	8,137	2,620	1,242	1,378	1,649	800	849
1851	22,259	10,855	11,404	17,928	8,781	9,146	2,889	1,376	1,513	1,443	698	745
1861	24,525	11,894	12,631	20,066	9,776	10,290	3,062	1,450	1,612	1,396	668	728
1871	27,431	13,309	14,122	22,712	11,059	11,653	3,360	1,603	1,757	1,359	647	712
1881	31,015	15,060	15,955	25,974	12,640	13,335	3,736	1,799	1,936	1,305	621	684
1891	34,264	16,593	17,671	29,003	14,060	14,942	4,026	1,943	2,083	1,236	590	646
1901	38,237	18,492	19,745	32,528	15,729	16,799	4,472	2,174	2,298	1,237	590	647
1911	42,082	20,357	21,725	36,070	17,446	18,625	4,761	2,309	2,452	1,251	603	648
1921	44,027	21,033	22,994	37,887	18,075	19,811	4,882	2,348	2,535	1,258	610	648
1931	46,038	22,060	23,978	39,952	19,133	20,819	4,843	2,326	2,517	1,243	601	642
1951	50,225	24,118	26,107	43,758	21,016	22,742	5,096	2,434	2,662	1,371	668	703
1961	52,709	25,481	27,228	46,105	22,304	23,801	5,179	2,483	2,697	1,425	694	731
1971	55,515	26,952	28,562	48,750	23,683	25,067	5,229	2,515	2,714	1,536	755	781
1981	55,848	27,104	28,742	49,155	23,873	25,281	5,131	2,466	2,664	1,533*	750	783
1991	56,467	27,344	29,123	49,890	24,182	25,707	4,999	2,392	2,607	1,578	769	809
2001	58,789	28,581	30,208	52,042	25,327	26,715	5,062	2,432	2,630	1,685	821	864

* Figure includes 44,500 non-enumerated persons

ISLANDS

	Isle of Man			Jersey			Guernsey†		
	Total	Male	Female	Total	Male	Female	Total	Male	Female
1901	54,752	25,496	29,256	52,576	23,940	28,636	40,446	19,652	20,794
1921	60,284	27,329	32,955	49,701	22,438	27,263	38,315	18,246	20,069
1951	55,123	25,749	29,464	57,296	27,282	30,014	43,652	21,221	22,431
1971	56,289	26,461	29,828	72,532	35,423	37,109	51,458	24,792	26,666
1991	69,788	33,693	36,095	84,082	40,862	43,220	58,867	28,297	30,570
2001	76,315	37,372	38,943	87,186	42,485	44,701	59,807	29,138	30,669
2006	80,058	39,523	40,535						

† Includes Herm, Jethou and Lithou

Source: ONS – Census Reports (Crown copyright)

RESIDENT POPULATION

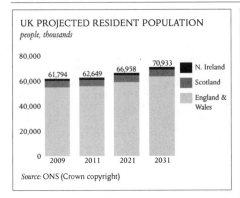

UK PROJECTED RESIDENT POPULATION
people, thousands

■ N. Ireland
■ Scotland
□ England & Wales

Source: ONS (Crown copyright)

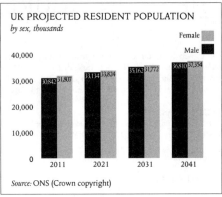

UK PROJECTED RESIDENT POPULATION
by sex, thousands

■ Female
■ Male

Source: ONS (Crown copyright)

BY AGE AND SEX (UK)

	Male	Female
	Thousands	
0–4	1,977	1,881
5–9	1,762	1,685
10–14	1,825	1,742
15–19	2,013	1,899
20–29	4,382	4,178
30–44	6,338	6,387
45–59	5,973	6,152
60–64	1,840	1,924
65–74	2,572	2,827
75–84	1,501	1,999
85+	460	951

Source: ONS (Crown copyright)

BY ETHNIC GROUP (ENGLAND AND WALES)

	Thousands
White	
British	45,682
Other	2,507
Mixed	
White and black Caribbean	311
White and black African	132
White and Asian	302
Other mixed	243
Asian	
Indian	1,434
Pakistani	1,007
Bangladeshi	392
Other Asian	386
Black	
Black Caribbean	615
Black African	799
Black other	126
Chinese	452
Other	423
ALL	54,809

Source: ONS (Crown copyright)

IMMIGRATION

ACCEPTANCES FOR SETTLEMENT IN THE UK

Geographical region	Number of persons	
	2007	2009
Europe*	8,660	10,580
Americas	10,435	15,120
Africa	34,050	47,730
Asia	67,955	116,740
Indian subcontinent	29,020	67,090
Middle East	10,655	9,390
Remainder of Asia	28,280	40,255
Oceania	3,615	4,365
Others	140	245
ALL NATIONALITIES	124,855	194,780

* Excluding European Economic Area and Swiss nationals
Source: Home Office

BIRTHS

	Live births	Birth rate*
United Kingdom	790,204	12.7
England and Wales	706,248	12.9
Scotland	59,046	11.4
Northern Ireland	24,910	13.9

* Live births per 1,000 population
Source: NISRA, ONS (Crown copyright), Scottish Government

FERTILITY RATES
Total fertility rate is the average number of children which would be born to a woman if she experienced the age-specific fertility rates of the period in question throughout her child-bearing life span. The figures for the years 1960–2 are estimates.

	1960–2	1998	2009
United Kingdom	2.80	1.71	1.94
England and Wales	2.77	1.72	1.95
Scotland	2.98	1.55	1.77
Northern Ireland	3.47	1.90	2.04

Source: ONS (Crown copyright)

MATERNITY RATES FOR ENGLAND AND WALES 2009

	All maternities*	Singleton	All multiple†	Twins	Triplets+
All ages	698,324	686,870	11,454	11,301	153
<20	43,216	42,920	296	294	2
20–24	135,404	134,068	1,336	1,323	13
25–29	192,422	189,832	2,590	2,562	28
30–34	188,767	185,074	3,693	3,639	54
35–39	112,134	109,382	2,752	2,712	40
40–44	24,906	24,275	631	619	12
45+	1,475	1,319	156	152	4

* Includes stillbirths
† Total inclues rates for twin, triplets, quads and above
Source: ONS (Crown copyright)

TOP TEN BABY NAMES

	1934		2009	
	Girls	Boys	Girls	Boys
1	Margaret	John	Olivia	Oliver
2	Jean	Peter	Ruby	Jack
3	Mary	William	Chloe	Harry
4	Joan	Brian	Emily	Alfie
5	Patricia	David	Sophie	Joshua
6	Sheila	James	Jessica	Thomas
7	Barbara	Michael	Grace	Charlie
8	Doreen	Ronald	Lily	William
9	June	Kenneth	Amelia	James
10	Shirley	George	Evie	Daniel

Source: ONS (Crown copyright)

LIVE BIRTHS BY AGE OF MOTHER AND REGISTRATION TYPE

Outside marriage

Year	under 20	20–29	30–39	40+	All ages
1971	21,600	33,500	9,500	1,100	65,700
1981	26,400	43,100	35,200	900	81,000
1991	43,400	130,200	35,500	2,100	211,300
2001	39,500	124,900	68,500	5,100	238,100
2009	40,900	185,700	89,900	9,600	326,200

Within marriage

1971	61,100	499,400	145,500	11,600	717,500
1981	30,100	367,200	150,200	6,000	553,500
1991	8,900	291,900	179,300	7,700	487,900
2001	4,600	143,800	196,900	11,100	356,500
2009	2,300	144,400	216,000	17,400	380,100

Source: ONS – *Social Trends 2011* (Crown copyright)

LEGAL ABORTIONS

	1998	2010
England and Wales	177,871	189,574
Scotland	12,458	12,826

Source: Department of Health, NHS Scotland

DEATHS

Men	Deaths
United Kingdom	270,804
England and Wales	238,062
Scotland	25,828
Northern Ireland	6,914
Women	
United Kingdom	288,813
England and Wales	253,286
Scotland	28,028
Northern Ireland	7,499

Source: ONS (Crown copyright)

INFANT MORTALITY RATE*

United Kingdom	4.5
England and Wales	4.5
Scotland	4.0
Northern Ireland	5.1

* Deaths of infants under one year of age per 1,000 live births
Source: General Register Office for Scotland, NISRA, ONS (Crown copyright)

MARRIAGE AND DIVORCE

	Marriages	Divorces
United Kingdom	266,950*	126,496
England and Wales	231,490*	113,949
Scotland	27,524	10,371
Northern Ireland	7,931	2,176

* Provisional figures
Source: ONS (Crown copyright)

HOUSEHOLDS

BY TYPE (GREAT BRITAIN)
Percentages

	1971	1991	2010
One person	18	27	29
One family households			
Couple			
No children	27	28	28
1–2 dependent children	26	20	18
3 or more dependent children	9	5	3
Non-dependent children only	8	8	6
Lone parent			
Dependent children	3	6	7
Non-dependent children only	4	4	3
Two or more unrelated adults	4	3	3
Multi-family households	1	1	1
All households (=100%) *(millions)*	18.6	22.4	25.3

Source: ONS – *Social Trends 2011* (Crown copyright)

BY SIZE (GREAT BRITAIN)
Percentages

	1971	1991	2010
One person	18	27	29
Two people	32	34	35
Three people	19	16	16
Four people	17	16	14
Five people	8	5	4
Six or more people	6	2	2
All households (=100%) *(millions)*	18.6	22.4	25.3
Average household size *(people)*	2.9	2.5	2.4

Source: ONS – *Social Trends 2011* (Crown copyright)

DEPENDENT CHILDREN LIVING IN DIFFERENT FAMILY TYPES
Millions

	1997	2005	2009
Married couple	9.6	8.6	8.3
Cohabiting couple	1.0	1.5	1.7
Female lone parent	2.5	2.8	2.9
Male lone parent	0.2	0.3	0.3

Source: ONS – *Social Trends 2010* (Crown copyright)

MORTGAGES

	1999	2005	2009
Mortgages* *(thousands)*	10,987	11,608	11,401
Loans in arrears at end-period* *(thousands)*			
By 6–12 months	57	39	92
By 12+ months	30	15	68
Properties repossessed in period	30	15	48

*Estimates cover only members of the Council of Mortgage Lenders, which account for 98 per cent of all outstanding mortgages

Source: ONS – *Annual Abstract of Statistics 2010* (Crown copyright)

TENURE BY HOUSEHOLD COMPOSITION (GREAT BRTAIN), 2009
Percentages

	Owned outright	Owned with mortgage	Privately rented*	Rented from social sector
One person households				
Under state pension age†	18.9	36.6	18.7	25.8
Over state pension age	59.5	4.4	7.9	28.2
One family households				
Couple				
No children	48.5	33.6	9.9	8.0
Dependent children	8.3	65.9	12.5	13.2
Non-dependent children	36.2	49.8	4.6	9.5
Lone parent				
Dependent children	5.0	30.3	23.6	41.0
Non-dependent children	31.1	31.7	10.2	27.0
Other households‡	20.3	28.2	37.9	13.6
All households	31.9	37.1	12.9	18.1

* Includes tenants in rent-free accommodation and squatters
† Stage pension age in 2009 is 65 for men and 60 for women
‡ Comprising two or more unrelated adults or two or more families or a small number of same-sex couples
Source: ONS – *Social Trends 2011* (Crown copyright)

HEALTH

DEATHS BY CAUSE, 2009

	England and Wales	Scotland	N. Ireland
Total deaths	491,348	53,856	14,413
Deaths from natural causes	473,470	51,658	13,608
Certain infectious and parasitic diseases	5,750	838	164
Intestinal infectious diseases	1861	109	69*
Respiratory and other tuberculosis	305	29	6*
Meningococcal infection	60	5	2*
Viral hepatitis	258	25	2*
AIDS (HIV – disease)	256	17	–
Neoplasms	140,497	15,484	3,992
Malignant neoplasms	137,420	15,187	3,885
Malignant neoplasm of trachea, bronchus and lung	30,018	4,147	927*
Malignant neoplasm of skin	2,325	253	57*
Malignant neoplasm of breast	10,440	1,010	312*
Malignant neoplasm of cervix uteri	830	124	28*
Malignant neoplasm of prostate	9.402	790	226*
Leukaemia	3,990	388	102*
Diseases of the blood and blood-forming organs and certain disorders involving the immune mechanism	1,026	113	28
Endocrine, nutritional and metabolic diseases	7,123	873	319
Diabetes mellitus	5,278	632	229
Mental and behavioural disorders	18,021	3,327	525
Vascular and unspecified dementia	16,911	2,585	472
Alcohol abuse	645	312	46*
Drug dependence and non-dependent abuse of drugs	1,340	410	2*
Diseases of the nervous system and sense organs	17,408	1,652	618
Meningitis (excluding meningococcal)	154	22	3*
Alzheimer's disease	6,194	634	241
Diseases of the circulatory system	159,779	16,769	4,485
Ischaemic heart diseases	72,120	8,274	2,305
Cerebrovascular diseases	43,595	4,906	1,175
Diseases of the respiratory system	67,559	7,125	2,017
Influenza	227	62	2*
Pneumonia	26,741	2,345	900*
Bronchitis, emphysema and other chronic obstructive pulmonary diseases	23,318	2,801	680*
Asthma	991	75	31*
Diseases of the digestive system	25,230	3,006	686
Gastric and duodenal ulcer	2,714	220	52*
Chronic liver disease	7,326	1,110	204*
Diseases of the skin and subcutaneous tissue	1,849	157	24*
Diseases of the musculo-skeletal system and connective tissue	4,141	344	85*
Osteoporosis	1,565	73	15*
Diseases of the genito-urinary system	11,998	1,269	367
Complications of pregnancy, childbirth and the puerperium	63	7	5
Certain conditions originating in the perinatal period†	237	123	60
Congenital malformations, deformations and chromosomal abnormalities†	1,261	153	82
Symptoms, signs and abnormal findings not classified elsewhere	9,243	414	138
Senility without mention of psychosis (old age)	7,531	236	107*
Sudden infant death syndrome	156	23	3*
Deaths from external causes	17,878	2,198	805
Suicide and intentional self-harm	3,457	568	252*
Homicide and assault	318‡	72	40*

* 2008 figures

† Excludes neonatal deaths (those at age under 28 days): for England and Wales neonatal deaths are included in the total number of deaths but excluded from the cause figures

‡ This will not be a true figure as registration of homicide and assault deaths in England and Wales is often delayed by adjourned inquests

Source: General Register Office for Scotland, NISRA, ONS (Crown copyright)

ALCOHOL CONSUMPTION* BY AGE (GREAT BRITAIN)
Percentages

	16–24	25–44	45–64	65+	All 16+
Men					
No units	37	28	26	34	30
Up to 4 units	21	30	33	44	33
4–8 units	12	15	20	14	16
8+ units	30	27	21	7	21
Women					
No units	48	41	40	57	45
Up to 3 units	16	22	28	33	26
3–6 units	12	16	19	8	15
6+ units	24	20	13	2	14

* Maximum consumed on any one day in the previous week. Department of Health guidelines recommend that men should not regularly drink more than three to four units of alcohol per day and women should not regularly drink more than two to three units per day. A unit of alcohol is 8 grams by weight or 10ml by volume of pure alcohol, ie the amount contained in half a pint of ordinary strength beer or lager, a single pub measure of spirits or a small glass of ordinary strength wine
Source: ONS – *Social Trends 2010* (Crown copyright)

PREVALENCE OF SMOKING, DRINKING AND BINGE-DRINKING AMONG ADULTS
Percentages

	Men			Women		
	Regular smoker	*Drank more than 4 units*	*Drank more than 8 units*	*Regular smoker*	*Drank more than 3 units*	*Drank more than 6 units*
2000–1	29	39	21	25	23	10
2001–2	28	40	22	26	23	10
2002–3	27	38	21	25	23	10
2003–4	28	40	23	24	23	9
2004–5	26	39	22	23	22	9
2005	25	35	19	23	20	8
2006	23	40	23	21	33	15
2007	22	41	24	20	34	15
2008	22	37	21	21	29	14
2009	22	37	20	20	29	13

Source: ONS – *Social Trends 2011* (Crown copyright)

NOTIFICATIONS OF INFECTIOUS DISEASES

	2000	2008
Measles	2,865	5,331
Mumps	3,367	8,682
Rubella	2,064	1,230
Whooping cough	866	1,676
Scarlet fever	2,544	3,983
Dysentery	1,613	1,289
Food poisoning	98,076	77,854
Typhoid and paratyphoid fevers	205	418
Hepatitis	4,530	6,515
Tuberculosis	7,100	7,878
Malaria	1,166	403

Source: ONS – *Annual Abstract of Statistics 2010* (Crown copyright)

CIGARETTE SMOKING HABITS
Percentages

	2000	2008
Men		
Current cigarette smoker	29	22
Light to moderate (fewer than 20 cigarettes a day)	18	15
Heavy (20 or more a day)	10	7
Ex-regular smoker	27	30
Never or only occasionally smoked	44	49
Women		
Current cigarette smoker	25	21
Light to moderate (fewer than 20 cigarettes a day)	19	15
Heavy (20 or more a day)	6	5
Ex-regular smoker	20	22
Never or only occasionally smoked	54	58

Source: ONS – *Social Trends 2010* (Crown copyright)

BODY MASS INDEX (BMI)* BY WEIGHT CLASSIFICATION (ENGLAND)
Percentages

	2000	2008
Underweight (BMI less than 18.5)	1.5	1.8
Normal (18.5 to less than 25)	38.6	36.8
Overweight (25 to less than 30)	38.8	36.9
Obese† (30 and over)	21.2	24.5
Morbidly obese (40 and over)	1.5	2.0

*BMI is the most widely used measure of obesity among adults aged 16 and over. BMI standardises weight for height and is calculated as weight (kg)/height (m)^2
† Includes morbidly obese
Source: ONS – *Social Trends 2010* (Crown copyright)

THE NATIONAL FLAG

The national flag of the United Kingdom is the Union Flag, generally known as the Union Jack.

The Union Flag is a combination of the cross of St George, patron saint of England, the cross of St Andrew, patron saint of Scotland and the cross of St Patrick, patron saint of Ireland.

Cross of St George: cross Gules in a field Argent (red cross on a white ground)

Cross of St Andrew: saltire Argent in a field Azure (white diagonal cross on a blue ground)

Cross of St Patrick: saltire Gules in a field Argent (red diagonal cross on a white ground)

The Union Flag was first introduced in 1606 after the union of the kingdoms of England and Scotland under one sovereign. The cross of St Patrick was added in 1801 after the union of Great Britain and Ireland.

See also Flags of the World colour plates.

FLYING THE UNION FLAG

The correct orientation of the Union Flag when flying is with the broader diagonal band of white uppermost in the hoist (ie near the pole) and the narrower diagonal band of white uppermost in the fly (ie furthest from the pole).

The flying of the Union Flag on government buildings is decided by the Department for Culture, Media and Sport (DCMS) at the Queen's command. There is no formal definition of a government building but it is generally accepted to mean a building owned or used by the Crown and/or predominantly occupied or used by civil servants or the Armed Forces.

The Scottish or Welsh governments are responsible for drawing up their own flag-flying guidance for their buildings. In Northern Ireland, the flying of flags is constrained by The Flags Regulations (Northern Ireland) 2000 and the Police Emblems and Flag Regulations (Northern Ireland) 2002. Individuals, local authorities and other organisations may fly the Union Flag whenever they wish, subject to compliance with any local planning requirement.

FLAGS AT HALF-MAST

Flags are flown at half-mast (ie two-thirds up between the top and bottom of the flagstaff) on the following occasions:

- from the announcement of the death of the sovereign until the funeral
- the death or funeral of a member of the royal family*
- the funerals of foreign rulers*
- the funerals of prime ministers and ex-prime ministers of the UK*
- the funerals of first ministers and ex-first ministers of Scotland, Wales and Northern Ireland (unless otherwise commanded by the sovereign, this only applies to flags in their respective countries)*
- other occasions by special command from the Queen

* By special command from the Queen in each case

DAYS FOR FLYING FLAGS

On 25 March 2008 the DCMS announced that UK government departments in England, Scotland and Wales may fly the Union Flag on their buildings whenever they choose and not just on the designated days listed below. In addition, on the patron saints' days of Scotland and Wales, the appropriate national flag may be flown alongside the Union Flag on UK government buildings in the wider Whitehall area. When flying on designated days flags are hoisted from 8am to sunset.

Countess of Wessex's birthday	20 Jan
Accession of the Queen	6 Feb
Duke of York's birthday	19 Feb
St David's Day (in Wales only)*	1 Mar
Earl of Wessex's birthday	10 Mar
Commonwealth Day (2012)	12 Mar
St Patrick's Day (in Northern Ireland only)†	17 Mar
The Queen's birthday	21 Apr
St George's Day (in England only)*	23 Apr
Europe Day†	9 May
Coronation Day	2 Jun
Duke of Edinburgh's birthday	10 Jun
The Queen's official birthday (2012)	16 Jun
Duchess of Cornwall's birthday	17 Jul
Princess Royal's birthday	15 Aug
Remembrance Day (2012)	11 Nov
Prince of Wales' birthday	14 Nov
Wedding Day of the Queen	20 Nov
St Andrew's Day (in Scotland only)*	30 Nov
Opening of parliament by the Queen‡	
Prorogation of parliament by the Queen‡	

* The appropriate national flag, or the European flag, may be flown in addition to the Union Flag (where there are two or more flagpoles), but not in a superior position

† Only the Union Flag should be flown

‡ Only in the Greater London area, whether or not the Queen performs the ceremony in person

THE ROYAL STANDARD

The Royal Standard comprises four quarterings – two for England (three lions passant), one for Scotland* (a lion rampant) and one for Ireland (a harp).

The Royal Standard is flown when the Queen is in residence at a royal palace, on transport being used by the Queen for official journeys and from Victoria Tower when the Queen attends parliament. It may also be flown on any building (excluding ecclesiastical buildings) during a visit by the Queen. If the Queen is to be present in a building advice on flag flying can be obtained from the DCMS.

The Royal Standard is never flown at half-mast, even after the death of the sovereign, as the new monarch immediately succeeds to the throne.

* In Scotland a version with two Scottish quarterings is used

THE ROYAL FAMILY

THE SOVEREIGN

ELIZABETH II, by the Grace of God, of the United Kingdom of Great Britain and Northern Ireland and of her other Realms and Territories Queen, Head of the Commonwealth, Defender of the Faith
Her Majesty Elizabeth Alexandra Mary of Windsor, elder daughter of King George VI and of HM Queen Elizabeth the Queen Mother
Born 21 April 1926, at 17 Bruton Street, London W1
Ascended the throne 6 February 1952
Crowned 2 June 1953, at Westminster Abbey
Married 20 November 1947, in Westminster Abbey, HRH the Prince Philip, Duke of Edinburgh
Official residences Buckingham Palace, London SW1A 1AA; Windsor Castle, Berks; Palace of Holyroodhouse, Edinburgh
Private residences Sandringham, Norfolk; Balmoral Castle, Aberdeenshire

HUSBAND OF THE QUEEN

HRH THE PRINCE PHILIP, DUKE OF EDINBURGH, KG, KT, OM, GBE, Royal Victorian Chain, AC, QSO, PC, Ranger of Windsor Park
Born 10 June 1921, son of Prince and Princess Andrew of Greece and Denmark, naturalised a British subject 1947, created Duke of Edinburgh, Earl of Merioneth and Baron Greenwich 1947

CHILDREN OF THE QUEEN

HRH THE PRINCE OF WALES (Prince Charles Philip Arthur George), KG, KT, GCB, OM and Great Master of the Order of the Bath, AK, QSO, PC, ADC(P)
Born 14 November 1948, created Prince of Wales and Earl of Chester 1958, succeeded as Duke of Cornwall, Duke of Rothesay, Earl of Carrick and Baron Renfrew, Lord of the Isles and Great Steward of Scotland 1952
Married (1) 29 July 1981 Lady Diana Frances Spencer (Diana, Princess of Wales (1961–97), youngest daughter of the 8th Earl Spencer and the Hon. Mrs Shand Kydd), marriage dissolved 1996; (2) 9 April 2005 Mrs Camilla Rosemary Parker Bowles, now HRH the Duchess of Cornwall (*born* 17 July 1947, daughter of Major Bruce Shand and the Hon. Mrs Rosalind Shand)
Residences Clarence House, London SW1A 1BA; Highgrove, Doughton, Tetbury, Glos GL8 8TN; Birkhall, Ballater, Aberdeenshire
Issue
1. HRH the Duke of Cambridge (Prince William Arthur Philip Louis), KG, *born* 21 June 1982, *created* Duke of Cambridge, Earl of Strathearn, and Baron Carrickfergus 2011 *married* 29 April 2011 Catherine Elizabeth Middleton, now HRH the Duchess of Cambridge (*born* 9 January 1982, eldest daughter of Michael and Carole Middleton)
2. HRH Prince Henry of Wales (Prince Henry Charles Albert David), *born* 15 September 1984

HRH THE PRINCESS ROYAL (Princess Anne Elizabeth Alice Louise), KG, KT, GCVO
Born 15 August 1950, declared the Princess Royal 1987
Married (1) 14 November 1973 Captain Mark Anthony

Peter Phillips, CVO (*born* 22 September 1948); marriage dissolved 1992; (2) 12 December 1992 Vice-Adm. Sir Timothy James Hamilton Laurence, KCVO, CB, ADC(P) (*born* 1 March 1955)
Residence Gatcombe Park, Minchinhampton, Glos GL6 9AT
Issue
1. Peter Mark Andrew Phillips, *born* 15 November 1977, *married* 17 May 2008 Autumn Patricia Kelly, and has issue, Savannah Phillips, *born* 29 December 2010
2. Zara Anne Elizabeth Phillips, MBE, *born* 15 May 1981, *married* 30 July 2011 Michael James Tindall, MBE

HRH THE DUKE OF YORK (Prince Andrew Albert Christian Edward), KG, GCVO, ADC(P)
Born 19 February 1960, created Duke of York, Earl of Inverness and Baron Killyleagh 1986
Married 23 July 1986 Sarah Margaret Ferguson, now Sarah, Duchess of York (*born* 15 October 1959, younger daughter of Major Ronald Ferguson and Mrs Hector Barrantes), marriage dissolved 1996
Residence Royal Lodge, Windsor Great Park, Berks
Issue
1. HRH Princess Beatrice of York (Princess Beatrice Elizabeth Mary), *born* 8 August 1988
2. HRH Princess Eugenie of York (Princess Eugenie Victoria Helena), *born* 23 March 1990

HRH THE EARL OF WESSEX (Prince Edward Antony Richard Louis), KG, GCVO, ADC(P)
Born 10 March 1964, created Earl of Wessex, Viscount Severn 1999
Married 19 June 1999 Sophie Helen Rhys-Jones, now HRH the Countess of Wessex, GCVO (*born* 20 January 1965, daughter of Mr and Mrs Christopher Rhys-Jones)
Residence Bagshot Park, Bagshot, Surrey GU19 5HS
Issue
1. Lady Louise Mountbatten-Windsor (Louise Alice Elizabeth Mary Mountbatten-Windsor), *born* 8 November 2003
2. Viscount Severn (James Alexander Philip Theo Mountbatten-Windsor), *born* 17 December 2007

NEPHEW AND NIECE OF THE QUEEN

Children of HRH the Princess Margaret, Countess of Snowdon and the Earl of Snowdon (*see* House of Windsor):

DAVID ALBERT CHARLES ARMSTRONG-JONES, VISCOUNT LINLEY, *born* 3 November 1961, *married* 8 October 1993 Hon. Serena Alleyne Stanhope, and has issue, Hon. Charles Patrick Inigo Armstrong-Jones, *born* 1 July 1999; Hon. Margarita Elizabeth Alleyne Armstrong-Jones, *born* 14 May 2002

LADY SARAH CHATTO (Sarah Frances Elizabeth), *born* 1 May 1964, *married* 14 July 1994 Daniel Chatto, and has issue, Samuel David Benedict Chatto, *born* 28 July 1996; Arthur Robert Nathaniel Chatto, *born* 5 February 1999

COUSINS OF THE QUEEN

Child of HRH the Duke of Gloucester and HRH Princess Alice, Duchess of Gloucester (*see* House of Windsor):

HRH THE DUKE OF GLOUCESTER (Prince Richard Alexander Walter George), KG, GCVO, Grand Prior of the Order of St John of Jerusalem
Born 26 August 1944
Married 8 July 1972 Birgitte Eva van Deurs, now HRH the Duchess of Gloucester, GCVO (*born* 20 June 1946, daughter of Asger Henriksen and Vivian van Deurs)
Residence Kensington Palace, London W8 4PU
Issue
1. Earl of Ulster (Alexander Patrick Gregers Richard), *born* 24 October 1974 *married* 22 June 2002 Dr Claire Alexandra Booth, and has issue, Lord Culloden (Xan Richard Anders), *born* 12 March 2007; Lady Cosima Windsor (Cosima Rose Alexandra), *born* 20 May 2010
2. Lady Davina Lewis (Davina Elizabeth Alice Benedikte), *born* 19 November 1977 *married* 31 July 2004 Gary Christie Lewis, and has issue, Senna Kowhai Lewis, *born* 22 June 2010
3. Lady Rose Gilman (Rose Victoria Birgitte Louise), *born* 1 March 1980 *married* 19 July 2008 George Edward Gilman, and has issue, Lyla Beatrix Christabel Gilman, *born* 30 May 2010

Children of HRH the Duke of Kent and Princess Marina, Duchess of Kent (*see* House of Windsor):

HRH THE DUKE OF KENT (Prince Edward George Nicholas Paul Patrick), KG, GCMG, GCVO, ADC(P)
Born 9 October 1935
Married 8 June 1961 Katharine Lucy Mary Worsley, now HRH the Duchess of Kent, GCVO (*born* 22 February 1933, daughter of Sir William Worsley, Bt.)
Residence Wren House, Palace Green, London W8 4PY
Issue
1. Earl of St Andrews (George Philip Nicholas), *born* 26 June 1962, *married* 9 January 1988 Sylvana Tomaselli, and has issue, Lord Downpatrick (Edward Edmund Maximilian George), *born* 2 December 1988; Lady Marina-Charlotte Windsor (Marina-Charlotte Alexandra Katharine Helen), *born* 30 September 1992; Lady Amelia Windsor (Amelia Sophia Theodora Mary Margaret), *born* 24 August 1995

2. Lady Helen Taylor (Helen Marina Lucy), *born* 28 April 1964, *married* 18 July 1992 Timothy Verner Taylor, and has issue, Columbus George Donald Taylor, *born* 6 August 1994; Cassius Edward Taylor, *born* 26 December 1996; Eloise Olivia Katharine Taylor, *born* 3 March 2003; Estella Olga Elizabeth Taylor, *born* 21 December 2004
3. Lord Nicholas Windsor (Nicholas Charles Edward Jonathan), *born* 25 July 1970, *married* 4 November 2006 Princess Paola Doimi de Lupis Frankopan Subic Zrinski, and has issue, Hon. Albert Louis Philip Edward Windsor, *born* 22 September 2007; Hon. Leopold Ernest Augustus Guelph Windsor, *born* 8 September 2009

HRH PRINCESS ALEXANDRA, THE HON. LADY OGILVY (Princess Alexandra Helen Elizabeth Olga Christabel), KG, GCVO
Born 25 December 1936
Married 24 April 1963 the Rt. Hon. Sir Angus Ogilvy, KCVO (1928–2004), second son of 12th Earl of Airlie
Residence Thatched House Lodge, Richmond Park, Surrey TW10 5HP
Issue
1. James Robert Bruce Ogilvy, *born* 29 February 1964, *married* 30 July 1988 Julia Rawlinson, and has issue, Flora Alexandra Ogilvy, *born* 15 December 1994; Alexander Charles Ogilvy, *born* 12 November 1996
2. Marina Victoria Alexandra Ogilvy, *born* 31 July 1966, *married* 2 February 1990 Paul Julian Mowatt (marriage dissolved 1997), and has issue, Zenouska May Mowatt, *born* 26 May 1990; Christian Alexander Mowatt, *born* 4 June 1993

HRH PRINCE MICHAEL OF KENT (Prince Michael George Charles Franklin), GCVO
Born 4 July 1942
Married 30 June 1978 Baroness Marie-Christine Agnes Hedwig Ida von Reibnitz, now HRH Princess Michael of Kent (*born* 15 January 1945, daughter of Baron Gunther von Reibnitz)
Residence Kensington Palace, London W8 4PU
Issue
1. Lord Frederick Windsor (Frederick Michael George David Louis), *born* 6 April 1979, *married* 12 September 2009 Sophie Winkleman
2. Lady Gabriella Windsor (Gabriella Marina Alexandra Ophelia), *born* 23 April 1981

ORDER OF SUCCESSION

1   HRH the Prince of Wales
2   HRH the Duke of Cambridge
3   HRH Prince Henry of Wales
4   HRH the Duke of York
5   HRH Princess Beatrice of York
6   HRH Princess Eugenie of York
7   HRH the Earl of Wessex
8   Viscount Severn
9   Lady Louise Mountbatten-Windsor
10 HRH the Princess Royal
11 Peter Phillips
12 Savannah Phillips
13 Zara Phillips
14 Viscount Linley
15 Hon. Charles Armstrong-Jones
16 Hon. Margarita Armstrong-Jones
17 Lady Sarah Chatto
18 Samuel Chatto
19 Arthur Chatto
20 HRH the Duke of Gloucester
21 Earl of Ulster
22 Lord Culloden
23 Lady Cosima Windsor
24 Lady Davina Lewis
25 Senna Lewis
26 Lady Rose Gilman
27 Lyla Gilman
28 HRH the Duke of Kent
29 Lady Amelia Windsor
30 Lady Helen Taylor
31 Columbus Taylor
32 Cassius Taylor
33 Eloise Taylor
34 Estella Taylor
35 Hon. Albert Windsor
36 Hon. Leopold Windsor
37 Lord Frederick Windsor
38 Lady Gabriella Windsor
39 HRH Princess Alexandra, the Hon. Lady Ogilvy

HRH Prince Michael of Kent, and the Earl of St Andrews both lost the right of succession to the throne through marriage to a Roman Catholic. Lord Nicholas Windsor, Lord Downpatrick and Lady Marina-Charlotte Windsor renounced their rights to the throne on converting to Roman Catholicism in 2001, 2003 and 2008 respectively. Their children remain in succession provided that they are in communion with the Church of England.

PRIVATE SECRETARIES

THE QUEEN
Office: Buckingham Palace, London SW1A 1AA
T 020-7930 4832 W www.royal.gov.uk
Private Secretary to the Queen, Rt. Hon. Sir Christopher Geidt, KCVO, OBE

PRINCE PHILIP, THE DUKE OF EDINBURGH
Office: Buckingham Palace, London SW1A 1AA
T 020-7930 4832
Private Secretary, Brig. Archie Miller-Bakewell

THE PRINCE OF WALES AND THE DUCHESS OF CORNWALL
Office: Clarence House, London SW1A 1BA
T 020-7930 4832
Principal Private Secretary, Sir Michael Peat, KCVO

THE DUKE AND DUCHESS OF CAMBRIDGE AND PRINCE HENRY OF WALES
Office: Clarence House, London SW1A 1BA
T 020-7930 4832
Private Secretary, James Lowther-Pinkerton, MVO, MBE

THE DUKE OF YORK
Office: Buckingham Palace, London SW1A 1AA
T 020-7930 4832
Private Secretary, Alastair Watson

THE EARL AND COUNTESS OF WESSEX
Office: Bagshot Park, Surrey GU19 5PL
T 01276-707040
Private Secretary, Brig. J. Smedley, LVO

THE PRINCESS ROYAL
Office: Buckingham Palace, London SW1A 1AA
T 020-7024 4199
Private Secretary, Capt. N. P. Wright, CVO, RN

THE DUKE AND DUCHESS OF GLOUCESTER
Office: Kensington Palace, London W8 4PU
T 020-7368 1000
Private Secretary, Alistair Wood, MBE

THE DUKE OF KENT
Office: St James's Palace, London SW1A 1BQ
T 020-7930 4872
Private Secretary, N. Marden

THE DUCHESS OF KENT
Office: Wren House, Palace Green, London W8 4PY
T 020-7937 2730
Personal Secretary, Chloe Hill

PRINCE AND PRINCESS MICHAEL OF KENT
Office: Kensington Palace, London W8 4PU
T 020-7938 3519
W www.princemichael.org.uk
Private Secretary, Nicholas Chance, LVO

PRINCESS ALEXANDRA, THE HON. LADY OGILVY
Office: Buckingham Palace, London SW1A 1AA
T 020-7024 4270
Private Secretary, Diane Duke

ROYAL HOUSEHOLD

The PRIVATE SECRETARY is responsible for:

- informing and advising the Queen on constitutional, governmental and political matters in the UK, her other Realms and the wider Commonwealth, including communications with the prime minister and government departments
- organising the Queen's domestic and overseas official programme
- the Queen's speeches, messages, patronage, photographs, portraits and official presents
- communications in connection with the role of the royal family
- dealing with correspondence to the Queen from members of the public
- royal travel policy
- coordinating and initiating research to support engagements by members of the royal family

The COMMUNICATIONS AND PRESS SECRETARY is in charge of Buckingham Palace's press office and reports to the private secretary. The press secretary is responsible for:

- developing communications strategies to enhance the public understanding of the role of the monarchy
- briefing the British and international media on the role and duties of the Queen and issues relating to the royal family
- responding to media enquiries
- arranging media facilities in the UK and overseas to support royal functions and engagements
- the management of the royal website

The private secretary is keeper of the royal archives and is responsible for the care of the records of the sovereign and the royal household from previous reigns, preserved in the royal archives at Windsor. As keeper, it is the private secretary's responsibility to ensure the proper management of the records of the present reign with a view to their transfer to the archives as and when appropriate. The private secretary is an *ex officio* trustee of the Royal Collection Trust.

The KEEPER OF THE PRIVY PURSE AND TREASURER to the Queen is responsible for:

- the Queen's Civil List, which is the money paid from the government's Consolidated Fund to meet official expenditure relating to the Queen's duties as head of state and head of the Commonwealth
- through the director of personnel, the planning and management of personnel policy across the royal household, the administration of all its pension schemes and private estates employees, and the allocation of employee and pensioner housing
- information technology systems
- internal audit services
- health and safety; insurance matters
- the privy purse, which is mainly financed by the net income of the Duchy of Lancaster, and meets both official and private expenditure incurred by the Queen
- liaison with other members of the royal family and their households on financial matters
- the Queen's private estates at Sandringham and Balmoral, the Queen's Racing Establishment and the Royal Studs and liaison with the Ascot Authority
- the Home Park at Windsor and liaison with the Crown Estate Commissioners concerning the Home Park and the Great Park at Windsor
- the Royal Philatelic Collection
- administrative aspects of the Military Knights of Windsor
- administration of the Royal Victorian Order, of which the keeper of the privy purse is secretary, Long and Faithful Service Medals, and the Queen's cups, medals and prizes, and policy on commemorative medals

The keeper of the privy purse is one of three royal trustees (in respect of his responsibilities for the Civil List) and is receiver-general of the Duchy of Lancaster and a member of the Duchy's Council.

The keeper of the privy purse is responsible for property services at occupied royal palaces in England, comprising Buckingham Palace, St James's Palace, Clarence House, Marlborough House Mews, the residential and office areas of Kensington Palace, Windsor Castle and buildings in the Home and Great Parks of Windsor and Hampton Court Mews and Paddocks. The costs of property services for occupied royal palaces are met from a grant-in-aid from the Department for Culture, Media and Sport (DCMS).

The keeper of the privy purse also oversees royal communications and information expenditure, which is met from the property services grant-in-aid, and the financial aspects of royal travel, met from a grant-in-aid provided by the Department for Transport.

The keeper of the privy purse is an *ex officio* trustee of the Historic Royal Palaces Trust and the Royal Collection Trust.

The Queen's Civil List and the grants-in-aid for property services and royal travel are provided by the government in return for the net surplus from the Crown Estate and other hereditary revenues.

The DIRECTOR OF THE PROPERTY SECTION has day-to-day responsibility for the royal household's property section:

- fire and health and safety
- repairs and refurbishment of buildings and new building work
- utilities and telecommunications
- putting up stages, tents and other work in connection with ceremonial occasions, garden parties and other official functions

The property section is also responsible, on a sub-contract basis from the DCMS, for the maintenance of Marlborough House (which is occupied by the Commonwealth Secretariat).

The MASTER OF THE HOUSEHOLD is responsible for:

- delivering the majority of the official and private entertaining in the Queen's annual programme at residences in the UK, and on occasion overseas
- periodic support for entertaining by other members of the royal family
- furnishings and internal decorative refurbishment in conjunction with the director of the Royal Collection and Property Services
- housekeeping, catering and service provision for the royal household

The COMPTROLLER, LORD CHAMBERLAIN'S OFFICE is responsible for:

- the organisation of all ceremonial engagements, including state visits to the Queen in the UK, royal weddings and funerals, the state opening of parliament, Guards of Honour at Buckingham Palace, investitures, and the Garter and Thistle ceremonies
- garden parties at Buckingham Palace and the Palace of Holyroodhouse (except for catering and tents)
- the Crown Jewels, which are part of the Royal Collection, when they are in use on state occasions
- coordination of the arrangements for the Queen to be represented at funerals and memorial services and at the arrival and departure of visiting heads of state
- delivery of all official and approved travel operations
- advising on matters of precedence, style and titles, dress, flying of flags, gun salutes, mourning and other ceremonial issues
- supervising the applications from tradesmen for Royal Warrants of Appointment
- advising on the commercial use of royal emblems and contemporary royal photographs
- the ecclesiastical household, the medical household, the body guards and certain ceremonial appointments such as Gentlemen Ushers and Pages of Honour
- the lords in waiting, who represent the Queen on various occasions and escort visiting heads of state during incoming state visits
- the Queen's bargemaster and watermen and the Queen's swans
- the Royal Almonry

The comptroller is also responsible for the Royal Mews, assisted by the CROWN EQUERRY, who has day-to-day responsibility for:

- the provision of carriage processions for the state opening of parliament, state visits, Trooping of the Colour, Royal Ascot, the Garter Ceremony, the Thistle Service, the presentation of credentials to the Queen by incoming foreign ambassadors and high commissioners, and other state and ceremonial occasions
- the provision of chauffeur-driven cars
- coordinating travel arrangements by road, air, rail or sea in respect of the royal household
- supervision and administration of the Royal Mews at Buckingham Palace, Windsor Castle, Hampton Court and the Palace of Holyroodhouse

The comptroller also has overall responsibility for the MARSHAL OF THE DIPLOMATIC CORPS, who is responsible for the relationship between the royal household and the Diplomatic Heads of Mission in London; and the SECRETARY OF THE CENTRAL CHANCERY OF THE ORDERS OF KNIGHTHOOD, who administers the Orders of Chivalry, makes arrangements for investitures and the distribution of insignia, and ensures the proper public notification of awards through *The London Gazette*.

The DIRECTOR OF THE ROYAL COLLECTION is responsible for:

- the administration and custodial control of the Royal Collection in all royal residences
- the care, display, conservation and restoration of items in the collection
- initiating and assisting research into the collection and publishing catalogues and books on the collection
- making the collection accessible to the public and educating and informing the public about the collection

The Royal Collection, which contains a large number of works of art, is held by the Queen as sovereign in trust for her successors and the nation and is not owned by her as an individual. The administration, conservation and presentation of the Royal Collection are funded by the Royal Collection Trust solely from income from visitors to Windsor Castle, Buckingham Palace and the Palace of Holyroodhouse. The Royal Collection Trust is chaired by the Prince of Wales. The Lord Chamberlain, the private secretary and the keeper of the privy purse are *ex officio* trustees and there are three external trustees appointed by the Queen.

The director of the Royal Collection is also at present the SURVEYOR OF THE QUEEN'S WORKS OF ART. The ROYAL LIBRARIAN is responsible for all books, manuscripts, coins and medals, insignia and works of art on paper including the watercolours, prints and drawings in the Print Room at Windsor Castle, and the SURVEYOR OF THE QUEEN'S PICTURES is responsible for pictures and miniatures.

Royal Collection Enterprises Limited is the trading subsidiary of the Royal Collection Trust. The company, whose chair is the Keeper of the Privy Purse, is responsible for:

- managing access by the public to Windsor Castle (including Frogmore House), Buckingham Palace (including the Royal Mews and the Queen's Gallery) and the Palace of Holyroodhouse (including the Queen's Gallery)
- running shops at each location
- managing the images and intellectual property rights of the Royal Collection

The director of the Royal Collection is also an *ex officio* trustee of the Historic Royal Palaces Trust.

SENIOR MANAGEMENT OF THE ROYAL HOUSEHOLD

Lord Chamberlain, Earl Peel, GCVO, PC

HEADS OF DEPARTMENT
Private Secretary to The Queen, Rt. Hon. Sir Christopher Geidt, KCVO, OBE
Keeper of the Privy Purse, Sir Alan Reid, KCVO
Master of the Household, Air Vice-Marshal Sir David Walker, KCVO, OBE
Comptroller, Lord Chamberlain's Office, Lt.-Col. Andrew Ford
Director of the Royal Collection, Jonathan Marsden, LVO

NON-EXECUTIVE MEMBERS
Private Secretary to the Duke of Edinburgh, Brig. Archie Miller-Bakewell
Private Secretary to the Prince of Wales and the Duchess of Cornwall, Sir Michael Peat, KCVO

THE POET LAUREATE

The post of Poet Laureate was officially established when John Dryden was appointed by royal warrant as Poet Laureate and Historiographer Royal in 1668. The post is attached to the royal household and was originally conferred on the holder for life; in 1999 the length of appointment was changed to a ten-year term. It is customary for the Poet Laureate to write verse to mark events of national importance. The postholder currently receives an honorarium of £5,750 a year.
The Poet Laureate, Carol Ann Duffy, *apptd* 2009

ROYAL SALUTES

ENGLAND

The basic royal salute is 21 rounds with an extra 20 rounds fired at Hyde Park because it is a royal park. At the Tower of London 62 rounds are fired on royal anniversaries (21 plus a further 20 because the Tower is a royal palace and a further 21 'for the City of London') and 41 on other occasions. When the Queen's official birthday coincides with the Duke of Edinburgh's birthday, 124 rounds are fired from the Tower (62 rounds for each birthday). Gun salutes occur on the following royal anniversaries:

• Accession Day
• The Queen's birthday
• Coronation Day
• Duke of Edinburgh's birthday
• The Queen's Official Birthday
• The Prince of Wales' birthday
• State opening of parliament

Gun salutes also occur when parliament is prorogued by the sovereign, on royal births and when a visiting head of state meets the sovereign in London, Windsor or Edinburgh.

In London, salutes are fired at Hyde Park and the Tower of London although on some occasions (state visits, state opening of parliament and the Queen's birthday parade) Green Park is used instead of Hyde Park. Other military saluting stations in England are at Colchester, Dover, Plymouth, Woolwich and York.

Constable of the Royal Palace and Fortress of London, Gen. Lord Dannatt, GCB, CBE, MC
Lieutenant of the Tower of London, Lt. Gen. Peter Pearson, CB, CBE
Resident Governor and Keeper of the Jewel House, Col. Richard Harrold, OBE
Master Gunner of St James's Park, Gen. Sir Alex Harley, KBE, CB
Master Gunner within the Tower, HRH Prince Michael of Kent, GCVO

SCOTLAND

Royal salutes are authorised at Edinburgh Castle and Stirling Castle. A salute of 21 guns is fired on the following occasions:

• the anniversaries of the birth, accession and coronation of the sovereign
• the anniversary of the birth of the Duke of Edinburgh

A salute of 21 guns is fired in Edinburgh on the occasion of the opening of the general assembly of the Church of Scotland. A salute of 21 guns may also be fired in Edinburgh on the arrival of HM The Queen or a member of the royal family who is a Royal Highness on an official visit.

Military saluting stations are also situated at Cardiff Castle in Wales, Hillsborough Castle in Northern Ireland and in Gibraltar.

ROYAL FINANCES

FUNDING

CIVIL LIST

The Civil List dates back to the late 17th century. It was originally used by the sovereign to supplement hereditary revenues for paying the salaries of judges, ambassadors and other government officers as well as the expenses of the royal household. In 1760, on the accession of George III, it was decided that the Civil List would be provided by parliament to cover all relevant expenditure in return for the king surrendering the hereditary revenues of the Crown (principally the net surplus of the Crown Estate). At that time parliament undertook to pay the salaries of judges, ambassadors etc. In 1831 parliament agreed also to meet the costs of the royal palaces in return for a reduction in the Civil List. Each sovereign has agreed to continue this arrangement. The Civil List now meets the central staff costs and running expenses of the Queen's official household.

Until 1972, the amount of money allocated annually under the Civil List was set for the duration of a reign. The system was then altered to a fixed annual payment for ten years but from 1975 high inflation made an annual review necessary. The system of payments reverted to the practice of a fixed annual payment of £7.9m for a ten-year period to 31 December 2000; during this period annual Civil List expenditure reached £6.5m, and a reserve of £35m was established. In order to draw down the reserve, the annual Civil List payment has remained at £7.9m since 2001.

The legislative requirement is for Civil List accounts to be submitted to parliament, in the form of Royal Trustees Reports, at ten-yearly intervals, but from June 2002 accounts have been published annually. The ninth annual accounts for the year ending 31 December 2010 were published in June 2011:

	2009	2010
Civil List payment	£7,900,000	£7,900,000
Draw-down from the Civil List reserve	£6,500,000	£5,600,000
Net Receipts	£14,400,000	£13,500,000
Net Civil List Expenditure	(£14,200,000)	(£13,700,000)

PARLIAMENTARY ANNUITIES

The Civil List Acts provide for other members of the royal family to receive parliamentary annuities from government funds to meet the expenses of carrying out their official duties. Since 1993 the Queen has reimbursed all the annuities except those paid to the late Queen Elizabeth the Queen Mother and the Duke of Edinburgh.

The Prince of Wales does not receive a parliamentary annuity. He derives his income from the revenues of the Duchy of Cornwall and these monies meet the official and private expenses of the Prince of Wales and his family (see Prince of Wales' Funding).

In 2000 the annual amounts payable to members of the royal family, excluding the Earl of Wessex, were reset at their 1990 levels for the next ten years. The Earl of

Wessex had his annuity increased by £45,000 to £141,000 on the occasion of his marriage in 1999.

The annual payments remain as follows until December 2011:

The Duke of Edinburgh	£359,000
The Duke of York	£249,000
The Earl of Wessex	£141,000
The Princess Royal	£228,000
The Duke and Duchess of Gloucester	£175,000
The Duke and Duchess of Kent	£236,000
Princess Alexandra	£225,000
Subtotal	£1,613,000
Refunded to the Treasury by the Queen	(£1,254,000)
TOTAL	£359,000

GRANTS-IN-AID

Grants-in-aid are provided to the royal household annually by the Department for Culture, Media and Sport for property services and communications and information, and by the Department for Transport for royal travel. Property services meets the cost of property maintenance, utilities, telephones and related services at the occupied royal palaces in England (*see* Royal Household section for a list of occupied palaces). Communications and Information meets the cost of these services in connection with official royal functions and engagements in England and Scotland. Royal travel meets the cost of official royal travel by air and rail.

GRANTS-IN-AID 2010–11:

	Grant-in-aid voted by parliament	Total net expenditure
Property Services	£14,600,000	£11,900,000
Communications and Information	£500,000	£500,000
Royal Travel	£7,000,000	£6,000,000

THE PRIVY PURSE AND THE DUCHY OF LANCASTER

The funds received by the privy purse pay for official expenses incurred by the Queen as head of state and for some of the Queen's private expenditure. The revenues of the Duchy of Lancaster are the principal source of income for the privy purse. The revenues of the Duchy were retained by George III in 1760 when the hereditary revenues were surrendered in exchange for the Civil List. The Duchy's affairs are the responsibility of the Duchy Council which reports to the Chancellor of the Duchy of Lancaster, who in turn is accountable directly to the sovereign rather than to parliament. However the chancellor does answer parliamentary questions on matters relating to the Duchy of Lancaster's responsibilities.

THE DUCHY OF LANCASTER, 1 Lancaster Place, London WC2E 7ED
E info@duchyoflancaster.co.uk
W www.duchyoflancaster.com
Chancellor of the Duchy of Lancaster, Rt. Hon. Lord Strathclyde, *apptd* 2010
Chair of the Council, Lord Shuttleworth
Clerk and Chief Executive, Paul Clarke, CVO, FRICS
Receiver-General, Sir Alan Reid, KCVO
Attorney-General, Robert Hildyard, QC

PERSONAL INCOME

The Queen's personal income derives mostly from investments, and is used to meet private expenditure.

EXPENDITURE MET BY GOVERNMENT DEPARTMENTS AND THE CROWN ESTATE 2010–11:

Administration of honours	£500,000
Equerries, orderlies and other personnel	£1,000,000
Maintenance of Holyroodhouse	£1,100,000
State visits to and by the Queen and liaison with the Diplomatic Corps	£100,000
Ceremonial occasions	£400,000
Maintenance of Home Park, Windsor Castle	£600,000
Other	£100,000
Total	£3,800,000

PRINCE OF WALES' FUNDING

The Duchy Estate was created in 1337 by Edward III for his son and heir Prince Edward (the Black Prince) who became the Duke of Cornwall. The Duchy's primary function is to provide an income from its assets for the Prince of Wales. Under a 1337 charter, confirmed by subsequent legislation, the Prince of Wales is not entitled to the proceeds or profit on the sale of Duchy assets but only to the annual income which is generated from these assets. The Duchy is responsible for the sustainable and commercial management of its properties, investment portfolio and approximately 54,090 hectares of land, based mostly in the south-west of England. The Prince of Wales has chosen to use a proportion of his income to meet the cost of his public and charitable work in addition to providing a private source of income. The Duchy also funds the public, charitable and private activities of the Duchess of Cornwall and princes William and Harry. Proceeds from the Duchy are voluntarily subject to income tax.

THE DUCHY OF CORNWALL, 10 Buckingham Gate, London SW1E 6LA
T 020-7834 7346 E London@duchyofcornwall.org
W www.duchyofcornwall.org
Lord Warden of the Stannaries, Sir Nicholas Bacon, Bt.
Receiver-General, James Leigh-Pemberton
Attorney-General, Jonathan Crow, QC
Secretary and Keeper of the Records, Bertie Ross

TAXATION

The sovereign is not legally liable to pay income tax or capital gains tax. After income tax was reintroduced in 1842, some income tax was paid voluntarily by the sovereign but over a long period these payments were phased out. In 1992 the Queen offered to pay income and capital gains tax on a voluntary basis from 6 April 1993, and the Prince of Wales offered to pay tax on a voluntary basis on his income from the Duchy of Cornwall (he was already taxed in all other respects).

The main provisions for the Queen and the Prince of Wales to pay tax, set out in a Memorandum of Understanding on Royal Taxation presented to parliament on 11 February 1993, are that the Queen will pay income tax and capital gains tax in respect of her private income and assets, and on the proportion of the income and capital gains of the Privy Purse used for private purposes. Inheritance tax will be paid on the Queen's assets, except for those which pass to the next sovereign, whether automatically or by gift or bequest. The Prince of Wales will pay income tax on income from the Duchy of Cornwall used for private purposes.

The Prince of Wales has confirmed that he intends to pay tax on the same basis following his accession to the throne. Other members of the royal family are subject to tax as for any taxpayer.

MILITARY RANKS AND TITLES

THE QUEEN

ARMY
Colonel-in-Chief
The Life Guards; The Blues and Royals (Royal Horse Guards and 1st Dragoons); The Royal Scots Dragoon Guards (Carabiniers and Greys); The Queen's Royal Lancers; Royal Tank Regiment; Corps of Royal Engineers; Grenadier Guards; Coldstream Guards; Scots Guards; Irish Guards; Welsh Guards; The Royal Regiment of Scotland; The Duke of Lancaster's Regiment (King's, Lancashire and Border); The Royal Welsh; Adjutant General's Corps; The Royal Mercian and Lancastrian Yeomanry; The Governor General's Horse Guards (of Canada); The King's Own Calgary Regiment (Royal Canadian Armoured Corps); Canadian Military Engineers Branch; Royal 22e Regiment (of Canada); Governor General's Foot Guards (of Canada); The Canadian Grenadier Guards; Le Régiment de la Chaudière (of Canada); 2nd Battalion Royal New Brunswick Regiment (North Shore); 48th Highlanders of Canada; The Argyll and Sutherland Highlanders of Canada (Princess Louise's); The Calgary Highlanders; Royal Australian Engineers; Royal Australian Infantry Corps; Royal Australian Army Ordnance Corps; Royal Australian Army Nursing Corps; The Corps of Royal New Zealand Engineers; Royal New Zealand Infantry Regiment; The Malawi Rifles; The Royal Malta Artillery

Affiliated Colonel-in-Chief
The Queen's Gurkha Engineers

Captain-General
Royal Regiment of Artillery; The Honourable Artillery Company; Combined Cadet Force; Royal Regiment of Canadian Artillery; Royal Regiment of Australian Artillery; Royal Regiment of New Zealand Artillery; Royal New Zealand Armoured Corps

Royal Colonel
The Argyll and Sutherland Highlanders, 5th Battalion The Royal Regiment of Scotland

Patron
Royal Army Chaplains' Department

ROYAL AIR FORCE
Air Commodore-in-Chief
Royal Auxiliary Air Force; Royal Air Force Regiment; Air Reserve of Canada; Royal Australian Air Force Reserve; Territorial Air Force (of New Zealand)

Commandant-in-Chief
RAF College, Cranwell

Royal Honorary Air Commodore
RAF Marham; 603 (City of Edinburgh) Squadron Royal Auxiliary Air Force

PRINCE PHILIP, DUKE OF EDINBURGH

ROYAL NAVY
Lord High Admiral of the United Kingdom

Admiral of the Fleet
Admiral of the Fleet, Royal Australian Navy
Admiral of the Fleet, Royal New Zealand Navy
Admiral of the Royal Canadian Sea Cadets

ROYAL MARINES
Captain-General

ARMY
Field Marshal
Field Marshal, Australian Military Forces
Field Marshal, New Zealand Army
Colonel-in-Chief
The Queen's Royal Hussars (Queen's Own and Royal Irish); The Rifles; Corps of Royal Electrical and Mechanical Engineers; Intelligence Corps; Army Cadet Force Association; The Royal Canadian Regiment; The Royal Hamilton Light Infantry (Wentworth Regiment of Canada); The Cameron Highlanders of Ottawa; The Queen's Own Cameron Highlanders of Canada; The Seaforth Highlanders of Canada; The Royal Canadian Army Cadets; The Royal Australian Corps of Electrical and Mechanical Engineers; The Australian Army Cadet Corps

Colonel
Grenadier Guards

Royal Colonel
The Highlanders, 4th Battalion The Royal Regiment of Scotland

Honorary Colonel
City of Edinburgh University Officers' Training Corps; The Trinidad and Tobago Regiment

Member
Honourable Artillery Company

ROYAL AIR FORCE
Marshal of the Royal Air Force
Marshal of the Royal Australian Air Force
Marshal of the Royal New Zealand Air Force
Air Commodore-in-Chief
Air Training Corps; Royal Canadian Air Cadets

THE PRINCE OF WALES

ROYAL NAVY
Admiral
Commodore-in-Chief
  Royal Naval Command Plymouth

ARMY
General
Colonel-in-Chief
  The Royal Dragoon Guards; The Parachute Regiment;
  The Royal Gurkha Rifles; Army Air Corps; The Royal
  Canadian Dragoons; Lord Strathcona's Horse (Royal
  Canadians); The Royal Regiment of Canada; Royal
  Winnipeg Rifles; Royal Australian Armoured Corps;
  The Royal Pacific Islands Regiment; 1st The Queen's
  Dragoon Guards; The Black Watch (Royal Highland
  Regiment) of Canada; The Toronto Scottish Regiment
  (Queen Elizabeth The Queen Mother's Own); The
  Mercian Regiment

Royal Colonel
  The Black Watch, 3rd Battalion The Royal Regiment of
  Scotland; 51st Highland, 7th Battalion The Royal
  Regiment of Scotland (Territorial Army)

Colonel
  The Welsh Guards

Royal Honorary Colonel
  The Queen's Own Yeomanry

ROYAL AIR FORCE
Air Chief Marshal
Honorary Air Commodore
  RAF Valley

Air Commodore-in-Chief
  Royal New Zealand Air Force

Colonel-in-Chief
  Air Reserve Canada

THE DUCHESS OF CORNWALL

ROYAL NAVY
Commodore-in-Chief
  Naval Medical Services; Royal Naval Chaplaincy
  Services

ARMY
Royal Colonel
  4th Battalion The Rifles

ROYAL AIR FORCE
Honorary AIr Commodore
  RAF Halton; RAF Leeming

THE DUKE OF CAMBRIDGE

ROYAL NAVY
Lieutenant
Commodore-in-Chief
  Scotland Command; Submarines Command

ARMY
Colonel
  Irish Guards

Captain
  The Blues and Royals (Royal Horse Guards and 1st
  Dragoons)

ROYAL AIR FORCE
Flight Lieutenant
Honorary Air Commandant
  RAF Coningsby

PRINCE HENRY OF WALES

ROYAL NAVY
Commodore-in-Chief
  Small Ships and Diving Command

ARMY
Lieutenant
  The Blues and Royals (Royal Horse Guards and 1st
  Dragoons)

ROYAL AIR FORCE
Honorary Air Commandant
  RAF Honington

THE DUKE OF YORK

ROYAL NAVY
Rear Admiral
Commodore-in-Chief
  Fleet Air Arm

Admiral of the Marine Society and Sea Cadets

ARMY
Colonel-in-Chief
  The Royal Irish Regiment (27th (Inniskilling), 83rd,
  87th and The Ulster Defence Regiment); 9th/12th
  Royal Lancers (The Prince of Wales's); The Royal
  Highland Fusiliers, 2nd Battalion The Royal Regiment
  of Scotland; The Yorkshire Regiment; Small Arms
  School Corps; The Queen's York Rangers (First
  Americans); Royal New Zealand Army Logistics
  Regiment; The Royal Highland Fusiliers of Canada;
  The Princess Louise Fusiliers (Canada)

ROYAL AIR FORCE
Honorary Air Commodore
  RAF Lossiemouth

THE EARL OF WESSEX

ROYAL NAVY
Commodore-in-Chief
  Royal Fleet Auxiliary

Patron
  Royal Fleet Auxiliary Association

ARMY
Colonel-in-Chief
  Hastings and Prince Edward Regiment; Saskatchewan
  Dragoons

Royal Colonel
  2nd Battalion, The Rifles

Royal Honorary Colonel
  Royal Wessex Yeomanry

ROYAL AIR FORCE
Honorary Air Commodore
  RAF Waddington

THE COUNTESS OF WESSEX
ARMY
Colonel-in-Chief
Queen Alexandra's Royal Army Nursing Corps; The Lincoln and Welland Regiment; South Alberta Light Horse Regiment

Royal Colonel
5th Battalion, The Rifles

ROYAL AIR FORCE
Honorary Air Commodore
RAF Wittering

THE PRINCESS ROYAL
ROYAL NAVY
Vice-Admiral
(Chief Commandant for Women in the Royal Navy)

Commodore-in-Chief
HM Naval Base Portsmouth

ARMY
Colonel-in-Chief
The King's Royal Hussars; Royal Corps of Signals; Royal Logistic Corps; The Royal Army Veterinary Corps; 8th Canadian Hussars (Princess Louise's); Royal Newfoundland Regiment; Canadian Forces Communications and Electronics Branch; The Grey and Simcoe Foresters (Royal Canadian Armoured Corps); The Royal Regina Rifle Regiment; Canadian Forces Medical Branch; Royal Australian Corps of Signals; Royal New Zealand Corps of Signals; Royal New Zealand Nursing Corps

Affiliated Colonel-in-Chief
The Queen's Gurkha Signals; The Queen's Own Gurkha Transport Regiment

Royal Colonel
1st Battalion The Royal Regiment of Scotland; 52nd Lowland, 6th Battalion The Royal Regiment of Scotland

Colonel
The Blues and Royals (Royal Horse Guards and 1st Dragoons)

Honorary Colonel
University of London Officers' Training Corps

Commandant-in-Chief
First Aid Nursing Yeomanry (Princess Royal's Volunteer Corps)

ROYAL AIR FORCE
Honorary Air Commodore
RAF Lyneham; University of London Air Squadron

THE DUKE OF GLOUCESTER
ARMY
Colonel-in-Chief
The Royal Anglian Regiment; Royal Army Medical Corps; Royal New Zealand Army Medical Corps

Deputy Colonel-in-Chief
The Royal Logistic Corps

Royal Colonel
6th Battalion, The Rifles

Honorary Royal Colonel
Royal Monmouthshire Royal Engineers (Militia)

ROYAL AIR FORCE
Honorary Air Marshal
Honorary Air Commodore
RAF Odiham; No. 501 (County of Gloucester) Squadron Royal Auxiliary Air Force

THE DUCHESS OF GLOUCESTER
ARMY
Colonel-in-Chief
Royal Army Dental Corps; Royal Australian Army Educational Corps; Royal New Zealand Army Educational Corps; Canadian Forces Dental Services

Deputy Colonel-in-Chief
Adjutant-General's Corps

Royal Colonel
7th Battalion, The Rifles

Vice-Patron
Adjutant General's Corps Regimental Association

Patron
Royal Army Educational Corps Association; Army Families Federation

THE DUKE OF KENT
ARMY
Field Marshal

Colonel-in-Chief
The Royal Regiment of Fusiliers; Lorne Scots (Peel, Dufferin and Hamilton Regiment)

Deputy Colonel-in-Chief
The Royal Scots Dragoon Guards (Carabiniers and Greys)

Royal Colonel
1st Battalion The Rifles

Colonel
Scots Guards

ROYAL AIR FORCE
Honorary Air Chief Marshal
Honorary Air Commodore
RAF Leuchars

THE DUCHESS OF KENT
ARMY
Deputy Colonel-in-Chief
The Royal Dragoon Guards; Adjutant-General's Corps; The Royal Logistic Corps

PRINCE MICHAEL OF KENT

ROYAL NAVY
Honorary Rear Admiral Royal Naval Reserve

ARMY
Colonel-in-Chief
  Essex and Kent Scottish Regiment (Ontario)

Regimental Colonel
  Honourable Artillery Company

Major (retired)
  King's Royal Hussars

ROYAL AIR FORCE
Honorary Air Commodore
  RAF Benson

PRINCESS ALEXANDRA, THE HON. LADY OGILVY

ROYAL NAVY
Patron
  Queen Alexandra's Royal Naval Nursing Service

ARMY
Colonel-in-Chief
  The Canadian Scottish Regiment (Princess Mary's)

Deputy Colonel-in-Chief
  The Queen's Royal Lancers

Royal Colonel
  3rd Battalion The Rifles

Royal Honorary Colonel
  The Royal Yeomanry

ROYAL AIR FORCE
Patron and Air Chief Commandant
  Princess Mary's RAF Nursing Service

Honorary Air Commodore
  RAF Cottesmore

KINGS AND QUEENS

ENGLISH KINGS AND QUEENS 927 TO 1603

HOUSES OF CERDIC AND DENMARK
Reign

927–939 ÆTHELSTAN
Son of Edward the Elder, by Ecgwynn, and grandson of Alfred
Acceded to Wessex and Mercia *c.*924, established direct rule over Northumbria 927, effectively creating the Kingdom of England
Reigned 15 years

939–946 EDMUND I
Born 921, son of Edward the Elder, by Eadgifu
Married (1) Ælfgifu (2) Æthelflæd
Killed aged 25, *reigned* 6 years

946–955 EADRED
Son of Edward the Elder, by Eadgifu
Reigned 9 years

955–959 EADWIG
Born before 943, son of Edmund and Ælfgifu
Married Ælfgifu
Reigned 3 years

959–975 EDGAR I
Born 943, son of Edmund and Ælfgifu
Married (1) Æthelflæd (2) Wulfthryth (3) Ælfthryth
Died aged 32, *reigned* 15 years

975–978 EDWARD I (the Martyr)
*Born c.*962, son of Edgar and Æthelflæd
Assassinated aged *c.*16, *reigned* 2 years

978–1016 ÆTHELRED (the Unready)
Born 968/969, son of Edgar and Ælfthryth
Married (1) Ælfgifu (2) Emma, daughter of Richard I, Count of Normandy
1013–14 dispossessed of kingdom by Swegn Forkbeard (King of Denmark 987–1014)
Died aged *c.*47, *reigned* 38 years

1016 EDMUND II (Ironside)
(Apr–Nov) *Born* before 993, son of Æthelred and Ælfgifu
Married Ealdgyth
Died aged over 23, *reigned* 7 months

1016–1035 CNUT (Canute)
*Born c.*995, son of Swegn Forkbeard, King of Denmark, and Gunhild
Married (1) Ælfgifu (2) Emma, widow of Æthelred the Unready
Gained submission of West Saxons 1015, Northumbrians 1016, Mercia 1016, King of all England after Edmund's death, King of Denmark 1019–35, King of Norway 1028–35
Died aged *c.*40, *reigned* 19 years

1035–1040 HAROLD I (Harefoot)
Born 1016/17, son of Cnut and Ælfgifu
Married Ælfgifu
1035 recognised as regent for himself and his brother Harthacnut; 1037 recognised as king
Died aged *c.*23, *reigned* 4 years

1040–1042 HARTHACNUT (Harthacanute)
*Born c.*1018, son of Cnut and Emma
Titular king of Denmark from 1028
Acknowledged King of England 1035–7 with Harold I as regent; effective king after Harold's death
Died aged *c.*24, *reigned* 2 years

1042–1066 EDWARD II (the Confessor)
Born between 1002 and 1005, son of Æthelred the Unready and Emma
Married Eadgyth, daughter of Godwine, Earl of Wessex
Died aged over 60, *reigned* 23 years

1066 HAROLD II (Godwinesson)
(Jan–Oct) *Born c.*1020, son of Godwine, Earl of Wessex, and Gytha
Married (1) Eadgyth (2) Ealdgyth
Killed in battle aged *c.*46, *reigned* 10 months

THE HOUSE OF NORMANDY

1066–1087 WILLIAM I (the Conqueror)
Born 1027/8, son of Robert I, Duke of Normandy; obtained the Crown by conquest
Married Matilda, daughter of Baldwin, Count of Flanders
Died aged *c.*60, *reigned* 20 years

1087–1100 WILLIAM II (Rufus)
Born between 1056 and 1060, third son of William I; succeeded his father in England only
Killed aged *c.*40, *reigned* 12 years

1100–1135 HENRY I (Beauclerk)
Born 1068, fourth son of William I
Married (1) Edith or Matilda, daughter of Malcolm III of Scotland (2) Adela, daughter of Godfrey, Count of Louvain
Died aged 67, *reigned* 35 years

1135–1154 STEPHEN
Born not later than 1100, third son of Adela, daughter of William I, and Stephen, Count of Blois
Married Matilda, daughter of Eustace, Count of Boulogne
1141 (Feb–Nov) held captive by adherents of Matilda, daughter of Henry I, who contested the crown until 1153
Died aged over 53, *reigned* 18 years

THE HOUSE OF ANJOU (PLANTAGENETS)

1154–1189 HENRY II (Curtmantle)
Born 1133, son of Matilda, daughter of Henry I, and Geoffrey, Count of Anjou
Married Eleanor, daughter of William, Duke of Aquitaine, and divorced queen of Louis VII of France
Died aged 56, *reigned* 34 years

1189–1199 RICHARD I (Coeur de Lion)
Born 1157, third son of Henry II
Married Berengaria, daughter of Sancho VI, King of Navarre
Died aged 42, *reigned* 9 years

1199–1216   JOHN (Lackland)
Born 1167, fifth son of Henry II
Married (1) Isabella or Avisa, daughter of
William, Earl of Gloucester (divorced)
(2) Isabella, daughter of Aymer, Count of
Angoulême
Died aged 48, *reigned* 17 years

1216–1272   HENRY III
Born 1207, son of John and Isabella of
Angoulême
Married Eleanor, daughter of Raymond,
Count of Provence
Died aged 65, *reigned* 56 years

1272–1307   EDWARD I (Longshanks)
Born 1239, eldest son of Henry III
Married (1) Eleanor, daughter of Ferdinand
III, King of Castile (2) Margaret, daughter
of Philip III of France
Died aged 68, *reigned* 34 years

1307–1327   EDWARD II
Born 1284, eldest surviving son of Edward I
and Eleanor
Married Isabella, daughter of Philip IV of
France
Deposed Jan 1327, *killed* Sep 1327 aged 43,
reigned 19 years

1327–1377   EDWARD III
Born 1312, eldest son of Edward II
Married Philippa, daughter of William,
Count of Hainault
Died aged 64, *reigned* 50 years

1377–1399   RICHARD II
Born 1367, son of Edward (the Black
Prince), eldest son of Edward III
Married (1) Anne, daughter of Emperor
Charles IV (2) Isabelle, daughter of Charles
VI of France
Deposed Sep 1399, *killed* Feb 1400 aged 33,
reigned 22 years

THE HOUSE OF LANCASTER
1399–1413   HENRY IV
Born 1366, son of John of Gaunt, fourth son
of Edward III, and Blanche, daughter of
Henry, Duke of Lancaster
Married (1) Mary, daughter of Humphrey,
Earl of Hereford (2) Joan, daughter of
Charles, King of Navarre, and widow of
John, Duke of Brittany
Died aged c.47, *reigned* 13 years

1413–1422   HENRY V
Born 1387, eldest surviving son of Henry
IV and Mary
Married Catherine, daughter of Charles VI
of France
Died aged 34, *reigned* 9 years

1422–1471   HENRY VI
Born 1421, son of Henry V
Married Margaret, daughter of René, Duke
of Anjou and Count of Provence
Deposed Mar 1461, *restored* Oct 1470
Deposed Apr 1471, *killed* May 1471 aged
49, *reigned* 39 years

THE HOUSE OF YORK
1461–1483   EDWARD IV
Born 1442, eldest son of Richard of York
(grandson of Edmund, fifth son of
Edward III; and son of Anne,
great-granddaughter of Lionel, third son
of Edward III)
Married Elizabeth Woodville, daughter
of Richard, Lord Rivers, and widow of
Sir John Grey
Acceded Mar 1461, *deposed* Oct 1470,
restored Apr 1471
Died aged 40, *reigned* 21 years

1483   EDWARD V
(Apr–Jun)   *Born* 1470, eldest son of Edward IV
Deposed Jun 1483, *died* probably Jul–Sep
1483, aged 12, *reigned* 2 months

1483–1485   RICHARD III
Born 1452, fourth son of Richard of York
Married Anne Neville, daughter of
Richard, Earl of Warwick, and widow
of Edward, Prince of Wales, son of
Henry VI
Killed in battle aged 32, *reigned* 2 years

THE HOUSE OF TUDOR
1485–1509   HENRY VII
Born 1457, son of Margaret Beaufort
(great-granddaughter of John of Gaunt,
fourth son of Edward III) and Edmund
Tudor, Earl of Richmond
Married Elizabeth, daughter of Edward IV
Died aged 52, *reigned* 23 years

1509–1547   HENRY VIII
Born 1491, second son of Henry VII
Married (1) Catherine, daughter of
Ferdinand II, King of Aragon, and widow of
his elder brother Arthur (divorced) (2) Anne,
daughter of Sir Thomas Boleyn (executed)
(3) Jane, daughter of Sir John Seymour
(died in childbirth) (4) Anne, daughter of
John, Duke of Cleves (divorced)
(5) Catherine Howard, niece of the Duke of
Norfolk (executed) (6) Catherine, daughter
of Sir Thomas Parr and widow of Lord
Latimer
Died aged 55, *reigned* 37 years

1547–1553   EDWARD VI
Born 1537, son of Henry VIII and Jane
Seymour
Died aged 15, *reigned* 6 years

1553   JANE
*(6/10–19 Jul)   *Born* 1537, daughter of Frances (daughter
of Mary Tudor, the younger daughter of
Henry VII) and Henry Grey, Duke of
Suffolk
Married Lord Guildford Dudley, son of the
Duke of Northumberland
Deposed Jul 1553, *executed* Feb 1554
aged 16, *reigned* 13/9 days

1553–1558   MARY I
Born 1516, daughter of Henry VIII and
Catherine of Aragon
Married Philip II of Spain
Died aged 42, *reigned* 5 years

1558–1603   ELIZABETH I
Born 1533, daughter of Henry VIII and
Anne Boleyn
Died aged 69, *reigned* 44 years

* Depending on whether the date of her predecessor's death
(6 July) or that of her official proclamation as Queen (10 July) is
taken as the beginning of her reign.

BRITISH KINGS AND QUEENS SINCE 1603

THE HOUSE OF STUART

Reign

1603–1625   JAMES I (VI OF SCOTLAND)
Born 1566, son of Mary, Queen of Scots (granddaughter of Margaret Tudor, elder daughter of Henry VII), and Henry Stewart, Lord Darnley
Married Anne, daughter of Frederick II of Denmark
Died aged 58, *reigned* 22 years

1625–1649   CHARLES I
Born 1600, second son of James I
Married Henrietta Maria, daughter of Henry IV of France
Executed 1649 aged 48, *reigned* 23 years

INTERREGNUM 1649–1660
1649–1653   Government by a council of state
1653–1658   Oliver Cromwell, Lord Protector
1658–1659   Richard Cromwell, Lord Protector

Reign

1660–1685   CHARLES II
Born 1630, eldest son of Charles I
Married Catherine, daughter of John IV of Portugal
Died aged 54, *reigned* 24 years

1685–1688   JAMES II (VII OF SCOTLAND)
Born 1633, second son of Charles I
Married (1) Lady Anne Hyde, daughter of Edward, Earl of Clarendon (2) Mary, daughter of Alphonso, Duke of Modena
Reign ended with flight from kingdom Dec 1688
Died 1701 aged 67, *reigned* 3 years

INTERREGNUM
11 Dec 1688 to 12 Feb 1689

Reign

1689–1702   WILLIAM III
Born 1650, son of William II, Prince of Orange, and Mary Stuart, daughter of Charles I
Married Mary, elder daughter of James II
Died aged 51, *reigned* 13 years

and

1689–1694   MARY II
Born 1662, elder daughter of James II and Anne
Died aged 32, *reigned* 5 years

1702–1714   ANNE
Born 1665, younger daughter of James II and Anne
Married Prince George of Denmark, son of Frederick III of Denmark
Died aged 49, *reigned* 12 years

THE HOUSE OF HANOVER

1714–1727   GEORGE I (Elector of Hanover)
Born 1660, son of Sophia (daughter of Frederick, Elector Palatine, and Elizabeth Stuart, daughter of James I) and Ernest Augustus, Elector of Hanover
Married Sophia Dorothea, daughter of George William, Duke of Lüneburg-Celle
Died aged 67, *reigned* 12 years

1727–1760   GEORGE II
Born 1683, son of George I
Married Caroline, daughter of John Frederick, Margrave of Brandenburg-Anspach
Died aged 76, *reigned* 33 years

1760–1820   GEORGE III
Born 1738, son of Frederick, eldest son of George II
Married Charlotte, daughter of Charles Louis, Duke of Mecklenburg-Strelitz
Died aged 81, *reigned* 59 years

REGENCY 1811–1820
Prince of Wales regent owing to the insanity of George III

Reign

1820–1830   GEORGE IV
Born 1762, eldest son of George III
Married Caroline, daughter of Charles, Duke of Brunswick-Wolfenbüttel
Died aged 67, *reigned* 10 years

1830–1837   WILLIAM IV
Born 1765, third son of George III
Married Adelaide, daughter of George, Duke of Saxe-Meiningen
Died aged 71, *reigned* 7 years

1837–1901   VICTORIA
Born 1819, daughter of Edward, fourth son of George III
Married Prince Albert of Saxe-Coburg and Gotha
Died aged 81, *reigned* 63 years

THE HOUSE OF SAXE-COBURG AND GOTHA

1901–1910   EDWARD VII
Born 1841, eldest son of Victoria and Albert
Married Alexandra, daughter of Christian IX of Denmark
Died aged 68, *reigned* 9 years

THE HOUSE OF WINDSOR

1910–1936   GEORGE V
Born 1865, second son of Edward VII
Married Victoria Mary, daughter of Francis, Duke of Teck
Died aged 70, *reigned* 25 years

1936   EDWARD VIII
(20 Jan–
11 Dec)   *Born* 1894, eldest son of George V
Married (1937) Mrs Wallis Simpson
Abdicated 1936, *died* 1972 aged 77, *reigned* 10 months

1936–1952   GEORGE VI
Born 1895, second son of George V
Married Lady Elizabeth Bowes-Lyon, daughter of 14th Earl of Strathmore and Kinghorne
Died aged 56, *reigned* 15 years

1952–   ELIZABETH II
Born 1926, elder daughter of George VI
Married Philip, son of Prince Andrew of Greece

KINGS AND QUEENS OF SCOTS 1016 TO 1603

Reign

1016–1034   MALCOLM II
Born c.954, son of Kenneth II
Acceded to Alba 1005, secured Lothian
c.1016, obtained Strathclyde for his
grandson Duncan c.1016, thus reigning
over an area approximately the same as that
governed by later rulers of Scotland
Died aged *c.80, reigned* 18 years

THE HOUSE OF ATHOLL

1034–1040   DUNCAN I
Son of Bethoc, daughter of Malcolm II,
and Crinan, Mormaer of Atholl
Married a cousin of Siward, Earl of
Northumbria
Reigned 5 years

1040–1057   MACBETH
Born c.1005, son of a daughter of
Malcolm II and Finlaec, Mormaer of Moray
Married Gruoch, granddaughter of
Kenneth III
Killed aged *c.52, reigned* 17 years

1057–1058   LULACH
(Aug–Mar)   *Born c.1032*, son of Gillacomgan, Mormaer
of Moray, and Gruoch (and stepson of
Macbeth)
Died aged *c.26, reigned* 7 months

1058–1093   MALCOLM III (Canmore)
Born c.1031, elder son of Duncan I
Married (1) Ingibiorg (2) Margaret
(St Margaret), granddaughter of Edmund II
of England
Killed in battle aged *c.62, reigned* 35 years

1093–1097   DONALD III BÁN
Born c.1033, second son of Duncan I
Deposed May 1094, *restored* Nov
1094, *deposed* Oct 1097, *reigned* 3 years

1094   DUNCAN II
(May–Nov)   *Born c.1060*, elder son of Malcolm III and
Ingibiorg
Married Octreda of Dunbar
Killed aged *c.34, reigned* 6 months

1097–1107   EDGAR
Born c.1074, second son of Malcolm III and
Margaret
Died aged *c.32, reigned* 9 years

1107–1124   ALEXANDER I (the Fierce)
Born c.1077, fifth son of Malcolm III and
Margaret
Married Sybilla, illegitimate daughter of
Henry I of England
Died aged *c.47, reigned* 17 years

1124–1153   DAVID I (the Saint)
Born c.1085, sixth son of Malcolm III and
Margaret
Married Matilda, daughter of Waltheof, Earl
of Huntingdon
Died aged *c.68, reigned* 29 years

1153–1165   MALCOLM IV (the Maiden)
Born c.1141, son of Henry, Earl of
Huntingdon, second son of David I
Died aged *c.24, reigned* 12 years

1165–1214   WILLIAM I (the Lion)
Born c.1142, brother of Malcolm IV
Married Ermengarde, daughter of Richard,
Viscount of Beaumont
Died aged *c.72, reigned* 49 years

1214–1249   ALEXANDER II
Born 1198, son of William I
Married (1) Joan, daughter of John, King of
England (2) Marie, daughter of Ingelram de
Coucy
Died aged 50, *reigned* 34 years

1249–1286   ALEXANDER III
Born 1241, son of Alexander II and Marie
Married (1) Margaret, daughter of Henry III
of England (2) Yolande, daughter of the
Count of Dreux
Killed accidentally aged 44, *reigned* 36 years

1286–1290   MARGARET (the Maid of Norway)
Born 1283, daughter of Margaret (daughter
of Alexander III) and Eric II of Norway
Died aged 7, *reigned* 4 years

FIRST INTERREGNUM 1290–1292

Throne disputed by 13 competitors. Crown awarded to
John Balliol by adjudication of Edward I of England

THE HOUSE OF BALLIOL

Reign

1292–1296   JOHN (Balliol)
Born c.1250, son of Dervorguilla,
great-great-granddaughter of David I, and
John de Balliol
Married Isabella, daughter of John, Earl of
Surrey
Abdicated 1296, *died* 1313 aged *c.63*,
reigned 3 years

SECOND INTERREGNUM 1296–1306

Edward I of England declared John Balliol to have
forfeited the throne for contumacy in 1296 and took the
government of Scotland into his own hands

THE HOUSE OF BRUCE

Reign

1306–1329   ROBERT I (Bruce)
Born 1274, son of Robert Bruce and
Marjorie, countess of Carrick, and
great-grandson of the second daughter of
David, Earl of Huntingdon, brother of
William I
Married (1) Isabella, daughter of Donald,
Earl of Mar (2) Elizabeth, daughter of
Richard, Earl of Ulster
Died aged 54, *reigned* 23 years

1329–1371   DAVID II
Born 1324, son of Robert I and Elizabeth
Married (1) Joanna, daughter of Edward II
of England (2) Margaret Drummond,
widow of Sir John Logie (divorced)
Died aged 46, *reigned* 41 years

1332 (Sep–   Edward Balliol, son of John
Dec)   Balliol

1333–1336   Edward Balliol

THE HOUSE OF STEWART

1371–1390   ROBERT II (Stewart)
Born 1316, son of Marjorie (daughter of
Robert I) and Walter, High Steward of
Scotland
Married (1) Elizabeth, daughter of
Sir Robert Mure of Rowallan
(2) Euphemia, daughter of Hugh,
Earl of Ross
Died aged 74, *reigned* 19 years

1390–1406   ROBERT III
Born c.1337, son of Robert II and
Elizabeth

	Married Annabella, daughter of Sir John Drummond of Stobhall
	Died aged c.69, reigned 16 years
1406–1437	JAMES I
	Born 1394, son of Robert III
	Married Joan Beaufort, daughter of John, Earl of Somerset
	Assassinated aged 42, reigned 30 years
1437–1460	JAMES II
	Born 1430, son of James I
	Married Mary, daughter of Arnold, Duke of Gueldres
	Killed accidentally aged 29, reigned 23 years
1460–1488	JAMES III
	Born 1452, son of James II
	Married Margaret, daughter of Christian I of Denmark
	Assassinated aged 36, reigned 27 years
1488–1513	JAMES IV
	Born 1473, son of James III
	Married Margaret Tudor, daughter of Henry VII of England
	Killed in battle aged 40, reigned 25 years
1513–1542	JAMES V
	Born 1512, son of James IV
	Married (1) Madeleine, daughter of Francis I of France (2) Mary of Lorraine, daughter of the Duc de Guise
	Died aged 30, reigned 29 years
1542–1567	MARY
	Born 1542, daughter of James V and Mary
	Married (1) the Dauphin, afterwards Francis II of France (2) Henry Stewart, Lord Darnley (3) James Hepburn, Earl of Bothwell
	Abdicated 1567, prisoner in England from 1568, executed 1587, reigned 24 years
1567–1625	JAMES VI (and I of England)
	Born 1566, son of Mary, Queen of Scots, and Henry, Lord Darnley
	Acceded 1567 to the Scottish throne, reigned 58 years
	Succeeded 1603 to the English throne, so joining the English and Scottish crowns in one person. The two kingdoms remained distinct until 1707 when the parliaments of the kingdoms became conjoined

WELSH SOVEREIGNS AND PRINCES

Wales was ruled by sovereign princes from the earliest times until the death of Llywelyn in 1282. The first English Prince of Wales was the son of Edward I, who was born in Caernarvon town on 25 April 1284. According to a discredited legend, he was presented to the Welsh chieftains as their prince, in fulfilment of a promise that they should have a prince who 'could not speak a word of English' and should be native born. This son, who afterwards became Edward II, was created 'Prince of Wales and Earl of Chester' at the Lincoln Parliament on 7 February 1301.

The title Prince of Wales is borne after individual conferment and is not inherited at birth, though some Princes have been declared and styled Prince of Wales but never formally so created (s.). The title was conferred on Prince Charles by the Queen on 26 July 1958. He was invested at Caernarvon on 1 July 1969.

INDEPENDENT PRINCES AD 844 TO 1282

844–878	Rhodri the Great
878–916	Anarawd, son of Rhodri
916–950	Hywel Dda, the Good
950–979	Iago ab Idwal (or Ieuaf)
979–985	Hywel ab Ieuaf, the Bad
985–986	Cadwallon, his brother
986–999	Maredudd ab Owain ap Hywel Dda
999–1008	Cynan ap Hywel ab Ieuaf
1018–1023	Llywelyn ap Seisyll
1023–1039	Iago ab Idwal ap Meurig
1039–1063	Gruffydd ap Llywelyn ap Seisyll
1063–1075	Bleddyn ap Cynfyn
1075–1081	Trahaern ap Caradog
1081–1137	Gruffydd ap Cynan ab Iago
1137–1170	Owain Gwynedd
1170–1194	Dafydd ab Owain Gwynedd
1194–1240	Llywelyn Fawr, the Great
1240–1246	Dafydd ap Llywelyn
1246–1282	Llywelyn ap Gruffydd ap Llywelyn

ENGLISH PRINCES SINCE 1301

1301	Edward (Edward II)
1343	Edward the Black Prince, son of Edward III
1376	Richard (Richard II), son of the Black Prince
1399	Henry of Monmouth (Henry V)
1454	Edward of Westminster, son of Henry VI
1471	Edward of Westminster (Edward V)
1483	Edward, son of Richard III (d. 1484)
1489	Arthur Tudor, son of Henry VII
1504	Henry Tudor (Henry VIII)
1610	Henry Stuart, son of James I (d. 1612)
1616	Charles Stuart (Charles I)
c.1638 (s.)	Charles Stuart (Charles II)
1688 (s.)	James Francis Edward Stuart (The Old Pretender), son of James II (d. 1766)
1714	George Augustus (George II)
1729	Frederick Lewis, son of George II (d. 1751)
1751	George William Frederick (George III)
1762	George Augustus Frederick (George IV)
1841	Albert Edward (Edward VII)
1901	George (George V)
1910	Edward (Edward VIII)
1958	Charles, son of Elizabeth II

PRINCESSES ROYAL

The style Princess Royal is conferred at the sovereign's discretion on his or her eldest daughter. It is an honorary title, held for life, and cannot be inherited or passed on. It was first conferred on Princess Mary, daughter of Charles I, in approximately 1642.

c.1642	Princess Mary (1631–60), daughter of Charles I
1727	Princess Anne (1709–59), daughter of George II
1766	Princess Charlotte (1766–1828), daughter of George III
1840	Princess Victoria (1840–1901), daughter of Victoria
1905	Princess Louise (1867–1931), daughter of Edward VII
1932	Princess Mary (1897–1965), daughter of George V
1987	Princess Anne (b. 1950), daughter of Elizabeth II

DESCENDANTS OF QUEEN VICTORIA

I. HRH Princess Victoria Adelaide Mary Louisa, Princess Royal (1840–1901) *m* Friedrich III (1831–88), later German Emperor

II. HRH Prince Albert Edward (HM KING EDWARD VII) (1841–1910) *succeeded* 22 Jan 1901 *m* HRH Princess Alexandra of Denmark (1844–1925)

III. HRH Princess Alice Maud Mary (1843–78) *m* Prince Ludwig (1837–92), later Grand Duke of Hesse

IV. HRH Prince Alfred Ernest Albert, Duke of Edinburgh (1844–1900) *succeeded* as Duke of Saxe-Coburg and Gotha 1893 *m* Grand Duchess Marie Alexandrovna of Russia (1853–1920)

1. HIM Wilhelm II (1859–1941), later German Emperor *m* (1) Princess Augusta Victoria of Schleswig-Holstein-Sonderburg-Augustenburg (1858–1921) (2) Princess Hermine of Reuss (1887–1947). *Issue* Wilhelm (1882–1951); Eitel-Friedrich (1883–1942); Adalbert (1884–1948); August Wilhelm (1887–1949); Oskar (1888–1958); Joachim (1890–1920); Viktoria Luise (1892–1980)

2. Charlotte (1860–1919) *m* Bernhard, Duke of Saxe-Meiningen (1851–1928). *Issue* Feodora (1879–1945)

1. Albert Victor, Duke of Clarence and Avondale (1864–92)

2. George (HM KING GEORGE V) (1865–1936) (*see* House of Windsor)

3. Louise (1867–1931), later Princess Royal *m* 1st Duke of Fife (1849–1912). *Issue* Alexandra (1891–1959); Maud (1893–1945)

4. Victoria (1868–1935)

5. Maud (1869–1938) *m* Prince Carl of Denmark (1872–1957), later King Haakon VII of Norway. *Issue* Olav V (1903–91)

6. Alexander (6–7 Apr 1871)

1. Victoria (1863–1950) *m* Prince Louis of Battenberg (1854–1921), later 1st Marquess of Milford Haven. *Issue* Alice (1885–1969); Louise (1889–1965); George (1892–1938); Louis (1900–79)

2. Elizabeth (1864–1918) *m* Grand Duke Sergius of Russia (1857–1905)

3. Irene (1866–1953) *m* Prince Heinrich of Prussia (*see* I.3)

4. Ernst Ludwig (1868–1937), Grand Duke of Hesse, *m* (1) Princess Victoria Melita of Saxe-Coburg (see IV.3) (2) Princess Eleonore of Solms-Hohensolms-Lich (1871–1937). *Issue* Elizabeth (1895–1903); George (1906–37); Ludwig (1908–68)

5. Frederick William (1870–3)

6. Alix (Tsaritsa of Russia) (1872–1918) *m* Nicholas II, Tsar of All the Russias (1868–1918). *Issue* Olga (1895–1918); Tatiana (1897–1918); Marie (1899–1918); Anastasia (1901–18); Alexis (1904–18)

7. Marie (1874–8)

3. Heinrich (1862–1929) *m* Princess Irene of Hesse (*see* III.3). *Issue* Waldemar (1889–1945); Sigismund (1896–1978); Heinrich (1900–4)

4. Sigismund (1864–6)

5. Victoria (1866–1929) *m* (1) Prince Adolf of Schaumburg-Lippe (1859–1916) (2) Alexander Zubkov (1900–36)

6. Waldemar (1868–79)

7. Sophie (1870–1932) *m* Constantine I (1868–1923), later King of the Hellenes. *Issue* George II (1890–1947); Alexander I (1893–1920); Helena (1896–1982); Paul I (1901–64); Irene (1904–74); Katherine (1913–2007)

8. Margarethe (1872–1954) *m* Prince Friedrich Karl of Hesse (1868–1940). *Issue* Friedrich Wilhelm (1893–1916); Maximilian (1894–1914); Philipp (1896–1980); Wolfgang (1896–1989); Richard (1901–69); Christoph (1901–43)

QUEEN VICTORIA (Alexandrina Victoria) (1819–1901) *succeeded* 20 Jun 1837 *m* (Francis) Albert Augustus Charles Emmanuel, Duke of Saxony, Prince of Saxe-Coburg and Gotha (HRH Albert, Prince Consort) (1819–61)

VI. HRH Princess Louise Caroline Alberta (1848–1939) *m* Marquess of Lorne (1845–1914), later 9th Duke of Argyll

VII. HRH Prince Arthur William Patrick Albert, Duke of Connaught (1850–1942) *m* Princess Louisa of Prussia (1860–1917)

VIII. HRH Prince Leopold George Duncan Albert, Duke of Albany (1853–84) *m* Princess Helena of Waldeck (1861–1922)

IX. HRH Princess Beatrice Mary Victoria Feodore (1857–1944) *m* Prince Henry of Battenberg (1858–96)

1. Alfred, Prince of Saxe-Coburg (1874–99)

2. Marie (1875–1938) *m* Ferdinand (1865–1927), later King of Roumania. *Issue* Carol II (1893–1953); Elisabeth (1894–1956); Marie (1900–61); Nicolas (1903–78); Ileana (1909–91); Mircea (1913–16)

3. Victoria Melita (1876–1936) *m* (1) Grand Duke Ernst Ludwig of Hesse (*see* III.4) (2) Grand Duke Kirill of Russia (1876–1938). *Issue* Marie (1907–51); Kira (1909–67); Vladimir (1917–92)

4. Alexandra (1878–1942) *m* Ernst, Prince of Hohenlohe Langenburg (1863–1950). *Issue* Gottfried (1897–1960); Maria (1899–1967); Alexandra (1901–63); Irma (1902–86)

5. Beatrice (1884–1966) *m* Alfonso of Orleans, Infante of Spain (1886–1975). *Issue* Alvaro (1910–97); Alonso (1912–36); Ataulfo (1913–74)

1. Margaret (1882–1920) *m* Crown Prince Gustaf Adolf (1882–1973), later King of Sweden. *Issue* Gustaf Adolf (1906–47); Sigvard (1907–2002); Ingrid (1910–2000); Bertil (1912–97); Count Carl Bernadotte (*b* 1916)

2. Arthur (1883–1938) *m* HH Duchess of Fife (1891–1959). *Issue* Alastair Arthur (1914–43)

3. (Victoria) Patricia (1886–1974) *m* Adm. Hon. Sir Alexander Ramsay (1881–1972). *Issue* Alexander (1919–2000)

1. Alice (1883–1981) *m* Prince Alexander of Teck (1874–1957), later 1st Earl of Athlone. *Issue* May (1906–94); Rupert (1907–28); Maurice (Mar–Sep 1910)

2. Charles Edward (1884–1954), Duke of Albany until title suspended 1917, Duke of Saxe-Coburg-Gotha, *m* Princess Victoria Adelheid of Schleswig-Holstein-Sonderburg-Glücksburg (1885–1970). *Issue* Johann Leopold (1906–72); Sibylla (1908–72); Dietmar Hubertus (1909–43); Caroline (1912–83); Friedrich Josias (1918–98)

1. Alexander, 1st Marquess of Carisbrooke (1886–1960) *m* Lady Irene Denison (1890–1956). *Issue* Iris (1920–82)

2. Victoria Eugénie (1887–1969) *m* Alfonso XIII, King of Spain (1886–1941). *Issue* Alfonso (1907–38); Jaime (1908–75); Beatriz (1909–2002); Maria (1911–96); Juan (1913–93); Gonzalo (1914–34)

3. Maj. Lord Leopold Mountbatten (1889–1922)

4. Maurice (1891–1914)

V. HRH Princess Helena Augusta Victoria (1846–1923) *m* Prince Christian of Schleswig-Holstein-Sonderburg-Augustenburg (1831–1917)

1. Christian Victor (1867–1900)

2. Albert (1869–1931), later Duke of Schleswig-Holstein

3. Helena (1870–1948)

4. Marie Louise (1872–1956), *m* Prince Aribert of Anhalt (1864–1933)

5. Harold (12–20 May 1876)

THE HOUSE OF WINDSOR

King George V assumed by royal proclamation (17 July 1917) for his House and family, as well as for all descendants in the male line of Queen Victoria who are subjects of these realms, the name of Windsor.

KING GEORGE V

(George Frederick Ernest Albert), second son of King Edward VII *born* 3 June 1865 *married* 6 July 1893 HSH Princess Victoria Mary Augusta Louise Olga Pauline Claudine Agnes of Teck (Queen Mary *born* 26 May 1867 *died* 24 March 1953) *succeeded* to the throne 6 May 1910 *died* 20 January 1936. *Issue*

1. HRH PRINCE EDWARD Albert Christian George Andrew Patrick David *born* 23 June 1894 *succeeded* to the throne as King Edward VIII, 20 January 1936 *abdicated* 11 December 1936 *created* Duke of Windsor 1937 *married* 3 June 1937 Mrs Wallis Simpson (Her Grace The Duchess of Windsor *born* 19 June 1896 *died* 24 April 1986) *died* 28 May 1972

2. HRH PRINCE ALBERT Frederick Arthur George *born* 14 December 1895 *created* Duke of York 1920 *married* 26 April 1923 Lady Elizabeth Bowes-Lyon, youngest daughter of the 14th Earl of Strathmore and Kinghorne (HM Queen Elizabeth the Queen Mother *born* 4 August 1900 *died* 30 March 2002) *succeeded* to the throne as King George VI, 11 December 1936 *died* 6 February 1952. *Issue*
   (1) HRH Princess Elizabeth Alexandra Mary *succeeded* to the throne as Queen Elizabeth II, 6 February 1952 (*see* Royal Family)
   (2) HRH Princess Margaret Rose (later HRH The Princess Margaret, Countess of Snowdon) *born* 21 August 1930 *married* 6 May 1960 Anthony Charles Robert Armstrong-Jones, GCVO *created* Earl of Snowdon 1961 (marriage dissolved 1978) *died* 9 February 2002, having had issue (*see* Royal Family)

3. HRH PRINCESS (Victoria Alexandra Alice) MARY *born* 25 April 1897 *created* Princess Royal 1932 *married* 28 February 1922 Viscount Lascelles, later the 6th Earl

of Harewood (1882–1947) *died* 28 March 1965. *Issue*
   (1) George Henry Hubert Lascelles, 7th Earl of Harewood, KBE *born* 7 February 1923 *married* (1) 1949 Maria (Marion) Stein (marriage dissolved 1967) *issue (a)* David Henry George, Viscount Lascelles *born* 1950 *(b)* James Edward *born* 1953 *(c)* (Robert) Jeremy Hugh *born* 1955 (2) 1967 Patricia Tuckwell *issue (d)* Mark Hubert *born* 1964
   (2) Gerald David Lascelles (1924–98) *married* (1) 1952 Angela Dowding (marriage dissolved 1978) *issue (a)* Henry Ulick *born* 1953 (2) 1978 Elizabeth Collingwood (Elizabeth Colvin) *issue (b)* Martin David *born* 1962

4. HRH PRINCE HENRY William Frederick Albert *born* 31 March 1900 *created* Duke of Gloucester, Earl of Ulster and Baron Culloden 1928 *married* 6 November 1935 Lady Alice Christabel Montagu-Douglas-Scott, daughter of the 7th Duke of Buccleuch and Queensberry (HRH Princess Alice, Duchess of Gloucester *born* 25 December 1901 *died* 29 October 2004) *died* 10 June 1974. *Issue*
   (1) HRH Prince William Henry Andrew Frederick *born* 18 December 1941 accidentally *killed* 28 August 1972
   (2) HRH Prince Richard Alexander Walter George (HRH The Duke of Gloucester, *see* Royal Family)

5. HRH PRINCE GEORGE Edward Alexander Edmund *born* 20 December 1902 *created* Duke of Kent, Earl of St Andrews and Baron Downpatrick 1934 *married* 29 November 1934 HRH Princess Marina of Greece and Denmark (*born* 30 November 1906 *died* 27 August 1968) *killed* on active service 25 August 1942. *Issue*
   (1) HRH Prince Edward George Nicholas Paul Patrick (HRH The Duke of Kent, *see* Royal Family)
   (2) HRH Princess Alexandra Helen Elizabeth Olga Christabel (HRH Princess Alexandra, the Hon. Lady Ogilvy, *see* Royal Family)
   (3) HRH Prince Michael George Charles Franklin (HRH Prince Michael of Kent, *see* Royal Family)

6. HRH PRINCE JOHN Charles Francis *born* 12 July 1905 *died* 18 January 1919

PRECEDENCE

ENGLAND AND WALES

The Sovereign
The Prince Philip, Duke of
  Edinburgh
The Prince of Wales
The Sovereign's younger sons
The Sovereign's grandsons
The Sovereign's cousins
Archbishop of Canterbury
Lord High Chancellor
Archbishop of York
The Prime Minister
Lord President of the Council
Speaker of the House of Commons
Speaker of the House of Lords
President of the Supreme Court
Lord Chief Justice of England and
  Wales
Lord Privy Seal
Ambassadors and High
  Commissioners
Lord Great Chamberlain
Earl Marshal
Lord Steward of the Household
Lord Chamberlain of the Household
Master of the Horse
Dukes, according to their patent of
  creation:
  1. of England
  2. of Scotland
  3. of Great Britain
  4. of Ireland
  5. those created since the Union
Eldest sons of Dukes of the Blood
  Royal
Ministers, Envoys, and other
  important overseas visitors
Marquesses, according to their patent
  of creation:
  1. of England
  2. of Scotland
  3. of Great Britain
  4. of Ireland
  5. those created since the Union
Dukes' eldest sons
Earls, according to their patent of
  creation:
  1. of England
  2. of Scotland
  3. of Great Britain
  4. of Ireland
  5. those created since the Union
Younger sons of Dukes of Blood
  Royal
Marquesses' eldest sons

Dukes' younger sons
Viscounts, according to their patent
  of creation:
  1. of England
  2. of Scotland
  3. of Great Britain
  4. of Ireland
  5. those created since the Union
Earls' eldest sons
Marquesses' younger sons
Bishop of London
Bishop of Durham
Bishop of Winchester
Other English Diocesan Bishops,
  according to seniority of
  consecration
Retired Church of England Diocesan
  Bishops, according to seniority of
  consecration
Suffragan Bishops, according to
  seniority of consecration
Secretaries of State, if of the degree
  of a Baron
Barons, according to their patent of
  creation:
  1. of England
  2. of Scotland (Lords of
  Parliament)
  3. of Great Britain
  4. of Ireland
  5. those created since the Union,
  including Life Barons
Master of the Rolls
Deputy President of the Supreme
  Court
Justices of the Supreme Court,
  according to seniority of
  appointment
Treasurer of the Household
Comptroller of the Household
Vice-Chamberlain of the Household
Secretaries of State under the degree
  of Baron
Viscounts' eldest sons
Earls' younger sons
Barons' eldest sons
Knights of the Garter
Privy Counsellors
Chancellor of the Order of the
  Garter
Chancellor of the Exchequer
Chancellor of the Duchy of Lancaster
President of the Queen's Bench
  Division
President of the Family Division
Chancellor of the High Court

Lord Justices of Appeal, according to
  seniority of appointment
Judges of the High Court, according
  to seniority of appointment
Viscounts' younger sons
Barons' younger sons
Sons of Life Peers
Baronets, according to date of
  patent
Knights of the Thistle
Knights Grand Cross of the Bath
Knights Grand Cross of St Michael
  and St George
Knights Grand Cross of the Royal
  Victorian Order
Knights Grand Cross of the British
  Empire
Knights Commanders of the Bath
Knights Commanders of St Michael
  and St George
Knights Commanders of the Royal
  Victorian Order
Knights Commanders of the British
  Empire
Knights Bachelor
Circuit Judges, according to priority
  and order of their respective
  appointments
Master of the Court of Protection
Companions of the Bath
Companions of St Michael and St
  George
Commanders of the Royal Victorian
  Order
Commanders of the British
  Empire
Companions of the Distinguished
  Service Order
Lieutenants of the Royal Victorian
  Order
Officers of the British Empire
Companions of the Imperial Service
  Order
Eldest sons of younger sons of
  peers
Baronets' eldest sons
Eldest sons of knights, in the same
  order as their fathers
Members of the Royal Victorian
  Order
Members of the British Empire
Baronets' younger sons
Knights' younger sons, in the same
  order as their fathers
Esquires
Gentlemen

WOMEN

Women take the same rank as their husbands or as their brothers; but the daughter of a peer marrying a commoner retains her title as Lady or Honourable. Daughters of peers rank next immediately after the wives of their elder brothers, and before their younger brothers' wives. Daughters of peers marrying peers of a lower degree take the same order of precedence as that of their husbands; thus the daughter of a Duke marrying a Baron becomes of the rank of Baroness only, while her sisters married to commoners retain their rank and take precedence over the Baroness. Merely official rank on the husband's part does not give any similar precedence to the wife.

Peeresses in their own right take the same precedence as peers of the same rank, ie from their date of creation.

SCOTLAND

The Sovereign
The Prince Philip, Duke of
  Edinburgh
The Lord High Commissioner to the
  General Assembly of the Church
  of Scotland (while that assembly is
  sitting)
The Duke of Rothesay (eldest son of
  the Sovereign)
The Sovereign's younger sons
The Sovereign's grandsons
The Sovereign's nephews
Lord-Lieutenants
Lord Provosts, during their term of
  office*
Sheriffs Principal, during their
  term of office and within the
  bounds of their respective
  sheriffdoms
Lord Chancellor of Great Britain
Moderator of the General Assembly
  of the Church of Scotland
Keeper of the Great Seal of Scotland
  (the First Minister)
Presiding Officer
The Secretary of State for Scotland
Hereditary High Constable of
  Scotland
Hereditary Master of the Household
  in Scotland
Dukes, as in England

Eldest sons of Dukes of the Blood
  Royal
Marquesses, as in England
Dukes' eldest sons
Earls, as in England
Younger sons of Dukes of Blood
  Royal
Marquesses' eldest sons
Dukes' younger sons
Lord Justice General
Lord Clerk Register
Lord Advocate
The Advocate General
Lord Justice Clerk
Viscounts, as in England
Earls' eldest sons
Marquesses' younger sons
Lords of Parliament or Barons, as in
  England
Eldest sons of Viscounts
Earls' younger sons
Eldest sons of Lords of Parliament or
  Barons
Knights and Ladies of the Garter
Knights and Ladies of the Thistle
Privy Counsellors
Senators of the College of Justice
  (Lords of Session)
Viscounts' younger sons
Younger sons of Lords of Parliament
  or Barons
Baronets
Knights and Dames Grand Cross and

Knights and Dames Grand
  Commanders of orders, as in
  England
Knights and Dames Commanders of
  orders, as in England
Solicitor-General for Scotland
Lord Lyon King of Arms
Sheriffs Principal, when not within
  own county
Knights Bachelor
Sheriffs
Companions of Orders, as in England
Commanders of the Royal Victorian
  Order
Commanders of the British Empire
Lieutenants of the Royal Victorian
  Order
Companions of the Distinguished
  Service Order
Officers of the British Empire
Companions of the Imperial Service
  Order
Eldest sons of younger sons of peers
Eldest sons of baronets
Eldest sons of knights, as in England
Members of the Royal Victorian
  Order
Members of the British Empire
Baronets' younger sons
Knights' younger sons
Queen's Counsel
Esquires
Gentlemen

* The Lord Provosts of Aberdeen, Dundee, Edinburgh and Glasgow are Lord-Lieutenants for these cities *ex officio* and take precedence as such

THE PEERAGE

ABBREVIATIONS AND SYMBOLS

S.	Scottish title	c.p.	civil partnership
I.	Irish title	w.	widower or widow
**	hereditary peer remaining in the House of Lords	M.	minor
°	there is no 'of' in the title	†	heir not ascertained at time of going to press
b.	born	F_	represents forename
s.	succeeded	S_	represents surname
m.	married	cr.	created

The rules which govern the creation and succession of peerages are extremely complicated. There are, technically, five separate peerages, the Peerage of England, of Scotland, of Ireland, of Great Britain, and of the United Kingdom. The Peerage of Great Britain dates from 1707 when an Act of Union combined the two kingdoms of England and Scotland and separate peerages were discontinued. The Peerage of the United Kingdom dates from 1801 when Great Britain and Ireland were combined under an Act of Union. Some Scottish peers have received additional peerages of Great Britain or of the United Kingdom since 1707, and some Irish peers additional peerages of the United Kingdom since 1801.

The Peerage of Ireland was not entirely discontinued from 1801 but holders of Irish peerages, whether pre-dating or created subsequent to the Union of 1801, were not entitled to sit in the House of Lords if they had no additional English, Scottish, Great Britain or United Kingdom peerage. However, they are eligible for election to the House of Commons and to vote in parliamentary elections. An Irish peer holding a peerage of a lower grade which enabled him to sit in the House of Lords was introduced there by the title which enabled him to sit, though for all other purposes he was known by his higher title.

In the Peerage of Scotland there is no rank of Baron; the equivalent rank is Lord of Parliament, abbreviated to 'Lord' (the female equivalent is 'Lady').

All peers of England, Scotland, Great Britain or the United Kingdom who are 21 years or over, and of British, Irish or Commonwealth nationality were entitled to sit in the House of Lords until the House of Lords Act 1999, when hereditary peers lost the right to sit. However, section two of the act provided an exception for 90 hereditary peers plus the holders of the office of Earl Marshal and Lord Great Chamberlain to remain as members of the House of Lords for their lifetime or pending further reform. Of the 90 hereditary peers, 75 were elected by the hereditary peers in their political party, or Crossbench grouping, and the remaining 15 by the whole house. Until 7 November 2002 any vacancy arising due to the death of one of the 90 excepted hereditary peers was filled by the runner-up to the original election. From 7 November 2002 any vacancy due to a death has been filled by holding a by-election. By-elections are conducted in accordance with arrangements made by the Clerk of the Parliaments and have to take place within three months of a vacancy occurring. If the vacancy is among the 75, only the excepted hereditary peers in the relevant party or Crossbench grouping are entitled to vote. If the vacancy is among the other 15, the whole house is entitled to vote.

In the list below, peers currently holding one of the 92 hereditary places in the House of Lords are indicated by ** .

HEREDITARY WOMEN PEERS
Most hereditary peerages pass on death to the nearest male heir, but there are exceptions, and several are held by women.

A woman peer in her own right retains her title after marriage, and if her husband's rank is the superior she is designated by the two titles jointly, the inferior one second. Her hereditary claim still holds good in spite of any marriage whether higher or lower. No rank held by a woman can confer any title or even precedence upon her husband but the rank of a hereditary woman peer in her own right is inherited by her eldest son (or in some cases daughter).

After the Peerage Act 1963, hereditary women peers in their own right were entitled to sit in the House of Lords, subject to the same qualifications as men, until the House of Lords Act 1999.

LIFE PEERS
From 1876 to 2009 non-hereditary or life peerages were conferred on certain eminent judges to enable the judicial functions of the House of Lords to be carried out. These lords were known as Lords of Appeal in Ordinary or law lords. The judicial role of the House of Lords as the highest appeal court in the UK ended on 30 July 2009 and since 1 October 2009, under the Constitutional Reform Act 2005, any peer who holds a senior judicial office is disqualified from sitting in the House of Lords until they retire from that office.

Justices of the Supreme Court currently disqualified from sitting or voting in the House of Lords until retirement are marked with a '§' in the list of life peerages which follows.

Since 1958 life peerages have been conferred upon distinguished men and women from all walks of life, giving them seats in the House of Lords in the degree of Baron or Baroness. They are addressed in the same way as hereditary lords and barons, and their children have similar courtesy titles.

PEERAGES EXTINCT SINCE THE LAST EDITION

EARLDOMS: Dunraven and Mount Earl (cr. 1822 I.); Halsbury (cr. 1898)

LIFE PEERAGES: Acton of Bridgnorth (cr. 2000); Bingham of Cornhill (cr. 1996); Boston of Faversham (cr. 1976); Carnegy of Lour (cr. 1982); Elliott of Morpeth (cr.1985); Fyfe of Fairfield (cr. 2000); Hennessy (cr. 1999); Livsey of Talgarth (cr. 2001); Marsh (cr.1981); Pilkington of Oxenford (cr.1996); Rodger of Earlsferry (cr. 1992)

DISCLAIMER OF PEERAGES

The Peerage Act 1963 enables peers to disclaim their peerages for life. Peers alive in 1963 could disclaim within twelve months after the passing of the act (31 July 1963); a person subsequently succeeding to a peerage may disclaim within 12 months (one month if an MP) after the date of succession, or of reaching 21, if later. The disclaimer is irrevocable but does not affect the descent of the peerage after the disclaimant's death, and children of a disclaimed peer may, if they wish, retain their precedence and any courtesy titles and styles borne as children of a peer. The disclaimer permitted the disclaimant to sit in the House of Commons if elected as an MP. As the House of Lords Act 1999 removed hereditary peers from the House of Lords, they are now entitled to sit in the House of Commons without having to disclaim their titles.

The following peerages are currently disclaimed:

EARLDOM: Selkirk (1994)
VISCOUNTCY: Stansgate (1963)
BARONIES: Merthyr (1977); Reith (1972); Sanderson of Ayot (1971); Silkin (2002)

PEERS WHO ARE MINORS (ie under 21 years of age)
VISCOUNT: Selby (*b.* 1993)
BARONS: Glenconner (*b.* 1994); Hawke (*b.* 1995)

FORMS OF ADDRESS

Forms of address are given under the style for each individual rank of the peerage. Both formal and social forms of address are given where usage differs; nowadays, the social form is generally preferred to the formal, which increasingly is used only for official documents and on very formal occasions.

ROLL OF THE PEERAGE

Crown Office, House of Lords, London SW1A 0PW

The Roll of the Peerage is kept at the Crown Office and maintained by the Registrar and Assistant Registrar of the Peerage in accordance with the terms of a 2004 royal warrant. The roll records the names of all living life peers and hereditary peers who have proved their succession to the satisfaction of the Lord Chancellor. The Roll of the Peerage is maintained in addition to the Clerk of the Parliaments' register of hereditary peers eligible to stand for election in House of Lords' by-elections.

A person whose name is not entered on the Roll of Peerage can not be addressed or mentioned by the title of a peer in any official document.

Registrar, Ian Denyer, MVO
Assistant Registrar, Grant Bavister

HEREDITARY PEERS

as at 31 August 2011

PEERS OF THE BLOOD ROYAL

Style, His Royal Highness the Duke of _/His Royal Highness the Earl of_/His Royal Highness the Lord_
Style of address (formal) May it please your Royal Highness; *(informal)* Sir

Created	Title, order of succession, name, etc	Heir
	Dukes	
1947	*Edinburgh (1st)*, HRH the Prince Philip, Duke of Edinburgh	The Prince of Wales *
1337	*Cornwall*, HRH the Prince of Wales, *s.* 1952	‡
1398 S.	*Rothesay*, HRH the Prince of Wales, *s.* 1952	‡
2011	*Cambridge (1st)*, HRH Prince William of Wales	None
1986	*York (1st)*, Prince Andrew, HRH the Duke of York	None
1928	*Gloucester (2nd)*, Prince Richard, HRH the Duke of Gloucester, *s.* 1974	Earl of Ulster
1934	*Kent (2nd)*, Prince Edward, HRH the Duke of Kent, *s.* 1942	Earl of St Andrews
	Earl	
2011	*Strathearn (1st)*, HRH Prince William of Wales	None
1999	*Wessex (1st)*, Prince Edward, HRH the Earl of Wesex	Viscount Severn
	Baron	
2011	*Carrickfergus (1st)*, HRH Prince William of Wales	None

* In June 1999 Buckingham Palace announced that the current Earl of Wessex will be granted the Dukedom of Edinburgh when the title reverts to the Crown. The title will only revert to the Crown on both the death of the current Duke of Edinburgh and the Prince of Wales' succession as king
‡ The title is held by the sovereign's eldest son from the moment of his birth or the sovereign's accession

DUKES

Coronet, Eight strawberry leaves

Style, His Grace the Duke of _
  Envelope (formal), His Grace the Duke of _; *(social)*, The Duke of _. *Letter (formal)*, My Lord Duke; *(social)*, Dear Duke. *Spoken (formal)*, Your Grace; *(social)*, Duke
Wife's style, Her Grace the Duchess of _
  Envelope (formal), Her Grace the Duchess of _; *(social)*, The Duchess of _. *Letter (formal)*, Dear Madam; *(social)*, Dear Duchess. *Spoken*, Duchess
Eldest son's style, Takes his father's second title as a courtesy title (*see* Courtesy Titles)
Younger sons' style, 'Lord' before forename (F_) and surname (S_)
  Envelope, Lord F_ S_. *Letter (formal)*, My Lord; *(social)*, Dear Lord F_. *Spoken (formal)*, My Lord; *(social)*, Lord F_
Daughters' style, 'Lady' before forename (F_) and surname (S_)
  Envelope, Lady F_ S_. *Letter (formal)*, Dear Madam; *(social)*, Dear Lady F_. *Spoken*, Lady F_

Created	Title, order of succession, name, etc	Heir
1868 I.	*Abercorn (5th)*, James Hamilton, KG, *b.* 1934, *s.* 1979, *m.*	Marquess of Hamilton, *b.* 1969
1701 S.	*Argyll (13th)*, Torquhil Ian Campbell, *b.* 1968, *s.* 2001	Marquess of Lorne, *b.* 2004
1703 S.	*Atholl (11th)*, John Murray, *b.* 1929, *s.* 1996, *m.*	Marquis of Tullibardine, *b.* 1960
1682	*Beaufort (11th)*, David Robert Somerset, *b.* 1928, *s.* 1984, *m.*	Marquess of Worcester, *b.* 1952
1694	*Bedford (15th)*, Andrew Ian Henry Russell, *b.* 1962, *s.* 2003, *m.*	Marquess of Tavistock, *b.* 2005
1663 S.	*Buccleuch (10th) and Queensberry (12th) (S. 1684)*, Richard Walter John Montagu Douglas Scott, KBE, *b.* 1954, *s.* 2007, *m.*	Earl of Dalkeith, *b.* 1984
1694	*Devonshire (12th)*, Peregrine Andrew Morny Cavendish, KCVO, CBE, *b.* 1944, *s.* 2004, *m.*	Earl of Burlington, *b.* 1969
1900	*Fife (3rd)*, James George Alexander Bannerman Carnegie, *b.* 1929, *s.* 1959	Earl of Southesk, *b.* 1961
1675	*Grafton (12th)*, Henry Oliver Charles FitzRoy, *b.* 1978, *s.* 2011, *m.*	Lord Charles P. H. F., *b.* 1957

1643 S.	*Hamilton (16th) and Brandon (13th) (1711)*, Alexander Douglas Douglas-Hamilton, *b.* 1978, *s.* 2010 *Premier Peer of Scotland*	Lord John W., *b.* 1979
1766 I.	*Leinster (9th)*, Maurice FitzGerald, *b.* 1948, *s.* 2004, *m. Premier Duke, Marquess and Earl of Ireland*	Lord John F., *b.* 1952
1719	*Manchester (13th)*, Alexander Charles David Drogo Montagu, *b.* 1962, *s.* 2002, *m.*	Lord Kimble W. D. M., *b.* 1964
1702	*Marlborough (11th)*, John George Vanderbilt Henry Spencer-Churchill, *b.* 1926, *s.* 1972, *m.*	Marquess of Blandford, *b.* 1955
1707 S.	** *Montrose (8th)*, James Graham, *b.* 1935, *s.* 1992, *m.*	Marquis of Graham, *b.* 1973
1483	** *Norfolk (18th)*, Edward Wiliam Fitzalan-Howard, *b.* 1956, *s.* 2002, *m. Premier Duke and Earl Marshal*	Earl of Arundel and Surrey, *b.* 1987
1766	*Northumberland (12th)*, Ralph George Algernon Percy, *b.* 1956, *s.* 1995, *m.*	Earl Percy, *b.* 1984
1675	*Richmond (10th) and Gordon (5th) (1876)*, Charles Henry Gordon Lennox, *b.* 1929, *s.* 1989, *m.*	Earl of March and Kinrara, *b.* 1955
1707 S.	*Roxburghe (10th)*, Guy David Innes-Ker, *b.* 1954, *s.* 1974, *m. Premier Baronet of Scotland*	Marquis of Bowmont and Cessford, *b.* 1981
1703	*Rutland (11th)*, David Charles Robert Manners, *b.* 1959, *s.* 1999, *m.*	Marquess of Granby, *b.*1999
1684	*St Albans (14th)*, Murray de Vere Beauclerk, *b.* 1939, *s.* 1988, *m.*	Earl of Burford, *b.* 1965
1547	*Somerset (19th)*, John Michael Edward Seymour, *b.* 1952, *s.* 1984, *m.*	Lord Seymour, *b.* 1982
1833	*Sutherland (7th)*, Francis Ronald Egerton, *b.* 1940, *s.* 2000, *m.*	Marquess of Stafford, *b.* 1975
1814	*Wellington (8th)*, Arthur Valerian Wellesley, KG, LVO, OBE, MC, *b.* 1915, *s.* 1972, *w.*	Marquess of Douro, *b.* 1945
1874	*Westminster (6th)*, Gerald Cavendish Grosvenor, KG, CB, OBE, *b.* 1951, *s.* 1979, *m.*	Earl Grosvenor, *b.* 1991

MARQUESSES

Coronet, Four strawberry leaves alternating with four silver balls

Style, The Most Hon. the Marquess (of) _ . In Scotland the spelling 'Marquis' is preferred for pre-Union creations
    Envelope (formal), The Most Hon. the Marquess of _; *(social)*, The Marquess of _. *Letter (formal)*, My Lord; *(social)*, Dear Lord _. *Spoken (formal)*, My Lord; *(social)*, Lord _
Wife's style, The Most Hon. the Marchioness (of) _
    Envelope (formal), The Most Hon. the Marchioness of _; *(social)*, The Marchioness of _. *Letter (formal)*, Madam; *(social)*, Dear Lady _. *Spoken*, Lady _
Eldest son's style, Takes his father's second title as a courtesy title (*see* Courtesy Titles)
Younger sons' style, 'Lord' before forename and surname, as for Duke's younger sons
Daughters' style, 'Lady' before forename and surname, as for Duke's daughter

Created	Title, order of succession, name, etc	Heir
1916	*Aberdeen and Temair (7th)*, Alexander George Gordon, *b.* 1955, *s.* 2002, *m.*	Earl of Haddo, *b.* 1983
1876	*Abergavenny (6th) and 10th Earl, Abergavenny, 1784*, Christopher George Charles Nevill, *b.* 1955, *s.* 2000, *m.*	To Earldom only, David M. R. N., *b.* 1941
1821	*Ailesbury (8th)*, Michael Sidney Cedric Brudenell-Bruce, *b.* 1926, *s.* 1974	Earl of Cardigan, *b.* 1952
1831	*Ailsa (8th)*, Archibald Angus Charles Kennedy, *b.* 1956, *s.* 1994	Lord David T. K., *b.* 1958
1815	*Anglesey (7th)*, George Charles Henry Victor Paget, *b.* 1922, *s.* 1947, *m.*	Earl of Uxbridge, *b.* 1950
1789	*Bath (6th)*, Alexander George Thynn, *b.* 1932, *s.* 1992, *m.*	Viscount Weymouth, *b.* 1974
1826	*Bristol (8th)*, Frederick William Augustus Hervey, *b.* 1979, *s.* 1999	Timothy H. H., *b.* 1960
1796	*Bute (7th)*, John Colum Crichton-Stuart, *b.* 1958, *s.* 1993, *m.*	Earl of Dumfries, *b.* 1989
1812	° *Camden (6th)*, David George Edward Henry Pratt, *b.* 1930, *s.* 1983	Earl of Brecknock, *b.* 1965
1815	** *Cholmondeley (7th)*, David George Philip Cholmondeley, KCVO, *b.* 1960, *s.* 1990, *m. Lord Great Chamberlain*	Earl of Rocksavage, *b.* 2010
1816 I.	° *Conyngham (8th)*, Henry Vivian Pierpoint Conyngham, *b.* 1951, *s.* 2009, *m.*	Earl of Mount Charles, *b.* 1975
1791 I.	*Donegall (8th)*, Arthur Patrick Chichester, *b.* 1952, *s.* 2007, *m.*	Earl of Belfast, *b.* 1990

1789 I.	*Downshire (9th)*, (Arthur Francis) Nicholas Wills Hill, *b.* 1959, *s.* 2003, *m.*	Earl of Hillsborough, *b.* 1996
1801 I.	*Ely (9th)*, Charles John Tottenham, *b.* 1943, *s.* 2006, *m.*	Lord Timothy C. T., *b.* 1948
1801	*Exeter (8th)*, (William) Michael Anthony Cecil, *b.* 1935, *s.* 1988, *m.*	Lord Burghley, *b.* 1970
1800 I.	*Headfort (7th)*, Thomas Michael Ronald Christopher Taylour, *b.* 1959, *s.* 2005, *m.*	Earl of Bective, *b.* 1989
1793	*Hertford (9th)*, Henry Jocelyn Seymour, *b.* 1958, *s.* 1997, *m.*	Earl of Yarmouth, *b.* 1993
1599 S.	*Huntly (13th)*, Granville Charles Gomer Gordon, *b.* 1944, *s.* 1987, *m.* *Premier Marquess of Scotland*	Earl of Aboyne, *b.* 1973
1784	*Lansdowne (9th)*, Charles Maurice Mercer Nairne Petty-Fitzmaurice, LVO *b.* 1941, *s.* 1999, *m.*	Earl of Kerry, *b.* 1970
1902	*Linlithgow (4th)*, Adrian John Charles Hope, *b.* 1946, *s.* 1987, *m.*	Earl of Hopetoun, *b.* 1969
1816 I.	*Londonderry (9th)*, Alexander Charles Robert Vane-Tempest-Stewart, *b.* 1937, *s.* 1955, *m.*	Viscount Castlereagh, *b.* 1972
1701 S.	*Lothian (13th) and Baron Kerr of Monteviot (life peerage 2010)*, Michael Andrew Foster Jude Kerr (Michael Ancram), PC, *b.* 1945, *s.* 2004, *m.*	Lord Ralph W. F. J. K., *b.* 1957
1917	*Milford Haven (4th)*, George Ivar Louis Mountbatten, *b.* 1961, *s.* 1970, *m.*	Earl of Medina, *b.* 1991
1838	*Normanby (5th)*, Constantine Edmund Walter Phipps, *b.* 1954, *s.* 1994, *m.*	Earl of Mulgrave, *b.* 1994
1812	*Northampton (7th)*, Spencer Douglas David Compton, *b.* 1946, *s.* 1978, *m.*	Earl Compton, *b.* 1973
1682 S.	*Queensberry (12th)*, David Harrington Angus Douglas, *b.* 1929, *s.* 1954	Viscount Drumlanrig, *b.* 1967
1926	*Reading (4th)*, Simon Charles Henry Rufus Isaacs, *b.* 1942, *s.* 1980, *m.*	Viscount Erleigh, *b.* 1986
1789	*Salisbury (7th) and Baron Gascoyne-Cecil (life peerage, 1999)*, Robert Michael James Gascoyne-Cecil, PC, *b.* 1946, *s.* 2003, *m.*	Viscount Cranborne, *b.* 1970
1800 I.	*Sligo (11th)*, Jeremy Ulick Browne, *b.* 1939, *s.* 1991, *m.*	Sebastian U. B., *b.* 1964
1787	° *Townshend (8th)*, Charles George Townshend, *b.* 1945, *s.* 2010, *m.*	Viscount Raynham, *b.* 1977
1694 S.	*Tweeddale (14th)*, Charles David Montagu Hay, *b.* 1947, *s.* 2005	(Lord) Alistair J. M. H., *b.* 1955
1789 I.	*Waterford (8th)*, John Hubert de la Poer Beresford, *b.* 1933, *s.* 1934, *m.*	Earl of Tyrone, *b.* 1958
1551	*Winchester (18th)*, Nigel George Paulet, *b.* 1941, *s.* 1968, *m.* *Premier Marquess of England*	Earl of Wiltshire, *b.* 1969
1892	*Zetland (4th)*, Lawrence Mark Dundas, *b.* 1937, *s.* 1989, *m.*	Earl of Ronaldshay, *b.* 1965

EARLS

Coronet, Eight silver balls on stalks alternating with eight gold strawberry leaves

Style, The Rt. Hon. the Earl (of) _
   Envelope *(formal)*, The Rt. Hon. the Earl (of) _; *(social)*, The Earl (of) _. Letter *(formal)*, My Lord; *(social)*, Dear Lord _. Spoken *(formal)*, My Lord; *(social)*, Lord _.
Wife's style, The Rt. Hon. the Countess (of) _
   Envelope *(formal)*, The Rt. Hon. the Countess (of) _; *(social)*, The Countess (of) _. Letter *(formal)*, Madam; *(social)*, Lady _. Spoken *(formal)*, Madam; *(social)*, Lady _.
Eldest son's style, Takes his father's second title as a courtesy title (*see* Courtesy Titles)
Younger sons' style, 'The Hon.' before forename and surname, as for Baron's children
Daughters' style, 'Lady' before forename and surname, as for Duke's daughter

Created	Title, order of succession, name, etc	Heir
1639 S.	*Airlie (13th)*, David George Coke Patrick Ogilvy, KT, GCVO, PC, Royal Victorian Chain, *b.* 1926, *s.* 1968, *m.*	Lord Ogilvy, *b.* 1958
1696	*Albemarle (10th)*, Rufus Arnold Alexis Keppel, *b.* 1965, *s.* 1979, *m.*	Viscount Bury, *b.* 2003
1952	° *Alexander of Tunis (2nd)*, Shane William Desmond Alexander, *b.* 1935, *s.* 1969, *m.*	Hon. Brian J. A., *b.* 1939
1662 S.	*Annandale and Hartfell (11th)*, Patrick Andrew Wentworth Hope Johnstone, *b.* 1941, *s.* 1983, *m.* claim established 1985	Lord Johnstone, *b.* 1971

1789 I.   ° *Annesley (11th)*, Philip Harrison Annesley, *b.* 1927, *s.* 2001, *m.*   Hon. Michael R. A., *b.* 1933
1785 I.   *Antrim (9th)*, Alexander Randal Mark McDonnell, *b.* 1935, *s.* 1977, *m.*   Viscount Dunluce, *b.* 1967
1762 I.   ** *Arran (9th)*, Arthur Desmond Colquhoun Gore, *b.* 1938, *s.* 1983, *m.*   Paul A. G., CMG, CVO, *b.* 1921
1955   ° ** *Attlee (3rd)*, John Richard Attlee, *b.* 1956, *s.* 1991, *m.*   None
1714   *Aylesford (12th)*, Charles Heneage Finch-Knightley, *b.* 1947,   Lord Guernsey, *b.* 1985
            s. 2008, *m.*
1937   ** *Baldwin of Bewdley (4th)*, Edward Alfred Alexander Baldwin, *b.* 1938,   Viscount Corvedale, *b.* 1973
            s. 1976, *w.*
1922   *Balfour (5th)*, Roderick Francis Arthur Balfour, *b.* 1948, *s.* 2003, *m.*   Charles G. Y. B., *b.* 1951
1772   ° *Bathurst (8th)*, Henry Allen John Bathurst, *b.* 1927, *s.* 1943, *m.*   Lord Apsley, *b.* 1961
1919   ° *Beatty (3rd)*, David Beatty, *b.* 1946, *s.* 1972, *m.*   Viscount Borodale, *b.* 1973
1797 I.   ° *Belmore (8th)*, John Armar Lowry-Corry, *b.* 1951, *s.* 1960, *m.*   Viscount Corry, *b.* 1985
1739 I.   *Bessborough (12th)*, Myles Fitzhugh Longfield Ponsonby, *b.* 1941,   Viscount Duncannon, *b.* 1974
            s. 2002, *m.*
1815   *Bradford (7th)*, Richard Thomas Orlando Bridgeman, *b.* 1947,   Viscount Newport, *b.* 1980
            s. 1981, *m.*
1469 S.   *Buchan (17th)*, Malcolm Harry Erskine, *b.* 1930, *s.* 1984, *m.*   Lord Cardross, *b.* 1960
1746   *Buckinghamshire (10th)*, (George) Miles Hobart-Hampden, *b.* 1944,   Sir John Hobart, Bt., *b.* 1945
            s. 1983, *m.*
1800   ° *Cadogan (8th)*, Charles Gerald John Cadogan, *b.* 1937, *s.* 1997, *m.*   Viscount Chelsea, *b.* 1966
1878   ° *Cairns (6th)*, Simon Dallas Cairns, CVO, CBE, *b.* 1939, *s.* 1989, *m.*   Viscount Garmoyle, *b.* 1965
1455 S.   ** *Caithness (20th)*, Malcolm Ian Sinclair, PC, *b.* 1948, *s.* 1965, *w.*   Lord Berriedale, *b.* 1981
1800 I.   *Caledon (7th)*, Nicholas James Alexander, *b.* 1955, *s.* 1980, *m.*   Viscount Alexander, *b.* 1990
1661   *Carlisle (13th)*, George William Beaumont Howard, *b.* 1949, *s.* 1994   Hon. Philip C. W. H., *b.* 1963
1793   *Carnarvon (8th)*, George Reginald Oliver Molyneux Herbert, *b.* 1956,   Lord Porchester, *b.* 1992
            s. 2001, *m.*
1748 I.   *Carrick (11th)*, Arion Thomas Piers Hamilton Butler, *b.* 1975, *s.* 2008   Hon. P. E. T. L. B., *b.* 1979
1800 I.   ° *Castle Stewart (8th)*, Arthur Patrick Avondale Stuart, *b.* 1928,   Viscount Stuart, *b.* 1953
            s. 1961, *m.*
1814   °** *Cathcart (7th)*, Charles Alan Andrew Cathcart, *b.* 1952, *s.* 1999, *m.*   Lord Greenock, *b.* 1986
1647 I.   *Cavan*, The 12th Earl died in 1988.   †Roger C. Lambart, *b.* 1944
1827   ° *Cawdor (7th)*, Colin Robert Vaughan Campbell, *b.* 1962, *s.* 1993, *m.*   Viscount Emlyn, *b.* 1998
1801   *Chichester (9th)*, John Nicholas Pelham, *b.* 1944, *s.* 1944, *m.*   Richard A. H. P., *b.* 1952
1803 I.   ** *Clancarty (9th)*, Nicholas Power Richard Le Poer Trench, *b.* 1952,   None
            s. 1995, *m.*
1776 I.   *Clanwilliam (8th)*, Patrick James Meade, *b.* 1960, *s.* 2009, *m.*   Lord Gillford, *b.* 1998
1776   *Clarendon (8th)*, George Edward Laurence Villiers, *b.* 1976,   Lord Hyde, *b.* 2008
            s. 2009, *m.*
1620 I.   *Cork and Orrery (15th)*, John Richard Boyle, *b.* 1945, *s.* 2003, *m.*   Viscount Dungarvan, *b.* 1978
1850   *Cottenham (9th)*, Mark John Henry Pepys, *b.* 1983, *s.* 2000   Hon. Sam R. P., *b.* 1986
1762 I.   ** *Courtown (9th)*, James Patrick Montagu Burgoyne Winthrop Stopford,   Viscount Stopford, *b.* 1988
            b. 1954, *s.* 1975, *m.*
1697   *Coventry (13th)*, George William Coventry, *b.* 1939, *s.* 2004, *m.*   David D. S. C., *b.* 1973
1857   ° *Cowley (7th)*, Garret Graham Wellesley, *b.* 1934, *s.* 1975, *w.*   Viscount Dangan, *b.* 1965
1892   *Cranbrook (5th)*, Gathorne Gathorne-Hardy, *b.* 1933, *s.* 1978, *m.*   Lord Medway, *b.* 1968
1801 M.   *Craven (9th)*, Benjamin Robert Joseph Craven, *b.* 1989, *s.* 1990   Rupert J. E. C., *b.* 1926
1398 S.   *Crawford (29th) and Balcarres (12th) (S. 1651) and Baron Balniel (life   Lord Balniel, *b.* 1958
            peerage, 1974)*, Robert Alexander Lindsay, KT, GCVO, PC, *b.* 1927,
            s. 1975, *m. Premier Earl on Union Roll*
1861   *Cromartie (5th)*, John Ruaridh Blunt Grant Mackenzie, *b.* 1948,   Viscount Tarbat, *b.* 1987
            s. 1989, *m.*
1901   *Cromer (4th)*, Evelyn Rowland Esmond Baring, *b.* 1946, *s.* 1991, *m.*   Viscount Errington, *b.* 1994
1633 S.   *Dalhousie (17th)*, James Hubert Ramsay, *b.* 1948, *s.* 1999, *m., Lord*   Lord Ramsay, *b.* 1981
            Steward
1725 I.   *Darnley (11th)*, Adam Ivo Stuart Bligh, *b.* 1941, *s.* 1980, *m.*   Lord Clifton, *b.* 1968
1711   *Dartmouth (10th)*, William Legge, *b.* 1949, *s.* 1997, *m.*   Hon. Rupert L., *b.* 1951
1761   ° *De La Warr (11th)*, William Herbrand Sackville, *b.* 1948, *s.* 1988, *m.*   Lord Buckhurst, *b.* 1979
1622   *Denbigh (12th) and Desmond (11th) (I. 1622)*, Alexander Stephen   Viscount Feilding, *b.* 2005
            Rudolph Feilding, *b.* 1970, *s.* 1995, *m.*
1485   *Derby (19th)*, Edward Richard William Stanley, *b.* 1962, *s.* 1994, *m.*   Lord Stanley, *b.* 1998
1553   *Devon (18th)*, Hugh Rupert Courtenay, *b.* 1942, *s.* 1998, *m.*   Lord Courtenay, *b.* 1975
1800 I.   *Donoughmore (8th)*, Richard Michael John Hely-Hutchinson, *b.* 1927,   Viscount Suirdale, *b.* 1952
            s. 1981, *w.*
1661 I.   *Drogheda (12th)*, Henry Dermot Ponsonby Moore, *b.* 1937,   Viscount Moore, *b.* 1983
            s. 1989, *m.*
1837   *Ducie (7th)*, David Leslie Moreton, *b.* 1951, *s.* 1991, *m.*   Lord Moreton, *b.* 1981
1860   *Dudley (4th)*, William Humble David Ward, *b.* 1920, *s.* 1969, *m.*   Viscount Ednam, *b.* 1947
1660 S.   ** *Dundee (12th)*, Alexander Henry Scrymgeour, *b.* 1949, *s.* 1983, *m.*   Lord Scrymgeour, *b.* 1982

1669 S.	*Dundonald (15th)*, Iain Alexander Douglas Blair Cochrane, *b.* 1961, *s.* 1986, *m.*	Lord Cochrane, *b.* 1991
1686 S.	*Dunmore (12th)*, Malcolm Kenneth Murray, *b.* 1946, *s.* 1995, *m.*	Hon. Geoffrey C. M., *b.*1949
1833	*Durham (7th)*, Edward Richard Lambton, *b.* 1961, *s.* 2006, *m.*	Viscount Lambton, *b.* 1985
1837	*Effingham (7th)*, David Mowbray Algernon Howard, *b.* 1939, *s.* 1996, *m.*	Lord Howard of Effingham, *b.* 1971
1507 S.	*Eglinton (18th) and Winton (9th) (S. 1600)*, Archibald George Montgomerie, *b.* 1939, *s.* 1966, *m.*	Lord Montgomerie, *b.* 1966
1733 I.	*Egmont (12th)*, Thomas Frederick Gerald Perceval, *b.* 1934, *s.* 2001, *m.*	Hon. Donald W. P., *b.* 1954
1821	*Eldon (5th)*, John Joseph Nicholas Scott, *b.* 1937, *s.* 1976, *m.*	Viscount Encombe, *b.* 1962
1633 S.	*Elgin (11th) and Kincardine (15th) (S. 1647)*, Andrew Douglas Alexander Thomas Bruce, KT, *b.* 1924, *s.* 1968, *m.*	Lord Bruce, *b.* 1961
1789 I.	*Enniskillen (7th)*, Andrew John Galbraith Cole, *b.* 1942, *s.* 1989, *m.*	Arthur G. C., *b.* 1920
1789 I.	*Erne (6th)*, Henry George Victor John Crichton, *b.* 1937, *s.* 1940, *m.*	Viscount Crichton, *b.* 1971
1452 S.	** *Erroll (24th)*, Merlin Sereld Victor Gilbert Hay, *b.* 1948, *s.* 1978, *m. Hereditary Lord High Constable and Knight Marischal of Scotland*	Lord Hay, *b.* 1984
1661	*Essex (11th)*, Frederick Paul de Vere Capell, *b.* 1944, *s.* 2005	William J. C., *b.* 1952
1711	° ** *Ferrers (13th)*, Robert Washington Shirley, PC, *b.* 1929, *s.* 1954, *m.*	Viscount Tamworth, *b.* 1952
1789	° *Fortescue (8th)*, Charles Hugh Richard Fortescue, *b.* 1951, *s.* 1993, *m.*	John A. F. F., *b.* 1955
1841	*Gainsborough (6th)*, Anthony Baptist Noel, *b.* 1950, *s.* 2009, *m.*	Viscount Campden, *b.* 1977
1623 S.	*Galloway (13th)*, Randolph Keith Reginald Stewart, *b.* 1928, *s.* 1978, *w.*	Andrew C. S., *b.* 1949
1703 S.	** *Glasgow (10th)*, Patrick Robin Archibald Boyle, *b.* 1939, *s.* 1984, *m.*	Viscount of Kelburn, *b.* 1978
1806 I.	*Gosford (7th)*, Charles David Nicholas Alexander John Sparrow Acheson, *b.* 1942, *s.* 1966, *m.*	Nicholas H. C. A., *b.* 1947
1945	*Gowrie (2nd)*, Alexander Patrick Greysteil Hore-Ruthven, PC, *b.* 1939, *s.* 1955, *m.*	Viscount Ruthven of Canberra, *b.* 1964
1684 I.	*Granard (10th)*, Peter Arthur Edward Hastings Forbes, *b.* 1957, *s.* 1992, *m.*	Viscount Forbes, *b.* 1981
1833	° *Granville (6th)*, Granville George Fergus Leveson-Gower, *b.* 1959, *s.* 1996, *m.*	Lord Leveson, *b.* 1999
1806	° *Grey (6th)*, Richard Fleming George Charles Grey, *b.* 1939, *s.* 1963, *m.*	Philip K. G., *b.* 1940
1752	*Guilford (10th)*, Piers Edward Brownlow North, *b.* 1971, *s.* 1999, *m.*	Lord North, *b.* 2002
1619 S.	*Haddington (13th)*, John George Baillie-Hamilton, *b.* 1941, *s.* 1986, *m.*	Lord Binning, *b.* 1985
1919	° *Haig (3rd)*, Alexander Douglas Derrick Haig, *b.* 1961, *s.* 2009, *m.*	None
1944	*Halifax (3rd)*, Charles Edward Peter Neil Wood, *b.* 1944, *s.* 1980, *m.*	Lord Irwin, *b.* 1977
1754	*Hardwicke (10th)*, Joseph Philip Sebastian Yorke, *b.* 1971, *s.* 1974, *m.*	Viscount Royston, *b.* 2009
1812	*Harewood (8th)*, David Henry George Lascelles, *b.* 1950, *s.* 2011, *m.*	Viscount Lascelles, *b.* 1978
1742	*Harrington (12th)*, Charles Henry Leicester Stanhope, *b.* 1945, *s.* 2009, *m.*	Viscount Petersham, *b.* 1967
1809	*Harrowby (8th)*, Dudley Adrian Conroy Ryder, *b.* 1951, *s.* 2007, *m.*	Viscount Sandon, *b.* 1981
1605 S.	** *Home (15th)*, David Alexander Cospatrick Douglas-Home, CVO, CBE, *b.* 1943, *s.* 1995, *m.*	Lord Dunglass, *b.* 1987
1821	° ** *Howe (7th)*, Frederick Richard Penn Curzon, *b.* 1951, *s.* 1984, *m.*	Viscount Curzon, *b.* 1994
1529	*Huntingdon (16th)*, William Edward Robin Hood Hastings Bass, LVO, *b.* 1948, *s.* 1990, *m.*	Hon. Simon A. R. H. H. B., *b.* 1950
1885	*Iddesleigh (5th)*, John Stafford Northcote, *b.* 1957, *s.* 2004, *m.*	Viscount St Cyres, *b.* 1985
1756	*Ilchester (10th)*, Robin Maurice Fox-Strangways, *b.* 1942, *s.* 2006, *m.*	Lord Stavordale, *b.* 1972
1929	*Inchcape (4th)*, (Kenneth) Peter (Lyle) Mackay, *b.* 1943, *s.* 1994, *m.*	Viscount Glenapp, *b.* 1979
1919	*Iveagh (4th)*, Arthur Edward Rory Guinness, *b.* 1969, *s.* 1992	Viscount Elveden, *b.* 2003
1925	° *Jellicoe (3rd)*, Patrick John Bernard Jellicoe, *b.* 1950, *s.* 2007	Viscount Brocas, *b.* 1970
1697	*Jersey (10th)*, George Francis William Child Villiers, *b.* 1976, *s.* 1998 *m.*	Hon. Jamie C. C. V., *b.* 1994
1822 I.	*Kilmorey (6th)*, Sir Richard Francis Needham, PC, *b.* 1942, *s.* 1977, *m.*, (does not use title)	Viscount Newry and Mourne, *b.* 1966
1866	*Kimberley (5th)*, John Armine Wodehouse, *b.* 1951, *s.* 2002, *m.*	Lord Wodehouse, *b.*1978
1768 I.	*Kingston (12th)*, Robert Charles Henry King-Tenison, *b.* 1969, *s.* 2002, *m.*	Viscount Kingsborough, *b.* 2000
1633 S.	*Kinnoull (15th)*, Arthur William George Patrick Hay, *b.* 1935, *s.* 1938, *m.*	Viscount Dupplin, *b.* 1962
1677 S.	*Kintore (14th)*, James William Falconer Keith, *b.* 1976, *s.* 2004	Lady Iona D. M. G. K., *b.* 1978
1914	° *Kitchener of Khartoum (3rd)*, Henry Herbert Kitchener, TD, *b.* 1919, *s.* 1937	None
1624 S.	*Lauderdale (18th)*, Ian Maitland, *b.* 1937, *s.* 2008, *m.*	Viscount Maitland, *b.* 1965
1837	*Leicester (7th)*, Edward Douglas Coke, *b.* 1936, *s.* 1994, *m.*	Viscount Coke, *b.* 1965

1641 S.	*Leven (14th) and Melville (13th) (S. 1690)*, Alexander Robert Leslie Melville, *b.* 1924, *s.* 1947, *m.*	Lord Balgonie, *b.* 1984
1831	*Lichfield (6th)*, Thomas William Robert Hugh Anson, *b.* 1978, *s.* 2005, *m.*	Viscount Anson, *b.* 2011
1803 I.	*Limerick (7th)*, Edmund Christopher Pery, *b.* 1963, *s.* 2003, *m.*	Viscount Glentworth, *b.* 1991
1572	*Lincoln (19th)*, Robert Edward Fiennes-Clinton, *b.* 1972, *s.* 2001	Hon. William R. F.-C., *b.* 1980
1633 S.	** *Lindsay (16th)*, James Randolph Lindesay-Bethune, *b.* 1955, *s.* 1989, *m.*	Viscount Garnock, *b.* 1990
1626	*Lindsey (14th) and Abingdon (9th) (1682)*, Richard Henry Rupert Bertie, *b.* 1931, *s.* 1963, *m.*	Lord Norreys, *b.* 1958
1776 I.	*Lisburne (8th)*, John David Malet Vaughan, *b.* 1918, *s.* 1965, *m.*	Viscount Vaughan, *b.* 1945
1822 I.	** *Listowel (6th)*, Francis Michael Hare, *b.* 1964, *s.* 1997, *m.*	Hon. Timothy P. H., *b.* 1966
1905	** *Liverpool (5th)*, Edward Peter Bertram Savile Foljambe, *b.* 1944, *s.* 1969, *m.*	Viscount Hawkesbury, *b.* 1972
1945	° *Lloyd George of Dwyfor (4th)*, David Richard Owen Lloyd George, *b.* 1951, *s.* 2010, *m.*	Viscount Gwynedd, *b.* 1986
1785 I.	*Longford (8th)*, Thomas Frank Dermot Pakenham, *b.* 1933, *s.* 2001, *m.*, (does not use title)	Hon. Edward M. P., *b.* 1970
1807	*Lonsdale (8th)*, Hugh Clayton Lowther, *b.* 1949, *s.* 2006, *m.*	Hon. William J. L., *b.* 1957
1633 S.	*Loudoun (14th)*, Michael Edward Abney-Hastings, *b.* 1942, *s.* 2002, *m.*	Lord Mauchline, *b.* 1974
1838	*Lovelace (5th)*, Peter Axel William Locke King, *b.* 1951, *s.* 1964, *m.*	None
1795 I.	*Lucan (7th)*, Richard John Bingham, *b.* 1934, *s.* 1964, *m.* (missing since 8 November 1974)	Lord Bingham, *b.* 1967
1880	** *Lytton (5th)*, John Peter Michael Scawen Lytton, *b.* 1950, *s.* 1985, *m.*	Viscount Knebworth, *b.* 1989
1721	*Macclesfield (9th)*, Richard Timothy George Mansfield Parker, *b.* 1943, *s.* 1992, *m.*	Hon. J. David G. P., *b.* 1945
1800	*Malmesbury (7th)*, James Carleton Harris, *b.* 1946, *s.* 2000, *m.*	Viscount FitzHarris, *b.* 1970
1776	*Mansfield and Mansfield (8th) (1792)*, William David Mungo James Murray, *b.* 1930, *s.* 1971, *m.*	Viscount Stormont, *b.* 1956
1565 S.	*Mar (14th) and Kellie (16th) (S. 1616) and Baron Erskine of Alloa Tower (life peerage, 2000)*, James Thorne Erskine, *b.* 1949, *s.* 1994, *m.*	Hon. Alexander D. E., *b.* 1952
1785 I.	*Mayo (11th)*, Charles Diarmuidh John Bourke, *b.* 1953, *s.* 2006, *m.*	Lord Naas, *b.* 1985
1627 I.	*Meath (15th)*, John Anthony Brabazon, *b.* 1941, *s.* 1998, *m.*	Lord Ardee, *b.* 1977
1766 I.	*Mexborough (8th)*, John Christopher George Savile, *b.* 1931, *s.* 1980, *m.*	Viscount Pollington, *b.* 1959
1813	*Minto (7th)*, Gilbert Timothy George Lariston Elliot-Murray-Kynynmound, *b.* 1953, *s.* 2005, *m.*	Viscount Melgund, *b.* 1984
1562 S.	*Moray (20th)*, Douglas John Moray Stuart, *b.* 1928, *s.* 1974, *m.*	Lord Doune, *b.* 1966
1815	*Morley (6th)*, John St Aubyn Parker, KCVO, *b.* 1923, *s.* 1962, *m.*	Viscount Boringdon, *b.* 1956
1458 S.	*Morton (22nd)*, John Charles Sholto Douglas, *b.* 1927, *s.* 1976, *m.*	Lord Aberdour, *b.* 1952
1789	*Mount Edgcumbe (8th)*, Robert Charles Edgcumbe, *b.* 1939, *s.* 1982	Piers V. E., *b.* 1946
1805	° *Nelson (10th)*, Simon John Horatio Nelson, *b.* 1971, *s.* 2009, *m.*	Viscount Merton, *b.* 1994
1660 S.	*Newburgh (12th)*, Don Filippo Giambattista Camillo Francesco Aldo Maria Rospigliosi, *b.* 1942, *s.* 1986, *m.*	Princess Donna Benedetta F. M. R., *b.* 1974
1827 I.	*Norbury (7th)*, Richard James Graham-Toler, *b.* 1967, *s.* 2000	None
1806 I.	*Normanton (6th)*, Shaun James Christian Welbore Ellis Agar, *b.* 1945, *s.* 1967, *w.*	Viscount Somerton, *b.* 1982
1647 S.	*Northesk (15th)*, Patrick Charles Carnegy, *b.* 1940, *s.* 2010	Colin D. C., *b.* 1942
1801	*Onslow (8th)*, Rupert Charles William Bullard Onslow, *b.* 1967, *s.* 2011, *m.*	Anthony E. E. O., *b.* 1955
1696 S.	*Orkney (9th)*, (Oliver) Peter St John, *b.* 1938, *s.* 1998, *m.*	Viscount Kirkwall, *b.* 1969
1328 I.	*Ormonde and Ossory (I. 1527)*, The 25th/18th Earl (7th Marquess) died in 1988	†Viscount Mountgarret *b.* 1961 (*see* that title)
1925	*Oxford and Asquith (3rd)*, Raymond Benedict Bartholomew Michael Asquith, OBE, *b.* 1952, *s.* 2011, *m.*	Viscount Asquith, *b.* 1979
1929	° ** *Peel (3rd)*, William James Robert Peel, GCVO, PC, *b.* 1947, *s.* 1969, *m.* Lord Chamberlain	Viscount Clanfield, *b.* 1976
1551	*Pembroke (18th) and Montgomery (15th) (1605)*, William Alexander Sidney Herbert, *b.* 1978, *s.* 2003, *m.*	Earl of Carnarvon *b.* 1956 (*see* that title)
1605 S.	*Perth (18th)*, John Eric Drummond, *b.* 1935, *s.* 2002, *m.*	Viscount Strathallan, *b.* 1965
1905	*Plymouth (3rd)*, Other Robert Ivor Windsor-Clive, *b.* 1923, *s.* 1943, *m.*	Viscount Windsor, *b.* 1951
1785	*Portarlington (7th)*, George Lionel Yuill Seymour Dawson-Damer, *b.* 1938, *s.* 1959, *m.*	Viscount Carlow, *b.* 1965
1689	*Portland (12th)*, Count Timothy Charles Robert Noel Bentinck, *b.* 1953, *s.* 1997, *m.*	Viscount Woodstock, *b.* 1984
1743	*Portsmouth (10th)*, Quentin Gerard Carew Wallop, *b.* 1954, *s.* 1984, *m.*	Viscount Lymington, *b.* 1981
1804	*Powis (8th)*, John George Herbert, *b.* 1952, *s.* 1993, *m.*	Viscount Clive, *b.* 1979
1765	*Radnor (9th)*, William Pleydell-Bouverie, *b.* 1955, *s.* 2008, *m.*	Viscount Folkestone, *b.* 1999

1831 I.	Ranfurly (7th), Gerald Françoys Needham Knox, b. 1929, s. 1988, m.	Viscount Northland, b. 1957
1771 I.	Roden (10th), Robert John Jocelyn, b. 1938, s. 1993, m.	Viscount Jocelyn, b. 1989
1801	Romney (8th), Julian Charles Marsham, b. 1948, s. 2004, m.	Viscount Marsham, b. 1977
1703 S.	Rosebery (7th), Neil Archibald Primrose, b. 1929, s. 1974, m.	Lord Dalmeny, b. 1967
1806 I.	Rosse (7th), William Brendan Parsons, b. 1936, s. 1979, m.	Lord Oxmantown, b. 1969.
1801	** Rosslyn (7th), Peter St Clair-Erskine, b. 1958, s. 1977, m.	Lord Loughborough, b. 1986
1457 S.	Rothes (22nd), James Malcolm David Leslie, b. 1958, s. 2005, m.	Hon. Alexander J. L., b. 1962
1861	° Russell (6th), Nicholas Lyulph Russell, b. 1968, s. 2004	Hon. John F. R., b. 1971
1915	° St Aldwyn (3rd), Michael Henry Hicks Beach, b. 1950, s. 1992, m.	Hon. David S. H. B., b. 1955
1815	St Germans (10th), Peregrine Nicholas Eliot, b. 1941, s. 1988	Lord Eliot, b. 2004
1660	** Sandwich (11th), John Edward Hollister Montagu, b. 1943, s. 1995, m.	Viscount Hinchingbrooke, b. 1969
1690	Scarbrough (13th), Richard Osbert Lumley, b. 1973, s. 2004	Hon. Thomas H. L., b. 1980
1701 S.	Seafield (13th), Ian Derek Francis Ogilvie-Grant, b. 1939, s. 1969, m.	Viscount Reidhaven, b. 1963
1882	** Selborne (4th), John Roundell Palmer, GBE, b. 1940, s. 1971, m.	Viscount Wolmer, b. 1971
1646 S.	Selkirk, Disclaimed for life 1994. (see Lord Selkirk of Douglas, Life Peers)	Master of Selkirk, b. 1978
1672	Shaftesbury (12th), Nicholas Edmund Anthony Ashley-Cooper, b. 1979, s. 2005, m.	Lord Ashley, b. 2011
1756 I.	Shannon (9th), Richard Bentinck Boyle, b. 1924, s. 1963	Viscount Boyle, b. 1960
1442	** Shrewsbury and Waterford (22nd) (I. 1446), Charles Henry John Benedict Crofton Chetwynd Chetwynd-Talbot, b. 1952, s. 1980, m. Premier Earl of England and Ireland	Viscount Ingestre, b. 1978
1961	Snowdon (1st) and Baron Armstrong-Jones (life peerage, 1999), Antony Charles Robert Armstrong-Jones, GCVO, b. 1930, m.	Viscount Linley, b. 1961
1765	° Spencer (9th), Charles Edward Maurice Spencer, b. 1964, s. 1992, m.	Viscount Althorp, b. 1994
1703 S.	** Stair (14th), John David James Dalrymple, b. 1961, s. 1996, m.	Viscount Dalrymple, b. 2008
1984	Stockton (2nd), Alexander Daniel Alan Macmillan, MEP, b. 1943, s. 1986, m.	Viscount Macmillan of Ovenden, b. 1974
1821	Stradbroke (6th), Robert Keith Rous, b. 1937, s. 1983, m.	Viscount Dunwich, b. 1961
1847	Strafford (8th), Thomas Edmund Byng, b. 1936, s. 1984, m.	Viscount Enfield, b. 1964
1606 S.	Strathmore and Kinghorne (18th) (S. 1677), Michael Fergus Bowes Lyon, b. 1957, s. 1987, m.	Lord Glamis, b. 1986
1603	Suffolk (21st) and Berkshire (14th) (1626), Michael John James George Robert Howard, b. 1935, s. 1941, m.	Viscount Andover, b. 1974
1955	Swinton (3rd), Nicholas John Cunliffe-Lister, b. 1939, s. 2006, m.	Lord Masham b. 1970
1714	Tankerville (10th), Peter Grey Bennet, b. 1956, s. 1980	Adrian G. B., b. 1958
1822	° Temple of Stowe (8th), (Walter) Grenville Algernon Temple-Gore-Langton, b. 1924, s. 1988, m.	Lord Langton, b. 1955
1815	Verulam (7th), John Duncan Grimston, b. 1951, s. 1973, m.	Viscount Grimston, b. 1978
1729	° Waldegrave (13th), James Sherbrooke Waldegrave, b. 1940, s. 1995, m.	Viscount Chewton, b. 1986
1759	Warwick (9th) and Brooke (9th) (1746), Guy David Greville, b. 1957, s. 1996, m.	Lord Brooke, b. 1982
1633 S.	Wemyss (13th) and March (9th) (S. 1697), James Donald Charteris, b. 1948, s. 2008, m.	Lord Elcho, b. 1984
1621 I.	Westmeath (13th), William Anthony Nugent, b. 1928, s. 1971, m.	Hon. Sean C. W. N., b. 1965
1624	Westmorland (16th), Anthony David Francis Henry Fane, b. 1951, s. 1993, m.	Hon. Harry St C. F., b. 1953
1876	Wharncliffe (5th), Richard Alan Montagu Stuart Wortley, b. 1953, s. 1987, m.	Viscount Carlton, b. 1980
1801	Wilton (8th), Francis Egerton Grosvenor, b. 1934, s. 1999, m.	Viscount Grey de Wilton, b.1959
1628	Winchilsea (17th) and Nottingham (12th) (1681), Daniel James Hatfield Finch Hatton, b. 1967, s. 1999, m.	Viscount Maidstone, b. 1998
1766	° Winterton (8th), (Donald) David Turnour, b. 1943, s. 1991, m.	Robert C. T., b. 1950
1956	Woolton (3rd), Simon Frederick Marquis, b. 1958, s. 1969, m.	None
1837	Yarborough (8th), Charles John Pelham, b. 1963, s. 1991, m.	Lord Worsley, b. 1990

COUNTESSES IN THEIR OWN RIGHT

Style, The Rt. Hon. the Countess (of) _
 Envelope (formal), The Rt. Hon. the Countess (of) _; *(social)*, The Countess (of) _. *Letter (formal)*, Madam; *(social)*,
 Lady _. *Spoken (formal)*, Madam; *(social)*, Lady _.
Husband, Untitled
Children's style, As for children of an Earl

Created	Title, order of succession, name, etc	Heir
1643 S.	*Dysart (12th in line)*, Katherine Grant of Rothiemurchus, *b.* 1918, *s.* 2003 *w.*	Lord Huntingtower, *b.* 1946
c.1115 S.	** *Mar (31st in line)*, Margaret of Mar, *b.* 1940, *s.* 1975, *m.* Premier Earldom of Scotland	Mistress of Mar, *b.* 1963
1947	° *Mountbatten of Burma (2nd in line)*, Patricia Edwina Victoria Knatchbull, CBE, *b.* 1924, *s.* 1979, *w.*	Lord Romsey, *(also* Lord Brabourne (8th) *see* that title)
c.1235 S.	*Sutherland (24th in line)*, Elizabeth Millicent Sutherland, *b.* 1921, *s.* 1963, *w.*	Lord Strathnaver, *b.* 1947

VISCOUNTS

Coronet, Sixteen silver balls

Style, The Rt. Hon. the Viscount _
 Envelope (formal), The Rt. Hon. the Viscount _; *(social)*, The Viscount _. *Letter (formal)*, My Lord; *(social)*, Dear Lord
 _. *Spoken*, Lord _.
Wife's style, The Rt. Hon. the Viscountess _
 Envelope (formal), The Rt. Hon. the Viscountess _; *(social)*, The Viscountess _. *Letter (formal)*, Madam; *(social)*, Dear
 Lady _. *Spoken*, Lady _.
Children's style, 'The Hon.' before forename and surname, as for Baron's children
In Scotland, the heir apparent to a Viscount may be styled 'The Master of _ (title of peer)'

Created	Title, order of succession, name, etc	Heir
1945	*Addison (4th)*, William Matthew Wand Addison, *b.* 1945, *s.* 1992, *m.*	Hon. Paul W. A., *b.* 1973
1946	*Alanbrooke (3rd)*, Alan Victor Harold Brooke, *b.* 1932, *s.* 1972	None
1919	** *Allenby (3rd)*, Lt.-Col. Michael Jaffray Hynman Allenby, *b.* 1931, *s.* 1984, *m.*	Hon. Henry J. H. A., *b.* 1968
1911	*Allendale (4th)*, Wentworth Peter Ismay Beaumont, *b.* 1948, *s.* 2002, *m.*	Hon. Wentworth A. I. B., *b.* 1979
1642 S.	*of Arbuthnott (16th)*, John Campbell Arbuthnott, KT, CBE, DSC, *b.* 1924, *s.* 1966, *m.*	Master of Arbuthnott, *b.* 1950
1751 I.	*Ashbrook (11th)*, Michael Llowarch Warburton Flower, *b.* 1935, *s.* 1995, *m.*	Hon. Rowland F. W. F., *b.* 1975
1917	** *Astor (4th)*, William Waldorf Astor, *b.* 1951, *s.* 1966, *m.*	Hon. William W. A., *b.* 1979
1781 I.	*Bangor (8th)*, William Maxwell David Ward, *b.* 1948, *s.* 1993, *m.*	Hon. E. Nicholas W., *b.* 1953
1925	*Bearsted (5th)*, Nicholas Alan Samuel, *b.* 1950, *s.* 1996, *m.*	Hon. Harry R. S., *b.* 1988
1963	*Blakenham (2nd)*, Michael John Hare, *b.* 1938, *s.* 1982, *m.*	Hon. Caspar J. H., *b.* 1972
1935	*Bledisloe (4th)*, Rupert Edward Ludlow Bathurst, *b.* 1964, *s.* 2009, *m.*	Hon. Benjamin B., *b.* 2004
1712	*Bolingbroke (8th) and St John (9th) (1716)*, Henry Fitzroy St John, *b.* 1957, *s.* 2010	Oliver J. B. St J., *b.* 1972
1960	*Boyd of Merton (2nd)*, Simon Donald Rupert Neville Lennox-Boyd, *b.* 1939, *s.* 1983, *m.*	Hon. Benjamin A. L.-B., *b.* 1964
1717 I.	*Boyne (11th)*, Gustavus Michael Stucley Hamilton-Russell, *b.* 1965, *s.* 1995, *m.*	Hon. Gustavus A. E. H.-R., *b.* 1999
1929	*Brentford (4th)*, Crispin William Joynson-Hicks, *b.* 1933, *s.* 1983, *m.*	Hon. Paul W. J.-H., *b.* 1971
1929	** *Bridgeman (3rd)*, Robin John Orlando Bridgeman, *b.* 1930, *s.* 1982, *m.*	Hon. Luke R. O. B., *b.* 1971

1868	*Bridport (4th) and 7th Duke, Bronte in Sicily, 1799,* Alexander Nelson Hood, *b.* 1948, *s.* 1969, *m.*	Hon. Peregrine A. N. H., *b.* 1974
1952	** *Brookeborough (3rd),* Alan Henry Brooke, *b.* 1952, *s.* 1987, *m.*	Hon. Christopher A. B., *b.* 1954
1933	*Buckmaster (4th),* Adrian Charles Buckmaster, *b.* 1949, *s.* 2007, *m.*	Hon. Andrew N. B., *b.* 1980
1939	*Caldecote (3rd),* Piers James Hampden Inskip, *b.* 1947, *s.* 1999, *m.*	Hon. Thomas J. H. I., *b.* 1985
1941	*Camrose (4th),* Adrian Michael Berry, *b.* 1937, *s.* 2001, *m.*	Hon. Jonathan W. B., *b.* 1970
1954	*Chandos (3rd) and Baron Lyttelton of Aldershot (life peerage, 2000),* Thomas Orlando Lyttelton, *b.* 1953, *s.* 1980, *m.*	Hon. Oliver A. L., *b.* 1986
1665 I.	*Charlemont (15th),* John Dodd Caulfeild, *b.* 1966, *s.* 2001, *m.*	Hon. Shane A. C., *b.* 1996
1921	*Chelmsford (4th)* Frederic Corin Piers Thesiger, *b.* 1962, *s.* 1999, *m.*	Hon. Frederic T. *b.* 2006
1717 I.	*Chetwynd (10th),* Adam Richard John Casson Chetwynd, *b.* 1935, *s.* 1965, *m.*	Hon. Adam D. C., *b.* 1969
1911	*Chilston (4th),* Alastair George Akers-Douglas, *b.* 1946, *s.* 1982, *m.*	Hon. Oliver I. A.-D., *b.* 1973
1902	*Churchill (3rd) and 5th UK Baron Churchill (1815),* Victor George Spencer, *b.* 1934, *s.* 1973	To Barony only, Richard H. R. S., *b.* 1926
1718	*Cobham (12th),* Christopher Charles Lyttelton, *b.* 1947, *s.* 2006, *m.*	Hon. Oliver C. L., *b.* 1976
1902	** *Colville of Culross (5th),* Charles Mark Townshend Colville, *b.* 1959, *s.* 2010	Hon. Richmond J. I. C., *b.* 1961
1826	*Combermere (6th),* Thomas Robert Wellington Stapleton-Cotton, *b.* 1969, *s.* 2000	Hon. Laszlo M. W. S.-C., *b.* 2010
1917	*Cowdray (4th),* Michael Orlando Weetman Pearson, *b.* 1944, *s.* 1995, *m.*	Hon. Peregrine J. D. P., *b.* 1994
1927	** *Craigavon (3rd),* Janric Fraser Craig, *b.* 1944, *s.* 1974	None
1943	*Daventry (4th),* James Edward FitzRoy Newdegate, *b.* 1960, *s.* 2000, *m.*	Hon. Humphrey J. F. N., *b.* 1995
1937	*Davidson (2nd),* John Andrew Davidson, *b.* 1928, *s.* 1970, *m.*	Hon. Malcolm W. M. D., *b.* 1934
1956	*De L'Isle (2nd),* Philip John Algernon Sidney, MBE, *b.* 1945, *s.* 1991, *m.*	Hon. Philip W. E. S., *b.* 1985
1776 I.	*De Vesci (7th),* Thomas Eustace Vesey, *b.* 1955, *s.* 1983, *m.*	Hon. Oliver I. V., *b.* 1991
1917	*Devonport (3rd),* Terence Kearley, *b.* 1944, *s.* 1973	Chester D. H. K., *b.* 1932
1964	*Dilhorne (2nd),* John Mervyn Manningham-Buller, *b.* 1932, *s.* 1980, *m.*	Hon. James E. M.-B., *b.* 1956
1622 I.	*Dillon (22nd),* Henry Benedict Charles Dillon, *b.* 1973, *s.* 1982	Hon. Richard A. L. D., *b.* 1948
1785 I.	*Doneraile (10th),* Richard Allen St Leger, *b.* 1946, *s.* 1983, *m.*	Hon. Nathaniel W. R. St J. St L., *b.* 1971
1680 I.	*Downe (12th),* Richard Henry Dawnay, *b.* 1967, *s.* 2002	Thomas P. D., *b.* 1978
1959	*Dunrossil (3rd),* Andrew William Reginald Morrison, *b.* 1953, *s.* 2000, *m.*	Hon. Callum A. B. M., *b.* 1994
1964	** *Eccles (2nd),* John Dawson Eccles, CBE, *b.* 1931, *s.* 1999, *m.*	Hon. William D. E., *b.* 1960
1897	*Esher (5th),* Christopher Lionel Baliol Brett, *b.* 1936, *s.* 2004, *m.*	Hon. Matthew C. A. B., *b.* 1963
1816	*Exmouth (10th),* Paul Edward Pellew, *b.* 1940, *s.* 1970, *m.*	Hon. Edward F. P., *b.* 1978
1620 S.	** *of Falkland (15th),* Lucius Edward William Plantagenet Cary, *b.* 1935, *s.* 1984, *m. Premier Scottish Viscount on the Roll*	Master of Falkland, *b.* 1963
1720	*Falmouth (9th),* George Hugh Boscawen, *b.* 1919, *s.* 1962, *w.*	Hon. Evelyn A. H. B., *b.* 1955
1720 I.	*Gage (8th),* (Henry) Nicolas Gage, *b.* 1934, *s.* 1993, *m.*	Hon. Henry W. G., *b.* 1975
1727 I.	*Galway (12th),* George Rupert Monckton-Arundell, *b.* 1922, *s.* 1980, *m.*	Hon. J. Philip M., *b.* 1952
1478 I.	*Gormanston (17th),* Jenico Nicholas Dudley Preston, *b.* 1939, *s.* 1940, *m. Premier Viscount of Ireland*	Hon. Jenico F. T. P., *b.* 1974
1816 I.	*Gort (9th),* Foley Robert Standish Prendergast Vereker, *b.* 1951, *s.* 1995, *m.*	Hon. Robert F. P. V., *b.* 1993
1900	** *Goschen (4th),* Giles John Harry Goschen, *b.* 1965, *s.* 1977, *m.*	Hon. Alexander J. E. G., *b.* 2001
1849	*Gough (5th),* Shane Hugh Maryon Gough, *b.* 1941, *s.* 1951	None
1929	*Hailsham (3rd),* Douglas Martin Hogg, PC, QC, *b.* 1945, *s.* 2001, *m.*	Hon. Quintin J. N. M. H., *b.* 1973
1891	*Hambleden (4th),* William Herbert Smith, *b.* 1930, *s.* 1948, *m.*	Hon. William H. B. S., *b.* 1955
1884	*Hampden (7th),* Francis Anthony Brand, *b.* 1970, *s.* 2008, *m.*	Hon. Lucian A. B., *b.* 2005
1936	** *Hanworth (3rd),* David Stephen Geoffrey Pollock, *b.* 1946, *s.* 1996, *m.*	Harold W. C. P., *b.* 1988
1791 I.	*Harberton (11th),* Henry Robert Pomeroy, *b.* 1958, *s.* 2004, *m.*	Hon. Patrick C. P., *b.* 1995
1846	*Hardinge (7th),* Andrew Hartland Hardinge, *b.* 1960, *s.* 2004, *m.*	Hon. Thomas H. de M. H., *b.* 1993
1791 I.	*Hawarden (9th),* (Robert) Connan Wyndham Leslie Maude, *b.* 1961, *s.* 1991, *m.*	Hon. Varian J. C. E. M., *b.* 1997
1960	*Head (2nd),* Richard Antony Head, *b.* 1937, *s.* 1983, *m.*	Hon. Henry J. H., *b.* 1980
1550	*Hereford (19th),* Charles Robin De Bohun Devereux, *b.* 1975, *s.* 2004, *Premier Viscount of England*	Hon. Edward M. de B. D., *b.* 1977
1842	*Hill (9th),* Peter David Raymond Charles Clegg-Hill, *b.* 1945, *s.* 2003	Hon. Michael C. D. C.-H., *b.* 1988

1796	*Hood (8th)*, Henry Lyttleton Alexander Hood, *b.* 1958, *s.* 1999, *m.*	Hon. Archibald L. S. H., *b.* 1993
1945	*Kemsley (3rd)*, Richard Gomer Berry, *b.* 1951, *s.* 1999, *m.*	Hon. Luke G. B., *b.* 1998
1911	*Knollys (3rd)*, David Francis Dudley Knollys, *b.* 1931, *s.* 1966, *m.*	Hon. Patrick N. M. K., *b.* 1962
1895	*Knutsford (6th)*, Michael Holland-Hibbert, *b.* 1926, *s.* 1986, *m.*	Hon. Henry T. H.-H., *b.* 1959
1954	*Leathers (3rd)*, Christopher Graeme Leathers, *b.* 1941, *s.* 1996, *m.*	Hon. James F. L., *b.* 1969
1781 I.	*Lifford (9th)*, (Edward) James Wingfield Hewitt, *b.* 1949, *s.* 1987, *m.*	Hon. James T. W. H., *b.* 1979
1921	*Long (4th)*, Richard Gerard Long, CBE, *b.* 1929, *s.* 1967, *m.*	Hon. James R. L., *b.* 1960
1957	*Mackintosh of Halifax (3rd)*, (John) Clive Mackintosh, *b.* 1958, *s.* 1980, *m.*	Hon. Thomas H. G. M., *b.* 1985
1955	*Malvern (3rd)*, Ashley Kevin Godfrey Huggins, *b.* 1949, *s.* 1978	Hon. M. James H., *b.* 1928
1945	*Marchwood (3rd)*, David George Staveley Penny, *b.* 1936, *s.* 1979, *w.*	Hon. Peter G. W. P., *b.* 1965
1942	*Margesson (2nd)*, Francis Vere Hampden Margesson, *b.* 1922, *s.* 1965, *m.*	Capt. Hon. Richard F. D. M., *b.* 1960
1660 I.	*Massereene (14th) and Ferrard (7th) (I. 1797)*, John David Clotworthy Whyte-Melville Foster Skeffington, *b.* 1940, *s.* 1992, *m.*	Hon. Charles J. C. W.-M. F. S., *b.* 1973
1802	*Melville (10th)*, Robert Henry Kirkpatrick Dundas, *b.* 1984, *s.* 2011	Hon. James D. B. D., *b.* 1986
1916	*Mersey (5th)*, Edward John Hallam Bigham, *b.* 1966, *s.* 2006, *m.*	Hon. David E. H. B., *b.* 1938
1717 I.	*Midleton (12th)*, Alan Henry Brodrick, *b.* 1949, *s.* 1988, *m.*	Hon. Ashley R. B., *b.* 1980
1962	*Mills (3rd)*, Christopher Philip Roger Mills, *b.* 1956, *s.* 1988, *m.*	None
1716 I.	*Molesworth (12th)*, Robert Bysse Kelham Molesworth, *b.* 1959, *s.* 1997	Hon. William J. C. M., *b.* 1960
1801 I.	*Monck (7th)*, Charles Stanley Monck, *b.* 1953, *s.* 1982 (Does not use title)	Hon. George S. M., *b.* 1957
1957	*Monckton of Brenchley (3rd)*, Christopher Walter Monckton, *b.* 1952, *s.* 2006, *m.*	Hon. Timothy D. R. M., *b.* 1955
1946	** *Montgomery of Alamein (2nd)*, David Bernard Montgomery, CMG, *b.* 1928, *s.* 1976, *m.*	Hon. Henry D. M., *b.* 1954
1550 I.	*Mountgarret (18th)*, Piers James Richard Butler, *b.* 1961, *s.* 2004	Hon. Edmund H. R. B., *b.* 1962
1952	*Norwich (2nd)*, John Julius Cooper, CVO, *b.* 1929, *s.* 1954, *m.*	Hon. Jason C. D. B. C., *b.* 1959
1651 S.	*of Oxfuird (14th)*, Ian Arthur Alexander Makgill, *b.* 1969, *s.* 2003	Hon. Robert E. G. M., *b.* 1969
1873	*Portman (10th)*, Christopher Edward Berkeley Portman, *b.* 1958, *s.* 1999, *m.*	Hon. Luke O. B. P., *b.* 1984
1743 I.	*Powerscourt (10th)*, Mervyn Niall Wingfield, *b.* 1935, *s.* 1973, *m.*	Hon. Mervyn A. W., *b.* 1963
1900	*Ridley (4th)*, Matthew White Ridley, KG, GCVO, TD, *b.* 1925, *s.* 1964, *w.*	Hon. Matthew W. R., *b.* 1958
1960	*Rochdale (2nd)*, St John Durival Kemp, *b.* 1938, *s.* 1993, *m.*	Hon. Jonathan H. D. K., *b.* 1961
1919	*Rothermere (4th)*, (Harold) Jonathan Esmond Vere Harmsworth, *b.* 1967, *s.* 1998, *m.*	Hon. Vere R. J. H. H., *b.* 1994
1937	*Runciman of Doxford (3rd)*, Walter Garrison Runciman (Garry), CBE, *b.* 1934, *s.* 1989, *m.*	Hon. David W. R., *b.* 1967
1918	*St Davids (4th)*, Rhodri Colwyn Philipps, *b.* 1966, *s.* 2009, *m.*	Hon. Roland A. J. E. P., *b.* 1970
1801	*St Vincent (8th)*, Edward Robert James Jervis, *b.* 1951, *s.* 2006, *m.*	Hon. James R. A. J., *b.* 1982
1937	*Samuel (3rd)*, David Herbert Samuel, OBE, PHD, *b.* 1922, *s.* 1978, *m.*	Hon. Dan J. S., *b.* 1925
1911	*Scarsdale (4th)*, Peter Ghislain Nathaniel Curzon, *b.* 1949, *s.* 2000, *m.*	Hon. David J. N. C., *b.* 1958
1905 M.	*Selby (6th)*, Christopher Rolf Thomas Gully, *b.* 1993, *s.* 2001	Hon. (James) Edward H. G. G., *b.* 1945
1805	*Sidmouth (8th)*, Jeremy Francis Addington, *b.* 1947, *s.* 2005, *w.*	Hon. Steffan A., *b.* 1966
1940	** *Simon (3rd)*, Jan David Simon, *b.* 1940, *s.* 1993, *m.*	None
1960	** *Slim (2nd)*, John Douglas Slim, OBE, *b.* 1927, *s.* 1970, *m.*	Hon. Mark W. R. S., *b.* 1960
1954	*Soulbury (4th)*, Oliver Peter Ramsbotham, *b.* 1943, *s.* 2010, *m.*	Hon. Edward H. R., *b.* 1966
1776 I.	*Southwell (7th)*, Pyers Anthony Joseph Southwell, *b.* 1930, *s.* 1960, *m.*	Hon. Richard A. P. S., *b.* 1956
1942	*Stansgate*, Anthony Neil Wedgwood Benn, *b.* 1925, *s.* 1960, *w.* Disclaimed for life 1963.	Stephen M. W. B., *b.* 1951
1959	*Stuart of Findhorn (3rd)*, James Dominic Stuart, *b.* 1948, *s.* 1999, *m.*	Hon. Andrew M. S., *b.* 1957
1957	** *Tenby (3rd)*, William Lloyd George, *b.* 1927, *s.* 1983, *m.*	Hon. Timothy H. G. L. G., *b.* 1962
1952	*Thurso (3rd)*, John Archibald Sinclair, MP, *b.* 1953, *s.* 1995, *m.*	Hon. James A. R. S., *b.* 1984
1721	*Torrington (11th)*, Timothy Howard St George Byng, *b.* 1943, *s.* 1961, *m.*	Colin H. C.-B., *b.* 1960
1936	** *Trenchard (3rd)*, Hugh Trenchard, *b.* 1951, *s.* 1987, *m.*	Hon. Alexander T. T., *b.* 1978
1921	** *Ullswater (2nd)*, Nicholas James Christopher Lowther, PC, LVO, *b.* 1942, *s.* 1949, *m.*	Hon. Benjamin J. L., *b.* 1975
1622 I.	*Valentia (16th)*, Frances William Dighton Annesley, *b.* 1959, *s.* 2005, *m.*	Hon. Peter J. A., *b.* 1967
1952	** *Waverley (3rd)*, John Desmond Forbes Anderson, *b.* 1949, *s.* 1990	Hon. Forbes A. R. A., *b.* 1996

1938	*Weir (3rd)*, William Kenneth James Weir, *b.* 1933, *s.* 1975, *m.*	Hon. James W. H. W., *b.* 1965
1918	*Wimborne (4th)*, Ivor Mervyn Vigors Guest, *b.* 1968, *s.* 1993	Hon. Julien J. G., *b.* 1945
1923	** *Younger of Leckie (5th)*, James Edward George Younger, *b.* 1955, *s.* 2003, *m.*	Hon. Alexander W. G. Y., *b.* 1993

BARONS/LORDS

Coronet, Six silver balls

Style, The Rt. Hon. the Lord _
   Envelope (formal), The Rt. Hon. Lord _; *(social)*, The Lord _. *Letter (formal)*, My Lord; *(social)*, Dear Lord _. *Spoken*, Lord _.
In the Peerage of Scotland there is no rank of Baron; the equivalent rank is Lord of Parliament and Scottish peers should always be styled 'Lord', never 'Baron'.
Wife's style, The Rt. Hon. the Lady _
   Envelope (formal), The Rt. Hon. Lady _; *(social)*, The Lady _. *Letter (formal)*, My Lady; *(social)*, Dear Lady _. *Spoken*, Lady _
Children's style, 'The Hon.' before forename (F_) and surname (S_)
   Envelope, The Hon. F_ S_. *Letter*, Dear Mr/Miss/Mrs S_. *Spoken*, Mr/Miss/Mrs S_
In Scotland, the heir apparent to a Lord may be styled 'The Master of _ (title of peer)'

Created	*Title, order of succession, name, etc*	*Heir*
1911	*Aberconway (4th)*, (Henry) Charles McLaren, *b.* 1948, *s.* 2003, *m.*	Hon. Charles S. M., *b.* 1984
1873	** *Aberdare (5th)*, Alastair John Lyndhurst Bruce, *b.* 1947, *s.* 2005, *m.*	Hon. Hector M. N. B., *b.* 1974
1835	*Abinger (9th)*, James Harry Scarlett, *b.* 1959, *s.* 2002, *m.*	Hon. Peter R. S., *b.* 1961
1869	*Acton (5th)*, John Charles Ferdinand Harold Lyon-Dalberg-Acton, *b.* 1966, *s.* 2010, *m.*	Hon. John C. L.-D.-A., *b.* 1943
1887	** *Addington (6th)*, Dominic Bryce Hubbard, *b.* 1963, *s.* 1982	Hon. Michael W. L. H., *b.* 1965
1896	*Aldenham (6th) and Hunsdon of Hunsdon (4th) (1923)*, Vicary Tyser Gibbs, *b.* 1948, *s.* 1986, *m.*	Hon. Humphrey W. F. G., *b.* 1989
1962	*Aldington (2nd)*, Charles Harold Stuart Low, *b.* 1948, *s.* 2000, *m.*	Hon. Philip T. A. L., *b.* 1990
1945	*Altrincham (3rd)*, Anthony Ulick David Dundas Grigg, *b.* 1934, *s.* 2001, *m.*	Hon. (Edward) Sebastian G., *b.* 1965
1929	*Alvingham (2nd)*, Maj.-Gen. Robert Guy Eardley Yerburgh, CBE, *b.* 1926, *s.* 1955, *m.*	Capt. Hon. Robert R. G. Y., *b.* 1956
1892	*Amherst of Hackney (5th)*, Hugh William Amherst Cecil, *b.* 1968, *s.* 2009, *m.*	Hon. Jack W. A. C., *b.* 2001
1881	*Ampthill (5th)*, David Whitney Erskine Russell, *b.* 1947, *s.* 2011	Hon. Anthony J. M. R., *b.* 1952
1947	*Amwell (3rd)*, Keith Norman Montague, *b.* 1943, *s.* 1990, *m.*	Hon. Ian K. M., *b.* 1973
1863	*Annaly (6th)*, Luke Richard White, *b.* 1954, *s.* 1990, *m.*	Hon. Luke H. W., *b.* 1990
1885	*Ashbourne (4th)*, Edward Barry Greynville Gibson, *b.* 1933, *s.* 1983, *m.*	Hon. Edward C. d'O. G., *b.* 1967
1835	*Ashburton (7th)*, John Francis Harcourt Baring, KG, KCVO, *b.* 1928, *s.* 1991, *m.*	Hon. Mark F. R. B., *b.* 1958
1892	*Ashcombe (4th)*, Henry Edward Cubitt, *b.* 1924, *s.* 1962, *m.*	Mark E. C., *b.* 1964
1911	** *Ashton of Hyde (4th)*, Thomas Henry Ashton, *b.* 1958, *s.* 2008, *m.*	Hon. John E. A., *b.* 1966
1800 I.	*Ashtown (8th)*, Roderick Nigel Godolphin Trench, *b.* 1944, *s.* 2010, *m.*	Hon. Timothy R. H. T., *b.* 1968
1956	** *Astor of Hever (3rd)*, John Jacob Astor, *b.* 1946, *s.* 1984, *m.*	Hon. Charles G. J. A., *b.* 1990
1789 I.	*Auckland (10th) and Auckland (10th) (1793)*, Robert Ian Burnard Eden, *b.* 1962, *s.* 1997, *m.*	Henry V. E., *b.* 1958
1313	*Audley*, Barony in abeyance between three co-heiresses since 1997	
1900	** *Avebury (4th)*, Eric Reginald Lubbock, *b.* 1928, *s.* 1971, *m.*	Hon. Lyulph A. J. L., *b.* 1954
1718 I.	*Aylmer (14th)*, (Anthony) Julian Aylmer, *b.* 1951, *s.* 2006, *m.*	Hon. Michael H. A., *b.* 1991
1929	*Baden-Powell (3rd)*, Robert Crause Baden-Powell, *b.* 1936, *s.* 1962, *w.*	Hon. David M. B.-P., *b.* 1940
1780	*Bagot (10th)*, (Charles Hugh) Shaun Bagot, *b.* 1944, *s.* 2001, *m.*	Richard C. V. B., *b.* 1941
1953	*Baillieu (3rd)*, James William Latham Baillieu, *b.* 1950, *s.* 1973, *m.*	Hon. Robert L. B., *b.* 1979
1607 S.	*Balfour of Burleigh (8th)*, Robert Bruce, *b.* 1927, *s.* 1967, *m.*	Hon. Victoria B., *b.* 1973
1945	*Balfour of Inchrye (2nd)*, Ian Balfour, *b.* 1924, *s.* 1988, *w.*	None
1924	*Banbury of Southam (3rd)*, Charles William Banbury, *b.* 1953, *s.* 1981, *m.*	None
1698	*Barnard (11th)*, Harry John Neville Vane, TD, *b.* 1923, *s.* 1964	Hon. Henry F. C. V., *b.* 1959

1887	*Basing (6th)*, Stuart Anthony Whitfield Sclater-Booth, *b.* 1969, *s.* 2007, *m.*	Hon. Luke W. S.-B., *b.* 2000
1917	*Beaverbrook (3rd)*, Maxwell William Humphrey Aitken, *b.* 1951, *s.* 1985, *m.*	Hon. Maxwell F. A., *b.* 1977
1647 S.	*Belhaven and Stenton (13th)*, Robert Anthony Carmichael Hamilton, *b.* 1927, *s.* 1961, *m.*	Master of Belhaven, *b.* 1953
1848 I.	*Bellew (8th)*, Bryan Edward Bellew, *b.* 1943, *s.* 2010, *m.*	Hon. Anthony R. B. B., *b.* 1972
1856	*Belper (5th)*, Richard Henry Strutt, *b.* 1941, *s.* 1999, *m.*	Hon. Michael H. S., *b.* 1969
1421	*Berkeley (18th) and Gueterbock (life peerage, 2000)*, Anthony Fitzhardinge Gueterbock, OBE, *b.* 1939, *s.* 1992, *m.*	Hon. Thomas F. G., *b.* 1969
1922	*Bethell (5th)*, James Nicholas Bethell, *b.* 1967, *s.* 2007, *m.*	Hon. Jacob N. D. B., *b.* 200–
1938	*Bicester (3rd)*, Angus Edward Vivian Smith, *b.* 1932, *s.* 1968	Hugh C. V. S., *b.* 1934
1903	*Biddulph (5th)*, (Anthony) Nicholas Colin Maitland Biddulph, *b.* 1959, *s.* 1988, *m.*	Hon. Robert J. M. B., *b.* 1994
1938	*Birdwood (3rd)*, Mark William Ogilvie Birdwood, *b.* 1938, *s.* 1962, *m.*	None
1958	*Birkett (2nd)*, Michael Birkett, *b.* 1929, *s.* 1962, *w.*	Hon. Thomas B., *b.* 1982
1907	*Blyth (5th)*, James Audley Ian Blyth, *b.* 1970, *s.* 2009, *m.*	Hon. Hugo A. J. B., *b.* 2006
1797	*Bolton (8th)*, Harry Algar Nigel Orde-Powlett, *b.* 1954, *s.* 2001, *m.*	Hon. Thomas O.-P., *b.* 1979
1452 S.	*Borthwick (24th)*, John Hugh Borthwick, *b.* 1940, *s.* 1996, *m.*	Hon. James H. A. B. of Glengelt, *b.* 1940
1922	*Borwick (5th)*, (Geoffrey Robert) James Borwick, *b.* 1955, *s.* 2007, *m.*	Hon. Edwin D. W. B., *b.* 1984
1761	*Boston (11th)*, George William Eustace Boteler Irby, *b.* 1971, *s.* 2007, *m.*	Hon. Thomas W. G. B. I., *b.* 1999
1942	** *Brabazon of Tara (3rd)*, Ivon Anthony Moore-Brabazon, *b.* 1946, *s.* 1974, *m.*	Hon. Benjamin R. M.-B., *b.* 1983
1880	*Brabourne (8th)*, Norton Louis Philip Knatchbull, *b.* 1947, *s.* 2005, *m.* (*also* Lord Romsey heir to Countess Mountbatten of Burma, *see* that title)	Hon. Nicholas L. C. N. K., *b.* 1981
1925	*Bradbury (3rd)*, John Bradbury, *b.* 1940, *s.* 1994, *m.*	Hon. John B., *b.* 1973
1962	*Brain (2nd)*, Christopher Langdon Brain, *b.* 1926, *s.* 1966, *m.*	Hon. Michael C. B., *b.* 1928
1938	*Brassey of Apethorpe (3rd)*, David Henry Brassey, OBE, *b.* 1932, *s.* 1967, *m.*	Hon. Edward B., *b.* 1964
1788	*Braybrooke (10th)*, Robin Henry Charles Neville, *b.* 1932, *s.* 1990, *m.*	Richard R. N., *b.* 1977
1957	** *Bridges (2nd)*, Thomas Edward Bridges, GCMG, *b.* 1927, *s.* 1969, *m.*	Hon. Mark T. B., *b.* 1954
1945	*Broadbridge (4th)*, Martin Hugh Broadbridge, *b.* 1929, *s.* 2000, *w.*	Hon. Richard J. M. B., *b.* 1959
1933	*Brocket (3rd)*, Charles Ronald George Nall-Cain, *b.* 1952, *s.* 1967, *w.*	Hon. Alexander C. C. N.-C., *b.* 1984
1860	** *Brougham and Vaux (5th)*, Michael John Brougham, CBE, *b.* 1938, *s.* 1967	Hon. Charles W. B., *b.* 1971
1776	*Brownlow (7th)*, Edward John Peregrine Cust, *b.* 1936, *s.* 1978, *m.*	Hon. Peregrine E. Q. C., *b.* 1974
1942	*Bruntisfield (3rd)*, Michael John Victor Warrender, *b.* 1949, *s.* 2007, *m.*	Hon. John M. P. C. W., *b.* 1996
1950	*Burden (4th)*, Fraser William Elsworth Burden, *b.* 1964, *s.* 2000, *m.*	Hon. Ian S. B., *b.* 1967
1529	*Burgh (8th)*, (Alexander) Gregory Disney Leith, *b.* 1958, *s.* 2001, *m.*	Hon. Alexander J. S. L., *b.* 1986
1903	*Burnham (7th)*, Harry Frederick Alan Lawson, *b.* 1968, *s.* 2005	None
1897	*Burton (3rd)*, Michael Evan Victor Baillie, *b.* 1924, *s.* 1962, *m.*	Hon. Evan M. R. B., *b.* 1949
1643	*Byron (13th)*, Robert James Byron, *b.* 1950, *s.* 1989, *m.*	Hon. Charles R. G. B., *b.* 1990
1937	*Cadman (3rd)*, John Anthony Cadman, *b.* 1938, *s.* 1966, *m.*	Hon. Nicholas A. J. C., *b.* 1977
1945	*Calverley (3rd)*, Charles Rodney Muff, *b.* 1946, *s.* 1971, *m.*	Hon. Jonathan E. M., *b.* 1975
1383	*Camoys (7th)*, (Ralph) Thomas Campion George Sherman Stonor, GCVO, PC, *b.* 1940, *s.* 1976, *m.*	Hon. R. William R. T. S., *b.* 1974
1715 I.	*Carbery (11th)*, Peter Ralfe Harrington Evans-Freke, *b.* 1920, *s.* 1970, *w.*	Hon. Michael P. E.-F., *b.* 1942
1834 I.	*Carew (7th) and Carew (7th) (1838)*, Patrick Thomas Conolly-Carew, *b.* 1938, *s.* 1994, *m.*	Hon. William P. C.-C., *b.* 1973
1916	*Carnock (5th)*, Adam Nicolson, *b.* 1957, *s.* 2008, *m.*	Hon. Thomas N., *b.* 1984
1796 I.	*Carrington (6th) and Carrington (6th) (1797) and Carington of Upton (life peerage, 1999)*, Peter Alexander Rupert Carington, KG, GCMG, CH, MC, PC, *b.* 1919, *s.* 1938, *w.*	Hon. Rupert F. J. C., *b.* 1948
1812 I.	*Castlemaine (8th)*, Roland Thomas John Handcock, MBE, *b.* 1943, *s.* 1973, *m.*	Hon. Ronan M. E. H., *b.* 1989
1936	*Catto (3rd)*, Innes Gordon Catto, *b.* 1950, *s.* 2001, *m.*	Hon. Alexander G. C., *b.* 1952
1918	*Cawley (4th)*, John Francis Cawley, *b.* 1946, *s.* 2001, *m.*	Hon. William R. H. C., *b.* 1981
1858	*Chesham (7th)*, Charles Gray Compton Cavendish, *b.* 1974, *s.* 2009, *m.*	Hon. Oliver N.B.C., *b.* 2007
1945	*Chetwode (2nd)*, Philip Chetwode, *b.* 1937, *s.* 1950, *m.*	Hon. Roger C., *b.* 1968
1945	** *Chorley (2nd)*, Roger Richard Edward Chorley, *b.* 1930, *s.* 1978, *m.*	Hon. Nicholas R. D. C., *b.* 1966
1858	*Churston (5th)*, John Francis Yarde-Buller, *b.* 1934, *s.* 1991, *m.*	Hon. Benjamin F. A. Y.-B., *b.* 1974

1800 I.	*Clanmorris (8th)*, Simon John Ward Bingham, *b*. 1937, *s*. 1988, *m*.	Robert D. de B. B., *b*. 1942
1672	*Clifford of Chudleigh (14th)*, Thomas Hugh Clifford, *b*. 1948, *s*. 1988, *m*.	Hon. Alexander T. H. C., *b*. 1985
1299	*Clinton (22nd)*, Gerard Nevile Mark Fane Trefusis, *b*. 1934, *s*. 1965, *m*.	Hon. Charles P. R. F. T., *b*. 1962
1955	*Clitheroe (2nd)*, Ralph John Assheton, *b*. 1929, *s*. 1984, *m*.	Hon. Ralph C. A., *b*. 1962
1919	*Clwyd (4th)*, (John) Murray Roberts, *b*. 1971, *s*. 2006	Hon. Jeremy T. R., *b*. 1973
1948	*Clydesmuir (3rd)*, David Ronald Colville, *b*. 1949, *s*. 1996, *m*.	Hon. Richard C., *b*. 1980
1960	** *Cobbold (2nd)*, David Antony Fromanteel Lytton Cobbold, *b*. 1937, *s*. 1987, *m*.	Hon. Henry F. L. C., *b*. 1962
1919	*Cochrane of Cults (4th)*, (Ralph Henry) Vere Cochrane, *b*. 1926, *s*. 1990, *m*.	Hon. Thomas H. V. C., *b*. 1957
1954	*Coleraine (2nd)*, (James) Martin (Bonar) Law, *b*. 1931, *s*. 1980, *m*.	Hon. James P. B. L., *b*. 1975
1873	*Coleridge (5th)*, William Duke Coleridge, *b*. 1937, *s*. 1984, *m*.	Hon. James D. C., *b*. 1967
1946	*Colgrain (4th)*, Alastair Colin Leckie Campbell, *b*. 1951, *s*. 2008, *m*.	Hon. Thomas C. D. C., *b*. 1984
1917	** *Colwyn (3rd)*, (Ian) Anthony Hamilton-Smith, CBE, *b*. 1942, *s*. 1966, *m*.	Hon. Craig P. H.-S., *b*. 1968
1956	*Colyton (2nd)*, Alisdair John Munro Hopkinson, *b*. 1958, *s*. 1996, *m*.	Hon. James P. M. H., *b*. 1983
1841	*Congleton (8th)*, Christopher Patrick Parnell, *b*. 1930, *s*. 1967, *m*.	Hon. John P. C. P., *b*. 1959
1927	*Cornwallis (4th)*, Fiennes Wykeham Jeremy Cornwallis, *b*. 1946, *s*. 2010, *m*.	Hon. Fiennes A. W. M. C., *b*. 1987
1874	*Cottesloe (5th)*, John Tapling Fremantle, *b*. 1927, *s*. 1994, *m*.	Hon. Thomas F. H. F., *b*. 1966
1929	*Craigmyle (4th)*, Thomas Columba Shaw, *b*. 1960, *s*. 1998, *m*.	Hon. Alexander F. S., *b*. 1988
1899	*Cranworth (3rd)*, Philip Bertram Gurdon, *b*. 1940, *s*. 1964, *m*.	Hon. Sacha W. R. G., *b*. 1970
1959	** *Crathorne (2nd)*, Charles James Dugdale, *b*. 1939, *s*. 1977, *w*.	Hon. Thomas A. J. D., *b*. 1977
1892	*Crawshaw (5th)*, David Gerald Brooks, *b*. 1934, *s*. 1997, *m*.	Hon. John P. B., *b*. 1938
1940	*Croft (3rd)*, Bernard William Henry Page Croft, *b*. 1949, *s*. 1997, *m*.	None
1797 I.	*Crofton (8th)*, Edward Harry Piers Crofton, *b*. 1988, *s*. 2007	Hon. Charles M. G. C., *b*. 1988
1375	*Cromwell (7th)*, Godfrey John Bewicke-Copley, *b*. 1960, *s*. 1982, *m*.	Hon. David G. B.-C., *b*. 1997
1947	*Crook (3rd)*, Robert Douglas Edwin Crook, *b*. 1955, *s*. 2001, *m*.	Hon. Matthew R. C., *b*. 1990
1920	*Cullen of Ashbourne (3rd)*, Edmund Willoughby Marsham Cokayne, *b*. 1916, *s*. 2000, *w*.	(Hon.) John O'B. M. C., *b*.1920
1914	*Cunliffe (3rd)*, Roger Cunliffe, *b*. 1932, *s*. 1963, *m*.	Hon. Henry C., *b*. 1962
1332	*Darcy de Knayth (19th)*, Caspar David Ingrams, *b*. 1962, *s*. 2008, *m*.	Hon. Thomas R. I., *b*. 1999
1927	*Daresbury (4th)*, Peter Gilbert Greenall, *b*. 1953, *s*. 1996, *m*.	Hon. Thomas E. G., *b*. 1984
1924	*Darling (3rd)*, (Robert) Julian Henry Darling, *b*. 1944, *s*. 2003, *m*.	Hon. Robert J. C. D., *b*. 1972
1946	*Darwen (4th)*, Paul Davies, *b*. 1962, *s*. 2011	Hon. Benjamin D., *b*. 1966
1932	*Davies (3rd)*, David Davies, *b*. 1940, *s*. 1944, *m*.	Hon. David D. D., *b*. 1975
1812 I.	*Decies (7th)*, Marcus Hugh Tristram de la Poer Beresford, *b*. 1948, *s*. 1992, *m*.	Hon. Robert M. D. de la P. B., *b*. 1988
1299	*de Clifford (27th)*, John Edward Southwell Russell, *b*. 1928, *s*. 1982, *m*.	Hon. William S. R., *b*. 1930
1851	*De Freyne (8th)*, Fulke Charles Arthur John French, *b*. 1957, *s*. 2009	Hon. Alexander J. C. F., *b*. 1988
1821	*Delamere (5th)*, Hugh George Cholmondeley, *b*. 1934, *s*. 1979, *m*.	Hon. Thomas P. G. C., *b*. 1968
1838	** *de Mauley (7th)*, Rupert Charles Ponsonby, *b*. 1957, *s*. 2002, *m*.	Ashley G. P., *b*. 1959
1937	** *Denham (2nd)*, Bertram Stanley Mitford Bowyer, KBE, PC, *b*. 1927, *s*. 1948, *m*.	Hon. Richard G. G. B., *b*. 1959
1834	*Denman (5th)*, Charles Spencer Denman, CBE, MC, TD, *b*. 1916, *s*. 1971, *w*.	Hon. Richard T. S. D., *b*. 1946
1887	*De Ramsey (4th)*, John Ailwyn Fellowes, *b*. 1942, *s*. 1993, *m*.	Hon. Freddie J. F., *b*. 1978
1264	*de Ros (28th)*, Peter Trevor Maxwell, *b*. 1958, *s*. 1983, *m*. Premier Baron of England	Hon. Finbar J. M., *b*. 1988
1881	*Derwent (5th)*, Robin Evelyn Leo Vanden-Bempde-Johnstone, LVO, *b*. 1930, *s*. 1986, *m*.	Hon. Francis P. H. V.-B.-J., *b*. 1965
1831	*de Saumarez (7th)*, Eric Douglas Saumarez, *b*. 1956, *s*. 1991, *m*.	Hon. Victor T. S., *b*. 1956
1910	*de Villiers (4th)*, Alexander Charles de Villiers, *b*. 1940, *s*. 2001, *m*.	None
1930	*Dickinson (2nd)*, Richard Clavering Hyett Dickinson, *b*. 1926, *s*. 1943, *m*.	Hon. Martin H. D., *b*. 1961
1620 I.	*Digby (12th) and Digby (5th) (1765)*, Edward Henry Kenelm Digby, KCVO, *b*. 1924, *s*. 1964, *m*.	Hon. Henry N. K. D., *b*. 1954
1615	*Dormer (17th)*, Geoffrey Henry Dormer, *b*. 1920, *s*. 1995, *m*.	Hon. William R. D., *b*. 1960
1943	*Dowding (3rd)*, Piers Hugh Tremenheere Dowding, *b*. 1948, *s*. 1992	Hon. Mark D. J. D., *b*. 1949
1439	*Dudley (15th)*, Jim Anthony Hill Wallace, *b*. 1930, *s*. 2002, *m*.	Hon. Jeremy W. G. W., *b*. 1964
1800 I.	*Dufferin and Clandeboye (11th)*, John Francis Blackwood, *b*. 1944, *s*. 1991 (claim to the peerage not yet established), *m*.	Hon. Francis S. B., *b*. 1979
1929	*Dulverton (3rd)*, (Gilbert) Michael Hamilton Wills, *b*. 1944, *s*. 1992, *m*.	Hon. Robert A. H. W., *b*. 1983
1800 I.	*Dunalley (7th)*, Henry Francis Cornelius Prittie, *b*. 1948, *s*. 1992, *m*.	Hon. Joel H. P., *b*. 1981
1324 I.	*Dunboyne (29th)*, John Fitzwalter Butler, *b*. 1951, *s*. 2004, *m*.	Hon. Richard P. T. B., *b*. 1983
1892	*Dunleath (6th)*, Brian Henry Mulholland, *b*. 1950, *s*. 1997, *m*.	Hon. Andrew H. M., *b*. 1981
1439 I.	*Dunsany (21st)*, Randal Plunkett, *b*. 1983, *s*. 2011	Hon. Oliver P., *b*. 1985

1780	*Dynevor (10th)*, Hugo Griffith Uryan Rhys, *b.* 1966, *s.* 2008	Robert D. A. R., *b.* 1963
1963	*Egremont (2nd) and Leconfield (7th) (1859)*, John Max Henry Scawen Wyndham, *b.* 1948, *s.* 1972, *m.*	Hon. George R. V. W., *b.* 1983
1643	*Elibank (14th)*, Alan D'Ardis Erskine-Murray, *b.* 1923, *s.* 1973, *w.*	Master of Elibank, *b.* 1964
1802	*Ellenborough (8th)*, Richard Edward Cecil Law, *b.* 1926, *s.* 1945, *m.*	Maj. Hon. Rupert E. H. L., *b.* 1955
1509 S.	*Elphinstone (19th) and Elphinstone (5th) (1885)*, Alexander Mountstuart Elphinstone, *b.* 1980, *s.* 1994, *m.*	Master of Elphinstone, *b.* 2011
1934	** *Elton (2nd)*, Rodney Elton, TD, *b.* 1930, *s.* 1973, *m.*	Hon. Edward P. E., *b.* 1966
1627 S.	*Fairfax of Cameron (14th)*, Nicholas John Albert Fairfax, *b.* 1956, *s.* 1964, *m.*	Hon. Edward N. T. F., *b.* 1984
1961	*Fairhaven (3rd)*, Ailwyn Henry George Broughton, *b.* 1936, *s.* 1973, *m.*	Maj. Hon. James H. A. B., *b.* 1963
1916	*Faringdon (3rd)*, Charles Michael Henderson, KCVO, *b.* 1937, *s.* 1977, *m.*	Hon. James H. H., *b.* 1961
1756 I.	*Farnham (13th)*, Simon Kenlis Maxwell, *b.* 1933, *s.* 2001, *m.*	Hon. Robin S. M., *b.* 1965
1856 I.	*Fermoy (6th)*, Patrick Maurice Burke Roche, *b.* 1967, *s.* 1984, *m.*	Hon. E. Hugh B. R., *b.* 1972
1826	*Feversham (7th)*, Jasper Orlando Slingsby Duncombe, *b.* 1968, *s.* 2009	Hon. Jake B. D., *b.* 1972
1798 I.	*ffrench (8th)*, Robuck John Peter Charles Mario ffrench, *b.* 1956, *s.* 1986, *m.*	Hon. John C. M. J. F. ff., *b.* 1928
1909	*Fisher (3rd)*, John Vavasseur Fisher, DSC, *b.* 1921, *s.* 1955, *m.*	Hon. Patrick V. F., *b.* 1953
1295	*Fitzwalter (22nd)*, Julian Brook Plumptre, *b.* 1952, *s.* 2004, *m.*	Hon. Edward B. P., *b.* 1989
1776	*Foley (8th)*, Adrian Gerald Foley, *b.* 1923, *s.* 1927, *m.*	Hon. Thomas H. F., *b.* 1961
1445	*Forbes (22nd)*, Nigel Ivan Forbes, KBE, *b.* 1918, *s.* 1953, *m. Premier Lord of Scotland*	Master of Forbes, *b.* 1946
1821	*Forester (9th)*, Charles Richard George Weld-Forester, *b.* 1975, *s.* 2004,	Wolstan W. W.-F., *b.* 1941
1922	*Forres (4th)*, Alastair Stephen Grant Williamson, *b.* 1946, *s.* 1978, *m.*	Hon. George A. M. W., *b.* 1972
1917	*Forteviot (4th)*, John James Evelyn Dewar, *b.* 1938, *s.* 1993, *w.*	Hon. Alexander J. E. D., *b.* 1971
1951	** *Freyberg (3rd)*, Valerian Bernard Freyberg, *b.* 1970, *s.* 1993	Hon. Joseph J. F., *b.* 2007
1917	*Gainford (3rd)*, Joseph Edward Pease, *b.* 1921, *s.* 1971, *m.*	Hon. George P., *b.* 1926
1818 I.	*Garvagh (5th)*, (Alexander Leopold Ivor) George Canning, *b.* 1920, *s.* 1956, *m.*	Hon. Spencer G. S. de R. C., *b.* 1953
1942	** *Geddes (3rd)*, Euan Michael Ross Geddes, *b.* 1937, *s.* 1975, *m.*	Hon. James G. N. G., *b.* 1969
1876	*Gerard (5th)*, Anthony Robert Hugo Gerard, *b.* 1949, *s.* 1992, *m.*	Hon. Rupert B. C. G., *b.* 1981
1824	*Gifford (6th)*, Anthony Maurice Gifford, *b.* 1940, *s.* 1961, *m.*	Hon. Thomas A. G., *b.* 1967
1917	*Gisborough (3rd)*, Thomas Richard John Long Chaloner, *b.* 1927, *s.* 1951, *m.*	Hon. T. Peregrine L. C., *b.* 1961
1960	*Gladwyn (2nd)*, Miles Alvery Gladwyn Jebb, *b.* 1930, *s.* 1996	None
1899	*Glanusk (5th)*, Christopher Russell Bailey, *b.* 1942, *s.* 1997, *m.*	Hon. Charles H. B., *b.* 1976
1918	** *Glenarthur (4th)*, Simon Mark Arthur, *b.* 1944, *s.* 1976, *m.*	Hon. Edward A. A., *b.* 1973
1911	*Glenconner (4th)*, Cody Charles Edward Tennant, *b.* 1994, *s.* 2010	Hon. Christopher C. T., *b.* 1967
1964	*Glendevon (3rd)*, Jonathan Charles Hope, *b.* 1952, *s.* 2009	None
1922	*Glendyne (4th)*, John Nivison, *b.* 1960, *s.* 2008	None
1939	** *Glentoran (3rd)*, (Thomas) Robin (Valerian) Dixon, CBE, *b.* 1935, *s.* 1995, *m.*	Hon. Daniel G. D., *b.* 1959
1909	*Gorell (5th)*, John Picton Gorell Barnes, *b.* 1959, *s.* 2007, *m.*	Hon. Oliver G. B., *b.* 1993
1953	** *Grantchester (3rd)*, Christopher John Suenson-Taylor, *b.* 1951, *s.* 1995, *m.*	Hon. Jesse D. S.-T., *b.* 1977
1782	*Grantley (8th)*, Richard William Brinsley Norton, *b.* 1956, *s.* 1995	Hon. Francis J. H. N., *b.* 1960
1794 I.	*Graves (10th)*, Timothy Evelyn Graves, *b.* 1960, *s.* 2002	None
1445 S.	*Gray (23rd)*, Andrew Godfrey Diarmid Stuart Campbell-Gray, *b.* 1964, *s.* 2003, *m.*	Master of Gray, *b.* 1996
1950	*Greenhill (3rd)*, Malcolm Greenhill, *b.* 1924, *s.* 1989	None
1927	** *Greenway (4th)*, Ambrose Charles Drexel Greenway, *b.* 1941, *s.* 1975, *m.*	Hon. Nigel. P. G., *b.* 1944
1902	*Grenfell (3rd) and Grenfell of Kilvey (life peerage, 2000)*, Julian Pascoe Francis St Leger Grenfell, *b.* 1935, *s.* 1976, *m.*	Francis P. J. G., *b.* 1938
1944	*Gretton (4th)*, John Lysander Gretton, *b.* 1975, *s.* 1989	Hon. John F. B. G., *b.* 2008
1397	*Grey of Codnor (6th)*, Richard Henry Cornwall-Legh, *b.* 1936, *s.* 1996, *m.*	Hon. Richard S. C. C.-L., *b.* 1976
1955	*Gridley (3rd)*, Richard David Arnold Gridley, *b.* 1956, *s.* 1996, *m.*	Peter A. C. G., *b.* 1940
1964	*Grimston of Westbury (3rd)*, Robert John Sylvester Grimston, *b.* 1951, *s.* 2003, *m.*	Hon. Gerald C. W. G., *b.* 1953
1886	*Grimthorpe (5th)*, Edward John Beckett, *b.* 1954, *s.* 2003, *m.*	Hon. Harry M. B., *b.* 1993
1945	*Hacking (3rd)*, Douglas David Hacking, *b.* 1938, *s.* 1971, *m.*	Hon. Douglas F. H., *b.* 1968
1950	*Haden-Guest (5th)*, Christopher Haden-Guest, *b.* 1948, *s.* 1996, *m.*	Hon. Nicholas H.-G., *b.* 1951

1886	*Hamilton of Dalzell (5th)*, Gavin Goulburn Hamilton, *b.* 1968, *s.* 2006, *m.*	Hon. Francis A. J. G. H., *b.* 2009
1874	*Hampton (7th)*, John Humphrey Arnott Pakington, *b.* 1964, *s.* 2003, *m.*	Hon. Charles R. C. P., *b.* 2005
1939	*Hankey (3rd)*, Donald Robin Alers Hankey, *b.* 1938, *s.* 1996, *m.*	Hon. Alexander M. A. H., *b.* 1947
1958	*Harding of Petherton (2nd)*, John Charles Harding, *b.* 1928, *s.* 1989, *m.*	Hon. William A. J. H., *b.* 1969
1910	*Hardinge of Penshurst (4th)*, Julian Alexander Hardinge, *b.* 1945, *s.* 1997	Hon. Hugh F. H., *b.* 1948
1876	*Harlech (6th)*, Francis David Ormsby-Gore, *b.* 1954, *s.* 1985, *m.*	Hon. Jasset D. C. O.-G., *b.* 1986
1939	*Harmsworth (3rd)*, Thomas Harold Raymond Harmsworth, *b.* 1939, *s.* 1990, *m.*	Hon. Dominic M. E. H., *b.* 1973
1815	*Harris (8th)*, Anthony Harris, *b.* 1942, *s.* 1996, *m.*	Rear-Adm. Michael G. T. H., *b.* 1941
1954	*Harvey of Tasburgh (3rd)*, Charles John Giuseppe Harvey, *b.* 1951, *s.* 2010, *m.*	Hon. John H., *b.* 1993
1295	*Hastings (23rd)*, Delaval Thomas Harold Astley, *b.* 1960, *s.* 2007, *m.*	Hon. Jacob A. A., *b.* 1991
1835	*Hatherton (8th)*, Edward Charles Littleton, *b.* 1950, *s.* 1985, *m.*	Hon. Thomas E. L., *b.* 1977
1776	*Hawke (12th)*, William Martin Theodore Hawke, *b.* 1995, *s.* 2010	None
1927	*Hayter (4th)*, George William Michael Chubb, *b.* 1943, *s.* 2003, *m.*	Hon. Thomas F. F. C., *b.*1986
1945	*Hazlerigg (3rd)*, Arthur Grey Hazlerigg, *b.* 1951, *s.* 2002, *m.*	Hon. Arthur W. G. H. *b.* 1987
1943	*Hemingford (3rd)*, (Dennis) Nicholas Herbert, *b.* 1934, *s.* 1982, *m.*	Hon. Christopher D. C. H., *b.* 1973
1906	*Hemphill (5th)*, Peter Patrick Fitzroy Martyn Martyn-Hemphill, *b.* 1928, *s.* 1957, *m.*	Hon. Charles A. M. M.-H., *b.* 1954
1799 I.	** *Henley (8th) and Northington (6th) (1885)*, Oliver Michael Robert Eden, *b.* 1953, *s.* 1977, *m.*	Hon. John W. O. E., *b.* 1988
1800 I.	*Henniker (9th) and Hartismere (6th) (1866)*, Mark Ian Philip Chandos Henniker-Major, *b.* 1947, *s.* 2004, *m.*	Hon. Edward G. M. H.-M., *b.* 1985
1461	*Herbert (19th)*, David John Seyfried Herbert, *b.* 1952, *s.* 2002, *m.*	Hon. Oliver R. S. H., *b.* 1976
1935	*Hesketh (3rd)*, Thomas Alexander Fermor-Hesketh, KBE, PC, *b.* 1950, *s.* 1955, *m.*	Hon. Frederick H. F.-H., *b.* 1988
1828	*Heytesbury (7th)*, James William Holmes à Court, *b.* 1967, *s.* 2004, *m.*	Peter M. H.. H. à. C., *b.* 1968
1886	*Hindlip (6th)*, Charles Henry Allsopp, *b.* 1940, *s.* 1993, *m.*	Hon. Henry W. A., *b.* 1973
1950	*Hives (3rd)*, Matthew Peter Hives, *b.* 1971, *s.* 1997	Hon. Michael B. H., *b.* 1926
1912	*Hollenden (4th)*, Ian Hampden Hope-Morley, *b.* 1946, *s.* 1999, *m.*	Hon. Edward H.-M., *b.* 1981
1897	*Holm Patrick (4th)*, Hans James David Hamilton, *b.* 1955, *s.* 1991, *m.*	Hon. Ion H. J. H., *b.* 1956
1797 I.	*Hotham (8th)*, Henry Durand Hotham, *b.* 1940, *s.* 1967, *m.*	Hon. William B. H., *b.* 1972
1881	*Hothfield (6th)*, Anthony Charles Sackville Tufton, *b.* 1939, *s.* 1991, *m.*	Hon. William S. T., *b.* 1977
1930	*Howard of Penrith (3rd)*, Philip Esme Howard, *b.* 1945, *s.* 1999, *m.*	Hon. Thomas Philip H., *b.* 1974
1960	*Howick of Glendale (2nd)*, Charles Evelyn Baring, *b.* 1937, *s.* 1973, *m.*	Hon. David E. C. B., *b.* 1975
1796 I.	*Huntingfield (7th)*, Joshua Charles Vanneck, *b.* 1954, *s.* 1994, *m.*	Hon. Gerard C. A. V., *b.* 1985
1866	** *Hylton (5th)*, Raymond Hervey Jolliffe, *b.* 1932, *s.* 1967, *m.*	Hon. William H. M. J., *b.* 1967
1933	*Iliffe (3rd)*, Robert Peter Richard Iliffe, *b.* 1944, *s.* 1996, *m.*	Hon. Edward R. I., *b.* 1968
1543 I.	*Inchiquin (18th)*, Conor Myles John O'Brien, *b.* 1943, *s.* 1982, *m.*	Conor J. A. O'B., *b.* 1952
1962	*Inchyra (3rd)*, Christian James Charles Hoyer Millar, *b.* 1962, *s.* 2011, *m.*	Hon. Jake C. R. M., *b.* 1996
1964	** *Inglewood (2nd)*, (William) Richard Fletcher-Vane, *b.* 1951, *s.* 1989, *m.*	Hon. Henry W. F. F.-V., *b.* 1990
1919	*Inverforth (4th)*, Andrew Peter Weir, *b.* 1966, *s.* 1982	Hon. Benjamin A. W., *b.* 1997
1941	*Ironside (2nd)*, Edmund Oslac Ironside, *b.* 1924, *s.* 1959, *m.*	Hon. Charles E. G. I., *b.* 1956
1952	*Jeffreys (3rd)*, Christopher Henry Mark Jeffreys, *b.* 1957, *s.* 1986, *m.*	Hon. Arthur M. H. J., *b.* 1989
1906	*Joicey (5th)*, James Michael Joicey, *b.* 1953, *s.* 1993, *m.*	Hon. William J. J., *b.* 1990
1937	*Kenilworth (4th)*, (John) Randle Siddeley, *b.* 1954, *s.* 1981, *m.*	Hon. William R. J. S., *b.* 1992
1935	*Kennet (3rd)*, William Aldus Thoby Young, *b.* 1957, *s.* 2009, *m.*	Hon. Archibald W. K. Y., *b.* 1992
1776 I.	*Kensington (8th) and Kensington (5th) (1886)*, Hugh Ivor Edwardes, *b.* 1933, *s.* 1981, *m.*	Hon. W. Owen A. E., *b.* 1964
1951	*Kenswood (2nd)*, John Michael Howard Whitfield, *b.* 1930, *s.* 1963, *m.*	Hon. Michael C. W., *b.* 1955
1788	*Kenyon (6th)*, Lloyd Tyrell-Kenyon, *b.* 1947, *s.* 1993, *m.*	Hon. Lloyd N. T.-K., *b.* 1972
1947	*Kershaw (4th)*, Edward John Kershaw, *b.* 1936, *s.* 1962, *m.*	Hon. John C. E. K., *b.* 1971
1943	*Keyes (3rd)*, Charles William Packe Keyes, *b.* 1951, *s.* 2005, *m.*	Hon. (Leopold R.) J. K., *b.* 1956
1909	*Kilbracken (4th)*, Christopher John Godley, *b.* 1945, *s.* 2006, *m.*	Hon. James J. G., *b.* 1972
1900	*Killanin (4th)*, (George) Redmond Fitzpatrick Morris, *b.* 1947, *s.* 1999, *m.*	Hon. Luke M. G. M., *b.* 1975
1943	*Killearn (3rd)*, Victor Miles George Aldous Lampson, *b.* 1941, *s.* 1996, *m.*	Hon. Miles H. M. L., *b.* 1977

1789 I.	*Kilmaine (7th)*, John David Henry Browne, *b.* 1948, *s.* 1978, *m.*	Hon. John F. S. B., *b.* 1983
1831	*Kilmarnock (8th)*, Dr Robin Jordan Boyd, *b.* 1941, *s.* 2009, *m.*	Hon. Simon J. B., *b.* 1978
1941	*Kindersley (3rd)*, Robert Hugh Molesworth Kindersley, *b.* 1929, *s.* 1976, *m.*	Hon. Rupert J. M. K., *b.* 1955
1223 I.	*Kingsale (36th)*, Nevinson Mark de Courcy, *b.* 1958, *s.* 2005, *m.*, *Premier Baron of Ireland*	Joseph K. C. de C., *b.* 1955
1902	*Kinross (5th)*, Christopher Patrick Balfour, *b.* 1949, *s.* 1985, *m.*	Hon. Alan I. B., *b.* 1978
1951	*Kirkwood (3rd)*, David Harvie Kirkwood, PHD, *b.* 1931, *s.* 1970, *m.*	Hon. James S. K., *b.* 1937
1800 I.	*Langford (9th)*, Col. Geoffrey Alexander Rowley-Conwy, OBE, *b.* 1912, *s.* 1953, *m.*	Hon. Owain G. R.-C., *b.* 1958
1942	*Latham (2nd)*, Dominic Charles Latham, *b.* 1954, *s.* 1970	Anthony M. L., *b.* 1954
1431	*Latymer (9th)*, Crispin James Alan Nevill Money-Coutts, *b.* 1955, *s.* 2003, *m.*	Hon. Drummond W. T. M.-C., *b.* 1986
1869	*Lawrence (5th)*, David John Downer Lawrence, *b.* 1937, *s.* 1968	None
1947	*Layton (3rd)*, Geoffrey Michael Layton, *b.* 1947, *s.* 1989, *m.*	Jonathan F., *b.* 1942
1839	*Leigh (6th)*, Christopher Dudley Piers Leigh, *b.* 1960, *s.* 2003, *m.*	Hon. Rupert D. L., *b.* 1994
1962	*Leighton of St Mellons (3rd)*, Robert William Henry Leighton Seager, *b.* 1955, *s.* 1998	Hon. Simon J. L. S., *b.* 1957
1797	*Lilford (8th)*, Mark Vernon Powys, *b.* 1975, *s.* 2005	Robert C. L. P., *b.* 1930
1945	*Lindsay of Birker (3rd)*, James Francis Lindsay, *b.* 1945, *s.* 1994, *m.*	Alexander S. L., *b.* 1940
1758 I.	*Lisle (9th)*, (John) Nicholas Geoffrey Lysaght, *b.* 1960, *s.* 2003	Hon. David J. L., *b.* 1963
1850	*Londesborough (9th)*, Richard John Denison, *b.* 1959, *s.* 1968, *m.*	Hon. James F. D., *b.* 1990
1541 I.	*Louth (16th)*, Otway Michael James Oliver Plunkett, *b.* 1929, *s.* 1950, *m.*	Hon. Jonathan O. P., *b.* 1952
1458 S.	*Lovat (16th) and Lovat (5th) (1837)*, Simon Fraser, *b.* 1977, *s.* 1995	Hon. Jack F., *b.* 1984
1946	*Lucas of Chilworth (3rd)*, Simon William Lucas, *b.* 1957, *s.* 2001, *m.*	Hon. John R. M. L., *b.* 1995
1663	** *Lucas (11th) and Dingwall (14th) (S. 1609)*, Ralph Matthew Palmer, *b.* 1951, *s.* 1991	Hon. Lewis E. P., *b.* 1987
1929	** *Luke (3rd)*, Arthur Charles St John Lawson-Johnston, *b.* 1933, *s.* 1996, *m.*	Hon. Ian J. St J. L.-J., *b.* 1963
1914	** *Lyell (3rd)*, Charles Lyell, *b.* 1939, *s.* 1943	None
1859	*Lyveden (7th)*, Jack Leslie Vernon, *b.* 1938, *s.* 1999, *m.*	Hon. Colin R. V., *b.* 1967
1959	*MacAndrew (3rd)*, Christopher Anthony Colin MacAndrew, *b.* 1945, *s.* 1989, *m.*	Hon. Oliver C. J. M., *b.* 1983
1776 I.	*Macdonald (8th)*, Godfrey James Macdonald of Macdonald, *b.* 1947, *s.* 1970, *m.*	Hon. Godfrey E. H. T. M., *b.* 1982
1937	*McGowan (4th)*, Harry John Charles McGowan, *b.* 1971, *s.* 2003, *m.*	Hon. Dominic J. W. McG., *b.* 1951
1922	*Maclay (3rd)*, Joseph Paton Maclay, *b.* 1942, *s.* 1969, *m.*	Hon. Joseph P. M., *b.* 1977
1955	*McNair (3rd)*, Duncan James McNair, *b.* 1947, *s.* 1989, *m.*	Hon. William S. A. M., *b.* 1958
1951	*Macpherson of Drumochter (3rd)*, James Anthony Macpherson, *b.* 1978, *s.* 2008	None
1937	** *Mancroft (3rd)*, Benjamin Lloyd Stormont Mancroft, *b.* 1957, *s.* 1987, *m.*	Hon. Arthur L. S. M., *b.* 1995
1807	*Manners (6th)*, John Hugh Robert Manners, *b.* 1956, *s.* 2008	Hon. Richard N. M., *b.* 1924
1922	*Manton (4th)*, Miles Ronald Marcus Watson, *b.* 1958, *s.* 2003, *m.*	Hon. Thomas N. C. D. W., *b.* 1985
1908	*Marchamley (4th)*, William Francis Whiteley, *b.* 1968, *s.* 1994	None
1964	*Margadale (3rd)*, Alastair John Morrison, *b.* 1958, *s.* 2003, *m.*	Hon. Declan J. M., *b.* 1993
1961	*Marks of Broughton (3rd)*, Simon Richard Marks, *b.* 1950, *s.* 1998, *m.*	Hon. Michael M., *b.* 1989
1964	*Martonmere (2nd)*, John Stephen Robinson, *b.* 1963, *s.* 1989	Hon. James I. R., *b.* 2003
1776 I.	*Massy (10th)*, David Hamon Somerset Massy, *b.* 1947, *s.* 1995	Hon. John H. M., *b.* 1950
1935	*May (4th)*, Jasper Bertram St John May, *b.* 1965, *s.* 2006	None
1928	*Melchett (4th)*, Peter Robert Henry Mond, *b.* 1948, *s.* 1973	None
1925	*Merrivale (4th)*, Derek John Philip Duke, *b.* 1948, *s.* 2007, *m.*	Hon. Thomas D., *b.* 1980
1911	*Merthyr*, Trevor Oswin Lewis, CBE, *b.* 1935, *s.* 1977, *m.* Disclaimed for life 1977	David T. L., *b.* 1977
1919	*Meston (3rd)*, James Meston, *b.* 1950, *s.* 1984, *m.*	Hon. Thomas J. D. M., *b.* 1977
1838	** *Methuen (7th)*, Robert Alexander Holt Methuen, *b.* 1931, *s.* 1994, *m.*	James P. A. M.-C., *b.* 1952
1711	*Middleton (12th)*, (Digby) Michael Godfrey John Willoughby, MC, *b.* 1921, *s.* 1970	Hon. Michael C. J. W., *b.* 1948
1939	*Milford (4th)*, Guy Wogan Philipps, *b.* 1961, *s.* 1999, *m.*	Hon. Archie S. P., *b.* 1997
1933	*Milne (3rd)*, George Alexander Milne, *b.* 1941, *s.* 2005	Hon. Iain C. L. M., *b.* 1949
1951	*Milner of Leeds (3rd)*, Richard James Milner, *b.* 1959, *s.* 2003, *m.*	None
1947	*Milverton (2nd)*, Revd Fraser Arthur Richard Richards, *b.* 1930, *s.* 1978, *m.*	Hon. Michael H. R., *b.* 1936
1873	*Moncreiff (6th)*, Rhoderick Harry Wellwood Moncreiff, *b.* 1954, *s.* 2002, *m.*	Hon. Harry J. W. M., *b.* 1986

1884	*Monk Bretton (3rd)*, John Charles Dodson, *b.* 1924, *s.* 1933, *m.*	Hon. Christopher M. D., *b.* 1958
1885	*Monkswell (5th)*, Gerard Collier, *b.* 1947, *s.* 1984, *m.*	Hon. James A. C., *b.* 1977
1728	*Monson (12th)*, Nicholas John Monson, *b.* 1955, *s.* 2011, *m.*	Hon. Alexander J. R. M., *b.* 1984
1885	** *Montagu of Beaulieu (3rd)*, Edward John Barrington Douglas-Scott-Montagu, *b.* 1926, *s.* 1929, *m.*	Hon. Ralph D.-S.-M., *b.* 1961
1839	*Monteagle of Brandon (6th)*, Gerald Spring Rice, *b.* 1926, *s.* 1946, *m.*	Hon. Charles J. S. R., *b.* 1953
1943	** *Moran (2nd)*, (Richard) John (McMoran) Wilson, KCMG, *b.* 1924, *s.* 1977, *m.*	Hon. James M. W., *b.* 1952
1918	*Morris (4th)*, Thomas Anthony Salmon Morris, *b.* 1982, *s.* 2011	Hon. John M. M., *b.* 1983
1950	*Morris of Kenwood (3rd)*, Jonathan David Morris, *b.* 1968, *s.* 2004, *m.*	Hon. Benjamin J. M., *b.* 1998
1831	*Mostyn (7th)*, Gregory Philip Roger Lloyd-Mostyn, *b.* 1984, *s.* 2011	Roger Hugh L.-M., *b.* 1941
1933	*Mottistone (4th)*, David Peter Seely, CBE, *b.* 1920, *s.* 1966, *w.*	Hon. Peter J. P. S., *b.* 1949
1945	*Mountevans (3rd)*, Edward Patrick Broke Evans, *b.* 1943, *s.* 1974, *m.*	Hon. Jeffrey de C. R. E., *b.* 1948
1283	*Mowbray (27th), Segrave (28th) (1295) and Stourton (24th) (1448)*, Edward William Stephen Stourton, *b.* 1953, *s.* 2006, *m.*	Hon. James C. P. S., *b.* 1991
1932	*Moyne (3rd)*, Jonathan Bryan Guinness, *b.* 1930, *s.* 1992, *m.*	Hon. Valentine G. B. G., *b.* 1959
1929	** *Moynihan (4th)*, Colin Berkeley Moynihan, *b.* 1955, *s.* 1997, *m.*	Hon. Nicholas E. B. M., *b.* 1994
1781 I.	*Muskerry (9th)*, Robert Fitzmaurice Deane, *b.* 1948, *s.* 1988, *m.*	Hon. Jonathan F. D., *b.* 1986
1627 S.	*Napier (14th) and Ettrick (5th) (1872)*, Francis Nigel Napier, KCVO, *b.* 1930, *s.* 1954, *m.*	Master of Napier, *b.* 1962
1868	*Napier of Magdala (6th)*, Robert Alan Napier, *b.* 1940, *s.* 1987, *m.*	Hon. James R. N., *b.* 1966
1940	*Nathan (3rd)*, Rupert Harry Bernard Nathan, *b.* 1957, *s.* 2007, *m.*	None
1960	*Nelson of Stafford (4th)*, Alistair William Henry Nelson, *b.* 1973, *s.* 2006	Hon. James J. N., *b.* 1947
1959	*Netherthorpe (3rd)*, James Frederick Turner, *b.* 1964, *s.* 1982, *m.*	Hon. Andrew J. E. T., *b.* 1993
1946	*Newall (2nd)*, Francis Storer Eaton Newall, *b.* 1930, *s.* 1963, *m.*	Hon. Richard H. E. N., *b.* 1961
1776 I.	*Newborough (8th)*, Robert Vaughan Wynn, *b.* 1949, *s.* 1998, *m.*	Antony C. V. W., *b.* 1949
1892	*Newton (5th)*, Richard Thomas Legh, *b.* 1950, *s.* 1992, *m.*	Hon. Piers R. L., *b.* 1979
1930	*Noel-Buxton (3rd)*, Martin Connal Noel-Buxton, *b.* 1940, *s.* 1980, *m.*	Hon. Charles C. N.-B., *b.* 1975
1957	*Norrie (2nd)*, (George) Willoughby Moke Norrie, *b.* 1936, *s.* 1977, *m.*	Hon. Mark W. J. N., *b.* 1972
1884	** *Northbourne (5th)*, Christopher George Walter James, *b.* 1926, *s.* 1982, *m.*	Hon. Charles W. H. J., *b.* 1960
1866	** *Northbrook (6th)*, Francis Thomas Baring, *b.* 1954, *s.* 1990, *m.*	To the Baronetcy, Peter B. *b.* 1939
1878	*Norton (8th)*, James Nigel Arden Adderley, *b.* 1947, *s.* 1993, *m.*	Hon. Edward J. A. A., *b.* 1982
1906	*Nunburnholme (6th)*, Stephen Charles Wilson, *b.* 1973, *s.* 2000	Hon. David M. W., *b.* 1954
1950	*Ogmore (3rd)*, Morgan Rees-Williams, *b.* 1937, *s.* 2004, *m.*	Hon. Tudor D. R.-W., *b.* 1991
1870	*O'Hagan (4th)*, Charles Towneley Strachey, *b.* 1945, *s.* 1961	Hon. Richard T. S., *b.* 1950
1868	*O'Neill (4th)*, Raymond Arthur Clanaboy O'Neill, KCVO, TD, *b.* 1933, *s.* 1944, *m.*	Hon. Shane S. C. O'N., *b.* 1965
1836 I.	*Oranmore and Browne (5th) and Mereworth (3rd) (1926)*, Dominick Geoffrey Thomas Browne, *b.* 1929, *s.* 2002	Hon. Martin M. D. B., *b.* 1931
1933	** *Palmer (4th)*, Adrian Bailie Nottage Palmer, *b.* 1951, *s.* 1990, *m.*	Hon. Hugo B. R. P., *b.* 1980
1914	*Parmoor (5th)*, Michael Leonard Seddon Cripps, *b.* 1942, *s.* 2008, *m.*	Hon. Henry W. A. C., *b.* 1976
1937	*Pender (3rd)*, John Willoughby Denison-Pender, *b.* 1933, *s.* 1965, *m.*	Hon. Henry J. R. D.-P., *b.* 1968
1866	*Penrhyn (7th)*, Simon Douglas-Pennant, *b.* 1938, *s.* 2003, *m.*	Hon. Edward S. D.-P., *b.* 1966
1603	*Petre (18th)*, John Patrick Lionel Petre, *b.* 1942, *s.* 1989, *m.*	Hon. Dominic W. P., *b.* 1966
1918	*Phillimore (5th)*, Francis Stephen Phillimore, *b.* 1944, *s.* 1994, *m.*	Hon. Tristan A. S. P., *b.* 1977
1945	*Piercy (3rd)*, James William Piercy, *b.* 1946, *s.* 1981	Hon. Mark E. P. P., *b.* 1953
1827	*Plunket (8th)*, Robin Rathmore Plunket, *b.* 1925, *s.* 1975, *m.*	Hon. Shaun A. F. S. P., *b.* 1931
1831	*Poltimore (7th)*, Mark Coplestone Bampfylde, *b.* 1957, *s.* 1978, *m.*	Hon. Henry A. W. B., *b.* 1985
1690 S.	*Polwarth (11th)*, Andrew Walter Hepburne-Scott, *b.* 1947, *s.* 2005, *m.*	Master of Polwarth, *b.* 1973
1930	*Ponsonby of Shulbrede (4th) and Ponsonby of Roehampton (life peerage, 2000)*, Frederick Matthew Thomas Ponsonby, *b.* 1958, *s.* 1990	None
1958	*Poole (2nd)*, David Charles Poole, *b.* 1945, *s.* 1993, *m.*	Hon. Oliver J. P., *b.* 1972
1852	*Raglan (6th)*, Geoffrey Somerset, *b.* 1932, *s.* 2010, *m.*	Hon. Arthur G. S., *b.* 1960
1932	*Rankeillour (5th)*, Michael Richard Hope, *b.* 1940, *s.* 2005, *m.*	James F. H., *b.* 1968
1953	*Rathcavan (3rd)*, Hugh Detmar Torrens O'Neill, *b.* 1939, *s.* 1994, *m.*	Hon. François H. N. O'N., *b.* 1968
1916	*Rathcreedan (3rd)*, Christopher John Norton, *b.* 1949, *s.* 1990, *m.*	Hon. Adam G. N., *b.* 1952
1868 I.	*Rathdonnell (5th)*, Thomas Benjamin McClintock-Bunbury, *b.* 1938, *s.* 1959, *m.*	Hon. William L. M.-B., *b.* 1966

1911	*Ravensdale (3rd)*, Nicholas Mosley, MC, *b.* 1923, *s.* 1966, *m.*	Daniel N. M., *b.* 1982
1821	*Ravensworth (9th)*, Thomas Arthur Hamish Liddell, *b.* 1954, *s.* 2004, *m.*	Hon. Henry A. T. L., *b.* 1987
1821	*Rayleigh (6th)*, John Gerald Strutt, *b.* 1960, *s.* 1988, *m.*	Hon. John F. S., *b.* 1993
1937	** *Rea (3rd)*, John Nicolas Rea, MD, *b.* 1928, *s.* 1981, *m.*	Hon. Matthew J. R., *b.* 1956
1628 S.	** *Reay (14th)*, Hugh William Mackay, *b.* 1937, *s.* 1963, *m.*	Master of Reay, *b.* 1965
1902	*Redesdale (6th) and Mitford (life peerage 2000)*, Rupert Bertram Mitford, *b.* 1967, *s.* 1991, *m.*	Hon. Bertram D. M., *b.* 2000
1940	*Reith*, Christopher John Reith, *b.* 1928, *s.* 1971, *m.* Disclaimed for life 1972.	Hon. James H. J. R., *b.* 1971
1928	*Remnant (3rd)*, James Wogan Remnant, CVO, *b.* 1930, *s.* 1967, *m.*	Hon. Philip J. R., CBE, *b.* 1954
1806 I.	*Rendlesham (9th)*, Charles William Brooke Thellusson, *b.* 1954, *s.* 1999, *m.*	Hon. Peter R. T., *b.* 1920
1933	*Rennell (4th)*, James Roderick David Tremayne Rodd, *b.* 1978, *s.* 2006	None
1964	*Renwick (2nd)*, Harry Andrew Renwick, *b.* 1935, *s.* 1973, *m.*	Hon. Robert J. R., *b.* 1966
1885	*Revelstoke (6th)*, James Cecil Baring, *b.* 1938, *s.* 2003, *m.*	Hon. Alexander R. B., *b.* 1970
1905	*Ritchie of Dundee (6th)*, Charles Rupert Rendall Ritchie, *b.* 1958, *s.* 2008, *m.*	Hon. Sebastian R., *b.* 2004
1935	*Riverdale (3rd)*, Anthony Robert Balfour, *b.* 1960, *s.* 1998	Arthur M. B., *b.* 1938
1961	*Robertson of Oakridge (3rd)*, William Brian Elworthy Robertson, *b.* 1975, *s.* 2009, *m.*	None
1938	*Roborough (3rd)*, Henry Massey Lopes, *b.* 1940, *s.* 1992, *m.*	Hon. Massey J. H. L., *b.* 1969
1931	*Rochester (2nd)*, Foster Charles Lowry Lamb, *b.* 1916, *s.* 1955, *w.*	Hon. David C. L., *b.* 1944
1934	*Rockley (3rd)*, James Hugh Cecil, *b.* 1934, *s.* 1976, *m.*	Hon. Anthony R. C., *b.* 1961
1782	*Rodney (11th)*, John George Brydges Rodney, *b.* 1999, *s.* 2011	Nicholas S. H. R., *b.* 1947
1651 S.	*Rollo (14th) and Dunning (5th) (1869)*, David Eric Howard Rollo, *b.* 1943, *s.* 1997, *m.*	Master of Rollo, *b.* 1972
1959	*Rootes (3rd)*, Nicholas Geoffrey Rootes, *b.* 1951, *s.* 1992, *m.*	William B. R., *b.* 1944
1796 I.	*Rossmore (7th) and Rossmore (6th) (1838)*, William Warner Westenra, *b.* 1931, *s.* 1958, *m.*	Hon. Benedict W. W., *b.* 1983
1939	** *Rotherwick (3rd)*, (Herbert) Robin Cayzer, *b.* 1954, *s.* 1996, *m.*	Hon. H. Robin C., *b.* 1989
1885	*Rothschild (4th)*, (Nathaniel Charles) Jacob Rothschild, OM, GBE, *b.* 1936, *s.* 1990, *m.*	Hon. Nathaniel P. V. J. R., *b.* 1971
1911	*Rowallan (4th)*, John Polson Cameron Corbett, *b.* 1947, *s.* 1993	Hon. Jason W. P. C. C., *b.* 1972
1947	*Rugby (3rd)*, Robert Charles Maffey, *b.* 1951, *s.* 1990, *m.*	Hon. Timothy J. H. M., *b.* 1975
1919	*Russell of Liverpool (3rd)*, Simon Gordon Jared Russell, *b.* 1952, *s.* 1981, *m.*	Hon. Edward C. S. R., *b.* 1985
1876	*Sackville (7th)*, Robert Bertrand Sackville-West, *b.* 1958, *s.* 2004, *m.*	Hon. Arthur S-W., *b.* 2000
1964	*St Helens (2nd)*, Richard Francis Hughes-Young, *b.* 1945, *s.* 1980, *m.*	Hon. Henry T. H.-Y., *b.* 1986
1559	** *St John of Bletso (21st)*, Anthony Tudor St John, *b.* 1957, *s.* 1978, *m.*	Hon. Oliver B. St J., *b.* 1995
1887	*St Levan (4th)*, John Francis Arthur St Aubyn, DSC, *b.* 1919, *s.* 1978, *w.*	James P. S. St. A., *b.* 1950
1885	*St Oswald (6th)*, Charles Rowland Andrew Winn, *b.* 1959, *s.* 1999, *m.*	Hon. Rowland C. S. H. W., *b.* 1986
1960	*Sanderson of Ayot (2nd)*, Alan Lindsay Sanderson, *b.* 1931, *s.* 1971, *m.* Disclaimed for life 1971.	Hon. Michael S., *b.* 1959
1945	*Sandford (3rd)*, James John Mowbray Edmondson, *b.* 1949, *s.* 2009, *m.*	Hon. Devon J. E., *b.* 1986
1871	*Sandhurst (6th)*, Guy Rees John Mansfield, *b.* 1949, *s.* 2002, *m.*	Hon. Edward J. M., *b.* 1982
1802	*Sandys (7th)*, Richard Michael Oliver Hill, *b.* 1931, *s.* 1961, *m.*	The Marquess of Downshire
1888	*Savile (4th)*, John Anthony Thornhill Lumley-Savile, *b.* 1947, *s.* 2008, *m.*	Hon. James G. A. L-S., *b.* 1975
1447	*Saye and Sele (21st)*, Nathaniel Thomas Allen Fiennes, *b.* 1920, *s.* 1968, *m.*	Hon. Martin G. F., *b.* 1961
1826	*Seaford (6th)*, Colin Humphrey Felton Ellis, *b.* 1946, *s.* 1999, *m.*	Hon. Benjamin F. T. E., *b.* 1976
1932	** *Selsdon (3rd)*, Malcolm McEacharn Mitchell-Thomson, *b.* 1937, *s.* 1963, *m.*	Hon. Callum M. M. M.-T., *b.* 1969
1489 S.	*Sempill (21st)*, James William Stuart Whitemore Sempill, *b.* 1949, *s.* 1995, *m.*	Master of Sempill, *b.* 1979
1916	*Shaughnessy (5th)*, Charles George Patrick Shaughnessy, *b.* 1955, *s.* 2007, *m.*	David J. S., *b.* 1957
1946	*Shepherd (3rd)*, Graham George Shepherd, *b.* 1949, *s.* 2001, *m.*	Hon. Patrick M. S., *b.* 19–
1964	*Sherfield (3rd)*, Dwight William Makins, *b.* 1951, *s.* 2006, *m.*	None
1902	*Shuttleworth (5th)*, Charles Geoffrey Nicholas Kay-Shuttleworth, KCVO, *b.* 1948, *s.* 1975, *m.*	Hon. Thomas E. K.-S., *b.* 1976
1950	*Silkin (3rd)*, Christopher Lewis Silkin, *b.* 1947, *s.* 2001. Disclaimed for life 2002.	Rory L. S., *b.* 1954
1963	*Silsoe (3rd)*, Simon Rupert Trustram Eve *b.* 1966, *s.* 2005	Hon. Peter N. T. E., *b.* 1930
1947	*Simon of Wythenshawe (3rd)*, Matthew Simon, *b.* 1955, *s.* 2002	Martin S., *b.* 1944

1449 S.	*Sinclair (18th)*, Matthew Murray Kennedy St Clair *b.* 1968, *s.* 2004, *m.*	Master of Sinclair, *b.* 2007
1957	*Sinclair of Cleeve (3rd)*, John Lawrence Robert Sinclair, *b.* 1953, *s.* 1985	None
1919	*Sinha (6th)*, Arup Kumar Sinha, *b.* 1966, *s.* 1999	Hon. Dilip K. S., *b.* 1967
1828	** *Skelmersdale (7th)*, Roger Bootle-Wilbraham, *b.* 1945, *s.* 1973, *m.*	Hon. Andrew B.-W., *b.* 1977
1916	*Somerleyton (3rd)*, Savile William Francis Crossley, GCVO, *b.* 1928, *s.* 1959, *m.*	Hon. Hugh F. S. C., *b.* 1971
1784	*Somers (9th)*, Philip Sebastian Somers Cocks, *b.* 1948, *s.* 1995	Alan B. C., *b.* 1930
1780	*Southampton (6th)*, Charles James FitzRoy, *b.* 1928, *s.* 1989, *m.*	Hon. Edward C. F., *b.* 1955
1959	*Spens (4th)*, Patrick Nathaniel George Spens, *b.* 1968, *s.* 2001, *m.*	Hon. Peter L. S., *b.* 2000
1640	*Stafford (15th)*, Francis Melfort William Fitzherbert, *b.* 1954, *s.* 1986, *m.*	Hon. Benjamin J. B. F., *b.* 1983
1938	*Stamp (4th)*, Trevor Charles Bosworth Stamp, MD, *b.* 1935, *s.* 1987, *m.*	Hon. Nicholas C. T. S., *b.* 1978
1839	*Stanley of Alderley (8th), Sheffield (8th) (I. 1738) and Eddisbury (7th) (1848)*, Thomas Henry Oliver Stanley, *b.* 1927, *s.* 1971, *m.*	Hon. Richard O. S., *b.* 1956
1318	*Strabolgi (12th)*, Andrew David Whitley Kenworthy, *b.* 1967, *s.* 2010, *m.*	Hon. Joel B. K., *b.* 2004
1954	*Strang (2nd)*, Colin Strang, *b.* 1922, *s.* 1978, *m.*	None
1628	*Strange (17th)*, Adam Humphrey Drummond of Megginch, *b.* 1953, *s.* 2005 *m.*	Hon. John A. H. D. of M. *b.* 1992
1955	*Strathalmond (3rd)*, William Roberton Fraser, *b.* 1947, *s.* 1976, *m.*	Hon. William G. F., *b.* 1976
1936	*Strathcarron (3rd)*, Ian David Patrick Macpherson, *b.* 1949, *s.* 2006, *m.*	Hon. Rory D. A. M., *b.* 1982
1955	** *Strathclyde (2nd)*, Thomas Galloway Dunlop du Roy de Blicquy Galbraith, PC, *b.* 1960, *s.* 1985, *m.*	Hon. Charles W. du R. de B. G., *b.* 1962
1900	*Strathcona and Mount Royal (4th)*, Donald Euan Palmer Howard, *b.* 1923, *s.* 1959, *m.*	Hon. D. Alexander S. H., *b.* 1961
1836	*Stratheden (6th) and Campbell (6th) (1841)*, Donald Campbell, *b.* 1934, *s.* 1987, *m.*	Hon. David A. C., *b.* 1963
1884	*Strathspey (6th)*, James Patrick Trevor Grant of Grant, *b.* 1943, *s.* 1992, *m.*	Hon. Michael P. F. G., *b.* 1953
1838	*Sudeley (7th)*, Merlin Charles Sainthill Hanbury-Tracy, *b.* 1939, *s.* 1941	D. Andrew J. H.-T., *b.* 1928
1786	*Suffield (11th)*, Anthony Philip Harbord-Hamond, MC, *b.* 1922, *s.* 1951, *w.*	Hon. Charles A. A. H.-H., *b.* 1953
1893	*Swansea (5th)*, Richard Anthony Hussey Vivian, *b.* 1957, *s.* 2005, *m.*	Hon. James H. H. V., *b.* 1999
1907	*Swaythling (5th)*, Charles Edgar Samuel Montagu, *b.* 1954, *s.* 1998, *m.*	Hon. Anthony T. S. M., *b.* 1931
1919	** *Swinfen (3rd)*, Roger Mynors Swinfen Eady, *b.* 1938, *s.* 1977, *m.*	Hon. Charles R. P. S. E., *b.* 1971
1831 I.	*Talbot of Malahide (10th)*, Reginald John Richard Arundell, *b.* 1931, *s.* 1987, *m.*	Hon. Richard J. T. A., *b.* 1957
1946	*Tedder (3rd)*, Robin John Tedder, *b.* 1955, *s.* 1994, *m.*	Hon. Benjamin J. T., *b.* 1985
1884	*Tennyson (6th)*, David Harold Alexander Tennyson, *b.* 1960, *s.* 2006	Alan J. D. T., *b.* 1965
1918	*Terrington (6th)*, Christopher Richard James Woodhouse, MB, *b.* 1946, *s.* 2001, *m.*	Hon. Jack H. L. W., *b.* 1978
1940	*Teviot (2nd)*, Charles John Kerr, *b.* 1934, *s.* 1968, *m.*	Hon. Charles R. K., *b.* 1971
1616	*Teynham (20th)*, John Christopher Ingham Roper-Curzon, *b.* 1928, *s.* 1972, *m.*	Hon. David J. H. I. R.-C., *b.* 1965
1964	*Thomson of Fleet (3rd)*, David Kenneth Roy Thomson, *b.* 1957, *s.* 2006, *m.*	Hon. Benjamin T., *b.* 2006
1792	*Thurlow (8th)*, Francis Edward Hovell-Thurlow-Cumming-Bruce, KCMG, *b.* 1912, *s.* 1971, *w.*	Hon. Roualeyn R. H.-T.-C.-B., *b.* 1952
1876	*Tollemache (5th)*, Timothy John Edward Tollemache, *b.* 1939, *s.* 1975, *m.*	Hon. Edward J. H. T., *b.* 1976
1564 S.	*Torphichen (15th)*, James Andrew Douglas Sandilands, *b.* 1946, *s.* 1975, *m.*	Robert P. S., *b.* 1950
1947	** *Trefgarne (2nd)*, David Garro Trefgarne, PC, *b.* 1941, *s.* 1960, *m.*	Hon. George G. T., *b.* 1970
1921	*Trevethin (4th) and Oaksey (2nd) (1947)*, John Geoffrey Tristram Lawrence, OBE, *b.* 1929, *s.* 1971, *m.*	Hon. Patrick J. T. L., *b.* 1960
1880	*Trevor (5th)*, Marke Charles Hill-Trevor, *b.* 1970, *s.* 1997, *m.*	Hon. Iain R. H.-T., *b.* 1971
1461 I.	*Trimlestown (21st)*, Raymond Charles Barnewall, *b.* 1930, *s.* 1997	None
1940	*Tryon (3rd)*, Anthony George Merrik Tryon, *b.* 1940, *s.* 1976	Hon. Charles G. B. T., *b.* 1976
1935	*Tweedsmuir (4th)*, John William de l'Aigle (Toby) Buchan, *b.* 1950, *s.* 2008, *m.*	Hon. John A. G. B., *b.* 1986
1523	*Vaux of Harrowden (11th)*, Anthony William Gilbey, *b.* 1940, *s.* 2002, *m.*	Hon. Richard H. G. G., *b.* 1965
1800 I.	*Ventry (8th)*, Andrew Wesley Daubeny de Moleyns, *b.* 1943, *s.* 1987, *m.*	Hon. Francis W. D. de M., *b.* 1965
1762	*Vernon (11th)*, Anthony William Vernon-Harcourt, *b.* 1939, *s.* 2000, *m.*	Hon. Simon A. V.-H., *b.* 1969

1922	*Vestey (3rd)*, Samuel George Armstrong Vestey, KCVO, *b.* 1941, *s.* 1954, *m.*	Hon. William G. V., *b.* 1983
1841	*Vivian (7th)*, Charles Crespigny Hussey Vivian, *b.* 1966, *s.* 2004	Hon. Victor A. R. B. V., *b.* 1940
1934	*Wakehurst (3rd)*, (John) Christopher Loder, *b.* 1925, *s.* 1970, *m.*	Hon. Timothy W. L., *b.* 1958
1723	** *Walpole (10th) and Walpole of Wolterton (8th) (1756)*, Robert Horatio Walpole, *b.* 1938, *s.* 1989, *m.*	Hon. Jonathan R. H. W., *b.* 1967
1780	*Walsingham (9th)*, John de Grey, MC, *b.* 1925, *s.* 1965, *m.*	Hon. Robert de. G., *b.* 1969
1936	*Wardington (3rd)*, William Simon Pease, *b.* 1925, *s.* 2005, *m.*	None
1792 I.	*Waterpark (7th)*, Frederick Caryll Philip Cavendish, *b.* 1926, *s.* 1948, *m.*	Hon. Roderick A. C., *b.* 1959
1942	*Wedgwood (4th)*, Piers Anthony Weymouth Wedgwood, *b.* 1954, *s.* 1970, *m.*	Antony J. W., *b.* 1944
1861	*Westbury (6th)*, Richard Nicholas Bethell, MBE, *b.* 1950, *s.* 2001, *m.*	Hon. Alexander B., *b.* 1986
1944	*Westwood (3rd)*, (William) Gavin Westwood, *b.* 1944, *s.* 1991, *m.*	Hon. W. Fergus W., *b.* 1972
1544/5	*Wharton (12th)*, Myles Christopher David Robertson, *b.* 1964, *s.* 2000, *m.*	Hon. Christopher J. R., *b.* 1969
1935	*Wigram (2nd)*, (George) Neville (Clive) Wigram, MC, *b.* 1915, *s.* 1960, *w.*	Maj. Hon. Andrew F. C. W., *b.* 1949
1491	** *Willoughby de Broke (21st)*, Leopold David Verney, *b.* 1938, *s.* 1986, *m.*	Hon. Rupert G. V., *b.* 1966
1937	*Windlesham (4th)*, James Rupert Hennessy, *b.* 1968, *s.* 2010, *m.*	Hon. George R. J. H., *b.* 2006
1951	*Wise (2nd)*, John Clayton Wise, *b.* 1923, *s.* 1968, *m.*	Hon. Christopher J. C. W., *b.* 1949
1869	*Wolverton (8th)*, Miles John Glyn, *b.* 1966, *s.* 2011	Jonathan C. G., *b.* 1990
1928	*Wraxall (3rd)*, Eustace Hubert Beilby Gibbs, KCVO, CMG, *b.* 1929, *s.* 2001, *m.*	Hon. Anthony H. G., *b.* 1958
1915	*Wrenbury (3rd)*, Revd John Burton Buckley, *b.* 1927, *s.* 1940, *m.*	Hon. William E. B., *b.* 1966
1838	*Wrottesley (6th)*, Clifton Hugh Lancelot de Verdon Wrottesley, *b.* 1968, *s.* 1977, *m.*	Hon. Victor E. F. de V. W., *b.* 2004
1829	*Wynford (9th)*, John Philip Robert Best, *b.* 1950, *s.* 2002, *m.*	Hon. Harry R. F. B., *b.* 1987
1308	*Zouche (18th)*, James Assheton Frankland, *b.* 1943, *s.* 1965, *m.*	Hon. William T. A. F., *b.* 1984

BARONESSES/LADIES IN THEIR OWN RIGHT

Style, The Rt. Hon. the Lady _ , *or* The Rt. Hon. the Baroness _ , according to her preference. Either style may be used, except in the case of Scottish titles (indicated by S.), which are not baronies (*see* page 44) and whose holders are always addressed as Lady.

Envelope, may be addressed in same way as a Baron's wife or, if she prefers *(formal)*, The Rt. Hon. the Baroness _; *(social)*, The Baroness _. Otherwise as for a Baron's wife

Husband, Untitled

Children's style, As for children of a Baron

Created	Title, order of succession, name, etc	Heir
1664	*Arlington*, Jennifer Jane Forwood, *b.* 1939, *s.* 1999, *w.* Title called out of abeyance 1999	Hon. Patrick J. D. F., *b.* 1967
1455	*Berners (16th)*, Pamela Vivien Kirkham, *b.* 1929, *s.* 1995, *m.*	Hon. Rupert W. T. K., *b.* 1953
1529	*Braye (8th)*, Mary Penelope Aubrey-Fletcher, *b.* 1941, *s.* 1985, *m.*	Two co-heirs
1321	*Dacre (27th)*, Rachel Leila Douglas-Home, *b.* 1929, *s.* 1970, *w.*	Hon. James T. A. D.-H., *b.* 1952
1490 S.	*Herries of Terregles (14th)*, Anne Elizabeth Fitzalan-Howard, *b.* 1938, *s.* 1975, *w.*	Lady Mary Mumford, *b.* 1940
1597	*Howard de Walden (10th)*, Mary Hazel Caridwen Czernin, *b.* 1935, *s.* 2004, *m.* Title called out of abeyance 2004	Hon. Peter J. J. C. *b.* 1966
1602 S.	*Kinloss (12th)*, Beatrice Mary Grenville Freeman-Grenville, *b.* 1922, *s.* 1944, *w.*	Master of Kinloss, *b.* 1953
1445 S.	** *Saltoun (20th)*, Flora Marjory Fraser, *b.* 1930, *s.* 1979, *w.*	Hon. Katharine I. M. I. F., *b.* 1957
1313	*Willoughby de Eresby (27th)*, (Nancy) Jane Marie Heathcote-Drummond-Willoughby, *b.* 1934, *s.* 1983	Two co-heirs

LIFE PEERS

Style, The Rt. Hon. the Lord _ /The Rt. Hon. the Lady _ , *or* The Rt. Hon. the Baroness _ , according to her preference
Envelope (formal), The Rt. Hon. Lord _/Lady_/ Baroness_; *(social),* The Lord _/Lady_/Baroness_
Letter (formal), My Lord/Lady; *(social),* Dear Lord/ Lady _. Spoken,* Lord/Lady _
Wife's style, The Rt. Hon. the Lady _
Husband, Untitled
Children's style, 'The Hon.' before forename (F_) and surname (S_)
Envelope, The Hon. F_ S_. *Letter,* Dear Mr/Miss/Mrs S_. *Spoken,* Mr/Miss/Mrs S_

NEW LIFE PEERAGES

1 September 2010 to 31 August 2011:
Tariq Mahmood Ahmad; Dame Joan Dawson Bakewell, DBE; Sir Robert George Alexander Balchin; Elizabeth Rose Berridge; Sir Michael David Bishop, CBE; Sarah Virginia Brinton; Raymond Edward Harry Collins; Alistair Basil Cooke, OBE; Sir Patrick Thomas Cormack; Gen. Sir (Francis) Richard Dannatt, GCB, CBE, MC; Michael John Dobbs; Elizabeth Deirdre Doocey, OBE; Robert Norman Edmiston; Sir Reginald Norman Morgan Empey, OBE; Andrew Simon Feldman; Julian Alexander Fellowes; Stanley Fink; Howard Emerson Flight; Rachel Heyhoe Flint, OBE; Maurice Mark Glasman; Michael Ian Grade; Stephen Keith Green; David Laurence Gold; Prof. Peter John Hennessy; Prof. Sheila Clare Hollins; Qurban Hussain; Anne Caroline Jenkin; Judith Anne Jolly; Jonathan Andrew Kestenbaum; Oona Tamsyn King; Susan Veronica Kramer; Margot Ruth Aline Lister, CBE; Rajinder Paul Loomba; Sir Michael Nicholson Lord; *Marquess of Lothian (Michael Ancram), PC, QC; David John Maclean, PC; George Morgan Magan; Jonathan Clive Marks, QC; Mair Eluned Morgan; Sir Gulam Kaderbhoy Noon, MBE; Monroe Edward Palmer; Jennifer Elizabeth Randerson; Sir Bernard Francisco Ribeiro, CBE; Fiona Sarah Shackleton, LVO; John Kevin Sharkey; Richard John Grenville Spring; Nicol Ross Stephen; Air Chief Marshal Sir Graham Eric Stirrup, GCB, AFC; Benjamin Russell Mackintosh Stoneham; Michael John Storey; Tina Wendy Stowell, MBE; Paul Cline Strasburger; Nicholas Edward True, CBE; Claire Tyler; Gordon Joshua Wasserman; Patience Jane Wheatcroft; Dafydd Wynne Wigley; Stewart Martin Wood; Bryony Katherine Worthington

SYMBOLS
* Hereditary peer who has been granted a life peerage. For further details, please refer to the Hereditary Peers section. For example, life peer *Balniel* can be found under his hereditary title *Earl of Crawford and Balcarres*
§ Justices of the Supreme Court currently disqualified from sitting or voting in the House of Lords until they retire from the supreme court. For further information *see* Law Courts and Offices
‡ Title not confirmed at time of going to press

CREATED UNDER THE APPELLATE JURISDICTION ACT 1876 (AS AMENDED)

BARONS
Created
2004 §*Brown of Eaton-under-Heywood,* Simon Denis Brown, PC, *b.* 1937, *m.*
1991 *Browne-Wilkinson,* Nicolas Christopher Henry Browne-Wilkinson, PC, *b.* 1930, *m.*
2004 *Carswell,* Robert Douglas Carswell, PC, *b.* 1934, *m.*
2009 §*Collins of Mapesbury,* Lawrence Antony Collins, PC, *b.* 1941
1986 *Goff of Chieveley,* Robert Lionel Archibald Goff, PC, *b.* 1926, *m.*
1985 *Griffiths,* (William) Hugh Griffiths, MC, PC, *b.* 1923, *m.*
1995 *Hoffmann,* Leonard Hubert Hoffmann, PC, *b.* 1934, *m.*
1997 *Hutton,* (James) Brian (Edward) Hutton, PC, *b.* 1931, *m.*
2009 §*Kerr of Tonaghmore,* Brian Francis Kerr, PC, *b.* 1948, *m.*
1993 *Lloyd of Berwick,* Anthony John Leslie Lloyd, PC, *b.* 1929, *m.*
2005 §*Mance,* Jonathan Hugh Mance, PC, *b.* 1943, *m.*
1998 *Millett,* Peter Julian Millett, PC, *b.* 1932, *m.*
1992 *Mustill,* Michael John Mustill, PC, *b.* 1931, *m.*
2007 *Neuberger of Abbotsbury,* David Edmond Neuberger, PC, *b.* 1948, *m., Master of the Rolls*
1994 *Nicholls of Birkenhead,* Donald James Nicholls, PC, *b.* 1933, *m.*
1999 §*Phillips of Worth Matravers,* Nicholas Addison Phillips, KG, *b.* 1938, *m.*
1997 §*Saville of Newdigate,* Mark Oliver Saville, PC, *b.* 1936, *m.*
2000 *Scott of Foscote,* Richard Rashleigh Folliott Scott, PC, *b.* 1934, *m.*
1995 *Steyn,* Johan van Zyl Steyn, PC, *b.* 1932, *m.*
1982 *Templeman,* Sydney William Templeman, MBE, PC, *b.* 1920, *w.*
2003 §*Walker of Gestingthorpe,* Robert Walker, PC, *b.* 1938, *m.*
1992 *Woolf,* Harry Kenneth Woolf, PC, *b.* 1933, *m.*

BARONESSES
2004 §*Hale of Richmond,* Brenda Marjorie Hale, DBE, PC, *b.* 1945, *m.*

CREATED UNDER THE LIFE PEERAGES ACT 1958

BARONS
Created
2001 *Adebowale,* Victor Olufemi Adebowale, CBE, *b.* 1962
2005 *Adonis,* Andrew Adonis, PC, *b.* 1963, *m.*
2011 *Ahmad of Wimbledon,* Tariq Mahmood Ahmad, *b.* 1968, *m.*

1998   *Ahmed*, Nazir Ahmed, *b. 1957, m.*

1996   *Alderdice*, John Thomas Alderdice, *b. 1955, m.*

2010   *Allan of Hallam*, Richard Beecroft Allan, *b. 1966*

1998   *Alli*, Waheed Alli, *b. 1964*

2004   *Alliance*, David Alliance, CBE, *b. 1932*

1997   *Alton of Liverpool*, David Patrick Paul Alton, *b. 1951, m.*

2005   *Anderson of Swansea*, Donald Anderson, PC, *b. 1939, m.*

1992   *Archer of Sandwell*, Peter Kingsley Archer, PC, QC, *b. 1926, m.*

1992   *Archer of Weston-super-Mare*, Jeffrey Howard Archer, *b. 1940, m.*

1988   *Armstrong of Ilminster*, Robert Temple Armstrong, GCB, CVO, *b. 1927, m.*

1999   **Armstrong-Jones*, Earl of Snowdon, GCVO, *b. 1930, m. (see* Hereditary Peers)

2000   *Ashcroft*, Michael Anthony Ashcroft, KCMG,

2001   *Ashdown of Norton-sub-Hamdon*, Jeremy John Durham (Paddy) Ashdown, GCMG, KBE, PC, *b. 1941, m.*

1992   *Ashley of Stoke*, Jack Ashley, CH, PC, *b. 1922, w.*

1993   *Attenborough*, Richard Samuel Attenborough, CBE, *b. 1923, m.*

1998   *Bach*, William Stephen Goulden Bach, *b. 1946, m.*

1997   *Bagri*, Raj Kumar Bagri, CBE, *b. 1930, m.*

1997   *Baker of Dorking*, Kenneth Wilfred Baker, CH, PC, *b. 1934, m.*

2004   *Ballyedmond*, Dr Edward Haughey, OBE, *b. 1944, m.*

1974   **Balniel*, The Earl of Crawford and Balcarres, *b. 1927, m. (see* Hereditary Peers)

2010   *Bannside*, Revd Ian Richard Kyle Paisley, PC, *b. 1926, m.*

1992   *Barber of Tewkesbury*, Derek Coates Barber, *b. 1918, m.*

1983   *Barnett*, Joel Barnett, PC, *b. 1923, m.*

1997   *Bassam of Brighton*, (John) Steven Bassam, PC, *b. 1953*

2008   *Bates*, Michael Walton Bates, *b. 1961*

2010   *Beecham*, Jeremy Hugh Beecham, *b. 1944, m.*

1998   *Bell*, Timothy John Leigh Bell, *b. 1941, m.*

2001   *Best*, Richard Stuart Best, OBE, *b. 1945, m.*

2007   *Bew*, Prof. Paul Anthony Elliott Bew, *b. 1950, m.*

2001   *Bhatia*, Amirali Alibhai Bhatia, OBE, *b. 1932, m.*

2004   *Bhattacharyya*, Prof. (Sushantha) Kumar Bhattacharyya, CBE *b. 1932, m.*

2010   *Bichard*, Michael George Bichard, KCB, *b. 1947*

2006   *Bilimoria*, Karan Faridoon Bilimoria, CBE, *b. 1961, m.*

2005   *Bilston*, Dennis Turner, *b. 1942, m.*

2000   *Birt*, John Francis Hodgess Birt, *b. 1944, m.*

2010   *Black of Brentwood*, Guy Vaughan Black, *b. 1964, c. p.*

2001   *Black of Crossharbour*, Conrad Moffat Black, OC, PC, *b. 1944, m.*

1997   *Blackwell*, Norman Roy Blackwell, *b. 1952, m.*

2010   *Blair of Boughton*, Ian Warwick Blair, QPM *b. 1953, m.*

2011   *Blencathra*, David John Maclean, PC, *b. 1953*

1995   *Blyth of Rowington*, James Blyth, *b. 1940, m.*

2010   *Boateng*, Paul Yaw Boateng, PC, *b. 1951, m.*

1996   *Borrie*, Gordon Johnson Borrie, QC, *b. 1931, w.*

2010   *Boswell of Aynho*, Timothy Eric Boswell, *b. 1942, m.*

1996   *Bowness*, Peter Spencer Bowness, CBE, *b. 1943, m.*

2003   *Boyce*, Michael Boyce, KG, GCB, OBE, *b. 1943*

2006   *Boyd of Duncansby*, Colin David Boyd, PC, *b. 1953, m.*

2006   *Bradley*, Keith John Charles Bradley, PC, *b. 1950, m.*

1999   *Bradshaw*, William Peter Bradshaw, *b. 1936, m.*

1998   *Bragg*, Melvyn Bragg, *b. 1939, m.*

1987   *Bramall*, Edwin Noel Westby Bramall, KG, GCB, OBE, MC, *b. 1923, m.*

2000   *Brennan*, Daniel Joseph Brennan, QC, *b. 1942, m.*

1999   *Brett*, William Henry Brett, *b. 1942, m.*

1976   *Briggs*, Asa Briggs, FBA, *b. 1921, m.*

2000   *Brittan of Spennithorne*, Leon Brittan, PC, QC, *b. 1939, m.*

2004   *Broers*, Prof. Alec (Nigel) Broers, *b. 1938, m.*

1997   *Brooke of Alverthorpe*, Clive Brooke, *b. 1942, m.*

2001   *Brooke of Sutton Mandeville*, Peter Leonard Brooke, CH, PC, *b. 1934, m.*

1998   *Brookman*, David Keith Brookman, *b. 1937, m.*

1979   *Brooks of Tremorfa*, John Edward Brooks, *b. 1927, m.*

2006   *Browne of Belmont*, Wallace Hamilton Browne, *b. 1947*

2010   *Browne of Ladyton*, Desmond Henry Browne, PC, *b. 1952*

2001   *Browne of Madingley*, Edmund John Phillip Browne, *b. 1948*

2006   *Burnett*, John Patrick Aubone Burnett, *b. 1945, m.*

1998   *Burns*, Terence Burns, GCB, *b. 1944, m.*

1998   *Butler of Brockwell*, (Frederick Edward) Robin Butler, KG, GCB, CVO, PC, *b. 1938, m.*

2004   *Cameron of Dillington*, Ewen (James Hanning) Cameron, *b. 1949, m.*

1984   *Cameron of Lochbroom*, Kenneth John Cameron, PC, *b. 1931, m.*

1981   *Campbell of Alloway*, Alan Robertson Campbell, QC, *b. 1917, m.*

2001   *Campbell-Savours*, Dale Norman Campbell-Savours, *b. 1943, m.*

2002   *Carey of Clifton*, Rt. Revd George Leonard Carey, PC, *b. 1935, m.*

1999   **Carington of Upton*, Lord Carrington, GCMG, *b. 1919, m. (see* Hereditary Peers)

1999   *Carlile of Berriew*, Alexander Charles Carlile, QC, *b. 1948, m.*

1975   *Carr of Hadley*, (Leonard) Robert Carr, PC, *b. 1916, m.*

2008   *Carter of Barnes*, Stephen Andrew Carter, CBE, *b. 1964, m.*

2004   *Carter of Coles*, Patrick Robert Carter, *b. 1946, m.*

1990   *Cavendish of Furness*, (Richard) Hugh Cavendish, *b. 1941, m.*

1996   *Chadlington*, Peter Selwyn Gummer, *b. 1942, m.*

1964   *Chalfont*, (Alun) Arthur Gwynne Jones, OBE, MC, PC, *b. 1919, w.*

2005   *Chidgey*, David William George Chidgey, *b. 1942, m.*

1987   *Chilver*, (Amos) Henry Chilver, FRS, FRENG, *b. 1926, m.*

1977   *Chitnis*, Pratap Chidamber Chitnis, *b. 1936, m.*

1998   *Christopher*, Anthony Martin Grosvenor Christopher, CBE, *b. 1925, m.*

2001   *Clark of Windermere*, David George Clark, PC, PHD, *b. 1939, m.*

1998   *Clarke of Hampstead*, Anthony James Clarke, CBE, *b. 1932, m.*

2009 §*Clarke of Stone-Cum-Ebony*, Anthony Peter Clarke, PC, *b.* 1943, *m.*

1998 *Clement-Jones*, Timothy Francis Clement-Jones, CBE, *b.* 1949, *m.*

1990 *Clinton-Davis*, Stanley Clinton Clinton-Davis, PC, *b.* 1928, *m.*

2000 *Coe*, Sebastian Newbold Coe, KBE, *b.* 1956, *m.*

2011 *Collins of Highbury*, Raymond Edward Harry Collins, *b.* 1954

2001 *Condon*, Paul Leslie Condon, QPM, *b.* 1947, *m.*

1997 *Cope of Berkeley*, John Ambrose Cope, PC, *b.* 1937, *m.*

2001 *Corbett of Castle Vale*, Robin Corbett, *b.* 1933, *m.*

2010 *Cormack*, Patrick Thomas Cormack, *b.* 1939, *m.*

2006 *Cotter*, Brian Joseph Michael Cotter, *b.* 1939, *m.*

1991 *Craig of Radley*, David Brownrigg Craig, GCB, OBE, *b.* 1929, *m.*

1987 *Crickhowell*, (Roger) Nicholas Edwards, PC, *b.* 1934, *m.*

2006 *Crisp*, (Edmund) Nigel (Ramsay) Crisp, KCB, *b.* 1952, *m.*

1978 *Croham*, Douglas Albert Vivian Allen, GCB, *b.* 1917, *w.*

2003 *Cullen of Whitekirk*, William Douglas Cullen, KT, PC, *b.* 1935, *m.*

2005 *Cunningham of Felling*, John Anderson Cunningham, PC, *b.* 1939, *m.*

1996 *Currie of Marylebone*, David Anthony Currie, *b.* 1946, *m.*

2011 *Dannatt*, Gen. (Francis) Richard Dannatt, GCB, CBE, MC, *b.* 1950, *m.*

2007 *Darzi of Denham*, Ara Warkes Darzi, KBE, *b.* 1960, *m.*

2006 *Davidson of Glen Clova*, Neil Forbes Davidson, QC, *b.* 1950, *m.*

2009 *Davies of Abersoch,* Evan Mervyn Davies, CBE, *b.* 1952, *m.*

1997 *Davies of Coity*, (David) Garfield Davies, CBE, *b.* 1935, *m.*

1997 *Davies of Oldham*, Bryan Davies, PC, *b.* 1939, *m.*

2010 *Davies of Stamford*, John Quentin Davies, *b.* 1944, *m.*

2006 *Dear*, Geoffrey (James) Dear, QPM, *b.* 1937, *m.*

2010 *Deben*, John Selwyn Gummer, PC, *b.* 1939, *m.*

1991 *Desai*, Prof. Meghnad Jagdishchandra Desai, PHD, *b.* 1940, *m.*

1997 *Dholakia*, Navnit Dholakia, OBE, PC, *b.* 1937, *m.*

1997 *Dixon*, Donald Dixon, PC, *b.* 1929, *m.*

1993 *Dixon-Smith*, Robert William Dixon-Smith, *b.* 1934, *m.*

2010 *Dobbs*, Michael John Dobbs, *b.* 1948, *m.*

1985 *Donoughue*, Bernard Donoughue, DPHIL, *b.* 1934

2004 *Drayson*, Paul Rudd Drayson, PC, *b.* 1960, *m.*

1994 *Dubs*, Alfred Dubs, *b.* 1932, *m.*

2004 *Dykes*, Hugh John Maxwell Dykes, *b.* 1939, *m.*

1995 *Eames*, Robert Henry Alexander Eames, OM, PHD, *b.* 1937, *m.*

1992 *Eatwell*, John Leonard Eatwell, PHD, *b.* 1945

1983 *Eden of Winton*, John Benedict Eden, PC, *b.* 1925, *m.*

2011 *Edmiston*, Robert Norman Edmiston, *b.* 1946, *m.*

1999 *Elder*, Thomas Murray Elder, *b.* 1950

1992 *Elis-Thomas*, Dafydd Elis Elis-Thomas, PC, *b.* 1946, *m.*

1981 *Elystan-Morgan*, Dafydd Elystan Elystan-Morgan, *b.* 1932, *w.*

2011 *Empey*, Reginald Norman Morgan Empey, OBE, *b.* 1947, *m.*

2000 **Erskine of Alloa Tower*, Earl of Mar and Kellie, *b.* 1949, *m.* (*see* Hereditary Peers)

1997 *Evans of Parkside*, John Evans, *b.* 1930, *m.*

2000 *Evans of Temple Guiting*, Matthew Evans, CBE, *b.* 1941, *m.*

1998 *Evans of Watford*, David Charles Evans, *b.* 1942, *m.*

1983 *Ezra*, Derek Ezra, MBE, *b.* 1919, *m.*

1997 *Falconer of Thoroton*, Charles Leslie Falconer, QC, *b.* 1951, *m.*

1999 *Faulkner of Worcester*, Richard Oliver Faulkner, *b.* 1946, *m.*

2010 *Faulks*, Edward Peter Lawless Faulks, QC, *b.* 1950, *m.*

2001 *Fearn*, Ronald Cyril Fearn, OBE, *b.* 1931, *m.*

1996 *Feldman*, Basil Feldman, *b.* 1926, *m.*

2010 *Feldman of Elstree*, Andrew Simon Feldman, *b.* 1966, *m.*

1999 *Fellowes*, Robert Fellowes, GCB, GCVO, PC, *b.* 1941, *m.*

2011 *Fellowes of West Stafford*, Julian Alexander Fellowes, *b.* 1949, *m.*

1999 *Filkin*, David Geoffrey Nigel Filkin, CBE, *b.* 1944

2011 *Fink*, Stanley Fink, *b.* 1957, *m.*

2011 *Flight*, Howard Emerson Flight, *b.* 1948, *m.*

1999 *Forsyth of Drumlean*, Michael Bruce Forsyth, *b.* 1954, *m.*

2005 *Foster of Bishop Auckland*, Derek Foster, PC, *b.* 1937, *m.*

1999 *Foster of Thames Bank*, Norman Robert Foster, OM, *b.* 1935, *m.*

2005 *Foulkes of Cumnock*, George Foulkes, PC, *b.* 1942, *m.*

2001 *Fowler*, (Peter) Norman Fowler, PC, *b.* 1938, *m.*

2011 *Framlingham*, Michael Nicholson Lord, *b.* 1938, *m.*

1989 *Fraser of Carmyllie*, Peter Lovat Fraser, PC, QC, *b.* 1945, *m.*

1997 *Freeman*, Roger Norman Freeman, PC, *b.* 1942, *m.*

2009 *Freud*, David Anthony Freud, *b.* 1950 *m.*

2010 *Gardiner of Kimble*, John Gardiner, *b.* 1956, *m.*

1997 *Garel-Jones*, (William Armand) Thomas Tristan Garel-Jones, PC, *b.* 1941, *m.*

1999* *Gascoyne-Cecil*, The Marquess of Salisbury, PC , *b.* 1946, *m.* (*see* Hereditary Peers)

1999 *Gavron*, Robert Gavron, CBE, *b.* 1930, *m.*

2010 *German*, Michael James German, OBE, *b.* 1945, *m.*

2004 *Giddens*, Prof. Anthony Giddens, *b.* 1938, *m.*

1997 *Gilbert*, John William Gilbert, PC, PHD, *b.* 1927, *m.*

2011 *Glasman*, Maurice Mark Glasman, *b.* 1961, *m.*

1977 *Glenamara*, Edward Watson Short, CH, PC, *b.* 1912, *m.*

2011 *Glendonbrook*, Michael David Bishop, CBE, *b.* 1942

2011 *Gold*, David Laurence Gold, *b.* 1951, *m.*

1999 *Goldsmith*, Peter Henry Goldsmith, QC, *b.* 1950, *m.*

1997 *Goodhart*, William Howard Goodhart, QC, *b.* 1933, *m.*

2005   *Goodlad,* Alastair Robertson Goodlad, KCMG,
        b. 1943, *m.*

1997   *Gordon of Strathblane,* James Stuart Gordon,
        CBE, *b.* 1936, *m.*

2004   *Gould of Brookwood,* Philip Gould *b.* 1950 *m.*

1999   *Grabiner,* Anthony Stephen Grabiner, QC,
        b. 1945, *m.*

2011   *Grade of Yarmouth,* Michael Ian Grade, CBE,
        b. 1943, *m.*

1983   *Graham of Edmonton,* (Thomas) Edward
        Graham, *b.* 1925, *m.*

2000   *Greaves,* Anthony Robert Greaves,
        b. 1942, *m.*

2010   *Green of Hurstpierpoint,* Stephen Keith Green,
        b. 1948, *m.*

2000   **Grenfell of Kilvey,* Lord Grenfell, *b.* 1935, *m.*
        (see Hereditary Peers)

2004   *Griffiths of Burry Port,* Revd Dr Leslie John
        Griffiths, *b.* 1942, *m.*

1991   *Griffiths of Fforestfach,* Brian Griffiths,
        b. 1941, *m.*

2001   *Grocott,* Bruce Joseph Grocott, PC, *b.* 1940, *m.*

2000   **Gueterbock,* Lord Berkeley, OBE, *b.* 1939, *m.* (*see*
        Hereditary Peers)

2000   *Guthrie of Craigiebank,* Charles Ronald
        Llewelyn Guthrie, GCB, LVO, OBE
        b. 1938, *m.*

1995   *Habgood,* Rt. Revd John Stapylton Habgood,
        PC, PHD, *b.* 1927, *m.*

2010   *Hall of Birkenhead,* Anthony William Hall, CBE,
        b. 1951, *m.*

2007   *Hameed,* Dr Khalid Hameed, *b.* 1941, *m.*

2005   *Hamilton of Epsom,* Archibald Gavin Hamilton,
        PC, *b.* 1941, *m.*

2001   *Hannay of Chiswick,* David Hugh Alexander
        Hannay, GCMG, CH, *b.* 1935, *m.*

1998   *Hanningfield,* Paul Edward Winston White,
        b. 1940

1997   *Hardie,* Andrew Rutherford Hardie, QC, PC,
        b. 1946, *m.*

2006   *Harries of Pentregarth,* Rt. Revd Richard Douglas
        Harries, *b.* 1936, *m.*

1998   *Harris of Haringey,* (Jonathan) Toby Harris,
        b. 1953, *m.*

1996   *Harris of Peckham,* Philip Charles Harris,
        b. 1942, *m.*

1999   *Harrison,* Lyndon Henry Arthur Harrison,
        b. 1947, *m.*

2004   *Hart of Chilton,* Garry Richard Rushby Hart,
        b. 1940, *m.*

1993   *Haskel,* Simon Haskel, *b.* 1934, *m.*

1998   *Haskins,* Christopher Robin Haskins,
        b. 1937, *m.*

2005   *Hastings of Scarisbrick,* Michael John Hastings,
        CBE, *b.* 1958, *m.*

1997   *Hattersley,* Roy Sidney George Hattersley, PC,
        b. 1932, *m.*

2004   *Haworth,* Alan Robert Haworth, *b.* 1948, *m.*

1992   *Hayhoe,* Bernard John (Barney) Hayhoe, PC,
        b. 1925, *m.*

1992   *Healey,* Denis Winston Healey, CH, MBE, PC,
        b. 1917, *w.*

2010   *Hennessy of Nympsfield,* Prof. Peter John
        Hennessy, *b.* 1947, *m.*

2001   *Heseltine,* Michael Ray Dibdin Heseltine, CH,
        PC, *b.* 1933, *m.*

1997   *Higgins,* Terence Langley Higgins, KBE, PC,
        b. 1928, *m.*

2010   *Hill of Oareford,* Jonathan Hopkin Hill, CBE,
        b. 1960, *m.*

2000   *Hodgson of Astley Abbotts,* Robin Granville
        Hodgson, CBE, *b.* 1942, *m.*

1991   *Hollick,* Clive Richard Hollick, *b.* 1945, *m.*

1979   *Hooson,* (Hugh) Emlyn Hooson, QC, *b.* 1925, *m.*

2005   *Hope of Thornes,* Rt. Revd David Michael Hope,
        KCVO, PC, *b.* 1940

1995   §*Hope of Craighead,* (James Arthur) David Hope,
        KT, PC, *b.* 1938, *m.*

2010   *Howard of Lympne,* Michael Howard, CH, PC,
        QC, *b.* 1941, *m.*

2004   *Howard of Rising,* Greville Patrick Charles
        Howard, *b.* 1941, *m.*

2005   *Howarth of Newport,* Alan Thomas Howarth,
        CBE, PC, *b.* 1944

1992   *Howe of Aberavon,* (Richard Edward) Geoffrey
        Howe, CH, PC, QC, *b.* 1926, *m.*

1997   *Howell of Guildford,* David Arthur Russell
        Howell, PC, *b.* 1936, *m.*

1978   *Howie of Troon,* William Howie, *b.* 1924, *w.*

1997   *Hoyle,* (Eric) Douglas Harvey Hoyle, *b.* 1930, *w.*

1997   *Hughes of Woodside,* Robert Hughes, *b.* 1932, *m.*

2000   *Hunt of Chesterton,* Julian Charles Roland Hunt,
        CBE, *b.* 1941, *m.*

1997   *Hunt of Kings Heath,* Philip Alexander Hunt,
        OBE, PC, *b.* 1949, *m.*

1997   *Hunt of Wirral,* David James Fletcher Hunt,
        MBE, PC, *b.* 1942, *m.*

1997   *Hurd of Westwell,* Douglas Richard Hurd, CH,
        CBE, PC, *b.* 1930, *w.*

2011   *Hussain,* Qurban Hussain, *m.*

1978   *Hutchinson of Lullington,* Jeremy Nicolas
        Hutchinson, QC, *b.* 1915, *w.*

2010   *Hutton of Furness,* John Matthew Patrick Hutton,
        PC, *b.* 1955, *m.*

1999   *Imbert,* Peter Michael Imbert, CVO, QPM, *b.*
        1933, *m.*

1997   *Inge,* Peter Anthony Inge, KG, GCB, PC,
        b. 1935, *m.*

1987   *Irvine of Lairg,* Alexander Andrew Mackay
        Irvine, PC, QC, *b.* 1940, *m.*

1997   *Jacobs,* (David) Anthony Jacobs, *b.* 1931, *m.*

2006   *James of Blackheath,* David Noel James, CBE,
        b. 1937, *m.*

1997   *Janner of Braunstone,* Greville Ewan Janner, QC,
        b. 1928, *w.*

2007   *Janvrin,* Robin Berry Janvrin, GCB, GCVO, PC,
        b. 1946, *m.*

2006   *Jay of Ewelme,* Michael (Hastings) Jay, GCMG,
        b. 1946, *m.*

1987   *Jenkin of Roding,* (Charles) Patrick (Fleeming)
        Jenkin, PC, *b.* 1926, *m.*

2000   *Joffe,* Joel Goodman Joffe, CBE, *b.* 1932, *m.*

2001   *Jones,* (Stephen) Barry Jones, *b.* 1937, *m.*

2007   *Jones of Birmingham,* Digby Marritt Jones,
        b. 1955, *m.*

2005,   *Jones of Cheltenham,* Nigel David Jones,
        b. 1948, *m.*

1997   *Jopling,* (Thomas) Michael Jopling, PC,
        b. 1930, *m.*

2000   *Jordan,* William Brian Jordan, CBE, *b.* 1936,
        m.

1991   *Judd,* Frank Ashcroft Judd, *b.* 1935, *m.*

2008   *Judge,* Igor Judge, PC, *b.* 1941, *m., Lord Chief
        Justice of England and Wales*

2010   *Kakkar,* Prof. Ajay Kumar Kakkar, *b.* 1964

2004   *Kalms,* Harold Stanley Kalms, *b.* 1931, *m.*

2010 *Kennedy of Southwark,* Roy Francis Kennedy, b. 1962

2004 *Kerr of Kinlochard,* John (Olav) Kerr, GCMG, b. 1942, m.

2010 **Kerr of Monteviot,* Marquess of Lothian (Michael Ancram), PC, QC, b. 1945, m. (*see* Hereditary Peers)

2011 *Kestenbaum,* Jonathan Andrew Kestenbaum, b. 1959, m.

2001 *Kilclooney,* John David Taylor, PC (NI), b. 1937, m.

1996 *Kilpatrick of Kincraig,* Robert Kilpatrick, CBE, b. 1926, m.

1985 *Kimball,* Marcus Richard Kimball, b. 1928, m.

2001 *King of Bridgwater,* Thomas Jeremy King, CH, PC, b. 1933, m.

1999 *King of West Bromwich,* Tarsem King, b. 1937

1993 *Kingsdown,* Robert (Robin) Leigh-Pemberton, KG, PC, b. 1927, m.

2005 *Kinnock,* Neil Gordon Kinnock, PC, b. 1942, m.

1999 *Kirkham,* Graham Kirkham, b. 1944, m.

1975 *Kirkhill,* John Farquharson Smith, b. 1930, m.

2005 *Kirkwood of Kirkhope,* Archibald Johnstone Kirkwood, b. 1946, m.

2007 *Krebs,* Prof. John (Richard) Krebs, FRS, b. 1945, m.

2010 *Knight of Weymouth,* James Philip Knight, PC, b. 1965, m.

1987 *Knights,* Philip Douglas Knights, CBE, QPM, b. 1920, m.

2004 *Laidlaw,* Irvine Alan Stewart Laidlaw, b. 1942, m.

1999 *Laird,* John Dunn Laird, b. 1944, m.

1998 *Laming,* (William) Herbert Laming, CBE, b. 1936, m.

1998 *Lamont of Lerwick,* Norman Stewart Hughson Lamont, PC, b. 1942, m.

1997 *Lang of Monkton,* Ian Bruce Lang, PC, b. 1940, m.

1992 *Lawson of Blaby,* Nigel Lawson, PC, b. 1932, m.

2000 *Layard,* Peter Richard Grenville Layard, b. 1934, m.

1999 *Lea of Crondall,* David Edward Lea, OBE, b. 1937

2006 *Leach of Fairford,* Charles Guy Rodney Leach, b. 1934, m.

2006 *Lee of Trafford,* John Robert Louis Lee, b. 1942, m.

2004 *Leitch,* Alexander Park Leitch, b. 1947, m.

1993 *Lester of Herne Hill,* Anthony Paul Lester, QC, b. 1936, m.

1997 *Levene of Portsoken,* Peter Keith Levene, KBE, b. 1941, m.

1997 *Levy,* Michael Abraham Levy, b. 1944, m.

1989 *Lewis of Newnham,* Jack Lewis, FRS, b. 1928, m.

2010 *Lexden,* Alistair Basil Cooke, OBE, b. 1945

2010 *Liddle,* Roger John Liddle, b. 1947, m.

2010 *Lingfield,* Robert George Alexander Balchin, b. 1942, m.

1999 *Lipsey,* David Lawrence Lipsey, b. 1948, m.

1997 *Lloyd-Webber,* Andrew Lloyd Webber, b. 1948, m.

1997 *Lofthouse of Pontefract,* Geoffrey Lofthouse, b. 1925, w.

2011 *Loomba,* Rajinder Paul Loomba, CBE, b. 1943, m.

2006 *Low of Dalston,* Prof. Colin Mackenzie Low, CBE, b. 1942, m.

2000 *Luce,* Richard Napier Luce, KG, GCVO, PC, b. 1936, m.

2000 **Lyttleton of Aldershot,* The Viscount Chandos, b. 1953, m. (*see* Hereditary Peers)

1984 *McAlpine of West Green,* (Robert) Alistair McAlpine, b. 1942, m.

2010 *McAvoy,* Thomas McLaughlin McAvoy, PC, b. 1943, m.

1988 *Macaulay of Bragar,* Donald Macaulay, QC, b. 1933, m.

1975 *McCarthy,* William Edward John McCarthy, DPHIL, b. 1925, m.

1976 *McCluskey,* John Herbert McCluskey, b. 1929, m.

1989 *McColl of Dulwich,* Ian McColl, CBE, FRCS, FRCSE, b. 1933, m.

2010 *McConnell of Glenscorrodale,* Dr Jack Wilson McConnell, PC, b. 1960, m.

2010 *MacDonald of River Glaven,* Kenneth Donald John MacDonald, QC, b. 1953, m.

1998 *Macdonald of Tradeston,* Angus John Macdonald, CBE, b. 1940, m.

2010 *McFall of Alcluith,* John Francis McFall, PC, b. 1944, m.

1991 *Macfarlane of Bearsden,* Norman Somerville Macfarlane, KT, FRSE, b. 1926, m.

2001 *MacGregor of Pulham Market,* John Roddick Russell MacGregor, CBE, PC, b. 1937, m.

1979 *Mackay of Clashfern,* James Peter Hymers Mackay, KT, PC, FRSE, b. 1927, m.

1995 *Mackay of Drumadoon,* Donald Sage Mackay, PC, b. 1946, m.

2004 *McKenzie of Luton,* William David McKenzie, b. 1946, m.

1999 *Mackenzie of Culkein,* Hector Uisdean MacKenzie, b. 1940

1998 *Mackenzie of Framwellgate,* Brian Mackenzie, OBE, b. 1943, m.

1974 *Mackie of Benshie,* George Yull Mackie, CBE, DSO, DFC, b. 1919, m.

1996 *MacLaurin of Knebworth,* Ian Charter MacLaurin, b. 1937, m.

2001 *Maclennon of Rogart,* Robert Adam Ross Maclennan, PC, b. 1936, m.

1995 *McNally,* Tom McNally, PC, b. 1943, m.

2011 *Magan of Castletown,* George Morgan Magan, b. 1945, m.

2001 *Maginnis of Drumglass,* Kenneth Wiggins Maginnis, b. 1938, m.

2007 *Malloch-Brown,* George Mark Malloch Brown, KCMG, PC, b. 1953, m.

2008 *Mandelson,* Peter Benjamin Mandelson, PC, b. 1953

2010 *Maples,* John Craddock Maples, b. 1943, m.

2011 *Marks of Henley-on-Thames,* Jonathan Clive Marks, QC, b. 1952, m.

2006 *Marland,* Jonathan Peter Marland, b. 1956, m.

1991 *Marlesford,* Mark Shuldham Schreiber, b. 1931, m.

1998 *Marshall of Knightsbridge,* Colin Marsh Marshall, b. 1933, m.

2009 *Martin of Springburn,* Michael Martin, PC, b. 1945, m.

1987 *Mason of Barnsley,* Roy Mason, PC, b. 1924, m.

2005 *Mawhinney,* Brian Stanley Mawhinney, PC, b. 1940, m.

2007   *Mawson*, Revd Andrew Mawson, OBE,
b. 1954, m.

2004   *Maxton*, John Alston Maxton, b. 1936, m.

2001   *May of Oxford*, Robert McCredie May, OM,
b. 1936, m.

1997   *Mayhew of Twysden*, Patrick Barnabas Burke
Mayhew, QC, PC, b. 1929, m.

2000   *Mitchell*, Parry Andrew Mitchell, b. 1943, m.

2000   *Mitford*, Lord Redesdale, b. 1967, m. (see
Hereditary Peers)

2008   *Mogg*, John (Frederick) Mogg, KCMG, b. 1943
m.

1997   *Molyneaux of Killead*, James Henry Molyneaux,
KBE, PC, b. 1920

2010   *Monks*, John Stephen Monks, b. 1945, m.

2005   *Moonie*, Dr. Lewis George Moonie, b. 1947, m.

1992   *Moore of Lower Marsh*, John Edward Michael
Moore, PC, b. 1937, w.

2000   *Morgan*, Kenneth Owen Morgan, b. 1934, m.

2001   *Morris of Aberavon*, John Morris, KG, QC,
b. 1931, m.

2006   *Morris of Handsworth*, William Manuel Morris,
b. 1938, m.

1997   *Morris of Manchester*, Alfred Morris, PC,
b. 1928, m.

2006   *Morrow*, Maurice George Morrow, m.

2001   *Moser*, Claus Adolf Moser, KCB, CBE,
b. 1922, m.

2008   *Myners*, Paul Myners, CBE, b. 1948, m.

1997   *Naseby*, Michael Wolfgang Laurence Morris, PC,
b. 1936, m.

1997   *Neill of Bladen*, (Francis) Patrick Neill, QC,
b. 1926, m.

1997   *Newby*, Richard Mark Newby, OBE,
b. 1953, m.

1997   *Newton of Braintree*, Antony Harold Newton,
OBE, PC, b. 1937, m.

1994   *Nickson*, David Wigley Nickson, KBE, FRSE,
b. 1929, m.

2011   *Noon*, Gulam Kaderbhoy Noon, MBE, b. 1936,
m.

1975   *Northfield*, (William) Donald Chapman, b. 1923

1998   *Norton of Louth*, Philip Norton, b. 1951

2000   *Oakeshott of Seagrove Bay*, Matthew Alan
Oakeshott, b. 1947, m.

2005   *O'Neill of Clackmannan*, Martin John O'Neill,
b. 1945, m.

2001   *Ouseley*, Herman George Ouseley, b. 1945, m.

1992   *Owen*, David Anthony Llewellyn Owen, CH,
PC, b. 1938, m.

1999   *Oxburgh*, Ernest Ronald Oxburgh, KBE, FRS,
PHD, b. 1934, m.

2011   *Palmer of Childs Hill*, Monroe Edward Palmer,
OBE, b. 1938, m.

1991   *Palumbo*, Peter Garth Palumbo, b. 1935, m.

2008   *Pannick*, David Philip Pannick, QC, b. 1956, m.

2000   *Parekh*, Bhikhu Chhotalal Parekh, b. 1935, m.

1992   *Parkinson*, Cecil Edward Parkinson, PC,
b. 1931, m.

1999   *Patel*, Narendra Babubhai Patel, b. 1938

2000   *Patel of Blackburn*, Adam Hafejee Patel, b. 1940

2006   *Patel of Bradford*, Prof. Kamlesh Kumar Patel,
OBE, b. 1960 m.

2005   *Patten of Barnes*, Christopher Francis Patten, CH,
PC, b. 1944, m.

1997   *Patten*, John Haggitt Charles Patten, PC,
b. 1945, m.

1996   *Paul*, Swraj Paul, PC, b. 1931, m.

1990   *Pearson of Rannoch*, Malcolm Everard MacLaren
Pearson, b. 1942, m.

2001   *Pendry*, Thomas Pendry, b. 1934, m.

1987   *Peston*, Maurice Harry Peston, b. 1931, m.

1998   *Phillips of Sudbury*, Andrew Wyndham Phillips,
OBE, b. 1939, m.

1992   *Plant of Highfield*, Prof. Raymond Plant, PHD,
b. 1945, m.

1987   *Plumb*, (Charles) Henry Plumb, b. 1925, m.

2000   *Ponsonby of Roehampton*, Lord Ponsonby of
Shulbrede, b. 1958 (see Hereditary Peers)

2010   *Popat*, Dolar Amarshi Popat, b. 1953, m.

2000   *Powell of Bayswater*, Charles David Powell,
KCMG, b. 1941

2010   *Prescott*, John Leslie Prescott, PC, b. 1938, m.

1987   *Prior*, James Michael Leathes Prior, PC,
b. 1927, m.

1982   *Prys-Davies*, Gwilym Prys Prys-Davies, b.
1923, m.

1997   *Puttnam*, David Terence Puttnam, CBE,
b. 1941, m.

1994   *Quirk*, Prof. (Charles) Randolph Quirk, CBE,
FBA, b. 1920, m.

2001   *Radice*, Giles Heneage Radice, PC, b. 1936

2005   *Ramsbotham*, Gen. David John Ramsbotham,
GCB, CBE, b. 1934, m.

2004   *Rana*, Dr Diljit Singh Rana, MBE, b. 1938, m.

1997   *Randall of St Budeaux*, Stuart Jeffrey Randall,
b. 1938, m.

1997   *Razzall*, (Edward) Timothy Razzall, CBE,
b. 1943, m.

2005   *Rees of Ludlow*, Prof. Martin John Rees, OM,
b. 1942, m.

1988   *Rees-Mogg*, William Rees-Mogg, b. 1928, m.

2010   *Reid of Cardowan*, Dr John Reid, PC, b. 1947, m.

1991   *Renfrew of Kaimsthorn*, (Andrew) Colin Renfrew,
FBA, b. 1937, m.

1999   *Rennard*, Christopher John Rennard, MBE,
b. 1960

1997   *Renton of Mount Harry*, (Ronald) Timothy
Renton, PC, b. 1932, m.

1997   *Renwick of Clifton*, Robin William Renwick,
KCMG, b. 1937, m.

2010   *Ribeiro*, Bernard Francisco Ribeiro, CBE,
b. 1944, m.

1990   *Richard*, Ivor Seward Richard, PC, QC,
b. 1932, m.

2010   *Risby*, Richard John Grenville Spring, b. 1946, m.

1992   *Rix*, Brian Norman Roger Rix, CBE,
b. 1924, m.

2004   *Roberts of Llandudno*, Revd John Roger Roberts,
b. 1935, m.

1997   *Roberts of Conwy*, (Ieuan) Wyn (Pritchard)
Roberts, PC, b. 1930, m.

1999   *Robertson of Port Ellen*, George Islay MacNeill
Robertson, KT, GCMG, PC, b. 1946, m.

1992   *Rodgers of Quarry Bank*, William Thomas
Rodgers, PC, b. 1928, w.

1999   *Rogan*, Dennis Robert David Rogan, b. 1942, m.

1996   *Rogers of Riverside*, Richard George Rogers, CH,
RA, RIBA, b. 1933, m.

2001   *Rooker*, Jeffrey William Rooker, PC, b. 1941, m.

2000   *Roper*, John Francis Hodgess Roper, PC,
b. 1935, m.

2004   *Rosser*, Richard Andrew Rosser, b. 1944, m.

2006   *Rowe-Beddoe*, David (Sydney) Rowe-Beddoe,
b. 1937, m.

2004   *Rowlands*, Edward Rowlands, CBE, b. 1940, m.

1997	*Ryder of Wensum*, Richard Andrew Ryder, OBE, PC, *b.* 1949, *m.*
1996	*Saatchi*, Maurice Saatchi, *b.* 1946, *w.*
2009	‡*Sacks*, Chief Rabbi Dr Jonathan Henry Sacks, *b.* 1948, *m.*
1989	*Sainsbury of Preston Candover*, John Davan Sainsbury, KG, *b.* 1927, *m.*
1997	*Sainsbury of Turville*, David John Sainsbury, *b.* 1940, *m.*
1987	*St John of Fawsley*, Norman Antony Francis St John-Stevas, PC, *b.* 1929
1997	*Sandberg*, Michael Graham Ruddock Sandberg, CBE, *b.* 1927, *m.*
1985	*Sanderson of Bowden*, Charles Russell Sanderson, *b.* 1933, *m.*
2010	*Sassoon*, James Meyer Sassoon, *b.* 1955, *m.*
1998	*Sawyer*, Lawrence (Tom) Sawyer, *b.* 1943
1997	*Selkirk of Douglas*, James Alexander Douglas-Hamilton, MSP, PC, QC, *b.* 1942, *m.*
1996	*Sewel*, John Buttifant Sewel, CBE, *b.* 1946
2010	*Sharkey*, John Kevin Sharkey, *b.* 1947, *m.*
1999	*Sharman*, Colin Morven Sharman, OBE, *b.* 1943, *m.*
1994	*Shaw of Northstead*, Michael Norman Shaw, *b.* 1920, *m.*
2006	*Sheikh*, Mohamed Iltaf Sheikh, *b.* 1941, *m.*
2001	*Sheldon*, Robert Edward Sheldon, PC, *b.* 1923, *m.*
1994	*Sheppard of Didgemere*, Allan John George Sheppard, KCVO, *b.* 1932, *m.*
2010	*Shipley*, John Warren Shipley, OBE, *b.* 1946
2000	*Shutt of Greetland*, David Trevor Shutt, OBE, PC, *b.* 1942
1997	*Simon of Highbury*, David Alec Gwyn Simon, CBE, *b.* 1939, *m.*
1997	*Simpson of Dunkeld*, George Simpson, *b.* 1942, *m.*
1991	*Skidelsky*, Robert Jacob Alexander Skidelsky, DPHIL, *b.* 1939, *m.*
1997	*Smith of Clifton*, Trevor Arthur Smith, *b.* 1937, *m.*
2005	*Smith of Finsbury*, Christopher Robert Smith, PC, *b.* 1951
2008	*Smith of Kelvin*, Robert (Haldane) Smith, *b.* 1944, *m.*
1999	*Smith of Leigh*, Peter Richard Charles Smith, *b.* 1945, *m.*
2004	*Snape*, Peter Charles Snape, *b.* 1942
2005	*Soley*, Clive Stafford Soley, *b.* 1939
1990	*Soulsby of Swaffham Prior*, Ernest Jackson Lawson Soulsby, PHD, *b.* 1926, *m.*
2010	*Spicer*, (William) Michael Hardy Spicer, *b.* 1943, *m.*
1997	*Steel of Aikwood*, David Martin Scott Steel, KT, KBE, PC, *b.* 1938, *m.*
2011	*Stephen*, Nicol Ross Stephen, *b.* 1960, *m.*
1991	*Sterling of Plaistow*, Jeffrey Maurice Sterling, GCVO, CBE, *b.* 1934, *m.*
2007	*Stern of Brentford*, Nicholas Herbert Stern, *b.* 1946, *m.*
2005	*Stevens of Kirkwhelpington*, John Arthur Stevens, *b.* 1942, *m.*
1987	*Stevens of Ludgate*, David Robert Stevens, *b.* 1936, *m.*
2010	*Stevenson of Balmacara*, Robert Wilfrid Stevenson, *b.* 1947, *m.*
1999	*Stevenson of Coddenham*, Henry Dennistoun Stevenson, CBE, *b.* 1945, *m.*

1992	*Stewartby*, (Bernard Harold) Ian (Halley) Stewart, RD, PC, FBA, FRSE, *b.* 1935, *m.*
2011	*Stirrup*, Air Chief Marshal Graham Eric Stirrup, GCB, AFC, *b.* 1949, *m.*
1983	*Stoddart of Swindon*, David Leonard Stoddart, *b.* 1926, *m.*
1997	*Stone of Blackheath*, Andrew Zelig Stone, *b.* 1942, *m.*
2011	*Stoneham of Droxford*, Benjamin Russell Mackintosh Stoneham 1940, *m.*
2011	*Storey*, Michael John Storey, CBE, *b.* 1949
2011	*Strasburger*, Paul Cline Strasburger, *b.* 1946
2009	*Sugar*, Alan Michael Sugar, *b.* 1947, *m.*
2001	*Sutherland of Houndwood*, Stewart Ross Sutherland, KT, *b.* 1941, *m.*
1971	*Tanlaw*, Simon Brooke Mackay, *b.* 1934, *m.*
1996	*Taverne*, Dick Taverne, QC, *b.* 1928, *m.*
2010	*Taylor of Goss Moor*, Matthew Owen John Taylor, *b.* 1963, *m.*
1978	*Taylor of Blackburn*, Thomas Taylor, CBE, *b.* 1929, *m.*
2006	*Taylor of Holbeach*, John Derek Taylor, CBE, *b.* 1943, *m.*
1996	*Taylor of Warwick*, John David Beckett Taylor, *b.* 1952, *m.*
1992	*Tebbit*, Norman Beresford Tebbit, CH, PC, *b.* 1931, *m.*
2001	*Temple-Morris*, Peter Temple-Morris, *b.* 1938, *m.*
2006	*Teverson*, Robin Teverson, *b.* 1952, *m.*
1996	*Thomas of Gresford*, Donald Martin Thomas, OBE, QC, *b.* 1937, *m.*
1997	*Thomas of Macclesfield*, Terence James Thomas, CBE, *b.* 1937, *m.*
1981	*Thomas of Swynnerton*, Hugh Swynnerton Thomas, *b.* 1931, *m.*
1990	*Tombs*, Francis Leonard Tombs, FENG, *b.* 1924, *w.*
1998	*Tomlinson*, John Edward Tomlinson, *b.* 1939
1994	*Tope*, Graham Norman Tope, CBE, *b.* 1943, *m.*
1981	*Tordoff*, Geoffrey Johnson Tordoff, *b.* 1928, *m.*
2010	*Touhig*, James Donnelly Touhig, PC, *b.* 1947, *m.*
2004	*Triesman*, David Maxim Triesman, *b.* 1943
2006	*Trimble*, William David Trimble, PC, *b.* 1944, *m.*
2010	*True*, Nicholas Edward True, CBE, *b.* 1951, *m.*
2004	*Truscott*, Dr Peter Derek Truscott, *b.* 1959, *m.*
1993	*Tugendhat*, Christopher Samuel Tugendhat, *b.* 1937, *m.*
2004	*Tunnicliffe*, Denis Tunnicliffe, CBE, *b.* 1943, *m.*
2000	*Turnberg*, Leslie Arnold Turnberg, MD, *b.* 1934, *m.*
2005	*Turnbull*, Andrew Turnbull, KCB, CVO, *b.* 1945, *m.*
2005	*Turner of Ecchinswell*, (Jonathan) Adair Turner, *b.* 1955, *m.*
2005	*Tyler*, Paul Archer Tyler, CBE, *b.* 1941, *m.*
2004	*Vallance of Tummel*, Iain (David Thomas) Vallance, *b.* 1943, *m.*
1996	*Vincent of Coleshill*, Richard Frederick Vincent, GBE, KCB, DSO, *b.* 1931, *m.*
1985	*Vinson*, Nigel Vinson, LVO, *b.* 1931, *m.*
1990	*Waddington*, David Charles Waddington, GCVO, PC, QC, *b.* 1929, *m.*
1990	*Wade of Chorlton*, (William) Oulton Wade, *b.* 1932, *m.*
1992	*Wakeham*, John Wakeham, PC, *b.* 1932, *m.*
1999	*Waldegrave of North Hill*, William Arthur Waldegrave, PC, *b.* 1946, *m.*

2007   *Walker of Aldringham,* Michael John Dawson Walker, GCB, CMG, CBE, *b.* 1944, *m.*

1995   *Wallace of Saltaire,* William John Lawrence Wallace, PHD, *b.* 1941, *m.*

2007   *Wallace of Tankerness,* James Robert Wallace, PC, QC, *b.* 1954, *m.*

1989   *Walton of Detchant,* John Nicholas Walton, TD, FRCP, *b.* 1922, *w.*

1998   *Warner,* Norman Reginald Warner, PC, *b.* 1940, *m.*

2011   *Wasserman,* Gordon Joshua Wasserman, *b.* 1938

1997   *Watson of Invergowrie,* Michael Goodall Watson, *b.* 1949, *m.*

1999   *Watson of Richmond,* Alan John Watson, CBE, *b.* 1941, *m.*

1977   *Wedderburn of Charlton,* (Kenneth) William Wedderburn, FBA, QC, *b.* 1927, *m.*

2010   *Wei,* Nathanael Ming-Yan Wei, *b.* 1977, *m.*

1976   *Weidenfeld,* (Arthur) George Weidenfeld, GBE, *b.* 1919, *m.*

2007   *West of Spithead,* Adm. Alan William John West, GCB, DSC, PC, *b.* 1948, *m.*

1996   *Whitty,* John Lawrence (Larry) Whitty, *b.* 1943, *m.*

2011   *Wigley,* Dafydd Wynne Wigley, *b.* 1943, *m.*

2010   *Williams of Baglan,* Michael Charles Williams, *b.* 1949

1985   *Williams of Elvel,* Charles Cuthbert Powell Williams, CBE, *b.* 1933, *m.*

1999   *Williamson of Horton,* David (Francis) Williamson, GCMG, CB, PC, *b.* 1934, *m.*

2010   *Willis of Knaresborough,* George Philip Willis, *b.* 1941, *m.*

2010   *Wills,* Michael David Wills, PC, *b.* 1952, *m.*

2002   *Wilson of Dinton,* Richard Thomas James Wilson, GCB, *b.* 1942, *m.*

1992   *Wilson of Tillyorn,* David Clive Wilson, KT, GCMG, PHD, *b.* 1935, *m.*

1995   *Winston,* Robert Maurice Lipson Winston, FRCOG, *b.* 1940, *m.*

2010   *Wolfson of Aspley Guise,* Simon David Wolfson, *b.* 1967

1991   *Wolfson of Sunningdale,* David Wolfson, *b.* 1935, *m.*

2011   *Wood of Anfield,* Stewart Martin Wood, *b.* 1968, *m.*

1999   *Woolmer of Leeds,* Kenneth John Woolmer, *b.* 1940, *m.*

1994   *Wright of Richmond,* Patrick Richard Henry Wright, GCMG, *b.* 1931, *m.*

2004   *Young of Norwood Green,* Anthony (Ian) Young, *b.* 1942, *m.*

1984   *Young of Graffham,* David Ivor Young, PC, *b.* 1932, *m.*

BARONESSES
Created

2005   *Adams of Craigielea,* Katherine Patricia Irene Adams, *b.* 1947, *w.*

1997   *Amos,* Valerie Ann Amos, *b.* 1954

2007   *Afshar,* Prof. Haleh Afshar, OBE, , *b.* 1944, *m.*

2000   *Andrews,* Elizabeth Kay Andrews, OBE, *b.* 1943, *m.*

1996   *Anelay of St Johns,* Joyce Anne Anelay, DBE, PC, *b.* 1947, *m.*

2010   *Armstrong of Hill Top,* Hilary Jane Armstrong, PC, *b.* 1945, *m.*

1999   *Ashton of Upholland,* Catherine Margaret Ashton, PC, *b.* 1956, *m.*

2011   *Bakewell,* Joan Dawson Bakewell, DBE, *b.* 1933

1999   *Barker,* Elizabeth Jean Barker, *b.* 1961

2010   *Benjamin,* Floella Karen Yunies Benjamin, OBE, *b.* 1949, *m.*

2011   *Berridge,* Elizabeth Rose Berridge, *b.* 1972

2000   *Billingham,* Angela Theodora Billingham, DPHIL, *b.* 1939, *w.*

1987   *Blackstone,* Tessa Ann Vosper Blackstone, PHD, *b.* 1942

1999   *Blood,* May Blood, MBE, *b.* 1938

2000   *Boothroyd,* Betty Boothroyd, OM, PC, *b.* 1929

2004   *Bonham-Carter of Yarnbury,* Jane Bonham Carter, *b.* 1957, *w.*

2005   *Bottomley of Nettlestone,* Virginia Hilda Brunette Maxwell Bottomley, PC, *b.* 1948, *m.*

2011   *Brinton,* Sarah Virginia Brinton, *b.* 1955, *m.*

2010   *Browning,* Angela Frances Browning, *b.* 1946, *m.*

1998   *Buscombe,* Peta Jane Buscombe, *b.* 1954, *m.*

2006   *Butler-Sloss,* (Ann) Elizabeth (Oldfield) Butler-Sloss, GBE, PC *b.* 1933, *m.*

1996   *Byford,* Hazel Byford, DBE, *b.* 1941, *m.*

2008   *Campbell of Loughborough,* Susan Catherine Campbell, CBE, *b.* 1948

2007   *Campbell of Surbiton,* Jane Susan Campbell, DBE, *b.* 1959, *m.*

1992   *Chalker of Wallasey,* Lynda Chalker, PC, *b.* 1942, *m.*

2005   *Clark of Calton,* Dr Lynda Margaret Clark, QC, *b.* 1949

2000   *Cohen of Pimlico,* Janet Cohen, *b.* 1940, *m.*

2005   *Corston,* Jean Ann Corston, PC, *b.* 1942, *w.*

2007   *Coussins,* Jean Coussins, *b.* 1950

1982   *Cox,* Caroline Anne Cox, *b.* 1937, *m.*

1998   *Crawley,* Christine Mary Crawley, *b.* 1950, *m.*

1990   *Cumberlege,* Julia Frances Cumberlege, CBE, *b.* 1943, *m.*

1993   *Dean of Thornton-le-Fylde,* Brenda Dean, PC, *b.* 1943, *m.*

2005   *Deech,* Ruth Lynn Deech, DBE, *b.* 1943, *m.*

2010   *Donaghy,* Rita Margaret Donaghy, CBE, *b.* 1944, *m.*

2010   *Doocey,* Elizabeth Deirdre Doocey, OBE, *m.*

2010   *Drake,* Jean Lesley Patricia Drake, CBE, *b.* 1948

2004   *D'Souza,* Dr Frances Gertrude Claire D'Souza, CMG, PC, *b.* 1944, *m.*

1990   *Dunn,* Lydia Selina Dunn, DBE, *b.* 1940, *m.*

2010   *Eaton,* Ellen Margaret Eaton, DBE

1990   *Eccles of Moulton,* Diana Catherine Eccles, *b.* 1933, *m.*

1997   *Emerton,* Audrey Caroline Emerton, DBE, *b.* 1935

1974   *Falkender,* Marcia Matilda Falkender, CBE, *b.* 1932

2004   *Falkner of Margravine,* Kishwer Falkner, *b.* 1955, *m.*

1994   *Farrington of Ribbleton,* Josephine Farrington, *b.* 1940, *m.*

2001   *Finlay of Llandaff,* Ilora Gillian Finlay, *b.* 1949, *m.*

1990   *Flather,* Shreela Flather, *m.*

1997   *Fookes,* Janet Evelyn Fookes, DBE, *b.* 1936

2006   *Ford,* Margaret Anne Ford, *b.* 1957, *m.*

2005   *Fritchie,* Irene Tordoff Fritchie, DBE, *b.* 1942, *m.*

1999   *Gale,* Anita Gale, *b.* 1940

2007   *Garden of Frognal,* Susan Elizabeth Garden, *b.* 1944, *m.*

1981   *Gardner of Parkes,* (Rachel) Trixie (Anne) Gardner, *b.* 1927, *w.*

2000   *Gibson of Market Rasen,* Anne Gibson, OBE, *b.* 1940, *m.*

2001   *Golding,* Llinos Golding, *b.* 1933, *m.*

1998   *Goudie,* Mary Teresa Goudie, *b.* 1946, *m.*

1993   *Gould of Potternewton,* Joyce Brenda Gould, *b.* 1932, *m.*

2001   *Greenfield,* Susan Adele Greenfield, CBE, *b.* 1950, *m.*

2000   *Greengross,* Sally Ralea Greengross, OBE, *b.* 1935, *m.*

2010   *Grey-Thompson,* Tanni Carys Davina Grey-Thompson, DBE, *b.* 1969, *m.*

1991   *Hamwee,* Sally Rachel Hamwee, *b.* 1947

1999   *Hanham,* Joan Brownlow Hanham, CBE, *b.* 1939, *m.*

1999   *Harris of Richmond,* Angela Felicity Harris, *b.* 1944

2011   *Heyhoe Flint,* Rachel Heyhoe Flint, OBE, *b.* 1939, *m.*

1996   *Hayman,* Helene Valerie Hayman, PC, *b.* 1949, *m.*

2010   *Hayter of Kentish Town,* Dr Dianne Hayter, *b.* 1949, *m.*

2010   *Healy of Primrose Hill,* Anna Healy, *b.* 1955, *m.*

2004   *Henig,* Ruth Beatrice Henig, CBE, *b.* 1943, *m.*

1991   *Hilton of Eggardon,* Jennifer Hilton, QPM, *b.* 1936

1995   *Hogg,* Sarah Elizabeth Mary Hogg, *b.* 1946, *m.*

2010   *Hollins,* Prof. Sheila Clare Hollins, *b.* 1946, *m.*

1990   *Hollis of Heigham,* Patricia Lesley Hollis, DPHIL, *b.* 1941, *m.*

1985   *Hooper,* Gloria Dorothy Hooper, CMG, *b.* 1939

2001   *Howarth of Breckland,* Valerie Georgina Howarth, OBE, *b.* 1940

2001   *Howe of Idlicote,* Elspeth Rosamond Morton Howe, CBE, *b.* 1932, *m.*

1999   *Howells of St Davids,* Rosalind Patricia-Anne Howells, *b.* 1931, *m.*

2010   *Hughes of Stretford,* Beverley Hughes, PC, *b.* 1950, *m.*

2010   *Hussein-Ece,* Meral Hussein Ece, OBE, *b.* 1953

1991   *James of Holland Park,* Phyllis Dorothy White (P. D. James), OBE, *b.* 1920, *w.*

1992   *Jay of Paddington,* Margaret Ann Jay, PC, *b.* 1939, *m.*

2011   *Jenkin of Kennington,* Anne Caroline Jenkin, *b.* 1955, *m.*

2010   *Jolly,* Judith Anne Jolly *m.*

2006   *Jones of Whitchurch,* Margaret Beryl Jones, *b.* 1955

1997   *Kennedy of the Shaws,* Helena Ann Kennedy, QC, *b.* 1950, *m.*

2011   *King of Bow,* Oona Tamsyn King, *b.* 1967, *m.*

2006   *Kingsmill,* Denise Patricia Byrne Kingsmill, CBE, *b.* 1947, *m.*

2009   *Kinnock of Holyhead,* Glenys Elizabeth Kinnock, *b.* 1944, *m.*

1997   *Knight of Collingtree,* (Joan Christabel) Jill Knight, DBE, *b.* 1927, *w.*

2010   *Kramer,* Susan Veronica Kramer, *b.* 1950, *w.*

2010   *Liddell of Coatdyke,* Helen Lawrie Liddell, PC, *b.* 1950, *m.*

1997   *Linklater of Butterstone,* Veronica Linklater, *b.* 1943, *m.*

2011   *Lister of Burtersett,* Margot Ruth Aline Lister, CBE, *b.* 1949, *m.*

1978   *Lockwood,* Betty Lockwood, *b.* 1924, *w.*

1997   *Ludford,* Sarah Ann Ludford, *b.* 1951

2004   *McDonagh,* Margaret Josephine McDonagh

1979   *McFarlane of Llandaff,* Jean Kennedy McFarlane, *b.* 1926

1999   *McIntosh of Hudnall,* Genista Mary McIntosh, *b.* 1946

1997   *Maddock,* Diana Margaret Maddock, *b.* 1945, *m.*

2008   *Manningham-Buller,* Elizabeth (Lydia) Manningham-Buller, DCB, *b.* 1948, *m.*

1991   *Mallalieu,* Ann Mallalieu, QC, *b.* 1945, *m.*

1970   *Masham of Ilton,* Susan Lilian Primrose Cunliffe-Lister, *b.* 1935, *w.*

1999   *Massey of Darwen,* Doreen Elizabeth Massey, *b.* 1938, *m.*

2006   *Meacher,* Molly Christine Meacher, *b.* 1940, *m.*

1998   *Miller of Chilthorne Domer,* Susan Elizabeth Miller, *b.* 1954

1993   *Miller of Hendon,* Doreen Miller, MBE, *b.* 1933, *m.*

2004   *Morgan of Drefelin,* Delyth Jane Morgan, *b.* 1961, *m.*

2011   *Morgan of Ely,* Mair Eluned Morgan, *b.* 1967, *m.*

2001   *Morgan of Huyton,* Sally Morgan, *b.* 1959, *m.*

2004   *Morris of Bolton,* Patricia Morris, OBE, *b.* 1953

2005   *Morris of Yardley,* Estelle Morris, PC, *b.* 1952

2004   *Murphy,* Elaine Murphy, *b.* 1947, *m.*

2004   *Neuberger,* Rabbi Julia (Babette Sarah) Neuberger, DBE, *b.* 1950, *m.*

2007   *Neville-Jones,* (Lilian) Pauline Neville-Jones, DCMG, PC, *b.* 1939

2010   *Newlove,* Helen Margaret Newlove, *w.*

1997   *Nicholson of Winterbourne,* Emma Harriet Nicholson, MEP, *b.* 1941, *m.*

1982   *Nicol,* Olive Mary Wendy Nicol, *b.* 1923, *m.*

2000   *Noakes,* Shiela Valerie Masters, DBE, *b.* 1949, *m.*

2000   *Northover,* Lindsay Patricia Granshaw, *b.* 1954

2010   *Nye,* Susan Nye, *b.* 1955, *m.*

1991   *O'Cathain,* Detta O'Cathain, OBE, *b.* 1938, *m.*

2009   *O'Loan,* Nuala Patricia, DBE, *b.* 1951, *m.*

1999   *O'Neill of Bengarve,* Onora Sylvia O'Neill, CBE, PHD, *b.* 1941

1989   *Oppenheim-Barnes,* Sally Oppenheim-Barnes, PC, *b.* 1930, *m.*

2006   *Paisley of St George's,* Eileen Emily Paisley, *m.*

2010   *Parminter,* Kathryn Jane Parminter, *b.* 1964, *m.*

1991   *Perry of Southwark,* Pauline Perry, *b.* 1931, *m.*

1997   *Pitkeathley,* Jill Elizabeth Pitkeathley, OBE, *b.* 1940

1981   *Platt of Writtle,* Beryl Catherine Platt, CBE, FENG, *b.* 1923, *m.*

1999   *Prashar,* Usha Kumari Prashar, CBE, PC, *b.* 1948, *m.*

2004   *Prosser,* Margaret Theresa Prosser, OBE, *b.* 1937

2006   *Quin,* Joyce Gwendoline Quin, PC *b.* 1944

1996   *Ramsay of Cartvale,* Margaret Mildred (Meta) Ramsay, *b.* 1936

2011   *Randerson,* Jennifer Elizabeth Randerson, *b.* 1948, *m.*

1994   *Rawlings,* Patricia Elizabeth Rawlings, *b.* 1939

1997   *Rendell of Babergh,* Ruth Barbara Rendell, CBE, *b.* 1930, *m.*

1998   *Richardson of Calow,* Kathleen Margaret Richardson, OBE, *b.* 1938, *m.*

2010   *Ritchie of Brompton,* Shireen Olive Ritchie,
        b. 1945
2004   *Royall of Blaisdon,* Janet Anne Royall, PC,
        b. 1955, *m.*
1997   *Scotland of Asthal,* Patricia Janet Scotland, QC,
        b. 1955, *m.*
2000   *Scott of Needham Market,* Rosalind Carol Scott,
        b. 1957
1991   *Seccombe,* Joan Anna Dalziel Seccombe, DBE,
        b. 1930, *m.*
2010   *Shackleton of Belgravia,* Fiona Sara Shackleton,
        LVO, *b.* 1956, *m.*
1998   *Sharp of Guildford,* Margaret Lucy Sharp,
        b. 1938, *m.*
1973   *Sharples,* Pamela Sharples, *b.* 1923, *m.*
2005   *Shephard of Northwold,* Gillian Patricia
        Shephard, PC, *b.* 1940, *m.*
2010   *Sherlock,* Maeve Christina Mary Sherlock, OBE,
        b. 1960
2010   *Smith of Basildon,* Angela Evans Smith, PC, *b.*
        1959, *m.*
1995   *Smith of Gilmorehill,* Elizabeth Margaret Smith,
        b. 1940, *w.*
2010   *Stedman-Scott,* Deborah Stedman-Scott, OBE,
        b. 1955
1999   *Stern,* Vivien Helen Stern, CBE, *b.* 1941
2011   *Stowell of Beeston,* Tina Wendy Stowell, MBE,
        b. 1967
1996   *Symons of Vernham Dean,* Elizabeth Conway
        Symons, *b.* 1951
2005   *Taylor of Bolton,* Winifred Ann Taylor, PC
        b. 1947, *m.*
1992   *Thatcher,* Margaret Hilda Thatcher, KG, OM,
        PC, FRS, *b.* 1925, *w.*
1994   *Thomas of Walliswood,* Susan Petronella
        Thomas, OBE, *b.* 1935, *m.*

2006   *Thomas of Winchester,* Celia Marjorie Thomas,
        MBE, *b.* 1945
1998   *Thornton,* (Dorothea) Glenys Thornton,
        b. 1952, *m.*
2005   *Tonge,* Dr. Jennifer Louise Tonge, *b.* 1941, *m.*
1980   *Trumpington,* Jean Alys Barker, DCVO, PC,
        b. 1922, *w.*
1985   *Turner of Camden,* Muriel Winifred Turner,
        b. 1927, *m.*
2011   *Tyler of Enfield,* Claire Tyler
1998   *Uddin,* Manzila Pola Uddin, *b.* 1959, *m.*
2007   *Vadera,* Shriti Vadera, PC
2005   *Valentine,* Josephine Clare Valentine
2006   *Verma,* Sandip Verma, *b.* 1959, *m.*
2004   *Wall of New Barnet,* Margaret Mary Wall,
        b. 1941, *m.*
2000   *Walmsley,* Joan Margaret Walmsley, *b.* 1943
1985   *Warnock,* Helen Mary Warnock, DBE,
        b. 1924, *w.*
2007   *Warsi,* Sayeeda Hussain Warsi, PC, *b.* 1971
1999   *Warwick of Undercliffe,* Diana Mary Warwick,
        b. 1945, *m.*
2010   *Wheatcroft,* Patience Jane Wheatcroft, *b.* 1951,
        m.
2010   *Wheeler,* Margaret Eileen Joyce Wheeler, MBE,
        b. 1949
1999   *Whitaker,* Janet Alison Whitaker, *b.* 1936
1996   *Wilcox,* Judith Ann Wilcox, *b.* 1940, *w.*
1999   *Wilkins,* Rosalie Catherine Wilkins, *b.* 1946
1993   *Williams of Crosby,* Shirley Vivien Teresa
        Brittain Williams, PC, *b.* 1930, *w.*
2011   *Worthington,* Bryony Katherine Worthington, *m.*
2004   *Young of Hornsey,* Prof. Margaret Omolola
        Young, OBE, *b.* 1951, *m.*
1997   *Young of Old Scone,* Barbara Scott Young,
        b. 1948

LORDS SPIRITUAL

The Lords Spiritual are the Archbishops of Canterbury and York and 24 diocesan bishops of the Church of England. The Bishops of London, Durham and Winchester always have seats in the House of Lords; the other 21 seats are filled by the remaining diocesan bishops in order of seniority. The Bishop of Sodor and Man and the Bishop of Gibraltar are not eligible to sit in the House of Lords.

ARCHBISHOPS

Style, The Most Revd and Rt. Hon. the Lord Archbishop of_
Addressed as Archbishop *or* Your Grace

INTRODUCED TO HOUSE OF LORDS

2003 *Canterbury* (104th), Rowan Douglas Williams, PC, DPHIL, *b.* 1950, *m., cons.* 1992, *elected* 2002
2005 *York* (97th), John Mugabi Tucker Sentamu, PC, PHD, *b.* 1949, *m., cons.* 1996, *elected* 2005, *trans.* 2005

BISHOPS

Style, The Rt. Revd the Lord Bishop of _
Addressed as My Lord
elected date of confirmation as diocesan bishop

INTRODUCED TO HOUSE OF LORDS
as at 31 August 2011

1996 *London* (132nd), Richard John Carew Chartres, KCVO, PC, *b.* 1947, *m., cons.* 1992, *elected* 1995
2011 *Durham* (72nd), Justin Welby, *b.* 1956, *m., cons.* 2011, *elected* 2011
1996 *Winchester* (96th), Michael Charles Scott-Joynt, *b.* 1943, *m., cons.* 1987, *elected* 1995
1997 *Manchester* (11th), Nigel Simeon McCulloch, *b.* 1942, *m., cons.* 1986, *elected* 1992, *trans.* 2002
2001 *Chester* (40th), Peter Robert Forster, PHD, *m., b.* 1950, *cons.* 1996, *elected* 1996
2003 *Newcastle* (11th), (John) Martin Wharton, *b.* 1944, *m., cons.* 1992, *elected* 1997
2003 *Liverpool* (7th), James Stuart Jones, *b.* 1948, *m., cons.* 1994, *elected* 1998
2003 *Leicester* (6th), Timothy John Stevens, *b.* 1946, *m., cons.* 1995, *elected* 1999
2004 *Norwich* (71st), Graham Richard James, *b.* 1951, *m., cons.* 1993, *elected* 1999
2005 *Exeter* (70th), Michael Lawrence Langrish, *b.* 1946, *m., cons.* 1993, *elected* 2000
2006 *Ripon and Leeds* (12th), John Richard Packer, *b.* 1946, *m., cons.* 1996, *elected* 2000
2008 *Chichester* (102nd), John William Hind, *b.* 1945, *m., cons.* 1991, *elected* 2001

2008 *Bath and Wells* (77th), Peter Bryan Price, *b.* 1944, *m., cons.* 1997, *elected* 2002
2009 *Wakefield* (12th), Stephen George Platten, *b.* 1947, *m., cons.* 2003, *elected* 2003
2009 *Bristol* (55th), Michael Arthur Hill, *b.* 1947, *m., cons.* 1998, *elected* 2003
2009 *Lichfield* (98th), Jonathan Michael Gledhill, *b.* 1949, *m., cons.* 1996, *elected* 2003
2009 *Blackburn* (8th), Nicholas Stewart Reade, *b.* 1946, *cons.* 2004, *elected* 2004
2009 *Hereford* (104th), Anthony Martin Priddis, *b.* 1948, *cons.* 1996, *elected* 2004
2009 *Gloucester* (40th), Michael Francis Perham, *b.* 1947, *m., cons.* 2004, *elected* 2004
2010 *Guildford* (9th), Christopher John Hill, *b.* 1945, *m., cons.* 1996, *elected* 2004
2010 *Derby* (7th), Alastair Llewellyn John Redfern, *b.* 1948, *m., cons.* 1997, *elected* 2005
2010 *Birmingham* (9th), David Andrew Urquhart, *b.* 1952, *cons.* 2000, *elected* 2006
2011 *Oxford* (42nd), John Lawrence Pritchard, *b.* 1948, *m., cons.* 2002, *elected* 2007
2011 *St Edmundsbury and Ipswich* (10th), (William) Nigel Stock, *b.* 1950, *m., cons.* 2000, *elected* 2007

BISHOPS AWAITING SEATS, in order of seniority
as at 31 August 2011

Worcester (113th), John Geoffrey Inge, PHD, *b.* 1955, *m., cons.* 2003, *elected* 2007
Coventry (9th), Christopher John Cocksworth, PHD, *b.* 1959, *m., cons.* 2008, *elected* 2008
Truro (15th), Timothy Martin Thornton, *b.* 1957, *m., cons.* 2001, *elected* 2008
Sheffield (7th), Stephen John Lindsey Croft, *b.* 1957, *m., cons.* 2009, *elected* 2009
St Albans (10th), Alan Gregory Clayton Smith, *b.* 1957, *cons.* 2001, *elected* 2009
Carlisle (66th), James Newcome, *b.* 1953, *m., cons.* 2002, *elected* 2009
Southwell and Nottingham (11th), Paul Butler, *b.* 1955, *m., cons.* 2004, *elected* 2009
Peterborough (38th), Donald Spargo Allister, *b.* 1952, *m., cons.* 2010, *elected* 2010
Portsmouth (9th), Christopher Richard James Foster, *b.* 1953, *m., cons.* 2001, *elected* 2010
Chelmsford (10th), Stephen Cottrell, *b.* 1958, *m., cons.* 2004, *elected* 2010
Rochester (107th), James Langstaff, *b.* 1956, *m., cons.* 2004, *elected* 2010
Ely (69th), Stephen Conway, *b.* 1957, *cons.* 2006, *elected* 2010
Southwark (10th), Christopher Chessun, *b.* 1956, *cons.* 2005, *elected* 2011
Bradford (10th), Nicholas Baines, *b.* 1957, *m., cons.* 2011, *elected* 2011
Salisbury (78th), Nicholas Holtam, *b.* 1954, *m., cons.* 2011, *elected* 2011
Lincoln (71st), Christopher Lowson, *b.* 1953, *m., cons.* 2011, *elected* 2011

COURTESY TITLES AND PEERS' SURNAMES

COURTESY TITLES

The heir apparent to a Duke, Marquess or Earl uses the highest of his father's other titles as a courtesy title. For example, the Marquess of Blandford is heir to the Dukedom of Marlborough, and Viscount Amberley to the Earldom of Russell. Titles of second heirs (when in use) are also given, and the courtesy title of the father of a second heir is indicated by * eg Earl of Mornington, eldest son of *Marquess of Douro.

The holder of a courtesy title is not styled 'the Most Hon.' or 'the Rt. Hon.', and in correspondence 'the' is omitted before the title. The heir apparent to a Scottish title may use the title 'Master'.

MARQUESSES
*Blandford – *Marlborough, D.*
Bowmont and Cessford – *Roxburghe, D.*
*Douro – *Wellington, D.*
Graham – *Montrose, D.*
*Hamilton – *Abercorn, D.*
Lorne – *Argyll, D.*
Stafford – *Sutherland, D.*
Tavistock – *Bedford, D.*
Tullibardine – *Atholl, D.*
*Worcester – *Beaufort, D.*

EARLS
Aboyne – *Huntly, M.*
Arundel and Surrey – *Norfolk, D.*
Bective – *Headfort, M.*
Belfast – *Donegall, M.*
Brecknock – *Camden, M.*
Burford – *St Albans, D.*
Burlington – *Devonshire, D.*
*Cardigan – *Ailesbury, M.*
Compton – *Northampton, M.*
*Dalkeith – *Buccleuch, D.*
Dumfries – *Bute, M.*
*Euston – *Grafton, D.*
Glamorgan – *Worcester, M.*
Grosvenor – *Westminster, D.*
Haddo – *Aberdeen and Temair, M.*
Hillsborough – *Downshire, M.*
Hopetoun – *Linlithgow, M.*
Kerry – *Lansdowne, M.*
March and Kinrara – *Richmond, D.*
Medina – *Milford Haven, M.*
*Mount Charles – *Conyngham, M.*
Mornington – *Douro, M.*
Mulgrave – *Normanby, M.*
Percy – *Northumberland, D.*

Rocksavage – *Cholmondley, M.*
Ronaldshay – *Zetland, M.*
*St Andrews – *Kent, D.*
*Southesk – *Fife, D.*
Sunderland – *Blandford, M.*
*Tyrone – *Waterford, M.*
Ulster – *Gloucester, D.*
*Uxbridge – *Anglesey, M.*
Wiltshire – *Winchester, M.*
Yarmouth – *Hertford, M.*

VISCOUNTS
Alexander – *Caledon, E.*
Althorp – *Spencer, E.*
Andover – *Suffolk and Berkshire, E.*
Anson – *Lichfield, E.*
Asquith – *Oxford and Asquith, E.*
Boringdon – *Morley, E.*
Borodale – *Beatty, E.*
Boyle – *Shannon, E.*
Brocas – *Jellicoe, E.*
Bury – *Albermarle, E.*
Campden – *Gainsborough, E.*
Carlow – *Portarlington, E.*
Carlton – *Wharncliffe, E.*
Castlereagh – *Londonderry, M.*
Chelsea – *Cadogan, E.*
Chewton – *Waldegrave, E.*
Clanfield – *Peel, E.*
Clive – *Powis, E.*
Coke – *Leicester, E.*
Corry – *Belmore, E.*
Corvedale – *Baldwin of Bewdley, E.*
Cranborne – *Salisbury, M.*
Cranley – *Onslow, E.*
Crichton – *Erne, E.*
Curzon – *Howe, E.*
Dalrymple – *Stair, E.*
Dangan – *Cowley, E.*
Drumlanrig – *Queensberry, M.*

Duncannon – *Bessborough, E.*
Dungarvan – *Cork and Orrery, E.*
Dunluce – *Antrim, E.*
Dunwich – *Stradbroke, E.*
Dupplin – *Kinnoull, E.*
Ednam – *Dudley, E.*
Elveden – *Iveagh, E.*
Emlyn – *Cawdor, E*
Encombe – *Eldon, E.*
Enfield – *Strafford, E.*
Erleigh – *Reading, M.*
Errington – *Cromer, E.*
Feilding – *Denbigh and Desmond, E.*
FitzHarris – *Malmesbury, E.*
Folkestone – *Radnor, E.*
Forbes – *Granard, E.*
Garmoyle – *Cairns, E.*
Garnock – *Lindsay, E.*
Glenapp – *Inchcape, E.*
Glentworth – *Limerick, E.*
Grey de Wilton – *Wilton, E.*
Grimstone – *Verulam, E.*
Gwynedd – *Lloyd George of Dwyfor, E.*
Hawkesbury – *Liverpool, E.*
Hinchingbrooke – *Sandwich, E.*
Ikerrin – *Carrick, E.*
Ingestre – *Shrewsbury, E.*
Jocelyn – *Roden, E.*
Kelburn – *Glasgow, E.*
Kingsborough – *Kingston, E.*
Kirkwall – *Orkney, E.*
Knebworth – *Lytton, E.*
Lambton – *Durham, E.*
Lascelles – *Harewood, E.*
Linley – *Snowdon, E.*
Lymington – *Portsmouth, E.*
Macmillan of Ovenden – *Stockton, E.*
Maidstone – *Winchilsea, E*
Maitland – *Lauderdale, E.*
Mandeville – *Manchester, D.*
Marsham – *Romney, E.*
Melgund – *Minto, E.*
Merton – *Nelson, E.*
Moore – *Drogheda, E.*
Newport – *Bradford, E.*
Northland – *Ranfurly, E*
Newry and Mourne – *Kilmorey, E.*
Petersham – *Harrington, E.*
Pollington – *Mexborough, E*

Raynham – *Townshend, M.*
Reidhaven – *Seafield, E.*
Royston – *Hardwicke, E.*
Ruthven of Canberra – *Gowrie, E.*
St Cyres – *Iddesleigh, E.*
Sandon – *Harrowby, E.*
Savernake – *Cardigan, E.*
Severn – *Wessex, E.*
Somerton – *Normanton, E.*
Stopford – *Courtown, E.*
Stormont – *Mansfield, E.*
Strabane – *Hamilton, M.*
Strathallan – *Perth, E.*
Stuart – *Castle Stewart, E.*
Suirdale – *Donoughmore, E.*
Tamworth – *Ferrers, E.*
Tarbat – *Cromartie, E.*
Vaughan – *Lisburne, E.*
Weymouth – *Bath, M.*
Windsor – *Plymouth, E.*
Wolmer – *Selborne, E.*
Woodstock – *Portland, E.*

BARONS (LORDS)
Aberdour – *Morton, E.*
Apsley – *Bathurst, E.*
Ardee – *Meath, E.*
Ashley – *Shaftesbury, E.*
Balgonie – *Leven and Melville, E.*
Balniel – *Crawford and Balcarres, E.*
Berriedale – *Caithness, E.*
Bingham – *Lucan, E.*
Binning – *Haddington, E.*
Brooke – *Warwick, E.*
Bruce – *Elgin, E.*
Burghley – *Exeter, M.*
Cardross – *Buchan, E.*
Carnegie – *Southesk, E.*
Clifton – *Darnley, E.*
Cochrane – *Dundonald, E.*
Courtenay – *Devon, E.*
Culloden – *Ulster, E.*
Dalmeny – *Rosebery, E.*
Doune – *Moray, E.*
Downpatrick – *St Andrews, E.*
Dunglass – *Home, E.*
Elcho – *Wemyss and March, E.*
Eliot – *St Germans, E.*
Formartine – *Haddo, E.*
Gillford – *Clanwilliam, E.*
Glamis – *Strathmore, E.*
Greenock – *Cathcart, E.*
Guernsey – *Aylesford, E.*
Hay – *Erroll, E.*
Howard of Effingham – *Effingham, E.*
Huntingtower – *Dysart, C.*

Irwin – *Halifax, E.*
Johnstone – *Annandale and Hartfell, E.*
Langton – *Temple of Stowe, E.*
La Poer – **Tyrone, E.*
Leveson – *Granville, E*
Loughborough – *Rosslyn, E.*

Masham – *Swinton, E.*
Mauchline – *Loudoun, C.*
Medway – *Cranbrook, E.*
Montgomerie – *Eglinton and Winton, E.*
Moreton – *Ducie, E.*
Naas – *Mayo, E.*
Norreys – *Lindsey and Abingdon, E.*

North – *Guilford, E.*
Ogilvy – *Airlie, E.*
Oxmantown – *Rosse, E.*
Paget de Beaudesert – **Uxbridge, E.*
Porchester – *Carnarvon, E.*
Ramsay – *Dalhousie, E.*
Romsey – *Mountbatten of Burma, C.*

Scrymgeour – *Dundee, E.*
Seymour – *Somerset, D.*
Stanley – *Derby, E.*
Stavordale – *Ilchester, E.*
Strathnaver – *Sutherland, C.*
Wodehouse – *Kimberley, E.*
Worsley – *Yarborough, E.*

PEERS' SURNAMES

The following symbols indicate the rank of the peer holding each title:

C.	Countess
D.	Duke
E.	Earl
M.	Marquess
V.	Viscount
*	Life Peer

Where no designation is given, the title is that of a hereditary Baron or Baroness.

Abney-Hastings – *Loudoun, C.*
Acheson – *Gosford, E.*
Adams – *A. of Craigielea**
Adderley – *Norton*
Addington – *Sidmouth, V.*
Adebowale – *A. of Thornes**
Agar – *Normanton, E.*
Ahmad – *A. of Wimbledon**
Aitken – *Beaverbrook*
Akers-Douglas – *Chilston, V.*
Alexander – *A. of Tunis, E.*
Alexander – *Caledon, E.*
Allan – *A. of Hallam**
Allen – *Croham**
Allsopp – *Hindlip*
Alton – *A. of Liverpool**
Ancram – *Kerr of Monteviot**
Anderson – *A. of Swansea**
Anderson – *Waverley, V.*
Anelay – *A. of St Johns**
Annesley – *Valentia, V.*
Anson – *Lichfield, E.*
Archer – *A. of Sandwell**
Archer – *A. of Weston-super-Mare**
Armstrong – *A. of Hill Top**
Armstrong – *A. of Ilminster**
Armstrong-Jones – *Snowdon, E.*
Arthur – *Glenarthur*
Arundell – *Talbot of Malahide*
Ashdown – *A. of Norton-sub-Hamdon**
Ashley – *A. of Stoke**

Ashley-Cooper – *Shaftesbury, E.*
Ashton – *A. of Hyde*
Ashton – *A. of Upholland**
Asquith – *Oxford and Asquith, E.*
Assheton – *Clitheroe*
Astley – *Hastings*
Astor – *A. of Hever*
Aubrey-Fletcher – *Braye*
Bailey – *Glanusk*
Baillie – *Burton*
Baillie Hamilton – *Haddington, E.*
Baker – *B. of Dorking**
Balchin – *Lingfield**
Baldwin – *B. of Bewdley, E.*
Balfour – *B. of Inchrye*
Balfour – *Kinross*
Balfour – *Riverdale*
Bampfylde – *Poltimore*
Banbury – *B. of Southam*
Barber – *B. of Tewkesbury**
Baring – *Ashburton*
Baring – *Cromer, E.*
Baring – *Howick of Glendale*
Baring – *Northbrook*
Baring – *Revelstoke*
Barker – *Trumpington**
Barnes – *Gorell*
Barnewall – *Trimlestown*
Bassam – *B. of Brighton**
Bathurst – *Bledisloe, V.*
Beauclerk – *St Albans, D.*
Beaumont – *Allendale, V.*
Beckett – *Grimthorpe*
Benn – *Stansgate, V.*
Bennet – *Tankerville, E.*
Bentinck – *Portland, E.*
Beresford – *Decies*
Beresford – *Waterford, M.*
Berry – *Camrose, V.*
Berry – *Kemsley, V.*
Bertie – *Lindsey, E.*
Best – *Wynford*
Bethell – *Westbury*
Bewicke-Copley – *Cromwell*
Bigham – *Mersey, V.*
Bingham – *Clanmorris*
Bingham – *Lucan, E.*
Bishop – *Glendonbrook**

Black – *B. of Brentwood**
Black – *B. of Crossharbour**
Blair – *B. of Boughton**
Bligh – *Darnley, E.*
Blyth – *B. of Rowington**
Bonham Carter – *B.-C. of Yarnbury**
Bootle-Wilbraham – *Skelmersdale*
Boscawen – *Falmouth, V.*
Boswell – *B. of Aynho**
Bottomley – *B. of Nettlestone**
Bourke – *Mayo, E.*
Bowes Lyon – *Strathmore, E.*
Bowyer – *Denham*
Boyd – *Kilmarnock*
Boyd – *B. of Duncansby**
Boyle – *Cork and Orrery, E.*
Boyle – *Glasgow, E.*
Boyle – *Shannon, E.*
Brabazon – *Meath, E.*
Brand – *Hampden, V.*
Brassey – *B. of Apethorpe*
Brett – *Esher, V.*
Bridgeman – *Bradford, E.*
Brittan – *B. of Spennithorne**
Brodrick – *Midleton, V.*
Brooke – *Alanbrooke, V.*
Brooke – *B. of Alverthorpe**
Brooke – *Brookeborough, V.*
Brooke – *B. of Sutton Mandeville**
Brooks – *B. of Tremorfa**
Brooks – *Crawshaw*
Brougham – *Brougham and Vaux*
Broughton – *Fairhaven*
Brown – *B. of Eaton-under-Heywood**
Browne – *B. of Belmont**
Browne – *B. of Ladyton**
Browne – *B. of Madingley**
Browne – *Kilmaine*
Browne – *Oranmore and Browne*
Browne – *Sligo, M.*
Bruce – *Aberdare*
Bruce – *Balfour of Burleigh*

Bruce – *Elgin and Kincardine, E.*
Brudenell-Bruce – *Ailesbury, M.*
Buchan – *Tweedsmuir*
Buckley – *Wrenbury*
Butler – *B. of Brockwell**
Butler – *Carrick, E.*
Butler – *Dunboyne*
Butler – *Mountgarret, V.*
Byng – *Strafford, E.*
Byng – *Torrington, V.*
Cambell-Savours – *C.-S. of Allerdale**
Cameron – *C. of Dillington**
Cameron – *C. of Lochbroom**
Campbell – *Argyll, D.*
Campbell – *C. of Alloway**
Campbell – *C. of Loughborough**
Campbell – *C. of Surbiton**
Campbell – *Cawdor, E.*
Campbell – *Colgrain*
Campbell – *Stratheden and Campbell*
Campbell-Gray – *Gray*
Canning – *Garvagh*
Capell – *Essex, E.*
Carey – *C. of Clifton**
Carington – *Carrington*
Carlisle – *C. of Berriew**
Carnegie – *Fife, D.*
Carnegy – *Northesk, E.*
Carr – *C. of Hadley**
Carter – *C. of Barnes**
Carter – *C. of Coles**
Cary – *Falkland, V.*
Caulfeild – *Charlemont, V.*
Cavendish – *C. of Furness**
Cavendish – *Chesham*
Cavendish – *Devonshire, D.*
Cavendish – *Waterpark*
Cayzer – *Rotherwick*
Cecil – *Amherst of Hackney*
Cecil – *Exeter, M.*
Cecil – *Rockley*
Chalker – *C. of Wallasey**
Chaloner – *Gisborough*
Chapman – *C. of Leeds**
Chapman – *Northfield**
Charteris – *Wemyss and March, E.*

Harbord-Hamond –
   Suffield
Harding – *H. of Petherton*
Hardinge – *H. of Penshurst*
Hare – *Blakenham, V.*
Hare – *Listowel, E.*
Harmsworth – *Rothermere,
   V.*
Harries – *H. of
   Pentregarth★*
Harris – *H. of Haringey★*
Harris – *H. of Peckham★*
Harris – *H. of Richmond★*
Harris – *Malmesbury, E.*
Hart – *H. of Chilton★*
Harvey – *H. of Tasburgh*
Hastings – *H. of
   Scarisbrick★*
Hastings Bass –
   Huntingdon, E.
Haughey – *Ballyedmond★*
Hay – *Erroll, E.*
Hay – *Kinnoull, E.*
Hay – *Tweeddale, M.*
Hayter – *H. of Kentish
   Town★*
Healy – *H. of Primrose
   Hill★*
Heathcote-Drummond-
   Willoughby –
   Willoughby de Eresby
Hely-Hutchinson –
   Donoughmore, E.
Henderson – *Faringdon*
Hennessy – *H. of
   Nympsfield★*
Hennessy – *Windlesham*
Henniker-Major –
   Henniker
Hepburne-Scott –
   Polwarth
Herbert – *Carnarvon, E.*
Herbert – *Hemingford*
Herbert – *Pembroke, E.*
Herbert – *Powis, E.*
Hervey – *Bristol, M.*
Heseltine – *H. of
   Thenford★*
Hewitt – *Lifford, V.*
Hicks Beach – *St Aldwyn,
   E.*
Hill – *Downshire, M.*
Hill – *H. of Oareford★*
Hill – *Sandys*
Hill-Trevor – *Trevor*
Hilton – *H. of Eggardon★*
Hobart-Hampden –
   Buckinghamshire, E.
Hodgson – *H. of Astley
   Abbotts★*
Hogg – *Hailsham, V.*
Holland-Hibbert –
   Knutsford, V.
Hollis – *H. of Heigham★*
Holmes à Court –
   Heytesbury
Hood – *Bridport, V.*
Hope – *Glendevon*

Hope – *H. of Craighead★*
Hope – *H. of Thornes★*
Hope – *Linlithgow, M.*
Hope – *Rankeillour*
Hope Johnstone –
   *Annandale and Hartfell,
   E.*
Hope-Morley – *Hollenden*
Hopkinson – *Colyton*
Hore Ruthven – *Gowrie, E.*
Hovell-Thurlow-
   Cumming-Bruce –
   Thurlow
Howard – *Carlisle, E.*
Howard – *Effingham, E.*
Howard – *H. of Lympne★*
Howard – *H. of Penrith*
Howard – *H. of Rising★*
Howard – *Strathcona*
Howard – *Suffolk and
   Berkshire, E.*
Howarth – *H. of
   Breckland★*
Howarth – *H. of Newport★*
Howe – *H. of Aberavon★*
Howe – *H. of Idlicote★*
Howell – *H. of Guildford★*
Howells – *H. of St.
   Davids★*
Howie – *H. of Troon★*
Hubbard – *Addington*
Huggins – *Malvern, V.*
Hughes – *H. of Stretford★*
Hughes – *H. of Woodside★*
Hughes-Young – *St Helens*
Hunt – *H. of Chesterton★*
Hunt – *H. of Kings Heath★*
Hunt – *H. of Wirral★*
Hurd – *H. of Westwell★*
Hutchinson – *H. of
   Lullington★*
Hutton – *H. of Furness★*
Ingrams – *Darcy de Knayth*
Innes-Ker – *Roxburghe, D.*
Inskip – *Caldecote, V.*
Irby – *Boston*
Irvine – *I. of Lairg★*
Isaacs – *Reading, M.*
James – *J. of Blackheath★*
James – *J. of Holland Park★*
James – *Northbourne*
Janner – *J. of Braunstone★*
Jay – *J. of Ewelme★*
Jay – *J. of Paddington★*
Jebb – *Gladwyn*
Jenkin – *J. of Kennington★*
Jenkin – *J. of Roding★*
Jervis – *St Vincent, V.*
Jocelyn – *Roden, E.*
Jolliffe – *Hylton*
Jones – *J. of Birmingham★*
Jones – *J. of Cheltenham★*
Jones – *J. of Deeside★*
Jones – *J. of Whitchurch★*
Joynson-Hicks – *Brentford,
   V.*
Kay-Shuttleworth –
   Shuttleworth

Kearley – *Devonport, V.*
Keith – *Kintore, E.*
Kemp – *Rochdale, V.*
Kennedy – *Ailsa, M*
Kennedy – *K. of the
   Shaws★*
Kennedy – *K. of
   Southwark★*
Kenworthy – *Strabolgi*
Keppel – *Albemarle, E.*
Kerr – *K. of Kinlochard★*
Kerr – *K. of Tonaghmore★*
Kerr – *Lothian, M.*
Kerr – *Teviot*
Kilpatrick – *K. of
   Kincraig★*
King – *K. of Bow★*
King – *K. of West
   Bromwich★*
King – *Lovelace, E.*
King-Tenison – *Kingston,
   E.*
Kinnock – *K. of
   Holyhead★*
Kirkham – *Berners*
Kirkwood – *K. of
   Kirkhope★*
Kitchener – *K. of
   Khartoum, E.*
Knatchbull – *Brabourne*
Knatchbull – *Mountbatten
   of Burma, C.*
Knight – *K. of Collingtree★*
Knight – *K. of Weymouth★*
Knox – *Ranfurly, E.*
Lamb – *Rochester*
Lambton – *Durham, E.*
Lamont – *L. of Lerwick★*
Lampson – *Killearn*
Lang – *L. of Monkton★*
Lascelles – *Harewood, E.*
Law – *Coleraine*
Law – *Ellenborough*
Lawrence – *Trevethin and
   Oaksey*
Lawson – *Burnham*
Lawson – *L. of Blaby★*
Lawson-Johnston – *Luke*
Lea – *L. of Crondall★*
Leach – *L. of Fairford★*
Lee – *L. of Trafford★*
Legge – *Dartmouth, E.*
Legh – *Grey of Codnor*
Legh – *Newton*
Leigh-Pemberton –
   Kingsdown★
Leith – *Burgh*
Lennox-Boyd – *Boyd of
   Merton, V.*
Le Poer Trench –
   Clancarty, E.
Leslie – *Rothes, E.*
Leslie Melville – *Leven and
   Melville, E.*
Lester – *L. of Herne Hill★*
Levene – *L. of Portsoken★*
Leveson-Gower –
   Granville, E.

Lewis – *L. of Newnham★*
Lewis – *Merthyr*
Liddell – *L. of Coatdyke★*
Liddell – *Ravensworth*
Lindesay-Bethune –
   Lindsay, E.
Lindsay – *Crawford,
   E.*
Lindsay – *L. of Birker*
Linklater – *L. of
   Butterstone★*
Lister – *L. of Burtersett★*
Littleton – *Hatherton*
Lloyd – *L. of Berwick★*
Lloyd George – *Lloyd
   George of Dwyfor, E.*
Lloyd George – *Tenby, V.*
Lloyd-Mostyn – *Mostyn*
Loder – *Wakehurst*
Lofthouse – *L. of
   Pontefract★*
Lopes – *Roborough*
Lord – *Framlingham★*
Lour – *Carneggy of Lour★*
Low – *Aldington*
Low – *L. of Dalston★*
Lowry-Corry – *Belmore, E.*
Lowther – *Lonsdale, E.*
Lowther – *Ullswater, V.*
Lubbock – *Avebury*
Lucas – *L. of Chilworth*
Lumley – *Scarbrough, E.*
Lumley-Savile – *Savile*
Lyon-Dalberg-Acton –
   Acton
Lysaght – *Lisle*
Lyttelton – *Chandos, V.*
Lyttelton – *Cobham, V.*
Lytton Cobbold – *Cobbold*
McAlpine – *M. of West
   Green★*
Macaulay – *M. of Bragar★*
Maclean – *Blencathra★*
McClintock-Bunbury –
   Rathdonnell
McColl – *M. of Dulwich★*
McConnell – *M. of
   Glenscorrodale★*
MacDonald – *M. of River
   Glaven★*
Macdonald – *M. of
   Tradeston★*
McDonnell – *Antrim, E.*
McFall – *M. of Alcluith★*
Macfarlane – *M. of
   Bearsden★*
McFarlane – *M. of
   Llandaff★*
MacGregor – *M. of
   Pulham Market★*
McIntosh – *M. of
   Hudnall★*
McKenzie – *M. of Luton★*
Mackay – *Inchcape, E.*
Mackay – *M. of Clashfern★*
Mackay – *M. of
   Drumadoon★*

Mackay – *Reay*
Mackay – *Tanlaw**
MacKenzie – *M. of Culkein**
MacKenzie – *M. of Framwellgate**
Mackenzie – *Cromartie, E.*
Mackie – *M. of Benshie**
Mackintosh – *M. of Halifax, V.*
McLaren – *Aberconway*
MacLaurin – *M. of Knebworth**
MacLennan – *M. of Rogart**
Macmillan – *Stockton, E.*
Macpherson – *M. of Drumochter*
Macpherson – *Strathcarron*
Maffey – *Rugby*
Magan – *M. of Castletown**
Maginnis – *M. of Drumglass**
Maitland – *Lauderdale, E.*
Makgill – *Oxfuird, V.*
Makins – *Sherfield*
Manners – *Rutland, D.*
Manningham-Buller – *Dilhorne, V.*
Mansfield – *Sandhurst*
Marks – *M. of Broughton*
Marks – *M. of Henley-on-Thames**
Marquis – *Woolton, E.*
Marshall – *M. of Knightsbridge**
Marsham – *Romney, E.*
Martin – *M. of Springburn**
Martyn-Hemphill – *Hemphill*
Mason – *M. of Barnsley**
Massey – *M. of Darwen**
Masters – *Noakes**
Maude – *Hawarden, V.*
Maxwell – *de Ros*
Maxwell – *Farnham*
May – *M. of Oxford**
Mayhew – *M. of Twysden**
Meade – *Clanwilliam, E.*
Mercer Nairne Petty-Fitzmaurice – *Lansdowne, M.*
Millar – *Inchyra*
Miller – *M. of Chiltorne Domer**
Miller – *M. of Hendon**
Milner – *M. of Leeds*
Mitchell-Thomson – *Selsdon*
Mitford – *Redesdale*
Molyneaux – *M. of Killead**
Monckton – *M. of Brenchley, V.*
Monckton-Arundell – *Galway, V.*

Mond – *Melchett*
Money-Coutts – *Latymer*
Montagu – *Manchester, D.*
Montagu – *Sandwich, E.*
Montagu – *Swaythling*
Montagu Douglas Scott – *Buccleuch, D.*
Montagu Stuart Wortley – *Wharncliffe, E.*
Montague – *Amwell*
Montgomerie – *Eglinton, E.*
Montgomery – *M. of Alamein, V.*
Moore – *Drogheda, E.*
Moore – *M. of Lower Marsh**
Moore-Brabazon – *Brabazon of Tara*
Moreton – *Ducie, E*
Morgan – *M. of Drefelin**
Morgan – *M. of Ely**
Morgan – *M. of Huyton**
Morris – *Killanin*
Morris – *M. of Aberavon**
Morris – *M. of Bolton**
Morris – *M. of Handsworth**
Morris – *M. of Manchester**
Morris – *M. of Kenwood*
Morris – *M. of Yardley**
Morris – *Naseby**
Morrison – *Dunrossil, V.*
Morrison – *Margadale*
Moser – *M. of Regents Park**
Mosley – *Ravensdale*
Mountbatten – *Milford Haven, M.*
Muff – *Calverley*
Mulholland – *Dunleath*
Murray – *Atholl, D.*
Murray – *Dunmore, E.*
Murray – *Mansfield and Mansfield, E.*
Nall-Cain – *Brocket*
Napier – *Napier and Ettrick*
Napier – *N. of Magdala*
Needham – *Kilmorey, E.*
Neill – *N. of Bladen**
Nelson – *N. of Stafford*
Neuberger – *N. of Abbotsbury**
Nevill – *Abergavenny, M.*
Neville – *Braybrooke*
Newton – *N. of Braintree**
Nicholls – *N. of Birkenhead**
Nicolson – *Carnock*
Nicholson – *N. of Winterbourne**
Nivison – *Glendyne*
Noel – *Gainsborough, E.*
North – *Guilford, E.*
Northcote – *Iddesleigh, E.*
Norton – *Grantley*
Norton – *N. of Louth**

Norton – *Rathcreedan*
Nugent – *Westmeath, E.*
Oakeshott – *O. of Seagrove Bay**
O'Brien – *Inchiquin*
Ogilvie-Grant – *Seafield, E.*
Ogilvy – *Airlie, E.*
O'Neill – *O'N. of Bengarve**
O'Neill – *O'N. of Clackmannan**
O'Neill – *Rathcavan*
Orde-Powlett – *Bolton*
Ormsby-Gore – *Harlech*
Ouseley – *O. of Peckham Rye**
Paget – *Anglesey, M.*
Paisley – *Bannside**
Paisley – *P. of St George's**
Pakenham – *Longford, E.*
Pakington – *Hampton*
Palmer – *Lucas and Dingwall*
Palmer – *P. of Childs Hill**
Palmer – *Selborne, E.*
Parker – *Macclesfield, E.*
Parker – *Morley, E.*
Parnell – *Congleton*
Parsons – *Rosse, E.*
Patel – *P. of Blackburn**
Patel – *P. of Bradford**
Patten – *P. of Barnes**
Paulet – *Winchester, M.*
Pearson – *Cowdray, V.*
Pearson – *P. of Rannoch**
Pease – *Gainford*
Pease – *Wardington*
Pelham – *Chichester, E.*
Pelham – *Yarborough, E.*
Pellew – *Exmouth, V*
Pendry – *P. of Stalybridge**.
Penny – *Marchwood, V.*
Pepys – *Cottenham, E.*
Perceval – *Egmont, E.*
Percy – *Northumberland, D.*
Perry – *P. of Southwark**
Pery – *Limerick, E.*
Philipps – *Milford*
Philipps – *St Davids, V.*
Phillips – *P. of Sudbury**
Phillips – *P. of Worth Matravers**
Phipps – *Normanby, M.*
Plant – *P. of Highfield**
Platt – *P. of Writtle**
Pleydell-Bouverie – *Radnor, E.*
Plumptre – *Fitzwalter*
Plunkett – *Dunsany*
Plunkett – *Louth*
Pollock – *Hanworth, V.*
Pomeroy – *Harberton, V.*
Ponsonby – *Bessborough, E.*
Ponsonby – *de Mauley*
Ponsonby – *P. of Shulbrede*
Powell – *P. of Bayswater**

Powys – *Lilford*
Pratt – *Camden, M.*
Preston – *Gormanston, V.*
Primrose – *Rosebery, E.*
Prittie – *Dunalley*
Ramsay – *Dalhousie, E.*
Ramsay – *R. of Cartvale**
Ramsbotham – *Soulbury, V.*
Randall – *R. of St. Budeaux**
Rees – *R. of Ludlow**
Rees-Williams – *Ogmore*
Reid – *R. of Cardowan**
Rendell – *R. of Babergh**
Renfrew – *R. of Kaimsthorn**
Renton – *R. of Mount Harry**
Renwick – *R. of Clifton**
Rhys – *Dynevor*
Richards – *Milverton*
Richardson – *R. of Calow**
Ritchie – *R. of Brompton**
Ritchie – *R. of Dundee*
Roberts – *Clwyd*
Roberts – *R. of Conway**
Roberts – *R. of Llandudno**
Robertson – *R. of Oakridge*
Robertson – *R. of Port Ellen**
Robertson – *Wharton*
Robinson – *Martonmere*
Roche – *Fermoy*
Rodd – *Rennell*
Rodgers – *R. of Quarry Bank**
Rogers – *R. of Riverside**
Roper-Curzon – *Teynham*
Rospigliosi – *Newburgh, E.*
Rous – *Stradbroke, E.*
Rowley-Conwy – *Langford*
Royall – *R. of Blaisdon**
Runciman – *R. of Doxford, V.*
Russell – *Ampthill*
Russell – *Bedford, D.*
Russell – *de Clifford*
Russell – *R. of Liverpool*
Ryder – *Harrowby, E.*
Ryder – *R. of Wensum**
Sackville – *De La Warr, E.*
Sackville-West – *Sackville*
Sainsbury – *S. of Preston Candover**
Sainsbury – *S. of Turville**
St Aubyn – *St Levan*
St Clair – *Sinclair*
St Clair-Erskine – *Rosslyn, E.*
St John – *Bolingbroke and St John, V.*
St John – *St John of Blesto*
St John-Stevas – *St John of Fawsley**

St Leger – *Doneraile, V.*
Samuel – *Bearsted, V.*
Sanderson – *S. of Ayot*
Sanderson – *S. of Bowden**
Sandilands – *Torphichen*
Saumarez – *De Saumarez*
Savile – *Mexborough, E.*
Saville – *S. of Newdigate**
Scarlett – *Abinger*
Schreiber – *Marlesford**
Sclater-Booth – *Basing*
Scotland – *S. of Asthal**
Scott – *Eldon, E*
Scott – *S. of Foscotte**
Scott – *S. of Needham Market**.
Scrymgeour – *Dundee, E.*
Seager – *Leighton of St Mellons*
Seely – *Mottistone*
Seymour – *Hertford, M.*
Seymour – *Somerset, D.*
Shackleton – *S. of Belgravia**
Sharp – *S. of Guildford**
Shaw – *Craigmyle*
Shaw – *S. of Northstead**
Shephard – *S. of Northwood**
Sheppard – *S. of Didgemere**
Shirley – *Ferrers, E.*
Short – *Glenamara**
Shutt – *S. of Greetland**
Siddeley – *Kenilworth*
Sidney – *De L'Isle, V.*
Simon – *S. of Highbury**
Simon – *S. of Wythenshawe*
Simpson – *S. of Dunkeld**
Sinclair – *Caithness, E.*
Sinclair – *S. of Cleeve*
Sinclair – *Thurso, V.*
Skeffington – *Massereene, V.*
Smith – *Bicester*
Smith – *Hambleden, V.*
Smith – *Kirkhill**
Smith – *S. of Basildon**
Smith – *S. of Clifton**
Smith – *Smith of Finsbury**
Smith – *S. of Gilmorehill**
Smith – *S. of Kelvin**
Smith – *S. of Leigh**
Somerset – *Beaufort, D.*
Somerset – *Raglan*
Soulsby – *S. of Swaffham Prior**
Spencer – *Churchill, V.*

Spencer-Churchill – *Marlborough, D.*
Spring – *Risby**
Spring Rice – *Monteagle of Brandon*
Stanhope – *Harrington, E.*
Stanley – *Derby, E.*
Stanley – *of Alderley and Sheffield*
Stapleton-Cotton – *Combermere, V.*
Steel – *S. of Aikwood**
Sterling – *S. of Plaistow**
Stern – *S. of Brentford**
Stevens – *S. of Kirkwhelpington**
Stevens – *S. of Ludgate**
Stevenson – *S. of Balmacara**
Stevenson – *S. of Coddenham**
Stewart – *Galloway, E.*
Stewart – *Stewartby**
Stoddart – *S. of Swindon**
Stone – *S. of Blackheath**
Stoneham – *S. of Droxford**
Stonor – *Camoys*
Stopford – *Courtown, E.*
Stourton – *Mowbray*
Stowell – *S. of Beeston**
Strachey – *O'Hagan*
Strutt – *Belper*
Strutt – *Rayleigh*
Stuart – *Castle Stewart, E.*
Stuart – *Moray, E.*
Stuart – *S. of Findhorn, V.*
Suenson-Taylor – *Grantchester*
Sutherland – *S. of Houndwood**
Symons – *S. of Vernham Dean**
Taylor – *Kilclooney**
Taylor – *T. of Blackburn**
Taylor – *T. of Bolton**
Taylor – *T. of Goss Moor**
Taylor – *T. of Holbeach**
Taylor – *T. of Warwick**
Taylour – *Headfort, M.*
Temple-Gore-Langton – *Temple of Stowe, E*
Temple-Morris – *Temple-Morris of Llandaff**
Tennant – *Glenconner*
Thellusson – *Rendlesham*
Thesiger – *Chelmsford, V.*

Thomas – *T. of Gresford**
Thomas – *T. of Macclesfield**
Thomas – *T. of Swynnerton**
Thomas – *T. of Walliswood**
Thomas – *T. of Winchester**
Thomson – *T. of Fleet*
Thynn – *Bath, M.*
Tottenham – *Ely, M.*
Trefusis – *Clinton*
Trench – *Ashtown*
Tufton – *Hothfield*
Turner – *Bilston**
Turner – *Netherthorpe*
Turner – *T. of Camden**
Turner – *T. of Ecchinswell**
Turnour – *Winterton, E.*
Tyler – *T. of Enfield**
Tyrell-Kenyon – *Kenyon*
Vanden-Bempde-Johnstone – *Derwent*
Vane – *Barnard*
Vane-Tempest-Stewart – *Londonderry, M.*
Vanneck – *Huntingfield*
Vaughan – *Lisburne, E.*
Vereker – *Gort, V.*
Verney – *Willoughby de Broke*
Vernon – *Lyveden*
Vesey – *De Vesci, V.*
Villiers – *Clarendon, E.*
Vincent – *V. of Coleshill**
Vivian – *Swansea*
Wade – *W. of Chorlton**
Waldegrave – *W. of North Hill**
Walker – *W. of Aldringham**
Walker – *W. of Gestingthorpe**
Wall – *W. of New Barnett**
Wallace – *Dudley*
Wallace – *W. of Saltaire**
Wallace – *W. of Tankerness**
Wallace – *W. of Tummel**
Wallop – *Portsmouth, E.*
Walton – *W. of Detchant**
Ward – *Bangor, V.*
Ward – *Dudley, E.*
Warrender – *Bruntisfield*
Warwick – *W. of Undercliffe**
Watson – *W. of Invergowrie**
Watson – *Manton*

Watson – *W. of Richmond**
Webber – *Lloyd-Webber**
Wedderburn – *W. of Charlton**
Weir – *Inverforth*
Weld-Forester – *Forester*
Wellesley – *Cowley, E.*
Wellesley – *Wellington, D.*
West – *W. of Spithead**
Westenra – *Rossmore*
White – *Annaly*
White – *Hanningfield**
Whiteley – *Marchamley*
Whitfield – *Kenswood*
Williams – *W. of Baglan**
Williams – *W. of Crosby**
Williams – *W. of Elve**
Williamson – *Forres*
Williamson – *W. of Horton**
Willis – *W. of Knaresborough**
Willoughby – *Middleton*
Wills – *Dulverton*
Wilson – *Moran*
Wilson – *Nunburnholme*
Wilson – *W. of Dinton**
Wilson – *W. of Tillyorn**
Windsor – *Gloucester, D.*
Windsor – *Kent, D.*
Windsor-Clive – *Plymouth, E.*
Wingfield – *Powerscourt, V.*
Winn – *St Oswald*
Wodehouse – *Kimberley, E.*
Wolfson – *W. of Aspley Guise**
Wolfson – *W. of Sunningdale**
Wood – *Halifax, E.*
Wood – *W. of Anfield**
Woodhouse – *Terrington*
Woolmer – *W. of Leeds**
Wright – *W. of Richmond**
Wyndham – *Egremont and Leconfield*
Wynn – *Newborough*
Yarde-Buller – *Churston*
Yerburgh – *Alvingham*
Yorke – *Hardwicke, E.*
Young – *Kennet*
Young – *Y. of Graffham**
Young – *Y. of Hornsey**
Young – *Y. of Norwood Green**
Young – *Y. of Old Scone**
Younger – *Y. of Leckie, V.*

ORDERS OF CHIVALRY

THE MOST NOBLE ORDER OF THE GARTER (1348)

KG
Ribbon, Blue
Motto, Honi soit qui mal y pense
(Shame on him who thinks evil of it)

The number of Knights and Lady Companions is limited to 24

SOVEREIGN OF THE ORDER
The Queen

LADIES OF THE ORDER
HRH The Princess Royal, 1994
HRH Princess Alexandra, The Hon. Lady Ogilvy, 2003

ROYAL KNIGHTS
HRH The Prince Philip, Duke of Edinburgh, 1947
HRH The Prince of Wales, 1958
HRH The Duke of Kent, 1985
HRH The Duke of Gloucester, 1997
HRH The Duke of York, 2006
HRH The Earl of Wessex, 2006
HRH The Duke of Cambridge, 2008

EXTRA KNIGHT COMPANIONS AND LADIES
Grand Duke Jean of Luxembourg, 1972
HM The Queen of Denmark, 1979
HM The King of Sweden, 1983
HM The King of Spain, 1988
HM The Queen of the Netherlands, 1989
HIM The Emperor of Japan, 1998
HM The King of Norway, 2001

KNIGHTS AND LADY COMPANIONS
Lord Carrington, 1985
Duke of Wellington, 1990
Lord Bramall, 1990
Viscount Ridley, 1992
Lord Sainsbury of Preston Candover, 1992
Lord Ashburton, 1994
Lord Kingsdown, 1994
Sir Ninian Stephen, 1994
Baroness Thatcher, 1995
Sir Timothy Colman, 1996
Duke of Abercorn, 1999
Sir William Gladstone, 1999
Lord Inge, 2001
Sir Anthony Acland, 2001
Duke of Westminster, 2003
Lord Butler of Brockwell, 2003
Lord Morris of Aberavon, 2003

Lady Soames, 2005
Sir John Major, 2005
Lord Luce, 2008
Sir Thomas Dunne, 2008
Lord Phillips of Worth Matravers, 2011
Lord Boyce, 2011

Prelate, Bishop of Winchester
Chancellor, Lord Carrington, KG, GCMG, CH, MC
Register, Dean of Windsor
Garter King of Arms, Thomas Woodcock, CVO
Gentleman Usher of the Black Rod, Lt.-Gen. David Leakey, CMG, CBE
Secretary, Patric Dickinson, LVO

THE MOST ANCIENT AND MOST NOBLE ORDER OF THE THISTLE (REVIVED 1687)

KT
Ribbon, Green
Motto, Nemo me impune lacessit
(No one provokes me with impunity)

The number of Knights and Ladies of the Thistle is limited to 16

SOVEREIGN OF THE ORDER
The Queen

ROYAL LADY OF THE ORDER
HRH The Princess Royal, 2000

ROYAL KNIGHTS
HRH The Prince Philip, Duke of Edinburgh, 1952
HRH The Prince of Wales, Duke of Rothesay, 1977

KNIGHTS AND LADIES
Earl of Elgin and Kincardine, 1981
Earl of Airlie, 1985
Viscount of Arbuthnott, 1996
Earl of Crawford and Balcarres, 1996
Lady Marion Fraser, 1996
Lord Macfarlane of Bearsden, 1996
Lord Mackay of Clashfern, 1997
Lord Wilson of Tillyorn, 2000
Lord Sutherland of Houndwood, 2002
Sir Eric Anderson, 2002
Lord Steel of Aikwood, 2004
Lord Robertson of Port Ellen, 2004

Lord Cullen of Whitekirk, 2007
Sir Garth Morrison, 2007
Lord Hope of Craighead, 2009
Lord Patel, 2009

Chancellor, Earl of Airlie, KT, GCVO, PC
Dean, Very Revd Gilleasbuig Macmillan, CVO
Secretary and Lord Lyon King of Arms, David Sellar
Gentleman Usher of the Green Rod, Rear-Adm. Christopher Layman, CB, DSO, LVO
Assistant Secretary, Mrs C. Roads, MVO

THE MOST HONOURABLE ORDER OF THE BATH (1725)

GCB *Military* GCB *Civil*

GCB	Knight (or Dame) Grand Cross
KCB	Knight Commander
DCB	Dame Commander
CB	Companion

Ribbon, Crimson
Motto, Tria juncta in uno
(Three joined in one)

Remodelled 1815, and enlarged many times since. The order is divided into civil and military divisions. Women became eligible for the order from 1 January 1971.

THE SOVEREIGN

GREAT MASTER AND FIRST OR PRINCIPAL KNIGHT GRAND CROSS
HRH The Prince of Wales, KG, KT, GCB, OM

Dean of the Order, Dean of Westminster
Bath King of Arms, Adm. Lord Boyce, KG, GCB, OBE
Registrar and Secretary, Rear-Adm. Iain Henderson, CB, CBE
Genealogist, Thomas Woodcock, CVO
Gentleman Usher of the Scarlet Rod, Maj.-Gen. Charles Vyvyan, CB, CBE
Deputy Secretary, Secretary of the Central Chancery of the Orders of Knighthood

Chancery, Central Chancery of the Orders of Knighthood, St James's Palace, London SW1A 1BH

THE ORDER OF MERIT (1902)

OM *Military*   OM *Civil*

OM
Ribbon, Blue and crimson

This order is designed as a special distinction for eminent men and women without conferring a knighthood upon them. The order is limited in numbers to 24, with the addition of foreign honorary members.

THE SOVEREIGN

HRH The Prince Philip, Duke of Edinburgh, 1968
Revd Prof. Owen Chadwick, KBE, 1983
Sir Andrew Huxley, 1983
Dr Frederick Sanger, 1986
Baroness Thatcher, 1990
Sir Michael Atiyah, 1992
Sir Aaron Klug, 1995
Lord Foster of Thames Bank, 1997
Sir Anthony Caro, 2000
Prof. Sir Roger Penrose, 2000
Sir Tom Stoppard, 2000
HRH The Prince of Wales, 2002
Lord May of Oxford, 2002
Lord Rothschild, 2002
Sir David Attenborough, 2005
Baroness Boothroyd, 2005
Sir Michael Howard, 2005
Sir Timothy Berners-Lee, KBE, 2007
Lord Eames, 2007
Lord Rees of Ludlow, 2007
Rt. Hon. Jean Chrétien, QC, 2009
Robert Neil MacGregor, 2010

Honorary Member, Nelson Mandela, 1995

Secretary and Registrar, Lord Fellowes, GCB, GCVO, PC, QSO
Chancery, Central Chancery of the Orders of Knighthood, St James's Palace, London SW1A 1BH

THE MOST DISTINGUISHED ORDER OF ST MICHAEL AND ST GEORGE (1818)

GCMG   KCMG

GCMG   Knight (or Dame) Grand Cross
KCMG   Knight Commander
DCMG   Dame Commander
CMG   Companion

Ribbon, Saxon blue, with scarlet centre
Motto, Auspicium melioris aevi
(Token of a better age)

THE SOVEREIGN

GRAND MASTER
HRH The Duke of Kent, KG, GCMG, GCVO, ADC

Prelate, Rt. Revd David Urquhart
Chancellor, Lord Robertson of Port Ellen, KT, GCMG
Secretary, Permanent Under-Secretary of State at the Foreign and Commonwealth Office and Head of the Diplomatic Service
Registrar, Sir David Manning, GCMG, CVO
King of Arms, Sir Jeremy Greenstock, GCMG
Gentleman Usher of the Blue Rod, Sir Anthony Figgis, KCVO, CMG
Dean, Dean of St Paul's
Deputy Secretary, Secretary of the Central Chancery of the Orders of Knighthood
Hon. Genealogist, Timothy Duke
Chancery, Central Chancery of the Orders of Knighthood, St James's Palace, London SW1A 1BH

THE IMPERIAL ORDER OF THE CROWN OF INDIA (1877) FOR LADIES

CI

Badge, the royal cipher of Queen Victoria in jewels within an oval, surmounted by an heraldic crown and attached to a bow of light blue watered ribbon, edged white

The honour does not confer any rank or title upon the recipient

No conferments have been made since 1947

HM The Queen, 1947

THE ROYAL VICTORIAN ORDER (1896)

GCVO   KCVO

GCVO   Knight or Dame Grand Cross
KCVO   Knight Commander
DCVO   Dame Commander
CVO   Commander
LVO   Lieutenant
MVO   Member

Ribbon, Blue, with red and white edges
Motto, Victoria

THE SOVEREIGN
GRAND MASTER
HRH The Princess Royal

Chancellor, Lord Chamberlain
Secretary, Keeper of the Privy Purse
Registrar, Secretary of the Central Chancery of the Orders of Knighthood
Chaplain, Chaplain of the Queen's Chapel of the Savoy
Hon. Genealogist, David White

THE MOST EXCELLENT ORDER OF THE BRITISH EMPIRE (1917)

GBE   KBE

The order was divided into military and civil divisions in December 1918

GBE   Knight or Dame Grand
       Cross
KBE   Knight Commander
DBE   Dame Commander
CBE   Commander
OBE   Officer
MBE   Member

Ribbon, Rose pink edged with pearl grey with vertical pearl stripe in centre (military division); without vertical pearl stripe (civil division)
Motto, For God and the Empire

THE SOVEREIGN

GRAND MASTER
HRH The Prince Philip, Duke of
   Edinburgh, KG, KT, OM, GBE,
   PC

Prelate, Bishop of London
King of Arms, Adm. Sir Peter Abbott,
   GBE, KCB
Registrar, Secretary of the Central
   Chancery of the Orders of
   Knighthood
Secretary, Secretary of the Cabinet
   and Head of the Home Civil
   Service
Dean, Dean of St Paul's
Gentleman Usher of the Purple Rod, Sir
   Alexander Michael Graham, GBE,
   DCL
Chancery, Central Chancery of the
   Orders of Knighthood, St James's
   Palace, London SW1A 1BH

ORDER OF THE COMPANIONS OF HONOUR (1917)

CH

Ribbon, Carmine, with gold edges

This order consists of one class only and carries with it no title. The number of awards is limited to 65 (excluding honorary members).

Anthony, Rt. Hon. John, 1981
Ashley of Stoke, Lord, 1975
Attenborough, Sir David, 1995
Baker, Dame Janet, 1993
Baker of Dorking, Lord, 1992
Birtwistle, Sir Harrison, 2000
Brenner, Sydney, 1986
Brook, Peter, 1998
Brooke of Sutton Mandeville, Lord,
   1992
Carrington, Lord, 1983
Christie, Sir George, 2001
Davis, Sir Colin, 2001
De Chastelain, Gen. John, 1999
Dench, Dame Judi, 2005
Fraser, Rt. Hon. Malcolm, 1977
Glenamara, Lord, 1976
Hamilton, Richard, 1999
Hannay of Chiswick, Lord, 2003
Hawking, Prof. Stephen, 1989
Healey, Lord, 1979
Heseltine, Lord, 1997
Hobsbawm, Prof. Eric, 1998
Hockney, David, 1997
Hodgkin, Sir Howard, 2002
Howard, Sir Michael, 2002
Howard of Lympne, Lord, 2011
Howe of Aberavon, Lord, 1996
Hurd of Westwell, Lord, 1995
King of Bridgwater, Lord, 1992
Lessing, Doris, 1999
Lovelock, Prof. James, 2002
McKellen, Sir Ian Murray, 2008
McKenzie, Prof. Dan Peter, 2003
Major, Rt. Hon. Sir John, 1998
Owen, Lord, 1994
Patten of Barnes, Rt. Hon. Lord,
   1997
Pawson, Prof. Anthony James, 2006
Riley, Bridget, 1998
Rogers of Riverside, Lord, 2008
Sanger, Dr. Frederick, 1981
Somare, Rt. Hon. Sir Michael, 1978
Talboys, Rt. Hon. Sir Brian, 1981
Tebbit, Lord, 1987

Honorary Members, Lee Kuan Yew,
   1970; Prof. Amartya Sen, 2000;
   Bernard Haitink, 2002
Secretary and Registrar, Secretary of
   the Central Chancery of the
   Orders of Knighthood

THE DISTINGUISHED SERVICE ORDER (1886)

DSO

Ribbon, Red, with blue edges

Bestowed in recognition of especial services in action of commissioned officers in the Navy, Army and Royal Air Force and (since 1942) Mercantile Marine. The members are Companions only. A bar may be awarded for any additional act of service.

THE IMPERIAL SERVICE ORDER (1902)

ISO

Ribbon, Crimson, with blue centre

Appointment as companion of this order is open to members of the civil services whose eligibility is determined by the grade they hold. The order consists of the sovereign and companions to a number not exceeding 1,900, of whom 1,300 may belong to the home civil services and 600 to overseas civil services. The then prime minister announced in March 1993 that he would make no further recommendations for appointments to the order.

Secretary, Secretary of the Cabinet
   and Head of the Home Civil
   Service
Registrar, Secretary of the Central
   Chancery of the Orders of
   Knighthood

THE ROYAL VICTORIAN CHAIN (1902)

It confers no precedence on its holders

HM THE QUEEN

HM The King of Thailand, 1960
HM The Queen of Denmark, 1974
HM The King of Sweden, 1975
HM The Queen of the Netherlands,
   1982
Gen. Antonio Eanes, 1985
HM The King of Spain, 1986
Dr Richard von Weizsäcker, 1992
HM The King of Norway, 1994
Earl of Airlie, 1997
Rt. Revd and Rt. Hon. Lord Carey of
   Clifton, 2002
HRH Prince Philip, Duke of
   Edinburgh, 2007
HM The King of Saudi Arabia, 2007
HM The Sultan of Oman, 2010

BARONETAGE AND KNIGHTAGE

BARONETS

Style, 'Sir' before forename and surname, followed by 'Bt'.
Envelope, Sir F_ S_, Bt. *Letter (formal),* Dear Sir; *(social),*
Dear Sir F_. *Spoken,* Sir F_
Wife's style, 'Lady' followed by surname
Envelope, Lady S_. *Letter (formal),* Dear Madam; *(social),*
Dear Lady S_. *Spoken,* Lady S_
Style of Baronetess, 'Dame' before forename and surname,
followed by 'Btss.' *(see also* Dames)

There are five different creations of baronetcies: Baronets
of England (creations dating from 1611); Baronets of
Ireland (creations dating from 1619); Baronets of
Scotland or Nova Scotia (creations dating from 1625);
Baronets of Great Britain (creations after the Act of Union
1707 which combined the kingdoms of England and
Scotland); and Baronets of the United Kingdom (creations
after the union of Great Britain and Ireland in 1801).

Badge of Baronets of the   *Badge of Baronets*
United Kingdom   *of Nova Scotia*

Badge of Ulster

The patent of creation limits the destination of a
baronetcy, usually to male descendants of the first
baronet, although special remainders allow the baronetcy
to pass, if the male issue of sons fail, to the male issue of
daughters of the first baronet. In the case of baronetcies of
Scotland or Nova Scotia, a special remainder of 'heirs
male and of tailzie' allows the baronetcy to descend to
heirs general, including women. There are four existing
Scottish baronets with such a remainder.

The Official Roll of the Baronetage is kept at the
Crown Office and maintained by the Registrar and
Assistant Registrar of the Baronetage. Anyone who
considers that he or she is entitled to be entered on the
roll may apply through the Crown Office to prove their
succession. Every person succeeding to a baronetcy must
exhibit proofs of succession to the Lord Chancellor. A
person whose name is not entered on the official roll will
not be addressed or mentioned by the title of baronet or
baronetess in any official document, nor will he or she be
accorded precedence as a baronet of baronetess.

BARONETCIES EXTINCT SINCE THE LAST EDITION
Beaumont (cr. 1661); Lawes (cr. 1882)

OFFICIAL ROLL OF THE BARONETAGE, Crown Office,
House of Lords, London SW1A 0PW **T** 020-7219 2632
Registrar, Ian Denyer, MVO
Assistant Registrar, Grant Bavister

KNIGHTS

Style, 'Sir' before forename and surname, followed by
appropriate post-nominal initials if a Knight Grand
Cross, Knight Grand Commander or Knight
Commander
Envelope, Sir F_ S_. *Letter (formal),* Dear Sir; *(social),* Dear
Sir F_. *Spoken,* Sir F_
Wife's style, 'Lady' followed by surname
'Envelope, Lady S_. *Letter (formal),* Dear Madam; *(social),*
Dear Lady S_. *Spoken,* Lady S_

The prefix 'Sir' is not used by knights who are clerics of
the Church of England, who do not receive the accolade.
Their wives are entitled to precedence as the wife of a
knight but not to the style of 'Lady'.

ORDERS OF KNIGHTHOOD
Knight Grand Cross, Knight Grand Commander, and
Knight Commander are the higher classes of the Orders
of Chivalry *(see* Orders of Chivalry). Honorary
knighthoods of these orders may be conferred on men
who are citizens of countries of which the Queen is not
head of state. As a rule, the prefix 'Sir' is not used by
honorary knights.

KNIGHTS BACHELOR

The Knights Bachelor do not constitute a royal order, but
comprise the surviving representation of the ancient state
orders of knighthood. The Register of Knights Bachelor,
instituted by James I in the 17th century, lapsed, and in
1908 a voluntary association under the title of the Society
of Knights (now the Imperial Society of Knights
Bachelor) was formed with the primary objectives of
continuing the various registers dating from 1257 and
obtaining the uniform registration of every created
Knight Bachelor. In 1926 a design for a badge to be worn
by Knights Bachelor was approved and adopted; in 1974
a neck badge and miniature were added.

THE IMPERIAL SOCIETY OF KNIGHTS BACHELOR,
1 Throgmorton Avenue, London EC2N 2BY
Knight Principal, Lord Lingfield
Prelate, Rt. Revd and Rt. Hon. Bishop of London
Registrar, Sir Paul Judge
Hon. Treasurer, Sir Colin Berry
Clerk to the Council, Col. Simon Doughty

LIST OF BARONETS AND KNIGHTS *as at 31 August 2011*

†	Not registered on the Official Roll of the Baronetage at the time of going to press
( )	The date of creation of the baronetcy is given in parentheses
I	Baronet of Ireland
NS	Baronet of Nova Scotia
S	Baronet of Scotland

A full entry in italic type indicates that the recipient of a knighthood died during the year in which the honour was conferred. The name is included for purposes of record. Peers are not included in this list.

Aaronson, Sir Michael John, Kt., CBE
Abbott, *Adm.* Sir Peter Charles, GBE, KCB
Abdy, Sir Valentine Robert Duff, Bt. (1850)
Abed, *Dr* Sir Fazle Hasan, KCMG
Ackroyd, Sir Timothy Robert Whyte, Bt. (1956)
Acland, Sir Antony Arthur, KG, GCMG, GCVO
Acland, *Lt.-Col.* Sir (Christopher) Guy (Dyke), Bt. (1890), MVO
†Acland, Sir Dominic Dyke, Bt. (1644)
Adam, Sir Kenneth Hugo, Kt., OBE
Adams, Sir Geoffrey Doyne, KCMG
Adams, Sir William James, KCMG
Adsetts, Sir William Norman, Kt., OBE
Adye, Sir John Anthony, KCMG
Aga Khan IV, HH Prince Karim, KBE
†Agnew, Sir Crispin Hamlyn, Bt. (S. 1629)
†Agnew, Sir George Anthony, Bt. (1895)
Agnew, Sir Rudolph Ion Joseph, Kt.
Agnew-Somerville, Sir James Lockett Charles, Bt. (1957)
Ah Koy, Sir James Michael, KBE
Aikens, *Rt. Hon.* Sir Richard John Pearson, Kt.
†Ainsworth, Sir Anthony Thomas Hugh, Bt. (1916)
Aird, Sir (George) John, Bt. (1901)
Airy, *Maj.-Gen.* Sir Christopher John, KCVO, CBE
Aitchison, Sir Charles Walter de Lancey, Bt. (1938)
Ajegbo, Sir Keith Onyema, Kt., OBE
Akenhead, *Hon.* Sir Robert, Kt.
Akers-Jones, Sir David, KBE, CMG
Alberti, *Prof.* Sir Kurt George Matthew Mayer, Kt.
Albu, Sir George, Bt. (1912)
Alcock, *Air Chief Marshal* Sir (Robert James) Michael, GCB, KBE
Aldous, *Rt. Hon.* Sir William, Kt.
†Alexander, Sir Richard, Bt. (1945)
Alexander, Sir Douglas, Bt. (1921)
Allen, *Prof.* Sir Geoffrey, Kt., PHD, FRS
Allen, Sir John Derek, Kt., CBE
Allen, Sir Mark John Spurgeon, Kt., CMG
Allen, *Hon.* Sir Peter Austin Philip Jermyn, Kt.
Allen, Sir Thomas Boaz, Kt., CBE
Allen, *Hon.* Sir William Clifford, KCMG

Allen, Sir William Guilford, Kt.
Alleyne, Sir George Allanmoore Ogarren, Kt.
Alleyne, *Revd* John Olpherts Campbell, Bt. (1769)
Allinson, Sir (Walter) Leonard, KCVO, CMG
Alliott, *Hon.* Sir John Downes, Kt.
Allison, *Air Chief Marshal* Sir John Shakespeare, KCB, CBE
Amet, *Hon.* Sir Arnold Karibone, Kt.
Amory, Sir Ian Heathcoat, Bt. (1874)
Anderson, *Dr* Sir James Iain Walker, Kt., CBE
Anderson, Sir John Anthony, KBE
Anderson, Sir Leith Reinsford Steven, Kt., CBE
Anderson, *Prof.* Sir Roy Malcolm, Kt.
Anderson, Sir (William) Eric Kinloch, KT.
Anderson, *Prof.* Sir (William) Ferguson, Kt., OBE
Anderton, Sir (Cyril) James, Kt., CBE, QPM
Andrew, Sir Robert John, KCB
Andrews, Sir Derek Henry, KCB, CBE
Andrews, Sir Ian Charles Franklin, Kt., CBE, TD
Annesley, Sir Hugh Norman, Kt., QPM
Anson, *Vice-Adm.* Sir Edward Rosebery, KCB
Anson, Sir John, KCB
Anson, *Rear-Adm.* Sir Peter, Bt. CB (1831)
Anstruther, Sir Sebastian Paten Campbell, Bt. (S. 1694)
Anstruther-Gough-Calthorpe, Sir Euan Hamilton, Bt. (1929)
Antrobus, Sir Edward Philip, Bt. (1815)
Appleyard, Sir Leonard Vincent, KCMG
Appleyard, Sir Raymond Kenelm, KBE
Arbib, Sir Martyn, Kt.
Arbuthnot, Sir Keith Robert Charles, Bt. (1823)
Arbuthnot, Sir William Reierson, Bt. (1964)
Arbuthnott, *Prof.* Sir John Peebles, Kt., PHD, FRSE
†Archdale, Sir Nicholas Edward, Bt. (1928)
Arculus, Sir Ronald, KCMG, KCVO
Arculus, Sir Thomas David Guy, Kt.

Armitage, *Air Chief Marshal* Sir Michael John, KCB, CBE
Armour, *Prof.* Sir James, Kt., CBE
Armstrong, Sir Christopher John Edmund Stuart, Bt. (1841), MBE
Armstrong, Sir Patrick John, Kt., CBE
Armstrong, Sir Richard, Kt., CBE
Armytage, Sir John Martin, Bt. (1738)
Arnold, *Hon.* Sir Richard David, Kt.
Arnold, Sir Thomas Richard, Kt.
Arnott, Sir Alexander John Maxwell, Bt. (1896)
†Arthur, Sir Benjamin Nathan Arthur, Bt. (1841)
Arthur, Sir Gavyn Farr, Kt.
Arthur, *Lt.-Gen.* Sir (John) Norman Stewart, KCB, CVO
Arthur, Sir Michael Anthony, KCMG
Arulkumaran, *Prof.* Sir Sabaratnam, Kt.
Asbridge, Sir Jonathan Elliott, Kt.
Ash, *Prof.* Sir Eric Albert, Kt., CBE, FRS, FRENG
Ashburnham, Sir James Fleetwood, Bt. (1661)
Ashmore, *Admiral of the Fleet* Sir Edward Beckwith, GCB, DSC
Ashworth, *Dr* Sir John Michael, Kt.
Aske, Sir Robert John Bingham, Bt. (1922)
Askew, Sir Bryan, Kt.
Asscher, *Prof.* Sir (Adolf) William, Kt., MD, FRCP
Astill, *Hon.* Sir Michael John, Kt.
Astley-Cooper, Sir Alexander Paston, Bt. (1821)
Astwood, *Hon.* Sir James Rufus, KBE
Atcherley, Sir Harold Winter, Kt.
Atiyah, Sir Michael Francis, Kt., OM, PHD, FRS
Atkins, *Rt. Hon.* Sir Robert James, Kt.
Atkinson, *Prof.* Sir Anthony Barnes, Kt.
Atkinson, *Air Marshal* Sir David William, KBE
Atkinson, Sir Frederick John, KCB
Atkinson, Sir John Alexander, KCB, DFC
Atkinson, Sir Robert, Kt., DSC, FRENG
Atkinson, Sir William Samuel, Kt.
Atopare, Sir Sailas, GCMG
Attenborough, Sir David Frederick, Kt., OM, CH, CVO, CBE, FRS
Aubrey-Fletcher, Sir Henry Egerton, Bt. (1782)

Audland, Sir Christopher John, KCMG
Augier, *Prof.* Sir Fitz-Roy Richard, Kt.
Auld, *Rt. Hon.* Sir Robin Ernest, Kt.
Austin, Sir Anthony Leonard, Bt. (1894)
Austin, *Air Marshal* Sir Roger Mark, KCB, AFC
Austen-Smith, *Air Marshal* Sir Roy David, KBE, CB, CVO, DFC
Avei, Sir Moi, KBE
Ayckbourn, Sir Alan, Kt., CBE
Aykroyd, Sir James Alexander Frederic, Bt. (1929)
†Aykroyd, Sir Henry Robert George, Bt. (1920)
Aylmer, Sir Richard John, Bt. (I. 1622)
Aylward, *Prof.* Sir Mansel, Kt., CB
Aynsley-Green, *Prof.* Sir Albert, Kt.

Bacha, Sir Bhinod, Kt., CMG
Backhouse, Sir Alfred James Stott, Bt. (1901)
Bacon, Sir Nicholas Hickman Ponsonby, Bt., OBE (1611 and 1627), *Premier Baronet of England*
Bacon, Sir Sidney Charles, Kt., CB, FRENG.
Baddeley, Sir John Wolsey Beresford, Bt. (1922)
Badge, Sir Peter Gilmour Noto, Kt.
Baer, Sir Jack Mervyn Frank, Kt.
Bagge, Sir (John) Jeremy Picton, Bt. (1867)
Bagnall, *Air Chief Marshal* Sir Anthony, GBE, KCB
Bailey, Sir Alan Marshall, KCB
Bailey, Sir Brian Harry, Kt., OBE
Bailey, Sir John Bilsland, KCB
†Bailey, Sir John Richard, Bt. (1919)
Bailhache, Sir Philip Martin, Kt.
Baillie, Sir Adrian Louis, Bt. (1823)
Bain, *Prof.* Sir George Sayers, Kt.
Baird, Sir Charles William Stuart, Bt. (1809)
†Baird, Sir James Andrew Gardiner, Bt. (S. 1695)
Baird, *Air Marshal* Sir John Alexander, KBE
Baird, *Vice-Adm.* Sir Thomas Henry Eustace, KCB
Bairsto, *Air Marshal* Sir Peter Edward, KBE, CB
Baker, Sir Bryan William, Kt.
Baker, *Prof.* Sir John Hamilton, Kt., QC
Baker, Sir John William, Kt., CBE
Baker, *Hon.* Sir Jonathan Leslie, Kt.
Baker, *Rt. Hon.* Sir (Thomas) Scott (Gillespie), Kt.
Balderstone, Sir James Schofield, Kt.
Baldwin, *Prof.* Sir Jack Edward, Kt., FRS
Ball, *Air Marshal* Sir Alfred Henry Wynne, KCB, DSO, DFC
Ball, Sir Christopher John Elinger, Kt.
Ball, *Prof.* Sir John Macleod, Kt.

Ball, Sir Richard Bentley, Bt. (1911)
Ball, *Prof.* Sir Robert James, Kt., PHD
Ballantyne, *Dr* Sir Frederick Nathaniel, GCMG
Bamford, Sir Anthony Paul, Kt.
Band, *Adm.* Sir Jonathon, GCB
Banham, Sir John Michael Middlecott, Kt.
Bannerman, Sir David Gordon, Bt., OBE (S. 1682)
Bannister, Sir Roger Gilbert, Kt., CBE, DM, FRCP
Barber, Sir Michael Bayldon, Kt.
Barber, Sir (Thomas) David, Bt. (1960)
Barbour, *Very Revd* Robert Alexander Stewart, KCVO, MC
Barclay, Sir David Rowat, Kt.
Barclay, Sir Frederick Hugh, Kt.
Barclay, Sir Peter Maurice, Kt., CBE
†Barclay, Sir Robert Colraine, Bt. (S. 1668)
Barder, Sir Brian Leon, KCMG
Baring, Sir John Francis, Bt. (1911)
Barker, Sir Colin, Kt.
Barker, *Hon.* Sir (Richard) Ian, Kt.
Barling, *Hon.* Sir Gerald Edward, Kt.
Barlow, Sir Christopher Hilaro, Bt. (1803)
Barlow, Sir Frank, Kt., CBE
Barlow, Sir (George) William, Kt., FRENG
Barlow, Sir James Alan, Bt. (1902)
Barlow, Sir John Kemp, Bt. (1907)
Barnes, *The Most Revd* Brian James, KBE
Barnes, Sir (James) David (Francis), Kt., CBE
Barnett, *Hon.* Sir Michael Lancelot Patrick, Kt.
Barnewall, Sir Reginald Robert, Bt. (I. 1623)
Baron, Sir Thomas, Kt., CBE
†Barran, Sir John Ruthven, Bt. (1895)
Barratt, Sir Lawrence Arthur, Kt.
Barratt, Sir Richard Stanley, Kt., CBE, QPM
Barrett, Sir Stephen Jeremy, KCMG
Barrett-Lennard, Sir Peter John, Bt. (1801)
Barrington, Sir Benjamin, Bt. (1831)
Barrington, Sir Nicholas John, KCMG, CVO
Barrington-Ward, *Rt. Revd* Simon, KCMG
Barron, Sir Donald James, Kt.
Barrow, Sir Anthony John Grenfell, Bt. (1835)
Barry, Sir (Lawrence) Edward (Anthony Tress), Bt. (1899)
Barter, Sir Peter Leslie Charles, Kt., OBE
†Bartlett, Sir Andrew Alan, Bt. (1913)
Barttelot, *Col.* Sir Brian Walter de Stopham, Bt. (1875), OBE
Bates, Sir James Geoffrey, Bt. (1880)
Bates, Sir Richard Dawson Hoult, Bt. (1937)

Bateson, *Prof.* Sir Patrick, Kt.
Bather, Sir John Knollys, KCVO
Batho, Sir Peter Ghislain, Bt. (1928)
Bathurst, *Admiral of the Fleet* Sir (David) Benjamin, GCB
Batten, Sir John Charles, KCVO
Battersby, *Prof.* Sir Alan Rushton, Kt., FRS
Battishill, Sir Anthony Michael William, GCB
Baulcombe, *Prof.* Sir David Charles, Kt., FRS
Baxendell, Sir Peter Brian, Kt., CBE, FRENG
Bayly, *Prof.* Sir Christopher Alan, Kt.
Bayne, Sir Nicholas Peter, KCMG
Baynes, Sir Christopher Rory, Bt. (1801)
Bazley, Sir Thomas John Sebastian, Bt. (1869)
Beach, *Gen.* Sir (William Gerald) Hugh, GBE, KCB, MC
Beache, *Hon.* Sir Vincent Ian, KCMG
Beale, *Lt.-Gen.* Sir Peter John, KBE, FRCP
Beamish, Sir Adrian John, KCMG
Bean, *Hon.* Sir David Michael, Kt
Beatson, *Hon.* Sir Jack, Kt.
Beavis, *Air Chief Marshal* Sir Michael Gordon, KCB, CBE, AFC
Beck, Sir Edgar Philip, Kt.
Beckett, Sir Richard Gervase, Bt. (1921), QC
Beckett, Sir Terence Norman, KBE, FRENG
Beckwith, Sir John Lionel, Kt., CBE
Beddington, *Prof.* Sir John Rex, Kt., CMG
Beecham, Sir John Stratford Roland, Bt. (1914)
Beetham, *Marshal of the Royal Air Force* Sir Michael James, GCB, CBE, DFC, AFC
Beevor, Sir Thomas Agnew, Bt. (1784)
Beith, *Rt. Hon.* Sir Alan James, Kt.
Beldam, *Rt. Hon.* Sir (Alexander) Roy (Asplan), Kt.
Belich, Sir James, Kt.
Bell, Sir David Charles Maurice, Kt.
Bell, Sir David Robert, KCB
Bell, *Prof.* Sir John Irving, Kt.
Bell, Sir John Lowthian, Bt. (1885)
Bell, *Prof.* Sir Peter Robert Frank, Kt.
Bell, *Hon.* Sir Rodger, Kt.
Bell, Sir Stuart, Kt.
Bellamy, *Hon.* Sir Christopher William, Kt.
Bellingham, Sir Anthony Edward Norman, Bt. (1796)
Bender, Sir Brian Geoffrey, KCB
Benn, Sir (James) Jonathan, Bt. (1914)
Bennett, *Air Vice-Marshal* Sir Erik Peter, KBE, CB
Bennett, *Hon.* Sir Hugh Peter Derwyn, Kt.
Bennett, *Gen.* Sir Phillip Harvey, KBE, DSO

Bennett, Sir Richard Rodney, Kt., CBE
Bennett, Sir Ronald Wilfrid Murdoch, Bt. (1929)
Benson, Sir Christopher John, Kt.
Benyon, Sir William Richard, Kt.
Beresford, Sir (Alexander) Paul, Kt.
Beresford-Peirse, Sir Henry Grant de la Poer, Bt. (1814)
Berghuser, *Hon.* Sir Eric, Kt., MBE
Beringer, *Prof.* Sir John Evelyn, Kt., CBE
Berman, Sir Franklin Delow, KCMG
Berners-Lee, Sir Timothy John, OM, KBE, FRS
Bernard, Sir Dallas Edmund, Bt. (1954)
Bernstein, Sir Howard, Kt.
Berney, Sir Julian Reedham Stuart, Bt. (1620)
Berridge, *Prof.* Sir Michael John, Kt., FRS
Berriman, Sir David, Kt.
Berry, *Prof.* Sir Colin Leonard, Kt., FRCPATH
Berry, *Prof.* Sir Michael Victor, Kt., FRS
Berthoud, Sir Martin Seymour, KCVO, CMG
Best, Sir Richard Radford, KCVO, CBE
Best-Shaw, Sir John Michael Robert, Bt. (1665)
Bethel, Sir Baltron Benjamin, KCMG
Bethlehem, Sir Daniel, KCMG
Bett, Sir Michael, Kt., CBE
Bettison, Sir Norman George, Kt., QPM
Bevan, Sir Martyn Evan Evans, Bt. (1958)
Bevan, Sir Nicolas, Kt., CB
Bevan, Sir Timothy Hugh, Kt.
Beverley, *Lt.-Gen.* Sir Henry York La Roche, KCB, OBE, RM
Bibby, Sir Michael James, Bt. (1959)
Bickersteth, *Rt. Revd* John Monier, KCVO
Biddulph, Sir Ian D'Olier, Bt. (1664)
Bidwell, Sir Hugh Charles Philip, GBE
Biggam, Sir Robin Adair, Kt.
Bilas, Sir Angmai Simon, Kt., OBE
Bill, *Lt.-Gen.* Sir David Robert, KCB
Billière, *Gen.* Sir Peter Edgar de la Cour de la, KCB, KBE, DSO, MC
Bindman, Sir Geoffrey Lionel, Kt.
Bingham, *Hon.* Sir Eardley Max, Kt.
Birch, Sir John Allan, KCVO, CMG
Birch, Sir Roger, Kt., CBE, QPM
Bird, Sir Richard Geoffrey Chapman, Bt. (1922)
Birkin, Sir John Christian William, Bt. (1905)
Birkin, Sir (John) Derek, Kt., TD
Birkmyre, Sir James, Bt. (1921)
Birrell, Sir James Drake, Kt.
Birtwistle, Sir Harrison, Kt., CH
Bischoff, Sir Winfried Franz Wilhelm, Kt.

Black, *Adm.* Sir (John) Jeremy, GBE, KCB, DSO
Black, Sir Robert David, Bt. (1922)
Blackburn, *Vice-Adm.* Sir David Anthony James, KCVO, CB
Blackburne, *Hon.* Sir William Anthony, Kt.
Blackett, Sir Hugh Francis, Bt. (1673)
Blackham, *Vice-Adm.* Sir Jeremy Joe, KCB
Blackman, Sir Frank Milton, KCVO, OBE
†Blair, Sir Patrick David Hunter, Bt. (1786)
Blair, *Hon.* Sir William James Lynton, Kt.
Blake, Sir Alfred Lapthorn, KCVO, MC
Blake, Sir Francis Michael, Bt. (1907)
Blake, *Hon.* Sir Nicholas John Gorrod, Kt.
Blake, Sir Peter Thomas, Kt., CBE
Blake, Sir Anthony Teilo Bruce, Bt. (I. 1622)
Blaker, Sir John, Bt. (1919)
Blakiston, Sir Ferguson Arthur James, Bt. (1763)
Blanch, Sir Malcolm, KCVO
Bland, Sir (Francis) Christopher (Buchan), Kt.
Bland, *Lt.-Col.* Sir Simon Claud Michael, KCVO
Blank, Sir Maurice Victor, Kt.
Blatherwick, Sir David Elliott Spiby, KCMG, OBE
Blelloch, Sir John Nial Henderson, KCB
Blennerhassett, Sir (Marmaduke) Adrian Francis William, Bt. (1809)
Blewitt, *Maj.* Sir Shane Gabriel Basil, GCVO
Blofeld, *Hon.* Sir John Christopher Calthorpe, Kt.
Blois, Sir Charles Nicholas Gervase, Bt. (1686)
Blom-Cooper, Sir Louis Jacques, Kt., QC
Blomefield, Sir Thomas Charles Peregrine, Bt. (1807)
Bloomfield, Sir Kenneth Percy, KCB
Blundell, Sir Thomas Leon, Kt., FRS
Blunden, Sir George, Kt.
†Blunden, Sir Hubert Chisholm, Bt. (I. 1766)
Blunt, Sir David Richard Reginald Harvey, Bt. (1720)
Blyth, Sir Charles (Chay), Kt., CBE, BEM
Boardman, *Prof.* Sir John, Kt., FSA, FBA
Bodey, *Hon.* Sir David Roderick Lessiter, Kt.
Bodmer, Sir Walter Fred, Kt., PHD, FRS
Body, Sir Richard Bernard Frank Stewart, Kt.
Bogan, Sir Nagora, KBE
Boileau, Sir Guy (Francis), Bt. (1838)
Boles, Sir Jeremy John Fortescue, Bt. (1922)

Boles, Sir John Dennis, Kt., MBE
Bolt, *Air Marshal* Sir Richard Bruce, KBE, CB, DFC, AFC
Bona, Sir Kina, KBE
Bonallack, Sir Michael Francis, Kt., OBE
Bond, Sir John Reginald Hartnell, Kt.
Bond, *Prof.* Sir Michael Richard, Kt., FRCPSYCH, FRCPGLAS, FRCSE
Bone, *Prof.* Sir James Drummond, Kt., FRSE
Bone, Sir Roger Bridgland, KCMG
Bonfield, Sir Peter Leahy, Kt., CBE, FRENG
†Bonham, Sir George Martin Antony, Bt. (1852)
Bonington, Sir Christian John Storey, Kt., CVO, CBE
Bonsall, Sir Arthur Wilfred, KCMG, CBE
Bonsor, Sir Nicholas Cosmo, Bt. (1925)
Boord, Sir Nicolas John Charles, Bt. (1896)
Boorman, *Lt.-Gen.* Sir Derek, KCB
Booth, Sir Christopher Charles, Kt., MD, FRCP
Booth, Sir Clive, Kt.
Booth, Sir Douglas Allen, Bt. (1916)
Booth, Sir Gordon, KCMG, CVO
Boothby, Sir Brooke Charles, Bt. (1660)
Bore, Sir Albert, Kt.
Boreel, Sir Stephan Gerard, Bt. (1645)
Borthwick, Sir Anthony Thomas, Bt. (1908)
Borysiewicz, *Prof.* Sir Leszek Krzysztof, Kt.
Bossom, *Hon.* Sir Clive, Bt. (1953)
Boswell, *Lt.-Gen.* Sir Alexander Crawford Simpson, KCB, CBE
Bosworth, Sir Neville Bruce Alfred, Kt., CBE
Botham, Sir Ian Terence, Kt., OBE
Bottoms, *Prof.* Sir Anthony Edward, Kt.
Bottomley, Sir James Reginald Alfred, KCMG
Bottomley, Sir Peter James, Kt.
Boughey, Sir John George Fletcher, Bt. (1798)
Boulton, Sir Clifford John, GCB
†Boulton, Sir John Gibson, Bt. (1944)
Bouraga, Sir Phillip, KBE
Bourn, Sir John Bryant, KCB
Bowater, Sir Euan David Vansittart, Bt. (1939)
†Bowater, Sir Michael Patrick, Bt. (1914)
Bowden, Sir Andrew, Kt., MBE
Bowden, Sir Nicholas Richard, Bt. (1915)
Bowen, Sir Barry Manfield, KCMG
Bowen, Sir Geoffrey Fraser, Kt.
Bowen, Sir Mark Edward Mortimer, Bt. (1921)

Bowes Lyon, Sir Simon Alexander, KCVO

†Bowlby, Sir Richard Peregrine Longstaff, Bt. (1923)

Bowman, Sir Edwin Geoffrey, KCB

Bowman, Sir Jeffery Haverstock, Kt.

Bowman-Shaw, Sir (George) Neville, Kt.

Bowness, Sir Alan, Kt., CBE

Bowyer-Smyth, Sir Thomas Weyland, Bt. (1661)

Boyce, Sir Graham Hugh, KCMG

Boyce, Sir Robert Charles Leslie, Bt. (1952)

Boyd, Sir Alexander Walter, Bt. (1916)

Boyd, Sir John Dixon Iklé, KCMG

Boyd, Prof. Sir Robert David Hugh, Kt.

Boyd-Carpenter, Sir (Marsom) Henry, KCVO

Boyd-Carpenter, Lt.-Gen. Hon. Sir Thomas Patrick John, KBE

Boyle, Prof. Sir Roger Michael, Kt., CBE

Boyle, Sir Stephen Gurney, Bt. (1904)

Boyson, Rt. Hon. Sir Rhodes, Kt.

Brabham, Sir John Arthur, Kt., OBE

Bracewell-Smith, Sir Charles, Bt. (1947)

Bradbeer, Sir John Derek Richardson, Kt., OBE, TD

Bradfield, Dr Sir John Richard Grenfell, Kt., CBE

Bradford, Sir Edward Alexander Slade, Bt. (1902)

Brady, Prof. Sir John Michael, Kt., FRS

Braithwaite, Sir Rodric Quentin, GCMG

Bramley, Prof. Sir Paul Anthony, Kt.

Branson, Sir Richard Charles Nicholas, Kt.

Braithwaite, Rt. Hon. Sir Nicholas Alexander, Kt., OBE

Bratza, Hon. Sir Nicolas Dušan, Kt.

Breckenridge, Prof. Sir Alasdair Muir, Kt., CBE

Brennan, Hon. Sir (Francis) Gerard, KBE

Brenton, Sir Anthony Russell, KCMG

Brewer, Sir David William, Kt., CMG

Brierley, Sir Ronald Alfred, Kt.

Briggs, Hon. Sir Michael Townley Featherstone, Kt.

Brighouse, Prof. Sir Timothy Robert Peter, Kt.

Bright, Sir Graham Frank James, Kt.

Bright, Sir Keith, Kt.

Brigstocke, Adm. Sir John Richard, KCB

Brinckman, Sir Theodore George Roderick, Bt. (1831)

†Brisco, Sir Campbell Howard, Bt. (1782)

Briscoe, Sir Brian Anthony, Kt.

Briscoe, Sir John Geoffrey James, Bt. (1910)

Brittan, Sir Samuel, Kt.

Britton, Sir Paul John James, Kt., CB

†Broadbent, Sir Andrew George, Bt. (1893)

Broadbent, Sir Richard John, KCB

Brocklebank, Sir Aubrey Thomas, Bt. (1885)

Brodie, Sir Benjamin David Ross, Bt. (1834)

Brooke, Sir Rodney George, Kt., CBE

Brooking, Sir Trevor, Kt., CBE

Bromhead, Sir John Desmond Gonville, Bt. (1806)

Bromley, Sir Michael Roger, KBE

Bromley, Sir Rupert Charles, Bt. (1757)

Bromley-Davenport, Sir William Arthur, KCVO

Brook, Prof. Sir Richard John, Kt. OBE

†Brooke, Sir Alistair Weston, Bt. (1919)

Brooke, Sir Francis George Windham, Bt. (1903)

Brooke, Rt. Hon. Sir Henry, Kt.

Brooke, Sir (Richard) David Christopher, Bt. (1662)

Brooking, Sir Trevor David, Kt., CBE

Brooks, Sir Timothy Gerald Martin, KCVO

Brooksbank, Sir (Edward) Nicholas, Bt. (1919)

Broomfield, Sir Nigel Hugh Robert Allen, KCMG

†Broughton, Sir David Delves, Bt. (1661)

Broughton, Sir Martin Faulkner, Kt.

Broun, Sir Wayne Hercules, Bt. (S. 1686)

Brown, Sir (Austen) Patrick, KCB

Brown, Adm. Sir Brian Thomas, KCB, CBE

Brown, Sir David, Kt.

Brown, Hon. Sir Douglas Dunlop, Kt.

Brown, Sir George Francis Richmond, Bt. (1863)

Brown, Sir Mervyn, KCMG, OBE

Brown, Sir Peter Randolph, Kt.

Brown, Rt. Hon. Sir Stephen, GBE

Brown, Sir Stephen David Reid, KCVO

Browne, Sir Nicholas Walker, KBE, CMG

Brownrigg, Sir Nicholas (Gawen), Bt. (1816)

Browse, Prof. Sir Norman Leslie, Kt., MD, FRCS

Bruce, Sir (Francis) Michael Ian, Bt. (S. 1628)

†Bruce-Clifton, Sir Hervey Hamish Peter, Bt. (1804)

Bruce-Gardner, Sir Robert Henry, Bt. (1945)

Brunner, Sir Hugo Laurence Joseph, KCVO

Brunner, Sir John Henry Kilian, Bt. (1895)

Brunton, Sir Gordon Charles, Kt.

†Brunton, Sir James Lauder, Bt. (1908)

Bryant, Air Chief Marshal Sir Simon, KCB, CBE, ADC

Bubb, Sir Stephen John Limrick, Kt.

Buchan-Hepburn, Sir John Alastair Trant Kidd, Bt. (1815)

Buchanan, Sir Andrew George, Bt. (1878), KCVO

Buchanan, Vice-Adm. Sir Peter William, KBE

Buchanan, Sir Robert Wilson (Robin), Kt.

†Buchanan-Jardine, Sir John Christopher Rupert, Bt. (1885)

Buckland, Sir Ross, Kt.

Buckley, Dr Sir George William, Kt.

Buckley, Sir Michael Sidney, Kt.

Buckley, Lt.-Cdr. Sir (Peter) Richard, KCVO

Buckley, Hon. Sir Roger John, Kt.

Buckworth-Herne-Soame, Sir Charles John, Bt. (1697)

Budd, Sir Alan Peter, Kt.

Budd, Sir Colin Richard, KCMG

Bull, Sir George Jeffrey, Kt.

Bull, Sir Simeon George, Bt. (1922)

Bullock, Sir Stephen Michael, Kt.

Bultin, Sir Bato, Kt., MBE

Bunbury, Sir Michael William, Bt. (1681), KCVO

Bunyard, Sir Robert Sidney, Kt., CBE, QPM

Burbidge, Sir Peter Dudley, Bt. (1916)

Burden, Sir Anthony Thomas, Kt., QPM

Burdett, Sir Savile Aylmer, Bt. (1665)

Burgen, Sir Arnold Stanley Vincent, Kt., FRS

Burgess, Gen. Sir Edward Arthur, KCB, OBE

Burgess, Sir (Joseph) Stuart, Kt., CBE, PHD, FRSC

Burgess, Prof. Sir Robert George, Kt.

Burgh, Sir John Charles, KCMG, CB

Burke, Sir James Stanley Gilbert, Bt. (I. 1797)

Burke, Sir (Thomas) Kerry, Kt.

Burn, Prof. Sir John, Kt.

Burnell-Nugent, Vice-Adm. Sir James Michael, KCB, CBE, ADC

Burnet, Sir James William Alexander (Sir Alastair Burnet), Kt.

Burnett, Air Chief Marshal Sir Brian Kenyon, GCB, DFC, AFC

Burnett, Sir Charles David, Bt., (1913)

Burnett, Hon. Sir Ian Duncan, Kt.

Burnett, Sir Walter John, Kt.

Burney, Sir Nigel Dennistoun, Bt. (1921)

Burns, Dr Sir Henry, Kt.

Burns, Sir (Robert) Andrew, KCMG

Burnton, Rt. Hon. Sir Stanley Jeffrey, Kt.

Burrell, Sir Charles Raymond, Bt. (1774)

Burridge, Air Chief Marshal Sir Brian Kevin, KCB, CBE, ADC

Burston, Sir Samuel Gerald Wood, Kt., OBE

Burt, Sir Peter Alexander, Kt.

Burton, Sir Carlisle Archibald, Kt., OBE

Burton, Lt.-Gen. Sir Edmund Fortescue Gerard, KBE

Burton, Sir Graham Stuart, KCMG

Burton, Hon. Sir Michael John, Kt.

Burton, Sir Michael St Edmund, KCVO, CMG

Bush, Adm. Sir John Fitzroy Duyland, GCB, DSC

Butler, Hon. Sir Arlington Griffith, KCMG

Butler, Dr Sir David Edgeworth, Kt., CBE

Butler, Sir Michael Dacres, GCMG

Butler, Sir (Reginald) Michael (Thomas), Bt. (1922)

Butler, Sir Percy James, Kt., CBE

Butler, Hon. Sir Richard Clive, Kt.

Butler, Sir Richard Pierce, Bt. (1628)

Butterfield, Hon. Sir Alexander Neil Logie, Kt.

Butterfill, Sir John Valentine, Kt.

Buxton, Sir Jocelyn Charles Roden, Bt. (1840)

Buxton, Rt. Hon. Sir Richard Joseph, Kt.

Buzzard, Sir Anthony Farquhar, Bt. (1929)

Byatt, Sir Ian Charles Rayner, Kt.

Byford, Sir Lawrence, Kt., CBE, QPM

Byron, Rt. Hon. Sir Charles Michael Dennis, Kt.

†Cable-Alexander, Sir Patrick Desmond William, Bt. (1809)

Cadbury, Sir (George) Adrian (Hayhurst), Kt.

Cadbury, Sir (Nicholas) Dominic, Kt.

Cadogan, Prof. Sir John Ivan George, Kt., CBE, FRS, FRSE

Cahn, Sir Albert Jonas, Bt. (1934)

Cahn, Sir Andrew Thomas, KCMG

Caine, Sir Michael (Maurice Micklewhite), Kt., CBE

Caines, Sir John, KCB

Caldwell, Sir Edward George, KCB

Callaghan, Sir William Henry, Kt.

Callan, Sir Ivan Roy, KCVO, CMG

Calman, Prof. Sir Kenneth Charles, KCB, MD, FRCP, FRCS, FRSE

Calne, Prof. Sir Roy Yorke, Kt., FRS

Calvert-Smith, Sir David, Kt., QC

Cameron, Sir Hugh Roy Graham, Kt., QPM

Campbell, Prof. Sir Colin Murray, Kt.

Campbell, Sir Ian Tofts, Kt., CBE, VRD

Campbell, Sir Ilay Mark, Bt. (1808)

Campbell, Sir James Alexander Moffat Bain, Bt. (S. 1668)

Campbell, Sir Lachlan Philip Kemeys, Bt. (1815)

Campbell, Sir Roderick Duncan Hamilton, Bt. (1831)

Campbell, Sir Robin Auchinbreck, Bt. (S. 1628)

Campbell, Rt. Hon. Sir Walter Menzies, Kt., CBE, QC

Campbell, Rt. Hon. Sir William Anthony, Kt.

Campbell-Orde, Sir John Alexander, Bt. (1790)

Cannadine, Prof. Sir David Nicholas, Kt.

†Carden, Sir Christopher Robert, Bt. (1887)

†Carden, Sir John Craven, Bt. (I. 1787)

Carew, Sir Rivers Verain, Bt. (1661)

Carey, Sir de Vic Graham, Kt.

Carleton-Smith, Maj.-Gen. Sir Michael Edward, Kt., CBE

Carlisle, Sir James Beethoven, GCMG

Carlisle, Sir John Michael, Kt.

Carlisle, Sir Kenneth Melville, Kt.

Carnegie, Sir Roderick Howard, Kt.

Carnwath, Rt. Hon. Sir Robert John Anderson, Kt., CVO

Caro, Sir Anthony Alfred, Kt., OM, CBE

Carr, Sir (Albert) Raymond (Maillard), Kt.

Carr, Very Revd Dr Arthur Wesley, KCVO

Carr, Sir Peter Derek, Kt., CBE

Carr, Sir Roger Martyn, Kt.

Carr-Ellison, Col. Sir Ralph Harry, KCVO, TD

Carrick, Hon. Sir John Leslie, KCMG

Carrick, Sir Roger John, KCMG, LVO

Carruthers, Sir Ian James, Kt., OBE

Carsberg, Prof. Sir Bryan Victor, Kt.

Carter, Prof. Sir David Craig, Kt., FRCSE, FRCSGLAS, FRCPE

Carter, Sir John Alexander, Kt.

Carter, Sir John Gordon Thomas, Kt.

Carter, Sir Philip David, Kt., CBE

Cartledge, Sir Bryan George, KCMG

Cary, Sir Roger Hugh, Bt. (1955)

Casey, Rt. Hon. Sir Maurice Eugene, Kt.

Cash, Sir Andrew John, Kt., OBE

Cass, Sir Geoffrey Arthur, Kt.

Cassel, Sir Timothy Felix Harold, Bt. (1920)

Cassels, Sir John Seton, Kt., CB

Cassels, Adm. Sir Simon Alastair Cassillis, KCB, CBE

Cassidi, Adm. Sir (Arthur) Desmond, GCB

Castell, Sir William Martin, Kt.

Castledine, Prof. Sir George, Kt.

Catherwood, Sir (Henry) Frederick (Ross), Kt.

Catto, Prof. Sir Graeme Robertson Dawson, Kt.

Cave, Sir John Charles, Bt. (1896)

Cave-Browne-Cave, Sir Robert, Bt. (1641)

Cayley, Sir Digby William David, Bt. (1661)

Cayzer, Sir James Arthur, Bt. (1904)

Cazalet, Hon. Sir Edward Stephen, Kt.

Cazalet, Sir Peter Grenville, Kt.

Cecil, Sir Henry, Kt.

Cecil, Rear-Adm. Sir (Oswald) Nigel Amherst, KBE, CB

Chadwick, Rt. Hon. Sir John Murray, Kt.

Chadwick, Sir Joshua Kenneth Burton, Bt. (1935)

Chadwick, Revd Prof. (William) Owen, OM, KBE, FBA

Chadwyck-Healey, Sir Charles Edward, Bt. (1919)

Chakrabarti, Sir Sumantra, KCB

Chalmers, Sir Iain Geoffrey, Kt.

Chalmers, Sir Neil Robert, Kt.

Chalstrey, Sir (Leonard) John, Kt., MD, FRCS

Chan, Rt. Hon. Sir Julius, GCMG, KBE

Chan, Sir Thomas Kok, Kt., OBE

Chance, Sir (George) Jeremy ffolliott, Bt. (1900)

Chandler, Sir Colin Michael, Kt.

Chantler, Prof. Sir Cyril, Kt., MD, FRCP

Chaplin, Sir Malcolm Hilbery, Kt., CBE

Chapman, Sir David Robert Macgowan, Bt. (1958)

Chapman, Sir Frank, Kt.

Chapman, Sir George Alan, Kt.

Chapman, Sir Sidney Brookes, Kt., MP

Chapple, Field Marshal Sir John Lyon, GCB, CBE

Charles, Hon. Sir Arthur William Hessin, Kt.

Charlton, Sir Robert (Bobby), Kt., CBE

Charnley, Sir (William) John, Kt., CB, FRENG

Chartres, Rt. Revd and Rt. Hon. Richard John Carew, KCVO

Chataway, Rt. Hon. Sir Christopher, Kt.

†Chaytor, Sir Bruce Gordon, Bt. (1831)

Checketts, Sqn. Ldr. Sir David John, KCVO

Checkland, Sir Michael, Kt.

Cheshire, Air Chief Marshal Sir John Anthony, KBE, CB

Chessells, Sir Arthur David (Tim), Kt.

†Chetwynd, Sir Robin John Talbot, Bt. (1795)

Cheyne, Sir Patrick John Lister, Bt. (1908)

Chichester, Sir James Henry Edward, Bt. (1641)

Chichester-Clark, Sir Robin, Kt.

Chilcot, Rt. Hon. Sir John Anthony, GCB

Child, Sir (Coles John) Jeremy, Bt. (1919)

Chilwell, Hon. Sir Muir Fitzherbert, Kt.

Chinn, Sir Trevor Edwin, Kt., CVO

Chipperfield, Prof. Sir David Alan, Kt., CBE

Chipperfield, Sir Geoffrey Howes, KCB

Chisholm, Sir John Alexander Raymond, Kt., FRENG

Chitty, Sir Thomas Willes, Bt. (1924)

Cholmeley, Sir Hugh John Frederick Sebastian, Bt. (1806)
Chow, Sir Chung Kong, Kt.
Chow, Sir Henry Francis, Kt., OBE
Christie, Sir George William Langham, Kt., CH
Christopher, Sir Duncan Robin Carmichael, KBE, CMG
Chung, Sir Sze-yuen, GBE, FRENG
Clark, Sir Francis Drake, Bt. (1886)
Clark, Sir John Arnold, Kt.
Clark, Sir Jonathan George, Bt. (1917)
Clark, Sir Robert Anthony, Kt., DSC
Clark, Sir Terence Joseph, KBE, CMG, CVO
Clarke, Sir (Charles Mansfield) Tobias, Bt. (1831)
Clarke, Hon. Sir Christopher Simon Courtenay Stephenson, Kt.
Clarke, Hon. Sir David Clive, Kt.
Clarke, Sir Jonathan Dennis, Kt.
Clarke, Sir Robert Cyril, Kt.
†Clarke, Sir Rupert Grant Alexander, Bt. (1882)
Clay, Sir Edward, KCMG
Clay, Sir Richard Henry, Bt. (1841)
Clayton, Sir David Robert, Bt. (1732)
Cleaver, Sir Anthony Brian, Kt.
Clementi, Sir David Cecil, Kt.
Clerk, Sir Robert Maxwell, Bt. (1679), OBE
Clerke, Sir John Edward Longueville, Bt. (1660)
Clifford, Sir Roger Joseph, Bt. (1887)
Clifford, Sir Timothy Peter Plint, Kt.
Coates, Sir Anthony Robert Milnes, Bt. (1911)
Coates, Sir David Frederick Charlton, Bt. (1921)
Coats, Sir Alastair Francis Stuart, Bt. (1905)
Cochrane, Sir (Henry) Marc (Sursock), Bt. (1903)
Cockburn, Sir John Elliot, Bt. (S. 1671)
Cockburn-Campbell, Sir Alexander Thomas, Bt. (1821)
Cockell, Sir Merrick, Kt.
Cockshaw, Sir Alan, Kt., FRENG
†Codrington, Sir Christopher George Wayne, Bt. (1876)
†Codrington, Sir Giles Peter, Bt. (1721)
Coghill, Sir Patrick Kendal Farley, Bt. (1778)
Coghlin, Rt. Hon. Sir Patrick, Kt.
Cohen, Sir Edward, Kt.
Cohen, Sir Ivor Harold, Kt., CBE, TD
Cohen, Prof. Sir Philip, Kt., PHD, FRS
Cohen, Sir Ronald, Kt.
Cole, Sir (Robert) William, Kt.
Coleman, Sir Robert John, KCMG
Coleridge, Hon. Sir Paul James Duke, Kt.
Coles, Sir (Arthur) John, GCMG
Colfox, Sir (William) John, Bt. (1939)

Collett, Sir Christopher, GBE
Collett, Sir Ian Seymour, Bt. (1934)
Collins, Sir Alan Stanley, KCVO, CMG
Collins, Hon. Sir Andrew David, Kt.
Collins, Sir Bryan Thomas Alfred, Kt., OBE, QFSM
Collins, Sir John Alexander, Kt
Collins, Sir Kenneth Darlingston, Kt.
Collins, Prof. Sir Rory Edwards, Kt.
Collyear, Sir John Gowen, Kt.
Colman, Hon. Sir Anthony David, Kt.
Colman, Sir Michael Jeremiah, Bt. (1907)
Colman, Sir Timothy, KG
†Colquhoun of Luss, Sir Malcolm Rory, Bt. (1786)
Colt, Sir Edward William Dutton, Bt. (1694)
Colthurst, Sir Charles St John, Bt. (1744)
Conant, Sir John Ernest Michael, Bt. (1954)
Connell, Hon. Sir Michael Bryan, Kt.
Conner, Rt. Revd Sir David John, KCVO
Connery, Sir Sean, Kt.
Connor, Sir William Joseph, Kt.
Conran, Sir Terence Orby, Kt.
Cons, Hon. Sir Derek, Kt.
Conway, Prof. Sir Gordon Richard, KCMG, FRS
Cook, Sir Christopher Wymondham Rayner Herbert, Bt. (1886)
Cook, Prof. Sir Peter Frederic Chester, Kt.
Cooke, Col. Sir David William Perceval, Bt. (1661)
Cooke, Sir Howard Felix Hanlan, GCMG, GCVO
Cooke, Hon. Sir Jeremy Lionel, Kt.
Cooke, Prof. Sir Ronald Urwick, Kt.
Cooksey, Sir David James Scott, GBE
Cooper, Gen. Sir George Leslie Conroy, GCB, MC
Cooper, Sir Richard Adrian, Bt. (1905)
Cooper, Maj.-Gen. Sir Simon Christie, GCVO
Cooper, Sir William Daniel Charles, Bt. (1863)
Coote, Sir Christopher John, Bt. (I. 1621), Premier Baronet of Ireland
Copas, Most Revd Virgil, KBE
Copisarow, Sir Alcon Charles, Kt.
Corbett, Maj.-Gen. Sir Robert John Swan, KCVO, CB
Cordy-Simpson, Lt.-Gen. Sir Roderick Alexander, KBE, CB
Corfield, Sir Kenneth George, Kt., FRENG
Corness, Sir Colin Ross, Kt.
Cornforth, Sir John Warcup, Kt., CBE, DPHIL, FRS
Corry, Sir James Michael, Bt. (1885)
Cortazzi, Sir (Henry Arthur) Hugh, GCMG
Cory, Sir (Clinton Charles) Donald, Bt. (1919)

Cory-Wright, Sir Richard Michael, Bt. (1903)
Cossons, Sir Neil, Kt., OBE
Cotter, Sir Patrick Laurence Delaval, Bt. (I. 1763)
Cotterell, Sir John Henry Geers, Bt. (1805)
Cottrell, Sir Alan Howard, Kt., PHD, FRS, FRENG
†Cotts, Sir Richard Crichton Mitchell, Bt. (1921)
Coulson, Hon. Sir Peter David William, Kt.
Couper, Sir James George, Bt. (1841)
Courtenay, Sir Thomas Daniel, Kt.
Cousins, Air Chief Marshal Sir David, KCB, AFC
Coville, Air Marshal Sir Christopher Charles Cotton, KCB
Cowan, Gen. Sir Samuel, KCB, CBE
Coward, Vice-Adm. Sir John Francis, KCB, DSO
Cowen, Rt. Hon. Prof. Sir Zelman, GCMG, GCVO
Cowie, Sir Thomas (Tom), Kt., OBE
Cowper-Coles, Sir Sherard Louis, KCMG, LVO
Cox, Sir Alan George, Kt., CBE
Cox, Prof. Sir David Roxbee, Kt.
Cox, Sir George Edwin, Kt.
Craft, Prof. Sir Alan William, Kt.
Craig, Sir (Albert) James (Macqueen), GCMG
Craig-Cooper, Sir (Frederick Howard) Michael, Kt., CBE, TD
Crane, Hon. Sir Peter Francis, Kt.
Crane, Prof. Sir Peter Robert, Kt.
Cranston, Hon. Sir Ross Frederick, Kt.
Craufurd, Sir Robert James, Bt. (1781)
Craven, Sir John Anthony, Kt.
Craven, Sir Philip Lee, Kt., MBE
Crawford, Prof. Sir Frederick William, Kt., FRENG
Crawford, Sir Robert William Kenneth, Kt. CBE
Crawley-Boevey, Sir Thomas Michael Blake, Bt. (1784)
Crew, Sir (Michael) Edward, Kt., QPM
Crewe, Prof. Sir Ivor Martin, Kt.
Cresswell, Hon. Sir Peter John, Kt.
Crichton-Brown, Sir Robert, KCMG, CBE, TD
Crisp, Sir John Charles, Bt. (1913)
Critchett, Sir Charles George Montague, Bt. (1908)
Crockett, Sir Andrew Duncan, Kt.
Croft, Sir Owen Glendower, Bt. (1671)
Croft, Sir Thomas Stephen Hutton, Bt. (1818)
†Crofton, Sir Hugh Denis, Bt. (1801)
†Crofton, Sir Julian Malby, Bt. (1838)
Crombie, Sir Alexander, Kt.
Crompton, Sir Dan, Kt., CBE, QPM
Cropper, Sir James Anthony, KCVO
Crosby, Sir James Robert, Kt.

Crossley, Sir Sloan Nicholas, Bt. (1909)

Crowe, Sir Brian Lee, KCMG

Cruickshank, Sir Donald Gordon, Kt.

Cruthers, Sir James Winter, Kt.

Cubbon, Sir Brian Crossland, GCB

Cubie, *Dr* Sir Andrew, Kt., CBE

Cubitt, Sir Hugh Guy, Kt., CBE

Cubitt, *Maj.-Gen.* Sir William George, KCVO, CBE

Cullen, Sir (Edward) John, Kt., FRENG

Culme-Seymour, Sir Michael Patrick, Bt. (1809)

Culpin, Sir Robert Paul, Kt.

Cummins, Sir Michael John Austin, Kt.

Cunliffe, *Prof.* Sir Barrington, Kt., CBE

Cunliffe, Sir David Ellis, Bt. (1759)

Cunliffe, Sir Jonathan Stephen, Kt., CB

Cunliffe-Owen, Sir Hugo Dudley, Bt. (1920)

Cunningham, *Lt.-Gen.* Sir Hugh Patrick, KBE

Cunningham, Sir Roger Keith, Kt., CBE

Cunynghame, Sir Andrew David Francis, Bt. (S. 1702)

†Currie, Sir Donald Scott, Bt. (1847)

Curry, Sir Donald Thomas Younger, Kt., CBE

Curtain, Sir Michael, KBE

Curtis, Sir Barry John, Kt.

Curtis, *Hon.* Sir Richard Herbert, Kt.

Curtis, Sir William Peter, Bt. (1802)

Curtiss, *Air Marshal* Sir John Bagot, KCB, KBE

Curwen, Sir Christopher Keith, KCMG

Cuschieri, *Prof.* Sir Alfred, Kt.

Dain, Sir David John Michael, KCVO

Dales, Sir Richard Nigel, KCVO

Dalrymple-Hay, Sir Malcolm John Robert, Bt. (1798)

†Dalrymple-White, Sir Jan Hew, Bt. (1926)

Dalton, *Vice-Adm.* Sir Geoffrey Thomas James Oliver, KCB

Dalton, Sir Richard John, KCMG

Dalton, *Air Chief Marshal* Sir Stephen Gary George, KCB

Dalyell, Sir Tam (Thomas), Bt. (NS 1685)

Daniel, Sir John Sagar, Kt., DSC

Darell, Sir Jeffrey Lionel, Bt. (1795), MC

Darling, Sir Clifford, GCVO

Darrington, Sir Michael John, Kt.

Darroch, Sir Nigel Kim, KCMG

Dasgupta, *Prof.* Sir Partha Sarathi, Kt.

†Dashwood, Sir Edward John Francis, Bt. (1707), *Premier Baronet of Great Britain*

Dashwood, Sir Richard James, Bt. (1684)

Daunt, Sir Timothy Lewis Achilles, KCMG

Davenport-Handley, Sir David John, Kt., OBE

David, Sir Jean Marc, Kt., CBE, QC

David, *His Hon.* Sir Robin (Robert) Daniel George, Kt.

Davies, Sir Alan Seymour, Kt.

Davies, Sir (Charles) Noel, Kt.

Davies, *Prof.* Sir David Evan Naughton, Kt., CBE, FRS, FRENG

Davies, *Hon.* Sir (David Herbert) Mervyn, Kt., MC, TD

Davies, Sir David John, Kt.

Davies, Sir Frank John, Kt., CBE

Davies, *Prof.* Sir Graeme John, Kt., FRENG

Davies, Sir John Howard, Kt.

Davies, Sir John Michael, KCB

Davies, Sir Peter Maxwell, Kt., CBE

Davies, Sir Rhys Everson, Kt., QC

Davis, Sir Andrew Frank, Kt., CBE

Davis, Sir Colin Rex, Kt., CH, CBE

Davis, Sir Crispin Henry Lamert, Kt.

Davis, Sir John Gilbert, Bt. (1946)

Davis, *Hon.* Sir Nigel Anthony Lambert, Kt.

Davis, Sir Peter John, Kt.

Davis-Goff, Sir Robert (William), Bt. (1905)

Davison, *Rt. Hon.* Sir Ronald Keith, GBE, CMG

†Davson, Sir George Trenchard Simon, Bt. (1927)

Dawanincura, Sir John Norbert, Kt., OBE

Dawbarn, Sir Simon Yelverton, KCVO, CMG

Dawson, *Hon.* Sir Daryl Michael, KBE, CB

Dawson, Sir Nicholas Antony Trevor, Bt. (1920)

Dawtry, Sir Alan (Graham), Kt., CBE, TD

Day, Sir Derek Malcolm, KCMG

Day, *Air Chief Marshal* Sir John Romney, KCB, OBE, ADC

Day, Sir (Judson) Graham, Kt.

Day, Sir Michael John, Kt., OBE

Day, Sir Simon James, Kt.

Deane, *Hon.* Sir William Patrick, KBE

Dearlove, Sir Richard Billing, KCMG, OBE

de Bellaigue, Sir Geoffrey, GCVO

†Debenham, Sir Thomas Adam, Bt. (1931)

de Deney, Sir Geoffrey Ivor, KCVO

Deeny, *Hon.* Sir Donnell Justin Patrick, Kt.

De Halpert, *Rear-Adm.* Sir Jeremy Michael, KCVO, CB

de Hoghton, Sir (Richard) Bernard (Cuthbert), Bt. (1611)

De la Bère, Sir Cameron, Bt. (1953)

de la Rue, Sir Andrew George Ilay, Bt. (1898)

De Silva, Sir George Desmond Lorenz, Kt., QC

Dellow, Sir John Albert, Kt., CBE

Delves, *Lt.-Gen.* Sir Cedric Norman George, KBE

Denholm, Sir John Ferguson (Ian), Kt., CBE

Denison-Smith, *Lt.-Gen.* Sir Anthony Arthur, KBE

Denny, Sir Anthony Coningham de Waltham, Bt. (I. 1782)

Denny, Sir Charles Alistair Maurice, Bt. (1913)

Derbyshire, Sir Andrew George, Kt.

†de Trafford, Sir John Humphrey, Bt. (1841)

Deverell, *Gen.* Sir John Freegard, KCB, OBE

Devesi, Sir Baddeley, GCMG, GCVO

De Ville, Sir Harold Godfrey Oscar, Kt., CBE

Devitt, Sir James Hugh Thomas, Bt. (1916)

de Waal, Sir (Constant Henrik) Henry, KCB, QC

Dewey, Sir Anthony Hugh, Bt. (1917)

De Witt, Sir Ronald Wayne, Kt.

Dick-Lauder, Sir Piers Robert, Bt. (S. 1690)

Dilke, Sir Charles John Wentworth, Bt. (1862)

Dillon, Sir Andrew Patrick, Kt., CBE

Dillwyn-Venables-Llewelyn, Sir John Michael, Bt. (1890)

Dixon, Sir Jeremy, Kt.

Dixon, Sir Jonathan Mark, Bt. (1919)

Dixon, Sir Peter John Bellett, Kt.

Djanogly, Sir Harry Ari Simon, Kt., CBE

Dobson, *Vice-Adm.* Sir David Stuart, KBE

Dodds, Sir Ralph Jordan, Bt. (1964)

Dollery, Sir Colin Terence, Kt.

Don-Wauchope, Sir Roger (Hamilton), Bt. (S. 1667)

Donald, Sir Alan Ewen, KCMG

Donald, *Air Marshal* Sir John George, KBE

Donaldson, *Prof.* Sir Liam Joseph, Kt.

Donne, Sir John Christopher, Kt.

Donnelly, Sir Joseph Brian, KBE, CMG

Dorey, Sir Graham Martyn, Kt.

Dorman, Sir Philip Henry Keppel, Bt. (1923)

Doughty, Sir William Roland, Kt.

Douglas, *Prof.* Sir Neil James, Kt.

Douglas, *Hon.* Sir Roger Owen, Kt.

Dowell, Sir Anthony James, Kt., CBE

Dowling, Sir Robert, Kt.

Downey, Sir Gordon Stanley, KCB

Downs, Sir Diarmuid, Kt., CBE, FRENG

Downward, *Maj.-Gen.* Sir Peter Aldcroft, KCVO, CB, DSO, DFC

Dowson, Sir Philip Manning, Kt., CBE, PRA

Doyle, Sir Reginald Derek Henry, Kt., CBE

D'Oyly, Sir Hadley Gregory Bt. (1663)

Drake, *Hon.* Sir (Frederick) Maurice, Kt., DFC

Drewry, *Lt.-Gen.* Sir Christopher Francis, KCB, CBE

Drinkwater, Sir John Muir, Kt., QC

Drury, Sir (Victor William) Michael, Kt., OBE

Dryden, Sir John Stephen Gyles, Bt. (1733 and 1795)

du Cann, *Rt. Hon.* Sir Edward Dillon Lott, KBE

†Duckworth, Sir James Edward Dyce, Bt. (1909)

du Cros, Sir Claude Philip Arthur Mallet, Bt. (1916)

Dudley-Williams, Sir Alastair Edgcumbe James, Bt. (1964)

Duff, *Prof.* Sir Gordon William, Kt.

Duff-Gordon, Sir Andrew Cosmo Lewis, Bt. (1813)

Duffell, *Lt.-Gen.* Sir Peter Royson, KCB, CBE, MC

Duffy, Sir (Albert) (Edward) Patrick, Kt., PHD

Dugdale, Sir William Stratford, Bt. (1936), MC

Duggin, Sir Thomas Joseph, Kt.

Dummett, *Prof.* Sir Michael Anthony Eardley, Kt., FBA

Dunbar, Sir Archibald Ranulph, Bt. (S. 1700)

Dunbar, Sir Robert Drummond Cospatrick, Bt. (S. 1698)

Dunbar, Sir James Michael, Bt. (S. 1694)

Dunbar of Hempriggs, Sir Richard Francis, Bt. (S. 1706)

Dunbar-Nasmith, *Prof.* Sir James Duncan, Kt., CBE

Duncan, Sir James Blair, Kt.

Dunlop, Sir Thomas, Bt. (1916)

Dunn, *Rt. Hon.* Sir Robin Horace Walford, Kt., MC

Dunne, Sir Thomas Raymond, KG, KCVO

Dunning, Sir Simon William Patrick, Bt. (1930)

Dunnington-Jefferson, Sir Mervyn Stewart, Bt. (1958)

Dunstan, *Lt.-Gen.* Sir Donald Beaumont, KBE, CB

Dunt, *Vice-Adm.* Sir John Hugh, KCB

Duntze, Sir Daniel Evans Bt. (1774)

Dupre, Sir Tumun, Kt., MBE

Dupree, Sir (Thomas William James) David, Bt. (1921)

Durand, Sir Edward Alan Christopher David Percy, Bt. (1892)

Durant, Sir (Robert) Anthony (Bevis), Kt.

Durie, Sir David Robert Campbell, KCMG

Durrant, Sir William Alexander Estridge, Bt. (1784)

Duthie, *Prof.* Sir Herbert Livingston, Kt.

Duthie, Sir Robert Grieve (Robin), Kt., CBE

Dutton, *Lt-Gen.* Sir James Benjamin, KCB, CBE

Dwyer, Sir Joseph Anthony, Kt.

Dyke, Sir David William Hart, Bt. (1677)

Dymock, *Vice-Adm.* Sir Anthony Knox, KBE, CB

Dyson, Sir James, Kt., CBE

Dyson, *Rt. Hon.* Sir John Anthony, Kt.

Eady, *Hon.* Sir David, Kt.

Eardley-Wilmot, Sir Michael John Assheton, Bt. (1821)

Earle, Sir (Hardman) George (Algernon), Bt. (1869)

Eaton, *Adm.* Sir Kenneth John, GBE, KCB

Eberle, *Adm.* Sir James Henry Fuller, GCB

Ebrahim, Sir (Mahomed) Currimbhoy, Bt. (1910)

Eddington, Sir Roderick Ian, Kt.

Eder, *Hon.* Sir Henry Bernard, Kt.

Edge, *Capt.* Sir (Philip) Malcolm, KCVO

†Edge, Sir William, Bt. (1937)

Edmonstone, Sir Archibald Bruce Charles, Bt. (1774)

Edward, *Rt. Hon.* Sir David Alexander Ogilvy, KCMG

Edwardes, Sir Michael Owen, Kt.

Edwards, Sir Christopher John Churchill, Bt. (1866)

Edwards, *Prof.* Sir Christopher Richard Watkin, Kt.

Edwards, Sir Llewellyn Roy, Kt.

Edwards, *Prof.* Sir Robert Geoffrey, Kt., CBE

Edwards, Sir Robert Paul, Kt.

Edwards, *Prof.* Sir Samuel Frederick, Kt., FRS

†Edwards-Moss, Sir David John, Bt. (1868)

Edwards-Stuart, *Hon.* Sir Antony James Cobham, Kt.

Egan, Sir John Leopold, Kt.

Ehrman, Sir William Geoffrey, KCMG

Eichelbaum, *Rt. Hon.* Sir Thomas, GBE

Elder, Sir Mark Philip, Kt., CBE

Eldon, Sir Stewart Graham, KCMG, OBE

Elias, *Rt. Hon.* Sir Patrick, Kt.

Eliott of Stobs, Sir Charles Joseph Alexander, Bt. (S. 1666)

Elliot, Sir Gerald Henry, Kt.

Elliott, Sir Clive Christopher Hugh, Bt. (1917)

Elliott, Sir David Murray, KCMG, CB

Elliott, *Prof.* Sir John Huxtable, Kt., FBA

Elliott, *Prof.* Sir Roger James, Kt., FRS

Ellis, Sir Vernon James, Kt.

Ellwood, Sir Peter Brian, Kt., CBE

Elphinstone, Sir John, Bt. (S. 1701)

Elphinstone, Sir John Howard Main, Bt. (1816)

Elton, Sir Arnold, Kt., CBE

Elton, Sir Charles Abraham Grierson, Bt. (1717)

Elton, Sir Leslie, Kt.

Elvidge, Sir John, KCB

Elwes, *Dr* Sir Henry William, KCVO

Elwes, Sir Jeremy Vernon, Kt., CBE

Elwood, Sir Brian George Conway, Kt., CBE

Elworthy, *Air Cdre. Hon.* Sir Timothy Charles, KCVO, CBE

Enderby, *Prof.* Sir John Edwin, Kt. CBE, FRS

Engle, Sir George Lawrence Jose, KCB, QC

English, Sir Terence Alexander Hawthorne, KBE, FRCS

Ennals, Sir Paul Martin, Kt., CBE

Epstein, *Prof.* Sir (Michael) Anthony, Kt., CBE, FRS

Errington, *Col.* Sir Geoffrey Frederick, Bt. (1963), OBE

Errington, Sir Lancelot, KCB

Erskine, Sir (Thomas) Peter Neil, Bt. (1821)

Erskine-Hill, Sir Alexander Rodger, Bt. (1945)

Esmonde, Sir Thomas Francis Grattan, Bt. (I. 1629)

Esplen, Sir John Graham, Bt. (1921)

Esquivel, *Rt. Hon.* Sir Manuel, KCMG

Essenhigh, *Adm.* Sir Nigel Richard, GCB

Etherington, Sir Stuart James, Kt.

Etherton, *Rt. Hon.* Sir Terence Michael Elkan Barnet, Kt.

Evans, Sir Anthony Adney, Bt. (1920)

Evans, *Rt. Hon.* Sir Anthony Howell Meurig, Kt., RD

Evans, *Prof.* Sir Christopher Thomas, Kt., OBE

Evans, *Air Chief Marshal* Sir David George, GCB, CBE

Evans, *Hon.* Sir David Roderick, Kt.

Evans, Sir Harold Matthew, Kt.

Evans, *Hon.* Sir Haydn Tudor, Kt.

Evans, *Prof.* Sir John Grimley, Kt., FRCP

Evans, Sir John Stanley, Kt., QPM

Evans, *Prof.* Sir Martin John, Kt., FRS

Evans, Sir Richard Harry, Kt., CBE

Evans, Sir Richard Mark, KCMG, KCVO

Evans, Sir Robert, Kt., CBE, FRENG

Evans-Lombe, *Hon.* Sir Edward Christopher, Kt.

†Evans-Tipping, Sir David Gwynne, Bt. (1913)

Eveleigh, *Rt. Hon.* Sir Edward Walter, Kt., ERD

†Everard, Sir Henry Peter Charles, Bt. (1911)

Every, Sir Henry John Michael, Bt. (1641)

Ewans, Sir Martin Kenneth, KCMG

Ewart, Sir William Michael, Bt. (1887)

Eyre, Sir Reginald Edwin, Kt.
Eyre, Sir Richard Charles Hastings, Kt., CBE

Fagge, Sir John Christopher Frederick, Bt. (1660)
Fairbairn, Sir (James) Brooke, Bt. (1869)
Fairlie-Cuninghame, Sir Robert Henry, Bt. (S. 1630)
Fairweather, Sir Patrick Stanislaus, KCMG
Faldo, Sir Nicholas Alexander, Kt., MBE
†Falkiner, Sir Benjamin Simon Patrick, Bt. (I. 1778)
Fall, Sir Brian James Proetel, GCVO, KCMG
Falle, Sir Samuel, KCMG, KCVO, DSC
Fang, Prof. Sir Harry, Kt., CBE
Fareed, Sir Djamil Sheik, Kt.
Farmer, Sir Thomas, Kt., CVO, CBE
Farquhar, Sir Michael Fitzroy Henry, Bt. (1796)
Farquharson, Sir Angus Durie Miller, KCVO, OBE
Farrell, Sir Terence, Kt., CBE
Farrer, Sir (Charles) Matthew, GCVO
Farrington, Sir Henry William, Bt. (1818)
Fat, Sir (Maxime) Edouard (Lim Man) Lim, Kt.
Faulkner, Sir (James) Dennis (Compton), Kt., CBE, VRD
Fay, Sir (Humphrey) Michael Gerard, Kt.
Fayrer, Sir John Lang Macpherson, Bt. (1896)
Feachem, Prof. Sir Richard George Andrew, KBE
Fean, Sir Thomas Vincent, KCVO
†Feilden, Sir Henry Rudyard, Bt. (1846)
Feldmann, Prof. Sir Marc, Kt.
Fell, Sir David, KCB
Fender, Sir Brian Edward Frederick, Kt., CMG, PHD
Fenn, Sir Nicholas Maxted, GCMG
Fenwick, Sir Leonard Raymond, Kt., CBE
Fergus, Sir Howard Archibald, KBE
Ferguson, Sir Alexander Chapman, Kt., CBE
Ferguson-Davie, Sir Michael, Bt. (1847)
Fergusson of Kilkerran, Sir Charles, Bt. (S. 1703)
Fergusson, Sir Ewan Alastair John, GCMG, GCVO
Fersht, Prof. Sir Alan Roy, Kt., FRS
Ferris, Hon. Sir Francis Mursell, Kt., TD
ffolkes, Sir Robert Francis Alexander, Bt. (1774), OBE
Field, Sir Malcolm David, Kt.
Field, Hon. Sir Richard Alan, Kt.

Fielding, Sir Leslie, KCMG
Fields, Sir Allan Clifford, KCMG
Fieldsend, Hon. Sir John Charles Rowell, KBE
Fiennes, Sir Ranulph Twisleton-Wykeham, Bt. (1916), OBE
Figg, Sir Leonard Clifford William, KCMG
Figgis, Sir Anthony St John Howard, KCVO, CMG
Finch, Sir Robert Gerard, Kt.
Finlay, Sir David Ronald James Bell, Bt. (1964)
Finlayson, Sir Garet Orlando, KCMG, OBE
Finney, Sir Thomas, Kt., OBE
†Fison, Sir Charles William, Bt. (1905)
†Fitzgerald, Revd Daniel Patrick, Bt. (1903)
FitzGerald, Sir Adrian James Andrew, Bt. (1880)
FitzHerbert, Sir Richard Ranulph, Bt. (1784)
Fitzpatrick, Air Marshal Sir John Bernard, KBE, CB
Flanagan, Sir Ronald, GBE
Flanagan, Sir Maurice, KBE
Flaux, Hon. Sir Julian Martin, Kt.
Floud, Prof. Sir Roderick Castle, Kt.
Floyd, Hon. Sir Christopher David, Kt.
Floyd, Sir Giles Henry Charles, Bt. (1816)
Foley, Lt.-Gen. Sir John Paul, KCB, OBE, MC
Follett, Prof. Sir Brian Keith, Kt., FRS
Forbes, Sir James Thomas Stewart, Bt. (1823)
Forbes, Adm. Sir Ian Andrew, KCB, CBE
Forbes, Vice-Adm. Sir John Morrison, KCB
Forbes, Hon. Sir Thayne John, Kt.
†Forbes Adam, Revd Stephen Timothy Beilby, Bt. (1917)
Forbes-Leith, Sir George Ian David, Bt. (1923)
Forbes of Craigievar, Sir Andrew Iain Ochoncar, Bt. (S. 1630)
Ford, Sir Andrew Russell, Bt. (1929)
Ford, Sir David Robert, KBE, LVO
Ford, Sir John Archibald, KCMG, MC
Ford, Gen. Sir Robert Cyril, GCB, CBE
Foreman, Sir Philip Frank, Kt., CBE, FRENG
Forestier-Walker, Sir Michael Leolin, Bt. (1835)
Forman, Sir John Denis, Kt., OBE
Forrest, Prof. Sir (Andrew) Patrick (McEwen), Kt.
Forsyth-Johnson, Sir Bruce Joseph, Kt., CBE (Bruce Forsyth)
Forte, Hon. Sir Rocco John Vincent, Kt.
Forwood, Sir Peter Noel, Bt. (1895)
Foskett, Hon. Sir David Robert, Kt.
Foster, Sir Andrew William, Kt.

Foster, Prof. Sir Christopher David, Kt.
†Foster, Sir Saxby Gregory, Bt. (1930)
Foulkes, Sir Arthur Alexander, GCMG
Foulkes, Sir Nigel Gordon, Kt.
Fountain, Hon. Sir Cyril Stanley Smith, Kt.
Fowke, Sir David Frederick Gustavus, Bt. (1814)
Fowler, Sir (Edward) Michael Coulson, Kt.
Fox, Sir Christopher, Kt., QPM
Fox, Sir Paul Leonard, Kt., CBE
France, Sir Christopher Walter, GCB
Francis, Sir Horace William Alexander, Kt., CBE, FRENG
Frank, Sir Robert Andrew, Bt. (1920)
Franklin, Sir Michael David Milroy, KCB, CMG
Fraser, Sir Alasdair MacLeod, Kt.
Fraser, Sir Charles Annand, KCVO
Fraser, Gen. Sir David William, GCB, OBE
Fraser, Sir Iain Michael Duncan, Bt. (1943)
Fraser, Sir James Murdo, KBE
Fraser, Sir William Kerr, GCB
Frayling, Prof. Sir Christopher John, Kt.
Frederick, Sir Christopher St John, Bt. (1723)
Freedman, Rt. Hon. Prof. Sir Lawrence David, KCMG, CBE
Freeland, Sir John Redvers, KCMG
Freeman, Sir James Robin, Bt. (1945)
Freer, Air Chief Marshal Sir Robert William George, GBE, KCB
French, Air Marshal Sir Joseph Charles, KCB, CBE
Frere, Vice-Adm. Sir Richard Tobias, KCB
Fretwell, Sir (Major) John (Emsley), GCMG
Friend Prof. Sir Richard Henry, Kt.
Froggatt, Sir Peter, Kt.
Frossard, Sir Charles Keith, KBE
Frost, Sir David Paradine, Kt., OBE
Fry, Sir Graham Holbrook, KCMG
Fry, Sir Peter Derek, Kt.
Fry, Lt.-Gen. Sir Robert Allan, KCB, CBE
Fulford, Hon. Sir Adrian Bruce, Kt.
Fuller, Sir James Henry Fleetwood, Bt. (1910)
Fulton, Lt.-Gen. Sir Robert Henry Gervase, KBE
Furness, Sir Stephen Roberts, Bt. (1913)

Gage, Rt. Hon. Sir William Marcus, Kt., QC
Gains, Sir John Christopher, Kt.
Gainsford, Sir Ian Derek, Kt.
Galsworthy, Sir Anthony Charles, KCMG
Galway, Sir James, Kt., OBE

Gamble, Sir David Hugh Norman, Bt. (1897)
Gambon, Sir Michael John, Kt., CBE
Gammell, Sir William Benjamin Bowring, Kt.
Gardiner, Sir John Eliot, Kt., CBE
Gardner, *Prof.* Sir Richard Lavenham, Kt.
Gardner, Sir Roy Alan, Kt.
Garland, *Hon.* Sir Patrick Neville, Kt.
Garland, *Hon.* Sir Ransley Victor, KBE
Garland, *Dr* Sir Trevor, KBE
Garner, Sir Anthony Stuart, Kt.
Garnett, *Adm.* Sir Ian David Graham, KCB
Garnier, *Rear-Adm.* Sir John, KCVO, CBE
Garrard, Sir David Eardley, Kt.
Garrett, Sir Anthony Peter, Kt., CBE
Garrick, Sir Ronald, Kt., CBE, FRENG
Garthwaite, Sir (William) Mark (Charles), Bt. (1919)
Gaskell, Sir Richard Kennedy Harvey, Kt.
Gass, Sir Simon Lawrance, KCMG, CVO
Geidt, *Rt. Hon.* Sir Christopher, KCVO, OBE
Geno, Sir Makena Viora, KBE
Gent, Sir Christopher Charles, Kt.
George, Sir Arthur Thomas, Kt.
George, *Prof.* Sir Charles Frederick, MD, FRCP
George, Sir Richard William, Kt., CVO
Gerken, *Vice-Adm.* Sir Robert William Frank, KCB, CBE
Gershon, Sir Peter Oliver, Kt., CBE
Gethin, Sir Richard Joseph St Lawrence, Bt. (I. 1665)
Gibb, Sir Francis Ross (Frank), Kt., CBE, FRENG
Gibbings, Sir Peter Walter, Kt.
Gibbons, Sir (John) David, KBE
Gibbons, Sir William Edward Doran, Bt. (1752)
Gibbs, *Hon.* Sir Richard John Hedley, Kt.
Gibbs, Sir Roger Geoffrey, Kt.
†Gibson, *Revd* Christopher Herbert, Bt. (1931)
Gibson, Sir Ian, Kt., CBE
Gibson, *Rt. Hon.* Sir Peter Leslie, Kt.
Gibson-Craig-Carmichael, Sir David Peter William, Bt. (S. 1702 and 1831)
Gieve, Sir Edward John Watson, KCB
Giffard, Sir (Charles) Sydney (Rycroft), KCMG
Gilbart-Denham, *Lt.-Col.* Sir Seymour Vivian, KCVO
Gilbert, *Air Chief Marshal* Sir Joseph Alfred, KCB, CBE
Gilbert, *Rt. Hon.* Sir Martin John, Kt., CBE

†Gilbey, Sir Walter Gavin, Bt. (1893)
Gill, Sir Anthony Keith, Kt.
Gill, Sir Arthur Benjamin Norman, Kt., CBE
Gill, Sir Robin Denys, KCVO
Gillam, Sir Patrick John, Kt.
Gillen, *Hon.* Sir John de Winter, Kt.
Gillett, Sir Nicholas Danvers Penrose, Bt. (1959)
Gillinson, Sir Clive Daniel, Kt., CBE
Gilmore, *Prof.* Sir Ian Thomas, Kt.
Gilmour, Sir John, Bt. (1897)
Gina, Sir Lloyd Maepeza, KBE
Giordano, Sir Richard Vincent, KBE
Girolami, Sir Paul, Kt.
Girvan, *Rt. Hon.* Sir (Frederick) Paul, Kt.
Gladstone, Sir (Erskine) William, Bt. (1846), KG
Glean, Sir Carlyle Arnold, GCMG
Glenn, Sir (Joseph Robert) Archibald, Kt., OBE
Glidewell, *Rt. Hon.* Sir Iain Derek Laing, Kt.
Glover, Sir Victor Joseph Patrick, Kt.
Glyn, Sir Richard Lindsay, Bt. (1759 and 1800)
Gobbo, Sir James Augustine, Kt., AC
Goldberg, *Prof.* Sir David Paul Brandes, Kt
Goldring, *Rt. Hon.* Sir John Bernard, Kt.
Gomersall, Sir Stephen John, KCMG
Gonsalves-Sabola, *Hon.* Sir Joaquim Claudino, Kt
Gooch, Sir Miles Peter, Bt. (1866)
Gooch, Sir Arthur Brian Sherlock Heywood, Bt. (1746)
Good, Sir John James Griffen, Kt. CBE
Goodall, Sir (Arthur) David Saunders, GCMG
Goodall, *Air Marshal* Sir Roderick Harvey, KBE, CB, AFC
Goode, *Prof.* Sir Royston Miles, Kt., CBE, QC
Goodenough, Sir Anthony Michael, KCMG
Goodenough, Sir William McLernon, Bt. (1943)
Goodhart, Sir Philip Carter, Kt.
Goodhart, Sir Robert Anthony Gordon, Bt. (1911)
Goodison, Sir Nicholas Proctor, Kt.
Goodman, Sir Patrick Ledger, Kt., CBE
Goodson, Sir Mark Weston Lassam, Bt. (1922)
Goodwin, Sir Frederick, KBE
Goodwin, Sir Frederick Anderson, Kt.
Goodwin, Sir Matthew Dean, Kt., CBE
Goody, *Prof.* Sir John Rankine, Kt.
†Goold, Sir George William, Bt. (1801)
Gordon, Sir Donald, Kt.
Gordon, Sir Gerald Henry, Kt., CBE, QC
Gordon, Sir Robert James, Bt. (S. 1706)

Gordon-Cumming, Sir Alexander Penrose, Bt. (1804)
Gore, Sir Hugh Frederick Corbet, Bt. (I. 1622)
Gore-Booth, Sir Josslyn Henry Robert, Bt. (I. 1760)
Goring, Sir William Burton Nigel, Bt. (1627)
Gorman, Sir John Reginald, Kt., CVO, CBE, MC
Goschen, Sir (Edward) Alexander, Bt. (1916)
Gosling, Sir (Frederick) Donald, KCVO
Goswell, Sir Brian Lawrence, Kt.
Gough, Sir Charles Brandon, Kt.
Goulden, Sir (Peter) John, GCMG
Goulding, Sir (William) Lingard Walter, Bt. (1904)
Gourlay, *Gen.* Sir (Basil) Ian (Spencer), KCB, OBE, MC, RM
Gourlay, Sir Simon Alexander, Kt.
Gow, *Gen.* Sir (James) Michael, GCB
Gowans, Sir James Learmonth, Kt., CBE, FRCP, FRS
Gozney, Sir Richard Hugh Turton, KCMG
†Graaff, Sir David de Villiers, Bt. (1911)
Grabham, Sir Anthony Henry, Kt.
Graham, Sir Alexander Michael, GBE
Graham, Sir James Bellingham, Bt. (1662)
Graham, Sir James Fergus Surtees, Bt. (1783)
Graham, Sir James Thompson, Kt., CMG
Graham, Sir John Alexander Noble, Bt. (1906), GCMG
Graham, Sir John Alistair, Kt.
Graham, Sir John Moodie, Bt. (1964)
Graham, Sir Peter, KCB, QC
Graham, *Lt.-Gen.* Sir Peter Walter, KCB, CBE
†Graham, Sir Ralph Stuart, Bt. (1629)
Graham-Moon, Sir Peter Wilfred Giles, Bt. (1855)
Graham-Smith, *Prof.* Sir Francis, Kt.
Grant, Sir Archibald, Bt. (S. 1705)
Grant, Sir Clifford, Kt.
Grant, Sir Ian David, Kt., CBE
Grant, Sir (John) Anthony, Kt.
Grant, Sir John Douglas Kelso, KCMG
Grant, Sir Patrick Alexander Benedict, Bt. (S. 1688)
Grant, Sir Paul Joseph Patrick, Kt.
Grant, *Lt.-Gen.* Sir Scott Carnegie, KCB
Grant-Suttie, Sir James Edward, Bt. (S. 1702)
Granville-Chapman, *Lt.-Gen.* Sir Timothy John, GBE, KCB, ADC
Gratton-Bellew, Sir Henry Charles, Bt. (1838)
Gray, *Hon.* Sir Charles Anthony St John, Kt.

Gray, Sir Charles Ireland, Kt., CBE

Gray, *Prof.* Sir Denis John Pereira, Kt., OBE, FRCGP

Gray, *Dr.* Sir John Armstrong Muir, Kt., CBE

Gray, Sir Robert McDowall (Robin), Kt.

Gray, Sir William Hume, Bt. (1917)

Graydon, *Air Chief Marshal* Sir Michael James, GCB, CBE

Grayson, Sir Jeremy Brian Vincent Harrington, Bt. (1922)

Green, Sir Allan David, KCB, QC

Green, Sir Andrew Fleming, KCMG

Green, Sir Edward Patrick Lycett, Bt. (1886)

Green, Sir Gregory David, KCMG

Green, *Hon.* Sir Guy Stephen Montague, KBE

Green, *Prof.* Sir Malcolm, Kt.

Green, Sir Owen Whitley, Kt.

Green, Sir Philip Green, Kt.

Green-Price, Sir Robert John, Bt. (1874)

Greenaway, Sir John Michael Burdick, Bt. (1933)

Greenbury, Sir Richard, Kt.

Greener, Sir Anthony Armitage, Kt.

Greengross, Sir Alan David, Kt.

Greenstock, Sir Jeremy Quentin, GCMG

Greenwell, Sir Edward Bernard, Bt. (1906)

Greenwood, *Prof.* Sir Christopher John, Kt., CMG

Gregory, *Prof.* Sir Michael John, Kt., CBE

Gregson, Sir Peter John, Kt.

Gregson, Sir Peter Lewis, GCB

Greig, Sir (Henry Louis) Carron, KCVO, CBE

Grey, Sir Anthony Dysart, Bt. (1814)

†Grey-Egerton, Sir William de Malpas, Bt. (1617), CB, OBE, MC

Grierson, Sir Ronald Hugh, Kt.

Griffiths, Sir Eldon Wylie, Kt.

Grigson, *Hon.* Sir Geoffrey Douglas, Kt.

Grimshaw, Sir Nicholas Thomas, Kt., CBE

Grimwade, Sir Andrew Sheppard, Kt., CBE

Grose, *Vice-Adm.* Sir Alan, KBE

Gross, *Rt. Hon.* Sir Peter Henry, Kt.

Grossart, Sir Angus McFarlane McLeod, Kt., CBE

Grotrian, Sir Philip Christian Brent, Bt. (1934)

Grove, Sir Charles Gerald, Bt. (1874)

Grundy, Sir Mark, Kt.

Guinness, Sir Howard Christian Sheldon, Kt., VRD

Guinness, Sir John Ralph Sidney, Kt., CB

†Guinness, Sir Kenelm Edward Lee, Bt. (1867)

†Guise, Sir Christopher James, Bt. (1783)

Gull, Sir Rupert William Cameron, Bt. (1872)

Gumbs, Sir Emile Rudolph, Kt.

Gunn, Sir Robert Norman, Kt.

†Gunning, Sir Charles Theodore, Bt. (1778)

Gunston, Sir John Wellesley, Bt. (1938)

Gurdon, *Prof.* Sir John Bertrand, Kt., DPHIL, FRS

Guthrie, Sir Malcolm Connop, Bt. (1936)

Haddacks, *Vice-Adm.* Sir Paul Kenneth, KCB

Hadfield, Sir Ronald, Kt., QPM

Hadlee, Sir Richard John, Kt., MBE

Hagart-Alexander, Sir Claud, Bt. (1886)

Hague, *Prof.* Sir Douglas Chalmers, Kt., CBE

Haines, *Prof.* Sir Andrew Paul, Kt.

Haji-Ioannou, Sir Stelios, Kt.

Halberg, Sir Murray Gordon, Kt., MBE

Hall, *Prof.* Sir David Michael Baldock, Kt.

Hall, Sir Ernest, Kt., OBE

Hall, Sir Graham Joseph, Kt.

Hall, Sir Iain Robert, Kt.

Hall, Sir (Frederick) John (Frank), Bt. (1923)

Hall, Sir John, Kt.

Hall, Sir John Bernard, Bt. (1919)

Hall, Sir John Douglas Hoste, Bt. (S. 1687)

Hall, HE *Prof.* Sir Kenneth Octavius, GCMG

Hall, Sir Peter Edward, KBE, CMG

Hall, *Prof.* Sir Peter Geoffrey, Kt., FBA

Hall, Sir Peter Reginald Frederick, Kt., CBE

Hall, Sir William Joseph, KCVO

Halpern, Sir Ralph Mark, Kt.

Halsey, *Revd* John Walter Brooke, Bt. (1920)

Halstead, Sir Ronald, Kt., CBE

Hamblen, *Hon.* Sir Nicholas Archibald, Kt.

†Hambling, Sir Herbert Peter Hugh, Bt. (1924)

Hamilton, Sir Andrew Caradoc, Bt. (S. 1646)

Hamilton, Sir James Arnot, KCB, MBE, FRENG

Hamilton, Sir Nigel, KCB

Hamilton-Dalrymple, *Maj.* Sir Hew Fleetwood, Bt. (S. 1697), GCVO

Hamilton-Spencer-Smith, Sir John, Bt. (1804)

Hammick, Sir Stephen George, Bt. (1834)

Hammond, Sir Anthony Hilgrove, KCB, QC

Hampel, Sir Ronald Claus, Kt.

Hampson, Sir Stuart, Kt.

Hampton, Sir (Leslie) Geoffrey, Kt.

Hampton, Sir Philip Roy, Kt.

Hanbury-Tenison, Sir Richard, KCVO

Hancock, Sir David John Stowell, KCB

†Hanham, Sir William John Edward, Bt. (1667)

Hankes-Drielsma, Sir Claude Dunbar, KCVO

Hanley, *Rt. Hon.* Sir Jeremy James, KCMG

Hanmer, Sir Wyndham Richard Guy, Bt. (1774)

Hannam, Sir John Gordon, Kt.

Hanson, Sir (Charles) Rupert (Patrick), Bt. (1918)

Hanson, Sir John Gilbert, KCMG, CBE

Harcourt-Smith, *Air Chief Marshal* Sir David, GBE, KCB, DFC

Hardie Boys, *Rt. Hon.* Sir Michael, GCMG

Harding, Sir George William, KCMG, CVO

Harding, *Marshal of the Royal Air Force* Sir Peter Robin, GCB

Harding, Sir Roy Pollard, Kt., CBE

Hardy, Sir David William, Kt.

Hardy, Sir James Gilbert, Kt., OBE

Hardy, Sir Richard Charles Chandos, Bt. (1876)

Hare, Sir David, Kt., FRSL

Hare, Sir Nicholas Patrick, Bt. (1818)

Haren, *Dr* Sir Patrick Hugh, Kt.

†Harford, Sir Mark John, Bt. (1934)

Harington, Sir Nicholas John, Bt. (1611)

Harkness, *Very Revd* James, KCVO, CB, OBE

Harland, *Air Marshal* Sir Reginald Edward Wynyard, KBE, CB

Harley, *Gen.* Sir Alexander George Hamilton, KBE, CB

Harman, *Hon.* Sir Jeremiah LeRoy, Kt.

Harman, Sir John Andrew, Kt.

Harmsworth, Sir Hildebrand Harold, Bt. (1922)

Harper, Sir Ewan William, Kt. CBE

Harper, *Prof.* Sir Peter Stanley, Kt., CBE

†Harris, Sir Christopher John Ashford, Bt. (1932)

Harris, *Prof.* Sir Henry, Kt., FRCP, FRCPATH, FRS

Harris, *Air Marshal* Sir John Hulme, KCB, CBE

Harris, *Prof.* Sir Martin Best, Kt., CBE

Harris, Sir Michael Frank, Kt.

Harris, Sir (Theodore) Wilson, Kt.

Harris, Sir Thomas George, KBE, CMG,

Harrison, *Prof.* Sir Brian Howard, Kt.

Harrison, Sir David, Kt., CBE, FRENG

Harrison, *Hon.* Sir Michael Guy Vicat, Kt.

Harrison, Sir Michael James Harwood, Bt. (1961)

Harrison, Sir (Robert) Colin, Bt. (1922)

Harrison, Sir Terence, Kt., FRENG

Harrop, Sir Peter John, KCB

Hart, *Hon.* Sir Anthony Ronald, Kt.

Hart, Sir David Michael, Kt., OBE

Hart, Sir Graham Allan, KCB

Hartwell, Sir (Francis) Anthony Charles Peter, Bt. (1805)

Harvey, Sir Charles Richard Musgrave, Bt. (1933)

Harvie, Sir John Smith, Kt., CBE

Harvie-Watt, Sir James, Bt. (1945)

Harwood, Sir Ronald, Kt., CBE

Haselhurst, *Rt. Hon.* Sir Alan Gordon Barraclough, Kt.

Haskard, Sir Cosmo Dugal Patrick Thomas, KCMG, MBE

Hastie, *Cdre* Sir Robert Cameron, KCVO, CBE, RD

Hastings, Sir Max Macdonald, Kt.

Hastings, *Dr* Sir William George, Kt., CBE

Hatter, Sir Maurice, Kt.

Havelock-Allan, Sir (Anthony) Mark David, Bt. (1858)

Hawkes, Sir John Garry, Kt., CBE

Hawkhead, Sir Anthony Gerard, Kt., CBE

Hawkins, Sir Richard Caesar, Bt. (1778)

†Hawley, Sir Henry Nicholas, Bt. (1795)

Hawley, Sir James Appleton, KCVO, TD

Haworth, Sir Philip, Bt. (1911)

Hawthorne, *Prof.* Sir William Rede, Kt., CBE, SCD, FRS, FRENG

Hay, Sir David Russell, Kt., CBE, FRCP, MD

Hay, Sir John Erroll Audley, Bt. (S. 1663)

†Hay, Sir Ronald Frederick Hamilton, Bt. (S. 1703)

Hayes, Sir Brian, Kt., CBE, QPM

Hayes, Sir Brian David, GCB

Hayman-Joyce, *Lt.-Gen.* Sir Robert John, KCB, CBE

Hayter, Sir Paul David Grenville, KCB, LVO

Hayward, Sir Jack Arnold, Kt., OBE

Head, Sir Richard Douglas Somerville, Bt. (1838)

Heap, Sir Peter William, KCMG

Heap, *Prof.* Sir Robert Brian, Kt., CBE, FRS

Hearne, Sir Graham James, Kt., CBE

Heathcote, *Brig.* Sir Gilbert Simon, Bt. (1733), CBE

†Heathcote, Sir Timothy Gilbert, Bt. (1733)

Heatley, Sir Peter, Kt., CBE

Hedley, *Hon.* Sir Mark, Kt.

Hegarty, Sir John Kevin, Kt.

Heiser, Sir Terence Michael, GCB

Henderson, Sir Denys Hartley, Kt.

Henderson, *Hon.* Sir Launcelot Dinadan James, Kt.

Henderson, *Maj.* Sir Richard Yates, KCVO

Hendry, *Prof.* Sir David Forbes, Kt.

Hennessy, Sir James Patrick Ivan, KBE, CMG

†Henniker, Sir Adrian Chandos, Bt. (1813)

Henniker-Heaton, Sir Yvo Robert, Bt. (1912)

Henriques, *Hon.* Sir Richard Henry Quixano, Kt.

Henry, *Hon.* Sir Geoffrey Arama, KBE

†Henry, Sir Patrick Denis, Bt. (1923)

Henshaw, Sir David George, Kt.

Hepple, *Prof.* Sir Bob Alexander, Kt.

Herbecq, Sir John Edward, KCB

Herbert, *Adm.* Sir Peter Geoffrey Marshall, KCB, OBE

Heron, Sir Conrad Frederick, KCB, OBE

Heron, Sir Michael Gilbert, Kt.

Heron-Maxwell, Sir Nigel Mellor, Bt. (S. 1683)

Hervey, Sir Roger Blaise Ramsay, KCVO, CMG

Hervey-Bathurst, Sir Frederick John Charles Gordon, Bt. (1818)

Heseltine, *Rt. Hon.* Sir William Frederick Payne, GCB, GCVO

Hewetson, Sir Christopher Raynor, Kt., TD

Hewett, Sir Richard Mark John, Bt. (1813)

Hewitt, Sir (Cyrus) Lenox (Simson), Kt., OBE

Hewitt, Sir Nicholas Charles Joseph, Bt. (1921)

Heygate, Sir Richard John Gage, Bt. (1831)

Heywood, Sir Peter, Bt. (1838)

Hickinbottom, *Hon.* Sir Gary Robert, Kt.

Hickman, Sir (Richard) Glenn, Bt. (1903)

Hicks, Sir Robert, Kt.

Hidden, *Hon.* Sir Anthony Brian, Kt.

Hielscher, Sir Leo Arthur, Kt.

Higgins, Sir Hartmann, Kt.

Higgins, *Rt. Hon.* Sir Malachy Joseph, Kt.

Higginson, Sir Gordon Robert, Kt., PHD, FRENG

Hill, Sir Arthur Alfred, Kt., CBE

Hill, Sir Brian John, Kt.

Hill, Sir James Frederick, Bt. (1917)

Hill, Sir John Alfred Rowley, Bt. (I. 1779)

Hill, *Vice-Adm.* Sir Robert Charles Finch, KBE, FRENG

Hill-Norton, *Vice-Adm. Hon.* Sir Nicholas John, KCB

Hill-Wood, Sir Samuel Thomas, Bt. (1921)

Hillhouse, Sir (Robert) Russell, KCB

Hills, Sir Graham John, Kt.

Hine, *Air Chief Marshal* Sir Patrick Bardon, GCB, GBE

Hirsch, *Prof.* Sir Peter Bernhard, Kt., PHD., FRS

Hirst, *Rt. Hon.* Sir David Cozens-Hardy, Kt.

Hirst, Sir Michael William, Kt.

Hoare, *Prof.* Sir Charles Anthony Richard, Kt., FRS

Hoare, Sir David John, Bt. (1786)

Hoare, Sir Charles James, Bt. (I. 1784)

Hobart, Sir John Vere, Bt. (1914)

Hobbs, *Maj.-Gen.* Sir Michael Frederick, KCVO, CBE

Hobday, Sir Gordon Ivan, Kt.

Hobhouse, Sir Charles John Spinney, Bt. (1812)

Hobson, Sir Ronald, KCVO

†Hodge, Sir Andrew Rowland, Bt. (1921)

Hodge, Sir James William, KCVO, CMG

Hodgkin, Sir (Gordon) Howard (Eliot), Kt., CH, CBE

Hodgkinson, Sir Michael Stewart, Kt.

Hodgson, Sir Maurice Arthur Eric, Kt., FRENG

Hodson, Sir Michael Robin Adderley, Bt. (I. 1789)

Hogg, Sir Christopher Anthony, Kt.

†Hogg, Sir Piers Michael James, Bt. (1846)

†Holcroft, Sir Charles Anthony Culcheth, Bt. (1921)

Holderness, Sir Martin William, Bt. (1920)

Holden, Sir Paul, Bt. (1893)

Holden, Sir John David, Bt. (1919)

Holden-Brown, Sir Derrick, Kt.

Holder, Sir John Henry, Bt. (1898)

Holdgate, Sir Martin Wyatt, Kt., CB, PHD

Holland, *Hon.* Sir Alan Douglas, Kt.

Holland, *Hon.* Sir Christopher John, Kt.

Holland, Sir Geoffrey, KCB

Holland, Sir John Anthony, Kt.

Holliday, *Prof.* Sir Frederick George Thomas, Kt., CBE, FRSE

Hollom, Sir Jasper Quintus, KBE

Holloway, *Hon.* Sir Barry Blyth, KBE

Holm, Sir Ian (Holm Cuthbert), Kt., CBE

Holman, *Hon.* Sir (Edward) James, Kt.

Holman, *Prof.* Sir John Stranger, Kt.

Holmes, *Prof.* Sir Frank Wakefield, Kt.

Holmes, Sir John Eaton, GCVO, KBE, CMG

Holroyd, *Air Marshal* Sir Frank Martyn, KBE, CB

Holroyd, Sir Michael De Courcy Fraser, Kt., CBE

Holroyde, *Hon.* Sir Timothy Victor, Kt.

Holt, *Prof.* Sir James Clarke, Kt.

Holt, Sir Michael, Kt., CBE

Home, Sir William Dundas, Bt. (S. 1671)

Honywood, Sir Filmer Courtenay William, Bt. (1660)

†Hood, Sir John Joseph Harold, Bt. (1922)

Hookway, Sir Harry Thurston, Kt.

Hooper, *Rt. Hon.* Sir Anthony, Kt.

Hope, Sir Colin Frederick Newton, Kt.

Hope, Sir Alexander Archibald Douglas, Bt. (S. 1628)

Hope-Dunbar, Sir David, Bt. (S. 1664)

Hopkin, *Prof.* Sir Deian Rhys, Kt.

Hopkin, Sir Royston Oliver, KCMG

Hopkins, Sir Anthony Philip, Kt., CBE

Hopkins, Sir Michael John, Kt., CBE, RA, RIBA

Hopwood, *Prof.* Sir David Alan, Kt., FRS

Hordern, *Rt. Hon.* Sir Peter Maudslay, Kt.

Horlick, *Vice-Adm.* Sir Edwin John, KBE, FRENG

Horlick, Sir James Cunliffe William, Bt. (1914)

Horlock, *Prof.* Sir John Harold, Kt., FRS, FRENG

Horn, *Prof.* Sir Gabriel, Kt., FRS

Horn-Smith, Sir Julian Michael, Kt.

Hornby, Sir Derek Peter, Kt.

Horne, Sir Alan Gray Antony, Bt. (1929)

Horne, *Dr* Sir Alistair Allan, Kt. CBE

Horsbrugh-Porter, Sir John Simon, Bt. (1902)

Horsfall, Sir Edward John Wright, Bt. (1909)

Hort, Sir Andrew Edwin Fenton, Bt. (1767)

Horton, Sir Robert Baynes, Kt.

Hosker, Sir Gerald Albery, KCB, QC

Hoskins, *Prof.* Sir Brian John, Kt. CBE, FRS

†Hoskyns, Sir Edwyn Wren, Bt. (1676)

Hoskyns, Sir John Austin Hungerford Leigh, Kt.

Hotung, Sir Joseph Edward, Kt.

Houghton, *Gen.* Sir John Nicholas Reynolds, GCB, CBE

Houghton, Sir John Theodore, Kt., CBE, FRS

Houldsworth, Sir Richard Thomas Reginald, Bt. (1887)

Hourston, Sir Gordon Minto, Kt.

Housden, Sir Peter James, KCB

House, *Lt.-Gen.* Sir David George, GCB, KCVO, CBE, MC

Houssemayne du Boulay, Sir Roger William, KCVO, CMG

Houstoun-Boswall, Sir (Thomas) Alford, Bt. (1836)

Howard, Sir David Howarth Seymour, Bt. (1955)

Howard, *Prof.* Sir Michael Eliot, Kt., OM, CH, CBE, MC

Howard-Lawson, Sir John Philip, Bt. (1841)

Howells, Sir Eric Waldo Benjamin, Kt., CBE

Howes, Sir Christopher Kingston, KCVO, CB

Howlett, *Gen.* Sir Geoffrey Hugh Whitby, KBE, MC

Hoy, Sir Christopher Andrew, Kt., MBE

Hugh-Jones, Sir Wynn Normington, Kt., LVO

Hugh-Smith, Sir Andrew Colin, Kt.

Hughes, *Rt. Hon.* Sir Anthony Philip Gilson, Kt.

Hughes, Sir Thomas Collingwood, Bt. (1773)

Hughes, Sir Trevor Poulton, KCB

†Hughes-Morgan, Sir (Ian) Parry David, Bt. (1925)

Hull, *Prof.* Sir David, Kt.

Hulse, Sir Edward Jeremy Westrow, Bt. (1739)

Hum, Sir Christopher Owen, KCMG

Humphreys, *Prof.* Sir Colin John, Kt., CBE

Hunt, Sir John Leonard, Kt.

Hunt, *Adm.* Sir Nicholas John Streynsham, GCB, LVO

Hunt, Sir Rex Masterman, Kt., CMG

Hunt, *Dr* Sir Richard Timothy, Kt.

Hunt-Davis, *Brig.* Sir Miles Garth, GCVO, CBE

Hunter, Sir Alistair John, KCMG

Hunter, *Prof.* Sir Laurence Colvin, Kt., CBE, FRSE

Hunter, *Dr* Sir Philip John, Kt., CBE

Hunter, Sir Thomas Blane, Kt.

Huntington-Whiteley, Sir Hugo Baldwin, Bt. (1918)

Hurn, Sir (Francis) Roger, Kt.

Hurst, Sir Geoffrey Charles, Kt., MBE

Husbands, Sir Clifford Straugh, GCMG

Hutchison, *Rt. Hon.* Sir Michael, Kt.

†Hutchison, Sir Peter Craft, CBE, Bt. (1956)

Hutchison, Sir Robert, Bt. (1939)

Hutt, Sir Dexter Walter, Kt.

Huxley, *Prof.* Sir Andrew Fielding, Kt., OM, FRS

Huxtable, *Gen.* Sir Charles Richard, KCB, CBE

Hytner, Sir Nicholas, Kt.

Ibbotson, *Vice-Adm.* Sir Richard Jeffrey, KBE, CB, DSC

Ibbs, Sir (John) Robin, KBE

Imbert-Terry, Sir Michael Edward Stanley, Bt. (1917)

Imray, Sir Colin Henry, KBE, CMG

Ingham, Sir Bernard, Kt.

Ingilby, Sir Thomas Colvin William, Bt. (1866)

Inglis, Sir Brian Scott, Kt.

Inglis of Glencorse, Sir Roderick John, Bt. (S. 1703)

Ingram, Sir James Herbert Charles, Bt. (1893)

Ingram, Sir John Henderson, Kt., CBE

Inkin, Sir Geoffrey David, Kt., OBE

†Innes, Sir Alastair Charles Deverell, Bt. (NS 1686)

Innes of Edingight, Sir Malcolm Rognvald, KCVO

Innes, Sir Peter Alexander Berowald, Bt. (S. 1628)

Insall, Sir Donald William, Kt., CBE

Irvine, Sir Donald Hamilton, Kt., CBE, MD, FRCGP

Irving, *Prof.* Sir Miles Horsfall, Kt., MD, FRCS, FRCSE

Irwin, *Lt.-Gen.* Sir Alistair Stuart Hastings, KCB, CBE

Irwin, *Hon.* Sir Stephen John, Kt.

Isaacs, Sir Jeremy Israel, Kt.

†Isham, Sir Norman Murray Crawford, Bt., OBE (1627)

Italeli, *HE* Sir Iakoba Taeia, GCMG

Ivory, Sir Brian Gammell, Kt., CBE

Jack, *Hon.* Sir Alieu Sulayman, Kt.

Jack, Sir David, Kt., CBE, FRS, FRSE

Jack, Sir Malcolm Roy, KCB

Jack, *Hon.* Sir Raymond Evan, Kt.

Jackling, Sir Roger Tustin, KCB, CBE

Jackson, Sir Barry Trevor, Kt.

Jackson, Sir Kenneth Joseph, Kt.

Jackson, *Gen.* Sir Michael David, GCB, CBE

Jackson, Sir Michael Roland, Bt. (1902)

†Jackson, Sir Neil Keith, Bt. (1815)

Jackson, Sir Nicholas Fane St George, Bt. (1913)

Jackson, *Hon.* Sir Peter Arthur Brian, Kt.

Jackson, *Rt. Hon.* Sir Rupert Matthew, Kt.

Jackson, Sir (William) Roland Cedric, Bt. (1869)

Jacob, *Rt. Hon.* Sir Robert Raphael Hayim (Robin), Kt.

Jacobi, Sir Derek George, Kt., CBE

Jacobs, Sir Cecil Albert, Kt., CBE

Jacobs, *Rt. Hon.* Sir Francis Geoffrey, KCMG, QC

Jacobs, *Hon.* Sir Kenneth Sydney, KBE

Jacomb, Sir Martin Wakefield, Kt.

Jaffray, Sir William Otho, Bt. (1892)

Jagger, Sir Michael Philip, Kt.

James, Sir Cynlais Morgan, KCMG

James, Sir Jeffrey Russell, KBE

James, Sir John Nigel Courtenay, KCVO, CBE

Jamieson, *Air Marshal* Sir David Ewan, KBE, CB

Jardine of Applegirth, Sir William Murray, Bt. (S. 1672)

Jardine, Sir Andrew Colin Douglas, Bt. (1916)

Jarman, *Prof.* Sir Brian, Kt., OBE

Jarratt, Sir Alexander Anthony, Kt., CB

Jawara, *Hon.* Sir Dawda Kairaba, Kt.

Jay, Sir Antony Rupert, Kt., CVO

Jeewoolall, Sir Ramesh, Kt.

Jefferson, Sir George Rowland, Kt., CBE, FRENG

Jeffrey, Sir William Alexander, KCB

Jeffreys, *Prof.* Sir Alec John, Kt., FRS

Jeffries, *Hon.* Sir John Francis, Kt.

Jehangir, Sir Cowasji, Bt. (1908)

†Jejeebhoy, Sir Jehangir, Bt. (1857)

Jenkins, Sir Brian Garton, GBE
Jenkins, Sir Elgar Spencer, Kt., OBE
Jenkins, Sir James Christopher, KCB, QC
Jenkins, Sir John, KCMG, LVO
Jenkins, Sir Michael Nicholas Howard, Kt., OBE
Jenkins, Sir Michael Romilly Heald, KCMG
Jenkins, Sir Simon, Kt.
Jenkinson, Sir John Banks, Bt. (1661)
Jenks, Sir (Richard) Peter, Bt. (1932)
Jenner, *Air Marshal* Sir Timothy Ivo, KCB
Jennings, Sir John Southwood, Kt., CBE, FRSE
Jennings, Sir Peter Neville Wake, Kt., CVO
Jephcott, Sir Neil Welbourn, Bt. (1962)
Jessel, Sir Charles John, Bt. (1883)
Jewkes, Sir Gordon Wesley, KCMG
Job, Sir Peter James Denton, Kt.
John, Sir David Glyndwr, KCMG
John, Sir Elton Hercules (Reginald Kenneth Dwight), Kt., CBE
Johns, *Vice-Adm.* Sir Adrian James, KCB, CBE, ADC
Johns, *Air Chief Marshal* Sir Richard Edward, GCB, KCVO, CBE
Johnson, Sir Colpoys Guy, Bt. (1755)
Johnson, *Gen.* Sir Garry Dene, KCB, OBE, MC
Johnson, Sir John Rodney, KCMG
†Johnson, Sir Patrick Eliot, Bt. (1818)
Johnson, *Hon.* Sir Robert Lionel, Kt.
Johnson-Ferguson, Sir Ian Edward, Bt. (1906)
Johnston, *Lt.-Gen.* Sir Maurice Robert, KCB, CVO, OBE
Johnston, Sir Thomas Alexander, Bt. (S. 1626)
Johnston, Sir William Ian Ridley, Kt., CBE, QPM
Johnstone, Sir Geoffrey Adams Dinwiddie, KCMG
Johnstone, Sir (George) Richard Douglas, Bt. (S. 1700)
Johnstone, Sir (John) Raymond, Kt., CBE
Jolliffe, Sir Anthony Stuart, GBE
Jolly, Sir Arthur Richard, KCMG
Jonas, Sir John Peter, Kt., CBE
Jones, Sir Alan Jeffrey, Kt.
Jones, Sir David Charles, Kt., CBE
Jones, Sir Harry George, Kt., CBE
Jones, Sir John Francis, Kt.
Jones, Sir Keith Stephen, Kt.
Jones, Sir Kenneth Lloyd, Kt., QPM
Jones, Sir Lyndon, Kt.
Jones, Sir Mark Ellis Powell, Kt.
Jones, Sir (Owen) Trevor, Kt.
Jones, Sir Richard Anthony Lloyd, KCB
Jones, Sir Robert Edward, Kt.
Jones, Sir Roger Spencer, Kt., OBE
Jones, Sir Simon Warley Frederick Benton, Bt. (1919)
†Joseph, *Hon.* Sir James Samuel, Bt. (1943)

Jowell, *Prof.* Sir Jeffrey Lionel, KCMG, QC
Jowell, *Prof.* Sir Roger Mark, Kt. CBE
Jowitt, *Hon.* Sir Edwin Frank, Kt.
Judge, Sir Paul Rupert, Kt.
Jugnauth, *Rt. Hon.* Sir Aneerood, KCMG
Jungius, *Vice-Adm.* Sir James George, KBE
Kaberry, *Hon.* Sir Christopher Donald, Bt. (1960)
Kabui, Sir Frank Utu Ofagioro, GCMG, OBE
Kadoorie, *Hon.* Sir Michael David, Kt.
Kakaraya, Sir Pato, KBE
Kamit, Sir Leonard Wilson, Kt., CBE
Kan Yuet-Keung, Sir, GBE
Kao, *Prof.* Sir Charles Kuen, KBE
Kaputin, Sir John Rumet, KBE, CMG
Kaufman, *Rt. Hon.* Sir Gerald Bernard, Kt.
Kavali, Sir Thomas, Kt., OBE
Kay, *Rt. Hon.* Sir Maurice Ralph, Kt.
Kaye, Sir Paul Henry Gordon, Bt. (1923)
†Keane, Sir John Charles, Bt. (1801)
Kearney, *Hon.* Sir William John Francis, Kt., CBE
Keegan, Sir John Desmond Patrick, Kt., OBE
Keene, *Rt. Hon.* Sir David Wolfe, Kt.
Keith, *Hon.* Sir Brian Richard, Kt.
Keith, *Prof.* Sir James, KBE
†Kellett, Sir Stanley Charles, Bt. (1801)
Kelly, Sir Christopher William, KCB
Kelly, Sir David Robert Corbett, Kt., CBE
Kemakeza, Sir Allan, Kt.
Kemball, *Air Marshal* Sir (Richard) John, KCB, CBE
Kemp-Welch, Sir John, Kt.
Kenilorea, *Rt. Hon.* Sir Peter, KBE
Kennaway, Sir John Lawrence, Bt. (1791)
Kennedy, Sir Francis, KCMG, CBE
Kennedy, *Hon.* Sir Ian Alexander, Kt.
Kennedy, *Prof.* Sir Ian McColl, Kt.
†Kennedy, Sir Michael Edward, Bt. (1836)
Kennedy, *Rt. Hon.* Sir Paul Joseph Morrow, Kt.
Kennedy, *Air Chief Marshal* Sir Thomas Lawrie, GCB, AFC
Kenny, Sir Anthony John Patrick, Kt., DPHIL, DLITT, FBA
Kenny, *Gen.* Sir Brian Leslie Graham, GCB, CBE
Kentridge, Sir Sydney Woolf, KCMG, QC
Kenyon, Sir Nicholas Roger, Kt., CBE
Keogh, *Prof.* Sir Bruce Edward, KBE
Kerr, *Adm.* Sir John Beverley, GCB
Kerr, Sir Ronald James, Kt., CB

Kerry, Sir Michael James, KCB, QC
Kershaw, *Prof.* Sir Ian, Kt.
Kerslake, Sir Robert Walker, Kt.
Keswick, Sir Henry Neville Lindley, Kt.
Keswick, Sir John Chippendale Lindley, Kt.
Kevau, *Prof.* Sir Isi Henao, Kt., CBE
Kikau, *Ratu* Sir Jone Latianara, KBE
Kimber, Sir Timothy Roy Henry, Bt. (1904)
King, *Prof.* Sir David Anthony, Kt., FRS
King, Sir John Christopher, Bt. (1888)
King, *Prof.* Sir Mervyn Allister, GBE
King, *Vice-Adm.* Sir Norman Ross Dutton, KBE
King, *Hon.* Sir Timothy Roger Alan, Kt.
King, Sir Wayne Alexander, Bt. (1815)
Kingman, *Prof.* Sir John Frank Charles, Kt., FRS
Kingsland, Sir Richard, Kt., CBE, DFC
Kingsley, Sir Ben, Kt.
Kinloch, Sir David, Bt. (S. 1686)
Kinloch, Sir David Oliphant, Bt. (1873)
Kipalan, Sir Albert, Kt.
Kirkpatrick, Sir Ivone Elliott, Bt. (S. 1685)
Kirkwood, *Hon.* Sir Andrew Tristram Hammett, Kt.
Kiszely, *Lt.-Gen.* Sir John Panton, KCB, MC
Kitchin, *Hon.* Sir David James Tyson, Kt.
Kitson, *Gen.* Sir Frank Edward, GBE, KCB, MC
Kitson, Sir Timothy Peter Geoffrey, Kt.
Kleinwort, Sir Richard Drake, Bt. (1909)
Klug, Sir Aaron, Kt., OM
Knight, Sir Harold Murray, KBE, DSC
Knight, Sir Kenneth John, Kt., CBE, QFSM
Knight, *Air Chief Marshal* Sir Michael William Patrick, KCB, AFC
Knight, *Prof.* Sir Peter, Kt.
Knill, Sir Thomas John Pugin Bartholomew, Bt. (1893)
Knowles, Sir Charles Francis, Bt. (1765)
Knowles, Sir Durward Randolph, Kt., OBE
Knowles, Sir Nigel Graham, Kt.
Knox, Sir David Laidlaw, Kt.
Knox, *Hon.* Sir John Leonard, Kt.
Knox-Johnston, Sir William Robert Patrick (Sir Robin), Kt., CBE, RD
Kohn, *Dr* Sir Ralph, Kt., FRS
Koraea, Sir Thomas, Kt.
Kornberg, *Prof.* Sir Hans Leo, Kt., DSC, SCD, PHD, FRS
Korowi, Sir Wiwa, GCMG

Kroto, *Prof.* Sir Harold Walter, Kt., FRS

Kulukundis, Sir Elias George (Eddie), Kt., OBE

Kurongku, *Most Revd* Peter, KBE

Kwok-Po Li, *Dr* Sir David, Kt., OBE

Lachmann, *Prof.* Sir Peter Julius, Kt.

Lacon, Sir Edmund Vere, Bt. (1818)

Lacy, Sir Patrick Brian Finucane, Bt. (1921)

Laing, Sir (John) Martin (Kirby), Kt., CBE

Laird, Sir Gavin Harry, Kt., CBE

Lake, Sir (Atwell) Graham, Bt. (1711)

Lakin, Sir Michael, Bt. (1909)

Lamb, Sir Albert Thomas, KBE, CMG, DFC

Lamb, *Lt.-Gen.* Sir Graeme Cameron Maxwell, KBE, CMG, DSO

Lambert, Sir John Henry, KCVO, CMG

†Lambert, Sir Peter John Biddulph, Bt. (1711)

Lambert, Sir Richard Peter, Kt.

Lampl, Sir Peter, Kt., OBE

Lamport, Sir Stephen Mark Jeffrey, KCVO

Landale, Sir David William Neil, KCVO

Landau, Sir Dennis Marcus, Kt.

Lander, Sir Stephen James, KCB

Lane, Prof. Sir David Philip, Kt.

Langham, Sir John Stephen, Bt. (1660)

Langlands, Sir Robert Alan, Kt.

Langley, *Hon.* Sir Gordon Julian Hugh, Kt.

Langrishe, Sir James Hercules, Bt. (I. 1777)

Langstaff, *Hon.* Sir Brian Frederick James, Kt.

Lankester, Sir Timothy Patrick, KCB

Lapli, Sir John Ini, GCMG

Lapthorne, Sir Richard Douglas, Kt., CBE

Large, Sir Andrew McLeod Brooks, Kt.

Latasi, *Rt. Hon.* Sir Kamuta, KCMG, OBE

Latham, *Rt. Hon.* Sir David Nicholas Ramsey, Kt.

Latham, Sir Michael Anthony, Kt.

Latham, Sir Richard Thomas Paul, Bt. (1919)

Latimer, Sir Graham Stanley, KBE

Latour-Adrien, *Hon.* Sir Maurice, Kt.

Laughton, Sir Anthony Seymour, Kt.

Laurence, *Vice-Adm.* Sir Timothy James Hamilton, KCVO, CB, ADC

Laurie, Sir Robert Bayley Emilius, Bt. (1834)

Lauterpacht, Sir Elihu, Kt., CBE, QC

Lauti, *Rt. Hon.* Sir Toaripi, GCMG

Lawler, Sir Peter James, Kt., OBE

Lawrence, Sir Clive Wyndham, Bt. (1906)

Lawrence, Sir Edmund Wickham, KCMG, OBE

Lawrence, Sir Henry Peter, Bt. (1858)

Lawrence, Sir Ivan John, Kt., QC

Lawrence, Sir John Patrick Grosvenor, Kt., CBE

Lawrence, Sir William Fettiplace, Bt. (1867)

Lawrence-Jones, Sir Christopher, Bt. (1831)

Laws, *Rt. Hon.* Sir John Grant McKenzie, Kt.

Laws, Sir Stephen Charles, KCB

Lawson, Sir Charles John Patrick, Bt. (1900)

Lawson, *Gen.* Sir Richard George, KCB, DSO, OBE

†Lawson-Tancred, Sir Andrew Peter, Bt. (1662)

Lawton, *Prof.* Sir John Hartley, Kt., CBE, FRS

Layard, *Adm.* Sir Michael Henry Gordon, KCB, CBE

Lea, *Vice-Adm.* Sir John Stuart Crosbie, KBE

Lea, Sir Thomas William, Bt. (1892)

Leahy, Sir Daniel Joseph, Kt.

Leahy, Sir John Henry Gladstone, KCMG

Leahy, Sir Terence Patrick, Kt.

Learmont, *Gen.* Sir John Hartley, KCB, CBE

Leaver, Sir Christopher, GBE

Le Cheminant, *Air Chief Marshal* Sir Peter de Lacey, GBE, KCB, DFC

†Lechmere, Sir Nicholas Anthony Hungerford, Bt. (1818)

Ledger, Sir Philip Stevens, Kt., CBE, FRSE

Lee, Sir Christopher Frank Carandini, Kt., CBE

Lee, Sir Quo-wei, Kt., CBE

†Leeds, Sir John Charles Hildyard, Bt. (1812)

Lees, Sir David Bryan, Kt.

Lees, Sir Thomas Edward, Bt. (1897)

Lees, Sir Thomas Harcourt Ivor, Bt. (1804)

Lees, Sir (William) Antony Clare, Bt. (1937)

Leese, Sir Richard Charles, Kt., CBE

le Fleming, Sir David Kelland, Bt. (1705)

Legard, Sir Charles Thomas, Bt. (1660)

Legg, Sir Thomas Stuart, KCB, QC

Leggatt, *Rt. Hon.* Sir Andrew Peter, Kt.

Leggatt, Sir Hugh Frank John, Kt.

Leggett, *Prof.* Sir Anthony James, KBE

Leigh, Sir Geoffrey Norman, Kt.

Leigh, Sir Richard Henry, Bt. (1918)

Leighton, Sir Michael John Bryan, Bt. (1693)

Leith-Buchanan, Sir Gordon Kelly McNicol, Bt. (1775)

Le Marchant, Sir Francis Arthur, Bt. (1841)

Lennox-Boyd, The Hon. Sir Mark Alexander, Kt.

Leon, Sir John Ronald, Bt. (1911)

Lepping, Sir George Geria Dennis, GCMG, MBE

Le Quesne, Sir (John) Godfray, Kt., QC

Leslie, Sir John Norman Ide, Bt. (1876)

Lester, Sir James Theodore, Kt.

Lethbridge, Sir Thomas Periam Hector Noel, Bt. (1804)

Lever, Sir Jeremy Frederick, KCMG, QC

Lever, Sir Paul, KCMG

Lever, Sir (Tresham) Christopher Arthur Lindsay, Bt. (1911)

Leveson, *Rt. Hon.* Sir Brian Henry, Kt.

Levi, Sir Wasangula Noel, Kt., CBE

Levine, Sir Montague Bernard, Kt.

Levinge, Sir Richard George Robin, Bt. (I. 1704)

Lewinton, Sir Christopher, Kt.

Lewis, Sir David Thomas Rowell, Kt.

Lewis, Sir John Anthony, Kt., OBE

Lewis, Sir Lawrence Vernon Harcourt, KCMG, GCM

Lewis, Sir Leigh Warren, KCB

Lewis, Sir Terence Murray, Kt., OBE, GM, QPM

Lewison, *Hon.* Sir Kim Martin Jordan, Kt.

Ley, Sir Ian Francis, Bt. (1905)

Li, Sir Ka-Shing, KBE

Lickiss, Sir Michael Gillam, Kt.

Liddington, Sir Bruce, Kt.

Lightman, *Hon.* Sir Gavin Anthony, Kt.

Lighton, Sir Thomas Hamilton, Bt. (I. 1791)

Likierman, *Prof.* Sir John Andrew, Kt.

Lilleyman, *Prof.* Sir John Stuart, Kt.

Limon, Sir Donald William, KCB

Linacre, Sir (John) Gordon (Seymour), Kt., CBE, AFC, DFM

Lindblom, *Hon.* Sir Keith John, Kt.

Lindop, Sir Norman, Kt.

Lindsay, *Hon.* Sir John Edmund Frederic, Kt.

†Lindsay, Sir James Martin Evelyn, Bt. (1962)

†Lindsay-Hogg, Sir Michael Edward, Bt. (1905)

Lipton, Sir Stuart Anthony, Kt.

Lipworth, Sir (Maurice) Sydney, Kt.

Lister, Sir Edward Julian, Kt.

Lister-Kaye, Sir John Phillip Lister, Bt. (1812)

Lithgow, Sir William James, Bt. (1925)

Little, *Most Revd* Thomas Francis, KBE

Llewellyn, Sir Roderic Victor, Bt. (1922)

Llewellyn-Smith, *Prof.* Sir Christopher Hubert, Kt.

Lloyd, *Prof.* Sir Geoffrey Ernest Richard, Kt., FBA

Lloyd, Sir Nicholas Markley, Kt.

Lloyd, *Rt. Hon.* Sir Peter Robert Cable, Kt.

Lloyd, Sir Richard Ernest Butler, Bt. (1960)

Lloyd, *Hon.* Sir Timothy Andrew Wigram, Kt.

Lloyd-Edwards, *Capt.* Sir Norman, KCVO, RD

Lloyd Jones, Sir David, Kt.

Loader, Air Marshal Sir Clive Robert, KCB, OBE

Lobo, Sir Rogerio Hyndman, Kt., CBE

Lockhead, Sir Moir, Kt., OBE

†Loder, Sir Edmund Jeune, Bt. (1887)

Logan, Sir David Brian Carleton, KCMG

Lokoloko, Sir Tore, GCMG, GCVO, OBE

Longmore, *Rt. Hon.* Sir Andrew Centlivres, Kt.

Lorimer, Sir (Thomas) Desmond, Kt.

Los, *Hon.* Sir Kubulan, Kt., CBE

Loughran, Sir Gerald Finbar, KCB

Lovell, Sir (Alfred Charles) Bernard, Kt., OBE, FRS

Lovelock, Sir Douglas Arthur, KCB

Lovill, Sir John Roger, Kt., CBE

Lowa, *Rt. Revd* Sir Samson, KBE

Lowe, *Air Chief Marshal* Sir Douglas Charles, GCB, DFC, AFC

Lowe, Sir Frank Budge, Kt.

Lowe, Sir Thomas William Gordon, Bt. (1918)

Lowson, Sir Ian Patrick, Bt. (1951)

Lowther, *Col.* Sir Charles Douglas, Bt. (1824)

Loyd, Sir Julian St John, KCVO

Lu, Sir Tseng Chi, Kt.

Lucas, *Prof.* Sir Colin Renshaw, Kt.

Lucas, Sir Thomas Edward, Bt. (1887)

Lucas-Tooth, Sir (Hugh) John, Bt. (1920)

Lumsden, Sir David James, Kt.

Lushington, Sir John Richard Castleman, Bt. (1791)

Lyall Grant, Sir Mark Justin, KCMG

Lygo, *Adm.* Sir Raymond Derek, KCB

Lyle, Sir Gavin Archibald, Bt. (1929)

Lynch-Blosse, *Capt.* Sir Richard Hely, Bt. (1622)

Lynch-Robinson, Sir Dominick Christopher, Bt. (1920)

Lyne, *Rt. Hon.* Sir Roderic Michael John, KBE, CMG

Lyons, Sir John, Kt.

Lyons, Sir Michael Thomas, Kt.

McAllister, Sir Ian Gerald, Kt., CBE

McAlpine, Sir William Hepburn, Bt. (1918)

Macara, Sir Alexander Wiseman, Kt., FRCP, FRCGP

McCaffrey, Sir Thomas Daniel, Kt.

McCallum, Sir Donald Murdo, Kt., CBE, FRENG

McCamley, Sir Graham Edward, KBE

McCarthy, Sir Callum, Kt.

McCartney, *Rt. Hon.* Sir Ian, Kt.

McCartney, Sir (James) Paul, Kt., MBE

Macartney, Sir John Ralph, Bt. (I. 1799)

McClement, *Vice-Admiral* Sir Timothy Pentreath, KCB, OBE

McClintock, Sir Eric Paul, Kt.

McCloskey, *Hon.* Sir John Bernard, Kt.

McColl, Sir Colin Hugh Verel, KCMG

McColl, *Gen.* Sir John Chalmers, KCB, CBE, DSO

McCollum, *Rt. Hon.* Sir William, Kt.

McCombe, *Hon.* Sir Richard George Bramwell, Kt.

McConnell, Sir Robert Shean, Bt. (1900)

MacCormac, Sir Richard Cornelius, Kt., CBE

†McCowan, Sir David William, Bt. (1934)

McCullough, *Hon.* Sir (Iain) Charles (Robert), Kt.

MacDermott, *Rt. Hon.* Sir John Clarke, Kt.

Macdonald, Sir Alasdair Uist, Kt., CBE

Macdonald, Sir Kenneth Carmichael, KCB

McDonald, Sir Trevor, Kt., OBE

Macdonald of Sleat, Sir Ian Godfrey Bosville, Bt. (S. 1625)

McDowell, Sir Eric Wallace, Kt., CBE

MacDuff, *Hon.* Sir Alistair Geoffrey, Kt.

Mace, *Lt.-Gen.* Sir John Airth, KBE, CB

McEwen, Sir John Roderick Hugh, Bt. (1953)

McFarland, Sir John Talbot, Bt. (1914)

MacFarlane, *Prof.* Sir Alistair George James, Kt., CBE, FRS

McFarlane, Sir Andrew Ewart, Kt.

Macfarlane, Sir (David) Neil, Kt.

McGeechan, Sir Ian Robert, Kt., OBE

McGrath, Sir Brian Henry, GCVO

Macgregor, Sir Ian Grant, Bt. (1828)

McGregor, Sir James David, Kt., OBE

MacGregor of MacGregor, Sir Malcolm Gregor Charles, Bt. (1795)

McGrigor, Sir James Angus Rhoderick Neil, Bt. (1831)

McIntosh, Sir Neil William David, Kt., CBE

McIntosh, Sir Ronald Robert Duncan, KCB

McIntyre, Sir Donald Conroy, Kt., CBE

McIntyre, Sir Meredith Alister, Kt.

Mackay, *Hon.* Sir Colin Crichton, Kt.

MacKay, *Prof.* Sir Donald Iain, Kt.

MacKay, Sir Francis Henry, Kt.

McKay, Sir Neil Stuart, Kt., CB

McKay, Sir William Robert, KCB

Mackay-Dick, *Maj.-Gen.* Sir Iain Charles, KCVO, MBE

Mackechnie, Sir Alistair John, Kt.

McKellen, Sir Ian Murray, Kt., CH, CBE

Mackenzie, Sir (James William) Guy, Bt. (1890)

Mackenzie, *Gen.* Sir Jeremy John George, GCB, OBE

†Mackenzie, Sir Peter Douglas, Bt. (S. 1673)

†Mackenzie, Sir Roderick McQuhae, Bt. (S. 1703)

Mackeson, Sir Rupert Henry, Bt. (1954)

McKillop, Sir Thomas Fulton Wilson, Kt.

McKinnon, *Rt. Hon.* Sir Donald Charles, GCVO

McKinnon, Sir James, Kt.

McKinnon, *Hon.* Sir Stuart Neil, Kt.

Mackintosh, Sir Cameron Anthony, Kt.

Mackworth, Sir Digby (John), Bt. (1776)

McLaughlin, Sir Richard, Kt.

Maclean of Dunconnell, Sir Charles Edward, Bt. (1957)

Maclean, Sir Lachlan Hector Charles, Bt. (NS 1631)

Maclean, Sir Murdo, Kt.

McLeod, Sir Charles Henry, Bt. (1925)

MacLeod, Sir (John) Maxwell Norman, Bt. (1924)

Macleod, Sir (Nathaniel William) Hamish, KBE

McLintock, Sir Michael William, Bt. (1934)

Maclure, Sir John Robert Spencer, Bt. (1898)

McMahon, Sir Brian Patrick, Bt. (1817)

McMahon, Sir Christopher William, Kt.

McMaster, Sir Brian John, Kt., CBE

McMichael, *Prof.* Sir Andrew James, Kt., FRS

MacMillan, *Lt.-Gen.* Sir John Richard Alexander, KCB, CBE

McMullin, *Rt. Hon.* Sir Duncan Wallace, Kt.

McMurtry, Sir David, Kt., CBE

Macnaghten, Sir Malcolm Francis, Bt. (1836)

McNair-Wilson, Sir Patrick Michael Ernest David, Kt.

McNamara, *Air Chief Marshal* Sir Neville Patrick, KBE

Macnaughton, *Prof.* Sir Malcolm Campbell, Kt.

McNee, Sir David Blackstock, Kt., QPM

McNulty, Sir (Robert William) Roy, Kt., CBE

MacPhail, Sir Bruce Dugald, Kt.

MacPherson, Sir Nicholas, KCB

Macpherson, Sir Ronald Thomas Steward (Tommy), CBE, MC, TD

Macpherson of Cluny, *Hon.* Sir William Alan, Kt., TD

McQuarrie, Sir Albert, Kt.

MacRae, Sir (Alastair) Christopher (Donald Summerhayes), KCMG

Macready, Sir Nevil John Wilfrid, Bt. (1923)

MacSween, *Prof.* Sir Roderick Norman McIver, Kt.

Mactaggart, Sir John Auld, Bt. (1938)

McWilliam, Sir Michael Douglas, KCMG

McWilliams, Sir Francis, GBE

Madden, Sir David Christopher Andrew, KCMG

†Madden, Sir Charles Jonathan, Bt. (1919)

Maddison, *Hon.* Sir David George, Kt.

Madejski, Sir John Robert, Kt., OBE

Madel, Sir (William) David, Kt.

Magee, Sir Ian Bernard Vaughan, Kt., CB

Magnus, Sir Laurence Henry Philip, Bt. (1917)

Mahon, Sir William Walter, Bt. (1819), LVO

Maiden, Sir Colin James, Kt., DPHIL

Maini, *Prof.* Sir Ravinder Nath, Kt.

Maino, Sir Charles, KBE

†Maitland, Sir Charles Alexander, Bt. (1818)

Major, *Rt. Hon.* Sir John, KG, CH

Malbon, *Vice-Adm.* Sir Fabian Michael, KBE

Malcolm, Sir James William Thomas Alexander, Bt. (S. 1665)

Malet, Sir Harry Douglas St Lo, Bt. (1791)

Mallaby, Sir Christopher Leslie George, GCMG, GCVO

Mallick, *Prof.* Sir Netar Prakash, Kt.

Mallinson, Sir William James, Bt. (1935)

Malpas, Sir Robert, Kt., CBE

Mancham, Sir James Richard Marie, KBE

†Mander, Sir (Charles) Nicholas, Bt. (1911)

Manduell, Sir John, Kt., CBE

Mann, *Hon.* Sir George Anthony, Kt.

Mann, *Rt. Revd* Michael Ashley, KCVO

Mann, Sir Rupert Edward, Bt. (1905)

Manning, Sir David Geoffrey, GCMG, CVO

Mano, Sir Koitaga, Kt., MBE

Mansel, Sir Philip, Bt. (1622)

Mansfield, *Prof.* Sir Peter, Kt.

Manuella, Sir Tulaga, GCMG, MBE

Manzie, Sir (Andrew) Gordon, KCB

Margetson, Sir John William Denys, KCMG

Margetts, Sir Robert John, Kt., CBE

Markesinis, *Prof.* Sir Basil Spyridonos, Kt. QC

Markham, *Prof.* Sir Alexander Fred, Kt.

Markham, Sir (Arthur) David, Bt. (1911)

Marling, Sir Charles William Somerset, Bt. (1882)

Marmot, Prof. Sir Michael Gideon, Kt.

Marr, Sir Leslie Lynn, Bt. (1919)

Marriner, Sir Neville, Kt., CBE

†Marsden, Sir Simon Neville Llewelyn, Bt. (1924)

Marsh, *Prof.* Sir John Stanley, Kt., CBE

Marshall, Sir Michael John, Kt., CBE

Marshall, *Prof.* Sir (Oshley) Roy, Kt., CBE

Marshall, Sir Peter Harold Reginald, KCMG

Marshall, *Prof. Emeritus* Sir Woodville Kemble, Kt.

Martin, Sir Clive Haydon, Kt., OBE

Martin, Sir George Henry, Kt., CBE

Martin, *Prof.* Sir Laurence Woodward, Kt.

Martin, Sir (Robert) Bruce, Kt., QC

Marychurch, Sir Peter Harvey, KCMG

Masefield, Sir Charles Beech Gordon, Kt.

Mason, *Hon.* Sir Anthony Frank, KBE

Mason, Sir (Basil) John, Kt., CB, DSC, FRS

Mason, *Prof.* Sir David Kean, Kt., CBE

Mason, Sir John Peter, Kt., CBE

Mason, Sir Peter James, KBE

Mason, *Prof.* Sir Ronald, KCB, FRS

Massey, *Vice-Adm.* Sir Alan, KCB, CBE, ADC

Massie, Sir Herbert William, Kt., CBE

Matane, HE Sir Paulias Nguna, GCMG, OBE

Matheson of Matheson, Sir Fergus John, Bt. (1882)

Mathewson, Sir George Ross, Kt., CBE, PHD, FRSE

Matthews, Sir Terence Hedley, Kt., OBE

Maud, *Hon.* Sir Humphrey John Hamilton, KCMG

Maughan, Sir Deryck, Kt.

Mawer, Sir Philip John Courtney, Kt.

Maxwell, Sir Michael Eustace George, Bt. (S. 1681)

†Maxwell Macdonald (formerly Stirling-Maxwell), Sir John Ronald, Bt. (NS 1682)

Maxwell-Scott, Sir Dominic James, Bt. (1642)

May, *Rt. Hon.* Sir Anthony Tristram Kenneth, Kt.

Mayhew-Sanders, Sir John Reynolds, Kt.

Meadow, *Prof.* Sir (Samuel) Roy, Kt., FRCP, FRCPE

Meale, Sir Joseph Alan, Kt.

Medlycott, Sir Mervyn Tregonwell, Bt. (1808)

Meeran, *His Hon.* Sir Goolam Hoosen Kader, Kt.

Meldrum, Sir Graham, Kt., CBE, QFSM

Melhuish, Sir Michael Ramsay, KBE, CMG

Mellars, *Prof.* Sir Paul Anthony, Kt., FBA

Mellon, Sir James, KCMG

Melmoth, Sir Graham John, Kt.

Melville, *Prof.* Sir David, Kt., CBE

Merifield, Sir Anthony James, KCVO, CB

†Meyer, Sir (Anthony) Ashley Frank, Bt. (1910)

Meyer, Sir Christopher John Rome, KCMG

Meyjes, Sir Richard Anthony, Kt.

†Meyrick, Sir Timothy Thomas Charlton, Bt. (1880)

Miakwe, *Hon.* Sir Akepa, KBE

Michael, Sir Duncan, Kt.

Michael, *Dr* Sir Jonathan, Kt.

Michael, Sir Peter Colin, Kt., CBE

Michels, Sir David Michael Charles, Kt.

Middleton, Sir John Maxwell, Kt.

Middleton, Sir Peter Edward, GCB

Miers, Sir (Henry) David Alastair Capel, KBE, CMG

Milbank, Sir Anthony Frederick, Bt. (1882)

Milborne-Swinnerton-Pilkington, Sir Thomas Henry, Bt. (S. 1635)

Milburn, Sir Anthony Rupert, Bt. (1905)

Miles, Sir Peter Tremayne, KCVO

†Miles, Sir Philip John, Bt. (1859)

Millais, Sir Geoffrey Richard Everett, Bt. (1885)

Millar, *Prof.* Sir Fergus Graham Burtholme, Kt.

Millard, Sir Guy Elwin, KCMG, CVO

Miller, Sir Albert Joel, KCMG, MVO, MBE, QPM, CPM

Miller, Sir Donald John, Kt., FRSE, FRENG

Miller, *Air Marshal* Sir Graham Anthony, KBE

†Miller, Sir Anthony Thomas, Bt. (1705)

Miller, Sir Hilary Duppa (Hal), Kt.

Miller, Sir Jonathan Wolfe, Kt., CBE

Miller, Sir Peter North, Kt.

Miller, Sir Robin Robert William, Kt.

Miller, Sir Ronald Andrew Baird, Kt., CBE

Miller of Glenlee, Sir Stephen William Macdonald, Bt. (1788)

Mills, Sir Ian, Kt.

Mills, Sir Keith, Kt.

Mills, Sir Peter Frederick Leighton, Bt. (1921)

Milman, Sir David Patrick, Bt. (1800)

Milne, Sir John Drummond, Kt.

Milne-Watson, Sir Andrew Michael, Bt. (1937)

Milner, Sir Timothy William Lycett, Bt. (1717)

Milton-Thompson, *Surgeon Vice-Adm.* Sir Godfrey James, KBE

Mirrlees, *Prof.* Sir James Alexander, Kt., FBA

Mitchell, Sir David Bower, Kt.

Mitchell, *Rt. Hon.* Sir James FitzAllen, KCMG

Mitchell, *Very Revd* Patrick Reynolds, KCVO

Mitchell, *Hon.* Sir Stephen George, Kt.

Mitting, *Hon.* Sir John Edward, Kt.

Moate, Sir Roger Denis, Kt.

Moberly, Sir Patrick Hamilton, KCMG

Moffat, Sir Brian Scott, Kt., OBE

Moffat, *Lt.-Gen.* Sir (William) Cameron, KBE

Moir, Sir Christopher Ernest, Bt. (1916)

†Molesworth-St Aubyn, Sir William, Bt. (1689)

†Molony, Sir Thomas Desmond, Bt. (1925)

Moncada, *Prof.* Sir Salvador, Kt.

Monck, Sir Nicholas Jeremy, KCB

Money-Coutts, Sir David Burdett, KCVO

Montagu, Sir Nicholas Lionel John, KCB

Montagu-Pollock, Sir Giles Hampden, Bt. (1872)

Montague, Sir Adrian Alastair, Kt., CBE

Montague-Browne, Sir Anthony Arthur Duncan, KCMG, CBE, DFC

Montgomery, Sir (Basil Henry) David, Bt. (1801), CVO

Montgomery, Sir (William) Fergus, Kt.

Montgomery-Cuninghame, Sir John Christopher Foggo, Bt. (NS 1672)

Moody-Stuart, Sir Mark, KCMG

Moollan, Sir Abdool Hamid Adam, Kt.

†Moon, Sir Roger, Bt. (1887)

Moorcroft, Sir William, Kt.

Moore, *Most Revd* Desmond Charles, KBE

Moore, Sir Francis Thomas, Kt.

Moore, Sir John Michael, KCVO, CB, DSC

Moore, *Vice Adm.* Sir Michael Antony Claës, KBE, LVO

Moore, *Prof.* Sir Norman Winfrid, Bt. (1919)

Moore, Sir Patrick Alfred Caldwell, Kt., CBE

Moore, Sir Patrick William Eisdell, Kt., OBE

Moore, Sir Roger George, KBE

Moore, Sir William Roger Clotworthy, Bt. (1932), TD

Moore-Bick, *Rt. Hon.* Sir Martin James, Kt.

Moores, Sir Peter, Kt., CBE

Morauta, Sir Mekere, KCMG

Mordaunt, Sir Richard Nigel Charles, Bt. (1611)

Moreton, Sir John Oscar, KCMG, KCVO, MC

Morgan, *Vice-Adm.* Sir Charles Christopher, KBE

Morgan, *Rt. Hon.* Sir (Charles) Declan, Kt.

Morgan, Sir Graham, Kt.

Morgan, Sir John Albert Leigh, KCMG

Morgan, *Hon.* Sir Paul Hyacinth, Kt.

Morgan-Giles, *Rear-Adm.* Sir Morgan Charles, Kt., DSO, OBE, GM

Morison, *Hon.* Sir Thomas Richard Atkin, Kt.

Morland, *Hon.* Sir Michael, Kt.

Morland, Sir Robert Kenelm, Kt.

Morpeth, Sir Douglas Spottiswoode, Kt., TD

†Morris, Sir Allan Lindsay, Bt. (1806)

Morris, *Air Marshal* Sir Arnold Alec, KBE, CB

Morris, Sir Derek James, Kt.

Morris, Sir Keith Elliot Hedley, KBE, CMG

Morris, *Prof.* Sir Peter John, Kt.

Morris, Sir Trefor Alfred, Kt., CBE, QPM

Morris, *Very Revd* William James, KCVO

Morrison, Sir (Alexander) Fraser, Kt., CBE

Morrison, Sir Kenneth Duncan, Kt., CBE

Morrison, Sir (William) Garth, KT, CBE

Morrison-Bell, Sir William Hollin Dayrell, Bt. (1905)

Morrison-Low, Sir James Richard, Bt. (1908)

Morritt, *Rt. Hon.* Sir (Robert) Andrew, Kt., CVO

Morse, Sir Christopher Jeremy, KCMG

Moseley, Sir George Walker, KCB

Moses, *Rt. Hon.* Sir Alan George, Kt.

Moses, *Very Revd* Dr John Henry, KCVO

Moss, Sir David Joseph, KCVO, CMG

Moss, Sir Stephen Alan, Kt.

Moss, Sir Stirling Craufurd, Kt., OBE

Mostyn, *Hon.* Sir Nicholas Anthony Joseph Ghislain, Kt.

Mostyn, Sir William Basil John, (1670)

Motion, Sir Andrew, Kt.

Mott, Sir John Harmer, Bt. (1930)

Mottram, Sir Richard Clive, GCB

†Mount, Sir (William Robert) Ferdinand, Bt. (1921)

†Mountain, Sir Edward Brian Stanford, Bt. (1922)

Mountfield, Sir Robin, KCB

Mowbray, Sir John Robert, Bt. (1880)

Moylan, *Hon.* Sir Andrew John Gregory, Kt.

†Muir, Sir Richard James Kay, Bt. (1892)

Muir-Mackenzie, Sir Alexander Alwyne Henry Charles Brinton, Bt. (1805)

Mulcahy, Sir Geoffrey John, Kt.

Mummery, *Rt. Hon.* Sir John Frank, Kt.

Munby, *Rt. Hon.* Sir James Lawrence, Kt.

Munro, Sir Alan Gordon, KCMG

†Munro, Sir Ian Kenneth, Bt. (S. 1634)

Munro, Sir Alasdair Thomas Ian, Bt. (1825)

Muria, *Hon.* Sir Gilbert John Baptist, Kt.

Murray, Sir David Edward, Kt.

Murray, *Rt. Hon.* Sir Donald Bruce, Kt.

Murray, *Prof.* Sir Kenneth, Kt.

Murray, Sir Nigel Andrew Digby, Bt. (S. 1628)

Murray, Sir Patrick Ian Keith, Bt. (S. 1673)

Murray, Sir Robert Sydney, Kt., CBE

Murray, Sir Robin MacGregor, Kt.

†Murray, Sir Rowland William, Bt. (S. 1630)

Musgrave, Sir Christopher John Shane, Bt. (1782)

Musgrave, Sir Christopher Patrick Charles, Bt. (1611)

Myers, Sir Philip Alan, Kt., OBE, QPM

Myers, *Prof.* Sir Rupert Horace, KBE

Mynors, Sir Richard Baskerville, Bt. (1964)

Naipaul, Sir Vidiadhar Surajprasad, Kt.

Nairn, Sir Michael, Bt. (1904)

Nairne, *Rt. Hon.* Sir Patrick Dalmahoy, GCB, MC

Naish, Sir (Charles) David, Kt.

Nalau, Sir Jerry Kasip, KBE

Nall, Sir Edward William Joseph Bt. (1954)

Namaliu, *Rt. Hon.* Sir Rabbie Langanai, KCMG

†Napier, Sir Charles Joseph, Bt. (1867)

Napier, Sir John Archibald Lennox, Bt. (S. 1627)

Naylor, Sir Robert, Kt.

Naylor-Leyland, Sir Philip Vyvyan, Bt. (1895)

Neal, Sir Eric James, Kt., CVO

Neale, Sir Gerrard Anthony, Kt.

Neave, Sir Paul Arundell, Bt. (1795)

Neill, *Rt. Hon.* Sir Brian Thomas, Kt.

Neill, Sir (James) Hugh, KCVO, CBE, TD

†Nelson, Sir Jamie Charles Vernon Hope, Bt. (1912)

Nelson, *Hon.* Sir Robert Franklyn, Kt.

Neubert, Sir Michael John, Kt.

New, *Maj.-Gen.* Sir Laurence Anthony Wallis, Kt., CB, CBE

Newall, Sir Paul Henry, Kt., TD

Newbigging, Sir David Kennedy, Kt., OBE

Newby, *Prof.* Sir Howard Joseph, Kt., CBE

Newey, *Hon.* Sir Guy Richard, Kt.

Newington, Sir Michael John, KCMG

Newman, Sir Francis Hugh Cecil, Bt. (1912)

Newman, Sir Geoffrey Robert, Bt. (1836)

Newman, *Hon.* Sir George Michael, Kt.

Newman, Sir Kenneth Leslie, GBE, QPM

Newman, *Vice-Adm.* Sir Roy Thomas, KCB

Newman Taylor, *Prof.* Sir Anthony John, Kt., CBE

Newsam, Sir Peter Anthony, Kt.

†Newson-Smith, Sir Peter Frank Graham, Bt. (1944)

Newton, Sir (Charles) Wilfred, Kt., CBE

†Newton, *Revd* George Peter Howgill, Bt. (1900)

Newton, Sir John Garnar, Bt. (1924)

Ngata, Sir Henare Kohere, KBE

Nice, Sir Geoffrey, Kt., QC

Nicol, *Hon.* Sir Andrew George Lindsay, Kt.

Nichol, Sir Duncan Kirkbride, Kt., CBE

Nicholas, Sir David, Kt., CBE

Nicholas, Sir John William, KCVO, CMG

Nicholls, Sir Nigel Hamilton, KCVO, CBE

Nichols, Sir Richard Everard, Kt.

Nicholson, Sir Bryan Hubert, GBE, Kt.

†Nicholson, Sir Charles Christian, Bt. (1912)

Nicholson, Sir David, KCB, CBE

Nicholson, *Rt. Hon.* Sir Michael, Kt.

Nicholson, Sir Paul Douglas, KCVO

Nicholson, Sir Robin Buchanan, Kt., PHD, FRS, FRENG

Nicoll, Sir William, KCMG

Nightingale, Sir Charles Manners Gamaliel, Bt. (1628)

Nixon, Sir Simon Michael Christopher, Bt. (1906)

Noble, Sir David Brunel, Bt. (1902)

†Noble, Sir Timothy Peter, Bt., OBE (1923)

Nombri, Sir Joseph Karl, Kt., ISO, BEM

Norman, Sir Arthur Gordon, KBE, DFC

Norman, Sir Mark Annesley, Bt. (1915)

Norman, Sir Ronald, Kt., OBE

Norman, Sir Torquil Patrick Alexander, Kt., CBE

Normington, Sir David John, GCB

Norrington, Sir Roger Arthur Carver, Kt., CBE

Norris, *Hon.* Sir Alastair Hubert, Kt.

Norriss, Air Marshal Sir Peter Coulson, KBE, CB, AFC

North, Sir Peter Machin, Kt., CBE, QC, DCL, FBA

North, Sir Thomas Lindsay, Kt.

North, Sir (William) Jonathan (Frederick), Bt. (1920)

Norton-Griffiths, Sir John, Bt. (1922)

Nossal, Sir Gustav Joseph Victor, Kt., CBE

Nott, *Rt. Hon.* Sir John William Frederic, KCB

Nourse, *Rt. Hon.* Sir Martin Charles, Kt.

†Nugent, Sir Christopher George Ridley, Bt. (1806)

†Nugent, Sir Nicholas Myles John, Bt. (I. 1795)

†Nugent, Sir (Walter) Richard Middleton, Bt. (1831)

Nunn, Sir Trevor Robert, Kt., CBE

Nunneley, Sir Charles Kenneth Roylance, Kt.

Nursaw, Sir James, KCB, QC

Nurse, Sir Paul Maxime, Kt.

†Nuttall, Sir Harry, Bt. (1922)

Nutting, Sir John Grenfell, Bt. (1903), QC

Oakeley, Sir John Digby Atholl, Bt. (1790)

Oakes, Sir Christopher, Bt. (1939)

†Oakshott, Hon. Sir Michael Arthur John, Bt. (1959)

Oates, Sir Thomas, Kt., CMG, OBE

O'Brien, Sir Frederick William Fitzgerald, Kt.

O'Brien, Sir Timothy John, Bt. (1849)

O'Brien, Sir William, Kt.

O'Brien, *Adm.* Sir William Donough, KCB, DSC

O'Connell, Sir Bernard, Kt.

O'Connell, Sir Maurice James Donagh MacCarthy, Bt. (1869)

O'Connor, Sir Denis Francis, Kt., CBE, QPM

Odell, Sir Stanley John, Kt.

Odgers, Sir Graeme David William, Kt.

O'Donnell, Sir Augustine Thomas, GCB

O'Donnell, Sir Christopher John, Kt.

O'Donoghue, *Lt.-Gen.* Sir Kevin, KCB, CBE

O'Dowd, Sir David Joseph, Kt., CBE, QPM

Ogden, *Dr* Sir Peter James, Kt.

Ogden, Sir Robert, Kt., CBE

Ogilvy, Sir Francis Gilbert Arthur, Bt. (S. 1626)

Ogilvy-Wedderburn, Sir Andrew John Alexander, Bt. (1803)

Ogio, *HE* Sir Michael, GCMG, CBE

Ognall, *Hon.* Sir Harry Henry, Kt.

Ohlson, Sir Brian Eric Christopher, Bt. (1920)

Oldham, *Dr* Sir John, Kt., OBE

Oliver, Sir James Michael Yorrick, Kt.

Oliver, Sir Stephen John Lindsay, Kt., QC

O'Loghlen, Sir Colman Michael, Bt. (1838)

Omand, Sir David Bruce, GCB

O'Nions, Prof. Sir Robert Keith, Kt., FRS, PHD

Ondaatje, Sir Christopher, Kt., CBE

†Onslow, Sir Richard Paul Atherton, Bt. (1797)

Oppenheimer, Sir Michael Bernard Grenville, Bt. (1921)

Oppenshaw, Sir Charles Peter Lawford, Kt., QC

Orde, Sir Hugh Stephen Roden, Kt., OBE, QPM

O'Regan, *Dr* Sir Stephen Gerard (Tipene), Kt.

O'Reilly, Sir Anthony John Francis, Kt.

O'Reilly, *Prof.* Sir John James, Kt.

Orr, Sir John, Kt., OBE

Orr-Ewing, Sir (Alistair) Simon, Bt. (1963)

Orr-Ewing, Sir Archibald Donald, Bt. (1886)

Osborn, Sir John Holbrook, Kt.

Osborn, Sir Richard Henry Danvers, Bt. (1662)

Osborne, Sir Peter George, Bt. (I. 1629)

O'Shea, *Prof.* Sir Timothy Michael Martin, Kt.

Osmotherly, Sir Edward Benjamin Crofton, Kt., CB

O'Sullevan, Sir Peter John, Kt., CBE

Oswald, Sir (William Richard) Michael, KCVO

Otton, Sir Geoffrey John, KCB

Otton, *Rt. Hon.* Sir Philip Howard, Kt.

Oulton, Sir Antony Derek Maxwell, GCB, QC

Ouseley, *Hon.* Sir Brian Walter, Kt.

Outram, Sir Alan James, Bt. (1858)

Owen, Sir Geoffrey, Kt.

Owen, *Hon.* Sir Robert Michael, Kt.

Owen-Jones, Sir Lindsay Harwood, KBE

Packer, Sir Richard John, KCB

Paget, Sir Julian Tolver, Bt. (1871), CVO

Paget, Sir Richard Herbert, Bt. (1886)

Paine, Sir Christopher Hammon, Kt., FRCP, FRCR

Pakenham, *Hon.* Sir Michael Aiden, KBE, CMG

Palin, *Air Chief Marshal* Sir Roger Hewlett, KCB, OBE

Palliser, *Rt. Hon.* Sir (Arthur) Michael, GCMG

Palmer, Sir Albert Rocky, Kt.

Palmer, Sir (Charles) Mark, Bt. (1886)

Palmer, Sir Geoffrey Christopher John, Bt. (1660)

Palmer, *Rt. Hon.* Sir Geoffrey Winston Russell, KCMG

Palmer, Sir John Edward Somerset, Bt. (1791)

Palmer, *Maj.-Gen.* Sir (Joseph) Michael, KCVO

Palmer, Sir Reginald Oswald, GCMG, MBE

Parbo, Sir Arvi Hillar, Kt.

Park, *Hon.* Sir Andrew Edward Wilson, Kt.

Parker, Sir Alan William, Kt., CBE

Parker, Sir Eric Wilson, Kt.

Parker, *Rt. Hon.* Sir Jonathan Frederic, Kt.

Parker, *Hon.* Sir Kenneth Blades, Kt.

Parker, *Maj.* Sir Michael John, KCVO, CBE

Parker, *Lt.-Gen.* Sir Nicholas Ralph, KCB, CBE

Parker, Sir Richard (William) Hyde, Bt. (1681)

Parker, Sir (Thomas) John, Kt.

Parker, Sir William Peter Brian, Bt. (1844)

Parkes, Sir Edward Walter, Kt., FRENG

Parkinson, Sir Michael, Kt., CBE

Parry, *Prof.* Sir Eldryd Hugh Owen, KCMG, OBE

Parry, Sir Emyr Jones, GCMG

Parry-Evans, *Air Chief Marshal* Sir David, GCB, CBE

Parsons, Sir John Christopher, KCVO

Parsons, Sir Richard Edmund (Clement Fownes), KCMG

Partridge, Sir Michael John Anthony, KCB

Partridge, Sir Nicholas Wyndham, Kt., OBE

Pascoe, *Gen.* Sir Robert Alan, KCB, MBE

Pasley, Sir Robert Killigrew Sabine, Bt. (1794)

†Paston-Bedingfeld, Sir Henry Edgar, Bt. (1661)

Paterson, Sir Dennis Craig, Kt.

Patey, Sir William Charters, KCMG

Patnick, Sir (Cyril) Irvine, Kt., OBE

Patten, *Rt. Hon.* Sir Nicholas John, Kt.

Pattie, *Rt. Hon.* Sir Geoffrey Edwin, Kt.

Pattison, *Prof.* Sir John Ridley, Kt., DM, FRCPATH

Pattullo, Sir (David) Bruce, Kt., CBE

Pauncefort-Duncombe, Sir Philip Digby, Bt. (1859)

Peace, Sir John Wilfrid, Kt.

Peach, Sir Leonard Harry, Kt.

Peach, *Air Marshal* Sir Stuart William, KCB, CBE

Peacock, *Prof.* Sir Alan Turner, Kt., DSC

Pearce, Sir (Daniel Norton) Idris, Kt., CBE, TD

Pearse, Sir Brian Gerald, Kt.

Pearson, Sir Francis Nicholas Fraser, Bt. (1964)

Pearson, Sir Keith, Kt.

Pearson, *Gen.* Sir Thomas Cecil Hook, KCB, CBE, DSO

Peart, *Prof.* Sir William Stanley, Kt., MD, FRS

Pease, Sir Joseph Gurney, Bt. (1882)

Pease, Sir Richard Thorn, Bt. (1920)

Peat, Sir Gerrard Charles, KCVO

Peat, Sir Michael Charles Gerrard, KCVO

Peckham, *Prof.* Sir Michael John, Kt., (1874)

Peek, Sir Richard Grenville, Bt. (1874)

Peirse, *Air Vice-Marshal* Sir Richard Charles Fairfax, KCVO, CB

Pelgen, Sir Harry Friedrich, Kt., MBE

Pelham, *Dr* Sir Hugh Reginald Brentnall, Kt., FRS

Peliza, Sir Robert John, KBE, ED

Pelly, Sir Richard John, Bt. (1840)

Pemberton, Sir Francis Wingate William, Kt., CBE

Pendry, *Prof.* Sir John Brian, Kt., FRS

Penrose, *Prof.* Sir Roger, Kt., OM, FRS

Penry-Davey, *Hon.* Sir David Herbert, Kt.

Pepper, *Dr.* Sir David Edwin, KCMG

Pepper, *Prof.* Sir Michael, Kt.

Perowne, *Vice-Adm.* Sir James Francis, KBE

Perring, Sir John Raymond, Bt. (1963)

Perris, Sir David (Arthur), Kt., MBE

Perry, Sir David Howard, KCB

Perry, Sir Michael Sydney, GBE

Pervez, Sir Mohammed Anwar, Kt., OBE

Peters, *Prof.* Sir David Keith, Kt., FRCP

Peterson, Sir Christopher Matthew, Kt., CBE, TD

†Petit, Sir Jehangir, Bt. (1890)

†Peto, Sir Francis Michael Morton, Bt. (1855)

Peto, Sir Henry Christopher Morton Bampfylde, Bt. (1927)

Peto, *Prof.* Sir Richard, Kt., FRS

Petrie, Sir Peter Charles, Bt. (1918), CMG

Pettigrew, Sir Russell Hilton, Kt.

†Philipson-Stow, Sir (Robert) Matthew, Bt. (1907)

Phillips, Sir (Gerald) Hayden, GCB

Phillips, Sir John David, Kt., QPM

Phillips, Sir Jonathan, KCB

Phillips, Sir Peter John, Kt., OBE

Phillips, Sir Robin Francis, Bt. (1912)

Phillips, Sir Tom Richard Vaughan, KCMG

Pickard, Sir (John) Michael, Kt.

Pickthorn, Sir James Francis Mann, Bt. (1959)

Pidgeon, Sir John Allan Stewart, Kt.

†Piers, Sir James Desmond, Bt. (I. 1661)

Piggott-Brown, Sir William Brian, Bt. (1903)

Pigot, Sir George Hugh, Bt. (1764)

Pigott, *Lt.-Gen.* Sir Anthony David, KCB, CBE

Pigott, Sir Berkeley Henry Sebastian, Bt. (1808)

Pike, *Lt.-Gen.* Sir Hew William Royston, KCB, DSO, MBE

Pike, Sir Michael Edmund, KCVO, CMG

Pike, Sir Philip Ernest Housden, Kt., QC

Pilditch, Sir Richard Edward, Bt. (1929)

†Pile, Sir Anthony John Devereux, Bt. (1900), MC

Pill, *Rt. Hon.* Sir Malcolm Thomas, Kt.

Pilling, Sir Joseph Grant, KCB

Pinsent, Sir Christopher Roy, Bt. (1938)

Pinsent, Sir Matthew Clive, Kt., CBE

Pitakaka, Sir Moses Puibangara, GCMG

Pitcher, Sir Desmond Henry, Kt.

Pitchers, *Hon.* Sir Christopher (John), Kt.

Pitchford, *Rt. Hon.* Sir Christopher John, Kt.

Pitoi, Sir Sere, Kt., CBE

Pitt, Sir Michael Edward, Kt.

Plastow, Sir David Arnold Stuart, Kt.

Platt, Sir Martin Philip, Bt. (1959)

Pledger, *Air Chief Marshal* Sir Malcolm David, KCB, OBE, AFC

Plender, *Hon.* Sir Richard Owen, Kt.

Plumbly, Sir Derek John, KCMG

Pogo, *Most Revd* Ellison Leslie, KBE

Pohai, Sir Timothy, Kt., MBE

†Pole, Sir John Chandos, Bt. (1791)

Pole, Sir (John) Richard (Walter Reginald) Carew, Bt. (1628)

Polkinghorne, *Revd Canon* John Charlton, KBE, FRS

Pollard, Sir Charles, Kt.

†Pollen, Sir Richard John Hungerford, Bt. (1795)

Pollock, Sir George Frederick, Bt. (1866)

Ponder, *Prof.* Sir Bruce Anthony John, Kt.

†Ponsonby, Sir Charles Ashley, Bt. (1956)

Poore, Sir Roger Ricardo, Bt. (1795)

Pope, Sir Joseph Albert, Kt., DSC, PHD

Popplewell, *Hon.* Sir Oliver Bury, Kt.

†Porritt, Sir Jonathon Espie, Bt. (1963)

Portal, Sir Jonathan Francis, Bt. (1901)

Porter, *Prof.* Sir Keith Macdonald Porter, Kt.

Porter, *Rt. Hon.* Sir Robert Wilson, Kt., PC (NI)

Potter, *Rt. Hon.* Sir Mark Howard, Kt.

Potts, *Hon.* Sir Francis Humphrey, Kt.

Pound, Sir John David, Bt. (1905)

Povey, Sir Keith, Kt., QPM

Powell, Sir John Christopher, Kt.

Powell, Sir Nicholas Folliott Douglas, Bt. (1897)

Power, Sir Alastair John Cecil, Bt. (1924)

Pownall, Sir Michael Graham, KCB

Prance, *Prof.* Sir Ghillean Tolmie, Kt., FRS

Pratchett, Sir Terence David John, Kt., OBE

Prendergast, Sir (Walter) Kieran, KCVO, CMG

Prescott, Sir Mark, Bt. (1938)

†Preston, Sir Philip Charles Henry Hulton, Bt. (1815)

Prevost, Sir Christopher Gerald, Bt. (1805)

Price, Sir David Ernest Campbell, Kt.

Price, Sir Francis Caradoc Rose, Bt. (1815)

Price, Sir Frank Leslie, Kt.

Prideaux, Sir Humphrey Povah Treverbian, Kt., OBE

Priestly, Sir Julian Gordon, KCMG

†Primrose, Sir John Ure, Bt. (1903)

Pringle, *Air Marshal* Sir Charles Norman Seton, KBE, FRENG

Pringle, *Hon.* Sir John Kenneth, Kt.

Pringle, *Lt.-Gen.* Sir Steuart (Robert), Bt. (S. 1683), KCB

†Prichard-Jones, Sir David John Walter, Bt. (1910)

Proby, Sir William Henry, Bt. (1952)

Proctor-Beauchamp, Sir Christopher Radstock, Bt. (1745)

Prosser, Sir David John, Kt.

Prosser, Sir Ian Maurice Gray, Kt.

Pryke, Sir Christopher Dudley, Bt. (1926)

Puapua, *Rt. Hon.* Sir Tomasi, GCMG, KBE

Purves, Sir William, Kt., CBE, DSO

Purvis, *Vice-Adm.* Sir Neville, KCB

Quan, Sir Henry (Francis), KBE

Quigley, Sir (William) George (Henry), Kt., CB, PHD

Quilter, Sir Anthony Raymond Leopold Cuthbert, Bt. (1897)

Quinton, Sir James Grand, Kt.

Radcliffe, Sir Sebastian Everard, Bt. (1813)

Radda, *Prof.* Sir George Karoly, Kt., CBE, FRS

Rae, Sir William, Kt., QPM

Raeburn, Sir Michael Edward Norman, Bt. (1923)

Raikes, *Vice-Adm.* Sir Iwan Geoffrey, KCB, CBE, DSC

Raison, *Rt. Hon.* Sir Timothy Hugh Francis, Kt.

Rake, Sir Michael Derek Vaughan, Kt.

†Ralli, Sir David Charles, Bt. (1912)

Ramdanee, Sir Mookteswar Baboolall Kailash, Kt.

Ramphal, Sir Shridath Surendranath, GCMG

Ramphul, Sir Baalkhristna, Kt.

Ramphul, Sir Indurduth, Kt.

Ramsay, Sir Alexander William Burnett, Bt. (1806)

Ramsay, Sir Allan John (Hepple), KBE, CMG

Ramsay-Fairfax-Lucy, Sir Edmund John William Hugh, Bt. (1836)

Ramsden, Sir John Charles Josslyn, Bt. (1689)

Ramsey, *Dr* Sir Frank Cuthbert, KCMG

Ramsey, *Hon.* Sir Vivian Arthur, Kt.

Rankin, Sir Ian Niall, Bt. (1898)

Rasch, Sir Simon Anthony Carne, Bt. (1903)

Rashleigh, Sir Richard Harry, Bt. (1831)

Ratford, Sir David John Edward, KCMG, CVO

Rattee, *Hon.* Sir Donald Keith, Kt.

Rattle, Sir Simon Dennis, Kt., CBE

Rawlins, *Prof.* Sir Michael David, Kt., FRCP, FRCPED

Rawlinson, Sir Anthony Henry John, Bt. (1891)

Rea, *Prof.* Sir Desmond, Kt., OBE

Read, *Air Marshal* Sir Charles Frederick, KBE, CB, DFC, AFC

Read, *Prof.* Sir David John, Kt.

Read, Sir John Emms, Kt.

†Reade, Sir Kenneth Ray, Bt. (1661)

Reardon-Smith, Sir (William) Antony (John), Bt. (1920)

Reay, *Lt.-Gen.* Sir (Hubert) Alan John, KBE

Redgrave, Sir Steven Geoffrey, Kt., CBE

Redmayne, Sir Giles Martin, Bt. (1964)

Redmond, Sir Anthony Gerard, Kt.

Redwood, Sir Peter Boverton, Bt. (1911)

Reed, *Prof.* Sir Alec Edward, Kt., CBE

Reedie, Sir Craig Collins, Kt., CBE

Rees, Sir David Allan, Kt., PHD, DSC, FRS

Rees, Sir Richard Ellis Meuric, Kt., CBE

Reeve, Sir Anthony, KCMG, KCVO

Reffell, *Adm.* Sir Derek Roy, KCB

Reich, Sir Erich Arieh, Kt.

Reid, Sir Alexander James, Bt. (1897)

Reid, Sir Hugh, Bt. (1922)

Reid, Sir (Philip) Alan, KCVO

Reid, Sir Robert Paul, Kt.

Reid, Sir William Kennedy, KCB

Reiher, Sir Frederick Bernard Carl, KCMG, KBE

Reilly, *Lt.-Gen.* Sir Jeremy Calcott, KCB, DSO

Renals, Sir Stanley, Bt. (1895)

Renouf, Sir Clement William Bailey, Kt.

Renshaw, Sir John David Bine, Bt. (1903)

Renwick, Sir Richard Eustace, Bt. (1921)

Reporter, Sir Shapoor Ardeshirji, KBE

Reynolds, Sir David James, Bt. (1923)

Reynolds, Sir Peter William John, Kt., CBE

Rhodes, Sir John Christopher Douglas, Bt. (1919)

Rice, *Prof.* Sir Charles Duncan, Kt.

Rice, *Maj.-Gen.* Sir Desmond Hind Garrett, KCVO, CBE

Rice, Sir Timothy Miles Bindon, Kt.

Richard, Sir Cliff, Kt., OBE

Richards, Sir Brian Mansel, Kt., CBE, PHD

Richards, *Hon.* Sir David Anthony Stewart, Kt.

Richards, Sir David Gerald, Kt.

Richards, *Gen.* Sir David, Julian, GCB, CBE, DSO

Richards, Sir Francis Neville, KCMG, CVO

Richards, *Prof.* Sir Michael Adrian, Kt., CBE

Richards, Sir Rex Edward, Kt., DSC, FRS

Richards, *Rt. Hon.* Sir Stephen Price, Kt.

Richardson, Sir Anthony Lewis, Bt. (1924)

Richardson, *Rt. Hon.* Sir Ivor Lloyd Morgan, Kt.

Richardson, *Lt.-Gen.* Sir Robert Francis, KCB, CVO, CBE

Richardson, Sir Thomas Legh, KCMG

Richardson-Bunbury, Sir (Richard David) Michael, Bt. (I. 1787)

Richmond, Sir David Frank, KBE, CMG

Richmond, *Prof.* Sir Mark Henry, Kt., FRS

Ricketts, Sir Peter Forbes, GCMG

Ricketts, Sir Stephen Tristram, Bt. (1828)

Ricks, *Prof.* Sir Christopher Bruce, Kt.

†Riddell, Sir Walter John, Bt. (S. 1628)

Ridgway, *Lt.-Gen.* Sir Andrew Peter, KBE, CB

Ridley, Sir Adam (Nicholas), Kt.

Ridley, Sir Michael Kershaw, KCVO

Rifkind, *Rt. Hon.* Sir Malcolm Leslie, KCMG

Rigby, Sir Anthony John, Bt. (1929)

Rigby, Sir Peter, Kt.

Rimer, *Hon.* Sir Colin Percy Farquharson, Kt.

Ripley, Sir William Hugh, Bt. (1880)

Risk, Sir Thomas Neilson, Kt.

Ritako, Sir Thomas Baha, Kt., MBE

Ritblat, Sir John Henry, Kt.

Ritchie, *Prof.* Sir Lewis Duthie, Kt., OBE

†Rivett-Carnac, Sir Jonathan James, Bt. (1836)

Rix, *Rt. Hon.* Sir Bernard Anthony, Kt.

Robb, Sir John Weddell, Kt.

Roberts, *Hon.* Sir Denys Tudor Emil, KBE,

Roberts, Sir Derek Harry, Kt., CBE, FRS, FRENG

Roberts, *Prof.* Sir Edward Adam, KCMG

Roberts, Sir Gilbert Howland Rookehurst, Bt. (1809)

Roberts, Sir Hugh Ashley, GCVO
Roberts, Sir Ivor Anthony, KCMG
Roberts, *Dr* Sir Richard John, Kt.
Roberts, *Maj.-Gen.* Sir Sebastian John Lechmere, KCVO, OBE
Roberts, Sir Samuel, Bt. (1919)
Roberts, Sir William James Denby, Bt. (1909)
Robertson, Sir Simon Manwaring, Kt.
Robins, Sir Ralph Harry, Kt., FRENG
Robinson, Sir Bruce, KCB
†Robinson, Sir Christopher Philipse, Bt. (1854)
Robinson, Sir Gerrard Jude, Kt.
Robinson, Sir Ian, Kt.
Robinson, Sir John James Michael Laud, Bt. (1660)
Robinson, *Dr* Sir Kenneth, Kt.
Robinson, Sir Wilfred Henry Frederick, Bt. (1908)
Robson, Sir John Adam, KCMG
Robson, Sir Stephen Arthur, Kt., CB
Roch, *Rt. Hon.* Sir John Ormond, Kt.
Roche, Sir David O'Grady, Bt. (1838)
Roche, Sir Henry John, Kt.
Rodgers, Sir (Andrew) Piers (Wingate Aikin-Sneath), Bt. (1964)
Rodley, *Prof.* Sir Nigel, KBE
Rogers, *Air Chief Marshal* Sir John Robson, KCB, CBE
Rogers, Sir Peter, Kt.
Rollo, *Lt.-Gen.* Sir William Raoul, KCB, CBE
Ropner, Sir John Bruce Woollacott, Bt. (1952)
Ropner, Sir Robert Clinton, Bt. (1904)
Rose, Sir Arthur James, Kt., CBE
Rose, *Rt. Hon.* Sir Christopher Dudley Roger, Kt.
Rose, Sir Clive Martin, GCMG
Rose, Sir David Lancaster, Bt. (1874)
Rose, *Gen.* Sir (Hugh) Michael, KCB, CBE, DSO, QGM
Rose, Sir John Edward Victor, Kt.
Rose, Sir Julian Day, Bt. (1872 and 1909)
Rose, Sir Stuart Alan Ransom, Kt.
Rosenthal, Sir Norman Leon, Kt.
Ross, *Maj.* Sir Andrew Charles Paterson, Bt. (1960)
Ross, *Lt.-Gen.* Sir Robert Jeremy, KCB, OBE
Ross, *Lt.-Col.* Sir Walter Hugh Malcolm, GCVO, OBE
Rossi, Sir Hugh Alexis Louis, Kt.
Roth, *Hon.* Sir Peter Marcel, Kt.
Rothschild, Sir Evelyn Robert Adrian de, Kt.
Rove, *Revd* Ikan, KBE
Rowe, *Rear-Adm.* Sir Patrick Barton, KCVO, CBE
Rowe-Ham, Sir David Kenneth, GBE
Rowland, Sir (John) David, Kt.
Rowland, Sir Geoffrey Robert, Kt.
Rowlands, Sir David, KCB
Rowley, Sir Richard Charles, Bt. (1836)

Rowling, Sir John Reginald, Kt.
Rowlinson, *Prof.* Sir John Shipley, Kt., FRS
Royce, *Hon.* Sir Roger John, Kt.
Royden, Sir Christopher John, Bt. (1905)
Rubin *Prof.* Sir Peter Charles, Kt.
Rudd, Sir (Anthony) Nigel (Russell), Kt.
Rudge, Sir Alan Walter, Kt., CBE, FRS
Rugge-Price, Sir James Keith Peter, Bt. (1804)
Ruggles-Brise, Sir Timothy Edward, Bt. (1935)
Rumbold, Sir Henry John Sebastian, Bt. (1779)
Runchorelal, Sir (Udayan) Chinubhai Madhowlal, Bt. (1913)
Rusby, *Vice-Adm.* Sir Cameron, KCB, LVO
Rushdie, Sir (Ahmed) Salman, Kt.
†Russell, Sir (Arthur) Mervyn, Bt. (1812)
Russell, Sir Charles Dominic, Bt. (1916)
Russell, Sir George, Kt., CBE
Russell, Sir Muir, KCB
Rutter, *Prof.* Sir Michael Llewellyn, Kt., CBE, MD, FRS
Ryan, Sir Derek Gerald, Bt. (1919)
Rycroft, Sir Richard John, Bt. (1784)
Ryder, *Hon.* Sir Ernest Nigel Ryder, Kt., TD
Ryrie, Sir William Sinclair, KCB

Sacranie, Sir Iqbal Abdul Karim Mussa, Kt., OBE
Sainsbury, *Rt. Hon.* Sir Timothy Alan Davan, Kt.
†St Clair-Ford, Sir Colin Anson, Bt. (1793)
St George, Sir John Avenel Bligh, Bt. (I. 1766)
St John-Mildmay, Sir Walter John Hugh, Bt. (1772)
St Omer, *Hon. Dr* Sir Dunstan Gerbert Raphael, KCMG
Sainty, Sir John Christopher, KCB
Sales, *Hon.* Sir Philip James, Kt.
Salisbury, Sir Robert William, Kt.
Salt, Sir Patrick MacDonnell, Bt. (1869)
Salt, Sir (Thomas) Michael John, Bt. (1899)
†Salusbury-Trelawny, Sir John William Richard, Bt. (1628)
Sampson, Sir Colin, Kt., CBE, QPM
Samuel, Sir John Michael Glen, Bt. (1898)
Samuelson, Sir James Francis, Bt. (1884)
Samuelson, Sir Sydney Wylie, Kt., CBE
Samworth, Sir David Chetwode, Kt., CBE
Sanders, Sir Robert Tait, KBE, CMG
Sanders, Sir Ronald Michael, KCMG
Sanderson, Sir Frank Linton, Bt. (1920)
Sands, Sir Roger Blakemore, KCB

Sarei, Sir Alexis Holyweek, Kt., CBE
Sargent, Sir William Desmond, Kt., CBE
Satchwell, Sir Kevin Joseph, Kt.
Saunders, *Hon.* Sir John Henry Boulton, Kt.
Savile, Sir James Wilson Vincent, Kt., OBE
Savill, *Prof.* Sir John Stewart, Kt.
Savory, Sir Michael Berry, Kt.
Sawers, Sir Robert John, KCMG
Saxby, *Prof.* Sir Robin Keith, Kt.
Scarlett, Sir John McLeod, KCMG, OBE
Scheele, Sir Nicholas Vernon, KCMG
Schiemann, *Rt. Hon.* Sir Konrad Hermann Theodor, Kt.
Scholar, Sir Michael Charles, KCB
Scholey, Sir David Gerald, Kt., CBE
Scholey, Sir Robert, Kt., CBE, FRENG
Schreier, Sir Bernard, Kt.
Schubert, Sir Sydney, Kt.
Scipio, Sir Hudson Rupert, Kt.
Scoon, Sir Paul, GCMG, GCVO, OBE
Scott, Sir Anthony Percy, Bt. (1913)
Scott, *Prof.* Sir George Peter, Kt.
Scott, Sir James Jervoise, Bt. (1962)
Scott, Sir John Hamilton, KCVO
Scott, Sir Kenneth Bertram Adam, KCVO, CMG
Scott, Sir Oliver Christopher Anderson, Bt. (1909)
Scott, *Prof.* Sir Philip John, KBE
Scott, Sir Ridley, Kt.
Scott, Sir Robert David Hillyer, Kt.
Scott, Sir Walter John, Bt. (1907)
Scott-Lee, Sir Paul Joseph, Kt., QPM
Seale, Sir Clarence David, Kt.
Seale, Sir John Henry, Bt. (1838)
Seaman, Sir Keith Douglas, KCVO, OBE
Sebastian, Sir Cuthbert Montraville, GCMG, OBE
†Sebright, Sir Rufus Hugo Giles, Bt. (1626)
Seccombe, Sir (William) Vernon Stephen, Kt.
Seconde, Sir Reginald Louis, KCMG, CVO
Sedley, *Rt. Hon.* Sir Stephen John, Kt.
Seely, Sir Nigel Edward, Bt. (1896)
Seeto, Sir Ling James, Kt., MBE
Seeyave, Sir Rene Sow Choung, Kt., CBE
Seligman, Sir Peter Wendel, Kt., CBE
Semple, Sir John Laughlin, KCB
Sergeant, Sir Patrick, Kt.
Serota, Sir Nicholas Andrew, Kt.
†Seton, Sir Charles Wallace, Bt. (S. 1683)
Seton, Sir Iain Bruce, Bt. (S. 1663)
Severne, *Air Vice-Marshal* Sir John de Milt, KCVO, OBE, AFC
Shaffer, Sir Peter Levin, Kt., CBE
Shakerley, Sir Geoffrey Adam, Bt. (1838)
Shakespeare, Sir Thomas William, Bt. (1942)

Sharp, Sir Adrian, Bt. (1922)
Sharp, Sir Leslie, Kt., QPM
Sharp, Sir Sheridan Christopher
 Robin, Bt. (1920)
Sharples, Sir James, Kt., QPM
Shaw, Sir Charles De Vere, Bt. (1821)
Shaw, *Prof.* Sir John Calman, Kt., CBE
Shaw, Sir Neil McGowan, Kt.
Shaw, Sir Roy, Kt.
Shaw, Sir Run Run, Kt., CBE
Shaw-Stewart, Sir Ludovic Houston,
 Bt. (S. 1667)
Shebbeare, Sir Thomas Andrew,
 KCVO
Sheehy, Sir Patrick, Kt.
Sheffield, Sir Reginald Adrian
 Berkeley, Bt. (1755)
Shehadie, Sir Nicholas Michael, Kt.,
 OBE
Sheil, *Rt. Hon.* Sir John, Kt.
Sheinwald, Sir Nigel Elton, GCMG
Shelley, Sir John Richard, Bt. (1611)
Shepherd, Sir Colin Ryley, Kt.
Shepherd, Sir John Alan, KCVO,
 CMG
Sher, Sir Antony, KBE
Sherbourne, Sir Stephen Ashley, Kt.,
 CBE
Sherston-Baker, Sir Robert George
 Humphrey, Bt. (1796)
Shiffner, Sir Henry David, Bt.
 (1818)
Silber, *Hon.* Sir Stephen Robert, Kt.
Shinwell, Sir (Maurice) Adrian, Kt.
Shirreff, *Lt.-Gen.* Sir Alexander
 Richard David, KCB, CBE
Shock, Sir Maurice, Kt.
Shortridge, Sir Jon Deacon, KCB
Shuckburgh, Sir Rupert Charles
 Gerald, Bt. (1660)
Sieff, *Hon.* Sir David, Kt.
Silber, *Rt. Hon.* Sir Stephen Robert,
 Kt.
Simeon, Sir Richard Edmund
 Barrington, Bt. (1815)
Simmonds, *Rt. Hon. Dr* Sir Kennedy
 Alphonse, KCMG
Simmons, *Air Marshal* Sir Michael
 George, KCB, AFC
Simmons, Sir Stanley Clifford, Kt.
Simms, Sir Neville Ian, Kt., FRENG
Simon, *Hon.* Sir Peregrine Charles
 Hugh, Kt.
Simonet, Sir Louis Marcel Pierre, Kt.,
 CBE
Simpson, Sir Peter Austin, Kt.,
 OBE
Simpson, *Dr* Sir Peter Jeffery, Kt.
Sims, Sir Roger Edward, Kt.
Sinclair, Sir Clive Marles, Kt.
Sinclair, Sir Ian McTaggart, KCMG,
 QC
Sinclair, Sir Robert John, Kt.
†Sinclair, Sir William Robert Francis,
 Bt. (S. 1704)
Sinclair-Lockhart, Sir Simon John
 Edward Francis, Bt. (S. 1636)
Sinden, Sir Donald Alfred, Kt.,
 CBE
Singer, *Hon.* Sir Jan Peter, Kt.
Singh, *His Hon.* Sir Mota, Kt., QC
Singh, Sir Pritpal, Kt.

Singleton, Sir Roger, Kt., CBE
Sione, Sir Tomu Malaefone, GCMG,
 OBE
†Sitwell, Sir George Reresby
 Sacheverell, Bt. (1808)
Skeggs, Sir Clifford George, Kt.
Skehel, Sir John James, Kt., FRS
Skingsley, *Air Chief Marshal* Sir
 Anthony Gerald, GBE, KCB
Skinner, Sir (Thomas) Keith (Hewitt),
 Bt. (1912)
Skipwith, Sir Patrick Alexander
 d'Estoteville, Bt. (1622)
Slack, Sir William Willatt, KCVO,
 FRCS
Slade, Sir Benjamin Julian Alfred, Bt.
 (1831)
Slade, *Rt. Hon.* Sir Christopher John,
 Kt.
Slaney, *Prof.* Sir Geoffrey, KBE
Slater, *Adm.* Sir John (Jock)
 Cunningham Kirkwood, GCB,
 LVO
Sleight, Sir Richard, Bt. (1920)
Sloman, Sir Albert Edward, Kt.,
 CBE
Smiley, *Lt.-Col.* Sir John Philip, Bt.
 (1903)
Smith, *Prof.* Sir Adrian Frederick
 Melhuish, Kt., FRS
Smith, Sir Alan, Kt., CBE, DFC
Smith, *Hon.* Sir Andrew Charles,
 Kt.
Smith, Sir Andrew Thomas, Bt.
 (1897)
Smith, *Prof.* Sir Colin Stansfield, Kt.,
 CBE
Smith, *Prof.* Sir David Cecil, Kt.,
 FRS
Smith, Sir David Iser, KCVO
Smith, Sir Dudley (Gordon), Kt.
Smith, *Prof.* Sir Eric Brian, Kt., PHD
Smith, Sir John Alfred, Kt., QPM
Smith, Sir Joseph William Grenville,
 Kt.
Smith, Sir Kevin, Kt., CBE
Smith, Sir Michael John Llewellyn,
 KCVO, CMG
Smith, Sir (Norman) Brian, Kt., CBE,
 PHD
Smith, Sir Paul Brierley, Kt., CBE
Smith, *Hon.* Sir Peter (Winston), Kt.
†Smith, Sir Robert Christopher
 Sydney Winwood, Bt. (1809)
Smith, Sir Robert Courtney, Kt., CBE
Smith, Sir Robert Hill, Bt. (1945)
Smith, *Gen.* Sir Rupert Anthony,
 KCB, DSO, OBE, QGM
Smith, Sir Steven Murray, Kt.
Smith-Dodsworth, Sir John
 Christopher, Bt. (1784)
Smith-Gordon, Sir (Lionel) Eldred
 (Peter), Bt. (1838)
Smith-Marriott, Sir Hugh Cavendish,
 Bt. (1774)
Smurfit, *Dr.* Sir Michael William
 Joseph, KBE
Smyth, Sir Timothy John, Bt.
 (1955)
Snyder, Sir Michael John, Kt.
Soar, *Vice-Adm.* Sir Trevor Alan,
 KCB, OBE

Sobers, Sir Garfield St Auburn, Kt.
Solomon, Sir Harry, Kt.
Somare, *Rt. Hon.* Sir Michael
 Thomas, GCMG, CH
Somerville, *Brig.* Sir John Nicholas,
 Kt., CBE
Songo, Sir Bernard Paul, Kt., CMG,
 OBE
Sorrell, Sir John William, Kt., CBE
Sorrell, Sir Martin Stuart, Kt.
Soulsby, Sir Peter Alfred, Kt.
Soutar, *Air Marshal* Sir Charles John
 Williamson, KBE
Souter, Sir Brian, Kt.
Southby, Sir John Richard Bilbe, Bt.
 (1937)
Southern, *Prof.* Sir Edwin Mellor, Kt.
Southgate, Sir Colin Grieve, Kt.
Southgate, Sir William David, Kt.
Southward, *Dr* Sir Nigel Ralph,
 KCVO
Sowrey, *Air Marshal* Sir Frederick
 Beresford, KCB, CBE, AFC
Sparrow, Sir John, Kt.
Spearman, Sir Alexander Young
 Richard Mainwaring, Bt. (1840)
Spedding, *Prof.* Sir Colin Raymond
 William, Kt., CBE
Speed, Sir (Herbert) Keith, Kt., RD
Speelman, Sir Cornelis Jacob, Bt.
 (1686)
Spencer, Sir Derek Harold, Kt., QC
Spencer, *Vice-Adm.* Sir Peter, KCB
Spencer, *Hon.* Sir Robin Godfrey,
 Kt.
Spencer-Nairn, Sir Robert Arnold,
 Bt. (1933)
Spicer, Sir James Wilton, Kt.
Spicer, Sir Nicholas Adrian Albert,
 Bt. (1906)
Spiers, Sir Donald Maurice, Kt., CB,
 TD
Spooner, Sir James Douglas, Kt.
Spratt, *Col.* Sir Greville Douglas,
 GBE, TD
Spring, Sir Dryden Thomas, Kt.
Squire, *Air Chief Marshal* Sir Peter
 Ted, GCB, DFC, AFC, ADC
Stadlen, *Hon.* Sir Nicholas Felix,
 Kt.
Stagg, Sir Charles Richard Vernon,
 KCMG
Stainton, Sir (John) Ross, Kt., CBE
Staite, Sir Richard John, Kt., OBE
Stamer, Sir (Lovelace) Anthony, Bt.
 (1809)
Stanhope, *Adm.* Sir Mark, GCB,
 OBE, ADC
Stanier, Sir Beville Douglas, Bt.
 (1917)
Stanley, *Rt. Hon.* Sir John Paul, Kt.,
 MP
Staples, Sir Richard Molesworth, Bt.
 (I. 1628)
Starkey, Sir John Philip, Bt. (1935)
Staughton, *Rt. Hon.* Sir Christopher
 Stephen Thomas Jonathan Thayer,
 Kt.
Stear, *Air Chief Marshal* Sir Michael
 James Douglas, KCB, CBE
Steel, *Hon.* Sir David William, Kt.
Steer, Sir Alan William, Kt.

Stephen, *Rt. Hon.* Sir Ninian Martin, KG, GCMG, GCVO, KBE
Stephens, Sir (Edwin) Barrie, Kt.
Stephens, Sir William Benjamin Synge, Kt.
Stephenson, Sir Henry Upton, Bt. (1936)
Stephenson, Sir Paul Robert, Kt., QPM
Sternberg, Sir Sigmund, Kt.
Stevens, Sir Jocelyn Edward Greville, Kt., CVO
Stevenson, Sir Hugh Alexander, Kt.
Stevenson, Sir Simpson, Kt.
Stewart, Sir Alan d'Arcy, Bt. (I. 1623)
Stewart, Sir Brian John, Kt., CBE
Stewart, Sir David James Henderson, Bt. (1957)
Stewart, Sir David John Christopher, Bt. (1803)
Stewart, Sir James Moray, KCB
Stewart, Sir (John) Simon (Watson), Bt. (1920)
Stewart, Sir John Young, Kt., OBE
Stewart, Sir Patrick, Kt., OBE
Stewart, *Lt.-Col.* Sir Robert Christie, KCVO, CBE, TD
Stewart, Sir Robin Alastair, Bt. (1960)
Stewart, *Prof.* Sir William Duncan Paterson, Kt., FRS, FRSE
Stewart-Clark, Sir John, Bt. (1918)
Stewart-Richardson, Sir Simon Alaisdair, Bt. (S. 1630)
Stibbon, *Gen.* Sir John James, KCB, OBE
Stirling, Sir Alexander John Dickson, KBE, CMG
Stirling, Sir Angus Duncan Aeneas, Kt.
Stirling-Hamilton, Sir Malcolm William Bruce, Bt. (S. 1673)
Stirling of Garden, *Col.* Sir James, KCVO, CBE, TD
Stockdale, Sir Thomas Minshull, Bt. (1960)
Stoddart, *Prof.* Sir James Fraser, Kt.
Stoker, *Prof.* Sir Michael George Parke, Kt., CBE, FRCP, FRS, FRSE
Stonhouse, *Revd* Michael Philip, Bt. (1628 and 1670)
Stonor, *Air Marshal* Sir Thomas Henry, KCB
Stoppard, Sir Thomas, Kt., OM, CBE
Storey, *Hon.* Sir Richard, Bt., CBE (1960)
Stothard, Sir Peter Michael, Kt.
Stott, Sir Adrian George Ellingham, Bt. (1920)
Stoute, Sir Michael Ronald, Kt.
Stowe, Sir Kenneth Ronald, GCB, CVO
Stracey, Sir John Simon, Bt. (1818)
Strachan, Sir Curtis Victor, Kt., CVO
Strachey, Sir Charles, Bt. (1801)
Straker, Sir Louis Hilton, KCMG
Strang Steel, Sir (Fiennes) Michael, Bt. (1938)
Street, *Hon.* Sir Laurence Whistler, KCMG

Streeton, Sir Terence George, KBE, CMG
Strickland-Constable, Sir Frederic, Bt. (1641)
Stringer, Sir Donald Edgar, Kt., CBE
Stringer, Sir Howard, Kt.
Strong, Sir Roy Colin, Kt., PHD, FSA
Stronge, Sir James Anselan Maxwell, Bt. (1803)
Stuart, Sir James Keith, Kt.
Stuart, Sir Kenneth Lamonte, Kt.
†Stuart, Sir Phillip Luttrell, Bt. (1660)
†Stuart-Forbes, Sir William Daniel, Bt. (S. 1626)
Stuart-Menteth, Sir Charles Greaves, Bt. (1838)
Stuart-Paul, *Air Marshal* Sir Ronald Ian, KBE
Stuart-Smith, *Rt. Hon.* Sir Murray, Kt.
Stubbs, Sir William Hamilton, Kt., PHD
Stucley, *Lt.* Sir Hugh George Coplestone Bampfylde, Bt. (1859)
Studd, Sir Edward Fairfax, Bt. (1929)
Studholme, Sir Henry William, Bt. (1956)
Sturridge, Sir Nicholas Anthony, KCVO
Stuttard, Sir John Boothman, Kt.
†Style, Sir William Frederick, Bt. (1627)
Sullivan, *Rt. Hon.* Sir Jeremy Mirth, Kt.
Sullivan, Sir Richard Arthur, Bt. (1804)
Sulston, Sir John Edward, Kt.
Sumner, *Hon.* Sir Christopher John, Kt.
Sunderland, Sir John Michael, Kt.
Supperstone, *Hon.* Sir Michael Alan, Kt.
Sutherland, Sir John Brewer, Bt. (1921)
Sutherland, Sir William George MacKenzie, Kt.
Sutton, *Air Marshal* Sir John Matthias Dobson, KCB
Sutton, Sir Richard Lexington, Bt. (1772)
Swaffield, Sir James Chesebrough, Kt., CBE, RD
Swaine, Sir John Joseph, Kt., CBE
Swan, Sir Conrad Marshall John Fisher, KCVO, PHD
Swan, Sir John William David, KBE
Swann, Sir Michael Christopher, Bt. (1906), TD
Sweeney, Sir George, Kt.
Sweeney, *Hon.* Sir Nigel Hamilton, Kt.
Sweeting, *Prof.* Sir Martin Nicholas, Kt., OBE, FRS
Sweetnam, Sir (David) Rodney, KCVO, CBE, FRCS
Swinburn, *Lt.-Gen.* Sir Richard Hull, KCB
Swinnerton-Dyer, *Prof.* Sir (Henry) Peter (Francis), Bt. (1678), KBE, FRS
Swinton, *Maj.-Gen.* Sir John, KCVO, OBE

Swire, Sir Adrian Christopher, Kt.
Swire, Sir John Anthony, Kt., CBE
Sykes, Sir David Michael, Bt. (1921)
Sykes, Sir Francis John Badcock, Bt. (1781)
Sykes, Sir Hugh Ridley, Kt.
Sykes, *Prof.* Sir (Malcolm) Keith, Kt.
Sykes, Sir Richard, Kt.
Sykes, Sir Tatton Christopher Mark, Bt. (1783)
Symons, *Vice-Adm.* Sir Patrick Jeremy, KBE
Synge, Sir Robert Carson, Bt. (1801)
Synnott, Sir Hilary Nicholas Hugh, KCMG

Talboys, *Rt. Hon.* Sir Brian Edward, CH, KCB
Tang, Sir David Wing-cheung, KBE
Tapps-Gervis-Meyrick, Sir George Christopher Cadafael, Bt. (1791)
Tapsell, Sir Peter Hannay Bailey, Kt., PC
Tate, Sir (Henry) Saxon, Bt. (1898)
Taureka, *Dr* Sir Reubeh, KBE
Tauvasa, Sir Joseph James, KBE
Tavare, Sir John, Kt., CBE
Tavener, *Prof.* Sir John Kenneth, Kt.
Taylor, Sir (Arthur) Godfrey, Kt.
Taylor, Sir Cyril Julian Hebden, GBE
Taylor, Sir Edward Macmillan (Teddy), Kt.
Taylor, Sir Hugh Henderson, KCB
Taylor, *Rt. Revd* John Bernard, KCVO
Taylor, *Dr* Sir John Michael, Kt., OBE
Taylor, *Prof.* Sir Martin John, Kt., FRS
Taylor, Sir Nicholas Richard Stuart, Bt. (1917)
Taylor, *Prof.* Sir William, Kt., CBE
Taylor, Sir William George, Kt.
Teagle, *Vice-Adm.* Sir Somerford Francis, KBE
Teare, *Hon.* Sir Nigel John Martin, Kt.
Teasdale, *Prof.* Sir Graham Michael, Kt.
Tebbit, Sir Kevin Reginald, KCB, CMG
Telito, *HE Revd* Filoimea, GCMG, MBE
Temple, *Prof.* Sir John Graham, Kt.
Temple, Sir Richard, Bt. (1876), Chartier
Temu, *Hon. Dr* Sir Puka, KBE, CMG
Tennyson-D'Eyncourt, Sir Mark Gervais, Bt. (1930)
Terry, *Air Marshal* Sir Colin George, KBE, CB
Terry, *Air Chief Marshal* Sir Peter David George, GCB, AFC
Thatcher, Sir Mark, Bt. (1990)
Thomas, Sir David John Godfrey, Bt. (1694)
Thomas, Sir Derek Morison David, KCMG
Thomas, Sir Gilbert Stanley, Kt., OBE

Thomas, Sir Jeremy Cashel, KCMG

Thomas, Sir (John) Alan, Kt.

Thomas, *Prof.* Sir John Meurig, Kt., FRS

Thomas, Sir Keith Vivian, Kt.

Thomas, *Dr* Sir Leton Felix, KCMG, CBE

Thomas, Sir Philip Lloyd, KCVO, CMG

Thomas, Sir Quentin Jeremy, Kt., CB

Thomas, *Rt. Hon.* Sir Roger John Laugharne, Kt.

Thomas, *Hon.* Sir Swinton Barclay, Kt.

Thomas, Sir William Michael, Bt. (1919)

Thomas, Sir (William) Michael (Marsh), Bt. (1918)

Thompson, Sir Christopher Peile, Bt. (1890)

Thompson, Sir Clive Malcolm, Kt.

Thompson, Sir David Albert, KCMG

Thompson, Sir Gilbert Williamson, Kt., OBE

Thompson, *Prof.* Sir Michael Warwick, Kt., DSC

Thompson, Sir Nicholas Annesley, Bt. (1963)

Thompson, Sir Nigel Cooper, KCMG, CBE

Thompson, Sir Paul Anthony, Bt. (1963)

Thompson, Sir Peter Anthony, Kt.

Thompson, *Dr* Sir Richard Paul Hepworth, KCVO

Thompson, Sir Thomas d'Eyncourt John, Bt. (1806)

Thomson, Sir (Frederick Douglas) David, Bt. (1929)

Thomson, Sir John Adam, GCMG

Thomson, Sir Mark Wilfrid Home, Bt. (1925)

Thomson, Sir Thomas James, Kt., CBE, FRCP

Thorne, Sir Neil Gordon, Kt., OBE, TD

Thornton, *Air Marshal* Sir Barry Michael, KCB

Thornton, Sir (George) Malcolm, Kt.

Thornton, Sir Peter Eustace, KCB

Thornton, Sir Richard Eustace, KCVO, OBE

†Thorold, Sir (Anthony) Oliver, Bt. (1642)

Thorpe, *Rt. Hon.* Sir Mathew Alexander, Kt.

Thurecht, Sir Ramon Richard, Kt., OBE

Thwaites, Sir Bryan, Kt., PHD

Tickell, Sir Crispin Charles Cervantes, GCMG, KCVO

Tidmarsh, Sir James Napier, KCVO, MBE

Tikaram, Sir Moti, KBE

Tilt, Sir Robin Richard, Kt.

Tiltman, Sir John Hessell, KCVO

Timmins, *Col.* Sir John Bradford, KCVO, OBE, TD

Tims, Sir Michael David, KCVO

Tindle, Sir Ray Stanley, Kt., CBE

Tirvengadum, Sir Harry Krishnan, Kt.

Tjoeng, Sir James Neng, KBE

Tod, *Vice-Adm.* Sir Jonathan James Richard, KCB, CBE

Todd, *Prof.* Sir David, Kt., CBE

Todd, Sir Ian Pelham, KBE, FRCS

Toka, Sir Mahuru Dadi, Kt., MBE

Tollemache, Sir Lyonel Humphry John, Bt. (1793)

Tomkys, Sir (William) Roger, KCMG

Tomlinson, *Prof.* Sir Bernard Evans, Kt., CBE

Tomlinson, Sir John Rowland, Kt., CBE

Tomlinson, Sir Michael John, Kt., CBE

Tomlinson, *Rt. Hon.* Sir Stephen Miles, Kt.

Tooke, *Prof.* Sir John Edward, Kt.

Tooley, Sir John, Kt.

ToRobert, Sir Henry Thomas, KBE

Torpy, *Air Marshal* Sir Glenn Lester, GCB, CBE, DSO

Torry, Sir Peter James, GCVO, KCMG

Tory, Sir Geofroy William, KCMG

Touche, Sir Anthony George, Bt. (1920)

Touche, Sir Rodney Gordon, Bt. (1962)

Toulson, *Rt. Hon.* Sir Roger Grenfell, Kt.

Tovadek, Sir Martin, Kt. CMG

Tovey, Sir Brian John Maynard, KCMG

ToVue, Sir Ronald, Kt., OBE

Towneley, Sir Simon Peter Edmund Cosmo William, KCVO

Townsend, Sir Cyril David, Kt.

Traill, Sir Alan Towers, GBE

Trainor, *Prof.* Sir Richard Hughes, KBE

Treacher, *Adm.* Sir John Devereux, KCB

Treacy, *Hon.* Sir Colman Maurice, Kt.

Treacy, *Hon.* Sir (James Mary) Seamus, Kt.

Treitel, *Prof.* Sir Guenter Heinz, Kt., FBA, QC

Trescowthick, Sir Donald Henry, KBE

†Trevelyan, Sir Andrew John, Bt. (1662 and 1874)

Trezise, Sir Kenneth Bruce, Kt., OBE

Trippier, Sir David Austin, Kt., RD

Tritton, Sir Anthony John Ernest, Bt. (1905)

Trollope, Sir Anthony Simon, Bt. (1642)

Trotman-Dickenson, Sir Aubrey Fiennes, Kt.

Trotter, Sir Neville Guthrie, Kt.

Troubridge, Sir Thomas Richard, Bt. (1799)

Trousdell, *Lt.-Gen.* Sir Philip Charles Cornwallis, KBE, CB

Truscott, Sir Ralph Eric Nicholson, Bt. (1909)

Tsang, Sir Donald Yam-keun, KBE

Tuamure-Maoate, *Dr* Sir Terepai, KBE

Tuck, Sir Bruce Adolph Reginald, Bt. (1910)

Tucker, *Hon.* Sir Richard Howard, Kt.

Tuckey, *Rt. Hon.* Sir Simon Lane, Kt.

Tugendhat, *Hon.* Sir Michael George, Kt.

Tuite, Sir Christopher Hugh, Bt. (1622), PHD

Tuivaga, Sir Timoci Uluiburotu, Kt.

Tully, Sir William Mark, KBE

†Tupper, Sir Charles Hibbert, Bt. (1888)

Turbott, Sir Ian Graham, Kt., CMG, CVO

Turing, Sir John Dermot, Bt. (S. 1638)

Turner, Sir Colin William Carstairs, Kt., CBE, DFC

Turner, *Hon.* Sir Michael John, Kt.

Turnquest, Sir Orville Alton, GCMG, QC

Tusa, Sir John, Kt.

Tweedie, *Prof.* Sir David Philip, Kt.

Tyree, Sir (Alfred) William, Kt., OBE

Tyrwhitt, Sir Reginald Thomas Newman, Bt. (1919)

Underhill, *Hon.* Sir Nicholas Edward, Kt.

Underwood, *Prof.* Sir James Cressee Elphinstone, Kt.

Unwin, Sir (James) Brian, KCB

Ure, Sir John Burns, KCMG, LVO

Urquhart, Sir Brian Edward, KCMG, MBE

Urwick, Sir Alan Bedford, KCVO, CMG

Usher, Sir Andrew John, Bt. (1899)

Utting, Sir William Benjamin, Kt., CB

Vardy, Sir Peter, Kt.

Varney, Sir David Robert, Kt.

Vasquez, Sir Alfred Joseph, Kt., CBE, QC

Vassar-Smith, Sir John Rathbone, Bt. (1917)

Vavasour, Sir Eric Michael Joseph Marmaduke, Bt. (1828)

Veness, Sir David, Kt., CBE, QPM

Venner, Sir Kenneth Dwight Vincent, KBE

Vereker, Sir John Michael Medlicott, KCB

†Verney, Sir John Sebastian, Bt. (1946)

Verney, *Hon.* Sir Lawrence John, Kt., TD

†Verney, Sir Edmund Ralph, Bt. (1818)

Vernon, Sir James William, Bt. (1914)

Vernon, Sir (William) Michael, Kt.

Vestey, Sir Paul Edmund, Bt. (1921)

Vickers, *Prof.* Sir Brian William, Kt.

Vickers, Sir John Stuart, Kt.

Vickers, *Lt.-Gen.* Sir Richard Maurice Hilton, KCB, CVO, OBE

Vickers, Sir Roger Henry, KCVO

Viggers, *Lt-Gen.* Sir Frederick Richard, KCB, CMG, MBE

Viggers, Sir Peter John, Kt.
Vincent, Sir William Percy Maxwell, Bt. (1936)
Vineall, Sir Anthony John Patrick, Kt.
Vos, *Hon.* Sir Geoffrey Michael, Kt.
†Vyvyan, Sir Ralph Ferrers Alexander, Bt. (1645)

Wade-Gery, Sir Robert Lucian, KCMG, KCVO
Waena, Sir Nathaniel Rahumaea, GCMG
Waine, *Rt. Revd* John, KCVO
Waite, *Rt. Hon.* Sir John Douglas, Kt.
Waka, Sir Lucas Joseph, Kt., OBE
Wake, Sir Hereward, Bt. (1621), MC
Wakefield, Sir (Edward) Humphry (Tyrell), Bt. (1962)
Wakefield, Sir Norman Edward, Kt.
Wakeford, Sir Geoffrey Michael Montgomery, Kt., OBE
Wakeham, *Prof.* Sir William Arnot, Kt.
Wakeley, Sir John Cecil Nicholson, Bt. (1952), FRCS
Wald, *Prof.* Sir Nicholas John, Kt.
Wales, Sir Robert Andrew, Kt.
Waley-Cohen, Sir Stephen Harry, Bt. (1961)
Walford, Sir Christopher Rupert, Kt.
Walker, *Gen.* Sir Antony Kenneth Frederick, KCB
†Walker, Sir Christopher Robert Baldwin, Bt. (1856)
Walker, Sir David Alan, Kt.
Walker, Air Vice-Marshal Sir David Allan, KCVO, OBE
Walker, Sir Harold Berners, KCMG
Walker, Sir John Ernest, Kt., DPHIL, FRS
Walker, *Air Marshal* Sir John Robert, KCB, CBE, AFC
Walker, Sir Miles Rawstron, Kt., CBE
Walker, Sir Patrick Jeremy, KCB
Walker, *Hon.* Sir Paul James, Kt.
Walker, Sir Rodney Myerscough, Kt.
Walker, Sir Roy Edward, Bt. (1906)
Walker, *Hon.* Sir Timothy Edward, Kt.
Walker, Sir Victor Stewart Heron, Bt. (1868)
Walker-Okeover, Sir Andrew Peter Monro, Bt. (1886)
Walker-Smith, Sir John Jonah, Bt. (1960)
Wall, Sir (John) Stephen, GCMG, LVO
Wall, *Rt. Hon.* Sir Nicholas Peter Rathbone, Kt.
Wall, *Gen.* Sir Peter Anthony, KCB, CBE
Wallace, *Lt.-Gen.* Sir Christopher Brooke Quentin, KBE
Wallace, *Prof.* David James, Kt., CBE, FRS
Waller, *Rt. Hon.* Sir (George) Mark, Kt.
Waller, Sir John Michael, Bt. (I. 1780)
Wallis, Sir Peter Gordon, KCVO

Wallis, Sir Timothy William, Kt.
Walmsley, *Vice-Adm.* Sir Robert, KCB
Walport, *Dr* Sir Mark Jeremy, Kt.
†Walsham, Sir Gerald Percy Robert, Bt. (1831)
Walters, Sir Dennis Murray, Kt., MBE
Walters, Sir Frederick Donald, Kt.
Walters, Sir Peter Ingram, Kt.
Wamiri, Sir Akapite, KBE
Wanless, Sir Derek, Kt.
Ward, *Rt. Hon.* Sir Alan Hylton, Kt.
Ward, Sir Austin, Kt., QC
Ward, *Prof.* Sir John MacQueen, Kt., CBE
Ward, Sir Joseph James Laffey, Bt. (1911)
Ward, Sir Timothy James, Kt.
Wardale, Sir Geoffrey Charles, KCB
Wardlaw, Sir Henry Justin, Bt. (NS. 1631)
Waring, Sir (Alfred) Holburt, Bt. (1935)
Warmington, Sir Rupert Marshall, Bt. (1908)
Warner, Sir Gerald Chierici, KCMG
†Warner, Sir Philip Courtenay Thomas, Bt. (1910)
Warren, Sir (Frederick) Miles, KBE
Warren, Sir Kenneth Robin, Kt.
Warren, Sir Nicholas Roger, Kt.
Wass, Sir Douglas William Gretton, GCB
Waterlow, Sir Christopher Rupert, Bt. (1873)
Waterlow, Sir (James) Gerard, Bt. (1930)
Waters, *Gen.* Sir (Charles) John, GCB, CBE
Waters, Sir (Thomas) Neil (Morris), Kt.
Waterworth, Sir Alan William, KCVO
Wates, Sir Christopher Stephen, Kt.
Watson, *Prof.* Sir David John, Kt., PHD
Watson, Sir Graham Robert, Kt.
Watson, Sir (James) Andrew, Bt. (1866)
Watson, Sir Ronald Matthew, Kt., CBE
Watson, Sir Simon Conran Hamilton, Bt. (1895)
Watt, *Gen.* Sir Charles Redmond, KCB, KCVO, CBE, ADC
Watts, Sir John Augustus Fitzroy, KCMG, CBE
Watts, Sir Philip Beverley, KCMG
Weatherall, *Prof.* Sir David John, Kt., FRS
Weatherall, *Vice-Adm.* Sir James Lamb, KCVO, KBE
Weatherup, *Hon.* Sir Ronald Eccles, Kt.
Webb, *Prof.* Sir Adrian Leonard, Kt.
Webb-Carter, *Gen.* Sir Evelyn John, KCVO, OBE

Webster, *Vice-Adm.* Sir John Morrison, KCB
†Wedgwood, Sir Ralph Nicholas, Bt. (1942)
Weekes, Sir Everton DeCourcey, KCMG, OBE
Weinberg, Sir Mark Aubrey, Kt.
Weir, *Hon.* Sir Reginald George, Kt.
Weir, Sir Roderick Bignell, Kt.
Welby, Sir (Richard) Bruno Gregory, Bt. (1801)
Welch, Sir John Reader, Bt. (1957)
Weldon, Sir Anthony William, Bt. (I. 1723)
Wellend, *Prof.* Sir Mark Edward, Kt.
Weller, Sir Arthur Burton, Kt., CBE
†Wells, Sir Christopher Charles, Bt. (1944)
Wells, Sir John Julius, Kt.
Wells, Sir William Henry Weston, Kt., FRICS
Wesker, Sir Arnold, Kt.
Westbrook, Sir Neil Gowanloch, Kt., CBE
Westmacott, Sir Peter John, KCMG
Weston, Sir Michael Charles Swift, KCMG, CVO
Weston, Sir (Philip) John, KCMG
Whalen, Sir Geoffrey Henry, Kt., CBE
Wheeler, Sir Harry Anthony, Kt., OBE
Wheeler, *Rt. Hon.* Sir John Daniel, Kt.
Wheeler, Sir John Frederick, Bt. (1920)
Wheeler, *Gen.* Sir Roger Neil, GCB, CBE
Wheeler-Booth, Sir Michael Addison John, KCB
Wheler, Sir Trevor Woodford, Bt. (1660)
Whitaker, Sir John James Ingham (Jack), Bt. (1936)
Whitbread, Sir Samuel Charles, KCVO
Whitchurch, Sir Graeme Ian, Kt., OBE
White, *Prof.* Sir Christopher John, Kt., CVO
White, Sir Christopher Robert Meadows, Bt. (1937)
White, Sir David (David Jason), Kt., OBE
White, Sir David Harry, Kt.
White, *Hon.* Sir Frank John, Kt.
White, Sir George Stanley James, Bt. (1904)
White, *Adm.* Sir Hugo Moresby, GCB, CBE
White, Sir John Woolmer, Bt. (1922)
White, Sir Nicholas Peter Archibald, Bt. (1802)
White, Sir Willard Wentworth, Kt., CBE
White-Spunner, *Lt.-Gen.* Sir Barnabas William Benjamin, KCB, CBE
Whitehead, Sir John Stainton, GCMG, CVO
Whitehead, Sir Philip Henry Rathbone, Bt. (1889)

Whiteley, *Gen.* Sir Peter John Frederick, GCB, OBE, RM

Whitfield, Sir William, Kt., CBE

Whitmore, Sir Clive Anthony, GCB, CVO

Whitmore, Sir John Henry Douglas, Bt. (1954)

Whitney, Sir Raymond William, Kt., OBE

Whitson, Sir Keith Roderick, Kt.

Wickerson, Sir John Michael, Kt.

Wicks, Sir Nigel Leonard, GCB, CVO, CBE

†Wigan, Sir Michael Iain, Bt. (1898)

Wiggin, Sir Alfred William (Jerry), Kt., TD

†Wiggin, Sir Charles Rupert John, Bt. (1892)

†Wigram, Sir John Woolmore, Bt. (1805)

Wilbraham, Sir Richard Baker, Bt. (1776)

Wild, Sir John Ralston, Kt., CBE

Wiles, *Prof.* Sir Andrew John, KBE

Wilkes, *Gen.* Sir Michael John, KCB, CBE

Wilkie, *Hon.* Sir Alan Fraser, Kt.

Wilkinson, Sir (David) Graham (Brook) Bt. (1941)

Wilkinson, *Prof.* Sir Denys Haigh, Kt., FRS

Willcocks, Sir David Valentine, Kt., CBE, MC

Willcocks, *Lt.-Gen.* Sir Michael Alan, KCB, CVO

Williams, Sir (Arthur) Gareth Ludovic Emrys Rhys, Bt. (1918)

Williams, Sir Charles Othniel, Kt.

Williams, Sir Daniel Charles, GCMG, QC

Williams, *Adm.* Sir David, GCB

Williams, Sir David Innes, Kt.

Williams, Sir David Reeve, Kt., CBE

Williams, *Hon.* Sir Denys Ambrose, KCMG

Williams, Sir Donald Mark, Bt. (1866)

Williams, *Prof.* Sir (Edward) Dillwyn, Kt., FRCP

Williams, Sir Francis Owen Garbett, Kt., CBE

Williams, *Hon.* Sir (John) Griffith, Kt.

Williams, Sir (Lawrence) Hugh, Bt. (1798)

Williams, Sir Osmond, Bt. (1909), MC

Williams, Sir Paul Michael, Kt., OBE

Williams, Sir Peter Michael, Kt.

Williams, Sir (Robert) Philip Nathaniel, Bt. (1915)

Williams, Sir Robin Philip, Bt. (1953)

Williams, *Prof.* Sir Roger, Kt.

Williams, Sir (William) Maxwell (Harries), Kt.

Williams, *Hon.* Sir Wyn Lewis

Williams-Bulkeley, Sir Richard Thomas, Bt. (1661)

Williams-Wynn, Sir David Watkin, Bt. (1688)

Williamson, Sir George Malcolm, Kt.

Williamson, *Marshal of the Royal Air Force* Sir Keith Alec, GCB, AFC

Williamson, Sir Robert Brian, Kt., CBE

Willink, Sir Edward Daniel, Bt. (1957)

Wills, Sir David James Vernon, Bt. (1923)

Wills, Sir David Seton, Bt. (1904)

Wilmot, Sir David, Kt., QPM

Wilmot, Sir Henry Robert, Bt. (1759)

Wilmut, *Prof.* Sir Ian, Kt., OBE

Wilsey, *Gen.* Sir John Finlay Willasey, GCB, CBE

Wilshaw, Sir Michael, Kt.

Wilson, *Prof.* Sir Alan Geoffrey, Kt.

Wilson, Sir Anthony, Kt.

Wilson, *Vice-Adm.* Sir Barry Nigel, KCB

Wilson, Sir David, Bt. (1920)

Wilson, Sir David Mackenzie, Kt.

Wilson, Sir James William Douglas, Bt. (1906)

Wilson, *Brig.* Sir Mathew John Anthony, Bt. (1874), OBE, MC

Wilson, *Rt. Hon.* Sir Nicholas Allan Roy, Kt.

Wilson, *Prof.* Sir Robert James Timothy, Kt.

Wilson, Sir Robert Peter, KCMG

Wilson, *Air Chief Marshal* Sir (Ronald) Andrew (Fellowes), KCB, AFC

Wingate, *Capt.* Sir Miles Buckley, KCVO

Winkley, Sir David Ross, Kt.

Winnington, Sir Anthony Edward, Bt. (1755)

Winship, Sir Peter James Joseph, Kt., CBE

Winter, *Dr* Sir Gregory Winter, Kt., CBE

Winterton, Sir Nicholas Raymond, Kt.

Wiseman, Sir John William, Bt. (1628)

Wolfendale, *Prof.* Sir Arnold Whittaker, Kt., FRS

Wolseley, Sir Charles Garnet Richard Mark, Bt. (1628)

†Wolseley, Sir James Douglas, Bt. (I. 1745)

†Wombell, Sir George Philip Frederick, Bt. (1778)

Womersley, Sir Peter John Walter, Bt. (1945)

Woo, Sir Leo Joseph, Kt.

Woo, Sir Po-Shing, Kt.

Wood, Sir Andrew Marley, GCMG

Wood, Sir Anthony John Page, Bt. (1837)

Wood, Sir Ian Clark, Kt., CBE

Wood, *Hon.* Sir John Kember, Kt., MC

Wood, Sir Martin Francis, Kt., OBE

Wood, Sir Michael Charles, KCMG

Wood, *Hon.* Sir Roderic Lionel James, Kt.

Woodard, *Rear Adm.* Sir Robert Nathaniel, KCVO

Woodcock, Sir John, Kt., CBE, QPM

Woodhead, *Vice-Adm.* Sir (Anthony) Peter, KCB

Woodhead, Sir Christopher Anthony, Kt.

Woodhouse, *Rt. Hon.* Sir (Arthur) Owen, KBE, DSC

Woodroffe, *Most Revd* George Cuthbert Manning, KBE

Woods, *Prof.* Sir Kent Linton, Kt.

Woods, Sir Robert Kynnersley, Kt., CBE

Woodward, Sir Clive Ronald, Kt., OBE

Woodward, *Adm.* Sir John Forster, GBE, KCB

Woodward, Sir Thomas Jones (Tom Jones), Kt., OBE

Worsley, *Gen.* Sir Richard Edward, GCB, OBE

Worsley, Sir (William) Marcus (John), Bt. (1838)

Worsthorne, Sir Peregrine Gerard, Kt.

Wratten, *Air Chief Marshal* Sir William John, GBE, CB, AFC

Wraxall, Sir Charles Frederick Lascelles, Bt. (1813)

Wrey, Sir George Richard Bourchier, Bt. (1628)

Wrigglesworth, Sir Ian William, Kt.

Wright, Sir Allan Frederick, KBE

Wright, Sir David John, GCMG, LVO

Wright, *Hon.* Sir (John) Michael, Kt.

Wright, *Prof.* Sir Nicholas Alcwyn, Kt.

Wright, Sir Peter Robert, Kt., CBE

Wright, *Air Marshal* Sir Robert Alfred, KBE, AFC

Wright, Sir Stephen John Leadbetter, KCMG

Wrightson, Sir Charles Mark Garmondsway, Bt. (1900)

Wrigley, *Prof.* Sir Edward Anthony (Sir Tony), Kt., PHD, PBA

Wrixon-Becher, Sir John William Michael, Bt. (1831)

Wroughton, Sir Philip Lavallin, KCVO

Wu, Sir Gordon Ying Sheung, KCMG

Wynne, Sir Graham Robert, Kt., CBE

Yacoub, *Prof.* Sir Magdi Habib, Kt., FRCS

Yaki, Sir Roy, KBE

Yang, *Hon.* Sir Ti Liang, Kt.

Yapp, Sir Stanley Graham, Kt.

Yardley, Sir David Charles Miller, Kt., LLD

Yarrow, Sir Eric Grant, Bt. (1916), MBE

Yocklunn, Sir John (Soong Chung), KCVO

Yoo Foo, Sir (François) Henri, Kt.

Young, Sir Brian Walter Mark, Kt.

Young, Sir Colville Norbert, GCMG, MBE

Young, Sir Dennis Charles, KCMG

Young, *Rt. Hon.* Sir George Samuel Knatchbull, Bt. (1813)

Young, Sir Jimmy Leslie Ronald, Kt., CBE

Young, Sir John Kenyon Roe, Bt. (1821)
Young, Sir John Robertson, GCMG
Young, Sir Leslie Clarence, Kt., CBE
Young, Sir Nicholas Charles, Kt.
Young, Sir Robin Urquhart, KCB

Young, Sir Roger William, Kt.
Young, Sir Stephen Stewart Templeton, Bt. (1945)
Young, Sir William Neil, Bt. (1769)
Younger, Sir Julian William Richard, Bt. (1911)
Yuwi, Sir Matiabe, KBE

Zeeman, *Prof.* Sir (Erik) Christopher, Kt., FRS
Zissman, Sir Bernard Philip, Kt.
Zochonis, Sir John Basil, Kt.
Zunz, Sir Gerhard Jacob (Jack), Kt., FRENG
Zurenuoc, Sir Zibang, KBE

THE ORDER OF ST JOHN

THE MOST VENERABLE ORDER OF THE HOSPITAL OF
ST JOHN OF JERUSALEM (1888)

GCStJ	Bailiff/Dame Grand Cross
KStJ	Knight of Justice/Grace
DStJ	Dame of Justice/Grace
CStJ	Commander
OstJ	Officer
SBStJ	Serving Brother
SSStJ	Serving Sister

Motto, Pro Fide, Pro Utilitate Hominum

The Order of St John, founded in the early 12th century in Jerusalem, was a religious order with a particular duty to care for the sick. In Britain the order was dissolved by Henry VIII in 1540 but the British branch was revived in the early 19th century. The branch was not accepted by the Grand Magistracy of the Order in Rome but its search for a role in the tradition of the hospitallers led to the founding of the St John Ambulance Association in 1877 and later the St John Ambulance Brigade; in 1882 the St John Ophthalmic Hospital was founded in Jerusalem. A royal charter was granted in 1888 establishing the Order of St John as a British Order of Chivalry with the sovereign as its head.

Since October 1999 the whole order worldwide has been governed by a Grand Council which includes a representative from each of the eight priories (England, Scotland, Wales, South Africa, New Zealand, Canada, Australia and the USA). In addition there are also two commanderies in Northern Ireland and Western Australia. There are also branches in about 30 other Commonwealth countries. Apart from the St John Ambulance Foundation, the Order is also responsible for the Jerusalem Eye Hospital. Admission to the order is usually conferred in recognition of service to either one of these institutions. Membership does not confer any rank, style, title or precedence on a recipient.

SOVEREIGN HEAD OF THE ORDER
HM The Queen

GRAND PRIOR
HRH The Duke of Gloucester, KG, GCVO

Lord Prior, Prof. Anthony Mellows, OBE, TD
Prelate, Rt. Revd John Nicholls
Deputy Lord Prior, vacant
Sub Prior, Prof. Villis Marshall, AC
Secretary General, Rear-Adm. Andrew Gough, CB
Headquarters, 3 Charterhouse Mews, London EC1M 6BB
T 020-7251 3292

DAMES

DAMES GRAND CROSS AND DAMES COMMANDERS

Style, 'Dame' before forename and surname, followed by appropriate post-nominal initials. Where such an award is made to a lady already in possession of a higher title, the appropriate initials follow her name
Envelope, Dame F_ S_, followed by appropriate post-nominal letters. *Letter (formal),* Dear Madam; *(social),* Dear Dame F_. *Spoken,* Dame F_
Husband, Untitled

Dame Grand Cross and Dame Commander are the higher classes for women of the Order of the Bath, the Order of St Michael and St George, the Royal Victorian Order, and the Order of the British Empire. Dames Grand Cross rank after the wives of Baronets and before the wives of Knights Grand Cross. Dames Commanders rank after the wives of Knights Grand Cross and before the wives of Knights Commanders.

Honorary Dames Commanders may be conferred on women who are citizens of countries of which the Queen is not head of state.

LIST OF DAMES
As at 31 August 2011

Women peers in their own right and life peers are not included in this list. Female members of the royal family are not included in this list; details of the orders they hold can be found within the Royal Family section.

If a dame has a double barrelled or hyphenated surname, she is listed under the first element of the name. *A full entry in italic type* indicates that the recipient of an honour died during the year in which the honour was conferred. The name is included for the purposes of record.

Abaijah, Dame Josephine, DBE
Abramsky, Dame Jennifer Gita, DBE
Airlie, The Countess of, DCVO
Albemarle, The Countess of, DBE
Alexander, Dame Helen Anne, DBE
Allen, *Prof.* Dame Ingrid Victoria, DBE
Andrews, Dame Julie, DBE
Angiolini, *Rt. Hon.* Dame Elish, DBE, QC
Anglesey, The Marchioness of, DBE
Anson, Lady (Elizabeth Audrey), DBE
Anstee, Dame Margaret Joan, DCMG
Arden, *Rt. Hon.* Dame Mary Howarth (Mrs Mance), DBE
Atkins, Dame Eileen, DBE
Bacon, Dame Patricia Anne, DBE
Baker, Dame Janet Abbott (Mrs Shelley), CH, DBE
Barbour, Dame Margaret (Mrs Ash), DBE
Baron, *Hon.* Dame Florence Jacqueline, DBE
Barrow, Dame Jocelyn Anita (Mrs Downer), DBE
Barstow, Dame Josephine Clare (Mrs Anderson), DBE
Bassey, Dame Shirley, DBE
Beasley, *Prof.* Dame Christine Joan, DBE
Beaurepaire, Dame Beryl Edith, DBE
Beer, *Prof.* Dame Gillian Patricia Kempster, DBE, FBA
Begg, Dame Anne, DBE

Beral, *Prof.* Dame Valerie, DBE
Bertschinger, *Dr* Dame Claire, DBE
Bevan, Dame Yasmin, DBE
Bewley, Dame Beulah Rosemary, DBE
Bibby, Dame Enid, DBE
Black, *Prof.* Dame Carol Mary, DBE
Black, *Rt. Hon.* Dame Jill Margaret, DBE
Blackadder, Dame Elizabeth Violet, DBE
Blaize, Dame Venetia Ursula, DBE
Blaxland, Dame Helen Frances, DBE
Blume, Dame Hilary Sharon Braverman, DBE
Booth, *Hon.* Dame Margaret Myfanwy Wood, DBE
Bowtell, Dame Ann Elizabeth, DCB
Boyd, Dame Vivienne Myra, DBE
Brain, Dame Margaret Anne (Mrs Wheeler), DBE
Brennan, Dame Maureen, DBE
Brewer, *Dr* Dame Nicola Mary, DCMG
Bridges, Dame Mary Patricia, DBE
Brindley, Dame Lynne Janie, DBE
Brittan, Dame Diana (Lady Brittan of Spennithorne), DBE
Browne, Lady Moyra Blanche Madeleine, DBE
Buckland, Dame Yvonne Helen Elaine, DBE
Burnell, *Prof.* Dame Susan Jocelyn Bell, DBE
Burslem, Dame Alexandra Vivien, DBE
Byatt, Dame Antonia Susan, DBE, FRSL
Bynoe, Dame Hilda Louisa, DBE
Caldicott, Dame Fiona, DBE, FRCP, FRCPSYCH
Cameron, *Prof.* Dame Averil Millicent, DBE
Campbell-Preston, Dame Frances Olivia, DCVO
Carnall, Dame Ruth, DBE
Cartwright, Dame Silvia Rose, DBE
Clark, *Prof.* Dame Jill MacLeod, DBE
Clark, *Prof.* Dame (Margaret) June, DBE, PHD
Cleverdon, Dame Julia Charity, DCVO, CBE
Collarbone, Dame Patricia, DBE
Contreras, *Prof.* Dame Marcela, DBE
Corsar, *Hon.* Dame Mary Drummond, DBE
Coward, Dame Pamela Sarah, DBE
Cox, *Hon.* Dame Laura Mary, DBE
Cramp, *Prof.* Dame Rosemary Jean, DBE
Dacon, Dame Monica Jessie, DBE, CMG
Davies, *Prof.* Dame Kay Elizabeth, DBE
Davies, *Hon.* Dame Nicola Velfor, DBE
Davies, *Prof.* Dame Sally Claire, DBE
Davies, Dame Wendy Patricia, DBE
Davis, Dame Karlene Cecile, DBE
Dawson, *Prof.* Dame Sandra Jane Noble, DBE
Dell, Dame Miriam Patricia, DBE
Dench, Dame Judith Olivia (Mrs Williams), CH, DBE
Descartes, Dame Marie Selipha Sesenne, DBE, BEM
Devonshire, The Duchess of, DCVO
Digby, Lady, DBE
Dobbs, *Hon.* Dame Linda Penelope, DBE
Docherty, Dame Jacqueline, DBE
Donald, *Prof.* Dame Athene Margaret, DBE, FRS
Dowling, *Prof.* Dame Ann Patricia, DBE
Duffield, Dame Vivien Louise, DBE
Dumont, Dame Ivy Leona, DCMG
Dunnell, Dame Karen, DCB

Dyche, Dame Rachael Mary, DBE
Elcoat, Dame Catherine Elizabeth, DBE
Ellison, Dame Jill, DBE
Elton, Dame Susan Richenda (Lady Elton), DCVO
Engel, Dame Pauline Frances (Sister Pauline Engel), DBE
Esteve-Coll, Dame Elizabeth Anne Loosemore, DBE
Evans, Dame Anne Elizabeth Jane, DBE
Evans, Dame Madeline Glynne Dervel, DBE, CMG
Farnham, Dame Marion (Lady Farnham), DCVO
Fawcett, Dame Amelia Chilcott, DBE
Fenner, Dame Peggy Edith, DBE
Fielding, Dame Pauline, DBE
Finch, *Prof.* Dame Janet Valerie, DBE
Fisher, Dame Jacqueline, DBE
Forgan, Dame Elizabeth Anne Lucy, DBE
Furse, Dame Clara Hedwig Frances, DBE
Fradd, Dame Elizabeth, DBE
Fraser, Lady Antonia, DBE
Fraser, Dame Dorothy Rita, DBE
Friend, Dame Phyllis Muriel, DBE
Fry, Dame Margaret Louise, DBE
Gallagher, Dame Monica Josephine, DBE
Gaymer, Dame Janet Marion, DBE, QC
Ghosh, Dame Helen Frances, DCB
Glen-Haig, Dame Mary Alison, DBE
Glenn, *Prof.* Dame Hazel Gillian, DBE
Glennie, *Dr* Dame Evelyn Elizabeth Ann, DBE
Gloster, *Hon.* Dame Elisabeth (Lady Popplewell), DBE
Glover, Dame Audrey Frances, DBE, CMG
Goodall, *Dr* Dame (Valerie) Jane, DBE
Goodfellow, *Prof.* Dame Julia Mary, DBE
Goodman, Dame Barbara, DBE
Gordon, Dame Minita Elmira, GCMG, GCVO
Gordon, *Hon.* Dame Pamela Felicity, DBE
Gow, Dame Jane Elizabeth (Mrs Whiteley), DBE
Grafton, The Duchess of, GCVO
Grant, Dame Mavis, DBE
Green, Dame Pauline, DBE
Grey, Dame Beryl Elizabeth (Mrs Svenson), DBE
Griffiths, Dame Anne, DCVO
Grimthorpe, The Lady, DCVO
Guilfoyle, Dame Margaret Georgina Constance, DBE
Guthardt, *Revd Dr* Dame Phyllis Myra, DBE
Hakin, *Dr* Dame Barbara Ann, DBE
Hall, *Prof.* Dame Wendy, DBE
Hallett, *Rt. Hon.* Dame Heather Carol, DBE
Harbison, Dame Joan Irene, DBE
Harper, Dame Elizabeth Margaret Way, DBE
Harris, Lady Pauline, DBE
Hassan, Dame Anna Patricia Lucy, DBE
Hay, Dame Barbara Logan, DCMG, MBE
Henderson, Dame Fiona Douglas, DCVO
Hercus, *Hon.* Dame (Margaret) Ann, DCMG
Higgins, *Prof.* Dame Joan Margaret, DBE
Higgins, *Prof.* Dame Julia Stretton, DBE, FRS
Higgins, *Prof.* Dame Rosalyn, DBE, QC
Hill, *Air Cdre* Dame Felicity Barbara, DBE
Hine, Dame Deirdre Joan, DBE, FRCP
Hodgson, Dame Patricia Anne, DBE
Hogg, *Hon.* Dame Mary Claire (Mrs Koops), DBE
Holborow, Lady Mary Christina, DCVO
Hollows, Dame Sharon, DBE
Holmes, Dame Kelly, DBE
Holroyd, Lady Margaret, DBE
Holt, Dame Denise Mary, DCMG
Hoodless, Dame Elisabeth Anne, DBE
Hufton, *Prof.* Dame Olwen, DBE
Humphrey, *Prof.* Dame Caroline, DBE

Husband, *Prof.* Dame Janet Elizabeth Siarey, DBE
Hussey, Dame Susan Katharine (Lady Hussey of North Bradley), DCVO
Hutton, Dame Deirdre Mary, DBE
Imison, Dame Tamsyn, DBE
Ion, *Dr* Dame Susan Elizabeth, DBE
Isaacs, Dame Albertha Madeline, DBE
James, Dame Naomi Christine (Mrs Haythorne), DBE
Jenkins, Dame (Mary) Jennifer (Lady Jenkins of Hillhead), DBE
John, Dame Susan, DBE
Johnson, *Prof.* Dame Louise Napier, DBE, FRS
Jonas, Dame Judith Mayhew
Jones, Dame Gwyneth (Mrs Haberfeld-Jones), DBE
Jordan, *Prof.* Dame Carole, DBE
Keeble, *Dr* Dame Reena, DBE
Keegan, Dame Elizabeth Mary, DBE
Keegan, Dame Geraldine Mary Marcella, DBE
Kekedo, Dame Rosalina Violet, DBE
Kelleher, Dame Joan, DBE
Kellett-Bowman, Dame (Mary) Elaine, DBE
Kelly, Dame Barbara Mary, DBE
Kelly, Dame Lorna May Boreland, DBE
Kershaw, Dame Janet Elizabeth Murray (Dame Betty), DBE
Kettlewell, *Comdt.* Dame Marion Mildred, DBE
Kidu, Lady, DBE
King, *Hon.* Dame Eleanor Warwick, DBE
Kinnair, Dame Donna, DBE
Kirby, Dame Carolyn Emma, DBE
Kirby, Dame Georgina Kamiria, DBE
Kramer, *Prof.* Dame Leonie Judith, DBE
Laine, Dame Cleo (Clementine) Dinah (Lady Dankworth), DBE
Lake-Tack, *HE* Dame Louise Agnetha, GCMG
Lamb, Dame Dawn Ruth, DBE
Leather, Dame Susan Catherine, DBE
Leslie, Dame Ann Elizabeth Mary, DBE
Lewis, Dame Edna Leofrida (Lady Lewis), DBE
Lott, Dame Felicity Ann Emwhyla (Mrs Woolf), DBE
Louisy, Dame (Calliopa) Pearlette, GCMG
Lynn, Dame Vera (Mrs Lewis), DBE
MacArthur, Dame Ellen Patricia, DBE
Macdonald, Dame Mary Beaton, DBE
McDonald, Dame Mavis, DCB
MacIntyre, *Prof.* Dame Sarah Jane, DBE
Macmillan of Ovenden, Katharine, Viscountess, DBE
Macur, *Hon.* Dame Julia Wendy, DBE
Mayhew, Dame Judith, DBE
Major, Dame Malvina Lorraine (Mrs Fleming), DBE
Major, Dame Norma Christina Elizabeth, DBE
Marsden, *Dr* Dame Rosalind Mary, DCMG
Marsh, Dame Mary Elizabeth, DBE
Mason, Dame Monica Margaret, DBE
Mellor, Dame Julie Thérèse Mellor, DBE
Metge, *Dr* Dame (Alice) Joan, DBE
Middleton, Dame Elaine Madoline, DCMG, MBE
Mirren, Dame Helen, DBE
Monroe, *Prof.* Dame Barbara, DBE
Moores, Dame Yvonne, DBE
Morgan, *Dr* Dame Gillian Margaret, DBE
Morrison, *Hon.* Dame Mary Anne, DCVO
Muirhead, Dame Lorna Elizabeth Fox, DBE
Muldoon, Lady Thea Dale, DBE, QSO
Mullally, *Revd* Dame Sarah Elisabeth, DBE
Mumford, Lady Mary Katharine, DCVO
Murdoch, Dame Elisabeth Joy, DBE
Murray, Dame Jennifer Susan, DBE

DECORATIONS AND MEDALS

PRINCIPAL DECORATIONS AND MEDALS
IN ORDER OF WEAR

VICTORIA CROSS (VC), 1856 (*see* below)
GEORGE CROSS (GC), 1940 (*see* below)

BRITISH ORDERS OF KNIGHTHOOD (*see also* Orders of Chivalry)
Order of the Garter
Order of the Thistle
Order of St Patrick
Order of the Bath
Order of Merit
Order of the Star of India
Order of St Michael and George
Order of the Indian Empire
Order of the Crown of India
Royal Victorian Order (Classes I, II and III)
Order of the British Empire (Classes I, II and III)
Order of the Companions of Honour
Distinguished Service Order
Royal Victorian Order (Class IV)
Order of the British Empire (Class IV)
Imperial Service Order
Royal Victorian Order (Class V)
Order of the British Empire (Class V)

BARONET'S BADGE

KNIGHT BACHELOR'S BADGE

INDIAN ORDER OF MERIT (MILITARY)

DECORATIONS
Conspicuous Gallantry Cross (CGC), 1995
Royal Red Cross Class I (RRC), 1883
Distinguished Service Cross (DSC), 1914
Military Cross (MC), December 1914
Distinguished Flying Cross (DFC), 1918
Air Force Cross (AFC), 1918
Royal Red Cross Class II (ARRC)
Order of British India
Kaisar-i-Hind Medal
Order of St John

MEDALS FOR GALLANTRY AND DISTINGUISHED CONDUCT
Union of South Africa Queen's Medal for Bravery, in Gold
Distinguished Conduct Medal (DCM), 1854
Conspicuous Gallantry Medal (CGM), 1874
Conspicuous Gallantry Medal (Flying)
George Medal (GM), 1940
Queen's Police Medal for Gallantry
Queen's Fire Service Medal for Gallantry
Royal West African Frontier Force Distinguished Conduct Medal
King's African Rifles Distinguished Conduct Medal
Indian Distinguished Service Medal
Union of South Africa Queen's Medal for Bravery, in Silver
Distinguished Service Medal (DSM), 1914
Military Medal (MM), 1916

Distinguished Flying Medal (DFM), 1918
Air Force Medal (AFM)
Constabulary Medal (Ireland)
Medal for Saving Life at Sea (Sea Gallantry Medal)
Indian Order of Merit (Civil)
Indian Police Medal for Gallantry
Ceylon Police Medal for Gallantry
Sierra Leone Police Medal for Gallantry
Sierra Leone Fire Brigades Medal for Gallantry
Colonial Police Medal for Gallantry (CPM)
Queen's Gallantry Medal (QGM), 1974
Royal Victorian Medal (RVM), Gold, Silver and Bronze
British Empire Medal (BEM)
Canada Medal
Queen's Police Medal for Distinguished Service (QPM)
Queen's Fire Service Medal for Distinguished Service (QFSM)
Queen's Volunteer Reserves Medal
Queen's Medal for Chiefs

CAMPAIGN MEDALS AND STARS
Including authorised United Nations, European Community/Union and North Atlantic Treaty Organisation medals (in order of date of campaign for which awarded)

POLAR MEDALS (in order of date)

IMPERIAL SERVICE MEDAL

POLICE MEDALS FOR VALUABLE SERVICE
Indian Police Medal for Meritorious Service
Ceylon Police Medal for Merit
Sierra Leone Police Medal for Meritorious Service
Sierra Leone Fire Brigades Medal for Meritorious Service
Colonial Police Medal for Meritorious Service

BADGE OF HONOUR

JUBILEE, CORONATION AND DURBAR MEDALS
Queen Victoria, King Edward VII, King George V, King George VI, Queen Elizabeth II, Visit Commemoration and Long and Faithful Service Medals

EFFICIENCY AND LONG SERVICE DECORATIONS AND MEDALS
Medal for Meritorious Service
Accumulated Campaign Service Medal
Medal for Long Service and Good Conduct (Military)
Naval Long Service and Good Conduct Medal
Medal for Meritorious Service (Royal Navy 1918–28)
Indian Long Service and Good Conduct Medal
Indian Meritorious Service Medal
Royal Marines Meritorious Service Medal (1849–1947)
Royal Air Force Meritorious Service Medal (1918–1928)
Royal Air Force Long Service and Good Conduct Medal
Medal for Long Service and Good Conduct (Ulster Defence Regiment)
Indian Long Service and Good Conduct Medal
Royal West African Frontier Force Long Service and Good Conduct Medal

Royal Sierra Leone Military Forces Long Service and Good Conduct Medal
King's African Rifles Long Service and Good Conduct Medal
Indian Meritorious Service Medal
Police Long Service and Good Conduct Medal
Fire Brigade Long Service and Good Conduct Medal
African Police Medal for Meritorious Service
Royal Canadian Mounted Police Long Service Medal
Ceylon Police Long Service Medal
Ceylon Fire Services Long Service Medal
Sierra Leone Police Long Service Medal
Colonial Police Long Service Medal
Sierra Leone Fire Brigades Long Service Medal
Mauritius Police Long Service and Good Conduct Medal
Mauritius Fire Services Long Service and Good Conduct Medal
Mauritius Prisons Service Long Service and Good Conduct Medal
Colonial Fire Brigades Long Service Medal
Colonial Prison Service Medal
Hong Kong Disciplined Services Medal
Army Emergency Reserve Decoration (ERD)
Volunteer Officers' Decoration (VD)
Volunteer Long Service Medal
Volunteer Officers' Decoration (for India and the Colonies)
Volunteer Long Service Medal (for India and the Colonies)
Colonial Auxiliary Forces Officers' Decoration
Colonial Auxiliary Forces Long Service Medal
Medal for Good Shooting (Naval)
Militia Long Service Medal
Imperial Yeomanry Long Service Medal
Territorial Decoration (TD), 1908
Ceylon Armed Services Long Service Medal
Efficiency Decoration (ED)
Territorial Efficiency Medal
Efficiency Medal
Special Reserve Long Service and Good Conduct Medal
Decoration for Officers of the Royal Navy Reserve (RD), 1910
Decoration for Officers of the Royal Naval Volunteer Reserve (VRD)
Royal Naval Reserve Long Service and Good Conduct Medal
Royal Naval Volunteer Reserve Long Service and Good Conduct Medal
Royal Naval Auxiliary Sick Berth Reserve Long Service and Good Conduct Medal
Royal Fleet Reserve Long Service and Good Conduct Medal
Royal Naval Wireless Auxiliary Reserve Long Service and Good Conduct Medal
Royal Naval Auxiliary Service Medal
Air Efficiency Award (AE), 1942
Volunteer Reserves Service Medal
Ulster Defence Regiment Medal
Northern Ireland Home Service Medal
Queen's Medal (for Champion Shots of the RN and RM)
Queen's Medal (for Champion Shots of the New Zealand Naval Forces)
Queen's Medal (for Champion Shots in the Military Forces)
Queen's Medal (for Champion Shots of the Air Forces)
Cadet Forces Medal, 1950
Coastguard Auxiliary Service Long Service Medal
Special Constabulary Long Service Medal
Canadian Forces Decoration
Royal Observer Corps Medal
Civil Defence Long Service Medal

Ambulance Service (Emergency Duties) Long Service and Good Conduct Medal
Royal Fleet Auxiliary Service Medal
Prison Services (Operational Duties) Long Service and Good Conduct Medal
Rhodesia Medal
Royal Ulster Constabulary Service Medal
Northern Ireland Prison Service Medal
Union of South Africa Commemoration Medal
Indian Independence Medal
Pakistan Medal
Ceylon Armed Services Inauguration Medal
Ceylon Police Independence Medal (1948)
Sierra Leone Independence Medal
Jamaica Independence Medal
Uganda Independence Medal
Malawi Independence Medal
Fiji Independence Medal
Papua New Guinea Independence Medal
Solomon Islands Independence Medal
Service Medal of the Order of St John
Badge of the Order of the League of Mercy
Voluntary Medical Service Medal (1932)
Women's Royal Voluntary Service Medal
South African Medal for War Services
Colonial Special Constabulary Medal

HONORARY MEMBERSHIP OF COMMONWEALTH ORDERS

OTHER COMMONWEALTH MEMBERS' ORDERS, DECORATIONS AND MEDALS

FOREIGN ORDERS

FOREIGN DECORATIONS

FOREIGN MEDALS

THE VICTORIA CROSS (1856)
FOR CONSPICUOUS BRAVERY

VC

Ribbon, Crimson, for all Services (until 1918 it was blue for the Royal Navy)

Instituted on 29 January 1856, the Victoria Cross was awarded retrospectively to 1854, the first being held by Lt. C. D. Lucas, RN, for bravery in the Baltic Sea on 21 June 1854 (gazetted 24 February 1857). The first 62 crosses were presented by Queen Victoria in Hyde Park, London, on 26 June 1857.

The Victoria Cross is worn before all other decorations, on the left breast, and consists of a cross-pattée of bronze, 3.8cm in diameter, with the royal crown surmounted by a lion in the centre, and beneath there is the inscription *For Valour.* Holders of the VC currently receive a tax-free annuity of £1,500, irrespective of need or other conditions. In 1911, the right to receive the cross was extended to Indian soldiers, and in 1920 to matrons, sisters and nurses, the staff of the nursing services and other services pertaining to hospitals and nursing, and to civilians of either sex regularly or temporarily under the orders, direction or supervision of the naval, military, or air forces of the crown.

SURVIVING RECIPIENTS OF THE VICTORIA CROSS
as at 31 August 2011

Apiata, *Cpl.* B. H. (New Zealand Special Air Service)
    2004 *Afghanistan*
Beharry, *Pte.* J. G. (Princess of Wales's Royal Regiment)
    2005 *Iraq*
Cruickshank, *Flt. Lt.* J. A. (RAFVR)
    1944 *World War*
Donaldson, *Trooper* M. G. S. (Australian Special Air Service)
    2008 *Afghanistan*
Payne, *WO* K., DSC (USA) (Australian Army Training Team)
    1969 *Vietnam*
Rambahadur Limbu, *Capt.,* MVO (10th Princess Mary's Gurkha Rifles)
    1965 *Sarawak*
Roberts-Smith, *Cpl.* B (Australian Special Air Service)
    2010 *Afghanistan*
Speakman-Pitts, *Sgt.* W. (Black Watch, attached KOSB)
    1951 *Korea*

THE GEORGE CROSS (1940)
FOR GALLANTRY

GC

Ribbon, Dark blue, threaded through a bar adorned with laurel leaves
Instituted 24 September 1940 (with amendments, 3 November 1942)

The George Cross is worn before all other decorations (except the VC) on the left breast (when worn by a woman it may be worn on the left shoulder from a ribbon of the same width and colour fashioned into a bow). It consists of a plain silver cross with four equal limbs, the cross having in the centre a circular medallion bearing a design showing St George and the Dragon. The inscription *For Gallantry* appears round the medallion and in the angle of each limb of the cross is the royal cypher 'G VI' forming a circle concentric with the medallion. The reverse is plain and bears the name of the recipient and the date of the award. The cross is suspended by a ring from a bar adorned with laurel leaves on dark blue ribbon 3.8cm wide.

The cross is intended primarily for civilians; awards to the fighting services are confined to actions for which purely military honours are not normally granted. It is awarded only for acts of the greatest heroism or of the most conspicuous courage in circumstances of extreme danger. From 1 April 1965, holders of the cross have received a tax-free annuity, which is currently £1,500. The cross has twice been awarded collectively rather than to an individual: to Malta (1942) and the Royal Ulster Constabulary (1999).

In October 1971 all surviving holders of the Albert Medal and the Edward Medal exchanged those decorations for the George Cross.

SURVIVING RECIPIENTS OF THE GEORGE CROSS
as at 31 August 2011

If the recipient originally received the Albert Medal (AM) or the Edward Medal (EM), this is indicated by the initials in parentheses.

Archer, *Col.* B. S. T., GC, OBE, ERD, 1941
Bamford, J., GC, 1952
Beaton, J., GC, CVO, 1974
Butson, *Lt.-Col.* A. R. C., GC, CD, MD (AM), 1948
Croucher, *Lance Cpl.* M., GC, 2008
Finney, C., GC, 2003
Flintoff, H. H., GC (EM), 1944
Gledhill, A. J., GC, 1967
Gregson, J. S., GC (AM), 1943
Hughes, *WO2* K. S., GC, 2010
Johnson, *WO1 (SSM)* B., GC, 1990
Kinne, D. G., GC, 1954
Lowe, A. R., GC (AM), 1949
Norton, *Maj.* P. A., GC, 2006
Pratt, M. K., GC, 1978
Purves, *Mrs* M., GC (AM), 1949
Raweng, Awang anak, GC, 1951
Stevens, H. W., GC, 1958
Walker, C., GC, 1972
Wooding, E. A., GC (AM), 1945

THE ELIZABETH CROSS (2009)

EC

Instituted 1 July 2009

The Elizabeth Cross consists of a silver cross with a laurel wreath passing between the arms, which bear the floral symbols of England (rose), Scotland (thistle), Ireland (shamrock) and Wales (daffodil). The centre of the cross bears the royal cypher and the reverse is inscribed with the name of the person for whom it is in honour. The cross is accompanied by a memorial scroll and a miniature.

The cross was created to commemorate UK armed forces personnel who have died on operations or as a result of an act of terrorism. It may be granted to and worn by the next of kin of any eligible personnel who died from 1 January 1948 to date. It offers the wearer no precedence. Those that are eligible include the next of kin of personnel who died while serving on a medal earning operation, as a result of an act of terrorism, or on a non-medal earning operation where death was caused by the inherent high risk of the task.

The Elizabeth Cross is not intended as a posthumous medal for the fallen but as an emblem of national recognition of the loss and sacrifice made by the personnel and their families.

CHIEFS OF CLANS IN SCOTLAND

Only chiefs of whole Names or Clans are included, except certain special instances (marked *) who, though not chiefs of a whole Name, were or are for some reason (eg the Macdonald forfeiture) independent. Under decision (*Campbell-Gray*, 1950) that a bearer of a 'double or triple-barrelled' surname cannot be held chief of a part of such, several others cannot be included in the list at present.

THE ROYAL HOUSE: HM The Queen

AGNEW: Sir Crispin Agnew of Lochnaw, Bt., QC
ANSTRUTHER: Tobias Anstruther of Anstruther and Balcaskie
ARBUTHNOTT: Viscount of Arbuthnott, KT, CBE, DSC
BANNERMAN: Sir David Bannerman of Elsick, Bt.
BARCLAY: Peter C. Barclay of Towie Barclay and of that Ilk
BORTHWICK: Lord Borthwick
BOYLE: Earl of Glasgow
BRODIE: Alexander Brodie of Brodie
BROUN OF COLSTOUN: Sir Wayne Broun of Colstoun, Bt.
BRUCE: Earl of Elgin and Kincardine, KT
BUCHAN: David Buchan of Auchmacoy
BURNETT: J. C. A. Burnett of Leys
CAMERON: Donald Cameron of Lochiel
CAMPBELL: Duke of Argyll
CARMICHAEL: Richard Carmichael of Carmichael
CARNEGIE: Duke of Fife
CATHCART: Earl Cathcart
CHARTERIS: Earl of Wemyss and March
CLAN CHATTAN: K. Mackintosh of Clan Chattan
CHISHOLM: Hamish Chisholm of Chisholm *(The Chisholm)*
COCHRANE: Earl of Dundonald
COLQUHOUN: Sir Malcolm Rory Colquhoun of Luss, Bt.
CRANSTOUN: David Cranstoun of that Ilk
CUMMING: Sir Alastair Cumming of Altyre, Bt.
DARROCH: Capt. Duncan Darroch of Gourock
DEWAR: Michael Dewar of that Ilk and Vogrie
DRUMMOND: Earl of Perth
DUNBAR: Sir James Dunbar of Mochrum, Bt.
DUNDAS: David Dundas of Dundas
DURIE: Andrew Durie of Durie, CBE
ELIOTT: Mrs Margaret Eliott of Redheugh
ERSKINE: Earl of Mar and Kellie
FARQUHARSON: Capt. A. Farquharson of Invercauld, MC
FERGUSSON: Sir Charles Fergusson of Kilkerran, Bt.
FORBES: Lord Forbes, KBE
FORSYTH: Alistair Forsyth of that Ilk
FRASER: Lady Saltoun
*FRASER (OF LOVAT): Lord Lovat
GAYRE: R. Gayre of Gayre and Nigg
GORDON: Marquess of Huntly
GRAHAM: Duke of Montrose
GRANT: Lord Strathspey
GUTHRIE: Alexander Guthrie of Guthrie
HAIG: Earl Haig

HALDANE: Martin Haldane of Gleneagles
HANNAY: David Hannay of Kirkdale and of that Ilk
HAY: Earl of Erroll
HENDERSON: Alistair Henderson of Fordell
HUNTER: Pauline Hunter of Hunterston
IRVINE OF DRUM: David Irvine of Drum
JARDINE: Sir William Jardine of Applegirth, Bt.
JOHNSTONE: Earl of Annandale and Hartfell
KEITH: Earl of Kintore
KENNEDY: Marquess of Ailsa
KERR: Marquess of Lothian, PC
KINCAID: Madam Arabella Kincaid of Kincaid
LAMONT: Revd Peter Lamont of that Ilk
LEASK: Jonathan Leask of that Ilk
LENNOX: Edward Lennox of that Ilk
LESLIE: Earl of Rothes
LINDSAY: Earl of Crawford and Balcarres, KT, GCVO, PC
LIVINGSTONE (or MACLEA): Niall Livingstone of the Bachuil
LOCKHART: Angus Lockhart of the Lee
LUMSDEN: Gillem Lumsden of that Ilk and Blanerne
MACALESTER: William St J. McAlester of Loup and Kennox
MACARTHUR; John MacArthur of that Ilk
MCBAIN: J. H. McBain of McBain
MACDONALD: Lord Macdonald *(The Macdonald of Macdonald)*
*MACDONALD OF CLANRANALD: Ranald Macdonald of Clanranald
*MACDONALD OF KEPPOCH: Ranald MacDonald of Keppoch
*MACDONALD OF SLEAT (CLAN HUSTEAIN): Sir Ian Macdonald of Sleat, Bt.
*MACDONELL OF GLENGARRY: Ranald MacDonell of Glengarry
MACDOUGALL: Morag MacDougall of MacDougall
MACDOWALL: Fergus Macdowall of Garthland
MACGREGOR: Sir Malcolm MacGregor of MacGregor, Bt.
MACINTYRE: Donald MacIntyre of Glenoe
MACKAY: Lord Reay
MACKENZIE: Earl of Cromartie
MACKINNON: Anne Mackinnon of Mackinnon
MACKINTOSH: John Mackintosh of Mackintosh *(The Mackintosh of Mackintosh)*
MACLACHLAN: Euan MacLachlan of MacLachlan
MACLAREN: Donald MacLaren of MacLaren and Achleskine
MACLEAN: Hon. Sir Lachlan Maclean of Duart, Bt., CVO
MACLENNAN: Ruaraidh MacLennan of MacLennan
MACLEOD: Hugh MacLeod of MacLeod
MACMILLAN: George MacMillan of MacMillan
MACNAB: J. C. Macnab of Macnab *(The Macnab)*
MACNAGHTEN: Sir Malcolm Macnaghten of Macnaghten and Dundarave, Bt.
MACNEACAIL: John Macneacail of Macneacail and Scorrybreac
MACNEIL OF BARRA: Rory Macneil of Barra *(The Macneil of Barra)*

MACPHERSON: Hon. Sir William Macpherson of
Cluny, TD
MACTAVISH: Steven MacTavish of Dunardry
MACTHOMAS: Andrew MacThomas of Finegand
MAITLAND: Earl of Lauderdale
MAKGILL: Viscount of Oxfuird
MALCOLM (MACCALLUM): Robin N. L. Malcolm of
Poltalloch
MAR: Countess of Mar
MARJORIBANKS: Andrew Marjoribanks of that Ilk
MATHESON: Maj. Sir Fergus Matheson of Matheson, Bt.
MENZIES: David Menzies of Menzies
MOFFAT: Madam Moffat of that Ilk
MONCREIFFE: Hon. Peregrine Moncreiffe of that Ilk
MONTGOMERIE: Earl of Eglinton and Winton
MORRISON: Dr Iain Morrison of Ruchdi
MUNRO: Hector Munro of Foulis
MURRAY: Duke of Atholl
NESBITT (or NISBET): Mark Nesbitt of that Ilk
OGILVY: Earl of Airlie, KT, GCVO, PC
OLIPHANT: Richard Oliphant of that Ilk
RAMSAY: Earl of Dalhousie

RIDDELL: Sir Walter Riddell of Riddell, Bt.
ROBERTSON: Alexander Robertson of Struan
(Struan-Robertson)
ROLLO: Lord Rollo
ROSE: Miss Elizabeth Rose of Kilravock
ROSS: David Ross of that Ilk and Balnagowan
RUTHVEN: Earl of Gowrie, PC
SCOTT: Duke of Buccleuch and Queensberry, KBE
SCRYMGEOUR: Earl of Dundee
SEMPILL: Lord Sempill
SHAW: John Shaw of Tordarroch
SINCLAIR: Earl of Caithness
SKENE: Danus Skene of Skene
STIRLING: Fraser Stirling of Cader
STRANGE: Maj. Timothy Strange of Balcaskie
SUTHERLAND: Countess of Sutherland
SWINTON: John Swinton of that Ilk
TROTTER: Alexander Trotter of Mortonhall
URQUHART: Kenneth Urquhart of Urquhart
WALLACE: Ian Wallace of that Ilk
WEDDERBURN: Master of Dundee
WEMYSS: Michael Wemyss of that Ilk

THE PRIVY COUNCIL

The sovereign in council, or Privy Council, was the chief source of executive power until the system of cabinet government developed in the 18th century. Now the Privy Council's main functions are to advise the sovereign and to exercise its own statutory responsibilities independent of the sovereign in council.

Membership of the Privy Council is automatic upon appointment to certain government and judicial positions in the UK, eg cabinet ministers must be Privy Counsellors and are sworn in on first assuming office. Membership is also accorded by the Queen to eminent people in the UK and independent countries of the Commonwealth of which she is Queen, on the recommendation of the prime minister. Membership of the council is retained for life, except for very occasional removals.

The administrative functions of the Privy Council are carried out by the Privy Council Office under the direction of the president of the council, who is always a member of the cabinet. (*See also* Parliament)
President of the Council, Rt. Hon. Nick Clegg
Clerk of the Council, Judith Simpson

Style The Right (or Rt.) Hon._
  Envelope, The Right (or Rt.) Hon. F_ S_
  Letter, Dear Mr/Miss/Mrs S_
  Spoken, Mr/Miss/Mrs S_
It is incorrect to use the letters PC after the name in conjunction with the prefix The Rt. Hon., unless the Privy Counsellor is a peer below the rank of Marquess and so is styled The Rt. Hon. because of his/her rank.

MEMBERS *as at August 2011*

HRH The Duke of Edinburgh, 1951
HRH The Prince of Wales, 1977

Abernethy, *Hon.* Lord (Alastair Cameron), 2005
Adonis, Lord, 2009
Aikens, Sir Richard, 2008
Ainsworth, Robert, 2005
Airlie, Earl of, 1984
Aldous, Sir William, 1995
Alebua, Ezekiel, 1988
Alexander, Douglas, 2005
Alexander, Danny, 2010
Amos, Baroness, 2003
Anderson of Swansea, Lord, 2000
Anelay of St Johns, Baroness, 2009
Angiolini, Dame Elish, 2006
Anthony, Douglas, 1971
Arbuthnot, James, 1998
Archer of Sandwell, Lord, 1977
Arden, Dame Mary, 2000
Armstrong of Hill Top, Baroness, 1999
Arthur, *Hon.* Owen, 1995
Ashdown of Norton-sub-Hamdon, Lord, 1989
Ashley of Stoke, Lord, 1979
Ashton of Upholland, Baroness, 2006
Atkins, Sir Robert, 1995
Auld, Sir Robin, 1995
Baker, Sir Thomas, 2002
Baker of Dorking, Lord, 1984
Balls, Ed, 2007
Bannside, Lord, 2005
Barnett, Lord, 1975
Barron, Kevin, 2001
Bassam of Brighton, Lord, 2009
Battle, John, 2002
Beckett, Margaret, 1993
Beith, Sir Alan, 1992
Beldam, Sir Roy, 1989
Benn, Anthony, 1964
Benn, Hilary, 2003
Bercow, John, 2009

Birch, William, 1992
Black, Dame Jill, 2011
Blackstone, Baroness, 2001
Blair, Anthony, 1994
Blanchard, Peter, 1998
Blears, Hazel, 2005
Blencathra, Lord, 1995
Blunkett, David, 1997
Boateng, Lord, 1999
Bolger, James, 1991
Bonomy, *Hon.* Lord (Iain Bonomy), 2010
Boothroyd, Baroness, 1992
Boscawen, *Hon.* Robert, 1992
Bottomley of Nettlestone, Baroness, 1992
Boyd of Duncansby, Lord, 2000
Boyson, Sir Rhodes, 1987
Bradley, Lord, 2001
Bradshaw, Ben, 2009
Brake, Thomas, 2011
Brathwaite, Sir Nicholas, 1991
Brittan of Spennithorne, Lord, 1981
Brooke, Sir Henry, 1996
Brooke of Sutton Mandeville, Lord, 1988
Brown, Gordon, 1996
Brown, Nicholas, 1997
Brown, Sir Stephen, 1983
Brown of Eaton-under-Heywood, Lord, 1992
Browne of Ladyton, Lord, 2005
Browne-Wilkinson, Lord, 1983
Bruce, Malcolm, 2006
Burnham, Andy, 2007
Burns, Simon, 2011
Burnton, Sir Stanley, 2008
Butler of Brockwell, Lord, 2004
Butler-Sloss, Baroness, 1988
Buxton, Sir Richard, 1997
Byers, Stephen, 1998
Byrne, Liam, 2008
Byron, Sir Dennis, 2004
Cable, Vincent, 2010
Caborn, Richard, 1999

Caithness, Earl of, 1990
Cameron, David, 2005
Cameron of Lochbroom, Lord, 1984
Camoys, Lord, 1997
Campbell, Sir Walter Menzies, 1999
Campbell, Sir William, 1999
Canterbury, Archbishop of, 2002
Carey of Clifton, Lord, 1991
Carloway, *Hon.* Lord (Colin Sutherland), 2008
Carmichael, Alistair, 2010
Carnwath, Sir Robert, 2002
Carr of Hadley, Lord, 1963
Carrington, Lord, 1959
Carswell, Lord, 1993
Casey, Sir Maurice, 1986
Chadwick, Sir John, 1997
Chalfont, Lord, 1964
Chalker of Wallasey, Baroness, 1987
Chan, Sir Julius, 1981
Chataway, Sir Christopher, 1970
Chilcot, Sir John, 2004
Christie, Perry, 2004
Clark, Greg, 2010
Clark, Helen, 1990
Clark of Windermere, Lord, 1997
Clarke, Charles, 2001
Clarke, Kenneth, 1984
Clarke, *Hon.* Lord (Matthew Clarke), 2008
Clarke, Thomas, 1997
Clarke of Stone-Cum-Ebony, Lord, 1998
Clegg, Nicholas, 2008
Clinton-Davis, Lord, 1998
Clwyd, Ann, 2004
Coghlin, Sir Patrick, 2009
Collins of Mapesbury, Lord, 2007
Cooper, Yvette, 2007
Cope of Berkeley, Lord, 1988
Corston, Baroness, 2003
Cosgrove, *Hon.* Lady (Hazel Cosgrove), 2003

Coulsfield, *Hon.* Lord (John Coulsfield), 2000
Cowen, Sir Zelman, 1981
Crawford and Balcarres, Earl of, 1972
Creech, *Hon.* Wyatt, 1999
Crickhowell, Lord, 1979
Cullen of Whitekirk, Lord, 1997
Cunningham of Felling, Lord, 1993
Curry, David, 1996
Darling, Alistair, 1997
Darzi of Denham, Lord, 2009
Davies, Denzil, 1978
Davies, Ronald, 1997
Davies of Oldham, Lord, 2006
Davis, David, 1997
Davis, Terence, 1999
Davison, Sir Ronald, 1978
de la Bastide, Michael, 2004
Dean of Thornton-le-Fylde, Baroness, 1998
Deben, Lord, 1985
Denham, John, 2000
Denham, Lord, 1981
Dholakia, Lord, 2010
Dixon, Lord, 1996
Dobson, Frank, 1997
Dodds, Nigel, 2010
Donaldson, Jeffrey, 2007
Dorrell, Stephen, 1994
Drayson, Lord, 2008
D'Souza, Baroness, 2009
du Cann, Sir Edward, 1964
Duncan, Alan, 2010
Duncan Smith, Iain, 2001
Dunn, Sir Robin, 1980
Dyson, Sir John, 2001
Eassie, *Hon.* Lord (Ronald Mackay), 2006
East, Paul, 1998
Eden of Winton, Lord, 1972
Edward, Sir David, 2005
Eggar, Timothy, 1995
Eichelbaum, Sir Thomas, 1989
Elias, Sir Patrick, 2009
Elias, *Hon.* Dame, Sian, 1999
Elis-Thomas, Lord, 2004
Emslie, *Hon.* Lord (George Emslie), 2011
Esquivel, Manuel, 1986
Etherton, Sir Terence, 2008
Evans, Sir Anthony, 1992
Eveleigh, Sir Edward, 1977
Falconer of Thoroton, Lord, 2003
Fellowes, Lord, 1990
Fergusson, Alexander, 2010
Ferrers, Earl, 1982
Field, Frank, 1997
Flint, Caroline, 2008
Forsyth of Drumlean, Lord, 1995
Foster, Donald, 2010
Foster of Bishop Auckland, Lord, 1993
Foulkes of Cumnock, Lord, 2002
Fowler, Lord, 1979
Fox, Liam, 2010
Francois, Mark, 2010
Fraser, Malcolm, 1976

Fraser of Carmyllie, Lord, 1989
Freedman, Sir Lawrence, 2009
Freeman, John, 1966
Freeman, Lord, 1993
Gage, Sir William, 2004
Garel-Jones, Lord, 1992
Gault, Thomas, 1992
Geidt, Sir Christopher, 2007
George, Bruce, 2000
Gibson, Sir Peter, 1993
Gilbert, Lord, 1978
Gilbert, Sir Martin, 2009
Gill, *Hon.* Lord (Brian Gill), 2002
Gillan, Cheryl, 2010
Girvan, Sir (Frederick) Paul, 2007
Glenamara, Lord, 1964
Glidewell, Sir Iain, 1985
Goff of Chieveley, Lord, 1982
Goggins, Paul, 2009
Goldring, Sir John, 2008
Goldsmith, Lord, 2002
Goodlad, Lord, 1992
Gove, Michael, 2010
Gowrie, Earl of, 1984
Graham, Sir Douglas, 1998
Graham of Edmonton, Lord, 1998
Grayling, Chris, 2010
Grieve, Dominic, 2010
Griffiths, Lord, 1980
Grocott, Lord, 2002
Gross, Sir Peter, 2011
Habgood, Rt. Revd Lord, 1983
Hague, William, 1995
Hain, Peter, 2001
Hale of Richmond, Baroness, 1999
Hallett, Dame Heather, 2005
Hamilton, *Hon.* Lord (Arthur Hamilton), 2002
Hamilton of Epsom, Lord, 1991
Hammond, Philip, 2010
Hanley, Sir Jeremy, 1994
Hanson, David, 2007
Hardie, Lord, 1997
Hardie Boys, Sir Michael, 1989
Harman, Harriet, 1997
Harrison, Walter, 1977
Haselhurst, Sir Alan, 1999
Hattersley, Lord, 1975
Hayhoe, Lord, 1985
Hayman, Baroness, 2000
Healey, John, 2008
Healey, Lord, 1964
Heathcoat-Amory, David, 1996
Henry, John, 1996
Herbert, Nick, 2010
Heseltine, Lord, 1979
Heseltine, Sir William, 1986
Hesketh, Lord, 1991
Hewitt, Patricia, 2001
Higgins, Lord, 1979
Higgins, Sir Malachy, 2007
Hill, Keith, 2003
Hirst, Sir David, 1992
Hodge, Margaret, 2003
Hoffmann, Lord, 1992
Hogg, *Hon.* Douglas, 1992
Hollis of Heigham, Baroness, 1999
Hoon, Geoffrey, 1999

Hooper, Sir Anthony, 2004
Hope of Craighead, Lord, 1989
Hope of Thornes, Lord, 1991
Hordern, Sir Peter, 1993
Howard of Lympne, Lord, 1990
Howarth, George, 2005
Howarth of Newport, Lord, 2000
Howe of Aberavon, Lord, 1972
Howell of Guildford, Lord, 1979
Howells, Kim, 2009
Hughes, Sir Anthony, 2006
Hughes, Simon, 2010
Hughes of Stretford, Baroness, 2004
Huhne, Chris, 2010
Hunt, Jeremy, 2010
Hunt, Jonathon, 1989
Hunt of Kings Heath, Lord, 2009
Hunt of Wirral, Lord, 1990
Hurd of Westwell, Lord, 1982
Hutchison, Sir Michael, 1995
Hutton, Lord, 1988
Hutton of Furness, Lord, 2001
Inge, Lord, 2004
Ingraham, Hubert, 1993
Ingram, Adam, 1999
Irvine of Lairg, Lord, 1997
Jack, Michael, 1997
Jackson, Sir Rupert, 2008
Jacob, Sir Robert, 2004
Jacobs, Francis, 2005
Janvrin, Lord, 1998
Jay of Paddington, Baroness, 1998
Jenkin of Roding, Lord, 1973
Johnson, Alan, 2003
Jones, Carwyn, 2010
Jones, Lord, 1999
Jopling, Lord, 1979
Jowell, Tessa, 1998
Judge, Lord, 1996
Jugnauth, Sir Anerood, 1987
Kaufman, Sir Gerald, 1978
Kay, Sir Maurice, 2004
Keene, Sir David, 2000
Keith, Sir Kenneth, 1998
Kelly, Ruth, 2004
Kenilorea, Sir Peter, 1979
Kennedy, Charles, 1999
Kennedy, Jane, 2003
Kennedy, Sir Paul, 1992
Kerr of Monteviot, Baron, 1996
Kerr of Tonaghmore, Lord, 2004
Khan, Sadiq, 2009
King of Bridgwater, Lord, 1979
Kingarth, *Hon.* Lord (Derek Emslie), 2006
Kingsdown, Lord, 1987
Kinnock, Lord, 1983
Kirkwood, *Hon.* Lord (Ian Kirkwood), 2000
Knight, Gregory, 1995
Knight of Weymouth, Lord, 2008
Lammy, David, 2008
Lamont of Lerwick, Lord, 1986
Lang of Monkton, Lord, 1990
Lansley, Andrew, 2010
Latasi, Sir Kamuta, 1996
Latham, Sir David, 2000
Lauti, Sir Toaripi, 1979

Laws, David, 2010
Laws, Sir John, 1999
Lawson of Blaby, Lord, 1981
Leggatt, Sir Andrew, 1990
Letwin, Oliver, 2002
Leveson, Sir Brian, 2006
Liddell of Coatdyke, Baroness, 1998
Lidington, David, 2010
Lilley, Peter, 1990
Lloyd of Berwick, Lord, 1984
Lloyd, Sir Peter, 1994
Lloyd, Sir Timothy, 2005
Llwyd, Elfyn, 2011
London, Bishop of, 1995
Longmore, Sir Andrew, 2001
Luce, Lord, 1986
Lyne, Sir Roderic, 2009
McAvoy, Lord, 2003
McCartney, Sir Ian, 1999
McCollum, Sir Liam, 1997
McConnell of Glenscorrodale, Lord, 2001
MacDermott, Sir John, 1987
Macdonald of Tradeston, Lord, 1999
McFadden, Patrick, 2008
McFall of Alcluith, Lord, 2004
MacGregor of Pulham Market, Lord, 1985
McGuire, Anne, 2008
Mackay, Andrew, 1998
McKay, Sir Ian, 1992
Mackay of Clashfern, Lord, 1979
Mackay of Drumadoon, Lord, 1996
McKinnon, Sir Donald, 1992
Maclean, Hon. Lord (Ranald MacLean), 2001
McLeish, Henry, 2000
Maclennan of Rogart, Lord, 1997
McLoughlin, Patrick, 2005
McMullin, Sir Duncan, 1980
McNally, Lord, 2005
McNulty, Anthony, 2007
MacShane, Denis, 2005
Major, Sir John, 1987
Malloch-Brown, Lord, 2007
Mance, Lord, 1999
Mandelson, Lord, 1998
Marnoch, Hon. Lord (Michael Marnoch), 2001
Martin of Springburn, Lord, 2000
Mason of Barnsley, Lord, 1968
Mates, Michael, 2004
Maude, Hon. Francis, 1992
Mawhinney, Lord, 1994
May, Sir Anthony, 1998
May, Theresa, 2003
Mayhew of Twysden, Lord, 1986
Meacher, Michael, 1997
Mellor, David, 1990
Michael, Alun, 1998
Milburn, Alan, 1998
Miliband, David, 2005
Miliband, Ed, 2007
Millan, Bruce, 1975
Millett, Lord, 1994
Mitchell, Andrew, 2010
Mitchell, Sir James, 1985
Mitchell, Dr Keith, 2004

Molyneaux of Killead, Lord, 1983
Moore, Michael, 1990
Moore, Michael, 2010
Moore of Lower Marsh, Lord, 1986
Moore-Bick, Sir Martin, 2005
Morgan, Sir Declan, 2009
Morgan, Rhodri, 2000
Morris, Charles, 1978
Morris of Aberavon, Lord, 1970
Morris of Manchester, Lord, 1979
Morris of Yardley, Baroness, 1999
Morritt, Sir Robert, 1994
Moses, Sir Alan, 2005
Moyle, Roland, 1978
Mulholland, Frank, 2011
Mummery, Sir John, 1996
Munby, Sir James, 2009
Mundell, David, 2010
Murphy, James, 2008
Murphy, Paul, 1999
Murray, Hon. Lord (Ronald Murray), 1974
Murray, Sir Donald, 1989
Musa, Wilbert, 2005
Mustill, Lord, 1985
Nairne, Sir Patrick, 1982
Namaliu, Sir Rabbie, 1989
Naseby, Lord, 1994
Needham, Sir Richard, 1994
Neill, Sir Brian, 1985
Neuberger of Abbotsbury, Lord, 2004
Neville-Jones, Baroness, 2010
Newton of Braintree, Lord, 1988
Nicholls of Birkenhead, Lord, 1995
Nicholson, Sir Michael, 1995
Nimmo Smith, Hon. Lord (William Nimmo Smith), 2005
Nott, Sir John, 1979
Nourse, Sir Martin, 1985
O'Brien, Mike, 2009
O'Donnell, Turlough, 1979
Oppenheim-Barnes, Baroness, 1979
Osborne, George, 2010
Osborne, Hon. Lord (Kenneth Osborne), 2001
Otton, Sir Philip, 1995
Owen, Lord, 1976
Paeniu, Bikenibeu, 1991
Paice, James, 2010
Palliser, Sir Michael, 1983
Palmer, Sir Geoffrey, 1986
Paraskeva, Dame Janet, 2010
Parker, Sir Jonathan, 2000
Parkinson, Lord, 1981
Paterson, Owen, 2010
Paton, Hon. Lady (Ann Paton), 2007
Patten, Lord, 1990
Patten, Sir Nicholas, 2009
Patten of Barnes, Lord, 1989
Patterson, Percival, 1993
Pattie, Sir Geoffrey, 1987
Paul, Lord, 2009
Peel, Earl, 2006
Pendry, Lord, 2000
Penrose, Hon. Lord (George Penrose), 2000

Peters, Winston, 1998
Philip, Hon. Lord (Alexander Philip), 2005
Phillips of Worth Matravers, Lord, 1995
Pickles, Eric, 2010
Pill, Sir Malcolm, 1995
Pitchford, Sir Christopher, 2010
Portillo, Michael, 1992
Potter, Sir Mark, 1996
Prashar, Baroness, 2009
Prescott, Lord, 1994
Price, George, 1982
Primarolo, Dawn, 2002
Prior, Lord, 1970
Prosser, Hon. Lord (William Prosser), 2000
Puapua, Sir Tomasi, 1982
Purnell, James, 2007
Quin, Baroness, 1998
Radice, Lord, 1999
Raison, Sir Timothy, 1982
Ramsden, James, 1963
Randall, John, 2010
Raynsford, Nick, 2001
Redwood, John, 1993
Reed, Lord, 2008
Reid, George, 2004
Reid of Cardowan, Lord, 1998
Renton of Mount Harry, Lord, 1989
Richard, Lord, 1993
Richards, Sir Stephen, 2005
Richardson, Sir Ivor, 1978
Riddell, Peter, 2010
Rifkind, Sir Malcolm, 1986
Rimer, Sir Colin, 2007
Rix, Sir Bernard, 2000
Robathan, Andrew, 2010
Roberts of Conwy, Lord, 1991
Robertson of Port Ellen, Lord, 1997
Robinson, Peter, 2007
Roch, Sir John, 1993
Rodgers of Quarry Bank, Lord, 1975
Rooker, Lord, 1999
Roper, Lord, 2005
Rose, Sir Christopher, 1992
Ross, Hon. Lord (Donald MacArthur), 1985
Royall of Blaisdon, Baroness, 2008
Ruddock, Joan, 2010
Ryan, Joan, 2007
Ryder of Wensum, Lord, 1990
Sainsbury, Sir Timothy, 1992
St John of Fawsley, Lord, 1979
Salisbury, Marquess of, 1994
Salmond, Alex, 2007
Sandiford, Erskine, 1989
Saville of Newdigate, Lord, 1994
Sawyer, Dame Joan, 2004
Schiemann, Sir Konrad, 1995
Scotland of Asthal, Baroness, 2001
Scott of Foscote, Lord, 1991
Seaga, Edward, 1981
Sedley, Sir Stephen, 1999
Selkirk of Douglas, Lord, 1996
Shapps, Grant, 2010
Sheldon, Lord, 1977

Shephard of Northwold, Baroness, 1992
Sheil, Sir John, 2005
Shipley, Jennifer, 1998
Short, Clare, 1997
Shutt of Greetland, Lord, 2009
Simmonds, Kennedy Sir, 1984
Sinclair, Ian, 1977
Slade, Sir Christopher, 1982
Smith, Andrew, 1997
Smith, Dame Janet, 2002
Smith, Jacqueline, 2003
Smith of Basildon, Baroness, 2009
Smith of Finsbury, Lord, 1997
Soames, *Hon.* (Arthur) Nicholas, 2011
Somare, Sir Michael, 1977
Spellar, John, 2001
Spelman, Caroline, 2010
Stanley, Sir John, 1984
Staughton, Sir Christopher, 1988
Steel of Aikwood, Lord, 1977
Stephen, Sir Ninian, 1979
Stewartby, Lord, 1989
Steyn, Lord, 1992
Strang, Gavin, 1997
Strathclyde, Lord, 1995
Straw, Jack, 1997
Stuart-Smith, Sir Murray, 1988
Sullivan, Sir Jeremy, 2009
Sutherland, *Hon.* Lord (Ranald Sutherland), 2000
Swayne, Desmond, 2011
Swire, Hugo, 2010

Symons of Vernham Dean, Baroness, 2001
Talboys, Sir Brian, 1977
Tapsell, Sir Peter, 2011
Taylor of Bolton, Baroness, 1997
Tebbit, Lord, 1981
Templeman, Lord, 1978
Thatcher, Baroness, 1970
Thomas, Edmund, 1996
Thomas, Sir Roger, 2003
Thomas, Sir Swinton, 1994
Thorpe, Jeremy, 1967
Thorpe, Sir Matthew, 1995
Timms, Stephen, 2006
Tipping, Andrew, 1998
Tizard, Robert, 1986
Tomlinson, Sir Stephen, 2011
Touhig, Lord, 2006
Toulson, Sir Roger, 2007
Trefgarne, Lord, 1989
Trimble, Lord, 1997
Trumpington, Baroness, 1992
Tuckey, Sir Simon, 1998
Ullswater, Viscount, 1994
Upton, Simon, 1999
Vadera, Baroness, 2009
Vaz, Keith, 2006
Villiers, Theresa, 2010
Waddington, Lord, 1987
Waite, Sir John, 1993
Wakeham, Lord, 1983
Waldegrave of North Hill, Lord, 1990

Walker of Gestingthorpe, Lord, 1997
Wall, Sir Nicholas, 2004
Wallace of Tankerness, Lord, 2000
Waller, Sir Mark, 1996
Ward, Sir Alan, 1995
Warner, Lord, 2006
Warsi, Baroness, 2010
West of Spithead, Lord, 2010
Wheatley, *Hon.* Lord (John Wheatley), 2007
Wheeler, Sir John, 1993
Whitty, Lord, 2005
Wicks, Malcolm, 2008
Widdecombe, Ann, 1997
Wigley, Dafydd, 1997
Willetts, David, 2010
Williams, Alan, 1977
Williams of Crosby, Baroness, 1974
Williamson of Horton, Lord, 2007
Wills, Lord, 2008
Wilson, Brian, 2003
Wilson, Sir Nicholas, 2005
Winterton, Rosie, 2006
Wingti, Paias, 1987
Withers, Reginald, 1977
Woodhouse, Sir Owen, 1974
Woodward, Shaun, 2007
Woolf, Lord, 1986
York, Archbishop of, 2005
Young, Sir George, 1993
Young of Graffham, Lord, 1984
Zacca, Edward, 1992

PRIVY COUNCIL OF NORTHERN IRELAND

The Privy Council of Northern Ireland had responsibilities in Northern Ireland similar to those of the Privy Council in Great Britain until the Northern Ireland Act 1974. Membership of the Privy Council of Northern Ireland is retained for life. Since the Northern Ireland Constitution Act 1973 no further appointments have been made. The postnominal initials PC (NI) are used to differentiate its members from those of the Privy Council.

MEMBERS *as at August 2011*
Bailie, Robin, 1971
Bleakley, David, 1971
Dobson, John, 1969
Kilclooney, Lord, 1970
Porter, Sir Robert, 1969

PARLIAMENT

The United Kingdom constitution is not contained in any single document but has evolved over time, formed partly by statute, partly by common law and partly by convention. A constitutional monarchy, the UK is governed by ministers of the crown in the name of the sovereign, who is head both of the state and of the government.

The organs of government are the legislature (parliament), the executive and the judiciary. The executive comprises HM government (the cabinet and other ministers), government departments and local authorities (*see* Government Departments, Public Bodies and Local Government sections). The judiciary (*see* Law Courts and Offices section) pronounces on the law, both written and unwritten, interprets statutes and is responsible for the enforcement of the law; the judiciary is independent of both the legislature and the executive.

THE MONARCHY

The sovereign personifies the state and is, in law, an integral part of the legislature, head of the executive, head of the judiciary, commander-in-chief of all armed forces of the crown and supreme governor of the Church of England. In the Channel Islands and the Isle of Man, which are crown dependencies, the sovereign is represented by a lieutenant-governor. In the member states of the Commonwealth of which the sovereign is head of state, her representative is a governor-general; in UK overseas territories the sovereign is usually represented by a governor, who is responsible to the British government.

Although in practice the powers of the monarchy are now very limited, and restricted mainly to the advisory and ceremonial, there are important acts of government which require the participation of the sovereign. These include summoning, proroguing and dissolving parliament, giving royal assent to bills passed by parliament, appointing important office-holders, eg government ministers, judges, bishops and governors, conferring peerages, knighthoods and other honours, and granting pardon to a person wrongly convicted of a crime. The sovereign appoints the prime minister; by convention this office is held by the leader of the political party which enjoys, or can secure, a majority of votes in the House of Commons. In international affairs the sovereign as head of state has the power to declare war and make peace, to recognise foreign states and governments, to conclude treaties and to annex or cede territory. However, as the sovereign entrusts executive power to ministers of the crown and acts on the advice of her ministers, which she cannot ignore, royal prerogative powers are in practice exercised by ministers, who are responsible to parliament.

Ministerial responsibility does not diminish the sovereign's importance to the smooth working of government. She holds meetings of the Privy Council (*see* below), gives audiences to her ministers and other officials at home and overseas, receives accounts of cabinet decisions, reads dispatches and signs state papers; she must be informed and consulted on every aspect of national life; and she must show complete impartiality.

COUNSELLORS OF STATE

If the sovereign travels abroad for more than a few days or suffers from a temporary illness, it is necessary to appoint members of the royal family, known as counsellors of state, under letters patent to carry out the chief functions of the monarch, including the holding of Privy Councils and giving royal assent to acts passed by parliament. The normal procedure is to appoint three or four members of the royal family among those members remaining in the UK, provided they are over 21. There are currently five counsellors of state.

In the event of the sovereign on accession being under the age of 18 years, or by infirmity of mind or body, rendered incapable of performing the royal functions, provision is made for a regency.

THE PRIVY COUNCIL

The sovereign in council, or Privy Council, was the chief source of executive power until the system of cabinet government developed. Its main function today is to advise the sovereign on the approval of various statutory functions and acts of the royal prerogative. These powers are exercised through orders in council and royal proclamations, approved by the Queen at meetings of the Privy Council. The council is also able to exercise a number of statutory duties without approval from the sovereign, including powers of supervision over the registering bodies for the medical and allied professions. These duties are exercised through orders of council.

Although appointment as a privy counsellor is for life, only those who are currently government ministers are involved in the day-to-day business of the council. A full council is summoned only on the death of the sovereign or when the sovereign announces his or her intention to marry. (For a full list of privy counsellors, *see* the Privy Council section.)

There are a number of advisory Privy Council committees whose meetings the sovereign does not attend. Some are prerogative committees, such as those dealing with legislative matters submitted by the legislatures of the Channel Islands and the Isle of Man or with applications for charters of incorporation; and some are provided for by statute, eg those for the universities of Oxford and Cambridge and some Scottish universities.

Administrative work is carried out by the Privy Council Office under the direction of the Lord President of the Council, a cabinet minister.

JUDICIAL COMMITTEE OF THE PRIVY COUNCIL
Supreme Court Building, Parliament Square, London SW1P 3BD
T 020-7960 1500 W www.jcpc.gov.uk

The Judicial Committee of the Privy Council is the court of final appeal from courts of the UK dependencies, courts of independent Commonwealth countries which have retained the right of appeal and courts of the Channel Islands and the Isle of Man. It also hears very occasional appeals from a number of ancient and ecclesiastical courts.

The committee is composed of privy counsellors who hold, or have held, high judicial office. Only three or five judges hear each case, and these are usually justices of the Supreme Court.

PARLIAMENT

Parliament is the supreme law-making authority and can legislate for the UK as a whole or for any parts of it separately (the Channel Islands and the Isle of Man are crown dependencies and not part of the UK). The main functions of parliament are to pass laws, to enable the government to raise taxes and to scrutinise government policy and administration, particularly proposals for expenditure. International treaties and agreements are customarily presented to parliament before ratification.

Parliament can trace its roots to two characteristics of Anglo-Saxon rule: the *witan* (a meeting of the king, nobles and advisors) and the *moot* (county meetings where local matters were discussed). However, it was the parliament that Simon de Montfort called in 1265 that is accepted as the forerunner to modern parliament, as it included non-noble representatives from counties, cities and towns alongside the nobility. The nucleus of early parliaments at the beginning of the 14th century were the officers of the king's household and the king's judges, joined by such ecclesiastical and lay magnates as the king might summon to form a prototype 'House of Lords', and occasionally by the knights of the shires, burgesses and proctors of the lower clergy. By the end of Edward III's reign a 'House of Commons' was beginning to appear; the first known Speaker was elected in 1377.

Parliamentary procedure is based on custom and precedent, partly formulated in the standing orders of both houses of parliament. Each house has the right to control its own internal proceedings and to commit for contempt. The system of debate in the two houses is similar; when a motion has been moved, the Speaker proposes the question as the subject of a debate. Members speak from wherever they have been sitting. Questions are decided by a vote on a simple majority. Draft legislation is introduced, in either house, as a bill. Bills can be introduced by a government minister or a private member, but in practice the majority of bills which become law are introduced by the government. To become law, a bill must be passed by each house (for parliamentary stages, *see* Parliamentary Information) and then sent to the sovereign for the royal assent, after which it becomes an act of parliament.

Proceedings of both houses are public, except on extremely rare occasions. The minutes (called *Votes and Proceedings in the Commons,* and *Minutes of Proceedings in the Lords*) and the speeches *(The Official Report of Parliamentary Debates,* Hansard) are published daily. Proceedings are also recorded for transmission on radio and television and stored in the Parliamentary Recording Unit before transfer to the National Sound Archive. Television cameras have been allowed into the House of Lords since 1985 and into the House of Commons since 1989; committee meetings may also be televised.

By the Parliament Act of 1911, the maximum duration of a parliament is five years (if not previously dissolved), the term being reckoned from the date given on the writs for the new parliament. The maximum life has been prolonged by legislation in such rare circumstances as the two world wars (31 January 1911 to 25 November 1918; 26 November 1935 to 15 June 1945). Dissolution and writs for a general election are ordered by the sovereign on the advice of the prime minister. The life of a parliament is divided into sessions, usually of one year in length, beginning and ending most often in October or November.

DEVOLUTION

The Scottish parliament and the National Assembly for Wales have legislative power over all devolved matters, ie matters not reserved to Westminster or otherwise outside its powers. The Northern Ireland Assembly has legislative authority in the fields previously administered by the Northern Ireland departments. The assembly was suspended in October 2002 and dissolved in April 2003, before being reinstated on 8 May 2007. For further information, *see* the Regional Government section.

THE HOUSE OF LORDS

London SW1A 0PW
T 020-7219 3000 Information Office 020-7219 3107
E hlinfo@parliament.uk W www.parliament.uk

The House of Lords is the second chamber, or 'Upper House', of the UK's bicameral parliament. Until the beginning of the 20th century, the House of Lords had considerable power, being able to veto any bill submitted to it by the House of Commons. Today the main functions of the House of Lords are to contribute to the legislative process, to act as a check on the government, and to provide a forum of independent expertise. Its judicial role as final court of appeal ended in 2009 as a result of the establishment of a new UK supreme court (*see* Law Courts and Offices section).

The House of Lords has a number of select committees. Some relate to the internal affairs of the house – such as its management and administration – while others carry out important investigative work on matters of public interest. The main areas of work are: Europe, science, the economy, the constitution and communications. House of Lords' investigative committees look at broader issues and do not mirror government departments as the select committees in the House of Commons do.

On 12 June 2003 the government announced reforms of the judicial function and the role of the Lord Chancellor as a judge and Speaker of the House of Lords. In 2006 the position of Lord Chancellor was significantly altered by the Constitutional Reform Act 2005. The office holder is no longer Speaker of the House of Lords nor head of the judiciary in England and Wales, but remains a cabinet minister (the Lord Chancellor and Secretary of State for Justice), currently in the House of Commons. The function of the Speaker of the House of Lords was devolved to the newly created post of Lord Speaker. The Rt. Hon. Baroness Hayman was elected as the first Lord Speaker by the house on 4 July 2006.

Members of the House of Lords comprise life peers created under the Life Peerages Act 1958, 92 hereditary peers under the House of Lords Act 1999 and Lords of Appeal in Ordinary, ie law lords, under the Appellate Jurisdiction Act 1876*. The Archbishops of Canterbury and York, the Bishops of London, Durham and Winchester, and the 21 senior diocesan bishops of the Church of England are also members.

The House of Lords Act provides for 90 elected hereditary peers to remain in the House of Lords until longer-term reform of the House has been carried out; 42 Conservative, 28 crossbench, three Liberal Democrat and two Labour. Elections for each of the party groups and the crossbenches were held in October and November 1999. Fifteen office holders were elected by the whole house. Two hereditary peers with royal duties, the Earl Marshal and the Lord Great Chamberlain, are also members.

Peers are disqualified from sitting in the house if they are:

- aliens, ie any peer who is not a British citizen, a Commonwealth citizen (under the British Nationality Act 1981) or a citizen of the Republic of Ireland
- under the age of 21
- undischarged bankrupts or, in Scotland, those whose estate is sequestered
- a non-domiciled resident in the UK for tax purposes
- convicted of treason

Bishops retire at the age of 70 and cease to be members of the house at that time.

Members who do not wish to attend sittings of the House of Lords may apply for leave of absence for the duration of a parliament.

Members of the House of Lords, who are not paid a salary, may claim a flat-rate daily attendance allowance of £300 (for peers that attend for a full sitting day) or £150 (for those peers that attend for less than a full sitting day), or may choose to make no claim for each sitting day they attend the house.

* Although the office of Lord of Appeal in Ordinary no longer exists, retired law lords remain in the House of Lords as life peers. Law lords who became justices of the UK supreme court are not permitted to sit or vote in the House of Lords until they retire.

COMPOSITION *as at 1 July 2011*

Archbishops and bishops	24
Life peers under the Appellate Jurisdiction Act 1876	23
Life peers under the Life Peerages Act 1958	690
Peers under the House of Lords Act 1999	90
Total	827

STATE OF THE PARTIES *as at 1 July 2011†*

Conservative	217
Labour	242
Liberal Democrat	92
Crossbench	184
Archbishops and bishops	24
Other	30
Total	789

† Excluding 22 peers on leave of absence, one currently suspended, 14 disqualified as senior members of the judiciary and one disqualified as an MEP

HOUSE OF LORDS PAY BANDS

Staff are placed in the following pay bands according to their level of responsibility and taking account of other factors such as experience and marketability.

Judicial group 4	£172,753
Senior band 3	£101,500–£145,629
Senior band 2	£82,900–£135,970
Senior band 1A	£67,600–£113,202
Senior band 1	£58,200–£100,374
Band A1	£56,723–£72,788
Band A2	£47,164–£60,221

OFFICERS AND OFFICIALS

The house is presided over by the Lord Speaker, whose powers differ from those of the Speaker of the House of Commons. The Lord Speaker has no power to maintain order because the House of Lords is self-regulating.

A panel of deputy speakers is appointed by Royal Commission. The first deputy speaker is the Chair of Committees, a salaried officer of the house appointed at the beginning of each session. He or she takes the chair when the whole house is in committee, as well as in some select committees. He or she is assisted by a panel of deputy chairs, headed by the salaried Principal Deputy Chair of Committees, who is also chair of the European Union Committee of the house.

The Clerk of the Parliaments is the accounting officer and the chief permanent official responsible for the administration of the house. The Gentleman Usher of the Black Rod is responsible for security and other services and also has royal duties as secretary to the Lord Great Chamberlain.

Lord Speaker (£101,038), Rt. Hon. Baroness Hayman
Chair of Committees (£84,524), Lord Brabazon of Tara
Principal Deputy Chair of Committees (£79,076), Lord Roper
Clerk of the Parliaments (Judicial Group 4), D. R. Beamish, LLM
Clerk Assistant (Senior Band 3), E. C. Ollard
Reading Clerk and Clerk of the Overseas Office (Senior Band 2), Dr R. H. Walters, DPHIL
Clerk of the Committees (Senior Band 2), Dr F. P Tudor
Director of Facilities (Senior Band 2), C. V. Woodall
Finance Director (Senior Band 1A), A. Makower
Head of Human Resources (Senior Band 1A), S. P. Burton
Clerk of the Judicial Office and Registrar of Members' Interests (Senior Band 1A), B. P. Keith
Director of Information Services and Librarian (Senior Band 2), Dr E. Hallam Smith
Clerk of Public and Private Bill Office and Examiner of Petitions for Private Bills in the House of Lords (Senior Band 1A), T. V. Mohan
Editor of the Official Report (Senior Band 1), A. S. Nicholls
Clerk of the Records (Senior Band 1), Dr C. Shenton
Deputy Finance Director and Head of Finance (Senior Band 1), J. P. Smith
Director of Public Information (Band A1), B. Hiscock
Counsel to the Chairman of Committees (Senior Band 2), M. Thomas
Second Counsel to the Chairman of Committees (Senior Band 2), A. Roberts
Legal Adviser to the Human Rights Committee (Senior Band 2), M. Hunt
Change Manager (Senior Band 1), Mrs M. E. Ollard
Clerk of the Journals (Senior Band 1), C. Johnson
Clerk of the European Union Committee (Senior Band 1A), J. Vaughan
Clerks of Select Committees (Senior Band 1), Ms C. Salmon Percival; Ms C. K. Mawson
Gentleman Usher of the Black Rod and Serjeant-at-Arms (Senior Band 2), Lt.-Gen. David Leakey, CMG, CBE
Yeoman Usher of the Black Rod and Deputy Serjeant-at-Arms (Band A2), T. Lloyd-Jukes

LORD GREAT CHAMBERLAIN'S OFFICE

Lord Great Chamberlain, Marquess of Cholmondeley
Secretary to the Lord Great Chamberlain, Lt.-Gen. David Leakey, CMG, CBE

SELECT COMMITTEES

The main House of Lords select committees, as at July 2011, are as follows:

Administration and Works Committee – Chair, vacant; *Clerk*, Tom Wilson
Communications Committee – Chair, Lord Inglewood; *Clerk*, Audrey Nelson

Constitution Committee – Chair, Baroness Jay of Paddington; Clerk, Emily Baldock

Delegated Powers and Regulatory Reform – Chair, Baroness Thomas of Winchester; Clerk, Kate Lawrence

Economic Affairs – Chair, Lord MacGregor of Pulham Market; Clerk, Bill Sinton

European Union – Chair, Lord Roper; Clerks, Jake Vaughan, Kate Meanwell

European Union – Sub-committees:

A (Economic and Financial Affairs and International Trade) – Chair, Lord Harrison; Clerk, Antony Willott

B (Internal Market, Energy and Transport) – Chair, Baroness O'Cathain; Clerk, John Turner

C (Foreign Affairs, Defence and Development Policy) – Chair, Lord Teverson; Clerk, Kathryn Colvin

D (Agriculture, Fisheries and Environment) – Chair, Lord Carter of Coles; Clerk, Paul Bristow

E (Justice and Institutions) – Chair, Lord Bowness; Clerk, John Turner

F (Home Affairs) – Chair, Lord Hannay of Chiswick; Clerk, Michael Collon

G (Social Policies and Consumer Protection) – Chair, Baroness Young of Hornsey; Clerk, Talitha Rowland

House Committee – Chair, Baroness Hayman; Clerk, Chris Clarke

Liaison Committee – Chair, Lord Brabazon of Tara; Clerk, Edward Ollard

Privileges and Conduct – Chair, Lord Brabazon of Tara; Clerk, vacant

Lords' Conduct Sub-committee – Chair, Baroness Manningham-Buller; Clerk, vacant

Merits of Statutory Instruments – Chair, Rt. Hon. Lord Goodlad; Clerk, Kate Lawrence

National Security Strategy Joint Commitee – Chair, Rt. Hon. Margaret Beckett, MP; Clerks, Michael Collon (Lords); Philippa Helme (Commons)

Refreshment Committee – Chair, Lord Brabazon of Tara; Clerk, vacant

Science and Technology – Chair, Lord Krebs; Clerk, Christine Salmon Percival

Science and Technology Sub-Committee I – Chair, Baroness Neuberger; Clerk, Daisy Ricketts

Selection Committee – Chair, Lord Brabazon of Tara; Clerk, vacant

Human Rights Joint Committee – Chair, Hywel Francis, MP; Clerk, Robert Whiteway (Lords)

Security Joint Committee – Chair, John Randall, MP; Clerks, Mr Wilson (Commons); Mr Clarke (Lords)

Statutory Instruments Joint Committee – Chair, George Mudie, MP; Clerk, John Whatley

THE HOUSE OF COMMONS

London SW1A 0AA
T 020-7219 3000 W www.parliament.uk

HOUSE OF COMMONS INFORMATION OFFICE
Norman Shaw Building (North), London SW1A 2TT
T 020-7219 4272 E hcinfo@parliament.uk

The members of the House of Commons are elected by universal adult suffrage. For electoral purposes, the UK is divided into constituencies, each of which returns one member to the House of Commons, the member being the candidate who obtains the largest number of votes cast in the constituency. To ensure equitable representation, the four Boundary Commissions keep constituency boundaries under review and recommend any re-distribution of seats which may seem necessary because of

population movements etc. At the 2010 general election the number of seats increased from 646 to 650. Of the present 650 seats, there are 533 for England, 40 for Wales, 59 for Scotland and 18 for Northern Ireland.

NUMBER OF SEATS IN THE HOUSE OF COMMONS BY COUNTRY

	2005	2010
England	529	533
Wales	40	40
Scotland	59	59
Northern Ireland	18	18
Total	646	650

ELECTIONS

Elections are by secret ballot, each elector casting one vote; voting is not compulsory. (For entitlement to vote in parliamentary elections, see Legal Notes.) When a seat becomes vacant between general elections, a by-election is held.

British subjects and citizens of the Irish Republic can stand for election as MPs provided they are 18 or over and not subject to disqualification. Those disqualified from sitting in the house include:

• undischarged bankrupts
• people sentenced to more than one year's imprisonment
• members of the House of Lords (but hereditary peers not sitting in the Lords are eligible)
• holders of certain offices listed in the House of Commons Disqualification Act 1975, eg members of the judiciary, civil service, regular armed forces, police forces, some local government officers and some members of public corporations and government commissions

A candidate does not require any party backing but his or her nomination for election must be supported by the signatures of ten people registered in the constituency. A candidate must also deposit £500 with the returning officer, which is forfeit if the candidate does not receive more than 5 per cent of the votes cast. All election expenses at a general election, except the candidate's personal expenses, are subject to a statutory limit of £7,150, plus five pence for each elector in a borough constituency or seven pence for each elector in a county constituency.

See pages 140–185 for an alphabetical list of MPs and results of the general election in 2010.

STATE OF THE PARTIES as at July 2011*

Party	Seats
Conservative	305
Labour	256
Liberal Democrats	57
Democratic Unionist Party	8
Scottish National Party	6
Sinn Fein (have not taken their seats)	5
Plaid Cymru	3
Social Democratic & Labour Party	3
Alliance	1
Green	1
Independent	1
The Speaker and three Deputy Speakers	4
Total	650

* Working majority of 84; 305 Conservative and 57 Liberal Democrat MPs less 279 of all other parties (excluding the speaker, deputy speakers and Sinn Fein)

BUSINESS

The week's business of the house is outlined each Thursday by the leader of the house, after consultation between the chief government whip and the chief opposition whip. A quarter to a third of the time will be taken up by the government's legislative programme and the rest by other business. As a rule, bills likely to raise political controversy are introduced in the Commons before going on to the Lords, and the Commons claims exclusive control in respect of national taxation and expenditure. Bills such as the finance bill, which imposes taxation, and the consolidated fund bills, which authorise expenditure, must begin in the Commons. A bill of which the financial provisions are subsidiary may begin in the Lords, and the Commons may waive its rights in regard to Lords' amendments affecting finance.

The Commons has a public register of MPs' financial and certain other interests; this is published annually as a House of Commons paper. Members must also disclose any relevant financial interest or benefit in a matter before the house when taking part in a debate, in certain other proceedings of the house, or in consultations with other MPs, with ministers or with civil servants.

MEMBERS' PAY AND ALLOWANCES

Since 1911 members of the House of Commons have received salary payments; facilities for free travel were introduced in 1924. Salary rates for the last 30 years are as follows:

1981 Jun	£13,950	1996 Jul	£43,000
1982 Jun	14,510	1997 Apr	43,860
1983 Jun	15,308	1998 Apr	45,066
1984 Jan	16,106	1999 Apr	47,008
1985 Jan	16,904	2000 Apr	48,371
1986 Jan	17,702	2001 Apr	49,822
1987 Jan	18,500	2002 Apr	55,118
1988 Jan	22,548	2003 Apr	56,358
1989 Jan	24,107	2004 Apr	57,485
1990 Jan	26,701	2005 Apr	59,095
1991 Jan	28,970	2006 Apr	59,686
1992 Jan	30,854	2007 Apr	61,181
1993 Jan	30,854	2008 Apr	63,291
1994 Jan	31,687	2009 Apr	64,766
1995 Jan	33,189	2010 Apr	65,738
1996 Jan	34,085	2011 Apr	65,738

The Independent Parliamentary Standards Authority (IPSA) was established under the Parliamentary Standards Act 2009 and is responsible for the independent regulation and administration of MPs' expenses, as well as for paying the salaries of MPs and their staff members. Since May 2011 IPSA has also been responsible for determining MPs' pay and setting the level of any increase to their salary.

For 2011–12, the office costs expenditure budget is £24,000 for London area MPs and £21,500 for non-London area MPs. The maximum annual staffing expenditure for each MP is set at £115,000.

Since 1972 MPs have been able to claim reimbursement for the additional cost of staying overnight away from their main residence while on parliamentary business. This is not payable to London area MPs and those MPs who reside in 'grace and favour' accommodation. Accommodation expenses for MPs claiming rental payments in the London area is capped at £19,900 per year; for MPs who own their own homes, mortgage

interest and associated expenses up to £17,500 are payable.

For ministerial salaries see Government Departments.

MEMBERS' PENSIONS

Pension arrangements for MPs were first introduced in 1964. Under the Parliamentary Contributory Pension Fund (PCPF), MPs receive a pension on retirement based upon their salary in their final year, and upon their number of years' service as an MP. Members may pay a contribution rate of 5.9, 7.9 or 11.9 per cent and build up a pension of 1.6, 2 or 2.5 per cent of salary for each year of service. Pensions are normally payable upon retirement at age 65; the pension payable is subject to a maximum of 66.6 per cent of salary, inclusive of pensions from employment or self-employment prior to becoming an MP. There are provisions in place for: early retirement for those MPs who cease to serve between the ages of 55 and 65; MPs of any age who retire due to ill health; and pensions for widows/widowers of MPs. All pensions are index-linked. There is also an Exchequer contribution; currently 28.7 per cent of an MP's salary.

The House of Commons Members' Fund provides for annual or lump sum grants to ex-MPs, their widows or widowers, and children of those who either ceased to serve as an MP prior to the PCPF being established or who are experiencing hardship. Members contribute £24 a year and the Exchequer £215,000 a year to the fund.

HOUSE OF COMMONS PAY BANDS

Staff are placed in the following Senior Civil Service pay bands. These pay bands apply to the most senior staff in departments and agencies.

Pay Band 1	£58,200–£93,380
Pay Band 1A	£67,600–£105,560
Pay Band 2	£82,900–£124,845
Pay Band 3	£101,500–£139,829

OFFICERS AND OFFICIALS

The House of Commons is presided over by the Speaker, who has considerable powers to maintain order. A deputy speaker, the Chairman of Ways and Means, and two deputy chairs may preside over sittings of the House of Commons; they are elected by the house, and, like the Speaker, neither speak nor vote other than in their official capacity.

The staff of the house are employed by a commission chaired by the Speaker. The heads of the six House of Commons departments are permanent officers of the house, not MPs. The Clerk of the House is the principal adviser to the Speaker on the privileges and procedures of the house, the conduct of the business of the house, and committees. The Serjeant-at-Arms is responsible for security and ceremonial functions of the house.

Speaker (£145,492)*, Rt. Hon. John Bercow, MP (Buckingham)

Chairman of Ways and Means (£107,108), Lindsay Hoyle, MP

First Deputy Chairman of Ways and Means (£102,098), Nigel Evans, MP

Second Deputy Chairman of Ways and Means (£102,098), Rt. Hon. Dawn Primarolo, MP

Parliamentary Commissioner for Standards in Public Life, John Lyon, CB

* Salaries in brackets are the maximum available. Ministers have opted not to take a pay rise for 2011–12

OFFICES OF THE SPEAKER AND CHAIRMAN OF WAYS AND MEANS
Acting Speaker's Secretary, P. Barratt
Chaplain to the Speaker, Revd Rose Hudson-Wilkin
Secretary to the Chairman of Ways and Means, E. Wilson
Clerk of the House of Commons and Chief Executive, Robert Rogers

OFFICE OF THE CHIEF EXECUTIVE
Head of Office, M. Hamlyn
Director of Internal Audit, P. Dillon-Robinson

DEPARTMENT OF CHAMBER AND COMMITTEE SERVICES
Director-General and Clerk Assistant, R. J. Rogers
Principal Clerks
    Table Office, A. R. Kennon
    Journals, L. Laurence Smyth
    Overseas Office, M. Hutton
Director of Departmental Services, N. Walker

VOTE OFFICE
Deliverer of the Vote, C. Fogarty
Deputy Deliverers of the Vote, O. B. T. Sweeney *(Parliamentary)*; T. P. McVeagh *(Production)*

COMMITTEE DIRECTORATE
Clerk of Committees, Ms J. Sharpe
Principal Clerk and Deputy Head of Committee Office, Ms P. Helme
Clerk of Domestic Committees/Secretary to the Commission, D. J. Gerhold
Select Committees, P. A. Evans; C. J. Poyser
Head of Scrutiny Unit, C. A. Shaw
Director of Broadcasting, T. Jeffes

LEGISLATION DIRECTORATE
Clerk of Legislation, D. Natzler
Principal Clerks
    Delegated Legislation, J. Benger
    Bills, S. J. Patrick
    National Parliament Office (Brussels), E. J. Beale
    Ways and Means Office, E. Wilson

OFFICIAL REPORT DIRECTORATE
Editor, Miss L. Sutherland
Deputy Editors, Ms V. Widgery; A. Newton

SERJEANT-AT-ARMS DIRECTORATE
Serjeant-at-Arms, Mrs J. Pay
Deputy Serjeant-at-Arms, M. Naworynsky
Assistant Serjeant-at-Arms, Mrs T. Cullen

LEGAL SERVICES OFFICE
Speaker's Counsel and Head of Legal Services Office, M. Carpenter
Counsel for European Legislation, P. Hardy
Counsel for Legislation, P. Davis
Deputy Counsel, P. Brooksbank; P. Davies; D. Greenberg
Senior Assistant Counsel, Ms V. Daly
Assistant Counsel, Ms H. Emes

DEPARTMENT OF FACILITIES
Director-General, J. Borley
Director of Business Management, J. Greenaway
Parliamentary Director of Estates, M. Barlex
Director of Accommodation Services, J. Robertson
Director of Facilities Finance, P. Collins

Executive Officer, M. Trott
Director of Catering Services, Mrs S. Harrison
Operations Manager, R. Gibbs
Executive Chef, M. Hill

DEPARTMENT OF FINANCE
Director of Finance, Mrs M. Barrett
Director of Financial Management, C. Ridley
Director of Commercial Services, vacant
Director of Savings, Ms. E. Honer
Head of Pensions, J. Walker

DEPARTMENT OF HUMAN RESOURCES AND CHANGE
Director-General of HR and Change, A. J. Walker
Director of Business and Capability, Ms J. Rissen
Director of Human Resource Services, Mrs H. Bryson
Director of Change, vacant
Director of Commercial Services, Ms B. Mohan
Head of Occupational Safety, Health and Wellbeing Service, Dr M. McDougall

DEPARTMENT OF INFORMATION SERVICES
Director-General and Librarian, J. Pullinger
Directors, vacant *(Service Delivery)*; Prof. D. Cope *(Parliamentary Office of Science and Technology)*; B. Morgan *(Research)*; R. Twigger *(Information Services)*; Ms A. Walker *(Public Information)*; S. Wise *(Information Management)*; Ms H. Wood *(SPIRE Programme)*
Media and Communications Adviser, Ms E. Parratt
Parliamentary Outreach Officer, Ms C. Cowan
Visitor and Information Manager, C. Weeds

PARLIAMENTARY INFORMATION AND COMMUNICATION TECHNOLOGY (ICT)
Director of Parliamentary ICT, Ms J. Miller
Director of Technology Directorate, S. O'Connor
Director of Operations and Members Services, M. Taylor
Director of Resources, F. Reid
Director of Programmes and Project Development, R. Ware
Director of Network Programme, I. Montgomery

SELECT COMMITTEES
The more significant committees, as at August 2011, are:

DEPARTMENTAL COMMITTEES
Business, Innovation and Skills – Chair, Adrian Bailey, MP; Clerk, James Davies
Communities and Local Government – Chair, Clive Betts, MP; Clerk, Huw Yardley
Culture, Media and Sport – Chair, John Whittingdale, MP; Clerk, Emily Commander
Defence – Chair, Rt. Hon. James Arbuthnot, MP; Clerk, Alda Barry
Education – Chair, Graham Stuart, MP; Clerk, Kenneth Fox
Energy and Climate Change – Chair, Tim Yeo, MP; Clerk, Nerys Welfoot
Environment, Food and Rural Affairs – Chair, Anne McIntosh, MP; Clerk, Richard Cooke
Foreign Affairs – Chair, Richard Ottaway, MP; Clerk, Dr Robin James
Health – Chair, Rt. Hon. Stephen Dorell, MP; Clerk, David Lloyd
Home Affairs – Chair, Rt. Hon. Keith Vaz, MP; Clerk, Elizabeth Flood
International Development – Chair, Rt. Hon. Malcolm Bruce, MP; Clerk, Dr David Harrison

Justice – *Chair,* Rt. Hon. Sir Alan Beith, MP; *Clerk,* Tom Goldsmith

Northern Ireland Affairs – *Chair,* Laurence Robertson, MP; *Clerk,* Mike Clark

Scottish Affairs – *Chair,* Ian Davidson, MP; *Clerk,* Dr Rebecca Davies

Transport – *Chair,* Louise Ellman, MP; *Clerk,* Dr Mark Egan

Treasury – *Chair,* Andrew Tyrie, MP; *Clerk,* Chris Stanton

Welsh Affairs – *Chair,* David T. C. Davies, MP; *Clerk,* Adrian Jenner

Work and Pensions – *Chair,* Dame Anne Begg, MP; *Clerk,* Carol Oxborough

NON-DEPARTMENTAL COMMITTEES

Environmental Audit – *Chair,* Joan Walley, MP; *Clerk,* Simon Fiander

Political and Constitutional Reform – *Chair,* Graham Allen, MP; *Clerk,* Steven Mark

Procedure – *Chair,* Rt. Hon. Greg Knight, MP; *Clerk,* Dr Lynn Gardner

Public Accounts – *Chair,* Rt. Hon. Margaret Hodge, MP; *Clerk,* Philip Aylett

Public Administration – *Chair,* Bernard Jenkin, MP; *Clerk,* Clive Porro

Science and Technology – *Chair,* Andrew Miller; *Clerk,* Glenn McKee

NATIONAL AUDIT OFFICE

157–197 Buckingham Palace Road, London SW1W 9SP
T 020-7798 7000
E enquiries@nao.gsi.gov.uk W www.nao.org.uk

The National Audit Office came into existence under the National Audit Act 1983 to replace and continue the work of the former Exchequer and Audit Department. The act reinforced the office's total financial and operational independence from the government and brought its head, the Comptroller and Auditor-General, into a closer relationship with parliament as an officer of the House of Commons.

The National Audit Office provides independent information, advice and assurance to parliament and the public about all aspects of the financial operations of government departments and many other bodies receiving public funds. It does this by examining and certifying the accounts of these organisations. It also regularly publishes reports to parliament on the results of its value for money investigations of the economy (the efficiency and effectiveness with which public resources have been used). The National Audit Office is also the auditor by agreement of the accounts of certain international and other organisations. In addition, the office authorises the issue of public funds to government departments.

Comptroller and Auditor-General, Amyas Morse
Private Secretary, Laura Brackwell
Chief Operating Officer, Michael Whitehouse
Leadership Team, Gabrielle Cohen; Ed Humpherson; Wendy Kenway-Smith; Martin Sinclair

PARLIAMENTARY INFORMATION

The following is a short glossary of aspects of the work of parliament. Unless otherwise stated, references are to House of Commons procedures.

BILL – Proposed legislation is termed a bill. The stages of a public bill (for private bills, *see* below) in the House of Commons are as follows:

First reading: This stage introduces the legislation to the house and, for government Bills, merely constitutes an order to have the bill printed.

Second reading: The debate on the principles of the bill.

Committee stage: The detailed examination of a bill, clause by clause. In most cases this takes place in a public bill committee, or the whole house may act as a committee. Public bill committees may take evidence before embarking on detailed scrutiny of the bill. Very rarely, a bill may be examined by a select committee.

Report stage: Detailed review of a bill as amended in committee, on the floor of the house, and an opportunity to make further changes.

Third reading: Final debate on the full bill in the Commons.

Public bills go through the same stages in the House of Lords, but with important differences: the committee stage is taken in committee of the whole house or in a grand committee, in which any peer may participate. There are no time limits, all amendments are debated, and further amendments can be made at third reading.

A bill may start in either house, and has to pass through both houses to become law. Both houses have to agree the final text of a bill, so that amendments made by the second house are then considered in the originating house, and if not agreed, sent back or themselves amended, until agreement is reached.

CHILTERN HUNDREDS – A nominal office of profit under the crown, the acceptance of which requires an MP to vacate his/her seat. The Manor of Northstead is similar. These are the only means by which an MP may resign.

CONSOLIDATED FUND BILL – A bill to authorise the issue of money to maintain government services. The bill is dealt with without debate.

EARLY DAY MOTION – A motion put on the notice paper by an MP without, in general, the real prospect of its being debated. Such motions are expressions of back-bench opinion.

FATHER OF THE HOUSE – The MP whose continuous service in the House of Commons is the longest. The present Father of the House is Sir Peter Tapsell, MP.

GRAND COMMITTEES – There are three grand committees in the House of Commons, one each for Northern Ireland, Scotland and Wales; they consider matters relating specifically to that country. In the House of Lords, bills may be sent to a grand committee instead of a committee of the whole house (*see also* Bill).

HOURS OF MEETING – The House of Commons normally meets on Mondays and Tuesdays at 2.30pm, Wednesdays at 11.30am, Thursdays at 10.30am and some Fridays at 9.30am. (*See also* Westminster Hall Sittings, below.) The House of Lords normally meets at 2.30pm Mondays and Tuesdays, 3pm on Wednesdays and at 11am on Thursdays. The House of Lords occasionally sits on Fridays at 10am.

LEADER OF THE OPPOSITION – In 1937 the office of leader of the opposition was recognised and a salary was assigned to the post. In 2011–12 this was £139,355 (including a parliamentary salary of £65,738). The present leader of the opposition is the Rt. Hon. Ed Miliband, MP.

THE LORD CHANCELLOR – The office of Lord High Chancellor of Great Britain was significantly altered by the Constitutional Reform Act 2005. Previously, the Lord Chancellor was (*ex officio*) the Speaker of the House of Lords, and took part in debates and voted in divisions in the House of Lords. The Department for Constitutional Affairs was created in 2003, which became the Ministry of Justice in 2007, incorporating most of the responsibilities of the Lord Chancellor's department. The role of Speaker has been transferred to the post of Lord Speaker. The Constitutional Reform Act 2005 also brought to an end the Lord Chancellor's role as head of the judiciary. A Judicial Appointments Commission was created in April 2006, and a supreme court (separate from the House of Lords) was established in 2009.

THE LORD SPEAKER – The first Lord Speaker of the House of Lords, the Rt. Hon. Baroness Hayman, took up office on 4 July 2006. Unlike in the case of the Lord Chancellor, the Lord Speaker is independent of the government and elected by members of the House of Lords rather than appointed by the prime minister. Although the Lord Speaker's primary role is to preside over proceedings in the House of Lords, she does not have the same powers as the Speaker of the House of Commons. For example, the Lord Speaker is not responsible for maintaining order during debates, as this is the responsibility of the house as a whole. The Lord Speaker sits in the Lords on one of the woolsacks, which are couches covered in red cloth and stuffed with wool.

THE LORD GREAT CHAMBERLAIN – The Lord Great Chamberlain is a Great Officer of State, the office being hereditary since the grant of Henry I to the family of De Vere, Earls of Oxford. It is now a joint hereditary office rotating on the death of the sovereign between the Cholmondeley, Carington and Ancaster families.

The Lord Great Chamberlain, currently the Marquess of Cholmondeley, is responsible for the royal apartments in the Palace of Westminster, the Royal Gallery, the administration of the Chapel of St Mary Undercroft and, in conjunction with the Lord Speaker and the Speaker of the House of Commons, Westminster Hall. The Lord Great Chamberlain has the right to perform specific services at a coronation, he carries out ceremonial duties in the Palace of Westminster when the sovereign visits the palace and has particular responsibility for the internal administrative arrangements within the House of Lords for state openings of parliament.

OPPOSITION DAY – A day on which the topic for debate is chosen by the opposition. There are 20 such days in a normal session. On 17 days, subjects are chosen by the leader of the opposition; on the remaining three days by the leader of the next largest opposition party.

PARLIAMENT ACTS 1911 AND 1949 – Under these acts, bills may become law without the consent of the Lords, though the House of Lords has the power to delay a public bill for a parliamentary session.

PRIME MINISTER'S QUESTIONS – The prime minister answers questions from 12 to 12.30pm on Wednesdays.

PRIVATE BILL – A bill promoted by a body or an individual to give powers additional to, or in conflict with, the general law, and to which a special procedure applies to enable people affected to object.

PRIVATE MEMBER'S BILL – A public bill promoted by an MP or peer who is not a member of the government.

PRIVATE NOTICE QUESTION – A question adjudged of urgent importance on submission to the Speaker (in the Lords, the Lord Speaker), answered at the end of oral questions.

PRIVILEGE – The House of Commons has rights and immunities to protect it from obstruction in carrying out its duties. These are known as parliamentary privilege and enable Members of Parliament to debate freely. The most important privilege is that of freedom of speech. MPs cannot be prosecuted for sedition or sued for libel or slander over anything said during proceedings in the house. This enables them to raise in the house questions affecting the public good which might be difficult to raise outside owing to the possibility of legal action against them. The House of Lords has similar privileges.

QUESTION TIME – Oral questions are answered by ministers in the Commons from 2.30 to 3.30pm on Mondays and Tuesdays, 11.30am to 12.30pm on Wednesdays, and 10.30 to 11.30am on Thursdays. Questions are also taken at the start of the Lords sittings, with a daily limit of four oral questions.

ROYAL ASSENT – The royal assent is signified by letters patent to such bills and measures as have passed both Houses of Parliament (or bills which have been passed under the Parliament Acts 1911 and 1949). The sovereign has not given royal assent in person since 1854. On occasion, for instance in the prorogation of parliament, royal assent may be pronounced to the two houses by Lords Commissioners. More usually royal assent is notified to each house sitting separately in accordance with the Royal Assent Act 1967. The old French formulae for royal assent are then endorsed on the acts by the Clerk of the Parliaments.

The power to withhold assent resides with the sovereign but has not been exercised in the UK since 1707.

SELECT COMMITTEES – Consisting usually of 10 to 15 members of all parties, select committees are a means used by both houses in order to investigate certain matters.

Most select committees in the House of Commons are tied to departments: each committee investigates subjects within a government department's remit. There are other select committees dealing with matters such as public accounts (ie the spending by the government of money voted by parliament) and European legislation, and also committees advising on procedures and domestic administration of the house. Major select committees usually take evidence in public; their evidence and reports are published on the parliament website and in hard copy by TSO (The Stationery Office). House of Commons select committees are reconstituted after a general election.

In the House of Lords, select committees do not mirror government departments but cover broader issues. There is a select committee on the European Union (EU), which has seven sub-committees dealing with specific areas of EU policy, a select committee on science and technology, a select committee on economic affairs and also one on the constitution. There is also a select committee on delegated powers and regulatory reform and one on privileges and conduct. In addition, *ad hoc* select committees have been set up from time to time to investigate specific subjects. There are also joint committees of the two houses, eg the committees on statutory instruments and on human rights.

THE SPEAKER – The Speaker of the House of Commons is the spokesperson and chair of the Chamber. He or she is elected by the house at the beginning of each parliament or when the previous Speaker retires or dies. The Speaker neither speaks in debates nor votes in divisions except when the voting is equal.

VACANT SEATS – When a vacancy occurs in the House of Commons during a session of parliament, the writ for the by-election is moved by a whip of the party to which the member whose seat has been vacated belonged. If the house is in recess, the Speaker can issue a warrant for a writ, should two members certify to him that a seat is vacant.

WESTMINSTER HALL SITTINGS – Following a report by the Modernisation of the House of Commons Select Committee, the Commons decided in May 1999 to set up a second debating forum. It is known as 'Westminster Hall' and sittings are in the Grand Committee Room on Tuesdays from 9.30 to 11.30am, Wednesdays from 9.30 to 11.30am and from 2 to 5pm, and Thursdays from 2.30 to 5.30pm. Sittings are open to the public at the times indicated.

WHIPS – In order to secure the attendance of members of a particular party in parliament, particularly on the occasion of an important vote, whips (originally known as 'whippers-in') are appointed. The written appeal or circular letter issued by them is also known as a 'whip', its urgency being denoted by the number of times it is underlined. Failure to respond to a three-line whip is tantamount in the Commons to secession (at any rate temporarily) from the party. Whips are provided with office accommodation in both houses, and government and some opposition whips receive salaries from public funds.

PARLIAMENTARY ARCHIVES

Houses of Parliament, London SW1A 0PW
T 020-7219 3074
E archives@parliament.uk W www.parliament.uk/archives

Since 1497, the records of parliament have been kept within the Palace of Westminster. They are in the custody of the Clerk of Parliaments. In 1946 the House of Lords Record Office, which became the Parliamentary Archives in 2006, was established to supervise their preservation and their availability to the public. Some three million documents are preserved, including acts of parliament from 1497, journals of the House of Lords from 1510, minutes and committee proceedings from 1610, and papers laid before parliament from 1531. Among the records are the Petition of Right, the death warrant of Charles I, the Declaration of Breda, and the Bill of Rights. Records are made available through a public search room.
Clerk of the Records, Dr Caroline Shenton

GOVERNMENT OFFICE

The government is the body of ministers responsible for the administration of national affairs, determining policy and introducing into parliament any legislation necessary to give effect to government policy. The majority of ministers are members of the House of Commons but members of the House of Lords, or of neither house, may also hold ministerial responsibility. The prime minister is, by current convention, always a member of the House of Commons.

THE PRIME MINISTER

The office of prime minister, which had been in existence for nearly 200 years, was officially recognised in 1905 and its holder was granted a place in the table of precedence. The prime minister, by tradition also First Lord of the Treasury and Minister for the Civil Service, is appointed by the sovereign and is usually the leader of the party which enjoys, or can secure, a majority in the House of Commons. Other ministers are appointed by the sovereign on the recommendation of the prime minister, who also allocates functions among ministers and has the power to dismiss ministers from their posts.

The prime minister informs the sovereign on state and political matters, advises on the dissolution of parliament, and makes recommendations for important crown appointments, ie the award of honours, etc.

As the chair of cabinet meetings and leader of a political party, the prime minister is responsible for translating party policy into government activity. As leader of the government, the prime minister is responsible to parliament and to the electorate for the policies and their implementation.

The prime minister also represents the nation in international affairs, eg summit conferences.

THE CABINET

The cabinet developed during the 18th century as an inner committee of the Privy Council, which was the chief source of executive power until that time. The cabinet is composed of about 20 ministers chosen by the prime minister, usually the heads of government departments (generally known as secretaries of state unless they have a special title, eg Chancellor of the Exchequer), the leaders of the two houses of parliament, and the holders of various traditional offices.

The cabinet's functions are the final determination of policy, control of government and coordination of government departments. The exercise of its functions is dependent upon the incumbent party's (or parties') majority support in the House of Commons. Cabinet meetings are held in private, taking place once or twice a week during parliamentary sittings and less often during a recess. Proceedings are confidential, the members being bound by their oath as privy counsellors not to disclose information about the proceedings.

The convention of collective responsibility means that the cabinet acts unanimously even when cabinet ministers do not all agree on a subject. The policies of departmental ministers must be consistent with the policies of the government as a whole, and once the government's policy has been decided, each minister is expected to support it or resign.

The convention of ministerial responsibility holds a minister, as the political head of his or her department, accountable to parliament for the department's work. Departmental ministers usually decide all matters within their responsibility, although on matters of political importance they normally consult their colleagues collectively. A decision by a departmental minister is binding on the government as a whole.

POLITICAL PARTIES

Before the reign of William and Mary the principal officers of state were chosen by and were responsible to the sovereign alone, and not to parliament or the nation at large. Such officers acted sometimes in concert with one another but more often independently, and the fall of one did not, of necessity, involve that of others, although all were liable to be dismissed at any moment.

In 1693 the Earl of Sunderland recommended to William III the advisability of selecting a ministry from the political party which enjoyed a majority in the House of Commons, and the first united ministry was drawn in 1696 from the Whigs, to which party the king owed his throne. This group became known as the 'junto' and was regarded with suspicion as a novelty in the political life of the nation, being a small section meeting in secret apart from the main body of ministers. It may be regarded as the forerunner of the cabinet and in the course of time it led to the establishment of the principle of joint responsibility of ministers, so that internal disagreement caused a change of personnel or resignation of the whole body of ministers.

The accession of George I, who was unfamiliar with the English language, led to a disinclination on the part of the sovereign to preside at meetings of his ministers and caused the emergence of a prime minister, a position first acquired by Robert Walpole in 1721 and retained by him without interruption for 20 years and 326 days. The office of prime minister was formally recognised in 1905 when it was established by royal warrant.

DEVELOPMENT OF PARTIES

In 1828 the Whigs became known as Liberals, a name originally given by opponents to imply laxity of principles, but gradually accepted by the party to indicate its claim to be pioneers and champions of political reform and progressive legislation. In 1861 a Liberal Registration Association was founded and Liberal Associations became widespread. In 1877 a National Liberal Federation was formed, with its headquarters in London. The Liberal Party was in power for long periods during the second half of the 19th century and for several years during the first quarter of the 20th century, but after a split in the party in 1931, the numbers elected remained small. In 1988 a majority of the Liberals agreed on a merger with the Social Democratic Party under the title Social and Liberal Democrats; since 1989 they have been known as the Liberal Democrats. A minority continue separately as the Liberal Party.

Soon after the change from Whig to Liberal, the Tory Party became known as Conservative, a name believed to have been invented by John Wilson Croker in 1830 and to have been generally adopted around the time of the passing of the Reform Act of 1832 – to indicate that the preservation of national institutions was the leading principle of the party. After the Home Rule crisis of 1886 the dissentient Liberals entered into a compact with the Conservatives, under which the latter undertook not to contest their seats, but a separate Liberal Unionist organisation was maintained until 1912, when it was united with the Conservatives.

Labour candidates for parliament made their first appearance at the general election of 1892, when there were 27 standing as Labour or Liberal-Labour. In 1900 the Labour Representation Committee (LRC) was set up in order to establish a distinct Labour group in parliament, with its own whips, its own policy, and a readiness to cooperate with any party which might be engaged in promoting legislation in the direct interests of labour. In 1906 the LRC became known as the Labour Party.

The Green Party was founded in 1973 and campaigns for social and environmental justice. The party began as 'People', was renamed the Ecology Party, and became the Green Party in 1985.

Plaid Cymru was founded in 1926 to provide an independent political voice for Wales and to campaign for self-government in Wales.

The Scottish National Party (SNP) was founded in 1934 to campaign for independence for Scotland.

The Social Democratic and Labour Party (SDLP) was founded in 1970, emerging from the civil rights movement of the 1960s, with the aim of promoting reform, reconciliation and partnership across the sectarian divide in Northern Ireland, and of opposing violence from any quarter.

The Democratic Unionist Party (DUP) was founded in 1971 to resist moves by the Ulster Unionist Party which were considered a threat to the Union. Its aim is to maintain Northern Ireland as an integral part of the UK.

The Alliance Party of Northern Ireland was formed in 1970 as a non-sectarian unionist party.

Sinn Fein first emerged in the 1900s as a federation of nationalist clubs. It is a left-wing republican and labour party that seeks to end British governance in Ireland and achieve a 32-county republic.

GOVERNMENT AND OPPOSITION

The government is formed by the party which wins the largest number of seats in the House of Commons at a general election, or which has the support of a majority of members in the House of Commons. By tradition, the leader of the majority party is asked by the sovereign to form a government, while the largest minority party becomes the official opposition with its own leader and a shadow cabinet. Leaders of the government and opposition sit on the front benches of the Commons with their supporters (the back-benchers) sitting behind them.

FINANCIAL SUPPORT

Financial support for opposition parties in the House of Commons was introduced in 1975 and is commonly known as Short Money, after Edward Short, the leader of the house at that time, who introduced the scheme. Short Money is only payable to those parties that have more than one sitting MP or 150,000 votes in total, and is only intended to provide assistance for parliamentary duties. Short Money allocations for 2011–12 are:

DUP	£149,823
Green	£59,501
Labour	£6,024,340
Plaid Cymru	£71,970
SDLP	£63,561
SNP	£168,795

A specific allocation for the leader of the opposition's office was introduced in April 1999 and has been set at £700,699 for the year 2011–12.

Financial support for opposition parties in the House of Lords was introduced in 1996 and is commonly known as Cranborne Money, after former leader of the house Viscount Cranborne.

The following list of parties are those with MPs elected to the present parliament.

ALLIANCE PARTY OF NORTHERN IRELAND

88 University Street, Belfast BT7 1HE
T 028-9032 4274 E alliance@allianceparty.org
W www.allianceparty.org
Party Leader, David Ford
Deputy Party Leader, Naomi Long, MP
President, Colm Cavanagh
Chair, Stewart Dickson
Hon. Treasurer, Dan McGuinness

CONSERVATIVE PARTY

Conservative Campaign Headquarters, 30 Millbank, London SW1P 4DP
T 020-7222 9000
W www.conservatives.com

Parliamentary Party Leader, Rt. Hon. David Cameron, MP
Leader in the Lords and Chancellor of the Duchy of Lancaster, Rt. Hon. Lord Strathclyde
Leader in the Commons and Lord Privy Seal, Rt. Hon. Sir George Young, Bt., MP
Chairs, Lord Feldman of Elstree; Baroness Warsi
Party Treasurer, Lord Fink

GREEN PARTY

Development House, 56–64 Leonard Street, London, EC2A 4LT
T 020-7549 0310
E office@greenparty.org.uk W www.greenparty.org.uk
Party Leader, Dr Caroline Lucas, MP
Deputy Leader, Adrian Ramsay
Chair of Party Executive, Jayne Forbes
Finance Coordinator, Dean Walton

LABOUR PARTY

39 Victoria Street, London SW1H 0HA
T 0870-590 0200 W www.labour.org.uk
General Secretary, Ray Collins
General Secretary, Welsh Labour, Dave Hagendyk
General Secretary, Scottish Labour Party, Colin Smyth

SHADOW CABINET AS AT AUGUST 2011
Leader of the Opposition, Rt. Hon. Ed Miliband, MP
Deputy Leader and Secretary of State for International Development, Rt. Hon. Harriet Harman, QC, MP
Chancellor of the Exchequer, Rt. Hon. Ed Balls, MP
Secretary of State for Foreign and Commonwealth Affairs, Rt. Hon. Douglas Alexander, MP
Secretary of State for the Home Department and Minister for Women and Equalities, Rt. Hon Yvette Cooper, MP
*Minister of State for the Cabinet Office, Jon Trickett, MP
Minister for the Cabinet Office and Olympics, Rt. Hon. Tessa Jowell, MP
Secretary of State for Communities and Local Government, Rt. Hon. Caroline Flint, MP
Secretary of State for Culture, Media and Sport, Ivan Lewis, MP
Secretary of State for Defence, Rt. Hon. Jim Murphy, MP
Secretary of State for Education and Election Co-ordinator, Rt. Hon. Andy Burnham, MP
Secretary of State for Energy and Climate Change, Meg Hiller, MP
Secretary of State for Environment, Food and Rural Affairs, Mary Creagh, MP
Secretary of State for Health, Rt. Hon. John Healey, MP
Lord Chancellor, Secretary of State for Justice (with responsibility for political/constitutional reform), Rt. Hon. Sadiq Khan, MP
Secretary of State for Northern Ireland, Rt. Hon. Shaun Woodward, MP
Secretary of State for Scotland, Ann McKechin, MP
Secretary of State for Transport, Maria Eagle, MP
Chief Secretary to the Treasury, Angela Eagle, MP
Secretary of State for Wales, Rt. Hon. Peter Hain, MP
Secretary of State for Work and Pensions, Rt. Hon. Liam Byrne, MP
Leader of the House of Commons, Rt. Hon. Hilary Benn, MP
Leader of the House of Lords, Baroness Royall of Blaisdon
Attorney-General, Baroness Scotland of Asthal, QC
Parliamentary Party Chair, Tony Lloyd, MP

LABOUR WHIPS
House of Commons, Rt. Hon. Rosie Winterton, MP
House of Lords, Lord Bassam of Brighton
* Attends Cabinet meetings but is not a Cabinet member

LIBERAL DEMOCRATS

4 Cowley Street, London SW1P 3NB
T 020-7222 7999
E info@libdems.org.uk W www.libdems.org.uk
Parliamentary Party Leader, Rt. Hon. Nick Clegg, MP
Deputy Party Leader, Simon Hughes, MP
Leader in the Lords, Rt. Hon. Lord McNally
Deputy Leader in the Commons, David Heath, MP
President, Baroness Ros Scott
Chief Executive (interim), Chris Fox
Hon. Treasurer, Lord Razzall

NORTHERN IRELAND DEMOCRATIC UNIONIST PARTY

91 Dundela Avenue, Belfast BT4 3BU
T 028-9047 1155
E info@dup.org.uk W www.dup.org.uk
Parliamentary Party Leader, Rt. Hon. Peter Robinson, MLA
Deputy Leader, Rt. Hon Nigel Dodds, OBE, MP, MLA
Chair, Lord Morrow, MLA
Treasurer, Gregory Campbell, MP, MLA
Party Secretary, Michelle McIlveen, MLA

PLAID CYMRU – THE PARTY OF WALES

Ty Gwynfor, Marine Chambers, Anson Court, Atlantic Wharf, Caerdydd CF10 4AL
T 029-2047 2272
E post@plaidcymru.org W www.plaidcymru.org
Party Leader, Ieuan Wyn Jones
Party President, Jill Evans, MEP
Parliamentary Group Leader, Elfyn Llwyd, MP
Chief Executive, vacant

SCOTTISH NATIONAL PARTY

Gordon Lamb House, 3 Jackson's Entry, Edinburgh EH8 8PJ
T 0800-633 5432
E info@snp.org W www.snp.org
Westminster Parliamentary Party Leader, Angus Robertson, MP
Westminster Parliamentary Party Chief Whip, Stewart Hosie, MP
Scottish Parliamentary Party Leader, Alex Salmond, MSP
Scottish Parliamentary Party Chief Whip, Brian Adam, MSP
National Treasurer, Cllr Colin Beattie
National Secretary, William Henderson
Chief Executive, Peter Murrell

SINN FEIN

53 Falls Road, Belfast BT12 4PD
T 028-9034 7350
E sfadmin@eircom.net W www.sinnfein.ie
Party President, Gerry Adams
Vice-President, Mary Lou McDonald
Chair, Declan Kearney
Treasurers, Rita O'Hare; Maurice Quinlivan
General Secretary, Dawn Doyle

SOCIAL DEMOCRATIC AND LABOUR PARTY

121 Ormeau Road, Belfast BT7 1SH
T 028-9024 7700 E info@sdlp.ie W www.sdlp.ie
Parliamentary Party Leader, Margaret Ritchie, MP, MLA
Deputy Leader, Patsy McGlone, MLA
Party Whip, Pat Ramsey, MLA
Chair, Joe Byrne, MLA
Treasurer, Peter McEvoy
General Secretary, Gerry Cosgrove

MEMBERS OF PARLIAMENT as at 10 August 2011

* New MP
† Previously MP in another seat
‡ Previously MP for another party

Abbott, Diane (*b.* 1953) *Lab., Hackney North & Stoke Newington*, Maj. 14,461
*Abrahams, Deborah (*b.* 1960) *Lab., Oldham East & Saddleworth*, Maj. 3,558
*Adams, Nigel (*b.* 1966) *C., Selby & Ainsty*, Maj. 12,265
Afriyie, Adam (*b.* 1965) *C., Windsor*, Maj. 19,054
Ainsworth, Rt. Hon. Robert (*b.* 1952) *Lab., Coventry North East*, Maj. 11,775
*Aldous, Peter (*b.* 1961) *C., Waveney*, Maj. 769
Alexander, Rt. Hon. Danny (*b.* 1972) *LD, Inverness, Nairn, Badenoch & Strathspey*, Maj. 8,765
Alexander, Rt. Hon. Douglas (*b.* 1967) *Lab., Paisley & Renfrewshire South*, Maj. 16,614
*Alexander, Heidi (*b.* 1975) *Lab., Lewisham East*, Maj. 6,216
*Ali, Rushanara, (*b.* 1975) *Lab., Bethnal Green & Bow*, Maj. 11,574
Allen, Graham (*b.* 1953) *Lab., Nottingham North*, Maj. 8,138
Amess, David (*b.* 1952) *C., Southend West*, Maj. 7,270
Anderson, David (*b.* 1953) *Lab., Blaydon*, Maj. 9,117
*Andrew, Stuart (*b.* 1971) *C., Pudsey*, Maj. 1,659
Arbuthnot, Rt. Hon. James (*b.* 1952) *C., Hampshire North East*, Maj. 18,597
*Ashworth, Jon (*b.* 1978) *Lab., Leicester South*, Maj. 12,078
Austin, Ian (*b.* 1965) *Lab., Dudley North*, Maj. 649
Bacon, Richard (*b.* 1962) *C., Norfolk South*, Maj. 10,940
*Bagshawe, Louise (*b.* 1971) *C., Corby*, Maj. 1,951
Bailey, Adrian (*b.* 1945) *Lab. (Co-op), West Bromwich West*, Maj. 5,651
Bain, William (*b.* 1972) *Lab., Glasgow North East*, Maj. 15,942
Baker, Norman (*b.* 1957) *LD, Lewes*, Maj. 7,647
*Baker, Steven (*b.* 1971) *C., Wycombe*, Maj. 9,560
Baldry, Tony (*b.* 1950) *C., Banbury*, Maj. 18,227
*Baldwin, Harriett (*b.* 1960) *C., West Worcestershire*, Maj. 6,804
Balls, Rt. Hon. Ed (*b.* 1967) *Lab. (Co-op), Morley & Outwood*, Maj. 1,101
Banks, Gordon (*b.* 1955) *Lab., Ochil & Perthshire South*, Maj. 5,187
*Barclay, Stephen (*b.* 1972) *C., Cambridgeshire North East*, Maj. 16,425
Barker, Gregory (*b.* 1966) *C., Bexhill & Battle*, Maj. 12,880
Baron, John (*b.* 1959) *C., Basildon & Billericay*, Maj. 12,398
Barron, Rt. Hon. Kevin (*b.* 1946) *Lab., Rother Valley*, Maj. 5,866
*Barwell, Gavin (*b.* 1972) *C., Croydon Central*, Maj. 2,969
Bayley, Hugh (*b.* 1952) *Lab., York Central*, Maj. 6,451
*Bebb, Guto (*b.* 1968) *C., Aberconwy*, Maj. 3,398
Beckett, Rt. Hon. Margaret (*b.* 1943) *Lab., Derby South*, Maj. 6,122
Begg, Anne (*b.* 1955) *Lab., Aberdeen South*, Maj. 3,506
Beith, Rt. Hon. Sir Alan (*b.* 1943) *LD, Berwick-upon-Tweed*, Maj. 2,690
Bell, Sir Stuart (*b.* 1938) *Lab., Middlesbrough*, Maj. 8,689

Bellingham, Henry (*b.* 1955) *C., Norfolk North West*, Maj. 14,810
Benn, Rt. Hon. Hilary (*b.* 1953) *Lab., Leeds Central*, Maj. 10,645
Benton, Joe (*b.* 1933) *Lab., Bootle*, Maj. 21,181
Benyon, Richard (*b.* 1960) *C., Newbury*, Maj. 12,248
Bercow, John (*b.* 1963) *The Speaker, Buckingham*, Maj. 12,529
Beresford, Sir Paul (*b.* 1946) *C., Mole Valley*, Maj. 15,653
*Berger, Luciana (*b.* 1981) *Lab. (Co-op), Liverpool, Wavertree*, Maj. 7,167
*Berry, Jake (*b.* 1978) *C., Rossendale & Darwen*, Maj. 4,493
Betts, Clive (*b.* 1950) *Lab., Sheffield South East*, Maj. 10,505
*Bingham, Andrew (*b.* 1962) *C., High Peak*, Maj. 4,677
Binley, Brian (*b.* 1942) *C., Northampton South*, Maj. 6,004
*Birtwistle, Gordon (*b.* 1943) *LD, Burnley*, Maj. 1,818
*Blackman, Bob (*b.* 1956) *C., Harrow East*, Maj. 3,403
Blackman-Woods, Dr Roberta (*b.* 1957) *Lab., Durham, City of*, Maj. 3,067
*Blackwood, Nicola (*b.* 1979) *C., Oxford West & Abingdon*, Maj. 176
Blears, Rt. Hon. Hazel (*b.* 1956) *Lab., Salford & Eccles*, Maj. 5,725
*Blenkinsop, Tom (*b.* 1980) *Lab., Middlesbrough South & East Cleveland*, Maj. 1,677
*Blomfield, Paul (*b.* 1953) *Lab., Sheffield Central*, Maj. 165
Blunkett, Rt. Hon. David (*b.* 1947) *Lab., Sheffield, Brightside & Hillsborough*, Maj. 13,632
Blunt, Crispin (*b.* 1960) *C., Reigate*, Maj. 13,591
*Boles, Nick (*b.* 1965) *C., Grantham & Stamford*, Maj. 14,826
Bone, Peter (*b.* 1952) *C., Wellingborough*, Maj. 11,787
Bottomley, Peter (*b.* 1944) *C., Worthing West*, Maj. 11,729
*Bradley, Karen (*b.* 1970) *C., Staffordshire Moorlands*, Maj. 6,689
Bradshaw, Ben (*b.* 1960) *Lab., Exeter*, Maj. 2,721
Brady, Graham (*b.* 1967) *C., Altrincham & Sale West*, Maj. 11,595
Brake, Tom (*b.* 1962) *LD, Carshalton & Wallington*, Maj. 5,260
*Bray, Angie (*b.* 1953) *C., Ealing Central & Acton*, Maj. 3,716
Brazier, Julian (*b.* 1953) *C., Canterbury*, Maj. 6,048
Brennan, Kevin (*b.* 1959) *Lab., Cardiff West*, Maj. 4,750
*Bridgen, Andrew (*b.* 1964) *C., Leicestershire North West*, Maj. 7,511
*Brine, Steve (*b.* 1974) *C., Winchester*, Maj. 3,048
†Brokenshire, James (*b.* 1968) *C., Old Bexley & Sidcup*, Maj. 15,857
Brooke, Annette (*b.* 1947) *LD, Dorset Mid & Poole North*, Maj. 269
Brown, Rt. Hon. Gordon (*b.* 1951) *Lab., Kirkcaldy & Cowdenbeath*, Maj. 23,009
Brown, Lyn (*b.* 1960) *Lab., West Ham*, Maj. 22,534
Brown, Rt. Hon. Nicholas (*b.* 1950) *Lab., Newcastle upon Tyne East*, Maj. 4,453
Brown, Russell (*b.* 1951) *Lab., Dumfries & Galloway*, Maj. 7,449
Browne, Jeremy (*b.* 1970) *LD, Taunton Deane*, Maj. 3,993

*Bruce, Fiona (b. 1957) C., Congleton, Maj. 7,063

Bruce, Rt. Hon. Malcolm (b. 1944) LD, Gordon, Maj. 6,748

Bryant, Chris (b. 1962) Lab., Rhondda, Maj. 11,553

Buck, Karen (b. 1958) Lab., Westminster North, Maj. 2,126

*Buckland, Robert (b. 1968) C., Swindon South, Maj. 3,544

Burden, Richard (b. 1954) Lab., Birmingham Northfield, Maj. 2,782

*Burley, Aidan (b. 1979) C., Cannock Chase, Maj. 3,195

Burnham, Rt. Hon. Andy (b. 1970) Lab., Leigh, Maj. 15,011

*Burns, Conor (b. 1972) C., Bournemouth West, Maj. 5,583

Burns, Simon (b. 1952) C., Chelmsford, Maj. 5,110

Burrowes, David (b. 1969) C., Enfield Southgate, Maj. 7,626

Burstow, Paul (b. 1962) LD, Sutton & Cheam, Maj. 1,608

Burt, Alistair (b. 1955) C., Bedfordshire North East, Maj. 18,942

Burt, Lorely (b. 1957) LD, Solihull, Maj. 175

*Byles, Daniel (b. 1974) C., Warwickshire North, Maj. 54

Byrne, Liam (b. 1970) Lab., Birmingham Hodge Hill, Maj. 10,302

Cable, Rt. Hon. Dr Vincent (b. 1943) LD, Twickenham, Maj. 12,140

*Cairns, Alun (b. 1970) C., Vale of Glamorgan, Maj. 4,307

Cameron, Rt. Hon. David (b. 1966) C., Witney, Maj. 22,740

Campbell, Alan (b. 1957) Lab., Tynemouth, Maj. 5,739

Campbell, Gregory (b. 1953) DUP, Londonderry East, Maj. 5,355

Campbell, Rt. Hon. Sir Menzies (b. 1941) LD, Fife North East, Maj. 9,048

Campbell, Ronnie (b. 1943) Lab., Blyth Valley, Maj. 6,668

Carmichael, Alistair (b. 1965) LD, Orkney & Shetland, Maj. 9,928

*Carmichael, Neil (b. 1961) C., Stroud, Maj. 1,299

Carswell, Douglas (b. 1971) C., Clacton, Maj. 12,068

Cash, Bill (b. 1940) C., Stone, Maj. 13,292

Caton, Martin (b. 1951) Lab., Gower, Maj. 2,683

*Chapman, Jenny (b. 1973) Lab., Darlington, Maj. 3,388

*Chishti, Rehman (b. 1978) C., Gillingham & Rainham, Maj. 8,680

Chope, Christopher (b. 1947) C., Christchurch, Maj. 15,410

Clappison, James (b. 1956) C., Hertsmere, Maj. 17,605

Clark, Greg (b. 1967) C., Tunbridge Wells, Maj. 15,576

Clark, Katy (b. 1967) Lab., Ayrshire North & Arran, Maj. 9,895

Clarke, Rt. Hon. Kenneth (b. 1940) C., Rushcliffe, Maj. 15,811

Clarke, Rt. Hon. Thomas (b. 1941) Lab., Coatbridge, Chryston & Bellshill, Maj. 20,714

Clegg, Rt. Hon. Nick (b. 1967) LD, Sheffield, Hallam, Maj. 15,284

Clifton-Brown, Geoffrey (b. 1953) C., The Cotswolds, Maj. 12,864

Clwyd, Rt. Hon. Ann (b. 1937) Lab., Cynon Valley, Maj. 9,617

Coaker, Vernon (b. 1953) Lab., Gedling, Maj. 1,859

Coffey, Ann (b. 1946) Lab., Stockport, Maj. 6,784

*Coffey, Thérèse (b. 1971) C., Suffolk Coastal, Maj. 9,128

*Collins, Damian (b. 1974) C., Folkestone & Hythe, Maj. 10,122

*Colvile, Oliver (b. 1959) C., Plymouth, Sutton & Devonport, Maj. 1,149

Connarty, Michael (b. 1947) Lab., Linlithgow & Falkirk East, Maj. 12,553

Cooper, Rosie (b. 1950) Lab., Lancashire West, Maj. 4,343

Cooper, Rt. Hon. Yvette (b. 1969) Lab., Pontefract & Castleford, Maj. 10,979

Corbyn, Jeremy (b. 1949) Lab., Islington North, Maj. 12,401

Cox, Geoffrey (b. 1960) C., Devon West & Torridge, Maj. 2,957

Crabb, Stephen (b. 1973) C., Preseli Pembrokeshire, Maj. 4,605

Crausby, David (b. 1946) Lab., Bolton North East, Maj. 4,084

Creagh, Mary (b. 1967) Lab., Wakefield, Maj. 1,613

*Creasy, Stella (b. 1977) Lab. (Co-op), Walthamstow, Maj. 9,478

*Crockart, Mike (b. 1966) LD, Edinburgh West, Maj. 3,803

*Crouch, Tracey (b. 1975) C., Chatham & Aylesford, Maj. 6,069

Cruddas, Jonathan (b. 1965) Lab., Dagenham & Rainham, Maj. 2,630

*Cryer, John (b. 1964) Lab., Leyton & Wanstead, Maj. 6,416

*Cunningham, Alex (b. 1955) Lab., Stockton North, Maj. 6,676

Cunningham, Jim (b. 1941) Lab., Coventry South, Maj. 3,845

Cunningham, Tony (b. 1952) Lab., Workington, Maj. 4,575

*Curran, Margaret (b. 1958) Lab., Glasgow East, Maj. 11,840

*Dakin, Nic (b. 1955) Lab., Scunthorpe, Maj. 2,549

*Danczuk, Simon (b. 1966) Lab., Rochdale, Maj. 889

Darling, Rt. Hon. Alistair (b. 1953) Lab., Edinburgh South West, Maj. 8,447

Davey, Edward (b. 1965) LD, Kingston & Surbiton, Maj. 7,560

David, Wayne (b. 1957) Lab., Caerphilly, Maj. 10,775

Davidson, Ian (b. 1950) Lab. (Co-op), Glasgow South West, Maj. 14,671

Davies, David (b. 1970) C., Monmouth, Maj. 10,425

*Davies, Geraint (b. 1960) Lab. (Co-op), Swansea West, Maj. 504

*Davies, Glyn (b. 1944) C., Montgomeryshire, Maj. 1,184

Davies, Philip (b. 1972) C., Shipley, Maj. 9,944

Davis, Rt. Hon. David (b. 1948) C., Haltemprice & Howden, Maj. 11,602

*de Bois, Nick (b. 1959) C., Enfield North, Maj. 1,692

*De Piero, Gloria (b. 1972) Lab., Ashfield, Maj. 192

Denham, Rt. Hon. John (b. 1953) Lab., Southampton Itchen, Maj. 192

*Dinenage, Caroline (b. 1971) C., Gosport, Maj. 14,413

Djanogly, Jonathan (b. 1965) C., Huntingdon, Maj. 10,819

Dobbin, Jim (b. 1941) Lab. (Co-op), Heywood & Middleton, Maj. 5,971

Dobson, Rt. Hon. Frank (b. 1940) Lab., Holborn & St Pancras, Maj. 9,942

*Docherty, Thomas (b. 1975) Lab., Dunfermline & Fife West, Maj. 5,470

Dodds, Nigel (b. 1958) DUP, Belfast North, Maj. 2,224

Doherty, Pat (b. 1945) SF, Tyrone West, Maj. 10,685

‡Donaldson, Rt. Hon. Jeffrey (b. 1962) DUP, Lagan Valley, Maj. 10,486

Donohoe, Brian (b. 1948) Lab., Ayrshire Central, Maj. 12,007

Doran, Frank (b. 1949) Lab., Aberdeen North, Maj. 8,361

Dorrell, Rt. Hon. Stephen (b. 1952) C., Charnwood, Maj. 15,029

Dorries, Nadine (b. 1958) C., Bedfordshire Mid, Maj. 15,152

Dowd, Jim (b. 1951) Lab., Lewisham West & Penge, Maj. 5,828

*Doyle, Gemma (b. 1981) Lab. (Co-op), Dunbartonshire West, Maj. 17,408

*Doyle-Price, Jackie (b. 1969) C., Thurrock, Maj. 92

*Drax, Richard (b. 1958) C., Dorset South, Maj. 7,443

*Dromey, Jack (b. 1948) Lab., Birmingham Erdington, Maj. 3,277

Duddridge, James (b. 1971) C., Rochford & Southend East, Maj. 11,050

*Dugher, Michael (b. 1975) Lab., Barnsley East, Maj. 11,090

Duncan, Alan (b. 1957) C., Rutland & Melton, Maj. 14,000

Duncan Smith, Rt. Hon. Iain (b. 1954) C., Chingford & Woodford Green, Maj. 12,963

Dunne, Philip (b. 1958) C., Ludlow, Maj. 9,749

Durkan, Mark (b. 1960) SDLP, Foyle, Maj. 4,824

Eagle, Angela (b. 1961) Lab., Wallasey, Maj. 8,507

Eagle, Maria (b. 1961) Lab., Garston & Halewood, Maj. 16,877

*Edwards, Jonathan (b. 1976) PC, Carmarthen East & Dinefwr, Maj. 3,481

Efford, Clive (b. 1958) Lab., Eltham, Maj. 1,663

*Elliott, Julie (b. 1963) Lab., Sunderland Central, Maj. 6,725

*Ellis, Michael (b. 1967) C., Northampton North, Maj. 1,936

*Ellison, Jane (b.1964) C., Battersea, Maj. 5,977

Ellman, Louise (b. 1945) Lab. (Co-op), Liverpool Riverside, Maj. 14,173

Ellwood, Tobias (b. 1966) C., Bournemouth East, Maj. 7,728

*Elphicke, Charlie (b. 1971) C., Dover, Maj. 5,274

Engel, Natascha (b. 1967) Lab., Derbyshire North East, Maj. 2,445

*Esterson, Bill (b. 1966) Lab., Sefton Central, Maj. 3,862

*Eustice, George (b. 1971) C., Camborne & Redruth, Maj. 66

*Evans, Chris (b. 1976) Lab. (Co-op), Islwyn, Maj. 12,215

*Evans, Graham (b. 1963) C., Weaver Vale, Maj. 991

*Evans, Jonathan (b. 1950) C., Cardiff North, Maj. 194

Evans, Nigel (b. 1957) C., Deputy Speaker, Ribble Valley, Maj. 14,769

Evennett, David (b. 1949) C., Bexleyheath & Crayford, Maj. 10,344

Fabricant, Michael (b. 1950) C., Lichfield, Maj. 17,683

Fallon, Michael (b. 1952) C., Sevenoaks, Maj. 17,515

Farrelly, Paul (b. 1962) Lab., Newcastle-under-Lyme, Maj. 1,552

Farron, Tim (b. 1970) LD, Westmorland & Lonsdale, Maj. 12,264

Featherstone, Lynne (b. 1951) LD, Hornsey & Wood Green, Maj. 6,875

Field, Rt. Hon. Frank (b. 1942) Lab., Birkenhead, Maj. 15,195

Field, Mark (b. 1934) C., Cities of London & Westminster, Maj. 11,076

Fitzpatrick, Jim (b. 1952) Lab., Poplar & Limehouse, Maj. 6,030

Flello, Robert (b. 1966) Lab., Stoke-on-Trent South, Maj. 4,130

Flint, Rt. Hon. Caroline (b. 1961) Lab., Don Valley, Maj. 3,595

Flynn, Paul (b. 1935) Lab., Newport West, Maj. 3,544

Foster, Don (b. 1947) LD, Bath, Maj. 11,883

*Fovargue, Yvonne (b. 1956) Lab., Makerfield, Maj. 12,490

Fox, Rt. Hon. Dr Liam (b. 1961) C., North Somerset, Maj. 7,862

Francis, Dr Hywel (b. 1946) Lab., Aberavon, Maj. 11,039

Francois, Mark (b. 1965) C., Rayleigh & Wickford, Maj. 22,338

*Freeman, George (b. 1967) C., Norfolk Mid, Maj. 13,856

*Freer, Mike (b. 1960) C., Finchley & Golders Green, Maj. 5,809

*Fullbrook, Lorraine (b. 1959) C., Ribble South, Maj. 5,554

*Fuller, Richard (b. 1962) C., Bedford, Maj. 1,353

Gale, Roger (b. 1943) C., Thanet North, Maj. 13,528

Gapes, Mike (b. 1952) Lab. (Co-op), Ilford South, Maj. 11,297

Gardiner, Barry (b. 1957) Lab., Brent North, Maj. 8,028

Garnier, Edward (b. 1952) C., Harborough, Maj. 9,877

*Garnier, Mark (b. 1963) C. Wyre Forest, Maj. 2,643

Gauke, David (b. 1971) C., Hertfordshire South West, Maj. 14,920

George, Andrew (b. 1958) LD, St Ives, Maj. 1,719

Gibb, Nick (b. 1960) C., Bognor Regis & Littlehampton, Maj. 13,063

*Gilbert, Stephen (b. 1976) LD, St Austell & Newquay, Maj. 1,312

Gildernew, Michelle (b. 1970) SF, Fermanagh & South Tyrone, Maj. 4

Gillan, Rt. Hon. Cheryl (b. 1952) C., Chesham & Amersham, Maj. 16,710

*Gilmore, Sheila (b. 1950) Lab., Edinburgh East, Maj. 9,181

*Glass, Pat (b. 1956) Lab., Durham North West, Maj. 7,612

*Glen, John (b. 1974) C., Salisbury, Maj. 5,966

*Glindon, Mary (b. 1957) Lab., Tyneside North, Maj. 12,884

Godsiff, Roger (b. 1946) Lab., Birmingham Hall Green, Maj. 3,799

Goggins, Paul (b. 1953) Lab., Wythenshawe & Sale East, Maj. 7,575

*Goldsmith, Zac (b. 1975) C., Richmond Park, Maj. 4,091

Goodman, Helen (b. 1958) Lab., Bishop Auckland, Maj. 5,218

Goodwill, Robert (b. 1956) C., Scarborough & Whitby, Maj. 8,130

Gove, Rt. Hon. Michael (b. 1967) C., Surrey Heath, Maj. 17,289

*Graham, Richard (b. 1958) C., Gloucester, Maj. 2,420

*Grant, Helen (b. 1961) C., Maidstone & The Weald, Maj. 5,889

Gray, James (b. 1954) C., Wiltshire North, Maj. 7,483

Grayling, Chris (b. 1962) C., Epsom & Ewell, Maj. 16,134

*Greatrex, Tom (b. 1974) Lab. (Co-op), Rutherglen & Hamilton West, Maj. 21,002

Green, Damian (b. 1956) C., Ashford, Maj. 17,297

*Green, Kate (b. 1960) Lab., Stretford & Urmston, Maj. 8,935

Greening, Justine (b. 1969) C., Putney, Maj. 10,053

Grieve, Rt. Hon. Dominic (*b.* 1956) *C., Beaconsfield*, Maj. 21,782

Griffith, Nia (*b.* 1956) *Lab., Llanelli*, Maj. 4,701

***Griffiths**, Andrew (*b.* 1970) *C., Burton*, Maj. 6,304

***Gummer**, Ben (*b.* 1978) *C., Ipswich*, Maj. 2,079

Gwynne, Andrew (*b.* 1974) *Lab., Denton & Reddish*, Maj. 9,831

***Gyimah**, Sam (*b.* 1976) *C., Surrey East*, Maj. 16,874

Hague, Rt. Hon. William (*b.* 1961) *C., Richmond (Yorks)*, Maj. 23,336

Hain, Rt. Hon. Peter (*b.* 1950) *Lab., Neath*, Maj. 9,775

***Halfon**, Robert (*b.* 1969) *C., Harlow*, Maj. 4,925

***Hames**, Duncan (*b.* 1977) *LD, Chippenham*, Maj. 2,470

Hamilton, David (*b.* 1950) *Lab., Midlothian*, Maj. 4,545

Hamilton, Fabian (*b.* 1955) *Lab., Leeds North East*, Maj. 10,349

Hammond, Rt. Hon. Philip (*b.* 1955) *C., Runnymede & Weybridge*, Maj. 16,509

Hammond, Stephen (*b.* 1962) *C., Wimbledon*, Maj. 11,408

***Hancock**, Matthew (*b.* 1978) *C., Suffolk West*, Maj. 13,050

Hancock, Mike (*b.* 1946) *LD, Portsmouth South*, Maj. 5,200

Hands, Greg (*b.* 1965) *C., Chelsea & Fulham*, Maj. 16,722

Hanson, Rt. Hon. David (*b.* 1957) *Lab., Delyn*, Maj. 2,272

Harman, Rt. Hon. Harriet (*b.* 1950) *Lab., Camberwell & Peckham*, Maj. 17,187

Harper, Mark (*b.* 1970) *C., Forest of Dean*, Maj. 11,064

***Harrington**, Richard (*b.* 1957) *C., Watford*, Maj. 1,425

***Harris**, Rebecca (*b.* 1967) *C., Castle Point*, Maj. 7,632

Harris, Tom (*b.* 1964) *Lab., Glasgow South*, Maj. 12,658

***Hart**, Simon (*b.* 1963) *C., Carmarthen West & Pembrokeshire South*, Maj. 3,423

Harvey, Nick (*b.* 1961) *LD, Devon North*, Maj. 5,821

Haselhurst, Rt. Hon. Sir Alan (*b.* 1937) *C., Saffron Walden*, Maj. 15,242

Havard, Dai (*b.* 1949) *Lab., Merthyr Tydfil & Rhymney*, Maj. 4,056

Hayes, John (*b.* 1958) *C., South Holland & The Deepings*, Maj. 21,880

Heald, Oliver (*b.* 1954) *C., Hertfordshire North East*, Maj. 15,194

Healey, Rt. Hon. John (*b.* 1960) *Lab., Wentworth & Dearne*, Maj. 13,920

Heath, David (*b.* 1954) *LD, Somerton & Frome*, Maj. 1,817

***Heaton-Harris**, Chris (*b.* 1967) *C., Daventry*, Maj. 19,188

Hemming, John (*b.* 1960) *LD, Birmingham Yardley*, Maj. 3,002

***Henderson**, Gordon (*b.* 1948) *C., Sittingbourne & Sheppey*, Maj. 12,383

Hendrick, Mark (*b.* 1958) *Lab. (Co-op), Preston*, Maj. 7,733

Hendry, Charles (*b.* 1959) *C., Wealden*, Maj. 17,179

Hepburn, Stephen (*b.* 1959) *Lab., Jarrow*, Maj. 12,908

Herbert, Nick (*b.* 1963) *C., Arundel & South Downs*, Maj. 16,691

‡**Hermon**, Lady Sylvia (*b.* 1956) *Ind., Down North*, Maj. 14,364

Heyes, David (*b.* 1946) *Lab., Ashton-under-Lyne*, Maj. 9,094

Hillier, Meg (*b.* 1969) *Lab. (Co-op), Hackney South & Shoreditch*, Maj. 14,288

***Hilling**, Julie (*b.* 1955) *Lab., Bolton West*, Maj. 92

***Hinds**, Damian (*b.* 1969) *C., Hampshire East*, Maj. 13,497

Hoban, Mark (*b.* 1964) *C., Fareham*, Maj. 17,092

Hodge, Rt. Hon. Margaret (*b.* 1944) *Lab., Barking*, Maj. 16,555

Hodgson, Sharon (*b.* 1966) *Lab., Washington & Sunderland West*, Maj. 11,458

Hoey, Kate (*b.* 1946) *Lab., Vauxhall*, Maj. 10,651

***Hollingbery**, George (*b.* 1963) *C., Meon Valley*, Maj. 12,125

Hollobone, Philip (*b.* 1964) *C., Kettering*, Maj. 9,094

Holloway, Adam (*b.* 1965) *C., Gravesham*, Maj. 9,312

Hood, Jim (*b.* 1948) *Lab., Lanark & Hamilton East*, Maj. 13,478

Hopkins, Kelvin (*b.* 1941) *Lab., Luton North*, Maj. 7,520

***Hopkins**, Kris (*b.* 1963) *C., Keighley*, Maj. 2,940

Horwood, Martin (*b.* 1962) *LD, Cheltenham*, Maj. 4,920

Hosie, Stewart (*b.* 1963) *SNP, Dundee East*, Maj. 1,821

Howarth, Rt. Hon. George (*b.* 1949) *Lab., Knowsley*, Maj. 25,690

Howarth, Gerald (*b.* 1947) *C., Aldershot*, Maj. 5,586

Howell, John (*b.* 1955) *C., Henley*, Maj. 16,588

Hoyle, Lindsay (*b.* 1957) *Lab., Deputy Speaker, Chorley*, Maj. 2,593

Hughes, Simon (*b.* 1951) *LD, Bermondsey & Old Southwark*, Maj. 8,530

Huhne, Rt. Hon. Chris (*b.* 1954) *LD, Eastleigh*, Maj. 3,864

Hunt, Rt. Hon. Jeremy (*b.* 1966) *C., Surrey South West*, Maj. 16,318

***Hunt**, Tristram (*b.* 1974) *Lab., Stoke-on-Trent Central*, Maj. 5,566

Hunter, Mark (*b.* 1957) *LD, Cheadle*, Maj. 3,272

***Huppert**, Julian (*b.* 1978) *LD, Cambridge*, Maj. 6,792

Hurd, Nick (*b.* 1962) *C., Ruislip, Northwood & Pinner*, Maj. 19,060

Irranca-Davies, Huw (*b.* 1963) *Lab., Ogmore*, Maj. 13,246

Jackson, Glenda (*b.* 1936) *Lab., Hampstead & Kilburn*, Maj. 42

Jackson, Stewart (*b.* 1965) *C., Peterborough*, Maj. 4,861

***James**, Margot (*b.* 1957) *C., Stourbridge*, Maj. 5,164

James, Siân (*b.* 1959) *Lab., Swansea East*, Maj. 10,838

***Jamieson**, Cathy (*b.* 1956) *Lab. (Co-op), Kilmarnock & Loudoun*, Maj. 12,378

***Jarvis**, Dan (*b.* 1972) *Lab., Barnsley Central*, Maj. 11,771

***Javid**, Sajid (*b.* 1969) *C., Bromsgrove*, Maj. 11,308

Jenkin, Bernard (*b.* 1959) *C., Harwich & Essex North*, Maj. 11,447

Johnson, Rt. Hon. Alan (*b.* 1950) *Lab., Hull West & Hessle*, Maj. 5,740

Johnson, Diana (*b.* 1966) *Lab., Hull North*, Maj. 641

***Johnson**, Gareth (*b.* 1969) *C., Dartford*, Maj. 24,428

***Johnson**, Jo (*b.* 1971) *C., Orpington*, Maj. 17,200

***Jones**, Andrew (*b.* 1963) *C., Harrogate & Knaresborough*, Maj. 1,039

Jones, David (*b.* 1952) *C., Clwyd West*, Maj. 6,419

***Jones**, Graham (*b.* 1966) *Lab., Hyndburn*, Maj. 3,090

Jones, Helen (*b.* 1954) *Lab., Warrington North*, Maj. 6,771

Jones, Kevan (*b.* 1964) *Lab., Durham North*, Maj. 12,076

***Jones**, Marcus (*b.* 1974) *C., Nuneaton*, Maj. 2,069

***Jones**, Susan (*b.* 1968) *Lab., Clwyd South*, Maj. 2,834

Jowell, Rt. Hon. Tessa (*b.* 1947) *Lab., Dulwich & West Norwood*, Maj. 9,365

Joyce, Eric (*b.* 1960) *Lab., Falkirk*, Maj. 7,843

Kaufman, Rt. Hon. Sir Gerald (*b.* 1930) *Lab., Manchester, Gorton*, Maj. 6,703

Kawczynski, Daniel (b. 1972) C., Shrewsbury & Atcham, Maj. 7,944

Keeley, Barbara (b. 1952) Lab., Worsley & Eccles South, Maj. 4,337

Keen, Alan (b. 1937) Lab. (Co-op), Feltham & Heston, Maj. 4,658

*Kelly, Chris (b. 1978) C., Dudley South, Maj. 3,856

*Kendall, Liz (b. 1971) Lab., Leicester West, Maj. 4,017

Kennedy, Rt. Hon. Charles (b. 1959) LD, Ross, Skye & Lochaber, Maj. 13,070

Khan, Rt. Hon. Sadiq (b. 1970) Lab., Tooting, Maj. 2,524

*Kirby, Simon (b. 1964) C., Brighton Kemptown, Maj. 1,328

Knight, Rt. Hon. Greg (b. 1949) C., Yorkshire East, Maj. 13,486

*Kwarteng, Kwasi (b. 1975) C., Spelthorne, Maj. 10,019

Laing, Eleanor (b. 1958) C., Epping Forest, Maj. 15,131

Lamb, Norman (b. 1957) LD, Norfolk North, Maj. 11,626

Lammy, Rt. Hon. David (b. 1972) Lab., Tottenham, Maj. 16,931

Lancaster, Mark (b. 1970) C., Milton Keynes North, Maj. 8,961

Lansley, Rt. Hon. Andrew (b. 1956) C., Cambridgeshire South, Maj. 7,838

*Latham, Pauline (b. 1948) C., Derbyshire Mid, Maj. 11,292

*Lavery, Ian (b. 1962) Lab., Wansbeck, Maj. 7,031

Laws, David (b. 1965) LD, Yeovil, Maj. 13,036

Lazarowicz, Mark (b. 1953) Lab. (Co-op), Edinburgh North & Leith, Maj. 1,724

*Leadsom, Andrea (b. 1963) C., Northamptonshire South, Maj. 20,478

*Lee, Jessica (b. 1976) C., Erewash, Maj. 2,501

*Lee, Phillip (b. 1970) C., Bracknell, Maj. 15,074

Leech, John (b. 1971) LD, Manchester Withington, Maj. 1,850

*Lefroy, Jeremy (b. 1959) C., Stafford, Maj. 5,460

Leigh, Edward (b. 1950) C., Gainsborough, Maj. 10,559

*Leslie, Charlotte (b. 1978) C., Bristol North West, Maj. 3,274

*Leslie, Chris (b. 1972) Lab. (Co-op), Nottingham East, Maj. 6,969

Letwin, Rt. Hon. Oliver (b. 1956) C., Dorset West, Maj. 3,923

*Lewis, Brandon (b. 1971) C., Great Yarmouth, Maj. 4,276

Lewis, Ivan (b. 1967) Lab., Bury South, Maj. 3,292

Lewis, Dr Julian (b. 1951) C., New Forest East, Maj. 11,307

Liddell-Grainger, Ian (b. 1959) C., Bridgwater & Somerset West, Maj. 9,249

Lidington, David (b. 1956) C., Aylesbury, Maj. 12,618

Lilley, Rt. Hon. Peter (b. 1943) C., Hitchin & Harpenden, Maj. 15,271

*Lloyd, Stephen (b. 1957) LD, Eastbourne, Maj. 3,435

Lloyd, Tony (b. 1950) Lab., Manchester Central, Maj. 10,439

Llwyd, Elfyn (b. 1951) PC, Dwyfor Meirionnydd, Maj. 6,367

*Long, Naomi (b. 1971) All. Belfast East, Maj. 1,533

*Lopresti, Jack (b. 1969) C., Filton & Bradley Stoke, Maj. 6,914

*Lord, Jonathan (b. 1962) C., Woking, Maj. 6,807

Loughton, Tim (b. 1962) C., Worthing East & Shoreham, Maj. 11,105

Love, Andy (b. 1949) Lab. (Co-op), Edmonton, Maj. 9,613

*Lucas, Caroline (b. 1960) Green, Brighton Pavilion, Maj. 1,252

Lucas, Ian (b. 1960) Lab., Wrexham, Maj. 3,658

Luff, Peter (b. 1955) C., Worcestershire Mid, Maj. 15,864

*Lumley, Karen (b. 1964) C., Redditch, Maj. 5,821

Maskey, Paul (b. 1967) SF, Belfast West, Maj. 13,123

McCabe, Steve (b. 1955) Lab., Birmingham Selly Oak, Maj. 3,482

*McCann, Michael (b. 1964) Lab., East Kilbride, Strathaven & Lesmahagow, Maj. 14,503

McCarthy, Kerry (b. 1965) Lab., Bristol East, Maj. 3,722

*McCartney, Jason (b. 1968) C., Colne Valley, Maj. 4,837

*McCartney, Karl (b. 1968) C., Lincoln, Maj. 1,058

*McClymont, Gregg (b. 1976) Lab., Cumbernauld, Kilsyth & Kirkintilloch East, Maj. 13,755

McCrea, Revd Dr William (b. 1948) DUP, Antrim South, Maj. 1,183

McDonagh, Siobhain (b. 1960) Lab., Mitcham & Morden, Maj. 13,666

McDonnell, Dr Alasdair (b. 1949) SDLP, Belfast South, Maj. 5,926

McDonnell, John (b. 1951) Lab., Hayes & Harlington, Maj. 10,824

McFadden, Rt. Hon. Pat (b. 1965) Lab., Wolverhampton South East, Maj. 6,593

*McGovern, Alison (b. 1980) Lab., Wirral South, Maj. 531

McGovern, James (b. 1956) Lab., Dundee West, Maj. 7,278

McGuinness, Martin (b. 1950) SF, Ulster Mid, Maj. 15,363

McGuire, Rt. Hon. Anne (b. 1949) Lab., Stirling, Maj. 8,354

McKechin, Ann (b. 1961) Lab., Glasgow North, Maj. 3,898

McKenzie, Iain (b. 1959) Lab., Inverclyde, Maj. 5,838

*McKinnell, Catherine (b. 1976) Lab., Newcastle upon Tyne North, Maj. 3,414

*MacLeod, Mary (b. 1969) C., Brentford & Isleworth, Maj. 1,958

McLoughlin, Rt. Hon. Patrick (b. 1957) C., Derbyshire Dales, Maj. 13,866

MacNeil, Angus (b. 1970) SNP, Na h-Eileanan an Iar, Maj. 1,885

*McPartland, Stephen (b. 1976) C., Stevenage, Maj. 3,578

MacShane, Rt. Hon. Denis (b. 1948) Lab., Rotherham, Maj. 10,462

Mactaggart, Fiona (b. 1953) Lab., Slough, Maj. 5,523

*McVey, Esther (b. 1967) C., Wirral West, Maj. 2,436

Mahmood, Khalid (b. 1961) Lab., Birmingham Perry Barr, Maj. 11,908

*Mahmood, Shabana (b. 1980) Lab., Birmingham Ladywood, Maj. 10,105

Main, Anne (b. 1957) C., St Albans, Maj. 2,305

Mann, John (b. 1960) Lab., Bassetlaw, Maj. 8,215

Marsden, Gordon (b. 1953) Lab., Blackpool South, Maj. 1,852

Maude, Rt. Hon. Francis (b. 1953) C., Horsham, Maj. 11,460

May, Rt. Hon. Theresa (b. 1956) C., Maidenhead, Maj. 16,769

*Maynard, Paul (b. 1975) C., Blackpool North & Cleveleys, Maj. 2,150

Meacher, Rt. Hon. Michael (b. 1939) Lab., Oldham West & Royton, Maj. 9,352

Meale, Alan (b. 1949) Lab., Mansfield, Maj. 6,012

*Mearns, Ian (b. 1957) Lab., Gateshead, Maj. 12,549

*Menzies, Mark (b. 1971) C., Fylde, Maj. 13,185

Mercer, Patrick (b. 1956) C., Newark, Maj. 16,152

*Metcalfe, Stephen (b. 1966) C., Basildon South & Thurrock East, Maj. 5,772

Michael, Rt. Hon. Alun (b. 1943) Lab. (Co-op), Cardiff South & Penarth, Maj. 4,709

Miliband, Rt. Hon. David (b. 1966) Lab., South Shields, Maj. 11,109

Miliband, Rt. Hon. Ed (b. 1969) Lab., Doncaster North, Maj. 10,909

Miller, Andrew (b. 1949) Lab., Ellesmere Port & Neston, Maj. 4,331

Miller, Maria (b. 1964) C., Basingstoke, Maj. 13,176

*Mills, Nigel (b. 1974) C., Amber Valley, Maj. 536

Milton, Anne (b. 1955) C., Guildford, Maj. 7,782

Mitchell, Rt. Hon. Andrew (b. 1956) C., Sutton Coldfield, Maj. 17,005

Mitchell, Austin (b. 1934) Lab., Great Grimsby, Maj. 714

Moon, Madeleine (b. 1950) Lab., Bridgend, Maj. 2,263

Moore, Rt. Hon. Michael (b. 1965) LD, Berwickshire, Roxburgh & Selkirk, Maj. 5,675

*Mordaunt, Penny (b. 1973) C., Portsmouth North, Maj. 7,289

Morden, Jessica (b. 1968) Lab., Newport East, Maj. 1,650

*Morgan, Nicky (b. 1972) C., Loughborough, Maj. 3,744

*Morrice, Graeme (b. 1959) Lab., Livingston, Maj. 10,791

*Morris, Anne Marie (b. 1957) C., Newton Abbot, Maj. 523

*Morris, David (b. 1966) C., Morecambe & Lunesdale, Maj. 866

*Morris, Grahame (b. 1961) Lab., Easington, Maj. 14,982

*Morris, James (b. 1967) C., Halesowen & Rowley Regis, Maj. 2,023

*Mosley, Stephen (b. 1972) C., Chester, City of, Maj. 2,583

*Mowat, David (b. 1957) C., Warrington South, Maj. 1,553

Mudie, George (b. 1945) Lab., Leeds East, Maj. 10,293

Mulholland, Greg (b. 1970) LD, Leeds North West, Maj. 9,103

Mundell, David (b. 1962) C., Dumfriesshire, Clydesdale & Tweeddale, Maj. 4,194

Munn, Meg (b. 1959) Lab. (Co-op), Sheffield Heeley, Maj. 5,807

*Munt, Tessa (b. 1959) LD, Wells, Maj. 800

Murphy, Conor (b. 1963) SF, Newry & Armagh, Maj. 8,331

Murphy, Rt. Hon. Jim (b. 1967) Lab., Renfrewshire East, Maj. 10,420

Murphy, Rt. Hon. Paul (b. 1948) Lab., Torfaen, Maj. 9,306

*Murray, Ian (b. 1976) Lab., Edinburgh South, Maj. 316

*Murray, Sheryll (b. 1956) C., Cornwall South East, Maj. 3,220

Murrison, Dr Andrew (b. 1961) C., Wiltshire South West, Maj. 10,367

*Nandy, Lisa (b. 1979) Lab., Wigan, Maj. 10,487

*Nash, Pamela (b. 1984) Lab., Airdrie & Shotts, Maj. 12,408

Neill, Robert (b. 1952) C., Bromley & Chislehurst, Maj. 13,900

Newmark, Brooks (b. 1958) C., Braintree, Maj. 16,121

*Newton, Sarah (b. 1962) C., Truro & Falmouth, Maj. 435

*Nokes, Caroline (b. 1972) C., Romsey & Southampton North, Maj. 4,156

*Norman, Jesse (b. 1962) C., Hereford & Herefordshire South, Maj. 2,481

*Nuttall, David (b. 1962) C., Bury North, Maj. 2,243

O'Brien, Stephen (b. 1957) C., Eddisbury, Maj. 13,255

*O'Donnell, Fiona (b. 1960) Lab., East Lothian, Maj. 12,258

*Offord, Matthew (b. 1969) C., Hendon, Maj. 106

*Ollerenshaw, Eric (b. 1950) C., Lancaster & Fleetwood, Maj. 333

*Onwurah, Chi (b. 1965) Lab., Newcastle upon Tyne Central, Maj. 7,464

*Opperman, Guy (b. 1965) C., Hexham, Maj. 5,788

Osborne, Rt. Hon. George (b. 1971) C., Tatton, Maj. 14,487

Osborne, Sandra (b. 1956) Lab., Ayr, Carrick & Cumnock, Maj. 9,911

Ottaway, Richard (b. 1945) C., Croydon South, Maj. 15,818

Owen, Albert (b. 1960) Lab., Ynys Mon, Maj. 2,461

Paice, James (b. 1949) C., Cambridgeshire South East, Maj. 5,946

*Paisley Jr, Ian (b. 1966) DUP, Antrim North, Maj. 12,558

*Parish, Neil (b. 1956) C., Tiverton & Honiton, Maj. 9,320

*Patel, Priti (b. 1972) C., Witham, Maj. 15,196

Paterson, Rt. Hon. Owen (b. 1956) C., Shropshire North, Maj. 15,828

*Pawsey, Mark (b. 1957) C., Rugby, Maj. 6,000

*Pearce, Teresa (b. 1955) Lab., Erith & Thamesmead, Maj. 5,703

Penning, Mike (b. 1957) C., Hemel Hempstead, Maj. 13,406

Penrose, John (b. 1964) C., Weston-Super-Mare, Maj. 2,691

*Percy, Andrew (b. 1977) C., Brigg & Goole, Maj. 5,147

*Perkins, Toby (b. 1970) Lab., Chesterfield, Maj. 549

*Perry, Claire (b. 1964) C., Devizes, Maj. 13,005

*Phillips, Stephen (b. 1970) C., Sleaford & Hykeham North, Maj. 19,905

*Phillipson, Bridget (b. 1983) Lab., Houghton & Sunderland South, Maj. 10,990

Pickles, Rt. Hon. Eric (b. 1952) C., Brentwood & Ongar, Maj. 16,920

*Pincher, Christopher (b. 1969) C., Tamworth, Maj. 6,090

*Poulter, Daniel (b. 1978) C., Suffolk Central & Ipswich North, Maj. 13,786

Pound, Stephen (b. 1948) Lab., Ealing North, Maj. 9,301

Primarolo, Rt. Hon. Dawn (b. 1954) Lab., Bristol South, Maj. 4,734

Prisk, Mark (b. 1962) C., Hertford & Stortford, Maj. 15,437

Pritchard, Mark (b. 1966) C., The Wrekin, Maj. 9,450

Pugh, Dr John (b. 1948) LD, Southport, Maj. 6,024

*Qureshi, Yasmin (b. 1963) Lab., Bolton South East, Maj. 8,634

*Raab, Dominic (b. 1974) C., Esher & Walton, Maj. 18,593

Randall, John (b. 1955) C., Uxbridge & Ruislip South, Maj. 11,216

Raynsford, Rt. Hon. Nick (b. 1945) Lab., Greenwich & Woolwich, Maj. 10,153

*Reckless, Mark (b. 1970) C., Rochester & Strood, Maj. 9,953

Redwood, Rt. Hon. John (b. 1951) C., Wokingham, Maj. 13,492

Reed, Jamie (b. 1973) Lab., Copeland, Maj. 3,833

*Rees-Mogg, Jacob (b. 1969) C., Somerset North East, Maj. 4,914

*Reevell, Simon (b. 1966) C., Dewsbury, Maj. 1,526

*Reeves, Rachel (*b.* 1979) *Lab., Leeds West,* Maj. 7,016

Reid, Alan (*b.* 1954) *LD, Argyll & Bute,* Maj. 3,431

*Reynolds, Emma (*b.* 1977) *Lab., Wolverhampton North East,* Maj. 2,484

*Reynolds, Jonathan (*b.* 1980) *Lab. (Co-op), Stalybridge & Hyde,* Maj. 2,744

Rifkind, Rt. Hon. Sir Malcolm (*b.* 1946) *C., Kensington,* Maj. 8,616

Riordan, Linda (*b.* 1953) *Lab. (Co-op), Halifax,* Maj. 1,472

*Ritchie, Margaret (*b.* 1958) *SDLP, South Down,* Maj. 8,412

Robathan, Andrew (*b.* 1951) *C., Leicestershire South,* Maj. 15,524

Robertson, Angus (*b.* 1969) *SNP, Moray,* Maj. 5,590

Robertson, Hugh (*b.* 1962) *C., Faversham & Kent Mid,* Maj. 17,088

Robertson, John (*b.* 1952) *Lab., Glasgow North West,* Maj. 13,611

Robertson, Laurence (*b.* 1958) *C., Tewkesbury,* Maj. 6,310

Robinson, Geoffrey (*b.* 1938) *Lab., Coventry North West,* Maj. 6,288

Rogerson, Dan (*b.* 1975) *LD, Cornwall North,* Maj. 2,981

Rosindell, Andrew (*b.* 1966) *C., Romford,* Maj. 16,954

*Rotheram, Steve (*b.* 1961) *Lab., Liverpool Walton,* Maj. 19,818

Roy, Frank (*b.* 1958) *Lab., Motherwell & Wishaw,* Maj. 16,806

Roy, Lindsay (*b.* 1949) *Lab., Glenrothes,* Maj. 16,455

Ruane, Chris (*b.* 1958) *Lab., Vale of Clwyd,* Maj. 2,509

*Rudd, Amber (*b.* 1963) *C., Hastings & Rye,* Maj. 1,993

Ruddock, Joan (*b.* 1943) *Lab., Lewisham Deptford,* Maj. 12,499

Ruffley, David (*b.* 1962) *C., Bury St Edmunds,* Maj. 12,380

Russell, Bob (*b.* 1946) *LD, Colchester,* Maj. 6,982

*Rutley, David (*b.* 1961) *C., Macclesfield,* Maj. 11,959

Sanders, Adrian (*b.* 1959) *LD, Torbay,* Maj. 4,078

*Sandys, Laura (*b.* 1964) *C., Thanet South,* Maj. 7,617

*Sarwar, Anas (*b.* 1983) *Lab., Glasgow Central,* Maj. 10,551

Scott, Lee (*b.* 1956) *C., Ilford North,* Maj. 5,404

Seabeck, Alison (*b.* 1954) *Lab., Plymouth Moor View,* Maj. 1,588

Selous, Andrew (*b.* 1962) *C., Bedfordshire South West,* Maj. 16,649

*Shannon, Jim (*b.* 1955) *DUP, Strangford,* Maj. 5,876

Shapps, Grant (*b.* 1968) *C., Welwyn Hatfield,* Maj. 7,423

*Sharma, Alok (*b.* 1967) *C., Reading West,* Maj. 6,004

Sharma, Virendra (*b.* 1947) *Lab., Ealing Southall,* Maj. 9,291

Sheerman, Barry (*b.* 1940) *Lab. (Co-op), Huddersfield,* Maj. 4,472

*Shelbrooke, Alec (*b.* 1976) *C., Elmet & Rothwell,* Maj. 4,521

Shepherd, Richard (*b.* 1942) *C., Aldridge-Brownhills,* Maj. 15,256

Sheridan, Jim (*b.* 1952) *Lab., Paisley & Renfrewshire North,* Maj. 15,280

*Shuker, Gavin (*b.* 1981) *Lab. (Co-op), Luton South,* Maj. 2,329

Simmonds, Mark (*b.* 1964) *C., Boston & Skegness,* Maj. 12,426

Simpson, David (*b.* 1959) *DUP, Upper Bann,* Maj. 3,361

†Simpson, Keith (*b.* 1949) *C., Broadland,* Maj. 7,292

Singh, Marsha (*b.* 1954) *Lab., Bradford West,* Maj. 5,763

*Skidmore, Chris (*b.* 1981) *C., Kingswood,* Maj. 2,445

Skinner, Dennis (*b.* 1932) *Lab., Bolsover,* Maj. 11,182

†Slaughter, Andrew (*b.* 1960) *Lab., Hammersmith,* Maj. 3,549

Smith, Rt. Hon. Andrew (*b.* 1951) *Lab., Oxford East,* Maj. 4,581

Smith, Angela C. (*b.* 1961) *Lab., Penistone & Stocksbridge,* Maj. 3,049

Smith, Chloe (*b.* 1982) *C., Norwich North,* Maj. 3,901

*Smith, Henry (*b.* 1969) *C., Crawley,* Maj. 5,928

*Smith, Julian (*b.* 1971) *C., Skipton & Ripon,* Maj. 9,950

*Smith, Nick (*b.* 1960) *Lab., Blaenau Gwent,* Maj. 10,516

*Smith, Owen (*b.* 1970) *Lab., Pontypridd,* Maj. 2,785

Smith, Sir Robert (*b.* 1958) *LD, Aberdeenshire West & Kincardine,* Maj. 6,684

Soames, Hon. Nicholas (*b.* 1948) *C., Sussex Mid,* Maj. 7,402

*Soubry, Anna (*b.* 1956) *C., Broxtowe,* Maj. 389

Spellar, Rt. Hon. John (*b.* 1947) *Lab., Warley,* Maj. 10,756

Spelman, Rt. Hon. Caroline (*b.* 1958) *C., Meriden,* Maj. 16,253

*Spencer, Mark (*b.* 1970) *C., Sherwood,* Maj. 214

Stanley, Rt. Hon. Sir John (*b.* 1942) *C., Tonbridge & Malling,* Maj. 18,178

*Stephenson, Andrew (*b.* 1981) *C., Pendle,* Maj. 3,585

*Stevenson, John (*b.* 1963) *C., Carlisle,* Maj. 853

*Stewart, Bob (*b.* 1949) *C., Beckenham,* Maj. 17,784

*Stewart, Iain (*b.* 1972) *C., Milton Keynes South,* Maj. 5,201

*Stewart, Rory (*b.* 1973) *C., Penrith & The Border,* Maj. 11,241

Straw, Rt. Hon. Jack (*b.* 1946) *Lab., Blackburn,* Maj. 9,856

Streeter, Gary (*b.* 1955) *C., Devon South West,* Maj. 15,874

*Stride, Mel (*b.* 1961) *C., Devon Central,* Maj. 9,230

Stringer, Graham (*b.* 1950) *Lab., Blackley & Broughton,* Maj. 12,303

Stuart, Gisela (*b.* 1955) *Lab., Birmingham, Edgbaston,* Maj. 1,274

Stuart, Graham (*b.* 1962) *C., Beverley & Holderness,* Maj. 12,987

Stunell, Andrew (*b.* 1942) *LD, Hazel Grove,* Maj. 6,371

*Sturdy, Julian (*b.* 1971) *C., York Outer,* Maj. 3,688

Sutcliffe, Gerry (*b.* 1953) *Lab., Bradford South,* Maj. 4,622

*Swales, Ian (*b.* 1953) *LD, Redcar,* Maj. 5,214

Swayne, Desmond (*b.* 1956) *C., New Forest West,* Maj. 16,896

Swinson, Jo (*b.* 1980) *LD, Dunbartonshire East,* Maj. 2,184

Swire, Hugo (*b.* 1959) *C., Devon East,* Maj. 9,114

Syms, Robert (*b.* 1956) *C., Poole,* Maj. 7,541

Tami, Mark (*b.* 1963) *Lab., Alyn & Deeside,* Maj. 2,919

Tapsell, Sir Peter (*b.* 1930) *C., Louth & Horncastle,* Maj. 13,871

Teather, Sarah (*b.* 1974) *LD, Brent Central,* Maj. 1,345

Thomas, Gareth (*b.* 1967) *Lab. (Co-op), Harrow West,* Maj. 3,143

Thornberry, Emily (*b.* 1960) *Lab., Islington South & Finsbury,* Maj. 3,569

Thurso, John (*b.* 1953) *LD, Caithness, Sutherland & Easter Ross,* Maj. 4,826

Timms, Rt. Hon. Stephen (*b.* 1955) *Lab., East Ham,* Maj. 27,826

Timpson, Edward (*b.* 1973) *C., Crewe & Nantwich,* Maj. 6,046

*Tomlinson, Justin (*b.* 1976) *C., Swindon North,* Maj. 7,060

Tredinnick, David (*b.* 1950) *C., Bosworth,* Maj. 5,032

Trickett, Jon (*b.* 1950) *Lab., Hemsworth,* Maj. 9,844

*Truss, Elizabeth (*b.* 1975) *C., Norfolk South West,* Maj. 13,140

Turner, Andrew (*b.* 1953) *C., Isle of Wight,* Maj. 10,527

*Turner, Karl (*b.* 1971) *Lab., Hull East,* Maj. 8,597

Twigg, Derek (*b.* 1959) *Lab., Halton,* Maj. 15,504

*Twigg, Stephen (*b.* 1966) *Lab. (Co-op), Liverpool Derby West,* Maj. 18,467

Tyrie, Andrew (*b.* 1957) *C., Chichester,* Maj. 15,877

*Umunna, Chuka (*b.* 1978) *Lab., Streatham,* Maj. 3,259

*Uppal, Paul (*b.* 1967) *C., Wolverhampton South West,* Maj. 691

Vaizey, Ed (*b.* 1969) *C., Wantage,* Maj. 13,547

Vara, Shailesh (*b.* 1960) *C., Cambridgeshire North West,* Maj. 16,677

Vaz, Rt. Hon. Keith (*b.* 1956) *Lab., Leicester East,* Maj. 14,082

*Vaz, Valerie (*b.* 1954) *Lab., Walsall South,* Maj. 1,755

*Vickers, Martin (*b.* 1950) *C., Cleethorpes,* Maj. 4,298

Villiers, Theresa (*b.* 1968) *C., Chipping Barnet,* Maj. 11,927

Walker, Charles (*b.* 1967) *C., Broxbourne,* Maj. 18,804

*Walker, Robin (*b.* 1978) *C., Worcester,* Maj. 2,982

Wallace, Ben (*b.* 1970) *C., Wyre & Preston North,* Maj. 15,844

Walley, Joan (*b.* 1949) *Lab., Stoke-on-Trent North,* Maj. 8,235

Walter, Robert (*b.* 1948) *C., Dorset North,* Maj. 7,625

*Ward, David, (*b.* 1953) *LD, Bradford East,* Maj. 365

Watkinson, Angela (*b.* 1941) *C., Hornchurch & Upminster,* Maj. 16,371

Watson, Tom (*b.* 1967) *Lab., West Bromwich East,* Maj. 6,696

Watts, Dave (*b.* 1951) *Lab., St Helens North,* Maj. 13,101

*Weatherley, Mike (*b.* 1957) *C., Hove,* Maj. 1,868

Webb, Prof. Steve (*b.* 1965) *LD, Thornbury & Yate,* Maj. 7,116

Weir, Mike (*b.* 1957) *SNP, Angus,* Maj. 3,282

*Wharton, James (*b.* 1984) *C., Stockton South,* Maj. 332

*Wheeler, Heather (*b.* 1959) *C., Derbyshire South,* Maj. 7,128

*White, Chris (*b.* 1967) *C., Warwick & Leamington,* Maj. 3,513

*Whiteford, Eilidh (*b.* 1969) *SNP, Banff & Buchan,* Maj. 4,027

Whitehead, Dr Alan (*b.* 1950) *Lab., Southampton, Test,* Maj. 2,413

*Whittaker, Craig (*b.* 1962) *C., Calder Valley,* Maj. 6,431

Whittingdale, John (*b.* 1959) *C., Maldon,* Maj. 19,407

Wicks, Malcolm (*b.* 1947) *Lab., Croydon North,* Maj. 16,483

Wiggin, Bill (*b.* 1966) *C., Herefordshire North,* Maj. 9,887

Willetts, David (*b.* 1956) *C., Havant,* Maj. 12,160

Williams, Hywel (*b.* 1953) *PC, Arfon,* Maj. 1,455

Williams, Mark (*b.* 1966) *LD, Ceredigion,* Maj. 8,324

Williams, Roger (*b.* 1948) *LD, Brecon & Radnorshire,* Maj. 3,747

Williams, Stephen (*b.* 1966) *LD, Bristol West,* Maj. 11,366

*Williamson, Chris (*b.* 1956) *Lab., Derby North,* Maj. 613

*Williamson, Gavin (*b.* 1976) *C., Staffordshire South,* Maj. 16,590

Willott, Jenny (*b.* 1974) *LD, Cardiff Central,* Maj. 4,576

Wilson, Phil (*b.* 1959) *Lab., Sedgefield,* Maj. 8,696

Wilson, Rob (*b.* 1965) *C., Reading East,* Maj. 7,605

Wilson, Sammy (*b.* 1953) *DUP, Antrim East,* Maj. 6,770

Winnick, David (*b.* 1933) *Lab., Walsall North,* Maj. 990

Winterton, Rt. Hon. Rosie (*b.* 1958) *Lab., Doncaster Central,* Maj. 6,229

Wishart, Peter (*b.* 1962) *SNP, Perth & Perthshire North,* Maj. 4,379

*Wollaston, Sarah (*b.* 1962) *C., Totnes,* Maj. 4,927

Wood, Mike (*b.* 1946) *Lab., Batley & Spen,* Maj. 4,406

*Woodcock, John (*b.* 1978) *Lab. (Co-op), Barrow & Furness,* Maj. 5,208

Woodward, Rt. Hon. Shaun (*b.* 1958) *Lab., St Helens South & Whiston,* Maj. 14,122

Wright, David (*b.* 1967) *Lab., Telford,* Maj. 981

Wright, Iain (*b.* 1972) *Lab., Hartlepool,* Maj. 5,509

Wright, Jeremy (*b.* 1972) *C., Kenilworth & Southam,* Maj. 12,552

*Wright, Simon (*b.* 1979) *LD, Norwich South,* Maj. 310

Yeo, Tim (*b.* 1945) *C., Suffolk South,* Maj. 8,689

Young, Rt. Hon. Sir George (*b.* 1941) *C., Hampshire North West,* Maj. 18,583

*Zahawi, Nadhim (*b.* 1967) *C., Stratford-on-Avon,* Maj. 11,346

GENERAL ELECTION RESULTS

The results of voting in each parliamentary division at the general election of 6 May 2010 are given below.

BOUNDARY CHANGES
The constituency boundaries were redrawn for the 2010 election in England, Wales and Northern Ireland. As a result of the review the number of constituencies increased from 646 to 650, with four new seats in England. Only 138 constituencies had no boundary changes, 59 of them in Scotland.

For the majority of constituencies where a boundary change has taken place, it is not appropriate to make a direct comparison between the results of 2005 and 2010. The seat of Hammersmith, for example, comprises 60 per cent of the old Hammersmith and Fulham constituency and 40 per cent of the old Ealing and Shepherds Bush constituency; it cannot therefore be described as a simple hold for the Labour party. The term 'notional' used here refers to a theoretical set of results, published by Professors Rallings and Thrasher of Plymouth University, which estimates the way each new constituency might have voted in the 2005 general election.

KEY
* New MP
† Previously MP in another seat
‡ Previously MP for another party
§ Notional result; *see* explanation of boundary changes
E. Electorate
T. Turnout

Abbreviations

AD	Apolitical Democrats
Alliance	Alliance
Animals	Animals Count
Anti-War	Fight for an Anti-War Government
APP	Animal Protection Party
Battersea	Putting the People of Battersea First
BB	A Better Britain for All
BCP	Basingstoke Common Man
Bean	New Millennium Bean
Beer	Reduce Tax on Beer Party
Best	The Best of a Bad Bunch
BIB	Bushra Irfan of Blackburn
BIC	Bromsgrove Independent Conservative
Blaenau Voice	Blaenau Gwent People's Voice
Blue	Blue Environment Party
BNP	British National Party
BP Elvis	Bus-Pass Elvis Party
C.	Conservative
Ch. M.	Christian Movement for Great Britain
Ch. P.	Christian Party
Christian	Christian
CIP	Campaign for Independent Politicians
City Ind.	City Independent
Clause 28	Clause 28, Children's Protection Christian Democrats
CNBPG	Community Need Before Private Greed
Comm.	Communist Party
Comm. Brit.	Communist Party of Britain
Comm. Lge	Communist League
Cornish D.	Cornish Democrats
CPA	Christian People's Alliance
CSP	Common Sense Party
Currency	Virtue Currency Cognitive Appraisal Party
D. Nat.	Democratic Nationalist
DDP	Direct Democracy Party
Deficit	Cut the Deficit Party
Dem. Lab.	Democratic Labour Party

DUP	Democratic Unionist Party
Eng. Dem.	English Democrats
Eng. Ind.	English Independence Party
F and R	For Freedom and Responsibility
FDP	Fancy Dress Party
Good	The Common Good
Green	Green
Green Belt	Independent Save Our Green Belt
Green Soc.	Alliance for Green Socialism
Humanity	Humanity
Impact	Impact Party
Ind.	Independent
Ind. CCF	New Independent Conservative Chelsea and Fulham
Ind. CHC	Independent Community and Health Concern
Ind. EACPS	Independent Ealing Action Communities Public Services
Ind. Fed.	Independents Federation UK
Ind. People	Independent People Together
Ind. Rantzen	Independent Rantzen
Ind. Voice	Independent Voice for Halifax
Integrity	Integrity UK
IZB	Islam Zinda Baad Platform
J & AC	Justice & Anti-Corruption Party
Jacobite	Scottish Jacobite Party
Joy	The Joy of Talk
JP	Justice Party
King George	Save King George Hospital
Lab.	Labour
Lab. (Co-op)	Labour and Co-operative
Land	Land is Power
LD	Liberal Democrat
Leave EU	Independent Leave the EU Alliance
Lib.	Liberal
Libertarian	Libertarian Party
Lincs. Ind.	Lincolnshire Independents

LLPBPP	Local Liberals People Before Politics Party
Loony	Monster Raving Loony Party
LTT	Lawfulness Trustworthiness and Transparency
Macc. Ind.	The Macclesfield Independent
Magna Carta	The Magna Carta Party
Mansfield Ind.	Mansfield Independent Forum
Meb. Ker.	Mebyon Kernow
Med. Ind.	Medway Independent
Mid.	Middle England Party
England	
MP Expense	A Vote Against MP Expense Abuse
MRP	Money Reform Party
Nat. Dem.	National Democrat
ND	No Description
New Party	The New Party
NF	National Front
NFP	Nationwide Reform Party
No Vote	No Candidate Deserves My Vote
Nobody	Nobody Party
NSPS	Northampton – Save Our Public Services
Parenting	Equal Parenting Alliance
PBP	People Before Profit
PC	Plaid Cymru
Pirate	Pirate Party UK
PNDP	People's National Democratic Party
Poetry	The True English (Poetry) Party
PP Essex	Peoples Party Essex
PPN-V	Peace Party Non-Violence Justice Environment
R and E	Citizens for Undead Rights and Equality
RA	Solihull and Meriden Residents' Association
Reform	Reform 2000
Respect	Respect the Unity Coalition
RP	The Restoration Party
RRG	Radical Reform Group

SACL	Scotland Against Crooked Lawyers	
Save QM	Independents to Save Queen Mary's Hospital	
Science	The Science Party	
SDLP	Social Democratic and Labour Party	
SEP	Socialist Equality Party	
SF	Sinn Fein	
SMA	Scrap Members Allowances	
Snouts	Get Snouts Out The Trough	
SNP	Scottish National Party	
Soc.	Socialist Party	
Soc. Alt.	Socialist Alternative Party	
Soc. Dem.	Social Democratic Party	
Soc. Lab.	Socialist Labour Party	

South	All the South Party
Speaker	The Speaker
SSP	Scottish Socialist Party
Staffs Ind.	Staffordshire Independent Group
Tendring	Tendring First
TOC	Tamsin Omond to the Commons
Trust	Trust
TUSC	Trade Unionist and Socialist Coalition
TUV	Traditional Unionist Voice
UCUNF	Ulster Conservatives and Unionists – New Force
UK Integrity	Independents Federation UK – Honest Integrity Democracy

UKIP	UK Independence Party
UPS	Unity for Peace and Socialism
Voice	United Voice
Wessex Reg.	Wessex Regionalist
Workers Lib.	Alliance for Workers Liberty
WP	Workers' Party
WRP	Workers' Revolutionary Party
You	You Party
Youth	Youth Party
YP	Go Mad and Vote For Yourself Party
YRDPL	Your Right to Democracy Party Limited

PARLIAMENTARY CONSTITUENCIES AS AT 6 MAY 2010 GENERAL ELECTION

UK Turnout
E. 45,533,536 T. 29,643,522 (65.1%)

ENGLAND

§ALDERSHOT
E. 71,469 T. 45,384 (63.50%) C. hold
Gerald Howarth, C. — 21,203
Adrian Collett, LD — 15,617
Jonathan Slater, Lab. — 5,489
Robert Snare, UKIP — 2,041
Gary Crowd, Eng. Ind. — 803
Juliana Brimicombe, Ch. P. — 231
C. majority 5,586 (12.31%)
Notional 1.41% swing C. to LD
(2005: C. majority 6,345 (15.12%))

§ALDRIDGE-BROWNHILLS
E. 59,355 T. 38,634 (65.09%) C. hold
Richard Shepherd, C. — 22,913
Ashiq Hussain, Lab. — 7,647
Ian Jenkins, LD — 6,833
Karl Macnaughton, Green — 847
Sue Gray, Ch. P. — 394
C. majority 15,266 (39.51%)
Notional 12.01% swing Lab. to C.
(2005: C. majority 5,732 (15.49%))

§ALTRINCHAM & SALE WEST
E. 71,254 T. 49,393 (69.32%) C. hold
Graham Brady, C. — 24,176
Jane Brophy, LD — 12,581
Tom Ross, Lab. — 11,073
Kenneth Bullman, UKIP — 1,563
C. majority 11,595 (23.47%)
Notional 0.83% swing C. to LD
(2005: C. majority 7,618 (17.57%))

§AMBER VALLEY
E. 70,171 T. 45,958 (65.49%) C. gain
*Nigel Mills, C. — 17,746
Judy Mallaber, Lab. — 17,210
Tom Snowdon, LD — 6,636
Michael Clarke, BNP — 3,195
Sue Ransome, UKIP — 906
Sam Thing, Loony — 265
C. majority 536 (1.17%)
Notional 6.85% swing Lab. to C.
(2005: Lab. majority 5,512 (12.53%))

§ARUNDEL & SOUTH DOWNS
E. 77,564 T. 55,982 (72.18%) C. hold
Nick Herbert, C. — 32,333
Derek Deedman, LD — 15,642
Tim Lunnon, Lab. — 4,835
Stuart Bower, UKIP — 3,172
C. majority 16,691 (29.81%)
Notional 3.00% swing LD to C.
(2005: C. majority 12,291 (23.81%))

§ASHFIELD
E. 77,379 T. 48,196 (62.29%) Lab. hold
*Gloria De Piero, Lab. — 16,239
Jason Zadrozny, LD — 16,047
Garry Hickton, C. — 10,698
Edward Holmes, BNP — 2,781
Tony Ellis, Eng. Dem. — 1,102
Terry Coleman, UKIP — 933
Eddie Smith, Ind. — 396
Lab. majority 192 (0.40%)
Notional 17.23% swing Lab. to LD
(2005: Lab. majority 10,370 (24.28%))

§ASHFORD
E. 81,269 T. 55,185 (67.90%) C. hold
Damian Green, C. — 29,878
Chris Took, LD — 12,581
Chris Clark, Lab. — 9,204
Jeffrey Elenor, UKIP — 2,508
Steve Campkin, Green — 1,014
C. majority 17,297 (31.34%)
Notional 2.25% swing C. to LD
(2005: C. majority 12,268 (25.02%))

§ASHTON UNDER LYNE
E. 67,564 T. 38,432 (56.88%) Lab. hold
David Heyes, Lab. — 18,604
Seema Kennedy, C. — 9,510
Paul Larkin, LD — 5,703
David Lomas, BNP — 2,929
Angela McManus, UKIP — 1,686
Lab. majority 9,094 (23.66%)
Notional 7.34% swing Lab. to C.
(2005: Lab. majority 13,199 (38.33%))

§AYLESBURY
E. 77,934 T. 53,162 (68.21%) C. hold
David Lidington, C. — 27,736
Steven Lambert, LD — 15,118
Kathryn White, Lab. — 6,695
Chris Adams, UKIP — 3,613
C. majority 12,618 (23.73%)
Notional 2.12% swing LD to C.
(2005: C. majority 9,314 (19.49%))

§BANBURY
E. 86,986 T. 56,241 (64.66%) C. hold
Tony Baldry, C. — 29,703
David Rundle, LD — 11,476
Les Sibley, Lab. — 10,773
Dr David Fairweather, UKIP — 2,806
Alastair White, Green — 959
Roseanne Edwards, Ind. — 524
C. majority 18,227 (32.41%)
Notional 1.51% swing LD to C.
(2005: C. majority 10,090 (18.79%))

§BARKING
E. 73,864 T. 45,343 (61.39%) Lab. hold
Margaret Hodge, Lab. — 24,628
Simon Marcus, C. — 8,073
Nick Griffin, BNP — 6,620
Dominic Carman, LD — 3,719
Frank Maloney, UKIP — 1,300
George Hargreaves, Ch. P. — 482
Jayne Forbes, Green — 317
Crucial Chris Dowling, Loony — 82
Thomas Darwood, Ind. — 77
Dapo Sijuwola, RP — 45
Lab. majority 16,555 (36.51%)
Notional 1.73% swing C. to Lab.
(2005: Lab. majority 12,183 (33.04%))

§BARNSLEY CENTRAL
E. 65,543 T. 37,001 (56.45%) Lab. hold
Eric Illsley, Lab. — 17,487
Christopher Wiggin, LD — 6,394
Piers Tempest, C. — 6,388
Ian Sutton, BNP — 3,307
David Silver, UKIP — 1,727
Donald Wood, Ind. — 732
Tony Devoy, Ind. — 610
Terry Robinson, Soc. Lab. — 356
Lab. majority 11,093 (29.98%)
Notional 4.17% swing Lab. to LD
(2005: Lab. majority 11,839 (38.32%))

§BARNSLEY EAST
E. 68,435 T. 38,386 (56.09%) Lab. hold
*Michael Dugher, Lab.   18,059
John Brown, LD   6,969
James Hockney, C.   6,329
Colin Porter, BNP   3,301
Tony Watson, UKIP   1,731
Kevin Hogan, Ind.   712
Eddie Devoy, Ind.   684
Ken Capstick, Soc. Lab.   601
Lab. majority 11,090 (28.89%)
Notional 14.02% swing Lab. to LD
(2005: Lab. majority 18,298 (56.94%))

§BARROW & FURNESS
E. 68,758 T. 44,124 (64.17%)
                       Lab. Co-op hold
*John Woodcock, Lab. Co-op   21,226
John Gough, C.   16,018
Barry Rabone, LD   4,424
John Smith, UKIP   841
Mike Ashburner, BNP   840
Christopher Loynes, Green   530
Brian Greaves, Ind.   245
Lab. Co-op majority 5,208 (11.80%)
Notional 0.37% swing Lab. to C.
(2005: Lab. majority 4,843 (12.54%))

§BASILDON & BILLERICAY
E. 65,482 T. 41,569 (63.48%) C. hold
John Baron, C.   21,922
Allan Davies, Lab.   9,584
Mike Hibbs, LD   6,538
Irene Bateman, BNP   1,934
Alan Broad, UKIP   1,591
C. majority 12,338 (29.68%)
Notional 9.23% swing Lab. to C.
(2005: C. majority 4,559 (11.22%))

§BASILDON SOUTH & THURROCK
EAST
E. 71,815 T. 44,735 (62.29%) C. gain
*Stephen Metcalfe, C.   19,624
Angela Smith, Lab. Co-op   13,852
Geoff Williams, LD   5,977
Kerry Smith, UKIP   2,639
Chris Roberts, BNP   2,518
None Of The Above X, ND   125
C. majority 5,772 (12.90%)
Notional 7.52% swing Lab. to C.
(2005: C. majority 905 (2.14%))

§BASINGSTOKE
E. 75,470 T. 50,654 (67.12%) C. hold
Maria Miller, C.   25,590
John Shaw, LD   12,414
Funda Pepperell, Lab.   10,327
Stella Howell, UKIP   2,076
Steve Saul, BCP   247
C. majority 13,176 (26.01%)
Notional 4.55% swing LD to C.
(2005: C. majority 2,651 (6.27%))

§BASSETLAW
E. 76,542 T. 49,577 (64.77%) Lab. hold
John Mann, Lab.   25,018
Keith Girling, C.   16,803
David Dobbie, LD   5,570
Andrea Hamilton, UKIP   1,779
Grahame Whithurst, Ind.   407
Lab. majority 8,215 (16.57%)
Notional 0.67% swing Lab. to C.
(2005: Lab. majority 8,256 (17.92%))

§BATH
E. 65,603 T. 47,086 (71.77%) LD hold
Don Foster, LD   26,651
Fabian Richter, C.   14,768
Hattie Ajderian, Lab.   3,251
Eric Lucas, Green   1,120
Ernie Warrender, UKIP   890
Steve Hewett, Ch. P.   250
ANON, ND   69
Sean Geddis, Ind.   56
Robert Craig, South   31
LD majority 11,883 (25.24%)
Notional 5.84% swing C. to LD
(2005: LD majority 5,624 (13.56%))

§BATLEY & SPEN
E. 76,732 T. 51,109 (66.61%) Lab. hold
Mike Wood, Lab.   21,565
Janice Small, C.   17,159
Neil Bentley, LD   8,095
David Exley, BNP   3,685
Matt Blakeley, Green   605
Lab. majority 4,406 (8.62%)
Notional 2.46% swing Lab. to C.
(2005: Lab. majority 6,060 (13.54%))

§BATTERSEA
E. 74,300 T. 48,792 (65.67%) C. gain
*Jane Ellison, C.   23,103
Martin Linton, Lab.   17,126
Layla Moran, LD   7,176
Guy Evans, Green   559
Christopher MacDonald, UKIP   505
Hugh Salmon, Battersea   168
Tom Fox, Ind.   155
C. majority 5,977 (12.25%)
Notional 6.53% swing Lab. to C.
(2005: Lab. majority 332 (0.81%))

§BEACONSFIELD
E. 74,982 T. 52,490 (70.00%) C. hold
Dominic Grieve, C.   32,053
John Edwards, LD   10,271
Jeremy Miles, Lab.   6,135
Delphine Gray-Fisk, UKIP   2,597
Jem Bailey, Green   768
Andrew Cowen, MP Expense   475
Quentin Baron, Ind.   191
C. majority 21,782 (41.50%)
Notional 4.70% swing LD to C.
(2005: C. majority 14,794 (32.09%))

§BECKENHAM
E. 66,219 T. 47,686 (72.01%) C. hold
*Bob Stewart, C.   27,597
Steve Jenkins, LD   9,813
Damien Egan, Lab.   6,893
Owen Brolly, UKIP   1,551
Roger Tonks, BNP   1,001
Ann Garrett, Green   608
Dan Eastgate, Eng. Dem.   223
C. majority 17,784 (37.29%)
Notional 3.15% swing C. to LD
(2005: C. majority 16,913 (40.40%))

§BEDFORD
E. 68,491 T. 45,102 (65.85%) C. gain
*Richard Fuller, C.   17,546
Patrick Hall, Lab.   16,193
Henry Vann, LD   8,957
Mark Adkin, UKIP   1,136
William Dewick, BNP   757
Ben Foley, Green   393
Samrat Bhandari, Ind.   120
C. majority 1,353 (3.00%)
Notional 5.52% swing Lab. to C.
(2005: Lab. majority 3,413 (8.04%))

§BEDFORDSHIRE MID
E. 76,023 T. 54,897 (72.21%) C. hold
Nadine Dorries, C.   28,815
Linda Jack, LD   13,663
David Reeves, Lab.   8,108
Bill Hall, UKIP   2,826
Malcolm Bailey, Green   773
John Cooper, Eng. Dem.   712
C. majority 15,152 (27.60%)
Notional 2.26% swing LD to C.
(2005: C. majority 11,593 (23.08%))

§BEDFORDSHIRE NORTH EAST
E. 78,060 T. 55,552 (71.17%) C. hold
Alistair Burt, C.   30,989
Mike Pitt, LD   12,047
Edward Brown,Lab.   8,957
Brian Capell, UKIP   2,294
Ian Seeby, BNP   1,265
C. majority 18,942 (34.10%)
Notional 2.55% swing LD to C.
(2005: C. majority 12,128 (24.59%))

BEDFORDSHIRE SOUTH WEST
E. 76,559 T. 50,774 (66.32%) C. hold
Andrew Selous, C.   26,815
Rod Cantrill, LD   10,166
Jennifer Bone, Lab.   9,948
Martin Newman, UKIP   2,142
Mark Tolman, BNP   1,703
C. majority 16,649 (32.79%)
0.69% swing LD to C.
(2005: C. majority 8,277 (18.07%))

§BERMONDSEY & OLD SOUTHWARK
E. 77,623 T. 44,651 (57.52%) LD hold
Simon Hughes, LD   21,590
Val Shawcross, Lab.   13,060
Loanna Morrison, C.   7,638
Stephen Tyler, BNP   1,370
Tom Chance, Green   718
Alan Kirkby, Ind.   155
Steve Freeman, ND   120
LD majority 8,530 (19.10%)
Notional 1.55% swing Lab. to LD
(2005: LD majority 5,769 (16.00%))

§BERWICK-UPON-TWEED
E. 57,403 T. 38,439 (66.96%) LD hold
Sir Alan Beith, LD   16,806
Anne-Marie Trevelyan, C.   14,116
Alan Strickland, Lab.   5,061
Michael Weatheritt, UKIP   1,243
Peter Mailer, BNP   1,213
LD majority 2,690 (7.00%)
Notional 8.29% swing LD to C.
(2005: LD majority 8,585 (23.58%))

§BETHNAL GREEN & BOW
E. 81,243 T. 50,728 (62.44%) Lab. gain
*Rushanara Ali, Lab.   21,784
Ajmal Masroor, LD   10,210
Abjol Miah, Respect   8,532
Zakir Khan, C.   7,071
Jeffrey Marshall, BNP   1,405
Farid Bakht, Green   856
Patrick Brooks, Ind.   277
Alexander Van Terheyden, Pirate   213
Hasib Hikmat, Voice   209
Haji Choudhury, Ind.   100
Ahmed Malik, Ind.   71
Lab. majority 11,574 (22.82%)
Notional 14.11% swing Respect to Lab.
(2005: Respect majority 804 (2.10%))

§BEVERLEY & HOLDERNESS
E. 79,611 T. 53,199 (66.82%) C. hold
Graham Stuart, C.   25,063
Craig Dobson, LD   12,076
Ian Saunders, Lab.   11,224
Neil Whitelam, BNP   2,080
Andrew Horsfield, UKIP   1,845
Bill Rigby, Green   686
Ron Hughes, Ind.   225
C. majority 12,987 (24.41%)
Notional 1.58% swing LD to C.
(2005: C. majority 3,097 (6.23%))

§BEXHILL & BATTLE
E. 79,208 T. 54,587 (68.92%) C. hold
Greg Barker, C.   28,147
Mary Varrall, LD   15,267
James Royston, Lab.   6,524
Stuart Wheeler, Trust   2,699
Neil Jackson, BNP   1,950
C. majority 12,880 (23.60%)
Notional 3.96% swing C. to LD
(2005: C. majority 15,893 (31.52%))

§BEXLEYHEATH & CRAYFORD
E. 64,985 T. 43,182 (66.45%) C. hold
David Evennett, C.   21,794
Howard Dawber, Lab.   11,450
Karelia Scott, LD   5,502
Stephen James, BNP   2,042
John Dunford, UKIP   1,557
John Griffiths, Eng. Dem.   466
Adrian Ross, Green   371
C. majority 10,344 (23.95%)
Notional 5.81% swing Lab. to C.
(2005: C. majority 5,167 (12.33%))

§BIRKENHEAD
E. 62,773 T. 35,323 (56.27%) Lab. hold
Frank Field, Lab.   22,082
Andrew Gilbert, C.   6,687
Stuart Kelly, LD   6,554
Lab. majority 15,395 (43.58%)
Notional 2.34% swing Lab. to C.
(2005: Lab. majority 14,638 (46.21%))

§BIRMINGHAM EDGBASTON
E. 68,573 T. 41,571 (60.62%) Lab. hold
Gisela Stuart, Lab.   16,894
Deirdre Alden, C.   15,620
Roger Harmer, LD   6,387
Trevor Lloyd, BNP   1,196
Greville Warwick, UKIP   732
Phil Simpson, Green   469
Harry Takhar, Impact   146
Charith Fernando, Ch. P.   127
Lab. majority 1,274 (3.06%)
Notional 0.47% swing Lab. to C.
(2005: Lab. majority 1,555 (4.01%))

§BIRMINGHAM ERDINGTON
E. 66,405 T. 35,546 (53.53%) Lab. hold
*Jack Dromey, Lab.   14,869
Robert Alden, C.   11,592
Ann Holtom, LD   5,742
Kevin McHugh, BNP   1,815
Maria Foy, UKIP   842
Tony Tomkins, Ind.   240
Terry Williams, NF   229
Timothy Gray, Ch. P.   217
Lab. majority 3,277 (9.22%)
Notional 10.43% swing Lab. to C.
(2005: Lab. majority 9,677 (30.07%))

§BIRMINGHAM HALL GREEN
E. 76,580 T. 48,727 (63.63%) Lab. hold
Roger Godsiff, Lab.   16,039
Salma Yaqoob, Respect   12,240
Jerry Evans, LD   11,988
Jo Barker, C.   7,320
Alan Blumenthal, UKIP   950
Andrew Gardner, Ind.   190
Lab. majority 3,799 (7.80%)
Notional 11.07% swing Lab. to Respect
(2005: Lab. majority 6,649 (15.90%))

§BIRMINGHAM HODGE HILL
E. 75,040 T. 42,472 (56.60%) Lab. hold
Liam Byrne, Lab.   22,077
Tariq Khan, LD   11,775
Shailesh Parekh, C.   4,936
Richard Lumby, BNP   2,333
Waheed Rafiq, UKIP   714
Peter Johnson, Soc. Dem.   637
Lab. majority 10,302 (24.26%)
Notional 3.61% swing LD to Lab.
(2005: Lab. majority 7,063 (17.05%))

§BIRMINGHAM LADYWOOD
E. 73,646 T. 35,833 (48.66%) Lab. hold
*Shabana Mahmood, Lab.   19,950
Ayoub Khan, LD   9,845
Nusrat Ghani, C.   4,277
Christopher Booth, UKIP   902
Peter Beck, Green   859
Lab. majority 10,105 (28.20%)
Notional 2.49% swing LD to Lab.
(2005: Lab. majority 6,804 (23.23%))

§BIRMINGHAM NORTHFIELD
E. 71,338 T. 41,814 (58.61%) Lab. hold
Richard Burden, Lab.   16,841
Keely Huxtable, C.   14,059
Mike Dixon, LD   6,550
Les Orton, BNP   2,290
John Borthwick, UKIP   1,363
Susan Pearce, Green   406
Dick Rodgers, Good   305
Lab. majority 2,782 (6.65%)
Notional 6.64% swing Lab. to C.
(2005: Lab. majority 7,879 (19.93%))

§BIRMINGHAM PERRY BARR
E. 71,304 T. 42,045 (58.97%) Lab. hold
Khalid Mahmood, Lab.   21,142
Karen Hamilton, LD   9,234
William Norton, C.   8,960
Melvin Ward, UKIP   1,675
John Tyrrell, Soc. Lab.   527
Deborah Hey-Smith, Ch. P.   507
Lab. majority 11,908 (28.32%)
Notional 4.05% swing LD to Lab.
(2005: Lab. majority 7,825 (20.22%))

§BIRMINGHAM SELLY OAK
E. 74,805 T. 46,563 (62.25%) Lab. hold
Steve McCabe, Lab.   17,950
Nigel Dawkins, C.   14,468
David Radcliffe, LD   10,371
Lynette Orton, BNP   1,820
Jeffery Burgess, UKIP   1,131
James Burn, Green   664
Samuel Leeds, Ch. P.   159
Lab. majority 3,482 (7.48%)
Notional 4.83% swing Lab. to C.
(2005: Lab. majority 7,564 (17.14%))

§BIRMINGHAM YARDLEY
E. 72,321 T. 40,850 (56.48%) LD hold
John Hemming, LD   16,162
Lynnette Kelly, Lab.   13,160
Meirion Jenkins, C.   7,836
Tanya Lumby, BNP   2,153
Graham Duffen, UKIP   1,190
Paul Morris, NF   349
LD majority 3,002 (7.35%)
Notional 0.02% swing Lab. to LD
(2005: LD majority 2,864 (7.30%))

§BISHOP AUCKLAND
E. 68,370 T. 41,136 (60.17%) Lab. hold
Helen Goodman, Lab.   16,023
Barbara Harrison, C.   10,805
Mark Wilkes, LD   9,189
Adam Walker, BNP   2,036
Sam Zair, LLPBPP   1,964
Dave Brothers, UKIP   1,119
Lab. majority 5,218 (12.68%)
Notional 7.20% swing Lab. to C.
(2005: Lab. majority 10,047 (26.35%))

§BLACKBURN
E. 72,331 T. 45,499 (62.90%) Lab. hold
Jack Straw, Lab.   21,751
Michael Law-Riding, C.   11,895
Paul English, LD   6,918
Robin Evans, BNP   2,158
Bushra Irfanullah, BIB   1,424
Bobby Anwar, UKIP   942
Grace Astley, Ind.   238
Janis Sharp, Ind.   173
Lab. majority 9,856 (21.66%)
Notional 1.11% swing C. to Lab.
(2005: Lab. majority 8,044 (19.45%))

§BLACKLEY & BROUGHTON
E. 69,489 T. 34,204 (49.22%) Lab. hold
Graham Stringer, Lab.   18,563
James Edsberg, C.   6,260
William Hobhouse, LD   4,861
Derek Adams, BNP   2,469
Kay Phillips, Respect   996
Bob Willescroft, Ind.   894
Shafiq-Uz Zaman, Ch. P.   161
Lab. majority 12,303 (35.97%)
Notional 6.74% swing Lab. to C.
(2005: Lab. majority 13,060 (43.35%))

§BLACKPOOL NORTH & CLEVELEYS
E. 65,888 T. 40,591 (61.61%) C. gain
*Paul Maynard, C.   16,964
Penny Martin, Lab.   14,814
Bill Greene, LD   5,400
Roy Hopwood, UKIP   1,659
James Clayton, BNP   1,556
Tony Davies, Loony   198
C. majority 2,150 (5.30%)
Notional 6.89% swing Lab. to C.
(2005: Lab. majority 3,241 (8.48%))

§BLACKPOOL SOUTH
E. 63,025 T. 35,191 (55.84%) Lab. hold
Gordon Marsden, Lab.   14,448
Ron Bell, C.   12,597
Doreen Holt, LD   5,082
Roy Goodwin, BNP   1,482
Hamish Howitt, UKIP   1,352
Si Thu Tun, Integrity   230
Lab. majority 1,851 (5.26%)
Notional 6.21% swing Lab. to C.
(2005: Lab. majority 5,911 (17.67%))

§BLAYDON
E. 67,808 T. 44,913 (66.24%) Lab. hold
Dave Anderson, Lab.   22,297
Neil Bradbury, LD   13,180
Glenn Hall, C.   7,159
Keith McFarlane, BNP   2,277
Lab. majority 9,117 (20.30%)
Notional 3.28% swing LD to Lab.
(2005: Lab. majority 5,748 (13.75%))

BLYTH VALLEY
E. 64,263 T. 38,566 (60.01%) Lab. hold
Ronnie Campbell, Lab.   17,156
Jeffrey Reid, LD   10,488
Barry Flux, C.   6,412
Steve Fairbairn, BNP   1,699
James Condon, UKIP   1,665
Barry Elliott, Ind.   819
Allan White, Eng. Dem.   327
Lab. majority 6,668 (17.29%)
3.27% swing Lab. to LD
(2005: Lab. majority 8,527 (23.84%))

§BOGNOR REGIS &
LITTLEHAMPTON
E. 70,812 T. 46,852 (66.16%) C. hold
Nick Gibb, C.   24,087
Simon McDougall, LD   11,024
Michael Jones, Lab.   6,580
Douglas Denny, UKIP   3,036
Andrew Moffat, BNP   1,890
Melissa Briggs, Ind.   235
C. majority 13,063 (27.88%)
Notional 2.31% swing LD to C.
(2005: C. majority 8,617 (20.15%))

§BOLSOVER
E. 72,766 T. 43,988 (60.45%) Lab. hold
Dennis Skinner, Lab.   21,994
Lee Rowley, C.   10,812
Denise Hawksworth, LD   6,821
Martin Radford, BNP   2,640
Ray Calladine, UKIP   1,721
Lab. majority 11,182 (25.42%)
Notional 11.23% swing Lab. to C.
(2005: Lab. majority 19,260 (47.68%))

§BOLTON NORTH EAST
E. 67,281 T. 43,277 (64.32%) Lab. hold
David Crausby, Lab.   19,870
Deborah Dunleavy, C.   15,786
Paul Ankers, LD   5,624
Neil Johnson, UKIP   1,815
Norma Armston, You   182
Lab. majority 4,084 (9.44%)
Notional 1.27% swing Lab. to C.
(2005: Lab. majority 4,527 (11.99%))

§BOLTON SOUTH EAST
E. 69,928 T. 39,604 (56.64%) Lab. hold
*Yasmin Qureshi, Lab.   18,782
Andy Morgan, C.   10,148
Donal O'Hanlon, LD   6,289
Sheila Spink, BNP   2,012
Ian Sidaway, UKIP   1,564
Alan Johnson, Green   614
Navaid Syed, CPA   195
Lab. majority 8,634 (21.80%)
Notional 5.61% swing Lab. to C.
(2005: Lab. majority 11,483 (33.03%))

§BOLTON WEST
E. 71,250 T. 47,576 (66.77%) Lab. hold
*Julie Hilling, Lab.   18,327
Susan Williams, C.   18,235
Jackie Pearcey, LD   8,177
Harry Lamb, UKIP   1,901
Rachel Mann, Green   545
Jimmy Jones, Ind.   254
Doug Bagnall, You   137
Lab. majority 92 (0.19%)
Notional 5.88% swing Lab. to C.
(2005: Lab. majority 5,041 (11.95%))

§BOOTLE
E. 71,426 T. 41,277 (57.79%) Lab. hold
Joe Benton, Lab.   27,426
James Murray, LD   6,245
Sohail Qureshi, C.   3,678
Paul Nuttall, UKIP   2,514
Charles Stewart, BNP   942
Pete Glover, TUSC   472
Lab. majority 21,181 (51.31%)
Notional 1.59% swing Lab. to LD
(2005: Lab. majority 20,125 (54.48%))

§BOSTON & SKEGNESS
E. 70,529 T. 43,125 (61.15%) C. hold
Mark Simmonds, C.   21,325
Paul Kenny, Lab.   8,899
Philip Smith, LD   6,371
Christopher Pain, UKIP   4,081
David Owens, BNP   2,278
Peter Wilson, Ind.   171
C. majority 12,426 (28.81%)
Notional 7.00% swing Lab. to C.
(2005: C. majority 6,391 (14.81%))

§BOSWORTH
E. 77,296 T. 54,274 (70.22%) C. hold
David Tredinnick, C.   23,132
Michael Mullaney, LD   18,100
Rory Palmer, Lab.   8,674
John Ryde, BNP   2,458
Dutch Veldhuizen, UKIP   1,098
James Lampitt, Eng. Dem.   615
Michael Brooks, Science   197
C. majority 5,032 (9.27%)
Notional 5.87% swing C. to LD
(2005: C. majority 5,335 (10.72%))

§BOURNEMOUTH EAST
E. 71,125 T. 44,024 (61.90%) C. hold
Tobias Ellwood, C.   21,320
Lisa Northover, LD   13,592
David Stokes, Lab.   5,836
David Hughes, UKIP   3,027
Steven Humphrey, Ind.   249
C. majority 7,728 (17.55%)
Notional 1.76% swing LD to C.
(2005: C. majority 5,874 (14.04%))

§BOURNEMOUTH WEST
E. 71,753 T. 41,659 (58.06%) C. hold
*Conor Burns, C.   18,808
Alasdair Murray, LD   13,225
Sharon Carr-Brown, Lab.   6,171
Philip Glover, UKIP   2,999
Harvey Taylor, Ind.   456
C. majority 5,583 (13.40%)
Notional 2.92% swing LD to C.
(2005: C. majority 2,766 (7.55%))

§BRACKNELL
E. 76,885 T. 52,140 (67.82%) C. hold
*Phillip Lee, C.   27,327
Ray Earwicker, LD   11,623
John Piasecki, Lab.   8,755
Murray Barter, UKIP   2,297
Mark Burke, BNP   1,253
David Young, Green   825
Dan Haycocks, SMA   60
C. majority 15,704 (30.12%)
Notional 0.97% swing C. to LD
(2005: C. majority 10,037 (21.96%))

§BRADFORD EAST
E. 65,116 T. 40,457 (62.13%) LD gain
*David Ward, LD   13,637
Terry Rooney, Lab.   13,272
Mohammed Riaz, C.   10,860
Neville Poynton, BNP   1,854
Raja Hussain, Ind.   375
Peter Shields, Ind.   237
Gerry Robinson, NF   222
LD majority 365 (0.90%)
Notional 7.57% swing Lab. to LD
(2005: Lab. majority 5,227 (14.24%))

§BRADFORD SOUTH
E. 63,580 T. 37,995 (59.76%) Lab. hold
Gerry Sutcliffe, Lab.   15,682
Matt Palmer, C.   11,060
Alun Griffiths, LD   6,948
Sharon Sutton, BNP   2,651
Jamie Illingworth, UKIP   1,339
James Lewthwaite, D Nat   315
Lab. majority 4,622 (12.16%)
Notional 5.91% swing Lab. to C.
(2005: Lab. majority 8,444 (23.99%))

§BRADFORD WEST
E. 62,519 T. 40,576 (64.90%) Lab. hold
Marsha Singh, Lab.   18,401
Zahid Iqbal, C.   12,638
David Hall-Matthews, LD   4,732
Jenny Sampson, BNP   1,370
Arshad Ali, Respect   1,245
David Ford, Green   940
Jason Smith, UKIP   812
Neil Craig, D. Nat.   438
Lab. majority 5,763 (14.20%)
Notional 2.93% swing C. to Lab.
(2005: Lab. majority 3,050 (8.34%))

§BRAINTREE
E. 71,162 T. 49,203 (69.14%) C. hold
Brooks Newmark, C.   25,901
Bill Edwards, Lab.   9,780
Steve Jarvis, LD   9,247
Michael Ford, UKIP   2,477
Paul Hooks, BNP   1,080
Daisy Blench, Green   718
C. majority 16,121 (32.76%)
Notional 6.74% swing Lab. to C.
(2005: C. majority 8,658 (19.28%))

§BRENT CENTRAL
E. 74,076 T. 45,324 (61.19%) LD gain
Sarah Teather, LD   20,026
Dawn Butler, Lab.   18,681
Sachin Rajput, C.   5,068
Shahar Ali, Green   668
Errol Williams, Ch. P.   488
Abdi Duale, Respect   230
Dean McCastree, Ind.   163
LD majority 1,345 (2.97%)
Notional 10.99% swing Lab. to LD
(2005: Lab. majority 7,469 (19.02%))

§BRENT NORTH
E. 83,896 T. 52,298 (62.34%) Lab. hold
Barry Gardiner, Lab.   24,514
Harshadbhai Patel, C.   16,486
James Allie, LD   8,879
Atiq Malik, Ind.   734
Martin Francis, Green   725
Sunita Webb, UKIP   380
Jannen Vamadeva, Ind.   333
Arvind Tailor, Eng. Dem.   247
Lab. majority 8,028 (15.35%)
Notional 2.35% swing Lab. to C.
(2005: Lab. majority 8,830 (20.04%))

§BRENTFORD & ISLEWORTH
E. 83,546 T. 53,765 (64.35%) C. gain
*Mary Macleod, C.   20,022
Ann Keen, Lab.   18,064
Andrew Dakers, LD   12,718
Jason Hargreaves, UKIP   863
John Hunt, Green   787
Paul Winnet, BNP   704
David Cunningham, Eng. Dem.   230
Aamir Bhatti, Ch. P.   210
Evangeline Pillai, CPA   99
Teresa Vanneck-Surplice, Ind.   68
C. majority 1,958 (3.64%)
Notional 5.96% swing Lab. to C.
(2005: Lab. majority 3,633 (8.29%))

§BRENTWOOD & ONGAR
E. 73,224 T. 50,592 (69.09%) C. hold
Eric Pickles, C.   28,793
David Kendall, LD   11,872
Heidi Benzing, Lab.   4,992
Michael McGough, UKIP   2,037
Paul Morris, BNP   1,447
Jess Barnecutt, Green   584
Robin Tilbrook, Eng. Dem.   491
James Sapwell, Ind.   263
Danny Attfield, ND   113
C. majority 16,921 (33.45%)
Notional 3.12% swing LD to C.
(2005: C. majority 12,522 (27.21%))

§BRIDGWATER & SOMERSET WEST
E. 76,560 T. 54,493 (71.18%) C. hold
Ian Liddell-Grainger, C.   24,675
Theo Butt Philip, LD   15,426
Kathryn Pearce, Lab.   9,332
Peter Hollings, UKIP   2,604
Donna Treanor, BNP   1,282
Charles Graham, Green   859
Bob Cudlipp, Ind.   315
C. majority 9,249 (16.97%)
Notional 2.88% swing C. to LD
(2005: C. majority 10,081 (19.77%))

§BRIGG & GOOLE
E. 67,345 T. 43,874 (65.15%) C. gain
*Andrew Percy, C.   19,680
Ian Cawsey, Lab.   14,533
Richard Nixon, LD   6,414
Nigel Wright, UKIP   1,749
Stephen Ward, BNP   1,498
C. majority 5,147 (11.73%)
Notional 9.79% swing Lab. to C.
(2005: Lab. majority 3,217 (7.84%))

§BRIGHTON KEMPTOWN
E. 66,017 T. 42,705 (64.69%) C. gain
*Simon Kirby, C.   16,217
Simon Burgess, Lab. Co-op   14,889
Juliet Williams, LD   7,691
Ben Duncan, Green   2,330
James Chamberlain-Webber, UKIP 1,384
Dave Hill, TUSC   194
C. majority 1,328 (3.11%)
Notional 3.97% swing Lab. to C.
(2005: Lab. majority 1,853 (4.83%))

§BRIGHTON PAVILION
E. 74,004 T. 51,834 (70.04%) Green gain
*Dr Caroline Lucas, Green   16,238
Nancy Platts, Lab.   14,986
Charlotte Vere, C.   12,275
Bernadette Millam, LD   7,159
Nigel Carter, UKIP   948
Ian Fyvie, Soc. Lab.   148
Soraya Kara, R and E   61
Leo Atreides, ND   19
Green majority 1,252 (2.42%)
Notional 8.45% swing Lab. to Green
(2005: Lab. majority 5,867 (13.11%))

§BRISTOL EAST
E. 69,448 T. 45,017 (64.82%) Lab. hold
Kerry McCarthy, Lab.   16,471
Adeela Shafi, C.   12,749
Mike Popham, LD   10,993
Brian Jenkins, BNP   1,960
Philip Collins, UKIP   1,510
Glenn Vowles, Green   803
Stephen Wright, Eng. Dem.   347
Rae Lynch, TUSC   184
Lab. majority 3,722 (8.27%)
Notional 4.54% swing Lab. to C.
(2005: Lab. majority 7,335 (17.35%))

§BRISTOL NORTH WEST
E. 73,469 T. 50,336 (68.51%) C. gain
*Charlotte Leslie, C.   19,115
Paul Harrod, LD   15,841
Sam Townend, Lab.   13,059
Robert Upton, UKIP   1,175
Ray Carr, Eng. Dem.   635
Alex Dunn, Green   511
C. majority 3,274 (6.50%)
Notional 8.86% swing Lab. to C.
(2005: Lab. majority 2,781 (5.69%))

§BRISTOL SOUTH
E. 78,579 T. 48,377 (61.56%) Lab. hold
Dawn Primarolo, Lab.   18,600
Mark Wright, LD   13,866
Mark Lloyd Davies, C.   11,086
Colin Chidsey, BNP   1,739
Colin McNamee, UKIP   1,264
Charlie Bolton, Green   1,216
Craig Clarke, Eng. Dem.   400
Tom Baldwin, TUSC   206
Lab. majority 4,734 (9.79%)
Notional 7.53% swing Lab. to LD
(2005: Lab. majority 10,928 (24.86%))

§BRISTOL WEST
E. 82,728 T. 55,347 (66.90%) LD hold
Stephen Williams, LD   26,593
Paul Smith, Lab.   15,227
Nick Yarker, C.   10,169
Ricky Knight, Green   2,090
Chris Lees, UKIP   655
Danny Kushlick, Ind.   343
Jon Baker, Eng. Dem.   270
LD majority 11,366 (20.54%)
Notional 9.00% swing Lab. to LD
(2005: LD majority 1,147 (2.55%))

§BROADLAND
E. 73,168 T. 52,676 (71.99%) C. hold
Keith Simpson, C.   24,338
Daniel Roper, LD   17,046
Allyson Barron, Lab.   7,287
Stuart Agnew, UKIP   2,382
Edith Crowther, BNP   871
Susan Curran, Green   752
C. majority 7,292 (13.84%)
Notional 0.06% swing C. to LD
(2005: C. majority 6,573 (13.97%))

§BROMLEY & CHISLEHURST
E. 65,427 T. 44,037 (67.31%) C. hold
Bob Neill, C.   23,569
Sam Webber, LD   9,669
Chris Kirby, Lab.   7,295
Emmett Jenner, UKIP   1,451
Rowena Savage, BNP   1,070
Roisin Robertson, Green   607
Jon Cheeseman, Eng. Dem.   376
C. majority 13,900 (31.56%)
Notional 5.13% swing LD to C.
(2005: C. majority 8,236 (20.57%))

BROMSGROVE
E. 73,086 T. 51,630 (70.64%) C. hold
*Sajid Javid, C.   22,558
Sam Burden, Lab.   11,250
Philip Ling, LD   10,124
Steven Morson, UKIP   2,950
Adrian Kriss, BIC   2,182
Elizabeth Wainwright, BNP   1,923
Mark France, Ind.   336
Ken Wheatley, Ind.   307
C. majority 11,308 (21.90%)
0.41% swing Lab. to C.
(2005: C. majority 10,080 (21.08%))

BROXBOURNE
E. 71,391 T. 45,658 (63.95%) C. hold
Charles Walker, C.   26,844
Michael Watson, Lab.   8,040
Allan Witherick, LD   6,107
Steve McCole, BNP   2,159
Martin Harvey, UKIP   1,890
Debbie LeMay, Eng. Dem.   618
C. majority 18,804 (41.18%)
6.43% swing Lab. to C.
(2005: C. majority 11,509 (28.33%))

§BROXTOWE
E. 72,042 T. 52,727 (73.19%) C. gain
*Anna Soubry, C.   20,585
Nick Palmer, Lab.   20,196
David Watts, LD   8,907
Mike Shore, BNP   1,422
Chris Cobb, UKIP   1,194
David Mitchell, Green   423
C. majority 389 (0.74%)
Notional 2.59% swing Lab. to C.
(2005: Lab. majority 2,139 (4.44%))

§BUCKINGHAM
E. 74,996 T. 48,335 (64.45%)
                               Speaker hold
‡John Bercow, Speaker   22,860
John Stevens, Ind.   10,331
Nigel Farage, UKIP   8,401
Patrick Phillips, Ind.   2,394
Debbie Martin, Ind.   1,270
Lynne Mozar, BNP   980
Colin Dale, Loony   856
Geoff Howard, Ind.   435
David Hews, Ch. P.   369
Anthony Watts, Ind.   332
Simon Strutt, Deficit   107
Speaker majority 12,529 (25.92%)
(2005: C. majority 18,716 (37.83%))

BURNLEY
E. 66,616 T. 41,845 (62.82%) LD gain
*Gordon Birtwistle, LD   14,932
Julie Cooper, Lab.   13,114
Richard Ali, C.   6,950
Sharon Wilkinson, BNP   3,747
Andrew Brown, Ind.   1,876
John Wignall, UKIP   929
Andrew Hennessey, Ind.   297
LD majority 1,818 (4.34%)
9.58% swing Lab. to LD
(2005: Lab. majority 5,778 (14.82%))

§BURTON
E. 74,874 T. 49,823 (66.54%) C. gain
*Andrew Griffiths, C.   22,188
Ruth Smeeth, Lab.   15,884
Michael Rodgers, LD   7,891
Alan Hewitt, BNP   2,409
Philip Lancaster, UKIP   1,451
C. majority 6,304 (12.65%)
Notional 8.73% swing Lab. to C.
(2005: Lab. majority 2,132 (4.81%))

§BURY NORTH
E. 66,759 T. 44,961 (67.35%) C. gain
*David Nuttall, C.   18,070
Maryam Khan, Lab.   15,827
Richard Baum, LD   7,645
John Maude, BNP   1,825
Stephen Evans, UKIP   1,282
Bill Brison, Ind.   181
Graeme Lambert, Pirate   131
C. majority 2,243 (4.99%)
Notional 5.02% swing Lab. to C.
(2005: Lab. majority 2,059 (5.05%))

§BURY SOUTH
E. 73,544 T. 48,267 (65.63%) Lab. hold
Ivan Lewis, Lab.   19,508
Michelle Wiseman, C.   16,216
Vic D'Albert, LD   8,796
Jean Purdy, BNP   1,743
Paul Chadwick, UKIP   1,017
Valerie Morris, Eng. Dem.   494
George Heron, Green   493
Lab. majority 3,292 (6.82%)
Notional 8.01% swing Lab. to C.
(2005: Lab. majority 9,779 (22.84%))

§BURY ST EDMUNDS
E. 84,727 T. 58,718 (69.30%) C. hold
David Ruffley, C.   27,899
David Chappell, LD   15,519
Kevin Hind, Lab.   9,776
John Howlett, UKIP   3,003
Mark Ereira-Guyer, Green   2,521
C. majority 12,380 (21.08%)
Notional 2.76% swing C. to LD
(2005: C. majority 10,080 (19.03%))

§CALDER VALLEY
E. 76,903 T. 51,780 (67.33%) C. gain
*Craig Whittaker, C.   20,397
Steph Booth, Lab.   13,966
Hilary Myers, LD   13,037
John Gregory, BNP   1,823
Greg Burrows, UKIP   1,173
Kate Sweeny, Green   858
Tim Cole, Ind.   194
Barry Greenwood, Ind.   175
Paul Rogan, Eng. Dem.   157
C. majority 6,431 (12.42%)
Notional 7.58% swing Lab. to C.
(2005: Lab. majority 1,303 (2.73%))

§CAMBERWELL & PECKHAM
E. 78,618 T. 46,659 (59.35%) Lab. hold
Harriet Harman, Lab.   27,619
Columba Blango, LD   10,432
Andy Stranack, C.   6,080
Jenny Jones, Green   1,361
Yohara Robby Munilla, Eng. Dem.   435
Joshua Ogunleye, WRP   211
Margaret Sharkey, Soc. Lab.   184
Decima Francis, Ind.   93
Steven Robbins, Ind.   87
Patricia Knox, ND   82
Jill Mountford, Workers Lib   75
Lab. majority 17,187 (36.84%)
Notional 3.00% swing Lab. to LD
(2005: Lab. majority 16,608 (42.83%))

§CAMBORNE & REDRUTH
E. 63,968 T. 42,493 (66.43%) C. gain
*George Eustice, C.   15,969
Julia Goldsworthy, LD   15,903
Jude Robinson, Lab.   6,945
Derek Elliott, UKIP   2,152
Loveday Jenkin, Meb. Ker.   775
Euan McPhee, Green   581
Robert Hawkins, Soc. Lab.   168
C. majority 66 (0.16%)
Notional 5.21% swing LD to C.
(2005: LD majority 2,733 (7.08%))

§CAMBRIDGE
E. 77,081 T. 50,130 (65.04%) LD hold
*Julian Huppert, LD   19,621
Nick Hillman, C.   12,829
Daniel Zeichner, Lab.   12,174
Tony Juniper, Green   3,804
Peter Burkinshaw, UKIP   1,195
Martin Booth, TUSC   362
Holborn Old, Ind.   145
LD majority 6,792 (13.55%)
Notional 6.98% swing LD to C.
(2005: LD majority 5,834 (12.27%))

§CAMBRIDGESHIRE NORTH EAST
E. 73,224 T. 52,264 (71.38%) C. hold
*Stephen Barclay, C.   26,862
Lorna Spenceley, LD   10,437
Peter Roberts, Lab.   9,274
Robin Talbot, UKIP   2,991
Susan Clapp, BNP   1,747
Debra Jordan, Ind.   566
Graham Murphy, Eng. Dem.   387
C. majority 16,425 (31.43%)
Notional 0.79% swing LD to C.
(2005: C. majority 7,726 (16.30%))

§CAMBRIDGESHIRE NORTH WEST
E. 88,857 T. 58,283 (65.59%) C. hold
Shailesh Vara, C.   29,425
Kevin Wilkins, LD   12,748
Chris York, Lab.   9,877
Robert Brown, UKIP   4,826
Stephen Goldspink, Eng. Dem.   1,407
C. majority 16,677 (28.61%)
Notional 2.64% swing C. to LD
(2005: C. majority 10,925 (20.62%))

§CAMBRIDGESHIRE SOUTH
E. 78,995 T. 59,056 (74.76%) C. hold
Andrew Lansley, C.   27,995
Sebastian Kindersley, LD   20,157
Tariq Sadiq, Lab.   6,024
Robin Page, Ind.   1,968
Helene Davies-Green, UKIP   1,873
Simon Saggers, Green   1,039
C. majority 7,838 (13.27%)
Notional 2.46% swing C. to LD
(2005: C. majority 9,634 (18.20%))

§CAMBRIDGESHIRE SOUTH EAST
E. 83,068 T. 57,602 (69.34%) C. hold
Jim Paice, C.   27,629
Jonathan Chatfield, LD   21,683
John Cowan, Lab.   4,380
Andy Monk, UKIP   2,138
Simon Sedgwick-Jell, Green   766
Geoffrey Woollard, Ind.   517
Daniel Bell, CPA   489
C. majority 5,946 (10.32%)
Notional 2.67% swing C. to LD
(2005: C. majority 8,110 (15.66%))

§CANNOCK CHASE
E. 74,509 T. 45,559 (61.15%) C. gain
*Aidan Burley, C.   18,271
Susan Woodward, Lab.   15,076
Jon Hunt, LD   7,732
Terence Majorowicz, BNP   2,168
Malcolm McKenzie, UKIP   1,580
Ron Turville, Ind.   380
Royston Jenkins, Snouts   259
Mike Walters, Ind.   93
C. majority 3,195 (7.01%)
Notional 14.01% swing Lab. to C.
(2005: Lab. majority 8,726 (21.00%))

§CANTERBURY
E. 76,808 T. 49,209 (64.07%) C. hold
Julian Brazier, C.   22,050
Guy Voizey, LD   16,002
Jean Samuel, Lab.   7,940
Howard Farmer, UKIP   1,907
Geoff Meaden, Green   1,137
Anne Belsey, MRP   173
C. majority 6,048 (12.29%)
Notional 5.36% swing C. to LD
(2005: C. majority 7,579 (16.37%))

§CARLISLE
E. 65,263 T. 42,200 (64.66%) C. gain
*John Stevenson, C.   16,589
Michael Boaden, Lab.   15,736
Neil Hughes, LD   6,567
Paul Stafford, BNP   1,086
Michael Owen, UKIP   969
John Reardon, Green   614
John Metcalfe, TUSC   376
Peter Howe, ND   263
C. majority 853 (2.02%)
Notional 7.74% swing Lab. to C.
(2005: Lab. majority 5,085 (13.46%))

§CARSHALTON & WALLINGTON
E. 66,520 T. 45,918 (69.03%) LD hold
Tom Brake, LD   22,180
Dr Ken Andrew, C.   16,920
Shafi Khan, Lab.   4,015
Frank Day, UKIP   1,348
Charlotte Lewis, BNP   1,100
George Dow, Green   355
LD majority 5,260 (11.46%)
Notional 4.26% swing C. to LD
(2005: LD majority 1,225 (2.93%))

CASTLE POINT
E. 67,284 T. 45,026 (66.92%) C. gain
*Rebecca Harris, C.   19,806
Bob Spink, Green Belt   12,174
Julian Ware-Lane, Lab.   6,609
Brendan D'Cruz, LD   4,232
Philip Howell, BNP   2,205
C. majority 7,632 (16.95%)
(2005: C. majority 8,201 (17.91%))

§CHARNWOOD
E. 74,473 T. 53,542 (71.89%) C. hold
Stephen Dorrell, C.   26,560
Robin Webber-Jones, LD   11,531
Eric Goodyer, Lab.   10,536
Cathy Duffy, BNP   3,116
Miles Storier, UKIP   1,799
C. majority 15,029 (28.07%)
Notional 0.10% swing C. to LD
(2005: C. majority 8,613 (18.05%))

§CHATHAM & AYLESFORD
E. 71,122 T. 43,807 (61.59%) C. gain
*Tracey Crouch, C.   20,230
Jonathan Shaw, Lab.   14,161
John McClintock, LD   5,832
Colin McCarthy-Stewart, BNP   1,365
Steve Newton, UKIP   1,314
Sean Varnham, Eng. Dem.   400
Dave Arthur, Green   396
Maureen Smith, Ch. P.   109
C. majority 6,069 (13.85%)
Notional 11.05% swing Lab. to C.
(2005: Lab. majority 3,289 (8.25%))

§CHEADLE
E. 72,458 T. 52,512 (72.47%) LD hold
Mark Hunter, LD   24,717
Ben Jeffreys, C.   21,445
Martin Miller, Lab.   4,920
Tony Moore, UKIP   1,430
LD majority 3,272 (6.23%)
Notional 0.59% swing LD to C.
(2005: LD majority 3,672 (7.41%))

§CHELMSFORD
E. 77,529 T. 54,593 (70.42%) C. hold
Simon Burns, C.   25,207
Stephen Robinson, LD   20,097
Peter Dixon, Lab.   5,980
Ken Wedon, UKIP   1,527
Mike Bateman, BNP   899
Angela Thomson, Green   476
Claire Breed, Eng. Dem.   254
Ben Sherman, Beer   153
C. majority 5,110 (9.36%)
Notional 0.08% swing LD to C.
(2005: C. majority 4,358 (9.20%))

§CHELSEA & FULHAM
E. 66,295 T. 39,856 (60.12%) C. hold
Greg Hands, C.   24,093
Alexander Hilton, Lab.   7,371
Dirk Hazell, LD   6,473
Julia Stephenson, Green   671
Timothy Gittos, UKIP   478
Brian McDonald, BNP   388
Roland Courtenay, Ind. CCF   196
George Roseman, Eng. Dem.   169
Godfrey Spickernell, Blue   17
C. majority 16,722 (41.96%)
Notional 6.08% swing Lab. to C.
(2005: C. majority 10,253 (29.79%))

§CHELTENHAM
E. 78,998 T. 52,786 (66.82%) LD hold
Martin Horwood, LD   26,659
Mark Coote, C.   21,739
James Green, Lab.   2,703
Peter Bowman, UKIP   1,192
Dancing Ken Hanks, Loony   493
LD majority 4,920 (9.32%)
Notional 4.33% swing C. to LD
(2005: LD majority 316 (0.66%))

§CHESHAM & AMERSHAM
E. 70,333 T. 52,444 (74.57%) C. hold
Cheryl Gillan, C.   31,658
Tim Starkey, LD   14,948
Anthony Gajadharsingh, Lab.   2,942
Alan Stevens, UKIP   2,129
Nick Wilkins, Green   767
C. majority 16,710 (31.86%)
Notional 2.28% swing LD to C.
(2005: C. majority 12,974 (27.31%))

§CHESTER, CITY OF
E. 68,874 T. 46,790 (67.94%) C. gain
*Stephen Mosley, C.   18,995
Christine Russell, Lab.   16,412
Elizabeth Jewkes, LD   8,930
Allan Weddell, UKIP   1,225
Ed Abrams, Eng. Dem.   594
Tom Barker, Green   535
John Whittingham, Ind.   99
C. majority 2,583 (5.52%)
Notional 3.86% swing Lab. to C.
(2005: Lab. majority 973 (2.20%))

§CHESTERFIELD
E. 71,878 T. 45,839 (63.77%) Lab. gain
*Toby Perkins, Lab.   17,891
Paul Holmes, LD   17,342
Carolyn Abbott, C.   7,214
David Phillips, UKIP   1,432
Ian Jerram, Eng. Dem.   1,213
Duncan Kerr, Green   600
John Noneoftheabove Daramy, Ind.   147
Lab. majority 549 (1.20%)
Notional 3.78% swing LD to Lab.
(2005: LD majority 2,733 (6.36%))

§CHICHESTER
E. 81,462 T. 56,787 (69.71%) C. hold
Andrew Tyrie, C.   31,427
Martin Lury, LD   15,550
Simon Holland, Lab.   5,937
Andrew Moncrieff, UKIP   3,873
C. majority 15,877 (27.96%)
Notional 3.82% swing LD to C.
(2005: C. majority 10,457 (20.32%))

CHINGFORD & WOODFORD GREEN
E. 64,831 T. 43,106 (66.49%) C. hold
Iain Duncan Smith, C.   22,743
Cath Arakelian, Lab.   9,780
Geoffrey Seeff, LD   7,242
Julian Leppert, BNP   1,288
Nick Jones, UKIP   1,133
Lucy Craig, Green   650
None of The Above, Ind.   202
Barry White, Ind.   68
C. majority 12,963 (30.07%)
1.27% swing Lab. to C.
(2005: C. majority 10,641 (27.53%))

§CHIPPENHAM
E. 72,105 T. 52,385 (72.65%) LD hold
*Duncan Hames, LD   23,970
Wilfred Emmanuel-Jones, C.   21,500
Greg Lovell, Lab.   3,620
Julia Reid, UKIP   1,783
Michael Simpkins, BNP   641
Samantha Fletcher, Green   446
John Maguire, Eng. Dem.   307
Richard Sexton, Ch. P.   118
LD majority 2,470 (4.72%)
Notional 0.01% swing C. to LD
(2005: LD majority 2,183 (4.70%))

§CHIPPING BARNET
E. 77,798 T. 50,608 (65.05%) C. hold
Theresa Villiers, C.   24,700
Damien Welfare, Lab.   12,773
Stephen Barber, LD   10,202
James Fluss, UKIP   1,442
Kate Tansley, Green   1,021
Philip Clayton, Ind.   470
C. majority 11,927 (23.57%)
Notional 5.77% swing Lab. to C.
(2005: C. majority 5,457 (12.02%))

§CHORLEY
E. 70,950 T. 49,774 (70.15%) Lab. hold
Lindsay Hoyle, Lab.   21,515
Alan Cullens, C.   18,922
Stephen Fenn, LD   6,957
Nick Hogan, UKIP   2,021
Chris Curtis, Ind.   359
Lab. majority 2,593 (5.21%)
Notional 5.60% swing Lab. to C.
(2005: Lab. majority 7,285 (16.41%))

§CHRISTCHURCH
E. 68,861 T. 49,416 (71.76%) C. hold
Christopher Chope, C.   27,888
Martyn Hurll, LD   12,478
Robert Deeks, Lab.   4,849
David Williams, UKIP   4,201
C. majority 15,410 (31.18%)
Notional 0.05% swing C. to LD
(2005: C. majority 14,640 (31.28%))

§CITIES OF LONDON &
WESTMINSTER
E. 66,489 T. 36,931 (55.54%) C. hold
Mark Field, C.   19,264
David Rowntree, Lab.   8,188
Naomi Smith, LD   7,574
Dr Derek Chase, Green   778
Paul Weston, UKIP   664
Frank Roseman, Eng. Dem.   191
Dennis Delderfield, Ind.   98
Jack Nunn, Pirate   90
Mad Cap'n Tom, Ind.   84
C. majority 11,076 (29.99%)
Notional 3.51% swing Lab. to C.
(2005: C. majority 7,352 (22.96%))

§CLACTON
E. 67,194 T. 43,123 (64.18%) C. hold
Douglas Carswell, C.   22,867
Ivan Henderson, Lab.   10,799
Michael Green, LD   5,577
Jim Taylor, BNP   1,975
Terry Allen, Tendring   1,078
Chris Southall, Green   535
Christopher Humphrey, Ind.   292
C. majority 12,068 (27.99%)
Notional 9.74% swing Lab. to C.
(2005: C. majority 3,629 (8.50%))

CLEETHORPES
E. 70,214 T. 44,966 (64.04%) C. gain
*Martin Vickers, C.   18,939
Shona McIsaac, Lab.   14,641
Malcolm Morland, LD   8,192
Stephen Harness, UKIP   3,194
C. majority 4,298 (9.56%)
7.81% swing Lab. to C.
(2005: Lab. majority 2,642 (6.06%))

§COLCHESTER
E. 74,062 T. 46,139 (62.30%) LD hold
Bob Russell, LD   22,151
Will Quince, C.   15,169
Jordan Newell, Lab.   5,680
John Pitts, UKIP   1,350
Sidney Chaney, BNP   705
Peter Lynn, Green   694
Eddie Bone, Eng. Dem.   335
Garryck Noble, PP Essex   35
Paul Shaw, ND   20
LD majority 6,982 (15.13%)
Notional 0.24% swing LD to C.
(2005: LD majority 6,388 (15.60%))

§COLNE VALLEY
E. 80,062 T. 55,296 (69.07%) C. gain
*Jason McCartney, C.   20,440
Nicola Turner, LD   15,603
Debbie Abrahams, Lab.   14,589
Barry Fowler, BNP   1,893
Melanie Roberts, UKIP   1,163
Chas Ball, Green   867
Dr Jackie Grunsell, TUSC   741
C. majority 4,837 (8.75%)
Notional 6.55% swing Lab. to C.
(2005: Lab. majority 1,267 (2.51%))

CONGLETON
E. 73,692 T. 50,780 (68.91%) C. hold
*Fiona Bruce, C.   23,250
Peter Hirst, LD   16,187
David Bryant, Lab.   8,747
Lee Slaughter, UKIP   2,147
Paul Edwards, Ind.   276
Paul Rothwell, ND   94
Adam Parton, Ind.   79
C. majority 7,063 (13.91%)
2.30% swing C. to LD
(2005: C. majority 8,246 (17.66%))

§COPELAND
E. 63,291 T. 42,787 (67.60%) Lab. hold
Jamie Reed, Lab.   19,699
Christopher Whiteside, C.   15,866
Frank Hollowell, LD   4,365
Clive Jefferson, BNP   1,474
Ted Caley-Knowles, UKIP   994
Jill Perry, Green   389
Lab. majority 3,833 (8.96%)
Notional 2.14% swing Lab. to C.
(2005: Lab. majority 5,157 (13.24%))

CORBY
E. 78,305 T. 54,236 (69.26%) C. gain
*Louise Bagshawe, C.   22,886
Phil Hope, Lab.   20,991
Portia Wilson, LD   7,834
Roy Davies, BNP   2,525
C. majority 1,895 (3.49%)
3.31% swing Lab. to C.
(2005: Lab. (Co-op) majority 1,517
(3.13%))

§CORNWALL NORTH
E. 68,662 T. 46,844 (68.22%) LD hold
Dan Rogerson, LD   22,512
Sian Flynn, C.   19,531
Miriel O'Connor, UKIP   2,300
Janet Hulme, Lab.   1,971
Joanie Willett, Meb. Ker.   530
LD majority 2,981 (6.36%)
Notional 0.25% swing LD to C.
(2005: LD majority 2,892 (6.87%))

§CORNWALL SOUTH EAST
E. 72,237 T. 49,617 (68.69%) C. gain
*Sheryll Murray, C.   22,390
Karen Gillard, LD   19,170
Michael Sparling, Lab.   3,507
Stephanie McWilliam, UKIP   3,083
Roger Creagh-Osborne, Green   826
Roger Holmes, Meb. Ker.   641
C. majority 3,220 (6.49%)
Notional 9.13% swing LD to C.
(2005: LD majority 5,485 (11.77%))

§COTSWOLDS, THE
E. 76,728 T. 54,832 (71.46%) C. hold
Geoffrey Clifton-Brown, C.   29,075
Mike Collins, LD   16,211
Mark Dempsey, Lab.   5,886
Adrian Blake, UKIP   2,292
Kevin Lister, Green   940
Alex Steel, Ind.   428
C. majority 12,864 (23.46%)
Notional 1.08% swing LD to C.
(2005: C. majority 10,742 (21.29%))

§COVENTRY NORTH EAST
E. 73,035 T. 43,383 (59.40%) Lab. hold
Bob Ainsworth, Lab.   21,384
Hazel Noonan, C.   9,609
Russell Field, LD   7,210
Tom Gower, BNP   1,863
Dave Nellist, Soc. Alt.   1,592
Chris Forbes, UKIP   1,291
Ron Lebar, Ch. M.   434
Lab. majority 11,775 (27.14%)
Notional 5.47% swing Lab. to C.
(2005: Lab. majority 14,621 (38.08%))

§COVENTRY NORTH WEST
E. 72,871 T. 46,560 (63.89%) Lab. hold
Geoffrey Robinson, Lab.   19,936
Gary Ridley, C.   13,648
Vincent McKee, LD   8,344
Edward Sheppard, BNP   1,666
Mark Nattrass, UKIP   1,295
John Clarke, Ind.   640
Justin Wood, Green   497
Nikki Downes, Soc. Alt.   370
William Sidhu, Ch. M.   164
Lab. majority 6,288 (13.51%)
Notional 3.92% swing Lab. to C.
(2005: Lab. majority 8,934 (21.35%))

§COVENTRY SOUTH
E. 73,652 T. 45,924 (62.35%) Lab. hold
Jim Cunningham, Lab.   19,197
Kevin Foster, C.   15,352
Brian Patton, LD   8,278
Mark Taylor, UKIP   1,767
Judy Griffiths, Soc. Alt.   691
Stephen Gray, Green   639
Lab. majority 3,845 (8.37%)
Notional 3.41% swing Lab. to C.
(2005: Lab. majority 6,237 (15.18%))

CRAWLEY
E. 72,781 T. 47,504 (65.27%) C. gain
*Henry Smith, C.   21,264
Chris Oxlade, Lab.   15,336
John Vincent, LD   6,844
Richard Trower, BNP   1,672
Chris French, UKIP   1,382
Phil Smith, Green   598
Arshad Khan, JP   265
Andrew Hubner, Ind.   143
C. majority 5,928 (12.48%)
6.28% swing Lab. to C.
(2005: Lab. majority 37 (0.09%))

§CREWE & NANTWICH
E. 77,460 T. 51,084 (65.95%) C. hold
Edward Timpson, C.   23,420
David Williams, Lab.   17,374
Roy Wood, LD   7,656
James Clutton, UKIP   1,414
Phil Williams, BNP   1,043
Mike Parsons, Ind.   177
C. majority 6,046 (11.84%)
Notional 13.67% swing Lab. to C.
(2005: Lab. majority 6,999 (15.50%))

§CROYDON CENTRAL
E. 78,880 T. 49,757 (63.08%) C. gain
*Gavin Barwell, C.   19,657
Gerry Ryan, Lab. (Co-op)   16,688
Peter Lambell, LD   6,553
Andrew Pelling, Ind.   3,239
Cliff Le May, BNP   1,448
Ralph Atkinson, UKIP   997
Bernice Golberg, Green   581
James Gitau, Ch. P.   264
John Cartwright, Loony   192
Michael Castle, Ind.   138
C. majority 2,969 (5.97%)
Notional 3.34% swing Lab. to C.
(2005: Lab. majority 328 (0.72%))

§CROYDON NORTH
E. 85,212 T. 51,678 (60.65%) Lab. hold
Malcolm Wicks, Lab.   28,949
Jason Hadden, C.   12,466
Gerry Jerome, LD   7,226
Shasha Khan, Green   1,017
Jonathan Serter, UKIP   891
Novlette Williams, Ch. P.   586
Mohommad Shaikh, Respect   272
Ben Stevenson, Comm.   160
Mohamed Seyed, Ind.   111
Lab. majority 16,483 (31.90%)
Notional 0.27% swing C. to Lab.
(2005: Lab. majority 14,185 (31.37%))

§CROYDON SOUTH
E. 81,301 T. 56,322 (69.28%) C. hold
Richard Ottaway, C.   28,684
Simon Rix, LD   12,866
Jane Avis, Lab.   11,287
Jeffrey Bolter, UKIP   2,504
Gordon Ross, Green   981
C. majority 15,818 (28.08%)
Notional 1.75% swing C. to LD
(2005: C. majority 14,228 (27.95%))

§DAGENHAM & RAINHAM
E. 69,764 T. 44,232 (63.40%) Lab. hold
Jon Cruddas, Lab.   17,813
Simon Jones, C.   15,183
Michael Barnbrook, BNP   4,952
Joseph Bourke, LD   3,806
Craig Litwin, UKIP   1,569
Gordon Kennedy, Ind.   308
Paula Watson, Ch. P.   305
Debbie Rosaman, Green   296
Lab. majority 2,630 (5.95%)
Notional 4.87% swing Lab. to C.
(2005: Lab. majority 6,372 (15.69%))

§DARLINGTON
E. 69,352 T. 42,896 (61.85%) Lab. hold
*Jenny Chapman, Lab.   16,891
Edward Legard, C.   13,503
Mike Barker, LD   10,046
Amanda Foster, BNP   1,262
Charlotte Bull, UKIP   1,194
Lab. majority 3,388 (7.90%)
Notional 9.14% swing Lab. to C.
(2005: Lab. majority 10,417 (26.18%))

§DARTFORD
E. 76,271 T. 50,080 (65.66%) C. gain
*Gareth Johnson, C.   24,428
John Adams, Lab.   13,800
James Willis, LD   7,361
Gary Rogers, Eng. Dem.   2,178
Richard Palmer, UKIP   1,842
Stephane Tindame, Ind.   264
John Crockford, FDP   207
C. majority 10,628 (21.22%)
Notional 11.56% swing Lab. to C.
(2005: Lab. majority 860 (1.90%))

§DAVENTRY
E. 71,451 T. 51,774 (72.46%) C. hold
*Chris Heaton-Harris, C.   29,252
Christopher McGlynn, LD   10,064
Paul Corazzo, Lab.   8,168
Jim Broomfield, UKIP   2,333
Alan Bennett-Spencer, Eng. Dem.   1,187
Steve Whiffen, Green   770
C. majority 19,188 (37.06%)
Notional 0.71% swing C. to LD
(2005: C. majority 11,776 (25.15%))

§DENTON & REDDISH
E. 64,765 T. 37,635 (58.11%) Lab. hold
Andrew Gwynne, Lab.   19,191
Julie Searle, C.   9,360
Stephen Broadhurst, LD   6,727
William Robinson, UKIP   2,060
Jeff Dennis, Ind.   297
Lab. majority 9,831 (26.12%)
Notional 6.25% swing Lab. to C.
(2005: Lab. majority 13,128 (38.62%))

§DERBY NORTH
E. 71,484 T. 45,080 (63.06%) Lab. hold
*Chris Williamson, Lab.   14,896
Stephen Mold, C.   14,283
Lucy Care, LD   12,638
Peter Cheeseman, BNP   2,000
Elizabeth Ransome, UKIP   829
David Gale, Ind.   264
David Geraghty, Pirate   170
Lab. majority 613 (1.36%)
Notional 7.39% swing Lab. to C.
(2005: Lab. majority 5,691 (14.58%))

§DERBY SOUTH
E. 71,012 T. 41,188 (58.00%) Lab. hold
Margaret Beckett, Lab.   17,851
Jack Perschke, C.   11,729
David Batey, LD   8,430
Stephen Fowke, UKIP   1,821
Alan Graves, Ind.   1,357
Lab. majority 6,122 (14.86%)
Notional 9.26% swing Lab. to C.
(2005: Lab. majority 11,655 (28.99%))

§DERBYSHIRE DALES
E. 63,367 T. 46,780 (73.82%) C. hold
Patrick McLoughlin, C.   24,378
Joe Naitta, LD   10,512
Colin Swindell, Lab.   9,061
Ian Guiver, UKIP   1,779
Josh Stockell, Green   772
Nick The Flying Brick Delves,
   Loony   228
Amila Y'mech, Humanity   50
C. majority 13,866 (29.64%)
Notional 3.74% swing LD to C.
(2005: C. majority 8,810 (20.82%))

§DERBYSHIRE MID
E. 66,297 T. 47,342 (71.41%) C. hold
*Pauline Latham, C.   22,877
Hardyal Dhindsa, Lab.   11,585
Sally McIntosh, LD   9,711
Lewis Allsebrook, BNP   1,698
Anthony Kay, UKIP   1,252
RU Seerius, Loony   219
C. majority 11,292 (23.85%)
Notional 5.66% swing Lab. to C.
(2005: C. majority 5,329 (12.54%))

§DERBYSHIRE NORTH EAST
E. 71,422 T. 47,034 (65.85%) Lab. hold
Natascha Engel, Lab.   17,948
Huw Merriman, C.   15,503
Richard Bull, LD   10,947
James Bush, UKIP   2,636
Lab. majority 2,445 (5.20%)
Notional 8.56% swing Lab. to C.
(2005: Lab. majority 9,564 (22.31%))

§DERBYSHIRE SOUTH
E. 70,610 T. 50,419 (71.40%) C. gain
*Heather Wheeler, C.   22,935
Michael Edwards, Lab.   15,807
Alexis Diouf, LD   8,012
Peter Jarvis, BNP   2,193
Charles Swabey, UKIP   1,206
Paul Liversuch, Soc. Lab.   266
C. majority 7,128 (14.14%)
Notional 9.80% swing Lab. to C.
(2005: Lab. majority 2,436 (5.45%))

§DEVIZES
E. 67,374 T. 46,340 (68.78%) C. hold
*Claire Perry, C.   25,519
Fiona Hornby, LD   12,514
Jurab Ali, Lab.   4,711
Patricia Bryant, UKIP   2,076
Mark Fletcher, Green   813
Martin Houlden, Ind.   566
Nic Coombe, Libertarian   141
C. majority 13,005 (28.06%)
Notional 0.33% swing C. to LD
(2005: C. majority 12,259 (28.63%))

§DEVON CENTRAL
E. 71,204 T. 53,873 (75.66%) C. hold
*Mel Stride, C.   27,737
Philip Hutty, LD   18,507
Moira Macdonald, Lab.   3,715
Bob Edwards, UKIP   2,870
Colin Mathews, Green   1,044
C. majority 9,230 (17.13%)
Notional 6.07% swing LD to C.
(2005: C. majority 2,338 (4.99%))

§DEVON EAST
E. 73,109 T. 53,092 (72.62%) C. hold
Hugo Swire, C.   25,662
Paull Robathan, LD   16,548
Gareth Manson, Lab.   5,721
Mike Amor, UKIP   4,346
Sharon Pavey, Green   815
C. majority 9,114 (17.17%)
Notional 1.03% swing C. to LD
(2005: C. majority 9,168 (19.23%))

§DEVON NORTH
E. 74,508 T. 51,321 (68.88%) LD hold
Nick Harvey, LD   24,305
Philip Milton, C.   18,484
Stephen Crowther, UKIP   3,720
Mark Cann, Lab.   2,671
L'Anne Knight, Green   697
Gary Marshall, BNP   614
Rodney Cann, Ind.   588
Nigel Vidler, Eng. Dem.   146
Gerrard Sables, Comm. Brit.   96
LD majority 5,821 (11.34%)
Notional 0.32% swing C. to LD
(2005: LD majority 5,276 (10.71%))

§DEVON SOUTH WEST
E. 70,059 T. 49,860 (71.17%) C. hold
Gary Streeter, C.   27,908
Anna Pascoe, LD   12,034
Luke Pollard, Lab.   6,193
Hugh Williams, UKIP   3,084
Vaughan Brean, Green   641
C. majority 15,874 (31.84%)
Notional 5.64% swing LD to C.
(2005: C. majority 9,442 (20.12%))

§DEVON WEST & TORRIDGE
E. 76,574 T. 55,257 (72.16%) C. hold
Geoffrey Cox, C.   25,230
Adam Symons, LD   22,273
Robin Julian, UKIP   3,021
Darren Jones, Lab.   2,917
Cathrine Simmons, Green   1,050
Nick Baker, BNP   766
C. majority 2,957 (5.35%)
Notional 0.01% swing C. to LD
(2005: C. majority 2,732 (5.37%))

§DEWSBURY
E. 78,901 T. 54,008 (68.45%) C. gain
*Simon Reevell, C.   18,898
Shahid Malik, Lab.   17,372
Andrew Hutchinson, LD   9,150
Khizar Iqbal, Ind.   3,813
Roger Roberts, BNP   3,265
Adrian Cruden, Green   849
Michael Felse, Eng. Dem.   661
C. majority 1,526 (2.83%)
Notional 5.85% swing Lab. to C.
(2005: Lab. majority 3,999 (8.88%))

§DON VALLEY
E. 73,214 T. 43,430 (59.32%) Lab. hold
Caroline Flint, Lab.   16,472
Matthew Stephens, C.   12,877
Edward Simpson, LD   7,422
Erwin Toseland, BNP   2,112
William Shaw, UKIP   1,904
Bernie Aston, Eng. Dem.   1,756
Martin Williams, Ind.   887
Lab. majority 3,595 (8.28%)
Notional 10.64% swing Lab. to C.
(2005: Lab. majority 11,333 (29.56%))

§DONCASTER CENTRAL
E. 75,207 T. 41,745 (55.51%) Lab. hold
Rosie Winterton, Lab.   16,569
Gareth Davies, C.   10,340
Patrick Wilson, LD   8,795
Lawrence Parramore, Eng. Dem.   1,816
John Bettney, BNP   1,762
Michael Andrews, UKIP   1,421
Scott Pickles, Ind.   970
Derek Williams, R and E   72
Lab. majority 6,229 (14.92%)
Notional 8.72% swing Lab. to C.
(2005: Lab. majority 10,325 (27.33%))

§DONCASTER NORTH
E. 72,381 T. 41,483 (57.31%) Lab. hold
Ed Miliband, Lab.   19,637
Sophie Brodie, C.   8,728
Edward Sanderson, LD   6,174
Pamela Chambers, BNP   2,818
Wayne Crawshaw, Eng. Dem.   2,148
Liz Andrews, UKIP   1,797
Bill Rawcliffe, TUSC
Lab. majority 10,909 (26.30%)
Notional 2.77% swing Lab. to C.
(2005: Lab. majority 12,027 (31.85%))

§DORSET MID & POOLE NORTH
E. 72,647 T. 46,788 (64.40%) LD hold
Annette Brooke, LD   21,100
Nick King, C.   20,831
Darren Brown, Lab.   2,748
Dave Evans, UKIP   2,109
LD majority 269 (0.57%)
Notional 6.27% swing LD to C.
(2005: LD majority 5,931 (13.12%))

§DORSET NORTH
E. 73,698 T. 54,141 (73.46%) C. hold
Bob Walter, C.   27,640
Emily Gasson, LD   20,015
Mike Bunney, Lab.   2,910
Jeremy Nieboer, UKIP   2,812
Anna Hayball, Green   546
Roger Monksummers, Loony   218
C. majority 7,625 (14.08%)
Notional 2.75% swing LD to C.
(2005: C. majority 4,200 (8.58%))

DORSET SOUTH
E. 73,838 T. 50,310 (68.14%) C. gain
*Richard Drax, C.   22,667
Jim Knight, Lab.   15,224
Ros Kayes, LD   9,557
Mike Hobson, UKIP   2,034
Brian Heatley, Green   595
Andy Kirkwood, YP   233
C. majority 7,443 (14.79%)
9.26% swing Lab. to C.
(2005: Lab. majority 1,812 (3.73%))

DORSET WEST
E. 76,869 T. 57,337 (74.59%) C. hold
Oliver Letwin, C.   27,287
Sue Farrant, LD   23,364
Dr Steve Bick, Lab.   3,815
Oliver Chisholm, UKIP   2,196
Susan Greene, Green   675
C. majority 3,923 (6.84%)
1.11% swing LD to C.
(2005: C. majority 2,461 (4.62%))

§DOVER
E. 71,832 T. 50,385 (70.14%) C. gain
*Charlie Elphicke, C.   22,174
Gwyn Prosser, Lab.   16,900
John Brigden, LD   7,962
Victor Matcham, UKIP   1,747
Dennis Whiting, BNP   1,104
Michael Walters, Eng. Dem.   216
David Clark, CPA   200
George Lee-Delisle, Ind.   82
C. majority 5,274 (10.47%)
Notional 10.43% swing Lab. to C.
(2005: Lab. majority 5,005 (10.40%))

§DUDLEY NORTH
E. 60,838 T. 38,602 (63.45%) Lab. hold
Ian Austin, Lab.   14,923
Graeme Brown, C.   14,274
Mike Beckett, LD   4,066
Malcolm Davis, UKIP   3,267
Ken Griffiths, BNP   1,899
Kevin Inman, NF   173
Lab. majority 649 (1.68%)
Notional 4.73% swing Lab. to C.
(2005: Lab. majority 4,106 (11.14%))

§DUDLEY SOUTH
E. 60,572 T. 38,165 (63.01%) C. gain
*Chris Kelly, C.   16,450
Rachel Harris, Lab.   12,594
Jonathan Bramall, LD   5,989
Philip Rowe, UKIP   3,132
C. majority 3,856 (10.10%)
Notional 9.51% swing Lab. to C.
(2005: Lab. majority 3,222 (8.91%))

§DULWICH & WEST NORWOOD
E. 72,817 T. 48,214 (66.21%) Lab. hold
Tessa Jowell, Lab.   22,461
Jonathan Mitchell, LD   13,096
Kemi Adegoke, C.   10,684
Shane Collins, Green   1,266
Elizabeth Jones, UKIP   707
Lab. majority 9,365 (19.42%)
Notional 0.84% swing Lab. to LD
(2005: Lab. majority 7,853 (19.75%))

DURHAM, CITY OF
E. 68,832 T. 46,252 (67.20%) Lab. hold
Roberta Blackman-Woods, Lab.   20,496
Carol Woods, LD   17,429
Nick Varley, C.   6,146
Ralph Musgrave, BNP   1,153
Nigel Coghill-Marshall, UKIP   856
Jonathan Collings, Ind.   172
Lab. majority 3,067 (6.63%)
0.37% swing Lab. to C.
(2005: Lab. majority 3,274 (7.38%))

§DURHAM NORTH
E. 67,548 T. 40,967 (60.65%) Lab. hold
Kevan Jones, Lab.   20,698
David Skelton, C.   8,622
Ian Lindley, LD   8,617
Pete Molloy, BNP   1,686
Bruce Reid, UKIP   1,344
Lab. majority 12,076 (29.48%)
Notional 8.93% swing Lab. to C.
(2005: Lab. majority 16,781 (44.94%))

§DURHAM NORTH WEST
E. 70,618 T. 43,815 (62.05%) Lab. hold
*Pat Glass, Lab.   18,539
Owen Temple, LD   10,927
Michelle Tempest, C.   8,766
Watts Stelling, Ind.   2,472
Michael Stewart, BNP   1,852
Andrew McDonald, UKIP   1,259
Lab. majority 7,612 (17.37%)
Notional 8.33% swing Lab. to LD
(2005: Lab. majority 13,443 (34.03%))

§EALING CENTRAL & ACTON
E. 63,489 T. 47,200 (74.34%) C. gain
*Angie Bray, C.   17,944
Bassam Mahfouz, Lab.   14,228
Jon Ball, LD   13,041
Julie Carter, UKIP   765
Sarah Edwards, Green   737
Suzanne Fernandes, Ch. P.   295
Sam Akaki, Ind. EACPS   190
C. majority 3,716 (7.87%)
Notional 5.02% swing Lab. to C.
(2005: Lab. majority 839 (2.16%))

§EALING NORTH
E. 67,902 T. 47,678 (70.22%) Lab. hold
Stephen Pound, Lab.   24,023
Ian Gibb, C.   14,722
Chris Lucas, LD   6,283
Dave Furness, BNP   1,045
Ian De Wulverton, UKIP   685
Christopher Warleigh-Lack, Green   505
Petar Ljubisic, Ch. P.   415
Lab. majority 9,301 (19.51%)
Notional 0.45% swing C. to Lab.
(2005: Lab. majority 8,126 (18.61%))

§EALING SOUTHALL
E. 60,379 T. 42,756 (70.81%) Lab. hold
Virendra Sharma, Lab.   22,024
Gurcharan Singh, C.   12,733
Nigel Bakhai, LD   6,383
Suneil Basu, Green   705
Mehboob Anil, Ch. P.   503
Sati Chaggar, Eng. Dem.   408
Lab. majority 9,291 (21.73%)
Notional 8.30% swing Lab. to C.
(2005: Lab. majority 13,140 (38.33%))

§EASINGTON
E. 63,873 T. 34,914 (54.66%) Lab. hold
*Grahame Morris, Lab.   20,579
Tara Saville, LD   5,597
Richard Harrison, C.   4,790
Cheryl Dunn, BNP   2,317
Martyn Aiken, UKIP   1,631
Lab. majority 14,982 (42.91%)
Notional 7.74% swing Lab. to LD
(2005: Lab. majority 18,874 (58.39%))

§EAST HAM
E. 90,675 T. 50,373 (55.55%) Lab. hold
Stephen Timms, Lab.   35,471
Paul Shea, C.   7,645
Chris Brice, LD   5,849
Barry O'Connor, Eng. Dem.   822
Judy Maciejowska, Green   586
Lab. majority 27,826 (55.24%)
Notional 7.71% swing C. to Lab.
(2005: Lab. majority 13,649 (33.08%))

§EASTBOURNE
E. 77,840 T. 52,124 (66.96%) LD gain
*Stephen Lloyd, LD   24,658
Nigel Waterson, C.   21,223
Dave Brinson, Lab.   2,497
Stephen Shing, Ind.   1,327
Roger Needham, UKIP   1,305
Colin Poulter, BNP   939
Michael Baldry, Ind.   101
Keith Gell, Ind.   74
LD majority 3,435 (6.59%)
Notional 4.00% swing C. to LD
(2005: C. majority 672 (1.41%))

§EASTLEIGH
E. 77,435 T. 53,650 (69.28%) LD hold
Chris Huhne, LD   24,966
Maria Hutchings, C.   21,102
Leo Barraclough, Lab.   5,153
Ray Finch, UKIP   1,933
Tony Stephen Pewsey, Eng. Dem.   249
Dave Stone, Ind.   154
Keith Low, Nat. Dem.   93
LD majority 3,864 (7.20%)
Notional 3.04% swing C. to LD
(2005: LD majority 534 (1.12%))

§EDDISBURY
E. 65,306 T. 45,414 (69.54%) C. hold
Stephen O'Brien, C.   23,472
Robert Thompson, LD   10,217
Pat Merrick, Lab.   9,794
Charles Dodman, UKIP   1,931
C. majority 13,255 (29.19%)
Notional 0.13% swing LD to C.
(2005: C. majority 6,408 (14.83%))

§EDMONTON
E. 63,902 T. 40,377 (63.19%)
                    Lab. (Co-op) hold
Andy Love, Lab. (Co-op)   21,665
Andrew Charalambous, C.   12,052
Iarla Kilbane-Dawe, LD   4,252
Roy Freshwater, UKIP   1,036
Jack Johnson, Green   516
Erol Basarik, Reform   379
Clive Morrison, Ch. P.   350
David Mclean, Ind.   127
Lab. (Co-op) majority 9,613 (23.81%)
Notional 2.26% swing Lab. (Co-op) to C.
(2005: Lab. (Co-op) majority 10,312
(28.33%))

§ELLESMERE PORT & NESTON
E. 63,097 T. 44,233 (70.10%) Lab. hold
Andrew Miller, Lab.   19,750
Stuart Penketh, C.   15,419
Denise Aspinall, LD   6,663
Henry Crocker, UKIP   1,619
Jonathan Starkey, Ind.   782
Lab. majority 4,331 (9.79%)
Notional 3.10% swing Lab. to C.
(2005: Lab. majority 6,713 (15.99%))

§ELMET & ROTHWELL
E. 77,724 T. 55,789 (71.78%) C. gain
*Alec Shelbrooke, C.   23,778
James Lewis, Lab.   19,257
Stewart Golton, LD   9,109
Sam Clayton, BNP   1,802
Darren Oddy, UKIP   1,593
Christopher Nolan, Ind.   250
C. majority 4,521 (8.10%)
Notional 9.77% swing Lab. to C.
(2005: Lab. majority 6,078 (11.43%))

§ELTHAM
E. 62,590 T. 41,964 (67.05%) Lab. hold
Clive Efford, Lab.   17,416
David Gold, C.   15,753
Steven Toole, LD   5,299
Roberta Woods, BNP   1,745
Ray Adams, UKIP   1,011
Arthur Hayles, Green   419
Mike Tibby, Eng. Dem.   217
Andrew Graham, Ind.   104
Lab. majority 1,663 (3.96%)
Notional 1.82% swing Lab. to C.
(2005: Lab. majority 2,904 (7.60%))

§ENFIELD NORTH
E. 66,258 T. 44,453 (67.09%) C. hold
*Nick de Bois, C.   18,804
Joan Ryan, Lab.   17,112
Paul Smith, LD   5,403
Tony Avery, BNP   1,228
Madge Jones, UKIP   938
Bill Linton, Green   489
Anthony Williams, Ch. P.   161
Raquel Weald, Eng. Dem.   131
Anna Athow, WRP   96
Gonul Daniels, Ind.   91
C. majority 1,692 (3.81%)
Notional 0.73% swing Lab. to C.
(2005: C. majority 937 (2.35%))

§ENFIELD SOUTHGATE
E. 64,138 T. 44,352 (69.15%) C. hold
David Burrowes, C.   21,928
Bambos Charalambous, Lab.   14,302
Johar Khan, LD   6,124
Peter Krakowiak, Green   632
Bob Brock, UKIP   505
Dr Asit Mukhopadhyay, Ind.   391
Samad Billoo, Respect   174
Ben Weald, Eng. Dem.   173
Mal Malakounides, ND   88
Jeremy Sturgess, BB   35
C. majority 7,626 (17.19%)
Notional 7.24% swing Lab. to C.
(2005: C. majority 1,127 (2.72%))

§EPPING FOREST
E. 72,198 T. 46,584 (64.52%) C. hold
Eleanor Laing, C.   25,148
Ann Haigh, LD   10,017
Katie Curtis, Lab.   6,641
Pat Richardson, BNP   1,982
Andrew Smith, UKIP   1,852
Simon Pepper, Green   659
Kim Sawyer, Eng. Dem.   285
C. majority 15,131 (32.48%)
Notional 1.08% swing C. to LD
(2005: C. majority 13,473 (31.33%))

§EPSOM & EWELL
E. 78,104 T. 54,955 (70.36%) C. hold
Chris Grayling, C.   30,868
Jonathan Lees, LD   14,734
Craig Montgomery, Lab.   6,538
Elizabeth Wallace, UKIP   2,549
Peter Ticher, RRG   266
C. majority 16,134 (29.36%)
Notional 2.05% swing C. to LD
(2005: C. majority 16,342 (33.47%))

§EREWASH
E. 69,654 T. 47,642 (68.40%) C. gain
*Jessica Lee, C.   18,805
Cheryl Pidgeon, Lab.   16,304
Martin Garnett, LD   8,343
Mark Bailey, BNP   2,337
Jodie Sutton, UKIP   855
Lee Fletcher, Green   534
Luke Wilkins, Ind.   464
C. majority 2,501 (5.25%)
Notional 10.45% swing Lab. to C.
(2005: Lab. majority 6,782 (15.66%))

§ERITH & THAMESMEAD
E. 69,918 T. 42,476 (60.75%) Lab. hold
*Teresa Pearce, Lab.   19,068
Colin Bloom, C.   13,365
Alexander Cunliffe, LD   5,116
Kevin Saunders, BNP   2,184
Pamela Perrin, UKIP   1,139
Laurence Williams, Eng. Dem.   465
Abbey Akinoshun, ND   438
Sid Cordle, CPA   379
Marek Powley, Green   322
Lab. majority 5,703 (13.43%)
Notional 6.34% swing Lab. to C.
(2005: Lab. majority 9,870 (26.11%))

ESHER & WALTON
E. 75,338 T. 54,543 (72.40%) C. hold
*Dominic Raab, C.   32,134
Lionel Blackman, LD   13,541
Francis Eldergill, Lab.   5,829
Bernard Collignon, UKIP   1,783
Tony Popham, Ind.   378
Chinners Chinnery, Loony   341
Mike Kearsley, Eng. Dem.   307
Andy Lear, Best   230
C. majority 18,593 (34.09%)
8.97% swing LD to C.
(2005: C. majority 7,727 (16.14%))

§EXETER
E. 77,157 T. 52,247 (67.72%) Lab. hold
Ben Bradshaw, Lab.   19,942
Hannah Foster, C.   17,221
Graham Oakes, LD   10,581
Keith Crawford, UKIP   1,930
Chris Gale, Lib.   1,108
Paula Black, Green   792
Robert Farmer, BNP   673
Lab. majority 2,721 (5.21%)
Notional 6.03% swing Lab. to C.
(2005: Lab. majority 8,559 (17.27%))

FAREHAM
E. 75,878 T. 54,345 (71.62%) C. hold
Mark Hoban, C.   30,037
Alex Bentley, LD   12,945
James Carr, Lab.   7,719
Steve Richards, UKIP   2,235
Peter Doggett, Green   791
Joe Jenkins, Eng. Dem.   618
C. majority 17,092 (31.45%)
1.73% swing LD to C.
(2005: C. majority 11,702 (24.09%))

§FAVERSHAM & KENT MID
E. 68,858 T. 46,712 (67.84%) C. hold
Hugh Robertson, C.   26,250
David Naghi, LD   9,162
Ash Rehal, Lab.   7,748
Sarah Larkins, UKIP   1,722
Tim Valentine, Green   890
Graham Kemp, NF   542
Hairy Knorm Davidson, Loony   398
C. majority 17,088 (36.58%)
Notional 1.62% swing LD to C.
(2005: C. majority 8,927 (21.00%))

§FELTHAM & HESTON
E. 81,058 T. 48,526 (59.87%)
Lab. (Co-op) hold

Alan Keen, Lab. (Co-op)	21,174
Mark Bowen, C.	16,516
Munira Wilson, LD	6,669
John Donnelly, BNP	1,714
Jerry Shadbolt, UKIP	992
Elizabeth Anstis, Green	530
Dharmendra Tripathi, Ind.	505
Asa Khaira, Ind.	180
Roger Williams, Ind.	168
Matthew Linley, WRP	78

Lab. (Co-op) majority 4,658 (9.60%)
Notional 4.83% swing Lab. (Co-op) to C.
(2005: Lab. (Co-op) majority 7,598
(19.25%))

§FILTON & BRADLEY STOKE
E. 69,003 T. 48,301 (70.00%) C. hold

*Jack Lopresti, C.	19,686
Ian Boulton, Lab.	12,772
Peter Tyzack, LD	12,197
John Knight, UKIP	1,506
David Scott, BNP	1,328
Jon Lucas, Green	441
Ruth Johnson, Ch. P.	199
Vote Zero None of the Above, ND	172

C. majority 6,914 (14.31%)
Notional 6.37% swing Lab. to C.
(2005: C. majority 653 (1.58%))

§FINCHLEY & GOLDERS GREEN
E. 77,198 T. 47,157 (61.09%) C. hold

*Mike Freer, C.	21,688
Alison Moore, Lab.	15,879
Laura Edge, LD	8,036
Susan Cummins, UKIP	817
Donald Lyven, Green	737

C. majority 5,809 (12.32%)
Notional 5.81% swing Lab. to C.
(2005: C. majority 294 (0.70%))

§FOLKESTONE & HYTHE
E. 78,003 T. 52,800 (67.69%) C. hold

*Damian Collins, C.	26,109
Lynne Beaumont, LD	15,987
Donald Worsley, Lab.	5,719
Frank McKenna, UKIP	2,439
Harry Williams, BNP	1,662
Penny Kemp, Green	637
David Plumstead, Ind.	247

C. majority 10,122 (19.17%)
Notional 2.58% swing C. to LD
(2005: C. majority 12,446 (24.33%))

FOREST OF DEAN
E. 68,419 T. 48,763 (71.27%) C. hold

Mark Harper, C.	22,853
Bruce Hogan, Lab.	11,789
Chris Coleman, LD	10,676
Tim Congdon, UKIP	2,522
James Greenwood, Green	923

C. majority 11,064 (22.69%)
9.19% swing Lab. to C.
(2005: C. majority 2,049 (4.30%))

§FYLDE
E. 65,917 T. 43,690 (66.28%) C. hold

*Mark Menzies, C.	22,826
Bill Winlow, LD	9,641
Liam Robinson, Lab.	8,624
Martin Bleeker, UKIP	1,945
Philip Mitchell, Green	654

C. majority 13,185 (30.18%)
Notional 4.15% swing C. to LD
(2005: C. majority 11,117 (28.67%))

§GAINSBOROUGH
E. 72,144 T. 49,251 (68.27%) C. hold

Edward Leigh, C.	24,266
Pat O'Connor, LD	13,707
Jamie McMahon, Lab.	7,701
Steve Pearson, UKIP	2,065
Malcolm Porter, BNP	1,512

C. majority 10,559 (21.44%)
Notional 1.80% swing LD to C.
(2005: C. majority 7,895 (17.73%))

§GARSTON & HALEWOOD
E. 71,312 T. 42,825 (60.05%) Lab. hold

Maria Eagle, Lab.	25,493
Paula Keaveney, LD	8,616
Richard Downey, C.	6,908
Tony Hammond, UKIP	1,540
Diana Raby, Respect	268

Lab. majority 16,877 (39.41%)
Notional 5.74% swing LD to Lab.
(2005: Lab. majority 10,814 (27.92%))

§GATESHEAD
E. 66,492 T. 38,257 (57.54%) Lab. hold

*Ian Mearns, Lab.	20,712
Frank Hindle, LD	8,163
Hazel Anderson, C.	5,716
Kevin Scott, BNP	1,787
John Tennant, UKIP	1,103
Andy Redfern, Green	379
Elaine Brunskill, TUSC	266
David Walton, Ch. P.	131

Lab. majority 12,549 (32.80%)
Notional 3.94% swing Lab. to LD
(2005: Lab. majority 14,245 (40.68%))

§GEDLING
E. 70,590 T. 48,190 (68.27%) Lab. hold

Vernon Coaker, Lab.	19,821
Bruce Laughton, C.	17,962
Julia Bateman, LD	7,350
Stephen Adcock, BNP	1,598
Dave Marshall, UKIP	1,459

Lab. majority 1,859 (3.86%)
Notional 2.89% swing Lab. to C.
(2005: Lab. majority 4,335 (9.63%))

§GILLINGHAM & RAINHAM
E. 70,865 T. 46,786 (66.02%) C. gain

*Rehman Chishti, C.	21,624
Paul Clark, Lab.	12,944
Andrew Stamp, LD	8,484
Robert Oakley, UKIP	1,515
Brian Ravenscroft, BNP	1,149
Dean Lacey, Eng. Dem.	464
Trish Marchant, Green	356
Gordon Bryan, ND	141
George Meegan, Med. Ind.	109

C. majority 8,680 (18.55%)
Notional 9.29% swing Lab. to C.
(2005: Lab. majority 15 (0.03%))

§GLOUCESTER
E. 79,322 T. 50,764 (64.00%) C. gain

*Richard Graham, C.	20,267
Parmjit Dhanda, Lab.	17,847
Jeremy Hilton, LD	9,767
Mike Smith, UKIP	1,808
Alan Platt, Eng. Dem.	564
Bryan Meloy, Green	511

C. majority 2,420 (4.77%)
Notional 8.86% swing Lab. to C.
(2005: Lab. majority 6,063 (12.95%))

GOSPORT
E. 72,720 T. 46,939 (64.55%) C. hold

*Caroline Dinenage, C.	24,300
Rob Hylands, LD	9,887
Graham Giles, Lab.	7,944
Andrew Rice, UKIP	1,496
Barry Bennett, BNP	1,004
Bob Shaw, Eng. Dem.	622
Andrea Smith, Green	573
David Smith, Ind.	493
Charles Read, Ind.	331
Brian Hart, Ind.	289

C. majority 14,413 (30.71%)
1.27% swing LD to C.
(2005: C. majority 5,730 (13.32%))

§GRANTHAM & STAMFORD
E. 78,000 T. 52,799 (67.69%) C. hold

*Nicholas Boles, C.	26,552
Harrish Bisnauthsing, LD	11,726
Mark Bartlett, Lab.	9,503
Christopher Robinson, BNP	2,485
Tony Wells, UKIP	1,604
Mark Horn, Lincs Ind.	929

C. majority 14,826 (28.08%)
Notional 1.18% swing C. to LD
(2005: C. majority 7,308 (15.77%))

GRAVESHAM
E. 70,195 T. 47,303 (67.39%) C. hold

Adam Holloway, C.	22,956
Kathryn Smith, Lab. (Co-op)	13,644
Anna Arrowsmith, LD	6,293
Geoffrey Clark, UKIP	2,265
Steven Uncles, Eng. Dem.	1,005
Richard Crawford, Green	675
Alice Dartnell, Ind.	465

C. majority 9,312 (19.69%)
9.12% swing Lab. (Co-op) to C.
(2005: C. majority 654 (1.45%))

GREAT GRIMSBY
E. 61,229 T. 32,954 (53.82%) Lab. hold

Austin Mitchell, Lab.	10,777
Victoria Ayling, C.	10,063
Andrew de Freitas, LD	7,388
Henry Hudson, UKIP	2,043
Steve Fyfe, BNP	1,517
Ernie Brown, Ind.	835
Adrian Howe, PNDP	331

Lab. majority 714 (2.17%)
10.53% swing Lab. to C.
(2005: Lab. majority 7,654 (23.22%))

GREAT YARMOUTH
E. 70,315 T. 43,057 (61.23%) C. gain

*Brandon Lewis, C.	18,571
Tony Wright, Lab.	14,295
Simon Partridge, LD	6,188
Alan Baugh, UKIP	2,066
Bosco Tann, BNP	1,421
Laura Biggart, Green	416
Margaret McMahon-Morris, LTT	100

C. majority 4,276 (9.93%)
8.66% swing Lab. to C.
(2005: Lab. majority 3,055 (7.38%))

§GREENWICH & WOOLWICH
E. 65,489 T. 41,188 (62.89%) Lab. hold
Nick Raynsford, Lab. 20,262
Spencer Drury, C. 10,109
Joseph Lee, LD 7,498
Lawrence Rustem, BNP 1,151
Andy Hewett, Green 1,054
Edward Adeleye, Ch. P. 443
Topo Wresniwiro, Eng. Dem. 339
Onay Kasab, TUSC 267
Dr Tammy Alingham, Ind. 65
Lab. majority 10,153 (24.65%)
Notional 5.12% swing Lab. to C.
(2005: Lab. majority 11,638 (32.77%))

§GUILDFORD
E. 77,082 T. 55,567 (72.09%) C. hold
Anne Milton, C. 29,618
Sue Doughty, LD 21,836
Tim Shand, Lab. 2,812
Mazhar Manzoor, UKIP 1,021
John Morris, PPN-V 280
C. majority 7,782 (14.00%)
Notional 6.91% swing LD to C.
(2005: C. majority 89 (0.17%))

§HACKNEY NORTH & STOKE
NEWINGTON
E. 73,874 T. 46,488 (62.93%) Lab. hold
Diane Abbott, Lab. 25,553
Keith Angus, LD 11,092
Darren Caplan, C. 6,759
Matt Sellwood, Green 2,133
Maxine Hargreaves, Ch. P. 299
Suzanne Moore, ND 285
Knigel Knapp, Loony 182
Paul Shaer, Ind. 96
Alessandra Williams, Ind. 61
Dr Jack Pope-De-Locksley, Magna
 Carta 28
Lab. majority 14,461 (31.11%)
Notional 2.61% swing LD to Lab.
(2005: Lab. majority 8,002 (25.88%))

§HACKNEY SOUTH & SHOREDITCH
E. 72,816 T. 42,858 (58.86%) Lab. hold
Meg Hillier, Lab. 23,888
Dave Raval, LD 9,600
Simon Nayyar, C. 5,800
Polly Lane, Green 1,493
Michael King, UKIP 651
Ben Rae, Lib. 539
John Williams, Ch. P. 434
Nusret Sen, DDP 202
Paul Davies, Comm. Lge 110
Denny De La Haye, Ind. 95
Jane Tuckett, Ind. 26
Michael Spinks, Ind. 20
Lab. majority 14,288 (33.34%)
Notional 0.99% swing LD to Lab.
(2005: Lab. majority 9,629 (31.37%))

§HALESOWEN & ROWLEY REGIS
E. 63,693 T. 43,979 (69.05%) C. gain
*James Morris, C. 18,115
Sue Hayman, Lab. 16,092
Philip Tibbets, LD 6,515
Derek Baddeley, UKIP 2,824
Derek Thompson, Ind. 433
C. majority 2,023 (4.60%)
Notional 7.13% swing Lab. to C.
(2005: Lab. majority 4,010 (9.66%))

§HALIFAX
E. 70,380 T. 43,555 (61.89%) Lab. hold
Linda Riordan, Lab. 16,278
Philip Allott, C. 14,806
Elisabeth Wilson, LD 8,335
Tom Bates, BNP 2,760
Diane Park, Ind. Voice 722
Jay Sangha, UKIP 654
Lab. majority 1,472 (3.38%)
Notional 2.69% swing Lab. to C.
(2005: Lab. majority 3,481 (8.75%))

§HALTEMPRICE & HOWDEN
E. 70,403 T. 48,737 (69.23%) C. hold
David Davis, C. 24,486
Jon Neal, LD 12,884
Danny Marten, Lab. 7,630
James Cornell, BNP 1,583
Joanne Robinson, Eng. Dem. 1,485
Shan Oakes, Green 669
C. majority 11,602 (23.81%)
Notional 6.64% swing LD to C.
(2005: C. majority 5,080 (10.52%))

§HALTON
E. 68,884 T. 41,338 (60.01%) Lab. hold
Derek Twigg, Lab. 23,843
Ben Jones, C. 8,339
Frank Harasiwka, LD 5,718
Andrew Taylor, BNP 1,563
John Moore, UKIP 1,228
Jim Craig, Green 647
Lab. majority 15,504 (37.51%)
Notional 2.87% swing Lab. to C.
(2005: Lab. majority 16,060 (43.25%))

§HAMMERSMITH
E. 72,348 T. 47,452 (65.59%) Lab. hold
Andy Slaughter, Lab. 20,810
Shaun Bailey, C. 17,261
Merlene Emerson, LD 7,567
Rollo Miles, Green 696
Vanessa Crichton, UKIP 551
Lawrence Searle, BNP 432
Stephen Brennan, Ind. 135
Lab. majority 3,549 (7.48%)
Notional 0.48% swing Lab. to C.
(2005: Lab. majority 3,673 (8.44%))

§HAMPSHIRE EAST
E. 72,250 T. 51,317 (71.03%) C. hold
*Damian Hinds, C. 29,137
Adam Carew, LD 15,640
Jane Edbrooke, Lab. 4,043
Hugh McGuinness, UKIP 1,477
Matt Williams, Eng. Dem. 710
Don Jerrard, J & AC 310
C. majority 13,497 (26.30%)
Notional 6.61% swing LD to C.
(2005: C. majority 5,968 (13.09%))

§HAMPSHIRE NORTH EAST
E. 72,196 T. 52,939 (73.33%) C. hold
James Arbuthnot, C. 32,075
Denzil Coulson, LD 13,478
Barry Jones, Lab. 5,173
Ruth Duffin, UKIP 2,213
C. majority 18,597 (35.13%)
Notional 4.52% swing LD to C.
(2005: C. majority 11,189 (26.09%))

§HAMPSHIRE NORTH WEST
E. 76,040 T. 53,292 (70.08%) C. hold
Sir George Young, C. 31,072
Thomas McCann, LD 12,489
Sarah Evans, Lab. 6,980
Stan Oram, UKIP 2,751
C. majority 18,583 (34.87%)
Notional 4.67% swing LD to C.
(2005: C. majority 12,683 (25.53%))

§HAMPSTEAD & KILBURN
E. 79,713 T. 52,822 (66.27%) Lab. hold
Glenda Jackson, Lab. 17,332
Chris Philp, C. 17,290
Edward Fordham, LD 16,491
Bea Campbell, Green 759
Magnus Nielsen, UKIP 408
Victoria Moore, BNP 328
Tamsin Omond, TOC 123
Gene Alcantara, Ind. 91
Lab. majority 42 (0.08%)
Notional 6.65% swing Lab. to C.
(2005: Lab. majority 474 (1.14%))

§HARBOROUGH
E. 77,917 T. 54,945 (70.52%) C. hold
Edward Garnier, C. 26,894
Zuffar Haq, LD 17,097
Kevin McKeever, Lab. 6,981
Geoff Dickens, BNP 1,715
Marrietta King, UKIP 1,462
David Ball, Eng. Dem. 568
Jeff Stephenson, Ind. 228
C. majority 9,797 (17.83%)
Notional 4.73% swing LD to C.
(2005: C. majority 4,047 (8.38%))

§HARLOW
E. 67,439 T. 43,878 (65.06%) C. gain
*Robert Halfon, C. 19,691
Bill Rammell, Lab. 14,766
David White, LD 5,990
Eddy Butler, BNP 1,739
John Croft, UKIP 1,591
Oluyemi Adeeko, Ch. P. 101
C. majority 4,925 (11.22%)
Notional 5.90% swing Lab. to C.
(2005: Lab. majority 230 (0.58%))

§HARROGATE & KNARESBOROUGH
E. 75,269 T. 53,134 (70.59%) C. gain
*Andrew Jones, C. 24,305
Claire Kelley, LD 23,266
Kevin McNerney, Lab. 3,413
Steven Gill, BNP 1,094
John Upex, UKIP 1,056
C. majority 1,039 (1.96%)
Notional 9.09% swing LD to C.
(2005: LD majority 7,980 (16.22%))

§HARROW EAST
E. 68,554 T. 48,006 (70.03%) C. gain
*Bob Blackman, C. 21,435
Tony McNulty, Lab. 18,032
Nahid Boethe, LD 6,850
Abhijit Pandya, UKIP 896
Madeleine Atkins, Green 793
C. majority 3,403 (7.09%)
Notional 6.99% swing Lab. to C.
(2005: Lab. majority 2,934 (6.89%))

§HARROW WEST
E. 71,510 T. 46,116 (64.49%)
Lab. (Co-op) hold
Gareth Thomas, Lab. (Co-op) 20,111
Dr Rachel Joyce, C. 16,968
Christopher Noyce, LD 7,458
Herbert Crossman, UKIP 954
Rowan Langley, Green 625
Lab. (Co-op) majority 3,143 (6.82%)
Notional 5.72% swing Lab. (Co-op) to C.
(2005: Lab. (Co-op) majority 7,742
(18.26%))

HARTLEPOOL
E. 68,923 T. 38,242 (55.49%) Lab. hold
Iain Wright, Lab. 16,267
Alan Wright, C. 10,758
Reg Clark, LD 6,533
Stephen Allison, UKIP 2,682
Ronnie Bage, BNP 2,002
Lab. majority 5,509 (14.41%)
12.82% swing Lab. to C.
(2005: Lab. majority 7,478 (21.10%))

§HARWICH & ESSEX NORTH
E. 70,743 T. 49,000 (69.26%) C. hold
Bernard Jenkin, C. 23,001
James Raven, LD 11,554
Darren Barrenger, Lab. 9,774
Simon Anselmi, UKIP 2,527
Stephen Robey, BNP 1,065
Chris Fox, Green 909
Peter Thompson Bates, Ind. 170
C. majority 11,447 (23.36%)
Notional 0.00% swing C. to LD
(2005: C. majority 5,583 (11.73%))

§HASTINGS & RYE
E. 78,000 T. 49,814 (63.86%) C. gain
*Amber Rudd, C. 20,468
Michael Foster, Lab. 18,475
Nicholas Perry, LD 7,825
Anthony Smith, UKIP 1,397
Nicholas Prince, BNP 1,310
Rodney Bridger, Eng. Dem. 339
C. majority 1,993 (4.00%)
Notional 3.27% swing Lab. to C.
(2005: Lab. majority 1,156 (2.54%))

§HAVANT
E. 69,712 T. 43,903 (62.98%) C. hold
David Willetts, C. 22,433
Alex Payton, LD 10,273
Robert Smith, Lab. 7,777
Gary Kerrin, UKIP 2,611
Fungus Addams, Eng. Dem. 809
C. majority 12,160 (27.70%)
Notional 1.79% swing LD to C.
(2005: C. majority 6,395 (15.58%))

§HAYES & HARLINGTON
E. 70,233 T. 42,637 (60.71%) Lab. hold
John McDonnell, Lab. 23,377
Scott Seaman-Digby, C. 12,553
Satnam Kaur Khalsa, LD 3,726
Chris Forster, BNP 1,520
Andrew Cripps, NF 566
Cliff Dixon, Eng. Dem. 464
Jessica Lee, Green 348
Aneel Shahzad, Ch. P. 83
Lab. majority 10,824 (25.39%)
Notional 1.65% swing Lab. to C.
(2005: Lab. majority 10,594 (28.68%))

§HAZEL GROVE
E. 63,074 T. 41,981 (66.56%) LD hold
Andrew Stunell, LD 20,485
Annesley Abercorn, C. 14,114
Richard Scorer, Lab. 5,234
John Whittaker, UKIP 2,148
LD majority 6,371 (15.18%)
Notional 2.37% swing LD to C.
(2005: LD majority 7,694 (19.92%))

§HEMEL HEMPSTEAD
E. 72,754 T. 49,471 (68.00%) C. hold
Mike Penning, C. 24,721
Dr Richard Grayson, LD 11,315
Ayfer Orhan, Lab. 10,295
Janet Price, BNP 1,615
David Alexander, UKIP 1,254
Mick Young, Ind. 271
C. majority 13,406 (27.10%)
Notional 1.94% swing LD to C.
(2005: C. majority 168 (0.36%))

§HEMSWORTH
E. 72,552 T. 43,840 (60.43%) Lab. hold
Jon Trickett, Lab. 20,506
Ann Myatt, C. 10,662
Alan Belmore, LD 5,667
Ian Womersley, Ind. 3,946
Ian Kitchen, BNP 3,059
Lab. majority 9,844 (22.45%)
Notional 7.03% swing Lab. to C.
(2005: Lab. majority 14,026 (36.51%))

§HENDON
E. 78,923 T. 46,374 (58.76%) C. gain
*Matthew Offord, C. 19,635
Andrew Dismore, Lab. 19,529
Matthew Harris, LD 5,734
Robin Lambert, UKIP 958
Andrew Newby, Green 518
C. majority 106 (0.23%)
Notional 4.14% swing Lab. to C.
(2005: Lab. majority 3,231 (8.06%))

§HENLEY
E. 75,005 T. 53,520 (71.36%) C. hold
John Howell, C. 30,054
Andrew Crick, LD 13,466
Richard McKenzie, Lab. 5,835
Laurence Hughes, UKIP 1,817
Mark Stevenson, Green 1,328
John Bews, BNP 1,020
C. majority 16,588 (30.99%)
Notional 1.93% swing LD to C.
(2005: C. majority 13,366 (27.13%))

§HEREFORD & HEREFORDSHIRE
SOUTH
E. 71,435 T. 48,381 (67.73%) C. gain
*Jesse Norman, C. 22,366
Sarah Carr, LD 19,885
Philippa Roberts, Lab. 3,506
Valentine Smith, UKIP 1,638
John Oliver, BNP 986
C. majority 2,481 (5.13%)
Notional 3.76% swing LD to C.
(2005: LD majority 1,089 (2.39%))

§HEREFORDSHIRE NORTH
E. 66,525 T. 47,568 (71.50%) C. hold
Bill Wiggin, C. 24,631
Lucy Hurds, LD 14,744
Neil Sabharwal, Lab. 3,373
Jonathan Oakton, UKIP 2,701
Felicity Norman, Green 1,533
John King, Ind. 586
C. majority 9,887 (20.78%)
Notional 3.82% swing C. to LD
(2005: C. majority 12,688 (28.43%))

§HERTFORD & STORTFORD
E. 78,459 T. 55,377 (70.58%) C. hold
Mark Prisk, C. 29,810
Andrew Lewin, LD 14,373
Steve Terry, Lab. 7,620
David Sodey, UKIP 1,716
Roy Harris, BNP 1,297
Loucas Xenophontos, Ind. 325
Martin Adams, Ind. 236
C. majority 15,437 (27.88%)
Notional 1.95% swing C. to LD
(2005: C. majority 12,756 (25.95%))

§HERTFORDSHIRE NORTH EAST
E. 72,200 T. 50,425 (69.84%) C. hold
Oliver Heald, C. 26,995
Hugh Annand, LD 11,801
David Kirkman, Lab. 8,291
Adrianne Smyth, UKIP 2,075
Rosemary Bland, Green 875
Richard Campbell, Ind. 209
David Ralph, YRDPL 143
Philip Reichardt, Ind. 36
C. majority 15,194 (30.13%)
Notional 1.19% swing LD to C.
(2005: C. majority 9,510 (19.75%))

§HERTFORDSHIRE SOUTH WEST
E. 78,248 T. 56,750 (72.53%) C. hold
David Gauke, C. 30,773
Christopher Townsend, LD 15,853
Harry Mann, Lab. 6,526
Mark Benson, UKIP 1,450
Deirdre Gates, BNP 1,302
James Hannaway, Ind. 846
C. majority 14,920 (26.29%)
Notional 4.66% swing LD to C.
(2005: C. majority 8,640 (16.97%))

HERTSMERE
E. 73,062 T. 47,270 (64.70%) C. hold
James Clappison, C. 26,476
Sam Russell, Lab. 8,871
Anthony Rowlands, LD 8,210
David Rutter, UKIP 1,712
Daniel Seabrook, BNP 1,397
Arjuna Krishna-Das, Green 604
C. majority 17,605 (37.24%)
5.59% swing Lab. to C.
(2005: C. majority 11,093 (26.06%))

§HEXHAM
E. 61,375 T. 43,483 (70.85%) C. hold
*Guy Opperman, C. 18,795
Andrew Duffield, LD 13,007
Antoine Tinnion, Lab. 8,253
Steve Ford, Ind. 1,974
Quentin Hawkins, BNP 1,205
Colin Moss, Ind. 249
C. majority 5,788 (13.31%)
Notional 1.70% swing C. to LD
(2005: C. majority 4,957 (12.03%))

§HEYWOOD & MIDDLETON
E. 80,171 T. 46,125 (57.53%) Lab. hold
Jim Dobbin, Lab. 18,499
Michael Holly, C. 12,528
Wera Hobhouse, LD 10,474
Peter Greenwood, BNP 3,239
Victoria Cecil, UKIP 1,215
Chrissy Lee, Ind. 170
Lab. majority 5,971 (12.95%)
Notional 6.82% swing Lab. to C.
(2005: Lab. majority 11,034 (26.58%))

§HIGH PEAK
E. 71,973 T. 50,337 (69.94%) C. gain
*Andrew Bingham, C.   20,587
Caitlin Bisknell, Lab.   15,910
Alistair Stevens, LD   10,993
Sylvia Hall, UKIP   1,690
Peter Allen, Green   922
Lance Dowson, Ind.   161
Tony Alves, ND   74
C. majority 4,677 (9.29%)
Notional 6.54% swing Lab. to C.
(2005: Lab. majority 1,750 (3.80%))

§HITCHIN & HARPENDEN
E. 73,851 T. 54,707 (74.08%) C. hold
Peter Lilley, C.   29,869
Nigel Quinton, LD   14,598
Oliver de Botton, Lab.   7,413
Graham Wilkinson, UKIP   1,663
Richard Wise, Green   807
Margaret Henderson, Ind.   109
Simon Byron, R and E   108
Eric Hannah, YRDPL   90
Peter Rigby, Ind.   50
C. majority 15,271 (27.91%)
Notional 2.50% swing LD to C.
(2005: C. majority 11,064 (22.90%))

§HOLBORN & ST PANCRAS
E. 86,863 T. 54,649 (62.91%) Lab. hold
Frank Dobson, Lab.   25,198
Jo Shaw, LD   15,256
George Lee, C.   11,134
Natalie Bennett, Green   1,480
Robert Carlyle, BNP   779
Max Spencer, UKIP   587
John Chapman, Ind.   96
Mikel Susperregi, Eng. Dem.   75
Iain Meek, Ind.   44
Lab. majority 9,942 (18.19%)
Notional 0.38% swing Lab. to LD
(2005: Lab. majority 8,348 (18.95%))

§HORNCHURCH & UPMINSTER
E. 78,487 T. 53,390 (68.02%) C. hold
Angela Watkinson, C.   27,469
Kath McGuirk, Lab.   11,098
Karen Chilvers, LD   7,426
William Whelpley, BNP   3,421
Lawrence Webb, UKIP   2,848
Melanie Collins, Green   542
David Durant, Ind.   305
Johnson Olukotun, Ch. P.   281
C. majority 16,371 (30.66%)
Notional 7.14% swing Lab. to C.
(2005: C. majority 8,058 (16.38%))

HORNSEY & WOOD GREEN
E. 79,916 T. 55,042 (68.87%) LD hold
Lynne Featherstone, LD   25,595
Karen Jennings, Lab.   18,720
Richard Merrin, C.   9,174
Pete McAskie, Green   1,261
Stephane De Roche, Ind.   201
Rohen Kapur, Ind.   91
LD majority 6,875 (12.49%)
3.72% swing Lab. to LD
(2005: LD majority 2,395 (5.06%))

§HORSHAM
E. 76,835 T. 55,841 (72.68%) C. hold
Francis Maude, C.   29,447
Godfrey Newman, LD   17,987
Andrew Skudder, Lab.   4,189
Harry Aldridge, UKIP   2,839
Nick Fitter, Green   570
Steve Lyon, Ch. P.   469
Jim Duggan, PPN-V   253
Derek Kissach, Ind.   87
C. majority 11,460 (20.52%)
Notional 0.57% swing C. to LD
(2005: C. majority 10,780 (21.66%))

§HOUGHTON & SUNDERLAND
SOUTH
E. 68,729 T. 38,021 (55.32%) Lab. hold
*Bridget Phillipson, Lab.   19,137
Robert Oliver, C.   8,147
Chris Boyle, LD   5,292
Colin Wakefield, Ind.   2,462
Karen Allen, BNP   1,961
Richard Elvin, UKIP   1,022
Lab. majority 10,990 (28.91%)
Notional 8.44% swing Lab. to C.
(2005: Lab. majority 16,986 (45.78%))

§HOVE
E. 71,708 T. 49,819 (69.47%) C. gain
*Mike Weatherley, C.   18,294
Celia Barlow, Lab.   16,426
Paul Elgood, LD   11,240
Ian Davey, Green   2,568
Paul Perrin, UKIP   1,206
Brian Ralfe, Ind.   85
C. majority 1,868 (3.75%)
Notional 2.37% swing Lab. to C.
(2005: Lab. majority 448 (1.00%))

§HUDDERSFIELD
E. 66,316 T. 40,524 (61.11%) Lab. hold
Barry Sheerman, Lab.   15,725
Karen Tweed, C.   11,253
James Blanchard, LD   10,023
Andrew Cooper, Green   1,641
Rachel Firth, BNP   1,563
Paul Cooney, TUSC   319
Lab. majority 4,472 (11.04%)
Notional 7.14% swing Lab. to C.
(2005: Lab. majority 7,883 (22.29%))

§HULL EAST
E. 67,530 T. 34,184 (50.62%) Lab. hold
*Karl Turner, Lab.   16,387
Jeremy Wilcock, LD   7,790
Christine Mackay, C.   5,667
Mike Hookem, UKIP   2,745
Joe Uttley, NF   880
Mike Burton, Eng. Dem.   715
Lab. majority 8,597 (25.15%)
Notional 5.35% swing Lab. to LD
(2005: Lab. majority 11,740 (35.84%))

§HULL NORTH
E. 64,082 T. 33,291 (51.95%) Lab. hold
Diana Johnson, Lab.   13,044
Denis Healy, LD   12,403
Victoria Aitken, C.   4,365
John Mainprize, BNP   1,443
Paul Barlow, UKIP   1,358
Martin Deane, Green   478
Michael Cassidy, Eng. Dem.   200
Lab. majority 641 (1.93%)
Notional 12.18% swing Lab. to LD
(2005: Lab. majority 7,384 (26.29%))

§HULL WEST & HESSLE
E. 69,017 T. 31,505 (45.65%) Lab. hold
Alan Johnson, Lab.   13,378
Mike Ross, LD   7,636
Gary Shores, C.   6,361
Ken Hordon, UKIP   1,688
Edward Scott, BNP   1,416
Peter Mawer, Eng. Dem.   876
Keith Gibson, TUSC   150
Lab. majority 5,742 (18.23%)
Notional 7.92% swing Lab. to LD
(2005: Lab. majority 9,430 (34.06%))

§HUNTINGDON
E. 83,557 T. 54,266 (64.94%) C. hold
Jonathan Djanogly, C.   26,516
Martin Land, LD   15,697
Anthea Cox, Lab.   5,982
Ian Curtis, UKIP   3,258
Jonathan Salt, Ind.   1,432
John Clare, Green   652
Lord Toby Jug, Loony   548
Carrie Holliman, APP   181
C. majority 10,819 (19.94%)
Notional 2.08% swing C. to LD
(2005: C. majority 11,652 (24.10%))

§HYNDBURN
E. 67,221 T. 42,672 (63.48%) Lab. hold
*Graham Jones, Lab.   17,531
Karen Buckley, C.   14,441
Andrew Rankine, LD   5,033
David Shapcott, BNP   2,137
Granville Barker, UKIP   1,481
The Revd Kevin Logan, CPA   795
Kerry Gormley, Green   463
Christopher Reid, Eng. Dem.   413
Craig Hall, Ind.   378
Lab. majority 3,090 (7.24%)
Notional 3.28% swing Lab. to C.
(2005: Lab. majority 5,528 (13.80%))

§ILFORD NORTH
E. 71,995 T. 47,018 (65.31%) C. hold
Lee Scott, C.   21,506
Sonia Klein, Lab.   16,102
Alex Berhanu, LD   5,966
Danny Warville, BNP   1,545
Henri van der Stighelen, UKIP   871
Caroline Allen, Green   572
The Revd Robert Hampson, CPA   456
C. majority 5,404 (11.49%)
Notional 3.68% swing Lab. to C.
(2005: C. majority 1,735 (4.14%))

ILFORD SOUTH
E. 75,246 T. 51,191 (68.03%)
                      Lab. (Co-op) hold
Mike Gapes, Lab. (Co-op)   25,301
Toby Boutle, C.   14,014
Anood Al-Samerai, LD   8,679
Wilson Chowdhry, Green   1,319
Terry Murray, UKIP   1,132
John Jestico, King George   746
Lab. (Co-op) majority 11,287 (22.05%)
0.22% swing C. to Lab. (Co-op)
(2005: Lab. (Co-op) majority 9,228
(21.61%))

§IPSWICH
E. 78,371 T. 46,941 (59.90%) C. gain
*Benedict Gummer, C.   18,371
Chris Mole, Lab.   16,292
Mark Dyson, LD   8,556
Chris Streatfield, UKIP   1,365
Dennis Boater, BNP   1,270
Tim Glover, Green   775
Kim Christofi, Ch. P.   149
Peter Turtill, Ind.   93
Sally Wainman, Ind.   70
C. majority 2,079 (4.43%)
Notional 8.12% swing Lab. to C.
(2005: Lab. majority 5,235 (11.81%))

ISLE OF WIGHT
E. 109,966 T. 70,264 (63.90%) C. hold
Andrew Turner, C.   32,810
Jill Wareham, LD   22,283
Mark Chiverton, Lab.   8,169
Mike Tarrant, UKIP   2,435
Geoff Clynch, BNP   1,457
Ian Dunsire, Eng. Dem.   1,233
Bob Keats, Green   931
Paul Martin, Mid. England   616
Pete Harris, Ind.   175
Paul Randle-Jolliffe, Ind.   89
Edward Corby, Ind.   66
C. majority 10,527 (14.98%)
2.22% swing C. to LD
(2005: C. majority 12,978 (19.42%))

ISLINGTON NORTH
E. 68,120 T. 44,554 (65.41%) Lab. hold
Jeremy Corbyn, Lab.   24,276
Rhodri Jamieson-Ball, LD   11,875
Adrian Berrill-Cox, C.   6,339
Emma Dixon, Green   1,348
Dominic Lennon, UKIP   716
Lab. majority 12,401 (27.83%)
3.25% swing LD to Lab.
(2005: Lab. majority 6,716 (21.32%))

ISLINGTON SOUTH & FINSBURY
E. 67,649 T. 43,555 (64.38%) Lab. hold
Emily Thornberry, Lab.   18,407
Bridget Fox, LD   14,838
Antonia Cox, C.   8,449
James Humphreys, Green   710
Rose-Marie McDonald, UKIP   701
John Dodds, Eng. Dem.   301
Richard Deboo, Animals   149
Lab. majority 3,569 (8.19%)
3.32% swing LD to Lab.
(2005: Lab. majority 484 (1.56%))

§JARROW
E. 64,350 T. 38,784 (60.27%) Lab. hold
Stephen Hepburn, Lab.   20,910
Jeffrey Milburn, C.   8,002
Tom Appleby, LD   7,163
Andy Swaddle, BNP   2,709
Lab. majority 12,908 (33.28%)
Notional 6.38% swing Lab. to C.
(2005: Lab. majority 12,749 (36.35%))

KEIGHLEY
E. 65,893 T. 47,692 (72.38%) C. gain
*Kris Hopkins, C.   20,003
Jane Thomas, Lab.   17,063
Nader Fekri, LD   7,059
Andrew Brons, BNP   1,962
Paul Latham, UKIP   1,470
Steven Smith, NF   135
C. majority 2,940 (6.16%)
8.32% swing Lab. to C.
(2005: Lab. majority 4,852 (10.48%))

§KENILWORTH & SOUTHAM
E. 59,630 T. 48,431 (81.22%) C. hold
Jeremy Wright, C.   25,945
Nigel Rock, LD   13,393
Nicholas Milton, Lab.   6,949
John Moore, UKIP   1,214
James Harrison, Green   568
Joe Rukin, Ind.   362
C. majority 12,552 (25.92%)
Notional 1.20% swing C. to LD
(2005: C. majority 10,956 (24.80%))

§KENSINGTON
E. 65,961 T. 35,150 (53.29%) C. hold
Sir Malcolm Rifkind, C.   17,595
Sam Gurney, Lab.   8,979
Robin Meltzer, LD   6,872
Lady Caroline Pearson, UKIP   754
Zahra-Melan Ebrahimi-Fardouee,
   Green   753
Eddie Adams, Green Soc.   197
C. majority 8,616 (24.51%)
Notional 5.19% swing Lab. to C.
(2005: C. majority 4,540 (14.13%))

§KETTERING
E. 68,837 T. 47,328 (68.75%) C. hold
Philip Hollobone, C.   23,247
Phil Sawford, Lab.   14,153
Chris Nelson, LD   7,498
Clive Skinner, BNP   1,366
Derek Hilling, Eng. Dem.   952
Dave Bishop, BP Elvis   112
C. majority 9,094 (19.21%)
Notional 9.41% swing Lab. to C.
(2005: C. majority 176 (0.39%))

§KINGSTON & SURBITON
E. 81,116 T. 57,111 (70.41%) LD hold
Edward Davey, LD   28,428
Helen Whately, C.   20,868
Max Freedman, Lab.   5,337
Jonathan Greensted, UKIP   1,450
Chris Walker, Green   555
Monkey the Drummer, Loony   247
Anthony May, CPA   226
LD majority 7,560 (13.24%)
Notional 2.43% swing LD to C.
(2005: LD majority 9,084 (18.11%))

§KINGSWOOD
E. 66,361 T. 47,906 (72.19%) C. gain.
*Chris Skidmore, C.   19,362
Roger Berry, Lab.   16,917
Sally Fitzharris, LD   8,072
Neil Dowdney, UKIP   1,528
Michael Carey, BNP   1,311
Nick Foster, Green   383
Michael Blundell, Eng. Dem.   333
C. majority 2,445 (5.10%)
Notional 9.43% swing Lab. to C.
(2005: Lab. majority 6,145 (13.76%))

§KNOWSLEY
E. 79,561 T. 44,658 (56.13%) Lab. hold
George Howarth, Lab.   31,650
Flo Clucas, LD   5,964
David Dunne, C.   4,004
Steven Greenhalgh, BNP   1,895
Anthony Rundle, UKIP   1,145
Lab. majority 25,686 (57.52%)
Notional 0.25% swing Lab. to LD
(2005: Lab. majority 24,333 (58.02%))

LANCASHIRE WEST
E. 75,975 T. 48,473 (63.80%) Lab. hold
Rosie Cooper, Lab.   21,883
Adrian Owens, C.   17,540
John Gibson, LD   6,573
Damon Noone, UKIP   1,775
Peter Cranie, Green   485
David Braid, Clause 28   217
Lab. majority 4,343 (8.96%)
2.57% swing Lab. to C.
(2005: Lab. majority 6,084 (14.10%))

§LANCASTER & FLEETWOOD
E. 69,908 T. 42,701 (61.08%) C. gain
*Eric Ollerenshaw, C.   15,404
Clive Grunshaw, Lab.   15,071
Stuart Langhorn, LD   8,167
Gina Dowding, Green   1,888
Fred McGlade, UKIP   1,020
Debra Kent, BNP   938
Keith Riley, Ind.   213
C. majority 333 (0.78%)
Notional 4.80% swing Lab. to C.
(2005: Lab. majority 3,428 (8.82%))

§LEEDS CENTRAL
E. 64,698 T. 37,394 (57.80%) Lab. hold
Hilary Benn, Lab.   18,434
Michael Taylor, LD   7,789
Alan Lamb, C.   7,541
Kevin Meeson, BNP   3,066
Dave Procter, Ind.   409
We Beat The Scum One-Nil, ND   155
Lab. majority 10,645 (28.47%)
Notional 4.76% swing Lab. to LD
(2005: Lab. majority 12,916 (37.98%))

§LEEDS EAST
E. 65,067 T. 37,813 (58.11%) Lab. hold
George Mudie, Lab.   19,056
Barry Anderson, C.   8,763
Andrew Tear, LD   6,618
Trevor Brown, BNP   2,947
Michael Davies, Green Soc.   429
Lab. majority 10,293 (27.22%)
Notional 5.49% swing Lab. to C.
(2005: Lab. majority 13,689 (38.21%))

§LEEDS NORTH EAST
E. 67,899 T. 47,535 (70.01%) Lab. hold
Fabian Hamilton, Lab.   20,287
Matthew Lobley, C.   15,742
Aqila Choudhry, LD   9,310
Warren Hendon, UKIP   842
Tom Redmond, BNP   758
Celia Foote, Green Soc.   596
Lab. majority 4,545 (9.56%)
Notional 2.97% swing Lab. to C.
(2005: Lab. majority 6,762 (15.51%))

§LEEDS NORTH WEST
E. 65,399 T. 43,483 (66.49%) LD hold
Greg Mulholland, LD   20,653
Julia Mulligan, C.   11,550
Judith Blake, Lab.   9,132
Geoffrey Bulmer, BNP   766
Mark Thackray, UKIP   600
Martin Hemingway, Green   508
Alan Procter, Eng. Dem.   153
Trevor Bavage, Green Soc.   121
LD majority 9,103 (20.93%)
Notional 5.44% swing C. to LD
(2005: LD majority 2,064 (4.96%))

§LEEDS WEST
E. 67,453 T. 38,752 (57.45%) Lab. hold
*Rachel Reeves, Lab.   16,389
Ruth Coleman, LD   9,373
Joe Marjoram, C.   7,641
Joanna Beverley, BNP   2,377
David Blackburn, Green   1,832
Jeff Miles, UKIP   1,140
Lab. majority 7,016 (18.10%)
Notional 10.36% swing Lab. to LD
(2005: Lab. majority 13,699 (38.83%))

§LEICESTER EAST
E. 72,986 T. 47,995 (65.76%) Lab. hold
Keith Vaz, Lab.   25,804
Jane Hunt, C.   11,722
Ali Asghar, LD   6,817
Colin Gilmore, BNP   1,700
Mo Taylor, Green   733
Felicity Ransome, UKIP   725
Avtar Sadiq, UPS   494
Lab. majority 14,082 (29.34%)
Notional 4.77% swing Lab. to C.
(2005: Lab. majority 16,400 (38.89%))

§LEICESTER SOUTH
E. 77,175 T. 47,124 (61.06%) Lab. hold
Sir Peter Soulsby, Lab.   21,479
Parmjit Singh Gill, LD   12,671
Ross Grant, C.   10,066
Adrian Waudby, BNP   1,418
Dave Dixey, Green   770
Christopher Lucas, UKIP   720
Lab. majority 8,808 (18.69%)
Notional 4.96% swing LD to Lab.
(2005: Lab. majority 3,727 (8.78%))

§LEICESTER WEST
E. 64,900 T. 35,819 (55.19%) Lab. hold
*Elizabeth Kendall, Lab.   13,745
Celia Harvey, C.   9,728
Peter Coley, LD   8,107
Gary Reynolds, BNP   2,158
Stephen Ingall, UKIP   883
Geoff Forse, Green   639
Steven Huggins, Ind.   181
Steve Score, TUSC   157
Shaun Dyer, Pirate   113
David Bowley, Ind.   108
Lab. majority 4,017 (11.21%)
Notional 7.60% swing Lab. to C.
(2005: Lab. majority 8,539 (26.42%))

LEICESTERSHIRE NORTH WEST
E. 71,219 T. 51,952 (72.95%) C. gain
*Andrew Bridgen, C.   23,147
Ross Willmott, Lab. (Co-op)   15,636
Paul Reynolds, LD   8,639
Ian Meller, BNP   3,396
Martin Green, UKIP   1,134
C. majority 7,511 (14.46%)
11.98% swing Lab. (Co-op) to C.
(2005: Lab. (Co-op) majority 4,477
(9.50%))

§LEICESTERSHIRE SOUTH
E. 76,639 T. 54,577 (71.21%) C. hold
Andrew Robathan, C.   27,000
Aladdin Ayesh, LD   11,476
Sally Gimson, Lab.   11,392
Paul Preston, BNP   2,721
John Williams, UKIP   1,988
C. majority 15,524 (28.44%)
Notional 1.03% swing LD to C.
(2005: C. majority 7,704 (15.77%))

§LEIGH
E. 76,350 T. 44,332 (58.06%) Lab. hold
Andy Burnham, Lab.   21,295
Shazia Awan, C.   9,284
Chris Blackburn, LD   8,049
Gary Chadwick, BNP   2,724
Mary Lavelle, UKIP   1,535
Norman Bradbury, Ind.   988
Terry Dainty, Ind.   320
Ryan Hessell, Ch. P.   137
Lab. majority 12,011 (27.09%)
Notional 7.17% swing Lab. to C.
(2005: Lab. majority 15,098 (38.73%))

§LEWES
E. 68,708 T. 50,088 (72.90%) LD hold
Norman Baker, LD   26,048
Jason Sugarman, C.   18,401
Hratche Koundarjian, Lab.   2,508
Peter Charlton, UKIP   1,728
Susan Murray, Green   729
David Lloyd, BNP   594
Ondrej Soucek, Ind.   80
LD majority 7,647 (15.27%)
Notional 0.81% swing LD to C.
(2005: LD majority 7,889 (16.89%))

§LEWISHAM DEPTFORD
E. 67,058 T. 41,220 (61.47%) Lab. hold
Joan Ruddock, Lab.   22,132
Tam Langley, LD   9,633
Gemma Townsend, C.   5,551
Darren Johnson, Green   2,772
Ian Page, Soc. Alt.   645
Malcolm Martin, CPA   487
Lab. majority 12,499 (30.32%)
Notional 3.56% swing Lab. to LD
(2005: Lab. majority 13,012 (37.43%))

§LEWISHAM EAST
E. 65,926 T. 41,719 (63.28%) Lab. hold
*Heidi Alexander, Lab.   17,966
Pete Pattisson, LD   11,750
Jonathan Clamp, C.   9,850
Roderick Reed, UKIP   771
Priscilla Cotterell, Green   624
James Rose, Eng. Dem.   426
George Hallam, CNBPG   332
Lab. majority 6,216 (14.90%)
Notional 6.41% swing Lab. to LD
(2005: Lab. majority 8,758 (23.31%))

§LEWISHAM WEST & PENGE
E. 69,022 T. 45,028 (65.24%) Lab. hold
Jim Dowd, Lab.   18,501
Alex Feakes, LD   12,673
Chris Phillips, C.   11,489
Peter Staveley, UKIP   1,117
Romayne Phoenix, Green   931
Stephen Hammond, CPA   317
Lab. majority 5,828 (12.94%)
Notional 3.10% swing Lab. to LD
(2005: Lab. majority 7,779 (19.15%))

§LEYTON & WANSTEAD
E. 63,541 T. 40,159 (63.20%) Lab. hold
*John Cryer, Lab.   17,511
Farooq Qureshi, LD   11,095
Ed Northover, C.   8,928
Graham Wood, UKIP   1,080
Ashley Gunstock, Green   562
Jim Clift, BNP   561
Sonika Bhatti, Ch. P.   342
Martin Levin, Ind. Fed.   80
Lab. majority 6,416 (15.98%)
Notional 2.57% swing Lab. to LD
(2005: Lab. majority 7,253 (21.11%))

§LICHFIELD
E. 72,586 T. 51,563 (71.04%) C. hold
Michael Fabricant, C.   28,048
Ian Jackson, LD   10,365
Steve Hyden, Lab.   10,230
Karen Maunder, UKIP   2,920
C. majority 17,683 (34.29%)
Notional 0.74% swing LD to C.
(2005: C. majority 7,791 (16.49%))

§LINCOLN
E. 73,540 T. 45,721 (62.17%) C. gain
*Karl McCartney, C.   17,163
Gillian Merron, Lab.   16,105
Reg Shore, LD   9,256
Robert West, BNP   1,367
Nick Smith, UKIP   1,004
Ernest Coleman, Eng. Dem.   604
Gary Walker, Ind.   222
C. majority 1,058 (2.31%)
Notional 5.89% swing Lab. to C.
(2005: Lab. majority 3,806 (9.47%))

§LIVERPOOL RIVERSIDE
E. 74,539 T. 38,801 (52.05%) Lab. hold
Louise Ellman, Lab.   22,998
Richard Marbrow, LD   8,825
Kegang Wu, C.   4,243
Tom Crone, Green   1,355
Peter Stafford, BNP   706
Pat Gaskell, UKIP   674
Lab. majority 14,173 (36.53%)
Notional 0.30% swing LD to Lab.
(2005: Lab. majority 11,731 (35.93%))

§LIVERPOOL WALTON
E. 62,612 T. 34,335 (54.84%) Lab. hold
*Steve Rotheram, Lab.   24,709
Patrick Moloney, LD   4,891
Adam Marsden, C.   2,241
Peter Stafford, BNP   1,104
Joe Nugent, UKIP   898
John Manwell, CPA   297
Daren Ireland, TUSC   195
Lab. majority 19,818 (57.72%)
Notional 1.47% swing LD to Lab.
(2005: Lab. majority 17,611 (54.77%))

§LIVERPOOL WAVERTREE
E. 62,518 T. 37,914 (60.64%)
                          Lab. (Co-op) hold
*Luciana Berger, Lab. (Co-op)   20,132
Colin Eldridge, LD   12,965
Andrew Garnett, C.   2,830
Neil Miney, UKIP   890
Rebecca Lawson, Green   598
Kim Singleton, Soc. Lab.   200
Steven McEllenborough, BNP   150
Frank Dunne, Ind.   149
Lab. (Co-op) majority 7,167 (18.90%)
Notional 5.00% swing LD to Lab. (Co-op)
(2005: Lab. (Co-op) majority 2,911
(8.91%))

§LIVERPOOL WEST DERBY
E. 63,082 T. 35,784 (56.73%)
                          Lab. (Co-op) hold
*Stephen Twigg, Lab. (Co-op)   22,953
Paul Twigger, LD   4,486
Stephen Radford, Lib   3,327
Pamela Hall, C.   3,311
Hilary Jones, UKIP   1,093
Kai Andersen, Soc. Lab.   614
Lab. (Co-op) majority 18,467 (51.61%)
Notional 3.16% swing LD to Lab. (Co-op)
(2005: Lab. majority 13,874
(45.29%))

§LOUGHBOROUGH
E. 77,502 T. 52,838 (68.18%) C. gain
*Nicky Morgan, C.   21,971
Andy Reed, Lab. (Co-op)   18,227
Mike Willis, LD   9,675
Kevan Stafford, BNP   2,040
John Foden, UKIP   925
C. majority 3,744 (7.09%)
Notional 5.48% swing Lab. (Co-op) to C.
(2005: Lab. (Co-op) majority 1,816
(3.88%))

§LOUTH & HORNCASTLE
E. 77,650 T. 50,494 (65.03%) C. hold
Sir Peter Tapsell, C.   25,065
Fiona Martin, LD   11,194
Patrick Mountain, Lab.   8,760
Julia Green, BNP   2,199
Pat Nurse, UKIP   2,183
Daniel Simpson, Lincs Ind.   576
Colin Mair, Eng. Dem.   517
C. majority 13,871 (27.47%)
Notional 0.80% swing LD to C.
(2005: C. majority 9,813 (21.08%))

LUDLOW
E. 66,631 T. 48,732 (73.14%) C. hold
Philip Dunne, C.   25,720
Heather Kidd, LD   15,971
Anthony Hunt, Lab.   3,272
Christopher Gill, UKIP   2,127
Christina Evans, BNP   1,016
Jacqui Morrish, Green   447
Alan Powell, Loony   179
C. majority 9,749 (20.01%)
7.82% swing LD to C.
(2005: C. majority 2,027 (4.36%))

§LUTON NORTH
E. 65,062 T. 43,018 (66.12%) Lab. hold
Kelvin Hopkins, Lab.   21,192
Jeremy Brier, C.   13,672
Rabi Martins, LD   4,784
Colin Brown, UKIP   1,564
Shelley Rose, BNP   1,316
Simon Hall, Green   490
Lab. majority 7,520 (17.48%)
Notional 0.55% swing C. to Lab.
(2005: Lab. majority 6,439 (16.39%))

§LUTON SOUTH
E. 59,962 T. 42,216 (70.40%)
                          Lab. (Co-op) hold
*Gavin Shuker, Lab. (Co-op)   14,725
Nigel Huddleston, C.   12,396
Qurban Hussain, LD   9,567
Esther Rantzen, Ind. Rantzen   1,872
Tony Blakey, BNP   1,299
Charles Lawman, UKIP   975
Stephen Rhodes, Ind.   463
Marc Scheimann, Green   366
Joe Hall, Ind.   264
Faruk Choudhury, Ind.   130
Stephen Lathwell, Ind.   84
Frank Sweeney, WRP   75
Lab. (Co-op) majority 2,329 (5.52%)
Notional 4.59% swing Lab. (Co-op) to C.
(2005: Lab. (Co-op) majority 5,698
(14.71%))

§MACCLESFIELD
E. 73,417 T. 50,059 (68.18%) C. hold
*David Rutley, C.   23,503
Roger Barlow, LD   11,544
Adrian Heald, Lab.   10,164
Brendan Murphy, Macc. Ind.   2,590
Jacqueline Smith, UKIP   1,418
John Knight, Green   840
C. majority 11,959 (23.89%)
Notional 3.11% swing C. to LD
(2005: C. majority 9,464 (20.66%))

§MAIDENHEAD
E. 72,844 T. 53,720 (73.75%) C. hold
Theresa May, C.   31,937
Tony Hill, LD   15,168
Pat McDonald, Lab.   3,795
Kenneth Wight, UKIP   1,243
Tim Rait, BNP   825
Peter Forbes, Green   482
Peter Prior, F and R   270
C. majority 16,769 (31.22%)
Notional 7.82% swing LD to C.
(2005: C. majority 7,650 (15.58%))

§MAIDSTONE & THE WEALD
E. 71,041 T. 48,928 (68.87%) C. hold
*Helen Grant, C.   23,491
Peter Carroll, LD   17,602
Rav Seeruthun, Lab.   4,769
Gareth Kendall, UKIP   1,637
Stuart Jeffery, Green   655
Gary Butler, NF   643
Heidi Simmonds, Ch. P.   131
C. majority 5,889 (12.04%)
Notional 8.48% swing C. to LD
(2005: C. majority 12,922 (28.99%))

§MAKERFIELD
E. 73,641 T. 43,771 (59.44%) Lab. hold
*Yvonne Fovargue, Lab.   20,700
Itrat Ali, C.   8,210
David Crowther, LD   7,082
Bob Brierley, Ind.   3,424
Ken Haslam, BNP   3,229
John Mather, Ind.   1,126
Lab. majority 12,490 (28.53%)
Notional 9.98% swing Lab. to C.
(2005: Lab. majority 17,903 (48.49%))

§MALDON
E. 68,861 T. 47,895 (69.55%) C. hold
John Whittingdale, C.   28,661
Elfreda Tealby-Watson, LD   9,254
Swatantra Nandanwar, Lab.   6,070
Jesse Pryke, UKIP   2,446
Len Blaine, BNP   1,464
C. majority 19,407 (40.52%)
Notional 0.40% swing C. to LD
(2005: C. majority 13,631 (32.13%))

§MANCHESTER CENTRAL
E. 90,110 T. 39,927 (44.31%) Lab. hold
Tony Lloyd, Lab.   21,059
Marc Ramsbottom, LD   10,620
Suhail Rahuja, C.   4,704
Tony Trebilcock, BNP   1,636
Gayle O'Donovan, Green   915
Nicola Weatherill, UKIP   607
Ron Sinclair, Soc. Lab.   153
John Cartwright, Ind.   120
Jonty Leff, WRP   59
Robert Skelton, SEP   54
Lab. majority 10,439 (26.15%)
Notional 6.11% swing Lab. to LD
(2005: Lab. majority 11,636 (38.36%))

§MANCHESTER GORTON
E. 75,933 T. 38,325 (50.47%) Lab. hold
Gerald Kaufman, Lab.   19,211
Qassim Afzal, LD   12,508
Caroline Healy, C.   4,224
Justine Hall, Green   1,048
Karen Reissman, TUSC   507
Mohammed Zulfikar, Respect   337
Peter Harrison, Ch. P.   254
Tim Dobson, Pirate   236
Lab. majority 6,703 (17.49%)
Notional 1.06% swing Lab. to LD
(2005: Lab. majority 6,355 (19.61%))

§MANCHESTER WITHINGTON
E. 74,371 T. 45,031 (60.55%) LD hold
John Leech, LD   20,110
Lucy Powell, Lab.   18,216
Christopher Green, C.   5,005
Brian Candeland, Green   798
Bob Gutfreund-Walmsley, UKIP   698
Yasmin Zalzala, Ind.   147
Marcus Farmer, Ind.   57
LD majority 1,894 (4.21%)
Notional 1.41% swing Lab. to LD
(2005: LD majority 531 (1.39%))

§MANSFIELD
E. 80,069 T. 48,395 (60.44%) Lab. hold
Joseph Meale, Lab.   18,753
Tracy Critchlow, C.   12,741
Michael Wyatt, LD   7,469
Andre Camilleri, Mansfield Ind.   4,339
David Hamilton, UKIP   2,985
Rachel Hill, BNP   2,108
Lab. majority 6,012 (12.42%)
Notional 9.49% swing Lab. to C.
(2005: Lab. majority 13,776 (31.39%))

§MEON VALLEY
E. 70,488 T. 51,238 (72.69%) C. hold
*George Hollingbery, C.   28,818
Liz Leffman, LD   16,693
Howard Linsley, Lab.   3,266
Steve Harris, UKIP   1,490
Pat Harris, Eng. Dem.   582
Sarah Coats, APP   255
Graeme Quar, Ind.   134
C. majority 12,125 (23.66%)
Notional 9.38% swing LD to C.
(2005: C. majority 2,378 (4.91%))

§MERIDEN
E. 83,826 T. 52,162 (62.23%) C. hold
Caroline Spelman, C.   26,956
Ed Williams, Lab.   10,703
Simon Slater, LD   9,278
Frank O'Brien, BNP   2,511
Barry Allcock, UKIP   1,378
Elly Stanton, Green   678
Nikki Sinclaire, RA   658
C. majority 16,253 (31.16%)
Notional 7.90% swing Lab. to C.
(2005: C. majority 7,412 (15.37%))

§MIDDLESBROUGH
E. 65,148 T. 33,455 (51.35%) Lab. hold
Sir Stuart Bell, Lab.   15,351
Chris Foote-Wood, LD   6,662
John Walsh, C.   6,283
Joan McTigue, Ind.   1,969
Michael Ferguson, BNP   1,954
Robert Parker, UKIP   1,236
Lab. majority 8,689 (25.97%)
Notional 6.45% swing Lab. to LD
(2005: Lab. majority 12,476 (38.87%))

§MIDDLESBROUGH SOUTH &
CLEVELAND EAST
E. 72,664 T. 46,214 (63.60%) Lab. hold
*Tom Blenkinsop, Lab.   18,138
Paul Bristow, C.   16,461
Nick Emmerson, LD   7,340
Stuart Lightwing, UKIP   1,881
Shaun Gatley, BNP   1,576
Mike Allen, Ind.   818
Lab. majority 1,677 (3.63%)
Notional 7.44% swing Lab. to C.
(2005: Lab. majority 8,096 (18.51%))

§MILTON KEYNES NORTH
E. 85,841 T. 53,888 (62.78%) C. gain
Mark Lancaster, C.   23,419
Andrew Pakes, Lab.   14,458
Jill Hope, LD   11,894
Michael Phillips, UKIP   1,772
Richard Hamilton, BNP   1,154
Alan Francis, Green   733
Revd John Lennon, CPA   206
Matt Bananamatt Fensome, Loony   157
Anant Vyas, Ind.   95
C. majority 8,961 (16.63%)
Notional 9.17% swing Lab. to C.
(2005: Lab. majority 848 (1.71%))

§MILTON KEYNES SOUTH
E. 90,487 T. 55,333 (61.15%) C. gain
*Iain Stewart, C.   23,034
Phyllis Starkey, Lab.   17,833
Peter Jones, LD   9,787
Philip Pinto, UKIP   2,074
Matthew Tait, BNP   1,502
Katrina Deacon, Green   774
Suzanne Nti, CPA   245
Jonathan Worth, NFP   84
C. majority 5,201 (9.40%)
Notional 6.22% swing Lab. to C.
(2005: Lab. majority 1,497 (3.04%))

§MITCHAM & MORDEN
E. 65,939 T. 43,797 (66.42%) Lab. hold
Siobhain McDonagh, Lab.   24,722
Melanie Hampton, C.   11,056
Diana Coman, LD   5,202
Tony Martin, BNP   1,386
Andrew Mills, UKIP   857
Smarajit Roy, Green   381
Rathy Alagaratnam, Ind.   155
Ernest Redgrave, Ind.   38
Lab. majority 13,666 (31.20%)
Notional 0.44% swing Lab. to C.
(2005: Lab. majority 12,739 (32.08%))

MOLE VALLEY
E. 72,612 T. 54,324 (74.81%) C. hold
Sir Paul Beresford, C.   31,263
Alice Humphreys, LD   15,610
James Dove, Lab.   3,804
Leigh Jones, UKIP   2,752
Rob Sedgwick, Green   895
C. majority 15,653 (28.81%)
2.27% swing LD to C.
(2005: C. majority 11,997 (24.28%))

§MORECAMBE & LUNESDALE
E. 69,965 T. 43,616 (62.34%) C. gain
*David Morris, C.   18,035
Geraldine Smith, Lab.   17,169
Leslie Jones, LD   5,971
Mark Knight, UKIP   1,843
Chris Coates, Green   598
C. majority 866 (1.99%)
Notional 6.86% swing Lab. to C.
(2005: Lab. majority 4,849 (11.74%))

§MORLEY & OUTWOOD
E. 74,200 T. 48,856 (65.84%)
                              Lab. (Co-op) hold
Ed Balls, Lab. (Co-op)   18,365
Antony Calvert, C.   17,264
James Monaghan, LD   8,186
Chris Beverley, BNP   3,535
David Daniel, UKIP   1,506
Lab. (Co-op) majority 1,101 (2.25%)
Notional 9.35% swing Lab. (Co-op) to C.
(2005: Lab. (Co-op) majority 8,669
(20.95%))

§NEW FOREST EAST
E. 72,858 T. 50,036 (68.68%) C. hold
Julian Lewis, C.   26,443
Terry Scriven, LD   15,136
Peter Sopowski, Lab.   4,915
Peter Day, UKIP   2,518
Beverley Golden, Green   1,024
C. majority 11,307 (22.60%)
Notional 3.20% swing LD to C.
(2005: C. majority 7,653 (16.21%))

§NEW FOREST WEST
E. 68,332 T. 47,572 (69.62%) C. hold
Desmond Swayne, C.   27,980
Mike Plummer, LD   11,084
Janice Hurne, Lab.   4,666
Martin Lyon, UKIP   2,783
Janet Richards, Green   1,059
C. majority 16,896 (35.52%)
Notional 0.60% swing C. to LD
(2005: C. majority 16,183 (36.71%))

§NEWARK
E. 71,785 T. 51,228 (71.36%) C. hold
Patrick Mercer, C.   27,590
Dr Ian Campbell, Lab.   11,438
Pauline Jenkins, LD   10,246
Tom Irvine, UKIP   1,954
C. majority 16,152 (31.53%)
Notional 4.68% swing Lab. to C.
(2005: C. majority 10,077 (22.17%))

§NEWBURY
E. 83,411 T. 58,589 (70.24%) C. hold
Richard Benyon, C.   33,057
David Rendel, LD   20,809
Hannah Cooper, Lab.   2,505
David Black, UKIP   1,475
Adrian Hollister, Green   490
Brian Burgess, Ind.   158
David Yates, AD   95
C. majority 12,248 (20.90%)
Notional 7.24% swing LD to C.
(2005: C. majority 3,452 (6.42%))

NEWCASTLE-UNDER-LYME
E. 69,433 T. 43,191 (62.21%) Lab. hold
Paul Farrelly, Lab.   16,393
Robert Jenrick, C.   14,841
Nigel Jones, LD   8,466
David Nixon, UKIP   3,491
Lab. majority 1,552 (3.59%)
8.39% swing Lab. to C.
(2005: Lab. majority 8,108 (20.38%))

§NEWCASTLE UPON TYNE CENTRAL
E. 60,507 T. 34,157 (56.45%) Lab. hold
*Chinyelu Onwurah, Lab.   15,694
Gareth Kane, LD   8,228
Nick Holder, C.   6,611
Ken Booth, BNP   2,302
Martin Davies, UKIP   754
John Pearson, Green   568
Lab. majority 7,466 (21.86%)
Notional 0.60% swing Lab. to LD
(2005: Lab. majority 7,509 (23.07%))

§NEWCASTLE UPON TYNE EAST
E. 64,487 T. 37,840 (58.68%) Lab. hold
Nicholas Brown, Lab.   17,043
Wendy Taylor, LD   12,590
Dominic Llewellyn, C.   6,068
Alan Spence, BNP   1,342
Andrew Gray, Green   620
Martin Levy, Comm.   177
Lab. majority 4,453 (11.77%)
Notional 4.60% swing Lab. to LD
(2005: Lab. majority 6,987 (20.97%))

§NEWCASTLE UPON TYNE NORTH
E. 67,110 T. 43,946 (65.48%) Lab. hold
*Catherine McKinnell, Lab.   17,950
Ronald Beadle, LD   14,536
Stephen Parkinson, C.   7,966
Terry Gibson, BNP   1,890
Ian Proud, UKIP   1,285
Anna Heyman, Green   319
Lab. majority 3,414 (7.77%)
Notional 4.54% swing Lab. to LD
(2005: Lab. majority 6,878 (16.84%))

§NEWTON ABBOT
E. 69,343 T. 48,283 (69.63%) C. gain
*Anne-Marie Morris, C.   20,774
Richard Younger-Ross, LD   20,251
Patrick Canavan, Lab.   3,387
Jackie Hooper, UKIP   3,088
Corinne Lindsey, Green   701
Keith Sharp, Ind.   82
C. majority 523 (1.08%)
Notional 5.79% swing LD to C.
(2005: LD majority 4,830 (10.50%))

§NORFOLK MID
E. 74,260 T. 50,765 (68.36%) C. hold
*George Freeman, C.   25,123
David Newman, LD   11,267
Elizabeth Hughes, Lab.   8,857
Toby Coke, UKIP   2,800
Tim Birt, Green   1,457
Christine Kelly, BNP   1,261
C. majority 13,856 (27.29%)
Notional 0.02% swing C. to LD
(2005: C. majority 7,793 (16.29%))

§NORFOLK NORTH
E. 67,841 T. 49,661 (73.20%) LD hold
Norman Lamb, LD   27,554
Trevor Ivory, C.   15,928
Phil Harris, Lab.   2,896
Michael Baker, UKIP   2,680
Andrew Boswell, Green   508
Simon Mann, Ind.   95
LD majority 11,626 (23.41%)
Notional 3.06% swing C. to LD
(2005: LD majority 8,575 (17.28%))

§NORFOLK NORTH WEST
E. 73,207 T. 47,800 (65.29%) C. hold
Henry Bellingham, C.   25,916
William Summers, LD   11,106
Manish Sood, Lab.   6,353
John Gray, UKIP   1,841
David Fleming, BNP   1,839
Michael de Whalley, Green   745
C. majority 14,810 (30.98%)
Notional 2.09% swing C. to LD
(2005: C. majority 8,417 (18.34%))

§NORFOLK SOUTH
E. 76,165 T. 54,993 (72.20%) C. hold
Richard Bacon, C.   27,133
Jacky Howe, LD   16,193
Mick Castle, Lab.   7,252
Evan Heasley, UKIP   2,329
Helen Mitchell, BNP   1,086
Jo Willcott, Green   1,000
C. majority 10,940 (19.89%)
Notional 3.25% swing LD to C.
(2005: C. majority 6,719 (13.39%))

§NORFOLK SOUTH WEST
E. 74,298 T. 49,150 (66.15%) C. hold
*Elizabeth Truss, C.   23,753
Stephen Gordon, LD   10,613
Peter Smith, Lab.   9,119
Kay Hipsey, UKIP   3,061
Dennis Pearce, BNP   1,774
Lori Allen, Green   830
C. majority 13,140 (26.73%)
Notional 0.48% swing LD to C.
(2005: C. majority 6,817 (15.00%))

§NORMANTON, PONTEFRACT &
CASTLEFORD
E. 82,239 T. 46,239 (56.23%) Lab. hold
Yvette Cooper, Lab.   22,293
Nick Pickles, C.   11,314
Chris Rush, LD   7,585
Graham Thewlis-Hardy, BNP   3,864
Gareth Allen, Ind.   1,183
Lab. majority 10,979 (23.74%)
Notional 12.49% swing Lab. to C.
(2005: Lab. majority 20,608 (48.73%))

§NORTHAMPTON NORTH
E. 64,230 T. 40,271 (62.70%) C. gain
*Michael Ellis, C.   13,735
Sally Keeble, Lab.   11,799
Andrew Simpson, LD   11,250
Ray Beasley, BNP   1,316
Jim Macarthur, UKIP   1,238
Tony Lochmuller, Green   443
Eamonn Fitzpatrick, Ind.   334
Timothy Webb, Ch. P.   98
Malcolm Mildren, Ind.   58
C. majority 1,936 (4.81%)
Notional 6.90% swing Lab. to C.
(2005: Lab. majority 3,340 (9.00%))

§NORTHAMPTON SOUTH
E. 66,923 T. 38,978 (58.24%) C. gain
*Brian Binley, C.   15,917
Clyde Loakes, Lab.   9,913
Paul Varnsverry, LD   7,579
Tony Clarke, Ind.   2,242
Derek Clark, UKIP   1,897
Kevin Sills, Eng. Dem.   618
Julie Hawkins, Green   363
Dave Green, NSPS   325
Kevin Willsher, Ind.   65
Liam Costello, SMA   59
C. majority 6,004 (15.40%)
Notional 9.59% swing Lab. to C.
(2005: Lab. majority 1,445 (3.78%))

§NORTHAMPTONSHIRE SOUTH
E. 82,032 T. 59,890 (73.01%) C. hold
*Andrea Leadsom, C.   33,081
Scott Collins, LD   12,603
Matthew May, Lab.   10,380
Barry Mahoney, UKIP   2,406
Tony Tappy, Eng. Dem.   735
Marcus Rock, Green   685
C. majority 20,478 (34.19%)
Notional 0.12% swing C. to LD
(2005: C. majority 11,356 (22.85%))

§NORWICH NORTH
E. 65,258 T. 42,573 (65.24%) C. gain
Chloe Smith, C.   17,280
John Cook, Lab.   13,379
John Stephen, LD   7,783
Glenn Tingle, UKIP   1,878
Jessica Goldfinch, Green   1,245
Thomas Richardson, BNP   747
Bill Holden, Ind.   143
Andrew Holland, Ch. P.   118
C. majority 3,901 (9.16%)
Notional 12.88% swing Lab. to C.
(2005: Lab. majority 6,769 (16.60%))

§NORWICH SOUTH
E. 73,649 T. 47,551 (64.56%) LD gain
*Simon Wright, LD   13,960
Charles Clarke, Lab.   13,650
Antony Little, C.   10,902
Adrian Ramsay, Green   7,095
Steve Emmens, UKIP   1,145
Leonard Heather, BNP   697
Gabriel Polley, WRP   102
LD majority 310 (0.65%)
Notional 4.03% swing Lab. to LD
(2005: Lab. majority 3,023 (7.40%))

§NOTTINGHAM EAST
E. 58,707 T. 33,112 (56.40%)
                         Lab. (Co-op) hold
*Christopher Leslie, Lab. (Co-op) 15,022
Sam Boote, LD   8,053
Ewan Lamont, C.   7,846
Pat Wolfe, UKIP   1,138
Benjamin Hoare, Green   928
Parvaiz Sardar, Ch. P.   125
Lab. (Co-op) majority 6,969 (21.05%)
Notional 1.89% swing Lab. (Co-op) to LD
(2005: Lab. (Co-op) majority 7,083
(24.22%))

§NOTTINGHAM NORTH
E. 63,240 T. 34,285 (54.21%) Lab. hold
Graham Allen, Lab.   16,646
Martin Curtis, C.   8,508
Tim Ball, LD   5,849
Bob Brindley, BNP   1,944
Irenea Marriott, UKIP   1,338
Lab. majority 8,138 (23.74%)
Notional 8.65% swing Lab. to C.
(2005: Lab. majority 12,870 (41.04%))

§NOTTINGHAM SOUTH
E. 67,441 T. 40,789 (60.48%) Lab. hold
*Lilian Greenwood, Lab.   15,209
Rowena Holland, C.   13,437
Tony Sutton, LD   9,406
Tony Woodward, BNP   1,140
Ken Browne, UKIP   967
Matthew Butcher, Green   630
Lab. majority 1,772 (4.34%)
Notional 7.43% swing Lab. to C.
(2005: Lab. majority 6,665 (19.20%))

§NUNEATON
E. 67,837 T. 44,646 (65.81%) C. gain
*Marcus Jones, C.   18,536
Jayne Innes, Lab.   16,467
Christina Jebb, LD   6,846
Martyn Findley, BNP   2,797
C. majority 2,069 (4.63%)
Notional 7.19% swing Lab. to C.
(2005: Lab. majority 3,894 (9.74%))

§OLD BEXLEY & SIDCUP
E. 65,665 T. 45,492 (69.28%) C. hold
James Brokenshire, C.   24,625
Rick Everitt, Lab.   8,768
Duncan Borrowman, LD   6,996
John Brooks, BNP   2,132
David Coburn, UKIP   1,532
Elaine Cheeseman, Eng. Dem.   520
John Hemming-Clark, Save QM   393
Jonathan Rooks, Green   371
Napoleon Dynamite, Loony   155
C. majority 15,857 (34.86%)
Notional 6.43% swing Lab. to C.
(2005: C. majority 9,309 (22.00%))

§OLDHAM EAST & SADDLEWORTH
E. 72,765 T. 44,520 (61.18%) Lab. hold
Phil Woolas, Lab.   14,186
Elwyn Watkins, LD   14,083
Kashif Ali, C.   11,773
Alwyn Stott, BNP   2,546
David Bentley, UKIP   1,720
Gulzar Nazir, Ch. P.   212
Lab. majority 103 (0.23%)
Notional 5.08% swing Lab. to LD
(2005: Lab. majority 4,245 (10.39%))

§OLDHAM WEST & ROYTON
E. 72,651 T. 42,910 (59.06%) Lab. hold
Michael Meacher, Lab.   19,503
Kamran Ghafoor, C.   10,151
Mark Alcock, LD   8,193
David Joines, BNP   3,049
Helen Roberts, UKIP   1,387
Shahid Miah, Respect   627
Lab. majority 9,352 (21.79%)
Notional 2.74% swing Lab. to C.
(2005: Lab. majority 10,454 (27.13%))

§ORPINGTON
E. 67,732 T. 48,911 (72.21%) C. hold
*Joseph Johnson, C.   29,200
David McBride, LD   12,000
Stephen Morgan, Lab.   4,400
Mick Greenhough, UKIP   1,360
Tess Culnane, BNP   1,241
Tamara Galloway, Green   511
Chriss Snape, Eng. Dem.   199
C. majority 17,200 (35.17%)
Notional 12.19% swing LD to C.
(2005: C. majority 5,221 (10.79%))

§OXFORD EAST
E. 81,886 T. 51,651 (63.08%) Lab. hold
Andrew Smith, Lab.   21,938
Steve Goddard, LD   17,357
Edward Argar, C.   9,727
Sushila Dhall, Green   1,238
Julia Gasper, UKIP   1,202
David O'Sullivan, SEP   116
Roger Crawford, Parenting   73
Lab. majority 4,581 (8.87%)
Notional 4.07% swing LD to Lab.
(2005: Lab. majority 332 (0.73%))

§OXFORD WEST & ABINGDON
E. 86,458 T. 56,480 (65.33%) C. gain
*Nicola Blackwood, C.   23,906
Evan Harris, LD   23,730
Richard Stevens, Lab.   5,999
Paul Williams, UKIP   1,518
Chris Goodall, Green   1,184
Keith Mann, APP   143
C. majority 176 (0.31%)
Notional 6.87% swing LD to C.
(2005: LD majority 6,816 (13.43%))

PENDLE
E. 66,417 T. 45,045 (67.82%) C. gain
*Andrew Stephenson, C.   17,512
Gordon Prentice, Lab.   13,927
Afzal Anwar, LD   9,095
James Jackman, BNP   2,894
Graham Cannon, UKIP   1,476
Richard Masih, Ch. P.   141
C. majority 3,585 (7.96%)
6.63% swing Lab. to C.
(2005: Lab. majority 2,180 (5.30%))

§PENISTONE & STOCKSBRIDGE
E. 68,501 T. 46,516 (67.91%) Lab. hold
Angela Smith, Lab.   17,565
Spencer Pitfield, C.   14,516
Ian Cuthbertson, LD   9,800
Paul James, BNP   2,207
Grant French, UKIP   1,936
Paul McEnhill, Eng. Dem.   492
Lab. majority 3,049 (6.55%)
Notional 7.45% swing Lab. to C.
(2005: Lab. majority 8,617 (20.43%))

§PENRITH & THE BORDER
E. 64,548 T. 45,087 (69.85%) C. hold
*Rory Stewart, C.   24,071
Peter Thornton, LD   12,830
Barbara Cannon, Lab.   5,834
John Stanyer, UKIP   1,259
Chris Davidson, BNP   1,093
C. majority 11,241 (24.93%)
Notional 0.32% swing C. to LD
(2005: C. majority 10,795 (25.58%))

§PETERBOROUGH
E. 70,316 T. 44,927 (63.89%) C. hold
Stewart Jackson, C.   18,133
Ed Murphy, Lab.   13,272
Nick Sandford, LD   8,816
Frances Fox, UKIP   3,007
Rob King, Eng. Dem.   770
Fiona Radic, Green   523
John Swallow, Ind.   406
C. majority 4,861 (10.82%)
Notional 0.94% swing Lab. to C.
(2005: C. majority 4,005 (8.93%))

§PLYMOUTH MOOR VIEW
E. 67,261 T. 41,526 (61.74%) Lab. hold
Alison Seabeck, Lab.   15,433
Matthew Groves, C.   13,845
Stuart Bonar, LD   7,016
Bill Wakeham, UKIP   3,188
Roy Cook, BNP   1,438
Wendy Miller, Green   398
David Marchesi, Soc. Lab.   208
Lab. majority 1,588 (3.82%)
Notional 7.77% swing Lab. to C.
(2005: Lab. majority 7,740 (19.37%))

§PLYMOUTH SUTTON &
DEVONPORT
E. 71,035 T. 43,894 (61.79%) C. gain
*Oliver Colville, C.   15,050
Linda Gilroy, Lab. (Co-op)   13,901
Judy Evans, LD   10,829
Andrew Leigh, UKIP   2,854
Tony Brown, Green   904
Brian Gerrish, Ind.   233
Robert Hawkins, Soc. Lab.   123
C. majority 1,149 (2.62%)
Notional 6.86% swing Lab. (Co-op) to C.
(2005: Lab. (Co-op) majority 4,472
(11.11%))

§POOLE
E. 64,661 T. 47,436 (73.36%) C. hold
Robert Syms, C.   22,532
Philip Eades, LD   14,991
Jason Sanderson, Lab.   6,041
Nick Wellstead, UKIP   2,507
David Holmes, BNP   1,188
Ian Northover, Ind.   177
C. majority 7,541 (15.90%)
Notional 0.79% swing LD to C.
(2005: C. majority 6,035 (14.32%))

§POPLAR & LIMEHOUSE
E. 74,956 T. 46,700 (62.30%) Lab. hold
Jim Fitzpatrick, Lab.   18,679
Tim Archer, C.   12,649
George Galloway, Respect   8,160
Jonathan Fryer, LD   5,209
Wayne Lochner, UKIP   565
Andrew Osborne, Eng. Dem.   470
Chris Smith, Green   449
Kabir Mahmud, Ind.   293
Mohammed Hoque, Ind.   167
Jim Thornton, Ind.   59
Lab. majority 6,030 (12.91%)
Notional 1.04% swing C. to Lab.
(2005: Lab. majority 3,823 (10.84%))

§PORTSMOUTH NORTH
E. 70,329 T. 44,118 (62.73%) C. gain
*Penny Mordaunt, C.   19,533
Sarah McCarthy-Fry, Lab.
  (Co-op)   12,244
Darren Sanders, LD   8,874
Mike Fitzgerald, UKIP   1,812
David Knight, Eng. Dem.   1,040
Iain Maclennan, Green   461
Mick Tosh, TUSC   154
C. majority 7,289 (16.52%)
Notional 8.64% swing Lab. (Co-op) to C.
(2005: Lab. (Co-op) majority 315 (0.77%))

§PORTSMOUTH SOUTH
E. 70,242 T. 41,264 (58.75%) LD hold
Mike Hancock, LD   18,921
Flick Drummond, C.   13,721
John Ferrett, Lab.   5,640
Christopher Martin, UKIP   876
Geoff Crompton, BNP   873
Tim Dawes, Green   716
Ian DuCane, Eng. Dem.   400
Les Cummings, J & AC   117
LD majority 5,200 (12.60%)
Notional 2.30% swing C. to LD
(2005: LD majority 2,955 (8.00%))

§PRESTON
E. 62,460 T. 32,505 (52.04%)
                        Lab. (Co-op) hold
Mark Hendrick, Lab. (Co-op)   15,668
Mark Jewell, LD   7,935
Nerissa Warner-O'Neill, C.   7,060
Richard Muirhead, UKIP   1,462
George Ambroze, Ch. P.   272
Krishna Tayya, Ind.   108
Lab. (Co-op) majority 7,733 (23.79%)
Notional 2.50% swing Lab. (Co-op) to LD
(2005: Lab. (Co-op) majority 8,338
(27.67%))

§PUDSEY
E. 69,257 T. 49,083 (70.87%) C. gain
*Stuart Andrew, C.   18,874
Jamie Hanley, Lab.   17,215
Jamie Matthews, LD   10,224
Ian Gibson, BNP   1,549
David Dews, UKIP   1,221
C. majority 1,659 (3.38%)
Notional 7.56% swing Lab. to C.
(2005: Lab. majority 5,204 (11.74%))

§PUTNEY
E. 63,370 T. 40,785 (64.36%) C. hold
Justine Greening, C.   21,223
Stuart King, Lab.   11,170
James Sandbach, LD   6,907
Bruce Mackenzie, Green   591
Peter Darby, BNP   459
Hugo Wareham, UKIP   435
C. majority 10,053 (24.65%)
Notional 9.92% swing Lab. to C.
(2005: C. majority 1,723 (4.80%))

§RAYLEIGH & WICKFORD
E. 75,905 T. 52,343 (68.96%) C. hold
Mark Francois, C.   30,257
Susan Gaszczak, LD   7,919
Michael Le-Surf, Lab.   7,577
John Hayter, Eng. Dem.   2,219
Tino Callaghan, UKIP   2,211
Anthony Evennett, BNP   2,160
C. majority 22,338 (42.68%)
Notional 2.13% swing LD to C.
(2005: C. majority 12,983 (27.37%))

§READING EAST
E. 74,922 T. 49,985 (66.72%) C. hold
Rob Wilson, C.   21,269
Gareth Epps, LD   13,664
Anneliese Dodds, Lab.   12,729
Adrian Pitfield, UKIP   1,086
Rob White, Green   1,069
Joan Lloyd, Ind.   111
Michael Turberville, Ind.   57
C. majority 7,605 (15.21%)
Notional 1.97% swing LD to C.
(2005: C. majority 739 (1.71%))

§READING WEST
E. 72,118 T. 47,530 (65.91%) C. gain
*Alok Sharma, C.   20,523
Naz Sarkar, Lab.   14,519
Daisy Benson, LD   9,546
Bruce Hay, UKIP   1,508
Howard Thomas, CSP   852
Adrian Windisch, Green   582
C. majority 6,004 (12.63%)
Notional 12.05% swing Lab. to C.
(2005: Lab. majority 4,931 (11.47%))

REDCAR
E. 67,125 T. 41,963 (62.51%) LD gain
*Ian Swales, LD   18,955
Vera Baird, Lab.   13,741
Steve Mastin, C.   5,790
Martin Bulmer, UKIP   1,875
Kevin Broughton, BNP   1,475
Hannah Walter, TUSC   127
LD majority 5,214 (12.43%)
21.80% swing Lab. to LD
(2005: Lab. majority 12,116 (31.18%))

§REDDITCH
E. 68,550 T. 44,018 (64.21%) C. gain
*Karen Lumley, C.   19,138
Jacqui Smith, Lab.   13,317
Nicholas Lane, LD   7,750
Anne Davis, UKIP   1,497
Andy Ingram, BNP   1,394
Kevin White, Green   393
Vincent Schittone, Eng. Dem.   255
Scott Beverley, Ch. P.   101
Paul Swansborough, Ind.   100
Derek Fletcher, Nobody   73
C. majority 5,821 (13.22%)
Notional 9.21% swing Lab. to C.
(2005: Lab. majority 2,163 (5.20%))

§REIGATE
E. 71,604   T. 49,978 (69.80%)   C. hold

Crispin Blunt, C.	26,688
Jane Kulka, LD	13,097
Robert Hull, Lab.	5,672
Joe Fox, UKIP	2,089
Keith Brown, BNP	1,345
Jonathan Essex, Green	1,087

C. majority 13,591 (27.19%)
Notional 0.89% swing LD to C.
(2005: C. majority 11,093 (25.41%))

§RIBBLE VALLEY
E. 78,068   T. 52,287 (66.98%)   C. hold

Nigel Evans, C.	26,298
Paul Foster, Lab.	11,529
Allan Knox, LD	10,732
Stephen Rush, UKIP	3,496
Tony Johnson, ND	232

C. majority 14,769 (28.25%)
Notional 6.58% swing Lab. to C.
(2005: C. majority 6,953 (15.09%))

§RICHMOND (YORKS)
E. 79,478   T. 53,412 (67.20%)   C. hold

William Hague, C.	33,541
Lawrence Meredith, LD	10,205
Eileen Driver, Lab.	8,150
Leslie Rowe, Green	1,516

C. majority 23,336 (43.69%)
Notional 0.64% swing LD to C.
(2005: C. majority 19,450 (38.73%))

§RICHMOND PARK
E. 77,060   T. 59,268 (76.91%)   C. gain

*Zac Goldsmith, C.	29,461
Susan Kramer, LD	25,370
Eleanor Tunnicliffe, Lab.	2,979
Peter Dul, UKIP	669
James Page, Green	572
Susan May, CPA	133
Charles Hill, Ind.	84

C. majority 4,091 (6.90%)
Notional 7.00% swing LD to C.
(2005: LD majority 3,613 (7.09%))

§ROCHDALE
E. 78,952   T. 45,907 (58.15%) Lab. hold

*Simon Danczuk, Lab.	16,699
Paul Rowen, LD	15,810
Mudasir Dean, C.	8,305
Chris Jackson, NF	2,236
Colin Denby, UKIP	1,999
Mohammed Salim, IZB	545
John Whitehead, Ind.	313

Lab. majority 889 (1.94%)
Notional 0.79% swing LD to Lab.
(2005: Lab. majority 149 (0.35%))

§ROCHESTER & STROOD
E. 73,882   T. 47,971 (64.93%)   C. hold

*Mark Reckless, C.	23,604
Teresa Murray, Lab.	13,651
Geoffrey Juby, LD	7,800
Ron Sands, Eng. Dem.	2,182
Simon Marchant, Green	734

C. majority 9,953 (20.75%)
Notional 9.81% swing Lab. to C.
(2005: C. majority 503 (1.14%))

§ROCHFORD & SOUTHEND EAST
E. 71,080   T. 41,631 (58.57%)   C. hold

James Duddridge, C.	19,509
Kevin Bonavia, Lab.	8,459
Graham Longley, LD	8,084
James Moyies, UKIP	2,405
Geoff Strobridge, BNP	1,856
Andrew Vaughan, Green	707
Anthony Chytry, Ind.	611

C. majority 11,050 (26.54%)
Notional 6.37% swing Lab. to C.
(2005: C. majority 5,307 (13.80%))

§ROMFORD
E. 71,193   T. 46,481 (65.29%)   C. hold

Andrew Rosindell, C.	26,031
Rachel Voller, Lab.	9,077
Helen Duffett, LD	5,572
Robert Bailey, BNP	2,438
Gerard Batten, UKIP	2,050
Dr Peter Thorogood, Eng. Dem.	603
Gary Haines, Green	447
Philip Hyde, Ind.	151
David Sturman, Ind.	112

C. majority 16,954 (36.48%)
Notional 3.94% swing Lab. to C.
(2005: C. majority 12,120 (28.59%))

§ROMSEY & SOUTHAMPTON NORTH
E. 66,901   T. 48,939 (73.15%)   C. gain

*Caroline Nokes, C.	24,345
Sandra Gidley, LD	20,189
Aktar Beg, Lab.	3,116
John Meropoulos, UKIP	1,289

C. majority 4,156 (8.49%)
Notional 4.48% swing LD to C.
(2005: LD majority 204 (0.46%))

§ROSSENDALE & DARWEN
E. 73,003   T. 47,128 (64.56%)   C. gain

*Jake Berry, C.	19,691
Janet Anderson, Lab.	15,198
Robert Sheffield, LD	8,541
David Duthie, UKIP	1,617
Kevin Bryan, NF	1,062
Michael Johnson, Eng. Dem.	663
Tony Melia, Impact	243
Mike Sivieri, Ind.	113

C. majority 4,493 (9.53%)
Notional 8.94% swing Lab. to C.
(2005: Lab. majority 3,696 (8.35%))

§ROTHER VALLEY
E. 72,841   T. 46,758 (64.19%) Lab. hold

Kevin Barron, Lab.	19,147
Lynda Donaldson, C.	13,281
Wesley Paxton, LD	8,111
Will Blair, BNP	3,606
Tina Dowdall, UKIP	2,613

Lab. majority 5,866 (12.55%)
Notional 7.96% swing Lab. to C.
(2005: Lab. majority 11,558 (28.47%))

§ROTHERHAM
E. 63,565   T. 37,506 (59.00%) Lab. hold

Denis MacShane, Lab.	16,741
Jackie Whiteley, C.	6,279
Rebecca Taylor, LD	5,994
Marlene Guest, BNP	3,906
Peter Thirlwall, Ind.	2,366
Caven Vines, UKIP	2,220

Lab. majority 10,462 (27.89%)
Notional 8.27% swing Lab. to C.
(2005: Lab. majority 13,865 (41.33%))

§RUGBY
E. 68,914   T. 47,468 (68.88%)   C. gain

*Mark Pawsey, C.	20,901
Andy King, Lab.	14,901
Jerry Roodhouse, LD	9,434
Mark Badrick, BNP	1,375
Roy Sandison, Green	451
Barry Milford, UKIP	406

C. majority 6,000 (12.64%)
Notional 8.92% swing Lab. to C.
(2005: Lab. majority 2,397 (5.20%))

§RUISLIP, NORTHWOOD & PINNER
E. 70,873   T. 50,205 (70.84%)   C. hold

Nick Hurd, C.	28,866
Anita McDonald, Lab.	9,806
Thomas Papworth, LD	8,345
Jason Pontey, UKIP	1,351
Ian Edward, NF	899
Graham Lee, Green	740
Ruby Akhtar, Ch. P.	198

C. majority 19,060 (37.96%)
Notional 3.63% swing Lab. to C.
(2005: C. majority 13,274 (30.71%))

RUNNYMEDE & WEYBRIDGE
E. 72,566   T. 48,150 (66.35%)   C. hold

Philip Hammond, C.	26,915
Andrew Falconer, LD	10,406
Paul Greenwood, Lab.	6,446
Toby Micklethwait, UKIP	3,146
Jenny Gould, Green	696
David Sammons, Ind.	541

C. majority 16,509 (34.29%)
0.38% swing LD to C.
(2005: C. majority 12,349 (28.37%))

§RUSHCLIFFE
E. 72,955   T. 53,687 (73.59%)   C. hold

Kenneth Clarke, C.	27,470
Karrar Khan, LD	11,659
Andrew Clayworth, Lab.	11,128
Matthew Faithfull, UKIP	2,179
Richard Mallender, Green	1,251

C. majority 15,811 (29.45%)
Notional 0.63% swing C. to LD
(2005: C. majority 9,932 (20.60%))

§RUTLAND & MELTON
E. 77,185   T. 55,220 (71.54%)   C. hold

Alan Duncan, C.	28,228
Grahame Hudson, LD	14,228
John Morgan, Lab.	7,893
Peter Baker, UKIP	2,526
Keith Addison, BNP	1,757
Leigh Higgins, Ind.	588

C. majority 14,000 (25.35%)
Notional 3.65% swing C. to LD
(2005: C. majority 12,998 (26.29%))

§SAFFRON WALDEN
E. 76,035   T. 54,369 (71.51%)   C. hold

Sir Alan Haselhurst, C.	30,155
Peter Wilcock, LD	14,913
Barbara Light, Lab.	5,288
Roger Lord, UKIP	2,228
Christine Mitchell, BNP	1,050
Reza Hossain, Green	735

C. majority 15,242 (28.03%)
Notional 3.39% swing LD to C.
(2005: C. majority 10,483 (21.25%))

§ST ALBANS
E. 70,058 T. 52,835 (75.42%) C. hold
Anne Main, C. 21,533
Sandy Walkington, LD 19,228
Roma Mills, Lab. 9,288
John Stocker, UKIP 2,028
Jack Easton, Green 758
C. majority 2,305 (4.36%)
Notional 3.74% swing C. to LD
(2005: C. majority 1,334 (2.94%))

§ST AUSTELL & NEWQUAY
E. 76,346 T. 47,238 (61.87%) LD hold
*Stephen Gilbert, LD 20,189
Caroline Righton, C. 18,877
Lee Jameson, Lab. 3,386
Dick Cole, Meb. Ker. 2,007
Clive Medway, UKIP 1,757
James Fitton, BNP 1,022
LD majority 1,312 (2.78%)
Notional 4.83% swing LD to C.
(2005: LD majority 5,723 (12.44%))

§ST HELENS NORTH
E. 74,984 T. 44,556 (59.42%) Lab. hold
Dave Watts, Lab. 23,041
Paul Greenall, C. 9,940
John Beirne, LD 8,992
Gary Robinson, UKIP 2,100
Stephen Whatham, Soc. Lab. 483
Lab. majority 13,101 (29.40%)
Notional 4.55% swing Lab. to C.
(2005: Lab. majority 15,265 (36.49%))

§ST HELENS SOUTH & WHISTON
E. 77,975 T. 46,081 (59.10%) Lab. hold
Shaun Woodward, Lab. 24,364
Brian Spencer, LD 10,242
Val Allen, C. 8,209
James Winstanley, BNP 2,040
John Sumner, UKIP 1,226
Lab. majority 14,122 (30.65%)
Notional 1.94% swing LD to Lab.
(2005: Lab. majority 10,987 (26.76%))

§ST IVES
E. 66,930 T. 45,921 (68.61%) LD hold
Andrew George, LD 19,619
Derek Thomas, C. 17,900
Philippa Latimer, Lab. 3,751
Mick Faulkner, UKIP 2,560
Tim Andrewes, Green 1,308
Jonathan Rogers, Cornish D. 396
Simon Reed, Meb. Ker. 387
LD majority 1,719 (3.74%)
Notional 10.39% swing LD to C.
(2005: LD majority 10,711 (24.52%))

§SALFORD & ECCLES
E. 75,482 T. 41,533 (55.02%) Lab. hold
Hazel Blears, Lab. 16,655
Norman Owen, LD 10,930
Matthew Sephton, C. 8,497
Tina Wingfield, BNP 2,632
Duran O'Dwyer, UKIP 1,084
David Henry, TUSC 730
Stephen Morris, Eng. Dem. 621
Richard Carvath, Ind. 384
Lab. majority 5,725 (13.78%)
Notional 9.43% swing Lab. to LD
(2005: Lab. majority 10,707 (32.64%))

§SALISBURY
E. 67,429 T. 48,481 (71.90%) C. hold
*John Glen, C. 23,859
Nick Radford, LD 17,893
Tom Gann, Lab. 3,690
Frances Howard, UKIP 1,392
Sean Witheridge, BNP 765
Nick Startin, Green 506
King Arthur, Ind. 257
John Holme, Ind. 119
C. majority 5,966 (12.31%)
Notional 3.60% swing C. to LD
(2005: C. majority 8,860 (19.50%))

SCARBOROUGH & WHITBY
E. 75,443 T. 49,282 (65.32%) C. hold
Robert Goodwill, C. 21,108
Annajoy David, Lab. 12,978
Tania Exley-Moore, LD 11,093
Michael James, UKIP 1,484
Trisha Scott, BNP 1,445
Dilys Cluer, Green 734
Peter Popple, Ind. 329
Juliet Boddington, Green Soc. 111
C. majority 8,130 (16.50%)
6.92% swing Lab. to C.
(2005: C. majority 1,245 (2.65%))

§SCUNTHORPE
E. 63,089 T. 37,034 (58.70%) Lab. hold
*Nic Dakin, Lab. 14,640
Caroline Johnson, C. 12,091
Neil Poole, LD 6,774
Jane Collins, UKIP 1,686
Douglas Ward, BNP 1,447
Natalie Hurst, Green 396
Lab. majority 2,549 (6.88%)
Notional 9.18% swing Lab. to C.
(2005: Lab. majority 8,638 (25.24%))

§SEDGEFIELD
E. 64,727 T. 40,222 (62.14%) Lab. hold
Phil Wilson, Lab. 18,141
Neil Mahapatra, C. 9,445
Alan Thompson, LD 8,033
Mark Walker, BNP 2,075
Brian Gregory, UKIP 1,479
Paul Gittins, Ind. 1,049
Lab. majority 8,696 (21.62%)
Notional 11.60% swing Lab. to C.
(2005: Lab. majority 18,198 (44.82%))

§SEFTON CENTRAL
E. 67,512 T. 48,463 (71.78%) Lab. hold
*Bill Esterson, Lab. 20,307
Debi Jones, C. 16,445
Richard Clein, LD 9,656
Peter Harper, UKIP 2,055
Lab. majority 3,862 (7.97%)
Notional 2.03% swing Lab. to C.
(2005: Lab. majority 4,950 (12.02%))

§SELBY & AINSTY
E. 72,789 T. 51,728 (71.07%) C. hold
*Nigel Adams, C. 25,562
Jan Marshall, Lab. 13,297
Tom Holvey, LD 9,180
Darren Haley, UKIP 1,635
Duncan Lorriman, BNP 1,377
Graham Michael, Eng. Dem. 677
C. majority 12,265 (23.71%)
Notional 9.70% swing Lab. to C.
(2005: C. majority 2,060 (4.31%))

§SEVENOAKS
E. 69,591 T. 49,408 (71.00%) C. hold
Michael Fallon, C. 28,076
Alan Bullion, LD 10,561
Gareth Siddorn, Lab. 6,541
Chris Heath, UKIP 1,782
Paul Golding, BNP 1,384
Louise Uncles, Eng. Dem. 806
Mark Ellis, Ind. 258
C. majority 17,515 (35.45%)
Notional 3.13% swing LD to C.
(2005: C. majority 13,060 (29.19%))

§SHEFFIELD BRIGHTSIDE &
HILLSBOROUGH
E. 68,186 T. 38,914 (57.07%) Lab. hold
David Blunkett, Lab. 21,400
Jonathan Harston, LD 7,768
John Sharp, C. 4,468
John Sheldon, BNP 3,026
Pat Sullivan, UKIP 1,596
Maxine Bowler, TUSC 656
Lab. majority 13,632 (35.03%)
Notional 10.77% swing Lab. to LD
(2005: Lab. majority 18,801 (56.58%))

§SHEFFIELD CENTRAL
E. 69,519 T. 41,468 (59.65%) Lab. hold
*Paul Blomfield, Lab. 17,138
Paul Scriven, LD 16,973
Andrew Lee, C. 4,206
Jillian Creasy, Green 1,556
Tracey Smith, BNP 903
Jeffrey Shaw, UKIP 652
Rod Rodgers, Ind. 40
Lab. majority 165 (0.40%)
Notional 7.36% swing Lab. to LD
(2005: Lab. majority 5,025 (15.12%))

§SHEFFIELD HALLAM
E. 69,378 T. 51,135 (73.70%) LD hold
Nick Clegg, LD 27,324
Nicola Bates, C. 12,040
Jack Scott, Lab. 8,228
Nigel James, UKIP 1,195
Steve Barnard, Green 919
David Wildgoose, Eng. Dem. 586
Martin Fitzpatrick, Ind. 429
Ray Green, Ch. P. 250
Mark Adshead, Loony 164
LD majority 15,284 (29.89%)
Notional 6.86% swing C. to LD
(2005: LD majority 7,416 (16.17%))

§SHEFFIELD HEELEY
E. 65,869 T. 40,871 (62.05%) Lab. hold
Meg Munn, Lab. 17,409
Simon Clement-Jones, LD 11,602
Anne Crampton, C. 7,081
John Beatson, BNP 2,260
Charlotte Arnott, UKIP 1,530
Gareth Roberts, Green 989
Lab. majority 5,807 (14.21%)
Notional 9.23% swing Lab. to LD
(2005: Lab. majority 12,340 (32.67%))

§SHEFFIELD SOUTH EAST
E. 67,284 T. 41,408 (61.54%) Lab. hold
Clive Betts, Lab. 20,169
Gail Smith, LD 9,664
Nigel Bonson, C. 7,202
Christopher Hartigan, BNP 2,345
Jonathan Arnott, UKIP 1,889
Steven Andrew, Comm. Brit. 139
Lab. majority 10,505 (25.37%)
Notional 9.00% swing Lab. to LD
(2005: Lab. majority 15,843 (43.36%))

§SHERWOOD
E. 71,043   T. 48,954 (68.91%)   C. gain
*Mark Spencer, C.   19,211
Emilie Oldknow, Lab.   18,997
Kevin Moore, LD   7,283
James North, BNP   1,754
Margot Parker, UKIP   1,490
Russ Swan, Ind.   219
C. majority 214 (0.44%)
Notional 8.17% swing Lab. to C.
(2005: Lab. majority 6,869 (15.90%))

§SHIPLEY
E. 67,689   T. 49,427 (73.02%)   C. hold
Philip Davies, C.   24,002
Susan Hinchcliffe, Lab.   14,058
John Harris, LD   9,890
Kevin Warnes, Green   1,477
C. majority 9,944 (20.12%)
Notional 9.58% swing Lab. to C.
(2005: C. majority 450 (0.97%))

SHREWSBURY & ATCHAM
E. 75,438   T. 53,045 (70.32%)   C. hold
Daniel Kawczynski, C.   23,313
Charles West, LD   15,369
Jon Tandy, Lab.   10,915
Peter Lewis, UKIP   1,627
James Whittall, BNP   1,168
Alan Whittaker, Green   565
James Gollings, Impact   88
C. majority 7,944 (14.98%)
0.06% swing LD to C.
(2005: C. majority 1,808 (3.59%))

SHROPSHIRE NORTH
E. 78,926   T. 51,869 (65.72%)   C. hold
Owen Paterson, C.   26,692
Ian Croll, LD   10,864
Ian McLaughlan, Lab.   9,406
Sandra List, UKIP   2,432
Phil Reddall, BNP   1,667
Steve Boulding, Green   808
C. majority 15,828 (30.52%)
0.33% swing LD to C.
(2005: C. majority 11,020 (23.69%))

§SITTINGBOURNE & SHEPPEY
E. 75,354   T. 48,578 (64.47%)   C. hold
*Gordon Henderson, C.   24,313
Angela Harrison, Lab.   11,930
Keith Nevols, LD   7,943
Ian Davison, UKIP   2,610
Lawrence Tames, BNP   1,305
Mad Mike Young, Loony   319
David Cassidy, Ind.   158
C. majority 12,383 (25.49%)
Notional 12.72% swing Lab. to C.
(2005: C. majority 22 (0.05%))

§SKIPTON & RIPON
E. 77,381   T. 54,724 (70.72%)   C. hold
*Julian Smith, C.   27,685
Helen Flynn, LD   17,735
Claire Hazelgrove, Lab.   5,498
Rodney Mills, UKIP   1,909
Bernard Allen, BNP   1,403
Roger Bell, Ind.   315
Dylan Gilligan, Youth   95
Robert Leakey, Currency   84
C. majority 9,950 (18.18%)
Notional 2.63% swing C. to LD
(2005: C. majority 11,596 (23.43%))

§SLEAFORD & NORTH HYKEHAM
E. 85,550   T. 59,530 (69.59%)   C. hold
*Stephen Phillips, C.   30,719
David Harding-Price, LD   10,814
James Normington, Lab.   10,051
Marianne Overton, Lincs Ind.   3,806
Rodger Doughty, UKIP   2,163
Mike Clayton, BNP   1,977
C. majority 19,905 (33.44%)
Notional 0.46% swing LD to C.
(2005: C. majority 12,687 (24.15%))

§SLOUGH
E. 77,068   T. 47,742 (61.95%)   Lab. hold
Fiona Mactaggart, Lab.   21,884
Diana Coad, C.   16,361
Chris Tucker, LD   6,943
Peter Mason-Apps, UKIP   1,517
Miriam Kennet, Green   542
Sunil Chaudhary, Ch. P.   495
Lab. majority 5,523 (11.57%)
Notional 4.14% swing Lab. to C.
(2005: Lab. majority 7,924 (19.86%))

§SOLIHULL
E. 77,863   T. 55,129 (70.80%)   LD gain
Lorely Burt, LD   23,635
Maggie Throup, C.   23,460
Sarah-Jayne Merrill, Lab.   4,891
Andrew Terry, BNP   1,624
John Ison, UKIP   1,200
Neill Watts, RA   319
LD majority 175 (0.32%)
Notional 0.28% swing C. to LD
(2005: C. majority 124 (0.25%))

§SOMERSET NORTH
E. 77,304   T. 57,941 (74.95%)   C. hold
Dr Liam Fox, C.   28,549
Brian Mathew, LD   20,687
Steven Parry-Hearn, Lab.   6,448
Susan Taylor, UKIP   2,257
C. majority 7,862 (13.57%)
Notional 0.98% swing LD to C.
(2005: C. majority 6,007 (11.61%))

§SOMERSET NORTH EAST
E. 67,412   T. 51,203 (75.96%)   C. hold
*Jacob Rees-Mogg, C.   21,130
Dan Norris, Lab.   16,216
Gail Coleshill, LD   11,433
Peter Sandell, UKIP   1,754
Michael Jay, Green   670
C. majority 4,914 (9.60%)
Notional 4.57% swing Lab. to C.
(2005: C. majority 212 (0.46%))

§SOMERTON & FROME
E. 81,548   T. 60,612 (74.33%)   LD hold
David Heath, LD   28,793
Annunziata Rees-Mogg, C.   26,976
David Oakensen, Lab.   2,675
Barry Harding, UKIP   1,932
Niall Warry, Leave EU   236
LD majority 1,817 (3.00%)
Notional 0.94% swing C. to LD
(2005: LD majority 595 (1.12%))

§SOUTH HOLLAND & THE DEEPINGS
E. 76,243   T. 50,188 (65.83%)   C. hold
John Hayes, C.   29,639
Jennifer Conroy, LD   7,759
Gareth Gould, Lab.   7,024
Richard Fairman, UKIP   3,246
Roy Harban, BNP   1,796
Ashley Baxter, Green   724
C. majority 21,880 (43.60%)
Notional 0.27% swing C. to LD
(2005: C. majority 15,127 (32.48%))

§SOUTH RIBBLE
E. 75,822   T. 51,458 (67.87%)   C. gain
*Lorraine Fullbrook, C.   23,396
David Borrow, Lab.   17,842
Peter Fisher, LD   7,271
David Duxbury, UKIP   1,895
Rosalind Gauci, BNP   1,054
C. majority 5,554 (10.79%)
Notional 8.11% swing Lab. to C.
(2005: Lab. majority 2,528 (5.42%))

§SOUTH SHIELDS
E. 63,294   T. 36,518 (57.70%)   Lab. hold
David Miliband, Lab.   18,995
Karen Allen, C.   7,886
Stephen Psallidas, LD   5,189
Donna Watson, BNP   2,382
Shirley Ford, Green   762
Siamak Kaikavoosi, Ind.   729
Victor Thompson, Ind.   316
Sam Navabi, Ind.   168
Roger Nettleship, Anti-War   91
Lab. majority 11,109 (30.42%)
Notional 6.36% swing Lab. to C.
(2005: Lab. majority 13,368 (41.61%))

§SOUTHAMPTON ITCHEN
E. 74,532   T. 44,412 (59.59%)   Lab. hold
John Denham, Lab.   16,326
Royston Smith, C.   16,134
David Goodall, LD   9,256
Alan Kebbell, UKIP   1,928
John Spottiswoode, Green   600
Tim Cutter, TUSC   168
Lab. majority 192 (0.43%)
Notional 10.28% swing Lab. to C.
(2005: Lab. majority 8,479 (21.00%))

§SOUTHAMPTON TEST
E. 71,931   T. 44,187 (61.43%)   Lab. hold
Alan Whitehead, Lab.   17,001
Jeremy Moulton, C.   14,588
David Callaghan, LD   9,865
Pearline Hingston, UKIP   1,726
Chris Bluemel, Green   881
Charles Sanderson, Ind.   126
Lab. majority 2,413 (5.46%)
Notional 6.86% swing Lab. to C.
(2005: Lab. majority 7,817 (19.17%))

§SOUTHEND WEST
E. 66,527   T. 43,606 (65.55%)   C. hold
David Amess, C.   20,086
Peter Welch, LD   12,816
Thomas Flynn, Lab.   5,850
Garry Cockrill, UKIP   1,714
Tony Gladwin, BNP   1,333
Barry Bolton, Green   644
Dr Vel, Ind.   617
Terry Phillips, Eng. Dem.   546
C. majority 7,270 (16.67%)
Notional 2.77% swing C. to LD
(2005: C. majority 9,008 (22.20%))

SOUTHPORT
E. 67,202   T. 43,757 (65.11%)   LD hold
John Pugh, LD   21,707
Brenda Porter, C.   15,683
Jim Conalty, Lab.   4,116
Terry Durrance, UKIP   2,251
LD majority 6,024 (13.77%)
2.23% swing C. to LD
(2005: LD majority 3,838 (9.32%))

SPELTHORNE
E. 70,479 T. 47,304 (67.12%) C. hold
*Kwasi Kwarteng, C.   22,261
Mark Chapman, LD   12,242
Adam Tyler-Moore, Lab.   7,789
Christopher Browne, UKIP   4,009
Ian Swinglehurst, Ind.   314
Rod Littlewood, Best   244
Paul Couchman, TUSC   176
John Gore, CIP   167
Grahame Leon-Smith, Ind. Fed.   102
C. majority 10,019 (21.18%)
6.11% swing C. to LD
(2005: C. majority 9,936 (23.20%))

§STAFFORD
E. 70,587 T. 50,239 (71.17%) C. gain
*Jeremy Lefroy, C.   22,047
David Kidney, Lab.   16,587
Barry Stamp, LD   8,211
Roy Goode, UKIP   1,727
Roland Hynd, BNP   1,103
Mike Shone, Green   564
C. majority 5,460 (10.87%)
Notional 7.44% swing Lab. to C.
(2005: Lab. majority 1,852 (4.01%))

§STAFFORDSHIRE MOORLANDS
E. 62,071 T. 43,815 (70.59%) C. hold
*Karen Bradley, C.   19,793
Charlotte Atkins, Lab.   13,104
Henry Jebb, LD   7,338
Steve Povey, UKIP   3,580
C. majority 6,689 (15.27%)
Notional 5.71% swing Lab. to C.
(2005: C. majority 1,618 (3.86%))

§STAFFORDSHIRE SOUTH
E. 73,390 T. 50,440 (68.73%) C. hold
*Gavin Williamson, C.   26,834
Kevin McElduff, Lab.   10,244
Sarah Fellows, LD   8,427
Mike Nattrass, UKIP   2,753
David Bradnock, BNP   1,928
Andrew Morris, Ind.   254
C. majority 16,590 (32.89%)
Notional 1.12% swing Lab. to C.
(2005: C. majority 8,346 (30.65%))

§STALYBRIDGE & HYDE
E. 69,037 T. 40,879 (59.21%) Lab. hold
*Jonathan Reynolds, Lab.   16,189
Rob Adlard, C.   13,445
John Potter, LD   6,965
Anthony Jones, BNP   2,259
John Cooke, UKIP   1,342
Ruth Bergan, Green   679
Lab. majority 2,744 (6.71%)
Notional 8.47% swing Lab. to C.
(2005: Lab. majority 8,455 (23.64%))

§STEVENAGE
E. 68,937 T. 44,651 (64.77%) C. gain
*Stephen McPartland, C.   18,491
Sharon Taylor, Lab. (Co-op)   14,913
Julia Davies, LD   7,432
Marion Mason, UKIP   2,004
Andrew Green, BNP   1,007
Charles Vickers, Eng. Dem.   366
Stephen Phillips, No Vote   327
David Cox, Ind.   80
Andrew Ralph, YRDPL   31
C. majority 3,578 (8.01%)
Notional 8.03% swing Lab. (Co-op) to C.
(2005: Lab. (Co-op) majority 3,288
(8.05%))

§STOCKPORT
E. 63,525 T. 39,128 (61.59%) Lab. hold
Ann Coffey, Lab.   16,697
Stephen Holland, C.   9,913
Stuart Bodsworth, LD   9,778
Duncan Warner, BNP   1,201
Mike Kelly, UKIP   862
Peter Barber, Green   677
Lab. majority 6,784 (17.34%)
Notional 5.74% swing Lab. to C.
(2005: Lab. majority 9,982 (28.82%))

§STOCKTON NORTH
E. 67,363 T. 39,498 (58.63%) Lab. hold
*Alex Cunningham, Lab.   16,923
Ian Galletley, C.   10,247
Philip Latham, LD   6,342
James Macpherson, BNP   1,724
Frank Cook, Ind.   1,577
Gordon Parkin, UKIP   1,556
Ian Saul, Eng. Dem.   1,129
Lab. majority 6,676 (16.90%)
Notional 8.35% swing Lab. to C.
(2005: Lab. majority 12,742 (33.60%))

§STOCKTON SOUTH
E. 74,552 T. 50,284 (67.45%) C. gain
*James Wharton, C.   19,577
Dari Taylor, Lab.   19,245
Jacquie Bell, LD   7,600
Neil Sinclair, BNP   1,553
Peter Braney, UKIP   1,471
Yvonne Hossack, Ind.   536
Ted Strike, Ch. P.   302
C. majority 332 (0.66%)
Notional 7.05% swing Lab. to C.
(2005: Lab. majority 5,834 (13.44%))

§STOKE-ON-TRENT CENTRAL
E. 60,995 T. 32,470 (53.23%) Lab. hold
*Tristram Hunt, Lab.   12,605
John Redfern, LD   7,039
Norsheen Bhatti, C.   6,833
Simon Darby, BNP   2,502
Carol Lovatt, UKIP   1,402
Paul Breeze, Ind.   959
Gary Elsby, Ind.   399
Brian Ward, City Ind.   303
Alby Walker, Ind.   295
Matthew Wright, TUSC   133
Lab. majority 5,566 (17.14%)
Notional 8.33% swing Lab. to LD
(2005: Lab. majority 9,717 (33.80%))

§STOKE-ON-TRENT NORTH
E. 72,052 T. 40,196 (55.79%) Lab. hold
Joan Walley, Lab.   17,815
Andy Large, C.   9,580
John Fisher, LD   7,120
Melanie Baddeley, BNP   3,196
Geoffrey Locke, UKIP   2,485
Lab. majority 8,235 (20.49%)
Notional 8.77% swing Lab. to C.
(2005: Lab. majority 13,666 (38.03%))

§STOKE-ON-TRENT SOUTH
E. 68,031 T. 39,852 (58.58%) Lab. hold
Rob Flello, Lab.   15,446
James Rushton, C.   11,316
Zulfiqar Ali, LD   6,323
Michael Coleman, BNP   3,762
Mark Barlow, UKIP   1,363
Terry Follows, Staffs Ind.   1,208
Mark Breeze, Ind.   434
Lab. majority 4,130 (10.36%)
Notional 6.15% swing Lab. to C.
(2005: Lab. majority 8,324 (22.67%))

§STONE
E. 66,979 T. 47,229 (70.51%) C. hold
Bill Cash, C.   23,890
Christine Tinker, LD   10,598
Jo Lewis, Lab.   9,770
Andrew Illsley, UKIP   2,481
Damon Hoppe, Green   490
C. majority 13,292 (28.14%)
Notional 0.81% swing C. to LD
(2005: C. majority 8,191 (18.72%))

§STOURBRIDGE
E. 69,637 T. 47,234 (67.83%) C. gain
*Margot James, C.   20,153
Lynda Waltho, Lab.   14,989
Christopher Bramall, LD   7,733
Maddy Westrop, UKIP   2,103
Robert Weale, BNP   1,696
Will Duckworth, Green   394
Alun Nicholas, Ind.   166
C. majority 5,164 (10.93%)
Notional 6.93% swing Lab. to C.
(2005: Lab. majority 1,280 (2.92%))

§STRATFORD-ON-AVON
E. 69,516 T. 50,542 (72.71%) C. hold
*Nadhim Zahawi, C.   26,052
Martin Turner, LD   14,706
Robert Johnston, Lab.   4,809
Brett Parsons, UKIP   1,846
George Jones, BNP   1,097
Neil Basnett, Ind.   1,032
Karen Varga, Green   527
Fred Bishop, Eng. Dem.   473
C. majority 11,346 (22.45%)
Notional 0.72% swing C. to LD
(2005: C. majority 10,928 (23.90%))

§STREATHAM
E. 74,531 T. 46,837 (62.84%) Lab. hold
*Chuka Umunna, Lab.   20,037
Chris Nicholson, LD   16,778
Rahoul Bhansali, C.   8,578
Rebecca Findlay, Green   861
Geoffrey Macharia, Ch. P.   237
Janus Polenceus, Eng. Dem.   229
Paul Lepper, WRP   117
Lab. majority 3,259 (6.96%)
Notional 5.25% swing Lab. to LD
(2005: Lab. majority 6,584 (17.47%))

§STRETFORD & URMSTON
E. 70,091 T. 44,910 (64.07%) Lab. hold
*Kate Green, Lab.   21,821
Alex Williams, C.   12,886
Steve Cooke, LD   7,601
David Owen, UKIP   1,508
Margaret Westbrook, Green   916
Samuel Jacob, Ch. P.   178
Lab. majority 8,935 (19.90%)
Notional 0.69% swing Lab. to C.
(2005: Lab. majority 8,310 (21.28%))

§STROUD
E. 78,305 T. 57,973 (74.03%) C. gain
*Neil Carmichael, C.   23,679
David Drew, Lab. (Co-op)   22,380
Dennis Andrewartha, LD   8,955
Martin Whiteside, Green   1,542
Steve Parker, UKIP   1,301
Alan Lomas, Ind.   116
C. majority 1,299 (2.24%)
Notional 2.05% swing Lab. (Co-op) to C.
(2005: Lab. (Co-op) majority 996
(1.85%))

§SUFFOLK CENTRAL & IPSWICH
NORTH
E. 75,848   T. 53,420 (70.43%)   C. hold
*Daniel Poulter, C.   27,125
Andrew Aalders-Dunthorne, LD   13,339
Bhavna Joshi, Lab.   8,636
Roy Philpot, UKIP   2,361
Andrew Stringer, Green   1,452
Mark Trevitt, Ind.   389
Richard Vass, New Party   118
C. majority 13,786 (25.81%)
Notional 0.76% swing LD to C.
(2005: C. majority 7,786 (16.07%))

§SUFFOLK COASTAL
E. 76,687   T. 54,893 (71.58%)   C. hold
*Therese Coffey, C.   25,475
Daisy Cooper, LD   16,347
Adam Leeder, Lab.   8,812
Prof. Stephen Bush, UKIP   3,156
Rachel Fulcher, Green   1,103
C. majority 9,128 (16.63%)
Notional 2.91% swing C. to LD
(2005: C. majority 9,674 (18.43%))

§SUFFOLK SOUTH
E. 72,498   T. 51,416 (70.92%)   C. hold
Tim Yeo, C.   24,550
Nigel Bennett, LD   15,861
Emma Bishton, Lab.   7,368
David Campbell Bannerman,
   UKIP   3,637
C. majority 8,689 (16.90%)
Notional 1.63% swing LD to C.
(2005: C. majority 6,664 (13.64%))

§SUFFOLK WEST
E. 74,413   T. 48,089 (64.62%)   C. hold
*Matthew Hancock, C.   24,312
Belinda Brooks-Gordon, LD   11,262
Ohid Ahmed, Lab.   7,089
Ian Smith, UKIP   3,085
Ramon Johns, BNP   1,428
Andrew Appleby, Ind.   540
Colin Young, CPA   373
C. majority 13,050 (27.14%)
Notional 2.28% swing C. to LD
(2005: C. majority 8,735 (19.92%))

§SUNDERLAND CENTRAL
E. 74,485   T. 42,463 (57.01%)   Lab. hold
*Julie Elliott, Lab.   19,495
Lee Martin, C.   12,770
Paul Dixon, LD   7,191
John McCaffrey, BNP   1,913
Pauline Featonby-Warren, UKIP   1,094
Lab. majority 6,725 (15.84%)
Notional 4.85% swing Lab. to C.
(2005: Lab. majority 9,464 (25.53%))

SURREY EAST
E. 76,855   T. 54,640 (71.09%)   C. hold
*Sam Gyimah, C.   31,007
David Lee, LD   14,133
Mathew Rodda, Lab.   4,925
Helena Windsor, UKIP   3,770
Martin Hogbin, Loony   422
Sandy Pratt, Ind.   383
C. majority 16,874 (30.88%)
0.72% swing C. to LD
(2005: C. majority 15,921 (32.32%))

SURREY HEATH
E. 77,690   T. 54,347 (69.95%)   C. hold
Michael Gove, C.   31,326
Alan Hilliar, LD   14,037
Matthew Willey, Lab.   5,552
Mark Stroud, UKIP   3,432
C. majority 17,289 (31.81%)
4.58% swing LD to C.
(2005: C. majority 10,845 (22.66%))

§SURREY SOUTH WEST
E. 77,980   T. 57,259 (73.43%)   C. hold
Jeremy Hunt, C.   33,605
Mike Simpson, LD   17,287
Richard Mollet, Lab.   3,419
Roger Meekins, UKIP   1,486
Cherry Allan, Green   690
Helen Hamilton, BNP   644
Luke Leighton, Pirate   94
Arthur Price, Ind.   34
C. majority 16,318 (28.50%)
Notional 8.63% swing LD to C.
(2005: C. majority 5,969 (11.23%))

§SUSSEX MID
E. 77,182   T. 55,855 (72.37%)   C. hold
Nicholas Soames, C.   28,329
Serena Tierney, LD   20,927
David Boot, Lab.   3,689
Marc Montgomery, UKIP   1,423
Paul Brown, Green   645
Stuart Minihane, BNP   583
Baron Von Thunderclap, Loony   259
C. majority 7,402 (13.25%)
Notional 0.32% swing LD to C.
(2005: C. majority 6,462 (12.62%))

§SUTTON & CHEAM
E. 66,658   T. 48,508 (72.77%)   LD hold
Paul Burstow, LD   22,156
Philippa Stroud, C.   20,548
Kathy Allen, Lab.   3,376
John Clarke, BNP   1,014
David Pickles, UKIP   950
Peter Hickson, Green   246
John Dodds, Eng. Dem.   106
Matthew Connolly, CPA   52
Martin Cullip, Libertarian   41
Dr Brian Hammond, UK Integrity   19
LD majority 1,608 (3.31%)
Notional 1.45% swing LD to C.
(2005: LD majority 2,689 (6.22%))

§SUTTON COLDFIELD
E. 74,489   T. 50,589 (67.91%)   C. hold
Andrew Mitchell, C.   27,303
Robert Pocock, Lab.   10,298
Richard Brighton, LD   9,117
Robert Grierson, BNP   1,749
Edward Siddall-Jones, UKIP   1,587
Joe Rooney, Green   535
C. majority 17,005 (33.61%)
Notional 3.44% swing Lab. to C.
(2005: C. majority 12,318 (26.72%))

§SWINDON NORTH
E. 78,391   T. 50,295 (64.16%)   C. gain
*Justin Tomlinson, C.   22,408
Victor Agarwal, Lab.   15,348
Jane Lock, LD   8,668
Stephen Halden, UKIP   1,842
Reginald Bates, BNP   1,542
Bill Hughes, Green   487
C. majority 7,060 (14.04%)
Notional 10.14% swing Lab. to C.
(2005: Lab. majority 2,675 (6.25%))

§SWINDON SOUTH
E. 72,622   T. 47,119 (64.88%)   C. gain
*Robert Buckland, C.   19,687
Anne Snelgrove, Lab.   16,143
Damon Hooton, LD   8,305
Robin Tingey, UKIP   2,029
Jenni Miles, Green   619
Alastair Kirk, Ch. P.   176
Karsten Evans, Ind.   160
C. majority 3,544 (7.52%)
Notional 5.51% swing Lab. to C.
(2005: Lab. majority 1,493 (3.50%))

TAMWORTH
E. 72,693   T. 46,390 (63.82%)   C. gain
*Christopher Pincher, C.   21,238
Brian Jenkins, Lab.   15,148
Jenny Pinkett, LD   7,516
Paul Smith, UKIP   2,253
Charlene Detheridge, Ch. P.   235
C. majority 6,090 (13.13%)
9.50% swing Lab. to C.
(2005: Lab. majority 2,569 (5.87%))

§TATTON
E. 65,689   T. 45,231 (68.86%)   C. hold
George Osborne, C.   24,687
David Lomax, LD   10,200
Richard Jackson, Lab.   7,803
Sarah Flannery, Ind.   2,243
Michael Gibson, Poetry   298
C. majority 14,487 (32.03%)
Notional 1.17% swing LD to C.
(2005: C. majority 11,537 (27.73%))

§TAUNTON DEANE
E. 82,537   T. 58,150 (70.45%)   LD hold
Jeremy Browne, LD   28,531
Mark Formosa, C.   24,538
Martin Jevon, Lab.   2,967
Tony McIntyre, UKIP   2,114
LD majority 3,993 (6.87%)
Notional 1.78% swing C. to LD
(2005: LD majority 1,868 (3.30%))

§TELFORD
E. 65,061   T. 41,310 (63.49%)   Lab. hold
David Wright, Lab.   15,974
Tom Biggins, C.   14,996
Phil Bennion, LD   6,399
Denis Allen, UKIP   2,428
Phil Spencer, BNP   1,513
Lab. majority 978 (2.37%)
Notional 6.32% swing Lab. to C.
(2005: Lab. majority 5,651 (15.01%))

§TEWKESBURY
E. 76,655   T. 53,961 (70.39%)   C. hold
Laurence Robertson, C.   25,472
Alistair Cameron, LD   19,162
Stuart Emmerson, Lab.   6,253
Brian Jones, UKIP   2,230
Matthew Sidford, Green   525
George Ridgeon, Loony   319
C. majority 6,310 (11.69%)
Notional 4.04% swing C. to LD
(2005: C. majority 9,130 (19.78%))

§THANET NORTH
E. 69,432   T. 43,343 (62.43%)   C. hold
Roger Gale, C.   22,826
Michael Britton, Lab.   9,298
Laura Murphy, LD   8,400
Rosamund Parker, UKIP   2,819
C. majority 13,528 (31.21%)
Notional 7.94% swing Lab. to C.
(2005: C. majority 6,118 (15.33%))

§THANET SOUTH
E. 71,596 T. 45,933 (64.16%) C. hold
*Laura Sandys, C.   22,043
Dr Stephen Ladyman, Lab.   14,426
Peter Bucklitsch, LD   6,935
Trevor Shonk, UKIP   2,529
C. majority 7,617 (16.58%)
Notional 7.41% swing Lab. to C.
(2005: C. majority 810 (1.76%))

§THIRSK & MALTON
E. 76,231 T. 38,142 (50.03%) C. hold
Anne McIntosh, C.   20,167
Howard Keal, LD   8,886
Jonathan Roberts, Lab.   5,169
Toby Horton, UKIP   2,502
John Clark, Lib.   1,418
C. majority 11,281 (29.58%)
Notional 1.75% swing C. to LD
(2005: C. majority 14,117 (28.50%))

§THORNBURY & YATE
E. 64,092 T. 48,226 (75.24%) LD hold
Steve Webb, LD   25,032
Matthew Riddle, C.   17,916
Roxanne Egan, Lab.   3,385
Jenny Knight, UKIP   1,709
Thomas Beacham, Ind. Fed.   126
Anthony Clements, ND   58
LD majority 7,116 (14.76%)
Notional 4.35% swing LD to C.
(2005: LD majority 11,060 (23.45%))

§THURROCK
E. 92,390 T. 45,821 (49.60%) C. gain
*Jackie Doyle-Price, C.   16,869
Carl Morris, Lab.   16,777
Carys Davis, LD   4,901
Emma Colgate, BNP   3,618
Clive Broad, UKIP   3,390
Arinola Araba, Ch. P.   266
C. majority 92 (0.20%)
Notional 6.61% swing Lab. to C.
(2005: Lab. majority 5,358 (13.02%))

§TIVERTON & HONITON
E. 76,810 T. 54,894 (71.47%) C. hold
*Neil Parish, C.   27,614
Jon Underwood, LD   18,294
Vernon Whitlock, Lab.   4,907
Daryl Stanbury, UKIP   3,277
Cathy Connor, Green   802
C. majority 9,320 (16.98%)
Notional 0.28% swing C. to LD
(2005: C. majority 9,007 (17.55%))

TONBRIDGE & MALLING
E. 71,790 T. 51,314 (71.48%) C. hold
Sir John Stanley, C.   29,723
Elizabeth Simpson, LD   11,545
Daniel Griffiths, Lab.   6,476
David Waller, UKIP   1,911
Steve Dawe, Green   764
Mike Easter, NF   505
Lisa Rogers, Eng. Dem.   390
C. majority 18,178 (35.43%)
1.02% swing LD to C.
(2005: C. majority 13,352 (28.99%))

§TOOTING
E. 73,836 T. 50,655 (68.60%) Lab. hold
Sadiq Khan, Lab.   22,038
Mark Clarke, C.   19,514
Nasser Butt, LD   7,509
Strachan McDonald, UKIP   624
Roy Vickery, Green   609
Susan John-Richards, Ind.   190
Shereen Paul, Ch. P.   171
Lab. majority 2,524 (4.98%)
Notional 3.60% swing Lab. to C.
(2005: Lab. majority 5,169 (12.17%))

§TORBAY
E. 76,151 T. 49,210 (64.62%) LD hold
Adrian Sanders, LD   23,126
Marcus Wood, C.   19,048
David Pedrick-Friend, Lab.   3,231
Julien Parrott, UKIP   2,628
Ann Conway, BNP   709
Sam Moss, Green   468
LD majority 4,078 (8.29%)
Notional 1.14% swing C. to LD
(2005: LD majority 2,727 (6.01%))

§TOTNES
E. 67,937 T. 47,843 (70.42%) C. hold
*Dr Sarah Wollaston, C.   21,940
Julian Brazil, LD   17,013
Carole Whitty, Lab.   3,538
Jeff Beer, UKIP   2,890
Lydia Somerville, Green   1,181
Mike Turner, BNP   624
Simon Drew, Ind.   390
Dr Stephen Hopwood, Ind.   267
C. majority 4,927 (10.30%)
Notional 2.27% swing LD to C.
(2005: C. majority 2,693 (5.76%))

TOTTENHAM
E. 69,933 T. 40,687 (58.18%) Lab. hold
David Lammy, Lab.   24,128
David Schmitz, LD   7,197
Sean Sullivan, C.   6,064
Jenny Sutton, TUSC   1,057
Anne Gray, Green   980
Winston McKenzie, UKIP   466
Neville Watson, Ind. People   265
Abimbola Kadara, Ch. P.   262
Sheik Thompson, Ind.   143
Errol Carr, Ind.   125
Lab. majority 16,931 (41.61%)
0.22% swing LD to Lab.
(2005: Lab. majority 13,034 (41.16%))

§TRURO & FALMOUTH
E. 70,598 T. 48,768 (69.08%) C. gain
*Sarah Newton, C.   20,349
Terrye Teverson, LD   19,914
Charlotte Mackenzie, Lab.   4,697
Harry Blakeley, UKIP   1,911
Loic Rich, Meb. Ker.   1,039
Ian Wright, Green   858
C. majority 435 (0.89%)
Notional 5.07% swing LD to C.
(2005: LD majority 3,931 (9.25%))

§TUNBRIDGE WELLS
E. 72,042 T. 50,320 (69.85%) C. hold
Greg Clark, C.   28,302
David Hallas, LD   12,726
Gary Heather, Lab.   5,448
Victor Webb, UKIP   2,054
Hazel Dawe, Green   914
Andrew McBride, BNP   704
Farel Bradbury, Ind.   172
C. majority 15,576 (30.95%)
Notional 2.79% swing LD to C.
(2005: C. majority 11,572 (25.38%))

TWICKENHAM
E. 79,861 T. 59,721 (74.78%) LD hold
Vince Cable, LD   32,483
Deborah Thomas, C.   20,343
Brian Tomlinson, Lab.   4,583
Brian Gilbert, UKIP   868
Steve Roest, Green   674
Chris Hurst, BNP   654
Harry Cole, R and E   76
Paul Armstrong, Magna Carta   40
LD majority 12,140 (20.33%)
0.52% swing C. to LD
(2005: LD majority 9,965 (19.28%))

§TYNEMOUTH
E. 75,680 T. 52,668 (69.59%) Lab. hold
Alan Campbell, Lab.   23,860
Wendy Morton, C.   18,121
John Appleby, LD   7,845
Dorothy Brooke, BNP   1,404
Natasha Payne, UKIP   900
Julia Erskine, Green   538
Lab. majority 5,739 (10.90%)
Notional 0.38% swing Lab. to C.
(2005: Lab. majority 5,490 (11.65%))

§TYNESIDE NORTH
E. 77,690 T. 46,405 (59.73%) Lab. hold
*Mary Glindon, Lab.   23,505
David Ord, LD   10,621
Gagan Mohindra, C.   8,514
John Burrows, BNP   1,860
Claudia Blake, UKIP   1,306
Bob Batten, NF   599
Lab. majority 12,884 (27.76%)
Notional 4.81% swing Lab. to LD
(2005: Lab. majority 14,929 (37.38%))

§UXBRIDGE & RUISLIP SOUTH
E. 71,168 T. 45,076 (63.34%) C. hold
John Randall, C.   21,758
Sidharath Garg, Lab.   10,542
Michael Cox, LD   8,995
Dianne Neal, BNP   1,396
Mark Wadsworth, UKIP   1,234
Mike Harling, Green   477
Roger Cooper, Eng. Dem.   403
Francis Mcallister, NF   271
C. majority 11,216 (24.88%)
Notional 3.44% swing Lab. to C.
(2005: C. majority 7,178 (18.01%))

§VAUXHALL
E. 74,811 T. 43,191 (57.73%) Lab. hold
Kate Hoey, Lab.   21,498
Caroline Pidgeon, LD   10,847
Glyn Chambers, C.   9,301
Joseph Healy, Green   708
Jose Navarro, Eng. Dem.   289
Lana Martin, Ch. P.   200
Daniel Lambert, Soc.   143
Jeremy Drinkall, WP   109
James Kapetanos, APP   96
Lab. majority 10,651 (24.66%)
Notional 0.06% swing LD to Lab.
(2005: Lab. majority 8,503 (24.54%))

§WAKEFIELD
E. 70,834 T. 44,444 (62.74%) Lab. hold
Mary Creagh, Lab.   17,454
Alex Story, C.   15,841
David Smith, LD   7,256
Ian Senior, BNP   2,581
Miriam Hawkins, Green   873
Mark Harrop, Ind.   439
Lab. majority 1,613 (3.63%)
Notional 6.94% swing Lab. to C.
(2005: Lab. majority 7,349 (17.50%))

§WALLASEY
E. 65,915 T. 41,654 (63.19%) Lab. hold
Angela Eagle, Lab.   21,578
Leah Fraser, C.   13,071
Steve Pitt, LD   5,693
Derek Snowden, UKIP   1,205
Emmanuel Mwaba, Ind.   107
Lab. majority 8,507 (20.42%)
Notional 1.78% swing Lab. to C.
(2005: Lab. majority 9,130 (23.98%))

§WALSALL NORTH
E. 65,183 T. 36,187 (55.52%) Lab. hold
David Winnick, Lab.   13,385
Helyn Clack, C.   12,395
Nadia Fazal, LD   4,754
Christopher Woodall, BNP   2,930
Elizabeth Hazell, UKIP   1,737
Peter Smith, Dem. Lab.   842
Babar Shakir, Ch. P.   144
Lab. majority 990 (2.74%)
Notional 9.03% swing Lab. to C.
(2005: Lab. majority 6,901 (20.79%))

§WALSALL SOUTH
E. 64,830 T. 40,882 (63.06%) Lab. hold
*Valerie Vaz, Lab.   16,211
Richard Hunt, C.   14,456
Dr Murli Sinha, LD   5,880
Derek Bennett, UKIP   3,449
Gulzaman Khan, Ch. P.   482
Mohammed Mulia, ND   404
Lab. majority 1,755 (4.29%)
Notional 8.24% swing Lab. to C.
(2005: Lab. majority 7,910 (20.77%))

WALTHAMSTOW
E. 64,625 T. 40,994 (63.43%) Lab. hold
*Stella Creasy, Lab.   21,252
Farid Ahmed, LD   11,774
Andy Hemsted, C.   5,734
Judith Chisholm-Benli, UKIP   823
Daniel Perrett, Green   767
Nancy Taaffe, TUSC   279
Ashar Mall, Ch. P.   248
Paul Warburton, Ind.   117
Lab. majority 9,478 (23.12%)
0.04% swing Lab. to LD
(2005: Lab. majority 7,993 (23.21%))

WANSBECK
E. 63,045 T. 38,273 (60.71%) Lab. hold
*Ian Lavery, Lab.   17,548
Simon Reed, LD   10,517
Campbell Storey, C.   6,714
Stephen Finlay, BNP   1,418
Linda Lee-Stokoe, UKIP   974
Nic Best, Green   601
Malcolm Reid, Ind.   359
Michael Flynn, Ch. P.   142
Lab. majority 7,031 (18.37%)
5.19% swing Lab. to LD
(2005: Lab. majority 10,581 (28.75%))

§WANTAGE
E. 80,456 T. 56,341 (70.03%) C. hold
Ed Vaizey, C.   29,284
Alan Armitage, LD   15,737
Steven Mitchell, Lab.   7,855
Jacqueline Jones, UKIP   2,421
Adam Twine, Green   1,044
C. majority 13,547 (24.04%)
Notional 4.30% swing LD to C.
(2005: C. majority 8,039 (15.44%))

§WARLEY
E. 63,106 T. 38,270 (60.64%) Lab. hold
John Spellar, Lab.   20,240
Jasbir Parmar, C.   9,484
Edward Keating, LD   5,929
Nigel Harvey, UKIP   2,617
Lab. majority 10,756 (28.11%)
Notional 1.94% swing Lab. to C.
(2005: Lab. majority 11,206 (31.99%))

§WARRINGTON NORTH
E. 71,601 T. 44,211 (61.75%) Lab. hold
Helen Jones, Lab.   20,135
Paul Campbell, C.   13,364
David Eccles, LD   9,196
Albert Scott, Ind.   1,516
Lab. majority 6,771 (15.32%)
Notional 6.61% swing Lab. to C.
(2005: Lab. majority 11,382 (28.53%))

§WARRINGTON SOUTH
E. 80,506 T. 54,874 (68.16%) C. gain
*David Mowat, C.   19,641
Nick Bent, Lab.   18,088
Jo Crotty, LD   15,094
James Ashington, UKIP   1,624
Steph Davies, Green   427
C. majority 1,553 (2.83%)
Notional 6.00% swing Lab. to C.
(2005: Lab. majority 4,337 (9.17%))

§WARWICK & LEAMINGTON
E. 58,030 T. 49,032 (84.49%) C. gain
*Chris White, C.   20,876
James Plaskitt, Lab.   17,363
Alan Beddow, LD   8,977
Christopher Lenton, UKIP   926
Ian Davison, Green   693
Jim Cullinane, Ind.   197
C. majority 3,513 (7.16%)
Notional 8.76% swing Lab. to C.
(2005: Lab. majority 4,393 (10.35%))

§WARWICKSHIRE NORTH
E. 70,143 T. 47,265 (67.38%) C. gain
*Dan Byles, C.   18,993
Mike O'Brien, Lab.   18,939
Stephen Martin, LD   5,481
Jason Holmes, BNP   2,106
Steven Fowler, UKIP   1,335
David Lane, Eng. Dem.   411
C. majority 54 (0.11%)
Notional 7.69% swing Lab. to C.
(2005: Lab. majority 6,684 (15.27%))

§WASHINGTON & SUNDERLAND
WEST
E. 68,910 T. 37,334 (54.18%) Lab. hold
Sharon Hodgson, Lab.   19,615
Ian Cuthbert, C.   8,157
Peter Andras, LD   6,382
Ian McDonald, BNP   1,913
Linda Hudson, UKIP   1,267
Lab. majority 11,458 (30.69%)
Notional 11.56% swing Lab. to C.
(2005: Lab. majority 17,060 (52.56%))

§WATFORD
E. 80,798 T. 55,208 (68.33%) C. gain
*Richard Harrington, C.   19,291
Sal Brinton, LD   17,866
Claire Ward, Lab.   14,750
Andrew Emerson, BNP   1,217
Graham Eardley, UKIP   1,199
Ian Brandon, Green   885
C. majority 1,425 (2.58%)
Notional 6.08% swing Lab. to C.
(2005: Lab. majority 1,151 (2.33%))

§WAVENEY
E. 78,532 T. 51,141 (65.12%) C. gain
*Peter Aldous, C.   20,571
Bob Blizzard, Lab.   19,802
Alan Dean, LD   6,811
Jack Tyler, UKIP   2,684
Graham Elliott, Green   1,167
Louis Barfe, Ind.   106
C. majority 769 (1.50%)
Notional 6.75% swing Lab. to C.
(2005: Lab. majority 5,950 (12.00%))

§WEALDEN
E. 76,537 T. 54,969 (71.82%) C. hold
Charles Hendry, C.   31,090
Chris Bowers, LD   13,911
Lorna Blackmore, Lab.   5,266
Dan Docker, UKIP   3,319
David Jonas, Green   1,383
C. majority 17,179 (31.25%)
Notional 2.79% swing LD to C.
(2005: C. majority 12,812 (25.66%))

§WEAVER VALE
E. 66,538 T. 43,990 (66.11%) C. gain
*Graham Evans, C.   16,953
John Stockton, Lab.   15,962
Peter Hampson, LD   8,196
Colin Marsh, BNP   1,063
Paul Remfry, UKIP   1,018
Howard Thorp, Green   338
Mike Cooksley, Ind.   270
Tom Reynolds, Ind.   133
Will Charlton, Ind.   57
C. majority 991 (2.25%)
Notional 8.14% swing Lab. to C.
(2005: Lab. majority 5,277 (14.03%))

§WELLINGBOROUGH
E. 76,857 T. 51,661 (67.22%) C. hold
Peter Bone, C.   24,918
Jayne Buckland, Lab.   13,131
Kevin Barron, LD   8,848
Adrian Haynes, UKIP   1,636
Rob Walker, BNP   1,596
Terry Spencer, Eng. Dem.   530
Jonathan Hornett, Green   480
Paul Crofts, TUSC   249
Gary Donaldson, Ind.   240
Marcus Lavin, Ind.   33
C. majority 11,787 (22.82%)
Notional 10.78% swing Lab. to C.
(2005: C. majority 610 (1.25%))

WELLS
E. 79,432 T. 55,864 (70.33%) LD gain
*Tessa Munt, LD   24,560
David Heathcoat-Amory, C.   23,760
Andy Merryfield, Lab.   4,198
Jake Baynes, UKIP   1,711
Richard Boyce, BNP   1,004
Chris Briton, Green   631
LD majority 800 (1.43%)
3.59% swing C. to LD
(2005: C. majority 3,040 (5.74%))

WELWYN HATFIELD
E. 72,058 T. 48,972 (67.96%) C. hold
Grant Shapps, C.   27,894
Mike Hobday, Lab.   10,471
Paul Zukowskyj, LD   8,010
David Platt, UKIP   1,643
Jill Weston, Green   796
Nigel Parker, Ind.   158
C. majority 17,423 (35.58%)
11.14% swing Lab. to C.
(2005: C. majority 5,946 (13.30%))

§WENTWORTH & DEARNE
E. 72,586 T. 42,106 (58.01%) Lab. hold
John Healey, Lab.   21,316
Michelle Donelan, C.   7,396
Nick Love, LD   6,787
John Wilkinson, UKIP   3,418
George Baldwin, BNP   3,189
Lab. majority 13,920 (33.06%)
Notional 7.49% swing Lab. to C.
(2005: Lab. majority 17,551 (45.55%))

§WEST BROMWICH EAST
E. 62,824 T. 37,950 (60.41%) Lab. hold
Tom Watson, Lab.   17,657
Alistair Thompson, C.   10,961
Ian Garrett, LD   4,993
Terry Lewin, BNP   2,205
Mark Cowles, Eng. Dem.   1,150
Steve Grey, UKIP   984
Lab. majority 6,696 (17.64%)
Notional 7.68% swing Lab. to C.
(2005: Lab. majority 11,947 (33.00%))

§WEST BROMWICH WEST
E. 65,013 T. 36,171 (55.64%) Lab. hold
Adrian Bailey, Lab.   16,263
Andrew Hardie, C.   10,612
Sadie Smith, LD   4,336
Russ Green, BNP   3,394
Mac Ford, UKIP   1,566
Lab. majority 5,651 (15.62%)
Notional 7.64% swing Lab. to C.
(2005: Lab. majority 9,821 (30.90%))

§WEST HAM
E. 85,313 T. 46,951 (55.03%) Lab. hold
Lyn Brown, Lab.   29,422
Virginia Morris, C.   6,888
Martin Pierce, LD   5,392
Stan Gain, CPA   1,327
Kamran Malik, Ind.   1,245
Michael Davidson, NF   1,089
Kim Gandy, UKIP   766
Jane Lithgow, Green   645
Grace Agbogun-Toko, Ind.   177
Lab. majority 22,534 (47.99%)
Notional 4.16% swing C. to Lab.
(2005: Lab. majority 12,274 (31.76%))

§WESTMINSTER NORTH
E. 66,739 T. 39,598 (59.33%) Lab. hold
Karen Buck, Lab.   17,377
Joanne Cash, C.   15,251
Mark Blackburn, LD   5,513
Tristan Smith, Green   478
Stephen Curry, BNP   334
Jasna Badzak, UKIP   315
Dr Ali Bahaijoub, Ind.   101
Edward Roseman, Eng. Dem.   99
Gabriela Fajardo, Ch. P.   98
Abby Dharamsey, Ind.   32
Lab. majority 2,126 (5.37%)
Notional 0.61% swing Lab. to C.
(2005: Lab. majority 2,120 (6.59%))

§WESTMORLAND & LONSDALE
E. 67,881 T. 51,487 (75.85%) LD hold
Tim Farron, LD   30,896
Gareth McKeever, C.   18,632
Jonathan Todd, Lab.   1,158
John Mander, UKIP   801
LD majority 12,264 (23.82%)
Notional 11.06% swing C. to LD
(2005: LD majority 806 (1.70%))

§WESTON-SUPER-MARE
E. 78,487 T. 52,716 (67.17%) C. hold
John Penrose, C.   23,356
Mike Bell, LD   20,665
David Bradley, Lab.   5,772
Paul Spencer, UKIP   1,406
Peryn Parsons, BNP   1,098
John Peverelle, Eng. Dem.   275
Steve Satch, Ind.   144
C. majority 2,691 (5.10%)
Notional 0.42% swing LD to C.
(2005: C. majority 2,088 (4.26%))

§WIGAN
E. 75,564 T. 44,140 (58.41%) Lab. hold
*Lisa Nandy, Lab.   21,404
Michael Winstanley, C.   10,917
Mark Clayton, LD   6,797
Alan Freeman, UKIP   2,516
Charles Mather, BNP   2,506
Lab. majority 10,487 (23.76%)
Notional 7.69% swing Lab. to C.
(2005: Lab. majority 15,501 (39.15%))

§WILTSHIRE NORTH
E. 66,313 T. 48,699 (73.44%) C. hold
James Gray, C.   25,114
Mike Evemy, LD   17,631
Jason Hughes, Lab.   3,239
Charles Bennett, UKIP   1,908
Phil Chamberlain, Green   599
Philip Allnatt, Ind.   208
C. majority 7,483 (15.37%)
Notional 0.01% swing LD to C.
(2005: C. majority 6,888 (15.34%))

§WILTSHIRE SOUTH WEST
E. 71,645 T. 49,018 (68.42%) C. hold
Andrew Murrison, C.   25,321
Trevor Carbin, LD   14,954
Rebecca Rennison, Lab.   5,613
Michael Cuthbert-Murray, UKIP   2,684
Crispin Black, Ind.   446
C. majority 10,367 (21.15%)
Notional 1.15% swing LD to C.
(2005: C. majority 8,568 (18.85%))

§WIMBLEDON
E. 65,723 T. 47,395 (72.11%) C. hold
Stephen Hammond, C.   23,257
Shas Sheehan, LD   11,849
Andrew Judge, Lab.   10,550
Mark McAleer, UKIP   914
Rajeev Thacker, Green   590
David Martin, Ch. P.   235
C. majority 11,408 (24.07%)
Notional 0.42% swing LD to C.
(2005: C. majority 2,480 (5.69%))

§WINCHESTER
E. 73,806 T. 55,955 (75.81%) C. gain
*Steve Brine, C.   27,155
Martin Tod, LD   24,107
Patrick Davies, Lab.   3,051
Jocelyn Penn-Bull, UKIP   1,139
Mark Lancaster, Eng. Dem.   503
C. majority 3,048 (5.45%)
Notional 9.09% swing LD to C.
(2005: LD majority 6,524 (12.74%))

§WINDSOR
E. 69,511 T. 49,588 (71.34%) C. hold
Adam Afriyie, C.   30,172
Julian Tisi, LD   11,118
Amanjit Jhund, Lab.   4,910
John-Paul Rye, UKIP   1,612
Peter Phillips, BNP   950
Derek Wall, Green   628
Peter Hooper, Ind.   198
C. majority 19,054 (38.42%)
Notional 8.05% swing LD to C.
(2005: C. majority 9,605 (22.32%))

§WIRRAL SOUTH
E. 56,099 T. 39,906 (71.13%) Lab. hold
*Alison McGovern, Lab.   16,276
Jeff Clarke, C.   15,745
Jamie Saddler, LD   6,611
David Scott, UKIP   1,274
Lab. majority 531 (1.33%)
Notional 3.98% swing Lab. to C.
(2005: Lab. majority 3,538 (9.30%))

§WIRRAL WEST
E. 55,050 T. 39,372 (71.52%) C. hold
*Esther McVey, C.   16,726
Phillip Davies, Lab.   14,290
Peter Reisdorf, LD   6,630
Philip Griffiths, UKIP   899
David Kirwan, Ind.   506
David James, CSP   321
C. majority 2,436 (6.19%)
Notional 2.34% swing Lab. to C.
(2005: C. majority 569 (1.51%))

§WITHAM
E. 66,750 T. 46,835 (70.16%) C. hold
*Priti Patel, C.   24,448
Margaret Phelps, LD   9,252
John Spademan, Lab.   8,656
David Hodges, UKIP   3,060
James Abbott, Green   1,419
C. majority 15,196 (32.45%)
Notional 1.06% swing C. to LD
(2005: C. majority 7,241 (17.29%))

§WITNEY
E. 78,766 T. 57,769 (73.34%) C. hold
David Cameron, C.   33,973
Dawn Barnes, LD   11,233
Joe Goldberg, Lab.   7,511
Stuart Macdonald, Green   2,385
Nikolai Tolstoy, UKIP   2,001
Howling Hope, Loony   234
Paul Wesson, Ind.   166
Johnnie Cook, Ind.   151
Colin Bex, Wessex Reg.   62
Aaron Barschak, Ind.   53
C. majority 22,740 (39.36%)
Notional 6.29% swing LD to C.
(2005: C. majority 13,874 (26.78%))

WOKING
E. 73,838 T. 52,786 (71.49%) C. hold
*Jonathan Lord, C.   26,551
Rosie Sharpley, LD   19,744
Tom Miller, Lab.   4,246
Rob Burberry, UKIP   1,997
Julie Roxburgh, PPN-V   204
Ruth Temple, Magna Carta   44
C. majority 6,807 (12.90%)
0.73% swing C. to LD
(2005: C. majority 6,612 (14.36%))

§WOKINGHAM
E. 76,219   T. 54,528 (71.54%)   C. hold
John Redwood, C.   28,754
Prue Bray, LD   15,262
George Davidson, Lab.   5,516
Mark Ashwell, Ind.   2,340
Ann Zebedee, UKIP   1,664
Marjory Bisset, Green   567
Top Cat Owen, Loony   329
Robin Smith, Ind.   96
C. majority 13,492 (24.74%)
Notional 4.65% swing LD to C.
(2005: C. majority 7,257 (15.44%))

§WOLVERHAMPTON NORTH EAST
E. 59,324   T. 34,894 (58.82%)   Lab. hold
*Emma Reynolds, Lab.   14,448
Julie Rook, C.   11,964
Colin Ross, LD   4,711
Simon Patten, BNP   2,296
Paul Valdmanis, UKIP   1,138
Shangara Bhatoe, Soc. Lab.   337
Lab. majority 2,484 (7.12%)
Notional 9.00% swing Lab. to C.
(2005: Lab. majority 8,628 (25.12%))

§WOLVERHAMPTON SOUTH EAST
E. 60,450   T. 34,707 (57.41%)   Lab. hold
Pat McFadden, Lab.   16,505
Ken Wood, C.   9,912
Richard Whitehouse, LD   5,277
Gordon Fanthom, UKIP   2,675
Sudhir Handa, Ind.   338
Lab. majority 6,593 (19.00%)
Notional 8.79% swing Lab. to C.
(2005: Lab. majority 12,309 (36.58%))

§WOLVERHAMPTON SOUTH WEST
E. 59,160   T. 40,160 (67.88%)   C. gain
*Paul Uppal, C.   16,344
Rob Marris, Lab.   15,653
Robin Lawrence, LD   6,430
Amanda Mobberley, UKIP   1,487
Raymond Barry, Parenting   246
C. majority 691 (1.72%)
Notional 3.52% swing Lab. to C.
(2005: Lab. majority 2,114 (5.31%))

WORCESTER
E. 72,831   T. 48,974 (67.24%)   C. gain
*Robin Walker, C.   19,358
Michael Foster, Lab.   16,376
Jackie Alderson, LD   9,525
Jack Bennett, UKIP   1,360
Spencer Lee Kirby, BNP   1,219
Louis Stephen, Green   735
Andrew Robinson, Pirate   173
Peter Nielsen, Ind.   129
Andrew Christian-Brookes, Ind.   99
C. majority 2,982 (6.09%)
6.43% swing Lab. to C.
(2005: Lab. majority 3,144 (6.78%))

§WORCESTERSHIRE MID
E. 72,171   T. 50,931 (70.57%)   C. hold
Peter Luff, C.   27,770
Margaret Rowley, LD   11,906
Robin Lunn, Lab.   7,613
John White, UKIP   3,049
Gordon Matthews, Green   593
C. majority 15,864 (31.15%)
Notional 0.04% swing LD to C.
(2005: C. majority 12,906 (27.33%))

§WORCESTERSHIRE WEST
E. 73,270   T. 54,093 (73.83%)   C. hold
*Harriett Baldwin, C.   27,213
Richard Burt, LD   20,459
Penelope Barber, Lab.   3,661
Caroline Bovey, UKIP   2,119
Malcolm Victory, Green   641
C. majority 6,754 (12.49%)
Notional 3.23% swing LD to C.
(2005: C. majority 3,053 (6.03%))

§WORKINGTON
E. 59,607   T. 39,259 (65.86%)   Lab. hold
Tony Cunningham, Lab.   17,865
Judith Pattinson, C.   13,290
Stan Collins, LD   5,318
Martin Wingfield, BNP   1,496
Stephen Lee, UKIP   876
Rob Logan, Eng. Dem.   414
Lab. majority 4,575 (11.65%)
Notional 5.66% swing Lab. to C.
(2005: Lab. majority 8,226 (22.97%))

§WORSLEY & ECCLES SOUTH
E. 72,473   T. 41,701 (57.54%)   Lab. hold
Barbara Keeley, Lab.   17,892
Iain Lindley, C.   13,555
Richard Gadsden, LD   6,883
Andrew Townsend, UKIP   2,037
Paul Whitelegg, Eng. Dem.   1,334
Lab. majority 4,337 (10.40%)
Notional 7.61% swing Lab. to C.
(2005: Lab. majority 10,001 (25.62%))

§WORTHING EAST & SHOREHAM
E. 74,001   T. 48,397 (65.40%)   C. hold
Tim Loughton, C.   23,458
James Doyle, LD   12,353
Emily Benn, Lab.   8,087
Mike Glennon, UKIP   2,984
Susan Board, Green   1,126
Clive Maltby, Eng. Dem.   389
C. majority 11,105 (22.95%)
Notional 1.70% swing LD to C.
(2005: C. majority 8,180 (18.37%))

§WORTHING WEST
E. 75,945   T. 49,123 (64.68%)   C. hold
Peter Bottomley, C.   25,416
Hazel Thorpe, LD   13,687
Ian Ross, Lab.   5,800
John Wallace, UKIP   2,924
David Aherne, Green   996
Stuart Dearsley, Christian   300
C. majority 11,729 (23.88%)
Notional 1.50% swing LD to C.
(2005: C. majority 9,383 (20.89%))

§WREKIN, THE
E. 65,544   T. 45,968 (70.13%)   C. hold
Mark Pritchard, C.   21,922
Paul Kalinauckas, Lab. (Co-op) 12,472
Ali Cameron-Daw, LD   8,019
Malcolm Hurst, UKIP   2,050
Susan Harwood, BNP   1,505
C. majority 9,450 (20.56%)
Notional 8.85% swing Lab. (Co-op) to C.
(2005: C. majority 1,187 (2.85%))

§WYCOMBE
E. 74,502   T. 48,151 (64.63%)   C. hold
*Steven Baker, C.   23,423
Steve Guy, LD   13,863
Andrew Lomas, Lab.   8,326
John Wiseman, UKIP   2,123
Madassar Khokar, Ind.   228
David Fitton, Ind.   188
C. majority 9,560 (19.85%)
Notional 4.83% swing C. to LD
(2005: C. majority 7,597 (17.29%))

§WYRE & PRESTON NORTH
E. 71,201   T. 51,308 (72.06%)   C. hold
*Ben Wallace, C.   26,877
Danny Gallagher, LD   11,033
Cat Smith, Lab.   10,932
Nigel Cecil, UKIP   2,466
C. majority 15,844 (30.88%)
Notional 3.86% swing C. to LD
(2005: C. majority 12,082 (27.51%))

§WYRE FOREST
E. 76,711   T. 50,899 (66.35%)   C. gain
*Mark Garnier, C.   18,793
Dr Richard Taylor, Ind. CHC   16,150
Nigel Knowles, Lab.   7,298
Neville Farmer, LD   6,040
Michael Wrench, UKIP   1,498
Gordon Howells, BNP   1,120
C. majority 2,643 (5.19%)
Notional 7.35% swing Ind. CHC to C.
(2005: Ind. CHC majority 4,613 (9.51%))

WYTHENSHAWE & SALE EAST
E. 79,923   T. 40,751 (50.99%)   Lab. hold
Paul Goggins, Lab.   17,987
Janet Clowes, C.   10,412
Martin Eakins, LD   9,107
Bernard Todd, BNP   1,572
Chris Cassidy, UKIP   1,405
Lynn Worthington, TUSC   268
Lab. majority 7,575 (18.59%)
5.67% swing Lab. to C.
(2005: Lab. majority 10,827 (29.92%))

§YEOVIL
E. 82,314   T. 57,160 (69.44%)   LD hold
David Laws, LD   31,843
Kevin Davis, C.   18,807
Lee Skevington, Lab.   2,991
Nigel Pearson, UKIP   2,357
Robert Baehr, BNP   1,162
LD majority 13,036 (22.81%)
Notional 2.74% swing C. to LD
(2005: LD majority 8,779 (17.33%))

§YORK CENTRAL
E. 74,908   T. 46,483 (62.05%)   Lab. hold
Hugh Bayley, Lab.   18,573
Susan Wade Weeks, C.   12,122
Christian Vassie, LD   11,694
Andy Chase, Green   1,669
Jeff Kelly, BNP   1,171
Paul Abbott, UKIP   1,100
Eddie Vee, Loony   154
Lab. majority 6,451 (13.88%)
Notional 6.02% swing Lab. to C.
(2005: Lab. majority 10,344 (25.92%))

§YORK OUTER
E. 74,965 T. 53,300 (71.10%) C. gain
*Julian Sturdy, C.   22,912
Madeleine Kirk, LD   19,224
James Alexander, Lab.   9,108
Judith Morris, UKIP   1,100
Cathy Smurthwaite, BNP   956
C. majority 3,688 (6.92%)
Notional 3.68% swing LD to C.
(2005: LD majority 203 (0.44%))

§YORKSHIRE EAST
E. 80,342 T. 51,254 (63.79%) C. hold
Greg Knight, C.   24,328
Robert Adamson, LD   10,842
Paul Rounding, Lab.   10,401
Chris Daniels, UKIP   2,142
Gary Pudsey, BNP   1,865
Ray Allerston, Soc. Dem.   914
Michael Jackson, Green   762
C. majority 13,486 (26.31%)
Notional 0.06% swing C. to LD
(2005: C. majority 6,284 (13.31%))

WALES

ABERAVON
E. 50,789 T. 30,958 (60.95%) Lab. hold
Hywel Francis, Lab.   16,073
Keith Davies, LD   5,034
Caroline Jones, C.   4,411
Paul Nicholls-Jones, PC   2,198
Kevin Edwards, BNP   1,276
Andrew Tutton, Ind.   919
Captain Beany, Bean   558
Joe Callan, UKIP   489
Lab. majority 11,039 (35.66%)
5.32% swing Lab. to LD
(2005: Lab. majority 13,937 (46.30%))

§ABERCONWY
E. 44,593 T. 29,966 (67.20%) C. gain
*Guto Bebb, C.   10,734
Ronald Hughes, Lab.   7,336
Mike Priestley, LD   5,786
Phil Edwards, PC   5,341
Mike Wieteska, UKIP   632
Louise Wynne-Jones, Ch. P.   137
C. majority 3,398 (11.34%)
Notional 7.63% swing Lab. to C.
(2005: Lab. majority 1,070 (3.93%))

ALYN & DEESIDE
E. 60,931 T. 39,923 (65.52%) Lab. hold
Mark Tami, Lab.   15,804
Will Gallagher, C.   12,885
Paul Brighton, LD   7,308
Maurice Jones, PC   1,549
John Walker, BNP   1,368
James Howson, UKIP   1,009
Lab. majority 2,919 (7.31%)
8.15% swing Lab. to C.
(2005: Lab. majority 8,378 (23.60%))

§ARFON
E. 41,198 T. 26,078 (63.30%) PC gain
Hywel Williams, PC   9,383
Alan Pugh, Lab.   7,928
Robin Millar, C.   4,416
Sarah Green, LD   3,666
Elwyn Williams, UKIP   685
PC majority 1,455 (5.58%)
Notional 3.70% swing Lab. to PC
(2005: Lab. majority 456 (1.82%))

BLAENAU GWENT
E. 52,438 T. 32,395 (61.78%) Lab. gain
*Nick Smith, Lab.   16,974
Dai Davies, Blaenau Voice   6,458
Matt Smith, LD   3,285
Liz Stevenson, C.   2,265
Rhodri Davies, PC   1,333
Anthony King, BNP   1,211
Mike Kocan, UKIP   488
Alyson O'Connell, Soc. Lab.   381
Lab. majority 10,516 (32.46%)
(2005: Ind. Law majority 9,121
(25.87%))(2006: Ind. Davies majority
2,484 (9.14%))

BRECON & RADNORSHIRE
E. 53,589 T. 38,845 (72.49%) LD hold
Roger Williams, LD   17,929
Suzy Davies, C.   14,182
Christopher Lloyd, Lab.   4,096
Janet Davies, PC   989
Clive Easton, UKIP   876
Dorienne Robinson, Green   341
Jeffrey Green, Ch. P.   222
Lord Offa, Loony   210
LD majority 3,747 (9.65%)
0.27% swing LD to C.
(2005: LD majority 3,905 (10.18%))

§BRIDGEND
E. 58,700 T. 38,347 (65.33%) Lab. hold
Madeleine Moon, Lab.   13,931
Helen Baker, C.   11,668
Wayne Morgan, LD   8,658
Nick Thomas, PC   2,269
Brian Urch, BNP   1,020
David Fulton, UKIP   801
Lab. majority 2,263 (5.90%)
Notional 5.98% swing Lab. to C.
(2005: Lab. majority 6,089 (17.87%))

§CAERPHILLY
E. 62,134 T. 38,992 (62.75%) Lab. hold
Wayne David, Lab.   17,377
Maria Caulfield, C.   6,622
Lindsay Whittle, PC   6,460
Kay David, LD   5,988
Laurence Reid, BNP   1,635
Tony Jenkins, UKIP   910
Lab. majority 10,755 (27.58%)
Notional 6.57% swing Lab. to C.
(2005: Lab. majority 13,517 (37.32%))

CARDIFF CENTRAL
E. 61,162 T. 36,151 (59.11%) LD hold
Jenny Willott, LD   14,976
Jenny Rathbone, Lab.   10,400
Karen Robson, C.   7,799
Chris Williams, PC   1,246
Susan Davies, UKIP   765
Sam Coates, Green   575
Ross Saunders, TUSC   162
Mark Beech, Loony   142
Alun Mathias, Ind.   86
LD majority 4,576 (12.66%)
1.41% swing LD to Lab.
(2005: LD majority 5,593 (15.48%))

CARDIFF NORTH
E. 65,553 T. 47,630 (72.66%) C. gain
*Jonathan Evans, C.   17,860
Julie Morgan, Lab.   17,666
John Dixon, LD   8,724
Llywelyn Rhys, PC   1,588
Lawrence Gwynn, UKIP   1,130
Christopher von Ruhland, Green   362
Derek Thomson, Ch. P.   300
C. majority 194 (0.41%)
1.47% swing Lab. to C.
(2005: Lab. majority 1,146 (2.53%))

§CARDIFF SOUTH & PENARTH
E. 73,704 T. 44,370 (60.20%)
                           Lab. (Co-op) hold
Alun Michael, Lab. (Co-op)   17,263
Simon Hoare, C.   12,553
Dominic Hannigan, LD   9,875
Farida Aslam, PC   1,851
Simon Zeigler, UKIP   1,145
George Burke, Ind.   648
Matt Townsend, Green   554
Clive Bate, Ch. P.   285
Robert Griffiths, Comm   196
Lab. (Co-op) majority 4,710 (10.62%)
Notional 6.03% swing Lab. (Co-op) to C.
(2005: Lab. (Co-op) majority 8,955
(22.68%))

§CARDIFF WEST
E. 62,787 T. 40,957 (65.23%) Lab. hold
Kevin Brennan, Lab.   16,893
Angela Jones-Evans, C.   12,143
Rachael Hitchinson, LD   7,186
Mohammed Sarul Islam, PC   2,868
Mike Henessey, UKIP   1,117
Jake Griffiths, Green   750
Lab. majority 4,750 (11.60%)
Notional 5.33% swing Lab. to C.
(2005: Lab. majority 8,361 (22.25%))

§CARMARTHEN EAST & DINEFWR
E. 52,385 T. 38,011 (72.56%) PC hold
*Jonathan Edwards, PC   13,546
Christine Gwyther, Lab.   10,065
Andrew Morgan, C.   8,506
Bill Powell, LD   4,609
John Atkinson, UKIP   1,285
PC majority 3,481 (9.16%)
Notional 4.19% swing PC to Lab.
(2005: PC majority 6,551 (17.54%))

§CARMARTHEN WEST &
PEMBROKESHIRE SOUTH
E. 57,519   T. 40,507 (70.42%)   C. gain
*Simon Hart, C.   16,649
Nick Ainger, Lab.   13,226
John Gossage, LD   4,890
John Dixon, PC   4,232
Ray Clarke, UKIP   1,146
Henry Langen, Ind.   364
C. majority 3,423 (8.45%)
Notional 6.88% swing Lab. to C.
(2005: Lab. majority 2,043 (5.32%))

§CEREDIGION
E. 59,043 T. 38,258 (64.80%) LD hold
Mark Williams, LD   19,139
Penri James, PC   10,815
Luke Evetts, C.   4,421
Richard Boudier, Lab.   2,210
Elwyn Williams, UKIP   977
Leila Kiersch, Green   696
LD majority 8,324 (21.76%)
Notional 10.57% swing PC to LD
(2005: LD majority 218 (0.61%))

§CLWYD SOUTH
E. 53,748 T. 34,681 (64.53%) Lab. hold
*Susan Elan Jones, Lab.   13,311
John Bell, C.   10,477
Bruce Roberts, LD   5,965
Janet Ryder, PC   3,009
Sarah Hynes, BNP   1,100
Nick Powell, UKIP   819
Lab. majority 2,834 (8.17%)
Notional 5.83% swing Lab. to C.
(2005: Lab. majority 6,220 (19.84%))

§CLWYD WEST
E. 57,913 T. 38,111 (65.81%) C. hold
David Jones, C.   15,833
Donna Hutton, Lab.   9,414
Llyr Huws Gruffydd, PC   5,864
Michele Jones, LD   5,801
Warwick Nicholson, UKIP   864
Revd Dr David Griffiths, Ch. P.   239
Joe Blakesley, Ind.   96
C. majority 6,419 (16.84%)
Notional 8.35% swing Lab. to C.
(2005: C. majority 51 (0.14%))

§CYNON VALLEY
E. 50,656 T. 29,876 (58.98%) Lab. hold
Ann Clwyd, Lab.   15,681
Dafydd Trystan Davies, PC   6,064
Lee Thacker, LD   4,120
Juliette Ash, C.   3,010
Frank Hughes, UKIP   1,001
Lab. majority 9,617 (32.19%)
Notional 8.65% swing Lab. to PC
(2005: Lab. majority 14,390 (49.48%))

DELYN
E. 53,470 T. 36,984 (69.17%) Lab. hold
David Hanson, Lab.   15,083
Antoinette Sandbach, C.   12,811
Bill Brereton, LD   5,747
Peter Ryder, PC   1,844
Jennifer Matthys, BNP   844
Andrew Haigh, UKIP   655
Lab. majority 2,272 (6.14%)
6.70% swing Lab. to C.
(2005: Lab. majority 6,644 (19.54%))

§DWYFOR MEIRIONNYDD
E. 45,354 T. 28,906 (63.73%) PC hold
Elfyn Llwyd, PC   12,814
Simon Baynes, C.   6,447
Alwyn Humphreys, Lab.   4,021
Steve Churchman, LD   3,538
Louise Hughes, Ind.   1,310
Frank Wykes, UKIP   776
PC majority 6,367 (22.03%)
Notional 7.28% swing PC to C.
(2005: PC majority 8,706 (29.02%))

§GOWER
E. 61,696 T. 41,671 (67.54%) Lab. hold
Martin Caton, Lab.   16,016
Byron Davies, C.   13,333
Mike Day, LD   7,947
Darren Price, PC   2,760
Adrian Jones, BNP   963
Gordon Triggs, UKIP   652
Lab. majority 2,683 (6.44%)
Notional 5.26% swing Lab. to C.
(2005: Lab. majority 6,703 (16.95%))

§ISLWYN
E. 54,826 T. 34,690 (63.27%)
                     Lab. (Co-op) hold
*Christopher Evans, Lab. (Co-op) 17,069
Daniel Thomas, C.   4,854
Steffan Lewis, PC   4,518
Asghar Ali, LD   3,597
Dave Rees, Ind.   1,495
John Voisey, BNP   1,320
Jason Crew, UKIP   936
Paul Taylor, Ind.   901
Lab. (Co-op) majority 12,215 (35.21%)
Notional 9.05% swing Lab. (Co-op) to C.
(2005: Lab. (Co-op) majority 17,582
(51.91%))

LLANELLI
E. 55,637 T. 37,461 (67.33%) Lab. hold
Nia Griffith, Lab.   15,916
Myfanwy Davies, PC   11,215
Christopher Salmon, C.   5,381
Myrddin Edwards, LD   3,902
Andrew Marshall, UKIP   1,047
Lab. majority 4,701 (12.55%)
3.96% swing Lab. to PC
(2005: Lab. majority 7,234 (20.47%))

MERTHYR TYDFIL & RHYMNEY
E. 54,715 T. 32,076 (58.62%) Lab. hold
Dai Havard, Lab.   14,007
Amy Kitcher, LD   9,951
Maria Hill, C.   2,412
Clive Tovey, Ind.   1,845
Glyndwr Cennydd Jones, PC   1,621
Richard Barnes, BNP   1,173
Adam Brown, UKIP   872
Alan Cowdell, Soc. Lab.   195
Lab. majority 4,056 (12.64%)
16.92% swing Lab. to LD
(2005: Lab. majority 13,934 (46.48%))

MONMOUTH
E. 62,768 T. 46,519 (74.11%) C. hold
David Davies, C.   22,466
Hamish Sandison, Lab.   12,041
Martin Blakebrough, LD   9,026
Jonathan Clark, PC   1,273
Derek Rowe, UKIP   1,126
Steve Millson, Green   587
C. majority 10,425 (22.41%)
6.25% swing Lab. to C.
(2005: C. majority 4,527 (9.92%))

§MONTGOMERYSHIRE
E. 48,730 T. 33,813 (69.39%) C. gain
*Glyn Davies, C.   13,976
Lembit Opik, LD   12,792
Heledd Fychan, PC   2,802
Nick Colbourne, Lab.   2,407
David Rowlands, UKIP   1,128
Milton Ellis, NF   384
Bruce Lawson, Ind.   324
C. majority 1,184 (3.50%)
Notional 13.15% swing LD to C.
(2005: LD majority 7,048 (22.80%))

§NEATH
E. 57,186 T. 37,122 (64.91%) Lab. hold
Peter Hain, Lab.   17,172
Alun Llewelyn, PC   7,397
Frank Little, LD   5,535
Emmeline Owens, C.   4,847
Michael Green, BNP   1,342
James Bevan, UKIP   829
Lab. majority 9,775 (26.33%)
Notional 4.58% swing Lab. to PC
(2005: Lab. majority 12,710 (35.49%))

NEWPORT EAST
E. 54,437 T. 34,448 (63.28%) Lab. hold
Jessica Morden, Lab.   12,744
Ed Townsend, LD   11,094
Dawn Parry, C.   7,918
Keith Jones, BNP   1,168
Fiona Cross, PC   724
David Rowlands, UKIP   677
Liz Screen, Soc. Lab.   123
Lab. majority 1,650 (4.79%)
8.35% swing Lab. to LD
(2005: Lab. majority 6,838 (21.49%))

NEWPORT WEST
E. 62,111 T. 39,720 (63.95%) Lab. hold
Paul Flynn, Lab.   16,389
Matthew Williams, C.   12,845
Veronica German, LD   6,587
Timothy Windsor, BNP   1,183
Hugh Moelwyn Hughes, UKIP   1,144
Jeff Rees, PC   1,122
Pippa Bartolotti, Green   450
Lab. majority 3,544 (8.92%)
3.18% swing Lab. to C.
(2005: Lab. majority 5,458 (15.27%))

§OGMORE
E. 55,527 T. 34,650 (62.40%) Lab. hold
Huw Irranca-Davies, Lab.   18,644
Emma Moore, C.   5,398
Jackie Radford, LD   5,260
Danny Clark, PC   3,326
Kay Thomas, BNP   1,242
Carolyn Passey, UKIP   780
Lab. majority 13,246 (38.23%)
Notional 4.28% swing Lab. to C.
(2005: Lab. majority 14,839 (46.29%))

§PONTYPRIDD
E. 58,219 T. 36,671 (62.99%) Lab. hold
*Owen Smith, Lab.   14,220
Michael Powell, LD   11,435
Lee Gonzalez, C.   5,932
Ioan Bellin, PC   2,673
David Bevan, UKIP   1,229
Simon Parsons, Soc. Lab.   456
Donald Watson, Ch. P.   365
John Matthews, Green   361
Lab. majority 2,785 (7.59%)
Notional 13.31% swing Lab. to LD
(2005: Lab. majority 11,694 (34.21%))

§PRESELI PEMBROKESHIRE
E. 57,419 T. 39,602 (68.97%) C. hold
Stephen Crabb, C.   16,944
Mari Rees, Lab.   12,339
Nick Tregoning, LD   5,759
Henry Jones-Davies, PC   3,654
Richard Lawson, UKIP   906
C. majority 4,605 (11.63%)
Notional 5.05% swing Lab. to C.
(2005: C. majority 601 (1.53%))

RHONDDA
E. 51,554 T. 31,072 (60.27%) Lab. hold
Chris Bryant, Lab.   17,183
Geraint Davies, PC   5,630
Paul Wasley, LD   3,309
Philip Howe, Ind.   2,599
Juliet Henderson, C.   1,993
Taffy John, UKIP   358
Lab. majority 11,553 (37.18%)
7.48% swing Lab. to PC
(2005: Lab. majority 16,242 (52.14%))

SWANSEA EAST
E. 59,823 T. 32,676 (54.62%) Lab. hold
Sian James, Lab. 16,819
Robert Speht, LD 5,981
Christian Holliday, C. 4,823
Dic Jones, PC 2,181
Clive Bennett, BNP 1,715
David Rogers, UKIP 839
Tony Young, Green 318
Lab. majority 10,838 (33.17%)
1.66% swing Lab. to LD
(2005: Lab. majority 11,249 (36.48%))

SWANSEA WEST
E. 61,334 T. 35,593 (58.03%) Lab. hold
*Geraint Davies, Lab. 12,335
Peter May, LD 11,831
Rene Kinzett, C. 7,407
Harri Roberts, PC 1,437
Alan Bateman, BNP 910
Tim Jenkins, UKIP 716
Keith Ross, Green 404
Ian McCloy, Ind. 374
Rob Williams, TUSC 179
Lab. majority 504 (1.42%)
5.74% swing Lab. to LD
(2005: Lab. majority 4,269 (12.90%))

TORFAEN
E. 61,178 T. 37,640 (61.53%) Lab. hold
Paul Murphy, Lab. 16,847
Jonathan Burns, C. 7,541
David Morgan, LD 6,264
Rhys ab Elis, PC 2,005
Jennifer Noble, BNP 1,657
Fred Wildgust, Ind. 1,419
Gareth Dunn, UKIP 862
Richard Turner-Thomas, Ind. 607
Owen Clarke, Green 438
Lab. majority 9,306 (24.72%)
8.19% swing Lab. to C.
(2005: Lab. majority 14,791 (41.11%))

§VALE OF CLWYD
E. 55,781 T. 35,534 (63.70%) Lab. hold
Chris Ruane, Lab. 15,017
Matt Wright, C. 12,508
Paul Penlington, LD 4,472
Caryl Wyn Jones, PC 2,068
Ian Si'Ree, BNP 827
Tom Turner, UKIP 515
Mike Butler, Green Soc. 127
Lab. majority 2,509 (7.06%)
Notional 3.56% swing Lab. to C.
(2005: Lab. majority 4,629 (14.18%))

§VALE OF GLAMORGAN
E. 70,262 T. 48,667 (69.27%) C. gain
*Alun Cairns, C. 20,341
Alana Davies, Lab. 16,034
Eluned Parrott, LD 7,403
Ian Johnson, PC 2,667
Kevin Mahoney, UKIP 1,529
Rhodri Thomas, Green 457
John Harrold, Ch. P. 236
C. majority 4,307 (8.85%)
Notional 6.11% swing Lab. to C.
(2005: Lab. majority 1,574 (3.37%))

WREXHAM
E. 50,872 T. 32,976 (64.82%) Lab. hold
Ian Lucas, Lab. 12,161
Tom Rippeth, LD 8,503
Gareth Hughes, C. 8,375
Arfon Jones, PC 2,029
Melvin Roberts, BNP 1,134
John Humberstone, UKIP 774
Lab. majority 3,658 (11.09%)
5.67% swing Lab. to LD
(2005: Lab. majority 6,819 (22.44%))

YNYS MON
E. 50,075 T. 34,444 (68.78%) Lab. hold
Albert Owen, Lab. 11,490
Dylan Rees, PC 9,029
Anthony Ridge-Newman, C. 7,744
Matt Wood, LD 2,592
Peter Rogers, Ind. 2,225
Elaine Gill, UKIP 1,201
The Rev David Owen, Ch. P. 163
Lab. majority 2,461 (7.14%)
1.82% swing PC to Lab.
(2005: Lab. majority 1,242 (3.50%))

SCOTLAND

ABERDEEN NORTH
E. 64,808 T. 37,701 (58.17%) Lab. hold
Frank Doran, Lab. 16,746
Joanna Strathdee, SNP 8,385
Kristian Chapman, LD 7,001
Stewart Whyte, C. 4,666
Roy Jones, BNP 635
Ewan Robertson, SSP 268
Lab. majority 8,361 (22.18%)
1.00% swing SNP to Lab.
(2005: Lab. majority 6,795 (18.55%))

ABERDEEN SOUTH
E. 64,031 T. 43,034 (67.21%) Lab. hold
Anne Begg, Lab. 15,722
John Sleigh, LD 12,216
Amanda Harvie, C. 8,914
Mark McDonald, SNP 5,102
Susan Ross, BNP 529
Rhonda Reekie, Green 413
Robert Green, SACL 138
Lab. majority 3,506 (8.15%)
2.45% swing LD to Lab.
(2005: Lab. majority 1,348 (3.24%))

ABERDEENSHIRE WEST &
KINCARDINE
E. 66,110 T. 45,195 (68.36%) LD hold
Sir Robert Smith, LD 17,362
Alex Johnstone, C. 13,678
Dennis Robertson, SNP 7,086
Greg Williams, Lab. 6,159
Gary Raikes, BNP 513
Anthony Atkinson, UKIP 397
LD majority 3,684 (8.15%)
4.89% swing LD to C.
(2005: LD majority 7,471 (17.94%))

AIRDRIE & SHOTTS
E. 62,364 T. 35,849 (57.48%) Lab. hold
*Pamela Nash, Lab. 20,849
Sophia Coyle, SNP 8,441
Ruth Whitfield, C. 3,133
John Love, LD 2,898
John McGeechan, Ind. 528
Lab. majority 12,408 (34.61%)
3.93% swing Lab. to SNP
(2005: Lab. majority 14,084 (42.48%))

ANGUS
E. 62,863 T. 37,960 (60.39%) SNP hold
Mike Weir, SNP 15,020
Alberto Costa, C. 11,738
Kevin Hutchens, Lab. 6,535
Sanjay Samani, LD 4,090
Martin Gray, UKIP 577
SNP majority 3,282 (8.65%)
2.22% swing C. to SNP
(2005: SNP majority 1,601 (4.20%))

ARGYLL & BUTE
E. 67,165 T. 45,207 (67.31%) LD hold
Alan Reid, LD 14,292
Gary Mulvaney, C. 10,861
David Graham, Lab. 10,274
Michael MacKenzie, SNP 8,563
Elaine Morrison, Green 789
George Doyle, Ind. 272
John Black, Jacobite 156
LD majority 3,431 (7.59%)
2.72% swing LD to C.
(2005: LD majority 5,636 (13.04%))

AYR, CARRICK & CUMNOCK
E. 73,320 T. 45,893 (62.59%) Lab. hold
Sandra Osborne, Lab. 21,632
William Grant, C. 11,721
Charles Brodie, SNP 8,276
James Taylor, LD 4,264
Lab. majority 9,911 (21.60%)
0.30% swing Lab. to C.
(2005: Lab. majority 9,997 (22.19%))

AYRSHIRE CENTRAL
E. 68,352 T. 43,915 (64.25%) Lab. hold
Brian Donohoe, Lab. 20,950
Maurice Golden, C. 8,943
John Mullen, SNP 8,364
Andrew Chamberlain, LD 5,236
James McDaid, Soc. Lab. 422
Lab. majority 12,007 (27.34%)
1.51% swing C. to Lab.
(2005: Lab. majority 10,423 (24.31%))

AYRSHIRE NORTH & ARRAN
E. 74,953 T. 46,116 (61.53%) Lab. hold

Katy Clark, Lab.	21,860
Patricia Gibson, SNP	11,965
Philip Lardner, C.	7,212
Gillian Cole-Hamilton, LD	4,630
Louise McDaid, Soc. Lab.	449

Lab. majority 9,895 (21.46%)
2.26% swing Lab. to SNP
(2005: Lab. majority 11,296 (25.55%))

BANFF & BUCHAN
E. 64,300 T. 38,466 (59.82%) SNP hold

*Eilidh Whiteford, SNP	15,868
Jimmy Buchan, C.	11,841
Glen Reynolds, Lab.	5,382
Galen Milne, LD	4,365
Richard Payne, BNP	1,010

SNP majority 4,027 (10.47%)
10.67% swing SNP to C.
(2005: SNP majority 11,837 (31.81%))

BERWICKSHIRE, ROXBURGH & SELKIRK
E. 73,826 T. 49,014 (66.39%) LD hold

Michael Moore, LD	22,230
John Lamont, C.	16,555
Ian Miller, Lab.	5,003
Paul Wheelhouse, SNP	4,497
Sherry Fowler, UKIP	595
Chris Black, Jacobite	134

LD majority 5,675 (11.58%)
0.71% swing LD to C.
(2005: LD majority 5,901 (13.00%))

CAITHNESS, SUTHERLAND & EASTER ROSS
E. 47,257 T. 28,768 (60.88%) LD hold

John Thurso, LD	11,907
John Mackay, Lab.	7,081
Jean Urquhart, SNP	5,516
Alastair Graham, C.	3,744
Gordon Campbell, Ind.	520

LD majority 4,826 (16.78%)
6.38% swing LD to Lab.
(2005: LD majority 8,168 (29.53%))

COATBRIDGE, CHRYSTON & BELLSHILL
E. 70,067 T. 41,635 (59.42%) Lab. hold

Tom Clarke, Lab.	27,728
Frances McGlinchey, SNP	7,014
Kenneth Elder, LD	3,519
Fiona Houston, C.	3,374

Lab. majority 20,714 (49.75%)
0.58% swing Lab. to SNP
(2005: Lab. majority 19,519 (50.90%))

CUMBERNAULD, KILSYTH & KIRKINTILLOCH EAST
E. 64,037 T. 41,150 (64.26%) Lab. hold

*Gregg McClymont, Lab.	23,549
Julie Hepburn, SNP	9,794
Rod Ackland, LD	3,924
Stephanie Fraser, C.	3,407
William O'Neill, SSP	476

Lab. majority 13,755 (33.43%)
1.92% swing SNP to Lab.
(2005: Lab. majority 11,562 (29.58%))

DUMFRIES & GALLOWAY
E. 74,581 T. 52,173 (69.95%) Lab. hold

Russell Brown, Lab.	23,950
Peter Duncan, C.	16,501
Andrew Wood, SNP	6,419
Richard Brodie, LD	4,608
William Wright, UKIP	695

Lab. majority 7,449 (14.28%)
4.27% swing C. to Lab.
(2005: Lab. majority 2,922 (5.74%))

DUMFRIESSHIRE, CLYDESDALE & TWEEDDALE
E. 66,627 T. 45,892 (68.88%) C. hold

David Mundell, C.	17,457
Claudia Beamish, Lab.	13,263
Catriona Bhatia, LD	9,080
Aileen Orr, SNP	4,945
Steven McKeane, UKIP	637
Alis Ballance, Green	510

C. majority 4,194 (9.14%)
2.62% swing Lab. to C.
(2005: C. majority 1,738 (3.90%))

DUNBARTONSHIRE EAST
E. 63,795 T. 47,948 (75.16%) LD hold

Jo Swinson, LD	18,551
Mary Galbraith, Lab.	16,367
Mark Nolan, C.	7,431
Iain White, SNP	5,054
James Beeley, UKIP	545

LD majority 2,184 (4.55%)
2.07% swing LD to Lab.
(2005: LD majority 4,061 (8.69%))

DUNBARTONSHIRE WEST
E. 66,085 T. 42,266 (63.96%) Lab. (Co-op) hold

*Gemma Doyle, Lab. (Co-op)	25,905
Graeme McCormick, SNP	8,497
Helen Watt, LD	3,434
Martyn McIntyre, C.	3,242
Mitch Sorbie, UKIP	683
Katharine McGavigan, Soc. Lab.	505

Lab. (Co-op) majority 17,408 (41.19%)
5.50% swing SNP to Lab. (Co-op)
(2005: Lab. (Co-op) majority 12,553 (30.18%))

DUNDEE EAST
E. 65,471 T. 40,568 (61.96%) SNP hold

Stewart Hosie, SNP	15,350
Katrina Murray, Lab.	13,529
Chris Bustin, C.	6,177
Clive Sneddon, LD	4,285
Shiona Baird, Green	542
Mike Arthur, UKIP	431
Angela Gorrie, SSP	254

SNP majority 1,821 (4.49%)
1.76% swing Lab. to SNP
(2005: SNP majority 383 (0.97%))

DUNDEE WEST
E. 63,013 T. 37,126 (58.92%) Lab. hold

Jim McGovern, Lab.	17,994
Jim Barrie, SNP	10,716
John Barnett, LD	4,233
Colin Stewart, C.	3,461
Andy McBride, Ind.	365
Jim McFarlane, TUSC	357

Lab. majority 7,278 (19.60%)
2.52% swing SNP to Lab.
(2005: Lab. majority 5,379 (14.56%))

DUNFERMLINE & FIFE WEST
E. 73,769 T. 48,947 (66.35%) Lab. gain

*Thomas Docherty, Lab.	22,639
Willie Rennie, LD	17,169
Joe McCall, SNP	5,201
Belinda Hacking, C.	3,305
Otto Inglis, UKIP	633

Lab. majority 5,470 (11.18%)
8.05% swing Lab. to LD
(2005: Lab. majority 11,562 (27.27%))(2006: LD majority 1,800 (5.21%))

EAST KILBRIDE, STRATHAVEN & LESMAHAGOW
E. 76,534 T. 50,946 (66.57%) Lab. hold

*Michael McCann, Lab.	26,241
John McKenna, SNP	11,738
Graham Simpson, C.	6,613
John Loughton, LD	5,052
Kirsten Robb, Green	1,003
John Houston, Ind.	299

Lab. majority 14,503 (28.47%)
1.19% swing Lab. to SNP
(2005: Lab. majority 14,723 (30.84%))

EAST LOTHIAN
E. 73,438 T. 49,161 (66.94%) Lab. hold

*Fiona O'Donnell, Lab.	21,919
Michael Veitch, C.	9,661
Stuart Ritchie, LD	8,288
Andrew Sharp, SNP	7,883
James Mackenzie, Green	862
Jon Lloyd, UKIP	548

Lab. majority 12,258 (24.93%)
0.28% swing Lab. to C.
(2005: Lab. majority 7,620 (16.65%))

EDINBURGH EAST
E. 60,941 T. 39,865 (65.42%) Lab. hold

*Sheila Gilmore, Lab.	17,314
George Kerevan, SNP	8,133
Beverley Hope, LD	7,751
Martin Donald, C.	4,358
Robin Harper, Green	2,035
Gary Clark, TUSC	274

Lab. majority 9,181 (23.03%)
0.01% swing SNP to Lab.
(2005: Lab. majority 6,202 (15.62%))

EDINBURGH NORTH & LEITH
E. 69,204 T. 47,356 (68.43%) Lab. (Co-op) hold

Mark Lazarowicz, Lab. (Co-op)	17,740
Kevin Lang, LD	16,016
Iain McGill, C.	7,079
Calum Cashley, SNP	4,568
Kate Joester, Green	1,062
John Hein, Lib.	389
Willie Black, TUSC	233
David Jacobsen, Soc. Lab.	141
Cameron MacIntyre, Ind.	128

Lab. majority 1,724 (3.64%)
0.70% swing Lab. (Co-op) to LD
(2005: Lab. (Co-op) majority 2,153 (5.05%))

EDINBURGH SOUTH
E. 59,354 T. 43,801 (73.80%) Lab. hold

*Ian Murray, Lab.	15,215
Fred Mackintosh, LD	14,899
Neil Hudson, C.	9,452
Sandy Howat, SNP	3,354
Steve Burgess, Green	881

Lab. majority 316 (0.72%)
0.11% swing Lab. to LD
(2005: Lab. majority 405 (0.95%))

EDINBURGH SOUTH WEST
E. 66,359 T. 45,462 (68.51%) Lab. hold
Alistair Darling, Lab.   19,473
Jason Rust, C.   11,026
Tim McKay, LD   8,194
Kaukab Stewart, SNP   5,530
Clare Cooney, Green   872
Colin Fox, SSP   319
Caroline Bellamy, Comm. Lge   48
Lab. majority 8,447 (18.58%)
1.05% swing C. to Lab.
(2005: Lab. majority 7,242 (16.49%))

EDINBURGH WEST
E. 65,161 T. 46,447 (71.28%) LD hold
*Michael Crockart, LD   16,684
Cameron Day, Lab.   12,881
Stewart Geddes, C.   10,767
Sheena Cleland, SNP   6,115
LD majority 3,803 (8.19%)
11.35% swing LD to Lab.
(2005: LD majority 13,600 (30.05%))

FALKIRK
E. 81,869 T. 50,777 (62.02%) Lab. hold
Eric Joyce, Lab.   23,207
John McNally, SNP   15,364
Katie Mackie, C.   5,698
Kieran Leach, LD   5,225
Brian Goldie, UKIP   1,283
Lab. majority 7,843 (15.45%)
7.00% swing Lab. to SNP
(2005: Lab. majority 13,475 (29.45%))

FIFE NORTH EAST
E. 62,969 T. 40,064 (63.62%) LD hold
Sir Menzies Campbell, LD   17,763
Miles Briggs, C.   8,715
Mark Hood, Lab.   6,869
Rod Campbell, SNP   5,685
Mike Scott-Hayward, UKIP   1,032
LD majority 9,048 (22.58%)
5.01% swing LD to C.
(2005: LD majority 12,571 (32.60%))

GLASGOW CENTRAL
E. 60,062 T. 30,580 (50.91%) Lab. hold
*Anas Sarwar, Lab.   15,908
Osama Saeed, SNP   5,357
Chris Young, LD   5,010
John Bradley, C.   2,158
Alastair Whitelaw, Green   800
Ian Holt, BNP   616
James Nesbitt, SSP   357
Ramsay Urquhart, UKIP   246
Finlay Archibald, Pirate   128
Lab. majority 10,551 (34.50%)
0.54% swing SNP to Lab.
(2005: Lab. majority 8,531 (30.43%))

GLASGOW EAST
E. 61,516 T. 32,164 (52.29%) Lab. gain
*Margaret Curran, Lab.   19,797
John Mason, SNP   7,957
Kevin Ward, LD   1,617
Hamira Khan, C.   1,453
Joseph Finnie, BNP   677
Frances Curran, SSP   454
Arthur Thackeray, UKIP   209
Lab. majority 11,840 (36.81%)
3.42% swing Lab. to SNP
(2005: Lab. majority 13,507
(43.66%))(2008: SNP majority 365
(1.39%))

GLASGOW NORTH
E. 51,416 T. 29,613 (57.59%) Lab. hold
Ann McKechin, Lab.   13,181
Katy Gordon, LD   9,283
Patrick Grady, SNP   3,530
Erin Boyle, C.   2,089
Martin Bartos, Green   947
Thomas Main, BNP   296
Angela McCormick, TUSC   287
Lab. majority 3,898 (13.16%)
0.60% swing LD to Lab.
(2005: Lab. majority 3,338 (11.96%))

GLASGOW NORTH EAST
E. 59,859 T. 29,409 (49.13%) Lab. hold
Willie Bain, Lab.   20,100
Billy McAllister, SNP   4,158
Eileen Baxendale, LD   2,262
Ruth Davidson, C.   1,569
Walter Hamilton, BNP   798
Graham Campbell, TUSC   187
Kevin McVey, SSP   179
Jim Berrington, Soc. Lab.   156
Lab. majority 15,942 (54.21%)
(2005: Speaker majority 10,134
(35.66%))(2009: Lab. majority 8,111
(39.38%))

GLASGOW NORTH WEST
E. 60,968 T. 35,582 (58.36%) Lab. hold
John Robertson, Lab.   19,233
Natalie McKee, LD   5,622
Mags Park, SNP   5,430
Richard Sullivan, C.   3,537
Moira Crawford, Green   882
Scott Mclean, BNP   699
Marc Livingstone, Comm.   179
Lab. majority 13,611 (38.25%)
4.31% swing LD to Lab.
(2005: Lab. majority 10,093 (29.63%))

GLASGOW SOUTH
E. 65,029 T. 40,094 (61.66%) Lab. hold
Tom Harris, Lab.   20,736
Malcolm Fleming, SNP   8,078
Shabnum Mustapha, LD   4,739
Davena Rankin, C.   4,592
Marie Campbell, Green   961
Mike Coyle, BNP   637
Brian Smith, TUSC   351
Lab. majority 12,658 (31.57%)
1.51% swing Lab. to SNP
(2005: Lab. majority 10,832 (28.19%))

GLASGOW SOUTH WEST
E. 58,182 T. 31,781 (54.62%)
                        Lab. (Co-op) hold
Ian Davidson, Lab. (Co-op)   19,863
Chris Stephens, SNP   5,192
Isabel Nelson, LD   2,870
Maya Henderson Forrest, C.   2,084
Tommy Sheridan, TUSC   931
David Orr, BNP   841
Lab. (Co-op) majority 14,671 (46.16%)
0.65% swing SNP to Lab. (Co-op)
(2005: Lab. (Co-op) majority 13,896
(44.86%))

GLENROTHES
E. 67,893 T. 40,501 (59.65%) Lab. hold
Lindsay Roy, Lab.   25,247
David Alexander, SNP   8,799
Harry Wills, LD   3,108
Sheila Low, C.   2,922
Kris Seunarine, UKIP   425
Lab. majority 16,448 (40.61%)
6.04% swing SNP to Lab.
(2005: Lab. majority 10,664
(28.54%))(2008: Lab. majority 6,737
(18.61%))

GORDON
E. 73,420 T. 48,775 (66.43%) LD hold
Malcolm Bruce, LD   17,575
Richard Thomson, SNP   10,827
Barney Crockett, Lab.   9,811
Ross Thomson, C.   9,111
Sue Edwards, Green   752
Elise Jones, BNP   699
LD majority 6,748 (13.83%)
7.61% swing LD to SNP
(2005: LD majority 11,026 (24.81%))

INVERCLYDE
E. 59,209 T. 37,502 (63.34%) Lab. hold
David Cairns, Lab.   20,993
Innes Nelson, SNP   6,567
Simon Hutton, LD   5,007
David Wilson, C.   4,502
Peter Campbell, UKIP   433
Lab. majority 14,426 (38.47%)
3.64% swing SNP to Lab.
(2005: Lab. majority 11,259 (31.19%))

INVERNESS, NAIRN, BADENOCH &
STRATHSPEY
E. 72,528 T. 47,086 (64.92%) LD hold
Danny Alexander, LD   19,172
Mike Robb, Lab.   10,407
John Finnie, SNP   8,803
Jim Ferguson, C.   6,278
Dr Donald Boyd, Ch. P.   835
Donnie MacLeod, Green   789
Ross Durance, UKIP   574
George MacDonald, TUSC   135
Kit Fraser, Joy   93
LD majority 8,765 (18.61%)
4.62% swing Lab. to LD
(2005: LD majority 4,148 (9.37%))

KILMARNOCK & LOUDOUN
E. 74,131 T. 46,553 (62.80%)
                       Lab. (Co-op) hold
*Cathy Jamieson, Lab. (Co-op)   24,460
George Leslie, SNP   12,082
Janette McAlpine, C.   6,592
Sebastian Tombs, LD   3,419
Lab. (Co-op) majority 12,378 (26.59%)
3.49% swing SNP to Lab. (Co-op)
(2005: Lab. (Co-op) majority 8,703
(19.61%))

KIRKCALDY & COWDENBEATH
E. 73,665 T. 45,802 (62.18%) Lab. hold
Gordon Brown, Lab.   29,559
Douglas Chapman, SNP   6,550
John Mainland, LD   4,269
Lindsay Paterson, C.   4,258
Peter Adams, UKIP   760
Susan Archibald, Ind.   184
Donald MacLaren of MacLaren, Ind. 165
Derek Jackson, Land   57
Lab. majority 23,009 (50.24%)
3.33% swing SNP to Lab.
(2005: Lab. majority 18,216 (43.58%))

LANARK & HAMILTON EAST
E. 74,773 T. 46,554 (62.26%) Lab. hold
Jim Hood, Lab.   23,258
Clare Adamson, SNP   9,780
Colin McGavigan, C.   6,981
Douglas Herbison, LD   5,249
Duncan McFarlane, Ind.   670
Rob Sale, UKIP   616
Lab. majority 13,478 (28.95%)
0.34% swing SNP to Lab.
(2005: Lab. majority 11,947 (27.41%))

LINLITHGOW & FALKIRK EAST
E. 80,907 T. 51,450 (63.59%) Lab. hold
Michael Connarty, Lab.   25,634
Tam Smith, SNP   13,081
Stephen Glenn, LD   6,589
Andrea Stephenson, C.   6,146
Lab. majority 12,553 (24.40%)
0.13% swing SNP to Lab.
(2005: Lab. majority 11,202 (24.15%))

LIVINGSTON
E. 75,924 T. 47,907 (63.10%) Lab. hold
*Graeme Morrice, Lab.   23,215
Lis Bardell, SNP   12,424
Charles Dundas, LD   5,316
Alison Adamson-Ross, C.   5,158
David Orr, BNP   960
Alistair Forrest, UKIP   443
Ally Hendry, SSP   242
Jim Slavin, Ind.   149
Lab. majority 10,791 (22.52%)
3.51% swing Lab. to SNP
(2005: Lab. majority 13,097
(29.54%))(2005: Lab. majority 2,680
(9.09%))

MIDLOTHIAN
E. 61,387 T. 39,242 (63.93%) Lab. hold
David Hamilton, Lab.   18,449
Colin Beattie, SNP   8,100
Ross Laird, LD   6,711
James Callander, C.   4,661
Ian Baxter, Green   595
Gordon Norrie, UKIP   364
George McCleery, Ind.   196
Willie Duncan, TUSC   166
Lab. majority 10,349 (26.37%)
1.07% swing Lab. to SNP
(2005: Lab. majority 7,265 (19.27%))

MORAY
E. 65,925 T. 41,004 (62.20%) SNP hold
Angus Robertson, SNP   16,273
Douglas Ross, C.   10,683
Kieron Green, Lab.   7,007
James Paterson, LD   5,956
Donald Gatt, UKIP   1,085
SNP majority 5,590 (13.63%)
0.50% swing SNP to C.
(2005: SNP majority 5,676 (14.63%))

MOTHERWELL & WISHAW
E. 66,918 T. 39,123 (58.46%) Lab. hold
Frank Roy, Lab.   23,910
Marion Fellows, SNP   7,104
Stuart Douglas, LD   3,840
Patsy Gilroy, C.   3,660
Ray Gunnion, TUSC   609
Lab. majority 16,806 (42.96%)
0.97% swing SNP to Lab.
(2005: Lab. majority 15,222 (41.02%))

NA H-EILEANAN AN IAR
E. 22,266 T. 14,717 (66.10%) SNP hold
Angus MacNeil, SNP   6,723
Donald John MacSween, Lab.   4,838
Murdo Murray, Ind.   1,412
Jean Davis, LD   1,097
Sheena Norquay, C.   647
SNP majority 1,885 (12.81%)
1.20% swing Lab. to SNP
(2005: SNP majority 1,441 (10.41%))

OCHIL & PERTHSHIRE SOUTH
E. 75,115 T. 50,469 (67.19%) Lab. hold
Gordon Banks, Lab.   19,131
Annabelle Ewing, SNP   13,944
Gerald Michaluk, C.   10,342
Graeme Littlejohn, LD   5,754
David Bushby, UKIP   689
Hilary Charles, Green   609
Lab. majority 5,187 (10.28%)
4.40% swing SNP to Lab.
(2005: Lab. majority 688 (1.47%))

ORKNEY & SHETLAND
E. 33,085 T. 19,346 (58.47%) LD hold
Alistair Carmichael, LD   11,989
Mark Cooper, Lab.   2,061
John Mowat, SNP   2,042
Frank Nairn, C.   2,032
Robert Smith, UKIP   1,222
LD majority 9,928 (51.32%)
6.98% swing Lab. to LD
(2005: LD majority 6,627 (37.35%))

PAISLEY & RENFREWSHIRE NORTH
E. 63,704 T. 43,707 (68.61%) Lab. hold
Jim Sheridan, Lab.   23,613
Mags MacLaren, SNP   8,333
Alistair Campbell, C.   6,381
Ruaraidh Dobson, LD   4,597
Gary Pearson, Ind.   550
Chris Rollo, SSP   233
Lab. majority 15,280 (34.96%)
4.03% swing SNP to Lab.
(2005: Lab. majority 11,001 (26.91%))

PAISLEY & RENFREWSHIRE SOUTH
E. 61,197 T. 39,998 (65.36%) Lab. hold
Douglas Alexander, Lab.   23,842
Andy Doig, SNP   7,228
Gordon McCaskill, C.   3,979
Ashay Ghai, LD   3,812
Paul Mack, Ind.   513
Jimmy Kerr, SSP   375
William Hendry, Ind.   249
Lab. majority 16,614 (41.54%)
3.27% swing SNP to Lab.
(2005: Lab. majority 13,232 (34.95%))

PERTH & PERTHSHIRE NORTH
E. 72,141 T. 48,268 (66.91%) SNP hold
Pete Wishart, SNP   19,118
Peter Lyburn, C.   14,739
Jamie Glackin, Lab.   7,923
Peter Barrett, LD   5,954
Douglas Taylor, Trust   534
SNP majority 4,379 (9.07%)
2.88% swing C. to SNP
(2005: SNP majority 1,521 (3.31%))

RENFREWSHIRE EAST
E. 66,249 T. 51,181 (77.26%) Lab. hold
Jim Murphy, Lab.   25,987
Richard Cook, C.   15,567
Gordon Macdonald, LD   4,720
Gordon Archer, SNP   4,535
Donald MacKay, UKIP   372
Lab. majority 10,420 (20.36%)
3.16% swing C. to Lab.
(2005: Lab. majority 6,657 (14.04%))

ROSS, SKYE & LOCHABER
E. 51,836 T. 34,838 (67.21%) LD hold
Charles Kennedy, LD   18,335
John McKendrick, Lab.   5,265
Alasdair Stephen, SNP   5,263
Donald Cameron, C.   4,260
Eleanor Scott, Green   777
Philip Anderson, UKIP   659
Ronnie Campbell, Ind.   279
LD majority 13,070 (37.52%)
3.14% swing LD to Lab.
(2005: LD majority 14,249 (43.79%))

RUTHERGLEN & HAMILTON WEST
E. 76,408 T. 46,981 (61.49%)
                      Lab. (Co-op) hold
*Tom Greatrex, Lab. (Co-op)   28,566
Graeme Horne, SNP   7,564
Ian Robertson, LD   5,636
Malcolm Macaskill, C.   4,540
Janice Murdoch, UKIP   675
Lab. (Co-op) majority 21,002 (44.70%)
1.51% swing SNP to Lab. (Co-op)
(2005: Lab. (Co-op) majority 16,112
(37.24%))

STIRLING
E. 66,080 T. 46,791 (70.81%) Lab. hold
Anne McGuire, Lab.   19,558
Bob Dalrymple, C.   11,204
Alison Lindsay, SNP   8,091
Graham Reed, LD   6,797
Mark Ruskell, Green   746
Paul Henke, UKIP   395
Lab. majority 8,354 (17.85%)
3.47% swing C. to Lab.
(2005: Lab. majority 4,767 (10.91%))

NORTHERN IRELAND

§ANTRIM EAST
E. 60,204 T. 30,502 (50.66%)

		DUP hold
Sammy Wilson, DUP		13,993
Rodney McCune, UCUNF		7,223
Gerry Lynch, Alliance		3,377
Oliver McMullan, SF		2,064
Justin McCamphill, SDLP		2,019
Samuel Morrison, TUV		1,826

DUP majority 6,770 (22.20%)
Notional 0.2% swing UCUNF to DUP
(2005: DUP majority 6,996 (21.76%))

§ANTRIM NORTH
E. 73,338 T. 42,397 (57.81%)

		DUP hold
*Ian Paisley Junior, DUP		19,672
Jim Allister, TUV		7,114
Daithi McKay, SF		5,265
Irwin Armstrong, UCUNF		4,634
Declan O'Loan, SDLP		3,738
Jayne Dunlop, Alliance		1,368
Lyle Cubitt, ND		606

DUP majority 12,558 (29.62%)
(2005: DUP majority 18,486 (41.80%))

§ANTRIM SOUTH
E. 63,054 T. 34,009 (53.94%)

		DUP hold
Revd William McCrea, DUP		11,536
Sir Reg Empey, UCUNF		10,353
Mitchel McLaughlin, SF		4,729
Michelle Byrne, SDLP		2,955
Alan Lawther, Alliance		2,607
Melwyn Lucas, TUV		1,829

DUP majority 1,183 (3.48%)
Notional 3.6% swing DUP to UCUNF
(2005: DUP majority 3,778 (10.74%))

§BELFAST EAST
E. 59,007 T. 34,488 (58.45%)

		Alliance gain
*Naomi Long, Alliance		12,839
Peter Robinson, DUP		11,306
Trevor Ringland, UCUNF		7,305
David Vance, TUV		1,856
Niall Donnelly, SF		817
Mary Muldoon, SDLP		365

Alliance majority 1,533 (4.45%)
Notional 22.87% swing DUP to Alliance
(2005: DUP majority 7,900 (22.87%))

§BELFAST NORTH
E. 65,504 T. 36,993 (56.47%)

		DUP hold
Nigel Dodds, DUP		14,812
Gerry Kelly, SF		12,588
Alban Maginness, SDLP		4,544
Fred Cobain, UCUNF		2,837
William Webb, Alliance		1,809
Martin McAuley, Ind.		403

DUP majority 2,224 (6.01%)
Notional 5.00% swing DUP to SF
(2005: DUP majority 5,832 (16.02%))

§BELFAST SOUTH
E. 59,524 T. 34,186 (57.43%)

		SDLP hold
Dr Alasdair McDonnell, SDLP		14,026
Jimmy Spratt, DUP		8,100
Paula Bradshaw, UCUNF		5,910
Anna Lo, Alliance		5,114
Adam McGibbon, Green		1,036

SDLP majority 5,926 (17.33%)
Notional 8.41% swing DUP to SDLP
(2005: SDLP majority 188 (0.52%))

§BELFAST WEST
E. 59,522 T. 32,133 (53.99%) SF hold

Gerry Adams, SF		22,840
Alex Attwood, SDLP		5,261
William Humphrey, DUP		2,436
Bill Manwaring, UCUNF		1,000
Maire Hendron, Alliance		596

SF majority 17,579 (54.71%)
Notional 1.07% swing SDLP to SF
(2005: SF majority 19,527 (52.57%))

DOWN NORTH
E. 60,698 T. 33,481 (55.16%)

		Ind. hold
Lady Sylvia Hermon, Ind.		21,181
Ian Parsley, UCUNF		6,817
Stephen Farry, Alliance		1,876
Mary Kilpatrick, TUV		1,634
Steven Agnew, Green		1,043
Liam Logan, SDLP		680
Vincent Parker, SF		250

Ind. majority 14,364 (42.90%)
(2005: UUP majority 4,944 (15.31%))

§DOWN SOUTH
E. 70,784 T. 42,589 (60.17%)

		SDLP hold
*Margaret Ritchie, SDLP		20,648
Caitriona Ruane, SF		12,236
Jim Wells, DUP		3,645
John McCallister, UCUNF		3,093
Ivor McConnell, TUV		1,506
Cadogan Enright, Green		901
David Griffin, Alliance		560

SDLP majority 8,412 (19.75%)
Notional 0.06% swing SDLP to SF
(2005: SDLP majority 8,801 (19.87%))

FERMANAGH & SOUTH TYRONE
E. 67,908 T. 46,803 (68.92%) SF hold

Michelle Gildernew, SF		21,304
Rodney Connor, Ind.		21,300
Fearghal McKinney, SDLP		3,574
Vasundhara Kamble, Alliance		437
John Stevenson, Ind.		188

SF majority 4 (0.01%)
(2005: SF majority 4,582 (9.39%))

§FOYLE
E. 65,843 T. 37,889 (57.54%)

		SDLP hold
Mark Durkan, SDLP		16,922
Martina Anderson, SF		12,098
Maurice Devenney, DUP		4,489
Eammon McCann, PBP		2,936
David Harding, UCUNF		1,221
Keith McGrellis, Alliance		223

SDLP majority 4,824 (12.73%)
Notional 0.17% swing SDLP to SF
(2005: SDLP majority 5,570 (13.08%))

§LAGAN VALLEY
E. 65,257 T. 36,540 (55.99%)

		DUP hold
Jeffrey Donaldson, DUP		18,199
Daphne Trimble, UCUNF		7,713
Trevor Lunn, Alliance		4,174
Keith Harbinson, TUV		3,154
Brian Heading, SDLP		1,835
Paul Butler, SF		1,465

DUP majority 10,486 (28.70%)
Notional 3.3% swing DUP to UCUNF
(2005: DUP majority 13,493 (35.33%))

§LONDONDERRY EAST
E. 63,220 T. 34,950 (55.28%)

		DUP hold
Gregory Campbell, DUP		12,097
Cathal O hOisin, SF		6,742
Lesley Macaulay, UCUNF		6,218
Thomas Conway, SDLP		5,399
William Ross, TUV		2,572
Bernard Fitzpatrick, Alliance		1,922

DUP majority 5,355 (15.32%)
Notional 4.13% swing DUP to SF
(2005: DUP majority 8,192 (21.26%))

NEWRY & ARMAGH
E. 74,308 T. 44,906 (60.43%) SF hold

Conor Murphy, SF		18,857
Dominic Bradley, SDLP		10,526
Danny Kennedy, UCUNF		8,558
William Irwin, DUP		5,764
William Frazer, Ind.		656
Andrew Muir, Alliance		545

SF majority 8,331 (18.55%)
1.19% swing SDLP to SF
(2005: SF majority 8,195 (16.16%))

§STRANGFORD
E. 60,539 T. 32,505 (53.69%)

		DUP hold
*Jim Shannon, DUP		14,926
Mike Nesbitt, UCUNF		9,050
Deborah Girvan, Alliance		2,828
Claire Hanna, SDLP		2,164
Terry Williams, TUV		1,814
Michael Coogan, SF		1,161
Barbara Haig, Green		562

DUP majority 5,876 (18.08%)
Notional 7.6% swing DUP to UCUNF
(2005: DUP majority 10,934 (33.32%))

TYRONE WEST
E. 61,148 T. 37,275 (60.96%) SF hold

Pat Doherty, SF		18,050
Thomas Buchanan, DUP		7,365
Ross Hussey, UCUNF		5,281
Joe Byrne, SDLP		5,212
Michael Bower, Alliance		859
Ciaran McClean, Ind.		508

SF majority 10,685 (28.67%)
3.79% swing DUP to SF
(2005: SF majority 5,005 (11.51%))

ULSTER MID
E. 64,594 T. 40,842 (63.23%) SF hold

Martin McGuinness, SF		21,239
Ian McCrea, DUP		5,876
Tony Quinn, SDLP		5,826
Sandra Overend, UCUNF		4,509
Walter Millar, TUV		2,995
Ian Butler, Alliance		397

SF majority 15,363 (37.62%)
6.73% swing DUP to SF
(2005: SF majority 10,976 (24.16%))

UPPER BANN
E. 74,732 T. 41,383 (55.38%)

		DUP hold
David Simpson, DUP		14,000
Harry Hamilton, UCUNF		10,639
John O'Dowd, SF		10,237
Dolores Kelly, SDLP		5,276
Brendan Heading, Alliance		1,231

DUP majority 3,361 (8.12%)
Notional 1.9% swing DUP to UCUNF
(2005: DUP majority 5,298 (11.93%))

BY-ELECTIONS 2010–11

For abbreviations of parties standing in the 2010–11 by-elections see also General Election results:

PBPA   People Before Profit Alliance

BARNSLEY CENTRAL
3 March 2011
E. 65,471   T. 24,252 (37%)   Lab. hold
Dan Jarvis, Lab.   14,724
Jane Collins, UKIP   2,953
James Hockney, C.   1,999
Enis Dalton, BNP   1,463
Tony Devoy, Ind.   1,266
Dominic Carman, LD   1,012
Kevin Riddiough, Eng. Dem.   544
Alan Hope, Loony   198
Michael Val Davies, Ind.   60
Lab. maj. 11,771 (48%)
3% swing UKIP to Lab.
(2010: Lab. maj. 11,093 (29.98%))

BELFAST WEST
9 June 2011
E. 61,441   T. 23,048 (37%)   SF hold
Paul Maskey, SF   16,211
Alex Attwood, SDLP   3,088
Gerry Carroll, PBPA   1,751
Brian Kingston, DUP   1,393
Bill Manwaring, UUP   386
Aaron McIntyre, Alliance   122
SF maj. 13,123 (56%)
1% swing SDLP to SF
(2010: SF maj. 17,579 (54.71%))

INVERCLYDE
30 June 2011
E. 61,856   T. 28,163 (45%)   Lab. hold
Iain McKenzie, Lab.   15,118
Anne McLaughlin, SNP   9,280
David Wilson, C.   2,784
Sophie Bridger, LD   627
Mitch Sorbie, UKIP   288
Lab. maj. 5,838 (20%)
8% swing Lab. to SNP
(2010: Lab. maj. 14,426 (38.47%))

LEICESTER SOUTH
5 May 2011
E. 77,880   T. 34,707 (44%)   Lab. hold
Jon Ashwurth, Lab.   19,771
Zuffar Haq, LD   7,693
Jane Hunt, C.   5,169
Abhijit Pandya, UKIP   994
Alan Hope, Loony   553
Lab. maj.12,078 (34%)
8% swing LD to Lab.
(2010: Lab. maj. 8,808 (18.69%))

OLDHAM EAST & SADDLEWORTH
13 January 2011
E. 72,788 T. 34,930 (47.99%) Lab. hold
Debbie Abrahams, Lab.   14,718
Elwyn Watkins, LD   11,160
Kashif Ali, C.   4,481
Paul Nuttall, UKIP   2,029
Derek Adams, BNP   1,560
Peter Allen, Green   530
The Flying Brick, Loony   145
Stephen Morris, Eng. Dem.   144
Loz Kaye, Pirate   96
David Bishop, Bus-Pass Elvis   67
Lab. maj. 3,558 (10.19%)
4.98% swing LD to Lab.
(2010: Lab. maj. 103 (0.23%))

GENERAL ELECTION FACTS AND FIGURES

TURNOUT

VOTER TURNOUT 1945 – 2010
per cent

* Average turnout – two elections were held in 1974

The UK parliamentary electorate on 6 May 2010 was 45,533,536. Overall turnout was 29,643,522, or 65.1 per cent. This excludes the 77,000 electors in the Thirsk & Malton constituency, where the election was held on 27 May 2010 owing to the death of a candidate.

HIGHEST TURNOUT

East Renfrewshire	77.3%
Westmorland & Lonsdale	76.9%
Richmond Park	76.2%
Winchester	75.8%
Devon Central	75.7%

LOWEST TURNOUT

Manchester Central	44.3%
Leeds Central	46.0%
Birmingham Ladywood	48.7%
Glasgow North East	49.1%
Blackley & Broughton	49.2%

WOMEN MPS
by party

Labour	81 (31 per cent)
Conservative	48 (16 per cent)
Liberal Democrat	7 (12 per cent)
Alliance	1 (100 per cent)
Green	1 (100 per cent)
SDLP	1 (33 per cent)
Sinn Fein	1 (20 per cent)
SNP	1 (17 per cent)
Other	1 (50 per cent)
DUP	0
Plaid Cymru	0
SDLP	0
Total	142 (22 per cent)

MAJORITIES
SMALLEST MAJORITIES

	Majority	Majority (per cent)
Fermanagh & South Tyrone,		
Michelle Gildernew, SF	4	0.0
Hampstead & Kilburn,		
Glenda Jackson, Lab.	42	0.1
Warwickshire North, Dan Byles, C.	54	
Camborne & Redruth,		
George Eustice, C.	66	0.2
Bolton West, Julie Hilling, Lab.	92	0.2

LARGEST MAJORITIES

Liverpool Walton,		
Steve Rotherham, Lab.	19,818	57.7
Knowsley, George Howarth, Lab.	25,686	57.5
East Ham, Stephen Timms, Lab.	27,826	55.2
Belfast West, Gerry Adams, SF	17,579	54.7
Glasgow North East, Willie Bain,		
Lab.	15,942	54.2

VOTES CAST 2001, 2005 AND 2010

	2001	2005	2010
Conservative	8,357,615	8,784,915	10,683,577
Labour	10,724,953	9,552,436	8,601,349
Liberal Democrat	4,814,321	5,985,454	6,827,312
UKIP	390,563	605,973	917,581
BNP	47,129	192,745	564,003
SNP	464,314	412,267	491,386
Green	166,477	283,414	284,823
Sinn Fein	175,933	174,530	171,942
DUP	181,999	241,856	168,216
Plaid Cymru	195,893	174,838	165,394
SDLP	169,865	125,626	110,970
UUP/ UCUNF*	216,839	127,414	102,361
Other	461,482	487,042	554,608
Total	26,367,383	27,148,510	29,643,522

* For the 2010 general election the Ulster Unionist Party formed an alliance with the Conservative Party in Northern Ireland and appeared on ballot papers as Ulster Conservatives and Unionists – New Force

AVERAGE AGE OF MPS
by party

Conservative	48
Liberal Democrat	50
Other	51
Labour	52
All Parties	50

Youngest MP: Pamela Nash (Lab.), Airdrie & Shotts, 25
Oldest MP: Sir Peter Tapsell (C.), Louth & Horncastle, 80

THE GOVERNMENT

A coalition government formed of the Conservative Party and Liberal Democrat Party (since 12 May 2010)

as at 1 September 2011

* Liberal Democrats

THE CABINET

Prime Minister, First Lord of the Treasury and Minister for the Civil Service
Rt. Hon. David Cameron, MP
Deputy Prime Minister, Lord President of the Council (with special responsibility for political and constitutional reform)
*Rt. Hon. Nick Clegg, MP
Chancellor of the Exchequer
Rt. Hon. George Osborne, MP
First Secretary of State, Secretary of State for Foreign and Commonwealth Affairs
Rt. Hon. William Hague, MP
Secretary of State for the Home Department and Minister for Women and Equalities
Rt. Hon. Theresa May, MP
Secretary of State for Business, Innovation and Skills and President of the Board of Trade
*Rt. Hon. Dr Vincent Cable, MP
Secretary of State for Communities and Local Government
Rt. Hon. Eric Pickles, MP
Secretary of State for Culture, Olympics, Media and Sport
Rt. Hon. Jeremy Hunt, MP
Secretary of State for Defence
Rt. Hon. Dr Liam Fox, MP
Secretary of State for Education
Rt. Hon. Michael Gove, MP
Secretary of State for Energy and Climate Change
*Rt. Hon. Chris Huhne, MP
Secretary of State for Environment, Food and Rural Affairs
Rt. Hon. Caroline Spelman, MP
Secretary of State for Health
Rt. Hon. Andrew Lansley, CBE, MP
Secretary of State for International Development
Rt. Hon. Andrew Mitchell, MP
Secretary of State for Justice and Lord Chancellor
Rt. Hon. Kenneth Clarke, QC, MP
Secretary of State for Northern Ireland
Rt. Hon. Owen Paterson, MP
Secretary of State for Scotland
*Rt. Hon. Michael Moore, MP
Secretary of State for Transport
Rt. Hon. Philip Hammond, MP
Secretary of State for Wales
Rt. Hon. Cheryl Gillan, MP
Secretary of State for Work and Pensions
Rt. Hon. Iain Duncan Smith, MP
Chief Secretary to the Treasury
*Rt. Hon. Danny Alexander, MP
Leader of the House of Lords, Chancellor of the Duchy of Lancaster
Rt. Hon. Lord Strathclyde
Minister without Portfolio (Minister of State)
Rt. Hon. Baroness Warsi

ALSO ATTENDING CABINET MEETINGS
Attorney-General
†Rt. Hon. Dominic Grieve, QC, MP

Leader of the House of Commons and Lord Privy Seal
Rt. Hon. Sir George Young, Bt., MP
Minister for the Cabinet Office and Paymaster General
Rt. Hon. Francis Maude, MP
Minister for the Cabinet Office (providing policy advice to the prime minister)
Rt. Hon. Oliver Letwin, MP
Minister of State for Universities and Science
Rt. Hon. David Willetts, MP
Parliamentary Secretary to the Treasury and Chief Whip
Rt. Hon. Patrick McLoughlin, MP

† Only attends cabinet meetings when ministerial responsibilities are on the agenda

LAW OFFICERS

Attorney-General
Rt. Hon. Dominic Grieve, QC, MP
Solicitor-General
Edward Garnier, QC, MP
Advocate-General for Scotland
*Rt. Hon. Lord Wallace of Tankerness, QC

MINISTERS OF STATE

Business, Innovation and Skills
Rt. Hon. Greg Clark, MP
†Lord Green of Hurstpierpoint
John Hayes, MP
Mark Prisk, MP
Rt. Hon. David Willetts, MP
Cabinet Office
Rt. Hon. Oliver Letwin, MP
Communities and Local Government
Rt. Hon. Greg Clark, MP
Rt. Hon. Grant Shapps, MP
Defence
*Nick Harvey, MP
Education
Nick Gibb, MP
John Hayes, MP
*Sarah Teather, MP
Energy and Climate Change
Gregory Barker, MP
Charles Hendry, MP
Environment, Food and Rural Affairs
Rt. Hon. James Paice, MP
Equalities Office
Rt. Hon. Theresa May, MP
Foreign and Commonwealth Office
*Jeremy Browne, MP
Rt. Hon. Lord Howell of Guildford
Rt. Hon. David Lidington, MP
‡Lord Green of Hurstpierpoint

† position held jointly with the Foreign and Commonwealth Office
‡ position held jointly with the Department of Business, Innovation and Skills

Health
    Rt. Hon. Simon Burns, MP
    *Paul Burstow, MP
Home Office
    Baroness Browning
    Damian Green, MP
    §Rt. Hon. Nick Herbert, MP
    Rt. Hon. Baroness Neville-Jones
International Development
    Rt. Hon. Alan Duncan, MP
Justice
    ¶Rt. Hon. Nick Herbert, MP
    *Rt. Hon. Lord McNally
Northern Ireland Office
    Rt. Hon. Hugo Swire, MP
Transport
    Rt. Hon. Theresa Villiers, MP
Work and Pensions
    Rt. Hon. Chris Grayling, MP
    *Steve Webb, MP

§ position held jointly with the Ministry of Justice
¶ position held jointly with the Home Office

UNDER-SECRETARIES OF STATE

Business, Innovation and Skills
    *Edward Davey, MP
    Baroness Wilcox
Communities and Local Government
    Baroness Hanham, CBE
    Bob Neill, MP
    *Andrew Stunell, OBE, MP
Culture, Media and Sport
    John Penrose, MP
    Hugh Robertson, MP
    Hon. Ed Vaizey, MP
Defence
    Lord Astor of Hever
    Gerald Howarth, MP
    Peter Luff, MP
    Rt. Hon. Andrew Robathan, MP
Education
    Lord Hill of Oareford, CBE
    Tim Loughton, MP
Energy and Climate Change
    Lord Marland
Environment, Food and Rural Affairs
    Richard Benyon, MP
    Lord Henley
Equalities Office
    *Lynne Featherstone, MP
Foreign and Commonwealth Office
    Henry Bellingham, MP
    Alistair Burt, MP
Health
    Earl Howe
    Anne Milton, MP
Home Office
    James Brokenshire, MP
International Development
    Stephen O'Brien, MP
Justice
    Crispin Blunt, MP
    Jonathan Djanogly, MP
Scotland Office
    Rt. Hon. David Mundell, MP

Transport
    *Norman Baker, MP
    Mike Penning, MP
Wales Office
    David Jones, MP
Work and Pensions
    Lord Freud
    Maria Miller, MP

OTHER MINISTERS

Parliamentary Private Secretary to the Prime Minister
    Desmond Swayne, MP
Cabinet Office
    Mark Harper, MP *(Parliamentary Secretary)*
    Nick Hurd, MP *(Parliamentary Secretary)*
Office of the Leader of the House of Commons
    *David Heath, CBE, MP *(Parliamentary Secretary and Deputy Leader of the Commons)*
Treasury
    Mark Hoban, MP *(Financial Secretary)*
    Justine Greening, MP *(Economic Secretary)*
    David Gauke, MP *(Exchequer Secretary)*
    Lord Sassoon *(Commercial Secretary)*

GOVERNMENT WHIPS

HOUSE OF LORDS
Captain of the Honourable Corps of the Gentlemen-at-Arms (Chief Whip)
    Rt. Hon. Baroness Anelay of St Johns, DBE
Captain of the Queen's Bodyguard of the Yeomen of the Guard (Deputy Chief Whip)
    *Rt. Hon. Lord Shutt of Greetland, OBE
Lords-in-Waiting
    Earl Attlee
    Lord Astor of Hever
    Lord De Mauley
    Lord Taylor of Holbeach, CBE
    *Lord Wallace of Saltaire
Baronesses-in-Waiting
    *Baroness Northover
    Baroness Rawlings
    Baroness Verma
    *Baroness Garden of Frognal

HOUSE OF COMMONS
Parliamentary Secretary to the Treasury (Chief Whip)
    Rt. Hon. Patrick McLoughlin, MP
Treasurer of HM Household (Deputy Chief Whip)
    Rt. Hon. John Randall, MP
Comptroller of HM Household (Deputy Chief Whip)
    *Rt. Hon. Alistair Carmichael, MP
Vice-Chamberlain of HM Household
    Rt. Hon. Mark Francois, MP
Lords Commissioners of HM Treasury
    James Duddridge, MP; Michael Fabricant, MP; Brooks Newmark, MP; Angela Watkinson, MP; Jeremy Wright, MP
Assistant Whips
    Stephen Crabb, MP; Philip Dunne, MP; Robert Goodwill, MP; *Mark Hunter, MP; *Norman Lamb, MP; Chloe Smith, MP; Shailesh Vara, MP; Bill Wiggin, MP

GOVERNMENT DEPARTMENTS

THE CIVIL SERVICE

Under the Next Steps programme, launched in 1988, many semi-autonomous executive agencies were established to carry out much of the work of the civil service. Executive agencies operate within a framework set by the responsible minister which specifies policies, objectives and available resources. All executive agencies are set annual performance targets by their minister. Each agency has a chief executive, who is responsible for the day-to-day operations of the agency and who is accountable to the minister for the use of resources and for meeting the agency's targets. The minister accounts to parliament for the work of the agency. Nearly 75 per cent of civil servants now work in executive agencies. In the first quarter of 2011 there were 471,000 permanent civil servants, down from about 537,000 in June 2005.

The Senior Civil Service was created in 1996 and comprises around 4,000 staff from permanent secretary to the former grade 5 level, including all agency chief executives. All government departments and executive agencies are now responsible for their own pay and grading systems for civil servants outside the Senior Civil Service.

SALARIES 2011–12

MINISTERIAL SALARIES *from 1 April 2011*
Ministers who are members of the House of Commons receive a parliamentary salary of £65,738 in addition to their ministerial salary.

Prime minister	£76,762
Cabinet minister (Commons)	£68,827
Cabinet minister (Lords)	£101,038
Minister of state (Commons)	£33,002
Minister of state (Lords)	£78,891
Parliamentary under-secretary (Commons)	£23,697
Parliamentary under-secretary (Lords)	£68,710

SPECIAL ADVISERS' SALARIES *from 1 April 2011*
Special advisers to government ministers are paid out of public funds; their salaries are negotiated individually, but are usually in the range of £40,352 to £106,864.

CIVIL SERVICE SALARIES *from 1 April 2011*

Senior Civil Servants	
Permanent secretary	£141,800–£277,300
Band 3	£101,500–£208,100
Band 2	£82,900–£162,500
Band 1A	£67,600–£128,900
Band 1	£58,200–£117,800

Staff are placed in pay bands according to their level of responsibility and taking account of other factors such as experience and marketability. Movement within and between bands is based on performance. Following the delegation of responsibility for pay and grading to government departments and agencies from 1 April 1996, it is no longer possible to show service-wide pay rates for staff outside the Senior Civil Service.

GOVERNMENT DEPARTMENTS

For more information on government departments, *see*
W www.cabinetoffice.gov.uk/resource-library/government-ministers-and-responsibilities

ATTORNEY-GENERAL'S OFFICE

Attorney-General's Office, 20 Victoria Street, London
SW1H 0NF
T 020-7271 2492
E correspondenceunit@attorneygeneral.gsi.gov.uk
W www.attorneygeneral.gov.uk

The law officers of the crown for England and Wales are the Attorney-General and the Solicitor-General. The Attorney-General, assisted by the Solicitor-General, is the chief legal adviser to the government and is also ultimately responsible for all crown litigation. He has overall responsibility for the work of the Law Officers' Departments (the Treasury Solicitor's Department, the Crown Prosecution Service incorporating the Revenue and Customs Prosecutions Office, the Serious Fraud Office, the Army Prosecuting Authority, HM Crown Prosecution Service Inspectorate and the Attorney-General's Office). He has a specific statutory duty to superintend the discharge of their duties by the Director of Public Prosecutions (who heads the Crown Prosecution Service) and the Director of the Serious Fraud Office. The Attorney-General has specific responsibilities for the enforcement of the criminal law and also performs certain public interest functions, eg protecting charities and appealing unduly lenient sentences. He also deals with questions of law arising in bills and with issues of legal policy.

Following the devolution of power to the Northern Ireland Assembly on 12 April 2010, the assembly now appoints the Attorney-General for Northern Ireland. The Attorney-General for England and Wales now holds the newly created office of Advocate-General for Northern Ireland, with significantly reduced responsibilities in Northern Ireland.

Attorney-General, Rt. Hon. Dominic Grieve, QC, MP
Private Secretary, D. Parish
Solicitor-General, Edward Garnier, QC, MP
Director-General, P. Fish
Director, Criminal Law, S. Patten

DEPARTMENT FOR BUSINESS, INNOVATION AND SKILLS

1 Victoria Street, London SW1H 0ET
T 020-7215 5000
W www.bis.gov.uk

The Department for Business, Innovation and Skills (BIS) was established in June 2009 by merging the Department for Business, Enterprise and Regulatory Reform and the Department for Innovation, Universities and Skills. It aims to build Britain's capabilities to compete in the global economy. The merger brought together expertise in enterprise, innovation, and world-class science and research. Among other roles, the department advocates the needs of business across government; promotes an enterprise environment; invests in the development of the higher education system; invests in the UK's science base; invests in skills through the further education system, aims to expand the number of apprenticeships; collaborates with regional development agencies to build economic growth in England; and encourages innovation in the UK.

Secretary of State for Business, Innovation and Skills and President of the Board of Trade, Rt. Hon. Dr Vince Cable, MP

Principal Private Secretary, Joanna Crellin

Senior Private Secretary, Bryan Payne

Special Advisers, Katie Waring; Giles Wilkes

Minister of State, Rt. Hon. David Willetts, MP *(Universities and Science)*

Senior Private Secretary, Emma Payne

Special Adviser, Nick Hillman

Minister of State, John Hayes *(Further Education, Skills and Lifelong Learning)**

Private Secretary, Kellie Hurst

Minister of State, Lord Green *(Trade and Investement)*

Private Secretary, Nick Whittingham

Minister of State, Mark Prisk, MP *(Business and Enterprise)*

Senior Private Secretary, Helen Mitchell

Parliamentary Under-Secretary of of State, Edward Davey, MP *(Employment Relations, Consumer and Postal Affairs)*

Private Secretary, Sarah Barraclough

Parliamentary Under-Secretary of State, Baroness Wilcox *(Business, Innovation and Skills)*

Private Secretary, Rachael Bishop

Permanent Secretary, Martin Donnelly

Senior Private Secretary, Karis Hewitt

Head of Parliamentary Unit, Ian Webster

* Jointly with the Department of Education

DEPARTMENTAL BOARD

Chair, Rt. Hon Dr Vince Cable, MP *(Secretary of State)*

Members, Tera Allas *(Economics, Strategy and Better Regulation);* Nick Baird *(Chief Executive UK Trade and Investment);* Martin Donnelly *(Permanent Secretary);* Bernadette Kelly *(Market Framework);* Stephen Lovegrove *(Shareholder Executive);* Howard Orme *(Finance and Commercial);* Philip Rutnam *(Business and Skills);* Rachel Sandby-Thomas *(Legal, People and Communications);* Adrian Smith *(Knowledge and Innovation)*

Non-Executive Members, Prof. Julia King; Andrew Witty; Dr Brian Woods-Scawen

BETTER REGULATION EXECUTIVE

1 Victoria Street, London SW1 0ET

T 020-7215 5000 E breadmin@bis.gsi.gov.uk

W www.bis.gov.uk/betterregulation

The Better Regulation Executive (BRE) is part of the Department for Business, Innovation and Skills (BIS) and leads the regulatory reform agenda across government. Working with other departments and regulators, the BRE helps to improve the design of new regulations and how they are communicated; to simplify and modernise existing regulations; and to change attitudes and approaches to regulation to become more risk-based.

Non-Executive Chair, Sir Don Curry

Chief Executive, Graham Turnock

SHAREHOLDER EXECUTIVE

1 Victoria Street, London SW1H 0ET

T 020-7215 3909

W www.shareholderexecutive.gov.uk

The Shareholder Executive was set up in September 2003 to work with other departments in government to improve the government's capabilities and performance as a shareholder, and to offer corporate finance expertise and advice across government. Its goal is to create a climate of ownership that, while challenging, is genuinely supportive and provides the framework for the 28 businesses under its remit to be successful. In addition, the Shareholder Executive's Government Property Unit is responsible for maximising value from the state's property portfolio.

Chair, vacant

Chief Executive, Stephen Lovegrove

CABINET OFFICE

70 Whitehall, London SW1A 2AS

T 020-7276 1234; Switchboard 020-7276 3000

W www.cabinet-office.gov.uk

The Cabinet Office, alongside the Treasury, sits at the centre of the government, with an overarching purpose of making government work better. It supports the prime minister and the cabinet, helping to ensure effective development, coordination and implementation of policy and operations across all government departments. The Cabinet Office also leads work to ensure that the Civil Service provides the most effective and efficient support to the government to meet its objectives. The department is headed by the Minister for the Cabinet Office.

Prime Minister, First Lord of the Treasury and Minister for the Civil Service, Rt. Hon. David Cameron, MP

Principal Private Secretary to the Prime Minister, James Bowler

Deputy Prime Minister, Rt. Hon. Nick Clegg, MP

Principal Private Secretary to the Deputy Prime Minister, Calum Miller

Minister for the Cabinet Office and Paymaster General, Rt. Hon. Francis Maude, MP

Principal Private Secretary, Sue Pither

Private Secretaries, Kitty von Bertele, Richard Stirling, Vicky Woodbine

Minister for Government Policy, Rt. Hon. Oliver Letwin, MP

Assistant Private Secretaries, Nasira Ashraf; Rose Jefferies

Parliamentary Secretary (Minister for Civil Society), Nick Hurd, MP

Private Secretary, Cameron Smith

Parliamentary Secretary (Minister for Political and Constitutional Reform), Mark Harper, MP

Private Secretary, Joanne Trimble-Bruce

Leader of the House of Lords and Chancellor of the Duchy of Lancaster, Rt. Hon. Lord Strathclyde

Private Secretary, Phil Lloyd *(Head of Office)*

Assistant Private Secretary, Sarah Kerr

Minister without Portfolio, Rt. Hon. Baroness Warsi

Private Secretary, Anna Shotbolt

Secretary of the Cabinet and Head of the Home Civil Service, Sir Gus O'Donnell, GCB

Principal Private Secretary, Rachel Hopcroft

Private Secretary, Lynne Charles

MANAGEMENT BOARD

Chair, Sir Gus O'Donnell, GCB *(Cabinet Secretary and Principal Accounting Officer for the Cabinet Office)*

Board Members, Ruth Carnall; Alexis Cleveland *(Corporate Services Group);* Sir Jon Cunliffe, CB *(Prime Minister's Adviser);* Sue Gray *(Head of Propriety and Ethics Team and Director of Private Offices Group);* Jeremy Heywood, CB, CVO *(Permanent Secretary, Prime*

Minister's Office); Bruce Mann *(Finance Director and Board Secretary);* Ian Watmore *(Chief Operating Officer for the Efficiency and Reform Group);* Chris Wormald *(Director-General and Head of the Deputy Prime Minister's Office)*
Non-Executive Directors, Lord Browne; Dame Barbara Stocking; Ian Davis; Rona Fairhead

HONOURS AND APPOINTMENTS SECRETARIAT
Ground Floor, Admiralty Arch, The Mall, London SW1A 2WH
T 020-7276 2777
Permanent Secretary, Alex Allan
Prime Minister's Appointments Secretary, Sir Paul Britton, CB
Ceremonial Officer, Denis Brennan

DOMESTIC POLICY GROUP
Comprising Economic and Domestic Affairs, Economic Policy Coordination, the Strategy Unit, and European and Global Issues.
Director-General, Chris Wormald

ECONOMIC AND DOMESTIC AFFAIRS SECRETARIAT
Director, Robin Fellgett, CB
Deputy Directors, Scott McPherson *(MoJ, Home Office, Devolution);* Hannah Tooze *(Legislation, Home Affairs – Olympics);* Patrick White *(Health and Social Justice)*
Parliamentary Adviser, John Healey

ECONOMIC POLICY COORDINATION
Director of the National Economic Council Secretariat and Deputy Head, Economic and Domestic Affairs Secretariat, Jeremy Pocklington
Deputy Directors, Caleb Deeks *(Public Spending, Labour Market);* Debbie Gillat *(Business Banking and Reform)*

STRATEGY UNIT
Director, Gareth Davies
Deputy Directors, Miatta Fahnbulleh *(Localism);* Hugh Harris *(Welfare);* Axel Heitmueller *(Economy);* Halima Khan *(Value for Money);* Sophia Oliver *(Health and Social Care);* Harvey Redgrave *(Home Affairs);* Matt Robinson *(Strategic Challenges);* Chloe Ross *(Education and Family)*

EUROPEAN AND GLOBAL ISSUES SECRETARIAT
Director, Paul Rankin
Prime Minister's Adviser, Sir Jon Cunliffe, CB *(Europe and Global Issues)*
Senior Adviser, Jonathan Portes *(Economic Policy Issues)*
Deputy Directors, Harold Freeman *(International Economic Affairs);* Hermione Gough *(Economic Reform, Energy and Climate Change, Employment and Social Affairs);* Matthew Taylor *(EU Issues)*

NATIONAL SECURITY
Comprises the Joint Intelligence Organisation, National Security Secretariat, Foreign Policy and Intelligence, Security and Resilience

JOINT INTELLIGENCE ORGANISATION
Chair, Joint Intelligence Committee and Professional Head of Intelligence Analysis, Alex Allan
Chief of the Assessments Staff and Deputy Head of Intelligence, Paul Rimmer

NATIONAL SECURITY SECRETARIAT
70 Whitehall, London SW1A 2AS
Prime Minister's National Security Adviser, Sir Peter Ricketts, GCMG

Deputy National Security Adviser, Julian Miller, CB *(Foreign Policy)*
Directors, Philip Barton, CMG, OBE *(Afghanistan and Pakistan);* Julian Miller, CB *(Foreign and Defence Policy)*

INTELLIGENCE, SECURITY AND RESILIENCE
Director, Oliver Robbins
Directors, Ciaran Martin *(Security and Intelligence);* Willam Nye *(Strategy and Counter-Terrorism);* Christina Scott *(Civil Contingencies Secretariat);* Neil Thompson *(Office of Cyber Security)*

EFFICIENCY AND REFORM GROUP
Chief Operating Officer, Ian Watmore
Director, Ben Jupp
Deputy Director, Paula McDonald, CBE *(Pay and Workforce Reform)*

OFFICE OF GOVERNMENT COMMERCE (OGC)
Rosebery Court, St Andrews Business Park, Norwich, Norfolk NR7 0HS
T 0845-000 4999 E servicedesk@ogc.gsi.gov.uk
W www.ogc.gov.uk

The Office of Government Commerce was set up in April 2000, and became part of the Efficiency and Reform Group in the Cabinet Office in June 2010. It is responsible for increasing the government's value for money by improving standards and capability in procurement, for example by delivering major capital projects, and maximising the effective use of government spending and a £30bn property estate.

CIVIL SERVICE CAPABILITY GROUP
Admiralty Arch, The Mall, London SW1A 2WH

Comprises Civil Service Reform, Civil Service Workforce and Leadership and Talent Management
Head, Gill Rider

CIVIL SERVICE REFORM
Director, Brian Etheridge, CBE
Deputy Directors, Liz McKeown *(Analysis and Insight);* Adam Pemberton *(Strategy and Performance);* Ian Wood *(Capability Review)*

CIVIL SERVICE WORKFORCE
Director, Dusty Amroliwala
Deputy Directors, Jennifer Hutton *(Diversity, Health and Wellbeing Strategy);* John Whittaker, CBE *(Employment Policy);* Julia Wood *(Pay and Reward)*

LEADERSHIP AND TALENT MANAGEMENT
Director, Helen Dudley, CBE
Deputy Directors, Jacquie Heany *(HR Profession);* Joanne Peel *(Fast Stream);* Esther Wallington *(Senior Appointments and Talent Management)*

CABINET OFFICE/NO. 10 COMMUNICATIONS
22 Whitehall, London SW1A 2WH
T 020-7276 1234
Director, Jenny Grey *(Policy Communication)*
Deputy Directors, John Toker *(Security, Intelligence and Counter-Terrorism);* Rishi Saha *(Digital Communication);* James Sorene *(Deputy Prime Minister's Spokesperson/Head of Communications);* Michael Warren *(Cross-Government Campaigns);* Emily Tofield, *(Efficiency and Reform Communication)*

OFFICE OF THE GOVERNMENT CHIEF INFORMATION OFFICER
Admiralty Arch, The Mall, London SW1A 2AH
HM Government Chief Information Officer, John Suffolk
Private Secretary and Secretary to the CIO Council, Sue Bateman
Special Projects, Andy Bloyce
Director, Martin Bellamy *(IT Strategy and Policy)*
Heads, Jo Clift *(Shared Services);* Owen Pengelly *(Central Sponsor for Information Assurance Unit)*

GOVERNMENT CLOUD PROGRAMME
Director, Chris Chant
Deputy Director, Andrew Tait *(Data Centre Strategy, G-Cloud and Apps Store)*

ICT STRATEGY AND POLICY
Deputy Government Chief Information Officer and Director, Bill McCluggage
Deputy Director, Rachel Gentry

SHARED ICT INFRASTRUCTURE
Director, Lesley Hume
Deputy Directors, Claire Baker *(Government IT Profession);* Kevin Doherty *(Cabinet Office ICT Strategy, Policy and Security);* Neill Goulder *(ICT Service Delivery);* John Stubley *(Public Service Network Programme);* Chris Thirkell *(Reliable Delivery)*

OFFICE FOR CIVIL SOCIETY
The Office for Civil Society replaced the Office for the Third Sector in May 2010 and takes a key role in delivering the government's Big Society agenda.
Executive Director, Gareth Davies
Programme Director, Juliet Mountford
Deputy Directors, Sarah Benioff *(Social Action);* Rannia Leontaridi *(Public Services);* Liz Liston-Jones *(Charities and Sector Support);* Juliet Mountford *(Strategy and Communications);* Helen Stephenson *(Bank and Investment Funds);* Annabel Turpie *(Big Society Policy and Analysis)*

CORPORATE SERVICES GROUP
Comprises Finance and Human Resources
Deputy Director, Karen Cadman *(Head of Civil Service Pensions)*
Head of Knowledge and Information Management, Roger Smethurst

FINANCE
Director, Bruce Mann, CB
Deputy Director Jerry Page *(Finance and Estates)*

HUMAN RESOURCES
Director, Janette Durbin
Deputy Director, Simon Fryer

NATIONAL SCHOOL OF GOVERNMENT
Sunningdale Park, Larch Avenue, Ascot, Berks SL5 0QE
T 01344-634000
E customer.services@nationalschool.gsi.gov.uk
W www.nationalschool.gov.uk

Since 1 April 2011, the National School of Government re-joined the Cabinet Office, and ceased to be a non-ministerial government department. The learning and development partner of the UK Civil Service, it is run by public servants for public servants, and aims to improve services for citizens by using learning and development to raise the bar for public services. Among these services are e-learning solutions, a range of open courses and qualifications and bespoke learning packages.
Principal and Chief Executive, Rod Clark

PRIME MINISTER'S OFFICE
10 Downing Street, London SW1A 2AA
T 020-7930 4433 W www.number-10.gov.uk
Prime Minister, Rt. Hon David Cameron, MP
Parliamentary Private Secretary, Desmond Swayne, MP
Permanent Secretary, Jeremy Heywood, CB, CVO
Principal Private Secretary, James Bowler
Private Secretaries, John Casson; Simon King; Gila Sacks; Matthew Style
Speech Writer to the Prime Minister, Tim Kiddell
Chief Operating Officer, Eric Hepburn
Director of Communications, Craig Oliver
Prime Minister's Official Spokesman, Steve Field
Head of News and Deputy Spokesperson, Vickie Sheriff
Chief of Staff (Political), Ed Llewellyn
Deputy Chief of Staff (Political), Catherine Fall
Director of Policy, James O'Shaughnessy
Political Press Secretary to the Prime Minister, Gabby Bertin

POLICY AND IMPLEMENTATION UNIT
Head of Policy Unit, Paul Kirby
Head of Implementation Unit, Kris Murrin
Head of Analytics Team, Ivan Collister

DEPUTY PRIME MINISTER'S OFFICE AND CONSTITUTIONAL REFORM
Principal Private Secretary to the Deputy Prime Minister, Calum Miller

CONSTITUTIONAL GROUP
Director-General, Rowena Collins-Rice
Director, Vijay Rangarajan
Deputy Directors, Judith Simpson *(Constitutional Settlement and Clerk of the Privy Council);* Mark Sweeney *(Elections and Democracy)*

CROSS GOVERNMENT UNITS in the Cabinet Office comprises the Committee on Standards in Public Life *(see* Public Bodies), Independent Offices and the Office of the Parliamentary Counsel.

INDEPENDENT OFFICES

THE COMMISSIONER FOR PUBLIC APPOINTMENTS
3rd Floor, 35 Great Smith Street, London SW1P 3BQ
T 020-7276 2625
E enquiries@publicappointmentscommissioner.org
W http://publicappointmentscommissioner.independent.gov.uk

The Commissioner for Public Appointments is responsible for monitoring, regulating and reporting on ministerial appointments to public bodies. The commissioner can investigate complaints about the way in which appointments were made.
Commissioner for Public Appointments, Sir David Normington, GCB
Head of Office, Leila Brosnan

CIVIL SERVICE COMMISSION
35 Great Smith Street, London SW1P 3BQ
T 020-7276 2617
W http://civilservicecommission.independent.gov.uk

The Civil Service Commission regulates the principle that selection for appointment to the Civil Service must be on merit on the basis of fair and open competition; the commission publishes its recruitment principles and audit departments and agencies' performance against these. They personally chair competitions for the most senior jobs in the civil service. In addition, the commission hears complaints from civil servants under the Civil Service Code.

The commission was established as a statutory body in November 2010 under the provisions of the Constitutional Reform and Governance Act 2010.
First Commissioner, Sir David Normington, GCB
Commissioners (part-time), Sir Michael Aaronson, CBE; Mark Addison; Adele Biss; Peter Blausten; Prof. Christine Hallett; Eliza Hermann; Bernard Knight, CBE; Sir Neil McIntosh; Anthea Millett, CBE; Ranjit Sondhi; Libby Watkins

OFFICE OF THE PARLIAMENTARY COUNSEL
36 Whitehall, London SW1A 2AY
T 020-7210 2588
W www.cabinetoffice.co.uk/parliamentarycounsel
First Parliamentary Counsel, Sir Stephen Laws, KCB
Chief Executive, Jim Barron, CBE

DEPARTMENT FOR COMMUNITIES AND LOCAL GOVERNMENT
Eland House, Bressenden Place, London SW1E 5DU
T 0303-444 0000
W www.communities.gov.uk

The Department for Communities and Local Government (CLG) was formed in May 2006 with a remit to promote community cohesion and prevent extremism, as well as responsibility for housing, urban regeneration and planning. It unites the communities and civil renewal functions previously undertaken by the Home Office, with responsibility for regeneration, neighbourhood renewal and local government (previously held by the Office of the Deputy Prime Minister, which was abolished following a cabinet reshuffle in May 2006).

The DCLG also has responsibility for equality policy on race and faith (functions that were previously split between several government departments).
Secretary of State for Communities and Local Government,
    Rt. Hon. Eric Pickles, MP
Principal Private Secretary, David Hill
Parliamentary Private Secretary, Stephen Hammond, MP
Minister of State, Rt. Hon. Grant Shapps, MP *(Housing)*
Private Secretary, Mark Livesey
Minister of State, Rt. Hon. Greg Clark, MP
    (Decentralisation and Cities)
Private Secretary, Fakruz Zaman
Parliamentary Under-Secretary of State, Bob Neill, MP
Private Secretary, Lee Burge
Parliamentary Under-Secretary of State, Andrew Stunell,
    OBE, MP
Private Secretary, Stella Michael-Sargeant
Parliamentary Under-Secretary of State, Baroness Hanham,
    CBE
Private Secretary, Elspeth Robinson
Permanent Secretary, Sir Bob Kerslake

Private Secretary, Caroline Winter
Chief Scientific Adviser, Jeremy Watson

MANAGEMENT BOARD
Chair, Rt. Hon. Eric Pickles, MP
Members, Andrew Campbell; Sue Higgins; Sir Bob
    Kerslake *(Permanent Secretary);* Richard McCarthy;
    David Prout
Non-Executive Members, Diana Brightmore-Armour;
    Stephen Hay; Sara Weller *(Lead)*

DEPARTMENT FOR CULTURE, MEDIA AND SPORT
2–4 Cockspur Street, London SW1Y 5DH
T 020-7211 6200
E enquiries@culture.gov.uk W www.culture.gov.uk

The Department for Culture, Media and Sport (DCMS) was established in July 1997 and aims to improve the quality of life for all those in the UK through cultural and sporting activities while championing the tourism, creative and leisure industries. It is responsible for government policy relating to the arts, sport, the National Lottery, tourism, libraries, museums and galleries, broadcasting, creative industries – including film and the music industry – press freedom and regulation, licensing, gambling and the historic environment.

The department is also responsible for 55 public bodies that help deliver the department's strategic aims and objectives, the 2012 Olympic Games and Paralympic Games, the listing of historic buildings and scheduling of ancient monuments, the export licensing of cultural goods, and the management of the Government Art Collection and the Royal Parks (its sole executive agency). It has the responsibility for humanitarian assistance in the event of a disaster, as well as for the organisation of the annual Remembrance Day ceremony at the Cenotaph. In May 2005 the DCMS assumed responsibility for fashion design, advertising and the arts market from the then Department for Trade and Industry – now the Department for Business, Innovation and Skills – which it also works jointly with on design issues (including sponsorship of the Design Council) and on relations with the computer games and publishing industries.
Secretary of State for Culture, Olympics, Media and Sport,
    Rt. Hon. Jeremy Hunt, MP
Principal Private Secretary, Paul Oldfield
Special Advisers, Sue Beeby; Adam Smith
Parliamentary Private Secretary, Rob Wilson, MP
Parliamentary Under-Secretary of State, John Penrose, MP
    (Tourism and Heritage)
Private Secretary, Leonie Phillips
Parliamentary Under-Secretary of State, Hugh Robertson,
    MP *(Sport and the Olympics)*
Private Secretary, Liz Wilson
Parliamentary Under-Secretary of State, Ed Vaizey, MP
    (Culture, Communications and Creative Industries)
Private Secretary, Craig Westwood
Permanent Secretary, Jonathan Stephens
Private Secretary, Helen Ewen

MANAGEMENT BOARD
Chair, Jonathan Stephens *(Permanent Secretary of State)*
Members, Jeremy Beeton *(Government Olympic Executive);*
    Simon Judge *(Finance)*

MINISTRY OF DEFENCE
see Defence section

DEPARTMENT FOR EDUCATION

Castle View House, East Lane, Runcorn, Cheshire WA7 2GJ
T 0870-001 2345 **Public Enquiries** 0370-000 2288
W www.education.gov.uk

The Department for Education (DfE) was established in May 2010 in place of the Department for Children, Schools and Families (DCSF), in order to refocus the department on its core purpose of supporting teaching and learning. The department is responsible for education and children's services, but the Department for Business, Innovation and Skills is responsible for higher education.

The department's objectives include the expansion of the academies programme, to allow schools to apply to become independent of their local authority, and the introduction of the free schools programme, to allow any suitable proposers, such as parents, businesses or charities, to set up their own school.

Secretary of State for Education, Rt. Hon. Michael Gove, MP
Principal Private Secretary, Hilary Spencer
Deputy Principal Private Secretary, Bernie Serieux
Private Secretary, Peter Walsh
Special Advisers, Dominic Cummings; Henry de Zoete
Parliamentary Private Secretary, David Evennett, MP
Minister of State, Sarah Teather, MP *(Children and Families)*
Private Secretary, Patrick Flack
Parliamentary Private Secretary, Duncan Hames, MP
Minister of State, Nick Gibb, MP *(Schools)*
Private Secretary, Camilla Frappell
Parliamentary Private Secretary, Nick Boles, MP
Minister of State, John Hayes, MP *(Further Education, Skills and Lifelong Learning)**
Private Secretary, Kellie Hurst
Parliamentary Under-Secretary of State, Lord Hill of Oareford, CBE *(Schools)*
Private Secretary, Jamie Weatherhead
Parliamentary Under-Secretary of State, Tim Loughton, MP *(Children and Families)*
Private Secretary, David Curtis
Parliamentary Clerk, Helen Heyden
Spokesperson in the House of Lords, Lord Hill of Oareford, CBE
Permanent Secretary, Sir David Bell, KCB
Private Secretary, Sophie Taylor

MANAGEMENT BOARD
Chair, David Bell *(Permanent Secretary of State)*
Members, Jon Coles; Sue Higgins; Tom Jeffery; Lesley Longstone
Non-Executive Members, Theodore Agnew; Sue John; John Nash; Anthony Saltz
*Jointly with the Department for Business, Innovation and Skills

DEPARTMENT OF ENERGY AND CLIMATE CHANGE

3 Whitehall Place, London SW1A 2AW
T 0300-060 4000 **E** correspondence@decc.gsi.gov.uk
W www.decc.gsi.gov.uk

The Department of Energy and Climate Change (DECC) was formed in 2008 to bring together energy policy, previously the responsibility of BERR (now the Department for Business, Innovation and Skills), and climate change mitigation policy, previously the responsibility of the Department for Environment, Food and Rural Affairs. DECC is responsible for tackling the threat of climate change by securing safe, clean and affordable energy in the UK, and by changing how we resource, manage and use our energy to create a low carbon and resource-efficient world.

Secretary of State for the Department for Energy and Climate Change, Rt. Hon. Chris Huhne, MP
Private Secretary, Ashley Ibbett
Parliamentary Private Secretary, Duncan Hames, MP
Minister of State, Charles Hendry, MP
Private Secretary, Emily Veitch
Parliamentary Private Secretary, Mark Menzies, MP
Minister of State, Gregory Barker, MP
Private Secretary, David Watson
Parliamentary Private Secretary, George Freeman, MP
Parliamentary Under-Secretary of State, Lord Marland
Private Secretary, Patrick Whitehead

EXECUTIVE TEAM
Private Secretary, Jen Goffin
Permanent Secretary, Moira Wallace
Members, Edmund Hosker *(Acting Chief Operating Officer);* Prof. David Mackay *(Chief Scientific Adviser);* Phil Wynn Owen *(Director General, International Climate Change and Energy Efficiency);* Simon Virley *(Director General, Energy Markets and Infrastructure)*

DEPARTMENT FOR ENVIRONMENT, FOOD AND RURAL AFFAIRS

Nobel House, 17 Smith Square, London SW1P 3JR
T 020-7238 3000 **Helpline** 0845-933 5577
E helpline@defra.gsi.gov.uk **W** www.defra.gov.uk

The Department for Environment, Food and Rural Affairs (DEFRA) is responsible for government policy on the environment, rural matters and farming and food production. In association with the agriculture departments of the Scottish government, the National Assembly for Wales and the Northern Ireland Office, and with the Intervention Board, the department is responsible for negotiations in the EU on the common agricultural and fisheries policies, and for single European market questions relating to its responsibilities. Its remit includes international agricultural and food trade policy.

The department's five strategic priorities are climate change, adaptation and mitigation; sustainable consumption and production; the protection of natural resources and the countryside; sustainable rural communities; and sustainable farming and food, including animal health and welfare. DEFRA is also the lead government department for emergencies in animal and plant diseases, flooding, food and water supply, dealing with the consequences of a chemical, biological, radiological or nuclear incident, and other threats to the environment.

Secretary of State for Environment, Food and Rural Affairs, Rt. Hon. Caroline Spelman, MP
Principal Private Secretary, Dr Jeremy Marlow
Private Secretaries, Alison Campbell; Mike Dowell; Emma Southard
Minister of State, Jim Paice, MP *(Agriculture and Food)*
Senior Private Secretary, Karen Morgan
Private Secretaries, Jaspreet Bassi; Ashwin Bolar; Caroline Jack;
Parliamentary Private Secretary, Mark Simmons, MP
Parliamentary Under-Secretary of State, Richard Benyon, MP *(Natural Environment and Fisheries)*
Senior Private Secretary, Simon Stannard
Private Secretaries, Emma Black; Sarah Nicholson; William Pryer

Parliamentary Under-Secretary of State, Lord Henley
Senior Private Secretary, Helena Busby
Private Secretaries, Samuel Evans; Helen Hazzledine;
Darryl Pearson
Permanent Secretary, Ms Bronwyn Hill
Senior Private Secretary, David Read
Private Secretaries, Lisa Lewis, Julie Little, Stratos Ttofis

MANAGEMENT BOARD
Chair, Ms Bronwyn Hill *(Permanent Secretary)*
Members, Alexis Cleveland; Iain Ferguson; Bill Griffiths;
Bill Stow *(Central Approvals Panel);* Peter Unwin
(Environment and Rural); Prof. Robert Watson *(Chief
Scientific Adviser);* Katrina Williams *(Food and Farming)*

FOREIGN AND COMMONWEALTH OFFICE

King Charles Street, London SW1A 2AH
T 020-7008 1500 W www.fco.gov.uk

The Foreign and Commonwealth Office (FCO) provides, through its staff in the UK and through its diplomatic missions abroad, the means of communication between the British government and other governments – and international governmental organisations – on all matters falling within the field of international relations.

It is responsible for alerting the British government to the implications of developments overseas; promoting British interests overseas; protecting British citizens abroad; explaining British policies to, and cultivating relationships with, governments overseas; the discharge of British responsibilities to the overseas territories; entry clearance UK visas (with the Home Office); and promoting British business overseas (jointly with the Department for Business, Innovation and Skills through UK Trade and Investment).

Secretary of State for Foreign and Commonwealth Affairs,
Rt. Hon. William Hague, MP
Principal Private Secretary, Lindsay Appleby
Special Advisers, Denzil Davidson; Arminka Helic; Will
Littlejohn
Parliamentary Private Secretary, Keith Simpson, MP
Minister of State, Rt. Hon. David Lidington, MP *(Europe
and NATO)*
Private Secretary, Paul Heardman
Minister of State, Jeremy Browne, MP
Private Secretary, Rachel Lloyd
Parliamentary Under-Secretary of State, Alistair Burt, MP
Private Secretary, Russ Dixon
Parliamentary Under-Secretary of State, Henry Bellingham,
MP
Private Secretary, Nick Heath
Minister of State, Rt. Hon. Lord Howell of Guildford
*(House of Lords; the Commonwealth; International Energy
Policy)*
Private Secretary, Ryder Thomas
Minister of State, Lord Green of Hurstpierpoint *(Trade and
Investment and the FCO's relations with British business)*
*Permanent Under-Secretary of State and Head of HM
Diplomatic Service,* Simon Fraser
Private Secretary, Anna Bradbury
Special Representatives, John Ashton *(Climate Change);* Sir
Andrew Burns *(Post-Holocaust Issues);* Sir Brian Fall
(South Caucasus); Michael Ryder *(Sudan);* Mark Sedwill
(Afghanistan and Pakistan)

BOARD
Chair, Simon Fraser

Members, Sir Geoffrey Adams *(Political);* Nick Baird
(Europe and Globalisation); Alison Currie *(Finance);*
Susan Haird *(acting Chief Executive, UKTI);* Robert
Hannigan *(Defence and Intelligence);* Susan le Jeune
(HR); Shan Morgan *(HM Ambassador, Buenos Aires);*
Matthew Rycroft *(Chief Operating Officer)*
Non-Executive Members, Julia Bond; Rudy Markham

DEPARTMENT OF HEALTH

Richmond House, 79 Whitehall, London SW1A 2NS
T 020-7210 4850 W www.dh.gov.uk

The Department of Health is responsible for the provision of the National Health Service (NHS) in England and for social care. The department's aims are to support, protect, promote and improve the nation's health; to secure the provision of comprehensive, high-quality care for all those who need it, regardless of their ability to pay, where they live or their age; and to provide responsive adult social care for those who lack the support they need.

The Department of Health is responsible for setting health and social care policy in England. The department's work sets standards and drives modernisation across all areas of the NHS, social care and public health.

Secretary of State for Health, Rt. Hon. Andrew Lansley,
CBE, MP
Principal Private Secretary, Paul Macnaught
Parliamentary Private Secretary, Dr Andrew Murrison, MP
Minister of State, Simon Burns, MP *(Health)*
Private Secretary, Guy Mayou
Minister of State, Paul Burstow, MP *(Care Services)*
Private Secretary, Ben Pledger
Parliamentary Under-Secretary of State, Anne Milton, MP
(Public Health)
Private Secretary, Giancarlo Laura
Parliamentary Under-Secretary, Lord Howe *(Quality)*
Parliamentary Clerk, Tim Elms

DEPARTMENTAL BOARD
Chair and Permanent Secretary, Una O'Brien
Members, David Behan, CBE *(Social Care, Local
Government and Care Partnerships);* Prof. Dame Sally
Davies *(Chief Medical Officer);* Richard Douglas, CB
(Principal Accounting Officer); Sir David Nicholson,
KCB, CBE *(Chief Executive, NHS);* Mike Wheeler
(Non-Executive Director)

NATIONAL CLINICAL DIRECTORS
Cancer, Prof. Sir Mike Richards, CBE
Children, Young People and Maternity Services, Dr Sheila
Shribman
Clinical Neurosciences (adviser), Dr Chris Clough
Dementia, Prof. Alistair Burns
Diabetes, Dr Rowan Hillson, MBE
Endoscopy, Roland Valori
Equality and Human Rights, Surinder Sharma
Health and Criminal Justice, Prof. Louis Appleby, CBE
Health and Work, Prof. Dame Carol Black
Imaging, Dr Erika Denton
Informatics, Dr Charles Gutteridge
Kidney Services, Dr Donal O'Donoghue
Learning Disabilities, Anne Williams, CBE
Liver Disease, Prof. Martin Lombard
Mental Health, Hugh Griffiths
Older People, Prof. David Oliver
Pathology, Dr Ian Barnes
Patient and Public Affairs, Joan Saddler, OBE
Pharmacy (Community), Jonathan Mason

Pharmacy (Hospitals), Martin Stephens
Respiratory Disease, Prof. Sue Hill; Robert Winter
Screening, Dr Anne Mackie
Transplantation, Chris J. Rudge
Trauma Care, Prof. Keith Willett
Urgent and Emergency Care, Prof. Matthew Cooke
Venous Thrombo-Embolism, Dr Mike Durkin

SOLICITOR'S OFFICE*
Solicitor, Gill Aitken
Director of DWP Legal Services, Greer Kerrigan
Director of DH Legal Services, Mark Wilson
* Also the solicitor's office for the Department for Work and Pensions

SPECIAL HEALTH AUTHORITIES
Health and Social Care Information Centre
W www.ic.nhs.uk
National Institute for Health and Clinical Excellence
W www.nice.org.uk
National Patient Safety Agency
W www.npsa.nhs.uk
National Treatment Agency for Substance Misuse
W www.nta.nhs.uk
NHS Blood and Transplant
W www.nhsbt.nhs.uk
NHS Business Services Authority
W www.nhsbsa.nhs.uk
NHS Institute for Innovation and Improvement
W www.institute.nhs.uk
NHS Litigation Authority
W www.nhsla.com

HOME OFFICE
2 Marsham Street, London SW1P 4DF
T 020-7035 4848 E public.enquiries@homeoffice.gsi.gov.uk
W www.homeoffice.gov.uk

The Home Office deals with those internal affairs in England and Wales which have not been assigned to other government departments. The Secretary of State for the Home Department is the link between the Queen and the public, and exercises certain powers on her behalf, including that of the royal pardon.

The Home Office aims to build a safe, just and tolerant society and to maintain and enhance public security and protection; to support and mobilise communities so that they are able to shape policy and improvement for their locality, overcome nuisance and anti-social behaviour, maintain and enhance social cohesion and enjoy their homes and public spaces peacefully; to deliver departmental policies and responsibilities fairly, effectively and efficiently; and to make the best use of resources. These objectives reflect the priorities of the government and the home secretary in areas of crime, citizenship and communities, namely to reduce crime and the fear of crime through visible, responsive and accountable policing; to reduce organised and international crime; to combat terrorism and other threats to national security; to ensure the effective delivery of justice; to reduce re-offending and protect the public; to reduce the availability and abuse of dangerous drugs; to regulate entry to, and settlement in, the UK in the interests of sustainable growth and social inclusion; and to support strong, active communities in which people of all races and backgrounds are valued and participate on equal terms.

The Home Office delivers these aims through the immigration services, its agencies and non-departmental public bodies, and by working with partners in private, public and voluntary sectors, individuals and communities. The home secretary is also the link between the UK government and the governments of the Channel Islands and the Isle of Man.

Secretary of State for the Home Department, Rt. Hon. Theresa May, MP
Principal Private Secretary, Gillian McGregor
Assistant Private Secretary, Alan Webster
Special Advisers, Fiona Cunningham; Nick Timothy
Minister of State, Rt. Hon. Baroness Browning (Crime Prevention and Anti-Social Behaviour)
Private Secretary, Nicola Payne
Minister of State, Damian Green, MP (Immigration)
Private Secretary, Benjamin Brown
Minister of State, Nick Herbert, MP (Policing and Criminal Justice)
Private Secretary, Christina Bankes
Parliamentary Under-Secretary of State, James Brokenshire, MP (Crime and Security)
Private Secretary, Katherine Richardson
Parliamentary Under-Secretary of State, Lynne Featherstone, MP (Equalities and Criminal Information)
Private Secretary, Mike Box
Permanent Secretary of State, Dame Helen Ghosh, DCB
Private Secretary, Rachel Hopcroft

MANAGEMENT BOARD
Chair, Sir David Normington, KCB (Permanent Secretary of State)
Members, Philip Augar; Val Gooding; Yasmin Diamond (Communications); Charles Farr (Office for Security and Counter Terrorism); Sarah Rapson (Identity and Passport Service); John Heywood; Lin Homer, CB (UK Border Agency); Helen Kilpatrick (Financial and Commercial); Peter Makeham, CB (Strategy and International Group); Stephen Rimmer (Crime and Policing Group); Kevin White, CB (Human Resources)

GOVERNMENT EQUALITIES OFFICE (GEO)
The GEO is responsible for the government's overall strategy on equality. Its work includes leading the development of a more integrated approach on equality across government with the aim of improving equality and reducing discrimination and disadvantage for all. The office is also responsible for leading policy on gender equality, sexual orientation and transgender equality matters.

Minister for Women and Equality, Rt. Hon. Theresa May, MP
Parliamentary Under-Secretary of State, Lynne Featherstone, MP (Equalities)

DEPARTMENT FOR INTERNATIONAL DEVELOPMENT
1 Palace Street, London SW1 5HE
T 020-7023 0000
Abercrombie House, Eaglesham Road, East Kilbride, Glasgow G75 8EA
T 01355-844000 Public Enquiries 0845-300 4100
E enquiry@dfid.gov.uk W www.dfid.gov.uk

The Department for International Development (DFID) is responsible for promoting sustainable development and reducing poverty. The central focus of the government's policy, based on the 1997, 2000 and 2006 white papers on international development, is a commitment to the internationally agreed Millennium Development Goals, to be achieved by 2015. These seek to eradicate extreme poverty and hunger; achieve universal primary education; promote gender equality and empower women; reduce child mortality; improve maternal health; combat HIV/AIDS, malaria and other diseases; ensure environmental sustainability; and encourage a global partnership for development.

DFID's assistance is concentrated in the poorest countries of sub-Saharan Africa and Asia, but also contributes to poverty reduction and sustainable development in middle-income countries, including those in Latin America and Eastern Europe. It also responds to overseas emergencies. The department works in partnership with governments of developing countries, charities, non-governmental organisations and businesses. It also works with multilateral institutions, including the World Bank, United Nations agencies and the European Commission. The department has headquarters in London and East Kilbride, offices in many developing countries, and staff based in British embassies and high commissions around the world.

Secretary of State for International Development, Rt. Hon. Andrew Mitchell, MP
Principal Private Secretary, Melanie Speight
Private Secretary, Mark Richardson
Special Advisers, Philippa Buckley; Richard Parr
Parliamentary Clerk, Jo Smith
Minister of State, Alan Duncan, MP
Private Secretary, Alice Mann
Parliamentary Under-Secretary of State, Stephen O'Brien, MP
Private Secretary, Greg Hicks
House of Lords Spokesperson, Baroness Verma
Whips, Chloe Smith, MP *(Commons);* Earl Attlee *(Lords)*
Permanent Secretary, Mark Lowcock

MANAGEMENT BOARD
Chair, Mark Lowcock
Members, Michael Anderson *(Policy and Global Issues);* Richard Calvert *(Finance and Corporate Performance);* Joy Hutcheon *(Country Programmes)*
Non-Executive Members, Vivienne Cox; Doreen Langston

CDC GROUP
Cardinal Place, 80 Victoria Street SW1E 5JL
T 020-7963 4700 E enquiries@cdcgroup.com
W www.cdcgroup.com

Founded in 1948, CDC is a government-owned Development Finance Institution that invests in the creation and growth of viable private businesses in poorer developing countries in order to contribute to economic growth and reduce poverty. In 2010 CDC invested £420m, with 44 per cent of new investments in Africa and 48 per cent in Asia. CDC is a public limited company with the Department for International Development as its 100 per cent shareholder.
Chair, Richard Gillingwater, CBE
Chief Executive (acting), Rod Evison

MINISTRY OF JUSTICE
102 Petty France, London SW1P 9AJ
T 020-3334 3555 E general.queries@justice.gsi.gov.uk
W www.justice.gov.uk

The Ministry of Justice (MoJ) was established in May 2007. MoJ is headed by the Lord Chancellor and Secretary of State for Justice who is responsible for improvements to the justice system so that it better serves the public. He is also responsible for some areas of constitutional policy (those not covered by the Deputy Prime Minister).

The MoJ's priorities are to reduce reoffending and protect the public; provide access to justice; increase confidence in the justice system; and uphold people's civil liberties. The Lord Chancellor is the government minister responsible to parliament for the judiciary, the court system and prisons and probation. The Lord Chief Justice has been the head of the judiciary since 2006.

MoJ incorporates the National Offender Management Service, which includes HM Prison Service and the National Probation Service, and Her Majesty's Courts and Tribunals Service.

MoJ has several associated departments, non-departmental public bodies and executive agencies, including Her Majesty's Land Registry, the National Archives, the Legal Services Commission, and the Public Guardianship Office. The administrative functions of the Scotland Office and the Wales Office fall under the MoJ but these offices report to the respective Secretaries of State for Scotland and Wales.

Lord Chancellor and Secretary of State for Justice, Rt. Hon. Kenneth Clarke, QC, MP
Principal Private Secretary, Mark Sweeney
Special Advisers, David Hass; Kathryn Laing
Parliamentary Private Secretary, Ben Wallace, MP
Minister of State and Deputy Leader of the House of Lords, Rt. Hon. Lord McNally
Private Secretary, Emma Douglas
Minister of State, Nick Herbert*, MP
Private Secretary, Christina Bankes
Parliamentary Under-Secretary of State, Jonathan Djanogly, MP
Private Secretary, Sally Jones
Parliamentary Under-Secretary of State, Crispin Blunt, MP
Private Secretary, David Young
Permanent Secretary, Sir Suma Chakrabarti, KCB
Private Secretary, Ben Connah
Parliamentary Clerk, Ann Nixon
* Nick Herbert, MP, is responsible for criminal justice strategy and reports jointly to the Lord Chancellor and the home secretary

DEPARTMENTAL BOARD
Chair, Rt. Hon. Kenneth Clarke, QC, MP *(Lord Chancellor and Secretary of State for Justice)*
Members, Anne Beasley *(Director-General, Finance);* Crispin Blunt, MP; Sir Suma Chakrabarti, KCB *(Permanent Secretary);* Jonathan Djanogly, MP; Nick Herbert, MP; Rt. Hon. Lord McNally; Jonathan Slater *(Director-General, Transforming Justice)*
Non-Executive Members, Anne Bulford; James Leng; David MacLeod; Dame Sue Street, DCB

NORTHERN IRELAND OFFICE
11 Millbank, London SW1P 4PN
Stormont House, Stormont Estate, Belfast BT4 3SH
T 028-9052 0700
W www.nio.gov.uk

The Northern Ireland Office was established in 1972, when the Northern Ireland (Temporary Provisions) Act transferred the legislative and executive powers of the Northern Ireland parliament and government to the UK parliament and a secretary of state.

The Northern Ireland Office is responsible primarily for security issues, and for matters relating to the political and constitutional future of the province. It also deals with international issues as they affect Northern Ireland. In April 2010 the office transferred responsibility for policing and criminal justice to the Northern Ireland Assembly and Executive.

Under the terms of the 1998 Good Friday Agreement, power was devolved to the Northern Ireland Assembly in 1999. The assembly took on responsibility for the relevant areas of work previously undertaken by the departments of the Northern Ireland Office, covering agriculture and rural development, the environment, regional development, social development, education, higher education, training and employment, enterprise, trade and investment, culture, arts and leisure, health, social services, public safety and finance and personnel. In October 2002 the Northern Ireland Assembly was suspended and Northern Ireland returned to direct rule, but despite repeated setbacks, devolution was restored on 8 May 2007. For further details, *see* Regional Government section.

Secretary of State for Northern Ireland, Rt. Hon. Owen Paterson, MP

Minister of State, Rt. Hon. Hugo Swire, MP

Permanent Secretary and Head of the Northern Ireland Civil Service, Sir Bruce Robinson, KCB

OFFICE OF THE ADVOCATE-GENERAL FOR SCOTLAND

Dover House, Whitehall, London SW1A 2AU
T 020-7270 6770
Office of the Solicitor to the Advocate-General, Victoria Quay, Leith, Edinburgh EH6 6QQ
T 0131-244 1635
E privateoffice@advocategeneral.gsi.gov.uk
W www.oag.gov.uk

The Advocate-General for Scotland is one of the three law officers of the crown, alongside the Attorney-General and the Solicitor-General for England and Wales. He is the legal adviser to the UK government on Scottish law and is supported by staff in the Office of the Advocate-General for Scotland. The office is divided into the Legal Secretariat, based mainly in London, and the Office of the Solicitor to the Advocate-General, based in Edinburgh.

The post was created as a consequence of the constitutional changes set out in the Scotland Act 1998, which created a devolved Scottish parliament. The Lord Advocate and the Solicitor-General for Scotland then became part of the Scottish government and the Advocate-General took over their previous role as legal adviser to the government on Scots law. *See also* Regional Government section and Ministry of Justice.

Advocate-General for Scotland, Lord Wallace of Tankerness, QC
Private Secretary, Alice Adamson

OFFICE OF THE LEADER OF THE HOUSE OF COMMONS

26 Whitehall, London SW1A 2WH
T 020-7276 1005
E leader@commonsleader.x.gsi.gov.uk
W www.commonsleader.gov.uk

The Office of the Leader of the House of Commons is responsible for the arrangement of government business in the House of Commons and for planning and supervising the government's legislative programme. The Leader of the House of Commons upholds the rights and privileges of the house and acts as a spokesperson for the government as a whole.

The leader reports regularly to the cabinet on parliamentary business and the legislative programme. In his capacity as leader of the house, he is a member of the Public Accounts Commission and of the House of Commons Commission. He also chairs the cabinet committee on the legislative programme. As Lord Privy Seal, he is chair of the board of trustees of the Chevening Estate.

The Deputy Leader of the House of Commons supports the leader in handling the government's business in the house. He is responsible for monitoring MPs' and peers' correspondence.

Leader of the House of Commons and Lord Privy Seal, Rt. Hon. Sir George Young, Bt., MP
Head of Office, Mike Winter
Private Secretary, Christine Hill
Assistant Private Secretaries, Robert Foot *(Parliamentary Business);* Ben Sneddon *(Parliamentary Reform)*
Deputy Leader of the House of Commons, David Heath, CBE, MP
Private Secretary, Ben Sneddon

PRIVY COUNCIL OFFICE

2 Carlton Gardens, London SW1Y 5AA
T 020-7747 5310 E pcosecretariat@pco.x.gsi.gov.uk
W www.privy-council.gov.uk

The primary function of the office is to act as the secretariat to the Privy Council. It is responsible for the arrangements leading to the making of all royal proclamations and orders in council; for certain formalities connected with ministerial changes; for considering applications for the granting (or amendment) of royal charters; for the scrutiny and approval of by-laws and statutes of chartered institutions and of the governing instruments of universities and colleges; and for the appointment of high sheriffs and Privy Council appointments to governing bodies. Under the relevant acts, the office is responsible for the approval of certain regulations and rules made by the regulatory bodies of the medical and certain allied professions.

The Lord President of the Council is the ministerial head of the office and presides at meetings of the Privy Council. The Clerk of the Council is the administrative head of the Privy Council office.

Lord President of the Council and Deputy Prime Minister, Rt. Hon. Nick Clegg, MP
Clerk of the Council, Judith Simpson
Head of Secretariat and Senior Clerk, Ceri King
Senior Clerk, Christopher Berry

SCOTLAND OFFICE

Dover House, Whitehall, London SW1A 2AU
T 020-7270 6754
1 Melville Crescent, Edinburgh EH3 7HW
T 0131-244 9010
E scottish.secretary@scotland.gsi.gov.uk
W www.scotlandoffice.gov.uk

The Scotland Office is the department of the Secretary of State for Scotland which represents Scottish interests within the UK government in matters reserved to the UK parliament. The Secretary of State for Scotland also exercises certain specific functions in relation to devolution, including those provided for in the Scotland Act 1998; maintains the stability of the devolution settlement for Scotland; and pays grants to the Scottish Consolidated Fund and manages other financial transactions.

Reserved matters include the constitution, foreign affairs, defence, international development, the civil service, financial and economic matters, national security, immigration and nationality, misuse of drugs, trade and industry, various aspects of energy regulation (eg coal, electricity, oil, gas and nuclear energy), various aspects of transport, social security, employment, abortion, genetics, surrogacy, medicines, broadcasting and equal opportunities. Devolved matters include health and social work, education and training, local government and housing, justice and police, agriculture, forestry, fisheries, the environment, tourism, sports, heritage, economic development and internal transport. *See also* Regional Government section and Ministry of Justice.

Secretary of State for Scotland, Michael Moore, MP
Principal Private Secretary, Kate Richards
Parliamentary Under-Secretary of State, David Mundell, MP
Private Secretary, Jennifer Manton
Advocate-General and Spokesperson in the House of Lords,
   Rt. Hon. Lord Wallace of Tankerness, QC
Private Secretary, Alice Adamson

DEPARTMENT FOR TRANSPORT

Great Minster House, 33 Horseferry Road, London SW1P 4DR
T 020-7944 8300 W www.dft.gov.uk

The Department for Transport (DfT) works to deliver a transport system that balances the needs of the economy, the environment and society. Its main responsibilities include aviation, public transport, freight, regional and local transport, social inclusion, railways, roads and road safety, science and research, shipping and vehicles and sustainable travel.

The department provides leadership across the transport sector to achieve its objectives, working with regional, local and private-sector partners to deliver many of the services. Much of the department's work is delivered by seven executive agencies that employ around 90 per cent of its staff.

Secretary of State for Transport, Rt. Hon. Philip Hammond, MP
Principal Private Secretary, Natasha Robinson
Minister of State, Rt. Hon. Theresa Villiers, MP
Private Secretary, Rosa Estevez
Parliamentary Under-Secretary of State, Norman Baker, MP
Private Secretary, Joanna Guthrie
Parliamentary Under-Secretary of State, Mike Penning, MP
Private Secretary, Claire McAllister
Permanent Secretary, Lin Homer
Private Secretary, Natasha Coates

MANAGEMENT BOARD
Chair, Rt. Hon Philip Hammond, MP *(Secretary of State)*
Members, Lucy Chadwick *(Major Projects and London);*
   Steve Gooding *(Domestic);* Richard Hatfield
   (International, Strategy and Environment); Lin Homer
   (Permanent Secretary); Claire Moriarty *(Corporate);*
   Christopher Muttukumaru *(General Counsel);* Rt. Hon
   Theresa Villiers, MP
Non-Executive Members, Alan Cook, Sally Davis; Sam
   Laidlaw; Ed Smith

HM TREASURY

1 Horse Guards Road, London SW1A 2HQ
T 020-7270 4558
E public.enquiries@hm-treasury.gov.uk
W www.hm-treasury.gov.uk

HM Treasury is the country's economics and finance ministry, and is responsible for formulating and implementing the government's financial and economic policy. It aims to raise the rate of sustainable growth, boost prosperity, and provide the conditions necessary for universal economic and employment opportunities. The Office of the Lord High Treasurer has been continuously in commission for over 200 years. The Lord High Commissioners of HM Treasury are the First Lord of the Treasury (who is also the prime minister), the Chancellor of the Exchequer and five junior lords. This board of commissioners is assisted at present by the chief secretary, the parliamentary secretary (who is also the government chief whip in the House of Commons), the financial secretary, the economic secretary, the exchequer secretary and the commercial secretary. The prime minister as first lord is not primarily concerned with the day-to-day aspects of Treasury business; neither are the parliamentary secretary and the junior lords as government whips. Treasury business is managed by the Chancellor of the Exchequer and the other Treasury ministers, assisted by the permanent secretary.

The chief secretary is responsible for public expenditure, including spending reviews and strategic planning; in-year control; public-sector pay and pensions; Annually Managed Expenditure and welfare reform; efficiency in public services; procurement and capital investment. He also has responsibility for the Treasury's interest in devolution.

The financial secretary is the departmental minister for HM Revenue and Customs and the Valuation Office Agency and has responsibility for financial services policy including banking and financial services reform and regulation; financial stability; city competitiveness; wholesale and retail markets in the UK, Europe and internationally; and the Financial Services Authority. His other responsibilities include banking support; bank lending; UK Financial Investments; Equitable Life; and personal savings and pensions policy. He also provides support to the chancellor on EU and wider international finance issues.

The exchequer secretary is a title only used occasionally, normally when the post of paymaster-general is allocated to a minister outside of the Treasury (as it is at present; Francis Maude, MP was appointed paymaster-general and minister of the Cabinet Office in May 2010). The exchequer secretary's responsibilities include strategic oversight of the UK tax system; corporate and small business taxation, with input from the commercial secretary; departmental minister for HM Revenue and Customs and the Valuation Office Agency; lead minister on European and international tax issues; and has overall responsibility for the finance bill.

The economic secretary's responsibilities include environmental issues such as taxation of transport, international climate change and energy; North Sea oil taxation; tax credits and child poverty; assisting the chief secretary on welfare reform; charities and the voluntary sector; excise duties and gambling; stamp duty land tax; EU Budget; the Royal Mint; minister for HM Treasury Group; and working with the exchequer secretary on the finance bill.

The role of commercial secretary was created in 2010. Responsibilities include enterprise and productivity; corporate finance; assisting the financial secretary on financial services, banking policy promoting the government's financial services policies and the competitiveness of the UK; asset freezing and financial crime; foreign exchange reserves and debt management policy; National Savings and Investments; and the Debt Management Office. The commercial secretary is also the treasury spokesperson in the House of Lords.

Prime Minister and First Lord of the Treasury, Rt. Hon. David Cameron, MP

Chancellor of the Exchequer, Rt. Hon. George Osborne, MP

Principal Private Secretary, Beth Russell

Private Secretary, Sophie Dean

Special Advisers, Ramesh Chhabra; Poppy Mitchell-Rose

Council of Economic Advisers, Rupert Harrison; Eleanor Shawcross

Chief Secretary to the Treasury, Rt. Hon. Danny Alexander, MP

Private Secretary, David Silk

Financial Secretary to the Treasury, Mark Hoban, MP

Private Secretary, Josh Fleming

Exchequer Secretary to the Treasury, David Gauke, MP

Private Secretary, Oliver Hayden

Economic Secretary to the Treasury, Justine Greening, MP

Private Secretary, Robin Tasker

Commercial Secretary to the Treasury, Lord Sassoon

Permanent Secretary to the Treasury, Sir Nicholas Macpherson

Private Secretary and Speechwriter, Helen Chamberlain

Lords Commissioners of HM Treasury (Whips), James Duddridge, MP; Michael Fabricant, MP; Brooks Newmark, MP; Angela Watkinson, MP; Jeremy Wright, MP

Assistant Whips, Stephen Crabb, MP; Philip Dunne, MP; Robert Goodwill, MP; Mark Hunter, MP; Norman Lamb, MP*; Chloe Smith, MP; Shailesh Vera, MP; Bill Wiggin, MP

* Also Chief Parliamentary and Political Adviser to the Deputy Prime Minister

MANAGEMENT BOARD

Chair, Sir Nicholas Macpherson *(Permanent Secretary)*

Members, Mark Bowman *(Strategy, Planning and Budget);* Alison Cottrell *(Corporate Services);* Michael Ellam *(International and EU);* Andrew Hudson *(Public Services);* Julian Kelly *(Finance and Commercial);* Dave Ramsden *(Chief Economic Adviser);* Tom Scholar *(Second Permanent Secretary);* Jonathan Taylor *(Financial Services);* Edward Troup *(Tax and Welfare)*

WALES OFFICE

Gwydyr House, Whitehall, London SW1A 2NP
T 020-7270 0534
E walesoffice@walesoffice.gsi.gov.uk
W www.walesoffice.gov.uk

The Wales Office was established in 1999 when most of the powers of the Welsh Office were handed over to the National Assembly for Wales. It is the department of the Secretary of State for Wales, who is the key government figure liaising with the devolved government in Wales and who represents Welsh interests in the cabinet and parliament. The secretary of state has the right to attend and speak at sessions of the National Assembly (and must consult the assembly on the government's legislative programme). *See also* Regional Government section and Ministry of Justice.

Secretary of State for Wales, Rt. Hon. Cheryl Gillan, MP

Principal Private Secretary, Stephen Hillcoat

Parliamentary Under-Secretary, David Jones, MP

Director of Office, Fiona Adams-Jones

DEPARTMENT FOR WORK AND PENSIONS

Caxton House, Tothill Street, London SW1H 9NA
T 020-7962 8000 E enquiries@dwp.gsi.gov.uk
W www.dwp.gov.uk

The Department for Work and Pensions was formed in June 2001 from parts of the former Department of Social Security, the Department for Education and Employment and the Employment Service. The department helps unemployed people of working age into work, helps employers to fill their vacancies and provides financial support to people unable to help themselves, through back-to-work programmes. The department also administers the child support system, social security benefits and the social fund. In addition, the department has reciprocal social security arrangements with other countries.

Secretary of State for Work and Pensions, Rt. Hon. Iain Duncan Smith, MP

Principal Private Secretary, John-Paul Marks

Private Secretaries, Jennifer Bradley; Matt Davies; Mark Swindells

Minister of State, Rt. Hon. Chris Grayling, MP *(Employment)*

Private Secretary, Debbie McMahon

Assistant Private Secretaries, Pippa Knott; Ann Lyle; John Mazzeo

Minister of State, Steve Webb, MP *(Pensions)*

Private Secretary, Michael Dynan-Oakley

Assistant Private Secretaries, Polly Fortune; Biba Hussain; Mark Swindells

Parliamentary Under-Secretary and Minister of State, Maria Miller, MP *(Disabled People)*

Private Secretary, Rachael Hunter

Assistant Private Secretaries, James Frew; Alice Simpson; Vicky Smith

Minister of State, Lord Freud *(Welfare Reform)*

Private Secretary, Jessica Yuille

Assistant Private Secretaries, Aisling Fox; Manjula Pelpola; Billy Street

EXECUTIVE TEAM

Permanent Secretary and Head of Department, Robert Devereux

Directors-General, Gill Aitken *(Legal Group);* Joe Harley *(IT and Chief Information Officer);* Richard Heaton *(Strategy, Information and Pensions);* Chris Last *(Human Resources);* Terry Moran *(Universal Credit Programme);* Hunada Nouss *(Finance);* Sue Owen *(Welfare and Wellbeing);* Adam Sharples *(Employment)*

Agencies Chief Executives, Vivien Hopkins *(Pension, Disability and Carers Service (acting));* Darra Singh *(Jobcentre Plus)*

EXECUTIVE AGENCIES

Executive agencies are well-defined business units that carry out services with a clear focus on delivering specific outputs within a framework of accountability to ministers. They can be set up or disbanded without legislation, and they are organisationally independent from the department they are answerable to. In the following list the agencies are shown in the accounts of their sponsor departments. Legally they act on behalf of the relevant secretary of state. Their chief executives also perform the role of accounting officers, which means they are responsible for the money spent by their organisations. Staff employed by agencies are civil servants.

CABINET OFFICE

COI (CENTRAL OFFICE OF INFORMATION)
Hercules Road, London SE1 7DU
T 020-7928 2345 W www.coi.gov.uk

The COI was created to improve the effectiveness of and add value to government publicity programmes, through consultancy, procurement and project management services across all communication channels. Administrative responsibility for the COI rests with the minister for the Cabinet Office.

Following recommendations by the former Permanent Secretary of Government Communications, Matt Tee, the Minister for the Cabinet Office, Francis Maude, announced in June 2011 that the COI will close by April 2012.
Chief Executives (acting), Graham Hooper; Emma Lochhead

GOVERNMENT PROCUREMENT SERVICE
3rd Floor, Royal Liver Building, Pier Head, Liverpool L3 1PE
T 0345-410 2222 E info@buyingsolutions.gsi.gov.uk
W www.buyingsolutions.gov.uk

The Government Procurement Service is an executive agency of the Cabinet Office, providing a professional procurement service to the UK public sector. As a result of the Strategic Review of Buying Solutions, published in July 2011, it will play a key role in delivering centralised procurement of common goods and services for central government departments. It was originally known as The Buying Agency when it was launched in 1991, and was later renamed Buying Solutions.
Chief Procurement Officer, John Collington
Managing Director, David Shields

ATTORNEY-GENERAL'S OFFICE

TREASURY SOLICITOR'S DEPARTMENT
1 Kemble Street, London WC2B 4TS
T 020-7210 3000
E thetreasurysolicitor@tsol.gsi.gov.uk
W www.tsol.gov.uk

The Treasury Solicitor's Department, which became an executive agency in 1996, provides legal services for many government departments and other publicly funded bodies, and is answerable to the Attorney-General. Those departments and bodies without their own lawyers are provided with legal advice and litigation services. The Treasury Solicitor is also the Queen's Proctor, and is responsible for collecting ownerless goods *(bona vacantia)* on behalf of the crown.
HM Procurator-General and Treasury Solicitor (Permanent Secretary), Paul Jenkins, QC
Deputy Treasury Solicitor, Jonathan Jones

BONA VACANTIA DIVISION
Head of Division, Zane Denton

CENTRAL ADVISORY DIVISION
Head of Division, Iain Macleod

EUROPEAN DIVISION
Head of Division, Paul Berman

LITIGATION AND EMPLOYMENT GROUP
Head of Division, Hugh Giles

DEPARTMENT FOR BUSINESS, INNOVATION AND SKILLS

COMPANIES HOUSE
Crown Way, Cardiff CF14 3UZ
T 0303-123 4500
E enquiries@companieshouse.gov.uk
W www.companieshouse.gov.uk

Companies House incorporates companies, registers company documents and provides company information.
Registrar of Companies for England and Wales, Gareth Jones
Registrar of Companies for Scotland, Dorothy Blair
Registrar of Companies for Northern Ireland, Helen Shilliday

THE INSOLVENCY SERVICE
21 Bloomsbury Street, London WC1B 3QW
Insolvency Enquiry Line 0845-602 9848
Redundancy Enquiry Line 0845-145 0004
E insolvency.enquiryline@insolvency.gsi.gov.uk
W www.bis.gov.uk/insolvency

The role of the service includes administration and investigation of the affairs of bankrupts, partners and companies in compulsory liquidation; dealing with the disqualification of directors in all corporate failures; authorising and regulating the insolvency profession; providing banking and investment services for bankruptcy and liquidation estate funds; assessing and paying statutory entitlement to redundancy payments when an employer cannot, or will not, pay its employees; and advising ministers on insolvency, redundancy and related issues. The service has around 2,100 staff, operating from 35 locations across Great Britain.
Inspector-General and Chief Executive, Stephen Speed
Deputy Chief Executive, Graham Horne
Deputy Inspector-General, Les Cramp, CBE
Inspector of Companies and Head of Investigation and Enforcement Services, Robert Burns

INTELLECTUAL PROPERTY OFFICE
Concept House, Cardiff Road, Newport NP10 8QQ
T 0300-300 2000 E information@ipo.gov.uk
W www.ipo.gov.uk

The Intellectual Property Office (an operating name of the Patent Office) was set up in 1852 to act as the UK's sole office for the granting of patents. It was established as an executive agency in 1990 and became a trading fund in 1991. The office is responsible for the granting of intellectual property (IP) rights which include patents, trade marks, designs and copyright.
Comptroller-General and Chief Executive, John Alty

NATIONAL MEASUREMENT OFFICE
Stanton Avenue, Teddington, Middx TW11 0JZ
T 020-8943 7272 E info@nmo.gov.uk
W www.bis.gov.uk/nmo

The National Measurement Office (NMO) was created in April 2009, merging the functions of the National Weights and Measures Laboratory and the National Measurement System. NMO is responsible for all aspects of the national measurement system and provides a legal metrology infrastructure necessary to facilitate fair competition, support innovation, promote international trade and protect consumers, health and the environment.
Chief Executive, Peter Mason

UK SPACE AGENCY

Polaris House, North Star Avenue, Swindon, Wiltshire
SN2 1SZ
T 020-7215 5000 E info@ukspaceagency.bis.gsi.gov.uk
W www.bis.gov.uk/ukspaceagency

The UK Space Agency was established on 23 March 2010 and became an executive agency on 1 April 2011. It was created to provide a single voice for UK space ambitions, and is responsible for all strategic decisions on the UK civil space programme. Responsibilities of the UK Space Agency include coordinating UK civil space activity; supporting academic research; nurturing the UK space industry; raising the profile of UK space activities at home and abroad; working to increase understanding of space science and its practical benefits; and inspiring the next generation of UK scientists and engineers.
Chief Executive, Dr David Williams

DEPARTMENT FOR COMMUNITIES AND LOCAL GOVERNMENT

FIRE SERVICE COLLEGE

Moreton-in-Marsh, Gloucestershire GL56 0RH
T 01608-650831 E enquiries@fireservicecollege.ac.uk
W www.fireservicecollege.ac.uk

The Fire Service College provides fire-related training, both practical and theoretical, consultancy, and library and information services to the UK fire and rescue service, other UK public sector organisations, the private sector, and the international market.
Chief Executive, Kim Robinson

ORDNANCE SURVEY

Adanac Drive, Southampton SO16 0AS
T 0845-605 0505
E customerservices@ordnancesurvey.co.uk
W www.ordnancesurvey.co.uk

Ordnance Survey is the national mapping agency for Great Britain. It is a government department and executive agency operating as a trading fund since 1999.
Director-General and Chief Executive, Vanessa Lawrence, CB

PLANNING INSPECTORATE

Temple Quay House, 2 The Square, Temple Quay, Bristol
BS1 6PN
T 0117-372 6372
E enquiries@planning-inspectorate.gsi.gov.uk
Crown Buildings, Cathays Park, Cardiff CF10 3NQ
T 029-2082 3866 E wales@planning-inspectorate.gsi.gov.uk
W www.planning-inspectorate.gov.uk

The main work of the inspectorate consists of the processing of planning and enforcement appeals, and holding examinations into development plan documents. It also deals with advertisement appeals; rights of way cases; cases arising from the Environmental Protection and Water acts, the Transport and Works Act 1992 and other highways legislation; and reporting on planning applications called in for decision by the Department for Communities and Local Government and the Welsh government
Chief Executive, Katrine Sporle

THE QUEEN ELIZABETH II CONFERENCE CENTRE

Broad Sanctuary, London SW1P 3EE
T 020-7222 5000 F 020-7798 4200
E info@qeiicc.co.uk W www.qeiicc.co.uk

The centre provides secure conference facilities for national and international government and private sector use.
Chief Executive, Ernest Vincent

DEPARTMENT FOR CULTURE, MEDIA AND SPORT

THE ROYAL PARKS

The Old Police House, Hyde Park, London W2 2UH
T 0300-061 2000 E hq@royalparks.gsi.gov.uk
W www.royalparks.org.uk

Royal Parks is responsible for maintaining and developing over 2,000 hectares (5,000 acres) of urban parkland contained within the eight royal parks in London: Bushy Park (with the Longford river); Green Park; Greenwich Park; Hyde Park; Kensington Gardens; Regent's Park (with Primrose Hill); Richmond Park and St James's Park.
Chief Executive, Mark Camley

DEPARTMENT FOR ENVIRONMENT, FOOD AND RURAL AFFAIRS

ANIMAL HEALTH

Corporate Centre, Block C, Government Buildings, Whittington Road, Worcester WR5 2LQ
T 01905-763355
E corporate.centre@ahvla.gsi.gov.uk
W www.defra.gov.uk/ahvla

The Animal Health and Veterinary Laboratories Agency (AHVLA) is an executive agency of DEFRA. It was formed on 1 April 2011 following the merger of Animal Health and The Veterinary Laboratories Agency.

The agency is responsible, on behalf of DEFRA, the Welsh government and the Scottish government for protecting the health and welfare of farmed animals, including playing a key role in the prevention, detection and management of exotic and endemic diseases in animals. It is also responsible for delivering research and laboratory services for animal and public health and for advising DEFRA regarding the veterinary evidence base for policy development.

The AHVLA's services include a wide range of core functions covering veterinary research, disease surveillance and specialised testing. This includes protecting the welfare of farmed animals; the eradication of endemic disease; import and export certification; animal by-product regulation; and preparedness for managing exotic animal diseases. The AHVLA also has an emergency response capability.

Animal Health is also reponsible for licensing the trade in endangered species for conservation purposes; for ensuring that eggs are correctly labelled and that marketing regulations are being complied with. It also monitors the standard of hygiene in dairies in relation to the nation's raw milk supply.
Chief Executive, Catherine Brown

CENTRE FOR ENVIRONMENT, FISHERIES AND
AQUACULTURE SCIENCE (CEFAS)
Pakefield Road, Lowestoft, Suffolk NR33 0HT
T 01502-562244 W www.cefas.defra.gov.uk

Established in April 1997, the agency provides research
and consultancy services in fisheries science and
management, aquaculture, fish health and hygiene,
environmental impact assessment, and environmental
quality assessment.
Chief Executive, Dr Richard Judge

FOOD AND ENVIRONMENT RESEARCH
AGENCY
Sand Hutton, York YO41 1LZ
T 01904-462000
E info@fera.gsi.gov.uk W wwwdefra.gov.uk/fera

The Food and Environment Research Agency was formed
on 1 April 2009 from the merger of the Central Science
Laboratory, the Government Decontamination Service,
and DEFRA's Plant Health division and Plant Varieties
office. The agency's purpose is to support and develop
a sustainable food chain, a healthy natural environment,
and to protect the community from biological and
chemical risks. It does this by providing evidence,
analysis and professional advice to the government,
international organisations and the private sector. The
agency brings together expertise in policy issues,
particularly relating to seed, plant and bee health;
inspection services necessary to ensure protection for
seeds, crops and horticulture; multi-disciplinary science
to rapidly diagnose threats, evaluate risk and inform
policy in food and environmental areas; and in
responding to and recovering from unforeseen or
emergency situations.
Chief Executive, Adrian Belton

RURAL PAYMENTS AGENCY
PO Box 69, Reading RG1 3YD
T 0845-603 7777
E enquiries@rpa.gsi.gov.uk W http://rpa.defra.gov.uk

The RPA was established in 2001. It is the single paying
agency responsible for Common Agricultural Policy
(CAP) schemes in England and for certain other schemes
throughout the UK; it is also responsible for operating
cattle tracing services across Great Britain, conducting
inspections of farms, processing plants and fresh produce
markets in England, and managing the Rural Land
Register.
Chief Executive, Mark Grimshaw

VETERINARY MEDICINES DIRECTORATE
Woodham Lane, New Haw, Addlestone, Surrey KT15 3LS
T 01932-336911 E postmaster@vmd.defra.gsi.gov.uk
W www.vmd.defra.gov.uk

The Veterinary Medicines Directorate is responsible for all
aspects of the authorisation and control of veterinary
medicines, including post-authorisation surveillance of
residues in animals and animal products. It is also
responsible for the development and enforcement of
legislation concerning veterinary medicines and the
provision of policy advice to ministers.
Chief Executive, Steve Dean

FOREIGN AND COMMONWEALTH
OFFICE

FCO SERVICES
Hanslope Park, Milton Keynes MK19 7BH
T 020-7008 02959 E fco.services@fco.gov.uk
W www.fcoservices.gov.uk

FCO Services was established as an executive agency in
April 2006 and became a trading fund in April 2008. It
provides a range of bespoke, secure services worldwide to
the FCO and other UK government departments. In
addition to the FCO, existing customers include foreign
governments and international organisations closely
linked to the UK.
Chief Executive, Chris Moxey

WILTON PARK CONFERENCE CENTRE
Wiston House, Steyning, W. Sussex BN44 3DZ
T 01903-815020 E admin@wiltonpark.org.uk
W www.wiltonpark.org.uk

Wilton Park organises international affairs conferences
and is hired out to government departments and
commercial users.
Chief Executive, Richard Burge

DEPARTMENT OF HEALTH

MEDICINES AND HEALTHCARE PRODUCTS
REGULATORY AGENCY (MHRA)
151 Buckingham Palace Road, London SW1W 9SS
E info@mhra.gsi.gov.uk
W www.mhra.gov.uk

The MHRA is responsible for protecting and promoting
public and patient safety by ensuring that medicines,
healthcare products and medical equipment meet
appropriate standards of safety, quality, performance and
effectiveness, and are used safely.
Chair, Prof. Sir Alasdair Breckenridge, CBE
Chief Executive, Prof. Kent Woods

HOME OFFICE

CRIMINAL RECORDS BUREAU
PO Box 110, Liverpool L69 3EF
T 0870-909 0811 E customerservices@crb.gov.uk
W www.homeoffice.gov.uk/crb

The Criminal Records Bureau was launched in March
2002 and provides access to criminal record information
to enable organisations in the public, private and
voluntary sectors to make safer recruitment decisions by
identifying candidates who may be unsuitable for certain
work – especially that which involves children or
vulnerable adults.
Chief Executive, Steve Long

IDENTITY AND PASSPORT SERVICE
2 Marsham Street, London SW1V 1PN
Passport Advice Line 0300-222 0000
General Register Office 0845-603 7788
W http://www.homeoffice.gov.uk/agencies-public-bodies/ips/

Established in April 2006, the Identity and Passport
Service (IPS) is an executive agency of the home
office and incorporates the UK Passport Service and the
General Register Office. The UK Passport Service issues,
renews and amends passports for UK nationals both at
home and abroad. The General Register Office is

responsible for overseeing the system of civil registration in England and Wales, which involves administering the marriage laws; securing an effective system for the registration of births, adoptions, civil partnerships, marriages and deaths; maintaining an archive of births, civil partnerships, marriages and deaths; maintaining the adopted children's register, adoption contact register and other registers; and supplying certificates from the registers and the archives for research or family history purposes.

Chief Executive and Registrar-General for England and Wales, Sarah Rapson

NATIONAL FRAUD AUTHORITY

PO Box 64170, London WC1A 9BP
T 020-3356 1000 E NFAcontact@attorneygeneral.gsi.gov.uk
W www.attorneygeneral.gov.uk/nfa

The National Fraud Authority (NFA) was established on 1 October 2008 to increase protection for the UK economy from the harm caused by fraud. It works with private, public and third sector organisations to initiate, co-ordinate and communicate counter-fraud activity across the economy. The authority's priorities are to tackle the key fraud threats to the UK, to act effectively to pursue fraudsters and hold them to account, and to improve the nation's long-term capability to prevent fraud. The NFA is also working to improve the support available to fraud victims and to build the UK's capability to share and act on knowledge about fraud, both nationally and internationally.

Chief Executive, Dr Bernard Herdan, CB

UK BORDER AGENCY

11th Floor, Lunar House, 40 Wellesley Road, Croydon CR9 2BY
T 0870-606 7766 E UKBApublicenquiries@ukba.gsi.gov.uk
W www.ukba.homeoffice.gov.uk

The UK Border Agency was established in April 2008 and became an executive agency of the Home Office in April 2009. The agency brings together the work previously carried out by the Border and Immigration Agency, and, following Royal Assent to the Borders, Citizenship and Immigration Act in July 2009, customs detection work at the border from HM Revenue and Customs, and UK visa services from the Foreign and Commonwealth Office.

Chief Executive, Rob Whiteman
Board Members, Jonathan Sedgwick *(Deputy Chief Executive);* Zilla Bowell *(Chief Executive's Chief of Staff);* Martin Baker, QPM; James Bevan; Kathryn Bishop; Brodie Clark; Matthew Coats; Melanie Dawes; Joe Dugdale; Mike Hawker; Justin Holliday; Martin Peach; Graham Sims; Mark Thomson; David Wood; Barbara Woodward; Rob Yeldham

MINISTRY OF JUSTICE

HER MAJESTY'S COURTS AND TRIBUNALS SERVICE

see Law Courts and Offices section

LAND REGISTRY

Trafalgar House, 1 Bedford Park, Croydon CR0 2AQ
T 0300-006 0001 E customersupport@landregistry.gsi.gov.uk
W www.landregistry.gov.uk

The registration of title to land was first introduced in England and Wales by the Land Registry Act 1862. Land Registry maintains and develops the Land Register for England and Wales, and is an executive agency and trading fund responsible to the Lord Chancellor and Secretary of State for Justice. The Land Register has been open to public inspection since 1990.

Chief Land Registrar and Chief Executive, Malcolm Dawson, OBE

NATIONAL ARCHIVES

Kew, Richmond, Surrey TW9 4DU
T 020-8876 3444
W www.nationalarchives.gov.uk

The National Archives is a non-ministerial government department and an executive agency of the Ministry of Justice. It incorporates the Public Records Office, Historical Manuscripts Commission, Office of Public Sector Information and Her Majesty's Stationery Office. As the official archive of the UK government, it preserves, protects and makes accessible the historical collection of official records.

The National Archives also manages digital information including the UK government web archive which contains over one billion digital documents, and devises solutions for keeping government records readable now and in the future.

The organisation administers the UK's public records system under the Public Records Acts of 1958 and 1967. The records it holds span 1,000 years – from the Domesday Book to the latest government papers to be released – and fill more than 167km (104 miles) of shelving.

Chief Executive, Oliver Morley

NATIONAL OFFENDER MANAGEMENT SERVICE

see Prison Service section

OFFICE OF THE PUBLIC GUARDIAN

PO Box 15118, Birmingham B16 6GX
T 0300-456 0300
E customerservices@publicguardian.gsi.gov.uk

The Office of the Public Guardian supports and promotes decision making for those who lack capacity or would like to plan for their future, within the framework of the Mental Capacity Act 2005.

Chief Executive and Public Guardian, Martin John

TRIBUNALS SERVICE

see Tribunals section

DEPARTMENT FOR TRANSPORT

DRIVER AND VEHICLE LICENSING AGENCY (DVLA)

Longview Road, Swansea SA6 7JL
T 01792-782341 W www.dft.gov.uk/dvla

The DVLA was established as an executive agency in 1990. It became a trading fund in 2004, but relinquished this status on 1 April 2011. The DVLA is responsible for registering and licensing drivers and vehicles, and for collection and enforcement of vehicle excise duty (£5.78bn in 2010–11). The DVLA also maintains records of all those who are entitled to drive various types of vehicle (currently over 44 million people), all vehicles entitled to travel on public roads (currently 36 million), and drivers' endorsements, disqualifications and medical conditions.

Chief Executive, Simon Tse

DRIVING STANDARDS AGENCY

The Axis Building, 112 Upper Parliament Street, Nottingham NG1 6LP

T 0115-936 6666 E customer.services@dsa.gsi.gov.uk
W www.dft.gov.uk/dsa

The agency is responsible for carrying out theory and practical driving tests for car drivers, motorcyclists, bus and lorry drivers, and for maintaining the statutory register of approved driving instructors and the voluntary register of large goods vehicle instructors and fleet driver trainers. It also supervises Compulsory Basic Training (CBT) for learner motorcyclists. There are two area offices, which manage over 400 practical driving test centres across Britain and 158 theory test centres.
Chief Executive, Rosemary Thew

GOVERNMENT CAR AND DESPATCH AGENCY

46 Ponton Road, London SW8 5AX
T 020-7217 3837 E info@gcda.gsi.gov.uk
W www.dft.gov.uk/gcda

The agency provides secure transport and mail distribution to government and the public sector.
Chief Executive, Marian Duncan

HIGHWAYS AGENCY

3rd Floor, 157–197 Buckingham Palace Road, London SW1W 9HA

T 0300-123 5000
E ha_info@highways.gsi.gov.uk W www.highways.gov.uk

The Highways agency is responsible for operating, maintaining and improving England's 7,000km (4,300 miles) of motorways and trunk roads – known as the strategic road network – on behalf of the Secretary of State for Transport.
Chief Executive, Graham Dalton

MARITIME AND COASTGUARD AGENCY

Spring Place, 105 Commercial Road, Southampton SO15 1EG
T 023-8032 9100
W www.dft.gov.uk/mca

The agency's aims are to prevent loss of life, continuously improve maritime safety and protect the marine environment.
Chief Executive, Sir Alan Massey
Chief Coastguard, Rod Johnson

VEHICLE CERTIFICATION AGENCY

1 Eastgate Office Centre, Eastgate Road, Bristol BS5 6XX
T 0117-951 5151 E enquiries@vca.gov.uk
W www.vca.gov.uk/vca/

The agency is the UK authority responsible for ensuring that vehicles and vehicle parts have been designed and constructed to meet internationally agreed standards of safety and environmental protection.
Chief Executive, Paul Markwick

VEHICLE AND OPERATOR SERVICES AGENCY

Berkeley House, Croydon Street, Bristol BS5 0DA
T 0300-123 9000
E enquiries@vosa.gov.uk W www.vosa.gov.uk

The Vehicle and Operator Services Agency was formed in April 2003 from the merger of the Vehicle Inspectorate and the Traffic Area Network. The agency works with the independent traffic commissioners to improve road safety and the environment; safeguard fair competition by promoting and enforcing compliance with commercial operator licensing requirements; process applications for licences to operate lorries and buses; register bus services; operate and administer testing schemes for all vehicles, including the supervision of the MOT testing scheme; enforce the law on vehicles to ensure that they comply with legal standards and regulations; enforce drivers' hours and licensing requirements; provide training and advice for commercial operators; investigate vehicle defects and recalls; and provide support to the police by examining vehicles involved in accidents for contributory defects.
Chief Executive, Alastair Peoples

HM TREASURY

NATIONAL SAVINGS AND INVESTMENTS

1 Drummond Gate, Pimlico, London SW1V 2QX
T 0500-007007 W www.nsandi.com

NS&I (National Savings and Investments) came into being in 1861 when the Palmerston government set up the Post Office Savings Bank, a savings scheme which aimed to encourage ordinary wage earners 'to provide for themselves against adversity and ill health'. NS&I was established as a government department in 1969. It became an executive agency of the Treasury in 1996 and is responsible for the design, marketing and administration of savings and investment products for personal savers and investors. It has over 26 million customers and almost £100bn invested. *See also* Banking and Finance, National Savings.
Chief Executive, Jane Platt

ROYAL MINT

PO Box 500, Llantrisant, Pontyclun CF72 8YT
T 01443-222111
W www.royalmint.com

The Royal Mint has operated as a trading fund since 1975, and was established as an executive agency in 1990.

The prime responsibility of the Royal Mint is the provision of United Kingdom coinage, but it actively competes in world markets for a share of the available circulating coin business and about half of the coins and blanks it produces annually are exported. It also manufactures special proof and uncirculated quality coins in gold, silver and other metals; military and civil decorations and medals; commemorative and prize medals; and royal and official seals.
Master of the Mint, Chancellor of the Exchequer *(ex officio)*
Chief Executive, Adam Lawrence

UK DEBT MANAGEMENT OFFICE

Eastcheap Court, 11 Philpot Lane, London EC3M 8UD
T 0845-357 6500
W www.dmo.gov.uk

The UK Debt Management Office (DMO) was launched as an executive agency of HM Treasury in April 1998. The Chancellor of the Exchequer determines the policy and financial framework within which the DMO operates, but delegates operational decisions on debt and cash management and the day-to-day running of the office to the chief executive. The DMO's remit is to carry out the government's debt management policy of minimising financing costs over the long term, and to minimise the cost of offsetting the government's net cash flows over time, while operating at a level of risk approved by ministers in both cases. The DMO is also responsible for providing loans to local authorities through the Public Works Loan Board, for managing the assets of certain public-sector bodies through the Commissioners for the Reduction of the National Debt, and for administering the operational delivery of the government's Credit Guarantee Scheme.

Chief Executive, Robert Stheeman

DEPARTMENT FOR WORK AND PENSIONS

JOBCENTRE PLUS
Level 6, Caxton House, Tothill Street, London SW1H 9NQ
T 0845-606 0234 W www.dwp.gov.uk/jobcentreplus

Jobcentre Plus was formed in April 2002 following the merger of the Employment Service and some parts of the Benefits Agency. The agency administers claims for, and payment of, social security benefits to help people gain employment or improve their prospects for work, as well as helping employers to fill their vacancies.

Chief Executive, Darra Singh

THE PENSION, DISABILITY AND CARERS SERVICE
Room 111, Block 1, Norcross, Blackpool, Lancs FY5 3TA
T 020-7271 2601
W www.dwp.gov.uk/about-dwp/customer-delivery/disability-and-carers-service

The Pension, Disability and Carers Service was formed in 2008 from the Pension Service and the Disability and Carers Service (DCS). The agency serves 16 million customers in Great Britain and abroad. The service administers benefits including disability living allowance, attendance allowance, carers allowance, state pension, pension credit and winter fuel payments.

Chief Executive, Vivien Hopkins, OBE

NON-MINISTERIAL GOVERNMENT DEPARTMENTS

Non-ministerial government departments are part of central government but are not headed by a minister and are not funded by a sponsor department. They are created to implement specific legislation, but do not have the ability to change it. Departments may have links to a minister, but the minister is not responsible for the department's overall performance. Staff employed by non-ministerial departments are civil servants.

CROWN ESTATE
16 New Burlington Place, London W1S 2HX
T 020-7851 5000 E enquiries@thecrownestate.co.uk
W www.thecrownestate.co.uk

The Crown Estate is part of the hereditary possessions of the sovereign 'in right of the crown', managed under the provisions of the Crown Estate Act 1961. It is valued at £7.0bn, and includes substantial blocks of urban property, primarily in London, almost 106,000 hectares (263,000 acres) of rural land, over half of the foreshore, and the sea bed out to the 12 nautical mile territorial limit throughout the UK. The Crown Estate has a duty to maintain and enhance the capital value of estate and the income obtained from it. Under the terms of the act, the estate

pays its revenue surplus to the Treasury every year.
Chair, Sir Stuart Hampson
Chief Executive, Roger Bright

CROWN PROSECUTION SERVICE
Rose Court, 2 Southwark Bridge Road, London SE1 9HS
T 020-7796 8000 E enquiries@cps.gsi.gov.uk
W www.cps.gov.uk

The Crown Prosecution Service (CPS) is the independent body responsible for prosecuting people in England and Wales. The CPS was established as a result of the Prosecution of Offences Act 1985. It works closely with the police to advise on lines of inquiry and to decide on appropriate charges and other disposals in all but minor cases. *See also* Law Courts and Offices.

The Revenue and Customs Prosecutions Office, which prosecutes major drug trafficking and tax fraud cases in the UK, was incorporated into the CPS on 1 January 2010.

Director of Public Prosecutions, Keir Starmer, QC
Chief Executive, Peter Lewis

EXPORT CREDITS GUARANTEE DEPARTMENT (ECGD)
PO Box 2200, 2 Exchange Tower, Harbour Exchange Square, London E14 9GS
T 020-7512 7887 E help@ecgd.gsi.gov.uk
W www.ecgd.gov.uk

ECGD is the UK export credit agency and was established in 1919. A separate government department reporting to the Secretary of State for Business, Innovation and Skills, it has more than 90 years' experience of working closely with exporters, project sponsors, banks and buyers to help UK exporters of capital equipment and project-related goods and services. ECGD does this by providing help in arranging finance packages for buyers of UK goods by guaranteeing bank loans; insurance against non-payment to UK exporters; and overseas investment insurance – a facility that gives UK investors up to 15 years' insurance against political risks such as war, expropriation and restrictions on remittances.

Chief Executive and Accounting Officer, Patrick Crawford
Non-Executive Chair, Guy Beringer, QC

FOOD STANDARDS AGENCY
Aviation House, 125 Kingsway, London WC2B 6NH
T 020-7276 8829
E helpline@foodstandards.gsi.gov.uk
W www.food.gov.uk

Established in April 2000, the FSA is a UK-wide non-ministerial government body responsible for food safety and hygiene. The agency has the general function of developing policy in these areas and provides information and advice to the government, other public bodies and consumers. It also sets standards for and monitors food safety and hygiene law enforcement by local authorities.

Chair, Lord Rooker
Chief Executive, Tim Smith
FOOD STANDARDS AGENCY NORTHERN
IRELAND, 10C Clarendon Road, Belfast BT1 3BG
T 028-9041 7700 E infofsani@foodstandards.gsi.gov.uk
FOOD STANDARDS AGENCY SCOTLAND,
St Magnus House, 6th Floor, 25 Guild Street, Aberdeen
AB11 6NJ T 01224-285100
E scotland@foodstandards.gsi.gov.uk

FOOD STANDARDS AGENCY WALES, 11th Floor,
Southgate House, Wood Street, Cardiff CF10 1EW
T 029-2067 8999 E wales@foodstandards.gsi.gov.uk

FORESTRY COMMISSION

Silvan House, 231 Corstorphine Road, Edinburgh
EH12 7AT
T 0131-334 0303 E enquiries@forestry.gsi.gov.uk
W www.forestry.gov.uk

The Forestry Commission is the government department
responsible for forestry policy in Great Britain. It reports
directly to forestry ministers (ie the Secretary of State for
Environment, Food and Rural Affairs, the Scottish
ministers and the National Assembly for Wales), to whom
it is responsible for advice on forestry policy and for the
implementation of that policy.

The commission's principal objectives are to protect
Britain's forests and woodlands; expand Britain's forest
area; enhance the economic value of forest resources;
conserve and improve the biodiversity, landscape and
cultural heritage of forests and woodlands; develop
opportunities for woodland recreation; and increase
public understanding of, and community participation in,
forestry.

Chair, Pamela Warhurst
Director-General and Deputy Chair, T. Rollinson

FORESTRY COMMISSION ENGLAND, 620 Bristol
Business Park, Coldharbour Lane, Bristol BS16 1EJ
T 0117-906 6000
FORESTRY COMMISSION SCOTLAND, Silvan House,
231 Corstorphine Road, Edinburgh EH12 7AT
T 0131-334 0303
FORESTRY COMMISSION WALES, Welsh Government,
Rhodfa Padarn, Llanbadarn Fawr, Aberystwyth SY23 3UR
T 0300-068 0300
NORTHERN RESEARCH STATION, Roslin, Midlothian
EH25 9SY T 0131-445 2176

FOREST ENTERPRISE

Forest Enterprise England, 620 Bristol Business Park,
Coldharbour Lane, Bristol BS16 1EJ
T 0117-906 6000
Forest Enterprise Scotland, 1 Highlander Way, Inverness Business
and Retail Park, Inverness IV2 7GB
T 01463-232811

Forest Enterprise was established as an executive agency
of the Forestry Commission in 1996 to manage the UK's
forest estate; it ceased to exist as a single executive agency
in March 2003, when three new agencies were created –
one each for England, Wales and Scotland. Forest
Enterprise Wales has since been wound up, with its
responsibilities reabsorbed by the Forestry Commission.

The agencies in England and Scotland take their
direction from their respective country governments but
their basic remit is to provide environmental, social and
economic benefits from the forests they manage.

Chief Executives, Simon Hodge *(Scotland);* Simon
Hodgson *(England)*

FOREST RESEARCH

Alice Holt Lodge, Farnham, Surrey GU10 4LH
T 01420-22255
E research.info@forestry.gsi.gov.uk
W www.forestresearch.gov.uk

Forest Research is also an executive agency of the Forestry
Commission. Its objectives are to inform and support
forestry's contribution to the development and delivery
of the policies of the government and devolved
administrations; to provide research, development and
monitoring services relevant to UK forestry interests; and
to transfer knowledge actively and appropriately.

Chief Executive, Dr James Pendlebury
Research Director, Dr Peter Freer-Smith

GOVERNMENT ACTUARY'S DEPARTMENT

Finlaison House, 15–17 Furnival Street, London EC4A 1AB
T 020-7211 2601
Abbey Business Centre, 83 Princes Street, Edinburgh EH2 2ER
T 0131-247 7510
E enquiries@gad.gov.uk W www.gad.gov.uk

The Government Actuary's Department was established in
1919 and provides actuarial advice to UK government
departments, the public sector, and overseas governments.
The actuaries provide valuations and advice for public-
service pensions and social security schemes, and advise
the government on occupational pension schemes and
private-sector pensions policy. They also provide advice
on the supervision of insurance companies, investment
and risk-related issues, demographic studies and
healthcare financing.

Government Actuary, T. J. Llanwarne
Deputy Government Actuary, G. Russell
Chief Actuaries (London), S. Bell; I. A. Boonin; H. Duckers;
D. Grenham; A. Hale; S. R. Humphrey; A. Smith;
N. Varma; S. Vivian
Chief Actuary (Edinburgh), K. Knelle

HM REVENUE AND CUSTOMS

Board of HM Revenue and Customs, 100 Parliament Street,
London SW1A 2BQ
T 020-7147 0000 W www.hmrc.gov.uk

HMRC was formed following the integration of the
Inland Revenue and HM Customs and Excise, which was
made formal by parliament in April 2005. It administers,
and advises the Chancellor of the Exchequer on, any
matters connected with the following areas: income,
corporation, capital gains, inheritance, insurance
premium, stamp, land and petroleum revenue taxes;
environmental taxes (climate change and aggregates levy,
landfill tax); value added tax (VAT); customs duties and
frontier protection; excise duties; National Insurance; tax
credits, child benefit and the Child Trust Fund;
enforcement of the minimum wage; and recovery of
student loan repayments.

Chair, Mike Clasper, CBE
Chief Executive and Permanent Secretary, Lesley Strathie

VALUATION OFFICE AGENCY

Wingate House, 93–107 Shaftesbury Avenue, London
W1D 5BU
T 0300-056 1700 E customerservices@voa.gsi.gov.uk
W www.voa.gov.uk

Established in 1991, the Valuation Office is an executive
agency of HM Revenue and Customs. It is responsible for
compiling and maintaining the business rating and
council tax valuation lists for England and Wales; valuing
property throughout Great Britain for the purposes of
taxes administered by the Inland Revenue; providing
statutory and non-statutory property valuation services in

England, Wales and Scotland; and giving policy advice to ministers on property valuation matters. In April 2009 the VOA assumed responsibility for the functions of The Rent Service, which provided a rental valuation service to local authorities in England, and fair rent determinations for landlords and tenants.
Chief Executive, Penny Ciniewicz

OFFICE OF FAIR TRADING (OFT)
Fleetbank House, 2–6 Salisbury Square, London EC4Y 8JX
T 020-7211 8000
E enquiries@oft.gsi.gov.uk W www.oft.gov.uk

The OFT is a non-ministerial government department established by statute in 1973, and it is the UK's consumer and competition authority. It encourages businesses to comply with competition and consumer law and to improve their trading practices through self-regulation. It acts decisively to stop serious or flagrant offenders, studies markets and recommends action where required, and empowers consumers with the knowledge and skills to make informed choices.
Chair, Philip Collins
Chief Executive Officer, John Fingleton

CHARITY COMMISSION
PO Box 1227, Liverpool L69 3UG
T 0845-300 0218
W www.charity-commission.gov.uk

The Charity Commission is established by law as the independent regulator and registrar of charities in England and Wales. Its aim is to provide the best possible regulation of these charities in order to ensure their legal compliance and increase their efficiency, accountability and effectiveness, as well as to encourage public trust and confidence in them. The commission maintains a register of over 160,000 charities. It is accountable to parliament and both the charity tribunal and the high court for decisions made in exercising its legal powers. The commission has offices in London, Liverpool, Taunton and Newport.
Chair, Dame Suzi Leather
Chief Executive, Sam Younger, CBE, FRSA

OFFICE OF GAS AND ELECTRICITY MARKETS (OFGEM)
9 Millbank, London SW1P 3GE
T 020-7901 7295 E consumeraffairs@ofgem.gov.uk
W www.ofgem.gov.uk

OFGEM is the regulator for Britain's gas and electricity industries. Its role is to protect and advance the interests of consumers by promoting competition where possible, and through regulation only where necessary. OFGEM operates under the direction and governance of the Gas and Electricity Markets Authority, which makes all major decisions and sets policy priorities for OFGEM. OFGEM's powers are provided for under the Gas Act 1986 and the Electricity Act 1989, as amended by the Utilities Act 2000. It also has enforcement powers under the Competition Act 1998 and the Enterprise Act 2002.
Chair, Lord Mogg, KCMG
Chief Executive, Alistair Buchanan

OFFICE OF RAIL REGULATION
1 Kemble Street, London WC2B 4AN
T 020-7282 2000 E contact.cct@orr.gsi.gov.uk
W www.rail-reg.gov.uk

The Office of the Rail Regulator was set up under the Railways Act 1993. It became the ORR in July 2004, under the provisions of the Railways and Transport Safety Act 2003. On 1 April 2006, in addition to its role as economic regulator, the ORR became the health and safety regulator for the rail industry. This transfer of responsibility from the Health and Safety Executive was given effect under the Railways Act 2005. The board and chair are appointed by the Secretary of State for Transport. The ORR's key roles are to ensure that Network Rail, the owner and operator of the national railway infrastructure (the track and signalling), manages the network efficiently and in a way that meets the needs of its users; to encourage continuous improvement in health and safety performance while securing compliance with relevant health and safety law, including taking enforcement action as necessary; and to develop policy and enhance relevant railway health and safety legislation. It is also responsible for licensing operators of railway assets, setting the terms for access by operators to the network and other railway facilities, and enforcing competition law in the rail sector.
Chair, Anna Walker
Chief Executive, Richard Price

OFFICE FOR STANDARDS IN EDUCATION, CHILDREN'S SERVICES AND SKILLS (OFSTED)
Royal Exchange Buildings, St Ann's Square, Manchester M2 7LA
T 0300-123 1231 E enquiries@ofsted.gov.uk
W www.ofsted.gov.uk

Ofsted was established under the Education (Schools Act) 1992 and was relaunched on 1 April 2007 with a wider remit, bringing together four formerly separate inspectorates. It works to raise standards in services through the inspection and regulation of care for children and young people, and inspects education and training for children of all ages. *See also* The Education System.
HM Chief Inspector, Miriam Rosen
Chair, Baroness Morgan of Huyton

SECURITY AND INTELLIGENCE SERVICES

GOVERNMENT COMMUNICATIONS HEADQUARTERS (GCHQ)
Hubble Road, Cheltenham GL51 0EX
T 01242-221491 E pressoffice@gchq.gsi.gov.uk
W www.gchq.gov.uk

GCHQ produces signals intelligence in support of national security and the UK's economic wellbeing, and in the prevention or detection of serious crime. Additionally, GCHQ's Information Assurance arm, CESG, is the national technical authority for information assurance, and provides advice and assistance to government departments, the armed forces and other national infrastructure bodies on the security of their communications and information systems. GCHQ was placed on a statutory footing by the Intelligence Services Act 1994 and is headed by a director who is directly accountable to the foreign secretary.
Director, Iain Lobban

SECRET INTELLIGENCE SERVICE (MI6)
PO Box 1300, London SE1 1BD
W www.sis.gov.uk

The Secret Intelligence Service produces secret intelligence in support of the government's security, defence, foreign and economic policies. It was placed on a statutory footing by the Intelligence Services Act 1994 and is headed by a chief, known as 'C', who is directly accountable to the foreign secretary.
Chief, Sir John Sawers

SECURITY SERVICE (MI5)
PO Box 3255, London SW1P 1AE
T 020-7930 9000
W www.mi5.gov.uk

The Security Service is responsible for security intelligence work against covertly organised threats to the UK. It is organised into seven branches, each with dedicated areas of responsibility, which include countering terrorism, espionage and the proliferation of weapons of mass destruction. The Security Service also provides security advice to a wide range of organisations to help reduce vulnerability to threats from individuals, groups or countries hostile to UK interests. The home secretary has parliamentary accountability for the Security Service.
Director-General, Jonathan Evans

SERIOUS FRAUD OFFICE
Elm House, 10–16 Elm Street, London WC1X 0BJ
T 020-7239 7272
E public.enquiries@sfo.gsi.gov.uk
W www.sfo.gov.uk

The Serious Fraud Office is an independent government department that investigates and prosecutes serious or complex fraud. It is part of the UK Criminal Justice System. The office is headed by a director who is appointed by and accountable to the Attorney-General, and has jurisdiction over England, Wales and Northern Ireland but not Scotland, the Isle of Man or the Channel Islands.
Director, Richard Alderman

UK STATISTICS AUTHORITY
Statistics House, Tredegar Park, Newport, Gwent NP10 8XG
T 0845-604 1857 E authority.enquiries@statistics.gov.uk
W www.statisticsauthority.gov.uk

The UK Statistics Authority was established on 1 April 2008 by the Statistics and Registration Service Act 2007 as an independent body operating at arm's length from government, reporting to the UK parliament and the devolved legislatures. Its overall objective is to promote and safeguard the production and publication of official statistics and ensure their quality and comprehensiveness. The authority's main functions are the oversight of the Office for National Statistics (ONS); monitoring and reporting on all UK official statistics; and independent assessment of official statistics.

BOARD
Chair, Sir Michael Scholar, KCB
Board Members, Richard Alldritt *(Head of Assessment);* Dr Colette Bowe; Partha Dasgupta; Moira Gibb, CBE; Prof. Sir Roger Jowell, CBE *(Deputy Chair, Statistical System);* Jil Matheson *(National Statistician);* Prof. Steve Nickell, FBA; Stephen Penneck *(Director-General, ONS);* Prof David Rhind, CBE, FRS, FBA; Lord Rowe-Beddoe *(Deputy Chair, ONS);* Sir John Shortridge, KCB

OFFICE FOR NATIONAL STATISTICS (ONS)
Cardiff Road, Newport NP10 8XG
T 0845-601 3034 E info@statistics.gov.uk
W www.statistics.gov.uk

The ONS was created in 1996 by the merger of the Central Statistical Office and the Office of Population Censuses and Surveys. On 1 April 2008 it became the executive office of the UK Statistics Authority. As part of these changes, the office's responsibility for the General Register Office transferred to the Identity and Passport Service of the Home Office.

The ONS is responsible for preparing, interpreting and publishing key statistics on the government, economy and society of the UK. Its key responsibilities include designing, managing and running the Census and providing statistics on health and other demographic matters in England and Wales; the production of the UK National Accounts and other economic indicators; the organisation of population censuses in England and Wales and surveys for government departments and public bodies.
National Statistician, Jil Matheson
Director-General, Stephen Penneck

UK TRADE AND INVESTMENT
Europa Building, 450 Argyle Street, Glasgow G2 8LH
T 020-7215 8000 W www.ukti.gov.uk

UK Trade and Investment is a government organisation that helps UK-based companies succeed in international markets. It assists overseas companies to bring high quality investment to the UK economy.
Chief Executive, Susan Haird

WATER SERVICES REGULATION AUTHORITY (OFWAT)
Centre City Tower, 7 Hill Street, Birmingham B5 4UA
T 0121-644 7500 E enquiries@ofwat.gsi.gov.uk
W www.ofwat.gov.uk

OFWAT is the independent economic regulator of the water and sewerage companies in England and Wales. It is responsible for ensuring that the water industry in England and Wales provides customers with a good quality service at a fair price. This is done by keeping bills for consumers as low as possible; monitoring and comparing the services that companies provide; scrutinising the companies' costs and investment; and encouraging competition where this benefits consumers.
Chair, Philip Fletcher
Chief Executive, Regina Finn

PUBLIC BODIES

The following section is a listing of public bodies and other civil service organisations: it is not a complete list of these organisations.

Whereas executive agencies are either part of a government department or are one in their own right (*see* Government Departments section), public bodies carry out their functions to a greater or lesser extent at arm's length from central government. Ministers are ultimately responsible to parliament for the activities of the public bodies sponsored by their department and in almost all cases (except where there is separate statutory provision) ministers make the appointments to their boards. Departments are responsible for funding and ensuring good governance of their public bodies.

The term 'public body' is a general one which includes public corporations, such as the BBC; NHS bodies; and non-departmental public bodies (NDPBs).

In October 2010, the government announced proposals to drastically reform public bodies or 'quangos' (quasi-autonomous non-governmental organisations, another term for NDPBs). In total, 901 bodies were reviewed – 679 NDPBs and 222 other statutory bodies. As a result of this review, 192 quangos were scheduled to be abolished, with a further 118 merged into exisiting NDPBs. While some of these have already disbanded, many others will only be abolished after the public bodies bill, due to be introduced to parliament on 28 October 2012, receives royal assent.

ADJUDICATOR'S OFFICE
8th Floor, Euston Tower, 286 Euston Road, London NW1 3US
T 0300-057 1111 **W** www.adjudicatorsoffice.gov.uk

The Adjudicator's Office investigates complaints about the way that HM Revenue and Customs, the Valuation Office Agency and the Insolvency Service have handled a person's affairs.
The Adjudicator, Judy Clements, OBE

ADMINISTRATIVE JUSTICE AND TRIBUNALS COUNCIL
81 Chancery Lane, London WC2A 1BQ
T 020-7855 5200 **E** enquiries@ajtc.gsi.gov.uk
W www.justice.gov.uk/ajtc

The Administrative Justice and Tribunals Council (AJTC) is a permanent standing advisory body set up under the Tribunals, Courts and Enforcement Act. It consists of 15 members appointed by the Lord Chancellor, Scottish and Welsh ministers. It has Scottish and Welsh Committees which discharge its responsibilities in their respective territories. The Parliamentary Ombudsman is an *ex officio* member of the council and of its Scottish and Welsh Committees.

The principal functions of the AJTC are to keep the administrative justice system under review; keep under review and report on the constitution and working of listed tribunals; and keep under review and report on the constitution and working of statutory inquiries. It is consulted by and advises government departments on a wide range of subjects relating to adjudicative procedures.

The public bodies bill introduced into the House of Lords in spring 2011 proposed that the ATJC be abolished. Subject to the bill's remaining stages in parliament and subsequent secondary legislation, the council may be abolished by spring 2012.
Chair, Richard Thomas, CBE
Members, The Parliamentary Ombudsman *(ex officio)*, Ann Abraham; Jodi Berg, OBE; Prof. Alice Brown, CBE; Prof. Andrew Coyle, CMG; Kate Dunlop; Richard Henderson, CB; Sukhvinder Kaur-Stubbs; Penny Letts, OBE; Bronwyn McKenna; Prof. Mary Seneviratne; Dr Jonathan Spencer, CB; Brian Thompson; Prof. Sir Adrian Webb

WELSH COMMITTEE OF THE ADMINISTRATIVE JUSTICE AND TRIBUNALS COUNCIL
81 Chancery Lane, London WC2A 1BQ
T 020-7855 5200 **E** enquiries@ajtc.gsi.gov.uk
W www.justice.gov.uk/ajtc/welsh/welsh.htm
Chair, Prof. Sir Adrian Webb
Members, The Parliamentary and Health Service Ombudsman *(ex officio);* The Public Services Ombudsman for Wales *(ex officio);* Bob Chapman; Gareth Lewis; Rhian Williams-Flew

SCOTTISH COMMITTEE OF THE ADMINISTRATIVE JUSTICE AND TRIBUNALS COUNCIL
George House, 126 George Street, Edinburgh EH2 4HH
T 0131-271 4300
W www.justice.gov.uk/ajtc/scottish/scottish.htm
Chair, Richard Henderson
Members, The Parliamentary Commissioner for Administration *(ex officio);* The Scottish Public Services Ombudsman *(ex officio);* Prof. Michael Adler; Prof. Andrew Coyle; Annabell Fowles; Michael Menlowe; Michael Scanlan

ADVISORY, CONCILIATION AND ARBITRATION SERVICE (ACAS)
22nd Floor, Euston Tower, 286 Euston Road, London NW1 3JJ
T 020-7396 0022 **Helpline** 0845-747 4747
W www.acas.org.uk

The Advisory, Conciliation and Arbitration Service was set up under the Employment Protection Act 1975 (the provisions now being found in the Trade Union and Labour Relations (Consolidation) Act 1992).

ACAS is largely funded by the Department for Business, Innovation and Skills. A council sets its strategic direction, policies and priorities, and ensures that the agreed strategic objectives and targets are met. It consists of a chair and 11 employer, trade union and independent members, appointed by the Secretary of State for Business, Innovation and Skills. ACAS aims to improve organisations and working life through better employment relations, to provide up-to-date information, independent advice and high-quality training, and to work with employers and employees to solve problems and improve performance.

ACAS has 13 regional offices, in Birmingham, Bristol, Bury St Edmonds, Cardiff, Fleet, Glasgow, Leeds, Liverpool, London, Manchester, Newcastle upon Tyne, Nottingham and Paddock Wood.
Chair, Ed Sweeney
Chief Executive, John Taylor

ADVISORY COUNCIL ON NATIONAL RECORDS AND ARCHIVES
The National Archives, Kew, Surrey TW9 4DU
T 020-8392 5377
W www.nationalarchives.gov.uk/advisorycouncil

The Advisory Council on National Records and Archives advises the Lord Chancellor on all matters relating to the preservation, use of and access to historical manuscripts, records and archives of all kinds. The council meets four times a year, and its main task is to consider requests for the extended closure of public records, or from departments that want to keep records. The council encompasses the statutory Advisory Council on Public Records and the Advisory Council on Historical Manuscripts.
Chair, Lord Neuberger of Abbotsbury, PC *(Master of the Rolls)*

AGRICULTURE AND HORTICULTURE DEVELOPMENT BOARD
Stoneleigh Park, Kenilworth, Warwickshire CV8 2TL
T 02476-692051 E info@ahdb.org.uk W www.ahdb.org.uk

The Agriculture and Horticulture Development Board (AHDB) is funded by the agriculture and horticulture industries through statutory levies, with the duty to improve efficiency and competitiveness within six sectors: pig meat in England; milk in Great Britain; beef and lamb in England; commercial horticulture in Great Britain; cereals and oilseeds in the UK; and potatoes in Great Britain. The AHDB represents about 75 per cent of total UK agricultural output. Levies raised from the six sectors are ring-fenced to ensure that they can only be used to the benefit of the sectors from which they were raised. The AHDB board consists of ten members: the chairs for each of the six sector organisations and four independent members.
Chair, John Godfrey, CBE
Independent members, Chris Bones; John Bridge; Lorraine Clinton; Clare Dodgson
Sector members, Tim Bennett (milk); Neil Bragg (horticulture); John Cross (beef and lamb); Stewart Houston (pig meat); Allan Stevenson (potatoes); Jonathan Tipples (cereals and oilseeds)
Chief Executive, Tom Taylor

ARCHITECTURE AND DESIGN SCOTLAND
Bakehouse Close, 146 Canongate, Edinburgh EH8 8DD
T 0131-556 6699 E info@ads.org.uk
W www.ads.org.uk

Architecture and Design Scotland (A+DS) was established in 2005 by the Scottish government as the national champion for good architecture, urban design and planning in the built environment; it works with a wide range of organisations at national, regional and local levels. A+DS also assumed the independent design review and advisory role of the Royal Fine Art Commission for Scotland.
Chair, Karen Anderson
Chief Executive, Jim MacDonald

ARMED FORCES' PAY REVIEW BODY
6th Floor, Victoria House, Southampton Row, London WC1B 4AD
T 020-7271 0469 W www.ome.uk.com

The Armed Forces' Pay Review Body was appointed in 1971. It advises the prime minister and the Secretary of State for Defence on the pay and allowances of members of naval, military and air forces of the Crown.
Chair, Prof. Alasdair Smith
Members, Mary Carter; Prof. Peter Dolton; Very Revd. Dr Graham Forbes, CBE; Vice-Adm. Sir Richard Ibbotson, KBE; Paul Kernaghan, CBE, QPM; Judy McKnight, CBE; John Steele

ARTS COUNCIL ENGLAND
14 Great Peter Street, London SW1P 3NQ
T 0845-300 6200 E enquiries@artscouncil.org.uk
W www.artscouncil.org.uk

Arts Council England is the national development agency for the arts in England. Using public money from government and the National Lottery, it supports a range of artistic activities, including theatre, music, literature, dance, photography, digital art, carnival and crafts. Between 2011 and 2015, Arts Council England will invest £1.4bn of public money from the government and a further £850m from the National Lottery.
In 2002, the Arts Council of England and nine regional arts boards joined together to form a single development organisation for the arts. The governing council's members and chair are appointed by the Secretary of State for Culture, Media, Olympics and Sport usually for a term of four years, and meet approximately five times a year.
Chair, Dame Liz Forgan
Members, Janet Barnes; Caroline Collier; Prof. Jon Cook; Joe Docherty; Ekow Eshun; Sheila Healy; Sir Nicholas Kenyon; Keith Khan; Francois Matarasso; Andrew Motion *(observer)*; Peter Phillips; Alice Rawsthorn; Anil Ruia, OBE; Alistair Spalding; Rosemary Squire, OBE; Veronica Wadley
Chief Executive, Alan Davey

ARTS COUNCIL OF NORTHERN IRELAND
77 Malone Road, Belfast BT9 6AQ
T 028-9038 5200 E info@artscouncil-ni.org
W www.artscouncil-ni.org

The Arts Council of Northern Ireland is the prime distributor of government funds in support of the arts in Northern Ireland. It is funded by the Department of Culture, Arts and Leisure and from National Lottery funds.
Chair, Rosemary Kelly
Members, Eithne Benson; Kate Bond; Damien Coyle *(Vice-Chair);* Raymond Fullerton; David Irvine; Anthony Kennedy; Bill Montgomery; Prof. Ian Montgomery; Sharon O'Connor; Joseph Rice; Prof. Paul Seawright; Brian Sore; Peter Spratt; Janine Walker
Chief Executive, Roisin McDonough

ARTS COUNCIL OF WALES
Bute Place, Cardiff CF10 5AL
T 0845-873 4900 E feedback@artswales.org.uk
W www.artswales.org.uk

The Arts Council of Wales was established in 1994 by royal charter and is the development body for the arts in Wales. It funds arts organisations with funding from the National Assembly for Wales and is the distributor of National Lottery funds to the arts in Wales. The grant-in-aid for 2011–12 was £30.6m from the National Assembly.

Chair, Prof. Dai Smith

Members, Emma Evans; John Geraint; Margaret Jervis, MBE; Robin Morrison; Osi Rhys Osmond; Ian Rees; Richard Turner; Alan Watkin; Gerwyn Wiliams; John Carey Williams; Dr Kate Woodward

Chief Executive, Nick Capaldi

AUDIT COMMISSION

1st Floor, Millbank Tower, London SW1P 4HQ
T 0844-798 1212
E public-enquiries@audit-commission.gov.uk
W www.audit-commission.gov.uk

The Audit Commission is a public corporation set up in 1983 to protect the public purse.

The commission appoints auditors to local authorities, NHS bodies (excluding NHS foundation trusts), police authorities and other local public services in England, and oversees their work. It also audits NHS foundation trusts under separate arrangements and helps public bodies to manage the financial challenges they face by providing authoritative, unbiased, evidence-based analysis and advice. The auditors are either Audit Commission employees or belong to one of the private audit firms

The commission has a chair, a deputy chair and a board of 10 commissioners who are appointed by the Department of Communities and Local Government following consultation with key stakeholders.

Following the public bodies' reform proposals, the Audit Commission will cease to exist as a public corporation, subject to legislation. The commission is working with the Department for Communities and Local Government to consider ways of transferring its in-house audit practice into the private sector.

Chair, Michael O'Higgins

Deputy Chair, Bahrat Shah

Commissioners, Lord Adebowale, CBE; Janet Baker; Cllr Sir Merrick Cockell; Dr Jennifer Dixon; Tony Harris; Cllr Stephen Houghton, CBE; Brian Landers; Cllr Chris White

Chief Executive, Eugene Sullivan

AUDIT SCOTLAND

110 George Street, Edinburgh EH2 4LH
T 0845-146 1010 E info@auditscotland.gov.uk
W www.audit-scotland.gov.uk

Audit Scotland was set up in 2000 to provide services to the Accounts Commission and the Auditor-General for Scotland. Together they help to ensure that public sector bodies in Scotland are held accountable for the proper, efficient and effective use of public funds.

Audit Scotland's work covers about 200 bodies including local authorities; police forces and fire rescue services; health boards; further education colleges; Scottish Water; the Scottish government; government agencies such as the Prison Service and non-departmental public bodies such as Scottish Enterprise.

Audit Scotland carries out financial and regularity audits to ensure that public sector bodies adhere to the highest standards of financial management and governance. It also performs audits to ensure that these bodies achieve the best value for money. All of Audit

Scotland's work in connection with local authorities, fire and police boards is carried out for the Accounts Commission; its other work is undertaken for the Auditor-General.

Auditor-General, R. W. Black

Chair of the Accounts Commission, J. Baillie

BANK OF ENGLAND

Threadneedle Street, London EC2R 8AH
T 020-7601 4444 E enquiries@bankofengland.co.uk
W www.bankofengland.co.uk

The Bank of England was incorporated in 1694 under royal charter. It was nationalised in 1946 under the Bank of England Act of that year which gave HM Treasury statutory powers over the bank. It is the banker of the government and it manages the issue of banknotes. Since 1998 it has been operationally independent and its Monetary Policy Committee has been responsible for setting short-term interest rates to meet the government's inflation target. Its responsibility for banking supervision was transferred to the Financial Services Authority in the same year. As the central reserve bank of the country, the Bank of England keeps the accounts of British banks, and of most overseas central banks; the larger banks and building societies are required to maintain with it a proportion of their cash resources. The bank's core purposes are monetary stability and financial stability. The Banking Act 2009 increased the responsibilities of the bank, including giving it a new financial stability objective and creating a special resolution regime for dealing with failing banks.

Governor, Sir Mervyn King, GBE

Deputy Governors, Charles Bean; Paul Tucker

Court of Directors, The Governor; the Deputy Governors; Brendan Barber; Roger Carr; Sir David Lees; Susan Rice; John Stewart; Mark Tucker; Lord Adair Turner; Harrison Young

Monetary Policy Committee, The Governor; the Deputy Governors; Ben Broadbent; Spencer Dale; Paul Fisher; David Miles; Adam Posen; Dr Martin Weale

Adviser to the Governor, Graham Nicholson

Chief Cashier and Executive Director, Banking Services, Andrew Bailey

The Auditor, Stephen Brown

BIG LOTTERY FUND

1 Plough Place, London EC4A 1DE
T 020-7211 1800 **Advice Line** 0845-410 2030
E general.enquiries@biglotteryfund.org.uk
W www.biglotteryfund.org.uk

The Big Lottery Fund was launched in 2004, merging the New Opportunities Fund and the Lottery Charities Board (Community Fund). The fund is responsible for giving out half of the money for good causes raised by the National Lottery. The money is distributed to charitable, benevolent and philanthropic organisations in the voluntary and community sectors, as well as health, education and environmental projects. The Big Lottery Fund also assumed the Millennium Commission's role of supporting large-scale regenerative projects.

Chair, Peter Ainsworth

Vice-Chair, Anna Southall

Regional Chairs, Nat Sloane *(England)*; Frank Hewitt *(Northern Ireland)*; Alison Magee *(Scotland)*; Janet Reed, OBE *(Wales, acting)*

Chief Executive, Peter Wanless

BOUNDARY COMMISSIONS

ENGLAND
35 Great Smith Street, London SW1P 3BQ
T 020-7276 1102 E information@bcommengland.gsi.gov.uk
W www.boundarycommissionforengland.independent.gov.uk
Deputy Chair, Hon. Mr Justice Sales

WALES
1st Floor, Caradog House, 1–6 St Andrews Place, Cardiff
CF10 3BE
T 029-2039 5031 E bcomm.wales@wales.gsi.gov.uk
W www.bcomm-wales.gov.uk
Deputy Chair, Hon. Justice Lloyd Jones

SCOTLAND
Thistle House, 91 Haymarket Terrace, Edinburgh EH12 5HD
T 0131-538 7510 F 0131-538 7511
E secretariat@scottishboundaries.gov.uk
W www.bcomm-scotland.gov.uk
Deputy Chair, Hon. Lord Woolman

NORTHERN IRELAND
Forestview, Purdy's Lane, Newtownbreda, Belfast BT8 7AR
T 028-9069 4800 E bcni@belfast.org.uk
W www.boundarycommission.org.uk
Deputy Chair, Hon. Mr Justice McLaughlin

The commissions, established in 1944, are constituted under the Parliamentary Constituencies Act 1986 (as amended). The Speaker of the House of Commons is the *ex officio* chair of all four commissions in the UK. Each of the four commissions is required by law to keep the parliamentary constituencies in their part of the UK under review (in the case of the Scottish Commission this includes constituencies for the Scottish parliament).

The Boundary Commission for England completed its fifth general review of parliamentary constituencies in England in 2006. The commissions for Wales and Northern Ireland completed their reviews in 2005 and 2007 respectively. The Parliamentary Constituencies (England) Order 2007, the Parliamentary Constituencies and Assembly Electoral Regions (Wales) Order 2006 and the Parliamentary Constituencies (Northern Ireland) Order 2008 made provisions for the new constituencies which were first used at the 2010 general election. The Boundary Commission for Scotland submitted its final report in 2004 and the new constituencies came into force at the 2005 general election. The review of constituencies for the Scottish parliament was completed in May 2010 and the new constituencies were first used in the 2011 Scottish parliament election.

The 2013 (sixth) general reviews of parliamentary constituences in England, Wales, Scotland and Northern Ireland are currently underway and initial proposals are due to be published by each of the boundary commissions in October 2011.

BRITISH BROADCASTING CORPORATION (BBC)
Television Centre, Wood Lane, London W12 7RJ
T 020-8743 8000
W www.bbc.co.uk

The BBC was incorporated under royal charter in 1926 as successor to the British Broadcasting Company Ltd. The BBC's current charter, which came into force on 1 January 2007 and extends to 31 December 2016, recognises the BBC's editorial independence and sets out its public purposes. The BBC Trust was formed under the new charter and replaces the Board of Governors; it sets the strategic direction of the BBC and has a duty to represent the interests of licence fee payers. The chair, vice-chair and other trustees are appointed by the Queen-in-Council. The BBC is financed by revenue from receiving licences for the home services and by grant-in-aid from parliament for the World Service (radio). *See also* Broadcasting.

BBC TRUST MEMBERS
Chair, Lord Patten, CH, PC
Vice-Chair, Diane Coyle
National Trustees, Alison Hastings *(England)*; Rotha Johnston *(Northern Ireland)*; Bill Matthews *(Scotland)*; Elan Closs Stephens *(Wales)*
Trustees, Richard Ayre; Anthony Fry; David Liddiment; Mehmuda Mian

EXECUTIVE BOARD
Director-General and Chair, Mark Thompson
Deputy Director-General, Mark Byford
Directors, Helen Boaden *(News)*; Tim Davie *(Audio and Music)*; George Entwistle *(Vision)*; Zarin Patel *(Chief Financial Officer)*; Ralph Rivera *(Future Media and Technology)*
Chief Executive, BBC Worldwide, John Smith
Chief Operating Officer, Caroline Thomson
Senior Non-Executive Director, Marcus Agius
Non-Executive Directors, Simon Burke; Val Gooding, CBE; Dr Mike Lynch, OBE; Robert Webb, QC

STATION CONTROLLERS
BBC1, Danny Cohen
BBC2, Janice Hadlow
BBC3, Zai Bennett
BBC4, Richard Klein
BBC News Channel, Kevin Bakhurst
BBC Parliament, Peter Knowles
BBC Northern Ireland, Peter Johnston
BBC Scotland, Ken MacQuarrie
BBC Wales, Menna Richards
CBBC, Damian Kavanagh
CBeebies, Kay Benbow
Radio 1, 1Xtra, Asian Network and Switch, Andy Parfitt
Radio 2 and 6 Music, Bob Shennan
Radio 3, Roger Wright
Radio 4, Gwyneth Williams
Radio 5 Live, Adrian Van Klaveren

BRITISH COUNCIL
Bridgewater House, 58 Whitworth Street, Manchester M1 6BB
T 0161-957 7755 E general.enquiries@britishcouncil.org
W www.britishcouncil.org

The British Council was established in 1934, incorporated by royal charter in 1940 and granted a supplemental charter in 1993. It is an independent, non-political organisation which promotes Britain abroad and is the UK's international organisation for educational and cultural relations. The British Council is represented in 216 towns and cities in 109 countries. Grant-in-aid received from the Foreign and Commonwealth Office in 2010-11 was £190m.
Chair, Vernon Ellis
Chief Executive, Martin Davidson, CMG

BRITISH FILM INSTITUTE (BFI)
21 Stephen Street, London W1T 1LN
T 020-7255 1444 W www.bfi.org.uk

The BFI, established in 1933, offers opportunities for people throughout the UK to experience, learn and discover more about the world of film and moving image culture. It incorporates the BFI National Archive, the BFI National Library, a range of DVD releases, publications and educational materials (including the monthly *Sight and Sound* magazine), BFI Southbank, BFI Distribution, the annual BFI London Film Festival as well as the BFI London Lesbian and Gay Film Festival, and the BFI IMAX cinema, and provides advice and support for regional cinemas and film festivals across the UK.

Following the closure of the UK Film Council in April 2011, the BFI has become the lead body for film in the UK. It is now in charge of allocating lottery money for the development and production of new British films, deciding which films should receive tax credits and overseeing support for the film in the English regions.
Chair, Greg Dyke
Director, Amanda Nevill

BRITISH LIBRARY
96 Euston Road, London NW1 2DB
T 0843-208 1144 E customer-services@bl.uk
W www.bl.uk

The British Library was established in 1973. It is the UK's national library and occupies a key position in the library and information network. It aims to serve scholarship, research, industry, commerce and all other major users of information. Its services are based on a collection of over 150 million separate items, including books, journals, manuscripts, maps, stamps, music, patents, newspapers and sound recordings in all written and spoken languages. The library is now based at three sites: London (St Pancras and Colindale) and Boston Spa, W. Yorks. The library's sponsoring department is the Department for Culture, Media and Sport.

Access to the reading rooms at St Pancras is limited to holders of a British Library reader's pass; information about eligibility is available from the reader admissions office. The exhibition galleries and public areas are open to all, free of charge.

BRITISH LIBRARY BOARD
Chair, Baroness Blackstone
Chief Executive and Deputy Chair, Dame L. Brindley, DBE
Members, Ms D. Airey; R. S. Broadhurst, CBE; Prof. R. Burgess; Sir K. Calman; Lord Fellowes; Ms S. Forbes, CBE; Prof. W. Hall, CBE; Ms E. Mackay, CB; Prof. K. McLuskie; Dr Stephen Page; M. Semple, OBE

SCHOLARSHIP AND COLLECTIONS
Americas Collections, T 020-7412 7743
Asia, Pacific and Africa Collections, T 020-7412 7873
British and Irish Collections, T 020-7412 7538
British Library Newspapers, Colindale Avenue, London NW9 5HE T 020-7412 7353
British Library Sound Archive, T 020-7412 7676
Early Printed Collections, T 020-7412 7564
Map Library, T 020-7412 7702
Music Library, T 020-7412 7772
Philatelic Collections, T 020-7412 7635
Reader Information, T 020-7412 7676
West European Collections, T 020-7412 7572/7569

OPERATIONS AND SERVICES
Permission Clearance, T 020-7412 7755
Research Services, T 020-7412 7903

SCIENCE, TECHNOLOGY AND INNOVATION
Business, T 020-7412 7454
National Preservation Office, T 020-7412 7612
Patents, T 020-7412 7454
Science and Technology, T 020-7412 7494/7288
Social Science, Law and Official Publications,
   T 020-7412 7536

BRITISH LIBRARY, BOSTON SPA
Boston Spa, Wetherby, W. Yorks LS23 7BQ
T 01937-546060

BRITISH MUSEUM
Great Russell Street, London WC1B 3DG
T 020-7323 8000
E information@britishmuseum.org
W www.britishmuseum.org

The British Museum houses the national collection of antiquities, ethnography, coins and paper money, medals, prints and drawings. The British Museum may be said to date from 1753, when parliament approved the holding of a public lottery to raise funds for the purchase of the collections of Sir Hans Sloane and the Harleian manuscripts, and for their proper housing and maintenance. The building (Montagu House) was opened in 1759. The existing buildings were erected between 1823 and the present day, and the original collection has increased to its current dimensions by gifts and purchases. Total government grant-in-aid for 2011–12 is £53.7m.

BOARD OF TRUSTEES
Appointed by the Sovereign, Chief Emeka Anyaoku
Appointed by the Prime Minister, Karen Armstrong; Prof. Sir Christopher Bayly; Sir Ronald Cohen; Francis Finlay; Val Gooding, CBE; Bonnie Greer; Penny Hughes; George Iacobescu, CBE; Baroness Kennedy, QC; Richard Lambert; David Norgrove; Lord Stern of Brentford, FBA; Baroness Wheatcroft of Blackheath
Appointed by the Trustees of the British Museum, Prof. Amartya Sen; Lord Broers of Cambridge, FRS, FRENG; Niall Fitzgerald *(Chair);* Edmee P. Leventis; Sir Martin Sorrell
Appointed by the Royal Society, Dr Olga Kennard, OBE
Appointed by the Royal Academy, Antony Gormley, OBE

OFFICERS
Director, Neil MacGregor
Deputy Director, Dr Andrew Burnett
Director of Public Engagement, Joanna Mackle
Director of Administration, Chris Yates
Director of Operations and Projects, Justin Morris
Heads of Departments, Carolyn Marsden-Smith
   (Exhibitions); Xerxes Mazda *(Learning and Audience)*

KEEPERS
Keeper of Africa, Oceania and the Americas (acting), Vivian Davies
Keeper of Ancient Egypt and Sudan, Vivian Davies
Keeper of Asia, Jan Stuart
Keeper of Coins and Medals, Philip Attwood
Keeper of Greece and Rome, J. Lesley Fitton
Keeper of the Middle East, John Curtis
Keeper of Prehistory and Europe, Jonathan Williams

Keeper of Prints and Drawings, Antony Griffiths
Conservation and Scientific Research, David Saunders

BRITISH PHARMACOPOEIA COMMISSION

151 Buckingham Palace Road, London SW1W 9SZ
T 020-3080 6561 E bpcom@mhra.gsi.gov.uk
W www.pharmacopoeia.gov.uk

The British Pharmacopoeia Commission sets standards for medicinal products used in human and veterinary medicines and is responsible for publication of the *British Pharmacopoeia* (a publicly available statement of the standard that a product must meet throughout its shelf-life), the *British Pharmacopoeia (Veterinary)* and the *British Approved Names.* It has 15 members, including two lay members, who are appointed by the Appointments Commission (the body responsible for appointments to all of the Medicines Act advisory bodies).
Chair, Prof. A. D. Woolfson
Vice-Chair, V'lain Fenton-May
Secretary and Scientific Director, Dr M. G. Lee

BRITISH WATERWAYS

64 Clarendon Road, Watford WD17 1DA
T 01923-201120
E enquiries.hq@britishwaterways.co.uk
W www.britishwaterways.co.uk

British Waterways conserves and manages the network of over 3,540km (2,200 miles) of canals and rivers in England, Scotland and Wales. Its sponsoring departments are the Department for Environment, Food and Rural Affairs in England and Wales, and the Scottish Government Transport Directive.

Its responsibilities include maintaining the waterways and structures on and around them; looking after wildlife and the waterway environment; and ensuring that canals and rivers are safe and enjoyable places to visit.

As part of the public bodies' reform proposals announced in October 2010, management of the network of inland waterways in England and Wales will transfer to a new charitable body. The government intends to have this new body established by April 2012.
Chair, Tony Hales, CBE
Vice-Chair, John Bridgeman, CBE, TD
Chief Executive, Robin Evans, FRICS

CARE QUALITY COMMISSION

Finsbury Tower, 103–105 Bunhill Row, London EC1Y 8TG
T 0300-061 6161 E enquiries@cqc.org.uk
W www.cqc.org.uk

The Care Quality Commission (CQC) was established on 1 April 2009, bringing together the work of the Healthcare Commission, the Mental Health Act Commission and the Commission for Social Care Inspection. CQC is the independent regulator of health and adult social care services in England, including care provided by the NHS, local authorities, private companies and voluntary organisations.
Chair (acting), Jo Williams
Chief Executive, Cynthia Bower
Board, John Harwood; Prof. Deirdre Kelly; Martin Marshall; Olu Olasode; Kay Sheldon; Jo Williams

CENTRAL ARBITRATION COMMITTEE

22nd Floor, Euston Tower, 286 Euston Road, London NW1 3JJ
T 020-7904 2300 E enquiries@cac.gov.uk
W www.cac.gov.uk

The Central Arbitration Committee (CAC) is a permanent independent body with statutory powers whose main function is to adjudicate on applications relating to the statutory recognition and de-recognition of trade unions for collective bargaining purposes, where such recognition or de-recognition cannot be agreed voluntarily. In addition, the CAC has a statutory role in determining disputes between trade unions and employers over the disclosure of information for collective bargaining purposes, and in resolving applications and complaints under the information and consultation regulations, and performs a similar role in relation to the legislation on the European Works Council, European companies, European cooperative societies and cross-border mergers. The CAC also provides voluntary arbitration in industrial disputes.

The committee consists of a chair and 10 deputy chairs, 25 members experienced as representatives of employers and 22 members experienced as representatives of workers. Members of the committee are appointed by the Secretary of State for Business, Innovation and Skills after consultation with the Advisory, Conciliation and Arbitration Service (ACAS).

Following the public bodies' reform proposals of October 2010, the CAC will merge with the Certification Office, subject to legislation.
Chair, Sir Michael Burton
Chief Executive, Simon Gouldstone

CERTIFICATION OFFICE FOR TRADE UNIONS AND EMPLOYERS' ASSOCIATIONS

Euston Tower, 286 Euston Road, London NW1 3JJ
T 020-7210 3734 E info@certoffice.org
W www.certoffice.org

The Certification Office is an independent statutory authority. The Certification Officer is appointed by the Secretary of State for Business, Innovation and Skills and is responsible for maintaining a list of trade unions and employers' associations; ensuring compliance with statutory requirements and keeping available for public inspection annual returns from trade unions and employers' associations; determining complaints concerning trade union elections, certain ballots and certain breaches of trade union rules; ensuring observance of statutory requirements governing mergers between trade unions and employers' associations; overseeing the political funds and finances of trade unions and employers' associations; and for certifying the independence of trade unions.

Following the public bodies' reform proposals of October 2010, the Certification Office will merge with the Central Arbitration Committee, subject to legislation.
Certification Officer, David Cockburn

SCOTLAND
69A George Street, Edinburgh EH2 2JG
T 0131-220 7660
Assistant Certification Officer for Scotland, Christine Stuart

CHURCH COMMISSIONERS

Church House, Great Smith Street, London SW1P 3AZ
T 020-7898 1000
E commissioners.enquiry@churchofengland.org
W www.churchofengland.org/about_us/structure/
churchcommissioners

The Church Commissioners were established in 1948 by the amalgamation of Queen Anne's Bounty (established 1704) and the Ecclesiastical Commissioners (established 1836). They are responsible for the management of some of the Church of England's assets, the income from which is predominantly used to help pay for the stipend and pension of the clergy and to support the church's work throughout the country. The commissioners own UK and global company shares, over 43,000ha (106,000 acres) of agricultural land, a residential estate in central London, and commercial property across Great Britain, plus an interest in overseas property via managed funds. They also carry out administrative duties in connection with pastoral reorganisation and closed churches.

The commissioners are: the Archbishops of Canterbury and of York; four bishops, three clergy and four lay persons elected by the respective houses of the General Synod; two deans elected by all the deans; three persons nominated by the Queen; three persons nominated by the Archbishops of Canterbury and York; three persons nominated by the archbishops after consultation with others including the Lord Mayors of London and York and the vice-chancellors of the universities of Oxford and Cambridge; the First Lord of the Treasury; the Lord President of the Council; the home secretary; the Secretary of State for Culture, Olympics, Media and Sport; and the Speakers of the House of Commons and the House of Lords.

CHURCH ESTATES COMMISSIONERS
First, A. Whittam Smith
Second, T. Baldry, MP
Third, T. E. H. Walker

OFFICERS
Secretary, A. C. Brown
Director of Investments, T. Joy
Assistant Secretary, Pastoral and Redundant Churches, P. Lewis
Official Solicitor, S. Slack

COAL AUTHORITY
200 Lichfield Lane, Mansfield, Notts NG18 4RG
T 01623-637000 E thecoalauthority@coal.gov.uk
W http://coal.decc.gov.uk

The Coal Authority was established under the Coal Industry Act 1994 to manage certain functions previously undertaken by British Coal, including ownership of unworked coal. It is responsible for licensing coal mining operations and for providing information on coal reserves and past and future coal mining. It settles subsidence damage claims which are not the responsibility of licensed coal mining operators. It deals with the management and disposal of property, and with surface hazards such as abandoned coal mine entries.
Chair, Dr Helen Mounsey
Chief Executive, Philip Lawrence

COMMISSION FOR RURAL COMMUNITIES
Unit 1, Saw Mill End, Corinium Avenue, Gloucester GL4 3DE
T 0845-933 5577 E info@ruralcommunities.gov.uk
W www.defra.gov.uk/crc

The Commission for Rural Communities (CRC) was established in October 2006 to promote awareness of rural needs. It was announced in June 2010 that the CRC would be abolished, and that the Department for Environment, Food and Rural Affairs internal rural policy capacity would be expanded to create a Rural Communities Policy Unit (RCPU). It was later agreed that from 1 April 2011, the CRC would significantly reduce its staffing levels and the scale of its operation, with some of its work and staff transferring to a new unit. The attenuated CRC will carry out its statutory functions of advice, advocacy and watchdog activity through its chair, commissioners and a small support team.
Chair, Dr Stuart Burgess
Commissioners, Prof. Sheena Asthana; Richard Childs, QPM; Elinor Goodman; John Mills, CBE; Howard Petch, CBE; Sue Prince, OBE; Rachel Purchase; Prof. Mark Shucksmith, OBE; Prof. Michael Winter, OBE

COMMITTEE ON STANDARDS IN PUBLIC LIFE
35 Great Smith Street, London SW1P 3BQ
T 020-7276 2595 E public@standards.x.gsi.gov.uk
W www.public-standards.org.uk

The Committee on Standards in Public Life was set up in October 1994. It is formed of 10 people appointed by the prime minister, comprising the chair, three political members nominated by the leaders of the three main political parties and six independent members. The committee's remit is to examine concerns about standards of conduct of all holders of public office, including arrangements relating to financial and commercial activities, and to make recommendations as to any changes in present arrangements which might be required to ensure the highest standards of propriety in public life. It is also charged with reviewing issues in relation to the funding of political parties. The committee does not investigate individual allegations of misconduct.
Chair, Sir Christopher Kelly, KCB
Members, Lord Alderdice; Lloyd Clarke, QPM; Oliver Heald, MP; Rt. Hon. Margaret Beckett, MP; Sir Derek Morris; Dame Denise Platt, DBE; David Prince, CBE; Dr Elizabeth Vallance; Dr Brian Woods-Scawen, CBE

COMMONWEALTH WAR GRAVES COMMISSION
2 Marlow Road, Maidenhead, Berks SL6 7DX
T 01628-634221 E casualty.enq@cwgc.org
W www.cwgc.org

The Commonwealth War Graves Commission (formerly Imperial War Graves Commission) was founded by royal charter in 1917. It is responsible for the commemoration of around 1.7 million members of the forces of the Commonwealth who lost their lives in the two world wars. More than one million graves are maintained in 23,274 burial grounds throughout the world. Over three-quarters of a million men and women who have no known grave or who were cremated are commemorated by name on memorials built by the commission.

The funds of the commission are derived from the six participating governments, ie the UK, Canada, Australia, New Zealand, South Africa and India.
President, HRH The Duke of Kent, KG, GCMG, GCVO, ADC
Chair, Secretary of State for Defence (UK)
Vice-Chair, Lt.-Gen. Sir Alistair Irwin, KCB, CBE
Members, High Commissioners in London for Australia, Canada, South Africa, New Zealand and India; Air Chief Marshal Sir Joe French, KCB, CBE; Kevan Jones, MP; Sara Jones, CBE; Keith Simpson, MP; Prof. Hew

Strachan, FRSE; Vice-Adm. Tim Laurence, CB, MVO; Duke of Westminster, KG, CB, OBE; Sir Rob Young, GCMG
Director-General and Secretary to the Commission, Alan Pateman-Jones
Deputy Director-General, T. Reeves
Director of Legal Services, Gillian Stedman

COMPETITION COMMISSION

Victoria House, Southampton Row, London WC1B 4AD
T 020-7271 0100 E info@cc.gsi.gov.uk
W www.competition-commission.org.uk

The commission was established in 1948 as the Monopolies and Restrictive Practices Commission (later the Monopolies and Mergers Commission); it became the Competition Commission in April 1999 under the Competition Act 1998. The commission conducts in-depth inquiries into mergers, markets and the regulation of major industries. Every inquiry the commission undertakes is in response to a reference made to it by another authority, usually the Office of Fair Trading. The commission has no power to conduct inquiries on its own initiative. The Enterprise Act 2002 introduced a new regime for the assessment of mergers and markets in the UK – in most related investigations the commission is responsible for making decisions on the competition questions and for making and implementing decisions on appropriate remedies.

The commission has a full-time chair and three deputy chairs. There are usually around 40 part-time commission members, who usually carry out investigations in groups of four or five after appointment by the chair. All are appointed by the Secretary of State for Business, Innovation and Skills for eight-year terms.

As part of the public bodies' reform proposals of October 2010, it was announced that the Competition Commission would merge with the Office of Fair Trading to form a single agency – the Competition and Markets Authority (CMA), subject to legislation.
Chair, Roger Witcomb
Deputy Chairs, Laura Carstensen; Dr Peter Davis
Non-Executive Directors, Grey Denham; Dame Patricia Hodgson, DBE; Lesley Watkins
Chief Executive and Secretary, David Saunders

COMPETITION SERVICE

Victoria House, Bloomsbury Place, London WC1A 2EB
T 020-7979 7979 E info@catribunal.org.uk
W www.catribunal.org.uk

The Competition Service is the financial corporate body by which the Competition Appeal Tribunal is administered and through which it receives funding for the performance of its judicial functions.
Director, Operations, Jeremy Straker
President, Hon. Mr Justice Barling
Registrar, Charles Dhanowa, OBE

CONSUMER COUNCIL FOR WATER

Victoria Square House, Victoria Square, Birmingham B2 4AJ
T 0121-345 1000 E enquiries@ccwater.org.uk
W www.ccwater.org.uk

The Consumer Council for Water was established in 2005 under the Water Act 2003 to represent consumers' interests in respect of price, service and value for money from their water and sewerage services, and to investigate complaints from customers about their water company. There are four regional committees in England and one in Wales.
Chair, Dame Yve Buckland, DBE

CONSUMER FOCUS

Fleetbank House, 1 Salisbury Square, London EC4Y 8JX
T 020-7799 7900 E contact@consumerfocus.org.uk
W www.consumerfocus.org.uk

Consumer Focus was formed from the merger of Energywatch, Postwatch and the National Consumer Council, and began operations in October 2008. The organisation works for the interests of consumers in private and public sectors throughout England, Scotland and Wales (and for postal services in Northern Ireland). Consumer Focus has legislative powers, including the right to investigate any complaint if it is of wider interest; the right to open up information from providers; and the ability to make an official 'super-complaint' about failing services. Consumer Focus is not a complaints-handling body or a statutory regulator; consumer complaints or requests for advice should be directed to Consumer Direct or Citizens Advice.

Following the public bodies' reform proposals of October 2010, Consumer Focus will be abolished, subject to legislation, with some of its functions likely to be transferred to Citizens Advice, Citizens Advice Scotland and the General Consumer Council for Northern Ireland. This is likely to happen in spring 2013.
Chair, Christine Farnish
Chief Executive, Mike O'Connor

CORPORATION OF TRINITY HOUSE

Trinity House, Tower Hill, London EC3N 4DH
T 020-7481 6900 E enquiries@thls.org
W www.trinityhouse.co.uk

The Corporation of Trinity House is the General Lighthouse Authority for England, Wales and the Channel Islands, and was granted its first charter by Henry VIII in 1514. Its remit is to assist the safe passage of a variety of vessels through some of the busiest sea-lanes in the world; it does this by deploying and maintaining approximately 600 aids to navigation, ranging from lighthouses to a satellite navigation service. The corporation also has certain statutory jurisdiction over aids to navigation maintained by local harbour authorities and is responsible for marking or dispersing wrecks dangerous to navigation, except those occurring within port limits or wrecks of HM ships.

The statutory duties of Trinity House are funded by the General Lighthouse Fund, which is provided from light dues levied on ships calling at ports of the UK and the Republic of Ireland. The corporation is a deep-sea pilotage authority, authorised by the Secretary of State for Transport to license deep-sea pilots. In addition Trinity House is a charitable organisation that maintains a number of retirement homes for mariners and their dependants, funds a four-year training scheme for those seeking a career in the merchant navy, and also dispenses grants to a wide range of maritime charities. The charity work is wholly funded by its own activities.

The corporation is controlled by a board of Elder Brethren; a separate board controls the Lighthouse Service. The Elder Brethren also act as nautical assessors in marine cases in the Admiralty Division of the High Court.

ELDER BRETHREN

Master, HRH the Princess Royal, KG, KT, GCVO
Deputy Master, Capt. Ian McNaught
Wardens, Capt. Duncan Glass, OBE *(Rental);*
   Capt. Nigel Pryke *(Nether)*
Elder Brethren, HRH The Prince of Wales, KG, KT, GCB;
   HRH The Duke of York, KG, GCVO, ADC; HRH The
   Princess Royal, KG, KT, GCVO; Capt. Roger Barker;
   Adm. Lord Boyce, KG, GCB, OBE; Lord Browne of
   Madingley; Capt. John Burton-Hall, RD; Lord
   Carrington, KG, GCMG, CH, PC; Viscount Cobham;
   Capt. Sir Malcolm Edge, KCVO; Capt. Ian Gibb; Lord
   Greenway; Lord Mackay of Clashfern, KT, PC; Capt.
   Peter Mason, CBE; Cdre. Peter Melson, CVO, CBE,
   RN; Capt. David Orr; Sir John Parker, FRENG;
   Douglas Potter; Capt. Derek Richards, RD, RNR; Lord
   Robertson of Port Ellen, KT, GCMG, PC; Rear-Adm.
   Sir Patrick Rowe, KCVO, CBE; Cdre. Jim Scorer;
   Simon Sherrard; Adm. Sir Jock Slater, GCB, LVO; Capt.
   David Smith, OBE, RN; Cdre. David Squire, CBE,
   RFA; Cdre. Lord Sterling of Plaistow, CBE, GCVO,
   RNR; Capt. Colin Stewart, LVO; Sir Adrian Swire, AE;
   Capt. Sir Miles Wingate, KCVO; Capt. Thomas
   Woodfield, OBE; Capt. Richard Woodman

OFFICERS

Secretary, Cdr Graham Hockley
Director of Finance, Jerry Wedge
Director of Navigation, Capt. Roger Barker
Director of Operations, Cdre. Jim Scorer

COUNTRYSIDE COUNCIL FOR WALES/CYNGOR CEFN GWLAD CYMRU

Maes-y-Ffynnon, Penrhosgarnedd, Bangor, Gwynedd LL57 2DW
T 0845-130 6229 **E** enquiries@ccw.gov.uk
W www.ccw.gov.uk

The Countryside Council for Wales is the government's
statutory adviser on sustaining natural beauty, wildlife and
the opportunity for outdoor enjoyment in Wales and its
inshore waters. It is funded by the National Assembly for
Wales and accountable to the First Secretary, who
appoints its members.
Chair, Morgan Parry
Chief Executive, Roger Thomas

COVENT GARDEN MARKET AUTHORITY

Covent House, New Covent Garden Market, London SW8 5BH
T 020-7720 2211 **E** info@cgma.co.uk
W www.newcoventgardenmarket.com

The Covent Garden Market Authority is constituted under
the Covent Garden Market Acts 1961 to 1977, the board
being appointed by the Department of Environment,
Food and Rural Affairs. The authority owns and operates
the 22.7ha (56 acre) New Covent Garden Markets (fruit,
vegetables, flowers), which have been trading at the site
since 1974.
Chair (part-time), Baroness Dean of Thornton-le-Fylde,
   PC
Chief Executive, Jan Lloyd

CREATIVE SCOTLAND

Waverley Gate, 2–4 Waterloo Place, Edinburgh EH3 1EG
T 0330-333 2000 **E** enquiries@creativescotland.com
W www.creativescotland.com

Creative Scotland is the organisation tasked with leading
the development of the arts, creative and screen industries

across Scotland. It was created in 2010 as an
amalgamation of the Scottish Arts Council and Scottish
Screen, and it encourages and sustains the arts through
investment in the form of grants, bursaries, loans and
equity. It aims to invest in talent; artistic production;
audiences, access and participation; and the cultural
economy. The intelligence it gathers from practitioners,
partners and sector peers will be used to guide its future
investments – the money for which is inherited from the
grant-in-aid budgets of its two predecessor organisations.
The draft budget for 2010–11 was £57.5m.
Chair, Sir Sandy Crombie
Board, Peter Cabrelli; Gwilym Gibbons; Steve Grimmond;
   Robin MacPherson; Prof. Gayle McPherson; Barclay
   Price; Dr Gary West; Ruth Wishart
Chief Executive, Andrew Dixon

CRIMINAL CASES REVIEW COMMISSION

5 Philip's Place, Birmingham B3 2PW
T 0121-233 1473 **E** info@ccrc.gov.uk
W www.ccrc.gov.uk

The Criminal Cases Review Commission is the
independent body set up under the Criminal Appeal Act
1995. It is a non-departmental public body reporting to
parliament via the Lord Chancellor and Secretary of State
for Justice. It is responsible for investigating possible
miscarriages of justice in England, Wales and Northern
Ireland, and deciding whether or not to refer cases
back to an appeal court. Membership of the commission
is by royal appointment; the senior executive staff are
appointed by the commission.
Chair, Richard Foster, CBE
Members, M. Allen; Ms P. Barrett; J. England;
   Ms J. Goulding; A. MacGregor, QC; I. Nicholl;
   E. Smith; J. Weeden
Chief Executive, Claire Bassett

CRIMINAL INJURIES COMPENSATION AUTHORITY (CICA)

Tay House, 300 Bath Street, Glasgow G2 4LN
Helpline: 0300-003 3601
W www.justice.gov.uk/guidance/compensation-schemes/cica

CICA is the government body responsible for
administering the Criminal Injuries Compensation
Scheme in England, Scotland and Wales (separate
arrangements apply in Northern Ireland). CICA deals
with every aspect of applications for compensation
under the 1996, 2001 and 2008 Criminal Injuries
Compensation Schemes. There is a separate avenue of
appeal to the First-tier Tribunal (Criminal Injuries
Compensation) (*see* Tribunals).
Chief Executive, Carole Oatway

CROFTERS COMMISSION

Great Glen House, Leachkin Road, Inverness IV3 8NW
T 01463-663450 **E** info@crofterscommission.org.uk
W www.crofterscommission.org.uk

The Crofters Commission, established in 1955 under
the Crofters (Scotland) Act, is a government-funded
organisation tasked with overseeing crofting legislation. It
works with communities to regulate crofting and advises
Scottish ministers on crofting matters. The commission
administers the Croft House Grant Scheme and the
Crofters' Cattle Improvement Scheme. It also provides a
free enquiry service.
Convener, Drew Ratter
Chief Executive, Nick Reiter

ENGLISH HERITAGE (HISTORIC BUILDINGS AND MONUMENTS COMMISSION FOR ENGLAND)

1 Waterhouse Square, 138–142 Holborn, London EC1N 2ST
T 020-7973 3000 W www.english-heritage.org.uk

English Heritage was established under the National Heritage Act 1983. On 1 April 1999 it merged with the Royal Commission on the Historical Monuments of England to become the new lead body for England's historic environment. It is sponsored by the Department for Culture, Media and Sport and its duties are to carry out and sponsor archaeological, architectural and scientific surveys and research designed to increase the understanding of England's past and its changing condition; to identify buildings, monuments and landscapes for protection while also offering expert advice, skills and grants to conserve these sites; to encourage town planners to make imaginative re-use of historic buildings to aid regeneration of the centres of cities, towns and villages; to manage and curate selected sites; and to curate and make publicly accessible the National Monuments Record, whose records of over one million historic sites and buildings, and extensive collections of photographs, maps, drawings and reports, constitute the central database and archive of England's historic environment.

Chair, Baroness Andrews, OBE
Commissioners, Lynda Addison, OBE; Maria Adebowale; Joyce Bridges, CBE; Manish Chande; Prof. Sir Barry Cunliffe, CBE; David Fursdon; Prof. Ronald Hutton; Jane Kennedy; John Walker, CBE; Chris Wilkinson, OBE; Elizabeth Williamson, FSA
Chief Executive, Dr Simon Thurley

CUSTOMER SERVICES DEPARTMENT, PO Box 569, Swindon SN2 2YP
T 0870-333 1181 E customers@english-heritage.org.uk
NATIONAL MONUMENTS RECORD CENTRE,
Kemble Drive, Swindon SN2 2GZ T 01793-414600

ENVIRONMENT AGENCY

National Customer Contact Centre, PO Box 544, Rotherham S60 1BY
T 0370-850 6506 E enquiries@environment-agency.gov.uk
W www.environment-agency.gov.uk

The Environment Agency was established in 1996 under the Environment Act 1995 and is a non-departmental public body sponsored by the Department for Environment, Food and Rural Affairs and the National Assembly for Wales – around 70 per cent of the agency's funding is from the government, with the rest raised from various charging schemes. The agency is responsible for pollution prevention and control in England and Wales and for the management and use of water resources, including flood defences, fisheries and navigation. Its remit also includes: scrutinising business operations which have the potential to be environmentally hazardous; helping businesses to use resources more efficiently; taking action against those who do not take environmental responsibilities seriously; looking after wildlife; and helping to improve the quality of inner city areas and parks.

The Environment Agency has head offices in London and Bristol, and seven regional offices.

THE BOARD
Chair, Lord Smith of Finsbury
Members, Andrew Brown; Prof. Ruth Hall; Julie Hill, MBE; Emma Howard Boyd; Robert Light; Dr Madeleine Harvard; John Varley; Jeremy Walker; Lady Warner, OBE; Lord Whitty
Chief Executive, Paul Leinster

EQUALITY AND HUMAN RIGHTS COMMISSION

Arndale House, The Arndale Centre, Manchester M4 3AQ
T 0161-829 8100 E info@equalityhumanrights.com
W www.equalityhumanrights.com

The Equality and Human Rights Commission (EHRC) is a statutory body, established under the Equality Act 2006 and launched in October 2007. It inherited the responsibilities of the Commission for Racial Equality, the Disability Rights Commission and the Equal Opportunities Commission. The EHRC's purpose is to reduce inequality, eliminate discrimination, strengthen relations between people, and promote and protect human rights. It enforces equality legislation on age, disability and health, gender, race, religion and belief, sexual orientation or transgender status, and encourages compliance with the Human Rights Act 1998 throughout England, Wales and Scotland. For information on how to contact the helpline, visit the EHRC website.

Chair, Trevor Phillips, OBE
Deputy Chair, Baroness Prosser, OBE
Commissioners, Stephen Alambritis; Ann Beynon, OBE; Prof. Geraldine Van Bueren; Kay Carberry, CBE; Meral Hussein Ece, OBE; Baroness Greengross, OBE; Dr Jean Irvine, OBE; Kaliani Lyle; Angela Mason; Michael Smith; Simon Woolley

EQUALITY COMMISSION FOR NORTHERN IRELAND

Equality House, 7–9 Shaftesbury Square, Belfast BT2 7DP
T 028-9089 0890 **Textphone** 028-9050 0589
E information@equalityni.org W www.equalityni.org

The Equality Commission was set up in 1999 under the Northern Ireland Act 1998 and is responsible for promoting equality, keeping the relevant legislation under review, eliminating discrimination on the grounds of race, disability, sexual orientation, gender (including marital and civil partner status, gender reassignment, pregnancy and maternity), age, religion and political opinion and for overseeing the statutory duty on public authorities to promote equality of opportunity.

Chief Commissioner, Bob Collins
Deputy Chief Commissioner, Jane Morrice
Chief Executive, Evelyn Collins, CBE, FRSA

GAMBLING COMMISSION

Victoria Square House, Victoria Square, Birmingham B2 4BP
T 0121-230 6666
E info@gamblingcommission.gov.uk
W www.gamblingcommission.gov.uk

The Gambling Commission was established under the Gambling Act 2005, and took over the role previously occupied by the Gaming Board for Great Britain in regulating and licensing all commercial gambling – apart from spread betting and the National Lottery – ie casinos, bingo, betting, remote gambling, gaming machines and lotteries. It also advises local and central government on related issues, and is responsible for the protection of children and the vulnerable from being exploited or harmed by gambling. The commission is sponsored by the Department for Culture, Media and Sport, with its work funded by licence fees paid by the gambling industry.

Following the public bodies' reform proposals of October 2010, the Gambling Commission will merge with the National Lottery Commission in 2012.

Chair, Philip Graf
Chief Executive, Jenny Williams

HEALTH AND SAFETY EXECUTIVE
Redgrave Court, Merton Road, Bootle, Merseyside L20 7HS
Incident Centre 0845-300 9923
W www.hse.gov.uk

The Health and Safety Commission (HSC) and the Health and Safety Executive (HSE) merged on 1 April 2008 to form a single national regulatory body responsible for promoting the cause of better health and safety at work.

HSE regulates all industrial and commercial sectors except operations in the air and at sea. This includes agriculture, construction, manufacturing, services, transport, mines, offshore oil and gas, nuclear, quarries and major hazard sites in chemicals and petrochemicals.

HSE is responsible for developing and enforcing health and safety law, providing guidance and advice, commissioning research, inspection including accident and ill-health investigation, developing standards and licensing or approving some work activities such as nuclear power and asbestos removal. HSE is sponsored by the Department for Work and Pensions.

Chair, Judith Hackitt, CBE
Board Members, Nick Baldwin; Sandy Blair; Robin Dahlberg; David Gartside; Paul Kenny; Frances Outram; Hugh Robertson; Elizabeth Snape; John Spanswick; Richard Taylor
Chief Executive, Geoffrey Podger

HEALTH PROTECTION AGENCY (HPA)
151 Buckingham Palace Road, London SW1W 9SZ
T 020-7811 7000 E hpa.enquiries@hpa.org.uk
W www.hpa.org.uk

The HPA was set up in 2003 and is responsible for providing an integrated approach to protecting public health through the provision of support and advice to the NHS, local authorities, emergency services, other non-departmental public bodies, the Department of Health and the devolved administrations.

The HPA works at local, regional, national and international levels to reduce the impact of infectious diseases and reduce exposure to chemicals, radiation and poisons, as well as ensure a rapid response when hazards occur. The HPA provides services in Northern Ireland and works closely with the devolved administrations, so that there is a coordinated response to incidents, trends and outbreaks on a national level. Research and development projects conducted by HPA scientists are primarily concerned with new methods of treating illness and assessing exposure to chemicals or radiation.

Following the public bodies' reform proposals of October 2010, the HPA will become part of Public Health England in April 2013.

Chair, Dr David Heymann
Board Members, Dr Barbara Bannister, FRCP; Michael Beaumont, CBE; James T. Brown; Michael Carroll; Prof. Charles Easmon, CBE, FMEDSCI (Deputy Chair); Helen Froud; Prof. William Gelletly, OBE; Martin Hindle; Prof. Alan Maryon Davis, FRCP

(adviser); Dr Vanessa Mayatt; Deborah Oakley; Dr Dipti Patel; Prof. Debby Reynolds; John Wyn Owen, CB; Dr Timothy Wyatt
Chief Executive, Justin McCracken

HER MAJESTY'S OFFICERS OF ARMS

COLLEGE OF ARMS (HERALDS' COLLEGE)
Queen Victoria Street, London EC4V 4BT
T 020-7248 2762 E enquiries@college-of-arms.gov.uk
W www.college-of-arms.gov.uk

The Sovereign's Officers of Arms (Kings, Heralds and Pursuivants of Arms) were first incorporated by Richard III in 1484. The powers vested by the crown in the Earl Marshal (the Duke of Norfolk) with regard to state ceremonial are largely exercised through the college. The college is also the official repository of the arms and pedigrees of English, Welsh, Northern Irish and Commonwealth (except Canadian) families and their descendants, and its records include official copies of the records of the Ulster King of Arms, the originals of which remain in Dublin. The 13 officers of the college specialise in genealogical and heraldic work for their respective clients.

Arms have long been, and still are, granted by letters patent from the Kings of Arms. A right to arms can only be established by the registration in the official records of the College of Arms of a pedigree showing direct male line descent from an ancestor already appearing therein as being entitled to arms, or by making application through the College of Arms for a grant of arms. Grants are made to corporations as well as to individuals.

Earl Marshal, Duke of Norfolk

KINGS OF ARMS
Garter, T. Woodcock, LVO, FSA
Clarenceux (and Earl Marshal's Secretary), P. L. Dickinson, LVO
Norroy and Ulster, H. Paston-Bedingfeld

HERALDS
Chester, T. H. S. Duke
Lancaster, R. J. B. Noel
Windsor (and Registrar), W. G. Hunt, TD
Somerset, D. V. White
Richmond, C. E. A. Cheesman
York, vacant

PURSUIVANT
Bluemantle, M. P. D. O'Donoghue

COURT OF THE LORD LYON
HM New Register House, Edinburgh EH1 3YT
T 0131-556 7255
W www.lyon-court.com

Her Majesty's Officers of Arms in Scotland perform ceremonial duties and in addition may be consulted by members of the public on heraldic and genealogical matters in a professional capacity.

KING OF ARMS
Lord Lyon King of Arms, David Sellar, FSA SCOT, FRHISTS

HERALDS
Rothesay, Sir Crispin Agnew of Lochnaw, Bt., QC
Ross, C. J. Burnett, FSA SCOT
Snawdoun, Mrs C. G. W. Roads, MVO, FSA SCOT

PURSUIVANTS
Unicorn, The Hon. Adam Bruce, WS
Ormond, Mark D. Dennis

EXTRAORDINARY OFFICERS
Orkney Herald Extraordinary, Sir Malcolm Innes of
    Edingight, KCVO, WS
Angus Herald Extraordinary, R. O. Blair, CVO, WS
Islay Herald Extraordinary, Alastair Campbell of Airds
Ross Herald Extraordinary, C. J. Burnett, FSA SCOT

HERALD PAINTER
Herald Painter, Mrs Y. Holton

HIGHLANDS AND ISLANDS ENTERPRISE

Cowan House, Inverness Retail and Business Park,
Inverness IV2 7GF
T 01463-234171 E info@hient.co.uk
W www.hie.co.uk

Highlands and Islands Enterprise (HIE) was set up under
the Enterprise and New Towns (Scotland) Act 1991. Its
role is to deliver community and economic development
in line with the Scottish government economic strategy. It
focuses on helping high-growth businesses, improving
regional competitiveness and strengthening communities.
HIE's budget for 2010–11 was £83m.
Chair, William Roe, CBE
Chief Executive, Alex Paterson

HISTORIC ROYAL PALACES

Apartment 39, Hampton Court Palace, Surrey KT8 9AU
T 0844-482 7777 E operators@hrp.org.uk
W www.hrp.org.uk

Historic Royal Palaces was established in 1998 as a royal
charter body with charitable status and is contracted by
the Secretary of State for Culture, Olympics, Media and
Sport to manage the palaces on his behalf. The palaces –
the Tower of London, Hampton Court Palace, the
Banqueting House, Kensington Palace and Kew Palace –
are owned by the Queen on behalf of the nation.
    The organisation is governed by a board comprising a
chair and 11 non-executive trustees. The chief executive is
accountable to the board of trustees and ultimately to
parliament. Historic Royal Palaces receives no funding
from the government or the Crown.

TRUSTEES
Chair, Charles Mackay
Appointed by the Queen, Jonathan Marsden, LVO, FSA;
    Sir Trevor McDonald, OBE; Sir Adrian Montague,
    CBE; Sir Alan Reid, KCVO
Appointed by the Secretary of State, Sophie Andreae;
    Dawn Austwick, OBE; Ian Barlow; Sue Farr; John
    Hamer, OBE; Malcolm Reading
Ex officio, Gen. Lord Dannatt, GCB, CBE, MC *(Constable
    of the Tower of London)*

OFFICERS
Chief Executive, Michael Day

HOMES AND COMMUNITIES AGENCY

Maple House, 149 Tottenham Court Road, London W1T 7BN
T 0300-1234 500 E mail@homesandcommunities.co.uk
W www.homesandcommunities.co.uk

The Homes and Communities Agency (HCA) is the
national housing regeneration agency for England. With a

capital investment budget of nearly £7bn, the HCA
contributes to economic growth by delivering
high-quality affordable housing. The HCA also provides
investment to improve existing social housing as well as
identifying and regenerating surplus public sector land.
Chair, Robert Napier
Chief Executive, Pat Richie

HUMAN FERTILISATION AND EMBRYOLOGY AUTHORITY (HFEA)

Finsbury Tower, 103–105 Bunhill Row, London EC1Y 8HF
T 020-7291 8200 E admin@hfea.gov.uk
W www.hfea.gov.uk

The HFEA was established in 1991 under the Human
Fertilisation and Embryology Act 1990. It is the UK's
independent regulator tasked with overseeing safe and
appropriate practice in fertility treatment and embryo
research, including licensing and monitoring centres
carrying out IVF, artificial insemination and human
embryo research. The HFEA also provides a range of
detailed information for patients, professionals and
government, and maintains a formal register of
information about donors, fertility treatments and
children born as a result of those treatments.
    In July 2010, the government announced proposals to
transfer the functions of the HFEA to the Care Quality
Commission and, by the end of the current parliament,
to abolish the authority.
Chair, Prof. Lisa Jardine, CBE
Chief Executive, Alan Doran, CB

HUMAN GENETICS COMMISSION

Area 605, Wellington House, 133–155 Waterloo Road,
London SE1 8UG
T 020-7972 4351 E hgc@dh.gsi.gov.uk
W www.hgc.gov.uk

The Human Genetics Commission (HGC) was established
in 1999, subsuming three previous advisory committees.
Its remit is to give ministers strategic advice on how
developments in human genetics will impact on people
and healthcare, focusing in particular on the social and
ethical implications.
    Following the government's public bodies reform
proposals of October 2010, the HGC is due to be
abolished by the end of the current parliament, with some
of its functions transferred to other regulators.
Chair, Prof. Jonathan Montgomery
Members, Prof. Tim Aitman; Prof. Thomas Baldwin;
    Prof. Angus Clarke; Prof. Sarah Cunningham-Burley;
    Dr Paul Darragh; Dr Paul Debenham; Nicola Drury;
    Dr Frances Flinter; Ros Gardner; Prof. John Harris;
    Caroline Harrison; Alastair Kent; Dr Anneke Lucassen;
    Dr Duncan McHale; Dr Alice Maynard; Dr Lola Oni;
    Dr Rosalind Skinner; Dr Anita Thomas

HUMAN TISSUE AUTHORITY (HTA)

2nd Floor, 151 Buckingham Palace Road,
London SW1W 9SZ
T 020-7269 1900 E enquiries@hta.gov.uk
W www.hta.gov.uk

The Human Tissue Authority (HTA) was established on
1 April 2005 under the Human Tissue Act 2004, and is
sponsored and part-funded by the Department of Health.
It regulates organisations that remove, store and use
tissue for research, medical treatment, post-mortem
examination, teaching and display in public. The HTA
also gives approval for organ and bone marrow donations

from living people. The HTA is the competent authority for the UK under the EU organ donation directive (ODD).

Chair, Baroness Diana Warwick
Chief Executive, Craig Muir

IMPERIAL WAR MUSEUM

Lambeth Road, London SE1 6HZ
T 020-7416 5000 E mail@iwm.org.uk
W www.iwm.org.uk

The museum, founded in 1917, illustrates and records all aspects of the two world wars and other military operations involving Britain and the Commonwealth since 1914. It was opened in its present home, formerly Bethlem Royal Hospital, in 1936. The museum is a multi-branch organisation that also includes the Churchill War Rooms in Whitehall; HMS *Belfast* in the Pool of London; Imperial War Museum Duxford in Cambridgeshire; and Imperial War Museum North in Trafford, Manchester.

The total grant-in-aid (including grants for special projects) for 2011–12 was £21.7m.

OFFICERS
Chair of Trustees, Air Chief Marshal Sir Peter Squire, GCB, DFC, AFC
Director-General, Diane Lees
Directors, Richard Ashton *(Imperial War Museum Duxford);* Jon Card *(Secretary, Business and Governance);* Sue Coleman *(Marketing and Development);* Jim Forrester *(Imperial War Museum North);* Samantha Heywood *(Learning and Interpretation);* Phil Reed *(Churchill War Rooms and HMS Belfast);* Alan Stoneman *(Corporate Services);* Mark Whitmore *(Collections and Research)*

INDEPENDENT REVIEW SERVICE FOR THE SOCIAL FUND

4th Floor, Centre City Podium, 5 Hill Street, Birmingham B5 4UB
T 0800-096 1926 E sfc@irs-review.org.uk
W www.irs-review.org.uk

The Social Fund Commissioner is appointed by the Secretary of State for Work and Pensions. The commissioner appoints Social Fund Inspectors, who provide an independent review for customers dissatisfied with decisions made in Jobcentre Plus offices throughout England, Scotland and Wales regarding the grants and loans available from the Discretionary Social Fund.
Social Fund Commissioner, Karamjit Singh, CBE

INDEPENDENT SAFEGUARDING AUTHORITY

PO Box 181, Darlington DL1 9FA
T 0300-123 1111 E info@vbs-info.org.uk
W www.isa.homeoffice.gov.uk

The Independent Safeguarding Authority (ISA) is a non-departmental public body sponsored by the Home Office. It was created in 2008 to help prevent unsuitable people working with children and vulnerable adults in England, Wales and Northern Ireland. Its role is to make fair, consistent and thorough barring decisions on people who have caused harm and those who pose a risk of harm. The ISA also manages the vulnerable adults' barred list and the children's barred list. Employers, local authorities, professional regulators and inspection bodies are under a duty to refer to the ISA any information about an employee that they believe has harmed or poses a risk of harm to children or vulnerable adults.

As a result of the government's vetting and barring scheme review in February 2011, the ISA is due to merge with the Criminal Records Bureau, subject to the introduction of legislation.

Chair, Sir Roger Singleton, CBE
Chief Executive, Adrian McAllister

INDUSTRIAL INJURIES ADVISORY COUNCIL

Second Floor, Caxton House, Tothill Street, London SW1H 9NA
T 020-7449 5618 E iiac@dwp.gsi.gov.uk
W www.iiac.independent.gov.uk

The Industrial Injuries Advisory Council was established under the National Insurance (Industrial Injuries) Act 1946, which came into effect on 5 July 1948. Statutory provisions governing its work are set out in section 171–173 of the Social Security Administration Act 1992 and corresponding Northern Ireland legislation. The council usually consists of 16 independent members appointed by the Secretary of State for Work and Pensions, and has three roles: to consider and advise on matters relating to industrial injuries benefit or its administration referred to it by the Secretary of State for Work and Pensions or the Department for Social Development in Northern Ireland; to consider and provide advice on any draft regulations that the secretary of state proposes to make on industrial injuries benefit or its administration; and to advise on any other matter relating to industrial injuries benefit or its administration.

Chair, Prof. Keith Palmer

INFORMATION COMMISSIONER'S OFFICE

Wycliffe House, Water Lane, Wilmslow, Cheshire SK9 5AF
T 0303-123 1113 W www.ico.gov.uk

The Information Commissioner's Office (ICO) is sponsored by the Ministry of Justice and oversees and enforces the Freedom of Information Act 2000 and the Data Protection Act 1998, with the objective of promoting public access to official information and protecting personal information.

The Data Protection Act 1998 sets out rules for the processing of personal information and applies to records held on computers and some paper files. It works in two ways: it dictates that those who record and use personal information (data controllers) must be open about how the information is used and must follow the eight principles of 'good information handling', and it gives individuals certain rights to access their personal information.

The Freedom of Information Act 2000 is designed to help end the culture of unnecessary secrecy and open up the inner workings of the public sector to citizens and businesses. Under the Freedom of Information Act, public authorities must produce a publication scheme that sets out what information the public authority is obliged to publish by law.

The Information Commissioner's Office also enforces and oversees the environmental information regulations, and the privacy and electronic communications regulations.

The Information Commissioner reports annually to parliament on the performance of his functions under the acts and has obligations to assess breaches of the acts.

As of April 2010, the ICO has been able to fine organisations up to £500,000 for serious breaches of the Data Protection Act.

Information Commissioner, Christopher Graham

JOINT NATURE CONSERVATION COMMITTEE

Monkstone House, City Road, Peterborough PE1 1JY
T 01733-562626 E communications@jncc.gov.uk
W www.jncc.defra.gov.uk

The committee was established under the Environmental Protection Act 1990 and was reconstituted by the Natural Environment and Rural Communities Act 2006. It advises the government and devolved administrations on UK and international nature conservation issues. Its work contributes to maintaining and enriching biological diversity, conserving geological features and sustaining natural systems.

Chair, Dr Peter Bridgewater
Deputy Chair, Prof. Lynda Warren

LAW COMMISSION

Steel House, 11 Tothill Street, London SW1H 9LJ
T 020-3334 0200
E chief.executive@lawcommission.gsi.gov.uk
W www.lawcom.gov.uk

The Law Commission was set up under the Law Commissions Act 1965 to make proposals to the government for the examination of the law in England and Wales and for its revision where it is unsuited for modern requirements, obscure or otherwise unsatisfactory. It recommends to the lord chancellor programmes for the examination of different branches of the law and suggests whether the examination should be carried out by the commission itself or by some other body. The commission is also responsible for the preparation of Consolidation and Statute Law (Repeals) Bills.

Chair, Rt. Hon. Lord Justice Munby
Commissioners, E. J. Cooke; David Hertzell; Prof. David Ormerod; Frances Patterson, QC
Chief Executive, Mark Ormerod

LEGAL SERVICES COMMISSION

4 Abbey Orchard Street, London SW1P 2BS
T 020-7783 7000
W www.legalservices.gov.uk

The Legal Services Commission (LSC) was created under the Access to Justice Act 1999 and replaced the Legal Aid Board in April 2000. It is a non-departmental public body which is sponsored by the Ministry of Justice (MoJ).

The commission is responsible for two schemes. The Community Legal Service funds the delivery of civil legal and advice services, identifies priorities and unmet needs, and develops suppliers and services to meet those needs. The Criminal Defence Service provides free legal advice and representation for people involved in criminal investigations or proceedings.

As part of the MoJ legal aid reform programme, the LSC will be replaced by a new executive agency of the MoJ. The government introduced legislation to give effect to this reform in June 2011.

Chief Executive, Carolyn Downs
Chair, Sir Bill Callaghan

MUSEUM OF LONDON

150 London Wall, London EC2Y 5HN
T 020-7001 9844
E info@museumoflondon.org.uk
W www.museumoflondon.org.uk

The Museum of London illustrates the history of London from prehistoric times to the present day. It opened in 1976 and is based on the amalgamation of the former Guildhall Museum and London Museum. The museum is controlled by a board of governors, appointed (ten each) by the prime minister and the City of London. The museum is currently funded by grants from the Greater London Authority and the City of London. The total grant-in-aid for 2010–11 was £17m.

Chair of Board of Governors, Michael Cassidy, CBE
Director, Prof. Jack Lohman

MUSEUMS, LIBRARIES AND ARCHIVES COUNCIL (MLA)

1st Floor, Grosvenor House, 14 Bennetts Hill,
Birmingham B2 5RS
T 0121-345 7300 E info@mla.gov.uk
W www.mla.gov.uk

The MLA was launched in April 2000 and is the lead strategic agency for museums, libraries and archives. It is a non-departmental public body sponsored by the Department for Culture, Media and Sport. The MLA replaced the Museums and Galleries Commission (MGC) and the Library and Information Commission (LIC).

It was announced in July 2010 that the MLA would be abolished; many of the key functions of the MLA are likely to transfer to Arts Council England by the end of Match 2012.

Chair, Sir Andrew Motion
Board Members, Geoffrey Bond, OBE; Patricia Cullen; Angela Dean; Yinnon Ezra, MBE; Helen Forde; Glen Lawes; Munira Mirza; Karen Tyerman; Robert Wand
Chief Executive (acting), Paul Lander

NATIONAL ARMY MUSEUM

Royal Hospital Road, London SW3 4HT
T 020-7730 0717 E info@nam.ac.uk
W www.nam.ac.uk

The National Army Museum was established by royal charter in 1960, and covers the history of five centuries of the British Army from the Middle Ages to the present. It chronicles the campaigns and battles fought over this time as well as the social history and development of the Army, and its impact on Britain, Europe and the world. The museum houses a wide array of artefacts, paintings, photographs, uniforms and equipment.

Chair, General Sir Jack Deverell, KCB, OBE
Council Members, Judith Anthony; Keith Baldwin; Mihir Bose; Patrick Bradley; Lord Freeman, PC, FCA; Richard Nunneley, MBE; Dr William Philpott; Maj.-Gen. C. Vyvyan, CB, CBE; Deborah Younger
Director, Janice Murray, FRSA

NATIONAL ENDOWMENT FOR SCIENCE, TECHNOLOGY AND THE ARTS (NESTA)

1 Plough Place, London EC4A 1DE
T 020-7438 2500 E information@nesta.org.uk
W www.nesta.org.uk

NESTA is an independent body helping to solve major economic and social challenges in the UK. It was established under the National Lottery Act 1998 with a £200m endowment from the proceeds of the National Lottery and operates at no cost to the taxpayer. NESTA carries out its work through experimental programmes, analytical research and investment in early-stage companies.

As part of the public bodies' reform proposals of October 2010, the government announced that, subject to legislation, NESTA will become a charitable company. It will continue to operate, as it has done since its creation, by virtue of its lottery endowment.

Chair, Sir John Chisholm
Chief Executive, Geoff Mulgan

NATIONAL GALLERIES OF SCOTLAND

The Dean Gallery, 73 Belford Road, Edinburgh EH4 3DS
T 0131-624 6200 E enquiries@nationalgalleries.org
W www.nationalgalleries.org

The National Galleries of Scotland comprise the National Gallery of Scotland, the Scottish National Portrait Gallery, the Scottish National Gallery of Modern Art, the Dean Gallery and the Royal Scottish Academy Building. There are also partner galleries at Paxton House, Berwickshire, and Duff House, Banffshire. Total government grant-in-aid for 2011–12 is £12m.

TRUSTEES
Chair, Ben Thomson
Trustees, Ian Barr; Richard Burns; Herbert Coutts, MBE; Prof. Ian Howard; James Knox; Lesley Knox; Ray Macfarlane; Alasdair Morton; Nicky Wilson

OFFICERS
Director-General, John Leighton
Directors, Nicola Caterall *(Chief Operating Officer);* Michael Clarke, CBE *(National Gallery of Scotland);* Dr Simon Groom *(Scottish National Gallery of Modern Art and Dean Gallery);* James Holloway *(Scottish National Portrait Gallery);* Jacqueline Ridge *(Keeper of Conservation);* Catrin Tilley *(Director of Development,Communications and Enterprise)*

NATIONAL GALLERY

Trafalgar Square, London WC2N 5DN
T 020-7747 2885 E information@ng-london.org.uk
W www.nationalgallery.org.uk

The National Gallery, which houses a permanent collection of western European painting from the 13th to the 20th century, was founded in 1824, following a parliamentary grant of £60,000 for the purchase and exhibition of the Angerstein collection of pictures. The present site was first occupied in 1838; an extension to the north of the building with a public entrance in Orange Street was opened in 1975; the Sainsbury Wing was opened in 1991; and the Getty Entrance opened off Trafalgar Square at the east end of the main building in 2004. Total government grant-in-aid for 2011–12 is £26.74m.

BOARD OF TRUSTEES
Chair, M. Getty
Trustees, L. Batchelor; G. Dalal; D. Dalwood; Prof. D. Ekserdjian; Lady Heseltine; M. Hintze; Prof. A. Hurlbert; P. Lankester; J. Nelson; Lady Normanby; H. Rothschild; C. Thomson

OFFICERS
Director, Dr N. Penny
Director of Collections and Deputy Director, Dr S. Foister
Director of Conservation, Larry Keith
Director of Education, Information and Access, Jillian Barker
Director of Operations and Administration, Greg Perry
Director of Public Affairs and Development, S. Ward
Director of Scientific Research, Dr A. Roy
Senior Curator, D. Jaffé

NATIONAL HERITAGE MEMORIAL FUND

7 Holbein Place, London SW1W 8NR
T 020-7591 6000 E enquire@hlf.org.uk
W www.nhmf.org.uk

The National Heritage Memorial Fund was set up under the National Heritage Act 1980 in memory of people who have given their lives for the United Kingdom. The fund provides grants to organisations based in the UK, mainly so that they can buy items of outstanding interest and of importance to the national heritage. These must either be at risk or have a memorial character. The fund is administered by a chair and 14 trustees who are appointed by the prime minister.

The National Heritage Memorial Fund receives an annual grant from the Department for Culture, Media and Sport. Under the National Lottery etc Act 1993, the trustees of the fund became responsible for the distribution of funds for both the National Heritage Memorial Fund and the Heritage Lottery Fund.

Chair, Jenny Abramsky
Chief Executive, Carole Souter

NATIONAL LIBRARY OF SCOTLAND

George IV Bridge, Edinburgh EH1 1EW
T 0131-623 3700 E enquiries@nls.uk
W www.nls.uk

The library, which was founded as the Advocates' Library in 1682, became the National Library of Scotland (NLS) in 1925. It is funded by the Scottish government. It contains about 14 million books and pamphlets, two million maps, 25,000 newspaper and magazine titles and 100,000 manuscripts, including the John Murray Archive. It has an unrivalled Scottish collection as well as online catalogues and digital resources which can be accessed through the NLS website.

Material can be consulted in the reading rooms, which are open to anyone with a valid library card.

Chair of the Trustees, Prof. Michael Anderson, OBE, FBA, FRSE
National Librarian and Chief Executive, Martyn Wade
Directors, Darryl Mead *(Collections and Research);* Duncan Campbell *(Corporate Services);* Alex Miller *(Customer Services)*

NATIONAL LIBRARY OF WALES/LLYFRGELL GENEDLAETHOL CYMRU

Aberystwyth, Ceredigion, Wales SY23 3BU
T 01970-632800
W www.llgc.org.uk

The National Library of Wales was founded by royal charter in 1907, and is funded by the National Assembly for Wales. It contains about five million printed books, 40,000 manuscripts, four million deeds and documents, numerous maps, prints and drawings, and a sound and moving image collection. It specialises in manuscripts and books relating to Wales and the Celtic peoples. It is the repository for pre-1858 Welsh probate records, manorial records and tithe documents, and certain legal records. Admission is by reader's ticket to the reading rooms but entry to the exhibition programme is free.

President, Rt. Hon. Dafydd Wigley

Trustees, David Barker *(Vice President)*; Tricia Carter; Arwel Ellis Owen; Roy Evans; John E. Gittins; Aled Gruffydd Jones; Gareth Haulfryn Williams; Colin John *(Treasurer)*; Elspeth Mitcheson; Enid Morgan; Wyn Penri Jones; Roy Roberts; Huw Williams

Heads of Departments, R. Arwel Jones *(Public Services);* Avril Jones *(Collection Services);* David Michael *(Finance)*

Librarian, A. M. W. Green

NATIONAL LOTTERY COMMISSION

101 Wigmore Street, London W1U 1QU
T 020-7016 3400 E publicaffairs@natlotcomm.gov.uk
W www.natlotcomm.gov.uk

The National Lottery Commission replaced the Office of the National Lottery (OFLOT) in 1999 under the National Lottery Act 1998. The commission is responsible for the granting, varying and enforcing of licences to run the National Lottery. It also runs the competition to award the next licence. Its duties are to ensure that the National Lottery is run with all due propriety, that the interests of players are protected and, subject to these two objectives, that returns to the good causes are maximised. The commission does not have a role in the distribution of funds to good causes: this is undertaken by 16 distributors; visit W www.lottery funding.org.uk for further information.

The Department for Culture, Media and Sport (DCMS) is responsible for gaming and lottery policy and laws. Empowered by the National Lottery Act 1993 (as amended), the DCMS directs the National Lottery Commission, which in turn regulates Camelot, the lottery operator. Camelot, a private company wholly owned by five shareholders, was granted a third licence to run the lottery from 1 February 2009 for ten years.

Following the government's public bodies' reform proposals of October 2010, the National Lottery Commission is due to merge with the Gambling Commission.

Chair, Dr Anne Wright, CBE

Chief Executive, Mark Harris

NATIONAL MARITIME MUSEUM

Romney Road, Greenwich, London SE10 9NF
T 020-8858 4422
W www.nmm.ac.uk

Established in 1934, the National Maritime Museum provides information on the maritime history of Great Britain and is the largest institution of its kind in the world, with over two million items in its collections related to seafaring, navigation and astronomy. The museum is in three groups of buildings in Greenwich Park: the main building, the Queen's House (built by Inigo Jones, 1616–35) and the Royal Observatory, Greenwich (including Christopher Wren's Flamsteed House). In 2007 a £16m project opened a new astronomy centre and planetarium (now the only public planetarium in London) at the Royal Observatory.

Director, Kevin Fewster, FRSA

Chair, Lord Sterling of Plaistow, GCVO, CBE

Trustees, Eleanor Boddington; Lord Boyce, GCB, OBE; Sir Robert Crawford, CBE; Prof. Geoffrey Crossick; Gilly Drummond, OBE; Sir John Guinness, CB; Linda Hutchinson; Jan Kopernicki; Dr Christopher Lintott; Nigel MacDonald; David Moorhouse, CBE; Dr David Quarmby, CBE

NATIONAL MUSEUM OF THE ROYAL NAVY

HM Naval Base (PP66), Portsmouth PO1 3NH
T 023-9272 7562 E info@nmrn.org.uk
W www.royalnavalmuseum.org

The National Museum of the Royal Navy and HMS *Victory* (formerly the Royal Naval Museum) is a subsidiary charity of the newly formed National Museum of the Royal Navy. It is located in Portsmouth Historic Dockyard alongside Nelson's flagship and is housed in three buildings offering exhibitions on the Navy from the 18th century onwards. The museum aims to provide an effective and accessible repository for the heritage of the Navy, and to raise public awareness of, and encourage scholarship and research into, the history and achievements of the Royal Navy.

Chair, Adm. Sir Peter Abbott, GBE, KCB

NATIONAL MUSEUMS AND GALLERIES NORTHERN IRELAND

Cultra, Holywood, Northern Ireland BT18 0EU
T 0845-608 0000 E info@nmni.com
W www.nmni.com

The organisation of National Museums and Galleries of Northern Ireland was established under the Museums and Galleries (Northern Ireland) Order in 1998 and comprises four sites: the Ulster Museum, the Armagh County Museum, the Ulster Folk and Transport Museum, the Ulster American Folk Park and W5 at the Odyssey compex in Belfast (a wholly owned subsidiary).

Legislation requires National Museums and Galleries of Northern Ireland's board of trustees to care for, preserve and add to the collections; ensure that the collections are exhibited to the public; ensure that the significance of the collections is interpreted; and promote the awareness, appreciation and understanding of the public in relation to art, history and science, to the culture and way of life of the people and to the migration and settlement of people.

Chair, Dan Harvey, OBE

Trustees, Linda Beers; Lt.-Col. Harvey Bicker, OBE, TD; Neil Bodger; Pat Carvill, CB; Dame Geraldine Keegan; Joe Kelly; Dr Richard Browne McMinn; David Moore; Wendy Osborne, OBE; Anne Peoples; Dr Brian Scott; Tom Shaw, CBE; Dr Alastair Walker

Chief Executive, Tim Cooke

NATIONAL MUSEUMS LIVERPOOL

127 Dale Street, Liverpool L2 2JH
T 0151-207 0001
W www.liverpoolmuseums.org.uk

The board of trustees of the National Museums Liverpool (formerly National Museums and Galleries on Merseyside) is responsible for World Museum, the Merseyside Maritime Museum (also home to the UK Border Agency National Museum, known as Seized! The Border and Customs Uncovered), the Lady Lever Art Gallery, the Walker Art Gallery, Sudley House, the International Slavery Museum and the Museum of Liverpool. Total government grant-in-aid for 2010–11 was £20.5m.

Chair of the Board of Trustees, Prof. P. Redmond, CBE
Director, Dr D. Fleming
Director of Art Galleries, R. King
Director, World Museum Liverpool, S. Judd
Director, Merseyside Maritime Museum, R. Mulhearn
Director, Museum of Liverpool, J. Dugdale
Director of Collections Management, Midland Railway
    Building, S. A. Yates
Head of International Slavery Museum, Dr R. Benjamin

NATIONAL MUSEUMS SCOTLAND
Chambers Street, Edinburgh EH1 1JF
T 0131-225 7534
E info@nms.ac.uk W www.nms.ac.uk

National Museums Scotland provides advice, expertise and support to the museums community across Scotland, and undertakes fieldwork that often involves collaboration at local, national and international levels. National Museums Scotland comprises the National Museum of Scotland, the National War Museum, the National Museum of Rural Life, the National Museum of Flight, the National Museum of Costume and the National Museums Collection Centre. Its collections represent more than two centuries of collecting and include Scottish and classical archaeology, decorative and applied arts, world cultures and social history and science, technology and the natural world. Total grant-in-aid funding from the Scottish government for 2011–12 was £20.4m.

Up to 15 trustees can be appointed by the Minister for Culture and External Affairs for a term of four years, and may serve a second term.

Chair, Sir Angus Grossart, CBE, LLD, DLITT, FRSE
Trustees, Dr Isabel Bruce, OBE; Dr Anna Gregor, CBE, FRCR, FRCP; Lesley Hart, MBE; Andrew Holmes; Michael Kirwan, FCA; Miller McLean, FCIBS, FIB; Prof. Malcolm McLeod, CBE, FRSE; Bruce Minto; Prof. Stuart Monro, OBE; James Troughton; Sir John Ward, CBE, FRSE, FRSA; Iain Watt, FCIBS
Director, Dr Gordon Rintoul

NATIONAL MUSEUM WALES – AMGUEDDFA CYMRU
Cathays Park, Cardiff CF10 3NP
T 029-2039 7951 E post@museumwales.ac.uk
W www.museumwales.ac.uk

National Museum Wales – Amgueddfa Cymru aims to provide a complete illustration of the geology, mineralogy, zoology, botany, ethnography, archaeology, art, history and special industries of Wales. It comprises the National Museum Cardiff; St Fagans National History Museum; Big Pit – National Coal Museum, Blaenafon; the National Roman Legion Museum, Caerleon; the National Slate Museum, Llanberis; the National Wool Museum, Dre-fach Felindre; the National Waterfront Museum, Swansea; and the National Collections Centre, Nantgarw. Total funding from the Welsh government for 2011–12 is £26.1m.

President, Elisabeth Elias
Director-General, David Anderson
Trustees, Prof. Anthony George Atkins; Carole-Anne Davies; Dr Haydn Edwards; Miriam Hazel Griffiths; Dr Iolo ap Gwynn; Emeritus Prof. Richard G. W. Jones, FLSW; Prof. J. W. Last, CBE; Christina Macaulay; W. Morgan, FCA (Treasurer); Prof. Jonathan Osmond; J. Peter; Victoria Mary Provis; Dr Keshav Singhal; David Beresford Vokes; Gareth Williams

NATIONAL PORTRAIT GALLERY
St Martin's Place, London WC2H 0HE
T 020-7306 0055
W www.npg.org.uk

The National Portrait Gallery was formed after a grant was made in 1856 to form a gallery of the portraits of the most eminent persons in British history. The present building was opened in 1896 and the Ondaatje Wing (including a new Balcony Gallery, Tudor Gallery, IT Gallery, lecture theatre and roof-top restaurant) opened in May 2000. There are three regional partnerships displaying portraits at Montacute House, Beningbrough Hall and Bodelwyddan Castle. Total government grant-in-aid for 2011–12 is £7.4m.

BOARD OF TRUSTEES
Chair, Prof. David Cannadine, FBA, FRSL
Trustees, Zeinab Badawi; Prof. Dame Carol Black, DBE; Sir Nicholas Blake, QC; Dr Rosalind P. Blakesley; Dr Augustus Casely-Hayford; Marchioness of Douro, OBE; Rt. Hon. Nick Clegg, MP; Amelia Fawcett, DBE; Sir Nicholas Grimshaw, CBE, PRA; Rt. Hon. Lord Janvrin, GCB, GCVO, QSO; Mary McCartney; Sir William Proby Bt., CBE; David Ross; Marina Warner, CBE, FBA
Director, Sandy Nairne

NATURAL ENGLAND
1 East Parade, Sheffield S1 2ET
T 0845-600 3078 E enquiries@naturalengland.org.uk
W www.naturalengland.org.uk

Natural England was established on 1 October 2006 after the Natural Environment and Rural Communities Act received royal assent in March 2006. It is the government's advisor on the natural environment, providing practical advice, grounded in science, on how best to safeguard England's natural wealth. The organisation's remit is to ensure sustainable stewardship of the land and sea and to ensure that England's environment can adapt and survive for future generations. Natural England works with farmers and land managers; business and industry; planners and developers; national, regional and local government; interest groups and local communities to help them improve their local environment.
Chief Executive, Dr Helen Phillips

NATURAL HISTORY MUSEUM
Cromwell Road, London SW7 5BD
T 020-7942 5000 W www.nhm.ac.uk

The Natural History Museum originates from the natural history departments of the British Museum, which grew extensively during the 19th century; in 1860 it was agreed that the natural history collections should be separated from the British Museum's collections of books, manuscripts and antiquities. Part of the site of the 1862 International Exhibition in South Kensington was acquired for the new museum, and the museum opened to the public in 1881. In 1963 the Natural History Museum became completely independent with its own board of trustees. The Natural History Museum at Tring, bequeathed by the second Lord Rothschild, has formed part of the museum since 1937. The Geological Museum merged with the Natural History Museum in 1985. In September 2009 the Natural History Museum opened the Darwin Centre, which contains public galleries, a high-tech audio-visual area known as the Attenborough

Studio, scientific research areas and space for 22 million zoological specimens, 17 million insect specimens and three million botanical specimens. Total government grant-in-aid for 2011–12 is £46.48m.

BOARD OF TRUSTEES
Chair, Oliver Stocken
Trustees, Daniel Alexander, QC; Prof. Sir Roy Anderson, FRS, FMEDSCI; Louise Charlton; Prof. David Drewry; Prof. Christopher Gilligan; Prof. Alex Halliday, FRS; Ian J. Henderson, CBE, FRICS; Dr Derek Langslow, CBE; Prof. Georgina Mace, CBE, FRS; Sir David Omand, GCB

SENIOR STAFF
Director, Dr Michael Dixon
Director of Estates and Services, David Sanders
Director of Finance and Administration, Neil Greenwood
Director of Human Resources, Paul Brereton
Director, Policy and Planning and Director of the Natural History Museum at Tring, Teresa Wild
Director of Public Engagement, Sharon Ament
Director of Science, Prof. Ian Owens
Head of Risk and Assurance, David Thorpe
Head of Library and Information Services, Graham Higley
Keeper of Botany, Dr Johannes Vogel
Interim Keeper of Entomology, Dr Andrew Polaszek
Keeper of Mineralogy, Dr Andy Fleet
Keeper of Palaeontology, Prof. Norman MacLeod
Keeper of Zoology, Prof. Phil Rainbow
Museum Manager, Ian Jenkinson

NHS PAY REVIEW BODY
6th Floor, Victoria House, Southampton Row, London WC1B 4AD
T 020-7271 0490 W www.ome.uk.com

The NHS Pay Review Body (NHSPRB) makes recommendations to the prime minister, Secretary of State for Health and ministers in Scotland, Wales and Northern Ireland on the remuneration of all paid staff under agenda for change and employed in the NHS. The review body was established in 1983 for nurses and allied health professionals. Its remit has since expanded to cover over 1.8 million staff; ie almost all staff in the NHS, with the exception of dentists, doctors and very senior managers.
Chair, Jerry Cope
Members, Philip Ashmore; Prof. David Blackaby; Dame Denise Holt; Graham Jagger; Ian McKay; Maureen Scott; Prof. Anna Vignoles

NORTHERN IRELAND HUMAN RIGHTS COMMISSION
Temple Court, 39 North Street, Belfast BT1 1NA
T 028-9024 3987 **Textphone** 028-9024 9066
E information@nihrc.org W www.nihrc.org

The Northern Ireland Human Rights Commission is a non-departmental public body, established by the Northern Ireland Act 1998 and set up in March 1999. Its purpose is to protect and promote human rights in Northern Ireland. Its main functions include reviewing the law and practice relating to human rights in Northern Ireland, advising government and the Northern Ireland Assembly, and promoting an awareness of human rights in Northern Ireland. It can also investigate human rights violations and take cases to court. The members of the commission are appointed by the Secretary of State for Northern Ireland.

Chief Commissioner, Michael O'Flaherty
Commissioners, Christine Collins; John Corey; Milton Kerr; Grainia Long; Alan McBride; Marion Reynolds; Paul Yam
Director, Virginia McVea

NORTHERN LIGHTHOUSE BOARD
84 George Street, Edinburgh EH2 3DA
T 0131-473 3100 E enquiries@nlb.org.uk
W www.nlb.org.uk

The Northern Lighthouse Board is the general lighthouse authority for Scotland and the Isle of Man and owes its origin to an act of parliament passed in 1786. At present there are 19 commissioners who operate under the Merchant Shipping Act 1995.

The commissioners control 208 lighthouses, many lighted and unlighted buoys, a DGPS (differential global positioning system) station and an ELORAN (long-range navigation) system. *See also* Transport.
Chair, Sheriff Principal Alistair Dunlop, QC
Commissioners, Lord Advocate; Solicitor-General for Scotland; Lord Provosts of Edinburgh, Glasgow and Aberdeen; Convener of Highland Council; Convener of Argyll and Bute Council; Sheriffs-Principal of North Strathclyde, Tayside, Central and Fife, Grampian, Highlands and Islands, South Strathclyde, Dumfries and Galloway, Lothians and Borders and Glasgow and Strathkelvin; Capt. Mike Close; Alistair MacKenzie; Robert Quayle; John Ross, CBE; Alistair Whyte
Chief Executive, Roger Lockwood, CB

NUCLEAR DECOMMISSIONING AUTHORITY
Herdus House, Westlakes Science and Technology Park, Moor Row, Cumbria CA24 3HU
T 01925-802001 E enquiries@nda.gov.uk
W www.nda.gov.uk

The Nuclear Decommissioning Authority (NDA) was created under the Energy Act 2004. It is a strategic authority that owns 19 sites and associated civil nuclear liabilities and assets of the public sector, previously under the control of the UK Energy Authority and British Nuclear Fuels. The NDA decommissions and cleans up civil nuclear facilities; ensures the safe management of waste products, both radioactive and non-radioactive; implements government policy on the long-term management of nuclear waste; develops UK-wide nuclear low-level waste strategy and plans; and scrutinises the decommissioning plans of British Energy.

Total planned expenditure for 2011–12 is £2.9bn, with total grant-in-aid standing at £2bn. The remaining £0.9bn will come from commercial operations.
Chair, Stephen Henwood
Chief Executive, Tony Fountain

OFFICE FOR BUDGET RESPONSIBILITY
20 Victoria Street, London SW1H 0NF
T 020-7271 2442 E obrenquiries@obr.gsi.gov.uk
W http://budgetresponsibility.independent.gov.uk

The Office for Budget Responsibility (OBR) was created in 2010 to provide independent and authoritative analysis of the UK's public finances. It has four main roles: producing forecasts for the economy and public finances; judging progress towards the government's fiscal targets; assessing the long-term sustainability of the public finances; and scrutinising HM Treasury's costing of Budget measures.

In support of these activities, the OBR undertakes a variety of research projects through the year. It also answers parliamentary questions on its forecasts and gives evidence to parliamentary committees.

Chair, Robert Chote
Committee Members, Steve Nickell, CBE; Graham Parker, CBE

OFFICE OF COMMUNICATIONS (OFCOM)

Riverside House, 2A Southwark Bridge Road, London SE1 9HA
T 0300-123 3000
W www.ofcom.org.uk

OFCOM was established in 2003 under the Office of Communications Act 2002 as the independent regulator and competition authority for the UK communications industries with responsibility for television, radio, telecommunications and wireless communications services.

Following the passing of the Post Services Act 2011, OFCOM has assumed regulatory responsibility for postal services from Postcomm, the Postal Services Commission.

Chief Executive, Ed Richards
Chair, Colette Bowe
Deputy Chair, Philip Graf, CBE
Board Members, Norman Blackwell; Tim Gardam; Stuart McIntosh; Mike McTighe; Peter Phillips; Jill Ainscough

OFFICE OF MANPOWER ECONOMICS (OME)

6th Floor, Victoria House, Southampton Row, London WC1B 4AD
T 020-7271 0497 **W** www.ome.uk.com

The Office of Manpower Economics (OME) was established in 1971. It is an independent non-statutory organisation which is responsible for servicing independent review bodies that advise on the pay of various public sector groups, the Police Negotiating Board and the Police Advisory Board for England and Wales. The OME is also responsible for servicing *ad hoc* bodies of inquiry and for undertaking research into pay and associated matters as requested by the government.

The OME has been allocated a total of £2.58m by the Department for Business, Innovation and Skills for 2011–12.

OME Director, Geoff Dart
Director, Doctors' and Dentists' and NHS Pay Review Body Secretariats, Research and Analysis Group and OME Deputy Director, Margaret McEvoy
Director, Armed Forces' and School Teachers' Secretariats, Jenny Eastabrook
Director, Senior Salaries', Prison Service and Police Board Secretariats, Keith Masson

OFFICE OF TAX SIMPLIFICATION

HM Treasury, 1 Horse Guards Road, London SW1A 2HQ
T 020-7270 4558 **E** ots@ots.gsi.gov.uk
W www.hm-treasury.gov.uk/ots.htm

The chancellor and exchequer secretary to HM Treasury launched the Office of Tax Simplification (OTS) on 20 July 2010 to provide the government with independent advice on simplifying the UK tax system. The chancellor has asked the OTS to carry out two initial reviews: a review of all tax reliefs, and a review of small business taxation.

The Office has been established as an independent office of HM Treasury for the life of the current parliament and draws together expertise from across the tax and legal professions, the business community and other interested parties.

Chair, Rt. Hon. Michael Jack
Tax Director, John Whiting

PARADES COMMISSION

Windsor House, 9–15 Bedford Street, Belfast BT2 7EL
T 028-9089 5900 **E** info@paradescommission.org
W www.paradescommission.org

The Parades Commission was set up under the Public Processions (Northern Ireland) Act 1998. Its function is to encourage and facilitate local accommodation of contentious parades; where this is not possible, the commission is empowered to make legal determinations about such parades, which may include imposing conditions on aspects of the notified parade (such as restrictions on routes/areas and exclusion of certain groups with a record of bad behaviour).

The chair and members are appointed by the Secretary of State for Northern Ireland; the membership must, as far as is practicable, be representative of the community in Northern Ireland.

Chair, Peter Osborne
Members, Douglas Bain; Delia Close; Revd Brian Kennaway; Dr Catriona King; Frances Nolan; Robin Percival

PAROLE BOARD FOR ENGLAND AND WALES

Grenadier House, 99–105 Horseferry Road, London SW1P 2DX
T 0845-251 2220 **E** info@paroleboard.gov.uk
W www.paroleboard.gov.uk

The Parole Board was established under the Criminal Justice Act 1967 and became an independent executive non-departmental public body under the Criminal Justice and Public Order Act 1994. It is the body that protects the public by making risk assessments about prisoners to decide who may safely be released into the community and who must remain in, or be returned to, custody. Board decisions are taken at two main types of panels of up to three members: 'paper panels' for the majority of cases, or oral hearings for decisions concerning prisoners serving life or indeterminate sentences for public protection.

Chair, Rt. Hon. Sir David Latham
Chief Executive, Linda Lennon, CBE

PAROLE BOARD FOR SCOTLAND

Saughton House, Broomhouse Drive, Edinburgh EH11 3XD
T 0131-244 8373
E paroleboardforscotlandexecutive@scotland.gsi.gov.uk
W www.scottishparoleboard.gov.uk

The board directs and advises the Scottish ministers on the release of prisoners on licence, and related matters.

Chair, Prof. A. Cameron
Vice-Chair, Ms H. Baillie

PENSION PROTECTION FUND (PPF)

Knollys House, 17 Addiscombe Road, Croydon CR0 6SR
T 0845-600 2541 **E** information@ppf.gsi.gov.uk
W www.pensionprotectionfund.org.uk

The PPF became operational in 2005. It was established to pay compensation to members of eligible defined-benefit

pension schemes where a qualifying insolvency event in relation to the employer occurs and where there is a lack of sufficient assets in the pension scheme. The PPF also administers the Financial Assistance Scheme, which helps members whose schemes wound-up before 2005. It is also responsible for the Fraud Compensation Fund (which provides compensation to occupational pension schemes that suffer a loss that can be attributed to dishonesty). The chair and board of the PPF are appointed by, and accountable to, the Secretary of State for Work and Pensions, and are responsible for paying compensation, calculating annual levies (which help fund the PPF), and setting and overseeing investment strategy.
Chair, Lady Barbara Judge
Chief Executive, Alan Rubenstein

PENSIONS REGULATOR

Napier House, Trafalgar Place, Brighton BN1 4DW
T 0870-606 3636
E customersupport@thepensionsregulator.gov.uk
W www.thepensionsregulator.gov.uk

The Pensions Regulator was established in 2005 as the regulator of work-based pension schemes in the UK, replacing the Occupational Pensions Regulatory Authority (OPRA). It aims to protect the benefits of occupational and personal pension scheme members by working with trustees, employers, pension providers and advisors. The regulator's work focuses on encouraging better management and administration of schemes, ensuring that final salary schemes have a sensible funding plan, and encouraging money purchase schemes to provide members with the information that they need to make informed choices about their pension fund. The pensions Acts of 2004 and 2008 gave the regulator a range of powers which can be used to protect scheme members, but a strong emphasis is placed on educating and enabling those responsible for managing pension schemes, and powers are used as a last resort. The regulator offers three free online resources to help trustees, employers, professionals and advisors understand their role, duties and obligations.
Chair, Michael O'Higgins
Chief Executive, Bill Galvin

POLICE ADVISORY BOARD FOR ENGLAND AND WALES

6th Floor, Victoria House, Southampton Row,
London WC1B 4AD
T 020-7271 0472 W www.ome.uk.com

The Police Advisory Board for England and Wales was established in 1965 and provides advice to the home secretary on general questions affecting the police in England and Wales. It also considers draft regulations which the secretary of state proposes to make with respect to matters other than hours of duty, leave, pay and allowances or the issue, use and return of police clothing, personal equipment and other effects.
Independent Chair, John Randall
Independent Deputy Chair, Prof. Gillian Morris

POLICE NEGOTIATING BOARD (PNB)

6th Floor, Victoria House, Southampton Row,
London WC1B 4AD
T 020-7271 0472 W www.ome.uk.com

The PNB was established in 1980 to negotiate pay; allowances; hours of duty; the issue, use and return of police clothing, personal equipment and accoutrements; leave; and pensions of UK police officers, and to make recommendations on these matters to the home secretary, Northern Ireland secretary and Scottish ministers.
Independent Chair, John Randall
Independent Deputy Chair, Prof. Gillian Morris

PRISON SERVICE PAY REVIEW BODY

6th Floor, Victoria House, Southampton Row,
London WC1B 4AD
T 020-7215 8369 W www.ome.uk.com

The Prison Service Pay Review Body was set up in 2001. It makes independent recommendations on the pay of prison governors, operational managers, prison officers and related grades for the Prison Service in England and Wales and for the Northern Ireland Prison Service.
Chair, Dr Peter Knight, CBE
Members, Prof. John Beath; Richard J. N. Childs, QPM; Bronwen Mary Curtis, CBE; John Davies, OBE; Joseph Magee; Vilma Patterson; Trevor Spires

REGIONAL DEVELOPMENT AGENCIES

5th Floor, Oceanic House, 1A Cockspur Street,
London SW1Y 5BG
T 020-7968 0600 W www.englandsrdas.com

Regional Development Agencies (RDAs) were established to help the English regions improve their relative economic performance and reduce social and economic disparities within and between regions. Their five statutory objectives are to further economic development and regeneration; to promote business efficiency and competitiveness; to promote employment; to enhance the development and application of skills relevant to employment; and to contribute to sustainable development. There are nine RDAs in England, and they are financed through a single fund provided by contributing government departments (BIS, DCLG, DECC, DEFRA and DCMS). The RDA's budget for 2011–12 is £711m.

The government has announced that the RDAs will close at the end of March 2012. Some of the RDAs current functions will be taken over by newly created local enterprise partnerships, while other functions are likely to be carried out at national, rather than local, level.

RDA REGIONS
NORTH WEST: Renaissance House, Centre Park, Warrington WA1 1QN T 01925-400100 *Chair,* Robert Hough
YORKSHIRE: Victoria House, Victoria Place, Leeds LS11 5AE T 0113-394 9600 *Chair,* Julie Kenny
NORTH EAST: Stella House, Goldcrest Way, Newburn Riverside, Newcastle upon Tyne NE15 8NY T 0191-229 6200 *Chair,* Paul Callaghan
WEST MIDLANDS: 3 Priestley Wharf, Holt Street, Aston Science Park, Birmingham B7 4BN T 0121-380 3500 *Chair,* Sir Roy McNulty
EAST MIDLANDS: Apex Court, City Link, Nottingham NG2 4LA T 0115-988 8300 *Chair,* Dr Bryan Jackson, OBE
EAST OF ENGLAND: Victory House, Vision Park, Chivers Way, Histon, Cambridgeshire CB24 9ZR T 01223-713900 *Chair,* Will Pope
SOUTH WEST: Sterling House, Dix's Field, Exeter EX1 1QA T 01392-214747 *Chair,* Sir Harry Studholme
LONDON: Palestra, 197 Blackfriars Road, London SE1 8AA T 020-7593 8000 *Chair,* Harvey McGrath
SOUTH EAST: Cross Lanes, Guildford GU1 1YA T 01483-484200 *Chair,* Robert Douglas, CBE

REGISTRAR OF PUBLIC LENDING RIGHT

Richard House, Sorbonne Close, Stockton on Tees TS17 6DA
T 01642-604699 E authorservices@plr.uk.com
W www.plr.uk.com

Under the Public Lending Right (PLR) system, in operation since 1983, payment is made from public funds to authors whose books are lent out from public libraries. Payment is made once a year and the amount that each author receives is proportionate to the number of times (established from a sample) that each registered book has been lent out during the previous year. The registrar of PLR, who is appointed by the Secretary of State for Culture, Olympics, Media and Sport, compiles the register of authors and books. Authors resident in all European Economic Area countries are eligible to apply. (The term 'author' covers writers, illustrators, translators and some editors/compilers.)

A payment of 6.25 pence was made in 2010–11 for each estimated loan of a registered book, up to a top limit of £6,600 for the books of any one registered author; the money for loans above this level is used to augment the remaining PLR payments. In 2010–11 the sum of £6.7m was paid out to 23,366 registered authors and assignees as the annual payment of PLR.

In October 2010, the government announced that the PLR would be abolished, subject to legislation, and that responsibility for the PLR scheme would transfer to another public body.
Registrar, Dr J. G. Parker

REVIEW BODY ON DOCTORS' AND DENTISTS' REMUNERATION

6th Floor, Victoria House, Southampton Row, London
WC1B 4AD
T 020-7271 0486 W www.ome.uk.com

The Review Body on Doctors' and Dentists' Remuneration was set up in 1971. It advises the prime minister, first ministers in Scotland, Wales and Northern Ireland, and the ministers for Health, in England, Scotland, Wales and Northern Ireland on the remuneration of doctors and dentists taking any part in the National Health Service.
Chair, Ron Amy, OBE
Members, Lucinda Bolton; Katrina Easterling; John Glennie; David Grafton; Sally Smedley; Prof. Steve Thompson; Prof. Ian Walker; David Williamson

ROYAL AIR FORCE MUSEUM

Grahame Park Way, London NW9 5LL
T 020-8205 2266 E london@rafmuseum.org
W www.rafmuseum.org.uk

The museum has two sites, one at the former airfield at Hendon and the second at Cosford, in the West Midlands, both of which illustrate the development of aviation from before the Wright brothers to the present-day RAF. The museum's collection across both sites consists of over 170 aircraft, as well as artefacts, aviation memorabilia, fine art and photographs. Total government grant-in-aid for 2011–12, provided by the Ministry of Defence, is £7.7m.
Director-General, Air Vice-Marshal Peter Dye, OBE

ROYAL BOTANIC GARDEN EDINBURGH

20A Inverleith Row, Edinburgh EH3 5LR
T 0131-552 7171 W www.rbge.org.uk

The Royal Botanic Garden Edinburgh (RBGE) originated as the Physic Garden, established in 1670 beside the Palace of Holyroodhouse. The garden moved to its present 28-hectare site at Inverleith, Edinburgh, in 1821. There are also three regional gardens: Benmore Botanic Garden, near Dunoon, Argyll; Logan Botanic Garden, near Stranraer, Wigtownshire; and Dawyck Botanic Garden, near Stobo, Peeblesshire. Since 1986 RBGE has been administered by a board of trustees established under the National Heritage (Scotland) Act 1985. It receives an annual grant from the Scottish government's Rural and Environmental Research and Analysis Directorate.

The RBGE is an international centre for scientific research on plant diversity and for horticulture education and conservation. It has an extensive library, a herbarium with almost three million preserved plant specimens, and over 15,000 species in the living collections.
Chair of the Board of Trustees, Sir George Mathewson, CBE, LLD, FRSE
Regius Keeper, Prof. Stephen Blackmore, FRSE

ROYAL BOTANIC GARDENS, KEW

Richmond, Surrey TW9 3AB
T 020-8332 5000
Wakehurst Place, Ardingly, W. Sussex RH17 6TN
T 01444-89000
E info@kew.org W www.kew.org

The Royal Botanic Gardens, Kew (RBG, Kew) were originally laid out as a private garden for the now demolished White House for George III's mother, Princess Augusta, in 1759. The gardens were much enlarged in the 19th century, notably by the inclusion of the grounds of the former Richmond Lodge. In 1965 Kew acquired the gardens at Wakehurst Place on a long lease from the National Trust. Under the National Heritage Act 1983 a board of trustees was set up to administer the gardens, which in 1984 became an independent body supported by grant-in-aid from the Department for Environment, Food and Rural Affairs.

The functions of RBG, Kew are to carry out research into plant sciences, to disseminate knowledge about plants and to provide the public with the opportunity to gain knowledge and enjoyment from the gardens' collections. There are extensive national reference collections of living and preserved plants and a comprehensive library and archive. The main emphasis is on plant conservation and biodiversity; Wakehurst Place houses the Millennium Seed Bank Partnership, which is the largest *ex situ* conservation project in the world – its aim is to save seed from 25 per cent of the earth's wild plant species by 2020.

BOARD OF TRUSTEES
Chair, Marcus Agius
Members, Prof. Michael Crawley; Prof. Jonathan Drori, CBE; Tessa Green; Dr Geoffrey Hawtin; Timothy Hornsby; Sir Henry Keswick; Mr George Loudon; Prof. Nicola Spence; Sir William Stewart, FRS; Ms Jennifer Ullman; Sir Ferrers Vyvyan
Director, Prof. Stephen D. Hopper

ROYAL COMMISSION ON THE ANCIENT AND HISTORICAL MONUMENTS OF SCOTLAND

John Sinclair House, 16 Bernard Terrace, Edinburgh EH8 9NX
T 0131-662 1456 E info@rcahms.gov.uk
W www.rcahms.gov.uk

The Royal Commission on the Ancient and Historical Monuments of Scotland (RCAHMS) was established by a royal warrant in 1908, which was revised in 1992, and is appointed to provide for the collecting, recording and interpretation of information on the architectural, industrial, archaeological and maritime heritage of Scotland, to give a picture of the human influence on Scotland's places from the earliest times to the present day. It is funded by the Scottish government. More than 15 million items, including photographs, maps, drawings and documents, are available through the search room, and online databases provide access to over 150,000 images and information on 300,000 buildings and sites. RCAHMS also holds Scotland's national collection of historical aerial photography as well as The Aerial Reconnaissance Archives (TARA) of international wartime photography.

Chair, Prof. John Hume, OBE, FSA SCOT

Commissioners, Kate Byrne, FRSA; Tom Dawson, FSA SCOT; Mark Hopton, FSA SCOT; Dr Jeremy Huggett, FSA, FSA SCOT; Prof. John Hunter, OBE, FSA, FSA SCOT; Paul Jardine; Dr Gordon Masterton, OBE; Jude Quartson-Mochrie; Elspeth Reid

Chief Executive, Diana Murray, FSA, FSA SCOT

ROYAL COMMISSION ON THE ANCIENT AND HISTORICAL MONUMENTS OF WALES

Crown Building, Plas Crug, Aberystwyth SY23 1NJ
T 01970-621200 E nmr.wales@rcahmw.gov.uk
W www.rcahmw.gov.uk

The Royal Commission on the Ancient and Historical Monuments of Wales, established in 1908, is responsible for developing and promoting understanding of the archaeological, built and maritime heritage of Wales. The Royal Commission holds a unique collection of photographs, maps, publications and reports within its archive, the National Monuments Record of Wales, which can be consulted via an online database or through the public enquiry service. The commission is funded by the National Assembly for Wales.

Chair, Dr Eurwyn William, FSA

Vice-Chair, Neil Harries, FCMI

Commissioners, Prof. Antony D. Carr, FRHISTS, FSA; Mrs Anne S. Eastham, FSA; Ms Catherine S. Hardman; Jonathan Hudson; John W. Lloyd, CB; Thomas O. S. Lloyd, OBE, FSA; John Newman, FSA; Henry Owen-John; Mark Redknap, FSA; Prof. C. M. Williams, FRHISTS

ROYAL MAIL GROUP

100 Victoria Embankment, London EC4Y 0HQ
T 020-7250 2888 W www.royalmailgroup.com

Crown services for the carriage of government dispatches were set up in about 1516. The conveyance of public correspondence began in 1635 and the mail service was made a parliamentary responsibility with the setting up of a Post Office in 1657. In 1840, Royal Mail launched the Penny Black, the world's first postage stamp. Telegraphs came under Post Office control in 1870 and the Post Office Telephone Service began in 1880. The National Girobank service of the Post Office began in 1968. The Post Office ceased to be a government department in 1969 when responsibility for the running of the postal, telecommunications, giro and remittance services was transferred to a public authority of the same name.

The British Telecommunications Act 1981 separated the functions of the Post Office, making it solely responsible for postal services and Girobank. Girobank was privatised in 1990. The Postal Services Act 2000 turned the Post Office into a wholly owned public limited company establishing a regulatory regime under the Postal Service Commission. The Post Office Group changed its name to Consignia plc in March 2001 when its new corporate structure took effect; in November 2002 the name was changed to Royal Mail Group plc. As of 1 January 2006 the UK postal service market was fully liberalised, and any licensed operator is now able to deliver mail to businesses and residential customers. Following the passing of the Postal Services Act 2011 on 13 June 2011, Royal Mail is now open to private ownership. A buyer will be able to own up to 90 per cent of the shares in the company, with Royal Mail staff offered the remaining 10 per cent.

Royal Mail processes and delivers around 62 million letters, packets and parcels to 28.8 million addresses every day; around 20 million customers are served in the 11,820 Post Office branches each week. The Royal Mail Group directly employs around 163,000 people in the UK.

The chair, chief executive and members of the board are appointed by the Secretary of State for Business, Innovation and Skills but responsibility for the running of Royal Mail Group as a whole rests with the board in its corporate capacity.

BOARD

Chair, Donald Brydon, CBE

Chief Executive, Moya Greene

Executive Directors, Mark Higson, Matthew Lester, David Smith, Paula Vannells

Non-Executive Directors, Lord Currie; Nick Horler; Cath Keers; Paul Murray; Orna Ni-Chionna; Les Owen

Company Secretary, Jon Millidge

SCHOOL TEACHERS' REVIEW BODY

6th Floor, Victoria House, Southampton Row,
London WC1B 4AD
T 020-7271 0474 W www.ome.uk.com

The School Teachers' Review Body was set up under the School Teachers' Pay and Conditions Act 1991. It is required to examine and report on such matters relating to the statutory conditions of employment of school teachers in England and Wales as may be referred to it by the education secretary.

Chair, vacant

Members, Dewi Jones; Elizabeth Kidd; Esmond Lindop; Stella Pantelides; Jill Pullen; Dr Patricia Rice; Anne Watts, CBE

SCIENCE MUSEUM

Exhibition Road, London SW7 2DD
T 0870-870 4868 E sciencem@sciencemuseum.org.uk
W www.sciencemuseum.org.uk

The Science Museum, part of the National Museum of Science & Industry (NMSI), houses the national collections of science, technology, industry and medicine. The museum began as the science collection of the South Kensington Museum and first opened in 1857. In 1883 it acquired the collections of the Patent Museum and in 1909 the science collections were transferred to the new Science Museum, leaving the art collections with the Victoria and Albert Museum. The Wellcome Wing was opened in July 2000.

The NMSI also incorporates the National Railway Museum, York; the National Media Museum, Bradford; and Locomotion: the National Railway Museum at Shildon.

Total government grant-in-aid for 2010–11 was £40m.

Chair, Dr Douglas Gurr
Trustees, Lady Chisholm; Howard Covington; Lord Faulkner of Worcester; Simon Linnett; Prof. Averil Macdonald; Sir Howard Newby, CBE; Dr Gill Samuels, CBE; Dr Maggie Semple, OBE; James Smith; Janet Street-Porter; Christopher Swinson, OBE; Michael G. Wilson, OBE
Director of NMSI, Ian Blatchford
Director of Science Museum, Ian Blatchford
Director of National Media Museum, Colin Philpott
Director of National Railway Museum, Steve Davies, MBE

SCOTTISH CRIMINAL CASES REVIEW COMMISSION

5th Floor, Portland House, 17 Renfield Street, Glasgow G2 5AH
T 0141-270 7030 E info@sccrc.org.uk
W www.sccrc.org.uk

The commission is a non-departmental public body, funded by the Scottish Government Criminal Justice Directorate, and established in April 1999. It assumed the role previously performed by the Secretary of State for Scotland to consider alleged miscarriages of justice in Scotland and refer cases meeting the relevant criteria to the high court for determination. Members are appointed by the Queen on the recommendation of the First Minister; senior executive staff are appointed by the commission.

Chair, Jean Couper, CBE
Members, Gerrard Bann; Graham Bell, QC; Prof. Brian Caddy; Stewart Campbell; Prof. George Irving, CBE; Gerard McClay; Francis McMenamin; Mhairi Richards, QC
Chief Executive, Gerard Sinclair

SCOTTISH ENTERPRISE

Atrium Court, 50 Waterloo Street, Glasgow G2 6HQ
T 0845-607 8787 E enquiries@scotent.co.uk
W www.scottish-enterprise.com

Scottish Enterprise was established in 1991 and its purpose is to stimulate the sustainable growth of Scotland's economy. It is mainly funded by the Scottish government and is responsible to the Scottish ministers. Working in partnership with the private and public sectors, Scottish Enterprise will invest £332m in 2011–12 to further the development of Scotland's economy by helping ambitious and innovative businesses grow and become more successful. Scottish Enterprise is particularly interested in supporting companies that provide renewable energy, encourage trade overseas, increase innovation, and those that will help Scotland become a low-carbon economy.

Chair, Crawford Gillies
Chief Executive, Lena C. Wilson

SCOTTISH ENVIRONMENT PROTECTION AGENCY (SEPA)

Erskine Court, Castle Business Park, Stirling FK9 4TR
T 01786-457700 **Hotline** 0800-807060
E info@sepa.org.uk W www.sepa.org.uk

SEPA was established in 1996 and is the public body responsible for environmental protection in Scotland. It regulates potential pollution to land, air and water; the storage, transport and disposal of controlled waste; and the safekeeping and disposal of radioactive materials. It does this within a complex legislative framework of acts of parliament, EU directives and regulations, granting licences to operations of industrial processes and waste disposal. SEPA also operates Floodline (T 0845-988 1188), a public service providing information on the possible risk of flooding 24 hours a day, 365 days a year.

Chair, David Sigsworth
Chief Executive, Campbell Gemmell
Directors, John Ford *(Finance and Corporate Services);* Calum MacDonald *(Operations);* James Curran *(Science and Strategy)*

SCOTTISH LAW COMMISSION

140 Causewayside, Edinburgh EH9 1PR
T 0131-668 2131 E info@scotlawcom.gsi.gov.uk
W www.scotlawcom.gov.uk

The Scottish Law Commission, established in 1965, keeps the law in Scotland under review and makes proposals for its development and reform. It is responsible to the Scottish ministers through the Scottish government law and courts directorate.

Chair (part-time), Hon. Lord Drummond Young
Chief Executive, M. McMillan
Commissioners, Ms L. Dunlop, QC; P. Layden, QC, TD; Prof. H. MacQueen

SCOTTISH LEGAL AID BOARD

44 Drumsheugh Gardens, Edinburgh EH3 7SW
T 0131-226 7061 **Helpline** 0845-122 8686
E general@slab.org.uk W www.slab.org.uk

The Scottish Legal Aid Board was set up under the Legal Aid (Scotland) Act 1986 to manage legal aid in Scotland. It reports to the Scottish government. Board members are appointed by Scottish ministers.

Chair, Iain A. Robertson, CBE
Members, Les Campbell; Joseph Hughes; Alastair Kinroy, QC; Denise Loney; Paul McBride, QC; Ray MacFarlane; Susan McPhee; Bill McQueen, CBE; Elaine Rosie; Sheriff Harry Small; Graham Watson
Chief Executive, Lindsay Montgomery, CBE

SCOTTISH NATURAL HERITAGE (SNH)

Great Glen House, Leachkin Road, Inverness IV3 8NW
T 01463-725000 E enquiries@snh.gov.uk
W www.snh.org.uk

SNH was established in 1992 under the Natural Heritage (Scotland) Act 1991. It is the government's adviser on all aspects of nature and landscape across Scotland and its role is to help the public understand, value and enjoy Scotland's nature.

Chair, Andrew Thin
Chief Executive, Ian Jardine
Director of Policy and Advice, Susan Davies
Directors of Operations, Andrew Bachell
Director of Corporate Services, Joe Moore

SEAFISH INDUSTRY AUTHORITY

18 Logie Mill, Logie Green Road, Edinburgh EH7 4HS
T 0131-558 3331 E seafish@seafish.co.uk
W www.seafish.org

Established under the Fisheries Act 1981, the authority on seafood works with all sectors of the UK seafood industry to satisfy consumers, raise standards, improve efficiency and secure a sustainable and profitable future. Services range from research and development, economic consulting, market research and training and accreditation through to legislative advice for the seafood industry. It is sponsored by the four UK fisheries departments, which appoint the board, and is funded by a levy on seafood.

Chair, John Whitehead, OBE

Chief Executive, Dr Paul Williams

SENIOR SALARIES REVIEW BODY

6th Floor, Victoria House, Southampton Row,
London WC1B 4AD
T 020-7271 0494 W www.ome.uk.com

The Senior Salaries Review Body (formerly the Top Salaries Review Body) was set up in 1971 to advise the prime minister on the remuneration of the judiciary, senior civil servants, senior officers of the armed forces and very senior managers in the NHS. In 1993 its remit was extended to cover the pay, pensions and allowances of MPs, ministers and others whose pay is determined by the Ministerial and Other Salaries Act 1975, and also the allowances of peers. If asked, it advises on the pay of officers and members of the devolved parliament and assemblies.

Chair, Bill Cockburn, CBE, TD

Members, Prof. Richard Disney; Martin Fish; Michael Langley; David Metcalf; Sir Peter North, CBE, QC; Alasdair Smith; Bruce Warman; Paul Williams

SERIOUS ORGANISED CRIME AGENCY (SOCA)

PO Box 8000, London SE11 5EN
T 0370-496 7622 W www.soca.gov.uk

SOCA was established in April 2006. It took over the functions of the National Criminal Intelligence Service and the National Crime Squad, as well as the role of HM Revenue and Customs in investigating drug trafficking and related criminal finance, and some of the functions of the UK Immigration Service in dealing with organised immigration crime. SOCA tackles serious organised crime affecting the UK and its citizens and is the custodian of a range of national and international capabilities. SOCA works to priorities set by the home secretary which currently include class A drugs, people smuggling and human trafficking, major gun crime, fraud, cyber crime and money laundering.

SOCA is due to become part of the new National Crime Agency in 2013.

Chair, Sir Ian Andrews, CBE, TD

Director-General, Trevor Pearce, QPM

Executive Directors, Malcolm Cornberg, OBE *(Capability and Service Delivery);* Brad Jones *(Operational Delivery);* Paul Evans *(Strategy and Prevention)*

Non-Executive Directors, Peter Clarke; Elizabeth France; Susan Garrard; Dame Janet Paraskeva, DBE; Francis Plowden

STUDENT LOANS COMPANY LTD

100 Bothwell Street, Glasgow G2 7JD
T 0141-306 2000 W www.slc.co.uk

The Student Loans Company (SLC) is wholly owned by the government. It processes and administers financial assistance for undergraduates who have secured a place at university or college, under the student loans scheme (established in 1990) and the income contingent student loans scheme (established in 1998). For 2010–11 support payments to students totalled £5.5bn, of which £3.6bn was in maintenance loans and £1.9bn was in maintenance grants and other non-repayable allowances. The SLC also paid £2.7bn in tuition fees to universities in 2010–11. At the end of 2010 the company had over 4 million borrowers.

Chair, Ed Smith

Chief Executive, Ed Lester

TATE BRITAIN

Millbank, London SW1P 4RG
T 020-7887 8888 E visiting.britain@tate.org.uk
W www.tate.org.uk/britain

Tate Britain displays the national collection of British art from 1500 to the present day – with special attention and dedicated space given to Blake, Turner and Constable. The gallery opened in 1897, the cost of building (£80,000) being defrayed by Sir Henry Tate, who also contributed the nucleus of the present collection. The Turner wing was opened in 1910, and further galleries and a new sculpture hall followed in 1937. In 1979 a further extension was built, and the Clore Gallery was opened in 1987. The Centenary Development was opened in 2001.

There are four Tate galleries: Tate Britain and Tate Modern in London, Tate Liverpool and Tate St Ives; the entire Tate collection is available to view online.

BOARD OF TRUSTEES

Chair, Lord Browne of Madingley

Trustees, Helen Alexander; Tom Bloxham; Howard Davies; Jeremy Deller; David Ekserdjian; Mala Gaonkar; Patricia Lankester; Elisabeth Murdoch; Franck Petitgas; Monisha Shah; Bob and Roberta Smith (Patrick Brill); Gareth Thomas; Wolfgang Tillmans

OFFICERS

Director, Sir Nicholas Serota

Director, Tate Britain, Dr Penelope Curtis

Director, Tate Liverpool, Dr Christoph Grunenberg

Director, Tate Modern, Chris Dercon

Artistic Director, Tate St Ives, Martin Clark

Executive Director, Tate St Ives, Mark Osterfield

TATE MODERN

Bankside, London SE1 9TG
T 020-7887 8888 E visiting.modern@tate.org.uk
W www.tate.org.uk/modern

Opened in May 2000, Tate Modern displays the Tate collection of international modern art dating from 1900 to the present day. It includes works by Dalí, Picasso, Matisse and Warhol as well as many contemporary works. It is housed in the former Bankside Power Station in London, which was redesigned by the Swiss architects Herzog and de Meuron.

Director, Chris Dercon

TENANT SERVICES AUTHORITY

Maple House, 149 Tottenham Court Road,
London W1T 7BN
T 0845-230 7000 E enquiries@tsa.gsi.gov.uk
W www.tenantservicesauthority.org

The Tenant Services Authority (TSA) was established on 1 December 2008 as the regulator for affordable housing.

It took over the regulatory powers of the Housing Corporation. The TSA's main aim is to raise the standards of services for tenants. In April 2010 the TSA became responsible for all affordable housing in England, whether it is provided by local authorities, housing associations or arm's-length management organisations.

The government announced in October 2010 that the TSA would be abolished by April 2012, and that its economic regulation and backstop consumer regulation functions would be transferred to the Homes and Communities Agency.

Chair, Anthony Mayer
Chief Executive, Claer Lloyd Jones

TOURISM BODIES

Visit Britain, Visit Scotland, Visit Wales and the Northern Ireland Tourist Board are responsible for developing and marketing the tourist industry in their respective regions. Visit Wales is not listed here as it is part of the Welsh government, within the Department for Heritage, and not a public body.

VISIT BRITAIN

1 Palace Street, Victoria SW1E 5HX **T** 020-7578 1000
W www.visitbritain.com
Chair, Christopher Rodrigues, CBE
Chief Executive, Sandie Dawe, MBE

VISIT SCOTLAND

Ocean Point One, 94 Ocean Drive, Leith, Edinburgh EH6 6JH
T 0131-472 2222
E info@visitscotland.com **W** www.visitscotland.com
Chair, Dr Mike Cantlay
Chief Executive, Malcolm Roughead, OBE

NORTHERN IRELAND TOURIST BOARD

St Anne's Court, 59 North Street, Belfast BT1 1NB
T 028-9023 1221
E info@nitb.com **W** www.discovernorthernireland.com
Chair, Howard Hastings
Chief Executive, Alan Clarke

TRAINING AND DEVELOPMENT AGENCY FOR SCHOOLS

Piccadilly Gate, Store Street, Manchester M1 2WD
T 0870-496 0123 **E** corporatecomms@tda.gov.uk
W www.tda.gov.uk

The Training and Development Agency for Schools (TDA) was launched in September 2005 and took on the role, and expanded the remit of, the Teacher Training Agency. The TDA aims to attract able and committed people to teaching, concentrating specifically on subjects where teachers are in short supply; provide schools and their staff with good information on training and development opportunities; and ensure that new teachers enter schools with appropriate skills and knowledge, through working closely with providers of initial teacher training. The government announced in November 2010 that from April 2012, the TDA will change in status from a non-departmental public body to an executive agency of the Department for Education.

Chief Executive, Stephen Hillier

TRANSPORT FOR LONDON (TFL)

Windsor House, 42–50 Victoria Street, London SW1H 0TL
T 020-7222 5600
E enquire@tfl.gov.uk **W** www.tfl.gov.uk

TfL was created in July 2000 and is the integrated body responsible for the capital's transport system. Its role is to implement the Mayor of London's transport strategy and manage the transport services across London for which the mayor has responsibility. These services include London's buses, London Underground, London Overground, the Docklands Light Railway (DLR), Tramlink, London River Services and Victoria Coach Station.

TfL is also responsible for managing the Congestion Charging scheme, maintaining 360 miles (580km) of main roads and all of London's traffic lights, regulating the city's taxis and private hire vehicles, promoting a range of walking and cycling initiatives and making London's transport system more accessible by coordinating schemes for people with impaired mobility and running Dial-a-ride alongside the London boroughs' Taxicard scheme.

Chair, Boris Johnson
Commissioner, Peter Hendy

UK ATOMIC ENERGY AUTHORITY

Culham Science Centre, Abingdon, Oxfordshire OX14 3DB
T 01235-528822
W www.uk-atomic-energy.org.uk

The UK Atomic Energy Authority (UKAEA) was established by the Atomic Energy Authority Act 1954 and took over responsibility for the research and development of the civil nuclear power programme. The authority reports to the Department for Business, Innovation and Skills and is responsible for managing UK fusion research, from its Culham Centre for Fusion Energy (CCFE). It also operates the Joint European Torus (JET) on behalf of the European Fusion Development Agency (EFDA) at its site in Culham, Oxfordshire, as well as managing the records service for the Nuclear Decommissioning Authority (NDA) at Harwell. In October 2009, as part of the government's Operation Efficiency Programme, the authority sold its commercial arm, UKAEA Limited; as a result, the UKAEA no longer provides nuclear decommissioning services.

Chair, Prof. Roger Cashmore
Chief Executive, Prof. Steven Cowley

UK SPORTS COUNCIL (UK SPORT)

40 Bernard Street, London WC1N 1ST
T 020-7211 5100
E info@uksport.gov.uk **W** www.uksport.gov.uk

UK Sport was established by royal charter in 1997 and is accountable to parliament through the Department for Culture, Media and Sport. Its mission is to lead sport in the UK to world-class success. This means working with partner organisations to deliver medals at the Olympic and Paralympic Games and organising, bidding for and staging major sporting events in the UK; increasing the UK's sporting activity and influence overseas; and promoting sporting conduct, ethics and diversity in society. UK Sport is funded by a mix of grant-in-aid and National Lottery income, as well as private investment through Team 2012. Projected government grant-in-aid for 2011–12 is £60.3m and National Lottery funding £60.45m.

As part of the public bodies' reform proposals, UK Sport and Sport England will merge into one body by 1 April 2013.

Chair, Baroness Sue Campbell, CBE

VICTORIA AND ALBERT MUSEUM

Cromwell Road, London SW7 2RL
T 020-7942 2000 W www.vam.ac.uk

The Victoria and Albert Museum (V&A) is the national museum of fine and applied art and design. It descends directly from the Museum of Manufactures, which opened in Marlborough House in 1852 after the Great Exhibition of 1851. The museum was moved in 1857 to become part of the South Kensington Museum. It was renamed the Victoria and Albert Museum in 1899. It also houses the National Art Library and Print Room.

The museum administers the V&A Museum of Childhood at Bethnal Green, which was opened in 1872; the building is the most important surviving example of the type of glass and iron construction used by Paxton for the Great Exhibition. Total government grant-in-aid for 2011–12 is £41.4m.

Chair, Paul Ruddock
Trustees, D. Adjaye, OBE; E. Davies, OBE; A. Hochhauser, QC; Ms B. Jackson, CBE; Prof. L. Jardine, CBE; S. McGuckin; Ms E. O' Connor; Ms M. Ogundehin; Rt. Hon. Sir T. Sainsbury; Dame M. Scardino, DBE; S. Shah, OBE; Sir John Sorrell; R. Stefanowski; Dr P. Thompson
Director of the V&A, Prof. M. Roth

WALLACE COLLECTION

Hertford House, Manchester Square, London W1U 3BN
T 020-7563 9500 E collections@wallacecollection.org
W www.wallacecollection.org

The Wallace Collection was bequeathed to the nation by the widow of Sir Richard Wallace, in 1897, and Hertford House was subsequently acquired by the government. The collection contains works by Titian and Rembrandt, and includes porcelain, furniture and an array of arms and armour. Total government grant-in-aid for 2010–11 was estimated at £4.21m.

Director, Dr Christoph Vogtherr

YOUNG PEOPLE'S LEARNING AGENCY

Cheylesmore House, Quinton Road, Coventry CV1 2WT
T 0845-377 2000 E enquiries@ypla.gov.uk
W www.ypla.gov.uk

The Young People's Learning Agency (YPLA) was launched in April 2010 with the mission of championing education and training for young people in England. It provides financial support to young learners, funds academies and supports local authorities to commission suitable education and training opportunities for all 16- to 19-year-olds.

The YPLA's board is made up of 12 members appointed by the Secretary of State for Education. Its budget for 2011 was £12.5bn. Subject to legislation, the YPLA will be replaced in April 2012 by the Education Funding Agency, an executive agency of the Department for Education.

Chair, Les Walton
Chief Executive, Peter Lauener

REGIONAL GOVERNMENT

LONDON

GREATER LONDON AUTHORITY (GLA)
City Hall, The Queen's Walk, London SE1 2AA
T 020-7983 4000 E mayor@london.gov.uk
W www.london.gov.uk

On 7 May 1998 London voted in favour of the formation of the Greater London Authority (GLA). The first elections to the GLA took place on 4 May 2000 and the new authority took over its responsibilities on 3 July 2000. In July 2002 the GLA moved to one of London's most spectacular buildings, newly built on a brownfield site on the south bank of the Thames, adjacent to Tower Bridge. The third and most recent election to the GLA took place on 1 May 2008.

The structure and objectives of the GLA stem from its main areas of responsibility: transport, policing, fire and emergency planning, economic development, planning, culture and health. There are four functional bodies that coordinate these functions and report to the GLA: the London Development Agency (LDA), the London Fire and Emergency Planning Authority (LFEPA), the Metropolitan Police Authority (MPA) and Transport for London (TfL).

The GLA consists of a directly elected mayor, the Mayor of London, and a separately elected assembly, the London Assembly. The mayor has the key role of decision making, with the assembly performing the tasks of regulating and scrutinising these decisions, and investigating issues of importance to Londoners. In addition, the GLA has around 600 permanent staff to support the activities of the mayor and the assembly, which are overseen by a head of paid service. The mayor may appoint two political advisers and no more than ten other members of staff, though he does not necessarily exercise this power, but he does not appoint the chief executive, the monitoring officer or the chief finance officer. These must be appointed jointly by the assembly and the mayor.

Every aspect of the assembly and its activities must be open to public scrutiny and therefore accountable. The assembly holds the mayor to account through scrutiny of his strategies, decisions and actions. This is carried out by direct questioning at assembly meetings and by conducting detailed investigations in committee.

People's Question Time and Mayor's Consultation Meetings give Londoners the chance to question the mayor and the London Assembly about plans, priorities and policies for London. Question time is held twice a year, and consultation meetings are held four times a year in different parts of London.

The role of the mayor can be broken down into a number of key areas:
• to represent and promote London at home and abroad and speak up for Londoners
• to devise strategies and plans to tackle London-wide issues, such as crime, transport, housing, planning, environment, accountability, business and skills, public services, society and culture, local government and the Olympic and Paralympic Games, sport and health; and

to set budgets for TfL, the LDA, the MPA and the LFEPA.
• the mayor is chair of TfL, and has the power to appoint the chair of the MPA and board members to TfL, the MPA and the LDA; he also makes appointments to the police and fire authorities
• with London's successful bid to host the 2012 Olympic and Paralympic Games, the previous mayor was the signatory to the contract with the International Olympic Committee undertaking that the games would be delivered

The role of the assembly can be broken down into a number of key areas:
• to check on and balance the mayor
• to scrutinise the mayor
• to have the power to amend the mayor's budget by a majority of two-thirds
• to have the power to summon the mayor, senior staff of the GLA and functional bodies
• to investigate issues of London-wide significance and make proposals to appropriate stakeholders
• to have representatives on the boards of the MPA, the LFEPA and the LDA

Mayor, Boris Johnson
Deputy Mayors, Richard Barnes (*Statutory Deputy Mayor*); Kit Malthouse (*Policing*); Sir Edward Lister (*Planning, and Chief of Staff*); Isabel Dedring (*Transport*)
Chair of the London Assembly, Jennette Arnold
Deputy Chair of the Assembly, Baroness Doocey

ELECTIONS AND VOTING SYSTEMS
The assembly is elected every four years at the same time as the mayor, and consists of 25 members. There is one member from each of the 14 GLA constituencies topped up with 11 London members who are either representatives of political parties or individuals standing as independent candidates. The last election was on 1 May 2008.

Two distinct voting systems are used to appoint the existing mayor and the assembly. The mayor is elected using the supplementary vote system (SVS). With SVS, electors have two votes: one to give a first choice for mayor and one to give a second choice. Electors can only have one effective vote and so cannot vote twice for the same candidate. If one candidate gets more than half of all the first-choice votes, he or she becomes mayor. If no candidate gets more than half of the first-choice votes, the two candidates with the most first-choice votes remain in the election and all the other candidates drop out. The second-choice votes on the ballot papers of the candidates who drop out are then counted. Where these second-choice votes are for the two remaining candidates they are added to the first-choice votes these candidates already have. The candidate with the most first- and second-choice votes combined becomes the Mayor of London.

The assembly is appointed using the additional member system (AMS). Under AMS, electors have two votes. The first vote is for a constituency candidate. The second vote is for a party list or individual candidate contesting the London-wide assembly seats. The

14 constituency members are elected under the first-past-the-post system, the same system used in general and local elections. Electors vote for one candidate and the candidate with the most votes wins. The additional (London) members are drawn from party lists or are independent candidates who stand as London members; they are chosen using a form of proportional representation.

The Greater London Returning Officer (GLRO) is the independent official responsible for running the election in London. He is supported in this by returning officers in each of the 14 London constituencies.

GLRO, John Bennett

TRANSPORT FOR LONDON (TFL)

TfL is the integrated body responsible for London's transport system. Its role is to implement the mayor's transport strategy for London and manage transport services across the capital for which the mayor has responsibility. TfL is directed by a management board whose members are chosen for their understanding of transport matters and are appointed by the mayor, who chairs the board. TfL's role is:
• to manage the London Underground, buses, Croydon Tramlink, London Overground and the Docklands Light Railway (DLR)
• to manage a network of main roads and all of London's traffic lights
• to regulate taxis and minicabs
• to run the London River Services, Victoria Coach Station and London Transport Museum
• to help to coordinate the Dial-a-Ride and Taxicard schemes for door-to-door services for transport users with mobility problems

The London Borough Councils maintain the role of highway and traffic authorities for 95 per cent of London's roads. A £5 congestion charge for motorists driving into central London between the hours of 7am and 6.30pm, Monday to Friday (excluding public holidays) was introduced on 17 February 2003, and was subsequently raised to £8 on 4 July 2005. On 19 February 2007, the charge zone roughly doubled in size after a westward expansion and the charging hours were shortened, to finish at 6pm. On 4 January 2011, the westward expansion was removed from the charging zone and the charge was increased to £10; an automated payment system was also introduced.

TfL introduced a low emission zone for London on 4 February 2008. It consisted of a £200 daily charge for polluting vehicles that entered the zone, which covered most of Greater London. Lorries over 12 tonnes that did not meet emissions standards were the first to be affected. Charges for vehicles exceeding three-and-a-half tonnes and buses and coaches exceeding five tonnes began on 7 July 2008; tougher emissions standards will be introduced in January 2012, which will extend to minibuses and vans.

Since 2 January 2009, Londoners over pensionable age (or over 60 if born before 1950) and those with eligible disabilities are entitled to free travel on the capital's transport network at any time. War veterans who are receiving ongoing payments under the war pensions scheme, or those receiving guaranteed income payments under the armed forces compensation scheme can travel free at any time on bus, underground, Docklands Light Railway, tram and London Overground services and at certain times on national rail services.

In the summer of 2010, the London cycle hire scheme launched with 6,000 new bicycles for hire from 400 docking stations across eight boroughs, the City and the Royal parks.

Transport Commissioner for London, Peter Hendy

METROPOLITAN POLICE AUTHORITY (MPA)

This body, which oversees the policing of London, consists of 23 members: 12 from the assembly and 11 independents. One of the independents is appointed directly by the home secretary. The role of the MPA is:
• to monitor and scrutinise the Metropolitan Police Service
• to maintain an efficient and effective police force
• to secure best value in the delivery of policing services
• to publish an annual policing plan
• to set police targets and monitor performance
• to be part of the appointment, discipline and removal of senior officers
• to be responsible for the police budget

The boundaries of the metropolitan police districts have been changed to be consistent with the 32 London boroughs. Areas beyond the GLA remit have been incorporated into the Surrey, Hertfordshire and Essex police areas. The City of London has its own police force.

Chair, Kit Malthouse

LONDON FIRE AND EMERGENCY PLANNING AUTHORITY (LFEPA)

In July 2000 the London Fire and Civil Defence Authority became the London Fire and Emergency Planning Authority. It consists of 17 members, eight drawn from the assembly, seven from the London boroughs and two mayoral appointees. The role of the LFEPA is:
• to set the strategy for the provision of fire services
• to ensure that the fire brigade can meet all the normal requirements efficiently
• to ensure that effective arrangements are made for the fire brigade to receive emergency calls and deal with them promptly
• to ensure members of the fire brigade are properly trained and equipped
• to ensure that information useful to the development of the fire brigades is gathered
• to ensure arrangements for advice and guidance on fire protection are made

Chair, Brian Coleman, FRSA

SALARIES *as at July 2011*	
Mayor	£143,911
Deputy Mayors	
Richard Barnes	£96,092
Kit Malthouse	£53,439
Sir Edward Lister	£127,784
Chair of the Assembly	£64,103
Assembly Members	£53,439

LONDON ASSEMBLY COMMITTEES

Chair, Audit Panel, Roger Evans
Chair, Budget and Performance Committee, John Biggs
Chair, Business Management and Administration Committee, Jennette Arnold
Chair, Confirmation Hearings Committee, various
Chair, Economy, Culture and Sport Committee, Baroness Doocey
Chair, Environment Committee, Murad Qureshi
Chair, Health and Public Services Committee, Victoria Borwick

Chair, Planning and Housing Committee, Jenny Jones
Chair, Standards Committee, Claer Lloyd-Jones
Chair, TIme for Action Panel, Joanne McCartney
Chair, Transport Committee, Caroline Pidgeon

LONDON ASSEMBLY MEMBERS
as at 1 July 2011

Arbour, Tony, C., South West, Maj. 26,928
Arnold, Jennette, Lab. North East, Maj. 28,437
Bacon, Gareth, C., London List
Barnbrook, Richard, Ind., London List
Barnes, Richard, C., Ealing and Hillingdon, Maj. 28,638
Biggs, John, Lab., City and East, Maj. 31,553
Boff, Andrew, C., London List
Borwick, Victoria, C., London List
Cleverly, James, C., Bexley and Bromley, Maj. 75,237
Coleman, Brian, C., Barnet and Camden, Maj. 19,693
Doocey, Baroness, LD, London List
Duvall, Len, Lab., Greenwich and Lewisham, Maj. 16,134
Evans, Roger, C., Havering and Redbridge, Maj. 43,025
Gavron, Nicky, Lab., London List
Johnson, Darren, Green, London List
Jones, Jenny, Green, London List
McCartney, Joanne, Lab., Enfield and Haringey, Maj. 1,402
Malthouse, Kit, C., West Central, Maj. 51,381
O'Connell, Steve, C., Croydon and Sutton, Maj. 42,665
Pidgeon, Caroline, LD, London List
Qureshi, Murad, Lab., London List
Shah, Navin, Lab., Brent and Harrow, Maj. 1,649
Shawcross, Valerie, Lab., Lambeth and Southwark, Maj. 23,648
Tracey, Richard, C., Merton and Wandsworth, Maj. 26,293
Tuffrey, Michael, LD, London List

STATE OF THE PARTIES as at 1 July 2011

Party	Seats
Conservative (C.)	11
Labour (Lab.)	8
Liberal Democrats (LD)	3
Green	2
Independent (Ind.)	1

MAYORAL ELECTION RESULTS
as at 1 May 2008

E. 5,419,913 T. 45.33%

Change in turnout from 2004: + 8.38%
Good votes: 1st choice 2,415,952 (98.32%); 2nd choice 2,004,078 (82.94%)
Rejected votes: 1st choice 41,032 (1.67%); 2nd choice 412,054 (17.05%)

First	Party	Votes	%
Boris Johnson	C.	1,043,761	42.48
Ken Livingstone	Lab.	893,877	36.38
Brian Paddick	LD	236,685	9.63
Sian Berry	Green	77,374	3.15
Richard Barnbrook	BNP	69,710	2.84
Alan Craig	CPA	39,249	1.60
Gerard Batten	UKIP	24,222	0.91
Lindsey German	Left List	16,796	0.68
Matt O'Connor	Eng. Dem.	10,695	0.44
Winston McKenzie	Ind.	5,389	0.22

Second	Party	Votes	%
Brian Paddick	LD	641,412	26.11
Sian Berry	Green	331,727	13.50
Ken Livingstone	Lab.	303,198	12.34
Boris Johnson	C.	257,792	10.49
Richard Barnbrook	BNP	128,609	5.23
Gerard Batten	UKIP	113,651	4.63
Alan Craig	CPA	80,140	3.26
Matt O'Connor	Eng. Dem.	73,538	2.99
Winston McKenzie	Ind.	38,954	1.59
Lindsey German	Left List	35,057	1.43

LONDON ASSEMBLY ELECTION RESULTS
as at 1 May 2008
E. Electorate T. Turnout
See General Election Results for a list of party abbreviations

CONSTITUENCIES
E. 5,419,913 T. 45.28%

BARNET AND CAMDEN
E. 376,818 T. 47.77%

Brian Coleman, C.		72,659
Nicky Gavron, Lab.		52,966
Nick Russell, LD		22,213
Miranda Dunn, Green		16,782
Magnus Nielsen, UKIP		3,678
Clement Adebayo, CPA		3,536
David Stevens, Eng. Dem.		2,146
Dave Hoefling, Left List		2,074
Graham Dare, Veritas		510
C. majority 19,693		

BEXLEY AND BROMLEY
E. 407,003 T. 49.85%

James Cleverly, C.		105,162
Alex Heslop, Lab.		29,925
Tom Papworth, LD,		21,244
Paul Winnett, NF		11,288
Ann Garrett, Green		9,261
Mick Greenhough, UKIP		8,021
John Hemming-Clark, Ind.		6,684
Miranda Suit, CPA		4,408
Steven Uncles, Eng. Dem.		2,907
David Davis, Left List		1,050
C. majority 75,237		

BRENT AND HARROW
E. 367,337 T. 43.10%

Navin Shah, Lab.		57,716
Bob Blackman, C.		56,067
James Allie, LD		19,299
Shahrar Ali, Green		10,129
Zena Sherman, CPA		4,180
Sunita Webb, UKIP		3,021
Pat McManus, Left List		2,287
Arvind Tailor, Eng. Dem.		2,150
Lab. majority 1,649		

CITY AND EAST
E. 470,863 T. 39.79%

John Biggs, Lab.	63,635
Philip Briscoe, C.	32,082
Hanif Abdulmuhit, Respect	26,760
Robert Bailey, BNP	18,020
Rajonuddin Jalal, LD	13,724
Heather Finlay, Green	11,478
Thomas Conquest, CPA	7,306
Michael McGough, UKIP	3,078
Graham Kemp, NF	2,350
Michael Gavan, Left List	2,274
John Griffiths, Eng. Dem.	2,048
Julie Crawford, Ind.	701

Lab. majority 31,553

CROYDON AND SUTTON
E. 360,221 T. 48.99%

Stephen O'Connell, C.	76,477
Shafi Khan, Lab.	33,812
Abigail Lock, LD	32,335
David Pickles, UKIP	9,440
Shasha Khan, Green	8,969
David Campanale, CPA	6,910
Richard Castle, Eng. Dem.	4,186
Zana Hussain, Left List	1,361

C. majority 42,665

EALING AND HILLINGDON
E. 401,671 T. 44.05%

Richard Barnes, C.	74,710
Ranjit Dheer, Lab.	46,072
Nigel Bakhai, LD	18,004
Sarah Edwards, Green	12,606
Ian Edward, NF	7,939
Mary Boyle, CPA	5,100
Lynnda Robson, UKIP	4,465
Salvinder Dhillon, Left List	2,390
Sati Chaggar, Eng. Dem.	1,853

C. majority 28,638

ENFIELD AND HARINGEY
E. 351,536 T. 46.04%

Joanne McCartney, Lab.	52,665
Matthew Laban, C.	51,263
Monica Whyte, LD	23,550
Pete McAskie, Green	12,473
Segun Johnson, CPA	5,779
Sait Akgul, Left List	5,639
Brian Hall, UKIP	4,682
Teresa Cannon, Eng. Dem.	2,282

Lab. majority 1,402

GREENWICH AND LEWISHAM
E. 347,252 T. 42.98%

Len Duvall, Lab.	53,174
Andy Jennings, C.	37,040
Brian Robson, LD	18,174
Susan Luxton, Green	15,607
Tess Culnane, NF	8,509
Stephen Hammond, CPA	5,079
Arnold Tarling, UKIP	3,910
Jennifer Jones, Left List	2,045
Johanna Munilla, Eng. Dem.	1,716
Chris Flood, Soc. Alt.	1,587

Lab. majority 16,134

HAVERING AND REDBRIDGE
E. 369,407 T. 45.46%

Roger Evans, C.	78,493
Balvinder Saund, Lab.	35,468
Farrukh Islam, LD	12,443
Lawrence Webb, UKIP	12,203
Ashley Gunstock, Green	9,126
Leo Brookes, Eng. Dem.	6,487
Paula Warren, CPA	5,533
Dr Peter Thorogood, Ind.	3,450
Carole Vincent, Left List	1,473

C. majority 43,025

LAMBETH AND SOUTHWARK
E. 395,202 T. 42.09%

Valerie Shawcross, Lab.	60,601
Caroline Pidgeon, LD	36,953
Shirley Houghton, C.	32,835
Shane Collins, Green	18,011
Geoffrey Macharia, CPA	4,432
Jens Winton, UKIP	3,012
Katt Young, Left List	1,956
Janus Polenceus, Eng. Dem.	1,867
Jasmijn De Boo, Animals Count	1,828
Daniel Lambert, Socialist	1,588

Lab. majority 23,648

MERTON AND WANDSWORTH
E. 362,542 T. 47.16%

Richard Tracey, C.	75,103
Leonie Cooper, Lab.	48,810
Shas Sheehan, LD	17,187
Roy Vickery, Green	14,124
Strachan McDonald, UKIP	4,286
Ellen Greco, CPA	4,053
Steve Scott, Eng. Dem.	2,160
Kris Stewart, Left List	1,714

C. majority 26,293

NORTH EAST
E. 451,787 T. 43.80%

Jennette Arnold, Lab.	73,551
Alexander Ellis, C.	45,114
Meral Ece, LD	28,973
Aled Fisher, Green	28,845
Unjum Mirza, Left List	6,019
Nicholas Jones, UKIP	5,349
Maxine Hargreaves, CPA	5,323
John Dodds, Eng. Dem.	3,637

Lab. majority 28,437

SOUTH WEST
E. 415,092 T. 46.15%

Tony Arbour, C.	76,913
Stephen Knight, LD	49,985
Ansuya Sodha, Lab.	30,190
John Hunt, Green	12,774
Andrew Cripps, NF	4,754
Peter Dul, UKIP	3,779
Sue May, CPA	3,718
Andrew Constantine, Free England Party	2,908
Roger Cooper, Eng. Dem.	1,874
Tansy Hoskins, Left List	1,526

C. majority 26,928

WEST CENTRAL
E. 343,182 T. 48.48%

Kit Malthouse, C.	86,651
Murad Qureshi, Lab.	35,270
Julia Stephenson, Green	16,874
Merlene Emerson, LD	15,934
Paul Wiffen, UKIP	3,060
Alex Vaughan, Eng. Dem.	1,858
Explo Nani-Kofi, Left List	1,630
Abby Dharamsey, Ind.	962

C. majority 51,381

TOP-UP MEMBERS

BRITISH NATIONAL PARTY
Richard Barnbrook

CONSERVATIVE
Andrew Boff
Victoria Borwick
Gareth Bacon

GREEN PARTY
Darren Johnson
Jenny Jones

LABOUR
Nicky Gavron
Murad Qureshi

LIBERAL DEMOCRAT
Baroness Doocey
Caroline Pidgeon
Michael Tuffrey

WALES

WELSH GOVERNMENT

Cathays Park, Cardiff CF10 3NQ
T 0845-010 3300 W http://wales.gov.uk

The Welsh government is the devolved government of Wales. It is accountable to the National Assembly for Wales, the Welsh legislature which represents the interests of the people of Wales, and makes laws for Wales. The Welsh government and the National Assembly for Wales were established as separate institutions under the Government of Wales Act 2006.

The Welsh government comprises the first minister, who is usually the leader of the largest party in the National Assembly for Wales; up to 12 ministers and deputy ministers; and a counsel general (the chief legal adviser).

Following the referendum on 3 March 2011 on granting further law-making powers to the national assembly, the Welsh government's functions now include the ability to propose bills to the national assembly on subjects within 20 set areas of policy. Subject to limitations prescribed by the Government of Wales Act 2006, acts of the National Assembly may make any provision that could be made by act of parliament. The 20 areas of responsibility devolved to the National Assembly for Wales (and within which Welsh ministers exercise executive functions) are: agriculture, fisheries, forestry and rural development; ancient monuments and historic buildings; culture; economic development; education and training; environment; fire and rescue services and promotion of fire safety; food; health and health services; highways and transport; housing; local government; the National Assembly for Wales; public administration; social welfare; sport and recreation; tourism; town and county planning; water and flood defence; and the Welsh language.

First Minister of Wales, Carwyn Jones, AM
Minister for Business, Enterprise, Technology and Science, Edwina Hart, MBE, AM
Minister for Education and Skills, Leighton Andrews, AM
Minister for Environment and Sustainable Development, John Griffiths, AM
Minister for Finance and Leader of the House, Jane Hutt, AM
Minister for Health and Social Services, Lesley Griffiths AM
Minister for Housing, Regeneration and Heritage, Huw Lewis, AM
Minister for Local Government and Communities, Carl Sargeant, AM
Deputy Minister for Agriculture, Food, Fisheries and European Programmes, Alun Davies, AM
Deputy Minister for Children and Social Services, Gwenda Thomas, AM
Deputy Minister for Skills, Jeff Cuthbert, AM
Counsel General, Theodore Huckle, QC
Chief Whip, Janice Gregory, AM

MANAGEMENT BOARD

Permanent Secretary, Dame Gillian Morgan
Director-General, Business, Enterprise, Technology and Science, James Price (acting)
Director-General, Education and Skills, Dr Emyr Roberts
Director-General, Health,Social Services and Children and Chief Executive of NHS Wales, David Sissling
Director-General, Local Government and Communities, Dr June Milligan
Director-General, People, Places and Corporate Services,, Bernard Galton
Director-General, Strategic Planning, Finance and Performance, Michael Hearty
Non-Executive Directors, Elan Cross Stephens; James Turner

DEPARTMENTS

Department for Education and Skills
Department for Health, Social Services and Children
Department for Business, Enterprise, Technology and Science
Department for Strategic Planning, Finance and Performance
People, Places and Corporate Services
Sustainable Futures
Local Government and Communities
Non-Directorate Services

ASSEMBLY COMMITTEES

Children and Young People
Communities, Equality and Local Government
Constitutional and Legislative Affairs
Enterprise and Business
Environment and Sustainability
Finance
Health and Social Care
Petitions
Public Accounts
Standards

ASSEMBLY COMMISSION

The Assembly Commission was created under the Government of Wales Act 2006 to ensure that the assembly is provided with the property, staff and services required for it to carry out its functions. The commission also sets the national assembly's strategic aims, objectives, standards and values. The Assembly Commission consists of the presiding officer, plus four other assembly members, one nominated by each of the four party groups. The five commissioners are accountable to the national assembly.

Presiding Officer, Rosemary Butler, AM
Commissioners, Peter Black, Angela Burns, Rhodri Glyn Thomas, Sandy Mewies
Chief Executive and Clerk to the Assembly, Claire Clancy

NATIONAL ASSEMBLY FOR WALES

Cardiff Bay, Cardiff CF99 1NA
T 0845-010 5500 W www.assemblywales.org

In July 1997 the government announced plans to establish a National Assembly for Wales. In a referendum in September 1997 about 50 per cent of the electorate voted, of whom 50.3 per cent voted in favour of a national assembly. Elections are held every four years and the first election took place on 6 May 1999. The fourth election took place on 5 May 2011.

National Assembly members are elected using the additional member system. Voters are given two votes: one for a constituency member and one for a regional member. The constituency members are elected under the first-past-the-post system, also used to elect constituency members to the London Assembly. Four regional members in each of the five constituencies are then chosen from party lists or independent candidates using a form of proportional representation.

Until 2007 the National Assembly for Wales was a corporate body comprising both the executive and legislative branches of government. It had no primary law-making powers and only had responsibility for exercising and implementing ministerial functions which had previously been vested in the Secretary of State for Wales.

The Government of Wales Act 2006 introduced a radical change to the functions and status of the National Assembly for Wales. With effect from 25 May 2007 the act formally separated the National Assembly for Wales (the legislature – made up of 60 elected assembly members) and the Welsh government (the executive – comprising the first minister, Welsh ministers, deputy Welsh ministers and the counsel general). It also made changes to the electoral process: candidates are no longer permitted to stand as both constituency and regional members. The act enabled the National Assembly for Wales to formulate its own legislation (assembly measures) on the 20 devolved areas for which it has responsibility (see Welsh government); the assembly was given legislative competence (the legal authority to pass measures) on a case-by-case basis by the UK parliament.

The act also included a mechanism that would allow for full transfer of legislative powers relating to all devolved matters to the National Assembly, provided that the people of Wales voted for such a proposal in a referendum. In a referendum held on 3 March 2011, 63.5 per cent voted in favour of giving the national assembly full legislative powers for all devolved matters. The National Assembly for Wales can now pass legislation (assembly acts) on the 20 devolved areas for which it has responsibility. An assembly act has the same powers as an act of the UK parliament and may be proposed by the Welsh government, assembly committees, an assembly member or the assembly commission.

The National Assembly for Wales also scrutinises and monitors the Welsh government. It meets in plenary in the Senedd debating chamber. The 60 assembly members examine and approve assembly bills and approve certain items of subordinate legislation; approve the Welsh government and assembly commmssion's budget; hold Welsh ministers to account; and analyse and debate their decisions and policies.

Presiding Officer, Rosemary Butler AM

SALARIES 2010–11	
First Minister*	£80,870
Minister/Presiding Officer*	£41,949
Deputy Minister/Deputy Presiding Officer*	£26,385
Assembly Members (AM)†	£53,852

* Also receives the assembly member salary
† Reduced by two-thirds if the member is already an MP or an MEP

MEMBERS OF THE NATIONAL ASSEMBLY FOR WALES

as at 16 June 2011

Andrews, Leighton, *Lab., Rhondda,* Maj. 6,739
Antoniw, Mick, *Lab., Pontypridd,* Maj. 7,694
Asghar, Mohammad, *C., South Wales East region*
Black, Peter, *LD, South Wales West region*
Burns, Angela, *C., Carmarthen West and South Pembrokeshire,* Maj. 1,504
Butler, Rosemary, *Lab., Newport W.,* Maj. 4,220
Chapman, Christine, *Lab., Cynon Valley,* Maj. 6,515
Cuthbert, Jeff, *Lab., Caerphilly,* Maj. 4,924
Davies, Alun, *Lab., Blaenau Gwent,*Maj. 9,120
Davies, Andrew R.T., *C., South Wales Central region*
Davies, Byron, *C., South Wales West region*

Davies, Jocelyn, *PC, South Wales East region*
Davies, Keith, *Lab., Llanelli,* Maj. 80
Davies, Paul, *C., Preseli Pembrokeshire,* Maj. 2,175
Davies, Suzy, *C., South Wales West region*
Drakeford, Mark, *Lab., Cardiff West,* Maj. 5,901
Elis-Thomas, Lord Dafydd, *PC, Dwyfor Meirionnydd,* Maj. 5,417
Evans, Rebecca, *Lab., Mid and West Wales region*
Finch-Saunders, Janet, *C., Aberconwy,* Maj. 1,567
George, Russell, *C., Montgomeryshire,* Maj. 2,324
Gething, Vaughan, *Lab., Cardiff South and Penarth,* Maj. 6,259
Graham, William, *C., South Wales East region*
Gregory, Janice, *Lab., Ogmore,* Maj. 9,576
Griffiths, John, *Lab., Newport East,* Maj. 5,388
Griffiths, Lesley, *Lab., Wrexham,* Maj. 3,337
Hart, Edwina, *Lab., Gower,* Maj. 4,864
Hedges, Mike, *Lab., Swansea East,* Maj. 8,281
Hutt, Jane, *Lab., Vale of Glamorgan,* Maj. 3,775
Huws Gruffydd, Llyr, *PC, North Wales region*
Isherwood, Mark, *C., North Wales region*
James, Julie, *Lab., Swansea West,* Maj. 4,654
Jenkins, Bethan, *PC, South Wales West region*
Jones, Alun Ffred, *PC, Arfon,* Maj. 5,394
Jones, Ann, *Lab., Vale of Clwyd,* Maj. 4,011
Jones, Carwyn Howell, *Lab., Bridgend,* Maj. 6,775
Jones, Elin, *PC, Ceredigion,* Maj. 1,777
Lewis, Huw, *Lab., Merthyr Tydfil and Rhymney,* Maj. 7,051
Melding, David, *C., South Wales Central region*
Mewies, Sandra Elaine, *Lab., Delyn,* Maj. 2,881
Millar, Darren, *C., Clwyd West,* Maj. 4,248
Morgan, Julie, *Lab., Cardiff North,* Maj. 1,782
Neagle, Lynne, *Lab., Torfaen,* Maj. 6,088
Parrott, Eluned, *LD, South Wales Central region*
Powell, William, *LD, Mid and West Wales region*
Price, Gwyn, *Lab., Islwyn,* Maj. 7,589
Ramsay, Nicholas, *C., Monmouth,* Maj. 8,469
Rathbone, Jenny, *Lab., Cardiff Central,* Maj. 38
Rees, David, *Lab., Aberavon,* Maj. 9,311
Roberts, Aled, *LD, North Wales region*
Sandbach, Antoinette, *C., North Wales region*
Sargeant, Carl, *Lab., Alyn and Deeside,* Maj. 3,362
Skates, Ken, *Lab., Clwyd South,* Maj. 2,659
Thomas, Gwenda, *Lab., Neath,* Maj. 1,944
Thomas, Rhodri, *PC, Carmarthen East and Dinefwr,* Maj. 8,469
Thomas, Simon, *PC, Mid and West Wales region*
Watson, Joyce, *Lab., Mid and West Wales region*
Whittle, Lindsay, *PC, South Wales East region*
Williams, Kirsty, *LD, Brecon and Radnorshire,* Maj. 5,354
Wood, Leanne, *PC, South Wales Central region*
Wyn Jones, Ieuan, *PC, Ynys Mon,* Maj. 2,937

STATE OF THE PARTIES

as at 16 June 2011

	Constituency AMs	Regional AMs	AM total
Labour (Lab.)	28	2	30
Conservative (C.)	6	8	14
Plaid Cymru (PC)	5	6	11
Liberal Democrats (LD)	1	4	5
The Presiding Officer	1	0	1
The Deputy Presiding Officer	1	0	1
Total	40	18	60

NATIONAL ASSEMBLY ELECTION RESULTS

As at 5 May 2011

E. Electorate T. Turnout

See General Election Results for a list of party abbreviations

CONSTITUENCIES

E. 2,289,555 T. 41.5%

ABERAVON (S. WALES WEST)
E. 50,754 T. 18,879 (37.20%)
David Rees, Lab.	12,104
Paul Nicholls-Jones, PC	2,793
Tamojen Morgan, C.	2,704
Helen Ceri Clarke, LD	1,278

Lab. majority 9,311 (49.32%)
8.65% swing PC to Lab.

ABERCONWY (WALES N.)
E. 44,978 T. 20,288 (45.11%)
Janet Finch-Saunders, C.	6,888
Iwan Huws, PC	5,321
Eifion Wyn Williams, Lab.	5,206
Mike Priestley, LD	2,873

C. majority 1,567 (7.72%)
7.95% swing PC to C.

ALYN AND DEESIDE (WALES N.)
E. 61,751 T. 22,769 (36.87%)
Carl Sargeant, Lab.	11,978
John Bell, C.	6,397
Pete Williams, LD	1,725
Shane Brennan, PC	1,710
Michael Whitby, BNP	959

Lab. majority 5,581 (24.51%)
4.29% swing C. to Lab.

ARFON (WALES N.)
E. 41,093 T. 17,664 (42.99%)
Alun Ffred Jones, PC	10,024
Christina Rees, Lab.	4,630
Aled Davies, C.	2,209
Rhys Jones, LD	801

PC majority 5,394 (30.54%)
2.45% swing Lab. to PC

BLAENAU GWENT (S. WALES EAST)
E. 53,230 T. 20,211 (37.97%)
Alun Davies, Lab.	12,926
Jayne Sullivan, Ind.	3,806
Darren Jones, PC	1,098
Bob Hayward, C.	1,066
Brian Urch, BNP	948
Martin Blakebrough, LD	367

Lab. majority 9,120 (45.12%)
33.95% swing Ind. to Lab.

BRECON AND RADNORSHIRE (WALES MID AND W.)
E. 53,546 T. 28,348 (52.94%)
Kirsty Williams, LD	12,201
Chris Davies, C.	9,444
Christopher Lloyd, Lab.	4,797
Gary Price, PC	1,906

LD majority 2,757 (9.73%)
4.45% swing LD to C.

BRIDGEND (S. WALES WEST)
E. 59,104 T. 24,035 (40.67%)
Carwyn Jones, Lab.	13,499
Alex Williams,C.	6,724
Tim Thomas, PC	2,076
Briony Davies, LD	1,736

Lab. majority 6,775 (28.19%)
8.89% swing C. to Lab.

CAERPHILLY (S. WALES EAST)
E. 62,049 T. 25,570 (41.21%)
Jeff Cuthbert, Lab.	12,521
Ron Davies, PC	7,597
Owen Meredith, C.	3,368
Kay David, LD	1,062
Anthony King, BNP	1,022

Lab. majority 4,924 (19.26%)
5.25% swing PC to Lab.

CARDIFF CENTRAL (S. WALES CENTRAL)
E. 64,347 T. 23,628 (36.72%)
Jenny Rathbone, Lab.	8,954
Nigel Howells, LD	8,916
Matt Smith, C.	3,559
Chris Williams, PC	1,690
Mathab Khan, Ind.	509

Lab. majority 38 (0.16%)
14.74% swing LD to Lab.

CARDIFF NORTH (S. WALES CENTRAL)
E. 66,934 T. 34,431 (51.44%)
Julie Morgan, Lab.	16,384
Jonathan Morgan, C.	14,602
Ben Foday, PC	1,850
Matt Smith, LD	1,595

Lab. majority 1,782 (5.18%)
9.77% swing C. to Lab.

CARDIFF SOUTH AND PENARTH (S. WALES CENTRAL)
E. 75,038 T. 27,479 (36.62%)
Vaughan Gething, Lab.	13,814
Ben Gray, C.	7,555
Liz Musa, PC	3,324
Sian Cliff, LD	2,786

Lab. majority 6,259 (22.78%)
6.24% swing C. to Lab.

CARDIFF WEST (S. WALES CENTRAL)
E. 64,219 T. 27,726 (43.17%)
Mark Drakeford, Lab.	13,067
Craig Williams, C.	7,167
Neil McEvoy, PC	5,551
David Morgan, LD	1,942

Lab. majority 5,901 (21.28%)
3.77% C. to Lab.

CARMARTHEN EAST AND DINEFWR (WALES MID AND W.)
E. 54,243 T. 27,828 (51.30%)
Rhodri Glyn Thomas, PC	12,501
Anthony Jones, Lab.	8,353
Henrietta Hensher, C.	5,635
Will Griffiths, LD	1,339

PC majority 4,148 (14.91%)
7.01% swing PC to Lab.

CARMARTHEN WEST AND SOUTH PEMBROKESHIRE
(WALES MID AND W.)
E. 58,435 T. 28,156 (48.18%)

Angela Burns, C.	10,095
Christine Gwyther, Lab.	8,591
Nerys Evans, PC	8,373
Selwyn Runnett, LD	1,097

C. majority 1,504 (5.34%)
2.50% swing Lab. to C.

CEREDIGION (WALES MID AND W.)
E. 56,983 T. 29,076 (51.03%)

Elin Jones, PC	12,020
Liz Evans, LD	10,243
Luke Evetts, C.	2,755
Richard Boudier, Lab.	2,544
Chris Simpson, Green	1,514

PC majority 1,777 (6.11%)
3.51% swing PC to LD

CLWYD SOUTH (WALES N.)
E. 54,499 T. 19,498 (37.59%)

Ken Skates, Lab.	8,500
Paul Rogers, C.	5,841
Mabon ap Gwynfor, PC	3,719
Bruce Roberts, LD	1,977

Lab. majority 2,659 (13.27%)
3.77% swing C. to Lab.

CLWYD WEST (WALES N.)
E. 57,980 T. 25,153 (43.38%)

Darren Millar, C.	10,890
Crispin Jones, Lab.	6,642
Eifion Lloyd Jones, PC	5,775
Brian Cossey, LD	1,846

C. majority 4,248 (16.89%)
5.40% swing Lab. to C.

CYNON VALLEY (S. WALES CENTRAL)
E. 52,133 T. 18,760 (35.98%)

Christine Chapman, Lab.	11,626
Dafydd Trystan Davies, PC	5,111
Dan Saxton, C.	1,531
Ian Walton, LD	492

Lab. majority 6,515 (34.73%)
2.96% swing PC to Lab.

DELYN (WALES N.)
E. 53,996 T. 23,194 (42.96%)

Sandy Mewies, Lab.	10,695
Matt Wright, C.	7,814
Carrie Harper, PC	2,918
Michele Jones, LD	1,767

Lab. majority 2,881 (12.42%)
5.03% swing C. to Lab.

DWYFOR MEIRONNYDD (WALES MID
AND W.)
E. 44,669 T. 20,743 (46.44%)

Dafydd Elis-Thomas, PC	9,656
Simon Baynes, C.	4,239
Louise Hughes, Llais Gwynedd	3,225
Martyn Stuart Singleton, Lab.	2,623
Steven William Churchman, LD	1,000

PC majority 5,417 (26.11%)
6.99% swing PC to C.

GOWER (S. WALES WEST)
E. 61,909 T. 26,773 (43.25%)

Edwina Hart, Lab.	12,866
Caroline Jones, C.	8,002
Darren Price, PC	3,249
Peter May, LD	2,656

Lab. majority 4,864 (18.17%)
6.92% swing C. to Lab.

ISLWYN (S. WALES EAST)
E. 54,893 T. 20,908 (38.09%)

Gwyn Price, Lab.	12,116
Steffan Lewis, PC	4,527
David Chipp, C.	2,497
Peter Whalley, BNP	1,115
Tom Sullivan, LD	653

Lab. majority 7,589 (36.30%)
10.09% swing PC to Lab.

LLANELLI (WALES MID AND W.)
E. 58,838 T. 26,070 (44.31%)

Keith Davies, Lab.	10,359
Helen Mary Jones, PC	10,279
Andrew Morgan, C.	2,880
Sian Caiach, Putting Llanelli First	2,004
Cheryl Philpott, LD	548

Lab. majority 80 (0.31%)
7.19% swing PC to Lab.

MERTHYR TYDFIL AND RHYMNEY (S. WALES EAST)
E. 55,031 T. 19,320 (35.11%)

Huw Lewis, Lab.	10,483
Tony Rogers, Ind.	3,432
Amy Kitcher, LD	2,480
Noel Turner, PC	1,701
Chris O'Brien, C.	1,224

Lab. majority 7,051 (36.50%)
0.14% swing Ind. to Lab.

MONMOUTH (S. WALES EAST)
E. 64,857 T. 30,001 (46.26%)

Nick Ramsay, C.	15,087
Mark Whitcutt, Lab.	8,970
Janet Ellard, LD	2,937
Fiona Cross, PC	2,263
Steve Uncles, Eng. Dem.	744

C. majority 6,117 (20.39%)
4.13% swing C. to Lab.

MONTGOMERYSHIRE (WALES MID AND W.)
E. 48,675 T. 22,933 (47.11%)

Russell George, C.	10,026
Wyn Williams, LD	7,702
Nick Colbourne, Lab.	2,609
David Senior, PC	2,596

C. majority 2,324 (10.13%)
9.50% swing LD to C.

NEATH (S. WALES WEST)
E. 57,533 T. 23,849 (41.45%)

Gwenda Thomas, Lab.	12,736
Alun Llewelyn, PC	6,346
Alex Powell, C.	2,780
Michael Green, BNP	1,004
Mathew McCarthy, LD	983

Lab. majority 6,390 (26.79%)
9.54% swing PC to Lab.

NEWPORT EAST (S. WALES EAST)
E. 55,120 T. 19,460 (35.30%)

John Griffiths, Lab.	9,888
Nick Webb, C.	4,500
Ed Townsend, LD	3,703
Chris Paul, PC	1,369

Lab. majority 5,388 (27.69%)
9.11% swing C. to Lab.

NEWPORT WEST (S. WALES EAST)
E. 63,180 T. 23,014 (36.43%)

Rosemary Butler, Lab.	12,011
David Williams, C.	7,791
Lyndon Binding, PC	1,626
Liz Newton, LD	1,586

Lab. majority 4,220 (18.34%)
6.21% swing C. to Lab.

OGMORE (S. WALES WEST)
E. 55,442 T. 20,264 (36.55%)

Janice Gregory, Lab.	12,955
Danny Clark, PC	3,379
Martyn Hughes, C.	2,945
Gerald Francis, LD	985

Lab. majority 9,576 (47.26%)
6.28% swing PC to Lab.

PONTYPRIDD (S. WALES CENTRAL)
E. 60,028 T. 23,333 (38.87%)

Mick Antoniw, Lab.	11,864
Michael Powell, LD	4,170
Joel James, C.	3,659
Ioan Bellin, PC	3,139
Ken Owen, ND	501

Lab. majority 7,694 (32.97%)
9.28% swing LD to Lab.

PRESELI PEMBROKESHIRE (WALES MID AND W.)
E. 57,758 T. 27,218 (47.12%)

Paul Davies, C.	11,541
Terry Mills (Lab.)	9,366
Rhys Sinnett, PC	4,226
Rob Kilmister, LD	2,085

C. majority 2,175 (7.99%)
1.58% swing C. to Lab.

RHONDDA (S. WALES CENTRAL)
E. 52,532 T. 20,027 (38.12%)

Leighton Andrews, Lab.	12,650
Sarah Evans-Fear, PC	5,911
James Jeffreys, C.	969
George Summers, LD	497

Lab. majority 6,739 (33.65%)
2.77% swing PC to Lab.

SWANSEA EAST (S. WALES WEST)
E. 60,246 T. 18,910 (58.36%)

Mike Hedges, Lab.	11,035
Daniel Boucher, C.	2,754
Dic Jones, PC	2,346
Sam Samuel, LD.	1,673
Joanne Shannon, BNP	1,102

Lab. majority 8,281 (43.79%)
6.05% swing C. to Lab.

SWANSEA WEST (S. WALES WEST)
E. 62,345 T. 21,805 (34.97%)

Julie James, Lab.	9,885
Steve Jenkins, C.	5,231
Rob Speht, LD	3,654
Carl Harris, PC	3,035

Lab. majority 4,654 (21.34%)
4.09% swing C. to Lab.

TORFAEN (S. WALES EAST)
E. 61,126 T. 22,328 (36.53%)

Lynne Neagle, Lab.	10,318
Elizabeth Haynes, Ind.	4,230
Natasha Asghar, C.	3,306
Jeff Rees, PC	2,716
Susan Harwood, BNP	906
Will Griffiths, LD	852

Lab. majority 6,088 (27.27%)
0.52% swing Lab. to Ind.

VALE OF CLWYD (WALES N.)
E. 56,232 T. 23,056 (41.00%)

Ann Jones, Lab.	11,691
Ian Gunning, C.	7,680
Alun Lloyd Jones, PC	2,597
Heather Prydderch, LD	1,088

Lab. majority 4,011 (17.40%)
8.49% swing C. to Lab.

VALE OF GLAMORGAN (S. WALES CENTRAL)
E. 71,602 T. 33,254 (46.80%)

Jane Hutt, Lab.	15,746
Angela Jones-Evans, C.	11,971
Ian Johnson, PC	4,024
Damian Chick, LD	1,513

Lab. majority 3,775 (11.35%)
5.55% swing C. to Lab.

WREXHAM (WALES N.)
E. 53,516 T. 18,687 (34.92%)

Lesley Griffiths, Lab.	8,368
John Marek, C.	5,031
Bill Brereton	2,692
Marc Jones, PC	2,596

Lab. majority 3,337 (17.86%)
3.15% swing C. to Lab.

YNYS MON (WALES N.)
E. 49,431 T. 24,067 (48.69%)

Ieuan Wyn Jones, PC	9,969
Paul Williams, C.	7,032
Joe Lock, Lab.	6,307
Rhys Taylor, LD	759

PC majority 2,937 (12.20%)
7.27% swing PC to C.

REGIONS
E. 2,289,555 T. 41.4%

MID AND WEST WALES
E. 433,147 T. 210,352 (48.56%)

PC	56,384	(26.7%)
C.	52,905	(25.1%)
Lab.	47,348	(22.5%)
LD	26,847	(12.7%)
UKIP	9,211	(4.4%)
Green	8,660	(4.1%)
Soc. Lab.	3,951	(1.9%)
BNP	2,821	(1.3%)
Welsh Christian Party	1,630	(0.8%)
Comm. Brit.	595	(0.3%)

PC majority 3,479 (1.65%)
3.25% swing PC to C. (2007 PC majority 17,652)

ADDITIONAL MEMBERS
Rebecca Evans, *Lab.*   William Powell, *LD*
Joyce Watson, *Lab.*   Simon Thomas, *PC*

NORTH WALES
E. 473,296 T. 194,798 (41.16%)

Lab.	62,677	(32.2%)
C.	52,201	(26.8%)
PC	41,701	(21,104)
LD	11,507	(5.9%)
UKIP	9,608	(4.9%)
Soc. Lab.	4,895	(2.5%)
BNP	4,785	(2.5%)
Green	4,406	(2.3%)
Welsh Christian Party	1,401	(0.7%)
Ind.	1,094	(0.6%)
Comm. Brit.	523	(0.3%)

Lab. majority 10,476 (5.38%)
5.05% swing PC to Lab. (2007 Lab. majority 1,273)

ADDITIONAL MEMBERS
Mark Isherwood, *C.*   Aled Roberts, *LD*
Antoinette Sandbach, *C.*   Llyr Huws Griffiths, *PC*

SOUTH WALES CENTRAL
E. 506,293 T. 208,333 (41.15%)

Lab.	85,445	(41.0%)
C.	45,751	(22.0%)
PC	28,606	(13.7%)
LD	16,514	(7.9%)
Green	10,774	(5.2%)
UKIP	8,292	(4.0%)
Soc. Lab.	4,690	(2.3%)
BNP	3,805	(1.8%)
Welsh Christian Party	1,873	(0.9%)
Loony	1,237	(0.6%)
TUSC	830	(0.4%)
Comm. Brit.	516	(0.2%)

Lab. majority 39,694 (19.05%)
6.55% swing LD to C. (2007 Lab. majority 25,652)

ADDITIONAL MEMBERS
David Melding, *C.*   Leanne Wood, *PC*
Andrew Davies, *C.*   John Dixon, *LD*

SOUTH WALES EAST
E. 469,486 T. 181,024 (38.56%)

Lab.	82,699	(45.7%)
C.	35,459	(19.6%)
PC	21,851	(12.1%)
LD	10,798	(6.0%)
UKIP	9,526	(5.3%)
BNP	6,485	(3.6%)
Green	4,857	(2.7%)
Soc. Lab.	4,427	(2.4%)
Welsh Christian Party	2,441	(1.3%)
Eng. Dem.	1,904	(1.1%)
Comm. Brit.	578	(0.3%)

Lab. majority 47,240 (26.10%)
5.95% swing LD to Lab. (2007 Lab. majority 30,063)

ADDITIONAL MEMBERS
William Graham, *C.*   Jocelyn Davies, *PC*
Mohammad Asghar, *C.*   Lindsay Whittle, *PC*

SOUTH WALES WEST
E. 407,333 T. 154,381 (37.90%)

Lab.	71,766	(46.5%)
Con.	27,457	(17.8%)
PC	21,258	(13.8%)
LD	10,683	(6.9%)
UKIP	6,619	(4.3%)
Soc. Lab.	5,057	(3.3%)
BNP	4,714	(3.1%)
Green	3,952	(2.6%)
Welsh Christian Party	1,602	(1.0%)
TUSC	809	(0.5%)
Comm. Brit.	464	(0.3%)

Lab. majority 44,309 (28.70%)
8.10% swing LD to Lab. (2007 Lab. majority 29,528)

ADDITIONAL MEMBERS
Suzy Davies, *C.*   Peter Black, *LD*
Byron Davies, *C.*   Bethan Jenkins, *PC*

SCOTLAND

SCOTTISH GOVERNMENT

St Andrew's House, Regent Road, Edinburgh EH1 3DG
T 0845-774 1741 **Enquiry Line** 0131-556 840
E ceu@scotland.gsi.gov.uk **W** www.scotland.gov.uk

The devolved government for Scotland is responsible for most of the issues of day-to-day concern to the people of Scotland, including health, education, justice, rural affairs and transport.

The Scottish government was known as the Scottish executive when it was established in 1999, following the first elections to the Scottish parliament. The current administration was formed after elections in May 2007.

The government is led by a first minister who is nominated by the parliament and in turn appoints the other Scottish ministers who make up the cabinet.

Civil servants in Scotland are accountable to Scottish ministers, who are themselves accountable to the Scottish parliament.

CABINET

First Minister, Rt. Hon. Alex Salmond, MSP
Deputy First Minister and Cabinet Secretary for Health, Wellbeing and Cities Strategy, Nicola Sturgeon, MSP
Cabinet Secretary for Culture and External Affairs, Fiona Hyslop, MSP
Cabinet Secretary for Education and Lifelong Learning, Michael Russell, MSP
Cabinet Secretary for Finance, Employment and Sustainable Growth, John Swinney, MSP
Cabinet Secretary for Infrastructure and Capital Investment, Alex Neill, MSP
Cabinet Secretary for Justice, Kenny MacAskill, MSP
Cabinet Secretary for Parliamentary Business and Government Strategy, Bruce Crawford, MSP
Cabinet Secretary for Rural Affairs and the Environment, Richard Lochhead, MSP
Minister for Children and Young People, Angela Constance, MSP
Minister for Commonwealth Games and Sport, Shona Robison, MSP
Minister for Community Safety and Legal Affairs (with responsibility for tackling sectarianism), Roseanna Cunningham, MSP
Minister for Energy, Enterprise and Tourism, Fergus Ewing, MSP
Minister for Environment and Climate Change, Stewart Stevenson, MSP
Minister for Housing and Transport, Keith Brown, MSP
Minister for Learning and Skills (with responsibility for Gaelic and Scots), Alasdair Allan, MSP
Minister for Local Government and Planning, Aileen Campbell, MSP
Minister for Parliamentary Business and Chief Whip, Brian Adam, MSP
Minister for Public Health, Michael Matheson, MSP

LAW OFFICERS

Lord Advocate, Frank Mulholland, QC
Solicitor-General for Scotland, Lesley Thomson

STRATEGIC BOARD

Permanent Secretary, Peter Housden
Director-General, Enterprise and Environment, Mike Neilson
Director-General, Finance, Alyson Stafford
Director-General, Governance and Communities, Paul Gray
Director-General, Health and Social Care, Derek Feeley
Director-General, Learning and Justice, Leslie Evans

NON-DEPARTMENTAL AGENCIES

HISTORIC SCOTLAND

Longmore House, Salisbury Place, Edinburgh EH9 1SH
T 0131-668 8600 **W** www.historic-scotland.gov.uk
Chief Executive, Ruth Parsons

NATIONAL RECORDS FOR SCOTLAND

HM General Register House, 2 Princes Street, Edinburgh EH1 3YY
T 0131-535 1314 **E** enquiries@nas.gov.uk
W www.nas.gov.uk
Keeper of the Records of Scotland, George MacKenzie

GOVERNMENT DEPARTMENTS

DIRECTOR-GENERAL ENTERPRISE AND ENVIRONMENT

Victoria Quay, Edinburgh EH6 6QQ
Directorates: Business; Chief Scientific Adviser for Rural Affairs and the Environment; DG Coordination – Enterprise and Environment; Energy and Climate Change; Marine Scotland; Rural and Environment; Rural Payments and Inspections
Director-General, Mike Neilson

EXECUTIVE AGENCY

Transport Scotland

DIRECTOR-GENERAL FINANCE

Victoria Quay, Edinburgh EH6 6QQ
Directorates: CAP and Risk; Corporate Reporting; Financial Policy; Financial Programme Management; Financial Services Division; FISC Responsibility; Internal Audit; Scottish Procurement and Commercial Directorate
Director-General, Alyson Stafford

EXECUTIVE AGENCY

Scottish Public Pensions Agency

DIRECTOR-GENERAL GOVERNANCE AND COMMUNITIES

Saughton House, Broomhouse Drive, Edinburgh, EH11 3XD
Directorates: Built Environment; Culture and Digital; Housing, Regeneration and Commonwealth Games; HR and Organisational Development; International and Constitution; Legal Services; Local Government and the Third Sector; Strategy and Performance; Inspectorate of Prosecution in Scotland; Office of the Scottish Parliamentary Counsel
Director-General, Paul Gray

EXECUTIVE AGENCY

Scottish Housing Regulator

DIRECTOR-GENERAL HEALTH AND SOCIAL CARE

St Andrew's House, Regent Road, Edinburgh EH1 3DG
Directorates: Coordination – Health and Social Care; Chief Medical Officer, Public Health and Sport; Chief Nursing Officer, Patients, Public and Health Professions; Children and Families; Health and Healthcare Improvement; Health and Social Care Integration; Health Delivery; Health Finance and Information; Health Workforce
Director-General Health and Social Care and Chief Executive, Derek Feeley

EXECUTIVE AGENCY
Disclosure Scotland

DIRECTOR-GENERAL LEARNING AND JUSTICE
Victoria Quay, Edinburgh, EH6 6QQ
Directorates: Coordination – Learning and Justice;
Education Analytical Services; Employability, Skills and
Lifelong Learning; Justice; Learning; Office of the
Chief Scientific Adviser; Safer Communities
Director-General, Leslie Evans

EXECUTIVE AGENCIES
Accountant in Bankruptcy
HM Inspectorate of Education
Scottish Prison Service
Student Awards Agency for Scotland

ASSOCIATED BODY
Scottish Courts Service

NON-DEPARTMENTAL OFFICES

AUDIT SCOTLAND
110 George Street, Edinburgh EH2 4LH
T 0845-146 1010 E info@audit-scotland.gov.uk
W www.audit-scotland.gov.uk
Auditor-General, Robert W. Black
Accounts Commission Chair, Prof. John Baillie

CROWN OFFICE AND PROCURATOR FISCAL
SERVICE
25 Chambers Street, Edinburgh EH1 1LA
T 0131-226 2626
Chief Executive and Crown Agent, Catherine Dyer

OFFICE OF THE PERMANENT SECRETARY
St Andrew's House, Regent Road, Edinburgh EH1 3DG
T 0131-556 8400
Permanent Secretary, Sir Peter Housden

SCOTTISH PARLIAMENT
Edinburgh EH99 1SP
T 0131-348 5000 **Textphone** 0800-092 7100
E sp.info@scottish.parliament.uk
W www.scottish.parliament.uk

In July 1997 the government announced plans to
establish a Scottish parliament. In a referendum on 11
September 1997 about 60 per cent of the electorate
voted. Of those who voted, 74.3 per cent voted in favour
of the parliament and 63.5 per cent in favour of it having
tax-raising powers. Elections are held every four years.
The first elections were held on 6 May 1999, when
around 59 per cent of the electorate voted. The first
meeting was held on 12 May 1999 and the Scottish
parliament was officially opened on 1 July 1999 at the
Assembly Hall, Edinburgh. A new building to house
parliament was opened, in the presence of the Queen, at
Holyrood on 9 October 2004. On 5 May 2011 the
fourth elections to the Scottish parliament took place.

The Scottish parliament has 129 members (including
the presiding officer), comprising 73 constituency
members and 56 additional regional members, mainly
from party lists. It can introduce primary legislation and
has the power to raise or lower the basic rate of income
tax by up to three pence in the pound. Members of the
Scottish parliament are elected using the additional
member system, the same system used to elect London
Assembly and Welsh Assembly members.

The areas for which the Scottish parliament is
responsible include: education, health, law, environment,
economic development, local government, housing,
police, fire services, planning, financial assistance to
industry, tourism, some transport, heritage and the arts,
agriculture, social work, sports, public registers and
records, forestry and food standards.

SALARIES *as at 1 May 2011*	
First Minister*	£83,326
Cabinet Secretaries*	£43,227
Lord Advocate*	£56,473
Solicitor-General for Scotland*	£40,837
Ministers*	£27,077
MSPs†	£57,521
Presiding Officer*	£43,227
Deputy Presiding Officer*	£27,077

* In addition to the MSP salary
† Reduced by two-thirds if the member is already an MP or an
MEP

MEMBERS OF THE SCOTTISH PARLIAMENT
as at 5 May 2011
Adam, Brian, *SNP, Aberdeen Donside,* Maj. 7,175
Adam, George, *SNP, Paisley,* Maj. 248
Adamson, Clare, *SNP, Central Scotland region*
Allan, Alisdair, *SNP, Na h-Eileanan an Iar,* Maj. 4,772
Baillie, Jackie, *Lab., Dumbarton,* Maj. 1,639
Baker, Claire, *Lab., Mid Scotland and Fife region*
Baker, Richard, *Lab., North East Scotland region*
Beamish, Claudia, *Lab., South Scotland region*
Beattie, Colin, *SNP, Midlothian North and Musselburgh,*
Maj. 2,996
Biagi, Marco, *SNP, Edinburgh Central,* Maj. 237
Bibby, Neil, *Lab., West Scotland region*
Boyack, Sarah, *Lab., Lothian region*
Brodie, Chic, *SNP, South Scotland region*
Brown, Gavin, *C., Lothian region*
Brown, Keith, *SNP, Clackmannanshire and Dunblane,*
Maj. 3,609
Burgess, Margaret, *SNP, Cunninghame South,* Maj. 2,348
Campbell, Aileen, *SNP, Clydesdale,* Maj. 4,216
Campbell, Roderick, *SNP, North East Fife,* Maj. 2,592
Carlaw, Jackson, *C., West Scotland region*
Chisholm, Malcolm, *Lab., Edinburgh Northern and Leith,*
Maj. 595
Coffey, Willie, *SNP, Kilmarnock and Irvine Valley,*
Maj. 5,993
Constance, Angela, *SNP, Almond Valley,* Maj. 5,542
Crawford, Bruce, *SNP, Stirling,* Maj. 5,671
Cunningham, Roseanna, *SNP, Perthshire South and
Kinross-shire,* Maj. 7,166
Davidson, Ruth, *C., Glasgow region*
Dey, Graeme, *SNP, Angus South,* Maj. 10,583
Don, Nigel, *SNP, Angus North and Mearns,* Maj. 7,286
Doris, Bob, *SNP, Glasgow region*
Dornan, James, *SNP, Glasgow Cathcart,* Maj. 1,592
Dugdale, Kezia, *Lab., Lothian region*
Eadie, Helen, *Lab., Cowdenbeath,* Maj. 1,247
Eadie, Jim, *SNP, Edinburgh Southern,* Maj. 693
Ewing, Annabelle, *SNP, Mid Scotland and Fife region*
Ewing, Fergus, *SNP, Inverness and Nairn,* Maj. 9,745
Fabiani, Linda, *SNP, East Kilbride,* Maj. 1,949
Fee, Mary, *Lab., West Scotland region*
Ferguson, Patricia, *Lab., Glasgow Maryhill and
Springburn,* Maj. 1,252
Fergusson, Alex, *C., Galloway and West Dumfries,,*
Maj. 862

Findlay, Neil, *Lab., Lothian region*
Finnie, John, *SNP, Highlands and Islands region*
FitzPatrick, Joe, *SNP, Dundee City West*, Maj. 6,405
Fraser, Murdo, *C., Mid Scotland and Fife region*
Gibson, Kenneth, *SNP, Cunninghame North*, Maj. 6,117
Gibson, Rob, *SNP, Caithness, Sutherland and Ross*, Maj. 7,458
Goldie, Annabel, *C., West Scotland region*
Grahame, Christine, *SNP, Midlothian South, Tweeddale and Lauderdale*, Maj. 4,924
Grant, Rhoda, *Lab., Highlands and Islands region*
Gray, Iain, *Lab., East Lothian*, Maj. 151
Griffin, Mark, *Lab., Central Scotland region*
Harvie, Patrick, *Green, Glasgow region*
Henry, Hugh, *Lab., Renfrewshire South*, Maj. 2,577
Hepburn, Jamie, *SNP, Cumbernauld and Kilsyth*, Maj. 3,459
Hume, Jim, *LD, South Scotland region*
Hyslop, Fiona, *SNP, Linlithgow*, Maj. 4,091
Ingram, Adam, *SNP, Carrick, Cumnock and Doon Valley*, Maj. 2,581
Johnstone, Alex, *C., North East Scotland region*
Johnstone, Alison, *Green, Lothian region*
Keir, Colin, *SNP, Edinburgh West*, Maj. 2,689
Kelly, James, *Lab., Rutherglen*, Maj. 1,779
Kidd, Bill, *SNP, Glasgow Anniesland*, Maj. 7
Lamont, Johann, *Lab., Glasgow Pollok*, Maj. 623
Lamont, John, *C., Ettrick, Roxburgh and Berwickshire*, Maj. 5,334
Lochhead, Richard, *SNP, Moray*, Maj. 10,944
Lyle, Richard, *SNP, Central Scotland region*
McAlpine, Joan, *SNP, South Scotland region*
McArthur, Liam, *LD, Orkney*, Maj. 860
MacAskill, Kenny, *SNP, Edinburgh Eastern*, Maj. 2,233
McCulloch, Margaret, *Lab., Central Scotland region*
MacDonald, Gordon, *SNP, Edinburgh Pentlands*, Maj. 1,758
Macdonald, Lewis, *Lab., North East Scotland region*
MacDonald, Margo, *Ind., Lothian region*
MacDonald, Angus, *SNP, Falkirk East*, Maj. 3,535
McDonald, Mark, *SNP, North East Scotland region*
McDougall, Margaret, *Lab., West Scotland region*
McGrigor, Jamie, *C., Highlands and Islands region*
McInnes, Alison, *LD, North East Scotland region*
Macintosh, Ken, *Lab., Eastwood*, Maj. 2,012
Mackay, Derek, *SNP Renfrewshire North and West*, Maj. 1,564
McKelvie, Christina, *SNP, Hamilton, Larkhall and Stonehouse*, Maj. 2,213
MacKenzie, Mike, *SNP, Highlands and Islands region*
McLeod, Aileen, *SNP, South Scotland region*
McLeod, Fiona, *SNP, Strathkelvin and Bearsden*, Maj. 1,802
McLetchie, David, *C., Lothian region*
McMahon, Michael, *Lab., Uddingston and Bellshill*, Maj. 714
McMahon, Siobhan, *Lab., Central Scotland region*
McMillan, Stuart, *SNP, West Scotland region*
McNeil, Duncan, *Lab., Greenock and Inverclyde*, Maj. 511
McTaggart, Anne, *Lab., Glasgow region*
Malik, Hanzala, *Lab., Glasgow region*
Marra, Jenny, *Lab., North East Scotland region*
Martin, Paul, *Lab., Glasgow Provan*, Maj. 2,079
Marwick, Tricia, *SNP, Mid Fife and Glenrothes*, Maj. 4,188
Mason, John, *SNP, Glasgow Shettleston*, Maj. 586
Matheson, Michael, *SNP, Falkirk West*, Maj. 5,745
Maxwell, Stewart, *SNP, West Scotland region*
Milne, Nanette, *C., North East Scotland region*

Mitchell, Margaret, *C., Central Scotland region*
Murray, Elaine, *Lab., Dumfriesshire*, Maj. 3,156
Neil, Alex, *SNP, Airdrie and Shotts*, Maj. 2,001
Park, John, *Lab., Mid Scotland and Fife region*
Paterson, Gil, *SNP, Clydebank and Milngavie*, Maj. 714
Pearson, Graeme, *Lab, South Scotland region*
Pentland, John, *Lab., Motherwell and Wishaw*, Maj. 587
Rennie, Willie, *LD, Mid Scotland and Fife region*
Robertson, Dennis, *SNP, Aberdeenshire West*, Maj. 4,112
Robison, Shona, *SNP, Dundee City East*, Maj. 10,679
Russell, Michael, *SNP, Argyll and Bute*, Maj. 8,543
Salmond, Alex, *SNP, Aberdeenshire East*, Maj. 15,295
Scanlon, Mary, *C., Highlands and Islands region*
Scott, John, *C., Ayr*, Maj. 1,113
Scott, Tavish, *LD, Shetland Islands*, Maj. 1,617
Simpson, Richard, *Lab., Mid Scotland and Fife region*
Smith, Drew, *Lab., Glasgow region*
Smith, Elaine, *Lab., Coatbridge and Chryston*, Maj. 2,741
Smith, Liz, *C., Mid Scotland and Fife region*
Stevenson, Stewart, *SNP, Banffshire and Buchan Coast*, Maj. 12,220
Stewart, David, *Lab., Highlands and Islands region*
Stewart, Kevin, *SNP, Aberdeen Central*, Maj. 617
Sturgeon, Nicola, *SNP, Glasgow Southside*, Maj. 4,349
Swinney, John, *SNP, Perthshire North*, Maj. 10,353
Thompson, Dave, *SNP, Skye, Lochaber and Badenoch* Maj. 4,995
Torrance, David, *SNP, Kirkcaldy*, Maj. 182
Urquhart, Jean, *SNP, Highlands and Islands region*
Walker, Bill, *SNP, Dunfermline*, Maj. 590
Watt, Maureen, *SNP, Aberdeen South and North Kincardine*, Maj. 6,323
Wheelhouse, Paul, *SNP, South Scotland region*
White, Sandra, *SNP, Glasgow Kelvin*, Maj. 882
Wilson, John, *SNP, Central Scotland region*
Yousaf, Humza, *SNP, Glasgow region*

STATE OF THE PARTIES
as at 5 May 2011

	Constituency MSPs	Regional MSPs	Total
Scottish National Party (SNP)	52	16	68
Scottish Labour Party (Lab.)	15	22	37
Scottish Conservative and Unionist Party (C.)	3	12	15
Scottish Liberal Democrats (LD)	2	3	5
Scottish Green Party (Green)	0	2	2
Independent (Ind.)	0	1	1
‡Presiding Officer	1	0	1
Total	73	56	129

‡The presiding officer was elected as a constituency member for the SNP but has no party allegiance while in post

The Presiding Officer, Tricia Marwick, MSP
Deputy Presiding Officers, John Scott, MSP *(C.)*; Elaine Smith, MSP *(Lab.)*

SCOTTISH PARLIAMENT ELECTION RESULTS

as at 5 May 2011

E. Electorate T. Turnout

See General Election Results for a list of party abbreviations

CONSTITUENCIES

E. 3,985,161 T. 50.4%

ABERDEEN CENTRAL
(Scotland North East Region)
E. 57,396 T. 25,149 (43.82%)

Kevin Stewart, SNP	10,058
Lewis Macdonald, Lab.	9,441
Sandy Wallace, C.	3,100
Sheila Thomson, LD	2,349
Mike Phillips, NF	201

SNP majority 617 (2.45%)
0.54% swing Lab. to SNP

ABERDEEN DONSIDE
(Scotland North East Region)
E. 56,145 T. 26,761 (47.66%)

Brian Adam, SNP	14,790
Barney Crockett, Lab.	7,615
Ross Thomson, C.	2,166
Millie McLeod, LD.	1,606
David Henderson, Ind.	371
Christopher Willett, NF	213

SNP majority 7,175 (26.81%)
6.87% swing Lab. to SNP

ABERDEEN SOUTH AND KINCARDINE NORTH
(Scotland North East Region)
E. 54,338 T. 28,697 (52.81%)

Maureen Watt, SNP	11,947
Greg Williams, Lab.	5,624
John Sleigh, LD	4,994
Stewart Whyte, C.	4,058

SNP majority 6,323 (22.03%)
15.77% swing LD to SNP

ABERDEENSHIRE EAST
(Scotland North East Region)
E. 57,591 T. 30,286 (52.59%)

Alex Salmond, SNP	19,533
Alison McInnes, LD	4,238
Geordie Burnett Stuart, C.	4,211
Peter Smyth, Lab.	2,304

SNP majority 15,295 (50.5%)
19.53% swing LD to SNP

ABERDEENSHIRE WEST
(Scotland North East Region)
E. 53,779 T. 28,636 (53.25%)

Dennis Robertson, SNP	12,186
Mike Rumbles, LD	8,074
Nanette Milne, C.	6,027
Jean Morrison, Lab.	2,349

SNP majority 4,112 (14.36%)
13.45% swing LD to SNP

AIRDRIE AND SHOTTS
(Scotland Central Region)
E. 51,336 T. 23,894 (46.54%)

Alex Neil, SNP	11,984
Karen Whitefield, Lab.	9,983
Robert Crozier, C.	1,396
John Love, LD	531

SNP majority 2,001 (8.37%)
5.50% swing Lab. to SNP

ALMOND VALLEY
(Lothian Region)
E. 59,896 T. 30,737 (51.32%)

Angela Constance, SNP	16,704
Lawrence Fitzpatrick, Lab.	11,162
Andrew Hardie, C.	1,886
Emma Sykes, LD	656
Neil McIvor, NF	329

SNP majority 5,542 (18.03%)
9.01% swing Lab. to SNP

ANGUS NORTH AND MEARNS
(Scotland North East Region)
E. 52,124 T. 24,920 (47.81%)

Nigel Don, SNP	13,660
Alex Johnstone, C.	6,374
Kevin Hutchens, Lab.	3,160
Sanjay Samani, LD	1,726

SNP majority 7,286 (29.24%)
4.15% swing C. to SNP

ANGUS SOUTH
(Scotland North East Region)
E. 54,922 T. 27,643 (50.33%)

Graeme Dey, SNP	16,164
Hughie Campbell Adamson, C.	5,581
William Campbell, Lab.	3,703
David Fairweather, AIR	1,321
Clive Sneddon, LD	874

SNP majority 10,583 (38.28%)
9.31% swing C. to SNP

ARGYLL AND BUTE
(Highlands and Islands Region)
E. 49,028 T. 26,476 (54.00%)

Michael Russell, SNP	13,390
Jamie McGrigor, C.	4,847
Mick Rice, Lab.	4,041
George Doyle, Ind.	542
George White, Lib.	436

SNP majority 8,543 (32.27%)
8.52% swing C. to SNP

AYR
(Scotland South Region)
E. 61,563 T. 33,373 (54.21%)

John Scott, C.	12,997
Chic Brodie, SNP	11,884
Gordon McKenzie, Lab.	7,779
Eileen Taylor, LD	713

C. majority 1,113 (3.34%)
5.16% swing C. to SNP

BANFFSHIRE AND BUCHAN COAST
(Scotland North East Region)
E. 53,698 T. 25,004 (46.56%)

Stewart Stevenson, SNP	16,812
Michael Watt, C.	4,592
Alan Duffill, Lab.	2,642
Galen Milne, LD	958

SNP majority 12,220 (48.87%)
3.48% swing C. to SNP

CAITHNESS, SUTHERLAND AND ROSS
(Highlands and Islands Region)
E. 55,116 T. 28,600 (51.89%)

Rob Gibson, SNP	13,843
Robbie Rowantree, LD	6,385
John MacKay, Lab.	5,438
Edward Mountain, C.	2,934

SNP majority 7,458 (26.08%)
17.32% swing LD to SNP

CARRICK, CUMNOCK AND DOON VALLEY
(Scotland South Region)
E. 59,368 T. 28,703 (48.35%)

Adam Ingram, SNP	13,250
Richard Leonard, Lab.	10,669
Peter Kennerley, C.	4,160
Andrew Chamberlain, LD	624

SNP majority 2,581 (8.99%)
11.77% Lab. to SNP

CLACKMANNANSHIRE & DUNBLANE
(Mid Scotland and Fife Region)
E. 49, 415 T. 27,416 (55.48%)

Keith Brown, SNP	13,253
Richard Simpson, Lab.	9,644
Callum Campbell, C.	3,501
Tim Brett, LD	1,018

SNP majority 3,609 (13.16%)
5.20% swing Lab. to SNP

CLYDEBANK AND MILNGAVIE
(Scotland West Region)
E. 53,018 T. 28,369 (53.51%)

Gils Paterson, SNP	12,278
Des McNulty, Lab.	11,564
Alice Struthers, C.	2,758
John Duncan, LD	1,769

SD majority 714 (2.52%)
6.56% swing Lab. to SNP

CLYDESDALE
(Scotland South Region)
E. 56,828 T. 29,937 (52.68%)

Aileen Campbell, SNP	14,931
Karen Gillon, Lab.	10,715
Colin McGavigan, C.	4,291

SNP majority 4,216 (14.08%)
8.89% swing Lab. to SNP

COATBRIDGE AND CHRYSTON
(Scotland Central Region)
E. 51,206 T. 23,279 (45.46%)

Elaine Smith, Lab.	12,161
John Wilson, SNP	9,420
Jason Lingiah, C.	1,317
Rod Ackland, LD	381

Lab. majority 2,741 (11.77%)
3.28% swing Lab. to SNP

COWDENBEATH
(Mid Scotland and Fife Region)
E. 54,284 T. 25,670 (47.29%)

Helen Eadie, Lab.	11,926
Ian Chisholm, SNP	10,679
Belinda Don, C.	1,792
Keith Legg, LD	997
Mike Heenan, Land Party	276

Lab. majority 1,247 (4.86%)
4.85% swing Lab. to SNP

CUMBERNAULD AND KILSYTH
(Scotland Central Region)
E. 48,006 T. 25,254 (52.61%)

Jamie Hepburn, SNP	13,595
Cathie Craigie, Lab.	10,136
James Boswell, C.	1,156
Martin Oliver, LD	367

SNP majority 3,459 (13.7%)
10.79% Lab. to SNP

CUNNINGHAME NORTH
(Scotland West Region)
E. 56,548 T. 29,536 (52.23%)

Kenneth Gibson, SNP	15,539
Allan Wilson, Lab.	9,422
Maurice Golden, C.	4,032
Mallika Punukollu, LD	543

SNP majority 6,117 (20.71%)
10.29% swing Lab. to SNP

CUNNINGHAME SOUTH
(Scotland South Region)
E. 50,926 T. 22,056 (43.31%)

Margaret Burgess, SNP	10,993
Irene Oldfather, Lab.	8,645
Alistair Haw, C.	1,871
Ruby Kirkwood, LD	547

SNP majority 2,348 (10.65%)
9.93% swing Lab. to SNP

DUMBARTON
(Scotland West Region)
E. 53,470 T. 28,508 (53.32%)

Jackie Baillie, Lab.	12,562
Iain Robertson, SNP	10,923
Graham Smith, C.	3,395
Helen Watt, LD	858
George Rice, Ind.	770

Lab. majority 1,639 (5.75%)
0.24% swing SNP to Lab.

DUMFRIESSHIRE
(Scotland South Region)
E. 59,716 T. 31,895 (53.41%)

Elaine Murray, Lab.	12,624
Gill Dykes, C.	9,468
Aileen Orr, SNP	8,384
Richard Brodie, LD	1,419

Lab. majority 3,156 (9.89%)
5.99% swing C. to Lab.

DUNDEE EAST
(Scotland North East Region)
E. 54,404 T. 25,753 (47.34%)
Shona Robison, SNP	16,541
Mohammed Asif, Lab.	5,862
Brian Docherty, C.	2,550
Allan Petrie, LD	800

SNP majority 10,679 (41.47%)
12.47% swing Lab. to SNP

DUNDEE WEST
(Scotland North East Region)
E. 53,841 T. 24,461 (45.43%)
Joe Fitzpatrick, SNP	14,089
Richard McCready, Lab.	7,684
Colin Stewart, C.	1,625
Alison Burns, LD	1,063

SNP majority 6,405 (26.18%)
8.88% swing Lab. to SNP

DUNFERMLINE
(Scotland Mid and Fife Region)
E. 55,479 T. 29,299 (52.81%)
Bill Walker, SNP	11,010
Alex Rowley, Lab.	10,420
Jim Tolson, LD	5,776
James Reekie, C.	2,093

SNP majority 599 (2.01%)
13.41% swing LD to SNP

EAST KILBRIDE
(Scotland Central Region)
E. 58,251 T. 29,911 (51.35%)
Linda Fabiani, SNP	14,359
Andy Kerr, Lab.	12,410
Graham Simpson, C.	2,260
Douglas Herbison, LD	468
John Houston, Ind.	414

SNP majority 1,949 (6.52%)
6.64% swing Lab. to SNP

EAST LOTHIAN
(Scotland South Region)
E. 56,333 T. 32,177 (57.12%)
Iain Gray, Lab.	12,536
David Berry, SNP	12,385
Derek Brownlee, C.	5,344
Ettie Spencer, LD	1,912

Lab. majority 151 (0.47%)
3.12% swing Lab. to SNP

EASTWOOD
(Scotland West Region)
E. 50,476 T. 31,924 (63.25%)
Ken Macintosh, Lab.	12,662
Jackson Carlaw, C.	10,650
Stewart Maxwell, SNP	7,777
Gordon Cochrane, LD	835

Lab. majority 2,012 (6.3%)
8.74% swing C. to Lab.

EDINBURGH CENTRAL
(Lothian Region)
E. 53,606 T. 29,014 (54.12%)
Marco Biagi, SNP	9,480
Sarah Boyack, Lab.	9,243
Alex Cole-Hamilton, LD	5,937
Iain McGill, C.	4,354

SNP majority 237 (0.82%)
10.16% swing Lab. to SNP

EDINBURGH EASTERN
(Lothian Region)
E. 55,773 T. 30,728 (55.09%)
Kenny MacAskill, SNP	14,552
Ewan Aitken, Lab.	12,319
Cameron Buchanan, C.	2,630
Martin Veart, LD	1,227

SNP majority 2,233 (7.27%)
4.53% swing Lab. to SNP

EDINBURGH NORTHERN AND LEITH
(Lothian Region)
E. 59,138 T. 30,885 (52.23%)
Malcolm Chisholm, Lab.	12,858
Shirley-Anne Somerville, SNP	12,263
Sheila Low, C.	2,928
Don Farthing, LD	2,836

Lab. majority 595 (1.93%)
2.66% swing Lab. to SNP

EDINBURGH PENTLANDS
(Lothian Region)
E. 52,620 T. 30,049 (57.11%)
Gordon MacDonald, SNP	11,197
David McLetchie, C.	9,439
Ricky Henderson, Lab.	7,993
Simon Clark, LD	1,420

SNP majority 1,758 (5.85%)
7.42% swing C. to SNP

EDINBURGH SOUTHERN
(Lothian Region)
E. 54,868 T. 33,796 (61.60%)
Jim Eadie, SNP	9,947
Paul Godzik, Lab.	9,254
Mike Pringle, LD	8,297
Gavin Brown, C.	6,298

SNP majority 693 (2.05%)
12.06% swing LD to SNP

EDINBURGH WESTERN
(Lothian Region)
E. 56,338 T. 33,452 (59.38%)
Colin Keir, SNP	11,965
Margaret Smith, LD	9,276
Lesley Hinds, Lab.	7,164
Gordon Lindhurst, C.	5,047

SNP majority 2,689 (8.04%)
12.60% swing LD to SNP

ETTRICK, ROXBURGH AND BERWICKSHIRE
(Scotland South Region)
E. 54,327 T. 28,816 (53.04%)

John Lamont, C.	12,933
Paul Wheelhouse, SNP	7,599
Euan Robson, LD	4,990
Rab Stewart, Lab.	2,986
Jesse Rae, Ind.	308

C. majority 5,334 (18.51%)
1.39% swing C. to SNP

FALKIRK EAST
(Scotland Central Region)
E. 56,408 T. 28,168 (49.94%)

Angus MacDonald, SNP	14,302
Cathy Peattie, Lab.	10,767
Lynn Munro, C.	2,372
Ross Laird, LD	727

SNP majority 3,535 (12.55%)
9.33% swing Lab. to SNP

FALKIRK WEST
(Scotland Central Region)
E. 55,739 T. 28,199 (50.59%)

Michael Matheson, SNP	15,607
Dennis Goldie, Lab.	9,862
Allan Finnie, C.	2,086
Callum Chomczuk, LD	644

SNP majority 5,745 (20.37%)
8.91% swing Lab. to SNP

FIFE MID AND GLENROTHES
(Scotland Mid and Fife Region)
E. 53,701 T. 26,313 (49.0%)

Tricia Marwick, SNP	13,761
Claire Baker, Lab.	9,573
Allan Smith, C.	1,676
Jim Parker, ASPP	673
Callum Leslie, LD	630

SNP majority 4,188 (15.92%)
3.43% swing Lab. to SNP

FIFE NORTH EAST
(Scotland Mid and Fife Region)
E. 58,858 T. 29,676 (50.42%)

Roderick Campbell, SNP	11,029
Iain Smith, LD	8,437
Miles Briggs, C.	5,618
Colin Davidson, Lab.	3,613
Mike Scott-Hayward, UKIP	979

SNP majority 2,592 (8.73%)
15.02% swing LD to SNP

GALLOWAY AND WEST DUMFRIES
(Scotland South Region)
E. 56,611 T. 29,997 (52.99%)

Alex Fergusson, C.	11,071
Aileen McLeod, SNP	10,209
Willie Scobie, Lab.	7,954
Joe Rosiejak, LD	763

C. majority 862 (2.87%)
2.40% swing C. to SNP

GLASGOW ANNIESLAND
(Glasgow Region)
E. 55,411 T. 23,918 (43.16%)

Bill Kidd, SNP	10,329
Bill Butler, Lab.	10,322
Matthew Smith, C.	2,011
Paul McGarry, LD	1,000
Marc Livingstone, Comm. Brit.	256

SNP majority 7 (0.03%)
10.09% swing Lab. to SNP

GLASGOW CATHCART
(Glasgow Region)
E. 58,525 T. 26,222 (44.8%)

James Dornan, SNP	11,918
Charlie Gordon, Lab.	10,326
Richard Sullivan, C.	2,410
Eileen Baxendale, LD	1,118
John McKee, Ind.	450

SNP majority 1,592 (6.07%)
6.53% swing Lab. to SNP

GLASGOW KELVIN
(Glasgow Region)
E. 61,893 T. 24,548 (39.66%)

Sandra White, SNP	10,640
Pauline McNeil, Lab.	9,758
Natalie McKee, LD	1,900
Ruth Davidson, C.	1,845
Tom Muirhead, Ind.	405

SNP majority 882 (3.59%)
4.03% swing Lab. to SNP

GLASGOW MARYHILL AND SPRINGBURN
(Glasgow Region)
E. 56,622 T. 20,531 (36.26%)

Patricia Ferguson, Lab.	9,884
Bob Doris, SNP	8,592
Stephanie Murray, C.	1,222
Sophie Bridger, LD	833

Lab. majority 1,292 (6.29%)
5.43% swing Lab. to SNP

GLASGOW POLLOK
(Glasgow Region)
E. 58,429 T. 22,915 (39.22%)

Johann Lamont, Lab.	10,875
Chris Stephens, SNP	10,252
Andrew Morrison, C.	1,298
Isabel Nelson, LD	490

Lab. majority 623 (2.72%)
8.53% swing Lab. to SNP

GLASGOW PROVAN
(Glasgow Region)
E. 55,118 T. 19,185 (34.81%)

Paul Martin, Lab.	10,037
Anne McLaughlin, SNP	7,958
Majid Hussain, C.	777
Michael O'Donnell, LD	413

Lab. majority 2,079 (10.84%)
8.68% swing Lab. to SNP

GLASGOW SHETTLESTON
(Glasgow Region)
E. 55,874 T. 21,204 (37.95%)

John Mason, SNP	10,128
Frank McAveety, Lab.	9,542
David Wilson, C.	1,163
Ruaraidh Dobson, LD	371

SNP majority 586 (2.76%)
12.61% swing Lab. to SNP

GLASGOW SOUTHSIDE
(Glasgow Region)
E. 52,325 T. 22,608 (43.21%)

Nicola Sturgeon, SNP	12,306
Stephen Curran, Lab.	7,957
David Meikle, C.	1,733
Kenneth Elder, LD	612

SNP majority 4,349 (19.24%)
9.68% swing Lab. to SNP

GREENOCK AND INVERCLYDE
(Scotland West Region)
E. 56,989 T. 28,298 (49.50%)

Duncan McNeil, Lab.	12,387
Stuart McMillan, SNP	11,876
Graeme Brooks, C.	2,011
Ross Finnie, LD	1,934

Lab. majority 511 (1.81%)
6.90% swing Lab. to SNP

HAMILTON, LARKHALL AND STONEHOUSE
(Scotland Central Region)
E. 56,123 T. 25,354 (45.18%)

Christina McKelvie, SNP	12,202
Tom McCabe, Lab.	9,989
Margaret Mitchell, C.	2,547
Ewan Hoyle, LD	616

SNP majority 2,213 (8.73%)
10.99% swing Lab. to SNP

INVERNESS & NAIRN
(Highlands and Islands Region)
E. 62,168 T. 32,731 (52.65%)

Fergus Ewing, SNP	16,870
David Stewart, Lab.	7,125
Mary Scanlon, C.	3,797
Christine Jardine, LD	3,763
Donald Boyd, Christian Party	646
Ross Durance, UKIP	530

SNP majority 9,745 (29.77%)
4.85% swing Lab. to SNP

KILMARNOCK AND IRVINE VALLEY
(Scotland Central Region)
E. 63,257 T. 31,858 (50.36%)

Willie Coffey, SNP	16,964
Matt McLaughlin, Lab.	10,971
Grant Fergusson, C.	3,309
Robbie Simpson, LD	614

SNP majority 5,993 (18.81%)
7.40% swing Lab. to SNP

KIRKCALDY
(Scotland Mid and Fife Region)
E. 60,079 T. 27,803 (46.28%)

David Torance, SNP	12,579
Marilyn Livingstone, Lab.	12,397
Ian McFarlane, C.	2,007
John Mainland, LD	820

SNP majority 182 (0.65%)
6.19% swing Lab. to SNP

LINLITHGOW
(Lothian Region)
E. 65,025 T. 34,182 (52.57%)

Fiona Hyslop, SNP	17,027
Mary Mulligan, Lab.	12,936
Christopher Donnelly, C.	2,646
Jennifer Lang, LD	1,015
Mike Coyle, NF	558

SNP majority 4,091 (11.97%)
6.42% swing Lab. to SNP

MIDLOTHIAN NORTH AND MUSSELBURGH
(Lothian Region)
E. 58,246 T. 29,818 (51.19%)

Colin Beattie, SNP	14,079
Bernard Harkins, Lab.	11,083
Scott Douglas, C.	2,541
Ian Younger, LD	1,254
Alan Hay, Ind.	861

SNP majority 2,996 (10.05%)
7.61% swing Lab. to SNP

MIDLOTHIAN SOUTH, TWEEDDALE AND
LAUDERDALE
(Lothian Region)
E. 57,781 T. 31,841 (55.11%)

Christine Grahame, SNP	13,855
Jeremy Purvis, LD	8,931
Ian Miller, Lab.	5,312
Peter Duncan, C.	3,743

SNP majority 4,924 (15.46%)
5.87% swing LD to SNP

MORAY
(Highlands and Islands Region)
E. 56,215 T. 28,596 (50.87%)

Richard Lochhead, SNP	16,817
Douglas Ross, C.	5,873
Kieron Green, Lab.	3,580
Jamie Paterson, LD	1,327
Donald Gatt, UKIP	999

SNP majority 10,944 (38.27%)
6.19% swing C. to SNP

MOTHERWELL AND WISHAW
(Scotland Central Region)
E. 53,610 T. 24,451 (45.61%)

John Pentland, Lab.	10,713
Clare Adamson, SNP	10,126
Bob Burgess, C.	1,753
John Swinburne, ASPP	945
Tom Selfridge, Christian Party	547
Beverley Hope, LD	367

Lab. majority 587 (2.4%)
10.20% swing Lab. to SNP

NA H-EILEANAN AN IAR
(Highlands and Islands Region)
E. 21,834 T. 13,011 (59.59%)

Alasdair Allan, SNP	8,496
Donald Crichton, Lab.	3,724
Charlie McGrigor, C.	563
Peter Morrison, LD	228

SNP majority 4,772 (36.68%)
15.82% swing Lab. to SNP

ORKNEY
(Highlands and Islands Region)
E. 16,393 T. 8,152 (49.73%)

Liam McArthur, LD	2,912
James Stockan, Ind.	2,052
George Adam, SNP	2,044
Jamie Halcro Johnston, C.	686
William Sharkey, Lab.	458

LD majority 860 (10.55%)
17.70% swing LD to Ind.

PAISLEY
(Scotland West Region)
E. 52,066 T. 25,590 (49.15%)

George Adam, SNP	10,913
Evan Williams, Lab.	10,665
Malcolm MacAskill, C.	2,229
Eileen McCartin, LD	1,783

SNP majority 248 (0.97%)
7.80% swing Lab. to SNP

PERTHSHIRE NORTH
(Scotland and Mid Fife Region)
E. 53,412 T. 29,953 (56.08%)

John Swinney, SNP	18,219
Murdo Fraser, C.	7,866
Pete Cheema, Lab.	2,672
Victor Clements, LD	1,196

SNP majority 10,353 (34.56%)
6.53% swing C. to SNP

PERTHSHIRE SOUTH AND KINROSS-SHIRE
(Scotland and Mid Fife Region)
E. 58,093 T. 31,216 (53.73%)

Roseanna Cunningham, SNP	16,073
Liz Smith, C.	8,907
Tricia Duncan, Lab.	3,980
Willie Robertson, LD	2,256

SNP majority 7,166 (22.96%)
9.25% swing C. to SNP

RENFREWSHIRE NORTH AND WEST
(Scotland West Region)
E. 49,060 T. 27,495 (56.04%)

Derek Mackay, SNP	11,510
Stuart Clark, Lab.	9,946
Annabel Goldie, C.	5,489
Andrew Page, LD	550

SNP majority 1,564 (5.69%)
8.42% swing Lab. to SNP

RENFREWSHIRE SOUTH
(Scotland West Region)
E. 50,221 T. 26,908 (53.58%)

Hugh Henry, Lab.	12,933
Andrew Doig, SNP	10,356
Alistair Campbell, C.	2,917
Gordon Anderson, LD	702

Lab. majority 2,577 (9.58%)
5.41% swing Lab. to SNP

RUTHERGLEN
(Glasgow Region)
E. 57,777 T. 27,122 (46.94%)

James Kelly, Lab.	12,489
Jim McGuigan, SNP	10,710
Martyn McIntyre, C.	2,096
Lisa Strachan, LD	1,174
Caroline Johnstone, Ind.	633

Lab. majority 1,779 (6.56%)
7.43% swing Lab. to SNP

SHETLAND ISLANDS
(Highlands and Islands Region)
E. 17,505 T. 9,391 (53.65%)

Tavish Scott, LD	4,462
Billy Fox, Ind.	2,845
Jean Urquhart, SNP	1,134
Jamie Kerr, Lab.	620
Sandy Cross, C.	330

LD majority 1,617 (17.22%)
5.5% swing LD to Ind.

SKYE, LOCHABER AND BADENOCH
(Highlands and Islands Region)
E. 57,024 T. 31,915 (55.97%)

Dave Thompson, SNP	14,737
Alan MacRae, LD	9,742
Linda Stewart, Lab.	4,112
Kerensa Carr, C.	2,834
Ronnie Campbell, Ind.	490

SNP majority 4,995 (15.65%)
12.97% swing LD to SNP

STIRLING
(Scotland and Mid Fife Region)
E. 51,458 T. 30,406 (59.09%)

Bruce Crawford, SNP	14,858
John Hendry, Lab.	9,188
Neil Benny, C.	4,610
Graham Reed, LD	1,296
Jack Black, Ind.	454

SNP majority 5,670 (18.65%)
9.93% swing Lab. to SNP

STRATHKELVIN AND BEARSDEN
(Scotland West Region)
E. 59,323 T. 33,752 (56.90%)

Fiona McLeod, SNP	14,258
David Whitton, Lab.	12,456
Jean Turner, Ind.	6,742
Stephanie Fraser, C.	4,438
Gordon Macdonald, LD	2,600

SNP majority 1,802 (5.34%)
7.69% swing Lab. to SNP

UDDINGSTON AND BELLSHILL
(Central Scotland Region)
E. 55,584 T. 24,995 (44.97%)

Michael McMahon, Lab.	11,531
Richard Lyle, SNP	10,817
Mark Brown, C.	2,117
Fraser Macgregor, LD	530

Lab. majority 714 (2.86%)
9.04% swing Lab. to SNP

REGIONS
E. 3,985,161 T. 50.4%

GLASGOW
E. 514,393 T. 208,712 (40.57%)

SNP	83,109	(39.82%)
Lab.	73,031	(35.0%)
C.	12,749	(6.1%)
Green	12,454	(6.0%)
Respect	6,972	(3.3%)
LD	5,312	(2.5%)
ASPP	3,750	(1.8%)
BNP	2,424	(1.2%)
Socialist Labour	2,276	(1.1%)
Christian Party	1,501	(0.7%)
Scottish Unionist Party	1,447	(0.7%)
SSP	1,362	(0.7%)
UKIP	1,123	(0.5%)
Pirate	581	(0.3%)
Ind. Johnstone	338	(0.2%)
SHP	283	(0.1%)

Lab. majority 10,078 (4.3%)
8.04% swing Lab. to SNP (2007 Lab. majority 23,006)

ADDITIONAL MEMBERS
Humza Yousaf, *SNP*
Bob Doris, *SNP*
Hanzala Malik, *Lab.*
Drew Smith, *Lab.*
Anne McTaggert, *Lab.*
Ruth Davidson, *C.*
Patrick Harvie, *Green*

HIGHLANDS AND ISLANDS
E. 337,588 T. 179,010 (53.03%)

SNP	85,082	(47.5%)
Lab.	25,884	(14.5%)
C.	21,729	(12.1%)
LD	20,843	(11.6%)
Green	9,076	(5.1%)
Christian Party	3,541	(2%)
UKIP	3,372	(1.9%)
ASPP	2,770	(1.5%)
Ban Bankers Bonuses	1,764	(1%)
Lib.	1,696	(0.9%)
Soc. Lab.	1,406	(0.8%)
BNP	1,134	(0.6%)
SSP	509	(0.3%)
Solidarity	204	(0.1%)

SNP majority 59,198 (33.07%)
8.16% swing Lab. to SNP (2007 SNP majority 26,978)

ADDITIONAL MEMBERS
John Finnie, *SNP*
Jean Urquhart, *SNP*
Mike MacKenzie, *SNP*
Rhoda Grant, *Lab.*
David Stewart, *Lab.*
Jamie McGrigor, *C.*
Mary Scanlon, *C.*

LOTHIAN
E. 515,978 T. 283,203 (54.89%)

SNP	110,953	(39.2%)
Lab.	70,544	(24.9%)
C.	33,019	(11.7%)
Green	21,505	(7.6%)
LD	15,588	(5.5%)
ASPP	3,218	(1.1%)
BNP	1,978	(0.7%)
UKIP	1,822	(0.6%)
Soc. Lab.	1,681	(0.6%)
SSP	1,183	(0.4%)
Christian Party	914	(0.3%)
Lib.	697	(0.2%)
CPA	553	(0.2%)
Solidarity	327	(0.1%)
Ind. Hogg	294	(0.1%)
Ind. O'Neill	134	(0.1%)
Ind. Brown	61	(0.1%)

SNP majority 40,409 (14.27%)
7.03% swing Lab. to SNP (2007 SNP majority 524)

ADDITIONAL MEMBERS
Sarah Boyack, *Lab.*
Kezia Dugdale, *Lab.*
Neil Findlay, *Lab.*
David McLetchie, *C.*
Gavin Brown, *C.*
Alison Johnstone, *Green*
Margo MacDonald, *Ind.*

SCOTLAND CENTRAL
E. 497,737 T. 233,560 (46.92%)

SNP	108,261	(46.4%)
Lab.	82,459	(35.3%)
C.	14,870	(6.4%)
ASPP	5,793	(2.5%)
Green	5,634	(2.4%)
LD	3,318	(1.4%)
Christian Party	3,173	(1.4%)
Soci. Lab.	2,483	(1.1%)
BNP	2,214	(0.9%)
Scottish Unionist Party	1,555	(0.7%)
UKIP	1,263	(0.5%)
Ind. O'Donnell	821	(0.4%)
SSP	820	(0.4%)
Solidarity	559	(0.2%)
SHP	337	(0.1%)

Lab. majority 25,802 (11.05%)
10.08% swing Lab. to SNP (2007 Lab. majority 23,386)

ADDITIONAL MEMBERS
Richard Lyle, *SNP*
John Wilson, *SNP*
Claire Adamson, *SNP*
Siobhan McMahon, *Lab.*
Mark Griffin, *Lab.*
Margaret McCulloch, *Lab.*
Margaret Mitchell, *C.*

SCOTLAND MID AND FIFE
E. 503,559 T. 258,163 (51.27%)

SNP	116,691	(25.0%)
Lab.	64,623	(26.3%)
C.	36,458	(14.1%)
LD	15,103	(5.9%)
Green	10,914	(4.2%)
ASPP	4,113	(1.6%)
UKIP	2,838	(1.1%)
Soc. Lab.	1,771	(0.7%)
BNP	1,726	(0.7%)
Ind. Rodger	1,466	(0.6%)
SSP	834	(0.3%)
Christian Party	786	(0.3%)
CPA	638	(0.2%)
Solidarity	202	(0.1%)

SNP majority 52,068 (20.17%)
7.43% swing Lab. to SNP (2007 Lab. majority 18,168)

ADDITIONAL MEMBERS
Annabelle Ewing, SNP
John Park, Lab.
Claire Brennan-Baker, Lab.
Richard Simpson, Lab.
Murdo Fraser, C.
Elizabeth Smith, C.
Willie Rennie, LD

SCOTLAND NORTH EAST
E. 550,162 T. 267,045 (48.54%)

SNP	140,749	(52.7%)
Lab.	43,893	(16.4%)
C.	37,681	(14.1%)
LD	18,178	(6.8%)
Green	10,407	(3.9%)
ASPP	4,420	(1.7%)
UKIP	2,477	(0.9%)
Christian Party	2,159	(0.8%)
BNP	1,925	(0.7%)
Soc. Lab.	1,459	(0.5%)
Ind. Cox	758	(0.3%)
NF	640	(0.2%)
AIR	471	(0.2%)
Solidarity	286	(0.1%)
Ind. Henderson	237	(0.1%)
Ind. McBride	190	(0.1%)

SNP majority 96,856 (36.27%)
7.68% swing Lab. to SNP (2007 SNP majority 53,140)

ADDITIONAL MEMBERS
Mark McDonald, SNP
Richard Baker, Lab.
Jenny Marra, Lab.
Lewis McDonald, Lab.
Alex Johnstone, C.
Nanette Milne, C.
Alison McInnes, LD

SCOTLAND SOUTH
E. 529,682 T. 278,987 (52.67%)

SNP	114,270	(41.0%)
Lab.	70,595	(25.3%)
C.	54,352	(19.5%)
LD	15,096	(5.4%)
Green	8,656	(3.1%)
ASPP	4,418	(1.6%)
UKIP	3,243	(1.2%)
Soc. Lab.	2,906	(1.0%)
BNP	2,017	(0.7%)
Christian Party	1,924	(0.7%)
Solidarity	813	(0.3%)
SSP	697	(0.2%)

SNP majority 43,675 (15.66%)
7.95% swing Lab. to SNP (2007 Lab. majority 2,709)

ADDITIONAL MEMBERS
Joan McAlpine, SNP
Aileen McLeod, SNP
Paul Wheelhouse, SNP
Chic Brodie, SNP
Claudia Beamish, Lab.
Graeme Pearson, Lab.
Jim Hume, LD

SCOTLAND WEST
E. 536,062 T. 282,371 (52.68%)

SNP	117,306	(32.8%)
Lab.	92,530	(32.8%)
C.	35,995	(12.7%)
LD	9,148	(3.2%)
Green	8,414	(3.0%)
ASPP	4,771	(1.7%)
Soc. Lab.	2,865	(1.0%)
Christian Party	2,468	(0.9%)
BNP	2,162	(0.8%)
UKIP	2,000	(0.7%)
SSP	1,752	(0.6%)
Ban Bankers Bonuses	1,204	(0.4%)
Pirate	850	(0.3%)
Ind. Vassie	460	(0.2%)
Solidarity	446	(0.2%)

SNP majority 24,776 (8.77%)
7.4% swing Lab. to SNP (2007 Lab. majority 15,772)

ADDITIONAL MEMBERS
Stewart Maxwell, SNP
Stuart McMillan, SNP
Mary Fee, Lab.
Neil Bibby, Lab.
Margaret McDougall, Lab.
Annabel Goldie, C.
Jackson Carlaw, C.

NORTHERN IRELAND

NORTHERN IRELAND EXECUTIVE

Stormont Castle, Stormont, Belfast BT4 3TT
T 028-9052 0700
W www.northernireland.gov.uk

The first minister and deputy first minister head the executive committee of ministers and, acting jointly, determine the total number of ministers in the executive. First and deputy first ministers are elected by Northern Ireland assembly members through a formula of parallel consent that requires a majority of designated unionists, a majority of designated nationalists and a majority of the whole assembly to vote in favour. The parties elected to the assembly select ministerial portfolios in proportion to party strengths using the d'Hondt nominating procedure.

The executive committee includes five DUP ministers, four SF ministers, two Alliance members, one Social Democratic and Labour Party minister and one Ulster Unionist minister alongside the first minister Peter Robinson, MLA of the DUP and the deputy first minister, Martin McGuinness, MLA, of SF.

EXECUTIVE COMMITTEE
First Minister, Rt. Hon. Peter Robinson, MLA
Deputy First Minister, Martin McGuinness, MP, MLA
Junior Ministers, Martina Anderson, MLA; Jonathan Bell, MLA
Minister for Agriculture and Rural Development, Michelle O'Neill, MLA
Minister for Culture, Arts and Leisure, Carai ni Chuilin, MLA
Minister for Education, John O'Dowd, MLA
Minister for Employment and Learning, Dr Stephen Farry, MLA
Minister for Enterprise, Trade and Investment, Arlene Foster, MLA
Minister for Environment, Alex Atwood, MLA
Minister for Finance and Personnel, Sammy Wilson, MP, MLA
Minister for Health, Social Services and Public Safety, Edwin Poots, MLA
Minister for Justice, David Ford, MLA
Minister for Regional Development, Danny Kennedy, MLA
Minister for Social Development, Nelson McCausland, MLA

OFFICE OF THE FIRST MINISTER AND DEPUTY FIRST MINISTER
Stormont Castle, Stormont, Belfast BT4 3TT
T 028-9052 8400 W www.ofmdfmni.gov.uk

DEPARTMENT OF AGRICULTURE AND RURAL DEVELOPMENT
Dundonald House, Upper Newtownards Road, Belfast BT4 3SB
T 028-9052 4420 W www.dardni.gov.uk

EXECUTIVE AGENCIES
Forest Service
Rivers Agency

DEPARTMENT OF CULTURE, ARTS AND LEISURE
Causeway Exchange, 1–7 Bedford Street, Belfast BT1 7FB
T 028-9025 8825 W www.dcalni.gov.uk

DEPARTMENT OF EDUCATION
Rathgael House, Balloo Road, Bangor, Co. Down BT19 7PR
T 028-9127 9279 W www.deni.gov.uk

DEPARTMENT FOR EMPLOYMENT AND LEARNING
Adelaide House, 39–49 Adelaide Street, Belfast BT2 8FD
T 028-9025 7777 W www.delni.gov.uk

DEPARTMENT OF ENTERPRISE, TRADE AND INVESTMENT
Netherleigh, Massey Avenue, Belfast BT4 2JP T 028-9052 9900
W www.detini.gov.uk

EXECUTIVE AGENCIES
General Consumer Council for Northern Ireland
Health and Safety Executive
Invest Northern Ireland
Northern Ireland Tourist Board

DEPARTMENT OF THE ENVIRONMENT
Clarence Court, 10–18 Adelaide Street, Belfast BT2 8GB
T 028-9054 0540 W www.doeni.gov.uk

EXECUTIVE AGENCIES
Driver and Vehicle Agency (Northern Ireland)
NI Environment Agency
Planning Service

DEPARTMENT OF FINANCE AND PERSONNEL
Rathgael House, Balloo Road, Bangor BT19 7PR
T 028-9185 8111 W www.dfpni.gov.uk

EXECUTIVE AGENCIES
Land and Property Services
Northern Ireland Statistics and Research Agency (Incorporates Land Registers of Northern Ireland and Ordnance Survey of Northern Ireland)

DEPARTMENT OF HEALTH, SOCIAL SERVICES AND PUBLIC SAFETY
Castle Buildings, Stormont, Belfast BT4 3SJ T 028-9052 0500
W www.dhsspsni.gov.uk

DEPARTMENT FOR REGIONAL DEVELOPMENT
Clarence Court, 10–18 Adelaide Street, Belfast BT2 8GB
T 028-9054 0540 W www.drdni.gov.uk

EXECUTIVE AGENCY
Roads Agency

DEPARTMENT FOR SOCIAL DEVELOPMENT
Lighthouse Building, 1 Cromac Place, Gasworks Business Park, Ormeau Road, Belfast BT7 2JB T 028-9082 9028
W www.dsdni.gov.uk

EXECUTIVE AGENCIES
Northern Ireland Housing Executive
Social Security Agency

DEPARTMENT OF JUSTICE
Block B, Castle Buildings, Stormont Estate, Belfast BT4 3SG
T 028-9076 3000 W www.dojni.gov.uk

EXECUTIVE AGENCIES
Compensation Agency
Forensic Science Agency
Northern Ireland Courts and Tribunals Service
Northern Ireland Prison Service
Youth Justice Agency

NORTHERN IRELAND AUDIT OFFICE

106 University Street, Belfast BT7 1EU
T 028-9025 1000 E info@niauditoffice.gov.uk
W www.niauditoffice.gov.uk
Comptroller and Auditor-General, Kieran Donnelly

NORTHERN IRELAND AUTHORITY FOR UTILITY REGULATION

Queens House, 14 Queen Street, Belfast BT1 6ED
T 028-9031 1575 E info@uregni.gov.uk W www.uregni.gov.uk
Chair, Prof. Peter Matthews

NORTHERN IRELAND ASSEMBLY

Parliament Buildings, Stormont, Belfast BT4 3XX
T 028-9052 1137 E info@niassembly.gov.uk
W www.niassembly.gov.uk

The Northern Ireland Assembly was established as a result of the Belfast Agreement (also known as the Good Friday Agreement) in April 1998. The agreement was endorsed through a referendum held in May 1998 and subsequently given legal force through the Northern Ireland Act 1998.

The Northern Ireland Assembly has full legislative and executive authority for all matters that are the responsibility of the government's Northern Ireland departments – known as transferred matters. Excepted and reserved matters are defined in schedules 2 and 3 of the Northern Ireland Act 1998 and remain the responsibility of UK parliament.

The first assembly election occurred on 25 June 1998 and the 108 members elected met for the first time on 1 July 1998. Members of the Northern Ireland Assembly are elected by the single transferable vote system from 18 constituencies – six per constituency. Under the single transferable vote system every voter has a single vote that can be transferred from one candidate to another. Voters number their candidates in order of preference. Where candidates reach their quota of votes and are elected, surplus votes are transferred to other candidates according to the next preference on each voter's ballot slip. The candidate in each round with the fewest votes is eliminated and their surplus votes are redistributed according to the voter's next preference. The process is repeated until the required number of members are elected.

On 29 November 1999 the assembly appointed ten ministers as well as the chairs and deputy chairs for the ten statutory departmental committees. Devolution of powers to the Northern Ireland Assembly occurred on 2 December 1999, following several delays concerned with Sinn Fein's inclusion in the executive while Irish Republican Army (IRA) weapons were yet to be decommissioned.

Since the devolution of powers, the assembly has been suspended by the Secretary of State for Northern Ireland on four occasions. The first was between 11 February and 30 May 2000, with two 24-hour suspensions on 10 August and 22 September 2001 – all owing to a lack of progress in decommissioning. The final suspension took place on 14 October 2002 after unionists walked out of the executive following a police raid on Sinn Fein's office investigating alleged intelligence gathering.

The assembly was formally dissolved in April 2003 in anticipation of an election, which eventually took place on 26 November 2003. The results of the election changed the balance of power between the political parties, with an increase in the number of seats held by the Democratic Unionist Party (DUP) and Sinn Fein (SF), so that they became the largest parties. The assembly was restored to a state of suspension following the November election while political parties engaged in a review of the Belfast Agreement aimed at fully restoring the devolved institutions.

In July 2005 the leadership of the IRA formally ordered an end to its armed campaign; it authorised a representative to engage with the Independent International Commission on Decommissioning in order to verifiably put the arms beyond use. On 26 September 2005 General John de Chastelain, the chair of the commission, along with two independent church witnesses confirmed that the IRA's entire arsenal of weapons had been decommissioned.

Following the passing of the Northern Ireland Act 2006 the secretary of state created a non-legislative fixed-term assembly, whose membership consisted of the 108 members elected in the 2003 election. It first met on 15 May 2006 with the remit of making preparations for the restoration of devolved government; its discussions informed the next round of talks called by the British and Irish governments held at St Andrews. The St Andrews agreement of 13 October 2006 led to the establishment of the transitional assembly.

The Northern Ireland (St Andrews Agreement) Act 2006 set out a timetable to restore devolution, and also set the date for the third election to the assembly as 7 March 2007. The DUP and SF again had the largest number of Members of the Legislative Assembly (MLAs) elected, and although the initial restoration deadline of 26 March was missed, the leaders of the DUP and SF (Revd Dr Ian Paisley, MP, MLA and Gerry Adams, MLA, respectively) took part in a historic meeting and made a joint commitment to establish an executive committee in the assembly to which devolved powers were restored on 8 May 2007. After completing a full four-year mandate, new assembly elections took place on 5 May 2011 to elect the 108 members of the legislative assembly.

SALARIES *as at May 2011*

Assembly Member	£43,101

NORTHERN IRELAND ASSEMBLY MEMBERS

as at May 2011

Agnew, Steven, *Green, North Down*
Allister, Jim, *TUV, North Antrim*
Anderson, Martina, *SF, Foyle*
Anderson, Sydney, *DUP, Upper Bann*
Attwood, Alex, *SDLP, Belfast West*
Beggs, Roy, *UUP, East Antrim*
Bell, Jonathan, *DUP, Strangford*
Boylan, Cathal, *SF, Newry and Armagh*
Boyle, Michaela, *SF, West Tyrone*
Bradley, Dominic, *SDLP, Newry and Armagh*
Bradley, Paula, *SDLP, South Down*
Brady, Mickey, *SF, Newry and Armagh*
Buchanan, Thomas, *DUP, West Tyrone*
Byrne, Joe, *SDLP, West Tyrone*
Campbell, Gregory, *DUP, East Londonderry*
Clarke, Trevor, *DUP, South Antrim*
Clarke, Willie, *SF, South Down*
Cochrane, Judith, *Alliance, Belfast East*
Copeland, Michael, *UUP, Belfast East*
Craig, Jonathan, *DUP, Lagan Valley*
Cree, Leslie, *UUP, North Down*
Dallat, John, *SDLP, East Londonderry*

Dickson, Stewart, *Alliance, East Antrim*
Dobson, Jo-Anne, *UUP, Upper Bann*
Doherty, Pat, *SF, West Tyrone*
Douglas, Sammy, *DUP, Belfast East*
Dunne, Gordon, *DUP, North Down*
Durkan, Mark, *SDLP, Foyle*
Easton, Alex, *DUP, North Down*
Eastwood, Colum, *SDLP, Foyle*
Elliot, Tom, *UUP, Fermanagh and South Tyrone*
Farry, Stephen, *Alliance, North Down*
Flanagan, Phil, *SF, Fermanagh and South Tyrone*
Ford, David, *Alliance, South Antrim*
Foster, Arlene, *DUP, Fermanagh and South Tyrone*
Frew, Paul, *DUP, North Antrim*
Gardiner, Samuel, *UUP, Upper Bann*
Gildernew, Michelle, *SF, Fermanagh and South Tyrone*
Girvan, Paul, *DUP, South Antrim*
Givan, Paul, *DUP, Lagan Valley*
Hale, Brenda, *DUP, Lagan Valley*
Hamilton, Simon, *DUP, Strangford*
Hay, William, *DUP, Foyle*
Hilditch, David, *DUP, East Antrim*
Humphrey, William, *DUP, Belfast North*
Hussey, Ross, *UUP, West Tyrone*
Irwin, William, *DUP, Newry and Armagh*
Kelly, Dolores, *SDLP, Upper Bann*
Kelly, Gerry, *SF, Belfast North*
Kennedy, Danny, *UUP, Newry and Armagh*
Kinahan, Danny, *UUP, South Antrim*
Lewis, Pam, *DUP, South Antrim*
Lo, Anna, *Alliance, Belfast South*
Lunn, Trevor, *Alliance, Lagan Valley*
Lyttle, Chris, *Alliance, Belfast East*
Lynch, Sean, *SDLP, Fermanagh and South Tyrone*
Maginness, Alban, *SDLP, Belfast North*
Maskey, Alex, *SF, Belfast South*
Maskey, Paul, *SF, Belfast West*
McCallister, John, *UUP, South Down*
McCann, Fra, *SF,Belfast West*
McCann, Jennifer, *SF, Belfast West*
McCarthy, Kieran, *Alliance, Strangford*
McCartney, Raymond, *SF, Foyle*
McCausland, Nelson, *DUP, Belfast North*
McClarty, David, *UUP, East Londonderry*
McCrea, Basil, *UUP, Lagan Valley*
McCrea, Ian, *DUP, Mid Ulster*
McDevitt, Conall, *SDLP, Belfast South*
McDonnell, Dr Alasdair, *SDLP, Belfast South*
McElduff, Barry, *SF, West Tyrone*
McGimpsey, Michael, *UUP, Belfast South*
McGlone, Patsy, *SDLP, Mid Ulster*
McGuinness, Martin, *SF, Mid Ulster*
McIlveen, David, *DUP, North Antrim*
McIlveen, Michelle, *DUP, Strangford*
McKay, Daithi, *SF, North Antrim*
McKevitt, Karen, *SDLP, South Down*
McLaughlin, Mitchel, *SF, South Antrim*
McMullan, Oliver, *SF, East Antrim*
McNarry, David, *UUP, Strangford*
McQuillan, Adrian, *DUP, East Londonderry*
Molloy, Francie, *SF, Mid Ulster*
Morrow, Lord, *DUP, Fermanagh and South Tyrone*
Moutray, Stephen, *DUP, Upper Bann*
Murphy, Conor, *SF, Newry and Armagh*
Nesbitt, Mike, *UUP, Strangford*
Newton, Robin, *DUP, Belfast East*
Ni Chuilin, Caral, *SF, Belfast North*
O'Dowd, John, *SF, Upper Bann*

O hOisin, Cathal, *SF, East Londonderry*
O'Neill, Michelle, *SF, Mid Ulster*
Overend, Sandra, *UUP, Mid Ulster*
Poots, Edwin, *DUP, Lagan Valley*
Ramsey, Pat, *SDLP, Foyle*
Ramsey, Sue, *SF, Belfast West*
Ritchie, Margaret, *SDLP, South Down*
Robinson, George, *DUP, East Londonderry*
Robinson, Peter, *DUP, Belfast East*
Ross, Alastair, *DUP, East Antrim*
Ruane, Caitriona, *SF, South Down*
Sheehan, Pat, *SF, Belfast West*
Spratt, Jimmy, *DUP, Belfast South*
Storey, Mervyn, *DUP, North Antrim*
Swann, Robin, *UUP, North Antrim*
Weir, Peter, *DUP, North Down*
Wells, Jim, *DUP, South Down*
Wilson, Sammy, *DUP, East Antrim*

STATE OF THE PARTIES *as at May 2011*

Party	Seats
Democratic Unionist Party (DUP)	38
Sinn Fein (SF)	29
Ulster Unionist Party (UUP)	16
Social Democratic and Labour Party (SDLP)	14
Alliance Party (Alliance)	8
Green Party	1
Independent (Ind.)	1
Traditional Unionist Voice (TUV)	1
Total	108

NORTHERN IRELAND ASSEMBLY ELECTION RESULTS
As at 5 May 2011
E. 1,210,009 T. 55.64%

E. Electorate T. Turnout
First = first-preference votes
Final = final total for that candidate, after all necessary transfers of lower-preference votes
R. = round
* = eliminated last
See General Election Results for a list of party abbreviations

ANTRIM EAST
E. 61,617 T. 29,430 (47.76%)

	First	Final	Elected (R.)
Sammy Wilson, DUP	7,181	7,181	First (1)
David Hilditch, DUP	3,288	4,219	Second (2)
Roy Beggs, UUP	3,042	4,194	Fifth (9)
Stewart Dickson, Alliance	2,889	4,777	Fourth (9)
Oliver McMullan, SF	2,369	3,389	Sixth (10)
*Rodney McCune, UUP	1,851	2,890	
Gerardine Mulvenna, Alliance	1,620		
Alastair Ross, DUP	1,608	4,267	Third (6)
Ruth Wilson, TUV	1,346		
Justin McCamphill, SDLP	1,333		
Gordon Lyons, DUP	1,321		
Daniel Donnelly, Green	664		
Steven Moore, BNP	511		

ANTRIM NORTH
E. 74,760 T. 40,983 (54.82%)

	First	Final	Elected (R.)
Paul Frew, DUP	6,581	6,581	First (1)
Daithi McKay, SF	6,152	6,152	Second (1)
Mervyn Storey, DUP	6,083	6,083	Third (1)
Jim Allister, TUV	4,061	5,430	Sixth (9)
*Declan O'Loan, SDLP	3,682	4,816	
David McIlveen, DUP	3,275	6,594	Fourth (8)
Evelyne Robinson, DUP	3,256		
Robin Swann, UUP	2,518	5,557	Fifth (9)
Bill Kennedy, UUP	2,189		
Jayne Dunlop, Alliance	1,848		
Audrey Patterson, TUV	668		

ANTRIM SOUTH
E. 65,231 T. 32,652 (50.06%)

	First	Final	Elected (R.)
Paul Girvan, DUP	4,844	4,844	First (1)
Mitchel McLaughlin, SF	4,662	4,662	Second (1)
Trevor Clarke, UUP	4,607	4,607	Third (1)
David Ford, Alliance	4,554	4,660	Fourth (2)
Danny Kinahan, UUP	3,445	5,585	Fifth (3)
*Thomas Burns, SDLP	3,406	3,591	
Pam Lewis, DUP	2,866	4,668	Sixth (4)
Adrian Cochrane-Watson, UUP	2,285		
Mel Lucas, TUV	1,091		
Stephen Parkes, BNP	404		

BELFAST EAST
E. 61,263 T. 32,828 (53.59%)

	First	Final	Elected (R.)
Peter Robinson, DUP	9,149	9,149	First (1)
Judith Cochrane, Alliance	4,329	4,755	Third (7)
Chris Lyttle, Alliance	4,183	4,696	Fourth (9)
Sammy Douglas, DUP	2,668	4,783	Fifth (11)
Robin Newton, DUP	2,436	4,801	Second (2)
Michael Copeland, UUP	2,194	3,723	Sixth (11)
*Dawn Purvis, Ind.	1,702	2,789	
Brian Ervine, PUP	1,493		
Niall O'Donnghaile, SF	1,030		
Philip Robinson, UUP	943		
Harry Toan, TUV	712		
Martin Gregg, Green	572		
Ann Cooper, BNP	337		
Magdalena Wolska, SDLP	250		
Tommy Black, SP	201		
Kevin McNally, WP	102		
Stephen Stewart, Ind.	46		

BELFAST NORTH
E. 68,119 T. 34,280 (50.32%)

	First	Final	Elected (R.)
Gerry Kelly, SF	6,674	6,674	First (1)
Nelson McCausland, DUP	5,200	5,200	Second (1)
Alban Maginness, SDLP	4,025	5,004	Fourth (6)
William Humphrey, DUP	3,724	4,332	Fifth (7)
Paula Bradley, DUP	3,488	4,065	Sixth (7)
Caral Ni Chuilin, SF	2,999	4,868	Third (6)
*Fred Cobain, UUP	2,758	3,623	
Billy Webb, Alliance	2,096		
Raymond McCord, Ind.	1,176		
JJ Magee, SF	998		
John Lavery, WP	332		

BELFAST SOUTH
E. 62,484 T. 32,752 (52.42%)

	First	Final	Elected (R.)
Anna Lo, Alliance	6,390	6,390	First (1)
Dr Alasdair McDonnell, SDLP	4,527	4,916	Second (2)
Jimmy Spratt, DUP	4,045	4,281	Sixth (5)
Alex Maskey, SF	4,038	4,452	Fourth (5)
*Ruth Patterson, DUP	3,800	4,163	
Connall McDevitt, SDLP	3,191	4,445	Fifth (5)
Michael McGimpsey, UUP	2,988	4,622	Third (5)
Mark Finlay, UUP	1,394		
Claire Bailey, Green	889		
Brian Faloon, PBP	414		
Paddy Meehan, SP	234		
Nico Torregrosa, UKIP	234		
Paddy Lynn, WP	135		
Charles Smyth, Pro-Capitalism	29		

BELFAST WEST
E. 61,520 T. 35,618 (57.89%)

	First	Final	Elected (R.)
Paul Maskey, SF	5,343	5,343	First (1)
Jennifer McCann, SF	5,239	5,239	Second (1)
Fra McCann, SF	4,481	5,167	Third (10)
Sue Ramsey, SF	4,116	4,823	Fifth (11)
Alex Atwood, SDLP	3,765	5,152	Fourth (10)
Pat Sheehan, SF	3,723	4,327	Sixth (11)
*Brian Kingston, DUP	2,587	3,867	
Gerry Carroll, PBP	1,661		
Bill Manwaring, UUP	1,471		
Colin Keenan, SDLP	802		
John Lowry, WP	586		
Pat Lawlor, SP	384		
Dan McGuinness, Alliance	365		
Brian Pelan, Ind.	122		

DOWN NORTH
E. 62,170 T. 28,528 (45.89%)

	First	Final	Elected (R.)
Alex Easton, DUP	5,175	5,175	First (1)
Gordon Dunne, DUP	3,741	4,121	Second (2)
Peter Weir, DUP	3,496	4,101	Third (2)
Stephen Farry, Alliance	3,131	4,078	Fourth (10)
Steven Agnew, Green	2,207	3,229	Sixth (11)
*Anne Wilson, Alliance	2,100	3,130	
Alan McFarland, Ind.	1,879		
Alan Chambers, Ind.	1,765		
Leslie Cree, UUP	1,585	4,015	Fifth (10)
Colin Breen, UUP	1,343		
Liam Logan, SDLP	768		
Fred McGlade, UKIP	615		
Conor Keenan, SF	293		

DOWN SOUTH
E. 73,240 T. 42,551 (58.10%)

	First	Final	Elected (R.)
Margaret Ritchie, SDLP	8,506	8,506	First (1)
Catriona Ruane, SF	5,955	6,192	Second (2)
Jim Wells, DUP	5,200	6,543	Third (5)
John McCallister, UUP	4,409	6,240	Fourth (6)
Willie Clarke, SF	3,882	6,777	Fifth (7)
Karen McKevitt, SDLP	3,758	5,347	Sixth (9)
Naomi Bailie, SF	3,050		
*Eamonn O'Neill, SDLP	2,663	4,883	
Henry Reilly, UKIP	2,332		
Cadogan Enright, Green	1,107		
David Griffin, Alliance	864		

FERMANAGH AND SOUTH TYRONE
E. 70,985 T. 48,949 (68.96%)

	First	Final	Elected (R.)
Michelle Gildernew, SF	9,110	9,110	First (1)
Tom Elliott, UUP	6,896	6,896	Second (1)
Arlene Foster, DUP	6,876	6,876	Third (3)
Sean Lynch, SF	5,146	6,476	Fifth (6)
Phil Flanagan, SF	5,082	6,137	Sixth (6)
Maurice Morrow, DUP	4,844	7,229	Fourth (5)
*Tommy Gallagher, SDLP	4,606	6,075	
Kenny Donaldson, UUP	2,366		
Alex Elliott, TUV	1,231		
Pat Cox, Ind.	997		
Hannah Su, Alliance	845		

FOYLE
E. 68,663 T. 39,686 (57.80%)

	First	Final	Elected (R.)
William Hay, DUP	7,154	7,154	First (1)
Martina Anderson, SF	6,950	6,950	Second (1)
Mark Durkan, SDLP	4,970	5,794	Third (4)
Raymond McCartney, SF	3,638	6,245	Fourth (7)
Pat Ramsey, SDLP	3,138	4,876	Sixth (7)
*Eamonn McCann (PBP)	3,120	3,916	
Colum Eastwood, SDLP	2,967	5,563	Fifth (7)
Pol Callaghan, SDLP	2,624		
Paul Fleming, SF	2,612		
Paul McFadden, Ind.	1,280		
Keith McGrellis, Alliance	334		
Terry Doherty, Ind.	60		

LAGAN VALLEY
E. 67,532 T. 35,842 (53.07%)

	First	Final	Elected (R.)
Edwin Poots, DUP	7,329	7,329	First (1)
Basil McCrea, UUP	5,771	5,771	Second (1)
Trevor Lunn, Alliance	4,389	5,120	Fourth (6)
Paul Givan, DUP	4,352	5,518	Fifth (7)
Jonathan Craig, DUP	4,263	5,081	Third (5)
Brenda Hale, DUP	2,910	4,791	Sixth (7)
*Pat Catney, SDLP	2,165	3,406	
Mark Hill, UUP	1,482		
Mary-Kate Quinn, SF	1,203		
Lyle Rea, TUV	1,031		
Conor Quinn, Green	592		

LONDONDERRY EAST
E. 65,226 T. 35,303 (54.12%)

	First	Final	Elected (R.)
Gregory Campbell, DUP	6,319	6,319	First (1)
Cathal O hOisin, SF	4,681	4,962	Third (6)
George Robinson, DUP	3,855	4,823	Fourth (7)
David McClarty (Ind.)	3,003	4,405	Fifth (7)
John Dallat, SDLP	2,967	5,207	Second (6)
Bernadette Archibald, SF	2,639		
Adrian McQuillan, DUP	2,633	3,782	Sixth (7)
Thomas Conway	2,222		
Barney Fitzpatrick, Alliance	1,905		
Boyd Douglas, TUV	1,568		
Lesley Macaulay, UUP	1,472		
*David Harding, UUP	1,458	3,460	

NEWRY AND ARMAGH
E. 77,544 T. 47,562 (61.34%)

	First	Final	Elected (R.)
Conor Murphy, SF	9,127	9,127	First (1)
Danny Kennedy, UUP	8,718	8,718	Second (1)
Dominic Bradley, SDLP	7,123	7,123	Third (1)
Cathal Boylan, SF	6,614	8,092	Fourth (2)
William Irwin, DUP	6,101	7,502	Fifth (3)
*Thomas O'Hanlon, SDLP	3,825	5,014	
Mickey Brady, SF	3,254	5,625	Sixth (6)
Barrie Halliday, TUV	830		
David Murphy, Alliance	734		
Robert Woods, UKIP	98		
James Malone, ND	90		

STRANGFORD
E. 62,178 T. 30,186 (48.55%)

	First	Final	Elected (R.)
Michelle McIlveen, DUP	4,573	4,573	First (1)
Kieran McCarthy, Alliance	4,284	4,284	Second (1)
Jonathan Bell, DUP	4,265	4,265	Third (1)
Simon Hamilton, DUP	3,456	5,745	Fourth (5)
Mike Nesbitt	3,273	4,072	Fifth (6)
David McNarry, UUP	2,733	3,767	Sixth (6)
*Joe Boyle, SDLP	2,525	3,308	
Billy Walker, DUP	2,175		
Mickey Coogan, SF	902		
Terry Williams, TUV	841		
Cecil Andrews, UKIP	601		

TYRONE WEST
E. 62,970 T. 40,323 (64.04%)

	First	Final	Elected (R.)
Barry McElduff, SF	6,008	6,008	First (1)
Pat Doherty, SF	5,630	5,630	Second (1)
Michaela Boyle, SF	5,053	7,792	Third (4)
Tom Buchanan, DUP	5,027	5,162	Fifth (5)
Ross Hussey, UUP	4,072	4,398	Sixth (5)
*Allan Bresland, DUP	4,059	4,124	
Joe Byrne, SDLP	3,353	5,321	Fourth (5)
Declan McAleer, SF	3,008		
Paddy McGowan, Ind.	1,145		
Eugene McMenamin, Ind.	1,096		
Eric Bullick, Ind.	852		

ULSTER MID
E. 66,602 T. 43,522 (65.35%)

	First	Final	Elected (R.)
Martin McGuinness, SF	8,957	8,957	First (1)
Ian McCrea, DUP	7,127	7,127	Second (1)
Michelle O'Neill, SF	5,178	5,735	Sixth (7)
Patsy McGlone, SDLP	5,065	6,110	Third (5)
Sandra Overend, UUP	4,409	7,130	Fourth (6)
Francie Molloy, SF	4,263	5,191	Fifth (7)
*Ian Milne, SF	2,635	4,412	
Walter Millar, TUV	2,075		
Austin Kelly, SDLP	1,214		
Hugh McCloy, Ind.	933		
Michael McDonald, Alliance	398		
Harry Hutchinson, PBP	243		
Gary McCann, Ind.	241		

UPPER BANN
E. 77,905 T. 43,113 (55.34%)

	First	Final	Elected (R.)
John O'Dowd, SF	6,649	6,649	First (1)
Sydney Anderson, DUP	5,584	6,163	Second (5)
Stephen Moutray, DUP	5,645	6,085	Third (5)
*Johnny McGibbon, SF	4,879	5,438	
Dolores Kelly, SDLP	4,846	5,787	Sixth (7)
Sam Gardiner, UUP	3,676	6,012	Fourth (7)
Colin McCusker, UUP	3,402		
Joanne Dobson, UUP	3,348	5,827	Fifth (7)
Harry Hamilton, Alliance	1,979		
David Vance, TUV	1,026		
Sheila McQuaid, Alliance	786		
Barbara Trotter, UKIP	272		

EUROPEAN PARLIAMENT

European parliament elections take place at five-yearly intervals; the first direct elections to the parliament were held in 1979. In mainland Britain, members of the European parliament (MEPs) were elected in all constituencies on a first-past-the-post basis until 1999, when a regional system of proportional representation was introduced; in Northern Ireland three MEPs have been elected by the single transferable vote system of proportional representation since 1979. From 1979 to 1994 the number of seats held by the UK in the European parliament was 81, which increased to 87 in the 1994 election, decreased to 78 following EU enlargement in 2004, and decreased to 72 (England 59, Wales 4, Scotland 6, Northern Ireland 3) for the 2009 election as a result of Bulgaria and Romania joining the EU in 2007. Under the Lisbon treaty, which came into force in December 2009, the UK will gain an extra seat. This seat will be added to the West Midlands region and will be filled by a Conservative MEP, based on the results from the 2009 European parliament elections; however, the earliest he/she could be installed was January 2012.

At the 2009 European parliament elections all UK MEPs were elected under a 'closed-list' regional system of proportional representation, with England being divided into nine regions* and Scotland, Wales and Northern Ireland each constituting a single region each. Parties submitted a list of candidates for each region in their own order of preference. Votes were cast for a party or an independent candidate, and the first seat in each region was allocated to the party or candidate with the highest number of votes. The rest of the seats in each region were then allocated broadly in proportion to each party's share of the vote. Each region returned the following number of members: East Midlands, 5; Eastern, 7; London, 8; North East, 3; North West, 8; South East, 10; South West, 6; West Midlands, 6; Yorkshire and the Humber, 6; Wales, 4; Northern Ireland, 3; Scotland, 6.

If a vacancy occurs due to the resignation or death of an MEP, it is filled by the next available person on that party's list. If an independent MEP resigns or dies, a by-election is held. Where an MEP leaves the party on whose list he/she was elected, there is no requirement to resign the post of MEP, and he/she can remain in office until the next election.

British subjects and nationals of member states of the European Union are eligible for election to the European parliament provided they are 18 or over and not subject to disqualification. Since 1994, eligible citizens have had the right to vote in elections to the European parliament in the UK as long as they are entered on the electoral register.

MEPs previously received a salary set at the level of the national parliamentary salary of their country. In July 2009 an MEP statute introduced a uniform salary for all MEPs, set at a rate of 38.5 per cent of the basic salary of a European court of justice judge. In 2011 this approximated an annual salary of €95,482 (£84,826).

The next elections to the European parliament will take place in 2014. For further information visit the UK's European parliament website (W www.europarl.org.uk).

* Since June 2004 residents of Gibraltar vote in the South West region.

UK MEMBERS *as at September 2011*

* Denotes membership of the last European parliament
† Previously sat as a member of the Conservative party
‡ Previously sat as a member of UUP

Agnew, John Stuart (*b.* 1949), *UKIP, Eastern*
Andreasen, Marta (*b.* 1954), *UKIP, South East*
***Ashworth**, Richard (*b.* 1947), *C., South East*
***Atkins**, Rt. Hon. Sir Robert (*b.* 1946), *C., North West*
***Batten**, Gerard (*b.* 1954), *UKIP, London*
Bearder, Catherine (*b.* 1949) *LD, South East*
***Bloom**, Godfrey (*b.* 1949), *UKIP, Yorkshire and the Humber*
***Bowles**, Sharon M. (*b.* 1953), *LD, South East*
***Bradbourn**, Philip, OBE (*b.* 1951), *C., West Midlands*
Brons, Andrew H. W. (*b.* 1947), *BNP, Yorkshire and the Humber*
Bufton, John (*b.* 1962), *UKIP, Wales*
***Callanan**, Martin (*b.* 1961), *C., North East*
Campbell Bannerman, David (*b.* 1960), *UKIP, Eastern*
***Cashman**, Michael (*b.* 1950), *Lab., West Midlands*
***Chichester**, Giles B. (*b.* 1946), *C., South West*
***Clark**, Derek Rowland (*b.* 1933), *UKIP, East Midlands*
Colman, Trevor (*b.* 1941), *UKIP, South West*
Dartmouth, Earl of (*b.* 1949), *UKIP, South West*
***Davies**, Chris G. (*b.* 1954), *LD, North West*
***de Brún**, Bairbre (*b.* 1954), *SF, Northern Ireland*
***Deva**, Nirj J. A. (*b.* 1948), *C., South East*
Dodds, Diane (*b.* 1958), *DUP, Northern Ireland*
***Duff**, Andrew N. (*b.* 1950), *LD, Eastern*
***Elles**, James E. M. (*b.* 1949), *C., South East*
***Evans**, Jill R. (*b.* 1959), *PC, Wales*
***Farage**, Nigel P. (*b.* 1964), *UKIP, South East*
Ford, Vicky (*b.* 1967), *C. Eastern*
Foster, Jacqueline (*b.* 1947), *C., North West*
Fox, Ashley (*b.* 1969), *C., South West*
Girling, Julie (*b.* 1956), *C., South West*
Griffin, Nick (*b.* 1959), *BNP, North West*
***Hall**, Fiona (*b.* 1955), *LD, North East*
***Hannan**, Daniel J. (*b.* 1971), *C., South East*
***Harbour**, Malcolm (*b.* 1947), *C., West Midlands*
***Helmer**, Roger (*b.* 1944), *C., East Midlands*
***Honeyball**, Mary (*b.* 1952), *Lab., London*
***Howitt**, Richard (*b.* 1961), *Lab., Eastern*
***Hudghton**, Ian (*b.* 1951), *SNP, Scotland*
***Hughes**, Stephen (*b.* 1952), *Lab., North East*
***Kamall**, Dr Syed S. (*b.* 1967), *C., London*
***Karim**, Sajjad (*b.* 1970), *C., North West*
***Kirkhope**, Timothy J. R. (*b.* 1945), *C., Yorkshire and the Humber*
***Lambert**, Jean D. (*b.* 1950), *Green, London*
***Ludford**, Baroness Sarah (*b.* 1951), *LD, London*
***Lynne**, Elizabeth (*b.* 1948), *LD, West Midlands*
Lyon, George (*b.* 1956), *LD, Scotland*
***McAvan**, Linda (*b.* 1962), *Lab., Yorkshire and the Humber*
***McCarthy**, Arlene (*b.* 1960), *Lab., North West*
McClarkin, Emma (*b.* 1978), *C., East Midlands*
*†**McMillan-Scott**, Edward H. C. (*b.* 1949), *LD, Yorkshire and the Humber*
***Martin**, David W. (*b.* 1954), *Lab., Scotland*
***Moraes**, Claude (*b.* 1965), *Lab., London*
***Nattrass**, Mike (*b.* 1945), *UKIP, West Midlands*
***Newton Dunn**, Bill F. (*b.* 1941), *LD, East Midlands*

*‡**Nicholson**, James (b. 1945), *UCUNF, Northern Ireland*
Nuttall, Paul (b. 1976), *UKIP, North West*
***Simpson**, Brian (b. 1953), *Lab., North West*
Sinclaire, Nikki (b. 1968), *Ind., West Midlands*
***Skinner**, Peter W. (b. 1959), *Lab., South East*
***Smith**, Alyn (b. 1973), *SNP, Scotland*
***Stevenson**, Struan (b. 1948), *C., Scotland*
***Stihler**, Catherine D. (b. 1973), *Lab., Scotland*
***Sturdy**, Robert W. (b. 1944), *C., Eastern*

Swinburne, Dr Kay (b. 1967), *C., Wales*
***Tannock**, Dr Charles (b. 1957), *C., London*
Taylor, Keith (b. 1953), *Green, South East*
***Van Orden**, Geoffrey (b. 1945), *C., Eastern*
Vaughan, Derek (b. 1961), *Lab., Wales*
***Wallis**, Diana (b. 1954), *LD, Yorkshire and the Humber*
***Watson**, Sir Graham R. (b. 1956), *LD, South West*
***Willmott**, Glenis (b. 1951), *Lab., East Midlands*
Yannakoudakis, Marina (b. 1956), *C., London*

UK REGIONS *as at 4 June 2009 election*

Abbreviations

AC	Animals Count
ChP	Christian Party
JT	Jury Team
Libertas	Libertas
No2EU	No2EU Yes to Democracy
Peace	Peace Party
Pensioners	Pensioners Party
Roman	Roman Party
SGB	Socialist Party of Great Britain
SLP	Socialist Labour Party
SSP	Scottish Socialist Party
TUV	Traditional Unionist Voice
UCUNF	Ulster Conservatives and Unionists – New Force
UKF	United Kingdom First
YD	Wai D (Your Decision)
Yes2EU	YES2EUROPE

For other abbreviations, *see* UK General Election Results. For detailed information on which areas of the country are covered by a particular region, please contact the Home Office.

E. 44,173,690   T. 34.48%

EASTERN
(Bedfordshire, Cambridgeshire, Essex, Hertfordshire, Luton, Norfolk, Peterborough, Southend-on-Sea, Suffolk, Thurrock)

E. 4,252,669		T. 38.0%
C.		500,331 (31.2%)
UKIP		313,921 (19.6%)
LD		221,235 (13.8%)
Lab.		167,833 (10.5%)
Green		141,016 (8.8%)
BNP		97,013 (6.1%)
UKF		38,185 (2.4%)
Eng. Dem.		32,211 (2.0%)
CPA		24,646 (1.5%)
No2EU		13,939 (0.9%)
SLP		13,599 (0.8%)
AC		13,201 (0.8%)
Libertas		9,940 (0.6%)
Ind.		9,916 (0.6%)
JT		6,354 (0.4%)
C. majority		186,410
(June 2004, C. maj. 169,366)		

MEMBERS ELECTED
1. *G. Van Orden, C. 2. D. Campbell Bannerman, *UKIP* 3. *R. Sturdy, C.

4. *A. Duff, *LD* 5. *R. Howitt, *Lab.*
6. V. Ford, C. 7. J. Agnew, *UKIP*

EAST MIDLANDS
(Derby, Derbyshire, Leicester, Leicestershire, Lincolnshire, Northamptonshire, Nottingham, Nottinghamshire, Rutland)

E. 3,312,944		T. 37.51%
C.		370,275 (30.2%)
Lab.		206,945 (16.9%)
UKIP		201,984 (16.4%)
LD		151,428 (12.3%)
BNP		106,319 (8.7%)
Green		83,939 (6.8%)
Eng. Dem.		28,498 (2.3%)
UKF		20,561 (1.7%)
CPA		17,907 (1.5%)
SLP		13,590 (1.1%)
No2EU		11,375 (0.9%)
Libertas		7,882 (0.6%)
JT		7,362 (0.6%)
C. majority		204,243
(June 2004, C. maj. 4,864)		

MEMBERS ELECTED
1. *R. Helmer, C. 2.*G. Willmott, *Lab.* 3. *D. Clark, *UKIP*
4. E. McClarkin, C. 5. *W. Newton Dunn, *LD*

LONDON

E. 5,257,624		T. 33.53%
C.		479,037 (27.4%)
Lab.		372,590 (21.3%)
LD		240,156 (13.7%)
Green		190,589 (10.9%)
UKIP		188,440 (10.8%)
BNP		86,420 (4.9%)
CPA		51,336 (2.9%)
Ind.		50,014 (2.9%)
Eng. Dem.		24,477 (1.4%)
No2EU		17,758 (1.0%)
SLP		15,306 (0.9%)
Libertas		8,444 (0.5%)
JT		7,284 (0.4%)
Ind, SC		4,918 (0.3%)
SGB		4,050 (0.2%)
Yes2EU		3,384 (0.2%)
Ind.		3,248 (0.2%)
Ind.		1,972 (0.1%)
Ind.		1,603 (0.1%)
C. majority		106,447
(June 2004, C. maj. 38,357)		

MEMBERS ELECTED
1. *C. Tannock, C. 2. *C. Moraes, *Lab.* 3. *Baroness Ludford, *LD*
4. *S. Kamall, C. 5. *J. Lambert, *Green*
6. *G. Batten, *UKIP* 7. *M. Honeyball, *Lab.* 8. M. Yannakoudakis, C.

NORTH EAST
(Co. Durham, Darlington, Hartlepool, Middlesbrough, Northumberland, Redcar and Cleveland, Stockton-on-Tees, Tyne and Wear)

E. 1,939,709		T. 30.50%
Lab.		147,338 (25.0%)
C.		116,911 (19.8%)
LD		103,644 (17.6%)
UKIP		90,700 (15.4%)
BNP		52,700 (8.9%)
Green		34,081 (5.8%)
Eng. Dem.		13,007 (2.2%)
SLP		10,238 (1.7%)
No2EU		8,066 (1.4%)
CPA		7,263 (1.2%)
Libertas		3,010 (0.5%)
JT		2,904 (0.5%)
Lab. majority		30,427
(June 2004, Lab. maj. 121,088)		

MEMBERS ELECTED
1. *S. Hughes, *Lab.* 2. *M. Callanan, C. 3. *Ms F. Hall, *LD*

NORTHERN IRELAND
(Northern Ireland forms a three-member seat with a single transferable vote system)

E. 1,141,979		T. 42.81%
		1st Pref. Votes
Bairbre de Brún,		126,184 (26.0%)
SF		
Diane Dodds, *DUP*		88,346 (18.2%)
Jim Nicholson,		82,893 (17.1%)
UCUNF		
Alban Maginness,		78,489 (16.2%)
SDLP		
Jim Allister, *TUV*		66,197 (13.7%)
Ian James Parsley,		26,699 (5.5%)
Alliance		
Steven Agnew,		15,764 (3.3%)
Green		

MEMBERS ELECTED
1. *B. de Brún, *SF* 2. *†J. Nicholson, *UCUNF* 3. D. Dodds, *DUP*

NORTH WEST
(Blackburn-with-Darwen, Blackpool, Cheshire, Cumbria, Greater Manchester, Halton, Lancashire, Merseyside, Warrington)

E. 1,651,825	T. 31.90%
C.	423,174 (25.6%)
Lab.	336,831 (20.4%)
UKIP	261,740 (15.8%)
LD	235,639 (14.3%)
BNP	132,094 (8.0%)
Green	127,133 (7.7%)
Eng. Dem.	40,027 (2.4%)
SLP	26,224 (1.6%)
CPA	25,999 (1.6%)
No2EU	23,580 (1.4%)
JT	8,783 (0.5%)
Libertas	6,980 (0.4%)
Ind.	3,621 (0.2%)
C. majority	86,343

(June 2004, Lab. maj. 66,942)

MEMBERS ELECTED
1. *Sir R. Atkins, C. 2. A. McCarthy, Lab. 3. P. Nuttall, UKIP
4. *C. Davies, LD 5. *S. Karim, C.
6. *B. Simpson, Lab. 7. J. Foster, C.
8. N. Griffin, BNP

SCOTLAND

E. 3,873,163	T. 28.60%
SNP	321,007 (29.1%)
Lab.	229,853 (20.8%)
C.	185,794 (16.8%)
LD	127,038 (11.5%)
Green	80,442 (7.3%)
UKIP	57,788 (5.2%)
BNP	27,174 (2.5%)
SLP	22,135 (2.0%)
CPA	16,738 (1.5%)
SSP	10,404 (0.9%)
Ind.	10,189 (0.9%)
No2EU	9,693 (0.9%)
JT	6,257 (0.6%)
SNP majority	91,154

(June 2004, Lab. maj. 79,360)

MEMBERS ELECTED
1. *I. Hudghton, SNP 2. *D. Martin, Lab. 3. *S. Stevenson, C. 4. *A. Smith, SNP 5. G. Lyon, LD 6. *C. Stihler, Lab.

SOUTH EAST
(Bracknell Forest, Brighton and Hove, Buckinghamshire, East Sussex, Hampshire, Isle of Wight, Kent, Medway, Milton Keynes, Newbury, Oxfordshire, Portsmouth, Reading, Slough, Southampton, Surrey, West Sussex, Windsor and Maidenhead, Wokingham)

E. 6,231,875	T. 38.19%
C.	812,288 (34.8%)
UKIP	440,002 (18.8%)
LD	330,340 (14.1%)
Green	271,506 (11.6%)

Lab.	192,592 (8.2%)
BNP	101,769 (4.4%)
Eng. Dem.	52,526 (2.2%)
CPA	35,712 (1.5%)
No2EU	21,455 (0.9%)
Libertas	16,767 (0.7%)
SLP	15,484 (0.7%)
UKF	15,261 (0.7%)
JT	14,172 (0.6%)
Peace Party	9,534 (0.4%)
Roman Party	5,450 (0.2%)
C. majority	372,286

(June 2004, C. maj. 345,259)

MEMBERS ELECTED
1. *D. Hannan, C. 2. *N. Farage, UKIP 3. *R. Ashworth, C.
4. *S. Bowles, LD 5. *Dr C. Lucas, Green 6. *N. Deva, C.
7. M. Andreasen, UKIP
8. *J. Elles, C. 9. *P. Skinner, Lab.
10. C. Bearder, LD

SOUTH WEST
(Bath and North East Somerset, Bournemouth, Bristol, Cornwall, Devon, Dorset, Gloucestershire, North Somerset, Plymouth, Poole, Somerset, South Gloucestershire, Swindon, Torbay, Wiltshire, Isles of Scilly, Gibraltar)

E. 3,998,479	T. 39.04%
C.	468,472 (30.2%)
UKIP	341,845 (22.1%)
LD	266,253 (17.2%)
Green	144,179 (9.3%)
Labour	118,716 (7.7%)
BNP	60,889 (3.9%)
Pensioners	37,785 (2.4%)
Eng. Dem.	25,313 (1.6%)
CPA	21,329 (1.4%)
Meb. Ker.	14,922 (1.0%)
SLP	10,033 (0.6%)
No2EU	9,741 (0.6%)
Ind.	8,971 (0.6%)
Libertas	7,292 (0.5%)
FPFT	7,151 (0.5%)
JT	5,758 (0.4%)
YD	789 (0.1%)
C. majority	126,627

(June 2004, C. maj. 130,587)

MEMBERS ELECTED
1. *G. Chichester, C. 2. T. Colman, UKIP 3. *G. Watson, LD
4. J. McCulloch Girling, C.
5. W. Dartmouth, UKIP 6. A. Fox, C.

WALES

E. 2,251,968	T. 30.50%
C.	145,193 (21.2%)
Lab.	138,852 (20.3%)
PC	126,702 (18.5%)
UKIP	87,585 (12.8%)
LD	73,082 (10.7%)
Green	38,160 (5.6%)
BNP	37,114 (5.4%)
ChP	13,037 (1.9%)

SLP	12,402 (1.8%)
No2EU	8,600 (1.3%)
JT	3,793 (0.6%)
C. majority	6,341

(June 2004, Lab. maj. 120,039)

MEMBERS ELECTED
1. K. Swinburne, C. 2. D. Vaughan. Lab. 3. *J. Evans, PC 4. J. Bufton, UKIP

WEST MIDLANDS
(Herefordshire, Shropshire, Staffordshire, Stoke-on-Trent, Telford and Wrekin, Warwickshire, West Midlands Metropolitan area, Worcestershire)

E. 4,056,370	T. 35.07%
C.	396,487 (28.1%)
UKIP	300,471 (21.3%)
Lab.	240,201 (17.0%)
LD	170,246 (12.0%)
BNP	121,967 (8.6%)
Green	88,244 (6.2%)
Eng. Dem.	32,455 (2.3%)
CPA	18,784 (1.3%)
SLP	14,724 (1.0%)
No2EU	13,415 (0.9%)
JT	8,721 (0.6%)
Libertas	6,961 (0.5%)
C. majority	96,016

(June 2004, C. maj. 56,324)

MEMBERS ELECTED
1. *P. Bradbourn, C. 2. *M. Nattrass, UKIP 3. *M. Cashman, Lab.
4. *M. Harbour, C. 5. *L. Lynne, LD
6. N. Sinclaire, UKIP

YORKSHIRE AND THE HUMBER
(East Riding of Yorkshire, Kingston-upon-Hull, North East Lincolnshire, North Lincolnshire, North Yorkshire, South Yorkshire, West Yorkshire, York)

E. 3,792,415	T. 32.51%
C.	299,802 (24.5%)
Lab.	230,009 (18.8%)
UKIP	213,750 (17.4%)
LD	161,552 (13.2%)
BNP	120,139 (9.8%)
Green	104,456 (8.5%)
Eng. Dem.	31,287 (2.6%)
SLP	19,380 (1.6%)
CPA	16,742 (1.4%)
No2EU	15,614 (1.3%)
JT	7,181 (0.6%)
Libertas	6,268 (0.5%)
C. majority	69,793

(June 1999, Lab. maj. 25,844)

MEMBERS ELECTED
1. *E. McMillan-Scott, C.
2. *L. McAvan, Lab. 3. *G. Bloom, UKIP 4. *D. Wallis, LD
5. *T. Kirkhope, C. 6. A. Brons, BNP

LOCAL GOVERNMENT

Major changes in local government were introduced in England and Wales in 1974 and in Scotland in 1975 by the Local Government Act 1972 and the Local Government (Scotland) Act 1973. Further significant alterations were made in England by the Local Government Acts of 1985, 1992 and 2000.

The structure in England was based on two tiers of local authorities (county councils and district councils) in the non-metropolitan areas; and a single tier of metropolitan councils in the six metropolitan areas of England and London borough councils in London.

Following reviews of the structure of local government in England by the Local Government Commission (now the Boundary Commission for England), 46 unitary (all-purpose) authorities were created between April 1995 and April 1998 to cover certain areas in the non-metropolitan counties. The remaining county areas continue to have two tiers of local authorities. The county and district councils in the Isle of Wight were replaced by a single unitary authority on 1 April 1995; the former counties of Avon, Cleveland, Humberside and Berkshire were replaced by unitary authorities; and Hereford and Worcester was replaced by a new county council for Worcestershire (with district councils) and a unitary authority for Herefordshire. On 1 April 2009 the county areas of Cornwall, Durham, Northumberland, Shropshire and Wiltshire were given unitary status and two new unitary authorities were created for Bedfordshire (Bedford and Central Bedfordshire) and Cheshire (Cheshire East and Cheshire West & Chester) replacing the two-tier county/district system in these areas.

The Local Government (Wales) Act 1994 and the Local Government etc (Scotland) Act 1994 abolished the two-tier structure in Wales and Scotland with effect from 1 April 1996, replacing it with a single tier of unitary authorities.

ELECTIONS

Local elections are normally held on the first Thursday in May. Generally, all British subjects, citizens of the Republic of Ireland, Commonwealth and other European Union citizens who are 18 years or over and resident on the qualifying date in the area for which the election is being held, are entitled to vote at local government elections. A register of electors is prepared and published annually by local electoral registration officers.

A returning officer has the overall responsibility for an election. Voting takes place at polling stations, arranged by the local authority and under the supervision of a presiding officer specially appointed for the purpose. Candidates, who are subject to various statutory qualifications and disqualifications designed to ensure that they are suitable to hold office, must be nominated by electors for the electoral area concerned.

In England, the Local Government Boundary Commission for England is responsible for carrying out periodic reviews of electoral arrangements, to consider whether the boundaries of wards or divisions within a local authority need to be altered to take account of changes in electorate; structural reviews, to consider

whether a single, unitary authority should be established in an area instead of an existing two-tier system; and administrative boundary reviews of district or county authorities.

The Local Government Boundary Commission for Wales, the Local Government Boundary Commission for Scotland and the local government boundary commissioner for Northern Ireland (appointed when required by the Boundary Commission for Northern Ireland) are responsible for reviewing the electoral arrangements and boundaries of local authorities within their respective regions.

The Local Government Act 2000 provided for the secretary of state to change the frequency and phasing of elections in England and Wales.

LOCAL GOVERNMENT BOUNDARY COMMISSION FOR ENGLAND, Layden House, 76–86 Turnmill Street, London EC1M 5LG **T** 020-7664 8534
E reviews@lgbce.org.uk **W** www.lgbce.org.uk

LOCAL GOVERNMENT BOUNDARY COMMISSION FOR WALES, Caradog House, 1–6 St Andrew's Place, Cardiff CF10 3BE **T** 029-2039 5031
E lgbc.wales@wales.gsi.gov.uk **W** www.lgbc-wales.gov.uk

LOCAL GOVERNMENT BOUNDARY COMMISSION FOR SCOTLAND, Thistle House, 91 Haymarket Terrace, Edinburgh EH12 5HD **T** 0131-538 7510
E lgbcs@scottishboundaries.gov.uk
W www.lgbc-scotland.gov.uk

BOUNDARY COMMISSION FOR NORTHERN IRELAND, Forestview, Purdy's Lane, Newtownbreda, Belfast BT8 7AR **T** 028-9069 4800 **E** bcni@belfast.org.uk
W www.boundarycommission.org.uk

INTERNAL ORGANISATION

The council as a whole is the final decision-making body within any authority. Councils are free to a great extent to make their own internal organisational arrangements. The Local Government Act, given royal assent on 28 July 2000, allows councils to adopt one of three broad categories of constitution which include a separate executive:

• A directly elected mayor with a cabinet selected by that mayor
• A cabinet, either elected by the council or appointed by its leader
• A directly elected mayor and council manager

Normally, questions of policy are settled by the full council, while the administration of the various services is the responsibility of committees of councillors. Day-to-day decisions are delegated to the council's officers, who act within the policies laid down by the councillors.

FINANCE

Local government in England, Wales and Scotland is financed from four sources: council tax, non-domestic rates, government grants and income from fees and charges for services.

COUNCIL TAX

Under the Local Government Finance Act 1992, from 1 April 1993 council tax replaced the community charge (which had been introduced in April 1989 in Scotland and April 1990 in England and Wales in place of domestic rates).

Council tax is a local tax levied by each local council. Liability for the council tax bill usually falls on the owner-occupier or tenant of a dwelling which is their sole or main residence. Council tax bills may be reduced because of the personal circumstances of people resident in a property, and there are discounts in the case of dwellings occupied by fewer than two adults.

In England, unitary and metropolitan authorities are responsible for collecting their own council tax from which the police authorities claim their share. In areas where there are two tiers of local authority, each county, district and police authority sets its own council tax rate; the district authorities collect the combined council tax and the county councils and police authorities claim their share from the district councils' collection funds. In Wales, each unitary authority and each police authority sets its own council tax rate. The unitary authorities collect the combined council tax and the police authorities claim their share from the funds. In Scotland, each local authority sets its own rate of council tax.

The tax relates to the value of the dwelling. In England and Scotland each dwelling is placed in one of eight valuation bands, ranging from A to H, based on the property's estimated market value as at 1 April 1991. In Wales there are nine bands, ranging from A to I, based on the estimated market value of property as at 1 April 2003.

The valuation bands and ranges of values in England, Wales and Scotland are:

England

A	Up to £40,000	E	£88,001–£120,000
B	£40,001–£52,000	F	£120,001–£160,000
C	£52,001–£68,000	G	£160,001–£320,000
D	£68,001–£88,000	H	Over £320,001

Wales

A	Up to £44,000	F	£162,001–£223,000
B	£44,001–£65,000	G	£223,001–£324,000
C	£65,001–£91,000	H	£324,001–£424,000
D	£91,001–£123,000	I	Over £424,001
E	£123,001–£162,000		

Scotland

A	Up to £27,000	E	£58,001–£80,000
B	£27,001–£35,000	F	£80,001–£106,000
C	£35,001–£45,000	G	£106,001–£212,000
D	£45,001–£58,000	H	Over £212,001

The council tax within a local area varies between the different bands according to proportions laid down by law. The charge attributable to each band as a proportion of the Band D charge set by the council is approximately:

A	67%	F	144%
B	78%	G	167%
C	89%	H	200%
D	100%	I	233%*
E	122%		

* Wales only

The average Band D council tax bill for each authority area is given in the tables on the following pages. There may be variations from the given figure within each district council area because of different parish or community precepts being levied.

NON-DOMESTIC RATES

Non-domestic (business) rates are collected by billing authorities; these are the district councils in those areas of England with two tiers of local government and are unitary authorities in other parts of England, in Wales and in Scotland. In respect of England and Wales, the Local Government Finance Act 1988 provides for liability for rates to be assessed on the basis of a poundage (multiplier) tax on the rateable value of property (hereditaments). Separate multipliers are set by the Department for Communities and Local Government (CLG) in England, the Welsh government and the Scottish government. Rates are collected by the billing authority for the area where a property is located. Rate income collected by billing authorities is paid into a national non-domestic rating (NNDR) pool and redistributed to individual authorities on the basis of the adult population figure as prescribed by CLG, the Welsh government or the Scottish government. The rates pools are maintained separately in England, Wales and Scotland. Actual payment of rates in certain cases is subject to transitional arrangements, to phase in the larger increases and reductions in rates resulting from the effects of the latest revaluation.

Rateable values for the 2010 rating lists came into effect on 1 April 2010. They are derived from the rental value of property as at 1 April 2003 and determined by certain statutory assumptions by the Valuation Office Agency in England and Wales, and by local area assessors in Scotland. New property which is added to the list, and significant changes to existing property, necessitate amendments to the rateable value on the same basis. Rating lists (valuation rolls in Scotland) remain in force until the next general revaluation. Such revaluations take place every five years, the next being in 2015.

Certain types of property are exempt from rates, eg agricultural land and buildings, certain businesses and some places of public religious worship. Charities and other non-profit-making organisations may receive full or partial relief. Empty commercial property in England and Wales is exempt from business rates for the first three months that the property is vacant (six months for an industrial property), after which full business rates are normally payable. In Scotland an empty commercial property is exempt from business rates for the first three months and entitled to a 50 per cent discount thereafter, except for some types of premises, such as factories, which are entirely exempt.

GOVERNMENT GRANTS

In addition to specific grants in support of revenue expenditure on particular services, central government pays a revenue support grant to local authorities. This grant is paid to each local authority so that if each authority spends at the level of its standard spending assessment, all authorities in the same class can set broadly the same council tax.

COMPLAINTS

ENGLAND

In England the Local Government Ombudsman investigates complaints of injustice arising from maladministration by local authorities and certain other bodies. The Local Government Ombudsman will not usually consider a complaint unless the local authority concerned has had an opportunity to investigate and reply to a complainant.

The Local Government Act 2000 established a standards board and an independent tribunal known as the Adjudication Panel for England. Under the Localism bill introduced to parliament in December 2010 responsibility for standards has been passed back to the local authorities and the board is due to be abolished in 2012. In addition, the functions of the Adjudication Panel to determine references and appeals about the conduct of members of local authorities have been subsumed by First-tier Tribunal (Local Government Standards in England), part of the general regulatory chamber of HM Courts and Tribunals Service.

FIRST-TIER TRIBUNAL (LOCAL GOVERNMENT STANDARDS IN ENGLAND), York House, 31–36 York Place, Leeds LS1 2ED T 0113-389 6086
E AP-enquiries@tribunals.gsi.gov.uk
LOCAL GOVERNMENT OMBUDSMAN, PO Box 4771, Coventry CV4 0EH T 0300-061 0614 E advice@lgo.org.uk
W www.lgo.org.uk
Ombudsmen, Jane Martin, Anne Seex

WALES

The office of Public Services Ombudsman for Wales came into force on 1 April 2006, incorporating the functions of the Local Government Ombudsman for Wales.

PUBLIC SERVICES OMBUDSMAN FOR WALES, 1 Ffordd yr Hen Gae, Pencoed CF35 5LJ T 01656-641150
E ask@ombudsman-wales.org.uk
W www.ombudsman-wales.org.uk
Ombudsman, Peter Tyndall

SCOTLAND

The Scottish Public Services Ombudsman is responsible for complaints regarding the maladministration of local government in Scotland.

SCOTTISH PUBLIC SERVICES OMBUDSMAN, 4 Melville Street, Edinburgh EH3 7NS T 0800-377 7330
W www.spso.org.uk
Ombudsman, Jim Martin

NORTHERN IRELAND

The Northern Ireland Commissioner for Complaints fulfils a similar function in Northern Ireland, investigating complaints about local authorities and certain public bodies. Complaints are made to the relevant local authority in the first instance but may also be made directly to the commissioner.

NORTHERN IRELAND COMMISSIONER FOR COMPLAINTS, Freepost BEL 1478, Belfast BT1 6BR
T 0800-343424 E ombudsman@ni-ombudsman.org.uk
W www.ni-ombudsman.org.uk
Northern Ireland Commissioner for Complaints, Tom Frawley, CBE

THE QUEEN'S REPRESENTATIVES

The lord-lieutenant of a county is the permanent local representative of the Crown in that county. The appointment of lord-lieutenants is now regulated by the Lieutenancies Act 1997. They are appointed by the sovereign on the recommendation of the prime minister. The retirement age is 75. The office of lord-lieutenant dates from 1551, and its holder was originally responsible for maintaining order and for local defence in the county. The duties of the post include attending on royalty during official visits to the county, performing certain duties in connection with the armed forces (and in particular the reserve forces), and making presentations of honours and awards on behalf of the Crown. In England, Wales and Northern Ireland, the lord-lieutenant usually also holds the office of *Custos Rotulorum.* As such, he or she acts as head of the county's commission of the peace (which recommends the appointment of magistrates).

The office of sheriff (from the Old English *shire-reeve*) of a county was created in the tenth century. The sheriff was the special nominee of the sovereign, and the office reached the peak of its influence under the Norman kings. The Provisions of Oxford (1258) laid down a yearly tenure of office. Since the mid-16th century the office has been purely civil, with military duties taken over by the lord-lieutenant of the county. The sheriff (commonly known as 'high sheriff') attends on royalty during official visits to the county, acts as the returning officer during parliamentary elections in county constituencies, attends the opening ceremony when a high court judge goes on circuit, executes high court writs, and appoints under-sheriffs to act as deputies. The appointments and duties of the sheriffs in England and Wales are laid down by the Sheriffs Act 1887.

The serving high sheriff submits a list of names of possible future sheriffs to a tribunal, which chooses three names to put to the sovereign. The tribunal nominates the high sheriff annually on 12 November and the sovereign picks the name of the sheriff to succeed in the following year. The term of office runs from 25 March to the following 24 March (the civil and legal year before 1752). No person may be chosen twice in three years if there is any other suitable person in the county.

CIVIC DIGNITIES

District councils in England and local councils in Wales may petition for a royal charter granting borough or 'city' status to the council.

In England and Wales the chair of a borough or county borough council may be called a mayor, and the chair of a city council may be called a lord mayor (if lord mayoralty has been conferred on that city). Parish councils in England and community councils in Wales may call themselves 'town councils', in which case their chair is the town mayor.

In Scotland the chair of a local council may be known as a convenor; a provost is the mayoral equivalent. The chair of the councils for the cities of Aberdeen, Dundee, Edinburgh and Glasgow are lord provosts.

ENGLAND

In April 2009 five county councils were given unitary status, abolishing the two-tier district/county system within these areas, and a further four unitary authorities were created from the division of the county areas of Bedfordshire and Cheshire. Plans to create unitary authorities at Exeter, Norwich and Suffolk were revoked by the coalition government in May 2010. There are 27 counties, divided into 201 districts, 55 unitary authorities (plus the Isles of Scilly) and 36 metropolitan boroughs. The populations of most of the unitary authorities are in the range of 100,000 to 300,000. The district councils have populations broadly in the range of 60,000 to 100,000; some, however, have larger populations, because of the need to avoid dividing large towns, and some in mainly rural areas have smaller populations.

The main conurbations outside Greater London – Tyne and Wear, West Midlands, Merseyside, Greater Manchester, West Yorkshire and South Yorkshire – are divided into 36 metropolitan boroughs, most of which have a population of over 200,000.

There are also about 8,700 town and parish councils with a population coverage of around 17 million.

ELECTIONS

For districts, counties and for around 8,700 parishes, there are elected councils, consisting of directly elected councillors. The councillors elect one of their number as chair annually.

In general, councils can have whole council elections, elections by thirds or elections by halves. However all metropolitan authorities must hold elections by thirds. The electoral cycle of any new unitary authority is specified in the appropriate statutory order under which it is established.

FUNCTIONS

In areas with a two-tier system of local governance, functions are divided between the district and county authorities, with those functions affecting the larger area or population generally being the responsibility of the county council. A few functions continue to be exercised over the larger area by joint bodies, made up of councillors from each authority within the area.

Generally the allocation of functions is as follows:
County councils: education; strategic planning; traffic, transport and highways; fire service; consumer protection; refuse disposal; smallholdings; social care; libraries
District councils: local planning; housing; highways (maintenance of certain urban roads and off-street car parks); building regulations; environmental health; refuse collection; cemeteries and crematoria; collection of council tax and non-domestic rates
Unitary and metropolitan councils: their functions are all those listed above, except that the fire service is exercised by a joint body
Concurrently by county and district councils: recreation (parks, playing fields, swimming pools); museums; encouragement of the arts, tourism and industry

PARISH COUNCILS

Parish or town councils are the most local tier of government in England. There are currently around 10,000 parishes in England, of which around 8,700 have councils served by approximately 70,000 councillors. Since 15 February 2008 local councils have been able to create new parish councils without seeking approval from the government. Around 80 per cent of parish councils represent populations of less than 2,500; parishes with no parish council can be grouped with neighbouring parishes under a common parish council. A parish council comprises at least five members, the number being fixed by the district council. Elections are held every four years, at the time of the election of the district councillor for the ward including the parish. Full parish councils must be formed for those parishes with more than 999 electors – below this number, parish meetings comprising the electors of the parish must be held at least twice a year.

Parish council functions include: allotments; encouragement of arts and crafts; community halls, recreational facilities (eg open spaces, swimming pools), cemeteries and crematoria; and many minor functions. They must also be given an opportunity to comment on planning applications. They may, like county and district councils, spend limited sums for the general benefit of the parish. They levy a precept on the district councils for their funds. Parish precepts for 2011–12 totalled £367m, an increase of 2.8 per cent on 2010–11.

FINANCE

The local government budget requirement (including parish precepts) for 2011–12 is £56.7bn; of this £26.5bn is to be raised through council tax, £19bn from redistributed business rates, £5.9bn from revenue support grant and £4.5bn from police grant.

In England, the average council tax per dwelling for 2011–12 is £1,196, an increase of just £1 from £1,195 in 2010–11. The average council tax bill for a Band D dwelling (occupied by two adults, including parish precepts) for 2011–12 is £1,439, the same as for 2010–11 – with the exception of parishes, no local authority has increased its Band D council tax for 2011–12. The average Band D council tax is £1,484 in shire areas, £1,399 in metropolitan areas and £1,308 in London. Since 2006–7 the London figure has included a levy to fund the 2012 Olympic Games, which equates to a £20 a year increase on a Band D council tax.

The provisional amount estimated to be raised from national non-domestic rates from central and local lists is £19bn. The non-domestic rating multiplier for England for 2011–12 is 43.3p (42.6p for small businesses). The City of London is able to set a different multiplier from the rest of England; for 2011–12 this is 43.7p (43.0p for small businesses).

Under the Local Government and Housing Act 1989, local authorities have four main ways of paying for capital expenditure: borrowing and other forms of extended credit; capital grants from central government towards some types of capital expenditure; 'usable' capital receipts from the sale of land, houses and other assets; and revenue.

The amount of capital expenditure which a local authority can finance by borrowing (or other forms of credit) is effectively limited by the credit approvals issued to it by central government. Most credit approvals can be used for any kind of local authority capital expenditure; these are known as basic credit approvals. Others (supplementary credit approvals) can be used only for the kind of expenditure specified in the approval, and so are often given to fund particular projects or services.

Local authorities can use all capital receipts from the sale of property or assets for capital spending, except in the case of sales of council houses. Generally, the 'usable' part of a local authority's capital receipts consists of

25 per cent of receipts from the sale of council houses and 50 per cent of other housing assets such as shops or vacant land. The balance has to be set aside as provision for repaying debt and meeting other credit liabilities.

EXPENDITURE

Local authority budgeted net expenditure for 2011–12 is:

Service	£ million
Education	43,002
Highways and transport	5,602
Social care	21,201
Housing (excluding HRA)	2,339
Cultural, environment and planning	9,796
Police	11,840
Fire and rescue	2,224
Central services	3,525
Mandatory rent allowances	13,925
Mandatory rent rebates	488
Rent rebates granted to HRA tenants	4,035
Other services	82
Net current expenditure	118,059
Capital financing	4,202
Capital expenditure charged to revenue account	1,171
Council tax benefit	4,141
Discretionary non-domestic rate relief	29
Bad debt provision	45
Flood defence payments to Environment Agency	32
Private Finance Initiative schemes	46
Less interest receipts	(390)
Less specific grants outside AEF	(25,229)
Less Business Rates Supplement	(222)
Gross revenue expenditure	101,885
Less specific grants inside AEF	(44,649)
Less Local Services Support Grant	(189)
NET REVENUE EXPENDITURE	57,048

HRA = Housing Revenue Account
AEF = aggregate external finance

LONDON

The Greater London Council was abolished in 1986 and London was divided into 32 borough councils, which have a status similar to the metropolitan borough councils in the rest of England, and the City of London Corporation.

In March 1998 the government announced proposals for a Greater London Authority (GLA) covering the area of the 32 London boroughs and the City of London, which would comprise a directly elected mayor and a 25-member assembly. A referendum was held in London on 7 May 1998; the turnout was approximately 34 per cent and 72 per cent of electors voted in favour of the GLA. A London mayor was elected on 4 May 2000 and the authority assumed its responsibilities on 3 July 2000 (*see also* Regional Government).

The GLA is responsible for transport, economic development, strategic planning, culture, health, the environment, the police and fire and emergency planning. The separately elected assembly scrutinises the mayor's activities and approves plans and budgets. There are 14 constituency assembly members, each representing a separate area of London (each constituency is made up of two or three complete London boroughs). Eleven additional members, making up the total assembly complement of 25 members, are elected on a London-wide basis, either as independents or from party political lists on the basis of proportional representation.

LONDON BOROUGH COUNCILS

The London boroughs have whole council elections every four years, in the year immediately following the county council election year. The most recent elections took place on 6 May 2010.

The borough councils have responsibility for the following functions: building regulations, cemeteries and crematoria, consumer protection, education, youth employment, environmental health, electoral registration, food, drugs, housing, leisure services, libraries, local planning, local roads, museums, parking, recreation (parks, playing fields, swimming pools), refuse collection and street cleaning, social services, town planning and traffic management.

CITY OF LONDON CORPORATION

The City of London Corporation is the local authority for the City of London. Its legal definition is the 'Mayor and Commonalty and Citizens of the City of London'. It is governed by the court of common council, which consists of the lord mayor, 25 other aldermen and 100 common councilmen. The lord mayor and two sheriffs are nominated annually by the City guilds (the livery companies) and elected by the court of common council. Aldermen and councilmen are elected from the 25 wards into which the City is divided; councilmen must stand for re-election annually. The council is a legislative assembly, and there are no political parties.

The corporation has the same functions as the London borough councils. In addition, it runs the City of London Police; is the health authority for the Port of London; has health control of animal imports throughout Greater London, including at Heathrow airport; owns and manages public open spaces throughout Greater London; runs the central criminal court; and runs Billingsgate, Smithfield and Spitalfields markets.

THE CITY GUILDS (LIVERY COMPANIES)

The livery companies of the City of London grew out of early medieval religious fraternities and began to emerge as trade and craft guilds, retaining their religious aspect, in the 12th century. From the early 14th century, only members of the trade and craft guilds could call themselves citizens of the City of London. The guilds began to be called livery companies, because of the distinctive livery worn by the most prosperous guild members on ceremonial occasions, in the late 15th century.

By the early 19th century the power of the companies within their trades had begun to wane, but those wearing the livery of a company continued to play an important role in the government of the City of London. Liverymen still have the right to nominate the lord mayor and sheriffs, and most members of the court of common council are liverymen.

WALES

The Local Government (Wales) Act 1994 abolished the two-tier structure of eight county and 37 district councils which had existed since 1974, and replaced it, from 1 April 1996, with 22 unitary authorities. The new authorities were elected in May 1995. Each unitary authority inherited all the functions of the previous county and district councils, except fire services (which are provided by three combined fire authorities, composed of representatives from the unitary authorities) and national parks (which are the responsibility of three independent national park authorities).

COMMUNITY COUNCILS
In Wales community councils are the equivalent of parishes in England. Unlike England, where many areas are not in any parish, communities have been established for the whole of Wales, approximately 865 communities in all. Community meetings may be convened as and when desired.

Community or town councils exist in around 740 of the communities and further councils may be established at the request of a community meeting. Community councils have broadly the same range of powers as English parish councils. Community councillors are elected for a term of four years.

ELECTIONS
Elections take place every four years; the last elections took place in May 2008.

FINANCE
Total budgeted revenue expenditure for 2011–12 is £7.6bn, an increase of 0.9 per cent on 2010–11. Total budget requirement, which excludes expenditure financed by specific and special government grants and any use of reserves, is £5.8bn. This comprises revenue support grant of £3.4bn, support from the national non-domestic rate pool of £787m, police grant of £246m and £1.3bn to be raised through council tax. The non-domestic rating multiplier for Wales for 2011–12 is 42.8p. The average Band D council tax levied in Wales for 2011–12 is £1,162, comprising unitary authorities £954, police authorities £183 and community councils £25.

EXPENDITURE
Local authority budgeted net revenue expenditure for 2011–12 is:

Service	£ million
Education	2,576
Social services	1,440
Council fund housing, including housing benefit	965
Local environmental services	419
Roads and transport	316
Libraries, culture, heritage, sport and recreation	264
Planning, economic and community development	134
Council tax collection	30
Debt financing costs: counties	326
Central administrative and other revenue expenditure	303
Police	663
Fire	149
National parks	16
Gross revenue expenditure	7,602
Less specific and special government grants	(1,826)
Net revenue expenditure	5,777
Less appropriations from reserves	(22)
BUDGET REQUIREMENT	5,755

SCOTLAND

The Local Government etc (Scotland) Act 1994 abolished the two-tier structure of nine regional and 53 district councils which had existed since 1975 and replaced it, from 1 April 1996, with 29 unitary authorities on the mainland; the three islands councils remained. The new authorities were elected in April 1995.

In July 1999 the Scottish parliament assumed responsibility for legislation on local government. The government had established a commission on local government and the Scottish parliament (the McIntosh Commission) to make recommendations on the relationship between local authorities and the Scottish parliament and on increasing local authorities' accountability.

The local government in Scotland bill was introduced to the Scottish parliament in May 2002. The bill focused on three integrated core elements:
- A power for local authorities to promote and improve the well-being of their area and/or persons in it
- Statutory underpinning for community planning through the introduction of a duty on local authorities and key partners, including police, health boards and enterprise agencies
- A duty to secure best value

ELECTIONS
The unitary authorities consist of directly elected councillors. The Scottish Local Government (Elections) Act 2002 moved elections from a three-year to a four-year cycle, but to avoid the local authority elections coinciding with the Scottish parliament elections in May 2011, local authority elections are now due to take place in May 2012. The last elections took place in May 2007.

FUNCTIONS
The functions of the councils and islands councils are: education; social work; strategic planning; the provision of infrastructure such as roads; consumer protection; flood prevention; coast protection; valuation and rating; the police and fire services; civil defence; electoral registration; public transport; registration of births, deaths and marriages; housing; leisure and recreation; development and building control; environmental health; licensing; allotments; public conveniences; and the administration of district courts.

COMMUNITY COUNCILS
Scottish community councils differ from those in England and Wales. Their purpose as defined in statute is to ascertain and express the views of the communities they represent, and to take in the interests of their communities such action as appears to be expedient or practicable. Around 1,200 community councils have been established under schemes drawn up by local authorities in Scotland.

FINANCE
Budgeted total revenue support for 2011–12 is £10.4bn, comprising £7.7bn general revenue funding, non-domestic rate income of £2.2bn and ring-fenced grants of £503m. The non-domestic rate multiplier or poundage for 2011–12 is 42.6p. All non-domestic properties with a rateable value of £18,000 or less may be eligible for non-domestic rates relief of up to 100 per cent. The average Band D council tax for 2011–12 is £1,149.

EXPENDITURE
Local authority budgeted net revenue expenditure for
2011–12 is:

Service	£ million
Education	4,623
Cultural and related services	607
Social work services	2,859
Police	951
Roads and transport	475
Environmental services	693
Fire	264
Planning and development services	280
Other	2,006
TOTAL	12,759

NORTHERN IRELAND

For the purpose of local government, Northern Ireland
has a system of 26 single-tier district councils.

ELECTIONS
Council members are elected for periods of four years at a
time on the principle of proportional representation. The
last elections took place in May 2011.

FUNCTIONS
The district councils have three main roles. These are:
Executive: responsibility for a wide range of local services
including building regulations; community services;
consumer protection; cultural facilities; environmental
health; miscellaneous licensing and registration
provisions, including dog control; litter prevention;
recreational and social facilities; refuse collection and
disposal; street cleaning; and tourist development
Representative: nominating representatives to sit as
members of the various statutory bodies responsible for
the administration of regional services such as drainage,
education, fire, health and personal social services,
housing, and libraries
Consultative: acting as the medium through which the
views of local people are expressed on the operation in
their area of other regional services – notably
conservation (including water supply and sewerage
services), planning and roads – provided by those
departments of central government which have an
obligation, statutory or otherwise, to consult the
district councils about proposals affecting their areas

FINANCE
Government in Northern Ireland is part-funded by a
system of rates, which supplement the Northern Ireland
budget from the UK government. The ratepayer receives a
combined tax bill consisting of the regional rate, set by
the Northern Ireland executive, and the district rate,
which is set by each district council. The regional and
district rates are both collected by the Land and Property
Services Agency (formerly the Rate Collection Agency).
The product of the district rates is paid over to each
council while the product of the regional rate supports
expenditure by the departments of the executive and
assembly.
   Since April 2007 domestic rates bills have been based
on the capital value of a property, rather than the rental
value. The capital value is defined as the price the
property might reasonably be expected to realise had it
been sold on the open market on 1 January 2005.
Non-domestic rates bills are based on 2001 rental values.
   Rate bills are calculated by multiplying the property's
net annual rental value (in the case of non-domestic
property), or capital value (in the case of domestic
property), by the regional and district rate poundages
respectively.
   For 2011–12 the overall average domestic poundage is
0.6888p compared to 0.6731p in 2010–11. The overall
average non-domestic rate poundage in 2011–12 is
55.61p compared to 54.33p in 2010–11.

POLITICAL COMPOSITION OF LOCAL COUNCILS

as at May 2011

Abbreviations

All.	Alliance
BNP	British National Party
C.	Conservative
DUP	Democratic Unionist Party
Green	Green
Ind.	Independent
Ind. Un.	Independent Unionist
Lab.	Labour
LD	Liberal Democrat
Lib.	Liberal
O.	Other
PC	Plaid Cymru
R	Residents Associations/Ratepayers
SD	Social Democrat
SDLP	Social Democratic and Labour Party
SF	Sinn Fein
SNP	Scottish National Party
Soc.	Socialist
UUP	Ulster Unionist Party
v.	Vacant

Total number of seats is given in parentheses after council name.

ENGLAND

COUNTY COUNCILS

Buckinghamshire (57)	C. 46; LD 11
Cambridgeshire (69)	C. 41; LD 21; Lab. 3; Ind. 2; Green 1; O. 1
Cumbria (84)	C. 39; Lab. 24; LD 15; Ind. 4; O. 2
Derbyshire (64)	C. 33; Lab. 21; LD 8; v. 2
Devon (62)	C. 41; LD 13; Lab. 5; Ind. 2; Green 1
Dorset (45)	C. 28; LD 16; Ind. 1
East Sussex (49)	C. 29; LD 13; Lab. 4; O. 2; Ind. 1
Essex (75)	C. 59; LD 11; Lab. 2; Ind. 2; v. I
Gloucestershire (63)	C. 40; LD 14; Lab. 5; O. 2; Ind. 1; Green 1
Hampshire (78)	C. 51; LD 25; Lab. 1; O. 1
Hertfordshire (77)	C. 55; LD 17; Lab. 3; Green 1; O. 1
Kent (84)	C. 73; LD 7; Lab. 3; O. 1
Lancashire (84)	C. 51; Lab. 17; LD 9; Ind. 3; Green 2; BNP 1; O. 1
Leicestershire (55)	C. 36; LD 14; Lab. 4; Ind. 1
Lincolnshire (77)	C. 61; Ind. 7; LD 5; Lab. 4
Norfolk (84)	C. 60; LD 13; Green 7; Lab. 3; O. 1
North Yorkshire (72)	C. 47; LD 11; Ind. 9; Lib. 2; O. 2; Lab. 1
Northamptonshire (73)	C. 56; LD 9; Lab. 6; Ind. 2
Nottinghamshire (67)	C. 35; Lab. 15; LD 9; O. 6; Ind. 2
Oxfordshire (74)	C. 52; LD 10; Lab. 9; Green 2; Ind. 1
Somerset (58)	C. 34; LD 22; Lab. 2
Staffordshire (62)	C. 48; O. 10; Lab. 2; v. 2
Suffolk (75)	C. 55; LD 11; Lab. 4; Green 2; Ind. 2; O. 1
Surrey (80)	C. 56; LD. 13; Ind. 10; Lab. 1
Warwickshire (62)	C. 39; LD 11; Lab. 11; Ind. 1
West Sussex (71)	C. 49; LD 19; Lab. 2; Ind. 1
Worcestershire (57)	C. 41; LD 8; Lab. 3; O. 3; Lib. 1; Ind. 1

DISTRICT COUNCILS

Adur (29)	C. 25; Ind. 2; LD. 2
Allerdale (56)	Lab. 28; C. 12; Ind. 10; O. 6
Amber Valley (45)	C. 28; Lab. 15; BNP 2
Arun (56)	C. 48; LD 4; Lab. 3; Ind. 1
Ashfield (33)	Lab. 24; LD 6; Ind. 3
Ashford (43)	C. 30; Lab. 5; O. 5; LD 2; Ind. 1
Aylesbury Vale (59)	C. 37; LD 17; Lab. 2; O. 2; Ind. 1
Babergh (43)	C. 18; LD 12; Ind. 9; lab. 3; O. 1
Barrow-in-Furness (36)	Lab. 29; C. 7
Basildon (42)	C. 29; Lab. 11; LD 2
Basingstoke and Deane (60)	C. 34; LD 13; Lab. 11; Ind. 2
Bassetlaw (48)	Lab. 27; C. 18; Ind. 3
Blaby (39)	C. 28; Lab. 6; LD 5
Bolsover (37)	Lab. 31; Ind. 4; R 1; Green 1
Boston (32)	C. 19; O. 6; Ind. 4; Lab. 3
Braintree (60)	C. 47; Lab. 9; Green 2; R 1; Ind. 1
Breckland (54)	C. 47; Lab. 4; Ind. 3
Brentwood (37)	C. 28; LD 7; Ind. 1; Lab. 1
Broadland (47)	C. 34; LD 12; Lab. 1
Bromsgrove (39)	C. 27; Lab. 10; R 2
Broxbourne (38)	C. 34; Lab. 3; v. 1
Broxtowe (44)	C. 18; Lab. 17; LD 9
Burnley (45)	LD 21; Lab. 18; C. 5; BNP 1
Cambridge (42)	LD 25; Lab. 14; Green 2; Ind. 1
Cannock Chase (41)	Lab. 17; C. 13; LD 11
Canterbury (50)	C. 37; LD 10; Lab. 3
Carlisle (52)	Lab. 24; C. 22; LD 4; Ind. 2
Castle Point (41)	C. 25; Ind. 16
Charnwood (52)	C. 33; Lab. 16; LD 1; BNP 1; Ind. 1
Chelmsford (57)	C. 40; LD 15; Lab. 1; Ind. 1
Cheltenham (40)	LD 25; C. 12; O. 3
Cherwell (50)	C. 43; Lab. 4; LD 3
Chesterfield (48)	Lab. 34; LD 14
Chichester (48)	C. 38; LD 8; Ind. 2
Chiltern (40)	C. 33; LD 5; Ind. 2
Chorley (47)	C. 23; Lab. 20; LD 2; Ind. 2
Christchurch (24)	C. 21; Ind. 2; LD 1
Colchester (60)	LD 26; C. 24; Lab. 7; Ind. 3
Copeland (51)	Lab. 34; C. 15; Ind. 2
Corby (29)	Lab. 22; C. 4; LD 3
Cotswolds (44)	C. 27; LD 12; Ind. 5
Craven (30)	C. 18; Ind. 9; LD 3
Crawley (37)	C. 24; Lab. 13
Dacorum (51)	C. 43; LD 6; Lab. 2
Dartford (44)	C. 31; Lab. 9; R 4
Daventry (38)	C. 34; LD 2; Lab. 2
Derbyshire Dales (39)	C. 28; Lab. 5; LD 4; Ind. 1; v. 1
Dover (45)	C. 26; Lab. 19
East Cambridgeshire (39)	C. 25; LD 10; Ind. 4
East Devon (59)	C. 43; LD 10; Ind. 6
East Dorset (36)	C. 30; LD 6
East Hampshire (44)	C. 39; LD 5
East Hertfordshire (50)	C. 46; LD 2; Ind. 2
East Lindsey (60)	C. 30; Ind. 15; Lab. 10; O. 5

East Northamptonshire (40)   C. 35; Ind. 3; Lab. 2

East Staffordshire (39)   C. 22; Lab. 16; LD 1

Eastbourne (27)   LD 15; C. 12

Eastleigh (44)   LD 38; C. 4; Ind. 2

Eden (38)   C. 16; Ind. 10; LD 9; O. 3

Elmbridge (60)   C. 35; R 18; LD 5; O. 2

Epping Forest (58)   C. 37; R 10; LD 6; Ind. 3; BNP 1; Lab. 1

Epsom and Ewell (38)   R 26; LD 6; C. 3; Lab.3

Erewash (51)   C. 26; Lab. 25

Exeter (40)   Lab. 19; C. 11; LD 9; Lib. 1

Fareham (31)   C. 23; LD 7; Ind. 1

Fenland (40)   C. 34; Ind. 4; LD 2

Forest Heath (27)   C. 23; LD 2; Ind. 1; Lab. 1

Forest of Dean (48)   C. 19; Lab. 17; Ind. 9; O. 2; LD 1

Fylde (51)   C. 28; Ind. 17; O. 3; LD 3

Gedling (50)   Lab. 32; C. 15; LD 3

Gloucester (36)   C. 19; LD 10; Lab. 7

Gosport (34)   C. 22; LD 5; Lab. 3; Ind. 2; O. 2

Gravesham (44)   Lab. 25; C. 19

Great Yarmouth (39)   C. 24; Lab. 14; Ind. 1

Guildford (48)   C. 34; LD 12; Lab. 2

Hambleton (44)   C. 39; Ind. 3; LD 2

Harborough (37)   C. 27; LD 10

Harlow (33)   C. 17; Lab. 14; LD 2

Harrogate (54)   C. 34; LD 17; Ind. 2; Lib. 1

Hart (35)   C. 20; LD 10; O. 5

Hastings (32)   Lab 17; C. 14; LD 1

Havant (38)   C. 35; LD 2; Lab. 1

Hertsmere (39)   C. 35; Lab. 4

High Peak (43)   Lab. 21; C. 15; LD 3; Ind. 3; O. 1

Hinckley and Bosworth (34)   LD 18; C. 15; Lab. 1

Horsham (44)   C. 34; LD 8; Ind. 2

Huntingdonshire (52)   C. 41; LD 8; O. 2; Ind. 1

Hyndburn (35)   Lab. 18; C. 14; Ind. 3

Ipswich (48)   Lab. 28; C. 16; LD 4

Kettering (36)   C. 26; Lab. 9; Ind. 1

King's Lynn and West Norfolk (62)   C. 42; Lab. 13; LD 3; Ind. 3; Green 1

Lancaster (60)   Lab. 24; C. 16; Ind. 12; Green 8

Lewes (41)   C. 22; LD 18; Ind. 1

Lichfield (56)   C. 46; LD 10

Lincoln City (33)   Lab. 17; C. 15; LD 1

Maidstone (55)   C. 30; LD 21; Ind. 4

Maldon (31)   C. 28; Ind. 3

Malvern Hills (38)   C. 21; LD 11; Ind. 4; Green 2

Mansfield (46)   Lab. 25; Ind. 10; v. 1

Melton (28)   C. 20; Lab. 7; Ind. 1

Mendip (47)   C. 31; LD 15; Ind. 1

Mid Devon (42)   C. 24; Ind. 10; LD 6; Lib. 1; O. 1

Mid Suffolk (40)   C. 22; LD 6; Ind. 5; Green 4; O. 2; Lab. 1

Mid Sussex (54)   C. 45; LD 8; Lab. 1

Mole Valley (41)   C. 18; LD 17; Ind. 5; O. 1

New Forest (60)   C. 54; LD 6

Newark and Sherwood (46)   C. 22; Lab. 15; Ind. 6; LD 3

Newcastle-under-Lyme (60)   Lab. 25; C. 21; LD 12; O. 2

North Devon (43)   C. 18; LD 14; Ind. 11

North Dorset (33)   C. 23; LD 6; Ind. 3; O. 1

North East Derbyshire (53)   Lab. 34; C. 17; Ind. 2

North Hertfordshire (49)   C. 34; LD 8; Lab. 7

North Kesteven (43)   C. 27; O. 9; Ind. 4; LD 3

North Norfolk (48)   C. 28; LD 18; Ind. 1; O. 1

North Warwickshire (35)   Lab. 18; C. 17

North West Leicestershire (38)   C. 21; Lab. 16; LD 1

Northampton (45)   C. 26; Lab. 15; LD 4

Norwich (39)   Lab. 18; Green 15; LD 4; C. 2

Nuneaton and Bedworth (34)   Lab. 17; C. 14; Ind. 2; BNP 1

Oadby and Wigston (26)   LD 23; C. 3

Oxford (48)   Lab. 26; LD 16; Green 5; O. 1

Pendle (49)   C. 18; Lab. 16; LD 12; BNP 2; Ind. 1

Preston (57)   Lab. 29; C. 21; LD 6; Ind. 1

Purbeck (24)   C. 11; LD 10; Ind. 2; v. 1

Redditch (29)   C. 17; Lab. 11; LD 1

Reigate and Banstead (51)   C. 35; R 7; LD 3; O. 3; Green 2; Ind. 1

Ribble Valley (40)   C. 33; LD 6; Ind. 1

Richmondshire (34)   Ind. 16; C. 14; LD 4

Rochford (39)   C. 31; LD 4; Green 2; R 2

Rossendale (36)   Lab. 17; C. 16 LD 2; O. 1

Rother (38)   C. 27; LD 5; Ind. 3; Lab. 2; O. 1

Rugby (48)   C. 29; Lab. 11; LD 8

Runnymede (42)   C. 36; Ind. 6

Rushcliffe (50)   C. 36; LD 6; Lab. 5; Green 2; Ind. 1

Rushmoor (42)   C. 32; Lab. 6; LD 4

Ryedale (30)   C. 20; Lib. 4; Ind. 3; LD 2; O. 1

St Albans (58)   C. 29; LD 24; Lab. 3; Ind. 1; Green 1

St Edmundsbury (45)   C. 38; Ind. 4; Lab. 3

Scarborough (50)   C. 25; Ind. 12; Lab. 6; LD 3; Green 2; O. 2

Sedgemoor (48)   C. 31; Lab. 13; LD 2; Ind. 2

Selby (41)   C. 29; Lab. 10; Ind. 2

Sevenoaks (54)   C. 47; Lab. 4; LD 2; Ind. 1

Shepway (46)   C. 44; O. 2

South Bucks (40)   C. 38; Ind. 1; LD 1

South Cambridgeshire (57)   C. 31; LD 18; Ind. 7; Lab. 1

South Derbyshire (36)   C. 19; Lab. 17

South Hams (40)   C. 30; LD 5; Green 3; Ind. 1; Lab. 1

South Holland (37)   C. 25; Ind. 12

South Kesteven (58)   C. 38; Ind. 12; Lab. 6; LD 1; O. 1

South Lakeland (51)   LD 32; C. 18; Lab. 1

South Norfolk (46)   C. 38; LD 8

South Northamptonshire (42)   C. 33; Ind. 7; LD 2

South Oxfordshire (48)   C. 33; LD 4; Ind. 4; Lab. 4; R 2; O. 1

South Ribble (55)   C. 33; Lab. 21; LD 1

South Somerset (60)   LD 31; C. 25; Ind. 4

South Staffordshire (49)   C. 42; Ind. 5; Lab. 2

Spelthorne (39)   C. 32; LD 6; Ind. 1

Stafford (59)   C. 38; Lab. 17; LD 3

Staffordshire Moorlands (56)   C. 25; Ind. 11; O. 9; Lab. 7; LD 4

Stevenage (39)   Lab. 27; C. 9; LD 3

Stratford-on-Avon (53)   C. 34; LD 16; Ind. 2; O. 1

Stroud (51)   C. 26; Lab. 11; LD 6; Green 6; Ind. 1; O. 1

Suffolk Coastal (55)   C. 44; LD 5; Lab. 4; Ind. 1; O. 1

Surrey Heath (40)   C. 35; Lab. 2; Ind. 2; LD 1

Swale (47) — C. 32; Lab. 13; Ind. 2
Tamworth (30) — C. 23; Lab. 6; Ind. 1
Tandridge (42) — C. 34; LD 6; Ind. 2
Taunton Deane (56) — C. 28; LD 23; lab. 3; Ind. 2
Teignbridge (46) — C. 26; LD 13; Ind. 7
Tendring (60) — C. 33; Lab. 9; Ind. 8; O. 8; LD 2
Test Valley (48) — C. 36; LD 12
Tewkesbury (38) — C. 24; LD 11; O. 2; Ind. 1
Thanet (56) — C. 27; Lab. 26; Ind. 3
Three Rivers (48) — LD 29; C. 14; Lab. 4; Ind. 1
Tonbridge and Malling (53) — C. 48; LD 4; Lab. 1
Torridge (36) — C. 18; Ind. 8; LD 6; O. 2; Lab. 1; Green 1
Tunbridge Wells (48) — C. 39; LD 6; Lab. 1; Ind. 1; O. 1
Uttlesford (44) — C. 34; LD 8; Ind. 2
Vale of White Horse (51) — C. 31; LD 19; Lab. 1
Warwick (46) — C. 25; LD 9; Lab. 8; R 3; Ind. 4
Watford (37) — LD 25; Lab. 6; C. 3; Green 3
Waveney (48) — C. 23; Lab. 23; Green 1; Ind. 1
Waverley (57) — C. 56; Ind. 1
Wealden (55) — C. 47; Ind. 4; LD 3; O. 1
Wellingborough (36) — C. 27; Lab. 9
Welwyn and Hatfield (48) — C. 37; Lab. 9; LD 2
West Devon (31) — C. 19; Ind. 8; LD 3; O. 1
West Dorset (48) — C. 32; LD 11; Ind. 5
West Lancashire (54) — C. 33; Lab. 21
West Lindsey (37) — C. 21; LD 11; Ind. 3; Lab. 2
West Oxfordshire (49) — C. 44; LD 4; Lab. 1
West Somerset (28) — C. 19; Ind. 7; Lab. 2
Weymouth and Portland (36) — C. 16; LD 10; Lab. 7; Ind. 3
Winchester (57) — C. 27; LD 27; Ind. 2; Lab. 1
Woking (36) — C. 20; LD 16
Worcester (35) — C. 18; Lab. 12; LD 3; Ind. 2
Worthing (37) — C. 25; LD 11; Lib. 1
Wychavon (45) — C. 39; LD 5; Lab. 1
Wycombe (60) — C. 42; Lab. 7; LD 8; Ind. 2; O. 1
Wyre (55) — C. 40; Lab. 15
Wyre Forest (42) — C. 24; Lab. 7; O. 5; Lib. 4; Ind. 2

LONDON BOROUGH COUNCILS

Barking and Dagenham (51) — Lab. 51
Barnet (63) — C. 39; Lab. 21; LD 3
Bexley (63) — C. 52; Lab. 11
Brent (63) — Lab. 40; LD 17; C. 6
Bromley (60) — C. 53; LD 4; Lab. 3
Camden (54) — Lab. 30; LD 13; C. 10; Green 1
Croydon (70) — C. 37; Lab. 33
Ealing (69) — Lab. 40; C. 24; LD 5
Enfield (63) — Lab. 36; C. 26; v. 1
Greenwich (51) — Lab. 40; C. 11
Hackney (57) — Lab. 49; C. 5; LD 3
Hammersmith and Fulham (46) — Lab. 31; C. 15
Haringey (57) — Lab. 34; LD 23
Harrow (63) — Lab. 34; C. 26; Ind. 2; LD 1
Havering (54) — C. 33; R 12; Lab. 5; Ind. 4
Hillingdon (65) — C. 46; Lab. 19
Hounslow (60) — Lab. 35; C. 25
Islington (48) — Lab. 35; LD 13

Kensington and Chelsea (54) — C. 40; Lab. 9; LD 3; v. 2
Kingston upon Thames (48) — LD 27; C. 21
Lambeth (63) — Lab. 44; LD 15; C. 4
Lewisham (55) — Lab. 39; LD 12; C. 2; Green 1
Merton (60) — Lab. 28; C. 27; R 3; LD 2
Newham (60) — Lab. 60
Redbridge (63) — C. 29; Lab. 26; LD 7; Ind. 1
Richmond upon Thames (54) — C. 30; LD 24
Southwark (63) — Lab. 35; LD 25; C. 3
Sutton (54) — LD 43; C. 11
Tower Hamlets (51) — Lab. 32; C. 8; Ind. 8; O. 2; LD 1
Waltham Forest (60) — Lab. 36; C. 18; LD 6
Wandsworth (60) — C. 47; Lab.13
Westminster (60) — C. 48; Lab. 12

METROPOLITAN BOROUGHS

Barnsley (63) — Lab. 43; Ind. 13; C. 6; O. 1
Birmingham (120) — Lab. 55; C. 39; LD 24; O. 2
Bolton (60) — Lab. 35; C. 20; LD 5
Bradford (90) — Lab. 44; C. 28; LD 11; Ind. 4; Green 3
Bury (51) — Lab. 26; C. 20 LD 8
Calderdale (51) — C. 21; LD 13; Lab. 13; Ind. 2; BNP 1; O. 1
Coventry (54) — Lab. 35; C. 17; LD 1; Soc. 1
Doncaster (64) — Lab. 43; C. 9; LD 6; O. 5; Ind. 1
Dudley (72) — C. 43; Lab. 28; O. 1
Gateshead (66) — Lab. 50; LD 15; Lib. 1
Kirklees (69) — Lab. 27; C. 22; LD 14; Green 4; Ind. 2
Knowsley (63) — Lab. 58; LD 4; v. 1
Leeds (99) — Lab. 55; C. 21; LD 16; O. 5; Green 2
Liverpool (90) — Lab. 62; LD 21; Lib. 3; Green 2; Ind. 1; O. 1
Manchester (96) — Lab. 75; LD 20; Ind. 1
Newcastle-upon-Tyne (78) — Lab. 45; LD 32; Ind.1
North Tyneside (60) — Lab. 35; C. 19; LD 6
Oldham (60) — Lab. 34; LD 21; C. 5
Rochdale (60) — Lab. 31; C. 17; LD 12
Rotherham (63) — Lab. 54; C. 7; Ind. 1; BNP 1
St Helens (48) — Lab. 35; LD 9; C. 4
Salford (60) — Lab. 44; C. 11; LD 3; Ind. 2
Sandwell (72) — Lab. 60; C. 9; Ind. 1; LD 1
Sefton (66) — LD 28; Lab. 23; C. 11; Ind. 3; O. 1
Sheffield (84) — Lab. 49; LD 32; Green 2; Ind. 1
Solihull (51) — C. 29; LD 12; Lab. 6; Green 3; Ind. 1
South Tyneside (54) — Lab. 39; O. 9; Ind. 4; C. 1; LD 1
Stockport (63) — LD 31; Lab. 18; C. 11; Ind. 3
Sunderland (75) — Lab. 56; C. 14; Ind. 3; LD 1; O. 1
Tameside (57) — Lab. 48; C. 8; Ind. 1
Trafford (63) — C. 37; Lab. 22; LD 4
Wakefield (63) — Lab. 39; C. 21; Ind. 3
Walsall (60) — C. 28; Lab. 26; LD 5; Ind. 1
Wigan (75) — Lab. 58; Ind. 8; C. 5; O. 2; LD 2
Wirral (66) — Lab. 30; C. 27; LD 9
Wolverhampton (60) — Lab. 35; C. 22; LD 3

UNITARY COUNCILS

Bath and North East Somerset (65)   C. 29; LD 29; Lab. 5; Ind. 2

Bedford (40)   LD 12; C. 12; Lab. 12; Ind. 4

Blackburn with Darwen (64)   Lab. 38; C. 17; LD 6; O. 2; Ind. 1

Blackpool (42)   Lab. 27; C. 14; LD 1

Bournemouth (54)   C. 46; LD 3; Lab. 3; Ind. 2

Bracknell Forest (42)   C. 40; Lab. 2

Brighton and Hove (54)   Green 23; C. 18; Lab. 13

Bristol (70)   LD 33; Lab 21; C. 14; Green 2

Central Bedfordshire (59)   C. 49; LD 5; Ind. 3; Lab. 1; O. 1

Cheshire East (82)   C. 52; Lab. 14; Ind. 10; LD 4; v. 2

Cheshire West and Chester (75)   C. 42; Lab. 32; LD 1

Cornwall (123)   C. 47; LD 40; Ind. 31; O. 4; Lab. 1

Darlington (53)   Lab. 34; C. 14; LD 5

Derby (51)   Lab. 22; C. 16; LD 12; Ind. 1

Durham (126)   Lab. 69; LD 23; Ind. 21; C. 10; O. 3

East Riding of Yorkshire (67)   C. 53; Lab. 6; Ind. 4; LD 3; SD 1

Halton (56)   Lab. 44; LD 6; C. 3; O. 2; Ind. 1

Hartlepool (48)   Lab. 29; Ind. 13; C. 4; LD 2

Herefordshire (58)   C. 30; Ind. 14; O. 9; LD 3; Lab. 1; Green 1

Isles of Scilly (21)*   Ind. 21

Isle of Wight (40)   C. 24; Ind. 10; LD 4; Lab. 1; v. 1

Kingston-upon-Hull (59)   Lab. 34; LD 22; C. 2; O. 1

Leicester (54)   Lab. 52; C. 1; LD 1

Luton (48)   Lab. 36; LD 8; C. 4

Medway (55)   C. 35; Lab. 15; LD 3; Ind. 2

Middlesbrough (49)   Lab. 30; Ind. 7; O. 6; C. 4; LD 1; Green 1

Milton Keynes (51)   C. 21; LD 18; Lab. 9; Ind. 3

North East Lincolnshire (42)   Lab. 20; C. 14; LD 8

North Lincolnshire (43)   C. 23; Lab. 20

North Somerset (61)   C. 42; Ind. 7; LD 6; Lab. 5; Green 1

Northumberland (67)   LD 25; C. 17; Lab. 17; Ind. 5; O. 3

Nottingham (55)   Lab. 50; C. 5

Peterborough (57)   C. 38; Ind. 9; Lab. 6; LD 3; O. 1

Plymouth (57)   C. 32; Lab. 25

Poole (42)   C. 21; LD 18; Ind. 3

Portsmouth (42)   LD 23; C. 17; Lab. 2

Reading (46)   Lab. 22; C. 16; LD 5; Green 2; O. 1

Redcar and Cleveland (59)   Lab. 32; LD 16; C. 6; Ind. 5

Rutland (26)   C. 16; Ind. 8; LD 2

Shropshire (74)   C. 52; LD 13; Lab. 7; Ind. 2

Slough (41)   Lab. 27; C. 9; O. 5

South Gloucestershire (70)   C. 34; LD 21; Lab. 15

Southampton (48)   C. 26; Lab. 19; LD 3

Southend-on-Sea (51)   C. 28; LD 10; Ind. 9; Lab. 4

Stockton-on-Tees (56)   Lab. 27; O. 13; C. 12; LD 4

Stoke-on-Trent (44)   Lab. 34; Ind. 7; C. 2; O. 1

Swindon (59)   C. 38; Lab. 17; LD 4

Telford and Wrekin (54)   Lab. 33; C. 17; LD 3; Ind. 1

Thurrock (49)   Lab. 24; C. 22; Ind. 2; O. 1

Torbay (37)   C. 22; LD 10; Ind. 4; Lab. 1

Warrington (57)   Lab. 27; LD 24; C. 6

West Berkshire (52)   C. 39; LD 13

Wiltshire (98)   C. 61; LD 24; Ind. 8; O. 3; Lab. 2

Windsor and Maidenhead (57)   C. 51; Ind. 5; LD 1

Wokingham (54)   C. 45; LD 9

York (47)   Lab. 26; C. 10; LD 8; Green 2; Ind. 1

* Thirteen councillors are elected by the residents of the isle of St Mary's and two councillors each are elected by the residents of the four other islands (Bryher, St Agnes, St Martins and Tresco)

WALES

Blaenau Gwent (42)   Ind. 42; Lab. 15; O. 2

Bridgend (54)   Lab. 27; Ind. 14; C. 6; LD 6; PC 1

Caerphilly (73)   PC 32; Lab. 30; Ind. 8; O. 3

Cardiff (75)   LD 35; C. 17; Lab. 13; PC 7; Ind. 3

Carmarthenshire (74)   PC 30; Ind. 28; Lab. 11; O. 3; LD 1; v. 1

Ceredigion (42)   PC 20; Ind. 12; LD 9; Lab. 1

Conwy (59)   C. 19; PC 14; Ind. 13; Lab. 7; LD 5; v. 1

Denbighshire (47)   C. 18; Ind. 10; PC 8; Lab. 6; O. 4; LD 1

Flintshire (70)   Lab. 22; Ind. 19; O. 10; C. 9; LD 9; PC 1

Gwynedd (75)   PC 37; Ind. 16; O. 13; LD 4; Lab. 4; v. 1

Merthyr Tydfil (33)   Ind. 13; Lab. 10; O. 6; LD 4

Monmouthshire (43)   C. 27; Lab. 7; LD 4; O. 5

Neath Port Talbot (64)   Lab. 39; PC 11; Ind. 6; LD 3; SD 3; O. 2

Newport (50)   Lab. 21; C. 17; LD 9; Ind. 2; PC 1

Pembrokeshire (60)   Ind. 39; O. 6; C. 5; Lab. 5; PC 5

Powys (73)   O. 45; LD 14; C. 9; Lab. 4; O. 1

Rhondda Cynon Taff (75)   Lab. 48; PC 18; Ind. 5; LD 3; C. 1

Swansea (72)   Lab. 27; LD 22; O. 11; Ind. 6; C. 5; PC 1

Torfaen (44)   Lab. 20; Ind. 8; O. 7; C. 5; PC 2; LD 1; v. 1

Vale of Glamorgan (47)   C. 25; Lab. 12; PC 6; Ind. 4

Wrexham (52)   O. 27; Lab. 12; C. 5; Ind. 4; PC 4

Ynys Mon (Isle of Anglesey) (40)   Ind. 14; O. 13; PC 8; Lab. 5

SCOTLAND

Aberdeen (43)	LD 13; SNP 13; Lab. 10; C. 4; Ind. 1; v. 2
Aberdeenshire (68)	LD 21; SNP 20; C. 13; Ind. 9; O. 5
Angus (29)	SNP 13; Ind. 6; C. 5; LD 3; Lab. 2
Argyll and Bute (36)	Ind. ; SNP 10; LD 6; O. 6; C. 2
Clackmannanshire (18)	Lab. 8; SNP 7; C. 1; Ind. 1; LD 1
Dumfries and Galloway (47)	C. 18; Lab. 14; SNP 10; LD 3; Ind. 2; O. 1
Dundee (29)	SNP 14; Lab. 8; C. 3; Ind. 2; LD 2
East Ayrshire (32)	Lab. 15; SNP 14; C. 3
East Dunbartonshire (24)	SNP 8; Lab. 6; C. 4; LD 4; Ind. 2
East Lothian (23)	SNP 9; Lab. 7; LD 4; C. 2; Ind. 1
East Renfrewshire (20)	C. 7; Lab. 7; SNP 3; Ind. 2; LD 1
Edinburgh (58)	LD 17; Lab. 15; SNP 12; C. 11; Green 3
Eilean Siar (Western Isles) (31)	Ind. 25; SNP 4; Lab. 2
Falkirk (32)	Lab. 14; SNP 13; Ind. 2; C. 2; O. 1
Fife (78)	Lab. 24; SNP 22; LD 21; Ind. 7; C. 4
Glasgow (79)	Lab. 47; SNP 19; LD 6; Green 5; C. 1; Ind. 1
Highland (80)	Ind. 25; LD 20; SNP 18; O. 10; Lab. 7
Inverclyde (20)	Lab. 8; SNP 5; LD 3; Ind. 2; C. 1; Lib. 1
Midlothian (18)	Lab. 10; SNP 6; LD 2
Moray (26)	Ind. 12; SNP 10; C. 2; Lab. 2
North Ayrshire (30)	Lab. 12; SNP 8; Ind. 6; C. 2; LD 2
North Lanarkshire (70)	Lab. 41; SNP 22; Ind. 4; C. 1; LD 1; O. 1
Orkney Islands (21)	Ind. 21
Perth and Kinross (41)	SNP 18; C. 11; LD 7; Lab. 3; Ind. 2
Renfrewshire (40)	Lab. 19; SNP 18; LD 2; C. 1
Scottish Borders (34)	C. 11; LD 10; SNP 6; Ind. 5; O. 2
Shetland Islands (22)	Ind. 11; O. 11
South Ayrshire (30)	C. 12; SNP 9; Lab. 6; Ind. 3
South Lanarkshire (67)	Lab. 32; SNP 23; C. 8; Ind. 2; LD 2
Stirling (22)	Lab. 8; SNP 7; C. 4; LD 3
West Dunbartonshire (22)	SNP 9; Lab. 8; Ind. 4; O. 1
West Lothian (32)	Lab. 14; SNP 13; O. 3; C. 1; Ind. 1

NORTHERN IRELAND

Antrim (19)	DUP 5; UUP 5; SF 4; SDLP 3; All. 2
Ards (23)	DUP 11; UUP 6; All. 4; SDLP 1; Ind. 1
Armagh City (22)	Sf 6; UUP 6; SDLP 5; DUP 4; Ind. 1
Ballymena (24)	DUP 12; UUP 6; SDLP 2; SF 2; O. 2; All. 1; Ind. 1
Ballymoney (16)	DUP 8; SF 3; UUP 2; SDLP 1; Ind. 1; O. 1
Banbridge (17)	UUP 7; DUP 5; SDLP 2; SF 2; All. 1
Belfast (51)	SF 16; DUP 15; SDLP 8; All. 6; UUP 3; O. 2
Carrickfergus (17)	DUP 8; UUP 4; All. 3; Ind. 2
Castlereagh (23)	DUP 11; All. 6; UUP 3; SDLP 2; Green 1
Coleraine (22)	DUP 9; UUP 5; SDLP 3; All. 2; Ind. 2; SF 1
Cookstown (16)	SF 6; SDLP 4; DUP 3; UUP 3
Craigavon (26)	DUP 9; SF 8; UUP 6; SDLP 2; All. 1
Derry City (30)	SDLP 14; SF 10; DUP 5; UUP 1
Down (23)	SDLP 9; SF 5; DUP 3; UUP 3; All. 1; Green 1; Ind. 1s
Dungannon and South Tyrone (22)	SF 8; DUP 6; UUP 4; SDLP 3; Ind. 1
Fermanagh (23)	SF 9; UUP 6; DUP 4; SDLP 3; Ind. 1
Larne (15)	DUP 4; UUP 4; All. 2; Ind. 2; SDLP 2; O. 1
Limavady (15)	SF 6; SDLP 3; DUP 3; UUP 2; O. 1
Lisburn (30)	DUP 14; UUP 5; SF 5; All. 3; SDLP 3;
Magherafelt (16)	SF 9; DUP 3; SDLP 2; UUP 2
Moyle (15)	Ind. 4; DUP 3; SDLP 3; SF 3; UUP 2
Newry and Mourne (30)	SF 14; SDLP 10; UUP 3; Ind. 2; DUP 1
Newtownabbey (25)	DUP 12; UUP 5; All. 5; SF 2; SDLP 1
North Down (25)	DUP 11; All. 6; UUP 4; Ind. 3; Green 1
Omagh (21)	SF 10; DUP 3; SDLP 3; UUP 3; Ind. 2
Strabane (16)	SF 8; DUP 4; Ind. 2; SDLP 1; UUP 1

ENGLAND

The region of England lies between 55° 46' and 49° 57' 30" N. latitude (from a few miles north of the mouth of the Tweed to the Lizard), and between 1° 46' E. and 5° 43' W. longitude (from Lowestoft to Land's End). England is bounded on the north by the Cheviot Hills; on the south by the English Channel; on the east by the Straits of Dover (Pas de Calais) and the North Sea; and on the west by the Atlantic Ocean, Wales and the Irish Sea. It has a total area of 130,432 sq. km (50,360 sq. miles): land 130,279 sq. km (50,301 sq. miles); inland water 153 sq. km (59 sq. miles).

POPULATION
The population at the 2001 census was 49,138,831. The average density of the population in 2001 was 377 persons per sq. km (976 per sq. mile).

FLAG
The flag of England is the cross of St George, a red cross on a white field (cross gules in a field argent). The cross of St George, the patron saint of England, has been used since the 13th century.

RELIEF
There is a marked division between the upland and lowland areas of England. In the extreme north the Cheviot Hills (highest point, the Cheviot, 815m/2,674ft) form a natural boundary with Scotland. Running south from the Cheviots, though divided from them by the Tyne Gap, is the Pennine range (highest point, Cross Fell, 893m/2,930ft), the main orological feature of the country. The Pennines culminate in the Peak District of Derbyshire (Kinder Scout, 636m/2,088ft). West of the Pennines are the Cumbrian mountains, which include Scafell Pike (978m/3,210ft), the highest peak in England, and to the east are the Yorkshire Moors, their highest point being Urra Moor (454m/1,490ft).

In the west, the foothills of the Welsh mountains extend into the bordering English counties of Shropshire (the Wrekin, 407m/1,334ft; Long Mynd, 516m/1,694ft) and Hereford and Worcester (the Malvern Hills – Worcestershire Beacon, 425m/1,394ft). Extensive areas of highland and moorland are also to be found in the south-western peninsula formed by Somerset, Devon and Cornwall, principally Exmoor (Dunkery Beacon, 519m/1,704ft), Dartmoor (High Willhays, 621m/2,038ft) and Bodmin Moor (Brown Willy, 420m/1,377ft). Ranges of low, undulating hills run across the south of the country, including the Cotswolds in the Midlands and south-west, the Chilterns to the north of London, and the North (Kent) and South (Sussex) Downs of the south-east coastal areas.

The lowlands of England lie in the Vale of York, East Anglia and the area around the Wash. The lowest-lying are the Cambridgeshire Fens in the valleys of the Great Ouse and the river Nene, which are below sea-level in places. Since the 17th century extensive drainage has brought much of the Fens under cultivation. The North Sea coast between the Thames and the Humber, low-lying and formed of sand and shingle for the most part, is subject to erosion, and defences against further incursion have been built along many stretches.

HYDROGRAPHY
The Severn is the longest river in Great Britain, rising in the north-eastern slopes of Plynlimon (Wales) and entering England in Shropshire, with a total length of 354km (220 miles) from its source to its outflow into the Bristol Channel, where it receives the Bristol Avon on the east and the Wye on the west; its other tributaries are the Vyrnwy, Tern, Stour, Teme and Upper (or Warwickshire) Avon. The Severn is tidal below Gloucester, and a high bore or tidal wave sometimes reverses the flow as high as Tewkesbury (21.75km/13.5 miles above Gloucester). The scenery of the greater part of the river is very picturesque, and the Severn is a noted salmon river, with some of its tributaries being famous for trout. Navigation is assisted by the Gloucester and Berkeley Ship Canal (26km/16.25 miles), which admits vessels of 350 tons to Gloucester. The Severn Tunnel was begun in 1873 and completed in 1886 at a cost of £2m and after many difficulties caused by flooding. It is 7km (4 miles 628 yards) in length (of which 3.67km/2.25 miles are under the river). The Severn road bridge between Haysgate, Gwent, and Almondsbury, Glos, with a centre span of 988m (3,240ft), was opened in 1966.

The longest river wholly in England is the Thames, with a total length of 346km (215 miles) from its source in the Cotswold hills to the Nore, and is navigable by ocean-going ships to London Bridge. The Thames is tidal to Teddington (111km/69 miles from its mouth) and forms county boundaries almost throughout its course; on its banks are situated London, Windsor Castle, Eton College and Oxford University. Of the remaining English rivers, those flowing into the North Sea are the Tyne, Wear, Tees, Ouse and Trent from the Pennine Range, the Great Ouse (257km/160 miles), which rises in Northamptonshire, and the Orwell and Stour from the hills of East Anglia. Flowing into the English Channel are the Sussex Ouse from the Weald, and the Itchen from the Hampshire Hills, and the Axe, Teign, Dart, Tamar and Exe from the Devonian hills. Flowing into the Irish Sea are the Mersey, Ribble and Eden from the western slopes of the Pennines and the Derwent from the Cumbrian mountains.

The English Lakes, notable for their picturesque scenery and poetic associations, lie in Cumbria's Lake District; the largest are Windermere (14.7 sq. km/5.7 sq. miles), Ullswater (8.8 sq. km/3.4 sq. miles) and Derwent Water (5.3 sq. km/2.0 sq. miles).

ISLANDS
The Isle of Wight is separated from Hampshire by the Solent. The capital, Newport, stands at the head of the estuary of the Medina, and Cowes (at the mouth) is the chief port. Other centres are Ryde, Sandown, Shanklin, Ventnor, Freshwater, Yarmouth, Totland Bay, Seaview and Bembridge.

Lundy (the name is derived from the Old Norse for 'puffin island'), 18km (11 miles) north-west of Hartland Point, Devon, is around 5km (3 miles) long and almost 1km (half a mile) wide on average, with a total area of around 452 hectares (1,116 acres), and a population of around 18. It became the property of the National Trust in 1969 and is now principally a bird sanctuary and the UK's first marine conservation zone.

The Isles of Scilly comprise around 140 islands and skerries (total area, 10 sq. km/6 sq. miles) situated 45 km (28 miles) south-west of Land's End in Cornwall. Only five are inhabited: St Mary's, St Agnes, Bryher, Tresco and St Martin's. The population at the 2001 census was 2,153. The entire group has been designated an Area of Outstanding Natural Beauty because of its unique flora and fauna. Tourism and the winter/spring flower trade for the home market form the basis of the economy of the islands. The island group is a recognised rural development area.

EARLY HISTORY

Archaeological evidence suggests that England has been inhabited since at least the Palaeolithic period, though the extent of the various Palaeolithic cultures was dependent upon the degree of glaciation. The succeeding Neolithic and Bronze Age cultures have left abundant remains throughout the country; the best-known of these are the henges and stone circles of Stonehenge (ten miles north of Salisbury, Wilts) and Avebury (Wilts), both of which are believed to have been of religious significance. In the latter part of the Bronze Age the Goidels, a people of the Celtic race, invaded the country and brought with them Celtic civilisation and dialects; as a result place names in England bear witness to the spread of the invasion across the whole region.

THE ROMAN CONQUEST
The Roman conquest of Gaul (57–50 BC) brought Britain into close contact with Roman civilisation, but although Julius Caesar raided the south of Britain in 55 and 54 BC, conquest was not undertaken until nearly 100 years later. In AD 43 the Emperor Claudius dispatched Aulus Plautius, with a well-equipped force of 40,000, and himself followed with reinforcements in the same year. Success was delayed by the resistance of Caratacus (Caractacus), the British leader from AD 48–51, who was finally captured and sent to Rome, and by a great revolt in AD 61 led by Boudicca (Boadicea), Queen of the Iceni, but the south of Britain was secured by AD 70, and Wales and the area north to the Tyne by about AD 80.

In AD 122, the Emperor Hadrian visited Britain and built a continuous rampart, since known as Hadrian's Wall, from Wallsend to Bowness (Tyne to Solway). The work was entrusted by the Emperor Hadrian to Aulus Platorius Nepos, legate of Britain from AD 122 to 126, and it was intended to form the northern frontier of the Roman Empire.

The Romans administered Britain as a province under a governor, with a well-defined system of local government, each Roman municipality ruling itself and its surrounding territory, while London was the centre of the road system and the seat of the financial officials of the Province of Britain. Colchester, Lincoln, York, Gloucester and St Albans stand on the sites of five Roman municipalities, and Wroxeter, Caerleon, Chester, Lincoln and York were at various times the sites of legionary fortresses. Well-preserved Roman towns have been uncovered at or near Silchester *(Calleva Atrebatum)*, ten miles south of Reading, Wroxeter *(Viroconium Cornoviorum)*, near Shrewsbury, and St Albans *(Verulamium)* in Hertfordshire.

Four main groups of roads radiated from London, and a fifth (the Fosse) ran obliquely from Lincoln through Leicester, Cirencester and Bath to Exeter. Of the four groups radiating from London, one ran south-east to Canterbury and the coast of Kent, a second to Silchester

and thence to parts of western Britain and south Wales, a third (later known as Watling Street) ran through St Albans to Chester, with various branches, and the fourth reached Colchester, Lincoln, York and the eastern counties.

In the fourth century Britain was subjected to raids along the east coast by Saxon pirates, which led to the establishment of a system of coastal defences from the Wash to Southampton Water, with forts at Brancaster, Burgh Castle (Yarmouth), Walton (Felixstowe), Bradwell, Reculver, Richborough, Dover, Lympne, Pevensey and Porchester (Portsmouth). The Irish (Scoti) and Picts in the north were also becoming more aggressive and from around AD 350 incursions became more frequent and more formidable. As the Roman Empire came increasingly under attack towards the end of the fourth century, many troops were removed from Britain for service in other parts of the empire. The island was eventually cut off from Rome by the Teutonic conquest of Gaul, and with the withdrawal of the last Roman garrison early in the fifth century, the Romano-British were left to themselves.

SAXON SETTLEMENT
According to legend, the British King Vortigern called in the Saxons to defend his lands against the Picts. The Saxon chieftains Hengist and Horsa landed at Ebbsfleet, Kent, and established themselves in the Isle of Thanet, but the events during the one-and-a-half centuries between the final break with Rome and the re-establishment of Christianity are unclear. However, it would appear that over the course of this period the raids turned into large-scale settlement by invaders traditionally known as Angles (England north of the Wash and East Anglia), Saxons (Essex and southern England) and Jutes (Kent and the Weald), which pushed the Romano-British into the mountainous areas of the north and west. Celtic culture outside Wales and Cornwall survives only in topographical names. Various kingdoms established at this time attempted to claim overlordship of the whole country, hegemony finally being achieved by Wessex (with the capital at Winchester) in the ninth century. This century also saw the beginning of raids by the Vikings (Danes), which were resisted by Alfred the Great (871–899), who fixed a limit on the advance of Danish settlement by the Treaty of Wedmore (878), giving them the area north and east of Watling Street on the condition that they adopt Christianity.

In the tenth century the kings of Wessex recovered the whole of England from the Danes, but subsequent rulers were unable to resist a second wave of invaders. England paid tribute *(Danegeld)* for many years, and was invaded in 1013 by the Danes and ruled by Danish kings (including Cnut) from 1016 until 1042, when Edward the Confessor was recalled from exile in Normandy. On Edward's death in 1066 Harold Godwinson (brother-in-law of Edward and son of Earl Godwin of Wessex) was chosen to be King of England. After defeating (at Stamford Bridge, Yorkshire, 25 September 1066) an invading army under Harald Hadraada, King of Norway (aided by the outlawed Earl Tostig of Northumbria, Harold's brother), Harold was himself defeated at the Battle of Hastings on 14 October 1066, and the Norman conquest secured the throne of England for Duke William of Normandy, a cousin of Edward the Confessor.

CHRISTIANITY
Christianity reached the Roman province of Britain from Gaul in the third century (or possibly earlier). Alban,

traditionally Britain's first martyr, was put to death as a Christian during the persecution of Diocletian (22 June 303) at his native town *Verulamium*, and the Bishops of *Londinium, Eboracum* (York), and *Lindum* (Lincoln) attended the Council of Arles in 314. However, the Anglo-Saxon invasions submerged the Christian religion in England until the sixth century: conversion was undertaken in the north from 563 by Celtic missionaries from Ireland led by St Columba, and in the south by a mission sent from Rome in 597 which was led by St Augustine, who became the first archbishop of Canterbury. England appears to have been converted again by the end of the seventh century and followed, after the Council of Whitby in 663, the practices of the Roman Church, which brought the kingdom into the mainstream of European thought and culture.

PRINCIPAL CITIES

There are 50 cities in England and space constraints prevent us from including profiles of them all. Below is a selection of England's principal cities with the date on which city status was conferred in parenthesis. Other cities are: Chichester (pre-1900), Derby (1977), Ely (pre-1900), Exeter (pre-1900), Gloucester (pre-1900), Hereford (pre-1900), Lancaster (1937), Lichfield (pre-1900), London (pre-1900), Peterborough (pre-1900), Plymouth (1928), Portsmouth (1926), Preston (2002), Ripon (pre-1900), Salford (1926), Sunderland (1992), Truro (pre-1900), Wakefield (pre-1900), Wells (pre-1900), Westminster (pre-1900), Wolverhampton (2000) and Worcester (pre-1900).

Certain cities have also been granted a lord mayoralty – this grant confers no additional powers or functions and is purely honorific. Cities with lord mayors are Birmingham, Bradford, Bristol, Canterbury, Chester, Coventry, Exeter, Kingston-upon-Hull, Leeds, Leicester, Liverpool, London, Manchester, Newcastle-upon-Tyne, Norwich, Nottingham, Oxford, Plymouth, Portsmouth, Sheffield, Stoke-on-Trent, Westminster and York.

BATH (PRE-1900)

Bath stands on the River Avon between the Cotswold Hills to the north and the Mendips to the south. In the early 18th century, Bath became England's premier spa town where the rich and celebrated members of fashionable society gathered to 'take the waters' and enjoy the town's theatres and concert rooms. During this period the architect John Wood laid the foundations for a new Georgian city to be built using the honey-coloured stone for which Bath is famous today.

Contemporary Bath is a thriving tourist destination and remains a leading cultural, religious and historical centre with many art galleries and historic sites including the Pump Room (1790); the Royal Crescent (1767); the Circus (1754); the 18th-century Assembly Rooms (housing the Museum of Costume); Pulteney Bridge (1771); the Guildhall and the Abbey, now over 500 years old, which is built on the site of a Saxon monastery. In 2006 the Bath Thermae Spa was completed and the hot springs re-opened to the public for the first time since 1978; combining five historic spa buildings with contemporary architecture, it is the only spa in the UK to utilise naturally occurring thermal waters.

BIRMINGHAM (PRE-1900)

Birmingham is Britain's second largest city, with a population of over one million. The generally accepted derivation of 'Birmingham' is the *ham* (dwelling-place) of the *ing* (family) of *Beorma*, presumed to have been Saxon. During the Industrial Revolution the town grew into a major manufacturing centre and in 1889 was granted city status.

Recent developments include Millennium Point, which houses Thinktank, the Birmingham science museum, and Brindleyplace, a development of shops, offices and leisure facilities on a former industrial site clustered around canals. In 2003 the Bullring shopping centre was officially opened as part of the city's urban regeneration programme.

The principal buildings are the Town Hall (1834–50), the Council House (1879), Victoria Law Courts (1891), the University of Birmingham (1906–9), the 13th-century Church of St Martin-in-the-Bull-Ring (rebuilt 1873), the cathedral (formerly St Philip's Church) (1711), the Roman Catholic cathedral of St Chad (1839–41), the Assay Office (1773), the Rotunda (1964) and the National Exhibition Centre (1976). There is also the Birmingham Museum and Art Gallery which was founded in 1885 and is home to a collection of Pre-Raphaelite paintings.

BRADFORD (PRE-1900)

During the Industrial Revolution of the 18th and 19th centuries Bradford expanded rapidly, largely as a result of the thriving wool industry.

Bradford city centre has a host of buildings with historical and cultural interest, including City Hall, with its 19th-century Lord Mayor's rooms and Victorian law court; Bradford Cathedral; the Priestley, a theatre and arts centre originally established as the Bradford Civic Playhouse by J. B. Priestley and friends; the National Media Museum which houses seven floors of interactive displays and three cinemas; Piece Hall Yard which incorporates the Bradford Club, a Victorian Gothic style building dating from 1837, and the Peace Museum.

BRIGHTON AND HOVE (2000)

Brighton and Hove is situated on the south coast of England, around 96 km (60 miles) south of London. Originally a fishing village called Brighthelmstone, it was transformed into a fashionable seaside resort in the 18th century when Dr Richard Russell popularised the benefits of his 'sea-water cure'; as one of the closest beaches to London, Brighton began to attract wealthy visitors. One of these was the Prince Regent (the future King George IV), who first visited in 1783 and became so fond of the city that in 1807 he bought the former farmhouse he had been renting, and gradually turned it into Brighton's most recognisable building, the Royal Pavilion. The Pavilion is renowned for its Indo-Saracenic exterior, featuring minarets and an enormous central dome designed by John Nash, combined with the lavish chinoiserie of Frederick Crace's and Robert Jones' interiors.

Brighton and Hove's Regency heritage can also be seen in the numerous elegant squares and crescents designed by Amon Wilds and Augustin Busby that dominate the seafront.

Brighton and Hove is once again a fashionable resort, known for its cafe culture, lively nightlife and thriving gay scene.

BRISTOL (PRE-1900)

Bristol was a royal borough before the Norman conquest. The earliest form of the name is *Bricgstow*.

The principal buildings include the 12th-century

Cathedral with Norman chapter house and gateway; the 14th-century Church of St Mary Redcliffe; Wesley's Chapel, Broadmead; the Merchant Venturers' Almshouses; the Council House (1956); the Guildhall; the Exchange (erected from the designs of John Wood in 1743); Cabot Tower; the University and Clifton College. The Roman Catholic cathedral at Clifton was opened in 1973.

The Clifton Suspension Bridge, with a span of 214m (702ft) over the Avon, was projected by Isambard Kingdom Brunel in 1836 but was not completed until 1864. Brunel's SS *Great Britain,* the first ocean-going propeller-driven ship, now forms a museum at the Western Dockyard, from where she was originally launched in 1843. The docks themselves have been extensively restored and redeveloped; the 19th-century two-storey former tea warehouse is now the Arnolfini centre for contemporary arts, and an 18th-century sail loft houses the Architecture Centre. Behind the baroque-domed facade of the former 'E' Shed are shops, cafes, restaurants and the Watershed Media Centre, and on Princes Wharf 1950s transit sheds, which formerly housed the Industrial Museum, have been renovated and converted into the new museum of Bristol, M Shed, which opened in June 2011.

CAMBRIDGE (1951)

Cambridge, a settlement far older than its ancient university, lies on the River Cam (or Granta). The city is a county town and regional headquarters. Its industries include technology research and development, and biotechnology. Among its open spaces are Jesus Green, Sheep's Green, Coe Fen, Parker's Piece, Christ's Pieces, the University Botanic Garden, and the 'Backs' – lawns and gardens through which the Cam winds behind the principal line of college buildings. Historical sites east of the Cam include King's Parade, Great St Mary's Church, Gibbs' Senate House and King's College Chapel.

University and college buildings provide the outstanding features of Cambridge's architecture but several churches (especially St Benet's, the oldest building in the city, and Holy Sepulchre or the Round Church) are also notable. The Guildhall (1937) stands on a site, of which at least part has held municipal buildings since 1224.

CANTERBURY (PRE-1900)

Canterbury, seat of the Archbishop of Canterbury, the primate of the Church of England, dates back to prehistoric times. It was the Roman *Durovernum Cantiacorum* and the Saxon *Cant-wara-byrig* (stronghold of the men of Kent). It was here in 597 that St Augustine began the conversion of the English to Christianity, when Ethelbert, King of Kent, was baptised.

Of the Benedictine St Augustine's Abbey, burial place of the Jutish Kings of Kent, only ruins remain. St Martin's Church, on the eastern outskirts of the city, is stated by Bede to have been the place of worship of Queen Bertha, the Christian wife of King Ethelbert, before the advent of St Augustine.

In 1170 the rivalry of Church and State culminated in the murder in Canterbury Cathedral, by Henry II's knights, of Archbishop Thomas Becket. His shrine became a great centre of pilgrimage, as described in Chaucer's *Canterbury Tales.* After the Reformation pilgrimages ceased, but the prosperity of the city was strengthened by an influx of Huguenot refugees, who introduced weaving. The poet and playwright Christopher Marlowe was born and raised in Canterbury (the city is home to the 1,000-seat Marlowe Theatre) and

there are also literary associations with Defoe, Dickens, Joseph Conrad and Somerset Maugham.

The cathedral, its architecture ranging from the 11th to the 15th centuries, is famous worldwide. Visitors are attracted particularly to the Martyrdom, the Black Prince's Tomb, the Warriors' Chapel and the many examples of medieval stained glass.

The medieval city walls are built on Roman foundations and the 14th-century West Gate is one of the finest buildings of its kind in the country.

The Canterbury Arts Festival takes place at a variety of venues throughout the city each autumn.

CARLISLE (PRE-1900)

Carlisle is situated at the confluence of the rivers Eden and Caldew, 497km (309 miles) north-west of London and around 16km (10 miles) from the Scottish border. It was granted a charter in 1158.

The city stands at the western end of Hadrian's Wall and dates from the original Roman settlement of *Luguvalium.* Granted to Scotland in the tenth century, Carlisle is not included in the Domesday Book. William Rufus reclaimed the area in 1092 and the castle and city walls were built to guard Carlisle and the western border; the citadel is a Tudor addition to protect the south of the city. Border disputes were common until the problem of the Debateable Lands was settled in 1552. During the Civil War the city remained Royalist; in 1745 Carlisle was besieged for the last time by the Young Pretender (Bonnie Prince Charlie).

The cathedral, originally a 12th-century Augustinian priory, was enlarged in the 13th and 14th centuries after the diocese was created in 1133. To the south is a restored tithe barn and nearby the 18th-century church of St Cuthbert, the third to stand on a site dating from the seventh century.

Carlisle is the major shopping, commercial and agricultural centre for the area, and industries include the manufacture of metal goods, biscuits and textiles. However, the largest employer is the services sector, most notably in central and local government, retailing and transport. The city occupies an important position at the centre of a network of major roads, as a stage on the main west coast rail services, and with its own airport at Crosby-on-Eden.

CHESTER (PRE-1900)

Chester is situated on the River Dee. Its recorded history dates from the first century when the Romans founded the fortress of *Deva.* The city's name is derived from the Latin *castra* (a camp or encampment). During the Middle Ages, Chester was the principal port of north-west England but declined with the silting of the Dee estuary and competition from Liverpool. The city was also an important military centre, notably during Edward I's Welsh campaigns and the Elizabethan Irish campaigns. During the Civil War, Chester supported the King and was besieged from 1643 to 1646. Chester's first charter was granted c.1175 and the city was incorporated in 1506. The office of sheriff is the earliest created in the country (1120s), and in 1992 the mayor was granted the title of Lord Mayor, who also enjoys the title 'Admiral of the Dee'.

The city's architectural features include the city walls (an almost complete two-mile circuit), the unique 13th-century Rows (covered galleries above the street-level shops), the Victorian Gothic Town Hall (1869), the castle (rebuilt 1788 and 1822) and numerous half-timbered buildings. The cathedral was a Benedictine abbey until the Dissolution of the Monasteries. Remaining monastic buildings include the chapter house, refectory and cloisters and there is a modern free-standing bell tower. The Norman church of St John the Baptist was a cathedral church in the early Middle Ages.

COVENTRY (PRE-1900)

Coventry is an important industrial centre, producing vehicles, machine tools, agricultural machinery, man-made fibres, aerospace components and telecommunications equipment. New investment has come from financial services, power transmission, professional services, leisure and education.

The city owes its beginning to Leofric, Earl of Mercia, and his wife Godiva who, in 1043, founded a Benedictine monastery. The guildhall of St Mary and three of the city's churches date from the 14th and 15th centuries, and 16th-century almshouses can still be seen. Coventry's first cathedral was destroyed during the Reformation, its second in the 1940 blitz (the walls and spire remain) and the new cathedral designed by Sir Basil Spence, consecrated in 1962, now draws numerous visitors.

Coventry is the home of the University of Warwick, Coventry University, Coventry Transport Museum, which specialises in British road transport, and the Skydome Arena.

DURHAM (PRE-1900)

The city of Durham is a major tourist attraction and its prominent Norman cathedral and castle are set high on a wooded peninsula overlooking the River Wear. The cathedral was founded as a shrine for the body of St Cuthbert in 995. The present building dates from 1093 and among its many treasures is the tomb of the Venerable Bede (673–735). Durham's prince bishops had unique powers up to 1836, being lay rulers as well as religious leaders. As a palatinate, Durham could have its own army, nobility, coinage and courts. The castle was the main seat of the prince bishops for nearly 800 years; it is now used as a college by the University of Durham. The university, founded in the early 19th century on the initiative of Bishop William Van Mildert, is England's third oldest.

Among other buildings of interest is the Guildhall in the Market Place which dates from the 14th century. Annual events include Durham's regatta in June (claimed to be the oldest rowing event in Britain) and the annual Gala (formerly Durham Miners' Gala) in July.

KINGSTON-UPON-HULL (PRE-1900)

Hull (officially Kingston-upon-Hull, so named by Edward I) lies at the junction of the River Hull with the Humber, 35km (22 miles) from the North Sea. It is one of the major seaports of the UK. The port provides a wide range of cargo services, including ro-ro and container traffic, and handles an estimated million passengers annually on daily sailings to Rotterdam and Zeebrugge. There is a variety of manufacturing and service industries. City status was accorded in 1897 and the office of mayor raised to the dignity of Lord Mayor in 1914.

The city, restored after heavy air raid damage during the Second World War, has good educational facilities with both the University of Hull and a campus of the University of Lincoln being within its boundaries. Hull is home to the world's only submarium, The Deep, which opened in 2002, and the state-of-the-art Truck Theatre, which opened in 2009.

Tourism is a growing industry; the old town area has been renovated and includes museums, a marina and a shopping complex. Just west of the city is the Humber Bridge, a suspension bridge, opened in 1981, which crosses the Humber Estuary.

LEEDS (PRE-1900)

Leeds, situated in the lower Aire Valley, is a junction for road, rail, canal and air services and an important commercial centre. It was first incorporated by Charles I in 1626. The earliest forms of the name are *Loidis* or *Ledes,* the origins of which are obscure.

The principal buildings are the Civic Hall (1933), the Town Hall (1858), the Municipal Buildings and Art Gallery (1884) with the Henry Moore Gallery (1982), the Corn Exchange (1863) and the University. The parish church (St Peter's) was rebuilt in 1841; the 17th-century St John's Church has a fine interior with a famous English Renaissance screen; the last remaining 18th-century church in the city is Holy Trinity in Boar Lane (1727). Kirkstall Abbey (about three miles from the centre of the city), founded by Henry de Lacy in 1152, is one of the most complete examples of a Cistercian house now remaining. Temple Newsam, birthplace of Lord Darnley and largely rebuilt by Sir Arthur Ingram *c.*1620, was acquired by the council in 1922. Adel Church, about five miles from the centre of the city, is a fine Norman structure. The Royal Armouries Museum forms part of a group of museums that house the national collection of antique arms and armour.

LEICESTER (1919)

Leicester is situated in central England. The city was an important Roman settlement and also one of the five Viking boroughs of Danelaw. In 1485 Richard III was buried in Leicester following his death at the nearby Battle of Bosworth. In 1589 Queen Elizabeth I granted a charter to the city and the ancient title was confirmed by letters patent in 1919.

The textile industry was responsible for Leicester's early expansion and the city still maintains a strong manufacturing base. Cotton mills and factories are now undergoing extensive regeneration and are being converted into offices, apartments, bars and restaurants. The principal buildings include the two universities (the University of Leicester and De Montfort University), as well as the Town Hall, the 13th-century Guildhall, De Montfort Hall, Leicester Cathedral, the Jewry Wall (the UK's highest standing Roman wall), St Nicholas Church and St Mary de Castro church. The motte and Great Hall of Leicester can be seen from the castle gardens, situated next to the River Soar.

Leicester is now one of the UK's most ethnically diverse cities – home to the only Jain temple in the West and hosting the country's second-largest Caribbean carnival.

LINCOLN (PRE-1900)

Situated 64km (40 miles) inland on the River Witham, Lincoln derives its name from a contraction of *Lindum Colonia,* the settlement founded in AD 48 by the Romans to command the crossing of Ermine Street and Fosse Way. Sections of the third-century Roman city wall can be seen, including an extant gateway (Newport Arch), and excavations have discovered traces of a sewerage system unique in Britain. The Romans also drained the surrounding fenland and created a canal system, laying the foundations of Lincoln's agricultural prosperity and also the city's importance in the medieval wool trade as a port and staple town.

As one of the five boroughs of Danelaw, Lincoln was an important trading centre in the ninth and tenth centuries and prosperity from the wool trade lasted until the 14th century. This wealth enabled local merchants to build parish churches, of which three survive, and there are also remains of a 12th-century Jewish community (Jew's House and Court, Aaron's House). However, the removal of the staple to Boston in 1369 heralded a decline, from which the city only recovered fully in the 19th century, when improved fen drainage made Lincoln agriculturally important. Improved canal and rail links led to industrial development, mainly in the manufacture of machinery, components and engineering products.

The castle was built shortly after the Norman Conquest and is unusual in having two mounds; on one motte stands a keep (Lucy's Tower) added in the 12th century. It currently houses one of the four surviving copies of the Magna Carta. The cathedral was begun c.1073 when the first Norman bishop moved the see of Lindsey to Lincoln, but was mostly destroyed by fire and earthquake in the 12th century. Rebuilding was begun by St Hugh and completed over a century later. Other notable architectural features are the 12th-century High Bridge, the oldest in Britain still to carry buildings, and the Guildhall, situated above the 15th-century Stonebow gateway.

LIVERPOOL (PRE-1900)

Liverpool, on the north bank of the river Mersey, 5km (3 miles) from the Irish Sea, is the United Kingdom's foremost port for Atlantic trade. Tunnels link Liverpool with Birkenhead and Wallasey.

There are 2,100 acres of dockland on both sides of the river and the Gladstone and Royal Seaforth Docks can accommodate tanker-sized vessels. Liverpool Free Port was opened in 1984.

Liverpool was created a free borough in 1207 and a city in 1880. From the early 18th century it expanded rapidly with the growth of industrialisation and the transatlantic slave trade. Surviving buildings from this period include the Bluecoat Chambers (1717, formerly the Bluecoat School), the Town Hall (1754, rebuilt to the original design 1795), and buildings in Rodney Street, Canning Street and the suburbs. Notable from the 19th and 20th centuries are the Anglican cathedral, built from the designs of Sir Giles Gilbert Scott (the foundation stone was laid in 1904, but the building was only completed in 1980); the Catholic Metropolitan Cathedral (designed by Sir Frederick Gibberd, consecrated 1967) and St George's Hall (1842), regarded as one of the finest modern examples of classical architecture. The refurbished Albert Dock (designed by Jesse Hartley) contains the Merseyside Maritime Museum, the International Slavery Museum and the Tate Liverpool art gallery.

In 1852 an act was passed establishing a public library, museum and art gallery; as a result Liverpool had one of the first public libraries in the country. The Brown, Picton and Hornby libraries form one of the country's major collections. The Victoria Building of Liverpool University; the Royal Liver, Cunard and Mersey Docks & Harbour Company buildings at the Pier Head; the Municipal Buildings and the Philharmonic Hall are other examples of the city's fine architecture.

Six areas of Liverpool's maritime mercantile city were designated as UNESCO World Heritage Sites in 2004.

MANCHESTER (PRE-1900)

Manchester (the *Mamucium* of the Romans, who occupied it in AD 79) is a commercial and industrial centre engaged in the engineering, chemical, clothing, food processing and textile industries and in education. Banking, insurance and a growing leisure industry are among its prime commercial activities. The city is connected with the sea by the Manchester Ship Canal, opened in 1894, 57km (35.5 miles) long, and accommodating ships up to 15,000 tons.

The principal buildings are the Town Hall, erected in 1877 from the designs of Alfred Waterhouse, with a large extension of 1938; the Royal Exchange (1869, enlarged 1921); the Central Library (1934); Heaton Hall; the 17th-century Chetham Library; the Rylands Library (1900), which includes the Althorp collection; the university precinct; the 15th-century cathedral (formerly the parish church); the Manchester Central conference and exhibition centre and the Bridgewater Hall (1996) concert venue. Manchester is the home of the Hallé Orchestra, the Royal Northern College of Music, the Royal Exchange Theatre and numerous public art galleries.

To accommodate the Commonwealth Games held in the city in 2002, new sports facilities were built including a stadium, swimming pool complex and the National Cycling Centre.

The town received its first charter of incorporation in 1838 and was created a city in 1853.

NEWCASTLE UPON TYNE (PRE-1900)

Newcastle upon Tyne, on the north bank of the River Tyne, is 13km (8 miles) from the North Sea. A cathedral and university city, it is the administrative, commercial and cultural centre for north-east England and the principal port. It is an important manufacturing centre with a wide variety of industries.

The principal buildings include the Castle Keep (12th century), Black Gate (13th century), Blackfriars (13th century), West Walls (13th century), St Nicholas's Cathedral (15th century, fine lantern tower), St Andrew's Church (12th–14th century), St John's (14th–15th century), All Saints (1786 by Stephenson), St Mary's Roman Catholic Cathedral (1844), Trinity House (17th century), Sandhill (16th-century houses), Guildhall (Georgian), Grey Street (1834–9), Central Station (1846–50), Laing Art Gallery (1904), University of Newcastle Physics Building (1962) and Medical Building (1985), Civic Centre (1963) and the Central Library (1969). Open spaces include the Town Moor (927 acres) and Jesmond Dene. Numerous bridges span the Tyne at Newcastle, including the Tyne Bridge (1928) and the tilting Millennium Bridge (2001) – which links the city with Gateshead to the south.

The city's name is derived from the 'new castle' (1080) erected as a defence against the Scots. In 1400 it was made a county, and in 1882 a city.

NORWICH (PRE-1900)

Norwich grew from an early Anglo-Saxon settlement near the confluence of the rivers Yare and Wensum, and now serves as the provincial capital for the predominantly agricultural region of East Anglia. The name is thought to relate to the most northerly of a group of Anglo-Saxon villages or *wics*. The city's first known charter was granted in 1158 by Henry II.

Norwich serves its surrounding area as a market town and commercial centre, with banking and insurance prominent among the city's businesses. From the 14th century until the Industrial Revolution, Norwich was the regional centre of the woollen industry, but now the biggest single industry is financial services and principal trades are engineering, printing, shoemaking, the production of chemicals and clothing, food processing and technology. Norwich is accessible to seagoing vessels by means of the River Yare, entered at Great Yarmouth, 32km (20 miles) to the east.

Among many historic buildings are the cathedral (completed in the 12th century and surmounted by a 15th-century spire 96m (315ft) in height); the keep of the Norman castle (now a museum and art gallery); the 15th-century flint-walled Guildhall; some thirty medieval parish churches; St Andrew's and Blackfriars' Halls; the Tudor houses preserved in Elm Hill and the Georgian Assembly House. The University of East Anglia is on the city's western boundary.

NOTTINGHAM (PRE-1900)

Nottingham stands on the River Trent. *Snotingaham* or *Notingeham,* literally the homestead of the people of Snot, is the Anglo-Saxon name for the Celtic settlement of *Tigguocobauc,* or the house of caves. In 878, Nottingham became one of the five boroughs of Danelaw. William the Conqueror ordered the construction of Nottingham Castle, while the town itself developed rapidly under Norman rule. Its laws and rights were later formally recognised by Henry II's charter in 1155. The castle became a favoured residence of King John. In 1642 King Charles I raised his personal standard at Nottingham Castle at the start of the Civil War.

Nottingham is home to Notts County FC (the world's oldest football league side), Nottingham Forest FC, Nottingham Racecourse, Trent Bridge cricket ground and the National Watersports Centre. The principal industries include textiles, pharmaceuticals, food manufacturing, engineering and telecommunications. There are two universities within the city boundaries.

Architecturally, Nottingham has a wealth of notable buildings, particularly those designed in the Victorian era by T. C. Hine and Watson Fothergill. The city council owns the castle, of Norman origin but restored in 1878, Wollaton Hall (1580–8), Newstead Abbey (once home of Lord Byron), the Guildhall (1888) and Council House (1929). St Mary's, St Peter's and St Nicholas' churches are of interest, as is the Roman Catholic cathedral (Pugin, 1842–4). Nottingham was granted city status in 1897.

OXFORD (PRE-1900)

Oxford is a university city, an important industrial centre and a market town. Industry played a minor part in Oxford until the motor industry was established in 1912.

Oxford is known for its architecture, its oldest specimens being the reputedly Saxon tower of St Michael's Church, the remains of the Norman castle and city walls, and the Norman church at Iffley. It also has many Gothic buildings, such as the Divinity Schools, the Old Library at Merton College, William of Wykeham's New College, Magdalen and Christ Church colleges and many other college buildings. Later centuries are represented by the Laudian quadrangle at St John's College, the Renaissance Sheldonian Theatre by Wren, Trinity College Chapel, All Saints Church, Hawksmoor's

mock-Gothic at All Souls College, and the 18th-century Queen's College. In addition to individual buildings, High Street and Radcliffe Square both form interesting architectural compositions. Most of the colleges have gardens, those of Magdalen, New College, St John's and Worcester being the largest.

The Oxford University Museum of Natural History, renowned for its spectacular neo-gothic architecture, houses the university's scientific collections of zoological, entomological and geological specimens and is attached to the neighbouring Pitt Rivers Museum which houses ethnographic and archaeological objects from around the world. The Ashmolean is the city's museum of art and archaeology and Modern Art Oxford hosts a programme of contemporary art exhibitions.

ST ALBANS (PRE-1900)

The origins of St Albans, situated on the River Ver, stem from the Roman town of *Verulamium.* Named after the first Christian martyr in Britain, who was executed there, St Albans has developed around the Norman abbey and cathedral church (consecrated 1115), built partly of materials from the old Roman city. The museums house Iron Age and Roman artefacts and the Roman theatre, unique in Britain, has a stage as opposed to an amphitheatre. Archaeological excavations in the city centre have revealed evidence of pre-Roman, Saxon and medieval occupation.

The town's significance grew to the extent that it was a signatory and venue for the drafting of the Magna Carta. It was also the scene of riots during the Peasants' Revolt, the French King John was imprisoned there after the Battle of Poitiers, and heavy fighting took place there during the Wars of the Roses.

Previously controlled by the Abbot, the town achieved a charter in 1553 and city status in 1877. The street market, first established in 1553, is still an important feature of the city, as are many hotels and inns, surviving from the days when St Albans was an important coach stop. Tourist attractions include historic churches and houses and a 15th-century clock tower.

The city is now home to a wide range of businesses, with special emphasis on information and legal services, and is home to the Royal National Rose Society.

SALISBURY (PRE-1900)

The history of Salisbury centres around the cathedral and cathedral close. The city evolved from an Iron Age camp a mile to the north of its current position which was strengthened by the Romans and called *Serviodunum.* The Normans built a castle and cathedral on the site and renamed it Sarum. In 1220 Bishop Richard Poore and the architect Elias de Derham decided to build a new Gothic style cathedral. The cathedral was completed 38 years later and a community known as New Sarum, now called Salisbury, grew around it. Originally the cathedral had a squat tower; the 123m (404ft) spire that makes the cathedral the tallest medieval structure in the world was added c.1315. A walled close with houses for the clergy was built around the cathedral; the Medieval Hall still stands today, alongside buildings dating from the 13th to the 20th century, including some designed by Sir Christopher Wren.

A prosperous wool and cloth trade allowed Salisbury to flourish until the 17th century. When the wool trade declined new crafts were established including cutlery, leather and basket work, saddlery, lacemaking, joinery and malting. By 1750 it had become an important road junction and coaching centre and in the Victorian era the railways enabled a new age of expansion and prosperity. Today Salisbury is a thriving tourist centre.

SHEFFIELD (PRE-1900)

Sheffield is situated at the junction of the Sheaf, Porter, Rivelin and Loxley valleys with the River Don and was created a city in 1893. Though its cutlery, silverware and plate have long been famous, Sheffield has other and now more important industries: special and alloy steels, engineering, tool-making, medical equipment and media-related industries (in its new cultural industries quarter). Sheffield has two universities and is an important research centre.

The parish church of St Peter and St Paul, founded in the 12th century, became the cathedral church of the Diocese of Sheffield in 1914. The Roman Catholic Cathedral Church of St Marie (founded 1847) was created a cathedral for the new diocese of Hallam in 1980. Parts of the present building date from c.1435. The principal buildings are the Town Hall (1897), the Cutlers' Hall (1832), City Hall (1932), Graves Art Gallery (1934), Mappin Art Gallery, the Crucible Theatre and the restored Lyceum theatre, which dates from 1897 and was reopened in 1990. Three major sporting and entertainment venues were opened between 1990 and 1991: Sheffield Arena, Don Valley Stadium and Pond's Forge. The Millennium Galleries opened in 2001.

SOUTHAMPTON (1964)

Southampton is a major seaport on the south coast of England, situated between the mouths of the Test and Itchen rivers. Southampton's natural deep-water harbour has made the area an important settlement since the Romans built the first port (known as *Clausentum*) in the first century, and Southampton's port has witnessed several important departures, including those of King Henry V in 1415 for the Battle of Agincourt, RMS *Titanic* in 1912, and the *Mayflower* in 1620.

The city's strategic importance, not only as a seaport but also as a centre for aircraft production, meant that it was heavily bombed during the Second World War; however, many historically significant structures remain, including the Wool House, dating from 1417 and now used as the Maritime Museum; parts of the Norman city walls which are among the most complete in the UK; the Bargate, which was originally the main gateway into the city; God's House Tower, now the Museum of Archaeology; St Michael's, the city's oldest church; and the Tudor Merchants Hall.

Home to the National Oceanography Centre, the international Southampton Boat Show and some of the country's principal watersports venues, Southampton's coastal setting and maritime history remain its main focus, but it also features extensive parks and a thriving entertainment scene.

STOKE-ON-TRENT (1925)

Stoke-on-Trent, standing on the River Trent and familiarly known as 'the potteries', is the main centre of employment for the population of north Staffordshire. The city is the largest clayware producer in the world (china, earthenware, sanitary goods, refractories, bricks and tiles) and also has a wide range of other manufacturing industries, including steel, chemicals, engineering and tyres. Extensive reconstruction has been carried out in recent years.

The city was formed by the federation of the separate municipal authorities of Tunstall, Burslem, Hanley, Stoke, Fenton, and Longton in 1910 and received its city status in 1925.

WINCHESTER (PRE-1900)

Winchester, the ancient capital of England, is situated on the River Itchen. The city is rich in architecture of all types, especially notable is the cathedral. Built in 1079–93 the cathedral exhibits examples of Norman, early English and Perpendicular styles and is the burial place of author Jane Austen. Winchester College, founded in 1382, is one of the country's most famous public schools, and the original building (1393) remains largely unaltered. St Cross Hospital, another great medieval foundation, lies one mile south of the city. The almshouses were founded in 1136 by Bishop Henry de Blois, and Cardinal Henry Beaufort added a new almshouse of 'Noble Poverty' in 1446. The chapel and dwellings are of great architectural interest, and visitors may still receive the 'Wayfarer's Dole' of bread and ale.

Excavations have done much to clarify the origins and development of Winchester. Part of the forum and several of the streets from the Roman town have been discovered. Excavations in the Cathedral Close have uncovered the entire site of the Anglo-Saxon cathedral (known as the Old Minster) and parts of the New Minster which was built by Alfred's son, Edward the Elder, and is the burial place of the Alfredian dynasty. The original burial place of St Swithun, before his remains were translated to a site in the present cathedral, was also uncovered.

Excavations in other parts of the city have thrown much light on Norman Winchester, notably on the site of the Royal Castle (adjacent to which the new Law Courts have been built) and in the grounds of Wolvesey Castle, where the great house built by Bishops Giffard and Henry de Blois in the 12th century has been uncovered. The Great Hall, built by Henry III between 1222 and 1236, survives and houses the Arthurian Round Table.

YORK (PRE-1900)

The city of York is an archiepiscopal seat. Its recorded history dates from AD 71, when the Roman Ninth Legion established a base under Petilius Cerealis that would later become the fortress of *Eburacum*, or *Eboracum*. In Anglo-Saxon times the city was the royal and ecclesiastical centre of Northumbria, and after capture by a Viking army in AD 866 it became the capital of the Viking kingdom of Jorvik. By the 14th century the city had become a great mercantile centre, mainly because of its control of the wool trade, and was used as the chief base against the Scots. Under the Tudors its fortunes declined, although Henry VIII made it the headquarters of the Council of the North. Excavations on many sites, including Coppergate, have greatly expanded knowledge of Roman, Viking and medieval urban life.

With its development as a railway centre in the 19th century the commercial life of York expanded, and today the city is home to the award-winning National Railway Museum. The principal industries are the manufacture of chocolate, scientific instruments and sugar.

The city is rich in examples of architecture of all periods. The earliest church was built in AD 627 and, from the 12th to 15th centuries, the present Minster was built in a succession of styles. Other examples within the city are the medieval city walls and gateways, churches and guildhalls. Domestic architecture includes the Georgian mansions of The Mount, Micklegate and Bootham.

LORD-LIEUTENANTS AND HIGH SHERIFFS

Area	Lord-Lieutenant	High Sheriff (2011–12)
Bedfordshire	Sir Samuel Whitbread, KCVO	Andrew Slack
Berkshire	Hon. Mary Bayliss	Robert Woods, CBE
Bristol	Mary Prior, MBE	John Cottrell
Buckinghamshire	Sir Henry Aubrey-Fletcher	James Naylor
Cambridgeshire	Hugh Duberly, CBE	Richard Barnwell
Cheshire	David Briggs, MBE	John Lea
Cornwall	Lady Mary Holborow, DCVO	Col. Edward Bolitho, OBE
Cumbria	Sir James Cropper, KCVO	Iona Frost-Pennington
Derbyshire	William Tucker	David Coke-Steel
Devon	Eric Dancer, CBE	Hon. Sarah Lopes
Dorset	Valerie Pitt-Rivers	Alan Frost
Durham	Sir Paul Nicholson, KCVO	Roger Howell
East Riding of Yorkshire	Hon. Susan Cunliffe-Lister	John Holtby
East Sussex	Peter Field	Kathleen Gore
Essex	Lord Petre	Rosemary Ruggles-Brise
Gloucestershire	Dame Janet Trotter, DBE	Marcus Heywood
Greater London	Sir David Brewer, CMG	Lady Elizabeth Arnold
Greater Manchester	Warren Smith	Christine Lee-Jones
Hampshire	Dame Mary Fagan, DCVO	Nigel Scott
Herefordshire	Countess of Darnley	Simon Arbuthnott
Hertfordshire	Countess of Verulam	Lord Charles Cecil
Isle of Wight	Maj.-Gen. Martin White, CB, CBE	Susan Sheldon
Kent	Allan Willett, CMG	Georgie Warner
Lancashire	Lord Shuttleworth, KCVO	Peter Mileham
Leicestershire	Lady Gretton	Resham Sandhu, MBE
Lincolnshire	Anthony Worth	Robin Battle
Merseyside	Dame Lorna Fox Muirhead, DBE	Prof. Helen Carty
Norfolk	Richard Jewson	Georgina Holloway
North Yorkshire	Lord Crathorne	Alexandra Holford
Northamptonshire	Lady Juliet Townsend, LVO	Penelope Escombe, MBE
Northumberland	Duchess of Northumberland	Revd Fiona Sample
Nottinghamshire	Sir Andrew Buchanan, Bt., KCVO	John Peace
Oxfordshire	Tim Stevenson, OBE	Penelope Glen
Rutland	Dr Laurence Howard, OBE	Peter Lawson
Shropshire	A. Heber-Percy	Richard Burbidge, OBE
Somerset	Lady Gass	John Cullum
South Yorkshire	David Moody	Andrew Coombe
Staffordshire	Sir James Hawley, KCVO, TD	Simon Clarke
Suffolk	Lord Tollemache	Stephen Miles
Surrey	Mrs S. Goad	Prof. Michael Joy, OBE
Tyne and Wear	N. Sherlock, OBE	Geoffrey Hodgson
Warwickshire	M. Dunne	Timothy Cox
West Midlands	Paul Sabapathy, CBE	David Grove, OBE
West Sussex	Susan Pyper	David Tupper
West Yorkshire	Dr Ingrid Roscoe	Anthony Grant, OBE
Wiltshire	John Bush, OBE	Robert Hiscox
Worcestershire	M. Brinton	Hon. Lady Morrison

COUNTY COUNCILS

Council & Administrative Headquarters	Telephone	Population*	Council Tax†	Chief Executive
Buckinghamshire, Aylesbury	01296-395000	494,700	£1,078	Chris Williams
Cambridgeshire, Cambridge	0345-045 5200	607,000	£1,048	Mark Lloyd
Cumbria, Carlisle	01228-606060	495, 000	£1,162	Jill Stannard
Derbyshire, Matlock	01629-580000	760,200	£1,077	Nick Hodgson
Devon, Exeter	0845-155 1015	747,400	£1,116	Phil Norrey
Dorset, Dorchester	01305-221000	404,000	£1,168	David Jenkins
East Sussex, Lewes	01273-481000	512,100	£1,158	Becky Shaw
Essex, Chelmsford	0845-743 0430	1,399,000	£1,087	Joanna Killian
Gloucestershire, Gloucester	01452-425000	589,100	£1,091	Peter Bungard
Hampshire, Winchester	01962-841841	1,289,400	£1,038	Andrew Smith
Hertfordshire, Hertford	01992-555644	1,095,500	£1,119	Caroline Tapster
Kent, Maidstone	01622-671411	1,411,100	£1,048	Katherine Kerswell
Lancashire, Preston	0545-053 0000	1,165,800	£1,108	Phil Halsall
Leicestershire, Leicester	0116-232 3232	644,700	£1,063	John Sinnott
Lincolnshire, Lincoln	01522-552222	697,900	£1,066	Tony McArdle
Norfolk, Norwich	0844-800 8020	853,400	£1,145	David White
North Yorkshire, Northallerton	01609-780780	597,700	£1,057	Richard Flinton
Northamptonshire, Northampton	01604-236236	683,800	£1,028	Paul Blantern
Nottinghamshire, Nottingham	0115-982 3823	776,600	£1,193	Mick Burrows
Oxfordshire, Oxford	01865-792422	640,300	£1,162	Joanna Simons
Somerset, Taunton	0845-345 9166	523,500	£1,027	Sheila Wheeler
Staffordshire, Stafford	01785-223121	828,700	£1,029	Nick Bell
Suffolk, Ipswich	0845-606 6067	714,000	£1,127	Lucy Robinson (acting)
Surrey, Kingston upon Thames	0845-600 9009	1,113,100	£1,116	David McNulty
Warwickshire, Warwick	01926-410410	535,100	£1,155	Jim Graham
West Sussex, Chichester	01243-777100	792,900	£1,162	Kieran Stigant
Worcestershire, Worcester	01905-763763	556,500	£1,039	Trish Haines

* Source: The Office of National Statistics – Mid-2009 Population Estimates (Crown copyright)
† Average 2011–12 Band D council tax in the county area exclusive of precepts for fire and police authorities. County councils claim their share of the combined council tax from the collection funds of the district authorities into whose area they fall. Average Band D council tax bills for the billing authority are given on the following pages

DISTRICT COUNCILS

District Council	Telephone	Population*	Council Tax†	Chief Executive
Adur	01273-263000	61,300	£1,588	Peter Latham
Allerdale	01900-702702	94,300	£1,539	Harry Dyke
Amber Valley	01773-570222	121,000	£1,495	Peter Carney
Arun	01903-737500	149,900	£1,520	Ian Sumnall
Ashfield	01623-450000	116,400	£1,596	Philip Marshall
Ashford	01233-331111	114,100	£1,413	John Bunnett
Aylesbury Vale	01296-585858	173,500	£1,493	Andrew Grant
Babergh	01473-822801	85,800	£1,490	Charlie Adan
Barrow-in-Furness	01229-876300	70,900	£1,562	Tom Campbell
Basildon	01268-533333	174,100	£1,544	Bala Mahendran
Basingstoke and Deane	01256-844844	163,300	£1,366	Tony Curtis
Bassetlaw	01909-533533	111,600	£1,598	David Hunter
Blaby	0116-275 0555	93,600	£1,497	Sandra Whiles
Bolsover	01246-240000	74,200	£1,563	Wesley Lumley
Boston	01205-314200	59,000	£1,427	Richard Harbord
Braintree	01376-552525	142,700	£1,480	Allan Reid
Breckland	01362-656870	129,900	£1,455	Terry Huggins
Brentwood	01277-312500	73,800	£1,467	Joanna Killian
Broadland	01603-431133	123,000	£1,507	Colin Bland
Bromsgrove	01527-881288	93,400	£1,502	Kevin Dicks
Broxbourne	01992-785555	90,200	£1,380	Mike Walker
Broxtowe	0115-917 7777	111,500	£1,607	Ruth Hyde, OBE
Burnley	01282-425011	85,600	£1,577	Steve Rumbelow
CAMBRIDGE	01223-457000	121,100	£1,442	Antoinette Jackson
Cannock Chase	01543-462621	94,500	£1,490	Stephen Brown
CANTERBURY	01227-862000	149,100	£1,444	Colin Carmichael
CARLISLE	01228-817000	104,700	£1,561	Maggie Mooney
Castle Point	01268-882200	89,200	£1,523	David Marchant
Charnwood	01509-263151	165,000	£1,459	Geoff Parker
Chelmsford	01245-606606	167,800	£1,481	Steve Packham
Cheltenham	01242-262626	113,900	£1,481	Andrew North
Cherwell	01295-252535	139,200	£1,519	Sue Smith
Chesterfield	01246-345345	100,900	£1,460	Huw Bowen
Chichester	01243-785166	112,600	£1,475	John Marsland
Chiltern	01494-729000	90,900	£1,506	Alan Goodrum
Chorley	01257-515151	104,800	£1,514	Gary Hall
Christchurch	01202-495000	47,000	£1,584	David McIntosh
Colchester	01206-282222	177,100	£1,477	Adrian Pritchard
Copeland	0845-054 8600	69,700	£1,555	Paul Walker
Corby	01536-464000	55,200	£1,402	Chris Mallender
Cotswold	01285-623000	83,500	£1,488	David Neudegg
Craven	01756-700600	55,500	£1,525	Paul Shevlin
Crawley	01293-438000	105,300	£1,488	Lee Harris
Dacorum	01442-228000	141,600	£1,447	Daniel Zammit
Dartford	01322-343434	93,600	£1,443	Graham Harris
Daventry	01327-871100	78,900	£1,407	Ian Vincent
Derbyshire Dales	01629-761100	70,100	£1,538	David Wheatcroft
Dover	01304-821199	106,100	£1,461	Nadeem Aziz
East Cambridgeshire	01353-665555	83,900	£1,463	John Hill
East Devon	01395-516551	132,700	£1,501	Mark Williams
East Dorset	01202-886201	87,600	£1,639	David McIntosh
East Hampshire	01730-266551	111,900	£1,433	Sandy Hopkins
East Hertfordshire	01279-655261	137,100	£1,486	Anne Freimanis
East Lindsey	01507-601111	140,800	£1,388	Nigel Howells
East Northamptonshire	01832-742000	85,000	£1,411	David Oliver
East Staffordshire	01283-508000	108,800	£1,485	Andy O'Brien
Eastbourne	01323-410000	96,400	£1,603	Robert Cottrill
Eastleigh	023-8068 8000	120,800	£1,434	Bernie Topham
Eden	01768-817817	51,800	£1,551	Robin Hooper *(acting)*
Elmbridge	01372-474474	130,600	£1,515	Robert Moran
Epping Forest	01992-564000	124,000	£1,491	Derek Macnab *(acting)*

District Council	Telephone	Population*	Council Tax†	Chief Executive
Epsom and Ewell	01372-732000	72,700	£1,478	Frances Rutter
Erewash	0115-907 2244	110,900	£1,480	Jeremy Jaroszek
EXETER	01392-277888	118,800	£1,470	Philip Bostock
Fareham	01329-236100	111,500	£1,386	Peter Grimwood
Fenland	01354-654321	91,700	£1,541	Sandra Claxton
Forest Heath	01638-719000	62,200	£1,499	David Burnip
Forest of Dean	01594-810000	82,800	£1,505	Sue Pangbourne (acting)
Fylde	01253-658658	76,300	£1,523	Phillip Woodward
Gedling	0115-901 3901	112,700	£1,577	John Robinson
GLOUCESTER	01452-522232	117,300	£1,476	Julian Wain
Gosport	023-9258 4242	80,000	£1,448	Ian Lycett
Gravesham	01474-337000	98,800	£1,427	Glyn Thomson
Great Yarmouth	01493-856100	96,300	£1,492	Richard Packham
Guildford	01483-505050	135,700	£1,481	David Hill
Hambleton	0845-121 1555	87,300	£1,445	Peter Simpson
Harborough	01858-828282	83,400	£1,490	Anna Graves
Harlow	01279-446655	80,600	£1,537	Malcolm Morley
Harrogate	01423-500600	157,900	£1,553	Wallace Sampson
Hart	01252-622122	91,200	£1,456	Geoff Bonner
Hastings	01424 451066	86,900	£1,614	Roy Mawford
Havant	023-9247 4174	116,500	£1,438	Sandy Hopkins
Hertsmere	020-8207 2277	98,900	£1,447	Donald Graham
High Peak	0845-129 7777	92,400	£1,500	Simon Baker
Hinckley and Bosworth	01455-238141	104,800	£1,438	Steve Atkinson
Horsham	01403-215100	129,800	£1,479	Tom Crowley
Huntingdonshire	01480-388388	165,800	£1,476	David Monks
Hyndburn	01254-388111	81,100	£1,549	David Welsby
Ipswich	01473-432000	126,600	£1,597	Russell Williams
Kettering	01536-410333	90,100	£1,429	David Cook, MBE
King's Lynn and West Norfolk	01553-616200	143,000	£1,491	Ray Harding
LANCASTER	01524-582000	139,800	£1,523	Mark Cullinan
Lewes	01273-471600	96,400	£1,643	Jenny Rowlands
Lichfield	01543-308000	98,300	£1,453	Nina Dawes
LINCOLN	01522-881188	88,500	£1,481	Andrew Taylor
Maidstone	01622-602000	148,200	£1,494	Alison Broom
Maldon	01621-854477	62,900	£1,495	Fiona Marshall
Malvern Hills	01684-862151	75,000	£1,478	Chris Bocock
Mansfield	01623-463463	99,700	£1,610	Ruth Marlow
Melton	01664-502502	48,900	£1,487	Lynn Aisbett
Mendip	01749-648999	118,700	£1,466	Stuart Brown
Mid Devon	01884-255255	76,000	£1,560	Kevin Finan
Mid Suffolk	01449-720711	94,200	£1,492	Charlie Adan
Mid Sussex	01444-458166	131,600	£1,505	Kathryn Hall
Mole Valley	01306-885001	83,800	£1,470	Darren Mepham
New Forest	023-8028 5000	176,400	£1,466	David Yates
Newark and Sherwood	01636-650000	113,000	£1,646	Andrew Muter
Newcastle-under-Lyme	01782-717717	124,200	£1,460	Mark Barrow
North Devon	01271-327711	91,500	£1,554	M. Mansell
North Dorset	01258-454111	64,300	£1,588	Elizabeth Goodall
North East Derbyshire	01246-231111	98,000	£1,566	Wes Lumley
North Hertfordshire	01462-474000	124,700	£1,481	John Campbell
North Kesteven	01529-414155	105,700	£1,444	Ian Fytche
North Norfolk	01263-513811	101,200	£1,510	Philip Burton
North Warwickshire	01827-715341	61,900	£1,579	Jeremy Hutchinson
North West Leicestershire	01530-454545	90,600	£1,506	Christine Fisher
Northampton	01604-837837	210,500	£1,445	David Kennedy
NORWICH	0344-980 3333	140,100	£1,562	Laura McGillivray
Nuneaton and Bedworth	02476-376376	122,000	£1,533	Alan Franks & Gareth Owens
Oadby and Wigston	0116-288 8961	58,500	£1,489	Mark Hall
OXFORD	01865-249811	149,300	£1,583	Peter Sloman
Pendle	01282-661661	89,300	£1,572	Stephen Barnes
PRESTON	01772-906900	134,600	£1,581	Lorraine Norris
Purbeck	01929-556561	45,200	£1,627	Steve Mackenzie
Redditch	01527-64252	78,700	£1,501	Kevin Dicks
Reigate and Banstead	01737-276000	136,100	£1,514	John Jory
Ribble Valley	01200-425111	57,700	£1,476	Marshal Scott
Richmondshire	01748-829100	52,800	£1,539	Peter Simpson

District Council	Telephone	Population*	Council Tax†	Chief Executive
Rochford	01702-546366	83,100	£1,521	Paul Warren
Rossendale	01706-217777	67,100	£1,574	Helen Lockwood
Rother	01424-787999	89,200	£1,588	Derek Stevens
Rugby	01788-533533	93,300	£1,517	Ian David & Andrew Gabbitas
Runnymede	01932-838383	83,900	£1,452	Paul Turrell
Rushcliffe	0115-981 9911	111,700	£1,598	Allen Graham
Rushmoor	01252-398398	91,100	£1,430	Andrew Lloyd
Ryedale	01653-600666	53,600	£1,534	Janet Waggott
ST ALBANS	01727-866100	137,200	£1,472	Daniel Goodwin
St Edmundsbury	01284-763233	103,500	£1,505	Geoff Rivers
Scarborough	01723-232323	108,500	£1,552	Jim Dillon
Sedgemoor	0845-408 2540	112,100	£1,445	Mr Kerry Rickards
Selby	01757-705101	82,200	£1,530	Martin Connor
Sevenoaks	01732-227000	113,200	£1,503	Robin Hales
Shepway	01303-853000	100,300	£1,535	Alistair Stewart
South Bucks	01895-837200	66,600	£1,489	Chris Furness
South Cambridgeshire	0345-0450500	144,500	£1,456	Jean Hunter
South Derbyshire	01283-221000	92,800	£1,476	Frank McArdle
South Hams	01803-861234	83,500	£1,520	Richard Sheard
South Holland	01775-761161	84,100	£1,430	Terry Huggins
South Kesteven	01476-406080	131,200	£1,408	Beverly Agass
South Lakeland	01539-733333	103,800	£1,557	Lawrence Conway
South Norfolk	01508-533633	119,700	£1,528	Sandra Dinneen
South Northamptonshire	01327-322322	88,500	£1,449	Sue Smith
South Oxfordshire	01491-823000	130,600	£1,508	David Buckle
South Ribble	01772-421491	108,200	£1,528	Mike Nuttall
South Somerset	01935-462462	158,600	£1,481	Mark Williams
South Staffordshire	01902-696000	106,300	£1,418	Steve Winterflood
Spelthorne	01784-451499	92,600	£1,482	Roberto Tambini
Stafford	01785-619000	125,500	£1,441	Ian Thompson
Staffordshire Moorlands	01538-483483	95,400	£1,454	Simon Baker
Stevenage	01438-242242	81,000	£1,455	Nick Parry
Stratford-on-Avon	01789-267575	118,900	£1,510	Paul Lankester
Stroud	01453-766321	111,100	£1,535	David Hagg
Suffolk Coastal	01394-383789	124,100	£1,481	Stephen Baker
Surrey Heath	01276-707100	83,900	£1,518	Karen Whelan
Swale	01795-417330	131,900	£1,430	Abdool Kara
Tamworth	01827-709709	75,700	£1,424	Tony Goodwin
Tandridge	01883-722000	82,200	£1,523	Stephen Weigel
Taunton Deane	01823-356356	108,700	£1,415	Penny James
Teignbridge	01626-361101	126,900	£1,540	Nicola Bulbeck
Tendring	01255-686868	148,000	£1,462	Ian Davidson
Test Valley	01264-368000	113,400	£1,397	Roger Tetstall
Tewkesbury	01684-295010	80,600	£1,434	Michael Dawson
Thanet	01843-577000	130,900	£1,480	Dr Sue McGonigal
Three Rivers	01923-776611	88,100	£1,459	Dr Steven Halls
Tonbridge and Malling	01732-844522	117,400	£1,466	David Hughes
Torridge	01237-428700	65,300	£1,524	Nicola Bulbeck
Tunbridge Wells	01892-526121	107,600	£1,434	William Benson
Uttlesford	01799-510510	75,600	£1,496	John Mitchell
Vale of White Horse	01235-520202	118,700	£1,493	David Buckle
Warwick	01926-450000	139,000	£1,497	Chris Elliott
Watford	01923-226400	83,800	£1,516	Manny Lewis
Waveney	01502-562111	117,700	£1,448	Stephen Baker
Waverley	01483-523333	119,300	£1,519	Mary Orton
Wealden	01323-443322	143,100	£1,631	Charles Lant
Wellingborough	01933-229777	75,700	£1,369	Joe Hubbard
Welwyn & Hatfield	01707-357000	112,800	£1,498	Michel Saminaden
West Devon	01822-813600	52,700	£1,584	Richard Sheard
West Dorset	01305-251010	96,500	£1,599	David Clarke
West Lancashire	01695-577177	110,200	£1,515	William Taylor, MBE
West Lindsey	01427-676676	88,600	£1,484	Manjeet Gill
West Oxfordshire	01993-861000	102,500	£1,455	David Neudegg
West Somerset	01643-703704	35,400	£1,453	Adrian Dyer
Weymouth and Portland	01305-838000	63,600	£1,678	David Clarke
WINCHESTER	01962-840222	113,300	£1,436	Simon Eden
Woking	01483-755855	92,400	£1,520	Ray Morgan, OBE

District Council	Telephone	Population*	Council Tax†	Chief Executive
WORCESTER	01905-723471	94,700	£1,457	Duncan Sharkey
Worthing	01903-239999	102,400	£1,516	Peter Latham
Wychavon	01386-565000	116,700	£1,440	Jack Hegarty
Wycombe	01494-461000	163,600	£1,457	Karen Satterford
Wyre	01253-891000	111,100	£1,507	Garry Payne
Wyre Forest	01562-732928	98,100	£1,502	Ian Miller

* Source: ONS – Mid-2009 Population Estimates (Crown copyright)
† Average Band D council tax bill for 2011–12
Councils in CAPITAL LETTERS have city status

METROPOLITAN BOROUGH COUNCILS

Metropolitan Borough Councils	Telephone	Population*	Council Tax†	Chief Executive
Barnsley	01226-770770	226,300	£1,401	Philip Coppard, OBE
BIRMINGHAM	0121-303 9944	1,028,700	£1,261	Stephen Hughes
Bolton	01204-333333	265,100	£1,414	Sean Harriss
BRADFORD	01274-432001	506,800	£1,283	Tony Reeves
Bury	0161-253 5000	182,600	£1,457	Mike Kelly
Calderdale	01422-357257	201,600	£1,417	Owen Williams
COVENTRY	024-7683 3333	312,800	£1,471	Martin Reeves
Doncaster	01302-734444	290,100	£1,316	Robert Vincent
Dudley	0300-555 2345	306,600	£1,273	John Polychronakis
Gateshead	0191-433 3000	190,800	£1,600	Roger Kelly
Kirklees	01484-221000	406,800	£1,405	Adrian Lythgo
Knowsley	0151-489 6000	149,400	£1,484	Sheena Ramsey
LEEDS	0113-222 4444	787,700	£1,312	Tom Riordan
LIVERPOOL	0151-233 3000	442,300	£1,519	Ged Fitzgerald
MANCHESTER	0161-234 5000	483,800	£1,327	Sir Howard Bernstein
NEWCASTLE UPON TYNE	0191-232 8520	284,300	£1,512	Barry Rowland
North Tyneside	0191-643 5991	197,200	£1,485	John Marsden
Oldham	0161-911 3000	218,800	£1,547	Charlie Parker
Rochdale	01706-647474	204,700	£1,482	Roger Ellis
Rotherham	01709-382121	253,900	£1,451	Martin Kimber
St Helens	01744-676789	177,100	£1,366	Carole Hudson
SALFORD	0161-794 4711	225,100	£1,523	Barbara Spicer
Sandwell	0121-569 2200	291,000	£1,323	Jan Britton (acting)
Sefton	0151-922 4040	273,300	£1,488	Margaret Carney
SHEFFIELD	0114-272 6444	547,000	£1,478	John Mothersole
Solihull	0121-704 6000	205,200	£1,337	Mark Rogers
South Tyneside	0191-427 1717	152,400	£1,448	Martin Swales
Stockport	0161-480 4949	283,700	£1,560	Eamonn Boylan
SUNDERLAND	0191-520 5555	281,700	£1,343	Dave Smith
Tameside	0161-342 8355	215,400	£1,366	Steven Pleasant
Trafford	0161-912 2000	215,300	£1,303	Janet Callender
WAKEFIELD	0845-8506 506	323,900	£1,306	Joanne Roney, OBE
Walsall	01922-650000	255,900	£1,532	Paul Sheehan
Wigan	01942-244991	306,500	£1,369	Joyce Redfearn
Wirral	0151-606 2000	308,500	£1,464	James Wilkie
WOLVERHAMPTON	01902-556556	238,500	£1,464	Simon Warren

* Source: ONS – Mid-2009 Population Estimates (Crown copyright)
† Average Band D council tax bill for 2011–12
Councils in CAPITAL LETTERS have city status

UNITARY COUNCILS

Unitary Councils	Telephone	Population*	Council Tax†	Chief Executive
Bath and North East Somerset	01225-477000	177,700	£1,462	John Everitt
Bedford	01234-267422	158,000	£1,556	Philip Simpkins
Blackburn with Darwen	01254-585585	139,900	£1,481	Graham Burgess
Blackpool	01253-477477	140,000	£1,516	Steve Weaver
Bournemouth	01202-451451	164,900	£1,499	Pam Donnellan
Bracknell Forest	01344-352000	115,100	£1,366	Timothy Wheadon
BRIGHTON AND HOVE	01273-290000	256,300	£1,483	John Barradell, OBE
BRISTOL	0117-922 2000	433,100	£1,567	Jan Ormondroyd
Central Bedfordshire	0300-300 8000	252,900	£1,641	Richard Carr
Cheshire East	0300-123 5500	362,700	£1,451	Erika Wenzel
Cheshire West and Chester	0300-123 8123	326,600	£1,486	Steve Robinson
Cornwall	0300-123 4100	531,100	£1,460	Kevin Lavery
Darlington	01325-380651	100,400	£1,394	Ada Burns
DERBY	01332-293111	244,100	£1,358	Adam Wilkinson
DURHAM	0300-123 7070	506,400	£1,602	George Garlick
East Riding of Yorkshire	01482-887700	337,000	£1,500	Nigel Pearson
Halton	0151-907 8300	118,700	£1,350	David Parr
Hartlepool	01429-266522	90,900	£1,671	Paul Walker
Herefordshire	01432-260000	179,100	£1,493	Chris Bull
Isle of Wight	01983-821000	140,200	£1,466	Joe Duckworth
Isles of Scilly‡	01720-422537	2,200	£1,187	Philip Hygate
KINGSTON-UPON-HULL	01482-609100	262,400	£1,341	Nicola Yates
LEICESTER	0116-254 9922	304,700	£1,409	Sheila Lock
Luton	01582-546000	194,300	£1,371	Trevor Holden
Medway	01634-333333	254,800	£1,330	Neil Davies
Middlesbrough	01642-245432	140,500	£1,514	Ian Parker
Milton Keynes	01908-691691	236,700	£1,390	David Hill
North East Lincolnshire	01472-313131	157,100	£1,503	Tony Hunter
North Lincolnshire	01724-296296	161,000	£1,555	Simon Driver
North Somerset	01934-888888	209,100	£1,423	Graham Turner
Northumberland	01670-533000	311,100	£1,496	Steve Stewart
NOTTINGHAM	0115-915 5555	300,800	£1,562	Jane Todd
PETERBOROUGH	01733-747474	171,200	£1,330	Gillian Beasley
PLYMOUTH	01752-668000	256,700	£1,473	Barry Keel
Poole	01202-633633	141,200	£1,450	John McBride
PORTSMOUTH	023-9282 2251	203,500	£1,357	David Williams
Reading	0118-9373737	151,800	£1,499	Michael Coughlin
Redcar and Cleveland	0164-277 4774	137,500	£1,556	Amanda Skelton
Rutland	01572-722577	38,400	£1,691	Helen Briggs
Shropshire	0345-678 9000	291,800	£1,495	Kim Ryley
Slough	01753-475111	128,400	£1,368	Ruth Bagley
South Gloucestershire	01454-868686	262,200	£1,529	Amanda Deeks
SOUTHAMPTON	023-8022 3855	236,700	£1,447	Alistair Neill
Southend-on-Sea	01702-215000	164,200	£1,320	Robert Tinlin
Stockton-on-Tees	01642-393939	191,100	£1,483	Neil Schneider
STOKE-ON-TRENT	01782-234567	238,900	£1,389	John van de Laarschot
Swindon	01793-445500	198,800	£1,393	Gavin Jones
Telford and Wrekin	01952-380000	162,300	£1,419	Richard Partington (interim)
Thurrock	01375-652652	157,200	£1,301	Graham Farrant
Torbay	01803-201201	134,000	£1,493	Elizabeth Raikes
Warrington	01925-444400	197,800	£1,369	Diana Terris
West Berkshire	01635-42400	153,000	£1,500	Nick Carter
Wiltshire	0300-456 0100	456,100	£1,514	Andrew Kerr
Windsor and Maidenhead	01628-683800	143,800	£1,218	Ian Trenholm
Wokingham	0118-974 6000	161,900	£1,462	Susan Law
YORK	01904-613161	198,800	£1,366	Kersten England

* Source: ONS – Mid-2009 Population Estimates (Crown copyright)
† Average Band D council tax bill for 2011–12
‡ Under the Isles of Scilly Clause the council has additional functions to other unitary authorities
Councils in CAPITAL LETTERS have city status

MAP OF COUNCILS IN ENGLAND

1	Stockton-on-Tees	22	Walsall
2	Middlesbrough	23	Sandwell
3	Blackpool	24	Dudley
4	Blackburn	25	Birmingham
	with Darwen	26	Solihull
5	Bolton	27	Coventry
6	Bury	28	Peterborough
7	Rochdale	29	South Glos
8	Salford	30	Bristol
9	Oldham	31	Bath and
10	Liverpool		NE Somerset
11	Knowsley	32	Windsor and
12	St Helens		Maidenhead
13	Halton	33	Slough
14	Warrington	34	Reading
15	Trafford	35	Wokingham
16	Manchester	36	Bracknell Forest
17	Tameside	37	Thurrock
18	Stockport	38	Southend
19	Nottingham	39	Medway
20	Telford and	40	Plymouth
	Wrekin	41	Torbay
21	Wolverhampton	42	Bournemouth

LONDON

1	Hillingdon	18	Kensington and Chelsea
2	Harrow	19	City of Westminster
3	Barnet	20	City of London
4	Enfield	21	Tower Hamlets
5	Waltham Forest	22	Richmond upon Thames
6	Redbridge	23	Wandsworth
7	Barking and Dagenham	24	Lambeth
8	Havering	25	Southwark
9	Ealing	26	Lewisham
10	Brent	27	Greenwich
11	Camden	28	Bexley
12	Haringey	29	Kingston upon Thames
13	Islington	30	Merton
14	Hackney	31	Sutton
15	Newham	32	Croydon
16	Hounslow	33	Bromley
17	Hammersmith and Fulham		

LONDON

THE CITY OF LONDON CORPORATION

The City of London is the historic centre at the heart of London known as 'the square mile' around which the vast metropolis has grown over the centuries. The City's residential population is roughly 8,000 and in addition, around a third of a million people work in the City. The civic government is carried on by the City of London Corporation through the court of Common Council.

The City is an international financial and business centre, generating about £30bn a year for the British economy. It includes the head offices of the principal banks, insurance companies and mercantile houses, in addition to buildings ranging from the historic Roman Wall and the 15th-century Guildhall, to the massive splendour of St Paul's Cathedral and the architectural beauty of Wren's spires.

The City of London was described by Tacitus in AD 62 as 'a busy emporium for trade and traders'. Under the Romans it became an important administration centre and hub of the road system. Little is known of London in Saxon times, when it formed part of the kingdom of the East Saxons. In 886 Alfred recovered London from the Danes and reconstituted it a burgh under his son-in-law. In 1066 the citizens submitted to William the Conqueror who in 1067 granted them a charter, which is still preserved, establishing them in the rights and privileges they had hitherto enjoyed.

THE MAYORALTY
The mayoralty was probably established about 1189, the first mayor being Henry Fitz Ailwyn who filled the office for 23 years and was succeeded by Fitz Alan (1212–14). A new charter was granted by King John in 1215, directing the mayor to be chosen annually, which has been done ever since, though in early times the same individual often held the office more than once. A familiar instance is that of 'Whittington, thrice Lord Mayor of London' (in reality four times: 1397, 1398, 1406 and 1419); and many modern cases have occurred. The earliest instance of the phrase 'lord mayor' in English is in 1414. It was used more generally in the latter part of the 15th century and became invariable from 1535 onwards. At Michaelmas the liverymen in Common Hall choose two aldermen who have served the office of sheriff for presentation to the Court of Aldermen, and one is chosen to be lord mayor for the following mayoral year.

LORD MAYOR'S DAY
The lord mayor of London was previously elected on the feast of St Simon and St Jude (28 October), and from the time of Edward I, at least, was presented to the King or to the Barons of the Exchequer on the following day, unless that day was a Sunday. The day of election was altered to 16 October in 1346, and after some further changes was fixed for Michaelmas Day in 1546, but the ceremonies of admittance and swearing-in of the lord mayor continued to take place on 28 and 29 October respectively until 1751. In 1752, at the reform of the calendar, the lord mayor was continued in office until 8 November, the 'new style' equivalent of 28 October. The lord mayor is now presented to the lord chief justice at the royal courts of justice on the second Saturday in November to make the final declaration of office, having been sworn in at Guildhall on the preceding day. The procession to the royal courts of justice is popularly known as the Lord Mayor's Show.

REPRESENTATIVES
Aldermen are mentioned in the 11th century and their office is of Saxon origin. They were elected annually between 1377 and 1394, when an act of parliament of Richard II directed them to be chosen for life. Aldermen now serve a six-year term of office before submitting themselves for re-election.

The Common Council was, at an early date, substituted for a popular assembly called the *Folkmote*. At first only two representatives were sent from each ward, but now each of the City's 25 wards is represented by an alderman and at least two Common Councilmen (the number depending on the size of the ward). Common Councilmen are elected every four years.

OFFICERS
Sheriffs were Saxon officers; their predecessors were the *wic-reeves* and *portreeves* of London and Middlesex. At first they were officers of the Crown, and were named by the Barons of the Exchequer; but Henry I (in 1132) gave the citizens permission to choose their own sheriffs, and the annual election of sheriffs became fully operative under King John's charter of 1199. The citizens lost this privilege, as far as the election of the sheriff of Middlesex was concerned, by the Local Government Act 1888; but the liverymen continue to choose two sheriffs of the City of London, who are appointed on Midsummer Day and take office at Michaelmas.

The office of chamberlain is an ancient one, the first contemporary record of which is 1237. The town clerk (or common clerk) is first mentioned in 1274.

ACTIVITIES
The work of the City of London Corporation is assigned to a number of committees which present reports to the Court of Common Council. These committees are: Administration of the Sir William Coxen Trust Fund; Audit and Risk Management; Barbican Centre; Barbican Residential; Board of Governors of the City of London Freeman's School, the City of London School, the City of London School for Girls, Emanuel Hospital Charitable Trust, the Guildhall School of Music and Drama and the Museum of London; Bridewell Royal Hospital; Christ's Hospital; City Bridge Trust; Community and Children's Services; Corporation Benevolent Association Management; Court of Aldermen; Court of Common Council; Culture, Heritage and Libraries; Epping Forest and Commons; Establishment; Finance; Freedom Applications; Gresham (city side); General Purposes; Guildhall Improvement; Hampstead Heath, Highgate Wood and Queen's Park Management; Joint Overview and Scrutiny; Joint Working Party of the Three Schools; Keats House Management; Licensing; Livery; London Drug Policy Forum; Markets; Open Spaces, City Gardens and West Ham Park; Planning and Transportation; Police;

Policy and Resources; Port Health and Environmental Services and Standards Committees.

The City's estate, in the possession of which the City of London Corporation differs from other municipalities, is managed by the City Lands and Bridge House Estates Committee, the chairmanship of which carries with it the title of chief commoner.

The Honourable the Irish Society, which manages the City Corporation's estates in Ulster, consists of a governor and five other aldermen, the recorder, and 19 common councilmen, of whom one is elected deputy governor.

THE LORD MAYOR 2011–12

The Rt. Hon. the Lord Mayor, David Wootton*
Private Secretary, William Chapman
* Provisional at time of going to press

THE SHERIFFS 2011–12

Wendy Mead *(Farringdon Wt.)*; Alderman Alan Yarrow *(Bridge & Bridge Wt.)*

OFFICERS, ETC

Town Clerk, Chris Duffield
Chamberlain, Chris Bilsland
Chief Commoner (2011), Richard Regan
Clerk, The Honourable the Irish Society, C. Fisher

THE ALDERMEN

with office held and date of appointment to that office

Name and Ward	Common Councilman	Alderman	Sheriff	Lord Mayor
Lord Levene of Portsoken, KBE, *Aldgate*	1983	1984	1995	1998
Sir David Howard, Bt., *Cornhill*	1972	1986	1997	2000
Sir Robert Finch, *Coleman Street*	–	1992	1999	2003
Sir Michael Savory, *Bread Street*	1980	1996	2001	2004
Sir John Stuttard, *Lime Street*	–	2001	2005	2006
Sir David Lewis, *Broad Street*	–	2001	2006	2007
Ian Luder, *Castle Baynard*	1998	2005	2007	2008
Nicholas Anstee, *Aldersgate*	1987	1996	2003	2009
Michael Bear, *Portsoken*	2003	2005	2007	2010

All the above have passed the Civic Chair

Simon Walsh, *Farringdon Wt.*	1989	2000
Dr Andrew Parmley, *Vintry*	1992	2001
Benjamin R. Hall, *Farringdon Wn.*	1995	2002
Alison Gowman, *Dowgate*	1991	2002
Gordon Haines, *Queenhithe*	–	2004
Roger Gifford, *Cordwainer*	–	2004	2008
David Wootton, *Langbourn*	2002	2005	2009
Alan Yarrow, *Bridge & Bridge Wt.*	–	2007
Jeffrey Evans, *Cheap*	–	2007
Sir Paul Judge, *Tower*	–	2007
Fiona Woolf, CBE, *Candlewick*	–	2007	2010
John White, TD, *Billingsgate*	–	2008
David Graves, *Cripplegate*	–	2008
John Garbutt, *Walbrook*	–	2009
Neil Redcliffe, *Bishopsgate*	–	2009
Philip Remnant, CBE, *Bassishaw*	–	2010

THE COMMON COUNCIL

Deputy: each common councilman so described serves as deputy to the alderman of her/his ward.

Abrahams, G. C. (2000)	*Farringdon Wt.*
Absalom, J. D. (1994)	*Farringdon Wt.*
Ayers, *Deputy* K. E., MBE (1996)	*Bassishaw*
Bain-Stewart, A. (2005)	*Farringdon Wn.*
Barker, *Deputy* J. A., OBE (1981)	*Cripplegate Wn.*
Barrow, *Deputy* D. (2007)	*Aldgate*
Bennett, *Deputy* J. A. (2005)	*Broad Street*
Bird, J. L., OBE (1977)	*Tower*
Boleat, M. J. (2002)	*Cordwainer*
Bradshaw, D. J. (1991)	*Cripplegate Wn.*
Cassidy, *Deputy* M. J., CBE (1989)	*Coleman Street*
Catt, R. M. (2004)	*Castle Baynard*
Chadwick, R. A. H. (1994)	*Tower*
Challis, N. K. (2005)	*Castle Baynard*
Chapman, J. D. (2006)	*Langbourn*
Cotgrove, D. (1991)	*Lime Street*
Cressey, N. (2009)	*Portsoken*
Currie, *Deputy* Miss S. E. M. (1985)	*Cripplegate Wt.*
Davies, P. S. (2009)	*Broad Street*
Day, M. J. (2005)	*Bishopsgate*
Deane, A. J. (2011)	*Farringdon Wt.*
Dove, W. H., MBE (1993)	*Bishopsgate*
Duckworth, S. D. (2000)	*Bishopsgate*
Dudley, Revd Dr M. R. (2002)	*Aldersgate*
Duffield, R. W. (2004)	*Farringdon Wn.*
Dunphy, P. G. (2009)	*Cornhill*
Eskenzi, *Deputy* A. N., CBE (1970)	*Farringdon Wn.*
Eve, *Deputy* R. A. (1980)	*Cheap*
Everett, K. M. (1984)	*Candlewick*
Farr, M. C. (1998)	*Walbrook*
Fernandes, S. A. (2009)	*Coleman Street*
Fraser, S. J. (1993)	*Coleman Street*
Fraser, *Deputy* W. B., OBE (1981)	*Vintry*
Fredericks, M. B. (2008)	*Tower*
Galloway, A. D., OBE (1981)	*Bishopsgate*
Gillon, G. M. F. (1995)	*Cordwainer*
Ginsburg, *Deputy* S. (1990)	*Bishopsgate*
Graves, A. C. (1985)	*Bishopsgate*
Haines, *Deputy* Revd S. D. (2005)	*Cornhill*
Halliday, *Deputy* Mrs P. A., OBE (1992)	*Walbrook*
Hardwick, Dr P. B. (1987)	*Aldgate*
Harris, B. N. (2004)	*Bridge*
Henderson-Begg, M. (1977)	*Coleman Street*
Hoffman, T. D. D. (2002)	*Vintry*
Howard, R. P. (2011)	*Lime Street*

Hudson, M. (2007)	*Castle Baynard*
Hughes-Penney, R. C. (2004)	*Farringdon Wn.*
Hunt, W. G., TD (2004)	*Castle Baynard*
James, Clare (2008)	*Farringdon Wn.*
Jones, *Deputy* H. L. M. (2004)	*Portsoken*
King, *Deputy* A. J. N. (1999)	*Queenhithe*
Knowles, *Deputy* S. K., MBE (1984)	*Candlewick*
Lawrence, *Deputy* G. A. (2002)	*Farringdon Wt.*
Leck, P. (1998)	*Aldersgate*
Littlechild, V. (2009)	*Cripplegate Wn.*
Llewelyn-Davies, A. (2009)	*Billingsgate*
Lodge, O. A. W., TD (2009)	*Bread Street*
Lord, C. E. (2009)	*Farringdon Wt.*
McGuinness, *Deputy* C. S. (1997)	*Castle Baynard*
Malins, *Deputy* J. H., QC (1981)	*Farringdon Wt.*
Martinelli, P. J. (2009)	*Farringdon Wt.*
Mayhew, J. P. (1996)	*Aldersgate*
Mead, Mrs W. (1997)	*Farringdon Wt.*
Merrett, R. A. (2009)	*Bassishaw*
Mooney, B. D. F. (1998)	*Queenhithe*
Moore, G. W. (2009)	*Cripplegate Wn.*
Morris, H. F. (2008)	*Aldgate*
Moys, Mrs S. D. (2001)	*Aldgate*
Nash, *Deputy* Mrs J. C., OBE (1983)	*Aldersgate*
Newman, Mrs B. P., CBE (1989)	*Aldersgate*
Owen, *Deputy* Mrs J., MBE (1975)	*Langbourn*
Owen-Ward, *Deputy* J. R., MBE (1983)	*Bridge*
Page, M. (2002)	*Farringdon Wn.*
Pembroke, Mrs A. M. F. (1978)	*Cheap*
Pollard, J. H. G. (2002)	*Dowgate*
Priest, H. J. S. (2009)	*Castle Baynard*
Pulman, *Deputy* G. A. G. (1983)	*Tower*
Punter, C. (1993)	*Cripplegate Wn.*
Quilter, S. D. (1998)	*Cripplegate Wt.*
Regan, *Deputy* R. D. (1998)	*Farringdon Wn.*
Regis, D. (2009)	*Portsoken*
Richardson, M. C. (2009)	*Coleman Street*
Robinson, Mrs D. C. (1989)	*Bishopsgate*
Rogula, E. (2008)	*Lime Street*
Rounding, V. (2011)	*Farringdon Wn.*
Scott, J. G. S. (1999)	*Broad Street*
Seaton, I. (2009)	*Bassishaw*
Sherlock, *Deputy* M. R. C. (1992)	*Dowgate*
Shilson, *Deputy*, G. R. E., DPHIL (2009)	*Bread Street*
Simons, J. L. (2004)	*Castle Baynard*
Snyder, *Deputy* Sir Michael (1986)	*Cordwainer*
Spanner, J. H., TD (2001)	*Farringdon Wt.*
Starling, Mrs A. J. (2006)	*Cripplegate Wt.*
Thompson, D. J. (2004)	*Aldgate*
Tomlinson, J. (2004)	*Cripplegate Wt.*
Tumbridge, J. R. (2009)	*Tower*
Twogood, M. (2004)	*Farringdon Wt.*
Welbank, *Deputy* M. (2005)	*Billingsgate*
Willoughby, *Deputy* P. J. (1985)	*Bishopsgate*

THE CITY GUILDS (LIVERY COMPANIES)

The constitution of the livery companies has been unchanged for centuries. There are three ranks of membership: freemen, liverymen and assistants. A person can become a freeman by patrimony (through a parent having been a freeman); by servitude (through having served an apprenticeship to a freeman); or by redemption (by purchase).

Election to the livery is the prerogative of the company, who can elect any of its freemen as liverymen. Assistants are usually elected from the livery and form a Court of Assistants which is the governing body of the company. The master (in some companies called the prime warden) is elected annually from the assistants.

The register for 2011–12 lists 24,971 liverymen of the guilds entitled to vote at elections at Common Hall.

The order of precedence, omitting extinct companies, is given in parentheses after the name of each company in the list below. In certain companies the election of master or prime warden for the year does not take place until the autumn. In such cases the master or prime warden for 2010–11, rather than 2011–12, is given.

THE TWELVE GREAT COMPANIES
In order of civic precedence

MERCERS *(1)*. *Hall*, Mercers' Hall, Ironmonger Lane, London EC2V 8HE *Livery*, 233. *Clerk*, Menna McGregor *Master*, Thomas Clifford Sheldon

GROCERS *(2)*. *Hall*, Grocers' Hall, Princes Street, London EC2R 8AD *Livery*, 342. *Clerk*, Brig. Robert Pridham, OBE *Master*, T. Stubbs

DRAPERS *(3)*. *Hall*, Drapers' Hall, Throgmorton Avenue, London EC2N 2DQ *Livery*, 300. *Clerk*, Rear-Adm. A. B. Ross, CB, CBE *Master*, A. H. R. Walker

FISHMONGERS *(4)*. *Hall*, Fishmongers' Hall, London Bridge, London EC4R 9EL *Livery*, 388. *Clerk*, Nigel Cox *Prime Warden*, Thomas Boyd, OBE

GOLDSMITHS *(5)*. *Hall*, Goldsmiths' Hall, Foster Lane, London EC2V 6BN *Livery*, 313. *Clerk*, Richard Melly *Prime Warden*, H. J. Miller

MERCHANT TAYLORS *(6/7)*. *Hall*, Merchant Taylors' Hall, 30 Threadneedle Street, London EC2R 8JB *Livery*, 330. *Clerk*, Rear-Adm. Nicholas Harris, CB, MBE *Master*, Eddie Charlton

SKINNERS *(6/7)*. *Hall*, Skinners' Hall, 8 Dowgate Hill, London EC4R 2SP *Livery*, 400. *Clerk*, Maj.-Gen. Brian Plummer, CBE *Master*, Andrew Boggis

HABERDASHERS *(8)*. *Hall*, Haberdashers' Hall, 18 West Smithfield, London EC1A 9HQ *Livery*, 314. *Clerk*, Rear-Adm. Richard Phillips, CB *Master*, Deborah Knight

SALTERS *(9)*. *Hall*, Salters' Hall, 4 Fore Street, London EC2Y 5DE *Livery*, 163. *Clerk*, Capt. David Morris, RN *Master*, Rt. Hon. Lord Butler of Brockwell, KG, GCB, CVO

IRONMONGERS *(10)*. *Hall*, Ironmongers' Hall, 1 Shaftesbury Place, London EC2Y 8AA *Livery*, 98. *Clerk*, Col. Hamon Massey *Master*, M. A. Hudson

VINTNERS *(11)*. *Hall*, Vintners' Hall, Upper Thames Street, London EC4V 3BG *Livery*, 310. *Clerk*, Brig. Michael Smythe, OBE *Master*, Michael Turner

CLOTHWORKERS *(12)*. *Hall*, Clothworkers' Hall, Dunster Court, Mincing Lane, London EC3R 7AH *Livery*, 200. *Clerk*, Andrew Blessley *Master*, John Stoddart-Scott

OTHER CITY GUILDS
In alphabetical order

ACTUARIES *(91)*. 3rd Floor Cheapside House, 138 Cheapside, London EC2V 6BW *Livery*, 234. *Clerk*, David Johnson *Master*, John Lockyer

AIR PILOTS AND AIR NAVIGATORS *(81)*. *Hall*, Cobham House, 9 Warwick Court, Gray's Inn, London WC1R 5DJ *Livery*, 600. *Clerk*, Paul Tacon *Grand Master*, HRH the Duke of York, KG, GCVO, ADC(P) *Master*, O. W. Epton

APOTHECARIES *(58)*. *Hall*, Apothecaries' Hall, 14 Black Friars Lane, London EC4V 6EJ *Livery*, 1,250. *Clerk*, Ann Wallington-Smith *Master*, Dr T. L. Chambers

ARBITRATORS *(93)*. 13 Hall Gardens, Colney Heath, St Albans, Herts AL4 0QF *Livery*, 108. *Clerk*, Gaye Duffy *Master*, Kay Linnell

ARMOURERS AND BRASIERS *(22)*. *Hall*, Armourers' Hall, 81 Coleman Street, London EC2R 5BJ *Livery*, 128. *Clerk*, Cdre Christopher Waite *Master*, Sir Timothy Ruggles Brise Bt.

BAKERS *(19)*. *Hall*, Bakers' Hall, 9 Harp Lane, London EC3R 6DP *Livery*, 350. *Clerk*, John Tompkins *Master*, Alan Cornwell

BARBERS *(17)*. *Hall*, Barber-Surgeons' Hall, Monkwell Square, Wood Street, London EC2Y 5BL *Livery*, 220. *Clerk*, Col. Peter Durrant, MBE *Master*, H. Harris Hughes, CBE

BASKETMAKERS *(52)*. Doric House, 108 Garstang Road West, Poulton le Fylde, Lancs FY6 7SN *Livery*, 300. *Clerk*, Roger de Pilkyngton *Prime Warden*, John Barker, OBE

BLACKSMITHS *(40)*. 9 Little Trinity Lane, London EC4V 2AD *Livery*, 235. *Clerk*, Christopher Jeal *Prime Warden*, Donald Banner

BOWYERS *(38)*. 46 The Haydens, Tonbridge, Kent TN9 1NS, *Livery*, 86. *Clerk*, Richard Sawyer *Master*, A. H. Mundy

BREWERS *(14)*. *Hall*, Brewers' Hall, Aldermanbury Square, London EC2V 7HR *Livery*, 190. *Clerk*, Brig. D. J. Ross, CBE *Master*, D. G. F. Thompson

BRODERERS *(48)*. Ember House, 35–37 Creek Road, East Molesey, Surrey KT8 9BE *Livery*, 125. *Clerk*, Peter J. C. Crouch *Master*, Lt-Col. G. T. R. Birdwood

BUILDERS MERCHANTS *(88)*. 4 College Hill, London EC4R 2RB *Livery*, 187. *Clerk*, T. Statham *Master*, Graham Ballinger

BUTCHERS *(24)*. *Hall*, Butchers' Hall, 87 Bartholomew Close, London EC1A 7EB *Livery*, 638. *Clerk*, Cdre Anthony Morrow, CVO *Master*, Ray Woodhouse

CARMEN *(77)*. Five Kings House, 1 Queen Street Place, London EC4R 1QS *Livery*, 500. *Clerk*, Walter Gill *Master*, John Older

CARPENTERS *(26)*. *Hall*, Carpenters' Hall, 1 Throgmorton Avenue, London EC2N 2JJ *Livery*, 196. *Clerk*, Brig. Tim Gregson, MBE *Master*, Giles Downes, CVO

CHARTERED ACCOUNTANTS *(86)*. Larksfield, Kent Hatch Road, Crockham Hill, Edenbridge, Kent TN8 6SX *Livery*, 286. *Clerk*, Peter Dickinson *Master*, Alderman Sir John Stuttard

CHARTERED ARCHITECTS *(98)*. 82A Muswell Hill Road, London N10 3JR *Livery*, 165. *Clerk*, David Cole-Adams *Master*, Michael Wilkey

CHARTERED SECRETARIES AND ADMINISTRATORS *(87)*. 3rd Floor, Saddlers' House, 40 Gutter Lane, London EC2V 6BR *Livery*, 279. *Clerk*, Col. Michael Dudding, OBE, TD *Master*, Ian Richardson

CHARTERED SURVEYORS *(85)*. 75 Meadway Drive, Horsell, Woking, Surrey GU21 4TF *Livery*, 345. *Clerk*, Amanda Jackson *Master*, Mickola Wilson

CLOCKMAKERS *(61)*. Salters' Hall, 4 Fore Street, London EC2Y 5DE *Livery*, 285. *Clerk*, Joe Buxton *Master*, Mark Elliott

COACHMAKERS AND COACH-HARNESS MAKERS *(72)*. 48 Aldernay Street,London SW1V 4EX *Livery*, 400. *Clerk*, Lt.-Col. Peter Henderson, OBE *Master*, Vice-Adm. Timothy Laurence, CB, MVO

CONSTRUCTORS *(99)*. 5 Delft Close, Locks Heath, Southampton SO31 7TQ *Livery*, 170. *Clerk*, Kim Tyrrell *Master*, Doug Barrat

COOKS *(35)*. 18 Solent Drive, Warsash, Southampton SO31 9HB *Livery*, 75. *Clerk*, Vice-Adm. P. J. Wilkinson, CB, CVO *Master*, Geoffrey J. Osborne

COOPERS *(36)*. *Hall*, Coopers' Hall, 13 Devonshire Square, London EC2M 4TH *Livery*, 260. *Clerk*, Lt.-Col. Adrian Carroll *Master*, Peter Timms

CORDWAINERS *(27)*. Clothworkers' Hall, Dunster Court, Mincing Lane, London EC3R 7AH *Livery*, 172. *Clerk*, John Miller *Master*, Geoffrey Branford

CURRIERS *(29)*. Hedgerley, 10 The Leaze, Ashton Keynes, Wiltshire SN6 6PE *Livery*, 92. *Clerk*, Simon Bevan *Master*, Richard Stewart

CUTLERS *(18)*. *Hall*, Cutlers' Hall, Warwick Lane, London EC4M 7BR *Livery*, 100. *Clerk*, J. P. Allen *Master*, C. C. Fisher

DISTILLERS *(69)*. 1 The Sanctuary, Westminster, London SW1P 3JT *Livery*, 260. *Clerk*, Edward Macey-Dare *Master*, Terence Barr

DYERS *(13)*. *Hall*, Dyers' Hall, 10 Dowgate Hill, London EC4R 2ST *Livery*, 136. *Clerk*, J. R. Vaizey *Prime Warden*, L. S. Mackintosh

ENGINEERS *(94)*. Wax Chandlers' Hall, 6 Gresham Street, London EC2V 7AD *Livery*, 320. *Clerk*, Wg Cdr A. G. Willenbruch, FRSE *Master*, John Banyard, OBE, FRENG

ENVIRONMENTAL CLEANERS *(97)*. 121 Hacton Lane, Upminster, Essex RM14 2NL *Livery*, 280. *Clerk*, Neil Morley *Master*, Peter D. Holt

FAN MAKERS *(76)*. Skinners' Hall, 8 Dowgate Hill, London EC4R 2SP *Livery*, 202. *Clerk*, Martin Davies *Master*, James Moore

FARMERS *(80)*. *Hall*, The Farmers' and Fletchers' Hall, 3 Cloth Street, London EC1A 7LD *Livery*, 330. *Clerk*, Col. David King, OBE *Master*, Peter Faulkner

FARRIERS *(55)*. 19 Queen Street, Chipperfield, Kings Langley, Herts WD4 9BT *Livery*, 342. *Clerk*, Charlotte Clifford *Master*, Stephen J. W. Scott

FELTMAKERS *(63)*. Post Cottage,Greywell, Hook, Hants RG29 1DA *Livery*, 173. *Clerk*, Maj. J. T. H. Coombs *Master*, Mrs E. M. B. Rose-Lawson

FIREFIGHTERS *(103)*. The Insurance Hall, 20 Aldermanbury, London EC2V 7HY *Livery*, 103. *Clerk*, Sir Martin Bonham *Master*, Peter Cowland

FLETCHERS *(39)*. *Hall*, The Farmers' and Fletchers' Hall, 3 Cloth Street, London EC1A 7LD *Livery*, 143. *Clerk*, Georgina Butler *Master*, John Owen-Ward, MBE

FOUNDERS *(33)*. *Hall*, Founders' Hall, 1 Cloth Fair, London EC1A 7JQ *Livery*, 175. *Clerk*, A. Gillett *Master*, Dr D. Cogan

FRAMEWORK KNITTERS *(64)*. 86 Park Drive, Upminster, Essex RM14 3AS *Livery*, 200. *Clerk*, Alan Clark *Master*, Paul Bethel

FRUITERERS *(45)*. Chapelstones, 84 High Street, Codford St Mary, Warminster BA12 0ND *Livery*, 283. *Clerk*, Lt.-Col. L. French *Master*, E. Dawes

FUELLERS *(95)*. 26 Merrick Square, London SE1 4JB *Livery*, 135. *Clerk*, Sir Anthony Reardon Smith, Bt. *Master*, Stuart Goldsmith

FURNITURE MAKERS *(83)*. *Hall*, Furniture Makers' Hall, 12 Austin Friars, London EC2N 2HE *Livery*, 228. *Clerk*, Charles Kerrigan *Master*, Hugh Garforth-Bles

GARDENERS *(66)*. 25 Luke Street, London EC2A 4AR *Livery*, 298. *Clerk*, Cdr Robert Woolgar, OBE *Master*, Daniel Caspi

GIRDLERS *(23)*. *Hall*, Girdlers' Hall, Basinghall Avenue, London EC2V 5DD *Livery*, 80. *Clerk*, Brig. I. D. O. Rees *Master*, J. J. Meade

GLASS SELLERS *(71)*. 57 Witley Court, Coram Street, London WC1N 1HD *Livery*, 230. *Clerk*, Col. Audrey Smith *Master*, Richard Lawman

GLAZIERS AND PAINTERS OF GLASS *(53)*. *Hall,* Glaziers' Hall, 9 Montague Close, London SE1 9DD *Livery,* 292. *Clerk,* Alex Galloway, CVO *Master,* David Ingmire

GLOVERS *(62)*. London SW3 *Livery,* 250. *Clerk,* C. Blackshaw *Master,* K. Ebsworth

GOLD AND SILVER WYRE DRAWERS *(74)*. 9A Prince of Wales Mansions, Prince of Wales Drive, London SW11 4BG *Livery,* 300. *Clerk,* Cdr. R. House *Master,* E. M. V. Knapper

GUNMAKERS *(73)*. The Proof House, 48–50 Commercial Road, London E1 1LP *Livery,* 350. *Clerk,* Col. William Chesshyre *Master,* W. Richards, OBE

HACKNEY CARRIAGE DRIVERS *(104)*. 25 The Grove, Parkfield, Latimer, Bucks HP5 1UE *Livery,* 98. *Clerk,* Mary Whitworth *Master,* James Rainbird

HORNERS *(54)*. St. Stephen's House, Hide Place, London SW1P 4NJ *Livery,* 225. *Clerk,* Raymond Layard *Master,* Georgina Scott

INFORMATION TECHNOLOGISTS *(100)*. *Hall,* Information Technologists' Hall, 39A Bartholomew Close, London EC1A 7JN *Livery,* 750. *Clerk,* Mike Jenkins *Master,* Jonathan Soar

INNHOLDERS *(32)*. *Hall,* Innholders' Hall, 30 College Street, London EC4R 2RH *Livery,* 154. *Clerk,* Dougal Bulger *Master,* Ian White, FRICS

INSURERS *(92)*. The Hall, 20 Aldermanbury, London EC2V 7HY *Livery,* 380. *Clerk,* Leonard Walters *Master,* Timothy Ablett

INTERNATIONAL BANKERS *(106)*. 12 Austin Friars, London EC2N 2HE *Livery,* 183. *Clerk,* Wg Cdr Tim Woods, BEM *Master,* Joseph King

JOINERS AND CEILERS *(41)*. 75 Meadway Drive, Horsell, Woking, Surrey GU21 4TF *Livery,* 128. *Clerk,* Amanda Jackson *Master,* Clive Turrell

LAUNDERERS *(89)*. *Hall,* Launderers' Hall, 9 Montague Close, London Bridge, London SE1 9DD *Livery,* 215. *Clerk,* Mrs J. Polek *Master,* Martyn Lewis

LEATHERSELLERS *(15)*. *Hall,* 21 Garlick Hill, London EC4V 2AU *Livery,* 150. *Clerk,* David Santa-Olalla *Master,* Miles Emley

LIGHTMONGERS *(96)*. 5 Rokefield House, Westcott Street, Dorking, Surrey RH4 3NZ *Livery,* 168. *Clerk,* Stephen Thomas *Master,* John Harding

LORINERS *(57)*. Hampton House, High Street, East Grinstead, West Sussex RH19 3AW *Livery,* 435. *Clerk,* Peter Lusty *Master,* Lady Milnes Coates

MAKERS OF PLAYING CARDS *(75)*. 256 St David's Square, London E14 3WE *Livery,* 147. *Clerk,* David Barrett *Master,* Lance Whitehouse

MANAGEMENT CONSULTANTS *(105)*. Skinners' Hall, 8 Dowgate Hill, London EC4R 2SP *Livery,* 177. *Clerk,* Leslie Johnson *Master,* Vicky Pryce

MARKETORS *(90)*. Plaisterers' Hall, 1 London Wall, London EC2Y 5JU *Livery,* 267. *Clerk,* Adele Thorpe *Master,* John Flynn

MASONS *(30)*. 22 Cannon Hill, Southgate, London N14 6LG *Livery,* 150. *Clerk,* Heather Rowell *Master,* Derek Sayer

MASTER MARINERS *(78)*. *Hall,* HQS Wellington, Temple Stairs, Victoria Embankment, London WC2R 2PN *Livery,* 197. *Clerk,* Rear-Adm. Nick Harris, CB, MBE *Master,* R. W. E. Charlton

MUSICIANS *(50)*. 6th Floor, 2 London Wall Building, London EC2M 5PP *Livery,* 385. *Clerk,* Margaret Alford *Master,* Alderman Dr Andrew Parmley

NEEDLEMAKERS *(65)*. PO Box 3682, Windsor, Berkshire SL4 3WR *Livery,* 200. *Clerk,* Philip Grant *Master,* Roger Staines

PAINTER-STAINERS *(28)*. *Hall,* Painters' Hall, 9 Little Trinity Lane, London EC4V 2AD *Livery,* 320. *Clerk,* Christopher Twyman *Master,* M. Lawson

PATTENMAKERS *(70)*. 3 The High Street, Sutton Valence, Kent ME17 3AG *Livery,* 200. *Clerk,* Col. R. Murfin, TD *Master,* John Timpson, CBE

PAVIORS *(56)*. 3 Ridgemount Gardens, Enfield, Middx EN2 8QL *Livery,* 283. *Clerk,* John White *Master,* John Price

PEWTERERS *(16)*. *Hall,* Pewterers' Hall, Oat Lane, London EC2V 7DE *Livery,* 120. *Clerk,* Capt. Paddy Watson, RN *Master,* Richard Boggis-Rolfe

PLAISTERERS *(46)*. *Hall,* Plaisterers' Hall, 1 London Wall, London EC2Y 5JU *Livery,* 236. *Clerk,* Nigel Bamping *Master,* Peter Baker

PLUMBERS *(31)*. Wax Chandlers' Hall, 6 Gresham Street, London EC2V 7AD *Livery,* 360. *Clerk,* Air Cdre Paul Nash, OBE *Master,* Lt-Col. Antony Paterson-Fox

POULTERS *(34)*. The Old Butchers, Station Road, Groombridge, Kent TN3 9QX *Livery,* 204. *Clerk,* Vernon Ashford *Master,* Brendan Tobin

SADDLERS *(25)*. *Hall,* Saddlers' Hall, 40 Gutter Lane, London EC2V 6BR *Livery,* 75. *Clerk,* Col. N. Lithgow, CBE *Master,* P. Laurie

SCIENTIFIC INSTRUMENT MAKERS *(84)*. 9 Montague Close, London SE1 9DD *Livery,* 185. *Clerk,* Neville Watson *Master,* B. D. Fishwick

SCRIVENERS *(44)*. HQS Wellington, Temple Stairs, Victoria Embankment, London WC2R 2PN *Livery,* 193. *Clerk,* Giles Cole *Master,* Peter Esslemont

SECURITY PROFESSIONALS *(108)*. 34 Tye Green, Glemsford, , Suffolk CO10 7RG *Livery,* 150. *Clerk,* Tricia Boswell *Master,* Nigel Churton, MBE

SHIPWRIGHTS *(59)*. Ironmongers Hall, Shaftesbury Place, London EC2Y 8AA *Livery,* 450. *Clerk,* Lt.-Col. Andy Milne, RN *Prime Warden,* HRH the Prince of Wales, KG, GCB, OM

SOLICITORS *(79)*. 4 College Hill, London EC4R 2RB *Livery,* 350. *Clerk,* Neil Cameron *Master,* Alderman John White, TD

SPECTACLE MAKERS *(60)*. Apothecaries' Hall, Black Friars Lane, London EC4V 6EL *Livery,* 390. *Clerk,* Lt.-Col. John Salmon, OBE *Master,* Prof. John Mardhall

STATIONERS AND NEWSPAPER MAKERS *(47)*. *Hall,* Stationers' Hall, Ave Maria Lane, London EC4M 7DD *Livery,* 476. *Clerk,* William Alden, MBE *Master,* Nigel Stapleton

TALLOW CHANDLERS *(21)*. *Hall,* Tallow Chandlers' Hall, 4 Dowgate Hill, London EC4R 2SH *Livery,* 180. *Clerk,* Brig. R. Wilde, CBE *Master,* Sir Christopher Pryke, Bt.

TAX ADVISERS *(107)*. 191 West End Road, Ruislip, Middx HA4 6LD *Freemen,* 142. *Clerk,* Paul Herbage *Master,* Peter Gravestock

TIN PLATE WORKERS (ALIAS WIRE WORKERS) *(67)*. Highbanks, Ferry Road, Surlingham, Norwich, Norfolk NR14 7AR *Livery,* 220. *Clerk,* Michael Henderson-Begg *Master,* Ian T. Chamberlain

TOBACCO PIPE MAKERS AND TOBACCO BLENDERS *(82)*. 108 Dorset Road, Bexhill on Sea, E. Sussex TN40 2HT *Livery,* 150. *Clerk,* Lt-Col. Peter Swanson *Master,* Fiona Adler

TURNERS *(51)*. Skinner's Hall, 8 Dowgate Hill, London EC4R 2SP *Livery,* 186. *Clerk,* Edward Windsor Clive *Master,* Ilan Krieger

TYLERS AND BRICKLAYERS *(37)*. 3 Farmers' Way, Seer Green, Bucks HP9 2YY *Livery,* 155. *Clerk,* John Brooks *Master,* Piers Nicholson

UPHOLDERS *(49)*. Hall in the Wood, 46 Quail Gardens, Selsdon Vale, Croydon CR2 8TF *Livery*, 209. *Clerk*, Jean Cody *Master*, James Kelly

WATER CONSERVATORS *(102)*. The Lark, 2 Bell Lane, Worlington, Bury St Edmunds, Suffolk IP28 8SE *Livery*, 210. *Clerk*, Ralph Riley *Master*, Barry Dennis

WAX CHANDLERS *(20)*. *Hall*, Wax Chandlers' Hall, 6 Gresham Street, London EC2V 7AD *Livery*, 120. *Clerk*, Georgina Brown *Master*, John Sleeman

WEAVERS *(42)*. Saddlers' House, Gutter Lane, London EC2V 6BR *Livery*, 125. *Clerk*, John Snowdon *Upper Bailiff*, His Honour Giles Forrester

WHEELWRIGHTS *(68)*. 7 Glengall Road, Bexleyheath, Kent DA7 4AL *Livery*, 220. *Clerk*, Brian François *Master*, Graham Westwell

WOOLMEN *(43)*. The Old Post Office, 56 Lower Way, Great Brickhill, Bucks MK17 9AG *Livery*, 150. *Clerk*, Gillian Wilson *Master*, William Wilson, CBE

WORLD TRADERS *(101)*. 13 Hall Gardens, Colney Heath, St. Albans, Herts AL4 0QF *Livery*, 240. *Clerk*, Mrs Gaye Duffy *Master*, Mei Sim Lai, OBE

PARISH CLERKS *(No Livery*)*. Acreholt, 33 Medstead Road, Beech, Alton, Hants GU34 4AD *Members*, 88. *Clerk*, Alana Coombes *Master*, Peter Maplestone

WATERMEN AND LIGHTERMEN *(No Livery*)*. *Hall*, Watermen's Hall, 16 St Mary-at-Hill, London EC3R 8EF *Craft Owning Freemen*, 600. *Clerk*, Colin Middlemiss *Master*, Paul Ludwig

* Parish Clerks and Watermen and Lightermen have requested to remain with no livery

LONDON BOROUGH COUNCILS

Council	Telephone	Population*	Council Tax†	Chief Executive
Barking and Dagenham	020-8592 4500	175,600	£1,326	Stella Manzie
Barnet	020-8359 2000	343,100	£1,423	Nick Walkley
Bexley	020-8303 7777	225,900	£1,438	Will Tuckley
Brent	020-8937 1234	255,500	£1,369	Gareth Daniel
Bromley	020-8464 3333	310,200	£1,301	Doug Patterson
Camden	020-7974 4444	231,200	£1,332	Moira Gibb, CBE
CITY OF LONDON CORPORATION	020-7606 3030	11,500	£939	Chris Duffield
Croydon	020-8726 6000	342,800	£1,460	Jon Rouse
Ealing	020-8825 5000	316,600	£1,370	Martin Smith
Enfield	020-8379 1000	291,200	£1,410	Rob Leak
Greenwich	020-8854 8888	226,100	£1,291	Mary Ney
Hackney	020-8356 5000	216,000	£1,308	Tim Shields
Hammersmith and Fulham	020-8748 3020	169,700	£1,122	Derek Myers
Haringey	020-8489 0000	225,500	£1,494	Kevin Crompton
Harrow	020-8863 5611	228,100	£1,496	Michael Lockwood
Havering	01708-434343	234,100	£1,505	Cheryl Coppell
Hillingdon	01895-250111	262,500	£1,423	Hugh Dunnachie
Hounslow	020-8583 2000	234,200	£1,400	Mary Harpley
Islington	020-7527 2000	191,800	£1,272	Lesley Seary
Kensington and Chelsea	020-7361 3000	169,900	£1,092	Derek Myers
Kingston upon Thames	020-8547 5757	166,700	£1,663	Bruce McDonald
Lambeth	020-7926 1000	283,300	£1,235	Derrick Anderson, CBE
Lewisham	020-8314 6000	264,500	£1,352	Barry Quirk, CBE
Merton	020-8543 2222	206,400	£1,416	Ged Curran
Newham	020-8430 2000	241,200	£1,255	Kim Bromley-Derry
Redbridge	020-8554 5000	267,700	£1,405	Roger Hampson
Richmond upon Thames	020-8891 1411	189,000	£1,597	Gillian Norton
Southwark	020-7525 5000	285,600	£1,222	Annie Shepperd
Sutton	020-8770 5000	192,200	£1,451	Niall Bolger
Tower Hamlets	020-7364 5000	234,800	£1,195	Dr. Kevan Collins
Waltham Forest	020-8496 3000	224,300	£1,462	Martin Esom
Wandsworth	020-8871 6000	286,600	£687	Paul Martin
WESTMINSTER	020-7641 6000	249,400	£688	Mike More

* *Source: ONS – Mid-2009 Population Estimates* (Crown copyright)
† Average Band D council tax bill for 2011–12
Councils in CAPITAL LETTERS have city status

WALES

Cymru

The principality of Wales (Cymru) occupies the extreme west of the central southern portion of the island of Great Britain, with a total area of 20,778 sq. km (8,022 sq. miles): land 20,733 sq. km (8,005 sq. miles); inland water 45 sq. km (17 sq. miles). It is bordered in the north by the Irish Sea, in the south by the Bristol Channel, in the east by the English counties of Cheshire West and Chester, Shropshire, Herefordshire and Gloucestershire, and in the west by St George's Channel.

Across the Menai Straits is Ynys Mon (Isle of Anglesey) (715 sq. km/276 sq. miles), communication with which is facilitated by the Menai Suspension Bridge (305m/1,000ft long) built by Telford in 1826, and by the Britannia Bridge (351m/1,151ft), a two-tier road and rail truss arch design, rebuilt in 1972 after a fire destroyed the original tubular railway bridge built by Stephenson in 1850. Holyhead harbour, on Holy Isle (north-west of Anglesey), provides ferry services to Dublin (113km/70 miles).

POPULATION

The population at the 2001 census was 2,903,085 (men 1,403,782; women 1,499,303). The average density of population in 2001 was 140 persons per sq. km (362 per sq. mile).

RELIEF

Wales is a country of extensive tracts of high plateau and shorter stretches of mountain ranges deeply dissected by river valleys. Lower-lying ground is largely confined to the coastal belt and the lower parts of the valleys. The highest mountains are those of Snowdonia in the north-west (Snowdon, 1,085m/3,559ft and Aran Fawddwy, 906m/2,971ft). Snowdonia is also home to Cader Idris (Pen y Gadair, 892m/2,928ft). Other high peaks are to be found in the Cambrian range (Plynlimon, 752m/2,467ft), and the Black Mountains, Brecon Beacons and Black Forest ranges in the south-east (Pen y Fan, 886m/2,906ft; Waun Fâch, 811m/2,660ft; Carmarthen Van, 802m/2,630ft).

HYDROGRAPHY

The principal river in Wales is the Severn, which flows from the slopes of Plynlimon to the English border. The Wye (209km/130 miles) also rises in the slopes of Plynlimon. The Usk (90km/56 miles) flows into the Bristol Channel through Gwent. The Dee (113km/70 miles) rises in Bala Lake and flows through the Vale of Llangollen, where an aqueduct (built by Telford in 1805) carries the Pontcysyllte branch of the Shropshire Union Canal across the valley. The estuary of the Dee is the navigable portion, it is 23km (14 miles) in length and about 8km (5 miles) in breadth. The Towy (109km/68 miles), Teifi (80km/50 miles), Taff (64km/40 miles), Dovey (48km/30 miles), Taf (40km/25 miles) and Conway (39km/24 miles) are wholly Welsh rivers.

The largest natural lake is Bala (Llyn Tegid) in Gwynedd, nearly 7km (4 miles) long and 1.6km (1 mile) wide. Lake Vyrnwy is an artificial reservoir, about the size of Bala, it forms the water supply of Liverpool;

Birmingham's water is supplied from reservoirs in the Elan and Claerwen valleys.

WELSH LANGUAGE

According to the 2001 census results, the percentage of people aged three years and over who are able to speak Welsh is:

Blaenau Gwent	9.1	Neath Port Talbot	17.8
Bridgend	10.6	Newport	9.6
Caerphilly	10.9	Pembrokeshire	21.5
Cardiff	10.9	Powys	20.8
Carmarthenshire	50.1	Rhondda Cynon Taf	12.3
Ceredigion	51.8	Swansea	13.2
Conwy	29.2	Torfaen	10.7
Denbighshire	26.1	Vale of Glamorgan	11.1
Flintshire	14.1	Wrexham	14.4
Gwynedd	67.8	Ynys Mon	
Merthyr Tydfil	10.0	(Isle of Anglesey)	59.8
Monmouthshire	9.0	*Total in Wales*	20.5

FLAG

The flag of Wales, the Red Dragon (*Y Ddraig Goch*), is a red dragon on a field divided white over green (per fess argent and vert a dragon passant gules). The flag was augmented in 1953 by a royal badge on a shield encircled with a riband bearing the words *Ddraig Goch Ddyry Cychwyn* and imperially crowned, but this augmented flag is rarely used.

EARLY HISTORY

The earliest inhabitants of whom there is any record appear to have been subdued or exterminated by the Goidels (a people of Celtic race) in the Bronze Age. A further invasion of Celtic Brythons and Belgae followed in the ensuing Iron Age. The Roman conquest of southern Britain and Wales was for some time successfully opposed by Caratacus (Caractacus or Caradog), chieftain of the Catuvellauni and son of Cunobelinus (Cymbeline). South-east Wales was subjugated and the legionary fortress at Caerleon-on-Usk established by around AD 75–7; the conquest of Wales was completed by Agricola around AD 78. Communications were opened up by the construction of military roads from Chester to Caerleon-on-Usk and Caerwent, and from Chester to Conwy (and thence to Carmarthen and Neath). Christianity was introduced in the fourth century, during the Roman occupation.

ANGLO-SAXON ATTACKS

The Anglo-Saxon invaders of southern Britain drove the Celts into the mountain stronghold of Wales, and into Strathclyde (Cumberland and south-west Scotland) and Cornwall, giving them the name of *Waelisc* (Welsh), meaning 'foreign'. The West Saxons' victory of Deorham (AD 577) isolated Wales from Cornwall and the battle of Chester (AD 613) cut off communication with Strathclyde and northern Britain. In the eighth century the boundaries of the Welsh were further restricted by the annexations of Offa, King of Mercia, and counter-attacks were largely prevented by the construction of an artificial boundary from the Dee to the Wye (Offa's Dyke).

In the ninth century Rhodri Mawr (844–878) united the country and successfully resisted further incursions of the Saxons by land and raids of Norse and Danish pirates by sea, but at his death his three provinces of Gwynedd (north), Powys (central) and Deheubarth (south) were divided among his three sons, Anarawd, Mervyn and Cadell. Cadell's son Hywel Dda ruled a large part of Wales and codified its laws but the provinces were not united again until the rule of Llewelyn ap Seisyllt (husband of the heiress of Gwynedd) from 1018 to 1023.

THE NORMAN CONQUEST

After the Norman conquest of England, William I created palatine counties along the Welsh frontier, and the Norman barons began to make encroachments into Welsh territory. The Welsh princes recovered many of their losses during the civil wars of Stephen's reign (1135–54), and in the early 13th century Owen Gruffydd, prince of Gwynedd, was the dominant figure in Wales. Under Llywelyn ap Iorwerth (1194–1240) the Welsh united in powerful resistance to English incursions and Llywelyn's privileges and de facto independence were recognised in the Magna Carta. His grandson, Llywelyn ap Gruffydd, was the last native prince; he was killed in 1282 during hostilities between the Welsh and English, allowing Edward I of England to establish his authority over the country. On 7 February 1301, Edward of Caernarvon, son of Edward I, was created Prince of Wales, a title subsequently borne by the eldest son of the sovereign.

Strong Welsh national feeling continued, expressed in the early 15th century in the rising led by Owain Glyndwr, but the situation was altered by the accession to the English throne in 1485 of Henry VII of the Welsh House of Tudor. Wales was politically annexed by England under the Act of Union of 1535, which extended English laws to the principality and gave it parliamentary representation for the first time.

EISTEDDFOD

The Welsh are a distinct nation, with a language and literature of their own; the national bardic festival (Eisteddfod), instituted by Prince Rhys ap Griffith in 1176, is still held annually.

PRINCIPAL CITIES

There are five cities in Wales (with date city status conferred): Bangor (pre-1900), Cardiff (1905), Newport (2002), St David's (1994) and Swansea (1969).

Cardiff and Swansea have also been granted Lord Mayoralities.

CARDIFF

Cardiff *(Caerdydd)*, at the mouth of the rivers Taff, Rhymney and Ely, is the capital city of Wales and at the 2001 census had a population of 305,353. The city has changed dramatically in recent years following the regeneration of Cardiff Bay and construction of a barrage, which has created a permanent freshwater lake and waterfront for the city. As the capital city, Cardiff is home to the National Assembly for Wales and is a major administrative, retail, business and cultural centre.

The city is home to many fine buildings including the City Hall, Cardiff Castle, Llandaff Cathedral, the National Museum of Wales, university buildings, law courts and the Temple of Peace and Health. The Millennium Stadium opened in 1999 and has hosted high-profile events since 2001.

SWANSEA

Swansea *(Abertawe)* is a seaport with a population of 223,293 at the 2001 census. The Gower peninsula was brought within the city boundary under local government reform in 1974.

The principal buildings are the Norman Castle (rebuilt c.1330), the Royal Institution of South Wales, founded in 1835 (including library), the University of Wales Swansea at Singleton and the Guildhall, containing Frank Brangwyn's British Empire panels. The Dylan Thomas Centre, formerly the old Guildhall, was restored in 1995. More recent buildings include the County Hall, the Maritime Quarter Marina, the Wales National Pool and the National Waterfront Museum.

Swansea was chartered by the Earl of Warwick (1158–84), and further charters were granted by King John, Henry III, Edward II, Edward III and James II, Oliver Cromwell and the Marcher Lord William de Breos. It was formally invested with city status in 1969 by HRH The Prince of Wales.

LORD-LIEUTENANTS AND HIGH SHERIFFS

Area	Lord-Lieutenant	High Sheriff (2011–12)
Clwyd	T. Jones, CBE	Edmund Fitzhugh, OBE
Dyfed	Hon. Robin Lewis, OBE	Thomas Lloyd, OBE
Gwent	S. Boyle	Lady Hayman-Joyce
Gwynedd	His Hon. Huw Daniel	Prof. Robin Grove-White
Mid Glamorgan	Kate Thomas, CVO	Dr Barbara Wilding, CBE, QPM
Powys	Hon. Mrs E. Legge-Bourke, LVO	Col. John Brunt, OBE, TD
South Glamorgan	Dr Peter Beck, MD, FRCP	Roger Thomas, OBE
West Glamorgan	D. Byron Lewis	Susan Thomas

LOCAL COUNCILS

Council	Administrative Headquarters	Telephone	Population*	Council Tax†	Chief Executive
Blaenau Gwent	Ebbw Vale	01495-350555	68,600	£1,426	David Waggett
Bridgend	Bridgend	01656-643643	134,200	£1,288	Dr Jo Farrar
Caerphilly	Hengoed	01443-815588	172,700	£1,095	Anthony O'Sullivan
CARDIFF	Cardiff	029-2087 2000	336,200	£1,086	Jonathan House
Carmarthenshire	Carmarthen	01267-234567	180,800	£1,188	Mark James
Ceredigion	Aberaeron	01545-570881	76,400	£1,133	Bronwen Morgan
Conwy	Conwy	01492-574000	111,400	£1,089	K. W. Finch *(acting)*
Denbighshire	Ruthin	01824-706000	96,700	£1,270	Dr Mohammed Mehmet
Flintshire	Mold	01352-752121	149,900	£1,151	Colin Everett
Gwynedd	Caernarfon	01766-771000	118,800	£1,237	Harry Thomas
Merthyr Tydfil	Merthyr Tydfil	01685-725000	55,700	£1,343	Gareth Chapman
Monmouthshire	Cwmbran	01633-644644	88,000	£1,225	Paul Matthews
Neath Port Talbot	Port Talbot	01639-763333	137,400	£1,384	Steven Phillips
NEWPORT	Newport	01633-656656	140,400	£995	Tracey Lee
Pembrokeshire	Haverfordwest	01437-764551	117,400	£923	Bryn Parry-Jones
Powys	Llandrindod Wells	01597-826000	131,700	£1,138	Jeremy Patterson
Rhondda Cynon Taff	Tonypandy	01443-424000	234,400	£1,303	Keith Griffiths
SWANSEA	Swansea	01792-636000	231,300	£1,162	Jack Straw
Torfaen	Pontypool	01495-762200	90,700	£1,180	Alison Ward
Vale of Glamorgan	Barry	01446-700111	124,600	£1,123	John Maitland-Evans
Wrexham	Wrexham	01978-292000	133,200	£1,135	Helen Paterson
Ynys Mon (Isle of Anglesey)	Ynys Mon	01248-750057	68,800	£1,094	Richard Parry Jones

* Source: ONS – *Mid-2009 Population Estimates* (Crown copyright)
† Average Band D council tax bill 2011–12
Councils in CAPITAL LETTERS have city status

Key	Council	Key	Council
1	Anglesey (Ynys Mon)	12	Merthyr Tydfil
2	Blaenau Gwent	13	Monmouthshire
3	Bridgend	14	Neath Port Talbot
4	Caerphilly	15	Newport
5	Cardiff	16	Pembrokeshire
6	Carmarthenshire	17	Powys
7	Ceredigion	18	Rhondda Cynon Taff
8	Conwy	19	Swansea
9	Denbighshire	20	Torfaen
10	Flintshire	21	Vale of Glamorgan
11	Gwynedd	22	Wrexham

SCOTLAND

Scotland occupies the northern portion of the main island of Great Britain and includes the Inner and Outer Hebrides, Orkney, Shetland and many other islands. It lies between 60° 51′ 30″ and 54° 38′ N. latitude and between 1° 45′ 32″ and 6° 14′ W. longitude, with England to the south-east, the North Channel and the Irish Sea to the south-west, the Atlantic Ocean on the north and west, and the North Sea on the east.

The greatest length of the mainland (Cape Wrath to the Mull of Galloway) is 441km (274 miles), and the greatest breadth (Buchan Ness to Applecross) is 248km (154 miles). The customary measurement of the island of Great Britain is from the site of John o' Groats house, near Duncansby Head, Caithness, to Land's End, Cornwall, a total distance of 970km (603 miles) in a straight line and approximately 1,448km (900 miles) by road.

The total area of Scotland is 78,807 sq. km (30,427 sq. miles): land 77,907 sq. km (30,080 sq. miles), inland water 900 sq. km (347 sq. miles).

POPULATION
The population at the 2001 census was 5,062,011 (men 2,432,494; women 2,629,517). The average density of the population in 2001 was 64 persons per sq. km (166 per sq. mile).

RELIEF
There are three natural orographic divisions of Scotland. The southern uplands have their highest points in Merrick (843m/2,766ft), Rhinns of Kells (814m/2,669ft) and Cairnsmuir of Carsphairn (797m/2,614ft), in the west; and the Tweedsmuir Hills in the east (Broad Law 840m/2,756ft; Dollar Law 817m/2,682ft; Hartfell 808m/2,651ft).

The central lowlands, formed by the valleys of the Clyde, Forth and Tay, divide the southern uplands from the Highlands, which extend from close to the extreme north of the mainland to the central lowlands, and are divided into a northern and a southern system by the Great Glen.

The Grampian Mountains, the southern Highland system, include in the west Ben Nevis (1,343m/4,406ft), the highest point in the British Isles, and in the east the Cairngorm Mountains (Ben Macdui 1,309m/4,296ft; Braeriach 1,295m/4,248ft; Cairn Gorm 1,245m/4,084ft). The North West Highlands area contains the mountains of Wester and Easter Ross (Carn Eige 1,183m/3,880ft; Sgurr na Lapaich 1,151m/3,775ft).

Created, like the central lowlands, by a major geological fault, the Great Glen (97km/60 miles long) runs between Inverness and Fort William, and contains Loch Ness, Loch Oich and Loch Lochy. These are linked to each other and to the north-east and south-west coasts of Scotland by the Caledonian Canal, providing a navigable passage between the Moray Firth and the Inner Hebrides.

HYDROGRAPHY
The western coast is fragmented by peninsulas and islands, and indented by fjords (sea-lochs), the longest of which is Loch Fyne (68km/42 miles long) in Argyll. Although the east coast tends to be less fractured and lower, there are several great drowned inlets (firths), including the Firth of Forth, the Firth of Tay and the Moray Firth, as well as the Firth of Clyde in the west.

The lochs are the principal hydrographic feature. The largest in Scotland and in Britain is Loch Lomond (70 sq. km/27 sq. miles), in the Grampian valleys and the longest and deepest is Loch Ness (39km/24 miles long and 244m/800ft deep), in the Great Glen.

The longest river is the Tay (188km/117 miles), noted for its salmon. It flows into the North Sea, with Dundee on the estuary, which is spanned by the Tay Bridge (3,136m/10,289ft) opened in 1887 and the Tay Road Bridge (2,245m/7,365ft) opened in 1966. Other noted salmon rivers are the Dee (145km/90 miles) which flows into the North Sea at Aberdeen, and the Spey (177km/110 miles), the swiftest flowing river in the British Isles, which flows into Moray Firth. The Tweed, which gave its name to the woollen cloth produced along its banks, marks in the lower stretches of its 154km (96 mile) course the border between Scotland and England.

The most important river commercially is the Clyde (171km/106 miles), formed by the junction of the Daer and Portrail water, which flows through the city of Glasgow to the Firth of Clyde. During its course it passes over the picturesque Falls of Clyde, Bonnington Linn (9m/30ft), Corra Linn (26m/84ft), Dundaff Linn (3m/10ft) and Stonebyres Linn (24m/80ft), above and below Lanark. The Forth (106km/66 miles), upon which stands Edinburgh, the capital, is spanned by the Forth Railway Bridge (1890), which is 1,625m (5,330ft) long, and the Forth Road Bridge (1964), which has a total length of 1,876m (6,156ft) (over water) and a single span of 914m (3,000ft).

The highest waterfall in Scotland, and the British Isles, is Eas a'Chùal Aluinn with a total height of 201m (658ft), which falls from Glas Bheinn in Sutherland. The Falls of Glomach, on a head-stream of the Elchaig in Wester Ross, have a drop of 113m (370ft).

GAELIC LANGUAGE
According to the 2001 census, 1.2 per cent of the population of Scotland, mainly in Eilean Siar (Western Isles), were able to speak the Scottish form of Gaelic.

LOWLAND SCOTTISH LANGUAGE
Several regional lowland Scottish dialects, known variously as Scots, Lallans or Doric, are widely spoken. The General Register Office (Scotland) estimated in 1996 that 1.5 million people, or 30 per cent of the population, are Scots speakers. A question on Scots was not included in the 2001 census.

FLAG
The flag of Scotland is known as the Saltire. It is a white diagonal cross on a blue field (saltire argent in a field azure) and represents St Andrew, the patron saint of Scotland.

THE SCOTTISH ISLANDS

ORKNEY

The Orkney Islands (total area 972 sq. km/376 sq. miles) lie about 10km (six miles) north of the mainland, separated from it by the Pentland Firth. Of the 90 islands and islets (holms and skerries) in the group, about one-third are inhabited.

The total population at the 2001 census was 19,245; the 2001 populations of the islands shown here include those of smaller islands forming part of the same council district.

Mainland, 15,339	Rousay, 267
Burray, 357	Sanday, 478
Eday, 121	Shapinsay, 300
Flotta, 81	South Ronaldsay, 854
Hoy, 392	Stronsay, 358
North Ronaldsay, 70	Westray, 563
Papa Westray, 65	

The islands are rich in prehistoric and Scandinavian remains, the most notable being the Stone Age village of Skara Brae, the burial chamber of Maes Howe, the many brochs (towers) and the 12th-century St Magnus Cathedral. Scapa Flow, between the Mainland and Hoy, was the war station of the British Grand Fleet from 1914 to 1919 and the scene of the scuttling of the surrendered German High Seas Fleet (21 June 1919).

Most of the islands are low-lying and fertile, and farming (principally beef cattle) is the main industry. Flotta, to the south of Scapa Flow, is the site of the oil terminal for the Piper, Claymore and Tartan fields in the North Sea.

The capital is Kirkwall (population 6,206) situated on Mainland.

SHETLAND

The Shetland Islands have a total area of 1,427 sq. km (551 sq. miles) and a population at the 2001 census of 21,988. They lie about 80km (50 miles) north of the Orkneys, with Fair Isle about half way between the two groups. Out Stack, off Muckle Flugga, 1.6km (one mile) north of Unst, is the most northerly part of the British Isles (60° 51′ 30″ N. lat.).

There are over 100 islands, of which 16 are inhabited. Populations at the 2001 census were:

Mainland, 17,575	Muckle Roe, 104
Bressay, 384	Trondra, 133
East Burra, 66	Unst, 720
Fair Isle, 69	West Burra, 784
Fetlar, 86	Whalsay, 1,034
Housay, 76	Yell, 957

Shetland's many archaeological sites include Jarlshof, Mousa and Clickhimin, and its long connection with Scandinavia has resulted in a strong Norse influence on its place names and dialect.

Industries include fishing, knitwear and farming. In addition to the fishing fleet there are fish processing factories, and the traditional handknitting of Fair Isle and Unst is now supplemented with machine-knitted garments. Farming is mainly crofting, with sheep being raised on the moorland and hills of the islands. Latterly the islands have become a centre of the North Sea oil industry, with pipelines from the Brent and Ninian fields

running to the terminal at Sullom Voe, the largest of its kind in Europe.

The capital is Lerwick (population 6,830) situated on Mainland. Lerwick is the main centre for supply services for offshore oil exploration and development.

THE HEBRIDES

Until the late 13th century the Hebrides included other Scottish islands in the Firth of Clyde, the peninsula of Kintyre (Argyll), the Isle of Man, and the (Irish) Isle of Rathlin. The origin of the name is probably the Greek *Eboudai*, latinised as *Hebudes* by Pliny, and corrupted to its present form. The Norwegian name *Sudreyjar* (Southern Islands) was latinised as *Sodorenses,* a name that survives in the Anglican bishopric of Sodor and Man.

There are over 500 islands and islets, of which about 100 are inhabited, though mountainous terrain and extensive peat bogs mean that only a fraction of the total area is under cultivation. Stone, Bronze and Iron Age settlement has left many remains, including those at Callanish on Lewis, and Norse colonisation influenced language, customs and placenames. Occupations include farming (mostly crofting and stock-raising), fishing and the manufacture of tweeds and other woollens. Tourism is also an important part of the economy.

The Inner Hebrides lie off the west coast of Scotland and are relatively close to the mainland. The largest and best-known is Skye (area 1,665 sq. km/643 sq. miles; pop. 9,251; chief town, Portree), which contains the Cuillin Hills (Sgurr Alasdair 993m/3,257ft), Bla Bheinn (928m/3,046ft), the Storr (719m/2,358ft) and the Red Hills (Beinn na Caillich 732m/2,403ft). Other islands in the Highland council area include Raasay (pop. 194), Rum, Eigg (pop. 131) and Muck.

Further south the Inner Hebridean islands include Arran (pop. 5,058) containing Goat Fell (874m/2,868ft); Coll and Tiree (pop. 934); Colonsay and Oronsay (pop. 113); Easdale (pop. 58); Gigha (pop. 110); Islay (area 608 sq. km/235 sq. miles; pop. 3,457); Jura (area 414 sq. km/160 sq. miles; pop. 188) with a range of hills culminating in the Paps of Jura (Beinn-an-Oir, 785m/2,576ft, and Beinn Chaolais, 755m/2,477ft); Lismore (pop. 146); Luing (pop. 220); and Mull (area 950 sq. km/367 sq. miles; pop. 2,696; chief town Tobermory) containing Ben More (967m/3,171ft).

The Outer Hebrides, separated from the mainland by the Minch, now form the Eilean Siar (Western Isles) council area (area 2,897 sq. km/1,119 sq. miles; pop. 26,502). The main islands are Lewis with Harris (area 1,994 sq. km/770 sq. miles, pop. 19,918), whose chief town, Stornoway, is the administrative headquarters; North Uist (pop. 1,320); South Uist (pop. 1,818); Benbecula (pop. 1,249) and Barra (pop. 1,078). Other inhabited islands include Bernera (233), Berneray (136), Eriskay (133), Grimsay (201), Scalpay (322) and Vatersay (94).

EARLY HISTORY

There is evidence of human settlement in Scotland dating from the third millennium BC, the earliest settlers being Mesolithic hunters and fishermen. Early in the second millennium BC, Neolithic farmers began to cultivate crops and rear livestock; their settlements were on the west coast and in the north, and included Skara Brae and Maeshowe (Orkney). Settlement by the early Bronze Age 'Beaker Folk', so-called from the shape of their drinking vessels, in eastern Scotland dates from about 1800 BC. Further settlement is believed to have occurred from 700 BC onwards, as tribes were displaced from further south by new incursions from the Continent and the Roman invasions from AD 43.

Julius Agricola, the Roman governor of Britain AD 77–84, extended the Roman conquests in Britain by advancing into Caledonia, culminating with a victory at Mons Graupius, probably in AD 84; he was recalled to Rome shortly afterwards and his forward policy was not pursued. Hadrian's Wall, mostly completed by AD 30, marked the northern frontier of the Roman empire except for the period between about AD 144 and 190 when the frontier moved north to the Forth-Clyde isthmus and a turf wall, the Antonine Wall, was manned.

After the Roman withdrawal from Britain, there were centuries of warfare between the Picts, Scots, Britons, Angles and Vikings. The Picts, generally accepted to be descended from the indigenous Iron Age people of northern Scotland, occupied the area north of the Forth. The Scots, a Gaelic-speaking people of northern Ireland, colonised the area of Argyll and Bute (the kingdom of Dalriada) in the fifth century AD and then expanded eastwards and northwards. The Britons, speaking a Brythonic Celtic language, colonised Scotland from the south from the first century BC; they lost control of south-eastern Scotland (incorporated into the kingdom of Northumbria) to the Angles in the early seventh century but retained Strathclyde (south-western Scotland and Cumbria). Viking raids from the late eighth century were followed by Norse settlement in the western and northern isles, Argyll, Caithness and Sutherland from the mid-ninth century onwards.

UNIFICATION

The union of the areas which now comprise Scotland began in AD 843 when Kenneth mac Alpin, king of the Scots from c.834, also became king of the Picts, joining the two lands to form the kingdom of Alba (comprising Scotland north of a line between the Forth and Clyde rivers). Lothian, the eastern part of the area between the Forth and the Tweed, seems to have been leased to Kenneth II of Alba (reigned 971–995) by Edgar of England c.973, and Scottish possession was confirmed by Malcolm II's victory over a Northumbrian army at Carham c.1016. At about this time Malcolm II (reigned 1005–34) placed his grandson Duncan on the throne of the British kingdom of Strathclyde, bringing under Scots rule virtually all of what is now Scotland.

The Norse possessions were incorporated into the kingdom of Scotland from the 12th century onwards. An uprising in the mid-12th century drove the Norse from most of mainland Argyll. The Hebrides were ceded to Scotland by the treaty of Perth in 1266 after a Norwegian expedition in 1263 failed to maintain Norse authority over the islands. Orkney and Shetland fell to Scotland in 1468–9 as a pledge for the unpaid dowry of Margaret of Denmark, wife of James III, although Danish claims of suzerainty were relinquished only with the marriage of Anne of Denmark to James VI in 1590.

From the 11th century, there were frequent wars between Scotland and England over territory and the extent of England's political influence. The failure of the Scottish royal line with the death of Margaret of Norway in 1290 led to disputes over the throne which were resolved by the adjudication of Edward I of England. He awarded the throne to John Balliol in 1292 but Balliol's refusal to be a puppet king led to war. Balliol surrendered to Edward I in 1296 and Edward attempted to rule Scotland himself. Resistance to Scotland's loss of independence was led by William Wallace, who defeated the English at Stirling Bridge (1297), and Robert Bruce, crowned in 1306, who held most of Scotland by 1311 and routed Edward II's army at Bannockburn (1314). England recognised the independence of Scotland in the treaty of Northampton in 1328. Subsequent clashes include the disastrous battle of Flodden (1513) in which James IV and many of his nobles fell.

THE UNION

In 1603 James VI of Scotland succeeded Elizabeth I on the throne of England (his mother, Mary Queen of Scots, was the great-granddaughter of Henry VII), his successors reigning as sovereigns of Great Britain. Political union of the two countries did not occur until 1707.

THE JACOBITE REVOLTS

After the abdication (by flight) in 1688 of James VII and II, the crown devolved upon William III (grandson of Charles I) and Mary II (elder daughter of James VII and II). In 1689 Graham of Claverhouse roused the Highlands on behalf of James VII and II, but died after a military success at Killiecrankie.

After the death of Anne (younger daughter of James VII and II), the throne devolved upon George I (great-grandson of James VI and I). In 1715, armed risings on behalf of James Stuart (the Old Pretender, son of James VII and II) led to the indecisive battle of Sheriffmuir, and the Jacobite movement died down until 1745, when Charles Stuart (the Young Pretender) defeated the Royalist troops at Prestonpans and advanced to Derby (1746). From Derby, the adherents of 'James VIII and III' (the title claimed for his father by Charles Stuart) fell back on the defensive and were finally crushed at Culloden (16 April 1746) by an army led by by the Duke of Cumberland, son of George II.

PRINCIPAL CITIES

ABERDEEN

Aberdeen, 209km (130 miles) north-east of Edinburgh, received its charter as a Royal Burgh in 1124. Scotland's third largest city, Aberdeen lies between two rivers, the Dee and the Don, facing the North Sea; the city has a strong maritime history and is today a major centre for offshore oil exploration and production. It is also an ancient university town and distinguished research centre. Other industries include engineering, food processing, textiles, paper manufacturing and chemicals.

Places of interest include King's College, St Machar's Cathedral, Brig o' Balgownie, Duthie Park and Winter Gardens, Hazlehead Park, the Kirk of St Nicholas, Mercat Cross, Marischal College and Marischal Museum, Provost Skene's House, Aberdeen Art Gallery, Gordon Highlanders Museum, Satrosphere Science Centre, and Aberdeen Maritime Museum.

DUNDEE

The Royal Burgh of Dundee is situated on the north bank of the Tay estuary. The city's port and dock installations are important to the offshore oil industry and the airport also provides servicing facilities. Principal industries include textiles, biotechnology and digital media, lasers, printing, tyre manufacture, food processing, engineering and tourism.

The unique City Churches – three churches under one roof, together with the 15th-century St Mary's Tower – are the most prominent architectural feature. Dundee is home to two historic ships: the Dundee-built RRS *Discovery* which took Capt. Scott to the Antarctic lies alongside Discovery Quay, and the frigate *Unicorn*, the only British-built wooden warship still afloat, is moored in Victoria Dock. Places of interest include Mills Public Observatory, the Tay road and rail bridges, Dundee Contemporary Arts centre, McManus Galleries, Claypotts Castle, Broughty Castle, Verdant Works (textile heritage centre) and the Sensation Science Centre.

EDINBURGH

Edinburgh is the capital city and seat of government in Scotland. The new Scottish parliament building designed by Enric Miralles was completed in 2004 and is open to visitors. The city is built on a group of hills and both the Old and New Towns are inscribed on the UNESCO World Cultural and Natural Heritage List for their cultural significance.

Other places of interest include the castle, which houses the Stone of Scone and also includes St Margaret's Chapel, the oldest building in Edinburgh, and near it, the Scottish National War Memorial; the Palace of Holyroodhouse, the Queen's official residence in Scotland; Parliament House, the present seat of the judicature; Princes Street; three universities (Edinburgh, Heriot-Watt, Napier); St Giles' Cathedral; St Mary's (Scottish Episcopal) Cathedral (Sir George Gilbert Scott); the General Register House (Robert Adam); the National and Signet libraries; the National Gallery of Scotland; the Royal Scottish Academy; the Scottish National Portrait Gallery and the Edinburgh International Conference Centre.

GLASGOW

Glasgow, a Royal Burgh, is Scotland's largest city and its principal commercial and industrial centre. The city occupies the north and south banks of the Clyde, formerly one of the chief commercial estuaries in the world. The main industries include engineering, electronics, finance, chemicals and printing. The city is also a key tourist and conference destination.

The chief buildings are the 13th-century Gothic cathedral, the university (Sir George Gilbert Scott), the City Chambers, the Royal Concert Hall, St Mungo Museum of Religious Life and Art, Pollok House, the School of Art (Charles Rennie Mackintosh), Kelvingrove Art Gallery and Museum, the Gallery of Modern Art, the Riverside Museum: Scotland's Museum of Transport and Travel (Zaha Hadid), the Burrell Collection museum and the Mitchell Library. The city is home to the Royal Scottish National Orchestra, Scottish Opera, Scottish Ballet and BBC Scotland and Scottish Television (STV).

INVERNESS

Inverness was granted city status in 2000. The city's name is derived from the Gaelic for 'the mouth of the Ness', referring to the river on which it lies. Inverness is recorded as being at the junction of the old trade routes since AD 565. Today the city is the main administrative centre for the north of Scotland and is the capital of the Highlands. Tourism is one of the city's main industries.

Among the city's most notable buildings is Abertarff House, built in 1593 and the oldest secular building remaining in Inverness. Balnain House, built as a town house in 1726, is a fine example of early Georgian architecture. The Old High Church, on St Michael's Mount, is the original parish church of Inverness and built on the site of the earliest Christian church in the city. Parts of the church date back to the 14th century.

Stirling was granted city status in 2002. Aberdeen, Dundee, Edinburgh and Glasgow have also been granted Lord Mayoralty/Lord Provostship.

LORD-LIEUTENANTS

Title	Name
Aberdeen City*	Lord Provost Peter Stephen
Aberdeenshire	James Ingleby
Angus	Mrs G. Osborne
Argyll and Bute	Patrick Stewart, MBE
Ayrshire and Arran	John Duncan, QPM
Banffshire	Clare Russell
Berwickshire	Maj. A. Trotter
Caithness	Miss M. Dunnett
Clackmannanshire	Rt. Hon. George Reid
Dumfries	Jean Tulloch
Dunbartonshire	Rear-Adm. Alexander Gregory, OBE
Dundee City*	Lord Provost John Letford
East Lothian	W. Garth Morrison, CBE
Edinburgh City*	Rt. Hon. Lord Provost George Grubb
Eilean Siar (Western Isles)	A. Matheson, OBE
Fife	Mrs C. Dean
Glasgow City*	Rt. Hon. Lord Provost Robert Winter
Inverness	Donald Angus Cameron of Lochiel
Kincardineshire	Carol Kinghorn
Lanarkshire	Mushtaq Ahmad, OBE
Midlothian	Patrick Prenter, CBE
Moray	Grenville Shaw Johnston, OBE, TD
Nairn	Ewen Brodie of Lethan
Orkney	Dr Anthony Trickett, MBE
Perth and Kinross	Brig. Melville Jameson, CBE
Renfrewshire	Guy Clark
Ross and Cromarty	Janet Bowen
Roxburgh, Ettrick and Lauderdale	Hon. Capt. Gerald Maitland-Carew
Shetland	Sir John Scott, KCVO
Stirling and Falkirk	Mrs M. McLachlan
Sutherland	Dr Monica Maitland Main
The Stewartry of Kirkcudbright	Lt.-Col. Sir Malcolm Walter Hugh Ross, GCVO, OBE
Tweeddale	Capt. D. Younger
West Lothian	Mrs I. Brydie, MBE
Wigtown	Marion Brewis

* The Lord Provosts of the four cities of Aberdeen, Dundee, Edinburgh and Glasgow are Lord-Lieutenants *ex officio* for those districts

LOCAL COUNCILS

Council	Administrative Headquarters	Telephone	Population*	Council Tax†	Chief Executive
ABERDEEN	Aberdeen	08456 08 09 10	213,800	£1,230	Sue Bruce
Aberdeenshire	Aberdeen	01467-620981	243,500	£1,141	Colin Mackenzie
Angus	Forfar	0845-277 7778	110,300	£1,072	David Sawers
Argyll and Bute	Lochgilphead	01546-602127	90,000	£1,178	Sally Loudon
Clackmannanshire	Alloa	01259-452000	50,500	£1,148	Angela Leitch
Dumfries and Galloway	Dumfries	01387-260000	148,500	£1,049	Gavin Stevenson
DUNDEE	Dundee	01382-434000	143,400	£1,211	David Dorward
East Ayrshire	Kilmarnock	01563-576000	120,200	£1,189	Fiona Lees
East Dunbartonshire	Kirkintilloch	0845-045 4510	104,700	£1,142	Gerry Cornes
East Lothian	Haddington	01620-827827	96,800	£1,118	Alan Blackie
East Renfrewshire	Giffnock	0141-577 3000	89,200	£1,126	Lorraine McMillan
EDINBURGH	Edinburgh	0131-200 2000	477,700	£1,169	Tom Aitchison, CBE
Eilean Siar (Western Isles)	Stornoway	01851-703773	26,200	£1,024	Malcolm Burr
Falkirk	Falkirk	01324-506070	152,500	£1,070	Mary Pitcaithly, OBE
Fife	Glenrothes	0845-555555	363,500	£1,118	Ronnie Hinds
GLASGOW	Glasgow	0141-287 2000	588,500	£1,213	George Black
Highland	Inverness	01463-702000	220,500	£1,163	Alistair Dodds
Inverclyde	Greenock	01475-717171	80,200	£1,198	John Mundell
Midlothian	Dalkeith	0131-270 7500	80,800	£1,210	Kenneth Lawrie
Moray	Elgin	01343-543451	87,700	£1,135	Alastair Keddie
North Ayrshire	Irvine	0845-603 0590	135,500	£1,152	Elma Murray
North Lanarkshire	Motherwell	01698-302222	326,300	£1,098	Gavin Whitefield
Orkney	Kirkwall	01856-873535	20,000	£1,037	Albert Tait
Perth and Kinross	Perth	01738-475000	145,900	£1,158	Bernadette Malone
Renfrewshire	Paisley	0141-842 5000	169,900	£1,165	David Martin
Scottish Borders	Melrose	01835-824000	112,700	£1,084	David Hume
Shetland	Lerwick	01595-693535	22,220	£1,053	vacant
South Ayrshire	Ayr	01292-612000	111,400	£1,154	David Anderson
South Lanarkshire	Hamilton	01698-454444	310,900	£1,101	Archie Strang
STIRLING	Stirling	0845-277 7000	88,700	£1,209	Bob Jack
West Dunbartonshire	Dumbarton	01389-737000	90,900	£1,163	David McMillan
West Lothian	Livingston	01506-775000	171,000	£1,128	Alex Linkston

* Source: ONS – Mid-2009 Population Estimates (Crown copyright)
† Average Band D council tax bill 2011–12
Councils in CAPITAL LETTERS have city status

Key	Council	Key	Council
1	Aberdeen City	18	Midlothian
2	Aberdeenshire	19	Moray
3	Angus	20	North Ayrshire
4	Argyll and Bute	21	North Lanarkshire
5	City of Edinburgh	22	Orkney
6	Clackmannanshire	23	Perth and Kinross
7	Dumfries and Galloway	24	Renfrewshire
8	Dundee City	25	Scottish Borders
9	East Ayrshire	26	Shetland
10	East Dunbartonshire	27	South Ayrshire
11	East Lothian	28	South Lanarkshire
12	East Renfrewshire	29	Stirling
13	Falkirk	30	West Dunbartonshire
14	Fife	31	Western Isles (Eilean Siar)
15	Glasgow City	32	West Lothian
16	Highland		
17	Inverclyde		

NORTHERN IRELAND

Northern Ireland has a total area of 14,149 sq. km (5,463 sq. miles): land, 13,576 sq. km (5,242 sq. miles); inland water, 573 sq. km (221 sq. miles).

The population of Northern Ireland at the 2001 census was 1,685,267 (men 821,449; women 863,818). The average density of population in 2001 was 119 persons per sq. km (308 per sq. mile).

At the 2001 census, the number of persons in the various religious denominations (expressed as percentages of the total population) were: Catholic, 40.26%; Presbyterian, 20.69%; Church of Ireland, 15.30%; Methodist Church in Ireland, 3.51%; other Christian (including Christian related), 6.07%; other religions and philosophies, 0.3%; no religion or religion not stated, 13.88%.

FLAG
The official national flag of Northern Ireland is the Union Flag.

PRINCIPAL CITIES

In addition to Belfast and Londonderry, three other places in Northern Ireland have been granted city status: Armagh (1994), Lisburn (2002) and Newry (2002).

BELFAST
Belfast, the administrative centre of Northern Ireland, is situated at the mouth of the River Lagan at its entrance to Belfast Lough. The city grew to be a great industrial centre, owing to its easy access by sea to Scottish coal and iron.

The principal buildings are of a relatively young age and include the parliament buildings at Stormont, the City Hall, Waterfront Hall, the Law Courts, the Public Library and the Museum and Art Gallery.

Belfast received its first charter of incorporation in 1613 and was created a city in 1888; the title of lord mayor was conferred in 1892.

LONDONDERRY
Londonderry (originally Derry) is situated on the River Foyle, and has important associations with the City of London. The Irish Society was created by the City of London in 1610, and under its royal charter of 1613 it fortified the city and was for a long time closely associated with its administration. Because of this connection the city was incorporated in 1613 under the new name of Londonderry.

The city is famous for the great siege of 1688–9, when for 105 days the town held out against the forces of James II. The city walls are still intact and form a circuit of 1.6 km (one mile) around the old city.

Interesting buildings are the Protestant cathedral of St Columb's (1633) and the Guildhall, reconstructed in 1912 and containing a number of beautiful stained glass windows, many of which were presented by the livery companies of London.

CONSTITUTIONAL HISTORY

Northern Ireland is subject to the same fundamental constitutional provisions which apply to the rest of the UK. It had its own parliament and government from 1921 to 1972, but after increasing civil unrest the Northern Ireland (Temporary Provisions) Act 1972 transferred the legislative and executive powers of the Northern Ireland parliament and government to the UK parliament and a secretary of state. The Northern Ireland Constitution Act 1973 provided for devolution in Northern Ireland through an assembly and executive, but a power-sharing executive formed by the Northern Ireland political parties in January 1974 collapsed in May 1974. Following the collapse of the power-sharing executive Northern Ireland returned to direct rule governance under the provisions of the Northern Ireland Act 1974, placing the Northern Ireland department under the direction and control of the Northern Ireland secretary.

In December 1993 the British and Irish governments published the Joint Declaration complementing their political talks, and making clear that any settlement would need to be founded on principles of democracy and consent.

On 12 January 1998 the British and Irish governments issued a joint document, *Propositions on Heads of Agreement,* proposing the establishment of various new cross-border bodies; further proposals were presented on 27 January. A draft peace settlement was issued by the talks' chairman, US Senator George Mitchell, on 6 April 1998 but was rejected by the Unionists the following day. On 10 April agreement was reached between the British and Irish governments and the eight Northern Ireland political parties still involved in the talks (the Good Friday Agreement). The agreement provided for an elected Northern Ireland Assembly, a North/South Ministerial Council, and a British-Irish Council comprising representatives of the British, Irish, Channel Islands and Isle of Man governments and members of the new assemblies for Scotland, Wales and Northern Ireland. Further points included the abandonment of the Republic of Ireland's constitutional claim to Northern Ireland; the decommissioning of weapons; the release of paramilitary prisoners and changes in policing.

The agreement was ratified in referendums held in Northern Ireland and the Republic of Ireland on 22 May 1998. In the UK, the Northern Ireland Act received royal assent in November 1998.

On 28 April 2003 the secretary of state again assumed responsibility for the direction of the Northern Ireland departments on the dissolution of the Northern Ireland Assembly, following its initial suspension from midnight on 14 October 2002. In 2006, following the passing of the Northern Ireland Act, the secretary of state created a non-legislative fixed-term assembly which would cease to operate either when the political parties agreed to restore devolution, or on 24 November 2006 (whichever occurred first). In October 2006 a timetable to restore devolution was drawn up (St Andrews Agreement) and a transitional Northern Ireland Assembly was formed on 24 November. The transitional assembly was dissolved in January 2007 in preparation for elections to be held on 7 March; following the elections a power-sharing executive was formed and the new 108-member Northern Ireland Assembly became operational on 8 May 2007.

See also Regional Government.

LORD-LIEUTENANTS AND HIGH SHERIFFS

County	Lord-Lieutenant	High Sheriff (2011)
Antrim	Joan Christie	David Traill
Armagh	The Earl of Caledon	Dr Peter Colvin
Belfast City	Dame Mary Peters, DBE	Cllr Ian Adamson, OBE
Down	David Lindsay	Ian Webb
Fermanagh	The Earl of Erne	Terence McCartney
Londonderry	Denis Desmond, CBE	John Burns
Londonderry City	Dr Donal Keegan, OBE	Steven Lindsay
Tyrone	Robert Scott, OBE	Gerard Broderick Francis Shields

LOCAL COUNCILS

Council	County Area	Map Key	Telephone	Population*	Chief Executive
Antrim	Down	1	028-9446 3113	54,000	David McCammick
Ards	Down	2	028-9182 4000	78,100	Ashley Boreland
ARMAGH	Armagh	3	028-3752 9600	58,800	John Briggs
Ballymena	Antrim	4	028-2566 0300	63,200	Anne Donaghy
Ballymoney	Antrim	5	028-2766 0200	30,400	John Dempsey
Banbridge	Down	6	028-4066 0600	47,600	Liam Hannaway
BELFAST	Antrim & Down	7	028-9032 0202	268,400	Peter McNaney
Carrickfergus	Antrim	8	028-9335 8000	40,100	Alan Cardwell
Castlereagh	Down	9	028-9046 4500	66,800	Stephen Reid
Coleraine	Londonderry	10	028-7034 7034	57,100	Roger Wilson
Cookstown	Tyrone	11	028-8676 2205	36,300	Michael McGuckin
Craigavon	Armagh	12	028-3831 2400	92,400	Dr Theresa Donaldson
DERRY	Londonderry	13	028-7136 5151	109,600	John Meehan (acting)
Down	Down	14	028-4461 0800	70,300	John Dumigan
Dungannon & South Tyrone	Tyrone	15	028-8772 0300	56,400	Alan Burke
Fermanagh	Fermanagh	16	028-6632 5050	62,400	Brendan Hegarty
Larne	Antrim	17	028-2827 2313	31,400	Geraldine McGahey
Limavady	Londonderry	18	028-7772 2226	34,000	Liam Flanigan
LISBURN	Antrim	19	028-9250 9250	116,500	Norman Davidson
Magherafelt	Londonderry	20	028-7939 7979	44,200	John McLaughlin
Moyle	Antrim	21	028-2076 2225	16,900	Richard Lewis
NEWRY & Mourne	Down & Armagh	22	028-3031 3031	98,700	Thomas McCall
Newtownabbey	Antrim	23	028-9034 0000	83,740	Jacqui Dixon
North Down	Down	24	028-9127 0371	79,600	Trevor Polley
Omagh	Tyrone	25	028 8224 5321	52,400	Daniel McSorley
Strabane	Tyrone	26	028-7138 2204	39,900	Philip Faithfull

* Source: ONS – Mid-2009 Population Estimates (Crown copyright)
Councils in CAPITAL LETTERS have city status

THE ISLE OF MAN

Ellan Vannin

The Isle of Man is an island situated in the Irish Sea, at latitude 54° 3'–54° 25' N. and longitude 4° 18'–4° 47' W., nearly equidistant from England, Scotland and Ireland. Although the early inhabitants were of Celtic origin, the Isle of Man was part of the Norwegian Kingdom of the Hebrides until 1266, when this was ceded to Scotland. Subsequently granted to the Stanleys (Earls of Derby) in the 15th century and later to the Dukes of Atholl, it was brought under the administration of the Crown in 1765. The island forms the bishopric of Sodor and Man.

The total land area is 572 sq. km (221 sq. miles). The 2006 census showed a resident population of 80,058 (men, 39,523; women, 40,535). The main language in use is English. Around 1,550 people are able to speak the Manx Gaelic language.

CAPITAL – ΨDouglas; population, 26,218 (2006). ΨCastletown (3,109) is the ancient capital; the other towns are ΨPeel (4,280) and ΨRamsey (7,309)

FLAG – A red flag charged with three conjoined armoured legs in white and gold

NATIONAL DAY – 5 July (Tynwald Day)

GOVERNMENT

The Isle of Man is a self-governing Crown dependency, with its own parliamentary, legal and administrative system. The British government is responsible for international relations and defence. Under the UK Act of Accession, Protocol 3, the island's relationship with the European Union is limited to trade alone and does not extend to financial aid. The Lieutenant-Governor is the Queen's personal representative on the island.

The legislature, Tynwald, is the oldest parliament in the world in continuous existence. It has two branches: the Legislative Council and the House of Keys. The council consists of the President of Tynwald, the Bishop of Sodor and Man, the Attorney-General (who does not have a vote) and eight members elected by the House of Keys. The House of Keys has 24 members, elected by universal adult suffrage. The branches sit separately to consider legislation and sit together, as Tynwald Court, for most other parliamentary purposes.

The presiding officer of Tynwald Court is the President of Tynwald, elected by the members, who also presides over sittings of the Legislative Council. The presiding officer of the House of Keys is the Speaker, who is elected by members of the house.

The principal members of the Manx government are the chief minister and nine departmental ministers, who comprise the Council of Ministers.

Lieutenant-Governor, HE Adam Wood
President of Tynwald, Hon. Clare Christian

Speaker, House of Keys, Hon. Steve Rodan, SHK
The First Deemster and Clerk of the Rolls,
  His Hon. David Doyle
Clerk of Tynwald, Secretary to the House of Keys and
  Counsel to the Speaker, Roger Phillips
Clerk of the Legislative Council and Deputy Clerk of
  Tynwald, Jonathan King
Attorney-General, Stephen Harding
Chief Minister, Hon. Tony Brown, MHK
Chief Secretary, Will Greenhow

ECONOMY

Most of the income generated in the island is earned in the services sector with financial and professional services accounting for just over half of the national income. Tourism and manufacturing are also major generators of income while the island's other traditional industries of agriculture and fishing now play a smaller role in the economy. Under the terms of protocol 3, the island has tariff-free access to EU markets for its goods.

In May 2011 the island's unemployment rate was 1.9 per cent and inflation (RPI) was 6.3 per cent.

FINANCE

The budget for 2011–12 provides for net revenue expenditure of £533m. The principal sources of government revenue are taxes on income and expenditure. Income tax is payable at a rate of 10 per cent on the first £10,500 of taxable income for single resident individuals and 20 per cent on the balance, after personal allowances of £9,300. These bands are doubled for married couples. The rate of income tax for trading companies is zero per cent except for income from banking and land and property, which is taxed at 10 per cent. By agreement with the British government, the island keeps most of its rates of indirect taxation (VAT and duties) the same as those in the UK. However, VAT on tourist accommodation, property, repairs and renovations is charged at 5 per cent. A reciprocal agreement on national insurance benefits and pensions exists between the governments of the Isle of Man and the UK. Taxes are also charged on property (rates), but these are comparatively low.

The major government expenditure items are health, social security, social care, which account for 67 per cent of the government budget. The island makes an annual contribution to the UK for defence and other external services.

The island has a special relationship with the European Union and neither contributes money to nor receives funds from the EU budget.

Ψ = sea port

THE CHANNEL ISLANDS

The Channel Islands, situated off the north-west coast of France (at a distance of 16km (10 miles) at their closest point), are the only portions of the Dukedom of Normandy still belonging to the Crown, to which they have been attached since the Norman Conquest of 1066. They were the only British territory to come under German occupation during the Second World War, following invasion on 30 June and 1 July 1940. The islands were relieved by British forces on 9 May 1945, and 9 May (Liberation Day) is now observed as a bank and public holiday.

The islands consist of Jersey (11,630ha/28,717 acres), Guernsey (6,340ha/15,654 acres), and the dependencies of Guernsey: Alderney (795ha/1,962 acres), Brecqhou (30ha/74 acres), Great Sark (419ha/1,035 acres), Little Sark (97ha/239 acres), Herm (130ha/320 acres), Jethou (18ha/44 acres) and Lihou (15ha/38 acres) – a total of 19,474ha/48,083 acres, or 195 sq. km/75 sq. miles.

The most recent estimate of the population of Jersey from the States of Jersey Statistics Unit was 92,500. The most recent official records for Guernsey and Alderney were estimated at 62,431 and 2,194 respectively. The 2001 census showed the population of Jersey as 87,186; Guernsey, 59,807 and Alderney, 2,294. Sark did not complete the same census but an informal census gave its population figure as 591. The official languages are English and French. In country districts of Jersey and Guernsey and throughout Sark a Norman-French *patois* is also in use, though to a lesser extent.

GOVERNMENT

The islands are Crown dependencies with their own legislative assemblies (the States in Jersey and Alderney, the States of Deliberation in Guernsey and the Chief Pleas in Sark), systems of local administration and law, and their own courts. *Projets de Loi* (Acts) passed by the States require the sanction of the Queen-in-council. The UK government is responsible for defence and international relations. The Channel Islands are not part of the European Union but, under protocol 3 of the UK's treaty of accession, have trading rights with the free movement of goods within the EU.

In both Jersey and Guernsey bailiwicks the Lieutenant-Governor and Commander-in-Chief, who is appointed by the Crown, is the personal representative of the Queen and the channel of communication between the Crown (via the Privy Council) and the island's government.

The head of government in both Jersey and Guernsey is the Chief Minister. Jersey has a ministerial system of government; the executive comprises the Council of Ministers and consists of a chief minister and nine other ministers. The ministers are assisted by up to 13 assistant ministers. Members of the States who are not in the executive are able to sit on a number of scrutiny panels and the Public Accounts Committee to examine the policy of the executive and hold ministers to account. Guernsey has a consensus form of government. There are ten States departments with mandated responsibilities, each department is constituted of a minister and four members of the States. Each of the ministers has a seat on the Policy Council which is presided over by the Chief Minister. The

States of Deliberation is the overarching executive. There are also five specialist committees, each led by a chair, responsible for scrutinising policy, finance and legislation, parliamentary procedural matters and public sector pay negotiations.

Justice is administered by the royal courts of Jersey and Guernsey, each consisting of the bailiff and 12 elected jurats. The bailiffs of Jersey and Guernsey, appointed by the Crown, are presidents of the states and of the royal courts of their respective islands.

Each bailiwick constitutes a deanery under the jurisdiction of the Bishop of Winchester.

ECONOMY

A mild climate and good soil have led to the development of intensive systems of agriculture and horticulture, which form a significant part of the economy. Equally important are earnings from tourism and banking and finance: the low rates of income and corporation tax and the absence of death duties make the islands an important offshore financial centre. The financial services sector contributes over 50 per cent of GDP in Jersey and around 40 per cent in Guernsey. In addition, there is no VAT or equivalent tax in Guernsey and only small goods and services tax in Jersey (set at 5 per cent from 1 June 2011). The Channel Islands stock exchange is located in Guernsey, which also has a thriving e-gaming sector.

Principal exports are agricultural produce and flowers; imports are chiefly machinery, manufactured goods, food, fuel and chemicals. Trade with the UK is regarded as internal.

British currency is legal tender in the Channel Islands but each bailiwick issues its own coins and notes (*see* Currency section). They also issue their own postage stamps; UK stamps are not valid.

JERSEY

Lieutenant-Governor and Commander-in-Chief of Jersey,
  HE Gen. Sir John McColl, KCB, CBE, DSO,
  apptd 2011
Secretary and ADC, Lt.-Col. A. Woodrow, OBE, MC
Bailiff of Jersey, Michael St J. Birt
Deputy Bailiff, W. Bailhache
Attorney-General, Timothy Le Cocq, QC
Receiver-General, P. Lewin
Solicitor-General, Howard Sharp, QC
Greffier of the States, M. de la Haye
States Treasurer, L. Rowley
Chief Minister, Senator T. Le Sueur

FINANCE

	2009	2010
Revenue income	£830,688,000	£745,741,000
Revenue expenditure	£784,603,000	£974,890,000
Capital expenditure	£123,531,000	£73,306,000

CHIEF TOWN – ΨSt Helier, on the south coast
FLAG – A white field charged with a red saltire cross, and the arms of Jersey in the upper centre

GUERNSEY AND DEPENDENCIES

Lieutenant-Governor and Commander-in-Chief of the Bailiwick of Guernsey and its Dependencies,
   HE Air Marshal Peter Walker, CB, CBE, *apptd* 2011
Presiding Officer of the Royal Court and of the States of Deliberation, Bailiff Sir Geoffrey Rowland
Deputy Presiding Officer of the Royal Court and States of Deliberation, Richard Collas
HM Procureur and Receiver-General (Attorney-General), Howard Roberts, QC
HM Comptroller (Solicitor-General), Richard McMahon, QC

GUERNSEY
Chief Minister, Deputy Lyndon Trott
Chief Executive, Mike Brown

FINANCE

	2009	2010
Revenue	£341m	£331m
Expenditure	£326m	£330m

CHIEF TOWNS – ΨSt Peter Port, on the east coast of Guernsey; St Anne on Alderney
FLAG – White, bearing a red cross of St George, with a gold cross of Normandy overall in the centre

ALDERNEY
President of the States, Stuart Trought
Chief Executive, Roy Burke
Greffier, Sarah Kelly

SARK
Sark was the last European territory to abolish feudal parliamentary representation. Elections for a democratic legislative assembly took place in December 2008, with the *conseillers* taking their seats in the newly constituted Chief Pleas in January 2009.
Seigneur of Sark, John Beaumont, OBE
Seneschal, Lt.-Col. R Guille, MBE
Greffier, Trevor Hamon

OTHER DEPENDENCIES
Herm and Lihou are owned by the States of Guernsey; Herm is leased, Lihou is uninhabited. Jethou is leased by the Crown to the States of Guernsey and is sub-let by the States. Brecqhou is within the legislative and judicial territory of Sark.

Ψ = seaport

LAW COURTS AND OFFICES

SUPREME COURT OF THE UNITED KINGDOM

The supreme court of the United Kingdom is the highest judicial authority; it replaced the House of Lords in its judicial capacity on 1 October 2009. It is the ultimate court of appeal for all courts in Great Britain and Northern Ireland (except criminal courts in Scotland) for all cases except those concerning the interpretation and application of European Union law, including preliminary rulings requested by British courts and tribunals, which are decided by the court of justice of the European Union (*see* European Union section). The UK supreme court also assumed jurisdiction in relation to devolution matters under the Scotland Act 1998, the Northern Ireland Act 1988 and the Government of Wales Act 2006; these powers were transferred from the Judicial Committee of the Privy Council. Ten of the 12 Lords of Appeal in Ordinary from the House of Lords transferred to the 12-member supreme court when it came into operation (at the same time one law lord retired and another was appointed Master of the Rolls). All new justices of the supreme court are now appointed by an independent UK Supreme Court Appointments Commission, and are not members of the House of Lords.

SUPREME COURT OF THE UNITED KINGDOM
President of the Supreme Court (£214,165), Rt. Hon. Lord Phillips of Worth Matravers, KG, *born* 1938, *apptd* 2008

Deputy President of the Supreme Court (£206,857), Rt. Hon. Lord Hope of Craighead, KT, *born* 1938, *apptd* 1996

JUSTICES OF THE SUPREME COURT *as at July 2011* (each £206,857)
Style, The Rt. Hon. Lord/Lady–

Rt. Hon. Lord Walker of Gestingthorpe, *born* 1938, *apptd* 2002
Rt. Hon. Lady Hale of Richmond, *born* 1945, *apptd* 2004
Rt. Hon. Lord Brown of Eaton-under-Heywood, *born* 1937, *apptd* 2004
Rt. Hon. Lord Mance, *born* 1943, *apptd* 2005
Rt. Hon. Lord Kerr of Tonaghmore, *born* 1948, *apptd* 2009
Rt. Hon. Lord Clarke of Stone-cum-Ebony, *born* 1943, *apptd* 2009
Rt. Hon. Lord Dyson, *born* 1943, *apptd* 2010
Rt. Hon. Lord Wilson of Culworth, *born* 1945, *apptd* 2011

UNITED KINGDOM SUPREME COURT
Parliament Square, London SW1P 3BD T 020-7960 1900
Chief Executive, Jenny Rowe

JUDICATURE OF ENGLAND AND WALES

The legal system in England and Wales is divided into criminal law and civil law. Criminal law is concerned with acts harmful to the community and the rules laid down by the state for the benefit of citizens, whereas civil law governs the relationships and transactions between individuals. Administrative law is a kind of civil law usually concerning the interaction of individuals and the state, and most cases are heard in tribunals specific to the subject (*see* Tribunals section). Scotland and Northern Ireland possess legal systems that differ from the system in England and Wales in law, judicial procedure and court structure, but retain the distinction between criminal and civil law.

Under the provisions of the Criminal Appeal Act 1995, a commission was set up to direct and supervise investigations into possible miscarriages of justice and to refer cases to the appeal courts on the grounds of conviction and sentence; these functions were formerly the responsibility of the home secretary.

SENIOR COURTS OF ENGLAND AND WALES
The senior courts of England and Wales (until September 2009 known as the supreme court of judicature of England and Wales) comprise the high court, the crown court and the court of appeal. The President of the Courts of England and Wales, a new title given to the Lord Chief Justice under the Constitutional Reform Act 2005, is the head of the judiciary.

The high court was created in 1875 and combined many previously separate courts. Sittings are held at the royal courts of justice in London or at around 120 district registries outside the capital. It is the superior civil court and is split into three divisions – the chancery division, the Queen's bench division and the family division – each of which is further divided. The chancery division is headed by the Chancellor of the High Court and is concerned mainly with equity, trusts, tax and bankruptcy, while also including two specialist courts, the patents court and the companies court. The Queen's bench division (QBD) is the largest of the three divisions, and is headed by its own president. It deals with common law (ie tort, contract, debt and personal injuries), some tax law, eg VAT tribunal appeals, and encompasses the admiralty court and the commercial court. The QBD also administers the technology and construction court. The family division was created in 1970 and is headed by its own president, who is also Head of Family Justice, and hears cases concerning divorce, access to and custody of children, and other family matters. The divisional court of the high court sits in the family and chancery divisions, and hears appeals from the magistrates' courts and county courts.

The crown court was set up in 1972 and sits at 77 centres throughout England and Wales. It deals with more serious (indictable) criminal offences, which are triable before a judge and jury, including treason, murder, rape, kidnapping, armed robbery and Official Secrets Act offences. It also handles cases transferred from the magistrates' courts where the magistrate decides his or her own power of sentence is inadequate, or where someone appeals against a magistrate's decision, or in a case that is triable 'either way' where the accused has chosen a jury trial. The crown court centres are divided into three tiers:

HIERARCHY OF ENGLISH COURTS

Court	Courts it binds	Courts it follows
European court of justice	The court making the preliminary reference	None
Supreme court	All English courts	None
Court of appeal	Divisional courts High court Crown court County courts Magistrates' courts	Supreme court
Divisional courts	High court Crown court County courts Magistrates' courts	Supreme court Court of appeal
High court	County courts Magistrates' courts	Supreme court Court of appeal Divisional courts
Crown court	None	Supreme court
County courts	None	Court of appeal
Magistrates' courts	None	Divisional courts High court

high court judges, circuit judges and sometimes recorders (part-time circuit judges), sit in first-tier centres, hearing the most serious criminal offences (eg murder, treason, rape, manslaughter) and some civil high court cases. The second-tier centres are presided over by high court judges, circuit judges or recorders and also deal with the most serious criminal cases. Third-tier courts deal with the remaining criminal offences, with circuit judges or recorders presiding.

The court of appeal hears appeals against both fact and law, and was last restructured in 1966 when it replaced the court of criminal appeal. It is split into the civil division (which hears appeals from the high court, tribunals and in certain cases, the county courts) and the criminal division (which hears appeals from the crown court). Cases are heard by Lords Justices of Appeal and high court judges if deemed suitable for reconsideration.

The Constitutional Reform Act 2005 instigated several key changes to the judiciary in England and Wales. These included the establishment of the independent supreme court, which opened in October 2009; the reform of the post of Lord Chancellor, transferring its judicial functions to the President of the Courts of England and Wales; a duty on government ministers to uphold the independence of the judiciary by barring them from trying to influence judicial decisions through any special access to judges; the formation of a fully transparent and independent Judicial Appointments Commission that is responsible for selecting candidates to recommend for judicial appointment to the Lord Chancellor and Secretary of State for Justice; and the creation of the post of Judicial Appointments and Conduct Ombudsman.

CRIMINAL CASES
In criminal matters the decision to prosecute (in the majority of cases) rests with the Crown Prosecution Service (CPS), which is the independent prosecuting body in England and Wales. The CPS is headed by the director of public prosecutions, who works under the superintendence of the Attorney-General. Certain categories of offence continue to require the Attorney-General's consent for prosecution.

Most minor criminal cases (summary offences) are dealt with in magistrates' courts, usually by a bench of three unpaid lay magistrates (justices of the peace) sitting without a jury and assisted on points of law and procedure by a legally trained clerk. There were 26,966 justices of the peace as at 1 April 2011. In some courts a full-time, salaried and legally qualified district judge (magistrates' court) – formerly known as a stipendiary judge – presides alone. There were 137 district judges (magistrates' courts) as at 1 April 2011. Magistrates' courts oversee the completion of 95 per cent of all criminal cases. Magistrates' courts also house some family proceedings courts (which deal with relationship breakdown and childcare cases) and youth courts. Cases of medium seriousness (known as 'offences triable either way') where the defendant pleads not guilty can be heard in the crown court for a trial by jury, if the defendant so chooses. Preliminary proceedings in a serious case to decide whether there is evidence to justify committal for trial in the crown court are dealt with in the magistrates' courts.

The 77 centres that the crown court sits in are divided into seven regions. There are 673 circuit judges and 1,221 recorders (part-time circuit judges); they must sit a minimum of 15 days per year and are usually subject to a maximum of 30. A jury is present in all trials that are contested.

Appeals from magistrates' courts against sentence or conviction are made to the crown court, and appeals upon a point of law are made to the high court, which may ultimately be appealed to the supreme court. Appeals from the crown court, either against sentence or conviction, are made to the court of appeal (criminal division). Again, these appeals may be brought to the supreme court if a point of law is contested, and if the house considers it is of sufficient importance.

CIVIL CASES
Most minor civil cases – including contract, tort (especially personal injuries), property, divorce and other family matters, bankruptcy etc – are dealt with by the county courts, of which there are 216 (see the Court

Service website, W www.justice.gov.uk, for further details). Cases are heard by circuit judges, recorders or district judges. For cases involving small claims (with certain exceptions, where the amount claimed is £5,000 or less) there are informal and simplified procedures designed to enable parties to present their cases themselves without recourse to lawyers. Where there are financial limits on county court jurisdiction, claims that exceed those limits may be tried in the county courts with the consent of the parties, subject to the court's agreement, or in certain circumstances on transfer from the high court. Outside London, bankruptcy proceedings can be heard in designated county courts. Magistrates' courts also deal with certain classes of civil case, and committees of magistrates license public houses, clubs and betting shops. For the implementation of the Children Act 1989, a new structure of hearing centres was set up in 1991 for family proceedings cases, involving magistrates' courts (family proceedings courts), divorce county courts, family hearing centres and care centres.

Appeals in certain family matters heard in the family proceedings courts go to the family division of the high court. Appeals from county courts may be heard in the court of appeal (civil division) or the high court, and may go on to the supreme court.

CORONERS' COURTS

The coroners' courts investigate violent and unnatural deaths or sudden deaths where the cause is unknown. Doctors, the police, various public authorities or members of the public may bring cases before a local coroner (a senior lawyer or doctor), in order to determine whether further criminal investigation is necessary. Where a death is sudden and the cause is unknown, the coroner may order a post-mortem examination to determine the cause of death rather than hold an inquest in court. An inquest must be held, however, if a person died in a violent or unnatural way, or died in prison or other unusual circumstances. If the coroner suspects murder, manslaughter or infanticide, he or she must summon a jury.

SENIOR JUDICIARY OF ENGLAND AND WALES

Lord Chief Justice of England and Wales (£239,845), Rt. Hon. Lord Judge, *born* 1941, *apptd* 2008
Master of the Rolls and Head of Civil Justice (£214,165), Rt. Hon. Lord Neuberger of Abbotsbury, *born* 1948, *apptd* 2009
President of the Queen's Bench Division (£206,857), Sir Anthony May, *born* 1940, *apptd* 2008
President of the Family Division and Head of Family Justice (£206,857), Rt. Hon. Sir Nicholas Wall, *born* 1945, *apptd* 2010
Chancellor of the High Court (£206,857), Rt. Hon. Sir Robert (Andrew) Morritt, CVO, *born* 1938, *apptd* 2000

SENIOR COURTS OF ENGLAND AND WALES

COURT OF APPEAL
Master of the Rolls (£214,165), Rt. Hon. Lord Neuberger of Abbotsbury, *born* 1948, *apptd* 2009
Secretary, Noella Roberts
Clerk, Graham Lister
Vice-President, Civil Division (£196,707), Rt. Hon. Sir Maurice Kay, *born* 1942, *apptd* 2010

Vice-President, Criminal Division (£196,707), Rt. Hon Sir Anthony Hughes, *born* 1948, *apptd* 2009

LORD JUSTICES OF APPEAL *as at July 2011* (each £196,707)
Style, The Rt. Hon. Lord/Lady Justice [surname]

Rt. Hon. Sir Malcolm Pill, *born* 1938, *apptd* 1995
Rt. Hon. Sir Alan Ward, *born* 1938, *apptd* 1995
Rt. Hon. Sir Mathew Thorpe, *born* 1938, *apptd* 1995
Rt. Hon. Sir John Mummery, *born* 1938, *apptd* 1996
Rt. Hon. Sir John Laws, *born* 1945, *apptd* 1999
Rt. Hon. Sir Bernard Rix, *born* 1944, *apptd* 2000
Rt. Hon. Dame Mary Arden, DBE, *born* 1947, *apptd* 2000
Rt. Hon. Sir Andrew Longmore, *born* 1944, *apptd* 2001
Rt. Hon. Sir Robert Carnwath, CVO, *born* 1945, *apptd* 2002
Rt. Hon. Sir Roger Thomas, *born* 1947, *apptd* 2003
Rt. Hon. Sir Maurice Kay, *born* 1942, *apptd* 2004
Rt. Hon. Sir Anthony Hooper, *born* 1937, *apptd* 2004
Rt. Hon. Sir Timothy Lloyd, *born* 1946, *apptd* 2005
Rt. Hon. Sir Martin Moore-Bick, *born* 1948, *apptd* 2005
Rt. Hon. Sir Alan Moses, *born* 1945, *apptd* 2005
Rt. Hon. Sir Stephen Richards, *born* 1950, *apptd* 2005
Rt. Hon. Dame Heather Hallett, DBE, *born* 1949, *apptd* 2005
Rt. Hon. Sir Anthony Hughes, *born* 1948, *apptd* 2006
Rt. Hon. Sir Brian Leveson, *born* 1949, *apptd* 2006
Rt. Hon. Sir Roger Toulson, *born* 1946, *apptd* 2007
Rt. Hon. Sir Colin Rimer, *born* 1944, *apptd* 2007
Rt. Hon. Sir Stanley Burnton, *born* 1942, *apptd* 2007
Rt. Hon. Sir Terence Etherton, *born* 1951, *apptd* 2008
Rt. Hon. Sir Rupert Jackson, *born* 1948, *apptd* 2008
Rt. Hon. Sir John Goldring, *born* 1944, *apptd* 2008
Rt. Hon. Sir Richard Aikens, *born* 1948, *apptd* 2008
Rt. Hon. Sir Jeremy Sullivan, *born* 1945, *apptd* 2009
Rt. Hon. Sir Patrick Elias, *born* 1947, *apptd* 2009
Rt. Hon. Sir Nicholas Patten, *born* 1950, *apptd* 2009
Rt. Hon. Sir James Munby, *born* 1948, *apptd* 2009
Rt. Hon. Sir Christopher Pitchford, *born* 1947, *apptd* 2010
Rt. Hon. Dame Jill Black, DBE, *born* 1954, *apptd* 2010
Rt. Hon. Sir Stephen Tomlinson, *born* 1952, *apptd* 2010
Rt. Hon. Sir Peter Gross, *born* 1952, *apptd* 2010
Rt. Hon. Dame Anne Rafferty, *born* 1950, *apptd* 2011
Rt. Hon. Sir Andrew McFarlane, *born* 1954, *apptd* 2011
Ex Officio Judges, Lord Chief Justice of England and Wales; Master of the Rolls; President of the Queen's Bench Division; President of the Family Division; and Chancellor of the High Court

COURTS-MARTIAL APPEAL COURT
Judges, Lord Chief Justice of England and Wales; Master of the Rolls; Lord Justices of Appeal; and Judges of the High Court of Justice

HIGH COURT OF JUSTICE

CHANCERY DIVISION
Chancellor of the High Court (£206,857), Rt. Hon. Sir Andrew Morritt, CVO, *born* 1938, *apptd* 2000
Secretary, Elaine Harbert
Clerk, Sheila Glasgow

JUDGES *as at July 2011* (each £172,753)
Style, The Hon. Mr/Mrs Justice [surname]

Hon. Sir Peter Smith, *born* 1952, *apptd* 2002
Hon. Sir Kim Lewison, *born* 1952, *apptd* 2003
Hon. Sir David Richards, *born* 1951, *apptd* 2003

Hon. Sir George Mann, *born* 1951, *apptd* 2004
Hon. Sir Nicholas Warren, *born* 1949, *apptd* 2005
Hon. Sir David Kitchin, *born* 1955, *apptd* 2005
Hon. Sir Michael Briggs, *born* 1954, *apptd* 2006
Hon. Sir Launcelot Henderson, *born* 1951, *apptd* 2006
Hon. Sir Paul Morgan, *born* 1952, *apptd* 2007
Hon. Sir Alastair Norris, *born* 1950, *apptd* 2007
Hon. Sir Gerald Barling, *born* 1949, *apptd* 2007
Hon. Sir Christopher Floyd, *born* 1951, *apptd* 2007
Hon. Sir Philip Sales, *born* 1962, *apptd* 2008
Hon. Dame Sonia Proudman, DBE, *born* 1949, *apptd* 2008
Hon. Sir Richard Arnold, *born* 1961, *apptd* 2008
Hon. Sir Peter Roth, *born* 1952, *apptd* 2009
Hon. Sir Geoffrey Vos, *born* 1955, *apptd* 2009
Hon. Sir Guy Newey, *born* 1959, *apptd* 2010

The Chancery Division also includes three specialist courts: the companies court, the patents court and the bankruptcy court.

QUEEN'S BENCH DIVISION
Lord Chief Justice of England and Wales (£239,845), Rt. Hon. Lord Judge, *born* 1941, *apptd* 2008
Secretary, Michèle Souris
Clerk, Linda Francis
President (£206,857), Rt. Hon. Sir Anthony May, *born* 1940, *apptd* 2008
Vice-President (£196,707), Rt. Hon. Sir Roger Thomas, *born* 1947, *apptd* 2008

JUDGES *as at July 2011* (each £172,753)
Style, The Hon. Mr/Mrs Justice [surname]

Hon. Sir Andrew Collins, *born* 1942, *apptd* 1994
Hon. Sir Alexander Butterfield, *born* 1942, *apptd* 1995
Hon. Sir David Eady, *born* 1943, *apptd* 1997
Hon. Sir David Steel, *born* 1943, *apptd* 1998
Hon. Sir Nicolas Bratza, *born* 1945, *apptd* 1998
Hon. Sir Michael Burton, *born* 1946, *apptd* 1998
Hon. Sir Stephen Silber, *born* 1944, *apptd* 1999
Hon. Sir Richard Henriques, *born* 1943, *apptd* 2000
Hon. Sir Andrew Smith, *born* 1947, *apptd* 2000
Hon. Sir Duncan Ouseley, *born* 1950, *apptd* 2000
Hon. Sir Richard McCombe, *born* 1952, *apptd* 2001
Hon. Sir Raymond Jack, *born* 1942, *apptd* 2001
Hon. Sir Robert Owen, *born* 1944, *apptd* 2001
Hon. Sir Colin Mackay, *born* 1943, *apptd* 2001
Hon. Sir John Mitting, *born* 1947, *apptd* 2001
Hon. Sir Roderick Evans, *born* 1946, *apptd* 2001
Hon. Sir Nigel Davis, *born* 1951, *apptd* 2001
Hon. Sir Brian Keith, *born* 1944, *apptd* 2001
Hon. Sir Jeremy Cooke, *born* 1949, *apptd* 2001
Hon. Sir Richard Field, *born* 1947, *apptd* 2002
Hon. Sir Colman Treacy, *born* 1949, *apptd* 2002
Hon. Sir Peregrine Simon, *born* 1950, *apptd* 2002
Hon. Sir Roger Royce, *born* 1944, *apptd* 2002
Hon. Dame Laura Cox, DBE, *born* 1951, *apptd* 2002
Hon. Sir Adrian Fulford, *born* 1953, *apptd* 2002
Hon. Sir Jack Beatson, *born* 1948, *apptd* 2003
Hon. Sir Michael Tugendhat, *born* 1944, *apptd* 2003
Hon. Dame Elizabeth Gloster, DBE, *born* 1949, *apptd* 2004
Hon. Sir David Bean, *born* 1954, *apptd* 2004
Hon. Sir Alan Wilkie, *born* 1947, *apptd* 2004
Hon. Dame Linda Dobbs, DBE, *born* 1951, *apptd* 2004
Hon. Sir Paul Walker, *born* 1954, *apptd* 2004
Hon. Sir David Calvert-Smith, *born* 1945, *apptd* 2005

Hon. Sir Christopher Clarke, *born* 1947, *apptd* 2005
Hon. Sir Charles Openshaw, *born* 1947, *apptd* 2005
Hon. Dame Caroline Swift, DBE, *born* 1955, *apptd* 2005
Hon. Sir Brian Langstaff, *born* 1948, *apptd* 2005
Hon. Sir David Lloyd Jones, *born* 1952, *apptd* 2005
Hon. Sir Vivian Ramsey, *born* 1950, *apptd* 2005
Hon. Sir Nicholas Underhill, *born* 1952, *apptd* 2006
Hon. Sir Stephen Irwin, *born* 1953, *apptd* 2006
Hon. Sir Nigel Teare, *born* 1952, *apptd* 2006
Hon. Sir Griffith Williams, *born* 1944, *apptd* 2007
Hon. Sir Wyn Williams, *born* 1951, *apptd* 2007
Hon. Sir Timothy King, *born* 1946, *apptd* 2007
Hon. Sir John Saunders, *born* 1959, *apptd* 2007
Hon. Sir Julian Flaux, *born* 1955, *apptd* 2007
Hon. Sir David Foskett, *born* 1949, *apptd* 2007
Hon. Sir Robert Akenhead, *born* 1949, *apptd* 2007
Hon. Sir Nicholas Stadlen, *born* 1950, *apptd* 2007
Hon. Sir Nicholas Blake, *born* 1949, *apptd* 2007
Hon. Sir Ross Cranston, *born* 1948, *apptd* 2007
Hon. Sir Peter Coulson, *born* 1958, *apptd* 2008
Hon. Sir David Maddison, *born* 1947, *apptd* 2008
Hon. Sir Richard Plender, *born* 1945, *apptd* 2008
Hon. Sir William Blair, *born* 1950, *apptd* 2008
Hon. Sir Alistair MacDuff, *born* 1945, *apptd* 2008
Hon. Sir Ian Burnett, *born* 1958, *apptd* 2008
Hon. Sir Nigel Sweeney, *born* 1954, *apptd* 2008
Hon. Dame Elizabeth Slade, DBE, *born* 1949, *apptd* 2008
Hon. Sir Nicholas Hamblen, *born* 1957, *apptd* 2008
Hon. Sir Gary Hickinbottom, *born* 1955, *apptd* 2009
Hon. Sir Timothy Holroyde, *born* 1955, *apptd* 2009
Hon. Dame Victoria Sharp, DBE, *born* 1956, *apptd* 2009
Hon. Sir Andrew Nicol, *born* 1951, *apptd* 2009
Hon. Sir Kenneth Parker, *born* 1945, *apptd* 2009
Hon. Sir Antony Edwards-Stuart, *born* 1946, *apptd* 2009
Hon. Dame Nicola Davies, DBE, *born* 1953, *apptd* 2010
Hon. Dame Kathryn Thirlwall, DBE, *born* 1957, *apptd* 2010
Hon. Sir Michael Supperstone, *born* 1950, *apptd* 2010
Hon. Sir Robin Spencer, *born* 1955, *apptd* 2010
Hon. Sir Keith Lindblom, *born* 1956, *apptd* 2010
Hon. Sir Henry Bernard Eder, *born* 1952, *apptd.* 2011

The Queen's Bench Division also includes three specialist courts – the commercial court, the admiralty court and the administration court – and administers the technology and construction court.

FAMILY DIVISION
President (£206,857), Rt. Hon. Sir Nicholas Wall, *born* 1945, *apptd* 2010
Secretary, Mrs Sarah Leung
Clerk, John Curtis

JUDGES *as at July 2011* (each £172,753)
Style, The Hon. Mr/Mrs Justice [surname]

Hon. Sir Jan Singer, *born* 1944, *apptd* 1993
Hon. Sir Edward Holman, *born* 1947, *apptd* 1995
Hon. Dame Mary Hogg, DBE, *born* 1947, *apptd* 1995
Hon. Sir Arthur Charles, *born* 1948, *apptd* 1998
Hon. Sir David Bodey, *born* 1947, *apptd* 1999
Hon. Sir Paul Coleridge, *born* 1949, *apptd* 2000
Hon. Sir Mark Hedley, *born* 1946, *apptd* 2002
Hon. Dame Anna Pauffley, DBE, *born* 1956, *apptd* 2003
Hon. Sir Roderic Wood, *born* 1951, *apptd* 2004
Hon. Dame Florence Baron, DBE, *born* 1952, *apptd* 2004
Hon. Sir Ernest Ryder, *born* 1957, *apptd* 2004
Hon. Dame Julia Macur, DBE, *born* 1957, *apptd* 2005

Hon. Sir Andrew Moylan, *born* 1953, *apptd* 2007
Hon. Dame Eleanor King, DBE, *born* 1957, *apptd*
  2008
Hon. Dame Judith Parker, DBE, *born* 1950, *apptd* 2008
Hon. Sir Jonathan Baker, *born* 1955, *apptd* 2009
Hon. Sir Nicholas Mostyn, *born* 1957, *apptd* 2010
Hon. Sir Peter Arthur Jackson, *born* 1955, *apptd* 2010
Hon. Dame Lucy Theis, *born* 1960, *apptd* 2010

DEPARTMENTS AND OFFICES OF THE SENIOR COURTS OF ENGLAND AND WALES
Royal Courts of Justice, London WC2A 2LL
T 020-7947 6000

ADMIRALTY, COMMERCIAL AND LONDON MERCANTILE COURT
T 020-7947 6112
Registrar (£102,921), J. Kay, QC
Admiralty Marshal and Court Manager, K. Houghton

BANKRUPTCY AND COMPANIES COURT REGISTRY
T 020-7947 6441
Chief Registrar (£128,296), S. Baister
Bankruptcy Registrars (£102,921), S. Barber; C. Derrett;
  G. W. Jaques; W. Nicholls; J. A. Simmonds
Court Manager, T. Pollen

CENTRAL OFFICE OF THE QUEEN'S BENCH DIVISION
Senior Master, and Queen's Remembrancer (£128,296),
  S. D. Whitaker
Masters of the Queen's Bench Division (£102,921), D.
  Cook; R. Eastman; P. G. A. Eyre; B. J. F. Fontaine;
  I. H. Foster; R. Kay; H. J. Leslie; R. Roberts;
  B. Yoxall
Court Manager, J. Ryan

CHANCERY CHAMBERS
T 020-7947 6148
Chief Master (£128,296), J. Winegarten
Masters of the Senior Courts (£102,921, T. J. Bowles;
  N. W. Bragge; J. A. Moncaster; N. S. Price;
  P. R. Teverson
Court Manager, T. Pollen

COURT OF APPEAL CIVIL DIVISION
T 020-7947 6916
Court Manager, Kim Langan

COURT OF APPEAL CRIMINAL DIVISION
T 020-7947 6011
Registrar (£102,921), R. A. Venne
Deputy Registrar, Mrs L. G. Knapman
Court Manager, Miss C. Brownbill

ADMINISTRATIVE COURT OFFICE
T 020-7947 6655
*Master of the Crown Office, and Queen's Coroner and
  Attorney* (£102,921), R. A. Venne
Deputy Master of the Crown Office, Mrs L. G. Knapman
Court Manager, Dave Brupbacher

EXAMINERS OF THE COURT
Empowered to take examination of witnesses in all
divisions of the High Court.

Examiners, His Hon. M. W. M. Chism; A. G. Dyer; A. W.
  Hughes; Mrs G. M. Keene; R. M. Planterose

COSTS OFFICE
T 020-7947 6423
Senior Costs Judge (£128,296), P. T. Hurst
Masters of the Senior Courts (£102,921), C. D. N.
  Campbell; A. Gordon-Saker; P. Haworth; C. Leonard;
  J. E. O'Hare; J. Simons; C. C. Wright
Court Manager, Helene Newman

COURT OF PROTECTION
11th Floor, Archway Tower, 2 Junction Road, London N19 5SZ
T 0300-456 4600
Senior Judge (£128,296), D. Lush

COURT OF PROTECTION VISITORS
Office of the Public Guardian, PO Box 15118, Birmingham
B16 6GX T 0845-330 2900

The Mental Capacity Act 2005 came into force on 1
October 2007, and it makes provision for two panels of
court of protection visitors (special visitors or general
visitors).

ELECTION PETITIONS OFFICE
Room E13, Royal Courts of Justice, London WC2A 2LL
T 020-7947 7529

The office accepts petitions and deals with all matters
relating to the questioning of parliamentary, European
parliament, local government and parish elections, and
with applications for relief under the 'representation of
the people' legislation.
Prescribed Officer (£128,296), Senior Master and Queen's
  Remembrancer, S. D. Whitaker
Chief Clerks, Helene Newman; Stuart Pycock

OFFICIAL RECEIVERS' DEPARTMENT (THE INSOLVENCY SERVICE)
21 Bloomsbury Street, London WC1B 3QW
T 020-7637 1110
Inspector General and Chief Executive, S. Speed
Deputy Inspector General, L. Cramp, CB

OFFICE OF COURT FUNDS
22 Kingsway, London WC2B 6LE
T 0845-223 8500
Head of Court Funds Office, E. Bloomfield

OFFICIAL SOLICITOR AND PUBLIC TRUSTEE
81 Chancery Lane, London WC2A 1DD
T 020-7911 7127
Official Solicitor to the Senior Courts, A. Pitblado
Public Trustee, E. Bloomfield

PRINCIPAL REGISTRY (FAMILY DIVISION)
First Avenue House, 42–49 High Holborn, London WC1V 6NP
T 020-7947 6000
Senior District Judge (£128,296), P. Waller
District Judges (£102,921), Mrs A. Aitken; A. R. S.
  Bassett-Cross; M. C. Berry; Ms S. M. Bowman;
  Ms H. C. Bradley; Ms P. Cushing; Ms Y. Gibson;
  Mrs L. Gordon-Saker; P. Greene; R. Harper; E. Hess;
  Ms H. MacGregor; K. Malik; C. Million; Ms C. Reid;
  Ms L. D. Roberts; R. Robinson; C. Simmonds;
  Ms S. Walker; K. J. White
Area Director, London Civil and Family, K. Launchbury
Head of Operations, London Family, J. Miller
Court Manager, J. Risk

PROBATE SERVICE

London Probate Department (Principal Registry)
7th Floor, PRFD, First Avenue House, 42–49 High Holborn, London WC1V 6NP T 020-7947 6939
Registrar, H. Whitby (Ipswich District)
Probate Manager, Tina Constantinou

DISTRICT PROBATE REGISTRARS/MANAGERS
Birmingham District Registrar, P. Walbeoff
Brighton District Probate Manager, S. Catt
Bristol District Registrar, B. Phillips
Cardiff District (Wales) Registrar, F. Herdman
Ipswich District Registrar, H. Whitby
Leeds District Probate Manager, S. Holding
Liverpool District Probate Manager, D. Shone
Manchester District Registrar, K. Murphy
Newcastle District Registrar, M. C. Riley
Oxford District Registrar, F. Herdman
Winchester District Registrar, A. Butler

JUDGE ADVOCATES GENERAL

The Judge Advocate General is the judicial head of the Service justice system, and the leader of the judges who preside over trials in the court martial and other Service courts. The defendants are service personnel from the Royal Navy, the army and the Royal Air Force, and civilians accompanying them overseas.

JUDGE ADVOCATE GENERAL OF THE FORCES
9th Floor, Thomas More Building, Royal Courts of Justice, Strand, London WC2A 2LL
T 020-7218 8095
Judge Advocate General (£138,548), His Hon. Judge Blackett
Vice Judge Advocate General (£120,785), Michael Hunter
Assistant Judge Advocates General (£106,921)*, J. P. Camp; M. R. Elsom; R. D. Hill; A. M. Large; A. J. B. McGrigor; E. Peters
Style, Judge [surname]

* Salary includes £2,000 London salary lead and a London allowance of £2,000

HIGH COURT AND CROWN COURT CENTRES

First-tier centres deal with both civil and criminal cases and are served by high court and circuit judges. Second-tier centres deal with criminal cases only and are served by high court and circuit judges. Third-tier centres deal with criminal cases only and are served only by circuit judges.

LONDON REGION
First-tier – None
Second-tier – Central Criminal Court
Third-tier – Blackfriars, Croydon, Harrow, Inner London, Isleworth, Kingston upon Thames, Snaresbrook, Southwark, Wood Green, Woolwich
Regional Director, Alan Eccles, 2nd Floor, Rose Court, 2 Southwark Bridge, London SE1 9HS T 020-7921 2006
Area Directors, Dave Weston *(Crime, Central and South);* Sandra Aston *(Crime, North and West);* Kelvin Launchbury *(Civil and Family)*

The high court (first-tier) in Greater London sits at the Royal Courts of Justice.

MIDLANDS REGION
First-tier – Birmingham, Lincoln, Nottingham, Stafford, Warwick
Second-tier – Leicester, Northampton, Shrewsbury, Worcester, Wolverhampton
Third-tier – Coventry, Derby, Hereford, Stoke on Trent
Delivery Director, Lucy Garrod, PO Box 11772, 6th Floor, Temple Court, Bull Street, Birmingham B4 6WF

NORTH-EAST REGION
First-tier – Leeds, Newcastle upon Tyne, Sheffield, Teesside
Second-tier – Bradford, York
Third-tier – Doncaster, Durham, Kingston upon Hull, Great Grimsby
Delivery Director, Sheila Proudlock, Old Elvet, Green Lane, Durham DH1 3RG T 0191-375 1815
Head of Crime, Dave Foley

NORTH-WEST REGION
First-tier – Carlisle, Chester, Liverpool, Manchester (Crown Square), Preston
Third-tier – Barrow in Furness, Bolton, Burnley, Knutsford, Lancaster, Manchester (Minshull Street), Warrington
Regional Director, Richard Knott, PO Box 4237, Manchester Civil Justice Centre, 1 Bridge Street West, Manchester M60 1TE T 0161-240 5000
Area Directors, Gill Hague *(Cumbria and Lancashire);* John Foley *(Greater Manchester);* Paul McGladrigan *(Merseyside and Cheshire)*

SOUTH-EAST REGION
First-tier – Cambridge, Chelmsford, Lewes, Norwich, Oxford
Second-tier – Guildford, Ipswich, Luton, Maidstone, Reading, St Albans
Third-tier – Aylesbury, Basildon, Canterbury, Chichester, Croydon, King's Lynn, Peterborough, Southend
Regional Director, Keith Budgen, 3rd Floor, Rose Court, 2 Southwark Bridge, London SE1 9HS T 020-7332 1831
Area Directors, Pauline Cornford *(Cambridgeshire, Norfolk and Suffolk);* Julia Eeles *(Surrey and Sussex);* Dr Jonathan Lane *(Thames Valley);* Mike Littlewood, OBE *(Bedfordshire, Essex and Hertfordshire);* Dave Weston *(Kent)*

SOUTH-WEST REGION
First-tier – Bristol, Exeter, Truro, Winchester
Second-tier – Dorchester & Weymouth, Gloucester, Plymouth
Third-tier – Barnstaple, Bournemouth, Newport (IoW), Portsmouth, Salisbury, Southampton, Swindon, Taunton
Regional Director, Peter Risk, Spectrum, 3rd Floor, Suite A, Bond Street, Bristol BS1 3LG T 0117-300 6238
Area Directors, David Gentry *(West);* Simon Townley *(East)*

WALES REGION
First-tier – Caernarfon, Cardiff, Merthyr Tydfil, Mold, Swansea
Second-tier – Carmarthen, Newport, Welshpool
Third-tier – Dolgellau, Haverfordwest
Delivery Director, Mark Swales, Churchill House, Churchill Way, Cardiff CF10 2HH T 029-2067 8311

CIRCUIT JUDGES
Circuit judges are barristers of at least seven years' standing or recorders of at least five years' standing. Circuit judges serve in the county courts and the crown court.
Style, His/Her Hon. Judge [surname]
Senior Presiding Judge, Rt. Hon. Lord Justice Goldring
Senior Circuit Judges, each £138,548
Circuit Judges at the Central Criminal Court, London (Old Bailey Judges), each £138,548
Circuit Judges, each £128,296

MIDLANDS CIRCUIT
Presiding Judges, Hon. Mr Justice Flaux; Hon. Mrs Justice Thirlwall

NORTH-EASTERN CIRCUIT
Presiding Judges, Hon. Mr Justice Coulson; Hon. Mr Justice Openshaw

NORTHERN CIRCUIT
Presiding Judges, Hon. Mr Justice Holroyde; Hon. Mr Justice Ryder

SOUTH-EASTERN CIRCUIT
Presiding Judges, Hon. Mr Justice Fulford; Hon. Mr Justice Nicol; Hon. Mr Justice Saunders; Mr Justice Sweeney

WALES CIRCUIT
Presiding Judges, Hon. Mr Justice Griffith Williams; Hon. Mr Justice Wyn Williams

WESTERN CIRCUIT
Presiding Judges, Hon. Mr Justice Burnett; Hon. Mr Justice Field

DISTRICT JUDGES
District judges, formerly known as registrars of the court, are solicitors of at least seven years' standing and serve in county courts.
District Judges, each £102,921

DISTRICT JUDGES (MAGISTRATES' COURTS)
District judges (magistrates' courts), formerly known as stipendiary magistrates, must be barristers or solicitors of at least seven years' standing (including at least two years' experience as a deputy district judge), and serve in magistrates' courts. All former provincial and metropolitan stipendiary magistrates can serve nationally within any district.
District Judges (Magistrates' Courts), each £102,921

CROWN PROSECUTION SERVICE
Rose Court, 2 Southwark Bridge Road, London SE1 9HS
T 020-7023 6539 E enquiries@cps.gsi.gov.uk
W www.cps.gov.uk

The Crown Prosecution Service (CPS) is responsible for prosecuting cases investigated by the police in England and Wales, with the exception of cases conducted by the Serious Fraud Office and certain minor offences.
The CPS is headed by the director of public prosecutions (DPP), who works under the superintendence of the attorney-general. The service is divided into 13 areas across England and Wales, with each area led by a chief crown prosecutor.
Director of Public Prosecutions, Keir Starmer, QC

Chief Executive, Peter Lewis
Chief Operating Officer, Mike Kennedy, CBE
Principal Legal Adviser, Alison Levitt
Directors, David Jones *(Business Information Systems);* Paul Staff *(Finance);* Sue Hemming, OBE *(Counter-Terrorism);* Simon Clements *(Special Crime);* Ros McCool *(Human Resources);* Roger Daw *(Policy);* Nick Hunt *(Strategy and Policy)*

CPS AREAS
WALES, 20th Floor, Capital Tower, Greyfriars Road, Cardiff CF10 3PL T 029-2080 3800
Chief Crown Prosecutor, Jim Brisbane
EAST MIDLANDS, 2 King Edward Court, King Edward Street, Nottingham NG1 1EL T 0115-852 3300
Chief Crown Prosecutor, Judith Walker
EASTERN, County House, 100 New London Road, Chelmsford, Essex CM2 0RG T 0124-455800
Chief Crown Prosecutor, Ken Caley
LONDON, 3rd Floor, New King's Beam House, 22 Upper Ground, London SE1 9BT T 020-3357 0000
Chief Crown Prosecutor, Alison Saunders
MERSEY/CHESHIRE, 7th Floor, Royal Liver Building, Pier Head, Liverpool L3 1HN T 0151-239 6400
Chief Crown Prosecutor, Paul Whittaker
NORTH EAST, St Ann's Quay, 112 Quayside, Newcastle Upon Tyne, NE1 3BD T 0191-260 4200
Chief Crown Prosecutor, Wendy Williams
NORTH WEST, 1st Floor, Stocklund House, Castle Street, Carlisle CA3 8SY T 01228-882900
Chief Crown Prosecutor, Nazir Afzal, OBE
SOUTH EAST, 29 Union Street, Maidstone, Kent ME14 1PT T 01622-356300
Chief Crown Prosecutor, Roger Coe-Salazar
SOUTH WEST, 2nd Floor, Froomsgate House, Rupert Street, Bristol BS1 2QJ T 0117-930 2800
Chief Crown Prosecutor, Barry Hughes
THAMES AND CHILTERN, Eaton Court, 112 Oxford Road, Reading, Berks RG1 7LL T 0118-951 3600
Chief Crown Prosecutor, Baljit Ubhey
WESSEX, 3rd Floor, Black Horse House, 8–10 Leigh Road, Eastleigh, Hants SO50 9FH T 02380-673 800
Chief Crown Prosecutor, Nick Hawkins
WEST MIDLANDS, Operations Centre, Colmore Gate, 2 Colmore Row, Birmingham B3 2QA T 0121-262 1300
Chief Crown Prosecutor, Harry Ireland
YORKSHIRE AND HUMBERSIDE, 27 Park Place, Leeds, LS1 2SZ T 0113-290 2700
Chief Crown Prosecutor, Martin Goldman

HER MAJESTY'S COURTS AND TRIBUNALS SERVICE
Zone C, 1st Floor, 102 Petty France, London SW1H 9AJ
T 0845-456 8770 W www.justice.gov.uk

Her Majesty's Courts Service and the Tribunals Service merged on 1 April 2011 to form HM Courts and Tribunals Service. It is an agency of the Ministry of Justice, operating as a partnership between the Lord Chancellor, the Lord Chief Justice and the Senior President of Tribunals. It is responsible for administering the criminal, civil and family courts and tribunals in England and Wales and non-devolved tribunals in Scotland and Northern Ireland.
Chief Executive, Peter Handcock

JUDICIAL APPOINTMENTS COMMISSION

Steel House, 11 Tothill Street, London SW1H 9LJ
T 020-3334 0453 E jaas@jac.gsi.gov.uk
W http://jac/judiciary.gov.uk

The Judicial Appointments Commission was established as an independent non-departmental public body in April 2006 by the Constitutional Reform Act 2005. Its role is to select judicial office holders independently of government (a responsibility previously held by the Lord Chancellor) for courts and tribunals in England and Wales, and for some tribunals whose jurisdiction extends to Scotland or Northern Ireland. It has a statutory duty to encourage diversity in the range of persons available for selection and is sponsored by the Ministry of Justice and accountable to parliament through the Lord Chancellor. It is made up of 15 commissioners, including a chair.

Chair, Christopher Stephens
Commissioners, Hon. Mr Justice Bean; Lady Justice Black, DBE; Dame Boreland-Kelly, DBE, FRSA; Dame Prof. Hazel Genn, DBE; Sir Geoffrey Inkin, OBE; Sara Nathan, OBE; Charles Newman; His Hon. Judge Pearl; Hon. Francis Plowden; Harriet Spicer; Jonathan Sumption, OBE, QC; Rt. Hon. Lord Justice Toulson
Chief Executive (interim), Nigel Reeder

DIRECTORATE OF JUDICIAL OFFICES

The Judicial Office was established in April 2006 to support the judiciary in discharging its responsibilities under the Constitutional Reform Act 2005. It is led by a chief executive, who reports to the Lord Chief Justice rather than to ministers, and its work is directed by the judiciary rather than by the administration of the day. The Judicial Office incorporates the Judicial College (formerly the Judicial Studies Board), the Judicial Communications Office, sponsorship of the Family and Civil Justice Councils, the Office for Judicial Complaints and the Tribunals Judicial Office.

CHIEF EXECUTIVE'S OFFICE
T 020-7947 7960
Chief Executive Officer, Anne Sharp
Personal Secretary, Maxine Fidler

HR FOR THE JUDICIARY
Head, Helen Wallace
Personal Secretary, Susan Holleran

JUDICIAL COLLEGE
T 020-3334 0700
Director of Studies, His Hon. Judge Phillips, CBE
Executive Director, Sheridan Greenland
Personal Secretary, Wendy Ford

OFFICE FOR JUDICIAL COMPLAINTS
T 020-3334 0145

STRATEGY, GOVERNANCE AND COMMUNICATIONS
Deputy Director, Jo Gordon
Personal Secretary, Susan Holleran
Head of News Stephen Ward

JUDICIAL COMMITTEE OF THE PRIVY COUNCIL

The Judicial Committee of the Privy Council is the final court of appeal for the United Kingdom overseas territories (*see* UK Overseas Territories section), crown dependencies and those independent Commonwealth countries which have retained this avenue of appeal (Antigua and Barbuda, Bahamas, Brunei, Cook Islands and Niue, Dominica, Grenada, Jamaica, Kiribati, Mauritius, St Christopher and Nevis, St Lucia, St Vincent and the Grenadines, Trinidad and Tobago, and Tuvalu) and the sovereign base areas of Akrotiri and Dhekelia in Cyprus. The committee also hears appeals against pastoral schemes under the Pastoral Measure 1983, and deals with appeals from veterinary disciplinary bodies.

Until October 2009, the Judicial Committee of the Privy Council was the final arbiter in disputes as to the legal competence of matters done or proposed by the devolved legislative and executive authorities in Scotland, Wales and Northern Ireland. This is now the responsibility of the new UK Supreme Court.

In 2010 the Judicial Committee dealt with a total of 33 appeals and 46 petitions for special leave to appeal.

The members of the Judicial Committee are the justices of the supreme court, and Privy Counsellors who hold or have held high judicial office in the United Kingdom or in certain designated courts of Commonwealth countries from which appeals are taken to committee.

JUDICIAL COMMITTEE OF THE PRIVY COUNCIL
Parliament Square, London SW1A 2AJ T 020-7960 1500
Registrar of the Privy Council, Louise di Mambro
Chief Clerk, Jackie Lindsay

SCOTTISH JUDICATURE

Scotland has a legal system separate from, and differing greatly from, the English legal system in enacted law, judicial procedure and the structure of courts.

In Scotland the system of public prosecution is headed by the Lord Advocate and is independent of the police, who have no say in the decision to prosecute. The Lord Advocate, discharging his functions through the Crown Office in Edinburgh, is responsible for prosecutions in the high court, sheriff courts and district courts. Prosecutions in the high court are prepared by the Crown Office and conducted in court by one of the law officers, by an advocate-depute, or by a solicitor advocate. In the inferior courts the decision to prosecute is made and prosecution is preferred by procurators fiscal, who are lawyers and full-time civil servants subject to the directions of the Crown Office. A permanent legally qualified civil servant, known as the crown agent, is responsible for the running of the Crown Office and the organisation of the Procurator Fiscal Service, of which he or she is the head.

Scotland is divided into six sheriffdoms, each with a full-time sheriff principal. The sheriffdoms are further divided into sheriff court districts, each of which has a legally qualified resident sheriff or sheriffs, who are the judges of the court.

In criminal cases sheriffs principal and sheriffs have the same powers; sitting with a jury of 15 members, they may try more serious cases on indictment, or, sitting alone, may try lesser cases under summary procedure. Minor summary offences are dealt with in Justice of the Peace Courts, which replaced district courts formerly operated by local authorities, and presided over by lay justices of the peace (of whom some 500 regularly sit in court) and, in Glasgow only, by stipendiary magistrates. Juvenile offenders (children under 16) may be brought before an informal children's hearing comprising three local lay people. The superior criminal court is the high court of justiciary which is both a trial and an appeal court. Cases on indictment are tried by a high court judge, sitting with a jury of 15, in Edinburgh and on circuit in other towns. Appeals from the lower courts against conviction or sentence are also heard by the high court, which sits as an appeal court only in Edinburgh. There is no further appeal to the supreme court in criminal cases.

In civil cases the jurisdiction of the sheriff court extends to most kinds of action. Appeals against decisions of the sheriff may be made to the sheriff principal and thence to the court of session, or direct to the court of session, which sits only in Edinburgh. The court of session is divided into the inner and the outer house. The outer house is a court of first instance in which cases are heard by judges sitting singly, sometimes with a jury of 12. The inner house, itself subdivided into two divisions of equal status, is mainly an appeal court. Appeals may be made to the inner house from the outer house as well as from the sheriff court. An appeal may be made from the inner house to the supreme court.

The judges of the court of session are the same as those of the high court of justiciary, with the Lord President of the court of session also holding the office of Lord Justice General in the high court. Senators of the College of Justice are Lords Commissioners of Justiciary as well as judges of the court of session. On appointment, a senator takes a judicial title, which is retained for life. Although styled The Hon./Rt. Hon. Lord, the senator is not a peer, although some judges are peers in their own right.

The office of coroner does not exist in Scotland. The local procurator fiscal inquires privately into sudden or suspicious deaths and may report findings to the crown agent. In some cases a fatal accident inquiry may be held before the sheriff.

COURT OF SESSION AND HIGH COURT OF JUSTICIARY

The Lord President and Lord Justice General (£214,165),
Rt. Hon. Lord Hamilton, *born* 1942, *apptd* 2005
Private Secretary, A. Maxwell

INNER HOUSE
Lords of Session (each £196,707)

FIRST DIVISION
The Lord President

Rt. Hon. Lord Eassie (Ronald Mackay), *born* 1945, *apptd* 2006
Rt. Hon. Lord Reed (Robert Reed), *born* 1956, *apptd* 2008
Rt. Hon. Lord Hardie (Andrew Hardie), *born* 1946, *apptd* 2009
Rt. Hon. Lord Bonomy (Iain Bonomy), *born* 1946, *apptd* 2010
Rt. Hon. Lord Emslie (George Emslie), *born* 1947, *apptd* 2010

SECOND DIVISION
Lord Justice Clerk (£206,857), Rt. Hon. Lord Gill (Brian Gill), *born* 1942, *apptd* 2001
Rt. Hon. Lady Paton (Ann Paton), *born* 1952, *apptd* 2007
Rt. Hon. Lord Carloway (Colin Sutherland), *born* 1954, *apptd* 2008
Rt. Hon. Lord Clarke (Matthew Clarke), *born* 1947, *apptd* 2008
Rt. Hon. Lord Mackay of Drumadoon (Donald Mackay), *born* 1946, *apptd* 2010

OUTER HOUSE
Lords of Session (each £172,753)
Hon. Lord Menzies (Duncan Menzies), *born* 1953, *apptd* 2001
Hon. Lord Drummond Young (James Drummond Young), *born* 1950, *apptd* 2001
Hon. Lady Smith (Anne Smith), *born* 1955, *apptd* 2001
Hon. Lord Brodie (Philip Brodie), *born* 1950, *apptd* 2002
Hon. Lord Bracadale (Alastair Campbell), *born* 1949, *apptd* 2003
Hon. Lady Dorrian (Leona Dorrian), *born* 1957, *apptd* 2005
Hon. Lord Hodge (Patrick Hodge), *born* 1953, *apptd* 2005
Hon. Lord Glennie (Angus Glennie), *born* 1950, *apptd* 2005
Hon. Lord Kinclaven (Alexander F. Wylie), *born* 1951, *apptd* 2005
Hon. Lord Turnbull (Alan Turnbull), *born* 1958, *apptd* 2006
Hon. Lady Clark of Calton (Lynda Clark), *born* 1949, *apptd* 2006
Hon. Lord Brailsford (Sidney Brailsford), *born* 1954, *apptd* 2006
Hon. Lord Uist (Roderick Macdonald), *born* 1951, *apptd* 2006
Hon. Lord Malcolm (Colin M. Campbell), *born* 1953, *apptd* 2007
Hon. Lord Matthews (Hugh Matthews), *born* 1953, *apptd* 2007
Hon. Lord Woolman (Stephen Woolman), *born* 1953, *apptd* 2008
Hon. Lord Pentland (Paul Cullen), *born* 1957, *apptd* 2008
Hon. Lord Bannatyne (Iain Peebles), *born* 1954, *apptd* 2008
Hon. Lady Stacey (Valerie E. Stacey), *born* 1954, *apptd* 2009
Hon. Lord Tyre (Colin Tyre), *born* 1956, *apptd* 2010
Hon. Lord Doherty (Raymond Doherty), *born* 1958, *apptd* 2010
Hon. Lord Stewart (Angus Stewart), *born* 1946, *apptd* 2010

COURT OF SESSION AND HIGH COURT OF JUSTICIARY
Parliament House, Parliament Square, Edinburgh EH1 1RQ
T 0131-225 2595
Principal Clerk of Session and Justiciary, G. Marwick
Deputy Principal Clerk of Justiciary, G. Prentice
Deputy Principal Clerk of Session and Principal Extractor, R. Cockburn
Depute in Charge of Offices of Court, Y. Anderson
Keeper of the Rolls, G. Combe
Division Clerks, D. Cullen; E. Dickson; R. Jenkins
Appeal Clerks, R. MacPherson; A. Mackay; R. Sinclair
Depute Clerks of Session and Justiciary Team Leaders,
W. Dunn; A. McArdle; L. McLachlan; D. MacLeod; C. Reid
Depute Clerks of Session and Justiciary R. Broome; A. Corr; K. Cumming; L. Curran; H. Fraser; C. Fyffe; A. Galloway; T. Kell; K. Kier; A. Lynch; E. McLeod; L. McNamara; N. Marchant; I. Martin; R. Martin; D. Morrison; R. Newlands; C. Richardson; N. Roberts; C. Scott; G. Slater; K. Todd; C. Truby; P. Weir

SHERIFF COURT OF CHANCERY

27 Chambers Street, Edinburgh EH1 1LB
T 0131-225 2525

The court deals with service of heirs and completion of title in relation to heritable property.
Sheriff of Chancery, M. Stephen

EDINBURGH SHERIFF COURT AND JUSTICE OF THE PEACE COURT

27 Chambers Street, Edinburgh EH1 1LB
T 0131-225 2525

The work of the Sheriff Courts and Justice of the Peace Courts can be divided into three main categories: civil, criminal and commissary, and is administered by local sheriff clerks and their staff.

SCOTTISH LAND COURT

126 George Street, Edinburgh EH2 4HH
T 0131-271 4360

The court deals with disputes relating to agricultural and crofting land in Scotland.
Chair (£138,548), Hon. Lord McGhie (James McGhie), QC
Deputy Chair, R. J. Macleod
Members, D. J. Houston; A. Macdonald *(part-time);*
J. A. Smith *(part-time)*
Principal Clerk, B. A. Brown, WS

SCOTTISH GOVERNMENT JUSTICE DIRECTORATE

Legal System Division, Room 2W, St Andrew's House, Edinburgh EH1 3DG
T 0131-244 2698

The Justice Directorate is responsible for the appointment of judges and sheriffs to meet the needs of the business of the supreme and sheriffs court in Scotland. It is also responsible for providing resources for the efficient administration of certain specialist courts and tribunals.
Deputy Director, C. McKay

JUDICIAL APPOINTMENTS BOARD FOR SCOTLAND

38–39 Drumsheugh Gardens, Edinburgh EH3 7SW
T 0131-528 5101

The board's remit is to provide the first minister with the names of candidates recommended for appointment to the posts of judge of the court of session chair of the Scottish Land Court, temporary judge, sheriff principal, sheriff and part-time sheriff.
Chair, Sir Muir Russell, KCB, FRSE

SCOTTISH COURT SERVICE

Saughton House, Broomhouse Drive, Edinburgh EH11 3XD
T 0131-444 3300 W www.scotcourts.gov.uk

The Scottish Court Service is responsible for the provision of staff, buildings and technology to support Scotland's courts, the independent judiciary, the courts' Rules Councils and the Office of the Public Guardian. On 1 April 2010 it was established by the Judiciary and Courts (Scotland) Act 2008 as an independent body, governed by a corporate board and chaired by the Lord President.
Chief Executive, E. Emberson

JUDICIAL OFFICE FOR SCOTLAND

1A Parliament Square, Edinburgh EH1 1RQ
T 0131-240 6672 W www.scotland-judiciary.org.uk

The Judicial Office for Scotland came into being on 1 April 2010 as part of the changes introduced by the Judiciary and Courts (Scotland) Act 2008. It provides support for the Lord President in his role as head of the Scottish judiciary with responsibility for the training, welfare, deployment and conduct of judges and the efficient disposal of business in the courts.
Executive Director, Steve Humphreys

SHERIFFDOMS

SALARIES

Sheriff Principal	£138,548
Sheriff	£128,296

GLASGOW AND STRATHKELVIN
Sheriff Principal, C. A. L. Scott
GRAMPIAN, HIGHLAND AND ISLANDS
Sheriff Principal, Sir Stephen S. T. Young, Bt., QC
LOTHIAN AND BORDERS
Sheriff Principal, M. M. Stephen
NORTH STRATHCLYDE
Sheriff Principal, B. A. Kerr, QC
SOUTH STRATHCLYDE, DUMFRIES AND GALLOWAY
Sheriff Principal, B. A. Lockhart
TAYSIDE, CENTRAL AND FIFE
Sheriff Principal, R. A. Dunlop, QC

JUSTICE OF THE PEACE AND STIPENDIARY MAGISTRATES COURT

GLASGOW
R. B. Christie, *apptd* 1985; A. Findlay, *apptd* 2008; Ms J. Kerr, *apptd* 2008; Mrs J. A. M. MacLean, *apptd* 1990

CROWN OFFICE AND PROCURATOR FISCAL SERVICE

CROWN OFFICE
25 Chambers Street, Edinburgh EH1 1LA
T 0131-226 2626 W www.crownoffice.gov.uk
Crown Agent, Catherine Oyer
Deputy Crown Agent, John Dunn

PROCURATORS FISCAL

SALARIES

Area Fiscals	£58,200–£162,500
District Procurator Fiscal	£48,899–£128,900

GRAMPIAN AREA
Area Procurator Fiscal, Mrs A. Currie *(Aberdeen)*
HIGHLAND AND ISLANDS AREA
Area Procurator Fiscal, A. Laing *(Inverness)*
LANARKSHIRE AREA
Area Procurator Fiscal, Ms J. Cameron *(Hamilton)*
CENTRAL AREA
Area Procurator Fiscal, D. Harvie *(Stirling)*
TAYSIDE AREA
Area Procurator Fiscal, J. Logue *(Dundee)*
FIFE AREA
Area Procurator Fiscal, D. Green *(Kirkcaldy)*
LOTHIAN AND BORDERS AREA
Area Procurator Fiscal, vacant *(Edinburgh)*
AYRSHIRE AREA
Area Procurator Fiscal, T. Dysart *(Kilmarnock)*

ARGYLL AND CLYDE AREA
Area Procurator Fiscal, J. Watt *(Paisley)*
DUMFRIES AND GALLOWAY AREA
Area Procurator Fiscal, Ms R. McQuaid *(Dumfries)*
GLASGOW AREA
Area Procurator Fiscal, Ms L. Thomson *(Glasgow)*

COURT OF THE LORD LYON

HM New Register House, Edinburgh EH1 3YT
T 0131-556 7255
W www.lyon-court.com

The Court of the Lord Lyon is the Scottish Court of Chivalry (including the genealogical jurisdiction of the *Ri-Sennachie* of Scotland's Celtic kings). The Lord Lyon King of Arms has jurisdiction, subject to appeal to the Court of Session and the House of Lords, in questions of heraldry and the right to bear arms. The court also administers the Public Register of All Arms and Bearings and the Public Register of All Genealogies in Scotland. Pedigrees are established by decrees of Lyon Court and by letters patent. As Royal Commissioner in Armory, the Lord Lyon grants patents of arms to virtuous and well-deserving Scots and to petitioners (personal or corporate) in the Queen's overseas realms of Scottish connection, and also issues birthbrieves. For information on Her Majesty's Officers of Arms in Scotland, *see* the Court of the Lord Lyon in the Public Bodies section.
Lord Lyon King of Arms, David Sellar, FSA SCOT, FRHISTS
Lyon Clerk and Keeper of the Records, Mrs C. G. W. Roads, MVO, FSA SCOT
Procurator Fiscal, Alexander M. S. Green
Macer, H. M. Love

NORTHERN IRELAND JUDICATURE

In Northern Ireland the legal system and the structure of courts closely resemble those of England and Wales; there are, however, often differences in enacted law.

The court of judicature of Northern Ireland comprises the court of appeal, the high court of justice and the crown court. The practice and procedure of these courts is similar to that in England. The superior civil court is the high court of justice, from which an appeal lies to the Northern Ireland court of appeal; the UK supreme court is the final civil appeal court.

The crown court, served by high court and county court judges, deals with criminal trials on indictment. Cases are heard before a judge and, except those certified by the Director of Public Prosecutions under the Justice and Security Act 2007, a jury. Appeals from the crown court against conviction or sentence are heard by the Northern Ireland court of appeal; the supreme court is the final court of appeal.

The decision to prosecute in criminal cases in Northern Ireland rests with the director of public prosecutions.

Minor criminal offences are dealt with in magistrates' courts by a legally qualified district judge (magistrates' courts) and, where an offender is under the age of 18, by youth courts each consisting of a district judge (magistrates' courts) and two lay magistrates (at least one of whom must be a woman). Appeals from magistrates' courts are heard by the county court, or by the court of appeal on a point of law or an issue as to jurisdiction.

Magistrates' courts in Northern Ireland can deal with certain classes of civil case but most minor civil cases are dealt with in county courts. Judgments of all civil courts are enforceable through a centralised procedure administered by the Enforcement of Judgments Office.

COURT OF JUDICATURE

The Royal Courts of Justice, Belfast BT1 3JF
T 028-9023 5111
Lord Chief Justice of Northern Ireland (£214,165), Rt. Hon. Sir Declan Morgan, *born* 1952, *apptd* 2009
Principal Secretary, Mrs Laurene McAlpine

LORD JUSTICES OF APPEAL (£196,707)
Style, The Rt. Hon. Lord Justice [surname]

Rt. Hon. Sir Malachy Higgins, *born* 1944, *apptd* 2007
Rt. Hon. Sir Paul Girvan, *born* 1948, *apptd* 2007
Rt. Hon. Sir Patrick Coghlin, *born* 1945, *apptd* 2008

PUISNE JUDGES (£172,753)
Style, The Hon. Mr Justice [surname]

Hon. Sir John Gillen, *born* 1947, *apptd* 1999
Hon. Sir Richard McLaughlin, *born* 1947, *apptd* 1999
Hon. Sir Ronald Weatherup, *born* 1947, *apptd* 2001
Hon. Sir Reginald Weir, *born* 1947, *apptd* 2003
Hon. Sir Donnell Deeny, *born* 1950, *apptd* 2004
Hon. Sir Anthony Hart, *born* 1946, *apptd* 2005
Hon. Sir Seamus Treacy, *born* 1956, *apptd* 2007
Hon. Sir William Stephens, *born* 1954, *apptd* 2007
Hon. Sir Bernard McCloskey, *born* 1956, *apptd* 2008

MASTERS OF THE SUPREME COURT (£102,921)
Master, Queen's Bench and Appeals, C. J. McCorry
Master, Office of Care and Protection, H. Wells
Master, Chancery and Probate, R. A. Ellison
Master, Matrimonial, C. W. G. Redpath
Master, Queen's Bench and Matrimonial, E. Bell
Master, Taxing Office, J. Baillie
Master, Bankruptcy, F. Kelly

OFFICIAL SOLICITOR
Official Solicitor to the Supreme Court of Northern Ireland, Miss B. M. Donnelly

COUNTY COURTS

JUDGES (£138,548)
Style, His/Her Hon. Judge [surname]

Judge Babington; Judge Devlin; Judge Finnegan, QC; Judge Fowler, QC; Her Hon. Judge Kennedy; Judge Loughran; Judge Lynch, QC; Judge McFarland; Judge McReynolds; Judge Marrinan, QC; Judge Miller, QC; Judge Philpott, QC; Judge Rodgers; Judge Smyth, QC; Her Hon. Judge Smyth

RECORDERS
Belfast (£149,631), Judge Burgess
Londonderry (£138,548), Judge Grant

MAGISTRATES' COURTS

DISTRICT JUDGES (MAGISTRATES' COURTS) (£102,921)
There are 21 district judges (magistrates' courts) in Northern Ireland.

NORTHERN IRELAND COURTS AND TRIBUNALS SERVICE
Laganside House, 23–25 Oxford Street, Belfast BT1 3LA
T 028-9032 8594 W www.courtsni.gov.uk
Director, D. A. Lavery

CROWN SOLICITOR'S OFFICE
Royal Courts of Justice, Chichester Street, Belfast BT1 3JE
T 028-9054 2555
Crown Solicitor, J. Conn

PUBLIC PROSECUTION SERVICE
93 Chichester Street, Belfast BT1 3JR
T 028-9054 2444 W www.ppsni.gov.uk
Director of Public Prosecutions (acting), Jim Scholes

TRIBUNALS

Information on all the tribunals listed here, with the exception of the independent tribunals and the tribunals based in Scotland, Wales and Northern Ireland can be found on the Ministry of Justice website (W www.justice.gov.uk).

HM COURTS AND TRIBUNALS SERVICE

5th Floor, 102 Petty France, London SW1H 9AJ
T 0845-600 0877 W www.justice.gov.uk

HM Courts Service and the Tribunals Service merged on 1 April 2011 to form HM Courts and Tribunals Service. This new service is an executive agency within the Ministry of Justice, operating as a partnership between the Lord Chancellor, the Lord Chief Justice and the Senior President of Tribunals. The agency provides common administrative support, including infrastructure and resources, to the non-devolved government tribunals in the UK for which the Lord Chancellor is responsible.

A two-tier tribunal system, comprising the First-tier Tribunal and Upper Tribunal, was established on 3 November 2008 as a result of radical reform under the Tribunals, Courts and Enforcement Act 2007. Both of these tiers are split into a number of separate chambers. These chambers group together individual tribunals (also known as 'jurisdictions') which deal with similar work or require similar skills. Cases start in the First-tier Tribunal and there is a right of appeal to the Upper Tribunal. Some tribunals transferred to the new two-tier system immediately, with many more transferring in 2010. The exception is employment tribunals, which remain outside this structure. The Act also allowed legally qualified tribunal chairs and adjudicators to swear the judicial oath and become judges.
Senior President, Lord Justice Carnwath, CVO
Chief Executive, Peter Handcock, CBE

FIRST-TIER TRIBUNAL

The main function of the First-tier Tribunal is to hear appeals by citizens against decisions of the government. In most cases appeals are heard by a panel made up of one judge and two specialists in their relevant field, known as 'members'. Both judges and members are appointed through the Independent Judicial Appointments Commission. Most of the tribunals administered by central government are part of the First-tier Tribunal, which is split into six separate chambers.

GENERAL REGULATORY CHAMBER
President (acting), Judge Warren

CHARITY
PO Box 9300, Leicester LE1 8DJ
T 0845-1234 504 E charitytribunal@tribunals.gsi.gov.uk

First-tier Tribunal (Charity) was established under the Charities Act 2006 to hear appeals against the decisions of the Charity Commission, applications for the review of decisions made by the Charity Commission and to consider references from the Attorney-General or the

Charity Commission on points of law. It became part of the General Regulatory Chamber on 1 September 2009. The tribunal consists of the principal judge, five legal members and seven non-legal members. The tribunal currently only has jurisdiction in respect of Charity Commission decisions made on or after 18 March 2008.
Principal Judge, Alison McKenna

CLAIMS MANAGEMENT SERVICES
PO Box 9300, Leicester LE1 8DJ
T 0300-1234 504 E cmst@tribunals.gsi.gov.uk

First-tier Tribunal (Claims Management Services) was established under the Compensation Act 2006 to hear appeals pertaining to decisions made by the Claims Regulator in relation to personal injury; criminal injuries compensation; employment matters; housing disrepair; financial products and services; and industrial injury disablement benefits. It was formerly known as the Claims Management Services Tribunal until it became part of the General Regulatory Chamber in January 2010.
Principal Judge, Judge Warren

CONSUMER CREDIT
PO Box 9300, Leicester LE1 8DJ T 0300-1234 504
E consumercreditappeals@tribunals.gsi.gov.uk

First-tier Tribunal (Consumer Credit) replaced the Consumer Credit Appeals Tribunal on 1 September 2009. It hears appeals against licensing decisions made by the Office of Fair Trading under the Consumer Credit Act 1974 and the amended Consumer Credit Act 2006. The tribunal also hears appeals relating to the implementation of requirements or a civil penalty on licensees under the Act; and the refusal to register, cancellation of registration, or imposition of a penalty under the Money Laundering Regulations 2007.
Principal Judge, His Hon. Judge Wulwik

ENVIRONMENT
PO Box 9300, Leicester LE1 8DJ T 0845-600 0877
E RegulatoryAppeals@tribunals.gsi.gov.uk

First-tier Tribunal (Environment) was created to decide appeals regarding civil sanctions made by environmental regulators. It forms part of the General Regulatory Chamber and was established in April 2010. Panels usually consist of a tribunal judge and two members, all of whom are appointed by the Lord Chancellor. The jurisdiction of the tribunal extends to England and Wales.
Principal Judge, Judge Warren

ESTATE AGENTS
PO Box 9300, Leicester LE1 8DJ T 0845-600 0877
E RegulatoryAppeals@tribunals.gsi.gov.uk

First-tier Tribunal (Estate Agents) hears appeals against decisions made by the Office of Fair Trading pertaining to orders preventing a person from being employed as an estate agent when that person has been, for example, convicted of fraud or another offence involving dishonesty. The tribunal also hears appeals relating to decisions refusing to revoke or vary a prohibition order or warning order under the 1979 Estate Agents Act, as

well as appeals regarding the issuing of a warning order when a person has not fulfilled their obligations under the Act.
Principal Judge, His Hon. Judge Wulwik

GAMBLING APPEALS

PO Box 9300, Leicester LE1 8DJ
T 0845-600 0877 E RegulatoryAppeals@tribunals.gsi.gov.uk

First-tier Tribunal (Gambling) hears and decides appeals against decisions made by the Gambling Commission. The cases heard by the tribunal involve the provision and withdrawal of both operating and personal management licenses. The tribunal comprises 12 judges, and each appeal is heard by one judicial member or a panel of members, depending on the complexity of the specific case.
Principal Judge, Judge Warren

IMMIGRATION SERVICES

7th Floor, Victory House, 30–34 Kingsway, London WC2B 6EX
T 020-3077 5860 E imset@tribunals.gsi.gov.uk

First-tier tribunal (Immigration Services) is an independent judicial body established in 2000 to provide a forum in which appeals against decisions of the Immigration Services Commissioner and complaints made by the Immigration Services Commissioner can be heard and determined.

There is a principal judge, who is the judicial head; other judicial members, who must be legally qualified; lay members, who must have substantial experience in immigration services or in the law and procedure relating to immigration; and a secretary, who is responsible for administration. The tribunal can sit anywhere in the UK.
Principal Judge, Judge Hunter, QC

INFORMATION RIGHTS

Arnhem House Support Centre, PO Box 9300, Leicester LE1 8DJ
T 0300-1234 504 E informationtribunal@tribunals.gsi.gov.uk

First-tier Tribunal (Information Rights) determines appeals against notices issued by the Information Commissioner. The principal judge and other judges are appointed by the Lord Chancellor and must be legally qualified. Members are appointed by the Lord Chancellor to represent the interests of data users or data subjects. A tribunal consists of the principal judge and one other judge sitting with two of the members.
Principal Judge, Judge Angel

LOCAL GOVERNMENT STANDARDS IN ENGLAND

York House, 31–36 York Place, Leeds, West Yorkshire LS1 2ED
T 0113-389 6086 E AP-enquiries@tribunals.gsi.gov.uk

First-tier Tribunal (Local Government Standards in England) was formed on 18 January 2010. It replaces the tribunal created by the Local Government Act 2000 to decide references and appeals regarding the conduct of members of local authorities.
Principal Judge, Judge Laverick

TRANSPORT

7th Floor, Victory House, 30–34 Kingsway, London WC2B 6EX
T 020-3077 5860 E transport@tribunals.gsi.gov.uk

First-tier Tribunal (Transport) hears appeals against decisions of the Registrar of Approved Driving Instructors, hears and decides appeals for London service permits against decisions made by Transport for London

and is able to resolve disputes over postal charges under the Postal Services Act 2000. The tribunal consists of a legally qualified principal judge, other judicial members, and lay members. The principal judge and legal members are appointed by the Lord Chancellor and the lay members by the transport secretary.
Principal Judge, Judge Brodrick

HEALTH, EDUCATION AND SOCIAL CARE CHAMBER

President, His Hon. Judge Sycamore

CARE STANDARDS

Mowden Hall, Staindrop Road, Darlington, Co Durham DL3 9BG
T 01325-392712 E cst@tribunals.gsi.gov.uk

First-tier Tribunal (Care Standards) was established under the Protection of Children Act 1999 and considers appeals in relation to decisions made about the inclusion of individuals' names on the list of those considered unsuitable to work with children or vulnerable adults, restrictions from teaching and employment in schools/further education institutions, and the registration of independent schools. It also deals with general registration decisions made about care homes, children's homes, childcare providers, nurses' agencies, social workers, residential family centres, independent hospitals and fostering agencies. The tribunal's principal judge appoints the panels for each case.
Deputy Chamber President, Judge Aitken

MENTAL HEALTH

Secretariat: PO Box 8793, 5th Floor, Leicester LE1 8BN
T 0300-123 2203

The First-tier Tribunal (Mental Health) hears applications and references for people detained under the Mental Health Act 1983 (as amended by the Mental Health Act 2007). The judiciary and members are appointed by the Lord Chancellor and the tribunal's jurisdiction covers the whole of England. There is a separate mental health tribunal for Wales, which is administered and based in Cardiff, and a separate mental health review tribunal for Scotland.
Deputy Chamber President, Judge Hinchliffe

PRIMARY HEALTH LISTS

Mowden Hall, Staindrop Road, Darlington DL3 9BG
T 01325-391 091

First-tier Tribunal (Primary Health Lists) took over the role of the Family Health Services Appeal Authority on 18 January 2010. The tribunal is independent of the Department of Health and considers appeals against the decisions of primary care trusts (PCTs), including appeals by GPs, dentists, pharmacists and opticians regarding action taken against them. The tribunal allocates appeals and applications to panels normally consisting of a tribunal judge, a specialist member and a lay member. All members are appointed by the Lord Chancellor following recommendation from the Judicial Appointments Commission, or may be assigned from other areas of the tribunal.
Deputy Chamber President, Judge Aitken

SPECIAL EDUCATIONAL NEEDS AND DISABILITY

Ground Floor, Mowden Hall, Staindrop Road DL3 9BG
T 01325-392760
E sendistqueries@tribunals.gsi.gov.uk

First-tier Tribunal (Special Educational Needs and Disability) considers parents' appeals against the decisions of local authorities (LAs) about children's special educational needs if parents cannot reach agreement with the LA. It also considers claims of disability discrimination in schools.

Deputy Chamber President, Judge Aitken

IMMIGRATION AND ASYLUM CHAMBER

Administrative Support Centre, Birmingham AIT, PO Box 14619, Birmingham B16 6FQ
T 0300-123 1711 E customer.service@tribunals.gsi.gov.uk

The Immigration and Asylum Chamber replaced the Asylum and Immigration Tribunal in February 2010. It is an independent tribunal dealing with appeals against decisions made by the Home Office, such as the decision to refuse a person asylum, or the decision to refuse a person leave to remain in the UK. Judges and non-legal members are appointed by the Lord Chancellor. Appeals are heard by one or more immigration judges, sometimes accompanied by non-legal members.

President (acting), Judge Arfon-Jones

SOCIAL ENTITLEMENT CHAMBER

President, His Hon. Judge Martin

ASYLUM SUPPORT

2nd Floor, Anchorage House, 2 Clove Crescent, London E14 2BE
T 020-7538 6171

First-tier Tribunal (Asylum Support) deals with appeals against decisions made by the UK Border Agency (UKBA). The UKBA decides whether asylum seekers, failed asylum seekers and/or their dependants are entitled to support and accommodation on the grounds of destitution, as provided by Section 4 and Part IV of the Immigration and Asylum Act 1999. The tribunal can only consider appeals against a refusal or termination of support. It can, if appropriate, require the Secretary of State for the Home Department to reconsider the original decision, substitute the original decision with the tribunal's own decision or dismiss the appeal.

Principal Judge, Sehba Storey

CRIMINAL INJURIES COMPENSATION

Head Office, Wellington House, 134–136 Wellington Street, Glasgow G2 2XL T 0141-354 8555
Judicial Review Enquiries, 5th Floor, Fox Court, 14 Gray's Inn Road, London WC1X 8HN T 020-3206 0664
E enquiries-cicap@tribunals.gsi.gov.uk

First-tier Tribunal (Criminal Injuries Compensation) determines appeals against review decisions made by the Criminal Injuries Compensation Authority on applications for compensation made by victims of violent crime. It only considers appeals on claims made on or after 1 April 1996 under the Criminal Injuries Compensation Scheme.

Principal Judge, Anthony Summers

SOCIAL SECURITY AND CHILD SUPPORT

Administrative Support Centre, PO Box 14620, Birmingham B16 6FR
T 0845-408 3500

First-tier Tribunal (Social Security and Child Support) arranges and hears appeals on a range of decisions made by the Department for Work and Pensions, HM Revenue and Customs, and local authorities. Appeals considered include those concerned with income support, jobseeker's allowance, child support, tax credits, retirement pensions, housing benefit, council tax benefit, disability living allowance, vaccine damage and compensation recovery. It is headed by the president of the Social Entitlement Chamber.

The tribunal also contains an executive agency responsible for the administration of appeals, headed by the chief executive of the HM Courts and Tribunals Service.

Judicial Lead, His Hon. Judge Martin

TAX CHAMBER

45 Bedford Square, London WC1B 3DN
T 0845-223 8080 E taxappeals@tribunals.gsi.gov.uk

The Tax Chamber, established on 1 April 2009, replaced four separate tax tribunals: the General Commissioners of Income Tax, the Special Commissioners, the VAT and Duties Tribunals, and section 706 tribunals. The chamber hears most appeals against decisions of HM Revenue and Customs in relation to tax. The chamber listens to appeals about income tax; corporation tax; capital gains tax; inheritance tax; national insurance contributions; and VAT or duties, and appeals can be made by individuals or organisations, single taxpayers or large multinational companies. Appeals are heard by legally qualified judges, non-legally qualified expert members or a mix of the two. The chamber has jurisdiction throughout the UK.

President, His Hon. Colin Bishopp, QC

WAR PENSIONS AND ARMED FORCES COMPENSATION CHAMBER

5th Floor, Fox Court, 14 Gray's Inn Road, London WC1X 8HN
T 020-3206 0705 E armedforces.chamber@hmcts.gsi.gov.uk

The War Pensions and Armed Forces Compensation Chamber of the First-tier Tribunal is the successor to the Pensions Appeal Tribunal which has existed in different forms since the War Pensions Act 1919. The tribunal hears appeals brought by ex-servicemen and women against decisions of the Secretary of State for Defence under the war pensions legislation for injuries sustained before 5th April 2005 and under the armed forces compensation scheme for injuries after that date. Under the war pensions legislation, the tribunal decides on entitlement to a war pension, the degree of disablement and entitlement to certain allowances (eg for mobility needs). Under the armed forces compensation scheme, the tribunal decides both the entitlement to an award and the tariff level of the award. The tribunal's jurisdiction covers England and Wales.

President, Judge Bano

PENSIONS APPEAL TRIBUNALS FOR SCOTLAND

George House, 126 George Street, Edinburgh EH2 4HH
T 0131-271 4340 E info@patscotland.org.uk
W www.patscotland.org.uk
President, C. M. McEachran, QC

UPPER TRIBUNAL

Comprising four separate chambers, the Upper Tribunal deals mostly with appeals from, and enforcement of, decisions taken by the First-tier Tribunal, but it also handles some cases that do not go through the First-tier Tribunal. Additionally, It has assumed some of the supervisory powers of the courts to deal with the actions of tribunals, government departments and some other public authorities. All the decision-makers of the Upper Tribunal are judges or expert members sitting in a panel chaired by a judge, and are specialists in the areas of law they handle. Over time their decisions are expected to build comprehensive case law for each area covered by the tribunals.

ADMINISTRATIVE APPEALS CHAMBER

5th Floor, Chichester Rents, 81 Chancery Lane, London WC2A 1DD

T 020-7911 7085 E adminappeals@tribunals.gsi.gov.uk

The Administrative Appeals Chamber deals with appeals from the Social Entitlement Chamber, the War Pensions and Armed Forces Compensation Chamber, the Health, Education and Social Care Chamber and the General Regulatory Chamber of the First-tier Tribunal, Forfeiture Act references and appeals in cases about safeguarding vulnerable groups. The Upper Tribunal in Northern Ireland deals with appeals from the Pensions Appeal Tribunal for Northern Ireland. There are 16 full-time judges and 17 deputy judges who sit part-time. Judges normally sit on their own and most of their cases are decided without oral hearings.
President, Mr Justice Walker

OFFICE OF THE SOCIAL SECURITY COMMISSIONERS AND CHILD SUPPORT COMMISSIONERS FOR NORTHERN IRELAND

Bedford House, 3rd Floor, 16–22 Bedford Street, Belfast BT2 7FD

T 028-9072 8731

E socialsecuritycommissioners@courtsni.gov.uk

W www.courtsni.gov.uk

The Social Security Commissioners and Child Support Commissioners in Northern Ireland are the specialised members of the judiciary appointed to determine appeals on points of law from appeal tribunals under the Social Security and Child Support legislation. They also have jurisdiction to deal with questions arising under the Forfeiture (NI) Order 1982. There are two Commissioners for Northern Ireland.
Chief Commissioner, Dr Kenneth Mullan

IMMIGRATION AND ASYLUM CHAMBER

Arnhem Support Centre, PO Box 6987, Leicester LE1 6ZX

T 0845-6000 877 E customer.service@tribunals.gsi.gov.uk

The Immigration and Asylum Chamber was created on 15 February 2010. It hears appeals against decisions made by the Immigration and Asylum Chamber in the First-tier Tribunal in matters of immigration, asylum and nationality. Appeals are heard by one or more senior or designated immigration judges, sometimes accompanied by non-legal members.
President, Mr Justice Blake

LANDS CHAMBER

45 Bedford Square, London WC1B 3AS

T 020-7612 9710 E lands@tribunals.gsi.gov.uk

The Lands Tribunal determines questions relating to the valuation of land, rating appeals from valuation tribunals, appeals from leasehold valuation tribunals and residential property tribunals, applications to discharge or modify restrictions on the use of land, and compulsory purchase compensation. The tribunal may also arbitrate under a reference by consent. Cases are usually heard by a single member of the tribunal but they may sometimes be heard by two or three members.
President, Judge Bartlett, QC

LANDS TRIBUNAL FOR SCOTLAND

George House, 126 George Street, Edinburgh EH2 4HH

T 0131-271 4350 E mailbox@lands-tribunal-scotland.org.uk

W www.lands-tribunal-scotland.org.uk

The Lands Tribunal for Scotland has much the same remit as the tribunal for England and Wales but also covers questions relating to tenants' rights to buy their homes under the Housing (Scotland) Act 1987 and appeals under the Land Registration (Scotland) Act 1979 and the Land Reform (Scotland) Act 2004. It is not part of HM Courts and Tribunals Service. The president is appointed by the Lord President of the Court of Session.
President, Hon. Lord McGhie, QC

TAX AND CHANCERY CHAMBER

45 Bedford Square, London WC1B 3DN

T 020-7612 9700 E financeandtaxappeals@tribunals.gsi.gov.uk

The Tax and Chancery Chamber decides applications for permission to appeal and appeals on point of law from decisions of the first-tier tribunal in tax or charity cases. The judiciary consists of high court judges and specialist tax judiciary, and the tribunal has jurisdiction throughout the UK. The jurisdiction of the former Financial Services and Markets tribunal transferred to the chamber in April 2010. As a result the chamber now hears appeals against decisions issued by the Financial Services Authority and from the Pensions Regulator.
President, Mr Justice Warren

EMPLOYMENT TRIBUNALS

ENGLAND AND WALES

Ground Floor, Victory House, 30–34 Kingsway, London WC2B 6EX

T 0845-795 9775

Employment Tribunals for England and Wales sit in 12 regions. The tribunals deal with matters of employment law, redundancy, dismissal, contract disputes, sexual, racial and disability discrimination and related areas of dispute which may arise in the workplace. A public register of judgments is held at 100 Southgate Street, Bury St Edmunds, Suffolk IP33 2AQ.

Chairs, who may be full-time or part-time, are legally qualified. They, along with the tribunal members, are appointed by the Ministry of Justice.
President, David John Latham

SCOTLAND

Central Office, Eagle Building, 215 Bothwell Street, Glasgow G2 7TS

T 0141-204 0730

Tribunals in Scotland have the same remit as those in England and Wales. Employment judges are appointed by the Lord President of the Court of Session and lay members by the Lord Chancellor.
President, Shona Simon

EMPLOYMENT APPEAL TRIBUNAL

London Office: Audit House, 58 Victoria Embankment, London EC4Y 0DS

T 020-7273 1041 E londoneat@tribunals.gsi.gov.uk

Edinburgh Office: 52 Melville Street, Edinburgh EH3 7HF

T 0131-225 3963 E edinburgheat@tribunals.gsi.gov.uk

The Employment Appeal Tribunal hears appeals (on points of law only) arising from decisions made by

employment tribunals. Hearings are conducted by a judge, either alone or accompanied by two lay members who have practical experience in employment relations.
President, Hon. Mr Justice Underhill
Registrar, Pauline Donleavy

SPECIAL IMMIGRATION APPEALS COMMISSION
PO Box 36469, London EC4A 1WR
T 0845-600 0877 E customer.service@tribunals.gsi.gov.uk

The commission was set up under the Special Immigration Appeals Commission Act 1997. It remains separate from the First-tier and Upper Tribunal structure but is part of HM Courts and Tribunals Service. Its main function is to consider appeals against orders for deportations in cases which involve, in the main, considerations of national security or the public interest. The commission also hears appeals against decisions to deprive persons of citizenship status. Members are appointed by the Lord Chancellor.
Chair, Hon. Mr Justice Mitting

INDEPENDENT TRIBUNALS

The following represents a selection of tribunals not administered by HM Courts and Tribunals Service.

AGRICULTURAL LAND TRIBUNALS
c/o DEFRA, Area 8E (Millbank), 17 Smith Square, London SW1P 3JR
T 0845-933 5577 E helpline@defra.gsi.gov.uk
W www.defra.gov.uk

Agricultural Land Tribunals settle disputes and other issues between landlords and tenants of agricultural holdings under the Agricultural Holdings Act 1986, mainly in relation to succession rights and notices to quit. The tribunals also settle drainage disputes between neighbours under the Land Drainage Act 1991.

There are seven tribunals covering England and one covering Wales. For each tribunal the Lord Chancellor appoints a chair and one or more deputies (barristers or solicitors of at least seven years' standing). The Lord Chancellor also appoints three panels of lay members: the 'landowners' panel, the 'farmers' panel and the 'drainage' panel.

Each tribunal is an independent statutory body with jurisdiction only within its own geographical area. A separate tribunal is constituted for each case, and consists of a chair and two lay members nominated by the chair.
Chairs (England), Shirley Evans; His Hon. John Machin; George Newsom; Paul de la Piquerie; His Hon. Robert Taylor; Nigel Thomas; Martin Wood
Chair (Wales), James Buxton

CIVIL AVIATION AUTHORITY
CAA House, 45–59 Kingsway, London WC2B 6TE
T 020-7453 6172 E legal@caa.co.uk
W www.caa.co.uk

The Civil Aviation Authority (CAA) does not have a separate tribunal department as such, but for certain purposes the CAA must conform to tribunal requirements. For example, to deal with appeals against the refusal or revocation of aviation licences and certificates issued by the CAA, and the allocation of routes outside of the EU to airlines.

The chair and four non-executive members who may sit on panels for tribunal purposes are appointed by the Secretary of State for Transport.
Chair, Dame Deirdre Hutton, DBE

COMPETITION APPEAL TRIBUNAL
Victoria House, Bloomsbury Place, London WC1A 2EB
T 020-7979 7979 E info@catribunal.org.uk
W www.catribunal.org.uk

The Competition Appeal Tribunal (CAT) is a specialist tribunal established to hear certain cases in the sphere of UK competition and economic regulatory law. It hears appeals against decisions of the Office of Fair Trading (OFT) and their sectoral regulators, and also decisions of the OFT, Secretary of State for Business, Innovation and Skills and the Competition Commission. The CAT also has jurisdiction to award damages in respect of infringements of EU or UK competition law and to hear appeals against decisions of OFCOM.

Cases are heard before a panel consisting of three members: either the president or a member of the panel of chairs and two ordinary members. The members of the panel of chairs are judges of the Chancery Division of the high court and other senior lawyers. The ordinary members have expertise in law and/or related fields. The president and chairs are appointed by the Lord Chancellor; the ordinary members are appointed by the secretary of state.
President, Hon. Mr Justice Barling

COPYRIGHT TRIBUNAL
21 Bloomsbury Street, London WC1B 3HF
T 020-7034 2836 E copyright.tribunal@ipo.gov.uk
W www.ipo.gov.uk/copy/tribunal

The Copyright Tribunal resolves disputes over the terms and conditions of licences offered by, or licensing schemes operated by, collective licensing bodies in the copyright and related rights area. Its decisions are appealable to the high court on points of law only.

The chair and two deputy chairs are appointed by the Lord Chancellor. Up to eight ordinary members are appointed by the Secretary of State for Business, Innovation and Skills. The tribunal operates on a panel basis and its members have wide expertise in copyright and rights, business and public administration.
Chair, His Hon. Judge Birss, QC

INDUSTRIAL TRIBUNALS AND THE FAIR EMPLOYMENT TRIBUNAL (NORTHERN IRELAND)
Killymeal House, 2 Cromac Quay, Ormeau Road, Belfast BT7 2JD
T 028-9032 7666 E mail@employmenttribunalsni.org
W www.employmenttribunalsni.co.uk

The industrial tribunal system in Northern Ireland was set up in 1965 and has a similar remit to the employment tribunals in the rest of the UK. There is also a Fair Employment Tribunal, which hears and determines individual cases of alleged religious or political discrimination in employment. Employers can appeal to the Fair Employment Tribunal if they consider the directions of the Equality Commission to be unreasonable, inappropriate or unnecessary, and the Equality Commission can make application to the tribunal for the enforcement of undertakings or directions with which an employer has not complied.

The president, vice-president and chairs of the Industrial Tribunal and the Fair Employment Tribunal are

appointed by the Lord Chancellor. The panel members to both the industrial tribunals and the Fair Employment Tribunal were appointed by the Department for Employment and Learning, but any future appointments will be made through a full public appointment process.
President of the Industrial Tribunals and the Fair Employment Tribunal, Eileen McBride

INVESTIGATORY POWERS TRIBUNAL

PO Box 33220, London SW1H 9ZQ

T 020-7035 3711 E info@ipt-uk.com W www.ipt-uk.com

The Investigatory Powers Tribunal replaced the Interception of Communications Tribunal, the Intelligence Services Tribunal, the Security Services Tribunal and the complaints function of the commissioner appointed under the Police Act 1997.

The Regulation of Investigatory Powers Act 2000 (RIPA) provides for a tribunal made up of senior members of the legal profession, independent of the government and appointed by the Queen, to consider all complaints against the intelligence services and those against public authorities in respect of powers covered by RIPA; and to consider proceedings brought under section 7 of the Human Rights Act 1998 against the intelligence services and law enforcement agencies in respect of these powers.
President, Rt. Hon. Lord Justice Mummery

NATIONAL HEALTH SERVICE TRIBUNAL (SCOTLAND)

Anderson Strathern LLP, 24 Blythswood Square, Glasgow G2 4BG

T 0141-242 6060 E nhstribunal@nhs.net

The Scottish National Health Service Tribunal considers representations that the continued inclusion of a family health service practitioner (eg a doctor, dentist, optometrist or pharmacist) on a health board's list would be prejudicial to the efficiency of the service concerned, by virtue either of fraudulent practices or unsatisfactory personal or professional conduct. If this is established, the tribunal has the power to disqualify practitioners from working in the NHS family health services. The tribunal sits when required and is composed of a chair, one lay member, and one practitioner member drawn from a representative professional panel. The chair is appointed by the Lord President of the Court of Session, and the lay member and the members of the professional panel are appointed by the Scottish ministers.
Chair, J. Michael D. Graham

RESIDENTIAL PROPERTY TRIBUNAL SERVICE

10 Alfred Place, London WC1E 7LR

T 0845-600 3178 E rptscorporateunit@communities.gsi.gov.uk W www.rpts.gov.uk

The Residential Property Tribunal Service provides members to sit on panels for the Rent Assessment Committees, Residential Property Tribunals and Leasehold Valuation Tribunals, and serves the private-rented and leasehold property market in England by resolving disputes between leaseholders, tenants and landlords. The president and chair are appointed by the Lord Chancellor and other members are appointed by the Department for Communities and Local Government and the Ministry of Justice.
Senior President, Siobhan McGrath

SOLICITORS' DISCIPLINARY TRIBUNAL

3rd Floor, Gate House, 1 Farringdon Street, London EC4M 7NS

T 020-7329 4808 E enquiries@solicitorsdt.com W www.solicitorstribunal.org.uk

The Solicitors' Disciplinary Tribunal is an independent statutory body whose members are appointed by the Master of the Rolls. The tribunal considers applications made to it alleging either professional misconduct and/or a breach of the statutory rules by which solicitors are bound against an individually named solicitor, former solicitor, registered foreign lawyer, or solicitor's clerk. The tribunal has around 60 members; two-thirds are solicitor members and one-third are lay members.
President, Jeremy Barnecutt

SOLICITORS' DISCIPLINE TRIBUNAL (SCOTTISH)

Unit 3.5, The Granary Business Centre, Coal Road, Cupar, Fife KY15 5YQ

T 01334-659088 W www.ssdt.org.uk

The Scottish Solicitors' Discipline Tribunal is an independent statutory body with a panel of 21 members, 11 of whom are solicitors; members are appointed by the Lord President of the Court of Session. Its principal function is to consider complaints of misconduct against solicitors in Scotland.
Chair, A. Cockburn

TRAFFIC PENALTY TRIBUNAL

Barlow House, Minshull Street, Manchester M1 3DZ

T 0161-242 5252 E info@trafficpenaltytribunal.gov.uk W www.trafficpenaltytribunal.gov.uk

The Traffic Penalty Tribunal considers appeals from motorists against penalty charge notices issued by Civil Enforcement Authorities in England (outside London) and Wales under the Traffic Management Act 2004, and considers appeals against bus lane contraventions in England (outside London) under the Bus Lane Contraventions Regulations 2005. Parking adjudicators are appointed with the express consent of the Lord Chancellor and must be lawyers of five years' standing. Cases are decided by a single adjudicator, either in a postal, telephone or a personal hearing.
Head of Service, Louise Hutchinson

VALUATION TRIBUNAL SERVICE

2nd Floor, Black Lion House, 45 Whitechapel Road, London E1 1DU

T 0300-123 2035 W www.valuationtribunal.gov.uk

The Valuation Tribunal Service (VTS) was created as a corporate body by the Local Government Act 2003, and is responsible for providing or arranging the services required for the operation of the Valuation Tribunal for England. The VTS board consists of a chair and members appointed by the secretary of state. The VTS is funded by the Department for Communities and Local Government.
Chair, VTS Board, Anne Galbraith, CBE

VALUATION TRIBUNAL FOR ENGLAND

President's Office, 2nd Floor, Black Lion House, 45 Whitechapel Road, London E1 1DU

T 020-7246 3900 W www.valuationtribunal.gov.uk

The Valuation Tribunal for England (VTE) came into being on 1 October 2009, replacing 56 valuation tribunals in England. Provision for the VTE was made in the Local Government and Public Involvement in Health Act 2007. The Valuation Tribunal for England hears appeals concerning council tax and non-domestic rating and land drainage rates. A separate tribunal is constituted for each hearing, and consists of a chair and two or three other members. A clerk, who is a paid employee of the VTS, is present to advise on points of procedure and law. The national president is the judicial head of a volunteer membership. Members will in future be appointed by the Judicial Appointments Commission.

President, Prof. Graham Zellick CBE, QC

VALUATION TRIBUNAL SERVICE FOR WALES

Governing Council of VTW, 22 Gold Tops, Newport, South Wales NP20 4PG

T 01633-266367 **E** VTWaleseast@vtw.gsi.gov.uk

The Valuation Tribunal for Wales (VTW) was established by the Valuation Tribunal for Wales Regulations 2010, and hears and determines appeals concerning council tax, non-domestic rating and drainage rates in Wales. The governing council, comprising the president, four regional representatives and one member who is appointed by the Welsh government, performs the management functions on behalf of the tribunal. Individual tribunal hearings are conducted by three members of the tribunal, supported by a clerk. These hearings are arranged locally.

Chief Executive, Simon Hill

OMBUDSMAN SERVICES

The following section is a listing of selected ombudsman services. Ombudsmen are a free, independent and impartial means of resolving certain disputes outside of the courts. These disputes are, in the majority of cases, concerned with whether something has been badly or unfairly handled (for example owing to delay, neglect, inefficiency or failure to follow proper procedures). Most ombudsman schemes are established by statute; they cover various public and private bodies and generally examine matters only after the relevant body has been given a reasonable opportunity to deal with the complaint.

After conducting an investigation an ombudsman will usually issue a written report, which normally suggests a resolution to the dispute and often includes recommendations concerning the improvement of procedures.

BRITISH AND IRISH OMBUDSMAN ASSOCIATION (BIOA)

PO Box 308, Twickenham TW1 9BE
T 020-8894 9272 E secretary@bioa.org.uk
W www.bioa.org.uk

The BIOA was established in 1994 and exists to provide information to the government, public bodies, and the public about ombudsmen and other complaint-handling services. An ombudsman scheme must meet four criteria in order to attain full BIOA membership: independence from the organisations the ombudsman has the power to investigate, fairness, effectiveness and public accountability. Associate membership is open to complaint-handling bodies that do not meet these criteria in full. Ombudsmen schemes from the UK, Ireland, British crown dependencies and overseas territories may apply to BIOA for membership.
Secretary, Ian Pattison

The following is a selection of organisations that are members of the BIOA.

FINANCIAL OMBUDSMAN SERVICE

South Quay Plaza, 183 Marsh Wall, London E14 9SR
T 020-7964 1000
E complaint.info@financial-ombudsman.org.uk
W www.financial-ombudsman.org.uk

The Financial Ombudsman Service settles individual disputes between businesses providing financial services and their customers. The service deals with around a million enquiries every year and settles over 100,000 disputes. The service examines complaints about most financial matters, including banking, insurance, mortgages, pensions, savings, loans and credit cards. *See also* Banking and Finance.
Chief Ombudsman and Chief Executive, Natalie Ceeney

HOUSING OMBUDSMAN SERVICE

81 Aldwych, London WC2B 4HN
T 020-7421 3800 E ihol@housing-ombudsman.org.uk
W www.housing-ombudsman.org.uk

The Housing Ombudsman Service, established in 1997, deals with complaints and disputes involving tenants and housing associations and social landlords, certain private-sector landlords and managing agents. The ombudsman has a statutory jurisdiction over all registered social landlords in England. Private and other landlords can join the service on a voluntary basis. Complaints from council/local authority tenants have to be made to the Local Government Ombudsman.
Ombudsman, Dr Mike Biles
Deputy Ombudsman, Rafael Runco

INDEPENDENT POLICE COMPLAINTS COMMISSION (IPCC)

90 High Holborn, London WC1V 6BH
T 0845-300 2002 E enquiries@ipcc.gsi.gov.uk
W www.ipcc.gov.uk

The IPCC succeeded the Police Complaints Authority in 2004. It was established under the Police Reform Act 2002. The IPCC has teams of investigators headed by commissioners in each of its regions to assist with the supervision and management of some police investigations. They also carry out independent investigations into serious incidents or allegations of misconduct by persons serving with the police. The IPCC decides on appeals against complaints investigated by the police service. It also has responsibility for investigating complaints of serious incidents, including death or injury, made against staff of HM Revenue and Customs, the Serious Organised Crime Agency and the United Kingdom Border Agency. The 12 commissioners of the IPCC must not previously have worked for the police.
Chair (interim), Len Jackson
Deputy Chairs, Deborah Glass
Chief Executive, Jane Furniss

LEGAL OMBUDSMAN

2nd Floor, Baskerville House, Centenary Square, Broad Street, Birmingham B1 2ND
T 0121-245 3100 E enquiries@legalombudsman.org.uk
W www.legalombudsman.org.uk

The Legal Ombudsman was set up by the Office for Legal Complaints under the Legal Services Act 2007 and replaced the Office of the Legal Services Ombudsman in 2010. The Legal Ombudsman is the single body for all consumer legal complaints in England and Wales. It aims to resolve disputes between individuals and authorised legal practitioners, including barristers, law costs draftsmen, legal executives, licensed conveyancers, notaries, patent attorneys, probate practitioners, registered European lawyers, solicitors and trade mark attorneys.
Chief Ombudsman, Adam Sampson

LOCAL GOVERNMENT OMBUDSMAN

Advice Team, PO Box 4771, Coventry CV4 OEH
T 0300-061 0614 W www.lgo.org.uk

The Local Government Ombudsman deals with complaints about councils and some other authorities and organisations, including education admission appeal panels and adult social care providers.

There are three ombudsmen in England, each with responsibility for different regions; they aim to provide satisfactory redress for complainants and better administration for the authorities. The ombudsmen investigate complaints about most council matters, including housing, planning, education, social care, consumer protection, drainage and council tax. *See also* Local Government.

Local Government Ombudsmen, Anne Seex; Jane Martin

NORTHERN IRELAND OMBUDSMAN

Progressive House, 33 Wellington Place, Belfast BT1 6HN
T 028-9023 3821 **E** ombudsman@ni-ombudsman.org.uk
W www.ni-ombudsman.org.uk

The ombudsman (also known as the Assembly Ombudsman for Northern Ireland and the Northern Ireland Commissioner for Complaints) is appointed under legislation with powers to investigate complaints by people claiming to have sustained injustice arising from action taken by a Northern Ireland government department, or any other public body within his remit. The ombudsman can investigate all local councils, education and library boards, health and social services boards and trusts, as well as all government departments and their agencies. As commissioner for complaints, the ombudsman can investigate complaints about doctors, dentists, pharmacists, optometrists and other healthcare professionals.

Ombudsman, Dr Tom Frawley, CBE
Deputy Ombudsman, Marie Anderson

OFFICE OF THE PENSIONS OMBUDSMAN

6th Floor, 11 Belgrave Road, London SW1V 1RB
T 020-7630 2200 **E** enquiries@pensions-ombudsman.org.uk
W www.pensions-ombudsman.org.uk

The Pensions Ombudsman is appointed by the Secretary of State for Work and Pensions, under the Pension Schemes Act 1993 as amended by the Pensions Act 1995. He investigates and decides complaints and disputes about the way that personal and occupational pension schemes are run. As the Ombudsman for the Board of the Pension Protection Fund, he can deal with disputes about the decisions made by the board or the actions of their staff. He also deals with appeals against decisions made by the scheme manager under the Financial Assistance Scheme.

Pensions Ombudsman, Tony King
Deputy Pensions Ombudsman, Jane Irvine

OMBUDSMAN SERVICES

Brew House, Wilderspool Park, Greenalls Avenue, Warrington WA4 6HL
W www.ombudsman-services.org

Ombudsman Services provides independent dispute resolution for the communications, copyright licensing, energy and property sectors.

Ombudsman Services: Communications investigates complaints from consumers about companies which provide communication services to the public.

Ombudsman Services: Copyright Licensing helps to resolve complaints from consumers regarding PRS for Music (formerly the Performing Right Society), its members, and those who may require or who have obtained a licence for the public performance of copyright music.

Ombudsman Services: Energy helps to resolve complaints from consumers about energy (gas and electricity companies).

Ombudsman Services: Property investigates complaints from consumers about chartered surveying companies, surveyors, estate agents and other property professionals.

Chair, Dame Janet Finch
Chief Ombudsman, Lewis Shand Smith
Ombudsmen, Andrew Walker *(Communications)*; Richard Sills *(Energy)*; Gillian Fleming *(Property)*

OMBUDSMAN SERVICES: COMMUNICATIONS

PO Box 730, Warrington WA4 6WU
T 0300-440 1614
E enquiries@os-communications.org

OMBUDSMAN SERVICES: COPYRIGHT LICENSING

PO Box 1124, Warrington WA4 9GH
T 0300-440 1601
E enquiries@os-cpl.org

OMBUDSMAN SERVICES: ENERGY

PO Box 966, Warrington WA4 9DF
T 0330-440 1624
E enquiries@os-energy.org

OMBUDSMAN SERVICES: PROPERTY

PO Box 1021, Warrington WA4 9FE
T 0300-440 1634
E enquiries@os-property.org

PARLIAMENTARY AND HEALTH SERVICE OMBUDSMAN

Millbank Tower, Millbank, London SW1P 4QP
T 0345-015 4033 **E** phso.enquiries@ombudsman.org.uk
W www.ombudsman.org.uk

The Parliamentary Ombudsman (also known as the Parliamentary Commissioner for Administration) is independent of government and is an officer of parliament. She is responsible for investigating complaints referred to her by MPs from members of the public who claim to have sustained injustice in consequence of maladministration by or on behalf of government departments and certain non-departmental public bodies in the UK. Certain types of action by government departments or bodies are excluded from investigation.

The Health Service Ombudsman is responsible for investigating complaints against National Health Service authorities and trusts in England that are not dealt with by those authorities to the satisfaction of the complainant. Complaints can be referred directly by the member of the public who claims to have sustained injustice or hardship in consequence of the failure in a service provided by a relevant body. The ombudsman's jurisdiction also covers complaints about family doctors, dentists, pharmacists and opticians, and complaints about actions resulting from clinical judgement.

The parliamentary and the health offices are traditionally held by the same person.

Parliamentary Ombudsman and Health Service Ombudsman, Ms A. Abraham
Deputy Ombudsman, Ms K.Hudson

PROPERTY OMBUDSMAN

Milford House, 43–55 Milford Street, Salisbury, Wiltshire SP1 2BP
T 01722-333306 **E** admin@tpos.co.uk
W www.tpos.co.uk

The Property Ombudsman service was established in 1998 and provides a service for dealing with disputes between estate agents (or residential letting agents) and consumers who are actual or potential buyers or sellers of residential property in the UK.

Complaints that the ombudsman considers include allegations of unfair treatment, maladministration and infringement of legal rights. The ombudsman's role is to resolve these complaints in full and final settlement and, where appropriate, make an award of financial compensation.

Ombudsman, Christopher Hamer

PUBLIC SERVICES OMBUDSMAN FOR WALES

1 Ffordd yr Hen Gae, Pencoed CF35 5LJ
T 01656-641150 E ask@ombudsman-wales.org.uk
W www.ombudsman-wales.org.uk

The office of Public Services Ombudsman for Wales was established, with effect from 1 April 2006, by the Public Services Ombudsman (Wales) Act 2005. The ombudsman, who is appointed by the Queen, investigates complaints of injustice caused by maladministration or service failure by the Assembly Commission (and public bodies sponsored by the assembly); Welsh government; National Health Service bodies, including GPs, family health service providers and hospitals; registered social landlords; local authorities, including community councils; fire and rescue authorities; police authorities; national park authorities; and countryside and environmental organisations. Free leaflets explaining the process of making a complaint are available from the ombudsman's office.

Ombudsman, Peter Tyndall

REMOVALS INDUSTRY OMBUDSMAN SCHEME

PO Box 3862, Gerrards Cross, Bucks SL9 7WG
T 01753-888206 E ombudsman@removalsombudsman.co.uk
W www.removalsombudsman.org.uk

The Removals Industry Ombudsman Scheme was established to resolve disputes between removal companies that are members of the scheme and their clients, both domestic and commercial. The ombudsman investigates complaints such as breaches of contract, unprofessional conduct, delays, or breaches in the code of practice.

Ombudsman, Matti Alderson

SCOTTISH PUBLIC SERVICES OMBUDSMAN

Freepost EH641, Edinburgh EH3 0BR
T 0800-377 7330 E ask@spso.org.uk
W www.spso.org.uk

The Scottish Public Services Ombudsman (SPSO) was established in 2002. The SPSO is the final stage for complaints about public services in Scotland. Its service is free and independent. SPSO investigates complaints about the Scottish government, its agencies and departments; colleges and universities; councils; housing associations; NHS Scotland; prisons; and most other Scottish public bodies. The Ombudsman looks at complaints regarding poor service or administrative failure and can only look at complaints that have been through the formal complaints process of the organisation concerned.

Scottish Public Services Ombudsman, Jim Martin

WATERWAYS OMBUDSMAN

PO Box 35, York YO60 6WW
T 01347-879075 E enquiries@waterways-ombudsman.org
W www.waterways-ombudsman.org

The Waterways Ombudsman considers complaints of maladministration or unfairness made against British Waterways or its subsidiaries, including British Waterways Marinas Limited. Complaints concerning the waterways responsibilities of the Environment Agency should be directed to the Parliamentary and Health Service Ombudsman.

Ombudsman, Hilary Bainbridge

THE POLICE SERVICE

There are 52 police forces in the United Kingdom: 43 in England and Wales, including the Metropolitan Police and the City of London Police, eight in Scotland and the Police Service of Northern Ireland. Forces' areas are coterminous with one or more local authority areas. The Isle of Man, Jersey and Guernsey have their own forces responsible for policing in their respective islands and bailiwicks. The Serious Organised Crime Agency (SOCA) is responsible for the investigation of national and international serious organised crime.

Police authorities are independent bodies, responsible for the supervision of local policing. There are 43 police authorities in England and Wales, plus an additional one for British Transport Police. Most police authorities have 17 members, comprising nine local councillors and eight independent members, of whom at least one must be a magistrate. Authorities which are responsible for larger areas may have more members, such as the Metropolitan Police Authority, which has 23 members: 12 drawn from the London Assembly, 10 independent members and one magistrate. The Corporation of London acts as the police authority for the City of London Police. In Scotland, six of the forces are maintained by joint police boards, made up of local councillors from each council in the force area; the other two constabularies (Dumfries & Galloway and Fife) are directly administered by their respective councils. The Northern Ireland Policing Board is an independent public body consisting of 19 political and independent members.

Police forces in England, Scotland and Wales are financed by central and local government grants and a precept on the council tax. The Police Service of Northern Ireland is wholly funded by central government. The police authorities, subject to the approval of the home secretary (in England and Wales), the Northern Ireland Minister of Justice and to regulations, are responsible for appointing the Chief Constable. In England and Wales the latter are responsible for the force's budget, levying the precept on the council tax, publishing annual policing plans and reports, setting local objectives, monitoring performance targets and appointing or dismissing senior officers. In Scotland the police authorities are responsible for setting the force's budget, providing the resources necessary to police the area adequately and appointing officers of the rank of Assistant Chief Constable and above. In Northern Ireland, the Northern Ireland Policing Board exercises similar functions.

The home secretary, the Northern Ireland Minister of Justice and the Scottish government are responsible for the organisation, administration and operation of the police service. They regulate police ranks, discipline, hours of duty and pay and allowances. All police forces are subject to inspection by HM Inspectors of Constabulary, who report to the home secretary, Scottish government or the Northern Ireland Minister of Justice.

COMPLAINTS

The Independent Police Complaints Commission (IPCC) was established under the Police Reform Act 2002 and became operational on 1 April 2004. The IPCC is responsible for carrying out independent investigations into serious incidents or allegations of misconduct by those serving with the police in England and Wales, HM Revenue and Customs, SOCA and the UK Border Agency. It has the power to initiate, undertake and oversee investigations and is also responsible for the way in which complaints are handled by local police forces. Complaints regarding local operational issues or quality of service should be made directly to the Chief Constable of the police force concerned or to the local police authority.

If a complaint is relatively minor, the police force will attempt to resolve it internally and an official investigation might not be required. In more serious cases the IPCC or police force may refer the case to the Crown Prosecution Service, which will decide whether to bring criminal charges against the officer(s) involved. An officer who is dismissed, required to resign or reduced in rank, whether as a result of a complaint or not, can appeal to a police appeals tribunal established by the relevant police authority.

Under the Police, Public Order and Criminal Justice (Scotland) Act 2006, which came into force on 1 April 2007, the Police Complaints Commissioner for Scotland is responsible for providing independent scrutiny of the way in which Scottish police forces, authorities and policing agencies handle complaints from the public. The commissioner also has the power to direct police forces to re-examine any complaints which are not considered to have been dealt with satisfactorily. If there is a suggestion of criminal activity, the complaint is investigated by a procurator fiscal.

The Police Ombudsman for Northern Ireland provides an independent police complaints system for Northern Ireland, dealing with all stages of the complaints procedure. Complaints that cannot be resolved informally are investigated and the ombudsman recommends a suitable course of action to the Chief Constable of the Police Service of Northern Ireland or the Northern Ireland Policing Board based on the investigation's findings. The ombudsman may recommend that a police officer be prosecuted, but the decision to prosecute a police officer rests with the Director of Public Prosecutions.

INDEPENDENT POLICE COMPLAINTS
  COMMISSION, 90 High Holborn, London WC1V 6BH
  T 0845-300 2002 E enquiries@ipcc.gsi.gov.uk
  W www.ipcc.gov.uk
POLICE COMPLAINTS COMMISSIONER FOR
  SCOTLAND, Hamilton House, Hamilton Business Park,
  ML3 0QA T 0808-178 5577 E enquiries@pcc-scotland.org
  W www.pcc-scotland.org
  Police Complaints Commissioner for Scotland, John
    McNeill
POLICE OMBUDSMAN FOR NORTHERN IRELAND,
  New Cathedral Buildings, St Anne's Square, 11 Church
  Street, Belfast BT1 1PG T 028-9082 8600
  E info@policeombudsman.org
  W www.policeombudsman.org
  Police Ombudsman, Al Hutchinson

POLICE SERVICES

FORENSIC SCIENCE SERVICE

Headquarters: Trident Court, 2920 Solihull Parkway, Birmingham Business Park, Birmingham B37 7YN
T 0121-329 5200 W www.forensic.gov.uk

The Forensic Science Service (FSS) is a government-owned company which is independent from the police service. It provides forensic science and technology services to police forces in England and Wales and other law enforcement agencies such as the Crown Prosecution Service, SOCA, MoD Police and Guarding Agency, British Transport Police and HM Revenue and Customs. Services are also available to defence lawyers and commercial companies. The FSS primarily covers England and Wales but can provide services worldwide.
Chair, Bill Griffiths

NATIONAL EXTREMISM TACTICAL COORDINATION UNIT

PO Box 525, Huntingdon PE29 9AL
T 01480-425091 E mailbox@netcu.pnn.police.uk
W www.netcu.org.uk

The National Extremism Tactical Coordination Unit (NETCU) provides the police service of England and Wales and other law enforcement agencies with tactical advice and guidance on policing domestic extremism and associated criminality. The unit also supports organisations and companies that are the targets of domestic extremism campaigns. NETCU is funded by the Home Office, is accountable to the National Coordinator for Domestic Extremism and forms part of the Association of Chief Police Officers' Terrorism and Allied Matters business unit.
National Coordinator for Domestic Extremism,
  Anton Setchell

NATIONAL POLICING IMPROVEMENT AGENCY

Fry Building, 2 Marsham Street, London SW1P 4DF
T 020-3113 6000 E enquiries@npia.pnn.police.uk
W www.npia.police.uk

The National Policing Improvement Agency (NPIA) was formed in April 2007 to make a unique contribution to improving public safety. The NPIA is owned and governed by the board which comprises representatives of the Association of Chief Police Officers, the Association of Police Authorities and the Home Office, in addition to the chair, chief executive and two independent members. The board is responsible for agreeing the budget and setting the objectives for the NPIA.

The NPIA's remit is to improve public safety through the provision of critical national services, building capability across the police service, and providing professional expertise to police forces and authorities. It is responsible for the procurement and deployment of information and communications technology systems to support and improve policing and works actively with police forces to develop a wide range of learning and professional development programmes. The NPIA is charged with improving policing in England and Wales but it is also connected to policing bodies in Scotland and Northern Ireland and collaborates with them on some initiatives.
Chief Executive, Nick Gargan
Chair, Peter Holland, CBE

NPIA MISSING PERSONS BUREAU

Foxley Hall, Bramshill, Hook, Hampshire RG27 0JW
T 01256-602979
E missingpersonsbureau@npia.pnn.police.uk
W www.npia.police.uk/en/10200.htm

The NPIA Missing Persons Bureau was launched in April 2008 within the National Policing Improvement Agency. The NPIA Missing Persons Bureau acts as the centre for the exchange of information connected with the search for missing persons nationally and internationally alongside the police and other related organisations. The unit focuses on cross-matching missing persons with unidentified persons or bodies by maintaining records, including a dental index of ante-mortem chartings of long-term missing persons and post-mortem chartings from unidentified bodies. The bureau also manages the missing children website (W www.missingkids.co.uk) and coordinates the child rescue alert services.

Information is supplied and collected for all persons who have been missing in the UK for over 72 hours (or fewer where police deem appropriate), foreign nationals reported missing in the UK, UK nationals reported missing abroad and all unidentified bodies and persons found within the UK.

SERIOUS ORGANISED CRIME AGENCY

PO Box 8000, London SE11 5EN T 0370-496 7622
W www.soca.gov.uk

The Serious Organised Crime Agency (SOCA) tackles serious organised crime affecting the UK and its citizens and is the custodian of a range of national and international capabilities. SOCA works to priorities set by the home secretary which currently include Class A drugs, people smuggling and human trafficking, major gun crime, fraud, cyber crime and money laundering. SOCA works to bring serious criminals to justice and uses many other tactics to disrupt crime and to make it harder to commit crime.

The National Crime Agency, to be established in 2013, will replace SOCA and the Child Exploitation and Online Protection Centre.
Chair, Sir Ian Andrews, CBE, TD
Director-General, Trevor Pearce, QPM

POLICE FORCES

ENGLAND*

Force	Telephone	Strength†	Chief Constable
Avon and Somerset	0845-456 7000	3,261	C. Port
Bedfordshire	01234-841212	1,260	Alfred Hitchcock, QPM
Cambridgeshire	0345-456 4564	1,421	Simon Parr
Cheshire	0845-458 0000	2,160	D. Whatton, QPM
Cleveland	01642-326326	1,695	Sean Price, QPM
Cumbria	0845-330 0247	1,236	Craig Mackey, QPM
Derbyshire	0345-123 3333	2,122	M. Creedon, QPM
Devon and Cornwall	0845-277 7444	3,469	Stephen Otter, QPM
Dorset	01202-222222	1,456	M. Baker, QPM
Durham	0345-606 0365	1,443	T. Stoddart, QPM
Essex	0300-333 4444	3,690	Jim Barker-McCardle, QPM
Gloucestershire	0845-090 1234	1,309	Tony Melville
Greater Manchester	0161-872 5050	7,849	Peter Fahy, QPM
Hampshire	0845-045 4545	3,615	Alex Marshall
Hertfordshire	0845-330 0222	2,055	Frank Whiteley, QPM
Humberside	0845-606 0222	2,011	Tim Hollis, QPM
Kent	01622-690690	3,766	Ian Learmonth
Lancashire	01772-614444	3,447	Stephen Finnigan, CBE, QPM
Leicestershire	0116-222 2222	2,216	Simon Cole
Lincolnshire	01522-532222	1,208	R. Crompton
Merseyside	0151-709 6010	4,461	J. Murphy, QPM
Norfolk	0845-456 4567	1,648	P. Gormley
North Yorkshire	0845-606 0247	1,547	Grahame Maxwell
Northamptonshire	03000-111222	1,279	Adrian Lee
Northumbria	01661-872555	4,145	S. Sim
Nottinghamshire	0115-967 0999	2,352	J. Hodson, QPM
South Yorkshire	0114-220 2020	2,979	M. Hughes, QPM
Staffordshire	0300-123 4455	2,150	Mike Cunningham
Suffolk	01473-613500	1,258	Simon Ash
Surrey	0845-125 2222	1,817	Mark Rowley, QPM
Sussex	0845-607 0999	3,167	Martin Richards
Thames Valley	0845-850 5505	4,257	Sara Thornton, CBE, QPM
Warwickshire	01926-415000	966	Keith Bristow, QPM
West Mercia	0300-333 3000	2,270	Paul West, QPM
West Midlands	0345-113 5000	8,567	C. Sims, OBE, QPM
West Yorkshire	01924-375222	5,670	Sir Norman Bettison
Wiltshire	0845-408 7000	1,169	Brian Moore, QPM

WALES

Dyfed-Powys	0845-330 2000	1,179	Ian Arundale, QPM
Gwent	01633-838111	1,531	Carmel Napier
North Wales	0845-607 1001	1,544	M. Polin, QPM
South Wales	01656-655555	3,105	Peter Vaughan

SCOTLAND

Central Scotland	01786-456000	840	Kevin Smith, QPM
Dumfries and Galloway	0845-600 5701	514	Patrick Shearer, QPM
Fife	0845-600 5702	1,099	Norma Graham, QPM
Grampian	0845-600 5700	1,535	Colin McKerracher, CBE, QPM
Lothian and Borders	0131-311 3131	3,053	David Strang, QPM
Northern	0845-603 3388	775	Ian Latimer
Strathclyde	0141-532 2000	7,949	Stephen House, QPM
Tayside	0300-111 2222	1,235	Justine Curran

NORTHERN IRELAND

Police Service of NI	0845-600 8000	7,172	Matt Baggott, CBE, QPM

ISLANDS

Isle of Man	01624-631212	236	Mike Langdon, QPM
States of Jersey	01534-612612	246	Mike Bowron
Guernsey	01481-725111	177	Patrick Rice

* For the City of London Police and the Metropolitan Police Service see London Forces

† Size of force as at February 2011

Source: R. Hazell & Co. Police and Constabulary Almanac 2011

LONDON FORCES

CITY OF LONDON POLICE
37 Wood Street, London EC2P 2NQ **T** 020-7601 2222
W www.cityoflondon.police.uk
Strength (February 2011), 823

Though small, the City of London has one of the most important financial centres in the world and the force has particular expertise in areas such as fraud investigation. The force has a wholly elected police authority, the police committee of the Corporation of London, which appoints the commissioner.
Commissioner, Adrian Leppard
Assistant Commissioner, Frank Armstrong
Commander, Ian Dyson

METROPOLITAN POLICE SERVICE
New Scotland Yard, 8–10 Broadway, London SW1H 0BG
T 020-7230 1212 **W** www.met.police.uk
Strength (February 2011), 31,865
Acting Commissioner, Tim Godwin, QPM
Acting Deputy Commissioner, Bernard Hogan-Howe, QPM

The Metropolitan Police Service is divided into four main areas for operational purposes:

TERRITORIAL POLICING
Most of the day-to-day policing of London is carried out by 33 borough operational command units; 32 command units operate within the same boundaries as the London borough councils, plus there is an additional unit which is responsible for policing Heathrow airport.
Assistant Commissioner, Ian McPherson, QPM

SPECIALIST CRIME DIRECTORATE
The Specialist Crime Directorate's main areas of focus are dismantling criminal networks of all levels, from neighbourhood street gangs to sophisticated international operations, and seizing their assets; safeguarding children and young people from physical, sexual and emotional abuse; and the investigation and prevention of homicide.
Assistant Commissioner, Cressida Dick, QPM

SPECIALIST OPERATIONS
Specialist Operations is divided into three commands:
• *Counter Terrorism Command* is responsible for the prevention and disruption of terrorist activity, domestic extremism and related offences both within London and nationally, providing an explosives disposal and chemical, biological, radiological and nuclear capability within London, assisting the security services in fulfilling their roles and providing a single point of contact for international partners in counter-terrorism matters.
• *Protection Command* is responsible for the protection and security of high-profile persons; key public figures, including the royal family; official delegations in the UK and overseas; and others where it is in the national interest or intelligence suggests that protection is necessary. It is also responsible for protecting royal residences and embassies, providing residential protection for visiting heads of state, heads of government and foreign ministers and advising the diplomatic community on security.
• *Protective Security Command* works in conjunction with authorities at the Houses of Parliament to provide security for peers, MPs, employees and visitors to the palace of Westminster. It is also responsible for policing Heathrow and London City airports.
Assistant Commissioner, Cressida Dick, QPM

CENTRAL OPERATIONS
Central Operations consists of a number of specialised units with a broad range of policing functions which provide an integrated, community-focused service to London. Central Operations also has the remit for delivering the security arrangements for the 2012 London Olympic Games.
Assistant Commissioner, Lynne Owens

SPECIALIST FORCES

BRITISH TRANSPORT POLICE
25–27 Camden Road, London NW1 9LN **T** 020-7830 8800
W www.btp.police.uk
Strength (February 2011), 2,835

British Transport Police is the national police force for the railways in England, Wales and Scotland, including the London Underground system, Docklands Light Railway, Glasgow Subway, Midland Metro Tram system and Croydon Tramlink. The chief constable reports to the British Transport Police Authority. The members of the authority are appointed by the transport secretary and include representatives from the rail industry as well as independent members. Officers are paid the same as other police forces.
Chief Constable, Andrew Trotter, OBE, QPM
Deputy Chief Constable, Paul Crowther

CIVIL NUCLEAR CONSTABULARY
Building F6, Culham Science Centre, Abingdon,
Oxfordshire OX14 3DB **T** 01235-466606 **W** www.cnc.police.uk
*Strength (March 2011), c.*1,000

The Civil Nuclear Constabulary (CNC) operates under the strategic direction of the Department of Energy and Climate Change. The CNC is a specialised armed force that protects civil nuclear sites and nuclear materials. The constabulary is responsible for policing UK civil nuclear industry facilities and for escorting nuclear material between establishments within the UK and worldwide.
Chief Constable, Richard Thompson
Deputy Chief Constable, John Sampson

MINISTRY OF DEFENCE POLICE
Ministry of Defence Police and Guarding Agency, Wethersfield,
Braintree, Essex CM7 4AZ **T** 01371-854000
W www.mod.police.uk
Strength (March 2011), 3,302

Part of the Ministry of Defence Police and Guarding Agency, the Ministry of Defence Police is a statutory civil police force with particular responsibility for the security and policing of the MoD environment. It contributes to the physical protection of property and personnel within its jurisdiction and provides a comprehensive police service to the MoD as a whole.
Chief Constable/Chief Executive, Stephen Love, QPM
Deputy Chief Constable, G. McAuley

THE SPECIAL CONSTABULARY
The Special Constabulary is a force of trained volunteers who support and work with their local police force, usually for a minimum of four hours a week (the

Metropolitan Police Special Constabulary usually asks for a minimum commitment of eight hours a week). Special constables are thoroughly grounded in the basic aspects of police work, such as self-defence, powers of arrest, common crimes and preparing evidence for court, before they can begin to carry out any police duties. Once they have completed their training, they have the same powers as a regular officer and wear a similar uniform. Information on the Special Constabulary can be found at W www.policespecials.com.

RATES OF PAY

London weighting of £2,277 per annum (as at August 2011) is awarded to all police officers working in London irrespective of their ranks and in addition to the salaries listed below:

BASIC RATES OF PAY *as at August 2011*

Chief Constables of Greater Manchester, Strathclyde and West Midlands*	£178,431–£181,455
Chief Constable*	£127,017–£169,359
Deputy Chief Constable*	£108,873–£139,119
Assistant Chief Constable and Commanders*	£90,726–£105,849
Chief Superintendent	£74,394–£78,636
Superintendent Range 2†	£71,331–£75,909
Superintendent	£62,298–£72,585
Chief Inspector‡§	£51,789 (£53,853)–£53,919 (£55,980)
Inspector‡§	£46,788 (£48,840)–£50,751 (£52,818)
Sergeant‡	£36,519–£41,040
Constable‡	£23,259–£36,519

Metropolitan Police

Commissioner	£260,088
Deputy Commissioner	£214,722

City of London Police

Commissioner	£160,902
Assistant Commissioner	£132,714

Police Service of Northern Ireland

Chief Constable	£193,548
Deputy Chief Constable	£157,257

* Chief Officers may receive a bonus of at least 5 per cent of pensionable pay if their performance is deemed exceptional

† For Superintendents who were not given the rank of Chief Superintendent on its re-introduction on 1 January 2002

‡ Officers who have been on the highest available salary for one year have access to a competence-related threshold payment of £1,212 per annum

§ London salary in parentheses (applicable only to officers in the Metropolitan and City of London police forces)

STAFF ASSOCIATIONS

Police officers are not permitted to join a trade union or to take strike action. All ranks have their own staff associations.

ASSOCIATION OF CHIEF POLICE OFFICERS OF ENGLAND, WALES AND NORTHERN IRELAND, 10 Victoria Street, London SW1H 0NN T 020-7084 8950
Chief Executive, Thomas Flaherty

ENGLAND AND WALES

POLICE FEDERATION OF ENGLAND AND WALES, Federation House, Highbury Drive, Leatherhead, Surrey KT22 7UY T 01372-352000 W www.polfed.org E gensec@polfed.org
General Secretary, Ian Rennie

POLICE SUPERINTENDENTS' ASSOCIATION OF ENGLAND AND WALES, 67A Reading Road, Pangbourne, Reading RG8 7JD T 0118-984 4005 E enquiries@policesupers.com W www.policesupers.com
National Secretary, Chief Supt. Graham Cassidy

SCOTLAND

ASSOCIATION OF CHIEF POLICE OFFICERS IN SCOTLAND, 26 Holland Street, Glasgow G2 4NH T 0141-435 1230 W www.acpos.police.uk
General Secretary, Cliff Anderson

ASSOCIATION OF SCOTTISH POLICE SUPERINTENDENTS, *Secretariat,* 99 Main Street, Glasgow G62 6JM T 0141-532 4022 E secretariat@scottishpolicesupers.org.uk W www.scottishpolicesupers.org.uk
General Secretary, Carol Forfar

SCOTTISH POLICE FEDERATION, 5 Woodside Place, Glasgow G3 7QF T 0141-332 5234 W www.spf.org.uk
General Secretary and Treasurer, Calum Steele

NORTHERN IRELAND

POLICE FEDERATION FOR NORTHERN IRELAND, 77–79 Garnerville Road, Belfast BT4 2NX T 028-9076 4200 E office.pfni@btconnect.com W www.policefed-ni.org.uk
Secretary, Stevie McCann

SUPERINTENDENTS' ASSOCIATION OF NORTHERN IRELAND, PSNI College, Garnerville Road, Belfast BT4 2NX T 028-9092 2201 E mail@policesuperintendentsni.org W www.policesuperintendentsni.org
Joint Secretary (interim), Ray Phillips; Wesley Wilson, QPM

THE PRISON SERVICE

The prison services in the United Kingdom are the responsibility of the Secretary of State for Justice, the Scottish Justice Department and the Minister of Justice in Northern Ireland. The chief directors-general (chief executive in Scotland, director-general in Northern Ireland), officers of the Prison Service, the Scottish Prison Service and the Northern Ireland Prison Service are responsible for the day-to-day running of the system.

There are 133 prison establishments in England and Wales, 15 in Scotland and three in Northern Ireland. Convicted prisoners are classified according to their assessed security risk and are housed in establishments appropriate to that level of security. There are no open prisons in Northern Ireland. Female prisoners are housed in women's establishments or in separate wings of mixed prisons. Remand prisoners are, where possible, housed separately from convicted prisoners. Offenders under the age of 21 are usually detained in a Young Offender Institution, which may be a separate establishment or part of a prison. Appellant and failed asylum seekers are held in Immigration Removal Centres, or in separate units of other prisons.

Eleven prisons are now run by the private sector in England and Wales, and in England, Wales and Scotland all escort services have been contracted out to private companies. In Scotland, two prisons (Kilmarnock and Addiewell) were built and financed by the private sector and are being operated by private contractors.

There are independent prison inspectorates in England, Wales and Scotland which report annually on conditions and the treatment of prisoners. The Chief Inspector of Criminal Justice in Northern Ireland and HM Chief Inspector of Prisons for England and Wales perform an inspectorate role for prisons in Northern Ireland. Every prison establishment also has an independent monitoring board made up of local volunteers.

Any prisoner whose complaint is not satisfied by the internal complaints procedures may complain to the prisons and probation ombudsman for England and Wales, the Scottish public services ombudsman or the prisoner ombudsman for Northern Ireland.

The 11 private sector prisons in England and Wales are the direct responsibility of the chief executive of the National Offender Management Service (NOMS). NOMS was created in January 2004, in order to integrate prisons and probation into a system whereby end-to-end management of offenders is provided; this is expected to reduce re-offending and cut the growth rate of the prison population. In May 2007 NOMS was amalgamated into the Ministry of Justice; in 2008 it was restructured with responsibilities for running HM Prison Service, overseeing the contracts of privately run prisons, managing probation performance and creating probation trusts. The prisons and probation inspectors, the prisons ombudsman and the independent monitoring boards report to the home secretary and to the Minister of Justice in Northern Ireland.

PRISON STATISTICS

The projected 'high scenario' prison population for 2016 in England and Wales is 93,600; the 'low scenario' is 83,100.

PRISON POPULATION (UK) *as at April 2011*

	Remand	Sentenced	Other
ENGLAND AND WALES			
Male	11,517	68,718	913
Female	783	3,448	21
Total	12,300	72,166	934
SCOTLAND*			
Male	1,042	5,553	–
Female	55	329	–
Total	1,097	5,882	–
N. IRELAND			
Male	553	1,054	2
Female	18	29	–
Total	571	1,083	2
UK TOTAL	13,968	79,131	938

* Figures from August 2011
Sources: Home Office; Scottish Prison Service; Northern Ireland Prison Service

PRISON CAPACITY (ENGLAND AND WALES)
as at April 2011

Male prisoners	81,148
Female prisoners	4,252
Total	85,400
Useable operational capacity	88,093
Number under home detention curfew supervision	3,002

SENTENCED PRISON POPULATION BY SEX AND OFFENCE (ENGLAND AND WALES) *as at July 2011*

	Male	Female
Violence against the person	19,520	911
Sexual offences	9,767	83
Burglary	6,931	171
Robbery	8,840	301
Theft, handling	3,747	451
Fraud and forgery	1,202	174
Drugs offences	9,899	722
Motoring offences	824	17
Other offences	7,219	536
Offence not recorded	475	45
*Total**	68,424	3,411

* Figures do not include civil (non-criminal) prisoners or fine defaulters
Source: Ministry of Justice – *Offender Management Statistics*

SENTENCED POPULATION BY LENGTH OF SENTENCE (ENGLAND AND WALES) as at June 2011

	Adults	Young offenders
Less than 12 months	6,394	1,420
12 months to less than 4 years	16,964	3,428
4 years to less than life	22,745	1,594
Indeterminate	13,286	358
Total*	59,389	6,800

* Figures do not include civil (non-criminal) prisoners or fine defaulters
Source: Ministry of Justice – Offender Management Statistics

AVERAGE DAILY SENTENCED POPULATION BY LENGTH OF SENTENCE 2010–11 (SCOTLAND)

	Adults	Young offenders
Less than 4 years	2,851	450
4 years or over (including life)	2,924	154
Total	5,775	604

Source: Scottish Prison Service – Annual Report and Accounts 2010–11

SUICIDES IN PRISON IN 2010 (ENGLAND AND WALES)

Men	57
Women	1
Total	58
Rate per 100,000 prisoners in custody	68

Source: www.justice.gov.uk

THE PRISON SERVICES

NATIONAL OFFENDER MANAGEMENT SERVICE

T 0300-047 6325 E public.enquiries@noms.gsi.gov.uk
W www.justice.gov.uk

HM Prison Service became part of the National Offender Management Service (NOMS) on 1 April 2008 as part of the reorganisation of the Ministry of Justice.

SALARIES from 1 April 2011

Senior manager A	£64,765–£82,892
Senior manager B	£60,980–£80,458
Senior manager C	£56,920–£72,451
Senior manager D	£45,700–£61,038
Manager E	£33,335–£46,024
Manager F	£29,685–£39,041
Manager G	£25,105–£32,140

THE NATIONAL OFFENDER MANAGEMENT SERVICE BOARD

Chief Executive Officer (SCS), Michael Spurr
Director of High Security Prisons (SCS), Danny McAllister
Director of Probation and Contracted Services (SCS), Colin Allars
Director of National Operational Sevices (SCS), Phil Copple
Director of Human Resources (SCS), Robin Wilkinson
Director of Information and Communications Technology, Martin Bellamy
Director of Commissioning and Commercial (SCS), Ian Poree
Director of Offender Health (SCS), Richard Bradshaw
Board Secretary and Head of Secretariat (SMB), Ken Everett
Director of Public Sector Prisons (SCS), Steve Wagstaffe

DEPUTY DIRECTORS OF CUSTODY

Andrew Cross (East Midlands); Adrian Smith (East of England); Paul Carroll (Kent and Sussex); Nick Pascoe (London); Alan Tallentire (North-East); Alan Scott (North-West); Claudia Sturt (South-Central); Roger Hill (South-East); Ferdie Parker (South-West); Ian Mullholland (Wales); Luke Serjeant (West Midlands); Amy Rice (Yorkshire and Humberside)

OPERATING COSTS OF PRISON SERVICE IN ENGLAND AND WALES 2010–11

Staff costs	£2,563,863,000
Other operating costs	£2,036,743,000
Operating income	(£409,483,000)
Net operating costs for the year	£4,192,180,000

Source: NOMS – Annual Report 2010–11

SCOTTISH PRISON SERVICE (SPS)

Calton House, 5 Redheughs Rigg, Edinburgh EH12 9HW
T 0131-244 8747 E gaolinfo@sps.pnn.gov.uk
W www.sps.gov.uk

SALARIES 2011–12

Senior managers in the Scottish Prison Service, including governors and deputy governors of prisons, are paid across three pay bands depending on the size of the establishment:

Band I	£54,930–£68,433
Band H	£43,601–£56,704
Band G	£34,333–£47,149

SPS BOARD

Chief Executive, John Ewing
Directors, Willie Pretswell (Finance); Dr Andrew Fraser (Health and Care); Stephen Swan (Human Resources); Eric Murch (Partnerships and Commissioning); Rona Sweeney (Prisons)
Non-Executive Directors, Allan Burns; Harry McGuigan; Jane Martin; Susan Matheson; Bill Morton; Zoe Van Zwanenberg

OPERATING COSTS OF SCOTTISH PRISON SERVICE 2010–11

Total income	£2,954,000
Total expenditure	£304,724,000
Staff costs	£139,374,000
Running costs	£130,550,000
Other current expenditure	£30,696,000
Operating cost	£301,770,000
Interest payable and similar charges	£8,254,000
Net operating cost	£310,024,000

Source: Scottish Prison Service – Annual Report and Accounts 2010–11

NORTHERN IRELAND PRISON SERVICE

Dundonald House, Upper Newtownards Road, Belfast BT4 3SU
T 028-9052 2922 E info@niprisonservice.gov.uk
W www.niprisonservice.gov.uk

SALARIES 2010–11

Governor 1	£74,747–£80,550
Governor 2	£67,983–£72,183
Governor 3	£58,824–£62,766
Governor 4	£51,156–£55,407
Governor 5	£44,934–£50,396

SENIOR STAFF
Director-General, Colin McConnell
Directors, Ronnie Armour *(Human Resources and Organisation Development)*; Max Murray *(Offender Policy and Regimes)*; Graeme Wilkinson *(Finance, Planning and Corporate Compliance)*

OPERATING COSTS OF NORTHERN IRELAND PRISON SERVICE 2010–11

Staff costs	£91,154,000
Net running costs	£25,704,000
Depreciation and Amortisation	£13,333,000
Operating expenditure	£130,191,000
Net operating costs for the year	£128,774,000

Source: Northern Ireland Prison Service – *Annual Report and Accounts 2010–11*

PRISON ESTABLISHMENTS

as at June 2011

ENGLAND AND WALES

Prison	Address	Prisoners	Governor/Director
ACKLINGTON	Northumberland NE65 9XF	823	Patrick Fox *(acting)*
ALTCOURSE (private prison)	Liverpool L9 7WU	1,162	John McLaughlin
††‡ASHFIELD (private prison)	Bristol BS16 9QJ	355	Wendy Sinclair
*‡ASKHAM GRANGE	York YO23 3FT	125	Marion Mahoney
‡AYLESBURY	Bucks HP20 1EH	420	Kevin Leggett
BEDFORD	Bedford MK40 1HG	480	Frank Flynn
BELMARSH	London SE28 0EB	842	Phil Wragg
BIRMINGHAM	Birmingham B18 4AS	1,459	James Shanley
BLANTYRE HOUSE	Kent TN17 2NH	121	Jim Carmichael
BLUNDESTON	Suffolk NR32 5BG	449	David Bamford
††‡BRINSFORD	Wolverhampton WV10 7PY	538	Steph Roberts-Bibby
‡BRISTOL	Bristol BS7 8PS	586	Kenny Brown
‡BRIXTON	London SW2 5XF	737	Edmond Tullett
*BRONZEFIELD (private prison)	Middlesex TW15 3JZ	499	Helga Swidenbank
BUCKLEY HALL	Lancs OL12 9DP	436	Susan Kennedy
BULLINGDON	Oxon OX25 1PZ	1,113	Andy Lattimore
‡BULLWOOD HALL	Essex SS5 4TE	223	Steve Bradford
BURE	Norfolk NR10 5GB	519	Sue Doolan
CANTERBURY	Kent CT1 1PJ	307	Chris Bartlett
†CARDIFF	Cardiff CF24 0UG	802	Richard Booty
‡CASTINGTON	Northumberland NE65 9XG	356	Patrick Fox
CHANNINGS WOOD	Devon TQ12 6DW	726	Jeannine Hendrick
‡CHELMSFORD	Essex CM2 6LQ	672	Rob Davis
COLDINGLEY	Surrey GU24 9EX	508	Glenn Knight
‡COOKHAM WOOD	Kent ME1 3LU	118	Emily Thomas
DARTMOOR	Devon PL20 6RR	504	Tony Corcoran
‡DEERBOLT	Co. Durham DL12 9BG	478	Jenny Mooney
‡DONCASTER (private prison)	Doncaster DN5 8UX	1,089	John Biggin
†DORCHESTER	Dorset DT1 1JD	199	Steve Hodson
DOVEGATE (private prison)	Staffs ST14 8XR	1,129	Wyn Jones
§DOVER	Kent CT17 9DR	270	Andy Bell
*DOWNVIEW	Surrey SM2 5PD	278	Louise Spencer
*‡DRAKE HALL	Staffs ST21 6LQ	309	Bridie Oakes-Richards
DURHAM	Durham DH1 3HU	881	Tim Allen *(acting)*
*‡EAST SUTTON PARK	Kent ME17 3DF	96	Jim Carmichael
*‡EASTWOOD PARK	Glos GL12 8DB	331	Andrea Albutt
ELMLEY	Kent ME12 4DZ	1,173	Nigel Foote
ERLESTOKE	Wilts SN10 5TU	369	Andy Rogers
EVERTHORPE	E. Yorks HU15 1RB	672	Alec McCrystal
††‡EXETER	Devon EX4 4EX	524	Jeannine Hendrick
FEATHERSTONE	Wolverhampton WV10 7PU	649	Deborah McGivern
††‡FELTHAM	Middx TW13 4ND	740	Cathy Robinson
FORD	W. Sussex BN18 0BX	505	Sharon Williams
‡FOREST BANK (private prison)	Manchester M27 8FB	1,340	Trevor Shortt
*FOSTON HALL	Derby DE65 5DN	271	Grey Riley-Smith
FRANKLAND	Durham DH1 5YD	813	Dave Thompson
FULL SUTTON	York YO41 1PS	608	Steve Tilley
GARTH	Preston PR26 8NE	829	Terry Williams
GARTREE	Leics LE16 7RP	672	Neil Richards
††‡GLEN PARVA	Leicester LE18 4TN	736	Michael Wood
††‡GLOUCESTER	Glos GL1 2JN	300	Mike Bolton

Prison	Address	Prisoners	Governor/Director
GRENDON/SPRING HILL	Bucks HP18 0TL	544	Dr Peter Bennett
‡GUYS MARSH	Dorset SP7 0AH	503	Duncan Burles
§HASLAR	Hampshire PO12 2AW	139	Vicky Baker
HAVERIGG	Cumbria LA18 4NA	639	Martin Farquhar
HEWELL	Worcs B97 6QS	1,399	Kieron Taylor
HIGH DOWN	Surrey SM2 5PJ	1,093	Peter Dawson
HIGHPOINT	Suffolk CB8 9YG	1,307	Michelle Jarman-Howe
†‡HINDLEY	Lancs WN2 5TH	338	Peter Francis
‡HOLLESLEY BAY	Suffolk IP12 3JW	365	Declan Moore
*‡HOLLOWAY	London N7 0NU	541	Julia Killick
HOLME HOUSE	Stockton-on-Tees TS18 2QU	1,053	Matt Spencer
‡HULL	Hull HU9 5LS	945	Paul Foweather
‡HUNTERCOMBE	Oxon RG9 5SB	367	Nigel Atkinson
ISIS	Thamesmead SE28 0NZ	424	Lisa Smitherman
ISLE OF WIGHT	Isle of Wight PO30 5RS	1,657	Barry Greenbury
KENNET	Merseyside L31 1HX	341	Derek Harrison
KINGSTON	Portsmouth PO3 6AS	197	Ian Telfer
KIRKHAM	Lancs PR4 2RN	590	John Hewitson
KIRKLEVINGTON GRANGE	Cleveland TS15 9PA	274	Gabrielle Lee (acting)
†‡LANCASTER FARMS	Lancaster LA1 3QZ	518	Steve Lawrence
LATCHMERE HOUSE	Surrey TW10 5HH	198	Phil Taylor
LEEDS	Leeds LS12 2TJ	1,018	Rob Kellett
LEICESTER	Leicester LE2 7AJ	335	Karen Head (acting)
‡LEWES	E. Sussex BN7 1EA	478	Robin Eldridge
LEYHILL	Glos GL12 8BT	476	Mick Bell
LINCOLN	Lincoln LN2 4BD	628	Ian Thomas
§LINDHOLME	Doncaster DN7 6EE	1,093	Bob Mullen
LITTLEHEY	Cambs PE28 0SR	1,132	Danny Spencer
LIVERPOOL	Liverpool L9 3DF	1,236	John Illingsworth
LONG LARTIN	Worcs WR11 8TZ	621	Simon Cartwright
*‡LOW NEWTON	Durham DH1 5YA	263	Alan Richer
LOWDHAM GRANGE (private prison)	Notts NG14 7DA	926	Gareth Sands
MAIDSTONE	Kent ME14 1UZ	593	Andy Hudson
MANCHESTER	Manchester M60 9AH	1,151	Richard Vince
‡MOORLAND/MOORLAND OPEN	Doncaster DN7 6BW	733	Rob Kellet
§MORTON HALL	Lincoln LN6 9PT	123	Jamie Bennett
THE MOUNT	Herts HP3 0NZ	758	Damian Evans
*‡NEW HALL	W. Yorks WF4 4XX	389	Marion Mahoney
NORTH SEA CAMP	Lincs PE22 0QX	367	Graham Batchford
‡NORTHALLERTON	N. Yorks DL6 1NW	189	Norman Griffin
‡NORWICH	Norfolk NR1 4LU	741	Will Styles
NOTTINGHAM	Notts NG5 3AG	993	Peter Wright
‡ONLEY	Warks CV23 8AP	697	Dave Harding
†‡PARC (private prison)	Bridgend CF35 6AP	1,446	Janet Wallsgrove
‡PENTONVILLE	London N7 8TT	1,213	Gary Monaghon
*†PETERBOROUGH (private prison)	Peterborough PE3 7PD	583	Nick Leader
‡PORTLAND	Dorset DT5 1DL	467	Steve Holland
PRESTON	Lancs PR1 5AB	759	Paul Holland
RANBY	Notts DN22 8EU	1,082	Louise Taylor
†‡READING	Berks RG1 3HY	231	Dave Rogers
RISLEY	Cheshire WA3 6BP	1,075	Bob McColm
‡ROCHESTER	Kent ME1 3QS	536	John Wilson
RYE HILL (private prison)	Warks CV23 8SZ	615	Tom Wheatley
*SEND	Surrey GU23 7LJ	282	Louise Spencer
SHEPTON MALLET	Somerset BA4 5LU	188	Nick Evans
‡SHREWSBURY	Shropshire SY1 2HR	331	Gerry Hendry
STAFFORD	Stafford ST16 3AW	736	Peter Small
STANDFORD HILL	Kent ME12 4AA	455	Nigel Foote
STOCKEN	Leics LE15 7RD	838	John O'Sullivan
‡STOKE HEATH	Shropshire TF9 2JL	247	John Huntington
*‡STYAL	Cheshire SK9 4HR	443	Clive Chatterton
SUDBURY	Derbys DE6 5HW	571	Ken Kan
SWALESIDE	Kent ME12 4AX	1,103	Jim Bourke
†‡SWANSEA	Swansea SA1 3SR	419	Neil Lavis
‡SWINFEN HALL	Staffs WS14 9QS	638	Tom Watson
‡THORN CROSS	Cheshire WA4 4RL	289	Bob McColm
USK/PRESCOED	Monmouthshire NP15 1XP	461	Steve Cross

Prison	Address	Prisoners	Governor/Director
VERNE	Dorset DT5 1EQ	591	James Lucas
WAKEFIELD	West Yorks WF2 9AG	738	Susan Howard
WANDSWORTH	London SW18 3HS	1,599	David Taylor
‡WARREN HILL	Suffolk IP12 3JW	116	Bev Bevan
WAYLAND	Norfolk IP25 6RL	1,015	Kevin Reilly
WEALSTUN	W. Yorks LS23 7AZ	820	Norma Harrington
WELLINGBOROUGH	Northants NN8 2NH	580	Peter Siddons
‡WERRINGTON	Stoke-on-Trent ST9 0DX	149	Carl Hardwick
‡WETHERBY	W. Yorks LS22 5ED	362	Will Styles
WHATTON	Nottingham NG13 9FQ	838	Lynn Saunders
WHITEMOOR	Cambs PE15 0PR	459	Paul Cawkwell
WINCHESTER	Winchester SO22 5DF	687	David Ward
WOLDS (private prison)	E. Yorks HU15 2JZ	351	Cathy James
WOODHILL	Bucks MK4 4DA	788	Nigel Smith
WORMWOOD SCRUBS	London W12 0AE	1,248	Phil Taylor
WYMOTT	Preston PR26 8LW	1,142	Paul Norbury

SCOTLAND *as at April 2011*

Prison	Address	Prisoners	Governor/Director
ABERDEEN	Aberdeen AB11 8FN	228	Audrey Mooney
ADDIEWELL(private prison)	West Lothian EH55 8QA	702	Audrey Park
†BARLINNIE	Glasgow G33 2QX	1,384	Derek McGill
*†‡CORNTON VALE	Stirling FK9 5NU	329	Teresa Medhurst
†DUMFRIES	Dumfries DG2 9AX	200	Martyn Bettel
†EDINBURGH	Edinburgh EH11 3LN	897	Sue Brookes
GLENOCHIL	Tullibody FK10 3AD	656	Dan Gunn
†‡GREENOCK	Greenock PA16 9AH	275	Jim Kerr
*†INVERNESS	Inverness IV2 3HH	139	Angus MacVicar
†‡KILMARNOCK (private prison)	Kilmarnock KA1 5AA	567	Sandy McEwan
OPEN ESTATE NORANSIDE	Angus DD8 3QY	256	Jim Farish
†PERTH	Perth PH2 8AT	640	Mike Inglis
PETERHEAD	Aberdeenshire AB42 2YY	245	Mike Hebden
†‡POLMONT	Falkirk FK2 0AB	732	Kate Donegan
SHOTTS	Lanarkshire ML7 4LE	536	Ian Whitehead

NORTHERN IRELAND *as at April 2011*

Prison	Address	Prisoners	Governor/Director
*†‡HYDEBANK WOOD	Belfast BT8 8NA	258	Gary Alcock
†§MAGHABERRY	Co. Antrim BT28 2NF	881	Pat Maguire
MAGILLIGAN	Co. Londonderry BT49 0LR	517	Alan Longwell

PRISON ESTABLISHMENTS KEY
* Women's establishment or establishment with units for women
† Remand Centre or establishment with units for remand prisoners
‡ Young Offender Institution or establishment with units for young offenders
§ Immigration Removal Centre or establishment with units for immigration detainees

DEFENCE

The armed forces of the United Kingdom comprise the Royal Navy, the Army and the Royal Air Force (RAF). The Queen is Commander-in-Chief of all the armed forces. The Secretary of State for Defence is responsible for the formulation and content of defence policy and for providing the means by which it is conducted. The formal legal basis for the conduct of defence in the UK rests on a range of powers vested by statute and letters patent in the Defence Council, chaired by the Secretary of State for Defence. Beneath the ministers lies the top management of the Ministry of Defence (MoD), headed jointly by the Permanent Secretary and the Chief of Defence Staff. The Permanent Secretary is the government's principal civilian adviser on defence and has the primary responsibility for policy, finance, management and administration. She is also personally accountable to parliament for the expenditure of all public money allocated to defence purposes. The Chief of the Defence Staff is the professional head of the armed forces in the UK and the principal military adviser to the secretary of state and the government.

The Defence Board is the executive of the Defence Council. Chaired by the Permanent Secretary, it acts as the main executive board of the Ministry of Defence, providing senior level leadership and strategic management of defence.

The Central Staff, headed by the Vice-Chief of the Defence Staff and the Second Permanent Under-Secretary of State, is the policy core of the department. Defence Equipment and Support, headed by the Chief of Defence Materiel, is responsible for purchasing defence equipment and providing logistical support to the armed forces.

A permanent Joint Headquarters for the conduct of joint operations was set up at Northwood in 1996. The Joint Headquarters connects the policy and strategic functions of the MoD head office with the conduct of operations and is intended to strengthen the policy/executive division.

The UK pursues its defence and security policies through its membership of NATO (to which most of its armed forces are committed), the European Union, the Organisation for Security and Cooperation in Europe and the UN (*see* International Organisations section).

STRENGTH OF THE ARMED FORCES

	Royal Navy	Army	RAF	All Services
1975 strength	76,200	167,100	95,000	338,300
2001 strength	42,420	109,530	53,700	205,650
2002 strength	41,630	110,050	53,000	204,680
2003 strength	41,550	112,130	53,240	206,920
2004 strength	40,880	112,750	53,390	207,020
2005 strength	39,940	109,290	51,870	201,100
2006 strength	39,390	107,730	48,730	195,850
2007 strength*	38,860	106,170	45,370	190,400
2008 strength*	38,570	105,090	43,390	187,060
2009 strength*	38,340	106,460	43,570	188,370
2010 strength*	38,730	108,870	44,050	191,660
2011 strength*	37,660	106,230	42,460	186,360

* Provisional figures apart from the 2007 Royal Navy data
Source: Defence Analytical Services and Advice (DASA) *National Statistics* (Crown copyright)

SERVICE PERSONNEL BY RANK AND GENDER

	Officers		Other ranks	
	Males	Females	Males	Females
All services	27,930	3,900	140,570	13,950
Royal Navy	6,690	720	27,430	2,810
Army	13,090	1,670	84,660	6,810
RAF	8,150	1,510	28,480	4,330

Source: DASA *National Statistics* (Crown copyright)

UK regular forces include trained and untrained personnel and nursing services, but exclude Gurkhas, full-time reserve service personnel, mobilised reservists and naval activated reservists. As at 1 April 2011 these groups provisionally numbered:

All Gurkhas	3,890
Full-time reserve service	2,050
Mobilised reservists	
Army	1,460
RAF	80
Naval activated reservists	140

Source: DASA *National Statistics* (Crown copyright)

CIVILIAN PERSONNEL

1993 level	159,600
2000 level	121,300
2001 level	118,200
2002 level	110,100
2003 level	107,600
2004 level	108,990
2005 level	107,680
2006 level	102,970
2007 level	95,790
2008 level	88,690
2009 level	85,730
2010 level	85,180
2011 level	83,100

Source: DASA *National Statistics* (Crown copyright)

UK REGULAR FORCES: DEATHS

In 2010 there were a total of 187 deaths among the UK regular armed forces, of which 30 were serving in the Royal Navy and Royal Marines, 136 in the Army and 21 in the RAF. The largest single cause of death was as a result of hostile action (killed in action and died of wounds), which accounted for 95 deaths (51 per cent of the total) in 2010. Land transport accidents accounted for 36 deaths (19 per cent) and other accidents accounted for a further 15 deaths (8 per cent). Suicides and open verdicts accounted for five deaths or 3 per cent of the total.

NUMBER OF DEATHS AND MORTALITY RATES

	2005	2007	2008	2009	2010
Total number	160	204	137	205	187
Royal Navy	27	27	40	23	30
Army	93	145	79	158	136
RAF	40	32	18	24	21
Mortality rates per thousand					
Tri-service rate	0.81	1.06	0.73	1.07	0.97
Navy	0.71	0.72	1.09	0.56	0.78
Army	0.87	1.29	0.73	1.34	1.16
RAF	0.72	0.71	0.36	0.53	0.49

Source: DASA *National Statistics* (Crown copyright)

NUCLEAR FORCES

The Vanguard Class SSBN (ship submersible ballistic nuclear) provides the UK's strategic nuclear deterrent. Each Vanguard Class submarine is capable of carrying 16 Trident D5 missiles equipped with nuclear warheads.

There is a ballistic missile early warning system station at RAF Fylingdales in North Yorkshire.

ARMS CONTROL

The 1990 Conventional Armed Forces in Europe (CFE) Treaty, which commits all NATO and former Warsaw Pact members to limiting their holdings of five major classes of conventional weapons, has been adapted to reflect the changed geo-strategic environment and negotiations continue for its implementation. The Open Skies Treaty, which the UK signed in 1992 and entered into force in 2002, allows for the overflight of states parties by other states parties using unarmed observation aircraft.

The UN Convention on Certain Conventional Weapons (as amended 2001), which bans or restricts the use of specific types of weapons that are considered to cause unnecessary or unjustifiable suffering to combatants, or to affect civilians indiscriminately, was ratified by the UK in 1995. In 1968 the UK signed and ratified the Nuclear Non-Proliferation Treaty, which came into force in 1970 and was indefinitely and unconditionally extended in 1995. In 1996 the UK signed the Comprehensive Nuclear Test Ban Treaty and ratified it in 1998. The UK is a party to the 1972 Biological and Toxin Weapons Convention, which provides for a worldwide ban on biological weapons, and the 1993 Chemical Weapons Convention, which came into force in 1997 and provides for a verifiable worldwide ban on chemical weapons.

DEFENCE BUDGET DEPARTMENTAL EXPENDITURE LIMITS (DEL) £ billion

	Resource budget	Capital budget	Total DEL
2010–11 (estimate)	28.4	9.6	38.0
2011–12 (plans)	27.3	10.0	37.3
2012–13 (plans)	25.2	9.1	34.3

Source: HM Treasury – *Budget 2011* (Crown copyright)

MINISTRY OF DEFENCE

Main Building, Whitehall, London SW1A 2HB
T 020-7218 9000 W www.mod.uk

Secretary of State for Defence, Rt. Hon. Liam Fox, MP
Private Secretary, Barry Burton
Special Advisers, Hayden Allen; Luke Coffey; Ollie Waghorn
Parliamentary Private Secretary, vacant
Minister of State, Nick Harvey, MP *(Armed Forces)*

Private Secretary, Gareth Martin
Parliamentary Under-Secretary of State, Gerald Howarth, MP *(International Security Strategy)*
Private Secretary, Austin Mitchell
Parliamentary Under-Secretary of State, Andrew Robathan, MP *(Defence Personnel, Welfare and Veterans)*
Private Secretary, Alan Nisbett
Parliamentary Under-Secretary of State, Peter Luff, MP *(Defence Equipment, Support and Technology)*
Private Secretary, Anna Platt
Parliamentary Under-Secretary of State for Defence and Lords Spokesman on Defence, Lord Astor
Private Secretary, Natasha Foskett

CHIEFS OF STAFF

Chief of the Defence Staff, Gen. Sir David Richards, GCB, CBE, DSO, ADC
Vice Chief of the Defence Staff, Gen. Sir Nick Houghton, GCB, CBE
Chief of the Naval Staff and First Sea Lord, Adm. Sir Mark Stanhope, GCB, OBE, ADC
Assistant Chief of the Naval Staff, Rear-Adm. Philip Jones
Chief of the General Staff, Gen. Sir Peter Wall, KCB, CBE, ADC
Assistant Chief of the General Staff, Maj.-Gen. James Everard, CBE
Chief of the Air Staff, Air Chief Marshal Sir Stephen Dalton, KCB, ADC
Assistant Chief of the Air Staff, Air Vice-Marshal Barry North, OBE

SENIOR OFFICIALS

Permanent Under-Secretary of State, Ursula Brennan
Second Permanent Under-Secretary of State, Jon Day
Chief of Defence Materiel, Bernard Gray
Chief Scientific Adviser, Prof. Mark Welland, FRS, FRENG
Director-General Finance, Jon Thompson

THE DEFENCE COUNCIL

The Defence Council is the senior committee of the MoD, and was established by royal prerogative under letters patent in April 1964. The letters patent confer on the Defence Council the command over all of the armed forces and charge the council with such matters relating to the administration of the armed forces as the Secretary of State for Defence should direct them to execute. It is chaired by the Secretary of State for Defence and consists of the Secretary of State for Defence, the Minister of State for the Armed Forces, the Minister of State for International Security Strategy, the Minister of State for Defence Personnel, Welfare and Veterans, the Minister of State for Defence Equipment, Support and Technology, the Parliamentary Under-Secretary of State for Defence and Lords Spokesman on Defence, the Chief of Defence Staff, the Permanent Under-Secretary of State, the Chief of the Naval Staff and First Sea Lord, the Chief of the General Staff, the Chief of the Air Staff, the Vice-Chief of the Defence Staff, the Chief of Defence Materiel, the Chief Scientific Adviser, the Second Permanent Under-Secretary of State and the Director-General Finance.

CENTRAL STAFF

Vice-Chief of the Defence Staff, Gen. Sir Nick Houghton, GCB, CBE
Second Permanent Under-Secretary of State, Jon Day

PERMANENT JOINT HQ

Chief of Joint Operations, Air Marshal Sir Stuart Peach, KCB, CBE

Chief of Staff (Operations), Maj.-Gen. Gordon Messenger, DSO, OBE

Chief of Staff (Joint Warfare Development), Maj.-Gen. Roddy Porter, MBE

FLEET COMMAND

Commander-in-Chief Fleet, Adm. Sir Trevor Soar, KCB, OBE

Deputy Commander-in-Chief Fleet, Vice-Adm. George Zambellas, DSC

NAVAL HOME COMMAND

Second Sea Lord and Commander-in-Chief Naval Home Command, Vice-Adm. Charles Montgomery,

Naval Secretary and Chief of Staff (Personnel), Rear-Adm. David Steel, CBE

LAND FORCES

Commander-in-Chief Land Forces, Gen. Sir Nick Parker, KCB, CBE

Chief of Staff Land Forces, Maj.-Gen. Mark Poffley, OBE

AIR COMMAND

Commander-in-Chief Air Command, Air Chief Marshal Sir Simon Bryant, KCB, CBE, ADC

Deputy Commander-in-Chief Operations, Air Marshal R. Garwood, CB

Deputy Commander-in-Chief Personnel, Air Marshal A. Pulford, CBE

DEFENCE EQUIPMENT AND SUPPORT

Chief of Defence Materiel, Bernard Gray

Chief Operating Officer, Dr Andrew Tyler

Chief of Corporate Services, Trevor Woolley

Chief of Materiel (Fleet), Vice-Adm. Andy Matthews, OBE

Chief of Materiel (Land), Lt.-Gen. Gary Coward, CB, OBE

Chief of Materiel (Air), Air Marshal Kevin Leeson, CBE

EXECUTIVE AGENCIES

DEFENCE SCIENCE AND TECHNOLOGY LABORATORY
Porton Down, Salisbury, Wiltshire SP4 0JQ T 01980-613121
E centralenquiries@dstl.gov.uk W www.dstl.gov.uk
Chief Executive, Dr Frances Saunders

DEFENCE SUPPORT GROUP
Building 203, Monxton Road, Andover, Hampshire SP11 8HT
T 01264-383295 E info@dsg.mod.uk W www.dsg.mod.uk
Chief Executive, Archie Hughes

MET OFFICE
Fitzroy Road, Exeter, Devon EX1 3PB T 0870-900 0100
E enquiries@metoffice.gov.uk W www.metoffice.gov.uk
Chief Executive, John Hirst

UK HYDROGRAPHIC OFFICE
Admiralty Way, Taunton, Somerset TA1 2DN T 01823-337900
E customerservices@ukho.gov.uk W www.ukho.gov.uk
Chief Executive, Mike Robinson

ARMED FORCES TRAINING AND RECRUITMENT

In April 2006 the MoD removed agency status from the three armed forces training agencies which now function as an integral part of their respective service.

Flag Officer Sea Training (FOST) is responsible for all Royal Navy and Royal Fleet Auxiliary training. FOST's International Defence Training provides the focal point for all aspects of naval training. Training is divided into five streams: Naval Core Training (responsible for new entry, command, leadership and management training); Royal Marine; Submarine; Surface and Aviation.

The Army Recruiting and Training Division (ARTD) is responsible for the four key areas of army training: soldier initial training, at the School of Infantry or at one of the army's four other facilities; officer initial training at the Royal Military Academy Sandhurst; trade training at one of the army's specialist facilities; and resettlement training for those about to leave the army. Trade training facilities include: the Armour Centre; the Defence College of Logistics and Personnel Administration; the Royal School of Artillery; the Royal School of Military Engineering and the Army Aviation Centre.

The Royal Air Force No. 22 (Training) Group exists to recruit RAF personnel and provide trained specialist personnel to the armed forces as a whole, such as providing the army air corps with trained helicopter pilots. The group is split into eight areas: RAF College Cranwell and Inspectorate of Recruiting; the Directorate of Flying Training (DFT); the Directorate of Joint Technical Training (DJTT); the Air Cadet Organisation (ACO); Core Headquarters; the Defence College of Aeronautical Engineering (DCAE); the Defence College of Communications and Information Systems (DCCIS) and the Defence College of Electro-Mechanical Engineering (DCEME).

USEFUL WEBSITES

W www.royalnavy.mod.uk
W www.army.mod.uk
W www.raf.mod.uk

THE ROYAL NAVY

In Order of Seniority

LORD HIGH ADMIRAL OF THE UNITED KINGDOM
HRH The Prince Philip, Duke of Edinburgh, KG, KT, OM, GBE, AC, QSO, PC, *apptd* 2011

ADMIRALS OF THE FLEET
HRH The Prince Philip, Duke of Edinburgh, KG, KT, OM, GBE, AC, QSO, PC, *apptd* 1953
Sir Edward Ashmore, GCB, DSC, *apptd* 1977
Sir Julian Oswald, GCB, *apptd* 1993
Sir Benjamin Bathurst, GCB, *apptd* 1995

ADMIRALS
(Former Chiefs or Vice Chiefs of Defence Staff and First Sea Lords who remain on the active list)
Slater, Sir Jock, GCB, LVO, *apptd* 1991
Boyce, Lord, KG, GCB, OBE, *apptd* 1995
Abbott, Sir Peter, GBE, KCB, *apptd* 1995
Essenhigh, Sir Nigel, GCB, *apptd* 1998
West of Spithead, Lord, GCB, DSC, PC, *apptd* 2000
Band, Sir Jonathon, GCB, *apptd* 2002

ADMIRALS
HRH The Prince of Wales, KG, KT, GCB, OM, AK, QSO, PC, ADC
Stanhope, Sir Mark, KCB, OBE, ADC *(First Sea Lord and Chief of Naval Staff)*
Soar, Sir Trevor, KCB, OBE *(Commander-in-Chief Fleet)*

VICE-ADMIRALS
HRH The Princess Royal, KG, KT, GCVO, QSO *(Chief Commandant for Women in the Royal Navy)*
Lambert, Paul, CB *(Deputy Chief of Defence Staff (Capability))*
Matthews, Andrew, CB *(Chief of Materiel (Fleet) and Chief of Fleet Support to the Navy Board)*
Cooling, Robert, CB *(Chief of Staff to the Supreme Allied Commander Transformation)*
Montgomery, Charles, CBE, ADC *(Second Sea Lord and Commander-in-Chief Naval Home Command)*
Zambellas, George, DSC, *(Deputy Commander-in-Chief Fleet, Chief of Staff Navy Command HQ and Chief Naval Warfare Officer)*

REAR-ADMIRALS
HRH The Duke of York, KG, GCVO, ADC
Mosisetti, Neil, CB *(MoD and FCO Climate and Energy Security Envoy)*
Hussain, Amjad, CB *(Director (Precision Attack) and Controller of the Navy)*
Johnstone-Burt, (Charles) Anthony, OBE *(Head of British Defence Staff (USA) and Defence Attaché)*
Richards, Alan *(Assistant Chief of Defence Staff (Strategy and Plans))*
Charlier, Simon *(Military Aviation Authority Operational Director)*
Jones, Philip *(Assistant Chief of Naval Staff)*
Lister, Simon, OBE *(Director Submarines and Chief Naval Engineering Officer)*
Lloyd, Stephen *(Chief Strategic Systems Executive)*
Corder, Ian *(Cdr (Operations) and Rear-Adm. Submarines (Head of Fighting Arm))*
Williams, Simon, OBE *(Senior Directing Staff (Navy), Royal College of Defence Studies)*
Hudson, Peter, CBE *(Chief of Staff (Capability))*

Williams, Bruce, CBE *(Deputy Director-General EU Military Staff)*
Cunningham, Thomas *(Chief of Staff (Aviation) and Rear-Adm. Fleet Air Arm (Head of Fighting Arm))*
Rymer, Alan *(Director Training, Education and Skills)*
Steel, David, CBE *(Naval Secretary and Chief of Staff (Personnel) and Chief Naval Logistics Officer)*
Mathias, Philip, MBE *(Strategic Defence and Security Review Nuclear Director)*
Lambert, Nicholas *(National Hydrographer and Deputy Chief Executive (Hydrography))*
Potts, D. *(Cdr UK Maritime Forces and Rear-Adm. Surface Ships as Head of Fighting Arm)*
Westbrook, Jonathan, MBE *(Chief of Staff to the Maritime Component Command and Senior Naval Representative, Naples)*
Harding, Russell, OBE *(Deputy Cdr Strike Force NATO)*
Johnstone, Clive, CBE *(Flag Officer Sea Training)*
Hockley, Christopher *(Flag Officer Scotland, Northern England and Northern Ireland and Flag Officer Reserve Forces)*

MEDICAL
Raffaelli, Philip, QHP, FRCP *(Surgeon Vice-Adm., Surgeon General)*
Jarvis, Lionel, QHS *(Assistant Chief of Defence Staff (Health), Chief Naval Medical Officer and Medical Director-General (Naval))*

ROYAL MARINES
CAPTAIN-GENERAL
HRH The Prince Philip, Duke of Edinburgh, KG, KT, OM, GBE, AC, QSO, PC

MAJOR-GENERALS
Thomas, Jeremy, DSO *(Assistant Chief of Defence Staff (Intelligence Capability))*
Salmon, Andrew, OBE *(Deputy Chief of Staff Force Readiness, Supreme HQ Allied Powers Europe)*
Capewell, David, OBE *(Assistant Chief of Defence Staff (Operations))*
Mason, Jeffrey, MBE *(Assistant Chief of Defence Staff (Operations), Permanent Joint HQ)*
Messenger, Gordon, DSO, OBE *(Chief of Defence Staff (Operations), Permanent Joint HQ)*
Howes, F., OBE *(Cdr UK Amphibious Forces and Commandant General Royal Marines)*
Hook, David, CBE *(Director Force Reintegration, HQ International Security and Assistance Force, Afghanistan)*

The Royal Marines were formed in 1664 and are part of the Naval Service. Their primary purpose is to conduct amphibious and land warfare. The principal operational units are:

- Three Commando Brigade, an amphibious all-arms brigade trained to operate in arduous environments (a core element of the UK's Joint Rapid Reaction Force). The commando units each have a strength of around 700 and are based in Taunton (40 Commando), Plymouth (42 Commando) and Arbroath (45 Commando)
- Fleet Protection Group, responsible for a wide range of tasks worldwide in support of the Royal Navy. The group is over 500 strong and is based at HM Naval Base Clyde on the west coast of Scotland

- Assault Group, which has its headquarters located in Devonport, Plymouth is responsible for ten landing craft training squadron at Poole, Dorset and 11 amphibious trials and training squadron at Instow, Devon

The Royal Marines also provide detachments for warships and land-based naval parties as required.

ROYAL MARINES RESERVES (RMR)

The Royal Marines Reserve is a commando-trained volunteer force with the principal role, when mobilised, of supporting the Royal Marines. The RMR consists of approximately 600 trained ranks who are distributed between the five RMR centres in the UK. Approximately 10 per cent of the RMR are working with the regular corps on long-term attachments within all of the Royal Marines regular units.

OTHER PARTS OF THE NAVAL SERVICE
FLEET AIR ARM

The Fleet Air Arm (FAA) provides the Royal Navy with a multi-role aviation combat capability able to operate autonomously at short notice worldwide in all environments, over the sea and land. The FAA numbers some 6,200 people, which comprises 11.5 per cent of the total Royal Naval strength. It operates some 200 combat aircraft and more than 50 support/training aircraft.

ROYAL FLEET AUXILIARY SERVICE (RFA)

The Royal Fleet Auxiliary Service is a civilian-manned flotilla of 13 ships owned by the MoD. Its primary role is to supply the Royal Navy and host nations while at sea with fuel, ammunition, food and spares, enabling them to maintain operations away from their home ports. It also provides amphibious support and secure sea transport for military units and their equipment. The ships routinely support and embark Royal Naval Air Squadrons.

ROYAL NAVAL RESERVE (RNR)

The Royal Naval Reserve is an integral part of the Naval Service. It is a part-time force of 2,300 trained men and women who are deployed with the Royal Navy in times of tension, humanitarian crisis or conflict.

The Royal Naval Reserve has 22 units throughout the UK; 19 of these provide initial training while three other specialist units provide intelligence and aviation training. Basic training is provided at HMS *Raleigh,* Torpoint in Cornwall for ratings and at the Britannia Royal Naval College, Dartmouth in Devon for officers; both these and most other RNR courses are of two weeks' duration or less.

QUEEN ALEXANDRA'S ROYAL NAVAL NURSING SERVICE

The first nursing sisters were appointed to naval hospitals in 1884 and the Queen Alexandra's Royal Naval Nursing Service (QARNNS) gained its current title in 1902. Nursing ratings were introduced in 1960 and men were integrated into the service in 1982; QARNNS recruits qualified nurses as both officers and ratings, and student nurse training can be undertaken in the service.

Patron, HRH Princess Alexandra, the Hon. Lady Ogilvy, KG, GCVO

Director of Naval Nursing Services and Matron-in-Chief, Capt. Helen Allkins, QARNNS

HM FLEET
as at 1 June 2011

Submarines	
Vanguard Class	Vanguard, Vengeance, Victorious, Vigilant
Trafalgar Class	Talent, Tireless, Torbay, Trafalgar, Trenchant, Triumph, Turbulent
Astute Class	Astute
Aircraft Carrier	Illustrious
Amphibious Assault Ships	Ocean, Albion, Bulwark
Destroyers	
Type 42 Batch 2	Liverpool
Type 42 Batch 3	Edinburgh, York
Type 45	Daring, Dauntless
Frigates	
Type 23	Argyll, Iron Duke, Kent, Lancaster, Monmouth, Montrose, Northumberland, Portland, Richmond, St Albans, Somerset, Sutherland, Westminster
Minehunters	
Hunt Class	Atherstone, Brocklesby, Cattistock, Chiddingfold, Hurworth, Ledbury, Middleton, Quorn
Sandown Class	Bangor, Blyth, Grimsby, Pembroke, Penzance, Ramsey, Shoreham
Patrol Class	
Archer Class P2000	Archer, Biter, Blazer,
Training Boats	Charger, Dasher, Example, Exploit, Explorer, Express, Puncher, Pursuer, Raider, Ranger, Smiter, Tracker, Trumpeter
Gibraltar Squadron 16m Fast Patrol Class	Sabre, Scimitar
River Class Patrol Vessels	Mersey, Severn, Tyne, Clyde
Survey Vessels	
Ice Patrol Ships	Endurance*, Protector
Ocean Survey Vessel	Scott
Coastal Survey Vessel	Gleaner
Multi-Role Survey Vessels	Echo, Enterprise

* HMS *Endurance* is currently non-operational

ROYAL FLEET AUXILIARY

Landing Ship Dock (Auxiliary)	RFA Cardigan Bay, RFA Mounts Bay, RFA Lyme Bay
Wave Class	RFA Wave Knight, RFA Wave Ruler
Rover Class	RFA Black Rover, RFA Gold Rover
Leaf Class	RFA Orangeleaf
Fort Class	RFA Fort Austin, RFA Fort Rosalie, RFA Fort Victoria
Forward Repair Ship	RFA Diligence
Joint Casualty Treatment Ship/Maritime Afloat Training Capability	RFA Argus

THE ARMY

In Order of Seniority

THE QUEEN

FIELD MARSHALS
HRH The Prince Philip, Duke of Edinburgh, KG, KT, OM, GBE, AC, QSO, PC, *apptd* 1953
Lord Bramall, KG, GCB, OBE, MC, *apptd* 1982
Lord Vincent of Coleshill, GBE, KCB, DSO, *apptd* 1991
Sir John Chapple, GCB, CBE, *apptd* 1992
HRH The Duke of Kent, KG, GCMG, GCVO, ADC, *apptd* 1993
Lord Inge, KG, GCB *apptd* 1994

FORMER CHIEFS OF STAFF
Gen. Lord Guthrie of Craigiebank, GCB, LVO, OBE, *apptd* 1994
Gen. Sir Roger Wheeler, GCB, CBE, *apptd* 1997
Gen. Lord Walker of Aldringham, GCB, CMG, CBE, *apptd* 2000
Gen. Sir Mike Jackson, GCB, CBE, DSO, *apptd* 2003
Gen. Lord Richard Dannatt, GCB, CBE, MC, *apptd* 2006

FORMER VICE-CHIEF OF STAFF
Gen. Sir Timothy Granville-Chapman, GBE, KCB, *apptd* 2005

GENERALS
HRH The Prince of Wales, KG, KT, GCB, OM, AK, QSO, PC, ADC
Richards, Sir David, GCB, CBE, DSO, ADC *(Chief of the Defence Staff)*
Houghton, Sir Nicholas, GCB, CBE, ADC *(Vice Chief of the Defence Staff)*
Wall, Sir Peter, KCB, CBE, ADC *(Chief of the General Staff)*
Parker, Sir Nick, KCB, CBE, ADC *(Commander-in-Chief Land Forces)*
Shirreff, Sir A., KCB, CBE *(Deputy Supreme Allied Cdr Europe)*

LIEUTENANT-GENERALS
Rollo, Sir William, KCB, CBE *(Deputy Chief of the Defence Staff (Personnel))*
Bill, Sir David, KCB *(UK Military Representative to NATO and the European Union)*
Brown, C., CBE *(Iraq Compendium Study Team Leader)*
Mayall, S., CB *(Defence Senior Adviser to the Middle East)*
White-Spunner, Sir Barney, KCB, CBE *(Cdr Field Army)*
Mans, M., CBE *(Adjutant-General)*
Coward, G., CB, OBE *(Chief of Materiel (Land), Defence Equipment and Support and Quartermaster General)*
Newton, P., CBE *(Cdr Force Development and Training, HQ Land Forces)*
Bucknall, J., CBE *(Cdr Allied Rapid Reaction Corps)*
Barrons, R., CBE *(Deputy Chief of the Defence Staff (Operations))*

MAJOR-GENERALS
Gregory, A., CB *(Military Secretary)*
Melvin, R., CB, OBE *(Royal College of Defence Studies)*
von Bertele, M., OBE, QHS *(Director-General Army Medical Services)*
Berragan, G., CB *(Director-General Personnel, HQ Land Forces)*

Shaw, J., CBE *(GOC 2nd Division)*
Page, J., CB, OBE *(MoD)*
Moore, W., CBE *(Director Battlespace Manoeuvre and Master General of the Ordnance)*
Rutledge, M., CB, OBE *(GOC 5th Division)*
Brealey, B., *(Director-General Reserves and Basing, HQ Land Forces)*
Bradshaw, A., CB, OBE *(Deputy Cdr International Security Assistance Force, Afghanistan)*
Inshaw, T., CB *(Director Information Systems and Services, Defence Equipment and Support)*
Boag, C., CBE *(GOC Support Command)*
Kennett, A., CBE *(Senior Directing Staff (Army), Royal College of Defence Studies)*
Caplin, N. *(GOC UK Support Command, Germany)*
Robbins, Ven. S., CB, QHC *(Chaplain-General to HM Land Forces)*
Dale, I., CBE *(Director Land Equipment, Defence Equipment and Support)*
Porter, R., MBE *(Chief of Staff (Joint Warfare Development), Permanent Joint HQ, UK)*
Gordon, J., CBE *(Senior British Loan Service Officer, Oman)*
Kirkland, R., CBE *(GOC 4th Division)*
Deverell, C., MBE *(Director Materiel Strategy, Defence Equipment and Support)*
Carter, N., CBE, DSO *(Director-General Land Warfare)*
Poffley, M., OBE *(Chief of Staff HQ Land Forces)*
Andrews, S., CBE *(Director Strategic Change, Defence Medical Services)*
Foster, A., MBE *(Deputy Force Cdr UN Mission, D. R. Congo)*
Everard, J., CBE *(Assistant Chief of the General Staff)*
Marriot, P., CBE *(Commandant Royal Military Academy Sandhurst)*
Evans, T., DSO, MBE *(Chief of Staff HQ International Security Assistance Force Joint Command, Afghanistan)*
Shaw, D. *(Assistant Chief of the Defence Staff (Global Issues))*
Smith, G. *(Assistant Chief of the Defence Staff (Reserves and Cadets))*
Jones, P., MBE *(Director Force Reintegration, HQ International Security Assistance Force, Afghanistan)*
Porter, S., CBE *(Supreme Allied Cdr Transformation Representative Europe)*
Beckett, T., CBE *(Deputy Cdr NATO Rapid Redeployment Corps, Italy)*
Chapman, C. *(Senior British Military Advisor, US Central Command)*
Conway, M. *(Director-General Army Legal Services)*
Lorimer, J., DSO, MBE *(GOC 3rd (UK) Division)*
Copeland, I. *(Director Joint Support Chain, Defence Equipment and Support)*
Davis, R., CBE *(Director-General Army Recruiting and Training)*
Jaques, P., *(Director-General Logistics, Support and Equipment, HQ Land Forces)*
Burley, S., MBE *(GOC Theatre Troops)*
Bashall, J., CBE *(GOC 1st (UK) Armoured Division)*
Wilks, C., CBE *(Director Land Equipment, Defence Equipment and Support)*
Pope, N., CBE *(Chief of the Defence Staff's Strategic Communications Officer)*
Norton, G., CBE *(GOC London District and Maj.-Gen. Commanding, The Household Division)*

CONSTITUTION OF THE ARMY

The army consists of the Regular Army, the Regular Reserve and the Territorial Army (TA). It is commanded by the Chief of the General Staff, who is the professional Head of Service and Chair of the Executive Committee of the Army Board, which provides overall strategic policy and direction to the Commander-in-Chief Land Forces. There are four subordinate commands that report to the Commander-in-Chief Land Forces: the Field Army; Personnel and Support Command, headed by the Adjutant-General; Force Development and Training Command and the Joint Helicopter Command. The army is divided into functional arms and services, subdivided into regiments and corps (listed below in order of precedence). During 2008, as part of the Future Army Structure (FAS) reform programme, the infantry was re-structured into large multi-battalion regiments, which involved amalgamations and changes in title for some regiments.

Members of the public can write for general information to Headquarters Adjutant General Secretariat, Trenchard Lines, Upavon, Wiltshire SN9 6BE. All enquiries with regard to records of serving personnel (Regular and Territorial Army) should be directed to The Army Personnel Centre Help Desk, Kentigern House, 65 Brown Street, Glasgow G2 8EX T 0141-224 2023/3303. Enquirers should note that the Army is governed in the release of personal information by various acts of parliament.

ORDER OF PRECEDENCE OF CORPS AND REGIMENTS OF THE BRITISH ARMY

ARMS

HOUSEHOLD CAVALRY
The Life Guards
The Blues and Royals (Royal Horse Guards and 1st Dragoons)

ROYAL HORSE ARTILLERY
(when on parade, the Royal Horse Artillery take precedence over the Household Cavalry)

ROYAL ARMOURED CORPS
1st the Queen's Dragoon Guards
The Royal Scots Dragoon Guards (Carabiniers and Greys)
The Royal Dragoon Guards
The Queen's Royal Hussars (The Queen's Own and Royal Irish)
9th/12th Royal Lancers (Prince of Wales')
The King's Royal Hussars
The Light Dragoons
The Queen's Royal Lancers
1st Royal Tank Regiment
2nd Royal Tank Regiment

ROYAL REGIMENT OF ARTILLERY
(with the exception of the Royal Horse Artillery (see above))

CORPS OF ROYAL ENGINEERS

ROYAL CORPS OF SIGNALS

REGIMENTS OF FOOT GUARDS
Grenadier Guards
Coldstream Guards
Scots Guards
Irish Guards
Welsh Guards

REGIMENTS OF INFANTRY
The Royal Regiment of Scotland
The Princess of Wales' Royal Regiment (Queen and Royal Hampshire's)
The Duke of Lancaster's Regiment (King's, Lancashire and Border)
The Royal Regiment of Fusiliers
The Royal Anglian Regiment
The Rifles
The Yorkshire Regiment
The Mercian Regiment
The Royal Welsh
The Royal Irish Regiment
The Parachute Regiment
The Royal Gurkha Rifles

SPECIAL AIR SERVICE

ARMY AIR CORPS

SERVICES

ROYAL ARMY CHAPLAINS' DEPARTMENT
THE ROYAL LOGISTIC CORPS
ROYAL ARMY MEDICAL CORPS
CORPS OF ROYAL ELECTRICAL AND MECHANICAL ENGINEERS
ADJUTANT-GENERAL'S CORPS
ROYAL ARMY VETERINARY CORPS
SMALL ARMS SCHOOL CORPS
ROYAL ARMY DENTAL CORPS
INTELLIGENCE CORPS
ARMY PHYSICAL TRAINING CORPS
QUEEN ALEXANDRA'S ROYAL ARMY NURSING CORPS
CORPS OF ARMY MUSIC
THE ROYAL MONMOUTHSHIRE ROYAL ENGINEERS (MILITIA) (TA)
THE HONOURABLE ARTILLERY COMPANY (TA)
REST OF THE TERRITORIAL ARMY (TA)

ARMY EQUIPMENT

Tanks	325
Challenger 2	325
Reconnaissance vehicles	738
Fuchs	11
Jackal	400
Scimitar	327
Armoured Infantry Fighting Vehicle	526
Warrior	526
Armoured Personnel Carrier	2,059+
AFV432	646
Bulldog	380
Mastiff	277
Ridgeback	118
Saxon (Northern Ireland only)	109
Spartan	394
Warthog	115
Wolfhound	20+
Light Forces Vehicle (Panther)	401
Artillery pieces	670
Anti-tank missile†	800+
Aircraft	8*
Defender	4
King Air	4

Helicopters	298
Apache	66
Gazelle	133
Lynx	99
Unmanned aerial vehicle	450
Surface-to-air missile	338+
Land radar	157
Amphibious craft	6
Logistics and support vehicles	5

* Includes 3 King Air and 1 Defender on order
† 2009 figure

THE TERRITORIAL ARMY (TA)

The Territorial Army is part of the UK's reserve land forces and provides support to the regular army at home and overseas. The TA is divided into three types of unit: national, regional, and sponsored. TA soldiers serving in regional units complete a minimum of 27 days training a year, comprising some evenings, weekends and an annual two-week camp. National units normally specialise in a specific role or trade, such as logistics, IT, communications or medical services. Members of national units have a lower level of training commitment and complete 19 days training a year. Sponsored reserves are individuals who will serve, as members of the workforce of a company contracted to the MoD, in a military capacity and have agreed to accept a reserve liability to be called up for active service in a crisis. The TA's total strength is around 35,000.

QUEEN ALEXANDRA'S ROYAL ARMY NURSING CORPS

The Queen Alexandra's Royal Army Nursing Corps (QARANC) was founded in 1902 as Queen Alexandra's Imperial Military Nursing Service and gained its present title in 1949. The QARANC has trained nurses for the register since 1950 and also trains and employs health care assistants to Level 2 NVQ, with the option to train to Level 3. The corps recruits qualified nurses as officers and other ranks and in 1992 male nurses already serving in the army were transferred to the QARANC.

Colonel-in-Chief, HRH The Countess of Wessex
Colonels Commandant, Col. Rosemary Kennedy, TD;
  Col. Bridget McEvilly, CBE

THE ROYAL AIR FORCE

In Order of Seniority

THE QUEEN

MARSHAL OF THE ROYAL AIR FORCE
HRH The Prince Philip, Duke of Edinburgh, KG, KT,
  OM, GBE, AC, QSO, PC, *apptd* 1953

FORMER CHIEFS OF THE AIR STAFF

MARSHALS OF THE ROYAL AIR FORCE
Sir Michael Beetham, GCB, CBE, DFC, AFC, *apptd*
  1982
Sir Keith Williamson, GCB, AFC, *apptd* 1985
Lord Craig of Radley, GCB, OBE, *apptd* 1988

AIR CHIEF MARSHALS
Sir Michael Graydon, GCB, CBE, *apptd* 1991
Sir Richard Johns, GCB, KCVO, OBE, *apptd* 1994
Sir Peter Squire, GCB, DFC, AFC *apptd* 1999
Sir Glenn Torpy, GCB, CBE, DSO *apptd* 2006

AIR RANK LIST

AIR CHIEF MARSHALS
HRH The Prince of Wales, KG, KT, GCB, OM, AK, QSO,
  PC, ADC
Dalton, Sir Stephen, KCB, ADC *(Chief of the Air Staff)*
Bryant, Sir Simon, KCB, CBE, ADC *(Commander-in-Chief,
  Air Command)*

AIR MARSHALS
Peach, Sir Stuart, KCB, CBE *(Chief of Joint Operations)*
Walker, D., CB, CBE, AFC *(Deputy Cdr Joint Force
  Command, Brunssum)*
Nickols, C., CB, CBE *(Chief of Defence Intelligence)*
Harper, Sir Christopher, KBE, *(UK Military Representative
  to NATO and the EU)*
Leeson, K., CBE *(Chief of Materiel (Air) / Air Member for
  Materiel)*
Anderson, T., CB, DSO *(Director-General of the Military
  Aviation Authority)*
Pulford, A., CBE *(Deputy Commander-in-Chief Personnel
  and Air Member for Personnel, Air Command)*
Garwood, R., CB *(Deputy Commander-in-Chief Operations,
  Air Command)*
Hillier, S., CBE, DFC *(Deputy Chief of the Defence Staff
  (Capability))*

AIR VICE-MARSHALS
Ness, C., CB *(Director of Technical Airworthiness in the
  Military Aviation Authority)*
Walker, Sir David, KCVO, OBE, MVO *(Master of the
  Royal Household)*
Bollom, S., CB *(Director Combat (Air) Defence Equipment
  and Support)*
Wiles, M., CBE, *(Executive Officer, HQ Air Command)*
Dixon, C., CB, OBE *(Cdr Joint Helicopter Command)*
Evans, C., QHP *(Cdr Joint Medical Command)*
Harwood, M., CBE *(Head of the British Defence Staff, USA
  and Defence Attaché)*
Bagwell, G., CBE *(Chief of Staff, Joint Warfare
  Development, Permanent Joint HQ)*
Stacey, G., CB, MBE *(Cdr British Forces Cyprus)*
Lloyd, M., *(Chief of Staff Personnel and Air Secretary)*

North, B., OBE *(Assistant Chief of the Air Staff)*
Irvine, L., *(Director RAF Legal Services)*
Bates, B., CBE *(Senior Directing Staff (Air), Royal College
  of Defence Studies)*
Young, J., OBE *(Chief of Staff (Support))*
Morris, C., QHS *(Chief of Staff Health and
  Director-General Medical Services (RAF))*
Pentland, R., QHC *(Chaplain Chief (RAF))*
Bushell, C., *(Director of the Oman Typhoon Project Team,
  UK Trade and Investment Defence and Security
  Organisation)*
Colley, M., OBE *(Assistant Chief of the Defence Staff
  Concepts and Doctrine)*
Green, M., CBE *(Air Officer Commanding, No. 22
  Group / Chief of Staff Training)*
Murray, D., OBE *(Assistant Chief of the Defence Staff
  (Personnel) and Defence Services Secretary)*
Lock, R., CBE *(Commandant Joint Services Command and
  Staff College)*
Osborn, P., CBE *(Air Officer Commanding No. 2 Group)*
Bell, S. *Director-General Saudi Armed Forces Project)*
Howard, G. *(Assistant Chief of the Defence Staff Logistics
  Operations)*
Atha, S., DSO *(Air Officer Commanding No. 1 Group)*

CONSTITUTION OF THE RAF

The RAF consists of a single command, Air Command,
based at RAF High Wycombe. RAF Air Command was
formed on 1 April 2007 from the amalgamation of Strike
Command and Personnel and Training Command.

Air Command consists of three groups, each organised
around specific operational duties. No. 1 Group is the
coordinating organisation for the tactical fast-jet forces
responsible for attack, offensive support and air defence
operations. No. 2 Group provides air combat support
including air transport and air to air refuelling;
intelligence surveillance; targeting and reconnaissance;
and force protection. No. 22 (Training) Group recruits
personnel and provides trained specialist personnel to the
RAF, as well as to the Royal Navy and the Army *(see also
Armed Forces Training and Recruitment).*

RAF EQUIPMENT

Aircraft	
BAe 125	6
BAe 146	2
Dominie	9
Firefly	38
Globemaster	7
Hawk	145
Hercules	43
Islander	2
Nimrod	14
Sentinel	5
Sentry	6
Shadow	4
Super King Air (leased)	7
Tornado	105
Tristar	9
Tucano	95
Tutor	101
Typhoon	72
VC10	16

Helicopters

Chinook	41
Griffin	16
Merlin	28
Puma	34
Sea King	25
Squirrel	31

ROYAL AUXILIARY AIR FORCE

The Auxiliary Air Force was formed in 1924 to train an elite corps of civilians to serve their country in flying squadrons in their spare time. In 1947 the force was awarded the prefix 'royal' in recognition of its distinguished war service and the Sovereign's Colour for the Royal Auxiliary Air Force (RAuxAF) was presented in 1989. The RAuxAF continues to recruit civilians who undertake military training in their spare time to support the Royal Air Force in times of emergency or war.

Air Commodore-in-Chief, HM The Queen
Honorary Inspector-General Royal Auxiliary Air Force, Air Vice-Marshal Lord Beaverbrook
Inspector Royal Auxiliary Air Force, Gp Capt. Gary Bunkell, QVRM, AE, ADC

PRINCESS MARY'S ROYAL AIR FORCE NURSING SERVICE

The Princess Mary's Royal Air Force Nursing Service (PMRAFNS) was formed on 1 June 1918 as the Royal Air Force Nursing Service. In June 1923, His Majesty King George V gave his royal assent for the Royal Air Force Nursing Service to be known as the Princess Mary's Royal Air Force Nursing Service. Men were integrated into the PMRAFNS in 1980.

Patron and Air Chief Commandant, HRH Princess Alexandra, The Hon. Lady Ogilvy, KG, GCVO
Director of Nursing Services and Matron-in-Chief, Gp Capt. Jacqueline Gross

SERVICE SALARIES

In line with the announcement made in the June 2010 Budget, all public sector workers earning £21,000 a year or less, received a pay increase of £250 for 2011–12. Those earning over £21,000 had their pay frozen for two years.

The following rates of pay apply from 1 April 2011 and are rounded to the nearest pound.

The pay rates shown are for army personnel. The rates also apply to personnel of equivalent rank and pay band in the other services (*see* below for table of relative ranks).

Rank	Annual salary
SECOND LIEUTENANT	£24,615
LIEUTENANT	
On appointment	£29,587
After 1 year in rank	£30,369
After 2 years in rank	£31,147
After 3 years in rank	£31,921
After 4 years in rank	£32,703
CAPTAIN	
On appointment	£37,916
After 1 year in rank	£38,932
After 2 years in rank	£39,959
After 3 years in rank	£40,991
After 4 years in rank	£42,011
After 5 years in rank	£43,039
After 6 years in rank	£44,059
After 7 years in rank	£44,579
After 8 years in rank	£45,090
MAJOR	
On appointment	£47,760
After 1 year in rank	£48,940
After 2 years in rank	£50,111
After 3 years in rank	£51,298
After 4 years in rank	£52,474
After 5 years in rank	£53,661
After 6 years in rank	£54,841
After 7 years in rank	£56,016
After 8 years in rank	£57,199
LIEUTENANT-COLONEL	
On appointment	£67,032
After 1 year in rank	£67,920
After 2 years in rank	£68,801
After 3 years in rank	£69,681
After 4 years in rank	£70,562
After 5 years in rank	£74,614
After 6 years in rank	£75,609
After 7 years in rank	£76,613
After 8 years in rank	£77,617
COLONEL	
On appointment	£81,310
After 1 year in rank	£82,321
After 2 years in rank	£83,336
After 3 years in rank	£84,347
After 4 years in rank	£85,357
After 5 years in rank	£86,368
After 6 years in rank	£87,379
After 7 years in rank	£88,394
After 8 years in rank	£89,408
BRIGADIER	
On appointment	£97,030
After 1 year in rank	£98,013
After 2 years in rank	£98,995
After 3 years in rank	£99,973
After 4 years in rank	£100,964

PAY SYSTEM FOR SENIOR MILITARY OFFICERS

Pay rates effective from 1 April 2011 for all military officers of 2* rank and above (excluding medical and dental officers). All pay rates are rounded to the nearest pound.

Rank	Annual salary
MAJOR-GENERAL (2*)	
Scale 1	£108,201
Scale 2	£110,317
Scale 3	£112,476
Scale 4	£114,678
Scale 5	£116,924
Scale 6	£119,214
LIEUTENANT-GENERAL (3*)	
Scale 1	£125,908
Scale 2	£132,084
Scale 3	£138,569
Scale 4	£144,016
Scale 5	£148,265
Scale 6	£152,642
GENERAL (4*)	
Scale 1	£165,284
Scale 2	£169,416
Scale 3	£173,652
Scale 4	£177,993
Scale 5	£181,553
Scale 6	£185,184

Field Marshal – appointments to this rank will not usually be made in peacetime. The salary for holders of the rank is equivalent to the salary of a 5-star General, a salary created only in times of war. In peacetime, the equivalent rank to Field Marshal is the Chief of the Defence Staff. From 1 April 2011, the annual salary range for the Chief of the Defence Staff is £238,123–£252,698.

OFFICERS COMMISSIONED FROM THE SENIOR RANKS

Rank	Annual salary
Level 15	£50,680
Level 14	£50,349
Level 13	£50,000
Level 12	£49,325
Level 11	£48,653
Level 10	£47,973
Level 9	£47,298
Level 8	£46,622
Level 7*	£45,778
Level 6	£45,258
Level 5	£44,730
Level 4†	£43,686
Level 3	£43,166
Level 2	£42,633
Level 1‡	£41,593

* Officers commissioned from the ranks with more than 15 years' service enter on level 7

† Officers commissioned from the ranks with between 12 and 15 years' service enter on level 4

‡ Officers commissioned from the ranks with less than 12 years' service enter on level 1

SOLDIERS' SALARIES

Under the Pay 2000 scheme, personnel are paid in either a high or low band in accordance with how their trade has been allocated to those bands at each rank. Pay is based on trade and rank, not on individual appointment, or in response to temporary changes in role.

Rates of pay effective from 1 April 2011 (rounded to the nearest pound) are:

Rank	Lower band	Higher band
PRIVATE		
Level 1	£17,265	£17,265
Level 2	£17,736	£18,592
Level 3	£18,207	£20,500
Level 4	£19,779	£21,773
LANCE CORPORAL (levels 5–7 also applicable to Privates)		
Level 5	£20,832	£24,074
Level 6	£21,441	£25,245
Level 7	£22,358	£26,404
Level 8	£23,382	£27,592
Level 9	£24,230	£28,939
CORPORAL		
Level 1	£26,404	£27,592
Level 2	£27,592	£28,939
Level 3	£28,939	£30,356
Level 4	£29,160	£31,064
Level 5	£29,389	£31,814
Level 6	£29,623	£32,473
Level 7	£29,840	£33,182

Rank	Lower band	Higher band
SERGEANT		
Level 1	£30,012	£32,756
Level 2	£30,798	£33,603
Level 3	£31,592	£34,455
Level 4	£31,892	£34,889
Level 5	£32,723	£35,569
Level 6	£33,853	£36,249
Level 7	£34,111	£36,929
STAFF SERGEANT		
Level 1	£33,223	£36,953
Level 2	£33,657	£37,846
Level 3	£34,750	£38,751
Level 4	£35,565	£39,648
WARRANT OFFICER II (levels 5–7 also applicable to Staff Sergeants)		
Level 5	£36,048	£40,549
Level 6	£37,678	£41,445
Level 7	£38,255	£42,043
Level 8	£38,751	£42,641
Level 9	£39,627	£43,251
WARRANT OFFICER I		
Level 1	£38,599	£42,080
Level 2	£39,349	£42,907
Level 3	£40,143	£43,644
Level 4	£40,938	£44,447
Level 5	£41,737	£45,242
Level 6	£42,907	£46,048
Level 7	£44,119	£46,783

RELATIVE RANK – ARMED FORCES

Royal Navy	Army	Royal Air Force
1 Admiral of the Fleet	1 Field Marshal	1 Marshal of the RAF
2 Admiral (Adm.)	2 General (Gen.)	2 Air Chief Marshal
3 Vice-Admiral (Vice-Adm.)	3 Lieutenant-General (Lt.-Gen.)	3 Air Marshal
4 Rear-Admiral (Rear-Adm.)	4 Major-General (Maj.-Gen.)	4 Air Vice-Marshal
5 Commodore (Cdre)	5 Brigadier (Brig.)	5 Air Commodore (Air Cdre)
6 Captain (Capt.)	6 Colonel (Col.)	6 Group Captain (Gp Capt.)
7 Commander (Cdr)	7 Lieutenant-Colonel (Lt.-Col.)	7 Wing Commander (Wg Cdr)
8 Lieutenant-Commander (Lt.-Cdr)	8 Major (Maj.)	8 Squadron Leader (Sqn Ldr)
9 Lieutenant (Lt.)	9 Captain (Capt.)	9 Flight Lieutenant (Flt Lt)
10 Sub-Lieutenant (Sub-Lt.)	10 Lieutenant (Lt.)	10 Flying Officer (FO)
11 Midshipman	11 Second Lieutenant (2nd Lt.)	11 Pilot Officer (PO)

SERVICE RETIRED PAY
on compulsory retirement

Those who leave the services having served at least five years, but not long enough to qualify for the appropriate immediate pension, now qualify for a preserved pension and terminal grant, both of which are payable at age 60. The tax-free resettlement grants shown below are payable on release to those who qualify for a preserved pension and who have completed nine years' service from age 21 (officers) or 12 years from age 18 (other ranks).

The annual rates for army personnel are given. The rates also apply to personnel of equivalent rank in the other services, including the nursing services.

OFFICERS

Applicable to officers who give full pay service on the active list on or after 31 March 2011. Pensionable earnings for senior officers (*) is defined as the total amount of basic pay received during the year ending on the day prior to retirement, or the amount of basic pay received during any 12-month period within 3 years prior to retirement, whichever is the higher. Figures for senior officers are percentage rates of pensionable earnings on final salary arrangements on or after 31 March 2011.

No. of years reckonable service	Capt. and below	Major	Lt.-Col.	Colonel	Brigadier	Major-General*	Lieutenant-General*	General*
16	£12,557	£14,955	£19,608	£23,751	£28,214	—	—	—
17	£13,135	£15,665	£20,610	£24,840	£29,313	—	—	—
18	£13,714	£16,376	£21,612	£25,930	£30,413	—	—	—
19	£14,293	£17,086	£22,614	£27,019	£31,513	—	—	—
20	£14,872	£17,797	£23,616	£28,109	£32,613	—	—	—
21	£15,450	£18,507	£24,618	£29,199	£33,713	—	—	—
22	£16,029	£19,217	£25,620	£30,288	£34,813	—	—	—
23	£16,608	£19,928	£26,622	£31,378	£35,913	—	—	—
24	£17,187	£20,638	£27,624	£32,467	£37,013	38.5%	—	—
25	£17,765	£21,348	£28,626	£33,557	£38,113	39.7%	—	—
26	£18,344	£22,059	£29,628	£34,646	£39,213	40.8%	—	—
27	£18,923	£22,769	£30,630	£35,736	£40,313	42.0%	42.0%	—
28	£19,502	£23,480	£31,632	£36,826	£41,413	43.1%	43.1%	—
29	£20,080	£24,190	£32,634	£37,915	£42,513	44.3%	44.3%	—
30	£20,659	£24,900	£33,636	£39,005	£43,613	45.4%	45.4%	45.4%
31	£21,238	£25,611	£34,638	£40,094	£44,713	46.6%	46.6%	46.6%
32	£21,817	£26,321	£35,640	£41,184	£45,813	47.7%	47.7%	47.7%
33	£22,395	£27,031	£36,642	£42,273	£46,913	48.9%	48.9%	48.9%
34	£22,974	£27,742	£37,644	£43,363	£48,012	50.0%	50.0%	50.0%

WARRANT OFFICERS, NCOS AND PRIVATES
(Applicable to soldiers who give full pay service on or after 31 March 2011)

No. of years reckonable service	Below Corporal	Corporal	Sergeant	Staff Sergeant	Warrant Officer Level II	Warrant Officer Level I
22	£7,431	£9,586	£10,509	£11,971	£12,781	£13,590
23	£7,690	£9,920	£10,876	£12,389	£13,227	£14,065
24	£7,950	£10,255	£11,243	£12,807	£13,673	£14,539
25	£8,209	£10,590	£11,610	£13,225	£14,119	£15,014
26	£8,469	£10,924	£11,977	£13,643	£14,565	£15,488
27	£8,728	£11,259	£12,344	£14,061	£15,011	£15,962
28	£8,987	£11,593	£12,710	£14,479	£15,458	£16,437
29	£9,247	£11,928	£13,077	£14,896	£15,904	£16,911
30	£9,506	£12,263	£13,444	£15,314	£16,350	£17,385
31	£9,765	£12,597	£13,811	£15,732	£16,796	£17,860
32	£10,025	£12,932	£14,178	£16,150	£17,242	£18,334
33	£10,284	£13,266	£14,545	£16,568	£17,688	£18,809
34	£10,544	£13,601	£14,911	£16,986	£18,134	£19,283
35	£10,803	£13,935	£15,278	£17,404	£18,580	£19,757
36	£11,062	£14,270	£15,645	£17,821	£19,026	£20,232
37	£11,322	£14,605	£16,012	£18,239	£19,473	£20,706

GRANTS AND GRATUITIES
Terminal grants are in each case three times the rate of retired pay or pension. There are special rates of retired pay for certain other ranks not shown above. Lower rates are payable in cases of voluntary retirement.

A gratuity of £4,270 is payable for officers with short service commissions for each year completed. Resettlement grants are £14,686 for officers and £10,038 for other ranks.

EDUCATION

THE UK EDUCATION SYSTEM

The structure of the education system in the UK is a devolved matter with each of the countries of the UK having separate systems under separate governments. There are differences between the school systems in terms of the curriculum, examinations and final qualifications and, at university level, in terms of the nature of some degrees and the matter of tuition fees. The systems in England, Wales and Northern Ireland are similar and have more in common with one another than the Scottish system, which differs significantly.

Education in England is overseen by the Department for Education (DfE) (formed by the coalition government on 12 May 2010 to replace the former government's Department for Children, Schools and Families (DCSF)) and by the Department for Business, Innovation and Skills (BIS).

In Wales, responsibility for education lies with the Department for Children, Education, Lifelong Learning and Skills (DCELLS) within the Welsh government. Ministers in the Scottish government are responsible for education in Scotland, led by the directorates of Learning and Lifelong Learning, while in Northern Ireland responsibility lies with the Department of Education (DENI) and the Department for Employment and Learning (DELNI) within the Northern Ireland government.

DEPARTMENT FOR EDUCATION T 0370-000 2288
   W www.education.gov.uk
DEPARTMENT FOR BUSINESS, INNOVATION AND
   SKILLS T 020-7215 5000 W www.bis.gov.uk
DEPARTMENT FOR CHILDREN, EDUCATION,
   LIFELONG LEARNING AND SKILLS (DCELLS)
   T 0300-060 3300; 0845-010 3300
   W www.wales.gov.uk/topics/educationandskills
SCOTTISH GOVERNMENT – EDUCATION
   T 08457-741741; 0131-556 8400
   W www.scotland.gov.uk/Topics/Education
DEPARTMENT OF EDUCATION (NI) T 028-9127 9279
   W www.deni.gov.uk
DEPARTMENT FOR EMPLOYMENT AND
   LEARNING (NI) T 028-9025 7777 W www.delni.gov.uk

RECENT DEVELOPMENTS

Many changes affecting the education sector in England have been introduced or announced by the Conservative and Liberal Democrat coalition government that took office in May 2010. These include:

- introducing a 'pupil premium' to allocate more money directly to poorer pupils and free early years care for two-year-olds from disadvantaged families
- enabling more schools to become academies and parent/teacher groups to set up 'free schools'
- giving schools greater autonomy
- giving teachers more disciplinary powers and restricting public reporting of allegations against teachers
- changing school inspection to focus on four core areas of achievement: teaching, leadership and management, behaviour and safety

- abolishing five bodies – the Qualifications and Curriculum Development Agency, the General Teaching Council for England, the Training and Development Agency for Schools, the School Support Staff Negotiating Body and the Young People's Learning Agency
- replacing the Education Maintenance Allowance, which paid 16- to 19-year-olds from low income families up to £30 a week to carry on studying, with a new bursary scheme

Schools will also be affected by the final outcomes of reviews of: the primary and secondary National Curriculum and associated programmes of study; national testing at the end of primary school; the Early Years Foundation Stage; music education; and arrangements for pupils with special educational needs.

Changes have been announced in teacher recruitment and training. From September 2012 only graduates with a 2:2 degree or above will be eligible for funding and trainees' basic skills will be tested at the start of courses. The Teach First scheme will double its intake, more ex-armed forces personnel will be sponsored to become teachers and in-school training will be increased.

Changes affecting higher education have been the most controversial. Cuts in funding mean that universities and colleges will cease to receive grants for teaching students starting courses from September 2012 – with the exception of science, technology and engineering courses. The government's decision to allow universities to compensate by raising tuition fees to a maximum of £9,000 a year led to protests by students and university staff. Government hopes that only a few universities would charge the maximum rate proved optimistic when, in April 2011, most universities announced that they would be setting their fees at or near £9,000. The higher education white paper published in June 2011 made clear that, to avoid unaffordable calls on student loan funding, controls over the numbers of students allowed to start higher education courses will be implemented. However, these controls will not apply to the 65,000 or so students admitted with top A-level grades (A ,A, B or better); and 20,000 places will be reserved for universities and colleges charging average tuition fees of £7,500 or less. Universities will also only be allowed to charge fees over £6,000 if they ensure access for students from poorer families by offering fee discounts or other financial support. Students will not have to start repaying loans until their income reaches £21,000 a year (formerly £15,000) and part-time students will no longer have to pay their tuition fees up front. In addition, all students are promised better information before they apply, better teaching while at university, greater transparency in areas such as feedback on their work and better preparation for the job market.

STATE SCHOOL SYSTEM

PRE-SCHOOL

Pre-school education for children from 3 to 5 years of age is not compulsory. Parents may take as little or as much of their entitlement as they choose, although a free place is available for every 3- and 4-year-old whose parents want one. All 3- and 4-year-olds in England are entitled to 15 hours a week of free early education over 38 weeks of the year until they reach compulsory school age (the term following their fifth birthday). This is delivered flexibly over a minimum of three days each week during normal term times. Free places are funded by local authorities and are delivered by a range of providers in the maintained and non-maintained sectors – nursery schools; nursery classes in primary schools; private schools; private day nurseries; voluntary playgroups; pre-schools; and registered childminders. In order to receive funding, providers must be working towards the early learning goals and other features of the Early Years Foundation Stage curriculum (though this curriculum has been reviewed and may change), must be inspected on a regular basis by Ofsted and must meet any conditions set by the local authority.

In Wales, every child is entitled to receive free Foundation Phase education for a minimum of two hours a day from the term following their third birthday.

In Scotland, councils have a duty to provide a pre-school education for all 3- and 4-year-olds whose parents request one. Education authorities must offer each child 475 hours of free pre-school education a year (less for children who start pre-school later in the year), although they may provide more if they choose. This is usually delivered as five 2.5 hour sessions a week.

In Northern Ireland, there are now free, part-time nursery places available for all 3- and 4-year-old children in their final pre-school year. Most places offer 2.5 hours a day, five days a week for 38 weeks a year.

PRIMARY AND SECONDARY SCHOOLS

By law, full-time education starts at the age of five for children in England, Scotland and Wales and at the age of four in Northern Ireland. In practice, most children in the UK start school before their fifth birthday: in England from 2011 all children will be entitled to a primary school place from the September after their fourth birthday. In all parts of the UK, compulsory schooling ends at age 16, but children born between certain dates may leave school before their 16th birthday. Most young people stay in some form of education until 17 or 18. From 2013, all pupils in England will be required to continue in education or training to 17 years and from 2015, to 18 years. Primary education consists mainly of infant schools for children aged 5 to 7, junior schools for those aged 7 to 11, and combined infant and junior schools for both age groups.

First schools in some parts of England cater for ages 5 to 10 as the first stage of a three-tier system of first (lower), middle and secondary (upper) schools. Scotland has only primary schools with no infant/junior division.

Children usually leave primary school and move on to secondary school at the age of 11 (or 12 in Scotland). In the few areas of England that have a three-tier system of schools, middle schools cater for children after they leave first schools for three to four years between the ages of 8 and 14, depending on the local authority.

Secondary schools cater for children aged 11 to 16 and, if they have a sixth form, for those who choose to stay on to age 17 or 18. From the age of 16, students may move instead to further education colleges or work-based training.

Most UK secondary schools are co-educational. The largest secondary schools have more than 1,500 pupils

and around 60 per cent of pupils in the UK are in schools that take more than 1,000 pupils.

Most state-maintained secondary schools in England, Wales and Scotland are comprehensive schools, whose admission arrangements are made without reference to ability or aptitude. In England there remain some areas with grammar schools, catering for pupils aged 11 to 18, which select pupils on the basis of high academic ability. Northern Ireland continues to have many grammar schools, though this is changing – see below.

More than 90 per cent of pupils in the UK attend publicly funded schools and receive free education. The rest attend privately funded 'independent' schools, which charge fees, or are educated at home. No fees are charged by any publicly maintained school in England, Wales or Scotland. In Northern Ireland, fees may be charged in the preparatory classes of grammar schools.

The bulk of the UK government's expenditure on school education is through local authorities (Education and Library Boards in Northern Ireland), who pass on state funding to schools and other educational institutions.

SPECIAL EDUCATION

Schools and local authorities in England and Wales, Education and Library Boards (ELBs) in Northern Ireland and education authorities in Scotland are required to identify and secure provision for children with special educational needs and to involve parents in decisions. Where appropriate, and taking parents' wishes into account, children with special educational needs are educated in ordinary mainstream schools, sometimes with supplementary help from outside specialists. Parents of children with special educational needs (referred to as additional support needs in Scotland) have a right of appeal to independent tribunals if their wishes are not met.

Special educational needs provision may be made in maintained special schools, special units attached to mainstream schools or in mainstream classes themselves, all funded by local authorities. There are also non-maintained special schools run by voluntary bodies, mainly charities, who may receive grants from central government for capital expenditure and equipment but whose other costs are met primarily from the fees charged to local authorities for pupils placed in the schools. Some independent schools also provide education wholly or mainly for children with special educational needs.

ADDITIONAL SUPPORT NEEDS TRIBUNALS FOR
SCOTLAND T 0845-120 2906
W www.asntscotland.gov.uk
FIRST-TIER TRIBUNAL (SPECIAL EDUCATIONAL
NEEDS AND DISABILITY) T 01325-392760
W www.justice.gov.uk/guidance/courts-and-tribunals/
tribunals/send/index.htm
SPECIAL EDUCATIONAL NEEDS TRIBUNAL FOR
WALES T 01597-829800 W http://wales.gov.uk/sentwsub

HOME EDUCATION

In England and Wales parents have the right to educate their children at home and do not have to be qualified teachers to do so. Home-educated children do not have to follow the National Curriculum or take national tests nor do they need a fixed timetable, formal lessons or to observe school hours, days or terms. However, by law parents must ensure that the home education provided is full-time and suitable for the child's age, ability and aptitude and, if appropriate, to any special educational needs. Parents have no legal obligation to notify the local authority that a child is being educated at home, but if they take a child out of school, they must notify the school in writing and the school must report this to the local authority. Local authorities can make informal enquiries of parents to establish that a suitable education is being provided. For children in special schools, parents must seek the consent of the local authority before taking steps to educate them at home.

In Northern Ireland, Education and Library Boards monitor the quality of home provision and provide general guidance on appropriate materials and exam types through regular home visits.

The home schooling law in Scotland is similar to that of England. One difference, however, is that if parents wish to take a child out of school they must have permission from the local education authority.

HOME EDUCATION ADVISORY SERVICE
T 01707-371854 W www.heas.org.uk
HOME EDUCATION IN NORTHERN IRELAND
W www.hedni.org
SCHOOLHOUSE HOME EDUCATION
ASSOCIATION (SCOTLAND) T 01307-463120
W www.schoolhouse.org.uk

FURTHER EDUCATION

In the UK, further education (FE) is generally understood as post-secondary education: ie any education undertaken after an individual leaves school that is below higher education level. FE therefore embraces a wide range of general and vocational study undertaken by people of all ages from 16 upwards, full-time or part-time, who may be self-funded, employer-funded or state-funded.

FE in the UK is often undertaken at further education colleges, although some takes place on employers' premises. Many of these colleges offer some courses at higher education level; some FE colleges teach certain subjects to 14- to 16-year-olds under collaborative arrangements with schools. Colleges' income comes from public funding, student fees and work for and with employers.

HIGHER EDUCATION

Higher education (HE) in the UK describes courses of study, provided in universities, specialist colleges of higher education and in some FE colleges, where the level of instruction is above that of A-level or equivalent exams.

All UK universities and colleges that provide HE are autonomous bodies with their own internal systems of governance. They are not owned by the state. However, most receive a portion of their income from state funds distributed by the separate HE funding councils for England, Scotland and Wales, and the Department for Employment and Learning in Northern Ireland. The rest of their income comes from a number of sources including fees from home and overseas students, government funding for research, endowments and work with or for business.

EXPENDITURE

UK-MANAGED EXPENDITURE ON EDUCATION
(Real terms) £bn

2001–2	61.8	2006–7	76.9
2002–3	64.0	2007–8	80.1
2003–4	69.4	2008–9	82.6
2004–5	72.0	2009–10	88.6
2005–6	75.7	2010–11 (est)	90.6

Source: Public Expenditure Statistical Analyses (PESA) 2011

SCHOOLS

ENGLAND AND WALES

In England and Wales, publicly funded schools are referred to as 'state schools'. The four main categories of state school – community, foundation, voluntary-aided and voluntary-controlled – are maintained by local authorities, which have a duty to ensure there is a suitable place for every school-age child resident in their area. Each school has a governing body, made up of volunteers elected or appointed by parents, staff, the community and the local authority, which is responsible for strategic management, ensuring accountability, monitoring school performance, setting budgets and appointing the headteacher and senior staff. The headteacher is responsible for the school's day-to-day management and operations and for decisions requiring professional teaching expertise.

In Community schools, which are non-denominational, local authorities are the employers of the staff, own the land and buildings and set the admissions criteria.

In Foundation schools, the governing body employs the staff and sets the admissions criteria. The land and buildings are usually owned by the governing body or a charitable foundation. A foundation school may have a religious character, although most do not. A trust school is a distinct type of foundation school that forms a charitable trust with an outside partner – for example, a business, a university, an educational charity or simply another school – that shares the school's aspirations. The decision to become a trust school is taken by the governing body while taking account of parents' views. Community schools can take on foundation status and set up a trust in a single process.

Most voluntary-aided schools are religious schools founded by Christian denominations or other faiths. As with foundation schools, the governing body employs the staff and sets the admissions criteria, which may include priority for members of the faith or denomination. The school buildings and land are normally owned and provided by a charitable foundation, often a religious organisation, which appoints a majority of the school's governors and makes a small contribution to major building costs.

Voluntary-controlled schools are similar to voluntary-aided schools in that they often have a particular religious ethos, commonly Church of England, and the school land and buildings are normally owned by a charity. However, as with community schools, the local authority employs the school's staff, sets the admissions criteria and bears all the costs.

Among the local authority-maintained schools are some with particular characteristics:

- Community and foundation special schools cater for children with specific special educational needs, which may include physical disabilities or learning difficulties
- Grammar schools are secondary schools catering for pupils aged 11 to 18 that select all of their pupils based on academic ability. In England there are 164 grammar schools, concentrated in certain local authority areas. Wales has none
- Maintained boarding schools are state-funded and offer free tuition but charge fees for board and lodging

In Wales, Welsh-medium primary and secondary schools were first established in the 1950s and 1960s, originally in response to the wishes of Welsh-speaking parents who wanted their children to be educated through the medium of the Welsh language. Now, many children who are not from Welsh-speaking homes also attend Welsh-medium and bilingual schools throughout Wales. Welsh language education has become increasingly important following the Welsh government's vision of creating a bilingual Wales. The latest statistics show that Wales has 428 Welsh-medium primary schools, where the main or sole medium of instruction is in the Welsh language, and 34 Welsh-medium secondary schools, where more than half of foundation subjects (other than English and Welsh) and religious education are taught wholly or partly in Welsh.

England now has increasing numbers of schools that are publicly funded and charge no fees but are not local authority-maintained. Almost all of these are *Academies*, sometimes called 'independent state schools'. Academies are all-ability schools set up by sponsors from business, faith or voluntary groups in partnership with the Department for Education. Together they fund the land and buildings, with the government covering the running costs at a level comparable to other local schools. The new coalition government has introduced legislation to enable more schools, including primaries for the first time, to apply for academy status in order to leave local authority control and have greater freedom over what they teach, the pay and conditions of their teachers and how they organise schooling. As at June 2011 there were 704 academies, of which 100 were primaries and 10 were 'all-through' schools taking pupils aged 3 or 5 to 18.

SCOTLAND

Most schools in Scotland, known as 'publicly funded' schools, are state-funded and charge no fees. Funding is met from resources raised by the Scottish local authorities and from an annual grant from the Scottish government. Scotland does not have school governing bodies like the rest of the UK: local authorities retain greater responsibility for the management and performance of publicly funded schools. Headteachers manage at least 80 per cent of a school's budget, covering staffing, furnishings, repairs, supplies, services and energy costs. Expenditure on new buildings, modernisation projects and equipment is financed by the local authority within the limits set by the Scottish government.

Scotland has approaching 400 state-funded *faith schools,* the majority of which are Catholic. It has no grammar schools.

Integrated community schools form part of the Scottish government's strategy to promote social inclusion and to raise educational standards. They encourage closer and better joint working among education, health and social work agencies and professionals, greater pupil and parental involvement in schools, and improved support and service provision for vulnerable children and young people.

Scotland has a number of *grant-aided schools* that are independent of local authorities but supported financially by the Scottish government. These schools are managed by boards and most of them provide education for children and young people with special educational needs.

NORTHERN IRELAND

Most schools in Northern Ireland are maintained by the state and generally charge no fees, though fees may be charged in preparatory departments of some grammar schools. There are different types of state-funded schools,

each under the control of management committees, which also employ the teachers.

Controlled schools (nursery, primary, special, secondary and grammar schools) are managed by Northern Ireland's five ELBs through boards of governors which consist of teachers, parents, members of the ELB and transferor representatives (mainly from the Protestant churches).

Catholic maintained schools (nursery, primary, special and secondary) are under the management of boards of governors that consist of teachers, parents and members nominated by the employing authority, the Council for Catholic Maintained Schools (CCMS).

Other maintained schools (primary, special and secondary) are, in the main, Irish-medium schools that provide education in an Irish-speaking environment. The Department of Education has a duty to encourage and facilitate the development of Irish-medium education. Northern Ireland has more than 20 standalone Irish-medium schools, most of them primary schools, and around a dozen Irish-medium units attached to English-medium host schools.

Voluntary schools are mainly grammar schools, which select pupils according to academic ability. They are managed by boards of governors consisting of teachers, parents and, in most cases, representatives from the Department of Education and the ELB.

Integrated schools (primary and secondary) educate pupils from both the Protestant and Catholic communities as well as those of other faiths and no faith; each school is managed by a board of governors. There are at present 62 integrated schools maintained by the state, 24 of which are controlled schools.

In 2008 Northern Ireland's Minister for Education proposed a phased ending of grammar schools' academic selection over a three-year period, but these proposals did not attract the necessary level of support to become law. As a result, post-primary transfer arrangements for September 2010 admissions were unregulated, although informed by guidance from the Department of Education which did not recommend the use of academic admissions criteria. From 2013 new post-primary arrangements will guarantee all pupils access to a much wider range of courses, with a minimum of 24 courses at Key Stage 4, and 27 at post-16. At least one-third of the courses on offer will be academic and another third will be vocational. Legislation is already in place to give effect to these changes and to enable schools to enter into collaborative arrangements with other schools, FE colleges or other providers.

INDEPENDENT SCHOOLS

Around 7 per cent of the UK's schoolchildren are educated by privately funded 'independent' schools that charge fees and set their own admissions policies. Independent schools are required to meet certain minimum standards but need not teach the National Curriculum. *See also* Independent Schools.

UK SCHOOLS BY CATEGORY (2009–10)

	England	Wales
Maintained nursery schools	430	25
Maintained primary and secondary schools (total)	20,098	1,685
Community	12,024	1,415
Voluntary-aided	4,246	161
Voluntary-controlled	2,618	97
Foundation	1,210	12

Pupil referral units	443	42
Maintained special schools	979	43
*Non-maintained special schools	75	–
†Academies, including City Technology Colleges	205	–
Independent schools	2,375	64
Total	24,605	1,859

* Excludes voluntary and private pre-school education centres
† Figure includes two hospital schools
Source: DfE; Welsh government

Scotland

Publicly funded schools (total)	2,667
Primary	2,119
Secondary	372
Special	176
Independent schools (total)*	159
Primary	59
Secondary	55
Special	45
Total	2,867

* 2008–9 figures
Source: Scottish government

Northern Ireland

State-maintained nursery schools	98
State-maintained primary and secondary schools (total)	1,068
Controlled	460
Voluntary	52
Catholic maintained	470
Other maintained	25
Integrated	61
Special schools	41
Independent schools	14
Total	1,221

Source: DENI

INSPECTION

ENGLAND

The Office for Standards in Education, Children's Services and Skills (Ofsted) is the main body responsible for inspecting education in English schools. As well as inspecting all publicly funded and some independent schools, Ofsted inspects a range of other services in England, including childcare, children's homes, pupil referral units, local authority children's services, further education, initial teacher training and publicly funded adult skills training.

Ofsted is an independent, non-ministerial government department that reports directly to parliament, headed by Her Majesty's Chief Inspector (HMCI). Ofsted is required to promote improvement in the public services that it inspects; ensure that these services focus on the interests of their users – children, parents, learners and employers; and see that these services are efficient, effective and promote value for money. The education bill of January 2011 established that Ofsted will now focus only on four core elements of schools – pupil achievement, teaching, leadership, and behaviour and safety (*see* also Recent Developments).

Ofsted publishes the findings of its inspection reports, its recommendations and statistical information on its website.

OFFICE FOR STANDARDS IN EDUCATION,
CHILDREN'S SERVICES AND SKILLS
T 0300-123 1231 W www.ofsted.gov.uk

WALES

Estyn is the office of Her Majesty's Inspectorate for Education and Training in Wales. It is independent of, but funded by, the Welsh government and is led by Her Majesty's Chief Inspector of Education and Training in Wales.

Estyn's role is to inspect quality and standards in education and training in Wales, including in primary, secondary, special and independent schools, and pupil referral units, publicly funded nursery schools and settings, further education, adult community-based and work-based learning, local authorities and teacher education and training.

Estyn also provides advice on quality and standards in education and training to the Welsh government and others and its remit includes making public good practice based on inspection evidence. Estyn publishes the findings of its inspection reports, its recommendations and statistical information on its website.

HER MAJESTY'S INSPECTORATE FOR EDUCATION
AND TRAINING IN WALES
T 029-2044 6446 W www.estyn.gov.uk

SCOTLAND

HM Inspectorate of Education (HMIE) merged with Learning and Teaching Scotland in July 2011 to become Education Scotland, an executive agency of the Scottish government. Education Scotland operates independently and impartially while being directly accountable to Scottish ministers for the standards of its work. The new agency's core business will continue to be inspection and review. It is responsible for delivering measurable year-on-year improvements, with maximum efficiency, by promoting excellence, building on strengths, and identifying and addressing under-performance.

Education Scotland is also responsible for supporting learners and their parents or carers and all those working in education. It will contribute to and support policy development, working with Scottish ministers and government officials who will continue to set policy and strategy for the education system at a national level.

Services it is responsible for include inspecting or reviewing all schools, pre-school centres, further education colleges, local authorities, teacher education and publicly funded training programmes. The agency will also take over responsibility for the Curriculum for Excellence Management Board and Excellence Groups from October 2011 and support continuing professional development at a national level. It will publish the findings of its inspection reports and reviews, its recommendations, examples of good practice and statistical information on its website.

EDUCATION SCOTLAND T 0141 282 5000
W www.educationscotland.gov.uk

NORTHERN IRELAND

The Education and Training Inspectorate (ETINI) provides inspection services for the Department of Education Northern Ireland, the Department for Employment and Learning, the Department of Culture, Arts and Leisure and Criminal Justice Inspection Northern Ireland. Its role is to promote improvement in the interests of all learners, through inspections and the dissemination of its findings.

ETINI carries out inspections of all schools, pre-school services, special education, further education colleges, initial teacher training, training organisations, and curriculum advisory and support services.

The inspectorate provides evidence-based advice to ministers in order to assist in the formulation of policies. It publishes the findings of its inspection reports, its recommendations and statistical information on its website.

EDUCATION AND TRAINING INSPECTORATE
T 028-9127 9726 W www.etini.gov.uk

THE NATIONAL CURRICULUM

ENGLAND

The National Curriculum, first introduced in 1988, is mandatory in all state schools. It is organised into blocks of years called 'Key Stages' and sets out the core subjects that must be taught and the standards or attainment targets for each subject at each Key Stage. In addition, there is also a mandatory curriculum for the Early Years Foundation Stage (EYFS).

The National Curriculum has four Key Stages:

- The Early Years Foundation Stage covers children from birth to age 5, or the end of Reception Year in primary school
- Key Stage 1 covers Years 1 and 2 of primary school, for children aged 5–7
- Key Stage 2 covers Years 3 to 6 of primary school, for children aged 7–11
- Key Stage 3 covers Years 7 to 9 of secondary school, for children aged 11–14
- Key Stage 4 covers Years 10 and 11 of secondary school, for children aged 14–16

Within the framework of the National Curriculum, schools may plan and organise teaching and learning in the way that best meets the needs of their pupils. However, the government is reviewing both EYFS and the National Curriculum for 5- to 16-year-olds (*see* also Recent Developments).

The present EYFS learning and development requirement, which all schools, nurseries and other registered early years providers must deliver, has three elements: the early learning goals, educational programmes and assessment arrangements. It sets out six areas covered by the early learning goals and educational programmes: personal, social and emotional development; communication, language and literacy; problem-solving, reasoning and numeracy; knowledge and understanding of the world; physical development; and creative development.

KEY STAGES 1 AND 2 COMPULSORY SUBJECTS
English
Mathematics
Science
Design and technology
Information and communication technology (ICT)
History
Geography
Art and design
Music
Physical education

Schools must also provide religious education (RE), although parents have the right to withdraw children for all or part of the RE curriculum. Schools are also advised to teach personal, social and health education (PSHE) and

citizenship, together with at least one modern foreign language.

The former Labour government intended to introduce, from September 2011, a new primary curriculum, which included a requirement for children to learn a modern foreign language from the age of seven. However, the new coalition government announced in June 2010 that it would not proceed with this. The existing primary curriculum will remain in force until 2012.

The government then intends to introduce a revised National Curriculum for 5- to 16-year-olds (*see* Recent Developments), the stated aims of which are to, ensure a focus on traditional, basic subjects and give teachers more freedom in what and how they teach.

New programmes of study for English, mathematics, science and physical education will be available to schools in September 2012 and become statutory in maintained schools in September 2013. Other subjects and programmes of study will be made available in September 2013 and become statutory in 2014. Until then, in Key Stage 3, compulsory subjects include those for Key Stages 1 and 2 plus modern foreign languages and citizenship. Sex and relationship education (SRE) and RE must also be provided, as must careers education and guidance during Year 9. Parents can choose to withdraw their children from all or part of the RE curriculum and from the non-statutory elements of SRE, but not from the statutory elements of SRE which form part of the National Curriculum for science.

Pupils in Key Stage 4 study a mix of compulsory and optional subjects in preparation for national examinations such as GCSEs.

KEY STAGE 4 COMPULSORY SUBJECTS
English
Mathematics
Science
ICT
Physical education
Citizenship

Pupils also have to undertake careers education and work-related learning. Schools must also offer RE, SRE and at least one subject from each of four 'entitlement' areas: arts subjects (art and design, music, dance, drama and media arts); design and technology; humanities (history and geography); and modern foreign languages. Other subjects such as classical languages are taught when school resources permit.

For each National Curriculum subject, there is a programme of study that describes the subject knowledge, skills and understanding that pupils are expected to develop during each Key Stage.

The programmes of study also map out a scale of attainment within the subject. In most subjects, these 'attainment targets' are split into eight levels plus an 'exceptional performance' level.

Schools inform parents what National Curriculum level their children have reached in any formal assessment. Parents can use these levels to get an idea of how their child is progressing compared to what is typical for their age. For example, by the end of Key Stage 2, most will be at level 4.

Statutory assessment takes place towards the end of the EYFS, when children's level of development is compared to and recorded against a Foundation Stage Profile. National tests and tasks take place in English and mathematics at the end of Key Stages 1 and 2; all pupils in publicly funded schools in the relevant years are expected to take these tests. At Key Stage 1 the results of tasks and tests are not reported, except to parents, but are used to underpin teachers' overall assessment of pupils. At Key Stages 2 and 3, separate teacher assessments of pupils' progress are made. In Key Stage 2 this is set alongside the test results. At Key Stage 4, national examinations are the main form of assessment.

Each year the DfE publishes on its website achievement and attainment tables, showing performance measures for every school and local authority. The tables for primary schools are based mainly on the results of the tests taken by children at the end of Key Stage 2 when they are usually aged 11; since 2010 the tables also include teacher assessment results. The tables for secondary schools and for attainment post-16 rely mainly on the results of national examinations. All tables include indicators of the progress that pupils have made since their last assessment.

DEPARTMENT FOR EDUCATION T 0370-000 2288
W www.education.gov.uk

WALES

Wales has introduced a Foundation Phase curriculum for 3- to 7-year-olds. Full implementation began for 3-year-olds from September 2008, for 4-year-olds from September 2009, for 5-year-olds from September 2010 and will begin for 6-year-olds from September 2011. The emphasis is on learning-by-doing and children's skills and knowledge are planned across seven areas of learning. They are:

- Personal and social development, well-being and cultural diversity
- Language, literacy and communication skills
- Mathematical development
- Welsh language development
- Knowledge and understanding of the world
- Physical development
- Creative development

Full details of the Foundation Phase can be found in *Framework for Children's Learning for 3- to 7-year-olds in Wales*, available on the Welsh government website (*see* below).

The National Curriculum exists for 7- to 16-year-olds. Originally it was broadly similar to that of England, with distinctive characteristics for Wales reflected in the programmes of study. From September 2008 a revised school curriculum was implemented, consisting of the National Curriculum subjects together with non-statutory frameworks for personal and social education, the world of work, religious education and skills.

The National Curriculum in Wales includes the following subjects:

- *Key Stage 2* – English, Welsh, mathematics, science, design and technology, ICT, history, geography, art and design, music, and physical education
- *Key Stage 3* – as Key Stage 2, plus a modern foreign language
- *Key Stage 4* – English, Welsh, mathematics, science and physical education

Welsh is compulsory for pupils at all key stages, either as a first or as a second language. The proportion of pupils taught Welsh as a first language rose from 16 per cent in 2009 to 16.5 per cent in 2010.

Statutory testing was removed for pupils in Wales at the end of Key Stage 2 from 2004–5. Only statutory teacher assessment remains. It is also done at the end of Key Stage 1 (in future, the Foundation Phase) and Key Stage 3, and is being strengthened by moderation and accreditation arrangements.

THE WELSH GOVERNMENT – EDUCATION AND SKILLS
W http://wales.gov.uk/topics/educationandskills/
schoolshome/curriculuminwales

SCOTLAND

The curriculum in Scotland is not prescribed by statute but is the responsibility of education authorities and individual schools. However, schools and authorities are expected to follow the Scottish government's guidance on management and delivery of the curriculum.

Advice and guidance are provided by the Scottish government primarily through new executive agency Education Scotland, after Learning and Teaching Scotland, an executive non-departmental public body sponsored by the government, merged with HMIE in May 2011.

Scotland is pursuing its biggest education reform for a generation by introducing a new curriculum – Curriculum for Excellence – which aims to provide more autonomy for teachers, greater choice and opportunity for pupils and a single coherent curriculum for all children and young people aged 3 to 18.

The purpose of Curriculum for Excellence is encapsulated in 'the four capacities': to enable each child or young person to be a successful learner, a confident individual, a responsible citizen and an effective contributor. It focuses on providing a broad curriculum that develops skills for learning, skills for life and skills for work, with a sustained focus on literacy and numeracy. The period of education from pre-school through to the end of secondary stage 3, when pupils reach age 14, has the particular purpose of providing each young person in Scotland with this broad general education.

Curriculum for Excellence sets out 'experiences and outcomes', which describe broad areas of learning and what is to be achieved within them. They are:

- Expressive arts (including art and design, dance, drama, music)
- Health and wellbeing (including physical education, food and health, relationships and sexual health, and mental, physical and social wellbeing)
- Languages
- Mathematics
- Religious and moral education
- Sciences
- Social studies (including history, geography, society and economy)
- Technologies (including business, computing, food and textiles, craft, design, engineering and graphics)

The experiences and outcomes are written at five levels with progression to examinations and qualifications during the senior phase, which covers secondary stages 4 to 6 when students are generally aged 14 to 17. The framework is designed to be flexible so that pupils can progress at their own pace.

Level	Stage
Early	The pre-school years and primary 1 (ages 3–5), or later for some
First	To the end of primary 4 (age 8), but earlier or later for some
Second	To the end of primary 7 (age 11), but earlier or later for some
Third and Fourth	Secondary 1 to secondary 3 (ages 12–14), but earlier for some. The fourth level experiences and outcomes are intended to provide possibilities for choice and young people's programmes will not include all of the Fourth level outcomes
Senior phase	Secondary 4 to secondary 6 (ages 15–18), and college or other means of study

Under the new curriculum, assessment of students' progress and achievements from ages 3 to 15 is carried out by teachers who are required to base their assessment judgements on a range of evidence rather than single assessment instruments such as tests. Teachers have access to an online National Assessment Resource (NAR) set up in 2010, which provides a range of assessment material and national exemplars across the curriculum areas.

In the senior phase, young people aged 16 to 18, including those studying outside school, build up a portfolio of national qualifications, awarded by the Scottish Qualifications Authority (SQA).

Provision is made for teaching in Gaelic in many parts of Scotland and the number of pupils, from nursery to secondary, in Gaelic-medium education is growing.

EDUCATION SCOTLAND T 0141-282 5000
   W www.educationscotland.gov.uk
SCOTTISH QUALIFICATIONS AUTHORITY
   T 0845-279 1000 W www.sqa.org.uk

NORTHERN IRELAND

Since September 2007 Northern Ireland has been phasing in a revised statutory curriculum that places greater emphasis than before on developing skills and preparing young people for life and work. The new curriculum has now been in place across Years 1 to 12 since September 2009.

The revised curriculum includes a new Foundation Stage to cover years one and two of primary school. This is to allow a more appropriate learning style for the youngest pupils and to ease the transition from pre-school. Key Stage 1 now covers primary years 3 and 4, until children are 8, and Key Stage 2 covers primary years 5, 6 and 7, until children are 11. At post-primary, Key Stage 3 covers Years 8, 9 and 10 and Key Stage 4 Years 11 and 12.

The revised primary curriculum is made up of RE and the following areas of learning:

• Language and literacy
• Mathematics and numeracy
• The arts
• The world around us
• Personal development and mutual understanding
• Physical education

The revised post-primary curriculum includes a new area of learning for life and work, made up of employability, personal development, local and global citizenship and home economics (at Key Stage 3). In addition, it is made up of RE and the following areas of learning:

• Language and literacy
• Mathematics and numeracy
• Modern languages
• The arts
• Environment and society
• Physical education
• Science and technology

At Key Stage 4, the statutory requirements have been significantly reduced to learning for life and work, Physical education, RE and developing skills and capabilities. The aim is to provide greater choice and flexibility for pupils and allow them access to a wider range of academic and vocational courses provided under the revised curriculum's 'entitlement framework' (EF). This should be fully in place by 2013.

From 2013, schools will be required to provide pupils with access to at least 24 courses at Key Stage 4 and at least 27 courses post-16. In both cases at least one-third of the courses must be academic and at least one-third applied (vocational/professional/technical). The remaining third is at the discretion of each school. Individual pupils decide on the number and mix of courses they wish to follow.

RE is a compulsory part of the Northern Ireland curriculum, although parents have the right to withdraw their children from part or all of RE or collective worship. Schools have to provide RE in accordance with a core syllabus drawn up by the province's four main churches (Church of Ireland, Presbyterian, Methodist and Roman Catholic) and specified by the Department of Education.

Revised assessment and reporting arrangements, expected to be fully in place by June 2012, are being introduced to support the revised curriculum. The focus from Foundation to Key Stage 3 is on 'assessment for learning'. This programme includes classroom-based teacher assessment, computer-based assessment of literacy and numeracy and pupils deciding on their strengths and weaknesses and how they might progress to achieve their potential. Assessment information is reported to parents using a new pupil profile. Pupils at Key Stage 4 and beyond continue to be assessed through public examinations.

The Council for the Curriculum, Examinations and Assessment (CCEA), a non-departmental public body reporting to the Department of Education in Northern Ireland, is unique in the UK in combining the functions of a curriculum advisory body, an awarding body and a qualifications regulatory body. It advises the government on what should be taught in Northern Ireland's schools and colleges, ensures that the qualifications and examinations offered by awarding bodies in Northern Ireland are of an appropriate quality and standard and, as the leading awarding body itself, offers a range of qualifications including GCSEs, A-levels and AS-levels.

The CCEA hosts a dedicated curriculum website covering all aspects of the revised curriculum, assessment and reporting – see below.

COUNCIL FOR THE CURRICULUM,
   EXAMINATIONS AND ASSESSMENT
   T 028-9026 1200 W www.ccea.org.uk
NORTHERN IRELAND CURRICULUM
   T 028-9028 1200 W www.nicurriculum.org.uk

QUALIFICATIONS

ENGLAND, WALES AND NORTHERN IRELAND

There is a very wide range of public examinations and qualifications available, accredited by the Office of Qualifications and Examinations Regulation (OFQUAL) in England; the Department for Children, Education, Lifelong Learning and Skills (DCELLS) in Wales; and the Council for the Curriculum, Examinations and Assessment (CCEA) in Northern Ireland. Up-to-date information on all accredited qualifications and awarding bodies is available online at the Register of Regulated Qualifications website.

The National Qualifications Framework (NQF) establishes the level of all accredited qualifications in England, Wales and Northern Ireland. The NQF comprises nine levels (entry level to level 8) and, at each level, groups together qualifications that place similar demands on individuals as learners. Entry level, for example, covers basic knowledge and skills in English, maths and ICT not geared towards specific occupations, while level 3 includes qualifications such as A-levels which are appropriate for people who plan to go to university, and level 7 covers Masters' degrees and vocational qualifications appropriate for senior professionals and managers.

Young people aged 14 to 19 in schools or (post-16) colleges or apprenticeships may gain academic qualifications such as GCSEs, AS-levels and A-levels; qualifications linked to particular career fields, like Diplomas; vocational qualifications such as BTECs and NVQs; and functional, key or basic skills qualifications.

COUNCIL FOR THE CURRICULUM,
    EXAMINATIONS AND ASSESSMENT
    (NORTHERN IRELAND) T 028-9026 1200
    W www.ccea.org.uk
DEPARTMENT FOR CHILDREN, EDUCATION,
    LIFELONG LEARNING AND SKILLS (DCELLS)
    T 0300-0603300; 0845-010 3300
    W http://wales.gov.uk/topics/educationandskills
DIRECTGOV W www.direct.gov.uk
REGISTER OF REGULATED QUALIFICATIONS
    T 0300-303 3346 W http://register.ofqual.gov.uk
OFFICE OF QUALIFICATIONS AND
    EXAMINATIONS REGULATION (OFQUAL)
    T 0300-303 3344 W www.ofqual.gov.uk

GCSE

The vast majority of pupils in their last year of compulsory schooling in England, Wales and Northern Ireland take at least one General Certificate of Secondary Education (GCSE) exam, though GCSEs may be taken at any age. GCSEs assess the performance of pupils on a subject-specific basis and are mostly taken after a two-year course. They are available in more than 50 subjects, most of them academic subjects, though some, known as vocational or applied GCSEs, involve the study of a particular area of employment and the development of work-related skills. Some subjects are also offered as short-course qualifications, equivalent to half a standard GCSE, or as double awards, equivalent to two GCSEs.

GCSEs have traditionally been assessed by exams at the end of the course and by coursework completed by students during the course. GCSE certificates are awarded on an eight-point scale from A* to G. In most subjects two different papers, foundation and higher, are provided for different ranges of ability with grades A*–D available from the higher tier and C–G available from the foundation tier.

All GCSE specifications, assessments and grading procedures are monitored by OFQUAL, DCELLS and the CCEA (which is currently revising the qualification and subject criteria). A key change is that coursework is being replaced in nearly all subjects by 'controlled assessment': extended tasks sat in exam conditions. The new specifications for many GCSE subjects were introduced in schools in September 2009 and in September 2010 for English, ICT and mathematics.

Since September 2010 the government has allowed state schools to offer pupils International GCSE (iGCSE) exams in key subjects including English, mathematics, science and ICT. The iGCSEs do not include coursework and are viewed by some experts as more rigorous than traditional GCSEs.

GCE A-LEVEL AND AS-LEVEL

GCE (General Certificate of Education) advanced levels (A-levels) are the qualifications that the majority of young people in England, Wales and Northern Ireland use to gain entry to university.

A-levels are subject-based qualifications mostly taken by UK students aged 16 to 19 over a two-year course in school sixth forms or at college, but they can be taken at any age. They are available in more than 45, mostly academic, subjects, though there are some A-levels in vocational areas, often known as applied A-levels.

An A-level qualification consists of advanced subsidiary (AS) and A2 units. The AS is a standalone qualification and is worth half a full A-level qualification. It normally consists of two units, assessed at the standard expected for a learner half way through an A-level course, that together contribute 50 per cent towards the full A-level.

The A2 is the second half of a full A-level qualification. It normally consists of two units, assessed at the standard expected for a learner at the end of a full A-level course, that together are worth 50 per cent of the full A-level qualification. Most units are assessed by examination but some are by internal assessment. Each unit is graded A–E. Revised A-level specifications were introduced in September 2008, with a new A* grade awarded from 2010 to reward exceptional candidates.

An extended project was introduced in September 2008 as a separate qualification. It is a single piece of work on a topic of the student's own choosing that requires a high degree of planning, preparation, research and autonomous working. Awards are graded A–E and the extended project is accredited as half an A-level.

INTERNATIONAL BACCALAUREATE

The International Baccalaureate (IB) offers three educational programmes for students aged 3 to 19.

Some 219 schools and colleges in the UK, both state and independent, now offer the IB diploma programme for students aged 16 to 19. Based around detailed academic study of a wide range of subjects, including languages, the arts, science, maths, history and geography, this leads to a single qualification recognised by UK universities.

The IB diploma is made up of a compulsory 'core' plus six separate subjects where individuals have some choice over what they study. The compulsory core contains three elements: theory of knowledge; creativity, action and service; and a 4,000-word extended essay.

The diploma normally takes two years to complete and most of the assessment is done through externally marked examinations. Candidates are awarded points for each part of the programme, up to a maximum of 45. A candidate must score 24 points or more to achieve a full diploma.

Successfully completing the diploma earns points on the 'UCAS tariff', the UK system for allocating points to qualifications used for entry to higher education. An IB diploma total of 24 points is worth 260 UCAS points – the same as a B and two C grades at A-level. The maximum of 45 points earns 720 UCAS points – equivalent to six A-levels at grade A.

WELSH BACCALAUREATE

The Welsh Baccalaureate (WBQ), available for 14- to 19-year-olds in Wales, combines a compulsory core, which incorporates personal development skills, with options from existing qualifications such as A-levels, GCSEs and NVQs to make one broader award. The WBQ can be studied in English or Welsh, or a combination of the two. Following positive evaluation of pilots, the WBQ is being rolled out across the 14 to 19 age range at Advanced, Intermediate and Foundation levels. From September 2011 the qualification will be available to some 70,000 learners in a total of over 240 centres across Wales.

DIPLOMAS

The Diploma is a new qualification for 14- to 19-year-olds that combines practical, hands-on experience with academic learning. It was introduced by the former Labour government to increase the qualification choices available to young people and to help them to develop the knowledge and skills that employers and universities demand. Consequently, all Diplomas were developed in partnership with employers. The Diploma is a flexible 'umbrella' qualification that can be gained by accruing other qualifications at the relevant level, so young people studying for a Diploma can include GCSEs and A-levels within their Diploma programme.

Diplomas in ten subject areas were introduced in selected schools and colleges from September 2009:

- business administration and finance
- construction and the built environment
- creative and media
- engineering
- environmental and land-based studies
- hair and beauty studies
- hospitality
- information technology
- manufacturing and product design
- society, health and development

A further four Diplomas – travel and tourism; public services; retail business; and sport and active leisure – began in September 2010. However, the Diplomas that the previous government planned to introduce in science, languages and humanities, to be taught from September 2011, have been cancelled. There are three levels of Diploma, each taking two years to complete:

- Foundation Diploma – a level 1 qualification, equivalent to five GCSEs at grades D to G
- Higher Diploma – a level 2 qualification, equivalent to seven GCSEs at grades A* to C
- Advanced Diploma – a level 3 qualification for those over 16, equivalent to 3.5 A-levels

All Diploma students continue to study English, maths and ICT and have some work experience with an employer. Advanced Diplomas can lead either to university or to a career.

BTECS, OCR NATIONALS AND OTHER VOCATIONAL QUALIFICATIONS

Vocational qualifications can range from general qualifications where a person learns skills relevant to a variety of jobs, to specialist qualifications designed for a particular sector. They are available from several awarding bodies, such as City & Guilds, Edexcel and OCR, and can be taken at many different levels.

BTEC qualifications and OCR Nationals are particular types of work-related qualifications, available in a wide range of subjects, including: art and design, business, health and social care, information technology, media, public services, science and sport. The qualifications offer a mix of theory and practice, can include work experience and can take the form of (or be part of) a technical certificate, one of the key components of an Apprenticeship. They can be studied full-time at college or school, or part-time at college. BTEC qualifications are available at various levels on the National Qualifications Framework (NQF), including Higher National Certificates and Diplomas (HNCs and HNDs), at higher education level; OCR Nationals are achieved at levels 1 to 3.

Learners complete a range of assignments, case studies and practical activities, as well as a portfolio of evidence that shows what work has been completed. Assessment is usually done by the teacher or trainer, sometimes externally. BTEC and OCR Nationals are graded as pass, merit or distinction. BTEC and OCR Nationals at level 3 can qualify the learner for university entry.

All vocational and work-related qualifications fit into the Qualifications and Credit Framework (QCF). QCF qualifications are made up of units that can be studied at each individual's own pace and built up to full qualifications over time. Every qualification and unit on the QCF has a credit value, showing how long it takes to complete. One credit is equivalent to ten hours. When an individual takes QCF units or qualifications, their learning is 'banked' and stored on their personal learner record, showing what they have completed and how they can progress further.

There are more than 2,500 new vocational qualifications on the QCF, available in a broad range of subjects from a wide range of learning providers and some employers. Available in England, Northern Ireland and Wales, they are also recognised in Scotland.

NVQS

A National Vocational Qualification (NVQ) is a 'competence-based' qualification that is recognised by employers. Individuals learn practical, work-related tasks designed to help them develop the skills and knowledge to do a particular job effectively. NVQs can be taken in school, at college or by people already in work. There are more than 1,300 different NVQs available from the vast majority of business sectors. NVQs exist at levels 1 to 5 on the NQF and as new vocational qualifications on the QCF, though some will continue to be called NVQs. An NVQ qualification at level 2 or 3 can also be taken as part of an apprenticeship.

FUNCTIONAL SKILLS

Functional skills are a new set of qualifications launched across England during 2010, available for all learners aged 14 and above. They test the practical skills in English, mathematics and ICT that allow people to work confidently, effectively and independently in life. These skills are an integral part of the secondary school curriculum and of other qualifications including Diplomas and apprenticeships. Stand-alone functional skills qualifications are also available. These skills are assessed mainly by a set of practical tasks completed within a given time limit, though new ways of assessment such as electronic and online methods are being considered. Functional skills replace previous skills for life qualifications and the three main key skills qualifications in England. In Wales these new qualifications are known as 'essential skills'.

APPRENTICESHIPS

An apprenticeship combines on-the-job training with nationally recognised qualifications, allowing individuals to gain skills and qualifications while working and earning a wage. Apprenticeships are available in more than 190 job roles across a wide variety of industry sectors and take between one and four years to complete. There are three levels available:

- Apprenticeships – at level 2 on the National Qualifications Framework (NQF), they are equivalent to five good GCSE passes
- Advanced Apprenticeships – at level 3 on the NQF, they are equivalent to two A-level passes
- Higher Apprenticeships – lead to qualifications at NVQ Level 4 or, in some cases, a foundation degree

In England, the National Apprenticeship Service (NAS), launched in 2009, has responsibility for the delivery of apprenticeships including the provision of an online vacancy matching system. Between April 2010 and March 2011, 257,000 young people started an apprenticeship in England. The Welsh government and the Department for Employment and Learning (DEL) are responsible for the apprenticeship programmes in Wales and Northern Ireland respectively.

NATIONAL APPRENTICESHIP SERVICE (NAS)
T 02476-826482 W www.apprenticeships.org.uk

SCOTLAND

Scotland has its own system of public examinations and qualifications. The Scottish Qualifications Authority (SQA) is Scotland's national body for qualifications, responsible for developing, accrediting, assessing and certificating all Scottish qualifications apart from university degrees and some professional body qualifications.

There are qualifications at all levels of attainment. Almost all school candidates gain SQA qualifications in the fourth year of secondary school and most obtain further qualifications in the fifth or sixth year or in further education colleges. Increasingly, people also take them in the workplace.

SQA, with partners such as Universities Scotland, has introduced the Scottish Credit and Qualifications Framework (SCQF) as a way of comparing and understanding Scottish qualifications. It includes qualifications across academic and vocational sectors and compares them by giving a level and credit points. There are 12 levels in the SCQF, level 1 being the least difficult and level 12 the most difficult. The number of SCQF credit points shows how much learning has to be done to achieve the qualification. For instance, one SCQF credit point equals about 10 hours of learning including assessment.

SQA is responsible for three main types of qualification: units, courses and group awards.

UNITS
NATIONAL UNITS

National Units can be taken at schools, colleges and in other training centres. There are more than 3,500 units available in a wide range of subjects such as science, engineering, agriculture and care. Most units are designed to take 40 hours of teaching time to complete. National Units can be built up into National Courses, National Progression Awards (NPAs) and National Certificates (NCs) – see below. The names for the National Units at the various SCQF levels are:

- level 1 – Access 1
- level 2 – Access 2
- level 3 – Access 3
- level 4 – Intermediate 1
- level 5 – Intermediate 2
- level 6 – Higher
- level 7 – Advanced Higher

HIGHER NATIONAL UNITS

Higher National Units, which cover the skills and knowledge that people need in jobs at middle management and technician levels, are mainly taken at college. They are the building blocks of Higher National Certificates (HNCs) and Higher National Diplomas (HNDs) – see below, though they are also qualifications in their own right. These units can sit at various SCQF levels but are normally between levels 6 and 9 and are often used for progression to courses in higher education.

SVQ UNITS

Scottish Vocational Qualifications units (SVQs) are based on national 'standards of competence' drawn up by government-sponsored bodies called 'sector skills councils', which are made up of trade bodies, employers and specialists. There are sector skills councils for most industries. Each SVQ unit defines one aspect of a job or a work-role, and says what it is to be competent in that aspect of the job. These units can be built into SVQs, see below, and are sometimes used in wider schemes such as apprenticeships.

COURSES
STANDARD GRADES

Standard Grades are generally taken over two years of study in years 3 and 4 at secondary school. These courses are made up of different parts called 'elements', usually with an exam at the end. There are Standard Grades at SCQF levels 3, 4 and 5 called:

- level 3 – Foundation
- level 4 – General
- level 5 – Credit

Candidates generally progress from Standard Grades to National Courses.

NATIONAL COURSES

National Courses are available at these levels:

- level 2 – Access 2
- level 3 – Access 3
- level 4 – Intermediate 1
- level 5 – Intermediate 2
- level 6 – Higher
- level 7 – Advanced Higher

Most National Courses are made up of three units plus an external assessment, usually an examination marked and checked by professional examiners appointed by the SQA. Candidates must pass all three units and are awarded grades A to D on the basis of how they did in their external assessment. Most young people who qualify for places at college and university do so on the basis of the Highers and Advanced Highers.

SKILLS FOR WORK COURSES

Skills for Work Courses are practical courses designed as an equivalent option to an existing qualification, such as Standard Grade, to help young people develop skills that are important to employment and life. These courses offer candidates practical experiences that are linked to particular careers and are normally delivered by a school and college working in partnership. They are assessed by the teacher or lecturer and have no final exam.

GROUP AWARDS

NATIONAL PROGRESSION AWARDS

National Progression Awards (NPAs) are designed to assess a defined set of skills and knowledge in specialist vocational areas and link to national occupational standards, the basis of SVQs. NPAs are at SCQF levels 2 to 6, and are mainly used in colleges for short programmes of study.

NATIONAL CERTIFICATES

National Certificates, also at SCQF levels 2 to 6, aim to develop a range of skills and knowledge, including transferable skills, such as core skills. Each National Certificate also has specific aims relating to a subject or occupational area and is designed to prepare candidates for further progression. They are primarily aimed at 16- to 18-year-olds and adults in full-time education, normally at a college. They prepare candidates for more advanced study at HNC/HND level or employment.

HNCS AND HNDS

HNCs and HNDs are qualifications introduced in the mid-1920s that provide the skills and knowledge needed for training towards jobs at middle management and technician level. They are made up of Higher National Units and cover a wide range of occupations. Many HNDs allow the holder entry to the second or third year of a degree course. HNCs are at SCQF level 7 and HNDs at level 8.

SVQS

SVQs are based on job competence, and recognise the skills and knowledge that people need in employment. There are SVQs in most occupations, and they are available for all types and levels of jobs. Primarily delivered to candidates in full-time employment, they are available at SCQF levels 4 to 12.

PDAS

Professional Development Awards (PDAs) are qualifications for people who are already in a career or vocation and who wish to extend or broaden their skills. People often take a PDA after completing a degree or vocational qualification. There are PDAs at SCQF levels 6 to 12. Customised Awards are vocational qualifications specially designed by SQA to meet an organisation's specific needs for skills and expertise.

THE SCOTTISH QUALIFICATIONS AUTHORITY (SQA) **T** 0845-279 1000 **W** www.sqa.org.uk
SCOTTISH CREDIT AND QUALIFICATIONS FRAMEWORK (SCQF) **T** 0845-270 7371 **W** www.scqf.org.uk

FURTHER EDUCATION AND LIFELONG LEARNING

ENGLAND

The further education (FE) system in England provides a wide range of education and training opportunities for young people and adults. From the age of 16, young people who wish to remain in education, but not in a school setting, can undertake further education (including skills training) in an FE college. There are two main types of college in the FE sector: sixth form colleges and general further education (GFE) colleges. Some FE colleges focus on a particular area, such as art and design or agriculture and horticulture. Each institution decides its own range of subjects and courses. Students at FE colleges can study for a wide and growing range of academic and/or work-related qualifications, from entry level to higher education level.

Though the Department for Business, Innovation and Skills is responsible for the FE sector and for funding FE for adults (19 or over), the Department for Education funds all education and training for 16- to 18-year-olds.

The proportion of 16- to 18-year-olds in education or training has risen steadily over recent years. In 2009–10 nearly 1.64 million 16- to 18-year-olds, 84.4 per cent of the age group, were in education or training, including 70.6 per cent in full-time education. By the time that England's education-leaving age rises to 18 in 2015, 100 per cent should be in education or training. It is assumed that most of the additional students will go into FE or work-based training rather than staying on at school.

The 'September Guarantee', introduced in 2007, offers a place in post-16 education or training to all 16- and 17-year-olds who want one. In 2010, 97 per cent of 16-year-olds and 91 per cent of 17-year-olds received an offer of a place.

Statutory responsibility for 16 to 19 education and training in England, formerly with the Learning and Skills Council (LSC), now rests with local authorities, supported by the Young People's Learning Agency (YPLA), a non-departmental public body. The agency's remit also includes funding and supporting academies and providing direct support for young learners.

The FE sector in England, as in other parts of the UK, also provides a range of opportunities for adults.

The Skills Funding Agency (SFA), part of the Department for Business, Innovation and Skills, is presently responsible for funding and regulating education and training for adults. It will invest government funding of £3.7bn in FE and skills training places for over 3 million adult learners (aged 19 or over) in the 2011/12 academic year.

In November 2010, the government announced a new strategy for FE, including more adult apprenticeships (provision for 200,000 adults by 2014–15 with £605m in funding in 2011–12); fully funded training for 19- to 24-year-olds undertaking their first full level 2 (GCSE equivalent) or first level 3 qualification when they do not already have one; and fully funded basic skills for people who left school without basic skills in reading, writing and mathematics. 'Train to Gain', the programme that funded trainees sponsored by employers, was replaced in July 2011 by a programme focused on helping small employers to train low-skilled staff.

There are currently 18 employer-led, funded and designed centres of training excellence called National Skills Academies in various stages of development. Each academy operates in a key sector of the economy, from financial services to construction, and operates in partnership with colleges, schools and independent training providers to offer specialist training within their sector.

Among the many voluntary bodies providing adult education, the Workers' Educational Association (WEA) is the UK's largest, operating throughout England and Scotland. It provides part-time courses to adults in response to local need in community centres, village halls, schools, pubs or workplaces. Similar but separate WEA organisations operate in Wales and Northern Ireland.

The National Institute of Adult Continuing Education (NIACE), a charitable non-governmental organisation, promotes lifelong learning opportunities for adults in England and Wales.

NATIONAL INSTITUTE OF ADULT CONTINUING EDUCATION (NIACE) T 0116-204 4200
W www.niace.org.uk
THE SKILLS FUNDING AGENCY T 0845-377 5000
W www.skillsfundingagency.bis.gov.uk
WORKERS' EDUCATIONAL ASSOCIATION (WEA)
T 020-7426 3450 W www.wea.org.uk
THE YOUNG PEOPLE'S LEARNING AGENCY
T 0845-337 2000 W www.ypla.gov.uk

WALES

In Wales, the aims and makeup of the FE system are similar to those outlined for England. The Welsh government funds a wide range of learning programmes for young people through colleges, local authorities and private organisations. Current thinking is outlined in *Skills That Work for Wales*, published in July 2008, which describes the 'one Wales' ambition for a highly educated, highly skilled and high-employment Wales, and *Transforming Education and Training Provision in Wales; Delivering Skills that Work for Wales*, published in November 2009. The Welsh government has set out plans to improve learning opportunities for all post-16 learners in the shortest possible time, to increase the engagement of disadvantaged young people in the learning process, and to transform the learning network to increase learner choice, reduce duplication of provision and encourage higher-quality learning and teaching in all post-16 provision. One goal is to ensure that, by 2015, 95 per cent of young people will be ready for high-skilled employment or higher education by the age of 25.

In Wales, responsibility for adult and continuing education lies with the Department for Children, Education, Lifelong Learning and Skills (DCELLS) within the Welsh government. Wales operates a range of programmes to support skills development, including subsidised work-based training courses for employees

and the Workforce Development Programme, where employers can use the free services of experienced skills advisers to develop staff training plans.
COLEG HARLECH WEA T 01248-353254
W www.harlech.ac.uk/en/
NIACE DYSGU CYMRU T 029-2037 0900
W www.niacedc.org.uk
WEA SOUTH WALES T 029-2023 5277
W www.swales.wea.org.uk

SCOTLAND

Scotland's 43 FE colleges (known simply as colleges) are at the forefront of lifelong learning, education, training and skills in Scotland. Colleges cater for the needs of learners both in and out of employment at all stages in their lives from middle secondary school and earlier to retirement. Colleges' courses span much of the range of learning needs, from specialised vocational education and training through to general educational programmes. The level of provision ranges from essential life skills and provision for students with learning difficulties to HNCs and HNDs. Some colleges, notably those in the Highlands and Islands, also deliver degrees and postgraduate qualifications.

The Scottish Funding Council (SFC) is the statutory body responsible for funding teaching and learning provision, research and other activities in Scotland's colleges. The 43 colleges were incorporated in 1993. Overall strategic direction for the sector is provided by the Lifelong Learning Directorate of the Scottish government, which provides annual guidance to the SFC and liaises closely with bodies such as Scotland's Colleges, the Scottish Qualifications Authority and the FE colleges themselves to ensure that its policies remain relevant and practical.

The Scottish government takes responsibility for community learning and development in Scotland while Skills Development Scotland, a non-departmental public body, is charged with improving Scotland's skills performance by linking skills supply and demand and helping people and organisations to learn, develop and make use of these skills to greater effect. ILA Scotland is a Scottish Government scheme delivered by Skills Development Scotland that provides funding for training to individuals over the age of 16 with an income of less than £22,000 a year.
ILA SCOTLAND T 0808-100 1090
W www.ilascotland.org.uk
SCOTLAND'S COLLEGES T 01786-892000
W www.scotlandscolleges.ac.uk
SCOTTISH FUNDING COUNCIL T 0131-313 6500
W www.sfc.ac.uk
SKILLS DEVELOPMENT SCOTLAND T 0141-285 6000
W www.skillsdevelopmentscotland.co.uk

NORTHERN IRELAND

FE in Northern Ireland is provided through six multi-campus colleges. Most secondary schools also provide a sixth form where students can choose to attend for two additional years to complete their AS-levels and A-levels.

Colleges Northern Ireland (CNI) acts as the representative body for the six FE colleges which, like their counterparts in the rest of the UK, are independent corporate bodies where management responsibility lies with each individual college's governing body. The range of courses that they offer spans essential skills, a wide choice of vocational and academic programmes and higher education programmes. The majority of full-time enrolments in the six colleges are in the 16 to 19 age group, while most part-time students are over 19.

The Department for Employment and Learning (DELNI) is responsible for the policy, strategic development and financing of the statutory FE sector and for lifelong learning, and also provides support to a small number of non-statutory FE providers. The Educational Guidance Service for Adults (EGSA), an independent, not-for-profit organisation, has a network of local offices based across Northern Ireland which provide services to adult learners, learning advisers, providers, employers and others interested in improving access to learning for adults.

COLLEGES NORTHERN IRELAND (CNI)
   T 028-9068 2296 W www.anic.ac.uk
THE EDUCATIONAL GUIDANCE SERVICE FOR
   ADULTS T 028-9024 4274 W www.egsa.org.uk
WEA NORTHERN IRELAND T 028-9032 9718
   W www.wea-ni.com

FINANCIAL SUPPORT

The *Education Maintenance Allowance* (EMA) in England, a scheme that paid 16- to 19-year-olds from low income families a weekly allowance to continue in education, closed in January 2011 (*see* Recent Developments). From September 2011 it will be replaced by a bursary scheme for full-time 16- to 19-year-old students facing financial hardship. Those in care, leaving care, on income support or on certain disability benefits will be guaranteed a bursary of £1,200 a year.

There are similar EMA schemes in Scotland, Wales and Northern Ireland, but with slightly different eligibility conditions. Students must apply to the EMA scheme for the part of the UK where they intend to study.

The *Adult Learning Grant* (ALG), a similar scheme to the EMA but for those aged 19 and over, has also closed. From 2011/12 colleges and learning providers will award learner support funds directly to new students.

Care to Learn is available in England to help young parents under the age of 20 who are caring for their own child or children with the costs of childcare and travel while they are in some form of publicly funded learning (below higher education level). The scheme is not income assessed and pays up to £160 a week (£175 in London) to cover costs. The Sixth Form College Childcare Scheme is similar to Care to Learn, also for the under-20s, and pays the same rates, but is income-assessed and available only to those learning in a school sixth form or sixth-form college.

Dance and Drama Awards (DaDA) are state-funded scholarships for students over the age of 16 enrolled at one of 22 private dance and drama schools in England, who are taking specified courses at National Certificate or National Diploma level. Awards cover most of a student's tuition fees but students also need to make a personal contribution – £1,275 for the 2011–12 academic year. DaDA is not income-assessed. Students from England, Scotland or Wales may get extra help with living costs and childcare if their family's annual income is below £33,000.

Young people studying away from home because their chosen course is not available locally may qualify for the *Residential Support Scheme* or *Residential Bursaries*.

Information and advice on funding support and applications are available from the Learner Support help-line on the Directgov website.

Discretionary Support Funds (DSF) are available in colleges and school sixth forms to help students who have trouble meeting the costs of participating in further education.

In Wales, students aged 19 or over on FE courses may be eligible for the *Assembly Learning Grant for Further Education Scheme* (ALG (FE)). This is a means-tested payment of up to £1,500 for full-time students and up to £750 for those studying part-time. *Discretionary Financial Contingency Funds* are also available to all students in Wales suffering hardship and are administered by the institutions themselves. *Individual Learning Accounts in Wales* closed in March 2011.

In Scotland, FE students can apply to their college for discretionary support in the form of *Further Education Bursaries*. These can include allowances for maintenance, travel, study, childcare and additional support needs. *Individual Learning Accounts* provide up to £500 for those with incomes of less than £22,000.

In Northern Ireland, FE students may be eligible for *Further Education Awards,* non-refundable assistance administered on behalf of the five Education and Library Boards by the Western Education and Library Board.

UK FE students over 18 whose costs are not fully met from the grants described above may also be eligible for *Professional and Career Development Loans*. These loans – also available to HE students – cover up to 80 per cent of course fees (up to 100 per cent for those unemployed for three months); other course costs, such as books, travel and childcare; and living expenses, such as rent, food and clothing (for those who are unemployed or working fewer than 30 hours a week). The loans, of between £300 and £10,000, are available from participating high street banks – currently Barclays and the Co-operative. The Young People's Learning Agency (YPLA) pays the interest on the loan while the student is studying and for one month afterwards. Once students complete their courses, they must pay interest at the rate fixed when they took out the loan, which will be competitive with other commercially available 'unsecured' personal loans.

CAREERS SCOTLAND
   W www.careers-scotland.org.uk/Education/Funding/
   Funding.asp
DIRECTGOV W www.direct.gov.uk
STUDENT FINANCE WALES T 0845-602 8845
   W www.studentfinancewales.co.uk
WESTERN EDUCATION AND LIBRARY BOARD
   T 028-8241 1411 W www.welbni.org

HIGHER EDUCATION

Publicly funded higher education (HE) in the UK is provided in 115 universities; 50 higher education colleges and other specialist HE institutions; and a significant number of FE colleges which offer higher education courses.

The Higher Education Funding Council for England (HEFCE) funds teaching and research in 130 English higher education institutions (HEIs), of which 91 are universities, and also funds the HE courses in 124 FE colleges.

The Higher Education Funding Council for Wales (HEFCW) distributes funding for HE in Wales through Wales's 12 HEIs and some FE colleges.

The Scottish Funding Council (SFC) – which is also responsible for FE in Scotland – is the national, strategic body responsible for funding HE teaching and research in Scotland's 20 HEIs, of which 16 are universities, and 43 colleges.

In Northern Ireland HE is provided by two universities,

the Open University (OU) and two university colleges, and six regional institutes of further and higher education. Unlike other parts of the UK, Northern Ireland has no higher education funding council; the Department for Employment and Learning fulfils that role.

All UK universities and a number of HE colleges award their own degrees and other HE qualifications. HE providers who do not have their own degree-awarding powers offer degrees under 'validation arrangements' with other institutions that do have those powers. The OU, for example, runs a validation service which enables a number of other institutions to award OU degrees, after the OU has assured itself that the academic standards of their courses are as high as the OU's own standards.

Each HE institution is responsible for the standards of the awards it makes and the quality of the education it provides to its students, and each has its own internal quality assurance procedures. External quality assurance for HE institutions throughout the UK is provided by the Quality Assurance Agency for Higher Education (QAA).

The QAA is independent of government, funded by subscriptions from all publicly funded UK universities and colleges of HE. Its main role is to safeguard the standards of HE qualifications. It does this by defining standards for HE through a framework known as the academic infrastructure. QAA also carries out reviews of the quality of UK HE institutions via a system known as 'institutional audits'. QAA also advises government on a range of HE quality issues, including applications for the grant of degree-awarding powers. It publishes reports on its review activities on its website.

DEPARTMENT FOR EMPLOYMENT AND
    LEARNING T 028-9025 7777 W www.delni.gov.uk
HIGHER EDUCATION FUNDING COUNCIL FOR
    ENGLAND T 0117-931 7317 W www.hefce.ac.uk
HIGHER EDUCATION FUNDING COUNCIL FOR
    WALES T 029-2076 1861 W www.hefcw.ac.uk
SCOTTISH FUNDING COUNCIL T 0131-313 6500
    W www.sfc.ac.uk
THE QUALITY ASSURANCE AGENCY FOR HIGHER
    EDUCATION T 01452-557000 W www.qaa.ac.uk
See also Universities for information on the Research Assessment Exercise (being replaced from 2011 by the Research Excellence Framework) and listings of universities in the UK.

STUDENTS IN HIGHER EDUCATION (2009–10)*			
	Full-time	Part-time	Total
HE students	–	–	2,493,415
Postgraduate students	298,255	284,450	578,705
Undergraduate students	1,333,900	580,810	1,914,710
*Includes UK, EU and non-EU students			
Source: Higher Education Statistics Agency 2010			

UK HIGHER EDUCATION QUALIFICATIONS AWARDED (2009–10)		
	Full-time	Part-time
First degrees	312,740	38,120
Other undergraduate qualifications	62,025	77,725
Postgraduate Certificate in Education (PGCE)	20,395	1,640
Other postgraduate qualifications	14,985	31,180
Total higher degrees including doctorates	118,235	39,900
Source: HESA 2010		

COURSES

HE institutions in the UK mainly offer courses leading to the following qualifications. These qualifications go from levels 4 to 8 on England's National Qualifications Framework, levels 7 to 12 on Scotland's Credit and Qualifications Framework (Scotland is reviewing its framework level descriptors until June 2012). Individual HEIs may not offer all of these.

Certificates of Higher Education (CertHE), awarded after one year's full-time study (or equivalent). If available to students on longer courses, they certify that students have reached a minimum standard in their first year.

Diplomas of Higher Education (DipHE) *and other Higher Diplomas,* awarded after two to three years' full-time study (or equivalent). They certify that a student has achieved a minimum standard in first- and second-year courses and, in the case of nursing, third-year courses. They can often be used for entry to the third year of a related degree course.

Foundation degrees, awarded after two years of full-time study (or equivalent). These degrees combine academic study with work-based learning, and have been designed jointly by universities, colleges and employers with a particular area of work in mind. They are usually accepted as a basis for entry to the third year of a related degree course.

Bachelor's degrees, also referred to as *first degrees.* There are different titles; Bachelor of Arts (BA) and Bachelor of Science (BSc) being the most common. In England, Wales and Northern Ireland most Bachelor's degree courses are typically 'with Honours' and awarded after three years of full-time study, although in some subjects the courses last longer. In Scotland, where young people often leave school and go to university a year younger, HE institutions typically offer Ordinary Bachelor's degrees after three years' study and Bachelor's degrees with Honours after four years. Honours degrees are graded as first, upper-second (2:1), lower second (2:2) or third. HEIs in England, Wales and Northern Ireland may allow students who fail the first year of an Honours degree by a small margin to transfer to an Ordinary degree course, if they have one. Ordinary degrees may also be awarded to Honours degree students who do not finish an Honours degree course but complete enough of it to earn a pass.

Postgraduate or *Higher degrees.* Graduates may go on to take *Master's degrees,* which involve one or two years' work and can be taught or research-based. They may also take one-year postgraduate diplomas and certificates, often linked to a specific profession, such as the *Postgraduate Certificate in Education* (PGCE) required to become a state school teacher. A *doctorate,* leading to a qualification such as a Doctor of Philosophy – a PHD or DPHIL – usually involves at least three years of full-time research.

The framework for HE qualifications in England, Wales and Northern Ireland (FHEQ) and the framework for qualifications of HE institutions in Scotland, can both be found on the QAA website (W www.qaa.ac.uk/academicinfrastructure/FHEQ/SCQF/), which describes the achievement represented by HE qualifications.

ADMISSIONS

When preparing to apply to a university or other HE college, individuals can compare facts and figures on institutions and courses using the government's Unistats website. This includes details of students' views from the annual National Student Survey.

For the vast majority of full-time undergraduate courses, individuals need to apply online through UCAS, the organisation responsible for managing applications to HE courses in the UK. More than half a million people wanting to study at a university or college each year use this UCAS service, which has useful online tools to help students find the right course.

UCAS also provides two specialist applications services used by more than 50,000 people each year: the Conservatoires UK Admissions Service (CUKAS), for those applying to UK music conservatoires, and the Graduate Teacher Training Registry (GTTR), for postgraduate applications for initial teacher training courses in England and Wales and some in Scotland. Details of initial teacher training courses in Scotland can also be obtained from Universities Scotland and from Teach in Scotland, the website created by the Scottish government to promote teaching.

Each university or college sets its own entry requirements. These can be in terms of particular exam grades or total points on the 'UCAS tariff' (UCAS's system for allocating points to different qualifications on a common basis), or be non-academic, like having a health check. HEIs will make 'firm offers' to candidates who have already gained the qualifications they present for entry, and 'conditional offers' to those who have yet to take their exams or obtain their results. Conditional offers often require a minimum level of achievement in a specified subject, for example '300 points to include grade A at A-level Chemistry'. If candidates' achievements are lower than specified in their conditional offers, the university or college may not accept them; then, if they still wish to go into HE, they need to find another institution through the UCAS 'clearing' process.

The OU conducts its own admissions. It is the UK's only university dedicated to distance learning and the UK's largest for part-time HE. Because it is designed to be 'open' to all, no qualifications are needed for entry to the majority of its courses.

Individuals can search more than 58,000 UK postgraduate courses and research opportunities on UK graduate careers website Prospects. The application process for postgraduate places can vary between institutions. Most universities and colleges accept direct applications and many accept applications through UKPASS, a free, centralised online service run by UCAS that allows individuals to submit up to ten different applications, track their progress and attach supporting material, such as references. Applications for postgraduate social work courses must also be made through UCAS.

UNISTATS W http://unistats.direct.gov.uk
UCAS T 0871-468 0468 W www.ucas.com
UNIVERSITIES SCOTLAND T 0131-226 1111
W www.universities-scotland.ac.uk
TEACH IN SCOTLAND T 0845-345 4745
W www.teachinginscotland.com
PROSPECTS T 0161-277 5200 W www.prospects.ac.uk
UKPASS T 0871-334 4447 W http://ukpass.ac.uk

TUITION FEES AND STUDENT SUPPORT
TUITION FEES
HE institutions in England, Wales and Northern Ireland are allowed to charge variable tuition fees for full-time HE courses. Although students from outside the EU can be charged the full cost of their courses, the amount that HEIs may charge students from the UK and other EU countries has been capped since 2006 at £3,000 a year plus inflationary increases. The maximum that an institution can charge new UK and EU students for the 2011–12 academic year is £3,375. From September 2012, universities will be able to charge up to £9,000 a year in tuition fees (see Recent Developments). The exact fee depends on the course studied and the institution attended. Full-time students do not have to pay their fees before or during their course, as tuition fee loans are available to cover the full cost; these do not have to be repaid until the student is working (see below).

In recent years, Scottish HE institutions have charged flat rate fees, set by the Scottish government, to undergraduate students classed as being ordinarily resident in England, Wales or Northern Ireland; though, as explained above, they can get repayable tuition fee loans to cover the cost. The fee for undergraduates starting courses in 2011–12 is £1,820 a year. However, the Scottish government has announced that it intends to allow universities to set their own fees, up to £9,000 a year, for these students from 2012–13. However, undergraduate students classed as being ordinarily resident in Scotland or another EU country do not have to pay tuition fees at Scottish HE institutions. All tuition fees are paid on their behalf by the Scottish government through the Student Awards Agency for Scotland (SAAS); students must apply for this funding every year.

STUDENT LOANS, GRANTS AND BURSARIES
ENGLAND
All students starting a full-time HE course in 2011–12 can apply through Student Finance England for financial support. Two student loans are available from the government: a *tuition fee loan* of up to £3,375 for 2011–12; and a *maintenance loan* to help with living expenses of up to £4,950 for those living away from home (£6,928 if studying away from home in London) and £3,838 for those living with their parents during term time.

The tuition fee loan is not affected by household income and is paid directly to the relevant HE institution. A proportion (currently 72 per cent) of the maximum maintenance loan is available irrespective of household income while the rest depends on an income assessment. Student Finance England usually pays the money into the student's own bank account in three instalments, one at the start of each term.

Repayment of both loans does not start until the April after the student has left university or college and is earning more than £15,000 a year. At this point the individual's employer will take 9 per cent of any salary above the £15,000 threshold through the Pay As You Earn (PAYE) system. The self-employed make repayments through their tax returns. Someone earning £20,000 a year, the average starting salary for graduates entering full-time employment, will have to pay back £8.65 a week. Student loans accrue interest from the date they are paid out, up until they are repaid in full. Generally, the interest rate for student loans is set in September each year. The latest rate can be found online (W www.studentloanrepayment.co.uk/interest).

Students can also apply for a *maintenance grant* towards living expenses which does not have to be repaid. The maximum grant available for 2011–12 is £2,906 for the academic year. This is available to full-time HE students with a household income of £25,000 or under. Those with a household income of £50,020 or under receive a partial grant. The exact amount paid depends upon income. Students eligible for help through the maintenance grant receive some of it instead of the maintenance loan. The amount they are eligible for through the maintenance loan is reduced by 50p for every £1 of maintenance grant that they are entitled to. This means that students from lower income households generally have less to repay when they finish studying and start work.

Certain groups of students who claim means-tested state benefits can get the *special support grant*, also worth up to £2,906, instead of the maintenance grant. Likely recipients include single parents and students with certain disabilities. If a student receives the special support grant, it does not affect the amount of maintenance loan that he or she receives.

Bursaries are an additional source of help available from universities and colleges. They do not have to be repaid. Institutions in England must offer at least a minimum bursary payment of £338 in 2011–12 to students paying maximum tuition fees and getting the full maintenance grant or special support grant.

Students can use the student finance calculator on the Student Finance England website to work out what financial support they may get.

PART-TIME HIGHER EDUCATION STUDENTS
Part-time HE students in England may be entitled to a grant towards their fees, and a grant towards their course costs. This help does not have to be repaid. Those with a household income of less than £28,066 may be able to get a maximum of £1,495 in 2011–12.

There are no regulations stating how much universities or colleges can charge in tuition fees for most part-time courses. The maximum *fee grant* is based on how 'intensive' the course is, or how long it takes to complete compared to the equivalent full-time course. Students on certain state benefits qualify for the maximum automatically. Otherwise the amount awarded depends on the student's household income. Separate applications for these grants must be made each academic year. Details are available on the Student Finance England website.

If the student's chosen HE institution runs the *additional fee support scheme*, it could provide extra financial help if the student is on a low income and in certain other circumstances. Help may also be available through the institution's *access to learning fund*, for students in financial difficulty.
STUDENT FINANCE ENGLAND T 0845-300 5090
    W www.direct.gov.uk/studentfinance

WALES
Welsh students starting a full-time HE course in 2011–12 can apply through Student Finance Wales for the forms of financial support described below.

A similar system of tuition fee loans and maintenance loans now operates in Wales as in England but with slightly lower maximum maintenance loans available: up to £4,715 for students living away from home (£6,618 if studying away from home in London) and £3,643 for those living with their parents during term time. Tuition fee loans of up to £3,375 are available to cover the exact amount that the institution charges for a course.

The Welsh government has made a commitment that all new Welsh-domiciled students who take out a maintenance loan from academic year 2011–12, irrespective of where they study in the UK, will receive up to £1,500 debt relief when they start repayment.

Welsh-domiciled students may apply for an *assembly learning grant* (ALG) of up to £5,600 to help meet general living costs. This is paid in three instalments, one at the start of each term, like the student maintenance loan. The amount that a student gets depends on household income. The maximum grant is available to those with a household income of £18,370 or under. Those with an income of £50,020 or under receive a partial grant.

Universities and colleges in Wales are committed to providing additional support for students under the *Welsh bursary scheme*. Every full-time HE student, regardless of where they live in the UK, may be considered for a means-tested bursary, which is paid in addition to other financial support received and is not offset by any reductions in other forms of support.

Institutions also hold *financial contingency funds* to provide discretionary assistance to students experiencing financial difficulties.

Students can use the student finance calculator on the Student Finance Wales website to work out what financial support they may be entitled to.

PART-TIME HIGHER EDUCATION STUDENTS
Part-time undergraduate students studying at least 50 per cent of an equivalent full-time course are entitled to receive a *fee grant*, depending on their household income (anyone earning over £28,181 will receive no support). The rate depends on how intensive the course is. For 2011–12, the maximum fee grant, which applies to students who study at a rate equivalent to 75 per cent of a full-time course, is £1,000 (less than 60 per cent is £670 and between 60 and 74 per cent is £800). Such students may also be entitled to receive *adult dependants' grant* (ADG), *childcare grant* (CCG) or *parents' learning allowance* (PLA). The amount received depends on the intensity of the course undertaken. The maximum grants paid to eligible students are £2,647 for ADG and £1,508 for PLA; CCG depends on the cost of childcare.

Part-time students can also apply for assistance with course-related costs worth up to £1,125. Students who already have a degree cannot normally apply for this support. Those on part-time teacher-training courses are not eligible for part-time grants but may qualify for full-time support.
STUDENT FINANCE WALES T 0845-602 8845
    W www.studentfinancewales.co.uk

SCOTLAND
All students starting a full-time HE course in 2011–12 can apply through the Student Awards Agency for Scotland for financial support. Living cost support is mainly provided through a *student loan*, the majority of which is income-assessed. The maximum loan for 2011–12 paid to students living away from home is £5,417 and for those living with their parents is £4,457 a year. If the family income is over approximately £62,000 a year, the student receives only the minimum loans of £915 and £605 respectively. Low-income students may also be eligible for an *additional loan* of up to £785 with the maximum lent to those whose household income is £18,000 or less a year.

The *young students' bursary* (YSB) is available to young students from low-income backgrounds and is non-repayable. Eligible students receive this bursary instead of part of the student loan, thus reducing their level of repayable debt. In 2011–12 the maximum annual support provided through YSB is £2,640 if household income is £18,000 or less a year.

The *independent students' bursary* (ISB) similarly replaces part of the loan and reduces repayable debt for low-income students classed as 'independent' of parental support. The maximum paid is £1,000 a year to those whose household income is £18,000 or less a year.

From 2011–12 travel expenses will be included within the student loan. There are also *supplementary grants* available to certain categories of students such as lone parents and those with dependants. Extra help is also available to those who have a disability, learning difficulty or mental health problem.

STUDENT AWARDS AGENCY FOR SCOTLAND
T 0300-555 0505
W www.saas.gov.uk/student_support/index.htm

NORTHERN IRELAND

All students starting a full-time HE course in 2011–12 can apply through Student Finance Northern Ireland for financial support. The arrangements for both full-time and part-time students are similar to those for England. The main difference is that the income-assessed *maintenance grant* (or *special support grant* for students on certain income-assessed benefits) for new full-time students studying at UK universities and colleges is worth up to £3,475 while continuing students are eligible instead for a *higher education bursary* of up to £2,000.

STUDENT FINANCE NORTHERN IRELAND
T 0845-600 0662 W www.studentfinanceni.co.uk

DISABLED STUDENTS' ALLOWANCES

Disabled Students' Allowances (DSAs) are grants available throughout the UK to help meet the extra course costs that students can face as a direct result of a disability, ongoing health condition, mental health condition or specific learning difficulty. They help disabled people to study in HE on an equal basis with other students. They are paid on top of the standard student finance package and do not have to be repaid. The amount that an individual gets depends on the type of extra help needed, not on household income. This amounts to £5,161 for specialist equipment for the entire course, non-medical helper allowance of £20,520 a year and a general allowance of £1,724 a year. Eligible individuals should apply as early as possible to their relevant UK awarding authority.

POSTGRADUATE AWARDS

In general, postgraduate students do not qualify for mandatory support like student loans. An exception to this is students taking a Postgraduate Certificate in Education (PGCE), who can qualify for the finance package usually available only to undergraduates.

There is heavy competition for any postgraduate funding available. Individuals can search for postgraduate awards and scholarships on two websites: Hot Courses and Prospects. They can also search for grants available from educational trusts, often reserved for students from poorer backgrounds or for those who have achieved academic excellence, on the Educational Grants Advisory Service (EGAS) website. Otherwise they need to fund their own fees and living expenses.

Postgraduates from Scotland on certain full-time vocational courses can apply through the Student Awards Agency for Scotland for funding under the *postgraduate students' allowances scheme*. In Northern Ireland, the Department for Employment and Learning and the Education and Library Boards provide postgraduate funding for certain courses. Postgraduate students with an impairment, health condition or learning difficulty can apply for disabled students' allowances (*see* above) for both taught courses and research places.

DEPARTMENT FOR EMPLOYMENT AND
LEARNING (DELNI) T 028-9025 7777
W www.delni.gov.uk
EDUCATIONAL GRANTS ADVISORY SERVICE
(EGAS) T 020-7254 6251 W www.family-action.org.uk
HOT COURSES W www.scholarship-search.org.uk
PROSPECTS W www.prospects.ac.uk
STUDENT AWARDS AGENCY FOR SCOTLAND
(SAAS) T 0300-555 0505
W www.student-support-saas.gov.uk

TEACHER TRAINING

See Professional Education.

EMPLOYEES AND SALARIES

EMPLOYEES

QUALIFIED TEACHERS IN MAINTAINED SCHOOLS
(2009–10)
Full-time equivalent, thousands

	England	Wales	Scotland	NI	UK
Nursery and primary schools	200.9	13.6	24.7	8.1	247.3
Secondary schools	225.6*	13.2	24.8	10.1	273.7
Special schools	15.1	0.7	1.9	0.8	18.5
Education elsewhere†	6.5	–	–	–	6.5
Total	448.1	27.5	51.4	19.0	546.0

* Includes academies and city technology colleges in England
† Figure includes pupil referral units and is a separate statistic for England only

SUPPORT STAFF IN MAINTAINED SCHOOLS (2009–10)
Full-time equivalent, thousands

	England	Wales	Scotland	NI*
Teaching assistants	194.2	15.5	11.6	N/A
Other support staff	168.6†	5.0	10.5	N/A

* Figures are not collated centrally for Northern Ireland
† Includes academies and city technology colleges in England

ACADEMIC STAFF IN UK HIGHER EDUCATION
INSTITUTIONS (2009–10)

	Full-time	Part-time	Total
Professors	15,320	2,055	17,375
Non-professors	102,605	61,610	164,220
Teaching only	8,360	38,115	46,475
Teaching and research	75,220	18,665	93,885
Research only	33,700	6,770	40,470
Neither teaching or research	650	120	770

Source: HESA 2010

SALARIES

State school teachers in England and Wales are employed by local authorities or the governing bodies of their schools, but their pay and conditions are set nationally. Classroom teachers start on the main pay scale which has different rates for different areas. Each September teachers move one point up on the main pay scale until they reach the maximum basic rate of pay (M6). Qualified teachers who reach the top of the main pay scale are eligible to apply and be assessed against national standards to 'cross the threshold' on to a three point upper pay scale. Progress along the upper pay scale is not automatic, but is based on performance recommendations made by the headteacher. Unqualified 'associate' teachers such as instructors are paid on a separate salary scale.

There are teaching and learning responsibility payments for specific posts, special needs work and recruitment and retention factors which may be awarded at the discretion of the school governing body or the local authority. An 'Excellent Teacher' scheme allows eligible teachers, who share their skills in classroom teaching for the benefit of professional development of other teachers within their own school, to access a higher salary. The Advanced Skills Teacher grade was introduced to enhance the prospects of the most able classroom teachers who disseminate good practice by working in other local schools. Advanced Skills Teachers have their own pay spine. Headteachers and other school leaders are paid on a separate leadership pay spine. All teachers are eligible for membership of the Teachers' Pension Scheme.

As at September 2010, salary scales for teachers in England and Wales were:

Headteacher	£42,379–£105,097
Excellent Teacher	£39,697–£52,090
Advanced Skills Teacher	£37,461–£56,950
Classroom teacher (upper pay scale)	£34,181–£36,755
Classroom teacher (main pay scale)	£21,588–£31,552
Associate teachers	£15,817–£25,016

Inner London	
Headteacher	£49,466–£112,181
Excellent Teacher	£48,600–£60,993
Advanced Skills Teacher	£44,540–£64,036
Classroom teacher (upper pay scale)	£41,497–£45,000
Classroom teacher (main pay scale)	£27,000–£36,387
Associate teachers	£19,893–£29,088

Pay structures for teachers in Scotland were agreed up until April 2011 when pay was frozen for two years until 2013. Teachers are paid on a seven-point scale where the entry point is for newly qualified teachers undertaking their probationary year. There is no equivalent in Scotland of the upper pay spine operated in England and Wales. Experienced, ambitious teachers who reach the top of the main pay scale are eligible to become chartered teachers

and earn more on a separate pay spine. However, to do so they must study for further professional qualifications and finance these studies. Headteachers and deputies have a separate pay spine as do 'principals' or heads of department. Additional allowances are payable to teachers under a range of circumstances, such as working in distant islands and remote schools.

As at September 2011, salary scales for teachers in Scotland were:

Headteacher/deputy headteacher	£42,288–£82,542
Principal teacher	£37,284–£48,120
Chartered teacher	£35,253–£41,925
Main grade	£21,438–£34,200

Teachers in Northern Ireland have broadly similar pay and working conditions to teachers in England and Wales, although there is neither an Advanced Skills Teacher grade nor an Excellent Teacher scheme. Classroom teachers who take on teaching and learning responsibilities outside their normal classroom duties may be awarded one of five teaching allowances.

As at September 2010, salary scales for teachers in Northern Ireland were:

Principal (headteacher)	£42,379–£105,379
Classroom teacher (upper pay scale)	£34,181–£36,756
Classroom teacher (main pay scale)	£21,588–£31,552
Associate teachers	£13,734
Teaching allowances	£1,847–£11,911

Since 2007, most academic staff in HE across the UK are paid on a single national pay scale as a result of a national framework agreement negotiated by the HE unions and HE institutions. The main features of the agreement are that all staff are paid according to rates on a 51-point national pay spine and that academic and academic-related staff are graded according to a national grading structure. Since August 2009 the pay spine has ranged from £13,150 to £55,535. As HE institutions are autonomous employers, precise job grades and salaries do vary to some extent from one institution to another but the following table gives a guide to the salaries that typically tally with certain job roles in HE.

Principal lecturer	£45,336–£52,556
Senior lecturer	£35,788–£44,016
Lecturer	£29,972–£34,745
Junior researcher	£23,661–£29,099

UNIVERSITIES

The following is a list of universities, which are those institutions that have been granted degree awarding powers by either a royal charter or an act of parliament, or have been permitted to use the word 'university' (or 'university college') by the Privy Council. There are other recognised bodies in the UK with degree awarding powers, as well as institutions offering courses leading to a degree from a recognised body. Further information is available at W www.bis.gov.uk

Student figures represent the number of undergraduate and postgraduate students based on information available at May 2011.

For information on tuition fees and student loans, *see* Education, Higher Education.

RESEARCH ASSESSMENT EXERCISE

The research assessment exercise (RAE) gives a rating to each university department or specialist college put forward for evaluation, based on the quality of its research. It enables the higher education funding bodies to distribute public funds for research selectively on the basis of quality. Institutions conducting the best research receive a larger proportion of the available grant so that the infrastructure for the top level of research in the UK is protected and developed. The table below shows the top five universities or specialist colleges for each discipline based on the mean average ranking of the overall quality of their research. The research excellence framework (REF) is the new system for assessing the quality of research in UK higher education institutions. It will replace the RAE and will be completed in 2014.

Subject	Universities or university colleges
Anthropology	LSE (1), SOAS (1), Cambridge (3), Roehampton (4), UCL (5)
Archaeology	Durham (1), Reading (2), Cambridge (3), Oxford (3), Liverpool (5)
Biological sciences	Institute of Cancer Research (1), Manchester (2), Oxford (2), Sheffield (2), Dundee (5), RHUL (5)
Business and management	London Business School (1), Imperial (2), Cambridge (3), Cardiff (4), Bath (5), King's (5), Lancaster (5), LSE (5), Oxford (5), Warwick (5)
Chemistry	Cambridge (1), Nottingham (2), Oxford (3), Bristol (4), Edinburgh (4), St Andrews (4)
Classics	Cambridge (1), Oxford (2), UCL (3), Durham (4), King's (4), Warwick (4)
Communication and media studies	Westminster (1), East Anglia (2), Goldsmiths (3), LSE (3), Cardiff (5)
Computer science	Cambridge (1), Edinburgh (2), Imperial (2), Southampton (2), Manchester (5), Oxford (5), UCL (5)
Dentistry	Manchester (1), Queen Mary (2), King's (3), Sheffield (4), Bristol (5), Cardiff (5)
Drama and performing arts	Queen Mary (1), St Andrews (1), Manchester (3), Warwick (4), Bristol (5), King's (5)
Economics	LSE (1), UCL (2), Essex (3), Oxford (3), Warwick (3)
Engineering (electronic)	Leeds (1), Bangor (2), Manchester (2), Surrey (2), Imperial (5)
Engineering (general)	Cambridge (1), Oxford (2), Leeds (3), Nottingham (3), Imperial (5), Swansea (5)
English	York (1), Edinburgh (2), Manchester (2), Queen Mary (2), Exeter (5), Nottingham (5), Oxford (5)
French	Oxford (1), King's (2), Warwick (2), Aberdeen (4), Cambridge (4), St Andrews (4)
Geography	Bristol (1), Cambridge (1), Durham (1), Oxford (1), Queen Mary (1)
German, Dutch and Scandinavian	Oxford (1), Cambridge (2), Durham (2), King's (2), Leeds (2), RHUL (2), St Andrews (2)
History	Imperial (1), Essex (2), Kent (2), Liverpool (2), Oxford (2), Warwick (2)
Law	LSE (1), UCL (2), Oxford (3), Durham (4), Nottingham (4)
Mathematics (applied)	Cambridge (1), Oxford (1), Bristol (3), Bath (4), Portsmouth (4), St Andrews (4)
Mathematics (pure)	Imperial (1), Warwick (2), Oxford (3), Cambridge (4), Bristol (5), Edinburgh (5), Heriot-Watt (5)
Music	RHUL (1), Birmingham (2), Manchester (2), Cambridge (4), King's (4), Sheffield (4), Southampton (4)
Philosophy	UCL (1), St Andrews (1), King's (3), Reading (3), Sheffield (3)
Physics	Lancaster (1), Bath (2), Cambridge (2), Nottingham (2), St Andrews (2)
Politics	Essex (1), Sheffield (1), Aberystwyth (3), Oxford (4), LSE (5)
Psychology	Cambridge (1), Oxford (2), Birmingham (3), UCL (4), Birkbeck (5), Cardiff (5)
Sociology	Essex (1), Goldsmiths (1), Manchester (1), York (1), Lancaster (5)
Sports-related subjects	Birmingham (1), Loughborough (1), Bristol (3), Liverpool John Moores (4), Stirling (5)
Theology and religious studies	Durham (1), Aberdeen (2), Cambridge (3), Oxford (3), UCL (3)

UG= undergraduate PG= postgraduate

UNIVERSITY OF ABERDEEN (1495)
King's College, Aberdeen AB24 3FX **T** 01224-272000
W www.abdn.ac.uk
Students: 11,610 UG; 3,925 PG
Chancellor, Lord Wilson of Tillyorn, KT, GCMG, FRSE
Vice-Chancellor and Principal, Prof. Ian Diamond
University Secretary, Dr Gillian Mackintosh

UNIVERSITY OF ABERTAY DUNDEE (1994)
Bell Street, Dundee DD1 1HG **T** 01382-308000
W www.abertay.ac.uk
Students: 3,719 UG; 463 PG
Chancellor, Lord Cullen of Whitekirk, KT, PC, FRSE
Vice-Chancellor, Prof. Bernard King, CBE, PHD
Registrar, Dr Colin Fraser, PHD

ANGLIA RUSKIN UNIVERSITY (1992)
Chelmsford Campus, Bishop Hall Lane, Chelmsford, Essex
CM1 1SQ **T** 0845-271 3333 **W** www.anglia.ac.uk
Students: 19,742 UG; 4,034 PG
Chancellor, Lord Ashcroft, KCMG
Vice-Chancellor, Prof. Michael Thorne, FRSA, PHD
Secretary and Clerk, Stephen Bennett

UNIVERSITY OF THE ARTS LONDON (Formerly The London Institute (1986), University of the Arts London was formed in 2004)
272 High Holborn, London WC1V 7EY **T** 020-7514 6000
W www.arts.ac.uk
Students: 13,161 UG; 2,774 PG
Chancellor, Lord Stevenson, CBE
Rector, Sir Michael Bichard, KCB
University Secretary, Martin Prince

COLLEGES

CAMBERWELL COLLEGE OF ARTS (1898)
Peckham Road, London SE5 8UF **T** 020-7514 6302
W www.camberwell.arts.ac.uk
Head of College, Chris Wainwright

CENTRAL SAINT MARTINS COLLEGE OF ART & DESIGN (1854)
Southampton Row, London WC1B 4AP **T** 020-7514 7022
W www.csm.arts.ac.uk
Head of College, Jane Rapley, OBE

CHELSEA COLLEGE OF ART & DESIGN (1895)
Millbank, London SW1P 4RJ **T** 020-7514 7751
W www.chelsea.arts.ac.uk
Head of College, Chris Wainwright

LONDON COLLEGE OF COMMUNICATION (1894)
Elephant & Castle, London SE1 6SB **T** 020-7514 6500
W www.lcc.arts.ac.uk
Head of College, Sandra Kemp

LONDON COLLEGE OF FASHION (1963)
20 John Princes Street, London W1G 0BJ **T** 020-7514 7500
W www.fashion.arts.ac.uk
Head of College, Dr Frances Corner

WIMBLEDON COLLEGE OF ART (1930)
Merton Hall Road, London SW19 3QA **T** 020-7514 9641
W www.wimbledon.arts.ac.uk
Head of College, Chris Wainwright

ASTON UNIVERSITY (1966)
Aston Triangle, Birmingham B4 7ET **T** 0121-204 3000
W www.aston.ac.uk
Students: 7,718 UG; 1,945 PG
Chancellor, Sir John Sunderland
Vice-Chancellor, Prof. Julia King, CBE, FRENG, FRSA
Registrar, John Walter

UNIVERSITY OF BATH (1966)
Bath BA2 7AY **T** 01225-388388 **W** www.bath.ac.uk
Students: 9,913 UG; 4,005 PG
Chancellor, Lord Tugendhat
Vice-Chancellor, Prof. Glynis Breakwell, FRSA
University Secretary, Mark Humphriss

BATH SPA UNIVERSITY (2005)
Newton Park, Newton St Loe, Bath BA2 9BN **T** 01225-875875
W www.bathspa.ac.uk
Students: 5,290 UG; 2,099 PG
Vice-Chancellor, Prof. Frank Morgan
Academic Registrar, Christopher Ellicott

UNIVERSITY OF BEDFORDSHIRE (1993)
Park Square, Luton LU1 3JU **T** 01234-400400
W www.beds.ac.uk
Students: 14,410 UG; 4,780 PG
Chancellor, Baroness Howells of St Davids, OBE
Vice-Chancellor, Prof. Les Ebdon, CBE
Registrar, Alice Hynes

UNIVERSITY OF BIRMINGHAM (1900)
Edgbaston, Birmingham B15 2TT **T** 0121-414 3344
W www.bham.ac.uk
Students: 17,355 UG; 8,718 PG
Chancellor, Sir Dominic Cadbury
Vice-Chancellor and Principal, Prof. David Eastwood
Registrar and Secretary, Lee Sanders

BIRMINGHAM CITY UNIVERSITY (1992)
City North Campus, Birmingham B42 2SU **T** 0121-331 5000
W www.bcu.ac.uk
Students: 20,610 UG; 4,225 PG
Chancellor, Lord Mayor of Birmingham, Anita Ward
Vice-Chancellor, Prof. David H. Tidmarsh
University Secretary, Ms Christine Abbott

UNIVERSITY OF BOLTON (2005)
Deane Road, Bolton BL3 5AB **T** 01204-900600
W www.bolton.ac.uk
Students: 10,327 UG; 2,295 PG
Chancellor, Rt. Hon. Baroness Morris of Bolton, OBE, DPHIL
Vice-Chancellor, Dr George Holmes

BOURNEMOUTH UNIVERSITY (1992)
Fern Barrow, Poole, Dorset BH12 5BB **T** 01202-524111
W www.bournemouth.ac.uk
Students: 15,670 UG; 2,645 PG
Chancellor, Rt. Hon. Lord Phillips of Worth Matravers, PC, QC
Vice-Chancellor, Prof. John Vinney
Clerk, Noel Richardson

UNIVERSITY OF BRADFORD (1966)
Bradford, W. Yorks BD7 1DP **T** 01274-232323
W www.brad.ac.uk
Students: 10,045 UG; 3,135 PG
Chancellor, Imran Khan
Vice-Chancellor, Prof. Mark Cleary
University Secretary, Adrian Pearce

UNIVERSITY OF BRIGHTON (1992)
Mithras House, Lewes Road, Brighton BN2 4AT
T 01273-600900 **W** www.bton.ac.uk
Students: 17,003 UG; 4,006 PG
Chairman, Lord Mogg
Vice-Chancellor, Prof. Julian Crampton
Registrar, Mrs Carol Burns

UNIVERSITY OF BRISTOL (1909)
Senate House, Tyndall Avenue, Bristol BS8 1TH
T 0117-928 9000 **W** www.bristol.ac.uk
Students: 13,468 UG; 5,147 PG
Chancellor, Baroness Hale of Richmond, DBE, PC
Vice-Chancellor, Prof. Eric Thomas
Registrar, Derek Pretty

BRUNEL UNIVERSITY (1966)
Uxbridge, Middx UB8 3PH **T** 01895-274000
W www.brunel.ac.uk
Students: 10,549 UG; 4,213 PG
Chancellor, Lord Wakeham
Vice-Chancellor and Principal, Prof. Chris Jenkins, FRSA
Interim Academic Registrar, Bob Westaway

UNIVERSITY OF BUCKINGHAM (1983)
Buckingham MK18 1EG **T** 01280-814080
W www.buckingham.ac.uk
Students: 835 UG; 448 PG
Chancellor, Lord Tanlaw of Tanlaw Hill
Vice-Chancellor, Dr Terence Kealey, DPHIL
Registrar, Anne Miller

**BUCKINGHAMSHIRE NEW UNIVERSITY
(2007)**
High Wycombe Campus, Queen Alexandra Road, High
Wycombe HP11 2JZ **T** 0800-0565 660 **W** www.bucks.ac.uk
Students: 6,017 UG; 527 PG
Vice-Chancellor, Prof. Ruth Farwell
Director of Academic Quality, Ellie Smith

UNIVERSITY OF CAMBRIDGE (1209)
The Old Schools, Trinity Lane, Cambridge CB2 1TN
T 01223-337733 **W** www.cam.ac.uk
Students: 12,192 UG; 5,795 PG
Chancellor, vacant
Vice-Chancellor, Prof. Sir Leszek Borysiewicz, FRS
  (Wolfson)
High Steward, Lord Watson of Richmond, CBE (Jesus)
Deputy High Steward, Mrs A. Lonsdale, CBE (Murray
  Edwards)
Commissary, Lord Mackay of Clashfern, KT, PC, FRSE
  (Trinity)
Pro-Vice-Chancellors, Dr J. C. Barnes (Murray Edwards);
  Prof. L. F. Gladden, CBE, FRS (Trinity); Prof. J. M.
  Rallison (Trinity); Prof. I. H. White, FRENG (Jesus);
  Prof. S. J. Young, FRENG (Emmanuel)
Proctors, Dr Oren Scherman (Jesus); Dr Alan Winter
  (Christ's)
Orator, Dr R. J. E. Thompson (Selwyn)
Registrary, Dr J. W. Nicholls (Emmanuel)
Librarian, Mrs A. E. Jarvis (Wolfson)
Director of the Fitzwilliam Museum, Dr T. F. Potts (Clare)
Academic Secretary, G. P. Allen (Wolfson)
Director of Finance, A. M. Reid (Wolfson)

COLLEGES AND HALLS *with dates of foundation*
CHRIST'S (1505)
Master, Prof. F. P. Kelly, FRS

CHURCHILL (1960)
Master, Prof. Sir David Wallace, CBE, FRS
CLARE (1326)
Master, Prof. A. J. Badger
CLARE HALL (1966)
President, Prof. Sir Martin Harris, CBE
CORPUS CHRISTI (1352)
Master, Mr S. Laing
DARWIN (1964)
Master, Prof. W. A. Brown, CBE
DOWNING (1800)
Master, Prof. B. J. Everitt, FRS
EMMANUEL (1584)
Master, Lord Wilson of Dinton, GCB
FITZWILLIAM (1966)
Master, Prof. R. D. Lethbridge
GIRTON (1869)
Mistress, Prof. S. J. Smith, FBA
GONVILLE AND CAIUS (1348)
Master, Sir Christopher Hum, KCMG
HOMERTON (1824)
Principal, Dr K. B. Pretty, CBE
HUGHES HALL (1985)
President, Mrs S. L. Squire
JESUS (1496)
Master, Prof. R. Mair, CBE, FRS
KING'S (1441)
Provost, Prof. T. R. Harrison
LUCY CAVENDISH (1965)
President, Prof. J. M. Todd
MAGDALENE (1542)
Master, Mr D. D. Robinson, CBE
MURRAY EDWARDS (1954)
President, Dr J. C. Barnes
NEWNHAM (1871)
Principal, Dame Patricia Hodgson, DBE
PEMBROKE (1347)
Master, Sir Richard Dearlove, KCMG, OBE
PETERHOUSE (1284)
Master, Prof. A. K. Dixon, FRCP
QUEENS' (1448)
President, Prof. Lord Eatwell
ROBINSON (1977)
Warden, Prof. A. D. Yates
ST CATHARINE'S (1473)
Master, Prof. Dame Jean Thomas, DBE, FRS
ST EDMUND'S (1896)
Master, Prof. J. P. Luzio, FRCPATH
ST JOHN'S (1511)
Master, Prof. C. M. Dobson, FRS
SELWYN (1882)
Master, Prof. R. J. Bowring
SIDNEY SUSSEX (1596)
Master, Prof. A. F. Wallace-Hadrill, OBE
TRINITY (1546)
Master, Prof. Lord Rees of Ludlow, OM, PRS
TRINITY HALL (1350)
Master, Prof. M. J. Daunton, FBA
WOLFSON (1965)
President, Prof. R. J. Evans, FBA

**CANTERBURY CHRIST CHURCH
UNIVERSITY (2005)**
North Holmes Road, Canterbury CT1 1QU **T** 01227-767700
W www.canterbury.ac.uk
Students: 4,407 UG; 13,571 PG
Chancellor, Most Revd Rowan Williams, PC, DPHIL
Vice-Chancellor and Principal, Prof. Robin Baker, CMG
Academic Registrar, Lorri Currie

CARDIFF UNIVERSITY (1883)
Cardiff CF10 3XQ **T** 029-2087 4000 **W** www.cardiff.ac.uk
Students: 21,243 UG; 7,597 PG
President, Prof. Sir Martin Evans, FRS
Vice-Chancellor, Dr David Grant, CBE
Chair of Council, Prof. Sir Keith Peters

UNIVERSITY OF CENTRAL LANCASHIRE (1992)
Preston PR1 2HE **T** 01772-201201 **W** www.uclan.ac.uk
Students: 27,660 UG; 4,635 PG
Chancellor, Sir Richard Evans, CBE
Vice-Chancellor, Dr Malcolm McVicar

UNIVERSITY OF CHESTER (2005)
Parkgate Road, Chester CH1 4BJ **T** 01244-511000
W www.chester.ac.uk
Students: 12,013 UG; 3,582 PG
Chancellor, His Grace, the Duke of Westminster, KG, OBE, DL
Vice-Chancellor, Canon Prof. Tim Wheeler, DL
Director of Registry Services, Jonathan Moores

UNIVERSITY OF CHICHESTER (2005)
Bishop Otter Campus, College Lane, Chichester PO19 6PE
T 01243-816000 **W** www.chi.ac.uk
Students: 3,670 UG; 477 PG
Vice-Chancellor, Prof. Clive Behagg, PHD

CITY UNIVERSITY LONDON (1966)
Northampton Square, London EC1V 0HB **T** 020-7040 5060
W www.city.ac.uk
Students: 9,763 UG; 6,945 PG
Chancellor, Michael Bear
Vice-Chancellor, Prof. Paul Curran

COVENTRY UNIVERSITY (1992)
Priory Street, Coventry CV1 5FB **T** 024-7688 7688
W www.coventry.ac.uk
Students: 18,772 UG; 3,473 PG
Chancellor, Sir John Egan
Vice-Chancellor, Prof. Madeleine Atkins
Academic Registrar and Secretary, Kate Quantrell

CRANFIELD UNIVERSITY (1969)
Cranfield, Bedfordshire MK43 0AL **T** 01234-750111
W www.cranfield.ac.uk
Students: 4,300 PG (postgraduate only)
Chancellor, Baroness Young of Old Scone
Vice-Chancellor, Prof. Sir John O'Reilly
Registrar, Prof. William Stephens

UNIVERSITY FOR THE CREATIVE ARTS (2008)
Falkner Road, Farnham, Surrey GU9 7DS **T** 01252-892883
W www.ucreative.ac.uk
Students: 5,500 UG; 350 PG
Chancellor, Zandra Rhodes, CBE
Vice-Chancellor, Prof. Elaine Thomas
Registrar, David Burt

UNIVERSITY OF CUMBRIA (2007)
Fusehill Street, Carlisle CA1 2HH **T** 01228-616234
W www.cumbria.ac.uk
Students: 9,695 UG; 2,715 PG
Chancellor, Most Revd and Rt. Hon. Dr John Sentamu, Archbishop of York
Interim Vice-Chancellor, Prof. Peter Strike
University Secretary, Neil Harris

DE MONTFORT UNIVERSITY (1992)
The Gateway, Leicester LE1 9BH **T** 0845-945 4647
W www.dmu.ac.uk
Students: 18,452 UG; 4,076 PG
Chancellor, Lord Waheed Alli
Vice-Chancellor, Prof. Dominic Shellard
Registrar, Joanne Cooke

UNIVERSITY OF DERBY (1992)
Kedleston Road, Derby DE22 1GB **T** 01332-590500
W www.derby.ac.uk
Students: 14,390 UG; 3,085 PG
Chancellor, The Duke of Devonshire, KCVO, CBE, DL
Vice-Chancellor, Prof. John Coyne
Registrar, June Hughes

UNIVERSITY OF DUNDEE (1967)
Nethergate, Dundee DD1 4HN **T** 01382-383000
W www.dundee.ac.uk
Students: 10,730 UG; 5,465 PG
Chancellor, Lord Patel, KT, FRSE
Vice-Chancellor and Principal, Prof. Peter Downes, OBE, FRSE
Secretary, Dr Jim McGeorge

DURHAM UNIVERSITY (1832)
The University Office, Old Elvet, Durham DH1 3HP
T 0191-334 2000 **W** www.dur.ac.uk
Students: 11,350 UG; 4,625 PG
Chancellor, Dr Bill Bryson
Vice-Chancellor and Warden, Prof. Christopher Higgins, FRSE
Registrar, Carolyn Fowler

COLLEGES
COLLINGWOOD (1972)
Principal, Prof. E. Corrigan, FRS
GREY
Master, Prof. J. M. Chamberlain, DPHIL
HATFIELD (1846)
Master, Prof. T. P. Burt, DSC
JOHN SNOW (2001)
Principal, Prof. Carolyn Summerbell
JOSEPHINE BUTLER (2006)
Principal, A. Simpson
ST AIDAN'S
Principal (acting), Dr Susan F. Frenk
ST CHAD'S (1904)
Principal, Revd Dr J. P. M. Cassidy
ST CUTHBERT'S SOCIETY (1888)
Principal, Prof. A. Broderick
ST HILD AND ST BEDE (1975)
Principal, Prof. C. J. Hutchinson
ST JOHN'S (1909)
Principal, Revd Dr D. Wilkinson
ST MARY'S
Principal, Prof. P. Gilmartin
STEPHENSON (2001)
Principal, Prof. A. C. Darnell
TREVELYAN (1966)
Principal, Prof. H. M. Evans
UNIVERSITY (1832)
Master, Prof. M. E. Tucker
USHAW
President, Fr. J. Marsland

USTINOV
Principal, Penelope B. Wilson, DPHIL
VAN MILDERT (1965)
Master, Prof. P. O'Meara, DPHIL

UNIVERSITY OF EAST ANGLIA (1963)
Norwich NR4 7TJ T 01603-456161 W www.uea.ac.uk
Students: 11,804 UG; 2,509 PG
Chancellor, Sir Brandon Gough
Vice-Chancellor, Prof. Edward Acton
Registrar, Brian Summers

UNIVERSITY OF EAST LONDON (1898)
University Way, London E16 2RD T 020-8223 3000
W www.uel.ac.uk
Students: 18,700 UG; 8,230 PG
Chancellor, Lord Rix
Vice-Chancellor, Prof. Patrick McGhee
Clerk to the Governors, Jill Grinstead

EDGE HILL UNIVERSITY (2006)
St Helens Road, Ormskirk, Lancs L39 4QP T 01695-575171
W www.edgehill.ac.uk
Students: 10,575 UG; 14,745 PG
Chancellor, Prof. Tanya Byron
Vice-Chancellor, Dr John Cater
University Secretary, Lesley Munro

UNIVERSITY OF EDINBURGH (1583)
Old College, South Bridge, Edinburgh EH8 9YL
T 0131-650 1000 W www.ed.ac.uk
Students: 17,955 UG; 7,735 PG
Chancellor, HRH the Princess Royal, KG, KT, GCVO
Vice-Chancellor and Principal, Prof. Sir Timothy O'Shea,
  FRSE
University Secretary, Dr Kim Waldron

EDINBURGH NAPIER UNIVERSITY (1992)
Craighouse Road, Edinburgh EH10 5LG T 0845-260 6040
W www.napier.ac.uk
Students: 13,107 UG; 2,584 PG
Chancellor, Tim Waterstone
Vice-Chancellor, Prof. Dame Joan Stringer, CBE
Secretary, Dr Gerry Webber

UNIVERSITY OF ESSEX (1965)
Wivenhoe Park, Colchester CO4 3SQ T 01206-873333
W www.essex.ac.uk
Students: 7,590 UG; 2,690 PG
Chancellor, Lord Phillips of Sudbury, OBE
Vice-Chancellor, Prof. Colin Riordan
Academic Registrar, Dr Tony Rich

UNIVERSITY OF EXETER (1955)
The Queen's Drive, Exeter EX4 4QJ T 01392-661000
W www.exeter.ac.uk
Students: 12,855 UG; 4,355 PG
Chancellor, Baroness Floella Benjamin, OBE
Vice-Chancellor, Prof. Steve Smith
Registrar, David Allen

UNIVERSITY OF GLAMORGAN (1992)
Pontypridd CF37 1DL T 0845-6434 030 W www.glam.ac.uk
Students: 17,140 UG; 3,930 PG
Chancellor, Lord Morris of Aberavon, KG, PC, QC
Vice-Chancellor, Julie Lydon
Academic Registrar, William Callaway

UNIVERSITY OF GLASGOW (1451)
University Avenue, Glasgow G12 8QQ T 0141-330 2000
W www.gla.ac.uk
Students: 20,000 UG; 5,600 PG
Chancellor, Prof. Sir Kenneth Calman, KCB, MD, FRCS
Vice-Chancellor, Prof. Anton Muscatelli, FRSE
Secretary of Court, David Newall

GLASGOW CALEDONIAN UNIVERSITY (1993)
City Campus, Cowcaddens Road, Glasgow G4 0BA
T 0141-331 3000 W www.gcu.ac.uk
Students: 15,427 UG; 3,049 PG
Chancellor, Rt. Hon. Lord Macdonald of Tradeston, CBE
Vice-Chancellor and Principal, Prof. Pamela Gillies,
  FRSA
Registrar, Brendan Ferguson

UNIVERSITY OF GLOUCESTERSHIRE (2001)
The Park, Cheltenham GL50 2RH T 0844-801 0001
W www.glos.ac.uk
Students: 7,065 UG; 2,655 PG
Vice-Chancellor, Stephen Marston
Academic Registrar, Julie Thackray

UNIVERSITY OF GREENWICH (1992)
Old Royal Naval College, Park Row, Greenwich, London
SE10 9LS T 020-8331 8000 W www.gre.ac.uk
Students: 22,658 UG; 6,145 PG
Chancellor, Lord Hart of Chilton
Vice-Chancellor, David Maguire
Secretary and Registrar, Linda Cording

HERIOT-WATT UNIVERSITY (1966)
Edinburgh EH14 4AS T 0131-449 5111 W www.hw.ac.uk
Students: 6,280 UG; 5,020 PG
Chancellor, Baroness Susan Greenfield, CBE, FRCP
Vice-Chancellor and Principal, Prof. Steve Chapman,
  FRSE
Secretary, Ann Marie Dalton

UNIVERSITY OF HERTFORDSHIRE (1992)
College Lane, Hatfield, Herts AL10 9AB T 01707-284000
W www.herts.ac.uk
Students: 21,650 UG; 6,000 PG
Chancellor, Marquess of Salisbury, PC
Vice-Chancellor, Prof. Quintin Mckellar, CBE
Registrar, Philip Waters, FRSA

UNIVERSITY OF HUDDERSFIELD (1992)
Queensgate, Huddersfield HD1 3DH T 01484-422288
W www.hud.ac.uk
Students: 18,064 UG; 4,070 PG
Chancellor, Sir Patrick Stewart, OBE
Vice-Chancellor, Prof. Bob Cryan, PHD, DSC
Head of Registry, Kathy Sherlock

UNIVERSITY OF HULL (1927)
Cottingham Road, Hull HU6 7RX T 01482-346311
W www.hull.ac.uk
Students: 19,700 UG; 3,375 PG
Chancellor, Baroness Bottomley, PC
Vice-Chancellor, Prof. Calie Pistorius, FRSA
Registrar and Secretary, Mrs Frances Owen

IMPERIAL COLLEGE LONDON (1907)
South Kensington, London SW7 2AZ T 020-7589 5111
W www.imperial.ac.uk

Students: 8,608 UG; 5,959 PG
Rector, Sir Keith O'Nions
Deputy Rector, Prof. Stephen Richardson
Academic Registrar, Nigel Wheatley

KEELE UNIVERSITY (1962)
Keele, Staffs ST5 5BG **T** 01782-732000 **W** www.keele.ac.uk
Students: 8,255 UG; 2,215 PG
Chancellor, Prof. Sir David Weatherall, DSC, MD, FRCP
Vice-Chancellor, Prof. Nick Foskett
Registrar and Secretary, Simon Morris

UNIVERSITY OF KENT (1965)
Canterbury, Kent CT2 7NZ **T** 01227-764000
W www.kent.ac.uk
Students: 17,825 UG; 2,840 PG
Chancellor, Prof. Sir Robert Worcester, KBE
Vice-Chancellor, Prof. Dame Julia Goodfellow, CBE
Registrar, Jon Pink

KINGSTON UNIVERSITY (1992)
River House, 53–57 High Street, Kingston upon Thames, Surrey KT1 1LQ **T** 020-8417 9000 **W** www.kingston.ac.uk
Students: 20,355 UG; 6,730 PG
Chancellor, Sir Peter Hall
Vice-Chancellor, Prof. Julius Weinberg
Acting Academic Registrar, Marie Sheehan

UNIVERSITY OF LANCASTER (1964)
Bailrigg, Lancaster LA1 4YW **T** 01524-65201
W www.lancs.ac.uk
Students: 8,780 UG; 3,345 PG
Chancellor, Sir Christian Bonington, CBE
Vice-Chancellor, Prof. Paul Wellings
University Secretary, Fiona Aiken

UNIVERSITY OF LEEDS (1904)
Leeds LS2 9JT **T** 0113-243 1751 **W** www.leeds.ac.uk
Students: 24,965 UG; 7,850 PG
Chancellor, Lord Bragg, LLD, DLITT, DCL
Vice-Chancellor, Prof. Michael Arthur, DM, FRCP
Registrar, Mr J. Roger Gair

LEEDS METROPOLITAN UNIVERSITY (1992)
Civic Quarter, Leeds LS1 3HE **T** 0113-812 0000
W www.leedsmet.ac.uk
Students: 23,628 UG; 4,796 PG
Chancellor, Lord Woolmer
Vice-Chancellor, Prof. Susan Price
Registrar, Steve Denton

UNIVERSITY OF LEICESTER (1957)
University Road, Leicester LE1 7RH **T** 0116-252 2522
W www.le.ac.uk
Students: 10,946 UG; 11,857 PG
Chancellor, vacant
Vice-Chancellor, Prof. Sir Robert Burgess
Registrar, Dave Hall

UNIVERSITY OF LINCOLN (1992)
Brayford Pool, Lincoln LN6 7TS **T** 01522-882000
W www.lincoln.ac.uk
Students: 9,597 UG; 1,085 PG
Chancellor, Lord Victor Adebowale
Vice-Chancellor, Prof. Mary Stuart
Registrar, Chris Spendlove

UNIVERSITY OF LIVERPOOL (1903)
Liverpool, Merseyside L69 7ZX **T** 0151-794 2000
W www.liv.ac.uk
Students: 14,049 UG; 3,036 PG
Chancellor, Prof. Sir David King, CH, PC, FRCP
Vice-Chancellor, Prof. Sir Howard Newby, FRSA
Chief Operating Officer, Patrick Hackett

LIVERPOOL HOPE UNIVERSITY (2005)
Hope Park, Liverpool L16 9JD **T** 0151-291 3000
W www.hope.ac.uk
Students: 4,674 UG; 1,774 PG
Chancellor, Baroness Cox of Queensbury, FRCN
Vice-Chancellor and Rector, Prof. Gerald Pillay, FRSA
Registrar, Neil McLaughlin-Cook

LIVERPOOL JOHN MOORES UNIVERSITY (1992)
Kingsway House, 2nd Floor, Hatton Garden, Liverpool L3 2AJ
T 0151-231 2121 **W** www.ljmu.ac.uk
Students: 21,000 UG; 4,860 PG
Chancellor, Dr Brian May, CBE
Vice-Chancellor and Chief Executive, Prof. Michael Brown, CBE, DL
Secretary, Denise Tipping

UNIVERSITY OF LONDON (1836)
Senate House, Malet Street, London WC1E 7HU
T 020-7862 8000 **W** www.london.ac.uk
Chancellor, HRH the Princess Royal, KG, KT, GCVO
Vice-Chancellor, Prof. Geoffrey Crossick
Chair of the Board of Trustees, Dame Jenny Abramsky
Director of Administration, Catherine Swarbrick

COLLEGES
BIRKBECK COLLEGE
Malet Street, London WC1E 7HX
Students: 14,240 UG; 4,435 PG
President, Prof. Eric Hobsbawm
Master, Prof. David Latchman

CENTRAL SCHOOL OF SPEECH AND DRAMA
Embassy Theatre, Eton Avenue, London NW3 3HY
Students: 555 UG; 300 PG
President, Michael Grandage, CBE
Principal, Prof. Gavin Henderson, CBE

COURTAULD INSTITUTE OF ART
North Block, Somerset House, Strand, London WC2R 0RN
Students: 150 UG; 255 PG
Director, Prof. Deborah Swallow

GOLDSMITHS COLLEGE
Lewisham Way, New Cross, London SE14 6NW
Students, 5,510 UG; 2,460 PG
Warden, Pat Loughrey

HEYTHROP COLLEGE
Kensington Square, London W8 5HN
Students: 515 UG; 420 PG
Principal, Revd Dr John McDade, SJ, BD

INSTITUTE OF CANCER RESEARCH
15 Cotswold Road, Belmont, Surrey SM2 5NG
Students: 300 PG (postgraduate only)
Chief Executive, Prof. Alan Ashworth

INSTITUTE OF EDUCATION
20 Bedford Way, London WC1H 0AL
Students: 540 UG; 6,830 PG
Director, Prof. Geoff Whitty, CBE

KING'S COLLEGE LONDON (includes Guy's, King's and St Thomas's Schools of Medicine, Dentistry and Biomedical Sciences)
Strand, London WC2R 2LS
Students: 14,970 UG; 9,525 PG
Principal, Prof. Rick Trainor

LONDON BUSINESS SCHOOL
Regent's Park, London NW1 4SA
Students: 2,050 PG (postgraduate only)
Dean, Sir Andrew Likierman

LONDON SCHOOL OF ECONOMICS AND POLITICAL SCIENCE
Houghton Street, London WC2A 2AE
Students: 4,000 UG; 5,560 PG
Director, Prof. Judith Rees, CBE

LONDON SCHOOL OF HYGIENE AND TROPICAL MEDICINE
50 Bedford Square, London WC1B 3DP
Students: 1,270 PG (postgraduate only)
Director, Peter Piot

QUEEN MARY (incorporating St Bartholomew's and the Royal London School of Medicine and Dentistry)
Mile End Road, London E1 4NS
Students: 11,085 UG; 3,640 PG
Principal, Prof. Simon Gaskell

ROYAL ACADEMY OF MUSIC
Marylebone Road, London NW1 5HT
Students: 330 UG; 385 PG
Principal, Prof. Jonathan Freeman-Attwood

ROYAL HOLLOWAY
Egham Hill, Egham, Surrey TW20 0EX
Students: 7,295 UG; 2,240 PG
Principal, Prof. Paul Layzell

ROYAL VETERINARY COLLEGE
Royal College Street, London NW1 0TU
Students: 1,535 UG; 530 PG
Principal, Prof. Stuart Reid

ST GEORGE'S
Cranmer Terrace, London SW17 0RE
Students: 4,590 UG; 535 PG
Principal, Prof. Peter Kopelman, FRCGP

SCHOOL OF ORIENTAL AND AFRICAN STUDIES
Thornhaugh Street, Russell Square, London WC1H 0XG
Students: 2,970 UG; 2,255 PG
Director, Prof. Paul Webley

SCHOOL OF PHARMACY
29–39 Brunswick Square, London WC1N 1AX
Students: 735 UG; 675 PG
Principal and Dean, Prof. Anthony Smith

UNIVERSITY COLLEGE LONDON (including UCL Medical School)
Gower Street, London WC1E 6BT
Students: 12,765 UG; 10,460 PG
Provost and President, Prof. Malcolm Grant, CBE

INSTITUTES
UNIVERSITY OF LONDON INSTITUTE IN PARIS
9–11 rue de Constantine, 75340 Paris Cedex 07
Dean, Prof. Andrew Hussey

UNIVERSITY MARINE BIOLOGICAL STATION
Millport, Isle of Cumbrae KA28 0EG
Director, Prof. Jim Atkinson

SCHOOL OF ADVANCED STUDY
Senate House, Malet Street, London WC1E 7HU
Dean and Chief Executive, Prof. Roger Kain, CBE

INSTITUTE OF ADVANCED LEGAL STUDIES
Charles Clore House, 17 Russell Square, London WC1B 5DR
Dean and Chief Executive, Prof. Roger Kain, CBE

INSTITUTE OF CLASSICAL STUDIES
Senate House, Malet Street, London WC1E 7HU
Director, Prof. M. Edwards

INSTITUTE OF COMMONWEALTH STUDIES
Senate House, Malet Street, London WC1E 7HU
Director, Prof. Philip Murphy

INSTITUTE OF ENGLISH STUDIES
Senate House, Malet Street, London WC1E 7HU
Director, Prof. Warwick Gould

INSTITUTE OF GERMANIC AND ROMANCE STUDIES
Senate House, Malet Street, London WC1E 7HU
Director, Prof. Naomi Segal

INSTITUTE OF HISTORICAL RESEARCH
Senate House, Malet Street, London WC1E 7HU
Director, Prof. Miles Taylor

INSTITUTE OF MUSICAL RESEARCH
Senate House, Malet Street, London WC1E 7HU
Director, Prof. John Irving

INSTITUTE OF PHILOSOPHY
Senate House, Malet Street, London WC1E 7HU
Director, Prof. Barry Smith

INSTITUTE FOR THE STUDY OF THE AMERICAS
Senate House, Malet Street, London WC1E 7HU
Director, Prof. Maxine Molyneux

WARBURG INSTITUTE
Woburn Square, London WC1H 0AB
Director, Prof. Peter Mack

LONDON METROPOLITAN UNIVERSITY (2002)
166–220 Holloway Road, London N7 8D8 T 020-7423 0000
W www.londonmet.ac.uk
Students: 19,485 UG; 7,750 PG
Patron, HRH the Prince Philip, Duke of Edinburgh, KG, KT, OM
Vice-Chancellor, Prof. Malcolm Gillies
Interim Secretary, Sally Neocosmos

LONDON SOUTH BANK UNIVERSITY (1992)
103 Borough Road, London SE1 0AA **T** 020-7815 7815
W www.lsbu.ac.uk
Students: 18,875 UG; 6,070 PG
Vice-Chancellor, Martin Earwicker

LOUGHBOROUGH UNIVERSITY (1966)
Ashby Road, Loughborough, Leics LE11 3TU **T** 01509-263171
W www.lboro.ac.uk
Students: 11,311 UG; 2,420 PG
Chancellor, Sir Nigel Rudd, CBE, FRSE, PHD
Vice-Chancellor, Prof. Shirley Pearce, CBE
Academic Registrar, Dr Jennifer Nutkins

UNIVERSITY OF MANCHESTER (2004)
Oxford Road, Manchester M13 9PL **T** 0161-306 6000
W www.manchester.ac.uk
Students: 28,313 UG; 11,125 PG
Chancellor, Tom Bloxham, MBE
Vice-Chancellor, Prof. Dame Nancy Rothwell, FRS
Registrar, Will Spinks

MANCHESTER METROPOLITAN UNIVERSITY
(1992)
All Saints, Manchester M15 6BH **T** 0161-247 2000
W www.mmu.ac.uk
Students: 27,904 UG; 7,822 PG
Chancellor, Dianne Thompson, CBE, FRSA
Vice-Chancellor, Prof. John Brooks, DSC
Registrar, Gwyn Arnold

MIDDLESEX UNIVERSITY (1992)
Hendon Campus, The Burroughs, London NW4 4BT
T 020-8411 5555 **W** www.mdx.ac.uk
Students: 13,867 UG; 7,955 PG
Chancellor, Lord Sheppard of Didgemere, KT, KCVO
Vice-Chancellor, Prof. Michael Driscoll
Academic Registrar, Colin Davies

NEWCASTLE UNIVERSITY (1963)
Newcastle upon Tyne NE1 7RU **T** 0191-222 6000
W www.ncl.ac.uk
Students: 14,383 UG; 5,284 PG
Chancellor, Sir Liam Donaldson
Vice-Chancellor, Prof. Chris Brink, FRS, DPHIL
Registrar, Dr John Hogan

UNIVERSITY OF NORTHAMPTON (2005)
Park Campus, Boughton Green Road, Northampton NN2 7AL
T 01604-735500 **W** www.northampton.ac.uk
Students: 11,415 UG; 2,510 PG
Chancellor, Baroness Falkner
Vice-Chancellor, Prof. Nick Petford
Registrar, Jane Bunce

NORTHUMBRIA UNIVERSITY AT
NEWCASTLE (1992)
Ellison Building, Ellison Place, Newcastle upon Tyne NE1 8ST
T 0191-232 6002 **W** www.northumbria.ac.uk
Students: 28,197 UG; 5,225 PG
Chancellor, Lord Stevens of Kirkwhelpington, QPM, DCL
Vice-Chancellor, Prof. Andrew Wathey, FRSA, DPHIL
Registrar, Prof. Jane Core

UNIVERSITY OF NOTTINGHAM (1948)
University Park, Nottingham NG7 2RD **T** 0115-951 5151
W www.nottingham.ac.uk
Students: 24,665 UG; 9,455 PG
Chancellor, Prof. Yang Fujia, LITTD

Vice-Chancellor, Prof. David Greenaway
Registrar, Dr Paul Greatrix

NOTTINGHAM TRENT UNIVERSITY (1992)
Burton Street, Nottingham NG1 4BU **T** 0115-941 8418
W www.ntu.ac.uk
Students: 21,365 UG; 5,090 PG
Chancellor, Sir Michael Parkinson, MBE
Vice-Chancellor, Prof. Neil Gorman
Registrar, David Samson

OPEN UNIVERSITY (1969)
Walton Hall, Milton Keynes MK7 6AA **T** 01908-274066
W www.open.ac.uk
Students: 190,272 UG; 16,300 PG
Chancellor, Lord Puttnam
Vice-Chancellor, Martin Bean
University Secretary, Fraser Woodburn

UNIVERSITY OF OXFORD (*c.*12th century)
University Offices, Wellington Square, Oxford OX1 2JD
T 01865-270000 **W** www.ox.ac.uk
Students: 11,723 UG; 9,327 PG
Chancellor, Lord Patten of Barnes, CH, PC (Balliol,
   St Antony's)
Vice-Chancellor, Prof. Andrew Hamilton, FRS (Kellogg,
   Harris Manchester, Wolfson)
High Steward, Lord Rodger of Earlsferry (Balliol, New,
   St Hugh's)
Pro-Vice-Chancellors, Prof. S. J. Goss (Wadham); Prof.
   W. James (Brasenose); Dr S. L. Mapstone (St Hilda's);
   Prof. J. N. P. Rawlins (Wolfson); Prof. I. A. Walmsley
   (St. Hugh's)
Registrar, Prof. E. G. McKendrick (Lady Margaret Hall)
Secretary of the Faculties and Academic Registrar, M. D.
   Sibly (St Anne's)
Public Orator, R. H. A. Jenkyns (Lady Margaret Hall)
*Director of University Library Services and Bodley's
   Librarian,* Dr S. E. Thomas (Balliol)
Director of the Ashmolean Museum, Dr C. Brown
   (Worcester)
Keeper of Archives, S. Bailey (Linacre)
Acting Director of Estates, M. Wigg
Director of Finance, G. F. B. Kerr (Keble)

COLLEGES AND HALLS *with dates of foundation*
ALL SOULS (1438)
Warden, Prof. Sir John Vickers, FBA
BALLIOL (1263)
Master, Prof. Sir Drummond Bone
BLACKFRIARS (1221)
Regent, Revd Dr Richard Finn
BRASENOSE (1509)
Acting Principal, Prof. Alan K. Bowman, FBA, FSA
CAMPION HALL (1896)
Master, Revd Brendan Callaghan
CHRIST CHURCH (1546)
Dean, Very Revd Dr Christopher A. Lewis
CORPUS CHRISTI (1517)
President, Prof. Richard Carwardine, FBA
EXETER (1314)
Rector, Ms Frances Cairncross, CBE, FRSE
GREEN TEMPLETON (2008)
Principal, Prof. Sir David Watson
HARRIS MANCHESTER (1889)
Principal, Revd Dr Ralph Waller, FRSE
HERTFORD (1740)
Principal, Will Hutton

JESUS (1571)
Principal, Lord Krebs, FRS
KEBLE (1870)
Warden, Sir Jonathan Phillips
KELLOGG (1990)
President, Prof. Jonathan M. Michie
LADY MARGARET HALL (1878)
Principal, Dr Frances Lannon
LINACRE (1962)
Principal, Dr Nick Brown
LINCOLN (1427)
Rector, Prof. Paul Langford, FBA
MAGDALEN (1458)
President, Prof. David Clary, FRS
MANSFIELD (1886)
Principal, Baroness Helena Kennedy, QC
MERTON (1264)
Warden, Prof. Sir Martin Taylor
NEW COLLEGE (1379)
Warden, Prof. Sir Curtis Price
NUFFIELD (1958)
Warden, Prof. Stephen Nickell, CBE, FBA
ORIEL (1326)
Provost, Sir Derek Morris
PEMBROKE (1624)
Master, Giles Henderson, CBE
QUEEN'S (1341)
Provost, Prof. Paul Madden, FRS, FRSE
REGENT'S PARK (1810)
Principal, Revd Dr Robert Ellis
ST ANNE'S (1878)
Principal, Tim Gardam
ST ANTONY'S (1953)
Warden, Prof. Margaret MacMillan
ST BENET'S HALL (1897)
Master, Revd J. Felix Stephens
ST CATHERINE'S (1963)
Master, Prof. Roger Ainsworth
ST CROSS (1965)
Master, Sir Mark Jones
ST EDMUND HALL (c.1278)
Principal, Prof. Keith Gull, CBE, FRS
ST HILDA'S (1893)
Principal, Sheila Forbes, CBE
ST HUGH'S (1886)
Principal, Andrew Dilnot, CBE
ST JOHN'S (1555)
President, Sir Michael Scholar, KCB
ST PETER'S (1929)
Principal, Mark Damazer
ST STEPHEN'S HOUSE (1876)
Principal, Revd Dr Robin Ward
SOMERVILLE (1879)
Principal, Dr Alice Prochaska
TRINITY (1554)
President, Sir Ivor Roberts, KCMG
UNIVERSITY (1249)
Master, Sir Ivor Crewe
WADHAM (1610)
Warden, Sir Neil Chalmers
WOLFSON (1981)
President, Prof. Hermione Lee, FBA, FRSL, CBE
WORCESTER (1714)
Provost, Prof. Jonathan Bate
WYCLIFFE HALL (1877)
Principal, Revd Dr Richard Turnbull

OXFORD BROOKES UNIVERSITY (1992)
Gipsy Lane, Oxford OX3 0BP T 01865-741111
W www.brookes.ac.uk
Students: 14,255 UG; 4,075 PG
Chancellor, Shami Chakrabarti, CBE
Vice-Chancellor, Prof. Janet Beer
Registrar, Paul Large

UNIVERSITY OF PLYMOUTH (1992)
Drake Circus, Plymouth PL4 8AA T 01752-600600
W www.plymouth.ac.uk
Students: 27,865 UG; 4,340 PG
Vice-Chancellor and Chief Executive, Prof. Wendy Purcell
Academic Registrar and Secretary, Jane Hopkinson

UNIVERSITY OF PORTSMOUTH (1992)
University House, Winston Churchill Avenue, Portsmouth
PO1 2UP T 023-9284 8484 W www.port.ac.uk
Students: 18,219 UG; 3,385 PG
Chancellor, Sheila Hancock, OBE
Vice-Chancellor, Prof. John Craven
Academic Registrar, Andrew Rees

QUEEN MARGARET UNIVERSITY (2007)
Queen Margaret University Drive, Musselburgh, Edinburgh
EH21 6UU T 0131-474 0000 W www.qmu.ac.uk
Students: 4,632 UG; 1,722 PG
Chancellor, Sir Tom Farmer, CVO, CBE
Vice-Chancellor, Prof. Petra Wend, FRSA
Registrar, Irene Hynd

QUEEN'S UNIVERSITY BELFAST (1908)
University Road, Belfast BT7 1NN T 028-9024 5133
W www.qub.ac.uk
Students: 17,209 UG; 5,497 PG
Chancellor, His Excellency Kamalesh Sharma
Vice-Chancellor, Prof. Sir Peter Gregson, FRENG, MRIA
Registrar and Chief Operating Officer, James O'Kane

UNIVERSITY OF READING (1926)
Whiteknights, PO Box 217, Reading RG6 6AH T 0118-987 5123
W www.reading.ac.uk
Students: 9,330 UG; 5,145 PG
Chancellor, Sir John Madejski, OBE, DL
Vice-Chancellor, Prof. Gordon Marshall, CBE, FBA
University Secretary, Keith Hodgson

ROBERT GORDON UNIVERSITY (1992)
Schoolhill, Aberdeen AB10 1FR T 01224-262000
W www.rgu.ac.uk
Students: 10,425 UG; 5,980 PG
Chancellor, Sir Ian Wood, CBE
Vice-Chancellor, Prof. Ferdinand non Prondzynski
Registrar, Hilary Douglas

ROEHAMPTON UNIVERSITY (2004)
Erasmus House, Roehampton Lane, London SW15 5PU
T 020-8392 3000 W www.roehampton.ac.uk
Students: 6,285 UG; 2,535 PG
Chancellor, John Simpson, CBE
Vice-Chancellor, Prof. Paul O'Prey
University Secretary and Registrar, Robin Geller

ROYAL COLLEGE OF ART (1967)
Kensington Gore, London SW7 2EU T 020-7590 4444
W www.rca.ac.uk
Students: 939 PG (postgraduate only)
Chancellor, Sir James Dyson
Vice-Chancellor, Dr Paul Thompson
Registrar, Jane Alexander

ROYAL COLLEGE OF MUSIC (1882)
Prince Consort Road, London SW7 2BS **T** 020-7591 4300
W www.rcm.ac.uk
Students: 365 UG; 315 PG
President, HRH the Prince of Wales, KG, KT, GCB
Director, Prof. Colin Lawson, DMUS, FRCM
Deputy Director, Kevin Porter

UNIVERSITY OF ST ANDREWS (1413)
College Gate, St Andrews, Fife KY16 9AJ **T** 01334-476161
W www.st-andrews.ac.uk
Students: 7,155 UG; 1,980 PG
Chancellor, Sir Menzies Campbell, CBE, QC, MP
Vice-Chancellor and Principal, Prof. Louise Richardson

UNIVERSITY OF SALFORD (1967)
The Crescent, Salford, Greater Manchester M5 4WT
T 0161-295 5000 **W** www.salford.ac.uk
Students: 16,385 UG; 4,388 PG
Chancellor, Dr Irene Khan
Vice-Chancellor, Prof. Martin Hall
Registrar, Dr Adrian Graves

UNIVERSITY OF SHEFFIELD (1905)
Western Bank, Sheffield S10 2TN **T** 0114-222 2000
W www.sheffield.ac.uk
Students: 18,357 UG; 6,559 PG
Chancellor, Sir Peter Middleton, GCB
Vice-Chancellor, Prof. Keith Burnett, CBE, DPHIL, FRS
Registrar and Secretary, Philip Harvey

SHEFFIELD HALLAM UNIVERSITY (1992)
City Campus, Howard Street, Sheffield S1 1WB
T 0114-225 5555 **W** www.shu.ac.uk
Students: 27,377 UG; 8,034 PG
Chancellor, Prof. Lord Winston, DSC, FRCOG, FRCP
Vice-Chancellor, Prof. Philip Jones, LLB, LLM
Secretary and Registrar, Elizabeth Winders

UNIVERSITY OF SOUTHAMPTON (1952)
Building 37, Highfield, Southampton SO17 1BJ
T 023-8059 5000 **W** www.soton.ac.uk
Students: 16,124 UG; 6,145 PG
Chancellor, Helen Alexander, CBE
Vice-Chancellor, Prof. Don Nutbeam
Registrar and Chief Operating Officer, Malcolm Ace

SOUTHAMPTON SOLENT UNIVERSITY (2005)
East Park Terrace, Southampton SO14 0YN **T** 023-8031 9000
W www.solent.ac.uk
Students: 11,730 UG; 810 PG
Chancellor, Adm. Lord West of Spithead, GCB, DSC, PC
Vice-Chancellor, Prof. Van Gore

STAFFORDSHIRE UNIVERSITY (1992)
College Road, Stoke-on-Trent, Staffs ST4 2DE **T** 01782-294000
W www.staffs.ac.uk
Students: 17,390 UG; 3,835 PG
Chancellor, Lord Morris of Handsworth
Vice-Chancellor and Chief Executive, Prof. Michael Gunn
University Secretary, Ken Sproston

UNIVERSITY OF STIRLING (1967)
Stirling FK9 4LA **T** 01786-473171 **W** www.stir.ac.uk
Students: 8,452 UG; 2,961 PG
Chancellor, Dr James Naughtie, OBE
Vice-Chancellor, Prof. Gerry McCormac, FRSE
Registrar, Kevin Clarke

UNIVERSITY OF STRATHCLYDE (1964)
16 Richmond Street, Glasgow G1 1XQ **T** 0141-552 4400
W www.strath.ac.uk
Students: 12,063 UG; 4,480 PG
Chancellor, Rt. Hon. Lord Hope of Craighead, KT, PC,
    FRSE
Vice-Chancellor and Principal, Prof. Jim McDonald,
    FRENG, FRSE
Chief Operating Officer, Hugh Hall

UNIVERSITY OF SUNDERLAND (1992)
Edinburgh Building, Chester Road, Sunderland SR1 3SD
T 0191-515 2000 **W** www.sunderland.ac.uk
Students: 16,085 UG; 2,845 PG
Chancellor, Steve Cram, MBE
Vice-Chancellor and Chief Executive, Prof. Peter Fidler
Secretary, John Pacey

UNIVERSITY OF SURREY (1966)
Guildford, Surrey GU2 7XH **T** 01483-300800
W www.surrey.ac.uk
Students: 10,190 UG; 5,225 PG
Chancellor, HRH the Duke of Kent, KG, GCMG, GCVO
Vice-Chancellor and Chief Executive, Prof. Christopher
    Snowden, FRS, FRENG
Registrar, Dr David Ashton

UNIVERSITY OF SUSSEX (1961)
Sussex House, Brighton BN1 9RH **T** 01273-606755
W www.sussex.ac.uk
Students: 8,362 UG; 3,479 PG
Chancellor, Sanjeev Bhaskar, OBE
Vice-Chancellor, Prof. Michael Farthing
Academic Registrar, John Duffy

UNIVERSITY OF TEESSIDE (1992)
Middlesbrough, Tees Valley TS1 3BA **T** 01642-218121
W www.tees.ac.uk
Students: 25,172 UG; 4,113 PG
Chancellor, Lord Sawyer
Vice-Chancellor, Prof. Graham Henderson, CBE
University Secretary, Morgan McClintock

UNIVERSITY OF ULSTER (1984)
Cromore Road, Coleraine, Co. Londonderry BT52 1SA
T 028-7012 3456 **W** www.ulster.ac.uk
Students: 20,610 UG; 5,420 PG
Chancellor, James Nesbitt
Vice-Chancellor, Prof. Richard Barnett
Registrar, Norma Cameron

UNIVERSITY OF WALES (1893)
King Edward VII Avenue, Cathays Park, Cardiff CF10 3NS
T 029-2037 6999 **W** www.wales.ac.uk
Chancellor, HRH the Prince of Wales, KG, KT, GCB
Vice-Chancellor and Chief Executive, Prof. Marc Clement

ACCREDITED INSTITUTIONS
ABERYSTWYTH UNIVERSITY
Old College, King Street, Aberystwyth SY23 2AX
T 01970-623111
Students: 9,030 UG; 1,775 PG
Vice-Chancellor, Prof. Noel G. Lloyd

BANGOR UNIVERSITY
Gwynedd LL57 2DG
T 01248-351151
Students: 8,685 UG; 2,770 PG
Vice-Chancellor, Prof. John Hughes

GLYNDWR UNIVERSITY
Mold Road, Wrexham LL11 2AW
T 01978-290666
Students: 6,865 UG; 1,135 PG
Vice-Chancellor, Prof. Michael Scott

UNIVERSITY OF WALES INSTITUTE, CARDIFF
Llandaff Campus, Western Avenue, Cardiff CF5 2YB
T 029-2041 6070
Students: 8,325 UG; 4,755 PG
Vice-Chancellor and Principal, Prof. Antony J. Chapman

UNIVERSITY OF WALES, NEWPORT
Caerleon Campus, Newport NP18 3QT
T 01633-432432
Students: 7,450 UG; 1,840 PG
Vice-Chancellor, Dr P. Noyes

UNIVERSITY OF WALES, TRINITY SAINT DAVID
Carmarthen SA31 3EP
T 01267-676767
Students: 4,775 UG; 1,335 PG
Vice-Chancellor, Prof. Medwin Hughes

SWANSEA UNIVERSITY
Singleton Park SA2 8PP
T 01792-205678
Students: 12,280 UG; 2,060 PG
Vice-Chancellor, Prof. Richard B. Davies

SWANSEA METROPOLITAN UNIVERSITY
Mount Pleasant, Swansea SA1 6ED
T 01792-481000
Students: 4,910 UG; 1,275 PG
Vice-Chancellor, Prof. David Warner

UNIVERSITY OF WARWICK (1965)
Coventry CV4 7AL T 024-7652 3523 W www.warwick.ac.uk
Students: 12,823 UG; 9,825 PG
Chancellor, Sir Richard Lambert
Vice-Chancellor, Prof. Nigel Thrift
Registrar, Jon Baldwin

UNIVERSITY OF WEST LONDON (1992)
St Mary's Road, Ealing, London W5 5RF T 020-8579 5000
W www.uwl.ac.uk
Students: 14,350 UG; 2,030 PG
Chancellor, Laurence Geller
Vice-Chancellor, Prof. Peter John
University Secretary, Maureen Skinner

UNIVERSITY OF WESTMINSTER (1992)
309 Regent Street, London W1B 2UW T 020-7911 5000
W www.westminster.ac.uk
Students: 17,175 UG; 6,785 PG
Chancellor, Lord Paul
Vice-Chancellor and Rector, Prof. Geoffrey Petts
Registrar and Secretary, Carole Mainstone

UNIVERSITY OF THE WEST OF ENGLAND
(1992)
Frenchay Campus, Coldharbour Lane, Bristol BS16 1QY
T 0117-965 6261 W www.uwe.ac.uk
Students: 21,826 UG; 6,411 PG
Chancellor, Rt. Hon. Baroness Butler-Sloss, GBE
Vice-Chancellor, Prof. Steven West, KB, CBE
Academic Registrar, Andrea Cheshire

UNIVERSITY OF THE WEST OF SCOTLAND
(1992)
Paisley PA1 2BE T 0141-848 3000 W www.uws.ac.uk
Students: 10,000 UG; 10,000 PG
Chancellor, Lord Smith of Kelvin
Vice-Chancellor and Principal, Prof. Seamus McDaid
Secretary, Kenneth Alexander

UNIVERSITY OF WINCHESTER (2005)
Winchester SO22 4NR T 01962-841515
W www.winchester.ac.uk
Students: 5,041 UG; 1,387 PG
Chancellor, Dame Mary Fagan
Vice-Chancellor, Prof. Joy Carter
Registrar, Malcolm Willis

UNIVERSITY OF WOLVERHAMPTON (1988)
Wulfruna Street, Wolverhampton WV1 1LY T 01902-321000
W www.wlv.ac.uk
Students: 18,740 UG; 3,870 PG
Chancellor, Rt. Hon. Lord Paul of Marylebone
Vice-Chancellor, Prof. Geoff Layer, OBE, FRSA

UNIVERSITY OF WORCESTER (2005)
Henwick Grove, Worcester WR2 6AJ T 01905-855000
W www.worcester.ac.uk
Students: 7,730 UG; 1,810 PG
Chancellor, HRH the Duke of Gloucester, KG, GCVO
Vice-Chancellor and Chief Executive, Prof. David Green
Registrar, John Ryan

UNIVERSITY OF YORK (1963)
Heslington, York YO10 5DD T 01904-320000
W www.york.ac.uk
Students: 10,383 UG; 2,881 PG
Chancellor, Greg Dyke
Vice-Chancellor, Prof. Brian Cantor, FRENG
Registrar, Dr David Duncan

YORK ST JOHN UNIVERSITY (2006)
Lord Mayor's Walk, York YO31 7EX T 01904-624624
W www.yorksj.ac.uk
Students: 4,449 UG; 887 PG
Chancellor, Most Revd Dr John Sentamu, Archbishop
  of York, PC
Vice-Chancellor, Prof. David Fleming
Registrar, vacant

PROFESSIONAL EDUCATION

The organisations selected below provide specialist training, conduct examinations or are responsible for maintaining a register of those with professional qualifications in their sector, thereby controlling entry into a profession.

EU RECOGNITION

It is possible for those with professional qualifications obtained in the UK to have these recognised in other European countries. Further information can be obtained from:

EUROPE OPEN UK NARIC, Oriel House, Oriel Road, Cheltenham, Glos GL50 1XP T 0871-226 2850
  W www.europeopen.org.uk

ACCOUNTANCY

Salary range for chartered accountants:
Certified £14,500–£25,000 (starting) rising to £29,000–£52,000+ (qualified), £40,000–£100,000+ at senior levels
Management £23,000 (starting), £25,000–£57,000 (newly qualified), £62,000–£106,000+ at senior levels
Public finance £23,000–£50,000 (newly qualified) rising to £35,000–£100,000+ at senior levels

Most chartered accountancy trainees are graduates, although some contracts are available to school-leavers. The undergraduate degree is followed by a three-year training contract with an approved employer culminating in professional exams provided by the Institute of Chartered Accountants of England and Wales (ICAEW), the Institute of Chartered Accountants of Scotland (ICAS) or the Institute of Chartered Accountants in Ireland (ICAI). Success in the examination and membership of one of the institutes allows the use of the designation 'chartered accountant' and the letters ACA or CA.

The Association of Chartered Certified Accountants (ACCA) is the global body for professional accountants. The ACCA aims to offer business-relevant qualifications to students in a range of business sectors and countries seeking a career in accountancy, finance and management. The ACCA Qualification consists of up to 14 examinations, practical experiences and a professional ethics module. Chartered certified accountants can use the designatory letters ACCA.

Chartered management accountants focus on accounting for businesses, and most do not work in accountancy practices but in industry, commerce, not-for-profit and public sector organisations. Graduates who have not studied a business or accounting undergraduate degree must gain the Chartered Institute of Management Accountants (CIMA) Certificate in Business Accounting before studying for the CIMA Professional Qualification which requires three years of practical experience, nine examinations and a pass in the Institute's Test of Professional Competence in Management Accounting (TOPCIMA). In May 2011, CIMA and the American Institute of Certified Public Accountants agreed on the creation of a new professional designation, the Chartered Global Management Accountant (CGMA),

which will represent a worldwide standard of professional excellence in management accounting.

Chartered public finance accountants usually work for public bodies, but they can also work in the private sector. To gain chartered public finance accountant status (CPFA), trainees must complete the three parts of the Chartered Institute of Public Finance and Accountancy (CIPFA) Professional Accountancy Qualification (PAQ), which takes approximately three years. The first stage is the certificate level, which leads to affiliate membership of CIPFA, the second is the diploma level which leads to associate membership, and finally completion of the Final Test of Professional Competence leads to full membership of CIPFA.

ASSOCIATION OF CHARTERED CERTIFIED ACCOUNTANTS (ACCA) 29 Lincoln's Inn Fields, London WC2A 3EE T 020-7059 5000
  E info@accaglobal.com W www.accaglobal.com
  Chief Executive, Helen Brand
CHARTERED INSTITUTE OF MANAGEMENT ACCOUNTANTS (CIMA) 26 Chapter Street, London SW1P 4NP T 020-8849 2251
  E cima.contact@cimaglobal.com W www.cimaglobal.com
  Chief Executive, Charles Tilley
CHARTERED INSTITUTE OF PUBLIC FINANCE AND ACCOUNTANCY (CIPFA) 3 Robert Street, London WC2N 6RL T 020-7543 5600
  E corporate@cipfa.org.uk W www.cipfa.org.uk
  Chief Executive, Steve Freer
INSTITUTE OF CHARTERED ACCOUNTANTS IN ENGLAND AND WALES (ICAEW) Chartered Accountants' Hall, Moorgate Place, London EC2R 6EA
  T 020-7920 8100 W www.icaew.com
  Chief Executive, Michael Izza
INSTITUTE OF CHARTERED ACCOUNTANTS IN IRELAND (ICAI) The Linenhall, 32–38 Linenhall Street, Belfast BT2 8BG T 028-9043 5840
  E ca@charteredaccountants.ie
  W www.charteredaccountants.ie
  Chief Executive, Pat Costello
INSTITUTE OF CHARTERED ACCOUNTANTS OF SCOTLAND (ICAS) CA House, 21 Haymarket Yards, Edinburgh EH12 5BH T 0131-347 0100
  E enquiries@icas.org.uk W www.icas.org.uk
  Chief Executive, Anton Colella

ACTUARIAL SCIENCE

Salary range: £25,000–£35,000 for graduate trainees; £45,000–£55,000 after qualification; £60,000–£100,000+ for senior roles

Actuaries apply financial and statistical theories to solve business problems. These problems usually involve analysing future financial events in order to assess investment risks. Following a vote of their respective members, the Faculty of Actuaries in Edinburgh and the Institute of Actuaries in London merged in August 2010 to form one professional body in the UK: the Institute and Faculty of Actuaries (IFA). The IFA develops actuarial techniques and sets examinations, professional codes and disciplinary standards. UK qualified actuaries are fellows and bear the designations FIA or FFA. On average, it takes five years to qualify as an actuary; examinations are held twice a year, and applicants to the profession must also have completed three years of actuarial work experience before gaining fellowship.

The Financial Reporting Council (FRC) is the unified independent regulator for corporate reporting, auditing, actuarial practice, corporate governance and the professionalism of accountants and actuaries. The FRC's Board for Actuarial Standards sets and maintains technical actuarial standards independently of the profession while the Professional Oversight Board of the FRC oversees the regulation of the accountancy and actuarial professions by their respective professional bodies. The Accountancy and Actuarial Discipline Board operates an investigation and discipline scheme in relation to members of the profession who raise issues affecting UK public interest.

FINANCIAL REPORTING COUNCIL (FRC) 5th Floor, Aldwych House, 71–91 Aldwych, London WC2B 4HN
T 020-7492 2300 W www.frc.org.uk
Chief Executive, Stephen Haddrill

INSTITUTE AND FACULTY OF ACTUARIES Staple Inn Hall, High Holborn, London WC1V 7QJ T 020-7632 2100
E info@actuaries.org.uk W www.actuaries.org.uk
Acting Chief Executive, Derek Cribb

ARCHITECTURE
Salary range: £17,000–£30,000 during training; newly registered £25,000–£35,000; project architect and senior roles £35,000–£80,000+

It takes a minimum of seven years to become an architect, involving three stages: a three-year first degree, a two-year second degree or diploma and two years of professional experience followed by the successful completion of a professional practice examination.

The Architects Registration Board (ARB) is the independent regulator for the profession. It was set up by an act of parliament in 1997 and is responsible for maintaining the register of UK architects, prescribing qualifications that lead to registration as an architect, investigating complaints about the conduct and competence of architects, and ensuring that only those who are registered with ARB offer their services as an architect. It is only following registration with ARB that an architect can apply for chartered membership of the Royal Institute of British Architects (RIBA). RIBA, the UK body for architecture and the architectural profession, received its royal charter in 1837 and validates courses at over 40 UK schools of architecture; it also validates overseas courses. RIBA provides support and guidance for its members in the form of training, technical services and events and sets standards for the education of architects.

The Chartered Institute of Architectural Technologists is the international qualifying body for chartered architectural technologists (MCIAT) and architectural technicians (TCIAT).

ARCHITECTS REGISTRATION BOARD (ARB)
8 Weymouth Street, London W1W 5BU T 020-7580 5861
E info@arb.org.uk W www.arb.org.uk
Registrar and Chief Executive, Alison Carr

CHARTERED INSTITUTE OF ARCHITECTURAL TECHNOLOGISTS 397 City Road, London EC1V 1NH
T 020-7278 2206 E info@ciat.org.uk W www.ciat.org.uk
Chief Executive, Francesca Berriman

ROYAL INCORPORATION OF ARCHITECTS IN SCOTLAND 15 Rutland Square, Edinburgh EH1 2BE
T 0131-229 7545 E info@rias.org.uk W www.rias.org.uk
Secretary and Treasurer, Neil Baxter

ROYAL INSTITUTE OF BRITISH ARCHITECTS (RIBA) 66 Portland Place, London W1B 1AD
T 020-7580 5533 E info@inst.riba.org W www.riba.org
Chief Executive, Harry Rich

ENGINEERING
Salary range:
Civil/structural £27,000–£34,000 (graduate); £32,000–£48,000 with experience, rising to £80,000+ in senior posts
Chemical £26,000 average (graduate); £44,000–£72,000+ (chartered)
Electrical £20,000–£23,000 (graduate); £45,000+ with experience

The Engineering Council sets standards of professional competence and ethics for engineers, technologists and technicians, and regulates the profession through the 36 institutions (Licensed Members) listed below, which are licensed to put suitably qualified members on the Engineering Council's Register of Engineers. All candidates for registration as chartered engineer, incorporated engineer, engineering technician or information and communication technology technicians must satisfy the competence standards set by the Engineering Council and be members of the appropriate institution. Applicants must show that they have a satisfactory educational base, have undergone approved professional development and, at interview, must demonstrate their professional competence against specific criteria.

ENGINEERING COUNCIL 246 High Holborn, London WC1V 7EX T 020-3206 0500 E info@engc.org.uk
W www.engc.org.uk
Chief Executive Officer, Jon Prichard

LICENSED MEMBERS
British Computer Society W www.bcs.org
British Institute of Non-destructive Testing
W www.bindt.org
Chartered Institution of Building Services Engineers
W www.cibse.org
Chartered Institution of Highways and Transportation
W www.ciht.org.uk
Chartered Institute of Plumbing and Heating Engineers
W www.ciphe.org.uk
Chartered Institution of Water and Environmental Management W www.ciwem.org
Energy Institute W www.energyinst.org.uk
Institute of Acoustics W www.ioa.org.uk
Institute of Cast Metals Engineers W www.icme.org.uk
Institute of Healthcare Engineering and Estate Management
W www.iheem.org.uk
Institute of Highway Engineers W www.theihe.org
Institute of Marine Engineering, Science and Technology
W www.imarest.org
Institute of Materials, Minerals and Mining
W www.iom3.org
Institute of Measurement and Control
W www.instmc.org.uk
Institute of Physics W www.iop.org
Institute of Physics and Engineering in Medicine
W www.ipem.ac.uk
Institute of Water W www.instituteofwater.org.uk
Institution of Agricultural Engineers W www.iagre.org
Institution of Chemical Engineers W www.icheme.org
Institution of Civil Engineers W www.ice.org.uk
Institution of Diesel and Gas Turbine Engineers
W www.idgte.org

Institution of Engineering Designers W www.ied.org.uk
Institution of Engineering and Technology
W www.theiet.org
Institution of Fire Engineers W www.ife.org.uk
Institution of Gas Engineers and Managers
W www.igem.org.uk
Institution of Lighting Professionals W www.theilp.org.uk
Institution of Mechanical Engineers W www.imeche.org
Institution of Railway Signal Engineers W www.irse.org
Institution of Royal Engineers W www.instre.org
Institution of Structural Engineers W www.istructe.org
Nuclear Institute W www.nuclearinst.com
Royal Aeronautical Society W www.aerosociety.com
Royal Institution of Naval Architects W www.rina.org.uk
Society of Environmental Engineers
W www.environmental.org.uk
Society of Operations Engineers W www.soe.org.uk
Welding Institute W www.twi.co.uk

HEALTHCARE

CHIROPRACTIC
Salary range: £22,000–£40,000 starting salary; with own practice up to £70,000

Chiropractors diagnose and treat conditions caused by problems with joints, ligaments, tendons and nerves of the body. The General Chiropractic Council (GCC) is the independent statutory regulatory body for chiropractors and its role and remit is defined in the Chiropractors Act 1994. The GCC sets the criteria for the recognition of chiropractic degrees and for standards of proficiency and conduct. Details of the institutions offering degree programmes are available on the GCC website (*see* below). It is illegal for anyone in the UK to use the title 'chiropractor' unless registered with the GCC.
   The British Chiropractic Association and the Scottish Chiropractic Association are two representative bodies for the profession and are sources of further information.
BRITISH CHIROPRACTIC ASSOCIATION 59 Castle
   Street, Reading RG1 7SN T 0118-950 5950
   E enquiries@chiropractic-uk.co.uk
   W www.chiropractic-uk.co.uk
   Executive Director, Sue Wakefield
GENERAL CHIROPRACTIC COUNCIL
   44 Wicklow Street, London WC1X 9HL T 020-7713 5155
   E enquiries@gcc-uk.org W www.gcc-uk.org
   Chief Executive and Registrar, Satjit Singh
SCOTTISH CHIROPRACTIC ASSOCIATION
   1 Chisholm Avenue, Bishopton, Renfrewshire PA7 5JH
   T 0141-404 0260 E admin@sca-chiropractic.org
   W www.sca-chiropractic.org
   Administrator, Morag Cairns

DENTISTRY
Salary range: see Health: Employees and Salaries

The General Dental Council (GDC) is the organisation that regulates dental professionals in the UK. All dentists, dental hygienists, dental therapists, clinical dental technicians, dental nurses and orthodontic therapists must be registered with the GDC to work in the UK.
   There are various different routes to qualify for registration as a dentist, including holding a degree from a UK university; completing the GDC's qualifying examination; or holding a relevant European Economic Area or overseas diploma. The GDC's purpose is to protect the public through the regulation of UK dental professionals. It keeps up-to-date registers of dental professionals, works to set standards of dental practice, behaviour and education, and helps to protect patients by hearing complaints and taking action against professionals where necessary.
   The British Dental Association is a membership organisation that provides dentists with professional and educational services.
BRITISH DENTAL ASSOCIATION 64 Wimpole Street,
   London W1G 8YS T 020-7935 0875 E enquiries@bda.org
   W www.bda.org
   Chief Executive, Peter Ward
GENERAL DENTAL COUNCIL 37 Wimpole Street,
   London W1G 8DQ T 020-7887 3800
   E information@gdc-uk.org W www.gdc-uk.org
   Chief Executive, Evlynne Gilvarry

MEDICINE
Salary range: see Health: Employees and Salaries

The General Medical Council (GMC) regulates medical education and training in the UK. This covers undergraduate study (usually five years), the two-year foundation programme taken by doctors directly after graduation and all subsequent postgraduate study, including specialty and GP training.
   All doctors must be registered with the GMC, which is responsible for protecting the public. It does this by setting standards for professional practice, overseeing medical education, keeping a register of qualified doctors and taking action where a doctor's fitness to practise is in doubt. Doctors are eligible for full registration upon successful completion of the first year of training after graduation.
   Following the foundation programme, many doctors undertake specialist training (provided by the colleges and faculties listed below) to become either a consultant or a GP. Once specialist training has been completed, doctors are awarded the Certificate of Completion of Training (CCT) and are eligible to be placed on either the GMC's specialist register or its GP register.
GENERAL MEDICAL COUNCIL (GMC) 350 Euston
   Road, London NW1 3JN T 0161-923 6602
   E gmc@gmc-uk.org W www.gmc-uk.org
   Chief Executive, Niall Dickson
SOCIETY OF APOTHECARIES OF LONDON
   Black Friars Lane, London EC4V 6EJ T 020-7236 1189
   E clerk@apothecaries.org W www.apothecaries.org
   Master, Dr T. Chambers

SPECIALIST TRAINING COLLEGES AND FACULTIES
College of Emergency Medicine
W www.collemergencymed.ac.uk
Faculty of Pharmaceutical Medicine W www.fpm.org.uk
Faculty of Public Health W www.fph.org.uk
Royal College of Anaesthetists W www.rcoa.ac.uk
Royal College of General Practitioners W www.rcgp.org.uk
Royal College of Obstetricians and Gynaecologists
W www.rcog.org.uk
Royal College of Opthalmologists W www.rcophth.ac.uk
Royal College of Paediatrics and Child Health
W www.rcpch.ac.uk
Royal College of Pathologists W www.rcpath.org
Royal College of Physicians, London W www.rcplondon.ac.uk
Royal College of Physicians and Surgeons of Glasgow
W www.rcpsg.ac.uk
Royal College of Physicians of Edinburgh W www.rcpe.ac.uk
Royal College of Psychiatrists W www.rcpsych.ac.uk

Royal College of Radiologists W www.rcr.ac.uk
Royal College of Surgeons of Edinburgh W www.rcsed.ac.uk
Royal College of Surgeons of England W www.rcseng.ac.uk

MEDICINE, SUPPLEMENTARY PROFESSIONS

The standard of professional education for arts therapists, biomedical scientists, chiropodists and podiatrists, clinical scientists, dietitians, occupational therapists, operating department practitioners, orthoptists, paramedics, physiotherapists, practitioner psychologists, prosthetists and orthotists, radiographers, and speech and language therapists is regulated by the Health Professions Council (HPC), which only registers those practitioners who meet certain standards of training, professional skills, behaviour and health. Other than biomedical science and clinical science, all the professions listed below are described by the NHS as 'allied health professions'. The HPC currently registers over 200,000 professionals.

HEALTH PROFESSIONS COUNCIL Park House, 184 Kennington Park Road, London SE11 4BU T 020-7582 0866 E registration@hpc-uk.org W www.hpc-uk.org
Chief Executive and Registrar, Marc Seale

ART, DRAMA AND MUSIC THERAPIES
Salary range: £25,000–£47,000

An art, drama or music therapist encourages people to express their feelings and emotions through art, such as painting and drawing, drama or music. A postgraduate qualification in the relevant therapy is required. Details of accredited training programmes in the UK can be obtained from the following organisations:

BRITISH ASSOCIATION FOR MUSIC THERAPY 24–27 White Lion Street, London N1 9PD T 020-7387 6100 E info@bamt.org W www.bamt.org
Chair, Angela Harrison
BRITISH ASSOCIATION OF ART THERAPISTS 24–27 White Lion Street, London N1 9PD T 020-7686 4216 E info@baat.org W www.baat.org
Chief Executive, Val Huet
BRITISH ASSOCIATION OF DRAMA THERAPISTS Waverley, Battledown Approach, Cheltenham, Gloucestershire GL52 6RE T 0124-2235 5155 E enquiries@badth.org.uk W www.badth.org.uk
Chair, Dr Bruce Bayley

BIOMEDICAL SCIENCES
Salary range: £21,000–£34,000, rising to £66,000+ in senior posts

Biomedical scientists analyse specimens from patients in order to help make diagnoses. Qualifications from higher education establishments and training in medical laboratories are required for membership of the Institute of Biomedical Science, which sets the professional standards of competence for those who practise biomedical science.

INSTITUTE OF BIOMEDICAL SCIENCE 12 Coldbath Square, London EC1R 5HL T 020-7713 0214 E mail@ibms.org W www.ibms.org
Chief Executive, Jill Rodney

CHIROPODY AND PODIATRY
Salary range: £21,000–£40,000

Chiropodists and podiatrists assess, diagnose and treat problems of the lower leg and foot. The Society of Chiropodists and Podiatrists is the professional body and trade union for the profession. Qualifications granted and

degrees recognised by the society are approved by the Health Professions Council (HPC). HPC registration is required in order to use the titles chiropodist and podiatrist.

SOCIETY OF CHIROPODISTS AND PODIATRISTS 1 Fellmonger's Path, Tower Bridge Road, London SE1 3LY T 020-7234 8620 E enq@scpod.org W www.feetforlife.org
Chief Executive, Joanna Brown

CLINICAL SCIENCE
Salary range: £25,000–£95,000+

Clinical scientists conduct tests in laboratories in order to diagnose and manage disease. The Association of Clinical Scientists is responsible for setting the criteria for competence of applicants to the HPC's register and to present a Certificate of Attainment to candidates following a successful assessment. This certificate will allow direct registration with the HPC.

ASSOCIATION OF CLINICAL SCIENTISTS c/o Association for Clinical Biochemistry, 130–132 Tooley Street, London SE1 2TU T 020-7940 8960 E info@assclinsci.org W www.assclinsci.org
Chair, Dr Iain Chambers

DIETETICS
Salary range: £21,000–£40,000

Dietitians advise patients on how to improve their health and counter specific health problems through diet. The British Dietetic Association, established in 1936, is the professional association for dietitians. Full membership is open to UK-registered dietitians, who must also be registered with the HPC.

BRITISH DIETETIC ASSOCIATION 5th Floor, Charles House, 148–149 Great Charles Street Queensway, Birmingham B3 3HT T 0121-200 8080 E info@bda.uk.com W www.bda.uk.com
Chief Executive, Andy Burman

OCCUPATIONAL THERAPY
Salary range: £20,000–£40,000, rising to £55,000 in senior posts

Occupational therapists work with people who have physical, mental and/or social problems, either from birth or as a result of accident, illness or ageing, and aim to make them as independent as possible. The professional qualification and eligibility for registration may be obtained upon successful completion of a validated course in any of the educational institutions approved by the British Association of Occupational Therapists, which is the professional body for occupational therapy in the UK. The courses are normally degree-level courses based in higher education institutions.

BRITISH ASSOCIATION OF OCCUPATIONAL THERAPISTS 106–114 Borough High Street, London SE1 1LB T 020-7357 6480 W www.cot.org.uk
Chief Executive, Julia Scott

MENTAL HEALTH
Salary range:
Clinical psychologist £24,000, rising to £50,000–£80,000+ at senior levels
Counsellor £18,000–£27,000, rising to £40,000–£50,000 with experience
Educational psychologist £21,000, rising to £31,000 when chartered and up to £63,000 at senior levels
Psychotherapist £20,000–£26,000 (starting), rising to £77,000+ at senior levels

Psychologists are mental health professionals who can work in a range of settings including prisons, schools and hospitals as well as businesses. The UK psychological profession is represented by the British Psychological Society (BPS). It accredits qualifications in psychology, and offers support to members through continuing professional development. The Association of Educational Psychologists (AEP) represents the interests of educational psychologists, while the British Association for Counselling and Psychotherapy (BACP) sets educational standards and provides professional support to those psychologists working in psychotherapy or counselling-related roles. The BPS website provides more information on the different specialisations that may be pursued by psychologists.

ASSOCIATION OF EDUCATIONAL
PSYCHOLOGISTS (AEP) 4 The Riverside Centre, Frankland Lane, Durham DH1 5TA T 0191-384 9512 E enquiries@aep.org.uk W www.aep.org.uk
General Secretary, Kate Fallon
BRITISH ASSOCIATION FOR COUNSELLING AND PSYCHOTHERAPY (BACP) BACP House, 15 St John's Business Park, Lutterworth, Leicestershire LE17 4HB T 01455-883300 E bacp@bacp.co.uk W www.bacp.co.uk
President, Laurie Clarke
BRITISH PSYCHOLOGICAL SOCIETY (BPS)
St Andrews House, 48 Princess Road East, Leicester LE1 7DR T 0116-254 9568 E enquiries@bps.org.uk W www.bps.org.uk
President, Dr Carole Allan

ORTHOPTICS
Salary range: £20,000–£38,000, rising to £38,000–£65,000 in senior posts

Orthoptists undertake the diagnosis and treatment of all types of squint and other anomalies of binocular vision, working in close collaboration with ophthalmologists. The all-graduate workforce comes from two universities: the University of Liverpool and University of Sheffield.

BRITISH AND IRISH ORTHOPTIC SOCIETY
62 Wilson Street, London EC2R 2BU T 01353-665541 W www.orthoptics.org.uk
Chair, Lesley-Anne Baxter

PARAMEDICAL SERVICES
Salary range: £21,000–£34,000

Paramedics deal with accidents and emergencies, assessing patients and carrying out any specialist treatment and care needed in the first instance. The body that represents ambulance professionals is the College of Paramedics.

COLLEGE OF PARAMEDICS The Exchange, Express Park, Bristol Road, Bridgwater TA6 4RR T 01278-420014 E help@collegeofparamedics.net W www.collegeofparamedics.net
Chief Executive, Roland Furber

PHYSIOTHERAPY
Salary range: £19,000–£37,000, rising to £62,000 in senior posts

Physiotherapists are concerned with movement and function and deal with problems arising from injury, illness and ageing. Full-time three- or four-year degree courses are available at around 35 higher education institutions in the UK. Information about courses leading to state registration is available from the Chartered Society of Physiotherapy.

CHARTERED SOCIETY OF PHYSIOTHERAPY
14 Bedford Row, London WC1R 4ED T 020-7306 6666 E enquiries@csp.org.uk W www.csp.org.uk
Chief Executive, Phil Gray

PROSTHETICS AND ORTHOTICS
Salary range: £21,000 on qualification up to £67,000 as a consultant

Prosthetists provide artificial limbs, while orthotists provide devices to support or control a part of the body. It is necessary to obtain an honours degree to become a prosthetist or orthotist. Training is centred at the universities of Salford and Strathclyde.

BRITISH ASSOCIATION OF PROSTHETISTS AND ORTHOTISTS Sir James Clark Building, Abbey Mill Business Centre, Paisley PA1 1TJ T 0141-561 7217 E enquiries@bapo.com W www.bapo.org
Chair, Peter Honeycombe

RADIOGRAPHY
Salary range: £20,000–£38,000, rising to £64,000 in senior posts

In order to practise both diagnostic and therapeutic radiography in the UK, it is necessary to have successfully completed a course of education and training recognised by the Health Professionals Council. Such courses are offered by universities throughout the UK and lead to the award of a degree in radiography. Further information is available from the Society and College of Radiographers.

SOCIETY AND COLLEGE OF RADIOGRAPHERS
207 Providence Square, Mill Street, London SE1 2EW T 020-7740 7200 E info@sor.org W www.sor.org
Chief Executive, Richard Evans

SPEECH AND LANGUAGE THERAPY
Salary range: £20,000 rising upwards of £53,000 in senior roles

Speech and language therapists (SLTs) work with people with communication, swallowing, eating and drinking problems. The Royal College of Speech and Language Therapists is the professional body for speech and language therapists and support workers. Alongside the Health Professions Council, it accredits education and training courses leading to qualification.

ROYAL COLLEGE OF SPEECH AND LANGUAGE THERAPISTS 2 White Hart Yard, London SE1 1NX T 020-7378 1200 E info@rcslt.org W www.rcslt.org
Chief Executive, Kamini Gadhok, MBE

NURSING
Salary range: see Health: Employees and Salaries

In order to practise in the UK, all nurses and midwives must be registered with the Nursing and Midwifery Council (NMC). The NMC is a statutory regulatory body that establishes and maintains standards of education, training, conduct and performance for nursing and midwifery. Courses leading to registration are currently at a minimum of diploma in higher education, with some offered at degree level. All are a minimum of three years if undertaken full-time. From September 2011 diplomas will be phased out, and by 2013 all new entrants to the nursing profession will have to study a degree. The NMC approves programmes run jointly by higher education institutions with their healthcare service partners who offer clinical placements. The nursing part of the register has four fields of practice: adult, children's, learning disability and mental health nursing. During the first year of a nursing course, the common foundation programme, students are taught across all four fields of practice. In addition, those studying to become adult nurses gain experience of nursing in relation to medicine, surgery, maternity care and nursing in the home. The NMC also sets standards for programmes leading to registration as a midwife and a range of post-registration courses including specialist practice programmes, nurse prescribing and those for teachers of nursing and midwifery. The NMC has a part of the register for specialist community public health nurses and approves programmes for health visitors, occupational health nurses and school nurses.

The Royal College of Nursing is the largest professional union for nursing in the UK, representing qualified nurses, healthcare assistants and nursing students in the NHS and the independent sector.

NURSING AND MIDWIFERY COUNCIL 23 Portland Place, London W1B 1PZ T 020-7333 9333
E communications@nmc-uk.org W www.nmc-uk.org
Chief Executive and Registrar, Prof. Dickon Weir-Hughes
ROYAL COLLEGE OF NURSING 20 Cavendish Square, London W1G 0RN T 020-740 3333 W www.rcn.org.uk
Chief Executive and General Secretary, Dr Peter Carter

OPTOMETRY AND DISPENSING OPTICS
Salary range:
Optometrist £19,000–£53,000 (up to £80,000 for consultant posts)
Dispensing Optician £18,000–£30,000+

There are various routes to qualification as a dispensing optician. Qualification takes three years in total, and can be completed by combining a distance learning course or day release while working as a trainee under the supervision of a qualified and registered optician. Alternatively, students can do a two-year full-time course followed by one year of supervised practice with a qualified and registered optician. Training must be done at a training establishment approved by the regulatory body – the General Optical Council (GOC). There are five training establishments which are approved by the GOC: Association of British Dispensing Opticians College, Anglia Ruskin University, Bradford College, City and Islington College and Glasgow Caledonian University. All routes are concluded by professional qualifying examinations, successful completion of which leads to registration with the GOC, which is compulsory for all practising dispensing opticians. After two years post-qualifying experience and completing training to fit contact lenses, students have the option to take a career progression course at the University of Bradford that allows them to graduate with a degree in optometry in one calendar year.

Optometrists must obtain an undergraduate optometry degree from one of the eight institutions approved by the GOC (Anglia Ruskin University, Aston University, the University of Bradford, Cardiff University, City University, Glasgow Caledonian University, the University of Manchester or the University of Ulster). Following graduation, trainees must complete a year of supervised

salaried training with a registered optometrist after which they must pass a series of assessments set by the College of Optometrists. As with dispensing opticians, optometrists must be registered with the GOC in order to practise.

ASSOCIATION OF BRITISH DISPENSING OPTICIANS Godmersham Park, Godmersham, Canterbury, Kent CT4 7DT T 01227-738829
E membership@abdo.org.uk W www.abdo.org.uk
General Secretary, Sir Anthony Garrett, CBE
COLLEGE OF OPTOMETRISTS 42 Craven Street, London WC2N 5NG T 020-7839 6000
E optometry@college-optometrists.org
W www.college-optometrists.org
Chief Executive, Bryony Pawinska
GENERAL OPTICAL COUNCIL (GOC) 1 Harley Street, London W1G 8DJ T 020-7580 3898
E goc@optical.org W www.optical.org
Chief Executive, Samantha Peters

OSTEOPATHY
Salary Range: £16,000–£65,000

Osteopathy is a system of diagnosis and treatment for a wide range of medical conditions. It works with the structure and function of the body, and is based on the principle that the well-being of an individual depends on the skeleton, muscles, ligaments and connective tissues functioning smoothly together. The General Osteopathic Council (GOsC) regulates the practice of osteopathy in the UK and maintains a register of those entitled to practise. It is a criminal offence for anyone to describe themselves as an osteopath unless they are registered with the GOsC.

To gain entry to the register, applicants must hold a recognised qualification from an osteopathic education institute accredited by the GOsC; this involves a four- to five-year honours degree programme combined with clinical training.

GENERAL OSTEOPATHIC COUNCIL Osteopathy House, 176 Tower Bridge Road, London SE1 3LU
T 020-7357 6655 E info@osteopathy.org.uk
W www.osteopathy.org.uk
Chief Executive and Registrar, Evlynne Gilvarry

PHARMACY
Salary range: £23,000–£68,000+

Pharmacists are involved in the preparation and use of medicines, from the discovery of their active ingredients to their use by patients. Pharmacists also monitor the effects of medicines, both for patient care and for research purposes.

The General Pharmaceutical Council (GPhC) is the independent regulatory body for pharmacists in England, Scotland and Wales, having taken over the regulating function of the Royal Pharmaceutical Society in 2010. The GPhC maintains the register of pharmacists, pharmacy technicians and pharmacy premises; it also sets national standards for training, ethics, proficiency and continuing professional development. The Pharmaceutical Society of Northern Ireland (PSNI) performs the same role in Northern Ireland. In order to register, students must complete a four-year degree in pharmacy that is accredited by either the GPhC or the PSNI followed by one year of pre-registration training at an approved pharmacy, and must then pass an entrance examination.

GENERAL PHARMACEUTICAL COUNCIL (GPHC)
129 Lambeth Road, London SE1 7BT T 020-3365 3400
E info@pharmacyregulation.org
W www.pharmacyregulation.org
Chief Executive and Registrar, Duncan Rudkin
PHARMACEUTICAL SOCIETY OF NORTHERN
IRELAND 73 University Street, Belfast BT7 1HL
T 028-9032 6927 E info@psni.org.uk W www.psni.org.uk
Director, Trevor Patterson
ROYAL PHARMACEUTICAL SOCIETY 1 Lambeth High
Street, London SE1 7JN T 020-7572 2737
E support@rpharms.com W www.rpharms.com
Chief Executive, Helen Gordon

INFORMATION MANAGEMENT

Salary range:
Archivist £21,000–£30,000 (starting); £30,000–
£55,000+ in senior posts
Information Officer £19,000–£28,000 (starting);
£28,000–£55,000+ in senior posts
Librarian £19,000–£24,000 (newly qualified); £49,000+
in senior posts

The Chartered Institute of Library and Information
Professionals (CILIP) is the professional body for
librarians, information specialists and knowledge
managers. The Archives and Records Association is the
professional body for archivists and record managers.
The Association of Special Libraries and Information
Bureau (ASLIB) is a membership association serving
people who manage information and knowledge in
organisations across all sectors.
ARCHIVES AND RECORDS ASSOCIATION Prioryfield
House, 20 Canon Street, Taunton, Somerset TA1 1SW
T 01823-327077 E ara@archives.org.uk
W www.archives.org.uk
Chief Executive, John Chambers
ASLIB Howard House, Wagon Lane, Bingley, West Yorkshire,
BD16 1WA T 01274-777700 E support@aslib.com
W www.aslib.com
Chief Executive, John Peters
CHARTERED INSTITUTE OF LIBRARY AND
INFORMATION PROFESSIONALS (CILIP)
7 Ridgmount Street, London WC1E 7AE T 020-7255 0500
E info@cilip.org.uk W www.cilip.org.uk
President, Brian Hall

JOURNALISM

Salary range: starting salaries £12,000 (trainee)–£18,000;
£22,000+ for established journalists, rising to £39,000–
£85,000 for senior journalists/editors

The National Council for the Training of Journalists
(NCTJ) accredits 70 courses for journalists run by 42
education providers; it also provides professional support
to journalists.
The Broadcast Journalism Training Council (BJTC) is
an association of the UK's main broadcast journalism
employers and accredits courses in broadcast journalism.
BROADCAST JOURNALISM TRAINING COUNCIL
(BJTC) 18 Miller's Close, Rippingale Nr. Bourne,
Lincolnshire PE10 0TH T 01778-440025 E sec@bjtc.org.uk
W www.bjtc.org.uk
Secretary, Jim Latham
NATIONAL COUNCIL FOR THE TRAINING OF
JOURNALISTS (NCTJ) The New Granary, Station Road,
Newport, Saffron Walden, Essex CB11 3PL T 01799-544014
E info@nctj.com W www.nctj.com
Chief Executive, Joanne Butcher

LAW

There are three types of practising lawyers: barristers,
notaries and solicitors. Solicitors tend to work as a group
in firms, and can be approached directly by individuals.
They advise on a variety of legal issues and must decide
the most appropriate course of action, if any. Notaries
have all the powers of a solicitor other than the conduct
of litigation. Most of them are primarily concerned with
the preparation and authentication of documents for
use abroad. Barristers are usually self-employed. If a
solicitor believes that a barrister is required, he or she will
instruct one on behalf of the client; the client will not
have contact with the barrister without the solicitor being
present.
When specialist expertise is needed, barristers give
opinions on complex matters of law, and when clients
require representation in the higher courts (crown courts,
the high court, the court of appeal and the supreme
court), barristers provide a specialist advocacy service.
However, solicitors – who represent their clients in the
lower courts such as tribunals, magistrates' courts and
county courts – can also apply for advocacy rights in the
higher courts instead of briefing a barrister.

THE BAR
Salary range: £10,000–£200,000+

The governing body of the Bar of England and Wales is
the General Council of the Bar, also known as the Bar
Council. Since January 2006, the regulatory functions of
the Bar Council (including regulating the education and
training requirements for those wishing to enter the
profession) have been undertaken by the Bar Standards
Board.
In the first (or 'academic') stage of training, aspiring
barristers must obtain a law degree of a good standard
(at least second class). Alternatively, those with a non-
law degree (at least second class) may complete a
one-year full-time or two-year part-time Common
Professional Examination (CPE) or Graduate Diploma in
Law (GDL).
The second (vocational) stage is the completion of the
Bar Professional Training Course (BPTC), which is
available at nine validated institutions in the UK and
must be applied for around one year in advance
(W www.barprofessionaltraining.org.uk). All barristers must
join one of the four Inns of Court prior to commencing
the BPTC.
Students are 'called to the Bar' by their Inn after
completion of the vocational stage, but cannot practise as
a barrister until completion of the third stage, which is
called 'pupillage'. Call to the Bar does not entitle a person
to practise as a barrister – successful completion of
pupillage is now a pre-requisite. Pupillage lasts for two
six-month periods: the 'non-practising six' and the
'practising six'. The former consists of shadowing an
experienced barrister, while the latter involves appearing
in court as a barrister.
Admission to the Bar of Northern Ireland is controlled
by the General Council of the Bar of Northern Ireland;
admission as an Advocate to the Scottish Bar is through
the Faculty of Advocates.
BAR STANDARDS BOARD address as above
E contactus@barstandardsboard.org.uk
W www.barstandardsboard.org.uk
Chair of the Bar Council, Peter Lodder, QC
Director Bar Standards Board, Dr Vanessa Davies

FACULTY OF ADVOCATES Parliament House, Edinburgh EH1 1RF **T** 0131-226 5071 **W** www.advocates.org.uk
Dean, Richard Keen, QC
GENERAL COUNCIL OF THE BAR (THE BAR COUNCIL) 289–293 High Holborn, London WC1V 7HZ
T 020-7242 0082 **E** contactus@barcouncil.org.uk
W www.barcouncil.org.uk
GENERAL COUNCIL OF THE BAR OF NORTHERN IRELAND The Bar Library, 91 Chichester Street, Belfast BT1 3JQ **T** 028-9056 2349 **W** www.barlibrary.com
Chief Executive, Brendan Garland

THE INNS OF COURT
HONOURABLE SOCIETY OF GRAY'S INN
8 South Square, London WC1R 5ET **T** 020-7458 7800
W www.graysinn.org.uk
Under-Treasurer, Brig. Anthony Faith, CBE
HONOURABLE SOCIETY OF LINCOLN'S INN
Treasury Office, Lincoln's Inn, London WC2A 3TL
T 020-7405 1393 **E** mail@lincolnsinn.org.uk
W www.lincolnsinn.org.uk
Under-Treasurer, Col. D. Hills, MBE
HONOURABLE SOCIETY OF THE INNER TEMPLE
Inner Temple, London EC4Y 7HL **T** 020-7797 8250
E enquiries@innertemple.org.uk
W www.innertemple.org.uk
Sub-Treasurer, Patrick Maddams
HONOURABLE SOCIETY OF THE MIDDLE TEMPLE
Middle Temple Lane, London EC4Y 9AT **T** 020-7427 4800
E members@middletemple.org.uk
W www.middletemple.org.uk
Under-Treasurer, Catherine Quinn

NOTARIES PUBLIC
Notaries are qualified lawyers with a postgraduate diploma in notarial practice. Once a potential notary has passed the postgraduate diploma, they can petition the Court of Faculties for a 'faculty'. After the faculty is granted, the notary is able to practise; however, for the first two years this must be under the supervision of an experienced notary. The admission and regulation of notaries in England and Wales is a statutory function of the Faculty Office. This jurisdiction was confirmed by the Courts and Legal Services Act 1990. The Notaries Society of England and Wales is the representative body for practising notaries.
THE FACULTY OFFICE 1 The Sanctuary, Westminster,
London SW1P 3JT **T** 020-7222 5381
E faculty.office@1thesanctuary.com
W www.facultyoffice.org.uk
Registrar, Peter Beesley
THE NOTARIES SOCIETY OF ENGLAND AND WALES PO Box 226, Melton Woodbridge IP12 1WX
T 01394-380436 **E** admin@the notariessociety.org.uk
W www.thenotariessociety.org.uk
Secretary, Christopher Vaughan

SOLICITORS
Salary range: £15,000–£23,000 (trainee); £42,000–£50,000 (associate or partner)

Graduates from any discipline can train to be a solicitor; however, if the undergraduate degree is not in law, a one-year conversion course – either the Common Professional Examination (CPE) or the Graduate Diploma in Law (GDL) – must be completed. The next stage, and the beginning of the vocational phase, is the Legal Practice Course (LPC), which takes one year and is obligatory for both law and non-law graduates. The LPC provides professional instruction for prospective solicitors and can be completed on a full-time or part-time basis. Trainee solicitors then enter the final stage, which is a paid period of supervised work that lasts two years for full-time contracts. The employer that provides the training contract must be authorised by the Solicitors Regulation Authority (SRA) (the regulatory body of the Law Society of England and Wales), the Law Society of Scotland or the Law Society of Northern Ireland. The SRA also monitors the training contract to ensure that it provides the trainee with the expertise to qualify as a solicitor.

Conveyancers are specialist property lawyers, dealing with the legal processes involved in transferring buildings, land and associated finances from one owner to another. This was the sole responsibility of solicitors until 1987 but under current legislation it is now possible for others to train as conveyancers.
COUNCIL FOR LICENSED CONVEYANCERS (CLC)
16 Glebe Road, Chelmsford, Essex CM1 1QG
T 01245-349599 **W** www.conveyancer.org.uk
Chief Executive, Victor Olowe
THE LAW SOCIETY OF ENGLAND AND WALES
The Law Society's Hall, 113 Chancery Lane, London
WC2A 1PL **T** 020-7242 1222 **E** enquiries@lawsociety.org.uk
W www.lawsociety.org.uk
Chief Executive, Des Hudson
LAW SOCIETY OF NORTHERN IRELAND
Law Society House, 96 Victoria Street, Belfast BT1 3GN
T 028-9023 1614 **E** info@lawsoc-ni.org
W www.lawsoc-ni.org
Chief Executive and Secretary, Alan Hunter
LAW SOCIETY OF SCOTLAND 26 Drumsheugh Gardens,
Edinburgh EH3 7YR **T** 0131-226 7411
E lawscot@lawscot.org.uk **W** www.lawscot.org.uk
Chief Executive, Lorna Jack
SOLICITORS REGULATION AUTHORITY Ipsley Court,
Berrington Close, Redditch, Worcs B98 0TD
T 0870-606 2555 **E** contactcentre@sra.org.uk
W www.sra.org.uk
Chief Executive, Antony Townsend

SOCIAL WORK
Salary range: £24,000–£30,000 (starting), rising to £42,000 as an experienced manager; £57,000+ at senior levels

Social workers tend to specialise in either adult or children's services. The General Social Care Council is responsible for setting standards of conduct and practice for social care workers and their employers; regulating the workforce and social work education and training. A degree or postgraduate qualification is needed in order to become a social worker. For more information *see* Social Welfare.
GENERAL SOCIAL CARE COUNCIL (GSCC)
Goldings House, 2 Hay's Lane, London SE1 2HB
T 020-7397 5100 **E** customer.service@gscc.org.uk
W www.gscc.org.uk
Chief Executive, Penny Thompson

SURVEYING
Salary range: £20,000–£26,000 (starting); £32,000+ (senior); £70,000+ (partner)

The Royal Institution of Chartered Surveyors (RICS) is the professional body that represents and regulates property professionals including land surveyors, valuers, auctioneers, quantity surveyors and project managers. Entry to the institution, following completion of a RICS-accredited degree, is through completion of the

Assessment of Professional Competence (APC), which involves a period of practical training concluded by a final assessment of competence. Entry as a technical surveyor requires completion of the Assessment of Technical Competence (ATC), which mirrors the format of the APC. The different levels of RICS membership are MRICS (member) or FRICS (fellow) for chartered surveyors, and AssocRICS for associate members.

Relevant courses can also be accredited by the Chartered Institute of Building (CIOB), which represents managers working in a range of construction disciplines. The CIOB offers four levels of membership to those who satisfy its requirements: FCIOB (fellow), MCIOB (member), ICIOB (incorporated) and ACIOB (associate).

CHARTERED INSTITUTE OF BUILDING Englemere, King's Ride, Ascot SL5 7TB T 01344-630700 E reception@ciob.org.uk W www.ciob.org.uk
Chief Executive, Chris Blythe

ROYAL INSTITUTION OF CHARTERED SURVEYORS (RICS) RICS Contact Centre, Surveyor Court, Westwood Way, Coventry CV4 8JE T 0870-333 1600 E contactrics@rics.org W www.rics.org
Chief Executive, Sean Tompkins

TEACHING

Salary range: £21,000–£64,000; headteacher £42,000–£112,000 (for more detailed information *see* Education, Employees and Salaries)

The General Teaching Councils (GTCs) for England, Northern Ireland, Scotland and Wales maintain registers of qualified teachers in their respective countries, and registration is a legal requirement in order to teach in local authority schools. The Graduate Teacher Training Registry (GTTR) processes applications for entry to postgraduate teaching courses in England, Wales and Scotland. All new entrants to the UK teaching profession must have qualified teacher status (QTS), which requires completing an initial teacher training (ITT) period. In order to gain QTS, individuals must be graduates.

Teachers in Further Education (FE) need not have QTS, though new entrants to FE are required to work towards a specified FE qualification recognised by the Learning and Skills Improvement Service. Similarly, academic staff in Higher Education require no formal teaching qualification, but are expected to obtain a qualification that meets standards set by the Higher Education Academy.

Details of routes to gaining QTS and funding for ITT are available in England from the Training and Development Agency for Schools (TDA), in Wales from the Teacher Training & Education Recruitment Forum Wales, in Scotland from Teach in Scotland and in Northern Ireland from the Department of Education.

The College of Teachers, under the terms of its royal charter, provides professional qualifications and membership to teachers and those involved in education in the UK and overseas.

COLLEGE OF TEACHERS Institute of Education, 20 Bedford Way, London WC1H 0AL T 020-7911 5536 W www.cot.ac.uk
Chief Executive and Registrar, Matthew Martin

DEPARTMENT OF EDUCATION NORTHERN IRELAND Rathgael House, Balloo Road, Bangor BT19 7PR T 028-9127 9279 E mail@deni.gov.uk W www.deni.gov.uk
Permanent Secretary, Paul Sweeney

GENERAL TEACHING COUNCIL FOR ENGLAND Whittington House, 19–30 Alfred Place, London WC1E 7EA T 0370-001 0308 E info@gtce.org.uk W www.gtce.org.uk
Chief Executive, Alan Meyrick

GENERAL TEACHING COUNCIL FOR NORTHERN IRELAND 4th Floor, Albany House, 73–75 Great Victoria Street, Belfast BT2 7AF T 028-9033 3390 E info@gtcni.org.uk W www.gtcni.org.uk
Chair, Sally McKee

GENERAL TEACHING COUNCIL FOR SCOTLAND Clerwood House, 96 Clermiston Road, Edinburgh EH12 6UT T 0131-314 6000 E gtcs@gtcs.org.uk W www.gtcs.org.uk
Chief Executive, Anthony Finn

GENERAL TEACHING COUNCIL FOR WALES 9th Floor, Eastgate House, 35–43 Newport Road, Cardiff CF24 0AB T 029-2046 0099 E information@gtcw.org.uk W www.gtcw.org.uk
Chief Executive, Gary Brace

GRADUATE TEACHER TRAINING REGISTRY Rosehill, New Barn Lane, Cheltenham GL52 3LZ T 0871-468 0469 E enquiries@gttr.ac.uk W www.gttr.ac.uk
Chief Executive, Mary Curnock Cook

HIGHER EDUCATION ACADEMY Innovation Way, York Science Park, Heslington, York YO10 5BR T 01904-717500 E enquiries@heacademy.ac.uk W www.heacademy.ac.uk
Chief Executive, Craig Mahoney

LEARNING AND SKILLS IMPROVEMENT SERVICE Friars House, Manor House Drive, Coventry CV1 2TE T 0247-662 7900 E enquiries@lsis.org.uk W www.lsis.org.uk
Chief Executive, Rob Wye

TRAINING AND DEVELOPMENT AGENCY FOR SCHOOLS Piccadilly Gate, Store Street, Manchester M1 2WD T 0870-496 0123 W www.tda.gov.uk
Chief Executive, Stephen Hillier

VETERINARY MEDICINE

Salary range: £30,000–£48,000

The regulatory body for veterinary surgeons in the UK is the Royal College of Veterinary Surgeons (RCVS), which keeps the register of those entitled to practise veterinary medicine as well as the list of qualified veterinary nurses. Holders of recognised degrees from any of the six UK university veterinary schools or from certain EU or overseas universities are entitled to be registered, and holders of certain other degrees may take a statutory membership examination. The UK's veterinary schools are located at the University of Bristol, the University of Cambridge, the University of Edinburgh, the University of Glasgow, the University of Liverpool and the Royal Veterinary College in London; all veterinary degrees last for five years except that offered at Cambridge, which lasts for six. A new course at the University of Nottingham's School of Veterinary Medicine and Science produced its first veterinary graduates in 2011.

The British Veterinary Association is the professional body representing veterinary surgeons. The British Veterinary Nursing Association is the professional body representing veterinary nurses.

BRITISH VETERINARY ASSOCIATION 7 Mansfield Street, London W1G 9NQ T 020-7636 6541 E bvahq@bva.co.uk W www.bva.co.uk
Secretary General, Henrietta Alderman

BRITISH VETERINARY NURSING ASSOCIATION 82 Greenway Business Centre, Harlow Business Park, Harlow CM19 5QE T 01279-408644 E bvna@bvna.co.uk W www.bvna.org.uk
Honorary Secretary, Kirstie Shield

ROYAL COLLEGE OF VETERINARY SURGEONS Belgravia House, 62–64 Horseferry Road, London SW1P 2AF T 020-7222 2001 E admin@rcvs.org.uk W www.rcvs.org.uk
Registrar, Jane Hern

INDEPENDENT SCHOOLS

Independent schools (non-maintained mainstream schools) charge fees and are owned and managed under special trusts, with profits being used for the benefit of the schools concerned. In 2009–10 there were 2,570 non-maintained mainstream schools in the UK, educating over 621,000 pupils, or around 6.4 per cent of the total school-age population. The approximate number of pupils at non-maintained mainstream schools in 2009–10 was:

UK	621,750
England	581,400
Wales	9,200
Scotland	30,500
Northern Ireland	650

The Independent Schools Council (ISC), formed in 1974, acts on behalf of the eight independent schools' associations which constitute it. These associations are:
Association of Governing Bodies of Independent Schools (AGBIS)
Council of British International Schools (COBIS)
Girls' Schools Association (GSA)
Headmasters' & Headmistresses' Conference (HMC)
Independent Association of Prep Schools (IAPS)
Independent Schools Association (ISA)
Independent Schools' Bursars Association (ISBA)
Society of Heads of Independent Schools (SHMIS)

In 2010–11 there were 506,500 pupils being educated in 1,234 schools in membership of associations within the Independent Schools Council (ISC). Most schools not in membership of an ISC association are likely to be privately owned. The Independent Schools Inspectorate (ISI) was demerged from ISC with effect from 1 January 2008 and is legally and operationally independent of ISC. ISI works as an accredited inspectorate of schools in membership of the ISC associations under a framework agreed with the Department for Education (DfE). A school must pass an ISI accreditation inspection to qualify for membership of an association within ISC.

In 2010 at GCSE 60.2 per cent of all exams taken by candidates in ISC associations' member schools achieved either an A* or A grade (compared to the national average of 22.6 per cent), and at A-level 18.2 per cent of entries were awarded the new A* grade (national average, 8.1 per cent). In 2010–11 a total of 164,105 pupils at schools in ISC associations received help with their fees, mainly in the form of bursaries and scholarships from the schools. These cost the schools more than £550m.

INDEPENDENT SCHOOLS COUNCIL
St Vincent House, 30 Orange Street, London WC2H 7HH
T 020-7766 7070 W www.isc.co.uk

The list of schools below was compiled from the Independent Schools Yearbook 2011–12 (ed. Judy Mott, published by A&C Black) which includes schools whose heads are members of one of the ISC's five Heads' Associations. Further details are available online (W www.isyb.co.uk).

The fees shown below represent the upper limits payable as at September 2011.

School	Web Address	Termly Fees Day	Board	Head
ENGLAND				
Abbey Gate College, Cheshire	www.abbeygatecollege.co.uk	£3,367	–	Mrs L. Horner
The Abbey School, Berks	www.theabbey.co.uk	£4,200	–	Mrs B. Stanley
Abbots Bromley School for Girls, Staffs	www.abbotsbromley.staffs.sch.uk	£4,775	£7,995	Mrs J. Dowling
Abbot's Hill School, Herts	www.abbotshill.herts.sch.uk	£4,880		Mrs K. Lewis
Abbotsholme School, Derbys	www.abbotsholme.com	£6,285	£9,225	S. Fairclough
Abingdon School, Oxon	www.abingdon.org.uk	£4,835	£9,915	Miss O. Lusk
Ackworth School, W. Yorks	www.ackworthschool.com	£3,920	£6,545	Mrs K. Bell
Aldenham School, Herts	www.aldenham.com	£6,083	£8,860	J. Fowler
Alderley Edge School for Girls, Cheshire	www.aesg.info	£3,067	–	Mrs S. Goff
Alleyn's School, London SE22	www.alleyns.org.uk	£4,867	–	Dr G. Savage
Amberfield School, Suffolk	www.amberfield.suffolk.sch.uk	£3,505	–	Mrs L. Ingram
Ampleforth College, N. Yorks	www.college.ampleforth.org.uk	£6,095	£9,472	Revd C. Everitt
Ardingly College, W. Sussex	www.ardingly.com	£6,880	£9,105	P. Green
Arnold School, Lancs	www.arnoldschool.com	£3,020	–	J. Keefe
Ashford School, Kent	www.ashfordschool.co.uk	£4,856	£9,401	M. Buchanan
Ashville College, N. Yorks	www.ashville.co.uk	£3,790	£7,420	D. Lauder
Austin Friars St Monica's Senior School, Cumbria	www.austinfriars.cumbria.sch.uk	£3,765	£3,765	C. Lumb
Bablake School, W. Midlands	www.bablake.com	£3,056	£3,056	J. Watson
Badminton School, Bristol	www.badminton.bristol.sch.uk	£5,270	£9,880	Mrs J. Scarrow
Bancroft's School, Essex	www.bancrofts.org	£4,396	£4,396	Mrs M. Ireland
Barnard Castle School, Durham	www.barnardcastleschool.org.uk	£3,660	£6,572	A. Stevens
Bearwood College, Berks	www.bearwoodcollege.co.uk	£5,455	£9,360	S. Aiano
Bedales School, Hants	www.bedales.org.uk	£7,850	£9,985	K. Budge

Bedford Girls' School, Beds	www.bedfordgirlsschool.co.uk	£3,561	–	Miss J. MacKenzie
Bedford Modern School, Beds	www.bedmod.co.uk	£3,561	–	M. Hall
Bedford School, Beds	www.bedfordschool.org.uk	£5,264	£8,649	J. Moule
Bedstone College, Shropshire	www.bedstone.org	£4,085	£7,410	M. Symonds
Beechwood Sacred Heart School, Kent	www.beechwood.org.uk	£4,835	£8,020	N. Beesley
Benenden School, Kent	www.benenden.kent.sch.uk	–	£9,980	Mrs C. Oulton
Berkhamsted School, Herts	www.berkhamstedschool.org	£5,600	£8,920	M. Steed
Bethany School, Kent	www.bethanyschool.org.uk	£5,040	£7,867	M. Healy
Birkdale School, S. Yorks	www.birkdaleschool.org.uk	£3,559	–	P. Owen
Birkenhead School, Merseyside	www.birkenheadschool.co.uk	£3,202	–	D. Clark
Bishop's Stortford College, Herts	www.bishops-stortford-college.herts.sch.uk	£3,999	£7,192	J. Gladwin
Blackheath High School, London SE3	www.blackheathhighschool.gdst.net	£4,171	–	Mrs E. Laws
Bloxham School, Oxon	www.bloxhamschool.com	£5,055	£9,255	M. Allbrook
Blundell's School, Devon	www.blundells.org	£5,830	£9,040	I. Davenport
Bolton School Boys' Division, Lancs	www.boltonschool.org/seniorboys	£3,290	–	P. Britton
Bolton School Girls' Division, Lancs	www.boltonschool.org/seniorgirls	£3,290	–	Miss S. Hincks
Bootham School, N. Yorks	www.boothamschool.com	£5,125	£8,600	J. Taylor
Bournemouth Collegiate School, Dorset	www.bournemouthcollegiateschool.co.uk	£4,070	£7,338	S. Duckitt
Box Hill School, Surrey	www.boxhillschool.com	£5,200	£8,750	M. Eagers
Bradfield College, Berks	www.bradfieldcollege.org.uk	£7,876	£9,845	S. Henderson
Bradford Girls' Grammar School, W. Yorks	www.bggs.com	£3,722	–	K. Matthews
Bradford Grammar School, W. Yorks	www.bradfordgrammar.com	£3,497	–	S. Davidson
Brentwood School, Essex	www.brentwoodschool.co.uk	£4,724	£8,481	D. Davies
Brighton and Hove High School, E. Sussex	www.bhhs.gdst.net	£3,459	–	Mrs L. Duggleby
Brighton College, E Sussex	www.brightoncollege.net	£6,225	£10,782	R. Cairns
Brigidine School Windsor, Berks	www.brigidine.org.uk	£4,585	–	Mrs E. Robinson
Bristol Grammar School, Bristol	www.bristolgrammarschool.co.uk	£3,711	–	R. MacKinnon
Bromley High School, Kent	www.bromleyhigh.gdst.net	£4,202	–	Ms L. Simpson
Bromsgrove School, Worcs	www.bromsgrove-school.co.uk	£3,985	£8,395	C. Edwards
Bruton School for Girls, Somerset	www.brutonschool.co.uk	£4,325	£7,820	J. Burrough
Bryanston School, Dorset	www.bryanston.co.uk	£8,192	£9,990	Ms S. Thomas
Burgess Hill School for Girls, W. Sussex	www.burgesshill-school.com	£4,520	£7,970	Mrs A. Aughwane
Bury Grammar School Boys, Lancs	www.bgsboys.co.uk	£2,912	–	Revd S. Harvey
Bury Grammar School Girls, Lancs	www.bgsg.bury.sch.uk	£2,912	–	Mrs R. Georghiou
Canford School, Dorset	www.canford.com	£7,245	£9,305	J. Lever
Casterton School, Lancs	www.castertonschool.co.uk	£5,082	£8,520	Mrs M. Lucas
Caterham School, Surrey	www.caterhamschool.co.uk	£4,817	£8,988	J. Thomas
Central Newcastle High School, Tyne and Wear	www.newcastlehigh.gdst.net	£3,370	–	Mrs H. French
Channing School, London N6	www.channing.co.uk	£4,680	–	Mrs B. Elliott
Charterhouse, Surrey	www.charterhouse.org.uk	£8,414	£10,178	Revd J. Witheridge
Cheadle Hulme School, Cheshire	www.cheadlehulmeschool.co.uk	£3,158	£3,158	Miss L. Pearson
Cheltenham College, Glos	www.cheltenhamcollege.org	£7,425	£9,909	Dr A. Peterken
The Cheltenham Ladies' College, Glos	www.cheltladiescollege.org	£6,455	£9,615	Miss E. Jardine-Young
Chetham's School of Music, Greater Manchester	www.chethams.com	sliding scale		Mrs C. Hickman
Chetwynde School, Cumbria	www.chetwynde.co.uk	£2,800	–	R. Collier
Chigwell School, Essex	www.chigwell-school.org	£4,846	£7,665	M. Punt
Christ's Hospital, W. Sussex	www.christs-hospital.org.uk	£5,665	£8,335	J. Franklin
Churcher's College, Hants	www.churcherscollege.com	£3,850	–	S. Williams
City of London Freemen's School, Surrey	www.clfs.surrey.sch.uk	£4,866	£7,746	P. MacDonald
City of London School, London EC4	www.clsb.org.uk	£4,350	–	D. Levin
City of London School for Girls, London EC2	www.clsg.org.uk	£4,377	–	Miss D. Vernon
Claremont Fan Court School, Surrey	www.claremont-school.co.uk	£4,550	–	J. Insall-Reid
Claysmore School, Dorset	www.claysmore.com	£6,993	£9,558	M. Cooke
Clifton College, Bristol	www.cliftoncollegeuk.com	£6,790	£9,750	M. Moore

Clifton High School, Bristol	www.cliftonhigh.bristol.sch.uk	£3,780	£6,795	Dr A. Neill
Cobham Hall, Kent	www.cobhamhall.com	£5,950	£8,950	P. Mitchell
Cokethorpe School, Oxon	www.cokethorpe.org.uk	£4,975	–	D. Ettinger
Colfe's School, London SE12	www.colfes.com	£4,371	–	R. Russell
Colston's School, Bristol	www.colstons.bristol.sch.uk	£3,445	£6,580	P. Fraser
Combe Bank School, Kent	www.combebank.kent.sch.uk	£4,870	–	Mrs E. Abbotts
Concord College, Shropshire	www.concordcollegeuk.com	£3,900	£8,850	N. Hawkins
Cranford House School, Oxon	www.cranford-house.org	£4,475	–	Mrs C. Hamilton
Cranleigh School, Surrey	www.cranleigh.org	£7,990	£9,805	G. Waller
Croydon High School, Surrey	www.croydonhigh.gdst.net	£4,203	–	Mrs D. Leonard
Culford School, Suffolk	www.culford.co.uk	£5,285	£8,555	J. Johnson-Munday
Dame Allan's Boys' School, Tyne and Wear	www.dameallans.co.uk	£3,291	–	Dr J. Hind
Dame Allan's Girls' School, Tyne and Wear	www.dameallans.co.uk	£3,291	–	Dr J. Hind
Dauntsey's School, Wilts	www.dauntseys.org	£5,195	£8,755	S. Roberts
Dean Close School, Glos	www.deanclose.org.uk	£6,790	£9,615	J. Lancashire
Denstone College, Staffs	www.denstonecollege.org	£4,061	£7,072	D. Derbyshire
Derby High School, Derbyshire	www.derbyhigh.derby.sch.uk	£3,360	–	C. Callaghan
Dodderhill School, Worcs	www.dodderhill.co.uk	£3,125	–	Mrs C. Mawston
Dover College, Kent	www.dovercollege.org.uk	£4,330	£8,650	S. Jones
d'Overbroeck's College, Oxon	www.doverbroecks.com	£6,175	£9,350	S. Cohen
Downe House, Berks	www.downehouse.net	£7,245	£10,010	Mrs E. McKendrick
Dulwich College, London SE21	www.dulwich.org.uk	£4,964	£10,213	Dr J. Spence
Dunottar School, Surrey	www.dunottarschool.com	£4,200	–	Mrs N. Matthews
Durham High School for Girls, Durham	www.dhsfg.org.uk	£3,315	–	A. Whelpdale
Durham School, Durham	www.durhamschool.co.uk	£5,000	£7,425	E. George
Eastbourne College, E. Sussex	www.eastbourne-college.co.uk	£5,995	£9,105	S. Davies
Edgbaston High School, W. Midlands	www.edgbastonhigh.co.uk	£3,176	–	Dr R. Weeks
Ellesmere College, Shropshire	www.ellesmere.com	£5,145	£8,679	B. Wignall
Eltham College, London SE9	www.eltham-college.org.uk	£4,260	–	P. Henderson
Emanuel School, London SW11	www.emanuel.org.uk	£4,861	–	M. Hanley-Browne
Epsom College, Surrey	www.epsomcollege.org.uk	£6,650	£9,730	S. Borthwick
Eton College, Berks	www.etoncollege.com	–	£10,327	A. Little
Ewell Castle School, Surrey	www.ewellcastle.co.uk	£4,150	–	A. Tibble
Exeter School, Devon	www.exeterschool.org.uk	£3,470	–	R. Griffin
Farlington School, W. Sussex	www.farlingtonschool.net	£4,831	£7,885	Mrs J. Goyer
Farnborough Hill, Hants	www.farnborough-hill.org.uk	£3,725	–	Mrs S. Buckle
Farringtons School, Kent	www.farringtons.org.uk	£3,920	£7,500	Mrs C. James
Felsted School, Essex	www.felsted.org	£6,470	£8,645	Dr M. Walker
Forest School, London E17	www.forest.org.uk	£4,650	–	Mrs S. Kerr-Dineen
Framlingham College, Suffolk	www.framlinghamcollege.co.uk	£5,318	£8,274	P. Taylor
Francis Holland School, London NW1	www.francisholland.org.uk	£4,800	–	Mrs V. Durham
Francis Holland School, London SW11	www.francisholland.org.uk	£4,880	–	Miss S. Pattenden
Frensham Heights, Surrey	www.frenshamheights.org	£5,300	£7,990	A. Fisher
Friends' School, Essex	www.friends.org.uk	£4,895	£7,790	G. Wigley
Fulneck School, W. Yorks	www.fulneckschool.co.uk	£3,530	£6,620	T. Kernohan
Gateways School, W. Yorks	www.gatewayschool.co.uk	£3,582	–	Y. Wilkinson
Giggleswick School, N. Yorks	www.giggleswickschool.co.uk	£6,150	£8,980	G. Boult
The Godolphin and Latymer School, London W6	www.godolphinandlatymer.com	£5,175	–	Mrs R. Mercer
The Godolphin School, Wilts	www.godolphin.org	£5,754	£8,273	Mrs S. Price
The Grange School, Cheshire	www.grange.org.uk	£3,040	–	C. Jeffery
Greenacre School for Girls, Surrey	www.greenacre.surrey.sch.uk	£4,100	–	Mrs L. Redding
Gresham's School, Norfolk	www.greshams.com	£6,975	£9,100	P. John
Guildford High School, Surrey	www.guildfordhigh.surrey.sch.uk	£4,434	–	Mrs F. Boulton
The Haberdashers' Aske's Boys' School, Herts	www.habsboys.org.uk	£4,889	–	P. Hamilton
Haberdashers' Aske's School for Girls, Herts	www.habsgirls.org.uk	£3,983	–	Miss B. O'Connor
Haileybury, Herts	www.haileybury.com	£6,855	£9,128	J. Davies
Halliford School, Middx	www.hallifordschool.co.uk	£3,807	–	P. Cottam

Hampshire Collegiate School, Hants	www.hampshirecs.org.uk	£4,438	£7,345	H. MacDonald
Hampton School, Middx	www.hamptonschool.org.uk	£4,870	–	B. Martin
Harrogate Ladies' College, N. Yorks	www.hlc.org.uk	£4,481	£7,825	Mrs R. Wilkinson
Harrow School, Middx	www.harrowschool.org.uk	–	£10,310	J. Hawkins
Headington School, Oxon	www.headington.org	£4,445	£8,606	Mrs C. Jordan
Heathfield School, Berks	www.heathfieldschool.net	–	£9,650	Mrs J. Heywood
Heathfield School, Middx	www.heathfield.gdst.net	£4,223	–	Mrs A. Stevens
Hereford Cathedral School, Herefordshire	www.herefordcs.com	£3,800	–	P. Smith
Hethersett Old Hall School, Norfolk	www.hohs.co.uk	£3,975	£7,400	S. Crump
Highgate School, London N6	www.highgateschool.org.uk	£5,290	–	A. Pettitt
Hipperholme Grammar School Foundation, W. Yorks	www.hgsf.org.uk	£3,150	–	J. Scarth
Hollygirt School, Notts	www.hollygirt.co.uk	£3,120	–	P. Hutley
Hull Collegiate School, E. Yorks	www.hullcollegiateschool.co.uk	£3,250	–	R. Haworth
Hurstpierpoint College, W. Sussex	www.hppc.co.uk	£6,345	£9,525	T. Manly
Hymers College, E. Yorks	www.hymerscollege.co.uk	£2,982	–	D. Elstone
Immanuel College, Herts	www.immanuelcollege.co.uk	£4,466	–	P. Skelker
Ipswich High School, Suffolk	www.ipswichhighschool.co.uk	£3,402	–	Ms E. Purves
Ipswich School, Suffolk	www.ipswich.suffolk.sch.uk	£3,895	£9,699	N. Weaver
James Allen's Girls' School (JAGS), London SE22	www.jags.org.uk	£4,520	–	Mrs M. Gibbs
The John Lyon School, Middx	www.johnlyon.org	£4,590	–	Miss K. Haynes
Kelly College, Devon	www.kellycollege.com	£4,875	£8,500	Dr G. Hawley
Kent College, Kent	www.kentcollege.com	£5,122	£9,109	D. Lamper
Kent College Pembury, Kent	www.kent-college.co.uk	£5,364	£8,648	Mrs S. Huang
Kimbolton School, Cambs	www.kimbolton.cambs.sch.uk	£4,215	£6,975	J. Belbin
King Edward VI High School for Girls, W. Midlands	www.kehs.org.uk	£3,405	–	Miss S. Evans
King Edward VI School, Hants	www.kes.hants.sch.uk	£3,870	–	A. Thould
King Edward VII and Queen Mary School, Lancs	www.keqms.co.uk	£2,900	–	R. Karling
King Edward's School, Somerset	www.kesbath.com	£3,775	–	M. Boden
King Edward's School, W. Midlands	www.kes.org.uk	£3,465	–	J. Claughton
King Edward's School, Surrey	www.kesw.org	£6,060	£8,660	J. Attwater
King Henry VIII School, W. Midlands	www.khviii.com	£3,056	–	J. Slack
King William's College, Isle of Man	www.kwc.im	£6,103	£8,888	M. Humphreys
Kingham Hill School, Oxon	www.kingham-hill.oxon.sch.uk	£5,145	£8,360	Revd N. Seward
King's College School, London SW19	www.kcs.org.uk	£5,840	–	A. Halls
King's College, Somerset	www.kings-taunton.co.uk	£5,910	£8,800	R. Biggs
King's High School, Warwicks	www.kingshighwarwick.co.uk	£3,252	–	Mrs E. Surber
King's School, Somerset	www.kingsbruton.com	£6,285	£8,782	I. Wilmshurst
The King's School, Canterbury, Kent	www.kings-school.co.uk	£7,470	£9,990	P. Roberts
The King's School, Chester, Cheshire	www.kingschester.co.uk	£3,544	–	C. Ramsey
The King's School, Cambs	www.kingsschoolely.co.uk	£5,615	£8,128	Mrs S. Freestone
The King's School, Glos	www.thekingsschool.co.uk	£5,320	–	A. Macnaughton
The King's School, Macclesfield, Cheshire	www.kingsmac.co.uk	£3,165	–	S. Hyde
King's Rochester, Kent	www.kings-rochester.co.uk	£5,270	£8,550	Dr I. Walker
The King's School, Tyne and Wear	www.kings-tynemouth.org.uk	£3,330	–	E. Wesson
The King's School, Worcs	www.ksw.org.uk	£3,697	–	T. Keyes
Kingsley School, Devon	www.kingsleyschoolbideford.co.uk	£3,880	£7,400	A. Waters
The Kingsley School, Warwicks	www.thekingsleyschool.com	£3,495	–	Ms H. Owens
Kingston Grammar School, Surrey	www.kgs.org.uk	£4,945	–	Mrs S. Fletcher
Kingswood School, Somerset	www.kingswood.bath.sch.uk	£3,853	£8,303	S. Morris
Kirkham Grammar School, Lancs	www.kirkhamgrammar.co.uk	£3,020	£5,726	D. Walker
The Lady Eleanor Holles School, Middx	www.lehs.org.uk	£4,900	–	Mrs G. Low
Lancing College, W. Sussex	www.lancingcollege.co.uk	£6,720	£9,615	J. Gillespie
Langley School, Norfolk	www.langleyschool.co.uk	£3,795	£7,715	D. Findlay

School	Website	Day fee	Boarding fee	Head
Latymer Upper School, London W6	www.latymer-upper.org	£4,985	–	P. Winter
Lavant House, W. Sussex	www.lavanthouse.org.uk	£4,470	£7,035	Mrs K. Bartholomew
The Grammar School at Leeds, W. Yorks	www.gsal.org.uk	£3,585	–	M. Gibbons
Leicester Grammar School, Leics	www.leicestergrammar.org.uk	£3,507	–	C. King
Leicester High School for Girls, Leics	www.leicesterhigh.co.uk	£3,175	–	Mrs J. Burns
Leighton Park School, Berks	www.leightonpark.com	£5,998	£9,154	A. McGrath
Leweston School, Dorset	www.leweston.co.uk	£5,295	£8,195	A. Aylward
The Leys School, Cambs	www.theleys.net	£5,750	£8,640	M. Slater
LVS Ascot (The Licensed Victuallers' School), Berks	www.lvs.ascot.sch.uk	£4,600	£8,080	Mrs C. Cunniffe
Lincoln Minster School, Lincs	www.lincolnminsterschool.co.uk	£3,749	£7,250	C. Rickart
Liverpool College, Merseyside	www.liverpoolcollege.org.uk	£3,225	–	H. van Mourik Broekman
Longridge Towers School, Northumberland	www.lts.org.uk	£3,653	£7,442	T. Manning
Lord Wandsworth College, Hants	www.lordwandsworth.org	£6,220	£8,770	F. Livingstone
Loughborough Grammar School, Leics	www.lesgrammar.org	£3,370	£6,182	P. Fisher
Loughborough High School, Leics	www.leshigh.org	£3,139	–	Mrs G. Byrom
Luckley-Oakfield School, Berks	www.luckley.wokingham.sch.uk	£4,492	£7,862	Miss V. Davis
Magdalen College School, Oxon	www.mcsoxford.org	£4,465	–	T. Hands
Malvern College, Worcs	www.malcol.org	£6,771	£10,572	A. Clark
Malvern St James, Worcs	www.malvernstjames.co.uk	£4,930	£9,645	Mrs P. Woodhouse
The Manchester Grammar School, Greater Manchester	www.mgs.org	£3,332	–	C. Ray
Manchester High School for Girls, Greater Manchester	www.manchesterhigh.co.uk	£3,214	–	Mrs A. Hewitt
Manor House School, Surrey	www.manorhouseschool.org	£4,420	–	Miss Z. Axton
The Marist Senior School, Berks	www.themaristschools.com	£3,565	–	K. McCloskey
Marlborough College, Wilts	www.marlboroughcollege.org	£8,150	£10,100	N. Sampson
Marymount International School, Surrey	www.marymountlondon.com	£6,320	£10,610	Ms S. Gallagher
The Maynard School, Devon	www.maynard.co.uk	£3,566	–	Ms B. Hughes
Merchant Taylors' Boys' School, Merseyside	www.merchanttaylors.com	£3,125	–	D. Cook
Merchant Taylors' Girls' School, Merseyside	www.merchanttaylors.com	£3,125	–	Mrs L. Robinson
Merchant Taylors' School, Middx	www.mtsn.org.uk	£5,340	–	S. Wright
Mill Hill School, London NW7	www.millhill.org.uk	£5,531	£8,739	Dr D. Luckett
Millfield, Somerset	www.millfieldschool.com	£6,500	£9,670	C. Considine
Milton Abbey School, Dorset	www.miltonabbey.co.uk	£7,350	£9,780	G. Doodes
Moira House Girls School, E. Sussex	www.moirahouse.co.uk	£4,765	£8,510	Mrs L. Watson
Monkton Combe School, Somerset	www.monktoncombeschool.com	£5,727	£9,045	R. Backhouse
More House School, London SW1	www.morehouse.org.uk	£4,685	–	R. Carlysle
Moreton Hall, Shropshire	www.moretonhall.org	£7,465	£9,115	J. Forster
Mount St Mary's College, Derbyshire	www.msmcollege.com	£3,705	£7,667	L. McKell
The Mount School, London NW7	www.mountschool.com	£3,775	–	Ms C. Cozens
The Mount School, N. Yorks	www.mountschoolyork.co.uk	£4,900	£7,625	Ms J. Lodrick
New Hall School, Essex	www.newhallschool.co.uk	£5,112	£7,901	Mrs K. Jeffrey
Newcastle School for Boys, Tyne and Wear	www.newcastleschool.co.uk	£3,495	–	L. Francis
Newcastle-under-Lyme School, Staffs	www.nuls.org.uk	£3,169	–	N. Rugg
The Newcastle upon Tyne Church High School, Tyne and Wear	www.churchhigh.com	£3,625	–	Mrs J. Gatenby
North Cestrian Grammar School, Cheshire	www.ncgs.co.uk	£2,767	–	D. Vanstone
North London Collegiate School, Middx	www.nlcs.org.uk	£4,841	–	Mrs B. McCabe
Northampton High School, Northants	www.gdst.net/northamptonhigh	£3,731	–	Mrs S. Dixon
Northwood College, Middx	www.northwoodcollege.co.uk	£4,350	–	Miss J. Pain
Norwich High School, Norfolk	www.norwichhigh.gdst.net	£3,420	–	J. Morrow
Norwich School, Norfolk	www.norwich-school.org.uk	£4,058	–	S. Griffiths

Notre Dame Senior School, Surrey	www.notredame.co.uk	£4,300	–	Mrs B. Williams
Notting Hill and Ealing High School, London W13	www.nhehs.gdst.net	£4,343	–	Ms L. Hunt
Nottingham Girls' High School, Notts	www.nottinghamgirlshigh.gdst.net	£3,370	–	Mrs S. Gorham
Nottingham High School, Notts	www.nottinghamhigh.co.uk	£3,724	–	K. Fear
Oakham School, Rutland	www.oakham.rutland.sch.uk	£5,450	£9,080	N. Lashbrook
Ockbrook School, Derbyshire	www.ockbrook.derby.sch.uk	£3,275	£6,220	Mrs A. Steele
Oldham Hulme Grammar Schools, Lancs	www.hulme-grammar.oldham.sch.uk	£2,940	–	Dr P. Neeson
The Oratory School, Berks	www.oratory.co.uk	£6,485	£8,980	C. Dytor
Oswestry School, Shropshire	www.oswestryschool.org.uk	£4,240	£7,380	D. Robb
Oundle School, Northants	www.oundleschool.org.uk	£6,160	£9,530	C. Bush
Our Lady of Sion School, W. Sussex	www.sionschool.org.uk	£3,345	–	M. Scullion
Our Lady's Abingdon Senior School, Oxon	www.olab.org.uk	£3,756	–	Mrs L. Renwick
Oxford High School, Oxon	www.oxfordhigh.gdst.net	£3,567	–	Mrs J. Carlisle
Padworth College, Berks	www.padworth.com	£3,950	£8,300	Mrs L. Melhuish
Palmers Green High School, London N21	www.pghs.co.uk	£3,945	–	Mrs C. Edmundson
Pangbourne College, Berks	www.pangbournecollege.com	£6,600	£9,330	T. Garnier
The Perse Upper School, Cambs	www.perse.co.uk	£4,549	–	E. Elliott
The Peterborough School, Cambs	www.thepeterboroughschool.co.uk	£3,986	£7,420	A. Meadows
Pipers Corner School, Bucks	www.piperscorner.co.uk	£4,490	£7,400	Mrs H. Ness-Gifford
Pitsford School, Northants	www.pitsfordschool.com	£3,927	–	N. Toone
Plymouth College, Devon	www.plymouthcollege.com	£4,070	£7,970	Dr S. Wormleighton
Pocklington School, E. Yorks	www.pocklingtonschool.com	£3,855	£6,898	M. Ronan
Polam Hall School, Durham	www.polamhall.com	£3,890	£7,475	J. Moreland
Portland Place School, London W1	www.portland-place.co.uk	£5,225	–	T. Cook
The Portsmouth Grammar School, Hants	www.pgs.org.uk	£4,186	–	J. Priory
Portsmouth High School, Hants	www.portsmouthhigh.co.uk	£3,467	–	Mrs J. Prescott
Princess Helena College, Herts	www.princesshelenacollege.co.uk	£5,680	£8,205	Mrs J. Duncan
Princethorpe College, Warwicks	www.princethorpe.co.uk	£3,118	–	E. Hester
Prior Park College, Somerset	www.thepriorfoundation.com	£4,061	£8,160	J. Murphy-O'Connor
Prior's Field, Surrey	www.priorsfieldschool.com	£4,995	£7,995	Mrs J. Roseblade
The Purcell School, Herts	www.purcell-school.org	£8,259	£10,562	P. Crook
Putney High School, London SW15	www.putneyhigh.gdst.net	£4,388	–	Dr D. Lodge
Queen Anne's School, Berks	www.qas.org.uk	£6,090	£8,975	Mrs J. Harrington
Queen Elizabeth Grammar School, W. Yorks	www.wgsf.org.uk	£3,332	–	D. Craig
Queen Elizabeth's Grammar School, Lancs	www.qegs.blackburn.sch.uk	£3,295	–	S. Corns
Queen Elizabeth's Hospital (QEH), Bristol	www.qehbristol.co.uk	£3,753	–	S. Holliday
Queen Margaret's School, N. Yorks	www.queenmargarets.com	£5,513	£8,700	Dr P. Silverwood
Queen Mary's School, N. Yorks	www.queenmarys.org	£4,640	£6,120	Mrs S. Lewis-Beckett
Queen's College, London, London W1	www.qcl.org.uk	£4,950	–	Dr F. Ramsey
Queen's College, Somerset	www.queenscollege.org.uk	£4,900	£7,800	C. Alcock
Queen's Gate School, London SW7	www.queensgate.org.uk	£5,100	–	Mrs R. Kamaryc
The Queen's School, Cheshire	www.queens.cheshire.sch.uk	£3,550	–	Mrs E. Clark
Queenswood, Herts	www.queenswood.org	£6,965	£9,165	Mrs P. Edgar
Radley College, Oxon	www.radley.org.uk	–	£9,875	A. McPhail
Ratcliffe College, Leics	www.ratcliffe-college.co.uk	£4,548	£6,954	G. Lloyd
The Read School, N. Yorks	www.readschool.co.uk	£3,060	£6,600	Mrs B. McCrea
Reading Blue Coat School, Berks	www.rbcs.org.uk	£4,320	–	M. Windsor
The Red Maids' School, Bristol	www.redmaids.co.uk	£3,480	–	Mrs I. Tobias
Redland High School for Girls, Bristol	www.redlandhigh.com	£3,400	–	Mrs C. Bateson
Reed's School, Surrey	www.reeds.surrey.sch.uk	£6,498	£8,595	D. Jarrett
Reigate Grammar School, Surrey	www.reigategrammar.org	£4,792	–	D. Thomas
Rendcomb College, Glos	www.rendcombcollege.org.uk	£6,180	£8,275	G. Holden

Repton School, Derbyshire	www.repton.org.uk	£6,980	£9,407	R. Holroyd
Rishworth School, W. Yorks	www.rishworth-school.co.uk	£3,480	£7,090	R. Baker
Roedean School, E. Sussex	www.roedean.co.uk	£5,820	£10,050	Mrs F. King
Rossall School, Lancs	www.rossallschool.org.uk	£3,900	£9,960	Dr S. Winkley
The Royal Grammar School, Surrey	www.rgs-guildford.co.uk	£4,540	–	J. Cox
Royal Grammar School, Tyne and Wear	www.rgs.newcastle.sch.uk	£3,332	–	B. Trafford
RGS Worcester, Worcs	www.rgsw.org.uk	£3,244	–	A. Rattue
The Royal High School, Bath, Somerset	www.royalhighbath.gdst.net	£3,419	£6,827	Mrs R. Dougall
The Royal Hospital School, Suffolk	www.royalhospitalschool.org	£4,153	£7,663	H. Blackett
The Royal Masonic School for Girls, Herts	www.royalmasonic.herts.sch.uk	£4,485	£7,480	Mrs D. Rose
Royal Russell School, Surrey	www.royalrussell.co.uk	£4,740	£9,370	C. Hutchinson
Royal School Hampstead, London NW3	www.royalschoolhampstead.net	£3,950	£7,850	Ms J. Ebner
The Royal Wolverhampton School, W. Midlands	www.theroyalschool.co.uk	£3,985	£8,540	M. Heywood
Rugby School, Warwicks	www.rugbyschool.net	£6,060	£9,725	P. Derham
Ryde School with Upper Chine, Isle of Wight	www.rydeschool.org.uk	£3,405	£7,000	Dr N. England
Rye St Antony, Oxon	www.ryestantony.co.uk	£4,100	£6,650	Miss A. Jones
St Albans High School for Girls, Herts	www.stahs.org.uk	£4,095	–	Mrs R. Martin
St Albans School, Herts	www.st-albans.herts.sch.uk	£4,598	–	A. Grant
St Andrew's School, Beds	www.standrewsschoolbedford.com	£3,492	–	S. Skehan
Saint Augustine's Priory School, London W5	www.saintaugustinespriory.org.uk	£3,730	–	Mrs F. Gumley-Mason
St Bede's College, Greater Manchester	www.stbedescollege.co.uk	£2,966	–	D. Kearney
St Bede's Senior School, E. Sussex	www.stbedesschool.org	£5,475	£9,115	Dr R. Maloney
St Bees School, Cumbria	www.st-bees-school.org	£4,998	£8,421	P. Capes
St Benedict's School, London W5	www.stbenedicts.org.uk	£4,120	–	C. Cleugh
St Catherine's School, Surrey	www.stcatherines.info	£4,780	£7,865	Mrs A. Phillips
St Catherine's School, Middx	www.stcatherineschool.co.uk	£3,705	–	Sister P. Thomas
St Christopher School, Herts	www.stchris.co.uk	£4,990	£8,830	R. Palmer
St Columba's College, Herts	www.stcolumbascollege.org	£3,770	–	D. Buxton
St Dominic's High School for Girls, Staffs	www.stdominicsschool.co.uk	£3,780	–	Mrs S. White
St Dominic's Priory School, Staffs	www.stdominicspriory.co.uk	£3,135	–	Mrs M. Adamson
St Dunstan's College, London SE6	www.stdunstans.org.ukintranet: www.sdonline.org.uk	£4,507	–	Mrs J. Davies
St Edmund's College & Prep School, Herts	www.stedmundscollege.org	£4,860	£8,010	C. Long
St Edmund's School, Kent	www.stedmunds.org.uk	£5,686	£8,849	Mrs L. Moelwyn-Hughes
St Edward's, Oxford, Oxon	www.stedwards.oxon.sch.uk	£7,948	£9,935	S. Jones
St Edward's School, Glos	www.stedwards.co.uk	£4,078	–	P. Harvey
Saint Felix School, Suffolk	www.stfelix.co.uk	£4,400	£7,775	S. Letman
St Francis' College, Herts	www.st-francis.herts.sch.uk	£3,925	£7,720	Mrs D. MacGinty
St Gabriel's School, Berks	www.stgabriels.co.uk	£4,410	–	A. Jones
St George's College, Surrey	www.st-georges-college.co.uk	£4,900	–	J. Peake
St George's School, W. Midlands	www.sgse.co.uk	£3,255	–	Sir Robert Dowling
St George's School, Berks	www.stgeorges-ascot.org.uk	£6,150	£9,460	Mrs R. Owens
St Helen & St Katharine, Oxon	www.shsk.org.uk	£3,945	–	Miss R. Edbrooke
St Helen's School, Middx	www.sthn.co.uk	£4,443	–	Dr M. Short
St James Senior Boys' School, Surrey	www.stjamesboys.co.uk	£4,220	–	D. Boddy
St James Senior Girls' School, London W14	www.stjamesgirls.co.uk	£4,360	–	Mrs L. Hyde
St John's College, Hants	www.stjohnscollege.co.uk	£3,100	£6,700	G. Best
St John's School, Surrey	www.stjohnsleatherhead.co.uk	£6,465	£8,865	M. Collier
St Joseph's College, Suffolk	www.stjos.co.uk	£4,075	£8,375	Mrs S. Grant
St Joseph's College, Berks	www.stjosephscollegereading.co.uk	£3,680	–	Mrs M. Sheridan
St Lawrence College, Kent	www.slcuk.com	£5,090	£8,835	Revd M. Aitken
St Leonards-Mayfield School, E. Sussex	www.mayfieldgirls.org	£5,540	£8,580	Miss A. Beary

St Margaret's School, Herts	www.stmargaretsbushey.org.uk	£4,500	£8,350	Mrs L. Crighton
St Margaret's School, Devon	www.stmargarets-school.co.uk	£3,395	–	Mrs S. Cooper
St Margaret's School, London NW3	www.st-margarets.co.uk	£3,542	–	M. Webster
St Martha's, Herts	www.st-marthas.co.uk	£3,720	–	J. Sheridan
Saint Martin's, W. Midlands	www.saintmartins-school.com	£3,485	–	Mrs J. Carwithen
St Mary's School Ascot, Berks	www.st-marys-ascot.co.uk	£6,930	£9,740	Mrs M. Breen
St Mary's Calne, Wilts	www.stmaryscalne.org	£7,350	£10,100	Mrs H. Wright
St Mary's School, Cambs	www.stmaryscambridge.co.uk	£4,230	£9,110	Miss C. Avery
St Mary's School, Essex	www.stmaryscolchester.org.uk	£3,255	–	Mrs H. Vipond
St Mary's College, Merseyside	www.stmarys.ac	£2,997	–	M. Kennedy
St Mary's School, Bucks	www.stmarysschool.co.uk	£4,260	–	Mrs J. Ross
St Mary's School, Dorset	www.st-marys-shaftesbury.co.uk	£5,450	£7,930	R. James
St Mary's, Worcs	www.stmarys.org.uk	£3,400	–	Mrs C. Jawaheer
St Nicholas' School, Hants	www.st-nicholas.hants.sch.uk	£3,701	–	Mrs A. Whatmough
St Paul's Girls' School, London W6	www.spgs.org	£5,842	–	Ms C. Farr
St Paul's School, London SW13	www.stpaulsschool.org.uk	£6,275	£9,297	M. Bailey
St Peter's School York, N. Yorks	www.st-peters.york.sch.uk	£4,839	£7,791	L. Winkley
St Swithun's School, Hants	www.stswithuns.com	£5,240	£8,640	Ms J. Gandee
St Teresa's School, Surrey	www.stteresasschool.com	£4,645	£3,360	Mrs J. Elburn
Scarborough College, N. Yorks	www.scarboroughcollege.co.uk	£3,743	£6,139	Mrs I. Nixon
Seaford College, W. Sussex	www.seaford.org	£5,555	£8,300	T. Mullins
Sedbergh School, Cumbria	www.sedberghschool.org	£6,675	£9,060	A. Fleck
Sevenoaks School, Kent	www.sevenoaksschool.org	£5,946	£9,537	Mrs C. Ricks
Shebbear College, Devon	www.shebbearcollege.co.uk	£3,495	£6,605	R. Barnes
Sheffield High School, S. Yorks	www.sheffieldhighschool.org.uk	£3,336	–	Mrs V. Dunsford
Sherborne Girls, Dorset	www.sherborne.com	£6,870	£9,450	Mrs J. Dwyer
Sherborne School, Dorset	www.sherborne.org	£7,875	£9,725	C. Davis
Shiplake College, Oxon	www.shiplake.org.uk	£5,740	£8,510	A. Davies
Shrewsbury High School, Shropshire	www.shrewsburyhigh.gdst.net	£3,434	–	Mrs M. Cass
Shrewsbury School, Shropshire	www.shrewsbury.org.uk	£6,595	£9,420	M. Turner
Sibford School, Oxon	www.sibford.oxon.sch.uk	£3,886	£7,550	M. Goodwin
Silcoates School, W. Yorks	www.silcoates.org.uk	£3,876	–	D. Wideman
Solihull School, W. Midlands	www.solsch.org.uk	£3,320	–	D. Lloyd
South Hampstead High School, London NW3	www.shhs.gdst.net	£4,343	–	Mrs J. Stephen
Stafford Grammar School, Staffs	www.stafford-grammar.co.uk	£3,249	–	M. Darley
Stamford High School, Lincs	www.ses.lincs.sch.uk	£4,084	£7,452	S. Roberts
Stamford School, Lincs	www.ses.lincs.sch.uk	£4,084	£7,452	S. Roberts
Stanbridge Earls School, Hants	www.stanbridgeearls.co.uk	£6,754	£8,920	P. Trythall
The Stephen Perse Foundation, Cambs	www.stephenperse.com	£4,675	–	Miss P. Kelleher
Stockport Grammar School, Cheshire	www.stockportgrammar.co.uk	£3,090	–	A. Chicken
Stonar School, Wilts	www.stonarschool.com	£4,455	£7,850	Mrs E. Thomas
Stonyhurst College, Lancs	www.stonyhurst.ac.uk	£5,151	£9,010	A. Johnson
Stover School, Devon	www.stover.co.uk	£3,497	£7,230	Mrs S. Bradley
Stowe School, Bucks	www.stowe.co.uk	£7,005	£9,655	A. Wallersteiner
Streatham & Clapham High School, London SW16	www.gdst.net/streathamhigh	£4,203	–	R. Hinton
Sunderland High School, Tyne and Wear	www.sunderlandhigh.co.uk	£2,778	–	Dr A. Slater
Surbiton High School, Surrey	www.surbitonhigh.com	£4,305	–	Ms E. Haydon
Sutton High School, Surrey	www.suttonhigh.gdst.net	£4,239	–	Mrs B. Goulding
Sutton Valence School, Kent	www.svs.org.uk	£5,800	£8,840	B. Grindlay
Sydenham High School, London SE26	www.sydenhamhighschool.gdst.net	£4,203	–	Mrs K. Pullen
Talbot Heath, Dorset	www.talbotheath.org	£3,555	£5,921	Mrs A. Holloway
Taunton School, Somerset	www.tauntonschool.co.uk	£5,150	£8,535	Dr J. Newton
Teesside High School, Cleveland	www.teessidehigh.co.uk	£3,545	–	M. Wilkinson
Tettenhall College, W. Midlands	www.tettenhallcollege.co.uk	£4,215	£7,680	M. Long
Thetford Grammar School, Norfolk	www.thetgram.norfolk.sch.uk	£3,516	–	G. Price
Thornton College, Bucks	www.thorntoncollege.com	£3,615	£5,925	Miss A. Williams
Tonbridge School, Kent	www.tonbridge-school.co.uk	£7,780	£10,421	T. Haynes
Tormead School, Surrey	www.tormeadschool.org.uk	£4,010	–	Mrs C. Foord
Trent College, Notts	www.trentcollege.net	£4,665	£7,905	Mrs G. Dixon

Tring Park School for the Performing Arts, Herts	www.tringpark.com	£6,105	£9,100	S. Anderson
Trinity School, Surrey	www.trinity-school.org	£4,154	–	M. Bishop
Truro High School for Girls, Cornwall	www.trurohigh.co.uk	£3,536	£6,721	Mrs C. Pascoe
Truro School, Cornwall	www.truroschool.com	£3,720	£7,120	P. Smith
Tudor Hall, Oxon	www.tudorhallschool.com	£5,725	£8,900	Miss W. Griffiths
University College School, London NW3	www.ucs.org.uk	£5,335	–	K. Durham
Uppingham School, Rutland	www.uppingham.co.uk	£6,860	£9,800	R. Harman
Wakefield Girls' High School, W. Yorks	www.wgsf.org.uk	£3,332	–	Mrs G. Wallwork
Walthamstow Hall, Kent	www.walthamstow-hall.co.uk	£5,080	–	Mrs J. Milner
Warminster School, Wilts	www.warminsterschool.org.uk	£4,340	£7,810	M. Priestley
Warwick School, Warwicks	www.warwickschool.org	£3,453	£7,369	E. Halse
Wellingborough School, Northants	www.wellingboroughschool.org	£4,202	–	G. Bowe
Wellington College, Berks	www.wellingtoncollege.org.uk	£7,515	£10,025	Dr A. Seldon
Wellington School, Somerset	www.wellington-school.org.uk	£4,010	£7,220	M. Reader
Wells Cathedral School, Somerset	www.wells-cathedral-school.com	£4,893	£8,218	Mrs E. Cairncross
West Buckland School, Devon	www.westbuckland.devon.sch.uk	£3,975	£7,510	J. Vick
Westfield School, Tyne and Wear	www.westfield.newcastle.sch.uk	£3,547	–	Mrs M. Farndale
Westholme School, Lancs	www.westholmeschool.com	£2,864	–	Mrs L. Croston
Westminster School, London SW1	www.westminster.org.uk	£7,026	£10,146	M. Spurr
Westonbirt, Glos	www.westonbirt.gloucs.sch.uk	£6,590	£9,990	Mrs M. Henderson
Whitgift School, Surrey	www.whitgift.co.uk	£4,808	–	C. Barnett
Wimbledon High School, London SW19	www.wimbledonhigh.gdst.net	£4,343	–	Mrs H. Hanbury
Winchester College, Hants	www.winchestercollege.org	–	£10,450	R. Townsend
Windermere School, Cumbria	www.windermereschool.co.uk	£4,589	£8,372	I. Lavender
Wisbech Grammar School, Cambs	www.wgs.cambs.sch.uk	£3,530	–	N. Hammond
Withington Girls' School, Greater Manchester	www.withington.manchester.sch.uk	£3,190	–	Mrs S. Marks
Woldingham School, Surrey	www.woldinghamschool.co.uk	£5,925	£9,470	Mrs J. Triffitt
Wolverhampton Grammar School, W Midlands	www.wgs.org.uk	£3,775	–	J. Darby
Woodbridge School, Suffolk	www.woodbridge.suffolk.sch.uk	£4,508	£8,050	S. Cole
Woodhouse Grove School, W. Yorks	www.woodhousegrove.co.uk	£3,520	£7,140	D. Humphreys
Worksop College, Notts	www.worksopcollege.notts.sch.uk	£5,115	£7,840	R. Collard
Worth School, W. Sussex	www.worthschool.co.uk	£6,517	£8,883	G. Carminati
Wrekin College, Shropshire	www.wrekincollege.com	£5,044	£8,325	R. Pleming
Wychwood School, Oxon	www.wychwood-school.org.uk	£3,840	£6,250	Mrs S. Wingfield Digby
Wycliffe College, Glos	www.wycliffe.co.uk	£5,600	£8,670	Mrs M. Burnet Ward
Wycombe Abbey School, Bucks	www.wycombeabbey.com	–	£10,200	Mrs C. Hall
Wykeham House School, Hants	www.wykehamhouse.com	£3,400	–	Mrs L. Clarke
Yarm School, Cleveland	www.yarmschool.org	£3,539	–	D. Dunn
The Yehudi Menuhin School, Surrey	www.yehudimenuhinschool.co.uk	sliding scale		Dr R. Hillier

WALES

Christ College, Brecon	www.christcollegebrecon.com	£4,725	£7,300	Mrs E. Taylor
Haberdashers' Monmouth School for Girls, Monmouth	www.habs-monmouth.org	£3,929	£7,381	Mrs H. Davy
Howell's School, Denbigh	www.howells.org	£3,900	£6,900	B. Routledge
Howell's School Llandaff, Cardiff	www.howells-cardiff.gdst.net	£3,404	–	Mrs S. Davis
Llandovery College, Llandovery	www.llandoverycollege.com	£4,695	£6,950	I. Hunt
Monmouth School, Monmouth	www.habs-monmouth.org	£4,238	£7,442	S. Connors
Rougemont School, Newport	www.rougemontschool.co.uk	£3,500	–	Dr J. Tribbick
Ruthin School, Ruthin	www.ruthinschool.co.uk	£3,917	£7,167	T. Belfield
Rydal Penrhos School, Colwyn Bay	www.rydal-penrhos.com	£4,500	£9,905	P. Lee-Browne

NORTHERN IRELAND

Bangor Grammar School, Bangor	www.bangorgrammarschool.org.uk	–	–	S. Connolly
Belfast Royal Academy, Belfast	www.belfastroyalacademy.com	£140	–	J. Dickson
Campbell College, Belfast	www.campbellcollege.co.uk	£2,200	£8,751	J. Piggot
Coleraine Academical Institution, Coleraine	www.coleraineai.com	£140	–	Dr D. Carruthers

Foyle and Londonderry College, Londonderry	www.foylenet.org	£135	–	W. Magill
Methodist College, Belfast	www.methody.org	£140	–	J. Naismith
The Royal Belfast Academical Institution, Belfast	www.rbai.org.uk	£795	–	Miss J. Williamson
The Royal School Dungannon, Dungannon	www.royaldungannon.com	£135	£7,335	D. Burnett

SCOTLAND

Dollar Academy, Dollar	www.dollaracademy.org.uk	£3,351	£4,296	D. Knapman
The High School of Dundee, Dundee	www.highschoolofdundee.org.uk	£3,350	–	Dr J. Halliday
The Edinburgh Academy, Edinburgh	www.edinburghacademy.org.uk	£3,012	–	M. Longmore
Fettes College, Edinburgh	www.fettes.com	£6,745	£9,050	M. Spens
George Heriot's School, Edinburgh	www.george-heriots.com	£3,233	–	A. Hector
George Watson's College, Edinburgh	www.gwc.org.uk	£3,202	–	G. Edwards
The Glasgow Academy, Glasgow	www.theglasgowacademy.org.uk	£3,360	–	P. Brodie
The High School of Glasgow, Glasgow	www.glasgowhigh.com	£2,957	–	C. Mair
Glenalmond College, Perth	www.glenalmondcollege.co.uk	£6,175	£9,054	G. Woods
Hutchesons' Grammar School, Glasgow	www.hutchesons.org	£3,153	–	Dr K. Greig
Kelvinside Academy, Glasgow	www.kelvinsideacademy.org.uk	£3,415	–	Mrs L. Douglas
Kilgraston, Bridge of Earn	www.kilgraston.com	£4,690	£7,995	M. Farmer
Lomond School, Helensburgh	www.lomond-school.org	£3,160	£6,760	S. Mills
Loretto School, Musselburgh	www.loretto.com	£6,100	£8,975	P. Hogan
The Mary Erskine School, Edinburgh	www.esms.edin.sch.uk	£3,032	£6,083	J. Gray
Merchiston Castle School, Edinburgh	www.merchiston.co.uk	£6,250	£8,585	A. Hunter
Morrison's Academy, Crieff	www.morrisonsacademy.org	£3,319	–	G. Pengelley
Robert Gordon's College, Aberdeen	www.rgc.aberdeen.sch.uk	£3,405	–	H. Ouston
St Aloysius' College, Glasgow	www.staloysius.org	£3,003	–	J. Stoer
St Columba's School, Kilmacolm	www.st-columbas.org	£3,147	–	D. Girdwood
St George's School for Girls, Edinburgh	www.st-georges.edin.sch.uk	£3,710	£7,530	Mrs A. Everest
St Leonards School, St Andrews	www.stleonards-fife.org	£3,650	£8,690	M. Carslaw
St Margaret's School for Girls, Aberdeen	www.st-margaret.aberdeen.sch.uk	£3,326	–	Dr J. Land
Stewart's Melville College, Edinburgh	www.esms.edin.sch.uk	£3,032	£6,083	J. Gray
Strathallan School, Perth	www.strathallan.co.uk	£5,955	£8,776	B. Thompson

CHANNEL ISLANDS

Elizabeth College, Guernsey	www.elizabethcollege.gg	£2,717	–	G. Hartley
The Ladies' College, Guernsey	www.ladiescollege.com	£2,110	–	Ms J. Riches
Victoria College, Jersey	www.victoriacollege.je	£1,482	–	A. Watkins

NATIONAL ACADEMIES OF SCHOLARSHIP

The national academies are self-governing bodies whose members are elected as a result of achievement and distinction in the academy's field. Within their discipline, the academies provide advice, support education and exceptional scholars, stimulate debate, promote UK research worldwide and collaborate with international counterparts.

Three of the national academies – the Royal Society, the British Academy and the Royal Academy of Engineering – receive grant-in-aid funding from the Department for Business, Innovation and Skills (BIS). The Academy for Medical Sciences receives core funding from the Department of Health, and the Royal Society of Edinburgh is aided by funds provided by the Scottish government. In addition to government funding, the national academies generate additional income from donations, membership contributions, trading and investments.

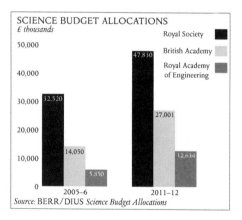

SCIENCE BUDGET ALLOCATIONS
£ thousands
Source: BERR/DIUS *Science Budget Allocations*

ACADEMY OF MEDICAL SCIENCES (1998)
41 Portland Place, London W1B 1QH
T 020-3176 2150
W www.acmedsci.ac.uk

The Academy of Medical Sciences was established in 1998 to promote advances in medical science and to ensure these are converted into healthcare benefits for society. It campaigns for the development, protection and promotion of careers for academics in the biomedical sciences and encourages good practice in training and development.

The academy is independent and self-governing and receives funding from a variety of sources including the fellowship, charitable donations, government and industry.

Fellows are elected from a broad range of medical sciences: biomedical, clinical and population based. The academy includes in its remit veterinary medicine, dentistry, nursing, medical law, economics, sociology and ethics. Elections are from nominations put forward by existing fellows.

As at May 2011 there were 1,023 fellows and 29 honorary fellows.
President, Prof. Sir John Bell, FRS, PMEDSCI
Vice-Presidents, Prof. Patrick Sissons FMEDSCI;
Prof. Ronald Laskey FRS, FMEDSCI
Executive Director, Dr Helen Munn

BRITISH ACADEMY (1902)
10–11 Carlton House Terrace, London SW1Y 5AH
T 020-7969 5200
W www.britac.ac.uk

The British Academy is an independent, self-governing learned society for the promotion of the humanities and social sciences. It was founded in 1901 and granted a royal charter in 1902. The British Academy supports advanced academic research and is a channel for the government's support of research in those disciplines.

The fellows are scholars who have attained distinction in one of the branches of study that the academy exists to promote. Candidates must be nominated by existing fellows. There are 902 fellows, 17 honorary fellows and 294 corresponding fellows overseas.
President, Prof. Sir Adam Roberts, KCMG
Chief Executive, Dr R. Jackson

ROYAL ACADEMY OF ENGINEERING (1976)
3 Carlton House Terrace, London SW1Y 5DG
T 020-7766 0600
W www.raeng.org.uk

The Royal Academy of Engineering was established as the Fellowship of Engineering in 1976. It was granted a royal charter in 1983 and its present title in 1992. It is an independent, self-governing body whose object is the pursuit, encouragement and maintenance of excellence in the whole field of engineering, in order to promote the advancement of science, art and practice of engineering for the benefit of the public.

Election to the fellowship is by invitation only, from nominations supported by the body of fellows. As at May 2011 there were 1,386 fellows. The Duke of Edinburgh is the senior fellow and the Duke of Kent is a royal fellow.
President, Lord Browne of Madingley, FRENG, FRS
Senior Vice-President, Prof. R. J. Mair, CBE, FRENG, FRS
Chief Executive, P. D. Greenish, CBE

ROYAL SOCIETY (1660)
6–9 Carlton House Terrace, London SW1Y 5AG
T 020-7451 2500
W www.royalsociety.org

The Royal Society is an independent academy promoting the natural and applied sciences. Founded in 1660 and granted a royal charter in 1662, the society has three roles, as the UK academy of science, as a learned society and as a funding agency. It is an independent, self-governing body under a royal charter, promoting and advancing all fields of physical and biological sciences, of mathematics and engineering, medical and agricultural sciences and their application.

Fellows are elected for their contributions to science, both in fundamental research resulting in greater understanding, and also in leading and directing scientific and technological progress in industry and research establishments. A maximum of 44 new fellows, who must be citizens or residents of the British Commonwealth countries or Ireland, may be elected annually.

Up to eight foreign members, who are selected from those not eligible to become fellows because of citizenship or residency, are elected annually for their contributions to science.

One honorary fellow may be elected each year from those not eligible for election as fellows or foreign members. There are approximately 1,400 fellows and foreign members covering all scientific disciplines.

President, Sir Paul Nurse, PRS

Executive Secretary, Dr Julie Maxton

ROYAL SOCIETY OF EDINBURGH (1783)

22–26 George Street, Edinburgh EH2 2PQ

T 0131-240 5000

W www.royalsoced.org.uk

The Royal Society of Edinburgh (RSE) is an educational charity and Scotland's National Academy. An independent body with charitable status, its multidisciplinary membership represents a knowledge resource for the people of Scotland. Granted its royal charter in 1783 for the 'advancement of learning and useful knowledge', the society organises conferences, debates and lectures; conducts independent inquiries; facilitates international collaboration and showcases the country's research and development capabilities; provides educational activities for primary and secondary school students and awards prizes and medals. The society also awards over £2m annually to Scotland's top researchers and entrepreneurs working in Scotland.

As at May 2011 there were 1,551 fellows.

President, Lord Wilson of Tillyorn, KT, GCMG, PRS

Vice-Presidents, Prof. Jean Beggs, CBE, FRSE;
   Prof. Hector MacQueen, FRSE; John McClelland,
   CBE; Prof. Wilson Sibbett, CBE, FRS, FRSE

General Secretary, Prof. Geoffrey Boulton, OBE, FRS,
   FRSE

PRIVATELY FUNDED ARTS ACADEMIES

The Royal Academy and the Royal Scottish Academy support the visual arts community in the UK, hold educational events and promote interest in the arts. They are entirely privately funded through contributions by 'friends' (regular donors who receive benefits such as free entry, previews and magazines), bequests, corporate donations and exhibitions.

ROYAL ACADEMY OF ARTS (1768)

Burlington House, Piccadilly, London W1J 0BD

T 020-7300 8000

W www.royalacademy.org.uk

The Royal Academy of Arts is an independent, self-governing society devoted to the encouragement and promotion of the fine arts.

Membership of the academy is limited to 80 academicians, all of whom are either painters, engravers, sculptors or architects. Candidates are nominated and elected by the existing academicians. The members are known as royal academicians (RAs) and are responsible for both the governance and direction of the academy.

The title of honorary academician is awarded to a small number of distinguished artists who are not UK citizens; as at May 2011, there were 21 honorary academicians. Unlike the RAs, they do not take part in the governance of the academy and are unable to vote.

President, Sir Nicholas Grimshaw, CBE, PRA

Secretary & Chief Executive, Charles Saumarez Smith,
CBE

ROYAL SCOTTISH ACADEMY (1838)

The Mound, Edinburgh EH2 2EL

T 0131-225 6671

W www.royalscottishacademy.org

Founded in 1826 and granted a Royal Charter in 1837, the Royal Scottish Academy is an independent institution led by prominent Scottish artists and architects. It promotes and supports the visual arts through an ongoing exhibitions programme, related educational events and through a series of awards, bursaries and scholarships for artists at all stages of their careers.

Academicians (members) have to be Scots by birth or domicile, and are elected from the disciplines of art and architecure following nominations put forward by the existing membership. There are also a small number of honorary academicians – distinguished artists and architects, writers, historians and musicians – who do not have to be Scottish. At mid 2011 there were 31 honorary academicians and 109 academicians.

President, Prof. Bill Scott, FRBS, PRSA

Secretary, Arthur Watson, RSA

RESEARCH COUNCILS

The government funds basic and applied civil science research, mostly through seven research councils, which are established under royal charter and supported by the Department for Business, Innovation and Skills (BIS). Research Councils UK is the strategic partnership of these seven councils* (for further information see W www.rcuk.ac.uk). The councils support research and training in universities and other higher education and research facilities.

The science budget, administered by BIS, is the main source of public sector funding for research councils, with further public funds provided through the Large Facilities Capital Fund and the Higher Education Innovation Fund. Additional funds may also be provided by other government departments, devolved administrations, European Commission and other international bodies. The councils also receive income for research specifically commissioned by government departments and the private sector, and income from charitable sources.

GOVERNMENT SCIENCE BUDGET
£ thousand

	2010–11	2011–12
Arts and Humanities Research Council	103,867	100,051
Biotechnology and Biological Sciences Research Council	435,737	415,806
Economic and Social Research Council	179,048	174,637
Engineering and Physical Sciences Research Council	829,306	801,720
Medical Research Council	702,229	615,467
Natural Environment Research Council	355,450	368,800
Science and Technology Facilities Council*	467,860	538,009
Large Facilities Capital Fund†	103,380	115,279
Higher Education Innovation Fund	113,000	113,000

* Includes cross-council facilities and international subscriptions budgets, which are managed by STFC on behalf of all research councils

† Allocations for 2011–12 are as follows: BBSRC £30.0m; EPSRC £15.0m; MRC £31.1m; NERC £20.0m; STFC £13.5m
Source: BIS – *The Allocation of Science and Research Funding 2011/12–2014/15*

ALCOHOL EDUCATION AND RESEARCH COUNCIL
4th Floor, Willow House, 17–23 Willow Place, London SW1P 1JH
T 020-7821 7880 W www.aerc.org.uk

The AERC was established by act of parliament in 1982 to administer the Alcohol Education and Research Fund. The government fund is used in UK education and research projects to develop new ways to help those with drinking problems. Every year, the AERC funds a small number of research projects of around £50,000, although funding of up to £70,000 is available depending on the nature of the project. The council also awards a number of research grants up to a maximum of £5,000. The AERC aims to increase awareness of alcohol issues, to reduce alcohol-related harm and to encourage best practice.
Chief Executive, Mr Dave Roberts
Research Director, Prof. Ray Hodgson

ARTS AND HUMANITIES RESEARCH COUNCIL*
Polaris House, North Star Avenue, Swindon SN2 1FL
T 01793-416000 W www.ahrc.ac.uk

Launched in April 2005 as the successor organisation to the Arts and Humanities Research Board, the AHRC provides funding for postgraduate training and research in the arts and humanities. In any one year, the AHRC makes approximately 700 research awards and around 1,500 postgraduate awards. Awards are made after a rigorous peer review process, which ensures the quality of applications.
Chair, Prof. Sir Alan Wilson
Chief Executive, Prof. Rick Rylance

BIOTECHNOLOGY AND BIOLOGICAL SCIENCES RESEARCH COUNCIL*
Polaris House, North Star Avenue, Swindon SN2 1UH
T 01793-413200 W www.bbsrc.ac.uk

Established by royal charter in 1994, the BBSRC is the UK funding agency for research in the life sciences. It funds research into how all living organisms function and behave, benefiting the agriculture, food, health, pharmaceutical and chemical sectors. To deliver its mission, the BBSRC supports research and training in universities and research centres throughout the UK, including providing strategic research grants to the institutes listed below.
Chair, Prof. Sir Tom Blundell
Chief Executive, Prof. D. Kell

INSTITUTES
BABRAHAM INSTITUTE, Babraham Hall, Babraham, Cambridge CB22 3AT T 01223-496000
Director, Prof. M. Wakelam
GENOME ANALYSIS CENTRE , Norwich Research Park, Colney, Norwich NR4 7UH T 01603-450861
Director, Dr J. Rogers
INSTITUTE FOR ANIMAL HEALTH, Pirbright Laboratory, Ash Road, Pirbright, Surrey GU24 0NF T 01483-232 441
Director, Prof. J. Fazakerley
INSTITUTE FOR BIOLOGICAL, ENVIRONMENTAL AND RURAL SCIENCES (ABERYSTWYTH UNIVERSITY), Penglais, Aberystwyth, Ceredigion SY23 3DA
T 01970-622316
Director, Prof. W. Powell
INSTITUTE OF FOOD RESEARCH, Norwich Research Park, Colney Lane, Norwich NR4 7UA T 01603-255000
Director, Prof. D. Boxer
JOHN INNES CENTRE, Norwich Research Park, Colney, Norwich NR4 7UH T 01603-450000
Director, Prof. D. Sanders

ROSLIN INSTITUTE (UNIVERSITY OF EDINBURGH), Roslin Biocentre, Roslin, Midlothian EH25 9PS
T 0131-651 9100
Director, Prof. D. Hume
ROTHAMSTED RESEARCH, Rothamsted, Harpenden, Herts AL5 2JQ T 01582-763133
Director, Prof. M. Moloney

ECONOMIC AND SOCIAL RESEARCH COUNCIL*

Polaris House, North Star Avenue, Swindon SN2 1UJ
T 01793-413000 E comms@esrc.ac.uk
W www.esrc.ac.uk

The purpose of the ESRC is to promote and support research and postgraduate training in the social sciences. It also provides advice, disseminates knowledge and promotes public understanding in these areas. The ESRC provides core funding to the centres listed below. Further information can be obtained on the ESRC website, including details of centres it funds in collaboration with other research councils.
Chair, Dr Alan Gillespie
Chief Executive, Prof. Paul Boyle

RESEARCH CENTRES
CENTRE FOR BUSINESS RELATIONSHIPS, ACCOUNTABILITY, SUSTAINABILITY AND SOCIETY, University of Cardiff, 55 Park Place, Cardiff CF10 3AT
T 029-2087 6562
Director, Prof. K. Peattie
CENTRE FOR CHARITABLE GIVING AND PHILANTHROPY, Cass Business School, 106 Bunhill Row, London EC1Y 8TZ T 020-7040 0136
Directors, Prof. J. Harrow; Prof. C. Pharoah
CENTRE FOR CLIMATE CHANGE, ECONOMICS AND POLICY, LSE, Houghton Street, London WC2 2AE
T 020-7955 6228
Directors, Prof. J. Rees; Prof. A. Gouldson
CENTRE FOR COMPETITION POLICY, University of East Anglia, Norwich NR4 7TJ T 01603-593715
Director, Prof. C. Waddams
CENTRE FOR COMPETITIVE ADVANTAGE IN THE GLOBAL ECONOMY, Department of Economics, University of Warwick, Coventry, Warks CV4 7AL T 02476-523468
Director, Prof. Nick Crafts
CENTRE FOR ECONOMIC AND SOCIAL ASPECTS OF GENOMICS, Cardiff University, 6 Museum Place, Cardiff CF10 3BG
Director, Prof. Ruth Chadwick
CENTRE FOR ECONOMIC PERFORMANCE, London School of Economics and Political Science, Houghton Street, London WC2A 2AE T 020-7955 7048
Director, Prof. J. Van Reenen
CENTRE FOR GENOMICS IN SOCIETY, Egenis Office, University of Exeter, Byrne House, St German's Road, Exeter EX4 4PJ T 01392-269127
Director, Prof. John Dupré
CENTRE FOR MARKET AND PUBLIC ORGANISATION , Bristol Institute of Public Affairs, 2 Priory Road, Bristol BS8 1TX T 0117-928 8436
Director, Prof. S. Burgess
CENTRE FOR MICRODATA METHODS AND PRACTICE, Department of Economics, UCL, Gower Street, London WC1E 6BT T 020-7679 5857
Director, Prof. Andrew Chesher
CENTRE FOR MICROECONOMIC ANALYSIS OF PUBLIC POLICY, Institute for Fiscal Studies, 7 Ridgmount Street, London WC1E 7AE T 020-7291 4820
Director, Prof. R. Blundell

CENTRE FOR POPULATION CHANGE, School of Social Sciences, University of Southampton SO17 1BJ
T 023-8059 3192
Director, Prof. J. Falkingham
CENTRE FOR RESEARCH ON SOCIO-CULTURAL CHANGE, University of Manchester, 178 Waterloo Place, Oxford Road, Manchester M13 9PL T 0161-275 8985
Directors, Prof. M. Savage
CENTRE FOR SOCIAL AND ECONOMIC RESEARCH ON INNOVATION IN GENOMICS, Innogen Centre, University of Edinburgh, Old Surgeon's Hall, High School Yards, Edinburgh EH1 1LZ T 0131-650 6385
Director, Prof. D. Wield
CENTRE FOR SOCIAL, TECHNOLOGICAL AND ENVIRONMENTAL PATHWAYS TO SUSTAINABILITY, Institute of Development Studies, Brighton BN1 9RE
T 01273-606261
Director, Prof. M. Leach
CENTRE FOR SPATIAL ECONOMICS, LSE, Houghton Street, London WC2A 2AE T 020-7955 6581
Director, Dr Henry Overman
CENTRE FOR THIRD SECTOR RESEARCH, Park House, 40 Edgbaston Park Road, University of Birmingham B15 2RT
T 0121-414 3171
Director, Prof. Peter Alcock
CENTRE OF MICRO-SOCIAL CHANGE, University of Essex, Colchester, Essex CO4 3SQ T 01206-873789
Director, Prof. S. Pudney
CENTRE ON MIGRATION, POLICY AND SOCIETY, University of Oxford, 58 Banbury Road, Oxford OX2 6QS
T 01865-274711
Director, Prof. M. Keith
CENTRE ON SKILLS, KNOWLEDGE AND ORGANISATIONAL PERFORMANCE, Department of Education, University of Oxford, 15 Norham Gardens, Oxford OX2 6PY T 01865-611030
Director, Mr K. Mayhew
ELECTRICITY POLICY RESEARCH GROUP, University of Cambridge, Trumpington Street CB2 1AG
T 01223-335246
Director, Prof. D. Newbery
INNOVATION RESEARCH CENTRE, Judge Business School Building, Trumpington Street, Cambridge CB2 1AG
T 01223-765335
Director, Prof. Alan Hughes
INTERNATIONAL CENTRE FOR LIFECOURSE STUDIES IN SOCIETY AND HEALTH, UCL Research Department of Epidemiology and Public Health, 1–19 Torrington Place, London WC1E 7HB
T 020-7679 1708
Director, Prof. M. Bartley
LANGUAGE-BASED AREA STUDIES CENTRES
T 01793-413089
Directors, Dr Robin Aizlewood; Dr Richard Berry; Prof. Anoush Ehteshami; Prof. Victor King; Dr Frank Pieke
LEARNING AND LIFE CHANCES IN KNOWLEDGE ECONOMIES AND SOCIETIES, Institute of Education, University of London, 20 Bedford Way, London WC1H 0AL
T 020-7911 5464
Director, Prof. A. Green
RESEARCH GROUP ON LIFESTYLES, VALUES AND ENVIRONMENT, Centre for Environmental Strategy, University of Surrey, Guildford, Surrey GU2 7XH
T 01483-689072
Director, Prof. T. Jackson

ENGINEERING AND PHYSICAL SCIENCES RESEARCH COUNCIL*
Polaris House, North Star Avenue, Swindon SN2 1ET
T 01793-444000 W www.epsrc.ac.uk

The EPSRC is the UK government's main agency for funding research and training in engineering and the physical sciences in universities and other organisations throughout the UK. It also provides advice, disseminates knowledge and promotes public understanding in these areas.
Chair, John Armitt, CBE, FRENG
Chief Executive, Prof. David Delpy, FRS

HEALTH PROTECTION AGENCY
151 Buckingham Palace Road, London SW1W 9SZ
T 020-7811 7000 E webteam@hpa.org.uk
W www.hpa.org.uk

The Health Protection Agency was established as a special health authority in 2003 and became a non-departmental public body, incorporating the National Radiological Board in 2005. The HPA gives advice to the public, health authorities and the government. It works to reduce the impact of infectious diseases and exposure to chemicals, poisons and radiation at local, national and regional levels and in emergency situations. The agency researches new ways to combat illness and to assess exposure to chemicals and radiation to determine whether treatment is needed. The HPA will become part of Public Health England from April 2012.
Chair, Dr David Heymann
Chief Executive, Justin McCracken

RESEARCH CENTRES
CENTRE FOR INFECTIONS, 61 Colindale Avenue, London NW9 5EQ T 020-8200 4400
CENTRE FOR EMERGENCY PREPAREDNESS AND RESPONSE, Porton Down, Salisbury, SP4 0JG
   T 01980-612100
CENTRE FOR RADIATION, CHEMICAL AND ENVIRONMENTAL HAZARDS, Chilton, Didcot OX11 0RQ
   T 01235-831600

MEDICAL RESEARCH COUNCIL*
20 Park Crescent, London W1B 1AL T 020-7636 5422
W www.mrc.ac.uk

The MRC is a publicly funded organisation dedicated to improving human health. The MRC supports research across the entire spectrum of medical sciences, in universities, hospitals, centres and institutes.
Chair, Sir John Chisholm
Chief Executive, Sir John Savill
Chair, Neurosciences and Mental Health Board, Prof. Chris Kennard
Chair, Molecular and Cellular Medicine Board, Prof. Paul Luzio
Chair, Infections and Immunity Board, Prof. Doreen Cantrell
Chair, Population and Systems Medicine Board, Prof. Jill Pell

MRC UNITS, CENTRES AND INSTITUTES
Anatomical Neuropharmacology Unit
   W mrcanu.pharm.ox.ac.uk
Asthma UK Centre in Allergic Mechanisms of Asthma
   W www.asthma-allergy.ac.uk
Centre for Behavioural and Clinical Neuroscience Institute (BCNI)
   W www.psychol.cam.ac.uk/bcni
Biostatistics Unit
   W www.mrc-bsu.cam.ac.uk

Centre for Brain Ageing and Vitality
   W www.ncl.ac.uk/cbav
Cancer Cell Unit
   W www.hutchison-mrc.cam.ac.uk
Cancer Research UK/BHF Clinical Trial Service Unit & Epidemiological Studies Unit (CTSU)
   W www.ctsu.ox.ac.uk
Cancer Research UK Gray Institute for Radiation Oncology and Biology, University of Oxford
   W www.rob.ox.ac.uk
Centre for Causal Analyses in Translational Epidemiology
   W www.bristol.ac.uk/caite
Cell Biology Unit
   W www.ucl.ac.uk/lmcb
Clinical Trials Unit
   W www.ctu.mrc.ac.uk
Cognition and Brain Sciences Unit
   W www.mrc-cbu.cam.ac.uk
Centre for Cognitive Ageing and Cognitive Epidemiology
   W www.ccace.ed.ac.uk
The Crucible Centre
   W www.ucl.ac.uk/crucible
Centre for Developmental and Biomedical Genetics
   W cdbg.shef.ac.uk
Centre for Developmental Neurobiology at King's College London
   W www.kcl.ac.uk/depsta/biomedical/mrc
Centre for Drug Safety Science
   W www.liv.ac.uk/drug-safety/
Centre for Environment and Health
   W www.environment-health.ac.uk
Centre of Epidemiology for Child Health
   W www.ich.ucl.ac.uk
Epidemiology Unit
   W www.mrc-epid.cam.ac.uk
Functional Genomics Unit
   W www.mrcfgu.ox.ac.uk
General Practice Research Framework (GPRF)
   W www.gprf.mrc.ac.uk
Centre in Genome Damage and Stability
   W www.sussex.ac.uk/gdsc
Centre for Genomics and Global Health
   W www.cggh.ox.ac.uk
Institute of Hearing Research
   W www.ihr.mrc.ac.uk
Institute of Hearing Research (Glasgow)
   T 0141-211 4695
Human Genetics Unit
   W www.hgu.mrc.ac.uk
Human Immunology Unit
   W www.imm.ox.ac.uk
Human Nutrition Research
   W www.mrc-hnr.cam.ac.uk
Human Reproductive Sciences Unit
   W www.hrsu.mrc.ac.uk
Centre for Immune Regulation
   W www.mrcbcir.bham.ac.uk
Centre for Inflammation Research
   W www.cir.med.ed.ac.uk
International Nutrition Group
   T 020-7958 8140
Laboratory of Molecular Biology (LMB)
   W www2.mrc-lmb.cam.ac.uk
Lifecourse Epidemiology Unit
   W www.mrc.soton.ac.uk
Unit for Lifelong Health and Ageing
   W www.nhsd.mrc.ac.uk
Mammalian Genetics Unit
   W www.har.mrc.ac.uk

Centre for Medical Molecular Virology
W www.ucl.ac.uk/infection-immunity/mrc_ucl-centre
National Institute for Medical Research (NIMR) including the
MRC Biomedical NMR Centre
W www.nimr.mrc.ac.uk
Mitochondrial Biology Unit
W www.mrc-mbu.cam.ac.uk
Molecular Haemotology Unit
T 01865-222398
Centre for Neurodegeneration Research
W cnr.iop.kcl.ac.uk
Centre for Neuromuscular Diseases
W www.cnmd.ac.uk
Centre for Neuropsychiatric Genetics and Genomics
W http://medicine.cf.ac.uk/research/research-groups/cngg/
Centre for Nutritional Epidemiology in Cancer Prevention and
Survival (CNC)
W www.srl.cam.ac.uk
Centre for Obesity and Related Metabolic Diseases
W www.mrc-cord.org
Centre for Outbreak Analysis and Modelling
W www1.imperial.ac.uk
Prion Unit
W www.prion.ucl.ac.uk
Protein Phosphorylation Unit
W www.ppu.mrc.ac.uk
Centre for Regenerative Medicine
W www.scrm.ed.ac.uk
Research Complex at Hawell (RCaH)
W www.rc-harwell.ac.uk
Scottish Collaboration for Public Health Research and Policy
W www.scphrp.ac.uk
Social and Public Health Sciences Unit
W www.sphsumrc.ac.uk
Social, Genetic and Developmental Psychiatry Research Centre
W www.iop.kcl.ac.uk/index.aspx
Centre for Stem Cell Biology and Regenerative Medicine
W www.stemcells.cam.ac.uk
Centre for Synaptic Plasticity
W www.bris.ac.uk/depts/synaptic
Toxicology Unit
W www.mrctox.le.ac.uk
Centre for Transplantation
W http://transplantation.kcl.ac.uk
Centre for Virus Research
W www.cvr.ac.uk
MRC (UK), the Gambia
W www.mrc.gm
UVRI Uganda Research Unit on AIDS
W www.mrcuganda.org

NATIONAL PHYSICAL LABORATORY

Hampton Road, Teddington, Middx TW11 0LW
T 020-8977 3222 W www.npl.co.uk

The National Physical Laboratory (NPL) was established in 1900 and is the UK's national measurement institute. It develops, maintains and disseminates national measurement standards for physical quantities such as mass, length, time, temperature, voltage and force. It also conducts underpinning research on engineering materials and information technology, and disseminates good measurement practice. It is government-owned but contractor-operated.
Managing Director, B. Bowsher

NATURAL ENVIRONMENT RESEARCH COUNCIL*

Polaris House, North Star Avenue, Swindon SN2 1EU
T 01793-411500 W www.nerc.ac.uk

The NERC funds and carries out impartial scientific research in the sciences relating to the natural environment. Its work covers the full range of atmospheric, earth, biological, terrestrial and aquatic sciences, from the depths of the oceans to the upper atmosphere. Its mission is to gather and apply knowledge, create understanding and predict the behaviour of the natural environment and its resources.
Chair, Edmund Wallis
Chief Executive, Prof. Alan Thorpe

RESEARCH CENTRES

BRITISH ANTARCTIC SURVEY, High Cross, Madingley
Road, Cambridge CB3 OET T 01223-221400
Director, Prof. Nick Owens
BRITISH GEOLOGICAL SURVEY, Kingsley Dunham Centre,
Keyworth, Nottingham NG12 5GG T 0115-936 3100
Executive Director, Prof. John Ludden
CENTRE FOR ECOLOGY AND HYDROLOGY, Maclean
Building, Benson Lane, Crowmarsh Gifford, Wallingford
OX10 8BB T 01491-838800
Director, Prof. Patricia Nuttall, OBE
NATIONAL CENTRE FOR ATMOSPHERIC SCIENCE,
NERC, Polaris House, North Star Avenue, Swindon SN2 1EU
T 01793-442543
Director, Prof. Stephen Mobbs
NATIONAL CENTRE FOR EARTH OBSERVATION,
Department of Meteorology, University of Reading, Building
58, Earley Gate, Reading RG6 6BB T 0118-378 6728
Director, Prof. Alan O'Neill
NATIONAL OCEANOGRAPHY CENTRE, Joseph Proudman
Building, 6 Brownlow Street, Liverpool L3 5DA
T 0151-795 4800
Director, Prof. Edward Hill

SCIENCE AND TECHNOLOGY FACILITIES COUNCIL*

Polaris House, North Star Avenue, Swindon SN2 1SZ
T 01793-442000 W www.stfc.ac.uk

Formed by royal charter on 1 April 2007, through the merger of the Council for the Central Laboratory of the Research Councils and the Particle Physics and Astronomy Research Council, the STFC is a non-departmental public body reporting to the Department for Business, Innovation and Skills.
The STFC invests in large national and international research facilities, while delivering science, technology and expertise for the UK. The council is involved in research projects including the Diamond Light Source Synchrotron and the Large Hadron Collider, and develops new areas of science and technology. The EPSRC has transferred its responsibility for nuclear physics to the STFC.
Chair, Prof. Michael Sterling
Chief Executive, Prof. Keith Mason

CHILBOLTON OBSERVATORY, Chilbolton, Stockbridge,
Hampshire SO20 6BJ T 01264-860391
DARESBURY LABORATORY, Daresbury Science and
Innovation Campus, Warrington WA4 4AD T 01925-603000

RUTHERFORD APPLETON LABORATORY, Harwell Science and Innovation Campus, Didcot OX11 0QX
T 01235-445000

UK ASTRONOMY TECHNOLOGY CENTRE, Royal Observatory, Edinburgh, Blackford Hill, Edinburgh EH9 3HJ
T 0131-668 8100

RESEARCH AND TECHNOLOGY ORGANISATIONS

Over 30 industrial and technological research bodies are members of the Association of Independent Research and Technology Organisations Limited (AIRTO). Members' activities span a wide range of disciplines from life sciences to engineering. Their work includes basic research, development and design of innovative products or processes, instrumentation testing and certification, and technology and management consultancy. AIRTO publishes a directory to help clients identify the organisations that might be able to assist them. For a full list of members, *see* AIRTO's website.

AIRTO LTD, c/o The National Physical Laboratory, Hampton Road, Teddington, Middlesex TW11 0LW
T 020-8943 6600 E enquiries@airto.co.uk
W www.airto.co.uk
President, Prof. R. Brook, OBE, FRENG

HEALTH

NATIONAL HEALTH SERVICE

The National Health Service (NHS) came into being on 5 July 1948 under the National Health Service Act 1946, covering England and Wales and, under separate legislation, Scotland and Northern Ireland. The NHS is now administered by the Secretary of State for Health (in England), the Welsh government, the Scottish government and the Secretary of State for Northern Ireland.

The function of the NHS is to provide a comprehensive health service designed to secure improvement in the physical and mental health of the people and to prevent, diagnose and treat illness. It was founded on the principle that treatment should be provided according to clinical need rather than ability to pay, and should be free at the point of delivery.

Hospital, mental, dental, nursing, ophthalmic and ambulance services and facilities for the care of expectant and nursing mothers and young children are provided by the NHS to meet all reasonable requirements. Rehabilitation services such as occupational therapy, physiotherapy, speech therapy and surgical and medical appliances are supplied where appropriate. Specialists and consultants who work in NHS hospitals can also engage in private practice, including the treatment of their private patients in NHS hospitals.

STRUCTURE

The structure of the NHS remained relatively stable for the first 30 years of its existence. In 1974, a three-tier management structure comprising regional health authorities, area health authorities and district management teams was introduced in England, and the NHS became responsible for community health services. In 1979 area health authorities were abolished and district management teams were replaced by district health authorities.

The National Health Service and Community Care Act 1990 provided for more streamlined regional health authorities and district health authorities, and for the establishment of family health services authorities (FHSAs) and NHS trusts. The concept of the 'internal market' was introduced into health care, whereby health was provided through NHS contracts where health authorities or boards and GP fundholders (the purchasers) were responsible for buying health care from hospitals, non-fundholding GPs, community services and ambulance services (the providers). The Act also paved the way for the community care reforms, which were introduced in April 1993, and changed the way care is administered for older people, the mentally ill, the physically disabled and people with learning disabilities.

ENGLAND

Regional health authorities in England were abolished in April 1996 and replaced by eight regional offices which, together with the headquarters in Leeds, formed the NHS executive (which has since been merged with the Department of Health). In April 2002, as an interim arrangement, the eight regional offices were replaced by four directorates of health and social care (DHSCs). In April 2003, the DHSCs were abolished.

HEALTH AUTHORITIES

In April 1996 the district health authorities and family health service authorities were merged to form 100 unified health authorities (HAs) in England. In April 2002, 28 new health authorities were formed from the existing HAs. In October 2002, as part of the new arrangements set out in the NHS Reform and Health Care Professions Act 2002, these new health authorities were renamed strategic health authorities (SHAs). The whole of England is now split into 10 strategic health authorities, each of which is divided into various types of trusts that take responsibilty for running different NHS services locally. The different types of trusts comprise acute trusts and foundation trusts (which are responsible for the management of NHS hospitals), ambulance trusts, care trusts, mental health trusts and primary care trusts. SHAs are charged with improving and monitoring the performance of the trusts in their area.

PRIMARY CARE TRUSTS

The first 17 primary care trusts (PCTs) became operational on 1 April 2000 and there are now around 150 PCTs in England. PCTs were created to give primary care professionals greater control over how resources are best used to benefit patients. PCTs are free-standing statutory bodies responsible for securing the provision of services and integrating health and social care locally. PCTs receive most of their funding directly from the Department of Health and can use this to purchase hospital and other services from NHS trusts and other healthcare providers. They are also responsible for making payments to independent primary care contractors such as GPs and dentists.

Each PCT is overseen by a board, typically comprising a chair; at least five non-executive directors who are appointed by the Appointments Commission; at least five executive members, including the chief executive, finance director and director of public health; and at least two members of the PCT's professional executive committee (PEC), which is made up of health professionals. Clinical expertise is provided by the PEC with representation from local GPs, nurses, other health professionals and social services. The board concentrates on the overall strategies for the trust and ensures that the trust meets its statutory, financial and legal obligations.

ACUTE TRUSTS AND FOUNDATION TRUSTS

Hospitals are managed by acute trusts that are responsible for the quality of hospital health care and for spending funds efficiently. There are 167 acute NHS trusts and 58 mental health NHS trusts which oversee around 1,600 NHS hospitals and specialist care centres.

First introduced in April 2004, there are now 129 foundation trusts in England. NHS foundation trusts are NHS hospitals, but have their own accountability and governance systems, which function outside of the Department of Health's framework, giving them greater freedom to run their own affairs. NHS foundation trusts treat patients according to NHS principles and standards and are regulated by the Care Quality Commission.

STRATEGIC HEALTH AUTHORITIES
EAST OF ENGLAND, Victoria House, Capital Park,
Fulbourn, Cambridge CB21 5XB T 01223-597500
W www.eoe.nhs.uk
Chief Executive, Sir Neil McKay, CB
EAST MIDLANDS, Octavia House, Bostocks Lane, Sandiacre,
Nottingham NG10 5QG T 0115-968 4444
W www.eastmidlands.nhs.uk
Chief Executive, Dame Barbara Hakin, DBE
LONDON, 4th Floor Southside, 105 Victoria Street, London
SW1E 6QT T 020-7932 3700 W www.london.nhs.uk
Chief Executive, Ruth Carnall, CBE
NORTH EAST, Riverside House, Goldcrest Way,
Newcastle upon Tyne NE15 8NY T 0191-210 6400
W www.northeast.nhs.uk
Chief Executive, Ian Dalton
NORTH WEST, 4th Floor, 3 Piccadilly Place, Manchester
M1 3BN T 0845-050 0194 W www.northwest.nhs.uk
Chief Executive, Mike Farrar, CBE
SOUTH CENTRAL, Newbury Business Park, London Road,
Newbury, Berks RG14 2PZ T 01635-275500
W www.southcentral.nhs.uk
Chief Executive, Andrea Young
SOUTH EAST, York House, 18–20 Masetts Road, Horley,
Surrey RH6 7DE T 01293-778899
W www.southeastcoast.nhs.uk
Chief Executive, Candy Morris, CBE
SOUTH WEST, South West House, Blackbrook Park Avenue,
Taunton, Somerset TA1 2PX T 01823-361000
W www.southwest.nhs.uk
Chief Executive, Sir Ian Carruthers, OBE
WEST MIDLANDS, St Chad's Court, 213 Hagley Road,
Edgbaston, Birmingham B16 9RG T 0121-695 2222
W www.westmidlands.nhs.uk
Chief Executive, Ian Cumming, OBE
YORKSHIRE AND THE HUMBER, Blenheim House,
Duncombe Street, Leeds LS1 4PL T 0113-295 2000
W www.yorksandhumber.nhs.uk
Chief Executive, Bill McCarthy

Contact details for PCTs and other NHS trusts in
England can be found on the NHS Choices website
(W www.nhs.uk).

WALES
The NHS Wales was reorganised according to Welsh
Assembly commitments laid out in the *One Wales* strategy
and came into effect in October 2009. There are now
seven local health boards (LHBs) that are responsible for
delivering all health care services within a geographical
area, rather than the trust and local health board system
that existed previously. Community health councils
(CHCs) are statutory lay bodies that represent the public
for the health service in their region. The number of
CHCs is being reduced to seven, contiguous with the
new LHBs. These seven CHCs are to be underpinned by
23 area associations with strong local links.

NHS TRUSTS
There are three NHS trusts in Wales. The Welsh
Ambulance Services NHS Trust is for emergency services;
the Velindre NHS Trust offers specialist services in cancer
care and other national support services; while Public
Health Wales serves as a unified public health organisation
for Wales.

REGIONAL HEALTH BOARDS
The websites of the seven LHBs, and contact details for
community health councils and NHS trusts, are available
in the *NHS Wales Directory* on the NHS Wales website
(W www.wales.nhs.uk).
ANEURIN BEVAN HEALTH BOARD, Mamhilad House,
Block A, Mamhilad Park Estate, Pontypool, Torfaen NP4 0YP
T 01873-732732
Chief Executive, Dr Andrew Goodall
ABERTAWE BRO MORGANNWG UNIVERSITY
HEALTH BOARD, One Talbot Gateway, Baglan Energy
Park, Baglan, Port Talbot SA12 7BR T 01639-683670
Chief Executive (acting), Alexandra Howells
BETSI CADWALADR UNIVERSITY HEALTH BOARD,
Ysbyty Gwynedd, Penrhosgarnedd, Bangor, Gwynedd
LL57 2PW T 01248-384384
Chief Executive, Mary Burrows
CARDIFF AND VALE UNIVERSITY HEALTH BOARD,
Whitchurch Hospital, Park Road, Whitchurch, Cardiff
CF14 7XB T 029-2074 7747
Chief Executive, Jan Williams
CWM TAF HEALTH BOARD, Ynysmeurig House,
Navigation Park, Abercynon, Mid Glamorgan CF45 4SN
T 01443-406834
Chief Executive, Allison Williams
HYWEL DDA HEALTH BOARD, Merlin's Court,
Winch Lane, Haverfordwest, Pembrokeshire SA61 1SB
T 01437-771220
Chief Executive, Trevor Purt
POWYS TEACHING HEALTH BOARD, Mansion House,
Bronllys, Brecon, Powys LD3 0LS T 01874-771661
Chief Executive, Andrew Cottom

SCOTLAND
The Scottish government Health Directorate is
responsible both for NHS Scotland and for the
development and implementation of health and
community care policy. The chief executive of NHS
Scotland leads the central management of the NHS,
is accountable to ministers for the efficiency and
performance of the service and heads the Health
Department which oversees the work of the 14 regional
health boards. These boards provide strategic
management for the entire local NHS system and are
responsible for ensuring that services are delivered
effectively and efficiently.
In addition to the 14 regional health boards there are a
further eight special boards which provide national
services, such as the Scottish ambulance service and NHS
National Services Scotland, the latter of which provides
national screening programmes, blood transfusion services
and monitors communicable diseases. A new health body,
Healthcare Improvement Scotland, was formed on 1 April
2011 by the Public Services Reform Act 2010 to improve
the quality of Scottish healthcare.

REGIONAL HEALTH BOARDS
AYRSHIRE AND ARRAN, Eglinton House, Ailsa Hospital,
Dalmellington Road, Ayr KA6 6AB T 0800-169 1441
W www.nhsayrshireandarran.com
Chief Executive, Dr Wai-yin Hatton
BORDERS, Newstead, Melrose TD6 9DA T 01896-826000
W www.nhsborders.org.uk
Chief Executive, Calum Campbell
DUMFRIES AND GALLOWAY, Ryan North, Crichton Hall,
Dumfries DG1 4TG T 01387-246246
W www.nhsdg.scot.nhs.uk
Chief Executive, John Burns
FIFE, Hayfield House, Hayfield Road, Kirkcaldy, Fife KY2 5AH
T 01592-643355 W www.nhsfife.scot.nhs.uk
Chief Executive, George Brechin

FORTH VALLEY, Carseview House, Castle Business Park, Stirling FK9 4SW T 01786-463031
W www.nhsforthvalley.com
Chief Executive, Prof. Fiona Mackenzie

GRAMPIAN, Summerfield House, 2 Eday Road, Aberdeen AB15 6RE T 0845-456 6000 W www.nhsgrampian.org
Chief Executive, Richard Carey

GREATER GLASGOW AND CLYDE, J B Russell House, Gartnavel Royal Hospital Campus, 1055 Great Western Road, Glasgow G12 0XH T 0141-201 4444
W www.nhsggc.org.uk
Chief Executive, Robert Calderwood

HIGHLAND, Assynt House, Beechwood Park, Inverness IV2 3BW T 01463-717123 W www.nhshighland.scot.nhs.uk
Chief Executive, Elaine Mead

LANARKSHIRE, Kirklands, Fallside Road, Bothwell G71 8BB T 0845-313 0130 W www.nhslanarkshire.org.uk
Chief Executive, Tim Davison

LOTHIAN, Waverley Gate, 2–4 Waterloo Place, Edinburgh EH1 3EG T 0131-536 9000 W www.nhslothian.scot.nhs.uk
Chief Executive, Prof. James Barbour, OBE

ORKNEY, Balfour Hospital, New Scapa Road, Kirkwall, Orkney KW15 1BH T 01856-888000 W www.ohb.scot.nhs.uk
Chief Executive, Cathie Cowan

SHETLAND, Brevik House, South Road, Lerwick ZE1 0TG T 01595-743060 W www.shb.scot.nhs.uk
Chief Executive, Ralph Roberts

TAYSIDE, Kings Cross, Clepington Road, Dundee DD3 8EA T 01382-818479 W www.nhstayside.scot.nhs.uk
Chief Executive, Gerry Marr

WESTERN ISLES, 37 South Beach Street, Stornoway, Isle of Lewis HS1 2BB T 01851-702997
W www.wihb.scot.nhs.uk
Chief Executive, Gordon Jamieson

NORTHERN IRELAND

On 1 April 2009 the four health and social services boards in Northern Ireland were replaced by a single health and social care board for the whole of Northern Ireland. The new board together with its local commissioning groups (whose boundaries are subject to review pending the outcome of local government reform) are responsible for improving the health and social wellbeing of people in the area for which they are responsible, planning and commissioning services, and coordinating the delivery of services in a cost-effective manner.

HEALTH AND SOCIAL CARE BOARD, 12–22 Linenhall Street, Belfast BT2 8BS T 028-9032 1313
W www.hscboard.hscni.net
Chief Executive, John Compton

NHS POLICY

In July 2000 the Labour government launched the NHS Plan, a ten-year strategy to modernise the health service. In June 2004 it also launched the NHS Improvement Plan, which set out the next stage of NHS reform, moving the focus from access to services towards the broader issues of public health and chronic disease management. The core aims were to sustain increased levels of investment in the NHS and to continue to focus on the improvements outlined in the NHS Plan, while delivering greater levels of choice and information to patients. In July 2004, the Department of Health published *National Standards, Local Action: Health and Social Care Standards and Planning Framework 2005/6–2007/8,* which cut the number of national targets from 62 to 20. The

national targets, which covered areas such as waiting times for accident and emergency treatment, became national core standards which all providers of care were required to maintain from April 2005. Alongside this, NHS providers were given power to set more locally relevant targets.

In June 2010 the coalition government published a white paper, *Liberating the NHS,* which set out its intentions for NHS reforms. In the lead up to 2013 it is proposed that GPs will be given increased control over budgets, which at present are controlled by the primary care trusts. The *Revision to the Operating Framework for the NHS in England 2010/11,* also published in June 2010, announced immediate changes to performance targets and plans for further changes to targets in 2011–12. The framework and further information on planned changes is available on the Department for Health website (W www.dh.gov.uk).

FINANCE

The NHS is still funded mainly through general taxation, although in recent years more reliance has been placed on the NHS element of national insurance contributions, patient charges and other sources of income.

The budgeted departmental expenditure limit for the NHS in England was set at £105.9bn for 2011–12. Expenditure for the NHS in Wales, Scotland and Northern Ireland is set by the devolved governments.

PRIVATE FINANCE INITIATIVE

The Private Finance Initiative (PFI) was launched in 1992, and involves the private sector in designing, building, financing and operating new hospitals and primary care premises, which are then leased to the NHS. Partnerships for Health, a public-private venture between the Department of Health and Partnerships UK plc was established in September 2001. Its role was to support the development of NHS Local Improvement Finance Trusts (LIFTs) by implementing a standard approach to procurement as well as providing some equity. LIFTs were set up as limited companies with the local NHS Partnerships for Health and the private sector as shareholders to build and refurbish primary care premises, which the schemes own and then rent to GPs on a lease basis (as well as other parties such as chemists, opticians, dentists etc).

EMPLOYEES AND SALARIES

NHS HEALTH SERVICE STAFF 2010 (ENGLAND)
Full-time equivalent

All hospital, community and dental staff	1,431,557
Consultants	37,752
Registrars	38,158
Qualified nursing and midwifery staff	410,615
General practitioners	39,409
Qualified scientific, therapeutic and technical staff	151,607

Source: NHS

SALARIES

Many general practitioners (GPs) are self-employed and hold contracts, either on their own or as part of a partnership, with their local PCT. The profit of GPs varies according to the services they provide for their patients and the way they choose to provide these services. The pay range for salaried GPs employed directly by PCTs for 2011–12 is £53,781–£81,158, dependent on, among other factors, length of service and experience. Most NHS dentists are self-employed contractors. A contract for dentists was introduced on 1 April 2006 which provides dentists with an annual income in return for carrying out an agreed amount, or units, of work. A salaried dentist employed directly by a PCT earns between £37,714 and £80,674.

BASIC SALARIES FOR HOSPITAL MEDICAL AND DENTAL STAFF*
from 1 April 2011

Consultant (2003 contract)	£74,504–£100,446
Consultant (pre-2003 contract)	£61,859–£80,186
Specialist registrar	£30,992–£46,708
Speciality registrar (full)	£29,705–£46,708
Speciality registrar (fixed term)	£29,705–£39,300
Senior house officer	£27,798–£38,705
House officer	£22,412–£25,209

* These figures do not include merit awards, discretionary points or banding supplements

NURSES
From 1 December 2004 the *Agenda for Change* pay system was introduced throughout the UK for all NHS staff with the exception of medical and dental staff, doctors in public health medicine and the community health service. Nurses' salaries are incorporated in the *Agenda for Change* nine pay band structure, which provides additional payments for flexible working such as providing out-of-hours services, working weekends and nights and being 'on-call'.

SALARIES FOR NURSES AND MIDWIVES

Nurse/Midwife consultant	£38,851–£67,134
Modern matron	£38,851–£46,621
Nurse advanced/team manager	£30,460–£40,157
Midwife higher level	£30,460–£40,157
Nurse specialist/team leader	£25,528–£34,189
Hospital/community midwife	£25,528–£34,189
Registered nurse/entry level midwife	£21,176–£27,625

HEALTH SERVICES

PRIMARY CARE
Primary care comprises the services provided by general practitioners, community health centres, pharmacies, dental surgeries and opticians. Primary nursing care includes the work carried out by practice nurses, community nurses, community midwives and health visitors.

PRIMARY MEDICAL SERVICES
In England, primary medical services are the responsibility of PCTs who contract with health care providers – GPs, dentists, pharmacists etc – to provide the service to the NHS.

In Wales, responsibility for primary medical services rests with local health boards (LHBs), in Scotland with the 14 regional health boards and in Northern Ireland with the health and social care board.

Any vocationally trained doctor may provide general or personal medical services. GPs may also have private fee-paying patients, but not if that patient is already an NHS patient on that doctor's patient list.

A person who is ordinarily resident in the UK is eligible to register with a GP (or PMS provider) for free primary care treatment. Should a patient have difficulty in registering with a doctor, he or she should contact the local PCT for help. When a person is away from home he/she can still access primary care treatment from a GP if they ask to be treated as a temporary resident. In an emergency any doctor in the service will give treatment and advice.

GPs or PCTs are responsible for the care of their patients 24 hours a day, seven days a week, but can fulfil the terms of their contract by delegating or transferring responsibility for out-of-hours care to an accredited provider.

Increasingly, some secondary care services, such as minor operations and consultations, can be provided in a primary care setting. The number of such practitioners is growing.

In addition there are around 93 NHS walk-in centres throughout England. Usually open seven days a week, from early in the morning until late in the evening, they are nurse-led and provide treatment for minor ailments and injuries, health information and self-help advice.

HEALTH COSTS
Some people are exempt from, or entitled to help with, health costs such as prescription charges, ophthalmic and dental costs, and in some cases help towards travel costs to and from hospital.

The following list is intended as a general guide to those who may be entitled to help, or who are exempt from some of the charges relating to the above:
- children under 16 and young people in full-time education who are under 19
- people aged 60 or over
- pregnant women and women who have had a baby in the last 12 months and have a valid maternity exemption certificate (MatEx)
- people, or their partners, who are in receipt of income support, income-based jobseeker's allowance and/or income-based employment and support allowance
- people in receipt of the pension credit
- diagnosed glaucoma patients, people who have been advised by an ophthalmologist that they are at risk of glaucoma and people aged 40 or over who have an immediate family member who is a diagnosed glaucoma patient
- NHS in-patients
- NHS out-patients for all prescribed contraceptives, medication given at a hospital, NHS walk-in centre, personally administered by a GP or supplied at a hospital or primary care trust clinic for the treatment of tuberculosis or a sexually transmissable infection
- patients of the Community Dental Service or an out-patient of the NHS Hospital Dental Service
- people registered blind or partially sighted
- people who need complex lenses
- war pensioners whose treatment/prescription is for their accepted disablement and who have a valid exemption certificate
- people who are entitled to, or named on, a valid NHS tax credit exemption or HC2 certificate
- people who have a medical exemption (MedEx) certificate, including those with cancer or diabetes
People in other circumstances may also be eligible for help; *see* booklet HC12 (England) and HCS2 (Scotland) for further information.

WALES
On 1 April 2007 all prescription charges (including those for medical supports and appliances and wigs) for people living in Wales were abolished. The above guide still applies for NHS dental and optical charges although all people aged under 25 living in Wales are also entitled to free dental examinations.

SCOTLAND
On 1 April 2011 all prescription charges in Scotland were abolished. Those entitled to free prescriptions in Scotland include patients registered with a Scottish GP and receiving a prescription from a Scottish pharmacy, and Scottish patients who have an English GP and an entitlement card.

NORTHERN IRELAND
On 1 April 2010 all prescription charges in Northern Ireland were abolished. All prescriptions dispensed in Northern Ireland are free, even for patients visiting from England, Wales or Scotland.

PHARMACEUTICAL SERVICES
Patients may obtain medicines and appliances under the NHS from any pharmacy whose owner has entered into arrangements with the PCT to provide this service. There are also some suppliers who only provide special appliances. In rural areas, where access to a pharmacy may be difficult, patients may be able to obtain medicines, etc, from a dispensing doctor.

In England, a charge of £7.40 is payable for each item supplied (except for contraceptives for which there is no charge), unless the patient is exempt and the declaration on the back of the prescription form is completed. Prepayment certificates (£29.10 valid for three months, £104.00 valid for a year) may be purchased by those patients not entitled to exemption who require frequent prescriptions.

DENTAL SERVICES
Dentists, like doctors, may take part in the NHS and also have private patients. Dentists are responsible to the local health provider in whose areas they provide services. Patients may go to any dentist who is taking part in the NHS and is willing to accept them. On 1 April 2006 the charging system for NHS dentistry in England and Wales was changed. There is now a three-tier payment system based on the individual course of treatment required.

COURSE OF TREATMENT COSTS 2010–11

	England / Wales
Examination, diagnosis, preventive care (A)* (eg x-rays, scale and polish)	£17.00/£12.00
A+ basic additional treatment (eg fillings and extractions)	£47.00/£39.00
A+ all other treatment (eg more complex procedures such as crowns, dentures etc)	£204.00/£177.00

* Urgent and out-of-hours treatment is also charged at this payment tier

The cost of individual treatment plans should be known prior to treatment and some dental practices may require payment in advance. There is no charge for writing a prescription or removing stitches and only one

charge is payable for each course of treatment even if more than one visit to the dentist is required. If additional treatment is required within two months of visiting the dentist and this is covered by the course of treatment most recently paid for (eg payment was made for the second tier of treatment but an additional filling is required) then this will be provided free of charge.

SCOTLAND AND NORTHERN IRELAND
Scotland and Northern Ireland have yet to simplify their charging systems. NHS dental patients pay 80 per cent of the cost of the individual items of treatment provided up to a maximum of £384. Patients in Scotland are entitled to free basic and extensive examinations.

GENERAL OPHTHALMIC SERVICES
General ophthalmic services are administered by local health providers. Testing of sight may be carried out by any ophthalmic medical practitioner or ophthalmic optician (optometrist). The optician must give the prescription to the patient, who can take this to any supplier of glasses to have them dispensed. Only registered opticians can supply glasses to children and to people registered as blind or partially sighted.

Free eyesight tests and help towards the cost are available to people in certain circumstances. Help is also available for the purchase of glasses or contact lenses (see Health Costs section). In Scotland eye examinations, which include a sight test, are free to all. Help is also available for the purchase of glasses or contact lenses to those entitled to help with health costs in the same way it is available to those in England and Wales.

CHILD HEALTH SERVICES
Pre-school services at GP surgeries or child health clinics provide regular monitoring of children's physical, mental and emotional health and development and advise parents on their children's health and welfare.

NHS DIRECT AND NHS 24
NHS Direct is a website and 24-hour nurse-led advice telephone service for England and Wales. It provides medical advice as well as directing people to the appropriate part of the NHS for treatment if necessary (W www.nhsdirect.nhs.uk T 0845-4647).

NHS 24 provides an equivalent service for Scotland (T 0845-424 2424).

SECONDARY CARE AND OTHER SERVICES

HOSPITALS
NHS hospitals provide acute and specialist care services, treating conditions which normally cannot be dealt with by primary care specialists, and provide for medical emergencies.

NUMBER OF BEDS 2010–11*

	Average daily	
	available beds	occupation of beds
England	141,019	121,614
Wales	12,868	10,449
Scotland	17,099	14,004
Northern Ireland	7,276	5,952

* Figures for Scotland, Wales and Northern Ireland are for 2009–10

Sources: Department of Health; Welsh government, NI Direct

HOSPITAL CHARGES

Acute or foundation trusts can provide hospital accommodation in single rooms or small wards, if not required for patients who need privacy for medical reasons. The patient is still an NHS patient, but there may be a charge for these additional facilities. Acute or foundation trusts can charge for certain patient services that are considered to be additional treatments over and above the normal hospital service provision. There is no blanket policy to cover this and each case is considered in the light of the patient's clinical need. However, if an item or service is considered to be an integral part of a patient's treatment by their clinician, then a charge should not be made.

In some NHS hospitals, accommodation and services are available for the treatment of private patients where it does not interfere with care for NHS patients. Income generated by treating private patients is then put back into local NHS services. Private patients undertake to pay the full costs of medical treatment, accommodation, medication and other related services. Charges for private patients are set locally.

WAITING LISTS

England

In July 2004 a target of an 18-week maximum wait, from start time (ie seeing a GP) to treatment, was introduced. For June 2011, 321,921 admitted patients and 937,205 non-admitted patients completed their referral to treatment. Of the admitted patients, 90.2 per cent were treated within 18 weeks, and for non-admitted patients 97.6 per cent were treated within 18 weeks. The *Revision to the Operating Framework for the NHS in England 2010/11*, published in June 2010, abolished the performance management of the 18-week waiting time target although referral-to-treatment data will continue to be published.

Wales

In Wales the main target is for referral to treatment to take no longer than 26 weeks. In February 2011, 87.3 per cent of patients were treated within 26 weeks and 97.4 per cent were treated within 36 weeks of the date the referral letter was received in the hospital. There are also operational standards for maximum waiting times for first outpatient appointments and inpatient or day-case treatment but these are not set targets. The standards are 14 weeks for inpatient or day case treatment, and ten weeks for a first outpatient appointment.

Scotland

An 18-week referral to treatment target, due to be delivered from December 2011, was set out in the publication *Better Health, Better Care*. In March 2011, 85.2 per cent of patients on an 18 week referral to treatment pathway were reported as being seen within 18 weeks, an increase from 83.7 per cent in February 2011.

Northern Ireland

From April 2009 the target is that no patient should wait more than nine weeks for a first out-patient appointment or 13 weeks for in-patient or day-case treatment. The total number of people waiting for a first out patient appointment at the end of 31 March 2011 was 106,227; of these, 31,909 had been waiting over nine weeks, an increase of 23,328 from the same quarter in 2010. The number of people waiting for in patient treatment during the quarter ending 31 March 2011 was 52,880; of these, 17,630 had been waiting for more than 13 weeks.

AMBULANCE SERVICE

The NHS provides emergency ambulance services free of charge via the 999 emergency telephone service. Air ambulances, provided through local charities and partially funded by the NHS, are used throughout the UK. They assist with cases where access may be difficult or heavy traffic could hinder road progress. Non-emergency ambulance services are provided free to patients who are deemed to require them on medical grounds.

Since 1 April 2001 all services have had a system of call prioritisation. The prioritisation procedures require all emergency calls to be classified as either immediately life threatening (category A) or other emergency (category B). Services are expected to reach 75 per cent of Category A (life threatening) calls within eight minutes and 95 per cent of category B calls within 19 minutes.

AMBULANCE STAFF

	Total staff	Number of paramedics
England	32,284	10,089
Wales	1,413*	847*
Scotland	3,836	1,323
Northern Ireland	1,033	635†

* 2008 figures
† Includes emergency medical technicians
Source: ONS – *Annual Abstract of Statistics 2009* (Crown copyright)

BLOOD AND TRANSPLANT SERVICES

There are four national bodies which coordinate the blood donor programme and transplant and related services in the UK. Donors give blood at local centres on a voluntary basis.

NHS BLOOD AND TRANSPLANT, Oak House, Reeds Crescent, Watford, Herts WD24 4QN
T 01923-486800 W www.nhsbt.nhs.uk
WELSH BLOOD SERVICE, Ely Valley Road, Talbot Green, Pontyclun CF72 9WB T 01443-622000
W www.welsh-blood.org.uk
SCOTTISH NATIONAL BLOOD TRANSFUSION SERVICE, 21 Ellen's Glen Road, Edinburgh EH17 7QT
T 0845-909 0999 W www.scotblood.co.uk
NORTHERN IRELAND BLOOD TRANSFUSION SERVICE, Lisburn Road, Belfast BT9 7TS T 028-9032 1414
W www.nibts.org

HOSPICES

Hospice or palliative care may be available for patients with life-threatening illnesses. It may be provided at the patient's home or in a voluntary or NHS hospice or in hospital, and is intended to ensure the best possible quality of life for the patient during their illness, and to provide help and support to both the patient and the patient's family. The National Council for Palliative Care coordinates NHS and voluntary services in England, Wales and Northern Ireland; the Scottish Partnership for Palliative Care performs the same function in Scotland.

NATIONAL COUNCIL FOR PALLIATIVE CARE, The Fitzpatrick Building, 188–194 York Way, London N7 9AS
T 020-7697 1520 W www.ncpc.org.uk

SCOTTISH PARTNERSHIP FOR PALLIATIVE CARE,
1A Cambridge Street, Edinburgh EH1 2DY T 0131-229 0538
W www.palliativecarescotland.org.uk

COMPLAINTS

Firstly, an attempt must be made to resolve the complaint at a local level directly with the health care provider concerned. Patient advice and liaison services (PALS) have been established for every NHS and PCT in England. PALS are not part of the complaints procedure itself, but can give advice on local complaints procedure, or resolve concerns informally. For more information, see W www.pals.nhs.uk. If the case is not resolved locally or the complainant is not satisfied with the way a local NHS body or practice has dealt with their complaint, they may approach the Health Service Ombudsman in England, the Scottish Public Services Ombudsman, Public Services Ombudsman for Wales or the Northern Ireland Commissioner for Complaints.

RECIPROCAL ARRANGEMENTS

The European Health Insurance Card (EHIC) allows UK residents access to state-provided health care that may become necessary while temporarily travelling in all European Economic Area countries and Switzerland either free or at a reduced cost. A card is free, valid for up to five years and should be obtained before travelling. Applications can be made by telephone (T 0845-606 2030), online (W www.ehic.org.uk) or by post (a form is available from the post office).

The UK also has bilateral agreements with several other countries, including Australia and New Zealand, for the free provision of urgent medical treatment.

European Economic Area nationals visiting the UK and visitors from other countries with which the UK has bilateral health care agreements are entitled to receive emergency health care on the NHS on the same terms as it is available to UK residents. For further information regarding health care abroad, see Travel Overseas.

SOCIAL WELFARE

SOCIAL SERVICES

The Secretary of State for Health (in England), the Welsh government, the Scottish government and the Secretary of State for Northern Ireland are responsible, under the Local Authority Social Services Act 1970, for the provision of social services for older people, disabled people, families and children, and those with mental disorders. Personal social services are administered by local authorities according to policies, with standards set by central and devolved government. Each authority has a director and a committee responsible for the social services functions placed upon them. Local authorities provide, enable and commission care after assessing the needs of their population. The private and voluntary sectors also play an important role in the delivery of social services, and an estimated 6 million people in the UK provide substantial regular care for a member of their family.

The Care Quality Commission (CQC) was established in April 2009, bringing together the independent regulation of health, mental health and adult social care. Prior to 1 April 2009 this work was carried out by three separate organisations: the Healthcare Commission, the Mental Health Act Commission and the Commission for Social Care Inspection. The CQC is responsible for the registration of health and social care providers, the monitoring and inspection of all health and adult social care, issuing fines, public warnings or closures if standards are not met and for undertaking regular performance reviews. Since April 2007 the Office for Standards in Education, Children's Services and Skills (Ofsted) has been responsible for inspecting and regulating all care services for children and young people in England. Both Ofsted and CQC collate information on local care services and make this information available to the public.

The Care and Social Services Inspectorate Wales (CSSIW), an operationally independent part of the Welsh government, is reponsible for the regulation and inspection of all social care services in Wales. A new unified body, Social Care and Social Work Improvement Scotland, was established on 1 April 2011, replacing the Scottish Commission for the Regulation of Care (the Care Commission) and is now the independent care services regulator for Scotland.

The Department of Health, Social Services and Public Safety is responsible for social care services in Northern Ireland.

CARE QUALITY COMMISSION (CQC), Citygate,
Gallowgate, Newcastle upon Tyne NE1 4PA
T 0300-061 6161 E enquiries@cqc.org.uk
W www.cqc.org.uk

OFFICE FOR STANDARDS IN EDUCATION,
CHILDREN'S SERVICES AND SKILLS (Ofsted),
Piccadilly Gate, Store Street, Manchester M1 2WD
T 0300-123 1231 E enquiries@ofsted.gov.uk
W www.ofsted.gov.uk

CARE AND SOCIAL SERVICES INSPECTORATE
WALES (CSSIW), Cathays Park, Cardiff CF10 3NQ
T 01443-848450 E cssiw@wales.gsi.gov.uk
W www.cssiw.org.uk

SOCIAL CARE AND SOCIAL WORK
IMPROVEMENT SCOTLAND, Compass House,
11 Riverside Drive, Dundee DD1 4NY T 0845-600 9527
E enquiries@scswis.com W www.scswis.com

DEPARTMENT OF HEALTH, SOCIAL SERVICES AND
PUBLIC SAFETY, Castle Buildings, Stormont, Belfast
BT4 3SJ T 028-9052 0500 E webmaster@dhsspsni.gov.uk
W www.dhsspsni.gov.uk

STAFF

Total Social Services Staff (England, full-time)	197,400
Area office/field work	110,700
Residential care staff	39,700
Day care staff	24,500
Central and strategic staff	20,200
Other staff	2,500

Source: Department of Health

OLDER PEOPLE

Services for older people are designed to enable them to remain living in their own homes for as long as possible. Local authority services include advice, domestic help, meals in the home, alterations to the home to aid mobility, emergency alarm systems, day and/or night attendants, laundry services and the provision of day centres and recreational facilities. Charges may be made for these services. Respite care may also be provided in order to allow carers temporary relief from their responsibilities.

Local authorities and the private sector also provide 'sheltered housing' for older people, sometimes with resident wardens.

If an older person is admitted to a residential home, charges are made according to a means test; if the person cannot afford to pay, the costs are met by the local authority.

DISABLED PEOPLE

Services for disabled people are designed to enable them to remain living in their own homes wherever possible. Local authority services include advice, adaptations to the home, meals in the home, help with personal care, occupational therapy, educational facilities and recreational facilities. Respite care may also be provided in order to allow carers temporary relief from their responsibilities.

Special housing may be available for disabled people who can live independently, and residential accommodation for those who cannot.

FAMILIES AND CHILDREN

Local authorities are required to provide services aimed at safeguarding the welfare of children in need and, wherever possible, allowing them to be brought up by their families. Services include advice, counselling, help in the home and the provision of family centres. Many authorities also provide short-term refuge accommodation for women and children.

DAY CARE

In allocating day care places to children, local authorities give priority to children with special needs, whether in terms of their health, learning abilities or social needs. Since September 2001 Ofsted has been responsible for the regulation and registration of all early years childcare and education provision in England (previously the responsibility of the local authorities). All day care and childminding services that care for children under eight years of age for more than two hours a day must register with Ofsted and are inspected at least every two years. As at 30 June 2011 there were 95,774 registered childcare providers in England.

CHILD PROTECTION
Children considered to be at risk of physical injury, neglect or sexual abuse are placed on the local authority's child protection register. Local authority social services staff, schools, health visitors and other agencies work together to prevent and detect cases of abuse. As at 31 March 2010, there was a total of 46,705 children on child protection registers or subject to a child protection plan in the UK. In England, there were 39,100 children on child protection registers, of these, 17,200 were at risk of neglect, 4,700 of physical abuse, 2,200 of sexual abuse and 11,400 of emotional abuse. At 31 March 2010 there were 2,730 children on child protection registers in Wales, 2,518 in Scotland and 2,357 in Northern Ireland.

LOCAL AUTHORITY CARE
Local authorities are required to provide accommodation for children who have no parents or guardians or whose parents or guardians are unable or unwilling to care for them. A family proceedings court may also issue a care order where a child is being neglected or abused, or is not attending school; the court must be satisfied that this would positively contribute to the well-being of the child.

The welfare of children in local authority care must be properly safeguarded. Children may be placed with foster families, who receive payments to cover the expenses of caring for the child or children, or in residential care.

Children's homes may be run by the local authority or by the private or voluntary sectors; all homes are subject to inspection procedures. As at 31 March 2010, 64,400 children in the UK were in the care of local authorities, of these, 47,200 were in foster placements and 6,200 were in children's homes, hostels or secure units.

ADOPTION
Local authorities are required to provide an adoption service, either directly or via approved voluntary societies. In 2009–10, there were 2,300 children aged under 18 entered in the adopted children register in the UK.

PEOPLE WITH LEARNING DISABILITIES
Services for people with learning disabilities are designed to enable them to remain living in the community wherever possible. Local authority services include short-term care, support in the home, the provision of day care centres, and help with other activities outside the home. Residential care is provided for the severely or profoundly disabled.

MENTALLY ILL PEOPLE
Under the care programme approach, mentally ill people should be assessed by specialist services and receive a care plan, and a key worker should be appointed for each patient. Regular reviews of the person's progress should be conducted. Local authorities provide help and advice to mentally ill people and their families, and places in day centres and social centres. Social workers can apply for a mentally disturbed person to be compulsorily detained in hospital. Where appropriate, mentally ill people are provided with accommodation in special hospitals, local authority accommodation, or at homes run by private or voluntary organisations. Patients who have been discharged from hospitals may be placed on a supervision register.

NATIONAL INSURANCE

The National Insurance (NI) scheme operates under the Social Security Contributions and Benefits Act 1992 and the Social Security Administration Act 1992, and orders and regulations made thereunder. The scheme is financed by contributions payable by earners, employers and others (*see* below). Money collected under the scheme is used to finance the National Insurance Fund (from which contributory benefits are paid) and to contribute to the cost of the National Health Service.

NATIONAL INSURANCE FUND
Estimated receipts, payments and statement of balances of the National Insurance Fund for 2011–12:

Receipts	£ million
Net national insurance contributions	80,195
Compensation from the Consolidated Fund for statutory sick, maternity, paternity and adoption pay recoveries	2,106
Income from investments	358
State scheme premiums	77
Other receipts	49
TOTAL RECEIPTS	82,784

Payments	£ million
Benefits	
At present rates	79,062
Increase due to proposed rate changes	3,233
Personal and stakeholder pensions contracted-out rebates	2,011
Age-related rebates for contracted-out money purchase schemes	195
Administration costs	1,377
Redundancy fund payments	308
Transfer to Northern Ireland	157
Other payments	137
TOTAL PAYMENTS	86,480

Balances	£ million
Opening balance	44,089
Excess of receipts over payments	(3,696)
BALANCE AT END OF YEAR	40,394

CONTRIBUTIONS
There are six classes of National Insurance contributions (NICs):

Class 1	paid by employees and their employers
Class 1A	paid by employers who provide employees with certain benefits in kind for private use, such as company cars
Class 1B	paid by employers who enter into a pay as you earn (PAYE) settlement agreement with HM Revenue and Customs
Class 2	paid by self-employed people
Class 3	voluntary contributions paid to protect entitlement to the state pension for those who do not pay enough NI contributions in another class
Class 4	paid by the self-employed on their taxable profits over a set limit. These are normally paid by self-employed people in addition to class 2 contributions. Class 4 contributions do not count towards benefits.

The lower and upper earnings limits and the percentage rates referred to below apply from April 2011 to April 2012.

CLASS 1
Class 1 contributions are paid where a person:
• is an employed earner (employee), office holder (eg company director) or employed under a contract of service in Great Britain or Northern Ireland
• is 16 or over and under state pension age
• earns at or above the earnings threshold of £139 per week (including overtime pay, bonus, commission, etc, without deduction of superannuation contributions)

Class 1 contributions are made up of primary and secondary contributions. Primary contributions are those paid by the employee and these are deducted from earnings by the employer. Since 6 April 2001 the employee's and employer's earnings thresholds have been the same and are referred to as the earnings threshold. Primary contributions are not paid on earnings below the earnings threshold of £139.00 per week. However, between the lower earnings limit of £102.00 per week and the earnings threshold of £139.00 per week, NI contributions are treated as having been paid to protect the benefit entitlement position of lower earners. Contributions are payable at the rate of 12 per cent on earnings between the earnings threshold and the upper earnings limit of £817.00 per week (10.4 per cent for contracted-out employment). Above the upper earnings limit 2 per cent is payable.

Some married women or widows pay a reduced rate of 5.85 per cent on earnings between the earnings threshold and upper earnings limits and 2 per cent above this. It is no longer possible to elect to pay the reduced rate but those who had reduced liability before 12 May 1977 may retain it for as long as certain conditions are met.

Secondary contributions are paid by employers of employed earners at the rate of 13.8 per cent on all earnings above the earnings threshold of £139.00 per week. There is no upper earnings limit for employers' contributions. Employers operating contracted-out salary related schemes pay reduced contributions of 10.1 per cent; those with contracted-out money-purchase schemes pay 12.4 per cent. The contracted-out rate applies only to that portion of earnings between the earnings threshold and the upper earnings limit. Employers' contributions below and above those respective limits are assessed at the appropriate not contracted-out rate.

CLASS 2
Class 2 contributions are paid where a person is self-employed and is 16 or over and under state pension age. Contributions are paid at a flat rate of £2.50 per week regardless of the amount earned. However, those with earnings of less than £5,315 a year can apply for small earnings exception. Those granted exemption from class 2 contributions may pay class 2 or class 3 contributions voluntarily. Self-employed earners (whether or not they pay class 2 contributions) may also be liable to pay class 4 contributions based on profits. There are special rules for those who are concurrently employed and self-employed.

Married women and widows can no longer choose not to pay class 2 contributions but those who elected not to pay class 2 contributions before 12 May 1977 may retain the right for as long as certain conditions are met.

Class 2 contributions are collected by the national insurance contributions department of HM Revenue and Customs (HMRC), by direct debit or quarterly bills.

CLASS 3

Class 3 contributions are voluntary flat-rate contributions of £12.60 per week payable by persons over the age of 16 who would otherwise be unable to qualify for retirement pension and certain other benefits because they have an insufficient record of class 1 or class 2 contributions. This may include those who are not working, those not liable for class 1 or class 2 contributions, or those excepted from class 2 contributions. Married women and widows who on or before 11 May 1977 elected not to pay class 1 (full rate) or class 2 contributions cannot pay class 3 contributions while they retain this right. Class 3 contributions are collected by HMRC by quarterly bills or direct debit.

CLASS 4

Self-employed people whose profits and gains are over £7,225 a year pay class 4 contributions in addition to class 2 contributions. This applies to self-employed earners over 16 and under the state pension age. Class 4 contributions are calculated at 9 per cent of annual profits or gains between £7,225 and £42,475 and 2 per cent above. Class 4 contributions are assessed and collected by HMRC. It is possible, in some circumstances, to apply for exceptions from liability to pay class 4 contributions or to have the amount of contribution reduced.

PENSIONS

Many people will qualify for a state pension; however, there are further pension choices available, such as personal and stakeholder pensions. There are also other non-pension savings and investment options. The following section provides background information on existing pension schemes.

STATE PENSION SCHEME
The state pension scheme consists of:
- basic state pension
- additional state pension

People may be able to get both or either when they reach state pension age and meet the qualifying conditions.

The state pension does not have to be claimed at state pension age, people can delay claiming it to earn extra weekly state pension or a lump sum payment.

Basic State Pension
The amount of basic state pension paid is dependent on the number of 'qualifying years' a person has established during their working life. In 2011–12, the full basic state pension is £102.15 a week (*see also* Benefits, State Pension: Categories A and B).

Working Life
Generally a working life is counted from the start of the tax year (6 April) in which a person reaches 16 to the end of the tax year (5 April) before the one in which they reach state pension age (*see* State Pension Age).

Qualifying Years
A 'qualifying year' is a tax year in which a person has sufficient earnings upon which they have paid, are treated as having paid, or have been credited with national insurance (NI) contributions (*see* National Insurance Credits section).

Since 6 April 2010, a person who has 30 qualifying years will be entitled to a full basic state pension. Someone with less than 30 qualifying years will be entitled to a proportion of the full basic state pension based on the number of qualifying years they have. Just one qualifying year, achieved through paid or credited contributions, will give entitlement to the basic state pension worth one-thirtieth of the full basic state pension.

Until 6 April 2010, women normally needed 39 qualifying years for a full basic state pension (£102.15 in 2011–12) and men normally needed 44 qualifying years. A reduced-rate basic state pension was payable if the number of qualifying years was less than 90 per cent of the working life, but to receive any basic state pension at all, a person must have had enough qualifying years, normally 10 or 11, to receive a basic state pension of at least 25 per cent of the standard rate.

National Insurance Credits
Those in receipt of carer's allowance, working tax credit (with a disability element), jobseeker's allowance, incapacity benefit, employment support allowance, unemployability supplement, statutory sick pay, statutory maternity pay or statutory adoption pay may have class 1 NI contributions credited to them each week. People may also get credits if they are unemployed and looking for work or too sick to work, even if they have not paid enough contributions to receive benefit. Since April 2010, spouses and civil partners of members of HM forces may get credits if they are on an accompanied assignment

outside the UK. Persons undertaking certain training courses or jury service or who have been wrongly imprisoned for a conviction which is quashed on appeal may also get class 1 NI credits for each week they fulfil certain conditions. Class 1 credits may also be available to men approaching state pension age. Until 5 April 2010, these credits were awarded for the tax years in which they reached age 60 and continued until age 64, if they were not liable to pay contributions and were not absent from the UK for more than six months in any tax year. Since 6 April 2010 these credits are being phased out in line with the increase in women's state pension age. Since 6 April 2010, spouses and civil partners who are accompanying members of HM forces on an assignment outside the UK can also apply for class 1 credits. Class 1 NI credits count toward all future contributory benefits. A class 3 NI credit for basic state pension and bereavement benefit purposes is awarded, where required, for each week the working tax credit (without a disability element) has been received or child benefit, for a child under 12, has been received. Class 3 credits may also be awarded, on application, to approved foster carers and people caring for at least 20 hours a week. Before 6 April 2010 class 3 credits were automatically awarded to young people in the tax years of their 16th, 17th and 18th birthdays if they did not work or earn enough to pay NI contributions. Since 6 April 2010 these credits are no longer awarded.

State Pension Age
State pension age is currently 60 for men and between 60 and 65 for women. However, this is planned to increase to 66 in 2020. Further information can be obtained from the online state pension calculator (W www.direct.gov.uk/en/pensionsandretirementplanning/statepension).

Using the NI Contribution Record of Another Person to Claim a State Pension
Married people or civil partners whose own NI record is incomplete may get a lower-rate basic state pension calculated using their partner's NI contribution record. This can be up to £61.20 a week in April 2011–12. Married men and civil partners may only be able to qualify if their wife or civil partner was born on or after 6 April 1950. A state pension may also be payable to widows, widowers, surviving civil partners, and people who are divorced or whose civil partnership has been dissolved, based on their late or ex-spouse's/civil partner's NI contributions.

Non-contributory State Pensions
A non-contributory state pension may be payable to those aged 80 or over who live in England, Scotland or Wales, and have done so for a total of ten years or more for any continuous period in the 20 years after their 60th birthday, if they are not entitled to another category of state pension, or are entitled to one below the rate of £61.20 a week in 2011–12 (*see also* Benefits, State Pension for people aged 80 and over).

Graduated Retirement Benefit
Graduated Retirement Benefit (GRB) is based on the amount of graduated NI contributions paid into the GRB scheme between April 1961 and April 1975 (*see also* Benefits, Graduated Retirement Benefit).

Home Responsibilities Protection
From 6 April 1978 until 5 April 2010, it was possible for people who had low income or were unable to work because they cared for children or a sick or disabled

person at home to reduce the number of qualifying years required for basic state pension. This was called home responsibilities protection (HRP); the number of years for which HRP was given was deducted from the number of qualifying years needed. HRP could, in some cases, also qualify the recipient for additional state pension. From April 2003 to April 2010 HRP was also available to approved foster carers.

From 6 April 2010, HRP was replaced by weekly credits for parents and carers. A class 3 national insurance credit is given, where eligible, towards basic pension and bereavement benefits for spouses and civil partners. An earnings factor credit towards additional state pension is also awarded. Any years of HRP accrued before 6 April 2010 have been converted into qualifying years of credits for people reaching state pension age after that date, up to a maximum of 22 years for basic state pension purposes.

Additional State Pension

The amount of additional state pension paid depends on the amount of earnings a person has, or is treated as having, between the lower and upper earnings limits (from April 2009, the upper accruals point replaced the upper earnings limit for additional pension) for each complete tax year between 6 April 1978 (when the scheme started) and the tax year before they reach state pension age. The right to additional state pension does not depend on the person's right to basic state pension.

From 1978 to 2002, additional state pension was called the State Earnings-Related Pension Scheme (SERPS). SERPS covered all earnings by employees from 6 April 1978 to 5 April 1997 on which standard rate class 1 NI contributions had been paid, and earnings between 6 April 1997 and 5 April 2002 if the standard rate class 1 NI contributions had been contracted-in.

In 2002, SERPS was reformed through the state second pension, by improving the pension available to low and moderate earners and extending access to certain carers and people with long-term illness or disability. If earnings on which class 1 NI contributions have been paid or can be treated as paid are above the annual NI lower earnings limit (£5,304 for 2011–12) but below the statutory low earnings threshold (£14,400 for 2011–12), the state second pension regards this as earnings of £14,400 and it is treated as equivalent. Certain carers and people with long-term illness and disability will be considered as having earned at the low earnings threshold for each complete tax year since 2002–3 even if they do not work at all, or earn less than the annual NI lower earnings limit.

The amount of additional state pension paid also depends on when a person reaches state pension age; changes phased in from 6 April 1999 mean that pensions are calculated differently from that date.

Inheritance

Men or women widowed before 6 October 2002 can inherit all of their late spouse's SERPS pension. From 6 October 2002, the maximum percentage of SERPS pension that a person can inherit from a late spouse or civil partner depends on their late spouse or civil partner's date of birth:

Maximum SERPS entitlement	d.o.b (men)	d.o.b (women)
100%	5/10/37 or earlier	5/10/42 or earlier
90%	6/10/37 to 5/10/39	6/10/42 to 5/10/44
80%	6/10/39 to 5/10/41	6/10/44 to 5/10/46
70%	6/10/41 to 5/10/43	6/10/46 to 5/10/48
60%	6/10/43 to 5/10/45	6/10/48 to 5/7/50
50%	6/10/45 or later	6/7/50 or later

The maximum state second pension a person can inherit from a late spouse or civil partner is 50 per cent. If a person is bereaved before they have reached their state pension age, inherited SERPS or state second pension can be paid as part of widowed parents allowance (in the case of a person who has dependent children) or otherwise only from state pension age.

Pension Forecasts

The Pension Service provides a state pension forecasting service. A state pension forecast provides an estimate of the current value of an individual's state pension, based on information held on their NI record, and an estimate of what it may be worth when they reach state pension age. There is also an online state pension profiler which, based on information input by individuals, tells the user their state pension age, an estimate of their basic state pension and how they are affected by changes to the state pension (T 0845-300 0168 W www.direct.gov.uk/pensionsandretirementplanning).

CONTRACTED-OUT PENSIONS

'Contracting-out' means leaving the state second pension scheme. There are two main types of contracting-out:
* occupational pension scheme
* personal pension scheme or stakeholder pension scheme (also known as an appropriate scheme)

Contracting-Out with an Occupational Pension Scheme

An occupational pension scheme is an arrangement some employers set up to give the people who work for them a pension when they retire. There are two main types of occupational pension schemes:
* salary-related (also known as defined benefit)
* money purchase (also known as defined contribution)

In contracting-out with a money purchase scheme, both the scheme member and the employer pay a reduced rate of NI contributions (the contracted-out rebate) to compensate for the state pension given up. In addition, at the end of each tax year, HM Revenue and Customs (HMRC) pays an additional age-related rebate direct to the scheme for investment on behalf of the employee.

In contracting-out with personal pension scheme or stakeholder pension schemes, an individual pays standard NI contributions and at the end of the tax year, HMRC pays an age-related rebate, together with tax relief on the employee's share of the rebate, directly into the scheme to be invested on behalf of the employee. These payments are known as 'minimum contributions'.

Contracting-out of the state second pension through money purchase, personal pension scheme and stakeholder pension scheme arrangements is to be abolished from 6 April 2012. From this date, employees will not be able to contract-out of the state second pension on this basis. Anyone contracted-out on this basis at that time will automatically be contracted back into the additional state pension. However, those rights built up before the abolition date will be used to provide pension benefits. These changes will not affect contracting-out via a salary-related occupational pension scheme.

Contracted-Out Salary-Related (COSR) Scheme

* these schemes (also known as contracted-out defined benefit (DB) schemes) provide a pension related to earnings and the length of pensionable service

- any notional additional state pension built up from 6 April 1978 to 5 April 1997 will be reduced by the amount of guaranteed minimum pension (GMP) accrued during that period (the contracted-out deduction)
- since 6 April 1997 these schemes no longer provide a GMP. Instead, as a condition of contracting-out they have to satisfy a reference scheme test to ensure that the benefits provided are at least as good as a prescribed standard
- when someone contracts-out of the additional state pension through a COSR scheme, both the scheme member and the employer pay a reduced rate of NI contributions (known as the contracted-out rebate) to compensate for the additional state pension given up

Contracted-Out Mixed Benefit (COMB) Scheme
A mixed benefit scheme is a single scheme with both a salary-related section and a money purchase section. Scheme rules set out which section individual employees may join and the circumstances (if any), in which members may move between sections. Each section must satisfy the respective contracting-out conditions for COSR and COMP schemes.

For more information on contracted-out pension schemes *see* the Department for Work and Pensions' leaflet *Contracted-out Pensions* (PM7).

STAKEHOLDER PENSION SCHEMES
Introduced in 2001, stakeholder pensions are available to everyone but are principally for moderate earners who do not have access to a good value company pension scheme. Stakeholder pensions must meet a number of minimum standards to make sure they are flexible, portable and annual management charges are capped. The minimum contribution is £20.

As with personal pensions it is possible to invest up to £3,600 (including tax relief) into stakeholder pensions each year without evidence of earnings. Contributions can be made on someone else's behalf, for example a non-working partner.

Stakeholder pensions can also be used by employees to contract-out of the additional state pension. For more information *see* Contracted-Out Appropriate Personal Pension Schemes (including Appropriate Stakeholder Pension Schemes).

COMPLAINTS
The Pensions Advisory Service provides information and guidance to members of the public, on state, company, personal and stakeholder schemes. They also help any member of the public who has a problem, complaint or dispute with their occupational or personal pensions.

There are two bodies for pension complaints. The Financial Ombudsman Service deals with complaints which predominantly concern the sale and/or marketing of occupational, stakeholder and personal pensions. The Pensions Ombudsman deals with complaints which predominantly concern the management (after sale or marketing) of occupational, stakeholder and personal pensions.

The Pensions Regulator is the UK regulator for work-based pension schemes; it concentrates its resources on schemes where there is the greatest risk to the security of members' benefits, promotes good administration practice for all work-based schemes and works with trustees, employers and professional advisers to put things right when necessary.

WAR PENSIONS AND THE ARMED FORCES COMPENSATION SCHEME

The Service Personnel and Veterans Agency (SPVA) is part of the Ministry of Defence. SPVA was formed on 1 April 2007 from the former Armed Forces Personnel Administration Agency and the Veterans Agency to provide services to both serving personnel and veterans.

SPVA is responsible for the administration of the war pensions scheme and the armed forces compensation scheme (AFCS) to members of the armed forces in respect of disablement or death due to service. There is also a scheme for civilians and civil defence workers in respect of the Second World War, and other schemes for groups such as merchant seamen and Polish armed forces who served under British command during the Second World War. The agency is also responsible for the administration of the armed forces pension scheme, which provides occupational pensions for ex-service personnel *(see* Defence).

THE WAR PENSIONS SCHEME
War disablement pension is awarded for the disabling effects of any injury, wound or disease which was the result of, or was aggravated by, service in the armed forces prior to 6 April 2005. Claims are only considered once the person has left the armed forces. The amount of pension paid depends on the severity of disablement, which is assessed by comparing the health of the claimant with that of a healthy person of the same age and sex. The person's earning capacity or occupation are not taken into account in this assessment. A pension is awarded if the person has a disablement of 20 per cent or more and a lump sum is usually payable to those with a disablement of less than 20 per cent. No award is made for noise-induced sensorineural hearing loss where the assessment of disablement is less than 20 per cent.

A pension is payable to war widows, widowers and surviving civil partners where the spouse's or civil partner's death was due to, or hastened by, service in the armed forces prior to 6 April 2005 or where the spouse or civil partner was in receipt of a war disablement pension constant attendance allowance (or would have been if not in hospital) at the time of death. A pension is also payable to widows, widowers or surviving civil partners if the spouse or civil partner was receiving the war disablement pension at the 80 per cent rate or higher in conjunction with unemployability supplement at the time of death. War widows, widowers and surviving civil partners receive a standard rank-related rate, but a lower weekly rate is payable to war widows, widowers and surviving civil partners of personnel of the rank of Major or below who are under the age of 40, without children and capable of maintaining themselves. This is increased to the standard rate at age 40. Allowances are paid for children (in addition to child benefit) and adult dependants. An age allowance is automatically given when the widow, widower or surviving civil partner reaches 65 and increased at ages 70 and 80.

Pensioners living overseas receive the same pension rates as those living in the UK. All war disablement pensions and allowances and pensions for war widows, widowers and surviving civil partners are tax-free in the UK; this does not always apply in overseas countries due to different tax laws.

SUPPLEMENTARY ALLOWANCES
A number of supplementary allowances may be awarded to a war pensioner and are intended to meet various needs.

The principal supplementary allowances are unemployability supplement, allowance for lowered standard of occupation and constant attendance allowance. Others include exceptionally severe disablement allowance, severe disablement occupational allowance, treatment allowance, mobility supplement, comforts allowance, clothing allowance, age allowance and widow/widower/surviving civil partner's age allowance. Rent and children's allowances are also available on pensions for war widows, widowers and surviving civil partners.

ARMED FORCES COMPENSATION SCHEME
The armed forces compensation scheme (AFCS) became effective on 6 April 2005 and covers all regular (including Gurkhas) and reserve personnel whose injury, ill health or death is caused by service on or after 6 April 2005. Ex-members of the armed forces who served prior to this date or who are in receipt of any pension under the war pensions scheme will continue to receive their pension and any associated benefits in the normal way.

The AFCS provides compensation where service in the armed forces is the only or main cause of injury, illness or death. Compensation can also be paid in certain exceptional circumstances to off-duty personnel; for example, to victims of a terrorist attack targeted owing to their position in the armed forces. Under the terms of the scheme a lump sum is payable to service or ex-service personnel based on a 15-level tariff, graduated according to the seriousness of the condition. A guaranteed income payment (GIP), payable for life, is received by those who could be expected to experience a serious loss of earning capability. A survivors GIP (SGIP) will also be paid to surviving spouses, civil partners and unmarried partners who meet certain criteria. GIP is calculated by multiplying the pensionable pay of the service person by a factor that depends on the age at the person's last birthday. The younger the person, the higher the factor, because there are more years to normal retirement age.

DEPARTMENT FOR WORK AND PENSIONS BENEFITS
Most benefits are paid in addition to those in receipt of payments under the AFCS and the war pensions scheme, but may be affected by any supplementary allowances in payment. Any state pension for which a war widow, widower or surviving civil partner qualifies for on their own NI contribution record can be paid in addition to monies received under the war pensions scheme.

CLAIMS AND QUESTIONS
Further information on the war pensions scheme, the armed forces compensation scheme and the nearest Veterans' Welfare Office can be obtained from the Service Personnel and Veterans Agency by telephone (T 0800-169 2277, if calling from the UK or, if living overseas, T (+44) (125) 386-6043).

SERVICE PERSONNEL AND VETERANS AGENCY,
Norcross, Thornton-Cleveleys FY5 3WP
E veterans.help@spva.gsi.gov.uk W www.veterans-uk.info

TAX CREDITS

Tax credits are administered by HM Revenue and Customs (HMRC). They are based on an individual's or couple's household income and current circumstances. Adjustments can be made during the year to reflect changes in income and/or circumstances. Further information regarding the qualifying conditions for tax credits, how to claim and the rates payable is available online on the HMRC website (W www.hmrc.gov.uk/taxcredits).

WORKING TAX CREDIT

Working tax credit is a payment from the government to support people on low incomes. It may be claimed by:

- those aged 25 or over who work at least 30 hours a week
- both partners in a couple who are responsible for a child or young person, who work at least 16 hours a week
- those aged 16 or over who work at least 16 hours a week, who are responsible for a child or young person, or have a disability that puts them at a disadvantage of getting a job
- from April 2011, those aged 60 or over, who work at least 16 hours a week
- from April 2012, couples who are responsible for a child or young person, who must work at least 24 hours per week between them with one partner working at least 16 hours a week

The amount received depends on the circumstances and number of hours worked a week.

WORKING TAX CREDIT FOR INDIVIDUALS WITHOUT CHILDREN 2011–12

Annual Income/Status	Tax Credit per annum
£4,996*	
Single	–
Couple	–
Single adult with a disability	£4,575
£9,368†	
Single	£1,500
Couple	£3,450
Single adult with a disability	£4,155
£10,000	
Single	£1,240
Couple	£3,195
Single adult with a disability	£3,895
£15,000	
Single	–
Couple	£1,145
Single adult with a disability	£1,845

* An annual income of £4,996 represents the 2011–2012 income of an adult working 16 hours a week at the national minimum wage: six months at the 2010–2011 rate of £5.93 a hour and six months at the rate of £6.08 a hour (national minimum wage from October 2011)

† Income of £9,368 represents the income of an adult working 30 hours a week at the national minimum wage rate (*see* above for explanation). For families with an income of £10,000 or above, it is assumed that at least one individual works 30 hours. From April 2012, couples who are responsible for a child or a young person have to be working at least 24 hours a week between them, with one partner working at least 16 hours a week

CHILDCARE

In families with children where a lone parent works at least 16 hours a week or both partners in a couple work at least 16 hours a week (from April 2012 couples must work at least 24 hours a week between them, with one partner working at least 16 hours a week) or where one partner works and the other is disabled, an in-patient in hospital, or in prison, the family is entitled to the childcare element of working tax credit. This payment can contribute up to 70 per cent of childcare costs up to a maximum of £175 a week for one child and up to £300 a week for two or more children. Families can only claim if they use an approved or registered childcare provider.

CHILD TAX CREDIT

Child tax credit combines all income-related support for children and is paid direct to the main carer. The credit is made up of a main 'family' payment with additional payments for each extra child in the household, for children with a disability and an extra payment for children who are severely disabled. Child tax credit is available to households where:

- there is at least one dependant under 16
- there is at least one dependant between 16 and 20 who is in relevant education or training or is registered for work, education or training with an approved body

CHILD TAX CREDIT AND WORKING TAX CREDIT
2011–12 *(£ per annum)*

Annual Income	One Child		Two Children	
	No Childcare	Maximum Childcare	No Childcare	Maximum Childcare
0	3,100	3,100	5,660	5,660
4.996*	6,975	13,345	9,530	20,450
9,368*	6,555	12,925	9,115	20,035
10,000†	6,295	12,665	8,855	19,775
15,000	4,245	10,615	6,805	17,725
20,000	2,195	8,565	4,755	15,675
25,000	545	6,515	2,705	13,625
30,000	545	4,465	655	11,575
35,000	545	2,415	545	9,525
40,000	545	545	545	7,475
45,000	–	–	–	5,425
50,000	–	–	–	5,015
60,000	–	–	–	4,605
65,000	–	–	–	4,195
70,000	–	–	–	3,785

* At income levels of £4,996 and £9,368 awards are shown for lone parents. At an income level of £4,996 the award is shown for a lone parent working part-time (between 16 and 30 hours a week). At an income level of £9,368 the award is shown for a lone parent working 30 hours a week

† At an income level of £10,000 and above awards are shown for a couple who are responsible for a child or young person, with both partners working at least 16 hours a week

BENEFITS

The following is intended as a general guide to the benefits system. Conditions of entitlement and benefit rates change annually and all prospective claimants should check exact entitlements and rates of benefit directly with their local Jobcentre Plus office, pension centre or online (W www.direct.gov.uk). Leaflets relating to the various benefits and contribution conditions for different benefits are available from local Jobcentre Plus offices.

CONTRIBUTORY BENEFITS
Entitlement to contributory benefits depends on national insurance contribution conditions being satisfied either by the claimant or by someone on the claimant's behalf (depending on the kind of benefit). The class or classes of national insurance contribution relevant to each benefit are:

Jobseeker's allowance (contribution-based)	Class 1
Incapacity benefit	Class 1 or 2
Employment and Support Allowance (contributory)	Class 1 or 2
Widow's benefit and bereavement benefit	Class 1, 2 or 3
State pensions, categories A and B	Class 1, 2 or 3

The system of contribution conditions relates to yearly levels of earnings on which national insurance (NI) contributions have been paid.

JOBSEEKER'S ALLOWANCE
Jobseeker's allowance (JSA) replaced unemployment benefit and income support for unemployed people under state pension age from 7 October 1996. There are two routes of entitlement. Contribution-based JSA is paid at a personal rate (ie additional benefit for dependants is not paid) to those who have made sufficient NI contributions in two particular tax years. Savings and partner's earnings are not taken into account and payment can be made for up to six months. Rates of JSA correspond to income support rates.

Claims are made through Jobcentre Plus. A person wishing to claim JSA must generally be unemployed or working on average less than 16 hours a week, capable of work and available for any work which he or she can reasonably be expected to do, usually for at least 40 hours a week. The claimant must agree and sign a 'jobseeker's agreement', which will set out his or her plans to find work, and must actively seek work. If the claimant refuses work or training the benefit may be sanctioned for between one and 26 weeks.

A person will be sanctioned from JSA for up to 26 weeks if he or she has left a job voluntarily without just cause or through misconduct. In these circumstances, it may be possible to receive hardship payments, particularly where the claimant or the claimant's family is vulnerable, eg if sick or pregnant, or with children or caring responsibilities.

Weekly Rates from April 2011
Person aged 16–24	£53.45
Person aged 25 to state pension age*	£67.50

* Since October 2003 people aged between 60 and state pension age can choose to claim pension credits instead of JSA

INCAPACITY BENEFIT
Since 31 January 2011 people can no longer make claims for incapacity benefit. Those seeking incapacity benefit should now claim employment and support allowance instead. Those claiming incapacity benefit prior to 31 January 2011 will continue to receive it for as long as they qualify, although it is intended that remaining recipients of incapacity benefit will be moved to employment and support allowance by 2014. There are three rates of incapacity benefit:
- short-term lower rate for the first 28 weeks of sickness
- short-term higher rate from weeks 29 to 52
- long-term rate from week 53 onwards

The terminally ill and those entitled to the highest rate care component of disability living allowance are paid the long-term rate after 28 weeks. Incapacity benefit is taxable after 28 weeks.

An age addition payment may be available where incapacity for work commenced before the age of 45. Increases are also available for adult dependants caring for children.

The 'personal capability' assessment is the main test for incapacity benefit claims. Claimants are assessed on their ability to carry out a range of work-related activities and may also be required to attend a medical examination. Incapacity benefit claimants (excluding people who are severely disabled and those who are terminally ill) are invited back for work-focused interviews at intervals of not longer than three years. The interviews do not include medical tests, but if the claimant is due for a medical test around the same time, their local office will aim to schedule both together.

Weekly Rates from April 2011
Short-term incapacity benefit lower rate
Person under state pension age	£71.10
Person over state pension age	£90.45

Short-term incapacity benefit higher rate
Person under state pension age	£84.15
Person over state pension age	£94.25

Long-term incapacity benefit
Person under state pension age	£94.25
Person over state pension age	–

EMPLOYMENT AND SUPPORT ALLOWANCE
From 27 October 2008, employment and support allowance (ESA) replaced incapacity benefit and income support paid on the grounds of incapacity or disability. The benefit consists of two strands, contribution-based benefit and income-related benefit, so that people no longer need to make two claims for benefit in order to gain their full entitlement. Contributory ESA is available to those who have limited capability for work but cannot get statutory sick pay from their employer. Those over pensionable age are not entitled to ESA. Apart from those who qualify under the special provisions for people incapacitated in youth, entitlement to contributory ESA is based on a person's NI contribution record. In order to qualify for contributory ESA, two contribution conditions, based on the last three years before the tax year in which benefit is claimed, must be satisfied. The amount of contributory ESA payable may be reduced where the person receives more than a specified amount of occupational or personal pension. Contributory ESA is paid only in respect of the person claiming the benefit – there are no additional amounts for dependants.

At the outset, new claimants are paid a basic allowance (the same rate as jobseeker's allowance) for 13 weeks while their medical condition is assessed and a work capability assessment is conducted. Following the completion of the assessment phase those claimants capable of engaging in work-related activities will receive a work-related activity component on top of the basic rate. The work-related activity component can be subject to sanctions if the claimant does not engage in the conditionality requirements without good reason. The maximum sanction is equal to the value of the work-related activity component of the benefit.

Those with the most severe health conditions or disabilities will receive the support component, which is more than the work-related activity component. Claimants in receipt of the support component are not required to engage in work-related activities, although they can volunteer to do so or undertake permitted work if their condition allows.

Weekly Rates from April 2011

ESA plus work-related activity component	up to £94.25
ESA plus support component	up to £99.85

BEREAVEMENT BENEFITS

Bereavement benefits replaced widow's benefit on 9 April 2001. Those claiming widow's benefit before this date will continue to receive it under the old scheme for as long as they qualify. The new system provides bereavement benefits for widows, widowers and, from 5 December 2005, surviving civil partners (providing that their deceased spouse or civil partner paid NI contributions). The new system offers benefits in three forms:

- *Bereavement payment* – may be received by a man or woman who is under the state pension age at the time of their spouse or civil partner's death, or whose husband, wife or civil partner was not entitled to a category A retirement pension when he or she died. It is a single tax-free lump sum of £2,000 payable immediately on widowhood or loss of a civil partner
- *Widowed parent's allowance* – a taxable benefit payable to the surviving partner if he or she is entitled or treated as entitled to child benefit, or to a widow if she is expecting her husband's baby at the time of his death
- *Bereavement allowance* – a taxable weekly benefit paid for 52 weeks after the spouse or civil partner's death. If aged over 55 and under state pension age the full allowance is payable, if aged between 45 and 54 a percentage of the full rate is paid. A widow, widower or surviving civil partner may receive this allowance if his or her widowed parent's allowance ends before 52 weeks

It is not possible to receive widowed parent's allowance and bereavement allowance at the same time. Bereavement benefits and widow's benefit, in any form, cease upon remarriage or a new civil partnership or are suspended during a period of cohabitation as partners without being legally married or in a civil partnership.

Weekly Rates from April 2011

Bereavement payment (lump sum)	£2,000
Widowed parent's allowance (or widowed mother's allowance)	£100.70
Bereavement allowance (or widow's pension), full entitlement (aged 55 and over at time of spouse's or civil partner's death)	£100.70

Amount of bereavement allowance (or widow's pension) by age of widow/widower or surviving civil partner at spouse's or civil partner's death:

aged 54	£93.65
aged 53	£86.60
aged 52	£79.55
aged 51	£72.50
aged 50	£65.46
aged 49	£58.41
aged 48	£51.36
aged 47	£44.31
aged 46	£37.26
aged 45	£30.21

STATE PENSION: CATEGORIES A AND B

Category A pension is payable for life to men and women who reach state pension age, who satisfy the contributions conditions and who claim for it. Category B pension may be payable to married women, married men and civil partners who are not entitled to a basic state pension on their own NI contributions or whose own basic state pension entitlement is less than £61.20 a week in 2011–12. It is based on their wife's, husband's or civil partner's NI contributions and is payable when both members of the couple have reached state pension age. Married men and civil partners may only be able to qualify for a category B pension if their wife or civil partner was born on or after 6 April 1950. Category B pension is also payable to widows, widowers and surviving civil partners who are bereaved before state pension age if they were previously entitled to widowed parent's allowance or bereavement allowance based on their late spouse's or civil partner's NI contributions. If they were receiving widowed parent's allowance on reaching state pension age, they could qualify for a category B pension payable at the same rate as their widowed parent's allowance comprising a basic pension, plus, if applicable, the appropriate share of their late spouse's or late civil partner's additional state pension. If their widowed parent's allowance had stopped before they reached state pension age, or they had been getting bereavement allowance at any time before state pension age, their category B pension will consist of inheritable additional state pension only. No basic state pension is included, although they may qualify for a basic state pension or have their own basic state pension improved by substituting their late spouse's or late civil partner's NI records for their own.

Widows who are bereaved when over state pension age can qualify for a category B pension regardless of the age of their husband when he died. This is payable at the same rate as the basic state pension the widow's late husband was entitled to (or would have been entitled to) at the time of his death. It can also be paid to widowers and civil partners who are bereaved when over state pension age if their wife or civil partner had reached state pension age when they died. Widowers and surviving civil partners who reached state pension age on or after 6 April 2010 and bereaved when over state pension age can qualify for a category B pension regardless of the age of their wife or civil partner when they died.

Where a person is entitled to both a category A and category B pension then they can be combined to give a composite pension, but this cannot be more than the full rate pension. Where a person is entitled to more than one category A or category B pension then only one can be paid. In such cases the person can choose which one to get; if no choice is made, the most favourable one is paid.

A person may defer claiming their pension beyond state pension age. In doing so they may earn increments which will increase the weekly amount paid by 1 per cent per five weeks of deferral (equivalent to 10.4 per cent/year) when they claim their state pension. If a person delays claiming for at least 12 months they are given the option of a one-off taxable lump sum, instead of a pension increase, based on the weekly pension deferred, plus interest of at least 2 per cent above the Bank of England base rate. Historically, if a married man deferred his category A pension, his wife could not claim a category B pension on his contributions but could earn increments on her state pension during this time. Since 6 April 2010, a category B pension has been treated independently of the spouse's or partner's pension. It is possible to take a category B pension even if the spouse or partner has deferred theirs.

It is no longer possible to claim an increase on a state pension for another adult (known as adult dependency increase). Those who received the increase before April 2010 can keep receiving it until the conditions are no longer met or until 5 April 2020, whichever is first.

Provision for children is made through child tax credits. An age addition of 25p a week is payable with a state pension if a pensioner is aged 80 or over.

Since 1989 pensioners have been allowed to have unlimited earnings without affecting their state pension. *See also* Pensions.

Weekly Rates from April 2011

Category A or B pension for a single person	£102.15
Maximum category B pension (married women)	£61.20
Increase for adult dependant	£61.20
Age addition at age 80	£0.25

GRADUATED RETIREMENT BENEFIT

Graduated retirement benefit (GRB) is based on the amount of graduated NI contributions paid into the GRB scheme between April 1961 and April 1975; however, it is still paid in addition to any state pension to those who made the relevant contributions. A person will receive graduated retirement benefit based on their own contributions, even if not entitled to a basic state pension. Widows, widowers and surviving civil partners may inherit half of their deceased spouse's or civil partner's entitlement, but none that the deceased spouse or civil partner may have been eligible for from a former spouse or civil partner. If a person defers making a claim beyond state pension age, they may earn an increase or a one-off lump sum payment in respect of their deferred graduated retirement benefit; calculated in the same way as for category A or B state pension.

NON-CONTRIBUTORY BENEFITS

These benefits are paid from general taxation and are not dependent on NI contributions.

JOBSEEKER'S ALLOWANCE (INCOME-BASED)

Those who do not qualify for contribution-based jobseeker's allowance (JSA), those who have exhausted their entitlement to contribution-based JSA or those for whom contribution-based JSA provides insufficient income may qualify for income-based JSA. The amount paid depends on age, whether they are single or a couple, number of dependants and amount of income and savings. Income-based JSA comprises three parts:

- a personal allowance for the jobseeker and his/her partner*
- premiums for people with special needs
- amounts for housing costs

* Since April 2003, child dependants have been provided for through the child tax credit system

The rules of entitlement are the same as for contribution-based JSA.

If one person in a couple was born after 28 October 1957 and neither person in the couple has responsibility for a child or children, then the couple will have to make a joint claim for JSA if they wish to receive income-based JSA.

Weekly Rates from April 2011

Person aged 16–24	£53.45
Person aged 25 to state pension age	£67.50
Couple with one or both under 18*	£53.45
Couple aged 18 to state pension age	£105.95
Lone parent aged under 18	£53.45
Lone parent aged 18 to state pension age	£67.50
* depending on circumstances	

MATERNITY ALLOWANCE

Maternity allowance (MA) is a benefit available for pregnant women who cannot get statutory maternity pay (SMP) from their employer or have been employed/self-employed during or close to their pregnancy. In order to qualify for payment, a woman must have been employed and/or self-employed for at least 26 weeks in the 66-week period up to and including the week before the baby is due (test period). These weeks do not have to be in a row and any part weeks worked will count towards the 26 weeks. She must also have an average weekly earning of at least £30 (maternity allowance threshold) over any 13 weeks of the woman's choice within the test period.

Self-employed women who pay class 2 NI contributions or who hold a small earnings exception certificate are deemed to have enough earnings to qualify for MA.

A woman can choose to start receiving MA from the 11th week before the week in which the baby is due (if she stops work before then) up to the day following the day of birth. The exact date MA starts will depend on when the woman stops work to have her baby or if the baby is born before she stops work. However, where the woman is absent from work wholly or partly due to her pregnancy in the four weeks before the week the baby is due to be born, MA will start the day following the first day of absence from work. MA is paid for a maximum of 39 weeks.

The woman may be entitled to get extra payments for her husband, civil partner or someone else who looks after her children.

Weekly Rate from April 2011

Standard rate	£128.73 or 90 per cent of the woman's average weekly earnings if less than £128.73

CHILD BENEFIT

Child benefit is payable for virtually all children aged under 16 and for those aged 16 and 17 if they are in relevant education or training or are registered for work, education or training with an approved body.

Weekly Rates from April 2011

Eldest/only child	£20.30
Each subsequent child	£13.40

GUARDIAN'S ALLOWANCE

Guardian's allowance is payable to a person who is bringing up a child or young person because the child's parents have died, or in some circumstances, where only one parent has died. To receive the allowance the person must be in receipt of child benefit for the child or young person, although they do not have to be the child's legal guardian.

Weekly Rate (in addition to child benefit) from April 2011

Each child	£14.75

CARER'S ALLOWANCE

Carer's allowance (CA) is a benefit payable to people who spend at least 35 hours a week caring for a severely disabled person. To qualify for CA a person must be caring for someone in receipt of one of the following benefits:

- attendance allowance
- disability living allowance care component at the middle or higher rate
- constant attendance allowance, paid at not less than the normal maximum rate with an industrial injuries disablement payment or basic (full-day) rate, under the industrial injuries or war pension schemes.

Weekly Rate from April 2011

Carer's allowance	£55.55

SEVERE DISABLEMENT ALLOWANCE

Since April 2001 severe disablement allowance (SDA) has not been available to new claimants. Those claiming SDA before that date will continue to receive it for as long as they qualify.

Weekly Rates from April 2011

Basic rate	£62.95
Age related addition*:	
Under 40	£13.80
40–49	£7.10
50–59	£5.60

* The age addition applies to the age when incapacity began

ATTENDANCE ALLOWANCE

This may be payable to people aged 65 or over who need help with personal care because they are physically or mentally disabled, and who have needed help for a period of at least six months. Attendance allowance has two rates: the lower rate is for day or night care, and the higher rate is for day and night care. People not expected to live for more than six months because of a progressive disease can receive the highest rate of attendance allowance straight away.

Weekly Rates from April 2011

Higher rate	£73.60
Lower rate	£49.30

DISABILITY LIVING ALLOWANCE

This may be payable to people aged under 65 who have had personal care and/or mobility needs because of an illness or disability for a period of at least three months and are likely to have those needs for a further six months or more. The allowance has two components: the care component, which has three rates, and the mobility component, which has two rates. The rates depend on the care and mobility needs of the claimant. People not expected to live for more than six months because of a progressive disease will automatically receive the highest rate of the care component.

Weekly Rates from April 2011

Care component	
Higher rate	£73.60
Middle rate	£49.30
Lowest rate	£19.55
Mobility component	
Higher rate	£51.40
Lower rate	£19.55

STATE PENSION FOR PEOPLE AGED 80 AND OVER

A state pension, also referred to as category D pension, is provided for people aged 80 and over if they are not entitled to another category of pension or are entitled to a state pension that is less than £58.50 a week. The person must also live in Great Britain and have done so for a period of ten years or more in any continuous 20-year period since their 60th birthday.

Weekly Rate from April 2010

Single person	£58.50

INCOME SUPPORT

Broadly speaking income support is a benefit for those between age 16 and the age they can receive pension credit, whose income is below a certain level, who work on average less than 16 hours a week and who are:

- bringing up children alone
- registered sick or disabled
- a student who is also a lone parent or disabled
- caring for someone who is sick or elderly

Income support is not payable if the claimant, or claimant and partner, have capital or savings in excess of £16,000 – and deductions are made for capital and savings in excess of £6,000. For people permanently in residential care and nursing homes deductions apply for capital in excess of £10,000.

Sums payable depend on fixed allowances laid down by law for people in different circumstances. If both partners are eligible for income support, either may claim it for the couple. People receiving income support may be able to receive housing benefit, help with mortgage or home loan interest and help with healthcare. They may also be eligible for help with exceptional expenses from the Social Fund. Special rates may apply to some people living in residential care or nursing homes.

INCOME SUPPORT PREMIUMS

Income support premiums are extra weekly payments for those with additional needs. People qualifying for more than one premium will normally only receive the highest single premium for which they qualify. However, family premium, disabled child premium, severe disability premium and carer premium are payable in addition to other premiums.

Child tax credit replaced premiums for people with children for all new income support claims from 6 April

2004. People with children who were already in receipt of income support in April 2004 and have not claimed child tax credit may qualify for:

- the family premium if they have at least one child
- the disabled child premium if they have a child who receives disability living allowance or is registered blind
- the enhanced disability child premium if they have a child in receipt of the higher rate disability living allowance care component

Carers may qualify for:

- the carer premium if they or their partner are in receipt of carer's allowance

Long-term sick or disabled people may qualify for:

- the disability premium if they or their partner are receiving certain benefits because they are disabled or cannot work; are registered blind; or if the claimant has been incapable of work or receiving statutory sick pay for at least 364 days (196 days if the person is terminally ill), including periods of incapacity separated by eight weeks or less
- the severe disability premium if the person lives alone and receives the middle or higher rate of disability living allowance care component and no one receives carer's allowance for caring for that person
- the enhanced disability premium if the person is in receipt of the higher rate disability living allowance care component

People with a partner aged over 60 may qualify for:

- the pensioner premium

WEEKLY RATES OF INCOME SUPPORT
from April 2011

Single person

aged 16–24	£53.45
aged 25+	£67.50
aged under 18 and a single parent	£53.45
aged 18+ and a single parent	£67.50

Couples

Both under 18	£53.45
Both under 18, in certain circumstances	£80.75
One under 18, one aged 18–24	£53.45
One under 18, one aged 25+	£67.50
Both aged 18+	£105.95

Premiums

Carer premium	£31.00
Severe disability premium	£55.30
Enhanced disability premium	
Single person	£14.05
Couples	£20.25
Pensioner premium (couple)	£103.75

PENSION CREDIT

Pension credit was introduced on 6 October 2003 and replaced income support for those aged 60 and over. Between April 2010 and April 2020 the pension credit qualifying age is increasing from 60 to 65 alongside the increase in women's state pension age.

There are two elements to pension credit:

THE GUARANTEE CREDIT

The guarantee credit guarantees a minimum income of £137.75 for single people and £209.70 for couples, with additional elements for people who have:

- eligible housing costs
- severe disabilities
- caring responsibilities

Income from state pension, private pensions, earnings, working tax credit and certain benefits are taken into account when calculating the pension credit. For savings and capital in excess of £10,000, £1 for every £500 or part of £500 held is taken into account as income when working out entitlement to pension credit.

People receiving the guarantee credit element of pension credit will be able to receive housing benefit, council tax benefit and help with healthcare costs.

Weekly Rates from April 2011

Additional amount for severe disability

Single person	£55.30
Couple (one qualifies)	£55.30
Couple (both qualify)	£110.60
Additional amount for carers	£31.00

THE SAVINGS CREDIT

Single people aged 65 or over (and couples where one member is 65 or over) may be entitled to a savings credit which provides additional support for pensioners who have made modest provision towards their retirement. The savings credit is calculated by taking into account any qualifying income above the savings credit threshold. For 2011–12 the threshold is £103.15 for single people and £164.55 for couples. The savings credit gives pensioners a cash addition calculated at 60p for every pound of qualifying income they have between the savings credit threshold and the guarantee credit. After this, the maximum savings credit will be reduced by 40p for every pound of income above the guarantee level. The maximum savings credit is £20.52 per week (£27.09 a week for couples).

Income that qualifies towards the savings credit includes state pensions, earnings, second pensions and income taken into account from capital above £10,000.

Some people will be entitled to the guarantee credit, some to the savings credit and some to both.

Where only the savings credit is in payment, people need to claim standard housing benefit or council tax benefit. Although local authorities take any savings credit into account in the housing benefit or council tax benefit assessment, for people aged 65 and over housing benefit or council tax benefit is enhanced to ensure that gains in pension credit are not depleted.

HOUSING BENEFIT

Housing benefit is designed to help people with rent (including rent for accommodation in guesthouses, lodgings or hostels). It does not cover mortgage payments. The amount of benefit paid depends on:

- the income of the claimant, and partner if there is one, including earned income, unearned income (any other income including some other benefits) and savings
- number of dependants
- certain extra needs of the claimant, partner or any dependants
- number and gross income of people sharing the home who are not dependent on the claimant
- how much rent is paid

Housing benefit is not payable if the claimant, or claimant and partner, have savings in excess of £16,000. The amount of benefit is affected if savings held exceed £6,000 (£10,000 for people living in residential care and nursing homes). Housing benefit is not paid for meals, fuel or certain service charges that may be included in the rent. Deductions are also made for most non-dependants who live in the same accommodation as the claimant (and their partner). If the claimant is living with a partner or civil partner there can only be one claim.

The maximum amount of benefit (which is not necessarily the same as the amount of rent paid) may be paid where the claimant is in receipt of income support, income-based jobseeker's allowance, the guarantee element of pension credit or where the claimant's income is less than the amount allowed for their needs. Any income over that allowed for their needs will mean that their benefit is reduced.

LOCAL HOUSING ALLOWANCE

Local housing allowance (LHA), which was rolled out nationally from 7 April 2008, is a way of calculating the rent element of housing benefit based on the area in which a person lives and household size. It affects people in the deregulated private rented sector who make a new claim for housing benefit or existing recipients who move address. LHA ensures that tenants in similar circumstances in the same area receive the same amount of financial support for their housing costs. It does not affect the way a person's income or capital is taken into account. LHA is paid to the tenant rather than the landlord in most circumstances. From 1 April 2011, the rates for LHA were reduced across England and the maximum £15 weekly excess was removed. A weekly limit on payments is now in place so LHA does not exceed:

- £250 for a one bedroom property
- £290 for a two bedroom property
- £340 for a three bedroom property
- £400 for a four bedroom property

COUNCIL TAX BENEFIT

Nearly all the rules that apply to housing benefit apply to council tax benefit, which helps people on low incomes to pay council tax bills. The amount payable depends on how much council tax is paid and who lives with the claimant. The benefit may be available to those receiving income support, income-based jobseeker's allowance, the guarantee element of pension credit or to those whose income is less than that allowed for their needs. Any income over that allowed for their needs will mean that their council tax benefit is reduced. Deductions are made for non-dependants.

The maximum amount that is payable for those living in properties in council tax bands A to E is 100 per cent of the claimant's council tax liability. This also applies to those living in properties in bands F to H who were in receipt of the benefit at 31 March 1998 if they have remained in the same property.

If a person shares a home with one or more adults (not their partner) who are on a low income, it may be possible to claim a second adult rebate. Those who are entitled to both council tax benefit and second adult rebate will be awarded whichever is the greater. Second adult rebate may be claimed by those not in receipt of or eligible for council tax benefit.

THE SOCIAL FUND

REGULATED PAYMENTS

Sure Start Maternity Grant

Sure start maternity grant (SSMG) is a one-off payment of £500 to help people on low incomes pay for essential items for new babies that are expected, born, adopted, the subject of a parental order (following a surrogate birth) or, in certain circumstances, the subject of a residency order. SSMG can be claimed any time from within 11 weeks of the expected birth and up to three months after the birth, adoption or date of parental or residency order. Those eligible are people in receipt of income support, income-based jobseeker's allowance, pension credit, child tax credit at a rate higher than the family element or working tax credit where a disability or severe disability element is in payment. Since 11 April 2011, new rules have been applied for babies due, born or adopted on this date. These are that SSMG is only available if there are no other children under 16 in the family or in the case of a dependent child's new baby, SSMG is only available if the dependent is under the age of 20 and has no other children.

Funeral Payments

Payable to help cover the necessary cost of burial or cremation, a new burial plot with an exclusive right of burial (where burial is chosen), certain other expenses, and up to £700 for any other funeral expenses, such as the funeral director's fees, the coffin or flowers. Those eligible are people receiving income support, income-based jobseeker's allowance, pension credit, child tax credit at a higher rate than the family element, working tax credit where a disability or severe disability element is in payment, council tax benefit or housing benefit who have good reason for taking responsibility for the funeral expenses. These payments are recoverable from any estate of the deceased.

Cold Weather Payments

A payment of £25.00 per seven day period between 1 November and 31 March when the average temperature is recorded at or forecast to be 0°C or below over seven consecutive days in the qualifying person's area. Payments are made to people on pension credit or child tax credit with a disability element, those on income support whose benefit includes a pensioner or disability premium, and those on income-based jobseeker's allowance or employment and support allowance who have a child who is disabled or under the age of five. Payments are made automatically and do not have to be repaid.

Winter Fuel Payments

For 2011–12 the winter fuel payment has been decreased to £200 for households with someone aged 60–79 and down to £300 for households with someone aged 80 or over. The rate paid is based on the person's age and circumstances in the 'qualifying week' between 19 and 25 September 2011. The majority of eligible people are paid automatically before Christmas, although a few need to claim. Payments do not have to be repaid.

Christmas Bonus

The Christmas bonus is a one-off tax-free £10 payment made before Christmas to those people in receipt of a qualifying benefit in the qualifying week.

DISCRETIONARY PAYMENTS

Community Care Grants

These are intended to help people in receipt of income support, income-based jobseeker's allowance or employment and support allowance, pension credit, or payments on account of such benefits (or those likely to receive these benefits within the next six weeks because they are leaving residential or institutional accommodation) to live as independently as possible in the community; ease exceptional pressures on families; care for a prisoner or young offender released on temporary licence; help people set up home as part of a resettlement programme and/or assist with certain travelling expenses. They do not have to be repaid.

Budgeting Loans
These are interest-free loans to people who have been receiving income support, income-based jobseeker's allowance or employment and support allowance, pension credit or payments on account of such benefits for at least 26 weeks, for intermittent expenses that may be difficult to budget for.

Crisis Loans
These are interest-free loans to anyone aged 16 or over, whether receiving benefits or not, who is without resources in an emergency or due to a disaster, where there is no other means of preventing serious damage or serious risk to their or their family members' health or safety.

SAVINGS
Savings over £500 (£1,000 for people aged 60 or over) are taken into account for community care grants and savings of £1,000 (£2,000 for people aged 60 or over) are taken into account for budgeting loans. All savings are taken into account for crisis loans. Savings are not taken into account for sure start maternity grant, funeral payments, cold weather payments, winter fuel payments or the Christmas bonus.

INDUSTRIAL INJURIES AND DISABLEMENT BENEFITS
The Industrial Injuries Scheme, administered under the Social Security Contributions and Benefits Act 1992, provides a range of benefits designed to compensate for disablement resulting from an industrial accident (ie an accident arising out of and in the course of an earner's employment) or from a prescribed disease due to the nature of a person's employment. Those who are self-employed are not covered by this scheme.

INDUSTRIAL INJURIES DISABLEMENT BENEFIT
A person may be able to claim industrial injuries disablement benefit if they are ill or disabled due to an accident or incident that happened at work or in connection with work in England, Scotland or Wales. The amount of benefit awarded depends on the person's age and the degree of disability as assessed by a doctor.

The benefit is payable whether the person works or not and those who are incapable of work are entitled to draw other benefits, such as statutory sick pay or incapacity benefit, in addition to industrial injuries disablement benefit. It may also be possible to claim the following allowances:

- reduced earnings allowance for those who are unable to return to their regular work or work of the same standard and who had their accident (or whose disease started) before 1 October 1990. At state pension age this is converted to retirement allowance
- constant attendance allowance for those with a disablement of 100 per cent who need constant care. There are four rates of allowance depending on how much care the person needs
- exceptionally severe disablement allowance can be claimed in addition to constant care attendance allowance at one of the higher rates for those who need constant care permanently

Weekly Rates of Benefit from April 2011

Degree of disablement	Aged 18+ or with dependants	Aged under 18 with no dependants
100 per cent	£150.30	£92.10
90	£135.27	£82.89
80	£120.24	£73.68
70	£105.21	£64.47
60	£90.18	£55.26
50	£75.15	£46.05
40	£60.12	£36.84
30	£45.09	£27.63
20	£30.06	£18.42
Unemployability supplement		£92.90
Reduced earnings allowance (maximum)		£60.12
Retirement allowance (maximum)		£15.03
Constant attendance allowance (normal maximum rate)		£60.20
Exceptionally severe disablement allowance		£60.20

OTHER BENEFITS
People who are disabled because of an accident or disease that was the result of work that they did before 5 July 1948 are not entitled to industrial injuries disablement benefit. They may, however, be entitled to payment under the Workmen's Compensation Scheme or the Pneumoconiosis, Byssinosis and Miscellaneous Diseases Benefit Scheme. People who suffer from certain industrial diseases caused by dust, or their dependants, can make a claim for an additional payment under the Pneumoconiosis Act 1979 if they are unable to get damages from the employer who caused or contributed to the disease.

Diffuse Mesothelioma Payment
Since 1 October 2008 any person suffering from the asbestos-related disease, diffuse mesothelioma, who is unable to make a claim under the Pneumoconiosis Act 1979, has not received payment in respect of the disease from an employer, via a civil claim or elsewhere, and are not entitled to compensation from a MoD scheme, can claim a one-off lump sum payment. The scheme covers people whose exposure to asbestos occurred in the UK and was not as a result of their work as an employee (ie they lived near a factory using asbestos). The amount paid depends on the age of the person when the disease was diagnosed, or the date of the claim if the diagnosis date is not known. The current rate is £77,506 for those aged 37 and under to £12,040 for persons aged 77 and over. From 1 October 2009 claims must be received within 12 months of the date of diagnosis. If the sufferer has died, their dependants may be able to claim, but must do so within 12 months of the date of death.

CLAIMS AND QUESTIONS
Entitlement to benefit and regulated Social Fund payments is determined by a decision maker on behalf of the Secretary of State for the Department for Work and Pensions. A claimant who is dissatisfied with that decision can ask for an explanation. He or she can dispute the decision by applying to have it revised or, in particular circumstances, superseded. The claimant can go to the Appeals Service where the case will be heard by an independent tribunal. There is a further right of appeal to a social security commissioner against the tribunal's decision but this is on a point of law only and leave to appeal must first be obtained.

Decisions on claims and applications for housing benefit and council tax benefit are made by local authorities. The explanation, dispute and appeals process is the same as for other benefits.

All decisions on applications to the discretionary Social Fund are made by Jobcentre Plus Social Fund decision makers. Applicants can ask for a review of the decision within 28 days of the date on the decision letter. The Social Fund review officer will review the case and there is a further right of review by an independent Social Fund inspector.

EMPLOYER PAYMENTS

STATUTORY MATERNITY PAY

Employers pay statutory maternity pay (SMP) to pregnant women who have been employed by them full or part-time continuously for at least 26 weeks into the 15th week before the week the baby is due, and whose earnings on average at least equal the lower earnings limit applied to NI contributions (£102 a week from April 2011). SMP can be paid for a maximum period of up to 39 weeks. If the qualifying conditions are met women will receive a payment of 90 per cent of their average earnings for the first six weeks, followed by 33 weeks at £128.73 or 90 per cent of the woman's average weekly earnings if this is less than £128.73. SMP can be paid, at the earliest, 11 weeks before the week in which the baby is due, up to the day following the birth. Women can decide when they wish their maternity leave and pay to start and can work until the baby is born. However, where the woman is absent from work wholly or partly due to her pregnancy in the four weeks before the week the baby is due to be born, SMP will start the day following the first day of absence from work.

Employers are reimbursed for 92 per cent of the SMP they pay. Small employers with annual gross NI payments of £45,000 or less recover 103 per cent of the SMP paid out.

STATUTORY PATERNITY PAY

Employers pay statutory paternity pay (SPP) to employees who are taking leave when a child is born or placed for adoption. To qualify the employee must:
• have responsibility for the child's upbringing
• be the biological father of the child (or the child's adopter), or the spouse/civil partner/partner of the mother or adopter
• have been employed by the same employer for at least 26 weeks ending with the 15th week before the baby is due (or the week in which the adopter is notified of having been matched with a child)
• continue working for the employer up to the child's birth (or placement for adoption)
• have earnings on average at least equal to the lower earnings limit applied to NI contributions (£102 a week from April 2011)

Employees who meet these conditions receive payment of £128.73 or 90 per cent of the employee's average weekly earnings if this is less than £128.73. The employee can choose to be paid for one or two consecutive weeks. The earliest the SPP period can begin is the date of the child's birth or placement for adoption. The SPP period must be completed within eight weeks of that date. SPP is not payable for any week in which the employee works. Employers are reimbursed in the same way as for statutory maternity pay.

ADDITIONAL PATERNITY LEAVE

Regulations introduced on 6 April 2010 give parents greater flexibility in how they use their maternity and paternity provisions. For births from 3 April 2011, additional paternity leave (APL) entitles eligible fathers to take up to 26 weeks' additional paternity leave, allowing for up to a total of one year's leave to be shared between the couple. APL entitlement requires the mother to have returned to work; it must also be taken between 20 weeks and one year after the child is born. APL may be paid if taken during the mother's statutory maternity pay period or maternity allowance period.

The APL entitlement will also apply to husbands, partners or civil partners who are not the child's father but expect to have the main responsibility (apart from the mother) for the child's upbringing.

Statutory paternity pay (see above) is due to be renamed ordinary paternity pay (OPL) but otherwise remains unchanged.

STATUTORY ADOPTION PAY

Employers pay statutory adoption pay (SAP) to employees taking adoption leave from their employers. To qualify for SAP the employee must:
• be newly matched with a child by an adoption agency
• have been employed by the same employer for at least 26 weeks ending the week in which they have been notified of being matched with a child
• have earnings at least equal to the lower earnings limit applied to NI contributions (£102 a week from April 2011)

Employees who meet these conditions receive payment of £128.73 or 90 per cent of their average weekly earnings if this is less than £128.73 for up to 39 weeks. The earliest SAP can be paid from is two weeks before the expected date of placement; the latest it can start is the date of the child's placement. Where a couple adopt a child, only one of them may receive SAP, the other may be able to receive statutory paternity pay (SPP) if they meet the eligibility criteria. Employers are reimbursed in the same way as for statutory maternity pay.

The additional paternity leave entitlement (see above) will also apply to adoptions where adoptive parents are notified of a match on or after 3 April 2011.

STATUTORY SICK PAY

Employers pay statutory sick pay (SSP) for up to a maximum of 28 weeks to any employee incapable of work for four or more consecutive days. Employees must have done some work under their contract of service and have average weekly earnings of at least £102 from April 2011. SSP is a daily payment and is usually paid for the days that an employee would normally work, these days are known as qualifying days. SSP is not paid for the first three qualifying days in a period of sickness. SSP is paid at £81.60 per week and is subject to PAYE and NI contributions. Employees who cannot obtain SSP may be able to claim incapacity benefit. Employers may be able to recover some SSP costs.

THE WATER INDUSTRY

In the UK, the water industry provides services to over 54 million consumers each day and has an annual turnover of around £10bn. It supplies around 17 billion litres of water a day to domestic and commercial customers and collects and treats more than 16 billion litres of wastewater a day. It also manages assets that include around 1,400 water treatment and 9,350 wastewater treatment works, 550 impounding reservoirs, over 6,500 service reservoirs/water towers and 800,000km of water mains and sewers.

Water services in England and Wales are provided by private companies. In Scotland and Northern Ireland there are single authorities, Scottish Water and Northern Ireland Water, that are publicly owned companies answerable to their respective governments. In drinking water quality tests carried out in 2010, the water industry in England and Wales achieved 99.96 per cent compliance with the standards required by the EU Drinking Water Directive; Scotland achieved 99.78 per cent and Northern Ireland 99.69 per cent.

Water UK is the industry association that represents all UK water and wastewater service suppliers at national and European level and is funded directly by its members, who are the service suppliers for England, Scotland, Wales and Northern Ireland; every member has a seat on the Water UK Council.

WATER UK, 1 Queen Anne's Gate, London SW1H 9BT
T 020-7344 1844 W www.water.org.uk
Chief Executive, Pamela Taylor

ENGLAND AND WALES

In England and Wales, the Secretary of State for Environment, Food and Rural Affairs and the National Assembly for Wales have overall responsibility for water policy and oversee environmental standards for the water industry.

The statutory consumer representative body for water services is the Consumer Council for Water.

CONSUMER COUNCIL FOR WATER, 1st Floor, Victoria Square House, Victoria Square, Birmingham B2 4AJ
T 0845-039 2837 W www.ccwater.org.uk

REGULATORY BODIES

The Water Services Regulation Authority (OFWAT) was established in 1989 when the water and sewerage industry in England and Wales was privatised. Its statutory role and duties are laid out under the Water Industry Act 1991 and it is the independent economic regulator of the water and sewerage companies in England and Wales. Overall responsibility for water policy and overseeing environmental standards for the water industry lies with DEFRA and the Welsh government. OFWAT's main duties are to ensure that the companies can finance and carry out their statutory functions and to protect the interests of water customers. OFWAT is a non-ministerial government department headed by a board following a change in legislation introduced by the Water Act 2003.

Under the Competition Act 1998, from 1 March 2000 the Competition Appeal Tribunal has heard appeals against the regulator's decisions regarding anti-competitive agreements and abuse of a dominant position in the marketplace. The Water Act 2003 placed a new duty on OFWAT to contribute to the achievement of sustainable development.

The Environment Agency has statutory duties and powers in relation to water resources, pollution control, flood defence, fisheries, recreation, conservation and navigation in England and Wales. It is also responsible for issuing permits, licences, consents and registrations such as industrial licences to extract water and fishing licences.

The Drinking Water Inspectorate (DWI) is the drinking water quality regulator for England and Wales, responsible for assessing the quality of the drinking water supplied by the water companies and investigating any incidents affecting drinking water quality, initiating prosecution where necessary. The DWI also provides scientific advice on drinking water policy issues to DEFRA and the Welsh government.

OFWAT, Centre City Tower, 7 Hill Street, Birmingham B5 4UA
T 0121-644 7500 E enquiries@ofwat.gsi.gov.uk
W www.ofwat.gov.uk
Chair, Philip Fletcher, CBE
Chief Executive, Regina Finn

METHODS OF CHARGING

In England and Wales, most domestic customers still pay for domestic water supply and sewerage services through charges based on the rateable value of their property. OFWAT estimates that the proportion of household customers in England and Wales to have metered supplies will increase from 41.5 per cent in 2011–12 to around 50 per cent in 2014–15. Nearly all non-household customers are charged according to consumption.

Under the Water Industry Act 1999, water companies can continue basing their charges on the old rateable value of the property. Domestic customers can continue paying on an unmeasured basis unless they choose to pay according to consumption. After having a meter installed (which is free of charge), a customer can revert to unmeasured charging within 12 months. However, water companies may charge by meter for new homes, or homes where there is a high discretionary use of water. Domestic, school and hospital customers cannot be disconnected for non-payment.

Price limits for the period 2010–15 were set by OFWAT in November 2009.

On average, prices for 2011–12 will increase by an average of 4.6 per cent. This takes into account a reduction in the average bill of 0.1 per cent before inflation of 4.7 per cent. Average household water bills in 2011–12 range from £91 for Portsmouth Water to £218 for Wessex Water; the overall average is £174. The average household sewerage bill costs £182, ranging from £123 for Thames Water up to £300 for South West Water.

WATER SUPPLY AND CONSUMPTION 2009–10 (ENGLAND AND WALES)

	Supply		Consumption			
	Distribution Input (megalitres/day)	Total Leakage (megalitres/day)	Household (litres/head/day) Unmetered	Metered	Non-household (litres/property/day) Unmetered	Metered
WATER AND SEWERAGE COMPANIES						
Anglian	1,145.4	210	178.7	138.8	626.2	2,691.5
Dwr Cymru	816.3	195	168.6	127.4	503.6	1,916.5
Northumbrian (NE)	710.0	155	166.3	151.5	810.0	3,220.2
Northumbrian (Essex & Suffolk)	455.1	67	173.7	159.4	645.0	2,462.7
Severn Trent	1,826.9	495	142.1	122.6	852.1	1,986.9
South West	421.1	82	177.1	133.6	1,156.0	1,411.4
Southern	560.4	95	157.0	138.1	806.9	2,481.8
Thames	2,574.6	670	195.7	151.5	650.9	2,836.4
United Utilities	1,785.0	460	151.0	121.6	714.5	2,490.2
Wessex	344.0	74	169.5	142.5	3,347.4	1,822.8
Yorkshire	1,284.7	295	173.3	125.9	175.8	2,364.3
Total	11,923.2	2,800	—	—	—	—
Average	—	—	167.3	135.0	778.5	2,358.5
WATER ONLY COMPANIES						
Total	2,670.4	480	—	—	—	—
Average	—	—	182.0	150.4	951.8	2,373.1

Source: OFWAT

SCOTLAND

Overall responsibility for national water policy in Scotland rests with the Scottish ministers. Until the Local Government (Scotland) Act 1994, water supply and sewerage services were local authority responsibilities. The Central Scotland Water Development Board had the function of developing new sources of water supply for the purpose of providing water in bulk to water authorities whose limits of supply were within the board's area. Under the act, three new public water authorities, covering the north, east and west of Scotland respectively, took over the provision of water and sewerage services from April 1996. The Central Scotland Water Development Board was then abolished. The act also established the Scottish Water and Sewerage Customers Council, representing consumer interests. It monitored the performance of the authorities; approved charges schemes; investigated complaints; and advised the secretary of state. The Water Industry Act 1999, whose Scottish provisions were accepted by the Scottish government, abolished the Scottish Water and Sewerage Customers Council and replaced it in November 1999 with a Water Industry Commissioner.

The Water Industry (Scotland) Act 2002 resulted from the Scottish government's proposal that a single authority was better placed than three separate authorities to harmonise changes across the Scottish water industry. In 2002 the three existing water authorities (East of Scotland Water, North of Scotland Water and West of Scotland Water) merged to form Scottish Water. Scottish Water, which serves around 2.4 million households, is a public sector company, structured and managed like a private company, but remains answerable to the Scottish parliament. Scottish Water is regulated by the Water Industry Commission for Scotland (established under the Water Services (Scotland) Act 2005), the Scottish Environment Protection Agency (SEPA) and the Drinking Water Quality Regulator for Scotland. The Water Industry Commissioner is responsible for regulating all aspects of economic and customer service performance, including water and sewerage charges. SEPA, created under the Environment Act 1995, is responsible for environmental issues, including controlling pollution and promoting the cleanliness of Scotland's rivers, lochs and coastal waters. Waterwatch Scotland is the consumer representative body for the water industry and the national complaints handling authority for water customers in Scotland.

METHODS OF CHARGING

Scottish Water sets charges for domestic and non-domestic water and sewerage provision through charges schemes which are regulated by the Water Industry Commission for Scotland. In February 2004 the harmonisation of all household charges across the country was completed following the merger of the separate authorities under Scottish Water. In November 2009 the Water Industry Commission for Scotland published *The Strategic Review of Charges 2010–2015*, stating that annual price rises would be kept at 5 per cent below the rate of inflation during this five-year period and for the year 2011–12 there would be a freeze on charges. The average household bill for 2011–12 therefore remains around £324.

SCOTTISH ENVIRONMENT PROTECTION

AGENCY, Erskine Court, Castle Business Park, Stirling FK9 4TR T 01786-457700 W www.sepa.org.uk

SCOTTISH WATER, PO Box 8855, Edinburgh EH10 6YQ T 0845-601 8855 W www.scottishwater.co.uk

WATER INDUSTRY COMMISSION FOR SCOTLAND, First Floor, Moray House, Forthside Way, Stirling FK8 1QZ T 01786-430200 W www.watercommission.co.uk

WATERWATCH SCOTLAND, Corporate Office, Forrester Lodge, Inglewood, Alloa FK10 2HU **T** 0845-850 3344 **W** www.waterwatchscotland.org

NORTHERN IRELAND

Formerly an executive agency of the Department for Regional Development, Northern Ireland Water is a government-owned company but with substantial independence from government. Northern Ireland Water was set up as a result of government reform of water and sewerage services in April 2007. It is responsible for policy and coordination with regard to the supply, distribution and cleanliness of water, and the provision and maintenance of sewerage services. The Northern Ireland Authority for Utility Regulation (known as the Utility Regulator) is responsible for regulating the water services provided by Northern Ireland Water. The Drinking Water Inspectorate, a unit in the Northern Ireland Environment Agency (NIEA), regulates drinking water quality. Another NIEA unit, the Water Management Unit, has responsibility for the protection of the aquatic environment. The Consumer Council for Northern Ireland is the consumer representative body for water services.

METHODS OF CHARGING
The water and sewerage used by domestic customers in Northern Ireland is currently paid for by the Department for Regional Development (DRD), a system which will continue during 2011–2012. In March 2010, the Northern Ireland Assembly passed the Water and Sewerage Services (Amendment) Act (Northern Ireland) 2010, which ensured that Northern Ireland Water would continue to receive DRD subsidy until 2013. Whether domestic billing will be introduced before this date is yet to be decided. Non-domestic customers in Northern Ireland became subject to water and sewerage charges and trade effluent charges where applicable in April 2008.

CONSUMER COUNCIL FOR NORTHERN IRELAND, 116 Holywood Road, Belfast BT4 1NY **T** 028-9067 2488 **W** www.consumercouncil.org.uk

NORTHERN IRELAND AUTHORITY FOR UTILITY REGULATION, Queens House, 14 Queen Street, Belfast BT1 6ED **T** 028-9031 1575 **W** www.uregni.gov.uk

NORTHERN IRELAND WATER, PO Box 1026, Belfast BT1 9DJ **T** 0845-744 0088 **W** www.niwater.com

WATER SERVICE COMPANIES

(* not a member of Water UK; † associate member of Water UK)

*ALBION WATER LTD, Harpenden Hall, Southdown Road, Harpenden, Herts AL5 1TE **T** 01582-767720 **W** www.albionwater.co.uk

ANGLIAN WATER SERVICES LTD, Customer Services, PO Box 10642, Harlow CM20 9HA **T** 0845-791 9155 **W** www.anglianwater.co.uk

BRISTOL WATER PLC, PO Box 218, Bridgwater Road, Bristol BS99 7AU **T** 0117-966 5881 **W** www.bristolwater.co.uk

CAMBRIDGE WATER PLC, 90 Fulbourn Road, Cambridge CB1 9JN **T** 01223-706050 **W** www.cambridge-water.co.uk

†CHOLDERTON & DISTRICT WATER COMPANY, Estate Office, Cholderton, Salisbury, Wiltshire SP4 0DR **T** 01980-629203 **W** www.choldertonwater.co.uk

DEE VALLEY WATER PLC, Packsaddle, Wrexham Road, Rhostyllen, Wrexham LL14 4EH **T** 01978-846946 **W** www.deevalleywater.co.uk

DWR CYMRU (WELSH WATER), PO Box 690, Cardiff CF3 5WL **T** 0800-052 0145 **W** www.dwrcymru.co.uk

ESSEX & SUFFOLK WATER PLC (subsidiary of Northumbrian Water Ltd), Customer Centre, PO Box 292, Durham DH1 9TX **T** 0845-782 0999 **W** www.eswater.co.uk

NORTHUMBRIAN WATER LTD, Customer Centre, PO Box 300, Durham DH1 9WQ **T** 0845-717 1100 **W** www.nwl.co.uk

PORTSMOUTH WATER LTD, PO Box 8, West Street, Havant, Hampshire PO9 1LG **T** 023-9249 9888 **W** www.portsmouthwater.co.uk

SEMBCORP BOURNEMOUTH WATER LTD, George Jessel House, Francis Avenue, Bournemouth, Dorset BH11 8NX **T** 01202-590059 **W** www.sembcorpbw.co.uk

SEVERN TRENT WATER LTD, PO Box 5310, Coventry CV3 9FJ **T** 0800-783 4444 **W** www.stwater.co.uk

SOUTH EAST WATER LTD, Rocfort Road, Snodland, Kent ME6 5AH **T** 0333-000 0002 **W** www.southeastwater.co.uk

SOUTH STAFFORDSHIRE WATER PLC, Green Lane, Walsall WS2 7PD **T** 0845-607 0456 **W** www.south-staffs-water.co.uk

SOUTH WEST WATER LTD, Peninsula House, Rydon Lane, Exeter EX2 7HR **T** 0800-169 1133 **W** www.southwestwater.co.uk

SOUTHERN WATER SERVICES LTD, Southern House, Yeoman Road, Worthing, W. Sussex BN13 3NX **T** 0845-278 0845 **W** www.southernwater.co.uk

SUTTON AND EAST SURREY WATER PLC, London Road, Redhill, Surrey RH1 1LJ **T** 01737-772000 **W** www.waterplc.com

THAMES WATER UTILITIES LTD, PO Box 286, Swindon SN38 2RA **T** 0845-920 0800 **W** www.thameswater.co.uk

UNITED UTILITIES WATER PLC, Haweswater House, Lingley Mere Business Park, Great Sankey, Warrington WA5 3LP **T** 01925-237000 **W** www.unitedutilities.com

VEOLIA WATER CENTRAL LTD, Tamblin Way, Hatfield, Herts AL10 9EZ **T** 0845-782 3333 **W** www.veoliawater.co.uk/central

VEOLIA WATER EAST LTD, Mill Hill, Manningtree, Essex CO11 2AZ **T** 0845-148 9288 **W** www.veoliawater.co.uk/east

VEOLIA WATER SOUTHEAST LTD, The Cherry Garden, Cherry Garden Lane, Folkestone, Kent CT19 4QB **T** 0845-888 5888 **W** www.veoliawater.co.uk/southeast

WESSEX WATER SERVICES LTD, Claverton Down, Bath BA2 7WW **T** 0845-600 3600 **W** www.wessexwater.co.uk

YORKSHIRE WATER SERVICES LTD, PO Box 52, Bradford BD3 7YD **T** 0845-124 2424 **W** www.yorkshirewater.com

ISLAND WATER AUTHORITIES
(not members of Water UK)

COUNCIL OF THE ISLES OF SCILLY, Town Hall, St Mary's, Isles of Scilly TR21 0LW **T** 01720-422537 **W** www.scilly.gov.uk

ISLE OF MAN WATER AND SEWERAGE AUTHORITY, Tromode Road, Douglas, Isle of Man IM2 5PA **T** 01624-695949 **W** www.gov.im/water

JERSEY WATER, PO Box 69, Mulcaster House, Westmount Road, St Helier, Jersey JE4 9PN **T** 01534-707301 **W** www.jerseywater.je

GUERNSEY WATER, PO Box 30, Brickfield House, St Andrew, Guernsey GY1 3AS **T** 01481-239500 **W** www.water.gg

ENERGY

The main primary sources of energy in Britain are coal, oil, natural gas, renewables and nuclear power. The main secondary sources (ie sources derived from the primary sources) are electricity, coke and smokeless fuels and petroleum products. The UK was a net importer of fuels in the 1970s, however as a result of growth in oil and gas production from the North Sea, the UK became a net exporter of energy for most of the 1980s. Output decreased in the late 1980s following the Piper Alpha disaster until the mid 1990s, after which the UK again became a net exporter. Since 2004, the UK reverted back to become a net importer of energy and has since continued to be so. In value terms, the total fuel deficit for 2010 was £7.5bn. The Department of Energy and Climate Change is responsible for promoting energy efficiency.

INDIGENOUS PRODUCTION OF PRIMARY FUELS
Million tonnes of oil equivalent

	2009	2010
Primary oils	74.7	69.0
Natural gas	59.7	57.2
Primary electricity	16.5	15.1
Coal	11.0	11.5
Renewable and waste	5.0	5.3
Total	167.0	158.1

Source: Department of Energy and Climate Change

INLAND ENERGY CONSUMPTION BY PRIMARY FUEL
Million tonnes of oil equivalent, seasonally adjusted

	2009	2010
Natural gas	86.0	93.2
Petroleum	71.1	70.7
Coal	31.5	32.2
Nuclear electricity	15.2	13.9
Renewables and waste	6.2	7.0
Wind and hydro electricity	1.3	1.2
Net Imports	0.2	0.2
Total	211.6	218.5

Source: Department of Energy and Climate Change

TRADE IN FUELS AND RELATED MATERIALS (2010)

	Quantity, million tonnes of oil equivalent	Value £m
Imports		
Crude oil	55.0	19,490
Petroleum products	28.9	12,291
Natural gas	50.7	6,849
Coal and other solid fuel	15.5	1,879
Electricity	0.6	326
Total	150.7	40,835
Exports		
Crude oil	45.2	15,744
Petroleum products	35.9	14,947
Natural gas	15.2	2,191
Coal and other solid fuel	1.0	220
Electricity	0.4	204
Total	97.6	33,306

Source: DECC/ONS

OIL

Until the 1960s Britain imported almost all its oil supplies. In 1969 oil was discovered in the Arbroath field in the North Sea. The first oilfield to be brought into production was Argyll in 1975, and since the mid-1970s Britain has been a major producer of crude oil.

At the end of 2009, there were a total of 317 offshore oil and gas fields in production. To date, the UK has produced around 3.5 billion tonnes of oil. It is estimated that there are 750 million tonnes remaining to be produced. Licences for exploration and production are granted to companies by the Department of Energy and Climate Change. At the end of 2004, 565 seaward production licences and 101 onshore petroleum exploration and development licenses had been awarded. At the end of 2009, there were a total of 317 offshore oil and gas fields in production. To date, the UK has produced around 26 billion barrels of oil. An estimated 4 to 12 billion barrels remain to be produced. Total UK oil production peaked in 1999 and is now declining. Profits from oil production are subject to a special tax regime with different taxes applying depending on the date of approval of each field.

DRILLING ACTIVITY (2010)
by number of wells started

	Offshore	Onshore
Exploration	28	8
Appraisal	34	1
Development	130	12

Source: Department of Energy and Climate Change

INDIGENOUS PRODUCTION AND REFINERY RECEIPTS
Thousand tonnes

	2009	2010
Indigenous production	68,199	62,962
Crude oil	62,820	58,047
NGLs*	5,378	4,915
Refinery receipts	79,078	77,335

* Natural Gas Liquids: condensates and petroleum gases derived at onshore treatment plants
Source: Department of Energy and Climate Change

DELIVERIES OF PETROLEUM PRODUCTS FOR INLAND CONSUMPTION BY ENERGY USE
Thousand tonnes

	2009	2010
Transport	49,601	49,087
Industry	4,505	4,529
Domestic	2,713	3,083
Other	1,145	1,155
Total	57,964	57,854

Source: Department of Energy and Climate Change

COAL

Mines were in private ownership until 1947 when they were nationalised and came under the management of the National Coal Board, later the British Coal Corporation. The corporation held a near monopoly on coal production until 1994 when the industry was restructured. Under the Coal Industry Act 1994, the Coal Authority was established to take over ownership of coal reserves and to issue licences to private mining companies. The Coal Authority is also responsible for the physical legacy of mining, eg subsidence damage claims, and for holding and making available all existing records. It also publishes current data on the coal industry.

The mines owned by the British Coal Corporation were sold as five separate businesses in 1994 and coal production is now undertaken entirely in the private sector. Coal output was around 50 million tonnes a year in 1994 but has since declined to just under 19 million tonnes. As at 31 March 2011 there were five large and twelve small underground mines as well as 34 surface mines in production or development in the UK.

The main consumer of coal in the UK is the electricity supply industry. Coal still supplies a third of the UK's electricity needs but as indigenous production has declined, imports have continued to make up the shortfall and now represent around 50 per cent of UK coal supply, 40 per cent of which is currently supplied from Russia.

UK government policy is to meet the long-term challenges posed by climate change while continuing to ensure secure, clean and affordable energy. Coal's availability, flexibility and reliability compared to other sources mean that it is expected to continue to play an important role in the future generating mix, but its carbon emissions will need to be managed through the introduction of abatement technologies including carbon capture and storage (CCS).

CCS attempts to mitigate the effects of global warming by capturing the carbon dioxide emissions from power stations that burn fossil fuels, preventing the gas from being released into the atmosphere, and storing it in underground geological formations. CCS is still in its infancy and only through its successful demonstration and development will it be possible for coal to remain a part of a low-carbon UK energy mix. The government is committed to public sector investment in CCS technology on four power stations and has made it clear that there can be no new coal power stations in England and Wales without CCS on a defined amount of capacity. As part of a wider package of reforms to the electricity market, the government will also be introducing an Emissions Performance Standard, which will limit the emissions from new fossil fuel power stations.

COAL PRODUCTION AND FOREIGN TRADE
Thousand tonnes

	2009	2010
Opencast	9,854	10,426
Deep-mined	7,520	7,390
Imports	38,167	26,521
Exports	(646)	(715)
Total supply	48,786*	51,429*
TOTAL	48,904	51,464

* Includes an estimate for slurry and stock change
Source: Department of Energy and Climate Change

INLAND COAL USE
Thousand tonnes

	2009	2010
Fuel producers		
Electricity generators	39,764	41,505
Coke manufacture	4,936	5,654
Blast furnaces	852	978
Heat generation	482	480
†Other conversion industries	341	351
Final consumption		
Industry	1,742	1,715
Domestic	689	718
Public administration	24	28
Commercial	49	4
Agriculture	–	1
Miscellaneous	3	6

† Mainly recycled products
Source: Department of Energy and Climate Change

GAS

From the late 18th century gas in Britain was produced from coal. In the 1960s town gas began to be produced from oil-based feedstocks using imported oil. In 1965 gas was discovered in the North Sea in the West Sole field, which became the first gasfield in production in 1967, and from the late 1960s natural gas began to replace town gas. From October 1998 Britain was connected to the continental European gas system via a pipeline from Bacton, Norfolk to Zeebrugge, Belgium. Gas is transported through 278,000km of mains pipeline including 7,600km of high-pressure gas pipelines owned and operated in the UK by National Grid Gas plc.

The gas industry in Britain was nationalised in 1949 and operated as the Gas Council. The Gas Council was replaced by the British Gas Corporation in 1972 and the industry became more centralised. The British Gas Corporation was privatised in 1986 as British Gas plc. In 1993 the Monopolies and Mergers Commission found that British Gas's integrated business in Great Britain as a gas trader and the owner of the gas transportation system could operate against the public interest. In February 1997, British Gas demerged its trading arm to become two separate companies, BG plc and Centrica plc. BG Group, as the company is now known, is an international natural gas company whose principal business is finding and developing gas reserves and building gas markets. Its core operations are located in the UK, South America, Egypt, Trinidad and Tobago, Kazakhstan and India. Centrica runs the trading and services operations under the British Gas brand name in Great Britain. In October 2000 BG demerged its pipeline business, Transco, which became part of Lattice Group, finally merging with the National Grid Group in 2002 to become National Grid Transco plc.

In July 2005 National Grid Transco plc changed its name to National Grid plc and Transco plc became National Grid Gas plc. In the same year National Grid Gas also completed the sale of four of its eight gas distribution networks. The distribution networks transport gas at lower pressures, which eventually supply the consumers such as domestic customers. The Scotland and south-east of England networks were sold to Scotia Gas Networks. The Wales and south-west network was sold to Wales

& West Utilities and the network in the north-east to Northern Gas Networks. This was the biggest change in the corporate structure of gas infrastructure since privatisation in 1986.

Competition was gradually introduced into the industrial gas market from 1986. Supply of gas to the domestic market was opened to companies other than British Gas, starting in April 1996 with a pilot project in the West Country and Wales, with the rest of the UK following soon after.

Declines in UK indigenous gas production and increasing demand led to the UK becoming a net importer of gas once more in 2004. In 2010, gross natural gas production was 4 per cent lower than in 2009 and 46 per cent lower than the record level seen in 2000. As part of the Energy Act 2008, the government planned to strengthen regulation of the offshore gas supply infrastructure, to allow private sector investment to help maintain UK energy supplies.

BG GROUP PLC, Thames Valley Park, Reading RG6 1PT
T 0118-935 3222 W www.bg-group.com
Chair, Sir Robert Wilson
Chief Executive, Sir Frank Chapman

CENTRICA PLC, Millstream, Maidenhead Road, Windsor, Berkshire SL4 5GD T 01753-494000 W www.centrica.com
Chair, Sir Roger Carr
Chief Executive, Sam Laidlaw

NATIONAL GRID PLC, Lakeside House, The Lakes, Northampton NN4 7HD T 0845-605 6677
W www.nationalgrid.com
Chair, Sir John Parker
Chief Executive, Steve Holliday

UK GAS CONSUMPTION BY INDUSTRY
GWh

	2009	2010
Domestic	332,499	389,595
Industry	116,409	121,963
Public administration	37,084	38,390
Commercial	29,305	31,758
Agriculture	1,860	1,969
Miscellaneous	15,485	16,507
Total gas consumption	540,643	608,683

Source: Department of Energy and Climate Change

ELECTRICITY

The first power station in Britain generating electricity for public supply began operating in 1882. In the 1930s a national transmission grid was developed and it was reconstructed and extended in the 1950s and 1960s. Power stations were operated by the Central Electricity Generating Board.

Under the Electricity Act 1989, 12 regional electricity companies, responsible for the distribution of electricity from the national grid to consumers, were formed from the former area electricity boards in England and Wales. Four companies were formed from the Central Electricity Generating Board: three generating companies (National Power plc, Nuclear Electric plc and Powergen plc) and the National Grid Company plc, which owned and operated the transmission system in England and Wales. National Power and Powergen were floated on the stock market in 1991.

National Power was demerged in October 2000 to form two separate companies: International Power plc and Innogy plc, which manages the bulk of National Power's UK assets. Nuclear Electric was split into two parts in 1996.

The National Grid Company was floated on the stock market in 1995 and formed a new holding company, National Grid Group. National Grid Group completed a merger with Lattice in 2002 to form National Grid Transco, a public limited company (*see* Gas).

Following privatisation, generators and suppliers in England and Wales traded via the Electricity Pool. A competitive wholesale trading market known as NETA (New Electricity Trading Arrangements) replaced the Electricity Pool in March 2001, and was extended to include Scotland via the British Electricity Transmissions and Trading Arrangements (BETTA) in 2005. As part of BETTA, National Grid became the system operator for all transmission. The introduction of competition into the domestic electricity market was completed in May 1999. Since competition was introduced, over 19 million of Britain's 28 million electricity customers have switched their supplier.

In Scotland, three new companies were formed under the Electricity Act 1989: Scottish Power plc and Scottish Hydro-Electric plc, which were responsible for generation, transmission, distribution and supply; and Scottish Nuclear Ltd. Scottish Power and Scottish Hydro-Electric were floated on the stock market in 1991. Scottish Hydro-Electric merged with Southern Electric in 1998 to become Scottish and Southern Energy plc. Scottish Nuclear was incorporated into British Energy in 1996. BETTA opened the Scottish market to the same competition that had applied in England and Wales.

In Northern Ireland, Northern Ireland Electricity plc (NIE) was set up in 1993 under a 1991 Order in Council. In 1993 it was floated on the stock market and in 1998 it became part of the Viridian Group and was responsible for distribution and supply until NIE was sold to ESB Independent Energy in December 2010. In June 2010, Airtricity became the first new electricity supplier since the Northern Ireland electricity market was opened to competition in 2007.

On 12 July 2011, the government published *Planning Our Electric Future: a White Paper for Secure, Affordable and Low-carbon Electricity* in response to the challenges set by increasing electricity demands. It has been agreed that over £110bn in investment is needed to update the grid and build new power stations.

On 30 September 2003 the Electricity Association, the industry's main trade association, was replaced with three separate trade bodies:

ASSOCIATION OF ELECTRICITY PRODUCERS, Charles House, 5–11 Regent Street, London SW1Y 4LR
T 020-7930 9390 W www.aepuk.com
ENERGY NETWORKS ASSOCIATION, 6th floor, Dean Bradley House, 52 Horseferry Road, London SW1P 2AF T 020-7706 5100
W www.energynetworks.org
ENERGY RETAIL ASSOCIATION, 1 Hobhouse Court, Suffolk Street, London SW1Y 4HH T 020-7104 4150
W www.energy-retail.org.uk

ELECTRICITY PRODUCTION, SUPPLY AND CONSUMPTION
GWh

	2009	2010
Electricity produced		
Nuclear	69,098	62,140
Hydro	5,262	3,603
Wind	9,324	10,216
Coal	103,038	107,694
Oil	6,042	4,860
Gas	166,494	175,003
Renewables	11,470	12,837
Other	2,327	1,625
Total	373,055	377,977
Electricity supplied		
Production	373,055	377,977
Other sources*	3,685	3,150
Imports	6,609	7,144
Exports	(3,748)	(4,481)
Total	379,601	383,791
Electricity consumed		
Industry	100,841	104,499
Transport	3,906	3,899
Other	217,970	219,920
Domestic	118,541	118,681
Public administration	19,442	18,773
Commercial	76,187	78,437
Agriculture	3,801	4,029
Total	322,717	328,318

* Pumped storage production
Source: Department of Energy and Climate Change

GAS AND ELECTRICITY SUPPLIERS

With the gas and electricity markets open, most suppliers offer their customers both services. The majority of gas/electricity companies have become part of larger multi-utility companies, often operating internationally.

As part of measures to reduce the UK's carbon output, the government has outlined plans to introduce 'smart meters' to all UK homes. Smart meters perform the traditional meter function of measuring energy consumption, in addition to more advanced functions such as allowing energy suppliers to communicate directly with their customers and removing the need for meter readings and bill estimates. The meters also allow domestic customers to have direct access to energy consumption information.

The following list comprises a selection of suppliers offering gas and electricity. Organisations in italics are subsidiaries of the companies listed in capital letters directly above.

ENGLAND, SCOTLAND AND WALES
CE ELECTRIC UK, W www.ce-electricuk.com
Northern Electric Distribution Ltd, Manor House, Station Road, Penshaw, Houghton-le-Spring DH4 7LA
T 0800-668877
Yorkshire Electricity Distribution, 98 Aketon Road, Castleford WF10 9DS T 0800-375675
CENTRICA PLC, Millstream, Maidenhead Road, Windsor, Berkshire SL4 5GD T 01753-494000 W www.centrica.com
British Gas/Scottish Gas, PO Box 4805, Worthing BN11 9QW
T 0800-048 0202 W www.britishgas.co.uk
EDF ENERGY, Osprey House, Osprey Road, Exeter, EX2 7WN
T 0800-096 9000 W www.edfenergy.com

E.ON, 6th Floor, 100 Pall Mall, London SW1Y 5NQ
T 024-7642 4000 W www.eon-uk.com
NPOWER, PO Box 93, Peterlee SR8 2XX T 0845-070 4851
W www.npower.com
SCOTTISH AND SOUTHERN ENERGY PLC,
Inveralmond House, 200 Dunkeld Road, Perth PH1 3AQ
T 01738-456000 W www.scottish-southern.co.uk
Scottish Hydro, T 0845-026 0655 W www.hydro.co.uk
Southern Electric, T 0845-026 0654
W www.southern-electric.co.uk
SWALEC, T 0800-026 0656 W www.swalec.co.uk
SCOTTISHPOWER, PO Box 8729, Bellshill ML4 3YD
T 0845-273 4444 W www.scottishpower.com

NORTHERN IRELAND
AIRTRICITY (a member of Scottish and Southern Energy), Airtricity House, Ravenscourt Office Park, Sandyford, Dublin 18 T 1850-812220 W www.airtricity.com
VIRIDIAN GROUP LTD, Greenwood House, 64 Newforge Lane, Belfast BT9 5NF T 028-9066 8416
W www.viridiangroup.co.uk
Energia, PO Box 1275, Belfast BT9 5WH T 1850-363744
W www.energia.ie
ESB INDEPENDENT ENERGY LTD (ELECTRIC IRELAND), Woodford Business Park, Santry, Dublin 17
T 1850-372999 W www.esbie.ie
Northern Ireland Electricity, 120 Malone Road, Belfast BT9 5HT T 08457-643643 W www.nie.co.uk

REGULATION OF THE GAS AND ELECTRICITY INDUSTRIES

The Office of the Gas and Electricity Markets (OFGEM) regulates the gas and electricity industries in Great Britain. It was formed in 1999 by the merger of the Office of Gas Supply and the Office of Electricity Regulation. OFGEM's overriding aim is to protect and promote the interests of all gas and electricity customers by promoting competition and regulating monopolies. It is governed by an authority and its powers are provided for under the Gas Act 1986, the Electricity Act 1989, the Competition Act 1998, the Utilities Act 2000 and the Enterprise Act 2002. Energywatch is the independent gas and electricity watchdog, set up in November 2000 through the Utility Act to protect and promote the interests of gas and electricity consumers. In October 2008 Energywatch merged with Postwatch and the National Consumer Council to form a new advocacy body, Consumer Focus. In October 2010, the government announced that Consumer Focus would be abolished and some of its functions would transfer to Citizens Advice, Citizens Advice Scotland and the General Consumer Council for Northern Ireland. This transfer is due to take place in spring 2013.

CONSUMER FOCUS, Fleetbank House, Salisbury Square, London EC4Y 8JX T 020-7799 7900
W www.consumerfocus.org.uk
THE OFFICE OF THE GAS AND ELECTRCITY MARKETS (OFGEM), 9 Millbank, London SW1 3GE
T 020-7901 7000 W www.ofgem.gov.uk

NUCLEAR POWER

Nuclear reactors began to supply electricity to the national grid in 1956. Nuclear power is currently generated in the UK at ten sites: two magnox reactors (shutdown expected in late 2012), seven advanced gas-cooled reactors (AGR) and one pressurised water reactor (PWR), Sizewell 'B' in Suffolk. The AGRs and PWR are owned by a private company, British Energy, while the two magnox reactors are state-owned by the Nuclear Decommissioning Authority. The first of a series of new-generation plants is expected to come on-line around 2018; all but one of the current sites (Sizewell 'B') will be retired by 2023.

In April 2005 the responsibility for the decommissioning of civil nuclear reactors and other nuclear facilities used in research and development was handed to the Nuclear Decommissioning Authority (NDA). The NDA is a non-departmental public body, funded mainly by the Department of Energy and Climate Change (DECC). Until April 2007, UK Nirex was responsible for the disposal of intermediate and some low-level nuclear waste. After this date Nirex was integrated into the NDA and renamed the Radioactive Waste Management Directorate.

There are currently nine non-operational magnox power stations and four nuclear research facilities undergoing decommissioning by the NDA, including the world's first commercial power station at Calder Hall on the Sellafield site in Cumbria. The decommissioning of these sites is scheduled for completion within the next 15 to 20 years. In the case of the Dounreay research facility in Scotland, controls on access to contaminated land are expected to remain in place until around 2300.

In 2010 electricity supplied from nuclear sources accounted for 16.4 per cent of the total electricity supply. The 2008 Energy Bill paved the way for the construction of up to ten new nuclear power stations by 2020. A number of factors have led to government backing for nuclear power: domestic gas supplies are running low; oil and gas prices are high; carbon emissions must be cut to comply with EU legislation and meet global climate change targets; and a number of coal-fired power stations that fail to meet clean air requirements are due to be closed.

Nuclear power has its advantages: reactors emit virtually no carbon dioxide and uranium prices remain relatively steady. However, the advantages of low emissions are countered by the high costs of construction and difficulties in disposing of nuclear waste. Currently, the only method is to store it securely until it has slowly decayed to safe levels. Public distrust persists despite the advances in safety technology.

SAFETY AND REGULATION

The Office for Nuclear Regulation (OCR), an agency of the Health and Safety Executive is the nuclear industry's regulator. Operations at all UK nuclear power stations are governed by a site licence which is issued under the Nuclear Installations Act. The OCR monitors compliance and has the jurisdiction to close down a reactor if the terms of the licence are breached. The DECC is responsible for security at all the UK's nuclear power stations, which are policed by the Civil Nuclear Constabulary, a specialised armed force created in April 2005. In 2009 Magnox Electric Ltd was found guilty of breaking the Radioactive Substances Act 2003: it had left a radioactive leak on a holding tank at Bradwell power station, Essex, unchecked for 14 years.

RENEWABLE SOURCES

Renewable sources of energy principally include biofuels, hydro, wind and solar. Renewable sources produced over 7.6 million tonnes of oil equivalent for primary energy usage in 2010; of this, about 5.2 million tonnes was used to generate electricity, 1.2 million tonnes to generate heat and 1.2 million tonnes was used as transport fuels. In 2010, the UK generated 6.8 per cent of its total energy production from renewable sources, up by 0.1 per cent from 2009.

The government's principal mechanism for developing renewable energy sources is the Renewables Obligation (RO), which aims to increase the contribution of electricity from renewables in the UK. There are separate RO schemes for England and Wales, Scotland and Northern Ireland. For both England and Wales and Scotland, the RO is set so that 9.7 per cent of licensed electricity sales should be from renewable sources eligible for the RO by 2009/10, and 15.4 per cent should be eligible by 2015/16. For Northern Ireland, these figures are 3.5 per cent and 6.3 per cent. In 2010, renewable sources accounted for 7.0 per cent of sales on an RO basis, an increase of 6.7 per cent from 2009.

A renewables obligation has been in place in England and Wales since April 2002 to give incentives to generators to supply progressively higher levels of renewable energy over time. These measures included exempting renewable energy sources from the climate change levy, capital grants, enhanced research funding and regional planning to meet renewables targets.

In addition to the RO, in April 2010, the government launched a Feed-in Tariff (FIT) scheme in Great Britain to encourage the uptake of small-scale low carbon electricity generation technologies, principally renewables such as solar photovoltaics, wind and hydro-electricity.

The government approved an EU-wide agreement in March 2007 to generate 20 per cent of energy production from renewable sources by 2020. It has since negotiated down the national share in this target to 15 per cent of energy production by 2020. In July 2009 the government published a Renewable Energy Strategy in order to meet this target. Other impediments to the expansion of renewable energy production include planning restrictions, rising raw material prices, and the possible redirection of funds to develop CCS technology and nuclear energy sources. For further information on renewable energy *see* The Environment.

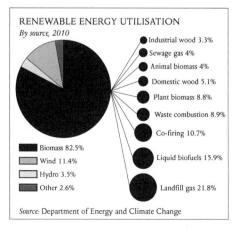

RENEWABLE ENERGY UTILISATION
By source, 2010

- Industrial wood 3.3%
- Sewage gas 4%
- Animal biomass 4%
- Domestic wood 5.1%
- Plant biomass 8.8%
- Waste combustion 8.9%
- Co-firing 10.7%
- Liquid biofuels 15.9%
- Landfill gas 21.8%

- Biomass 82.5%
- Wind 11.4%
- Hydro 3.5%
- Other 2.6%

Source: Department of Energy and Climate Change

TRANSPORT

CIVIL AVIATION

Since the privatisation of British Airways in 1987, UK airlines have been operated entirely by the private sector. In 2010, total capacity of British airlines amounted to 47 billion tonne-km, of which 38 billion tonne-km was on scheduled services. UK airlines carried around 124 million passengers; 103 million on scheduled services and 21 million on charter flights. Passenger traffic through UK airports decreased by 3.4 per cent; the third consecutive year traffic had decreased. Traffic at the six main London area airports (Gatwick, Heathrow, London City, Luton, Southend and Stansted) decreased by 5 per cent over 2010 and other UK regional airports saw a decrease of 6 per cent.

Leading British airlines include BMI, British Airways, EasyJet, Monarch, Thomas Cook Airlines, Thomson Airways and Virgin Atlantic. Irish airline Ryanair also operates frequent flights from the UK.

There are around 140 licensed civil aerodromes in Britain, with Heathrow and Gatwick handling the highest volume of passengers. BAA plc owns and operates six major airports: Heathrow, Stansted, Southampton, Glasgow, Edinburgh and Aberdeen. BAA sold Gatwick to an investment group in December 2009 for £1.5bn. Other airports are controlled by local authorities or private companies.

The Civil Aviation Authority (CAA), an independent statutory body, is responsible for the regulation of UK airlines. This includes economic and airspace regulation, air safety, consumer protection and environmental research and consultancy. All commercial airline companies must be granted an air operator's certificate, which is issued by the CAA to operators meeting the required safety standards. The CAA issues airport safety licences, which must be obtained by any airport used for public transport and training flights. All British-registered aircraft must be granted an airworthiness certificate, and the CAA issues professional licences to pilots, flight crew, ground engineers and air traffic controllers. The CAA also manages the Air Travel Organiser's Licence (ATOL), the UK's principal travel protection scheme. The CAA's costs are met entirely from charges on those whom it regulates; there is no direct government funding of the CAA's work.

The Transport Act, passed by parliament on 29 November 2000, separated the CAA from its subsidiary, National Air Traffic Services (NATS), which provides air traffic control services to aircraft flying in UK airspace and over the eastern part of the North Atlantic. NATS is a public-private partnership (PPP) between the Airline Group (a consortium of UK airlines), which holds 42 per cent of the shares; NATS staff, who hold 5 per cent; BAA, which holds 4 per cent, and the government, which holds 49 per cent and a golden share. In 2010 NATS handled a total of 2,106,689 flights, a decrease of 4.3 per cent compared with 2009 figures. The effect of the severe winter weather and the ash cloud resulting from the eruption of the Eyjafjallajokull volcano in Iceland in spring 2010 contributed to the decrease in the number of aircraft in UK controlled airspace in 2010.

AIR PASSENGERS 2010

All UK Airports: Total	211,830,788
Aberdeen (BAA)	2,763,708
Barra (HIAL)	10,192
Belfast City	2,740,341
Belfast International	4,016,170
Benbecula (HIAL)	30,406
Birmingham	8,572,398
Blackpool	235,340
Bournemouth	751,331
Bristol	5,747,604
Cambridge	916
Campbeltown (HIAL)	8,682
Cardiff	1,404,613
City of Derry (Eglinton)	339,432
Doncaster Sheffield	876,153
Dundee	70,398
Durham Tees Valley	226,209
East Midlands	4,113,501
Edinburgh (BAA)	8,596,715
Exeter	744,957
Gatwick (BAA)	31,375,290
Glasgow (BAA)	6,548,865
Gloucestershire	16,533
Heathrow (BAA)	65,881,660
Humberside	283,160
Inverness (HIAL)	530,213
Islay (HIAL)	25,009
Isle of Man	675,871
Isles of Scilly (St Mary's)	115,194
Isles of Scilly (Tresco)	34,310
Kent International	15,580
Kirkwall (HIAL)	141,399
Lands End (St Just)	30,214
Leeds Bradford	2,755,110
Lerwick (Tingwall)	4,609
Liverpool	5,013,940
London City	2,780,582
Luton	8,738,717
Lydd	485
Manchester	17,759,015
Newcastle	4,356,130
Newquay	315,107
Norwich	425,821
Oxford (Kidlington)	2,186
Penzance Heliport	89,469
Plymouth	128,603
Prestwick	1,662,744
Scatsta	279,482
Shoreham	886
Southampton (BAA)	1,733,690
Southend	3,583
Stansted (BAA)	18,573,803
Stornoway (HIAL)	113,680
Sumburgh (HIAL)	140,129
Tiree (HIAL)	7,943
Wick (HIAL)	22,710
Channel Islands Airports: Total	2,456,916
Alderney	70,012
Guernsey	923,683
Jersey	1,463,221

HIAL = Highlands and Islands Airports Ltd
Source: Civil Aviation Authority

CAA, CAA House, 45–59 Kingsway, London WC2B 6TE
T 020-7379 7311 W www.caa.co.uk
BAA, The Compass Centre, Nelson Road, London Heathrow
Airport, Hounslow TW6 2GW T 020-8745 9800
W www.baa.com

Heathrow Airport	T 0844-335 1801
Southampton Airport	T 0844-481 7777
Stansted Airport	T 0844-335 1803
Aberdeen Airport	T 0844-481 6666
Edinburgh Airport	T 0844 481 8989
Glasgow Airport	T 0844 481 5555

BMI, Donington Hall, Castle Donington, Derby DE74 2SB
T 01332-854000 W www.flybmi.com
BRITISH AIRWAYS, PO Box 365, Waterside,
Harmondsworth UB7 0GB T 01805-266522
W www.britishairways.com
EASYJET, Hangar 89, London Luton Airport LU2 9PF
T 0871-244 2366 W www.easyjet.com
MONARCH, Prospect House, Prospect Way, London Luton
Airport LU2 9NU T 0871-225 0250 W www.monarch.co.uk
THOMAS COOK AIRLINES, Thomas Cook Business Park,
Coningsby Road, Peterborough PE3 8SB T 0844-855 0515
W www.thomascookairlines.co.uk
THOMSON AIRWAYS, Wigmore House, Wigmore Place,
Wigmore Lane, Luton, Bedfordshire LU2 9TN
T 0844-871 1603 W www.thomson.co.uk
VIRGIN ATLANTIC, PO Box 747, Dunstable LU6 9AH
T 0844-811 0000 W www.virgin-atlantic.com

RAILWAYS

The railway network in Britain was developed by private
companies in the 19th century. In 1948 the main railway
companies were nationalised and were run by a public
authority, the British Transport Commission. The
commission was replaced by the British Railways Board
in 1963, operating as British Rail. On 1 April 1994,
responsibility for managing the track and railway
infrastructure passed to a newly formed company,
Railtrack plc. In October 2001 Railtrack was put into
administration under the Railways Act 1993 and Ernst
and Young was appointed as administrator. In October
2002 Railtrack was taken out of administration and
replaced by the not-for-profit company Network Rail.
The British Railways Board continued as operator of all
train services until 1996–7, when they were sold or
franchised to the private sector.

The Strategic Rail Authority (SRA) was created to provide strategic leadership to the rail industry and formally
came into being on 1 February 2001 following the passing
of the Transport Act 2000. In January 2002 it published
its first strategic plan, setting out the strategic priorities for
Britain's railways over the next ten years. In addition to its
coordinating role, the SRA was responsible for allocating
government funding to the railways and awarding and
monitoring the franchises for operating rail services.

On 15 July 2004 the transport secretary announced a
new structure for the rail industry in the white paper *The
Future of Rail*. These proposals were implemented under
the Railways Act 2005, which abolished the Strategic
Rail Authority, passing most of its functions to the
Department for Transport; established the Rail Passengers
Council (RPC) as a single national body, dissolving the
regional committees; and gave devolved governments in
Scotland and Wales more say in decisions at a local level.

In addition, responsibility for railway safety regulation
was transferred to the Office of Rail Regulation from the
Health and Safety Executive.

OFFICE OF RAIL REGULATION
The Office of Rail Regulation (ORR) was established on
5 July 2004 by the Railways and Transport Safety Act
2003, replacing the Office of the Rail Regulator. As the
railway industry's economic and safety regulator, the
ORR's principal function is to regulate Network Rail's
stewardship of the national network. The ORR also
licenses operators of railway assets, approves agreements
for access by operators to track, stations and light
maintenance depots, and enforces domestic competition
law. The ORR is led by a board appointed by the
Secretary of State for Transport and chaired by Anna
Walker.

SERVICES
For privatisation, under the Railways Act 1993, domestic
passenger services were divided into 25 train operating
units, which were franchised to private sector operators
via a competitive tendering process. The train operators
formed the Association of Train Operating Companies
(ATOC) to act as the official voice of the passenger rail
industry and provide its members with a range of services
enabling them to comply with conditions imposed on
them through their franchise agreements and operating
licences.

As at July 2011 there were 23 passenger train
operating companies: Arriva Trains Wales, c2c, Chiltern
Railways, CrossCountry, East Coast, East Midlands
Trains, Eurostar, First Capital Connect, First Great
Western, First Hull Trains, First TransPennine Express,
Grand Central, Heathrow Express, London Midland,
London Overground, Merseyrail, National Express East
Anglia, Northern Rail, ScotRail, South West Trains,
Southeastern, Southern and Virgin Trains.

Network Rail publishes a national timetable which
contains details of rail services operated over the UK
network and sea ferry services which provide connections
with Ireland, the Isle of Man, the Isle of Wight, the
Channel Islands and some European destinations.

The national rail enquiries service offers information
about train times and fares for any part of the country,
Transport for London (TfL) provides London-specific
travel information for all modes of travel and Eurostar
provides information for international channel tunnel rail
services:

NATIONAL RAIL ENQUIRIES
T 0845-748 4950 W www.nationalrail.co.uk
TRANSPORT FOR LONDON
T 0843-222 1234 W www.tfl.gov.uk
EUROSTAR
T 08432-186186 W www.eurostar.com

PASSENGER FOCUS AND LONDON
TRAVELWATCH
Passenger Focus is the operating name of the Passengers'
Council, a single national consumer body for rail, which is
funded by the Department for Transport but whose
independence is guaranteed by an act of parliament.
Under the Passengers' Council (non-railway functions)
Order of February 2010, Passenger Focus also represents
bus passengers in England, outside London. Included in
this remit are local bus services and scheduled domestic
coach journeys.

Established in July 2000, London TravelWatch is the operating name of the official watchdog organisation representing the interests of transport users in and around the capital. Officially known as the London Transport Users' Committee, it is sponsored and funded by the London Assembly and is independent of the transport operators. London TravelWatch represents users of buses, the Underground, river and rail services in and around London, including Eurostar and Heathrow Express, Croydon Tramlink and the Docklands Light Railway. The interests of pedestrians, cyclists and motorists are also represented, as are those of taxi users.

FREIGHT

On privatisation in 1996, British Rail's bulk freight operations were sold to North and South Railways – subsequently called English, Welsh and Scottish Railways (EWS). In 2007, EWS was bought by Deutsche Bahn and in January 2009 was re-named DB Schenker. The other major companies in the rail freight sector are: Colas Rail, Direct Rail Services, Freightliner, Freight Europe and GB Railfreight (GBRf). In 2010–11 freight moved by rail amounted to 19.23 billion tonne-kilometres, a 0.9 per cent increase from 2009–10.

NETWORK RAIL

Network Rail is responsible for the tracks, bridges, tunnels, level crossings, viaducts and 18 main stations that form Britain's rail network. In addition to providing the timetables for the passenger and freight operators, Network Rail is also responsible for all the signalling and electrical control equipment needed to operate the rail network and for monitoring and reporting performance across the industry.

Network Rail is a private company run as a commercial business; it is directly accountable to its members and regulated by the ORR. The members have similar rights to those of shareholders in a public company except they do not receive dividends or share capital and thereby have no financial or economic interest in Network Rail. All of Network Rail's profits are reinvested into maintaining and upgrading the rail infrastructure.

ASSOCIATION OF TRAIN OPERATING

COMPANIES, 3rd Floor, 40 Bernard Street, London WC1N 1BY T 020-7841 8000 W www.atoc.org
LONDON TRAVELWATCH, 6 Middle Street, London EC1A 7JA T 020-7505 9000
W www.londontravelwatch.org.uk
NETWORK RAIL, Kings Place, 90 York Way, London N1 9AG T 020-7557 8000 W www.networkrail.co.uk
OFFICE OF RAIL REGULATION, 1 Kemble Street, London WC2B 4AN T 020-7282 2000
W www.rail-reg.gov.uk
PASSENGER FOCUS, Freepost (RRRE-ETTC-LEET), PO Box 4257, Manchester M60 3AR T 0300-123 2350
W www.passengerfocus.org.uk

RAIL SAFETY

On 1 April 2006 responsibility for health and safety policy and enforcement on the railways transferred from the Health and Safety Executive to the Office of Rail Regulation (ORR).

In 2010–11 a total of 40 passengers, railway staff and other members of the public were fatally injured in all rail incidents (excluding suicides), compared with 70 in 2009–10.

ACCIDENTS ON RAILWAYS

	2009–10	2010–11
Rail incident fatalities	70	40
Passengers	5	8
Railway employees	3	1
Public	62	31
Rail incident major injuries	396	395
Passengers	235	240
Railway employees	122	122
Public	39	33

SUICIDES AND ATTEMPTED SUICIDES 2010–11
Fatalities 208
Major Injuries 36
Source: ORR – National Rail Trends 2010–11 Yearbook

OTHER RAIL SYSTEMS

Responsibility for the London Underground passed from the government to the Mayor and Transport for London on 15 July 2003, with a public-private partnership already in place. Plans for a public-private partnership for London Underground were pushed through by the government in February 2002 despite opposition from the Mayor of London and a range of transport organisations. Under the PPP, long-term contracts with private companies were estimated to enable around £16bn to be invested in renewing and upgrading the London Underground's infrastructure over 15 years. In July 2007, Metronet, which was responsible for two of three PPP contracts, went into administration; TfL took over both contracts. Responsibility for stations, trains, operations, signalling and safety remains in the public sector. In 2008–9 there were 1,089 million passenger journeys on the London Underground.

In addition to Glasgow Subway, which is classified as an underground system, Britain has eight other light rail and tram systems: Blackpool Trams, Croydon Tramlink, Docklands Light Railway (DLR), Manchester Metrolink, Midland Metro, Nottingham Express Transit (NET), Sheffield Supertram and Tyne and Wear Metro.

In 2009–10 there were 186.2 million passenger light rail and tram journeys in Great Britain; a decrease of 1.3 per cent on 2008–9 figures, and the first year-on-year decrease in light rail passenger journeys since 1991–2.

THE CHANNEL TUNNEL

The earliest recorded scheme for a submarine transport connection between Britain and France was in 1802. Tunnelling began simultaneously on both sides of the Channel three times: in 1881, in the early 1970s, and on 1 December 1987, when construction workers bored the first of the three tunnels which form the Channel Tunnel. Engineers 'holed through' the first tunnel (the service tunnel) on 1 December 1990 and tunnelling was completed in June 1991. The tunnel was officially inaugurated by the Queen and President Mitterrand of France on 6 May 1994.

The submarine link comprises two rail tunnels, each carrying trains in one direction, which measure 7.6m (24.93ft) in diameter. Between them lies a smaller service tunnel, measuring 4.8m (15.75ft) in diameter. The service tunnel is linked to the rail tunnels by 130 cross-passages for maintenance and safety purposes. The tunnels are 50km (31 miles) long, 38km (24 miles) of which is under the seabed at an average depth of 40m (132ft). The rail terminals are situated at Folkestone and Calais, and the tunnels go underground at Shakespeare Cliff, Dover and Sangatte, west of Calais.

RAIL LINKS

The British Channel Tunnel Rail Link route runs from Folkestone to St Pancras station, London, with intermediate stations at Ashford and Ebbsfleet in Kent.

Construction of the rail link was financed by the private sector with a substantial government contribution. A private sector consortium, London and Continental Railways Ltd (LCR), comprising Union Railways and the UK operator of Eurostar, owns the rail link and was responsible for its design and construction. The rail link was constructed in two phases: phase one, from the Channel Tunnel to Fawkham Junction, Kent, began in October 1998 and opened to fare-paying passengers on 28 September 2003; phase two, from Southfleet Junction to St Pancras, was completed in November 2007.

There are direct services from the UK to Calais, Disneyland Paris, Lille and Paris in France and Brussels in Belgium. There are also direct services to Avignon in the south of France between July and September and during the winter months (December to April) to the French Alps. High-speed trains also run from Lille to the south of France.

Eurostar, the high-speed passenger train service, connects London with Paris in 2 hours 15 minutes, Brussels in 1 hour 51 minutes and Lille in 1 hour 20 minutes. There are Eurostar terminals at London St Pancras, Ashford and Ebbsfleet in Kent, Paris Gare Du Nord, Brussels-South and Lille in France, and Brussels-South in Belgium.

ROADS

HIGHWAY AUTHORITIES

The powers and responsibilities of highway authorities in England and Wales are set out in the Highways Act 1980; for Scotland there is separate legislation.

Responsibility for motorways and other trunk roads in Great Britain rests in England with the Secretary of State for Transport, in Scotland with the Scottish government, and in Wales with the Welsh government. The highway authority for non-trunk roads in England, Wales and Scotland is, in general, the local authority in whose area the roads lie. With the establishment of the Greater London Authority in July 2000, Transport for London became the highway authority for roads in London.

In Northern Ireland the Department of Regional Development is the statutory road authority responsible for public roads and their maintenance and construction; the Roads Service executive agency carries out these functions on behalf of the department.

FINANCE

In England all aspects of trunk road and motorway funding are provided directly by the government to the Highways Agency, which operates, maintains and improves a network of motorways and trunk roads around 7,050km (4,381 miles) long, on behalf of the secretary of state. Since 2001 the length of the network that the Highways Agency is responsible for has been decreasing owing to a policy of de-trunking, which transfers responsibility for non-core roads to local authorities. For the financial year 2011–12 the Highways Agency's total planned expenditure is £4,211m: £417m for maintenance, £797m for major schemes and the remainder for traffic management, technology improvements, other programmes and administration costs.

Government support for local authority capital expenditure on roads and other transport infrastructure is provided through grant and credit approvals as part of the Local Transport Plan (LTP). Local authorities bid for resources on the basis of a five-year programme built around delivering integrated transport strategies. As well as covering the structural maintenance of local roads and the construction of major new road schemes, LTP funding also includes smaller-scale safety and traffic management measures with associated improvements for public transport, cyclists and pedestrians.

For the financial year 2011–12, total allocated LTP funding amounted to £1,106m: £806m for maintenance and £300m for integrated transport measures.

Total budgeted expenditure by the Welsh government in 2010–11 to improve and maintain the trunk road network is £116m, a further £41m is allocated to improve and maintain local roads.

Since 1 July 1999 all decisions on Scottish transport expenditure have been devolved to the Scottish government. Total expenditure on motorways and trunk roads in Scotland during 2010–11 was £592m (including depreciation and other annually managed expenditure charges). Planned expenditure for 2011–12 is £560m. The cost of capital charges was abolished by HM Treasury during 2010–11; at the start of the year these had originally been forecast at £650m.

In Northern Ireland total expenditure by the Roads Service on all roads in 2010–11 was £284.5m, with £237.8m spent on trunk roads and motorways. Planned expenditure for 2011–12 is £122.5m, with £57.9m allocated for trunk roads and motorways.

The Transport Act 2000 gave English and Welsh local authorities (outside London) powers to introduce road-user charging or workplace parking levy schemes. The act requires that the net revenue raised is used to improve local transport services and facilities for at least ten years. The aim is to reduce congestion and encourage greater use of alternative modes of transport. Schemes developed by local authorities require government approval. The UK's first toll road, the M6 Toll, opened in December 2003 and runs for 43.5km (27 miles) around Birmingham from junction 3a to junction 11a on the M6.

Charging schemes in London are allowed under the 1999 Greater London Authority Act. The Central London Congestion Charge Scheme began on 17 February 2003 (see also Regional Government).

ROAD LENGTHS 2010
Miles

	England	Wales	Scotland	Great Britain
Major Roads	21,918.1	2,674.9	6,639.9	31,233.0
Motorways	1,870.1	87.8	252.6	2,210.6
Minor Roads	165,193.0	18,349.6	30,202.0	213,744.5
Total	187,111.1	21,024.5	36,841.9	244,977.5

Source: Department for Transport

FREIGHT TRANSPORT BY ROAD (GREAT BRITAIN) 2009
GOODS MOVED
By mode of working (billion tonne kilometres)

All modes	131.7
Own account	50.4
Public haulage	81.4

By gross weight of vehicle (billion tonne kilometres)

All vehicles	131.7
3.5–25 tonnes	13.8
Over 25 tonnes	117.9

GOODS LIFTED
By mode of working (million tonnes)

All modes	1,422
Own account	699
Public haulage	723

By gross weight of vehicle (million tonnes)

All vehicles	1,422
3.5–25 tonnes	207
Over 25 tonnes	1,215

Source: Department for Transport

ROAD TRAFFIC BY TYPE OF VEHICLE (GREAT BRITAIN) 2009
Million vehicle kilometres

All motor vehicles	504,000
Cars and taxis	400,700
Light vans	66,600
Goods vehicles	26,400
Buses and coaches	5,200
Motorcycles	5,200
Pedal cycles	5,000

Source: Department for Transport

BUSES

The majority of bus services outside London are provided on a commercial basis by private operators. Local authorities have powers to subsidise services where needs are not being met by a commercial service.

Since April 2008 people aged 60 and over and disabled people who qualify under the categories listed in the Transport Act 2000 have been able to travel for free on any local bus across England between 9.30am and 11pm Monday to Friday and all day on weekends and bank holidays. Local authorities recompense operators for the reduced fare revenue. A similar scheme operates in Wales and within London, although there is no time restriction. In Scotland, people aged 60 and over and disabled people have been able to travel for free on any local or long-distance bus since April 2006.

In London, Transport for London (TfL) has overall responsibility for setting routes, service standards and fares for the bus network. Almost all routes are competitively tendered to commercial operators.

In Northern Ireland, passenger transport services are provided by Ulsterbus and Metro (formerly Citybus), two wholly owned subsidiaries of the Northern Ireland Transport Holding Company. Along with Northern Ireland Railways, Ulsterbus and Metro operate under the brand name of Translink and are publicly owned. Ulsterbus is responsible for virtually all bus services in Northern Ireland except Belfast city services, which are operated by Metro. People living in Northern Ireland aged 65 and over can travel on buses and trains for free once they have obtained a Senior SmartPass from Translink.

LOCAL BUS PASSENGER JOURNEYS 2009–10
No. of journeys (millions)

England	4,604
London	2,238
Scotland	467
Wales	117
Total	5,188

Source: Department for Transport

TAXIS AND PRIVATE HIRE VEHICLES

A taxi is a public transport vehicle with fewer than nine passenger seats, which is licensed to 'ply for hire'. This distinguishes taxis from private hire vehicles which must be booked in advance through an operator. In London, taxis and private hire vehicles are licensed by the Public Carriage Office (PCO), part of TfL. Outside London, local authorities are responsible for the licensing of taxis and private hire vehicles operational in their respective administrative areas. At the end of March 2009 there were 71,000 licensed taxis in England.

ROAD SAFETY

In March 2000, the government published a new road safety strategy, *Tomorrow's Roads – Safer for Everyone*, which set casualty reduction targets for 2010. The targets included a 40 per cent reduction in the overall number of people killed or seriously injured in road accidents, a 50 per cent reduction in the number of children killed or seriously injured and a 10 per cent reduction in the slight casualty rate (per 100 million vehicle kilometres), all compared with the average for 1994–8.

There were 208,648 reported casualties on roads in Great Britain in 2010, 6 per cent fewer than in 2009. Child casualties (0–15 years) fell by 5 per cent to 19,569 in 2010, with 55 child fatalities: a 32 per cent reduction. Car user casualties decreased by 7 per cent on the 2009 level to 133,205 and fatalities decreased by 24 per cent to 835. Pedestrian casualties were 25,845 in 2010, 4 per cent less than 2009, while pedestrian deaths were 19 per cent lower compared to 2009 at 405. Compared to 2009, pedal cyclist casualties increased slightly by 1 per cent to 17,185 and the number of pedal cyclists killed on British roads increased by 7 per cent to 111.

ROAD ACCIDENT CASUALTIES 2010

	Fatal	Serious	Slight	All Severities
Average for				
1994–8	3,578	44,078	272,272	319,928
England	1,553	19,702	164,114	185,369
Wales	89	998	8,868	9,955
Scotland	208	1,960	11,156	13,324
Great Britain	1,850	22,660	184,138	208,648

Source: Department for Transport

ROAD ACCIDENT CASUALTIES

injured □   ➔ killed

Source: Department for Transport

DRIVING LICENCES

It is necessary to hold a valid full licence in order to drive unaccompanied on public roads in the UK. Learner drivers must obtain a provisional driving licence before starting to learn to drive and must then pass theory and practical tests to obtain a full driving licence.

There are separate tests for driving motorcycles, cars, passenger-carrying vehicles (PCVs) and large goods vehicles (LGVs). Drivers must hold full car entitlement before they can apply for PCV or LGV entitlements.

The Driver and Vehicle Licensing Agency (DVLA) ceased the issue of paper licences in March 2000, but those currently in circulation will remain valid until they expire or the details on them change. The photocard driving licence was introduced to comply with the second EC directive on driving licences. This requires a photograph of the driver to be included on all UK licences issued from July 2001.

To apply for a first photocard driving licence, individuals are required to complete the form *Application for a Driving Licence* (D1).

The minimum age for driving motor cars, light goods vehicles up to 3.5 tonnes and motorcycles is 17 (moped, 16). Since June 1997, drivers who collect six or more penalty points within two years of qualifying lose their licence and are required to take another test. All forms and leaflets including *What You Need to Know About Driving Licences* (D100), are available from post offices, DVLA local offices and online (W www.dvla.gov.uk or W www.direct.gov.uk).

The DVLA is responsible for issuing driving licences, registering and licensing vehicles, and collecting excise duty in Great Britain. Driver and Vehicle Licensing Northern Ireland (DVLNI), part of the Driver and Vehicle Agency (DVA), has similar responsibilities in Northern Ireland.

DRIVING LICENCE FEES
As at August 2011

Provisional licence	
Car, motorcycle or moped	£50.00
Bus or lorry	Free
After disqualification until passing re-test	Free
Changing a provisional licence to a full licence	Free
Renewal	
Renewing the photo on the licence (must be renewed every 10 years)	£20.00
At age 70 and over	Free
For medical reasons	Free
Bus or lorry licence	Free
After disqualification	£65.00
After disqualification for some drink driving offences*	£90.00
After revocation (under the New Drivers Act)	£50.00
Replacing a lost or stolen licence	£20.00
Adding an entitlement to a full licence	Free
Exchanging	
a paper licence for a photocard licence†	£20.00
a photocard for a photocard licence†	£20.00
a full GB licence for a full Northern Ireland licence	Free
a full GB licence for a full EU/EEA or other foreign licence (including Channel Islands and Isle of Man)	Free
a full EU/EEA or other foreign licence (including Channel Islands and Isle of Man) for a full GB licence	£50.00
Change of name or address (existing licence must be surrendered)	Free

* For an alcohol-related offence where the DVLA needed to arrange medical enquiries

† Including removing expired endorsements

DRIVING TESTS
The Driving Standards Agency (DSA) is responsible for carrying out driving tests and approving driving instructors in Great Britain. Driver and Vehicle Testing, part of the Driver and Vehicle Agency, is responsible for testing drivers and vehicles in Northern Ireland.

DRIVING TESTS TAKEN AND PASSED
April 2010–March 2011

	Number Taken	Percentage Passed
Practical Test		
Car	1,605,599	46
Motorcycle Module 1	57,711	65
Motorcycle Module 2	49,644	67
Large goods vehicle	43,894	52
Passenger-carrying vehicle	8,546	54
Theory Test		
Car	1,346,192	63
Motorcycle	58,133	81
Large goods vehicle		
Multiple choice	26,606	80
Hazard perception	26,478	82
Driver CPC*	10,874	62
Passenger-carrying vehicle		
Multiple choice	7,421	77
Hazard perception	7,291	81
Driver CPC*	5,348	49

* Driver Certificate of Professional Competence – legal requirement for all professional bus, coach and lorry drivers
Source: DSA

The theory and practical driving tests can be booked with a postal application, online (W www.direct.gov.uk/drivingtest) or by phone (T 0300-200 1122).

DRIVING TEST FEES (WEEKDAY/EVENING* AND WEEKEND)
As at June 2010

Theory tests	
Car and motorcycle	£31.00
Bus and lorry	
Multiple choice test	£35.00
Hazard perception test	£15.00
Driver Certificate of Professional Competence (CPC)	£30.00
Practical tests	
Car	£62.00/£75.00
Tractor and other specialist vehicles	£62.00/£75.00
Motorcycle	
Module 1	£15.50/£15.50
Module 2	£75.00/£88.50
Lorry and bus	£115.00/£141.00
Driver Certificate of Professional Competence (CPC)	£55.00/£63.00
Car and trailer	£115.00/£141.00
Extended tests for disqualified drivers	
Car	£124.00/£150.00
Motorcycle	
Module 1	£15.50/£15.50
Module 2	£150.00/£177.00

* After 4.30pm

RATES OF DUTY
Cars registered on or after 1 March 2001 and first-year* rates

Band	CO_2 Emissions (g/km)	Petrol and Diesel Car		Alternative Fuel Car	
		6 months	12 months	6 months	12 months
A	Up to 100	–	–	–	–
B	101–110	£20.00	–	£10.00	–
C	111–120	£30.00	–	£20.00	–
D	121–130	£95.00	£52.25	£85.00	£46.75
E	131–140	£115.00	£63.25	£105.00	£57.75
F	141–150	£130.00	£71.50	£120.00	£66.00
G	151–165	£165.00	£90.75	£155.00	£85.25
H	166–175	£190.00 (£265.00)	£104.50	£180.00 (£255.00)	£99.00
I	176–185	£210.00 (£315.00)	£115.50	£200.00 (£305.00)	£110.00
J	186–200	£245.00 (£445.00)	£134.75	£233.00 (£435.00)	£129.25
K†	201–225	£260.00 (£580.00)	£143.00	£250.00 (£570.00)	£137.50
L	226–255	£445.00 (£790.00)	£244.75	£435.00 (£780.00)	£239.25
M	255+	£460.00 (£1,000.00)	£253.00	£450.00 (£990.00)	£247.50

* First-year rates (figures in parentheses) are payable for some vehicles' first tax disc taken out at first registration
† Includes cars that have a CO_2 emission figure over 225g/km but were registered before 23 March 2006

VEHICLE LICENCES
Registration and first licensing of vehicles is through local offices of the DVLA in Swansea. Local facilities for relicensing are available at any post office which deals with vehicle licensing. Applicants will need to take their vehicle registration document (V5C) or, if this is not available, the applicant must complete form V62. Postal applications can be made to the post offices shown in the V100 booklet, which also provides guidance on registering and licensing vehicles. All forms and booklets are available at post offices, DVLA local offices and online (W www.dvla.gov.uk or W www.direct.gov.uk)

MOTOR VEHICLES LICENSED 2010 (GREAT BRITAIN)

	Thousands
All cars	28,421
Light goods vehicles	3,208
Motorcycles	1,234
Heavy goods vehicles	470
Buses and coaches	171
Other vehicles*	616
Total	34,120

* Includes rear diggers, lift trucks, rollers, ambulances, Hackney Carriages, three-wheelers and agricultural vehicles
Source: Department for Transport

VEHICLE EXCISE DUTY
Details of the present duties chargeable on motor vehicles are available at DVLA local offices, post offices and online (W www.dvla.gov.uk or W www.direct.gov.uk). The Vehicle Excise and Registration Act 1994 provides *inter alia* that any vehicle kept on a public road but not used on roads is chargeable to excise duty as if it were in use. All non-commercial vehicles constructed before 1 January 1973 are exempt from vehicle excise duty. Any vehicle licensed on or after 31 January 1998, not in use and not kept on public roads must be registered as SORN (Statutory Off Road Notification) to be exempted from vehicle excise duty. From 1 January 2004 the registered keeper of a vehicle remains responsible for taxing a vehicle or making a SORN declaration until that liability is formally transferred to a new keeper.

RATES OF DUTY *from April 2011*

	12 months	6 months
Cars (private/light goods) registered before 1 March 2001		
Under 1,549cc	£130.00	£71.50
Over 1,549cc	£215.00	£118.25
Cars (private/light goods) registered on or after 1 March 2001	£210.00	£115.00
Euro 4 light goods vehicles registered between 1 March 2003 and 31 December 2006	£130.00	£71.50
Euro 5 light goods vehicles registered between 1 January 2009 and 31 December 2010	£130.00	£71.50
Motorcycles (with or without sidecar)		
Not over 150cc	£16.00	–
151–400cc	£35.00	–
401–600cc	£53.00	£29.15
600cc+	£74.00	£40.70
Tricycles		
Not over 150cc	£16.00	–
All others	£74.00	£40.70
Buses*		
Seating 10–17	£165.00	£90.75
Seating 18–36	£220.00	£121.00
Seating 37–61	£330.00	£181.50
Seating 62+	£500.00	£275.00

* Seating capacity includes driver. The 12-month rate for all reduced pollution buses is £165.00 and the 6-month rate is £90.75

MOT TESTING
Cars, motorcycles, motor caravans, light goods and dual-purpose vehicles more than three years old must be covered by a current MOT test certificate. However, some vehicles (ie minibuses, ambulances and taxis) may require a certificate at one year old. All certificates must be renewed annually. The MOT testing scheme is administered by the Vehicle and Operator Services Agency (VOSA) on behalf of the Secretary of State for Transport.

A fee is payable to MOT testing stations, which must be authorised to carry out tests. The current maximum fees are:

For cars, private hire and public service vehicles, motor caravans, dual purpose vehicles, ambulances and taxis (all up to eight passenger seats)	£54.85
For motorcycles	£29.65
For motorcycles with sidecar	£37.80
For three-wheeled vehicles (up to 450kg unladen weight)	£37.80
*Private passenger vehicles and ambulances with:	
9–12 passenger seats	£57.30 (£64.00)
13–16 passenger seats	£59.55 (£80.50)
16+ passenger seats	£80.65 (£124.50)
Goods vehicles (3,000–3,500kg)	£58.60

* Figures in parentheses include seatbelt installation check

SHIPPING AND PORTS

Sea trade has always played a central role in Britain's economy. By the 17th century Britain had built up a substantial merchant fleet and by the early 20th century it dominated the world shipping industry. Until the late 1990s the size and tonnage of the UK-registered trading fleet had been steadily declining. By the end of 2010* the number of ships in the UK-flagged merchant fleet had increased by 76 per cent while gross tonnage had more than quadrupled since 1999. The UK-flagged merchant fleet now constitutes 1.2 per cent of the world merchant fleet in terms of vessels and 1.8 per cent in terms of gross tonnage.

Freight is carried by liner and bulk services, almost all scheduled liner services being containerised. About 95 per cent by weight of Britain's overseas trade is carried by sea; this amounts to 75 per cent of its total value. Passengers and vehicles are carried by roll-on, roll-off ferries, hovercraft, hydrofoils and high-speed catamarans. There were around 44 million ferry passengers in 2010, of whom 22 million travelled internationally.

Lloyd's of London provides the most comprehensive shipping intelligence service in the world. *Lloyd's Shipping Index,* published daily, lists some 25,000 ocean-going vessels and gives the latest known report of each.

PORTS

There are more than 650 ports in Great Britain for which statutory harbour powers have been granted. Of these about 120 are commercially significant ports. In 2010* the largest ports in terms of freight tonnage were Grimsby and Immingham (54.0 million tonnes), London (48.1 million tonnes), Milford Haven (42.8 million tonnes), Southampton (39.4 million tonnes), Tees and Hartlepool (35.7 million tonnes), Forth (34.3 million tonnes), Liverpool (30.1 million tonnes), Felixstowe (25.8 million tonnes) and Dover (24.1 million tonnes). Belfast (12.8 million tonnes) is the principal freight port in Northern Ireland.

Broadly speaking, ports are owned and operated by private companies, local authorities or trusts. The largest operator is Associated British Ports which owns 21 ports. Provisional port traffic results show that 510 million tonnes were handled by UK ports in 2010, an increase of 2 per cent on the previous year's figure of 501 million tonnes.

* Provisional data

MARINE SAFETY

The Maritime and Coastguard Agency is an executive agency of the Department for Transport. Working closely with the shipping industry and the public, it aims to:

- reduce accidents and accident-related deaths within UK search and rescue waters and coastline
- reduce accidents and accident-related deaths from UK-registered merchant ships and fishing vessels
- reduce the number of incidents of pollution from shipping activities in the UK pollution control zone

HM Coastguard maintains a 24-hour search and rescue response and coordination capability for the whole of the UK coast and the internationally agreed search and rescue region. HM Coastguard is responsible for mobilising and organising resources in response to people in distress at sea, or at risk of injury or death on the UK's cliffs or shoreline.

Locations hazardous to shipping in coastal waters are marked by lighthouses and other lights and buoys. The lighthouse authorities are the Corporation of Trinity House (for England, Wales and the Channel Islands), the Northern Lighthouse Board (for Scotland and the Isle of Man), and the Commissioners of Irish Lights (for Northern Ireland and the Republic of Ireland). Trinity House maintains 69 lighthouses, 10 light vessels/floats, 412 buoys, 19 beacons, 48 radar beacons and seven DGPS (Differential Global Positioning System) stations*. The Northern Lighthouse Board maintains 208 lighthouses, 160 buoys, 31 beacons, 27 radar beacons, 26 AIS (automatic identification system) stations, four DGPS stations and one LORAN (long-range navigation) station; and Irish Lights looks after 80 lighthouses, 148 buoys, 45 beacons, 22 radar beacons, three DGPS stations, one LANBY (large automatic navigational buoy) with AIS in operation on ten lighthouses.

Harbour authorities are responsible for pilotage within their harbour areas; and the Ports Act 1991 provides for the transfer of lights and buoys to harbour authorities where these are used mainly for local navigation.

* DGPS is a satellite-based navigation system

UK-OWNED TRADING VESSELS
500 gross tons and over, as at end 2009

Type of vessel	No.	Gross tonnage
Tankers	153	6,374,000
Fully cellular container	108	5,341,000
Dry bulk carriers	65	3,185,000
Ro-Ro (passenger and cargo)	106	1,535,000
Passenger	25	1,207,000
Other general cargo	116	685,000
Specialised carriers	26	1,250,000
All vessels	599	19,577,000

Source: Department for Transport

UK SEA PASSENGER MOVEMENTS 2009

Type of journey	No. of passenger movements
International	
Ro-Ro Passengers on short sea routes	21,626,000
Passengers on cruises beginning or ending at UK ports*	1,347,000
Passengers on long sea journeys	55,000
Total	23,028,000

* Passengers are included at both departure and arrival if their journeys begin and end at a UK seaport
Source: Department for Transport

MARINECALL WEATHER FORECAST SERVICE

Marinecall offers a wide range of inshore, offshore and European forecasts from the Met Office which include gale and strong wind warnings, the general situation, wind speed and direction, probability and strength of gusts, developing weather conditions, visibility and sea state. Information is provided by various means including telephone, fax, SMS etc. Marinecall 10-day forecasts contain a 48-hour inshore waters forecast for the coastal area and up to 12 miles offshore, followed by a 1–5 day forecast for the local sea area, 6–10 day national forecast and an outlook for the month ahead. In addition fax forecasts provide an Atlantic surface pressure chart and 24-hour offshore forecast maps. Other services such as area specific, current weather reports and 48-hour forecasts are also available.

MARINECALL 10-DAY FORECAST

INSHORE AREA	By Phone 09068-500+	By Fax 09065-300+
Cape Wrath – Rattray Head	451	251
Rattray Head – Berwick	452	252
Berwick – Whitby	453	253
Whitby – Gibraltar Point	454	254
Gibraltar Point – North Foreland	455	255
North Foreland – Selsey Bill	456	256
Selsey Bill – Lyme Regis	457	257
Lyme Regis – Hartland Point	458	258
Hartland Point – St David's Head	459	259
St David's Head – Great Ormes Head	460	260
Great Ormes Head – Mull of Galloway	461	261
Mull of Galloway – Mull of Kintyre	462	262
Mull of Kintyre – Ardnamurchan	463	263
Ardnamurchan – Cape Wrath	464	264
Lough Foyle – Carlingford Lough	465	265
Channel Islands	432	–
OFFSHORE AREA		
English Channel	992	270
Southern North Sea	991	271
Irish Sea	954	273
Biscay	953	274
North-west Scotland	955	275
Northern North Sea	985	276

Marinecall by UK landline is charged at 60p per minute and Marinecall by fax at £1.50 per minute. Calls from mobiles may be subject to network operator surcharges. Subscription packages are available.

UK SHIPPING FORECAST AREAS

Weather bulletins for shipping are broadcast daily on BBC Radio 4 at 00h 48m, 05h 20m, 12h 01m and 17h 54m. All transmissions are broadcast on long wave at 1515m (198kHz) and the 00h 48m and 05h 20m transmissions are also broadcast on FM. The bulletins consist of a gale warning summary, general synopsis, sea-area forecasts and coastal station reports. In addition, gale warnings are broadcast at the first available programme break after receipt. If this does not coincide with a news bulletin, the warning is repeated after the next news bulletin. Shipping forecasts and gale warnings are also available on the Met Office and BBC Weather websites.

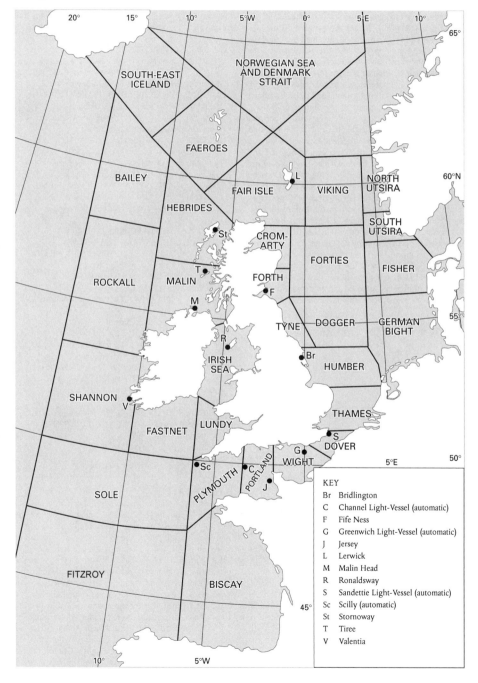

KEY
Br Bridlington
C   Channel Light-Vessel (automatic)
F   Fife Ness
G   Greenwich Light-Vessel (automatic)
J   Jersey
L   Lerwick
M   Malin Head
R   Ronaldsway
S   Sandettie Light-Vessel (automatic)
Sc Scilly (automatic)
St Stornoway
T   Tiree
V   Valentia

RELIGION IN THE UK

The 2001 census included a voluntary question on religion for the first time (although the question had been included in previous censuses in Northern Ireland); 92 per cent of people chose to answer the question. In the UK, 71.6 per cent of people in Britain identified themselves as Christian (42.1 million people). After Christianity, the next most prevalent faith was Islam with 2.7 per cent describing their religion as Muslim (1.6 million people). The next largest religious groups were Hindus (559,000), followed by Sikhs (336,000), Jews (267,000), Buddhists (152,000) and people from other religions (179,000). Together, these groups accounted for less than 3 per cent of the total UK population. People in Northern Ireland were most likely to say that they identified with a religion (86 per cent) compared with 77 per cent in England and Wales and 67 per cent in Scotland. The English counties with the highest proportion of Christians are Durham, Merseyside and Cumbria, each with 82 per cent or more; in Wales it is Ynys Mon (Isle of Anglesey) (79 per cent). London has the highest proportion of Muslims (8.5 per cent), Hindus (4.1 per cent), Jews (2.1 per cent), Buddhists (0.8 per cent) and people of other religions (0.5 per cent). Around 16 per cent of the UK population stated that they had no religion. The districts with the highest proportions of people with no religion were Norwich, Brighton and Hove and Cambridge, all with over 25 per cent. This category included those who identified themselves as agnostics, atheists, heathens and Jedi Knights.

CENSUS 2001 RESULTS – RELIGIONS IN THE UK

	thousands	per cent
Christian	42,079	71.6
Buddhist	152	0.3
Hindu	559	1.0
Jewish	267	0.5
Muslim	1,591	2.7
Sikh	336	0.6
Other religion	179	0.3
All religions	45,163	76.8
No religion	9,104	15.5
Not stated	4,289	7.3
All no religion/not stated	13,626	23.2
TOTAL	58,789	100

Source: Census 2001

INTER-CHURCH AND INTER-FAITH COOPERATION

The main umbrella body for the Christian churches in the UK is Churches Together in Britain and Ireland. There are also ecumenical bodies in each of the constituent countries of the UK: Churches Together in England, Action of Churches Together in Scotland, CYTUN (Churches Together in Wales), and the Irish Council of Churches. The Free Churches Group (formerly the Free Churches Council), which is closely associated with Churches Together in England, represents most of the free churches in England and Wales, and the Evangelical Alliance represents evangelical Christians.

The Inter Faith Network for the United Kingdom promotes cooperation between faiths, and the Council of Christians and Jews works to improve relations between the two religions. Churches Together in Britain and Ireland also has a commission on inter-faith relations.

ACTION OF CHURCHES TOGETHER IN SCOTLAND, Inglewood House, Alloa, Clackmannanshire FK10 2HU T 01259-216980 W www.acts-scotland.org
  General Secretary, Brother Stephen Smyth
CHURCHES TOGETHER IN BRITAIN AND IRELAND, 39 Ecclestone Square, London SW1V 1BX T 020-7901 4890 E info@ctbi.org.uk W www.ctbi.org.uk
  General Secretary, Revd Bob Fyffe
CHURCHES TOGETHER IN ENGLAND, 27 Tavistock Square, London WC1H 9HH T 020-7529 8131
  E office@cte.org.uk W www.churches-together.net
  General Secretary, Revd Dr David Cornick
COUNCIL OF CHRISTIANS AND JEWS, 1st Floor, Camelford House, 87–89 Albert Embankment, London SE1 7TP T 020-7820 0090 E cjrelations@ccj.org.uk
  W www.ccj.org.uk
  Chief Executive, David Gifford
CYTUN (CHURCHES TOGETHER IN WALES), 58 Richmond Road, Cardiff CF24 3UR T 029-2046 4204 E post@scytun.org.uk W www.cytun.org.uk
  Chief Executive, Revd Aled Edwards, OBE
EVANGELICAL ALLIANCE, 186 Kennington Park Road, London SE11 4BT T 020-7207 2100 E info@eauk.org W www.eauk.org
  General Director, Steve Clifford
FREE CHURCHES GROUP, 27 Tavistock Square, London WC1H 9HH T 020-7529 8131 E freechurch@cte.org.uk
  Executive Secretary, Revd Mark Fisher
INTERFAITH NETWORK FOR THE UK, 8A Lower Grosvenor Place, London SW1W 0EN T 020-7931 7766 E ifnet@interfaith.org.uk W www.interfaith.org.uk
  Director, Dr Harriet Crabtree
IRISH COUNCIL OF CHURCHES, Inter-Church Centre, 48 Elmwood Avenue, Belfast BT9 6AZ T 028-9066 3145 E info@irishchurches.org W www.irishchurches.org
  Executive Officer, Mervyn McCullagh

RELIGIONS AND BELIEFS

BAHA'I FAITH

Mirza Husayn-'Ali, known as Baha'u'llah (Glory of God) was born in Iran in 1817 and became a follower of the Bab, a religious reformer and prophet who was imprisoned for his beliefs and executed on the grounds of heresy in 1850. Baha'u'llah was himself imprisoned in 1852, and in 1853 he had a vision that he was the 'promised one' foretold by the Bab. He was exiled after his release from prison and eventually arrived in Acre, now in Israel, where he continued to compose the Baha'i sacred scriptures. He died in 1892 and was succeeded by his son, Abdu'l-Baha, as spiritual leader, under whose guidance the faith spread to Europe and North America. He was followed by Shoghi Effendi, his grandson, who translated many of Baha'u'llah's works into English. Upon his death in 1957, a democratic system of leadership was brought into operation.

The Baha'i faith espouses the unity and relativity of religious truth and teaches that there is only one God, whose will has been revealed to mankind by a series of messengers, such as Zoroaster, Abraham, Moses, Buddha, Krishna, Christ, Muhammad, the Bab and Baha'u'llah, who were seen as the founders of separate religions, but whose common purpose was to bring God's message to mankind. It teaches that all races and both sexes are equal and deserving of equal opportunities and treatment, that education is a fundamental right and encourages a fair distribution of wealth. In addition, the faith exhorts mankind to establish a world federal system to promote peace and tolerance.

A feast is held every 19 days, which consists of prayer and readings of Baha'i scriptures, consultation on community business, and social activities. Music, food and beverages usually accompany the proceedings. There is no clergy; each local community elects a local assembly, which coordinates community activities (such as devotional gatherings, study circles and classes for children and young people), enrols new members, counsels and assists members in need, and conducts Baha'i marriages and funerals. A national assembly is elected annually by locally elected delegates, and every five years the national spiritual assemblies meet together to elect the Universal House of Justice, the supreme international governing body of the Baha'i Faith. Worldwide there are over 13,000 local spiritual assemblies; there are around five million members residing in about 235 countries, of which 179 have national organisations.

BAHA'I COMMUNITY OF THE UK,
27 Rutland Gate, London SW7 1PD T 020-7584 2566
E oea@bahai.org.uk W www.bahai.org.uk
Director, Office of External Affairs, Dr Kishan Manocha

BUDDHISM

Buddhism originated in what is now the Bihar area of northern India in the teachings of Siddhartha Gautama, who became the *Buddha* (Enlightened One). In the Thai or Suriyakati calendar the beginning of the Buddhist era is dated from death of Buddha; the year 2011 is therefore 2554 by the Thai Buddhist reckoning.

Fundamental to Buddhism is the concept of rebirth, whereby each life carries with it the consequences of the conduct of earlier lives (known as the law of *karma*) and this cycle of death and rebirth is broken only when the state of *nirvana* has been reached. Buddhism steers a middle path between belief in personal continuity and the belief that death results in total extinction.

While doctrine does not have a pivotal position in Buddhism, a statement of four 'Noble Truths' is common to all its schools and varieties. These are: suffering is inescapable in even the most fortunate of existences; craving is the root cause of suffering; abandonment of the selfish mindset is the way to end suffering; and bodily and mental discipline, accompanied by the cultivation of wisdom and compassion, provides the spiritual path ('Noble Eightfold Path') to accomplish this. Buddhists deny the idea of a creator and prefer to emphasise the practical aspects of moral and spiritual development.

The schools of Buddhism can be broadly divided into three: *Theravada,* the generally monastic-led tradition practised in Sri Lanka and South-East Asia; *Mahayana,* the philosophical and popular traditions of the Far East; and *Esoteric,* the Tantric-derived traditions found in Tibet and Mongolia and, to a lesser extent, China and Japan. The extensive Theravada scriptures are contained in the *Pali Canon,* which dates in its written form from the first century BC. Mahayana and Esoteric schools have Sanskrit-derived translations of these plus many more additional scriptures as well as exegetical material.

In the East the new and full moons and the lunar quarter days were (and to a certain extent, still are) significant in determining the religious calendar. Most private homes contain a shrine where offerings, worship and other spiritual practices (such as meditation, chanting or mantra recitation) take place on a daily basis. Buddhist festivals vary according to local traditions within the different schools and there is little uniformity – even in commemorating the birth, enlightenment and death of the Buddha.

There is no governing authority for Buddhism in the UK. Communities representing all schools of Buddhism operate independently. The Buddhist Society was established in 1924; it runs courses, lectures and meditation groups, and publishes books about Buddhism. The Network of Buddhist Organisations was founded in 1993 to promote fellowship and dialogue between Buddhist organisations and to facilitate cooperation in matters of common interest.

There are estimated to be at least 300 million Buddhists worldwide. Of the 152,000 Buddhists in the UK (according to the 2001 census), 60,000 are white British (the majority are converts), 36,000 Chinese, 15,000 Asian and 36,000 'other ethnic'.

THE BUDDHIST SOCIETY, 58 Eccleston Square, London SW1V 1PH T 020-7834 5858 E info@thebuddhistsociety.org W www.thebuddhistsociety.org

LONDON BUDDHIST CENTRE,
51 Roman Road, London E2 0HU T 0845-458 4716
E info@lbc.org.uk W www.lbc.org.uk

THE NETWORK OF BUDDHIST ORGANISATIONS,
PO Box 4147, Maidenhead SL60 1DN T 0845-345 8978
E secretary@nbo.org.uk W www.nbo.org.uk

THE OFFICE OF TIBET, Tibet House, 1 Culworth Street, London NW8 7AF T 020-7722 5378 E samdup@tibet.com W www.tibet.com
Representative of HH the Dalai Lama, Thubten Samdup

SOKA GAKKAI INTERNATIONAL (UK), Taplow Court Grand Cultural Centre, Taplow, Berkshire SL6 0ER
T 01628-773163 W www.sgi-uk.org

CHRISTIANITY

Christianity is a monotheistic faith based on the person and teachings of Jesus Christ, and all Christian denominations claim his authority. Central to its teaching is the concept of God and his son Jesus Christ, who was crucified and resurrected in order to enable mankind to attain salvation.

The Jewish scriptures predicted the coming of a *Messiah,* an 'anointed one', who would bring salvation. To Christians, Jesus of Nazareth, a Jewish rabbi (teacher) who was born in Palestine, was the promised Messiah. Jesus' birth, teachings, crucifixion and subsequent resurrection are recorded in the *Gospels,* which, together with other scriptures that summarise Christian belief, form the *New Testament.* This, together with the Hebrew scriptures – entitled the *Old Testament* by Christians – makes up the Bible, the sacred texts of Christianity.

Christians believe that sin distanced mankind from God, and that Jesus was the son of God, sent to redeem mankind from sin by his death. In addition, many believe that Jesus will return again at some future date, triumph over evil and establish a kingdom on earth, thus inaugurating a new age. The Gospel assures Christians that those who believe in Jesus and obey his teachings will be forgiven their sins and will be resurrected from the dead.

The Apostles were Jesus' first converts and are recognised by Christians as the founders of the Christian community. Early Christianity spread rapidly throughout the eastern provinces of the Roman Empire but was subjected to great persecution until AD 313, when Emperor Constantine's Edict of Toleration confirmed its right to exist. Christianity was established as the religion of the Roman Empire in AD 381.

Between AD 325 and 787 there were seven Oecumenical Councils at which bishops from the entire Christian world assembled to resolve various doctrinal disputes. The estrangement between East and West began after Constantine moved the centre of the Roman Empire from Rome to Constantinople, and it grew after the division of the Roman Empire into eastern and western halves. Linguistic and cultural differences between Greek East and Latin West served to encourage separate ecclesiastical developments which became pronounced in the tenth and early 11th centuries. Administration of the church was divided between five ancient patriarchates: Rome and all the West, Constantinople (the imperial city – the 'New Rome'), Jerusalem and all of Palestine, Antioch and all the East, and Alexandria and all of Africa. Of these, only Rome was in the Latin West and after the schism in 1054, Rome developed a structure of authority centralised on the Papacy, while the Orthodox East maintained the style of localised administration. Papal authority over the doctrine and jurisdiction of the church in Western Europe was unrivalled after the split with the Eastern Orthodox Church until the Protestant Reformation in the 16th century.

Christian practices vary widely between different Christian churches, but prayer, charity and giving (for the maintenance of the church buildings, for the work of the church, and to those in need) are common to all. In addition, certain days of observance, ie the *Sabbath, Easter* and *Christmas,* are celebrated by most Christians. The Orthodox, Roman Catholic and Anglican churches celebrate many more days of observance, based on saints and significant events in the life of Jesus. The belief in sacraments, physical signs believed to have been ordained by Jesus Christ to symbolise and convey spiritual gifts, varies greatly between Christian denominations; *baptism* and the *Eucharist* are practised by most Christians. Baptism, symbolising repentance and faith in Jesus, is an act marking entry into the Christian community; the Eucharist, the ritual re-enactment of the Last Supper, Jesus' final meal with his disciples, is also practised by most denominations. Other sacraments, such as anointing the sick, the laying on of hands to symbolise the passing on of the office of priesthood or to heal the sick, and speaking in tongues, where it is believed that the person is possessed by the Holy Spirit, are less common. In denominations where infant baptism is practised, confirmation (where the person confirms the commitments made on their behalf in infancy) is common. Matrimony and the ordination of priests are also widely believed to be sacraments. Many Protestants regard only baptism and the Eucharist to be sacraments; the Quakers and the Salvation Army reject the use of sacraments.

See Churches for contact details of the Church of England, the Roman Catholic Church and other Christian churches in the UK.

HINDUISM

Hinduism has no historical founder but had become highly developed in India by *c.*2500 BC. Its adherents originally called themselves Aryans; Muslim invaders first called the Aryans 'Hindus' (derived from 'Sindhu', the name of the river Indus) in the eighth century.

Most Hindus hold that *satya* (truthfulness), honesty, sincerity and devotion to God are essential for good living. They believe in one supreme spirit *(Brahman),* and in the transmigration of *atman* (the soul). Most Hindus accept the doctrine of *karma* (consequences of actions), the concept of *samsara* (successive lives) and the possibility of all atmans achieving *moksha* (liberation from samsara) through *jnana* (knowledge), *yoga* (meditation), *karma* (work or action) and *bhakti* (devotion).

Most Hindus offer worship to *murtis* (images of deities) representing different incarnations or aspects of Brahman, and follow their *dharma* (religious and social duty) according to the traditions of their *varna* (social class), *ashrama* (stage in life), *jaiti* (caste) and *kula* (family).

Hinduism's sacred texts are divided into *shruti* ('that which is heard'), including the *Vedas,* and *smriti* ('that which is remembered'), including the *Ramayana,* the *Mahabharata,* the *Puranas* (ancient myths), and the sacred law books. Most Hindus recognise the authority of the *Vedas,* the oldest holy books, and accept the philosophical teachings of the *Upanishads,* the *Vedanta Sutras* and the *Bhagavad-Gita.*

Hindus believe Brahman to be omniscient, omnipotent, limitless and all-pervading. Brahman is usually worshipped in its deity form. Brahma, Vishnu and Shiva are the most important deities or aspects of Brahman worshipped by Hindus; their respective consorts are Saraswati, Lakshmi and Durga or Parvati, also known as Shakti. There are believed to have been ten *avatars* (incarnations) of Vishnu, of whom the most important are Rama and Krishna. Other popular gods are Ganesha, Hanuman and Subrahmanyam. All Hindu gods are seen as aspects of the supreme spirit (Brahman), not as competing deities.

Orthodox Hindus revere all gods and goddesses equally, but there are many denominations, including the Hare-Krishna movement (ISKCon), the Arya Samaj and the Swaminarayan Hindu mission, in which worship is concentrated on one deity. The *guru* (spiritual teacher) is seen as the source of spiritual guidance.

Hinduism does not have a centrally trained and ordained priesthood. The pronouncements of the *shankaracharyas* (heads of monasteries) of Shringeri, Puri, Dwarka and Badrinath are heeded by the orthodox but may be ignored by the various sects.

The commonest form of worship is *puja,* in which water, flowers, food, fruit, incense and light are offered to the deity. Puja may be done either in a home shrine or a *mandir* (temple). Many British Hindus celebrate *samskars* (purification rites), to name a baby, for the sacred thread (an initiation ceremony), marriage and cremation.

The largest communities of Hindus in Britain are in Leicester, London, Birmingham and Bradford, and developed as a result of immigration from India, eastern Africa and Sri Lanka.

There are an estimated 800 million Hindus worldwide; there are around 559,000 adherents, according to the 2001 UK census, and over 140 temples in the UK.

ARYA SAMAJ LONDON, 69A Argyle Road, London
W13 0LY **T** 020-8991 1732
E aryasamajlondon@yahoo.co.uk
Vice President, Amrit Lal Bhardwaj

BHARATIYA VIDYA BHAVAN, Institute of Indian Art and Culture, 4A Castletown Road, London W14 9HE
T 020-7381 3086/4608 E info@bhavan.net
W www.bhavan.net
Executive Director, Dr M. N. Nandakumara

INTERNATIONAL SOCIETY FOR KRISHNA CONSCIOUSNESS (ISKCON), Bhaktivedanta Manor, Dharam Marg, Hilfield Lane, Aldenham, Watford, Herts WD25 8EZ T 01923-851000 E info@krishnatemple.com
W www.krishnatemple.com
Temple President, Sruti Dharma Das

NATIONAL COUNCIL OF HINDU TEMPLES (UK), 1 Hans Close, Stoke, Coventry CV2 4WA T 0780-505 4776 E sanjay.jagatia@ntlworld.com W www.nchtuk.org
General Secretary, Sanjay Jagatia

SWAMINARAYAN HINDU MISSION (SHRI SWAMINARAYAN MANDIR), 105–119 Brentfield Road, London NW10 8LD T 020-8965 2651 E info@mandir.org
W www.mandir.org

HUMANISM

Humanism traces its roots back to ancient times, with Indian, Chinese, Greek and Roman philosophers expressing Humanist ideas some 2,500 years ago. Confucius, the Chinese philosopher who lived *c.*500 BC, believed that religious observances should be replaced with moral values as the basis of social and political order and that 'the true way' is based on reason and humanity. He also stressed the importance of benevolence and respect for others, and believed that the individual situation should be considered rather than the global application of traditional rules.

Humanists believe that there is no God or other supernatural being, that humans have only one life (Humanists do not believe in an afterlife or reincarnation) and that humans can live ethical and fulfilling lives without religious beliefs through a moral code derived from a shared history, personal experience and thought. There are no sacred Humanist texts. Particular emphasis is placed on science as the only reliable source of knowledge of the universe. Many Humanists recognise a need for ceremonies to mark important occasions in life and the British Humanist Association has a network of celebrants who are trained and accredited to conduct baby namings, weddings and funerals. The British Humanist Association's campaigns for a secular society (a society based on freedom of religious or non-religious belief with no privileges for any particular set of beliefs) are based on equality and human rights. The association also campaigns for inclusive schools that meet the needs of all parents and pupils, regardless of their religious or non-religious beliefs.

BRITISH HUMANIST ASSOCIATION, 1 Gower Street, London WC1E 6HD T 020-7079 3580 E 020-7079 3588 E info@humanism.org.uk W www.humanism.org.uk
Chief Executive, Andrew Copson

ISLAM

Islam (which means 'peace arising from submission to the will of Allah' in Arabic) is a monotheistic religion which was taught in Arabia by the Prophet Muhammad, who was born in Mecca (Al-Makkah) in 570 AD. Islam spread to Egypt, north Africa, Spain and the borders of China in the century following the Prophet's death, and is now the predominant religion in Indonesia, the near and Middle East, northern and parts of western Africa, Pakistan, Bangladesh, Malaysia and some of the former Soviet republics. There are also large Muslim communities in other countries.

For Muslims (adherents of Islam), there is one God (*Allah*), who holds absolute power. Muslims believe that Allah's commands were revealed to mankind through the prophets, who include Abraham, Moses and Jesus, but that Allah's message was gradually corrupted until revealed finally and in perfect form to Muhammad through the angel *Jibril* (Gabriel) over a period of 23 years. This last, incorruptible message is said to have been recorded in the *Qur'an* (Koran), which contains 114 divisions called *surahs*, each made up of *ayahs* of various lengths, and is held to be the essence of all previous scriptures. The *Ahadith* are the records of the Prophet Muhammad's deeds and sayings (the *Sunnah*) as practised and recounted by his immediate followers. A culture and a system of law and theology gradually developed to form a distinctive Islamic civilisation. Islam makes no distinction between sacred and worldly affairs and provides rules for every aspect of human life. The *Shariah* is the sacred law of Islam based primarily upon prescriptions derived from the *Qur'an* and the *Sunnah* of the Prophet.

The 'five pillars of Islam' are *shahadah* (a declaration of faith in the oneness and supremacy of Allah and the messengership of Muhammad); *salat* (formal prayer, to be performed five times a day facing the *Ka'bah* (the most sacred shrine in the holy city of Mecca)); *zakat* (welfare due, paid annually on all savings at the rate of 2.5 per cent); *sawm* (fasting during the month of Ramadan from dawn until sunset); and *hajj* (pilgrimage to Mecca made once in a lifetime if the believer is financially and physically able). Some Muslims would add *jihad* as the sixth pillar (striving for the cause of good and resistance to evil).

Two main groups developed among Muslims. *Sunni* Muslims accept the legitimacy of Muhammad's first four *caliphs* (successors as head of the Muslim community) and of the authority of the Muslim community as a whole. About 90 per cent of Muslims are Sunni Muslims.

Shi'ites recognise only Muhammad's son-in-law Ali as his rightful successor and the *Imams* (descendants of Ali, not to be confused with *imams,* who are prayer leaders or religious teachers) as the principal legitimate religious authority. The largest group within Shi'ism is *Twelver Shi'ism*, which has been the official school of law and theology in Iran since the 16th century; other subsects include the *Ismailis*, the *Druze* and the *Alawis*, the latter two differing considerably from the main body of Muslims. The *Ibadis* of Oman are neither Sunni nor Shia, deriving from the strictly observant *Khariji* (Seceders). There is no organised priesthood, but learned men such as imams, *ulama,* and *ayatollahs* are accorded great respect. The *Sufis* are the mystics of Islam. Mosques are centres for worship and teaching and also for social and welfare activities.

Islam was first recorded in western Europe in the eighth century AD when 800 years of Muslim rule began in Spain. Later, Islam spread to eastern Europe. More recently, Muslims came to Europe from Africa, the Middle East and Asia in the late 19th century. Both the Sunni and Shi'a traditions are represented in Britain, but the majority of Muslims in Britain adhere to Sunni Islam. Efforts to establish a representative national body for Muslims in Britain resulted in the founding, in 1997, of the Muslim Council of Britain. In addition, there are many other Muslim organisations in the UK. There are around 1,200 million Muslims worldwide, with nearly two million adherents and about 1,650 mosques in the UK.

IMAMS AND MOSQUES COUNCIL, 20–22 Creffield Road, London W5 3RP T 020-8992 6636
E msraza@muslimcollege.ac.uk
Director, Moulana M. S. Raza

ISLAMIC CULTURAL CENTRE – THE LONDON CENTRAL MOSQUE, 146 Park Road, London NW8 7RG T 020-7725 2213 E info@iccuk.org W www.iccuk.org
Director, Dr Ahmad Al-Dubayan

MUSLIM WORLD LEAGUE LONDON, 46 Goodge Street, London W1T 4LU T 020-7636 7568
Director, Dr Ahmad Makhoodom

UNION OF MUSLIM ORGANISATIONS OF THE UK AND IRELAND, 109 Campden Hill Road, London W8 7TL T 020-7581 9236
Secretary-General, Dr Syed A. Pasha

JAINISM

Jainism traces its history to Vardhamana Jnatriputra, known as *Tirthankara Mahavira* (the Great Hero) whose traditional dates were 599–527 BC. Jains believe he was the last of a series of 24 *Jinas* (those who overcome all passions and desires) or *Tirthankaras* (those who show a way across the ocean of life) stretching back to remote antiquity. Born to a noble family in north-eastern India (the state of Bihar), he renounced the world for the life of a wandering ascetic and after 12 years of austerity and meditation he attained enlightenment. He then preached his message until, at the age of 72, he left the mortal world and achieved total liberation *(moksha)* from the cycle of death and rebirth.

Jains declare that the Hindu rituals of transferring merit are not acceptable as each living being is responsible for its own actions. They recognise some of the minor deities of the Hindu pantheon, but the supreme objects of worship are the Tirthankaras. The pious Jain does not ask favours from the Tirthankaras, but seeks to emulate their example in his or her own life.

Jains believe that the universe is eternal and self-subsisting, that there is no omnipotent creator God ruling it and the destiny of the individual is in his or her own hands. *Karma,* the fruit of past actions, is believed to determine the place of every living being and rebirth may be in the heavens, on earth as a human, an animal or other lower being, or in the hells. The ultimate goal of existence for Jains is *moksha,* a state of perfect knowledge and tranquility for each individual soul, which can be achieved only by gaining enlightenment.

The Jainist path to liberation is defined by the three jewels: *Samyak Darshan* (right perception), *Samyak Jnana* (right knowledge) and *Samyak Charitra* (right conduct). Of the five fundamental precepts of the Jains, *Ahimsa* (non-injury to any form of being, in any mode: thought, speech or action) is the first and foremost, and was popularised by Gandhi as *Ahimsa paramo dharma* (non-violence is the supreme religion).

The largest population of Jains can be found in India but there are approximately 30,000 Jains in Britain, sizeable communities in North America, East Africa, Australia and smaller groups in many other countries.

INSTITUTE OF JAINOLOGY, Unit 18, Silicon Business Centre, 28 Wadsworth Road, Perivale, Greenford, Middx UB6 7JZ T 020-8997 2300 E secretary@jainology.org W www.jainology.org
Hon. Secretary, Dr Harshad Sanghrajka

JUDAISM

Judaism is the oldest monotheistic faith. The primary text of Judaism is the Hebrew bible or *Tanakh,* which records how the descendants of Abraham were led by Moses out of their slavery in Egypt to Mount Sinai where God's law *(Torah)* was revealed to them as the chosen people. The *Talmud,* which consists of commentaries on the *Mishnah* (the first text of rabbinical Judaism), is also held to be authoritative, and may be divided into two main categories: the *halakah* (dealing with legal and ritual matters) and the *aggadah* (dealing with theological and ethical matters not directly concerned with the regulation of conduct). The *midrash* comprises rabbinic writings containing biblical interpretations in the spirit of the aggadah. The halakah has become a source of division: orthodox Jews regard Jewish law as derived from God and therefore unalterable; progressive Jews seek to interpret it in the light of contemporary considerations; and conservative Jews aim to maintain most of the traditional rituals but to allow changes in accordance with tradition. Reconstructionist Judaism, a 20th-century movement, regards Judaism as a culture rather than a theological system and accepts all forms of Jewish practice.

The family is the basic unit of Jewish ritual, with the synagogue playing an important role as the centre for public worship and religious study. A synagogue is led by a group of laymen who are elected to office. The Rabbi is primarily a teacher and spiritual guide. The *Sabbath* is the central religious observance. Most British Jews are descendants of either the *Ashkenazim* of central and eastern Europe or the *Sephardim* of Spain, Portugal and the Middle East.

The Chief Rabbi of the United Hebrew Congregations of the Commonwealth is appointed by a Chief Rabbinate Conference, and is the rabbinical authority of the mainstream Orthodox sector of the Ashkenazi Jewish community, the largest body of which is the United Synagogue. His formal ecclesiastical authority is not recognised by the Reform Synagogues of Great Britain (the largest progressive group), the Union of Liberal and Progressive Synagogues, the Sephardi community or the Assembly of Masorti Synagogues. He is, however, generally recognised both outside the Jewish community and within it as the public religious representative of the totality of British Jewry. The Chief Rabbi is President of the London *Beth Din* (Court of Judgment), a rabbinic court. The *Dayanim* (Assessors) adjudicate in disputes or on matters of Jewish law and tradition; they also oversee dietary law administration, marriage, divorce and issues of personal status.

The Board of Deputies of British Jews, established in 1760, is the representative body of British Jewry. The basis of representation is through the election of deputies by synagogues and communal organisations. It protects and promotes the interests of British Jewry, acts as the central voice of the community and seeks to counter anti-Jewish discrimination and anti-Semitic activities.

There are over 12.5 million Jews worldwide; in the UK there are an estimated 300,000 adherents and over 400 synagogues.

OFFICE OF THE CHIEF RABBI, 305 Ballards Lane, London N12 8GB T 020-8343 6301
E info@chiefrabbi.org W www.chiefrabbi.org
Chief Rabbi, Lord Sacks

BETH DIN (COURT OF THE CHIEF RABBI), 305 Ballards Lane, London N12 8GB T 020-8343 6270 E info@bethdin.org.uk W www.theus.org.uk
Registrar, David Frei
Dayanim, Rabbi Chanoch Ehrentreu *(Consultant Dayan);* Menachem Gelley *(Senior Dayan);* Ivan Binstock; Yonason Abraham; Shmuel Simons

ASSEMBLY OF MASORTI SYNAGOGUES,
Alexander House, 3 Shakespeare Road, London N3 1XE
T 020-8349 6650 E enquiries@masorti.org.uk
W www.masorti.org.uk
Executive Director, Michael Gluckman

BOARD OF DEPUTIES OF BRITISH JEWS,
6 Bloomsbury Square, London WC1A 2LP T 020-7543 5400
F 020-7543 0010 E info@bod.org.uk W www.bod.org.uk
President, Vivian Wineman

FEDERATION OF SYNAGOGUES, 65 Watford Way,
London NW4 3AQ T 020-8202 2263
E info@federationofsynagogues.com
W www.federationofsynagogues.com
President, Alan Finlay
Chief Executive, Dr Eli Kienwald

LIBERAL JUDAISM, The Montagu Centre, 21 Maple Street,
London W1T 4BE T 020-7580 1663
E montagu@liberaljudaism.org W www.liberaljudaism.org
Chief Executive, Rabbi Danny Rich

THE MOVEMENT FOR REFORM JUDAISM, The
Sternberg Centre for Judaism, 80 East End Road, London
N3 2SY T 020-8349 5640 E admin@reformjudaism.org.uk
W www.reformjudaism.org.uk
Chief Executive, Ben Rich

SPANISH AND PORTUGUESE JEWS'
CONGREGATION, 2 Ashworth Road, London W9 1JY
T 020-7289 2573 E howardmiller@spsyn.org.uk
W www.sandp.org.uk
Chief Executive, Howard Miller

UNION OF ORTHODOX HEBREW
CONGREGATIONS, 140 Stamford Hill, London N16 6QT
T 020-8802 6226
Executive Coordinator, Chanoch Kesselman
Secretary, Chayim Schneck

UNITED SYNAGOGUE HEAD OFFICE, Adler House,
735 High Road, London N12 0US T 020-8343 8989
E info@theus.org.uk W www.theus.org.uk
Chief Executive, Jeremy Jacobs

PAGANISM

Paganism draws on the ideas of the Celtic people of pre-Roman Europe and is closely linked to Druidism. The first historical record of Druidry comes from classical Greek and Roman writers of the third century BC, who noted the existence of Druids among a people called the Keltoi who inhabited central and southern Europe. The word druid may derive from the Indo-European 'dreo-vid', meaning 'one who knows the truth'. In practice it was probably understood to mean something like 'wise-one' or 'philosopher-priest'.

Paganism is a pantheistic nature-worshipping religion which incorporates beliefs and ritual practices from ancient times. Pagans place much emphasis on the natural world and the ongoing cycle of life and death is central to their beliefs. Most Pagans believe that they are part of nature and not separate from, or superior to it, and seek to live in a way that minimises harm to the natural environment (the word Pagan derives from the Latin *Paganus,* meaning 'rural'). Paganism strongly emphasises the equality of the sexes, with women playing a prominent role in the modern Pagan movement and goddess worship featuring in most ceremonies. Paganism cannot be defined by any principal beliefs because it is shaped by each individual's experiences.

The Pagan Federation was founded in 1971 to provide information on Paganism, campaigns on issues which affect Paganism and provides support to members of the Pagan community. Within the UK the Pagan Federation is divided into 13 districts each with a district manager, regional and local coordinators. Local meetings are called 'moots' and take place in private homes, pubs or coffee bars. The Pagan Federation publishes a quarterly journal, *Pagan Dawn,* formerly *The Wiccan* (founded in 1968). The federation also publishes other material, arranges members-only and public events and maintains personal contact by letter with individual members and the wider Pagan community. Regional gatherings and conferences are held throughout the year.

THE PAGAN FEDERATION, BM Box 7097, London
WC1N 3XX E secretary@paganfed.org
W www.paganfed.org
President, Chris Crowley
General Secretary, Lee-Anne Haye

SIKHISM

The Sikh religion dates from the birth of Guru Nanak in the Punjab in 1469. 'Guru' means teacher but in Sikh tradition has come to represent the divine presence of God giving inner spiritual guidance. Nanak's role as the human vessel of the divine guru was passed on to nine successors, the last of whom (Guru Gobind Singh) died in 1708. The immortal guru is now held to reside in the sacred scripture, Guru Granth Sahib, and so to be present in all Sikh gatherings.

Guru Nanak taught that there is one God and that different religions are like different roads leading to the same destination. He condemned religious conflict, ritualism and caste prejudices. The fifth Guru, Guru Arjan Dev, largely compiled the Sikh Holy scripture, a collection of hymns *(gurbani)* known as the *Adi Granth.* It includes the writings of the first five gurus and the ninth guru, and selected writings of Hindu and Muslim saints whose views are in accord with the gurus' teachings. Guru Arjan Dev also built the Golden Temple at Amritsar, the centre of Sikhism. The tenth guru, Guru Gobind Singh, passed on the guruship to the sacred scripture, *Guru Granth Sahib* and founded the *Khalsa,* an order intended to fight against tyranny and injustice. Male initiates to the order added 'Singh' to their given names and women added 'Kaur'. Guru Gobind Singh also made the wearing of five symbols obligatory: *kaccha* (a special undergarment), *kara* (a steel bangle), *kirpan* (a small sword), *kesh* (long unshorn hair, and consequently the wearing of a turban) and *kangha* (a comb). These practices are still compulsory for those Sikhs who are initiated into the Khalsa (the *Amritdharis*). Those who do not seek initiation are known as *Sehajdharis.*

There are no professional priests in Sikhism; anyone with a reasonable proficiency in the Punjabi language can conduct a service. Worship can be offered individually or communally, and in a private house or a *gurdwara* (temple). Sikhs are forbidden to eat meat prepared by ritual slaughter; they are also asked to abstain from smoking, alcohol and other intoxicants. Such abstention is compulsory for the Amritdharis.

There are about 20 million Sikhs worldwide and, according to the 2001 census, there are 336,000 adherents in the UK. Every gurdwara manages its own affairs; there is no central body in the UK. The Sikh Missionary Society provides an information service.

SIKH MISSIONARY SOCIETY UK, 10 Featherstone Road,
Southall, Middx UB2 5AA T 020-8574 1902
E info@sikhmissionarysociety.org
W www.sikhmissionarysociety.org
Hon. General Secretary, Teja Singh Manget

ZOROASTRIANISM

Zoroastrians are followers of the Iranian prophet Spitaman Zarathushtra (or Zoroaster in its hellenised form) who lived *c.*1200 BC. Zoroastrians were persecuted in Iran following the Arab invasion of Persia in the seventh century AD and a group (who are known as Parsis) migrated to India in the eighth century AD to avoid harassment and persecution. Zarathushtra's words are recorded in five poems called the *Gathas*, which, together with other scriptures, form the *Avesta*.

Zoroastrianism teaches that there is one God, *Ahura Mazda* (Wise Lord), and that all creation stems ultimately from God; the Gathas teach that human beings have free will, are responsible for their own actions and can choose between good and evil. It is believed that choosing *Asha* (truth or righteousness), with the aid of *Vohu Manah* (good mind), leads to happiness for the individual and society, whereas choosing evil leads to unhappiness and conflict. The *Gathas* also encourage hard work, good deeds and charitable acts. Zoroastrians believe that after death the immortal soul is judged by God, and is then sent to paradise or hell, where it will stay until the end of time to be resurrected for the final judgment.

In Zoroastrian places of worship, an urn containing fire is the central feature; the fire symbolises purity, light and truth and is a visible symbol of the *Fravashi* or *Farohar* (spirit), the presence of Ahura Mazda in every human being. Zoroastrians respect nature and much importance is attached to cultivating land and protecting air, earth and water.

The Zoroastrian Trust Funds of Europe is the main body for Zoroastrians in the UK. Founded in 1861 as the Religious Funds of the Zoroastrians of Europe, it disseminates information on the Zoroastrian faith, provides a place of worship and maintains separate burial grounds for Zoroastrians. It also holds religious and social functions and provides assistance to Zoroastrians as considered necessary, including the provision of loans and grants to students of Zoroastrianism.

There are approximately 140,000 Zoroastrians worldwide, of which around 7,000 reside in Britain, mainly in London and the South East.

ZOROASTRIAN TRUST FUNDS OF EUROPE, Zoroastrian Centre, 440 Alexandra Avenue, Harrow, Middx HA2 9TL T 020-8866 0765 E secretary@ztfe.com W www.ztfe.com
President, Malcolm Deboo

CHURCHES

There are two established (ie state) churches in the United Kingdom: the Church of England and the Church of Scotland. There are no established churches in Wales or Northern Ireland, though the Church in Wales, the Scottish Episcopal Church and the Church of Ireland are members of the Anglican Communion.

CHURCH OF ENGLAND

The Church of England is divided into the two provinces of Canterbury and York, each under an archbishop. The two provinces are subdivided into 44 dioceses.

Legislative provision for the Church of England is made by the General Synod, established in 1970. It also discusses and expresses opinion on any other matter of religious or public interest. The General Synod has 467 members in total, divided between three houses: the House of Bishops, the House of Clergy and the House of Laity. It is presided over jointly by the Archbishops of Canterbury and York and normally meets twice a year. The synod has the power, delegated by parliament, to frame statute law (known as a 'measure') on any matter concerning the Church of England. A measure must be laid before both houses of parliament, who may accept or reject it but cannot amend it. Once accepted the measure is submitted for royal assent and then has the full force of law. In addition to the General Synod, there are synods at diocesan level. The entire General Synod is re-elected once every five years. The ninth General Synod was inaugurated by the Queen on 23 November 2010.

The Archbishops' Council was established in January 1999. Its creation was the result of changes to the Church of England's national structure proposed in 1995 and subsequently approved by the synod and parliament. The council's purpose, set out in the National Institutions Measure 1998, is 'to coordinate, promote and further the work and mission of the Church of England'. It reports to the General Synod. The Archbishops' Council comprises the Archbishops of Canterbury and York, *ex officio*, the prolocutors elected by the convocations of Canterbury and York, the chair and vice-chair of the House of Laity, two bishops, two clergy and two lay persons elected by their respective houses of the General Synod, the Church Estates Commissioner, and up to six persons appointed jointly by the two archbishops.

There are also a number of national boards, councils and other bodies working on matters such as social responsibility, mission, Christian unity and education which report to the General Synod through the Archbishops' Council.

GENERAL SYNOD OF THE CHURCH OF ENGLAND/ ARCHBISHOPS' COUNCIL, Church House, Great Smith Street, London SW1P 3NZ T 020-7898 1000

Secretary-General, William Fittall

THE ORDINATION OF WOMEN
The canon making it possible for women to be ordained to the priesthood was promulgated in the General Synod in February 1994 and the first 32 women priests were ordained on 12 March 1994.

PORVOO DECLARATION
The Porvoo Declaration was approved by the General Synod of the Church of England in July 1995. Churches that approve the declaration regard baptised members of each other's churches as members of their own, and allow free interchange of episcopally ordained ministers within the rules of each church.

MEMBERSHIP
In 2009, 138,300 people were baptised, 52,700 people were married in parish churches, the Church of England had an electoral roll membership of 1.2 million, and each week over 1.1 million people attended services. As at December 2010 there were over 16,000 churches and places of worship; 118 dignitaries (including bishops, archdeacons and cathedral clergy); 7,296 full-time parochial stipendiary clergy; 340 full-time non parochial stipendiary clergy; 3,110 self-supporting ministers; 1,570 chaplains; 320 lay workers and Church Army evangelists; 7,090 licensed readers and 2,690 readers with permission to officiate and active emeriti; and approximately 5,670 active retired ordained clergy.

	Full-time Equivalent Diocesan Clergy 2010		Electoral Roll Membership
	Male	Female	2009
Bath and Wells	152	53	36,200
Birmingham	125	47	17,200
Blackburn	157	21	32,500
Bradford	83	18	11,700
Bristol	100	23	15,800
Canterbury	118	24	20,700
Carlisle	95	26	20,400
Chelmsford	289	85	46,500
Chester	188	55	44,900
Chichester	268	24	52,200
Coventry	100	22	16,800
Derby	107	37	18,300
Durham	147	43	23,200
Ely	96	44	18,900
Europe	–	–	10,900
Exeter	170	38	30,900
Gloucester	103	36	23,600
Guildford	139	36	29,500
Hereford	65	27	17,500
Leicester	100	41	16,800
Lichfield	246	60	43,700
Lincoln	135	36	25,800
Liverpool	154	55	28,000
London	456	81	74,100
Manchester	178	64	32,400
Newcastle	101	33	16,000
Norwich	156	37	19,300
Oxford	300	93	54,500
Peterborough	108	28	19,400
Portsmouth	83	22	17,000
Ripon and Leeds	90	36	16,500
Rochester	179	33	30,100
St Albans	174	81	37,600

St Edmundsbury and Ipswich	108	42	23,100
Salisbury	166	52	41,400
Sheffield	115	39	17,900
Sodor and Man	11	0	2,500
Southwark	261	88	47,600
Southwell and Nottingham	102	45	18,900
Truro	89	18	15,600
Wakefield	101	39	19,300
Winchester	170	26	38,000
Worcester	103	27	19,200
York	174	44	33,900
Total	6,354	1,774	1,197,000

STIPENDS*

	2011–12	2012–13
Archbishop of Canterbury	£71,870	£73,310
Archbishop of York	£61,600	£62,830
Bishop of London	£56,460	£57,590
Other diocesan bishops	£39,020	£39,800
Suffragan bishops	£31,830	£32,470
Assistant bishops (full-time)	£30,810	£31,430
Deans	£31,830	£32,470
Archdeacons (recommended)	£31,110	£31,730
Residentiary canons	£24,640†	£25,130†
Incumbents and clergy of similar status	£22,810†	£23,270†

* For those appointed on or after 1 April 2004; transitional arrangements are in place for those appointed prior to this date.
† Adjusted regionally to reflect variations in the cost of living

CANTERBURY
104TH ARCHBISHOP AND PRIMATE OF ALL ENGLAND
Most Revd and Rt. Hon. Rowan Williams, *cons.* 1992, *apptd* 2002; Lambeth Palace, London SE1 7JU
Signs Rowan Cantuar:

BISHOPS SUFFRAGAN
Dover, Rt. Revd Trevor Willmott, *cons.* 2002, *apptd* 2009; Upway, St Martin's Hill, Canterbury, Kent CT1 1PR
Ebbsfleet, vacant
Richborough, vacant

DEAN
Very Revd Robert Willis, *apptd* 2001

Organist, D. Flood, FRCO, *apptd* 1988

ARCHDEACONS
Ashford, Ven. Philip Down, *apptd* 2011
Canterbury, Ven. Sheila Watson *apptd* 2007
Maidstone, Ven. Stephen Taylor, *apptd* 2011

Vicar-General of Province and Diocese, Chancellor Sheila Cameron, QC
Commissary-General, Morag Ellis, QC
Joint Registrars of the Province, Canon John Rees; Stephen Slack
Diocesan Registrar and Legal Adviser, Owen Carew Jones
Diocesan Secretary, Julian Hills, Diocesan House, Lady Wootton's Green, Canterbury CT1 1NQ T 01227-459401

YORK
97TH ARCHBISHOP AND PRIMATE OF ENGLAND
Most Revd and Rt. Hon. Dr John Sentamu, *cons.* 1996, *trans.* 2005; Bishopthorpe, York YO23 2GE
Signs Sentamu Ebor:

BISHOPS SUFFRAGAN
Hull, Rt. Revd Richard Frith, *cons.* 1998, *apptd* 1998; Hullen House, Woodfield Lane, Hessle, Hull HU13 0ES
Selby, Rt. Revd Martin Wallace, *cons.* 2003, *apptd* 2003; Bishop's House, Barton le Street, Malton, York YO17 6PL
Whitby, Rt. Revd Martin Warner, PHD, *cons.* 2010, *apptd* 2009; 60 West Green, Stokesley, Middlesbrough TS9 5BD

PRINCIPAL EPISCOPAL VISITOR
Rt. Revd Martyn Jarrett (*Bishop Suffragan of Beverley*), *cons.* 1994, *apptd* 2000; 3 North Lane, Roundhay, Leeds LS8 2QJ

DEAN
Very Revd Keith Jones, *apptd* 2004

Director of Music, Robert Sharpe, *apptd* 2008

ARCHDEACONS
Cleveland, Ven. Paul Ferguson, *apptd* 2001
East Riding, Ven. David Butterfield, *apptd* 2006
York, Ven. Richard Seed, *apptd* 1999

Chancellor of the Diocese, His Hon. Judge Collier, QC, *apptd* 2006
Registrar and Legal Secretary, Lionel Lennox
Diocesan Secretary, Peter Warry, Diocesan House, Aviator Court, Clifton Moor, York YO30 4WJ T 01904-699500

LONDON *(CANTERBURY)*
132ND BISHOP
Rt. Revd and Rt. Hon. Richard Chartres, KCVO, *cons.* 1992, *apptd* 1995; The Old Deanery, Dean's Court, London EC4V 5AA
Signs Richard Londin:

AREA BISHOPS
Edmonton, Rt. Revd Peter Wheatley, *cons.* 1999, *apptd* 1999; 27 Thurlow Road, London NW3 5PP
Kensington, Rt. Revd Paul Williams, *cons.* 2009, *apptd* 2008; Dial House, Riverside, Twickenham, Middlesex TW1 3DT
Stepney, Rt. Revd Adrian Newman, *cons.* 2011, *apptd* 2011; 63 Coburn Road, London E3 2DB
Willesden, Rt. Revd Peter Broadbent, *cons.* 2001, *apptd* 2001; 173 Willesden Lane, London NW6 7YN

BISHOP SUFFRAGAN
Fulham, vacant

DEAN OF ST PAUL'S
Rt. Revd Graeme Knowles, *apptd* 2007

Director of Music, Andrew Carwood, *apptd* 2007

ARCHDEACONS
Charing Cross, Ven. Dr William Jacob, *apptd* 1996
Hackney, vacant
Hampstead, Ven. Luke Miller, *apptd* 2011
London, Ven. David Meara, *apptd* 2009
Middlesex, Ven. Stephan Welch, *apptd* 2006
Northolt, Ven. Rachel Treweek, *apptd* 2006

Chancellor, Nigel Seed, QC, *apptd* 2002
Registrar and Legal Secretary, Paul Morris
Diocesan Secretary, Andrew Brookes, London Diocesan House, 36 Causton Street, London SW1P 4AU T 020-7932 1100

DURHAM *(YORK)*
72ND BISHOP
Rt. Revd Justin Welby, *cons.* 2011, *apptd* 2011;
Auckland Castle, Bishop Auckland DL14 7NR
Signs Justin Dunelm:

BISHOP SUFFRAGAN
Jarrow, Rt. Revd Mark Bryant, *cons.* 2007, *apptd* 2007;
Bishop's House, 25 Ivy Lane, Low Fell, Gateshead NE9 6QD

DEAN
Very Revd Michael Sadgrove, *apptd* 2003

Organist, James Lancelot, FRCO, *apptd* 1985

ARCHDEACONS
Auckland, Ven. Nicholas Barker, *apptd* 2007
Durham, Ven. Ian Jagger, *apptd* 2006
Sunderland, Ven. Stuart Bain, *apptd* 2002

Chancellor, The Worshipful Revd Dr Rupert Bursell, QC,
  apptd 1989
Registrar and Legal Secretary, Hilary Monckton-Milnes
Diocesan Secretary, Ian Boothroyd, Diocesan Office,
  Auckland Castle, Bishop Auckland, Co. Durham DL14 7QJ
  T 01388-604515

WINCHESTER *(CANTERBURY)*
97TH BISHOP
vacant

BISHOPS SUFFRAGAN
Basingstoke, Rt. Revd Peter Hancock, *apptd* 2010, *cons.*
  2010; Bishop's Lodge, Colden Lane, Old Alresford,
  Hants SO24 9DY
Southampton, Rt. Revd Jonathan Frost, *apptd* 2010;
  Old Alresford Place, Alresford, Hants SO24 9DH

DEAN
Very Revd James Atwell, *apptd* 2005
Dean of Jersey (A Peculiar), Very Revd Robert Key,
  apptd 2005
Dean of Guernsey (A Peculiar), Very Revd Paul Mellor,
  apptd 2003
Director of Music, Andrew Lumsden, *apptd* 2002

ARCHDEACONS
Bournemouth, vacant
Winchester, Ven. Michael Harley, *apptd* 2009

Chancellor, His Hon. Judge Clark, QC, *apptd* 1993
Registrar and Legal Secretary, Andrew Johnson
Diocesan Secretary, Andrew Robinson, Old Alresford Place,
  Alresford, Hants SO24 9DH T 01962-737300

BATH AND WELLS *(CANTERBURY)*
78TH BISHOP
Rt. Revd Peter Price, *cons.* 1997, *apptd* 2003; The Palace,
  Wells BA5 2PD
Signs Peter Bath & Wells

BISHOP SUFFRAGAN
Taunton, Rt. Revd Peter Maurice, *cons.* 2006, *apptd* 2006;
  The Palace, Wells BA5 2PD

DEAN
Very Revd John Clarke, *apptd* 2004

Organist, Matthew Owens, *apptd* 2005

ARCHDEACONS
Bath, Ven. Andrew Piggott, *apptd* 2005
Taunton, Ven. John Reed, *apptd* 1999
Wells, Ven. Nicola Sullivan, *apptd* 2006

Chancellor, Timothy Briden, *apptd* 1993
Registrar and Legal Secretary, Tim Berry
Diocesan Secretary, Nick Denison, The Old Deanery, Wells,
  Somerset BA5 2UG T 01749-670777

BIRMINGHAM *(CANTERBURY)*
8TH BISHOP
Rt. Revd David Urquhart, *cons.* 2000, *apptd* 2006;
  Bishop's Croft, Old Church Road, Harborne, Birmingham
  B17 0BG
Signs David Birmingham:

BISHOP SUFFRAGAN
Aston, Rt. Revd Andrew Watson, *cons.* 2008, *apptd* 2008;
  175 Harborne Park Road, Birmingham B17 0BH

DEAN
Very Revd Catherine Ogle, *apptd* 2010

Director of Music, Marcus Huxley, FRCO, *apptd* 1986

ARCHDEACONS
Aston, Ven. Dr Brian Russell, *apptd* 2005
Birmingham, Ven. Hayward Osborne, *apptd* 2001

Chancellor, His Hon. Judge Cardinal, *apptd* 2005
Registrar and Legal Secretary, Hugh Carslake
Diocesan Secretary, Andrew Halstead, 175 Harborne Park
  Road, Harborne, Birmingham B17 0BH T 0121-426 0400

BLACKBURN *(YORK)*
8TH BISHOP
Rt. Revd Nicholas Reade, *apptd* 2003, *cons.* March 2004;
  Bishop's House, Ribchester Road, Blackburn BB1 9EF
Signs Nicholas Blackburn

BISHOPS SUFFRAGAN
Burnley, Rt. Revd John Goddard, *cons.* 2000, *apptd* 2000;
  All Saints House, Padiham Road, Burnley BB12 6PA
Lancaster, Rt. Revd Geoffrey Pearson, *cons.* 2006, *apptd*
  2006; The Vicarage, Whinney Brow Lane, Shireshead,
  Forton, Preston PR3 0AE

DEAN
Very Revd Christopher Armstrong, *apptd* 2001

Organist and Director of Music, vacant

ARCHDEACON
Blackburn, Ven. John Hawley, *apptd* 2002
Lancaster, Ven. Michael Everitt, *apptd* 2011

Chancellor, His Hon. Judge Bullimore, *apptd* 1990
Registrar and Legal Secretary, Thomas Hoyle
Diocesan Secretary, Graeme Pollard, Diocesan Office,
  Cathedral Close, Blackburn BB1 5AA T 01254-503070

BRADFORD *(YORK)*
10TH BISHOP
Rt. Revd Nicholas Baines, *cons.* 2003, *apptd* 2010;
  Bishopscroft, Ashwell Road, Heaton, Bradford BD9 4AU
Signs Nicholas Bradford

DEAN
Very Revd Dr David Ison, *apptd* 2005

Organist, Andrew Teague, FRCO, *apptd* 2003

ARCHDEACONS
Bradford, Ven. David Lee, *apptd* 2004
Craven, Ven. Paul Slater, *apptd* 2005

Chancellor, His Hon. Judge Walford, *apptd* 1999
Registrar and Legal Secretary, Peter Foskett
Diocesan Secretary (acting), Debbie Child, Kadugli House,
   Elmsley Street, Steeton, Keighley BD20 6SE **T** 01535-650555

BRISTOL *(CANTERBURY)*
55TH BISHOP
Rt. Revd Michael Hill, *cons.* 1998, *apptd* 2003;
   58A High Street, Winterbourne, Bristol BS36 1JQ
Signs Michael Bristol

BISHOP SUFFRAGAN
Swindon, Rt. Revd Dr Lee Rayfield, *cons.* 2005, *apptd*
   2005; Mark House, Field Rise, Swindon, Wiltshire, SN1 4HP

DEAN
Very Revd David Hoyle, *apptd* 2010

Organist and Director of Music, Mark Lee, *apptd* 1998

ARCHDEACONS
Bristol, Ven. Tim McClure, *apptd* 1999
Malmesbury, Ven. Christine Froude, *apptd* 2011

Acting Chancellor, Timothy Briden
Registrar and Legal Secretary, Tim Berry
Diocesan Secretary, Lesley Farrall, Diocesan Church House,
   23 Great George Street, Bristol BS1 5QZ **T** 0117-906 0100

CARLISLE *(YORK)*
67TH BISHOP
Rt. Revd James Newcome, *cons.* 2002, *apptd* 2009;
   Bishop's House, Ambleside Road, Keswick CA12 4DD
Signs James Carliol

BISHOP SUFFRAGAN
Penrith, vacant; Holm Croft, Castle Road, Kendal, Cumbria
   LA9 7AU

DEAN
Very Revd Mark Boyling, *apptd* 2004

Organist, Jeremy Suter, FRCO, *apptd* 1991

ARCHDEACONS
Carlisle, Ven. Kevin Roberts, *apptd* 2009
West Cumberland, Ven. Dr Richard Pratt, *apptd* 2009
Westmorland and Furness, vacant

Chancellor, Geoffrey Tattersall, QC, *apptd* 2003
Registrar and Legal Secretary, Jane Lowdon
Diocesan Secretary, Derek Hurton, Church House,
   West Walls, Carlisle CA3 8UE **T** 01228-522573

CHELMSFORD *(CANTERBURY)*
10TH BISHOP
Rt. Revd Stephen Cottrell, *cons.* 2004, *apptd.* 2010;
   Bishopscourt, Main Road, Margaretting, Ingatestone,
   Essex CM4 0HD
Signs Stephen Chelmsford

BISHOPS SUFFRAGAN
Barking, Rt. Revd David Hawkins, *cons.* 2002, *apptd*
   2003; Barking Lodge, Verulam Avenue, London, E17 8ES
Bradwell, vacant
Colchester, Rt. Revd Christopher Morgan, *cons.* 2001,
   apptd 2001; 1 Fitzwalter Road, Colchester, Essex CO3 3SS

DEAN
Very Revd Peter S. M. Judd, *apptd* 1997

Master of Music, Peter Nardone, *apptd* 2000

ARCHDEACONS
Colchester, Ven. Annette Cooper, *apptd* 2004
Harlow, Ven. Martin Webster, *apptd* 2009
Southend, Ven. David Lowman, *apptd* 2001
West Ham, Ven. Elwin Cockett, *apptd* 2007

Chancellor, George Pulman QC, *apptd* 2001
Registrar and Legal Secretary, Brian Hood
Chief Executive, John Ball, 53 New Street, Chelmsford, Essex
   CM1 1AT **T** 01245-294400

CHESTER *(YORK)*
40TH BISHOP
Rt. Revd Peter Forster, PHD, *cons.* 1996, *apptd* 1996;
   Bishop's House, Abbey Square, Chester CH1 2JD
Signs Peter Cestr:

BISHOPS SUFFRAGAN
Birkenhead, Rt. Revd Keith Sinclair, *cons.* 2007, *apptd*
   2007; Bishop's Lodge, 67 Bidston Road, Prenton CH43 6TR
Stockport, Rt. Revd Robert Atwell, *cons.* 2008, *apptd*
   2008; Bishop's Lodge, Back Lane, Dunham Town,
   Altrincham WA14 4SG

DEAN
Very Revd Dr Gordon McPhate, *apptd* 2002

Organist and Director of Music, Philip Rushforth, FRCO,
   apptd 2008

ARCHDEACONS
Chester, Ven. Dr Michael Gilbertson, *apptd* 2010
Macclesfield, Ven. Ian Bishop, *apptd* 2011

Chancellor, His Hon. Judge Turner, QC, *apptd* 1998
Registrar and Legal Secretary, Helen McFall
Diocesan Secretary, George Colville, Church House,
   Lower Lane, Aldford, Chester CH3 6HP **T** 01244-681973

CHICHESTER *(CANTERBURY)*
102ND BISHOP
Rt. Revd Dr John Hind, *cons.* 1991, *apptd* 2001;
   The Palace, Chichester PO19 1PY
Signs John Cicestr:

BISHOPS SUFFRAGAN
Horsham, Rt. Revd Mark Sowerby, *cons.* 2009, *apptd*
   2009
Lewes, Rt. Revd Wallace Benn, *cons.* 1997, *apptd* 1997;
   Bishop's Lodge, 16A Prideaux Road, Eastbourne,
   E. Sussex BN21 2NB

DEAN
Very Revd Nicholas Frayling, *apptd* 2002

Organist, Sarah Baldock, *apptd* 2007

ARCHDEACONS
Chichester, Ven. Douglas McKittrick, *apptd* 2002
Horsham, Ven. Roger Combes, *apptd* 2003
Lewes and Hastings, Ven. Philip Jones, *apptd* 2005

Chancellor, Mark Hill
Registrar and Legal Secretary, John Stapleton
Diocesan Secretary, Angela Sibson, OBE, Diocesan Church
   House, 211 New Church Road, Hove, E. Sussex BN3 4ED
   T 01273-421021

COVENTRY *(CANTERBURY)*
9TH BISHOP
Rt. Revd Dr Christopher Cocksworth, *cons.* 2008, *apptd*
2008; The Bishop's House, 23 Davenport Road, Coventry
CV5 6PW
Signs Christopher Coventry

BISHOP SUFFRAGAN
Warwick, Rt. Revd John Stroyan, *cons.* 2005, *apptd* 2005;
Warwick House, 139 Kenilworth Road, Coventry CV4 7AP

DEAN
Very Revd John Irvine, *apptd* 2001

Director of Music, Mr Kerry Beaumont, *apptd* 2006

ARCHDEACONS
Coventry, Ven. Ian Watson, *apptd* 2007
Warwick, Ven. Morris Rodham, *apptd* 2010

Chancellor, Stephen Eyre, *apptd* 2009
Registrar and Legal Secretary, Mary Allanson
Diocesan Secretary, Simon Lloyd, Cathedral & Diocesan
Offices, 1 Hilltop, Coventry CV1 5AB **T** 024-7652 1200

DERBY *(CANTERBURY)*
7TH BISHOP
Rt. Revd Dr Alastair Redfern, *cons.* 1997, *apptd* 2005;
The Bishop's House, 6 King Street, Duffield, Belper,
Derbyshire DE56 4EU
Signs Alastair Derby

BISHOP SUFFRAGAN
Repton, Rt. Revd Humphrey Southern, *cons.* 2007, *apptd*
2007; Repton House, Lea, Matlock, Derbyshire DE4 5JP

DEAN
Very Revd Dr John Davies *apptd* 2010

Organist, Peter Gould, *apptd* 1982

ARCHDEACONS
Chesterfield, Ven. Christine Wilson, *apptd* 2010
Derby, Ven. Dr Christopher Cunliffe, *apptd* 2006

Chancellor, His Hon. Judge Bullimore, *apptd* 1981
Registrar and Legal Secretary, Mrs Nadine Waldron
Diocesan Secretary, Bob Carey, Derby Church House,
Full Street, Derby DE1 3DR **T** 01332-388650

ELY *(CANTERBURY)*
69TH BISHOP
Rt. Revd Stephen Conway, *cons.* 2006, *apptd* 2011;
The Bishop's House, Ely CB7 4DW
Signs Stephen Ely

BISHOP SUFFRAGAN
Huntingdon, Rt. Revd David Thomson, DPHIL, *cons.*
2008, *apptd* 2008; 14 Lynn Road, Ely, Cambs CB6 1DA

DEAN
Very Revd Dr Michael Chandler, *apptd* 2003

Director of Music, Paul Trepte, FRCO, *apptd* 1991

ARCHDEACONS
Cambridge, Ven. John Beer, *apptd* 2004
Huntingdon and Wisbech, Ven. Hugh McCurdy, *apptd*
2005

Chancellor, Rt. Hon. Sir William Gage, QC
Registrar, Peter Beesley

Diocesan Secretary, Graham Shorter, Bishop Woodford
House, Barton Road, Ely, Cambs CB7 4DX **T** 01353-652700

EXETER *(CANTERBURY)*
70TH BISHOP
Rt. Revd Michael Langrish, *cons.* 1993, *apptd* 2000;
The Palace, Exeter EX1 1HY
Signs Michael Exon:

BISHOPS SUFFRAGAN
Crediton, Rt. Revd Robert Evens, *cons.* 2004, *apptd* 2004;
32 The Avenue, Tiverton EX16 4HW
Plymouth, Rt. Revd John Ford, *cons.* 2006, *apptd* 2005;
31 Riverside Walk, Tamerton Foliot, Plymouth PL5 4AQ

DEAN
vacant

Director of Music, Andrew Millington, *apptd* 1999

ARCHDEACONS
Barnstaple, Ven. David Gunn-Johnson, *apptd* 2003
Exeter, Ven. Penny Driver, *apptd* 2006
Plymouth, Ven. Ian Chandler, *apptd* 2010
Totnes, Ven. John Rawlings, *apptd* 2006

Chancellor, Hon. Sir Andrew McFarlane
Registrar and Legal Secretary, M. Follett
Diocesan Secretary, Mark Beedell, The Old Deanery,
The Cloisters, Exeter EX1 1HS **T** 01392-272686

GIBRALTAR IN EUROPE *(CANTERBURY)*
3RD BISHOP
Rt. Revd Dr Geoffrey Rowell, *cons.* 1994, *apptd* 2001;
Bishop's Lodge, Church Road, Worth, Crawley, West Sussex
RH10 7RT

BISHOP SUFFRAGAN
In Europe, Rt. Revd David Hamid, *cons.* 2002, *apptd*
2002; 14 Tufton Street, London SW1P 3QZ
Dean, Cathedral Church of the Holy Trinity, Gibraltar,
Very Revd Dr John Paddock

Chancellor, Pro-Cathedral of St Paul, Valletta, Malta,
Canon Simon Godfrey
Chancellor, Pro-Cathedral of the Holy Trinity, Brussels,
Belgium, Canon Dr Robert Innes

ARCHDEACONS
Eastern, Ven. Patrick Curran
North-West Europe, Ven. John de Wit
France, Ven. Kenneth Letts
Gibraltar, Ven. David Sutch
Italy, Ven. Jonathan Boardman
Scandinavia and Germany, Ven. Jonathan Lloyd
Switzerland, Ven. Peter Potter

Chancellor, Mark Hill
Registrar and Legal Secretary, Aiden Hargreaves-Smith
Diocesan Secretary, Adrian Mumford, 14 Tufton Street,
London SW1P 3QZ **T** 020-7898 1155

GLOUCESTER *(CANTERBURY)*
40TH BISHOP
Rt. Revd Michael Perham, *cons.* 2004, *apptd* 2004;
2 College Green, Gloucester GL1 2LR
Signs Michael Gloucestr

BISHOP SUFFRAGAN
Tewkesbury, Rt. Revd John Went, *cons.* 1995, *apptd* 1995;
2 College Green, Gloucester GL1 2LR

DEAN
Very Revd Stephen Lake, *apptd* 2011

Director of Music, Adrian Partington, *apptd* 2007

ARCHDEACONS
Cheltenham, Ven. Robert Springett, *apptd* 2010
Gloucester, Ven. Geoffrey Sidaway, *apptd* 2000

Chancellor and Vicar-General, June Rodgers, *apptd* 1990
Registrar and Legal Secretary, Chris Peak
Diocesan Secretary, Dr Kevin Brown, Church House,
   College Green, Gloucester GL1 2LY T 01452-410022

GUILDFORD *(CANTERBURY)*
9TH BISHOP
Rt. Revd Christopher Hill, *cons.* 1996, *apptd* 2004;
   Willow Grange, Woking Road, Guildford GU4 7QS
   Signs Christopher Guildford

BISHOP SUFFRAGAN
Dorking, Rt. Revd Ian Brackley, *cons.* 1996, *apptd* 1995;
   Dayspring, 13 Pilgrims Way, Guildford GU4 8AD

DEAN
Very Revd Victor Stock, *apptd* 2002

Organist, Katherine Dienes-Williams, *apptd* 2007

ARCHDEACONS
Dorking, Ven. Julian Henderson, *apptd* 2005
Surrey, Ven. Stuart Beake, *apptd* 2005

Chancellor, Andrew Jordan
Registrar and Legal Secretary, Peter Beesley
Diocesan Secretary, Stephen Marriott, Diocesan House,
   Quarry Street, Guildford GU1 3AG T 01483-571826

HEREFORD *(CANTERBURY)*
104TH BISHOP
Rt. Revd Anthony Priddis, *cons.* 1996, *apptd* 2004;
   The Bishop's House, Hereford HR4 9BN
   Signs Anthony Hereford

BISHOP SUFFRAGAN
Ludlow, Rt. Revd Alistair Magowan, *cons.* 2009, *apptd*
   2009; Bishop's House, Corvedale Road, Craven Arms,
   Shropshire SY7 9BT

DEAN
Very Revd Michael Tavinor, *apptd* 2002

Organist and Director of Music, Geraint Bowen, FRCO,
apptd 2001

ARCHDEACONS
Hereford, Ven. Paddy Benson, *apptd* 2011
Ludlow, Rt. Revd Alistair Magowan, *apptd* 2009

Chancellor, His Hon. Judge Kaye, QC
Registrar and Legal Secretary, Peter Beesley
Diocesan Secretary, John Clark, The Palace, Hereford HR4 9BL
   T 01432-373300

LEICESTER *(CANTERBURY)*
6TH BISHOP
Rt. Revd Timothy Stevens, *cons.* 1995, *apptd* 1999;
   Bishop's Lodge, 10 Springfield Road, Leicester LE2 3BD
   Signs Timothy Leicester

ASSISTANT BISHOP
Rt. Revd Christopher Boyle, *cons.* 2000, *apptd* 2009;
   Church House, St Martin' East, Leicester LE1 5FX

DEAN
Very Revd Vivienne Faull, *apptd* 2000

Director of Music, Dr Christopher Johns

ARCHDEACONS
Leicester, Ven. Richard Atkinson, *apptd* 2002
Loughborough, Ven. David Newman, *apptd* 2009

Chancellor, Dr James Behrens
Registrar and Legal Secretary, Revd Trevor Kirkman
Diocesan Secretary, Jonathan Kerry, St Martin's House,
   7 Peacock Lane, Leicester LE1 5PZ T 0116-261 5200

LICHFIELD *(CANTERBURY)*
98TH BISHOP
Rt. Revd Jonathan Gledhill *cons.* 1996, *apptd* 2003;
   Bishop's House, The Close, Lichfield WS13 7LG
   Signs Jonathan Lichfield

BISHOPS SUFFRAGAN
Shrewsbury, Rt. Revd Mark Rylands, *cons.* 2009, *apptd*
   2009; Athlone House, 66 London Road, Shrewsbury
   SY2 6PG
Stafford, Rt. Revd Geoffrey Annas, *cons.* 2010, *apptd*
   2010; Ash Garth, Broughton Crescent, Barlaston,
   Stoke-on-Trent ST12 9DD
Wolverhampton, Rt. Revd Clive Gregory, *cons.* 2007,
   apptd 2007; 61 Richmond Road, Wolverhampton WV3 9JH

DEAN
Very Revd Adrian Dorber, *apptd* 2005

Directors of Music, Ben and Cathy Lamb, *apptd* 2010
Organist, Martyn Rawles, *apptd* 2010

ARCHDEACONS
Lichfield, Ven. Christopher Liley, *apptd* 2001
Salop, Ven. Paul Thomas, *apptd* 2011
Stoke-on-Trent, Ven. Godfrey Owen Stone, *apptd* 2002
Walsall, Ven. Christopher Sims, *apptd* 2009

Chancellor, vacant
Registrar and Legal Secretary, N. Blackie
Diocesan Secretary, Julie Jones, St Mary's House, The Close,
   Lichfield, Staffs WS13 7LD T 01543-306030

LINCOLN *(CANTERBURY)*
72ND BISHOP
Rt. Revd Christopher Lowson *cons.* 2011, *apptd* 2011;
   Bishop's House, Eastgate, Lincoln LN2 1QQ
   Signs Christopher Lincoln

BISHOPS SUFFRAGAN
Grantham, Rt. Revd Dr Timothy Ellis, *cons.* 2006, *apptd*
   2006; Saxonwell Vicarage, Church Street, Long
   Bennington, Newark NG23 5ES
Grimsby, Rt. Revd David D. J. Rossdale, *cons.* 2000, *apptd*
   2000; Bishop's House, Church Lane, Irby-upon-Humber,
   Grimsby DN37 7JR

DEAN
Very Revd Philip Buckler, *apptd* 2007

Director of Music, A. Prentice, *apptd* 2003

ARCHDEACONS
Lincoln, Ven. Timothy Barker, *apptd* 2009
Lindsey and Stow, Ven. Jane Sinclair, *apptd* 2007

Chancellor, His Hon. Judge Mark Bishop, QC, *apptd* 2007
Registrar and Legal Secretary, Caroline Mockford, *apptd*
   2008

Diocesan Secretary, Max Manin, The Old Palace, Lincoln
LN2 1PU **T** 01522-504050

LIVERPOOL *(YORK)*
7TH BISHOP
Rt. Revd James Jones, *cons.* 1994, *apptd* 1998; Bishop's
Lodge, Woolton Park, Liverpool L25 6DT
Signs James Liverpool

BISHOP SUFFRAGAN
Warrington, Rt. Revd Richard Blackburn, *cons.* 2009,
apptd 2009; 34 Central Avenue, Eccleston Park, Liverpool
L34 2QP

DEAN
vacant

Director of Music, David Poulter, *apptd* 2008

ARCHDEACONS
Liverpool, Ven. Richard Panter, *apptd* 2002
Warrington, Ven. Peter Bradley, *apptd* 2001

Chancellor, Hon. Sir Mark Hedley
Registrar and Legal Secretary, Howard Dellar
Diocesan Secretary, Mike Eastwood, St James House,
20 St James Street, Liverpool L1 7BY **T** 0151-709 9722

MANCHESTER *(YORK)*
11TH BISHOP
Rt. Revd Nigel McCulloch, *cons.* 1986, *apptd* 2002, *trans.*
2002; Bishopscourt, Bury New Road, Manchester M7 4LE
Signs Nigel Manchester

BISHOPS SUFFRAGAN
Bolton, Rt. Revd Christopher Edmondson, *cons.* 2008,
apptd 2008; Bishop's Lodge, Walkden Road, Worsley,
Manchester M28 2WH
Middleton, Rt. Revd Mark Davies, *cons.* 2008, *apptd*
2008; The Hollies, Manchester Road, Rochdale OL11 3QY

DEAN
Revd Rogers Govender, *apptd* 2006

Organist, Christopher Stokes, *apptd* 1992

ARCHDEACONS
Bolton, Ven. David Bailey, *apptd* 2008
Manchester, Ven. Mark Ashcroft, *apptd* 2009
Rochdale, Ven. Cherry Vann, *apptd* 2008
Salford, Ven. David Sharples, *apptd* 2009

Chancellor, Geoffrey Tattersall, QC
Registrar and Legal Secretary, Jane Monks
Diocesan Secretary, Martin Miller, Diocesan Church House,
90 Deansgate, Manchester M3 2GH **T** 0161-828 1400

NEWCASTLE *(YORK)*
11TH BISHOP
Rt. Revd J. Martin Wharton, CBE, *cons.* 1992, *apptd*
1997; Bishop's House, 29 Moor Road South, Gosforth,
Newcastle upon Tyne NE3 1PA
Signs Martin Newcastle

ASSISTANT BISHOP
Rt. Revd Frank White, *cons.* 2002, *apptd* 2010

DEAN
Very Revd Christopher C. Dalliston, *apptd* 2003

Director of Music, Michael Stoddart, *apptd* 2009

ARCHDEACONS
Lindisfarne, Ven. Dr Peter Robinson, *apptd* 2008
Northumberland, Ven. Geoffrey Miller, *apptd* 2004

Chancellor, His Hon. Judge David Hodson, *apptd* 2009
Registrar and Legal Secretary, Jane Lowdon
Diocesan Secretary, Graham Barnard, Church House,
St John's Terrace, North Shields NE29 6HS **T** 0191-270 4100

NORWICH *(CANTERBURY)*
71ST BISHOP
Rt. Revd Graham R. James, *cons.* 1993, *apptd* 2000;
Bishop's House, Norwich NR3 1SB
Signs Graham Norvic:

BISHOPS SUFFRAGAN
Lynn, Rt. Revd Jonathan Meyrick, *cons.* 2011, *apptd*
2011; The Old Vicarage, Castle Acre, King's Lynn PE32 2AA
Thetford, Rt. Revd Alan Winton PHD, *cons.* 2009, *apptd*
2009; The Red House, 53 Norwich Road, Stoke Holy Cross,
Norwich NR14 8AB

DEAN
Very Revd Graham Smith, *apptd* 2004

Master of Music, David Lowe, *apptd* 2007

ARCHDEACONS
Lynn, Ven. John Ashe, *apptd* 2009
Norfolk, Ven. David Hayden, *apptd* 2002
Norwich, Ven. Jan McFarlane, *apptd* 2008

Chancellor, His Hon. Judge Downes, *apptd* 2007
Registrar and Legal Secretary, Stuart Jones
Diocesan Secretary, Richard Butler, Diocesan House,
109 Dereham Road, Easton, Norwich, Norfolk NR9 5ES
T 01603-880853

OXFORD *(CANTERBURY)*
42ND BISHOP
Rt. Revd John Pritchard *cons.* 2002, *apptd* 2007; Diocesan
Church House, North Hinksey Lane, Oxford OX2 0NB
Signs John Oxon:

AREA BISHOPS
Buckingham, Rt. Revd Dr Alan Wilson *cons.* 2003, *apptd*
2003; Sheridan, Grimms Hill, Great Missenden, Bucks
HP16 9BD
Dorchester, Rt. Revd Colin Fletcher, *cons.* 2000, *apptd*
2000; Arran House, Sandy Lane, Yarnton, Oxon OX5 1PB
Reading, Rt. Revd Andrew Proud, *cons.* 2011 *apptd* 2011;
Bishop's House, Tidmarsh Lane, Tidmarsh, Reading RG8 8HA

DEAN OF CHRIST CHURCH
Very Revd Dr Christopher Lewis, *apptd* 2003

Organist, Dr Stephen Darlington, FRCO, *apptd* 1985

ARCHDEACONS
Berkshire, Ven. Norman Russell, *apptd* 1998
Buckingham, Ven. Karen Gorham, *apptd* 2007
Oxford, Ven. Julian Hubbard, *apptd* 2005

Chancellor, Revd Dr Rupert Bursell, *apptd* 2001
Registrar and Legal Secretary, Revd Canon John Rees
Diocesan Secretary, Rosemary Pearce, Diocesan Church
House, North Hinksey, Oxford OX2 0NB **T** 01865-208202

PETERBOROUGH *(CANTERBURY)*
38TH BISHOP
Rt. Revd Donald Allister, *cons.* 2010, *apptd* 2009; Bishop's
Lodging, The Palace, Peterborough PE1 1YA
Signs Donald Petriburg:

BISHOP SUFFRAGAN
Brixworth, Rt. Revd John Holbrook, *cons.* 2011, *apptd*
2011; Orchard Acre, 11 North Street, Mears Ashby,
Northants NN6 0DW

DEAN
Very Revd Charles Taylor, *apptd* 2007

Director of Music, Andrew Reid, *apptd* 2004

ARCHDEACONS
Northampton, Ven. Christine Allsopp, *apptd* 2005
Oakham, Ven. David Painter, *apptd* 2000

Chancellor, David Pittaway, QC, *apptd* 2005
Registrar and Legal Secretary, Revd Raymond Hemingray
Diocesan Secretary, Canon Richard Pestell, Diocesan Office,
The Palace, Peterborough PE1 1YB T 01733-887000

PORTSMOUTH *(CANTERBURY)*
9TH BISHOP
Rt. Revd Christopher Foster, *cons.* 2010, *apptd* 2010;
Bishopsgrove, 26 Osborn Road, Fareham, Hants PO16 7DQ
Signs Christopher Portsmouth

DEAN
Very Revd David Brindley, *apptd* 2002

Organist, David Price, *apptd* 1996

ARCHDEACONS
Isle of Wight, Ven. Caroline Baston, *apptd* 2006
Portsdown, Ven. Trevor Reader, *apptd* 2006
The Meon, Ven. Gavin Collins, *apptd* 2011

Chancellor, C. Clark, QC
Registrar and Legal Secretary, Hilary Tyler
Diocesan Secretary, Wendy Kennedy, Diocesan Offices,
1st Floor, Peninsular House, Wharf Road, Portsmouth
PO2 8HB T 023-9289 9664

RIPON AND LEEDS *(YORK)*
12TH BISHOP
Rt. Revd John Packer, *cons.* 1996, *apptd* 2000;
Hollin House, Weetwood Avenue LS16 5NG
Signs John Ripon and Leeds

BISHOP SUFFRAGAN
Knaresborough, Rt. Revd James Bell, *cons.* 2004, *apptd*
2004; Thistledown, Main Street, Exelby, Bedale DL8 2HD

DEAN
Revd Keith Jukes, *apptd* 2007

Director of Music, Andrew Bryden, *apptd* 2003

ARCHDEACONS
Leeds, Ven. Peter Burrows, *apptd* 2005
Richmond, Ven. Janet Henderson, *apptd* 2007

Chancellor, His Hon. Judge Simon Grenfell, *apptd* 1992
Registrars and Legal Secretaries, Nicola Harding;
Christopher Tunnard
Diocesan Secretary, Dr Sue Proctor, Diocesan Office,
St Mary's Street, Leeds LS9 7DP T 0113-200 0540

ROCHESTER *(CANTERBURY)*
107TH BISHOP
Rt. Revd James Langstaff, *cons.* 2004 *apptd.* 2010;
Bishopscourt, 24 St Margaret's Street, Rochester ME1 1TS

BISHOP SUFFRAGAN
Tonbridge, Rt. Revd Dr Brian C. Castle, *cons.* 2002, *apptd*
2002; Bishop's Lodge, 48 St Botolph's Road, Sevenoaks
TN13 3AG

DEAN
Very Revd Adrian Newman, *apptd* 2004

Director of Music, Scott Farrell, *apptd* 2008

ARCHDEACONS
Bromley, Ven. Dr Paul Wright, *apptd* 2003
Rochester, Ven. Simon Burton-Jones, *apptd* 2010
Tonbridge, Ven. Clive Mansell, *apptd* 2002

Chancellor, John Gallagher, *apptd* 2006
Registrar and Legal Secretary, Owen Carew-Jones
Diocesan Secretary, Canon Louise Gilbert, St Nicholas
Church, Boley Hill, Rochester ME1 1SL T 01634-560000

ST ALBANS *(CANTERBURY)*
10TH BISHOP
Rt. Revd Dr Alan Smith, *cons.* 2001, *apptd* 2009, *trans.*
2009; Abbey Gate House, St Albans AL3 4HD
Signs Alan St Albans

BISHOPS SUFFRAGAN
Bedford, Rt. Revd Richard N. Inwood, *cons.* 2003,
apptd 2003; Bishop's Lodge, Bedford Road, Cardington,
Bedford MK44 3SS
Hertford, Rt. Revd Paul Bayes, *cons.* 2010, *apptd* 2010;
Bishopswood, 3 Stobarts Close, Knebworth, Herts SG3 6ND

DEAN
Very Revd Dr Jeffrey John, *apptd* 2004

Organist, Andrew Lucas, *apptd* 1998

ARCHDEACONS
Bedford, Ven. Paul Hughes, *apptd* 2004
Hertford, Ven. Trevor Jones, *apptd* 1997
St Albans, Ven. Jonathan Smith, *apptd* 2008

Chancellor, Roger Kaye, *apptd* 2002
Registrar and Legal Secretary, Lee Coley
Diocesan Secretary, Susan Pope, Holywell Lodge,
41 Holywell Hill, St Albans AL1 1HE T 01727-854532

ST EDMUNDSBURY AND IPSWICH *(CANTERBURY)*
10TH BISHOP
Rt. Revd Nigel Stock, *cons.* 2000, *apptd* 2007;
Bishop's House, 4 Park Road, Ipswich IP1 3ST
Signs Nigel St Edum and Ipswich

BISHOP SUFFRAGAN
Dunwich, Rt. Revd Clive Young, *cons.* 1999, *apptd* 1999;
28 Westerfield Road, Ipswich IP4 2UJ

DEAN
Very Revd Frances Ward, *apptd* 2010

Director of Music, James Thomas, *apptd* 1997

ARCHDEACONS
Sudbury, Ven. Dr David Jenkins, *apptd* 2010
Suffolk, Ven. Dr Judy Hunt, *apptd* 2009

Chancellor, David Etherington, QC
Registrar and Legal Secretary, James Hall
Diocesan Secretary, Nicholas Edgell, Diocesan Office,
   St Nicholas Centre, 4 Cutler Street, Ipswich IP1 1UQ
   T 01473-298500

SALISBURY *(CANTERBURY)*
78TH BISHOP
Rt. Revd Nicholas Holtam, *cons.* 2011, *apptd* 2011;
   South Canonry, 71 The Close, Salisbury SP1 2ER

BISHOPS SUFFRAGAN
Ramsbury, vacant
Sherborne, Rt. Revd Graham Kings, PHD, *cons.* 2009,
   apptd 2009; Sherborne Area Office, St Nicholas'
   Church Centre, Wareham Road, Corfe Mullen BH21 3LE

DEAN
Very Revd June Osborne, *apptd* 2004

Organist, David Halls, *apptd* 2005

ARCHDEACONS
Dorset, Ven. Stephen Waine, *apptd* 2010
Sarum, Ven. Alan Jeans, *apptd* 2003
Sherborne, Ven. Paul Taylor, *apptd* 2004
Wilts, Ven. John Wraw, *apptd* 2004

Chancellor, His Hon. Judge Wiggs, *apptd* 1997
Registrar and Legal Secretary, Andrew Johnson
Diocesan Secretary, Lucinda Herklots, Church House,
   Crane Street, Salisbury SP1 2QB T 01722-411922

SHEFFIELD *(YORK)*
7TH BISHOP
Rt. Revd Steven Croft, PHD, *cons.* 2009, *apptd* 2008;
   Bishopscroft, Snaithing Lane, Sheffield S10 3LG
   Signs Steven Sheffield

BISHOP SUFFRAGAN
Doncaster, vacant

DEAN
Very Revd Peter Bradley, *apptd* 2003

Master of Music, Neil Taylor, *apptd* 1997

ARCHDEACONS
Doncaster, Ven. Robert Fitzharris, *apptd* 2001
Sheffield and Rotherham, Ven. Martyn Snow, *apptd* 2010

Chancellor, Prof. David McClean, *apptd* 1992
Registrar and Legal Secretary, Andrew Vidler
Diocesan Secretary, Malcolm Fair, Diocesan Church House,
   95–99 Effingham Street, Rotherham S65 1BL
   T 01709-309100

SODOR AND MAN *(YORK)*
81ST BISHOP
Rt. Revd Robert Paterson, *cons.* 2008, *apptd* 2008;
   The Bishop's House, The Falls, Tromode Road, Douglas,
   Isle of Man IM4 4PZ
   Signs Robert Sodor as Mannin

ARCHDEACON OF MAN
Ven. Brian Smith, *apptd* 2005
Vicar-General and Chancellor, Clare Faulds

Registrar, Timothy Mann
Diocesan Secretary, Mrs S. Lawrinson, 8 Hilary Wharf,
   South Quay, Douglas, Isle of Man IM1 5BL
   T 01624-673477

SOUTHWARK *(CANTERBURY)*
10TH BISHOP
Rt. Revd Christopher Chessun, *cons.* 2005, *apptd* 2011;
   Trinity House, 4 Chapel Court, Borough High Street, London
   SE1 1HW
   Signs Christopher Southwark

AREA BISHOPS
Croydon, vacant
Kingston upon Thames, Rt. Revd Richard Cheetham, *cons.*
   2002, *apptd* 2002 ; Kingston Episcopal Area Office,
   620 Kingston Road, London SW20 8DN
Woolwich, vacant

DEAN (ACTING)
Revd Canon Andrew Nunn

Organist, Peter Wright, FRCO, *apptd* 1989

ARCHDEACONS
Croydon, Ven. Barry Goodwin, *apptd* 2011
Lambeth, Ven. Christopher Skilton, *apptd* 2003
Lewisham, Ven. Christine Hardman, *apptd* 2001
Reigate, Ven. Daniel Kajumba, *apptd* 2001
Southwark, Ven. Dr Michael Ipgrave, *apptd* 2004
Wandsworth, Ven. Stephen Roberts, *apptd* 2005

Chancellor, Philip Petchey
Registrar and Legal Secretary, Paul Morris
Diocesan Secretary, Simon Parton, Trinity House,
   4 Chapel Court, Borough High Street, London SE1 1HW
   T 020-7939 9400

SOUTHWELL AND NOTTINGHAM *(YORK)*
11TH BISHOP
Rt. Revd Paul Butler, *cons.* 2004, *apptd* 2009;
   Bishop's Manor, Southwell NG25 0JR
   Signs Paul Southwell and Nottingham

BISHOP SUFFRAGAN
Sherwood, Rt. Revd Anthony Porter, *cons.* 2006,
   apptd 2006; Dunham House, 8 Westgate, Southwell
   NG25 0JL

DEAN
Very Revd John Guille, *apptd* 2007

Organist, Paul Hale, *apptd* 1989

ARCHDEACONS
Newark, Ven. Nigel Peyton, *apptd* 1999
Nottingham, Ven. Peter Hill, *apptd* 2007

Chancellor, Linda Box, *apptd* 2005
Registrar and Legal Secretary, Christopher Hodson
Chief Executive, Nigel Spraggins, Dunham House,
   8 Westgate, Southwell, Notts NG25 0JL T 01636-814331

TRURO *(CANTERBURY)*
15TH BISHOP
Rt. Revd Tim Thornton, *cons.* 2001, *apptd* 2008; Lis Escop,
   Truro TR3 6QQ
   Signs Tim Truro

BISHOP SUFFRAGAN
St Germans, Rt. Revd Royden Screech, *cons.* 2000, *apptd;* 2000 32 Falmouth Road, Truro, Cornwall TR1 2HX

DEAN
Very Revd Dr Christopher Hardwick, *apptd* 2005

Organist and Director of Music, Chris Gray, *apptd* 2008

ARCHDEACONS
Cornwall, Ven. Roger Bush, *apptd* 2006
Bodmin, Ven. Audrey Elkington, *apptd* 2011

Chancellor, Timothy Briden, *apptd* 1998
Registrar and Legal Secretary, Martin Follett
Deputy Diocesan Secretary, Esther Pollard, Diocesan House, Kenwyn, Truro TR1 1JQ **T** 01872-274351

WAKEFIELD *(YORK)*
12TH BISHOP
Rt. Revd Stephen Platten, *cons.* 2003, *apptd* 2003; Bishop's Lodge, Woodthorpe Lane, Wakefield WF2 6JL
Signs Stephen Wakefield

BISHOP SUFFRAGAN
Pontefract, Rt. Revd Tony Robinson, *cons.* 2003, *apptd* 2002; Pontefract House, Manygates Lane, Sandal, Wakefield WF2 7DR

DEAN
Very Revd Jonathan Greener, *apptd* 2007

Organist, Thomas Moore, *apptd* 2010

ARCHDEACONS
Halifax, Ven. Robert Freeman, *apptd* 2003
Pontefract, Ven. Peter Townley, *apptd* 2008

Chancellor, His Hon. Judge Downes, *apptd* 2006
Registrars and Legal Secretaries, Julian Gill; Julia Wilding
Diocesan Secretary, Ashley Ellis, Church House, 1 South Parade, Wakefield WF1 1LP **T** 01924-371802

WORCESTER *(CANTERBURY)*
113TH BISHOP
Rt. Revd Dr John Inge, *cons.* 2003, *apptd* 2007; The Bishop's Office, The Old Palace, Deansway, Worcester WR1 2JE
Signs John Wigorn

SUFFRAGAN BISHOP
Dudley, Rt. Revd David Walker, *cons.* 2000, *apptd* 2000; The Bishop's House, Bishop's Walk, Cradley Heath B64 7JF

DEAN
Very Revd Peter Atkinson, *apptd* 2006

Organist, Dr Adrian Lucas, *apptd* 1996

ARCHDEACONS
Dudley, Ven. Fred Trethewey, *apptd* 2001
Worcester, Ven. Roger Morris, *apptd* 2008

Chancellor, Charles Mynors, *apptd* 1999
Registrar and Legal Secretary, Michael Huskinson
Diocesan Secretary, Robert Higham, The Old Palace, Deansway, Worcester WR1 2JE **T** 01905-20537

ROYAL PECULIARS
WESTMINSTER
The Collegiate Church of St Peter
Dean, Very Revd Dr John Hall
Sub Dean, Revd Canon Robert Reiss
Archdeacon, Ven. Dr June Hedges
Chapter Clerk, Receiver-General and Registrar, Sir Stephen Lamport, KCVO, Chapter Office, 20 Dean's Yard, London SW1P 3PA
Organist, James O'Donnell, *apptd* 1999
Legal Secretary, Christopher Vyse, *apptd* 2000

WINDSOR
The Queen's Free Chapel of St George within Her Castle of Windsor
Dean, Rt. Revd David Conner, KCVO, *apptd* 1998
Chapter Clerk, Charlotte Manley, LVO, OBE, *apptd* 2003; Chapter Office, The Cloisters, Windsor Castle, Windsor, Berks SL4 1NJ
Director of Music, Timothy Byram-Wigfield, *apptd* 2004

OTHER ANGLICAN CHURCHES

THE CHURCH IN WALES
The Anglican Church was the established church in Wales from the 16th century until 1920, when the estrangement of the majority of Welsh people from Anglicanism resulted in disestablishment. Since then the Church in Wales has been an autonomous province consisting of six sees. The bishops are elected by an electoral college comprising elected lay and clerical members, who also elect one of the diocesan bishops as Archbishop of Wales.

The legislative body of the Church in Wales is the Governing Body, which has 143 members divided between the three orders of bishops, clergy and laity. Its president is the Archbishop of Wales and it meets twice annually. Its decisions are binding upon all members of the church. The church's property and finances are the responsibility of the Representative Body. There are 58,136 members of the Church in Wales, with 518 stipendiary clergy and 923 parishes.

THE REPRESENTATIVE BODY OF THE CHURCH IN WALES, 39 Cathedral Road, Cardiff CF11 9XF **T** 029-2034 8200 *Secretary,* John Shirley

12TH ARCHBISHOP OF WALES, Most Revd Dr Barry Morgan (Bishop of Llandaff), *elected* 2003
Signs Barry Cambrensis

BISHOPS
Bangor (81st), Rt. Revd Andrew John, *b.* 1964 *cons.* 2008, *elected* 2008; Ty'r Esgob, Upper Garth Road, Bangor, Gwynedd LL57 2SS *Signs* Andrew Bangor. *Stipendiary clergy,* 52
Llandaff (102nd), Most Revd Dr Barry Morgan (*also* Archbishop of Wales), *b.* 1947, *cons.* 1993, *trans.* 1999; Llys Esgob, The Cathedral Green, Llandaff, Cardiff CF5 2YE *Signs* Barry Cambrensis. *Stipendiary clergy,* 118
Monmouth (9th), Rt. Revd Dominic Walker, *b.* 1948, *cons.* 1997, *elected* 2003; Bishopstow, Stow Hill, Newport NP20 4EA *Signs* Dominic Monmouth. *Stipendiary clergy,* 87
St Asaph (76th), Rt. Revd Gregory Cameron, *b.* 1959, *cons.* 2009, *elected* 2009; Esgobty, Upper Denbigh Road, St Asaph, Denbighshire LL17 0TW *Signs* Gregory Llanelwy. *Stipendiary clergy,* 92
St David's (128th), Rt. Revd (John) Wyn Evans, *b.* 1946, *cons.* 2008, *elected* 2008; Llys Esgob, Abergwili,

Carmarthen SA31 2JG *Signs* Wyn St Davids. *Stipendiary clergy,* 98

Swansea and Brecon (9th), Rt. Revd John Davies, *b.* 1953, *cons.* 2008, *elected* 2008; Ely Tower, Castle Square, Brecon, Powys LD3 9DJ *Signs* John Swansea & Brecon. *Stipendiary clergy,* 71

The stipend for a diocesan bishop of the Church in Wales is £39,576 a year for 2011–12.

SCOTTISH EPISCOPAL CHURCH

The Scottish Episcopal Church was founded after the Act of Settlement (1690) established the presbyterian nature of the Church of Scotland. The Scottish Episcopal Church is a member of the worldwide Anglican Communion. The governing authority is the General Synod, an elected body of 140 members (70 from the clergy and 70 from the laity) which meets once a year. The bishop who convenes and presides at meetings of the General Synod is called the 'primus' and is elected by his fellow bishops.

There are 35,780 members of the Scottish Episcopal Church, seven bishops, 524 serving clergy and around 309 churches and places of worship.

THE GENERAL SYNOD OF THE SCOTTISH EPISCOPAL CHURCH, 21 Grosvenor Crescent, Edinburgh EH12 5EE T 0131-225 6357
W www.scotland.anglican.org
Secretary-General, John Stuart

PRIMUS OF THE SCOTTISH EPISCOPAL CHURCH, Most Revd David Chillingworth (Bishop of St Andrews, Dunkeld and Dunblane), *elected* 2009

BISHOPS

Aberdeen and Orkney, Rt. Revd Dr Bob Gillies, *b.* 1951, *cons.* 2007, *elected* 2007. *Clergy,* 50

Argyll and the Isles, Rt. Revd Kevin Pearson, *b.* 1954, *cons.* 2011, *elected* 2010. *Clergy* 27

Brechin, vacant. *Clergy,* 35

Edinburgh, Rt. Revd Brian Smith, *b.* 1943, *cons.* 1993, *elected* 2001. *Clergy,* 170

Glasgow and Galloway, Rt. Revd Dr Gregor Duncan, *b.* 1950, *cons.* 2010, *elected* 2010. *Clergy,* 113

Moray, Ross and Caithness, Rt. Revd Mark Strange, *b.* 1961, *cons.* 2007, *elected* 2007. *Clergy,* 56

St Andrews, Dunkeld and Dunblane, Most Revd David Chillingworth, *b.* 1951, *cons.* 2005, *elected* 2005. *Clergy,* 89

The minimum stipend of a diocesan bishop of the Scottish Episcopal Church for 2011 is £34,215 (ie 1.5 times the standard clergy stipend of £22,810).

CHURCH OF IRELAND

The Anglican Church was the established church in Ireland from the 16th century but never secured the allegiance of the majority and was disestablished in 1871. The Church of Ireland is divided into the provinces of Armagh and Dublin, each under an archbishop. The provinces are subdivided into 12 dioceses.

The legislative body is the General Synod, which has 660 members in total, divided between the House of Bishops (12 members) and the House of Representatives (216 clergy and 432 laity). The Archbishop of Armagh is elected by the House of Bishops; other episcopal elections are made by an electoral college.

There are around 390,000 members of the Church of Ireland, 275,000 in Northern Ireland and 115,000 in the Republic of Ireland. There are two archbishops, ten bishops and over 500 stipendiary clergy.

CENTRAL OFFICE, Church of Ireland House, Church Avenue, Rathmines, Dublin 6 T (+353) (1) 497 8422
Chief Officer and Secretary of the Representative Church Body, D. C. Reardon

PROVINCE OF ARMAGH
Archbishop of Armagh, Primate of all Ireland and Metropolitan, Most Revd Alan Harper, OBE, *b.* 1944, *cons.* 2002, *trans.* 2007. *Clergy,* 55

BISHOPS

Clogher, Rt. Revd John McDowell, *b.* 1956, *cons.* 2011, *apptd* 2011. *Clergy,* 32

Connor, Rt. Revd Alan Abernethy, *b.* 1957, *cons.* 2007, *apptd* 2007. *Clergy,* 106

Derry and Raphoe, Rt. Revd Kenneth Good, *b.* 1952, *cons.* 2002, *apptd* 2002. *Clergy,* 51

Down and Dromore, Rt. Revd Harold Miller, *b.* 1950, *cons.* 1997, *apptd* 1997. *Clergy,* 116

Kilmore, Elphin and Ardagh, Rt. Revd Kenneth Clarke, *b.* 1949, *cons.* 2001, *apptd* 2001. *Clergy,* 21

Tuam, Killala and Achonry, Rt. Revd Patrick Rooke, *b.* 1955, *cons.* 2011, *apptd* 2011. *Clergy,* 13

PROVINCE OF DUBLIN
Archbishop of Dublin, Bishop of Glendalough, Primate of Ireland and Metropolitan, Most Revd Michael Jackson, PHD, DPHIL, *b.* 1956, *apptd* 2011. *Clergy,* 86

BISHOPS

Cashel and Ossory, Most Revd Michael Burrows, *b.* 1961, *cons.* 2006, *apptd* 2006. *Clergy,* 42

Cork, Cloyne and Ross, Rt. Revd William Colton, *b.* 1960, *cons.* 1999, *apptd* 1999. *Clergy,* 30

Limerick, Killaloe and Ardfert, Rt. Revd Trevor Williams, *b.* 1948, *cons.* 2008. *Clergy,* 19

Meath and Kildare, Most Revd Richard Clarke, PHD, *b.* 1949, *cons.* 1996, *apptd* 1996. *Clergy,* 26

OVERSEAS

PRIMATES

Primate and Presiding Bishop of Aotearoa, New Zealand and Polynesia, Most Revd William Turei

Primate of Australia, Most Revd Phillip Aspinall

Primate of Brazil, Most Revd Maurício Araújo de Andrade

Archbishop of the Province of Burundi, Most Revd Bernard Ntahoturi

Archbishop and Primate of Canada, Most Revd Frederick Hiltz

Archbishop of the Province of Central Africa, Rt. Revd Albert Chama

Primate of the Central Region of America, Most Revd Armando Soria

Archbishop of the Province of Congo, Most Revd Henry Isingoma

Primate of the Province of Hong Kong Sheng Kung Hui, Most Revd Paul Kwong

Archbishop of the Province of the Indian Ocean, Most Revd Gerald Ernest

Primate of Japan (Nippon Sei Ko Kai), Most Revd Nathaniel Uematsu

President-Bishop of Jerusalem and the Middle East, Most Revd Dr Mouneer Anis

Archbishop of the Province of Kenya, Most Revd Eliud Wabukala

Archbishop of the Province of Korea, Rt. Revd Paul
  Keun-Sang Kim
Archbishop of the Province of Melanesia, Most Revd David
  Vunagi
Archbishop of Mexico, Most Revd Carlos Touche-Porter
Archbishop of the Province of Myanmar (Burma), Most
  Revd Stephen Oo
Archbishop of the Province of Nigeria, Most Rt. Revd
  Nicholas Okoh
Archbishop of Papua New Guinea, Most Revd Joseph
  Kopapa
Prime Bishop of the Philippines, Rt. Revd Edward Malecdan
Archbishop of the Province of Rwanda, Most Revd
  Onesphore Rwaje
Primate of the Province of South East Asia, Most Revd Dr
  John Chew
Metropolitan of the Province of Southern Africa, Most Revd
  Thabo Makgoba
Presiding Bishop of the Southern Cone of America, Most
  Revd Hector Zavala
Archbishop of the Province of the Sudan, Most Revd Daniel
  Yak
Archbishop of the Province of Tanzania, Most Revd
  Valentino Mokiwa
Archbishop of the Province of Uganda, Most Revd Henry
  Orombi
Presiding Bishop and Primate of the USA, Most Revd
  Katharine Schori
Archbishop of the Province of West Africa, Most Revd
  Justice Ofei Akrofi
Archbishop of the Province of the West Indies, Most Revd Dr
  John Holder

OTHER CHURCHES AND EXTRA-PROVINCIAL DIOCESES

*Anglican Church of Bermuda, extra-provincial to
  Canterbury*
  Bishop, Rt. Revd Patrick White
Church of Ceylon, extra-provincial to Canterbury
  Bishop of Colombo, Rt. Revd Duleep de Chickera
  Bishop of Kurunagala, Rt. Revd Kumara Illangasinghe
Episcopal Church of Cuba, Rt. Revd Miguel Tamayo
  (interim)
Falkland Islands, extra-provincial to Canterbury
Episcopal Commissary, Rt. Revd Stephen Venner (Bishop
  to the Forces)
*Lusitanian Church (Portuguese Episcopal Church),
  extra-provincial to Canterbury*
  Bishop, Rt. Revd Fernando Soares
*Reformed Episcopal Church of Spain, extra-provincial to
  Canterbury*
  Bishop, Rt. Revd Carlos López-Lozano

MODERATION OF CHURCHES IN FULL COMMUNION WITH THE ANGLICAN COMMUNION

Church of Bangladesh, Rt. Revd Paul Sarkar
Church of North India, Most Revd Purely Lyngdoh
Church of South India, Most Revd Suputhrappa Kumar
Church of Pakistan, Rt. Revd Samuel Azariah

CHURCH OF SCOTLAND

The Church of Scotland is the national church of
Scotland. The church is reformed in doctrine, and
presbyterian in constitution; ie based on a hierarchy of
courts of ministers and elders and, since 1990, of
members of a diaconate. At local level the Kirk Session

consists of the parish minister and ruling elders. At district
level the presbyteries, of which there are 44 in Britain,
consist of all the ministers in the district, one ruling elder
from each congregation, and those members of the
diaconate who qualify for membership. The General
Assembly is the supreme authority, and is presided over by
a Moderator chosen annually by the Assembly. The
sovereign, if not present in person, is represented by a
Lord High Commissioner who is appointed each year by
the Crown.

The Church of Scotland has around 600,000 members,
1,200 parish ministers and 1,464 churches. There are
about 20 ministers and other personnel working overseas.
Lord High Commissioner (2011–12), Rt. Hon. Lord
  Wilson of Tillyorn, KT, GCMG
Moderator of the General Assembly (2011–12), Rt. Revd
  David Arnott
Principal Clerk, Revd John Chalmers
Depute Clerk, vacant
Procurator, Laura Dunlop
Law Agent and Solicitor of the Church, Janette Wilson
Parliamentary Officer, Chloe Clemmons
General Treasurer, Iain Grimmond
Secretary, Church and Society Council, Revd Ewan Aitken
CHURCH OFFICE, 121 George Street, Edinburgh EH2 4YN
  T 0131-225 5722

PRESBYTERIES AND CLERKS
Aberdeen, Revd Dr Ian McLean
Abernethy, Revd James MacEwan
Annandale and Eskdale, Revd C. Haston
Angus, Revd Mike Goss
Ardrossan, Revd Johnston Mackay
Argyll, Ian MacLagan
Ayr, Revd Kenneth Elliott
Buchan, George Berstan
Caithness, Revd Ronald Johnstone
Dumbarton, Revd Colin Caskie
Dumfries and Kirkcudbright, Revd Gordon Savage
Dundee, Revd James Wilson
Dunfermline, Revd Elizabeth Kenny
Dunkeld and Meigle, Revd John Russell
Duns, Peter Johnson
Edinburgh, Revd George Whyte
England, Revd Dr P. Mills
Europe, Revd John Cowie
Falkirk, Revd Jerome O'Brien
Glasgow, Revd Dr Angus Kerr
Gordon, Gerald Moore
Greenock and Paisley, Revd Alastair Cherry
Hamilton, Revd Shaw Paterson
Inverness, Revd Alastair Younger
Irvine and Kilmarnock, Revd Colin Brockie
Jedburgh, Revd W. Frank Campbell
Kincardine and Deeside, Revd Hugh Conkey
Kirkcaldy, Revd Rosemary Frew
Lanark, Revd Helen Jamieson
Lewis, Revd Thomas Sinclair
Lochaber, Ella Gill
Lochcarron-Skye, Revd Allan MacArthur
Lothian, John McCulloch
Melrose and Peebles, Jack Stewart
Moray, Revd Hugh Smith
Orkney, Revd James Wishart
Perth, Revd Derek Lawson
Ross, Ronald Gunstone
St Andrews, Revd James Redpath
Shetland, Revd Charles Greig

Stirling, Dorothy Kinloch
Sutherland, Mrs Mary Stobo
Uist, Wilson McKinlay
West Lothian, Revd Duncan Shaw
Wigtown and Stranraer, Nicola Steel

The stipends for ministers in the Church of Scotland in 2011 range from £23,139–£30,426, depending on length of service.

ROMAN CATHOLIC CHURCH

The Roman Catholic Church is a worldwide Christian church acknowledging as its head the Bishop of Rome, known as the Pope (father). Despite its widespread usage, 'Pope' is actually an unofficial term, the *Annuario Pontificio,* (Pontifical Yearbook) lists eight official titles: Bishop of Rome, Vicar of Jesus Christ, Successor of the Prince of the Apostles, Supreme Pontiff of the Universal Church, Primate of Italy, Archbishop and Metropolitan of the Roman Province, Sovereign of the State of the Vatican City and Servant of the Servants of God.

The Pope leads a communion of followers of Christ, who believe they continue his presence in the world as servants of faith, hope and love to all society. The Pope is held to be the successor of St Peter and thus invested with the power which was entrusted to St Peter by Jesus Christ. A direct line of succession is therefore claimed from the earliest Christian communities. With the fall of the Roman Empire the Pope also became an important political leader. His territory is now limited to the 0.44 sq. km (0.17 sq. miles) of the Vatican City State, created to provide some independence to the Pope from Italy and other nations. The episcopal jurisdiction of the Roman Catholic Church is called the Holy See.

The Pope exercises spiritual authority over the church with the advice and assistance of the Sacred College of Cardinals, the supreme council of the church. The number of cardinals was fixed at 70 by Pope Sixtus V in 1586 but has been steadily increasing since the pontificate of John XXIII and in May 2011 stood at 198.

Following the death of the Pope, the members of the College of Cardinals under the age of 80 are called to the Vatican to elect a successor. They are known as cardinal electors and as at May 2011 numbered 115. The assembly of cardinal electors is known as the conclave, and, in complete seclusion, they vote by a secret ballot. A two-thirds majority is necessary before the vote can be accepted as final. When a cardinal receives the necessary number of votes, the Dean of the Sacred College formally asks him if he will accept election and the name by which he wishes to be known. On his acceptance of the office of Supreme Pontiff, the conclave is dissolved and the first Cardinal Deacon announces the election to the assembled crowd in St Peter's Square.

The Pope has full legislative, judicial and administrative power over the whole Roman Catholic Church. He is aided in his administration by the curia, which is made up of a number of departments. The Secretariat of State is the central office for carrying out the Pope's instructions and is presided over by the Cardinal Secretary of State. It maintains relations with the departments of the curia, with the episcopate, with the representatives of the Holy See in various countries, governments and private persons. The congregations and pontifical councils are the Pope's ministries and include departments such as the Congregation for the Doctrine of Faith, whose field of competence concerns faith and morals; the Congregation for the Clergy and the Congregation for the Evangelisation of Peoples, the Pontifical Council for the Family and the Pontifical Council for the Promotion of Christian Unity.

The Holy See, composed of the Pope and those who help him in his mission for the church, is recognised by the Conventions of Vienna as an international moral body. Apostolic nuncios are the Pope's diplomatic representatives; in countries where no formal diplomatic relations exist between the Holy See and that country, the papal representative is known as an apostolic delegate.

The Roman Catholic Church has over one billion adherents under the care of around 5,000 diocesan bishops worldwide.

SUPREME PONTIFF

His Holiness Pope Benedict XVI (Joseph Ratzinger), *born* Bavaria, Germany, 16 April 1927; *ordained priest* 1951; *appointed Archbishop* (of Munich), March 1977; *created Cardinal* June 1977; *assumed pontificate* 19 April 2005

SECRETARIAT OF STATE

Secretary of State, HE Cardinal Tarcisio Bertone
First Section (General Affairs), Most Revd Fernando Filoni
    (Titular Archbishop of Volturno)
Second Section (Relations with Other States), Most Revd
    Dominique Mamberti (Titular Archbishop of Sagona)

BISHOPS' CONFERENCE

The Catholic Church in England and Wales consists of a total of 22 dioceses. The Bishops' Conference, which coordinates common activity, includes the diocesan bishops, the Personal Ordinary of the Ordinariate of Our Lady of Walsingham, the Apostolic Exarch of the Ukrainians, the Bishop of the Forces and the auxiliary bishops. The conference is headed by the president (the Most Revd Vincent Nichols, Archbishop of Westminster) and vice-president (the Most Revd Peter Smith, Archbishop of Southwark). There are six departments, each with an episcopal chair: the Department for Christian Life and Worship (the Bishop of Leeds), the Department for Dialogue and Unity (the Archbishop of Birmingham), the Department for Catholic Education and Formation (the Bishop of Nottingham), the Department for Christian Responsibility and Citizenship (the Archbishop of Southwark), the Department for International Affairs (the Bishop of Clifton) and the Department for Evangelisation and Catechesis (the Bishop of Arundel and Brighton).

The Bishops' Conference Standing Committee is made up of two directly elected bishops in addition to the Metropolitan Archbishops and chairs from each of the above departments. The committee has general responsibility for continuity of policy between the plenary sessions of the conference, preparing the conference agenda and implementing its decisions.

The administration of the Bishops' Conference is funded by a levy on each diocese, according to income. A general secretariat in London coordinates and supervises the Bishops' Conference administration activities. There are also other agencies and consultative bodies affiliated to the conference.

The Bishops' Conference of Scotland is the permanently constituted assembly of the bishops of Scotland. The conference is headed by the president (HE Cardinal Keith Patrick O'Brien, Archbishop of St. Andrews and Edinburgh). The conference establishes various agencies which perform advisory functions in relation to the conference. The more important of these agencies are called commissions; each one is headed by a bishop president who, with the other members of the commissions, are appointed by the conference.

The Irish Catholic Bishops' Conference (also known as the Irish Episcopal Conference) has as its president Cardinal Sean Brady of Armagh. Its membership comprises all 31 of the archbishops and bishops of Ireland. It appoints various commissions and agencies to assist with the work of the Catholic Church in Ireland.

The Catholic Church in the UK has over 900,000 mass attendees, 5,599 priests and 4,583 churches.

Bishops' Conferences secretariats:

ENGLAND AND WALES, 39 Eccleston Square, London SW1V 1BX T 020-7630 8220 E secretariat@cbcew.org.uk W www.catholicchurch.org.uk
General Secretary, Fr Marcus Stock
SCOTLAND, 64 Aitken Street, Airdrie ML6 6LT
T 01236-764061 W www.bpsconfscot.com
General Secretary, Very Revd Mgr Paul Conroy
IRELAND, Columba Centre, Maynooth, County Kildare
T (+353) (1) 505 3000 E info@catholicbishops.ie
W www.catholicbishops.ie
Secretary, Most Revd William Lee (Bishop of Waterford and Lismore)
Executive Secretary, Revd Gearoid Dullea

GREAT BRITAIN
APOSTOLIC NUNCIO TO GREAT BRITAIN
Most Revd Antonio Mennini, 54 Parkside, London SW19 5NE T 020-8944 7189

ENGLAND AND WALES
THE MOST REVD ARCHBISHOPS
Westminster, Vincent Nichols, cons. 1992, apptd 2009
Archbishop Emeritus, Cardinal Cormac Murphy-O'Connor, cons. 1977, elevated 2001
Auxiliaries, Alan Hopes cons. 2003; John Arnold cons. 2006. Clergy, 690. Archbishop's Residence, Archbishop's House, Ambrosden Avenue, London SW1P 1QJ
T 020-7798 9033
Birmingham, Bernard Longley, cons. 2003, apptd 2009
Auxiliaries, David McGough, cons. 2005; William Kenney, cons. 1987; Philip Pargeter (retd), cons. 1990.
Clergy, 430. Archbishop's Residence, Archbishop's House, 8 Shadwell Street, Birmingham B4 6EY T 0121-236 9090
Cardiff, George Stack cons. 2001, apptd 2011. Clergy, 95.
Archbishop's Residence, Archbishop's House, 41–43 Cathedral Road, Cardiff CF11 9HD T 029-2022 0411
Liverpool, Patrick Kelly, cons. 1984, apptd 1996 Auxiliary, Thomas Williams, cons. 2003. Clergy, 434. Diocesan Curia, Archdiocese of Liverpool, Centre for Evangelisation, Croxteth Drive, Sefton Park, Liverpool L17 1AA
T 0151-522 1000
Southwark, Peter Smith, cons. 1995, apptd 2010
Auxiliaries, John Hine, cons. 2001; Patrick Lynch, cons. 2006; Paul Hendricks, cons. 2006. Clergy, 546.
Diocesan Curia, Archbishop's House, 150 St George's Road, London SE1 6HX T 020-7928 5592

THE RT. REVD BISHOPS
Arundel and Brighton, Kieran Conry, cons. 2001, apptd 2001. Clergy, 96. Diocesan Curia, Bishop's House, The Upper Drive, Hove, E. Sussex BN3 6NB
T 01273-506387
Brentwood, Thomas McMahon, cons. 1980, apptd 1980.
Clergy, 121. Bishop's Office, Cathedral House, Ingrave Road, Brentwood, Essex CM15 8AT T 01277-232266

Clifton, Declan Lang, cons. 2001, apptd 2001.
Clergy, 251. Bishop's House, St Ambrose, North Road, Leigh Woods, Bristol BS8 3PW T 0117-973 3072
East Anglia, Michael Evans, cons 2003, apptd 2003.
Clergy, 129. Diocesan Curia, The White House, 21 Upgate, Poringland, Norwich NR14 7SH T 01508-492202
Hallam, John Rawsthorne, cons. 1981, apptd 1997.
Clergy, 75. Bishop's House, 75 Norfolk Road, Sheffield S2 2SZ T 0114-278 7988
Hexham and Newcastle, Seamus Cunningham, cons. 2009, apptd 2009. Clergy, 185. Diocesan Curia, Bishop's House, East Denton Hall, 800 West Road, Newcastle upon Tyne NE5 2BJ T 0191-228 0003
Lancaster, Michael Campbell, cons. 2008, apptd 2009.
Clergy, 170. Bishop's Office, The Pastoral Centre, Balmoral Road, Lancaster LA1 3BT T 01524-596050
Leeds, Arthur Roche, cons. 2001, apptd 2004. Clergy, 193.
Diocesan Curia, Hinsley Hall, 62 Headingley Lane, Leeds LS6 2BX T 0113-261 8022
Menevia (Wales), Thomas Burns, cons. 2002, apptd 2008.
Clergy, 60. Diocesan Curia, 27 Convent Street, Swansea SA1 2BX T 01792-644017
Middlesbrough, Terence Drainey, cons. 2008, apptd 2007.
Clergy, 98. Diocesan Curia, 50A The Avenue, Linthorpe, Middlesbrough TS5 6QT T 01642-850505
Northampton, Peter Doyle, cons. 2005, apptd 2005. Clergy, 122. Diocesan Curia, Bishop's House, Marriott Street, Northampton NN2 6AW T 01604-715635
Nottingham, Malcolm McMahon, cons. 2000, apptd 2000.
Clergy, 162. Bishop's House, 27 Cavendish Road East, The Park, Nottingham NG7 1BB T 0115-947 4786
Plymouth, Christopher Budd, cons. 1986, apptd 1985.
Clergy, 130. Bishop's Residence, Bishop's House, 31 Wyndham Street West, Plymouth PL1 5RZ T 01752-224414
Portsmouth, Crispian Hollis, cons. 1987, apptd 1989.
Clergy, 282. Bishop's Residence, Bishop's House, Bishop Crispian Way, Portsmouth, Hants PO1 3HG
T 023-9282 0894
Salford, Terence Brain, cons. 1991, apptd 1997. Clergy, 254. Diocesan Curia, Wardley Hall, Worsley, Manchester M28 2ND T 0161-794 2825
Shrewsbury, Mark Davies, cons. 2010, apptd 2011. Clergy 123. Diocesan Curia, 2 Park Road South, Prenton, Wirral CH43 4UX T 0151-652 9855
Wrexham (Wales), Edwin Regan, cons.1994, apptd 1994.
Clergy, 45. Diocesan Curia, Bishop's House, Sontley Road, Wrexham LL13 7EW T 01978-262726

SCOTLAND
THE MOST REVD ARCHBISHOPS
St Andrews and Edinburgh, HE Cardinal Keith Patrick O'Brien, cons. 1985, apptd 1985, elevated 2003. Clergy, 170. Diocesan Office, 100 Strathearn Road, Edinburgh EH9 1BB T 0131-447 3377
Glasgow, Mario Joseph Conti, cons. 1977, apptd 2002.
Clergy, 225. Diocesan Curia, 196 Clyde Street, Glasgow G1 4JY T 0141-226 5898

THE RT. REVD BISHOPS
Aberdeen, Peter Moran, cons. 2003, apptd 2003. Clergy, 43. Diocesan Curia, 3 Queen's Cross, Aberdeen AB15 4XU T 01224-319154
Argyll and the Isles, Joseph Toal, cons. 2008, apptd 2008.
Clergy, 32. Bishop's House, Esplanade, Oban, Argyll PA34 5AB T 01631-567436
Dunkeld, Vincent Logan, cons. 1981. Clergy, 49. Diocesan Curia, 24–28 Lawside Road, Dundee DD3 6XY T 01382-225453

Galloway, John Cunningham, *cons.* 2004, *apptd* 2004. *Clergy* 56. *Diocesan Curia,* 8 Corsehill Road, Ayr KA7 2ST T 01292-266750

Motherwell, Joseph Devine, *cons.* 1977, *apptd* 1983. *Clergy,* 123. *Diocesan Curia,* Coursington Road, Motherwell ML1 1PP T 01698-269114

Paisley, Philip Tartaglia, *cons.* 2005, *apptd* 2005. *Clergy,* 83. *Diocesan Curia,* Diocesan Centre, Cathedral Precincts, Incle Street, Paisley PA1 1HR T 0141-847 6130

BISHOPRIC OF THE FORCES
Rt. Revd Richard Moth, *cons.* 2009, *apptd* 2009. *Administration,* RC Bishopric of the Forces, Wellington House, St Omer Barracks, Thornhill Road, Aldershot, Hants GU11 2BG T 01252-348234

IRELAND
There is one hierarchy for the whole of Ireland. Several of the dioceses have territory partly in the Republic of Ireland and partly in Northern Ireland.

APOSTOLIC NUNCIO TO IRELAND
HE Most Revd Giuseppe Leanza (Titular Archbishop of Lilybaeum), 183 Navan Road, Dublin 7
T (+353) (1) 838 0577 F (+353) (1) 838 0276

THE MOST REVD ARCHBISHOPS
Armagh, Cardinal Sean Brady (*also* Primate of all Ireland), *cons.* 1995, *apptd* 1996. *Auxiliary Bishop,* Most Revd Gerard Clifford, *cons.* 1991. *Clergy,* 156. *Bishop's Residence,* Ara Coeli, Armagh BT61 7QY T 028-3752 2045

Cashel and Emly, Dermot Clifford, *cons.* 1986, *apptd* 1988. *Clergy,* 95. *Archbishop's House,* Thurles, Co. Tipperary T (+353) (504) 21512

Dublin, Diarmuid Martin, *cons.* 1999, *apptd* Coadjutor Archbishop 2003, *succeeded as Archbishop* 2004. *Archbishop Emeritus,* HE Cardinal Desmond Connell, *cons.* 1988, *elevated* 2001. *Auxiliary,* vacant. *Clergy,* 994. *Archbishop's House,* Drumcondra, Dublin 9 T (+353) (1) 837 3732

Tuam, Dr Michael Neary, *cons.* 1992, *apptd* 1995. *Clergy,* 128. *Archbishop's House,* Tuam, Co. Galway T (+353) (93) 24166

THE MOST REVD BISHOPS
Achonry, Brendan Kelly, *cons.* 2008, *apptd* 2007. *Clergy,* 53. *Bishop's House,* Edmondstown, Ballaghaderreen, Co. Roscommon T (+353) (94) 986 0021

Ardagh and Clonmacnois, Colm O'Reilly, *cons.* 1983, *apptd* 1983. *Clergy,* 61. *Diocesan Office,* St Michael's, Longford, Co. Longford T (+353) (43) 46432

Clogher, Liam MacDaid *cons.* 2010, *apptd* 2010. *Clergy,* 74. *Bishop's House,* Monaghan T (+353) (47) 81019

Clonfert, John Kirby, *cons.* 1988 *apptd* 1988. *Clergy,* 39. *Bishop's Residence,* Coorheen, Loughrea, Co. Galway T (+353) (91) 841560

Cloyne, vacant. *Clergy,* 132. *Diocesan Office,* Cobh, Co. Cork T (+353) (21) 481 1430

Cork and Ross, John Buckley, *cons.* 1984, *apptd* 1998. *Clergy,* 136. *Diocesan Office,* Cork and Ross Offices, Redemption Road, Cork T (+353) (21) 430 1717

Derry, Seamus Hegarty, *cons.* 1982, *apptd* 1994. *Clergy,* 120. *Bishop's House,* St Eugene's Cathedral, Derry BT48 9YG T 028-7126 2302

Down and Connor, Noel Treanor, *cons.* 2008, *apptd* 2008. *Auxiliaries,* Anthony Farquhar, *cons.* 1983; Donal McKeown, *cons.* 2001. *Clergy,* 218. *Bishop's Residence,* Lisbreen, 73 Somerton Road, Belfast, Co. Antrim BT15 4DE T 028-9077 6185

Dromore, John McAreavey, *cons.* 1999, *apptd* 1999. *Clergy,* 43. *Bishop's House,* 44 Armagh Road, Newry, Co. Down BT35 6PN T 028-3026 2444

Elphin, Christopher Jones, *cons.* 1994, *apptd* 1994. *Clergy,* 70. *Bishop's Residence,* St Mary's, Sligo T (+353) (71) 916 2670

Ferns, Denis Brennan, *cons.* 2006, *apptd* 2006. *Clergy,* 92. *Bishop's House,* Summerhill, Wexford T (+353) (53) 912 2177

Galway, Kilmacduagh and Kilfenora, Martin Drennan, *cons.* 1997, *apptd* 2005. *Clergy,* 57. *Bishop's Residence,* Mount Saint Mary's, Taylor's Hill, Galway T (+353) (91) 563566

Kerry, William Murphy, *cons.* 1995, *apptd* 1995. *Clergy,* 104. *Bishop's House,* Killarney, Co. Kerry T (+353) (64) 663 1168

Kildare and Leighlin, vacant. *Clergy,* 110. *Bishop's House,* Carlow T (+353) (59) 917 6725

Killala, John Fleming, *cons.* 2002, *apptd* 2002. *Clergy,* 54. *Bishop's House,* Ballina, Co. Mayo T (+353) (96) 21518

Killaloe, Dr Keiran O'Reilly, *cons.* 2010, *apptd* 2010 *Clergy,* 118. *Diocesan Office,* Westbourne, Ennis, Co. Clare T (+353) (65) 682 8638

Kilmore, Leo O'Reilly, *cons.* 1997, *apptd* 1998. *Clergy,* 75. *Bishop's House,* Cullies, Co. Cavan T (+353) (49) 433 1496

Limerick, vacant. *Clergy,* 109. *Diocesan Office,* Social Service Centre, Henry Street, Limerick T (+353) (61) 315856

Meath, Michael Smith, *cons.* 1984, *apptd* 1990. *Clergy,* 131. *Bishop's House,* Dublin Road, Mullingar, Co. Westmeath T (+353) (44) 934 8841

Ossory, Seamus Freeman, *cons.* 2007, *apptd* 2007. *Clergy,* 65. *Bishop's Residence,* Sion House, Kilkenny T (+353) (56) 776 2448

Raphoe, Dr Philip Boyce, *cons.* 1995, *apptd* 1995. *Clergy,* 82. *Bishop's Residence,* Ard Adhamhnáin, Letterkenny, Co. Donegal T (+353) (74) 912 1208

Waterford and Lismore, William Lee, *cons.* 1993, *apptd* 1993. *Clergy,* 114. *Bishop's House,* John's Hill, Waterford T (+353) (51) 874463

OTHER CHURCHES IN THE UK

ASSOCIATED PRESBYTERIAN CHURCHES OF SCOTLAND

The Associated Presbyterian Churches came into being in 1989 as a result of a division within the Free Presbyterian Church of Scotland. The Associated Presbyterian Churches is reformed and evangelistic in nature and emphasises the importance of doctrine based primarily on the Bible and secondly on the Westminster Confession of Faith. There are an estimated 500 members, 8 ministers and 12 congregations in Scotland. There are also congregations in Canada.

ASSOCIATED PRESBYTERIAN CHURCHES OF SCOTLAND, APC Manse, Polvinster Road, Oban PA34 5TN T 01631-567076 E archibald.mcphail@virgin.net W www.apchurches.org

Moderator of Presbytery, Revd Dr Wayne Pearce
Clerk of Presbytery, Revd Archibald McPhail

BAPTIST CHURCH

Baptists trace their origins to John Smyth, who in 1609 in Amsterdam reinstituted the baptism of conscious believers as the basis of the fellowship of a gathered church. Members of Smyth's church established the first Baptist church in England in 1612. They came to be known as 'General' Baptists and their theology was Arminian, whereas a later group of Calvinists who adopted the baptism of believers came to be known as 'Particular' Baptists. The two sections of the Baptists were united into one body, the Baptist Union of Great Britain and Ireland, in 1891. In 1988 the title was changed to the Baptist Union of Great Britain.

Baptists emphasise the complete autonomy of the local church, although individual churches are linked in various kinds of associations. There are international bodies (such as the Baptist World Alliance) and national bodies, but some Baptist churches belong to neither. However, in Great Britain the majority of churches and associations belong to the Baptist Union of Great Britain. There are also Baptist Unions in Wales, Scotland and Ireland, which are much smaller than the Baptist Union of Great Britain, and there is some overlap of membership.

There are currently around 140,000 members, 2,500 ministers and 2,000 churches associated with the Baptist Union of Great Britain. The Baptist Union of Great Britain is one of the founder members of the European Baptist Federation (1948) and the Baptist World Alliance (1905), which represents around 40 million members worldwide.

In the Baptist Union of Scotland there are 11,450 members, 140 pastors and 165 churches.

In the Baptist Union of Wales (Undeb Bedyddwyr Cymru) there are 13,326 members, 105 pastors and 417 churches, including those in England.

BAPTIST UNION OF GREAT BRITAIN, Baptist House, PO Box 44, 129 Broadway, Didcot, Oxon OX11 8RT T 01235-517700 E info@baptist.org.uk W www.baptist.org.uk

General Secretary, Revd Jonathan Edwards

BAPTIST UNION OF SCOTLAND, 14 Aytoun Road, Glasgow G41 5RT T 0141-423 6169 E director@scottishbaptist.org.uk

General Director, Revd A. J. Donaldson

BAPTIST UNION OF WALES, Y Llwyfan, Trinity Saint David University College, College Road, Carmarthen SA31 3EQ T 01267-245660 E peter@bedyddwyrcymru.co.uk W www.buw.org.uk

President of the English Assembly (2011–12), Revd John P. R. Davies
President of the Welsh Assembly (2011–12), Glyndwr Prideaux
General Secretary of the Baptist Union of Wales, Revd Peter Thomas

THE BRETHREN

The Brethren was founded in Dublin in 1827–8, basing itself on the structures and practices of the early church and rejecting denominationalism and clericalism. Many groups sprang up; the group at Plymouth became the best known, resulting in its designation by others as the 'Plymouth Brethren'. Early worship had a prescribed form but quickly assumed an unstructured, non-liturgical format.

There are services devoted to worship, usually involving the breaking of bread, and separate preaching meetings. There is no salaried ministry.

A theological dispute led in 1848 to schism between the Open Brethren and the Closed or Exclusive Brethren, each branch later suffering further divisions.

Open Brethren churches are run by appointed elders and are completely independent, but freely cooperate with each other. Exclusive Brethren churches believe in a universal fellowship between congregations. They do not have appointed elders, but use respected members of their congregation to perform certain administrative functions.

The Brethren are established throughout the UK, Ireland, Europe, India, Africa and Australasia. In the UK there are over 70,000 members, 1,250 assembly halls and over 200 full-time Bible teachers, evangelists and administrators. There are a number of publishing houses that publish Brethren-related literature. Chapter Two is the main supplier of such literature in the UK; it also has a Brethren history archive which is available for use by appointment.

CHAPTER TWO, Conduit Mews, London SE18 7AP T 020-8316 5389 E info@chaptertwobooks.org.uk W www.chaptertwobooks.org.uk

CONGREGATIONAL FEDERATION

The Congregational Federation was founded by members of Congregational churches in England and Wales who did not join the United Reformed Church in 1972. There are also churches in Scotland and France affiliated to the federation. The federation exists to encourage congregations of believers to worship in free assembly, but it has no authority over them and emphasises their right to independence and self-governance.

The federation has 8,325 members, 67 accredited ministers and 282 churches in England, Wales and Scotland.

CONGREGATIONAL FEDERATION, 6 Castle Gate, Nottingham NG1 7AS T 0115-911 1460 E admin@congregational.org.uk W www.congregational.org.uk

President of the Federation (2011–12), Revd Brian Gist
General Secretary, Revd M. Heaney

FELLOWSHIP OF INDEPENDENT EVANGELICAL CHURCHES

The Fellowship of Independent Evangelical Churches was founded by Revd E. J. Poole-Connor (1872–1962) in 1922. In 1923 the fellowship published its first register of non-denominational pastors, evangelists and congregations who had accepted the doctrinal basis for the fellowship.

Members of the fellowship have two primary convictions: firstly to defend the evangelical faith, and secondly that evangelicalism is the bond that unites the fellowship, rather than forms of worship or church government.

The Fellowship of Independent Evangelical Churches exists to promote the welfare of non-denominational Bible churches and to give expression to the fundamental doctrines of evangelical Christianity. It supports individual churches by gathering and disseminating information and resources, advising churches on current theological, moral, social and practical issues and seeking to uphold the quality and integrity of church leaders through the Pastors' Association.

More than 500 churches throughout the UK are linked through the fellowship. There are more than 350 pastors, and approximately 38,000 people worship in fellowship churches every Sunday.

FELLOWSHIP OF INDEPENDENT EVANGELICAL CHURCHES, 39 The Point, Market Harborough, Leics LE16 7QU **T** 01858-434540 **E** admin@fiec.org.uk **W** www.fiec.org.uk

Director, John Stevens

FREE CHURCH OF ENGLAND

The Free Church of England, otherwise called the Reformed Episcopal Church, is an independent church, constituted according to the historic faith, tradition and practice of the Church of England. Its roots lie in the 18th century, but it started to grow significantly from the 1840s onwards, as clergy and congregations joined it from the established church in protest against the Oxford Movement. The historic episcopate was conferred on the English church in 1876 through bishops of the Reformed Episcopal Church (which had broken away from the Protestant Episcopal Church in the USA in 1873). A branch of the Reformed Episcopal Church was founded in the UK and this merged with the Free Church of England in 1927 to create the present church.

Worship is according to the *Book of Common Prayer* and some modern liturgy is permissible. Only men are ordained to the orders of deacon, presbyter and bishop.

The Free Church of England has 29 ministers, 17 congregations and around 1,150 members, now mainly confined to England with one congregation in St Petersburg, Russia.

THE FREE CHURCH OF ENGLAND, St Andrews Church, Wolverhampton Road West, Bentley, Walsall WV13 2RL **T** 01902-607335 **W** www.fcofe.org.uk

General Secretary, Rt. Revd Paul Hunt

FREE CHURCH OF SCOTLAND

The Free Church of Scotland was formed in 1843 when over 400 ministers withdrew from the Church of Scotland as a result of interference in the internal affairs of the church by the civil authorities. In 1900, all but 26 ministers joined with others to form the United Free Church (most of which rejoined the Church of Scotland in 1929). In 1904 the remaining 26 ministers were recognised by the House of Lords as continuing the Free Church of Scotland.

The church maintains strict adherence to the Westminster Confession of Faith (1648) and accepts the Bible as the sole rule of faith and conduct. Its general assembly meets annually. It also has links with reformed churches overseas. The Free Church of Scotland has about 12,000 members, 90 ministers and 100 congregations.

FREE CHURCH OF SCOTLAND, 15 North Bank Street, The Mound, Edinburgh EH1 2LS **T** 0131-226 5286 **E** offices@freechurchofscotland.org.uk **W** www.freechurch.org

Chief Administrative Officer, Rod Morrison

FREE PRESBYTERIAN CHURCH OF SCOTLAND

The Free Presbyterian Church of Scotland was formed in 1893 by two ministers of the Free Church of Scotland who refused to accept a Declaratory Act passed by the Free Church General Assembly in 1892. The Free Presbyterian Church of Scotland is Calvinistic in doctrine and emphasises observance of the Sabbath. It adheres strictly to the Westminster Confession of Faith (1648).

The church has about 1,000 members in Scotland and about 4,000 in overseas congregations. It has 20 ministers and 50 churches in the UK.

FREE PRESBYTERIAN CHURCH OF SCOTLAND, 133 Woodlands Road, Glasgow G3 6LE **T** 0141-332 9283 **W** www.fpchurch.org.uk

Moderator (2011–12), Revd Kenneth Macleod *Clerk of the Synod,* Revd John MacLeod

HOLY APOSTOLIC CATHOLIC ASSYRIAN CHURCH OF THE EAST

The Holy Apostolic Catholic Assyrian Church of the East traces its beginnings to the middle of the first century. It spread from Upper Mesopotamia throughout the territories of the Persian Empire. The Assyrian Church of the East became theologically separated from the rest of the Christian community following the Council of Ephesus in 431. The church is headed by the Catholicos Patriarch and is episcopal in government. The liturgical language is Syriac (Aramaic). The Assyrian Church of the East and the Roman Catholic Church agreed a common Christological declaration in 1994, and a process of dialogue between the Assyrian Church of the East and the Chaldean Catholic Church, which is in communion with Rome but shares the Syriac liturgy, was instituted in 1996.

The church has about 400,000 members in the Middle East, India, Europe, North America and Australasia. In Great Britain there are three congregations, 15 priests and around 7,000 members. The church in Great Britain forms part of the diocese of Europe under Mar Odisho Oraham.

HOLY APOSTOLIC CATHOLIC ASSYRIAN CHURCH OF THE EAST, St Mary's Church, Westminster Road, Hanwell, London W7 3TU **T** 020-8567 1814

Representative in Great Britain, Revd Tony

INDEPENDENT METHODIST CHURCHES

The Independent Methodist Churches were formed in 1805 and remained independent when the Methodist Church in Great Britain was formed in 1932. They are mainly concentrated in the industrial areas of the north of England.

The churches are Methodist in doctrine but their organisation is congregational. All the churches are members of the Independent Methodist Connexion of Churches. The controlling body of the Connexion is the Annual Meeting, to which churches send delegates. The Connexional President is elected annually. Between annual meetings the affairs of the Connexion are handled by departmental committees. Ministers are appointed by the churches and trained through the Connexion.

The ministry is open to both men and women and is unpaid.

There are 1,700 members, 86 ministers and 82 churches in Great Britain.

INDEPENDENT METHODIST RESOURCE CENTRE,
Fleet Street, Pemberton, Wigan WN5 0DS
T 01942-223526 E resourcecentre@imcgb.org.uk
W www.imcgb.org.uk
President, Eric Southwick
General Secretary, Brian Rowney

LUTHERAN CHURCH

Lutheranism is based on the teachings of Martin Luther, the German leader of the Protestant Reformation. The authority of the scriptures is held to be supreme over church tradition. The teachings of Lutheranism are explained in detail in 16th-century confessional writings, particularly the Augsburg Confession. Lutheranism is one of the largest Protestant denominations and it is particularly strong in northern Europe and the USA. Some Lutheran churches are episcopal, while others have a synodal form of organisation; unity is based on doctrine rather than structure. Most Lutheran churches are members of the Lutheran World Federation, based in Geneva.

Lutheran services in Great Britain are held in 18 languages to serve members of different nationalities. Services usually follow ancient liturgies. English-language congregations are members either of the Lutheran Church in Great Britain or of the Evangelical Lutheran Church of England. The Lutheran Church in Great Britain and other Lutheran churches in Britain are members of the Lutheran Council of Great Britain, which represents them and coordinates their common work.

There are over 70 million Lutherans worldwide; in Great Britain there are about 170,000 members, 45 clergy and 100 congregations.

THE LUTHERAN COUNCIL OF GREAT BRITAIN,
30 Thanet Street, London WC1H 9QH T 020-7554 2900
E enquiries@lutheran.org.uk W www.lutheran.org.uk
Acting General Secretary, Revd Timothy Fletcher

METHODIST CHURCH

The Methodist movement started in England in 1729 when the Revd John Wesley, an Anglican priest, and his brother Charles met with others in Oxford and resolved to conduct their lives and study by 'rule and method'. In 1739 the Wesleys began evangelistic preaching and the first Methodist chapel was founded in Bristol in the same year. In 1744 the first annual conference was held, at which the Articles of Religion were drawn up. Doctrinal emphases included repentance, faith, the assurance of salvation, social concern and the priesthood of all believers. After John Wesley's death in 1791 the Methodists withdrew from the established church to form the Methodist Church. Methodists gradually drifted into many groups, but in 1932 the Wesleyan Methodist Church, the United Methodist Church and the Primitive Methodist Church united to form the Methodist Church of Great Britain.

The governing body of the Methodist Church is the Conference. The Conference meets annually in June or July and consists of two parts: the ministerial and representative sessions. The Methodist Church is structured as a 'Connexion' of churches, circuits and districts. The local churches in a defned area form a circuit, and a number of these circuits make up each of the 31 districts. There are around 70 million Methodists worldwide; at the last count in 2007 there were 267,257 members, 3,509 ministers, 226 Deacons and 6,402 churches in Great Britain.

THE METHODIST CHURCH OF GREAT BRITAIN,
Methodist Church House, 25 Marylebone Road, London NW1 5JR T 020-7486 5502
E helpdesk@methodistchurch.org.uk
W www.methodist.org.uk
President of the Conference (2011–12),
Revd Lionel E. Osborne
General Secretary and Secretary of the Conference,
Revd Dr Martyn Atkins

THE METHODIST CHURCH IN IRELAND
The Methodist Church in Ireland is autonomous but has close links with British Methodism. It has a community roll of 51,425 members, 126 ministers, 233 lay preachers and 230 churches.
1 Fountainville Avenue, Belfast BT9 6AN T 028-9032 4554
E secretary@irishmethodist.org W www.irishmethodist.org
President (2011–12), Revd Ian D. Henderson
Secretary (2011–12), Donald P. Ket

ORTHODOX CHURCHES

EASTERN ORTHODOX CHURCH
The Eastern (or Byzantine) Orthodox Church is a communion of self-governing Christian churches that recognises the honorary primacy of the Ecumenical Patriarch of Constantinople.

The position of Orthodox Christians is that the faith was fully defined during the period of the Oecumenical Councils. In doctrine it is strongly trinitarian, and stresses the mystery and importance of the sacraments. It is episcopal in government. The structure of the Orthodox Christian year differs from that of western churches.

Orthodox Christians throughout the world are estimated to number about 300 million; there are around 300,000 in the UK.

GREEK ORTHODOX CHURCH (PATRIARCHATE OF ANTIOCH)
The Archdiocese of Europe is led by HE Metropolitan John (Yazigi), based in Paris.
St George's Cathedral Church, 1A Redhill Street, London NW1 4BG T 020-7383 0403
E fr.samir@antiochianorth.co.uk
W www.antiochianorth.co.uk
Archpriest, Fr. Samir Gholam
Antiochian Orthodox Deanery of the United Kingdom and Ireland, St Aidan's Orthodox Church, Clare Road, Levenshulme, Manchester T 0161-476 4847
E orthodox@.clara.net W www.antiochian-orthodox.co.uk
Dean, Archpriest Fr. Gregory Hallam

GREEK ORTHODOX CHURCH (PATRIARCHATE OF CONSTANTINOPLE)
The presence of Greek Orthodox Christians in Britain dates back at least to 1677 when Archbishop Joseph Geogirenes of Samos fled from Turkish persecution and came to London. The present Greek cathedral in Moscow Road, Bayswater, was opened for public worship in 1879, and the Diocese of Thyateira and Great Britain was established in 1922. There are now 116 parishes and other communities (including monasteries) in the UK, served by four bishops, 106 clergy, nine cathedrals and 109 parishes. .
The Patriarchate Of Constantinople In Great Britain,
Thyateira House, 5 Craven Hill, London W2 3EN
T 020-7723 4787 E mail@thyateira.org.uk
W www.thyateira.org.uk
Archbishop, Gregorios of Thyateira and Great Britain

THE RUSSIAN ORTHODOX CHURCH (PATRIARCHATE OF MOSCOW) AND THE RUSSIAN ORTHODOX CHURCH OUTSIDE RUSSIA

The records of Russian Orthodox Church activities in Britain date from the visit to England of Tsar Peter I in the early 18th century. Clergy were sent from Russia to serve the chapel established to minister to the staff of the Imperial Russian Embassy in London.

In 2007, after an 80-year division, the Russian Orthodox Church Outside Russia agreed to become an autonomous part of the Russian Orthodox Church, Patriarchate of Moscow. The reunification agreement was signed by Patriarch Alexy II, 15th Patriarch of Moscow and All Russia and Metropolitan Laurus, leader of the Russian Orthodox Church Outside Russia on 17 May at a ceremony at Christ the Saviour Cathedral in Moscow. Patriarch Alexy II died on 5 December 2008. Metropolitan Kirill of Smolensk and Kaliningrad was enthroned as the 16th Patriarch of Moscow and All Russia on 1 February 2009, having been elected by a secret ballot of clergy on 27 January 2009.

The diocese of Sourozh is the diocese of the Russian Orthodox Church in Great Britain and Ireland and is led by Archbishop Elisey of Sourozh.

Diocese of Sourozh, Diocesan Office, Cathedral of the Dormition, 67 Ennismore Gardens, London SW7 1NH
T 020-7584 0096 W www.sourozh.org
Diocesan Bishop, Most Revd Elisey (Ganaba) of Sourozh
Assistant Diocesan Bishop, Most Revd Anatoly (Kuznetsov) of Kerch

SERBIAN ORTHODOX CHURCH (PATRIARCHATE OF SERBIA)

There are seven parishes in Great Britain and around 4,000 members. Great Britain is part of the Diocese of Great Britain and Scandinavia, which is led by Bishop Dositej. The church can be contacted via the church of St Sava in London.

Serbian Orthodox Church in Great Britain, Church of Saint Sava, 89 Lancaster Road, London W11 1QQ
T 020-7727 8367 E crkva@spclondon.org
W www.spclondon.org
Priest, Very Revd Milun Kostic

OTHER NATIONALITIES

The Patriarchates of Romania and Bulgaria (Diocese of Western Europe) have memberships estimated at 20,000 and 2,000 respectively, while the Georgian Orthodox Church has around 500 members. The Belarusian (membership estimated at 2,400) and Latvian (membership of around 100) Orthodox churches are part of the Patriarchate of Constantinople.

ORIENTAL ORTHODOX CHURCHES

The term 'Oriental Orthodox Churches' is now generally used to describe a group of six ancient eastern churches (Armenian, Coptic, Eritrean, Ethiopian, Indian (Malankara) and Syrian) which rejected the Christological definition of the Council of Chalcedon (AD 451). There are around 50 million members worldwide of the Oriental Orthodox Churches and about 20,075 in the UK.

ARMENIAN ORTHODOX CHURCH (CATHOLICOSATE OF ETCHMIADZIN)

The Armenian Orthodox Church is led by HH Karekin II, Catholicos of All Armenians. The Very Revd Dr Vahan Hovhanessian is the Primate of the Armenian Church of Great Britain and President of the Armenian Community and Church Council.

Armenian Church of Great Britain, The Armenian Vicarage, Iverna Gardens, London W8 6TP T 020-7937 0152
E information@armenianchurch.org.uk
W www.armenianchurch.co.uk
Primate, Very Revd Dr Vahan Hovhanessian

COPTIC ORTHODOX CHURCH

The Coptic Orthodox Church is led by HH Pope Shenouda III and is represented in Great Britain by Bishop Angaelos at the Coptic Orthodox Cathedral of St George at the Coptic Orthodox Church Centre. The Coptic Orthodox Church is the largest Oriental Orthodox community in Great Britain.

Coptic Orthodox Church Centre, Shephalbury Manor, Broadhall Way, Stevenage, Herts SG2 8NP T 01438-745232
E admin@copticcentre.com W www.copticcentre.com
Bishop, HG Bishop Angaelos

BRITISH ORTHODOX CHURCH

The British Orthodox Church is canonically part of the Coptic Orthodox Patriarchate of Alexandria. As it ministers to British people, all of its services are in English.

The British Orthodox Church, 10 Heathwood Gardens, Charlton, London SE7 8EP T 020-8854 3090
E info@britishorthodox.org W www.britishorthodox.org
Metropolitan, Abba Seraphim

INDIAN ORTHODOX CHURCH

The Indian Orthodox Church, also known as the Malankara Orthodox Church, traces its origins to the first century. The UK is part of the Diocese of Europe, UK and Africa.

Indian Orthodox Church, St Gregorios Indian Orthodox Church, Cranfield Road, Brockley, London SE4 1UF
T 020-8691 9456 E vicar@indian-orthodox.co.uk
W www.indian-orthodox.co.uk
Diocesan Metropolitan, HG Dr Mathews Mar Thimotios
Vicar, Fr. John Samuel

SYRIAN ORTHODOX CHURCH

The Patriarchate Vicariate of the Syrian Orthodox Church in the United Kingdom is represented by HE Mor Athanasius Toma Dawood.

Syrian Orthodox Church in the UK, St Thomas Cathedral, 7–11 Armstrong Road, London W3 7JL T 020-8654 7531
E enquiry-uk@syrianorthodoxchurch.net
W www.syrianorthodoxchurch.net
Patriarchal Vicar, HE Mor Athanasius Toma Dawood

PENTECOSTAL CHURCHES

Pentecostalism is inspired by the descent of the Holy Spirit upon the apostles at Pentecost. The movement began in Los Angeles, USA, in 1906 and is characterised by baptism with the Holy Spirit, divine healing, speaking in tongues (glossolalia), and a literal interpretation of the scriptures.

The Pentecostal movement in Britain dates from 1907. Initially, groups of Pentecostalists were led by laymen and did not organise formally. However, in 1915 the Elim Foursquare Gospel Alliance (more commonly called the Elim Pentecostal Church) was founded in Ireland by George Jeffreys and currently has about 550 churches, 68,500 adherents and 650 accredited ministers. In 1924 about 70 independent assemblies formed a fellowship called the Assemblies of God in Great Britain and Ireland, which now incorporates 591 churches, around 70,000 adherents and 720 ministers.

The Apostolic Church grew out of the 1904–5 Christian revivals in South Wales and was established in 1916. The Apostolic Church has around 109 churches, 5,400 adherents and 103 ministers in the UK. The New Testament Church of God was established in England in 1953 and has around 125 congregations, 28,137 members and 320 ministers across England and Wales. The Church of God of Prophecy was founded in 1923 in Cleveland, Tennessee. The UK branch was established in 1953 and now incorporates around 90 churches, 100 ministers and 25,000 adherents.

In recent years many aspects of Pentecostalism have been adopted by the growing charismatic movement within the Roman Catholic, Protestant and Eastern Orthodox churches. There are about 105 million Pentecostalists worldwide, with over 350,000 adherents in the UK.

THE APOSTOLIC CHURCH, International Administration Offices, PO Box 51298, London SE11 9AJ T 020-7587 1802

E admin@apostolic-church.org

National Leader, Emmanuel Mbakwe

THE ASSEMBLIES OF GOD INCORPORATED, PO Box 7634, Nottingham NG11 6ZY T 0115-921 7272

E info@aog.org.uk W www.aog.org.uk

National leader, John Partington

THE CHURCH OF GOD OF PROPHECY, 6 Beacon Court, Birmingham Road, Great Barr, Birmingham B43 6NN T 0121-358 2231

E admin@cogop.org.uk

National Overseer, Bishop Wilton Powell, OBE

THE ELIM PENTECOSTAL CHURCH, Elim International Centre, De Walden Road, West Malvern, Worcestershire WR14 4DF T 0845-302 6750 E info@elimhq.net

W www.elim.org.uk

General Superintendent, Revd John Glass

THE NEW TESTAMENT CHURCH OF GOD, 3 Cheyne Walk, Northampton NN1 5PT T 01604-824222

W www.ntcg.org.uk

Administrative Bishop, Eric Brown

PRESBYTERIAN CHURCH IN IRELAND

Irish Presbyterianism traces its origins back to the Plantation of Ulster in 1606, when English and Scottish Protestants began to settle on the land confiscated from the Irish chieftains. The first presbytery was established in Ulster in 1642 by chaplains of a Scottish army that had been sent to crush a Catholic rebellion in 1641.

The Presbyterian Church in Ireland is reformed in doctrine and belongs to the World Alliance of Reformed Churches. Structurally, the 549 congregations are grouped in 19 presbyteries under the General Assembly. This body meets annually and is presided over by a moderator who is elected for one year. The ongoing work of the church is undertaken by 15 boards under which there are specialist committees.

There are around 250,000 members of Irish presbyterian churches in the UK and Ireland.

THE PRESBYTERIAN CHURCH IN IRELAND, Church House, Belfast BT1 6DW T 028-9032 2284

E info@presbyterianireland.org

W www.presbyterianireland.org

Moderator (2011–12), Rt. Revd Dr Ivan Patterson

Clerk of Assembly and General Secretary,
Revd Dr Donald Watts

PRESBYTERIAN CHURCH OF WALES

The Presbyterian Church of Wales or Calvinistic Methodist Church of Wales is Calvinistic in doctrine and presbyterian in constitution. It was formed in 1811 when Welsh Calvinists severed the relationship with the established church by ordaining their own ministers. It secured its own confession of faith in 1823 and a Constitutional Deed in 1826, and since 1864 the General Assembly has met annually, presided over by a moderator elected for a year. The doctrine and constitutional structure of the Presbyterian Church of Wales was confirmed by act of parliament in 1931–2.

The Church has 28,687 members, 65 ministers and 676 congregations.

THE PRESBYTERIAN CHURCH OF WALES, Tabernacle Chapel, 81 Merthyr Road, Whitchurch, Cardiff CF14 1DD T 029-2062 7465

E swyddfa.office@ebcpcw.org.uk W www.ebcpcw.org.uk

Moderator (2011–12), Revd R. Roberts

General Secretary, Revd Bryn Williams

RELIGIOUS SOCIETY OF FRIENDS (QUAKERS)

Quakerism is a religious denomination which was founded in the 17th century by George Fox and others in an attempt to revive what they saw as the original 'primitive Christianity'. The movement, at first called Friends of the Truth, started in the Midlands, Yorkshire and north-west England, but there are now Quakers all over the UK and in 36 countries around the world. The colony of Pennsylvania, founded William Penn, was originally a Quaker settlement.

Quakers place an emphasis on the experience of God in daily life rather than on sacraments or religious occasions. There is no church calendar. Worship is largely silent and there are no appointed ministers; the responsibility for conducting a meeting is shared equally among those present. Religious tolerance and social reform have always been important to Quakers, together with a commitment to peace and non-violence in resolving disputes.

There are more than 23,000 'friends' or Quakers in Great Britain. There are about 470 places where Quaker meetings are held, many of them Quaker-owned Friends Meeting Houses. The Britain Yearly Meeting is the name given to the central organisation of Quakers in Britain.

THE RELIGIOUS SOCIETY OF FRIENDS (QUAKERS) IN BRITAIN, Friends House, 173–177 Euston Road, London NW1 2BJ T 020-7663 1000

E enquiries@quaker.org.uk W www.quaker.org.uk

Recording Clerk, Paul Parker

SALVATION ARMY

The Salvation Army is an international Christian organisation working in 124 countries worldwide. As a church and registered charity, the Salvation Army is funded through donations from its members, the general public and, where appropriate, government grants.

The Salvation Army was founded by a Methodist minister, William Booth, in the East End of London in 1865, and now has 709 local church and community centres, more than 70 residential support centres for homeless people, 17 care homes for older people and six substance-misuse centres. It also runs a clothing recycling programme, charity shops, a prison-visiting service and a family-tracing service. In 1878 it adopted a quasi-military command structure intended to inspire and regulate its endeavours and to reflect its view that the church was engaged in spiritual warfare. There are around 50,000 members and 1,350 Salvation Army officers (full-time ministers) in the UK. Salvationists emphasise evangelism and the provision of social welfare.

UK TERRITORIAL HEADQUARTERS,
101 Newington Causeway, London SE1 6BN
T 020-7367 4500 E info@salvationarmy.org.uk
W www.salvationarmy.org.uk
UK Territorial Commander, Commissioner John Matear

SEVENTH-DAY ADVENTIST CHURCH
The Seventh-day Adventist Church is a worldwide Christian church marked by its observance of Saturday as the Sabbath and by its emphasis on the imminent second coming of Jesus Christ. Adventists summarise their faith in '28 fundamental beliefs'.

The church grew out of the Millerite movement in the USA during the mid-19th century and was formally established in 1863. The church has an ethnically and culturally diverse worldwide membership of over 16 million, with a presence in more than 200 countries. In the UK and Ireland there are approximately 31,000 members worshipping in 299 churches and companies.

BRITISH UNION CONFERENCE OF SEVENTH-DAY ADVENTISTS, Stanborough Park, Watford WD25 9JZ
T 01923-672251 W www.adventist.org.uk
President, Pastor Ian Sweeney

THE (SWEDENBORGIAN) NEW CHURCH
The New Church is based on the teachings of the 18th-century Swedish scientist and theologian Emanuel Swedenborg (1688–1772), who believed that Jesus Christ appeared to him and instructed him to reveal the spiritual meaning of the Bible. He claimed to have visions of the spiritual world, including heaven and hell, and conversations with angels and spirits. He published several theological works, including descriptions of the spiritual world and a Bible commentary.

Swedenborgians believe that the second coming of Jesus Christ is taking place, being not an actual physical reappearance of Christ, but rather his return in spirit. It is also believed that concurrent with our life on earth is life in a parallel spiritual world, of which we are usually unconscious until death. There are around 30,000 Swedenborgians worldwide, with 8,470 members, 21 Churches and 20 ministers in the UK.

THE GENERAL CONFERENCE OF THE NEW CHURCH, Swedenborg House, 20 Bloomsbury Way, London WC1A 2TH T 0845-686 0086
E enquiries@generalconference.org.uk
W www.generalconference.org.uk
Chief Executive, Michael Hindley

UNDEB YR ANNIBYNWYR CYMRAEG
Undeb Yr Annibynwyr Cymraeg (the Union of Welsh Independents) was formed in 1872 and is a voluntary association of Welsh Congregational churches and personal members. It is mainly Welsh-speaking. Congregationalism in Wales dates back to 1639 when the first Welsh Congregational church was opened in Gwent.

Member churches are traditionally congregationalist in organisation and Calvinistic in doctrine, although a wide range of interpretations are permitted. Each church has complete independence in the governance and administration of its affairs.

The Union has 28,892 members, 98 ministers and 449 member churches.

UNDEB YR ANNIBYNWYR CYMRAEG, 5 Axis Court, Riverside Business Park, Swansea Vale, Swansea SA7 0AJ
T 01792-795888 E undeb@annibynwyr.org
W www.annibynwyr.org
President of the Union (2010–12), Revd Andrew Lenny
General Secretary, Revd Dr Geraint Tudur

UNITED REFORMED CHURCH
The United Reformed Church (URC) was first formed by the union of most of the Congregational churches in England and Wales with the Presbyterian Church of England in 1972. Congregationalism dates from the mid-16th century. It is Calvinistic in doctrine, and its followers form independent self-governing congregations bound under God by covenant, a principle laid down in the writings of Robert Browne (1550–1633). From the late 16th century the movement was driven underground by persecution, but the cause was defended at the Westminster Assembly in 1643 and the Savoy Declaration of 1658 laid down its principles. Congregational churches formed county associations for mutual support and in 1832 these associations merged to form the Congregational Union of England and Wales.

Presbyterianism in England also dates from the mid 16th century, and was Calvinistic and evangelical in its doctrine. It was governed by a hierarchy of courts.

In the 1960s there was close cooperation locally and nationally between congregational and presbyterian churches. This led to union negotiations and a Scheme of Union, supported by act of parliament in 1972. In 1981 a further unification took place, with the Reformed Association of Churches of Christ becoming part of the URC. In 2000 a third union took place, with the Congregational Union of Scotland. In its basis the United Reformed Church reflects local church initiative and responsibility with a conciliar pattern of oversight.

The United Reformed Church is divided into 13 synods, each with a synod moderator. There are around 1,550 congregations which serve around 67,000 adults and 54,000 children and young people. There are around 660 ministers in active service.

The General Assembly is the central body, and comprises around 400 representatives, mainly appointed by the synods, of which half are lay persons and half are ministers. From 2010 the General Assembly will meet biennially to elect two moderators, both lay and ordained, who will then become the public representatives of the URC. This will replace the current arrangement where one lay or ordained moderator is elected annually by the General Assembly. As a transitional arrangement the moderator will remain in office for two years from 2008.

UNITED REFORMED CHURCH, 86 Tavistock Place, London WC1H 9RT T 020-7916 2020 E info@urc.org.uk
W www.urc.org.uk
Moderators of the General Assembly (2010–12), Val Morrison; Revd Dr Kirsty Thorpe
General Secretary, Revd Roberta Rominger

WESLEYAN REFORM UNION

The Wesleyan Reform Union was founded by Methodists who left or were expelled from Wesleyan Methodism in 1849 following a period of internal conflict. Its doctrine is conservative evangelical and its organisation is congregational, each church having complete independence in the government and administration of its affairs. The union has around 1,540 members, 20 ministers and 96 churches.

THE WESLEYAN REFORM UNION, Wesleyan Reform Church House, 123 Queen Street, Sheffield S1 2DU
T 0114-272 1938 E admin@thewru.co.uk
W www.thewru.com
President (2011–12), Graham Evans
General Secretary, Revd Colin Braithwaite

NON-TRINITARIAN CHURCHES

CHRISTADELPHIAN

Christadelphians believe that the Bible is the word of God and that it reveals both God's dealings with mankind in the past and his plans for the future. These plans centre on the work of Jesus Christ, who it is believed will return to Earth to establish God's kingdom. The Christadelphian group was founded in the USA in the 1850s by the Englishman, Dr John Thomas.

THE CHRISTADELPHIAN, 404 Shaftmoor Lane, Hall Green, Birmingham B28 8SZ T 0121-777 6328
E enquiries@thechristadelphian.com
W www.thechristadelphian.com

CHURCH OF CHRIST, SCIENTIST

The Church of Christ, Scientist was founded by Mary Baker Eddy in the USA in 1879 to 'reinstate primitive Christianity and its lost element of healing'. Christian Science teaches the need for spiritual regeneration and salvation from sin, but it is best known for its reliance on prayer alone in the healing of sickness. Adherents believe that such healing is the result of divine laws, or divine science, and is in direct line with that practised by Jesus Christ (revered, not as God, but as the son of God) and by the early Christian church.

The denomination consists of The First Church of Christ, Scientist, in Boston, Massachusetts, USA ('The Mother Church') and its branch churches in almost 80 countries worldwide. The Bible and Mary Baker Eddy's book, *Science and Health with Key to the Scriptures,* are used for daily spiritual guidance and healing by all members and are read at services. There are no clergy; those engaged in full-time healing are called Christian Science practitioners, of whom there are 1,500 worldwide. The church also publishes *The Christian Science Monitor.*

No membership figures are available, since Mary Baker Eddy felt that numbers are no measure of spiritual vitality and ruled that such statistics should not be published. There are almost 2,000 branch churches worldwide, including over 100 in the UK.

CHRISTIAN SCIENCE COMMITTEE ON PUBLICATION, Unit T10, Tideway Yard, 125 Mortlake High Street, London SW14 8SN
T 020-8150 0245 E londoncs@csps.com
W www.christianscience.com
District Manager for the UK and the Republic of Ireland, Tony Lobl

CHURCH OF JESUS CHRIST OF LATTER-DAY SAINTS

The Church of Jesus Christ of Latter-Day Saints (often referred to as 'Mormons') was founded in New York State, USA, in 1830, and came to Britain in 1837. The oldest continuous congregation of the church is in Preston, Lancashire.

Mormons are Christians who claim to belong to the 'restored church' of Jesus Christ. They believe that true Christianity died when the last original apostle died, but that it was given back to the world by God and Jesus Christ through Joseph Smith, the church's founder and first president. They accept and use the Bible as scripture, but believe in continuing revelation from God; Mormons also use additional scriptures, including *The Book of Mormon: Another Testament of Jesus Christ.* The importance of the family is central to the church's beliefs and practices. Church members set aside Monday evenings as family home evenings when Christian family values are taught. Polygamy was formally discontinued in 1890.

The church has no paid ministry: local congregations are headed by a leader chosen from among their number. The world governing body, based in Utah, USA, is led by a president, believed to be the chosen prophet, and his two counsellors. There are more than 14 million members worldwide, with over 190,000 adherents and 411 congregations in the UK.

THE CHURCH OF JESUS CHRIST OF LATTER-DAY SAINTS, British Headquarters, 751 Warwick Road, Solihull, W. Midlands B91 3DQ T 0121-712 1200
W www.lds.org.uk

JEHOVAH'S WITNESSES

The movement now known as Jehovah's Witnesses grew from a Bible study group formed by Charles Taze Russell in 1872 in Pennsylvania, USA. In 1896 it adopted the name of the Watch Tower Bible and Tract Society, and in 1931, its members became known as Jehovah's Witnesses.

Jehovah's (God's) Witnesses believe in the Bible as the word of God, and consider it to be inspired and historically accurate. They take the scriptures literally, except where there are obvious indications that they are figurative or symbolic, and reject the doctrine of the Trinity. Witnesses also believe that all those approved of by Jehovah will have eternal life on a cleansed and beautified earth; only 144,000 will go to heaven to rule with Jesus Christ. They believe that the second coming of Christ began in 1914, that his thousand-year reign over the earth is imminent, and that armageddon (a final battle in which evil will be defeated) will precede Christ's rule of peace. Jehovah's Witnesses refuse to take part in military service and do not accept blood transfusions.

The seven-member world governing body is based in New York, USA. There is no paid ministry, but each congregation has elders assigned to look after various duties and every Witness takes part in the public ministry in their neighbourhood. There are over 7.5 million Jehovah's Witnesses worldwide, with 134,000 Witnesses in the UK organised into more than 1,500 congregations.

BRITISH ISLES HEADQUARTERS, Watch Tower, The Ridgeway, London NW7 1RN T 020-8906 2211
E opi@uk.jw.org W www.watchtower.org

UNITARIAN AND FREE CHRISTIAN CHURCHES

Unitarianism has its historical roots in the Judaeo-Christian tradition but rejects the deity of Christ and the doctrine of the Trinity. It allows the individual to embrace insights from all of the world's faiths and philosophies, as there is no fixed creed. It is accepted that beliefs may evolve in the light of personal experience.

Unitarian communities first became established in Poland and Transylvania in the 16th century. The first avowedly Unitarian place of worship in the British Isles opened in London in 1774. The General Assembly of Unitarian and Free Christian Churches came into existence in 1928 as the result of the amalgamation of two earlier organisations.

There are around 5,000 Unitarians in Great Britain and about 76 Unitarian ministers. Nearly 200 self-governing congregations and fellowship groups, including a small number overseas, are members of the General Assembly.

GENERAL ASSEMBLY OF UNITARIAN AND FREE CHRISTIAN CHURCHES, Essex Hall, 1–6 Essex Street, London WC2R 3HY T 020-7240 2384
E ga@unitarian.org.uk W www.unitarian.org.uk
President (2011–12), Revd Dr Ann Peart
Vice-President (2011–12), Lis Dyson-Jones

COMMUNICATIONS

POSTAL SERVICES

The Royal Mail Group plc operates Parcelforce Worldwide, General Logistics Systems (GLS), the Post Office and Royal Mail. Each working day Royal Mail processes and delivers more than 71 million items to 28 million addresses. Following the passing of the Post Services Act 2011, OFCOM assumed regulatory responsibility for postal services from the Postal Services Commission (Postcomm). It is responsible for promoting effective competition between postal operators after the market was opened to full competition in 2006. All 54 of the UK's current operators, including Royal Mail, are licensed by Postcomm to ensure that the mail they handle is secure and that they maintain certain standards. In October 2008 Postwatch merged with Energywatch and the National Consumer Council to form Consumer Focus, a consumer representation and advocacy body. Consumer Focus is responsible for postal services and takes up complaints on behalf of consumers against any licensed provider of postal services. In October 2010 the government announced that Consumer Focus would be abolished, most likely by spring 2013.

CONSUMER FOCUS, Fleetbank House, Salisbury Square, London EC4Y 8JX T 020-7799 7900
W www.consumerfocus.org.uk
POSTCOMM, Hercules House, 6 Hercules Road, London SE1 7DB T 020-7593 2100 W www.psc.gov.uk

PRICING IN PROPORTION
Since August 2006 Royal Mail has priced mail according to its size as well as its weight. The system is intended to reflect the fact that larger, bulkier items cost more to handle than smaller, lighter ones. There are three basic categories of correspondence:

LETTER
Length up to 240mm, *width* up to 165mm, *thickness* up to 5mm, *weight* up to 100g; eg most cards, postcards and bills

LARGE LETTER
Length up to 353mm, *width* up to 250mm, *thickness* up to 25mm, *weight* up to 750g; eg most A4 documents, CDs and magazines

PACKET
Length over 353mm, *width* over 250mm, *thickness* over 25mm, *weight* over 750g; eg books, clothes, gifts, prints and posters in cylindrical packaging

INLAND POSTAL SERVICES
Following are details of a number of popular postal services along with prices correct as at April 2011.

FIRST AND SECOND CLASS

Format	Maximum weight	First class	Second class†
Letter*	100g	£0.46	£0.36
Large letter	100g	£0.75	£0.58
	250g	£1.09	£0.92
	500g	£1.46	£1.23
	750g	£2.07	£1.76
Packet	100g	£1.58	£1.33
	250g	£1.96	£1.72
	500g	£2.48	£2.16
	750g	£3.05	£2.61
	1,000g‡	£3.71	£3.15

* Includes postcards
† First class post is normally delivered on the following working day and second class within three working days
‡ Packets heavier than 1,000g must be sent first class. For a full list of prices *see* W www.royalmail.com

STANDARD PARCEL RATES*

Maximum weight	Standard tariff
2kg	£4.41
4kg	£7.62
6kg	£10.34
8kg	£12.67
10kg	£13.61
20kg	£15.86

* Standard parcels may be up to 1.5m long and 20kg in weight with a combined length and width of less than 3m. They are normally delivered within three to five working days

OVERSEAS POSTAL SERVICES
Royal Mail divides the world into two zones: **Europe** (Albania, Andorra, Armenia, Austria, Azerbaijan, Azores, Balearic Islands, Belarus, Belgium, Bosnia and Hercegovina, Bulgaria, Canary Islands, Corsica, Croatia, Cyprus, Czech Republic, Denmark, Estonia, Faroe Islands, Finland, France, Georgia, Germany, Gibraltar, Greece, Greenland, Hungary, Iceland, Rep. of Ireland, Italy, Kazakhstan, Kosovo, Kyrgyzstan, Latvia, Liechtenstein, Lithuania, Luxembourg, Macedonia, Madeira, Malta, Moldova, Monaco, Montenegro, Netherlands, Norway, Poland, Portugal, Romania, Russia, San Marino, Serbia, Slovakia, Slovenia, Spain, Sweden, Switzerland, Tajikistan, Turkey, Turkmenistan, Ukraine, Uzbekistan, Vatican City State) and **Rest of the World** (all countries that are not listed under Europe).

OVERSEAS SURFACE MAIL RATES*
Letters

Maximum weight	Standard tariff	Maximum weight	Standard tariff
20g†	£0.66	450g	£6.05
60g	£1.14	500g	£6.68
100g	£1.60	750g	£9.68
150g	£2.27	1,000g	£12.68
200g	£2.89	1,250g	£15.68
250g	£3.54	1,500g	£18.68
300g	£4.16	1,750g	£21.68
350g	£4.79	2,000g	£24.68
400g	£5.43		

* Letters and postcards to Europe are sent by Airmail
† Includes postcards

Small packets and printed papers

Maximum weight	Standard tariff	Maximum weight	Standard tariff
100g	£1.12	450g	£3.79
150g	£1.50	500g	£4.16
200g	£1.89	750g	£5.86
250g	£2.28	1,000g	£7.56
300g	£2.64	1,500g	£10.96
350g	£3.02	2,000g*	£14.36
400g	£3.42		

* Maximum weight. For printed papers only: add £0.28 for each additional 50g up to a maximum weight of 5,000g

AIRMAIL LETTERS

Europe:

Maximum weight	Standard tariff	Maximum weight	Standard tariff
20g*	£0.68	300g	£4.20
40g	£1.00	400g	£4.96
60g	£1.30	500g	£5.72
80g	£1.49	600g	£6.71
100g	£1.73	700g	£7.70
120g	£2.01	800g	£8.69
140g	£2.29	900g	£9.68
160g	£2.58	1,000g	£10.67
180g	£2.86	1,200g	£12.39
200g	£3.11	1,400g	£14.11
220g	£3.38	1,600g	£15.83
240g	£3.64	1,800g	£17.55
260g	£3.89	2,000g	£19.27
280g	£4.13		

* Includes postcards

Rest of the World:

Maximum weight	Standard tariff
Postcards	£0.76
20g	£1.10
40g	£1.65
60g	£2.07
80g	£2.51
100g	£3.19
500g	£10.80
1,000g	£18.70
2,000g	£32.90

Note that there are different rates for small packets and printed matter, and that the latter has a greater maximum weight allowance. *See* W www.royalmail.com for further details.

SPECIAL DELIVERY SERVICES

INTERNATIONAL SIGNED FOR AND AIRSURE

Express airmail services (maximum weight 2kg) that include £41 compensation in case of loss or damage. The fee for International Signed For is £4.95 plus airmail or surface mail postage. The fee for Airsure is £5.30 plus airmail postage.

RECORDED SIGNED FOR

Provides a record of posting and delivery of letters and ensures a signature on delivery. This service is recommended for items of little or no monetary value. All packets must be handed to the post office and a receipt issued as proof of posting. The charge is 77p plus the standard first or second class postage with up to £41 compensation in case of loss or damage.

SPECIAL DELIVERY NEXT DAY

A guaranteed next working day delivery service by 1pm to 99 per cent of the UK (maximum item weight is 10kg). Prices start at £5.45. There is also a service that guarantees delivery by 9am (maximum item weight is 2kg). Prices start at £15.25. There is also a Saturday guarantee for mail sent out on a Friday, which costs an additional £2.70 an item. Note that size restrictions apply on these services.

OTHER SERVICES

BUSINESS SERVICES

A range of postal services are available to businesses, including business collection, freepost, business reply services, secure mail opening, international bulk and sustainable mailing options. Smartstamp allows businesses to print postage directly from a computer using a pre-pay system.

COMPENSATION

Compensation for loss or damage to an item sent varies according to the service used to send the item.

KEEPSAFE

Mail is held for up to two months while the addressee is away, and is delivered when the addressee returns. Prices start at £11.25 for 17 days. Recorded items are held for a week before being returned to the sender, and special delivery items for three weeks beyond the Keepsafe expiry date.

PASSPORT APPLICATIONS

Many post offices process passport applications. To find your nearest post office offering this service and for further information *see* W www.postoffice.co.uk

POST OFFICE BOX

A PO Box provides a short and memorable alternative address. Mail is held at a local delivery office until the addressee is ready to collect it, or delivered to a street address for an extra fee. Prices start at £95 for six months or £170 for a year.

POSTCODE FINDER

Customers can search an online database to find UK postcodes and addresses. For more information *see* Royal Mail's postcode finder W http://postcode.royalmail.com

REDIRECTION

Customers may arrange the redirection of their mail via phone, post, at the Post Office or online, subject to verification of their identity. A fee is payable for each different surname on the application form, and the service may be renewed up to a maximum of two years. The charges are: one month, £8.00; three months, £17.62; six months, £27.20; 12 months, £40.85. Prices for redirection overseas vary depending on location, beginning at £27 for one month to a non-EU address, up to £150 for 12 months to an EU address.

TRACK AND TRACE

An online service for customers to track the progress of items sent using special delivery. It is accessible from W http://track.royalmail.com and W http://track.postoffice.co.uk.

CONTACTS

Parcelforce Worldwide
T 08448-004466 W www.parcelforce.com

Post Office enquiries
T 08457-223344 W www.postoffice.co.uk

Postcode enquiry line
T 0906-302 1222 / 08457-111222

Royal Mail business enquiries
T 08457-950950 W www.royalmail.com/business-customers

Royal Mail general enquiries
T 08457-740740 W www.royalmail.com

TELECOMMUNICATIONS

The 1984 Telecommunications Act set the framework for a competitive market for telecommunications by abolishing British Telecom's (BT) exclusive right to provide services. The early 1990s saw the market open up and a number of new national public telecommunications operators (PTOs) received licences. This ended the duopoly that had existed in the 1980s when only BT and Mercury were licensed to provide fixed-line telecoms networks in the UK.

Four EU directives were agreed in March 2002 with the aim of further developing a pro-competitive regulatory structure. These directives were provided for in the Communications Act which came into force in July 2003. Under the act, licences are no longer required for providing communications networks or services in the UK. All persons providing such networks and services are subject to 'general conditions of entitlement', which constitute a set of rules they are obliged to observe.

Mobile network technology has improved dramatically since the launch in 1985 of the first-generation global system for mobile communications (GSM), which offered little or no data capability. In 1992 Vodafone launched a new GSM network, usually referred to as 2G or second generation, which used digital encoding and allowed voice and low-speed data communications. This technology has now been extended, via the enhanced data transfer rate of 2.5G, to 3G – a family of mobile standards that provide high bandwidth support to applications such as voice- and video-calling, high-speed data transfer, television streaming and full internet access.

RECENT DEVELOPMENTS

The four GSM operators, namely Orange, O2, T-Mobile and Vodafone, were joined in March 2003 by the first 3G operator, '3' (Hutchison 3UK). Orange, T-Mobile and Vodafone all launched their own 3G services in 2004, and O2 in February 2005. In 2009 the number of 3G subscriptions increased by 7.1 million, with 31.8 per cent of mobile users using 3G at the end of the year compared to 24 per cent in 2008.

In April 2010 T-Mobile and Orange merged their UK operations becoming the largest mobile phone network in Britain with 28.4 million customers, or 37 per cent of the market, overtaking both O2 and Vodafone. Both T-Mobile and Orange remain separate brands, but from October 2010 they began signal-sharing, allowing customers to 'roam' across both mobile networks.

In March 2011 OFCOM announced plans for the auction of additional spectrum (the airwaves on which all communications rely) to provide the necessary capacity for 4G technology in the UK. The auction will be for two spectrum bands – 800 MHz and 2.6 GHz – which lie within the 'sweetspot', the frequency in greatest demand. This combination of low and high frequencies provides

the potential to cope with high demand of 4G services. OFCOM aims to begin the auction in early 2012 and expects operators to start offering 4G services in 2013.

The use of Wi-Fi (wireless fidelity) expanded rapidly in 2010 as the UK overtook the USA and China as the largest provider of public Wi-Fi locations with over 143,000 active hotspots; 24,000 in London alone. Deregulation has allowed public network operators to use certain parts of the spectrum, which are exempt from licensing, for wireless LAN (Wi-Fi) type systems. Initially only personal use was permitted in these bands, but this has been expanded to a full commercial service. Twelve city centres offer continuous Wi-Fi coverage using a network, or 'mesh', of 300m-range Wi-Fi signals.

FIXED-LINE COMMUNICATIONS

In the year to December 2009 there was a decrease in both the total fixed-line telephony revenue, down by £0.3bn to £8.8bn, and the number of fixed-line connections, down by 1.1 million to 32.1 million. BT's share of the fixed-line market decreased to under 60 per cent for the first time. Fixed-line telephony, which accounted for 60 per cent of telecoms revenue in 1998, contributed less than 30 per cent in 2009 as a result of the rise in the use of mobiles phones, email and voice over internet protocol (VoIP) services, such as Skype.

The average headline speed of residential fixed broadband connections increased in 2009 to 8.2Mbit/s, an increase of 1.8Mbit/s from 2008 as the average monthly cost decreased by 2 per cent to £13.31. There were 31.5 fixed broadband connections per 100 people in the UK at the end of 2009.

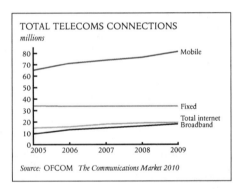

TOTAL TELECOMS CONNECTIONS
millions

Source: OFCOM *The Communications Market 2010*

MOBILE COMMUNICATIONS

In *The Communications Market 2010* report, revenue from mobile services declined sharply representing the first decrease since mobile telephony was established as a mass-market service in the late 1990's, falling to £14.9bn, a decrease of 3.5 per cent. OFCOM attributed the decline to falling prices, as a result of 'bundled' voice minutes and text messages being included within monthly rental fees. There was a rise in the amount of active mobile connections in the UK, with 132 connections per every 100 people, representing the increase in people using 3G dongles and multiple mobile phones for business purposes.

The number of people using the internet on mobile phones continued to grow – to 13.5 million – in the first quarter of 2010, due, in part, to the increase in the number of people using smartphones such as iPhones, Blackberrys and android operating systems.

MOBILE SUBSCRIPTIONS
There are two basic types of mobile subscription: contracts and pre-pay or 'pay as you go'. The proportion of contract to pay-as-you-go customers in the UK has remained relatively constant over the last few years. At the end of 2009 there were 33 million active contract subscribers and 47.3 million pre-pay customers.

MOBILE SUBSCRIPTIONS BY NETWORK
Active subscriptions, millions

Source: OFCOM *The Communications Market 2010*

HEALTH
In 1999 the Independent Expert Group on Mobile Phones (IEGMP) was established to examine the possible effects on health of mobile phones, base stations and transmitters. The main findings of the IEGMP's report *Mobile Phones and Health,* published in May 2000, were:
- exposure to radio frequency radiation below guideline levels did not cause adverse health effects to the general population
- the use of mobile phones by drivers of any vehicle can increase the chance of accidents
- the widespread use of mobile phones by children for non-essential calls should be discouraged because if there are unrecognised adverse health effects children may be more vulnerable
- there is no general risk to the health of people living near to base stations on the basis that exposures are expected to be much lower than guidelines set by the International Commission on Non-Ionising Radiation Protection (ICNIRP)

As part of its response to the research recommendations contained in the IEGMP's report, the government set up the Mobile Telecommunications Health and Research (MTHR) programme in 2001 to undertake independent research into the possible health risks from mobile telephone technology. The MTHR programme published its report in September 2007 concluding that, in the short term, neither mobile phones nor base stations have been found to be associated with any biological or adverse health effects. An international cohort study into the possible long-term health effects of mobile phone use was launched by the MTHR in April 2010. The study is known as COSMOS and aims to follow the health of 250,000 mobile phone users from five countries over 20 to 30 years. The full 2007 report and details of COSMOS can be found on the MTHR website (W www.mthr.org.uk).

A national measurement programme, to ensure that emissions from mobile phone base stations do not exceed the ICNIRP guideline levels, is overseen by OFCOM and annual audits of these levels can be found on the sitefinder part of its website. The Health Protection Agency is responsible for providing information and advice in relation to the health effects of electromagnetic fields, including those emitted from mobile phones and base stations (W www.hpa.org.uk).

SAFETY WHILE DRIVING
Under legislation that came into effect in December 2003 it is illegal for drivers to use a hand-held mobile phone while driving. Since February 2007, under the Road Safety Act 2006, the fixed penalty for using a hand-held mobile device while driving is £60 and three penalty points. The same fixed penalty can also be issued to a driver for not having proper control of a vehicle while using a hands-free device. If the police or driver chooses to take the case to court rather than issue or accept a fixed penalty notice, the maximum fine is £1,000 for car drivers and £2,500 for drivers of buses, coaches or heavy goods vehicles.

REGULATION
Under the Communications Act 2003, OFCOM is the independent regulator and competition authority for the UK communications industries, with responsibilities across television, radio, telecommunications and wireless communications services. Competition in the communications market is also regulated by the Office of Fair Trading, although OFCOM takes the lead in competition investigations in the UK market. The Competition Appeal Tribunal hears appeals against OFCOM's decisions, and price-related appeals are referred to the Competition Commission.

CONTACTS
DEPARTMENT FOR BUSINESS, INNOVATION AND SKILLS, 1 Victoria Street, London SW1H 0ET T 020-7215 5000 W www.bis.gov.uk

OFCOM, Riverside House, 2A Southwark Bridge Road, London SE1 9HA T 020-7981 3040 W www.ofcom.org.uk

INTERNATIONAL DIRECT DIALLING

When dialling add two zeros before the IDD code, followed by the area code and the telephone number. Also add two zeros before the IDD code when dialling into the UK unless otherwise indicated.

* No extra zeros should be added
† Varies depending on area and/or carrier
‡ used to dial between Ireland and Northern Ireland; cheaper than using the UK code

	IDD from UK	IDD to UK
Afghanistan	93	44
Albania	355	44
Algeria	213	44
American Samoa	1 684	011 44*
Andorra	376	44
Angola	244	44
Anguilla	1 264	011 44*
Antigua and Barbuda	1 268	011 44*
Argentina	54	44
Armenia	374	44
Aruba	297	44
Ascension Island	247	44
Australia	61	11 44
Austria	43	44
Azerbaijan	994	44
Azores	351	44
Bahamas	1 242	011 44*
Bahrain	973	44
Bangladesh	880	44
Barbados	1 246	011 44*
Belarus	375	810 44*
Belgium	32	44
Belize	501	44
Benin	229	44
Bermuda	1 441	011 44*
Bhutan	975	44
Bolivia	591	10 44†
		11 44†
		12 44†
		13 44†
Bosnia and Hercegovina	387	44
Botswana	267	44
Brazil	55	14 44†
		15 44†
		21 44†
		23 44†
		31 44†
British Virgin Islands	1 284	011 44*
Brunei	673	44
Bulgaria	359	44
Burkina Faso	226	44
Burundi	257	44
Cambodia	855	1 44
Cameroon	237	44
Canada	1	011 44*
Cape Verde	238	44
Cayman Islands	1 345	011 44*
Central African Republic	236	44
Chad	235	15 44*
Chile	56	44
China	86	44
Colombia	57	5 44†
		7 44†
		9 44†
The Comoros	269	44
Congo, Dem. Rep. of	243	44
Congo, Rep. of	242	44
Cook Islands	682	44
Costa Rica	506	44
Côte d'Ivoire	225	44
Croatia	385	44
Cuba	53	119 44*
Cyprus	357	44
Czech Rep.	420	44
Denmark	45	44
Djibouti	253	44
Dominica	1 767	011 44*
Dominican Rep.	1 809	011 44*
	1 829	
Ecuador	593	44
Egypt	20	44
El Salvador	503	44
Equatorial Guinea	240	44
Eritrea	291	44
Estonia	372	44
Ethiopia	251	44
Falkland Islands	500	44
Faeroe Islands	298	44
Fiji	679	44
Finland	358	44
France	33	44
French Guiana	594	44
French Polynesia	689	44
Gabon	241	44
The Gambia	220	44
Georgia	995	810 44*
Germany	49	44
Ghana	233	44
Gibraltar	350	44
Greece	30	44
Greenland	299	44
Grenada	1 473	011 44*
Guadeloupe	590	44
Guam	1 671	011 44*
Guatemala	502	44
Guinea	224	44
Guinea-Bissau	245	44
Guyana	592	1 44
Haiti	509	44
Honduras	504	44
Hong Kong	852	1 44
Hungary	36	44
Iceland	354	44
India	91	44
Indonesia	62	1 44†
		8 44†
Iran	98	44
Iraq	964	44
Ireland	353	44
		048*‡
Israel	972	44†
		012*†
		013*†
		014*†
Italy	39	44
Jamaica	1 876	011 44*
Japan	81	1 44†
		010 44*†
		41 44†
		61 44†
Jordan	962	44
Kazakhstan	7	810 44*
Kenya	254	0 44

Kiribati	686	44		Puerto Rico	1 787	011 44*
Korea, Dem. People's	850	44			1 939	
Rep. Of				Qatar	974	44
Korea, Republic Of	82	1 44†		Réunion	262	44
		2 44†		Romania	40	44
Kuwait	965	44		Russia	7	810 44*
Kyrgyzstan	996	44		Rwanda	250	44
Laos	856	44		St Christopher and Nevis	1 869	011 44*
Latvia	371	44		St Helena	290	44
Lebanon	961	44		St Lucia	1 758	011 44*
Lesotho	266	44		St Pierre and Miquelon	508	44
Liberia	231	44		St Vincent and the	1 784	011 44*
Libya	218	44		Grenadines		
Liechtenstein	423	44		Samoa	685	0 44*
Lithuania	370	44		San Marino	378	44
Luxembourg	352	44		São Tomé and Príncipe	239	44
Macao	853	44		Saudi Arabia	966	44
Macedonia	389	44		Senegal	221	44
Madagascar	261	44		Serbia	381	44
Madeira	351	44		Seychelles	248	44
Malawi	265	44		Sierra Leone	232	44
Malaysia	60	44		Singapore	65	1 44†
Maldives	960	44				2 44†
Mali	223	44				8 44†
Malta	356	44		Slovakia	421	44
Marshall Islands	692	011 44*		Slovenia	386	44
Martinique	596	44		Solomon Islands	677	44
Mauritania	222	44		Somalia	252	44
Mauritius	230	44		South Africa	27	44
Mayotte	262	44		Spain	34	44
Mexico	52	44		Sri Lanka	94	44
Micronesia, Federated	691	011 44*		Sudan	249	44
States of				Suriname	597	44
Midway Island	1 808	011 44*		Swaziland	268	44
Moldova	373	44		Sweden	46	44
Monaco	377	44		Switzerland	41	44
Mongolia	976	1 44		Syria	963	44
Montenegro	382	44		Taiwan	886	2 44
Montserrat	1 664	011 44*		Tajikistan	992	810 44*
Morocco	212	44		Tanzania	255	0 44
Mozambique	258	44		Thailand	66	1 44
Myanmar	95	44		Timor-Leste	670	44
Namibia	264	44		Togo	228	44
Nauru	674	44		Tokelau	690	44
Nepal	977	44		Tonga	676	44
The Netherlands	31	44		Trinidad and Tobago	1 868	011 44*
Netherlands Antilles	599	44		Tristan de Cunha	290	44
New Caledonia	687	44		Tunisia	216	44
New Zealand	64	44		Turkey	90	44
Nicaragua	505	44		Turkmenistan	993	810 44*
Niger	227	44		Turks and Caicos	1 649	011 44*
Nigeria	234	9 44		Islands		
Niue	683	44		Tuvalu	688	44
Norfolk Island	672	44		Uganda	256	0 44
Northern Mariana Islands	1 670	011 44*		Ukraine	380	44
Norway	47	44		United Arab Emirates	971	44
Oman	968	44		United States of America	1	011 44*
Pakistan	92	44		Uruguay	598	44
Palau	680	011 44*		Uzbekistan	998	810 44*
Palestinian Territories	970	44		Vanuatu	678	44
Panama	507	44		Vatican City State	39	44
Papua New Guinea	675	44		Venezuela	58	44
Paraguay	595	44		Vietnam	84	44
Peru	51	44		Virgin Islands	1 340	011 44*
The Philippines	63	44		Yemen	967	44
Poland	48	44		Zambia	260	44
Portugal	351	44		Zimbabwe	263	44

INTERNET DOMAIN NAMES

The domain name system (DNS) helps users to find their way around the internet. Just as a telephone line has an identifying number attached to it, each computer connected to the internet has a unique numerical address known as its IP address. The DNS means users seldom need to recall the string of numbers in an IP address, since they can instead access internet content via the more memorable domain names (for example, whitakersalmanack.com).

Top-level domains (TLDs) are the rightmost element of an internet domain name (in the above example .com is the website's TLD) and their management is delegated by the Internet Corporation for Assigned Names and Numbers (ICANN). There are two types of TLD: generic top-level domains (gTLDs) and country code top-level domains (ccTLDs).

Generic TLDs designate general categories of organisation, such as .org for public interest or .jobs for human resources. Some gTLDs, such as .com and .net, can be registered without restriction while others, such as .edu and .gov, have limited purposes.

Country code TLDs are usually two letters long and identify the website's country or territory of origin. In May 2010 the first ccTLDs using characters outside of the basic Latin alphabet were implemented by ICANN; as at March 2011, 17 territories had been granted permission to use a ccTLD composed of native script. The rules and policies for registering domain names within a ccTLD vary significantly, although registration of a ccTLD is always limited to citizens of the corresponding country.

The list below is of active two-letter domain names for countries only.

ad	Andorra	dz	Algeria	kz	Kazakhstan
ae	United Arab Emirates	ec	Ecuador	la	Laos
af	Afghanistan	ee	Estonia	lb	Lebanon
ag	Antigua and Barbuda	eg	Egypt	lc	St Lucia
al	Albania	er	Eritrea	li	Liechtenstein
am	Armenia	es	Spain	lk	Sri Lanka
ao	Angola	et	Ethiopia	lr	Liberia
ar	Argentina	fi	Finland	ls	Lesotho
at	Austria	fj	Fiji	lt	Lithuania
au	Australia	fm	Micronesia, Federated States	lu	Luxembourg
az	Azerbaijan		of	lv	Latvia
ba	Bosnia and Hercegovina	fr	France	ly	Libya
bb	Barbados	ga	Gabon	ma	Morocco
bd	Bangladesh	gd	Grenada	mc	Monaco
be	Belgium	ge	Georgia	md	Moldova
bf	Burkina Faso	gh	Ghana	me	Montenegro
bg	Bulgaria	gm	The Gambia	mg	Madagascar
bh	Bahrain	gn	Guinea	mh	Marshall Islands
bi	Burundi	gq	Equatorial Guinea	mk	Macedonia
bj	Benin	gr	Greece	ml	Mali
bn	Brunei	gt	Guatemala	mm	Myanmar
bo	Bolivia	gw	Guinea-Bissau	mn	Mongolia
br	Brazil	gy	Guyana	mr	Mauritania
bs	The Bahamas	hn	Honduras	mt	Malta
bt	Bhutan	hr	Croatia	mu	Mauritius
bw	Botswana	ht	Haiti	mv	Maldives
by	Belarus	hu	Hungary	mw	Malawi
bz	Belize	id	Indonesia	mx	Mexico
ca	Canada	ie	Ireland	my	Malaysia
cd	Congo, Dem. Rep. of	il	Israel	mz	Mozambique
cf	Central African Republic	in	India	na	Namibia
cg	Congo, Rep. of	iq	Iraq	ne	Niger
ch	Switzerland	ir	Iran	ng	Nigeria
ci	Côte d'Ivoire	is	Iceland	ni	Nicaragua
cl	Chile	it	Italy	nl	The Netherlands
cm	Cameroon	jm	Jamaica	no	Norway
cn	China	jo	Jordan	np	Nepal
co	Colombia	jp	Japan	nr	Nauru
cr	Costa Rica	ke	Kenya	nz	New Zealand
cu	Cuba	kg	Kyrgyzstan	om	Oman
cv	Cape Verde	kh	Cambodia	pa	Panama
cy	Cyprus	ki	Kiribati	pe	Peru
cz	Czech Republic	km	The Comoros	pg	Papua New Guinea
de	Germany	kn	St Christopher and Nevis	ph	The Philippines
dj	Djibouti	kp	Korea, Dem. People's	pk	Pakistan
dk	Denmark		Republic of	pl	Poland
dm	Dominica	kr	Korea, Republic of	pt	Portugal
do	Dominican Republic	kw	Kuwait	pw	Palau

py	Paraguay	sr	Suriname	tz	Tanzania
qa	Qatar	st	São Tomé and Príncipe	ua	Ukraine
ro	Romania	sv	El Salvador	ug	Uganda
rs	Serbia	sy	Syria	uk	United Kingdom
ru	Russian Federation	sz	Swaziland	us	United States of America
rw	Rwanda	td	Chad	uy	Uruguay
sa	Saudi Arabia	tg	Togo	uz	Uzbekistan
sb	Solomon Islands	th	Thailand	va	Vatican City State (Holy See)
sc	Seychelles	tj	Tajikistan	vc	St Vincent and the
sd	Sudan	tl	Timor-Leste		Grenadines
se	Sweden	tm	Turkmenistan	ve	Venezuela
sg	Singapore	tn	Tunisia	vn	Vietnam
si	Slovenia	to	Tonga	vu	Vanuatu
sk	Slovakia	tp	Timor-Leste*	ws	Samoa
sl	Sierra Leone	tr	Turkey	ye	Yemen
sm	San Marino	tt	Trinidad and Tobago	za	South Africa
sn	Senegal	tv	Tuvalu	zm	Zambia
so	Somalia	tw	Taiwan	zw	Zimbabwe

* No new registrations are being accepted for the code .tp, which is active but being phased out in favour of .tl

THE ENVIRONMENT

The past two decades have witnessed a reduction in the production of chemicals that damage the ozone layer by 95 per cent, the establishment of carbon trading and a greenhouse gas emissions reduction treaty, and the introduction of much legislation. However, there remain persistent and intractable problems.

The average temperature over the first decade of the 21st century was significantly warmer than any previous decade. There is a clear underlying trend of increasing global temperature from the late 1970s onwards at about 0.16°C per decade, although this rate of warming has decreased slightly in the last 10 years, according to the UK Met Office. A report by the US National Oceanic and Atmospheric Administration concluded that 2010 tied with 2005 as the warmest year on record for global surface temperature.

A best estimate for temperature rise in the 21st century is between 1.8°C and 4°C; with an increase of at least 0.6 per cent attributable to past emissions. A rise of more than 2°C above pre-industrial levels is the level at which major, irreversible damage becomes more likely. According to the European Environment Agency, past legislation has been effective. Water and air have been cleaned up, ozone-depleting substances have been phased out and more waste is recycled. However, this is potentially being undermined by changes in individual consumption patterns. Europeans are living longer and more of them live alone, increasing the demand on living space and associated resources. For example, consumption of electricity in a household of one is 55 per cent more than for an individual in a four-person household. Additionally, 75 per cent of Europe's population live in urban areas and this is expected to rise to 80 per cent by 2020. Cities emit 69 per cent of Europe's carbon dioxide.

Transport is the fastest-growing contributor to greenhouse gas emissions and is likely to be so for the foreseeable future; emissions from transport in Europe increased by 24 per cent between 1990 and 2008. Road transport produced 25 per cent of UK carbon dioxide emissions in 2010. The issue is being addressed both by legislation and the government's commitment to a national recharging network for electric and plug-in hybrid vehicles through the 'plugged-in places' programme. The programme offers funding to local consortia of businesses and public sector partners to install electric vehicle recharging infrastructure in key places across the UK. So far, London, Milton Keynes and the North East are installing recharging points in their areas and funding has been allocated for five additional 'plugged-in places' projects in Greater Manchester, the Midlands, the East of England, Scotland and Northern Ireland. In 2009 average CO_2 emissions from new cars in the UK decreased 5.4 per cent to 149g/km. However, an EU strategy to reduce this to 120g/km by 2012 looks unlikely to be met. Instead it is considering a target of 70g/km by 2025.

By 2020, 10 per cent of transport fuel must be from renewable sources. Biodiesel is the most common biofuel in Europe, while ethanol is the most common worldwide. The usage of biofuels helps to reduce fossil fuel use, decrease greenhouse gas emissions and promote rural development; the downside is that using farmland for biofuel production pushes up prices for food crops such as corn, reduces farmland biodiversity and contributes to soil erosion and deforestation. The challenge is to support biofuel production with policies to help ensure that biofuel commercialisation is sustainable. The government has a set of sustainability standards for biofuels, but currently just 31 per cent meet these standards, against a target of 50 per cent.

Attention is also on individuals and what they can do to reduce their carbon footprint. This is a measure of the amount of carbon dioxide emitted by the fossil fuels burned as part of a person's daily life or, in the case of an organisation, as part of its everyday operations. More than 40 per cent of the UK's carbon dioxide emissions come from people's homes and travel requirements, and 80 per cent of the energy used in homes is for heating.

The UK emitted 473.7 million tonnes of carbon dioxide in 2009 and has an average carbon footprint of 10 tonnes per person. To put this into context, the average American generates 20 tonnes of carbon dioxide a year, against a global average of around four tonnes per person.

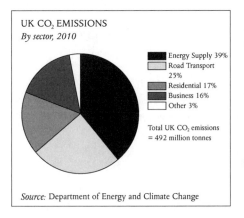

UK CO₂ EMISSIONS
By sector, 2010

Energy Supply 39%
Road Transport 25%
Residential 17%
Business 16%
Other 3%

Total UK CO₂ emissions = 492 million tonnes

Source: Department of Energy and Climate Change

SELECTED UK TARGETS

AIR
• Reduce particulates (also referred to as fine particles or soot) in urban areas by 20 per cent by 2020

CLIMATE CHANGE
• Reduce carbon dioxide emissions to 20 per cent below 1990 levels by 2010, 34 per cent by 2020, and 80 per cent by 2050
• Reduce greenhouse gas emissions to 12.5 per cent below 1990 levels by 2008–12

ENERGY
• Provide 10 per cent of UK electricity from renewable sources by 2010 and 15 per cent by 2020
• Scotland to generate 80 per cent of electricity from renewable sources by 2020

- Around 40 per cent of UK electricity to be from low carbon sources (ie renewable, nuclear or clean coal) by 2020
- Produce 10 per cent of transport energy from renewable sources by 2020
- Improve energy efficiency by 20 per cent by 2020

WASTE
- Recycle 50 per cent of household waste by 2020
- Reduce amount of household waste not reused, recycled or composted from 22.2 million tonnes in 2000 to 12.2 million tonnes by 2020, a reduction of 45 per cent
- Reduce biodegradable municipal waste sent to landfill to 50 per cent by 2013 and 35 per cent by 2020
- Recycle or compost 50 per cent of municipal waste in Scotland by 2013, 60 per cent by 2020 and 70 per cent by 2025
- Recover 70 per cent of construction and demolition waste by 2020

EUROPEAN UNION MEASURES

Environmental legislation in the EU is based around the principle that the polluter pays and policies are formulated at the level of international conventions and protocols, European directives, and national legislation and strategies. The interlinked sixth environment action programme, the EU sustainable development strategy and the Cardiff process (which aims to integrate environmental concerns into other policies) are being developed as a framework for more detailed strategies.

The first environment action programme began in the 1970s and the EU adopted the sixth programme, Environment 2010: Our Future, Our Choice, in January 2001. Focusing on the topics of climate change, nature and biodiversity, environment and health, and natural resources and waste, it is the cornerstone of EU policy. Work has started on the seventh plan.

The European Commission (EC) is also using more diverse methods, in particular market-based instruments such as environmental taxes and voluntary measures. These are increasingly being adopted across Europe. Taxing energy consumption and selling the right to emit greenhouse gases are key ways of tackling climate change, and both follow the 'polluter pays' principle. Environmental taxes account for 2–6 per cent of GDP in most European countries. Items subject to environmental taxes in Europe include plastic bags (Belgium, Ireland and Italy), plastic mineral water bottles (Italy), milk and fruit juice cartons (Norway), tyres (Denmark and Finland), disposable cutlery (Belgium) and paper and cardboard (France).

SUSTAINABLE DEVELOPMENT

The environmental agenda is part of the wider issue of addressing sustainability that incorporates social, environmental and economic development. During the World Summit on Sustainable Development, held in Johannesburg in 2002, governments agreed on a series of commitments in five priority areas: water and sanitation, energy, health, agriculture and biodiversity. Targets and timetables included halving the number of people who lack access to clean water or proper sanitation by 2015, and reducing biodiversity loss by 2010. Following the summit, the United Nations Commission on Sustainable Development agreed its programme for the next 15 years.

In addition, 2005–15 has been named as the 'Water for Life' decade.

Countries have started to prepare for the next World Summit on Sustainable Development to be held in Brazil in 2012. Key themes emerging for the summit include concern about the potential toxicity of plastics when broken down in the sea, and phosphorus pollution. Phosphorus, a valuable fertiliser, is being lost to the oceans partly from a lack of recycling waste water. Sweden, for example, aims to recycle 60 per cent of phosphorus in municipal wastewater by 2015. The idea of a transition to a low-carbon resource efficient global economy will also be top of the agenda.

In June 2010, the EU committed to the Europe 2020 strategy that supports a shift to a resource efficient economy. It has set objectives on employment, innovation, education, social inclusion and climate/energy to be reached by 2020. Each member state will adopt its own national targets in each of these areas. In March 2011, as part of this framework, the EC published a roadmap for moving to a competitive low-carbon economy by 2050.

CLIMATE CHANGE AND AIR POLLUTION

Temperature in central England has risen by about 1°C since the 1970s, with 2010 being one of the warmest years on record. Sea levels around the UK rose by 1mm a year in the 20th century, although the rate for the 1990s and 2000s is higher.

The government's response to climate change has been driven by the UN framework convention on climate change. This is a binding agreement that aims to reduce the risks of global warming by limiting greenhouse gas emissions.

Annual global carbon dioxide emissions in 2009 were 1.3 per cent below 2008 figures, partly because of the global financial crisis. However, the concentration of carbon dioxide in the atmosphere rose to 387ppm (parts per million), up from 385ppm in 2008.

Progress towards the UN framework convention's targets is assessed at regular conferences. At Kyoto in 1997, the Kyoto protocol was adopted. It covers the six main greenhouse gases: carbon dioxide, methane, nitrous oxide, hydrofluorocarbons (HFCs), perfluorocarbons (PFCs) and sulphur hexafluoride. Under the protocol, industrialised countries agreed to a legally binding target of cutting emissions of greenhouse gases to 5.2 per cent below 1990 levels by 2008–12. The protocol came into force in February 2005 after it was ratified by Russia. The USA has not ratified the treaty, while the UK set its own target at a 12.5 per cent reduction on 1990.

A legally binding post-Kyoto agreement was expected at the Copenhagen climate change conference in December 2009, however, no consensus was reached. Instead, a political agreement was drawn up – known as the Copenhagen Accord – that recognises the objective to cap the global temperature rise to below 2°C (445–490ppm carbon dioxide equivalents). The accord also outlines developed countries' commitments to provide additional funding to help the developing world address climate change. Countries have made pledges to cut emissions, but the UN says these are unlikely to keep temperatures below the target of a 2°C temperature rise by 2050. At the UN climate change conference in Cancun, Mexico, in December 2010 an agreement was reached that builds on the decisions made at Copenhagen, but the UN says that there is still a gap between this and what is needed to cap temperature rises at 2°C. One of the major challenges for the next conference, to be held in Durban, South Africa, in November 2011 will be to bridge this gap.

To keep climate change below 2°C, the EU has an objective of reducing greenhouse gas emissions by 80–95 per cent by 2050 compared to 1990. In 2007, the EU heads of state and government agreed a firm target of cutting 20 per cent of the EU's greenhouse gas emissions by 2020, rising to 30 per cent if the USA, Canada and India make similar commitments. The UK, France and Germany are pushing for the EU to adopt a 30 per cent target.

Greenhouse gas emissions in the 27 EU member states are decreasing. Between 1990 and 2009, they decreased by 17 per cent with a particularly large decrease between 2008 and 2009, largely due to the economic crisis. The EU is currently on track to meet the 20 per cent target.

Scientists are also looking at ways to avoid global warming by reducing other emissions such as methane, black carbon (formed when fossil and biofuels are not completely combusted) and tropospheric ozone.

In 2008 the UK already had a goal to reduce its carbon dioxide emissions to 20 per cent below 1990 levels by 2010. However, the Climate Change Act proposed two further goals: an interim target of a 34 per cent reduction in carbon dioxide emissions below 1990 levels by 2020 and a legally binding target of an 80 per cent reduction by 2050. The government must also set binding limits on carbon dioxide emissions during five-year budget periods; budgets have been set until 2022 and the UK is on track to meet the first. Provisional figures show that UK greenhouse gas emissions rose by 2.8 per cent in 2010, with CO_2 emissions increasing by 3.8 per cent. Residential sector use contributed to this with an increase of 13 per cent, mainly attributable to the cold winter.

Measures to tackle climate change in the UK are also covered by the climate change programme, launched in March 2006. It targets every sector of the economy and includes: a stricter emissions cap for industry; measures to encourage the uptake of biofuels in petrol; tighter building regulations; measures to improve household energy efficiency; a renewed emphasis on encouraging and enabling the general public, businesses and public authorities to help achieve the government's targets; and increased levels of microgeneration.

The UK has a voluntary greenhouse gas emissions trading scheme that allows businesses to buy an emission allowance to meet emission targets, or to sell surplus emission allowances. The carbon reduction commitment (CRC) energy efficiency scheme, which came into force in April 2010, aims to improve energy efficiency and significantly reduce emissions from non-energy related businesses in the UK, such as supermarkets and banks.

A mandatory EU emissions trading scheme for carbon dioxide applies at a company level. The companies covered by the ruling account for around half of the EU's total carbon dioxide emissions. From 2012, airlines will be included in the scheme, covering emissions from all domestic and international flights arriving at, or departing from, an EU airport. Emissions of other pollutants are also regulated within the EU. Countries have legally binding targets for emissions of sulphur dioxide, nitrogen oxides, non-methane volatile organic compounds and ammonia, which harm both human health and the environment. These targets were due to be met by 2010, however, around half of the member states did not meet one or more of the targets, with emissions of nitrogen oxides, in particular, causing problems for most of the 27 EU countries. A revision of the limits is likely to introduce tougher targets for 2020.

WASTE

By 2020 the EU could be generating 45 per cent more waste than in 1995. In the UK the uncoupling of waste growth from economic growth is a key objective along with placing greater emphasis on prevention and reuse, putting less non-municipal waste into landfill and investing in the infrastructure necessary to divert waste from landfill.

In the year to June 2010, the UK generated about 456kg of municipal waste per person (a total of 23.6 million tonnes), a figure that has been decreasing each year since 2006–7. To put this into context, the average municipal waste generation in Europe is 524kg per person (ranging from 400kg to 800kg), while in the USA it is 750kg and in Japan 400kg. The majority of municipal waste across Europe went into landfill (41 per cent); the rest is recycled (22 per cent), incinerated (20 per cent) or composted (17 per cent). In the UK, the proportion of household waste recycled or composted has been increasing steadily, reaching 40 per cent in the year to June 2010 in contrast to 6 per cent in 1995–6. This meets the UK's 2010 waste recycling target. The UK is still behind countries such as Denmark, Belgium and Germany who recycle or compost around 60 per cent of their municipal waste. Others, such as Romania, Bulgaria, and Malta landfill over 80 per cent.

Meanwhile, 48 million tonnes of commercial and industrial waste was generated in 2009, a decrease of 29 per cent since the last survey in 2002–3. Of this, 52 per cent was recycled or reused.

A full review of waste policy is currently underway and is looking at what policies are needed to reduce the amount of waste generated and to maximise reuse and recycling. The review is also taking into consideration how waste policies affect local communities, individual households and businesses. It will also consider anaerobic digestion, and other energy from waste technologies, as part of the UK's long-term goal of becoming a zero-waste economy.

EU directives help to shape UK policy, particularly in relation to commercial and industrial waste. For instance, the EU's European Integrated Products Policy aims to

UK MUNICIPAL WASTE GENERATION
million tonnes

Municipal waste not sent for recycling/composting/refuse
Municipal waste sent for recycling/composting/refuse

40,000
35,000
30,000
25,000
20,000
15,000
10,000
5,000
0

96/97 97/98 98/99 99/00 00/01 01/02 02/03 03/04 04/05 05/06 06/07 07/08 08/09 09/10

Source: DEFRA, Northern Ireland Environment Agency, Scottish Environment Protection Agency, Welsh government minimise the environmental impact of a product by looking at all phases of its life-cycle and encouraging each one to improve its environmental performance. A series of directives on waste packaging, vehicles, electrical waste and electronic equipment and batteries is intended to promote greater responsibility for products at the end of their life. The EU is also examining the issue of bio-waste (ie biodegradable garden, kitchen and food waste) which accounts for around one third of municipal waste.

WATER

Climate change alters rainfall patterns in ways that can put pressure on water resources, resulting in certain regions having more droughts. The EU flagship water legislation, the Water Framework Directive, takes this into account. Among its policy suggestions is the pricing of water in ways that would encourage efficient water use, thereby addressing water scarcity and drought. A substantial proportion of Europe's freshwater (40 per cent of surface water and 30 per cent of groundwater) is at risk of not achieving 'good status' under the terms of the directive by 2015. Water strategy in the UK tackles similar issues: the sustainable delivery of secure water supplies; an improved and protected water environment; fair, affordable and cost-reflective water charges; reduced water industry greenhouse gas emissions; and more sustainable and effective management of surface water.

For drinking water, wastewater discharges, rivers, coastal water and bathing water, quality targets are set at both EU and UK level: the aim is again to achieve 'good status' throughout the EU by 2015. The EU has an interactive internet tool, WISE (Water Information System for Europe), which provides water data and allows users to monitor water quality in their neighbourhood. In 2010, nearly 98 per cent of bathing water in the UK met the EU directive's minimum requirements, compared to two-thirds in 1988, while over 72 per cent achieved a newer, tighter standard.

ENERGY

The Climate Change Act 2008 sets out four energy policy goals for the UK: cutting carbon dioxide emissions by 80 per cent by 2050, maintaining reliable energy supplies, promoting competitive energy markets, and ensuring homes are adequately and affordably heated. In terms of renewable energy, the UK target was to increase the contribution of renewables to 10 per cent of electricity by 2010, with a further target (set by the EU) of 15 per cent by 2020. In reality, renewables accounted for around 7 per cent of electricity generated in the UK in 2010.

The UK's Carbon Plan, launched in March 2011, sets out what the UK needs to do to meet carbon targets. It includes the changes needed as to how electricity is generated, how homes and businesses are heated and the way people need to change the way they travel. The UK also intends to turn more food waste into power; it produces more than 100 million tonnes of organic waste, which could be turned into heat and power for over 2 million homes.

The EU has also adopted a number of targets. These are to improve energy efficiency by 20 per cent by 2020; increase the level of renewables used in transport fuel to 10 per cent by 2020 (the target was originally just for biofuels); and for 20 per cent of the EU's energy consumption to come from renewables by 2020. If all member states keep on track, the EU will meet and slightly exceed the 20 per cent renewables target. In 2008, renewable energy accounted for 8.4 per cent of EU primary energy consumption, including nearly one third of energy consumed in Sweden and more than a quarter in Austria, Latvia and Finland. At the end of 2009, a quarter of global power capacity was renewables (1,230GW). Grid connected photovoltaic capacity rose 53 per cent, wind 32 per cent, solar water/heating 21 per cent and geothermal by 4 per cent. For the second year running more renewable capacity than traditional capacity was added in the USA and Europe. In 2010, renewables accounted for 60 per cent of new capacity in Europe.

ENVIRONMENT AND HEALTH

Particulate matter in the air (also known as fine particles or soot), noise and ground-level ozone damages the health of thousands of people each year. Environmental pollutants, including pesticides, endocrine disruptors, dioxins and PCBs persist in the environment and their long-term effect on health is not fully understood. Emerging evidence suggests that air pollution may not only damage lungs but might also contribute to diseases such as Type 1 diabetes and multiple sclerosis. There are concerns about the effects of electromagnetic fields on human health and whether the use of nanotechnology in food could be dangerous for the human body.

In 2008, the EU set binding limits on emissions of fine particles. Under the new law, which takes effect in 2011, countries will have to reduce exposure to fine particles in urban areas by an average of 20 per cent by 2020, based on 2010 levels.

A chemicals policy, under which industry has to provide information on the effects of chemicals on human health and the environment, as well as on safe ways of handling them, has also been established.

CONTACTS

DEPARTMENT FOR ENVIRONMENT, FOOD AND RURAL AFFAIRS (DEFRA), Nobel House, 17 Smith Square, London SW1P 3JR T 0845-933 5577 W www.defra.gov.uk

DEPARTMENT OF ENERGY AND CLIMATE CHANGE, 3 Whitehall Place, London SW1A 2AW T 0300-060 4000 W www.decc.gov.uk

ENVIRONMENT AGENCY, National Customer Contact Centre, PO Box 544, Rotherham S60 1BY T 0870-850 6506 W www.environment-agency.gov.uk

EUROPEAN ENVIRONMENT AGENCY, Kongens Nytorv 6, DK-1050 Copenhagen K, Denmark T +45 3336 7100 W www.eea.europa.eu

SCOTTISH GOVERNMENT, RURAL AND ENVIRONMENT DIRECTORATE, Victoria Quay, Edinburgh EH6 6QQ T 0131-556 8400 W www.scotland.gov.uk

CONSERVATION AND HERITAGE

NATIONAL PARKS

© Natural England – material is reproduced
with the permission of Natural England

ENGLAND AND WALES

There are nine national parks in England, and three in Wales. In addition, the Norfolk and Suffolk Broads are considered to have equivalent status to a national park. Under the provisions of the National Parks and Access to the Countryside Act 1949, as clarified by the Natural Environment and Rural Communities Act 2006, the two purposes of the national parks are to conserve and enhance the natural beauty, wildlife and cultural heritage, and to promote opportunities for the understanding and enjoyment of the special qualities of national parks by the public. If there is a conflict between the two purposes, then conservation takes precedence.

Natural England is the statutory body that has the power to designate national parks in England, and the Countryside Council for Wales is responsible for national parks in Wales. Designations in England are confirmed by the Secretary of State for Environment, Food and Rural Affairs and those in Wales by the Welsh government. The designation of a national park does not affect the ownership of the land or remove the rights of the local community. The majority of the land in the national parks is owned by private landowners (around 75 per cent) or by bodies such as the National Trust and the Forestry Commission. The national park authorities own only a small percentage of the land themselves.

The Environment Act 1995 replaced the existing national park boards and committees with free-standing national park authorities (NPAs). NPAs are the sole local planning authorities for their areas and as such influence land use and development, and deal with planning applications. NPAs are responsible for carrying out the statutory purposes of national parks stated above. In pursuing these purposes they have a statutory duty to seek to foster the economic and social well-being of the communities within national parks. The NPAs publish management plans setting out overarching policies for their area and appoint their own officers and staff.

The Broads Authority was established under the Norfolk and Suffolk Broads Act 1988 and meets the requirement for the authority to have a navigation function in addition to a regard for the needs of agriculture, forestry and the economic and social interests of those who live or work in the Broads.

MEMBERSHIP

Membership of English NPAs comprises local authority appointees, members directly appointed by the environment secretary of state and members appointed by her after a consultation with local parishes. Under the Natural Environment and Rural Communities Act 2006 every district, county or unitary authority with land in a national park is entitled to appoint at least one member unless it chooses to opt out. The total number of local authority and parish members must exceed the number of national members. The majority of the English NPAs currently have 22 members, except the Peak District which has 30 and the South Downs which has 27 members.

The Broads Authority has 21 members: nine appointed by the constituent local authorities, two appointed by the Navigation Committee and ten appointed by the secretary of state. The secretary of state's appointees include at least three which are appointed after consultation with representatives of boating interests and at least two which are appointed after consultation with representatives of landowning and farming interests.

In Wales, two-thirds of NPA members are appointed by the constituent local authorities and one-third by the Welsh government, advised by the Countryside Council for Wales.

FUNDING

The English NPAs and the Broads Authority are funded by central government. In the financial year 2011–12 a core grant totalling £55.2m was allocated between the authorities.

In Wales, national parks are funded via a grant from the Welsh government. The grant for 2011–12 amounted to £10.9m. The three NPAs in Wales receive further funding via a local authority levy.

All NPAs and the Broads Authority can take advantage of grants from other bodies including lottery and European grants.

The national parks (with date that designation was confirmed) are:

BRECON BEACONS (1957), Powys (66 per cent)/ Carmarthenshire/Rhondda, Cynon and Taff/Merthyr Tydfil/Blaenau Gwent/Monmouthshire, 1,347 sq. km/520 sq. miles – The park is centred on the Brecon Beacons mountain range, which includes the three highest mountains in southern Britain (Pen y Fan, Corn Du and Cribyn), but also includes the valley of the rivers Usk and Wye, the Black Mountains to the east and the Black Mountain to the west. There are information centres at the visitor centre at Libanus (near Brecon), Abergavenny and Llandovery.
National Park Authority, Plas y Ffynnon, Cambrian Way, Brecon, Powys LD3 7HP **T** 01874-624437
E enquiries@breconbeacons.org **W** www.breconbeacons.org
Chief Executive, John Cook

BROADS (1989), Norfolk/Suffolk, 303 sq. km/117 sq. miles – The Broads are located between Norwich and Great Yarmouth on the flood plains of the six rivers flowing through the area to the sea. The area is one of fens, winding waterways, woodland and marsh. The 60 or so broads are man-made, and many are connected to the rivers by dykes, providing over 200km (124 miles) of navigable waterways. There are information centres at Hoveton, Whitlingham and Toad Hole Cottage at How Hill.
Broads Authority, Dragonfly House, 2 Gilders Way, Norwich NR3 1UB **T** 01603-610734
E broads@broads-authority.gov.uk
W www.broads-authority.gov.uk
Chief Executive, Dr John Packman

DARTMOOR (1951), Devon, 953 sq. km/368 sq. miles – The park consists of moorland and rocky granite tors, and is rich in prehistoric remains. There are information centres at Haytor, Princetown (main visitor centre) and Postbridge.
National Park Authority, Parke, Bovey Tracey, Devon TQ13 9JQ **T** 01626-832093 **E** hq@dartmoor-npa.gov.uk
W www.dartmoor-npa.gov.uk
Chief Executive, Kevin Bishop

EXMOOR (1954), Somerset (71 per cent)/Devon, 692 sq. km/267 sq. miles – Exmoor is a moorland plateau inhabited by wild Exmoor ponies and red deer. There are many ancient remains and burial mounds. There are national park centres at Dunster, Dulverton and Lynmouth.
National Park Authority, Exmoor House, Dulverton, Somerset TA22 9HL **T** 01398-323665
E info@exmoor-nationalpark.gov.uk
W www.exmoor-nationalpark.gov.uk
Chief Executive/National Park Officer, Dr Nigel Stone

LAKE DISTRICT (1951), Cumbria, 2,292 sq. km/885 sq. miles – The Lake District includes England's highest mountains (Scafell Pike, Helvellyn and Skiddaw) but it is most famous for its glaciated lakes. There are national park information centres at Bowness Bay, Keswick, Ullswater and a visitor centre at Brockhole, Windermere.
National Park Authority, Murley Moss, Oxenholme Road, Kendal, Cumbria LA9 7RL **T** 01539-724555
E hq@lakedistrict.gov.uk **W** www.lakedistrict.gov.uk
Chief Executive, Richard Leafe

NEW FOREST (2005), Hampshire, 570 sq. km/220 sq. miles – The forest has been protected since 1079 when it was declared a royal hunting forest. The area consists of forest, ancient woodland and heathland. Much of the forest is managed by the Forestry Commission, which provides several campsites. The main villages are Brockenhurst, Burley and Lyndhurst, which has a visitor centre.
National Park Authority, Town Hall, Avenue Road, Lymington, Hants SO41 9ZG **T** 01590-646600
E enquiries@newforestnpa.gov.uk
W www.newforestnpa.gov.uk
Chief Executive, Alison Barnes

NORTH YORK MOORS (1952), North Yorkshire (96 per cent)/Redcar and Cleveland, 1,434 sq. km/554 sq. miles – The park consists of woodland and moorland, and includes the Hambleton Hills and the Cleveland Way. There are information centres at Danby and Sutton Bank.
National Park Authority, The Old Vicarage, Bondgate, Helmsley, York YO62 5BP **T** 01439-770657
E info@northyorkmoors-npa.gov.uk
W www.northyorkmoors.org.uk
Chief Executive, Andrew Wilson

NORTHUMBERLAND (1956), Northumberland, 1,049 sq. km/405 sq. miles – The park is an area of hill country stretching from Hadrian's Wall to the Scottish border. There are information centres at Ingram, Once Brewed and Rothbury.
National Park Authority, Eastburn, South Park, Hexham, Northumberland NE46 1BS **T** 01434-605555
E enquiries@nnpa.org.uk
W www.northumberlandnationalpark.org.uk
Chief Executive, Tony Gates

PEAK DISTRICT (1951), Derbyshire (64 per cent)/ Staffordshire/South Yorkshire/Cheshire/West Yorkshire/Greater Manchester, 1,437 sq. km/555 sq. miles – The Peak District includes the gritstone moors of the 'Dark Peak' and the limestone dales of the 'White Peak'. There are information centres at Bakewell, Castleton, Edale and Upper Derwent.
National Park Authority, Aldern House, Baslow Road, Bakewell, Derbyshire DE45 1AE **T** 01629-816200
E customer.service@peakdistrict.gov.uk
W www.peakdistrict.gov.uk
Chief Executive, Jim Dixon

PEMBROKESHIRE COAST (1952 and 1995), Pembrokeshire, 621 sq. km/240 sq. miles – The park includes cliffs, moorland and a number of islands, including Skomer and Ramsey. There are information centres in Newport and Tenby and a gallery and visitor centre, Oriel y Parc, in St Davids. The park also manages sites at Castell Henllys and Carew Castle and Tidal Mill.
National Park Authority, Llanion Park, Pembroke Dock, Pembrokeshire SA72 6DY **T** 0845-345 7275
E info@pembrokeshirecoast.org.uk
W www.pembrokeshirecoast.org.uk
Chief Executive/National Park Officer, Tegryn Jones

SNOWDONIA/ERYRI (1951), Gwynedd/Conwy, 2,132 sq. km/823 sq. miles – Snowdonia, which takes its name from Snowdon – the highest peak in England and Wales – is an area of deep valleys and rugged mountains. There are information centres at Aberdyfi, Beddgelert, Betws y Coed, Dolgellau and Harlech.
National Park Authority, Penrhyndeudraeth, Gwynedd LL48 6LF **T** 01766-770274 **E** parc@snowdonia-npa.gov.uk
W www.snowdonia-npa.gov.uk
Chief Executive, Aneurin Phillips

THE SOUTH DOWNS (2010), West Sussex/Hampshire,1,648 sq. km/636 sq. miles – The South Downs contains a diversity of natural habitats, including flower-studded chalk grassland, ancient woodland, flood meadow, lowland heath and rare chalk heathland. The South Downs National Park Authority acquired statutory powers on 1 April 2011 and is now responsible for planning the future of the park.

National Park Authority, Rosemary's Parlour, North Street, Midhurst, W. Sussex GU29 9SB
T 0300-303 1053 E info@southdowns.gov.uk
W www.southdowns.gov.uk
Chair, Margaret Paren

YORKSHIRE DALES (1954), North Yorkshire (88 per cent)/Cumbria, 1,762 sq. km/680 sq. miles – The Yorkshire Dales is composed primarily of limestone overlaid in places by millstone grit. The three peaks of Ingleborough, Whernside and Pen-y-ghent are within the park. There are information centres at Grassington, Hawes, Aysgarth Falls, Malham and Reeth.

National Park Authority, Yoredale, Bainbridge, Leyburn, N. Yorks DL8 3EL T 0300-456 0030
E info@yorkshiredales.org.uk W www.yorkshiredales.org.uk
Chief Executive, David Butterworth

SCOTLAND

On 9 August 2000 the national parks (Scotland) bill received royal assent, giving parliament the ability to create national parks in Scotland. The first two Scottish national parks became operational in 2002 and 2003 respectively. The Act gives Scottish parks wider powers than in England and Wales, including statutory responsibilities for the local economy and rural communities. The board of each Scottish NPA consists of 25 members, of which five are directly elected by a postal ballot of the local electorate. The remaining 20 members, ten of which are nominated by the constituent local authorities, are chosen by the Scottish ministers. In Scotland, the national parks are central government bodies and are wholly funded by the Scottish government. Funding for 2010–11 totals £12.9m.

CAIRNGORMS (2003), North-East Scotland, 4,528 sq. km/1,748 sq. miles – The Cairngorms national park is the largest in the UK. It displays a vast collection of landforms, including five of the six highest mountains in the UK. The near natural woodlands contain remnants of the original ancient Caledonian pine forest.

National Park Authority, 14 The Square, Grantown-on-Spey, Morayshire PH26 3HG T 01479-873535
E enquiries@cairngorms.co.uk W www.cairngorms.co.uk
Chief Executive, Jane Hope

LOCH LOMOND AND THE TROSSACHS (2002), Argyll and Bute/Perth and Kinross/Stirling/West Dunbartonshire, 1,865 sq. km/720 sq. miles – The park boundaries encompass lochs, rivers, forests, 20 mountains above 914m (3,000ft) including Ben More and a further 20 mountains between 762m (2,500ft) and 914m (3,000ft).

National Park Authority, Carrochan, Carrochan Road, Balloch G83 8EG T 01389-722600
E info@lochlomond-trossachs.org
W www.lochlomond-trossachs.org
Chief Executive, Fiona Logan

NORTHERN IRELAND

There is a power to designate national parks in Northern Ireland under the Nature Conservation and Amenity Lands Order (Northern Ireland) 1985, but there are currently no national parks in Northern Ireland.

AREAS OF OUTSTANDING NATURAL BEAUTY

ENGLAND AND WALES

Under the National Parks and Access to the Countryside Act 1949, provision was made for the designation of areas of outstanding natural beauty (AONBs). Natural England is responsible for AONBs in England and the Countryside Council for Wales for the Welsh AONBs. Designations in England are confirmed by the Secretary of State for Environment, Food and Rural Affairs and those in Wales by the National Assembly for Wales. The Countryside and Rights of Way (CROW) Act 2000 placed greater responsibility on local authorities to protect AONBs and made it a statutory duty for relevant authorities to produce a management plan for their AONB area. The CROW Act also provided for the creation of conservation boards for larger and more complex AONBs. The first two conservation boards for the Cotswolds and Chilterns AONBs were established in July 2004.

The primary objective of the AONB designation is to conserve and enhance the natural beauty of the area. Where an AONB has a conservation board, it has the additional purpose of increasing public understanding and enjoyment of the special qualities of the area; the board has greater weight should there be a conflict of interests between the two. In addition, the board is also required to foster the economic and social well-being of the local communities but without incurring significant expenditure in doing so. Overall responsibility for AONBs lies with the relevant local authorities or conservation board. To coordinate planning and management responsibilities between local authorities in whose area they fall, AONBs are overseen by a joint advisory committee (or similar body) which includes representatives from the local authorities, landowners, farmers, residents and conservation and recreation groups. Core funding for AONBs is provided by central government through Natural England and the Countryside Council for Wales.

The 40 AONBs (with date designation confirmed) are:

ARNSIDE AND SILVERDALE (1972), Cumbria/Lancashire, 75 sq. km/29 sq. miles
BLACKDOWN HILLS (1991), Devon/Somerset, 370 sq. km/143 sq. miles
CANNOCK CHASE (1958), Staffordshire, 70 sq. km/27 sq. miles
CHICHESTER HARBOUR (1964), Hampshire/West Sussex, 73 sq. km/28 sq. miles
CHILTERNS (1965; extended 1990), Bedfordshire/Buckinghamshire/Herefordshire/Oxfordshire, 839 sq. km/324 sq. miles
CLWYDIAN RANGE (1985), Denbighshire/Flintshire, 157 sq. km/61 sq. miles
CORNWALL (1959; Camel Estuary 1983), 963 sq. km/372 sq. miles
COTSWOLDS (1966; extended 1990), Gloucestershire/Oxfordshire/Warwickshire/Wiltshire/Worcestershire, 2,041 sq. km/788 sq. miles
CRANBORNE CHASE AND WEST WILTSHIRE DOWNS (1983), Dorset/Hampshire/Somerset/Wiltshire, 987 sq. km/381 sq. miles
DEDHAM VALE (1970; extended 1978, 1991), Essex/Suffolk, 90 sq. km/35 sq. miles
DORSET (1959), Dorset/Somerset, 1,129 sq. km/436 sq. miles
EAST DEVON (1963), 269 sq. km/104 sq. miles

EAST HAMPSHIRE (1962), 383 sq. km/148 sq. miles
FOREST OF BOWLAND (1964), Lancashire/North
Yorkshire, 805 sq. km/311 sq. miles
GOWER (1956), Swansea, 188 sq. km/73 sq. miles
HIGH WEALD (1983), East Sussex/Kent/Surrey/West
Sussex, 1,460 sq. km/564 sq. miles
HOWARDIAN HILLS (1987), North Yorkshire, 204 sq.
km/79 sq. miles
ISLE OF WIGHT (1963), 192 sq. km/74 sq. miles
ISLES OF SCILLY (1976), 16 sq. km/6 sq. miles
KENT DOWNS (1968), 878 sq. km/339 sq. miles
LINCOLNSHIRE WOLDS (1973), 559 sq. km/216 sq.
miles
LLYN (1957), Gwynedd, 161 sq. km/62 sq. miles
MALVERN HILLS (1959), Gloucestershire/
Worcestershire, 105 sq. km/41 sq. miles
MENDIP HILLS (1972; extended 1989), Somerset,
199 sq. km/77 sq. miles
NIDDERDALE (1994), North Yorkshire, 601 sq.
km/232 sq. miles
NORFOLK COAST (1968), 445 sq. km/172 sq. miles
NORTH DEVON (1960), 171 sq. km/66 sq. miles
NORTH PENNINES (1988), Cumbria/Durham/North
Yorkshire/Northumberland, 1,983 sq. km/766 sq.
miles
NORTH WESSEX DOWNS (1972), Hampshire/
Oxfordshire/Wiltshire, 1,730 sq. km/668 sq. miles
NORTHUMBERLAND COAST (1958), 132 sq. km/
51 sq. miles
QUANTOCK HILLS (1957), Somerset, 99 sq. km/38 sq.
miles
SHROPSHIRE HILLS (1959), 808 sq. km/
312 sq. miles
SOLWAY COAST (1964), Cumbria, 122 sq. km/47 sq.
miles
SOUTH DEVON (1960), 339 sq. km/131 sq. miles
SUFFOLK COAST AND HEATHS (1970), 403 sq. km/
156 sq. miles
SURREY HILLS (1958), 422 sq. km/163 sq. miles
SUSSEX DOWNS (1966), 983 sq. km/379 sq. miles
TAMAR VALLEY (1995), Cornwall/Devon, 197 sq. km/
76 sq. miles
WYE VALLEY (1971), Gloucestershire/Herefordshire/
Monmouthshire, 326 sq. km/126 sq. miles
YNYS MON (ISLE OF ANGLESEY) (1967), 221 sq. km/
85 sq. miles

NORTHERN IRELAND

The Department of the Environment for Northern
Ireland, with advice from the Council for Nature
Conservation and the Countryside, designates AONBs in
Northern Ireland. At present there are eight and these
cover a total area of 2,849 sq. km (1,100 sq. miles). Dates
given are those of designation.

ANTRIM COAST AND GLENS (1988), Co. Antrim,
706 sq. km/272 sq. miles
BINEVENAGH (2006), Co. Londonderry, 166 sq. km/
64 sq. miles
CAUSEWAY COAST (1989), Co. Antrim, 42 sq. km/
16 sq. miles
LAGAN VALLEY (1965), Co. Down, 39 sq. km/15 sq.
miles
MOURNE (1986), Co. Down, 570 sq. km/220 sq. miles
RING OF GULLION (1991), Co. Armagh, 154 sq. km/
59 sq. miles
SPERRIN (1968; extended 2008), Co. Tyrone/
Co. Londonderry, 1,182 sq. km/456 sq. miles

STRANGFORD LOUGH AND LECALE (2010)*, Co.
Down, 528 sq. km/204 sq. miles

*Strangford Lough (1972) and Lecale Coast (1967) merged in
2010

NATIONAL SCENIC AREAS

In Scotland, national scenic areas have a broadly
equivalent status to AONBs. Scottish Natural Heritage
recognises areas of national scenic significance. At the end
of May 2011 there were 40, covering a land area of
1,020,500 hectares (2,521,710 acres) and a marine area
of 357,900 hectares (884,390 acres).

Development within national scenic areas is dealt with
by local authorities, who are required to consult Scottish
Natural Heritage concerning certain categories of
development. Disagreements between Scottish Natural
Heritage and local authorities are referred to the Scottish
government. Land management uses can also be modified
in the interest of scenic conservation.

ASSYNT-COIGACH, Highland, 90,200ha/222,884
acres
BEN NEVIS AND GLEN COE, Highland, 101,600ha/
251,053 acres
CAIRNGORM MOUNTAINS, Highland/
Aberdeenshire/Moray, 67,200ha/ 166,051 acres
CUILLIN HILLS, Highland, 21,900ha/54,115 acres
DEESIDE AND LOCHNAGAR, Aberdeenshire,
40,000ha/98,840 acres
DORNOCH FIRTH, Highland, 7,500ha/18,532 acres
EAST STEWARTRY COAST, Dumfries and Galloway,
4,500ha/11,119 acres
EILDON AND LEADERFOOT, Borders, 3,600ha/
8,896 acres
FLEET VALLEY, Dumfries and Galloway, 5,300ha/
13,096 acres
GLEN AFFRIC, Highland, 19,300ha/47,690 acres
GLEN STRATHFARRAR, Highland, 3,800ha/9,390
acres
HOY AND WEST MAINLAND, Orkney Islands,
14,800ha/36,571 acres
JURA, Argyll and Bute, 21,800ha/53,868 acres
KINTAIL, Highland, 15,500ha/38,300 acres
KNAPDALE, Argyll and Bute, 19,800ha/48,926 acres
KNOYDART, Highland, 39,500ha/97,604 acres
KYLE OF TONGUE, Highland, 18,500ha/45,713 acres
KYLES OF BUTE, Argyll and Bute, 4,400ha/10,872
acres
LOCH LOMOND, Argyll and Bute, 27,400ha/67,705
acres
LOCH NA KEAL, Mull, Argyll and Bute, 12,700ha/
31,382 acres
LOCH RANNOCH AND GLEN LYON, Perthshire and
Kinross, 48,400ha/119,596 acres
LOCH SHIEL, Highland, 13,400ha/33,111 acres
LOCH TUMMEL, Perthshire and Kinross, 9,200ha/
22,733 acres
LYNN OF LORN, Argyll and Bute, 4,800ha/11,861
acres
MORAR, MOIDART AND ARDNAMURCHAN,
Highland, 13,500ha/33,358 acres
NITH ESTUARY, Dumfries and Galloway, 9,300ha/
22,980 acres
NORTH ARRAN, North Ayrshire, 23,800ha/58,810
acres

NORTH-WEST SUTHERLAND, Highland, 20,500ha/ 50,655 acres

RIVER EARN, Perthshire and Kinross, 3,000ha/7,413 acres

RIVER TAY, Perthshire and Kinross, 5,600ha/13,838 acres

ST KILDA, Eilean Siar (Western Isles), 900ha/2,224 acres

SCARBA, LUNGA AND THE GARVELLACHS, Argyll and Bute, 1,900ha/4,695 acres

SHETLAND, Shetland Isles, 11,600ha/28,664 acres

SMALL ISLANDS, Highland, 15,500ha/38,300 acres

SOUTH LEWIS, HARRIS AND NORTH UIST, Eilean Siar (Western Isles), 109,600ha/270,822 acres

SOUTH UIST MACHAIR, Eilean Siar (Western Isles), 6,100ha/15,073 acres

THE TROSSACHS, Stirling, 4,600ha/11,367 acres

TROTTERNISH, Highland, 5,000ha/12,355 acres

UPPER TWEEDDALE, Borders, 10,500ha/25,945 acres

WESTER ROSS, Highland, 145,300ha/359,036 acres

THE NATIONAL FOREST

The National Forest is being planted across 517 sq. km (200 sq. miles) of Derbyshire, Leicestershire and Staffordshire. Nearly 8 million trees, of mixed species but mainly broadleaved, covering over 6,230ha (15,394 acres) have been planted. The aim is to eventually cover about one-third of the designated area.

The project was developed in 1992–5 by the Countryside Commission and is now run by the National Forest Company, which was established in April 1995. The National Forest Company is responsible for the delivery of the government-approved National Forest Strategy and is funded by DEFRA.

NATIONAL FOREST COMPANY, Bath Lane, Moira, Swadlincote, Derbyshire DE12 6BD T 01283-551211 E enquiries@nationalforest.org W www.nationalforest.org

Chief Executive, Sophie Churchill

SITES OF SPECIAL SCIENTIFIC INTEREST

Site of special scientific interest (SSSIs) is a legal notification applied to land in England, Scotland or Wales which Natural England (NE) (formerly English Nature), Scottish Natural Heritage (SNH) or the Countryside Council for Wales (CCW) identifies as being of special interest because of its flora, fauna, geological, geomorphological or physiographical features. In some cases, SSSIs are managed as nature reserves.

NE, SNH and CCW must notify the designation of an SSSI to the local planning authority, every owner/ occupier of the land, and the environment secretary, the Scottish ministers or the National Assembly for Wales. Forestry and agricultural departments and a number of other interested parties are also formally notified.

Objections to the notification of an SSSI can be made and ultimately considered at a full meeting of the Council of NE or CCW. In Scotland an objection will be dealt with by the main board of SNH or an appropriate subgroup, depending on the nature of the objection.

The protection of these sites depends on the cooperation of individual landowners and occupiers. Owner/occupiers must consult NE, SNH or CCW and gain written consent before they can undertake certain listed activities on the site. Funds are available through management agreements and grants to assist owners and occupiers in conserving sites' interests. Sites can also be protected by management schemes, management notices and other enforcement mechanisms. As a last resort a site can be purchased.

The number and area of SSSIs in Britain as at May 2011 was:

	Number	Hectares	Acres
England	4,118	1,077,168	2,661,740
Scotland	1,447	1,023,237	2,528,474
Wales	1,045	266,681	658,995

NORTHERN IRELAND
In Northern Ireland 305 areas of special scientific interest (ASSIs) have been declared by the Department of the Environment for Northern Ireland.

NATIONAL NATURE RESERVES

National nature reserves are defined in the National Parks and Access to the Countryside Act 1949 as modified by the Natural Environment and Rural Communities Act 2006. National nature reserves may be managed solely for the purpose of conservation, or for both the purposes of conservation and recreation, providing this does not compromise the conservation purpose.

NE, SNH or CCW can declare as a national nature reserve land which is held and managed as a nature reserve under an agreement; land held and managed by NE, SNH or CCW; or land held and managed as a nature reserve by an approved body. NE, SNH or CCW can make by-laws to protect reserves from undesirable activities; these are subject to confirmation by the Secretary of State for Environment, Food and Rural Affairs, the National Assembly for Wales or the Scottish ministers.

The number and area of national nature reserves in Britain as at May 2011 was:

	Number	Hectares	Acres
England	224	94,400	233,267
Scotland	62	133,736	330,469
Wales	72	25,623	63,316

NORTHERN IRELAND
Nature reserves are established and managed by the Department of the Environment for Northern Ireland, with advice from the Council for Nature Conservation and the Countryside. Nature reserves are declared under the Nature Conservation and Amenity Lands (Northern Ireland) Order 1985; to date, 49 nature reserves have been declared.

LOCAL NATURE RESERVES

Local nature reserves are defined in the National Parks and Access to the Countryside Act 1949 (as amended by the Natural Environment and Rural Communities Act 2006) as land designated for the study and preservation of flora and fauna, or of geological or physiographical features. Local nature reserves also have a statutory obligation to provide opportunities for the enjoyment of nature or open air recreation, providing this does not compromise the conservation purpose of the reserve. Local authorities in England, Scotland and Wales have the power to acquire, declare and manage reserves in consultation with NE, SNH and CCW. There is similar legislation in Northern Ireland, where the consulting organisation is the Environment Agency.

Any organisation, such as water companies, educational trusts, local amenity groups and charitable nature conservation bodies, such as wildlife trusts, may manage local nature reserves, provided that a local authority has a legal interest in the land. This means that the local authority must either own it, lease it or have a management agreement with the landowner.

The number and area of designated local nature reserves in Britain as at May 2011 was:

	Number	Hectares	Acres
England	1,475	35,527	87,751
Scotland	58	10,023	24,767
Wales	82	5,840	14,431

There are 11 local nature reserves in Northern Ireland.

FOREST RESERVES

The Forestry Commission is the government department responsible for forestry policy throughout Great Britain. Forestry is a devolved matter, with the separate Forestry Commissions for England, Scotland and Wales reporting directly to their appropriate minister. The equivalent body in Northern Ireland is the Forest Service, an agency of the Department of Agriculture and Rural Development for Northern Ireland. The Forestry Commission in each country is led by a director who is also a member of the GB Board of Commissioners. As at March 2011, UK woodland certified by the Forestry Commission (including Forestry Commission-managed woodland) amounted to around 1,325,000 hectares (3,274,146 acres): 335,000 hectares (827,803 acres) in England, 133,000 hectares (328,650 acres) in Wales, 793,000 hectares (1,959,545 acres) in Scotland and 63,000 hectares (155,676 acres) in Northern Ireland. For more information, see W www.forestry.gov.uk

There are 34 forest nature reserves in Northern Ireland, covering 1,512 hectares (3,736 acres), designated and administered by the Forest Service. There are also 16 national nature reserves on Forest Service-owned property.

MARINE NATURE RESERVES

Marine protected areas provide protection for marine flora and fauna, and geological and physiographical features on land covered by tidal waters or parts of the sea in or adjacent to the UK. These areas also provide opportunities for study and research.

The Marine and Coastal Access Act 2009 created a new kind of statutory protection for marine protected areas in England and Wales, marine conservation zones (MCZs), which are designed to increase the protection of species and habitats deemed to be of national importance. Individual MCZs can have varying levels of protection: some include specific activities that are appropriately managed, while others prohibit all damaging and disturbing activities. The act converted the waters around Lundy Island, a former marine protected area, to MCZ status and it is expected that further designations, including the waters around Skomer Island off the coast of Pembrokeshire, Wales, will be made in 2012.

The Secretary of State for Environment, Food and Rural Affairs and the National Assembly for Wales have the power to designate MCZs. Natural England and the Countryside Council for Wales have set up four regional projects covering the south-west, Irish Sea, North Sea and eastern channel to deliver recommendations for potential MCZ designations.

Under the Marine (Scotland) Act 2010 there are new statutory powers for the Scottish government to designate marine protected areas (MPAs) in the seas around Scotland; Scottish Natural Heritage is currently advising on potential MPA designations.

In Northern Ireland, marine nature reserves may be established under the Nature Conservation and Amenity Lands Order (Northern Ireland) 1985.

Marine Conservation Zone:
LUNDY (2010), Bristol Channel

Marine Nature Reserve:
STRANGFORD LOUGH (1995), Northern Ireland

CONSERVATION OF WILDLIFE AND HABITATS

The UK is party to a number of international conventions.

BERN CONVENTION

The 1979 Bern Convention on the Conservation of European Wildlife and Natural Habitats came into force in the UK in June 1982. Currently there are 50 contracting parties and a number of other states attend meetings as observers.

The aims are to conserve wild flora and fauna and their natural habitats, especially where this requires the cooperation of several countries, and to promote such cooperation. The convention gives particular emphasis to endangered and vulnerable species.

All parties to the convention must promote national conservation policies and take account of the conservation of wild flora and fauna when setting planning and development policies. Reports on contracting parties' conservation policies must be submitted to the standing committee every four years.

SECRETARIAT OF THE BERN CONVENTION STANDING COMMITTEE, Council of Europe, 67075 Strasbourg-Cedex, France T (+33) (3) 8841 2000 W www.coe.int

BIODIVERSITY

The UK ratified the Convention on Biological Diversity in June 1994. As at June 2011 there were 193 parties to the convention.

The objectives are the conservation of biological diversity, the sustainable use of its components and the fair and equitable sharing of the benefits arising out of the use of genetic resources. There are seven thematic work programmes addressing agricultural biodiversity, marine and coastal biodiversity and the biodiversity of inland waters, dry and sub-humid lands, islands, mountains and forests. The Conference of the Parties to the Convention on Biological Diversity adopted a supplementary agreement to the convention known as the Cartagena Protocol on Biosafety on 29 January 2000. The protocol seeks to protect biological diversity from potential risks that may be posed by introducing modified living organisms, resulting from biotechnology, into the environment. As at June 2011, 160 countries were party to the protocol; the UK joined on 17 February 2004.

The UK Biodiversity Action Plan (UKBAP) is the UK government's response to the Convention on Biological Diversity and constitutes a record of UK biological resources and a detailed plan for their protection. The list of priority species and habitats under the UKBAP covers 1,150 species and 65 habitats. The UK Biodiversity Partnership Standing Committee guides and supports the UK Biodiversity Partnership in implementing UKBAP; it also coordinates between the four UK country groups which form the partnership and are responsible for implementing UKBAP at a national level. In addition, the UK Biodiversity Partnership includes two support groups: the Biodiversity Research Advisory Group and the Biodiversity Reporting and Information Group. Information on UKBAP is available from the Joint Nature Conservation Committee (JNCC).

JNCC, Monkstone House, City Road, Peterborough PE1 1JY T 01733-562626 W www.jncc.defra.gov.uk

BONN CONVENTION

The 1979 Convention on Conservation of Migratory Species of Wild Animals (also known as the CMS or Bonn Convention) came into force in the UK in October 1985. As at 1 March 2011, 115 countries were party to the convention.

It requires the protection of listed endangered migratory species and encourages international agreements covering these and other threatened species. International agreements can range from legally binding treaties to less formal memoranda of understanding.

Seven agreements have been concluded to date under the convention. They aim to conserve seals in the Wadden Sea; bat populations in Europe; small cetaceans of the Baltic, north-east Atlantic, Irish and North Seas; African-Eurasian migratory waterbirds; cetaceans of the Mediterranean Sea, Black Sea and contiguous Atlantic area; albatrosses and petrels; and gorillas and their habitats. A further 19 memorandums of understanding have been agreed for the Siberian crane, slender-billed curlews, marine turtles of the Atlantic coast of Africa, Indian Ocean and South-East Asia, the middle-European population of the great bustard, bukhara deer, aquatic warblers, West-African populations of the African elephant, the saiga antelope, cetaceans of the Pacific Islands, dugongs (large marine mammals), Mediterranean monk seals, the ruddy-headed goose, grassland birds of southern South America, birds of prey of Africa and Eurasia, small cetaceans and manatees of West Africa, sharks, huemuls (Andean deer) and high Andean flamingoes.

UNEP/CMS SECRETARIAT, United Nations Premises, Hermann-Ehlers-Str. 10, 53113 Bonn, Germany T (+49) (228) 815 2426 E secretariat@cms.int W www.cms.int

CITES

The 1973 Convention on International Trade in Endangered Species of Wild Fauna and Flora (CITES) is an agreement between governments to ensure that international trade in specimens of wild animals and plants does not threaten their survival. The convention came into force in the UK in October 1976 and there are currently 175 member countries. Countries party to the convention ban commercial international trade in an agreed list of endangered species and regulate and monitor trade in other species that might become endangered. The convention accords varying degrees of protection to more than 30,000 species of animals and plants whether they are traded as live specimens or as products derived from them, such as fur coats and dried herbs.

The Conference of the Parties to CITES meets every two to three years to review the convention's implementation. The Animal Health agency at the Department for Environment, Food and Rural Affairs carries out the government's responsibilities under CITES.

CITES SECRETARIAT, International Environment House, 11 Chemin des Anémones, CH-1219 Châtelaine, Geneva, Switzerland T (+41) (22) 917 8139/8140 E info@cites.org W www.cites.org

EUROPEAN WILDLIFE TRADE REGULATION

The Council (EC) Regulation on the Protection of Species of Wild Fauna and Flora by Regulating Trade Therein came into force in the UK on 1 June 1997. It is intended to standardise wildlife trade regulations across Europe and to improve the application of CITES.

RAMSAR CONVENTION

The 1971 Ramsar Convention on Wetlands of International Importance entered into force in the UK in May 1976. As at June 2011, 160 countries were party to the convention.

The aim of the convention is the conservation and wise use of wetlands and their resources. Governments that are party to the convention must designate wetlands and include wetland conservation considerations in their land-use planning; 1,933 wetland sites, totalling 189 million hectares, have been designated for inclusion in the list of wetlands of international importance. The UK currently has 168 designated sites covering 1,274,323 hectares. The member countries meet every three years to assess the progress of the convention and the next meeting is scheduled to be held in Bucharest in June 2012.

The UK has set targets under the Ramsar Strategic Plan, 2009–15. Progress towards these is monitored by the UK Ramsar Committee, known as the Joint Working Party. The UK and the Republic of Ireland have established a formal protocol to ensure common monitoring standards for waterbirds in the two countries.

RAMSAR CONVENTION SECRETARIAT,
Rue Mauverney 28, CH-1196 Gland, Switzerland
T (+41) (22) 999 0170 E ramsar@ramsar.org
W www.ramsar.org

UK LEGISLATION

The Wildlife and Countryside Act 1981 gives legal protection to a wide range of wild animals and plants. Every five years the statutory nature conservation agencies (Natural England, Countryside Council for Wales and Scottish Natural Heritage) are required to review schedules 5 (animals, other than birds) and 8 (plants) of the Wildlife and Countryside Act 1981. They make recommendations to the Secretary of State for Environment, Food and Rural Affairs, the National Assembly for Wales and the Scottish government for changes to these schedules. The most recent variation of schedule 5 for England came into effect in February 2008 (the fourth quinquennial review recommended no changes to schedule 8; the fifth is currently under way).

Under section 9 of the act it is an offence to kill, injure, take, possess or sell (whether alive or dead) any wild animal included in schedule 5 of the act and to disturb its place of shelter and protection or to destroy that place. However certain species listed on schedule 5 are protected against some, but not all, of these activities.

Under section 13 of the act it is illegal without a licence to pick, uproot, sell or destroy plants listed in schedule 8. Since January 2001, under the Countryside and Rights of Way Act 2000, persons found guilty of an offence under part 1 of the Wildlife and Countryside Act 1981 face a maximum penalty of up to £5,000 and/or up to a six-month custodial sentence per specimen.

BIRDS

The act lays down a close season for birds (listed on Schedule 2, part 1) from 1 February to 31 August inclusive, each year. Exceptions to these dates are made for:

Capercaillie and (except Scotland) Woodcock – 1 February to 30 September
Snipe – 1 February to 11 August
Birds listed on schedule 2, part 1 (below high water mark) (see below) – 21 February to 31 August
Wild duck and wild geese, in or over any area below the high-water mark of ordinary spring tides – 21 February to 31 August
Birds listed on schedule 2, part 1, which may be killed or taken outside the close season are: capercaillie; coot; certain wild duck (gadwall, goldeneye, mallard, pintail, pochard, shoveler, teal, tufted duck, wigeon); certain wild geese (Canada, greylag, pink-footed, white-fronted (in England and Wales only); golden plover; moorhen; snipe; and woodcock.

Section 16 of the 1981 act allows licences to be issued on either an individual or general basis, to allow the killing, taking and sale of certain birds for specified reasons such as public health and safety. All other wild birds are fully protected by law throughout the year.

ANIMALS PROTECTED BY SCHEDULE 5

Adder (Vipera berus)
Allis Shad (Alosa alosa)
Anemone, Ivell's Sea (Edwardsia ivelli)
Anemone, Starlet Sea (Nematosella vectensis)
Bat, Horseshoe, all species (Rhinolophidae)
Bat, Typical, all species (Vespertilionidae)
Beetle (Hypebaeus flavipes)
Beetle, Bembridge Water (Paracymus aeneus)
Beetle, Lesser Silver Water (Hydrochara caraboides)
Beetle, Mire Pill (Curimopsis nigrita)
Beetle, Moccas (Hypebaeus flavipes)
Beetle, Rainbow Leaf (Chrysolina cerealis)
Beetle, Spangled Water (Graphoderus zonatus)
Beetle, Stag (Lucanus cervus)
Beetle, Violet Click (Limoniscus violaceus)
Beetle, Water (Paracymus aeneus)
Burbot (Lota lota)
Butterfly, Adonis Blue (Lysandra bellargus)
Butterfly, Black Hairstreak (Strymonidia pruni)
Butterfly, Brown Hairstreak (Thecla betulae)
Butterfly, Chalkhill Blue (Lysandra coridon)
Butterfly, Chequered Skipper (Carterocephalus palaemon)
Butterfly, Duke of Burgundy Fritillary (Hamearis lucina)
Butterfly, Glanville Fritillary (Melitaea cinxia)
Butterfly, Heath Fritillary (Mellicta athalia or Melitaea athalia)
Butterfly, High Brown Fritillary (Argynnis adippe)
Butterfly, Large Blue (Maculinea arion)
Butterfly, Large Copper (Lycaena dispar)
Butterfly, Large Heath (Coenonympha tullia)
Butterfly, Large Tortoiseshell (Nymphalis polychloros)
Butterfly, Lulworth Skipper (Thymelicus acteon)
Butterfly, Marsh Fritillary (Eurodryas aurinia)
Butterfly, Mountain Ringlet (Erebia epiphron)
Butterfly, Northern Brown Argus (Aricia artaxerxes)
Butterfly, Pearl-bordered Fritillary (Boloria euphrosyne)
Butterfly, Purple Emperor (Apatura iris)
Butterfly, Silver Spotted Skipper (Hesperia comma)
Butterfly, Silver-studded Blue (Plebejus argus)
Butterfly, Small Blue (Cupido minimus)
Butterfly, Swallowtail (Papilio machaon)

Butterfly, White Letter Hairstreak *(Stymonida w-album)*
Butterfly, Wood White *(Leptidea sinapis)*
Cat, Wild *(Felis silvestris)*
Cicada, New Forest *(Cicadetta montana)*
Crayfish, Atlantic Stream *(Austropotamobius pallipes)*
Cricket, Field *(Gryllus campestris)*
Cricket, Mole *(Gryllotalpa gryllotalpa)*
Cricket, Wart-biter *(Decticus verrucivorus)*
Damselfly, Southern *(Coenagrion mercuriale)*
Dolphin, all species *(Cetacea)*
Dormouse *(Muscardinus avellanarius)*
Dragonfly, Norfolk Aeshna *(Aeshna isosceles)*
Frog, Common *(Rana temporaria)*
Goby, Couch's *(Gobius couchii)*
Goby, Giant *(Gobius cobitis)*
Hatchet Shell, Northern *(Thyasira gouldi)*
Hydroid, Marine *(Clavopsella navis)*
Lagoon Snail *(Paludinella littorina)*
Lagoon Snail, De Folin's *(Caecum armoricum)*
Lagoon Worm, Tentacled *(Alkmaria romijni)*
Leech, Medicinal *(Hirudo medicinalis)*
Lizard, Sand *(Lacerta agilis)*
Lizard, Viviparous *(Lacerta vivipara)*
Marten, Pine *(Martes martes)*
Moth, Barberry Carpet *(Pareulype berberata)*
Moth, Black-veined *(Siona lineata* or *Idaea lineata)*
Moth, Essex Emerald *(Thetidia smaragdaria)*
Moth, Fiery Clearwing *(Bembecia chrysidiformis)*
Moth, Fisher's Estuarine *(Gortyna borelii)*
Moth, New Forest Burnet *(Zygaena viciae)*
Moth, Reddish Buff *(Acosmetia caliginosa)*
Moth, Sussex Emerald *(Thalera fimbrialis)*
Mussel, Fan *(Atrina fragilis)*
Mussel, Freshwater Pearl *(Margaritifera margaritifera)*
Newt, Great Crested (or Warty) *(Triturus cristatus)*
Newt, Palmate *(Triturus helveticus)*
Newt, Smooth *(Triturus vulgaris)*
Otter, Common *(Lutra lutra)*
Porpoise, all species *(Cetacea)*
Sandworm, Lagoon *(Armandia cirrhosa)*
Sea Fan, Pink *(Eunicella verrucosa)*
Sea Slug, Lagoon *(Tenellia adspersa)*
Sea-mat, Trembling *(Victorella pavida)*
Seahorse, Short Snouted (England only) *(Hippocampus hippocampus)*
Seahorse, Spiny (England only) *(Hippocampus guttulatus)*
Shad, Twaite *(Alosa fallax)*
Shark, Angel (England only) *(Squatina squatina)*
Shark, Basking *(Cetorhinus maximus)*
Shrimp, Fairy *(Chirocephalus diaphanus)*
Shrimp, Lagoon Sand *(Gammarus insensibilis)*
Shrimp, Tadpole (Apus) *(Triops cancriformis)*
Slow-worm *(Anguis fragilis)*
Snail, Glutinous *(Myxas glutinosa)*
Snail, Roman (England only) *(Helix pomatia)*
Snail, Sandbowl *(Catinella arenaria)*
Snake, Grass *(Natrix natrix* or *Natrix helvetica)*
Snake, Smooth *(Coronella austriaca)*
Spider, Fen Raft *(Dolomedes plantarius)*
Spider, Ladybird *(Eresus niger)*
Squirrel, Red *(Sciurus vulgaris)*
Sturgeon *(Acipenser sturio)*
Toad, Common *(Bufo bufo)*
Toad, Natterjack *(Bufo calamita)*
Turtle, Flatback *(Cheloniidae/Natator Depressus)*
Turtle, Green Sea *(Chelonia mydas)*
Turtle, Hawksbill *(Eretmochelys imbricate)*
Turtle, Kemp's Ridley Sea *(Lepidochelys kempii)*

Turtle, Leatherback Sea *(Dermochelys coriacea)*
Turtle, Loggerhead Sea *(Caretta caretta)*
Turtle, Olive Ridley *(Lepidochelys olivacea)*
Vendace *(Coregonus albula)*
Vole, Water *(Arvicola terrestris)*
Walrus *(Odobenus rosmarus)*
Whale, all species *(Cetacea)*
Whitefish *(Coregonus lavaretus)*

PLANTS PROTECTED BY SCHEDULE 8

Adder's Tongue, Least *(Ophioglossum lusitanicum)*
Alison, Small *(Alyssum alyssoides)*
Anomodon, Long-leaved *(Anomodon longifolius)*
Beech-lichen, New Forest *(Enterographa elaborata)*
Blackwort *(Southbya nigrella)*
Bluebell *(Hyacinthoides non-scripta)*
Bolete, Royal *(Boletus regius)*
Broomrape, Bedstraw *(Orobanche caryophyllacea)*
Broomrape, Oxtongue *(Orobanche loricata)*
Broomrape, Thistle *(Orobanche reticulata)*
Cabbage, Lundy *(Rhynchosinapis wrightii)*
Calamint, Wood *(Calamintha sylvatica)*
Caloplaca, Snow *(Caloplaca nivalis)*
Catapyrenium, Tree *(Catapyrenium psoromoides)*
Catchfly, Alpine *(Lychnis alpina)*
Catillaria, Laurer's *(Catellaria laureri)*
Centaury, Slender *(Centaurium tenuiflorum)*
Cinquefoil, Rock *(Potentilla rupestris)*
Cladonia, Convoluted *(Cladonia convoluta)*
Cladonia, Upright Mountain *(Cladonia stricta)*
Clary, Meadow *(Salvia pratensis)*
Club-rush, Triangular *(Scirpus triquetrus)*
Colt's-foot, Purple *(Homogyne alpina)*
Cotoneaster, Wild *(Cotoneaster integerrimus)*
Cottongrass, Slender *(Eriophorum gracile)*
Cow-wheat, Field *(Melampyrum arvense)*
Crocus, Sand *(Romulea columnae)*
Crystalwort, Lizard *(Riccia bifurca)*
Cudweed, Broad-leaved *(Filago pyramidata)*
Cudweed, Jersey *(Gnaphalium luteoalbum)*
Cudweed, Red-tipped *(Filago lutescens)*
Cut-grass *(Leersia oryzoides)*
Diapensia *(Diapensia lapponica)*
Dock, Shore *(Rumex rupestris)*
Earwort, Marsh *(Jamesoniella undulifolia)*
Eryngo, Field *(Eryngium campestre)*
Fern, Dickie's Bladder *(Cystopteris dickieana)*
Fern, Killarney *(Trichomanes speciosum)*
Flapwort, Norfolk *(Leiocolea rutheana)*
Fleabane, Alpine *(Erigeron borealis)*
Fleabane, Small *(Pulicaria vulgaris)*
Fleawort, South Stack *(Tephroseris integrifolia ssp maritima)*
Frostwort, Pointed *(Gymnomitrion apiculatum)*
Fungus, Hedgehog *(Hericium erinaceum)*
Galingale, Brown *(Cyperus fuscus)*
Gentian, Alpine *(Gentiana nivalis)*
Gentian, Dune *(Gentianella uliginosa)*
Gentian, Early *(Gentianella anglica)*
Gentian, Fringed *(Gentianella ciliata)*
Gentian, Spring *(Gentiana verna)*
Germander, Cut-leaved *(Teucrium botrys)*
Germander, Water *(Teucrium scordium)*
Gladiolus, Wild *(Gladiolus illyricus)*
Goblin Lights *(Catolechia wahlenbergii)*
Goosefoot, Stinking *(Chenopodium vulvaria)*
Grass-poly *(Lythrum hyssopifolia)*
Grimmia, Blunt-leaved *(Grimmia unicolor)*
Gyalecta, Elm *(Gyalecta ulmi)*

Hare's-ear, Sickle-leaved *(Bupleurum falcatum)*
Hare's-ear, Small *(Bupleurum baldense)*
Hawk's-beard, Stinking *(Crepis foetida)*
Hawkweed, Northroe *(Hieracium northroense)*
Hawkweed, Shetland *(Hieracium zetlandicum)*
Hawkweed, Weak-leaved *(Hieracium attenuatifolium)*
Heath, Blue *(Phyllodoce caerulea)*
Helleborine, Red *(Cephalanthera rubra)*
Helleborine, Young's *(Epipactis youngiana)*
Horsetail, Branched *(Equisetum ramosissimum)*
Hound's-tongue, Green *(Cynoglossum germanicum)*
Knawel, Perennial *(Scleranthus perennis)*
Knotgrass, Sea *(Polygonum maritimum)*
Lady's-slipper *(Cypripedium calceolus)*
Lecanactis, Churchyard *(Lecanactis hemisphaerica)*
Lecanora, Tarn *(Lecanora archariana)*
Lecidea, Copper *(Lecidea inops)*
Leek, Round-headed *(Allium sphaerocephalon)*
Lettuce, Least *(Lactuca saligna)*
Lichen, Arctic Kidney *(Nephroma arcticum)*
Lichen, Ciliate Strap *(Heterodermia leucomelos)*
Lichen, Coralloid Rosette *(Heterodermia propagulifera)*
Lichen, Ear-lobed Dog *(Peltigera lepidophora)*
Lichen, Forked Hair *(Bryoria furcellata)*
Lichen, Golden Hair *(Teloschistes flavicans)*
Lichen, Orange-fruited Elm *(Caloplaca luteoalba)*
Lichen, River Jelly *(Collema dichotomum)*
Lichen, Scaly Breck *(Squamarina lentigera)*
Lichen, Starry Breck *(Buellia asterella)*
Lily, Snowdon *(Lloydia serotina)*
Liverwort, Lindenberg's Leafy *(Adelanthus lindenbergianus)*
Marsh-mallow, Rough *(Althaea hirsuta)*
Marshwort, Creeping *(Apium repens)*
Milk-parsley, Cambridge *(Selinum carvifolia)*
Moss *(Drepanocladius vernicosus)*
Moss, Alpine Copper *(Mielichoferia mielichoferi)*
Moss, Baltic Bog *(Sphagnum balticum)*
Moss, Blue Dew *(Saelania glaucescens)*
Moss, Blunt-leaved Bristle *(Orthotrichum obtusifolium)*
Moss, Bright Green Cave *(Cyclodictyon laetevirens)*
Moss, Cordate Beard *(Barbula cordata)*
Moss, Cornish Path *(Ditrichum cornubicum)*
Moss, Derbyshire Feather *(Thamnobryum angustifolium)*
Moss, Dune Thread *(Bryum mamillatum)*
Moss, Flamingo *(Desmatodon cernuus)*
Moss, Glaucous Beard *(Barbula glauca)*
Moss, Green Shield *(Buxbaumia viridis)*
Moss, Hair Silk *(Plagiothecium piliferum)*
Moss, Knothole *(Zygodon forsteri)*
Moss, Large Yellow Feather *(Scorpidium turgescens)*
Moss, Millimetre *(Micromitrium tenerum)*
Moss, Multi-fruited River *(Cryphaea lamyana)*
Moss, Nowell's Limestone *(Zygodon gracilis)*
Moss, Polar Feather *(Hygrohypnum polare)*
Moss, Rigid Apple *(Bartramia stricta)*
Moss, Round-leaved Feather *(Rhyncostegium rotundifolium)*
Moss, Schleicher's Thread *(Bryum schleicheri)*
Moss, Slender Green Feather *(Drepanocladus vernicosus)*
Moss, Triangular Pygmy *(Acaulon triquetrum)*
Moss, Vaucher's Feather *(Hypnum vaucheri)*
Mudwort, Welsh *(Limosella austeralis)*
Naiad, Holly-leaved *(Najas marina)*
Naiad, Slender *(Najas flexilis)*
Orache, Stalked *(Halimione pedunculata)*

Orchid, Early Spider *(Ophrys sphegodes)*
Orchid, Fen *(Liparis loeselii)*
Orchid, Ghost *(Epipogium aphyllum)*
Orchid, Lapland Marsh *(Dactylorhiza lapponica)*
Orchid, Late Spider *(Ophrys fuciflora)*
Orchid, Lizard *(Himantoglossum hircinum)*
Orchid, Military *(Orchis militaris)*
Orchid, Monkey *(Orchis simia)*
Pannaria, Caledonia *(Panneria ignobilis)*
Parmelia, New Forest *(Parmelia minarum)*
Parmentaria, Oil Stain *(Parmentaria chilensis)*
Pear, Plymouth *(Pyrus cordata)*
Penny-cress, Perfoliate *(Thlaspi perfoliatum)*
Pennyroyal *(Mentha pulegium)*
Pertusaria, Alpine Moss *(Pertusaria bryontha)*
Petalwort *(Petallophyllum ralfsi)*
Physcia, Southern Grey *(Physcia tribacioides)*
Pigmyweed *(Crassula aquatica)*
Pine, Ground *(Ajuga chamaepitys)*
Pink, Cheddar *(Dianthus gratianopolitanus)*
Pink, Childing *(Petroraghia nanteuilii)*
Pink, Deptford (England and Wales only) *(Dianthus armeria)*
Polypore, Oak *(Buglossoporus pulvinus)*
Pseudocyphellaria, Ragged *(Pseudocyphellaria lacerata)*
Psora, Rusty Alpine *(Psora rubiformis)*
Puffball, Sandy Stilt *(Battarraea phalloides)*
Ragwort, Fen *(Senecio paludosus)*
Ramping-fumitory, Martin's *(Fumaria martinii)*
Rampion, Spiked *(Phyteuma spicatum)*
Restharrow, Small *(Ononis reclinata)*
Rock-cress, Alpine *(Arabis alpina)*
Rock-cress, Bristol *(Arabis stricta)*
Rustwort, Western *(Marsupella profunda)*
Sandwort, Norwegian *(Arenaria norvegica)*
Sandwort, Teesdale *(Minuartia stricta)*
Saxifrage, Drooping *(Saxifraga cernua)*
Saxifrage, Tufted *(Saxifraga cespitosa)*
Saxifrage, Yellow Marsh *(Saxifrage hirulus)*
Solenopsora, Serpentine *(Solenopsora liparina)*
Solomon's-seal, Whorled *(Polygonatum verticillatum)*
Sow-thistle, Alpine *(Cicerbita alpina)*
Spearwort, Adder's-tongue *(Ranunculus ophioglossifolius)*
Speedwell, Fingered *(Veronica triphyllos)*
Speedwell, Spiked *(Veronica spicata)*
Spike-rush, Dwarf *(Eleocharis parvula)*
Star-of-Bethlehem, Early *(Gagea bohemica)*
Starfruit *(Damasonium alisma)*
Stonewort, Bearded *(Chara canescens)*
Stonewort, Foxtail *(Lamprothamnium papulosum)*
Strapwort *(Corrigiola litoralis)*
Sulphur-tresses, Alpine *(Alectoria ochroleuca)*
Threadmoss, Long-leaved *(Bryum neodamense)*
Turpswort *(Geocalyx graveolens)*
Violet, Fen *(Viola persicifolia)*
Viper's-grass *(Scorzonera humilis)*
Water-plantain, Floating *(Luronium natans)*
Water-plantain, Ribbon-leaved *(Alisma gramineum)*
Wood-sedge, Starved *(Carex depauperata)*
Woodsia, Alpine *(Woodsia alpina)*
Woodsia, Oblong *(Woodsia ilvenis)*
Wormwood, Field *(Artemisia campestris)*
Woundwort, Downy *(Stachys germanica)*
Woundwort, Limestone *(Stachys alpina)*
Yellow-rattle, Greater *(Rhinanthus serotinus)*

WORLD HERITAGE SITES

The Convention Concerning the Protection of the World Cultural and Natural Heritage was adopted by the United Nations Educational, Scientific and Cultural Organization (UNESCO) in 1972 and ratified by the UK in 1984. As at June 2011, 187 states were party to the convention. The convention provides for the identification, protection and conservation of cultural and natural sites of outstanding universal value.

Cultural sites may be:
• sites representing architectural and technological innovation or cultural interchange
• sites of artistic, historic, aesthetic, archaeological, scientific, ethnologic or anthropologic value
• 'cultural landscapes', ie sites whose characteristics are marked by significant interactions between human populations and their natural environment
• exceptional examples of traditional settlement or land- or sea-use; especially those threatened by irreversible change.

Natural sites may be:
• those with remarkable physical, biological or geological formations
• those with outstanding universal value from the point of view of science, conservation or natural beauty
• the habitat of threatened species and plants.

Governments which are party to the convention nominate sites in their country for inclusion in the World Cultural and Natural Heritage List. Nominations are considered by the World Heritage Committee, an inter-governmental committee composed of 21 representatives of the parties to the convention. The committee is advised by the International Council on Monuments and Sites (ICOMOS), the International Centre for the Study of the Preservation and Restoration of Cultural Property (ICCROM) and the International Union for the Conservation of Nature (IUCN). ICOMOS evaluates and reports on proposed cultural and mixed sites, ICCROM provides expert advice and training on how to conserve and restore cultural property and IUCN provides technical evaluations of natural heritage sites and reports on the state of conservation of listed sites. The Department for Culture, Media and Sport represents the UK government in matters relating to the convention.

A prerequisite for inclusion in the World Heritage List is the existence of an effective legal protection system in the country in which the site is situated and a detailed management plan to ensure the conservation of the site. Inclusion in the list does not confer any greater degree of protection on the site than that offered by the national protection framework.

If a site is considered to be in serious danger of decay or damage, the committee may add it to the World Heritage in Danger List. Sites on this list may benefit from particular attention or emergency measures to allay threats and allow them to retain their world heritage status, or in extreme cases of damage or neglect they may lose their world heritage status completely.

Financial support for the conservation of sites on the World Cultural and Natural Heritage List is provided by the World Heritage Fund, administered by the World Heritage Committee. The fund's income is derived from compulsory and voluntary contributions from the states party to the convention and from private donations.

DESIGNATED SITES

As at 29 June 2011, following the 35th session of the World Heritage Committee, 936 sites were inscribed on the World Cultural and Natural Heritage List. Of these, 25 are in the UK and three in British overseas territories; 23 are listed for their cultural significance (†), four for their natural significance (*) and one for both cultural and natural significance. The year in which sites were designated appears in parentheses. In 2005 Hadrian's Wall, a World Heritage Site in its own right since 1987, was joined by the upper German-Raetian Limes to form the first section of a trans-national world heritage site, Frontiers of the Roman Empire.

UNITED KINGDOM
†Bath – the city (1987)
†Blaenarvon industrial landscape, Wales (2000)
†Blenheim Palace and Park, Oxfordshire (1987)
†Canterbury Cathedral, St Augustine's Abbey, St Martin's Church, Kent (1988)
†Castle and town walls of King Edward I, north Wales – Beaumaris, Caernarfon Castle, Conwy Castle, Harlech Castle, Ynys Mon (Isle of Anglesey) (1986)
†Cornwall and west Devon mining landscape (2006)
†Derwent Valley Mills, Derbyshire (2001)
*Dorset and east Devon coast (2001)
†Durham Cathedral and Castle (1986)
†Edinburgh old and new towns (1995)
†Frontiers of the Roman Empire, Hadrian's Wall, northern England (1987, 2005)
*Giant's Causeway and Causeway coast, Co. Antrim (1986)
†Greenwich, London – maritime Greenwich, including the Royal Naval College, Old Royal Observatory, Queen's House, town centre (1997)
†Heart of Neolithic Orkney (1999)
†Ironbridge Gorge, Shropshire – the world's first iron bridge and other early industrial sites (1986)
†Liverpool – six areas of the maritime mercantile city (2004)
†New Lanark, South Lanarkshire, Scotland (2001)
†Pontcysyllte Aqueduct and Canal, Wrexham, Wales (2009)
†Royal Botanic Gardens, Kew (2003)
†*St Kilda, Eilean Siar (Western Isles) (1986)
†Saltaire, West Yorkshire (2001)
†Stonehenge, Avebury and related megalithic sites, Wiltshire (1986)
†Studley Royal Park, Fountains Abbey, St Mary's Church, N. Yorkshire (1986)
†Tower of London (1988)
†Westminster Abbey, Palace of Westminster, St Margaret's Church, London (1987)

BRITISH OVERSEAS TERRITORIES
*Henderson Island, Pitcairn Islands, South Pacific Ocean (1988)
*Gough Island and Inaccessible Island (part of Tristan da Cunha), South Atlantic Ocean (1995)
†St George town and related fortifications, Bermuda (2000)

WORLD HERITAGE CENTRE, UNESCO, 7 Place de Fontenoy, 75352 Paris 07 SP, France
W http://whc.unesco.org

HISTORIC BUILDINGS AND MONUMENTS

ENGLAND

Under the Planning (Listed Buildings and Conservation Areas) Act 1990, the Secretary of State for Culture, Media and Sport has a statutory duty to approve lists of buildings or groups of buildings in England which are of special architectural or historic interest. In November 2009 responsibility for compiling the list of buildings was passed to English Heritage. Under the Ancient Monuments and Archaeological Areas Act 1979 as amended by the National Heritage Act 1983, the secretary of state is also responsible for compiling a schedule of ancient monuments. Decisions are taken on the advice of English Heritage. On 1 April 2005 responsibility for the administration of the listing system was transferred from the secretary of state to English Heritage. This marked the start of a programme of changes designed to increase the involvement and awareness of the property owner and make the listing process more straightforward and more accountable.

LISTED BUILDINGS

Listed buildings are classified into Grade I, Grade II* and Grade II. There are around 374,000 individual listed buildings in England, of which approximately 92 per cent are Grade II listed. Almost all pre-1700 buildings are listed, as are most buildings of 1700 to 1840. English Heritage carries out thematic surveys of particular types of buildings with a view to making recommendations for listing, and members of the public may propose a building for consideration. The main purpose of listing is to ensure that care is taken in deciding the future of a building. No changes which affect the architectural or historic character of a listed building can be made without listed building consent (in addition to planning permission where relevant). Applications for listed building consent are normally dealt with by the local planning authority, although English Heritage is always consulted about proposals affecting Grade I and Grade II* properties. It is a criminal offence to demolish a listed building, or alter it in such a way as to affect its character, without consent.

SCHEDULED MONUMENTS

There are around 19,700 scheduled monuments in England. English Heritage is carrying out a Monuments Protection Programme assessing archaeological sites with a view to making recommendations for scheduling, and members of the public may propose a monument for consideration. All monuments proposed for scheduling are considered to be of national importance. Where buildings are both scheduled and listed, ancient monuments legislation takes precedence. The main purpose of scheduling a monument is to preserve it for the future and to protect it from damage, destruction or any unnecessary interference. Once a monument has been scheduled, scheduled monument consent is required before any works can be carried out. The scope of the control is more extensive and more detailed than that applied to listed buildings, but certain minor works, as detailed in the Ancient Monuments (Class Consents) Order 1994, may be carried out without consent. It is a criminal offence to carry out unauthorised work to scheduled monuments.

WALES

Under the Planning (Listed Buildings and Conservation Areas) Act 1990 and the Ancient Monuments and Archaeological Areas Act 1979, the National Assembly for Wales is responsible for listing buildings and scheduling monuments in Wales on the advice of Cadw (the Welsh Assembly's historic environment division), the Historic Buildings Advisory Council for Wales, the Ancient Monuments Advisory Board for Wales and the Royal Commission on the Ancient and Historical Monuments of Wales (RCAHMW). The criteria for evaluating buildings are similar to those in England and the same listing system is used. There are approximately 29,900 listed buildings and 4,134 scheduled monuments in Wales.

SCOTLAND

Under the Planning (Listed Buildings and Conservation Areas) (Scotland) Act 1997 and the Ancient Monuments and Archaeological Areas Act 1979, Scottish ministers are responsible for listing buildings and scheduling monuments in Scotland on the advice of Historic Scotland, the Historic Environment Advisory Council for Scotland (HEACS) and the Royal Commission on the Ancient and Historical Monuments of Scotland (RCAHMS). The criteria for evaluating buildings are similar to those in England but an A, B, C(S) categorisation is used. As at March 2011 there were 47,643 listed buildings and 8,170 scheduled monuments in Scotland.

NORTHERN IRELAND

Under the Planning (Northern Ireland) Order 1991 and the Historic Monuments and Archaeological Objects (Northern Ireland) Order 1995, the Northern Ireland Environment Agency (part of the Department of the Environment of the Northern Ireland) is responsible for listing buildings and scheduling monuments. The Historic Buildings Council for Northern Ireland and the relevant district council must be consulted on listing proposals, and the Historic Monuments Council for Northern Ireland must be consulted on scheduling proposals. The criteria for evaluating buildings are similar to those in England but an A, B+, B1 and B2 categorisation is used. As at March 2011 there were 8,742 listed buildings and 1,897 scheduled monuments in Northern Ireland.

ENGLAND

For more information on English Heritage properties, including those listed below, the official website is www.english-heritage.org.uk
For more information on National Trust properties in England, including those listed below, the official website is www.nationaltrust.org.uk
(EH) English Heritage property
(NT) National Trust property

A LA RONDE (NT), Exmouth, Devon EX8 5BD
  T 01395-265514
  Unique 16-sided house completed c.1796
ALNWICK CASTLE, Alnwick, Northumberland NE66 1NQ
  T 01665-510777 W www.alnwickcastle.com
  Seat of the Dukes of Northumberland since 1309; Italian Renaissance-style interior; gardens with spectacular water features
ALTHORP, Northants NN7 4HQ T 01604-770107
  W www.althorp.com
  Spencer family seat; Diana, Princess of Wales memorabilia
ANGLESEY ABBEY (NT), Lode, Cambs CB25 9EJ
  T 01223-810080
  House built c.1600; houses many paintings and a unique clock collection; gardens and Lode Mill
APSLEY HOUSE (EH), London W1J 7NT T 020-7499 5676
  Built by Robert Adam 1771–8, home of the Dukes of Wellington since 1817 and known as 'No. 1 London'; collection of fine and decorative arts
ARUNDEL CASTLE, Arundel, W. Sussex BN18 9AB
  T 01903-882173 W www.arundelcastle.org
  Castle dating from the Norman Conquest; seat of the Dukes of Norfolk
AVEBURY (EH/NT), Wilts SN8 1RF T 01672-539250
  Remains of stone circles constructed 4,000 years ago surrounding the later village of Avebury
BANQUETING HOUSE, Whitehall, London SW1A 2ER
  T 0844-482 7777 W www.hrp.org.uk
  Designed by Inigo Jones; ceiling paintings by Rubens; site of the execution of Charles I
BASILDON PARK (NT), Reading, Berks RG8 9NR
  T 0118-984 3040
  Palladian mansion built in 1776–83 by John Carr
BATTLE ABBEY (EH), Battle, E. Sussex TN33 0AD
  T 01424-775705
  Remains of the abbey founded by William the Conqueror on the site of the Battle of Hastings
BEAULIEU, Brockenhurst, Hants SO42 7ZN T 01590-612345
  W www.beaulieu.co.uk
  House and gardens; Beaulieu Abbey and exhibition of monastic life; National Motor Museum
BEESTON CASTLE (EH), Cheshire CW6 9TX
  T 01829-260464
  Built in the 13th century by Ranulf, sixth Earl of Chester
BELTON HOUSE (NT), Grantham, Lincs NG32 2LS
  T 01476-566116
  17th-century house; formal gardens in landscaped park
BELVOIR CASTLE, Grantham, Lincs NG32 1PE
  T 01476-871002 W www.belvoircastle.com
  Seat of the Dukes of Rutland; 19th-century Gothic-style castle
BERKELEY CASTLE, Glos GL13 9BQ T 01453-810332
  W www.berkeley-castle.com
  Completed 1153; site of the murder of Edward II (1327)

BIRDOSWALD FORT (EH), Cumbria CA8 7DD
  T 01697-747602
  Stretch of Hadrian's Wall with Roman wall fort, turret and milecastle
BLENHEIM PALACE, Woodstock, Oxon OX20 1PX
  T 01993-810500 W www.blenheimpalace.com
  Seat of the Dukes of Marlborough and Winston Churchill's birthplace; designed by Vanbrugh
BLICKLING ESTATE (NT), Blickling, Norfolk NR11 6NF
  T 01263-738030
  Jacobean house with state rooms; extensive gardens, temple and 18th-century orangery
BODIAM CASTLE (NT), Bodiam, E. Sussex TN32 5UA
  T 01580-830196
  Well-preserved medieval moated castle built in 1385
BOLSOVER CASTLE (EH), Bolsover, Derbys S44 6PR
  T 01246-822844
  17th-century building on site of medieval castle
BOSCOBEL HOUSE (EH), Bishops Wood, Staffs ST19 9AR
  T 01902-850244
  Timber-framed 17th-century hunting lodge; refuge of fugitive Charles II
BOUGHTON HOUSE, Kettering, Northants NN14 1BJ
  T 01536-515731 W www.boughtonhouse.org.uk
  A 17th-century house with French-style additions; home of the Dukes of Buccleuch and Queensbury
BOWOOD HOUSE, Calne, Wilts SN11 0LZ
  T 01249-812102 W www.bowood-house.co.uk
  An 18th-century house in Capability Brown park, with lake, temple and arboretum
BRONTË PARSONAGE, Haworth, W. Yorks BD22 8DR
  T 01535-642323 W www.bronte.org.uk
  Home of the Brontë sisters; museum and memorabilia
BUCKFAST ABBEY, Buckfastleigh, Devon TQ11 0EE
  T 01364-645500 W www.buckfast.org.uk
  Benedictine monastery on medieval foundations
BUCKINGHAM PALACE, London SW1A 1AA
  T 020-7766 7300 W www.royalcollection.org.uk
  Purchased by George III in 1761, and the Sovereign's official London residence since 1837; 18 state rooms, including the Throne Room, and Picture Gallery
BUCKLAND ABBEY (NT), Yelverton, Devon PL20 6EY
  T 01822-853607
  13th-century Cistercian monastery; home of Sir Francis Drake
BURGHLEY HOUSE, Stamford, Lincs PE9 3JY
  T 01780-752451 W www.burghley.co.uk
  Late Elizabethan house built by William Cecil, first Lord Burghley
CALKE ABBEY (NT), Ticknall, Derbys DE73 7LE
  T 01332-863822
  Baroque 18th-century mansion
CARISBROOKE CASTLE (EH), Newport, Isle of Wight
  PO30 1XY T 01983-522107
  W www.carisbrookecastlemuseum.org.uk
  Norman castle; museum; prison of Charles I 1647–8
CARLISLE CASTLE (EH), Carlisle, Cumbria CA3 8UR
  T 01228-591922
  Medieval castle; prison of Mary Queen of Scots
CARLYLE'S HOUSE (NT), Chelsea, London SW3 5HL
  T 020-7352 7087
  Home of Thomas and Jane Carlyle
CASTLE ACRE PRIORY (EH), Swaffham, Norfolk
  PE32 2XD T 01760-755394
  Remains include 12th-century church and prior's lodgings
CASTLE DROGO (NT), Drewsteignton, Devon EX6 6PB
  T 01647-433306
  Granite castle designed by Lutyens

CASTLE HOWARD, N. Yorks YO60 7DA T 01653-648333
W www.castlehoward.co.uk
Designed by Vanbrugh 1699–1726; mausoleum
designed by Hawksmoor

CASTLE RISING CASTLE (EH), King's Lynn, Norfolk
PE31 6AH T 01553-631330 W www.castlerising.co.uk
12th-century keep in a massive earthwork with
gatehouse and bridge

CHARLES DARWIN'S HOUSE (EH), Down House, Luxted
Road, Downe, Kent BR6 7JT T 01689-859119
The family home where Darwin wrote *On the Origin
of Species*

CHARTWELL (NT), Westerham, Kent TN16 1PS
T 01732-868381
Home of Sir Winston Churchill

CHATSWORTH, Bakewell, Derbys DE45 1PP
T 01246-565300 W www.chatsworth.org
Tudor mansion set in magnificent parkland

CHESTERS ROMAN FORT (EH), Chollerford,
Northumberland NE46 4EU T 01434-681379
Roman cavalry fort built to guard Hadrian's Wall

CHYSAUSTER ANCIENT VILLAGE (EH), Penzance,
Cornwall TR20 8XA T 07831-757934
Remains of Celtic settlement; eight stone-walled
homesteads

CLANDON PARK (NT), West Clandon, Guildford, Surrey
GU4 7RQ T 01483-222482 W www.clandonpark.co.uk
18th-century Palladian mansion and gardens, which
contain a Maori meeting house, removed from New
Zealand in 1892

CLIFFORD'S TOWER (EH), York YO1 9SA
T 01904-646940 W www.cliffordstower.com
13th-century tower built on a mound; remains of
a castle built by William the Conqueror

CLIVEDEN (NT), Taplow, Bucks SL6 0JA T 01494-755562
Former home of the Astors, now a hotel set in garden
and woodland

CORBRIDGE ROMAN SITE (EH), Corbridge,
Northumberland NE45 5NT T 01434-632349
Excavated central area of a Roman town and successive
military bases

CORFE CASTLE (NT), Wareham, Dorset BH20 5EZ
T 01929-481294
Ruined former royal castle dating from the 11th
century

CROFT CASTLE AND PARKLAND (NT), Yarpole,
Herefordshire HR6 9PW T 01568-780246
Pre-Conquest border castle with Georgian-Gothic
interior

DEAL CASTLE (EH), Deal, Kent CT14 7BA T 01304-372762
Largest of the coastal defence forts built by Henry VIII

DICKENS HOUSE, Doughty Street, London WC1N 2LX
T 020-7405 2127 W www.dickensmuseum.com
House occupied by Dickens 1837–9; manuscripts,
furniture and portraits

DOVE COTTAGE, Grasmere, Cumbria LA22 9SH
T 01539-435544 W www.wordsworth.org.uk
Wordsworth's home 1799–1808; museum

DOVER CASTLE (EH), Dover, Kent CT16 1HU
T 01304-211067
Castle with Roman, Saxon and Norman features;
wartime operations rooms

DR JOHNSON'S HOUSE, Gough Square, London
EC4A 3DE T 020-7353 3745 W www.drjohnsonshouse.org
Home of Samuel Johnson 1748–59

DUNSTANBURGH CASTLE (EH/NT), Craster,
nr Alnwick, Northumberland NE66 3TT T 01665-576231
14th-century castle ruins on a cliff with a substantial
gatehouse-keep

ELTHAM PALACE (EH), Eltham, London SE9 5QE
T 020-8294 2548
Combines an Art Deco country house and remains of
medieval palace set in moated gardens

FARLEIGH HUNGERFORD CASTLE (EH), Bath,
Somerset BA2 7RS T 01225-754026
Late 14th-century castle with two courts; chapel with
tomb of Sir Thomas Hungerford

FARNHAM CASTLE KEEP (EH), Farnham, Surrey
GA9 0AG T 01252-721194 W www.farnhamcastle.com
Large 12th-century castle keep with motte and
bailey wall

FISHBOURNE ROMAN PALACE, Salthill Road,
Fishbourne, Chichester, W. Sussex PO19 3QR
T 01243-789829 W www.sussexpast.co.uk
Excavated Roman palace with largest collection of
in-situ mosaics in Britain

FOUNTAINS ABBEY (NT), nr Ripon, N. Yorks HG4 3DY
T 01765-608888 W www.fountainsabbey.org.uk
Deer park; St Mary's Church; ruined Cistercian
monastery; Georgian water garden

FRAMLINGHAM CASTLE (EH), Woodbridge, Suffolk
IP13 9BP T 01728-724189
Castle (*c.*1200) with high curtain walls enclosing an
almshouse (1639)

FURNESS ABBEY (EH), Barrow-in-Furness, Cumbria
LA13 0PJ T 01229-823420
Remains of church and cloister buildings founded
in 1123

GLASTONBURY ABBEY, Glastonbury, Somerset BA6 9EL
T 01458-831631 W www.glastonburyabbey.com
Ruins of a 12th-century abbey rebuilt after fire; site of
an early Christian settlement

GOODRICH CASTLE (EH), Ross-on-Wye, Herefordshire
HR9 6HY T 01600-890538
Remains of 13th-century castle with 12th-century
keep

GREENWICH, London SE10 9NF
W www.visitgreenwich.org.uk
Former Royal Observatory (founded 1675) housing
the time ball and zero meridian of longitude; the
Queen's House, designed for Queen Anne, wife of
James I, by Inigo Jones; Painted Hall and Chapel (Old
Royal Naval College)

GRIMES GRAVES (EH), Brandon, Norfolk IP26 5DE
T 01842-810656
Neolithic flint mines; one shaft can be descended

GUILDHALL, London EC2P 2EJ T 020-7606 3030
W www.cityoflondon.gov.uk
Centre of civic government of the City built *c.* 1441;
facade built 1788–9

HADDON HALL, Bakewell, Derbys DE45 1LA
T 01629-812855 W www.haddonhall.co.uk
Well-preserved 12th-century manor house

HAILES ABBEY (EH), Cheltenham, Glos GL54 5PB
T 01242-602398
Ruins of a 13th-century Cistercian monastery

HAM HOUSE AND GARDEN (NT), Richmond-upon-
Thames, Surrey TW10 7RS T 020-8940 1950
Stuart house with lavish interiors and formal gardens

HAMPTON COURT PALACE, East Molesey, Surrey
KT8 9AU T 0844-482 7777 W www.hrp.org.uk
16th-century palace with additions by Wren

HARDWICK HALL (NT), Chesterfield, Derbys S44 5QJ
T 01246-850430
Built 1591–7 for Bess of Hardwick

HARDY'S BIRTHPLACE (NT), Higher Bockhampton,
Dorset DT2 8QJ T 01305-262366
Birthplace and home of Thomas Hardy

HAREWOOD HOUSE, Harewood, W. Yorks LS17 9LG
T 0113-218 1010 W www.harewood.org
18th-century house designed by John Carr and Robert
Adam; park by Capability Brown

HATFIELD HOUSE, Hatfield, Herts AL9 5NQ
T 01707-287010 W www.hatfield-house.co.uk
Jacobean house built by Robert Cecil; surviving wing
of Royal Palace of Hatfield (c.1485)

HELMSLEY CASTLE (EH), Helmsley, N. Yorks YO62 5AB
T 01439-770442
12th-century keep and curtain wall with 16th-century
buildings; spectacular earthwork defences

HEVER CASTLE, nr Edenbridge, Kent TN8 7NG
T 01732-865224 W www.hevercastle.co.uk
13th-century double-moated castle; childhood home
of Anne Boleyn

HOLKER HALL, Cumbria LA11 7PL T 01539-558328
W www.holker.co.uk
Former home of the Dukes of Devonshire;
award-winning gardens

HOLKHAM HALL, Wells-next-the-Sea, Norfolk NR23 1AB
T 01328-710227 W www.holkham.co.uk
Palladian mansion; notable fine art collection

HOUSESTEADS ROMAN FORT (EH), Hexham,
Northumberland NE47 6NN T 01434-344363
Excavated infantry fort on Hadrian's Wall with
museum

HUGHENDEN MANOR (NT), High Wycombe, Bucks
HP14 4LA T 01494-755565
Home of Disraeli; small formal garden

JANE AUSTEN'S HOUSE, Chawton, Hants GU34 1SD
T 01420-83262
W www.jane-austens-house-museum.org.uk
Jane Austen's home from 1809 to 1817

KEDLESTON HALL (NT), Derbys DE22 5JH
T 01332-842191
Classical Palladian mansion built 1759–65; complete
Robert Adam interiors

KELMSCOTT MANOR, nr Lechlade, Glos GL7 3HJ
T 01367-252486 W www.kelmscottmanor.org.uk
Summer home of William Morris, with products of
Morris and Co.

KENILWORTH CASTLE (EH), Kenilworth, Warks CV8 1NE
T 01926-852078
Largest castle ruin in England

KENSINGTON PALACE, Kensington Gardens, London
W8 4PX T 0870-482 7777 W www.hrp.org.uk
Built in 1605 and enlarged by Wren; birthplace of
Queen Victoria; 'Enchanted Palace' exhibition

KENWOOD HOUSE (EH), Hampstead Lane, London
NW3 7JR T 020-8348 1286
Neo-classical villa housing the Iveagh bequest of
paintings and furniture

KEW PALACE, Richmond-upon-Thames, Surrey TW9 3AB
T 0870-482 7777 W www.hrp.org.uk
Includes Queen Charlotte's Cottage, used by King
George III and family as a summerhouse

KINGSTON LACY (NT), Wimborne Minster, Dorset
BH21 4EA T 01202-883402
17th-century house with 19th-century alterations;
important art collection

KNEBWORTH HOUSE, Knebworth, Herts SG3 6PY
T 01438-812661 W www.knebworthhouse.com
Tudor manor house concealed by 19th-century Gothic
decoration; Lutyens gardens

KNOLE (NT), Sevenoaks, Kent TN15 0RP T 01732-450608
House dating from 1456 set in parkland; fine art
collection; birthplace of Vita Sackville-West

LAMBETH PALACE, London SE1 7JU T 020-7898 1200
W www.archbishopofcanterbury.org
Official residence of the Archbishop of Canterbury
since the 13th century

LANERCOST PRIORY (EH), Brampton, Cumbria CA8 2HQ
T 01697-73030
The nave of the Augustinian priory church, c.1166, is
still used; remains of other claustral buildings

LANHYDROCK (NT), Bodmin, Cornwall PL30 5AD
T 01208-265950
House dating from the 17th century; 50 rooms,
including kitchen and nursery

LEEDS CASTLE, nr Maidstone, Kent ME17 1PL
T 01622-765400 W www.leeds-castle.com
Castle dating from the 12th century, on two islands
in lake

LEVENS HALL, Kendal, Cumbria LA8 0PD T 01539-560321
W www.levenshall.co.uk
Elizabethan house with unique topiary garden (1694);
steam engine collection

LINCOLN CASTLE, Lincoln, Lincs LN1 3AA
T 01522-511068 W www.lincolnshire.gov.uk
Built by William the Conqueror in 1068

LINDISFARNE PRIORY (EH), Holy Island,
Northumberland TD15 2RX T 01289-389200
Founded in AD 635; re-established in the 12th century
as a Benedictine priory, now ruined

LITTLE MORETON HALL (NT), Congleton, Cheshire
CW12 4SD T 01260-272018
Timber-framed moated Tudor manor house with
knot garden

LONGLEAT HOUSE, Warminster, Wilts BA12 7NW
T 01985-844400 W www.longleat.co.uk
Elizabethan house in Italian Renaissance style;
safari park

LULLINGSTONE ROMAN VILLA (EH), Eynsford, Kent
DA4 0JA T 01322-863467
Large villa occupied for much of the Roman period;
fine mosaics

MARBLE HILL HOUSE (EH), Twickenham, Middx
TW1 2NL T 020-8892 5115
English Palladian villa with Georgian paintings
and furniture

MICHELHAM PRIORY, Hailsham, E. Sussex BN27 3QS
T 01323-844224 W www.sussexpast.co.uk
Tudor house built onto an Augustinian priory

MIDDLEHAM CASTLE (EH), Leyburn, N. Yorks DL8 4QG
T 01969-623899
12th-century keep within later fortifications;
childhood home of Richard III

MONTACUTE HOUSE (NT), Montacute, Somerset
TA15 6XP T 01935-823289
Elizabethan house with National Portrait Gallery
collection of portraits from the period

MOUNT GRACE PRIORY (EH), Northallerton, N. Yorks
DL6 3JG T 01609-883494
Carthusian priory with remains of monastic buildings

OLD SARUM (EH), Salisbury, Wilts SP1 3SD
T 01722-335398
Earthworks enclosing remains of Norman castle
and cathedral

ORFORD CASTLE (EH), Orford, Suffolk IP12 2ND
T 01394-450472
Polygonal tower keep of c.1170 and remains of coastal
defence castle built by Henry II

OSBORNE HOUSE (EH), East Cowes, Isle of Wight
PO32 6JX T 01983-200022
Queen Victoria's seaside residence

OSTERLEY PARK (NT), Isleworth, Middx TW7 4RB
T 020-8232 5050 W www.osterleypark.org.uk
    Elizabethan mansion set in parkland
PENDENNIS CASTLE (EH), Falmouth, Cornwall TR11 4LP
T 01326-316594
    Well-preserved 16th-century coastal defence castle
PENSHURST PLACE, Penshurst, Kent TN11 8DG
T 01892-870307 W www.penshurstplace.com
    House with medieval Baron's Hall and 14th-century
    gardens
PETWORTH HOUSE (NT), Petworth, W. Sussex GU28 0AE
T 01798-343929
    Late 17th-century house set in Capability Brown
    landscaped deer park
PEVENSEY CASTLE (EH), Pevensey, E. Sussex BN24 5LE
T 01323-762604
    Walls of a fourth-century Roman fort; remains of an
    11th-century castle
PEVERIL CASTLE (EH), Castleton, Derbys S33 8WQ
T 01433-620613
    12th-century castle defended on two sides by
    precipitous rocks
POLESDEN LACEY (NT), nr Dorking, Surrey RH5 6BD
T 01372-458203
    Regency villa remodelled in the Edwardian era; fine
    paintings and furnishings
PORTCHESTER CASTLE (EH), Portchester, Hants
PO16 9QW T 02392-378291
    Walls of a late Roman fort enclosing a Norman keep
    and an Augustinian priory church
POWDERHAM CASTLE, Kenton, Devon EX6 8JQ
T 01626-890243 W www.powderham.co.uk
    Medieval castle with 18th- and 19th-century
    alterations
RABY CASTLE, Staindrop, Co. Durham DL2 3AH
T 01833-660202 W www.rabycastle.com
    14th-century castle with walled gardens
RAGLEY HALL, Alcester, Warks B49 5NJ T 01789-762090
W www.ragleyhall.com
    17th-century house with gardens, park and lake
RICHBOROUGH ROMAN FORT (EH), Richborough,
Kent CT13 9JW T 01304-612013
    Landing-site of the Claudian invasion in AD 43
RICHMOND CASTLE (EH), Richmond, N. Yorks
DL10 4QW T 01748-822493
    12th-century keep with 11th-century curtain wall
RIEVAULX ABBEY (EH), nr Helmsley, N. Yorks YO62 5LB
T 01439-798228
    Remains of a Cistercian abbey founded c.1132
ROCHESTER CASTLE (EH), Rochester, Kent ME1 1SW
T 01634-402276
    11th-century castle partly on the Roman city wall, with
    a square keep of c. 1127
ROCKINGHAM CASTLE, Market Harborough, Leics
LE16 8TH T 01536-770240 W www.rockinghamcastle.com
    Built by William the Conqueror
ROYAL PAVILION, Brighton BN1 1EE T 03000-290900
W www.royalpavilion.org.uk
    Palace of George IV, in Chinese style with Indian
    exterior and Regency gardens
RUFFORD OLD HALL (NT), nr Ormskirk, Lancs L40 1SG
T 01704-821254
    16th-century hall with unique screen
ST AUGUSTINE'S ABBEY (EH), Canterbury, Kent CT1 1PF
T 01227-378100
    Remains of Benedictine monastery founded AD 597
ST MAWES CASTLE (EH), St Mawes, Cornwall TR2 5DE
T 01326-270526
    Coastal defence castle built by Henry VIII

ST MICHAEL'S MOUNT (NT), Cornwall TR17 0HT
T 01736-710507 W www.stmichaelsmount.co.uk
    12th-century castle with later additions, off the coast
    at Marazion
SANDRINGHAM, Norfolk PE35 6EN T 01485-545408
W www.sandringhamestate.co.uk
    The Queen's private residence; a neo-Jacobean house
    built in 1870
SCARBOROUGH CASTLE (EH), Scarborough, N. Yorks
YO11 1HY T 01723-372451
    Remains of 12th-century keep and curtain walls
SHERBORNE CASTLE, Sherborne, Dorset DT9 5NR
T 01935-812072 W www.sherbornecastle.com
    16th-century castle built by Sir Walter Raleigh set in
    landscaped gardens
SHUGBOROUGH ESTATE (NT), Milford, Staffs ST17 0XB
T 01889-881388 W www.shugborough.org.uk
    House set in 18th-century park with monuments,
    temples and pavilions in the Greek Revival style;
    arboretum; seat of the Earls of Lichfield
SKIPTON CASTLE, Skipton, N. Yorks BD23 1AW
T 01756-792442 W www.skiptoncastle.co.uk
    D-shaped castle with six round towers and inner
    courtyard
SMALLHYTHE PLACE (NT), Tenterden, Kent TN30 7NG
T 01580-762334
    Half-timbered 16th-century house; home of Ellen
    Terry 1899–1928; the Barn Theatre
STONEHENGE (EH), nr Amesbury, Wilts SP4 7DE
T 0870-333 1181
    Prehistoric monument consisting of concentric stone
    circles surrounded by a ditch and bank
STONOR PARK, Henley-on-Thames, Oxon RG9 6HF
T 01491-638587 W www.stonor.com
    Medieval house with Georgian facade; centre of
    Roman Catholicism after the Reformation
STOURHEAD (NT), Stourton, Wilts BA12 6QD
T 01747-841152
    English 18th-century Palladian mansion with
    landscape gardens
STRATFIELD SAYE HOUSE, Hants RG7 2BT
T 01256-882694 W www.stratfield-saye.co.uk
    House built 1630–40; home of the Dukes of
    Wellington since 1817
STRATFORD-UPON-AVON, Warks T 01789-204016
W www.shakespeare.org.uk
    Shakespeare's Birthplace Trust with Shakespeare
    Centre; Anne Hathaway's Cottage, home of
    Shakespeare's wife; Mary Arden's House, home of
    Shakespeare's mother; grammar school attended by
    Shakespeare; Holy Trinity Church, where Shakespeare
    is buried; Royal Shakespeare Theatre (burnt down
    1926, rebuilt 1932) and Swan Theatre (opened 1986)
SUDELEY CASTLE, Winchcombe, Glos GL54 5JD
T 01242-602308 W www.sudeleycastle.co.uk
    Castle built in 1442; restored in the 19th century
SULGRAVE MANOR, nr Banbury, Oxon OX17 2SD
T 01295-760205 W www.sulgravemanor.org.uk
    Home of George Washington's family
SUTTON HOUSE (NT), 2 & 4 Homerton High Street,
Hackney, London E9 6JQ T 020-8986 2264
    Tudor house, built in 1535 by Sir Ralph Sadleir
SYON HOUSE, Brentford, Middx TW8 8JF T 020-8560 0882
W www.syonpark.co.uk
    Built on the site of a former monastery; Robert Adam
    interior; Capability Brown park
TILBURY FORT (EH), Tilbury, Essex RM18 7NR
T 01375-858489
    16th-century coastal fort

TINTAGEL CASTLE (EH), Tintagel, Cornwall PL34 0HE
T 01840-770328
13th-century cliff-top castle and Dark Age settlement site; linked with Arthurian legend

TOWER OF LONDON, London EC3N 4AB
T 0870-482 7777 W www.hrp.org.uk
Royal palace and fortress begun by William the Conqueror in 1078; houses the Crown Jewels

TRERICE (NT), nr Newquay, Cornwall TR8 4PG
T 01637-875404
Elizabethan manor house

TYNEMOUTH PRIORY AND CASTLE (EH), Tyne and Wear NE30 4BZ T 0191-257 1090
Remains of a Benedictine priory, founded c. 1090, on Saxon monastic site

UPPARK (NT), South Harting, W. Sussex GU31 5QR
T 01730-825857
Late 17th-century house, completely restored after fire; Fetherstonhaugh art collection

WALMER CASTLE (EH), Walmer, Kent CT14 7LJ
T 01304-364288
One of Henry VIII's coastal defence castles, now the residence of the Lord Warden of the Cinque Ports

WARKWORTH CASTLE (EH), Warkworth, Northumberland NE65 0UJ T 01665-711423
14th-century keep amid earlier ruins, with hermitage upstream

WHITBY ABBEY (EH), Whitby, N. Yorks YO22 4JT
T 01947-603568
Remains of Norman church on the site of a monastery founded in AD 657

WILTON HOUSE, nr Salisbury, Wilts SP2 0BJ
T 01722-746714 W www.wiltonhouse.co.uk
17th-century house on the site of a Tudor house and ninth-century nunnery

WINDSOR CASTLE, Windsor, Berks SL4 1NJ
T 020-7766 7304 W www.royalcollection.org.uk
Official residence of the Queen; oldest royal residence still in regular use; largest inhabited castle in the world. Also St George's Chapel

WOBURN ABBEY, Woburn, Beds MK17 9WA
T 01525-290333 W www.woburn.co.uk
Built on the site of a Cistercian abbey; seat of the Dukes of Bedford; art collection; antiques centre

WROXETER ROMAN CITY (EH), nr Shrewsbury, Shropshire SY5 6PH T 01743-761330
Second-century public baths and part of the forum of the Roman town of Viroconium; replica Roman town house

WALES

For more information on Cadw properties, including those listed below, the official website is
www.cadw.wales.gov.uk
For more information on National Trust properties in Wales, including those listed below, the official website is
www.nationaltrust.org.uk
(C) Property of Cadw: Welsh Historic Monuments
(NT) National Trust property

BEAUMARIS CASTLE (C), Anglesey LL58 8AP
T 01248-810361
Concentrically planned castle, still virtually intact

CAERLEON ROMAN BATHS AND AMPHITHEATRE
(C), Newport NP18 1AE T 01633-422518
Rare example of a legionary bath-house and late first-century arena surrounded by bank for spectators

CAERNARFON CASTLE (C), Gwynedd LL55 2AY
T 01286-677617
Castle built between 1283 and 1330, initially for King Edward I of England; setting for the investiture of Prince Charles in 1969

CAERPHILLY CASTLE (C), Caerphilly CF83 1JD
T 029-2088 3143
Concentrically planned castle (c. 1270) notable for its scale and use of water defences

CARDIFF CASTLE, Cardiff CF10 3RB T 029-2087 8100
W www.cardiffcastle.com
Castle built on the site of a Roman fort

CASTELL COCH (C), Tongwynlais, Cardiff CF15 7JS
T 029-2081 0101
'Fairytale'-style castle, rebuilt 1875–90 on medieval foundations

CHEPSTOW CASTLE (C), Monmouthshire NP16 5EZ
T 01291-624065
Rectangular keep amid extensive fortifications; developed throughout the Middle Ages

CONWY CASTLE (C), Gwynedd LL32 8AY
T 01492-592358
Built for Edward I, 1283–7, on a narrow rocky outcrop

CRICCIETH CASTLE (C), Gwynedd LL55 0DP
T 01766-522227
Native Welsh 13th-century castle, altered by Edward I and Edward II

DENBIGH CASTLE (C), Denbighshire LL16 3NB
T 01745-813385
Remains of the castle (begun 1282), including triple-towered gatehouse

HARLECH CASTLE (C), Gwynedd LL46 2YH
T 01766-780552
Well-preserved Edwardian castle, constructed 1283–9, on an outcrop above the former shoreline

PEMBROKE CASTLE, Pembrokeshire SA71 4LA
T 01646-684585 W www.pembrokecastle.co.uk
Castle founded in 1093; Great Tower built in late 12th century; birthplace of King Henry VII

PENRHYN CASTLE (NT), Bangor, Gwynedd LL57 4HN
T 01248-363219
Neo-Norman castle built in the 19th century; railway museum; private art collection

PORTMEIRION, Gwynedd LL48 6ER T 01766-770000
W www.portmeirion-village.com
Village in Italianate style built by Clough Williams-Ellis

POWIS CASTLE (NT), Welshpool, Powys SY21 8RF
T 01938-551944
Medieval castle with interior in variety of styles; 17th-century gardens; Clive of India museum

RAGLAN CASTLE (C), Monmouthshire NP15 2BT
T 01291-690228
Remains of 15th-century castle with moated hexagonal keep

ST DAVIDS BISHOP'S PALACE (C), Pembrokeshire
SA62 6PE T 01437-720517
Remains of residence of Bishops of St Davids built 1328–47

TINTERN ABBEY (C), nr Chepstow, Monmouthshire
NP16 6SE T 01291-689251
Remains of 13th-century church and conventual buildings of a 12th-century Cistercian monastery

TRETOWER COURT AND CASTLE (C), nr Crickhowell,
Powys NP8 1RF T 01874-730279
Medieval house rebuilt in the 15th century, with remains of 12th-century castle nearby

MUSEUMS AND GALLERIES

There are approximately 2,500 museums and galleries in the United Kingdom. Around 1,400 of these are accredited by the Museums, Libraries and Archives Council (MLA), which indicates that they have an appropriate constitution, are soundly financed, have adequate collection management standards and public services, and have access to professional curatorial advice. A further 400 museums and galleries have applied for, or are in the process of obtaining accreditation, and these applications are assessed by either the relevant regional agency in England; Museums, Archives and Libraries Wales (CyMAL); Museums Galleries Scotland or the Northern Ireland Museums Council.

The following is a selection of museums and art galleries in the UK. Opening hours and admission charges vary. Further information about museums and galleries in the UK is available from the Museums Association (W www.museumsassociation.org T 020-7426 6910)

W www.culture24.org.uk includes a database of all the museums and galleries in the UK.

ENGLAND

* England's national museums and galleries, which receive funding from a government department, such as the DCMS or MOD. These institutions are deemed to have collections of national importance, and the government is able to call upon their staff for expert advice

BARNARD CASTLE
The Bowes Museum, Co. Durham DL12 8NP T 01833-690606
W www.thebowesmuseum.org.uk
European art from the late medieval period to the 19th century; music and costume galleries; English period rooms from Elizabeth I to Victoria; local archaeology
BATH
American Museum, Claverton Manor BA2 7BD
T 01225-460503 W www.americanmuseum.org
American decorative arts from the 17th to 19th centuries; American heritage exhibition
Fashion Museum, Bennett Street BA1 2QH T 01225-477173
W www.museumofcostume.co.uk
Fashion from the 18th century to the present day
Roman Baths Museum, Pump Room, Stall Street BA1 1LZ
T 01225-477785 W www.romanbaths.co.uk
Museum adjoins the remains of a Roman baths and temple complex
Victoria Art Gallery, Bridge Street BA2 4AT T 01225-477233
W www.victoriagal.org.uk
European Old Masters and British art since the 15th century
BEAMISH
Beamish Museum, Co. Durham DH9 0RG T 0191-370 4000
W www.beamish.org.uk
Northern town recreated in 1825 and 1913
BEAULIEU
National Motor Museum, Hants SO42 7ZN T 01590-614650
W www.nationalmotormuseum.org.uk
Displays of over 250 vehicles dating from 1895 to the present day

BIRMINGHAM
Aston Hall, Trinity Road B6 6JD T 0121-675 4722
W www.bmag.org.uk
Jacobean House containing paintings, furniture and tapestries from the 17th to 19th centuries
Barber Institute of Fine Arts, University of Birmingham, Edgbaston B15 2TS T 0121-414 7333 W www.barber.org.uk
Fine arts, including Old Masters
Birmingham Museum and Art Gallery, Chamberlain Square B3 3DH T 0121-303 1966 W www.bmag.org.uk
Includes notable collection of Pre-Raphaelite art
Museum of the Jewellery Quarter, Vyse Street, Hockley B18 6HA T 0121-554 3598 W www.bmag.org.uk
Built around a real jewellery workshop
BOVINGTON
Tank Museum, Dorset BH20 6JG T 01929-405096
W www.tankmuseum.org
Collection of 200 tanks from the earliest days of tank warfare to the present
BRADFORD
Bradford Industrial Museum and Horses at Work, Moorside Road, Eccleshill BD2 3HP T 01274-435900
W www.bradfordmuseums.org
Engineering, textiles, transport and social history exhibits
Cartwright Hall Art Gallery, Lister Park BD9 4NS
T 01274-431212 W www.bradfordmuseums.org
British 19th- and 20th-century fine art
National Media Museum, Princes Way BD1 1NQ
T 0870-701 0200 W www.nationalmediamuseum.org.uk
Photography, film and television interactive exhibits; features an IMAX cinema and the only public Cinerama screen in Europe
BRIGHTON
Booth Museum of Natural History, Dyke Road BN1 5AA
T 03000-290900 W www.brighton-hove-rpml.org.uk/Museums/boothmuseum
Zoology, botany and geology collections; British birds in recreated habitats
Brighton Museum and Art Gallery, Royal Pavilion Gardens BN1 1EE T 03000-290900
W www.brighton-hove-rpml.org.uk/Museums/brightonmuseum
Includes fine art and design, fashion, non-Western art; Brighton history
BRISTOL
Arnolfini, Narrow Quay BS1 4QA T 0117-917 2300
W www.arnolfini.org.uk
Contemporary visual arts, dance, performance, music, talks and workshops
Blaise Castle House Museum, Henbury BS10 7QS
T 0117-903 9818 W www.bristol-city.gov.uk/museums
Agricultural and social history collections in an 18th-century mansion
City Museum and Art Gallery, Queen's Road BS8 1RL
T 0117-922 3571 W www.bristol-city.gov.uk/museums
Includes fine and decorative art, oriental art, Egyptology and Bristol ceramics and paintings
M Shed, Prince's Wharf BS1 4RN T 0117-352 6600
W www.mshed.org
The story of Bristol's heritage of engineering, transport, music and industry

CAMBRIDGE
Fitzwilliam Museum, Trumpington Street CB2 1RB
  T 01223-332900 W www.fitzmuseum.cam.ac.uk
  Antiquities, fine and applied arts, clocks, ceramics,
  manuscripts, furniture, sculpture, coins and medals
*Imperial War Museum Duxford, Duxford CB22 4QR
  T 01223-835000 W duxford.iwm.org.uk
  Displays of military and civil aircraft, tanks, guns and
  naval exhibits
Sedgwick Museum of Earth Sciences, Downing Street CB2 3EQ
  T 01223-333456 W www.sedgwickmuseum.org
  Extensive geological collection
University Museum of Archaeology and Anthropology,
  Downing Street CB2 3DZ T 01223-333516
  W www.maa.cam.ac.uk
  Due to reopen in 2012, extensive global archaeological
  and anthropological collections
University Museum of Zoology, Downing Street CB2 3EJ
  T 01223-336650 W www.museum.zoo.cam.ac.uk
  Extensive zoological collection
Whipple Museum of the History of Science, Free School Lane
  CB2 3RH T 01223-330906 W www.hps.cam.ac.uk/whipple
  Scientific instruments from the 14th century to the
  present
CARLISLE
Tullie House Museum and Art Gallery, Castle Street CA3 8TP
  T 01228-618718 W www.tulliehouse.co.uk
  Prehistoric archaeology, Hadrian's Wall, Viking and
  medieval Cumbria, and the social history of Carlisle
CHATHAM
The Historic Dockyard, ME4 4TZ T 01634-823800
  W www.thedockyard.co.uk
  Maritime attractions including HMS *Cavalier,* the UK's
  last Second World War destroyer
Royal Engineers Museum and Library, Prince Arthur Road,
  Gillingham ME4 4UG T 01634-822839
  W www.remuseum.org.uk
  Regimental history, ethnography, decorative art and
  photography
CHELTENHAM
Art Gallery and Museum, Clarence Street GL50 3JT
  T 01242-237431 W www.cheltenhammuseum.org.uk
  Paintings, arts and crafts
CHESTER
Grosvenor Museum, Grosvenor Street CH1 2DD
  T 01244-402033 W www.cheshirewestandchester.gov.uk/
  visiting
  Roman collections, natural history, art, Chester silver,
  local history and costume
CHICHESTER
Weald and Downland Open Air Museum, Singleton
  PO18 0EU T 01243-811348 W www.wealddown.co.uk
  Rebuilt vernacular buildings from south-east England;
  includes medieval houses, agricultural and rural craft
  buildings and a working watermill
COLCHESTER
Colchester Castle Museum, Castle Park CO1 1TJ
  T 01206-282939 W www.colchestermuseums.org.uk
  Largest Norman keep in Europe standing on
  foundations of the Roman Temple of Claudius; tours
  of the Roman vaults, castle walls and chapel
COVENTRY
Coventry Transport Museum, Hales Street CV1 1JD
  T 024-7623 4270 W www.transport-museum.com
  Hundreds of motor vehicles and bicycles
Herbert Art Gallery and Museum, Jordan Well CV1 5QP
  T 024-7683 2386 W www.theherbert.org
  Local history, archaeology and industry, and fine and
  decorative art

DERBY
Derby Museum and Art Gallery, The Strand DE1 1BS
  T 01332-641901 W www.derby.gov.uk/museums
  Includes paintings by Joseph Wright of Derby and
  Derby porcelain
Pickford's House Museum, Friar Gate DE1 1DA
  T 01332-715181 W www.derby.gov.uk/museums
  Georgian town house by architect Joseph Pickford;
  museum of Georgian life and costume
The Silk Mill, Derby's Museum of Industry and History,
  Silk Mill Lane DE1 3AF T 01332-642234
  W www.derby.gov.uk/museums
  Rolls-Royce aero engine collection and railway
  engineering gallery; on the site of two silk mills built
  in the early 1700s
DEVIZES
Wiltshire Heritage Museum, Long Street SN10 1NS
  T 01380-727369 W www.wiltshireheritage.org.uk
  Natural and local history; art gallery; archaeological
  finds from prehistoric, Roman and Saxon sites
DORCHESTER
Dorset County Museum, High West Street DT1 1XA
  T 01305-262735 W www.dorsetcountymuseum.org
  Includes a collection of Thomas Hardy's manuscripts,
  books, notebooks and drawings; local history, geology
  and Roman mosaics
DOVER
Dover Museum, Market Square CT16 1PB T 01304-201066
  W www.dover.gov.uk/museum
  Contains the Dover Bronze Age Boat Gallery and
  archaeological finds from Bronze Age, Roman and
  Saxon sites
EXETER
Royal Albert Memorial Museum and Art Gallery,
  Queen Street EX4 3RX T 01392-665858
  W www.rammuseum.org.uk
  Natural history, archaeology, worldwide fine and
  decorative art including Exeter silver
GATESHEAD
Baltic Centre for Contemporary Art, South Shore Road
  NE8 3BA T 0191-478 1810 W www.balticmill.com
  Contemporary art exhibitions and events
Shipley Art Gallery, Prince Consort Road NE8 4JB
  T 0191-477 1495 W www.twmuseums.org.uk/shipley
  Contemporary crafts
GAYDON
Heritage Motor Centre, Banbury Road, Warks CV35 0BJ
  T 01926-641188 W www.heritage-motor-centre.co.uk
  History of British motor industry from 1895 to
  present; classic vehicles; engineering gallery; Corgi
  and Lucas collections
GLOUCESTER
Gloucester Waterways Museum, Gloucester Docks GL1 2EH
  T 01452-318200
  W www.gloucesterwaterwaysmuseum.org.uk
  Two-hundred-year history of Britain's canals and
  inland waterways
GOSPORT
Royal Navy Submarine Museum, Haslar Jetty Road, Hants
  PO12 2AS T 023-9251 0354 W www.submarine-
  museum.co.uk
  Underwater warfare, including the submarine *Alliance;*
  first Royal Navy submarine
GRASMERE
Dove Cottage and the *Wordsworth Museum,* Cumbria
  LA22 9SH T 01539-435544 W www.wordsworth.org.uk
  William Wordsworth's manuscripts, home and
  garden

HULL

Ferens Art Gallery, Queen Victoria Square HU1 3RA
T 01482-300300 W www.hullcc.gov.uk
European art, especially Dutch 17th-century paintings, British portraits from 17th to 20th centuries, and marine paintings

Hull Maritime Museum, Queen Victoria Square HU1 3DX
T 01482-300300 W www.hullcc.gov.uk
Whaling, fishing and navigation exhibits

HUNTINGDON

The Cromwell Museum, Grammar School Walk PE29 3LF
T 01480-375830 W www.cambridgeshire.gov.uk/cromwell
Portraits and memorabilia relating to Oliver Cromwell

IPSWICH

Christchurch Mansion and *Wolsey Art Gallery*, Soane Street IP4 2BE T 01473-433554 W www.ipswich.gov.uk
Tudor house with paintings by Gainsborough, Constable and other Suffolk artists; furniture and 18th-century ceramics; temporary exhibitions

KESWICK

Pencil Museum, Southey Works CA12 5NG T 017687-73626
W www.pencilmuseum.co.uk
500-year history of the pencil; demonstration events and workshops throughout the year

LEEDS

Armley Mills, Leeds Industrial Museum, Canal Road, Armley LS12 2QF T 0113-263 7861
W www.leeds.gov.uk/armleymills
World's largest woollen mill, now a museum for textiles, clothing and engine manufacture

Leeds City Art Gallery, The Headrow LS1 3AA
T 0113-247 8256 W www.leeds.gov.uk/artgallery
Includes English watercolours; modern sculpture; Henry Moore gallery; print room

Lotherton Hall, Aberford LS25 3EB T 0113-281 3259
W www.leeds.gov.uk/lothertonhall
Costume, ceramics and furniture collections in furnished Edwardian house; deer park and bird garden

Royal Armouries Museum, Armouries Drive LS10 1LT
T 0113-220 1999 W www.royalarmouries.org
National collection of arms and armour from BC to present; demonstrations of foot combat in museum's five galleries; falconry and mounted combat in the tiltyard

Temple Newsam, LS15 0AE T 0113-264 5535
W www.leeds.gov.uk/templenewsam
Old Masters and 17th- and 18th-century decorative art in furnished Jacobean/Tudor house

LEICESTER

Jewry Wall Museum, St Nicholas Circle LE1 4LB
T 0116-225 4971 W www.leicester.gov.uk
Archaeology; Roman Jewry Wall and baths; mosaics

New Walk Museum and Art Gallery, 53 New Walk LE1 7EA
T 0116-255 4900 W www.leicester.gov.uk
Natural history and geology; ancient Egypt gallery; European art and decorative arts

LINCOLN

The Collection, Danes Terrace LN2 1LP T 01522-550990
W www.lincolnshire.gov.uk
Artefacts from the Stone Age to the Viking and Medieval eras; adjacent art gallery with decorative and contemporary visual arts

Museum of Lincolnshire Life, Burton Road LN1 3LY
T 01522-528448 W www.lincolnshire.gov.uk
Social history and agricultural collection

LIVERPOOL

International Slavery Museum, Albert Dock L3 4AX
T 0151-478 4499 W www.liverpoolmuseums.org.uk/ism
Explores historical and contemporary aspects of slavery

Lady Lever Art Gallery, Wirral CH62 5EQ T 0151-478 4136
W www.liverpoolmuseums.org.uk/ladylever
Paintings, furniture and porcelain

Merseyside Maritime Museum, Albert Dock L3 4AQ
T 0151-478 4499
W www.liverpoolmuseums.org.uk/maritime
Floating exhibits, working displays and craft demonstrations; incorporates *HM Customs and Excise National Museum*

Museum of Liverpool, Pier Head L3 1PZ
T 0151-478 4499 W www.liverpoolmuseums.org.uk/mol
Formerly the *Museum of Liverpool Life*; explores the significance of the city's geography, history and culture

Sudley House, Mossley Hill Road L18 8BX T 0151-724 3245
W www.liverpoolmuseums.org.uk/sudley
Late 18th- and 19th-century paintings in former shipowner's home

Tate Liverpool, Albert Dock L3 4BB T 0151-702 7400
W www.tate.org.uk/liverpool
Twentieth-century paintings and sculpture

Walker Art Gallery, William Brown Street L3 8EL
T 0151-478 4199 W www.liverpoolmuseums.org.uk/walker
Paintings from the 13th to 20th centuries

World Museum Liverpool, William Brown Street L3 8EN
T 0151-478 4393 W www.liverpoolmuseums.org.uk/wml
Includes Egyptian mummies, weapons and classical sculpture; planetarium, aquarium, vivarium and natural history centre

LONDON: GALLERIES

Barbican Art Gallery, Barbican Centre, Silk Street EC2Y 8DS
T 020-7638 4141 W www.barbican.org.uk
Temporary exhibitions

Courtauld Institute of Art Gallery, Somerset House, Strand WC2R 0RN T 020-7848 2526 W www.courtauld.ac.uk
Impressionist and post-impressionist paintings

Dulwich Picture Gallery, Gallery Road, Dulwich Village SE21 7AD T 020-8693 5254
W www.dulwichpicturegallery.org.uk
England's first public art gallery; designed by Sir John Soane to house 17th- and 18th-century paintings

Estorick Collection of Modern Italian Art, Canonbury Square N1 2AN T 020-7704 9522 W www.estorickcollection.com
Early 20th-century Italian drawings, paintings, sculptures and etchings, with an emphasis on Futurism

Hayward Gallery, Belvedere Road SE1 8XX T 020-7960 4200
W www.southbankcentre.co.uk
Temporary exhibitions

National Gallery, Trafalgar Square WC2N 5DN
T 020-7747 2885 W www.nationalgallery.org.uk
Western painting from the 13th to 19th centuries; early Renaissance collection in the Sainsbury Wing

National Portrait Gallery, St Martin's Place WC2H 0HE
T 020-7306 0055 W www.npg.org.uk
Portraits of eminent people in British history

Photographers' Gallery, Ramillies Street W1F 7LW
T 0845-262 1618 W www.photonet.org.uk
Temporary exhibitions

The Queen's Gallery, Buckingham Palace SW1A 1AA
T 020-7766 7301 W www.royalcollection.org.uk
Art from the Royal Collection

Royal Academy of Arts, Burlington House, Piccadilly W1J 0BD
T 020-7300 8000 W www.royalacademy.org.uk
British art since 1750 and temporary exhibitions; annual Summer Exhibition

Saatchi Gallery, Duke of York's HQ, King's Road, SW3 4SQ
  T 020-7823 2363 W www.saatchi-gallery.co.uk
  Contemporary art including paintings, photographs,
  sculpture and installations

Serpentine Gallery, Kensington Gardens W2 3XA
  T 020-7402 6075 W www.serpentinegallery.org
  Temporary exhibitions of British and international
  contemporary art

Tate Britain, Millbank SW1P 4RG T 020-7887 8888
  W www.tate.org.uk/britain
  British painting and 20th-century painting and
  sculpture

Tate Modern, Bankside SE1 9TG T 020-7887 8888
  W www.tate.org.uk/modern
  International modern art from 1900 to the present

Wallace Collection, Manchester Square W1U 3BN
  T 020-7563 9500 W www.wallacecollection.org
  Paintings and drawings, French 18th-century furniture,
  armour, porcelain, clocks and sculpture

Whitechapel Art Gallery, Whitechapel High Street E1 7QX
  T 020-7522 7888 W www.whitechapel.org
  Temporary exhibitions of modern art

LONDON: MUSEUMS

Bank of England Museum, Threadneedle Street EC2R 8AH
  (entrance on Bartholomew Lane) T 020-7601 5545
  W www.bankofengland.co.uk/museum
  History of the Bank of England since 1694

British Museum, Great Russell Street WC1B 3DG
  T 020-7323 8000 W www.thebritishmuseum.org
  Antiquities, coins, medals, prints and drawings;
  temporary exhibitions; home of the Sir Percival David
  collection of Chinese ceramics

Brunel Museum, Rotherhithe SE16 4LF T 020-7231 3840
  W www.brunel-museum.org.uk
  Explores the engineering achievements of
  Isambard Kingdom Brunel and his father, Marc
  Brunel

Churchill War Rooms, King Charles Street SW1A 2AQ
  T 020-7930 6961 W cwr.iwm.org.uk
  Underground rooms used by Churchill and the
  government during the Second World War

Cutty Sark, Greenwich SE10 9BG T 020-8858 2698
  W www.cuttysark.org.uk
  The world's last remaining tea clipper due to reopen in
  spring 2012 with new exhibitions

Design Museum, Shad Thames SE1 2YD T 020-7940 8790
  W www.designmuseum.org
  The development of design and the mass-production of
  consumer objects

Firepower, the Royal Artillery Museum, Royal Arsenal,
  Woolwich SE18 6ST T 020-8855 7755
  W www.firepower.org.uk
  The history and development of artillery over the last
  700 years including the collections of the Royal
  Regiment of Artillery

Garden Museum, Lambeth Palace Road SE1 7LB
  T 020-7401 8865 W www.gardenmuseum.org.uk
  History and development of gardens and gardening;
  temporary exhibitions, symposia and events

Geffrye Museum, Kingsland Road E2 8EA T 020-7739 9893
  W www.geffrye-museum.org.uk
  English urban domestic interiors from 1600 to the
  present day; also paintings, furniture, decorative arts,
  walled herb garden and period garden rooms

HMS Belfast, Morgan's Lane, Tooley Street SE1 2JH
  T 020-7940 6300 W hmsbelfast.iwm.org.uk
  Life on a Second World War cruiser

Horniman Museum, London Road SE23 3PQ
  T 020-8699 1872 W www.horniman.ac.uk
  Museum of anthropology, musical instruments and
  natural history; aquarium; reference library; gardens

Imperial War Museum, Lambeth Road SE1 6HZ
  T 020-7416 5320 W www.iwm.org.uk
  All aspects of the two World Wars and other military
  operations involving Britain and the Commonwealth
  since 1914

Jewish Museum, Albert Street NW1 7NB T 020-7284 7384
  W www.jewishmuseum.org.uk
  Jewish life, history and religion

London Metropolitan Archives , Northampton Road EC1R
  0HB T 020-7332 3820 W www.cityoflondon.gov.uk/lma
  Material on the history of London and its people
  dating 1067–2006

London Transport Museum, Covent Garden Piazza WC2E 7BB
  T 020-7379 6344 W www.ltmuseum.co.uk
  Vehicles, photographs and graphic art relating to the
  history of transport in London

MCC Museum, Lord's, St John's Wood NW8 8QN
  T 020-7616 8656 W www.lords.org/mcc
  Cricket museum; guided tours by appointment

Museum in Docklands, West India Quay, Hertsmere Road
  E14 4AL T 020-7001 9844
  W www.museumindocklands.org.uk
  Explores the story of London's river, port and people
  over 2,000 years, from Roman times through to the
  recent regeneration of London's Docklands

Museum of Childhood at Bethnal Green (V&A),
  Cambridge Heath Road E2 9PA T 020-8983 5200
  W www.vam.ac.uk/moc
  Toys, games and exhibits relating to the social history
  of childhood

Museum of London, London Wall EC2Y 5HN
  T 020-7001 9844 W www.museumoflondon.org.uk
  History of London from prehistoric times to the
  present day

National Archives Museum, Kew TW9 4DU T 020-8876 3444
  W www.nationalarchives.gov.uk
  Displays treasures from the archives, including the
  Domesday Book and Magna Carta

National Army Museum, Royal Hospital Road SW3 4HT
  T 020-7730 0717 W www.national-army-museum.ac.uk
  Five-hundred-year history of the British soldier;
  exhibits include model of the Battle of Waterloo and
  recreated First World War trench

National Maritime Museum, Greenwich SE10 9NF
  T 020-8858 4422 W www.nmm.ac.uk
  Maritime history of Britain; collections include globes,
  clocks, telescopes and paintings; comprises the main
  building, the Royal Observatory and the Queen's House

Natural History Museum, Cromwell Road SW7 5BD
  T 020-7942 5000 W www.nhm.ac.uk
  Natural history collections and interactive Darwin
  Centre

Petrie Museum of Egyptian Archaeology, University College
  London, Malet Place WC1E 6BT T 020-7679 2884
  W www.ucl.ac.uk/museums/petrie
  Egyptian archaeology collection

Royal Air Force Museum, Hendon NW9 5LL
  T 020-8205 2266 W www.rafmuseum.org.uk
  Aviation from before the Wright brothers to the
  present-day RAF

Royal Mews, Buckingham Palace SW1A 1AA T 020-7766 7302
  W www.royalcollection.org.uk
  State vehicles, including the Queen's gold state coach;
  home to the Queen's horses

*Science Museum, Exhibition Road SW7 2DD T 0870 870 4868
W www.sciencemuseum.org.uk
Science, technology, industry and medicine collections;
children's interactive gallery; IMAX cinema

Shakespeare's Globe Exhibition, Bankside SE1 9DT
T 020-7902 1400 W www.shakespearesglobe.com
Recreation of Elizabethan theatre using 16th-century
techniques; includes a tour of the theatre

*Sir John Soane's Museum, Lincoln's Inn Fields WC2A 3BP
T 020-7405 2107 W www.soane.org
Art and antiquities collected by Soane throughout his
lifetime; house designed by Soane

Tower Bridge Experience, SE1 2UP T 020-7403 3761
W www.towerbridge.org.uk
History of the bridge and display of Victorian steam
machinery; panoramic views from walkways

*Victoria and Albert Museum, Cromwell Road SW7 2RL
T 020-7942 2000 W www.vam.ac.uk
Includes National Art Library and Print Room; fine and
applied art and design; furniture, glass, textiles, theatre
and dress collections

Wellcome Collection, Euston Road NW1 2BE
T 020-7611 2222 W www.wellcomecollection.org
Contemporary and historic exhibitions and collections
including the Wellcome Library

Wimbledon Lawn Tennis Museum, Church Road SW19 5AE
T 020-8946 6131 W www.wimbledon.com/visiting/museum
Tennis trophies, fashion and memorabilia; view of
Centre Court

MALTON
Eden Camp, N. Yorks YO17 6RT T 01653-697777
W www.edencamp.co.uk
Restored POW camp and Second World War
memorabilia

MANCHESTER
Gallery of Costume, Platt Hall, Rusholme M14 5LL
T 0161-245 7245 W www.manchestergalleries.org
Exhibits from the 17th century to the present day

*Imperial War Museum North, Trafford Wharf Road M17 1TZ
T 0161-836 4000 W north.iwm.org.uk
History of war in the 20th and 21st centuries

Manchester Art Gallery, Mosley Street M2 3JL
T 0161-235 8888 W www.manchestergalleries.org
Six centuries of European fine and decorative art

Manchester Museum, Oxford Road M13 9PL T 0161-275 2634
W www.museum.manchester.ac.uk
Collections include archaeology, decorative arts,
Egyptology, natural history and zoology

*Museum of Science and Industry, Liverpool Road, Castlefield
M3 4FP T 0161-832 2244 W www.mosi.org.uk
On site of world's oldest passenger railway station;
galleries relating to space, energy, power, transport,
aviation, textiles and social history

National Football Museum, Cathedral Gardens M4 3BG
T 0161-870 9275 W www.nationalfootballmuseum.com
Home to the FIFA, FA and Football League collections
including the 1966 World Cup final ball

People's History Museum, Left Bank, Spinningfields M3 3ER
T 0161-838 9190 W www.phm.org.uk
British political and working life history

Whitworth Art Gallery, Oxford Road M15 6ER
T 0161-275 7450 W www.whitworth.manchester.ac.uk
Watercolours, drawings, prints, textiles, wallpapers and
British art

MILTON KEYNES
Bletchley Park National Codes Centre, Bucks MK3 6EB
T 01908-640404 W www.bletchleypark.org.uk

Home of British codebreaking during the Second
World War; Enigma machine; computer museum;
wartime toys and memorabilia

MONKWEARMOUTH
Monkwearmouth Station Museum, North Bridge Street,
Sunderland SR5 1AP T 0191-567 7075
W www.twmuseums.org.uk/monkwearmouth
Victorian train station; interactive galleries

NEWCASTLE UPON TYNE
Discovery Museum, Blandford Square NE1 4JA
T 0191-232 6789 W www.twmuseums.org.uk/discovery
Science and industry, local history, fashion; Tyneside's
maritime history; Turbinia (first steam-driven vessel)
gallery

Great North Museum: Hancock, Barras Bridge NE2 4PT
T 0191-222 6765
W www.twmuseums.org.uk/greatnorthmuseum
Natural history and ancient history

Laing Art Gallery, New Bridge Street NE1 8AG
T 0191-232 7734 W www.twmuseums.org.uk/laing
18th- and 19th-century collection; watercolour
gallery

NEWMARKET
National Horseracing Museum, High Street CB8 8JH
T 01638-667333 W www.nhrm.co.uk
The story of people and horses involved in racing;
temporary exhibitions

NORTH SHIELDS
Stephenson Railway Museum, Middle Engine Lane NE29 8DX
T 0191-200 7146 W www.twmuseums.org.uk/stephenson
Locomotive engines and rolling stock

NOTTINGHAM
Castle Museum and Art Gallery, Friar Lane NG1 6EL
T 0115-915 3700 W www.nottinghamcity.gov.uk
Paintings, ceramics, silver and glass; history of
Nottingham

Museum of Nottingham Life, Brewhouse Yard,
Castle Boulevard NG7 1FB T 0115-915 3600
W www.nottinghamcity.gov.uk
Social history from the 17th to 20th centuries

Natural History Museum, Wollaton Hall, Wollaton NG8 2AE
T 0115-915 3900 W www.nottinghamcity.gov.uk
Local natural history and wildlife dioramas

OXFORD
Ashmolean Museum, Beaumont Street OX1 2PH
T 01865-278000 W www.ashmolean.org
European and Oriental fine and applied arts,
archaeology, Egyptology and numismatics

Modern Art Oxford, Pembroke Street OX1 1BP
T 01865-722733 W www.modernartoxford.org.uk
Temporary exhibitions

Museum of the History of Science, Broad Street OX1 3AZ
T 01865-277280 W www.mhs.ox.ac.uk
Displays include early scientific instruments, chemical
apparatus, clocks and watches

Oxford University Museum of Natural History, Parks Road
OX1 3PW T 01865-272950 W www.oum.ox.ac.uk
Entomology, geology, mineralogy and
zoology

Pitt Rivers Museum, South Parks Road OX1 3PP
T 01865-270927 W www.prm.ox.ac.uk
Ethnographic and archaeological artefacts

PLYMOUTH
City Museum and Art Gallery, Drake Circus PL4 8AJ
T 01752-304774 W www.plymouthmuseum.gov.uk
Local and natural history; ceramics; silver; Old Masters;
world artefacts; temporary exhibitions

PORTSMOUTH
Charles Dickens Birthplace, Old Commercial Road PO1 4QL
    T 023-9282 7261 W www.charlesdickensbirthplace.co.uk
    Dickens memorabilia
D-Day Museum, Clarence Esplanade, Southsea PO5 3NT
    T 023-9282 7261 W www.ddaymuseum.co.uk
    Includes the Overlord embroidery
Portsmouth Historic Dockyard, HM Naval Base PO1 3LJ
    T 023-9283 9766 W www.historicdockyard.co.uk
    Incorporates the *Royal Naval Museum* (PO1 3NH
    T 023-9272 7562 W www.royalnavalmuseum.org), *HMS
    Victory* (PO1 3NH T 023-9272 3111
    W www.hms-victory.com), *HMS Warrior* (PO1 3QX
    T 023-9277 8600 W www.hmswarrior.org), the *Mary Rose*
    (PO1 3LX T 023-9281 2931 W www.maryrose.org) and
    Action Stations (PO1 3LJ T 023-9289 3338
    W www.actionstations.org)
    History of the Royal Navy and of the dockyard;
    warships and technology spanning 500 years
PRESTON
Harris Museum and Art Gallery, Market Square PR1 2PP
    T 01772-258248 W www.harrismuseum.org.uk
    British art since the 18th century; ceramics, glass,
    costume and local history; contemporary exhibitions
ST ALBANS
Verulamium Museum, St Michael's Street AL3 4SW
    T 01727-751810 W www.stalbansmuseums.org.uk
    Remains of Iron Age settlement and the third-largest
    city in Roman Britain; exhibits include Roman wall
    plasters, jewellery, mosaics and room reconstructions
ST IVES
Tate St Ives, Porthmeor Beach, Cornwall TR26 1TG
    T 01736-796226 W www.tate.org.uk/stives
    Modern art, much by artists associated with St Ives;
    includes the Barbara Hepworth Museum and Sculpture
    Garden
SALISBURY
Salisbury & South Wiltshire Museum, The Close SP1 2EN
    T 01722-332151 W www.salisburymuseum.org.uk
    Archaeology collection
SHEFFIELD
Graves Art Gallery, Surrey Street S1 1XZ T 0114-278 2600
    W www.museums-sheffield.org.uk
    Twentieth-century British art, Grice Collection of
    Chinese ivories
Millennium Galleries, Arundel Gate S1 2PP T 0114-278 2600
    W www.museums-sheffield.org.uk
    Incorporates four different galleries: the Special
    Exhibition Gallery, the Craft and Design Gallery, the
    Metalwork Gallery and the Ruskin Gallery, which
    houses John Ruskin's collection of paintings, drawings,
    books and medieval manuscripts
Weston Park Museum, Western Bank S10 2TP
    T 0114-278 2600 W www.museums-sheffield.org.uk
    World history for families
SOUTHAMPTON
City Art Gallery, Commercial Road SO14 7LP
    T 023-8083 2277 W www.southampton.gov.uk/art
    Fine art collection spanning six centuries of European
    art
Maritime Museum, Town Quay Road SO14 2AR
    T 023-8083 2706 W www.southampton.gov.uk
    Southampton maritime history; Titanic exhibition
Museum of Archaeology (God's House Tower), Winkle Street
    SO14 2NY T 023-8091 5732 W www.southampton.gov.uk
    Roman, Saxon and medieval archaeology
Tudor House Museum and Garden, Bugle Street SO14 2AD
    T 023-8063 5904 W www.southampton.gov.uk

Story of the 15th-century house and the people who
    lived and worked in it
SOUTH SHIELDS
Arbeia Roman Fort, Baring Street NE33 2BB T 0191-456 1369
    W www.twmuseums.org.uk/arbeia
    Excavated ruins; reconstructions of original buildings
South Shields Museum and Art Gallery, Ocean Road
    NE33 2JA T 0191-456 8740
    W www.twmuseums.org.uk/southshields
    South Tyneside history; interactive art gallery
STOKE-ON-TRENT
Etruria Industrial Museum, Lower Bedford Street ST4 7AF
    T 01782-233144 W www.stokemuseums.org.uk/eim
    Britain's sole surviving steam-powered potter's
    mill
Gladstone Pottery Museum, Longton ST3 1PQ
    T 01782-237777 W www.stokemuseums.org.uk/gpm
    A working Victorian pottery
Potteries Museum and Art Gallery, Bethesda Street ST1 3DW
    T 01782-232323 W www.stokemuseums.org.uk/pmag
    Pottery, china and porcelain collections and a
    Mark XVI Spitfire
The Wedgwood Museum, Barlaston ST12 9ER
    T 01782-371900 W www.wedgwoodmuseum.org.uk
    The story of Josiah Wedgwood and the company
    he founded
SUNDERLAND
Sunderland Museum & Winter Gardens, Burdon Road
    SR1 1PP T 0191-553 2323
    W www.twmuseums.org.uk/sunderland
    Fine and decorative art, local history and gardens
TELFORD
Ironbridge Gorge Museums, TF8 7DQ T 01952-433424
    W www.ironbridge.org.uk
    World's first iron bridge; Blists Hill (late Victorian
    working town); Museum of Iron; Jackfield Tile
    Museum; Coalport China Museum; Tar Tunnel;
    Broseley Pipeworks
WAKEFIELD
Hepworth Wakefield, Gallery Walk WF1 5AW
    T 01924-247360 W www.hepworthwakefield.org
    Historic and modern art, temporary exhibitions of
    contemporary art
National Coal Mining Museum for England, Overton
    WF4 4RH T 01924-848806 W www.ncm.org.uk
    Includes underground tours of one of Britain's oldest
    working mines
Yorkshire Sculpture Park, West Bretton WF4 4LG
    T 01924-832631 W www.ysp.co.uk
    Open-air sculpture gallery including works by Moore,
    Hepworth, Frink and others in 202 hectares
    (500 acres) of parkland
WEYBRIDGE
Brooklands Museum, KT13 0QN T 01932-857381
    W www.brooklandsmuseum.com
    Birthplace of British motorsport; world's first
    purpose-built motor racing circuit
WILMSLOW
Quarry Bank Mill, Styal SK9 4LA T 01625-527468
    W www.quarrybankmill.org.uk
    Working mill owned by the National Trust illustrating
    history of cotton industry; costumed guides at restored
    Apprentice House
WINCHESTER
INTECH, Telegraph Way, Hampshire SO21 1HZ
    T 01962-863791 W www.intech-uk.com
    Interactive science centre and planetarium

WORCESTER
City Art Gallery and Museum, Foregate Street WR1 1DT
T 01905-25371 W www.worcestercitymuseums.org.uk
Includes a military museum, 19th-century chemist
shop and changing art exhibitions
Museum of Worcester Porcelain, Severn Street WR1 2ND
T 01905-21247 W www.worcesterporcelainmuseum.org.uk
Worcester porcelain from 1751 to the present day
YEOVIL
Fleet Air Arm Museum, Royal Naval Air Station, Yeovilton,
Somerset BA22 8HT T 01935-840565
W www.fleetairarm.com
History of naval aviation; historic aircraft, including
Concorde 002
YORK
Beningbrough Hall, Beningbrough YO30 1DD
T 01904-472027 W www.nationaltrust.org.uk
18th-century house with portraits from the National
Portrait Gallery
JORVIK Viking Centre, Coppergate YO1 9WT
T 01904-615505 W www.jorvik-viking-centre.co.uk
Reconstruction of Viking York based on archaeological
evidence
National Railway Museum, Leeman Road YO26 4XJ
T 0844-815 3139 W www.nrm.org.uk
Includes locomotives, rolling stock and carriages
York Art Gallery, Exhibition Square YO1 7EW
T 01904-687687 W www.yorkartgallery.org.uk
European and British painting spanning seven
centuries; modern pottery; decorative arts
York Castle Museum, Eye of York YO1 9RY T 01904-687687
W www.yorkcastlemuseum.org.uk
Reconstructed streets and rooms; costume and military
collections
Yorkshire Museum & Gardens, Museum Gardens YO1 7FR
T 01904-687687 W www.yorkshiremuseum.org.uk
Yorkshire life from Roman to medieval times; geology
and biology; York observatory

WALES

* Members of National Museum Wales, a public body that
receives its funding through grant-in-aid from the Welsh
Assembly

ABERYSTWYTH
Ceredigion Museum, Terrace Road SY23 2AQ T 01970-633088
W www.ceredigion.gov.uk
Local history, housed in a restored Edwardian theatre
Llywernog Silver-Lead Mine, Ponterwyd
SY23 3AB T 01970-890620 W www.silverminetours.co.uk
Tours of an 18th-century silver mine, exhibitions
containing artefacts used therein
BLAENAFON
Big Pit National Coal Museum, Torfaen NP4 9XP
T 01495-790311 W www.museumwales.ac.uk
Colliery with underground tour
BODELWYDDAN
Bodelwyddan Castle, Denbighshire LL18 5UY T 01745-584060
W www.bodelwyddan-castle.co.uk
Portraits from the National Portrait Gallery; furniture
from the Victoria and Albert Museum; sculptures from
the Royal Academy
CAERLEON
National Roman Legion Museum, NP18 1AE
T 01633-423134 W www.museumwales.ac.uk
Material from the site of the Roman fortress of Isca and
its suburbs

CARDIFF
National Museum Cardiff, Cathays Park CF10 3NP
T 029-2039 7951 W www.museumwales.ac.uk
Includes natural sciences, archaeology and
Impressionist paintings
St Fagans: National History Museum, St Fagans CF5 6XB
T 029-2057 3500 W www.museumwales.ac.uk
Open-air museum with re-erected buildings,
agricultural equipment and costume
TECHNIQUEST, Stuart Street CF10 5BW T 029-2047 5475
W www.techniquest.org
Interactive science exhibits, planetarium and science
theatre
CRICCIETH
Lloyd George Museum, Llanystumdwy LL52 0SH
T 01766-522071 W www.gwynedd.gov.uk
Childhood home of David Lloyd George; museum
commemorates his life
DRE-FACH FELINDRE
National Wool Museum, nr Llandysul SA44 5UP
T 01559-370929 W www.museumwales.ac.uk
Exhibitions, a working woollen mill and craft
workshops
LLANBERIS
National Slate Museum, Gwynedd LL55 4TY
T 01286-870630 W www.museumwales.ac.uk
Former slate quarry with original machinery and plant;
slate crafts demonstrations; working waterwheel
LLANDRINDOD WELLS
National Cycle Collection, Automobile Palace, Temple Street
LD1 5DL T 01597-825531 W www.cyclemuseum.org.uk
Over 200 bicycles on display, from 1819–present
PRESTEIGNE
Judge's Lodging Museum, Broad Street LD8 2AD
T 01544-260650 W www.judgeslodging.org.uk
Restored apartments, courtroom, cells and servants'
quarters
SWANSEA
Glynn Vivian Art Gallery, Alexandra Road SA1 5DZ
T 01792-516900 W www.swansea.gov.uk/glynnvivian
Paintings, ceramics, Swansea pottery and porcelain,
clocks, glass and Welsh art
National Waterfront Museum, Oystermouth Road SA1 3RD
T 01792-638950 W www.museumwales.ac.uk
Wales during the Industrial Revolution
Swansea Museum, Victoria Road SA1 1SN T 01792-653763
W www.swansea.gov.uk/swanseamuseum
Archaeology, social history, Swansea pottery
TENBY
Tenby Museum and Art Gallery, Castle Hill SA70 7BP
T 01834-842809 W www.tenbymuseum.org.uk
Local archaeology, history, geology and art

SCOTLAND

* Members of National Museums of Scotland or National
Galleries of Scotland, which are non-departmental public bodies
funded by, and accountable to, the Scottish government

ABERDEEN
Aberdeen Art Gallery, Schoolhill AB10 1FQ T 01224-523700
W www.aagm.co.uk
Paintings, sculptures and graphics from the 15th
century to the present day
Aberdeen Maritime Museum, Shiprow AB11 5BY
T 01224-337700 W www.aagm.co.uk
Maritime history, including shipbuilding and
North Sea oil

DUMFRIES
*National Museum of Costume, New Abbey DG2 8HQ
T 0300-123 6789 W www.nms.ac.uk/costume
History of fashion from the 1850s to the 20th century
EDINBURGH
Britannia, Leith EH6 6JJ T 0131-555 5566
W www.royalyachtbritannia.co.uk
Former royal yacht with royal barge and royal family
picture gallery
City Art Centre, Market Street EH1 1DE T 0131-529 3993
W www.edinburghmuseums.org.uk
Scottish late 19th- and 20th-century art, worldwide
collections and temporary exhibitions
*Modern Art Galleries, 75 Belford Road EH4 3DR
T 0131-624 6200 W www.nationalgalleries.org
Includes the Gallery of Modern Art and the Dean Gallery
Museum of Childhood, High Street EH1 1TG T 0131-529 4142
W www.edinburghmuseums.org.uk
Toys, games, clothes and exhibits relating to the social
history of childhood
Museum of Edinburgh, Canongate EH8 8DD
T 0131-529 4143 W www.edinburghmuseums.org.uk
Local history, silver, glass and Scottish pottery
*Museum of Flight, East Fortune Airfield, East Lothian
EH39 5LF T 0300-123 6789 W www.nms.ac.uk/flight
Display of aircraft
*National Gallery Complex, The Mound EH2 2EL
T 0131-624 6200 W www.nationalgalleries.org
Paintings, drawings and prints from the early
Renaissance to the end of the 19th century
*National Museum of Scotland, Chambers Street EH1 1JF
T 0131-225 7534 W www.nms.ac.uk/scotland
Scottish history from prehistoric to present day
through 16 galleries
*National War Museum of Scotland, Edinburgh Castle
EH1 2NG T 0300-123 6789 W www.nms.ac.uk/war
History of Scottish military and conflicts
*Scottish National Portrait Gallery, Queen Street EH2 1JD
T 0131-624 6200 W www.nationalgalleries.org
Due to reopen in late 2011: portraits of eminent people
in Scottish history; the national collection of
photography
The Writers' Museum, Lawnmarket EH1 2PA
T 0131-529 4901 W www.edinburghmuseums.org.uk
Exhibitions relating to Robert Louis Stevenson, Walter
Scott and Robert Burns
FORT WILLIAM
West Highland Museum, Cameron Square PH33 6AJ
T 01397-702169 W www.westhighlandmuseum.org.uk
Includes tartan collections and exhibits relating to
1745 uprising
GLASGOW
Burrell Collection, Pollokshaws Road G43 1AT
T 0141-287 2550 W www.glasgowlife.org.uk/museums
Paintings, textiles, furniture, ceramics, stained glass and
silver from classical times to the 19th century
Gallery of Modern Art, Royal Exchange Square G1 3AH
T 0141-287 3005 W www.glasgowlife.org.uk/museums
Collection of contemporary Scottish and world art
Hunterian Museum & Art Gallery, University of Glasgow
G12 8QQ T 0141-330 4221 W www.hunterian.gla.ac.uk
Rennie Mackintosh and Whistler collections; Old
Masters; Scottish paintings; archaeology; medicine;
zoology
Kelvingrove Art Gallery & Museum, Argyle Street G3 8AG
T 0141-276 9599 W www.glasgowlife.org.uk/museums
Includes Old Masters, 19th-century French paintings
and armour collection

Museum of Piping, McPhater Street G4 0HW
T 0141-353 0220 W www.thepipingcentre.co.uk
The history and origins of bagpiping
*Museum of Rural Life, East Kilbride G76 9HR
T 0300-123 6789 W www.nms.ac.uk
History of rural life and work
People's Palace and Winter Gardens, Glasgow Green G40 1AT
T 0141-276 0788 W www.glasgowlife.org.uk/museums
Social history of Glasgow since 1750
*Riverside Museum, 100 Pointhouse Place G3 8RS
T 0141-287 2720 W www.glasgowlife.org.uk/museums
Scotland's museum of transport and travel; the Tall
Ship, a Clyde-built sailing ship, is berthed alongside
St Mungo Museum of Religious Life and Art, Castle Street
G4 0RH T 0141-276 1625 W www.glasgowlife.org.uk/
museums
Explores universal themes through objects from the
main world religions

NORTHERN IRELAND

* Members of National Museums Northern Ireland, a
non-departmental public body of the Northern Ireland Office

ARMAGH
*Armagh County Museum, The Mall East BT61 9BE
T 028-3752 3070 W www.nmni.com/acm
Local history; archaeology; crafts
BANGOR
North Down Museum, Town Hall BT20 4BT T 028-9127 1200
W www.northdown.gov.uk/heritage
Presents the history of North Down, including its
early-Christian monastery
BELFAST
*W5, Odyssey, Queen's Quay BT3 9QQ T 028-9046 7700
W www.w5online.co.uk
Interactive science and technology centre
HOLYWOOD
*Ulster Folk and Transport Museum, Cultra, Co. Down
BT18 0EU T 028-9042 8428 W www.nmni.com/uftm
Open-air museum with original buildings from Ulster
town and rural life c.1900; indoor galleries including
Irish rail and road transport
LONDONDERRY
The Tower Museum, Union Hall Place BT48 6LU
T 028-7137 2411 W www.derrycity.gov.uk/museums
Tells the story of Ireland through the history of
Londonderry
Workhouse Museum, Glendermott Road BT48 6BG
T 028-7131 8328 W www.derrycity.gov.uk/museums
Exhibitions on the Second World War, workhouse life,
19th-century poverty and the famine
NEWTOWNARDS
The Somme Heritage Centre, 233 Bangor Road BT23 7PH
T 01247-823202 W www.irishsoldier.org
Commemorates the part played by Irish forces in the
First World War
OMAGH
*Ulster American Folk Park, Castletown, Co. Tyrone
BT78 5QU T 028-8224 3292 W www.nmni.com/uafp
Open-air museum telling the story of Ulster's
emigrants to America; restored or recreated dwellings
and workshops; ship and dockside gallery
*Ulster Museum, Botanic Gardens BT9 5AB T 0845-608 0000
W www.nmni.com/um
Irish antiquities; natural and local history; fine and
applied arts

SIGHTS OF LONDON

For historic buildings, museums and galleries in London, *see* the Historic Buildings and Monuments, and Museums and Galleries sections.

BRIDGES

The bridges over the Thames in London, from east to west, are:

Queen Elizabeth II Bridge (2,872m/9,423ft), engineer: Sir William Halcrow and partners, opened 1991

Tower Bridge (268m/880ft by 18m/60ft), architect: Horace Jones, engineer: John Wolfe Barry, opened 1894

London Bridge (262m/860ft by 32m/105ft), original 13th-century stone bridge rebuilt and opened 1831 (engineer: John Rennie), reconstructed in Arizona when current London Bridge opened 1973 (architect: Lord Holford, engineer: Mott, Hay and Anderson)

Cannon Street Railway Bridge (261m/855ft), engineers: John Hawkshaw and John Wolfe Barry, originally named the Alexandra Bridge, opened 1866; renovated 1979–82

Southwark Bridge (244m/800ft by 17m/55ft), engineer: John Rennie, opened 1819; rebuilt 1912–21 (architect: Ernest George, engineer: Mott, Hay and Anderson)

Millennium Bridge (325m/1,066ft by 4m/13ft), architect: Foster and Partners, engineer: Ove Arup and Partners, opened 2000; reopened after modification 2002

Blackfriars Railway Bridge (284m/933ft), engineers: John Wolfe Barry and Henri Marc Brunel, opened 1886

London, Chatham and Dover Railway Bridge (234m/933ft), engineer: Joseph Cubitt, opened in 1864; only the columns remain, the rest of the structure was removed in 1985

Blackfriars Bridge (294m/963ft by 32m/105ft), engineer: Robert Mylne, opened 1769; rebuilt 1869 (engineer: Joseph Cubitt); widened 1909

Waterloo Bridge (366m/1,200ft by 24m/80ft), engineer: John Rennie, opened 1817; rebuilt 1945 (architect: Sir Giles Gilbert Scott, engineer: Rendel, Palmer and Triton)

Golden Jubilee Bridges (325m/1,066ft by 4.7m/15ft), architect: Lifschutz Davidson, engineer: WSP Group, opened 2002; commonly known as the Hungerford Footbridges

Hungerford Railway Bridge (366m/1,200ft), engineer: Isambard Kingdom Brunel, suspension bridge opened 1845; present railway bridge opened 1864 (engineer: John Hawkshaw); widened in 1886

Westminster Bridge (228m/748ft by 26m/85ft), engineer: Charles Labelye, opened 1750; rebuilt 1862 (architect: Charles Barry, engineer: Thomas Page)

Lambeth Bridge (237m/776ft by 18m/60ft), engineer: Peter W. Barlow, original suspension bridge opened 1862; current structure opened 1932 (architect: Reginald Blomfield, engineer: George W. Humphreys)

Vauxhall Bridge (231m/759ft by 24m/80ft), engineer: James Walker, opened 1816; redesigned and opened 1906 (architect: William Edward Riley, engineers: Alexander Binnie and Maurice Fitzmaurice)

Grosvenor Railway Bridge (213m/700ft), engineer: John Fowler, opened 1860; rebuilt 1965; also known as the Victoria Railway Bridge

Chelsea Bridge (213m/698ft by 25m/83ft), original suspension bridge opened 1858 (engineer: Thomas Page); rebuilt 1937 (architects: George Topham Forrest and E. P. Wheeler, engineer: Rendel, Palmer and Triton)

Albert Bridge (216m/710ft, by 12m/40ft), engineer: Rowland M. Ordish, opened 1873; restructured 1884 (engineer: Joseph Bazalgette); strengthened 1971–3

Battersea Bridge (204m/670ft by 17m/55ft), engineer: Henry Holland, opened 1771; rebuilt 1890 (engineer: Joseph Bazalgette)

Battersea Railway Bridge (204m/670ft), engineer: William Baker, opened 1863, also known as Cremorne Bridge

Wandsworth Bridge (189m/619ft by 18m/60ft), engineer: Julian Tolmé, opened 1873; rebuilt 1940 (architect: E. P. Wheeler, engineer: T. Peirson Frank)

Putney Railway Bridge (229m/750ft), engineers: W. H. Thomas and William Jacomb, opened 1889, also known as the Fulham Railway Bridge or the Iron Bridge – it has no official name

Putney Bridge (213m/700ft by 23m/74ft), architect: Jacob Ackworth, original wooden bridge opened 1729; current granite structure completed in 1886 (engineer: Joseph Bazalgette)

Hammersmith Bridge (210m/688ft by 10m/33ft), engineer: William Tierney Clarke; the first suspension bridge in London, originally built 1827; rebuilt 1887 (engineer: Joseph Bazalgette)

Barnes Railway Bridge (also footbridge, 110m/360ft), engineer: Joseph Locke, opened 1849; rebuilt 1895 (engineers: London and South Western Railway); the original structure stands unused

Chiswick Bridge (137m/450ft by 21m/70ft), architect: Herbert Baker, engineer: Alfred Dryland, opened 1933

Kew Railway Bridge (175m/575ft), engineer: W. R. Galbraith, opened 1869

Kew Bridge (110m/360ft by 17m/56ft), engineer: Robert Tunstall, original timber bridge built 1759; replaced by a Portland stone structure in 1789 (engineer: James Paine); current granite bridge renamed King Edward VII Bridge in 1903, but still known as Kew Bridge (engineers: John Wolfe Barry and Cuthbert Brereton)

Richmond Lock (91m/300ft by 11m/36ft), engineer: F. G. M. Stoney, lock and footbridge opened 1894

Twickenham Bridge (85m/280ft by 21m/70ft), architect: Maxwell Ayrton, engineer: Alfred Dryland, opened 1933

Richmond Railway Bridge (91m/300ft), engineer: Joseph Locke, opened 1848; rebuilt 1906–8 (engineer: J. W. Jacomb-Hood)

Richmond Bridge (85m/280ft by 10m/33ft), architect: James Paine, engineer: Kenton Couse, built 1777; widened 1939

Teddington Lock (198m/650ft), engineer: G. Pooley, two footbridges opened 1889; marks the end of the tidal reach of the Thames

Kingston Railway Bridge, architects: J. E. Errington and W. R. Galbraith, engineer: Thomas Brassey, opened 1863

Kingston Bridge (116m/382ft), engineer: Edward Lapidge, built 1825–8; widened 1911–14 (engineers: Basil Mott and David Hay) and 1999–2001

Hampton Court Bridge, engineers: Samuel Stevens and Benjamin Ludgator, built 1753; replaced by iron bridge 1865; present bridge opened 1933 (architect: Edwin Lutyens, engineer: W. P. Robinson)

CEMETERIES

In 1832, in response to the overcrowding of burial grounds in London, the government authorised the establishment of seven non-denominational cemeteries that would encircle the city. These large cemeteries, known as the 'magnificent seven', were seen by many Victorian families as places in which to demonstrate their wealth and stature, and as a result there are some highly ornate graves and tombs.

THE MAGNIFICENT SEVEN

Abney Park, Stamford Hill, N16 (13ha/32 acres), established 1840; tomb of General Booth, founder of the Salvation Army, and memorials to many nonconformists and dissenters

Brompton, Old Brompton Road, SW10 (16ha/40 acres), established 1840; graves of Sir Henry Cole, Emmeline Pankhurst, John Wisden. Managed by the Royal Parks, it is the only Crown cemetery

Highgate, Swains Lane, N6 (15ha/38 acres), established 1839; graves of Douglas Adams, George Eliot, Michael Faraday, Karl Marx, Christina Rossetti and Radclyffe Hall; western side only accessible as part of a guided tour

Kensal Green, Harrow Road, W10 (31.5ha/79 acres), established 1832; tombs of William Makepeace Thackeray, Anthony Trollope, Sydney Smith, Wilkie Collins, Tom Hood, George Cruikshank, Leigh Hunt, Isambard Kingdom Brunel and Charles Kemble

Nunhead, Linden Grove, SE15 (21ha/52 acres), established 1840; closed in 1969, subsequently restored and opened for burials

Tower Hamlets, Southern Grove, E3 (11ha/27 acres), established 1841; bombed heavily during the Second World War and closed to burials in 1966; now a nature reserve

West Norwood Cemetery and Crematorium, Norwood High Street, SE27 (17ha/42 acres), established 1837; tombs of Sir Henry Bessemer, Mrs Beeton, Sir Henry Tate and Joseph Whitaker *(Whitaker's Almanack)*

OTHER CEMETERIES

Bunhill Fields, City Road, EC1 (1.6ha/4 acres), 17th-century nonconformist burial ground containing the graves of William Blake, John Bunyan and Daniel Defoe

City of London Cemetery and Crematorium, Aldersbrook Road, E12 (81ha/200 acres), established 1856; grave of Bobby Moore

Golders Green Crematorium, Hoop Lane, NW11 (5ha/12 acres), established 1902; retains the ashes of Kingsley Amis, Peter Sellers, Marc Bolan, Sigmund Freud, Ivor Novello, Bram Stoker, H. G. Wells, Anna Pavlova and Joe Orton

Hampstead, Fortune Green Road, NW6 (10.5ha/26 acres), established 1876; graves of Kate Greenaway, Lord Lister and Marie Lloyd

MARKETS

Billingsgate (fish), a market site for over 1,000 years, with the Lower Thames Street site dating from 1876; moved to the Isle of Dogs (Trafalgar Way, E14) in 1982; owned and run by the Corporation of London

Borough, Southwark Street, SE1 (vegetables, fruit, gourmet food, flowers), established on present site in 1756; privately owned and run

Brick Lane, E1 (jewellery, vintage clothes, bric-a-brac, food), open Sunday

Brixton, SW8 (African-Caribbean food, music, clothes), open Monday to Saturday

Broadway, E8 (food, fashion, crafts), re-established in 2004, open Saturday

Camden Lock, NW1 (second-hand clothing, jewellery, alternative fashion, crafts), established in 1973

Columbia Road, E2 (flowers), dates from 19th century; became dedicated flower market in the 20th century

Covent Garden, WC2 (antiques, handicrafts, jewellery, clothing, food), originally a fruit and vegetable market *(see* New Covent Garden market), it has been trading in its current form since 1980

Grays, Davies Street, W1 (antiques), indoor market in listed building, established 1977

Greenwich, SE10 (crafts, fashion, food), market revived in the 1980s

Leadenhall, Leadenhall Street, EC3 (meat, poultry, cheese, etc), site of market since 14th century; present hall built 1881; owned and run by the Corporation of London

New Covent Garden Nine Elms, SW8 (wholesale vegetables, fruit and flowers) owned and run by the Covent Garden Market Authority, established in 1670 under a charter of Charles II; relocated from central London in 1974

Petticoat Lane, Middlesex Street, E1, a market has existed on the site for over 500 years, now a Sunday morning market selling almost anything

Portobello Road, W11, originally for herbs and horse-trading from 1870; became famous for antiques after the closure of the Caledonian Market in 1948

Smithfield, EC1 (meat, poultry), built 1866–8, refurbished 1993–4; the site of St Bartholomew's Fair from 12th to 19th century; owned and run by the Corporation of London

New Spitalfields, E10 (vegetables, fruit), established 1682, modernised 1928, moved out of the City to Leyton in 1991

Old Spitalfields, E1, continues to trade on the original Spitalfields site on Commercial Street, selling arts, crafts, books, clothes, organic food and antiques on Sundays

MONUMENTS

CENOTAPH

Whitehall, SW1. The Cenotaph (from the Greek meaning 'empty tomb') was built to commemorate 'The Glorious Dead' and is a memorial to all ranks of the sea, land and air forces who gave their lives in the service of the Empire during the First World War. Designed by Sir Edwin Lutyens and constructed in plaster as a temporary memorial in 1919, it was replaced by a permanent structure of Portland stone and unveiled by George V on 11 November 1920, Armistice Day. An additional inscription was made in 1946 to commemorate those who gave their lives in the Second World War

FOURTH PLINTH

Trafalgar Square, WC2. The fourth plinth (1841) was designed for an equestrian statue that was never built due to lack of funds. From 1999 temporary works have been displayed on the plinth including *Ecce Homo* (Mark Wallinger), *Regardless of History* (Bill Woodrow), *Monument* (Rachel Whiteread), *Alison Lapper Pregnant* (Marc Quinn) and *Model for a Hotel* (Thomas Schütte). Antony Gormley's project *One & Other* occupied the plinth from July–October 2009. This was followed in November 2009 by a memorial statue to Second World War hero Air Chief Marshal Sir Keith Park and from May 2010 by *Nelson's Ship in a Bottle* by Yinka Shonibare

LONDON MONUMENT

(Commonly called the Monument), Monument Street, EC3. Built to designs by Sir Christopher Wren and Robert Hooke between 1671 and 1677, the Monument commemorates the Great Fire of London, which broke out in Pudding Lane on 2 September 1666. The fluted Doric column is 36.6m (120ft) high, the moulded cylinder above the balcony supporting a flaming vase of gilt bronze is an additional 12.8 m (42ft), and the column is based on a square plinth 12.2m (40ft) high (with fine carvings on the west face), making a total height of 61.6m (202ft) – the tallest isolated stone column in the world, with views of London from a gallery at the top (311 steps)

OTHER MONUMENTS

(sculptor's name in parentheses):
7 July Memorial (Carmody Groarke), Hyde Park
Viscount Alanbrooke (Roberts-Jones), Whitehall
Albert Memorial (Scott), Kensington Gore
Battle of Britain (Day), Victoria Embankment
Beatty (Wheeler), Trafalgar Square
Belgian Gratitude (setting by Blomfield, statue by Rousseau), Victoria Embankment
Boadicea (or Boudicca), *Queen of the Iceni* (Thornycroft), Westminster Bridge
Brunel (Marochetti), Victoria Embankment
Burghers of Calais (Rodin), Victoria Tower Gardens, Westminster
Burns (Steell), Embankment Gardens
Canada Memorial (Granche), Green Park
Carlyle (Boehm), Chelsea Embankment
Cavalry (Jones), Hyde Park
Edith Cavell (Frampton), St Martin's Place
Charles I (Le Sueur), Trafalgar Square
Charles II (Gibbons), Royal Hospital, Chelsea
Churchill (Roberts-Jones), Parliament Square
Cleopatra's Needle (20.9m/68.5ft high, c.1500BC, erected in London in 1878; the sphinxes are Victorian), Thames Embankment
Clive (Tweed), King Charles Street
Captain Cook (Brock), The Mall
Oliver Cromwell (Thornycroft), outside Westminster Hall
Cunningham (Belsky), Trafalgar Square
Gen. Charles de Gaulle (Conner), Carlton Gardens
Diana, Princess of Wales Memorial Fountain (Gustafson Porter), Hyde Park
Disraeli, Earl of Beaconsfield (Raggi), Parliament Square
Lord Dowding (Winter), Strand
Duke of Cambridge (Jones), Whitehall
Duke of York (37.8m/124ft column, with statue by Westmacott), Carlton House Terrace
Edward VII (Mackennal), Waterloo Place

Elizabeth I (Kerwin, 1586, oldest outdoor statue in London; from Ludgate), Fleet Street
Eros (Shaftesbury Memorial) (Gilbert), Piccadilly Circus
Marechal/Marshall Foch (Mallisard, copy of one in Cassel, France), Grosvenor Gardens
Charles James Fox (Westmacott), Bloomsbury Square
Yuri Gagarin (Novikov, copy of the one in Russia), The Mall
George III (Cotes Wyatt), Cockspur Street
George IV (Chantrey), Trafalgar Square
George V (Reid Dick and Scott), Old Palace Yard
George VI (McMillan), Carlton Gardens
Gladstone (Thornycroft), Strand
Guards' (Crimea) (Bell), Waterloo Place
Guards Division (Ledward, figures, Bradshaw, cenotaph), Horse Guards' Parade
Haig (Hardiman), Whitehall
Sir Arthur (Bomber) Harris (Winter), Strand
Gen. Henry Havelock (Behnes), Trafalgar Square
International Brigades Memorial (Spanish Civil War) (Ian Walters), Jubilee Gardens, South Bank
Irving (Brock), north side of National Portrait Gallery
Isis (Gudgeon), Hyde Park
James II (Gibbons), Trafalgar Square
Jellicoe (McMillan), Trafalgar Square
Samuel Johnson (Fitzgerald), opposite St Clement Danes
Kitchener (Tweed), Horse Guards' Parade
Abraham Lincoln (Saint-Gaudens, copy of one in Chicago), Parliament Square
Mandela (Walters), Parliament Square
Milton (Montford), St Giles, Cripplegate
Mountbatten (Belsky), Foreign Office Green
Gen. Charles James Napier (Adams), Trafalgar Square
Nelson (Railton), Trafalgar Square, with Landseer's lions (cast from guns recovered from the wreck of the *Royal George*)
Florence Nightingale (Walker), Waterloo Place
Palmerston (Woolner), Parliament Square
Sir Keith Park (Johnson), Waterloo Place
Peel (Noble), Parliament Square
Pitt (Chantrey), Hanover Square
Portal (Nemon), Embankment Gardens
Prince Albert (Bacon), Holborn Circus
Queen Elizabeth Gate (Lund and Wynne), Hyde Park Corner
Queen Mother (Jackson), Carlton Gardens
Raleigh (McMillan), Greenwich
Richard I (Coeur de Lion) (Marochetti), Old Palace Yard
Roberts (Bates), Horse Guards' Parade
Royal Air Force (Blomfield), Victoria Embankment
Franklin D. Roosevelt (Reid Dick), Grosvenor Square
Royal Artillery (Great War) (Jagger and Pearson), Hyde Park Corner
Royal Artillery (South Africa) (Colton), The Mall; *Captain Scott* (Lady Scott), Waterloo Place; *Shackleton* (Jagger), Kensington Gore
Shakespeare (Fontana, copy of one by Scheemakers in Westminster Abbey), Leicester Square
Smuts (Epstein), Parliament Square
Sullivan (Goscombe John), Victoria Embankment
Trenchard (McMillan), Victoria Embankment
Victoria Memorial (Webb and Brock), in front of Buckingham Palace
Raoul Wallenberg (Jackson), Great Cumberland Place
George Washington (Houdon copy), Trafalgar Square
Wellington (Boehm), Hyde Park Corner
Wellington (Chantrey), outside Royal Exchange
John Wesley (Adams Acton), City Road
Westminster School (Crimea) (Scott), Broad Sanctuary
William III (Bacon), St James's Square
Wolseley (Goscombe John), Horse Guards' Parade

PARKS, GARDENS AND OPEN SPACES

CORPORATION OF LONDON OPEN SPACES
W www.cityoflondon.gov.uk
Ashtead Common (202ha/500 acres), Surrey
Burnham Beeches and *Fleet Wood* (219ha/540 acres), Bucks.
    Purchased by the Corporation for the benefit of the
    public in 1880, Fleet Wood (26ha/65 acres) being
    presented in 1921
Coulsdon Common (51ha/127 acres), Surrey
Epping Forest (2,476ha/6,118 acres), Essex. Purchased by
    the Corporation and opened to the public in 1882. The
    Queen Elizabeth Hunting Lodge, built for Henry VIII
    in the mid-16th century, lies at the edge of the forest.
    The present forest is 19.3km (12 miles) long by around
    3km (2 miles) wide, approximately one-tenth of its
    original area
*Epping Forest Buffer Land (718ha/1,774 acres), Waltham
    Abbey/Epping
Farthing Downs and New Hill (95ha/235 acres), Surrey
Hampstead Heath (275ha/680 acres), NW3. Including
    Golders Hill (15ha/36 acres) and Parliament Hill
    (110ha/271 acres)
Highgate Wood (28ha/70 acres), N6/N10
Kenley Common (56ha/139 acres), Surrey
Queen's Park (12ha/30 acres), NW6
Riddlesdown (43ha/107 acres), Surrey
Spring Park (21ha/51 acres), Kent
Stoke Common (83ha/206 acres), Bucks. Ownership was
    transferred to the Corporation in 2007
West Ham Park (31ha/77 acres), E15
West Wickham Common (11ha/26 acres), Kent
Also over 150 smaller open spaces within the City of
London, including *Finsbury Circus* and *St
Dunstan-in-the-East*
* Includes Copped Hall Park, Woodredon Estate and Warlies
Park

OTHER PARKS AND GARDENS
CHELSEA PHYSIC GARDEN, 66 Royal Hospital Road SW3
4HS T 020-7352 5646 W www.chelseaphysicgarden.co.uk
    A garden of general botanical research and education,
    maintaining a wide range of rare and unusual plants;
    established in 1673 by the Society of Apothecaries
HAMPTON   COURT   PARK   AND   GARDENS
(303.5ha/750 acres), Surrey KT8 9AU T 0844-482 7777
W www.hrp.org.uk Also known as Home Park, the park
lies beyond the palace's formal gardens. It contains a
herd of deer and a 1,000-year-old oak tree from the
original park
KEW, ROYAL BOTANIC GARDENS (120ha/300 acres),
Richmond, Surrey TW9 3AB T 020-8332 5655
W www.kew.org Officially inscribed on the UNESCO
list of World Heritage Sites
THAMES   BARRIER   PARK   (9ha/22acres),   North
Woolwich E16 2HP T 020-7476 3741
W www.thamesbarrierpark.org.uk Opened in 2000,
landscaped gardens with spectacular views of the
Thames Barrier

ROYAL PARKS
W www.royalparks.gov.uk
Bushy Park (450ha/1,099 acres), Middx. Adjoins Hampton
    Court; contains an avenue of horse-chestnuts enclosed
    in a fourfold avenue of limes planted by William III
Green Park (19ha/47 acres), W1. Between Piccadilly and
    St James's Park, with Constitution Hill leading to Hyde
    Park Corner

Greenwich Park (74ha/183 acres), SE10. Enclosed by
    Humphrey, Duke of Gloucester, and laid out by Charles
    II from the designs of Le Nôtre. On a hill in Greenwich
    Park is the Royal Observatory (founded 1675). Its
    buildings are now managed by the National Maritime
    Museum (T 020-8858 4422 W www.nmm.ac.uk) and the
    earliest building is named Flamsteed House, after John
    Flamsteed (1646–1719), the first astronomer royal
Hyde Park (142ha/350 acres), W1/W2. From Park Lane to
    Kensington Gardens and incorporating the Serpentine
    lake, Apsley House, the Achilles Statue, Rotten Row
    and the Ladies' Mile; fine gateway at Hyde Park
    Corner. To the north-east is Marble Arch, originally
    erected by George IV at the entrance to Buckingham
    Palace and re-erected in the present position in 1851
Kensington Gardens (111ha/275 acres), W2/W8. From the
    western boundary of Hyde Park to Kensington Palace;
    contains the Albert Memorial, Serpentine Gallery and
    Peter Pan statue
Regent's Park and *Primrose Hill* (197ha/487 acres), NW1.
    From Marylebone Road to Primrose Hill surrounded
    by the Outer Circle; divided by the Broad Walk leading
    to the Zoological Gardens
Richmond Park (1,000ha/2,500 acres), Surrey. Designated
    a National Nature Reserve, a Site of Special Scientific
    Interest and a Special Area of Conservation
St James's Park (23ha/58 acres), SW1. From Whitehall
    to Buckingham Palace; ornamental lake of 4.9ha
    (12 acres); the Mall leads from Admiralty Arch to
    Buckingham Palace, Birdcage Walk from Storey's Gate
    to Buckingham Palace

PLACES OF HISTORICAL AND CULTURAL INTEREST

1 Canada Square
    Canary Wharf E14 5DY T 020-7418 2000
    W www.canarywharf.com
    Also known as 'Canary Wharf', the steel and glass sky-
    scraper is designed to sway 35cm in the strongest winds
30 St Mary Axe
    EC3A 8EP W www.30stmaryaxe.com
    Completed in 2004 and commonly known as the
    'Gherkin', each of the floors rotates five degrees from
    the one below
Alexandra Palace
    Alexandra Palace Way, Wood Green N22 7AY
    T 020-8365 2121 W www.alexandrapalace.com
    The Victorian palace was severely damaged by fire in
    1980 but was restored, and reopened in 1988.
    Alexandra Palace now provides modern facilities for
    exhibitions, conferences, banquets and leisure activities.
    There is a winter ice rink, a boating lake, the Phoenix
    Bar and a conservation area
Barbican Centre
    Silk Street EC2Y 8DS T 020-7638 4141
    W www.barbican.org.uk
    Owned, funded and managed by the Corporation of
    London, the Barbican Centre opened in 1982 and
    houses the Barbican Theatre, a studio theatre called
    The Pit and the Barbican Hall; it is also home to the
    London Symphony Orchestra. There are three cinemas,
    seven conference rooms, two art galleries, a sculpture
    court, a lending library, trade and banqueting facilities,
    a conservatory, shops, restaurants, cafes and bars
British Library
    St Pancras, 96 Euston Road NW1 2DB T 0843-208 1144
    W www.bl.uk

The largest building constructed in the UK in the 20th century with basements extending 24.5m underground. Holdings include the *Magna Carta*, the *Lindisfarne Gospels*, Mozart manuscripts and the world's earliest dated printed book, the *Diamond Sutra*. Holds temporary exhibitions on a range of topics

Central Criminal Court
Old Bailey EC4M 7EH **T** 020-7248 3277
W www.cityoflondon.gov.uk
The highest criminal court in the UK, the 'Old Bailey' is located on the site of the old Newgate Prison. Trials held here have included those of Oscar Wilde, Dr Crippen and the Yorkshire Ripper. The courthouse has been rebuilt several times since 1674; Edward VII officially opened the current neo-baroque building in 1907

Charterhouse
Charterhouse Square EC1M 6AN **T** 020-7253 9503
W www.thecharterhouse.org
A Carthusian monastery from 1371 to 1538, purchased in 1611 by Thomas Sutton, who endowed it as a residence for aged men 'of gentle birth' and a school for poor scholars (removed to Godalming in 1872)

Downing Street SW1
Number 10 Downing Street is the official town residence of the prime minister, number 11 of the chancellor of the exchequer and number 12 is the office of the government whips. The street was named after Sir George Downing, Bt., soldier and diplomat, who was MP for Morpeth 1660–84

George Inn
Borough High Street SE1 1NH **T** 020-7407 2056
W www.nationaltrust.org.uk
The last galleried inn in London, built in 1677. Now owned by the National Trust and run as an ordinary public house

Horse Guards, Whitehall SW1
Archway and offices built about 1753. The changing of the guard takes place daily at 11am (10am on Sundays) and the inspection at 4pm. Only those with the Queen's permission may drive through the gates and archway into *Horse Guards' Parade*, where the colour is 'trooped' on the Queen's official birthday

HOUSES OF PARLIAMENT
House of Commons, Westminster SW1A 0AA **T** 020-7219 4272
W www.parliament.uk
House of Lords, Westminster SW1A 0PW **T** 020-7219 3107
W www.parliament.uk
The royal palace of Westminster, originally built by Edward the Confessor, was the normal meeting place of Parliament from about 1340. St Stephen's Chapel was used from about 1550 for the meetings of the House of Commons, which had previously been held in the Chapter House or Refectory of Westminster Abbey. The House of Lords met in an apartment of the royal palace. The fire of 1834 destroyed much of the palace, and the present Houses of Parliament were erected on the site from the designs of Sir Charles Barry and Augustus Welby Pugin between 1840 and 1867. The chamber of the House of Commons was destroyed by bombing in 1941, and a new chamber designed by Sir Giles Gilbert Scott was used for the first time in 1950. *Westminster Hall and the Crypt Chapel* was the only part of the old palace of Westminster to survive the fire of 1834. It was built by William II from 1097 to 1099 and altered by Richard II between 1394 and 1399. The hammerbeam roof of carved oak dates

from 1396–8. The Hall was the scene of the trial of Charles I. *The Victoria Tower* of the House of Lords is 98.5m (323ft) high, and *The Clock Tower* of the House of Commons is 96.3m (316ft) high and contains 'Big Ben', the hour bell said to be named after Sir Benjamin Hall, First Commissioner of Works when the original bell was cast in 1856. This bell, which weighed 16 tons 11 cwt, was found to be cracked in 1857. The present bell (13.5 tons) is a recasting of the original and was first brought into use in 1859. The dials of the clock are 7m (23ft) in diameter, the hands being 2.7m (9ft) and 4.3m (14ft) long (including balance piece).

During session, tours of the Houses of Parliament are only available to UK residents who have made advance arrangements through an MP or peer. Overseas visitors are no longer provided with permits to tour the Houses of Parliament during session, although they can tour on Saturdays and during the summer opening and attend debates for both houses in the Strangers' Galleries. During the summer recess, tickets for tours of the Houses of Parliament can be booked by telephone (**T** 0844-847 1672) or bought on site at the ticket office on Abingdon Green opposite Parliament and the Victoria Tower Gardens. The Strangers' Gallery of the House of Commons is open to the public when the house is sitting. To acquire tickets in advance, UK residents should write to their local MP and overseas visitors should apply to their embassy or high commission in the UK for a permit. If none of these arrangements has been made, visitors should join the public queue outside St Stephen's Entrance, where there is also a queue for entry to the House of Lords Gallery

INNS OF COURT
The Inns of Court are ancient unincorporated bodies of lawyers which for more than five centuries have had the power to call to the Bar those of their members who have qualified for the rank or degree of Barrister-at-Law. There are four Inns of Court as well as many lesser inns

Lincoln's Inn, Chancery Lane/Lincoln's Inn Fields WC2A 3TL **T** 020-7405 1393 **W** www.lincolnsinn.org.uk
The most ancient of the inns with records dating back to 1422. The hall and library buildings are from 1845, although the library is first mentioned in 1474; the old hall (late 15th century) and the chapel were rebuilt c.1619–23

Inner Temple, King's Bench Walk EC4Y 7HL
T 020-7797 8250 **W** www.innertemple.org.uk
Middle Temple, Middle Temple Lane EC4Y 9AT
T 020-7427 4800 **W** www.middletemple.org.uk
Records for the Middle and Inner Temple date back to the beginning of the 16th century. The site was originally occupied by the Order of Knights Templar c.1160–1312. The two inns have separate halls thought to have been formed c.1350. The division between the two societies was formalised in 1732 with Temple Church and the Masters House remaining in common. The Inner Temple Garden is normally open to the public on weekdays between 12.30pm and 3pm

Temple Church, EC4Y 7BB **T** 020-7353 8559
W www.templechurch.com
The nave forms one of five remaining round churches in England

Gray's Inn, South Square WC1R 5ET **T** 020-7458 7800
W www.graysinn.info
Founded early 14th century; hall 1556–8

No other 'Inns' are active, but there are remains of *Staple Inn*, a gabled front on Holborn (opposite Gray's Inn Road). *Clement's Inn* (near St Clement Danes Church), *Clifford's Inn*, Fleet Street, and *Thavies Inn*, Holborn Circus, are all rebuilt. *Serjeants' Inn*, Fleet Street, and another (demolished 1910) of the same name in Chancery Lane, were composed of Serjeants-at-Law, the last of whom died in 1922

Institute of Contemporary Arts
The Mall SW1Y 5AH **T** 020-7930 3647 **W** www.ica.org.uk
Exhibitions of modern art in the fields of film, theatre, new media and the visual arts

Lloyd's
Lime Street EC3M 7HA **T** 020-7327 1000
W www.lloyds.com
International insurance market which evolved during the 17th century from Lloyd's Coffee House. The present building was opened for business in May 1986, and houses the Lutine Bell. Underwriting is on three floors with a total area of 10,591 sq. m (114,000 sq. ft). The Lloyd's building is not open to the general public

London Central Mosque and the Islamic Cultural Centre
Park Road NW8 7RG **T** 020-7725 2213 **W** www.iccuk.org
The focus for London's Muslims; established in 1944 but not completed until 1977, the mosque can accommodate about 5,000 worshippers; guided tours are available

London Eye
South Bank SE1 7PB **T** 0870-990 8883
W www.londoneye.com
Opened in March 2000 as London's millennium landmark, this 450ft observation wheel is the tallest cantilevered observation wheel in the world. The wheel provides a 30-minute ride offering panoramic views of the capital

London Zoo
Regent's Park NW1 4RY **T** 020-7722 3333
W www.londonzoo.org

Madame Tussauds
Marylebone Road NW1 5LR **T** 0871-894 3000
W www.madametussauds.com
Waxwork exhibition

Marlborough House
Pall Mall SW1Y 5HX **T** 020-7747 6500
W www.thecommonwealth.org
Built by Sir Christopher Wren for the first Duke of Marlborough and completed in 1711, the house reverted to the Crown in 1835. In 1863 it became the London house of the Prince of Wales and was the London home of Queen Mary until her death in 1953. In 1959 Marlborough House was given by the Queen as the headquarters for the Commonwealth Secretariat and it was opened as such in 1965. The Queen's Chapel, Marlborough Gate, was begun in 1623 from the designs of Inigo Jones for the Infanta Maria of Spain, and completed for Queen Henrietta Maria. Marlborough House is not open to the public

Mansion House
Cannon Street EC4N 8BH **T** 020-7626 2500
W www.cityoflondon.gov.uk
The official residence of the Lord Mayor. Built in the 18th century in the Palladian style. Open to groups by appointment only

Neasden Temple
BAPS Shri Swaminarayan Mandir, 105–119 Brentfield Road, Neasden NW10 8LD **T** 020-8965 2651 **W** www.mandir.org
The first and largest traditional Hindu Mandir outside of India; opened in 1995

Olympic Park
Stratford E20 **T** 0845-267 2012 **W** www.london2012.com
The heart of the London 2012 Olympic Games, the purpose-built park comprises nine sporting venues including the Olympic Stadium, Velodrome and Aquatics Centre in addition to the Olympic Village

Port of London
Port of London Authority, Bakers' Hall, 7 Harp Lane
EC3R 6LB **T** 01474-562200 **W** www.pla.co.uk
The Port of London covers the tidal section of the river Thames from Teddington to the seaward limit (the outer Tongue buoy and the Sunk light vessel), a distance of 150km. The governing body is the Port of London Authority (PLA). Cargo is handled at privately operated riverside terminals between Fulham and Canvey Island, including the enclosed dock at Tilbury, 40km below London Bridge. Passenger vessels and cruise liners can be handled at moorings at Greenwich, Tower Bridge and Tilbury

Roman Remains
The city wall of Roman *Londinium* was largely rebuilt during the medieval period but sections may be seen near the White Tower in the Tower of London; at Tower Hill; at Coopers' Row; at All Hallows, London Wall, its vestry being built on the remains of a semi-circular Roman bastion; at St Alphage, London Wall, showing a succession of building repairs from the Roman until the late medieval period; and at St Giles, Cripplegate. Sections of the great forum and basilica, more than 165 sq. m, have been encountered during excavations in the area of Leadenhall, Gracechurch Street and Lombard Street. Traces of Roman activity along the river include a massive riverside wall built in the late Roman period, and a succession of Roman timber quays along Lower and Upper Thames Street. Finds from these sites can be seen at the Museum of London.

Other major buildings are the amphitheatre at Guildhall, remains of bath-buildings in Upper and Lower Thames Street, and the temple of Mithras in Walbrook

Royal Albert Hall
Kensington Gore SW7 2AP **T** 020-7589 8212
W www.royalalberthall.com
The elliptical hall, one of the largest in the world, was completed in 1871; since 1941 it has been the venue each summer for the Promenade Concerts founded in 1895 by Sir Henry Wood. Other events include pop and classical music concerts, dance, opera, sporting events, conferences and banquets

Royal Courts of Justice
Strand WC2A 2LL **T** 020-7947 6000
W www.hmcourts-service.gov.uk
Victorian Gothic building that is home to the high court. Visitors are free to watch proceedings

Royal Hospital, Chelsea
Royal Hospital Road SW3 4SR **T** 020-7881 5200
W www.chelsea-pensioners.co.uk
Founded by Charles II in 1682 and built by Sir Christopher Wren; opened in 1692 for old and disabled soldiers. The extensive grounds include the former Ranelagh Gardens and are the venue for the Chelsea Flower Show each May

Royal Naval College
Greenwich SE10 9LW **T** 020-8269 4747
W www.oldroyalnavalcollege.org
The building was the Greenwich Hospital until 1869. It was built by Charles II, largely from designs by John

Webb, and by Queen Mary II and William III, from designs by Wren. It stands on the site of an ancient abbey, a royal house and Greenwich Palace, which was constructed by Henry VII. Henry VIII, Mary I and Elizabeth I were born in the royal palace and Edward VI died there

Royal Opera House
Covent Garden WC2E 9DD T 020-7240 1200
W www.roh.org.uk
Home of The Royal Ballet (1931) and The Royal Opera (1946). The Royal Opera House is the third theatre to be built on the site, opening 1858; the first was opened in 1732

St James's Palace
Pall Mall SW1A 1BQ T 020-7930 4832
W www.royal.gov.uk
Built by Henry VIII, only the Gatehouse and Presence Chamber remain; later alterations were made by Wren and Kent. Representatives of foreign powers are still accredited 'to the Court of St James's'. *Clarence House* (1825), the official London residence of the Prince of Wales and his sons, stands within the St James's Palace estate

St Paul's Cathedral
St Paul's Churchyard EC4M 8AD T 020-7236 4128
E chapter@stpaulscathedral.org.uk W www.stpauls.co.uk
Built 1675–1710. The cross on the dome is 111m (365ft) above ground level, the inner cupola 66.4m (218ft) above the floor. 'Great Paul' in the south-west tower weighs nearly 17 tons. The organ by Father Smith (enlarged by Willis and rebuilt by Mander) is in a case carved by Grinling Gibbons, who also carved the choir stalls

Shard
London Bridge SE1 T 020-7493 5311
W www.the-shard.com
Due to be completed in May 2012, the skyscraper standing at 310m (1,016ft) possesses a unique facade of 11,000 glass panels and a 360-degree viewing gallery

Somerset House
Strand WC2R 1LA T 020 7845 4600
W www.somersethouse.org.uk
The river facade (183m/600ft long) was built in 1776–1801 from the designs of Sir William Chambers; the eastern extension, which houses part of King's College, was built by Smirke in 1829–35. Somerset House was the property of Lord Protector Somerset, at whose attainder in 1552 the palace passed to the Crown, and it was a royal residence until 1692. Somerset House has recently undergone extensive renovation and is home to the Gilbert Collection, Embankment Galleries and the Courtauld Institute Gallery. Open-air concerts and ice-skating (Dec–Jan) are held in the courtyard

SOUTH BANK, SE1
Arts complex on the south bank of the river Thames which consists of:
The *Royal Festival Hall* T 020-7960 4200
W www.southbankcentre.co.uk
Opened in 1951 for the Festival of Britain, adjacent are the *Queen Elizabeth Hall,* the *Purcell Room* and the *Hayward Gallery*
BFI Southbank T 020-7633 0274 W www.bfi.org.uk
Opened in 1952 and is administered by the British Film Institute, has three auditoria and an IMAX cinema. The London Film Festival is held there every November
The *Royal National Theatre,* T 020-7452 3000
W www.nationaltheatre.org.uk

Opened in 1976; comprises the Olivier, the Lyttelton and the Cottesloe theatres

Southwark Cathedral
London Bridge SE1 9DA T 020-7367 6700
W www.cathedral.southwark.anglican.org
Mainly 13th century, but the nave is largely rebuilt. The tomb of John Gower (1330–1408) is between the Bunyan and Chaucer memorial windows in the north aisle; Shakespeare's effigy, backed by a view of Southwark and the Globe Theatre, is in the south aisle; the tomb of Bishop Andrewes (d.1626) is near the screen. The Lady Chapel was the scene of the consistory courts of the reign of Mary (Gardiner and Bonner) and is still used as a consistory court. John Harvard, after whom Harvard University is named, was baptised here in 1607, and the chapel by the north choir aisle is his memorial chapel

Thames Embankments
Sir Joseph Bazalgette (1819–91) constructed the *Victoria Embankment,* on the north side from Westminster to Blackfriars for the Metropolitan Board of Works, 1864–70; (the seats, of which the supports of some are a kneeling camel, laden with spicery, and of others a winged sphinx, were presented by the Grocers' Company and by W. H. Smith, MP, in 1874); the *Albert Embankment,* on the south side from Westminster Bridge to Vauxhall, 1866–9, and the Chelsea Embankment, 1871–4. The total cost exceeded £2m. Bazalgette also inaugurated the London main drainage system, 1858–65. A medallion *(Flumini vincula posuit)* has been placed on a pier of the *Victoria Embankment* to commemorate the engineer

Thames Flood Barrier
W www.environment-agency.gov.uk
Officially opened in May 1984, though first used in February 1983, the barrier consists of ten rising sector gates which span approximately 570 yards from bank to bank of the Thames at Woolwich Reach. When not in use the gates lie horizontally, allowing shipping to navigate the river normally; when the barrier is closed, the gates turn through 90 degrees to stand vertically more than 50 feet above the river bed. The barrier took eight years to complete and can be raised within about 30 minutes

Trafalgar Tavern
Park Row, Greenwich SE10 9NW T 020-8858 2909
W www.trafalgartavern.co.uk
Regency-period riverside public house built in 1837. Charles Dickens and William Gladstone were patrons

Westminster Abbey
Broad Sanctuary SW1P 3PA T 020-7222 5152
E info@westminster-abbey.org
W www.westminster-abbey.org
Founded as a Benedictine monastery over 1,000 years ago, the church was rebuilt by Edward the Confessor in 1065 and again by Henry III in the 13th century. The abbey is the resting place for monarchs including Edward I, Henry III, Henry V, Henry VII, Elizabeth I, Mary I and Mary Queen of Scots, and has been the setting of coronations since that of William the Conqueror in 1066. In Poets' Corner there are memorials to many literary figures, and many scientists and musicians are also remembered here. The grave of the Unknown Warrior is to be found in the nave

Westminster Cathedral
Francis Street SW1P 1QW T 020-7798 9055
W www.westminstercathedral.org.uk
Roman Catholic cathedral built 1895–1903 from the designs of J. F. Bentley. The campanile is 284ft high

LONDON 2012 OLYMPIC GAMES VENUES

Venue   *Event*

Olympic Park, Stratford E20
  Aquatics Centre   swimming, synchronised swimming, diving
  Basketball Arena   basketball, handball
  BMX Circuit   cycling (BMX)
  Handball Arena   handball
  Hockey Centre   hockey
  Olympic Stadium   opening/closing ceremony, athletics
  Velodrome   cycling (track)
  Water Polo Arena   water polo

Greater London
  Earls Court, SW5 9TA   volleyball
  ExCel Arena, E16 1XL   boxing, fencing, judo, table tennis, taekwondo, weightlifting,
                                           wrestling (freestyle/Greco-Roman)
  Greenwich Park, SE10   equestrian (dressage/eventing/jumping)
  Hampton Court Palace, KT8 9AU   cycling (road)
  Horse Guards' Parade, SW1   beach volleyball
  Hyde Park, W1/W2   swimming (marathon), triathlon
  Lords Cricket Ground, NW8 8QN   archery
  The Mall, SW1A   athletics (marathon/walk), cycling (road)
  North Greenwich Arena, SE10 0DX   gymnastics (artistic/trampoline), basketball
  The Royal Artillery Barracks, SE18   shooting
  Wembley Arena, HA9 0AA   badminton, gymnastics (rhythmic)
  Wembley Stadium, HA9 0WS   football
  Wimbledon, SW19 5AE   tennis

Modern pentathlon takes place at the Handball Arena, Aquatics Centre and Greenwich Park

Rest of UK
  City of Coventry Stadium, W. Midlands CV6 6GE   football
  Eton Dorney, Bucks SL4 6QP   rowing, canoe sprint
  Hadleigh Farm, Essex SS7   cycling (mountain bike)
  Hampden Park, Glasgow G42 9BA   football
  Lee Valley White Water Centre, Herts E9 1AB   canoe slalom
  Millennium Stadium, Cardiff CF10 1NS   football
  Old Trafford, Manchester M16 0RA   football
  St James' Park, Newcastle NE1 4ST   football
  Weymouth and Portland, Dorset DT5 1SA   sailing

HALLMARKS

Hallmarks are the symbols stamped on gold, silver, palladium or platinum articles to indicate that they have been tested at an official Assay Office and that they conform to one of the legal standards. The marking of gold and silver articles to identify the maker was instituted in England in 1363 under a statute of Edward III. In 1478 the Assay Office in Goldsmiths' Hall was established and all gold and silversmiths were required to bring their wares to be date-marked by the Hall, hence the term 'hallmarked'.

With certain exceptions, all gold, silver, palladium or platinum articles are required by law to be hallmarked before they are offered for sale. Current hallmarking requirements come under the UK Hallmarking Act 1973 and subsequent amendments. The act is built around the principle of description, where it is an offence for any person to apply to an unhallmarked article a description indicating that it is wholly or partly made of gold, silver, palladium or platinum. There is an exemption by weight: compulsory hallmarks are not needed on gold and palladium under 1g, silver under 7.78g and platinum under 0.5g. Also, some descriptions, such as rolled gold and gold plate, are permissible. The British Hallmarking Council is a statutory body created as a result of the Hallmarking Act. It ensures adequate provision for assaying and hallmarking, supervises the assay offices and ensures the enforcement of hallmarking legislation. The four assay offices at London, Birmingham, Sheffield and Edinburgh operate under the act.

BRITISH HALLMARKING COUNCIL Secretariat, 1 Colmore Square, Birmingham B4 6AA T 0800-763 1414 W www.britishhallmarkingcouncil.gov.uk

COMPULSORY MARKS

Since January 1999 UK hallmarks have consisted of three compulsory symbols – the sponsor's mark, the millesimal fineness (purity) mark and the assay office mark. The distinction between UK and foreign articles has been removed, and more finenesses are now legal, reflecting the more common finenesses elsewhere in Europe.

SPONSOR'S MARK
Formerly known as the maker's mark, the sponsor's mark was instituted in England in 1363. Originally a device such as a bird or fleur-de-lis, now it consists of a combination of at least two initials (usually a shortened form of the manufacturer's name) and a shield design. The London Assay Office offers 45 standard shield designs but other designs are possible by arrangement.

MILLESIMAL FINENESS MARK
The millesimal fineness (purity) mark indicates the number of parts per thousand of pure metal in the alloy. The current finenesses allowed in the UK are:

Gold	999; 990; 916.6 (22 carat); 750 (18 carat); 585 (14 carat); 375 (9 carat)
Silver	999; 958.4 (Britannia); 925 (sterling); 800
Palladium	999; 950; 500
Platinum	999; 950; 900; 850

ASSAY OFFICE MARK
This mark identifies the particular assay office at which the article was tested and marked. The British assay offices are:

 LONDON, Goldsmiths' Hall, Gutter Lane, London EC2V 8AQ T 020-7606 8971 W www.thegoldsmiths.co.uk

 BIRMINGHAM, PO Box 151, Newhall Street, Birmingham B3 1SB T 0121-236 6951 W www.theassayoffice.co.uk

 SHEFFIELD, Guardians' Hall, Beulah Road, Hillsborough, Sheffield S6 2AN T 0114-231 2121 W www.assayoffice.co.uk

 EDINBURGH, Goldsmiths' Hall, 24 Broughton Street, Edinburgh EH1 3RH T 0131-556 1144 W www.assayofficescotland.com

Assay offices formerly existed in other towns, eg Chester, Exeter, Glasgow, Newcastle, Norwich and York, each having its own distinguishing mark.

OPTIONAL MARKS

Since 1999 traditional pictorial marks such as a crown for gold, the Britannia for 958 silver, the lion passant for 925 silver (lion rampant in Scotland) and the orb for 950 platinum may be added voluntarily to the millesimal mark. In 2010 a pictorial mark for 950 palladium was introduced.

 Gold – a crown

 Sterling silver (Scotland)

 Britannia silver

 Platinum – an orb

 Sterling silver (England)

 Palladium – the Greek goddess Pallas Athene

DATE LETTER

The date letter shows the year in which an article was assayed and hallmarked. Each alphabetical cycle has a distinctive style of lettering or shape of shield. The date letters were different at the various assay offices and the particular office must be established from the assay office mark before reference is made to tables of date letters. Date letter marks became voluntary from 1 January 1999.

The table which follows shows one specimen shield and letter used by the London Assay Office on silver articles for each alphabetical cycle from 1498. The same letters are found on gold articles but the surrounding shield may differ. Until 1 January 1975 two calendar years are given for each specimen date letter as the letter changed annually in May on St Dunstan's Day (the patron saint of silversmiths). Since 1 January 1975, each date letter has indicated a calendar year from January to December and each office has used the same style of date letter and shield for all articles:

LONDON (GOLDSMITHS' HALL) DATE LETTERS FROM 1498

from	to		from	to
1498–9	1517–18		1756–7	1775–6
1518–19	1537–8		1776–7	1795–6
1538–9	1557–8		1796–7	1815–16
1558–9	1577–8		1816–17	1835–6
1578–9	1597–8		1836–7	1855–6
1598–9	1617–18		1856–7	1875–6
1618–19	1637–8		1876–7 (A to M square shield, N to Z as shown)	1895–6
1638–9	1657–8		1896–7	1915–16
1658–9	1677–8		1916–17	1935–6
1678–9	1696–7		1936–7	1955–6
1697	1715–16		1956–7	1974
1716–17	1735–6		1975	1999
1736–7	1738–9		2000	
1739–40	1755–6			

OTHER MARKS

FOREIGN GOODS

Foreign goods imported into the UK are required to be hallmarked before sale, unless they already bear a convention mark (*see* below) or a hallmark struck by an independent assay office in the European Economic Area which is deemed to be equivalent to a UK hallmark.

The following are the assay office marks used for gold imported articles until the end of 1998. For silver and platinum the symbols remain the same but the shields differ in shape.

 London   *Sheffield*

 Birmingham   *Edinburgh*

CONVENTION HALLMARKS

The UK has been a signatory to the International Convention on Hallmarks since 1972. A convention hallmark struck by the UK assay offices is recognised by all member countries in the convention and, similarly, convention marks from member countries are legally recognised in the UK. There are currently 19 members of the hallmarking convention: Austria, Cyprus, Czech Republic, Denmark, Finland, Hungary, Ireland, Israel, Latvia, Lithuania, the Netherlands, Norway, Poland, Portugal, Slovakia, Slovenia, Sweden, Switzerland, and the UK.

A convention hallmark comprises four marks: a sponsor's mark, a common control mark, a fineness mark, and an assay office mark.

Examples of common control marks (figures differ according to fineness, but the style of each mark remains the same for each article):

GOLD	SILVER	PALLADIUM	PLATINUM

COMMEMORATIVE MARKS

There are other marks to commemorate special events: the silver jubilee of King George V and Queen Mary in 1935, the coronation of Queen Elizabeth II in 1953, her silver jubilee in 1977, and her golden jubilee in 2002. During 1999 and 2000 there was a voluntary additional Millennium Mark. A mark to commemorate the Queen's diamond jubilee in 2012 is available from July 2011 to October 2012:

   Diamond Jubilee Hallmark

BRITISH CURRENCY

The unit of currency is the pound sterling (£) of 100 pence. The decimal system was introduced on 15 February 1971.

COIN

Gold Coins	Bi-colour Coins ‡
One hundred pounds £100*	Two pounds £2
Fifty pounds £50*	Nickel-Brass Coins
Twenty-five pounds £25*	Two pounds £2 (pre-1997)§
Ten pounds £10*	One pound £1
Five pounds £5	
Two pounds £2	Cupro-Nickel Coins
Sovereign £1	Crown £5 (since 1990)§
Half-sovereign 50p	50 pence 50p
	Crown 25p (pre-1990)§
Silver Coins	20 pence 20p
(Britannia coins*)	10 pence 10p
Two pounds £2	5 pence 5p
One pound £1	
50 pence 50p	Bronze Coins
Twenty pence 20p	2 pence 2p
	1 penny 1p
Maundy Money†	
Fourpence 4p	Copper-plated Steel Coins ¶
Threepence 3p	2 pence 2p
Twopence 2p	1 penny 1p
Penny 1p	

* Britannia coins: gold bullion coins introduced 1987; silver coins introduced 1997

† Gifts of special money distributed by the sovereign annually on Maundy Thursday to the number of elderly men and women corresponding to the sovereign's own age

‡ Cupro-nickel centre and nickel-brass outer ring

§ Commemorative coins; not intended for general circulation

¶ Since September 1992, although in 1998 the 2p was struck in both copper-plated steel and bronze

GOLD COIN

Gold ceased to circulate during the First World War. Since then controls on buying, selling and holding gold coins have been imposed at various times but have subsequently been revoked. Under the Exchange Control (Gold Coins Exemption) Order 1979, gold coins may now be imported and exported without restriction, except gold coins which are more than 50 years old and valued at a sum in excess of £8,000; these cannot be exported without specific authorisation from the Department for Business, Innovation and Skills.

Value Added Taxation on the sale of gold coins was revoked in 2000.

SILVER COIN

Prior to 1920 silver coins were struck from sterling silver, an alloy of which 925 parts in 1,000 were silver. In 1920 the proportion of silver was reduced to 500 parts. Since 1947 all 'silver' coins, except Maundy money, have been struck from cupro-nickel, an alloy of 75 parts copper and 25 parts nickel, except for the 20p, composed of 84 parts copper, 16 parts nickel. Maundy coins continue to be struck from sterling silver.

BRONZE COIN

Bronze, introduced in 1860 to replace copper, is an alloy consisting mainly of copper with small amounts of zinc and tin. Bronze was replaced by copper-plated steel in September 1992 with the exception of 1998 when the 2p was made in both copper-plated steel and bronze.

LEGAL TENDER

Gold (dated 1838 onwards, if not below least current weight)	to any amount
£5 (Crown since 1990)*	to any amount
£2	to any amount
£1	to any amount
50p	up to £10
25p (Crown pre-1990)*	up to £10
20p	up to £10
10p	up to £5
5p	up to £5
2p	up to 20p
1p	up to 20p

* Only redeemable at the Post Office

The £1 coin was introduced in 1983 to replace the £1 note. The following coins have ceased to be legal tender:

Farthing	31 Dec 1960
Halfpenny (½d)	31 Jul 1969
Half-crown	31 Dec 1969
Threepence	31 Aug 1971
Penny (1d)	31 Aug 1971
Sixpence	30 Jun 1980
Halfpenny (½p)	31 Dec 1984
Old 5 pence	31 Dec 1990
Old 10 pence	30 Jun 1993
Old 50 pence	28 Feb 1998

The Channel Islands and the Isle of Man issue their own coinage, which is legal tender only in the island of issue.

COIN STANDARDS

	Metal	Standard weight (g)	Standard diameter (mm)
1p	bronze	3.56	20.3
1p	copper-plated steel	3.56	20.3
2p	bronze	7.13	25.9
2p	copper-plated steel	7.13	25.9
5p	cupro-nickel	3.25	18.0
10p	cupro-nickel	6.5	24.5
20p	cupro-nickel	5.0	21.4
25p Crown	cupro-nickel	28.28	38.6
50p	cupro-nickel	8.00	27.3
£1	nickel-brass	9.5	22.5
£2	nickel-brass	15.98	28.4
£2	cupro-nickel, nickel-brass	12.00	28.4
£5 Crown	cupro-nickel	28.28	38.6

The 'remedy' is the amount of variation from standard permitted in weight and fineness of coins when first issued from the Royal Mint.

THE TRIAL OF THE PYX

The Trial of the Pyx is the examination by a jury to ascertain that coins made by the Royal Mint, which have been set aside in the pyx (or box), are of the proper weight, diameter and composition required by law. The trial is held annually, presided over by the Queen's Remembrancer, with a jury of freemen of the Company of Goldsmiths.

BANKNOTES

Bank of England notes are issued in denominations of £5, £10, £20 and £50 for the amount of the fiduciary note issue, and are legal tender in England and Wales. No £1 notes have been issued since 1984 and in March 1998 the outstanding notes were written off in accordance with the provision of the Currency Act 1983.

The current E series of notes was introduced from June 1990, replacing the D series (*see* below). A new-style £20 note, the first in series F, was introduced on 13 March 2007. The historical figures portrayed in these series are:

£5	May 2002–date	Elizabeth Fry
£5	Jun 1990–2003	George Stephenson*
£10	Nov 2000–date	Charles Darwin
£10	Apr 1992–2003	Charles Dickens*
£20	Mar 2007–date	Adam Smith
£20	Jun 1999–2010	Sir Edward Elgar*
£20	Jun 1991–2001	Michael Faraday*
£50	Apr 1994–date	Sir John Houblon

* These notes have been withdrawn from circulation

NOTE CIRCULATION

Note circulation is highest at the two peak spending periods of the year: around Christmas and during the summer holiday period.

The value of notes in circulation (£ million) at the end of February 2010 and 2011 was:

	2010	2011
£5	1,245	1,355
£10	6,399	6,493
£20	30,048	30,973
£50	9,248	9,940
Other notes*	3,280	3,433
TOTAL	50,220	52,194

* Includes higher value notes used internally in the Bank of England, eg as cover for the note issues of banks in Scotland and Northern Ireland in excess of their permitted issue

LEGAL TENDER

Banknotes which are no longer legal tender are payable when presented at the head office of the Bank of England in London.

The white notes for £10, £20, £50, £100, £500 and £1,000, which were issued until April 1943, ceased to be legal tender in May 1945, and the white £5 note in March 1946.

The white £5 note issued between October 1945 and September 1956, the £5 notes issued between 1957 and 1963 (bearing a portrait of Britannia) and the first series to bear a portrait of the Queen, issued between 1963 and 1971, ceased to be legal tender in March 1961, June 1967 and September 1973 respectively.

The series of £1 notes issued during the years 1928 to 1960 and the 10 shilling notes issued from 1928 to 1961 (those without the royal portrait) ceased to be legal tender in May and October 1962 respectively. The £1 note first issued in March 1960 (bearing on the back a representation of Britannia) and the £10 note first issued in February 1964 (bearing a lion on the back), both bearing a portrait of the Queen on the front, ceased to be legal tender in June 1979. The £1 note first issued in 1978 ceased to be legal tender on 11 March 1988. The 10 shilling note was replaced by the 50p coin in October 1969, and ceased to be legal tender on 21 November 1970.

The D series of banknotes was introduced from 1970 and ceased to be legal tender from the dates shown below. The predominant identifying feature of each note was the portrayal on the back of a prominent figure from British history:

£1	Feb 1978–Mar 1988	Sir Isaac Newton
£5	Nov 1971–Nov 1991	Duke of Wellington
£10	Feb 1975–May 1994	Florence Nightingale
£20	Jul 1970–Mar 1993	William Shakespeare
£50	Mar 1981–Sep 1996	Sir Christopher Wren

The £1 coin was introduced on 21 April 1983 to replace the £1 note.

OTHER BANKNOTES

Scotland – Banknotes are issued by three Scottish banks. The Royal Bank of Scotland issues notes for £1, £5, £10, £20, £50 and £100. Bank of Scotland and the Clydesdale Bank issue notes for £5, £10, £20, £50 and £100. Scottish notes are not legal tender in the UK but they are an authorised currency.

Northern Ireland – Banknotes are issued by four banks in Northern Ireland. The Bank of Ireland, the Northern Bank and the Ulster Bank issue notes for £5, £10, £20, £50 and £100. The First Trust Bank issues notes for £10, £20, £50 and £100. Northern Ireland notes are not legal tender in Northern Ireland but they circulate widely and enjoy a status comparable to that of Bank of England notes.

Channel Islands – The States of Guernsey issues its own currency notes and coinage. The notes are for £1, £5, £10, £20 and £50, and the coins are for 1p, 2p, 5p, 10p, 20p, 50p, £1 and £2. The States of Jersey issues its own currency notes and coinage. The notes are for £1, £5, £10, £20 and £50, and the coins are for 1p, 2p, 5p, 10p, 20p, 50p, £1 and £2.

The Isle of Man – The Isle of Man government issues notes for £1, £5, £10, £20 and £50. Although these notes are only legal tender in the Isle of Man, they are accepted at face value in branches of the clearing banks in the UK. The Isle of Man issues coins for 1p, 2p, 5p, 10p, 20p, 50p, £1, £2 and £5.

Although none of the series of notes specified above is legal tender in the UK, they are generally accepted by banks irrespective of their place of issue. At one time banks made a commission charge for handling Scottish and Irish notes but this was abolished some years ago.

BANK FAMILY TREE

Includes the major retail banks operating in the UK as at
April 2011. Financial results for these banks are given on
the following page. Building societies are only included in
instances where they demutualised to become a bank.

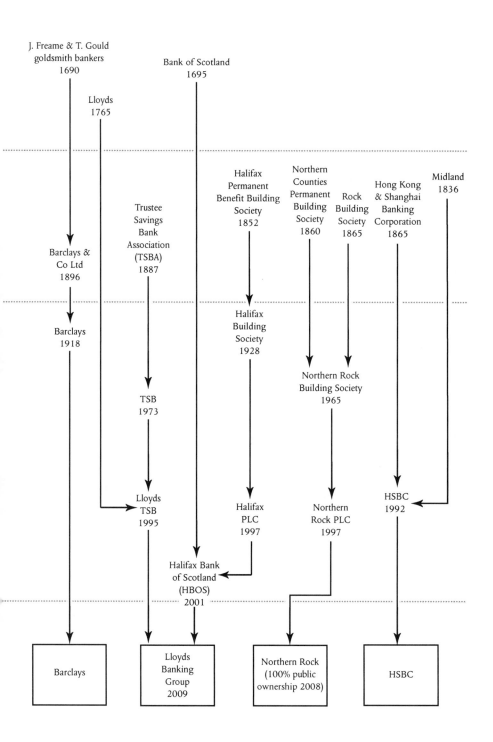

BANKING AND PERSONAL FINANCE

There are two main types of deposit-taking institutions: banks and building societies, although National Savings and Investments also provides savings products. Banks and building societies are supervised by the Financial Services Authority (*see* Financial Services Regulation) and National Savings and Investments is accountable to the Treasury. As a result of the conversion of several building societies into banks in the 1990s, the size of the banking sector, which was already substantially greater than the non-bank deposit-taking sector, increased further.

The main institutions within the British banking system are the Bank of England (the central bank), retail banks, investment banks and overseas banks. In its role as the central bank, the Bank of England acts as banker to the government and as a note-issuing authority; it also oversees the efficient functioning of payment and settlement systems.

Since May 1997, the Bank of England has had operational responsibility for monetary policy. At monthly meetings of its monetary policy committee the Bank sets the interest rate at which it will lend to the money markets.

OFFICIAL INTEREST RATES 2005–11

4 August 2005	4.50%
3 August 2006	4.75%
9 November 2006	5.00%
11 January 2007	5.25%
10 May 2007	5.50%
5 July 2007	5.75%
6 December 2007	5.50%
7 February 2008	5.25%
10 April 2008	5.00%
8 October 2008	4.50%
6 November 2008	3.00%
4 December 2008	2.00%
8 January 2009	1.50%
5 February 2009	1.00%
5 March 2009	0.50%

RETAIL BANKING

Retail banks offer a wide variety of financial services to individuals and companies, including current and deposit accounts, loan and overdraft facilities, credit and debit cards, investment services, pensions, insurance and mortgages. All banks offer telephone and internet banking facilities in addition to traditional branch services.

The Financial Ombudsman Service provides independent and impartial arbitration in disputes between banks and their customers (*see* Financial Services Regulation).

PAYMENT CLEARINGS

The UK Payments Administration (UKPA) is a trade body that brings together the organisations responsible for delivering payment services. It also provides information on payment issues such as card fraud, cheques, plastic cards, electronic payments and cash. The Payments Council sets strategy for UK payments to ensure they meet the needs of users, payment service providers and the wider economy. Membership of the Payments Council is open to any member of a payment scheme that is widely used or significant in the UK. As at April 2011 the Payments Council had 30 members, comprising banks, financial services providers, one building society and the Post Office.

There are three organisations, overseen by UKPA, that manage the majority of payment clearings in the UK:
- BACS manages the schemes under which electronic payments are made, processing direct debits, direct credits and standing orders (W www.bacs.co.uk)
- CHAPS Clearing Company provides electronic same-day clearing and real-time settlement services for sterling payments (W www.chapsco.co.uk)
- The Cheque and Credit Clearing Company manages the cheque clearing system (W www.chequeandcredit.co.uk)

PAYMENTS COUNCIL/UKPA, 2 Thomas More Square, London E1W 1YN T 020-3217 8200
W www.ukpayments.org.uk

GLOSSARY OF FINANCIAL TERMS

AER (ANNUAL EQUIVALENT RATE) – A notional rate quoted on savings and investment products which demonstrates the return on interest, when compounded and paid annually.

APR (ANNUAL PERCENTAGE RATE) – Calculates the total amount of interest payable over the whole term of a product (such as investment or loan), allowing consumers to compare rival products on a like-for-like basis. Companies offering loans, credit cards

MAJOR RETAIL BANKS' FINANCIAL RESULTS 2010

Bank group	Profit/(loss) before taxation £ million	Profit/(loss) after taxation £ million	Total assets £ million
Banco Santander Group	10,681	7,251	1,079,341
Barclays	6,065	4,549	1,489,645
Cooperative Bank	109	79	45,581
HSBC	11,601	8,648	1,495,956
Lloyds Banking Group	281	(258)	991,574
Northern Rock*	(224)	(224)	18,562
RBS Group	(239)	(902)	1,452,634
* In February 2008 Northern Rock was taken into public ownership			

mortgages or overdrafts are required by law to provide the APR rate. Where typical APR is shown, it refers to the company's typical borrower and so is given as a best example; rate and costs may vary depending on individual circumstances.

ANNUITY – A type of insurance policy that provides regular income in exchange for a lump sum. The annuity can be bought from a company other than the existing pension provider.

ASU – Accident, sickness and unemployment insurance taken out by a borrower to protect against being unable to work for these reasons. The policy will usually pay a percentage of the normal monthly mortgage repayment if the borrower is unable to work.

ATM (AUTOMATED TELLER MACHINES) – Commonly referred to as cash machines. Users can access their bank accounts using a card for simple transactions such as withdrawing and depositing cash. Some banks and independent ATM deployers charge for transactions.

BANKER'S DRAFT – A cheque drawn on a bank against a cash deposit. Considered to be a secure way of receiving money in instances where a cheque could 'bounce' or where it is not desirable to receive cash.

BASE RATE – The interest rate set by the Bank of England at which it will lend to financial institutions. This acts as a benchmark for all other interest rates.

BASIS POINT – Unit of measure (usually one-hundredth of a percentage point) used to express movements in interest rates, foreign rates or bond yields.

BUY-TO-LET – The purchase of a residential property for the sole purpose of letting to a tenant. Not all lenders provide mortgage finance for this purpose. Buy-to-let lenders assess projected rental income (typical expectations are between 125 and 130 per cent of the monthly interest payment) in addition to, or instead of, the borrower's income. Buy-to-let mortgages are available as either interest only or repayment.

CAPITAL GAIN/LOSS – Increase/decrease in the value of a capital asset when it is sold or transferred compared to its initial worth.

CAPPED RATE MORTGAGE – The interest rate applied to a loan is guaranteed not to rise above a certain rate for a set period of time; the rate can therefore fall but will not rise above the capped rate. The level at which the cap is fixed is usually higher than for a fixed rate mortgage for a comparable period of time. The lender normally imposes early redemption penalties within the first few years.

CASH CARD – Issued by banks and building societies for withdrawing cash from ATMs.

CHARGE CARD – Charge cards, eg American Express and Diners Club, can be used in a similar way to credit cards but the debt must be settled in full each month.

CHIP AND PIN CARD – A credit/debit card which incorporates an embedded chip containing unique owner details. When used with a PIN, such cards offer greater security as they are less prone to fraud. Since 14 February 2006, most card transactions in the UK have required the use of a chip and pin card.

CREDIT CARD – Normally issued with a credit limit, credit cards can be used for purchases until the limit is reached. There is normally an interest-free period on the outstanding balance of up to 56 days. Charges can be avoided if the balance is paid off in full within the interest-free period. Alternatively part of the balance can be paid and in most cases there is a minimum

amount set by the issuer (normally a percentage of the outstanding balance) which must be paid on a monthly basis. Some card issuers charge an annual fee and most issuers belong to a least one major credit card network, eg Mastercard or Visa.

CREDIT RATING – Overall credit worthiness of a borrower based on information from a credit reference agency, such as Experian or Equifax, which holds details of credit agreements, payment records, county court judgements etc for all adults in the UK. This information is supplied to lenders who use it in their credit scoring or underwriting systems to calculate the risk of granting a loan to an individual and the probability that it will be repaid. Each lender sets their own criteria for credit worthiness and may accept or reject a credit application based on an individual's credit rating.

CRITICAL ILLNESS COVER – Insurance that covers borrowers against critical illnesses such as stroke, heart attack or cancer and is designed to protect mortgage or other loan payments.

DEBIT CARD – Debit cards were introduced on a large scale in the UK in the mid-1980s, replacing cash and cheques to purchase goods and services. They can be used to withdraw cash from ATMs in the UK and abroad and may also function as a cheque guarantee card. Funds are automatically withdrawn from an individual's bank account after making a purchase and no interest is charged.

DIRECT DEBIT – An instruction from a customer to their bank, which authorises the payee to charge costs to the customer's bank account.

DISCOUNTED MORTGAGE – Discounted mortgages guarantee an interest rate set at a margin below the standard variable rate for a period of time. The discounted rate will move up or down with the standard variable rate, but the payment rate will retain the agreed differential below the standard variable rate. The lender normally imposes early redemption penalties within the first few years.

EARLY REDEMPTION PENALTY – see Redemption Penalty

ENDOWMENT MORTGAGE – Only the interest on a property loan is paid back to the lender each month as long as an endowment life insurance policy is taken out for an agreed amount of time, typically 25 years. When the policy matures the lender will take repayment of the money owed on the property loan and any surplus goes to the policyholder. If the endowment policy shows a shortfall on projected returns, the policy holder must make further provision to pay off the mortgage.

EQUITY – When applied to real estate, equity is the difference between the value of a property and the amount outstanding on any loan secured against it. Negative equity occurs when the loan is greater than the market value of the property.

FIXED RATE MORTGAGE – A repayment mortgage where the interest rate on the loan is fixed for a set amount of time, normally a period of between one and ten years. The interest rate does not vary with changes to the base rate resulting in the monthly mortgage payment remaining the same for the duration of the fixed period. The lender normally imposes early redemption penalties within the first few years.

ISA (INDIVIDUAL SAVINGS ACCOUNT) – A means by which investors can save (in a cash ISA) and invest (in a stocks and shares ISA) without paying any tax on the proceeds. There are limits on the amount that can be invested during any given tax year (*see* Taxation).

INTEREST ONLY MORTGAGE – Only interest is paid by the borrower and capital remains constant for the term of the loan. The onus is on the borrower to make provision to repay the capital at the end of the term. This is usually achieved through an investment vehicle such as an endowment policy or pension.

LOAN TO VALUE (LTV) – This is the ratio between the size of a mortgage loan sought and the mortgage lender's valuation. On a loan of £55,000, for example, on a property valued at £100,000 the loan to value is 55 per cent. This means that there is sufficient equity in the property for the lender to be reassured that if interest or capital repayments were stopped, it could sell the property and recoup the money owed. Fewer options are available to borrowers requiring high LTV.

LONDON INTERBANK OFFERED RATE (LIBOR) – Is the interest rate that London banks charge when lending to one another on the wholesale money market. LIBOR is set by supply and demand of money as banks lend to each other in order to balance their books on a daily basis.

MIG (MORTGAGE INDEMNITY GUARANTEE) – An insurance for the lender paid by the borrower on high LTV mortgages (typically more than 90 per cent). It is a policy designed to protect the lender against loss in the event of the borrower defaulting or ceasing to repay a mortgage and is usually paid as a one-off premium or can be added to the value of the loan. It offers no protection to the borrower. Not all lenders charge MIG premiums.

OVERDRAFT – An 'authorised' overdraft is an arrangement made between customer and bank allowing the balance of the customer's account to go below zero; interest is normally charged at an agreed rate and sometimes an arrangement fee is charged. If the negative balance exceeds the agreed terms or a prior arrangement for an overdraft facility has not been made (an 'unauthorised' overdraft) then additional penalty fees may be charged and higher interest rates may apply. Interest-free overdrafts are availble for customers in certain circumstances, such as full-time higher education students and recent graduates.

PERSONAL PENSION PLAN (PPP) – Designed for the self-employed or those in non-pensionable employment. Contributions made to a PPP are exempt from tax and the retirement age may be selected at any time from age 50 to 75. Up to 25 per cent of the pension fund may be taken as a tax-free cash sum on retirement.

PHISHING – A fraudulent attempt to obtain bank account details and security codes through an email. The email purports to come from a *bona fide* bank or building society and attempts to steer the recipient, usually under the pretext that the banking institution is updating its security arrangements, to a website which requests personal details.

PIN (PERSONAL IDENTIFICATION NUMBER) – A PIN is issued alongside a cash card to allow the user to access a bank account via an ATM. PINs are also issued with smart, credit and debit cards and, since 14 February 2006, have been requested in the majority of shops and restaurants as a security measure when making a purchase.

PORTABLE MORTGAGE – A mortgage product that can be transferred to a different property in the event of a house move. Preferable where early redemption penalties are charged.

REDEMPTION PENALTY – A charge levied for paying off a loan, debt balance or mortgage before a date agreed with the lender.

REPAYMENT MORTGAGE – In contrast to the interest only mortgage, the monthly repayment includes an element of the capital sum borrowed in addition to the interest charged.

SELF-CERTIFICATION – Some lenders allow borrowers to self-certify their income. This type of scheme is useful to the self-employed who may not have accounts available or any other person who has difficulty proving their regular income.

SHARE – A share is a divided-up unit of the value of a company. If a company is worth £100m, and there are 50 million shares in issue, then each share is worth £2 (usually listed as pence). As the overall value of the company fluctuates so does the share price.

SMART CARD – *see* chip and pin card

STANDING ORDER – An instruction made by the customer to their bank, which allows the transfer of a set amount to a payee at regular intervals.

TELEPHONE BANKING – Banking facilities which can be accessed via the telephone.

UNIT TRUST – A 'pooled' fund of assets, usually shares, owned by a number of individuals. Managed by professional, authorised fund-management groups, unit trusts have traditionally delivered better returns than average cash deposits, but do rise and fall in value as their underlying investment varies in value.

VARIABLE RATE MORTGAGE – Repayment mortgages where the interest rate set by the lender increases or decreases in relation to the base interest rate which can result in fluctuating monthly repayments.

WITH-PROFITS – Usually applies to pensions, endowments, savings schemes or bonds. The intention is to smooth out the rises and falls in the stock market for the benefit of the investor. Actuaries working for the insurance company, or fund managers, hold back some profits in good years in order to make up the difference in years when shares perform badly.

FINANCIAL SERVICES REGULATION

FINANCIAL SERVICES AUTHORITY

The FSA has been the single regulator for financial services in the UK since 1 December 2001, when the Financial Services and Markets Act 2000 (FSMA) came into force. Under the FSMA the FSA has four main statutory objectives:
- maintaining market confidence
- contributing to financial stability
- protecting consumers
- reducing financial crime

In June 2010, the Chancellor of the Exchequer announced the government's intention to restructure the UK's financial regulatory framework and replace the FSA with two new regulatory bodies by 2013:
- The Prudential Regulation Authority (PRA), a subsidiary of the bank of England, will be responsible for promoting the stable and prudent operation of the financial system through the regulation of all deposit-taking institutions, insurers and investment banks
- The Financial Conduct Authority (FCA) will be responsible for regulation of conduct in retail, wholesale and financial markets and the infrastructure that supports these markets. The FCA will also have responsibility for the regulation of firms that do not fall under the PRA's scope.

On 4 April 2011, in order to ensure a smooth transition to the new regulatory framework, the FSA changed it's organisational structure, replacing the supervision and risk business units with a prudential business unit and a conduct business unit.

FUNDING
The FSA is a company limited by guarantee and financed by levies on the industry. It receives no funds from the public purse. It is accountable to treasury ministers and, through them, to parliament. The FSA must report annually on the achievement of its statutory objectives to the Treasury, which is required to lay the report before parliament. The FSA's budget for 2011–12 is £500.5m.

FSA REGISTER
The FSA register is a public record of financial services firms, individuals and other bodies who come under the FSA's regulatory jurisdiction as defined in the FSMA. The register has information on all authorised firms currently doing business in the UK. It includes firms that are UK registered as well as those authorised in other European economic area states that conduct business in the UK. Each entry outlines exactly what regulated activities the firm or individual is authorised to carry out.

FINANCIAL SERVICES AUTHORITY, 25 The North Colonnade, Canary Wharf, London E14 5HS T 020-7066 1000
W www.fsa.gov.uk
Chair, Lord Turner of Ecchinswell
Chief Executive, Hector Sants

COMPENSATION

Created under the FSMA, the Financial Services Compensation Scheme (FSCS) is the UK's statutory fund of last resort for customers of authorised financial services firms. It provides compensation if a firm authorised by the FSA is unable, or likely to be unable, to pay claims against it. In general this is when a firm has stopped trading and has insufficient assets to meet claims, or is in insolvency. The FSCS covers deposits, insurance policies, insurance broking, investment business and mortgage advice and arranging. The FSCS is independent of the FSA, with separate staff and premises. However, the FSA appoints the board of the FSCS and sets its guidelines. The FSCS is funded by levies on authorised firms.

The Pension Protection Fund (PPF) is a statutory fund established under the Pensions Act 2004 and became operational on 6 April 2005. The fund was set up to pay compensation to members of eligible defined benefit pension schemes, where there is a qualifying insolvency event in relation to the employer and where there are insufficient assets in the pension scheme to cover PPF levels of compensation. Compulsory annual levies are charged on all eligible schemes to help fund the PPF, in addition to investment of PPF assets.

FINANCIAL SERVICES COMPENSATION SCHEME, 7th Floor, Lloyds Chambers, Portsoken Street, London E1 8BN
T 020-7741 4100/0800-678 1100 E enquiries@fscs.org.uk
W www.fscs.org.uk
Chair, David Hall
Chief Executive, Mark Neale
PENSION PROTECTION FUND, Knollys House, 17 Addiscombe Road, Croydon, Surrey CR0 6SR T 0845-600 2541
E information@ppf.gsi.gov.uk
W www.pensionprotectionfund.org.uk
Chair, Lady Judge, CBE
Chief Executive, Alan Rubenstein

DESIGNATED PROFESSIONAL BODIES

Professional firms are exempt from requiring direct regulation by the FSA if they carry out only certain restricted activities that arise out of, or are complementary to, the provision of professional services, such as arranging the sale of shares on the instructions of executors or trustees, or providing services to small, private companies. These firms are, however, supervised by designated professional bodies (DPBs). There are a number of safeguards to protect consumers dealing with firms that do not require direct regulation. These arrangements include:
- the FSA's power to ban a specific firm from taking advantage of the exemption and to restrict the regulated activities permitted to the firms
- rules which require professional firms to ensure that their clients are aware that they are not authorised persons
- a requirement for the DPBs to supervise and regulate the firms and inform the FSA on how the professional firms carry on their regulated activities

See Professional Education section for contact details of the following DPBs:

Association of Chartered Certified Accountants
Council for Licensed Conveyancers
Institute and Faculty of Actuaries
Institute of Chartered Accountants in England and Wales
Institute of Chartered Accountants in Ireland
Institute of Chartered Accountants of Scotland
Law Society of England and Wales
Law Society of Northern Ireland
Law Society of Scotland
Royal Institution of Chartered Surveyors

RECOGNISED INVESTMENT EXCHANGES

The FSA currently supervises six recognised investment exchanges (RIEs) in the UK; under the FSMA, recognition confers an exemption from the need to be authorised to carry out regulated activities in the UK. The RIEs are organised markets on which member firms can trade investments such as equities and derivatives. As a regulator the FSA must focus on the impact of changes brought about by the continued growth in electronic trading by exchanges and other organisations. Issues such as how these changes affect market quality, reliability and access are important and the FSA works with the exchanges to ensure that new systems meet regulatory requirements. The RIEs are listed with their year of recognition in parentheses:

EUROPEAN DERIVATIVES EXCHANGE (EDX) LONDON (2003), 10 Paternoster Square, London EC4M 7LS T 020-7797 4683 W www.londonstockexchange.com/edx/home/homepage.htm
INTERCONTINENTAL EXCHANGE (ICE) FUTURES EUROPE (2001), 5th Floor, Milton Gate, 60 Chiswell Street, London EC1Y 4SA T 020-7065 7700 W www.theice.com
LONDON INTERNATIONAL FINANCIAL FUTURES (LIFFE) ADMINISTRATION AND MANAGEMENT (2001), Cannon Bridge House, 1 Cousin Lane, London EC4R 3XX T 020-7623 0444 W www.liffe.com
LONDON METAL EXCHANGE (2001), 56 Leadenhall Street, London EC3A 2BJ T 020-7264 5555 W www.lme.co.uk
LONDON STOCK EXCHANGE (LSE) (2001), 10 Paternoster Square, London EC4M 7LS T 020-7797 1000 W www.londonstockexchange.com
PLUS STOCK EXCHANGE (2007), 33 Queen Street, London EC4R 1AP T 020-7429 7800 W www.plusmarketsgroup.com

RECOGNISED CLEARING HOUSES

The FSA is also responsible for recognising and supervising recognised clearing houses (RCHs), which organise the settlement of transactions on recognised investment exchanges. There are currently five RCHs in the UK:

CME CLEARING EUROPE (2010), Watling House, 33 Cannon Street, London EC4M 5SB T 020-7796 7150 W www.cmeclearingeurope.co.uk
EUROCLEAR UK AND IRELAND (2001), Watling House, 33 Cannon Street, London EC4M 5SB T 020-7849 0000 W www.crestco.co.uk
EUROPEAN CENTRAL COUNTERPARTY (2008), Broadgate West, 1 Snowdon Street, London EC2A 2DQ T 020-7650 1401 W www.euroccp.co.uk
ICE CLEAR EUROPE (2008), 5th Floor, Milton Gate, 60 Chiswell Street, London EC1Y 4SA T 020-7265 3648 W www.theice.com/clear_europe

LONDON CLEARING HOUSE (LCH) CLEARNET (2001), Aldgate House, 33 Aldgate High Street, London EC3N 1EA T 020-7426 7000 W www.lchclearnet.com

OMBUDSMAN SCHEMES

The Financial Ombudsman Service was set up by the Financial Services and Markets Act 2000 to provide consumers with a free, independent service for resolving disputes with authorised financial firms. The Financial Ombudsman Service can consider complaints about most financial matters including: banking; credit cards and store cards; financial advice; hire purchase and pawnbroking; insurance; loans and credit; money transfer; mortgages; pensions; savings and investments; stocks, shares, unit trusts and bonds.

Complainants must first complain to the firm involved. They do not have to accept the ombudsman's decision and are free to go to court if they wish, but if a decision is accepted, it is binding for both the complainant and the firm.

The Pensions Ombudsman can investigate and decide complaints and disputes about the way that occupational and personal pension schemes are administered and managed. The Pensions Ombudsman is also the Ombudsman for the Pension Protection Fund (PPF) and the Financial Assistance Scheme (which offers help to those who were a member of an under-funded defined benefit pension scheme that started to wind-up in specific financial circumstances between 1 January 1997 and 5 April 2005).

FINANCIAL OMBUDSMAN SERVICE, South Quay Plaza, 183 Marsh Wall, London E14 9SR Helpline 0845-080 1800 T 020-7964 1000 E complaint.info@financial-ombudsman.org.uk W www.financial-ombudsman.org.uk
Chief Executive and Chief Ombudsman, Natalie Ceeney, CBE
Principal Ombudsmen, Tony Boorman; David Thomas; Caroline Wayman
PENSIONS OMBUDSMAN, 11 Belgrave Road, London SW1V 1RB T 020-7630 2200 E enquiries@pensions-ombudsman.org.uk W www.pensions-ombudsman.org.uk
Pensions Ombudsman, Tony King
Deputy Pensions Ombudsman, Jane Irvine

PANEL ON TAKEOVERS AND MERGERS

The Panel on Takeovers and Mergers is an independent body, established in 1968, whose main functions are to issue and administer the City code and to ensure equality of treatment and opportunity for all shareholders in takeover bids and mergers. The panel's statutory functions are set out in the Companies Act 2006.

The panel comprises up to 35 members drawn from major financial and business institutions. The chair, deputy chair and up to 20 other members are nominated by the panel's own nomination committee. The remaining members are nominated by professional bodies representing the banking, insurance, investment, pension and accountancy industries and the CBI.

PANEL ON TAKEOVERS AND MERGERS, 10 Paternoster Square, London EC4M 7DY T 020-7382 9026 W www.thetakeoverpanel.org.uk
Chair, Sir Gordon Langley

NATIONAL SAVINGS AND INVESTMENTS

NS&I (National Savings and Investments) is an executive agency of HM Treasury and one of the UK's largest financial providers, with almost 27 million customers and over £98bn invested. NS&I offers savings and investment products to personal savers and investors and the money is used to manage the national debt. When people invest in NS&I they are lending money to the government which pays them interest or prizes in return. All products are financially secure because they are guaranteed by HM Treasury.

TAX-FREE PRODUCTS

SAVINGS CERTIFICATES

Index-linked Saving Certificates
Otherwise known as inflation-beating savings, index-inked saving certificates are fixed rate investments that pay tax-free returns guaranteed to be above inflation. They are sold in limited issues with a minimum and maximum investment.

Fixed Interest Saving Certificates
Fixed interest saving certificates are fixed rate investments that pay tax-free returns. They are sold in limited issues with a minimum and maximum investment.

PREMIUM BONDS
Introduced in 1956, premium bonds enable savers to enter a regular draw for tax-free prizes, while retaining the right to get their money back. A sum equivalent to interest on each bond is put into a prize fund and distributed by monthly prize draws. The prizes are drawn by ERNIE (electronic random number indicator equipment) and are free of all UK income tax and capital gains tax. A £1m jackpot is drawn each month in addition to other tax-free prizes ranging in value from £25 to £100,000.

Bonds are in units of £1, with a minimum purchase of £100; above this, purchases must be in multiples of £10, up to a maximum holding limit of £30,000 per person. Bonds become eligible for prizes once they have been held for one clear calendar month following the month of purchase. Each £1 unit can win only one prize per draw, but it will be awarded the highest for which it is drawn. Bonds remain eligible for prizes until they are repaid.

The scheme offers a facility to reinvest prize wins automatically. Upon completion of an automatic prize reinvestment mandate, holders receive new bonds which are immediately eligible for future prize draws. Bonds can only be held in the name of an individual and not by organisations.

As at April 2011, over 225 million prizes totalling £13bn had been distributed since the first prize draw in 1957.

CHILDREN'S BONUS BONDS
Children's bonus bonds were introduced in 1991. The bonds are sold in five-year issues at multiples of £25. For each issue the minimum holding is £25 and the maximum holding is £3,000 per child. They can be bought for any child under 16, but must be held by a parent or guardian.

All returns are totally exempt from UK income tax and a bonus is payable if the bond is held for the full five years.

OTHER PRODUCTS

GUARANTEED EQUITY BONDS
Guaranteed equity bonds are five-year investments where the returns are linked to the performance of the FTSE-100 index with a guarantee that the original capital invested will be returned even if the FTSE-100 index fell over the five years. They are sold in limited issues with a minimum investment of £1,000 and a maximum of £1m. The returns are subject to income tax on maturity, unless they are held in a self-invested pension plan (SIPP).

SAVINGS AND INVESTMENT ACCOUNTS
The direct saver account was launched in March 2010. Customers are able to invest between £1 and £2m per person. The account can be managed online or by telephone. Interest is paid without deduction of tax at source.

The easy access savings account offers access to savings via Post Office counters, an ATM card, telephone and online. It can be opened with a minimum balance of £100 and has a maximum limit of £2m (£4m jointly). The interest is paid without deduction of tax at source.

The investment account is a passbook account which pays tiered rates of interest. It can be opened with a minimum balance of £20 and has a maximum limit of £100,000. The interest is paid without deduction of tax at source.

Since April 1999 NS&I has offered cash individual savings accounts (ISAs). Its Direct ISA, launched in April 2006, can be opened and managed online and by telephone with a minimum investment of £100. Interest for the Direct ISA is calculated daily and is free of tax.

INCOME BONDS
NS&I income bonds were introduced in 1982. They are suitable for those who want to receive regular monthly payments of interest while preserving the full cash value of their capital. The bonds are sold in multiples of £500. The minimum holding is £500 and the maximum £1m (sole or joint holding). A variable rate of interest is calculated on a day-to-day basis and paid monthly. Interest is taxable but is paid without deduction of tax at source.

GUARANTEED INCOME BONDS
Guaranteed income bonds were introduced in February 2008. They are designed for those who want to receive regular monthly payments of interest while preserving the full cash value of their capital. The minimum holding is £500 and the maximum £1m, including any amount held in guaranteed growth bonds and fixed rate savings bonds. A fixed rate of interest is calculated on a day-to-day basis and paid monthly on these bonds. Interest is taxable and tax is deducted at source.

GUARANTEED GROWTH BONDS
Guaranteed growth bonds were introduced in February 2008. They are suitable for those who want to receive

regular monthly payments of interest while preserving the full cash value of their capital. The minimum holding is £500 and the maximum £1m, including any amount held in guaranteed income bonds and fixed rate savings bonds. A fixed rate of interest is calculated on a day-to-day basis and is paid annually on the anniversary of the date of investment. Interest is taxable and tax is deducted at source.

FURTHER INFORMATION

Further information regarding products and their current availability can be obtained online (W www.nsandi.com), by telephone (T 0500-007007) or at Post Office counters.

NATIONAL DEBT

The UK Debt Management Office (DMO), an executive agency of HM Treasury, was created in April 1998 following the transfer of operational responsibility for monetary policy from HM Treasury to the Bank of England. Initially the DMO was responsible only for the management of government marketable debt and for issuing gilts. In April 2000 responsibility for exchequer cash management and for issuing Treasury bills (short-dated securities with maturities of less than one year) was transferred from the Bank of England to the DMO. The national debt also includes the (non-marketable) liabilities of National Savings and Investments and other public sector and foreign currency debt.

In 2002 the operations of the long-standing statutory functions of the Public Works Loan Board, which lends capital to local authorities, and the Commissioners for the Reduction of the National Debt, which manages the investment portfolios of certain public funds, were integrated within the DMO (see also Government Departments).

Since 2008 the DMO has undertaken a range of activities at the request of HM Treasury to help stabilise the financial markets and support the UK banking sector. These include administering the credit guarantee scheme and the asset-backed securities guarantee scheme. Since November 2008, the DMO has also undertaken auctions of EU allowances on behalf of the Department of Energy and Climate Change as part of the emissions trading system.

UK NATIONAL DEBT

	£ billion	per cent of GDP
2009–10 (outturn)	741.1	52.7
2010–11 (forecast)	888.2	60.3
2011–12 (forecast)	1,020.6	66.1

Source: HM Treasury: Budget 2011 (Crown copyright)

THE LONDON STOCK EXCHANGE

The London Stock Exchange serves the needs of companies and investors by providing facilities for raising capital and a central marketplace for securities trading. This marketplace covers UK and overseas company shares and other instruments such as: exchange traded funds (ETFs) and exchange traded commodities (ETCs), international equity derivative products (through EDX London) and both corporate and government bonds.

Over 400 member firms trading on the London Stock Exchange buy and sell securities on behalf of the public, as well as institutions such as pension funds or insurance companies.

The London Stock Exchange is a subsidiary, along with Borsa Italiana, of the London Stock Exchange Group (LSEG).

HISTORY

The London Stock Exchange is one of the world's oldest stock exchanges dating back more than 300 years when it began in the coffee houses of 17th-century London. It was formally established as a membership organisation in 1801.

RECENT DEVELOPMENTS

'BIG BANG'
What has come to be known as 'Big Bang' was a package of reforms in 1986 that transformed the Exchange and the City, liberalising the way in which banks and stock-broking firms operated and bringing in foreign investment. The Exchange ceased granting voting rights to individual members and became a private company. Big Bang also saw the start of a move towards fully electronic trading and the closure of the trading floor.

INTRODUCTION OF SETS
In October 1997, the Exchange introduced SETS, its electronic order book. The system enhanced the efficiency and transparency of trading on the Exchange, allowing trades to be executed automatically and anonymously rather than negotiated by telephone.

DEMUTALISATION AND LISTING
The London Stock Exchange became demutualised in 2000 and listed on its own main market in 2001 in order to allow further commercialisation.

EDX LONDON
In 2003 the London Stock Exchange created EDX London (European derivatives exchange), a recognised investment exchange for international equity derivatives.

MERGER WITH BORSA ITALIANA
On 1 October 2007 the Exchange merged with the Italian stock exchange Borsa Italiana and London Stock Exchange Group PLC replaced the London Stock Exchange as the listed entity.

PRIMARY MARKETS

The London Stock Exchange enables UK and overseas companies to raise capital for development and growth through the issue of securities. For a company entering the market the Exchange offers a choice of four differently regulated markets, depending upon the size, history and requirements of the company:

• the main market enables established companies to raise capital, widen their investor base and have their shares traded on a global stock market. The market is regulated by the FSA's UK Listing Authority (UKLA). The FTSE 100 index is based on main market stocks
• the Alternative Investment Market (AIM), established in June 1995, is specially designed to meet the needs of small, young and growing companies, enabling them to raise capital, broaden their investor base and benefit from being traded on an internationally recognised market. AIM is regulated by the London Stock Exchange and quoted companies must adhere to the AIM rules and retain a Nominated Adviser (or 'Nomad') at all times, who is responsible for ensuring the company's suitability for the market. The AIM model has been extended to AIM Italia, launched in Italy at the end of 2008, and AIM Tokyo, launched in collaboration with the Tokyo Stock Exchange in spring 2009
• the Professional Securities Market (PSM), established in July 2005 and regulated by the FSA, offers international companies that wish to access an exclusively institutional investor base an option to list equity and debt securities in London on a market that offers greater flexibility in accounting standards
• the Specialist Fund Market (SFM), established in November 2007, is the Exchange's market for highly specialised investment entities, such as hedge funds or private equity funds, that wish to target institutional investors. This market is regulated by the FSA in accordance with standards set out in EU directives

At April 2011 there were 2,612 companies quoted on the London Stock Exchange: 1,086 on the UK main market, with a combined market capitalisation of £2,007.1bn; 323 on the international main market, with a combined market capitalisation of £1,897.8bn; 1,164 on AIM, with a combined market capitalisation of £81.3bn; 31 on the PSM, with a combined market capitalisation of £10.2bn; and eight companies listed on the SFM.

LONDON STOCK EXCHANGE, 10 Paternoster Square, London EC4M 7LS T 020-7797 1000
W www.londonstockexchange.com
Chair, Chris Gibson-Smith, PHD
Chief Executive, Xavier Rolet

ECONOMIC STATISTICS

THE BUDGET (MARCH 2011)

GOVERNMENT EXPENDITURE

DEPARTMENTAL EXPENDITURE LIMITS
£ billion

	Estimate 2010–11	Projection 2011–12	Projection 2012–13
Resource DEL			
Education	51.3	51.2	52.1
Health	100	101.5	104.0
of which NHS England	98.4	101.5	104.0
Transport	5.2	5.3	5.0
Business, Innovation and Skills	17.2	16.5	15.7
Communities	3.6	2.0	1.7
Local Government	26.0	26.1	24.4
Home Office	8.9	8.9	8.5
Justice	8.6	8.2	7.8
Law Officers' Departments	0.7	0.6	0.6
Defence	28.4	27.3	25.2
Foreign and Commonwealth Office	2.1	1.5	1.5
International Development	5.9	6.7	7.2
Energy and Climate Change	1.3	1.5	1.4
Environment, Food and Rural Affairs	2.2	2.2	2.1
Culture, Media and Sport	1.5	1.4	1.9
Work and Pensions	8.7	7.6	7.4
Scotland	25.2	24.8	25.1
Wales	13.4	13.3	13.4
Northern Ireland	9.7	9.4	9.4
Chancellor's departments	3.8	3.8	3.7
Cabinet Office	2.0	2.1	2.1
Independent bodies	1.6	1.7	1.5
Reserve	0.0	0.0	0.2
Special reserve	0.0	2.4	2.5
Allowance for shortfall	(1.1)	0.0	0.0
TOTAL RESOURCE DEL	326.1	326.3	327.1
Capital DEL			
Education	7.3	5.1	4.2
Health	4.5	4.4	4.4
of which NHS England	4.5	4.4	4.4
Transport	7.1	7.7	8.1
Business, Innovation and Skills	2.1	1.3	1.1
Communities	6.4	3.5	2.3
Local Government	0.0	0.0	0.0
Home Office	0.8	0.5	0.5
Justice	0.6	0.4	0.3
Law Officers' Departments	0.0	0.0	0.0
Defence	9.6	10.0	9.1
Foreign and Commonwealth Office	0.2	0.1	0.1
International Development	1.6	1.4	1.6
Energy and Climate Change	2.0	1.5	2.0
Environment, Food and Rural Affairs	0.6	0.4	0.4
Culture, Media and Sport	0.6	1.3	0.4
Work and Pensions	0.3	0.2	0.3
Scotland	3.3	2.5	2.5
Wales	1.8	1.3	1.2
Northern Ireland	1.2	0.9	0.9
Chancellor's departments	0.2	0.3	0.2
Cabinet Office	0.4	0.4	0.4
Independent bodies	0.1	0.1	0.1
Reserve	0.0	0.9	1.0
Special reserve	0.0	0.2	0.8
Green investment bank	0.0	0.0	0.8
Allowance for shortfall	(0.6)	0.0	0.0
TOTAL CAPITAL DEL	50.0	44.5	42.6
TOTAL DEL	376.1	370.8	369.7

Source: HM Treasury – *Budget 2011* (Crown copyright)

TOTAL MANAGED EXPENDITURE
£ billion

	Estimate 2010–11	Projection 2011–12	Projection 2012–13
Current Expenditure			
Resource Annually Managed Expenditure	287.4	314.4	324.9
Implied Resource DELs	345.4	342.3	344.7
Capital Expenditure			
Capital Annually Managed Expenditure (AME)	11.5	9.2	8.0
Implied Capital DELs	50.0	44.5	42.6
TOTAL MANAGED EXPENDITURE	694.4	710.4	720.2

Source: HM Treasury – *Budget 2011* (Crown copyright)

GOVERNMENT RECEIPTS
£ billion

	Outturn 2009–10	Forecast 2010–11	Forecast 2011–12
HM Revenue and Customs (HMRC)			
Income tax (gross of tax credits)[1]	147.5	151.5	156.6
Income tax credits	(5.6)	(5.5)	(4.7)
National insurance contributions (NIC)	96.6	96.5	100.7
Value added tax	73.5	86.1	100.3
Corporation tax[2]	36.5	42.7	49.0
Corporation tax credits[3]	(0.7)	(0.9)	(0.9)
Petroleum revenue tax	0.9	1.5	2.0
Fuel duties	26.2	27.3	26.9

	Outturn 2009–10	Forecast 2010–11	Forecast 2011–12
Business rates	23.4	23.8	25.5
Council tax	25.3	25.7	26.1
VAT refunds	11.2	13.2	15.0
Capital gains tax	2.5	3.2	3.4
Inheritance tax	2.4	2.7	2.7
Stamp duties	7.9	9.0	9.1
Tobacco duties	8.8	9.1	9.3
Spirits duties	2.7	2.7	2.7
Wine duties	3.0	3.1	3.3
Beer and cider duties	3.5	3.7	3.7
Air passenger duty	1.9	2.2	2.5
Insurance premium tax	2.3	2.5	2.9
Climate change levy	0.7	0.7	0.7
Other HMRC taxes[4]	5.4	6.0	6.4
Vehicle excise duties	5.6	5.7	5.9
Temporary bank payroll tax	0.0	3.5	0.0
Bank levy	0.0	0.0	1.9
Licence fee recipts	3.0	3.1	3.1
Enviromental levies	0.5	0.6	1.8
EU ETS Auction recipts	0.0	0.4	0.3
Other taxes	5.3	5.3	5.3
National Accounts Taxes	490.3	525.3	562.4
Less own resources contribution to EU budget	(3.8)	(4.8)	(4.9)
Interest and dividends	3.4	3.3	5.2
Other receipts	23.4	24.7	25.9
CURRENT RECEIPTS	513.3	548.5	588.6
UK oil and gas revenues[5]	6.5	8.8	13.4

[1] Income tax includes PAYE and Self Assessment recipts, and also includes tax on savings income and other minor income tax components
[2] National Accounts measure, gross of enhanced and payable credits
[3] Includes enhanced company tax credits
[4] Consists of landfill tax, aggregates levy, betting and gaming duties, and customs duties and levies
[5] Consitis of offshore corporation tax and petroleum revenue tax
Source: HM Treasury – *Budget 2011* (Crown copyright)

TRADE

TRADE IN GOODS
£ million

	Exports	Imports	Balance
1999	166,166	195,217	(29,051)
2000	187,936	220,912	(32,976)
2001	189,093	230,305	(41,212)
2002	186,524	234,229	(47,705)
2003	188,320	236,927	(48,607)
2004	190,874	251,774	(60,900)
2005	211,608	280,197	(68,589)
2006	243,633	319,945	(76,312)
2007	220,858	310,612	(89,754)
2008	252,068	345,202	(93,116)
2009	227,645	310,010	(82,365)
2010	266,079	363,278	(97,199)

Source: ONS (Crown copyright)

BALANCE OF PAYMENTS, 2010

Current Account	£ million
Trade in goods and services	
Trade in goods	(98,816)
Trade in services	49,515
Total trade in goods and services	(49,301)

Income	
Compensation of employees	(360)
Investment income	23,218
Total income	22,858
Total current transfers	(19,823)
TOTAL (CURRENT BALANCE)	(46,266)

Source: ONS (Crown copyright)

UK GDP GROWTH
volume % change on previous quarter

Source: ONS

EMPLOYMENT

DISTRIBUTION OF THE WORKFORCE

	Mar 2009	Mar 2011
Workforce jobs	31,696,000	31,354,000
HM forces	196,000	193,000
Self-employment jobs	4,208,000	4,349,000
Employees jobs	27,247,000	26,780,000
Government-supported trainees	45,000	32,000

Source: ONS – *Labour Market Statistics 2011* (Crown copyright)

EMPLOYMENT, 2010–2011
thousands
Mar–May 2010

Age	Male	Female
16–17	175	214
18–24	1,175	1,629
25–34	3,448	2,848
35–49	5,684	5,119
50–64	3,931	3,346
65+	469	331
All aged 16+	15,483	13,487

Mar–May 2011

Age	Male	Female
16-17	161	194
18–24	1,789	1,605
25–34	3,573	2,943
35–49	5,691	5,040
50–64	3,966	3,422
65+	533	362
All aged 16+	15,713	13,566

Source: ONS – *Labour Market Statistics 2011* (Crown copyright)

UNEMPLOYMENT, 2009–10
per cent

Age	2009	2010
16–17	29.3	35.0
18–24	16.2	18.0
25–49	5.5	6.5
50+	4.2	4.6
All aged 16+	7.1	8.0

Source: ONS – *Social Trends 2011* (Crown copyright)

UNEMPLOYMENT RATES BY REGION
per cent
Mar–May 2011

North East	9.8
North West	8.6
Yorkshire and The Humber	8.6
East Midlands	7.9
West Midlands	8.5
East	6.5
London	9.3
South East	5.7
South West	6.4
England	7.8
Wales	7.9
Scotland	7.6
Northern Ireland	7.1

Source: ONS (Crown copyright)

DURATION OF UNEMPLOYMENT, APR–JUN 2011
thousands

All unemployed	2,494
Duration of unemployment	
Less than 6 months	1,228
6 months–1 year	428
1 year +	838
1 year + *as percentage of total*	33.6

Source: ONS – *Labour Market Statistics 2011* (Crown copyright)

MEDIAN EARNINGS, 2010

	All	Male	Female
Median gross annual earnings (£, thousands)	25.9	28.1	22.5
Median gross weekly earnings (£)	498.8	538.21	439.0
Median hourly earnings, excluding overtime (£)	12.50	13.01	11.68

Source: ONS – *Annual Survey of Hours and Earnings 2010* (Crown copyright)

NUMBER OF TAXPAYERS BY ANNUAL INCOME*, 2010–11

	Number of taxpayers (thousands)
£6,475†–£7,499	939
£7,500–£9,999	2,620
£10,000–£14,999	6,440
£15,000–£19,999	5,210
£20,000–£29,999	6,910
£30,000–£49,999	5,680
£50,000–£99,999	2,050
£100,000–£149,999	342
£150,000–£199,999	145
£200,000–£499,999	143
£500,000–£999,999	26
£1,000,000+	13
All incomes	30,500

* Includes investment income

† Basic personal tax-free allowance for 2010–11

Source: ONS – *Social Trends 2011* (Crown copyright)

LABOUR STOPPAGES BY DURATION, 2009

Under 5 days	80
5–10 days	11
11–20 days	4
21–30 days	0
31–50 days	0
50+ days	3
All stoppages	98

Source: ONS – *Economic and Labour Market Review 2010* (Crown copyright)

WORKING DAYS LOST THROUGH LABOUR DISPUTES BY INDUSTRY, 2009

Mining and energy	200
Manufacturing	1,100
Services	394,600
Sewage, waste management and water supply	86,100
Construction	59,200
Transport, storage, information and communication	296,200
Financial, insurance and other administrative activites	600
Public administration and defence	5,100
Education	6,700

Source: ONS – *Economic & Labour Market Review 2010* (Crown copyright)

TRADE UNIONS

Year	No. of unions	Total membership
2000–1	237	7,897,519
2001–2	226	7,779,393
2002–3	216	7,750,990
2003–4	213	7,735,983
2004–5	206	7,559,062
2005–6	193	7,473,000
2006–7	192	7,602,842
2007–8	193	7,627,693
2008–9	185	7,656,156
2009–10	176	7,328,905

Source: Annual Report of the Certification Officer 2010–11

HOUSEHOLD INCOME AND EXPENDITURE

AVERAGE HOUSEHOLD INCOME, 2009–10

Income by source	£ per year	Percentage of total
Wages and Salaries	23,717	65.2
Imputed income from benefits in kind	325	0.9
Self-employment	2,937	8.1
Investments	910	2.5
Annuities and pensions	2,743	7.5
Social security benefits*	5,448	14.9
Other sources	293	0.8
Total	36,373	100

* Excluding council tax benefit

Source: ONS – *The Effects of Taxes and Benefits on Household Income 2009–10* (Crown copyright)

WEEKLY HOUSEHOLD INCOME: BY ETHNIC GROUP OF HOUSEHOLD REFERENCE PERSON, 2006/7–8/9

	Wages and salaries	Self-employed income	Investments	Tax credits	State pension	Other pension	Social security	Other benefits
White	64	9	3	1	7	7	7	2
Mixed	71	8	1	2	2	2	9	4
Asian or Asian British	70	9	1	4	2	2	8	4
Indian	74	9	1	1	2	2	5	4
Pakistani and Bangladeshi	56	10	1	10	4	1	15	4
Black or Black British	69	7	0	3	3	1	11	4
Black Caribbean	70	5	1	3	5	2	12	2
Black non-Caribbean	69	8	0	4	1	1	12	5
Chinese or other	70	8	1	2	2	3	6	7
All households	64	9	3	2	6	7	7	2

Source: ONS – Social Trends 2011 (Crown copyright)

AVERAGE HOUSEHOLD EXPENDITURE, 2009

Commodity or service	£ per week	Percentage of total
Transport	58.40	12.8
Recreation and culture	57.90	12.7
Housing, fuel and power	57.30	12.6
Food and non-alcoholic drinks	52.20	11.5
Restaurants and hotels	38.40	8.4
Miscellaneous goods and services	35.00	7.7
Household goods and servies	27.90	6.1
Clothing and footwear	20.90	4.6
Communication	11.70	2.6
Alcoholic drinks, tobacco and narcotics	11.20	2.5
Education	7.00	1.5
Health	5.30	1.1
Other expenditure items	71.80	15.8
Total	455.00	100

Source: ONS – Family Spending 2009 (Crown copyright)

HOUSEHOLD OWNERSHIP OF SELECTED DURABLE GOODS

percentages

	2000–1	2009
Car/van	72	76
Central heating (full or partial)	91	95
Washing machine	93	96
Tumble dryer	53	58
Dishwasher	25	39
Microwave	84	93
Telephone	93	88
Mobile phone	47	81
Home computer	44	75
Video recorder	87	61
DVD player	–	90
CD player	77	84
Internet connection	32	71

Source: ONS – Family Spending 2009 (Crown copyright)

INDIVIDUAL INSOLVENCIES

	2000	2005	2009
England and Wales	29,528	67,584	134,142
Scotland	5,766	11,846	23,482
Northern Ireland	616	1,454	1,959
Total	35,910	80,884	159,583

Source: ONS – Annual Abstract of Statistics 2010 (Crown copyright)

COST OF LIVING AND INFLATION RATES

The first cost of living index to be calculated took July 1914 as 100 and was based on the pattern of expenditure of working-class families in 1914. The cost of living index was superseded in 1947 by the general index of retail prices (RPI), although the older term is still popularly applied.

The Harmonised Index of Consumer Prices (HICP) was introduced in 1997 to enable comparisons within the European Union using an agreed methodology. In 2003 the National Statistician renamed the HICP as the Consumer Prices Index (CPI) to reflect its role as the main target measure of inflation for macroeconomic purposes. The RPI and indices based on it continue to be published alongside the CPI. Some pensions, and index-linked gilts continue to be calculated with reference to RPI or its derivatives.

CPI AND RPI

The CPI and RPI measure the changes month by month in the average level of prices of goods and services purchased by households in the UK. The indices are compiled using a selection of around 650 goods and services, and the prices charged for these items are collected at regular intervals at about 150 locations throughout the country. The Office for National Statistics (ONS) reviews the components of the indices once every year to reflect changes in consumer preferences and the establishment of new products. The table below shows changes made by the ONS to the CPI 'shopping basket' in 2011.

CPI excludes a number of items that are included in RPI, mainly related to housing such as council tax and a range of owner-occupier housing costs, such as mortgage payments. The CPI covers all private households, whereas RPI excludes the top 4 per cent by income and pensioner households who derive at least three-quarters of their income from state benefits. The two indices use different methodologies to combine the prices of goods and services, which means that since 1996 the CPI inflation measure is less than the RPI inflation measure.

INFLATION RATE

The 12-monthly percentage change in the 'all items' index of the RPI or CPI is referred to as the rate of inflation. As the most familiar measure of inflation, RPI is often referred to as the 'headline rate of inflation'. CPI is the main measure of inflation for macroeconomic purposes and forms the basis for the government's inflation target, which is currently 2 per cent. The percentage change in prices between any two months/years can be obtained using the formula overleaf.

CHANGES TO THE 2011 'SHOPPING BASKET' OF GOODS AND SERVICES

The table below shows changes to the 2011 CPI* basket of goods and services made by the ONS in order to reflect changes in consumer preferences and the establishment of new products.

Goods and services group	Removed items	New items
Alcoholic beverages	canned lager (4-pack)	sparkling wine
Audio-visual equipment	flat panel TVs (14″–25″; 26″–42″)	flat panel TVs (14″–22″; 23″–32″; 33″+)
Books and newspapers	evening provincial newspaper; morning provincial newspaper	hardback book (fiction); provincial newspaper
Clothing	girls' summer jacket; girl's winter jacket; men's casual shirt (long-sleeved); women's casual outer jacket (eg fleece); women's premium branded dress	girl's jacket; men's casual shirt (long or short-sleeved); women's blouse/shirt;
Food	pork shoulder	oven-ready joint; dried fruit
Footwear	women's high-heeled party shoe; women's high-heeled sensible shoes	women's high heeled shoes
Maintenance and repair of dwelling	hardboard	medium density fibreboard (MDF)
Medical products, appliances and equipment	spectacle frames (without lenses)	spectacle frames with single-vision lens
Personal care	–	hair conditioner
Recreational items, gardens and pets	rosebush; vet fees for spaying a kitten	craft kit
Telephone equipment and services	mobile phone downloads	mobile phone applications; smart phone handsets
Tobacco	–	vending machine cigarettes
Other services (not elsewhere classified)	–	dating agency fees

* RPI goods and services are grouped together under different classifications

$$\frac{\text{Later date RPI/CPI} - \text{Earlier date RPI/CPI}}{\text{Earlier date RPI/CPI}} \times 100$$

eg to find the CPI rate of inflation for 2006, using the annual averages for 2005 and 2006:

$$\frac{102.3 - 100.0}{100.0} \times 100 = 2.3$$

From 14 February 2006 the reference year for CPI was re-based to 2005=100 to improve price comparison clarity across the EU. None of the underlying data, from which the re-referenced series was calculated, was revised. Historical rates of change (such as annual inflation figures), calculated from the re-based rounded index levels, were revised due to the effect of rounding. The CPI rate of inflation figure given in the table below may differ by plus or minus 0.1 percentage points from the figure calculated by the above equation. The change of reference period and revision due to rounding does not apply to the RPI which remains unchanged.

The RPI and CPI figures are published by the Office for National Statistics on either the second or third Tuesday of each month in an indices bulletin

and electronically on the national statistics website (W www.statistics.gov.uk).

PURCHASING POWER OF THE POUND

Changes in the internal purchasing power of the pound may be defined as the 'inverse' of changes in the level of prices: when prices go up, the amount which can be purchased with a given sum of money goes down. To find the purchasing power of the pound in one month or year, given that it was 100p in a previous month or year, the calculation would be:

$$100p \times \frac{\text{Earlier month/year RPI}}{\text{Later month/year RPI}}$$

Thus, if the purchasing power of the pound is taken to be 100p in 1975, the comparable purchasing power in 2000 would be:

$$100p \times \frac{34.2}{170.3} = 20.1p$$

For longer term comparisons, it has been the practice to use an index which has been constructed by linking together the RPI for the period 1962 to date; an index derived from the consumers' expenditure deflator for the period from 1938 to 1962; and the pre-war 'cost of living' index for the period 1914 to 1938. This long-term index enables the internal purchasing power of the pound to be calculated for any year from 1914 onwards. It should be noted that these figures can only be approximate.

PLACEHOLDER

	Annual average RPI (1987 = 100)	Purchasing power of £ (1998 = 1.00)	Annual average CPI (2005 = 100)*	Rate of inflation (RPI/CPI)
1914	2.8	58.18		
1915	3.5	46.54		
1920	7.0	23.27		
1925	5.0	32.58		
1930	4.5	36.20		
1935	4.0	40.72		
1938	4.4	37.02		
There are no official figures for 1939–45				
1946	7.4	22.01		
1950	9.0	18.10		
1955	11.2	14.54		
1960	12.6	12.93		
1965	14.8	11.00		
1970	18.5	8.80		
1975	34.2	4.76		
1980	66.8	2.44	18.0	
1985	94.6	1.72	6.1	
1990	126.1	1.29	71.5	9.5/7.0
1995	149.1	1.09	86.0	3.5/2.6
1998	162.9	1.00	91.1	3.4/1.6
2000	170.3	0.96	93.1	3.0/0.8
2005	192.0	0.85	100.0	2.8/2.1
2006	198.1	0.82	102.3	3.2/2.3
2007	206.6	0.79	104.7	4.3/2.3
2008	214.8	0.76	108.5	4.0/3.6
2009	213.7	0.76	110.8	−0.5/2.2
2010	223.6	0.73	114.5	4.6/3.3

* In accordance with an EU Commission regulation all published CPI figures were re-based to 2005 = 100 with effect from 14 February 2006, replacing the 1996 = 100 series

INSURANCE

AUTHORISATION AND REGULATION OF INSURANCE COMPANIES

Since 2001, the Financial Services Authority (FSA) has been the authorising, enforcement, supervisory and rule-making body of insurers. Since 2005, this has also included insurance brokers and intermediaries.

The FSA's powers are primarily conferred by the Financial Services and Markets Act 2000, which unified the previous sectoral arrangements and regulators.

AUTHORISATION

The FSA's current role is to ensure that firms to which it grants authorisation satisfy the necessary financial criteria, that the senior management of the company are 'fit and proper persons' and that unauthorised firms are not permitted to trade. This part of the FSA's role was previously undertaken by HM Treasury under the Insurance Companies Act 1982, which was repealed when the Financial Services and Markets Act came fully into force. At the end of 2009 there were over 1,400 insurance organisations and friendly societies with authorisation from the FSA to transact one or more classes of insurance business in the UK. However, the single European insurance market, established in 1994, gave insurers authorised in any other European Union country automatic UK authorisation without further formality. This means a potential market of over 5,000 insurers.

In June 2010, the Chancellor of the Exchequer announced the government's intention to replace the FSA with two successor bodies, and to restructure the UK's financial regulatory framework by 2013 (see Financial Services Regulation).

REGULATION

All life insurers, general insurers, re-insurers, insurance and reinsurance brokers, financial advisers and composite firms are statutorily regulated. This is achieved through the formulation (after consultation) by the FSA of rules and guidance for regulated organisations. The FSA is also responsible for consumer education and the reduction of financial crime, particularly money laundering (see also Financial Services Regulation).

COMPLAINTS

Disputes between policyholders and insurers can be referred to the Financial Ombudsman Service (FOS). Policyholders with a complaint against their financial services provider must firstly take the matter to the highest level within the company. Thereafter, if it remains unresolved and it involves an amount below £100,000, they can refer, free of charge, to the FOS, which examines the facts of a complaint and delivers a decision binding on the provider (but not the policyholder). Small businesses with a turnover of up to €2m (£1.7m) and fewer than ten employees also have access to the scheme. The Financial Ombudsman Service also covers other areas of the financial services industry including banks, building societies and investment firms. In 2010 the FOS handled around 1 million enquires and around 150,000 complaints regarding financial services companies.

See also Financial Services Regulation.

ASSOCIATION OF BRITISH INSURERS

Over 90 per cent of the domestic business of UK insurance companies is transacted by the 300 members of the Association of British Insurers (ABI). ABI is a trade association which protects and promotes the interests of all its insurance company members. Only insurers authorised in the EU are eligible for membership. Brokers, intermediaries, financial advisers and claims handlers may not join ABI but may have their own trade associations.

ASSOCIATION OF BRITISH INSURERS (ABI),
51 Gresham Street, London EC2V 7HQ
T 020-7600 3333 W www.abi.org.uk
Chair, Tim Breedon
Director-General, Otto Thoresen

BALANCE OF PAYMENTS

The financial services industry contributes around 10 per cent of the UK's gross domestic product (GDP). In 2009 insurance companies' net exports rose to £8.3bn, a 10 per cent increase on 2008.

WORLDWIDE MARKET

The UK insurance industry is the largest in Europe and the third largest in the world behind the USA and Japan.

Market	Premium Income ($bn)	Percentage of total
United States	1,140	28
Japan	506	12
United Kingdom	309	8

TAKEOVERS AND MERGERS

Despite a few high profile attempts, such as the Prudential bid for the Asian operation of AIG and RSA's hostile bid for AVIVA, the only major activity in 2010 was the purchase of the UK life business of French insurer AXA by Resolution, the closed life fund specialist, for £2.75bn. The Royal Bank of Scotland also began the process of consolidating its UK insurance business to prepare it for sale by 2013, as mandated by the European Commission.

INDUSTRY ISSUES

Since 2002 the insurance industry has been negotiating with the European Commission (EC) on 'Solvency II' which aims to establish an EU-wide set of requirements for capital adequacy and management standards. The Solvency II directive is scheduled to come into force on 1 November 2012, although this is likely to be extended into 2013. The intention is that in all 27 European Union member states and in three European Economic Area countries a consistent standard will be established for insurers, which will reduce the possibility of company failures and consumer loss. In 2010 insurers spent a great deal of time convincing the EC that the financial problems suffered by the banks in 2009 were not a justification for increased capital adequacy requirements for insurers; this seems to have been accepted by the commission.

GENERAL INSURANCE

Extended periods of snow and freezing temperatures at the start and end of 2010 resulted in claims totalling £650m in January and £900m in November and December. In addition, £67m in travel cancellation claims resulted from the Eyjafjallajokull volcanic eruption in Iceland.

Motor insurance grabbed the headlines with claim costs rising 216 per cent to £1.6bn in the UK at a time when the competitive market meant UK premiums fell on average by around 7 per cent. Given that general insurers have also seen a fall in overall investment returns, motor premium increases in 2011–12 are inevitable, with rises of up to 40 per cent being suggested.

Personal injury claims under motor policies also contributed to these record claim levels; during 2010 insurers pressed for a reform of the legal system used for small claims of this kind. The average personal injury claim is around £2,430 but insurers point to the fact that they also have to pay a further £2,100 in legal fees to settle the claim. This could be drastically reduced if a simplified settlement system could be established to prevent small cases having to go to court. It is estimated that these legal costs add £40 a year to every UK driver's premium.

Fraud continues to be a problem for insurers but the number of fraudsters being caught continues to rise. It's impossible to accurately quantify the total cost of insurance fraud in the UK, but the number of bogus claims detected in 2010 increased to 335 a day (1.2 million a year) representing claims worth £2.3m a day. Fraudulent motor claims are the most costly, while bogus home insurance claims are the most common.

Government public spending cuts revived fears over the maintenance of flood and sea defences throughout the UK. In the past 10 years insurers have paid over £4.5bn in flood claims and although the UK insurance industry currently has an agreement with the government to offer flood cover to every home in the UK, this expires in 2013. It is estimated that one home in six is at risk of flooding and nearly 500,000 people face a significant flood risk.

Other general insurance areas, such as theft and fire, recorded a reduction in claims in 2010. Theft claims decreased by 4.5 per cent to £530m and fire claims totalled £1.07bn; a decrease of 10 per cent on 2009.

LONDON INSURANCE MARKET

The London Insurance Market is a unique wholesale marketplace and a distinct, separate sector of the UK insurance and reinsurance industry. It is the world's leading market for internationally traded insurance and reinsurance, its business comprising mainly overseas non-life large and high-exposure risks. It is the only place in the world where all 20 of the world's largest insurance companies have an office. The market is centred on the square mile of the City of London, which provides the required financial, banking, legal and other support services. Around 61 per cent of London market business is transacted at Lloyd's of London, 36 per cent through insurance companies and the remainder through protection and indemnity clubs. In 2009 the market had a written gross premium income of over £31.9bn. Around 170 Lloyd's brokers service the market.

The trade association for the international insurers and reinsurers writing primarily non-marine insurance and all classes of reinsurance business in the London market is the International Underwriting Association (IUA).

INTERNATIONAL UNDERWRITING ASSOCIATION, London Underwriting Centre, 3 Mincing Lane, London EC3R 7DD T 020-7617 4444 W www.iua.co.uk
Chair, Stephen Riley
Chief Executive, Dave Matcham

CLAIMS STATISTICS *(£m)*

	2006	2007	2008	2009	2010
Theft	517	525	531	555	530
Fire	1,139	1,102	1,273	1,205	1,073
Weather	475	2,459	904	662	706
Domestic subsidence	302	162	137	175	172
Business interruption	168	320	193	128	179
Total	2,601	4,568	3,038	2,725	2,660

WORLDWIDE GENERAL BUSINESS TRADING RESULTS *(£m)*

	2008	2009
Net written premiums	47,213	43,791
Underwriting results	1,115	(356)
Investment income	3,368	3,963
Overall trading profit	4,483	3,606
Profit as percentage of premium income	9.5	8.2

BRITISH INSURANCE COMPANIES

The following insurance company figures refer to members and certain non-members of the ABI.

WORLDWIDE GENERAL BUSINESS UNDERWRITING RESULTS *(£m)*

	2008			2009		
	UK	Overseas	Total	UK	Overseas	Total
Motor						
Premiums	10,676	4,086	14,783	9,894	4,447	14,341
Profit (loss)	(503)	264	(240)	(1,592)	123	(1,469)
Percentage of premiums	4.7	6.5	1.6	16	2.8	10.2
Non-motor						
Premiums	20,945	8,708	29,653	18,595	8,162	26,757
Profit (loss)	1,076	160	1,236	804	258	1,062
Percentage of premiums	5.1	1.8	4.2	4.3	4.2	4.0

NET PREMIUM INCOME BY SECTOR 2009 *(£m)*

	UK	Overseas
Motor	9,894	4,447
Non-motor	18,595	8,162
Marine, aviation and transport	665	128
Reinsurance	1,219	549
Total general business	30,373	13,286
Ordinary long-term	123,895	40,286
Total long-term business	123,895	40,286

LLOYD'S OF LONDON

Lloyd's of London is an international market for almost all types of general insurance. Lloyd's currently has a capacity to accept insurance premiums of around £23bn. Much of this business comes from outside the UK and makes a valuable contribution to the balance of payments.

A policy is underwritten at Lloyd's by a mixture of private and corporate members – corporate members having been admitted for the first time in 1992. Specialist underwriters accept insurance risks at Lloyd's on behalf of members (referred to as 'Names') grouped in syndicates. There are currently 86 syndicates of varying sizes, each managed by one of the 51 underwriting agents approved by the Council of Lloyd's.

Members divide into three categories: corporate organisations, individuals who have no limit to their liability for losses, and those who have an agreed limit (known as NameCos).

Lloyd's is incorporated by an act of parliament (Lloyd's Acts 1871 onwards) and is governed by an 18-person council, made up of six working, six external and six nominated members. The structure immediately below this changed when, in 2002, Lloyd's members voted at an extraordinary general meeting to implement a new franchise system for the market with the aim of improving profitability. The first move was the introduction of a new governance structure, replacing the Lloyd's Market Board and the Lloyd's Regulatory Board with an 11-person Lloyd's Franchise Board. Four main committees report to this board.

The corporation is a non-profit making body chiefly financed by its members' subscriptions. It provides the premises, administrative staff and services enabling Lloyd's underwriting syndicates to conduct their business. It does not, however, assume corporate liability for the risks accepted by its members. Individual members are responsible to the full extent of their personal means for their underwriting affairs unless they have converted to limited liability companies.

Lloyd's syndicates have no direct contact with the public. All business is transacted through insurance brokers accredited by the Corporation of Lloyd's. In addition, non-Lloyd's brokers in the UK, when guaranteed by Lloyd's brokers, are able to deal directly with Lloyd's motor syndicates, a facility that has made the Lloyd's market more accessible to the insuring public.

The FSA has ultimate responsibility for the regulation of the Lloyd's market. However, in situations where Lloyd's internal regulatory and compensation arrangements are more far-reaching – as for example with the Lloyd's Central Fund which safeguards claim payments to policyholders – the regulatory role is delegated to the Council of Lloyd's.

Lloyd's also provides the most comprehensive shipping intelligence service in the world. The shipping and other information received from Lloyd's agents, shipowners, news agencies and other sources throughout the world is collated and distributed to the media as well as to the maritime and commercial sectors in general. *Lloyd's List* is London's oldest daily newspaper and contains news of general commercial interest as well as shipping information. It has been independent of Lloyd's since a management buy-out in 1992. *Lloyd's Shipping Index,* published weekly, lists some 23,000 ocean-going merchant vessels in alphabetical order and gives the latest known report of each.

DEVELOPMENTS IN 2010
It was a mixed year for Lloyd's in 2010, with natural disasters having a strong influence on the final result. None of the year's Atlantic storms made landfall, but three major earthquakes in Chile, Haiti and New Zealand, in addition to the Deepwater Horizon oil rig explosion and resulting spill in the Gulf of Mexico, did lead to substantial claims.

Overall the Lloyd's market recorded a profit before tax of £2.2bn; a 43 per cent decrease from the 2009 figure (£3.9bn). Despite this decrease, it still represented a healthy profit considering the market had seen a 29 per cent decrease in investment returns and a 16 per cent increase in net incurred claims.

LLOYD'S OF LONDON, One Lime Street, London EC3M 7HA T 020-7327 1000 W www.lloyds.com
Chair, John Nelson
Chief Executive, Richard Ward

LLOYD'S MEMBERSHIP

	2009	2010
Individual	773	700
Corporate	1,238	1,443

LLOYD'S SEGMENTAL RESULTS 2010 *(£m)*

	Gross premiums written	Net earned premium	Result
Reinsurance	8,388	6,112	590
Casualty	4,397	3,353	113
Property	4,908	3,786	283
Marine	1,671	1,408	128
Motor	1,103	1,009	(520)
Energy	1,419	983	164
Aviation	642	458	115
Life	63	51	3
Total from syndicate operations	22,591	17,111	1,143

LIFE AND LONG-TERM INSURANCE AND PENSIONS

The economic climate, low interest rates and poor investment returns continued to have an effect on life insurance sales. New business figures for regular premium investment and saving products decreased by 25 per cent in 2010, with single premium new business decreasing by 19 per cent.

Following an independent review, auto-enrolment for pensions is due to be phased-in (beginning with larger companies) over a four-year period from October 2012. This system will mean that all employers will have to automatically enrol their staff into a private pension scheme or the National Employment Savings Trust (NEST). Not surprisingly, this was warmly welcomed by the pensions industry but concerns were expressed elsewhere over the administration costs, particularly to small businesses. The Government estimated that for a small business employing four people the administrative cost would be £46 per person, but the Federation of Small Business (FSB) claimed the cost would be much higher at £2,550 per person. Although a number of issues remain to be fine-tuned, auto-enrolment is a reality and pension providers are updating their systems to cope with the workload it will bring.

After a consultation period lasting over two and a half years, the FSA's final proposals following their *Retail Distribution Review* were published in March 2010. When they are implemented in late 2012, the payment of commission to advisers will be replaced by a fee-paying structure. This is designed to eliminate fears that products have been recommended because of the commission rate rather than their suitability. It also provides remuneration for advisers who spend time and money researching for a client who subsequently decides not to go ahead with their purchase. The proposals from the review are designed to increase professional standards among advisers and re-establish consumer confidence in an industry harmed by scandals and mis-selling.

Regulatory changes, the introduction of Solvency II and automatic enrolment for workplace pensions combined with low consumer confidence and reduced disposable income present significant challenges for the UK life insurance and pensions market in 2012.

PAYMENTS TO POLICYHOLDERS *(£m)*

	2008	2009
Payments to UK policyholders	180,757	152,539
Payments to overseas policyholders	31,954	25,843
Total	212,108	178,382

WORLDWIDE LONG-TERM PREMIUM INCOME *(£m)*

	2005	2006	2007	2008	2009
UK Life Insurance					
Regular Premium	10,585	9,414	8,927	7,895	7,912
Single Premium	25,421	32,088	40,256	27,598	11,958
Total	36,032	41,502	49,183	35,493	19,870
Individual Pensions					
Regular Premium	8,548	8,628	8,714	9,547	9,629
Single Premium	12,311	24,906	24,368	18,721	15,177
Total	20,859	33,534	33,082	28,268	24,806
Other Pensions					
Regular Premium	4,577	5,752	5,687	5,863	5,695
Single Premium	54,383	59,410	93,020	57,013	64,032
Total	58,960	60,162	98,707	62,876	69,727
Other (eg income protection, annuities)	4,343	9,852	4,425	2,580	2,799
TOTAL UK PREMIUM INCOME	120,194	145,050	183,772	129,217	117,202
Overseas Premium Income					
Regular Premium	8,171	8,191	7,877	10,386	11,322
Single Premium	16,814	21,104	25,693	26,709	28,964
Total	24,985	29,295	33,571	37,095	40,286
TOTAL WORLDWIDE PREMIUM INCOME	145,178	174,345	218,968	166,312	157,488

PRIVATE MEDICAL INSURANCE

	2005	2006	2007	2008	2009
Number of people covered (thousand)	5,820	5,879	6,004	6,224	5,938
Corporate	4,125	4,188	4,341	4,571	4,384
Personal	1,695	1,691	1,663	1,653	1,554
Gross Earned Premiums (£m)	2,942	3,070	3,241	3,468	3,444
Corporate	1,493	1,561	1,696	1,831	1,838
Personal	1,449	1,509	1,545	1,637	1,606
Gross Claims Incurred (£m)	2,255	2,376	2,501	2,653	2,679

INVESTMENTS OF INSURANCE COMPANIES 2009

Investment of funds	Long-term business (£m)	General business (£m)
Index-linked British government securities	71,253	3,001
Non-index-linked British government securities	107,055	10,356
Other UK public sector debt securities	6,859	56
Overseas government, provincial and municipal securities	73,099	15,184
Debentures, loan shares, preference and guaranteed stocks and shares		
UK	157,789	14,585
Overseas	205,813	24,554
Ordinary stocks and shares UK	239,922	3,905
Overseas	236,014	8,400
Unit trusts		
Equities	160,272	6,167
Fixed interest	46,859	1,826
Loans secured on property	28,943	12,810
Real property and ground rents	52,490	2,680
Other invested assets	116,381	18,259
Total invested assets	1,495,750	109,450
NET INVESTMENT INCOME	61,588	3,963

NEW BUSINESS

	2006	2007	2008	2009	2010
New regular premiums					
Investment and savings	92	88	75	77	57
Individual protection	905	867	858	883	804
Group protection	311	318	290	313	256
Individual pension	3,024	3,273	3,363	2,805	3,184
Group pension	753	821	989	962	910
Offshore business	22	21	19	21	37
TOTAL REGULAR	5,107	5,388	5,594	5,060	5,248
New single premiums					
Investments and savings	30,540	38,903	23,769	12,444	10,034
Individual protection	1,634	1,266	1,019	236	225
Individual pensions	18,758	22,165	18,389	14,811	15,155
Retirement income products	12,157	14,061	13,916	12,673	13,183
Occupational pensions	10,796	10,986	12,097	10,039	12,802
Offshore business	7,150	7,594	7,777	4,267	6,404
TOTAL SINGLE	81,034	94,970	76,967	54,830	57,803

TAXATION

The government raises money to pay for public services such as education, health and the social security system through tax. Each year the Chancellor of the Exchequer's budget sets out how much it will cost to provide these services and how much tax is therefore needed to pay for them. HM Revenue and Customs (HMRC) is the government department that collects it. There are several different types of tax. The varieties that individuals may have to pay include income tax payable on earnings, pensions, state benefits, savings and investments; capital gains tax (CGT) payable on the disposal of certain assets; inheritance tax (IHT) payable on estates upon death and certain lifetime gifts; stamp duty payable when purchasing property and shares; and value added tax (VAT) payable on goods and services, plus certain other duties such as fuel duty on petrol and excise duty on alcohol and tobacco. Government funds are also raised from companies and small businesses through corporation tax.

In July 2010 the Chancellor of the Exchequer launched the Office of Tax Simplification (OTS), an independent office of the Treasury which draws together expertise from across the tax and legal professions to provide the government with independent advice on simplifying the UK tax system with the objective of reducing compliance burdens on both businesses and individual taxpayers. In March 2011 the OTS reported to the government on two initial reviews, one on all tax reliefs and one on small business taxation. As a result the government announced in the 2011 Budget that it will be abolishing 43 tax reliefs as their rationale is no longer valid. It will also consult on options for merging the operation of National Insurance and Income Tax. Details of the OTS and its work can be found on the Treasury website (W www.hm-treasury.gov.uk). The OTS welcomes views from individuals and can be contacted via email (E ots@ots.gsi.gov.uk).

HELP AND INFORMATION ON TAXATION
For detailed information on any aspect of taxation individuals may contact their local tax office or enquiry centre. The HMRC website (W www.hmrc.gov.uk) provides wide-ranging information online. All HMRC forms, leaflets and guides are listed on, and can be downloaded from, the website or ordered by telephone. A list of all HMRC telephone helplines and order lines is also on the website. Those most relevant to topics covered in this section on taxation are included at pertinent points throughout. Information on taxation is also available in the Money, Tax and Benefits section of the government's public information website for individuals (W www.direct.gov.uk), and the Tax, Payroll and Company Information section of the equivalent information website for companies (W www.businesslink.gov.uk).

INCOME TAX

Income tax is levied on different sorts of income. Not all types of income are taxable, however, and individuals are only taxed on their 'taxable income' above a certain level. Reliefs and allowances can also reduce or, in some cases, cancel out an individual's income tax bill.

An individual's taxable income is assessed each tax year, starting on 6 April and ending on 5 April the following year. The information below relates specifically to the year of assessment 2011–12, ending on 5 April 2012, and has only limited application to earlier years. Changes due to come into operation at a later date are briefly mentioned where information is available. Types of income that are taxable include:

- earnings from employment or self-employment
- most pensions income including state, company and personal pensions
- interest on most savings
- income (dividends) from shares
- income from property
- income received from a trust
- certain state benefits
- an individual's share of any joint income

There are certain sorts of income on which individuals never pay tax. These are ignored altogether when working out how much income tax an individual may need to pay. Types of income that are not taxable include:

- certain state benefits and tax credits such as child benefit, working tax credit, child tax credit, pension credit, attendance allowance, disability living allowance, housing benefit and the first 28 weeks of incapacity benefit
- winter fuel payments
- income from National Savings and Investments savings certificates
- interest, dividends and other income from various tax-free investments, notably individual savings accounts (ISAs)
- premium bond and national lottery prizes

PERSONAL ALLOWANCE
Every individual resident in the UK for tax purposes has a 'personal allowance'. This is the amount of taxable income that an individual can earn or receive each year tax-free. This tax year (2011–12) the basic personal allowance or tax-free amount is £7,475. Individuals may be entitled to a higher personal allowance if they are 65 or over. Income tax is only due on an individual's taxable income that is above his or her tax-free allowance. Husbands and wives are taxed separately, with each entitled to his or her personal allowance. Each spouse may obtain other allowances and reliefs where the required conditions are satisfied.

The amount of personal allowance depends on an individual's age on 5 April 2012 and, if he or she is 65 or over, the total income received from all taxable sources. There are three age-related levels of personal allowance – see table below. If an individual became 65 or 75 during the year to 5 April 2012, he or she is entitled to the allowance for that age group.

If an individual aged 65 or over has an income over the £24,000 'income limit' for age-related allowances but not more than £100,000, their age-related allowance reduces by half the amount (£1 for every £2) he or she has over the £24,000 limit, until the basic rate allowance for those aged under 65 is reached. For a 66-year-old with an income of £24,400 (£400 over the limit), for example, the age-related allowance would reduce by £200 to £9,740.

Since April 2010 all three levels of personal allowance have been subject to a single income limit of £100,000, meaning that the personal allowance is reduced for individuals with an 'adjusted net income' (see below) over £100,000. Those individuals with an 'adjusted net income' below or equal to the £100,000 limit are entitled to the full amount of personal allowance. However, where an individual's adjusted net income is above the £100,000 limit, their personal allowance is reduced by half the amount (£1 for every £2) they have over that limit, irrespective of age, until their personal allowance is reduced to nil.

'Adjusted net income' is the measure of an individual's income that is used for the calculation of the existing income-related reductions to personal allowances for those aged between 65 and 74 and for those 75 and over. It is calculated in a series of steps. The starting point is 'net income', which is the total of the individual's income subject to income tax less specified deductions such as payments made gross to pension schemes. This net income is then reduced by the grossed-up amount of the individual's Gift Aid contributions to charities and the grossed-up amount of the individual's pension contributions that have received tax relief at source. The final step is to add back any relief for payments to trade unions or police organisations deducted in arriving at the individual's net income. The result is the individual's adjusted net income.

LEVELS OF PERSONAL ALLOWANCE FOR 2011–12

	Personal allowance	Income limit
Age under 65	£7,475	£100,000
Age 65–74	£9,940	£24,000
Age 75 and over	£10,090	£24,000

BLIND PERSON'S ALLOWANCE
If an individual is registered blind or is unable to perform any work for which eyesight is essential, he or she can claim blind person's allowance, an extra amount of tax-free income added to the personal allowance. In 2011–12 the blind person's allowance is £1,980. It is the same for everyone who can claim it, whatever his or her age or level of income. If an individual is married or in a civil partnership and cannot use all of his or her blind person's allowance because of insufficient income, the unused part of the allowance can be passed to the spouse or civil partner.

Other deductible allowances and reliefs that have the effect of reducing an income tax bill are available to taxpayers in certain circumstances and will be explained in more detail later in this section.

CALCULATING INCOME TAX DUE
Individuals' liability to pay income tax is determined by establishing their level of taxable income for the year. For married couples and civil partners, income must be allocated between the couple by reference to the individual who is beneficially entitled to that income. Where income arises from jointly held assets, it is normally apportioned equally between the partners. If, however, the beneficial interests in jointly held assets are

not equal, in most cases couples can make a special declaration to have income apportioned by reference to the actual interests in that income.

To work out an individual's liability for tax, his or her taxable income must be allocated between three different types: earned income (excluding income from savings and dividends); income from savings; and company dividends from shares and other equity-based investments.

After the tax-free allowance plus any deductible allowances and reliefs have been taken into account, the amount of tax an individual pays is calculated using different tax rates and a series of tax bands. The tax band applies to an individual's income after tax allowances and any reliefs have been taken into account. Individuals are not taxed on all of their income.

There were significant changes to income tax rates for 2008–9. The basic rate of income tax was reduced from 22 per cent to 20 per cent and a previous 10 per cent starting rate was removed for earned income and pensions. This created a simpler structure of two rates: a 20 pence (in the pound) basic rate and a 40 pence (in the pound) higher rate. From 2010–11 an additional income tax rate of 50 per cent was introduced, which applies on both savings and non-savings income over £150,000.

The 10 per cent starting rate continues to be available for savings income only, with a limit of £2,560 for 2011–12. If an individual's taxable non-savings income is above £2,560, the 10 per cent savings rate is not applicable.

The personal allowance for people aged under 65 has been increased by £1,000 in cash terms to £7,475 for the tax year 2011–12. The basic rate band above which tax is payable at the higher rate of 40 per cent has been simultaneously reduced to ensure that higher rate taxpayers do not benefit from this change.

In the 2011 budget it was announced that the personal allowance for people aged under 65 will increase by £630 on 6 April 2012 to £8,105 for the 2012–13 tax year. The basic rate limit will simultaneously fall by £630, taking it down to £34,370 in 2012–13. All other income tax personal allowances and limits that are subject to indexation will be increased in line with the retail prices index (RPI) for the 2012–13 tax year.

INCOME TAX RATES (PER CENT) AND TAX BANDS FOR 2011–12

Band	Earned income	Band	Savings	Dividends
£0–£35,000	20%	£0–£2,560*	10%	10%
£35,000+	40%	£2,560–£35,000	20%	10%
£150,000+	50%	£35,000+	40%	32.5%
		£150,000+	50%	42.5%

* If an individual's taxable non-savings income is above £2,560 the 20 per cent tax band applies to savings income from £0–£35,000

The first calculation is applied to earned income which includes income from employment or self-employment, most pension income and rental income plus the value of a wide range of employee fringe benefits such as company cars, living accommodation and private medical insurance (for more information on fringe benefits, see later section on payment of income tax). In working out the amount of an individual's net taxable earnings, all expenses incurred 'wholly, exclusively and necessarily' in the performance of his or her work duties, together with the cost of business travel, may be deducted. Fees and subscriptions to certain professional bodies may also be deducted. Redundancy payments and other sums paid on the termination of an employment are assessable income, but the first £30,000 is normally tax-free provided the payment is not linked with the recipient's retirement or performance.

The first £35,000 of taxable income remaining after the tax-free allowance plus any deductible allowances and reliefs have been taken into account, is taxed at the basic rate of 20 per cent. Taxable income between £35,000 and £150,000 is taxed at the higher rate of 40 per cent. Taxable income above £150,000 is taxed at the additional rate of 50 per cent.

Savings and dividends income is added to an individual's other taxable income and taxed last. This means that tax on such sorts of income is based on an individual's highest income tax band.

SAVINGS INCOME

The second calculation is applied to any income from savings received by an individual. The appropriate rate at which it must be taxed is determined by adding income from savings to an individual's other taxable income, excluding dividends.

There is a 10 per cent starting rate for savings income only, with a limit of £2,560. If an individual's taxable non-savings income exceeds this limit, the 10 per cent savings rate is not applicable. Savings income above £2,560 and below the £35,000 basic rate limit is taxable at 20 per cent. Savings income between £35,000 and £150,000 is taxable at 40 per cent. Savings income over £150,000 is taxed at 50 per cent. If savings income falls on both sides of a tax band, the relevant amounts are taxed at the rates for each tax band.

Most savings income, such as interest paid on bank and building society accounts, already has tax at a rate of 20 per cent deducted from it 'at source' – that is, before it is paid out to individuals. This is confirmed by the entry 'net interest' on bank and building society statements.

Higher rate taxpayers whose income is sufficient to pay 40 or 50 per cent tax on their savings income must let their tax office know what savings income they have received so that the extra tax they owe can be collected.

Non taxpayers – ie individuals, including most children, whose taxable income is less than their tax allowances – can register to have their savings interest paid 'gross' without any tax being deducted from it at source. To do this, they must complete form R85, available at all banks and building societies. Parents or guardians need to fill in this form on behalf of those under 16. For individuals who are unsure whether they qualify as non-taxpayers and, therefore, whether they are able to register to have their savings interest paid gross, HMRC offers an 'R85 checker' on its website (W www.hmrc.gov.uk/calcs/r85/).

Non-taxpayers who have already had tax deducted from their savings interest can claim it back from HMRC by filling in form R40. For help or information about registering to get interest paid tax-free or to claim tax back on savings interest, individuals may visit W www.hmrc.gov.uk/taxon/bank.htm or call a dedicated savings helpline on T 0845-980 0645. Further information is available in the leaflet *IR111: Bank and building society interest – Are you paying tax when you don't need to?*

DIVIDEND INCOME

The third and final income tax calculation is on UK dividends, which means income from shares in UK companies and other share-based investments including unit trusts and open-ended investment companies (OEICs).

Dividend tax rates differ from those on savings income. The rate that an individual pays on his or her dividends depends on the amount of his or her overall taxable income (after allowances). Dividend income at or below the £35,000 basic rate tax limit is taxable at 10 per cent, between £35,000 and £150,000 at 32.5 per cent, and above £150,000 at 42.5 per cent.

When dividends are paid, a voucher is sent that shows the dividend paid and the amount of associated 'tax credit'. Companies pay dividends out of profits on which they have already paid or are due to pay tax. The tax credit takes account of this and is available to the shareholder to offset against any income tax that may be due on their dividend income. The dividend paid represents 90 per cent of their dividend income. The remaining 10 per cent is made up of the tax credit. In other words the tax credit represents 10 per cent of the dividend income.

Individuals who pay tax at the basic rate have no tax to pay on their dividend income because the tax liability is 10 per cent – the same amount as the tax credit. Higher rate taxpayers pay a total of 32.5 per cent tax on dividend income above the £35,000 basic rate income tax limit, but because the first 10 per cent of the tax due on their dividend income is already covered by the tax credit, in practice they owe only 22.5 per cent. For the same reason, additional rate taxpayers who pay a total of 42.5 per cent on dividend income above the £150,000 additional rate tax limit, owe only 32.5 per cent in practice.

Non-taxpayers cannot claim the 10 per cent tax credit. This is because income tax has not been deducted from the dividends paid to them. The view is that they have simply been given a 10 per cent credit against any income tax due.

If there is significant change to an individual's savings or other income, whatever his or her current tax bracket, it is the individual's responsibility to contact the relevant tax office immediately, even if he or she does not normally complete a tax return. This enables the tax office to work out whether extra or less tax should be paid.

INDIVIDUAL SAVINGS ACCOUNTS

There is a small selection of savings and investment products that are tax-free. This means that there is no tax to pay on any income generated in the form of interest or dividends nor on any increase in the value of the capital invested. Their tax-efficient status has been granted by the government in order to give people an incentive to save more. For this reason there are usually limits and restrictions on the amount of money an individual may invest in such savings and investments. Individual savings accounts (ISAs) are the best known among tax-efficient savings and investments. They were introduced in 1999 to replace other similar schemes called PEPs and TESSAs. Individuals can use an ISA to save cash, or invest in stocks and shares.

Changes were made to the ISA rules which took effect from April 2008. These reforms removed the distinction between what were previously known as maxi and mini ISAs and simplified an individual's options.

For the 2011–12 tax year individuals may save up to £10,680 each tax year in an ISA and receive all profits free of tax provided that they are UK residents and are over 18 (over 16 for cash ISAs). An ISA must be in an individual's name and cannot be held jointly with another person.

Individuals may invest in two separate ISAs each tax year: a cash ISA and a stocks and shares ISA (an umbrella term covering investments in unit trusts, company shares, bonds, investment-type life insurance and so on). Up to £5,340 of an individual's ISA allowance may be saved in one cash ISA with one provider. The remainder of the £10,680 can be invested in one stocks and shares ISA with either the same or a different provider. Alternatively an individual may open a single stocks and shares ISA and invest the full £10,680 into it. Various non-cash assets can be held in a stocks and shares ISA including unit trusts, company shares, bonds, investment-type life insurance and investment trusts.

The government has announced that annually, over the course of this parliament, the ISA limits will increase in line with the retail prices index (RPI). Each September's RPI figure will be used to set the ISA limits for the following tax year. The limits will be rounded each year to the nearest multiple of £120 to enable savers to plan monthly savings more easily.

Under the simplified ISA regime, what used to be known as mini cash ISAs, TESSA-only ISAs (TOISAs) and the cash component of a maxi ISA have become cash ISAs. Similarly, mini stocks and shares ISAs, the stocks and shares component of a maxi ISA and all Personal Equity Plans (PEPs) have become stocks and shares ISAs.

ISA savers have the option to transfer some or all of the money they have saved in previous tax years in cash ISAs to their stocks and shares ISA without affecting their annual ISA investment allowance. They may also choose to transfer all the money they have saved to date in a cash ISA in the current tax year to a stocks and shares ISA. However, the rules do not allow the reverse; that is, the transfer of monies saved in a stocks and shares ISA to a cash ISA.

Further details are available via HMRC's savings helpline (T 0845-604 1701).

DEDUCTIBLE ALLOWANCES AND RELIEF

Income taxpayers may be entitled to certain tax-deductible allowances and reliefs as well as their personal allowances. Examples include the married couple's allowance and maintenance payments relief, both of which are explained below. Unlike the tax-free allowances, these are not amounts of income that an individual can receive tax-free but amounts by which their tax bill can be reduced.

MARRIED COUPLE'S ALLOWANCE

A married couple's allowance (MCA) is available to taxpayers who are married or are in a civil partnership only where one or other partner was born before 6 April 1935. Eligible couples can start to claim the MCA from the year of marriage or civil partnership registration.

The MCA is restricted to give relief at a fixed rate of 10 per cent, which means that – unlike the personal allowance – it is not income that can be received without paying tax. Instead, it reduces an individual's tax bill by up to a fixed amount calculated as 10 per cent of the amount of the allowance to which they are entitled.

In 2011–12, the MCA is £7,295 at 10 per cent, worth up to £729.50 off a couple's tax bill. The MCA is made up of two parts. There is a minimum amount (£2,800 in 2011–12) which will always be due. The remaining amount (£4,495 in 2011–12) can be reduced if the husband's income exceeds certain limits.

The husband will normally receive the allowance, but

the couple can jointly decide which of them will get the minimum amount of the allowance. Alternatively, they can decide to have the minimum amount of the allowance split equally between them. They must inform their tax office of their decision before the start of the new tax year in which they want the decision to take effect. Once this is done, the change will apply until the couple decides to alter it. The remaining part of the allowance must go to the husband unless he lacks sufficient income to use it.

If an individual does not have enough income to use all his or her share of the married couple's allowance, the tax office can transfer the unused part of it to his or her spouse or civil partner.

Like the personal allowance, the MCA can be gradually reduced at the rate of £1 of the allowance for every £2 of income above the income limit (£24,000 in 2011–12). The amount of MCA can only be affected by the husband's income, and it only starts to be affected if his personal allowance has already been reduced back to the basic level for people under 65. The wife's income never affects the amount of MCA. It does not matter whether all or part of the minimum amount of the allowance has been transferred to her. Whatever the level of the husband's income, the MCA can never be reduced below the minimum amount: in 2011–12 this is £2,800 at 10 per cent.

The same system of allowance allocation applies to civil partners based on the income of the highest earner.

MAINTENANCE PAYMENTS RELIEF

An allowance is available to reduce an individual's tax bill for maintenance payments he or she makes to his or her ex spouse or former civil partner in certain circumstances. To be eligible one or other partner must have been born before 6 April 1935; the couple must be legally separated or divorced; the maintenance payments being made must be under a court order; and the payments must be for the maintenance of an ex-spouse or former civil partner (provided he or she is not now remarried or in a new civil partnership) or for children who are under 21. For the tax year 2011–12, this allowance can reduce an individual's tax bill by:

- 10 per cent of £2,800 (maximum £280) – this applies where an individual makes maintenance payments of £2,800 or more a year
- 10 per cent of the amount the individual has actually paid – this applies where an individual makes maintenance payments of less than £2,800 a year

An individual cannot claim a tax reduction for any voluntary payments he or she makes for a child, ex-spouse or former civil partner. To claim maintenance payments relief, individuals should contact their tax office.

CHARITABLE DONATION

A number of charitable donations qualify for tax relief. Individuals can increase the value of regular or one-off charitable gifts of money, however small, by using the Gift Aid scheme that allows charities or community amateur sports clubs (CASCs) to reclaim 20 per cent basic rate tax relief on donations they receive.

The way the scheme works means that if a taxpayer gives £10 using Gift Aid, for example, the donation is worth £12.50 to the charity or CASC.

Individuals who pay 40 per cent higher rate income tax can claim back the difference between the 40 per cent and the 20 per cent basic rate of income tax on the total (gross) value of their donations. For example, a 40 per cent tax payer donates £100. The total value of this donation to the charity or CASC is £125, of which the individual can claim back 20 per cent (£25) for themself. Similarly, those who pay 50 per cent additional rate income tax can claim back the difference between the 50 per cent and the 20 per cent basic rate on the total (gross) value of their donations. On a £100 donation, this means they can claim back £37.50.

Individuals who claim the age-related personal allowance, married couple's allowance or tax credits should tell HMRC about any Gift Aid donations they make because these can sometimes increase the amount of allowance or tax credit to which they are entitled.

In order to make a Gift Aid donation, individuals need to make a Gift Aid declaration. The charity or CASC will normally ask an individual to complete a simple form. One form can cover every gift made to the same charity or CASC for whatever period chosen, including both gifts made in the past and in the future. It was announced in the 2011 budget that the government intends to introduce a new scheme in April 2013 where charities will be able to claim Gift Aid on small donations, up to a total of £5,000 a year per charity, without the need for donors to fill in any forms at all. This will mean Gift Aid could be claimed on the contents of collecting tins, for example.

Individuals can use Gift Aid provided the amount of income tax and/or capital gains tax they have paid in the tax year in which their donations are made is at least equal to the amount of basic rate tax the charity or CASC is reclaiming on their gifts. It is the responsibility of the individual to make sure this is the case. If an individual makes Gift Aid donations and has not paid sufficient tax, they may have to pay the shortfall to HMRC. The Gift Aid scheme is not suitable for non-taxpayers.

Individuals who complete a tax return and are due a tax refund can ask HMRC to treat all or part of it as a Gift Aid donation.

For employees or those in receipt of an occupational pension, a tax-efficient way of making regular donations to charities is to use the Payroll Giving scheme. It allows the donations to be paid from a salary or pension before income tax is deducted. This effectively reduces the cost of giving for donors, which may allow them to give more.

For example, it costs a basic-rate taxpayer only £8 in take-home pay to give £10 to charity from their pre-tax pay. Where a donor pays 40 per cent higher rate tax, that same £10 donation costs the taxpayer £6 and for donors who pay the additional 50 per cent rate tax, it costs £5.

Anyone who pays tax through the PAYE system can give to any charity of their choosing in this way, providing their employer or pension provider offers a payroll giving scheme. There is no limit to the amount individuals can donate.

It was announced in the 2011 budget that a reduced rate of inheritance tax (IHT) will apply where an individual, in their will, leaves 10 per cent or more of their net estate to charity. In such cases the current IHT 40 per cent rate will be reduced to 36 per cent. The new rate will apply where death occurs on or after 6 April 2012.

Details of tax-efficient charitable giving methods can be found at W www.direct.gov.uk/en/MoneyTaxAndBenefits/ManagingMoney and W www.hmrc.gov.uk/individuals/giving

TAX RELIEF ON PENSION CONTRIBUTIONS

Pensions are long-term investments designed to help ensure that people have enough income in retirement. The government encourages individuals to save towards a pension by offering tax relief on their contributions. Tax relief reduces an individual's tax bill or increases their pension fund.

The way tax relief is given on pension contributions depends on whether an individual pays into a company, public service or personal pension scheme.

For employees who pay into a company or public service pension scheme, most employers take the pension contributions from the employee's pay before deducting tax, which means that the individual – whether they pay income tax at the basic or higher rate – gets full tax relief straight away. Some employers, however, use the same method of paying pension contributions as that used by personal pension scheme payers described below.

Individuals who pay into a personal pension scheme make contributions from their net salary; that is, after tax has been deducted. For each pound that individuals contribute to their pension from net salary, the pension provider claims tax back from the government at the basic rate of 20 per cent and reinvests it on behalf of the individual into the scheme. In practice this means that for every £80 an individual pays into their pension, they receive £100 in their pension fund.

Higher rate taxpayers currently get 40 per cent tax relief on money they put into a pension. On contributions made from net salary, the first 20 per cent is claimed back from HMRC by the pension scheme in the same way as for a lower rate taxpayer. It is then up to individuals to claim back the other 20 per cent from their tax office, either when they fill in their annual tax return or by telephone or letter. In a similar fashion, individuals subject to the 50 per cent additional rate of income tax can get 50 per cent tax relief on their pension contributions.

Most providers of retirement annuities, which are a type of personal pension scheme set up before July 1988, do not offer a 'tax relief at source' scheme whereby they claim back tax at the basic rate as is the case with more modern personal pensions. In such cases, contributing individuals need to claim the tax relief they are due through their tax return or by telephoning or writing to HMRC.

Non taxpayers can still pay into a personal pension scheme and benefit from 20 per cent basic rate relief on the first £2,880 a year they contribute. In practice this means that the government tops up their £2,880 contribution to make it £3,600 which is the current universal pension allowance. Such pension contributions may be made on behalf of a non-taxpayer by another individual. An individual may, for example, contribute to a pension on behalf of a husband, wife, civil partner, child or grandchild. Tax relief will be added to their contribution at the basic rate, again on up to £2,880 a year benefiting the recipient, but their own tax bill will not be affected.

In any one tax year, individuals can get tax relief on pension contributions made into any number and type of registered pension schemes of 100 per cent of their annual earnings, irrespective of age, up to a maximum 'annual allowance'. For the tax year 2011–12 the annual allowance is £50,000, a dramatic reduction from the £255,000 allowance for tax-privileged pension saving in 2010–11. Individuals pay tax at 40 per cent on any contributions they make above the annual allowance. Everyone now also has a 'lifetime allowance' (£1.8m for 2011–12) which means taxpayers can save up to a total of

£1.8m in their pension fund and still get tax relief at their highest income tax rate on all their contributions. It was announced in the 2011 budget that the lifetime allowance will drop to £1.5 million in 2012–13.

For information on pensions and tax relief visit W www.direct.gov.uk/en/Pensionsandretirementplanning Another useful source of information and advice is The Pensions Advisory Service (TPAS), an independent voluntary organisation grant-aided by the Department for Work and Pensions at W www.pensionsadvisory service.org.uk; its Pensions Helpline is on T 0845-601 2923.

PAYMENT OF INCOME TAX

Employees have their income tax deducted from their wages throughout the year by their employer who sends it on to HMRC. Those in receipt of a company pension have their due tax deducted in the same way by their pension provider. This system of collecting income tax is known as 'pay as you earn' (PAYE).

BENEFITS IN KIND

The PAYE system is also used to collect tax on certain fringe benefits or 'benefits in kind' that employees or directors receive from their employer, but are not included in their salary cheque or wages. These include company cars, private medical insurance paid for by the employer or cheap or free loans from the employer. Some fringe benefits are tax-free, including employer-paid contributions into an employee's pension fund, cheap or free canteen meals, works buses, in-house sports facilities, reasonable relocation expenses, provision of a mobile phone and workplace nursery places provided for the children of employees. For taxable fringe benefits, tax is paid on the 'taxable value' of the benefit.

Employers submit returns for individual employees earning at or above the £8,500 per annum threshold (including the value of expenses and benefits) to the tax office on the form P11D, with details of any fringe benefits they have been given. For those earning less than the £8,500 threshold (part-time employees) a P9D form is submitted. Employees should get a copy of this form by 6 July following the end of the tax year and must enter the value of the fringe benefits they have received on their tax return for the relevant year, even if tax has already been paid on them under PAYE. Fringe benefits may be taxed under PAYE by being offset against personal tax allowances in an individual's PAYE code. Otherwise tax will be collected after the end of the tax year by the issue of an assessment on the fringe benefits.

SELF-ASSESSMENT

Individuals who are not on PAYE, notably the self-employed, need to complete a self-assessment tax return each year, in paper form or online at the HMRC website (W www.hmrc.gov.uk), and pay any income tax owed in twice-yearly instalments. Some individuals with more complex tax affairs such as those who earn money from rents or investments above a certain level may also need to fill out a self-assessment return, even if they are on PAYE. HMRC uses the figures supplied on the tax return to work out the individual's tax bill, or they can choose to work it out themselves. It is called 'self-assessment' because individuals are responsible for making sure the details they provide are correct.

Tax returns are usually sent out in early April, following the end of the tax year to which they apply. They may also go out at other times, for example if an individual wants to claim an allowance or repayment or to register for self-assessment for the first time.

Individuals with simple tax affairs may receive a short four-page return. Those with more complex affairs must fill out a full return that has 12 core pages plus extra pages, depending on the sorts of income received.

Central to the self-assessment system is the requirement for individuals to contact their tax office if they do not receive a self-assessment return but think they should or if their financial circumstances change. Individuals have six months from when the tax year ends to report any new income, for example. If an individual becomes self-employed, they have three months after the calendar month in which they began self-employed work to let HMRC know. This can be done by telephoning the helpline number for the newly self-employed on T 0845-915 4515.

TAX RETURN FILING AND PAYMENT DEADLINES

There are also key deadlines for filing (sending in) completed tax returns and paying the tax due. Failure to do so can incur penalties, interest charges and surcharges.

KEY FILING DATES FOR SELF-ASSESSMENT RETURNS

Date	Why the date is important
31 Oct*	Deadline for filing paper returns* for tax year ending the previous 5 April
30 Dec	Deadline for online filing where the amount owed for tax year ending the previous 5 April is less than £2,000 and the taxpayer wants HMRC to collect any tax due through their PAYE tax code
31 Jan†	Deadline for online filing of returns for tax year ending the previous 5 April

* Or three months from the date the return was requested if this was after 31 July

† Or three months from the date the return was requested if this was after 31 October

KEY SELF-ASSESSMENT PAYMENT DATES

Date	What payment is due?
31 Jan	Deadline for paying the balance of any tax owed – the 'balancing payment' – for the tax year ending the previous 5 April. It is also the date by which a taxpayer must make any first 'payment on account' (advance payment) for the current tax year. For example, on 31 January 2011 a taxpayer may have to pay both the balancing payment for the year 2010–11 and the first payment on account for 2011–12
31 Jul	Deadline for making a second payment on account for the current tax year

LATE FILING AND PAYMENT PENALTIES

Late filing of tax returns incurs an automatic £100 penalty although individuals may appeal against the penalty if they have a reasonable excuse. For late filing of 2010–11 tax returns the following additional penalties also apply:

• Over three months late – £10 each day, up to a maximum of £900
• Over six months late – an additional £300 or 5 per cent of the tax due, whichever is the higher
• Over 12 months late – a further £300 or 5 per cent of the tax due, whichever is the higher

Late payment of tax owing for 2010-11 incurs the following penalties:

- Over 30 days – 5 per cent of the tax unpaid at that date
- Over six months – an additional 5 per cent of the tax unpaid at that date
- Over 12 months – a further 5 per cent of the tax unpaid at that date

Interest is due on all outstanding amounts, including any unpaid penalties until payment is received in full.

TAX CREDITS

Child tax credit and working tax credit are paid to qualifying individuals. Although the title of both credits incorporates the word 'tax', neither affects the amount of income tax payable or repayable. Both are forms of social security benefits. *See* Social Welfare.

CAPITAL GAINS TAX

Capital gains tax (CGT) is a tax on the gain or profit that an individual makes when they sell, give away or otherwise dispose of an asset – that is, something they own such as shares, land or buildings. An individual potentially has to pay CGT on gains they make from any disposal of assets during a tax year. There is, however, a tax-free allowance and some additional reliefs that may reduce an individual's CGT bill. The following information relates to the tax year 2011–12 ending on 5 April 2012.

CGT is paid by individuals who are either resident or ordinarily resident in the UK for the tax year, executors or administrators – 'personal representatives' – responsible for a deceased person's financial affairs and trustees of a settlement. Non-residents are not usually liable to CGT unless they carry on a business in the UK through a branch or agency. Special CGT rules may apply to individuals who used to live and work in the UK but have since left the country.

CAPITAL GAINS CHARGEABLE TO CGT

Typically, individuals have made a gain if they sell an asset for more than they paid for it. It is the gain that is taxed, not the amount the individual receives for the asset. For example, a man buys shares for £1,000 and later sells them for £2,000 (£3,000 less £1,000). If someone gives an asset away, the gain will be based on the difference between what the asset was worth when originally acquired compared with its worth at the time of disposal. The same is true when an asset is sold for less than its full worth in order to give away part of the value. For example, a woman buys a property for £120,000 and three years later, when the property's market value has risen to £180,000, she gives it to her son. The son may pay nothing for the property or pay less than its true worth, eg £100,000. Either way, she has made a gain of £60,000 (£180,000 less £120,000).

If an individual disposes of an asset he or she received as a gift, the gain is worked out according to the market value of the asset when it was received. For example, a man gives his sister a painting worth £8,000. She pays nothing for it. Later she sells the painting for £10,000. For CGT purposes, she is treated as making a gain of £2,000 (£10,000 less £8,000). If an individual inherits an asset, the estate of the person who died does not pay CGT at the time. If the inheritor later disposes of the asset, the gain is worked out by looking at the market value at the time of the death. For example, a woman acquires some shares for £5,000 and leaves them to her niece when she dies. No CGT is payable at the time of death when the shares are worth £8,000. Later the niece sells the shares for £10,000. She has made a gain of £2,000 (£10,000 less £8,000).

Individuals may also have to pay CGT if they dispose of part of an asset or exchange one asset for another. Similarly, CGT may be payable if an individual receives a capital sum of money from an asset without disposing of it, for example where he or she receives compensation when an asset is damaged.

Assets that may lead to a CGT charge when they are disposed of include:

- shares in a company
- units in a unit trust
- land and buildings (though not normally an individual's main home – *see* 'disposal of a home' section for details)
- higher value jewellery, paintings, antiques and other personal effects assets used in business such as goodwill

EXEMPT GAINS

Certain kinds of assets do not give rise to a chargeable gain when they are disposed of. Assets exempt from CGT include:

- an individual's private car
- an individual's main home, provided certain conditions are met
- tax-free investments such as assets held in an individual savings account (ISA)
- UK government gilts or 'bonds'
- personal belongings including jewellery, paintings, antiques individually worth £6,000 or less
- cash in sterling or foreign currency held for an individual or his/her family's own personal use
- betting, lottery or pools winnings
- personal injury compensation

DISPOSAL OF A HOME: PRIVATE RESIDENCE RELIEF

Individuals do not have to pay CGT when they sell their main home if all the following conditions are met:

- they bought it and made any expenditure on it, primarily for use as their home rather than with a view to making a profit
- the property was their only home throughout the period they owned it (ignoring the last three years of ownership)
- the property was actually used as their home all the time that they owned it and, throughout the period, it was not used for any purpose other than as a home for the individual, his or her family and no more than one lodger
- the garden and area of grounds sold with the property does not exceed 5,000 sq. m (1.24 acres) including the site of the property

Even if all these conditions are not met, individuals may still be entitled to CGT relief when they sell the home. They may, for example, qualify for relief if they lived away from home temporarily while working abroad. Married couples or couples in a civil partnership may have relief from CGT on only one home. There is a special exception, however, where the spouse or partner each had a qualifying home before marriage or civil partnership and both live together in one of these homes after marriage or civil partnership and sell the other. Provided that it is sold within three years of marriage or the civil partnership, they may not have to pay any CGT (subject to the normal rules for this relief). If they sell it after more than three years it may qualify for partial relief. There are special rules on divorce and separation.

Certain other kinds of disposal similarly do not give rise to a chargeable gain. For example, individuals who are married or in a civil partnership and who live together may sell or give assets to their spouse or civil partner without having to pay CGT. Individuals may not, however, give or sell assets cheaply to their children without having to consider CGT. There is no CGT to pay on assets given to a registered charity.

CALCULATING CGT

CGT is worked out for each tax year and is charged on the total of an individual's taxable gains after taking into account certain costs and reliefs that can reduce or defer chargeable gains, allowable losses made on assets to which CGT normally applies and an annual exempt (tax-free) amount that applies to every individual. If the total of an individual's net gains in a tax year is less than the annual exempt amount (AEA), the individual will not have to pay CGT. For the tax year 2011–12 the AEA is £10,600. If an individual's net gains are more than the AEA, they pay CGT on the excess. Should any part of the exemption remain unused, this cannot be carried forward to a future year. A smaller exemption amount (£5,300 for 2011–12) applies to most trusts.

There are certain reliefs available that may eliminate, reduce or defer CGT. Some reliefs are available to many people while others are available only in special circumstances. Some reliefs are given automatically while others are given only if they are claimed. Some of the costs of buying, selling and improving assets may be deducted from total gains when working out an individual's chargeable gain.

RATES OF TAX

The net gains remaining, if any, calculated after subtracting the AEA, deducting costs and taking into account all CGT reliefs, incur liability to capital gains tax. There was a single rate of CGT of 18 per cent for individuals, trustees and personal representatives on taxable gains until the coalition government's budget on 22 June 2010 when it was announced that, from 23 June 2010, CGT would rise to 28 per cent for higher and additional rate taxpayers. Basic rate taxpayers continue to pay CGT at a rate of 18 per cent.

CGT for 2011–12 is due for payment in full on 31 January 2013. If payment is delayed, interest or surcharges may be imposed. A husband and wife or registered civil partners who live together are separately assessed to CGT. Each partner must independently calculate his or her gains and losses with each entitled to the AEA of £10,600 for 2011–12.

VALUATION OF ASSETS

The disposal proceeds – ie the amount received as consideration for the disposal of an asset – are the sum used to establish the gain or loss once certain allowable costs have been deducted. In most cases this is straightforward because the disposal proceeds are the amount actually received for disposing of the asset. This may include cash payable now or in the future and the value of any asset received in exchange for the asset disposed of. However, in certain circumstances, the disposal proceeds may not accurately reflect the value of the asset and the individual may be treated as disposing of an asset for an amount other than the actual amount (if any) that they received. This applies, in particular, where an asset is transferred as a gift or sold for a price known to be below market value. Disposal proceeds in such transactions are deemed to be equal to the market value of the asset at the time it was disposed of rather than the actual amount (if any) received for it.

Market value represents the price that an asset might reasonably be expected to fetch upon sale in the open market. In the case of unquoted shares or securities, it is to be assumed that the hypothetical purchaser in the open market would have available all the information that a prudent prospective purchaser of shares or securities might reasonably require if that person were proposing to purchase them from a willing vendor by private treaty and at arm's length. The market value of unquoted shares or securities will often be established following negotiations with the specialist HMRC Shares & Assets Valuation department. The valuation of land and interests in land in the UK is dealt with by the Valuation Office Agency. Special rules apply to determine the market value of shares quoted on the London Stock Exchange.

ALLOWABLE COSTS

When working out a chargeable gain, once the actual or notional disposal proceeds have been determined, certain allowable costs may be deducted. There is a general rule that no costs that could be taken into account when working out income or losses for income tax purposes may be deducted. Subject to this, allowable costs are:

- acquisition costs – the actual amount spent on acquiring the asset or, in certain circumstances, the equivalent market value
- incidental costs of acquiring the asset such as fees paid for professional advice, valuation costs, stamp duty and advertising costs to find a seller
- enhancement costs – incurred for the purpose of enhancing the value of the asset (not including normal maintenance and repair costs)
- expenditure on defending or establishing a person's rights over the asset
- incidental costs of disposing of the asset such as fees paid for professional advice, valuation costs, stamp duty and advertising costs to find a buyer

If an individual disposes of part of his or her interest in an asset, or part of a holding of shares of the same class in the same company, or part of a holding of units in the same unit trust, he or she can deduct part of the allowable costs of the asset or holding when working out the chargeable gain. Allowable costs may also be reduced by some reliefs.

ENTREPRENEURS' RELIEF

Entrepreneurs' Relief allows individuals in business and some trustees to claim relief on the first £10m of gains (£5m prior to 6 April 2011) made on the disposal of any of the following: all or part of a business; the assets of a business after it has ceased; and shares in a company. The relief is available to taxpayers as individuals if they are in business, for example as a sole trader or as a partner in a trading business, or if they hold shares in their own personal trading company. This relief is not available for companies.

Depending on the type of disposal, certain qualifying conditions need to be met throughout a qualifying one-year period. For example, if an individual is selling all or part of their business, they must have owned the business during a one-year period that ends on the date of the disposal.

Where Entrepreneurs' Relief applies, qualifying gains liable to CGT on or after 23 June 2010, are charged at 10 per cent. An individual can make claims for this relief on more than one occasion as long as the lifetime total of all their claims does not exceed £10m of gains qualifying for relief.

BUSINESS ASSET ROLL-OVER RELIEF

When certain types of business asset are sold or disposed of and the proceeds reinvested in new qualifying trading assets, business asset roll-over relief makes it possible to 'roll-over' or postpone the payment of any CGT that would normally be due. The gain is deducted from the base cost of the new asset and only becomes chargeable to CGT on the eventual disposal of that replacement asset unless a further roll-over situation then develops. Full relief is available if all the proceeds from the original asset are reinvested in the qualifying replacement asset.

For example, a trader sells a freehold office for £75,000 and makes a gain of £30,000. All of the proceeds are reinvested in a new freehold business premises costing £90,000. The trader can postpone the whole of the £30,000 gain made on the sale of the old office, as all of the proceeds have been reinvested. When the trader eventually sells the new business premises and the CGT bill becomes payable, the cost of the new premises will be treated as £60,000 (£90,000 less the £30,000 gain).

If only part of the proceeds from the disposal of an old asset is reinvested in a new one, it may still be possible to postpone paying tax on part of the gain until the eventual disposal of the new asset.

Relief is only available if the acquisition of the new asset takes place within a period between 12 months before, and 36 months after, the disposal of the old asset. However, HMRC may extend this time limit at their discretion where there is a clear intention to acquire a replacement asset. The most common types of business assets that qualify for roll-over relief are land, buildings occupied and used for the purposes of trade, fixed plant and machinery. Assets used for the commercial letting of furnished holiday accommodation qualify if certain conditions are satisfied.

GIFTS HOLD-OVER RELIEF

The gift of an asset is treated as a disposal made for a consideration equal to market value, with a corresponding acquisition by the transferee at an identical value. In the case of gifts of business assets made by individuals and a limited range of trustees, a form of hold-over relief may be available. This relief, which must be claimed, in effect enables liability for CGT to be deferred and passed to the person to whom the gift is made. Relief is limited to the transfer of certain assets including the following:

- gifts of assets used for the purposes of a business carried on by the donor or his or her personal company
- gifts of shares in trading companies that are not listed on a stock exchange
- gifts of shares or securities in the donor's personal trading company

- gifts of agricultural land and buildings that would qualify for inheritance tax agricultural property relief
- gifts that are chargeable transfers for inheritance tax purposes
- certain types of gifts that are specifically exempted from inheritance tax

Hold-over relief is automatically due on certain sorts of gifts including gifts to charities and community amateur sports clubs, and gifts of works of art where certain undertakings have been given. There are certain rules to prevent gifts hold-over relief being used for tax-avoidance purposes. For example, restrictions may apply where an individual gifts assets to trustees administering a trust in which the individual retains an interest or the assets transferred comprise a dwelling-house. Subject to these exceptions, the effect of a valid claim for hold-over relief is similar to that following a claim for roll-over relief on the disposal of business assets.

OTHER CGT RELIEFS

There are certain other CGT reliefs available on the disposal of property, shares and business assets. For detailed information on all CGT reliefs and for more general guidance on CGT, see the capital gains tax pages on the HMRC website (**W** www.hmrc.gov.uk/cgt).

REPORTING AND PAYING CGT

Individuals are responsible for telling HMRC about capital gains on which they have to pay tax. Individuals who receive a self-assessment tax return may report capital gains by filling in the capital gains supplementary pages – the return explains how to obtain these pages if needed.

Individuals who do not normally complete a tax return but who need to report capital gains or losses should contact their local tax office. If an individual has CGT to pay, they must tell their tax office in writing by 5 October after the end of the tax year for which the CGT is due.

There is a time limit for claiming capital losses. The deadline is five years from 31 January after the end of the tax year in which the loss was made.

INHERITANCE TAX

Inheritance tax (IHT) is a tax on the value of a person's estate on death and on certain gifts made by an individual during his or her lifetime, usually payable within six months of death. Broadly speaking, a person's estate is everything he or she owned at the time of death including property, possessions, money and investments, less his or her debts. Not everyone pays IHT. It only applies if the taxable value of an estate is above the current inheritance tax threshold. If an estate, including any assets held in trust and gifts made within seven years of death, is less than the threshold, no IHT will be due. See table for the lower threshold limit, known as the nil rate band.

It was announced in the 2009 pre-Budget report that the nil rate band for 2010–11 would be frozen at £325,000 and it was further announced in the 2010 Budget that this freeze would extend until 2014–15.

2007–8	£300,000
2008–9	£312,000
2009–10	£325,000
2010–11	£325,000

A claim can be made to transfer any unused IHT nil-rate band on a person's death to the estate of their surviving spouse or civil partner. This applies where the IHT nil-rate band of the first deceased spouse or civil partner was not fully used in calculating the IHT liability of their estate. When the surviving spouse or civil partner dies, the unused amount may be added to their own nil-rate band (*see* below for details).

IHT used to be something only very wealthy individuals needed to consider. This is no longer the case. The fact that the IHT threshold has not kept pace with house price inflation in recent years means that the estates of some 'ordinary' taxpayers, who would not consider themselves wealthy, are now liable for IHT purely because of the value of their home. However, there are a number of ways that individuals – while still alive – can legally reduce the IHT bill that will apply to their estates on death. Several valuable IHT exemptions are available (explained further below) which allow individuals to pass on assets during their lifetime or in their will without any IHT being due. Detailed information on IHT is available on the HMRC website (W www.hmrc.gov.uk/inheritancetax/index.htm). Further help is also available from the IHT & Probate Helpline (T 0845-302 0900).

DOMICILE

Liability to IHT depends on an individual's domicile at the time of any gift or on death. Domicile is a complex legal concept and what follows explains some of the main issues. An individual is domiciled in the country where he or she has a permanent home. Domicile is different from nationality or residence, and an individual can only have one domicile at any given time.

A 'domicile of origin' is normally acquired from the individual's father on birth, though this may not be the country in which he or she is born. For example, a child born in Germany while his or her father is working there, but whose permanent home is in the UK, will have the UK as his or her domicile of origin. Until a person legally changes his or her domicile, it will be the same as that of the person on whom they are legally dependent.

Individuals can legally acquire a new domicile – a 'domicile of choice' – from the age of 16 by leaving the current country of domicile and settling in another country and providing strong evidence of intention to live there permanently or indefinitely. Women who were married before 1974 acquired their husband's domicile and still retain it until they legally acquire a new domicile.

For IHT purposes, there is a concept of 'deemed domicile'. This means that even if a person is not domiciled in the UK under general law, he or she is treated as domiciled in the UK at the time of a transfer (ie at the time of a lifetime gift or on death) if he or she (a) was domiciled in the UK within the three years immediately before the transfer, or (b) was 'resident' in the UK in at least 17 of the 20 income tax years of assessment ending with the year in which a transfer is made. Where a person is domiciled, or treated as domiciled, in the UK at the time of a gift or on death, the location of assets is immaterial and full liability to IHT arises. A non-UK domiciled individual is also liable to IHT but only on chargeable property in the UK.

The assets of husband and wife and registered civil partners are not merged for IHT purposes, except that the IHT value of assets owned by one spouse or civil partner may be affected if the other also owns similar assets (eg shares in the same company or a share in their jointly owned house). Each spouse or partner is treated as a separate individual entitled to receive the benefit of his or her exemptions, reliefs and rates of tax.

IHT EXEMPTIONS

There are some important exemptions that allow individuals to legally pass assets on to others, both before and after their death – without being subject to IHT.

Exempt Beneficiaries

Assets can be given away to certain people and organisations without any IHT having to be paid. These gifts, which are exempt whether individuals make them during their lifetime or in their will, include gifts to:

- a husband, wife or civil partner, even if the couple is legally separated (but not if they are divorced or the civil partnership has dissolved), as long as both partners have a permanent home in the UK. Note that gifts to an unmarried partner or a partner with whom the donor has not formed a civil partnership are not exempt
- UK charities
- some national institutions, including national museums, universities and the National Trust
- UK political parties

Annual Exemption

The first £3,000 of gifts made each tax year by each individual is exempt from IHT. If this exemption is not used, or not wholly used in any year, the balance may be carried forward to the following year only. A couple, therefore, may give away a total of £6,000 per tax year between them or £12,000 if they have not used their previous year's annual exemptions.

Wedding gifts/civil partnership ceremony gifts

Some gifts are exempt from IHT because of the type of gift or reason for making it. Wedding or civil partnership ceremony gifts made to either of the couple are exempt from IHT up to certain amounts:

- gifts by a parent, £5,000
- gifts by a grandparent or other relative, £2,500
- gifts by anyone else, £1,000

The gift must be made on or shortly before the date of the wedding or civil partnership ceremony. If the ceremony is called off but the gift is made, this exemption will not apply.

Small Gifts

An individual can make small gifts, up to the value of £250, to any number of people in any one tax year without them being liable for IHT. However, a larger sum such as £500 cannot be given and exemption claimed for the first £250. In addition, this exemption cannot be used with any other exemption when giving to the same person. For example, a parent cannot combine a 'small gifts exemption' with a 'wedding/civil partnership ceremony gift exemption' to give a child £5,250 when he or she gets married or forms a civil partnership. Neither may an individual combine a 'small gifts exemption' with the 'annual exemption' to give someone £3,250. Note that it is possible to use the 'annual exemption' with any other exemption, such as the 'wedding/civil partnership ceremony gift exemption'. For example, if a child marries or forms a civil partnership, the parent can give him or her a total IHT-free gift of £8,000 by combining £5,000 under the wedding/civil partnership gift exemption and £3,000 under the annual exemption.

Normal Expenditure
Any gifts made out of individuals' after-tax income (not capital) are exempt from IHT if they are part of their normal expenditure and do not result in a fall in their standard of living. These can include regular payments to someone, such as an allowance or gifts for Christmas or a birthday and regular premiums paid on a life insurance policy for someone else.

Maintenance Gifts
An individual can make IHT-free maintenance payments to his or her spouse or registered civil partner, ex-spouse or former civil partner, relatives dependent because of old age or infirmity, and children (including adopted children and step-children) who are under 18 or in full-time education.

POTENTIALLY EXEMPT TRANSFERS
If an individual makes a gift to either another individual or certain types of trust and it is not covered by one of the above exemptions, it is known as a 'potentially exempt transfer' (PET). A PET is only free of IHT on two strict conditions: (a) the gift must be made at least seven years before the donor's death. If the donor does not survive seven years after making the gift, it will be liable for IHT and (b) the gift must be made as a true gift with no strings attached (technically known as a 'gift with reservation of benefit'). This means that the donor must give up all rights to the gift and stop benefiting from it in any way.

If a gift is made and the donor does retain some benefit from it then it will still count as part of his or her estate no matter how long he or she lives after making it. For example, a father could make a lifetime gift of his home to his child. However, HMRC would not accept this as a true gift if the father continued to live in the home (unless he paid his child a full commercial rent to do so) because he would be considered to still have a material interest in the gifted home. Its value, therefore, would still be liable for IHT.

In some circumstances a gift with strings attached might give rise to an income tax charge on the donor based on the value of the benefit he or she retains. In this case the donor can choose whether to pay the income tax or have the gift treated as a gift with reservation.

CHARGEABLE TRANSFERS
Any remaining lifetime gifts that are not (potentially or otherwise) exempt transfers are chargeable transfers or 'chargeable gifts', meaning that they incur liability to IHT. Chargeable transfers comprise mainly gifts to or from companies and gifts to particular types of trust. There is an immediate claim for IHT on chargeable gifts, and additional tax may be payable if the donor dies within seven years of making a chargeable gift.

DEATH
Immediately before the time of death an individual is deemed to make a transfer of value. This transfer will comprise the value of assets forming part of the deceased's estate after subtracting most liabilities. Any exempt transfers may be excluded such as transfers for the benefit of a surviving spouse or civil partner, and charities. Death may also trigger three additional liabilities:

- a PET made within the seven years before the death loses its potential status and becomes chargeable to IHT
- the value of gifts made with reservation may incur liability if any benefit was enjoyed within the seven years before the death
- additional tax may become payable for chargeable lifetime transfers made within the seven years before the death

The 'personal representative' (the person nominated to handle the affairs of the deceased person) arranges to value the estate and pay any IHT that is due. One or more personal representatives can be nominated in a person's will, in which case they are known as the 'executors'. If a person dies without leaving a will a court can nominate the personal representative, who is then known as the 'administrator'. Valuing the deceased person's estate is one of the first things his or her personal representative needs to do. The representative will not normally be able to take over management of the estate (called 'applying for probate') until all or some of any IHT that is due has been paid.

VALUATIONS
When valuing a deceased person's estate all assets (property, possessions and money) owned at the time of death and certain assets given away during the seven years before death must be included. The valuation must accurately reflect what those assets would reasonably fetch in the open market at the date of death. The value of all of the assets that the deceased owned should include:

- his or her share of any assets owned jointly with someone else, for example a house owned with a partner
- any assets that are held in a trust, from which the deceased had the right to benefit
- any assets given away, but in which he or she kept an interest (gifts with reservation)
- PETs given away within the last seven years

Most estate assets can be valued quite easily, for example money in bank accounts or stocks and shares. In other instances the help of a professional valuer may be needed. Advice on how to value different assets including joint or trust assets is available at W www.hmrc.gov.uk. When valuing an estate, special relief is made available for certain assets. The two main reliefs are business relief and agricultural property relief outlined below. Once all assets have been valued, the next step is to deduct from the total assets everything that the deceased person owed such as unpaid bills, outstanding mortgages and other loans plus their funeral expenses. The value of all of the assets, less the deductible debts, is their estate. IHT is only payable on any value above £325,000 for the tax year 2011–12 at the current rate of 40 per cent.

RELIEF FOR SELECTED ASSETS

Agricultural Property
Relief from IHT is available on the agricultural value of agricultural property that is transferred. Agricultural property generally includes land or pasture used in the growing of crops or intensive rearing of animals for food consumption. It can also include farmhouses and farm cottages. The agricultural property can be owner-occupied or let. Relief is only due if the transferor has owned the property and it has been occupied for agricultural purposes for a minimum period.

The chargeable value transferred, either on a lifetime gift or on death, must be determined. This value may then be reduced by a percentage. Under current rates, a 100 per cent deduction will be available if the transferor retained vacant possession or could have obtained that possession within a period of 12 months following the transfer. In other cases, notably including land let to tenants, a lower deduction of 50 per cent is usually available. However, this lower deduction may be increased to 100 per cent if the letting was made after 31 August 1995.

To qualify for the relief, the agricultural property must either have been occupied by the transferor for the purposes of agriculture throughout a two-year period ending on the date of the transfer, or have been owned by the transferor throughout a period of seven years ending on that date and also occupied for agricultural purposes.

Business Relief
Business relief is available on transfers of certain types of business and of business assets if they qualify as relevant business property and the transferor has owned them for a minimum period. The relief can be claimed for transfers made during the person's lifetime and on death and on chargeable occasions arising on relevant business property held in trust. Where the chargeable value transferred is attributable to relevant business property, the business relief reduces that value by a percentage. Business relief may be claimed on relevant business property including:

- a business or an interest in a business such as a partnership
- unquoted shares and securities
- shares or securities of a quoted company which themselves or with other listed shares or securities give the transferor control of a company
- any land, buildings, plant or machinery owned by a partner or controlling shareholder and used wholly or mainly in the business of the partnership or company immediately before the transfer; this applies only if the partnership interest or shareholding would itself, if it were transferred, qualify for business relief
- any land, buildings, plant or machinery that were used wholly or mainly for the purpose of a business carried on by the transferor

If an asset qualifies for business relief, the rates at which it is currently allowed are as follows:

A business or interest in a business	100%
A holding of shares in an unquoted company	100%
Control holding of shares in a quoted company (more than 50 per cent of the voting rights)	50%
Land, buildings, plant or machinery used in a business of which the deceased was a partner at the date of death or used by a company controlled by the deceased	50%
Land, buildings, plant or machinery held in a trust where the deceased had the right to benefit from the trust and the asset was used in a business carried on by the deceased	50%

It is a general requirement that the property must have been retained for a period of two years before the transfer or death, and restrictions may be necessary if the property has not been used wholly for business purposes. The same property cannot obtain both business property relief and the relief available for agricultural property.

CALCULATION OF TAX PAYABLE
The calculation of IHT payable adopts the use of a cumulative or 'running' total. Looking back seven years from the death the chargeable value of gifts in that period is added to the total value of the estate at death. The gifts will use up all or part of the inheritance tax threshold (the 'nil-rate band' above which IHT becomes payable) first.

Lifetime Chargeable Transfers
The value transferred by lifetime chargeable transfers must be added to the seven-year running total to calculate whether any IHT is due. If the nil-rate band is exceeded, tax will be imposed on the excess at the rate of 20 per cent. However, if the donor dies within a period of seven years from the date of the chargeable lifetime transfer, additional tax may be due. This is calculated by applying tax at the full rate of 40 per cent in substitution for the rate of 20 per cent previously paid. The amount of tax is then reduced to a percentage by applying tapering relief. This percentage is governed by the number of years from the date of the lifetime gift to the date of death, as follows:

PERIOD OF YEARS BEFORE DEATH

Not more than 3	100%
More than 3 but not more than 4	80%
More than 4 but not more than 5	60%
More than 5 but not more than 6	40%
More than 6 but not more than 7	20%

Should this exercise produce liability greater than that previously paid at the 20 per cent rate on the lifetime transfer, additional tax, representing the difference, must be paid. Where the calculation shows an amount falling below tax paid on the lifetime transfer, no additional liability can arise nor will the shortfall become repayable.

Tapering relief is, of course, only available if the calculation discloses a liability to IHT. There is no liability if the lifetime transfer falls within the nil-rate band.

Potentially Exempt Transfers
Where a PET loses immunity from liability to IHT because the donor dies within seven years of making the transfer, the value transferred enters into the running total. Any liability to IHT will be calculated by applying the full rate of 40 per cent, reduced to the percentage governed by tapering relief if the original transfer occurred more than three years before death. Again, liability to IHT can only arise if the nil-rate band is exceeded.

Death
On death, IHT is due on the value of the deceased's estate plus the running total of gifts made in the seven years before death if they come to more than the nil-rate band. IHT is then charged at the full rate of 40 per cent on the amount in excess of the nil-rate band.

Settled Property and Trusts
Trusts are special legal arrangements that can be used by individuals to control how their assets are distributed to their beneficiaries and minimise their IHT liability. Complex rules apply to establish IHT liability on settled property which includes property held in trust, and individuals are advised to take expert legal advice when setting up trusts.

RATES OF TAX
Since 1988 there have been three rates:

• a nil rate
• a lifetime rate of 20 per cent
• a full rate of 40 per cent

The nil-rate band usually changes on an annual basis, but has been frozen at £325,000 since 2009–10. Any excess over this level is taxable at 20 per cent or 40 per cent as the case may be.

The Government has announced that from April 2012 a reduced rate of IHT will apply where 10 per cent or more of a deceased's net estate (after deducting IHT exemptions, reliefs and the nil rate band) is left to charity. In those cases the current 40 per cent rate will be reduced to 36 per cent. The new rate will apply where death occurs on or after 6 April 2012.

TRANSFER OF NIL-RATE BAND
Transfers of property between spouses or civil partners are generally exempt from IHT. This means that someone who dies leaving some or all of their property to their spouse or civil partner may not have fully used up their nil-rate band. Under rules introduced in autumn 2007, any nil-rate band unused on the first death can be used when the surviving spouse or civil partner dies. A transfer of unused nil-rate band from a deceased spouse or civil partner (no matter what the date of their death) may be made to the estate of their surviving spouse or civil partner who dies on or after 9 October 2007.

Where a valid claim to transfer unused nil-rate band is made, the nil-rate band that is available when the surviving spouse or civil partner dies is increased by the proportion of the nil-rate band unused on the first death. For example, if on the first death the chargeable estate is £150,000 and the nil-rate band is £300,000, 50 per cent of the nil-rate band would be unused. If the nil-rate band when the survivor dies is £325,000, then that would be increased by 50 per cent to £487,500. The amount of the nil-rate band that can be transferred does not depend on the value of the first spouse or civil partner's estate. Whatever proportion of the nil-rate band is unused on the first death is available for transfer to the survivor.

The amount of additional nil-rate band that can be accumulated by any one surviving spouse or civil partner is limited to the value of the nil-rate band in force at the time of their death. This may be relevant, for example, where a person dies having survived more than one spouse or civil partner.

Where these rules have effect, personal representatives do not have to claim for the unused nil-rate band to be transferred at the time of the first death. Any claims for transfer of unused nil-rate band amounts are made by the personal representatives of the estate of the second spouse or civil partner to die when they make an IHT return.

Detailed guidance on how to transfer the nil-rate band can be found on the HMRC website (W www.hmrc.gov.uk).

PAYMENT OF TAX
IHT is normally due six months after the end of the month in which the death occurs or the chargeable transaction takes place. This is referred to as the 'due date'. Tax on some assets such as business property, certain shares and securities and land and buildings (including the deceased person's home) can be deferred and paid in equal instalments over ten years, though interest will be

charged in most cases. If IHT is due on lifetime gifts and transfers, the person or transferee who received the gift or assets is normally liable to pay the IHT, though any IHT already paid at the time of a transfer into a trust or company will be taken into account. If tax owed is not paid by the due date, interest is charged on any unpaid IHT, no matter what caused the delay in payment.

CORPORATION TAX

Corporation tax is a tax on a company's profits, including all its income and gains. This tax is payable by UK resident companies and by non-resident companies carrying on a trade in the UK through a permanent establishment. The following comments are confined to companies resident in the UK. The word 'company' is also used to include:

• members' clubs, societies and associations
• trade associations
• housing associations
• groups of individuals carrying on a business but not as a partnership (for example, cooperatives)

A company's taxable income is charged by reference to income or gains arising in its 'accounting period', which is normally 12 months long. In some circumstances accounting periods can be shorter than 12 months, but never longer. The accounting period is also normally the period for which a company's accounts are drawn up, but the two periods do not have to coincide.

If a company is liable to pay corporation tax on its profits, several things must be done. HMRC must be informed that the company exists and is liable for tax. A self-assessment company tax return plus full accounts and calculation of tax liability must be filed by the statutory filing date, normally 12 months after the end of the accounting period. Companies have to work out their own tax liability and have to pay their tax without prior assessment by HMRC. Records of all company expenditure and income must be kept in order to work out the tax liability correctly. Companies are liable to penalties if they fail to carry out these obligations.

Extensive corporation tax information is available on the HMRC website (W www.hmrc.gov.uk/businesses) and companies may file their company tax returns online (W www.hmrc.gov.uk/ct/ct-online/file-return/online.htm).

RATE OF TAX
The rate of corporation tax is fixed for a financial year starting on 1 April and ending on the following 31 March. If a company's accounting period does not coincide with the financial year, its profits must be apportioned between the financial years and the tax rates for each financial year applied to those profits. The corporation tax liability is the total tax for both financial years.

The main rate of corporation tax for 2011–12 is 26 per cent, a decrease from 28 per cent in 2010–11. North Sea oil and gas ringfence activities but retain a main corporation tax rate of 30 per cent. The main rate of corporation tax applies when profits (including ringfence profits) are at a rate exceeding £1.5m, or where there is no claim to another rate, or where another rate does not apply.

It was announced in the 2011 March budget that the main rate of corporation tax will be reduced by one percentage point each forthcoming tax year until it reaches 23 per cent in 2014–15.

SMALL COMPANIES' RATE

Where the profits of a company do not exceed stated limits, corporation tax becomes payable at the small companies' rate. It is the amount of profits and not the size of the company that governs the application of the small companies' rate.

The small companies' rate for 2011–12 is 20 per cent, a decrease from 21 per cent in 2010–11. North Sea oil and gas ringfence activities retain a small companies' rate of 19 per cent.

A company can make profits of up to £300,000 without losing the benefit of the small companies' rate. If, however, its profits exceed £300,000 but fall below £1.5m, then marginal small companies' rate relief applies to ease the transition. The effect of marginal relief is that the average rate of corporation tax imposed on all profits steadily increases from the lower small companies' rate of 20 per cent to the main rate of 26 per cent, with tax being imposed on profits in the margin at an increased rate. HMRC has produced an easy-to-use corporation tax marginal relief rate calculator (W www.hmrc.gov.uk/calcs/mrr.htm).

Where a change in the rate of tax is introduced and the accounting period of a company overlaps 31 March, profits must be apportioned to establish the appropriate rate for each part of those profits.

The lower limit of £300,000 and the upper limit of £1.5m apply to a period of 12 months and must be proportionately reduced for shorter periods. Some restriction in the small companies' rate and the marginal rate may be necessary if there are two or more associated companies, namely companies under common control.

CORPORATION TAX ON PROFITS

£ per year	2010–11	2011–12
£0–£300,000	21%	20%
£300,001–£1,500,000	Marginal relief	Marginal relief
£1,500,001 or more	28%	26%

CAPITAL ALLOWANCES

Businesses can claim tax allowances, called capital allowances, on certain purchases or investments. This means that a proportion of these costs can be deducted from a business' taxable profits and reduce its tax bill. Capital allowances are currently available on plant and machinery, buildings and research and development. The amount of the allowance depends on what is being claimed for.

Detailed information on capital allowances is available from the Enhanced Capital Allowances website (W www.eca.gov.uk).

PAYMENT OF TAX

Corporation tax liabilities are normally due and payable in a single lump sum not later than nine months and one day after the end of the accounting period. For 'large' companies – those with profits over £1.5m which pay corporation tax at the main rate – there is a requirement to pay corporation tax in four quarterly instalments. Where a company is a member of a group, the profits of the entire group must be merged to establish whether the company is large.

In November 2008 HMRC launched a Business Payment Support Service (BPSS) which allows businesses facing temporary financial difficulties more time to pay their tax bills. Traders concerned about their ability to meet corporation tax, VAT or other payments owed to HMRC can call the Business Payment Support Line (T 0845-302 1435) seven days a week. This helpline is for new enquiries only, not for traders who have already been contacted by HMRC about an overdue payment. For details of the service visit W www.hmrc.gov.uk/pbr2008/business-payment.htm

CAPITAL GAINS

Chargeable gains arising to a company are calculated in a manner similar to that used for individuals. However, companies are not entitled to the CGT annual exemption. Companies do not suffer capital gains tax on chargeable gains but incur liability to corporation tax instead. Tax is due on the full chargeable gain of an accounting period after subtracting relief for any losses.

GROUPS OF COMPANIES

Each company within a group is separately charged to corporation tax on profits, gains and income. However, where one group member realises a loss for which special rules apply, other than a capital loss, a claim may be made to offset the deficiency against profits of some other member of the same group. The transfer of capital assets from one member of a group to a fellow member will usually incur no liability to tax on chargeable gains.

SPORTS CLUBS

Though corporation tax is payable by unincorporated associations including most clubs, a substantial exemption from liability to corporation tax, introduced in April 2002, is available to qualifying registered community amateur sports clubs (CASCs). Sports clubs that are registered as CASCs are exempt from liability to corporation tax on:

- profits from trading where the turnover of the trade is less than £30,000 in a 12-month period
- income from letting property where the gross rental income is less than £20,000 in a 12-month period
- bank and building society interest received
- chargeable gains

All of the exemptions depend upon the club having been a registered CASC for the whole of the relevant accounting period and the income or gains being used only for qualifying purposes. If the club has only been a registered CASC for part of an accounting period the exemption amounts of £30,000 (for trading) and £20,000 (for income from property) are reduced proportionately. Only interest and gains received after the club is registered are exempted.

Among other advantages available to registered clubs is that donations may be received under the Gift Aid arrangements. Charities are also generally exempt from corporation tax where they operate through a company structure.

VALUE ADDED TAX

Value added tax (VAT) is a tax on consumer expenditure charged when an individual buys goods and services in the European Union, including the UK. It is normally included in the sale price of goods and services and paid at the point of purchase. Each EU country has its own rate of VAT. From a business point of view, VAT is charged on most business transactions involving the supply of goods and services by a registered trader in the UK and Isle of

Man. It is also charged on goods and some services imported from places outside the EU and on goods and some services coming into the UK from the other EU countries. VAT is administered by HMRC. A wide range of information on VAT, including VAT forms, is available online at W www.hmrc.gov.uk/vat/index.htm. HMRC also runs a VAT and Excise helpline (T 0845-010 9000).

RATES OF TAX

There are three rates of VAT in the UK. The standard rate, payable on most goods and services in the UK, has been 20 per cent since 4 January 2011 when it was increased from 17.5 per cent.

The reduced rate – currently 5 per cent – is payable on certain goods and services including, for example, domestic fuel and power, children's car seats, women's sanitary products, contraceptive products and the installation of energy-saving materials such as wall insulation and solar panels. Since 1 January 2008 renovations and alterations to residential properties that have been empty for at least two years have been eligible for the 5 per cent rate.

A zero, or nil, rate applies to certain items including, for example, children's clothes, books, newspapers, most food and drink, and drugs and aids for disabled people. There are numerous exceptions to the zero-rated categories, however. While most food and drink is zero-rated, items including ice creams, chocolates, sweets, potato crisps and alcoholic drinks are not. Neither are drinks or items sold for consumption in a restaurant or cafe. Takeaway cold items such as sandwiches are zero-rated, while takeaway hot foods like fish and chips are not.

REGISTRATION

All traders, including professional persons and companies, must register for VAT if they are making 'taxable supplies' of a value exceeding stated limits. All goods and services that are VAT-rated are defined as 'taxable supplies' including zero-rated items which must be included when calculating the total value of a trader's taxable supplies – his or her 'taxable turnover'. The limits that govern mandatory registration are amended periodically.

An unregistered trader must register for VAT if:

- at the end of any month the total value of his or her taxable turnover (not just profit) for the past 12 months or less is more than the current VAT threshold of £70,000 – and
- at any time he or she has reasonable grounds to expect that his or her taxable turnover will be more than the current registration threshold of £70,000 in the next 30 days alone

To register for VAT, one or more forms must be completed and sent to HMRC within 30 days of any of the above. Basic VAT registration can currently be completed online (W https://online.hmrc.gov.uk/registration/). Traders who do not register at the correct time can be fined. Traders must charge VAT on their taxable supplies from the date they first need to be registered. Traders who only supply zero-rated goods may not have to register for VAT even if their taxable turnover goes above the registration threshold. However, a trader in this position must inform HMRC first and apply to be 'exempt from registration'. A trader whose taxable turnover does not reach the mandatory registration limit may choose to register for VAT voluntarily if what he or she does counts as a business for VAT purposes. This step may be thought advisable to recover input tax (see below) or to compete with other registered traders. Registered traders may submit an application for deregistration if their taxable turnover subsequently falls. An application for deregistration can be made if the taxable turnover for the year beginning on the application date is not expected to exceed £71,000.

INPUT TAX

Registered traders suffer input tax when buying in goods or services for the purposes of their business. It is the VAT that traders pay out to their suppliers on goods and services coming in to their business. Relief can usually be obtained for input tax suffered, either by setting that tax against output tax due or by repayment. Most items of input tax can be relieved in this manner. Where a registered trader makes both exempt supplies and taxable supplies to his customers or clients, there may be some restriction in the amount of input tax that can be recovered.

OUTPUT TAX

When making a taxable supply of goods or services, registered traders must account for output tax, if any, on the value of that supply. Output tax is the term used to describe the VAT on the goods and services that they supply or sell – the VAT on supplies going out of the business and collected from customers on each sale made. Usually the price charged by the registered trader will be increased by adding VAT, but failure to make the required addition will not remove liability to account for output tax. The liability to account for output tax, and also relief for input tax, may be affected where a trader is using a special secondhand goods scheme.

EXEMPT SUPPLIES

VAT is not chargeable on certain goods and services because the law deems them 'exempt' from VAT. These include the provision of burial and cremation facilities, insurance, loans of money, certain types of education and training and some property transactions. The granting of a lease to occupy land or the sale of land will usually comprise an exempt supply, for example, but there are numerous exceptions. Exempt supplies do not enter into the calculation of taxable turnover that governs liability to mandatory registration (see above). Such supplies made by a registered trader may, however, limit the amount of input tax that can be relieved. It is for this reason that the exemption may be useful.

COLLECTION OF TAX

Registered traders submit VAT returns for accounting periods usually of three months in duration, but arrangements can be made to submit returns on a monthly basis. Very large traders must account for tax on a monthly basis, but this does not affect the three-monthly return. The return will show both the output tax due for supplies made by the trader in the accounting period and also the input tax for which relief is claimed. If the output tax exceeds input tax the balance must be remitted with the VAT return. Where input tax suffered exceeds the output tax due, the registered trader may claim the excess from HMRC.

This basis for collecting tax explains the structure of VAT. Where supplies are made between registered traders the supplier will account for an amount of tax that will usually be identical to the tax recovered by the person to whom the supply is made. However, where the supply is made to a person who is not a registered trader there can be no recovery of input tax and it is on this person that the final burden of VAT eventually falls. Where goods are acquired by a UK trader from a supplier within the EU, the trader must also account for the tax due on acquisition. There are a number of simplified arrangements to make VAT accounting easier for businesses, particularly small businesses, and there is advice on the HMRC website about how to choose the most appropriate scheme for a business:

Cash Accounting
This scheme allows businesses to only pay VAT on the basis of payments received from their customers rather than on invoice dates or time of supply. It can therefore be useful for businesses with cash flow problems that cannot pay their VAT as a result. Businesses may use the cash accounting scheme if taxable turnover is under £1.35m. There is no need to apply for the scheme – eligible businesses may start using it at the beginning of a new tax period. If a trader opts to use this scheme, he or she can do so until the taxable turnover reaches £1.6m.

Annual Accounting
If taxable turnover is under £1.35m a year, the trader may join the annual accounting scheme which allows them to make nine monthly or three quarterly instalments during the year based on an estimate of their total annual VAT bill. At the end of the year they submit a single return and any balance due. The advantages of this scheme for businesses are easier budgeting and cash flow planning because fixed payments are spread regularly throughout the year. Once a trader has joined the annual accounting scheme, membership may continue until the annual taxable turnover reaches £1.6m.

Flat Rate Scheme
First introduced in the 2002 budget, this scheme allows small businesses with an annual taxable turnover of less than £150,000 to save on administration by paying VAT as a set flat percentage of their annual turnover instead of accounting internally for VAT on each individual 'in and out'. The percentage rate used is governed by the trade sector into which the business falls. The scheme can no longer be used once annual income exceeds £230,000.

Retail Schemes
There are special schemes that offer retailers an alternative if it is impractical for them to issue invoices for a large number of supplies direct to the public. These schemes include a provision to claim relief from VAT on bad debts where goods or services are supplied to a customer who does not pay for them.

VAT FACT SUMMARY
from 1 April 2011

Standard rate	20%
Reduced rate	5%
Registration (last 12 months or next 30 days)	£73,000
Deregistration (next 12 months under)	£71,000
Cash accounting scheme – up to	£1,350,000
Flat rate scheme – up to	£150,000
Annual accounting scheme – up to	£1,350,000

STAMP DUTY

For the majority of people, contact with stamp duty arises when they buy a property. Stamp duty is payable by the buyer as a way of raising revenue for the government based on the purchase price of a property, stocks and shares. This section aims to provide a broad overview of stamp duty as it may affect the average person.

STAMP DUTY LAND TAX
Stamp duty land tax was introduced on 1 December 2003 and covers the purchase of houses, flats and other land, buildings and certain leases in the UK.

Before 1 December 2003 property purchasers had to submit documents providing all details of the purchase to the Stamp Office for 'stamping'. The purchaser's solicitor or licensed conveyancer would then send the stamped documentation to the appropriate land registry to register ownership of the property. Under stamp duty land tax, purchasers do not have to send documents for stamping. Instead, a land transaction return form SDLT1, which contains all information regarding the purchase that is relevant to HMRC, is signed by the purchaser. Buyers of property are responsible for completing the land transaction return and payment of stamp duty, though the solicitor or licensed conveyancer acting for them in a land transaction will normally complete the relevant paperwork. Once HMRC has received the completed land transaction return and the payment of any stamp duty due, a certificate will be issued that enables a solicitor or licensed conveyancer to register the property in the new owner's name at the Land Registry.

The threshold for notification of residential property is currently £40,000. This means that taxpayers entering into a transaction involving residential or non-residential property where the chargeable consideration is less than £40,000 do not need to notify HMRC about the transaction.

RATES OF STAMP DUTY LAND TAX
Stamp duty is charged at different rates and has thresholds for different types of property and different values of transaction. The tax rate and payment threshold can vary according to whether the property is in residential or non-residential use and whether it is freehold or leasehold.

Below a certain threshold, currently £125,000, no stamp duty is payable on residential property purchases. A two-year holiday period from stamp duty for first-time property buyers was announced by the Labour government in its 2010 budget. The relief is equivalent to a reduction in the average deposit for first-time buyers of £1,500 and is available where:

- an individual or individuals jointly purchase a major interest in land which is wholly residential, and
- the consideration is more than £125,000 but not more than £250,000, and
- that individual (or all of them) intends to occupy the property as their only or main residence, and
- that individual (or all of them) has not previously purchased such an interest, or its equivalent, anywhere in the world, and
- the effective date of the transaction is on or after 25 March 2010 and before 25 March 2012

In order to fund this first-time buyer stamp duty holiday, it was also announced in the 2010 budget that a new 5 per cent rate of stamp duty would apply to purchases of residential property over £1m from April 2011. The current coalition government has so far stuck with these plans and made no changes to the main rates and thresholds for stamp duty in its March 2011 budget.

The following table shows the rates of stamp duty and payment thresholds that apply on residential property purchase prices during 2011–12:

Purchase price	Rate of tax (% of purchase price)
up to £125,000*	0%
over £125,000 to £250,000**	1%
over £250,000 to £500,000	3%
over £500,000 to £1,000,000	4%
over £1,000,000	5%

* Up to £150,000 for residential property transactions in certain designated disadvantaged areas, a full list of which can be found at W www.hmrc.gov.uk. For transactions of non-residential land and property, the zero per cent rate applies for purchases up to £150,000; a 1 per cent rate is payable for transactions of £150,001 to £250,000; thereafter, rates are as per residential property transactions except there is no higher 5 per cent rate.
** First-time buyers can claim relief from stamp duty on residential transactions up to £250,000 between 25 March 2010 and 25 March 2012

When assessing how much stamp duty is payable, the entire purchase price must be taken into account so the relevant stamp duty rate is paid on the whole sum, not just on the amount over each tax threshold. For example, on a property bought for £250,000, 1 per cent (£2,500) is payable in stamp duty. On a property bought for £250,001, however, 3 per cent of the whole price (£7,500) is payable.

RELIEF FOR NEW ZERO CARBON HOMES
A relief from stamp duty land tax was introduced on 1 October 2007 for the vast majority of new-build 'zero carbon' homes in the UK. The relief was time limited for five years and is due to expire on 30 September 2012. Qualifying criteria for the relief require zero carbon emissions from all energy use in the home over a year. To achieve this, the fabric of the home is required to reach a very high energy efficiency standard and to be able to provide onsite renewable heat and power. New homes which are liable to stamp duty land tax on the first sale are eligible to qualify. The relief provides complete removal of stamp duty liabilities for all homes up to a purchase price of £500,000. Where the purchase price is in excess of £500,000 then the stamp duty liability is reduced by £15,000. The balance of the stamp duty is due in the normal way. Relief is not available on second and subsequent sales of new-build zero carbon homes.

FIXTURES AND CHATTELS
As well as buying a property a purchaser may buy items inside the property. Some things inside a property are, in law, part of the land. These are called 'fixtures'. Examples are fitted kitchen units and bathroom suites. Because these fixtures are part of the land, any price paid for them must be taken into account for stamp duty purposes. Other things inside a property are not part of the land. These are called 'chattels'. Examples are free-standing cookers, curtains and fitted carpets. The purchase of chattels is not chargeable to stamp duty. However, where both a property and chattels are purchased, the amount shown on the land transaction return as the purchase price of the property must be a 'just and reasonable' apportionment of the total amount paid. As with other entries on the form, the purchaser is responsible for the accuracy of this information. HMRC pays especial attention to residential property purchases just below stamp duty thresholds to prevent arrangements between buyer and seller to hand over cash so that the purchase price on paper looks lower, or where the buyer has paid an unreasonably high amount to buy chattels.

STAMP DUTY RESERVE TAX
Stamp duty or stamp duty reserve tax (SDRT) is payable at the rate of 0.5 per cent when shares are purchased. Stamp duty is payable when the shares are transferred using a stock transfer form, whereas SDRT is payable on 'paperless' share transactions where the shares are transferred electronically without using a stock transfer form. Most share transactions nowadays are paperless and settled by stockbrokers through CREST (the electronic settlement and registration system). SDRT therefore now accounts for the majority of taxation collected on share transactions effected through the London Stock Exchange.

The flat rate of 0.5 per cent is based on the amount paid for the shares, not what they are worth. If, for example, shares are bought for £2,000, £10 SDRT is payable, whatever the value of the shares themselves. If shares are transferred for free, no SDRT is payable.

A higher rate of 1.5 per cent is payable where shares are transferred into a 'depositary receipt scheme' or a 'clearance service'. These are special arrangements where the shares are held by a third party.

CREST automatically deducts the SDRT and sends it to the HMRC. A stockbroker will settle up with CREST for the cost of the shares and the SDRT and then bill the purchaser for these and the broker's fees. If shares are not purchased through CREST, the stamp duty must be paid by the purchaser to HMRC.

UK stamp duty or SDRT is not payable on the purchase of foreign shares, though there may be foreign taxes to pay. SDRT is already accounted for in the price paid for units in unit trusts or shares in open-ended investment companies.

HELP AND INFORMATION
Further information on stamp duty land tax is available via the stamp taxes helpline on T 0845-603 0135 (open 8.30am to 5pm Monday to Friday) or the HMRC website (W www.hmrc.gov.uk), where a stamp duty calculator for both shares and land and property can be found.

LEGAL NOTES

These notes outline certain aspects of the law as they might affect the average person. They are intended only as a broad guideline and are by no means definitive. The law is constantly changing so expert advice should always be taken. In some cases, sources of further information are given in these notes.

It is always advisable to consult a solicitor without delay. Anyone who does not have a solicitor can contact the following for assistance in finding one: Citizens Advice (W www.citizensadvice.org.uk), the Community Legal Service (W www.direct.gov.uk) or the Law Society of England and Wales. For assistance in Scotland, contact Citizens Advice Scotland (W www.cas.org.uk) or the Law Society of Scotland.

Legal aid schemes exist to make the help of a lawyer available to those who would not otherwise be able to afford one. Entitlement for most types of legal aid depends on an individual's means but a solicitor or Citizens Advice will be able to advise on this.

LAW SOCIETY OF ENGLAND AND WALES
  113 Chancery Lane, London WC2A 1PL T 020-7242 1222
  W www.lawsociety.org.uk
LAW SOCIETY OF SCOTLAND
  26 Drumsheugh Gardens, Edinburgh EH3 7YR
  T 0131-226 7411 W www.lawscot.org.uk

ABORTION

Abortion is governed by the Abortion Act 1967. Under its provisions, a legally induced abortion must be:
- performed by a registered medical practitioner
- carried out in an NHS hospital or other approved premises
- certified by two registered medical practitioners as justified on one or more of the following grounds:
  (a) that the pregnancy has not exceeded its 24th week and that the continuance of the pregnancy would involve risk, greater than if the pregnancy were terminated, of injury to the physical or mental health of the pregnant woman or any existing children of her family
  (b) that the termination is necessary to prevent grave permanent injury to the physical or mental health of the pregnant woman
  (c) that the continuance of the pregnancy would involve risk to the life of the pregnant woman, greater than if the pregnancy were terminated
  (d) that there is a substantial risk that if the child were born it would suffer from such physical or mental abnormalities as to be seriously handicapped.

In determining whether the continuance of a pregnancy would involve such risk of injury to health as is mentioned in grounds (a) or (b), account may be taken of the pregnant woman's actual or reasonably foreseeable environment.

The requirements relating to the opinion of two registered medical practitioners and to the performance of the abortion at an NHS hospital or other approved place cease to apply in circumstances where a registered medical practitioner is of the opinion, formed in good faith, that a termination is immediately necessary to save the life, or to prevent grave permanent injury to the physical or mental health, of the pregnant woman.

The Abortion Act 1967 does not apply to Northern Ireland, where abortion is not legal.

FAMILY PLANNING ASSOCIATION (UK)
  50 Featherstone Street, London EC1Y 8QU T 020-7608 5240
  W www.fpa.org.uk
BRITISH PREGNANCY ADVISORY SERVICE (BPAS)
  T 0845-730 4030 W www.bpas.org

ADOPTION OF CHILDREN

The Adoption and Children Act 2002 reformed the framework for domestic and intercountry adoption in England and Wales and some parts of it extend to Scotland and Northern Ireland. The Children and Adoption Act 2006 introduces further provisions for adoptions involving a foreign element.

WHO MAY APPLY FOR AN ADOPTION ORDER

A couple (whether married or two people living as partners in an enduring family relationship) may apply for an adoption order where both of them are over 21 or where one is only 18 but the natural parent and the other is 21. An adoption order may be made for one applicant where that person is 21 and: a) the court is satisfied that person is the partner of a parent of the person to be adopted; or b) they are not married and are not civil partners; or c) married or in a civil partnership but they are separated from their spouse or civil partner and living apart with the separation likely to be permanent; or d) their spouse/civil partner is either unable to be found, or their spouse/civil partner is incapable by reason of ill-health of making an application. There are certain qualifying conditions an applicant must meet eg residency in the British Isles.

ARRANGING AN ADOPTION

Adoptions may generally only be arranged by an adoption agency or by way of an order from the high court; breach of the restrictions on who may arrange an adoption would constitute a criminal offence. When deciding whether a child should be placed for adoption, the court or adoption agency must consider all the factors set out in the 'welfare checklist' – the paramount consideration being the child's welfare, throughout his or her life. These factors include the child's wishes, needs, age, sex, background and any harm which the child has suffered or is likely to suffer. At all times, the court or adoption agency must bear in mind that delay is likely to prejudice a child's welfare.

ADOPTION ORDER

Once an adoption has been arranged, a court order is necessary to make it legal; this may be obtained from the high court, county court or magistrates' court (including the family proceedings court). An adoption order may not be given unless the court is satisfied that the consent of the child's natural parents (or guardians) has been given correctly. Consent can be dispensed with on two grounds: where the parent or guardian cannot be found or is incapable of giving consent, or where the welfare of the child so demands.

An adoption order extinguishes the parental responsibility that a person other than the adopters (or adopter) has for the child. Where an order is made on the application of the partner of the parent, that parent keeps parental responsibility. Once adopted the child has the same status as a child born to the adoptive parents, but may lose rights to the estates of those losing their parental responsibility.

REGISTRATION AND CERTIFICATES

All adoption orders made in England and Wales are required to be registered in the Adopted Children Register which also contains particulars of children adopted under registrable foreign adoptions. The General Register Office keeps this register from which certificates may be obtained in a similar way to birth certificates. The General Register Office also has equivalents in Scotland and Northern Ireland.

TRACING NATURAL PARENTS OR CHILDREN WHO HAVE BEEN ADOPTED

An adult adopted person may apply to the Registrar-General to obtain a certified copy of his/her birth certificate. Adoption agencies and adoption support agencies should provide services to adopted persons to assist them in obtaining information about their adoption and facilitate contact with their relatives. There is an Adoption Contact Register which provides a safe and confidential way for birth parents and other relatives to assure an adopted person that contact would be welcome. The BAAF (*see* below) can provide addresses of organisations which offer advice, information and counselling to adopted people, adoptive parents and people who have had their children adopted.

BRITISH ASSOCIATION FOR ADOPTION AND FOSTERING (BAAF)
Saffron House, 6–10 Kirkby Street, London EC1N 8TS
T 020-7421 2600 W www.baaf.org.uk

SCOTLAND

The relevant legislation is the Adoption and Children (Scotland) Act 2007. Previously adoption was governed in Scotland by the Adoption (Scotland) Act 1978, as amended by the Children (Scotland) Act 1995. In September 2009, the 2007 act made further amendments to the 1995 act and repealed the 1978 act – but for Part IV – when its final provisions took effect. The provisions of the 2007 act are similar to those described above. In Scotland, petitions for adoption are made to the sheriff court or the court of session.

BRITISH ASSOCIATION FOR ADOPTION AND FOSTERING (BAAF)
BAAF Scottish Centre, 113 Rose Street, Edinburgh EH2 3DT
T 0131-226 9270

BIRTHS (REGISTRATION)

It is the duty of the parents of a child born in England or Wales to register the birth within 42 days of the date of birth at the register office in the district in which the baby was born. If it is inconvenient to go to the district where the birth took place, the information for the registration may be given to a registrar in another district, who will send your details to the appropriate register office. Failure to register the birth within 42 days without reasonable cause may leave the parents liable to a penalty. If a birth

has not been registered within 12 months of its occurrence it is possible for the late registration of the birth to be authorised by the Registrar-General, provided certain requirements can be met.

Births that take place in England may only be registered in English, but births that take place in Wales may be registered bilingually in Welsh and English. In order to do this, the details must be given in Welsh and the registrar must be able to understand and write in Welsh.

If the parents of the child were married to each other at the time of the birth (or conception), either the mother or the father may register the birth. If the parents were not married to each other at the time of the child's birth (or conception), the father's particulars may be entered in the register only where he attends the register office with the mother and they sign the birth register together. Where an unmarried parent is unable to attend the register office either parent may submit to the registrar a statutory declaration on Form 16 (or Form 16W for births which took place in Wales) acknowledging the father's paternity (this form may be obtained from any registrar in England or Wales or online at W www.gro.gov.uk); alternatively a parental responsibility agreement or appropriate court order may be produced to the registrar.

If the father's details are not included in the birth register, it may be possible to re-register the birth at a later date. If the parents do not register the birth of their child the following people may do so:

- the occupier of the house or hospital where the child was born
- a person who was present at the birth
- a person who is responsible for the child

Upon registration of the birth a short certificate is issued. It may be possible to register the birth while still at hospital. Hospitals will advise individually whether this is possible.

BIRTHS ABROAD

There are certain countries where birth registrations may be made for British citizens overseas (for more details on British citizenship *see* below). The British consul or high commission may register the births and issue certificates which are then sent to the General Register Office. If a birth is registered by the British consul or high commission, the registration would show the person's claim to British citizenship, British overseas territories citizenship or British overseas citizenship.

SCOTLAND

In Scotland the birth of a child must be registered within 21 days at the registration office of any registration district in Scotland.

If the child is born, either in or out of Scotland, on a ship, aircraft or land vehicle that ends its journey at any place in Scotland, the child, in most cases, will be registered as if born in that place.

CERTIFICATES OF BIRTHS, DEATHS OR MARRIAGES

Certificates of births, marriages and deaths that have taken place in England and Wales since 1837 can be obtained from the General Register Office (GRO).

Marriage or death certificates may also be obtained from the minister of the church in which the marriage or funeral took place. Any register office can advise about the best way to obtain certificates.

The fees for certificates are:

Online application:
- full certificate of birth, marriage, death or adoption, £9.25
- full certificate of birth, marriage, death or adoption with GRO reference supplied, £9.25

By postal/phone/fax application:
- full certificate of birth, marriage, death or adoption, £9.25
- full certificate of birth, marriage, death or adoption with GRO reference supplied, £9.25
- extra copies of the same birth, marriage or death certificate issued at the same time, £9.25

A priority service is available for an additional fee.

A complete set of the GRO indexes including births, deaths and marriages, civil partnerships, adoptions and provisional indexes for births and deaths from January 2010 to March 2011 are available at the British Library, City of Westminster Archives Centre, London Metropolitan Archives, Manchester City Library, Birmingham Central Library, Bridgend Reference and Information Library and Plymouth Central Library. Copies of GRO indexes may also be held at some libraries, family history societies, local records offices and The Church of Jesus Christ of Latter Day Saints family history centres. Some organisations may not hold a complete record of indexes and a small fee may be charged by some of them. GRO indexes are also available online.

The Society of Genealogists has many records of baptisms, marriages and deaths prior to 1837.

SCOTLAND

Certificates of births, deaths or marriages that have taken place in Scotland since 1855 can be obtained from the National Records of Scotland (formerly the General Register Office for Scotland) or from the appropriate local registrar.

Applicable fees – local registrar:
- each extract or abbreviated certificate of birth, death, marriage, civil partnership or adoption within the year of registration, £10.00
- each extract or abbreviated certificate of birth, death, marriage, civil partnership or adoption outwith the current year of registration, £15.00

A priority service is available for an additional fee.

The National Records of Scotland also keeps the Register of Divorces (including decrees of declaration of nullity of marriage), and holds parish registers dating from before 1855.

Applicable fees – National Records of Scotland:
- personal application, or postal, telephone or fax order: £15.00

A priority service for a response within 24 hours is available for an additional fee of £15.00.

General search in the indexes to the statutory registers and parochial registers, per day or part thereof:
- full or part-day search pass: £15.00
- Quarterly search pass: £490.00
- annual search pass: £1,450.00

Online searching is also available. For more information, visit W www.scotlandspeople.gov.uk.

THE GENERAL REGISTER OFFICE
General Register Office, Certificate Services Section, PO Box 2, Southport PR8 2JD T 0845-603 7788
W www.gro.gov.uk/gro/content/certificates

THE NATIONAL RECORDS OF SCOTLAND
New Register House, 3 West Register Street, Edinburgh
EH1 3YT T 0131-334 0380 W www.gro-scotland.gov.uk
THE SOCIETY OF GENEALOGISTS
14 Charterhouse Buildings, Goswell Road, London EC1M 7BA
T 020-7251 8799 W www.sog.org.uk

BRITISH NATIONALITY

There are different types of British nationality status: British citizenship; British overseas citizenship; British overseas territories citizenship; British protected persons; and British subjects. The most widely held of these is British citizenship. Everyone born in the UK before 1 January 1983 became a British citizen when the British Nationality Act 1981 came into force, with the exception of children born to certain diplomatic staff working in the UK at the time. Individuals born outside the UK before 1 January 1983 but who at that date were citizens of the UK and colonies and had a right of abode in the UK also became British citizens. British citizens have the right to live permanently in the UK and are free to leave and re-enter the UK at any time.

A person born on or after 1 January 1983 in the UK (including, for this purpose, the Channel Islands and the Isle of Man) is entitled to British citizenship if he/she falls into one of the following categories:
- he/she has a parent who is a British citizen
- he/she has a parent who is settled in the UK
- he/she is a newborn infant found abandoned in the UK
- his/her parents subsequently settle in the UK or become British citizens and an application is made before he/she is 18
- he/she lives in the UK for the first ten years of his/her life and is not absent for more than 90 days in each of those years
- he/she is adopted in the UK and one of the adopters is a British citizen
- the home secretary consents to his/her registration while he/she is a minor
- if he/she has always been stateless and lives in the UK for a period of five years before his/her 22nd birthday

A person born outside the UK may acquire British citizenship if he/she falls into one of the following categories:
- he/she has a parent who is a British citizen otherwise than by descent, eg a parent who was born in the UK
- he/she has a parent who is a British citizen serving the crown or a European community institution overseas and was recruited to that service in the UK (including qualifying territories for those born on or after 21 May 2002) or in the European Community (for services within an EU institution)
- the home secretary consents to his/her registration while he/she is a minor
- he/she is a British overseas territories citizen, a British overseas citizen, a British subject or a British protected person and has been lawfully resident in the UK for five years
- he/she is a British overseas territories citizen who acquired that citizenship from a connection with Gibraltar
- he/she is adopted or naturalised

Where parents are married, the status of either may confer citizenship on their child. Since July 2006, both parents are able to pass on nationality even if they are not married, provided that there is satisfactory evidence of paternity. For children born before July 2006, it must be shown that there is parental consent and that the child would have an automatic claim to citizenship or entitlement to registration had the parents been married. Where parents are not married, the status of the mother determines the child's citizenship.

Under the 1981 act, Commonwealth citizens and citizens of the Republic of Ireland were entitled to registration as British citizens before 1 January 1983. In 1983, citizens of the Falkland Islands were granted British citizenship.

Renunciation of British citizenship must be registered with the home secretary and will be revoked if no new citizenship or nationality is acquired within six months. If the renunciation was required in order to retain or acquire another citizenship or nationality, the citizenship may be reacquired only once. If the renunciation was for another reason, the home secretary may allow reacquisition more than once, depending on the circumstances. The secretary of state may deprive a person of a citizenship status if he or she is satisfied that the person has done anything seriously prejudicial to the vital interests of the UK, or a British overseas territory, unless making the order would have the effect of rendering such a person stateless. A person may also be deprived of a citizenship status which results from his registration or naturalisation if the secretary of state is satisfied that the registration or naturalisation was obtained by fraud, false representation or concealment of a material fact.

BRITISH DEPENDENT TERRITORIES CITIZENSHIP

Since 26 February 2006, this category of nationality no longer exists and has been replaced by British overseas territory citizenship.

If a person had this class of nationality only by reason of a connection to the territory of Hong Kong, they lost it automatically when Hong Kong was returned to the People's Republic of China. However, if after 30 June 1997, they had no other nationality and would have become stateless, or were born after 30 June 1997 and would have been born stateless (but had a parent who was a British national (overseas) or a British overseas citizen), they became a British overseas citizen.

BRITISH OVERSEAS CITIZENSHIP

Under the 1981 act, as amended by the British Overseas Territories Act 2002, this type of citizenship was conferred on any UK and colonies citizens who did not become either a British citizen or a British overseas territories citizen on 1 January 1983 and as such is now, for most purposes, only acquired by persons who would otherwise be stateless.

BRITISH OVERSEAS TERRITORIES CITIZENSHIP

This category of nationality replaced British dependent territories citizenship. Most commonly, this form of nationality is acquired where, after 31 December 1982, a person was a citizen of the UK and colonies and did not become a British citizen, and that person, and their parents or grandparents, were born, registered or naturalised in the specified British overseas territory. However, on 21 May 2002, people became British citizens if they had British overseas territories citizenship by connection with any British overseas territory except for the sovereign base areas of Akrotiri and Dhekelia in Cyprus.

RESIDUAL CATEGORIES

British subjects, British protected persons and British nationals (overseas) may be entitled to registration as British citizens on completion of five years' legal residence in the UK.

Citizens of the Republic of Ireland who were also British subjects before 1 January 1949 can retain that status if they fulfil certain conditions.

EUROPEAN UNION CITIZENSHIP

British citizens (including Gibraltarians who are registered for this purpose) are also EU citizens and are entitled to travel freely to other EU countries to work, study, reside and set up a business. EU citizens have the same rights with respect to the UK.

NATURALISATION

Naturalisation is granted at the discretion of the home secretary. The basic requirements are five years' residence (three years if the applicant is married to, or is the civil partner of a British citizen), good character, adequate knowledge of the English, Welsh or Scottish Gaelic language, passing the UK citizenship test (if the applicant is not married to, or is the civil partner of a British citizen) and an intention to reside permanently in the UK.

STATUS OF ALIENS

Aliens, being persons without any of the above forms of British nationality, may not hold public office or vote in Britain and they may not own a British ship or aircraft. Citizens of the Republic of Ireland are not deemed to be aliens. Certain provisions of the Immigration and Asylum Act 1999 make provision about immigration and asylum and about procedures in connection with marriage by superintendent registrar's certificate.

CONSUMER LAW

SALE OF GOODS

A sale of goods contract is the most common type of contract. It is governed by the Sale of Goods Act 1979 (as amended by the Sale and Supply of Goods Act 1994). The act provides protection for buyers by implying terms into every sale of goods contract. These terms include:

- an implied term that the seller will pass good title to the buyer (unless it appears from the contract or is to be inferred from the circumstances that there is an intention that the seller should transfer only such title as he has)
- where the seller sells goods by reference to a description, an implied term that the goods will match that description and, where the sale is by sample and description, it will not be sufficient that the bulk of the goods correspond with the sample if the goods do not also correspond with the description
- where goods are sold by a business seller, an implied term that the goods will be of satisfactory quality ie they meet the standard that a reasonable person would regard as satisfactory, taking into account any description of the goods, the price, and all other relevant circumstances. The quality of the goods includes their state and condition, relevant aspects being whether they are fit for all the purposes for which such goods are commonly supplied, their appearance and finish, freedom from minor defects and their safety and durability. This term will not be implied, however, if a buyer has examined the goods (including in a sale by sample) and should have noticed the defect or if the

seller specifically drew the buyer's attention to the defect

- where goods are sold by a business seller, an implied term that the goods are reasonably fit for any purpose made known to the seller by the buyer (either expressly or by implication), unless it is shown that the buyer does not rely on the seller's judgment, or it is not reasonable for him/her to do so
- where goods are sold by sample, implied terms that the bulk of the sample will correspond with the sample in quality, and that the goods are free from any defect rendering them unsatisfactory which would not have been apparent on a reasonable examination of the sample

Some of the above terms can be excluded from contracts by the seller. The seller's right to do this is, however, restricted by the Unfair Contract Terms Act 1977. The act offers more protection to a buyer who 'deals as a consumer' (that is where the seller is selling in the course of a business, the goods are of a type ordinarily bought for private use and the goods are bought by a buyer who is not a business buyer) and does not allow for the implied terms described above to be excluded. In a sale of secondhand goods by auction (at which individuals have the opportunity of attending the sale in person), a buyer does not deal as a consumer.

HIRE-PURCHASE AGREEMENTS

Terms similar to those implied in contracts of sales of goods are implied into contracts of hire-purchase, under the Supply of Goods (Implied Terms) Act 1973. The 1977 act limits the exclusion of these implied terms as before.

SUPPLY OF GOODS AND SERVICES

Under the Supply of Goods and Services Act 1982, similar terms are also implied in other types of contract under which ownership of goods passes, and contracts for the hire of goods (though not hire-purchase agreements). These types of contracts have additional implied terms:

- that the supplier will use reasonable care and skill in carrying out the service
- that the supplier will carry out the service in a reasonable time (unless the time has been agreed)
- that the supplier will make a reasonable charge (unless the charge has already been agreed)

The 1977 act limits the exclusion of these implied terms in a similar manner as before.

UNFAIR TERMS

The Unfair Terms in Consumer Contracts Regulations 1999 apply to contracts between business sellers (or suppliers of goods and services) and consumers. Where the terms have not been individually negotiated (ie where the terms were drafted in advance so that the consumer was unable to influence those terms), a term will be deemed unfair if it operates to the detriment of the consumer (ie causes a significant imbalance in the parties' rights and obligations arising under the contract). An unfair term does not bind the consumer but the contract may continue to bind the parties if it is capable of existing without the unfair term. The regulations contain a non-exhaustive list of terms that are regarded as potentially unfair. When a term does not fall into such a category, whether it will be regarded as fair or not will depend on many factors, including the nature of the goods or services, the surrounding circumstances (such as the bargaining strength of both parties) and the other terms in the contract.

CONSUMER PROTECTION

The Consumer Protection from Unfair Trading Regulations 2008 (CPRs) replaced much previous consumer protection regulation including the majority of the Trade Descriptions Act 1968. CPRs prohibit 31 specific practices, including pyramid schemes. In addition CPRs prohibit business sellers from making misleading actions and misleading omissions, which cause, or are likely to cause, the average consumer to take a different transactional decision. There is also a general duty not to trade unfairly.

Under the Consumer Protection Act 1987, producers of goods are liable for any injury, death or damage to any property exceeding £275 caused by a defect in their product (subject to certain defences).

Consumers are also afforded protection under the Consumer Protection (Distance Selling) Regulations 2000 and the Cancellation of Contracts made in a Consumer's Home or Place of Work etc Regulations 2008 in relation to cancellation rights.

CONSUMER CREDIT

In matters relating to the provision of credit (or the supply of goods on hire or hire-purchase), consumers are also protected by the Consumer Credit Act 1974 (as amended by the Consumer Credit Act 2006). Under this act, a licence, issued by the Office of Fair Trading, is required in order to conduct a consumer credit or consumer hire business or an ancillary credit business, subject to certain exemptions. Any 'fit' person as defined within the act may apply to the Office of Fair Trading for a licence. The provisions of the act only apply to 'regulated' agreements; there are a number of exemptions under which consumer credit agreements are not regulated by the act (such as first charge mortgages which are regulated instead by the FSA). Provisions include:

- in order for a creditor to enforce a regulated agreement, the agreement must comply with certain formalities and must be properly executed. An improperly executed regulated agreement is enforceable only on an order of the court. The debtor must also be given specified information by the creditor or his/her broker or agent during the negotiations which take place before the signing of the agreement. The agreement must also state certain information to ensure that the debtor or hirer is aware of the rights and duties conferred or imposed on him/her and the protection and remedies available to him/her under the act
- the right to withdraw from or cancel some contracts depending on the circumstances. For example, subject to certain exceptions, a borrower may withdraw from a regulated credit agreement within 14 days without giving any reason. The exceptions include agreements for credit exceeding £60,260 and agreements secured on land. The right to withdraw applies only to the credit agreement itself and not to goods or services purchased with it. The borrower must also repay the credit and any interest
- if the debtor is in breach of the agreement, the creditor must serve a default notice before taking any action such as repossessing the goods
- if the agreement is a hire-purchase or conditional sale agreement, the creditor cannot repossess the goods without a court order if the debtor has paid one third of the total price of the goods
- in agreements where the relationship between the creditor and the debtor is unfair to the debtor, the court

may alter or set aside some of the terms of the agreement

Where a credit reference agency has been used to check the debtor's financial standing, the creditor may be required to give the agency's name to the debtor, who is entitled to see the agency's file on him. A fee of £2 is payable to the agency.

SCOTLAND

The legislation governing the sale and supply of goods applies to Scotland as follows:
- the Sale of Goods Act 1979 applies with some modifications and it has been amended by the Sale and Supply of Goods Act 1994
- the Supply of Goods (Implied Terms) Act 1973 applies
- the Supply of Goods and Services Act 1982 does not extend to Scotland but some of its provisions were introduced by the Sale and Supply of Goods Act 1994
- only Parts II and III of the Unfair Contract Terms Act 1977 apply
- the Trade Descriptions Act 1968 applies with minor modifications
- the Consumer Credit Act 1974 applies
- the Consumer Credit Act 2006 applies
- the Consumer Protection Act 1987 applies
- the General Product Safety Regulations 2005 apply
- the Unfair Terms in Consumer Contracts Regulations 1999 apply
- the Unfair Terms in Consumer Contracts (Amendment) Regulations 2001 apply
- the Consumer Protection (Distance Selling) Regulations 2000 apply
- the Sale and Supply of Goods to Consumers Regulations 2002 apply
- the Consumer Protection from Unfair Trading Regulations 2008 apply

PROCEEDINGS AGAINST THE CROWN

Until 1947, proceedings against the Crown were generally possible only by a procedure known as a petition of right, which put the private litigant at a considerable disadvantage. The Crown Proceedings Act 1947 placed the Crown (not the sovereign in his/her private capacity, but as the embodiment of the state) largely in the same position as a private individual and made proceedings in the high court involving the Crown subject to the same rules as any other case. The act did not, however, extinguish or limit the Crown's prerogative or statutory powers, and it continued the immunity of HM ships and aircraft. It also left certain Crown privileges unaffected. The act largely abolished the special procedures which previously applied to civil proceedings by and against the Crown. Civil proceedings may be initiated against the appropriate government department or if there is doubt regarding which is the appropriate department, against the attorney-general.

In Scotland proceedings against the Crown founded on breach of contract could be taken before the 1947 act and no special procedures applied. The Crown could, however, claim certain special pleas. The 1947 act applies in part to Scotland and brings the practice of the two countries as closely together as the different legal systems permit. As a result of the Scotland Act 1998 actions against government departments should be raised against the Lord Advocate or the advocate-general. Actions should be raised against the Lord Advocate where the department involved administers a devolved matter. Devolved matters include agriculture, education, housing, local government, health and justice. Actions should be raised against the advocate-general where the department is dealing with a reserved matter. Reserved matters include defence, foreign affairs and social security.

DEATHS

WHEN A DEATH OCCURS

If the death (including stillbirth) was expected, the doctor who attended the deceased during their final illness should be contacted. If the death was sudden or unexpected, the family doctor (if known) and police should be contacted. If the cause of death is quite clear the doctor will provide:
- a medical certificate that shows the cause of death
- a formal notice that states that the doctor has signed the medical certificate and that explains how to get the death registered
- if the death was known to be caused by a natural illness but the doctor wishes to know more about the cause of death, he/she may ask the relatives for permission to carry out a post-mortem examination

In England and Wales a coroner is responsible for investigating deaths occurring:
- when there is no doctor who can issue a medical certificate of cause of death
- no doctor has treated the deceased during his or her last illness or when the doctor attending the patient did not see him or her within 14 days before death, or after death
- the death occurred during an operation or before recovery from the effect of an anaesthetic
- the death was sudden and unexplained or attended by suspicious circumstances
- the death might be due to an industrial injury or disease, or to accident, violence, neglect or abortion
- the death occurred in prison or in police custody

The doctor will write on the formal notice that the death has been referred to the coroner; if the post-mortem shows that death was due to natural causes, the coroner may issue a notification which gives the cause of death so that the death can be registered. If the cause of death was violent or unnatural, is still undetermined after a post-mortem, or took place in prison or police custody, the coroner must hold an inquest. The coroner must hold an inquest in these circumstances even if the death occurred abroad (and the body has been returned to England or Wales).

In Scotland the office of coroner does not exist. The local procurator fiscal inquires into sudden or suspicious deaths. A fatal accident inquiry will be held before the sheriff where the death has resulted from an accident during the course of the employment of the person who has died, or where the person who has died was in legal custody, or where the Lord Advocate deems it in the public interest that an inquiry be held.

REGISTERING A DEATH

In England and Wales the death must be registered by the registrar of births and deaths for the district in which it occurred. A death which occurs in Scotland can be registered in any registration district in Scotland. Information concerning a death can be given before any registrar of births and deaths in England and Wales. The registrar will pass the relevant details to the registrar for the district where the death occurred, who will then register the death.

In England and Wales the death must normally be registered within five days (unless the registrar says this period can be extended); in Scotland within eight days. If the death has been referred to the coroner/local procurator fiscal it cannot be registered until the registrar has received authority from the coroner/local procurator fiscal to do so. Failure to register a death involves a penalty in England and Wales and may lead to a court decree being granted by a sheriff in Scotland.

If the death occurred at a house or hospital, the death may be registered by:
• any relative of the deceased
• any person present at the death
• the occupier or any inmate of the house or hospital if he/she knew of the occurrence of the death
• any person making the funeral arrangements (but not the funeral director)
• an official from the hospital
• in Scotland, the deceased's executor or legal representative
For deaths that took place elsewhere, the death may be registered by:
• any relative of the deceased
• someone present at the death
• someone who found the body
• a person in charge of the body
• any person making the funeral arrangements
The majority of deaths are registered by a relative of the deceased. The registrar would normally allow one of the other listed persons to register the death only if there were no relatives available.

The person registering the death should take the medical certificate of the cause of death with them; it is also useful, though not essential, to take the deceased's birth and marriage/civil partnership certificates, NHS medical card, pension documentation and life assurance details. The details given to the registrar must be absolutely correct, otherwise it may be difficult to change them later. The person registering the death should check the entry carefully before it is signed. The registrar will issue a certificate for burial or cremation, and a certificate of registration of death (commonly known as a 'death certificate' which is issued for social security purposes if the deceased received a state pension or benefits) – both free of charge. A death certificate is a certified copy of the entry in the death register; copies can be provided on payment of a fee and may be required for the following purposes, in particular by the executor or administrator when sorting out the deceased's affairs:
• the will
• bank and building society accounts
• savings bank certificates and premium bonds
• insurance policies
• pension claims
If the death occurred abroad or on a foreign ship or aircraft, the death should be registered according to the local regulations of the relevant country and a death certificate should be obtained. In many countries the death can also be registered with the British consulate in that country and a record will be kept at the General Register Office. This avoids the expense of bringing the body back.

After 12 months (three months in Scotland) of death or the finding of a dead body, no death can be registered without the consent of the registrar-general.

BURIAL AND CREMATION

In most circumstances in England and Wales a certificate for burial or cremation must be obtained from the registrar before the burial or cremation can take place. If the death has been referred to the coroner, an order for burial or a certificate for cremation must be obtained. In Scotland a body may be buried (but not cremated) before the death is registered.

Funeral costs can normally be repaid out of the deceased's estate and will be given priority over any other claims. If the deceased has left a will it may contain directions concerning the funeral; however, these directions need not be followed by the executor.

The deceased's papers should also indicate whether a grave space had already been arranged. This information will be contained in a document known as a 'Deed of Grant'. Most town churchyards and many suburban churchyards are no longer open for burial because they are full. Most cemeteries are non-denominational and may be owned by local authorities or private companies; fees vary.

If the body is to be cremated, an application form, two cremation certificates (for which there is a charge) or a certificate for cremation if the death was referred to the coroner, and a certificate signed by the medical referee must be completed in addition to the certificate for burial or cremation (the form is not required if the coroner has issued a certificate for cremation). All the forms are available from the funeral director or crematorium. Most crematoria are run by local authorities; the fees usually include the medical referee's fee and the use of the chapel. Ashes may be scattered, buried in a churchyard or cemetery, or kept.

The registrar must be notified of the date, place and means of disposal of the body within 96 hours (England and Wales) or three days (Scotland).

If the death occurred abroad or on a foreign ship or aircraft, a local burial or cremation may be arranged. If the body is to be brought back to England or Wales, a death certificate from the relevant country or an authorisation for the removal of the body from the country of death from the coroner or relevant authority, together with a certificate of embalming will be required. The British consulate can help to arrange this documentation. To arrange a funeral in England or Wales, an authenticated translation of a foreign death certificate or a death certificate issued in Scotland or Northern Ireland which must show the cause of death, is needed, together with a certificate of no liability to register from the registrar in England and Wales in whose sub-district it is intended to bury or cremate the body. If it is intended to cremate the body, a cremation order will be required from the Home Office or a certificate for cremation. If the body is to be cremated in Scotland, an order from the Scottish government Health Department must be obtained.

THE GENERAL REGISTER OFFICE
General Register Office, PO Box 2, Southport PR8 2JD
T 0845-603 7788
W www.gro.gov.uk/gro/content/certificates
THE NATIONAL RECORDS OF SCOTLAND
New Register House, 3 West Register Street, Edinburgh
EH1 3YT T 0131-334 0380 W www.gro-scotland.gov.uk

DIVORCE, DISSOLUTION AND RELATED MATTERS

Divorce is a legal process carried out by the civil courts to end the marriage of an opposite sex couple whilst dissolution is a similar process which ends a civil partnership. Divorce should be distinguished from judicial separation which is a court order confirming that the parties have separated but it does not legally dissolve the marriage/civil partnership. It is often applied for due to moral, religious or ethical grounds but it does allow for financial provision to be made as divorce does.

DIVORCE

The process for divorce begins with a petition and ends with what is known as a 'decree absolute' which dissolves the marriage.

The process begins with the lodging of a standard court form (known as an application for a matrimonial order) at any divorce county court or at the principal registry in London. This must be accompanied by a court form outlining the current and proposed arrangements for any children of the family under 16 or between 16 and 18 and in full-time education.

An application for a matrimonial order for divorce may only be presented to the court after one year of marriage and it must be based on matters which occurred within that time. The spouse who lodges this document is known as the 'petitioner' throughout the divorce proceedings and the other spouse is the 'respondent'.

The issue of where the petitioner normally lives or the connections the parties have abroad may have to be considered by the court to determine whether a court has authority to deal with a particular divorce (whether the court has jurisdiction). These matters concern the law relating to domicile and habitual residence and can be complex.

There is only one ground for divorce, namely that the marriage has broken down irretrievably. This ground must be 'proved' by one of the following facts:

- the respondent has committed adultery and the petitioner finds it intolerable to live with him/her
- the respondent has behaved in such a way that the petitioner cannot reasonably be expected to live with him/her
- the respondent has deserted the petitioner for a continuous period of at least two years
- the two spouses have lived apart for at least two years and the respondent agrees to a divorce
- the two spouses have lived apart for at least five years

If the court is satisfied that the petitioner has proved one of those facts then it must grant a decree nisi (*see* below) unless it is satisfied that the marriage has not broken down.

The procedure is more complex if the divorce is defended, although this is very rare.

DECREE NISI

If the judge is satisfied that the petitioner has proved the contents of the divorce petition, a date will be set for the pronouncement of the decree nisi in open court. The decree nisi is a preliminary decree of divorce which must be obtained but the marriage will not be legally dissolved until the decree absolute. Neither party needs to attend and all the proceedings up to this point are usually carried out on paper.

DECREE ABSOLUTE

The final step in the divorce procedure is to obtain a decree absolute which formally ends the marriage. The petitioner can apply for this six weeks and one day after the date of the decree nisi. If the petitioner does not apply the respondent can apply, but only after three months

from the earliest date on which the petitioner could have applied.

A decree absolute will not normally be granted until the parties have agreed, or the court has dealt with, the parties' financial situation (*see* below for details of financial provision).

DISSOLUTION OF CIVIL PARTNERSHIPS

The legal process for dissolution of a civil partnership follows a model closely based on divorce. Irretrievable breakdown of the partnership is the sole ground for dissolution. The facts to be proved to establish this are the same as for divorce, with the exception of adultery which, due to its legal definition, can only apply to opposite sex couples. Adultery can, however, be used as an example of unreasonable behaviour.

FINANCIAL RELIEF ANCILLARY TO DIVORCE, NULLITY AND JUDICIAL SEPARATION

Following a petition for divorce, nullity or judicial separation, it is open to either spouse or former spouse to make a claim for financial provision provided they have not remarried. It is common practice for such an application to be made at the same time, or shortly after, a divorce petition has been issued. The courts have wide powers to make financial provision where a marriage breaks down. Orders can be made for:

- spousal maintenance (periodical payments) which can be capitalised into a lump sum
- lump sum payments
- payments of school fees
- adjustment or transfer of interests in property
- adjustment of interests in trusts and settlements
- orders relating to pensions

EXERCISE OF THE COURT'S POWERS TO ORDER FINANCIAL PROVISION

The court must exercise its powers so as to achieve an outcome which is fair between the parties, although it has a wide discretion in determining what is a fair financial outcome. It will consider the worldwide assets of both parties, whether liquid or illiquid. In exercising its discretion, the court has to consider a range of statutory factors including:

- the income, earning capacity, property and other financial resources which either party has or is likely to have in the foreseeable future
- the financial needs, obligations and responsibilities which each of the parties to the marriage has or is likely to have in the foreseeable future
- the standard of living enjoyed by the family
- the age of each party and the duration of the marriage
- any physical or mental disability of either party
- the contribution which each of the parties has made or is likely to make in the foreseeable future to the welfare of the family, including any contribution by looking after the home or caring for the family
- the conduct of parties
- loss of benefits

When considering the above factors, however, the court must give paramount consideration to the welfare of any child of the family.

The court has a wide discretion in considering these factors in order to achieve an outcome it considers to be fair. However, the court has emphasised that a 50:50 division of assets is frequently the correct result unless there are compelling reasons to the contrary. It is important to bear in mind that the House of Lords (now the supreme court) in *White v White* said that if each spouse contributed equally in their different sphere it does not matter in principle which of them earned the money and built up the assets. The contributions of the 'breadwinner' and 'homemaker' are considered equal.

The Law Commission's Marital Property Agreements project began in October 2009 and a consultation paper was published on 11 January 2011. The project is examining the status and enforceability of agreements made between spouses or civil partners (or those contemplating marriage or civil partnership) concerning their property or finances.

In October 2010, the supreme court gave judgement in *Radmacher v Granatino* and made it clear that a person now entering into a pre-nuptial agreement will be considered to have intended to be held to that agreement. However, the court will still be able to decide as to whether the agreement is fair and whether it should govern all the financial results of divorce. The supreme court did not give clear guidelines on when a pre-nuptial agreement would be considered 'fair' and it is likely to depend on the facts of an individual case.

In *Miller v Miller* and *MacFarlane v MacFarlane*, the House of Lords said that fairness required the court to consider three strands:
• the needs of the parties going forwards
• compensation for any economic disparity between the parties (such as where one party has sacrificed their career to become a full-time parent)
• sharing
The court also has a duty to consider making an order which will settle once and for all the parties' financial responsibilities towards each other, known as a 'clean break'.

FINANCIAL PROVISION ON DISSOLUTION OF A CIVIL PARTNERSHIP

The Civil Partnership Act 2004 makes provisions for financial relief for civil partners generally and extends the same rights and responsibilities invoked by marriage. Again the court must consider a number of factors when exercising its discretion and must take into account all of the circumstances of the case while giving first consideration to the welfare of any child of the family who is under 18. The list of statutory factors the court must consider resemble those for marriage and it is likely that the interpretation of these factors will be based on the courts' interpretation of the factors relating to marriage.

COHABITING COUPLES

Rights of unmarried couples are not the same as for married couples. Agreements, whether express or inferred by conduct, often determine interest in money and property. Reliance upon inferences is problematic, therefore it is advisable to consider entering into a contract, or 'cohabitation agreement', which establishes how money and property should be divided in the event of a relationship breakdown.

This area of law is still developing. In July 2007, the Law Commission published its report to parliament, recommending a scheme to provide remedies for eligible candidates. The Cohabitation Bill was subsequently introduced to parliament in December 2008 and the first day of the committee stage took place in April 2009. The next day of the committee stage is yet to be determined. In the meantime, cohabitation agreements continue to be governed by the general principles of contract law.

FINANCIAL PROVISION FOR CHILDREN

All parents are under a legal obligation to support their children financially and the live-in parent with care of the child can make claims against the non-resident parent for maintenance for the child.

The Child Maintenance and Other Payments Act 2008 changed the law with regard to child maintenance and set up the Child Maintenance and Enforcement Commission ('CMEC') which took over responsibility from the Child Support Agency. Since October 2008, all parents have been able to choose either a private or statutory maintenance arrangement, thereby removing the compulsion for benefit claimants to use the Child Support Agency.

If a parent chooses a statutory maintenance calculation, the CMEC will assess the amount that the non-resident parent must pay based on a new gross income scheme. This bases the amount payable on the gross income as per the latest available tax information held by HMRC. Parents using the old scheme (based on a percentage formula relating to net income) are to be encouraged to move to the new scheme or to come to their own arrangements privately.

If a non-resident parent does not make the payments due, CMEC has a wide variety of enforcement powers which include the power to seize a passport or driving licence, without the need to refer to the court.

An application can be made to the court for child maintenance only in certain circumstances as the court's jurisdiction in this area has been limited by the statute. The circumstances include where the income of the non-resident parent exceeds the limit dealt with by CMEC or the parents have already come to a written agreement about child support; or where one parent is seeking additional maintenance to cover, for example, school fees.

Provision is also made under Schedule 1 of the Children Act 1989 for unmarried parents to apply to the court for lump sum and property adjustment orders and, in limited circumstances, orders for child maintenance.

SCOTLAND

Although some provisions are similar to those for England and Wales, there is separate legislation for Scotland covering nullity of marriage, judicial separation, divorce and ancillary matters. The principal legislation in relation to family law in Scotland is the Family Law (Scotland) Act 1985. The Family Law (Scotland) Act 2006 came in to force on 4 May 2006, and introduced reforms to various aspects of Scottish family law. The following is confined to major points on which the law in Scotland differs from that of England and Wales.

An action for judicial separation or divorce may be raised in the court of session; it may also be raised in the sheriff court if either party was resident in the sheriffdom for 40 days immediately before the date of the action or for 40 days ending not more than 40 days before the date of the action. The fee for starting a divorce petition in the sheriff court is £140.

The grounds for raising an action of divorce in Scotland have been subject to reform in terms of the 2006 act. The current grounds for divorce are:
• the defender has committed adultery. When adultery is cited as proof that the marriage has broken down irretrievably, it is not necessary in Scotland to prove that it is also intolerable for the pursuer to live with the defender

- the defender's behaviour is such that the pursuer cannot reasonably be expected to cohabit with the defender
- there has been no cohabitation between the parties for one year prior to the raising of the action for divorce, and the defender consents to the granting of decree of divorce
- there has been no cohabitation between the parties for two years prior to the raising of the action for divorce
- an interim gender recognition certificate under the Gender Recognition Act 2004 has, after the date of marriage, been issued to either party to the marriage

The previously available ground of desertion was abolished by the 2006 act.

A simplified procedure for 'do-it-yourself divorce' was introduced in 1983 for certain divorces. If the action is based on one or two years' separation and will not be opposed, and if there are no children under 16 and no financial claims, and there is no sign that the applicant's spouse is unable to manage his or her affairs through mental illness or handicap, the applicant can write directly to the local sheriff court or to the court of session for the appropriate forms to enable him or her to proceed. The fee is £105, unless the applicant receives income support or legal advice and assistance, in which case there may be no fee.

Where a divorce action has been raised, it may be put on hold for a variety of reasons. In all actions for divorce an extract decree, which brings the marriage to an end, will be made available 14 days after the divorce has been granted. Unlike in England, there is no decree nisi, only a final decree of divorce. Parties must ensure that all financial issues have been resolved prior to divorce, as it is not possible to seek further financial provision after divorce has been granted.

FINANCIAL PROVISION

In relation to financial provision on divorce, the first, and most important, principle is fair sharing of the matrimonial property. In terms of Scots law matrimonial property is defined as all property acquired by either spouse from the date of marriage up to the date of separation. Property acquired before the marriage is not deemed to be matrimonial unless it was acquired for use by the parties as a family home or as furniture for that home. Property acquired after the date of separation is not matrimonial property. Any property acquired by either of the parties by way of gift or inheritance during the marriage is excluded and does not form part of the matrimonial property.

When considering whether to make an award of financial provision a court shall also take account of any economic advantage derived by either party to the marriage as a result of contributions, financial or otherwise, by the other, and of any economic disadvantage suffered by either party for the benefit of the other party. The court must also ensure that the economic burden of caring for a child under the age of 16 is shared fairly between the parties.

A court can also consider making an order requiring one party to pay the other party a periodical allowance for a certain period of time following divorce. Such an order may be appropriate in cases where there is insufficient capital to effect a fair sharing of the matrimonial property. Orders for periodical allowance are uncommon, as courts will favour a 'clean break' where possible.

CHILDREN

The court has the power to award a residence order in respect of any children of the marriage or to make an order regulating the child's contact with the non-resident parent. The court will only make such orders if it is deemed better for the child to do so than to make no order at all, and the welfare of the children is of paramount importance. The fact that a spouse has caused the breakdown of the marriage does not in itself preclude him/her from being awarded residence.

NULLITY

An action for 'declaration of nullity' can be brought if someone with a legitimate interest is able to show that the marriage is void or voidable. The action can only be brought in the court of session. Although the grounds on which a marriage may be void or voidable are similar to those on which a marriage can be declared invalid in England, there are some differences. Where a spouse is capable of sexual intercourse but refuses to consummate the marriage, this is not a ground for nullity in Scots law, though it could be a ground for divorce. Where a spouse was suffering from venereal disease at the time of marriage and the other spouse did not know, this is not a ground for nullity in Scots law, neither is the fact that a wife was pregnant by another man at the time of marriage without the knowledge of her husband.

COHABITING COUPLES

The law in Scotland now provides certain financial and property rights for cohabiting couples in terms of the Family Law (Scotland) Act 2006, or 'the 2006 Act'. The relevant 2006 act provisions do not place cohabitants in Scotland on an equal footing with married couples or civil partners, but provide some rights for cohabitants in the event that the relationship is terminated by separation or death. The provisions relate to couples who cease to cohabit after 4 May 2006.

The legislation provides for a presumption that any contents of the home shared by the cohabitants are owned in equal shares. A former cohabitant can also seek financial provision on termination of the relationship in the form of a capital payment if they can successfully demonstrate that they have been financially disadvantaged, and that conversely the other cohabitant has been financially advantaged, as a consequence of contributions made (financial or otherwise). Such a claim must be made no later than one year after the day on which the cohabitants cease to cohabit.

The 2006 act also provides that a cohabitant may make a claim on their partner's estate in the event of that partner's death, providing that there is no will. A claim of this nature must be made no later than six months after the date of the partner's death.

THE PRINCIPAL REGISTRY
First Avenue House, 42–49 High Holborn, London WC1 6NP
THE COURT OF SESSION
Parliament House, Parliament Square, Edinburgh EH1 1RQ
T 0131-225 2595 W www.scotcourts.gov.uk
THE CHILD SUPPORT AGENCY
T 08457-133133 W www.csa.gov.uk

EMPLOYMENT LAW

EMPLOYEES

A fundamental distinction in UK employment law is that drawn between an employee and someone who is self-employed. Further, there is an important, intermediate category introduced by legislation: 'workers' covers all employees but also catches some of those who are self-employed. An 'employee' is someone who has entered into or works under a contract of employment, while a 'worker' has entered into or works under a contract whereby he undertakes to do or perform personally any work or services for another party whose status is not that of a client or customer. Whether or not someone is an employee or a worker as opposed to being genuinely self-employed is an important and complex question, for it determines that person's statutory rights and protections.

The greater the level of control that the employer has over the work carried out, the greater the depth of integration of the employee in the employer's business, and the closer the obligations to provide and perform work between the parties, the more likely it is that the parties will be employer and employee.

PAY AND CONDITIONS

The Employment Rights Act 1996 consolidated the statutory provisions relating to employees' rights. Employers must give each employee employed for one month or more a written statement containing the following information:

- names of employer and employee
- date when employment began and the date on which the employee's period of *continuous* employment began (taking into account any employment with a previous employer which counts towards that period)
- the scale, rate or other method of calculating remuneration and intervals at which it will be paid
- job title or description of job
- hours and the permitted place(s) of work and, where there are several such places, the address of the employer
- holiday entitlement and holiday pay
- provisions concerning incapacity for work due to sickness and injury, including provisions for sick pay
- details of pension scheme(s)
- length of notice period that employer and employee need to give to terminate employment
- if the employment is not intended to be permanent, the period for which it is expected to continue or, if it is for a fixed term, the end date of the contract
- details of any collective agreement (including the parties to the agreement) which affects the terms of employment
- details of disciplinary and grievance procedures (including the individual to whom a complaint should be made and the process of making that complaint)
- if the employee is to work outside the UK for more than one month, the period of such work and the currency in which payment is made
- a note stating whether a contracting-out certificate is in force

This must be given to the employee within two months of the start of their employment.

If the employer does not provide the written statement within two months (or a statement of any changes to these particulars within one month of the changes being made) then the employee can complain to an employment tribunal, which can specify the information that the employer should have given. When, in the context of an employee's successful tribunal claim, the employer is also found to have been in breach of the duty to provide the written statement at the time proceedings were commenced, the tribunal must award the employee two weeks' pay, and may award four weeks' pay, unless it would be unjust or inequitable to do so.

The Working Time Regulations 1998, the National Minimum Wage Act 1998, the Employment Rights (Dispute Resolution) Act 1998, Employment Relations Act 1999, the Employment Act 2002 and the Employment Act 2008 now supplement the 1996 act.

FLEXIBLE WORKING

The Employment Act 2002 (and regulations made under it) gives employees who are responsible for the upbringing of a child the right to apply for flexible working for the purpose of caring for that child. The right has been extended to carers of adults. Whether or not an employee has this right depends on both the employee and the child/adult cared for meeting a number of criteria. If an application under the act is rejected, the employee may complain to an employment tribunal.

SICK PAY

Employees absent from work through illness or injury are entitled to receive Statutory Sick Pay (SSP) from the employer for a maximum period of 28 weeks in any three-year period.

MATERNITY AND PARENTAL RIGHTS

Under the Employment Relations Act 1999, the Employment Act 2002, the Maternity and Parental Leave Regulations 1999 (as amended in 2002 and 2006) and the Paternity and Adoption Leave Regulations 2002 and 2003, both men and women are entitled to take leave when they become a parent. Women are protected from discrimination, detriment or dismissal by reason of their pregnancy or maternity, including discrimination by association and by perception. Men are protected from suffering a detriment or dismissal for taking paternity or parental leave.

Any woman who needs to attend an antenatal appointment on the advice of a registered medical professional is entitled to paid leave from work to attend the appointment. All pregnant women are entitled to a maximum period of maternity leave of 52 weeks. This comprises 26 weeks' ordinary maternity leave, followed immediately by 26 weeks' additional maternity leave. A woman who takes ordinary maternity leave normally has the right to return to the job in which she was employed before her absence. If she takes additional maternity leave, she is entitled to return to the same job or, if that is not reasonably practicable, to another job that is suitable and appropriate for her to do. There is a two-week period of compulsory maternity leave, immediately following the birth of the child, wherein the employer is not permitted to allow the mother to work.

A woman will qualify for Statutory Maternity Pay (SMP), which is payable for up to 39 weeks, if she has been continuously employed for not less than 26 weeks prior to the 15th week before the expected week of childbirth. For further information *see* Social Welfare, Employer Payments.

Employees are entitled to adoption leave and adoption pay (at the same rates as SMP) subject to fulfilment of similar criteria in relation to maternity leave and pay, but note that there is a 26-week qualifying period for adoption leave. Where a couple is adopting a child, either one (but not both) of the parents may take adoption leave, and the other may take paternity leave.

Certain employees are entitled to paternity leave on the birth or adoption of a child. To be eligible, the employee must be the child's father, or the partner of the mother or adopter, and meet other conditions. These conditions are, firstly, that they must have been continuously employed for not less than 26 weeks prior to the 15th week before the expected week of childbirth (or, in the case of adoptions, 26 weeks ending with the week in which notification of the adoption match is given) and, secondly, that the employee must have or expect to have responsibility for the upbringing of the child. The employee may take either one week's leave, or two consecutive weeks' leave. This leave may be taken at any time between the date of the child's birth (or placement for adoption) and 56 days later.

For births and adoptions from 3 April 2011, an eligible employee may take additional paternity leave at the end of the mother's or adopter's leave period. For more information *see* Social Welfare, Employer Payments.

Any employee with one year's service who has, or expects to have, responsibility for a child may take parental leave to care for the child. Each parent is entitled to a total of 13 weeks' parental leave for each of their children (or 18 weeks if the child is disabled). This leave must be taken (at the rate of no more than four weeks a year, and in blocks of whole weeks only) before the child's fifth birthday (18th birthday if the child is disabled) or before the fifth anniversary of the date of placement of an adopted child.

SUNDAY TRADING

The Sunday Trading Act 1994 allows shops to open on Sunday for serving retail customers. The Employment Rights Act 1996 gives shop workers and betting workers the right not to be dismissed, selected for redundancy or to suffer any detriment (such as the denial of overtime, promotion or training) if they refuse to work on Sundays. This does not apply to those who, under their contracts, are employed to work on Sundays.

TERMINATION OF EMPLOYMENT

An employee may be dismissed without notice if guilty of gross misconduct but in other cases a period of notice must be given by the employer. The minimum periods of notice specified in the Employment Rights Act 1996 are:

- one week if the employee has been continuously employed for one month or more but for less than two years
- an additional week for each complete year of continuous employment from and including two to 12 years (making the maximum statutory notice period 12 weeks after 12 years' continuous employment)
- longer periods apply if these are specified in the contract of employment

If an employee is dismissed with less notice than he/she is entitled to by statute, or under their contract if longer, he/she will have a wrongful dismissal claim (unless the employer paid the employee in lieu of notice in accordance with a contractual provision entitling it to do so). This claim for wrongful dismissal can be brought by the employee either in the civil courts or the employment tribunal, but if brought in the tribunal the maximum amount that can be awarded is £25,000.

REDUNDANCY

An employee dismissed because of redundancy may be entitled to redundancy pay. This applies if:

- the employee has at least two years' continuous service

- the employee is dismissed by the employer (this can include cases of voluntary redundancy)
- dismissal is due to redundancy.

Redundancy can mean closure of the entire business, closure of a particular site of the business, or a reduction in the need for employees to carry out work of a particular kind.

An employee may not be entitled to a redundancy payment if offered a suitable alternative job by the same employer. The amount of statutory redundancy pay depends on the length of service, age, and their earnings, subject to a weekly maximum of (currently) £400. The maximum payment that can be awarded is £12,000. The redundancy payment is guaranteed by the government in cases where the employer becomes insolvent.

UNFAIR DISMISSAL

Complaints of unfair dismissal are dealt with by an employment tribunal. Any employee with one year's continuous service (subject to exceptions, including in relation to whistleblowers – *see* below) can make a complaint to the tribunal. At the tribunal, it is for the employer to prove that the dismissal was due to one or more potentially fair reasons: a legal restriction preventing the continuation of the employee's contract; the employee's capability or qualifications for the job he/she was employed to do; the employee's conduct; redundancy; or some other substantial reason.

If the employer succeeds in showing this, the tribunal must then decide whether the employer acted reasonably in dismissing the employee for that reason. If the employee is found to have been unfairly dismissed, the tribunal can order that he/she be reinstated, re-engaged or compensated. Any person believing that they may have been unfairly dismissed should contact their local Citizens Advice bureau or seek legal advice. A claim must be brought within three months of the date of termination of employment.

The normal maximum compensatory award for unfair dismissal is £68,400 (as at 1 February 2011). If the dismissal occurred after 6 April 2009 and the employer unreasonably failed to follow the ACAS Code of Practice on Disciplinary and Grievance Procedures in carrying out the dismissal, the tribunal may increase the employee's compensation by up to 25 per cent.

WHISTLEBLOWING

Under the whistleblowing legislation (Public Interest Disclosure Act 1998, which inserted provisions into the Employment Rights Act 1996) dismissal of an employee is automatically unfair if the reason or principal reason for the dismissal is that the employee has made a protected disclosure. The legislation also makes it unlawful to subject workers (a broad category that includes employees and certain other individuals, such as agency workers) who have made a protected disclosure to any detriment on the ground that they have done so.

For a disclosure to qualify for protection, the claimant must show that he has disclosed information, which in his reasonable belief tends to show one or more of the following six categories of wrongdoing: criminal offences; breach of any legal obligation; miscarriages of justice; danger to the health and safety of any individual; damage to the environment; or the deliberate concealing of information about any of the other categories. The malpractices can be past, present, prospective or merely alleged.

A qualifying disclosure will only be protected if the manner of the disclosure fulfills certain conditions, including being made in good faith and being made to a defined category of persons, which varies according to the type of disclosure.

Any whistleblower claim in the employment tribunal must normally be brought within three months of the date of dismissal or other act leading to a detriment.

An individual does not need to have been working with the employer for any particular period of time to be able to bring such a claim and compensation is uncapped (and can include an amount for injury to feelings).

DISCRIMINATION

Discrimination in employment on the grounds of sex (including gender reassignment), sexual orientation, race, colour, nationality, ethnic or national origins, religion or belief, marital or civil partnership status, age or disability is unlawful. Discrimination legislation generally covers direct discrimination, indirect discrimination, harassment and victimisation. Only in limited circumstances can such discrimination be justified (rendering it lawful).

An individual does not need to be employed for any particular period of time to be able to claim discrimination (discrimination can be alleged at the recruitment phase), and discrimination compensation is uncapped (and can include an amount for injury to feelings). These features distinguish the discrimination laws from, for example, the unfair dismissal laws.

The Equality Act 2010 was passed on 8 April 2010 and the main provisions came into force on 1 October 2010. The Act unifies several pieces of discrimination legislation, providing one definition of direct discrimination, indirect discrimination, harassment and victimisation. The Equality Act applies to those employed in Great Britain but not to employees in Northern Ireland or (subject to EC exceptions) to those who work mainly abroad, and provides that:

• it is unlawful to discriminate on the grounds of sex, gender reassignment or marital/civil partner status, including discrimination by association and by perception. This covers all aspects of employment (including advertising for jobs), but there are some limited exceptions, such as where the essential nature of the job requires it to be given to someone of a particular sex, or where decency and privacy requires it. The act entitles men and women to equality of remuneration for equivalent work or work of the same value

• individuals have the right not to be discriminated against on the grounds of race, colour, nationality, or ethnic or national origins and this applies to all aspects of employment. Employers may also take lawful positive action, including in relation to recruitment and promotion

• discrimination against a disabled person in all aspects of employment is unlawful. This includes protecting carers from discrimination by association with the disabled persons that they look after. In certain circumstances, the employer may show that the less favourable treatment is justified and so does not constitute discrimination. The act also imposes a duty on employers to make 'reasonable adjustments' to the arrangements and physical features of the workplace if these place disabled people at a substantial disadvantage compared with those who are not disabled. The definition of a 'disabled person' is wide and includes people diagnosed with HIV, cancer and multiple sclerosis

• discrimination against a person on the grounds of religion or belief (or lack of belief) including discrimination by association and by perception, in all aspects of employment, is unlawful

• discrimination against an individual on the grounds of sexual orientation, including discrimination by association and by perception, in all aspects of employment, is unlawful

• age discrimination in the workplace is unlawful, and an employer may no longer dismiss an employee by reason of retirement once they have reached a certain age

The responsibility for monitoring equality in society rests with the Equality and Human Rights Commission.

In Northern Ireland similar provisions exist to those that were in force in Great Britain prior to the coming into force of the Equality Act but are contained in separate legislation (although the Disability Discrimination Act does extend to Northern Ireland). As such, there is a general perception that Northern Ireland now offers less protection to individuals against discrimination than Great Britain.

In Northern Ireland there is one combined body working towards equality and eliminating discrimination, the Equality Commission for Northern Ireland.

WORKING TIME

The Working Time Regulations 1998 impose rules that limit working hours and provide for rest breaks and holidays. The regulations apply to workers and so cover not only employees but also other individuals who undertake to perform personally any work or services (eg freelancers). The regulations are complex and subject to various exceptions and qualifications but the basic provisions relating to adult day workers are as follows:

• No worker is permitted to work more than an average of 48 hours per week (unless they have made a genuine voluntary opt-out of this limit – it is not sufficient to make it a term of the contract that the worker opts out), and a worker is entitled to, but is not required to take, the following breaks:

• 11 consecutive hours' rest in every 24-hour period

• an uninterrupted rest period of at least 24 hours in each 7-day period or 48 hours in each fortnight (in addition to the daily rest period)

• 20 minutes' rest break provided that the working day is longer than 6 hours

• 5.6 weeks' paid annual leave (28 days full-time). This equates to 4 weeks plus public holidays

There are specific provisions relating to night work, young workers (ie those over school leaving age but under 18) and a variety of workers in specialised sectors (such as off-shore oil rig workers).

HUMAN RIGHTS

On 2 October 2000 the Human Rights Act 1998 came into force. This act incorporates the European Convention on Human Rights into the law of the UK. The main principles of the act are as follows:

• all legislation must be interpreted and given effect by the courts as compatible with the Convention so far as it is possible to do so. Before the second reading of a new bill the minister responsible for the bill must provide a statement regarding its compatibility with the Human Rights Act

• subordinate legislation (eg statutory instruments) which are incompatible with the Convention can be struck down by the courts

- primary legislation (eg an act of parliament) which is incompatible with the Convention cannot be struck down by a court, but the higher courts can make a declaration of incompatibility which is a signal to parliament to change the law
- all public authorities (including courts and tribunals) must not act in a way which is incompatible with the Convention
- individuals whose Convention rights have been infringed by a public authority may bring proceedings against that authority, but the act is not intended to create new rights as between individuals

The main human rights protected by the Convention are the right to life (article 2); protection from torture and inhuman or degrading treatment (article 3); protection from slavery or forced labour (article 4); the right to liberty and security of the person (article 5); the right to a fair trial (article 6); the right not to be subject to retrospective criminal offences (article 7); the right to respect for private and family life (article 8); freedom of thought, conscience and religion (article 9); freedom of expression (article 10); freedom of peaceful association and assembly (article 11); the right to marry and found a family (article 12); protection from discrimination (article 14); the right to property (article 1 protocol No.1); the right to education (article 2 protocol No.1); and the right to free elections (article 3 protocol No.1). Most of the Convention rights are subject to limitations which deem the breach of the right acceptable on the basis it is 'necessary in a democratic society'.

Human rights are also enshrined in the common law (of tort). Although this is of historical significance, the common law (for example the duty of confidentiality) remains especially important regarding violations of human rights that occur between private parties, where the Human Rights Act 1998 does not apply.

PARENTAL RESPONSIBILITY

The Children Act 1989 gives both the mother and father parental responsibility for the child if the parents are married to each other at the time of the child's birth. If the parents are not married, only the mother has parental responsibility. The father may acquire it in accordance with the provisions of section 4 of the Children Act 1989. He can do this in one of four ways: a) by being registered as the father on the child's birth certificate with the consent of the mother (only for fathers of children born after 1 December 2003, following changes to the Adoption and Children Act 2002); b) by applying to the court for a parental responsibility order; c) by entering into a parental responsibility agreement with the mother which must be in the prescribed form; or d) by obtaining a residence order from the court. Otherwise, a father can gain parental responsibility by marrying the mother of the child.

Where a child's parent, who has parental responsibility, marries a person who is not the child's parent, the child's parent(s) with parental responsibility can agree for the step-parent to have parental responsibility or, the step-parent may acquire parental responsibility by order of the court (section 4A(1) Children Act 1989).

Where a child is adopted, parental responsibility will be given to the adopter of the child. However, before an order for adoption can be made, the court must be satisfied that every parent or guardian consents. The consent of a father without parental responsibility is not required, although adoption agencies and local authorities must be careful to establish, if possible, the identity of the father and satisfy themselves that any person claiming to be the father either has no intention to apply for parental responsibility or that if he did apply, the application would be likely to be refused.

In Scotland, the relevant legislation is the Children (Scotland) Act 1995, which also gives the mother parental responsibility for her child whether or not she is married to the child's father. A father who is married to the mother, either at the time of the child's conception or subsequently, will also have automatic parental rights. Section 23 of the 2006 act provides that an unmarried father will obtain automatic parental responsibilities and rights if he is registered as the father on the child's birth certificate. For unmarried fathers who are not named on the birth certificate, or whose children were born before the 2006 act came into force, it is possible to acquire parental responsibilities and rights by applying to the court or by entering into a parental responsibilities and rights agreement with the mother. The father of any child, regardless of parental rights, has a duty to aliment that child until he/she is 18 (25 if the child is still at an educational establishment).

LEGITIMATION

Under the Legitimacy Act 1976, an illegitimate person automatically becomes legitimate when his/her parents marry. This applies even where one of the parents was married to a third person at the time of the birth. In such cases it is necessary to re-register the birth of the child. In Scotland, the status of illegitimacy has been abolished by section 21 of the 2006 act. The Law Reform Act 1987 reformed the law so as to remove so far as possible the legal disadvantages of illegitimacy.

JURY SERVICE

In England and Wales, the law concerning juries is largely consolidated in the Juries Act 1974. In England and Wales a person charged with a serious criminal offence is entitled to have their trial heard by a jury in a crown court, except in some complex fraud cases where the evidence is too complex to be usefully considered by a jury, or where there is a real risk of jury tampering. In such cases a judge may be entitled to order a trial by judge alone.

In civil cases, there is a right to a jury in the Queen's Bench Division of the high court in cases where the person applying for a jury has been accused of fraud, as well as in cases of libel, slander, malicious prosecution or false imprisonment. The same applies to the county court. In all other cases in the Queen's Bench Division only the judge has discretion to order trial with a jury, though such an order is seldom made. In the chancery division of the high court a jury is never used. The same is true in the family division of the high court.

No right to a jury trial exists in Scotland, although more serious offences are heard before a jury. In England and Wales there must be at least nine, and no more than 12 members of a jury in a criminal case. Civil cases held in the county court must have eight members but those held in the high court may have any number of members up to a maximum of 12. At an inquest, there must be at least seven and no more than 11 members. In Scotland there are 12 members of a jury in a civil case in the court of session (the civil jury being confined to the court of session and a restricted number of actions), and 15 in a criminal trial in the high court of justiciary. Jurors are normally asked to serve for ten working days, during which time they could sit on more than one case. Jurors selected for longer cases are expected to sit for the duration of the trial.

Every 'registered' parliamentary or local government elector between the ages of 18 and 70 who has lived in the UK (including, for this purpose, the Channel Islands and the Isle of Man) for any period of at least five years since reaching the age of 13 is qualified to serve on a jury unless he/she is 'mentally disordered' or disqualified.

Those disqualified from jury service include:

• those who have at any time been sentenced by a court in the UK (including, for this purpose, the Channel Islands and the Isle of Man) to a term of imprisonment or youth custody of five years or more
• those who have been imprisoned for life, detained at Her Majesty's, or the Secretary of State's pleasure, detained for a period of at least five years, imprisoned or detained for public protection, or received an 'extended sentence' under the relevant provisions of the Criminal Justice Act 2003 or the Criminal Procedure (Scotland) Act 1995
• those who have within the previous ten years served any part of a sentence of imprisonment, youth custody or detention, been detained in a young offenders' institution, received a suspended sentence of imprisonment or order for detention, or received a community order
• those who are on bail in criminal proceedings

The court has the discretion to excuse a juror from service, or defer the date of service, if the juror can show there is good reason why he/she should be excused from attending or good reason why his attendance should be deferred. It is an offence (punishable by a fine) to fail to attend when summoned, to serve knowing that you are disqualified from service, or to make false representations in an attempt to evade service. If a juror fails to turn up for service, or attends but cannot serve due to being under the influence of drink or drugs, this is punishable as contempt of court. Any party can object to any juror if he/she can show cause to the trial judge.

It may be appropriate for a judge to excuse a juror from a particular case if he is personally concerned in the facts of the particular case, or closely connected with a party to the proceedings or with a prospective witness. The judge may also discharge any juror who, from a mental or physical incapacity, temporary or permanent, cannot pay proper attention to the evidence.

An individual juror (or the entire jury) can be discharged if it is shown that they or any of their number have, among other things, separated from the rest of the jury without the leave of the court; talked to any person out of court who is not a member of the jury; determined the verdict of the trial by drawing lots; come to a compromise on the verdict; been drunk, or otherwise incapacitated, while carrying out their duties as a juror; exerted improper pressure on the other members of the jury (eg harassment or bullying); declined to take part in the jury's functions; displayed actual or apparent bias (eg racism, sexism or other discriminatory or deliberate hostility); or inadvertently possessed knowledge of the bad character of a party to the proceedings which has not been adduced as evidence in the proceedings. The factual situations that arise are many, and include consulting an ouija board in the course of deliberations, making telephone calls after retirement, and lunching with a barrister not connected with the proceedings.

A jury's verdict need not be unanimous. In criminal proceedings the agreement of 10 jurors will suffice when there are not fewer than 11 people on the jury (or 9 in a jury of 10). In civil proceedings in the county court the agreement of seven or eight jurors will suffice. However, where a majority verdict is given, the court must be satisfied that the jury had reasonable time to consider its verdict based on the nature and complexity of the case. In criminal proceedings this must be no less than two hours.

A juror is immune from prosecution or civil claim in respect of anything said or done by him or her in the discharge of their office. It is a contempt of court for a juror to disclose what happened in the jury room even after the trial is over. A juror may claim travelling expenses, a subsistence allowance and an allowance for other financial loss (eg loss of earnings or benefits, fees paid to carers or child-minders) up to a stated limit. For more information on jury service, visit W www.direct.gov.uk/en/crimejusticeandthelaw/juryservice

SCOTLAND

Qualification criteria for jury service in Scotland are similar to those in England and Wales, except that members of the judiciary are ineligible for ten years after ceasing to hold their post, and others concerned with the administration of justice are only eligible for service five years after ceasing to hold office. Certain persons who have the right to be excused include full-time members of the medical, dental, nursing, veterinary and pharmaceutical professions, full-time members of the armed forces, ministers of religion, persons who have served on a jury within the previous five years, members of the Scottish parliament, members of the Scottish government, junior Scottish ministers, those who have recently served on a jury and those aged over 71 years. For civil trials there is an age limit of 65 years. Those convicted of a serious crime are automatically disqualified. Those who are incapable by reason of a mental disorder may also be excused. The maximum fine for a person serving on a jury knowing himself/herself to be ineligible is £1,000. The maximum fine for failing to attend without good cause is also £1,000.

HER MAJESTY'S COURTS AND TRIBUNALS SERVICE
    102 Petty France, London SW1H 9AJ T 0845-456 8770
JURY CENTRAL SUMMONING BUREAU
    T 0845-803 8003 E jurysummoning@hmcts.gsi.gov.uk
SCOTTISH COURTS SERVICE
    Courts of Session, Parliament House, Parliament Square,
    Edinburgh EH1 1RQ T 0131-225 2595
    W www.scotcourts.gov.uk
THE CLERK OF JUSTICIARY
    High Court of Justiciary, Lawnmarket, Edinburgh EH2 2NS
    T 0131-240 6900

LANDLORD AND TENANT

RESIDENTIAL LETTINGS

The provisions outlined here apply only where the tenant lives in a separate dwelling from the landlord and where the dwelling is the tenant's only or main home. It does not apply to licensees such as lodgers, guests or service occupiers.

The 1996 Housing Act radically changed certain aspects of the legislation referred to below; in particular, the grant of assured and assured shorthold tenancies under the Housing Act 1988.

ASSURED SHORTHOLD TENANCIES

If a tenancy was granted on or after 15 January 1989 and before 28 February 1997, the tenant would have an assured tenancy unless the landlord served notice under section 20 in the prescribed form prior to the commencement of the tenancy, stating that the tenancy is to be an assured shorthold tenancy and the tenancy is for a minimum fixed term period of six months (*see* below). An assured tenancy gives that tenant greater security. The tenant could, for example, stay in possession of the dwelling for as long as the tenant observed the terms of the tenancy. The landlord cannot obtain possession from such a tenant unless the landlord can establish a specific ground for possession (set out in the Housing Act 1988) and obtains a court order. The rent payable is that agreed with the landlord at the start of the tenancy. The landlord has the right to increase the rent annually by serving a notice. If that happens the tenant can apply to have the rent fixed by the rent assessment committee of the local authority. The tenant or the landlord may request that the committee sets the rent in line with open market rents for that type of property.

Under the Housing Act 1996, all new lettings (below an annual rent threshold of £100,000 since October 2010) entered into on or after 28 February 1997 (for whatever term) will be assured shorthold tenancies unless the landlord serves a notice stating that the tenancy is not to be an assured shorthold tenancy. This means that the landlord is entitled to possession at the end of the tenancy provided he serves a notice under section 21 Housing Act 1988 and commences the proceedings in accordance with the correct procedure. The landlord must obtain a court order, however, to obtain possession if the tenant refuses to vacate at the end of the tenancy. If the tenancy is an assured shorthold tenancy, the court must grant the order. For both assured and assured shorthold tenancies, if the tenant is more than eight weeks in arrears, the landlord can serve notice and, if the tenant is still in arrears at the date of the hearing, the court must make an order for possession.

REGULATED TENANCIES

Before the Housing Act 1988 came into force on 15 January 1989 there were regulated tenancies; some are still in existence and are protected by the Rent Act 1977. Under this act it is possible for the landlord or the tenant to apply to the local rent officer to have a 'fair' rent registered. The fair rent is then the maximum rent payable.

SECURE TENANCIES

Secure tenancies are generally given to tenants of local authorities, housing associations (before 15 January 1989) and certain other bodies. This gives the tenant security of tenure unless the terms of the agreement are broken by the tenant and it is reasonable to make an order for possession. Those with secure tenancies may have the right to buy their property. In practice this right is generally only available to council tenants.

AGRICULTURAL PROPERTY

Tenancies in agricultural properties are governed by the Agricultural Holdings Act 1986, the Agricultural Tenancies Act 1995 (both amended by the Regulatory Reform (Agricultural Tenancies) (England and Wales) Order 2006), the Tribunals, Courts and Enforcement Act 2007, the Legal Services Act 2007 and the Rent (Agriculture) Act 1976, which give similar protections to those described above, eg security of tenure, right to

compensation for disturbance, etc. The Agricultural Holdings (Scotland) Act 1991 along with Agricultural Holdings (Scotland) Act 2003 and the Housing (Scotland) Act 2006 apply similar provisions to Scotland.

EVICTION

The Protection from Eviction Act 1977 (as amended by the Housing Act 1988 and Nationality, Immigration and Asylum Act 2002) sets out the procedure a landlord must follow in order to obtain possession of property. It is unlawful for a landlord to evict a tenant otherwise than in accordance with the law. For common law tenancies and for Rent Act tenants a notice to quit in the prescribed form giving 28 days notice is required. For secure and assured tenancies a notice seeking possession must be served. It is unlawful for the landlord to evict a person by putting their belongings on to the street, by changing the locks and so on. It is also unlawful for a landlord to harass a tenant in any way in order to persuade him/her to give up the tenancy. The tenant may be able to obtain an injunction to restrain the actions of the landlord and get back into the property and be awarded damages.

LANDLORD RESPONSIBILITIES

Under the Landlord and Tenant Act 1985, where the term of the lease is less than seven years, the landlord is responsible for maintaining the structure and exterior of the property, for sanitation, for heating and hot water, and all installations for the supply of water, gas and electricity.

LEASEHOLDERS

Strictly speaking, leaseholders have bought a long lease rather than a property and in certain limited circumstances the landlord can end the tenancy. Under the Leasehold Reform Act 1967 (as amended by the Housing Acts 1969, 1974, 1980 and 1985), leaseholders of houses may have the right to buy the freehold or to take an extended lease for a term of 50 years. This applies to leases where the term of the lease is over 21 years, at a low rent, and where the leaseholder has occupied the house as his/her only or main residence for the last two years, or for a total of two years over the last ten. The tenant must give the landlord written notice of his desire to acquire the freehold or extend the leasehold.

The Leasehold Reform, Housing and Urban Development Act came into force in 1993 and allows the leaseholders of flats in certain circumstances to buy the freehold of the building in which they live.

Responsibility for maintenance of the structure, exterior and interior of the building should be set out in the lease. Usually the upkeep of the interior of his/her part of the property is the responsibility of the leaseholder, and responsibility for the structure, exterior and common interior areas is shared between the freeholder and the leaseholder(s).

If leaseholders are dissatisfied with charges made in respect of lease extensions, they are entitled to have their situation evaluated by the Leasehold Valuation Tribunal.

The Commonhold and Leasehold Reform Act 2002 makes provision for the freehold estate in land to be registered as commonhold land and for the legal interest in the land to be vested in a 'commonhold association' ie a private limited company.

BUSINESS LETTINGS

The Landlord and Tenant Acts 1927 and 1954 (as amended) give security of tenure to the tenants of most business premises. The landlord can only evict the tenant on one of the grounds laid down in the 1954 act, and in some cases where the landlord repossesses the property the tenant may be entitled to compensation.

SCOTLAND

In Scotland assured and short assured tenancies exist for lettings after 2 January 1989 and are similar to assured tenancies in England and Wales. The relevant legislation is the Housing (Scotland) Act 1988.

Most tenancies created before 2 January 1989 were regulated tenancies and the Rent (Scotland) Act 1984 still applies where these exist. The act defines, among other things, the circumstances in which a landlord can increase the rent when improvements are made to the property. The provisions of the Rent Act do not apply to tenancies where the landlord is the Crown, a local authority or a housing corporation.

The Housing (Scotland) Acts of 1987 and 2001 relate to local authority responsibilities for housing, the right to buy, and local authority secured tenancies. The provisions are broadly similar to England and Wales. The Housing (Scotland) Act 2010 is expected to come fully into force by April 2012. When fully in force, the act will reform the existing right-to-buy provisions, modernise social housing regulation and replace the regulatory framework established by the 1988 and 2001 acts.

In Scotland, business premises are not controlled by statute to the same extent as in England and Wales, although the Tenancy of Shops (Scotland) Act 1949 gives some security to tenants of shops. Tenants of shops can apply to the sheriff, within 21 days of being served a notice to quit, for a renewal of tenancy if threatened with eviction. This application may be dismissed on various grounds including where the landlord has offered to sell the property to the tenant at an agreed price or, in the absence of agreement as to price, at a price fixed by a single arbiter appointed by the parties or the sheriff. The act extends to properties where the Crown or government departments are the landlords or the tenants.

Under the Leases Act 1449 the landlord's successors (either purchasers or creditors) are bound by the agreement made with any tenants so long as the following conditions are met:
- the lease, if for more than one year, must be in writing
- there must be a rent
- there must be a term of expiry
- the tenant must have entered into possession
- the subjects of the lease must be land
- the landlord, if owner, must be the proprietor with a recorded title, ie the title deeds recorded in the Register of Sasines or registered in the Land Register

The Antisocial Behaviour etc (Scotland) Act 2004 provides that all landlords letting property in Scotland must register with the local authority in which the let property is situated. Exceptions apply to holiday lets, owner-occupied accommodation and agricultural holdings. The act applies to partnerships, trusts and companies as well as to individuals.

LEGAL AID

The Access to Justice Act 1999 has transformed what used to be known as the Legal Aid system. The Legal Aid Board has been replaced by the Legal Services Commission, which is responsible for the development and administration of two legal funding schemes in England and Wales, namely the Criminal Defence Service and the Community Legal Service. The Criminal Defence Service assists people who are under police investigation or facing criminal charges. The Community Legal Service is designed to increase access to legal information and advice by involving a much wider network of funders and providers in giving publicly funded legal services. In Scotland, provision of legal aid is governed by the Legal Aid (Scotland) Act 1986 and the Legal Profession and Legal Aid (Scotland) Act 2007 and administered by the Scottish Legal Aid Board.

LEGAL SERVICES COMMISSION
  4 Abbey Orchard Street, London SW1P 2BS T 020-7783 7000
  W www.legalservices.gov.uk

CIVIL LEGAL AID

From 1 January 2000, only organisations (such as solicitors or Citizens Advice) with a contract with the Legal Services Commission have been able to give initial help in any civil matter. Moreover, from that date decisions about funding were devolved from the Legal Services Commission to contracted organisations in relation to any level of publicly funded service in family and immigration cases. For other types of case, applications for public funding are made through a solicitor (or other contracted legal services providers) in much the same way as the former Legal Aid. On 1 April 2001 the so-called civil contracting scheme was extended to cover all levels of service for all types of cases.

Under the civil funding scheme there are broadly six levels of service available:
- legal help
- help at court
- family help – either family help (lower) or family help (higher)
- legal representation – either investigative help or full representation
- family mediation
- such other services as authorised by specific orders

ELIGIBILITY

Eligibility for funding from the Community Legal Service depends broadly on five factors:
- the level of service sought (see above)
- whether the applicant qualifies financially
- the merits of the applicant's case
- a costs-benefits analysis (if the costs are likely to outweigh any benefit that might be gained from the proceedings, funding may be refused)
- whether there is any public interest in the case being litigated (ie whether the case has a wider public interest beyond that of the parties involved, eg a human rights case)

The limits on capital and income above which a person is not entitled to public funding vary with the type of service sought.

CONTRIBUTIONS

Some of those who qualify for Community Legal Service funding will have to contribute towards their legal costs. Contributions must be paid by anyone who has a disposable income or disposable capital exceeding a prescribed amount. The rules relating to applicable contributions are complex and detailed information can be obtained from the Legal Services Commission.

STATUTORY CHARGE

A statutory charge is made if a person keeps or gains money or property in a case for which they have received legal aid. This means that the amount paid by the Community Legal Service fund on their behalf is deducted from the amount that the person receives. This does not apply if the court has ordered that the costs be paid by the other party (unless the amount paid by the other party does not cover all of the costs). In certain circumstances, the Legal Services Commission may waive or postpone payment.

CONTINGENCY OR CONDITIONAL FEES

This system was introduced by the Courts and Legal Services Act 1990. It can offer legal representation on a 'no win, no fee' basis. It provides an alternative form of assistance, especially for those cases which are ineligible for funding by the Community Legal Service. The main area for such work is in the field of personal injuries.

Not all solicitors offer such a scheme and different solicitors may well have different terms. The effect of the agreement is that solicitors may not make any charges, or may waive some of their charges, until the case is concluded successfully. If a case is won then the losing party will usually have to pay towards costs, with the winning party contributing around one third.

SCOTLAND

Civil legal aid is available for cases in the following:
- the sheriff courts
- the court of session
- the House of Lords
- the lands valuation appeal court
- the Scottish land court
- the Lands Tribunal for Scotland
- the Employment Appeal Tribunals
- the Judicial Committee of the Privy Council
- the Proscribed Organisations Appeal Commissioner
- proceedings before the Social Security Commissioners
- proceedings before the Child Support Commissioners

Civil legal aid is not available for defamation actions, small claims or simplified divorce procedures or petitions by a debtor for his own sequestration.

Eligibility for civil legal aid is assessed in a similar way to that in England and Wales, though the financial limits differ in some respects. A person shall be eligible for civil legal aid if their disposable income does not exceed £26,239 a year. A person may be refused civil aid if their disposable capital exceeds £13,017 and it appears to the Legal Aid board that they can afford to pay without legal aid. Additionally:
- if disposable income is between £3,521 and £11,540, a contribution of one third of the difference between £3,521 and the disposable income may be payable
- if disposable income is between £11,541 and £15,743, one third of the difference between £3,521 and £11,540 plus half the difference between £11,541 and the disposable income may be payable
- if disposable income is between £15,743 and £26,239, a contribution of the following: one third of the difference between £3,521 and £11,540, plus half the difference between £11,541 and £15,743, plus all the remaining disposable income between £15,744 and £26,239 – will be payable

CRIMINAL LEGAL AID

The Legal Services Commission provides defendants facing criminal charges with free legal representation if they pass a merits test and a means test.

Criminal legal aid covers the cost of preparing a case and legal representation in criminal proceedings. It is also available for appeals against verdicts or sentences in magistrates' courts, the crown court or the court of appeal. It is not available for bringing a private prosecution in a criminal court.

If granted criminal legal aid, either the person may choose their own solicitor or the court will assign one. Contributions to the legal costs may be required. The rules relating to applicable contributions are complex and detailed information can be obtained from the Legal Services Commission.

DUTY SOLICITORS

The Legal Aid Act 1988 also provides free advice and assistance to anyone questioned by the police (whether under arrest or helping the police with their enquiries). No means test or contributions are required for this.

SCOTLAND

Legal advice and assistance operates in a similar way in Scotland. A person is eligible:
- if disposable income does not exceed £245 a week. If disposable income is between £105 and £245 a week, contributions are payable
- if disposable capital does not exceed £1,716 (if the person has dependent relatives, the savings allowance is higher)
- if receiving income support or income-related job seeker's allowance they qualify automatically provided they have no savings over the limit

The procedure for application for criminal legal aid depends on the circumstances of each case. In solemn cases (more serious cases, such as murder) heard before a jury, a person is automatically entitled to criminal legal aid until they are given bail or placed in custody. Thereafter, it is for the court to decide whether to grant legal aid. The court will do this if the person accused cannot meet the expenses of the case without undue hardship on him or his dependants. In less serious cases the procedure depends on whether the person is in custody:
- anyone taken into custody has the right to free legal aid from the duty solicitor up to and including the first court appearance
- if the person is not in custody and wishes to plead guilty, they are not entitled to criminal legal aid but may be entitled to legal advice and assistance, including assistance by way of representation
- if the person is not in custody and wishes to plead not guilty, they can apply for criminal legal aid. This must be done within 14 days of the first court appearance at which they made the plea

The criteria used to assess whether or not criminal legal aid should be granted is similar to the criteria for England and Wales. When meeting with your solicitor, take evidence of your financial position such as details of savings, bank statements, pay slips, pension book or benefits book.

THE SCOTTISH LEGAL AID BOARD
44 Drumsheugh Gardens, Edinburgh EH3 7SW
T 0131-226 7061 W www.slab.org.uk

MARRIAGE

Any two persons may marry provided that:
- they are at least 16 years old on the day of the marriage (in England and Wales persons under the age of 18 must generally obtain the consent of their parents or guardian; if consent is refused an appeal may be made

to the high court, the county court or a court of summary jurisdiction)

- they are not related to one another in a way which would prevent their marrying
- they are unmarried (a person who has already been married must produce documentary evidence that the previous marriage has been ended by death, divorce or annulment)
- they are not of the same sex (though same sex couples can register a civil partnership instead)
- they are capable of understanding the nature of a marriage ceremony and of consenting to marriage

The parties should check the marriage will be recognised as valid in their home country if either is not a British citizen.

DEGREES OF RELATIONSHIP

A marriage between persons within the prohibited degrees of consanguinity, affinity or adoption is void.

A man may not marry his mother, daughter, grandmother, granddaughter, sister, aunt, niece, adoptive mother, former adoptive mother, adopted daughter or former adopted daughter.

A woman may not marry her father, son, grandfather, grandson, brother, uncle, nephew, adoptive father, former adoptive father, adopted son or former adopted son. Under the Marriage (Prohibited Degrees of Relationship) Act 1986, some exceptions to the law permit a man or a woman to marry certain step-relatives or in-laws.

In addition to the above, a person may not marry a child of their former civil partner, a child of a former spouse, the former civil partner of a grandparent, the former civil partner of a parent, the former spouse of a grandparent, the former spouse of a parent, the grandchild of a former civil partner or the grandchild of a former spouse, unless the only reason they cannot marry is the affinity mentioned above and both persons are over 21 and the younger party has not at any time before attaining the age of 18 been a child of the family in relation to the other party. All references to brothers/sisters include half-brothers/sisters.

ENGLAND AND WALES

TYPES OF MARRIAGE CEREMONY

It is possible to marry by either religious or civil ceremony. A religious ceremony can take place at a church or chapel of the Church of England or the Church in Wales, or at any other place of worship which has been formally registered by the Registrar-General.

A civil ceremony can take place at a register office, a registered building or any other premises approved by the local authority.

An application for an approved premises licence must be made by the owners or trustees of the building concerned; it cannot be made by the prospective marriage couple. Approved premises must be regularly open to the public so that the marriage can be witnessed; the venue must be deemed to be a permanent and immovable structure. Open-air ceremonies are prohibited.

Non-Anglican marriages may also be solemnised following the issue of a Registrar-General's licence in unregistered premises where one of the parties is seriously ill, is not expected to recover, and cannot be moved to registered premises. Detained and housebound persons may be married at their place of residence.

MARRIAGE IN THE CHURCH OF ENGLAND OR THE CHURCH IN WALES

Marriage by banns

The marriage can take place in a parish in which one of the parties lives, or in a church in another parish if it is the usual place of worship of either or both of the parties. New regulations introduced in October 2008 also allow marriages to take place in a parish where one of the parties was baptised or prepared for confirmation (but not if combined rite); a parish where one of the parties lived or attended worship for six months or more; a parish where one of the parents of either of the parties lived for six months or more; a parish where one of the parents of either of the parties has attended public worship for six months or more in the child's lifetime; or a parish where the parents or grandparents of either of the parties were married. The banns (ie the announcement of the marriage ceremony) must be called in the parish in which the marriage is to take place on three Sundays before the day of the ceremony; if either or both of the parties lives in a different parish the banns must also be called there. After three months the banns are no longer valid. The minister will not perform the marriage unless satisfied that the banns have been properly called.

Marriage by common licence

The vicar who is to conduct the marriage will arrange for a common licence to be issued by the diocesan bishop; this dispenses with the necessity for banns. One of the parties must have lived in the parish for 15 days immediately before the issuing of the licence or must usually worship at the church. Eligibility requirements vary from diocese to diocese, but it is not normally required that the parties should have been baptised. The licence is valid for three months.

Marriage by special licence

A special licence is granted by the Archbishop of Canterbury in special circumstances for the marriage to take place at any place, with or without previous residence in the parish, or at any time. It is usually required that at least one of the parties has been baptised. The special licence will expire after three months. Application must be made to the registrar of the Faculty Office: 1 The Sanctuary, London SW1P 3JT T 020-7222 5381.

Marriage by certificate

The marriage can be conducted on the authority of the superintendent registrar's certificate, provided that the vicar's consent is obtained (the vicar is not obliged to accept the certificate). One of the parties must live in the parish or must usually worship at the church.

MARRIAGE BY OTHER RELIGIOUS CEREMONY

One of the parties must normally live in the registration district where the marriage is to take place. If the building where the parties wish to be married has not been registered, the couple can still have a religious ceremony there, but will also need to have a separate civil ceremony for the marriage to be valid. If the building is registered, in addition to giving notice to the superintendent registrar it may also be necessary to book a registrar, or authorised person to be present at the ceremony.

CIVIL MARRIAGE

A marriage may be solemnised at any register office, registered building or approved premises in England and Wales, without either of the parties being resident in the same district. The superintendent registrar of the district should be contacted, and, if the marriage is to take place at approved premises, the necessary arrangements at the venue must also be made.

NOTICE OF MARRIAGE

Unless it is to take place by banns or under common or special licence in the Church of England or the Church in Wales, a notice of the marriage must be given in person to the superintendent registrar. Notice of marriage may be given in the following ways:

- by certificate. Both parties must have lived in a registration district in England or Wales for at least seven days immediately before giving notice personally at the local register office. If they live in different registration districts, notice must be given in both districts by the respective party in person. The marriage can take place in any register office or other approved premises in England and Wales no sooner than 16 days after notice has been given, when the superintendent registrar issues a certificate
- by licence. One of the parties must have lived in a registration district in England or Wales for at least 15 days before giving notice at the register office; the other party need only be a resident of, or be physically in, England and Wales on the day notice is given

A notice of marriage is valid for 12 months, unless it is for the marriage of a detained or housebound person, when it will usually only be accepted within three months of publication. Notice for marriages taking place within the Church of England or Church of Wales are also only valid for three months following publication. It should be possible to make an advance (provisional) booking 12 months before the ceremony. In this case it is still necessary to give formal notice three months before the marriage. When giving notice of the marriage it is necessary to produce official proof, if relevant, that any previous marriage has ended in divorce or death by producing a decree absolute or death certificate; it is also necessary to provide proof of age, identity and nationality for each of the parties, for example, with a passport. If either party is under 18 years old, evidence of consent by their parent or guardian is required. There are special procedures for those wishing to get married in the UK that are subject to immigration control; the register office will be able to advise on these.

SOLEMNISATION OF THE MARRIAGE

On the day of the wedding there must be at least two other people present who are prepared to act as witnesses and sign the marriage register. A registrar of marriages must be present at a marriage in a register office or at approved premises, but an authorised person may act in the capacity of registrar in a registered building.

If the marriage takes place at approved premises, the room must be separate from any other activity on the premises at the time of the ceremony, and no food or drink can be sold or consumed in the room during the ceremony or for one hour beforehand.

The marriage must be solemnised between 8am and 6pm, with open doors. At some time during the ceremony the parties must make a declaration that they know of no legal impediment to the marriage and they must also say the contracting words; the declaratory and contracting words may vary according to the form of service. A civil marriage cannot contain any religious aspects, but it may be possible for non-religious music and/or readings to be included. It may also be possible to embellish the marriage vows taken by the couple.

CIVIL FEES

Notice and registration of Marriage at a Register Office

By superintendent registrar's certificate, £33.50 per person for the notice of the marriage (which is not refundable if the marriage does not in fact take place) and £40 for the registration of the marriage.

Marriage at a Register Office / Approved Premises

Fees for marriage at a register office are set by the local authority responsible. An additional fee will also be payable for the superintendent registrar's and registrar's attendance at the marriage on an approved premises. This is also set locally by the local authority responsible. A further charge is likely to be made by the owners of the building for the use of the premises. For marriages taking place in a religious building other than the Church of England or Church of Wales, an additional fee of £80 is payable for the registrar's attendance at the marriage unless an 'Authorised Person' appointed by the trustees of the building has agreed to register the marriage. Additional fees may be charged by the trustees of the building for the wedding and by the person who performs the ceremony.

ECCLESIASTICAL FEES

(Church of England and Church in Wales)

Marriage by banns

For publication of banns, £22*

For certificate of banns issued at time of publication, £12.00*

For marriage service, £262*

For marriage certificate at registration if required £3.50**

* These fees are revised from 1 January each calendar year. Some may not apply to the Church in Wales

** This fee is revised from 1 April each calendar year

SCOTLAND

REGULAR MARRIAGES

A regular marriage is one which is celebrated by a minister of religion or authorised registrar or other celebrant. Each of the parties must complete a marriage notice form and return it to the district registrar for the area in which they are to be married, irrespective of where they live, within the three month period prior to the date of the marriage and not later than 15 days prior to that date. The district registrar must then enter the date of receipt and certain details in a marriage book kept for this purpose, and must also enter the names of the parties and the proposed date of marriage in a list which is displayed in a conspicuous place at the registration office until the date of the marriage has passed. All persons wishing to enter into a regular marriage in Scotland must follow the same preliminary procedure regardless of whether they intend to have a religious or civil ceremony. Before the marriage ceremony takes place any person may submit an objection in writing to the district registrar.

A marriage schedule, which is prepared by the registrar, will be issued to one or both of the parties in person up to seven days before a religious marriage; for a civil marriage the schedule will be available at the ceremony. The schedule must be handed to the celebrant before the ceremony starts; it must be signed immediately after the wedding and the marriage must be registered within three days.

The authority to conduct a religious marriage is deemed to be vested in the authorised celebrant rather than the building in which it takes place; open-air religious ceremonies are therefore permissible in Scotland.

From 10 June 2002 it has been possible, under the Marriage (Scotland) Act 2002, for venues or couples to apply to the local council for a licence to allow a civil ceremony to take place at a venue other than a registration office. To obtain further information, a venue or couple should contact the district registrar in the area they wish to marry. A list of licensed venues is also available on the National Records of Scotland website.

MARRIAGE BY COHABITATION WITH HABIT AND REPUTE

Prior to the enactment of the 2006 act, if two people had lived together constantly as husband and wife and were generally held to be such by the neighbourhood and among their friends and relations, a presumption could arise from which marriage could be inferred. Before such a marriage could be registered, however, a decree of declarator of marriage had to be obtained from the court of session. Section 3 of the 2006 act provides that it will no longer be possible for a marriage to be constituted by cohabitation with habit and repute, but it will still be possible for couples whose period of cohabitation began before commencement of the 2006 act to seek a declarator under the old rule of law.

CIVIL FEES

The fee for submitting a notice of marriage to the district registrar is £30.00 a person. Solemnisation of a civil marriage costs £55.00, while the extract of the entry in the register of marriages attracts a fee of £10.00. The costs of religious marriage ceremonies can vary.

THE GENERAL REGISTER OFFICE
PO Box 2, Southport PR8 2JD **T** 0845-603 7788
W www.gro.gov.uk/gro/content/certificates
THE NATIONAL RECORDS OF SCOTLAND
New Register House, 3 West Register Street, Edinburgh
EH1 3YT **T** 0131-314 4452 **W** www.gro-scotland.gov.uk

TOWN AND COUNTRY PLANNING

The planning system can help to protect the environment and assist individuals in assessing their land rights. There are a number of acts governing the development of land and buildings in England and Wales and advice should always be sought from Citizens Advice or the local planning authority before undertaking building works on any land or property. If development takes place which requires planning permission without permission being given, enforcement action may take place and the situation may need to be rectified. Planning law in Scotland is similar but certain Scotland-specific legislation applies so advice should always be sought.

PLANNING PERMISSION

Planning permission is needed if the work involves:
• making a material change in use, such as dividing off part of the house or garden so that it can be used as a separate home or dividing off part of the house for commercial use, eg for a workshop
• going against the terms of the original planning permission, eg there may be a restriction on fences in front gardens on an open-plan estate
• building, engineering or mining, except for the permitted developments below
• new or wider access to a main road

• additions or extensions to flats or maisonettes
• work which might obstruct the view of road users

Planning permission is not needed to carry out internal alterations or work which does not affect the external appearance of the building, and are not works for making good war damage or works begun after 5 December 1968 for the alteration of a building by providing additional space in it underground.

Under regulations which came into effect on 1 October 2008, there are certain types of development for which the Secretary of State for the Environment, Food and Rural Affairs has granted general permissions (permitted development rights). These include house extensions and additions, outbuildings and garages, other ancillary garden buildings such as swimming pools or ponds, and laying patios, paths or driveways for domestic use. All developments are subject to a number of conditions.

Before carrying out any of the above permitted developments you should contact your local planning authority to find out whether the general permission has been modified in your area. For more information, visit **W** www.planningportal.gov.uk

OTHER RESTRICTIONS

It may be necessary to obtain other types of permissions before carrying out any development. These permissions are separate from planning permission and apply regardless of whether or not planning permission is needed, eg:
• building regulations will probably apply if a new building is to be erected, if an existing one is to be altered or extended, or if the work involves building over a drain or sewer. The building control department of the local authority will advise on this
• any alterations to a listed building or the grounds of a listed building must be approved by the local authority. Listing will include not only the main building but everything in the curtilage of the building
• local authority approval is necessary if a building (or, in some circumstances, gates, walls, fences or railings) in a conservation area is to be demolished; each local authority keeps a register of all local buildings that are in conservation areas
• a council order is required if your proposed development would obstruct a public path which crosses your property, and you should discuss any such proposals with the council at an early stage
• many trees are protected by tree preservation orders and must not be pruned or taken down without local authority consent
• bats and many other species are protected, and Natural England, the Countryside Council for Wales or Scottish Natural Heritage must be notified before any work is carried out that will affect the habitat of protected species, eg timber treatment, renovation or extensions of lofts
• developments in areas with special designations, such as National Parks, Areas of Outstanding Natural Beauty, National Scenic Areas or in the Norfolk or Suffolk Broads, are subject to greater restrictions. The local planning authority will advise or refer enquirers to the relevant authority

There may also be restrictions contained in the title to the property which require you to get someone else's agreement before carrying out certain developments, and which should be considered when works are planned.

VOTERS' QUALIFICATIONS

Those entitled to vote at parliamentary, and local government elections are those who, at the date of taking the poll, are:
- on the electoral roll
- aged 18 years or older
- British citizens, Commonwealth citizens or citizens of the Irish Republic who are resident in the UK
- those who suffer from no other legal bar to voting (eg prisoners). It should be noted that following a decision taken by the European Court of Human Rights, prisoners' voting rights are currently under review by the government
- in Northern Ireland electors must have been resident in Northern Ireland during the whole of the three-month period prior to the relevant date
- citizens of any EU member state may vote in local elections if they meet the criteria listed above (save for the nationality requirements)

British citizens resident abroad are entitled to vote for 15 years after leaving Britain, as overseas electors in domestic parliamentary elections in the constituency in which they were last resident if they are on the electoral roll of the relevant constituency. Members of the armed forces, Crown servants and employees of the British Council who are overseas and their spouses are entitled to vote regardless of how long they have been abroad. British citizens who had never been registered as an elector in the UK are not eligible to register as an overseas voter unless they left the UK before they were 18, providing they left the country no more than 15 years ago. Overseas electors may opt to vote by proxy or by postal vote. Overseas voters may not vote in local government elections.

The main categories of people who are not entitled to vote at general elections are:
- sitting peers in the House of Lords
- convicted persons detained in pursuance of their sentences (though remand prisoners, unconvicted prisoners and civil prisoners can vote if on the electoral register). This is currently subject to review, as detailed above
- those convicted within the previous five years of corrupt or illegal election practices
- EU citizens (who may only vote in EU and local government elections)

Under the Representation of the Peoples Act 2000, several new groups of people are permitted to vote for the first time. These include: people who live on barges; people in mental health hospitals (other than those with criminal convictions) and homeless people who have made a 'declaration of local connection'.

REGISTERING TO VOTE

Voters must be entered on an electoral register. The Electoral Registration Officer (ERO) for each council area is responsible for preparing and publishing the register for his area by 1 December each year. Names may be added to the register to reflect changes in people's circumstances as they occur and each month during December to August, the ERO publishes a list of alterations to the published register.

A registration form is sent to all households in the autumn of each year and the householder is required to provide details of all occupants who are eligible to vote, including ones who will reach their 18th birthday in the year covered by the register. Anyone failing to supply information to the ERO when requested, or supplying false information, may be fined by up to £1,000. Application forms and more information are available from the Electoral Commission (W www.aboutmyvote.co.uk).

VOTING

Voting is not compulsory in the UK. Those who wish to vote do so in person at the allotted polling station. Postal votes are now available to anyone on request and you do not need to give a reason for using a postal vote.

A proxy (whereby the voter nominates someone to vote in person on their behalf) can be appointed to act in a specific election, for a specified period of time or indefinitely. For the appointment of an indefinite or long-term proxy, the voter needs to specify physical employment or study reasons as to why they are making an application. With proxy votes where a particular election is specified, the voter needs to provide details of the circumstances by which they cannot reasonably be expected to go to the polling station.

Further information can be obtained from the local authority's ERO in England and Wales or the electoral registration office in Scotland, or the Chief Electoral Officer in Northern Ireland.

WILLS

A will is used to appoint executors (who will administer the estate), give directions as to the disposal of the body, appoint guardians for children, and determine how and to whom property is to be passed. A well-drafted will can operate to reduce the level of inheritance tax which the estate pays. It is best to have a will drawn up by a solicitor, but if a solicitor is not employed the following points must be taken into account:
- if possible the will must not be prepared on behalf of another person by someone who is to benefit from it or who is a close relative of a major beneficiary
- the language used must be clear and unambiguous and it is better to avoid the use of legal terms where the same thing can be expressed in plain language
- it is better to rewrite the whole document if a mistake is made. If necessary, alterations can be made by striking through the words with a pen, and the signature or initials of the testator and the witnesses must be put in the margin opposite the alteration. No alteration of any kind should be made after the will has been executed
- if the person later wishes to change the will or part of it, it is better to write a new will revoking the old. The use of codicils (documents written as supplements or containing modifications to the will) should be left to a solicitor
- the will should be typed or printed, or if handwritten be legible and preferably in ink

The form of a will varies to suit different cases – a solicitor will be able to advise as to wording, however, 'DIY' will-writing kits can be purchased from good stationery shops and many banks offer a will-writing service.

LAPSED LEGATEES

If a person who has been left property in a will dies before the person who made the will, the gift fails and will pass to the person entitled to everything not otherwise disposed of (the residuary estate).

If the person left the residuary estate dies before the person who made the will, their share will pass to the closest relative(s) of the testator under the intestacy rules.

It is always better to draw up a new will if a beneficiary predeceases the person who made the will.

EXECUTORS

It is usual to appoint two executors, although one is sufficient. No more than four persons can deal with the estate of the person who has died. The name and address of each executor should be given in full (the addresses are not essential but including them adds clarity to the document). Executors should be 18 years of age or over. An executor may be a beneficiary of the will.

WITNESSES

A person who is a beneficiary of a will, or the spouse or civil partner of a beneficiary at the time the will is signed, must not act as a witness or else he/she will be unable to take his/her gift except in some limited circumstances. Husband and wife can both act as witnesses provided neither benefits from the will.

It is better that a person does not act as an executor and as a witness, as he/she can take no benefit under a will to which he/she is witness. The identity of the witnesses should be made as explicit as possible.

EXECUTION OF A WILL

The person making the will should sign his/her name in the presence of the two witnesses. It is advisable to sign at the foot of the document, so as to avoid uncertainty about the testator's intention. The witnesses must then sign their names while the person making the will looks on. If this procedure is not adhered to, the will may be considered invalid. There are certain exceptional circumstances where these rules are relaxed, eg where the person may be too ill to sign.

CAPACITY TO MAKE A WILL

Anyone aged 18 or over can make a will. However, if there is any suspicion that the person making the will is not, through reasons of infirmity or age, fully in command of his/her faculties, it is advisable to arrange for a medical practitioner to examine the person making the will at the time it is to be executed (to verify his/her mental capacity and to record that medical opinion in writing), and to ask the examining practitioner to act as a witness. If a person is not mentally able to make a will, the court may do this for him/her by virtue of the Mental Health Act 2005.

REVOCATION

A will may be revoked or cancelled in a number of ways:
- a later will revokes an earlier one if it says so; otherwise the earlier will is by implication revoked by the later one to the extent that it contradicts or repeats the earlier one
- a will is revoked if the physical document on which it is written is destroyed by the person whose will it is. There must be an intention to revoke the will and an act of destruction. It may not be sufficient to obliterate the will with a pen
- a will is revoked by the testator making a written declaration to this effect executed in the same way as a will
- a will is also revoked when the person marries or forms a civil partnership, unless it is clear from the will that the person intended the will to stand after that particular marriage or civil partnership
- where a marriage or civil partnership ends in divorce or dissolution or is annulled or declared void, gifts to the spouse or civil partner and the appointment of the

spouse or civil partner as executor fail unless the will says that this is not to happen. A former spouse or civil partner is treated as having predeceased the testator. A separation does not change the effect of a married person's will.

PROBATE AND LETTERS OF ADMINISTRATION

Probate is granted to the executors named in a will and once granted, the executors are obliged to carry out the instructions of the will. Letters of administration are granted where no executor is named in a will or is willing or able to act or where there is no will or no valid will; this gives a person, often the next of kin, similar powers and duties to those of an executor.

Applications for probate or for letters of administration can be made to the Principal Registry of the Family Division, to a district probate registry or to a probate sub-registry. Applicants will need the following documents: the Probate Application Form; the original will and codicils (if any); a certificate of death; oath for executors or administrators; and the appropriate tax form (an 'IHT 205' if no inheritance tax is owed; otherwise an 'IHT 400' and 'IHT 421'), in addition to a cheque for the relevant probate fee. Certain property, up to the value of £5,000, may be disposed of without a grant of probate or letters of administration, as can assets that do not pass under the will such as jointly owned assets which pass automatically on the death of one of the joint holders to the survivor.

WHERE TO FIND A PROVED WILL

Since 1858 wills which have been proved, that is wills on which probate or letters of administration have been granted, must have been proved at the Principal Registry of the Family Division or at a district probate registry. The Lord Chancellor has power to direct where the original documents are kept but most are filed where they were proved and may be inspected there and a copy obtained. The Principal Registry also holds copies of all wills proved at district probate registries and these may be inspected at First Avenue House, High Holborn, London. An index of all grants, both of probate and of letters of administration, is compiled by the Principal Registry and may be seen either at the Principal Registry or at a district probate registry.

It is also possible to discover when a grant of probate or letters of administration is issued by requesting a standing search. In response to a request and for a small fee, a district probate registry will supply the names and addresses of executors or administrators and the registry in which the grant was made, of any grant in the estate of a specified person made in the previous 12 months or following six months. This is useful for creditors of the deceased and for applicants who may be beneficiaries to a will but who have lost contact with the deceased.

INTESTACY

Intestacy occurs when someone dies without leaving a will or leaves a will which is invalid or which does not take effect for some reason. Intestacy can be partial, for instance, if there is a will which disposes of some but not all of the testator's property. In such cases the person's estate (property, possessions, other assets following the payment of debts) passes to certain members of the family. If a will has been written that disposes of only part of a person's property, these rules apply to the part which is undisposed of.

INTELLECTUAL PROPERTY

Intellectual property is a broad term covering a number of legal rights provided by the government to help people protect their creative works and encourage further innovation. By using these legal rights people can own the things they create and control the way in which others use their innovations. Intellectual property owners can take legal action to stop others using their intellectual property, they can license their intellectual property to others or they can sell it on. Different types of intellectual property utilise different forms of protection including copyright, designs, patents and trade marks, which are all covered below in more detail.

COPYRIGHT

Copyright protects all original literary, dramatic, musical and artistic works, as well as sound and film recordings and broadcasts. Among the works covered by copyright are novels, computer programs, newspaper articles, sculptures, technical drawings, websites, maps and photographs. Under copyright the creators of these works can control the various ways in which their material may be exploited, the rights broadly covering copying, adapting, issuing (including renting and lending) copies to the public, performing in public, and broadcasting the material. The transfer of copyright works to formats accessible to visually impaired persons without infringement of copyright was enacted in 2002.

Copyright protection in the United Kingdom is automatic and there is no official registration system. The creator of a work can help to protect it by including the copyright symbol (©), the name of the copyright owner, and the year in which the work was created. In addition, steps can be taken by the work's creator to provide evidence that he/she had the work at a particular time (eg by depositing a copy with a bank or solicitor). The main legislation is the Copyright, Designs and Patents Act 1988 (as amended). As a result of an EU directive effective from January 1996, the term of copyright protection for literary, dramatic, musical (including song lyrics and musical compositions) and artistic works lasts for 70 years after the death of the creator. For film, copyright lasts for 70 years after the director, authors of the screenplay and dialogue, or the composer of any music specially created for the film have all died. Sound recordings are protected for 50 years after their publication (or their first performance if they are not published), and broadcasts for 50 years from the end of the year in which the broadcast/transmission was made. The typographical arrangement of published editions remains under copyright protection for 25 years from the end of the year in which the particular edition was published.

The main international treaties protecting copyright are the Berne Convention for the Protection of Literary and Artistic Works (administered by the World Intellectual Property Organisation (WIPO)), the Rome Convention for the Protection of Performers, Producers of Phonograms and Broadcasting Organisations (administered by UNESCO, the International Labour Organisation and WIPO), the Geneva Phonograms Convention (administered by WIPO), and the Universal Copyright Convention (developed by UNESCO); the UK is a signatory to these conventions. Copyright material created by UK nationals or residents is protected in the countries that have signed one of the above-named conventions by the national law of that country. A list of participating countries may be obtained from the UK Intellectual Property Office. The World Trade Organisation's Trade-Related Aspects of Intellectual Property Rights (TRIPS) agreement, signed in 1995, may also provide copyright protection abroad.

Two treaties which strengthen and update international standards of protection, particularly in relation to new technologies, were agreed in December 1996: the WIPO copyright treaty, and the WIPO performances and phonograms treaty. In May 2001 the European Union passed a new directive (which in 2003 became law in the UK) aimed at harmonising copyright law throughout the EU to take account of the internet and other technologies. More information can be found online (W www.ipo.gov.uk).

The government commissioned a major independent review of intellectual property laws in November 2010 to tackle the concern that the current framework does not adequately promote growth and innovation in the UK economy. The review was published in May 2011.

LICENSING

Use of copyright material without seeking permission in each instance may be permitted under 'blanket' licences available from national copyright licensing agencies. The International Federation of Reproduction Rights Organisations facilitates agreements between its member licensing agencies and on behalf of its members with organisations such as WIPO, UNESCO, the European Union and the Council of Europe. More information can be found online (W www.ifrro.org).

DESIGN PROTECTION

Design protection covers the outward appearance of an article and in the UK takes two forms: registered design and design right, which are not mutually exclusive. Registered design protects the aesthetic appearance of an article, including shape, configuration, pattern or ornament, although artistic works such as sculptures are excluded, being generally protected by copyright. To achieve design protection the owner of the design must apply to the Intellectual Property Office. In order to qualify for protection, a design must be new and materially different from earlier UK published designs. Initial registration lasts for five years and can be extended in five-year increments to a maximum of 25 years. The current legislation is the Registered Designs Act 1949 which has been amended several times, most recently by the Regulatory Reform Order 2006.

UK applicants wishing to protect their designs in the EU can do so by applying for a Registered Community Design with the Office for Harmonisation in the Internal Market. Outside the EU separate applications must be made in each country in which protection is sought.

Design right is an automatic right which applies to the shape or configuration of articles and does not require registration. Unlike registered design, two-dimensional designs do not qualify for protection but designs of electronic circuits are protected by design right. Designs must be original and non-commonplace. The term of design right is ten years from first marketing of the design, or 15 years after the creation of the design, whichever is earlier. This right is effective only in the UK. After five years anyone is entitled to apply for a licence of right, which allows others to make and sell products copying the design. The current legislation is Part 3 of the Copyright, Designs and Patents Act 1988, amended on 9 December 2001 to incorporate the European designs directive, and again in 2006.

PATENTS

A patent is a document issued by the UK Intellectual Property Office relating to an invention. It gives the proprietor the right for a limited period to stop others from making, using, importing or selling the invention without the inventor's permission. In return the patentee pays a fee to cover the costs of processing the patent and publicly discloses details of the invention.

To qualify for a patent an invention must be new, must be functional or technical, must exhibit an inventive step, and must be capable of industrial application. The patent is valid for a maximum of 20 years from the date on which the application was filed, subject to payment of annual fees from the end of the fifth year.

The UK Intellectual Property Office, established in 1852, is responsible for ensuring that all stages of an application comply with the Patents Act 1977, and that the invention meets the criteria for a patent.

WIPO is responsible for administering many of the international conventions on intellectual property. The Patent Cooperation Treaty allows inventors to file a single application for patent rights in some or all of the contracting states. This application is searched by an International Searching Authority to confirm the invention is novel and that the same concept has not already been made publicly available. The application and search report are then published by the International Bureau of WIPO. It may also be the subject of an (optional) international preliminary examination. Applicants must then deal directly with the patent offices in the countries where they are seeking patent rights. The European Patent Convention allows inventors to obtain patent rights in all the contracting states by filing a single application with the European Patent Office. More information can be found online (W www.ipo.gov.uk).

RESEARCH DISCLOSURES

Research disclosures are publicly disclosed details of inventions. Once published, an invention is considered no longer novel and becomes 'prior art'. Publishing a disclosure is significantly cheaper than applying for a patent; however, unlike a patent, it does not entitle the author to exclusive rights to use or license the invention. Instead, research disclosures are primarily published to ensure the inventor the freedom to use the invention. This works because publishing legally prevents other parties from patenting the disclosed innovation and in the UK, patent law dictates that by disclosing details of an invention, even the inventor relinquishes their right to a patent.

In theory, publishing details of an invention anywhere should be enough to constitute a research disclosure. However, to be effective, a research disclosure needs to be published in a location which patent examiners will include in their prior art searches. To ensure global legal precedent it must be included in a publication with a recognised date stamp and made publicly available throughout the world.

The *Research Disclosure* journal, established in 1960 and published by KMP Ltd, is the primary publisher of research disclosures. It is the only disclosure service recognised by the Patent Cooperation Treaty as a mandatory search resource which must be consulted by the international search authorities. More information can be found online (W www.researchdisclosure.com).

TRADE MARKS

Trade marks are a means of identification, which enable traders to make their goods and services readily distinguishable from those supplied by others. Trade marks can take the form of words, a logo or a combination of both. Registration prevents other traders using the same or similar trade marks for similar products or services for which the mark is registered.

In the UK trade marks are registered at the UK Intellectual Property Office. In order to qualify for registration a trade mark must be capable of distinguishing its proprietor's goods or services from those of other undertakings; it should be non-deceptive, should not describe the goods and services or any characteristics of them, should not be contrary to law or morality and should not be similar or identical to any earlier trade marks for the same or similar goods or services. The owner of a registered trade mark may include an ® symbol next to it, and must renew their registration every ten years to keep it in force. The relevant current legislation is the Trade Marks Act 1994 (as amended).

It is possible to obtain an international trade mark registration, effective in 81 countries, under the Madrid system for the international registration of marks, to which the UK is party. British companies can obtain international trade mark registration in those countries party to the system through a single application to WIPO.

EU trade mark regulation is administered by the Office for Harmonisation in the Internal Market (Trade Marks and Designs) in Alicante, Spain. The office registers Community trade marks, which are valid throughout the European Union. The registration of trade marks in individual member states continues in parallel with EU trade mark standards.

DOMAIN NAMES

An internet domain name (eg www.whitakersalmanack.com) has to be registered separately from a trade mark, and this can be done through a number of registrars which charge varying rates and compete for business. For each top-level domain name (eg .uk, .com), there is a central registry to store the unique internet names and addresses using that suffix. A list of accredited registrars can be found online (W www.icann.org).

CONTACTS

COPYRIGHT LICENSING AGENCY LTD,
  Saffron House, 6–10 Kirby Street, London EC1N 8TS
  T 020-7400 3100 W www.cla.co.uk
EUROPEAN PATENT OFFICE, 80298 Munich, Germany
  T (+49) 89 2399-0 W www.epo.org
THE UK INTELLECTUAL PROPERTY OFFICE,
  Concept House, Cardiff Road, Newport NP10 8QQ
  T 0300-300 2000 W www.ipo.gov.uk
WORLD INTELLECTUAL PROPERTY
  ORGANISATION, 34 chemin des Colombettes,
  CH-1211 Geneva 20, Switzerland T (+41) 22 338 9111
  W www.wipo.int

THE MEDIA

CROSS-MEDIA OWNERSHIP

The rules surrounding cross-media ownership were overhauled as part of the 2003 Communications Act. The act simplified and relaxed existing rules to encourage dispersion of ownership and new market entry while preventing the most influential media in any community being controlled by too narrow a range of interests. However, transfers and mergers are not solely subject to examination on competition grounds by the competition authorities. The Secretary of State for Culture, Olympics, Media and Sport has a broad remit to decide if a transaction is permissible and can intervene on public interest grounds (relating both to newspapers and cross-media criteria, if broadcasting interests are also involved). The Office of Communications (OFCOM) has an advisory role in this context. Government and parliamentary assurances were given that any intervention into local newspaper transfers would be rare and exceptional. Following a request from the Secretary of State for Culture, Olympics, Media and Sport in June 2010 for a removal of all restrictions from the ownership of local media, OFCOM recommended the liberalisation of local cross-media regulations to enable a single owner to control newspapers, a TV licence and radio stations in one area.

REGULATION

OFCOM is the regulator for the communication industries in the UK and has responsibility for television, radio, telecommunications and wireless communications services. It replaced the Broadcasting Standards Commission, the Independent Television Commission, the Radio Authority, the Radio Communications Agency and OFTEL. OFCOM is required to report annually to parliament and exists to further the interests of consumers by balancing choice and competition with the duty to foster plurality; protect viewers and listeners and promote cultural diversity in the media; and to ensure full and fair competition between communications providers.

OFFICE OF COMMUNICATIONS (OFCOM)
Riverside House, 2A Southwark Bridge Road, London SE1 9HA
T 020-7981 3000 W www.ofcom.org.uk
Chief Executive, Ed Richards

COMPLAINTS

Under the Communications Act 2003 OFCOM's licensees are obliged to adhere to the provisions of its codes (including advertising, programme standards, fairness, privacy and sponsorship). Complainants should contact the broadcaster in the first instance (details can be found on OFCOM's website); however, if the complainant wishes the complaint to be considered by OFCOM, it will do so. Complaints should be made within a reasonable time, as broadcasters are only required to keep recordings for the following periods: radio, 42 days; television, 90 days; and cable and satellite, 60 days. OFCOM can fine a broadcaster, revoke a licence or take programmes

off the air. Since November 2004 complaints relating to individual advertisements on TV or radio have been dealt with by the Advertising Standards Authority.

ADVERTISING STANDARDS AUTHORITY
Mid City Place, 71 High Holborn, London WC1V 6QT
T 020-7492 2222 W www.asa.org.uk
Chief Executive, Guy Parker

TELEVISION

There are six major television broadcasters operating in the UK. Four of these – the BBC, ITV, Channel 4 and Channel 5 – launched as free-to-air analogue terrestrial networks. BSkyB and Virgin Media Television provide satellite television services.

The BBC is the oldest broadcaster in the world. The corporation began a London-only television service from Alexandra Palace in 1936 and achieved nationwide coverage 15 years later. A second station, BBC Two, was launched in 1964. The BBC's digital services comprise BBC Three, BBC Four, BBC News, BBC Parliament and the children's channels, CBeebies and CBBC. The services are funded by the licence fee. The corporation also has a commercial arm, BBC Worldwide, which was formed in 1994 and exists to maximise the value of the BBC's programme and publishing assets for the benefit of the licence payer. Its businesses include international programming distribution, magazines, other licensed products, live events and media monitoring.

The ITV (Independent Television) network was set up on a regional basis in 1955 to provide competition for the BBC. ITV began broadcasting on Channel 3 in the London area, following the Television Act of 1954 which made commercial television possible. It comprised a number of independent licensees, the majority of which have now merged to form ITV plc. The network generates funds through broadcasting television advertisements. Its flagship analogue channel was renamed ITV1 in 2001 as part of a rebranding exercise to coincide with the creation of a number of digital-only channels. These now include ITV2, ITV3, ITV4 and CiTV. ITV Network Centre is wholly owned by the ITV companies and undertakes commissioning and scheduling of programmes shown across the ITV network and, as with the other terrestrial channels, 25 per cent of programmes must come from independent producers.

Channel 4 and S4C were launched in 1982 to provide programmes with a distinctive character that appeal to interests not catered for by ITV. Although publicly owned, Channel 4 receives no public funding and is financed by commercial activities, including advertising. It has expanded to create the digital stations E4, More4, Film4 and 4Music. S4C receives annual funding from the Department for Culture, Olympics, Media and Sport. In March 2010 the S4C analogue service was closed and its digital service, S4C Digidol, became the default S4C channel across Wales, broadcasting entirely in the Welsh language.

Channel 5 began broadcasting in 1997. It was rebranded Five in 2002 but reverted to its original name, Channel 5, after the station was acquired by Northern &

Shell in July 2010. Digital stations 5USA and 5* (formerly Five Life, then Fiver) were launched in October 2006.

BSkyB was formed after the merger in 1990 of Sky Television and British Sky Broadcasting. The company operates a satellite television service and has around 40 television channels, including Sky One and the Sky Sports and Sky Movies ranges. It is part-owned by Rupert Murdoch's News Corporation. Sky Digital was launched in 1998 and offers access to over 500 channels. With the 2005 acquisition of Easynet, an internet access provider and network operator, BSkyB now offers voice over IP (VoIP) telephony, video on demand and internet-based TV. With a special box, Sky+ allows viewers to pause and rewind live TV and record up to 40 hours of programming. In July 2010 BSkyB acquired Virgin Media Television, including its portfolio of channels such as Bravo, Challenge and Virgin1. It was subsequently rebranded as the Living TV Group.

VIEWING TRENDS, TERRESTRIAL TELEVISION
- National news and weather accounts for 22 per cent of viewing on BBC One
- Sport makes up 19 per cent of television watched on BBC Two
- 24 per cent of viewing on ITV1 is entertainment programmes
- 65 per cent of viewing on Channel 4 is factual and entertainment programming
- Drama accounts for 21 per cent of viewing on Channel 5

Source: OFCOM Public Service Broadcasting Annual Report 2011

THE TELEVISION LICENCE
In the UK and its dependencies, a television licence is required to receive any publicly broadcast television service, regardless of its source, including commercial, satellite and cable programming.

The TV licence is classified as a tax, therefore non-payment is a criminal offence. A fine of up to £1,000 can be imposed on those successfully prosecuted. The TV licence is issued on behalf of the BBC as the licensing authority under the Communications Act 2003. TV Licensing is the name of the agent contracted to collect the licence fee on behalf of the BBC. An additional 142,000 licence fees were collected in the year 2010–11 increasing the number of licences in force in the UK to over 25 million. In 2011 an annual colour television licence cost £145.50 and a black and white licence £49. Concessions are available for the elderly and people with disabilities. Further details can be found at W www.tvlicensing.co.uk/information

DIGITAL TELEVISION
Digital broadcasting has dramatically increased the number and reception quality of television channels. Sound and pictures are converted into a digital format and compressed, using as few bits as possible to convey the information on a digital signal. This technique enables several television channels to be carried in the space used by the current analogue signals to carry one channel. Digital signals can be received by standard aerials using Freeview (*see* below), satellite dishes or cable. The signals are decoded and turned back into sound and pictures by either a set-top box or a decoder built into the television set (iDTV). A basic package of channels is available without charge and services are also offered by cable and satellite companies.

The Broadcasting Act 1996 provided for the licensing of 20 or more digital terrestrial television channels (on six frequency channels or 'multiplexes'). The first digital services went on air in autumn 1998.

In June 2002, following the collapse of ITV Digital, the digital terrestrial television licence was awarded to a consortium made up of the BBC, BSkyB and transmitter company Crown Castle by the Independent Television Commission. Freeview was launched on 30 October 2002: it offers around 50 digital channels and requires the purchase of a set-top box, but is subsequently free of charge.

As at March 2011, 93 per cent of British homes had access to digital TV. The digital channels combined have a greater share of viewing than any of the five main channels and continue to increase this lead.

DIGITAL SWITCHOVER
The digital switchover involves the turning off of the analogue terrestrial transmissions network that has been in place since the 1930s and replacing it with an all-digital terrestrial network. Viewers who receive television through an aerial will need to upgrade their sets with a set-top box (typically costing between £20 and £100) or use integrated digital television (iDTV), cable or satellite digital services. A Switchover Help Scheme is available for those who have difficulty in making the switch to digital TV such as people aged 75 or over, those on disability living allowance and people registered blind. The switchover has started and is due to be completed in 2012. For more information, *see* W www.digitaluk.co.uk.

Region	Expected switchover date
Border, West Country, Granada	Complete
Wales, West, STV North	Complete
STV Central	Complete
Central, Yorkshire, Anglia	2011
London, Meridian, Tyne Tees, UTV	2012

Source: Digital UK

RECENT DEVELOPMENTS
The advent of digital television has coincided with the emergence of the internet as a viable alternative means of watching TV. Channel 4's 4oD (4 On Demand) service allows viewers to revisit and download programmes from the previous 28 days and access an archive of older footage using their PC. The BBC launched its iPlayer on Christmas Day 2007, enabling viewers to watch programmes broadcast in the previous seven days via the streaming option or download and store programmes for up to 30 days on their computer. An integrated service, launched in June 2008, allows viewers to access BBC

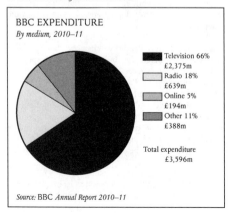

BBC EXPENDITURE
By medium, 2010–11

Television 66% £2,375m
Radio 18% £639m
Online 5% £194m
Other 11% £388m

Total expenditure £3,596m

Source: BBC *Annual Report 2010–11*

radio programmes in addition to televisual output. The iPlayer service also allows viewers to watch live TV using the On Now facility. In 2009 iPlayer was extended to more than 20 devices, including mobile phones, televisions and games consoles. A high definition (HD) service was launched in the same year. ITV has a similar service called ITV Player, and Channel 5's service is called Demand Five. Online streaming of TV has been a major success, especially with a younger demographic. BBC iPlayer averaged over 100 million programme requests each month for the year 2010–11 and more than 1.6 billion programmes were viewed during the year, boosted by the iPlayer app released on smartphones and tablets.

HD TV is the latest development in TV picture quality, providing more vibrant colours, greater detail and picture clarity in addition to improved sound quality. While a standard television picture is made up of 576 lines of 720 pixels, an HD television screen uses 1,280 by 720 pixels up to 1,920 by 1,080 pixels. Sky Digital, ITV and the BBC all provide HD channels, with a growing number becoming available. To access HD channels, viewers need an 'HD ready' TV set and HD TV decoder, available through satellite services or a cable connection. It is expected that four HD channels will become nationally available through Freeview by 2012. In April 2010 Samsung released the first consumer 3D TV; in the same month Sky launched the UK's first dedicated 3D channel. Several sporting events have been broadcast in 3D including the Wimbledon men's final in July 2011.

In June 2010 the BBC Trust gave permission for the BBC to participate in the development of Project Canvas, now known as YouView, a proposed standard for internet protocol television (IPTV) in partnership with ITV, BT, Channel 4, TalkTalk and Arqiva. Through the IPTV platform, viewers will be able to watch programmes (including on-demand), browse the internet and listen to digital radio via a special set-top box connected to a broadband connection. The subscription-free service is due to begin in 2012.

In February 2011, a new version of OFCOM's Broadcasting Code came into force, permitting product placement for the first time in UK-produced television programmes. A large 'P' logo designed by OFCOM and broadcasters is displayed at the beginning and end of each programme containing product placement. The first instance of product placement occurred on 28 February 2011.

CONTACTS

THE BRITISH BROADCASTING CORPORATION

BBC TV Centre, Wood Lane, London W12 7RJ
T 020-8743 8000 W www.bbc.co.uk

BBC North, Media City UK, Salford Quays, Manchester
M50 2BH T 0161-886 5300
W www.bbc.co.uk/aboutthebbc/bbcnorth
Chair, Lord Patten of Barnes

BBC Worldwide, 201 Wood Lane, London W12 7TQ
W www.bbcworldwide.com

INDEPENDENT TELEVISION NETWORK

ITV Network Centre, 200 Gray's Inn Road, London WC1X 8HF
T 020-7156 6000 W www.itv.com
Chair, Archie Norman

INDEPENDENT TELEVISION NETWORK REGIONS AND COMPANIES

Anglia (eastern England), Anglia House, Norwich NR1 3JG
   T 0844-881 6900 W www.itv.com/anglia
Border (Borders and the Isle of Man), Television House,
   The Watermark, Gateshead NE11 9SZ T 0844-881 51000
   W www.itv.com/border
Central (east, west and south Midlands), Gas Street,
   Birmingham B1 2JT T 0844-881 4121
   W www.itv.com/central
Channel (Channel Islands), The Television Centre, St Helier,
   Jersey JE1 3ZD T 01534-816816 W www.channelonline.tv
Granada (north-west England), Quay Street, Manchester
   M60 9EA T 0161-952 6018 W www.itv.com/granada
London, 200 Gray's Inn Road, London WC1X 8XZ
   T 020-7430 4000 W www.itv.com/london
Meridian (south and south-east England), Parkway Solent
   Business Park, Whiteley, Hants PO15 7PA T 0844-881 2000
   W www.itv.com/meridian
STV (Scotland), Pacific Quay, Glasgow G51 1PQ
   T 0141-300 3704 W www.stv.tv
Tyne Tees (north-east England), Television House,
   The Watermark, Gateshead, Tyne and Wear NE11 9SZ
   T 0844-881 51000 W www.itv.com/tynetees
Ulster (Northern Ireland), Ormeau Road, Belfast BT7 1EB
   T 028-9032 8122 W www.u.tv
Wales, Media Centre, Culverhouse Cross, Cardiff CF5 6XJ
   T 0844-881 0100 W www.itv.com/wales
West, Television Centre, Bath Road, Bristol BS4 3HG
   T 0808-101 0185 W www.itv.com/westcountry
Yorkshire, 104 Kirkstall Road, Leeds LS3 1JS T 0113-222 8885
   W www.itv.com/yorkshire

OTHER TELEVISION COMPANIES

Channel 4 Television, 124 Horseferry Road, London
   SW1P 2TX T 020-7396 4444 W www.channel4.com
Channel 5 Broadcasting Ltd, 22 Long Acre, London WC2E 9LY
   T 020-7421 7270 W www.channel5.com
Independent Television News (ITN), 200 Gray's Inn Road,
   London WC1X 8XZ T 020-7833 3000 W www.itn.co.uk
   Provides news programming for ITV and Channel 4.
Sianel Pedwar Cymru (S4C), Parc Ty Glas, Llanishen, Cardiff
   CF14 5DU T 0870-600 4141 W www.s4c.co.uk
Teletext Ltd, 10 Chiswick Park, 566 Chiswick High Road,
   London W4 5TS T 020-8323 5000 W www.teletext.co.uk
   Its analogue news service closed in 2009, but Teletext
   Ltd continues to offer holiday and other commercial
   services on digital channels.

ESTIMATED AUDIENCE SHARE

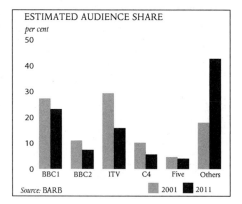

per cent

Source: BARB   ▨ 2001 ■ 2011

DIRECT BROADCASTING BY SATELLITE
TELEVISION
British Sky Broadcasting Ltd, Grant Way, Isleworth, Middx
TW7 5QD **T** 020-7705 3000 **W** www.sky.com
Chair, James Murdoch

RADIO

UK domestic radio services are broadcast across three
wavebands: FM, medium wave and long wave (used by
BBC Radio 4). In the UK the FM waveband extends in
frequency from 87.5MHz to 108MHz and the medium
waveband from 531kHz to 1602kHz. A number of radio
stations are broadcast in both analogue and digital as well
as a growing number in digital alone. As at March 2011,
the BBC Radio network controlled 55 per cent of the
listening market (*see* BBC Radio section), and the
independent sector (*see* Independent Radio section) just
over 42 per cent.

ESTIMATED AUDIENCE SHARE

			Percentage
	Jan–Mar 2009	*Jan–Mar 2010*	*Jan–Mar 2011*
BBC Radio 1	10.3	9.5	8.7
BBC Radio 2	15.9	17.2	16.0
BBC Radio 3	1.1	1.2	1.3
BBC Radio 4	12.5	12.2	12.3
BBC Radio Five Live	4.7	4.6	4.5
Five Live Sports Extra	0.1	0.2	0.2
6 Music	0.4	0.8	1.0
BBC Radio 7	0.5	0.6	0.6
Asian Network	0.2	0.2	0.3
1Xtra	0.3	0.3	0.4
BBC Local/Regional	9.4	9.3	8.8
BBC World Service	0.8	0.6	0.9
All BBC	56.3	56.5	55.0
All independent	41.6	41.3	42.6
All national independent	10.2	10.3	11.6
All local independent	31.3	31.1	31.0
Other	2.1	2.2	2.4

Source: RAJAR

DIGITAL RADIO

DAB (digital audio broadcasting) allows more services to
be broadcast to a higher technical quality and provides
the data facility for text and pictures. It improves the
robustness of high fidelity radio services, especially
compared with current FM and AM radio transmissions. It
was developed in a collaborative research project under
the pan-European Eureka 147 initiative and has been
adopted as a world standard by the International
Telecommunication Union for new digital radio systems.
The frequencies allocated for terrestrial digital radio in the
UK are 174 to 239MHz. Additional spectrum (in the
'L-Band' range: 1452–1478MHz) was introduced in 2007.

Digital radios are available as standalone portable units,
hi-fi stacks, car radios and PC cards, or inbuilt within a
mobile phone. Newer DAB radios allow the listener to
rewind, pause and record broadcasts and then upload
them to a computer using a USB cable. Some portable sets
now combine MP3 playback with DAB. An alternative
method is to listen to digital radio through television sets
via Freeview, cable or satellite.

The possibility of a switchover to entirely digital
radio services remains uncertain as takeup is still

proportionately low. Over 26 per cent of listening is now
on a digital platform. DAB accounts for 63 per cent of
total digital listening, 14 per cent is on the internet and
15 per cent on digital TV. In June 2009 the government
published the white paper *Digital Britain,* which
recommended that most services carried on the national
and local DAB multiplexes should cease broadcasting on
analogue radio by 2015. Ultra-local radio, consisting of
small independent and community stations, would
continue to broadcast on FM. There are two criteria that
must be met for digital migration to occur:

• at least 50 per cent of radio listening is digital
• national DAB coverage is comparable to FM coverage,
  and local DAB reaches 90 per cent of the population
  and all major roads

LICENSING
The Broadcasting Act 1996 provided for the licensing of
digital radio services (on multiplexes, where a number of
stations share one frequency to transmit their services). To
allocate the multiplexes, OFCOM advertises licences for
which interested parties can bid. Once the licence has
been awarded, the new owner seeks out services to
broadcast on the multiplex. The BBC has a separate
national multiplex for its services. There are local

multiplexes around the country, each broadcasting an
average of seven services, plus the local BBC station.
There are also several regional multiplexes covering a
wider area and broadcasting up to 11 services each.

INNOVATIONS
As with television, the opportunities offered by digital
services and the internet have made important changes to
radio. The internet offers a number of advantages
compared to other digital platforms such as DAB
including higher sound quality, a greater range of channel
availability and flexibility in listening opportunity.
Listeners can tune in to the majority of radio stations
live on the internet or listen again online for seven days
after broadcast. DAB radio does not allow the same
interactivity: the data is only able to travel one-way from
broadcaster to listener whereas the internet allows a
two-way flow of information.

Since 2005 increasing numbers of radio stations offer
all or part of their programmes as downloadable files,
known as podcasts, to listen to on computers or mobile
devices such as mp3 players or phones. Podcasting
technology allows listeners to subscribe in order to
receive automatically the latest episodes of regularly
transmitted programmes as soon as they become available.

The relationship between radio stations and their
audiences is also undergoing change. The quantity and
availability of music on the internet has led to the creation
of shows dedicated entirely to music sent in by listeners.
Another new development in internet-based radio has
been personalised radio stations, such as last.fm and
Spotify. Last.fm 'recommends' songs based on the
favourite artists and previous choices of the user. Spotify
allows listeners access to the track, artist or genre of
their choice, or to share and create playlists; either
advertisements are played at set intervals or there is a
subscription charge. Radioplayer, a joint-venture between
the BBC and UK commercial radio allows audiences to
listen to live and on demand radio from one place. The
service attracted 5.7 million listeners in May 2011 after
its launch eight weeks previously. WiFi technology is also

making changes to radio-listening behaviour. WiFi internet radios and media adaptors (which plug into a hi-fi) mean that people are not limited to listening to internet radio stations, podcasts or on demand programmes solely when using their computer.

BBC RADIO

BBC Radio broadcasts network services to the UK, Isle of Man and the Channel Islands. There is also a tier of national services in Wales, Scotland and Northern Ireland and 40 local radio stations in England and the Channel Islands. In Wales and Scotland there are also dedicated language services in Welsh and Gaelic respectively. The frequency allocated for digital BBC broadcasts is 225.648MHz.

BBC Radio, Broadcasting House, Portland Place, London W1A 1AA T 020-7580 4468 W www.bbc.co.uk/radio

BBC NETWORK RADIO STATIONS

Radio 1 (contemporary pop music and entertainment news) – 24 hours a day, *Frequencies:* 97–99 FM and digital

Radio 2 (popular music, entertainment, comedy and the arts) – 24 hours a day, *Frequencies:* 88–91 FM and digital

Radio 3 (classical music, classic drama, documentaries and features) – 24 hours a day, *Frequencies:* 90–93 FM and digital

Radio 4 (news, documentaries, drama, entertainment and cricket on long wave in season) – 5.20am–1am daily, with BBC World Service overnight, *Frequencies:* 92–95 FM and 198 LW and digital

Radio Five Live (news and sport) – 24 hours a day, *Frequencies:* 693/909 MW and digital

Five Live Sports Extra (live sport) – schedule varies, digital only

6 Music (contemporary and classic pop and rock music) – 24 hours a day, digital only

Radio 7 (comedy, drama and children's) – 24 hours a day, digital only

Asian Network (news, music and sport) – 5am–1am, with Radio Five Live overnight, *Frequencies:* various MW frequencies in Midlands and digital

1Xtra (urban music: drum & bass, garage, hip hop, R&B) – 24 hours a day, digital only

BBC NATIONAL RADIO STATIONS

Radio Cymru (Welsh-language), *Frequencies:* 92–105 FM and digital

Radio Foyle, Frequencies: 93.1 FM and 792 MW and digital

Radio Nan Gaidheal (Gaelic service), *Frequencies:* 103.5–105 FM and digital

Radio Scotland, Frequencies: 92–95 FM and 810 MW and digital. Local programmes for Orkney and Shetland

Radio Ulster, Frequencies: 1341 MW and 92–95 FM and digital. Local programmes on Radio Foyle

Radio Wales, Frequencies: 657/882 MW and 93–104 FM and digital

BBC LOCAL RADIO STATIONS

In England, BBC local radio has an average weekly reach of 7.7 million listeners. There are 40 local stations serving England and the Channel Islands, all of which are available via the internet:

Berkshire, PO Box 104.4, Reading RG4 8FH
T 0118-946 4200 *Frequencies:* 95.4/104.1 FM and digital

Bristol, Broadcasting House, Whiteladies Road, Bristol, BS8 2LR
T 0117-974 1111 *Frequencies:* 94.9/104.6 and digital

Cambridgeshire, 104 Hills Road, Cambridge CB2 1LQ
T 01223-259696 *Frequencies:* 95.7/96 FM and digital

Cornwall, Phoenix Wharf, Truro TR1 1UA
T 01872-275421 *Frequencies:* 95.2/103.9 FM and digital

Coventry and Warwickshire, Priory Place, Coventry CV1 5SQ
T 024-7655 1000 *Frequencies:* 94.8/103.7 FM and digital

Cumbria, Annetwell Street, Carlisle CA3 8BB
T 01228-592444 *Frequencies:* 95.6/96.1 FM

Derby, PO Box 269, Derby DE1 3HL
T 01332-361111 *Frequencies:* 95.3/96.0/104.5 FM

Devon, PO Box 5, Broadcasting House, Seymour Road, Plymouth PL3 5YQ
T 01752-260323 *Frequencies:* 95.7/103.4 FM and digital

Essex, 198 New London Road, Chelmsford CM2 9XB
T 01245-616000 *Frequencies:* 95.3/103.5 FM, 765 AM and digital

Gloucestershire, London Road, Gloucester GL1 1SW
T 01452-308585 *Frequencies:* 95.0/95.8/104.7 FM, 1413 AM

Guernsey, Broadcasting House, Bulwer Avenue, St Sampson's GY2 4lA
T 01481-200373 *Frequencies:* 93.2/99.0 FM, 1116 AM

Hereford and Worcester, Hylton Road, Worcester WR2 5WW
T 01905-748485 *Frequencies:* 94.7/104.0/104.4, 738 AM

Humberside, Queen's Court, Hull HU1 3RH
T 01482-323232 *Frequencies:* 95.9 FM, 1485 AM and digital

Jersey, 18 Parade Road, St Helier JE2 3PL
T 01534-720255 *Frequencies:* 88.8 FM, 1026 AM

Kent, The Great Hall, Mount Pleasant Road, Tunbridge Wells TN1 1QQ
T 01892-670000 *Frequencies:* 96.7/104.2 FM, 774 AM and digital

Lancashire, 26 Darwen Street, Blackburn BB2 2EA
T 01254-583583 *Frequencies:* 95.5/103.9/104.5 FM, 1557 AM and digital

Leeds, 2 St Peter's Square, Leeds LS9 8AH
T 0113-244 2131 *Frequencies:* 92.4/95.3 FM, 774 AM and digital

Leicester, 9 St Nicholas Place, Leicester LE1 5LB
T 0116-251 1049 *Frequency:* 104.9 FM and digital

Lincolnshire, PO Box 219, Newport, Lincoln LN1 3XY
T 01522-511411 *Frequencies:* 94.9/104.7 FM

London, 2nd Floor, Egton Wing, BBC Broadcasting House, Portland Place, London W1A 1AA
T 020-7224 2424 *Frequency:* 94.9 FM and digital

Manchester, New Broadcasting House, Oxford Road, Manchester M60 1SJ
T 0161-200 2000 *Frequency:* 95.1 FM and digital

Merseyside, PO Box 95.8, Liverpool L69 1ZJ
T 0151-708 5500 *Frequencies:* 95.8 FM, 1485 AM and digital

Newcastle, Broadcasting Centre, Barrack Road, Newcastle upon Tyne NE99 1RN
T 0191-232 4141 *Frequencies:* 95.4/96.0/103.7/104.4 FM, 1458 AM and digital

Norfolk, The Forum, Millennium Plain, Norwich NR2 1BH
T 01603-617321 *Frequencies:* 95.1/95.6/104.4 FM, 855 AM and digital

Northampton, Broadcasting House, Abington Street, Northampton NN1 2BH
T 01604-239100 *Frequencies:* 103.6/104.2 FM

Nottingham, London Road, Nottingham NG2 4UU
T 0115-955 0500 *Frequencies:* 95.1/95.5/103.8 FM, 1584 AM and digital

Oxford, PO Box 95.2, Oxford OX2 7YL
T 0845-931 1444 *Frequency:* 95.2 FM

Sheffield, 54 Shoreham Street, Sheffield S1 4RS
T 0114-273 1177 *Frequencies:* 88.6/104.1 FM, 1035 AM
and digital
Shropshire, 2–4 Boscobel Drive, Shrewsbury SY1 3TT
T 01743-248484 *Frequencies:* 90.0/95.0/96.0/104.1 FM
and digital
Solent, Havelock Road, Southampton SO14 7PW
T 023-8063 1311 *Frequencies:* 96.1/103.8 FM, 999 AM
and digital
Somerset, Broadcasting House, Park Street, Taunton TA1 4DA
T 01823-323956 *Frequencies:* 95.5 FM,1566 AM
Stoke, Cheapside, Hanley, Stoke-on-Trent ST1 1JJ
T 01782-208080 *Frequencies:* 94.6/104.1 FM and digital
Suffolk, Broadcasting House, St Matthew's Street, Ipswich
IP1 3EP
T 01473-250000 *Frequencies:* 95.5/95.9/103.9/104.6 FM
Surrey, Broadcasting Centre, Guildford, Surrey GU2 7AP
T 01483-306306 *Frequencies:* 104/104.6 FM, 1368 AM
Sussex, 40–42 Queens Road, Brighton, East Sussex BN1 3XB
T 01273-320428 *Frequencies:* 95.3/104.5/104.8 FM,
1161 AM and digital
Tees, PO Box 95FM, Broadcasting House, Newport Road,
Middlesborough TS1 5DG
T 01642-225211 *Frequency:* 95 FM and digital
Three Counties, PO Box 3CR, Luton LU1 5XL
T 01582-637400 *Frequencies:* 95.5/103.8/104.5 FM,
630/1161 AM
Wiltshire, PO Box 1234, Swindon SN1 3RW
T 01793-513626 *Frequencies:* 103.5/104.3/104.9 FM, 1332
AM and digital
WM (West Midlands), The Mailbox, Birmingham B1 1RF
T 0121-567 6000 *Frequency:* 95.6 FM and digital
York, 20 Bootham Row, York YO3 7BR
T 01904-641351 *Frequencies:* 95.5/103.7/104.3 FM,
666/1260 AM

BBC WORLD SERVICE

The BBC World Service broadcasts to an estimated
weekly audience of 180 million worldwide, in 28
languages including English, and is now available in 154
capital cities. It no longer broadcasts in Dutch, French for
Europe, German, Hebrew, Italian, Japanese or Malay
because it was found that most speakers of these
languages preferred to listen to the English broadcasts. In
2006 services in ten languages (Bulgarian, Croatian,
Czech, Greek, Hungarian, Kazakh, Polish, Slovak,
Slovene and Thai) were terminated to provide funding for
a new Arabic television channel, which was launched in
March 2008. In August 2008 the BBC's Romanian World
Service broadcasts were discontinued after 68 years. In
January 2011 the BBC announced five more language
services would be terminated: Albanian, Caribbean
English, Macedonian, Portuguese for Africa and Serbian.
The BBC World Service website offers interactive news
services in English, Arabic, Chinese, Hindi, Persian,
Portuguese for Brazil, Russian, Spanish and Urdu with
audiostreaming available in 27 languages.

LANGUAGES
Arabic, Azeri, Bangla, Burmese, Chinese, English, French,
Hausa, Hindi, Indonesian, Kinyarwanda, Kirundi, Kyrgyz,
Nepali, Pashto, Persian, Portuguese, Russian, Sinhala,
Somali, Spanish, Swahili, Tamil, Turkish, Ukrainian,
Urdu, Uzbek and Vietnamese.

UK frequencies: digital; overnight on BBC Radio 4.
BBC Learning English teaches English worldwide through
radio, television and a wide range of published and
online courses.

BBC Monitoring tracks the global media for the latest
news reports emerging around the world.
BBC World Service Trust is a registered charity established
in 1999 by BBC World Service. It promotes
development through the innovative use of the media
in the developing world. The trust presently works in
over 40 countries worldwide and focuses on health,
education and good governance.
BBC WORLD SERVICE, Bush House, Strand, London
WC2B 4PH T 020-7240 3456

INDEPENDENT RADIO

Until 1973, the BBC had a legal monopoly on radio
broadcasting in the UK. During this time, the
corporation's only competition came from pirate stations
located abroad, such as Radio Luxembourg. Christopher
Chataway, Minister for Post and Telecommunications in
Edward Heath's government, changed this by creating
the first licences for commercial radio stations. The
Independent Broadcasting Authority (IBA) awarded the
first of these licences to the London Broadcasting
Company (LBC) to provide London's news and
information service. LBC was followed by Capital Radio,
to offer the city's entertainment service, Radio Clyde in
Glasgow and BRMB in Birmingham.

The IBA was dissolved when the Broadcasting Act of
1990 de-regulated broadcasting, to be succeeded by the
less rigid Radio Authority (RA). The RA began
advertising new licences for the development of
independent radio in January 1991. It awarded national
and local radio, satellite and cable services licences, and
long-term restricted service licences for stations serving
non-commercial establishments such as hospitals and
universities. The first national commercial digital
multiplex licence was awarded in October 1998 and a
number of local digital multiplex licences followed.

At the end of 2003 the RA was replaced by OFCOM,
which now carries out the licensing administration.

The RadioCentre was formed in July 2006 as a result
of the merger between the Radio Advertising Bureau
(RAB) and the Commercial Radio Companies Association
(CRCA), the former non-profit trade body for commercial
radio companies in the UK, to operate essentially as a
union for commercial radio stations. According to a 2008
audit, it is possible to listen to 93 per cent of independent
radio stations online, while 48 per cent can be listened to
on DAB radios.
THE RADIOCENTRE, 4th Floor, 5 Golden Square, London
W1F 9BS T 020-3206 7800 W www.radiocentre.org
Chief Executive, Andrew Harrison

INDEPENDENT NATIONAL RADIO STATIONS

Absolute Radio, 1 Golden Square, London W1F 9DJ
T 020-7434 1215 – 24 hours a day, *Frequencies:* 105.8 FM,
1197/1215/1233/1242/1260 AM and digital
Amazing Radio, Church Street, Gateshead NE8 2AT –
24 hours a day, *Frequencies:* digital only
BFBS Radio UK, Chalfont Grove, Narcot Lane, Chalfont St
Peter, Bucks SL9 8TN T 01494-878354 *Frequency:* digital
only
Classic FM, 30 Leicester Square, London WC2H 7LA
T 020-7343 9000 – 24 hours a day, *Frequencies:*
100–102 FM and digital
Planet Rock, 54 Lisson Street, London NW1 5DF
T 020-7453 1600 – 24 hours a day, *Frequency:* digital
only

Talk Sport, 18 Hatfields, London SE1 8DJ T 020-7959 7800 – 24 hours a day, *Frequencies:* 1053/1089 AM and digital

INDEPENDENT LOCAL RADIO STATIONS
ENGLAND

2BR, 2ᴀ Petre Court, Accrington, Lancs BB5 5HY T 01282-690000 *Frequency:* 99.8 FM

96.2 The Revolution, Sarah Moor Studios, Henshaw Street, Oldham OL1 3EN T 0161-621 6500 *Frequency:* 96.2 FM

96.2 Touch FM, Holly Farm Business Park, Honiley, Kenilworth, Warks CV8 1NP T 01926-485600 *Frequency:* 96.2 FM

96.3 Radio Aire, 51 Burley Road, Leeds LS3 1LR T 0113-283 5500 *Frequency:* 96.3 FM and digital

96.4 Eagle Radio, Dolphin House, North Street, Guildford, Surrey GU1 4AA T 01483-300964 *Frequency:* 96.4 FM

96.4 FM BRMB, Nine Brindleyplace, 4 Oozells Square, Birmingham B1 2DJ T 0121-566 5200 *Frequency:* 96.4 FM

96.9 Viking FM, The Boathouse, Commercial Road, Hull, E. Yorks HU1 2SG T 01482-325141 *Frequency:* 96.9 FM and digital

97.2 Stray FM, The Hamlet, Hornbeam Park Avenue, Harrogate HG2 8RE T 01423-522972 *Frequency:* 97.2 FM

97.4 Rock FM, St. Paul's Square, Preston, Lancs PR1 1XA T 01772-477700 *Frequency:* 97.4 FM and digital

99.9 Radio Norwich, Stanton House, 29 Yarmouth Road, Norwich NR7 0EE T 01603-703300 *Frequency:* 99.9 FM

102 Touch FM, Holly Farm Business Park, Honiley, Kenilworth, Warks CV8 1NP T 01926-485600 *Frequency:* 102 FM

102.4 Wish FM, Orrell Lodge, Orrell Road, Wigan, Lancs WN5 8HJ T 01942-761024 *Frequency:* 102.4 FM

103.4 Sun FM, PO Box 1034, Sunderland, Tyne and Wear SR5 2YL T 0191-548 6767 *Frequency:* 103.4 FM

107 The Bee, 2ᴀ Petre Court, Petre Road, Clayton-le-Moors BB5 5HY T 01254-350350 *Frequency:* 107 FM

107.2 The Wyre, 13 Oxford Street, Kidderminster DY10 1BQ T 03331-231072 *Frequency:* 107.2 FM

107.5 Sovereign Radio, 14 St Mary's Walk, Hailsham, E. Sussex BN27 1AF T 01323-442700 *Frequency:* 107.5 FM

107.6 Banbury Sound, Holly Farm Business Park, Honiley, Kenilworth, Warks CV8 1NP T 01295-661076 *Frequency:* 107.6 FM

107.6 FM Juice Liverpool, 27 Fleet Street, Liverpool L1 4AR T 0151-707 3107 *Frequency:* 107.6 FM

107.6 Touch Banbury, Unit 9A, Manor Park, Banbury, Oxfordshire OX16 3TB T 0129-566 1076 *Frequency:* 107.6 FM

107.7 Splash FM, Guildbourne Centre, Worthing, W. Sussex BN11 1LZ T 01903-233005 *Frequency:* 107.7 FM

107.7 The Wolf, 2nd Floor, Mander House, Wolverhampton WV1 3NB T 01902-571070 *Frequency:* 107.7 FM

107.8 Arrow FM, Priory Meadow Shopping Centre, Hastings, E. Sussex TN34 1PJ T 01424-461177 *Frequency:* 107.8 FM

107.8 Radio Jackie, 110 Tolworth Broadway, Surbiton, Surrey KT6 7JD T 020-8288 1300 *Frequency:* 107.8 FM

107.9 Dune FM, The Power Station, Victoria Way, Southport, Merseyside PR8 1RR T 01704-502500 *Frequency:* 107.9 FM

Absolute Radio 80s, 1 Golden Square, London W1F 9DJ T 020-7434 1215 *Frequency:* digital only

Absolute Radio 90s, 1 Golden Square, London W1F 9DJ T 020-7434 1215 *Frequency:* digital only

Absolute Radio 00s, 1 Golden Square, London W1F 9DJ T 020-7434 1215 *Frequency:* digital only

Absolute Radio Classic Rock, 1 Golden Square, London W1F 9DJ T 020-7434 1215 *Frequency:* digital only

Absolute Radio London, 1 Golden Square, London W1F 9DJ T 020-7434 1215 *Frequency:* 105.8 FM, 1215 AM (nationwide) and digital

The Arrow, 30 Leicester Square, London WC2H 7LA T 020-7766 6000 *Frequency:* digital only

Asian Sound Radio, Globe House, Southall Street, Manchester M3 1LG T 0161-288 1000 *Frequencies:* 963/1377 AM and digital

Atlantic FM, Unit 10, Wheal Kitty Workshops, St Agnes, Cornwall TR5 0RD T 01872-554400 *Frequencies:* 105.1/107 FM

The Bay, PO Box 969, St George's Quay, Lancaster LA1 3LD T 01524-848747 *Frequencies:* 96.9/102.3/103.2 FM

The Beach, 10 Oulton Road, Lowestoft, Suffolk NR32 4QP T 0845-345 1035 *Frequencies:* 97.4/103.4 FM and digital

Beacon Radio, 267 Tettenhall Road, Wolverhampton WV6 0DE T 01902-461300 *Frequencies:* 97.2/103.1 FM and digital

Big L, 8 Manchester Park, Tewkesbury Road, Cheltenham GL51 9EJ T 01242-699555 *Frequency:* 1395 AM and digital

The Breeze, Roman Landing, Kingsway, Soton SO14 1BN T 0845-466 1107 *Frequencies:* 107.2/107.4/107.8 FM

Bright 106.4, 11A The Market Place Shopping Centre, Burgess Hill, W. Sussex RH15 9NP T 01444-248127 *Frequency:* 106.4 FM

Buzz Asia, Radio House, Southall, Middx UB2 4AT T 020-8574 6666 *Frequencies:* 963/972 AM

Capital FM: Birmingham, 1 The Square, 111 Broad Street, Birmingham B15 1AS T 0121-695 0000 *Frequency:* 102.2 FM and digital

Capital FM: East Midlands, Level 6, Chapel Quarter, Maid Marian Way, Nottingham NG1 6JR T 0115-873 1500 *Frequencies:* 96.2/96.5/102.8/105.4 FM and digital

Capital FM: London, 30 Leicester Square, London WC2H 7LA T 020-7766 6000 *Frequency:* 95.8 FM and digital

Capital FM: Manchester, Suite 1.1, 4 Exchange Way, Salford, Manchester M5 3EE T 0161-662 4700 *Frequency:* 102 FM and digital

Capital FM: North East, Kingfisher Way, Silverlink Business Park, Tyne & Wear NE28 9NX T 0191-206 8000 *Frequencies:* 105.3/105.6/105.8/106.4 FM and digital

Capital FM: South Coast, Radio House, Whittle Avenue, Segensworth West, Fareham PO15 5SH T 01489-589911 *Frequency:* 103.2 FM and digital

Capital FM: Yorkshire, Joseph's Well, Westgate, Leeds LS3 1AB T 0113-308 5100 *Frequencies:* 105.1/105.6/105.8 FM and digital

CFM (Carlisle and West Cumbria), PO Box 964, Carlisle, Cumbria CA1 3NG T 01228-818964 *Frequencies:* 96.4/102.5 FM (Carlisle); 102.2/103.4 FM (West Cumbria)

Chelmsford Radio 107.7, Icon Building, Western Esplanade, Southend-on-Sea, Essex SS1 1EE T 01702-455344 *Frequency:* 107.7 FM

Cheshire's Silk 106.9, 140 Moss Lane, Macclesfield, Cheshire SK11 7XE T 01625 268000 *Frequency:* 106.9 FM

Choice 96.9/107.1 FM, 30 Leicester Square, London WC2H 7LA T 020-7766 6000 *Frequency:* 96.9/107.1 FM and digital

Compass FM, 26A Wellowgate, Grimsby, Lincs DN32 0RA T 01472-346666 *Frequency:* 96.4 FM

Connect FM, 55 Headlands, Kettering, Northants NN15 7EY T 01733-704106 *Frequencies:* 97.2/106.8/107.4 FM

County Sound Radio 1566 AM, Dolphin House, North Street, Guildford, Surrey GU1 4AA T 01483-300964 *Frequency:* 1566 AM

Dearne FM, Unit 7, Network Centre, Zenith Park, Whaley Road, Barnsley S75 1HT T 01226-321733 *Frequencies:* 97.1/102 FM

Dee 106.3, 2 Chantry Court, Chester CH1 4QN T 01244-391000 *Frequency:* 106.3 FM

Dream 100 FM, Northgate House, St Peter's Street, Colchester, Essex CO1 1HT **T** 01206-764466 *Frequency:* 100.2 FM

Fire 107.6 FM, 307 Holdenhurst Road, Bournemouth, Dorset BH8 8BX **T** 01202-835107 *Frequency:* 107.6 FM

Fresh Radio, The Watermill, Broughton Hall, Skipton, N. Yorks BD23 3AG **T** 0845-224 2052 *Frequencies:* 936/1413/1431 AM; 102.6/107.1 FM

Gaydar Radio, PO Box 113, Twickenham, Middx TW1 4WY **T** 020-8744 1287 *Frequency:* digital only

Gem 106, City Link, Nottingham NG2 4NG **T** 0115-910 6100 *Frequency:* 106 FM

Glide FM, 270 Woodstock Road, Oxford OX2 7NW **T** 01865-315980 *Frequency:* 107.9 FM

Gold, 30 Leicester Square, London WC2H 7LA **T** 020-7776 6000 *Frequencies:* 603 AM (East Kent); 774 AM (Gloucester); 792 AM (Bedford); 828 AM (Bournemouth, Luton); 936 AM (West Wiltshire); 945 AM (Eastbourne, Derby); 999 AM (Nottingham); 1152 AM (Norfolk, Plymouth); 1161 AM (Swindon); 1170 AM (Portsmouth, Ipswich); 1242 AM (West Kent); 1251 AM (Bury St. Edmunds); 1260 AM (Bristol, Bath); 1323 AM (Brighton); 1332 AM (Peterborough); 1359 AM (Chelmsford); 1431 AM (Southend, Reading); 1458 AM (Manchester); 1485 AM (Newbury); 1548 AM (London); 1557 AM (Northampton) and digital

Gold: Midlands, Nine Brindleyplace, 4 Oozells Square, Birmingham B1 2DJ **T** 0121-566 5200 *Frequencies:* 990 AM (Wolverhampton); 1017 AM (Shrewsbury & Telford); 1152 AM (Birmingham); 1359 AM (Coventry & Warwickshire) and digital

Hallam FM, Radio House, 900 Herries Road, Sheffield S6 1RH **T** 0114-209 1000 *Frequencies:* 97.4/102.9/103.4 FM and digital

Heart (Cambridgeshire), PO Box 225, Queensgate Centre, Peterborough PE1 1XJ **T** 01733-460460 *Frequencies:* 97.4/102.7/103 FM and digital

Heart (Devon), Exeter Business Park, Exeter, Devon EX1 3QS **T** 01392-444444 *Frequency:* 96.2/96.4/96.6/97/97.3/100.5/ 100.8/101.2/101.9/103 FM and digital

Heart (East Anglia), 47–49 Colegate, Norwich, Norfolk NR3 1DB **T** 01603-671180 *Frequencies:* 96.4/97.1/102.4 FM and digital

Heart (Essex), Radio House, 31 Glebe Road, Chelmsford, Essex CM1 1QG **T** 01245-524500 *Frequencies:* 96.1/96.3/97.5/101.7/102.6 FM and digital

Heart (Four Counties), Broadcast Centre, 14 Vincent Avenue, Milton Keynes MK8 0AB **T** 01908-269111 *Frequencies:* 96.6/96.9/97.6/103.3 FM and digital

Heart (Gloucestershire), Bridge Studios, Eastgate Centre, Gloucester, Gloucestershire GL1 1SS **T** 01452-313200 *Frequencies:* 102.4/103 FM

Heart (Hertfordshire), Unit 5, The Metro Centre, Dwight Road, Watford WD18 9UD **T** 01923-205470 *Frequency:* 96.6 FM

Heart (Kent), Radio House, John Wilson Business Park, Whitstable, Kent CT5 3QX **T** 01227-772004 *Frequencies:* 95.9/96.1/97/102.8/103.1 FM and digital

Heart (London), 30 Leicester Square, London WC2H 7LA **T** 020-7468 1062 *Frequency:* 106.2 FM and digital

Heart (South Coast), Radio House, Whittle Avenue, Segensworth West, Fareham PO15 5SH **T** 01489-589911 *Frequencies:* 96.7/97.5/102.3 FM

Heart (Sussex), Radio House, PO Box 2000, Brighton BN41 2SS **T** 01273-430111 *Frequencies:* 96.9/97.5/102/102.4/102.7/103.5 FM and digital

Heart (Thames Valley), PO Box 2020, The Chase, Reading, Berks RG31 7FG **T** 0118-945 4400 *Frequencies:* 97/97.4/102.6/102.9/103.4 FM

Heart (West Country), One Passage Street, Bristol BS2 0JF **T** 0117-984 3200 *Frequencies:* 96.3/96.5/97.1/102.6/103 FM and digital

Heart (West Midlands), 1 The Square, 111 Broad Street, Birmingham B15 1AS **T** 0121-695 0000 *Frequency:* 100.7 and digital

Heart (Wiltshire), PO Box 2000, Swindon SN4 7EX **T** 01793-842600 *Frequencies:* 96.5/97.2/102.2 FM and digital

High Peak Radio, PO Box 106, High Peak, Derbys SK23 0QD **T** 01298-813144 *Frequencies:* 103.3/106.4 FM

Imagine FM, Waterloo Place, Watson Square, Stockport SK1 3AZ **T** 0161-476 7340 *Frequency:* 104.9 FM

Isle Of Wight Radio, Dodnor Park, Newport, IOW PO30 5XE **T** 01983-822557 *Frequencies:* 102/107 FM

Jack FM (Bristol), County Gates, Ashton Road, Bristol BS3 2JH **T** 0117-966 1065 *Frequency:* 106.5 FM

Jack FM (Hertfordshire), The Pump House, Knebworth Park, Hertfordshire SG3 6HQ **T** 01438-810900 *Frequency:* 106 FM

Jack FM (Oxfordshire), 270 Woodstock Road, Oxford, Oxfordshire OX2 7NW **T** 01865-315980 *Frequency:* 106.8/106.4 FM

Jack FM (South Coast), Roman Landing, Kingsway, Soton SO14 1BN **T** 023-8038 4100 *Frequencies:* 106/106.6 FM

Juice 107.2, 170 North Street, Brighton BN1 1EA **T** 01273-386107 *Frequency:* 107.2 FM and digital

Kerrang! 105.2 FM, Kerrang! House, 20 Lionel Street, Birmingham B3 1AQ **T** 0845-053 1052 *Frequency:* 105.2 FM and digital

Kestrel FM, Suite 2, Paddington House, Festival Place, Basingstoke, Hants RG21 7LJ **T** 01256-694000 *Frequency:* 107.6 FM

Key 103, Castle Quay, Castlefield, Manchester M15 4PR **T** 0161-288 5000 *Frequency:* 103 FM and digital

Kismat, Radio House, Southall, Middx UB2 4AT **T** 020-8574 6666 *Frequency:* 1035 AM and digital

Kiss, Mappin House, 4 Winsley Street, London W1W 8HF **T** 020-7436 1515 *Frequencies:* 97.2/100/101/105.6/106.1/106.4/107.7 FM and digital

KL.FM 96.7, 18 Blackfriars Street, King's Lynn, Norfolk PE30 1NN **T** 01553-772777 *Frequency:* 96.7 FM

KMFM (Ashford), 34–36 North Street, Ashford, Kent TN24 8JR **T** 01233-623232 *Frequency:* 107.6 FM

KMFM (Canterbury), 183 Northdown Road, Cliftonville, Margate, Kent CT9 2PA **T** 01227-475950 *Frequency:* 106 FM

KMFM (Maidstone), Medway House, Ginsbury Close, Sir Thomas Longley Road, Medway City Estate, Strood, Rochester, Kent ME2 4DU **T** 01622-662500 *Frequency:* 105.6 FM

KMFM (Medway), Medway House, Ginsbury Close, Sir Thomas Longley Road, Medway City Estate, Strood, Rochester, Kent ME2 4DU **T** 01634-227808 *Frequencies:* 100.4/107.9 FM

KMFM (Shepway and White Cliffs Country), 34–36 North Street, Ashford, Kent TN24 8JR **T** 01303-220303 *Frequencies:* 96.4/106.8 FM

KMFM (Thanet), 2–14 High Street, Margate, Kent CT9 1DH **T** 01843-220222 *Frequency:* 107.2 FM

KMFM (West Kent), Medway House, Ginsbury Close, Sir Thomas Langley Road, Medway City Estate, Strood, Rochester, Kent ME2 4DU **T** 01732-369200 *Frequencies:* 96.2/101.6 FM

KMFM extra, Medway House, Ginsbury Close, Sir Thomas Langley Road, Medway City Estate, Strood, Rochester, Kent ME2 4DU **T** 0844-967 1000 *Frequency:* digital only

Lakeland Radio, Plumgarths, Crook Road, Kendal, Cumbria LA8 8QJ T 01539-737380 Frequencies: 100.1/100.8 FM

LBC 97.3 FM, 30 Leicester Square, London WC2H 7LA T 020-7766 6000 Frequency: 97.3 FM and digital

LBC News 1152, 30 Leicester Square, London WC2H 7LA T 020-7766 6000 Frequency: 1152 AM and digital

Lincs FM, Witham Park, Waterside South, Lincoln LN5 7JN T 01522-549900 Frequencies: 96.7/97.6/102.2 FM and digital

London Greek Radio, LGR House, 437 High Road, London N12 0AP T 0871-288 1000 Frequency: 103.3 FM

London Turkish Radio, 185B High Road, Wood Green, London N22 6BA T 020-8881 0606 Frequency: 1584 AM

Magic 105.4, Mappin House, 4 Winsley Street, London W1W 8HF T 020-7975 8100 Frequency: 105.4 FM and digital

Magic 828, 51 Burley Road, Leeds LS3 1LR T 0113-283 5500 Frequency: 828 AM and digital

Magic 999, St Paul's Square, Preston, Lancs PR1 1XS T 01772-477700 Frequency: 999 AM and digital

Magic 1152 (Manchester), Castle Quay, Castlefield, Manchester M15 4PR T 0161-288 5000 Frequency: 1152 AM and digital

Magic 1152 (Tyne & Wear), 55 Degrees North, Pilgrim Street, Newcastle upon Tyne NE1 6BF T 0191-230 6100 Frequency: 1152 AM and digital

Magic 1161 AM, Commercial Road, Hull, E. Yorks HU1 2SG T 01482-325141 Frequency: 1161 AM and digital

Magic 1170, Radio House, Yale Crescent, Thornaby, Stockton-on-Tees TS17 6AA T 01642-888222 Frequency: 1170 AM and digital

Magic 1548 AM, St John's Beacon, 1 Houghton Street, Liverpool L1 1RL T 0151-472 6800 Frequency: 1548 AM and digital

Magic AM (South Yorkshire), Radio House, 900 Herries Road, Sheffield S6 1RH T 0114-285 2121 Frequencies: 990/1305/1548 AM and digital

Mansfield 103.2 FM, The Media Suite, Brunts Business Centre, Samuel Brunts Way, Mansfield, Notts NG18 2AH T 01623-646666 Frequency: 103.2 FM

Mercia, Hertford Place, Coventry CV1 3TT T 024-7686 8200 Frequencies: 97/102.9 FM and digital

Metro Radio, 55 Degrees North, Pilgrim Street, Newcastle upon Tyne NE1 6BF T 0191-230 6100 Frequencies: 97.1/102.6/103/103.2 FM and digital

Midwest Radio (Blandford & The Vale) Longmead, Shaftesbury, Dorset SP7 8QQ T 01747-855711 Frequencies: 96.6/97.4 FM

Midwest Radio (Somerset & West Dorset), The Studios, Middle Street, Yeovil, Somerset BA20 1DJ T 01935-848488 Frequencies: 105.6/106.6 FM

Minster FM, PO Box 123, Dunnington, York YO19 5ZX T 01904-488888 Frequencies: 102.3/104.7 FM

Mix 96, Friars Square Studios, 11 Bourbon Street, Aylesbury, Bucks HP20 2PZ T 01296-399396 Frequency: 96.2 FM

Newbury Sound, 42 Bone Lane, Newbury, Berks RG14 5SD T 01635-841600 Frequencies: 105.6/107.4 FM

North Norfolk Radio, PO Box 962, Norfolk NR24 2ER T 01263-860808 Frequencies: 96.2/103.2 FM

Oak FM, Unit 3 Martins Court, Telford Way, Coalville LE67 3HD T 01530-835107 Frequencies: 107.9 FM

Palm 105.5, Marble Court, Lymington Road, Torquay TQ1 4FB T 01803-321 055 Frequency: 105.5 FM

Passion Radio, PO Box 4738, Worthing, West Sussex BN11 9LR T 01903-685555 Frequency: digital only

Peak FM, Radio House, Foxwood Road, Chesterfield, Derbys S41 9RF T 01246-269107 Frequencies: 102/107.4 FM

Pirate FM, Carn Brea Studios, Wilson Way, Redruth, Cornwall TR15 3XX T 0870-800 0007 Frequencies: 102.2/102.8 FM and digital

Polish Radio London, Unit 6, King Street Cloisters, Clifton Walk, London W6 0GY T 0870-041 3636 Frequency: digital only

Premier Christian Radio, 22 Chapter Street, London SW1P 4NP T 020-7316 1300 Frequencies: 1305/1332/1413 AM and digital

The Pulse of West Yorkshire, Forster Square, Bradford, W. Yorks BD1 5NE T 01274-203040 Frequencies: 97.5/102.5 FM and digital

Pulse 2, Forster Square, Bradford, W. Yorks BD1 5NE T 01274-203040 Frequencies: 1278/1530 AM and digital

Radio City 96.7, St John's Beacon, 1 Houghton Street, Liverpool L1 1RL T 0151-472 6800 Frequency: 96.7 FM and digital

Radio Wave 96.5, 965 Mowbray Drive, Blackpool, Lancs FY3 7JR T 01253-304965 Frequency: 96.5 FM

Radio XL 1296 AM, KMS House, Bradford Street, Birmingham B12 0JD T 0121-753 5353 Frequency: 1296 AM and digital

Ram FM, 35/36 Irongate, Derby DE1 3GA T 01332-324000 Frequency: 102.8 FM

Reading 107 FM, Radio House, Madejski Stadium, Reading, Berks RG2 0FN T 0118-986 2555 Frequency: 107 FM

Real Radio (Northeast), Marquis Court, Team Valley, Trading Estate, Gateshead NE11 0RU T 0191-440 7500 Frequencies 96.2/96.4/100.7/101.8 FM and digital

Real Radio (Northwest), Laser House, Waterfront Quay, Manchester M50 3XW T 0161-886 8800 Frequency: 105.4 FM and digital

Real Radio (Yorkshire), 1 Sterling Court, Tingley, Wakefield WF3 1EL T 0113-238 1114 Frequencies: 106.2/107.6/107.7 FM and digital

Ridings FM, PO Box 333, Wakefield WF2 7YQ T 01924-367177 Frequency: 106.8 FM and digital

Rother FM, Aspen Court, Bessemer Way, Rotherham S60 1FB T 01709-369994 Frequency: 96.1 FM

Rugby FM, Holly Farm Business Park, Honiley, Kenilworth CV8 1NP T 0845-094 9780 Frequency: 107.1 FM

Rutland Radio, 40 Melton Road, Oakham, Rutland, Leics LE15 6AY T 01572-757868 Frequencies: 97.4/107.2 FM

Sabras Radio, Radio House, 63 Melton Road, Leicester LE4 6PN T 0116-261 0666 Frequency: 1260 AM and digital

The Severn, Shropshire Star Building, Waterloo Road, Ketley, Telford TF1 5HU T 0333-456 0777 Frequencies: 106.5/107.1/107.4 FM

Signal 1, Stoke Road, Stoke-on-Trent ST4 2SR T 01782-441300 Frequencies: 96.4/96.9/102.6 FM and digital

Signal 2, Stoke Road, Stoke-on-Trent ST4 2SR T 01782-441300 Frequency: 1170 AM and digital

Smooth Radio Northwest, Laser House, Waterfront Quay, Salford Quays, Manchester M50 3XW T 0845-050 1004 Frequencies: 100.4 FM (North West); 101.4 FM (Derby); 102.2 FM (London); 105.7 FM (West Midlands); 106.6 FM (East Midlands) and digital

Southend Radio 105.1, The Icon Building, Western Esplanade, Southend-on-Sea, Essex SS1 1EE T 01702-455060, Frequency: 105.1 FM and digital

Spectrum Radio, 4 Ingate Place, Battersea, London SW8 3NS T 020-7627 4433 Frequency: 558 AM and digital

Spire FM, City Hall Studios, Malthouse Lane, Salisbury, Wilts SP2 7QQ T 01722-416644 Frequency: 102 FM

Spirit FM, 9 Dukes Court, Bognor Road, Chichester, W. Sussex PO19 8FX T 01243-773600 Frequencies: 96.6/102.3/106.6 FM

Star Radio (Cambridge and Ely), 20 Mercers Row, Cambridge CB5 8HY T 01223-305107 Frequencies: 107.1/107.9 FM

Star Radio (North East), Radio House, 11 Woodland Road, Darlington, Co. Durham DL3 7BJ T 01325-341810 Frequencies: 102.3/102.8/103.2/103.5/106.8 FM

Sunshine Radio, Penn House, Broad Street, Hereford HR4 9AP T 01432-360246 Frequencies: 106.2/107/107.8 FM

Sunrise Radio (London), Sunrise House, Sunrise Road, Southall, Middx UB2 4AT T 020-8574 6666 Frequency: 1458 AM and digital

Sunrise Radio (Yorkshire), Sunrise House, 55 Leeds Road, Little Germany, Bradford BD1 5AF T 01274-735043 Frequency: 103.2 FM and digital

Telford FM, MNA Broadcasting, Shropshire Newspapers, Waterloo Road, Ketley TF1 5HU T 01952-280011 Frequency: 107.4 FM

TFM, Radio House, Yale Crescent, Thornaby, Stockton-on-Tees TS17 6AA T 01642-888222 Frequency: 96.6 FM and digital

Time 106.6, Radio House, Southall, Middlesex UB2 4AT T 0845-194 1066 Frequency: 106.6 FM

Time 107.5, 7th Floor, Lambourne House, 7 Western Road, Romford, Essex RM1 3LD T 0870-607 1075 Frequency: 107.5 FM

Total Star Gloucestershire, 8 Manchester Park, Tewkesbury Road, Cheltenham GL51 9EJ T 01242-252333 Frequency: 107.5 FM

Total Star Somerset, 8 Manchester Park, Tewkesbury Road, Cheltenham GL51 9EJ T 01242-252333 Frequencies: 100.8/102.4/107.4 FM

Tower FM, The Mill, Brownlow Way, Bolton BL1 2RA T 01204-387000 Frequency: 107.4 FM

Town FM, First Floor, Radio House, Orion Court, Great Blakenham, Ipswich, Suffolk IP6 0LW T 01473-836102 Frequency: 102 FM

Touch FM, 5–6 Aldergate, Tamworth, Staffordshire B79 7DJ T 01827-318000 Frequencies: 101.6/102.4 FM and digital

Trax FM, 5 Sidings Court, White Rose Way, Doncaster DN4 5NU T 01302-341166 Frequencies: 107.1/107.9 FM and digital

Wave 105 FM, 5 Manor Court, Barnes Wallis Road, Fareham, Hampshire PO15 5TH T 01489-481057 Frequencies: 105.2/105.8 FM and digital

Wessex FM, Radio House, Trinity Street, Dorchester, Dorset DT1 1DJ T 01305-250333 Frequencies: 96/97.2 FM

Wire FM, Warrington Business Park, Long Lane, Warrington WA2 8TX T 01925-445545 Frequency: 107.2 FM

Wyvern FM, First Floor, Kirkham House, John Comyn Drive, Worcester WR3 7NS T 01905-545510 Frequencies: 96.7/97.6/102.8 FM

XFM Manchester, Suite 1.1, 4 Exchange Quay, Manchester M5 3EE T 0161-662 4700 Frequency: 97.7 FM and digital

XFM UK, 30 Leicester Square, London WC2H 7LA T 020-7766 6000 Frequency: 104.9 FM and digital

Yorkshire Coast Radio, Unit 2B, Newchase Business Centre, Hopper Hill Road, Scarborough, N. Yorks YO11 3YS T 01723-500962 Frequencies: 96.2/102.4/103.1 FM

Yorkshire Radio, PO Box 197 Elland Road, Leeds LS11 1AZ T 0871-521 2288 Frequency: digital only

WALES

96.4 The Wave, PO Box 964, Victoria Road, Gowerton, Swansea SA4 3AB T 01792-511964 Frequency: 96.4 FM and digital

97.1 Radio Carmarthenshire, PO Box 971, Llanelli, Carmarthenshire SA15 1YH T 0845-890 7000 Frequencies: 97.1/97.5 FM

97.5 Scarlet FM, PO Box 971, Llanelli, Carmarthenshire SA15 1YH T 0845-890 7000 Frequency: 97.5 FM

102.1 Bay Radio, Newby House, Neath Abbey Business Park, Neath SA10 7DR T 0845-890 4000 Frequency: 102.1 FM

102.5 Radio Pembrokeshire, Unit 14, Old School Estate, Station Road, Narberth, Pembrokeshire SA67 7DU T 01834-869384 Frequencies: 102.5/107.5 FM

106.3 Bridge FM, PO Box 1063, Bridgend CF35 6WY T 0845-890 4000 Frequency: 106.3 FM

Capital FM: South Wales, The Red Dragon Centre, Cardiff CF10 4DJ T 029-2066 2066 Frequencies: 97.4/103.2 FM and digital

Gold (Wales), Red Dragon Centre, Atlantic Wharf, Cardiff CF10 4DJ T 029-2066 2066 Frequencies: 1305/1359 AM and digital

Heart (North West and Wales), The Studios, Mold Road, Wrexham LL11 4AF T 01978-722 200 Frequencies: 96.3/97.1/103/103.4 FM

Nation Radio, Newby House, Neath Abbey Business Park, Neath SA10 7DR T 0845-025 1000 Frequencies: 106.8/107.3 FM and digital

NME, The Media Centre, Culverhouse Cross, Cardiff CF5 6XJ T 029-2141 4100 Frequency: digital only

Radio Ceredigion, Glan Yr Afon Industrial Estate, Aberystwyth, Ceredigion SY23 3FF T 01970-229113 Frequencies: 96.6/97.4/103.3 FM

Radio Hafren, The Studios, The Park, Newtown, Powys SY16 2NZ T 01686-623777 Frequency: 756 AM

Real Radio (Wales), Ty-Nant Court, Ty-Nant Road, Morganstown, Cardiff CF15 8LW T 029-2031 5100 Frequencies: 88/102.3/102.8/105.2/105.4/105.6/105.7/105.9/106/106.1/ 106.2/106.9/107.2/107.3/107.7 FM and digital

Red Dragon FM, Atlantic Wharf, Cardiff CF10 4DJ T 029-2066 2066 Frequencies: 97.4/103.2 FM and digital

Swansea Sound, Victoria Road, Gowerton, Swansea SA4 3AB T 01792-511170 Frequency: 1170 AM and digital

XS Wales, Unit 5, Water Street Business Centre, Water Street, Port Talbot SA12 6LF T 01639-262025 Frequency: 97.4/107.9 FM

SCOTLAND

Argyll FM, 27–29 Longrow, Campbelltown, Argyll PA28 6ER T 01586-551800 Frequencies: 106.5/107.1/107.7 FM

Central 103.1 FM, 201 High Street, Falkirk FK1 1DU T 01324-611164 Frequency: 103.1 FM

Clyde 1, Clydebank Business Park, Clydebank, Glasgow G81 2RX T 0141-565 2200 Frequencies: 97/102.3/102.5/103.3 FM and digital

Clyde 2, Clydebank Business Park, Clydebank, Glasgow G81 2RX T 0141-565 2200 Frequency: 1152 AM and digital

Cuillin FM, Stormyhill Road, Portree, Isle of Skye IV51 9DY T 01478-611797 Frequencies: 102.7/106.2 FM

Forth One, Forth House, Forth Street, Edinburgh EH1 3LE T 0131-556 9255 Frequencies: 97.3/97.6/102.2 FM and digital

Forth 2, Forth House, Forth Street, Edinburgh EH1 3LE T 0131-556 9255 Frequency: 1548 AM and digital

Heartland FM, 9 Alba Place, Pitlochry, Perthshire PH16 5BU T 01796-474040 Frequency: 97.5 FM

Isles FM, PO Box 333, Stornoway, Isle of Lewis HS1 2PU T 01851-703333 Frequency: 103 FM

Kingdom FM, Haig House, Haig Business Park, Balgonie Road, Markinch, Fife KY7 6AQ T 01592-753753 Frequencies: 95.2/96.1/96.6/105.4/106.3 FM

Lanarkshire's L107, Radio House, 69 Bothwell Road, Hamilton, Lanarkshire ML3 0DW **T** 01698-303420 *Frequencies:* 107.5/107.9 FM

Lochbroom FM, Radio House, Mill Street, Ullapool, Ross-shire IV26 2UN **T** 01854-613131 *Frequencies:* 96.8/102.2 FM

Moray Firth Radio (MFR), PO Box 271, Scorguie Place, Inverness IV3 8UJ **T** 01463-224433 *Frequencies:* 97.4 FM, 1107 AM and digital

NECR, The Shed, School Road, Kintore, Inverurie, Aberdeenshire AB51 0UX **T** 01467-632909 *Frequencies:* 97.1/101.9/102.1/102.6/103.2/106.4 FM and digital

Nevis Radio, Ben Nevis Estate, Claggan, Fort William PH33 6PR **T** 01397-700007 *Frequencies:* 96.6/97/102.3/102.4 FM

Northsound 1, Abbotswell Road, West Tullos, Aberdeen AB12 3AJ **T** 01224-337000 *Frequencies:* 96.9/97.6/103 FM and digital

Northsound 2, Abbotswell Road, West Tullos, Aberdeen AB12 3AJ **T** 01224-337000 *Frequency:* 1035 AM and digital

Oban FM, 132 George Street, Oban, Argyll PA34 5NT **T** 01631-570057 *Frequency:* 103.3 FM

Original 106, Craigshaw Road, West Tullos, Aberdeen AB12 3AR **T** 01224-294860 *Frequency:* 106.3/106.8 FM

Radio Borders, Tweedside Park, Galashiels TD1 3TD **T** 01896-759444 *Frequencies:* 96.8/97.5/103.1/103.4 FM

Real Radio (Scotland), Parkway Court, Glasgow Business Park, Glasgow G69 6GA **T** 0141-781 1011 *Frequencies:* 100.3/101.1 FM and digital

RNA (Radio North Angus), Rosemount Road, Arbroath, Angus DD11 2AT **T** 01241-879660 *Frequencies:* 96.6/87.7 FM and digital

Rock Radio, Glasgow Business Park, Glasgow G69 6GA **T** 0141-781 1011 *Frequency:* 96.3 FM and digital

SIBC, Market Street, Lerwick, Shetland ZE1 0JN **T** 01595-695299 *Frequencies:* 96.2/102.2 FM

Smooth 105.2, PO Box 105, Glasgow G69 1AQ **T** 0141-781 1011 *Frequency:* 105.2 FM and digital

Tay AM, 6 North Isla Street, Dundee DD3 7JQ **T** 01382-200800 *Frequencies:* 1161/1584 AM and digital

Tay FM, 6 North Isla Street, Dundee DD3 7JQ **T** 01382-200800 *Frequencies:* 96.4/102.8 FM and digital

Two Lochs Radio, Gairloch, Ross-shire IV21 2LR **T** 01445-712106 *Frequencies:* 106/106.6 FM

Wave 102, 8 South Tay Street, Dundee DD1 1PA **T** 01382-901000 *Frequency:* 102 FM and digital

Waves Radio, 7 Blackhouse Circle, Blackhouse Industrial Estate, Peterhead, Aberdeenshire AB42 1BN **T** 01779-491012 *Frequency:* 101.2 FM and digital

West FM, Radio House, 54A Holmston Road, Ayr KA7 3BE **T** 01292-283662 *Frequencies:* 96.7/97.5/106.7 FM and digital

West Sound AM, Radio House, 54A Holmston Road, Ayr KA7 3BE **T** 01292-283662 *Frequency:* 1035 AM and digital

West Sound FM, Unit 40, Loreburn Centre, Dumfries DG1 2BD **T** 01387-250999 *Frequencies:* 96.5/97/103 FM

Your Radio, Unit 3, 80 Castlegreen Street, Dumbarton G82 1JB **T** 01389-734411 *Frequencies:* 103 FM (Dumbarton), 106.9 FM (Helensburgh)

NORTHERN IRELAND

Citybeat 96.7 FM, 2nd Floor, Arena Building, 85 Ormeau Road, Belfast, Antrim BT7 1SH **T** 028-9023 4967 *Frequency:* 96.7/102.5 FM and digital

Cool FM, Kiltonga Industrial Estate, Newtownards, Belfast BT23 4ES **T** 028-9181 7181 *Frequency:* 97.4 FM and digital

Downtown Radio, Newtownards, Co. Down BT23 4ES **T** 028-9181 5555 *Frequencies:* 96.4 FM (Limavady); 96.6 FM (Enniskillen); 97.1 FM (Larne); 102.3 FM (Ballymena); 102.4 FM (Londonderry); 103.1 FM (South Newry); 103.4 FM (Newcastle), 1026 AM and digital

Q97.2 FM , 24 Cloyfin Road, Coleraine, Co. Londonderry BT52 2NU **T** 028-7035 9100 *Frequency:* 97.2 FM

Q101.2 West FM, 42 Market Street, Omagh, Co. Tyrone BT78 1EH **T** 028-8224 5777 *Frequency:* 101.2 FM

Q102.9 FM (Londonderry), The Riverview Suite, 87 Rossdowney Road, Waterside, Londonderry BT47 5SU **T** 028-7134 4449 *Frequency:* 102.9 FM and digital

Seven FM, 1 Millennium Park, Woodside Industrial Estate, Woodside Road, Ballymena, Co. Antrim BT42 4PT **T** 028-2564 8777 *Frequency:* 107 FM

Six FM, 2C Park Avenue, Cookstown, Co. Tyrone BT80 8AH **T** 028-8675 8696 *Frequencies:* 106/107.2 FM

U105, UTV, Ormeau Road, Belfast BT7 1EB **T** 028-9032 8122 *Frequency:* 105.8 FM

CHANNEL ISLANDS AND ISLE OF MAN

3FM, 45 Victoria Street, Douglas, Isle of Man IM1 3RS **T** 01624-616333 *Frequencies:* 104–106 FM

Channel 103 FM, 6 Tunnell Street, St Helier, Jersey JE2 4LU **T** 01534-888103 *Frequency:* 103.7 FM

Energy FM, 100 Market Street, Douglas, Isle of Man IM1 2PH **T** 01624-611936 *Frequencies:* 91.2 FM (Laxey); 93.4 FM (north Isle of Man); 98.4 FM (Ramsey); 98.6 FM

Island FM, 12 Westerbrook, St Sampsons, Guernsey GY2 4QQ **T** 01481-242000 *Frequencies:* 93.7/104.7 FM

Manx Radio, Broadcasting House, Douglas, Isle of Man IM99 1SW **T** 01624-682600 *Frequencies:* 89.0/97.2/103.7 FM, 1368 AM

THE PRESS

The newspaper and periodical press in the UK is large and diverse, catering for a wide variety of views and interests. There is no state control or censorship of the press; however, it is subject to the laws on publication, and the Press Complaints Commission (PCC) was set up by the industry as a means of self-regulation.

The press is not state-subsidised and receives few tax concessions. The income of most newspapers and periodicals is derived largely from sales and from advertising; the press remains one of the largest advertising mediums in the UK with around 18 per cent of the market share.

SELF-REGULATION

The PCC was founded by the newspaper and magazine industry in January 1991 to replace the Press Council (established in 1953). It is a voluntary, non-statutory body set up to operate the press' self-regulation system following the Calcutt report in 1990 on privacy and related matters, when the industry feared that failure to regulate itself might lead to statutory regulation of the press. The performance of the PCC was reviewed in February 2010 by the Culture, Media and Sport Select Committee, which concluded in favour of continuing self-regulation. In July 2010 an independent review into the commission's governance made 75 recommendations for enhancing the system of press self-regulation. In July 2011, following the News of the World phone-hacking scandal, prime minister David Cameron announced that an inquiry would be held regarding the regulation of the press.

The commission is funded by the industry through the Press Standards Board of Finance.

COMPLAINTS

The PCC's aims are to consider, adjudicate, conciliate, and resolve complaints of unfair treatment by the press; and to ensure that the press maintains the highest professional standards and shows respect for generally recognised freedoms, including freedom of expression, the public's right to know, and the right of the press to operate free from improper pressure. The commission judges newspaper and magazine conduct by a code of practice drafted by editors, agreed by the industry and ratified by the commission.

The PCC has three classes of members: the chair, public members and press members. Although a number of the commision's members are newspaper or magazine editors, the majority of the 17 members have no connection with the press in order to ensure that the PCC maintains independence from the newspaper industry. In 2010 the PCC processed 750 'complaints with merit', an increase of just 1.6 per cent from 2009, and received around 7,000 complaints in total, including multiple complaints about the same article. The PCC successfully mediated or ruled on 557 cases that related to privacy in 2010.

PRESS COMPLAINTS COMMISSION
Halton House, 20–23 Holborn, London EC1N 2JD
T 020-7831 0022 E complaints@pcc.org.uk
W www.pcc.org.uk
Chair, Baroness Peta Buscombe

NEWSPAPERS

Newspapers are mostly financially independent of any political party, though most adopt a political stance in their editorial comments, usually reflecting proprietorial influence. Ownership of the national and regional daily newspapers is concentrated in the hands of large corporations whose interests cover publishing and communications, although *The Guardian* and *The Observer* are owned by the Scott Trust, formed in 1936 to protect the financial and editorial independence of *The Guardian* in perpetuity. The rules on cross-media ownership, as amended by the Broadcasting Act 1996, which limited the extent to which newspaper organisations may become involved in broadcasting, have been relaxed by the Communications Act 2003: newspapers with over a 20 per cent share of national circulation may own national and/or local radio licences.

In October 2010, *The Independent* launched a concise newspaper, *i*, the first new daily newspaper since 1986. In July 2011, *News of the World* was closed by its parent company, News International, following accusations of phone-hacking (*see* Events of the Year: Arts and Media). There are around 14 daily and 13 Sunday national papers and several hundred local papers that are published daily, weekly or twice-weekly. Scotland, Wales and Northern Ireland all have at least one daily and one Sunday national paper.

UK CIRCULATION

National Daily Newspapers	June 2010	June 2011
The Sun	2,797,972	2,806,746
Daily Mail	1,924,051	2,047,206
Daily Mirror	1,119,135	1,170,541
Daily Star	703,365	708,163
The Daily Telegraph	635,719	622,719
Daily Express	624,288	621,871
The Times	463,177	440,581
Financial Times	110,684	356,194
Daily Record	307,574	305,840
The Guardian	261,738	256,283
The Independent	162,232	176,681
i	–	173,165
The Herald	53,228	48,465
The Scotsman	44,315	40,390

National Sunday Newspapers	June 2010	June 2011
News of the World	2,610,900	2,667,428
The Mail on Sunday	1,676,088	1,927,791
Sunday Mirror	1,052,230	1,087,796
The Sunday Times	920,681	1,000,848
Sunday Express	524,699	539,478
The Sunday Telegraph	475,995	474,722
The People	471,681	474,549
Sunday Mail	368,978	360,475
Daily Star Sunday	287,478	305,978
Sunday Post	323,742	302,420
The Observer	299,492	288,928
The Independent on Sunday	127,730	151,229
Scotland on Sunday	55,657	51,053
Sunday Herald	40,715	29,233

Source: Audit Bureau of Circulations Ltd

Newspapers are usually published in either broadsheet or smaller, tabloid format. The 'quality' daily papers – ie those providing detailed coverage of a wide range of public matters – have traditionally been broadsheets, the more populist newspapers tabloid. In 2004 this correlation between format and content was redefined when three traditionally broadsheet newspapers, *The Times*, *The Independent* and *The Scotsman*, switched to tabloid-sized editions, while *The Guardian* launched a 'Berliner' format in September 2005. In October 2005 *The Independent on Sunday* became the first Sunday broadsheet to be published in the tabloid (or 'compact') size, and *The Observer*, like its daily counterpart *The Guardian*, began publishing in the Berliner format in January 2006.

NATIONAL DAILY NEWSPAPERS

DAILY EXPRESS
Northern & Shell Building, 10 Lower Thames Street, London
  EC3R 6EN **T** 020-8612 7000 **W** www.express.co.uk
  Editor, Peter Hill
DAILY MAIL
Northcliffe House, 2 Derry Street, London W8 5TT
  T 020-7938 6000 **W** www.dailymail.co.uk
  Editor, Paul Dacre
DAILY MIRROR
1 Canada Square, Canary Wharf, London E14 5AP
  T 020-7293 3000 **W** www.mirror.co.uk
  Editor, Richard Wallace
DAILY RECORD
1 Central Quay, Glasgow G3 8DA **T** 0141-309 3000
  W www.dailyrecord.co.uk
  Editor, Bruce Waddell
DAILY STAR
Express Newspapers, Northern & Shell Building, 10 Lower
  Thames Street, London EC3R 6EN **T** 020-8612 7000
  W www.dailystar.co.uk
  Editor, Dawn Neesom
THE DAILY TELEGRAPH
111 Buckingham Palace Road, London SW1W 0DT
  T 020-7931 2000 **W** www.telegraph.co.uk
  Editor, Tony Gallagher
FINANCIAL TIMES
1 Southwark Bridge, London SE1 9HL **T** 020-7873 3000
  W www.ft.com
  Editor, Lionel Barber
THE GUARDIAN
King's Place, 90 York Way, London N1 9GU
  T 020-3353 2000 **W** www.guardian.co.uk
  Editor, Alan Rusbridger
THE HERALD
Herald & Times Group, 200 Renfield Street, Glasgow G2 3QB
  T 0141-302 7000 **W** www.heraldscotland.com
  Editor, Jonathan Russell
THE INDEPENDENT AND I
2 Derry Street, London W8 5HF **T** 020-7005 2000
  W www.independent.co.uk
  Editor-in-Chief, Simon Kelner
MORNING STAR
People's Press Printing Society Ltd, William Rust House, 52
  Beachey Road, London E3 2NS **T** 020-8510 0815
  W www.morningstaronline.co.uk
  Editor, John Haylett
THE SCOTSMAN
Barclay House, 108 Holyrood Road, Edinburgh EH8 8AS
  T 0131-620 8620 **W** www.scotsman.com
  Editor, John McLellan

THE SUN
News Group Newspapers Ltd, 1 Virginia Street, London E1 9XP
  T 020-7782 4000 **W** www.the-sun.co.uk
  Editor, Dominic Mohan
THE TIMES
1 Pennington Street, London E98 1TT **T** 020-7782 5000
  W www.thetimes.co.uk
  Editor, James Harding

WEEKLY NEWSPAPERS

DAILY STAR SUNDAY
Express Newspapers, The Northern and Shell Building,
  10 Lower Thames Street, London EC3R 6EN
  T 0871-520 7424 **W** www.dailystarsunday.co.uk
  Editor, Gareth Morgan
INDEPENDENT ON SUNDAY
2 Derry Street, London W8 5HF **T** 020-7005 2000
  W www.independent.co.uk
  Executive Editor, Lisa Markwell
MAIL ON SUNDAY
Northcliffe House, 2 Derry Street, London W8 5TT
  T 020-7938 6000 **W** www.mailonsunday.co.uk
  Editor, Peter Wright
THE OBSERVER
Kings Place, 90 York Way, London N1 9GU **T** 020-3353 2000
  W www.observer.co.uk
  Editor, John Mulholland
THE PEOPLE
1 Canada Square, Canary Wharf, London E14 5AP
  T 020-7293 3000 **W** www.people.co.uk
  Editor, Lloyd Embley
SCOTLAND ON SUNDAY
108 Holyrood Road, Edinburgh EH8 8AS **T** 0131-620 8620
  W www.scotlandonsunday.co.uk
  Editor, Ian Stewart
SUNDAY EXPRESS
Northern & Shell Building, 10 Lower Thames Street,
  London EC4R 6EN **T** 020-8612 7000
  W www.express.co.uk/sunday
  Editor, Martin Townsend
SUNDAY HERALD
200 Renfield Street, Glasgow G2 3QB **T** 0141-302 7800
  W www.sundayherald.com
  Editor, Richard Walker
SUNDAY MAIL
1 Central Quay, Glasgow G3 8DA **T** 0141-309 3000
  W www.sundaymail.com
  Editor, Allan Rennie
SUNDAY MIRROR
1 Canada Square, Canary Wharf, London E14 5AP
  T 020-7293 3000 **W** www.sundaymirror.co.uk
  Editor, Tina Weaver
SUNDAY POST
D.C. Thomson & Co. Ltd, 144 Port Dundas Road, Glasgow
  G4 0HZ **T** 0141-332 9933 **W** www.sundaypost.com
  Editor, Donald Martin
SUNDAY TELEGRAPH
111 Buckingham Palace Road, London SW1W 0DT
  T 020-7931 2000 **W** www.telegraph.co.uk
  Editor, Ian MacGregor
THE SUNDAY TIMES
3 Thomas More Square, London E98 1XY **T** 020-7782 5000
  W www.thesundaytimes.co.uk
  Editor, John Witherow
THE SUNDAY TIMES SCOTLAND
6th Floor, Guildhall, 57 Queen Street, Glasgow G1 3EN
  T 0141-420 5100 **W** www.timesonline.co.uk
  Editor, Carlos Alba

WALES ON SUNDAY
6 Park Street, Cardiff CF10 1XR **T** 029-2024 3600
  W www.icwales.co.uk
  Editor, Alison Gow

REGIONAL DAILY NEWSPAPERS

EAST ANGLIA
CAMBRIDGE EVENING NEWS
Winship Road, Milton, Cambs. CB24 6PP **T** 01223-434437
  W www.cambridge-news.co.uk
  Group Editor-in-Chief, Colin Grant
EAST ANGLIAN DAILY TIMES
30 Lower Brook Street, Ipswich, Suffolk IP4 1AN
  T 01473-230023 **W** www.eadt.co.uk
  Editor, Terry Hunt
EASTERN DAILY PRESS
Prospect House, Rouen Road, Norwich NR1 1RE
  T 01603-628311 **W** www.edp24.co.uk
  Editor, Peter Waters
EVENING STAR
Archant Regional, Press House, 30 Lower Brook Street, Ipswich,
  Suffolk IP4 1AN **T** 01473-230023 **W** www.eveningstar.co.uk
  Editor, Nigel Pickover
NORWICH EVENING NEWS
Prospect House, Rouen Road, Norwich NR1 1RE
  T 01603-628311 **W** www.eveningnews24.co.uk
  Editor, Tim Williams

EAST MIDLANDS
BURTON MAIL
Burton Daily Mail Ltd, 65–68 High Street, Burton on Trent
  DE14 1LE **T** 01283-524855 **W** www.burtonmail.co.uk
  Editor, Andy Parker
CHRONICLE & ECHO, NORTHAMPTON
Northamptonshire Newspapers Ltd, Upper Mounts,
  Northampton NN1 3HR **T** 01604-467000
  Editor, David Summers
DERBY EVENING TELEGRAPH
Northcliffe House, Meadow Road, Derby DE1 2BH
  T 01332-291111 **W** www.thisisderbyshire.co.uk
  Editor, Steve Hall
THE LEICESTER MERCURY
St George Street, Leicester LE1 9FQ **T** 0116-251 2512
  W www.thisisleicestershire.co.uk
  Editor, Keith Perch
LINCOLNSHIRE ECHO
Brayford Wharf East, Lincoln LN5 7AT **T** 01522-820000
  W www.thisislincolnshire.co.uk
  Editor, Jon Grubb
NOTTINGHAM POST
Castle Wharf House, Nottingham NG1 7EU **T** 0115-948 2000
  W www.thisisnottingham.co.uk
  Editor, Malcolm Pheby

LONDON
EVENING STANDARD
Northcliffe House, 2 Derry Street, London W8 5EE
  T 020-3367 7000 **W** www.thisislondon.com
  Editor, Geordie Greig
METRO
Northcliffe House, 2 Derry Street, London W8 5TT
  T 020-7651 5200 **W** www.metro.co.uk
  Editor, Sarah Getty

NORTH EAST
EVENING CHRONICLE
ncjMedia Ltd, Groat Market, Newcastle upon Tyne NE1 1ED
  T 0191-232 7500 **W** www.chroniclelive.co.uk
  Editor, Paul Robertson
EVENING GAZETTE
Gazette Media Company Ltd, 105–111 Borough Road,
  Middlesbrough TS1 3AZ **T** 01642-245401
  W www.gazettelive.co.uk
  Editor, Darren Thwaites
HARTLEPOOL MAIL
Northeast Press Ltd, New Clarence House, Wesley Square,
  Hartlepool TS24 8BX **T** 01429-239333
  W www.hartlepoolmail.co.uk, www.peterleemail.co.uk
  Editor, Joy Yates
THE JOURNAL
Groat Market, Newcastle upon Tyne NE1 1ED **T** 0191-232 7500
  W www.journallive.co.uk
  Editor, Brian Aitken
THE NORTHERN ECHO
Priestgate, Darlington, Co. Durham DL1 1NF **T** 01325-381313
  W www.thenorthernecho.co.uk
  Editor, Peter Barron
THE SHIELDS GAZETTE
Chapter Row, South Shields, Tyne & Wear NE33 1BL
  T 0191-427 4800 **W** www.shieldsgazette.com
  Editor, John Szymanski
THE SUNDAY SUN
Groat Market, Newcastle upon Tyne NE1 1ED **T** 0191-201 6201
  W www.sundaysun.co.uk
  Editor, Matt McKenzie
SUNDERLAND ECHO
Echo House, Pennywell, Sunderland, Tyne & Wear SR4 9ER
  T 0191-501 5800 **W** www.sunderlandecho.com
  Editor, Rob Lawson

NORTH WEST
THE BLACKPOOL GAZETTE
Blackpool Gazette & Herald Ltd, Avroe House, Avroe Crescent,
  Blackpool Business Park, Squires Gate, Blackpool FY4 2DP
  T 01253-400888 **W** www.blackpoolgazette.co.uk
  Editor, David Helliwell
THE BOLTON NEWS
Newspaper House, Churchgate, Bolton, Lancs. BL1 1DE
  T 01204-537270 **W** www.thisisbolton.co.uk
  Editor-in-Chief, Ian Savage
CARLISLE NEWS AND STAR
CN Group, Newspaper House, Dalston Road, Carlisle CA2 5UA
  T 01228-612600 **W** www.newsandstar.co.uk
  Editorial Director, Neil Hodgkinson
LANCASHIRE EVENING POST
Oliver's Place, Preston PR2 9ZA **T** 01772-254841
  W www.lep.co.uk
  Editor, Simon Reynolds
LANCASHIRE TELEGRAPH
Newspaper House, High Street, Blackburn, Lancs. BB1 1HT
  T 01254-678678 **W** www.lancashiretelegraph.co.uk
  Editor, Kevin Young
LIVERPOOL DAILY POST
PO Box 48, Old Hall Street, Liverpool L69 3EB **T** 0151-227 2000
  W www.liverpooldailypost.co.uk
  Editor, Mark Thomas
LIVERPOOL ECHO
PO Box 48, Old Hall Street, Liverpool L69 3EB **T** 0151-227 2000
  W www.liverpoolecho.co.uk
  Editor, Alastair Machray

MANCHESTER EVENING NEWS
MEN Media, Mitchell Henry House, Hollinwood Avenue,
 Chadderton OL9 8EF **T** 0161-832 7200
 W www.manchestereveningnews.co.uk
 Editor, Maria McGeoghan
NORTH-WEST EVENING MAIL
Newspaper House, Abbey Road, Barrow-in-Furness, Cumbria
 LA14 5QS **T** 01229-840150 **W** www.nwemail.co.uk
 Editor, Jonathan Lee
OLDHAM EVENING CHRONICLE
PO Box 47, 172 Union Street, Oldham, Lancs. OL1 1EQ
 T 0161-633 2121 **W** www.oldham-chronicle.co.uk
 Editor, David Whaley

SOUTH EAST
THE ARGUS
Argus House, Crowhurst Road, Hollingbury, Brighton BN1 8AR
 T 01273-544544 **W** www.theargus.co.uk
 Group Editor, Michael Beard
ECHO
Newspaper House, Chester Hall Lane, Basildon, Essex SS14 3BL
 T 01268-522792 **W** www.echo-news.co.uk
 Editor, Martin McNeill
MEDWAY MESSENGER
Medway House, Ginsbury Close, Sir Thomas Longley Road,
 Medway City Estate, Strood, Kent ME2 4DU
 T 01634-227800 **W** www.kentonline.co.uk
 Editor, Bob Bounds
THE NEWS, PORTSMOUTH
The News Centre, London Road, Hilsea, Portsmouth PO2 9SX
 T 023-9266 4488 **W** www.portsmouth.co.uk
 Editor, Mark Waldron
OXFORD MAIL
Newspaper House, Osney Mead, Oxford OX2 0EJ
 T 01865-425262 **W** www.oxfordmail.co.uk
 Editor, Simon O'Neill
READING EVENING POST
8 Tessa Road, Reading, Berks. RG1 8NS **T** 0118-918 3000
 W www.getreading.co.uk
 Editor, Andy Murrill
THE SOUTHERN DAILY ECHO
Newspaper House, Test Lane, Redbridge, Southampton
 SO16 9JX **T** 023-8042 4777 **W** www.dailyecho.co.uk
 Editor, Ian Murray

SOUTH WEST
BRISTOL EVENING POST
Temple Way, Old Market, Bristol BS99 7HD **T** 0117-934 3000
 W www.thisisbristol.co.uk
 Editor-in-Chief, Mike Norton
THE CITIZEN
1 Clarence Parade, Cheltenham GL50 3NY **T** 01452-420621
 W www.thisisgloucestershire.co.uk
 Editor, Ian Mean
DAILY ECHO
Richmond Hill, Bournemouth BH2 6HH **T** 01202-554601
 W www.bournemouthecho.co.uk
 Editor, Neal Butterworth
DORSET ECHO
Fleet House, Hampshire Road, Weymouth, Dorset DT4 9XD
 T 01305-830930 **W** www.dorsetecho.co.uk
 Editor, Toby Granville
EXPRESS & ECHO
Express & Echo News & Media, Heron Road, Sowton, Exeter
 EX2 7NF **T** 01392-442211 **W** www.thisisexeter.co.uk
 Editor, Marc Astley

GLOUCESTERSHIRE ECHO
Third Floor, St James's House, St James's Square, Cheltenham,
 Glos. GL50 3PR **T** 01242-278000
 W www.thisisgloucestershire.co.uk
 Editor, Kevan Blackadder
THE HERALD
17 Brest Road, Derriford Business Park, Plymouth PL6 5AA
 T 01752-765500 **W** www.thisisplymouth.co.uk
 Editor, Bill Martin
HERALD EXPRESS
Harmsworth House, Barton Hill Road, Torquay, Devon TQ2 8JN
 T 01803-676000 **W** www.thisissouthdevon.co.uk
 Editor, Andy Phelan
SUNDAY INDEPENDENT
The Sunday Independent Newspapers Ltd, Webbs House,
 Tindle Suite, Liskeard, Cornwall PL14 6AH **T** 01579-342174
 Editor, John Noble
SWINDON ADVERTISER
100 Victoria Road, Old Town, Swindon SN1 3BE
 T 01793-528144 **W** www.swindonadvertiser.co.uk
 Editor, Dave King
WESTERN DAILY PRESS
Bristol Evening Post and Press Ltd, Temple Way, Bristol
 BS99 7HD **T** 0117-934 3000
 W www.westerndailypress.co.uk
 Editor, Tim Dixon
THE WESTERN MORNING NEWS
17 Brest Road, Derriford, Plymouth PL6 5AA **T** 01752-765500
 W www.thisiswesternmorningnews.co.uk
 Editor, Alan Qualtrough

WEST MIDLANDS
BIRMINGHAM MAIL
6th Floor, Fort Dunlop, Fort Parkway, Birmingham B24 9FF
 T 0121-236 3366 **W** www.birminghammail.net
 Editor, David Brookes
THE BIRMINGHAM POST
6th Floor, Fort Dunlop, Fort Parkway, Birmingham B24 9FF
 T 0121-234 5301 **W** www.birminghampost.net
 Editor, David Brookes
COVENTRY TELEGRAPH
Corporation Street, Coventry CV1 1FP **T** 024-7663 3633
 W www.coventrytelegraph.net
 Editor, Darren Parkin
EXPRESS & STAR
51–53 Queen Street, Wolverhampton WV1 1ES
 T 01902-313131 **W** www.expressandstar.com
 Editor, Adrian Faber
THE SENTINEL
Staffordshire Sentinel News & Media Ltd, Sentinel House,
 Etruria, Stoke-on-Trent ST1 5SS **T** 01782-602525
 W www.thisisthesentinel.co.uk
 Editor, Michael Sassi
SHROPSHIRE STAR
Waterloo Road, Ketley, Telford TF1 5HU **T** 01952-242424
 W www.shropshirestar.com
 Editor, Sarah Jane Smith
WORCESTER NEWS
Berrows House, Hylton Road, Worcester WR2 5JX
 T 01905-748200 **W** www.worcesternews.co.uk
 Editor, Kevin Ward

YORKSHIRE AND HUMBERSIDE
EVENING COURIER
PO Box 19, King Cross Street, Halifax HX1 2SF **T** 01422-260200
 W www.halifaxcourier.co.uk
 Editor, Tim Robinson

EVENING NEWS
17–23 Aberdeen Walk, Scarborough, North Yorkshire YO11 1BB
T 01723-363636 W www.scarboroughmeveningnews.co.uk
Editor, Ed Asquith
GRIMSBY TELEGRAPH
80 Cleethorpe Road, Grimsby, North East Lincolnshire
DN31 3EH T 01472-360360 W www.thisisgrimsby.co.uk
Editor, Michelle Lalor
THE HUDDERSFIELD DAILY EXAMINER
Trinity Mirror Huddersfield Ltd, Queen Street South,
Huddersfield HD1 3DU T 01484-430000
W www.examiner.co.uk
Editor, Roy Wright
HULL DAILY MAIL
Blundell's Corner, Beverley Road, Hull HU3 1XS
T 01482-327111 W www.thisishullandeastriding.co.uk
Editor, John Meehan
THE PRESS
Newsquest York, PO Box 29, 76–86 Walmgate, York YO1 9YN
T 01904-653051 W www.yorkpress.co.uk
Managing Editor, Steve Hughes
SHEFFIELD STAR
York Street, Sheffield S1 1PU T 0114-276 7676
W www.thestar.co.uk
Editor, Alan Powell
TELEGRAPH & ARGUS
Hall Ings, Bradford BD1 1JR T 01274-729511
W www.telegraphandargus.co.uk
Editor, Perry Austin-Clarke
YORKSHIRE EVENING POST
PO Box 168, Wellington Street, Leeds LS1 1RF T 0113-2432701
W www.yorkshireeveningpost.co.uk
Editor, Paul Napier
YORKSHIRE POST
Wellington Street, Leeds LS1 1RF T 0113-243 2701
W www.yorkshirepost.co.uk
Editor, Peter Charlton

SCOTLAND
THE COURIER AND ADVERTISER
D.C. Thomson & Co. Ltd, 80 Kingsway East, Dundee DD4 8SL
T 01382-223131 W www.thecourier.co.uk
Editor, Mike Alexander
DUNDEE EVENING TELEGRAPH AND POST
80 Kingsway East, Dundee DD4 8SL T 01382-223131
W www.eveningtelegraph.co.uk
EVENING EXPRESS
Aberdeen Journals Ltd, PO Box 43, Lang Stracht, Mastrick,
Aberdeen AB15 6DF T 01224-690222
W www.eveningexpress.co.uk
Editor, Alan McCabe
EVENING NEWS
108 Holyrood Road, Edinburgh EH8 8AS T 0131-620 8620
W www.edinburghnews.com
Editor, Tom Little
GLASGOW EVENING TIMES
200 Renfield Street, Glasgow G2 3QB T 0141-302 7000
W www.eveningtimes.co.uk
Editor, Tony Carlin
INVERNESS COURIER
New Century House, Stadium Road, Inverness IV1 1FG
T 01463-233059 W www.inverness-courier.co.uk
Editor, Robert Taylor
PAISLEY DAILY EXPRESS
Scottish and Universal Newspapers Ltd, 14 New Street, Paisley,
Renfrewshire PA1 1YA T 0141-887 7911
W www.paisleydailyexpress.co.uk
Editor, Anne Dalrymple

THE PRESS AND JOURNAL
Lang Stracht, Aberdeen AB15 6DF T 01224-690222
W www.pressandjournal.co.uk
Editor, Damian Bates

WALES
THE LEADER
NWN Media Ltd, Mold Business Park, Wrexham Road, Mold,
Flintshire CH7 1XY T 01352-707707
W www.leaderlive.co.uk
Editor, Barrie Jones
SOUTH WALES ARGUS
South Wales Argus, Cardiff Road, Maesglas, Newport, Gwent
NP20 3QN T 01633-810000
W www.southwalesargus.co.uk
Editor, Gerry Keighley
SOUTH WALES ECHO
6 Park Street, Cardiff CF10 1XR T 02920-223333
W www.walesonline.co.uk
Editor, Tim Gordon
SOUTH WALES EVENING POST
PO Box 14, Adelaide Street, Swansea SA1 1QT
T 01792-510000 W www.thisissouthwales.co.uk
Editor-in-Chief, Spencer Feeney
WESTERN MAIL
6 Park Street, Cardiff CF10 1XR T 029-2022 3333
W www.walesonline.co.uk
Editor, Alan Edmunds

NORTHERN IRELAND
BELFAST TELEGRAPH
124–144 Royal Avenue, Belfast BT1 1EB T 028-9026 4000
W www.belfasttelegraph.co.uk
Editor, Mike Gilson
IRISH NEWS
113–117 Donegall Street, Belfast BT1 2GE T 028-9032 2226
W www.irishnews.com
Editor, Noel Doran
NEWS LETTER
2 Esky Drive, Portadown, Craigavon, Belfast BT63 5YY
T 028-9089 7720 W www.newsletter.co.uk
Editor, Darwin Templeton
SUNDAY LIFE
124–144 Royal Avenue, Belfast BT1 1EB T 028-9026 4000
W www.sundaylife.co.uk
Editor, Martin Breen

CHANNEL ISLANDS
GUERNSEY PRESS AND STAR
PO Box 57, Braye Road, Vale, Guernsey GY1 3BW
T 01481-240240 W www.guernseypress.com
Editor, Richard Digard
JERSEY EVENING POST
PO Box 582, Five Oaks, St Saviour, Jersey JE4 8XQ
T 01534-611611 W www.thisisjersey.com
Editor, Chris Bright

PERIODICALS

ACCOUNTANCY AGE
Incisive Media, 32–34 Broadwick Street, London W1A 2HG
T 020-7316 9000 W www.accountancyage.com
Editor, Gavin Hinks
ACCOUNTING & BUSINESS
Association of Chartered Certified Accountants, 29 Lincolns Inn
Fields, London WC2A 3EE T 020-7059 5000
W www.accaglobal.com
Editor, Chris Quick

AEROPLANE MONTHLY
IPC Media Ltd, The Blue Fin Building, 110 Southwark Street,
London SE1 0SU **T** 020-3148 4100
W www.aeroplanemonthly.com
Editor, Michael Oakey

AESTHETICA MAGAZINE
PO Box 371, York YO23 1WL **T** 01904-479168
W www.aestheticamagazine.com
Editor, Cherie Federico

AFRICA CONFIDENTIAL
Asempa Ltd, 73 Farringdon Road, London EC1M 3JQ
T 020-7831 3511 **W** www.africa-confidential.com
Editor, Patrick Smith

ALL OUT CRICKET
Unit 3–23 Kennington Court, 1–3 Brixton Road, London
SW9 6DE **T** 020-3176 0187 **W** www.alloutcricket.com
Editor, Andy Afford

AMATEUR GARDENING
IPC Media Ltd, Westover House, West Quay Road, Poole,
Dorset BH15 1JG **T** 01202-440840
W www.amateurgardening.com
Editor, Tim Rumball

AMATEUR PHOTOGRAPHER
IPC Media, The Blue Fin Building, 110 Southwark Street,
London SE1 0SU **T** 020-3148 5000
W www.amateurphotographer.co.uk
Editor, Damien Demolder

AMBIT
17 Priory Gardens, London N6 5QY **T** 020-8340 3566
W www.ambitmagazine.co.uk
Editor, Martin Bax

ANGLING TIMES
Bauer Consumer Media, Bushfield House, Orton Centre,
Peterborough PE2 5UW **T** 01733-395106
W www.gofishing.co.uk/Angling-Times
Editor, Richard Lee

APOLLO
22 Old Queen Street, London SW1H 9HP **T** 020-7961 0150
W www.apollo-magazine.com
Editor, Oscar Humphries

THE ARCHITECTS' JOURNAL
EMAP Construct, Greater London House, Hampstead Road,
London NW1 7EJ **T** 020-7728 5000
W www.architectsjournal.co.uk
Editor, Kieran Long

ART MONTHLY
4th Floor, 28 Charing Cross Road, London WC2H 0DB
T 020-7240 0389 **W** www.artmonthly.co.uk
Editor, Patricia Bickers

THE ART NEWSPAPER
70 South Lambeth Road, London SW8 1RL **T** 020-7735 3331
W www.theartnewspaper.com
Editor, Jane Morris

ART QUARTERLY
The Art Fund, Millais House, 7 Cromwell Place, London SW7 2JN
T 020-7225 4800 **W** www.artfund.org
Editor, Caroline Bugler

ASTRONOMY NOW
Pole Star Publications, PO Box 175, Tonbridge, Kent TN10 4ZY
T 01732-446110 **W** www.astronomynow.com
Editor, Keith Cooper

ATTITUDE
Ground Floor, 211 Old Street, London EC1V 9NR
T 020-7608 6446 **W** www.attitude.co.uk
Editor, Matthew Todd

BBC HISTORY MAGAZINE
Bristol Magazines Ltd, Tower House, Fairfax Street, Bristol
BS1 3BN **T** 0117-927 9009 **W** www.historyextra.com
Editor, Dave Musgrove

THE BEANO
D.C. Thomson & Co. Ltd, 2 Albert Square, Dundee DD1 9QJ
W www.beano.com
Editor, Alan Digby

THE BIG ISSUE
1–5 Wandsworth Road, London SW8 2LN **T** 020-7526 3200
W www.bigissue.com
Editor-in-Chief, Charles Howgego

BIKE
Bauer Consumer Media, Media House, Lynchwood,
Peterborough PE2 6EA **T** 01733-468181
W www.bikemagazine.co.uk
Editor, Tim Thompson

BIRDWATCH
Solo Publishing Ltd, The Chocolate Factory, 5 Clarendon
Road, London N22 6XJ **T** 020-8881 0550
W www.birdwatch.co.uk
Editor, Dominic Mitchell

BIZARRE
Dennis Publishing, 30 Cleveland Street, London W1T 4JD
T 020-7907 6000 **W** www.bizarremag.com
Editor, David McComb

THE BOOKSELLER
Endeavour House, 189 Shaftesbury Avenue, London WC2H 8TJ
T 020-7420 6006 **W** www.thebookseller.com
Editor-in-Chief, Neill Denny

BRITISH CHESS MAGAZINE
44 Baker Street, London W1U 7RT **T** 020-7486 8222
W www.bcmchess.co.uk
Editor, John Saunders

BRITISH DEAF NEWS
British Deaf Association, Bushell Street Mill, Bushell Street,
Preston, Lancs PR1 2SP **T** 01772-259725
W www.bda.org.uk
Editor, Alison Gudgeon

THE BRITISH JOURNAL OF PHOTOGRAPHY
32–34 Broadwick Street, London W1A 2HG **T** 020-7316 9000
W www.bjp-online.com
Editor, Simon Bainbridge

BRITISH JOURNALISM REVIEW
Sage Publications, 1 Oliver's Yard, 55 City Road, London
EC1Y 1SP **T** 020-7324 8500 **W** www.bjr.org.uk
Editor, Bill Hagerty

BRITISH MEDICAL JOURNAL
BMJ Publishing Group, BMA House, Tavistock Square, London
WC1H 9JR **T** 020-7387 4499 **W** www.bmj.com
Editor, Dr Fiona Godlee

BRITISH PHILATELIC BULLETIN
Royal Mail, 35–50 Rathbone Place, London W1T 1HQ
W www.royalmail.com/stamps
Editor, J.R. Holman

BUILDING DESIGN
UBM Information Ltd, Ludgate House, 245 Blackfriars
Road, London SE1 9UY **T** 020-7921 5000
W www.bdonline.co.uk
Editor, Amanda Baillieu

CANALS & RIVERS
PO Box 618, Norwich NR7 0QT **T** 01603-708930
W www.canalsandrivers.co.uk
Editor, Chris Cattrall

CAR
Bauer Consumer Media, 3rd Floor, Media House, Lynchwood,
Peterborough PE2 6EA **T** 01733-468379
Editor, Phil McNamara

CARAVAN MAGAZINE
IPC Inspire, Leon House, 233 High Street, Croydon CR9 1HZ
T 020-8726 8000 **W** www.caravanmagazine.co.uk
Editor, Victoria Bentley

CHURCH TIMES
13–17 Long Lane, London EC1A 9DJ **T** 020-7776 1060
    W www.churchtimes.co.uk
    Editor, Paul Handley
CLASSIC CARS
Bauer Consumer Media, Media House, Lynchwood,
    Peterborough Business Park, Peterborough PE2 6EA
    T 01733-468000 **W** www.classiccarsmagazine.co.uk
    Editor, Phil Bell
CLASSIC ROCK
Future Publishing Ltd, 2 Balcombe Street, London NW1 6NW
    T 020-7042 4000 **W** www.classicrockmagazine.com
    Editor-in-Chief, Scott Rowley
CLASSICAL MUSIC
Rhinegold Publishing Ltd, 241 Shaftesbury Avenue,
    London WC2H 8TF **T** 020-7333 1742
    W www.rhinegold.co.uk
    Editor, Keith Clarke
CLIMB MAGAZINE
160–164 Barkby Road, Leicester LE16 8FZ **T** 0116-202 2600
    W www.climbmagazine.com
    Editor, David Pickford
COIN NEWS
Token Publishing Ltd, Orchard House, Duchy Road, Heathpark,
    Honiton, Devon EX14 1YD **T** 01404-46972
    Editor, John Mussell
COMMUNITY CARE
Reed Business Information Ltd, Quadrant House, The Quadrant,
    Sutton, Surrey SM2 5AS **T** 020-8652 3500
    W www.communitycare.co.uk
    Editor, Bronagh Miskelly
COMPUTER WEEKLY
Marble Arch Tower, 55 Bryanston Street, London W1H 7AA
    T 020-7868 4282 **W** www.computerweekly.com
    Editor, Brian McKenna
CONDÉ NAST TRAVELLER
Vogue House, Hanover Square, London W1S 1JU
    T 020-7499 9080 **W** www.cntraveller.com
    Editor, Sarah Miller
CONTEMPORARY
Studio 56, 4 Montpelier Street, London SW7 1EE
    T 020-7019 6205 **W** www.contemporary-magazines.com
    Editor, Brian Muller
CONTEMPORARY REVIEW
Contemporary Review Co. Ltd, PO Box 1242, Oxford OX1 4FJ
    T 01865-201529 **W** www.contemporaryreview.co.uk
    Editor, Dr Richard Mullen
COSMOPOLITAN
National Magazine House, 72 Broadwick Street, London
    W1F 9EP **T** 020-7439 5000
    Editor-in-Chief, Louise Court
COUNTRYFILE
9th Floor, Tower House, Fairfax Street, Bristol BS1 3BN
    T 0117-927 9009 **W** www.countryfile.com
    Editor, Fergus Collins
COUNTRY LIFE
IPC Media Ltd, The Blue Fin Building, 110 Southwark Street,
    London SE1 0SU **T** 020-3148 4444
    W www.countrylife.co.uk
    Editor, Mark Hedges
CYCLING WEEKLY
IPC Media, Leon House, 233 High Street, Croydon CR9 1HZ
    T 020-8726 8462 **W** www.cyclingweekly.co.uk
    Editor, Robert Garbutt
DARTS WORLD
MB Graphics, 25 Orlestone View, Ham Street, Ashford, Kent
    TN26 2LB **T** 01233-733558 **W** www.dartsworld.com
    Editor, Michael Beeken

DIGITAL CAMERA
Future Publishing Ltd, 30 Monmouth Street, Bath BA1 2BW
    W www.magazine.photoradar.com
    Editor, Geoff Harris
DISABILITY NOW
6 Market Road, London N7 9PW **T** 020-7619 7323
    W www.disabilitynow.org.uk
    Editor, Ian Macrae
THE ECOLOGIST
Unit 102, Lana House Studios, 116–118 Commercial Street,
    London E1 6NF **T** 020-7422 8100 **W** www.theecologist.org
    Editor, Mark Anslow
THE ECONOMIST
25 St James's Street, London SW1A 1HG **T** 020-7830 7000
    W www.economist.com
    Editor, John Micklethwait
ELLE
Hachette Filipacchi UK, 64 North Row, London W1K 7LL
    T 020-7150 7000 **W** www.elleuk.com
    Editor, Lorraine Candy
EMPIRE
Bauer Consumer Media, Mappin House, 4 Winsley Street,
    London W1W 8HF **T** 020-7182 8000
    W www.empireonline.com
    Editor, Mark Dinning
THE ENGINEER
Centaur Communications Ltd, St Giles House, 50 Poland Street,
    London W1F 7AX **T** 020-7970 4437
    W www.theengineer.com
    Editor, Jon Excell
ESQUIRE
National Magazine House, 72 Broadwick Street, London
    W1F 9EP **T** 020-7439 5000 **W** www.esquire.co.uk
    Editor, Alex Bilmes
ESSENTIALS
IPC Media, The Blue Fin Building, 110 Southwark Street,
    London SE1 0SU **T** 020-3148 7211
    Editor, Jules Barton-Breck
FAMILY TREE
61 Great Whyte, Ramsey, Huntingdon, Cambs PE26 1HJ
    T 01487-814050 **W** www.family-tree.co.uk
    Editor, Helen Tovey
FARMERS WEEKLY
Reed Business Information, Quadrant House, The Quadrant,
    Sutton, Surrey SM2 5AS **T** 020-8652 4911 **W** www.fwi.co.uk
    Editor, Jane King
FHM
Bauer Consumer Media, Endeavour House, 189 Shaftesbury
    Avenue, London WC2H 8JG **T** 020-7182 8000
    W www.fhm.com
    Editor, Joe Barnes
FOCUS
Bristol Magazines Ltd, Tower House, Fairfax Street, Bristol
    BS1 3BN **T** 0117-927 9009 **W** www.sciencefocus.com
    Editor, Jheni Osman
FOLIO
2nd Floor, Bristol News and Media, Temple Way, Bristol
    BS99 7HD **T** 0117-942 8491 **W** www.foliomagazine.co.uk
    Editor, Mike Gartside
FORTEAN TIMES
Box 2409, London NW5 4NP **T** 020-7907 6235
    W www.forteantimes.com
    Editor, David Sutton
FOURFOURTWO
Haymarket, Teddington Studios, Broom Road, Teddington,
    Middlesex TW11 9BE **T** 020-8267 5848
    W www.fourfourtwo.magazine.co.uk
    Editor, David Hall

FRANCE
Archant House, Oriel Road, Cheltenham, Glos. GL50 1BB
T 01242-216050 W www.francemag.com
Editor, Carolyn Boyd

GAMESMASTER
Future Publishing Ltd, 30 Monmouth Street, Bath BA1 2BW
T 01225-442244
Editor-in-Chief, Robin Alway

GARDEN NEWS
Bauer Consumer Media Ltd, Lincoln Road, Peterborough
PE1 2RF T 01733-237111
W www.gardennewsmagazine.co.uk
Editor, Clare Foggett

GAY TIMES – GT
Spectrum House, 32–34 Gordon House Road, London
NW5 1LP T 020-7424 7400 W www.gaytimes.co.uk
Editor, Tris Reid-Smith

GEOGRAPHICAL JOURNAL
1 Kensington Gore, London SW7 2AR T 020-7591 3026
Editor, Prof. Klaus Dodds

GLAMOUR
6–8 Old Bond Street, London W1S 4PH T 020-7499 9080
W www.glamourmagazine.com
Editor, Jo Elvin

GOLF WORLD
Bauer Media, Media House, Lynchwood, Peterborough
Business Park, Peterborough PE2 6EA T 01733-468000
W www.golf-world.co.uk
Editor, Chris Jones

GOOD HOUSEKEEPING
National Magazine House, 72 Broadwick Street, London W1F 9EP
T 020-7439 5000 W www.goodhousekeeping.co.uk
Editorial Director, Lindsay Nicholson

GQ
Condé Nast Publications, Vogue House, Hanover Square,
London W1S 1JU T 020-7499 9080
W www.gq-magazine.co.uk
Editor, Dylan Jones

GRANTA
12 Addison Avenue, London W11 4QR T 020-7605 1360
W www.granta.com
Editor, John Freeman

GRAZIA
BauerConsumer Media, Endeavour House, 189 Shaftesbury
Avenue, London WC2H 8JG T 020-7437 9011
W www.graziadaily.co.uk
Editor-in-Chief, Jane Bruton

THE GROCER
William Reed Publishing Ltd, Broadfield Park, Crawley, West
Sussex RH11 9RT T 01293-613400 W www.thegrocer.co.uk
Editor, Adam Leyland

GUITARIST
Future Publishing UK, 30 Monmouth Street, Bath BA1 2BW
T 01225-442244 W www.guitarist.co.uk
Editor, Mick Taylor

HARPER'S BAZAAR
National Magazine House, 72 Broadwick Street, London
W1F 9EP T 020-7439 5000 W www.harpersbazaar.co.uk
Editor, Lucy Yeomans

HEAT
Bauer Consumer Media, Endeavour House, 189 Shaftesbury
Avenue, London WC2H 8JG T 020-7437 9011
W www.heatworld.com
Editor, Sam Delaney

HELLO!
Wellington House, 69–71 Upper Ground, London SE1 9PQ
T 020-7667 8700 W www.hellomagazine.com
Editor-in-Chief, Eduardo Sanchez Perez

HISTORY TODAY
25 Bedford Avenue, London WC1B 3AT T 020-3219 7810
W www.historytoday.com
Editor, Paul Lay

HORSE & HOUND
IPC Inspire, 9th Floor, The Blue Fin Building, 110 Southwark
Street, London SE1 0SU T 020-3148 4562
W www.horseandhound.co.uk
Editor, Lucy Higginson

HOUSE & GARDEN
Vogue House, 1 Hanover Square, London W1S 1JU
T 020-7499 9080
Editor, Susan Crewe

ICON MAGAZINE
Media 10, National House, High Street, Epping, Essex
CM16 4BD T 01992-570030 W www.iconeye.com
Editor, Justin McGuirk

IN STYLE
IPC Southbank, The Blue Fin Building, 110 Southwark Street,
London SE1 0SU T 020-3148 5000
Editor, Eilidh MacAskill

INTERNATIONAL AFFAIRS
The Royal Institute of International Affairs, Chatham
House, 10 St James's Square, London SW1Y 4LE
T 020-7957 5728
Editor, Caroline Soper

JEWISH CHRONICLE
25 Furnival Street, London EC4A 1JT T 020-7415 1500
W www.thejc.com
Editor, Stephen Pollard

KERRANG!
Endeavour House, Shaftesbury Avenue, London WC2H 8JG
T 020-7182 8406 W www.kerrang.com
Editor, Nichola Browne

THE LADY
39–40 Bedford Street, London WC2E 9ER T 020-7379 4717
W www.lady.co.uk
Editor, Rachel Johnson

LANCET
32 Jamestown Road, London NW1 7BY T 020-7424 4910
W www.thelancet.com
Editor, Dr Richard Horton

THE LAWYER
Centaur Communications Group, St Giles House, 50 Poland
Street, London W1F 7AX T 020-7970 4000
W www.thelawyer.com
Editor, Catrin Griffiths

LEGAL WEEK
32–34 Broadwick Street, London W1A 2HG T 020-7316 9000
W www.legalweek.com
Editor, Alex Novarese

THE LIST
14 High Street, Edinburgh EH1 1TE T 0131-550 3050
W www.list.co.uk
Editor, Jonathan Ensall

THE LITERARY REVIEW
44 Lexington Street, London W1F 0LW T 020-7437 9392
W www.literaryreview.co.uk
Editor, Nancy Sladek

LOADED
IPC Ignite, The Blue Fin Building, 110 Southwark Street, London
SE1 0SU T 020-3148 5000 W www.loaded.co.uk
Editor, Andy Sherwood

THE LONDON MAGAZINE: A REVIEW OF LITERATURE
AND THE ARTS
Administration Flat 5, 11 Queen's Gate, London SW7 5EL
W www.thelondonmagazine.net
Editor, Steven O'Brien

LONDON REVIEW OF BOOKS
28 Little Russell Street, London WC1A 2HN **T** 020-7209 1101
W www.lrb.co.uk
Editor, Mary-Kay Wilmers
MACWORLD
101 Euston Road, London NW1 2RA **T** 020-7756 2877
W www.macworld.co.uk
Editor, Karen Haslam
MARIE CLAIRE
European Magazines Ltd, 7th Floor, The Blue Fin Building,
110 Southwark Street, London SE1 0SU **T** 020-3148 7513
W www.marieclaire.co.uk
Editor, Trish Halpin
MEDIA WEEK
Haymarket Publishing Ltd, 174 Hammersmith Road, London
W6 7JP **T** 020-8267 8034 **W** www.mediaweek.co.uk
Editor, Harriet Dennys
MEN'S HEALTH
Natmag Rodale Ltd, 33 Broadwick Street, London W1F 0DQ
T 020-7339 4400 **W** www.menshealth.co.uk
Editor, Morgan Rees
MODEL ENGINEER
MyHobbyStore Ltd, PO Box 718, Orpington, Kent BR6 1AP
T 01847-821136
Editor, David Clark
MOJO
Bauer Consumer Media, Mappin House, 4 Winsley Street,
London W1W 8HF **T** 020-7182 8616
W www.mojo4music.com
Editor, Phil Alexander
MOTOR BOAT AND YACHTING
IPC Media Ltd, The Blue Fin Building, 110 Southwark Street,
London SE1 0SU **T** 020-3148 4651 **W** www.mby.com
Editor, Hugo Andreae
MUSCLE & FITNESS
Weider Publishing, 10 Windsor Court, Clarence Drive,
Harrogate, North Yorkshire HG1 2PE **T** 01423-504516
W www.muscle-fitness-europe.com
Editor, Chris Lund
MUSIC WEEK
CMPi, 1st Floor, Ludgate House, 245 Blackfriars Road, London
SE1 9UY **W** www.musicweek.com
Editor, Paul Williams
THE NATIONAL TRUST MAGAZINE
The National Trust, Heelis, Kemble Drive, Swindon SN2 2NA
T 01793-817400 **W** www.nationaltrust.org.uk
Editor, Sue Herdman
NATURE
Macmillan Magazines Ltd, The Macmillan Building, 4 Crinan
Street, London N1 9XW **T** 020-7833 4000
W www.nature.com/nature
Editor, Philip Campbell
NB MAGAZINE
RNIB, 105 Judd Street, London WC1H 9NE **T** 020-7391 2070
Editor, Ann Lee
NEW HUMANIST
1 Gower Street, London WC1E 6HD **T** 020-7436 1171
W www.newhumanist.org.uk
Editor, Caspar Melville
NEW MUSICAL EXPRESS (NME)
IPC Ignite, The Blue Fin Building, 110 Southwark Street,
London SE1 0SU **T** 020-3148 5000
W www.nme.com/magazine
Editor, Krissi Murison
NEW SCIENTIST
Lacon House, 84 Theobalds Road, London WC1X 8NS
T 020-7611 1200 **W** www.newscientist.com
Editor, Jeremy Webb

NEW STATESMAN
7th Floor, John Carpenter House, John Carpenter Street,
London EC4Y 0AN **T** 020-7730 3444
W www.newstatesman.co.uk
Editor, Jason Cowley
THE NEWSPAPER
Young Media Holdings Ltd, PO Box 400, Bridgwater TA6 9DT
T 0845-094 0646 **W** www.thenewspaper.org.uk
Managing Editor, Phil Wood
NOW
IPC Connect, The Blue Fin Building, 110 Southwark Street,
London SE1 0SU **T** 020-3148 5000
W www.nowmagazine.co.uk
Editor, Sally Eyden
OK!
Northern & Shell Building, 10 Lower Thames Street, London
EC3R 6EN **T** 0871-434 1010 **W** www.ok-magazine.com
Editor, Lisa Byrne
THE OLDIE
65 Newman Street, London W1T 3EG **T** 020-7436 8801
W www.theoldie.co.uk
Editor, Richard Ingrams
OPERA
36 Black Lion Lane, London W6 9BE **T** 020-8563 8893
W www.opera.co.uk
Editor, John Allison
OPERA NOW
241 Shaftesbury Avenue, London WC2H 8TF **T** 020-7333 1740
W www.rhinegold.co.uk
Editor, Ashutosh Khandekar
PC PRO
Dennis Publishing Ltd, 30 Cleveland Street, London W1T 4JD
T 020-7907 6000 **W** www.pcpro.co.uk
Editor, Barry Collins
PEACE NEWS
5 Caledonian Road, London N1 9DY **T** 020-7278 3344
W www.peacenews.info
Editors, Emily Johns and Milan Rai
THE PHOTOGRAPHER
PO Box 9337, Witham, Essex CM8 2UT **T** 01279-503871
W www.bipp.com
Editor, Jonathan Briggs
PICK ME UP
IPC Connect Ltd, The Blue Fin Building, 110 Southwark Street,
London SE1 0SU **T** 020-3148 5000
W www.pickmeupmagazine.co.uk
Editor, Rachel Tompkins
POETRY LONDON
81 Lambeth Walk, London SE11 6DX **T** 020-7735 8880
W www.poetrylondon.co.uk
Editor, Colette Bryce
POETRY REVIEW
22 Betterton Street, London WC2H 9BX **T** 020-7420 9883
W www.poetrysociety.org.uk
Editor, Fiona Sampson
THE POLITICAL QUARTERLY
Wiley-Blackwell, 9600 Garsington Road, Oxford OX4 2DQ
T 01865-776868 **W** www.wiley.com
Editor, Andrew Gamble
PRACTICAL PARENTING
Magicalia Limited, 15–18 White Lion Street, Islington,
London N1 9PD **T** 020-7843 8800
W www.practicalparenting.co.uk
Editor, Daniella Delaney
PRACTICAL PHOTOGRAPHY
Bauer, Media House, Lynchwood, Peterborough PE2 6EA
T 01733-468000 **W** www.practicalphotography.co.uk
Editor-in-Chief, Andrew James

PRESS GAZETTE
John Carpenter House, John Carpenter Street, London
   EC4Y 0AN **T** 020-7936 6432 **W** www.pressgazette.co.uk
   Editor, Dominic Ponsford
PRIDE
Pride House, 55 Battersea Bridge Road, London SW11 3AX
   T 020-7228 3110 **W** www.pridemagazine.com
   Publisher, C. Cushnie
PRIVATE EYE
6 Carlisle Street, London W1D 3BN **T** 020-7437 4017
   W www.private-eye.co.uk
   Editor, Ian Hislop
PROSPECT MAGAZINE
Prospect Publishing Ltd, 2 Bloomsbury Place, London
   WC1A 2QA **T** 020-7255 1281
   W www.prospect-magazine.co.uk
   Editor, Bronwen Maddox
PSYCHOLOGIES
Hachette Filipacchi UK Ltd, 64 North Row, London W1K 7LL
   T 020-7150 7000 **W** www.psychologies.co.uk
   Editor, Louise Chunn
PULSE
CMP Medica Ltd, Ludgate House, 245 Blackfriars Road, London
   SE1 9UY **T** 020-7921 8102 **W** www.pulsetoday.co.uk
   Editor, Jo Haynes
Q MAGAZINE
Endeavour House, 189 Shaftesbury Avenue, London
   WC2H 8JG **T** 020-7182 8000 **W** www.qthemusic.com
   Editor, Paul Rees
RA MAGAZINE
Royal Academy of Arts, Burlington House, Piccadilly, London
   W1J 0BD **T** 020-7300 5820 **W** www.ramagazine.org.uk
   Acting Editor, Sarah Greenberg
RADIO TIMES
BBC Worldwide Ltd, 201 Wood Lane, London W12 7TQ
   T 020-8433 3400 **W** www.radiotimes.com
   Editor, Ben Preston
RAILWAY MAGAZINE
Media Centre, Morton Way, Horncastle, Lincs LN9 6JR
   T 01507-529589 **W** www.railwaymagazine.co.uk
   Editor, Nick Pigott
READER'S DIGEST
The Reader's Digest Association Ltd, 11 Westferry Circus,
   Canary Wharf, London E14 4HE **T** 020-7715 8000
   W www.readersdigest.co.uk
   Editor-in-Chief, Gill Hudson
RED
Hachette Filipacchi UK Ltd, 64 North Row, London W1K 7LL
   T 020-7150 7600 **W** www.redonline.co.uk
   Editor-in-Chief, Sam Baker
RUGBY WORLD
IPC Media Ltd, 9th Floor, The Blue Fin Building, 110 Southwark
   Street, London SE1 0SU **T** 020-3148 5000
   Editor, Paul Morgan
RUNNER'S WORLD
Natmag Rodale Ltd, 33 Broadwick Street, London W1F 0DG
   T 020-7339 4400 **W** www.runnersworld.co.uk
   Editor, Andy Dixon
SAGA MAGAZINE
Saga Publishing Ltd, The Saga Building, Enbrook Park,
   Sandgate, Folkestone, Kent CT20 3SE **T** 01303-771523
   W www.saga.co.uk/saga-magazine
   Editor, Katy Bravery
SCREEN INTERNATIONAL
EMAP Media, Greater London House, 1 Hampstead Road,
   London NW1 7EJ **T** 020-7728 5000
   W www.screendaily.com
   Editor, Conor Dignam

SFX MAGAZINE
Future Publishing Ltd, 30 Monmouth Street, Bath BA1 2BW
   T 01225-442244 **W** www.sfx.co.uk
   Editor, Dave Bradley
SHOOTING TIMES AND COUNTRY MAGAZINE
IPC Inspire, The Blue Fin Building, 110 Southwark Street,
   London SE1 0SU **T** 020-3148 4741
   W www.shootingtimes.co.uk
   Editor, Camilla Clark
SIGHT AND SOUND
BFI, 21 Stephen Street, London W1T 1LN **T** 020-7255 1444
   W www.bfi.org.uk/sightandsound
   Editor, Nick James
SKI + BOARD
The Ski Club of Great Britain, The White House, 57–63 Church
   Road, London SW19 5SB **T** 020-8410 2010
   W www.skiclub.co.uk
   Editor, Arnie Wilson
SMARTPHONE ESSENTIALS
Imagine Publishing Ltd, Richmond House, 33 Richmond Hill,
   Bournemouth BH2 6EZ **W** www.smartphonedaily.co.uk
   Editor, Andy Betts
SNOOKER SCENE
Hayley Green Court, 130 Hagley Road, Halesowen, West
   Midlands B63 1DY **T** 0121-585 9188
   W www.snookerscene.com
   Editor, Clive Everton
THE SPECTATOR
22 Old Queen Street, London SW1H 9HP **T** 020-7961 0200
   W www.spectator.co.uk
   Editor, Fraser Nelson
SPECTATOR BUSINESS
22 Old Queen Street, London SW1H 9HP **T** 020-7961 0200
   W www.spectator.co.uk/business
   Editor, Martin Vander Weyer
SPIRIT & DESTINY
H. Bauer Publishing, Academic House, 24–28 Oval Road,
   London NW1 7DT **T** 020-7241 8000
   Editor, Rhiannon Powell
THE STAGE
Stage House, 47 Bermondsey Street, London SE1 3XT
   T 020-7403 1818 **W** www.thestage.co.uk
   Editor, Brian Attwood
THE TABLET
1 King Street Cloisters, Clifton Walk, London W6 0GY
   T 020-8748 8484 **W** www.thetablet.co.uk
   Editor, Catherine Pepinster
TAKE A BREAK
H. Bauer Publishing, Academic House, 24–28 Oval Road,
   London NW1 7DT **T** 020-7241 8000
   W www.takeabreak.co.uk
   Editor, Rebecca Fleming
TATE ETC
20 John Islip Street, London SW1P 4RG **T** 020-7887 8724
   W www.tate.org.uk/tateetc
   Editor, Simon Grant
TATLER
Vogue House, Hanover Square, London W1S 1JU
   T 020-7499 9080 **W** www.tatler.co.uk
   Editor, Catherine Ostler
THE TEACHER
National Union of Teachers, Hamilton House, Mabledon Place,
   London WC1H 9BD **T** 020-7380 4708
   Editor, Elyssa Campbell-Barr
THE TES
26 Red Lion Square, Holborn WC1R 4HQ **T** 020-3194 3000
   W www.tes.co.uk
   Editor, Gerard Kelly

TGO (THE GREAT OUTDOORS) MAGAZINE
Newsquest, 200 Renfield Street, Glasgow G2 3QB
   T 0141-302 7736 W www.tgomagazine.co.uk
   Editor, Emily Rodway
TIME OUT LONDON
Time Out Group Ltd, Universal House, 251 Tottenham Court
   Road, London W1T 7AB T 020-7813 3000
   W www.timeout.com
   Acting Editor, Mark Frith
TLS (THE TIMES LITERARY SUPPLEMENT)
3 Thomas More Square, London E98 1BS T 020-7782 5000
   W www.the-tls.co.uk
   Editor, Peter Stothard
TOTAL FILM
2 Balcombe Street, London NW1 6NW T 020-7042 4000
   W www.totalfilm.com
   Editor, Aubrey Day
TRIBUNE
9 Arkwright Road, London NW3 6AN T 020-7433 6410
   Editor, Chris McLaughlin
VANITY FAIR
The Condé Nast Publications Ltd, Vogue House, Hanover
   Square, London W1S 1JU T 020-7499 9080
   W www.vanityfair.com
   Editor-in-Chief, Graydon Carter
VENUE
Bristol News & Media, Temple Way, Bristol BS99 7HD
   T 0117-942 8491 W www.venue.co.uk
   Editor, Joe Spurgeon
VIZ
Dennis Publishing, 30 Cleveland Street, London W1T 4JD
   T 020-7907 6000 W www.viz.co.uk
   Editor, Hampton Doubleday
VOGUE
Vogue House, 1 Hanover Square, London W1S 1JU
   T 020-7499 9080 W www.vogue.co.uk
   Editor, Alexandra Shulman
THE VOICE
6th Floor, Northern & Shell Tower, 4 Selsdon Way,
   London E14 9GL T 020-7510 0340
   W www.voice-online.co.uk
   Editor, Steve Pope
WALK
The Ramblers' Association, 2nd Floor, Camelford House, 87–90
   Albert Embankment, London SE1 7TW T 020-7339 8540
   W www.walkmag.co.uk
   Editor, Dominic Bates
WALLPAPER
IPC Media, The Blue Fin Building, 110 Southwark Street,
   London SE1 0SU T 020-3148 5000 W www.wallpaper.com
   Editor-in-Chief, Tony Chambers
WATERSTONE'S BOOKS QUARTERLY
Seven Squared, Sea Containers House, 20 Upper Ground,
   London SE1 9PD T 020-7775 5777
   W www.subscribeonline.com/wbq
   Editor, Keeley Young
WEDDING MAGAZINE
Hubert Burda Media Ltd, Swan House, 37–39 High Holborn,
   London WC1V 6AA T 020-7421 5000
   W www.weddingmagazine.co.uk
   Editor, Catherine Westwood
THE WEEK
The Week Ltd, 6th Floor, Compass House, 22 Redan Place,
   London W2 4SA T 020-7907 6180 W www.theweek.co.uk
   Editor, Caroline Law
WEIGHT WATCHERS MAGAZINE
River Publishing Ltd, 1 Neal Street, London WC2H 9QL
   T 020-7306 0304
   Editor, Mary Frances

WHAT CAR?
Haymarket Motoring Magazines Ltd, Teddington Studios,
   Broom Road, Teddington, Middlesex TW11 9BE
   T 020-8267 5688 W www.whatcar.com
   Group Editor, Steve Fowler
WHO DO YOU THINK YOU ARE?
BBC Magazines Bristol, 9th Floor, Tower House, Fairfax Street,
   Bristol BS1 3BN T 0117-314 7400
   W www.whodoyouthinkyouaremagazine.com
   Editor, Sarah Williams
THE WISDEN CRICKETER
2nd Floor, 123 Buckingham Palace Road, London SW1W 9SL
   T 020-7705 4911 W www.wisdencricketer.com
   Editor, John Stern
WOMAN'S OWN
IPC Connect Ltd, The Blue Fin Building, 110 Southwark Street,
   London SE1 0SU T 020-3148 5000
   Editor, Vicky Mayer
WOMAN'S WEEKLY
IPC Connect Ltd, The Blue Fin Building, 110 Southwark Street,
   London SE1 0SU T 020-3148 5000
   Editor, Diane Kenwood
THE WORD
Development Hell Ltd, 90–92 Pentonville Road, London N1 9HS
   T 020-7078 8400 W www.wordmagazine.co.uk
   Editor, Mark Ellen
WORLD SOCCER
IPC Inspire, The Blue Fin Building, 110 Southwark Street,
   London SE1 0SU T 020-3148 5000
   W www.worldsoccer.com
   Editor, Gavin Hamilton
THE WORLD TODAY
Chatham House, 10 St James's Square, London SW1Y 4LE
   T 020-7957 5712 W www.theworldtoday.org
   Editor, Graham Walker
WRITING MAGAZINE
5th Floor, 31–32 Park Row, Leeds LS1 5JD T 0113-200 2929
   W www.writersnews.co.uk
   Editor, Jonathan Telfer
YACHTING MONTHLY
IPC Media, The Blue Fin Building, 110 Southwark Street,
   London SE1 0SU T 020-3148 5000
   W www.yachtingmonthly.com
   Editor, Paul Gelder
YOGA & HEALTH
Yoga Today Ltd, PO Box 2130, Seaford, Sussex BN25 9BF
   T 01323-872466 W www.yogaandhealthmag.co.uk
   Editor, Jane Sill
YOUNG WRITER MAGAZINE
5th Floor, 31–32 Park Row, Leeds LS1 5JD T 0113-200 2929
   W www.youngwriter.org
   Editor, Matthew Hill
YOUR CAT MAGAZINE
BPG (Stamford) Ltd, Roebuck House, 33 Broad Street, Stamford,
   Lincs. PE9 1RB T 01780-766199 W www.yourcat.co.uk
   Editor, Sue Parslow
YOUR DOG MAGAZINE
BPG (Stamford) Ltd, Roebuck House, 33 Broad Street, Stamford,
   Lincs. PE9 1RB T 01780-766199 W www.yourdog.co.uk
   Editor, Sarah Wright
YOURS
Bauer Publishing, Media House, Peterborough Business Park,
   Peterborough PE2 6EA T 01733-468000
   W www.yours.co.uk
   Editor, Valery McConnell
ZEST
National Magazine House, 72 Broadwick Street, London
   W1F 9EP T 020-7439 5000 W www.zest.co.uk
   Editor, Mandie Gower

INTERNET

INTERNET TRENDS

The number of UK households with an internet connection continued to increase in 2010, with 900,000 connecting since 2009. This brought the UK's total up to 73 per cent – some 19.2 million households. Of the total number of new internet users in 2010, over half (around 1 million people) were 50 years or older. However, 60 per cent of over 65 year-olds had still never used the internet.

The steady increase in home-based internet has coincided with a drop in the use of internet cafes: only 3 per cent of users had accessed the internet this way in 2010, down by half since 2009. Conversely, the number of users connecting via wifi hotspots had quadrupled since 2007, while the number of UK adults going online on their mobile phone went from one quarter in 2009 to nearly one third.

TOP 10 BROADBAND SUBSCRIBERS BY COUNTRY

Country (2009 position)	2010
1. China (all territories) (1)	136,496,883
2. USA (2)	87,172,827
3. Japan (3)	34,467,000
4. Germany (4)	26,715,350
5. France (5)	19,887,530
6. UK (6)	19,607,600
7. South Korea (7)	17,202,641
8. Italy (8)	14,257,650
9. Brazil (9)	12,656,200
10. Russia (13)	11,619,000

Source: www.point-topic.com

With the proliferation of connection methods came the ability to log on more frequently, and for longer periods. The number of UK adults connecting to the internet at least once a day has increased steadily over the two years since 2008, from 69 per cent to 78 per cent in 2010.

The year also saw an increase in average broadband speeds, which in turn precipitated a shift in usage trends. With the average UK speed increasing by over 25 per cent, more users could take advantage of bandwidth-hungry services, such as watching TV and films, downloading music or uploading images. Of all online media consumption, it was gaming that proved most popular, usurping film- and music-downloading on the top spot. Being more immersive than web-browsing or email, these activities, in addition to the time spent on social networking sites and blogs, added significantly to the time users spent connected: the average UK user was online for over 22 hours a month in 2010.

Despite these various media applications, it was communication that once again proved most popular among users: 90 per cent of all users had sent or received email, and the most popular internet application was Microsoft's instant messenger programme, Windows Live Messenger. Social networking also showed no sign of losing its appeal: nearly a quarter of all web time was spent browsing these sites.

• The internet's second most popular use in 2010 was information gathering: three quarters of users had searched the web to find information on goods and services

• 56 per cent of the total UK population visited Google during May 2010

• One fifth of internet users believed that, by virtue of its inclusion on a search engine, information found online was accurate and unbiased

Sources: ONS, *Statistical Bulletin: Internet Access 2010;* Ofcom, *The Communications Market 2010*

GLOSSARY OF TERMS

The following is a list of selected internet terms. It is by no means exhaustive but is intended to cover those that the average computer user might encounter.

BANNER AD: An advertisement on a web page that links to a corresponding website when clicked.

BLOG: Short for 'web log' – an online personal journal that is frequently updated and intended to be read by the public. Blogs are kept by 'bloggers' and are commonly available as RSS feeds.

BROWSER: Typically refers to a 'web browser' program that allows a computer user to view web page content on their computer, eg Firefox, Internet Explorer or Safari.

CLICK-THROUGH: The number of times a web user 'clicks through' a paid advertisement link to the corresponding website.

CLOUD COMPUTING: The use of IT resources as an on-demand service across a network; through cloud computing, software, advanced computation and archived information can be accessed remotely, without the user needing local dedicated hardware.

COOKIE: A piece of information placed on a user's hard disk by a web server. Cookies contain data about the user's activity on a website, and are returned to the server whenever a browser makes further requests. They are important for remembering information such as login and registration details, 'shopping cart' data, user preferences etc, and are often set to expire after a fixed period.

CSS: Cascading Style Sheet – a standard for specifying the appearance of text. It provides a single 'library' of styles that are used throughout a large number of related documents.

DOMAIN: A set of words or letters, separated by dots, used to identify an internet server, eg www.whitakersalmanack.co.uk, where 'www' denotes a web (http) server, 'whitakersalmanack' denotes the organisation name, 'co' denotes that the organisation is a company and 'uk' indicates United Kingdom. (For a complete list of country suffixes *see* Internet Domain Names).

FTP: File Transfer Protocol – a set of network rules enabling a user to exchange files with a remote server.

HACKER: A person who attempts to break or 'hack' into websites. Motives typically involve the desire to procure personal information such as addresses, passwords or credit card details. Hackers may also delete code or incorporate traces of malicious code to damage the functionality of a website. The malicious activities of a hacker might be simulated by a 'penetration tester', someone legitimately employed to test the security of information systems.

HIT: A single request from a web browser for a single item from a web server. In order for a web browser to display a page that contains three graphics, four 'hits' would occur at the server: one for the HTML page and one for each of the three graphics. Therefore the number of hits on a website is not synonymous with the number of visitors.

HTML: HyperText Mark-up Language – a programming language used to denote or mark up how an internet page should be presented to a user from an HTTP server via a web browser.

HTTP: HyperText Transfer Protocol – an internet protocol whereby a web server sends web pages, images and files to a web browser.

HYPERLINK: A piece of specially coded text that users can click on to navigate to the web page, or element of a web page, associated with that link's code. Links are typically distinguished through the use of bold, underlined, or differently coloured text.

MALWARE: A combination of the words 'malicious' and 'software'. Malware is software designed with the specific intention of infiltrating a computer and damaging its system.

META TAG: A type of HTML tag that contains information not normally displayed to the user. Meta tags are typically used to include information for search engines to help them categorise a page.

MP3: A popular audio compression format allowing quicker transmission of files for later playback on personal computers and music players.

MPEG: Motion Picture Encoding Group – a popular format standard for compressing video and audio information for transmission over the internet and later playback on personal computers and hand-held devices.

OPEN CONTENT: Copyrighted information that is made available by the owner to the general public under licence terms that allow reuse of the material, often with the requirement that the reuser grant the public the same rights to the modified version. Information that is in the 'public domain' might also be considered a form of open content.

OPEN-SOURCE: Describes a computer program that has its source code (the instructions that make up a program) freely available for viewing and modification.

P2P: Peer to peer – the act of a computer on one network communicating to a computer on a different network. The communication usually involves the sharing of files between computers.

PAGERANK: A link analysis algorithm used by search engines that assigns a numerical value based on a website's relevance and reputation. In general, a site with a higher pagerank has more traffic than a site with a lower one.

PODCASTING: A form of audio and video broadcasting using the internet. Although the word is a portmanteau of 'iPod' and broadcasting, podcasting does not require the use of an iPod. A podcaster creates a list of files and makes it available in the RSS 2.0 format. The list can then be obtained using podcast 'retriever' software which makes the files available to digital devices (including, but not limited to, iPods); users may then listen or watch at their convenience.

RSS FEED: Rich Site Summary or RDF Site Summary or Real Simple Syndication – a commonly used protocol for syndication and sharing of content, originally developed to facilitate the syndication of news articles, now widely used to share the content of blogs.

SEO: Search engine optimisation – the process of optimising the content of a web page to ensure that a website is properly set up and structured to be indexed by search engines.

SERVER: A node on a network that provides service to the terminals on the network. These computers have higher hardware specifications, ie more resources and greater speed, in order to handle large amounts of data.

SOCIAL NETWORKING: The practice of using a web-hosted service such as Facebook or MySpace to upload and share content and build friendship networks.

SPAM: A term used for unsolicited, generally junk, email. Junk email is becoming a major issue, with some estimates suggesting that spam is becoming more prevalent than legitimate email. Many legislatures around the globe are taking steps to ban or regulate spam.

SPOTIFY: A peer-to-peer music streaming service that allows users to share songs and playlists.

TRAFFIC: The number of visitors to a website.

TROLL: Someone who posts controversial, inflammatory or irrelevant messages on a blog or other online discussion forum in order to disrupt on-topic discussion or provoke other users into an emotional response.

TWITTER: An online microblogging service that allows users to stay connected through the exchange of 140-character posts, known as 'tweets'.

URL: Uniform Resource Locator – address of a file accessible on the internet, eg http://www. whitakersalmanack.com

USER-GENERATED CONTENT (UGC): Refers to various media content produced or primarily influenced by end-users, as opposed to traditional media producers such as licensed broadcasters and production companies. These forms of media include digital video, blogging, podcasting, mobile phone photography and wikis.

VISIBILITY: How visible a website is to search engines and browsers.

VOIP: Voice Over Internet Protocol – various technologies used to make telephone calls over computer networks, especially the internet. Just as modems allow computers to connect to the internet over regular telephone lines, VOIP technology allows telephone calls to take place over internet connections. Costs for VOIP calls are usually much lower than for traditional telephone calls.

WEB 2.0: Generally refers to a second generation of services available on the web that lets people collaborate and share information online. In contrast to the static web pages of the first generation, Web 2.0 gives users an experience closer to that of desktop applications.

WIDGET: A piece of software that provides access to online information items or to functions which the user accesses on a regular basis.

WIKI: Software that allows users to freely create and edit web page content using any web browser. Theoretically this encourages the democratic use of the internet and promotes content composition by non-technical users.

TIME AND SPACE

ASTRONOMY

The following pages give astronomical data for each month of the year 2012. There are four pages of data for each month. All data are given for 0h Greenwich Mean Time (GMT), ie at the midnight at the beginning of the day named. This applies also to data for the months when British Summer Time is in operation (for dates, *see* below).

The astronomical data are given in a form suitable for observation with the naked eye or with a small telescope. These data do not attempt to replace the *Astronomical Almanac* for professional astronomers.

A fuller explanation of how to use the astronomical data is given on pages 683–5.

CALENDAR FOR EACH MONTH

The calendar for each month comprises dates of general interest plus the dates of birth or death of well-known people. For key religious, civil and legal dates *see* page 9. For details of flag-flying days *see* page 23. For royal birthdays *see* pages 23 and 24–5. Public holidays are given in italics. *See* also pages 10 and 11.

Fuller explanations of the various calendars can be found under Time Measurement and Calendars.

The zodiacal signs through which the Sun is passing during each month are illustrated. The date of transition from one sign to the next, to the nearest hour, is given under Astronomical Phenomena.

JULIAN DATE

The Julian date on 2012 January 0.0 is 2455926.5. To find the Julian date for any other date in 2012 (at 0h GMT), add the day-of-the-year number on the extreme right of the calendar for each month to the Julian date for January 0.0.

SEASONS

The seasons are defined astronomically as follows:

Spring from the vernal equinox to the summer solstice
Summer from the summer solstice to the autumnal equinox
Autumn from the autumnal equinox to the winter solstice
Winter from the winter solstice to the vernal equinox

The time when seasons start in 2012 (to the nearest hour) are:

Northern Hemisphere

Vernal equinox	March 20d 05h GMT
Summer solstice	June 20d 23h GMT
Autumnal equinox	September 22d 15h GMT
Winter solstice	December 21d 11h GMT

Southern Hemisphere

Autumnal equinox	March 20d 05h GMT
Winter solstice	June 20d 23h GMT
Vernal equinox	September 22d 15h GMT
Summer solstice	December 21d 11h GMT

The longest day of the year, measured from sunrise to sunset, is at the summer solstice. The longest day in the United Kingdom will fall on 20 June in 2012.

The shortest day of the year is at the winter solstice. The shortest day in the United Kingdom will fall on 21 December in 2012.

The equinox is the point at which day and night are of equal length all over the world.

In popular parlance, the seasons in the northern hemisphere comprise the following months:

Spring	March, April, May
Summer	June, July, August
Autumn	September, October, November
Winter	December, January, February

BRITISH SUMMER TIME

British Summer Time is the legal time for general purposes during the period in which it is in operation (*see also* pages 687–8). During this period, clocks are kept one hour ahead of Greenwich Mean Time. The hour of changeover is 01h Greenwich Mean Time. The duration of Summer Time in 2012 is from March 25 01h GMT to October 28 01h GMT.

JANUARY 2012

FIRST MONTH, 31 DAYS. *Janus*, god of the portal, facing two ways, past and future

1	Sunday	Giuseppe Piazzi, Italian astronomer, discovered the first asteroid, Ceres 1801	day 1

2	Monday	Construction of the Brooklyn Bridge, New York, commenced 1870	week 1 day 2
3	Tuesday	The first battery-powered watch, the Hamilton Electric 500, was released 1957	3
4	Wednesday	Sir Isaac Newton, physicist and mathematician who discovered the law of gravitation *b.* 1642	4
5	Thursday	X-rays first demonstrated by German physicist Wilhelm Konrad von Röntgen 1896	5
6	Friday	Demonstration by Samuel Morse of the first electric telegraph system 1838	6
7	Saturday	Nikola Tesla, Serbian inventor, mechanical and electrical engineer *d.* 1943	7
8	Sunday	Professor Stephen Hawking, theoretical physicist and cosmologist *b.* 1942	8

9	Monday	Jean Pierre Blanchard made first successful balloon flight in the USA 1793	week 2 day 9
10	Tuesday	London Underground railway opened, carrying 30,000 passengers on the first day 1863	10
11	Wednesday	Insulin was used to successfully treat diabetes for the first time 1922	11
12	Thursday	Jean Joseph Lenoir, inventor of the first practical internal combustion engine *b.* 1822	12
13	Friday	The Wham-O Company introduced the Pluto Platter, later to become famous as the Frisbee 1957	13
14	Saturday	Edmond Halley, Astronomer Royal after whom Halley's Comet is named *d.* 1742	14
15	Sunday	Construction completed of the Pentagon in Virginia, consisting of 17.5 miles of corridors 1943	15

16	Monday	Nylon, the 'miracle fibre', was patented by Wallace Carothers of the Dupont company 1937	week 3 day 16
17	Tuesday	Benjamin Franklin, author, statesman, inventor and scientist *b.* 1706	17
18	Wednesday	Airbus' 840-passenger A380, the world's biggest passenger jet, was unveiled in France 2005	18
19	Thursday	James Watt, inventor after whom the unit of power is named *b.* 1736	19
20	Friday	Dr Edwin 'Buzz' Aldrin, the second man to walk on the Moon *b.* 1930	20
21	Saturday	First Concorde flight carrying commercial passengers 1976	21
22	Sunday	Dr Roberta Bondar became the first Canadian woman in space 1992	22

23	Monday	Charles King, biochemist who discovered and isolated vitamin C *d.* 1988	week 4 day 23
24	Tuesday	The Macintosh 128K, the first computer built by Apple Macintosh, was released 1984	24
25	Wednesday	Robert Boyle, physicist and chemist, most widely known for Boyle's Law *b.* 1627	25
26	Thursday	The electric dental drill was patented by George F. Green of Kalamazoo, Michigan 1875	26
27	Friday	John Logie Baird, electrical engineer, gave the first public demonstration of television 1926	27
28	Saturday	The space shuttle *Challenger* exploded shortly after lift-off, killing all crew 1986	28
29	Sunday	Lewis Urry, chemical engineer who invented the alkaline and lithium battery *b.* 1927	29

30	Monday	Orville Wright, aviation pioneer and aeroplane inventor *d.* 1948	week 5 day 30
31	Tuesday	Ham, a chimp, returned safely to Earth after being sent into space 1961	31

ASTRONOMICAL PHENOMENA

d h
2 23 Jupiter in conjunction with Moon. Jupiter 5°S.
5 01 Earth at perihelion (147 million km.)
14 01 Mars in conjunction with Moon. Mars 8°N.
16 15 Saturn in conjunction with Moon. Saturn 6°N.
20 16 Sun's longitude 300° ♒
22 12 Mercury in conjunction with Moon. Mercury 5°S.
24 01 Mars at stationary point
26 13 Venus in conjunction with Moon. Venus 6°S.
30 11 Jupiter in conjunction with Moon. Jupiter 4°S.

MINIMA OF ALGOL

d	h	d	h	d	h
3	00.3	14	11.5	25	22.8
5	21.1	17	08.4	28	19.7
8	17.9	20	05.2	31	16.5
11	14.7	23	02.0		

CONSTELLATIONS

The following constellations are near the meridian at

	d	h		d	h
December	1	24	January	16	21
December	16	23	February	1	20
January	1	22	February	15	19

Draco (below the Pole), Ursa Minor (below the Pole), Camelopardalis, Perseus, Auriga, Taurus, Orion, Eridanus and Lepus

THE MOON

Phases, Apsides and Node	d	h	m
☽ First Quarter	1	06	15
○ Full Moon	9	07	30
☾ Last Quarter	16	09	08
● New Moon	23	07	39
☽ First Quarter	31	04	10

Apogee (404,618km)	2	20	17
Perigee (369,851km)	17	21	16
Apogee (404,363km)	30	17	42

Mean longitude of ascending node on January 1, 253°

THE SUN

s.d. 16′.3

Day	Right Ascension h m s	Dec. ° ′	Equation of time m s	Rise 52° h m	Rise 56° h m	Transit h m	Set 52° h m	Set 56° h m	Sidereal time h m s	Transit of first point of Aries h m s
1	18 43 20	23 04	−3 05	8 08	8 31	12 03	15 59	15 36	6 40 15	17 16 54
2	18 47 45	22 59	−3 33	8 08	8 31	12 04	16 00	15 37	6 44 12	17 12 58
3	18 52 10	22 54	−4 01	8 08	8 31	12 04	16 01	15 38	6 48 09	17 09 02
4	18 56 34	22 48	−4 29	8 08	8 30	12 05	16 02	15 39	6 52 05	17 05 06
5	19 00 58	22 42	−4 56	8 07	8 30	12 05	16 03	15 41	6 56 02	17 01 11
6	19 05 21	22 35	−5 23	8 07	8 29	12 06	16 04	15 42	6 59 58	16 57 15
7	19 09 44	22 28	−5 49	8 07	8 29	12 06	16 06	15 44	7 03 55	16 53 19
8	19 14 07	22 21	−6 15	8 06	8 28	12 06	16 07	15 45	7 07 51	16 49 23
9	19 18 29	22 13	−6 41	8 06	8 27	12 07	16 08	15 47	7 11 48	16 45 27
10	19 22 50	22 04	−7 06	8 05	8 27	12 07	16 10	15 48	7 15 44	16 41 31
11	19 27 11	21 56	−7 30	8 05	8 26	12 08	16 11	15 50	7 19 41	16 37 35
12	19 31 31	21 46	−7 54	8 04	8 25	12 08	16 13	15 52	7 23 38	16 33 39
13	19 35 51	21 37	−8 17	8 03	8 24	12 08	16 14	15 53	7 27 34	16 29 43
14	19 40 10	21 27	−8 40	8 02	8 23	12 09	16 16	15 55	7 31 31	16 25 47
15	19 44 29	21 16	−9 02	8 02	8 22	12 09	16 17	15 57	7 35 27	16 21 51
16	19 48 47	21 05	−9 23	8 01	8 21	12 10	16 19	15 59	7 39 24	16 17 56
17	19 53 04	20 54	−9 44	8 00	8 20	12 10	16 20	16 01	7 43 20	16 14 00
18	19 57 21	20 42	−10 04	7 59	8 18	12 10	16 22	16 03	7 47 17	16 10 04
19	20 01 37	20 30	−10 23	7 58	8 17	12 11	16 24	16 05	7 51 14	16 06 08
20	20 05 52	20 18	−10 42	7 57	8 16	12 11	16 25	16 07	7 55 10	16 02 12
21	20 10 06	20 05	−11 00	7 56	8 14	12 11	16 27	16 09	7 59 07	15 58 16
22	20 14 20	19 51	−11 17	7 55	8 13	12 11	16 29	16 11	8 03 03	15 54 20
23	20 18 33	19 38	−11 33	7 53	8 11	12 12	16 31	16 13	8 07 00	15 50 24
24	20 22 45	19 24	−11 49	7 52	8 10	12 12	16 32	16 15	8 10 56	15 46 28
25	20 26 57	19 09	−12 04	7 51	8 08	12 12	16 34	16 17	8 14 53	15 42 32
26	20 31 08	18 55	−12 18	7 50	8 07	12 12	16 36	16 19	8 18 49	15 38 36
27	20 35 17	18 40	−12 31	7 48	8 05	12 13	16 38	16 21	8 22 46	15 34 40
28	20 39 26	18 24	−12 44	7 47	8 03	12 13	16 39	16 23	8 26 43	15 30 45
29	20 43 35	18 09	−12 56	7 45	8 01	12 13	16 41	16 25	8 30 39	15 26 49
30	20 47 42	17 53	−13 06	7 44	8 00	12 13	16 43	16 27	8 34 36	15 22 53
31	20 51 49	17 36	−13 16	7 42	7 58	12 13	16 45	16 30	8 38 32	15 18 57

DURATION OF TWILIGHT (in minutes)

Latitude	52°	56°	52°	56°	52°	56°	52°	56°
	1 January		11 January		21 January		31 January	
Civil	41	47	40	45	38	43	37	41
Nautical	84	96	82	93	80	90	78	87
Astronomical	125	141	123	138	120	134	117	130

THE NIGHT SKY

Mercury begins the year as a difficult morning object visible low above the south-eastern horizon at about the beginning of morning civil twilight. Its magnitude is then −0.4. It is getting closer to the Sun and is unlikely to be visible after the first two days of the month. Unfortunately its low declination means that observers in Scotland will not be able to see it at all.

Venus, magnitude −0.4, is a magnificent evening object in the south-western sky, and by the end of the month can still be seen for as long as 3 hours after sunset. On the evening of the 26th the thin waxing crescent Moon passes 5 degrees north of the planet.

Mars begins the year as a morning object, though by the end of the month it is becoming visible low above the eastern horizon shortly after 21h. During January its magnitude brightens from +0.2 to −0.5. Mars is moving eastwards from Leo into Virgo, reaching its first stationary point on the 24th, commencing its retrograde motion. On the morning of the 14th the waning gibbous Moon passes about 9 degrees south of the planet.

Jupiter, magnitude −2.5, is an evening object, visible in the southern sky, shortly after sunset. Jupiter is in the constellation of Aries. On the evening of the 2nd, the waxing Moon, just after First Quarter, passes 4 degrees north of the planet: there is a repeat performance on the 30th.

Saturn, magnitude +0.7, is a morning object, visible in the south-eastern sky after about 03h at the beginning of the month and 01h by the end of the month. Saturn is moving very slowly eastwards in the constellation of Virgo, and is easily located since it is less than 10 degrees west-north-west of Spica. On the 16th the waning Moon, at Last Quarter, passes 7 degrees south of the planet.

THE MOON

Day	R.A.		Dec.	Hor. Par.	Semi-diam.	Sun's Co-Long.	PA of Br. Limb	Ph.	Age	Rise				Transit		Set			
										52°		56°				52°		56°	
	h	m	°	'	'	°	°	%	d	h	m	h	m	h	m	h	m	h	m
1	0	18	+ 7.3	54.5	14.8	354	246	48	7.3	11	10	11	02	18	09	0	16	0	22
2	1	04	+11.4	54.3	14.8	6	248	57	8.3	11	30	11	18	18	52	1	22	1	33
3	1	50	+15.1	54.2	14.8	18	251	66	9.3	11	53	11	38	19	37	2	28	2	43
4	2	37	+18.2	54.3	14.8	31	254	75	10.3	12	21	12	02	20	24	3	34	3	52
5	3	27	+20.6	54.6	14.9	43	257	83	11.3	12	56	12	34	21	13	4	37	4	59
6	4	19	+22.1	54.9	15.0	55	261	89	12.3	13	40	13	16	22	04	5	36	6	00
7	5	12	+22.5	55.4	15.1	67	264	95	13.3	14	33	14	10	22	57	6	29	6	53
8	6	07	+21.9	56.0	15.2	79	265	98	14.3	15	36	15	15	23	49	7	14	7	36
9	7	01	+20.0	56.5	15.4	91	241	100	15.3	16	46	16	28	—		7	51	8	10
10	7	55	+17.2	57.1	15.6	103	124	99	16.3	18	01	17	48	0	41	8	21	8	36
11	8	48	+13.3	57.6	15.7	115	117	97	17.3	19	18	19	09	1	32	8	47	8	57
12	9	40	+8.8	58.0	15.8	128	117	92	18.3	20	35	20	32	2	21	9	09	9	15
13	10	32	+3.7	58.4	15.9	140	117	85	19.3	21	54	21	55	3	10	9	30	9	32
14	11	23	−1.6	58.7	16.0	152	116	76	20.3	23	13	23	19	3	59	9	51	9	48
15	12	15	−6.8	59.0	16.1	164	115	66	21.3	—		—		4	49	10	13	10	05
16	13	08	−11.8	59.1	16.1	176	113	54	22.3	0	34	0	45	5	41	10	38	10	25
17	14	04	−16.1	59.3	16.1	188	110	43	23.3	1	54	2	10	6	35	11	07	10	50
18	15	02	−19.4	59.3	16.2	200	105	32	24.3	3	13	3	33	7	32	11	45	11	24
19	16	02	−21.6	59.2	16.1	213	101	22	25.3	4	26	4	50	8	31	12	33	12	08
20	17	03	−22.5	59.1	16.1	225	96	13	26.3	5	30	5	54	9	30	13	32	13	07
21	18	03	−21.9	58.8	16.0	237	92	7	27.3	6	21	6	44	10	29	14	40	14	18
22	19	02	−20.0	58.4	15.9	249	93	2	28.3	7	02	7	21	11	25	15	55	15	37
23	19	59	−16.9	57.8	15.8	261	121	0	29.3	7	34	7	48	12	18	17	11	16	58
24	20	52	−13.0	57.2	15.6	274	227	1	0.7	7	59	8	09	13	07	18	26	18	17
25	21	43	−8.6	56.6	15.4	286	238	3	1.7	8	20	8	26	13	54	19	39	19	35
26	22	31	−3.9	55.9	15.2	298	240	8	2.7	8	39	8	41	14	38	20	49	20	50
27	23	17	+0.9	55.4	15.1	310	242	14	3.7	8	57	8	55	15	21	21	58	22	03
28	0	03	+5.5	54.9	14.9	322	243	22	4.7	9	15	9	09	16	04	23	06	23	14
29	0	48	+9.8	54.5	14.8	334	245	30	5.7	9	35	9	25	16	47	—		—	
30	1	34	+13.7	54.3	14.8	347	248	39	6.7	9	56	9	43	17	31	0	12	0	25
31	2	21	+17.1	54.2	14.8	359	251	49	7.7	10	22	10	05	18	17	1	18	1	35

MERCURY

Day	R.A.		Dec.	Diam.	Phase	Transit		5° high			
								52°		56°	
	h	m	°	"	%	h	m	h	m	h	m
1	17	16	−22.1	6	80	10	37	7	26	7	59
3	17	28	−22.6	6	83	10	40	7	34	8	08
5	17	40	−23.0	5	85	10	45	7	41	8	17
7	17	52	−23.3	5	87	10	49	7	49	8	25
9	18	05	−23.6	5	89	10	54	7	56	8	33
11	18	17	−23.8	5	90	10	59	8	02	8	40
13	18	30	−23.9	5	92	11	04	8	08	8	47
15	18	44	−23.9	5	93	11	09	8	14	8	52
17	18	57	−23.8	5	94	11	15	8	19	8	57
19	19	10	−23.7	5	95	11	21	8	23	9	00
21	19	24	−23.5	5	96	11	26	8	26	9	03
23	19	38	−23.1	5	96	11	32	8	29	9	04
25	19	51	−22.7	5	97	11	38	8	31	9	05
27	20	05	−22.2	5	98	11	44	8	32	9	05
29	20	19	−21.6	5	98	11	50	8	33	9	04
31	20	33	−20.9	5	99	11	56	8	33	9	02

VENUS

Day	R.A.		Dec.	Diam.	Phase	Transit		5° high			
								52°		56°	
	h	m	°	"	%	h	m	h	m	h	m
1	21	07	−18.4	13	83	14	28	18	09	17	46
6	21	32	−16.5	13	82	14	32	18	27	18	07
11	21	56	−14.4	14	80	14	36	18	45	18	28
16	22	19	−12.2	14	79	14	40	19	03	18	48
21	22	41	−9.8	14	78	14	43	19	20	19	08
26	23	04	−7.3	15	76	14	45	19	36	19	27
31	23	26	−4.8	15	75	14	47	19	52	19	45

MARS

Day	R.A.		Dec.	Diam.	Phase	Transit		5° high			
								52°		56°	
	h	m	°	"	%	h	m	h	m	h	m
1	11	28	+6.6	9	92	4	47	22	44	22	42
6	11	33	+6.3	9	92	4	32	22	30	22	28
11	11	36	+6.1	10	93	4	16	22	15	22	13
16	11	39	+6.0	10	93	3	59	21	58	21	56
21	11	40	+6.0	11	94	3	40	21	39	21	38
26	11	40	+6.1	11	95	3	21	21	19	21	17
31	11	40	+6.4	12	96	3	00	20	57	20	55

SUNRISE AND SUNSET

	London 0° 05' 51° 30'		Bristol 2° 35' 51° 28'		Birmingham 1° 55' 52° 28'		Manchester 2° 15' 53° 28'		Newcastle 1° 37' 54° 59'		Glasgow 4° 14' 55° 52'		Belfast 5° 56' 54° 35'	
d	h m	h m	h m	h m	h m	h m	h m	h m	h m	h m	h m	h m	h m	h m
1	8 06	16 01	8 16	16 12	8 18	16 04	8 25	16 00	8 31	15 48	8 47	15 53	8 46	16 08
2	8 06	16 03	8 16	16 13	8 18	16 05	8 25	16 01	8 31	15 50	8 47	15 55	8 46	16 09
3	8 06	16 04	8 16	16 14	8 18	16 06	8 25	16 02	8 31	15 51	8 47	15 56	8 46	16 10
4	8 06	16 05	8 15	16 15	8 18	16 07	8 24	16 03	8 31	15 52	8 46	15 57	8 45	16 12
5	8 05	16 06	8 15	16 16	8 17	16 08	8 24	16 05	8 30	15 53	8 46	15 58	8 45	16 13
6	8 05	16 07	8 15	16 17	8 17	16 10	8 24	16 06	8 30	15 55	8 45	16 00	8 45	16 14
7	8 05	16 08	8 14	16 19	8 17	16 11	8 23	16 07	8 29	15 56	8 45	16 01	8 44	16 16
8	8 04	16 10	8 14	16 20	8 16	16 12	8 23	16 09	8 29	15 58	8 44	16 03	8 43	16 17
9	8 04	16 11	8 14	16 21	8 16	16 14	8 22	16 10	8 28	15 59	8 44	16 04	8 43	16 19
10	8 03	16 12	8 13	16 23	8 15	16 15	8 21	16 11	8 27	16 01	8 43	16 06	8 42	16 20
11	8 03	16 14	8 12	16 24	8 14	16 17	8 21	16 13	8 26	16 02	8 42	16 08	8 41	16 22
12	8 02	16 15	8 12	16 25	8 14	16 18	8 20	16 15	8 26	16 04	8 41	16 09	8 41	16 23
13	8 01	16 17	8 11	16 27	8 13	16 20	8 19	16 16	8 25	16 06	8 40	16 11	8 40	16 25
14	8 01	16 18	8 10	16 28	8 12	16 21	8 18	16 18	8 24	16 07	8 39	16 13	8 39	16 27
15	8 00	16 20	8 10	16 30	8 11	16 23	8 17	16 19	8 23	16 09	8 38	16 15	8 38	16 28
16	7 59	16 21	8 09	16 31	8 11	16 24	8 17	16 21	8 22	16 11	8 37	16 17	8 37	16 30
17	7 58	16 23	8 08	16 33	8 10	16 26	8 16	16 23	8 21	16 13	8 36	16 18	8 36	16 32
18	7 57	16 24	8 07	16 35	8 09	16 28	8 14	16 24	8 19	16 15	8 34	16 20	8 35	16 34
19	7 56	16 26	8 06	16 36	8 08	16 29	8 13	16 26	8 18	16 16	8 33	16 22	8 33	16 36
20	7 55	16 28	8 05	16 38	8 06	16 31	8 12	16 28	8 17	16 18	8 32	16 24	8 32	16 38
21	7 54	16 29	8 04	16 40	8 05	16 33	8 11	16 30	8 16	16 20	8 30	16 26	8 31	16 39
22	7 53	16 31	8 03	16 41	8 04	16 35	8 10	16 32	8 14	16 22	8 29	16 28	8 30	16 41
23	7 52	16 33	8 02	16 43	8 03	16 36	8 08	16 33	8 13	16 24	8 28	16 30	8 28	16 43
24	7 51	16 35	8 00	16 45	8 02	16 38	8 07	16 35	8 11	16 26	8 26	16 32	8 27	16 45
25	7 49	16 36	7 59	16 46	8 00	16 40	8 06	16 37	8 10	16 28	8 24	16 34	8 25	16 47
26	7 48	16 38	7 58	16 48	7 59	16 42	8 04	16 39	8 08	16 30	8 23	16 36	8 24	16 49
27	7 47	16 40	7 57	16 50	7 58	16 44	8 03	16 41	8 07	16 32	8 21	16 39	8 22	16 51
28	7 45	16 42	7 55	16 52	7 56	16 45	8 01	16 43	8 05	16 34	8 20	16 41	8 21	16 53
29	7 44	16 43	7 54	16 53	7 55	16 47	8 00	16 45	8 04	16 36	8 18	16 43	8 19	16 55
30	7 43	16 45	7 52	16 55	7 53	16 49	7 58	16 47	8 02	16 38	8 16	16 45	8 17	16 57
31	7 41	16 47	7 51	16 57	7 52	16 51	7 57	16 49	8 00	16 40	8 14	16 47	8 16	16 59

JUPITER

Day	R.A.		Dec.		Transit		5° high 52°		56°	
	h	m	°	'	h	m	h	m	h	m
1	1	55.0	+10	28	19	12	1	36	1	41
11	1	56.4	+10	39	18	34	0	59	1	04
21	1	59.0	+10	56	17	57	0	24	0	29
31	2	02.8	+11	20	17	22	23	47	23	53

Diameters – equatorial 41″ polar 39″

SATURN

Day	R.A.		Dec.		Transit		5° high 52°		56°	
	h	m	°	'	h	m	h	m	h	m
1	13	48.6	–8	36	7	07	2	27	2	38
11	13	50.8	–8	46	6	30	1	50	2	02
21	13	52.3	–8	51	5	52	1	13	1	25
31	13	53.2	–8	54	5	14	0	35	0	46

Diameters – equatorial 17″ polar 15″
Rings – major axis 39″ minor axis 10″

URANUS

Day	R.A.		Dec.		Transit		10° high 52°		56°	
	h	m	°	'	h	m	h	m	h	m
1	0	04.2	–0	20	17	21	22	13	22	06
11	0	05.1	–0	14	16	43	21	35	21	28
21	0	06.2	–0	06	16	05	20	58	20	51
31	0	07.5	+0	03	15	27	20	21	20	14

Diameter 4″

NEPTUNE

Day	R.A.		Dec.		Transit		10° high 52°		56°	
	h	m	°	'	h	m	h	m	h	m
1	22	04.9	–12	22	15	22	19	03	18	42
11	22	06.0	–12	16	14	44	18	25	18	04
21	22	07.3	–12	09	14	06	17	48	17	27
31	22	08.6	–12	02	13	28	17	11	16	50

Diameter 2″

FEBRUARY 2012

SECOND MONTH, 28 or 29 DAYS. *Februa*, Roman festival of Purification

1	*Wednesday*	The space shuttle *Columbia* broke up as it re-entered the Earth's atmosphere 2003	day 32
2	*Thursday*	Dmitry Mendeleyev, chemist who created periodic table of elements arranged by atomic mass *d.* 1907	33
3	*Friday*	The Soviet Union's *Luna 9* became the first controlled spacecraft to land on the Moon 1966	34
4	*Saturday*	Charles Lindbergh, pilot of first one-man flight across the Atlantic *b.* 1902	35
5	*Sunday*	John Dunlop, inventor who developed and patented the first pneumatic tyre *b.* 1840	36
6	*Monday*	Alan Shepard became the first man to hit a golf ball on the Moon 1971	week 6 day 37
7	*Tuesday*	Concorde crossed the Atlantic (between New York and London) in record time 1996	38
8	*Wednesday*	The astronaut crew of the final Skylab mission returned to Earth 1974	39
9	*Thursday*	Mintonette, now known as volleyball, was invented by William G. Morgan 1895	40
10	*Friday*	Gary Kasparov, the world chess champion, lost a game to Deep Blue, an IBM computer 1996	41
11	*Saturday*	Thomas Edison, physicist whose inventions included the light bulb and phonograph *b.* 1847	42
12	*Sunday*	Albert Alexander became the first human test subject to be treated with penicillin 1941	43
13	*Monday*	France carried out its first atomic-bomb test in Algeria 1960	week 7 day 44
14	*Tuesday*	Dolly the sheep, the first mammal cloned from an adult, was euthanised due to premature ageing 2003	45
15	*Wednesday*	Galileo Galilei, mathematician and astronomer, the first man to use a telescope to study the skies *b.* 1564	46
16	*Thursday*	The Kyoto Protocol, aimed at cutting air pollution, came into force 2005	47
17	*Friday*	Christopher Latham Sholes, inventor of the first commercially successful typewriter *d.* 1890	48
18	*Saturday*	Pluto, then regarded as our solar system's ninth planet, was discovered by Clyde Tombaugh 1930	49
19	*Sunday*	Nicolaus Copernicus, astronomer who proposed the Earth and other planets revolved around the Sun *b.* 1473	50
20	*Monday*	The Soviet Union launched *Mir*, the world's biggest space station 1986	week 8 day 51
21	*Tuesday*	Jethro Tull, agriculturalist who invented a horse-drawn seed drill *d.* 1741	52
22	*Wednesday*	Heinrich Hertz, physicist after whom the unit of frequency is named *b.* 1857	53
23	*Thursday*	Passenger railway service linking Perth with Sydney (3,961 kilometres) opened 1970	54
24	*Friday*	Paris and Brussels became the first two cities to be connected by telephone link 1887	55
25	*Saturday*	Gunsmith Samuel Colt patented the first revolving barrel firearm 1836	56
26	*Sunday*	First factory for production of Volkswagen, the 'people's car', is opened by Adolf Hitler 1936	57
27	*Monday*	Ivan Petrovich Pavlov, physiologist, best known for studies of animal behaviour *d.* 1936	week 9 day 58
28	*Tuesday*	James Watson and Frances Crick announced they had determined the double-helix structure of DNA 1953	59
29	*Wednesday*	John Holland, engineer who designed the modern submarine *b.* 1840	60

ASTRONOMICAL PHENOMENA

h d
7 09 Mercury in superior conjunction
7 14 Saturn at stationary point
10 05 Mars in conjunction with Moon. Mars 9°N.
12 21 Saturn in conjunction with Moon. Saturn 6°N.
19 06 Sun's longitude 330° ♓
19 21 Neptune in conjunction
23 01 Mercury in conjunction with Moon. Mercury 6°S.
25 19 Venus in conjunction with Moon. Venus 3°S.
27 04 Jupiter in conjunction with Moon. Jupiter 4°S.

MINIMA OF ALGOL

d	*h*	*d*	*h*	*d*	*h*
3	13.3	15	00.6	26	11.9
6	10.1	17	21.4	29	08.7
9	07.0	20	18.2		
12	03.8	23	15.1		

CONSTELLATIONS

The following constellations are near the meridian at

	d	*h*		*d*	*h*
January	1	24	February	15	21
January	16	23	March	1	20
February	1	22	March	16	19

Draco (below the Pole), Camelopardalis, Auriga, Taurus, Gemini, Orion, Canis Minor, Monoceros, Lepus, Canis Major and Puppis

THE MOON

Phases, Apsides and Node		*d*	*h*	*m*
○	Full Moon	7	21	54
☾	Last Quarter	14	17	04
●	New Moon	21	22	35
Perigee (367,891km)		11	18	44
Apogee (404,899km)		27	14	05

Mean longitude of ascending node on February 1, 251°

THE SUN

s.d. 16′.2

Day	Right Ascension			Dec.		Equation of time		Rise 52°		Rise 56°		Transit		Set 52°		Set 56°		Sidereal time			Transit of first point of Aries		
	h	m	s	°	′	m	s	h	m	h	m	h	m	h	m	h	m	h	m	s	h	m	s
1	20	55	54	17	20	−13	26	7	41	7	56	12	13	16	47	16	32	8	42	29	15	15	01
2	20	59	59	17	03	−13	34	7	39	7	54	12	14	16	49	16	34	8	46	25	15	11	05
3	21	04	03	16	45	−13	41	7	38	7	52	12	14	16	50	16	36	8	50	22	15	07	09
4	21	08	06	16	28	−13	48	7	36	7	50	12	14	16	52	16	38	8	54	18	15	03	13
5	21	12	09	16	10	−13	54	7	34	7	48	12	14	16	54	16	40	8	58	15	14	59	17
6	21	16	10	15	52	−13	59	7	33	7	46	12	14	16	56	16	43	9	02	12	14	55	21
7	21	20	11	15	33	−14	03	7	31	7	44	12	14	16	58	16	45	9	06	08	14	51	25
8	21	24	11	15	15	−14	06	7	29	7	42	12	14	17	00	16	47	9	10	05	14	47	30
9	21	28	10	14	56	−14	09	7	27	7	40	12	14	17	02	16	49	9	14	01	14	43	34
10	21	32	09	14	37	−14	11	7	26	7	38	12	14	17	03	16	51	9	17	58	14	39	38
11	21	36	06	14	17	−14	12	7	24	7	36	12	14	17	05	16	54	9	21	54	14	35	42
12	21	40	03	13	58	−14	12	7	22	7	33	12	14	17	07	16	56	9	25	51	14	31	46
13	21	43	59	13	38	−14	12	7	20	7	31	12	14	17	09	16	58	9	29	47	14	27	50
14	21	47	54	13	18	−14	11	7	18	7	29	12	14	17	11	17	00	9	33	44	14	23	54
15	21	51	49	12	57	−14	09	7	16	7	27	12	14	17	13	17	02	9	37	41	14	19	58
16	21	55	43	12	37	−14	06	7	14	7	24	12	14	17	15	17	05	9	41	37	14	16	02
17	21	59	36	12	16	−14	03	7	12	7	22	12	14	17	17	17	07	9	45	34	14	12	06
18	22	03	29	11	55	−13	59	7	10	7	20	12	14	17	18	17	09	9	49	30	14	08	10
19	22	07	21	11	34	−13	54	7	08	7	17	12	14	17	20	17	11	9	53	27	14	04	15
20	22	11	12	11	12	−13	49	7	06	7	15	12	14	17	22	17	13	9	57	23	14	00	19
21	22	15	02	10	51	−13	43	7	04	7	13	12	14	17	24	17	16	10	01	20	13	56	23
22	22	18	52	10	29	−13	36	7	02	7	10	12	14	17	26	17	18	10	05	16	13	52	27
23	22	22	41	10	08	−13	29	7	00	7	08	12	13	17	28	17	20	10	09	13	13	48	31
24	22	26	30	9	46	−13	21	6	58	7	05	12	13	17	29	17	22	10	13	09	13	44	35
25	22	30	18	9	23	−13	12	6	56	7	03	12	13	17	31	17	24	10	17	06	13	40	39
26	22	34	05	9	01	−13	03	6	54	7	01	12	13	17	33	17	26	10	21	03	13	36	43
27	22	37	52	8	39	−12	53	6	52	6	58	12	13	17	35	17	28	10	24	59	13	32	47
28	22	41	38	8	16	−12	43	6	49	6	56	12	13	17	37	17	31	10	28	56	13	28	51
29	22	45	24	7	54	−12	32	6	47	6	53	12	12	17	39	17	33	10	32	52	13	24	56

DURATION OF TWILIGHT (in minutes)

Latitude	52°	56°	52°	56°	52°	56°	52°	56°
	1 February		11 February		21 February		31 February	
Civil	37	41	35	39	34	38	34	37
Nautical	77	86	75	83	74	81	73	80
Astronomical	117	130	114	126	113	124	112	124

THE NIGHT SKY

Mercury passes through superior conjunction on the 7th and is thus unsuitably placed for observation until the last week of the month, when it becomes visible as an evening object very low in the western sky, at the end of evening civil twilight. During this period its magnitude fades from −1.2 to −0.8.

Venus continues to be visible as a brilliant object in the early evenings in the southwestern sky, shortly after sunset. Its magnitude is −4.1. The waxing crescent Moon passes 2 degrees north of the planet on the evening of the 25th.

Mars, its magnitude brightening from −0.6 to −1.2 as it approaches opposition early next month, is becoming visible for the greater part of the night. Its retrograde motion takes it back into the constellation of Leo. The waning gibbous Moon will be seen passing about 9 degrees south of the planet on February 9–11.

Jupiter, magnitude −2.3, continues to be visible in the south-western sky in the early part of the evening. On the 27th the waxing crescent Moon passes 3 degrees north of the planet.

Saturn, in the constellation of Virgo, continues to be visible as a morninig object in the south-eastern sky and by the end of the month should be visible by about 23h. Its magnitude is +0.5. It reaches its first stationary point on the 7th and then moves very slowly retrograde. On the 12th the waning gibbous Moon passes about 7 degrees south of the planet.

Zodiacal Light. The evening cone may be observed stretching up from the western horizon, along the ecliptic, after the end of twilight, from the 9th to the 22nd. This faint phenomenon is only visible under good conditions and in the absence of both moonlight and artificial lighting.

THE MOON

Day	R.A. h	R.A. m	Dec. °	Hor. par. ′	Semi-diam. ′	Sun's Co-Long. °	PA of Br. Limb °	Ph. %	Age d	Rise 52° h	Rise 52° m	Rise 56° h	Rise 56° m	Transit h	Transit m	Set 52° h	Set 52° m	Set 56° h	Set 56° m
1	3	10	+19.7	54.4	14.8	11	255	58	8.7	10	54	10	33	19	04	2	22	2	42
2	4	00	+21.5	54.7	14.9	23	259	67	9.7	11	33	11	10	19	54	3	22	3	45
3	4	53	+22.4	55.1	15.0	35	263	76	10.7	12	21	11	58	20	45	4	18	4	42
4	5	46	+22.1	55.7	15.2	47	267	84	11.7	13	20	12	57	21	37	5	06	5	29
5	6	41	+20.8	56.4	15.4	60	271	90	12.7	14	26	14	07	22	30	5	47	6	07
6	7	35	+18.3	57.1	15.6	72	272	96	13.7	15	40	15	24	23	22	6	20	6	37
7	8	29	+14.8	57.8	15.8	84	265	99	14.7	16	57	16	46	—		6	49	7	01
8	9	23	+10.5	58.5	15.9	96	184	100	15.7	18	16	18	11	0	13	7	13	7	21
9	10	16	+5.5	59.0	16.1	108	130	98	16.7	19	37	19	36	1	04	7	35	7	38
10	11	08	+0.1	59.4	16.2	120	122	94	17.7	20	58	21	02	1	54	7	57	7	55
11	12	02	−5.3	59.6	16.2	132	119	88	18.7	22	20	22	29	2	45	8	19	8	13
12	12	56	−10.4	59.6	16.2	145	116	79	19.7	23	42	23	56	3	38	8	44	8	33
13	13	51	−14.9	59.5	16.2	157	112	69	20.7	—		—		4	32	9	12	8	57
14	14	49	−18.6	59.3	16.2	169	107	58	21.7	1	01	1	20	5	28	9	47	9	27
15	15	48	−21.0	59.0	16.1	181	102	47	22.7	2	16	2	39	6	25	10	31	10	08
16	16	48	−22.2	58.7	16.0	193	97	36	23.7	3	22	3	46	7	24	11	25	11	01
17	17	48	−22.0	58.3	15.9	205	92	26	24.7	4	16	4	40	8	21	12	29	12	06
18	18	46	−20.5	57.9	15.8	217	88	17	25.7	5	00	5	20	9	17	13	40	13	20
19	19	42	−17.9	57.4	15.7	230	85	9	26.7	5	34	5	50	10	10	14	54	14	38
20	20	35	−14.3	57.0	15.5	242	85	4	27.7	6	01	6	13	10	59	16	08	15	57
21	21	26	−10.2	56.5	15.4	254	94	1	28.7	6	24	6	32	11	47	17	20	17	14
22	22	14	−5.6	56.0	15.2	266	167	0	0.1	6	44	6	48	12	32	18	32	18	30
23	23	01	−0.9	55.5	15.1	278	226	1	1.1	7	02	7	02	13	15	19	41	19	43
24	23	47	+3.8	55.0	15.0	291	236	4	2.1	7	21	7	17	13	58	20	49	20	56
25	0	33	+8.2	54.6	14.9	303	241	9	3.1	7	40	7	32	14	41	21	56	22	07
26	1	19	+12.3	54.3	14.8	315	244	15	4.1	8	01	7	49	15	25	23	02	23	17
27	2	06	+15.8	54.2	14.8	327	248	23	5.1	8	25	8	10	16	10	—		—	
28	2	54	+18.7	54.2	14.8	339	252	31	6.1	8	54	8	35	16	57	0	07	0	25
29	3	43	+20.7	54.3	14.8	352	257	40	7.1	9	30	9	08	17	45	1	08	1	30

MERCURY

Day	R.A. h	R.A. m	Dec. °	Diam. ″	Phase %	Transit h	Transit m	5° high 52° h	5° high 52° m	5° high 56° h	5° high 56° m
1	20	40	−20.5	5	99	11	59	8	33	9	01
3	20	54	−19.6	5	99	12	05	15	38	15	12
5	21	08	−18.7	5	100	12	11	15	52	15	28
7	21	22	−17.6	5	100	12	17	16	05	15	43
9	21	36	−16.5	5	100	12	23	16	20	15	59
11	21	50	−15.2	5	99	12	29	16	34	16	16
13	22	04	−13.9	5	99	12	35	16	49	16	32
15	22	17	−12.4	5	98	12	41	17	04	16	49
17	22	31	−10.9	5	96	12	47	17	19	17	06
19	22	45	−9.3	5	94	12	53	17	34	17	22
21	22	58	−7.7	5	91	12	58	17	48	17	39
23	23	11	−6.0	6	88	13	03	18	03	17	55
25	23	23	−4.3	6	83	13	08	18	16	18	10
27	23	35	−2.6	6	77	13	11	18	29	18	24
29	23	46	−0.9	6	70	13	14	18	40	18	37
31	23	56	+0.6	7	62	13	16	18	49	18	47

VENUS

Day	R.A. h	R.A. m	Dec. °	Diam. ″	Phase %	Transit h	Transit m	5° high 52° h	5° high 52° m	5° high 56° h	5° high 56° m
1	23	30	−4.3	15	74	14	48	19	55	19	49
6	23	51	−1.6	16	73	14	49	20	11	20	06
11	0	12	+1.0	16	71	14	51	20	26	20	23
16	0	33	+3.6	17	69	14	52	20	40	20	40
21	0	54	+6.2	17	67	14	53	20	54	20	56
26	1	15	+8.7	18	65	14	54	21	08	21	12
31	1	36	+11.1	19	63	14	55	21	22	21	28

MARS

Day	R.A. h	R.A. m	Dec. °	Diam. ″	Phase %	Transit h	Transit m	5° high 52° h	5° high 52° m	5° high 56° h	5° high 56° m
1	11	39	+6.4	12	96	2	56	20	52	20	50
6	11	37	+6.8	12	97	2	34	20	28	20	26
11	11	33	+7.3	13	98	2	11	20	02	19	59
16	11	29	+7.9	13	99	1	47	19	35	19	31
21	11	23	+8.6	13	99	1	21	19	05	19	02
26	11	16	+9.3	14	100	0	55	18	35	18	31
31	11	09	+10.0	14	100	0	28	18	05	18	00

SUNRISE AND SUNSET

d	London 0° 05′ 51° 30′				Bristol 2° 35′ 51° 28′				Birmingham 1° 55′ 52° 28′				Manchester 2° 15′ 53° 28′				Newcastle 1° 37′ 54° 59′				Glasgow 4° 14′ 55° 52′				Belfast 5° 56′ 54° 35′			
	h	m	h	m	h	m	h	m	h	m	h	m	h	m	h	m	h	m	h	m	h	m	h	m	h	m	h	m
1	7	40	16	49	7	49	16	59	7	50	16	53	7	55	16	51	7	58	16	42	8	12	16	49	8	14	17	01
2	7	38	16	51	7	48	17	01	7	49	16	55	7	53	16	53	7	56	16	44	8	10	16	51	8	12	17	03
3	7	36	16	52	7	46	17	02	7	47	16	57	7	52	16	55	7	55	16	46	8	09	16	54	8	10	17	05
4	7	35	16	54	7	45	17	04	7	45	16	58	7	50	16	56	7	53	16	49	8	07	16	56	8	09	17	07
5	7	33	16	56	7	43	17	06	7	44	17	00	7	48	16	58	7	51	16	51	8	05	16	58	8	07	17	09
6	7	32	16	58	7	41	17	08	7	42	17	02	7	46	17	00	7	49	16	53	8	03	17	00	8	05	17	11
7	7	30	17	00	7	40	17	10	7	40	17	04	7	44	17	02	7	47	16	55	8	01	17	02	8	03	17	14
8	7	28	17	01	7	38	17	12	7	38	17	06	7	43	17	04	7	45	16	57	7	58	17	04	8	01	17	16
9	7	26	17	03	7	36	17	13	7	36	17	08	7	41	17	06	7	43	16	59	7	56	17	07	7	59	17	18
10	7	25	17	05	7	35	17	15	7	35	17	10	7	39	17	08	7	41	17	01	7	54	17	09	7	57	17	20
11	7	23	17	07	7	33	17	17	7	33	17	12	7	37	17	10	7	39	17	03	7	52	17	11	7	55	17	22
12	7	21	17	09	7	31	17	19	7	31	17	14	7	35	17	12	7	37	17	05	7	50	17	13	7	53	17	24
13	7	19	17	11	7	29	17	21	7	29	17	16	7	33	17	14	7	35	17	08	7	48	17	15	7	51	17	26
14	7	17	17	12	7	27	17	23	7	27	17	17	7	31	17	16	7	32	17	10	7	45	17	18	7	49	17	28
15	7	15	17	14	7	25	17	24	7	25	17	19	7	29	17	18	7	30	17	12	7	43	17	20	7	46	17	30
16	7	13	17	16	7	23	17	26	7	23	17	21	7	27	17	20	7	28	17	14	7	41	17	22	7	44	17	32
17	7	12	17	18	7	21	17	28	7	21	17	23	7	25	17	22	7	26	17	16	7	39	17	24	7	42	17	34
18	7	10	17	20	7	20	17	30	7	19	17	25	7	23	17	24	7	24	17	18	7	36	17	26	7	40	17	36
19	7	08	17	22	7	18	17	32	7	17	17	27	7	20	17	26	7	21	17	20	7	34	17	28	7	38	17	38
20	7	06	17	23	7	16	17	33	7	15	17	29	7	18	17	28	7	19	17	22	7	32	17	31	7	35	17	40
21	7	04	17	25	7	14	17	35	7	13	17	31	7	16	17	30	7	17	17	24	7	29	17	33	7	33	17	42
22	7	02	17	27	7	12	17	37	7	11	17	33	7	14	17	32	7	15	17	26	7	27	17	35	7	31	17	45
23	7	00	17	29	7	09	17	39	7	09	17	34	7	12	17	34	7	12	17	28	7	25	17	37	7	29	17	47
24	6	57	17	31	7	07	17	41	7	06	17	36	7	10	17	36	7	10	17	31	7	22	17	39	7	26	17	49
25	6	55	17	32	7	05	17	42	7	04	17	38	7	07	17	38	7	08	17	33	7	20	17	41	7	24	17	51
26	6	53	17	34	7	03	17	44	7	02	17	40	7	05	17	40	7	05	17	35	7	17	17	44	7	22	17	53
27	6	51	17	36	7	01	17	46	7	00	17	42	7	03	17	42	7	03	17	37	7	15	17	46	7	19	17	55
28	6	49	17	38	6	59	17	48	6	58	17	44	7	01	17	44	7	00	17	39	7	12	17	48	7	17	17	57
29	6	47	17	39	6	57	17	50	6	56	17	46	6	58	17	46	6	58	17	41	7	10	17	50	7	15	17	59

JUPITER

Day	R.A.		Dec.		Transit		5° high			
							52°		56°	
	h	m	°	′	h	m	h	m	h	m
1	2	03.3	+11	23	17	18	23	44	23	50
11	2	08.2	+11	51	16	44	23	12	23	18
21	2	14.1	+12	24	16	11	22	41	22	48
31	2	20.7	+13	01	15	38	22	12	22	19

Diameters – equatorial 37″ polar 35″

SATURN

Day	R.A.		Dec.		Transit		5° high			
							52°		56°	
	h	m	°	′	h	m	h	m	h	m
1	13	53.3	−8	54	5	10	0	31	0	42
11	13	53.4	−8	52	4	31	23	48	0	03
21	13	52.9	−8	46	3	51	23	07	23	19
31	13	51.8	−8	37	3	11	22	26	22	37

Diameters – equatorial 18″ polar 16″
Rings – major axis 41″ minor axis 11″

URANUS

Day	R.A.		Dec.		Transit		10° high			
							52°		56°	
	h	m	°	′	h	m	h	m	h	m
1	0	07.7	+0	04	15	23	20	17	20	10
11	0	09.3	+0	14	14	45	19	40	19	34
21	0	11.0	+0	26	14	08	19	04	18	57
31	0	13.0	+0	39	13	30	18	27	18	21

Diameter 4″

NEPTUNE

Day	R.A.		Dec.		Transit		10° high			
							52°		56°	
	h	m	°	′	h	m	h	m	h	m
1	22	08.7	−12	01	13	24	17	07	16	47
11	22	10.2	−11	53	12	46	16	30	16	10
21	22	11.6	−11	45	12	08	15	53	15	33
31	22	13.1	−11	37	11	31	15	16	14	56

Diameter 2″

MARCH 2012

THIRD MONTH, 31 DAYS. *Mars*, Roman god of battle

1	*Thursday*	The USA tested a hydrogen bomb in the Pacific (at the time, the biggest-ever man-made explosion) 1954	day 61
2	*Friday*	NASA launched *Pioneer 10*, which became the first space probe to exit the solar system 1972	62
3	*Saturday*	Alexander Graham Bell, inventor of the electric telephone *b.* 1847	63
4	*Sunday*	Emile Berliner received a patent for his invention – the gramophone 1887	64

5	*Monday*	The Britannia Bridge, designed and built by Robert Stephenson, opened 1850	week 10 day 65
6	*Tuesday*	German pharmaceutical company Friedrich Bayer & Co patented aspirin 1899	66
7	*Wednesday*	Queen Elizabeth II officially opened the Victoria Line on the London Underground 1969	67
8	*Thursday*	Abraham Darby, ironmaster who first used coke in the smelting of iron ore *d.* 1717	68
9	*Friday*	Yuri Gagarin, cosmonaut who was the first human to travel into space *b.* 1934	69
10	*Saturday*	Marcello Malpighi, regarded as the founder of microscopic anatomy *b.* 1628	70
11	*Sunday*	Cai Lun, a Chinese eunuch, revolutionised papermaking, allowing it to be mass produced AD 105	71

12	*Monday*	Sir William Henry Perkin, chemist made famous for his discovery of mauveine *b.* 1838	week 11 day 72
13	*Tuesday*	Uranus was discovered by astronomer Sir William Herschel 1781	73
14	*Wednesday*	Albert Einstein, regarded as the father of modern physics *b.* 1879	74
15	*Thursday*	Jesse Reno, an engineer, received a patent for the first escalator – the Reno Inclined Elevator 1892	75
16	*Friday*	Georg Simon Ohm, physicist after whom the unit of electrical resistance is named *b.* 1789	76
17	*Saturday*	University of California scientists announced the discovery of a new element, californium 1950	77
18	*Sunday*	Rudolf Diesel, mechanical engineer best known for the invention of the diesel engine *b.* 1858	78

19	*Monday*	The Sydney Harbour Bridge, known locally as the 'Coathanger', was opened 1932	week 12 day 79
20	*Tuesday*	Sir Isaac Newton, physicist and mathematician who discovered the law of universal gravitation *d.* 1727	80
21	*Wednesday*	The first driverless trains on the London Underground were demonstrated to the public 1963	81
22	*Thursday*	Robert Millikan, Nobel laureate physicist who devised the Millikan oil-drop experiment *b.* 1868	82
23	*Friday*	The USA announced plans to develop a space-based system to defend against nuclear missiles 1983	83
24	*Saturday*	Bacteriologist Robert Koch announced the discovery of mycobacterium tuberculosis 1882	84
25	*Sunday*	Astronomer Christiaan Huygens discovered Titan, the largest moon of Saturn 1655	85

26	*Monday*	Jonas Salk announces the successful test of the first safe and effective polio vaccine 1953	week 13 day 86
27	*Tuesday*	Sir Frederick Henry Royce, car manufacturer and co-founder of the Rolls-Royce company *b.* 1863	87
28	*Wednesday*	Henri Fabre, aviator and inventor, succeeded in taking off from water in his seaplane *Le Canard* 1910	88
29	*Thursday*	John Pemberton brewed the first batch of Coca-Cola (originally used for medicinal purposes) 1886	89
30	*Friday*	Hymen Lipman registered the first patent for a lead pencil with an attached rubber 1858	90
31	*Saturday*	Robert Bunsen, chemist credited with inventing the Bunsen burner *b.* 1811	91

ASTRONOMICAL PHENOMENA

d	h	
3	20	Mars at opposition
5	09	Mercury at greatest elongation E. 18°
7	23	Mars in conjunction with Moon. Mars 9°N.
11	03	Saturn in conjunction with Moon. Saturn 6°N.
12	08	Mercury at stationary point
14	06	Jupiter in conjunction with Venus. Jupiter 3°S.
20	05	Sun's longitude 0° ♈
21	19	Mercury in inferior conjunction
22	12	Mercury in conjunction with Moon. Mercury 1°S.
24	18	Uranus in conjunction
25	22	Jupiter in conjunction with Moon. Jupiter 3°S.
26	19	Venus in conjunction with Moon. Venus 2°N.
27	07	Venus at greatest elongation E. 46°

MINIMA OF ALGOL

d	h	d	h	d	h
3	05.5	14	16.8	26	04.1
6	02.4	17	13.6	29	00.9
8	23.2	20	10.5	31	21.8
11	20.0	23	07.3		

CONSTELLATIONS

The following constellations are near the meridian at

	d	h		d	h
February	1	24	March	16	21
February	15	23	April	1	20
March	1	22	April	15	19

Cepheus (below the Pole), Camelopardalis, Lynx, Gemini, Cancer, Leo, Canis Minor, Hydra, Monoceros, Canis Major and Puppis

THE MOON

Phases, Apsides and Node		d	h	m
☽	First Quarter	1	01	21
○	Full Moon	8	09	39
☾	Last Quarter	15	01	25
●	New Moon	22	14	37
☽	First Quarter	30	19	41

	d	h	m
Perigee (362,383km)	10	10	08
Apogee (405,801km)	26	06	12

Mean longitude of ascending node on March 1, 250°

THE SUN

s.d. 16′.1

Day	Right Ascension h m s			Dec. ° ′		Equation of time m s		Rise 52° h m	Rise 56° h m	Transit h m	Set 52° h m	Set 56° h m	Sidereal time h m s			Transit of first point of Aries h m s		
1	22	49	09	−7	31	−12	20	6 45	6 51	12 12	17 40	17 35	10	36	49	13	21	00
2	22	52	54	−7	08	−12	08	6 43	6 48	12 12	17 42	17 37	10	40	45	13	17	04
3	22	56	38	−6	45	−11	56	6 41	6 46	12 12	17 44	17 39	10	44	42	13	13	08
4	23	00	22	−6	22	−11	43	6 38	6 43	12 12	17 46	17 41	10	48	38	13	09	12
5	23	04	05	−5	59	−11	30	6 36	6 40	12 11	17 47	17 43	10	52	35	13	05	16
6	23	07	47	−5	35	−11	16	6 34	6 38	12 11	17 49	17 45	10	56	32	13	01	20
7	23	11	30	−5	12	−11	02	6 32	6 35	12 11	17 51	17 48	11	00	28	12	57	24
8	23	15	12	−4	49	−10	47	6 29	6 33	12 11	17 53	17 50	11	04	25	12	53	28
9	23	18	53	−4	25	−10	32	6 27	6 30	12 10	17 55	17 52	11	08	21	12	49	32
10	23	22	34	−4	02	−10	17	6 25	6 28	12 10	17 56	17 54	11	12	18	12	45	36
11	23	26	15	−3	38	−10	01	6 23	6 25	12 10	17 58	17 56	11	16	14	12	41	41
12	23	29	56	−3	15	−9	45	6 20	6 22	12 10	18 00	17 58	11	20	11	12	37	45
13	23	33	36	−2	51	−9	29	6 18	6 20	12 09	18 02	18 00	11	24	07	12	33	49
14	23	37	16	−2	27	−9	12	6 16	6 17	12 09	18 03	18 02	11	28	04	12	29	53
15	23	40	56	−2	04	−8	55	6 13	6 15	12 09	18 05	18 04	11	32	01	12	25	57
16	23	44	36	−1	40	−8	38	6 11	6 12	12 08	18 07	18 06	11	35	57	12	22	01
17	23	48	15	−1	16	−8	21	6 09	6 09	12 08	18 09	18 08	11	39	54	12	18	05
18	23	51	54	−0	53	−8	04	6 07	6 07	12 08	18 10	18 10	11	43	50	12	14	09
19	23	55	33	−0	29	−7	47	6 04	6 04	12 08	18 12	18 12	11	47	47	12	10	13
20	23	59	12	−0	05	−7	29	6 02	6 01	12 07	18 14	18 14	11	51	43	12	06	17
21	0	02	51	+0	19	−7	11	6 00	5 59	12 07	18 15	18 17	11	55	40	12	02	21
22	0	06	30	+0	42	−6	53	5 57	5 56	12 07	18 17	18 19	11	59	36	11	58	26
23	0	10	08	+1	06	−6	35	5 55	5 53	12 06	18 19	18 21	12	03	33	11	54	30
24	0	13	47	+1	30	−6	17	5 53	5 51	12 06	18 21	18 23	12	07	30	11	50	34
25	0	17	25	+1	53	−5	59	5 50	5 48	12 06	18 22	18 25	12	11	26	11	46	38
26	0	21	04	+2	17	−5	41	5 48	5 46	12 06	18 24	18 27	12	15	23	11	42	42
27	0	24	42	+2	40	−5	23	5 46	5 43	12 05	18 26	18 29	12	19	19	11	38	46
28	0	28	21	+3	04	−5	05	5 43	5 40	12 05	18 28	18 31	12	23	16	11	34	50
29	0	31	59	+3	27	−4	47	5 41	5 38	12 05	18 29	18 33	12	27	12	11	30	54
30	0	35	38	+3	50	−4	29	5 39	5 35	12 04	18 31	18 35	12	31	09	11	26	58
31	0	39	17	+4	14	−4	11	5 36	5 32	12 04	18 33	18 37	12	35	05	11	23	02

DURATION OF TWILIGHT (in minutes)

Latitude	52°	56°	52°	56°	52°	56°	52°	56°
	1 March		11 March		21 March		31 March	
Civil	34	37	34	37	34	37	34	38
Nautical	73	80	73	80	74	81	75	84
Astronomical	112	124	113	125	115	128	120	135

THE NIGHT SKY

Mercury reaches its greatest eastern elongation (18 degrees) on the 5th and therefore is visible in the evenings for the first 10 days of the month. It may be detected low above the west-south-western horizon around the beginning of evening civil twilight. At first its magnitude is −0.8 but this has diminished to about +1.1 by the end of its period of visibility.

Venus, magnitude −4.5, reaches its greatest eastern elongation (46 degrees) on the 27th and completely dominates the southwestern sky for about 4 hours after sunset. On the 14th the planet passes 3 degrees north of Jupiter while on the evening of the 26th the waxing crescent Moon passes 2 degrees south of Venus.

Mars reaches opposition on the 3rd and is therefore visible throughout the hours of darkness. Its retrograde motion takes it back in the direction of Regulus, in Leo, though it reaches its second stationary point next month, still about 5 degrees from that star. During the month its magnitude fades from −1.2 to −0.9. The Full Moon passes about 9 degrees south of the planet on the night of the 7th–8th.

Jupiter, magnitude −2.1, is now only visible low above the south-western horizon for a short while after sunset. On the 25th the crescent Moon, only 3 days old, passes about 3 degrees north of the planet.

Saturn continues to be visible from the late evenings onwards, magnitude +0.4, in the constellation of Virgo. By the end of the month it should be visible low above the eastern horizon by about 21h as it moves towards opposition next month. During the night of the 10th–11th the waning gibbous Moon passes about 7 degrees south of the planet.

Zodiacal Light. The evening cone may be observed stretching up from the western horizon, along the ecliptic, after the end of twilight, from the 9th to the 23rd. This faint phenomenon is only visible under good conditions and in the absence of both moonlight and artificial lighting. The proximity of Venus will make detection of this faint phenomenon more difficult.

THE MOON

Day	R.A. h	m	Dec. °	Hor. par. '	Semi-diam. '	Sun's Co-Long. °	PA of Br. Limb °	Ph. %	Age d	Rise 52° h	m	Rise 56° h	m	Transit h	m	Set 52° h	m	Set 56° h	m
1	4	34	+21.9	54.6	14.9	4	262	50	8.1	10	13	9	50	18	35	2	05	2	29
2	5	27	+22.1	55.1	15.0	16	266	59	9.1	11	06	10	43	19	26	2	56	3	19
3	6	20	+21.2	55.8	15.2	28	271	69	10.1	12	08	11	47	20	17	3	39	4	01
4	7	13	+19.2	56.6	15.4	40	275	78	11.1	13	17	12	59	21	08	4	16	4	34
5	8	07	+16.2	57.4	15.6	52	278	86	12.1	14	31	14	18	22	00	4	47	5	01
6	9	00	+12.3	58.3	15.9	65	279	92	13.1	15	49	15	41	22	51	5	13	5	23
7	9	54	+7.6	59.1	16.1	77	276	97	14.1	17	10	17	07	23	42	5	37	5	42
8	10	47	+2.3	59.8	16.3	89	250	100	15.1	18	33	18	34	—		5	59	6	00
9	11	41	−3.2	60.2	16.4	101	143	99	16.1	19	57	20	03	0	34	6	22	6	18
10	12	37	−8.5	60.5	16.5	113	123	96	17.1	21	21	21	33	1	28	6	46	6	38
11	13	34	−13.4	60.5	16.5	125	116	90	18.1	22	45	23	02	2	23	7	14	7	01
12	14	33	−17.4	60.2	16.4	137	110	82	19.1	—		—		3	20	7	48	7	30
13	15	33	−20.3	59.8	16.3	150	104	73	20.1	0	03	0	25	4	19	8	31	8	09
14	16	34	−21.8	59.2	16.1	162	98	62	21.1	1	14	1	37	5	19	9	22	8	59
15	17	34	−21.9	58.6	16.0	174	93	51	22.1	2	12	2	36	6	17	10	24	10	01
16	18	33	−20.7	58.0	15.8	186	87	40	23.1	2	59	3	20	7	13	11	32	11	12
17	19	29	−18.4	57.4	15.6	198	83	30	24.1	3	36	3	53	8	06	12	44	12	28
18	20	22	−15.1	56.8	15.5	211	80	20	25.1	4	05	4	18	8	56	13	57	13	45
19	21	13	−11.2	56.3	15.3	223	78	13	26.1	4	28	4	37	9	43	15	09	15	01
20	22	01	−6.8	55.8	15.2	235	78	7	27.1	4	49	4	54	10	28	16	19	16	16
21	22	48	−2.2	55.3	15.1	247	83	3	28.1	5	08	5	09	11	12	17	28	17	29
22	23	34	+2.4	54.9	15.0	259	102	1	29.1	5	27	5	24	11	55	18	36	18	41
23	0	19	+6.8	54.6	14.9	272	202	0	0.4	5	46	5	39	12	38	19	43	19	52
24	1	05	+11.0	54.3	14.8	284	234	2	1.4	6	06	5	56	13	21	20	49	21	03
25	1	52	+14.6	54.1	14.7	296	243	5	2.4	6	29	6	15	14	06	21	54	22	11
26	2	39	+17.7	54.0	14.7	308	250	10	3.4	6	57	6	39	14	52	22	57	23	17
27	3	28	+20.0	54.1	14.7	320	255	17	4.4	7	30	7	09	15	39	23	55	—	
28	4	19	+21.4	54.2	14.8	333	260	24	5.4	8	10	7	47	16	28	—		0	17
29	5	10	+21.9	54.6	14.9	345	265	33	6.4	8	58	8	35	17	17	0	47	1	10
30	6	02	+21.4	55.0	15.0	357	271	42	7.4	9	55	9	33	18	07	1	33	1	55
31	6	54	+19.8	55.7	15.2	9	275	52	8.4	10	59	10	40	18	57	2	11	2	31

MERCURY

Day	R.A. h	m	Dec. °	Diam. "	Phase %	Transit h	m	5° high 52° h	m	5° high 56° h	m
1	23	51	−0.1	6	66	13	15	18	45	18	42
3	0	00	+1.4	7	57	13	16	18	53	18	51
5	0	08	+2.7	7	48	13	15	18	59	18	58
7	0	14	+3.9	8	39	13	13	19	01	19	02
9	0	18	+4.8	8	31	13	08	19	01	19	01
11	0	20	+5.4	9	23	13	02	18	56	18	58
13	0	20	+5.7	9	16	12	53	18	49	18	50
15	0	18	+5.7	10	10	12	43	18	38	18	39
17	0	14	+5.4	10	5	12	31	18	23	18	24
19	0	09	+4.8	11	2	12	18	18	07	18	07
21	0	03	+4.0	11	1	12	04	17	48	17	48
23	23	57	+3.0	11	1	11	50	6	09	6	10
25	23	51	+2.0	11	2	11	36	6	01	6	03
27	23	46	+0.9	11	4	11	24	5	53	5	56
29	23	42	−0.1	11	8	11	12	5	47	5	50
31	23	39	−0.9	11	11	11	01	5	40	5	45

VENUS

Day	R.A. h	m	Dec. °	Diam. "	Phase %	Transit h	m	5° high 52° h	m	5° high 56° h	m
1	1	31	+10.7	18	64	14	55	21	19	21	25
6	1	52	+13.0	19	62	14	56	21	33	21	40
11	2	13	+15.3	20	59	14	56	21	45	21	55
16	2	33	+17.4	21	57	14	57	21	58	22	10
21	2	53	+19.3	22	55	14	58	22	10	22	23
26	3	14	+21.1	23	52	14	58	22	20	22	36
31	3	34	+22.7	25	49	14	59	22	30	22	48

MARS

Day	R.A. h	m	Dec. °	Diam. "	Phase %	Transit h	m	5° high 52° h	m	5° high 56° h	m
1	11	11	+9.9	14	100	0	34	6	51	6	55
6	11	03	+10.6	14	100	0	07	6	27	6	32
11	10	56	+11.2	14	100	23	34	6	03	6	09
16	10	49	+11.8	14	99	23	07	5	40	5	46
21	10	42	+12.3	13	99	22	42	5	16	5	23
26	10	37	+12.6	13	98	22	17	4	53	5	00
31	10	32	+12.8	13	97	21	53	4	30	4	37

SUNRISE AND SUNSET

	London 0° 05′ 51° 30′		Bristol 2° 35′ 51° 28′		Birmingham 1° 55′ 52° 28′		Manchester 2° 15′ 53° 28′		Newcastle 1° 37′ 54° 59′		Glasgow 4° 14′ 55° 52′		Belfast 5° 56′ 54° 35′	
d	h m	h m	h m	h m	h m	h m	h m	h m	h m	h m	h m	h m	h m	h m
1	6 45	17 41	6 55	17 51	6 53	17 47	6 56	17 47	6 56	17 43	7 07	17 52	7 12	18 01
2	6 43	17 43	6 53	17 53	6 51	17 49	6 54	17 49	6 53	17 45	7 05	17 54	7 10	18 03
3	6 40	17 45	6 50	17 55	6 49	17 51	6 51	17 51	6 51	17 47	7 02	17 56	7 07	18 05
4	6 38	17 47	6 48	17 57	6 47	17 53	6 49	17 53	6 48	17 49	7 00	17 58	7 05	18 07
5	6 36	17 48	6 46	17 58	6 44	17 55	6 47	17 55	6 46	17 51	6 57	18 00	7 03	18 09
6	6 34	17 50	6 44	18 00	6 42	17 57	6 44	17 57	6 43	17 53	6 55	18 03	7 00	18 11
7	6 32	17 52	6 42	18 02	6 40	17 58	6 42	17 59	6 41	17 55	6 52	18 05	6 58	18 13
8	6 29	17 53	6 39	18 04	6 37	18 00	6 40	18 01	6 38	17 57	6 50	18 07	6 55	18 15
9	6 27	17 55	6 37	18 05	6 35	18 02	6 37	18 03	6 36	17 59	6 47	18 09	6 53	18 17
10	6 25	17 57	6 35	18 07	6 33	18 04	6 35	18 04	6 33	18 01	6 44	18 11	6 50	18 19
11	6 23	17 59	6 33	18 09	6 31	18 06	6 32	18 06	6 31	18 03	6 42	18 13	6 48	18 20
12	6 20	18 00	6 30	18 10	6 28	18 07	6 30	18 08	6 28	18 05	6 39	18 15	6 45	18 22
13	6 18	18 02	6 28	18 12	6 26	18 09	6 28	18 10	6 26	18 07	6 37	18 17	6 43	18 24
14	6 16	18 04	6 26	18 14	6 24	18 11	6 25	18 12	6 23	18 09	6 34	18 19	6 40	18 26
15	6 14	18 06	6 24	18 16	6 21	18 13	6 23	18 14	6 21	18 11	6 31	18 21	6 38	18 28
16	6 11	18 07	6 21	18 17	6 19	18 14	6 20	18 16	6 18	18 13	6 29	18 23	6 35	18 30
17	6 09	18 09	6 19	18 19	6 17	18 16	6 18	18 17	6 16	18 15	6 26	18 25	6 33	18 32
18	6 07	18 11	6 17	18 21	6 14	18 18	6 16	18 19	6 13	18 17	6 24	18 27	6 30	18 34
19	6 05	18 12	6 15	18 22	6 12	18 20	6 13	18 21	6 11	18 19	6 21	18 29	6 28	18 36
20	6 02	18 14	6 12	18 24	6 10	18 22	6 11	18 23	6 08	18 21	6 18	18 31	6 25	18 38
21	6 00	18 16	6 10	18 26	6 07	18 23	6 08	18 25	6 05	18 23	6 16	18 33	6 23	18 40
22	5 58	18 17	6 08	18 27	6 05	18 25	6 06	18 27	6 03	18 25	6 13	18 35	6 20	18 42
23	5 55	18 19	6 05	18 29	6 02	18 27	6 03	18 29	6 00	18 27	6 10	18 38	6 18	18 44
24	5 53	18 21	6 03	18 31	6 00	18 29	6 01	18 30	5 58	18 29	6 08	18 40	6 15	18 46
25	5 51	18 22	6 01	18 32	5 58	18 30	5 59	18 32	5 55	18 31	6 05	18 42	6 13	18 48
26	5 49	18 24	5 59	18 34	5 55	18 32	5 56	18 34	5 53	18 33	6 03	18 44	6 10	18 50
27	5 46	18 26	5 56	18 36	5 53	18 34	5 54	18 36	5 50	18 34	6 00	18 46	6 08	18 51
28	5 44	18 28	5 54	18 37	5 51	18 36	5 51	18 38	5 48	18 36	5 57	18 48	6 05	18 53
29	5 42	18 29	5 52	18 39	5 48	18 37	5 49	18 40	5 45	18 38	5 55	18 50	6 03	18 55
30	5 40	18 31	5 50	18 41	5 46	18 39	5 46	18 41	5 43	18 40	5 52	18 52	6 00	18 57
31	5 37	18 33	5 47	18 43	5 44	18 41	5 44	18 43	5 40	18 42	5 49	18 54	5 58	18 59

JUPITER

Day	R.A.		Dec.		Transit		5° high 52°		56°	
	h	m	°	′	h	m	h	m	h	m
1	2	20.0	+12	57	15	41	22	15	22	22
11	2	27.3	+13	35	15	09	21	46	21	54
21	2	35.3	+14	15	14	38	21	18	21	27
31	2	43.7	+14	56	14	07	20	51	21	00

Diameters – equatorial 35″ polar 33″

SATURN

Day	R.A.		Dec.		Transit		5° high 52°		56°	
	h	m	°	′	h	m	h	m	h	m
1	13	51.9	−8	38	3	15	22	30	22	41
11	13	50.3	−8	27	2	34	21	48	21	59
21	13	48.1	−8	13	1	52	21	05	21	16
31	13	45.6	−7	58	1	10	20	22	20	32

Diameters – equatorial 19″ polar 17″
Rings – major axis 42″ minor axis 11″

URANUS

Day	R.A.		Dec.		Transit		10° high 52°		56°	
	h	m	°	′	h	m	h	m	h	m
1	0	12.8	+0	38	13	34	18	31	18	25
11	0	14.8	+0	51	12	57	17	55	17	49
21	0	16.9	+1	04	12	19	17	19	17	13
31	0	19.0	+1	18	11	42	16	43	16	37

Diameter 4″

NEPTUNE

Day	R.A.		Dec.		Transit		10° high 52°		56°	
	h	m	°	′	h	m	h	m	h	m
1	22	12.9	−11	38	11	34	7	49	8	09
11	22	14.3	−11	30	10	56	7	10	7	30
21	22	15.7	−11	23	10	18	6	31	6	51
31	22	16.9	−11	16	9	40	5	52	6	12

Diameter 2″

APRIL 2012

FOURTH MONTH, 30 DAYS. *Aperire*, to open; Earth opens to receive seed.

1	*Sunday*	William Harvey, physician best known for his description of blood circulation *b.* 1578	day 92

2	*Monday*	Samuel Morse, inventor of Morse Code (communications system of dots and dashes) *d.* 1872	week 14 day 93
3	*Tuesday*	RAF officer David McIntyre completed the first aerial photographic survey of Mt Everest 1933	94
4	*Wednesday*	Microsoft, the computer technology corporation, was founded by Bill Gates and Paul Allen 1975	95
5	*Thursday*	Joseph Lister, surgeon and medical scientist credited as the founder of antiseptic medicine *b.* 1827	96
6	*Friday*	*Early Bird* became the first commercial communications satellite to be placed in geosynchronous orbit 1965	97
7	*Saturday*	Congreves – the original friction matches – were first sold by their inventor, John Walker 1827	98
8	*Sunday*	The steamship *Great Western*, designed by Isambard K. Brunel, made her maiden transatlantic voyage 1838	99

9	*Monday*	The space shuttle *Endeavour* was launched on an 11-day mission 1994	week 15 day 100
10	*Tuesday*	Walter Hunt, a mechanic and inventor, received a patent for the safety pin 1849	101
11	*Wednesday*	The Ryan X-13 Vertijet, the first jet to take off and land vertically, completed a full flight 1957	102
12	*Thursday*	Yuri Gagarin became the first man to travel in space; the Soviet Union declared the space race won 1961	103
13	*Friday*	Joseph Bramah, engineer and inventor best known for inventing the hydraulic press *b.* 1748	104
14	*Saturday*	Christiaan Huygens, mathematician, astronomer and physicist who invented the pendulum clock *b.* 1629	105
15	*Sunday*	Leonardo da Vinci, polymathic artist, engineer and scientist *b.*1452	106

16	*Monday*	Isaac Newton was knighted by Queen Anne at Trinity College, London 1705	week 16 day 107
17	*Tuesday*	The crew of Apollo 13 safely landed on Earth after experiencing a major malfunction while en route to the Moon 1970	108
18	*Wednesday*	Albert Einstein, physicist awarded the Nobel Prize for Physics for his theories of relativity *d.* 1955	109
19	*Thursday*	Charles Darwin, naturalist best known for his study of evolution and *On the Origin of Species d.* 1882	110
20	*Friday*	Marie Curie, physicist and chemist, isolated the radioactive element radium 1902	111
21	*Saturday*	Crew from Apollo 16 landed in the previously unexplored Descartes Highlands area of the Moon 1972	112
22	*Sunday*	James Hargreaves, carpenter and inventor, credited with inventing the spinning jenny *d.* 1778	113

23	*Monday*	Max Planck, physicist who formulated the quantum theory of radiation *b.* 1858	week 17 day 114
24	*Tuesday*	The Hubble Space Telescope was launched 1990	115
25	*Wednesday*	Construction of the 163km Suez Canal (connecting the Mediterranean with the Red Sea) began 1859	116
26	*Thursday*	Charles Richter, seismologist best known for inventing the earthquake-measuring Richter scale *b.* 1900	117
27	*Friday*	Francis Clarke and M. G. Foster received a patent for the electric hearing aid 1880	118
28	*Saturday*	Dennis Tito, a businessman, made history by becoming the first paying passenger to go into space 2001	119
29	*Sunday*	Harold Urey, scientist who was a key figure in developing the atomic bomb *b.* 1893	120

30	*Monday*	J. J. Thomson announced his discovery of the first subatomic particle, the electron 1897	week 18 day 121

ASTRONOMICAL PHENOMENA

d	h	
3	21	Mars in conjunction with Moon. Mars 8°N.
4	10	Mercury at stationary point
7	10	Saturn in conjunction with Moon. Saturn 6°N.
10	16	Pluto at stationary point
14	04	Mars at stationary point
15	18	Saturn at opposition
18	17	Mercury at greatest elongation W. 27°
18	19	Mercury in conjunction with Moon. Mercury 7°S.
19	16	Sun's longitude 30° ♉
22	17	Jupiter in conjunction with Moon. Jupiter 2°S.
25	04	Venus in conjuction with Moon. Venus 6°N.
30	01	Venus at greatest brilliancy

MINIMA OF ALGOL

d	h	d	h	d	h
3	18.6	15	05.9	26	17.1
6	15.4	18	02.7	29	14.0
9	12.2	20	23.5		
12	09.0	23	20.3		

CONSTELLATIONS

The following constellations are near the meridian at

	d	h		d	h
March	1	24	April	15	21
March	16	23	May	1	20
April	1	22	May	16	19

Cepheus (below the Pole), Cassiopeia (below the Pole), Ursa Major, Leo Minor, Leo., Sextans, Hydra and Crater

THE MOON

Phases, Apsides and Node	d	h	m
○ Full Moon	6	19	19
☾ Last Quarter	13	10	50
● New Moon	21	07	18
☽ First Quarter	29	09	57

Perigee (358,306km)	7	17	06
Apogee (406,429km)	22	14	03

Mean longitude of ascending node on April 1, 248°

THE SUN

s.d. 16'.0

Day	Right Ascension			Dec.		Equation of time		Rise 52°		Rise 56°		Transit		Set 52°		Set 56°		Sidereal time			Transit of first point of Aries		
	h	m	s	°	′	m	s	h	m	h	m	h	m	h	m	h	m	h	m	s	h	m	s
1	0	42	55	4	37	−3	53	5	34	5	30	12	04	18	34	18	39	12	39	02	11	19	07
2	0	46	34	5	00	−3	35	5	32	5	27	12	03	18	36	18	41	12	42	58	11	15	11
3	0	50	13	5	23	−3	18	5	30	5	25	12	03	18	38	18	43	12	46	55	11	11	15
4	0	53	52	5	46	−3	00	5	27	5	22	12	03	18	40	18	45	12	50	52	11	07	19
5	0	57	31	6	09	−2	43	5	25	5	19	12	03	18	41	18	47	12	54	48	11	03	23
6	1	01	10	6	31	−2	26	5	23	5	17	12	02	18	43	18	49	12	58	45	10	59	27
7	1	04	50	6	54	−2	09	5	20	5	14	12	02	18	45	18	51	13	02	41	10	55	31
8	1	08	30	7	16	−1	52	5	18	5	12	12	02	18	46	18	53	13	06	38	10	51	35
9	1	12	10	7	39	−1	35	5	16	5	09	12	01	18	48	18	55	13	10	34	10	47	39
10	1	15	50	8	01	−1	19	5	14	5	06	12	01	18	50	18	57	13	14	31	10	43	43
11	1	19	31	8	23	−1	03	5	11	5	04	12	01	18	51	18	59	13	18	27	10	39	47
12	1	23	11	8	45	−0	47	5	09	5	01	12	01	18	53	19	01	13	22	24	10	35	52
13	1	26	53	9	07	−0	32	5	07	4	59	12	00	18	55	19	03	13	26	21	10	31	56
14	1	30	34	9	28	−0	17	5	05	4	56	12	00	18	57	19	05	13	30	17	10	28	00
15	1	34	16	9	50	−0	02	5	03	4	54	12	00	18	58	19	08	13	34	14	10	24	04
16	1	37	58	10	11	+0	12	5	00	4	51	12	00	19	00	19	10	13	38	10	10	20	08
17	1	41	41	10	32	+0	26	4	58	4	49	11	59	19	02	19	12	13	42	07	10	16	12
18	1	45	24	10	53	+0	39	4	56	4	46	11	59	19	03	19	14	13	46	03	10	12	16
19	1	49	08	11	14	+0	52	4	54	4	44	11	59	19	05	19	16	13	50	00	10	08	20
20	1	52	51	11	35	+1	05	4	52	4	41	11	59	19	07	19	18	13	53	56	10	04	24
21	1	56	36	11	55	+1	17	4	50	4	39	11	59	19	09	19	20	13	57	53	10	00	28
22	2	00	21	12	16	+1	29	4	48	4	36	11	58	19	10	19	22	14	01	50	9	56	32
23	2	04	06	12	36	+1	40	4	46	4	34	11	58	19	12	19	24	14	05	46	9	52	37
24	2	07	51	12	56	+1	51	4	44	4	32	11	58	19	14	19	26	14	09	43	9	48	41
25	2	11	38	13	15	+2	02	4	42	4	29	11	58	19	15	19	28	14	13	39	9	44	45
26	2	15	24	13	35	+2	12	4	40	4	27	11	58	19	17	19	30	14	17	36	9	40	49
27	2	19	11	13	54	+2	21	4	38	4	25	11	58	19	19	19	32	14	21	32	9	36	53
28	2	22	59	14	13	+2	30	4	36	4	22	11	57	19	20	19	34	14	25	29	9	32	57
29	2	26	47	14	31	+2	38	4	34	4	20	11	57	19	22	19	36	14	29	25	9	29	01
30	2	30	36	14	50	+2	46	4	32	4	18	11	57	19	24	19	38	14	33	22	9	25	05

DURATION OF TWILIGHT (in minutes)

Latitude	52°	56°	52°	56°	52°	56°	52°	56°
	1 April		11 April		21 April		31 April	
Civil	34	38	35	39	37	42	39	44
Nautical	76	84	79	89	83	96	89	106
Astronomical	120	136	127	147	137	165	152	204

THE NIGHT SKY

Mercury, despite being at greatest western elongation (27 degrees) on the 18th, is unsuitably placed for observation throughout the month.

Venus, magnitude −4.5, reaches its greatest brilliancy on the last day of the month and therefore continues to dominate the western sky in the evenings for several hours after sunset. The waxing crescent Moon will be seen passing about 6 degrees south of the planet on April 24–25.

Mars, its magnitude fading from −0.7 to 0.0 during the month, is in the constellation of Leo, reaching its second stationary point on the 14th. By the end of the month it will be too low in the west-north-western sky to be visible after about 02h. On the night of April 3–4

the waxing gibbous Moon passes about 9 degrees south of the planet.

Jupiter, magnitude −2.0, is only visible for about the first 3 weeks of April, low in the western sky after sunset. However, it may be possible to detect it on the evening of the 22nd as the thin crescent Moon passes 2 degrees north of it.

Saturn, reaches opposition on the 15th, and therefore is visible throughout the hours of darkness. It is in the constellation of Virgo, and has a magnitude of +0.2. The rings of Saturn are getting more easily visible in smaller telescopes as the minor axis is now 10 arcseconds. The Full Moon is in the vicinity of the planet on the night of April 6–7, passing 7 degrees south of it.

THE MOON

Day	R.A. h	m	Dec. °	Hor. Par. '	Semi-diam. '	Sun's Co-Long. °	PA of Br. Limb °	Ph. %	Age d	Rise 52° h	m	Rise 56° h	m	Transit h	m	Set 52° h	m	Set 56° h	m
1	7	46	+17.3	56.5	15.4	21	279	62	9.4	12	09	11	54	19	47	2	44	2	59
2	8	39	+13.8	57.4	15.6	34	283	72	10.4	13	23	13	13	20	37	3	11	3	23
3	9	31	+9.5	58.3	15.9	46	285	81	11.4	14	41	14	35	21	27	3	36	3	43
4	10	23	+4.6	59.2	16.1	58	285	89	12.4	16	01	16	01	22	19	3	59	4	02
5	11	17	-0.8	60.1	16.4	70	283	95	13.4	17	25	17	29	23	12	4	21	4	20
6	12	12	-6.2	60.7	16.5	82	272	99	14.4	18	50	18	59	—		4	45	4	39
7	13	10	-11.4	61.1	16.7	94	165	100	15.4	20	16	20	31	0	07	5	12	5	01
8	14	09	-15.8	61.2	16.7	107	118	98	16.4	21	40	22	00	1	05	5	44	5	29
9	15	11	-19.2	60.9	16.6	119	108	93	17.4	22	57	23	20	2	06	6	24	6	04
10	16	14	-21.2	60.4	16.5	131	100	85	18.4	—		—		3	07	7	14	6	51
11	17	17	-21.8	59.7	16.3	143	94	76	19.4	0	03	0	26	4	08	8	15	7	51
12	18	17	-20.9	58.9	16.1	155	87	66	20.4	0	55	1	17	5	07	9	23	9	02
13	19	15	-18.8	58.1	15.8	167	82	55	21.4	1	36	1	54	6	02	10	35	10	18
14	20	10	-15.7	57.3	15.6	180	78	44	22.4	2	08	2	22	6	54	11	48	11	35
15	21	01	-11.9	56.5	15.4	192	75	34	23.4	2	33	2	43	7	42	13	00	12	52
16	21	50	-7.7	55.9	15.2	204	73	25	24.4	2	55	3	01	8	27	14	11	14	06
17	22	37	-3.2	55.3	15.1	216	73	17	25.4	3	14	3	16	9	11	15	19	15	19
18	23	22	+1.4	54.9	14.9	228	73	10	26.4	3	33	3	31	9	53	16	27	16	30
19	0	08	+5.8	54.5	14.9	241	76	5	27.4	3	51	3	46	10	36	17	33	17	41
20	0	53	+10.0	54.2	14.8	253	82	2	28.4	4	11	4	02	11	19	18	40	18	51
21	1	39	+13.7	54.1	14.7	265	112	0	29.4	4	34	4	21	12	03	19	45	20	00
22	2	27	+16.9	54.0	14.7	277	235	0	0.7	5	00	4	43	12	49	20	48	21	07
23	3	15	+19.4	54.0	14.7	290	251	3	1.7	5	31	5	11	13	36	21	48	22	09
24	4	05	+21.0	54.0	14.7	302	259	6	2.7	6	09	5	47	14	24	22	42	23	05
25	4	56	+21.7	54.2	14.8	314	265	12	3.7	6	54	6	31	15	13	23	29	23	52
26	5	48	+21.4	54.6	14.9	326	270	19	4.7	7	48	7	26	16	02	—		—	
27	6	39	+20.2	55.0	15.0	339	275	27	5.7	8	48	8	29	16	51	0	10	0	30
28	7	31	+18.0	55.6	15.1	351	280	36	6.7	9	55	9	38	17	40	0	43	1	00
29	8	22	+14.8	56.3	15.3	3	284	46	7.7	11	05	10	53	18	28	1	12	1	25
30	9	12	+10.9	57.2	15.6	15	287	56	8.7	12	19	12	11	19	16	1	37	1	46

MERCURY

Day	R.A. h	m	Dec. °	Diam. "	Phase %	Transit h	m	5° high 52° h	m	5° high 56° h	m
1	23	38	-1.3	11	13	10	57	5	38	5	42
3	23	37	-2.0	10	17	10	48	5	32	5	37
5	23	38	-2.5	10	21	10	41	5	28	5	33
7	23	39	-2.8	10	25	10	35	5	23	5	29
9	23	42	-2.9	9	29	10	31	5	19	5	25
11	23	46	-2.9	9	33	10	27	5	15	5	21
13	23	51	-2.7	9	37	10	24	5	11	5	17
15	23	57	-2.4	8	40	10	23	5	08	5	13
17	0	04	-2.0	8	44	10	21	5	04	5	09
19	0	11	-1.4	8	47	10	21	5	01	5	05
21	0	19	-0.8	8	50	10	21	4	57	5	01
23	0	27	0.0	7	53	10	22	4	54	4	57
25	0	36	+0.9	7	56	10	23	4	50	4	53
27	0	46	+1.9	7	58	10	25	4	47	4	49
29	0	56	+2.9	7	61	10	27	4	44	4	45
31	1	07	+4.0	6	64	10	30	4	41	4	41

VENUS

Day	R.A. h	m	Dec. °	Diam. "	Phase %	Transit h	m	5° high 52° h	m	5° high 56° h	m
1	3	38	+23.0	25	49	14	59	22	32	22	50
6	3	57	+24.3	26	46	14	58	22	40	23	00
11	4	16	+25.4	28	42	14	57	22	46	23	07
16	4	33	+26.3	30	39	14	55	22	49	23	12
21	4	49	+27.0	32	35	14	51	22	50	23	14
26	5	04	+27.5	35	31	14	45	22	47	23	12
31	5	16	+27.8	37	27	14	38	22	41	23	06

MARS

Day	R.A. h	m	Dec. °	Diam. "	Phase %	Transit h	m	5° high 52° h	m	5° high 56° h	m
1	10	31	+12.8	13	97	21	48	4	25	4	33
6	10	29	+12.9	12	96	21	26	4	03	4	10
11	10	27	+12.8	12	95	21	05	3	41	3	49
16	10	26	+12.6	11	94	20	45	3	20	3	27
21	10	27	+12.4	11	93	20	26	3	00	3	07
26	10	29	+12.0	10	92	20	08	2	40	2	46
31	10	32	+11.5	10	91	19	52	2	21	2	27

SUNRISE AND SUNSET

	London 0° 05′	51° 30′	Bristol 2° 35′	51° 28′	Birmingham 1° 55′	52° 28′	Manchester 2° 15′	53° 28′	Newcastle 1° 37′	54° 59′	Glasgow 4° 14′	55° 52′	Belfast 5° 56′	54° 35′
d	h m	h m	h m	h m	h m	h m	h m	h m	h m	h m	h m	h m	h m	h m
1	5 35	18 34	5 45	18 44	5 41	18 43	5 42	18 45	5 37	18 44	5 47	18 56	5 55	19 01
2	5 33	18 36	5 43	18 46	5 39	18 44	5 39	18 47	5 35	18 46	5 44	18 58	5 53	19 03
3	5 30	18 38	5 41	18 48	5 37	18 46	5 37	18 49	5 32	18 48	5 42	19 00	5 50	19 05
4	5 28	18 39	5 38	18 49	5 34	18 48	5 34	18 50	5 30	18 50	5 39	19 02	5 48	19 07
5	5 26	18 41	5 36	18 51	5 32	18 50	5 32	18 52	5 27	18 52	5 36	19 04	5 45	19 09
6	5 24	18 43	5 34	18 53	5 30	18 51	5 30	18 54	5 25	18 54	5 34	19 06	5 43	19 11
7	5 22	18 44	5 32	18 54	5 27	18 53	5 27	18 56	5 22	18 56	5 31	19 08	5 40	19 12
8	5 19	18 46	5 29	18 56	5 25	18 55	5 25	18 58	5 20	18 58	5 29	19 10	5 38	19 14
9	5 17	18 48	5 27	18 58	5 23	18 56	5 23	19 00	5 17	19 00	5 26	19 12	5 35	19 16
10	5 15	18 49	5 25	18 59	5 21	18 58	5 20	19 01	5 15	19 02	5 24	19 14	5 33	19 18
11	5 13	18 51	5 23	19 01	5 18	19 00	5 18	19 03	5 12	19 04	5 21	19 16	5 30	19 20
12	5 10	18 53	5 21	19 03	5 16	19 02	5 16	19 05	5 10	19 06	5 18	19 18	5 28	19 22
13	5 08	18 54	5 18	19 04	5 14	19 03	5 13	19 07	5 07	19 08	5 16	19 20	5 26	19 24
14	5 06	18 56	5 16	19 06	5 12	19 05	5 11	19 09	5 05	19 10	5 13	19 22	5 23	19 26
15	5 04	18 58	5 14	19 08	5 09	19 07	5 09	19 10	5 03	19 11	5 11	19 24	5 21	19 28
16	5 02	18 59	5 12	19 09	5 07	19 09	5 06	19 12	5 00	19 13	5 08	19 26	5 18	19 30
17	5 00	19 01	5 10	19 11	5 05	19 10	5 04	19 14	4 58	19 15	5 06	19 28	5 16	19 32
18	4 58	19 03	5 08	19 13	5 03	19 12	5 02	19 16	4 55	19 17	5 03	19 30	5 14	19 34
19	4 56	19 04	5 06	19 14	5 01	19 14	4 59	19 18	4 53	19 19	5 01	19 32	5 11	19 35
20	4 53	19 06	5 03	19 16	4 58	19 16	4 57	19 20	4 51	19 21	4 59	19 34	5 09	19 37
21	4 51	19 08	5 01	19 18	4 56	19 17	4 55	19 21	4 48	19 23	4 56	19 36	5 07	19 39
22	4 49	19 09	4 59	19 19	4 54	19 19	4 53	19 23	4 46	19 25	4 54	19 38	5 04	19 41
23	4 47	19 11	4 57	19 21	4 52	19 21	4 51	19 25	4 44	19 27	4 51	19 40	5 02	19 43
24	4 45	19 13	4 55	19 23	4 50	19 23	4 48	19 27	4 41	19 29	4 49	19 42	5 00	19 45
25	4 43	19 14	4 53	19 24	4 48	19 24	4 46	19 29	4 39	19 31	4 47	19 44	4 58	19 47
26	4 41	19 16	4 51	19 26	4 46	19 26	4 44	19 30	4 37	19 33	4 44	19 46	4 55	19 49
27	4 39	19 18	4 49	19 28	4 44	19 28	4 42	19 32	4 35	19 35	4 42	19 48	4 53	19 51
28	4 37	19 19	4 47	19 29	4 42	19 30	4 40	19 34	4 32	19 37	4 40	19 50	4 51	19 53
29	4 35	19 21	4 46	19 31	4 40	19 31	4 38	19 36	4 30	19 39	4 37	19 52	4 49	19 55
30	4 34	19 23	4 44	19 32	4 38	19 33	4 36	19 38	4 28	19 41	4 35	19 55	4 47	19 56

JUPITER

Day	R.A. h	R.A. m	Dec. °	Dec. ′	Transit h	Transit m	5° high 52° h	52° m	56° h	56° m
1	2	44.5	+15	00	14	04	20	48	20	58
11	2	53.4	+15	41	13	33	20	22	20	32
21	3	02.6	+16	21	13	03	19	55	20	06
31	3	12.0	+17	00	12	33	19	29	19	40

Diameters – equatorial 33″ polar 31″

SATURN

Day	R.A. h	R.A. m	Dec. °	Dec. ′	Transit h	Transit m	5° high 52° h	52° m	56° h	56° m
1	13	45.3	−7	56	1	06	5	50	5	40
11	13	42.5	−7	39	0	24	5	10	5	00
21	13	39.7	−7	23	23	38	4	29	4	19
31	13	36.8	−7	07	22	56	3	48	3	39

Diameters – equatorial 19″ polar 17″
Rings – major axis 43″ minor axis 10″

URANUS

Day	R.A. h	R.A. m	Dec. °	Dec. ′	Transit h	Transit m	10° high 52° h	52° m	56° h	56° m
1	0	19.2	+1	19	11	38	6	38	6	43
11	0	21.2	+1	33	11	01	5	59	6	05
21	0	23.2	+1	46	10	24	5	21	5	26
31	0	25.1	+1	58	9	46	4	42	4	47

Diameter 4″

NEPTUNE

Day	R.A. h	R.A. m	Dec. °	Dec. ′	Transit h	Transit m	10° high 52° h	52° m	56° h	56° m
1	22	17.1	−11	16	9	37	5	49	6	08
11	22	18.2	−11	09	8	58	5	10	5	29
21	22	19.2	−11	04	8	20	4	31	4	50
31	22	20.0	−11	00	7	41	3	52	4	11

Diameter 2″

648   Astronomy

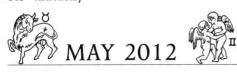

MAY 2012

FIFTH MONTH, 31 DAYS. *Maia*, goddess of growth and increase

1	*Tuesday*	The Empire State Building, at the time, the tallest skyscraper in the world, dedicated 1931	day 122
2	*Wednesday*	Sir William Bayliss, physiologist who discovered the first known hormone, secretin *b.* 1860	123
3	*Thursday*	A team of 18 doctors led by Donald Ross successfully completed the UK's first heart transplant 1968	124
4	*Friday*	Bartolomeo Cristofori, inventor of the pianoforte, precursor of the piano *b.* 1655	125
5	*Saturday*	*Ariel 3*, the first artificial satellite designed and built in Britain, was launched from the USA 1967	126
6	*Sunday*	Yale's self-detaching and attaching key-lock was patented by Linus Yale, Jr 1851	127

7	*Monday*	Edwin Land, inventor of the Polaroid camera *b.* 1909	week 19 day 128
8	*Tuesday*	The Thames Barrier was officially opened by HM Queen Elizabeth II 1984	129
9	*Wednesday*	Albert Michelson, physicist who became the first American to win the Nobel prize in sciences *d.* 1931	130
10	*Thursday*	The First Transcontinental Railroad, revolutionising transportation in the USA, was completed 1869	131
11	*Friday*	Ottmar Mergenthaler, inventor whose Linotype typesetting machine revolutionised publishing *b.* 1854	132
12	*Saturday*	Dorothy Hodgkin, biochemist whose research into chemical structures led to her 1964 Nobel prize *b.* 1910	133
13	*Sunday*	Marie Curie, Nobel prize winning physicist, became the first female professor at the Sorbonne 1906	134

14	*Monday*	H. J. Heinz, founder of the H. J. Heinz Co., producer of ketchup and other foods *d.* 1919	week 20 day 135
15	*Tuesday*	The W-1 turbojet engine, the first Allied aircraft to use jet propulsion, was tested in Britain 1941	136
16	*Wednesday*	Bouncing bombs, developed by Barnes Wallis, were used in Operation Chastise by the RAF 1943	137
17	*Thursday*	Edward Jenner, surgeon who received worldwide recognition for developing a smallpox vaccine *b.* 1749	138
18	*Friday*	Helen Sharman became the first Briton in space after answering an advert for an astronaut vacancy 1991	139
19	*Saturday*	Balamurali Ambati, aged 17 years and 294 days, graduated to become the world's youngest doctor 1995	140
20	*Sunday*	Levi Strauss and Jacob Davis received a patent to create 'waist overalls', now known as blue jeans 1873	141

21	*Monday*	Charles Lindbergh landed in Paris, completing the first solo non-stop transatlantic flight 1927	week 21 day 142
22	*Tuesday*	Apollo 10's lunar module flew within 14 miles of the Moon's surface in a rehearsal for Apollo 11 1969	143
23	*Wednesday*	Franz Mesmer, a forerunner of modern hypnotists who used to 'mesmerise' his patients *b.* 1734	144
24	*Thursday*	Samuel Morse sent the first telegraph – 'What hath God wrought!' – from Baltimore to Washington 1844	145
25	*Friday*	Igor Sikorsky, pilot and pioneer of aviation in fixed-wing aircraft and helicopters *b.* 1889	146
26	*Saturday*	Sally Ride, the first American woman to go into space (aboard the *Challenger* in 1983) *b.* 1951	147
27	*Sunday*	John Howard Northrop, biochemist whose study of enzymes led to his 1946 Nobel prize *d.* 1987	148

28	*Monday*	Two monkeys, Able and Baker, became the first living creatures to survive space flight 1959	week 22 day 149
29	*Tuesday*	Sir Humphry Davy, chemist who discovered several chemical elements, including magnesium *d.* 1829	150
30	*Wednesday*	The first hovercraft, the SR. N1 designed by Sir Christopher Cockerell, made its maiden trip 1959	151
31	*Thursday*	John Harvey Kellogg applied for a patent for 'flaked cereal', now known as Corn Flakes 1884	152

ASTRONOMICAL PHENOMENA

d	h	
1	08	Mars in conjunction with Moon. Mars 7°N.
4	18	Saturn in conjunction with Moon. Saturn 6°N.
13	13	Jupiter in conjunction
15	15	Venus at stationary point
20	05	Mercury in conjunction with Moon. Mercury 2°S.
20	13	Jupiter in conjunction with Moon. Jupiter 2°S.
20	15	Sun's longitude 60° ♊
21	00	Annular eclipse of Sun (see page 682)
22	06	Jupiter in conjunction with Mercury. Jupiter 0°.4 S.
22	21	Venus in conjunction with Moon. Venus 5°N.
27	11	Mercury in superior conjunction
29	06	Mars in conjunction with Moon. Mars 6°N.

MINIMA OF ALGOL

Algol is inconveniently situated for observation during May

CONSTELLATIONS

The following constellations are near the meridian at

	d	h		d	h
April	1	24	May	16	21
April	15	23	June	1	20
May	1	22	June	15	19

Cepheus (below the Pole), Cassiopeia (below the Pole), Ursa Minor, Ursa Major, Canes Venatici, Coma Berenices, Bootes, Leo, Virgo, Crater, Corvus and Hydra

THE MOON

Phases, Apsides and Node	d	h	m
○ Full Moon	6	03	35
☾ Last Quarter	12	21	47
● New Moon	20	23	47
☽ First Quarter	28	20	16
Perigee (356,955 km)	6	03	40
Apogee (406,439 km)	19	16	28

Mean longitude of ascending node on May 1, 247°

THE SUN

s.d. 15′.8

Day	Right Ascension			Dec. +		Equation of time		Rise 52°		Rise 56°		Transit		Set 52°		Set 56°		Sidereal time			Transit of first point of Aries		
	h	m	s	°	′	m	s	h	m	h	m	h	m	h	m	h	m	h	m	s	h	m	s
1	2	34	25	15	08	+2	54	4	30	4	15	11	57	19	25	19	40	14	37	19	9	21	09
2	2	38	14	15	26	+3	01	4	28	4	13	11	57	19	27	19	42	14	41	15	9	17	13
3	2	42	04	15	44	+3	07	4	26	4	11	11	57	19	29	19	44	14	45	12	9	13	17
4	2	45	55	16	01	+3	13	4	24	4	09	11	57	19	30	19	46	14	49	08	9	09	22
5	2	49	46	16	18	+3	18	4	22	4	07	11	57	19	32	19	48	14	53	05	9	05	26
6	2	53	38	16	35	+3	23	4	20	4	04	11	57	19	34	19	50	14	57	01	9	01	30
7	2	57	30	16	52	+3	27	4	19	4	02	11	57	19	35	19	52	15	00	58	8	57	34
8	3	01	23	17	08	+3	31	4	17	4	00	11	56	19	37	19	54	15	04	54	8	53	38
9	3	05	17	17	24	+3	34	4	15	3	58	11	56	19	39	19	56	15	08	51	8	49	42
10	3	09	11	17	40	+3	37	4	14	3	56	11	56	19	40	19	58	15	12	48	8	45	46
11	3	13	06	17	56	+3	39	4	12	3	54	11	56	19	42	20	00	15	16	44	8	41	50
12	3	17	01	18	11	+3	40	4	10	3	52	11	56	19	43	20	02	15	20	41	8	37	54
13	3	20	57	18	26	+3	41	4	09	3	50	11	56	19	45	20	04	15	24	37	8	33	58
14	3	24	53	18	40	+3	41	4	07	3	48	11	56	19	46	20	05	15	28	34	8	30	02
15	3	28	50	18	55	+3	40	4	06	3	47	11	56	19	48	20	07	15	32	30	8	26	07
16	3	32	48	19	09	+3	39	4	04	3	45	11	56	19	50	20	09	15	36	27	8	22	11
17	3	36	46	19	22	+3	38	4	03	3	43	11	56	19	51	20	11	15	40	23	8	18	15
18	3	40	45	19	35	+3	35	4	01	3	41	11	56	19	53	20	13	15	44	20	8	14	19
19	3	44	44	19	48	+3	33	4	00	3	40	11	56	19	54	20	15	15	48	17	8	10	23
20	3	48	44	20	01	+3	29	3	59	3	38	11	57	19	55	20	16	15	52	13	8	06	27
21	3	52	44	20	13	+3	25	3	57	3	36	11	57	19	57	20	18	15	56	10	8	02	31
22	3	56	45	20	25	+3	21	3	56	3	35	11	57	19	58	20	20	16	00	06	7	58	35
23	4	00	47	20	37	+3	16	3	55	3	33	11	57	20	00	20	21	16	04	03	7	54	39
24	4	04	49	20	48	+3	11	3	54	3	32	11	57	20	01	20	23	16	07	59	7	50	43
25	4	08	51	20	59	+3	05	3	52	3	30	11	57	20	02	20	25	16	11	56	7	46	47
26	4	12	54	21	09	+2	58	3	51	3	29	11	57	20	04	20	26	16	15	52	7	42	52
27	4	16	57	21	20	+2	52	3	50	3	28	11	57	20	05	20	28	16	19	49	7	38	56
28	4	21	01	21	29	+2	44	3	49	3	26	11	57	20	06	20	29	16	23	46	7	35	00
29	4	25	06	21	39	+2	36	3	48	3	25	11	57	20	07	20	31	16	27	42	7	31	04
30	4	29	10	21	48	+2	28	3	47	3	24	11	58	20	08	20	32	16	31	39	7	27	08
31	4	33	15	21	56	+2	20	3	47	3	23	11	58	20	10	20	34	16	35	35	7	23	12

DURATION OF TWILIGHT (in minutes)

Latitude	52°	56°	52°	56°	52°	56°	52°	56°
	1 May		11 May		21 May		31 May	
Civil	39	44	41	48	44	53	46	57
Nautical	89	106	97	120	106	141	115	187
Astronomical	152	204	176	TAN	TAN	TAN	TAN	TAN

THE NIGHT SKY

Mercury remains unsuitably placed for observation throughout the month.

Venus, magnitude −4.4, continues to be visible in the west-northwestern sky in the evenings after sunset. The period available for observation is decreasing day by day so that by the end of the month Venus will only be seen for a very short while after sunset. Observers with small telescopes will notice a significant change in the size and shape of the planet during the month. On the 1st it is about a quarter illuminated with a diameter of 37 arc-seconds while at the end of May it is an incredibly thin sliver, only 1% illuminated but with a diameter of 57 seconds – if it can be seen at all! On the evening of May 22nd the waxing crescent moon passes 5 degrees south of the planet.

Mars continues to be visible in the southwestern sky in the evenings, but by the end of the month it will be lost to view soon after midnight. During May its magnitude fades from 0.0 to +0.5. On the first day of the month the Moon, just past First Quarter, passes 8 degrees south of the planet: again, on the 29th, it passes 7 degrees south of the planet.

Jupiter remains too close to the Sun for observation throughout the month.

Saturn continues to be visible in the southern skies, in the constellation of Virgo, moving slowly retrograde a few degrees north of Spica. Its magnitude is +0.4. On the 4th the waxing gibbous Moon passes 7 degrees south of Saturn.

THE MOON

Day	R.A. h	R.A. m	Dec. °	Hor. Par. '	Semi-diam. '	Sun's Co-Long. °	PA of Bright Limb °	Ph. %	Age d	Rise 52° h	Rise 52° m	Rise 56° h	Rise 56° m	Transit h	Transit m	Set 52° h	Set 52° m	Set 56° h	Set 56° m
1	10	03	+6.4	58.1	15.8	27	289	67	9.7	13	35	13	32	20	06	1	59	2	04
2	10	55	+1.3	59.0	16.1	40	289	77	10.7	14	54	14	56	20	56	2	21	2	22
3	11	48	−3.9	59.9	16.3	52	289	86	11.7	16	17	16	24	21	49	2	44	2	40
4	12	43	−9.1	60.7	16.5	64	286	93	12.7	17	42	17	54	22	45	3	09	3	00
5	13	41	−13.9	61.2	16.7	76	281	98	13.7	19	08	19	25	23	45	3	38	3	25
6	14	43	−17.8	61.4	16.7	88	246	100	14.7	20	30	20	51	—		4	14	3	56
7	15	46	−20.5	61.3	16.7	100	105	99	15.7	21	44	22	07	0	47	5	00	4	38
8	16	51	−21.7	60.9	16.6	113	95	95	16.7	22	44	23	07	1	51	5	57	5	34
9	17	55	−21.3	60.2	16.4	125	88	88	17.7	23	32	23	51	2	53	7	05	6	42
10	18	56	−19.5	59.3	16.2	137	82	80	18.7	—		—		3	52	8	19	8	00
11	19	53	−16.6	58.4	15.9	149	77	70	19.7	0	08	0	23	4	47	9	34	9	20
12	20	47	−12.9	57.4	15.6	161	74	60	20.7	0	36	0	48	5	37	10	49	10	39
13	21	37	−8.7	56.6	15.4	174	71	49	21.7	1	00	1	07	6	25	12	01	11	55
14	22	25	−4.2	55.8	15.2	186	70	39	22.7	1	20	1	23	7	09	13	10	13	09
15	23	11	+0.3	55.2	15.0	198	69	30	23.7	1	39	1	38	7	52	14	18	14	21
16	23	57	+4.8	54.7	14.9	210	70	21	24.7	1	58	1	53	8	35	15	25	15	32
17	0	42	+9.0	54.3	14.8	222	71	14	25.7	2	17	2	09	9	18	16	31	16	42
18	1	28	+12.9	54.1	14.7	235	74	8	26.7	2	38	2	27	10	01	17	36	17	51
19	2	15	+16.2	54.0	14.7	247	77	4	27.7	3	03	2	48	10	46	18	40	18	58
20	3	03	+18.8	54.0	14.7	259	82	1	28.7	3	33	3	14	11	33	19	41	20	02
21	3	53	+20.7	54.0	14.7	271	181	0	0.1	4	08	3	47	12	21	20	38	21	00
22	4	44	+21.6	54.2	14.8	284	266	1	1.1	4	52	4	29	13	10	21	27	21	50
23	5	35	+21.6	54.4	14.8	296	272	4	2.1	5	43	5	20	13	59	22	10	22	31
24	6	27	+20.5	54.8	14.9	308	277	8	3.1	6	41	6	21	14	48	22	45	23	03
25	7	18	+18.5	55.2	15.0	320	281	14	4.1	7	46	7	28	15	37	23	15	23	30
26	8	09	+15.7	55.7	15.2	333	285	22	5.1	8	54	8	41	16	24	23	41	23	51
27	8	59	+12.0	56.3	15.4	345	288	31	6.1	10	05	9	56	17	12	—		—	
28	9	48	+7.7	57.1	15.5	357	291	41	7.1	11	19	11	14	17	59	0	04	0	10
29	10	38	+2.9	57.9	15.8	9	292	52	8.1	12	34	12	34	18	47	0	25	0	27
30	11	29	−2.1	58.7	16.0	21	292	63	9.1	13	52	13	57	19	37	0	46	0	44
31	12	22	−7.2	59.5	16.2	34	291	73	10.1	15	13	15	23	20	30	1	09	1	03

MERCURY

Day	R.A. h	R.A. m	Dec. °	Diam. "	Phase %	Transit h	Transit m	5° high 52° h	5° high 52° m	5° high 56° h	5° high 56° m
1	1	07	+4.0	6	64	10	30	4	41	4	41
3	1	18	+5.2	6	67	10	33	4	38	4	37
5	1	29	+6.5	6	70	10	37	4	35	4	33
7	1	41	+7.8	6	73	10	41	4	32	4	29
9	1	53	+9.2	6	77	10	46	4	30	4	26
11	2	07	+10.6	6	80	10	51	4	28	4	22
13	2	20	+12.0	6	83	10	57	4	26	4	19
15	2	35	+13.5	5	86	11	04	4	25	4	17
17	2	49	+14.9	5	90	11	11	4	24	4	15
19	3	05	+16.4	5	93	11	19	4	24	4	13
21	3	21	+17.8	5	95	11	27	4	24	4	12
23	3	38	+19.2	5	98	11	37	4	26	4	12
25	3	56	+20.5	5	99	11	47	4	28	4	13
27	4	14	+21.6	5	100	11	57	4	31	4	15
29	4	33	+22.7	5	100	12	08	19	42	20	00
31	4	51	+23.6	5	98	12	19	19	58	20	17

VENUS

Day	R.A. h	R.A. m	Dec. °	Diam. "	Phase %	Transit h	Transit m	5° high 52° h	5° high 52° m	5° high 56° h	5° high 56° m
1	5	16	+27.8	37	27	14	38	22	41	23	06
6	5	25	+27.8	41	22	14	27	22	30	22	55
11	5	31	+27.7	44	18	14	13	22	14	22	39
16	5	33	+27.3	48	13	13	54	21	52	22	16
21	5	31	+26.6	51	8	13	32	21	25	21	48
26	5	24	+25.7	54	4	13	05	20	51	21	12
31	5	13	+24.6	57	1	12	34	20	13	20	32

MARS

Day	R.A. h	R.A. m	Dec. °	Diam. "	Phase %	Transit h	Transit m	5° high 52° h	5° high 52° m	5° high 56° h	5° high 56° m
1	10	32	+11.5	10	91	19	52	2	21	2	27
6	10	35	+10.9	10	91	19	36	2	02	2	07
11	10	40	+10.3	9	90	19	21	1	43	1	48
16	10	45	+9.6	9	90	19	06	1	25	1	30
21	10	51	+8.9	9	90	18	52	1	07	1	11
26	10	57	+8.1	8	89	18	39	0	50	0	53
31	11	04	+7.2	8	89	18	27	0	33	0	35

SUNRISE AND SUNSET

	London 0° 05' | 51° 30'		Bristol 2° 35' | 51° 28'		Birmingham 1° 55' | 52° 28'		Manchester 2° 15' | 53° 28'		Newcastle 1° 37' | 54° 59'		Glasgow 4° 14' | 55° 52'		Belfast 5° 56' | 54° 35'	
d	h m	h m	h m	h m	h m	h m	h m	h m	h m	h m	h m	h m	h m	h m
1	4 32	19 24	4 42	19 34	4 36	19 35	4 34	19 39	4 26	19 43	4 33	19 57	4 45	19 58
2	4 30	19 26	4 40	19 36	4 34	19 36	4 32	19 41	4 24	19 44	4 31	19 58	4 42	20 00
3	4 28	19 27	4 38	19 37	4 32	19 38	4 30	19 43	4 22	19 46	4 28	20 00	4 40	20 02
4	4 26	19 29	4 36	19 39	4 30	19 40	4 28	19 45	4 19	19 48	4 26	20 02	4 38	20 04
5	4 24	19 31	4 34	19 41	4 28	19 41	4 26	19 47	4 17	19 50	4 24	20 04	4 36	20 06
6	4 23	19 32	4 33	19 42	4 26	19 43	4 24	19 48	4 15	19 52	4 22	20 06	4 34	20 08
7	4 21	19 34	4 31	19 44	4 25	19 45	4 22	19 50	4 13	19 54	4 20	20 08	4 32	20 09
8	4 19	19 35	4 29	19 45	4 23	19 46	4 20	19 52	4 11	19 56	4 18	20 10	4 30	20 11
9	4 17	19 37	4 28	19 47	4 21	19 48	4 18	19 54	4 09	19 58	4 16	20 12	4 28	20 13
10	4 16	19 39	4 26	19 48	4 19	19 50	4 17	19 55	4 07	19 59	4 14	20 14	4 27	20 15
11	4 14	19 40	4 24	19 50	4 18	19 51	4 15	19 57	4 06	20 01	4 12	20 16	4 25	20 17
12	4 13	19 42	4 23	19 52	4 16	19 53	4 13	19 59	4 04	20 03	4 10	20 18	4 23	20 18
13	4 11	19 43	4 21	19 53	4 14	19 55	4 11	20 00	4 02	20 05	4 08	20 20	4 21	20 20
14	4 10	19 45	4 20	19 55	4 13	19 56	4 10	20 02	4 00	20 07	4 06	20 22	4 19	20 22
15	4 08	19 46	4 18	19 56	4 11	19 58	4 08	20 04	3 58	20 08	4 04	20 24	4 18	20 24
16	4 07	19 48	4 17	19 58	4 10	19 59	4 07	20 05	3 57	20 10	4 02	20 25	4 16	20 25
17	4 05	19 49	4 15	19 59	4 08	20 01	4 05	20 07	3 55	20 12	4 01	20 27	4 14	20 27
18	4 04	19 51	4 14	20 01	4 07	20 02	4 03	20 08	3 53	20 14	3 59	20 29	4 13	20 29
19	4 02	19 52	4 13	20 02	4 05	20 04	4 02	20 10	3 52	20 15	3 57	20 31	4 11	20 30
20	4 01	19 54	4 11	20 03	4 04	20 05	4 01	20 12	3 50	20 17	3 56	20 33	4 10	20 32
21	4 00	19 55	4 10	20 05	4 03	20 07	3 59	20 13	3 49	20 19	3 54	20 34	4 08	20 34
22	3 59	19 56	4 09	20 06	4 01	20 08	3 58	20 15	3 47	20 20	3 52	20 36	4 07	20 35
23	3 57	19 58	4 08	20 07	4 00	20 10	3 56	20 16	3 46	20 22	3 51	20 38	4 05	20 37
24	3 56	19 59	4 06	20 09	3 59	20 11	3 55	20 17	3 44	20 23	3 49	20 39	4 04	20 38
25	3 55	20 00	4 05	20 10	3 58	20 12	3 54	20 19	3 43	20 25	3 48	20 41	4 02	20 40
26	3 54	20 01	4 04	20 11	3 57	20 14	3 53	20 20	3 42	20 26	3 47	20 42	4 01	20 41
27	3 53	20 03	4 03	20 13	3 56	20 15	3 52	20 22	3 40	20 28	3 45	20 44	4 00	20 43
28	3 52	20 04	4 02	20 14	3 55	20 16	3 51	20 23	3 39	20 29	3 44	20 45	3 59	20 44
29	3 51	20 05	4 01	20 15	3 54	20 17	3 49	20 24	3 38	20 31	3 43	20 47	3 58	20 46
30	3 50	20 06	4 00	20 16	3 53	20 19	3 48	20 25	3 37	20 32	3 42	20 48	3 57	20 47
31	3 49	20 07	4 00	20 17	3 52	20 20	3 48	20 27	3 36	20 33	3 41	20 50	3 56	20 48

JUPITER

Day	R.A.		Dec.		Transit		5° high		
							52°		56°
	h	m	°	'	h	m	h m		h m
1	3	12.0	+17	00	12	33	5 38		5 26
11	3	21.5	+17	38	12	03	5 04		4 52
21	3	31.2	+18	14	11	34	4 31		4 19
31	3	40.8	+18	47	11	04	3 58		3 45

Diameters – equatorial 33" polar 31"

SATURN

Day	R.A.		Dec.		Transit		5° high		
							52°		56°
	h	m	°	'	h	m	h m		h m
1	13	36.8	−7	07	22	56	3 48		3 39
11	13	34.2	−6	53	22	14	3 08		2 58
21	13	32.0	−6	42	21	32	2 27		2 18
31	13	30.2	−6	33	20	51	1 47		1 38

Diameters – equatorial 19" polar 17"
Rings – major axis 42" minor axis 9"

URANUS

Day	R.A.		Dec.		Transit		10° high		
							52°		56°
	h	m	°	'	h	m	h m		h m
1	0	25.1	+1	58	9	46	4 42		4 47
11	0	26.9	+2	09	9	09	4 04		4 09
21	0	28.4	+2	18	8	31	3 25		3 30
31	0	29.8	+2	27	7	53	2 46		2 51

Diameter 4"

NEPTUNE

Day	R.A.		Dec.		Transit		10° high		
							52°		56°
	h	m	°	'	h	m	h m		h m
1	22	20.0	−11	00	7	41	3 52		4 11
11	22	20.6	−10	57	7	03	3 13		3 32
21	22	21.0	−10	55	6	24	2 34		2 52
31	22	21.2	−10	54	5	45	1 54		2 13

Diameter 2"

Ⅱ JUNE 2012

SIXTH MONTH, 30 DAYS. *Junius*, Roman *gens* (family)

1	Friday	Sir Frank Whittle, pilot and aviation engineer who invented the jet engine *b.* 1907	day 153
2	Saturday	Guglielmo Marconi secured the first patent for a system of communication by electromagnetic waves 1896	154
3	Sunday	Major Edward White II became the first American astronaut to complete a spacewalk 1965	155

4	Monday	The first shopping trolleys were introduced at a supermarket in Oklahoma City, USA 1937	week 23 day 156
5	Tuesday	Dr Michael Gottlieb first described the epidemic disease which was later to become known as AIDS 1981	157
6	Wednesday	Henry Seely received a patent for his electric flatiron 1882	158
7	Thursday	The first domestic videocassette recorder, the Betamax produced by Sony, went on sale in Japan 1975	159
8	Friday	Sir Tim Berners-Lee, computer scientist credited with inventing the world wide web *b.* 1955	160
9	Saturday	George Stephenson, engineer and inventor of the famous *Rocket* locomotive *b.* 1781	161
10	Sunday	The ballpoint pen was patented by Laslo Biro; commercial production began two years later 1943	162

11	Monday	Jacques-Yves Cousteau, diving innovator who co-invented the aqualung *b.* 1910	week 24 day 163
12	Tuesday	Carl Elsener patented the multi-function penknife, later known as the 'Swiss Army knife' 1897	164
13	Wednesday	Space probe *Pioneer 10*, launched in 1972, became the first man-made object to exit the solar system 1983	165
14	Thursday	John Logie Baird, engineer, the first person to televise pictures of objects in motion *d.* 1946	166
15	Friday	Benjamin Franklin demonstrated the electrical nature of lightning by flying a kite during a storm 1752	167
16	Saturday	US aviation pioneer Henry Berliner conducted the first manned, controlled helicopter flight 1922	168
17	Sunday	Charles Goodyear obtained a patent for a procedure he discovered to stop rubber melting in heat 1837	169

18	Monday	Waterloo Bridge was opened in London, on the second anniversary of the Battle of Waterloo 1817	week 25 day 170
19	Tuesday	Valentina Tereshkova returned to Earth, three days after becoming the first woman in space 1963	171
20	Wednesday	Sir Frederick G. Hopkins, who won the 1929 Nobel Prize for Physiology for his study of vitamins *b.* 1861	172
21	Thursday	The first stored-program computer, the Small-Scale Experimental Machine, ran its first program 1948	173
22	Friday	The Royal Greenwich Observatory, a centre for practical astronomy, was created by Royal Warrant 1675	174
23	Saturday	Christopher Latham Sholes, with two colleagues, received a patent for the typewriter 1868	175
24	Sunday	Sir Fred Hoyle, astronomer who formulated a basis for the steady-state theory of the universe *b.* 1915	176

25	Monday	Lucien B. Smith patented barbed wire, which was intended to enclose livestock 1867	week 26 day 177
26	Tuesday	Samuel Crompton, inventor of the spinning mule, which revolutionised cotton production *d.* 1827	178
27	Wednesday	The world's first atomic power station began producing electricity in Obninsk, Russia 1954	179
28	Thursday	Adolphe Sax patented the saxophone, which was a combination of a clarinet and an oboe 1846	180
29	Friday	The space shuttle *Atlantis* docked with *Mir* to form the largest man-made satellite to orbit Earth 1995	181
30	Saturday	The Prince of Wales officially opened Tower Bridge 1894	182

ASTRONOMICAL PHENOMENA

d h
1 02 Saturn in conjunction with Moon. Saturn 6°N.
1 21 Venus in conjunction with Mercury. Venus 0°.2 S.
4 11 Partial eclipse of Moon (see page 682)
4 21 Neptune at stationary point
6 01 Venus in inferior conjunction (transit)
17 08 Jupiter in conjunction with Moon. Jupiter 1°S.
18 00 Venus in conjunction with Moon. Venus 2°S.
20 23 Sun's longitude 90° ♋
21 17 Mercury in conjunction with Moon. Mercury 6°N.
25 08 Saturn at stationary point
26 11 Mars in conjunction with Moon. Mars 5°N.
27 15 Venus at stationary point
28 08 Saturn in conjunction with Moon. Saturn 6°N.
29 15 Pluto at opposition

MINIMA OF ALGOL
Algol is inconveniently situated for observation during June

CONSTELLATIONS
The following constellations are near the meridian at

d	*h*		*d*	*h*
May	1	24	June	15	21
May	16	23	July	1	20
June	1	22	July	16	19

Cassiopeia (below the Pole), Ursa Minor, Draco, Ursa Major, Canes Venatici, Bootes, Corona, Serpens, Virgo and Libra

THE MOON

Phases, Apsides and Node	*d*	*h*	*m*
○ Full Moon	4	11	12
☾ Last Quarter	11	10	41
● New Moon	19	15	02
☽ First Quarter	27	03	30
Perigee (358,492km)	3	13	23
Apogee (405,762km)	16	01	33

Mean longitude of ascending node on June 1, 245°

THE SUN

s.d. 15'.8

Day	Right Ascension			Dec.		Equation of time		Rise 52°		Rise 56°		Transit		Set 52°		Set 56°		Sidereal time			Transit of first point of Aries		
	h	m	s	°	'	+ m	s	h	m	h	m	h	m	h	m	h	m	h	m	s	h	m	s
1	4	37	21	22	05	+2	11	3	46	3	22	11	58	20	11	20	35	16	39	32	7	19	16
2	4	41	27	22	13	+2	02	3	45	3	21	11	58	20	12	20	36	16	43	28	7	15	20
3	4	45	33	22	20	+1	52	3	44	3	20	11	58	20	13	20	38	16	47	25	7	11	24
4	4	49	40	22	27	+1	42	3	44	3	19	11	58	20	14	20	39	16	51	21	7	07	28
5	4	53	47	22	34	+1	31	3	43	3	18	11	59	20	15	20	40	16	55	18	7	03	32
6	4	57	54	22	40	+1	21	3	42	3	17	11	59	20	16	20	41	16	59	15	6	59	37
7	5	02	01	22	46	+1	10	3	42	3	16	11	59	20	17	20	42	17	03	11	6	55	41
8	5	06	09	22	52	+0	58	3	41	3	16	11	59	20	17	20	43	17	07	08	6	51	45
9	5	10	17	22	57	+0	47	3	41	3	15	11	59	20	18	20	44	17	11	04	6	47	49
10	5	14	26	23	01	+0	35	3	40	3	15	12	00	20	19	20	45	17	15	01	6	43	53
11	5	18	34	23	06	+0	23	3	40	3	14	12	00	20	20	20	46	17	18	57	6	39	57
12	5	22	43	23	10	+0	11	3	40	3	14	12	00	20	20	20	46	17	22	54	6	36	01
13	5	26	52	23	13	−0	02	3	40	3	13	12	00	20	21	20	47	17	26	50	6	32	05
14	5	31	02	23	16	−0	15	3	40	3	13	12	00	20	21	20	48	17	30	47	6	28	09
15	5	35	11	23	19	−0	27	3	39	3	13	12	01	20	22	20	48	17	34	44	6	24	13
16	5	39	20	23	21	−0	40	3	39	3	13	12	01	20	22	20	49	17	38	40	6	20	17
17	5	43	30	23	23	−0	53	3	39	3	13	12	01	20	23	20	49	17	42	37	6	16	21
18	5	47	40	23	24	−1	06	3	39	3	13	12	01	20	23	20	50	17	46	33	6	12	26
19	5	51	49	23	25	−1	20	3	39	3	13	12	01	20	23	20	50	17	50	30	6	08	30
20	5	55	59	23	26	−1	33	3	40	3	13	12	02	20	24	20	50	17	54	26	6	04	34
21	6	00	09	23	26	−1	46	3	40	3	13	12	02	20	24	20	50	17	58	23	6	00	38
22	6	04	19	23	26	−1	59	3	40	3	13	12	02	20	24	20	51	18	02	19	5	56	42
23	6	08	28	23	25	−2	12	3	40	3	14	12	02	20	24	20	51	18	06	16	5	52	46
24	6	12	38	23	24	−2	25	3	41	3	14	12	03	20	24	20	51	18	10	13	5	48	50
25	6	16	47	23	23	−2	38	3	41	3	15	12	03	20	24	20	51	18	14	09	5	44	54
26	6	20	56	23	21	−2	51	3	42	3	15	12	03	20	24	20	50	18	18	06	5	40	58
27	6	25	05	23	19	−2	03	3	42	3	16	12	03	20	24	20	50	18	22	02	5	37	02
28	6	29	14	23	16	−3	15	3	43	3	16	12	03	20	24	20	50	18	25	59	5	33	06
29	6	33	23	23	13	−3	28	3	43	3	17	12	04	20	24	20	50	18	29	55	5	29	11
30	6	37	31	23	09	−3	39	3	44	3	18	12	04	20	23	20	49	18	33	52	5	25	15

DURATION OF TWILIGHT (in minutes)

Latitude	52°	56°	52°	56°	52°	56°	52°	56°
	1 June		11 June		21 June		31 June	
Civil	46	58	48	61	49	63	48	61
Nautical	116	TAN	124	TAN	127	TAN	124	TAN
Astronomical	TAN	TAN	TAN	TAN	TAN	TAN	TAN	TAN

THE NIGHT SKY

Mercury is only visible under good conditions for about 5 days around the 19th, its magnitude falling from −0.4 to +0.2 during this period. The planet may be seen very low above the west-northwestern horizon at the end of evening civil twilight. The long duration of twilight means that it is very unlikely to be seen at all from as far north as Scotland.

Venus is too close to the Sun for observation at first, but passes rapidly through inferior conjunction on the 6th. By the middle of the month it becomes visible in the east-north-eastern sky, in the early mornings for a short while before sunrise, magnitude −4.1. Venus will transit the Sun on the morning of the 6th (see page 682 for details).

Mars continues to be visible as an evening object, passing from Leo into Virgo during the month. During this period its magnitude fades from +0.6 to +0.9. On the 26th the Moon, at First Quarter, passes 6 degrees south of the planet.

Jupiter, is now moving away from the Sun, becoming visible low in the east-northeastern sky before dawn, after the first three weeks of the month. It is moving steadily eastwards in the constellation of Taurus, magnitude −2.0. Note its proximity to the much brighter planet Venus.

Saturn, magnitude +0.6, continues to be visible in the western sky in the evenings. On the 25th it reaches its second stationary point and resumes its direct motion. Saturn is still in the constellation of Virgo. The Moon passes 7 degrees south of the planet on the morning of the 1st and again on the 28th.

Twilight. Reference to the section above shows that astronomical twilight lasts all night for a period around the summer solstice (i.e. in June and July), even in southern England. Under these conditions the sky never gets completely dark as the Sun is always less than 18 degrees below the horizon.

THE MOON

Day	R.A. h	R.A. m	Dec. °	Hor. Par. '	Semi-diam. '	Sun's Co-Long. °	PA. of Br. Limb °	Ph. %	Age d	Rise 52° h	Rise 52° m	Rise 56° h	Rise 56° m	Transit h	Transit m	Set 52° h	Set 52° m	Set 56° h	Set 56° m
1	13	17	−12.0	60.2	16.4	46	289	83	11.1	16	37	16	51	21	26	1	35	1	24
2	14	16	−16.2	60.8	16.6	58	286	91	12.1	18	00	18	19	22	26	2	06	1	51
3	15	18	−19.4	61.1	16.7	70	282	97	13.1	19	18	19	41	23	29	2	46	2	26
4	16	22	−21.3	61.1	16.7	82	281	100	14.1	20	26	20	50	—		3	37	3	15
5	17	27	−21.6	60.8	16.6	95	82	100	15.1	21	21	21	42	0	33	4	40	4	17
6	18	30	−20.4	60.3	16.4	107	80	97	16.1	22	04	22	21	1	35	5	53	5	32
7	19	31	−17.9	59.5	16.2	119	76	91	17.1	22	36	22	50	2	33	7	11	6	54
8	20	27	−14.4	58.6	16.0	131	72	83	18.1	23	03	23	12	3	28	8	29	8	16
9	21	20	−10.2	57.6	15.7	143	69	74	19.1	23	25	23	30	4	18	9	44	9	37
10	22	10	−5.6	56.7	15.5	156	68	65	20.1	23	45	23	45	5	05	10	57	10	53
11	22	58	−1.0	55.9	15.2	168	67	55	21.1	—		—		5	49	12	07	12	08
12	23	44	+3.6	55.2	15.0	180	67	45	22.1	0	03	0	01	6	33	13	15	13	20
13	0	30	+7.9	54.7	14.9	192	68	35	23.1	0	23	0	16	7	15	14	21	14	30
14	1	16	+11.9	54.3	14.8	204	70	26	24.1	0	44	0	33	7	59	15	27	15	40
15	2	02	+15.3	54.1	14.7	217	72	18	25.1	1	07	0	53	8	43	16	31	16	48
16	2	50	+18.2	54.0	14.7	229	75	12	26.1	1	35	1	17	9	29	17	34	17	54
17	3	40	+20.3	54.1	14.7	241	78	6	27.1	2	08	1	48	10	17	18	32	18	54
18	4	30	+21.5	54.2	14.8	253	80	2	28.1	2	49	2	26	11	06	19	24	19	47
19	5	22	+21.7	54.5	14.8	266	74	0	29.1	3	37	3	15	11	55	20	09	20	31
20	6	14	+20.9	54.8	14.9	278	302	0	0.4	4	34	4	13	12	45	20	48	21	07
21	7	06	+19.1	55.2	15.0	290	289	2	1.4	5	37	5	19	13	34	21	20	21	35
22	7	57	+16.5	55.6	15.2	302	289	6	2.4	6	45	6	30	14	22	21	46	21	58
23	8	47	+13.0	56.1	15.3	315	291	11	3.4	7	56	7	45	15	10	22	10	22	18
24	9	37	+8.8	56.7	15.4	327	293	19	4.4	9	08	9	02	15	57	22	31	22	35
25	10	26	+4.2	57.3	15.6	339	294	27	5.4	10	22	10	20	16	44	22	52	22	52
26	11	16	−0.7	57.9	15.8	351	294	38	6.4	11	38	11	40	17	32	23	14	23	09
27	12	07	−5.7	58.5	15.9	4	294	48	7.4	12	55	13	03	18	22	23	37	23	28
28	13	00	−10.5	59.1	16.1	16	292	60	8.4	14	15	14	27	19	15	—		23	52
29	13	56	−14.8	59.7	16.3	28	289	71	9.4	15	36	15	53	20	12	0	05	—	
30	14	54	−18.3	60.2	16.4	40	285	81	10.4	16	54	17	15	21	11	0	40	0	22

MERCURY

Day	R.A. h	R.A. m	Dec. °	Diam. "	Phase %	Transit h	Transit m	5° high 52° h	5° high 52° m	5° high 56° h	5° high 56° m
1	5	01	+24.0	5	97	12	24	20	05	20	25
3	5	19	+24.6	5	95	12	35	20	20	20	40
5	5	38	+25.0	5	91	12	45	20	33	20	53
7	5	56	+25.3	5	87	12	55	20	44	21	05
9	6	13	+25.4	6	83	13	05	20	53	21	14
11	6	30	+25.3	6	79	13	13	21	01	21	22
13	6	46	+25.1	6	74	13	21	21	07	21	27
15	7	01	+24.7	6	70	13	28	21	11	21	31
17	7	16	+24.2	6	66	13	35	21	14	21	33
19	7	29	+23.7	6	62	13	40	21	15	21	33
21	7	42	+23.0	7	58	13	44	21	15	21	32
23	7	53	+22.3	7	55	13	48	21	14	21	30
25	8	04	+21.6	7	51	13	51	21	12	21	27
27	8	14	+20.8	7	48	13	52	21	08	21	23
29	8	23	+19.9	8	44	13	53	21	04	21	18
31	8	31	+19.1	8	41	13	53	20	59	21	12

VENUS

Day	R.A. h	R.A. m	Dec. °	Diam. "	Phase %	Transit h	Transit m	5° high 52° h	5° high 52° m	5° high 56° h	5° high 56° m
1	5	11	+24.3	57	1	12	28	4	51	4	31
6	4	58	+22.8	58	0	11	56	4	27	4	10
11	4	46	+21.3	57	1	11	24	4	05	3	49
16	4	35	+19.9	55	4	10	54	3	43	3	29
21	4	28	+18.8	52	7	10	28	3	23	3	10
26	4	25	+18.0	48	12	10	06	3	05	2	53
31	4	26	+17.5	45	17	9	47	2	49	2	37

MARS

Day	R.A. h	R.A. m	Dec. °	Diam. "	Phase %	Transit h	Transit m	5° high 52° h	5° high 52° m	5° high 56° h	5° high 56° m
1	11	06	+7.0	8	89	18	24	0	29	0	32
6	11	13	+6.1	8	89	18	12	0	12	0	14
11	11	21	+5.1	7	89	18	00	23	52	23	53
16	11	29	+4.1	7	89	17	49	23	36	23	36
21	11	38	+3.1	7	89	17	38	23	20	23	19
26	11	47	+2.0	7	89	17	27	23	03	23	01
31	11	56	+0.9	7	89	17	17	22	47	22	44

SUNRISE AND SUNSET

	London 0° 05′	51° 30′	Bristol 2° 35′	51° 28′	Birmingham 1° 55′	52° 28′	Manchester 2° 15′	53° 28′	Newcastle 1° 37′	54° 59′	Glasgow 4° 14′	55° 52′	Belfast 5° 56′	54° 35′
d	h m	h m	h m	h m	h m	h m	h m	h m	h m	h m	h m	h m	h m	h m
1	3 49	20 08	3 59	20 18	3 51	20 21	3 47	20 28	3 35	20 35	3 39	20 51	3 55	20 49
2	3 48	20 10	3 58	20 19	3 50	20 22	3 46	20 29	3 34	20 36	3 38	20 52	3 54	20 51
3	3 47	20 11	3 57	20 20	3 49	20 23	3 45	20 30	3 33	20 37	3 38	20 54	3 53	20 52
4	3 47	20 11	3 57	20 21	3 49	20 24	3 44	20 31	3 32	20 38	3 37	20 55	3 52	20 53
5	3 46	20 12	3 56	20 22	3 48	20 25	3 44	20 32	3 31	20 39	3 36	20 56	3 51	20 54
6	3 45	20 13	3 56	20 23	3 47	20 26	3 43	20 33	3 31	20 40	3 35	20 57	3 51	20 55
7	3 45	20 14	3 55	20 24	3 47	20 27	3 42	20 34	3 30	20 41	3 34	20 58	3 50	20 56
8	3 44	20 15	3 55	20 25	3 46	20 28	3 42	20 35	3 29	20 42	3 34	20 59	3 49	20 57
9	3 44	20 16	3 54	20 26	3 46	20 29	3 41	20 36	3 29	20 43	3 33	21 00	3 49	20 58
10	3 44	20 16	3 54	20 26	3 45	20 29	3 41	20 37	3 28	20 44	3 33	21 01	3 48	20 59
11	3 43	20 17	3 53	20 27	3 45	20 30	3 40	20 37	3 28	20 45	3 32	21 02	3 48	20 59
12	3 43	20 18	3 53	20 28	3 45	20 31	3 40	20 38	3 28	20 46	3 32	21 02	3 48	21 00
13	3 43	20 18	3 53	20 28	3 45	20 31	3 40	20 39	3 27	20 46	3 31	21 03	3 47	21 01
14	3 43	20 19	3 53	20 29	3 44	20 32	3 40	20 39	3 27	20 47	3 31	21 04	3 47	21 01
15	3 43	20 19	3 53	20 29	3 44	20 32	3 40	20 40	3 27	20 47	3 31	21 04	3 47	21 02
16	3 43	20 20	3 53	20 30	3 44	20 33	3 40	20 40	3 27	20 48	3 31	21 05	3 47	21 02
17	3 42	20 20	3 53	20 30	3 44	20 33	3 39	20 41	3 27	20 48	3 31	21 05	3 47	21 03
18	3 43	20 21	3 53	20 30	3 44	20 34	3 39	20 41	3 27	20 49	3 31	21 06	3 47	21 03
19	3 43	20 21	3 53	20 31	3 44	20 34	3 40	20 41	3 27	20 49	3 31	21 06	3 47	21 03
20	3 43	20 21	3 53	20 31	3 45	20 34	3 40	20 42	3 27	20 49	3 31	21 06	3 47	21 04
21	3 43	20 21	3 53	20 31	3 45	20 34	3 40	20 42	3 27	20 49	3 31	21 07	3 48	21 04
22	3 43	20 22	3 53	20 31	3 45	20 34	3 40	20 42	3 27	20 50	3 31	21 07	3 48	21 04
23	3 44	20 22	3 54	20 31	3 45	20 35	3 41	20 42	3 28	20 50	3 32	21 07	3 48	21 04
24	3 44	20 22	3 54	20 31	3 46	20 35	3 41	20 42	3 28	20 50	3 32	21 07	3 48	21 04
25	3 44	20 22	3 55	20 31	3 46	20 35	3 41	20 42	3 29	20 50	3 33	21 07	3 49	21 04
26	3 45	20 22	3 55	20 31	3 47	20 34	3 42	20 42	3 29	20 49	3 33	21 06	3 49	21 04
27	3 45	20 21	3 55	20 31	3 47	20 34	3 42	20 42	3 30	20 49	3 34	21 06	3 50	21 04
28	3 46	20 21	3 56	20 31	3 48	20 34	3 43	20 42	3 30	20 49	3 34	21 06	3 50	21 04
29	3 46	20 21	3 57	20 31	3 48	20 34	3 44	20 41	3 31	20 49	3 35	21 06	3 51	21 03
30	3 47	20 21	3 57	20 31	3 49	20 34	3 44	20 41	3 32	20 48	3 36	21 05	3 52	21 03

JUPITER

Day	R.A.		Dec.		Transit		5° high			
							52°		56°	
	h	m	°	′	h	m	h	m	h	m
1	3	41.8	+18	51	11	01	3	55	3	42
11	3	51.3	+19	21	10	31	3	22	3	09
21	4	00.6	+19	49	10	01	2	49	2	35
31	4	09.7	+20	14	9	31	2	17	2	02

Diameters – equatorial 33″ polar 31″

SATURN

Day	R.A.		Dec.		Transit		5° high			
							52°		56°	
	h	m	°	′	h	m	h	m	h	m
1	13	30.0	−6	33	20	47	1	43	1	34
11	13	28.8	−6	28	20	06	1	03	0	54
21	13	28.2	−6	27	19	27	0	23	0	14
31	13	28.1	−6	29	18	47	23	39	23	30

Diameters – equatorial 18″ polar 16″
Rings – major axis 41″ minor axis 9″

URANUS

Day	R.A.		Dec.		Transit		10° high			
							52°		56°	
	h	m	°	′	h	m	h	m	h	m
1	0	29.9	+2	28	7	49	2	43	2	47
11	0	31.0	+2	34	7	11	2	04	2	08
21	0	31.8	+2	39	6	32	1	25	1	29
31	0	32.3	+2	42	5	54	0	46	0	50

Diameter 4″

NEPTUNE

Day	R.A.		Dec.		Transit		10° high			
							52°		56°	
	h	m	°	′	h	m	h	m	h	m
1	22	21.2	−10	54	5	41	1	50	2	09
11	22	21.2	−10	54	5	01	1	11	1	30
21	22	21.0	−10	56	4	22	0	32	0	51
31	22	20.6	−10	58	3	42	23	48	0	11

Diameter 2″

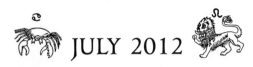

JULY 2012

SEVENTH MONTH, 31 DAYS. *Julius* Caesar, formerly *Quintilis*, fifth month of Roman pre-Julian calendar

1	*Sunday*	The Wallace–Darwin theory of evolution was first published at the Linnean Society 1858	day 183

2	*Monday*	The first directed flight of a zeppelin was made in Germany; the *LZ-1* flew for 18 minutes 1900	week 27 day 184
3	*Tuesday*	André-Gustave Citroën, engineer who introduced Ford's method of car mass-production to Europe *d*. 1935	185
4	*Wednesday*	Marie Curie died, almost certainly due to her exposure to radiation 1934	186
5	*Thursday*	Dolly the sheep, the first mammal to be cloned from an adult cell, was born 1996	187
6	*Friday*	Louis Pasteur began the modern era of immunisation by vaccinating a boy bitten by a rabid dog 1885	188
7	*Saturday*	Henry Phillips received several patents for the Phillips-head screw and screwdriver 1936	189
8	*Sunday*	John Pemberton, pharmacist who invented Coca-Cola *b*. 1831	190

9	*Monday*	Elias Howe, inventor who designed and patented the first sewing machine *b*. 1819	week 28 day 191
10	*Tuesday*	*Telstar 1*, the first satellite to relay TV and telephone signals across the Atlantic, was launched 1962	192
11	*Wednesday*	US space station Skylab re-entered Earth's atmosphere and disintegrated 1979	193
12	*Thursday*	The Panama Canal, which cost US $347m to complete, was formally dedicated 1920	194
13	*Friday*	William Hedley, engineer who built the first commercially used steam locomotive, *Puffing Billy b*. 1779	195
14	*Saturday*	Alfred Nobel, engineer and innovator, demonstrated dynamite for the first time 1867	196
15	*Sunday*	Hippolyte Mège Mouriés patented margarine, which was created after a request from Napoleon III 1869	197

16	*Monday*	The first atom bomb was successfully tested in New Mexico, USA 1945	week 29 day 198
17	*Tuesday*	Georges Lemaître, astronomer and cosmologist who proposed the modern big-bang theory *b*. 1894	199
18	*Wednesday*	Hendrik Lorentz, physicist whose work on electromagnetic radiation inspired Albert Einstein *b*. 1853	200
19	*Thursday*	Chief engineer Fulgence Bienvenüe oversaw the opening of the Métropolitan subway in Paris 1900	201
20	*Friday*	Neil Armstrong became the first person to walk on the surface of the Moon 1969	202
21	*Saturday*	The 7,414 kilometre Trans-Siberian railway was completed, becoming the longest railway in the world 1904	203
22	*Sunday*	Gregor Mendel, pioneer in the study of heredity and regarded as the father of genetics *b*. 1822	204

23	*Monday*	Sir William Ramsay, chemist who discovered elements including neon and krypton *d*. 1916	week 30 day 205
24	*Tuesday*	Amelia Earhart, who in 1932 became the first woman to fly solo over the Atlantic *b*. 1897	206
25	*Wednesday*	Louise Brown, the first baby to be conceived via the method of in-vitro fertilisation, was born 1978	207
26	*Thursday*	Apollo 15 launched, the first mission to the Moon which used the lunar rover 1971	208
27	*Friday*	The de Havilland Comet, the first jet-propelled airliner, made its maiden flight 1949	209
28	*Saturday*	A water tricycle was pedalled across the English Channel in under eight hours by Mr Ferry 1883	210
29	*Sunday*	The National Aeronautics and Space Administration (NASA) was founded 1958	211

30	*Monday*	Henry Ford, industrialist whose Model T cars revolutionised the industry *b*. 1863	week 31 day 212
31	*Tuesday*	Stephanie Kwolek, inventor of Kevlar, which is used in aircraft parts and body armour *b*. 1923	213

ASTRONOMICAL PHENOMENA
d h
1 02 Mercury at greatest elongation E. 26°
5 04 Earth at aphelion (152 million km.)
12 16 Venus at greatest brilliancy
13 10 Uranus at stationary point
15 02 Mercury at stationary point
15 03 Jupiter in conjunction with Moon. Jupiter 0°.5 S.
15 15 Venus in conjunction with Moon. Venus 4°S.
20 08 Mercury in conjunction with Moon. Mercury 0°.5 N.
22 10 Sun's longitude 120° ♌
24 19 Mars in conjunction with Moon. Mars 4°N.
25 15 Saturn in conjunction with Moon. Saturn 6°N.
28 20 Mercury in inferior conjunction

MINIMA OF ALGOL

d	h	d	h	d	h
1	15.9	13	03.1	24	14.4
4	12.7	16	00.0	27	11.2
7	09.5	18	20.8	30	08.0
10	06.3	21	17.6		

CONSTELLATIONS
The following constellations are near their meridian at

	d	h		d	h
June	1	24	July	16	21
June	15	23	August	1	20
July	1	22	August	16	19

Ursa Minor, Draco, Corona, Hercules, Lyra, Serpens, Ophiuchus, Libra, Scorpius and Sagittarius

THE MOON

Phases, Apsides and Node		d	h	m
○	Full Moon	3	18	52
☾	Last Quarter	11	01	48
●	New Moon	19	04	24
☽	First Quarter	26	08	56

Perigee (362,384km)	1	18	10
Apogee (404,744km)	13	16	51
Perigee (367,343km)	29	08	37

Mean longitude of ascending node on July 1, 243°

THE SUN

s.d. 15′.8

Day	Right Ascension h m s	Dec. + ° ′	Equation of time m s	Rise 52° h m	Rise 56° h m	Transit h m	Set 52° h m	Set 56° h m	Sidereal time h m s	Transit of first point of Aries h m s
1	6 41 40	23 05	−3 51	3 45	3 19	12 04	20 23	20 49	18 37 48	5 21 19
2	6 45 47	23 01	−4 02	3 45	3 20	12 04	20 23	20 48	18 41 45	5 17 23
3	6 49 55	22 56	−4 13	3 46	3 20	12 04	20 22	20 48	18 45 42	5 13 27
4	6 54 02	22 51	−4 24	3 47	3 21	12 04	20 22	20 47	18 49 38	5 09 31
5	6 58 09	22 46	−4 35	3 48	3 22	12 05	20 21	20 46	18 53 35	5 05 35
6	7 02 16	22 40	−4 45	3 49	3 24	12 05	20 20	20 45	18 57 31	5 01 39
7	7 06 22	22 34	−4 54	3 50	3 25	12 05	20 20	20 45	19 01 28	4 57 43
8	7 10 28	22 27	−5 04	3 51	3 26	12 05	20 19	20 44	19 05 24	4 53 47
9	7 14 34	22 20	−5 13	3 52	3 27	12 05	20 18	20 43	19 09 21	4 49 51
10	7 18 39	22 12	−5 21	3 53	3 28	12 05	20 18	20 42	19 13 18	4 45 56
11	7 22 44	22 05	−5 30	3 54	3 30	12 06	20 17	20 41	19 17 14	4 42 00
12	7 26 48	21 56	−5 37	3 55	3 31	12 06	20 16	20 39	19 21 11	4 38 04
13	7 30 52	21 48	−5 45	3 56	3 32	12 06	20 15	20 38	19 25 07	4 34 08
14	7 34 55	21 39	−5 51	3 57	3 34	12 06	20 14	20 37	19 29 04	4 30 12
15	7 38 58	21 29	−5 58	3 58	3 35	12 06	20 13	20 36	19 33 00	4 26 16
16	7 43 00	21 20	−6 04	4 00	3 37	12 06	20 12	20 34	19 36 57	4 22 20
17	7 47 02	21 10	−6 09	4 01	3 38	12 06	20 11	20 33	19 40 53	4 18 24
18	7 51 04	20 59	−6 14	4 02	3 40	12 06	20 10	20 31	19 44 50	4 14 28
19	7 55 05	20 48	−6 18	4 03	3 42	12 06	20 08	20 30	19 48 47	4 10 32
20	7 59 05	20 37	−6 22	4 05	3 43	12 06	20 07	20 28	19 52 43	4 06 36
21	8 03 05	20 26	−6 25	4 06	3 45	12 06	20 06	20 27	19 56 40	4 02 41
22	8 07 04	20 14	−6 28	4 08	3 47	12 06	20 05	20 25	20 00 36	3 58 45
23	8 11 02	20 02	−6 30	4 09	3 48	12 07	20 03	20 24	20 04 33	3 54 49
24	8 15 00	19 49	−6 31	4 10	3 50	12 07	20 02	20 22	20 08 29	3 50 53
25	8 18 58	19 36	−6 32	4 12	3 52	12 07	20 00	20 20	20 12 26	3 46 57
26	8 22 54	19 23	−6 32	4 13	3 54	12 07	19 59	20 18	20 16 22	3 43 01
27	8 26 51	19 10	−6 32	4 15	3 55	12 07	19 57	20 16	20 20 19	3 39 05
28	8 30 46	18 56	−6 30	4 16	3 57	12 07	19 56	20 15	20 24 16	3 35 09
29	8 34 41	18 42	−6 29	4 18	3 59	12 06	19 54	20 13	20 28 12	3 31 13
30	8 38 35	18 27	−6 27	4 19	4 01	12 06	19 53	20 11	20 32 09	3 27 17
31	8 42 29	18 13	−6 24	4 21	4 03	12 06	19 51	20 09	20 36 05	3 23 21

DURATION OF TWILIGHT (in minutes)

Latitude	52°	56°	52°	56°	52°	56°	52°	56°
	1 July		11 July		21 July		31 July	
Civil	48	61	47	58	44	53	42	49
Nautical	124	TAN	117	TAN	107	146	98	123
Astronomical	TAN	TAN	TAN	TAN	TAN	TAN	182	TAN

THE NIGHT SKY

Mercury reaches greatest eastern elongation (26 degrees) on the 1st but the long duration of twilight means that it remains unsuitably placed for observation throughout the month.

Venus, magnitude −4.5, is rapidly moving away from the Sun and is visible as a morning object, dominating the eastern sky for several hours before dawn. It will attain its greatest brilliancy on the 12th. Locating Venus in daylight is a challenge for keen sighted naked-eye observers, ideally standing in shade from the Sun. A good opportunity comes within a few hours after sunrise on the 15th when Venus will be about 2 degrees to the left and 5 degrees below the waning crescent Moon.

Mars, its magnitude fading from +0.9 to +1.1 during the month, is moving steadily eastwards towards Spica, in Virgo. By the end of the month it will be too low in the western sky to be seen after 21h. On the 24th the Moon, shortly before First Quarter, passes 4 degrees south of the planet.

Jupiter, magnitude −2.1, continues to be visible as a bright morning object in the south-eastern sky. By the end of the month it is becoming visible low above the eastern horizon shortly after midnight. On the morning of the 15th the waning crescent Moon will be seen approaching Jupiter and observers in southeast England will be able to see an actual occultation of the planet between about 01h 45m and 02h 00m. Those with telescopes may be able to see the satellites Io and Europa being occulted as well. Good observing conditions are required in the ENE sky since the altitude is then only around 10 degrees.

Saturn, magnitude +0.7, continues to be visible in the evenings, low above the western horizon although by the end of the month the long evening twilight severely restricts the time available for observation before the planet sets. On the 25th, the Moon, just before First Quarter, passes 6 degrees south of the planet.

THE MOON

Day	R.A. h	R.A. m	Dec. °	Hor. Par. '	Semi-diam. '	Sun's Co-Long. °	PA. of Br. Limb °	Ph. %	Age d	Rise 52° h	Rise 52° m	Rise 56° h	Rise 56° m	Transit h	Transit m	Set 52° h	Set 52° m	Set 56° h	Set 56° m
1	15	56	−20.7	60.4	16.5	52	281	89	11.4	18	06	18	29	22	13	1	24	1	02
2	16	59	−21.7	60.5	16.5	65	278	95	12.4	19	07	19	30	23	16	2	20	1	56
3	18	03	−21.2	60.3	16.4	77	282	99	13.4	19	55	20	15	—		3	27	3	05
4	19	05	−19.2	59.9	16.3	89	34	100	14.4	20	33	20	49	0	16	4	43	4	24
5	20	04	−16.0	59.2	16.1	101	64	98	15.4	21	03	21	14	1	13	6	02	5	47
6	20	59	−12.0	58.5	15.9	113	65	93	16.4	21	28	21	34	2	06	7	20	7	10
7	21	52	−7.5	57.6	15.7	126	65	87	17.4	21	49	21	52	2	56	8	36	8	31
8	22	41	−2.8	56.8	15.5	138	64	79	18.4	22	09	22	07	3	43	9	49	9	48
9	23	29	+1.9	56.0	15.2	150	65	70	19.4	22	28	22	23	4	27	10	59	11	02
10	0	15	+6.4	55.3	15.1	162	66	61	20.4	22	49	22	40	5	11	12	07	12	15
11	1	02	+10.6	54.8	14.9	174	67	51	21.4	23	11	22	59	5	55	13	14	13	26
12	1	48	+14.3	54.4	14.8	187	70	41	22.4	23	37	23	21	6	39	14	20	14	35
13	2	36	+17.3	54.2	14.8	199	73	32	23.4	—		23	49	7	25	15	23	15	42
14	3	25	+19.6	54.2	14.8	211	76	24	24.4	0	08	—		8	12	16	23	16	44
15	4	15	+21.1	54.3	14.8	223	80	16	25.4	0	46	0	24	9	00	17	18	17	40
16	5	07	+21.7	54.5	14.9	236	83	10	26.4	1	31	1	09	9	49	18	06	18	28
17	5	59	+21.2	54.9	15.0	248	85	5	27.4	2	25	2	03	10	39	18	47	19	07
18	6	51	+19.7	55.3	15.1	260	82	2	28.4	3	27	3	07	11	29	19	22	19	39
19	7	43	+17.3	55.8	15.2	272	39	0	29.4	4	34	4	18	12	19	19	51	20	04
20	8	34	+14.0	56.3	15.3	285	309	1	0.9	5	44	5	32	13	07	20	16	20	25
21	9	25	+10.0	56.8	15.5	297	300	4	1.9	6	57	6	50	13	55	20	38	20	43
22	10	15	+5.4	57.3	15.6	309	298	9	2.9	8	11	8	08	14	43	21	00	21	00
23	11	05	+0.5	57.8	15.7	321	297	16	3.9	9	27	9	28	15	30	21	21	21	18
24	11	56	−4.5	58.2	15.9	334	296	25	4.9	10	44	10	50	16	20	21	44	21	36
25	12	48	−9.3	58.6	16.0	346	294	35	5.9	12	02	12	12	17	11	22	10	21	58
26	13	42	−13.7	59.0	16.1	358	291	46	6.9	13	21	13	36	18	05	22	41	22	25
27	14	38	−17.3	59.3	16.2	10	288	57	7.9	14	38	14	57	19	02	23	20	23	00
28	15	38	−20.0	59.6	16.2	23	283	68	8.9	15	51	16	13	20	01	—		23	47
29	16	39	−21.4	59.7	16.3	35	278	79	9.9	16	54	17	17	21	01	0	09	—	
30	17	41	−21.4	59.7	16.3	47	274	87	10.9	17	47	18	08	22	01	1	10	0	47
31	18	42	−20.0	59.5	16.2	59	271	94	11.9	18	29	18	46	22	59	2	20	2	00

MERCURY

Day	R.A. h	R.A. m	Dec. °	Diam. "	Phase %	Transit h	Transit m	5° high 52° h	5° high 52° m	5° high 56° h	5° high 56° m
1	8	31	+19.1	8	41	13	53	20	59	21	12
3	8	38	+18.3	8	37	13	52	20	53	21	05
5	8	44	+17.4	9	34	13	49	20	46	20	57
7	8	49	+16.7	9	30	13	46	20	38	20	49
9	8	52	+15.9	9	27	13	42	20	30	20	39
11	8	55	+15.2	10	23	13	36	20	20	20	30
13	8	56	+14.6	10	20	13	29	20	10	20	19
15	8	56	+14.1	10	16	13	21	19	59	20	08
17	8	55	+13.7	11	13	13	12	19	48	19	56
19	8	53	+13.4	11	10	13	01	19	36	19	44
21	8	50	+13.3	11	7	12	50	19	24	19	32
23	8	45	+13.3	11	5	12	37	19	12	19	19
25	8	40	+13.4	12	3	12	24	18	59	19	07
27	8	34	+13.6	11	1	12	11	18	47	18	55
29	8	28	+14.0	11	1	11	57	5	19	5	11
31	8	23	+14.4	11	2	11	44	5	03	4	54

VENUS

Day	R.A. h	R.A. m	Dec. °	Diam. "	Phase %	Transit h	Transit m	5° high 52° h	5° high 52° m	5° high 56° h	5° high 56° m
1	4	26	+17.5	45	17	9	47	2	49	2	37
6	4	31	+17.4	41	21	9	32	2	35	2	23
11	4	39	+17.5	38	26	9	21	2	22	2	11
16	4	49	+17.8	35	30	9	12	2	11	1	59
21	5	02	+18.2	33	34	9	05	2	02	1	50
26	5	17	+18.6	30	38	9	00	1	54	1	42
31	5	33	+19.1	28	41	9	57	1	48	1	35

MARS

Day	R.A. h	R.A. m	Dec. °	Diam. "	Phase %	Transit h	Transit m	5° high 52° h	5° high 52° m	5° high 56° h	5° high 56° m
1	11	56	+0.9	7	89	17	17	22	47	22	44
6	12	05	−0.2	6	89	17	06	22	31	22	27
11	12	15	−1.4	6	89	16	56	22	15	22	11
16	12	25	−2.6	6	89	16	47	21	59	21	54
21	12	35	−3.7	6	89	16	38	21	44	21	37
26	12	46	−4.9	6	90	16	28	21	28	21	20
31	12	57	−6.2	6	90	16	19	21	13	21	04

SUNRISE AND SUNSET

	London 0° 05' 51° 30'		Bristol 2° 35' 51° 28'		Birmingham 1° 55' 52° 28'		Manchester 2° 15' 53° 28'		Newcastle 1° 37' 54° 59'		Glasgow 4° 14' 55° 52'		Belfast 5° 56' 54° 35'	
d	h m	h m	h m	h m	h m	h m	h m	h m	h m	h m	h m	h m	h m	h m
1	3 48	20 21	3 58	20 30	3 50	20 33	3 45	20 41	3 32	20 48	3 37	21 05	3 52	21 02
2	3 48	20 20	3 59	20 30	3 50	20 33	3 46	20 40	3 33	20 47	3 37	21 04	3 53	21 02
3	3 49	20 20	3 59	20 30	3 51	20 32	3 46	20 40	3 34	20 47	3 38	21 04	3 54	21 01
4	3 50	20 19	4 00	20 29	3 52	20 32	3 47	20 39	3 35	20 46	3 39	21 03	3 55	21 01
5	3 51	20 19	4 01	20 29	3 53	20 31	3 48	20 38	3 36	20 46	3 40	21 02	3 56	21 00
6	3 52	20 18	4 02	20 28	3 54	20 31	3 49	20 38	3 37	20 45	3 41	21 01	3 57	20 59
7	3 53	20 18	4 03	20 27	3 55	20 30	3 50	20 37	3 38	20 44	3 43	21 01	3 58	20 59
8	3 54	20 17	4 04	20 27	3 56	20 29	3 51	20 36	3 39	20 43	3 44	21 00	3 59	20 58
9	3 55	20 16	4 05	20 26	3 57	20 29	3 52	20 36	3 40	20 42	3 45	20 59	4 00	20 57
10	3 56	20 15	4 06	20 25	3 58	20 28	3 53	20 35	3 42	20 41	3 46	20 58	4 01	20 56
11	3 57	20 15	4 07	20 24	3 59	20 27	3 55	20 34	3 43	20 40	3 48	20 57	4 03	20 55
12	3 58	20 14	4 08	20 23	4 00	20 26	3 56	20 33	3 44	20 39	3 49	20 55	4 04	20 54
13	3 59	20 13	4 09	20 23	4 01	20 25	3 57	20 32	3 46	20 38	3 50	20 54	4 05	20 53
14	4 00	20 12	4 10	20 22	4 02	20 24	3 58	20 31	3 47	20 37	3 52	20 53	4 07	20 52
15	4 01	20 11	4 11	20 21	4 04	20 23	4 00	20 30	3 48	20 36	3 53	20 52	4 08	20 51
16	4 02	20 10	4 13	20 20	4 05	20 22	4 01	20 28	3 50	20 34	3 55	20 50	4 09	20 49
17	4 04	20 09	4 14	20 18	4 06	20 21	4 02	20 27	3 51	20 33	3 56	20 49	4 11	20 48
18	4 05	20 08	4 15	20 17	4 07	20 20	4 04	20 26	3 53	20 32	3 58	20 48	4 12	20 47
19	4 06	20 06	4 16	20 16	4 09	20 18	4 05	20 25	3 54	20 30	3 59	20 46	4 14	20 45
20	4 07	20 05	4 18	20 15	4 10	20 17	4 07	20 23	3 56	20 29	4 01	20 45	4 15	20 44
21	4 09	20 04	4 19	20 14	4 12	20 16	4 08	20 22	3 57	20 27	4 03	20 43	4 17	20 42
22	4 10	20 03	4 20	20 12	4 13	20 14	4 09	20 21	3 59	20 26	4 04	20 41	4 18	20 41
23	4 11	20 01	4 22	20 11	4 14	20 13	4 11	20 19	4 01	20 24	4 06	20 40	4 20	20 39
24	4 13	20 00	4 23	20 10	4 16	20 12	4 12	20 18	4 02	20 23	4 08	20 38	4 22	20 38
25	4 14	19 58	4 24	20 08	4 17	20 10	4 14	20 16	4 04	20 21	4 09	20 36	4 23	20 36
26	4 16	19 57	4 26	20 07	4 19	20 09	4 16	20 14	4 05	20 19	4 11	20 34	4 25	20 35
27	4 17	19 56	4 27	20 05	4 20	20 07	4 17	20 13	4 07	20 18	4 13	20 33	4 27	20 33
28	4 19	19 54	4 29	20 04	4 22	20 05	4 19	20 11	4 09	20 16	4 15	20 31	4 28	20 31
29	4 20	19 53	4 30	20 02	4 23	20 04	4 20	20 09	4 11	20 14	4 17	20 29	4 30	20 29
30	4 22	19 51	4 32	20 01	4 25	20 02	4 22	20 08	4 12	20 12	4 18	20 27	4 32	20 28
31	4 23	19 49	4 33	19 59	4 27	20 01	4 24	20 06	4 14	20 10	4 20	20 25	4 33	20 26

JUPITER

Day	R.A.		Dec.		Transit		5° high		
							52°		56°
	h	m	°	'	h	m	h	m	h	m
1	4	09.7	+20	14	9	31	2	17	2	02
11	4	18.4	+20	36	9	00	1	44	1	29
21	4	26.7	+20	56	8	29	1	11	0	56
31	4	34.4	+21	12	7	57	0	38	0	22

Diameters – equatorial 35" polar 33"

SATURN

Day	R.A.		Dec.		Transit		5° high		
							52°		56°
	h	m	°	'	h	m	h	m	h	m
1	13	28.1	−6	29	18	47	23	39	23	30
11	13	28.7	−6	36	18	09	23	00	22	51
21	13	29.9	−6	46	17	31	22	21	22	12
31	13	31.7	−6	59	16	53	21	42	21	33

Diameters – equatorial 17" polar 15"
Rings – major axis 39" minor axis 9"

URANUS

Day	R.A.		Dec.		Transit		10° high		
							52°		56°
	h	m	°	'	h	m	h	m	h	m
1	0	32.3	+2	42	5	54	0	46	0	50
11	0	32.5	+2	43	5	14	0	07	0	11
21	0	32.5	+2	42	4	35	23	23	23	28
31	0	32.1	+2	40	3	55	22	44	22	48

Diameter 4"

NEPTUNE

Day	R.A.		Dec.		Transit		10° high		
							52°		56°
	h	m	°	'	h	m	h	m	h	m
1	22	20.6	−10	58	3	42	23	48	0	11
11	22	20.0	−11	02	3	02	23	09	23	28
21	22	19.2	−11	07	2	22	22	29	22	48
31	22	18.4	−11	12	1	42	21	50	22	09

Diameter 2"

AUGUST 2012

EIGHTH MONTH, 31 DAYS. *Augustus*, formerly *Sextilis*, sixth month of Roman pre-Julian calendar

1	Wednesday	Joseph Priestley identified a gas which he called 'dephlogisticated air' (oxygen) 1774	day 214
2	Thursday	The Tower Subway, a tunnel running beneath the River Thames, was officially opened 1870	215
3	Friday	Elisha Otis, inventor of a safety device for lifts which made high-rise buildings practical *b.* 1811	216
4	Saturday	Étienne Lenoir, who developed the first commercially successful internal combustion engine *d.* 1900	217
5	Sunday	The UK, USA and USSR signed the Nuclear Test Ban Treaty to prohibit above-ground nuclear tests 1963	218

6	Monday	Sir Alexander Fleming, bacteriologist best known for his discovery of penicillin *b.* 1881	week 32 day 219
7	Tuesday	Alan Hazeltine, inventor of the neutrodyne circuit which made commercial radio possible *b.* 1886	220
8	Wednesday	The LZ-127 *Graf Zeppelin* embarked on the first round-the-world flight by airship 1929	221
9	Thursday	Nathan Ames patented the first escalator-type idea, which he named 'revolving stairs' 1859	222
10	Friday	*Magellan*, a space probe tasked with mapping the surface of Venus, arrived at its destination 1990	223
11	Saturday	Christiaan Eijkman, physician whose part in discovering vitamins won him the 1929 Nobel prize *b.* 1858	224
12	Sunday	IBM introduced its personal computer for $1,600, which quickly came to dominate the market 1981	225

13	Monday	Johann Christoph Denner, inventor of the clarinet *b.* 1655	week 33 day 226
14	Tuesday	Enzo Ferrari, founder of the sports car manufacturer which bears his name *b.* 1898	227
15	Wednesday	M. W. Hanchett patented his invention, a dental chair with adjustable elevation and tilting options 1848	228
16	Thursday	Chemists met in Ottawa to name the element 110, which they decided to call Darmstadtium 2003	229
17	Friday	Three Americans made the first transatlantic crossing in a hot air balloon, taking six days 1978	230
18	Saturday	Astronomer Pierre Janssen discovered helium in the solar spectrum 1868	231
19	Sunday	Orville Wright, aviation pioneer who, with his brother Wilbur, invented the first aeroplane *b.* 1871	232

20	Monday	The first round-the-world telegram was sent; it read 'This message sent around the world' 1911	week 34 day 233
21	Tuesday	William Murdock, inventor and pioneer in steam power who made use of coal gas for lighting *b.* 1754	234
22	Wednesday	*Voyager 2* discovered Neptune's first complete ring, about 27,360 kilometres above its atmosphere 1989	235
23	Thursday	Bryan Allen piloted the first human-powered flight, for 1.9 kilometres, using the *Gossamer Condor* 1977	236
24	Friday	The International Astronomical Union reclassified Pluto as a dwarf planet rather than a planet 2006	237
25	Saturday	Hans Adolf Krebs, biochemist who discovered the citric acid cycle and won the 1953 Nobel prize *b.* 1900	238
26	Sunday	Electricity was first transmitted commercially, utilising power generated by Niagara Falls 1895	239

27	Monday	The world's biggest battery was connected (to supply emergency power to Fairbanks, Alaska) 2003	week 35 day 240
28	Tuesday	Paul MacCready, inventor of the first human-powered flying machines (*see* 23 August) *d.* 2007	241
29	Wednesday	The USSR tested its first atomic device, 'First Lightning', escalating nuclear arms development 1949	242
30	Thursday	Sir Ernest Rutherford, nuclear physics pioneer who achieved the 'splitting' of light atoms *b.* 1871	243
31	Friday	General Motors demonstrated the first solar-powered car, built by William Cobb, in Chicago, USA 1955	244

ASTRONOMICAL PHENOMENA

d   h

8 06 Mercury at stationary point
11 21 Jupiter in conjunction with Moon. Jupiter 0°.1 N.
13 20 Venus in conjunction with Moon. Venus 0°.6 S.
15 09 Venus at greatest elongation W. 46°
15 11 Saturn in conjunction with Mars. Saturn 3°N.
16 03 Mercury in conjunction with Moon. Mercury 3°N.
16 12 Mercury at greatest elongation W. 19°
22 00 Saturn in conjunction with Moon. Saturn 5°N.
22 06 Mars in conjunction with Moon. Mars 2°N.
22 17 Sun's longitude 150° ♍
24 13 Neptune at opposition

MINIMA OF ALGOL

d	h	d	h	d	h
2	04.8	13	16.1	25	03.3
5	01.6	16	12.9	28	00.1
7	22.4	19	09.7	30	20.9
10	19.2	22	06.5		

CONSTELLATIONS

The following constellations are near their meridian at

	d	h		d	h
July	1	24	August	16	21
July	16	23	September	1	20
August	1	22	September	15	19

Draco, Hercules, Lyra, Cygnus, Sagitta, Ophiuchus, Serpens, Aquila and Sagittarius

THE MOON

Phases, Apsides and Node	d	h	m
○ Full Moon	2	03	27
☾ Last Quarter	9	18	55
● New Moon	17	15	54
☽ First Quarter	24	13	54
○ Full Moon	31	13	58
Apogee (404,084km)	10	10	52
Perigee (369,764km)	23	19	23

Mean longitude of ascending node on August 1, 242°

THE SUN

s.d. 15′.8

Day	Right Ascension			Dec. +		Equation of time		Rise 52°		56°		Transit		Set 52°		56°		Sidereal time			Transit of first point of Aries		
	h	m	s	°	′	m	s	h	m	h	m	h	m	h	m	h	m	h	m	s	h	m	s
1	8	46	22	17	58	−6	20	4	22	4	05	12	06	19	49	20	07	20	40	02	3	19	25
2	8	50	14	17	43	−6	16	4	24	4	06	12	06	19	48	20	05	20	43	58	3	15	30
3	8	54	06	17	27	−6	11	4	25	4	08	12	06	19	46	20	03	20	47	55	3	11	34
4	8	57	57	17	11	−6	06	4	27	4	10	12	06	19	44	20	01	20	51	51	3	07	38
5	9	01	48	16	55	−6	00	4	29	4	12	12	06	19	42	19	58	20	55	48	3	03	42
6	9	05	38	16	38	−5	53	4	30	4	14	12	06	19	41	19	56	20	59	45	2	59	46
7	9	09	27	16	22	−5	46	4	32	4	16	12	06	19	39	19	54	21	03	41	2	55	50
8	9	13	16	16	05	−5	39	4	33	4	18	12	06	19	37	19	52	21	07	38	2	51	54
9	9	17	04	15	48	−5	30	4	35	4	20	12	05	19	35	19	50	21	11	34	2	47	58
10	9	20	52	15	30	−5	21	4	36	4	22	12	05	19	33	19	47	21	15	31	2	44	02
11	9	24	39	15	12	−5	12	4	38	4	24	12	05	19	31	19	45	21	19	27	2	40	06
12	9	28	26	14	55	−5	02	4	40	4	26	12	05	19	29	19	43	21	23	24	2	36	10
13	9	32	12	14	36	−4	52	4	41	4	28	12	05	19	27	19	41	21	27	20	2	32	15
14	9	35	58	14	18	−4	41	4	43	4	30	12	05	19	25	19	38	21	31	17	2	28	19
15	9	39	43	13	59	−4	29	4	45	4	32	12	04	19	23	19	36	21	35	14	2	24	23
16	9	43	27	13	40	−4	17	4	46	4	33	12	04	19	21	19	34	21	39	10	2	20	27
17	9	47	11	13	21	−4	05	4	48	4	35	12	04	19	19	19	31	21	43	07	2	16	31
18	9	50	55	13	02	−3	51	4	49	4	37	12	04	19	17	19	29	21	47	03	2	12	35
19	9	54	38	12	42	−3	38	4	51	4	39	12	04	19	15	19	26	21	51	00	2	08	39
20	9	58	20	12	23	−3	24	4	53	4	41	12	03	19	13	19	24	21	54	56	2	04	43
21	10	02	02	12	03	−3	09	4	54	4	43	12	03	19	11	19	21	21	58	53	2	00	47
22	10	05	44	11	43	−2	54	4	56	4	45	12	03	19	08	19	19	22	02	49	1	56	51
23	10	09	25	11	22	−2	39	4	58	4	47	12	03	19	06	19	16	22	06	46	1	52	56
24	10	13	05	11	02	−2	23	4	59	4	49	12	02	19	04	19	14	22	10	42	1	49	00
25	10	16	46	10	41	−2	06	5	01	4	51	12	02	19	02	19	11	22	14	39	1	45	04
26	10	20	25	10	20	−1	50	5	02	4	53	12	02	19	00	19	09	22	18	36	1	41	08
27	10	24	05	10	00	−1	32	5	04	4	55	12	01	18	58	19	06	22	22	32	1	37	12
28	10	27	44	9	38	−1	15	5	06	4	57	12	01	18	55	19	04	22	26	29	1	33	16
29	10	31	22	9	17	−0	57	5	07	4	59	12	01	18	53	19	01	22	30	25	1	29	20
30	10	35	00	8	56	−0	39	5	09	5	01	12	00	18	51	18	59	22	34	22	1	25	24
31	10	38	38	8	34	−0	20	5	11	5	03	12	00	18	49	18	56	22	38	18	1	21	28

DURATION OF TWILIGHT (in minutes)

Latitude	52°	56°	52°	56°	52°	56°	52°	56°
	1 August		11 August		21 August		31 August	
Civil	41	49	39	45	37	42	35	40
Nautical	97	121	90	107	84	97	79	90
Astronomical	179	TAN	154	210	139	168	128	148

THE NIGHT SKY

Mercury is at greatest western elongation (19 degrees) on the 16th and is visible as a morning object, low above the east-north-eastern horizon for about 8 days either side of the 20th. During this period its magnitude brightens from +1.1 to −1.2. On the morning of the 16th the old waning Moon passes 4 degrees south of the planet.

Venus, magnitude −4.3, reaches its greatest western elongation (46 degrees) on the 15th and thus continues to be a magnificent object in the eastern skies before dawn. On the 13th the waning crescent Moon will be seen near Venus on the mornings of the 13th and 14th.

Mars, magnitude +1.1, is coming to the end of its evening apparition after about the first 3 weeks of the month, though it could possibly be detected very low above the south-western horizon as the thin waning crescent Moon passes about 3 degrees south of the planet on August 22–23. Earlier in the month Mars passes 2 degrees north of Spica (magnitude +1.0) on the 13th,

and 3 degrees south of Saturn (magnitude +0.8) on the 15th.

Jupiter continues to be visible as a brilliant object, magnitude −2.2, in the south-eastern sky in the late evenings. On the 3rd Jupiter will be seen passing 5 degrees north of Aldebaran, in Taurus. The waning crescent Moon passes 1 degree south of the planet on the evening of the 11th.

Saturn, magnitude +0.8, is visible low above the south-western horizon for a short while in the evenings. On the 22nd the waxing crescent Moon passes 6 degrees south of the planet. Do not confuse Saturn with Mars which is very slightly fainter.

Neptune is at opposition on the 24th, in the constellation of Aquarius. It is not visible to the naked-eye since its magnitude is +7.9.

Meteors. The maximum of the famous Perseid meteor shower occurs on the 12th, though there will be interference from the waning gibbous Moon after midnight.

THE MOON

Day	R.A.		Dec.	Hor. Par.	Semi-diam.	Sun's Co-Long.	PA. of Br. Limb	Ph.	Age	Rise 52°		56°		Transit		Set 52°		56°	
	h	m	°	'	'	°	°	%	d	h	m	h	m	h	m	h	m	h	m
1	19	41	−17.4	59.1	16.1	71	275	98	12.9	19	02	19	15	23	54	3	37	3	20
2	20	38	−13.8	58.6	16.0	84	323	100	13.9	19	29	19	38	—		4	55	4	43
3	21	31	−9.4	58.0	15.8	96	47	99	14.9	19	52	19	57	0	45	6	12	6	05
4	22	22	−4.8	57.3	15.6	108	57	96	15.9	20	13	20	14	1	33	7	27	7	24
5	23	11	0.0	56.5	15.4	120	60	90	16.9	20	33	20	30	2	20	8	39	8	41
6	23	59	+4.7	55.9	15.2	132	62	84	17.9	20	53	20	46	3	05	9	50	9	55
7	0	46	+9.0	55.3	15.1	144	65	76	18.9	21	15	21	04	3	49	10	58	11	08
8	1	33	+12.9	54.8	14.9	157	67	67	19.9	21	40	21	26	4	34	12	05	12	18
9	2	21	+16.2	54.4	14.8	169	71	58	20.9	22	09	21	51	5	19	13	09	13	26
10	3	09	+18.8	54.3	14.8	181	74	48	21.9	22	44	22	23	6	05	14	11	14	31
11	3	59	+20.5	54.3	14.8	193	78	39	22.9	23	26	23	04	6	53	15	07	15	29
12	4	50	+21.4	54.5	14.8	206	83	30	23.9	—		23	54	7	42	15	58	16	21
13	5	42	+21.3	54.8	14.9	218	87	21	24.9	0	16	—		8	31	16	43	17	03
14	6	34	+20.2	55.2	15.1	230	90	14	25.9	1	14	0	53	9	21	17	20	17	38
15	7	26	+18.1	55.8	15.2	242	92	8	26.9	2	18	2	01	10	11	17	52	18	06
16	8	18	+15.1	56.4	15.4	255	91	3	27.9	3	28	3	15	11	00	18	19	18	29
17	9	09	+11.3	57.0	15.5	267	77	1	28.9	4	41	4	32	11	49	18	43	18	49
18	10	00	+6.9	57.6	15.7	279	340	0	0.4	5	56	5	51	12	38	19	05	19	08
19	10	51	+2.0	58.2	15.8	291	308	2	1.4	7	13	7	12	13	27	19	27	19	25
20	11	43	−3.0	58.6	16.0	303	301	7	2.4	8	30	8	35	14	17	19	50	19	44
21	12	35	−8.0	58.9	16.1	316	297	14	3.4	9	49	9	58	15	08	20	16	20	05
22	13	30	−12.5	59.2	16.1	328	294	22	4.4	11	09	11	22	16	02	20	45	20	31
23	14	26	−16.4	59.3	16.1	340	289	32	5.4	12	27	12	45	16	57	21	22	21	03
24	15	24	−19.3	59.3	16.2	352	285	43	6.4	13	40	14	02	17	55	22	07	21	45
25	16	24	−21.0	59.2	16.1	5	279	55	7.4	14	46	15	09	18	54	23	03	22	40
26	17	25	−21.3	59.1	16.1	17	274	66	8.4	15	41	16	03	19	53	—		23	47
27	18	25	−20.4	58.9	16.0	29	269	76	9.4	16	26	16	45	20	50	0	08	—	
28	19	23	−18.2	58.6	16.0	41	266	85	10.4	17	01	17	16	21	44	1	20	1	02
29	20	20	−15.0	58.2	15.9	53	264	92	11.4	17	30	17	41	22	36	2	36	2	22
30	21	13	−11.0	57.8	15.7	66	266	97	12.4	17	55	18	01	23	25	3	52	3	43
31	22	04	−6.5	57.2	15.6	78	284	99	13.4	18	17	18	19	—		5	07	5	02

MERCURY

Day	R.A.		Dec.	Diam.	Phase	Transit		5° high 52°		56°	
	h	m	°	"	%	h	m	h	m	h	m
1	8	20	+14.7	11	2	11	37	4	55	4	47
3	8	16	+15.2	11	4	11	26	4	41	4	31
5	8	13	+15.8	10	7	11	15	4	27	4	17
7	8	12	+16.3	10	11	11	06	4	15	4	04
9	8	12	+16.8	9	16	10	59	4	04	3	53
11	8	14	+17.3	9	22	10	54	3	56	3	45
13	8	18	+17.6	8	29	10	50	3	51	3	39
15	8	24	+17.9	8	36	10	49	3	48	3	36
17	8	32	+18.0	7	43	10	49	3	47	3	35
19	8	41	+17.9	7	51	10	51	3	49	3	37
21	8	53	+17.7	7	59	10	55	3	54	3	42
23	9	05	+17.2	6	67	10	59	4	01	3	50
25	9	18	+16.6	6	75	11	05	4	10	4	00
27	9	33	+15.8	6	81	11	12	4	21	4	11
29	9	47	+14.9	6	87	11	19	4	34	4	25
31	10	02	+13.7	5	91	11	26	4	47	4	39

VENUS

Day	R.A.		Dec.	Diam.	Phase	Transit		5° high 52°		56°	
	h	m	°	"	%	h	m	h	m	h	m
1	5	36	+19.2	28	42	8	56	1	47	1	34
6	5	54	+19.6	26	45	8	54	1	43	1	30
11	6	13	+19.8	25	48	8	54	1	41	1	27
16	6	33	+20.0	23	50	8	54	1	41	1	26
21	6	54	+20.0	22	53	8	55	1	42	1	28
26	7	16	+19.8	21	56	8	57	1	45	1	31
31	7	38	+19.4	20	58	9	00	1	49	1	36

MARS

Day	R.A.		Dec.	Diam.	Phase	Transit		5° high 52°		56°	
	h	m	°	"	%	h	m	h	m	h	m
1	12	59	−6.4	6	90	16	18	21	10	21	01
6	13	10	−7.6	6	90	16	09	20	54	20	44
11	13	21	−8.8	6	90	16	01	20	39	20	28
16	13	33	−10.0	5	91	15	53	20	24	20	11
21	13	45	−11.2	5	91	15	45	20	09	19	55
26	13	57	−12.4	5	91	15	37	19	55	19	39
31	14	09	−13.6	5	91	15	30	19	40	19	23

SUNRISE AND SUNSET

	London 0° 05' 51° 30'		Bristol 2° 35' 51° 28'		Birmingham 1° 55' 52° 28'		Manchester 2° 15' 53° 28'		Newcastle 1° 37' 54° 59'		Glasgow 4° 14' 55° 52'		Belfast 5° 56' 54° 35'	
d	h m	h m	h m	h m	h m	h m	h m	h m	h m	h m	h m	h m	h m	h m
1	4 25	19 48	4 35	19 58	4 28	19 59	4 25	20 04	4 16	20 08	4 22	20 23	4 35	20 24
2	4 26	19 46	4 36	19 56	4 30	19 57	4 27	20 02	4 18	20 06	4 24	20 21	4 37	20 22
3	4 28	19 44	4 38	19 54	4 31	19 55	4 29	20 01	4 20	20 04	4 26	20 19	4 39	20 20
4	4 29	19 43	4 39	19 53	4 33	19 54	4 30	19 59	4 21	20 02	4 28	20 17	4 40	20 18
5	4 31	19 41	4 41	19 51	4 34	19 52	4 32	19 57	4 23	20 00	4 30	20 15	4 42	20 16
6	4 32	19 39	4 42	19 49	4 36	19 50	4 34	19 55	4 25	19 58	4 32	20 13	4 44	20 14
7	4 34	19 37	4 44	19 47	4 38	19 48	4 35	19 53	4 27	19 56	4 33	20 10	4 46	20 12
8	4 35	19 35	4 45	19 45	4 39	19 46	4 37	19 51	4 29	19 54	4 35	20 08	4 47	20 10
9	4 37	19 34	4 47	19 43	4 41	19 44	4 39	19 49	4 30	19 52	4 37	20 06	4 49	20 08
10	4 38	19 32	4 49	19 42	4 43	19 42	4 40	19 47	4 32	19 50	4 39	20 04	4 51	20 06
11	4 40	19 30	4 50	19 40	4 44	19 40	4 42	19 45	4 34	19 48	4 41	20 02	4 53	20 04
12	4 42	19 28	4 52	19 38	4 46	19 38	4 44	19 43	4 36	19 46	4 43	19 59	4 55	20 01
13	4 43	19 26	4 53	19 36	4 48	19 36	4 46	19 41	4 38	19 43	4 45	19 57	4 57	19 59
14	4 45	19 24	4 55	19 34	4 49	19 34	4 47	19 39	4 40	19 41	4 47	19 55	4 58	19 57
15	4 46	19 22	4 56	19 32	4 51	19 32	4 49	19 36	4 42	19 39	4 49	19 52	5 00	19 55
16	4 48	19 20	4 58	19 30	4 52	19 30	4 51	19 34	4 43	19 37	4 51	19 50	5 02	19 52
17	4 50	19 18	5 00	19 28	4 54	19 28	4 53	19 32	4 45	19 34	4 53	19 48	5 04	19 50
18	4 51	19 16	5 01	19 26	4 56	19 26	4 54	19 30	4 47	19 32	4 55	19 45	5 06	19 48
19	4 53	19 14	5 03	19 24	4 57	19 24	4 56	19 28	4 49	19 30	4 57	19 43	5 08	19 46
20	4 54	19 12	5 04	19 22	4 59	19 22	4 58	19 26	4 51	19 27	4 59	19 40	5 09	19 43
21	4 56	19 10	5 06	19 20	5 01	19 19	5 00	19 23	4 53	19 25	5 01	19 38	5 11	19 41
22	4 57	19 08	5 08	19 18	5 02	19 17	5 01	19 21	4 55	19 23	5 03	19 35	5 13	19 39
23	4 59	19 06	5 09	19 15	5 04	19 15	5 03	19 19	4 57	19 20	5 05	19 33	5 15	19 36
24	5 01	19 03	5 11	19 13	5 06	19 13	5 05	19 17	4 58	19 18	5 07	19 30	5 17	19 34
25	5 02	19 01	5 12	19 11	5 07	19 11	5 07	19 14	5 00	19 15	5 08	19 28	5 19	19 32
26	5 04	18 59	5 14	19 09	5 09	19 08	5 08	19 12	5 02	19 13	5 10	19 25	5 20	19 29
27	5 05	18 57	5 16	19 07	5 11	19 06	5 10	19 10	5 04	19 10	5 12	19 23	5 22	19 27
28	5 07	18 55	5 17	19 05	5 12	19 04	5 12	19 07	5 06	19 08	5 14	19 20	5 24	19 24
29	5 09	18 53	5 19	19 02	5 14	19 02	5 13	19 05	5 08	19 05	5 16	19 18	5 26	19 22
30	5 10	18 50	5 20	19 00	5 16	18 59	5 15	19 03	5 10	19 03	5 18	19 15	5 28	19 19
31	5 12	18 48	5 22	18 58	5 17	18 57	5 17	19 00	5 11	19 01	5 20	19 13	5 30	19 17

JUPITER

Day	R.A.	Dec.	Transit	5° high 52°	5° high 56°
	h m	° '	h m	h m	h m
1	4 35.1	+21 13	7 54	0 34	0 19
11	4 42.0	+21 26	7 22	0 00	23 41
21	4 48.0	+21 37	6 48	23 23	23 07
31	4 53.0	+21 45	6 14	22 47	22 31

Diameters – equatorial 37" polar 35"

SATURN

Day	R.A.	Dec.	Transit	5° high 52°	5° high 56°
	h m	° '	h m	h m	h m
1	13 31.9	-7 00	16 49	21 39	21 29
11	13 34.3	-7 16	16 12	21 00	20 50
21	13 37.1	-7 35	15 36	20 22	20 12
31	13 40.4	-7 56	15 00	19 44	19 34

Diameters – equatorial 16" polar 15"
Rings – major axis 37" minor axis 9"

URANUS

Day	R.A.	Dec.	Transit	10° high 52°	10° high 56°
	h m	° '	h m	h m	h m
1	0 32.0	+2 39	3 51	22 40	22 44
11	0 31.4	+2 35	3 11	22 00	22 05
21	0 30.5	+2 29	2 31	21 21	21 25
31	0 29.3	+2 21	1 51	20 41	20 45

Diameter 4"

NEPTUNE

Day	R.A.	Dec.	Transit	10° high 52°	10° high 56°
	h m	° '	h m	h m	h m
1	22 18.3	-11 12	1 38	21 46	22 05
11	22 17.3	-11 18	0 58	21 06	21 26
21	22 16.3	-11 24	0 17	20 26	20 46
31	22 15.2	-11 30	23 33	19 47	20 06

Diameter 2"

SEPTEMBER 2012

NINTH MONTH, 30 DAYS. *Septem* (seven), seventh month of Roman pre-Julian calendar

| 1 | Saturday | A solar flare was observed for the first time by astronomer Richard Carrington 1859 | day 245 |
| 2 | Sunday | The first non-stop aeroplane flight from Europe to the USA was completed, taking 37 hours 1930 | 246 |

3	Monday	Carl D. Anderson, Nobel prize-winning physicist who discovered the positive electron *b.* 1905	week 36 day 247
4	Tuesday	The Forth Road Bridge opened (at the time, Europe's longest suspension bridge) 1964	248
5	Wednesday	James Glaisher and Henry Coxwell set a new altitude record when their balloon ascended 11 kilometres 1862	249
6	Thursday	John Derry, piloting a de Havilland DH 108, became the first Briton to break the sound barrier 1948	250
7	Friday	James Van Allen, physicist who discovered Earth's magnetosphere (Van Allen radiation belts) *b.* 1914	251
8	Saturday	Scotch tape, the first transparent adhesive tape was marketed for the first time by 3M 1930	252
9	Sunday	Scientists stated that the hole in the ozone layer had reached record size (28 million sq. kilometres) 2000	253

10	Monday	Geneticist Sir Alec Jeffreys developed the techniques required for DNA fingerprinting 1984	week 37 day 254
11	Tuesday	Carl Zeiss, manufacturer of high-quality optical instruments (lenses, microscopes etc) *b.* 1816	255
12	Wednesday	Dr Richard Gatling, inventor of the Gatling gun, the first successful machine gun *b.* 1818	256
13	Thursday	A rail detector car which found faults in railroad tracks was demonstrated in New York, USA 1928	257
14	Friday	Ivan Petrovich Pavlov, physiologist famed for his research into the 'conditioned reflex' *b.* 1849	258
15	Saturday	The first weather balloon used for meteorological research in the USA was released in Missouri 1904	259
16	Sunday	Gabriel Fahrenheit, inventor of the mercury thermometer and the eponymous temperature scale *d.* 1736	260

17	Monday	Thomas Etholen Selfridge became the first person to die in a powered aeroplane crash 1908	week 38 day 261
18	Tuesday	Léon Foucault, physicist who experimentally proved that the Earth rotates on its axis *b.* 1819	262
19	Wednesday	Ötzi, the mummified body of a man who lived in about 3,300 BC, was discovered in the Ötztal Alps 1991	263
20	Thursday	Sir James Dewar, chemist who invented the Dewar flask by creating a vacuum in a container *b.* 1842	264
21	Friday	*Galileo*'s eight-year mission to Jupiter ended when the probe burnt up in the planet's atmosphere 2003	265
22	Saturday	Michael Faraday, physicist who contributed towards the understanding of electromagnetism *b.* 1791	266
23	Sunday	Johan Galle discovered Neptune after using calculations predicting the planet's location 1846	267

24	Monday	John Young, astronaut who became the first person to make six spaceflights *b.* 1930	week 39 day 268
25	Tuesday	The first transfusion using human blood took place at Guy's Hospital, London 1818	269
26	Wednesday	Nils Bohlin, inventor of the three-point lap and shoulder seatbelt, present in most cars *d.* 2002	270
27	Thursday	Europe's first travelator (moving walkway) opened at Bank Underground station in London 1960	271
28	Friday	Dr Elizabeth Garrett Anderson became the first woman to obtain a medical qualification in Britain 1865	272
29	Saturday	Enrico Fermi, physicist known for his nuclear research, including on induced radioactivity *b.* 1901	273
30	Sunday	The world's first hydroelectric power plant was opened on the Fox River in Wisconsin, USA 1882	274

ASTRONOMICAL PHENOMENA

d h
8 11 Jupiter in conjunction with Moon. Jupiter 0°.6 N.
10 13 Mercury in superior conjunction
12 15 Venus in conjunction with Moon. Venus 4°N.
16 11 Mercury in conjunction with Moon. Mercury 6°N.
18 05 Pluto at stationary point
18 11 Saturn in conjunction with Moon. Saturn 5°N.
19 21 Mars in conjunction with Moon. Mars 0°.1 N.
22 15 Sun's longitude 180° ♎
29 07 Uranus at opposition

MINIMA OF ALGOL

d	h	d	h	d	h
2	17.7	14	05.0	25	16.2
5	14.5	17	01.8	28	13.0
8	11.4	19	22.6		
11	08.2	22	19.4		

CONSTELLATIONS

The following constellations are near their meridian at

	d	h		d	h
August	1	24	September	15	21
August	16	23	October	1	20
September	1	22	October	16	19

Draco, Cepheus, Lyra, Cygnus, Vulpecula, Sagitta, Delphinus, Equuleus, Aquila, Aquarius and Capricornus

THE MOON

Phases, Apsides and Node	d	h	m
☾ Last Quarter	8	13	15
● New Moon	16	02	11
☽ First Quarter	22	19	41
○ Full Moon	30	03	19
Apogee (404,256km)	7	05	58
Perigee (365,775km)	19	02	41

Mean longitude of ascending node on September 1, 240°

THE SUN

s.d. 15′.9

Day	Right Ascension			Dec.		Equation of time		Rise 52°		Rise 56°		Transit		Set 52°		Set 56°		Sidereal time			Transit of first point of Aries		
	h	m	s	°	′	m	s	h	m	h	m	h	m	h	m	h	m	h	m	s	h	m	s
1	10	42	16	+8	12	-0	01	5	12	5	05	12	00	18	46	18	54	22	42	15	1	17	32
2	10	45	53	+7	51	+0	18	5	14	5	07	12	00	18	44	18	51	22	46	11	1	13	36
3	10	49	30	+7	29	+0	38	5	15	5	09	11	59	18	42	18	48	22	50	08	1	09	41
4	10	53	07	+7	07	+0	58	5	17	5	11	11	59	18	40	18	46	22	54	05	1	05	45
5	10	56	43	+6	44	+1	18	5	19	5	13	11	59	18	37	18	43	22	58	01	1	01	49
6	11	00	20	+6	22	+1	38	5	20	5	15	11	58	18	35	18	41	23	01	58	0	57	53
7	11	03	56	+6	00	+1	58	5	22	5	17	11	58	18	33	18	38	23	05	54	0	53	57
8	11	07	32	+5	37	+2	19	5	24	5	19	11	58	18	30	18	35	23	09	51	0	50	01
9	11	11	08	+5	15	+2	40	5	25	5	20	11	57	18	28	18	33	23	13	47	0	46	05
10	11	14	43	+4	52	+3	01	5	27	5	22	11	57	18	26	18	30	23	17	44	0	42	09
11	11	18	19	+4	29	+3	22	5	28	5	24	11	56	18	23	18	27	23	21	40	0	38	13
12	11	21	54	+4	06	+3	43	5	30	5	26	11	56	18	21	18	25	23	25	37	0	34	17
13	11	25	30	+3	43	+4	04	5	32	5	28	11	56	18	19	18	22	23	29	34	0	30	21
14	11	29	05	+3	20	+4	25	5	33	5	30	11	55	18	16	18	19	23	33	30	0	26	26
15	11	32	40	+2	57	+4	47	5	35	5	32	11	55	18	14	18	17	23	37	27	0	22	30
16	11	36	15	+2	34	+5	08	5	37	5	34	11	55	18	12	18	14	23	41	23	0	18	34
17	11	39	51	+2	11	+5	29	5	38	5	36	11	54	18	09	18	11	23	45	20	0	14	38
18	11	43	26	+1	48	+5	51	5	40	5	38	11	54	18	07	18	09	23	49	16	0	10	42
19	11	47	01	+1	24	+6	12	5	42	5	40	11	54	18	05	18	06	23	53	13	0	06	46
20	11	50	36	+1	01	+6	33	5	43	5	42	11	53	18	02	18	03	23	57	09	0	02	50
																					23	58	54
21	11	54	12	+0	38	+6	54	5	45	5	44	11	53	18	00	18	01	0	01	06	23	54	58
22	11	57	47	+0	14	+7	16	5	46	5	46	11	53	17	58	17	58	0	05	03	23	51	02
23	12	01	22	-0	09	+7	37	5	48	5	48	11	52	17	55	17	55	0	08	59	23	47	07
24	12	04	58	-0	32	+7	58	5	50	5	50	11	52	17	53	17	53	0	12	56	23	43	11
25	12	08	34	-0	56	+8	18	5	51	5	52	11	52	17	51	17	50	0	16	52	23	39	15
26	12	12	10	-1	19	+8	39	5	53	5	54	11	51	17	48	17	48	0	20	49	23	35	19
27	12	15	46	-1	42	+9	00	5	55	5	56	11	51	17	46	17	45	0	24	45	23	31	23
28	12	19	22	-2	06	+9	20	5	56	5	58	11	51	17	44	17	42	0	28	42	23	27	27
29	12	22	58	-2	29	+9	40	5	58	6	00	11	50	17	41	17	40	0	32	38	23	23	31
30	12	26	35	-2	52	+10	00	6	00	6	02	11	50	17	39	17	37	0	36	35	23	19	35

DURATION OF TWILIGHT (in minutes)

Latitude	52°	56°	52°	56°	52°	56°	52°	56°
	1 September		11 September		21 September		31 September	
Civil	35	39	34	38	34	37	34	37
Nautical	79	89	76	85	74	82	73	80
Astronomical	127	147	120	136	116	129	113	125

THE NIGHT SKY

Mercury passes through superior conjunction on the 10th and is therefore unsuitably placed for observation throughout the month.

Venus, magnitude -4.1, continues to be visible as a magnificent object in the eastern sky for three hours before sunrise. The old crescent Moon passes south of the planet on the 12th.

Mars is unsuitably placed for observation during the month, and will not be seen again for the rest of the year.

Jupiter, magnitude -2.4, is moving slowly eastwards in Taurus, and by the end of the month is visible low above the eastern horizon by 21h. The Moon, at Last Quarter, passes about 1 degree south of the planet on the 8th.

Saturn has now moved closer to the Sun and will not be available for observation again until early in the New Year.

Uranus is at opposition on the 29th, in the constellation of Pisces. The planet is barely visible to the naked-eye as its magnitude is +5.7, but it is readily located with only small optical aid.

Zodiacal Light. The morning cone may be observed stretching up from the eastern horizon, along the ecliptic, before the beginning of morning twilight, from the 14th to the 27th. This faint phenomenon is only visible under good conditions and in the absence of both moonlight and artificial lighting.

THE MOON

Day	R.A. h	m	Dec. °	Hor. Par. ′	Semi-diam. ′	Sun's Co-Long. °	PA. of Br. Limb °	Ph. %	Age d	Rise 52° h	m	Rise 56° h	m	Transit h	m	Set 52° h	m	Set 56° h	m
1	22	54	−1.8	56.7	15.4	90	24	100	14.4	18	37	18	36	0	12	6	20	6	19
2	23	42	+2.9	56.1	15.3	102	52	98	15.4	18	58	18	52	0	57	7	31	7	35
3	0	29	+7.4	55.5	15.1	114	60	94	16.4	19	19	19	10	1	42	8	40	8	48
4	1	17	+11.4	55.0	15.0	126	64	88	17.4	19	43	19	30	2	27	9	48	10	00
5	2	05	+14.9	54.6	14.9	139	68	81	18.4	20	11	19	54	3	13	10	54	11	09
6	2	53	+17.7	54.4	14.8	151	73	73	19.4	20	43	20	24	3	59	11	57	12	16
7	3	43	+19.8	54.2	14.8	163	77	65	20.4	21	22	21	00	4	46	12	56	13	17
8	4	33	+21.0	54.3	14.8	175	82	55	21.4	22	08	21	46	5	34	13	49	14	11
9	5	24	+21.2	54.5	14.9	187	86	46	22.4	23	02	22	41	6	23	14	35	14	57
10	6	15	+20.5	54.9	15.0	200	91	36	23.4	—		23	44	7	12	15	15	15	34
11	7	07	+18.8	55.4	15.1	212	95	27	24.4	0	03	—		8	01	15	49	16	05
12	7	58	+16.2	56.1	15.3	224	98	19	25.4	1	09	0	54	8	50	16	18	16	30
13	8	50	+12.7	56.8	15.5	236	100	11	26.4	2	20	2	09	9	39	16	44	16	52
14	9	41	+8.6	57.6	15.7	249	99	6	27.4	3	34	3	28	10	28	17	07	17	11
15	10	32	+3.8	58.4	15.9	261	93	2	28.4	4	51	4	49	11	17	17	30	17	30
16	11	25	−1.2	59.0	16.1	273	38	0	29.4	6	10	6	12	12	08	17	53	17	49
17	12	18	−6.3	59.5	16.2	285	311	1	0.9	7	30	7	37	13	00	18	19	18	10
18	13	13	−11.0	59.8	16.3	298	299	5	1.9	8	51	9	03	13	55	18	48	18	35
19	14	10	−15.2	59.9	16.3	310	292	11	2.9	10	12	10	28	14	51	19	23	19	06
20	15	10	−18.4	59.9	16.3	322	286	20	3.9	11	29	11	49	15	50	20	06	19	46
21	16	10	−20.4	59.6	16.3	334	280	30	4.9	12	38	13	00	16	49	20	59	20	37
22	17	11	−21.1	59.3	16.2	346	274	41	5.9	13	37	13	59	17	48	22	02	21	40
23	18	12	−20.5	58.9	16.0	359	269	52	6.9	14	24	14	44	18	45	23	12	22	53
24	19	10	−18.6	58.4	15.9	11	264	63	7.9	15	02	15	18	19	40	—		—	
25	20	06	−15.7	57.9	15.8	23	260	73	8.9	15	33	15	45	20	31	0	25	0	10
26	20	59	−11.9	57.4	15.6	35	258	82	9.9	15	58	16	06	21	20	1	39	1	29
27	21	50	−7.7	56.9	15.5	47	257	90	10.9	16	21	16	25	22	07	2	53	2	47
28	22	39	−3.2	56.4	15.4	59	258	95	11.9	16	42	16	42	22	52	4	05	4	03
29	23	27	+1.5	56.0	15.2	72	266	99	12.9	17	02	16	58	23	37	5	16	5	18
30	0	14	+5.9	55.5	15.1	84	315	100	13.9	17	23	17	16	—		6	25	6	31

MERCURY

Day	R.A. h	m	Dec. °	Diam. ″	Phase %	Transit h	m	5° high 52° h	m	5° high 56° h	m
1	10	10	+13.1	5	93	11	29	4	54	4	47
3	10	25	+11.8	5	96	11	37	5	08	5	02
5	10	40	+10.4	5	98	11	43	5	23	5	18
7	10	54	+8.9	5	99	11	50	5	37	5	33
9	11	09	+7.4	5	100	11	56	5	51	5	49
11	11	22	+5.8	5	100	12	02	17	57	17	58
13	11	36	+4.2	5	100	12	08	17	55	17	54
15	11	49	+2.6	5	99	12	13	17	52	17	50
17	12	02	+1.1	5	99	12	18	17	48	17	45
19	12	15	−0.5	5	98	12	23	17	45	17	41
21	12	27	−2.1	5	97	12	27	17	41	17	36
23	12	39	−3.6	5	96	12	31	17	37	17	30
25	12	51	−5.1	5	95	12	35	17	33	17	25
27	13	03	−6.6	5	94	12	39	17	29	17	19
29	13	14	−8.0	5	93	12	42	17	25	17	14
31	13	25	−9.4	5	91	12	46	17	20	17	08

VENUS

Day	R.A. h	m	Dec. °	Diam. ″	Phase %	Transit h	m	5° high 52° h	m	5° high 56° h	m
1	7	42	+19.3	20	58	9	00	1	50	1	37
6	8	05	+18.7	19	61	9	03	1	57	1	44
11	8	27	+17.9	18	63	9	06	2	04	1	52
16	8	50	+16.8	18	65	9	09	2	13	2	02
21	9	13	+15.6	17	67	9	12	2	23	2	14
26	9	36	+14.2	16	69	9	15	2	34	2	26
31	9	58	+12.6	16	71	9	18	2	46	2	39

MARS

Day	R.A. h	m	Dec. °	Diam. ″	Phase %	Transit h	m	5° high 52° h	m	5° high 56° h	m
1	14	12	−13.8	5	91	15	29	19	37	19	20
6	14	24	−14.9	5	92	15	22	19	23	19	05
11	14	37	−16.0	5	92	15	15	19	10	18	49
16	14	51	−17.1	5	92	15	09	18	56	18	34
21	15	04	−18.1	5	93	15	03	18	43	18	19
26	15	18	−19.1	5	93	14	57	18	30	18	05
31	15	33	−20.0	5	93	14	51	18	18	17	51

SUNRISE AND SUNSET

	London 0° 05'	51° 30'	Bristol 2° 35'	51° 28'	Birmingham 1° 55'	52° 28'	Manchester 2° 15'	53° 28'	Newcastle 1° 37'	54° 59'	Glasgow 4° 14'	55° 52'	Belfast 5° 56'	54° 35'
d	h m	h m	h m	h m	h m	h m	h m	h m	h m	h m	h m	h m	h m	h m
1	5 13	18 46	5 23	18 56	5 19	18 55	5 19	18 58	5 13	18 58	5 22	19 10	5 31	19 15
2	5 15	18 44	5 25	18 54	5 21	18 52	5 20	18 55	5 15	18 56	5 24	19 08	5 33	19 12
3	5 17	18 41	5 27	18 51	5 22	18 50	5 22	18 53	5 17	18 53	5 26	19 05	5 35	19 10
4	5 18	18 39	5 28	18 49	5 24	18 48	5 24	18 51	5 19	18 51	5 28	19 02	5 37	19 07
5	5 20	18 37	5 30	18 47	5 26	18 46	5 26	18 48	5 21	18 48	5 30	19 00	5 39	19 05
6	5 21	18 35	5 31	18 45	5 27	18 43	5 27	18 46	5 23	18 45	5 32	18 57	5 41	19 02
7	5 23	18 32	5 33	18 42	5 29	18 41	5 29	18 43	5 25	18 43	5 34	18 55	5 42	19 00
8	5 25	18 30	5 35	18 40	5 31	18 39	5 31	18 41	5 26	18 40	5 36	18 52	5 44	18 57
9	5 26	18 28	5 36	18 38	5 32	18 36	5 33	18 39	5 28	18 38	5 38	18 49	5 46	18 55
10	5 28	18 26	5 38	18 35	5 34	18 34	5 34	18 36	5 30	18 35	5 40	18 47	5 48	18 52
11	5 29	18 23	5 39	18 33	5 36	18 31	5 36	18 34	5 32	18 33	5 41	18 44	5 50	18 50
12	5 31	18 21	5 41	18 31	5 37	18 29	5 38	18 31	5 34	18 30	5 43	18 41	5 52	18 47
13	5 32	18 19	5 43	18 29	5 39	18 27	5 40	18 29	5 36	18 28	5 45	18 39	5 53	18 44
14	5 34	18 16	5 44	18 26	5 41	18 24	5 41	18 26	5 38	18 25	5 47	18 36	5 55	18 42
15	5 36	18 14	5 46	18 24	5 42	18 22	5 43	18 24	5 39	18 22	5 49	18 34	5 57	18 39
16	5 37	18 12	5 47	18 22	5 44	18 20	5 45	18 21	5 41	18 20	5 51	18 31	5 59	18 37
17	5 39	18 09	5 49	18 19	5 46	18 17	5 47	18 19	5 43	18 17	5 53	18 28	6 01	18 34
18	5 40	18 07	5 51	18 17	5 47	18 15	5 48	18 17	5 45	18 15	5 55	18 26	6 02	18 32
19	5 42	18 05	5 52	18 15	5 49	18 12	5 50	18 14	5 47	18 12	5 57	18 23	6 04	18 29
20	5 44	18 03	5 54	18 13	5 51	18 10	5 52	18 12	5 49	18 10	5 59	18 20	6 06	18 27
21	5 45	18 00	5 55	18 10	5 52	18 08	5 54	18 09	5 51	18 07	6 01	18 18	6 08	18 24
22	5 47	17 58	5 57	18 08	5 54	18 05	5 55	18 07	5 52	18 04	6 03	18 15	6 10	18 22
23	5 49	17 56	5 59	18 06	5 56	18 03	5 57	18 04	5 54	18 02	6 05	18 12	6 12	18 19
24	5 50	17 53	6 00	18 03	5 57	18 01	5 59	18 02	5 56	17 59	6 07	18 10	6 14	18 17
25	5 52	17 51	6 02	18 01	5 59	17 58	6 01	17 59	5 58	17 57	6 09	18 07	6 15	18 14
26	5 53	17 49	6 03	17 59	6 01	17 56	6 02	17 57	6 00	17 54	6 11	18 04	6 17	18 12
27	5 55	17 46	6 05	17 56	6 03	17 54	6 04	17 55	6 02	17 52	6 13	18 02	6 19	18 09
28	5 57	17 44	6 07	17 54	6 04	17 51	6 06	17 52	6 04	17 49	6 15	17 59	6 21	18 06
29	5 58	17 42	6 08	17 52	6 06	17 49	6 08	17 50	6 06	17 47	6 16	17 57	6 23	18 04
30	6 00	17 40	6 10	17 50	6 08	17 46	6 09	17 47	6 08	17 44	6 18	17 54	6 25	18 01

JUPITER

Day	R.A.		Dec.		Transit		5° high 52°		56°	
	h	m	°	'	h	m	h m		h m	
1	4	53.5	+21	45	6	10	22 44		22 28	
11	4	57.3	+21	51	5	35	22 08		21 51	
21	4	59.9	+21	54	4	58	21 31		21 14	
31	5	01.1	+21	55	4	20	20 52		20 36	

Diameters – equatorial 41" polar 38"

SATURN

Day	R.A.		Dec.		Transit		5° high 52°		56°	
	h	m	°	'	h	m	h m		h m	
1	13	40.7	−7	58	14	56	19 40		19 30	
11	13	44.4	−8	21	14	21	19 02		18 52	
21	13	48.4	−8	45	13	45	18 25		18 14	
31	13	52.7	−9	10	13	10	17 48		17 36	

Diameters – equatorial 16" polar 14"
Rings – major axis 35" minor axis 9"

URANUS

Day	R.A.		Dec.		Transit		10° high 52°		56°	
	h	m	°	'	h	m	h m		h m	
1	0	29.2	+2	20	1	47	20 37		20 42	
11	0	27.9	+2	12	1	06	19 57		20 02	
21	0	26.5	+2	03	0	25	19 17		19 22	
31	0	25.0	+1	53	23	40	18 37		18 42	

Diameter 4"

NEPTUNE

Day	R.A.		Dec.		Transit		10° high 52°		56°	
	h	m	°	'	h	m	h m		h m	
1	22	15.1	−11	30	23	29	3 19		3 00	
11	22	14.1	−11	36	22	49	2 38		2 18	
21	22	13.2	−11	41	22	08	1 58		1 37	
31	22	12.3	−11	46	21	28	1 17		0 57	

Diameter 2"

OCTOBER 2012

TENTH MONTH, 31 DAYS. *Octo* (eighth), eighth month of Roman pre-Julian calendar

1	*Monday*	Ford's Model T, the first assembly line car, was introduced to the US market 1908	week 40 day 275
2	*Tuesday*	Charles Darwin returned from his momentous voyage to the Pacific aboard *HMS Beagle* 1836	276
3	*Wednesday*	The UK tested its first nuclear weapon, named 'Hurricane', in Australia 1952	277
4	*Thursday*	The Soviet Union launched *Sputnik*, the first man-made satellite, which commenced the space age 1957	278
5	*Friday*	Robert Goddard, inventor and physicist credited as the father of modern rocketry *b.* 1882	279
6	*Saturday*	Benjamin Hanks received a patent for the self-winding clock 1783	280
7	*Sunday*	The Soviet space probe *Luna 3* photographed the far side of the Moon for the first time 1959	281

8	*Monday*	The Post Office Tower, then the tallest building in London, was officially opened 1965	week 41 day 282
9	*Tuesday*	The first generator at the Hoover Dam began transmitting electricity to Los Angeles 1936	283
10	*Wednesday*	Henry Cavendish, scientist who measured the density and mass of the Earth *b.* 1731	284
11	*Thursday*	Kathryn D. Sullivan, a NASA astronaut, became the first woman to walk in space 1984	285
12	*Friday*	Robert Stephenson, civil engineer who built many bridges, including the Britannia Bridge *d.* 1859	286
13	*Saturday*	At the International Meridian Conference, Greenwich was adopted as the universal meridian 1884	287
14	*Sunday*	George Eastman, founder of Kodak, received a patent for the paper-strip photographic film 1884	288

15	*Monday*	Evangelista Torricelli, physicist credited with inventing the barometer *b.* 1608	week 42 day 289
16	*Tuesday*	Samuel Franklin Cody completed the first aeroplane flight in the UK 1908	290
17	*Wednesday*	Dr Ernest Goodpasture, pathologist who developed vaccines against influenza and smallpox *b.* 1886	291
18	*Thursday*	Thomas Edison, inventor of the phonograph who held over 1,000 patents *d.* 1931	292
19	*Friday*	Auguste Lumière, pioneer of photographic equipment, including a motion-picture camera *b.* 1862	293
20	*Saturday*	The metre was redefined as the distance that light travels in a vacuum in 1/299,792,458 of a second 1983	294
21	*Sunday*	Alfred Nobel, chemist and inventor of dynamite whose funds instituted the famed annual prizes *b.* 1833	295

22	*Monday*	The Campaign for Nuclear Disarmament held its biggest ever protest against nuclear weapons 1983	week 43 day 296
23	*Tuesday*	The first modern rhinoplasty was performed by surgeon Joseph Carpue in London 1814	297
24	*Wednesday*	Concorde made its last commercial passenger flight, landing at Heathrow airport 2003	298
25	*Thursday*	The first domestic microwave oven, manufactured by the Tappan Stove Company, went on sale 1955	299
26	*Friday*	A patent was issued by Hamilton Smith for a rotary washing machine, which cycled reheated water 1858	300
27	*Saturday*	Isaac Singer, inventor whose company was the world's largest sewing machine manufacturer *b.* 1811	301
28	*Sunday*	John Wallis, mathematician credited with introducing the mathematical symbol for infinity *d.* 1703	302

29	*Monday*	John Glenn became the oldest person to go into space, aboard the shuttle *Discovery*, at 77 1998	week 44 day 303
30	*Tuesday*	Daniel Cooper patented a time clock which recorded employees' hours of work 1888	304
31	*Wednesday*	Michael Collins, astronaut who orbited the Moon in the momentous Apollo 11 mission *b.* 1930	305

ASTRONOMICAL PHENOMENA

	d	*h*	
4	13	Jupiter at stationary point	
5	10	Saturn in conjunction with Mercury. Saturn 3°N.	
5	21	Jupiter in conjunction with Moon. Jupiter 0°.9 N.	
12	15	Venus in conjunction with Moon. Venus 6°N.	
16	02	Saturn in conjunction with Moon. Saturn 4°N.	
17	02	Mercury in conjunction with Moon. Mercury 1°S.	
18	14	Mars in conjunction with Moon. Mars 2°S.	
23	00	Sun's longitude 210° ♏	
25	09	Saturn in conjunction	
26	15	Mercury at greatest elongation E. 24°	

MINIMA OF ALGOL

d	*h*	*d*	*h*	*d*	*h*
1	09.8	12	21.1	24	08.3
4	06.7	15	17.9	27	05.2
7	03.5	18	14.7	30	02.0
10	00.3	21	11.5		

CONSTELLATIONS

The following constellations are near their meridian at

	d	*h*		*d*	*h*
September	1	24	October	16	21
September	15	23	November	1	20
October	1	22	November	15	19

Ursa Major (below the Pole), Cepheus, Cassiopeia, Cygnus, Lacerta, Andromeda, Pegasus, Capricornus, Aquarius and Piscis Austrinus

THE MOON

Phases, Apsides and Node	*d*	*h*	*m*
☾ Last Quarter	8	07	33
● New Moon	15	12	02
☽ First Quarter	22	03	32
○ Full Moon	29	19	49
Apogee (405,128km)	5	00	37
Perigee (360,685km)	17	00	53

Mean longitude of ascending node on October 1, 238°

THE SUN

Day	Right Ascension			Dec.		Equation of time		Rise				Transit		Set				Sidereal time			Transit of first point of Aries		
								52°		56°				52°		56°							
	h	m	s	°	′	m	s	h	m	h	m	h	m	h	m	h	m	h	m	s	h	m	s
1	12	30	12	3	16	+10	19	6	01	6	04	11	49	17	37	17	34	0	40	31	23	15	39
2	12	33	49	3	39	+10	39	6	03	6	06	11	49	17	34	17	32	0	44	28	23	11	43
3	12	37	27	4	02	+10	58	6	05	6	08	11	49	17	32	17	29	0	48	25	23	07	47
4	12	41	05	4	25	+11	16	6	06	6	10	11	49	17	30	17	27	0	52	21	23	03	52
5	12	44	43	4	48	+11	34	6	08	6	12	11	48	17	28	17	24	0	56	18	22	59	56
6	12	48	22	5	11	+11	52	6	10	6	14	11	48	17	25	17	21	1	00	14	22	56	00
7	12	52	01	5	34	+12	10	6	11	6	16	11	48	17	23	17	19	1	04	11	22	52	04
8	12	55	41	5	57	+12	27	6	13	6	18	11	47	17	21	17	16	1	08	07	22	48	08
9	12	59	20	6	20	+12	43	6	15	6	20	11	47	17	18	17	14	1	12	04	22	44	12
10	13	03	01	6	43	+13	00	6	17	6	22	11	47	17	16	17	11	1	16	00	22	40	16
11	13	06	42	7	05	+13	15	6	18	6	24	11	47	17	14	17	09	1	19	57	22	36	20
12	13	10	23	7	28	+13	30	6	20	6	26	11	46	17	12	17	06	1	23	54	22	32	24
13	13	14	05	7	50	+13	45	6	22	6	28	11	46	17	10	17	03	1	27	50	22	28	28
14	13	17	48	8	13	+13	59	6	23	6	30	11	46	17	07	17	01	1	31	47	22	24	32
15	13	21	31	8	35	+14	12	6	25	6	32	11	46	17	05	16	58	1	35	43	22	20	37
16	13	25	14	8	57	+14	25	6	27	6	34	11	45	17	03	16	56	1	39	40	22	16	41
17	13	28	59	9	19	+14	38	6	29	6	36	11	45	17	01	16	54	1	43	36	22	12	45
18	13	32	43	9	41	+14	50	6	31	6	38	11	45	16	59	16	51	1	47	33	22	08	49
19	13	36	29	10	03	+15	01	6	32	6	40	11	45	16	57	16	49	1	51	29	22	04	53
20	13	40	15	10	24	+15	11	6	34	6	42	11	45	16	55	16	46	1	55	26	22	00	57
21	13	44	01	10	46	+15	21	6	36	6	44	11	45	16	53	16	44	1	59	23	21	57	01
22	13	47	49	11	07	+15	30	6	38	6	46	11	44	16	50	16	41	2	03	19	21	53	05
23	13	51	37	11	28	+15	39	6	39	6	49	11	44	16	48	16	39	2	07	16	21	49	09
24	13	55	25	11	49	+15	47	6	41	6	51	11	44	16	46	16	37	2	11	12	21	45	13
25	13	59	14	12	10	+15	54	6	43	6	53	11	44	16	44	16	34	2	15	09	21	41	17
26	14	03	04	12	30	+16	01	6	45	6	55	11	44	16	42	16	32	2	19	05	21	37	22
27	14	06	55	12	51	+16	07	6	46	6	57	11	44	16	40	16	30	2	23	02	21	33	26
28	14	10	47	13	11	+16	12	6	48	6	59	11	44	16	39	16	28	2	26	58	21	29	30
29	14	14	39	13	31	+16	16	6	50	7	01	11	44	16	37	16	25	2	30	55	21	25	34
30	14	18	32	13	50	+16	20	6	52	7	03	11	44	16	35	16	23	2	34	52	21	21	38
31	14	22	25	14	10	+16	23	6	54	7	06	11	44	16	33	16	21	2	38	48	21	17	42

DURATION OF TWILIGHT (in minutes)

Latitude	52°	56°	52°	56°	52°	56°	52°	56°
	1 October		11 October		21 October		31 October	
Civil	34	37	34	37	34	38	35	39
Nautical	73	80	73	80	74	81	75	83
Astronomical	113	125	112	124	113	124	114	126

THE NIGHT SKY

Mercury, although reaching greatest eastern elongation (24 degrees) on the 26th remains unsuitably placed for observation throughout October.

Venus is still a magnificent object in the eastern sky in the early mornings for about three hours before dawn, magnitude −4.1. The planet passes only about 0.1 degrees below Regulus, closest approach being around 2 hours after sunrise on the morning of the 3rd. On the 12th the thin crescent Moon passes 6 degrees south of Venus.

Mars is unsuitably placed for observation.

Jupiter continues to be visible in the evening skies as a brilliant object, magnitude −2.6. It reaches its first stationary point on the 4th and then moves slowly retrograde in the constellation of Taurus. On the 5th the waning gibbous Moon passes about 1 degree south of the planet. The four Galilean satellites are readily observable with a small telescope or even a good pair of binoculars provided that they are held rigidly.

Saturn remains too close to the Sun for observation throughout October as it passes through conjunction on the 25th.

THE MOON

Day	R.A.		Dec.	Hor. Par.	Semi-diam.	Sun's Co-Long.	PA. of Br. Limb	Ph.	Age	Rise 52°		Rise 56°		Transit		Set 52°		Set 56°	
	h	m	°	'	'	°	°	%	d	h	m	h	m	h	m	h	m	h	m
1	1	02	+10.1	55.1	15.0	96	49	99	14.9	17	46	17	35	0	22	7	33	7	43
2	1	49	+13.7	54.7	14.9	108	63	97	15.9	18	13	17	58	1	07	8	40	8	54
3	2	38	+16.8	54.4	14.8	120	70	92	16.9	18	43	18	25	1	53	9	44	10	01
4	3	27	+19.0	54.2	14.8	132	76	87	17.9	19	20	18	59	2	40	10	44	11	04
5	4	17	+20.5	54.1	14.7	145	81	80	18.9	20	03	19	41	3	27	11	39	12	01
6	5	08	+21.0	54.2	14.8	157	86	72	19.9	20	53	20	32	4	16	12	28	12	50
7	5	58	+20.6	54.4	14.8	169	91	63	20.9	21	50	21	31	5	04	13	10	13	30
8	6	49	+19.3	54.8	14.9	181	95	53	21.9	22	53	22	37	5	52	13	46	14	03
9	7	40	+17.0	55.4	15.1	193	99	43	22.9	—		23	48	6	40	14	16	14	30
10	8	30	+14.0	56.1	15.3	206	102	34	23.9	0	00	—		7	28	14	43	14	53
11	9	20	+10.2	56.9	15.5	218	105	24	24.9	1	11	1	03	8	16	15	07	15	13
12	10	11	+5.7	57.8	15.8	230	106	16	25.9	2	26	2	21	9	05	15	30	15	32
13	11	02	+0.9	58.7	16.0	242	105	9	26.9	3	42	3	42	9	54	15	53	15	51
14	11	55	−4.2	59.6	16.2	254	102	3	27.9	5	02	5	07	10	46	16	18	16	11
15	12	50	−9.1	60.2	16.4	267	87	0	28.9	6	24	6	34	11	40	16	46	16	35
16	13	48	−13.6	60.6	16.5	279	309	0	0.5	7	47	8	02	12	38	17	19	17	04
17	14	48	−17.3	60.8	16.6	291	290	3	1.5	9	09	9	27	13	38	18	01	17	41
18	15	50	−19.8	60.7	16.5	303	282	9	2.5	10	24	10	45	14	39	18	52	18	30
19	16	53	−20.9	60.3	16.4	315	275	17	3.5	11	29	11	51	15	40	19	53	19	31
20	17	56	−20.6	59.7	16.3	328	269	27	4.5	12	21	12	41	16	40	21	02	20	43
21	18	56	−19.0	59.1	16.1	340	263	37	5.5	13	03	13	20	17	36	22	16	22	00
22	19	53	−16.2	58.4	15.9	352	259	48	6.5	13	36	13	49	18	28	23	30	23	19
23	20	47	−12.7	57.6	15.7	4	256	59	7.5	14	02	14	11	19	18	—		—	
24	21	38	−8.6	57.0	15.5	16	253	70	8.5	14	26	14	31	20	05	0	44	0	36
25	22	27	−4.1	56.4	15.4	29	252	79	9.5	14	47	14	48	20	50	1	55	1	52
26	23	15	+0.4	55.8	15.2	41	252	86	10.5	15	07	15	05	21	34	3	06	3	06
27	0	02	+4.8	55.4	15.1	53	253	92	11.5	15	28	15	22	22	19	4	14	4	19
28	0	49	+9.0	54.9	15.0	65	256	97	12.5	15	50	15	40	23	03	5	22	5	31
29	1	36	+12.7	54.6	14.9	77	264	99	13.5	16	15	16	02	23	49	6	29	6	41
30	2	24	+15.9	54.3	14.8	89	32	100	14.5	16	44	16	27	—		7	33	7	49
31	3	13	+18.4	54.1	14.8	102	73	99	15.5	17	19	16	59	0	35	8	35	8	54

MERCURY

Day	R.A.		Dec.	Diam.	Phase	Transit		5° high 52°		56°	
	h	m	°	"	%	h	m	h	m	h	m
1	13	25	−9.4	5	91	12	46	17	20	17	08
3	13	37	−10.7	5	90	12	49	17	16	17	02
5	13	48	−12.0	5	89	12	52	17	11	16	56
7	13	59	−13.3	5	87	12	56	17	07	16	50
9	14	10	−14.5	5	86	12	59	17	02	16	44
11	14	21	−15.7	5	84	13	01	16	57	16	37
13	14	31	−16.8	5	82	13	04	16	53	16	31
15	14	42	−17.8	6	80	13	07	16	49	16	25
17	14	52	−18.8	6	78	13	09	16	44	16	19
19	15	02	−19.7	6	76	13	12	16	40	16	13
21	15	12	−20.5	6	73	13	14	16	35	16	06
23	15	22	−21.3	6	70	13	15	16	31	16	00
25	15	31	−21.9	6	67	13	16	16	27	15	55
27	15	40	−22.5	7	63	13	17	16	23	15	49
29	15	48	−23.0	7	58	13	17	16	19	15	43
31	15	55	−23.3	7	53	13	15	16	15	15	38

VENUS

Day	R.A.		Dec.	Diam.	Phase	Transit		5° high 52°		56°	
	h	m	°	"	%	h	m	h	m	h	m
1	9	58	+12.6	16	71	9	18	2	46	2	39
6	10	21	+10.8	15	73	9	21	2	58	2	53
11	10	44	+8.9	15	74	9	24	3	11	3	07
16	11	06	+6.9	14	76	9	27	3	24	3	22
21	11	29	+4.7	14	78	9	29	3	38	3	37
26	11	51	+2.5	14	79	9	32	3	52	3	53
31	12	13	+0.3	13	81	9	35	4	06	4	10

MARS

Day	R.A.		Dec.	Diam.	Phase	Transit		5° high 52°		56°	
	h	m	°	"	%	h	m	h	m	h	m
1	15	33	−20.0	5	93	14	51	18	18	17	51
6	15	47	−20.8	5	94	14	46	18	07	17	37
11	16	02	−21.6	5	94	14	41	17	56	17	24
16	16	17	−22.3	5	94	14	37	17	45	17	12
21	16	33	−22.9	5	94	14	33	17	36	17	01
26	16	48	−23.4	5	95	14	29	17	27	16	50
31	17	04	−23.9	5	95	14	25	17	20	16	41

SUNRISE AND SUNSET

d	London 0° 05'	51° 30'	Bristol 2° 35'	51° 28'	Birmingham 1° 55'	52° 28'	Manchester 2° 15'	53° 28'	Newcastle 1° 37'	54° 59'	Glasgow 4° 14'	55° 52'	Belfast 5° 56'	54° 35'
	h m	h m	h m	h m	h m	h m	h m	h m	h m	h m	h m	h m	h m	h m
1	6 01	17 37	6 11	17 47	6 09	17 44	6 11	17 45	6 09	17 41	6 20	17 51	6 26	17 59
2	6 03	17 35	6 13	17 45	6 11	17 42	6 13	17 42	6 11	17 39	6 22	17 49	6 28	17 56
3	6 05	17 33	6 15	17 43	6 13	17 39	6 15	17 40	6 13	17 36	6 24	17 46	6 30	17 54
4	6 06	17 30	6 16	17 41	6 14	17 37	6 17	17 38	6 15	17 34	6 26	17 44	6 32	17 51
5	6 08	17 28	6 18	17 38	6 16	17 35	6 18	17 35	6 17	17 31	6 28	17 41	6 34	17 49
6	6 10	17 26	6 20	17 36	6 18	17 32	6 20	17 33	6 19	17 29	6 30	17 38	6 36	17 47
7	6 11	17 24	6 21	17 34	6 20	17 30	6 22	17 31	6 21	17 26	6 32	17 36	6 38	17 44
8	6 13	17 22	6 23	17 32	6 21	17 28	6 24	17 28	6 23	17 24	6 34	17 33	6 40	17 42
9	6 15	17 19	6 25	17 29	6 23	17 26	6 26	17 26	6 25	17 21	6 36	17 31	6 42	17 39
10	6 16	17 17	6 26	17 27	6 25	17 23	6 27	17 23	6 27	17 19	6 38	17 28	6 43	17 37
11	6 18	17 15	6 28	17 25	6 27	17 21	6 29	17 21	6 29	17 16	6 40	17 26	6 45	17 34
12	6 20	17 13	6 30	17 23	6 28	17 19	6 31	17 19	6 31	17 14	6 42	17 23	6 47	17 32
13	6 21	17 11	6 31	17 21	6 30	17 17	6 33	17 16	6 33	17 12	6 45	17 21	6 49	17 29
14	6 23	17 08	6 33	17 19	6 32	17 14	6 35	17 14	6 35	17 09	6 47	17 18	6 51	17 27
15	6 25	17 06	6 35	17 16	6 34	17 12	6 37	17 12	6 37	17 07	6 49	17 16	6 53	17 25
16	6 27	17 04	6 36	17 14	6 35	17 10	6 38	17 10	6 39	17 04	6 51	17 13	6 55	17 22
17	6 28	17 02	6 38	17 12	6 37	17 08	6 40	17 07	6 41	17 02	6 53	17 11	6 57	17 20
18	6 30	17 00	6 40	17 10	6 39	17 06	6 42	17 05	6 43	17 00	6 55	17 08	6 59	17 18
19	6 32	16 58	6 42	17 08	6 41	17 03	6 44	17 03	6 44	16 57	6 57	17 06	7 01	17 15
20	6 33	16 56	6 43	17 06	6 43	17 01	6 46	17 01	6 47	16 55	6 59	17 03	7 03	17 13
21	6 35	16 54	6 45	17 04	6 44	16 59	6 48	16 59	6 49	16 53	7 01	17 01	7 05	17 11
22	6 37	16 52	6 47	17 02	6 46	16 57	6 50	16 56	6 51	16 50	7 03	16 59	7 07	17 09
23	6 39	16 50	6 49	17 00	6 48	16 55	6 52	16 54	6 53	16 48	7 05	16 56	7 09	17 06
24	6 40	16 48	6 50	16 58	6 50	16 53	6 53	16 52	6 55	16 46	7 07	16 54	7 11	17 04
25	6 42	16 46	6 52	16 56	6 52	16 51	6 55	16 50	6 57	16 44	7 09	16 52	7 13	17 02
26	6 44	16 44	6 54	16 54	6 53	16 49	6 57	16 48	6 59	16 41	7 11	16 49	7 15	17 00
27	6 46	16 42	6 56	16 52	6 55	16 47	6 59	16 46	7 01	16 39	7 14	16 47	7 17	16 57
28	6 47	16 40	6 57	16 50	6 57	16 45	7 01	16 44	7 03	16 37	7 16	16 45	7 19	16 55
29	6 49	16 38	6 59	16 48	6 59	16 43	7 03	16 42	7 05	16 35	7 18	16 43	7 21	16 53
30	6 51	16 36	7 01	16 46	7 01	16 41	7 05	16 40	7 07	16 33	7 20	16 40	7 23	16 51
31	6 53	16 34	7 03	16 45	7 03	16 39	7 07	16 38	7 09	16 31	7 22	16 38	7 25	16 49

JUPITER

Day	R.A. h m	Dec. ° '	Transit h m	5° high 52° h m	56° h m
1	5 01.1	+21 55	4 20	20 52	20 36
11	5 00.9	+21 55	3 40	20 13	19 56
21	4 59.2	+21 52	2 59	19 32	19 15
31	4 56.2	+21 47	2 17	18 50	18 34

Diameters – equatorial 45" polar 42"

SATURN

Day	R.A. h m	Dec. ° '	Transit h m	5° high 52° h m	56° h m
1	13 52.7	−9 10	13 10	17 48	17 36
11	13 57.1	−9 35	12 35	17 10	16 58
21	14 01.7	−10 00	12 01	16 33	16 20
31	14 06.3	−10 25	11 26	15 56	15 43

Diameters – equatorial 15" polar 14"
Rings – major axis 35" minor axis 10"

URANUS

Day	R.A. h m	Dec. ° '	Transit h m	10° high 52° h m	56° h m
1	0 25.0	+1 53	23 40	4 48	4 43
11	0 23.5	+1 44	23 00	4 07	4 01
21	0 22.1	+1 35	22 19	3 25	3 20
31	0 20.9	+1 27	21 38	2 44	2 38

Diameter 4"

NEPTUNE

Day	R.A. h m	Dec. ° '	Transit h m	10° high 52° h m	56° h m
1	22 12.3	−11 46	21 28	1 17	0 57
11	22 11.6	−11 50	20 48	0 36	0 16
21	22 11.1	−11 53	20 08	23 52	23 32
31	22 10.8	−11 55	19 29	23 12	22 52

Diameter 2"

NOVEMBER 2012

ELEVENTH MONTH, 30 DAYS. *Novem* (nine), ninth month of Roman pre-Julian calendar

1	*Thursday*	The USA tested the first hydrogen bomb, codenamed 'Ivy Mike', detonated in the Pacific 1952	day 306
2	*Friday*	Aviation pioneer Howard Hughes flew his eight-engine wooden aeroplane *Spruce Goose* for one minute 1947	307
3	*Saturday*	The Soviet Union launched the first living creature into space, a dog named Laika 1957	308
4	*Sunday*	Benjamin Palmer was granted the first patent in the USA for an artificial leg 1846	309
5	*Monday*	Fred Whipple, astronomer who proposed the 'dirty snowball' hypothesis for comets *b.* 1906 week 45 day 310
6	*Tuesday*	Adolphe Sax, musical instrument designer best known for inventing the saxophone *b.* 1814	311
7	*Wednesday*	Marie Curie, chemist and physicist who discovered radium and won two Nobel prizes *b.* 1867	312
8	*Thursday*	Wilhelm Conrad Röntgen, physicist, observed x-rays for the first time 1895	313
9	*Friday*	Physicist Gordon Gould wrote down the principles for his invention, the laser, but failed to patent his idea 1957	314
10	*Saturday*	Fred Cohen presented his creation, the computer virus, to a security seminar in the USA 1983	315
11	*Sunday*	Construction began on the Manchester Ship Canal, which took just over six years to complete 1887	316
12	*Monday*	*Voyager 1* began sending images of Saturn's rings 1.5 billion kilometres back to Earth 1980 week 46 day 317
13	*Tuesday*	An aeroplane spread pellets of dry ice at 4,000 metres creating artificial snow for the first time 1946	318
14	*Wednesday*	Edward H. White II became the first to walk in space, during the orbital flight of Gemini 4 *b.* 1930	319
15	*Thursday*	King Camp Gillette received a patent for his safety razor, which used disposable blades 1904	320
16	*Friday*	The discovery of Americium (atomic number 95) and curium (96), two new elements, was announced 1945	321
17	*Saturday*	Doug Engelbart, inventor and computer pioneer, was issued a patent for the computer mouse 1970	322
18	*Sunday*	Alan Shepard Jr, the USA's first man in space and one of 12 men to have walked on the Moon *b.* 1923	323
19	*Monday*	Blackfriars Bridge, designed by Robert Mylne, was opened 1769 week 47 day 324
20	*Tuesday*	Edwin Powell Hubble, astronomer who provided evidence of the expansion of the universe *b.* 1889	325
21	*Wednesday*	Two Frenchmen made the first manned hot-air balloon flight, travelling 8 kilometres in 25 minutes 1783	326
22	*Thursday*	Concorde began operating flights between New York and Europe with a flight time under 3.5 hours 1977	327
23	*Friday*	Octave Chanute, pioneer of aviation who heavily influenced Orville and Wilbur Wright *d.* 1910	328
24	*Saturday*	Charles Darwin's groundbreaking *On the Origin of Species* was published and sold out immediately 1859	329
25	*Sunday*	In the USA, Leroy Parsons established cable television 1948	330
26	*Monday*	John Newlands, chemist who first ordered chemical elements by their atomic weights week 48 day 331 *b.* 1837
27	*Tuesday*	Anders Celsius, physicist who developed the eponymous temperature scale *b.* 1701	332
28	*Wednesday*	Skywriting was demonstrated in the USA for the first time 1922	333
29	*Thursday*	The first US underground atomic bomb test, codenamed 'Uncle', was detonated 1951	334
30	*Friday*	A 4 kilogram meteorite hit Elizabeth Hodges after it crashed through her roof in Alabama, USA 1954	335

ASTRONOMICAL PHENOMENA

d h
2 01 Jupiter in conjunction with Moon. Jupiter 0°.9 N.
6 23 Mercury at stationary point
11 08 Neptune at stationary point
11 14 Venus in conjunction with Moon. Venus 5°N.
12 18 Saturn in conjunction with Moon. Saturn 4°N.
13 22 Total eclipse of Sun (see page 682)
14 11 Mercury in conjunction with Moon. Mercury 1°S.
16 10 Mars in conjunction with Moon. Mars 4°S.
17 16 Mercury in inferior conjunction
21 22 Sun's longitude 240° ♐
26 23 Mercury at stationary point
27 01 Saturn in conjunction with Venus. Saturn 0°.5 N.
29 01 Jupiter in conjunction with Moon. Jupiter 0°.6 N.

MINIMA OF ALGOL

d	h	d	h	d	h
1	22.8	13	10.1	24	21.3
4	19.6	16	06.9	27	18.1
7	16.4	19	03.7	30	15.0
10	13.2	22	00.5		

CONSTELLATIONS

The following constellations are near their meridian at

d	h		d	h
October	1	24	November	15	21
October	16	23	December	1	20
November	1	22	December	16	19

Ursa Major (below the Pole), Cepheus, Cassiopeia, Andromeda, Pegasus, Pisces, Aquarius and Cetus

THE MOON

Phases, Apsides and Node	d	h	m
☾ Last Quarter	7	00	36
● New Moon	13	22	08
☽ First Quarter	20	14	31
○ Full Moon	28	14	46
Apogee (406,030km)	1	15	18
Perigee (357,365km)	14	10	15
Apogee (406,360km)	28	19	19

Mean longitude of ascending node on November 1, 237°

SUNRISE AND SUNSET

	London 0° 05′	51° 30′	Bristol 2° 35′	51° 28′	Birmingham 1° 55′	52° 28′	Manchester 2° 15′	53° 28′	Newcastle 1° 37′	54° 59′	Glasgow 4° 14′	55° 52′	Belfast 5° 56′	54° 35′
d	h m	h m	h m	h m	h m	h m	h m	h m	h m	h m	h m	h m	h m	h m
1	6 54	16 33	7 04	16 43	7 04	16 37	7 09	16 36	7 11	16 28	7 24	16 36	7 27	16 47
2	6 56	16 31	7 06	16 41	7 06	16 35	7 11	16 34	7 13	16 26	7 26	16 34	7 29	16 45
3	6 58	16 29	7 08	16 39	7 08	16 34	7 12	16 32	7 15	16 24	7 28	16 32	7 31	16 43
4	7 00	16 27	7 10	16 37	7 10	16 32	7 14	16 30	7 17	16 22	7 31	16 30	7 33	16 41
5	7 01	16 26	7 11	16 36	7 12	16 30	7 16	16 28	7 19	16 20	7 33	16 28	7 35	16 39
6	7 03	16 24	7 13	16 34	7 14	16 28	7 18	16 26	7 21	16 19	7 35	16 26	7 37	16 37
7	7 05	16 22	7 15	16 33	7 15	16 27	7 20	16 25	7 23	16 17	7 37	16 24	7 39	16 35
8	7 07	16 21	7 17	16 31	7 17	16 25	7 22	16 23	7 25	16 15	7 39	16 22	7 41	16 34
9	7 09	16 19	7 18	16 29	7 19	16 23	7 24	16 21	7 27	16 13	7 41	16 20	7 43	16 32
10	7 10	16 18	7 20	16 28	7 21	16 22	7 26	16 19	7 29	16 11	7 43	16 18	7 45	16 30
11	7 12	16 16	7 22	16 26	7 23	16 20	7 28	16 18	7 31	16 09	7 45	16 16	7 47	16 28
12	7 14	16 15	7 24	16 25	7 25	16 19	7 30	16 16	7 33	16 08	7 47	16 14	7 49	16 26
13	7 15	16 13	7 25	16 23	7 26	16 17	7 31	16 15	7 35	16 06	7 49	16 12	7 51	16 25
14	7 17	16 12	7 27	16 22	7 28	16 16	7 33	16 13	7 37	16 04	7 51	16 11	7 53	16 23
15	7 19	16 11	7 29	16 21	7 30	16 14	7 35	16 12	7 39	16 03	7 54	16 09	7 55	16 22
16	7 21	16 09	7 30	16 19	7 32	16 13	7 37	16 10	7 41	16 01	7 56	16 07	7 56	16 20
17	7 22	16 08	7 32	16 18	7 33	16 11	7 39	16 09	7 43	15 59	7 58	16 06	7 58	16 19
18	7 24	16 07	7 34	16 17	7 35	16 10	7 41	16 07	7 45	15 58	8 00	16 04	8 00	16 17
19	7 26	16 05	7 36	16 16	7 37	16 09	7 42	16 06	7 47	15 57	8 02	16 03	8 02	16 16
20	7 27	16 04	7 37	16 14	7 39	16 08	7 44	16 05	7 49	15 55	8 04	16 01	8 04	16 14
21	7 29	16 03	7 39	16 13	7 40	16 07	7 46	16 03	7 51	15 54	8 06	16 00	8 06	16 13
22	7 31	16 02	7 40	16 12	7 42	16 05	7 48	16 02	7 52	15 52	8 07	15 58	8 08	16 12
23	7 32	16 01	7 42	16 11	7 44	16 04	7 49	16 01	7 54	15 51	8 09	15 57	8 10	16 10
24	7 34	16 00	7 44	16 10	7 45	16 03	7 51	16 00	7 56	15 50	8 11	15 56	8 11	16 09
25	7 35	15 59	7 45	16 09	7 47	16 02	7 53	15 59	7 58	15 49	8 13	15 55	8 13	16 08
26	7 37	15 58	7 47	16 08	7 48	16 01	7 54	15 58	8 00	15 48	8 15	15 53	8 15	16 07
27	7 38	15 57	7 48	16 08	7 50	16 00	7 56	15 57	8 01	15 47	8 17	15 52	8 17	16 06
28	7 40	15 57	7 50	16 07	7 52	16 00	7 58	15 56	8 03	15 46	8 18	15 51	8 18	16 05
29	7 41	15 56	7 51	16 06	7 53	15 59	7 59	15 55	8 05	15 45	8 20	15 50	8 20	16 04
30	7 43	15 55	7 53	16 05	7 55	15 58	8 01	15 54	8 06	15 44	8 22	15 49	8 21	16 03

JUPITER

Day	R.A.		Dec.		Transit		5° high			
							52°		56°	
	h	m	°	′	h	m	h	m	h	m
1	4	55.9	+21	47	2	13	18	46	18	29
11	4	51.6	+21	40	1	29	18	03	17	47
21	4	46.4	+21	32	0	45	17	19	17	03
31	4	40.7	+21	23	0	00	16	35	16	19

Diameters – equatorial 48″ polar 45″

SATURN

Day	R.A.		Dec.		Transit		5° high			
							52°		56°	
	h	m	°	′	h	m	h	m	h	m
1	14	06.8	−10	28	11	22	6	53	7	06
11	14	11.4	−10	51	10	48	6	20	6	34
21	14	15.9	−11	14	10	13	5	47	6	01
31	14	20.2	−11	35	9	38	5	15	5	29

Diameters – equatorial 15″ polar 14″
Rings – major axis 35″ minor axis 10″

URANUS

Day	R.A.		Dec.		Transit		10° high			
							52°		56°	
	h	m	°	′	h	m	h	m	h	m
1	0	20.8	+1	26	21	34	2	40	2	34
11	0	19.7	+1	20	20	54	1	59	1	53
21	0	18.9	+1	15	20	14	1	18	1	12
31	0	18.3	+1	12	19	34	0	38	0	32

Diameter 4″

NEPTUNE

Day	R.A.		Dec.		Transit		10° high			
							52°		56°	
	h	m	°	′	h	m	h	m	h	m
1	22	10.7	−11	55	19	25	23	08	22	48
11	22	10.6	−11	55	18	45	22	29	22	09
21	22	10.7	−11	55	18	06	21	50	21	29
31	22	11.0	−11	53	17	27	21	11	20	51

Diameter 2″

DECEMBER 2012

TWELFTH MONTH, 31 DAYS. *Decem* (ten), tenth month of Roman pre-Julian calendar

1	Saturday	Workers broke through the final wall to link the Channel Tunnel between the UK and France 1990	day 336
2	Sunday	Barney Clark became the first recipient of a permanent artificial heart, surviving for 112 days 1982	337

3	Monday	Samuel Crompton, inventor of the spinning mule *b.* 1753	week 49 day 338
4	Tuesday	Glenn L. Martin, aviation pioneer whose bomber planes played major parts in the Second World War *d.* 1955	339
5	Wednesday	The UK's first stretch of motorway, the Preston bypass (now part of the M6), was opened 1958	340
6	Thursday	Thomas Edison completed the first sound recording when he recited 'Mary Had a Little Lamb' 1877	341
7	Friday	Apollo 17, the sixth and final US mission to land men on the Moon, launched 1972	342
8	Saturday	Harrison Brown, best known for isolating plutonium for its use in the first atomic bombs *d.* 1986	343
9	Sunday	Astronauts completed repairs on the faulty Hubble Space Telescope by correcting a faulty lens 1993	344

10	Monday	The first Nobel prizes were awarded, on the fifth anniversary of Alfred Nobel's death 1901	week 50 day 345
11	Tuesday	The first dental anaesthetic, nitrous oxide ('laughing gas'), was used for a tooth extraction 1844	346
12	Wednesday	Radio pioneer Guglielmo Marconi sent the first radio transmission across the Atlantic 1901	347
13	Thursday	Gordo, a monkey, was lost in the Atlantic due to a technical problem after a 482 kilometre space journey 1958	348
14	Friday	*Rutan Voyager*, the first plane to fly non-stop around the world without refuelling, took off 1986	349
15	Saturday	The Chernobyl nuclear plant in Ukraine was shut down, 14 years after the infamous disaster 2000	350
16	Sunday	The Underground link from Heathrow airport to central London opened 1977	351

17	Monday	Sir Francis Beaufort, creator of the eponymous scale used to measure wind speeds *d.* 1857	week 51 day 352
18	Tuesday	Sir John Alcock, pilot who, in 1919, made the first non-stop transatlantic flight *d.*1919	353
19	Wednesday	The Williamsburg Bridge opened in New York City, becoming the world's longest suspension bridge 1903	354
20	Thursday	New York's Broadway became known as the 'Great White Way' after being lit by electricity 1880	355
21	Friday	Dried human blood serum was prepared for the first time; it was later used in the Second World War 1933	356
22	Saturday	Electric lights were first used to decorate Christmas trees by Edward Johnson 1882	357
23	Sunday	Apollo 8 astronauts became the first to orbit the Moon and escape the influence of Earth's gravity 1968	358

24	Monday	James Prescott Joule, physicist after whom the unit of energy is named *b.* 1818	week 52 day 359
25	Tuesday	Scientists failed to make contact with Beagle 2, a British probe which should have landed on Mars 2003	360
26	Wednesday	Charles Babbage, pioneer of mechanical computation who proposed the difference engine *b.* 1791	361
27	Thursday	*HMS Beagle*, with Charles Darwin aboard, left Plymouth on a voyage of scientific discovery 1831	362
28	Friday	The first commercial movie screening, *Workers Leaving The Lumière Factory in Lyon*, takes place 1895	363
29	Saturday	Cosmonaut Yuri Romanenko returned to Earth having spent a record 326 days aboard *Mir* 1987	364
30	Sunday	A second full moon of the month was visible (a 'blue moon') at the same time as a total lunar eclipse 1982	365

31	Monday	Donald Campbell broke the water speed record with an average 276.33mph in *Bluebird* 1964	week 53 day 366

ASTRONOMICAL PHENOMENA

d h
3 02 Jupiter at opposition
4 23 Mercury at greatest elongation W. 21°
10 10 Saturn in conjunction with Moon. Saturn 4°N.
11 13 Venus in conjunction with Moon. Venus 2°N.
12 00 Mercury in conjunction with Moon. Mercury 1°N.
13 12 Uranus at stationary point
15 08 Mars in conjunction with Moon. Mars 5°S.
21 11 Sun's longitude 270° ♑
26 00 Jupiter in conjunction with Moon. Jupiter 0°.4 N.
30 14 Pluto in conjunction

MINIMA OF ALGOL

d	h	d	h	d	h
3	11.8	14	23.1	26	10.3
6	08.6	17	19.9	29	07.2
9	05.4	20	16.7		
12	02.2	23	13.5		

CONSTELLATIONS

The following constellations are near their meridian at

	d	h		d	h
November	1	24	December	16	21
November	15	23	January	1	20
December	1	22	January	16	19

Ursa Major (below the Pole), Ursa Minor (below the Pole), Cassiopeia, Andromeda, Perseus, Triangulum, Aries, Taurus, Cetus and Eridanus

THE MOON

Phases, Apsides and Node	d	h	m
☾ Last Quarter	6	15	31
● New Moon	13	08	42
☽ First Quarter	20	05	19
○ Full Moon	28	10	21

Perigee (357,071km)	12	23	07
Apogee (406,117 km)	25	21	06

Mean longitude of ascending node on December 1, 235°

THE SUN

s.d. 16'.3

Day	Right Ascension			Dec.		Equation of time		Rise 52°		Rise 56°		Transit		Set 52°		Set 56°		Sidereal time			Transit of first point of Aries		
	h	m	s	°	'	m	s	h	m	h	m	h	m	h	m	h	m	h	m	s	h	m	s
1	16	30	01	21	50	+11	00	7	46	8	07	11	49	15	52	15	31	4	41	01	19	15	49
2	16	34	21	21	59	+10	37	7	47	8	09	11	50	15	51	15	30	4	44	58	19	11	53
3	16	38	41	22	07	+10	14	7	49	8	11	11	50	15	51	15	29	4	48	54	19	07	57
4	16	43	01	22	15	+9	50	7	50	8	12	11	50	15	50	15	28	4	52	51	19	04	01
5	16	47	22	22	23	+9	25	7	51	8	14	11	51	15	50	15	28	4	56	48	19	00	05
6	16	51	44	22	31	+9	00	7	53	8	15	11	51	15	49	15	27	5	00	44	18	56	09
7	16	56	06	22	37	+8	35	7	54	8	16	11	52	15	49	15	27	5	04	41	18	52	13
8	17	00	29	22	44	+8	09	7	55	8	18	11	52	15	49	15	26	5	08	37	18	48	17
9	17	04	52	22	50	+7	42	7	56	8	19	11	53	15	49	15	26	5	12	34	18	44	22
10	17	09	15	22	55	+7	15	7	57	8	20	11	53	15	48	15	25	5	16	30	18	40	26
11	17	13	39	23	01	+6	47	7	58	8	21	11	53	15	48	15	25	5	20	27	18	36	30
12	17	18	04	23	05	+6	19	7	59	8	23	11	54	15	48	15	25	5	24	23	18	32	34
13	17	22	29	23	09	+5	51	8	00	8	24	11	54	15	48	15	25	5	28	20	18	28	38
14	17	26	54	23	13	+5	23	8	01	8	25	11	55	15	48	15	25	5	32	17	18	24	42
15	17	31	19	23	16	+4	54	8	02	8	26	11	55	15	49	15	25	5	36	13	18	20	46
16	17	35	45	23	19	+4	25	8	03	8	26	11	56	15	49	15	25	5	40	10	18	16	50
17	17	40	11	23	21	+3	55	8	04	8	27	11	56	15	49	15	25	5	44	06	18	12	54
18	17	44	37	23	23	+3	26	8	04	8	28	11	57	15	49	15	26	5	48	03	18	08	58
19	17	49	03	23	25	+2	56	8	05	8	29	11	57	15	50	15	26	5	51	59	18	05	02
20	17	53	29	23	26	+2	26	8	05	8	29	11	58	15	50	15	26	5	55	56	18	01	07
21	17	57	56	23	26	+1	57	8	06	8	30	11	58	15	51	15	27	5	59	52	17	57	11
22	18	02	22	23	26	+1	27	8	06	8	30	11	59	15	51	15	27	6	03	49	17	53	15
23	18	06	49	23	26	+0	57	8	07	8	31	11	59	15	52	15	28	6	07	46	17	49	19
24	18	11	15	23	25	+0	27	8	07	8	31	12	00	15	52	15	29	6	11	42	17	45	23
25	18	15	41	23	23	−0	02	8	08	8	31	12	00	15	53	15	29	6	15	39	17	41	27
26	18	20	07	23	21	−0	32	8	08	8	31	12	01	15	54	15	30	6	19	35	17	37	31
27	18	24	33	23	19	−1	02	8	08	8	32	12	01	15	55	15	31	6	23	32	17	33	35
28	18	28	59	23	16	−1	31	8	08	8	32	12	02	15	56	15	32	6	27	28	17	29	39
29	18	33	25	23	13	−2	00	8	08	8	32	12	02	15	56	15	33	6	31	25	17	25	43
30	18	37	50	23	09	−2	29	8	08	8	32	12	03	15	57	15	34	6	35	21	17	21	47
31	18	42	16	23	05	−2	58	8	08	8	31	12	03	15	58	15	35	6	39	18	17	17	51

DURATION OF TWILIGHT (in minutes)

Latitude	52°	56°	52°	56°	52°	56°	52°	56°
	1 December		11 December		21 December		31 December	
Civil	40	45	41	47	41	47	41	47
Nautical	82	93	84	96	85	97	84	96
Astronomical	123	138	125	141	126	142	125	141

THE NIGHT SKY

Mercury reaches greatest western elongation (21 degrees) on the 4th and continues to be visible as a morning object during the first half of the month, low above the east-north-eastern horizon. During this period its magnitude brightens from −0.3 to −0.5.

Venus, magnitude −4.0, is still visible as a magnificent object in the south-eastern sky in the mornings before dawn. It is now moving more rapidly towards the Sun and consequently rising later and later until by the end of December observers in southern England will have to wait until shortly after 07h, while those in Scotland will have to wait until about half-an-hour before sunrise. Given favourable conditions and a clear horizon observers may be able to see a line up of three planets, a star and the Moon low above the SE-SSE horizon around 07h on the morning of the 9th. From left to right they are Mercury, Venus, Saturn, Spica, and the waning crescent Moon.

However, atmospheric extinction may make it too difficult to spot Mercury at such a low altitude.

Mars remains unsuitably placed for observation.

Jupiter, magnitude −2.8, reaches opposition on the 3rd and is therefore visible throughout the hours of darkness. On the 7th Jupiter passes 5 degrees north of Aldebaran as it moves slowly retrograde in the constellation of Taurus. During the night of the 25th–26th the waxing gibbous Moon passes about 1 degree south of the planet.

Saturn, magnitude +0.6, can now be seen in the early mornings in the south-eastern quadrant of the sky after about 04h. Early in the month Saturn passes from Virgo into Libra. On the 10th the waning crescent Moon passes 5 degrees south of the planet.

Meteors. The maximum of the well known Geminid meteor shower occurs on the 13th. As there is a New Moon that day it will provide no interference.

THE MOON

Day	R.A.		Dec.	Hor. Par.	Semi- diam.	Sun's Co- Long.	PA. of Br. Limb	Ph.	Age	Rise				Transit		Set			
										52°		56°				52°		56°	
	h	m	°	'	'	°	°	%	d	h	m	h	m	h	m	h	m	h	m
1	6	21	+20.0	54.2	14.8	119	99	95	17.1	18	34	18	15	1	43	9	46	10	05
2	7	11	+18.3	54.4	14.8	131	102	90	18.1	19	36	19	21	2	31	10	19	10	35
3	8	01	+15.7	54.8	14.9	143	106	84	19.1	20	42	20	30	3	18	10	48	11	00
4	8	49	+12.5	55.2	15.1	155	109	76	20.1	21	50	21	43	4	04	11	12	11	22
5	9	37	+8.6	55.8	15.2	167	111	67	21.1	23	00	22	57	4	49	11	35	11	40
6	10	25	+4.3	56.6	15.4	179	112	57	22.1	—		—		5	35	11	56	11	58
7	11	14	−0.3	57.4	15.6	192	113	46	23.1	0	13	0	13	6	22	12	18	12	16
8	12	05	−5.1	58.3	15.9	204	112	36	24.1	1	27	1	32	7	10	12	41	12	35
9	12	57	−9.7	59.2	16.1	216	111	25	25.1	2	45	2	54	8	02	13	08	12	57
10	13	53	−14.0	60.1	16.4	228	108	16	26.1	4	06	4	19	8	57	13	40	13	25
11	14	53	−17.5	60.8	16.6	240	105	8	27.1	5	26	5	45	9	57	14	21	14	02
12	15	56	−19.9	61.2	16.7	253	103	3	28.1	6	43	7	05	10	59	15	13	14	51
13	17	01	−20.9	61.4	16.7	265	115	0	29.1	7	51	8	13	12	04	16	17	15	55
14	18	06	−20.4	61.2	16.7	277	251	1	0.7	8	47	9	07	13	07	17	31	17	12
15	19	10	−18.4	60.7	16.5	289	254	4	1.7	9	31	9	48	14	07	18	51	18	35
16	20	10	−15.2	60.0	16.3	301	251	10	2.7	10	05	10	18	15	03	20	10	19	59
17	21	06	−11.2	59.1	16.1	313	249	18	3.7	10	33	10	41	15	55	21	28	21	21
18	21	59	−6.7	58.1	15.8	326	247	28	4.7	10	57	11	01	16	44	22	42	22	40
19	22	50	−2.1	57.1	15.6	338	246	38	5.7	11	19	11	19	17	30	23	54	23	56
20	23	38	+2.5	56.3	15.3	350	246	48	6.7	11	40	11	36	18	15	—		—	
21	0	25	+6.9	55.5	15.1	2	247	58	7.7	12	01	11	53	18	59	1	03	1	09
22	1	12	+10.9	54.9	15.0	14	249	67	8.7	12	24	12	13	19	44	2	10	2	20
23	1	59	+14.3	54.5	14.8	26	251	76	9.7	12	50	12	35	20	29	3	16	3	29
24	2	48	+17.2	54.2	14.8	39	254	84	10.7	13	20	13	03	21	16	4	19	4	36
25	3	37	+19.3	54.0	14.7	51	256	90	11.7	13	56	13	36	22	03	5	19	5	39
26	4	27	+20.6	54.0	14.7	63	259	95	12.7	14	39	14	18	22	52	6	15	6	36
27	5	17	+20.9	54.1	14.7	75	258	98	13.7	15	29	15	08	23	40	7	04	7	25
28	6	08	+20.4	54.2	14.8	87	238	100	14.7	16	26	16	07	—		7	46	8	06
29	6	59	+18.9	54.4	14.8	99	127	100	15.7	17	28	17	11	0	28	8	22	8	39
30	7	49	+16.5	54.7	14.9	111	115	98	16.7	18	33	18	20	1	16	8	52	9	06
31	8	38	+13.4	55.1	15.0	123	114	94	17.7	19	41	19	32	2	02	9	18	9	29

MERCURY

Day	R.A.		Dec.	Diam.	Phase	Transit		5° high			
								52°		56°	
	h	m	°	"	%	h	m	h	m	h	m
1	15	11	−15.1	7	48	10	30	6	28	6	47
3	15	17	−15.6	7	56	10	28	6	30	6	49
5	15	24	−16.2	7	62	10	27	6	33	6	54
7	15	33	−16.9	6	68	10	28	6	39	7	01
9	15	42	−17.7	6	73	10	30	6	46	7	09
11	15	52	−18.4	6	77	10	33	6	54	7	18
13	16	03	−19.2	6	81	10	36	7	03	7	29
15	16	15	−20.0	6	84	10	39	7	12	7	39
17	16	26	−20.7	5	86	10	43	7	22	7	51
19	16	38	−21.4	5	88	10	48	7	31	8	02
21	16	51	−22.0	5	90	10	52	7	41	8	14
23	17	03	−22.6	5	92	10	57	7	50	8	25
25	17	16	−23.1	5	93	11	02	8	00	8	36
27	17	29	−23.5	5	94	11	07	8	09	8	46
29	17	43	−23.9	5	95	11	13	8	17	8	56
31	17	56	−24.1	5	96	11	18	8	25	9	05

VENUS

Day	R.A.		Dec.	Diam.	Phase	Transit		5° high			
								52°		56°	
	h	m	°	"	%	h	m	h	m	h	m
1	14	37	−13.6	12	88	9	56	5	45	6	01
6	15	01	−15.5	12	89	10	01	6	02	6	21
11	15	26	−17.3	11	90	10	06	6	19	6	41
16	15	51	−18.8	11	91	10	12	6	36	7	01
21	16	17	−20.2	11	92	10	18	6	52	7	20
26	16	44	−21.3	11	93	10	25	7	08	7	38
31	17	10	−22.2	11	94	10	32	7	22	7	55

MARS

Day	R.A.		Dec.	Diam.	Phase	Transit		5° high			
								52°		56°	
	h	m	°	"	%	h	m	h	m	h	m
1	18	46	−24.2	4	97	14	05	16	58	16	19
6	19	03	−23.8	4	97	14	02	16	59	16	21
11	19	20	−23.3	4	97	13	59	17	00	16	24
16	19	37	−22.8	4	97	13	56	17	02	16	28
21	19	53	−22.1	4	97	13	53	17	05	16	33
26	20	10	−21.3	4	98	13	50	17	08	16	38
31	20	26	−20.4	4	98	13	46	17	12	16	44

SUNRISE AND SUNSET

	London				Bristol				Birmingham				Manchester				Newcastle				Glasgow				Belfast			
	0° 05'		51° 30'		2° 35'		51° 28'		1° 55'		52° 28'		2° 15'		53° 28'		1° 37'		54° 59'		4° 14'		55° 52'		5° 56'		54° 35'	
d	h	m	h	m	h	m	h	m	h	m	h	m	h	m	h	m	h	m	h	m	h	m	h	m	h	m	h	m
1	7	44	15	55	7	54	16	05	7	56	15	57	8	02	15	54	8	08	15	43	8	24	15	48	8	23	16	03
2	7	45	15	54	7	55	16	04	7	57	15	57	8	04	15	53	8	09	15	42	8	25	15	48	8	25	16	02
3	7	47	15	54	7	57	16	04	7	59	15	56	8	05	15	52	8	11	15	42	8	27	15	47	8	26	16	01
4	7	48	15	53	7	58	16	03	8	00	15	56	8	07	15	52	8	12	15	41	8	28	15	46	8	27	16	00
5	7	49	15	53	7	59	16	03	8	01	15	55	8	08	15	51	8	14	15	40	8	30	15	45	8	29	16	00
6	7	51	15	52	8	00	16	02	8	03	15	55	8	09	15	51	8	15	15	40	8	31	15	45	8	30	15	59
7	7	52	15	52	8	02	16	02	8	04	15	54	8	11	15	51	8	17	15	39	8	33	15	44	8	32	15	59
8	7	53	15	52	8	03	16	02	8	05	15	54	8	12	15	50	8	18	15	39	8	34	15	44	8	33	15	59
9	7	54	15	51	8	04	16	02	8	06	15	54	8	13	15	50	8	19	15	39	8	35	15	44	8	34	15	58
10	7	55	15	51	8	05	16	01	8	07	15	54	8	14	15	50	8	20	15	38	8	36	15	43	8	35	15	58
11	7	56	15	51	8	06	16	01	8	08	15	54	8	15	15	50	8	21	15	38	8	38	15	43	8	36	15	58
12	7	57	15	51	8	07	16	01	8	09	15	54	8	16	15	49	8	23	15	38	8	39	15	43	8	37	15	58
13	7	58	15	51	8	08	16	01	8	10	15	54	8	17	15	49	8	24	15	38	8	40	15	43	8	38	15	58
14	7	59	15	51	8	09	16	02	8	11	15	54	8	18	15	50	8	25	15	38	8	41	15	43	8	39	15	58
15	8	00	15	51	8	10	16	02	8	12	15	54	8	19	15	50	8	25	15	38	8	42	15	43	8	40	15	58
16	8	01	15	52	8	10	16	02	8	13	15	54	8	20	15	50	8	26	15	38	8	42	15	43	8	41	15	58
17	8	01	15	52	8	11	16	02	8	14	15	54	8	21	15	50	8	27	15	38	8	43	15	43	8	42	15	58
18	8	02	15	52	8	12	16	02	8	14	15	55	8	21	15	50	8	28	15	39	8	44	15	43	8	43	15	58
19	8	03	15	53	8	12	16	03	8	15	15	55	8	22	15	51	8	28	15	39	8	45	15	44	8	43	15	59
20	8	03	15	53	8	13	16	03	8	16	15	55	8	22	15	51	8	29	15	39	8	45	15	44	8	44	15	59
21	8	04	15	54	8	14	16	04	8	16	15	56	8	23	15	52	8	30	15	40	8	46	15	45	8	44	16	00
22	8	04	15	54	8	14	16	04	8	17	15	56	8	24	15	52	8	30	15	40	8	46	15	45	8	45	16	00
23	8	05	15	55	8	14	16	05	8	17	15	57	8	24	15	53	8	30	15	41	8	47	15	46	8	45	16	01
24	8	05	15	55	8	15	16	05	8	17	15	58	8	24	15	53	8	31	15	42	8	47	15	46	8	46	16	01
25	8	05	15	56	8	15	16	06	8	18	15	58	8	25	15	54	8	31	15	42	8	47	15	47	8	46	16	02
26	8	06	15	57	8	15	16	07	8	18	15	59	8	25	15	55	8	31	15	43	8	48	15	48	8	46	16	03
27	8	06	15	58	8	16	16	08	8	18	16	00	8	25	15	56	8	31	15	44	8	48	15	49	8	46	16	04
28	8	06	15	58	8	16	16	09	8	18	16	01	8	25	15	57	8	32	15	45	8	48	15	50	8	46	16	05
29	8	06	15	59	8	16	16	09	8	18	16	02	8	25	15	58	8	32	15	46	8	48	15	51	8	46	16	06
30	8	06	16	00	8	16	16	10	8	18	16	03	8	25	15	59	8	31	15	47	8	48	15	52	8	46	16	07
31	8	06	16	01	8	16	16	11	8	18	16	04	8	25	16	00	8	31	15	48	8	47	15	53	8	46	16	08

JUPITER

Day	R.A.		Dec.		Transit		5° high			
							52°		56°	
	h	m	°	'	h	m	h	m	h	m
1	4	40.7	+21	23	0	00	7	20	7	36
11	4	34.9	+21	13	23	10	6	34	6	50
21	4	29.5	+21	03	22	26	5	48	6	04
31	4	24.9	+20	55	21	42	5	04	5	19

Diameters – equatorial 48" polar 45"

SATURN

Day	R.A.		Dec.		Transit		5° high			
							52°		56°	
	h	m	°	'	h	m	h	m	h	m
1	14	20.2	−11	35	9	38	5	15	5	29
11	14	24.2	−11	54	9	03	4	41	4	56
21	14	28.0	−12	11	8	27	4	07	4	22
31	14	31.3	−12	26	7	51	3	33	3	48

Diameters – equatorial 16" polar 14"
Rings – major axis 36" minor axis 11"

URANUS

Day	R.A.		Dec.		Transit		10° high			
							52°		56°	
	h	m	°	'	h	m	h	m	h	m
1	0	18.3	+1	12	19	34	0	38	0	32
11	0	18.1	+1	10	18	55	23	54	23	49
21	0	18.2	+1	11	18	15	23	15	23	10
31	0	18.5	+1	14	17	36	22	37	22	31

Diameter 4"

NEPTUNE

Day	R.A.		Dec.		Transit		10° high			
							52°		56°	
	h	m	°	'	h	m	h	m	h	m
1	22	11.0	−11	53	17	27	21	11	20	51
11	22	11.6	−11	50	16	48	20	33	20	12
21	22	12.3	−11	45	16	10	19	55	19	34
31	22	13.2	−11	40	15	32	19	17	18	57

Diameter 2"

RISING AND SETTING TIMES

TABLE 1. SEMI-DIURNAL ARCS (HOUR ANGLES AT RISING/SETTING)

Dec.	Latitude 0°	10°	20°	30°	40°	45°	50°	52°	54°	56°	58°	60°	Dec.
	h m	h m	h m	h m	h m	h m	h m	h m	h m	h m	h m	h m	
0°	6 00	6 00	6 00	6 00	6 00	6 00	6 00	6 00	6 00	6 00	6 00	6 00	0°
1°	6 00	6 01	6 01	6 02	6 03	6 04	6 05	6 05	6 06	6 06	6 06	6 07	1°
2°	6 00	6 01	6 03	6 05	6 07	6 08	6 10	6 10	6 11	6 12	6 13	6 14	2°
3°	6 00	6 02	6 04	6 07	6 10	6 12	6 14	6 15	6 17	6 18	6 19	6 21	3°
4°	6 00	6 03	6 06	6 09	6 13	6 16	6 19	6 21	6 22	6 24	6 26	6 28	4°
5°	6 00	6 04	6 07	6 12	6 17	6 20	6 24	6 26	6 28	6 30	6 32	6 35	5°
6°	6 00	6 04	6 09	6 14	6 20	6 24	6 29	6 31	6 33	6 36	6 39	6 42	6°
7°	6 00	6 05	6 10	6 16	6 24	6 28	6 34	6 36	6 39	6 42	6 45	6 49	7°
8°	6 00	6 06	6 12	6 19	6 27	6 32	6 39	6 41	6 45	6 48	6 52	6 56	8°
9°	6 00	6 06	6 13	6 21	6 31	6 36	6 44	6 47	6 50	6 54	6 59	7 04	9°
10°	6 00	6 07	6 15	6 23	6 34	6 41	6 49	6 52	6 56	7 01	7 06	7 11	10°
11°	6 00	6 08	6 16	6 26	6 38	6 45	6 54	6 58	7 02	7 07	7 12	7 19	11°
12°	6 00	6 09	6 18	6 28	6 41	6 49	6 59	7 03	7 08	7 13	7 20	7 26	12°
13°	6 00	6 09	6 19	6 31	6 45	6 53	7 04	7 09	7 14	7 20	7 27	7 34	13°
14°	6 00	6 10	6 21	6 33	6 48	6 58	7 09	7 14	7 20	7 27	7 34	7 42	14°
15°	6 00	6 11	6 22	6 36	6 52	7 02	7 14	7 20	7 27	7 34	7 42	7 51	15°
16°	6 00	6 12	6 24	6 38	6 56	7 07	7 20	7 26	7 33	7 41	7 49	7 59	16°
17°	6 00	6 12	6 26	6 41	6 59	7 11	7 25	7 32	7 40	7 48	7 57	8 08	17°
18°	6 00	6 13	6 27	6 43	7 03	7 16	7 31	7 38	7 46	7 55	8 05	8 17	18°
19°	6 00	6 14	6 29	6 46	7 07	7 21	7 37	7 45	7 53	8 03	8 14	8 26	19°
20°	6 00	6 15	6 30	6 49	7 11	7 25	7 43	7 51	8 00	8 11	8 22	8 36	20°
21°	6 00	6 16	6 32	6 51	7 15	7 30	7 49	7 58	8 08	8 19	8 32	8 47	21°
22°	6 00	6 16	6 34	6 54	7 19	7 35	7 55	8 05	8 15	8 27	8 41	8 58	22°
23°	6 00	6 17	6 36	6 57	7 23	7 40	8 02	8 12	8 23	8 36	8 51	9 09	23°
24°	6 00	6 18	6 37	7 00	7 28	7 46	8 08	8 19	8 31	8 45	9 02	9 22	24°
25°	6 00	6 19	6 39	7 02	7 32	7 51	8 15	8 27	8 40	8 55	9 13	9 35	25°
26°	6 00	6 20	6 41	7 05	7 37	7 57	8 22	8 35	8 49	9 05	9 25	9 51	26°
27°	6 00	6 21	6 43	7 08	7 41	8 03	8 30	8 43	8 58	9 16	9 39	10 08	27°
28°	6 00	6 22	6 45	7 12	7 46	8 08	8 37	8 52	9 08	9 28	9 53	10 28	28°
29°	6 00	6 22	6 47	7 15	7 51	8 15	8 45	9 01	9 19	9 41	10 10	10 55	29°
30°	6 00	6 23	6 49	7 18	7 56	8 21	8 54	9 11	9 30	9 55	10 30	12 00	30°
35°	6 00	6 28	6 59	7 35	8 24	8 58	9 46	10 15	10 58	12 00	12 00	12 00	35°
40°	6 00	6 34	7 11	7 56	8 59	9 48	12 00	12 00	12 00	12 00	12 00	12 00	40°
45°	6 00	6 41	7 25	8 21	9 48	12 00	12 00	12 00	12 00	12 00	12 00	12 00	45°
50°	6 00	6 49	7 43	8 54	12 00	12 00	12 00	12 00	12 00	12 00	12 00	12 00	50°
55°	6 00	6 58	8 05	9 42	12 00	12 00	12 00	12 00	12 00	12 00	12 00	12 00	55°
60°	6 00	7 11	8 36	12 00	12 00	12 00	12 00	12 00	12 00	12 00	12 00	12 00	60°
65°	6 00	7 29	9 25	12 00	12 00	12 00	12 00	12 00	12 00	12 00	12 00	12 00	65°
70°	6 00	7 56	12 00	12 00	12 00	12 00	12 00	12 00	12 00	12 00	12 00	12 00	70°
75°	6 00	8 45	12 00	12 00	12 00	12 00	12 00	12 00	12 00	12 00	12 00	12 00	75°
80°	6 00	12 00	12 00	12 00	12 00	12 00	12 00	12 00	12 00	12 00	12 00	12 00	80°

Note: If latitude and declination are of the same sign, take out the respondent directly. If they are of opposite signs, subtract the respondent from 12h.

Table 1 gives the complete range of declinations in case any user wishes to calculate semi-diurnal arcs for bodies other than the Sun and Moon.

Example:

Lat.	Dec.	Semi-diurnal arc
+52°	+20°	7h 51m
+52°	−20°	4h 09m

TABLE 2. CORRECTION FOR REFRACTION AND SEMI-DIAMETER

	m	m	m	m	m	m	m	m	m	m	m	m	m	
0°	3	3	4	4	4	5	5	5	6	6	6	7	0°
10°	3	3	4	4	4	5	5	6	6	6	7	7	10°
20°	4	4	4	4	5	5	6	7	7	8	8	9	20°
25°	4	4	4	4	5	6	7	8	8	9	11	13	25°
30°	4	4	4	5	6	7	8	9	11	14	21	—	30°

SUNRISE AND SUNSET

The local mean time of sunrise or sunset may be found by obtaining the hour angle from Table 1 and applying it to the time of transit. The hour angle is negative for sunrise and positive for sunset. A small correction to the hour angle, which always has the effect of increasing it numerically, is necessary to allow for the Sun's semi-diameter (16') and for refraction (34'); it is obtained from Table 2. The resulting local mean time may be converted into the standard time of the country by taking the difference between the longitude of the standard meridian of the country and that of the place, adding it to the local mean time if the place is west of the standard meridian, and subtracting it if the place is east.

Example – Required the New Zealand Mean Time (12h fast on GMT) of sunset on May 23 at Auckland, latitude 36° 50' S. (or minus), longitude 11h 39m E. Taking the declination as +20°.6 (page 649), we find

	h	*m*
New Zealand Standard Time	+ 12	00
Longitude	− 11	39
Longitudinal Correction	+ 0	21
Tabular entry for Lat. 30° and Dec. 20°, opposite signs	+ 5	11
Proportional part for 6° 50' of Lat.	−	15
Proportional part for 0°.6 of Dec.	−	2
Correction (Table 2)	+	4
Hour angle	4	58
Sun transits (page 649)	11	57
Longitudinal correction	+	21
New Zealand Mean Time	17	16

MOONRISE AND MOONSET

It is possible to calculate the times of moonrise and moonset using Table 1, though the method is more complicated because the apparent motion of the Moon is much more rapid and also more variable than that of the Sun.

TABLE 3. LONGITUDE CORRECTION

X	40m	45m	50m	55m	60m	65m	70m
A							
h	*m*	*m*	*m*	*m*	*m*	*m*	*m*
1	2	2	2	2	3	3	3
2	3	4	4	5	5	5	6
3	5	6	6	7	8	8	9
4	7	8	8	9	10	11	12
5	8	9	10	11	13	14	15
6	10	11	13	14	15	16	18
7	12	13	15	16	18	19	20
8	13	15	17	18	20	22	23
9	15	17	19	21	23	24	26
10	17	19	21	23	25	27	29
11	18	21	23	25	28	30	32
12	20	23	25	28	30	33	35
13	22	24	27	30	33	35	38
14	23	26	29	32	35	38	41
15	25	28	31	34	38	41	44
16	27	30	33	37	40	43	47
17	28	32	35	39	43	46	50
18	30	34	38	41	45	49	53
19	32	36	40	44	48	51	55
20	33	38	42	46	50	54	58
21	35	39	44	48	53	57	61
22	37	41	46	50	55	60	64
23	38	43	48	53	58	62	67
24	40	45	50	55	60	65	70

The parallax of the Moon, about 57', is near to the sum of the semi-diameter and refraction but has the opposite effect on these times. It is thus convenient to neglect all three quantities in the method outlined below.

Notation

ϕ	= latitude of observer
λ	= longitude of observer (measured positively towards the west)
T_{-1}	= time of transit of Moon on previous day
T_0	= time of transit of Moon on day in question
T_1	= time of transit of Moon on following day
δ_0	= approximate declination of Moon
δ_R	= declination of Moon at moonrise
δ_S	= declination of Moon at moonset
h_0	= approximate hour angle of Moon
h_R	= hour angle of Moon at moonrise
h_S	= hour angle of Moon at moonset
t_R	= time of moonrise
t_S	= time of moonset

Method

1. With arguments ϕ, δ_0 enter Table 1 on page 680 to determine h_0 where h_0 is negative for moonrise and positive for moonset.

2. Form approximate times from
$$t_R = T_0 + \lambda + h_0$$
$$t_S = T_0 + \lambda + h_0$$

3. Determine δ_R, δ_S for times t_R, t_S respectively.

4. Re-enter Table 1 (as above) with
   (*a*) arguments ϕ, δ_R to determine h_R
   (*b*) arguments ϕ, δ_S to determine h_S

5. Form $t_R = T_0 + \lambda + h_R + AX$
   $$t_S = T_0 + \lambda + h_S + AX$$

   where $A = (\lambda + h)$

   and $X = (T_0 - T_{-1})$ if $(\lambda + h)$ is negative
   $X = (T_1 - T_0)$ if $(\lambda + h)$ is positive

   AX is the respondent in Table 3.

Example – To find the times (GMT) of moonrise and moonset at Vancouver ($\phi = +49°$, $\lambda = +8h\ 12m$) on 2012 January 19. The starting data (page 634) are

T_{-1}	= 7h 32m
T_0	= 8h 31m
T_1	= 9h 30m
δ_0	= −22°

1. h_0 = 4h 09m
2. Approximate values
   t_R = 19d 08h 31m + 8h 12m + (−4h 09m)
   = 19d 12h 34m
   t_S = 19d 08h 31m + 8h 12m + (+4h 09m)
   = 19d 20h 52m
3. δ_R = −22°.0
   δ_S = −22°.4
4. h_R = −4h 09m
   h_S = +4h 12m
5. t_R = 19d 08h 31m + 8h 12m + (−4h 09m) + 10m
   = 19d 12h 44m
   t_S = 19d 08h 31m + 8h 12m + (+4h 09m) + 31m
   = 19d 21h 23m

To get the LMT of the phenomenon the longitude is subtracted from the GMT thus:

Moonrise = 19d 12h 44m − 8h 12m = 19d 04h 32m
Moonset = 19d 21h 23m − 8h 12m = 19d 13h 11m

ECLIPSES 2012

During 2012 there will be three eclipses, two of the Sun and one of the Moon. (Penumbral eclipses of the Moon are not mentioned in this section as they are so difficult to observe.)

1. An annular eclipse of the Sun on May 20–21 is visible as a partial eclipse from North America, the Pacific Ocean, Asia, and the north polar regions, beginning at 20h 56m and ending at 02h 49m. The track of the annular eclipse starts at 22h 06m in southeastern China, crosses southern Japan, crosses the Pacific Ocean and ends at 01h 39m in Texas, U.S.A. The maximum duration of annularity is 5m 46s.

2. A partial eclipse of the Moon on June 4 begins at 10h 00m and ends at 12h 06m. It is visible from the Americas, eastern Asia and Australasia.

3. A total eclipse of the Sun occurs on November 13–14. The partial phase is visible from Australasia, the Pacific Ocean, the extreme south of South America, and Antarctica, beginning at 20h 25m and ending at 23h 48m. The track of totality starts at 20h 35m in the extreme north of Australia, crosses the South Pacific Ocean and ends at 23h 48m off the coast of South America. The maximum duration of totality is 4m 2s.

TRANSIT

A transit of Venus occurs on June 5–6, visible from extreme western Europe, northeast Africa, north and central America, northwest of south America, Australasia and Asia. From the British Isles the beginning occurs before sunrise on June 6, which occurs at 03h 45m at Greenwich and 03h 30m at Edinburgh. For both places the interior egress occurs at 04h 37m, and exterior egress at 04h 55m. However, the Sun is still at a very low altitude (7 degrees at Greenwich and 9 degrees at Edinburgh).

POSITIONS OF STARS

The positions of heavenly bodies on the celestial sphere are defined by two co-ordinates, right ascension and declination, which are analogous to longitude and latitude on the surface of the Earth. If we imagine the plane of the terrestrial equator extended indefinitely, it will cut the celestial sphere in a great circle known as the celestial equator. Similarly the plane of the Earth's orbit, when extended, cuts in the great circle called the ecliptic. The two intersections of these circles are known as the First Point of Aries and the First Point of Libra. If from any star a perpendicular is drawn to the celestial equator, the length of this perpendicular is the star's declination. The arc, measured eastwards along the equator from the First Point of Aries to the foot of this perpendicular, is the right ascension. An alternative definition of right ascension is that it is the angle at the celestial pole (where the Earth's axis, if prolonged, would meet the sphere) between the great circles to the First Point of Aries and to the star.

The plane of the Earth's equator has a slow movement, so that our reference system for right ascension and declination is not fixed. The consequent alteration in these quantities from year to year is called precession. In right ascension it is an increase of about 3 seconds a year for equatorial stars, and larger or smaller changes in either direction for stars near the poles, depending on the right ascension of the star. In declination it varies between +20″ and −20″ according to the right ascension of the star.

A star or other body crosses the meridian when the sidereal time is equal to its right ascension. The altitude is then a maximum, and may be deduced by remembering that the altitude of the elevated pole is numerically equal to the latitude, while that of the equator at its intersection with the meridian is equal to the co-latitude, or complement of the latitude.

Thus in London (lat. 51° 30′) the meridian altitude of Sirius is found as follows:

	°	′
Altitude of equator	38	30
Declination south	16	43
Difference	21	47

The altitude of Capella (Dec. +46° 00′) at lower transit is:

	°	′
Altitude of pole	51	30
Polar distance of star	44	00
Difference	7	30

The brightness of a heavenly body is denoted by its magnitude. Omitting the exceptionally bright stars Sirius and Canopus, the twenty brightest stars are of the first magnitude, while the faintest stars visible to the naked eye are of the sixth magnitude. The magnitude scale is a precise one, as a difference of five magnitudes represents a ratio of 100 to 1 in brightness. Typical second magnitude stars are Polaris and the stars in the belt of Orion. The scale is most easily fixed in memory by comparing the stars with Norton's *Star Atlas*. The stars Sirius and Canopus and the planets Venus and Jupiter are so bright that their magnitudes are expressed by negative numbers. A small telescope will show stars down to the ninth or tenth magnitude, while stars fainter than the twentieth magnitude may be photographed by long exposures with the largest telescopes.

MEAN AND SIDEREAL TIME

The length of a sidereal day in mean time is 23h 56m 04s.09. Hence 1h MT = 1h+9ˢ.86 ST and 1h ST = 1h − 9ˢ.83 MT.

Acceleration						Retardation					
h	m	s	m	s	s	h	m	s	m	s	s
1	0	10	0	00	0	1	0	10	0	00	0
2	0	20	3	02		2	0	20	3	03	
3	0	30	9	07	1	3	0	29	9	09	1
4	0	39	15	13	2	4	0	39	15	15	2
5	0	49	21	18	3	5	0	49	21	21	3
6	0	59	27	23	4	6	0	59	27	28	4
7	1	09	33	28	5	7	1	09	33	34	5
8	1	19	39	34	6	8	1	19	39	40	6
9	1	29	45	39	7	9	1	28	45	46	7
10	1	39	51	44	8	10	1	38	51	53	8
11	1	48	57	49	9	11	1	48	57	59	9
12	1	58	60	00	10	12	1	58	60	00	10
13	2	08				13	2	08			
14	2	18				14	2	18			
15	2	28				15	2	27			
16	2	38				16	2	37			
17	2	48				17	2	47			
18	2	57				18	2	57			
19	3	07				19	3	07			
20	3	17				20	3	17			
21	3	27				21	3	27			
22	3	37				22	3	36			
23	3	47				23	3	46			
24	3	57				24	3	56			

To convert an interval of mean time to the corresponding interval of sidereal time, enter the acceleration table with the given mean time (taking the hours and the minutes and seconds separately) and add the acceleration obtained to the given mean time. To convert an interval of sidereal time to the corresponding interval of mean time, take out the retardation for the given sidereal time and subtract.

The columns for the minutes and seconds of the argument are in the form known as critical tables. To use these tables, find in the appropriate left-hand column the two entries between which the given number of minutes and seconds lies; the quantity in the right-hand column between these two entries is the required acceleration or retardation. Thus the acceleration for 11m 26s (which lies between the entries 9m 07s and 15m 13s) is 2s. If the given number of minutes and seconds is a tabular entry, the required acceleration or retardation is the entry in the right-hand column above the given tabular entry, eg the retardation for 45m 46s is 7s.

Example – Convert 14h 27m 35s from ST to MT

	h	m	s
Given ST	14	27	35
Retardation for 14h		2	18
Retardation for 27m 35s			5
Corresponding MT	14	25	12

EXPLANATION OF ASTRONOMICAL DATA

Positions of the heavenly bodies are given only to the degree of accuracy required by amateur astronomers for setting telescopes, or for plotting on celestial globes or star atlases. Where intermediate positions are required, linear interpolation may be employed.

Definitions of the terms used cannot be given here. They must be sought in astronomical literature and textbooks.

A special feature has been made of the times when the various heavenly bodies are visible in the British Isles. Since two columns, calculated for latitudes 52° and 56°, are devoted to risings and settings, the range 50° to 58° can be covered by interpolation and extrapolation. The times given in these columns are Greenwich Mean Times for the meridian of Greenwich. An observer west of this meridian must add his/her longitude (in time) and vice versa.

In accordance with the usual convention in astronomy, + and − indicate respectively north and south latitudes or declinations.

All data are, unless otherwise stated, for 0h Greenwich Mean Time (GMT), ie at the midnight at the beginning of the day named. Allowance must be made for British Summer Time during the period that this is in operation.

PAGE ONE OF EACH MONTH
The calendar for each month is explained on page 631.

Under the heading Astronomical Phenomena will be found particulars of the more important conjunctions of the Sun, Moon and planets with each other, and also the dates of other astronomical phenomena of special interest.

Times of Minima of Algol are approximate times of the middle of the period of diminished light.

The Constellations listed each month are those that are near the meridian at the beginning of the month at 22h local mean time. Allowance must be made for British Summer Time if necessary. The fact that any star crosses the meridian 4m earlier each night or 2h earlier each month may be used, in conjunction with the lists given each month, to find what constellations are favourably placed at any moment. The table preceding the list of constellations may be extended indefinitely at the rate just quoted.

The principal phases of the Moon are the GMTs when the difference between the longitude of the Moon and that of the Sun is 0°, 90°, 180° or 270°. The times of perigee and apogee are those when the Moon is nearest to, and farthest from, the Earth, respectively. The nodes or points of intersection of the Moon's orbit and the ecliptic make a complete retrograde circuit of the ecliptic in about 19 years. From a knowledge of the longitude of the ascending node and the inclination, whose value does not vary much from 5°, the path of the Moon among the stars may be plotted on a celestial globe or star atlas.

PAGE TWO OF EACH MONTH
The Sun's semi-diameter, in arc, is given once a month.

The right ascension and declination (Dec.) is that of the true Sun. The right ascension of the mean Sun is obtained by applying the equation of time, with the sign given, to the right ascension of the true Sun, or, more easily, by applying 12h to the Sidereal Time. The direction in which the equation of time has to be applied in different problems is a frequent source of confusion and error. Apparent Solar Time is equal to the Mean Solar Time plus the Equation of Time. For example, at 12h GMT on August 8 the Equation of Time is −5m 35s and thus at 12h Mean Time on that day the Apparent Time is 12h − 5m 35s = 11h 54m 23s.

The Greenwich Sidereal Time at 0h and the Transit of the First Point of Aries (which is really the mean time when the sidereal time is 0h) are used for converting mean time to sidereal time and vice versa.

The GMT of transit of the Sun at Greenwich may also be taken as the local mean time (LMT) of transit in any longitude. It is independent of latitude. The GMT of transit in any longitude is obtained by adding the longitude to the time given if west, and vice versa.

LIGHTING-UP TIME
The legal importance of sunrise and sunset is that the Road Vehicles Lighting Regulations 1989 (SI 1989 No. 1796) as amended, make the use of front and rear position lamps on vehicles compulsory during the period between sunset and sunrise. Headlamps on vehicles are required to be used during the hours of darkness on unlit roads, on lit roads with a speed limit exceeding 30mph, or whenever visibility is seriously reduced. The hours of darkness are defined in these regulations as the period between half an hour after sunset and half an hour before sunrise.

In all laws and regulations 'sunset' refers to the local sunset, ie the time at which the Sun sets at the place in question. This common-sense interpretation has been upheld by legal tribunals.

SUNRISE AND SUNSET
The times of sunrise and sunset are those when the Sun's upper limb, as affected by refraction, is on the true horizon of an observer at sea-level. Assuming the mean refraction to be 34′, and the Sun's semi-diameter to be 16′, the time given is that when the true zenith distance of the Sun's centre is 90°+34′+16′ or 90° 50′, or, in other words, when the depression of the Sun's centre below the true horizon is 50′. The upper limb is then 34′ below

the true horizon, but is brought there by refraction. An observer on a ship might see the Sun for a minute or so longer, because of the dip of the horizon, while another viewing the sunset over hills or mountains would record an earlier time. Nevertheless, the moment when the true zenith distance of the Sun's centre is 90° 50' is a precise time dependent only on the latitude and longitude of the place, and independent of its altitude above sea-level, the contour of its horizon, the vagaries of refraction or the small seasonal change in the Sun's semi-diameter; this moment is suitable in every way as a definition of sunset (or sunrise) for all statutory purposes.

TWILIGHT
Light reaches us before sunrise and continues to reach us for some time after sunset. The interval between darkness and sunrise or sunset and darkness is called twilight. Astronomically speaking, twilight is considered to begin or end when the Sun's centre is 18° below the horizon, as no light from the Sun can then reach the observer. As thus defined twilight may last several hours; in high latitudes at the summer solstice the depression of 18° is not reached, and twilight lasts from sunset to sunrise.

The need for some sub-division of twilight is met by dividing the gathering darkness into four stages.

(1) *Sunrise or Sunset*, defined as above
(2) *Civil twilight*, which begins or ends when the Sun's centre is 6° below the horizon. This marks the time when operations requiring daylight may commence or must cease. In England it varies from about 30 to 60 minutes after sunset and the same interval before sunrise
(3) *Nautical twilight*, which begins or ends when the Sun's centre is 12° below the horizon. This marks the time when it is, to all intents and purposes, completely dark
(4) *Astronomical twilight*, which begins or ends when the Sun's centre is 18° below the horizon. This marks theoretical perfect darkness. It is of little practical importance, especially if nautical twilight is tabulated

To assist observers the durations of civil, nautical and astronomical twilights are given at intervals of ten days. The beginning of a particular twilight is found by subtracting the duration from the time of sunrise, while the end is found by adding the duration to the time of sunset. Thus the beginning of astronomical twilight in latitude 52°, on the Greenwich meridian on March 11 is found as 06h 23m − 113m = 04h 30m and similarly the end of civil twilight as 17h 58m +34m = 18h 32m. The letters TAN (twilight all night) are printed when twilight lasts all night.

Under the heading The Night Sky will be found notes describing the position and visibility of the planets and other phenomena.

PAGE THREE OF EACH MONTH
The Moon moves so rapidly among the stars that its position is given only to the degree of accuracy that permits linear interpolation. The right ascension (RA) and declination (Dec.) are geocentric, ie for an imaginary observer at the centre of the Earth. To an observer on the surface of the Earth the position is always different, as the altitude is always less on account of parallax, which may reach 1°.

The lunar terminator is the line separating the bright from the dark part of the Moon's disk. Apart from irregularities of the lunar surface, the terminator is elliptical, because it is a circle seen in projection. It becomes the full circle forming the limb, or edge, of the Moon at New and Full Moon. The selenographic longitude of the terminator is measured from the mean centre of the visible disk, which may differ from the visible centre by as much as 8°, because of libration.

Instead of the longitude of the terminator the Sun's selenographic co-longitude (Sun's co-long.) is tabulated. It is numerically equal to the selenographic longitude of the morning terminator, measured eastwards from the mean centre of the disk. Thus its value is approximately 270° at New Moon, 360° at First Quarter, 90° at Full Moon and 180° at Last Quarter.

The Position Angle (PA) of the Bright Limb is the position angle of the midpoint of the illuminated limb, measured eastwards from the north point on the disk. The Phase column shows the percentage of the area of the Moon's disk illuminated; this is also the illuminated percentage of the diameter at right angles to the line of cusps. The terminator is a semi-ellipse whose major axis is the line of cusps, and whose semi-minor axis is determined by the tabulated percentage; from New Moon to Full Moon the east limb is dark, and vice versa.

The times given as moonrise and moonset are those when the upper limb of the Moon is on the horizon of an observer at sea-level. The Sun's horizontal parallax (Hor. par.) is about 9", and is negligible when considering sunrise and sunset, but that of the Moon averages about 57'. Hence the computed time represents the moment when the true zenith distance of the Moon is 90° 50' (as for the Sun) minus the horizontal parallax. The time required for the Sun or Moon to rise or set is about four minutes (except in high latitudes).

See also page 681 and footnote on page 685.

The GMT of transit of the Moon over the meridian of Greenwich is given; these times are independent of latitude but must be corrected for longitude. For places in the British Isles it suffices to add the longitude if west, and vice versa. For other places a further correction is necessary because of the rapid movement of the Moon relative to the stars. The entire correction is conveniently determined by first finding the west longitude λ of the place. If the place is in west longitude, λ is the ordinary west longitude; if the place is in east longitude λ is the complement to 24h (or 360°) of the longitude and will be greater than 12h (or 180°). The correction then consists of two positive portions, namely λ and the fraction $\lambda/24$ (or $\lambda°/360$) multiplied by the difference between consecutive transits. Thus for Christchurch, New Zealand, the longitude is 11h 31m east, so λ = 12h 29m and the fraction $\lambda/24$ is 0.52. The transit on the local date 11 October 2012 is found as follows:

		d	h	m
GMT of transit at Greenwich	October 10	07	28
λ			12	29
0.52 × (7h 28m − 6h 40m)				25
GMT of transit at Christchurch		10	20	22
Corr. to NZ Standard Time			12	00
Local standard time of transit	October 11	08	22

As is evident, for any given place the quantities λ and the correction to local standard time may be combined permanently, being here 24h 29m.

Positions of Mercury are given for every second day, and those of Venus and Mars for every fifth day; they may be interpolated linearly. The diameter (Diam.) is given in seconds of arc. The phase is the illuminated percentage of the disk. In the case of the inner planets this approaches 100 at superior conjunction and 0 at inferior conjunction. When the phase is less than 50 the planet is crescent-shaped or horned; for greater phases it is gibbous. In the case of the exterior planet Mars, the phase approaches 100 at conjunction and opposition, and is a minimum at the quadratures.

Since the planets cannot be seen when on the horizon, the actual times of rising and setting are not given; instead, the time when the planet has an apparent altitude of 5° has been tabulated. If the time of transit is between 00h and 12h the time refers to an altitude of 5° above the eastern horizon; if between 12h and 24h, to the western horizon. The phenomenon tabulated is the one that occurs between sunset and sunrise. The times given may be interpolated for latitude and corrected for longitude, as in the case of the Sun and Moon.

PAGE FOUR OF EACH MONTH

The GMTs of sunrise and sunset for seven cities, whose adopted positions in longitude (W.) and latitude (N.) are given immediately below the name, may be used not only for these phenomena, but also for lighting-up times (*see* page 683 for a fuller explanation).

The particulars for the four outer planets resemble those for the planets on Page Three of each month, except that, under Uranus and Neptune, times when the planet is 10° high instead of 5° high are given; this is because of the inferior brightness of these planets. The diameters given for the rings of Saturn are those of the major axis (in the plane of the planet's equator) and the minor axis respectively. The former has a small seasonal change due to the slightly varying distance of the Earth from Saturn, but the latter varies from zero when the Earth passes through the ring plane every 15 years to its maximum opening half-way between these periods. The rings were last open at their widest extent (and Saturn at its brightest) in 2002; this will occur again in 2017. The Earth passed through the ring plane in 2009.

TIME

From the earliest ages, the natural division of time into recurring periods of day and night has provided the practical time-scale for the everyday activities of the human race. Indeed, if any alternative means of time measurement is adopted, it must be capable of adjustment

---

SUNRISE, SUNSET, MOONRISE AND MOONSET

The tables have been constructed for the meridian of Greenwich and for latitudes 52° and 56°. They give Greenwich Mean Time (GMT) throughout the year. To obtain the GMT of the phenomenon as seen from any other latitude and longitude in the British Isles, first interpolate or extrapolate for latitude by the usual rules of proportion. To the time thus found, the longitude (expressed in time) is to be added if west (as it usually is in Great Britain) or subtracted if east. If the longitude is expressed in degrees and minutes of arc, it must be converted to time at the rate of 1° = 4m and 15′ = 1m. A method of calculating rise and set time for other places in the world is given on page 681.

The GMT at which the planet transits the Greenwich meridian is also given. The times of transit are to be corrected to local meridians in the usual way, as already described.

so as to remain in general agreement with the natural time-scale defined by the diurnal rotation of the Earth on its axis. Ideally the rotation should be measured against a fixed frame of reference; in practice it must be measured against the background provided by the celestial bodies. If the Sun is chosen as the reference point, we obtain Apparent Solar Time, which is the time indicated by a sundial. It is not a uniform time but is subject to variations which amount to as much as a quarter of an hour in each direction. Such wide variations cannot be tolerated in a practical time-scale, and this has led to the concept of Mean Solar Time in which all the days are exactly the same length and equal to the average length of the Apparent Solar Day.

The positions of the stars in the sky are specified in relation to a fictitious reference point in the sky known as the First Point of Aries (or the Vernal Equinox). It is therefore convenient to adopt this same reference point when considering the rotation of the Earth against the background of the stars. The time-scale so obtained is known as Apparent Sidereal Time.

GREENWICH MEAN TIME

The daily rotation of the Earth on its axis causes the Sun and the other heavenly bodies to appear to cross the sky from east to west. It is convenient to represent this relative motion as if the Sun really performed a daily circuit around a fixed Earth. Noon in Apparent Solar Time may then be defined as the time at which the Sun transits across the observer's meridian. In Mean Solar Time, noon is similarly defined by the meridian transit of a fictitious Mean Sun moving uniformly in the sky with the same average speed as the true Sun. Mean Solar Time observed on the meridian of the transit circle telescope of the Royal Observatory at Greenwich is called Greenwich Mean Time (GMT). The mean solar day is divided into 24 hours and, for astronomical and other scientific purposes, these are numbered 0 to 23, commencing at midnight. Civil time is usually reckoned in two periods of 12 hours, designated am (*ante meridiem,* ie before noon) and pm (*post meridiem,* ie after noon), although the 24 hour clock is increasingly being used.

UNIVERSAL TIME

Before 1925 January 1, GMT was reckoned in 24 hours commencing at noon; since that date it has been reckoned from midnight. To avoid confusion in the use of the designation GMT before and after 1925, since 1928 astronomers have tended to use the term Universal Time (UT) or Weltzeit (WZ) to denote GMT measured from Greenwich Mean Midnight.

In precision work it is necessary to take account of small variations in Universal Time. These arise from small irregularities in the rotation of the Earth. Observed astronomical time is designated UT0. Observed time corrected for the effects of the motion of the poles (giving rise to a 'wandering' in longitude) is designated UT1. There is also a seasonal fluctuation in the rate of rotation of the Earth arising from meteorological causes, often called the annual fluctuation. UT1 corrected for this effect is designated UT2 and provides a time-scale free from short-period fluctuations. It is still subject to small secular and irregular changes.

APPARENT SOLAR TIME

As mentioned above, the time shown by a sundial is called Apparent Solar Time. It differs from Mean Solar Time by an amount known as the Equation of Time, which is the total effect of two causes which make the length of the apparent solar day non-uniform. One cause of variation is that the orbit of the Earth is not a circle but an ellipse, having the Sun at one focus. As a consequence, the angular speed of the Earth in its orbit is not constant; it is greatest at the beginning of January when the Earth is nearest the Sun.

The other cause is due to the obliquity of the ecliptic; the plane of the equator (which is at right angles to the axis of rotation of the Earth) does not coincide with the ecliptic (the plane defined by the apparent annual motion of the Sun around the celestial sphere) but is inclined to it at an angle of 23° 26′. As a result, the apparent solar day is shorter than average at the equinoxes and longer at the solstices. From the combined effects of the components due to obliquity and eccentricity, the equation of time reaches its maximum values in February (−14 minutes) and early November (+16 minutes). It has a zero value on four dates during the year, and it is only on these dates (approximately April 15, June 14, September 1 and December 25) that a sundial shows Mean Solar Time.

SIDEREAL TIME

A sidereal day is the duration of a complete rotation of the Earth with reference to the First Point of Aries. The term sidereal (or 'star') time is a little misleading since the time-scale so defined is not exactly the same as that which would be defined by successive transits of a selected star, as there is a small progressive motion between the stars and the First Point of Aries due to the precession of the Earth's axis. This makes the length of the sidereal day shorter than the true period of rotation by 0.008 seconds. Superimposed on this steady precessional motion are small oscillations (nutation), giving rise to fluctuations in apparent sidereal time amounting to as much as 1.2 seconds. It is therefore customary to employ Mean Sidereal Time, from which these fluctuations have been removed. The conversion of GMT to Greenwich sidereal time (GST) may be performed by adding the value of the GST at 0h on the day in question (page two of each month) to the GMT converted to sidereal time using the table on page 682.

Example – To find the GST at August 8d 02h 41m 11s GMT

	h	*m*	*s*
GST at 0h	21	07	38
GMT	2	41	11
Acceleration for 2h			20
Acceleration for 41m 11s			7
Sum = GST =	23	49	16

If the observer is not on the Greenwich meridian then his/her longitude, measured positively westwards from Greenwich, must be subtracted from the GST to obtain Local Sidereal Time (LST). Thus, in the above example, an observer 5h east of Greenwich, or 19h west, would find the LST as 4h 49m 16s.

EPHEMERIS TIME

An analysis of observations of the positions of the Sun, Moon and planets taken over an extended period is used in preparing ephemerides. (An ephemeris is a table giving the apparent position of a heavenly body at regular intervals of time, eg one day or ten days, and may be used to compare current observations with tabulated positions.)

Discrepancies between the positions of heavenly bodies observed over a 300-year period and their predicted positions arose because the time-scale to which the observations were related was based on the assumption that the rate of rotation of the Earth is uniform. It is now known that this rate of rotation is variable. A revised time-scale, Ephemeris Time (ET), was devised to bring the ephemerides into agreement with the observations.

The second of ET is defined in terms of the annual motion of the Earth in its orbit around the Sun (1/31556925.9747 of the tropical year for 1900 January 0d 12h ET). The precise determination of ET from astronomical observations is a lengthy process as the requisite standard of accuracy can only be achieved by averaging over a number of years.

In 1976 the International Astronomical Union adopted Terrestrial Dynamical Time (TDT), a new dynamical time-scale for general use whose scale unit is the SI second (*see* Atomic Time, below). TDT was renamed Terrestrial Time (TT) in 1991. ET is now of little more than historical interest.

TERRESTRIAL TIME

The uniform time system used in computing the ephemerides of the solar system is Terrestrial Time (TT), which has replaced ET for this purpose. Except for the most rigorous astronomical calculations, it may be assumed to be the same as ET. During 2012 the estimated difference TT − UT is about 67 seconds.

ATOMIC TIME

The fundamental standards of time and frequency must be defined in terms of a periodic motion adequately uniform, enduring and measurable. Progress has made it possible to use natural standards, such as atomic or molecular oscillations. Continuous oscillations are generated in an electrical circuit, the frequency of which is then compared or brought into coincidence with the frequency characteristic of the absorption or emission by the atoms or molecules when they change between two selected energy levels. Since the 13th General Conference on Weights and Measures in October 1967, the unit of time, the second, has been defined in the International System of units (SI) as 'the duration of 9 192 631 770 periods of the radiation corresponding to the transition between the two hyperfine levels of the ground state of the caesium-133 atom'.

In the UK, the national time scale is maintained by the National Physical Laboratory (NPL), using an ensemble of atomic clocks based on either caesium or hydrogen atoms. In addition the NPL (along with several other national laboratories) has constructed and operates a caesium fountain primary frequency standard, which utilises the cooling of caesium atoms by laser light to determine the duration of the SI second at the highest attainable level of accuracy. Caesium fountain primary standards typically achieve an accuracy of around 1 part in 1,000 000 000 000 000, which is equivalent to one second in 30 million years.

Timekeeping worldwide is based on two closely related atomic time scales that are established through international collaboration. International Atomic Time (TAI) is formed by combining the readings of more than 250 atomic clocks located in about 55 institutes and set close to the astronomically based Universal Time (UT) near the beginning of 1958. It was formally recognised in 1971 and since 1988 January 1 has been maintained by the International Bureau of Weights and Measures

(BIPM). Civil time in almost all countries is now based on Coordinated Universal Time (UTC), which differs from TAI by an integer number of seconds and was designed to make both atomic time and UT available with accuracy appropriate for most users. On 1 January 1972 UTC was set to be exactly 10 seconds behind TAI, and since then the UTC time-scale has been adjusted by the insertion (or, in principle, omission) of leap seconds in order to keep it within ±0.9 s of UT. These leap seconds are introduced, when necessary, at the same instant throughout the world, either at the end of December or at the end of June. The last leap second occurred immediately prior to 0h UTC on 2009 January 1 and was the 24th leap second. All leap seconds so far have been positive, with 61 seconds in the final minute of the UTC month. The time 23h 59m 60s UTC is followed one second later by 0h 0m 00s of the first day of the following month. Notices concerning the insertion of leap seconds are issued by the International Earth Rotation and Reference Systems Service (IERS).

The computation of UTC is carried out monthly by the BIPM and takes place in three stages. First, a weighted average known as Echelle Atomique Libre (EAL) is calculated from all of the contributing atomic clocks. In the second stage, TAI is generated by applying small corrections, derived from the results contributed by primary frequency standards, to the scale interval of EAL to maintain its value close to that of the SI second. Finally, UTC is formed from TAI by the addition of an integer number of seconds. The results are published monthly in the BIPM Circular T in the form of offsets at 5-day intervals between UTC and the time scales of contributing organisations.

RADIO TIME-SIGNALS
UTC is made generally available through time-signals and standard frequency broadcasts such as MSF in the UK, CHU in Canada and WWV and WWVH in the USA. These are based on national time-scales that are maintained in close agreement with UTC and provide traceability to the national time-scale and to UTC. The markers of seconds in the UTC scale coincide with those of TAI.

To disseminate the national time-scale in the UK, special signals (call-sign MSF) are broadcast by the National Physical Laboratory. From 2007 April 1 the MSF service, previously broadcast from British Telecom's radio station at Rugby, has been transmitted from Anthorn radio station in Cumbria. The signals are controlled from a caesium beam atomic frequency standard and consist of a precise frequency carrier of 60 kHz which is switched off, after being on for at least half a second, to mark every second. The first second of the minute begins with a period of 500 ms with the carrier switched off, to serve as a minute marker. In the other seconds the carrier is always off for at least one tenth of a second at the start and then it carries an on-off code giving the British clock time and date, together with information identifying the start of the next minute. Changes to and from summer time are made following government announcements. Leap seconds are inserted as announced by the IERS and information provided by them on the difference between UTC and UT is also signalled. Other broadcast signals in the UK include the BBC six pips signal, the BT Timeline ('speaking clock'), the NPL telephone and internet time services for computers, and a coded time-signal on the BBC 198 kHz transmitters which is used for timing in the electricity supply industry. From 1972 January 1 the six

pips on the BBC have consisted of five short pips from second 55 to second 59 (six pips in the case of a leap second) followed by one lengthened pip, the start of which indicates the exact minute. From 1990 February 5 these signals have been controlled by the BBC with seconds markers referenced to the satellite-based US navigation system GPS (Global Positioning System) and time and day referenced to the MSF transmitter. Formerly they were generated by the Royal Greenwich Observatory. The NPL telephone and internet services are directly connected to the national time scale.

Accurate timing may also be obtained from the signals of international navigation systems such as the ground-based eLORAN, or the satellite-based American GPS or Russian GLONASS systems.

STANDARD TIME
Since 1880 the standard time in Britain has been Greenwich Mean Time (GMT); a statute that year enacted that the word 'time' when used in any legal document relating to Britain meant, unless otherwise specifically stated, the mean time of the Greenwich meridian. Greenwich was adopted as the universal meridian on 13 October 1884. A system of standard time by zones is used worldwide, standard time in each zone differing from that of the Greenwich meridian by an integral number of hours or, exceptionally, half-hours or quarter-hours, either fast or slow. The large territories of the USA and Canada are divided into zones approximately 7.5° on either side of central meridians.

Variations from the standard time of some countries occur during part of the year; they are decided annually and are usually referred to as Summer Time or Daylight Saving Time.

At the 180th meridian the time can be either 12 hours fast on Greenwich Mean Time or 12 hours slow, and a change of date occurs. The internationally recognised date or calendar line is a modification of the 180th meridian, drawn so as to include islands of any one group on the same side of the line, or for political reasons. The line is indicated by joining up the following coordinates:

Lat.	Long.	Lat.	Long.
90° S.	180°	48° N.	180°
51° S.	180°	53° N.	170° E.
45° S.	172.5° W.	65.5° N.	169° W.
15° S.	172.5° W.	68° N.	169° W.
5° S.	180°	90° N.	180°

Changes to the date line would require an international conference.

BRITISH SUMMER TIME
In 1916 an Act ordained that during a defined period of that year the legal time for general purposes in Great Britain should be one hour in advance of Greenwich Mean Time. The Summer Time Acts 1922 and 1925 defined the period during which Summer Time was to be in force, stabilising practice until the Second World War.

During the Second World War (1941–5) and in 1947 Double Summer Time (two hours in advance of Greenwich Mean Time) was used for the period in which ordinary Summer Time would have been in force. During these years clocks were also kept one hour in advance of Greenwich Mean Time in the winter. After the war, ordinary Summer Time was invoked each year from 1948–68.

Between 1968 October 27 and 1971 October 31

clocks were kept one hour ahead of Greenwich Mean Time throughout the year. This was known as British Standard Time.

The most recent legislation is the Summer Time Act 1972, which enacted that 'the period of summer time for the purposes of this Act is the period beginning at two o'clock, Greenwich Mean Time, in the morning of the day after the third Saturday in March or, if that day is Easter Day, the day after the second Saturday in March, and ending at two o'clock, Greenwich Mean Time, in the morning of the day after the fourth Saturday in October.'

The duration of Summer Time can be varied by Order in Council and in recent years alterations have been made to synchronise the period of Summer Time in Britain with that used in Europe. The rule for 1981–94 defined the period of Summer Time in the UK as from the last Sunday in March to the day following the fourth Saturday in October and the hour of changeover was altered to 01h Greenwich Mean Time.

There was no rule for the dates of Summer Time between 1995–7. Since 1998 the 9th European Parliament and Council Directive on Summer Time has harmonised the dates on which Summer Time begins and ends across member states as the last Sundays in March and October respectively. Under the directive Summer Time begins and ends at 01hr Greenwich Mean Time in each member state. Amendments to the Summer Time Act to implement the directive came into force in 2002.

The duration of Summer Time in 2012 is:
March 25 01h GMT to October 28 01h GMT

MEAN REFRACTION

Alt.	Ref.	Alt.	Ref.	Alt.	Ref.
° ′	′	° ′	′	° ′	′
1 20	21	3 12	13	7 54	6
1 30		3 34		9 27	
1 41	20	4 00	12	11 39	5
1 52	19	4 30	11	15 00	4
2 05	18	5 06	10	20 42	3
2 19	17	5 50	9	32 20	2
2 35	16	6 44	8	62 17	1
2 52	15	7 54	7	90 00	0
3 12	14				

The refraction table is in the form of a critical table (*see* page 682).

ASTRONOMICAL CONSTANTS

Solar parallax	8″.794
Astronomical unit	149597870 km
Precession for the year 2012	50″.291
Precession in right ascension	3ˢ.075
Precession in declination	20″.043
Constant of nutation	9″.202
Constant of aberration	20″.496
Mean obliquity of ecliptic (2012)	23° 26′ 17″
Moon's equatorial hor. parallax	57′ 02″.70
Velocity of light in vacuo per second	299792.5 km
Solar motion per second	20.0 km
Equatorial radius of the Earth	6378.140 km
Polar radius of the Earth	6356.755 km
North galactic pole (IAU standard)	
	RA 12h 49m (1950.0). Dec.+27°.4 N.
Solar apex	RA 18h 06m Dec. + 30°

Length of year (in mean solar days)

Tropical	365.24219
Sidereal	365.25636
Anomalistic (perihelion to perihelion)	365.25964
Eclipse	346.62003

Length of month (mean values)	d	h	m	s
New Moon to New	29	12	44	02.9
Sidereal	27	07	43	11.5
Anomalistic (perigee to perigee)	27	13	18	33.4

THE EARTH

The shape of the Earth is that of an oblate spheroid or solid of revolution whose meridian sections are ellipses not differing much from circles, while the sections at right angles are circles. The length of the equatorial axis is about 12,756 km, and that of the polar axis is 12,714 km. The mean density of the Earth is 5.5 times that of water, although that of the surface layer is less. The Earth and Moon revolve about their common centre of gravity in a lunar month; this centre in turn revolves round the Sun in a plane known as the ecliptic, that passes through the Sun's centre. The Earth's equator is inclined to this plane at an angle of 23.4°. This tilt is the cause of the seasons. In mid-latitudes, and when the Sun is high above the Equator, not only does the high noon altitude make the days longer, but the Sun's rays fall more directly on the Earth's surface; these effects combine to produce summer. In equatorial regions the noon altitude is large throughout the year, and there is little variation in the length of the day. In higher latitudes the noon altitude is lower, and the days in summer are appreciably longer than those in winter.

The average velocity of the Earth in its orbit is 30km a second. It makes a complete rotation on its axis in about 23h 56m of mean time, which is the sidereal day. Because of its annual revolution round the Sun, the rotation with respect to the Sun, or the solar day, is more than this by about four minutes. The extremity of the axis of rotation, or the North Pole of the Earth, is not rigidly fixed, but wanders over an area roughly 20 metres in diameter.

ELEMENTS OF THE SOLAR SYSTEM

Orb	Mean distance from Sun (Earth = 1)	km 10⁶	Sidereal period days	Synodic period days	Incl. of orbit to ecliptic °	'	Diameter km	Mass (Earth = 1)	Period of rotation on axis days
Sun	—	—	—	—		—	1,392,000	332,981	25–35*
Mercury	0.39	58	88.0	116	7	00	4,879	0.0553	58.646
Venus	0.72	108	224.7	584	3	24	12,104	0.8150	243.019r
Earth	1.00	150	365.3	—		—	12,756e	1.0000	0.997
Mars	1.52	228	687.0	780	1	51	6,794e	0.1074	1.026
Jupiter	5.20	778	4,332.6	399	1	18	{ 142,984e / 133,708p	317.83	{ 0.410e
Saturn	9.55	1429	10,759.2	378	2	29	{ 120,536e / 108,728p	95.16	{ 0.426e
Uranus	19.22	2875	30,684.6	370	0	46	51,118e	14.54	0.718r
Neptune	30.11	4504	60,191.2	367	1	46	49,528e	17.15	0.671
Pluto†	39.80	5954	91,708.2	367	17	09	2,390	0.002	6.387

e equatorial, *p* polar, *r* retrograde, * depending on latitude, † reclassified as a dwarf planet since August 2006

THE SATELLITES

Name		Star mag.	Mean distance from primary km	Sidereal period of revolution d
EARTH				
I	Moon	—	384,400	27.322
MARS				
I	Phobos	11	9,378	0.319
II	Deimos	12	23,459	1.262
JUPITER				
XVI	Metis	17	127,960	0.295
XV	Adrastea	19	128,980	0.298
V	Amalthea	14	181,300	0.498
XIV	Thebe	16	221,900	0.675
I	Io	5	421,600	1.769
II	Europa	5	670,900	3.551
III	Ganymede	5	1,070,000	7.155
IV	Callisto	6	1,883,000	16.689
XIII	Leda	20	11,165,000	240.92
VI	Himalia	15	11,460,000	250.57
X	Lysithea	18	11,717,000	259.22
VII	Elara	17	11,741,000	259.65
XII	Ananke	19	21,276,000	629.77r
XI	Carme	18	23,404,000	734.17r
VIII	Pasiphae	17	23,624,000	743.68r
IX	Sinope	18	23,939,000	758.90r
SATURN				
XVIII	Pan	20	133,583	0.575
XV	Atlas	18	137,640	0.602
XVI	Prometheus	16	139,353	0.613
XVII	Pandora	16	141,700	0.629
XI	Epimetheus	15	151,422	0.694
X	Janus	14	151,472	0.695
I	Mimas	13	185,520	0.942
II	Enceladus	12	238,020	1.370
III	Tethys	10	294,660	1.888
XIII	Telesto	19	294,660	1.888
XIV	Calypso	19	294,660	1.888
IV	Dione	10	377,400	2.737
XII	Helene	18	377,400	2.737
V	Rhea	10	527,040	4.518
VI	Titan	8	1,221,850	15.945

Name		Star mag.	Mean distance from primary km	Sidereal period of revolution d
SATURN				
VII	Hyperion	14	1,481,000	21.277
VIII	Iapetus	11	3,561,300	79.330
IX	Phoebe	16	12,952,000	550.48r
URANUS				
VI	Cordelia	24	49,770	0.335
VII	Ophelia	24	53,790	0.376
VIII	Bianca	23	59,170	0.435
IX	Cressida	22	61,780	0.464
X	Desdemona	22	62,680	0.474
XI	Juliet	21	64,350	0.493
XII	Portia	21	66,090	0.513
XIII	Rosalind	22	66,940	0.558
XIV	Belinda	22	75,260	0.624
XV	Puck	20	86,010	0.762
V	Miranda	16	129,390	1.413
I	Ariel	14	191,020	2.520
II	Umbriel	15	266,300	4.144
III	Titania	14	435,910	8.706
IV	Oberon	14	583,520	13.463
XVI	Caliban	22	7,230,000	579.5r
XX	Stephano	24	8,002,000	676.5r
XVII	Sycorax	21	12,179,000	1,283.4r
XVIII	Prospero	23	16,418,000	1,992.8r
XIX	Setebos	23	17,459,000	2,202.2r
NEPTUNE				
III	Naiad	25	48,230	0.294
IV	Thalassa	24	50,080	0.311
V	Despina	23	52,530	0.335
VI	Galatea	22	61,950	0.429
VII	Larissa	22	73,550	0.555
VIII	Proteus	20	117,650	1.122
I	Triton	13	354,760	5.877
II	Nereid	19	5,513,400	360.136
PLUTO				
I	Charon	17	19,600	6.387

Currently the total number of satellites of the outer planets are: Jupiter 62, Saturn 60, Uranus 27, Neptune 13, Pluto 3.

TERRESTRIAL MAGNETISM

The Earth's main magnetic field corresponds approximately to that of a very strong small bar magnet near the centre of the Earth, but with appreciable smooth spatial departures. The origin of the main field is generally ascribed to electric currents associated with fluid motions in the Earth's core. As a result not only does the main field vary in strength and direction from place to place, but also with time. Superimposed on the main field are local and regional anomalies whose magnitudes may in places approach that of the main field; these are due to the influence of mineral deposits in the Earth's crust. A small proportion of the field is of external origin, mostly associated with electric currents in the ionosphere. The configuration of the external field and the ionisation of the atmosphere depend on the incident particle and radiation flux from the Sun. There are, therefore, short-term and non-periodic as well as diurnal, 27-day, seasonal and 11-year periodic changes in the magnetic field, dependent upon the position of the Sun and the degree of solar activity.

A magnetic compass points along the horizontal component of a magnetic line of force. These lines of force converge on the 'magnetic dip-poles', the places where the Earth's magnetic field is vertical. These poles move with time, and their present approximate adopted mean positions are 85.5° N., 140.2° W. and 64.4° S., 137.1° E.

There is also a 'magnetic equator', at all points of which the vertical component of the Earth's magnetic field is zero and a magnetised needle remains horizontal. This line runs between 2° and 12° north of the geographical equator in Asia and Africa, turns sharply south off the west African coast, and crosses South America through Brazil, Bolivia and Peru; it re-crosses the geographical equator in mid-Pacific.

Reference has already been made to secular changes in the Earth's field. The following table indicates the changes in magnetic declination (or variation of the compass). Declination is the angle in the horizontal plane between the direction of true north and that in which a magnetic compass points. Similar, though much smaller, changes have occurred in 'dip' or magnetic inclination. Secular changes differ throughout the world. Although the London observations suggest a cycle with a period of several hundred years, an exact repetition is unlikely.

London			Greenwich		
1580	11°	15′ E.	1900	16°	29′ W.
1622	5°	56′ E.	1925	13°	10′ W.
1665	1°	22′ W.	1950	9°	07′ W.
1730	13°	00′ W.	1975	6°	39′ W.
1773	21°	09′ W.	1998	3°	32′ W.
1850	22°	24′ W.			

In order that up-to-date information on declination may be available, many governments publish magnetic charts on which there are lines (isogonic lines) passing through all places at which specified values of declination will be found at the date of the chart.

In the British Isles, isogonic lines now run approximately north-east to south-west. Though there are considerable local deviations due to geological causes, a rough value of magnetic declination may be obtained by assuming that at 50° N. on the meridian of Greenwich, the value in 2012 is 0° 49′ west and allowing an increase of 11′ for each degree of latitude northwards and one of 26′ for each degree of longitude westwards. For example, at 53° N., 5° W., declination will be about 0° 49′ + 33′ + 130′, ie 3° 32′ west. The average annual change at the present time is about 11′ decrease.

The number of magnetic observatories is about 180, irregularly distributed over the globe. There are three in Great Britain, run by the British Geological Survey: at Hartland, north Devon; at Eskdalemuir, Dumfries and Galloway; and at Lerwick, Shetland Islands. The following are some recent annual mean values of the magnetic elements for Hartland.

Year	Declination West		Dip or inclination		Horizontal intensity nanoTesla (nT)	Vertical intensity nT
	°	′	°	′		
1960	9	58.8	66	43.9	18707	43504
1965	9	30.1	66	34.0	18872	43540
1970	9	06.5	66	26.1	19033	43636
1975	8	32.3	66	17.0	19212	43733
1980	7	43.8	66	10.3	19330	43768
1985	6	56.1	66	07.9	19379	43796
1990	6	15.0	66	09.7	19539	43896
1995	5	33.2	66	07.3	19457	43951
2000	4	43.6	66	06.9	19508	44051
2005	3	56.4	66	06.0	19576	44177
2010	3	09.5	66	02.1	19670	44251

As well as navigation at sea, in the air and on land by compass the oil industry depends on the Earth's magnetic field as a directional reference. They use magnetic survey tools when drilling well-bores and require accurate estimates of the local magnetic field, taking into account the crustal and external fields.

MAGNETIC STORMS

Occasionally, sometimes with great suddenness, the Earth's magnetic field is subject for several hours to marked disturbance. During a severe storm in October 2003 the declination at Eskdalemuir changed by over 5° in six minutes. In many instances such disturbances are accompanied by widespread displays of aurorae, marked changes in the incidence of cosmic rays, an increase in the reception of 'noise' from the Sun at radio frequencies, and rapid changes in the ionosphere and induced electric currents within the Earth which adversely affect satellite operations, telecommunications and electric power transmission systems. The disturbances are caused by changes in the stream of ionised particles which emanates from the Sun and through which the Earth is continuously passing. Some of these changes are associated with visible eruptions on the Sun, usually in the region of sun-spots. There is a marked tendency for disturbances to recur after intervals of about 27 days, the apparent period of rotation of the Sun on its axis, which is consistent with the sources being located on particular areas of the Sun.

TIME MEASUREMENT AND CALENDARS

MEASUREMENTS OF TIME

Measurements of time are based on the time taken by the earth to rotate on its axis (day); by the moon to revolve around the earth (month); and by the earth to revolve around the sun (year). From these, which are not commensurable, certain average or mean intervals have been adopted for ordinary use.

THE DAY

The day begins at midnight and is divided into 24 hours of 60 minutes, each of 60 seconds. The hours are counted from midnight up to 12 noon (when the sun crosses the meridian), and these hours are designated am *(ante meridiem)*; and again from noon up to 12 midnight, which hours are designated pm *(post meridiem)*, except when the 24-hour reckoning is employed. The 24-hour reckoning ignores am and pm, numbering the hours 0 to 23 from midnight.

Colloquially the 24 hours are divided into day and night, day being the time while the sun is above the horizon (including the four stages of twilight defined in the Astronomy section). Day is subdivided into morning, the early part of daytime, ending at noon; afternoon, from noon to about 6pm; and evening, which may be said to extend from 6pm until midnight. Night begins at the close of astronomical twilight (*see* the Astronomy section) and extends beyond midnight to sunrise the next day.

The names of the days are derived from Old English translations or adaptations of the Roman titles.

Sunday	Sol	Sun
Monday	Luna	Moon
Tuesday	Tiw/Tyr (god of war)	Mars
Wednesday	Woden/Odin	Mercury
Thursday	Thor	Jupiter
Friday	Frigga/Freyja (goddess of love)	Venus
Saturday	Saeterne	Saturn

THE MONTH

The month in the ordinary calendar is approximately the twelfth part of a year, but the lengths of the different months vary from 28 (or 29) days to 31.

THE YEAR

The equinoctial or tropical year is the time that the earth takes to revolve around the sun from equinox to equinox, ie 365.24219 mean solar days, or 365 days 5 hours 48 minutes and 45 seconds.

The calendar year usually consists of 365 days but a year containing 366 days is called a bissextile (*see* Roman calendar) or leap year, one day being added to the month of February so that a date 'leaps over' a day of the week. In the Roman calendar the day that was repeated was the sixth day before the beginning of March, the equivalent of 24 February.

A year is a leap year if the date of the year is divisible by four without remainder, unless it is the last year of the century. The last year of a century is a leap year only if its number is divisible by 400 without remainder, eg the years 1800 and 1900 had only 365 days but the year 2000 had 366 days.

THE SOLSTICE

A solstice is the point in the tropical year at which the sun attains its greatest distance, north or south, from the Equator. In the northern hemisphere the furthest point north of the Equator marks the summer solstice and the furthest point south marks the winter solstice.

The date of the solstice varies according to locality. For example, if the summer solstice falls on 21 June late in the day by Greenwich time, that day will be the longest of the year at Greenwich though it may be by only a second, but it will fall on 22 June, local date, in Japan, and so 22 June will be the longest day there. The date of the solstice is also affected by the length of the tropical year, which is 365 days 6 hours less about 11 minutes 15 seconds. If a solstice happens late on 21 June in one year, it will be nearly 6 hours later in the next (unless the next year is a leap year), ie early on 22 June, and that will be the longest day.

This delay of the solstice does not continue because the extra day in a leap year brings it back a day in the calendar. However, because of the 11 minutes 15 seconds mentioned above, the additional day in a leap year brings the solstice back too far by 45 minutes, and the time of the solstice in the calendar is earlier, in a four-year pattern, as the century progresses. The last year of a century is in most cases not a leap year, and the omission of the extra day puts the date of the solstice later by about 6 hours. Compensation for this is made by the fourth centennial year being a leap year. The solstice has become earlier in date throughout the last century and, because the year 2000 was a leap year, the solstice will get earlier still throughout the 21st century. The date of the winter solstice, the shortest day of the year, is affected by the same factors as the longest day.

At Greenwich the sun sets at its earliest by the clock about ten days before the shortest day. The daily change in the time of sunset is due in the first place to the sun's movement southwards at this time of the year, which diminishes the interval between the sun's transit and its setting. However, the daily decrease of the Equation of Time causes the time of apparent noon to be continuously later day by day, which to some extent counteracts the first effect. The rates of the change of these two quantities are not equal or uniform; their combination causes the date of earliest sunset to be 12 or 13 December at Greenwich. In more southerly latitudes the effect of the movement of the sun is less, and the change in the time of sunset depends on that of the Equation of Time to a greater degree, and the date of earliest sunset is earlier than it is at Greenwich, eg on the Equator it is about 1 November.

THE EQUINOX

The equinox is the point at which the sun crosses the Equator and day and night are of equal length all over the world. This occurs in March and September.

DOG DAYS

The days about the heliacal rising of the Dog Star, noted from ancient times as the hottest period of the year in the northern hemisphere, are called the Dog Days. Their incidence has been variously calculated as depending on the Greater or Lesser Dog Star (Sirius or Procyon) and their duration has been reckoned as from 30 to 54 days. A generally accepted period is from 3 July to 15 August.

CHRISTIAN CALENDAR

In the Christian chronological system the years are distinguished by cardinal numbers before or after the birth of Christ, the period being denoted by the letters BC (Before Christ) or, more rarely, AC *(Ante Christum)*, and AD *(Anno Domini* – In the Year of Our Lord). The correlative dates of the epoch are the fourth year of the 194th Olympiad, the 753rd year from the foundation of Rome, AM 3761 in Jewish chronology, and the 4,714th year of the Julian period. The actual date of the birth of Christ is somewhat uncertain.

The system was introduced into Italy in the sixth century. Though first used in France in the seventh century, it was not universally established there until about the eighth century. It has been said that the system was introduced into England by St Augustine (AD 596), but it was probably not generally used until some centuries later. It was ordered to be used by the bishops at the Council of Chelsea (AD 816).

THE JULIAN CALENDAR
In the Julian calendar (adopted by the Roman Empire in 45 BC) all the centennial years were leap years, and for this reason towards the close of the 16th century there was a difference of ten days between the tropical and calendar years; the equinox fell on 11 March of the calendar, whereas at the time of the Council of Nicaea (AD 325), it had fallen on 21 March. In 1582 Pope Gregory ordained that 5 October should be called 15 October and that of the end-century years only the fourth should be a leap year.

THE GREGORIAN CALENDAR
The Gregorian calendar was adopted by Italy, France, Spain and Portugal in 1582, by Prussia, the Roman Catholic German states, Switzerland, Holland and Flanders on 1 January 1583, by Poland in 1586, Hungary in 1587, the Protestant German and Netherland states and Denmark in 1700, and by Great Britain and its Dominions (including the North American colonies) in 1752, by the omission of 11 days (3 September being reckoned as 14 September). Sweden omitted the leap day in 1700 but observed leap days in 1704 and 1708, and reverted to the Julian calendar by having two leap days in 1712; the Gregorian calendar was adopted in 1753 by the omission of 11 days (18 February being reckoned as 1 March). Japan adopted the calendar in 1872, China in 1912, Bulgaria in 1916, Turkey and Soviet Russia in 1918, Yugoslavia and Romania in 1919, and Greece in 1923.

In the same year that the change was made in England from the Julian to the Gregorian calendar, the start of the new year was also changed from 25 March to 1 January.

THE ORTHODOX CHURCHES
Some Orthodox churches still use the Julian reckoning but the majority of Greek Orthodox churches and the Romanian Orthodox Church have adopted a modified 'New Calendar', observing the Gregorian calendar for fixed feasts and the Julian for movable feasts.

The Orthodox Church year begins on 1 September. There are four fast periods and, in addition to Pascha (Easter), twelve great feasts, as well as numerous commemorations of the saints of the Old and New Testaments throughout the year.

THE DOMINICAL LETTER
The dominical letter is one of the letters A–G which are used to denote the Sundays in successive years. If the first day of the year is a Sunday the letter is A; if the second, B; the third, C; and so on. A leap year requires two letters, the first for 1 January to 29 February, the second for 1 March to 31 December.

EPIPHANY
The feast of the Epiphany, commemorating the manifestation of Christ, later became associated with the offering of gifts by the Magi. The day was of great importance from the time of the Council of Nicaea (AD 325), as the primate of Alexandria was charged at every Epiphany feast with the announcement in a letter to the churches of the date of the forthcoming Easter. The day was also of importance in Britain as it influenced dates, ecclesiastical and lay, eg Plough Monday, when work was resumed in the fields, fell on the Monday in the first full week after Epiphany.

LENT
The Teutonic word *Lent,* which denotes the fast preceding Easter, originally meant no more than the spring season; but from Anglo-Saxon times, at least, it has been used as the equivalent of the more significant Latin term *Quadragesima,* meaning the 'forty days' or, more literally, the fortieth day. Ash Wednesday is the first day of Lent, which ends at midnight before Easter Day.

PALM SUNDAY
Palm Sunday, the Sunday before Easter and the beginning of Holy Week, commemorates the triumphal entry of Christ into Jerusalem and is celebrated in Britain (when palm is not available) by branches of willow gathered for use in the decoration of churches on that day.

MAUNDY THURSDAY
Maundy Thursday is the day before Good Friday, the name itself being a corruption of *dies mandati* (day of the mandate) when Christ washed the feet of the disciples and gave them the mandate to love one another.

EASTER DAY
Easter Day is the first Sunday after the full moon which happens on, or next after, the 21st day of March; if the full moon happens on a Sunday, Easter Day is the Sunday after.

This definition is contained in an Act of Parliament (24 Geo. II c. 23) and explanation is given in the preamble to the Act that the day of full moon depends on certain tables that have been prepared. These tables are summarised in the early pages of the Book of Common Prayer. The moon referred to is not the real moon of the heavens, but a hypothetical moon on whose 'full' the date of Easter depends, and the lunations of this 'calendar' moon consist of 29 and 30 days alternately, with certain necessary modifications to make the date of its full agree as nearly as possible with that of the real moon, which is known as the Paschal Full Moon.

A FIXED EASTER
In 1928 the House of Commons agreed to a motion for the third reading of a bill proposing that Easter Day shall, in the calendar year next but one after the commencement of the Act and in all subsequent years, be the first Sunday after the second Saturday in April. Easter would thus fall on the second or third Sunday in April, ie

between 9 and 15 April (inclusive). A clause in the bill provided that before it shall come into operation, regard shall be had to any opinion expressed officially by the various Christian churches. Efforts by the World Council of Churches to secure a unanimous choice of date for Easter by its member churches have so far been unsuccessful.

ROGATION DAYS
Rogation Days are the Monday, Tuesday and Wednesday preceding Ascension Day and from the fifth century were observed as public fasts with solemn processions and supplications. The processions were discontinued as religious observances at the Reformation, but survive in the ceremony known as 'beating the parish bounds'. Rogation Sunday is the Sunday before Ascension Day.

EMBER DAYS
The Ember days occur on the Wednesday, Friday and Saturday of the same week, four times a year. Used for the ordination of clergy, these days are set aside for fasting and prayer. The weeks in which they fall are: (a) after the third Sunday in Advent, (b) before the second Sunday in Lent, (c) before Trinity Sunday and (d) after Holy Cross day.

TRINITY SUNDAY
Trinity Sunday is eight weeks after Easter Day, on the Sunday following Pentecost (Whit Sunday). Subsequent Sundays are reckoned in the Book of Common Prayer calendar of the Church of England as 'after Trinity'.

Thomas Becket (1118–70) was consecrated Archbishop of Canterbury on the Sunday after Whit Sunday and his first act was to ordain that the day of his consecration should be held as a new festival in honour of the Holy Trinity. This observance spread from Canterbury throughout the whole of Christendom.

MOVEABLE FEASTS TO THE YEAR 2035

Year	Ash Wednesday	Easter	Ascension	Pentecost (Whit Sunday)	Advent Sunday
2012	22 February	8 April	17 May	27 May	2 December
2013	13 February	31 March	9 May	19 May	1 December
2014	5 March	20 April	29 May	8 June	30 November
2015	18 February	5 April	14 May	24 May	29 November
2016	10 February	27 March	5 May	15 May	27 November
2017	1 March	16 April	25 May	4 June	3 December
2018	14 February	1 April	10 May	20 May	2 December
2019	6 March	21 April	30 May	9 June	1 December
2020	26 February	12 April	21 May	31 May	29 November
2021	17 February	4 April	13 May	23 May	28 November
2022	2 March	17 April	26 May	5 June	27 November
2023	22 February	9 April	18 May	28 May	3 December
2024	14 February	31 March	9 May	19 May	1 December
2025	5 March	20 April	29 May	8 June	30 November
2026	18 February	5 April	14 May	24 May	29 November
2027	10 February	28 March	6 May	16 May	28 November
2028	1 March	16 April	25 May	4 June	3 December
2029	14 February	1 April	10 May	20 May	2 December
2030	6 March	21 April	30 May	9 June	1 December
2031	26 February	13 April	22 May	1 June	30 November
2032	11 February	28 March	6 May	16 May	28 November
2033	2 March	17 April	26 May	5 June	27 November
2034	22 February	9 April	18 May	28 May	3 December
2035	7 February	25 March	3 May	13 May	2 December

NOTES
Ash Wednesday (first day in Lent) can fall at earliest on 4 February and at latest on 10 March

Mothering Sunday (fourth Sunday in Lent) can fall at earliest on 1 March and at latest on 4 April

Easter Day can fall at earliest on 22 March and at latest on 25 April

Ascension Day is forty days after Easter Day and can fall at earliest on 30 April and at latest on 3 June

Pentecost (Whit Sunday) is seven weeks after Easter and can fall at earliest on 10 May and at latest on 13 June

Trinity Sunday is the Sunday after Whit Sunday

Corpus Christi falls on the Thursday after Trinity Sunday

Sundays after Pentecost – there are not less than 18 and not more than 23

Advent Sunday is the Sunday nearest to 30 November

EASTER DAYS AND DOMINICAL LETTERS 1500 TO 2035

Dates up to and including 1752 are according to the Julian calendar. For dominical letters in leap years, *see* note below

		1500–1599	1600–1699	1700–1799	1800–1899	1900–1999	2000–2035
March							
d	22	1573	1668	1761	1818		
e	23	1505/16	1600	1788	1845/56	1913	2008
f	24	1611/95	1706/99	1940			
g	25	1543/54	1627/38/49	1722/33/44	1883/94	1951	2035
A	26	1559/70/81/92	1654/65/76	1749/58/69/80	1815/26/37	1967/78/89	
b	27	1502/13/24/97	1608/87/92	1785/96	1842/53/64	1910/21/32	2005/16
c	28	1529/35/40	1619/24/30	1703/14/25	1869/75/80	1937/48	2027/32
d	29	1551/62	1635/46/57	1719/30/41/52	1807/12/91	1959/64/70	
e	30	1567/78/89	1651/62/73/84	1746/55/66/77	1823/34	1902/75/86/97	
f	31	1510/21/32/83/94	1605/16/78/89	1700/71/82/93	1839/50/61/72	1907/18/29/91	2002/13/24
April							
g	1	1526/37/48	1621/32	1711/16	1804/66/77/88	1923/34/45/56	2018/29
A	2	1553/64	1643/48	1727/38	1809/20/93/99	1961/72	
b	3	1575/80/86	1659/70/81	1743/63/68/74	1825/31/36	1904/83/88/94	
c	4	1507/18/91	1602/13/75/86/97	1708/79/90	1847/58	1915/20/26/99	2010/21
d	5	1523/34/45/56	1607/18/29/40	1702/13/24/95	1801/63/74/85/96	1931/42/53	2015/26
e	6	1539/50/61/72	1634/45/56	1729/35/40/60	1806/17/28/90	1947/58/69/80	
f	7	1504/77/88	1667/72	1751/65/76	1822/33/44	1901/12/85/96	
g	8	1509/15/20/99	1604/10/83/94	1705/87/92/98	1849/55/60	1917/28	2007/12
A	9	1531/42	1615/26/37/99	1710/21/32	1871/82	1939/44/50	2023/34
b	10	1547/58/69	1631/42/53/64	1726/37/48/57	1803/14/87/98	1955/66/77	
c	11	1501/12/63/74/85/96	1658/69/80	1762/73/84	1819/30/41/52	1909/71/82/93	2004
d	12	1506/17/28	1601/12/91/96	1789	1846/57/68	1903/14/25/36/98	2009/20
e	13	1533/44	1623/28	1707/18	1800/73/79/84	1941/52	2031
f	14	1555/60/66	1639/50/61	1723/34/45/54	1805/11/16/95	1963/68/74	
g	15	1571/82/93	1655/66/77/88	1750/59/70/81	1827/38	1900/06/79/90	2001
A	16	1503/14/25/36/87/98	1609/20/82/93	1704/75/86/97	1843/54/65/76	1911/22/33/95	2006/17/28
b	17	1530/41/52	1625/36	1715/20	1808/70/81/92	1927/38/49/60	2022/33
c	18	1557/68	1647/52	1731/42/56	1802/13/24/97	1954/65/76	
d	19	1500/79/84/90	1663/74/85	1747/67/72/78	1829/35/40	1908/81/87/92	
e	20	1511/22/95	1606/17/79/90	1701/12/83/94	1851/62	1919/24/30	2003/14/25
f	21	1527/38/49	1622/33/44	1717/28	1867/78/89	1935/46/57	2019/30
g	22	1565/76	1660	1739/53/64	1810/21/32	1962/73/84	
A	23	1508	1671		1848	1905/16	2000
b	24	1519	1603/14/98	1709/91	1859		2011
c	25	1546	1641	1736	1886	1943	

No dominical letter is placed against the intercalary day 29 February, but since it is still counted as a weekday and given a name, the series of letters moves back one day every leap year after intercalation. Thus, a leap year beginning with the dominical letter C will change to a year with the dominical letter B on 1 March

HINDU CALENDAR

The Hindu calendar is a luni-solar calendar of 12 months, each containing 29 days, 12 hours. Each month is divided into a light fortnight (Shukla or Shuddha) and a dark fortnight (Krishna or Vadya) based on the waxing and waning of the moon. In most parts of India the month starts with the light fortnight, ie the day after the new moon, although in some regions it begins with the dark fortnight, ie the day after the full moon.

The new year according to the civil calendar begins on the first day of the month of Chaitra (March/April) and ends in the month of Phalgun (March). The financial new year begins on the first day of Kartik (Diwali day). For most Hindus, the first day of Chaitra and the first day of Kartik are equally important.

The 12 months – Chaitra, Vaishakh, Jyeshtha, Ashadh, Shravan, Bhadrapad, Ashvin, Kartik, Margashirsh, Paush, Magh and Phalgun – have Sanskrit names derived from 12 asterisms (constellations). There are regional variations to the names of the months but the Sanskrit names are understood throughout India.

Every lunar month that has a solar transit is termed pure *(shuddha)*. The lunar month without a solar transit is impure *(mala)* and called an intercalary month. An intercalary month occurs approximately every 32 lunar months, whenever the difference between the Hindu year of 360 lunar days (354 days 8 hours solar time) and the 365 days 6 hours of the solar year reaches the length of one Hindu lunar month (29 days 12 hours).

The leap month may be added at any point in the Hindu year. The name given to the month varies according to when it occurs but is taken from the month immediately following it. The leap month in 2012 is Bhadrapad.

The days of the week are called Raviwar (Sunday), Somawar (Monday), Mangalwar (Tuesday), Budhawar (Wednesday), Guruwar (Thursday), Shukrawar (Friday) and Shaniwar (Saturday). The names are derived from the Sanskrit names of the sun, the moon and five planets, Mars, Mercury, Jupiter, Venus and Saturn.

Most fasts and festivals are based on the lunar calendar but a few are determined by the apparent movement of the sun, eg Sankranti and Pongal (in southern India), which are celebrated on 14/15 January to mark the start of the Sun's apparent journey northwards and a change of season.

Festivals celebrated throughout India are Chaitra (the New Year), Raksha-bandhan (the renewal of the kinship bond between brothers and sisters), Navaratri (a nine-night festival dedicated to the goddess Parvati), Dasara (the victory of Rama over the demon army), Diwali (a festival of lights), Makara Sankranti, Shivaratri (dedicated to Shiva), and Holi (a spring festival). British Hindus commonly celebrate the festival of Diwali as the start of the financial new year.

Regional festivals are Durga-puja (dedicated to the goddess Durga (Parvati)), Sarasvati-puja (dedicated to the goddess Sarasvati), Ganesh Chaturthi (worship of Ganesh on the fourth day (Chaturthi) of the light half of Bhadrapad), Ramanavami (the birth festival of the god Rama) and Janmashtami (the birth festival of the god Krishna).

The main festivals celebrated in Britain are Navaratri, Dasara, Durga-puja, Diwali, Holi, Sarasvati-puja, Ganesh Chaturthi, Raksha-bandhan, Ramanavami and Janmashtami.

For dates of the main festivals in 2012, *see* page 9.

JEWISH CALENDAR

The story of the Flood in the Book of Genesis indicates the use of a calendar of some kind and that the writers recognised 30 days as the length of a lunation. However, after the diaspora, Jewish communities were left in considerable doubt as to the times of fasts and festivals. This led to the formation of the Jewish calendar as used today. It is said that this was done in AD 358 by Rabbi Hillel II, though some assert that it did not happen until much later.

The calendar is luni-solar, and is based on the lengths of the lunation and of the tropical year as found by Hipparchus (*c*.120 BC), which differ little from those adopted at the present day. The year AM 5772 (2011–12) is the 15th year of the 304th Metonic (Minor or Lunar) cycle of 19 years and the 4th year of the 207th Solar (or Major) cycle of 28 years since the Era of the Creation. Jews hold that the Creation occurred at the time of the autumnal equinox in the year known in the Christian calendar as 3760 BC (954 of the Julian period). The epoch or starting point of Jewish chronology corresponds to 7 October 3761 BC. At the beginning of each solar cycle, the Tekufah of Nisan (the vernal equinox) returns to the same day and to the same hour.

The hour is divided into 1,080 minims, and the month between one new moon and the next is reckoned as 29 days 12 hours 793 minims. The normal calendar year, called a regular common year, consists of 12 months of 30 days and 29 days alternately. Since 12 months such as these comprise only 354 days, in order that each of them shall not diverge greatly from an average place in the solar year, a 13th month is occasionally added after the fifth month of the civil year (which commences on the first day of the month Tishri), or as the penultimate month of the ecclesiastical year (which commences on the first day of the month Nisan). The years when this happens are called Embolismic or leap years.

Of the 19 years that form a Metonic cycle, seven are leap years; they occur at places in the cycle indicated by the numbers 3, 6, 8, 11, 14, 17 and 19, these places being chosen so that the accumulated excesses of the solar years should be as small as possible.

A Jewish year is of one of the following six types:

minimal common	353 days
regular common	354 days
full common	355 days
minimal leap	383 days
regular leap	384 days
full leap	385 days

The regular year has alternate months of 30 and 29 days. In a Full year Marcheshvan, the second month of the civil year, has 30 days instead of 29; in minimal years Kislev, the third month, has 29 instead of 30. The additional month in leap years is called Adar Sheni (Adar II) and follows the month called Adar Rishon; the usual Adar festivals are observed in Adar Sheni. In a leap year Adar I has 30 days, in all other years it has 29. None of the variations mentioned are allowed to change the number of days in the other months, which still follow the alternation of the normal 12.

These are the main features of the Jewish calendar, which must be considered permanent because as a Jewish law it cannot be altered except by a Great Sanhedrin.

The Jewish day begins between sunset and nightfall. The time used is that of the meridian of Jerusalem, which is 2h 21m in advance of Greenwich Mean Time. Rules for the beginning of sabbaths and festivals were laid down for the latitude of London in the 18th century and hours for nightfall are fixed annually by the Chief Rabbi.

JEWISH CALENDAR 5772–73

AM 5772 is a regular common year of 12 months, 51 sabbaths and 354 days. AM 5773 is a minimal common year of 12 months, 50 sabbaths and 353 days.

Month (length)	AM 5772	AM 5773
Tishri 1 (30)	29 September 2011	17 September 2012
Marcheshvan 1 (29)	29 October	17 October
Kislev 1 (30/29)	27 November	15 November
Tebet 1 (29)	27 December	14 December
Shebat 1 (30)	25 January 2012	12 January 2013
*Adar 1 (29)	24 February	
Nisan 1 (30)	24 March	
Iyar 1 (29)	23 April	
Sivan 1 (30)	22 May	
Tammuz 1 (29)	21 June	
Ab 1 (30)	20 July	
Elul 1 (29)	19 August	

* Known as Adar Rishon in leap years

JEWISH FASTS AND FESTIVALS

For dates of principal festivals in 2012, *see* page 9.

Tishri 1–2	Rosh Hashanah (New Year)
Tishri 3	*Fast of Gedaliah
Tishri 10	Yom Kippur (Day of Atonement)
Tishri 15–21	Succoth (Feast of Tabernacles)
Tishri 21	Hoshana Rabba
Tishri 22	Shemini Atseret (Solemn Assembly)
Tishri 23	Simchat Torah (Rejoicing of the Law)
Kislev 25	Hanukkah (Dedication of the Temple) begins
Tebet 10	Fast of Tebet
†*Adar 13*	§Fast of Esther
†*Adar 14*	Purim
†*Adar 15*	Shushan Purim
Nisan 15–22	Pesach (Passover)
Sivan 6–7	Shavuoth (Feast of Weeks)
Tammuz 17	*Fast of Tammuz
Ab 9	*Fast of Ab

* If these dates fall on the sabbath the fast is kept on the following day
† Adar Sheni in leap years
§ This fast is observed on Adar 11 (or Adar Sheni 11 in leap years) if Adar 13 falls on a sabbath

MUSLIM CALENDAR

The Muslim era is dated from the *Hijrah,* or flight of the Prophet Muhammad from Mecca to Medina, the corresponding date of which in the Julian calendar is 16 July AD 622. The lunar *hijri* calendar is used principally in Iran, Egypt, Malaysia, Pakistan, Mauritania, various Arab states and certain parts of India. Iran uses the solar hijri calendar as well as the lunar hijri calendar. The dating system was adopted about AD 639, commencing with the first day of the month Muharram.

The lunar calendar consists of 12 months of either 30 or 29 days, with the intercalation of one day at the end of the 12th month at stated intervals in each cycle of 30 years. The object of the intercalation is to reconcile the date of the first day of the month with the date of the actual new moon.

Some adherents still take the date of the evening of the first physical sighting of the crescent of the new moon as that of the first of the month. If cloud obscures the moon the present month may be extended to 30 days, after which the new month will begin automatically regardless of whether the moon has been seen. (Under religious law a month must have less than 31 days.) This means that the beginning of a new month and the date of religious festivals can vary from the published calendars.

In each cycle of 30 years, 19 years are common and contain 354 days, and 11 years are intercalary (leap years) of 355 days, the latter being called *kabisah.* The mean length of the Hijrah years is 354 days 8 hours 48 minutes and the period of mean lunation is 29 days 12 hours 44 minutes.

To ascertain if a year is common or kabisah, divide it by 30: the quotient gives the number of completed cycles and the remainder shows the place of the year in the current cycle. If the remainder is 2, 5, 7, 10, 13, 16, 18, 21, 24, 26 or 29, the year is kabisah and consists of 355 days.

MUSLIM CALENDAR 1433–34

Hijrah 1433 (remainder 23) is a common year and Hijrah 1434 (remainder 24) is a kabisah year. Calendar dates below are estimates based on calculations of moon phases.

Month (length)	1433 AH	1434 AH
Muharram 1	26 November	15 November
(30/29)	2011	2012
Safar 1 (29/30)	26 December	14 December
Rabi' I 1 (30/29)	24 January 2012	13 January 2013
Rabi' II 1 (30)	23 February	
Jumada I 1 (29)	24 March	
Jumada II 1 (30)	22 April	
Rajab 1 (30)	22 May	
Sha'ban 1 (29)	21 June	
Ramadan 1 (30)	20 July	
Shawwal 1 (29)	19 August	
Dhu'l Qa'da 1 (30)	17 September	
Dhu'l Hijjah 1 (29)	17 October	

MUSLIM FESTIVALS

Ramadan is a month of fasting for all Muslims because it is the month in which the revelation of the *Qur'an* (Koran) began. During Ramadan, Muslims abstain from food, drink and sexual pleasure from dawn until after sunset throughout the month.

The two major festivals are *Eid ul-Fitr* and *Eid ul-Adha.* Eid ul-Fitr marks the end of the Ramadan fast and is celebrated on the day after the sighting of the new moon of the following month. Eid ul-Adha, the festival of

sacrifice (also known as the great festival), celebrates the submission of the Prophet Ibrahim (Abraham) to God. Eid ul-Adha falls on the tenth day of Dhu'l-Hijjah, coinciding with the day when those on *hajj* (pilgrimage to Mecca) sacrifice animals.

Other days accorded special recognition are:

Muharram 1	New Year's Day
Muharram 10	Ashura (the day Prophet Noah left the Ark and Prophet Moses was saved from Pharaoh (Sunni), the death of the Prophet's grandson Husain (Shi'ite))
Rabi'u-l-Awwal (Rabi' I) 12	Mawlid ul-Nabi (birthday of the Prophet Muhammad)
Rajab 27	Laylat ul-Isra' wa'l-Mi'raj (The Night of Journey and Ascension)
Ramadan *	Laylat ul-Qadr (Night of Power)
Dhu'l-Hijjah 10	Eid ul-Adha (Festival of Sacrifice)
* Moveable feast	

For dates of the major celebrations in 2012, *see* page 9.

SIKH CALENDAR

The Sikh calendar is a lunar calendar of 365 days divided into 12 months. The length of the months varies between 29 and 32 days.

There are no prescribed feast days and no fasting periods. The main celebrations are Baisakhi Mela (the new year and the anniversary of the founding of the Khalsa), Diwali Mela (festival of light), Hola Mohalla Mela (a spring festival held in the Punjab), and the Gurpurbs (anniversaries associated with the ten Gurus).

For dates of the major celebrations in 2012, *see* page 9.

THAI CALENDAR

Thailand adopted the Suriyakati calendar, a modified version of the Gregorian calendar, during the reign of King Rama V in 1888, using 1 April as the first day of the year. In 1940 the date of the new year was changed to 1 January. The years are counted from the beginning of the Buddhist era (BE), which is calculated to have commenced upon the death of the Lord Buddha, taken to have occurred in 543 BC, so AD 2012 is BE 2555. The Chinese system of associating years with one of twelve animals is also in use in Thailand. The Chantarakati lunar calendar is used to determine religious holidays; the new year begins on the first day of the waxing moon in November or, if there is a leap month, in December.

CIVIL AND LEGAL CALENDAR

THE HISTORICAL YEAR

Before 1752, two calendar systems were used in England. The civil or legal year began on 25 March and the historical year on 1 January. Thus the civil or legal date 24 March 1658 was the same day as the historical date 24 March 1659; a date in that portion of the year is written as 24 March 1658/9, the earlier date showing the civil or legal year.

THE NEW YEAR

In England in the seventh century, and as late as the 13th, the year was reckoned from Christmas Day, but in the 12th century the Church in England began the year with the feast of the Annunciation of the Blessed Virgin ('Lady

Day') on 25 March, and this practice was adopted generally in the 14th century. The civil or legal year in the British dominions (exclusive of Scotland) began with Lady Day until 1751. But in and since 1752 the civil year has begun with 1 January. New Year's Day in Scotland was changed from 25 March to 1 January in 1600.

Elsewhere in Europe, 1 January was adopted as the first day of the year by Venice in 1522, German states in 1544, Spain, Portugal and the Roman Catholic Netherlands in 1556, Prussia, Denmark and Sweden in 1559, France in 1564, Lorraine in 1579, the Protestant Netherlands in 1583, Russia in 1725, and Tuscany in 1751.

REGNAL YEARS

Regnal years are the years of a sovereign's reign and each begins on the anniversary of his or her accession, eg regnal year 61 of the present queen begins on 6 February 2012.

The system was used for dating Acts of Parliament until 1962. The Summer Time Act 1925, for example, is quoted as 15 and 16 Geo. V c. 64, because it became law in the parliamentary session which extended over part of both of those regnal years. Acts of a parliamentary session during which a sovereign died were usually given two year numbers, the regnal year of the deceased sovereign and the regnal year of his or her successor, eg those passed in 1952 were dated 16 Geo. VI and 1 Elizabeth II. Since 1962 Acts of Parliament have been dated by the calendar year.

QUARTER AND TERM DAYS

Holy days and saints days were the usual means in early times for setting the dates of future and recurrent appointments. The quarter days in England and Wales are the feast of the Nativity (25 December), the feast of the Annunciation (25 March), the feast of St John the Baptist (24 June) and the feast of St Michael and All Angels (29 September).

The term days in Scotland are Candlemas (the feast of the Purification), Whitsunday, Lammas (Loaf Mass) and Martinmas (St Martin's Day). These fell on 2 February, 15 May, 1 August and 11 November respectively. However, by the Term and Quarter Days (Scotland) Act 1990, the dates of the term days were changed to 28 February (Candlemas), 28 May (Whitsunday), 28 August (Lammas) and 28 November (Martinmas).

RED-LETTER DAYS

Red-letter days were originally the holy days and saints days indicated in early ecclesiastical calendars by letters printed in red ink. The days to be distinguished in this way were approved at the Council of Nicaea in AD 325.

These days still have a legal significance, as judges of the Queen's Bench Division wear scarlet robes on red-letter days falling during the law sittings. The days designated as red-letter days for this purpose are:

Holy and saints days
The Conversion of St Paul, the Purification, Ash Wednesday, the Annunciation, the Ascension, the feasts of St Mark, SS Philip and James, St Matthias, St Barnabas, St John the Baptist, St Peter, St Thomas, St James, St Luke, SS Simon and Jude, All Saints, St Andrew.

Civil calendar (for dates, *see* page 9)
The anniversaries of the Queen's accession, the Queen's birthday and the Queen's coronation, the Queen's official birthday, the birthday of the Duke of Edinburgh, the birthday of the Prince of Wales, St David's Day and Lord Mayor's Day.

PUBLIC HOLIDAYS

Public holidays are divided into two categories, common law and statutory. Common law holidays are holidays 'by habit and custom'; in England, Wales and Northern Ireland these are Good Friday and Christmas Day.

Statutory public holidays, known as bank holidays, were first established by the Bank Holidays Act 1871. They were, literally, days on which the banks (and other public institutions) were closed and financial obligations due on that day were payable the following day. The legislation currently governing public holidays in the UK, which is the Banking and Financial Dealings Act 1971, stipulates the days that are to be public holidays in England, Wales, Scotland and Northern Ireland.

If a public holiday falls on a Saturday or a Sunday then another day will be given in lieu, usually the following Monday. For example, Christmas Day 2011 falls on a Sunday, so Monday 26 December is a 'substitute' holiday. For dates of public holidays in 2012 and 2013, *see* pages 10–11. The public holidays are:

England and Wales
*New Year's Day
Good Friday
Easter Monday
*The first Monday in May
The last Monday in May
†The Queen's Diamond Jubilee
The last Monday in August
Christmas Day
Boxing Day

Scotland
New Year's Day
*2 January
Good Friday
The first Monday in May
*The last Monday in May
†The Queen's Diamond Jubilee
The first Monday in August
‡St Andrew's Day
Christmas Day
Boxing Day

Northern Ireland
*New Year's Day
Good Friday
17 March
Easter Monday
*The first Monday in May
The last Monday in May
†The Queen's Diamond Jubilee
§12 July
The last Monday in August
Christmas Day
Boxing Day

* Granted annually by royal proclamation
† 2012 only
‡ Voluntary public holiday in exchange for an existing local holiday
§ Subject to proclamation by the Secretary of State for Northern Ireland

CHRONOLOGICAL CYCLES AND ERAS

SOLAR (OR MAJOR) CYCLE
The solar cycle is a period of 28 years; in any corresponding year of each cycle the days of the week recur on the same day of the month.

METONIC (LUNAR, OR MINOR) CYCLE
In 432 BC, Meton, an Athenian astronomer, found that 235 lunations are very nearly, though not exactly, equal in duration to 19 solar years and so after 19 years the phases of the Moon recur approximately on the same days of the month. The dates of full moon in a cycle of 19 years were inscribed in figures of gold on public monuments in Athens, and the number showing the position of a year in the cycle is called the golden number of that year.

JULIAN PERIOD
The Julian period was proposed by Joseph Scaliger in 1582. The period is 7,980 Julian years, and its first year coincides with the year 4713 BC. The figure of 7,980 is the product of the number of years in the solar cycle, the Metonic cycle and the cycle of the Roman indiction (28 × 19 × 15).

ROMAN INDICTION
The Roman indiction is a period of 15 years, instituted for fiscal purposes about AD 300.

EPACT
The epact is the age of the calendar Moon, diminished by one day, on 1 January, in the ecclesiastical lunar calendar.

CHINESE CALENDAR
A lunar calendar was the sole calendar in use in China until 1911, when the government adopted the new (Gregorian) calendar for official and most business activities. The Chinese tend to follow both calendars, the lunar calendar playing an important part in personal life, eg birth celebrations, festivals, marriages; and in rural villages the lunar calendar dictates the cycle of activities, denoting the change of weather and farming activities.

The lunar calendar is used in Hong Kong, Singapore, Malaysia, Tibet and elsewhere in south-east Asia. The calendar has a cycle of 60 years. The new year begins at the first new moon after the sun enters the sign of Aquarius, ie the new year falls between 21 January and 19 February in the Gregorian calendar.

Each year in the Chinese calendar is associated with one of 12 animals: the rat, the ox, the tiger, the rabbit, the dragon, the snake, the horse, the goat or sheep, the monkey, the chicken or rooster, the dog, and the pig.

The date of the Chinese new year and the astrological sign for the years 2012–15 are:

2012	23 January	Dragon
2013	10 February	Snake
2014	31 January	Horse
2015	19 February	Goat or Sheep

COPTIC CALENDAR
In the Coptic calendar, which is used in parts of Egypt and Ethiopia, the year is made up of 12 months of 30 days each, followed, in general, by five complementary days. Every fourth year is an intercalary or leap year and in these years there are six complementary days. The intercalary year of the Coptic calendar immediately precedes the leap year of the Julian calendar. The era is that of Diocletian or the Martyrs, the origin of which is fixed at 29 August AD 284 (Julian date).

INDIAN ERAS
In addition to the Muslim reckoning, other eras are used in India. The Saka era of southern India, dating from 3 March AD 78, was declared the national calendar of the Republic of India with effect from 22 March 1957, to be used concurrently with the Gregorian calendar. As revised, the year of the new Saka era begins at the spring equinox, with five successive months of 31 days and seven of 30 days in ordinary years, and six months of each length in leap years. The year AD 2012 is 1934 of the revised Saka era.

The year AD 2012 corresponds to the following years in other eras:

Year 2069 of the Vikram Samvat era
Year 1419 of the Bengali San era
Year 1188 of the Kollam era
Year 5113 of the Kaliyuga era
Year 2555 of the Buddha Nirvana era

JAPANESE CALENDAR
The Japanese calendar is essentially the same as the Gregorian calendar, the years, months and weeks being of the same length and beginning on the same days as those of the Gregorian calendar. The numeration of the years is different, based on a system of epochs or periods, each of which begins at the accession of an emperor or other important occurrence. The method is not unlike the British system of regnal years, except that each year of a period closes on 31 December. The Japanese chronology begins about AD 650 and the three latest epochs are defined by the reigns of emperors, whose actual names are not necessarily used:

Epoch
Taisho – 1 August 1912 to 25 December 1926
Showa – 26 December 1926 to 7 January 1989
Heisei – 8 January 1989

The year Heisei 24 begins on 1 January 2012.

The months are known as First Month, Second Month, etc, First Month being equivalent to January. The days of the week are Nichiyobi (Sun-day), Getsuyobi (Moon-day), Kayobi (Fire-day), Suiyobi (Water-day), Mokuyobi (Wood-day), Kinyobi (Metal-day) and Doyobi (Earth-day).

THE MASONIC YEAR
Two dates are quoted in warrants, dispensations, etc, issued by the United Grand Lodge of England, those for the current year being expressed as *Anno Domini* 2012 – *Anno Lucis* 6012. This *Anno Lucis* (year of light) is based on the Book of Genesis 1:3, the 4,000-year difference being derived, in modified form, from *Ussher's Notation,* published in 1654, which places the Creation of the World in 4004 BC.

OLYMPIADS
Ancient Greek chronology was reckoned in Olympiads, cycles of four years corresponding with the periodic Olympic Games held on the plain of Olympia, in Elis, once every four years. The intervening years were the first, second, etc, of the Olympiad, which received the name of the victor at the Games. The first recorded Olympiad is that of Choroebus, 776 BC.

ZOROASTRIAN CALENDAR
Zoroastrians, followers of the Iranian prophet Zarathushtra (known to the Greeks as Zoroaster) are mostly to be found in Iran and in India, where they are known as Parsees.

The Zoroastrian era dates from the coronation of the last Zoroastrian Sasanian king in AD 631. The Zoroastrian calendar is divided into 12 months, each comprising 30 days, followed by five holy days of the Gathas at the end of each year to make the year consist of 365 days.

In order to synchronise the calendar with the solar year of 365 days, an extra month was intercalated once every 120 years. However, this intercalation ceased in the 12th century and the new year, which had fallen in the spring, slipped back to August. Because intercalation ceased at different times in Iran and India, there was one month's difference between the calendar followed in Iran (Kadmi calendar) and that followed by the Parsees (Shenshai calendar). In 1906 a group of Zoroastrians decided to bring the calendar back in line with the seasons again and restore the new year to 21 March each year (Fasli calendar).

The Shenshai calendar (new year in August) is mainly used by Parsees. The Fasli calendar (new year, 21 March) is mainly used by Zoroastrians living in Iran, in the Indian subcontinent, or away from Iran.

ROMAN CALENDAR

Roman historians adopted as an epoch the foundation of Rome, which is believed to have happened in the year 753 BC. The ordinal number of the years in Roman reckoning is followed by the letters AUC *(ab urbe condita)*, so that the year 2012 is 2765 AUC (MMDCCLXV). The calendar that we know has developed from one said to

have been established by Romulus using a year of 304 days divided into ten months, beginning with March. To this Numa added January and February, making the year consist of 12 months of 30 and 29 days alternately, with an additional day so that the total was 355. It is also said that Numa ordered an intercalary month of 22 or 23 days in alternate years, making 90 days in eight years, to be inserted after 23 February.

However, there is some doubt as to the origination and the details of the intercalation in the Roman calendar. It is certain that some scheme of this kind was inaugurated and not fully carried out, for in the year 46 BC Julius Caesar found that the calendar had been allowed to fall into some confusion. He sought the help of the Egyptian astronomer Sosigenes, which led to the construction and adoption (45 BC) of the Julian calendar, and, by a slight alteration, to the Gregorian calendar now in use. The year 46 BC was made to consist of 445 days and is called the Year of Confusion.

In the Roman (Julian) calendar the days of the month were counted backwards from three fixed points, or days, and an intervening day was said to be so many days before the next coming point, the first and last being counted. These three points were the Kalends, the Nones, and the Ides. Their positions in the months and the method of counting from them will be seen in the table below. The year containing 366 days was called *bissextilis annus*, as it had a doubled sixth day *(bissextus dies)* before the March Kalends on 24 February – *ante diem sextum Kalendas Martias*, or a.d. VI Kal. Mart.

Present days of the month	March, May, July, October have thirty-one days	January, August, December have thirty-one days	April, June, September, November have thirty days	February has twenty-eight days, and in leap year twenty-nine
1	Kalendis	Kalendis	Kalendis	Kalendis
2	VI	IV ⎫ ante	IV ⎫ ante	IV ⎫ ante
3	V ⎱ ante	III ⎭ Nonas	III ⎭ Nonas	III ⎭ Nonas
4	IV ⎰ Nonas	pridie Nonas	pridie Nonas	pridie Nonas
5	III ⎭	Nonis	Nonis	Nonis
6	pridie Nonas	VIII ⎫	VIII ⎫	VIII ⎫
7	Nonis	VII	VII	VII
8	VIII ⎫	VI ⎱ ante	VI ⎱ ante	VI ⎱ ante
9	VII	V ⎰ Idus	V ⎰ Idus	V ⎰ Idus
10	VI ⎱ ante	IV	IV	IV
11	V ⎰ Idus	III ⎭	III ⎭	III ⎭
12	IV	pridie Idus	pridie Idus	pridie Idus
13	III ⎭	Idibus	Idibus	Idibus
14	pridie Idus	XIX ⎫	XVIII ⎫	XVI ⎫
15	Idibus	XVIII	XVII	XV
16	XVII ⎫	XVII	XVI	XIV
17	XVI	XVI	XV	XIII
18	XV	XV	XIV	XII
19	XIV	XIV	XIII	XI
20	XIII	XIII	XII	X ⎱ ante Kalendas
21	XII	XII ⎱ ante Kalendas	XI ⎱ (of the month	IX ⎰ Martias
22	XI ⎱ ante Kalendas	XI ⎰ (of the month	X ⎰ following)	VIII
23	X ⎰ (of the month	X ⎰ following)	IX	VII
24	IX ⎰ following)	IX	VIII	*VI
25	VIII	VIII	VII	V
26	VII	VII	VI	IV
27	VI	VI	V	III ⎭
28	V	V	IV	pridie Kalendas
29	IV	IV	III ⎭	Martias
30	III ⎭	III ⎭	pridie Kalendas	
31	pridie Kalendas (Aprilis, Iunias, Sextilis, Novembris)	pridie Kalendas (Februarias, Septembris, Ianuarias)	(Maias, Quinctilis, Octobris, Decembris)	

* Repeated in leap year

CALENDAR FOR ANY YEAR 1780–2040

To select the correct calendar for any year between 1780 and 2040, consult the index below
*leap year

1780 N*	1813 K	1846 I	1879 G	1912 D*	1945 C	1978 A	2011 M		
1781 C	1814 M	1847 K	1880 J*	1913 G	1946 E	1979 C	2012 B*		
1782 E	1815 A	1848 N*	1881 M	1914 I	1947 G	1980 F*	2013 E		
1783 G	1816 D*	1849 C	1882 A	1915 K	1948 J*	1981 I	2014 G		
1784 J*	1817 G	1850 E	1883 C	1916 N*	1949 M	1982 K	2015 I		
1785 M	1818 I	1851 G	1884 F*	1917 C	1950 A	1983 M	2016 L*		
1786 A	1819 K	1852 J*	1885 I	1918 E	1951 C	1984 B*	2017 A		
1787 C	1820 N*	1853 M	1886 K	1919 G	1952 F*	1985 E	2018 C		
1788 F*	1821 C	1854 A	1887 M	1920 J*	1953 I	1986 G	2019 E		
1789 I	1822 E	1855 C	1888 B*	1921 M	1954 K	1987 I	2020 H*		
1790 K	1823 G	1856 F*	1889 E	1922 A	1955 M	1988 L*	2021 K		
1791 M	1824 J*	1857 I	1890 G	1923 C	1956 B*	1989 A	2022 M		
1792 B*	1825 M	1858 K	1891 I	1924 F*	1957 E	1990 C	2023 A		
1793 E	1826 A	1859 M	1892 L*	1925 I	1958 G	1991 E	2024 D*		
1794 G	1827 C	1860 B*	1893 A	1926 K	1959 I	1992 H*	2025 G		
1795 I	1828 F*	1861 E	1894 C	1927 M	1960 L*	1993 K	2026 I		
1796 L*	1829 I	1862 G	1895 E	1928 B*	1961 A	1994 M	2027 K		
1797 A	1830 K	1863 I	1896 H*	1929 E	1962 C	1995 A	2028 N*		
1798 C	1831 M	1864 L*	1897 K	1930 G	1963 E	1996 D*	2029 C		
1799 E	1832 B*	1865 A	1898 M	1931 I	1964 H*	1997 G	2030 E		
1800 G	1833 E	1866 C	1899 A	1932 L*	1965 K	1998 I	2031 G		
1801 I	1834 G	1867 E	1900 C	1933 A	1966 M	1999 K	2032 J*		
1802 K	1835 I	1868 H*	1901 E	1934 C	1967 A	2000 N*	2033 M		
1803 M	1836 L*	1869 K	1902 G	1935 E	1968 D*	2001 C	2034 A		
1804 B*	1837 A	1870 M	1903 I	1936 H*	1969 G	2002 E	2035 C		
1805 E	1838 C	1871 A	1904 L*	1937 K	1970 I	2003 G	2036 F*		
1806 G	1839 E	1872 D*	1905 A	1938 M	1971 K	2004 J*	2037 I		
1807 I	1840 H*	1873 G	1906 C	1939 A	1972 N*	2005 M	2038 K		
1808 L*	1841 K	1874 I	1907 E	1940 D*	1973 C	2006 A	2039 M		
1809 A	1842 M	1875 K	1908 H*	1941 G	1974 E	2007 C	2040 B*		
1810 C	1843 A	1876 N*	1909 K	1942 I	1975 G	2008 F*			
1811 E	1844 D*	1877 C	1910 M	1943 K	1976 J*	2009 I			
1812 H*	1845 G	1878 E	1911 A	1944 N*	1977 M	2010 K			

A

	January	February	March
Sun.	1 8 15 22 29	5 12 19 26	5 12 19 26
Mon.	2 9 16 23 30	6 13 20 27	6 13 20 27
Tue.	3 10 17 24 31	7 14 21 28	7 14 21 28
Wed.	4 11 18 25	1 8 15 22	1 8 15 22 29
Thur.	5 12 19 26	2 9 16 23	2 9 16 23 30
Fri.	6 13 20 27	3 10 17 24	3 10 17 24 31
Sat.	7 14 21 28	4 11 18 25	4 11 18 25

	April	May	June
Sun.	2 9 16 23 30	7 14 21 28	4 11 18 25
Mon.	3 10 17 24	1 8 15 22 29	5 12 19 26
Tue.	4 11 18 25	2 9 16 23 30	6 13 20 27
Wed.	5 12 19 26	3 10 17 24 31	7 14 21 28
Thur.	6 13 20 27	4 11 18 25	1 8 15 22 29
Fri.	7 14 21 28	5 12 19 26	2 9 16 23 30
Sat.	1 8 15 22 29	6 13 20 27	3 10 17 24

	July	August	September
Sun.	2 9 16 23 30	6 13 20 27	3 10 17 24
Mon.	3 10 17 24 31	7 14 21 28	4 11 18 25
Tue.	4 11 18 25	1 8 15 22 29	5 12 19 26
Wed.	5 12 19 26	2 9 16 23 30	6 13 20 27
Thur.	6 13 20 27	3 10 17 24 31	7 14 21 28
Fri.	7 14 21 28	4 11 18 25	1 8 15 22 29
Sat.	1 8 15 22 29	5 12 19 26	2 9 16 23 30

	October	November	December
Sun.	1 8 15 22 29	5 12 19 26	3 10 17 24 31
Mon.	2 9 16 23 30	6 13 20 27	4 11 18 25
Tue.	3 10 17 24 31	7 14 21 28	5 12 19 26
Wed.	4 11 18 25	1 8 15 22 29	6 13 20 27
Thur.	5 12 19 26	2 9 16 23 30	7 14 21 28
Fri.	6 13 20 27	3 10 17 24	1 8 15 22 29
Sat.	7 14 21 28	4 11 18 25	2 9 16 23 30

EASTER DAYS

March 26	1815, 1826, 1837, 1967, 1978, 1989
April 2	1809, 1893, 1899, 1961
April 9	1871, 1882, 1939, 1950, 2023, 2034
April 16	1786, 1797, 1843, 1854, 1865, 1911
	1922, 1933, 1995, 2006, 2017
April 23	1905

B (LEAP YEAR)

	January	February	March
Sun.	1 8 15 22 29	5 12 19 26	4 11 18 25
Mon.	2 9 16 23 30	6 13 20 27	5 12 19 26
Tue.	3 10 17 24 31	7 14 21 28	6 13 20 27
Wed.	4 11 18 25	1 8 15 22 29	7 14 21 28
Thur.	5 12 19 26	2 9 16 23	1 8 15 22 29
Fri.	6 13 20 27	3 10 17 24	2 9 16 23 30
Sat.	7 14 21 28	4 11 18 25	3 10 17 24 31

	April	May	June
Sun.	1 8 15 22 29	6 13 20 27	3 10 17 24
Mon.	2 9 16 23 30	7 14 21 28	4 11 18 25
Tue.	3 10 17 24	1 8 15 22 29	5 12 19 26
Wed.	4 11 18 25	2 9 16 23 30	6 13 20 27
Thur.	5 12 19 26	3 10 17 24 31	7 14 21 28
Fri.	6 13 20 27	4 11 18 25	1 8 15 22 29
Sat.	7 14 21 28	5 12 19 26	2 9 16 23 30

	July	August	September
Sun.	1 8 15 22 29	5 12 19 26	2 9 16 23 30
Mon.	2 9 16 23 30	6 13 20 27	3 10 17 24
Tue.	3 10 17 24 31	7 14 21 28	4 11 18 25
Wed.	4 11 18 25	1 8 15 22 29	5 12 19 26
Thur.	5 12 19 26	2 9 16 23 30	6 13 20 27
Fri.	6 13 20 27	3 10 17 24 31	7 14 21 28
Sat.	7 14 21 28	4 11 18 25	1 8 15 22 29

	October	November	December
Sun.	7 14 21 28	4 11 18 25	2 9 16 23 30
Mon.	1 8 15 22 29	5 12 19 26	3 10 17 24 31
Tue.	2 9 16 23 30	6 13 20 27	4 11 18 25
Wed.	3 10 17 24 31	7 14 21 28	5 12 19 26
Thur.	4 11 18 25	1 8 15 22 29	6 13 20 27
Fri.	5 12 19 26	2 9 16 23 30	7 14 21 28
Sat.	6 13 20 27	3 10 17 24	1 8 15 22 29

EASTER DAYS

April 1	1804, 1888, 1956, 2040
April 8	1792, 1860, 1928, 2012
April 22	1832, 1984

C

	January	February	March
Sun.	7 14 21 28	4 11 18 25	4 11 18 25
Mon.	1 8 15 22 29	5 12 19 26	5 12 19 26
Tue.	2 9 16 23 30	6 13 20 27	6 13 20 27
Wed.	3 10 17 24 31	7 14 21 28	7 14 21 28
Thur.	4 11 18 25	1 8 15 22	1 8 15 22 29
Fri.	5 12 19 26	2 9 16 23	2 9 16 23 30
Sat.	6 13 20 27	3 10 17 24	3 10 17 24 31

	April	May	June
Sun.	1 8 15 22 29	6 13 20 27	3 10 17 24
Mon.	2 9 16 23 30	7 14 21 28	4 11 18 25
Tue.	3 10 17 24	1 8 15 22 29	5 12 19 26
Wed.	4 11 18 25	2 9 16 23 30	6 13 20 27
Thur.	5 12 19 26	3 10 17 24 31	7 14 21 28
Fri.	6 13 20 27	4 11 18 25	1 8 15 22 29
Sat.	7 14 21 28	5 12 19 26	2 9 16 23 30

	July	August	September
Sun.	1 8 15 22 29	5 12 19 26	2 9 16 23 30
Mon.	2 9 16 23 30	6 13 20 27	3 10 17 24
Tue.	3 10 17 24 31	7 14 21 28	4 11 18 25
Wed.	4 11 18 25	1 8 15 22 29	5 12 19 26
Thur.	5 12 19 26	2 9 16 23 30	6 13 20 27
Fri.	6 13 20 27	3 10 17 24 31	7 14 21 28
Sat.	7 14 21 28	4 11 18 25	1 8 15 22 29

	October	November	December
Sun.	7 14 21 28	4 11 18 25	2 9 16 23 30
Mon.	1 8 15 22 29	5 12 19 26	3 10 17 24 31
Tue.	2 9 16 23 30	6 13 20 27	4 11 18 25
Wed.	3 10 17 24 31	7 14 21 28	5 12 19 26
Thur.	4 11 18 25	1 8 15 22 29	6 13 20 27
Fri.	5 12 19 26	2 9 16 23 30	7 14 21 28
Sat.	6 13 20 27	3 10 17 24	1 8 15 22 29

EASTER DAYS
March 25	1883, 1894, 1951, 2035
April 1	1866, 1877, 1923, 1934, 1945, 2018, 2029
April 8	1787, 1798, 1849, 1855, 1917, 2007
April 15	1781, 1827, 1838, 1900, 1906, 1979, 1990, 2001
April 22	1810, 1821, 1962, 1973

E

	January	February	March
Sun.	6 13 20 27	3 10 17 24	3 10 17 24 31
Mon.	7 14 21 28	4 11 18 25	4 11 18 25
Tue.	1 8 15 22 29	5 12 19 26	5 12 19 26
Wed.	2 9 16 23 30	6 13 20 27	6 13 20 27
Thur.	3 10 17 24 31	7 14 21 28	7 14 21 28
Fri.	4 11 18 25	1 8 15 22	1 8 15 22 29
Sat.	5 12 19 26	2 9 16 23	2 9 16 23 30

	April	May	June
Sun.	7 14 21 28	5 12 19 26	2 9 16 23 30
Mon.	1 8 15 22 29	6 13 20 27	3 10 17 24
Tue.	2 9 16 23 30	7 14 21 28	4 11 18 25
Wed.	3 10 17 24	1 8 15 22 29	5 12 19 26
Thur.	4 11 18 25	2 9 16 23 30	6 13 20 27
Fri.	5 12 19 26	3 10 17 24 31	7 14 21 28
Sat.	6 13 20 27	4 11 18 25	1 8 15 22 29

	July	August	September
Sun.	7 14 21 28	4 11 18 25	1 8 15 22 29
Mon.	1 8 15 22 29	5 12 19 26	2 9 16 23 30
Tue.	2 9 16 23 30	6 13 20 27	3 10 17 24
Wed.	3 10 17 24 31	7 14 21 28	4 11 18 25
Thur.	4 11 18 25	1 8 15 22 29	5 12 19 26
Fri.	5 12 19 26	2 9 16 23 30	6 13 20 27
Sat.	6 13 20 27	3 10 17 24 31	7 14 21 28

	October	November	December
Sun.	6 13 20 27	3 10 17 24	1 8 15 22 29
Mon.	7 14 21 28	4 11 18 25	2 9 16 23 30
Tue.	1 8 15 22 29	5 12 19 26	3 10 17 24 31
Wed.	2 9 16 23 30	6 13 20 27	4 11 18 25
Thur.	3 10 17 24 31	7 14 21 28	5 12 19 26
Fri.	4 11 18 25	1 8 15 22 29	6 13 20 27
Sat.	5 12 19 26	2 9 16 23 30	7 14 21 28

EASTER DAYS
March 24	1799
March 31	1782, 1793, 1839, 1850, 1861, 1907
	1918, 1929, 1991, 2002, 2013
April 7	1822, 1833, 1901, 1985
April 14	1805, 1811, 1895, 1963, 1974
April 21	1867, 1878, 1889, 1935, 1946, 1957, 2019, 2030

D (LEAP YEAR)

	January	February	March
Sun.	7 14 21 28	4 11 18 25	3 10 17 24 31
Mon.	1 8 15 22 29	5 12 19 26	4 11 18 25
Tue.	2 9 16 23 30	6 13 20 27	5 12 19 26
Wed.	3 10 17 24 31	7 14 21 28	6 13 20 27
Thur.	4 11 18 25	1 8 15 22 29	7 14 21 28
Fri.	5 12 19 26	2 9 16 23	1 8 15 22 29
Sat.	6 13 20 27	3 10 17 24	2 9 16 23 30

	April	May	June
Sun.	7 14 21 28	5 12 19 26	2 9 16 23 30
Mon.	1 8 15 22 29	6 13 20 27	3 10 17 24
Tue.	2 9 16 23 30	7 14 21 28	4 11 18 25
Wed.	3 10 17 24	1 8 15 22 29	5 12 19 26
Thur.	4 11 18 25	2 9 16 23 30	6 13 20 27
Fri.	5 12 19 26	3 10 17 24 31	7 14 21 28
Sat.	6 13 20 27	4 11 18 25	1 8 15 22 29

	July	August	September
Sun.	7 14 21 28	4 11 18 25	1 8 15 22 29
Mon.	1 8 15 22 29	5 12 19 26	2 9 16 23 30
Tue.	2 9 16 23 30	6 13 20 27	3 10 17 24
Wed.	3 10 17 24 31	7 14 21 28	4 11 18 25
Thur.	4 11 18 25	1 8 15 22 29	5 12 19 26
Fri.	5 12 19 26	2 9 16 23 30	6 13 20 27
Sat.	6 13 20 27	3 10 17 24 31	7 14 21 28

	October	November	December
Sun.	6 13 20 27	3 10 17 24	1 8 15 22 29
Mon.	7 14 21 28	4 11 18 25	2 9 16 23 30
Tue.	1 8 15 22 29	5 12 19 26	3 10 17 24 31
Wed.	2 9 16 23 30	6 13 20 27	4 11 18 25
Thur.	3 10 17 24 31	7 14 21 28	5 12 19 26
Fri.	4 11 18 25	1 8 15 22 29	6 13 20 27
Sat.	5 12 19 26	2 9 16 23 30	7 14 21 28

EASTER DAYS
March 24	1940
March 31	1872, 2024
April 7	1844, 1912, 1996
April 14	1816, 1968

F (LEAP YEAR)

	January	February	March
Sun.	6 13 20 27	3 10 17 24	2 9 16 23 30
Mon.	7 14 21 28	4 11 18 25	3 10 17 24 31
Tue.	1 8 15 22 29	5 12 19 26	4 11 18 25
Wed.	2 9 16 23 30	6 13 20 27	5 12 19 26
Thur.	3 10 17 24 31	7 14 21 28	6 13 20 27
Fri.	4 11 18 25	1 8 15 22 29	7 14 21 28
Sat.	5 12 19 26	2 9 16 23	1 8 15 22 29

	April	May	June
Sun.	6 13 20 27	4 11 18 25	1 8 15 22 29
Mon.	7 14 21 28	5 12 19 26	2 9 16 23 30
Tue.	1 8 15 22 29	6 13 20 27	3 10 17 24
Wed.	2 9 16 23 30	7 14 21 28	4 11 18 25
Thur.	3 10 17 24	1 8 15 22 29	5 12 19 26
Fri.	4 11 18 25	2 9 16 23 30	6 13 20 27
Sat.	5 12 19 26	3 10 17 24 31	7 14 21 28

	July	August	September
Sun.	6 13 20 27	3 10 17 24 31	7 14 21 28
Mon.	7 14 21 28	4 11 18 25	1 8 15 22 29
Tue.	1 8 15 22 29	5 12 19 26	2 9 16 23 30
Wed.	2 9 16 23 30	6 13 20 27	3 10 17 24
Thur.	3 10 17 24 31	7 14 21 28	4 11 18 25
Fri.	4 11 18 25	1 8 15 22 29	5 12 19 26
Sat.	5 12 19 26	2 9 16 23 30	6 13 20 27

	October	November	December
Sun.	5 12 19 26	2 9 16 23 30	7 14 21 28
Mon.	6 13 20 27	3 10 17 24	1 8 15 22 29
Tue.	7 14 21 28	4 11 18 25	2 9 16 23 30
Wed.	1 8 15 22 29	5 12 19 26	3 10 17 24 31
Thur.	2 9 16 23 30	6 13 20 27	4 11 18 25
Fri.	3 10 17 24 31	7 14 21 28	5 12 19 26
Sat.	4 11 18 25	1 8 15 22 29	6 13 20 27

EASTER DAYS
March 23	1788, 1856, 2008
April 6	1828, 1980
April 13	1884, 1952, 2036
April 20	1924

G

	January	February	March
Sun.	5 12 19 26	2 9 16 23	2 9 16 23 30
Mon.	6 13 20 27	3 10 17 24	3 10 17 24 31
Tue.	7 14 21 28	4 11 18 25	4 11 18 25
Wed.	1 8 15 22 29	5 12 19 26	5 12 19 26
Thur.	2 9 16 23 30	6 13 20 27	6 13 20 27
Fri.	3 10 17 24 31	7 14 21 28	7 14 21 28
Sat.	4 11 18 25	1 8 15 22	1 8 15 22 29

	April	May	June
Sun.	6 13 20 27	4 11 18 25	1 8 15 22 29
Mon.	7 14 21 28	5 12 19 26	2 9 16 23 30
Tue.	1 8 15 22 29	6 13 20 27	3 10 17 24
Wed.	2 9 16 23 30	7 14 21 28	4 11 18 25
Thur.	3 10 17 24	1 8 15 22 29	5 12 19 26
Fri.	4 11 18 25	2 9 16 23 30	6 13 20 27
Sat.	5 12 19 26	3 10 17 24 31	7 14 21 28

	July	August	September
Sun.	6 13 20 27	3 10 17 24 31	7 14 21 28
Mon.	7 14 21 28	4 11 18 25	1 8 15 22 29
Tue.	1 8 15 22 29	5 12 19 26	2 9 16 23 30
Wed.	2 9 16 23 30	6 13 20 27	3 10 17 24
Thur.	3 10 17 24 31	7 14 21 28	4 11 18 25
Fri.	4 11 18 25	1 8 15 22 29	5 12 19 26
Sat.	5 12 19 26	2 9 16 23 30	6 13 20 27

	October	November	December
Sun.	5 12 19 26	2 9 16 23 30	7 14 21 28
Mon.	6 13 20 27	3 10 17 24	1 8 15 22 29
Tue.	7 14 21 28	4 11 18 25	2 9 16 23 30
Wed.	1 8 15 22 29	5 12 19 26	3 10 17 24 31
Thur.	2 9 16 23 30	6 13 20 27	4 11 18 25
Fri.	3 10 17 24 31	7 14 21 28	5 12 19 26
Sat.	4 11 18 25	1 8 15 22 29	6 13 20 27

EASTER DAYS
March 23	1845, 1913
March 30	1823, 1834, 1902, 1975, 1986, 1997
April 6	1806, 1817, 1890, 1947, 1958, 1969
April 13	1800, 1873, 1879, 1941, 2031
April 20	1783, 1794, 1851, 1862, 1919, 1930, 2003, 2014, 2025

H (LEAP YEAR)

	January	February	March
Sun.	5 12 19 26	2 9 16 23	1 8 15 22 29
Mon.	6 13 20 27	3 10 17 24	2 9 16 23 30
Tue.	7 14 21 28	4 11 18 25	3 10 17 24 31
Wed.	1 8 15 22 29	5 12 19 26	4 11 18 25
Thur.	2 9 16 23 30	6 13 20 27	5 12 19 26
Fri.	3 10 17 24 31	7 14 21 28	6 13 20 27
Sat.	4 11 18 25	1 8 15 22 29	7 14 21 28

	April	May	June
Sun.	5 12 19 26	3 10 17 24 31	7 14 21 28
Mon.	6 13 20 27	4 11 18 25	1 8 15 22 29
Tue.	7 14 21 28	5 12 19 26	2 9 16 23 30
Wed.	1 8 15 22 29	6 13 20 27	3 10 17 24
Thur.	2 9 16 23 30	7 14 21 28	4 11 18 25
Fri.	3 10 17 24	1 8 15 22 29	5 12 19 26
Sat.	4 11 18 25	2 9 16 23 30	6 13 20 27

	July	August	September
Sun.	5 12 19 26	2 9 16 23 30	6 13 20 27
Mon.	6 13 20 27	3 10 17 24 31	7 14 21 28
Tue.	7 14 21 28	4 11 18 25	1 8 15 22 29
Wed.	1 8 15 22 29	5 12 19 26	2 9 16 23 30
Thur.	2 9 16 23 30	6 13 20 27	3 10 17 24
Fri.	3 10 17 24 31	7 14 21 28	4 11 18 25
Sat.	4 11 18 25	1 8 15 22 29	5 12 19 26

	October	November	December
Sun.	4 11 18 25	1 8 15 22 29	6 13 20 27
Mon.	5 12 19 26	2 9 16 23 30	7 14 21 28
Tue.	6 13 20 27	3 10 17 24	1 8 15 22 29
Wed.	7 14 21 28	4 11 18 25	2 9 16 23 30
Thur.	1 8 15 22 29	5 12 19 26	3 10 17 24 31
Fri.	2 9 16 23 30	6 13 20 27	4 11 18 25
Sat.	3 10 17 24 31	7 14 21 28	5 12 19 26

EASTER DAYS
March 29	1812, 1964
April 5	1896
April 12	1868, 1936, 2020
April 19	1840, 1908, 1992

I

	January	February	March
Sun.	4 11 18 25	1 8 15 22	1 8 15 22 29
Mon.	5 12 19 26	2 9 16 23	2 9 16 23 30
Tue.	6 13 20 27	3 10 17 24	3 10 17 24 31
Wed.	7 14 21 28	4 11 18 25	4 11 18 25
Thur.	1 8 15 22 29	5 12 19 26	5 12 19 26
Fri.	2 9 16 23 30	6 13 20 27	6 13 20 27
Sat.	3 10 17 24 31	7 14 21 28	7 14 21 28

	April	May	June
Sun.	5 12 19 26	3 10 17 24 31	7 14 21 28
Mon.	6 13 20 27	4 11 18 25	1 8 15 22 29
Tue.	7 14 21 28	5 12 19 26	2 9 16 23 30
Wed.	1 8 15 22 29	6 13 20 27	3 10 17 24
Thur.	2 9 16 23 30	7 14 21 28	4 11 18 25
Fri.	3 10 17 24	1 8 15 22 29	5 12 19 26
Sat.	4 11 18 25	2 9 16 23 30	6 13 20 27

	July	August	September
Sun.	5 12 19 26	2 9 16 23 30	6 13 20 27
Mon.	6 13 20 27	3 10 17 24 31	7 14 21 28
Tue.	7 14 21 28	4 11 18 25	1 8 15 22 29
Wed.	1 8 15 22 29	5 12 19 26	2 9 16 23 30
Thur.	2 9 16 23 30	6 13 20 27	3 10 17 24
Fri.	3 10 17 24 31	7 14 21 28	4 11 18 25
Sat.	4 11 18 25	1 8 15 22 29	5 12 19 26

	October	November	December
Sun.	4 11 18 25	1 8 15 22 29	6 13 20 27
Mon.	5 12 19 26	2 9 16 23 30	7 14 21 28
Tue.	6 13 20 27	3 10 17 24	1 8 15 22 29
Wed.	7 14 21 28	4 11 18 25	2 9 16 23 30
Thur.	1 8 15 22 29	5 12 19 26	3 10 17 24 31
Fri.	2 9 16 23 30	6 13 20 27	4 11 18 25
Sat.	3 10 17 24 31	7 14 21 28	5 12 19 26

EASTER DAYS
March 22	1818
March 29	1807, 1891, 1959, 1970
April 5	1795, 1801, 1863, 1874, 1885, 1931, 1942, 1953, 2015, 2026, 2037
April 12	1789, 1846, 1857, 1903, 1914, 1925, 1998, 2009
April 19	1829, 1835, 1981, 1987

J (LEAP YEAR)

	January	February	March
Sun.	4 11 18 25	1 8 15 22 29	7 14 21 28
Mon.	5 12 19 26	2 9 16 23	1 8 15 22 29
Tue.	6 13 20 27	3 10 17 24	2 9 16 23 30
Wed.	7 14 21 28	4 11 18 25	3 10 17 24 31
Thur.	1 8 15 22 29	5 12 19 26	4 11 18 25
Fri.	2 9 16 23 30	6 13 20 27	5 12 19 26
Sat.	3 10 17 24 31	7 14 21 28	6 13 20 27

	April	May	June
Sun.	4 11 18 25	2 9 16 23 30	6 13 20 27
Mon.	5 12 19 26	3 10 17 24 31	7 14 21 28
Tue.	6 13 20 27	4 11 18 25	1 8 15 22 29
Wed.	7 14 21 28	5 12 19 26	2 9 16 23 30
Thur.	1 8 15 22 29	6 13 20 27	3 10 17 24
Fri.	2 9 16 23 30	7 14 21 28	4 11 18 25
Sat.	3 10 17 24	1 8 15 22 29	5 12 19 26

	July	August	September
Sun.	4 11 18 25	1 8 15 22 29	5 12 19 26
Mon.	5 12 19 26	2 9 16 23 30	6 13 20 27
Tue.	6 13 20 27	3 10 17 24 31	7 14 21 28
Wed.	7 14 21 28	4 11 18 25	1 8 15 22 29
Thur.	1 8 15 22 29	5 12 19 26	2 9 16 23 30
Fri.	2 9 16 23 30	6 13 20 27	3 10 17 24
Sat.	3 10 17 24 31	7 14 21 28	4 11 18 25

	October	November	December
Sun.	3 10 17 24 31	7 14 21 28	5 12 19 26
Mon.	4 11 18 25	1 8 15 22 29	6 13 20 27
Tue.	5 12 19 26	2 9 16 23 30	7 14 21 28
Wed.	6 13 20 27	3 10 17 24	1 8 15 22 29
Thur.	7 14 21 28	4 11 18 25	2 9 16 23 30
Fri.	1 8 15 22 29	5 12 19 26	3 10 17 24 31
Sat.	2 9 16 23 30	6 13 20 27	4 11 18 25

EASTER DAYS
March 28	1880, 1948, 2032
April 4	1920
April 11	1784, 1852, 2004
April 18	1824, 1976

K

	January	February	March
Sun.	3 10 17 24 31	7 14 21 28	7 14 21 28
Mon.	4 11 18 25	1 8 15 22	1 8 15 22 29
Tue.	5 12 19 26	2 9 16 23	2 9 16 23 30
Wed.	6 13 20 27	3 10 17 24	3 10 17 24 31
Thur.	7 14 21 28	4 11 18 25	4 11 18 25
Fri.	1 8 15 22 29	5 12 19 26	5 12 19 26
Sat.	2 9 16 23 30	6 13 20 27	6 13 20 27

	April	May	June
Sun.	4 11 18 25	2 9 16 23 30	6 13 20 27
Mon.	5 12 19 26	3 10 17 24 31	7 14 21 28
Tue.	6 13 20 27	4 11 18 25	1 8 15 22 29
Wed.	7 14 21 28	5 12 19 26	2 9 16 23 30
Thur.	1 8 15 22 29	6 13 20 27	3 10 17 24
Fri.	2 9 16 23 30	7 14 21 28	4 11 18 25
Sat.	3 10 17 24	1 8 15 22 29	5 12 19 26

	July	August	September
Sun.	4 11 18 25	1 8 15 22 29	5 12 19 26
Mon.	5 12 19 26	2 9 16 23 30	6 13 20 27
Tue.	6 13 20 27	3 10 17 24 31	7 14 21 28
Wed.	7 14 21 28	4 11 18 25	1 8 15 22 29
Thur.	1 8 15 22 29	5 12 19 26	2 9 16 23 30
Fri.	2 9 16 23 30	6 13 20 27	3 10 17 24
Sat.	3 10 17 24 31	7 14 21 28	4 11 18 25

	October	November	December
Sun.	3 10 17 24 31	7 14 21 28	5 12 19 26
Mon.	4 11 18 25	1 8 15 22 29	6 13 20 27
Tue.	5 12 19 26	2 9 16 23 30	7 14 21 28
Wed.	6 13 20 27	3 10 17 24	1 8 15 22 29
Thur.	7 14 21 28	4 11 18 25	2 9 16 23 30
Fri.	1 8 15 22 29	5 12 19 26	3 10 17 24 31
Sat.	2 9 16 23 30	6 13 20 27	4 11 18 25

EASTER DAYS

March 28	1869, 1875, 1937, 2027
April 4	1790, 1847, 1858, 1915, 1926, 1999, 2010, 2021
April 11	1819, 1830, 1841, 1909, 1971, 1982, 1993
April 18	1802, 1813, 1897, 1954, 1965
April 25	1886, 1943, 2038

M

	January	February	March
Sun.	2 9 16 23 30	6 13 20 27	6 13 20 27
Mon.	3 10 17 24 31	7 14 21 28	7 14 21 28
Tue.	4 11 18 25	1 8 15 22	1 8 15 22 29
Wed.	5 12 19 26	2 9 16 23	2 9 16 23 30
Thur.	6 13 20 27	3 10 17 24	3 10 17 24 31
Fri.	7 14 21 28	4 11 18 25	4 11 18 25
Sat.	1 8 15 22 29	5 12 19 26	5 12 19 26

	April	May	June
Sun.	3 10 17 24	1 8 15 22 29	5 12 19 26
Mon.	4 11 18 25	2 9 16 23 30	6 13 20 27
Tue.	5 12 19 26	3 10 17 24 31	7 14 21 28
Wed.	6 13 20 27	4 11 18 25	1 8 15 22 29
Thur.	7 14 21 28	5 12 19 26	2 9 16 23 30
Fri.	1 8 15 22 29	6 13 20 27	3 10 17 24
Sat.	2 9 16 23 30	7 14 21 28	4 11 18 25

	July	August	September
Sun.	3 10 17 24 31	7 14 21 28	4 11 18 25
Mon.	4 11 18 25	1 8 15 22 29	5 12 19 26
Tue.	5 12 19 26	2 9 16 23 30	6 13 20 27
Wed.	6 13 20 27	3 10 17 24 31	7 14 21 28
Thur.	7 14 21 28	4 11 18 25	1 8 15 22 29
Fri.	1 8 15 22 29	5 12 19 26	2 9 16 23 30
Sat.	2 9 16 23 30	6 13 20 27	3 10 17 24

	October	November	December
Sun.	2 9 16 23 30	6 13 20 27	4 11 18 25
Mon.	3 10 17 24 31	7 14 21 28	5 12 19 26
Tue.	4 11 18 25	1 8 15 22 29	6 13 20 27
Wed.	5 12 19 26	2 9 16 23 30	7 14 21 28
Thur.	6 13 20 27	3 10 17 24	1 8 15 22 29
Fri.	7 14 21 28	4 11 18 25	2 9 16 23 30
Sat.	1 8 15 22 29	5 12 19 26	3 10 17 24 31

EASTER DAYS

March 27	1785, 1842, 1853, 1910, 1921, 2005
April 3	1825, 1831, 1983, 1994
April 10	1803, 1814, 1887, 1898, 1955, 1966, 1977, 2039
April 17	1870, 1881, 1927, 1938, 1949, 2022, 2033
April 24	1791, 1859, 2011

L (LEAP YEAR)

	January	February	March
Sun.	3 10 17 24 31	7 14 21 28	6 13 20 27
Mon.	4 11 18 25	1 8 15 22 29	7 14 21 28
Tue.	5 12 19 26	2 9 16 23	1 8 15 22 29
Wed.	6 13 20 27	3 10 17 24	2 9 16 23 30
Thur.	7 14 21 28	4 11 18 25	3 10 17 24 31
Fri.	1 8 15 22 29	5 12 19 26	4 11 18 25
Sat.	2 9 16 23 30	6 13 20 27	5 12 19 26

	April	May	June
Sun.	3 10 17 24	1 8 15 22 29	5 12 19 26
Mon.	4 11 18 25	2 9 16 23 30	6 13 20 27
Tue.	5 12 19 26	3 10 17 24 31	7 14 21 28
Wed.	6 13 20 27	4 11 18 25	1 8 15 22 29
Thur.	7 14 21 28	5 12 19 26	2 9 16 23 30
Fri.	1 8 15 22 29	6 13 20 27	3 10 17 24
Sat.	2 9 16 23 30	7 14 21 28	4 11 18 25

	July	August	September
Sun.	3 10 17 24 31	7 14 21 28	4 11 18 25
Mon.	4 11 18 25	1 8 15 22 29	5 12 19 26
Tue.	5 12 19 26	2 9 16 23 30	6 13 20 27
Wed.	6 13 20 27	3 10 17 24 31	7 14 21 28
Thur.	7 14 21 28	4 11 18 25	1 8 15 22 29
Fri.	1 8 15 22 29	5 12 19 26	2 9 16 23 30
Sat.	2 9 16 23 30	6 13 20 27	3 10 17 24

	October	November	December
Sun.	2 9 16 23 30	6 13 20 27	4 11 18 25
Mon.	3 10 17 24 31	7 14 21 28	5 12 19 26
Tue.	4 11 18 25	1 8 15 22 29	6 13 20 27
Wed.	5 12 19 26	2 9 16 23 30	7 14 21 28
Thur.	6 13 20 27	3 10 17 24	1 8 15 22 29
Fri.	7 14 21 28	4 11 18 25	2 9 16 23 30
Sat.	1 8 15 22 29	5 12 19 26	3 10 17 24 31

EASTER DAYS

March 27	1796, 1864, 1932, 2016
April 3	1836, 1904, 1988
April 17	1808, 1892, 1960

N (LEAP YEAR)

	January	February	March
Sun.	2 9 16 23 30	6 13 20 27	5 12 19 26
Mon.	3 10 17 24 31	7 14 21 28	6 13 20 27
Tue.	4 11 18 25	1 8 15 22 29	7 14 21 28
Wed.	5 12 19 26	2 9 16 23	1 8 15 22 29
Thur.	6 13 20 27	3 10 17 24	2 9 16 23 30
Fri.	7 14 21 28	4 11 18 25	3 10 17 24 31
Sat.	1 8 15 22 29	5 12 19 26	4 11 18 25

	April	May	June
Sun.	2 9 16 23 30	7 14 21 28	4 11 18 25
Mon.	3 10 17 24	1 8 15 22 29	5 12 19 26
Tue.	4 11 18 25	2 9 16 23 30	6 13 20 27
Wed.	5 12 19 26	3 10 17 24 31	7 14 21 28
Thur.	6 13 20 27	4 11 18 25	1 8 15 22 29
Fri.	7 14 21 28	5 12 19 26	2 9 16 23 30
Sat.	1 8 15 22 29	6 13 20 27	3 10 17 24

	July	August	September
Sun.	2 9 16 23 30	6 13 20 27	3 10 17 24
Mon.	3 10 17 24 31	7 14 21 28	4 11 18 25
Tue.	4 11 18 25	1 8 15 22 29	5 12 19 26
Wed.	5 12 19 26	2 9 16 23 30	6 13 20 27
Thur.	6 13 20 27	3 10 17 24 31	7 14 21 28
Fri.	7 14 21 28	4 11 18 25	1 8 15 22 29
Sat.	1 8 15 22 29	5 12 19 26	2 9 16 23 30

	October	November	December
Sun.	1 8 15 22 29	5 12 19 26	3 10 17 24 31
Mon.	2 9 16 23 30	6 13 20 27	4 11 18 25
Tue.	3 10 17 24 31	7 14 21 28	5 12 19 26
Wed.	4 11 18 25	1 8 15 22 29	6 13 20 27
Thur.	5 12 19 26	2 9 16 23 30	7 14 21 28
Fri.	6 13 20 27	3 10 17 24	1 8 15 22 29
Sat.	7 14 21 28	4 11 18 25	2 9 16 23 30

EASTER DAYS

March 26	1780
April 2	1820, 1972
April 9	1944
April 16	1876, 2028
April 23	1848, 1916, 2000

GEOLOGICAL TIME

The earth is thought to have come into existence approximately 4,600 million years ago, but for nearly half this time, the Archean era, it was uninhabited. Life is generally believed to have emerged in the succeeding Proterozoic era. The Archean and the Proterozoic eras are often together referred to as the Precambrian.

Although primitive forms of life, eg algae and bacteria, existed during the Proterozoic era, it is not until the strata of Palaeozoic rocks are reached that abundant fossilised remains appear. Since the Precambrian, there have been three great geological eras:

PALAEOZOIC ('ANCIENT LIFE')
c.542–c.251 million years ago
Cambrian – Mainly sandstones, slate and shales; limestones in Scotland. Shelled fossils and invertebrates, eg trilobites and brachiopods appear, as do the earliest known vertebrates (jawless fish)
Ordovician – Mainly shales and mudstones, eg in north Wales; limestones in Scotland. First fish
Silurian – Shales, mudstones and some limestones, found mostly in Wales and southern Scotland
Devonian – Old red sandstone, shale, limestone and slate, eg in south Wales and the West Country
Carboniferous – Coal-bearing rocks, millstone grit, limestone and shale. First traces of land-living creatures
Permian – Marls, sandstones and clays. First reptile fossils

There were two great phases of mountain building in the Palaeozoic era: the Caledonian, characterised in Britain by NE–SW lines of hills and valleys; and the later Hercynian, widespread in west Germany and adjacent areas, and in Britain exemplified in E–W lines of hills and valleys.

The end of the Palaeozoic era was marked by the extensive glaciations of the Permian period in the southern continents and the decline of amphibians. It was succeeded by an era of warm conditions.

MESOZOIC ('MIDDLE FORMS OF LIFE')
c.251–c.65.5 million years ago
Triassic – Mostly sandstone, eg in the West Midlands; primitive mammals appear
Jurassic – Mainly limestones and clays, typically displayed in the Jura mountains, and in England in a NE–SW belt from Lincolnshire and the Wash to the Severn and the Dorset coast
Cretaceous – Mainly chalk, clay and sands, eg in Kent and Sussex

Giant reptiles were dominant during the Mesozoic era, but it was at this time that marsupial mammals first appeared, as well as *Archaeopteryx lithographica,* the earliest known species of bird. Coniferous trees and flowering plants also developed during the era and, with the birds and the mammals, were the main species to survive into the Cenozoic era. The giant reptiles became extinct.

CENOZOIC ('RECENT LIFE')
from c.65.5 million years ago

Palaeocene ⎫ The emergence of new forms of life,
Eocene ⎭ including existing species; primate appear
Oligocene – Fossils of a few still existing species
Miocene – Fossil remains show a balance of existing and extinct species
Pliocene – Fossil remains show a majority of still existing species
Pleistocene – The majority of remains are those of still existing species
Holocene – The present, post-glacial period. Existing species only, except for a few exterminated by humans

In the last 25 million years, from the Miocene through the Pliocene periods, the Alpine-Himalayan and the circum-Pacific phases of mountain building reached their climax. During the Pleistocene period ice-sheets repeatedly locked up masses of water as land ice; its weight depressed the land, but the locking-up of the water lowered the sea level by 100–200 metres. The glaciations and interglacials of the Ice Age are difficult to date and classify, but recent scientific opinion considers the Pleistocene period to have begun approximately 1.64 million years ago. The last glacial retreat, merging into the Holocene period, was c. 10,000 years ago.

HUMAN DEVELOPMENT

Any consideration of the history of humans must start with the fact that all members of the human race belong to one species of animal, ie *Homo sapiens,* the definition of a species being in biological terms that all its members can interbreed. As a species of mammal it is possible to group humans with other similar types, known as the primates. Amongst these is found a sub-group, the apes, which includes, in addition to humans, the chimpanzees, gorillas, orangutans and gibbons. All lack a tail, have shoulder blades at the back, and a Y-shaped chewing pattern on the surface of their molars, as well as showing the more general primate characteristics of four incisors, a thumb which is able to touch the fingers of the same hand, and finger and toe nails instead of claws. The factors available to scientific study suggest that human beings have chimpanzees and gorillas as their nearest relatives in the animal world. However, there once lived creatures, now extinct, which were closer to modern man than the chimpanzees and gorillas, and which shared with modern man the characteristics of having flat faces (ie the absence of a pronounced muzzle), being bipedal, and possessing large brains.

The debate surrounding evidence for the oldest human ancestors is ongoing. The fossil record becomes more patchy as time stretches backward, which makes new hominid discoveries harder to confirm. The earliest putative hominin for which there is significant fossil evidence is *Ardipithecus ramidus,* for which an almost complete skeleton, dating to at least 4.4 million years ago, was discovered in the Afar Rift, Ethiopia in 1992. Analysis of the *Ardipithecus ramidus* skeleton suggests the creature had characteristics of both humans and apes; able to climb trees and walk on two feet.

The subsequent Australopithecines have left more numerous remains in south and east Africa, among which sub-groups may be detected. Living between 4.2 and 1.5 million years ago, they were relatives of modern humans in respect of the fact that they walked upright, did not have an extensive muzzle and had similar types of pre-molars. The first australopithecine remains were recognised at Taung in South Africa in 1924 and named *Australopithecus africanus,* dating between 3.3 and 2.3 million years ago. The most impressive discovery was made at Hadar, Ethiopia, in 1974 when about half a skeleton of *Australopithecus afarensis,* known as 'Lucy', was found. Some 3.2 million years ago, 'Lucy' (who is now considered to be male) certainly walked upright.

Also in east Africa, especially at Olduvai Gorge in

Tanzania, between *c.* 2.5 and 1.8 million years ago, lived a hominid group which not only walked upright, had a flat face, and a large brain case, but also made simple pebble and flake stone tools. These early pebble tool users, because of their distinctive characteristics, have been grouped as a separate sub-species, now extinct, of the genus *Homo* and are known as *Homo habilis* or 'handy man'.

The use of fire, again a human characteristic, is associated with another group of extinct hominids whose remains, about a million years old, are found in south and east Africa, China, Indonesia, north Africa and Europe. Mastery of the techniques of making fire probably helped the colonisation of the colder northern areas and in this respect the site of Vertesszollos in Hungary is of particular importance. *Homo ergaster* in Africa and *Homo erectus* in Asia are the names given to this group of fossils and they relate to a number of famous individual discoveries, eg Solo Man, Heidelberg Man, and especially Peking Man who lived at the cave site at Choukoutien which has yielded evidence of fire and burnt bone.

The well-known group the Neanderthals, or *Homo neanderthalensis,* is an extinct form of human that lived between about 350,000 and 24,000 years ago, thus spanning the last Ice Age and living alongside modern humans. The Neanderthals' ability to adapt to the cold climate on the edge of the ice-sheets is one of their characteristic features, with remains being found only in Europe, Asia and the Middle East. Complete Neanderthal skeletons were found during excavations at Tabun in Israel, together with evidence of tool-making and the use of fire. Distinguished by very large brains, it seems that Neanderthals were the first to develop recognisable social customs, especially deliberate burial rites. Why the Neanderthals became extinct is not clear but it may be connected with the climatic changes at the end of the Ice Ages, which would have seriously affected their food supplies; possibly they became too specialised for their own good.

The shin bone of Boxgrove Man found in 1993 – *Homo heidelbergensis* – and the Swanscombe skull are the best known early human fossil remains found in England. Some specialists prefer to group Swanscombe Man (or, more probably, woman) together with the Steinheim skull from Germany, seeing both as a separate sub-species. There is too little evidence as yet on which to form a final judgement.

Anatomically modern humans – *Homo sapiens sapiens* ('doubly wise man') – had evolved to our present physical condition and had colonised much of the world by about 40,000 years ago. There are many previously distinguished individual specimens, eg Cromagnon Man, the first early *Homo sapiens sapiens* of the European Upper Palaeolithic. It was such modern humans that spread to the American continent, potentially by crossing the landbridge between Siberia and Alaska and from there moved south through North America and into South America.

One of the problems for those studying human fossils is the lack in many cases of sufficient quantities of fossil bone for analysis. It is important that theories should be tested against evidence, rather than the evidence being made to fit the theory. The Piltdown hoax of 1912 (and not fully exposed until the 1970s) is a well-known example of 'fossils' being forged to fit what was seen in some quarters as the correct theory of human evolution.

The discovery of the structure of DNA in 1953 has come to have a profound effect upon the study of human evolution. For example, it was claimed in 1987 that a common ancestor of all human beings was a person who lived in Africa some 200,000 years ago, thus encouraging the 'out of Africa' theory of hominid migration from east Africa to the Middle East and then throughout the world. There is no doubt that the studies based on DNA have vast potential to elucidate further the course of human evolution.

CULTURAL DEVELOPMENT

The Eurocentric bias of early archaeologists meant that the search for a starting point for the development and transmission of cultural ideas, especially by migration, trade and warfare, concentrated unduly on Europe and the Near East. The Three Age system, whereby prehistory was divided into a Stone Age, a Bronze Age and an Iron Age, was devised by Christian Thomsen, curator of the National Museum of Denmark in the early 19th century, to facilitate the classification of the museum's collections. The descriptive adjectives referred to the materials from which the implements and weapons were made and came to be regarded as the dominant features of the societies to which they related. The refinement of the Three Age system once dominated archaeological thought and remains a generally accepted concept in the popular mind. However, it is now seen by archaeologists as an inadequate model for human development.

Common sense suggests that there were no complete breaks between one so-called Age and another, any more than contemporaries would have regarded 1485 as a complete break between medieval and modern English history. Nor can the Three Age system be applied universally. In some areas it is necessary to insert a Copper Age, while in South Africa there would seem to be no Bronze Age at all; in Australia, Old Stone Age societies survived, while in South America, New Stone Age communities exist into modern times.

The concept of the 'Neolithic revolution', associated with the domestication of plants and animals, was a development of particular importance in the human cultural pattern. It reflected change from the hunter-gatherer economies to a more settled agricultural way of life and therefore, so the argument goes, made possible the development of urban civilisation. However, it can no longer be argued that this change was an instantaneous 'revolution' – it was typically a more gradual process – or that it took place only in one area from which all development stemmed. Though it appears that the cultivation of wheat and barley was first undertaken, together with the domestication of cattle and goats/sheep, around 10,000 years ago in the Fertile Crescent (the area bounded by the rivers Tigris and Euphrates), there is evidence that sorghum was first domesticated in Africa, rice was first deliberately planted and pigs domesticated in south-east Asia, maize first cultivated in Central America and llamas first domesticated in South America. Cultural change took place independently in different parts of the world at different rates and different times.

The Neolithic period of cultural development has been difficult to date reliably because the transition to agriculture took place long before writing was invented. The development and refinement of radio-carbon dating and other scientific methods of producing absolute chronologies is enabling the cross-referencing of societies to be undertaken. It may eventually be possible to obtain a reliable chronological framework, in absolute terms of years, against which the cultural development of any particular area may be set.

GEOLOGICAL TIME

Era	Period	Epoch	Dates*	Evolutionary Stages
Cenozoic	Quarternary	Holocene	11,700 BP†–present	
		Pleistocene	2,588,000–11,700 BP	First humans
	Neogene	Pliocene	5.332–2.588 Mya ‡	Majority of still existing species
		Miocene	23.03–5.332 Mya	
	Paleogene	Oligocene	33.9–23.03 Mya	
		Eocene	55.8–33.9 Mya	} First modern mammals
		Palaeocene	65.5–55.8 Mya	
Mesozoic	Cretaceous		145.5–65.5 Mya	
	Jurassic		199.6–145.5 Mya	First birds
	Triassic		251–199.6 Mya	First mammals
Palaeozoic	Permian		299–251 Mya	First reptiles
	Carboniferous		359.2–299 Mya	First traces of land-living creatures
	Devonian		416–359.2 Mya	
	Silurian		443.7–416 Mya	
	Ordovician		488.3–443.7 Mya	First fish
	Cambrian		542–488.3 Mya	First invertebrates
Precambrian	Proterozoic		2,500–542 Mya	First primitive life forms, eg algae and bacteria
	Archaean		3,800–2,500 Mya	} Earth uninhabited
	Hadean		4,600–3,800 Mya	

* approximate   †BP = Before Present   ‡Mya = million years ago

TIDES AND TIDAL PREDICTIONS

TIDES

Tides are the periodic rise and fall of the sea level caused mainly by the gravitational pull, or tide raising force (TRF), of the Moon and the Sun. The Moon's TRF accounts for 70 per cent of the total; the Sun's for 30 per cent. When the Moon and the Sun are in line with the Earth they are said to be 'in conjunction' (or syzygy) and their combined TRFs are greatest. This produces the largest rise and fall of the tide, otherwise known as spring tides; they occur just after a full or new moon. The opposite effect, just after the Moon's first and last quarters, when the Sun and Moon form a right angle with the Earth, produces neap tides, with a relatively small tidal range between high water and low water.

A lunar day is about 24 hours and 50 minutes, giving two complete tidal cycles, with about 12 hours and 25 minutes between successive high waters. These are known as semi-diurnal tides and are applicable to the Atlantic Ocean and around the coasts of north-west Europe. Other parts of the world have diurnal tides, with only one high water and one low water each (lunar) day, or mixed tides which are partly diurnal and partly semi-diurnal.

Land and seabed conditions influence the tides locally. On the south coast of England, for example, double high waters occur between Swanage and Selsey Bill, and low water is much more sharply defined than high water. Tides can also be greatly affected by the Coriolis force, which is induced by the Earth's rotation and, in the northern hemisphere, tends to deflect any moving object to the right. Thus the easterly flood tidal stream in the English Channel is deflected towards the French coast causing higher high waters; on the ebb the opposite happens causing lower low waters. This, coupled with local geography, means that the mean spring range of the tide at St Malo is nearly 11m while the range on the English coast at Portland, 120 miles to the north, is a mere 2m.

Meteorological conditions also affect the tides. Prolonged strong winds and unusually high (or low) atmospheric pressure can significantly lower (or raise) the height of the tide; the wind alone can affect the predicted times of high and low water by as much as an hour. Variation of pressure by 34 millibars from the norm can cause a height difference of 0.3m. Intense minor depressions, line squalls, or other abrupt changes in the weather can cause wave oscillations known as seiches. The wave period of a seiche can vary from a few minutes to about 2 hours, with heights of up to a metre. Wick on the north-east coast of Scotland and Fishguard in south-west Wales are particularly prone to seiches.

TIDAL STREAMS

Tidal streams are the horizontal movements of water caused by the rise and fall of the tide. They normally change direction about every 6 hours. Tidal streams should not be confused with ocean currents, such as the Gulf Stream, which run indefinitely in the same direction. The rate, or set, of the stream at any particular place is proportional to the range of the tide. Thus, the rate during spring tides is greater than that at neaps. In the central English Channel the maximum spring rate is nearly 5 knots while the neap rate at the same position is just 3 knots. As with tidal heights, local geography plays a significant role in the rate of the tidal stream. For example, in the narrow waters of the Pentland Firth between mainland Scotland and the Orkney Islands, rates of 16 knots have been recorded.

The tidal stream does not necessarily turn at the same time as high or low water. In the English Channel the stream turns at approximately high and low water at Dover. However, high water at Dover is at about the same time as low water at Plymouth, and vice versa.

Around the UK, the main flood tidal stream sets eastward up the English Channel, north-east into the Bristol Channel, and north up the west coasts of Ireland and Scotland. However, the flood sets south-east through the North Channel and south into the Irish Sea, where it meets the northerly flood through St George's Channel at the Isle of Man. Off the east coasts of Scotland and England the stream sets south as far as the Thames Estuary before meeting the north-going stream from the eastern part of the Dover Strait.

DEFINITIONS

Chart Datum (CD) is the reference level from which tidal levels are predicted. **Ordnance Datum** at Newlyn is the datum of the land levelling system on mainland England, Scotland and Wales. This is the datum from which heights on UK land maps are measured. CD varies from about 5m above Ordnance Datum to about 6.5m below. **Highest Astronomical Tide (HAT)** and **Lowest Astronomical Tide (LAT)** are the highest and lowest levels of the tide that can be predicted to occur under average meteorological, and any combination of astronomical, conditions. **Duration** of the tide is the interval between low water and the next high water. It can be used to calculate the approximate time of low water when only the time of high water is known. **Mean Sea Level (MSL or ML)** is the average level of the sea's surface over a long period, normally observed over 18.6 years. The **Range** of the tide is the difference between heights of successive high waters and low waters. It is greatest at spring tides, least at neaps. The range may be indicated by **Tidal Coefficients** which are proportional to, but not the same as, the range on a particular day. A coefficient of 95 indicates an average spring tide, while 45 is an average neap tide.

PREDICTIONS

The following data are daily predictions of the time and height of high water at London Bridge, Liverpool, Greenock and Leith. The time of the data is Greenwich Mean Time; this applies also to data for the months when British Summer Time is in operation and the hour's time difference should be added. The datum of predictions for each port shows the difference of height, in metres from Ordnance datum (Newlyn).

The tidal information for London Bridge, Liverpool, Greenock and Leith is reproduced by permission of the Controller of Her Majesty's Stationery Office and the UK Hydrographic Office. © Crown copyright. All rights reserved. The section was compiled with the assistance of Andy Du Port and Chris Stevens.

JANUARY 2012   *High Water*   GMT

	LONDON BRIDGE *Datum of Predictions 3.20m below				LIVERPOOL (Gladstone Dock) *Datum of Predictions 4.93m below				GREENOCK *Datum of Predictions 1.62m below				LEITH *Datum of Predictions 2.90m below			
	hr	m	hr	m	hr	m	hr	m	hr	m	hr	m	hr	m	hr	m
SU 1	06 25	6.2	19 00	6.1	03 54	7.7	16 19	7.9	05 16	3.1	17 32	3.3	07 54	4.6	20 11	4.6
M 2	07 13	6.0	19 52	5.8	04 50	7.4	17 19	7.5	06 03	3.0	18 23	3.1	08 47	4.4	21 08	4.5
TU 3	08 18	5.8	20 55	5.7	05 57	7.2	18 27	7.4	06 56	3.0	19 23	3.0	09 43	4.4	22 08	4.4
W 4	09 29	5.7	22 00	5.8	07 10	7.3	19 37	7.5	07 59	3.0	20 36	2.9	10 43	4.4	23 11	4.4
TH 5	10 35	5.9	23 06	6.0	08 14	7.6	20 37	7.7	09 11	3.0	21 51	3.0	11 45	4.6	—	—
F 6	11 37	6.2	—	—	09 06	8.0	21 27	8.1	10 14	3.2	22 50	3.1	00 14	4.6	12 43	4.8
SA 7	00 06	6.2	12 30	6.4	09 49	8.4	22 09	8.4	11 03	3.4	23 37	3.2	01 07	4.8	13 29	5.0
SU 8	00 56	6.5	13 15	6.7	10 27	8.7	22 48	8.7	11 44	3.5	—	—	01 51	5.0	14 10	5.2
M 9	01 40	6.6	13 56	6.8	11 04	9.0	23 25	8.9	00 19	3.2	12 20	3.6	02 30	5.2	14 47	5.4
TU 10	02 20	6.7	14 36	7.0	11 40	9.2	—	—	00 58	3.3	12 55	3.7	03 07	5.4	15 22	5.5
W 11	02 59	6.8	15 15	7.1	00 02	9.1	12 18	9.4	01 36	3.3	13 32	3.8	03 44	5.5	15 57	5.6
TH 12	03 36	6.9	15 55	7.2	00 41	9.2	12 56	9.4	02 14	3.3	14 11	3.8	04 22	5.5	16 34	5.6
F 13	04 12	6.9	16 34	7.1	01 21	9.2	13 36	9.4	02 53	3.3	14 52	3.8	05 02	5.5	17 13	5.5
SA 14	04 49	6.9	17 15	6.9	02 03	9.0	14 18	9.2	03 33	3.4	15 34	3.8	05 44	5.4	17 56	5.4
SU 15	05 29	6.8	17 59	6.7	02 47	8.8	15 05	8.9	04 14	3.3	16 17	3.7	06 30	5.2	18 43	5.3
M 16	06 12	6.6	18 48	6.5	03 37	8.4	15 59	8.6	04 57	3.2	17 04	3.6	07 21	5.0	19 39	5.1
TU 17	07 05	6.5	19 48	6.2	04 36	8.1	17 05	8.2	05 46	3.1	17 58	3.4	08 21	4.8	20 51	4.9
W 18	08 12	6.3	21 00	6.1	05 49	7.9	18 25	8.0	06 49	3.0	19 05	3.2	09 34	4.7	22 12	4.8
TH 19	09 34	6.2	22 15	6.1	07 08	7.9	19 46	8.0	08 26	3.0	20 43	3.1	10 48	4.8	23 28	4.9
F 20	10 51	6.3	23 32	6.2	08 21	8.3	20 57	8.4	09 51	3.1	22 12	3.1	11 57	4.9	—	—
SA 21	12 04	6.5	—	—	09 23	8.7	21 56	8.7	10 51	3.3	23 16	3.2	00 35	5.1	12 57	5.2
SU 22	00 39	6.5	13 05	6.8	10 16	9.1	22 46	9.0	11 41	3.5	—	—	01 33	5.3	13 48	5.4
M 23	01 33	6.7	13 56	7.0	11 02	9.4	23 30	9.2	00 09	3.3	12 27	3.6	02 21	5.5	14 33	5.6
TU 24	02 19	6.8	14 41	7.1	11 44	9.6	—	—	00 57	3.3	13 10	3.7	03 05	5.6	15 16	5.7
W 25	03 01	6.9	15 23	7.1	00 10	9.2	12 23	9.6	01 39	3.3	13 49	3.7	03 47	5.5	15 57	5.7
TH 26	03 38	7.0	16 01	7.1	00 47	9.1	12 59	9.5	02 16	3.3	14 27	3.7	04 27	5.4	16 37	5.6
F 27	04 12	7.0	16 35	6.9	01 20	8.9	13 33	9.2	02 50	3.3	15 02	3.7	05 05	5.3	17 15	5.4
SA 28	04 44	6.8	17 06	6.7	01 53	8.7	14 08	8.9	03 24	3.3	15 38	3.6	05 43	5.1	17 53	5.2
SU 29	05 16	6.7	17 36	6.4	02 27	8.4	14 44	8.5	04 00	3.3	16 14	3.4	06 21	4.9	18 32	5.0
M 30	05 47	6.4	18 09	6.2	03 04	8.0	15 26	8.0	04 37	3.2	16 53	3.3	07 03	4.6	19 17	4.7
TU 31	06 23	6.2	18 48	5.9	03 48	7.5	16 16	7.5	05 17	3.1	17 36	3.1	07 50	4.4	20 10	4.4

FEBRUARY 2012   *High Water*   GMT

	LONDON BRIDGE				LIVERPOOL (Gladstone Dock)				GREENOCK				LEITH			
W 1	07 08	5.9	19 41	5.7	04 47	7.1	17 24	7.1	06 02	3.0	18 28	2.9	08 45	4.3	21 12	4.3
TH 2	08 15	5.6	21 00	5.5	06 05	7.0	18 45	7.0	06 57	2.9	19 34	2.7	09 48	4.2	22 19	4.2
F 3	09 44	5.6	22 21	5.6	07 28	7.1	20 02	7.3	08 10	2.9	21 07	2.7	10 57	4.3	23 31	4.4
SA 4	10 58	5.9	23 33	6.0	08 34	7.6	21 02	7.7	09 36	3.0	22 28	2.9	12 07	4.6	—	—
SU 5	12 00	6.3	—	—	09 24	8.1	21 48	8.2	10 37	3.2	23 20	3.0	00 38	4.6	13 04	4.9
M 6	00 31	6.4	12 52	6.6	10 06	8.6	22 28	8.7	11 21	3.3	—	—	01 28	4.9	13 48	5.1
TU 7	01 19	6.6	13 36	6.9	10 44	9.1	23 06	9.1	00 03	3.2	11 59	3.5	02 09	5.2	14 26	5.4
W 8	02 01	6.8	14 18	7.1	11 21	9.4	23 44	9.4	00 43	3.2	12 37	3.6	02 46	5.4	15 02	5.6
TH 9	02 41	7.0	14 59	7.2	11 59	9.7	—	—	01 21	3.3	13 15	3.7	03 23	5.6	15 37	5.7
F 10	03 19	7.1	15 38	7.3	00 22	9.5	12 38	9.8	01 58	3.3	13 56	3.8	04 01	5.7	16 14	5.8
SA 11	03 56	7.2	16 18	7.2	01 02	9.5	13 18	9.7	02 35	3.4	14 37	3.8	04 40	5.7	16 54	5.8
SU 12	04 33	7.1	16 57	7.0	01 42	9.4	13 59	9.5	03 13	3.4	15 18	3.8	05 22	5.5	17 37	5.6
M 13	05 11	7.0	17 38	6.7	02 25	9.1	14 44	9.1	03 51	3.4	16 00	3.7	06 06	5.3	18 25	5.4
TU 14	05 54	6.8	18 23	6.4	03 12	8.6	15 36	8.6	04 31	3.3	16 45	3.5	06 55	5.0	19 20	5.1
W 15	06 44	6.5	19 19	6.1	04 10	8.1	16 43	8.0	05 15	3.2	17 34	3.2	07 53	4.7	20 33	4.8
TH 16	07 49	6.2	20 31	5.9	05 25	7.7	18 10	7.6	06 10	3.0	18 35	3.0	09 09	4.6	21 59	4.6
F 17	09 14	6.0	21 56	5.8	06 51	7.7	19 39	7.7	07 54	2.8	20 42	2.8	10 31	4.6	23 21	4.7
SA 18	10 40	6.1	23 24	6.0	08 11	8.0	20 54	8.1	09 40	3.0	22 17	2.9	11 47	4.8	—	—
SU 19	11 58	6.4	—	—	09 15	8.5	21 50	8.5	10 40	3.2	23 13	3.1	00 33	4.9	12 50	5.0
M 20	00 30	6.4	12 57	6.8	10 05	8.9	22 35	8.9	11 28	3.4	—	—	01 28	5.2	13 39	5.3
TU 21	01 22	6.7	13 45	7.0	10 48	9.3	23 14	9.1	00 00	3.2	12 13	3.6	02 12	5.3	14 21	5.5
W 22	02 04	6.8	14 26	7.0	11 25	9.4	23 49	9.2	00 42	3.3	12 53	3.6	02 50	5.4	14 59	5.6
TH 23	02 41	6.9	15 02	7.0	12 00	9.5	—	—	01 19	3.3	13 31	3.6	03 26	5.4	15 36	5.6
F 24	03 14	7.0	15 35	7.0	00 20	9.1	12 33	9.4	01 55	3.3	14 05	3.6	04 01	5.4	16 11	5.5
SA 25	03 45	7.1	16 04	6.9	00 51	9.0	13 04	9.2	02 21	3.3	14 38	3.5	04 34	5.3	16 46	5.4
SU 26	04 15	7.0	16 31	6.7	01 20	8.8	13 36	9.0	02 52	3.3	15 10	3.5	05 08	5.1	17 20	5.2
M 27	04 45	6.8	17 00	6.5	01 51	8.6	14 08	8.6	03 26	3.4	15 44	3.4	05 43	4.9	17 56	5.0
TU 28	05 15	6.6	17 30	6.3	02 23	8.2	14 43	8.1	04 00	3.3	16 20	3.2	06 20	4.7	18 37	4.7
W 29	05 48	6.3	18 05	6.0	02 59	7.8	15 25	7.6	04 36	3.2	17 01	3.0	07 02	4.5	19 24	4.5

MARCH 2012 *High Water* GMT

	LONDON BRIDGE *Datum of Predictions 3.20m below*				LIVERPOOL (Gladstone Dock) *Datum of Predictions 4.93m below*				GREENOCK *Datum of Predictions 1.62m below*				LEITH *Datum of Predictions 2.90m below*			
	hr m	ht	hr m	ht	hr m	ht	hr m	ht	hr m	ht	hr m	ht	hr m	ht	hr m	ht
TH 1	06 27	6.0	18 49	5.7	03 47	7.3	16 23	7.1	05 17	3.0	17 50	2.8	07 54	4.3	20 22	4.3
F 2	07 19	5.7	19 51	5.5	04 59	6.9	17 48	6.8	06 08	2.9	18 53	2.6	08 58	4.2	21 32	4.2
SA 3	08 38	5.5	21 29	5.4	06 33	6.9	19 19	7.0	07 14	2.8	20 22	2.6	10 11	4.2	22 47	4.3
SU 4	10 14	5.7	22 54	5.8	07 53	7.4	20 28	7.5	08 42	2.8	22 02	2.8	11 27	4.4	—	—
M 5	11 24	6.2	23 58	6.3	08 50	8.0	21 19	8.2	10 00	3.0	22 56	3.0	00 01	4.5	12 31	4.7
TU 6	12 21	6.6	—	—	09 36	8.6	22 01	8.7	10 50	3.2	23 39	3.1	00 57	4.9	13 19	5.1
W 7	00 49	6.6	13 09	6.9	10 17	9.1	22 41	9.2	11 32	3.4	—	—	01 41	5.2	13 59	5.4
TH 8	01 34	6.9	13 54	7.1	10 56	9.6	23 20	9.6	00 19	3.2	12 14	3.5	02 20	5.5	14 36	5.7
F 9	02 15	7.1	14 36	7.3	11 35	9.9	23 59	9.8	00 58	3.3	12 56	3.6	02 58	5.7	15 13	5.9
SA 10	02 55	7.3	15 17	7.3	12 16	10.0	—	—	01 36	3.4	13 38	3.7	03 36	5.8	15 53	6.0
SU 11	03 34	7.4	15 57	7.2	00 40	9.8	12 58	9.9	02 13	3.4	14 21	3.8	04 17	5.8	16 35	5.9
M 12	04 14	7.4	16 37	7.0	01 21	9.6	13 41	9.6	02 51	3.5	15 03	3.7	04 59	5.6	17 21	5.7
TU 13	04 54	7.2	17 18	6.7	02 05	9.2	14 27	9.1	03 29	3.5	15 46	3.6	05 44	5.4	18 11	5.4
W 14	05 38	6.9	18 03	6.4	02 53	8.7	15 21	8.5	04 09	3.4	16 30	3.4	06 34	5.1	19 09	5.0
TH 15	06 29	6.6	18 57	6.0	03 52	8.2	16 31	7.8	04 53	3.2	17 19	3.1	07 34	4.7	20 25	4.7
F 16	07 35	6.2	20 10	5.8	05 09	7.7	17 59	7.4	05 48	2.9	18 22	2.8	08 53	4.5	21 49	4.5
SA 17	09 00	6.0	21 39	5.8	06 35	7.6	19 29	7.5	07 33	2.8	20 51	2.7	10 16	4.5	23 10	4.6
SU 18	10 26	6.1	23 05	6.0	07 54	7.9	20 41	8.0	09 20	2.9	22 05	2.9	11 32	4.7	—	—
M 19	11 42	6.5	—	—	08 57	8.4	21 33	8.4	10 19	3.2	22 56	3.0	00 20	4.8	12 34	5.0
TU 20	00 11	6.4	12 39	6.8	09 45	8.8	22 15	8.7	11 07	3.4	23 39	3.1	01 13	5.1	13 22	5.2
W 21	01 00	6.7	13 24	6.9	10 25	9.0	22 50	8.9	11 50	3.5	—	—	01 54	5.2	14 02	5.3
TH 22	01 40	6.8	14 02	6.9	11 01	9.2	23 22	9.0	00 17	3.2	12 31	3.5	02 29	5.3	14 38	5.4
F 23	02 15	6.9	14 35	6.9	11 33	9.3	23 52	9.1	00 50	3.2	13 07	3.5	03 01	5.3	15 12	5.4
SA 24	02 46	7.0	15 04	6.9	12 05	9.2	—	—	01 20	3.3	13 40	3.4	03 33	5.3	15 46	5.4
SU 25	03 16	7.1	15 31	6.9	00 21	9.0	12 36	9.1	01 49	3.3	14 11	3.4	04 05	5.2	16 19	5.3
M 26	03 46	7.1	15 59	6.8	00 51	8.9	13 07	8.9	02 21	3.4	14 43	3.3	04 36	5.1	16 53	5.2
TU 27	04 16	6.9	16 28	6.6	01 20	8.7	13 39	8.5	02 53	3.4	15 16	3.3	05 10	5.0	17 28	5.0
W 28	04 47	6.7	16 59	6.4	01 51	8.4	14 13	8.2	03 26	3.4	15 52	3.2	05 45	4.8	18 07	4.8
TH 29	05 20	6.4	17 33	6.1	02 25	8.0	14 52	7.7	04 00	3.3	16 33	3.0	06 25	4.6	18 52	4.5
F 30	05 59	6.2	18 15	5.9	03 08	7.6	15 45	7.3	04 39	3.1	17 21	2.8	07 12	4.4	19 46	4.3
SA 31	06 47	5.9	19 10	5.6	04 11	7.2	17 00	7.0	05 26	2.9	18 22	2.6	08 12	4.2	20 51	4.2

APRIL 2012 *High Water* GMT

	LONDON BRIDGE				LIVERPOOL (Gladstone Dock)				GREENOCK				LEITH			
SU 1	07 53	5.7	20 33	5.5	05 39	7.1	18 28	7.1	06 28	2.8	19 42	2.6	09 26	4.2	22 05	4.3
M 2	09 27	5.8	22 07	5.8	07 03	7.4	19 44	7.5	07 48	2.8	21 22	2.7	10 43	4.4	23 18	4.5
TU 3	10 43	6.2	23 17	6.2	08 07	7.9	20 41	8.2	09 12	2.9	22 22	2.9	11 49	4.7	—	—
W 4	11 44	6.6	—	—	08 59	8.6	21 28	8.8	10 12	3.2	23 08	3.1	00 19	4.9	12 42	5.1
TH 5	00 12	6.7	12 38	6.9	09 44	9.1	22 11	9.3	11 00	3.3	23 49	3.2	01 08	5.2	13 26	5.4
F 6	01 02	7.0	13 25	7.1	10 28	9.6	22 53	9.6	11 47	3.5	—	—	01 50	5.5	14 07	5.7
SA 7	01 46	7.2	14 10	7.2	11 11	9.9	23 35	9.8	00 30	3.3	12 33	3.6	02 31	5.7	14 49	5.9
SU 8	02 30	7.4	14 54	7.3	11 55	10.0	—	—	01 11	3.4	13 20	3.7	03 12	5.8	15 32	6.0
M 9	03 13	7.5	15 37	7.2	00 18	9.9	12 40	9.8	01 50	3.5	14 05	3.7	03 54	5.8	16 19	5.9
TU 10	03 55	7.5	16 19	7.0	01 03	9.7	13 27	9.5	02 30	3.6	14 50	3.6	04 39	5.7	17 08	5.7
W 11	04 39	7.3	17 02	6.7	01 49	9.3	14 16	9.0	03 10	3.5	15 35	3.5	05 27	5.4	18 01	5.4
TH 12	05 26	7.0	17 49	6.4	02 39	8.8	15 12	8.4	03 52	3.4	16 22	3.2	06 19	5.1	19 03	5.0
F 13	06 20	6.6	18 43	6.1	03 39	8.3	16 21	7.8	04 39	3.2	17 15	3.0	07 22	4.8	20 15	4.7
SA 14	07 25	6.3	19 53	5.9	04 52	7.9	17 41	7.5	05 37	3.0	18 27	2.7	08 38	4.6	21 30	4.6
SU 15	08 41	6.1	21 14	5.9	06 10	7.7	19 03	7.5	07 10	2.8	20 24	2.7	09 54	4.6	22 45	4.6
M 16	09 58	6.2	22 32	6.1	07 25	7.9	20 13	7.8	08 46	2.9	21 35	2.8	11 05	4.7	23 52	4.7
TU 17	11 12	6.4	23 38	6.4	08 27	8.2	21 05	8.2	09 48	3.1	22 25	3.0	12 06	4.9	—	—
W 18	12 10	6.6	—	—	09 16	8.5	21 46	8.5	10 38	3.3	23 07	3.1	00 45	4.9	12 55	5.0
TH 19	00 29	6.6	12 56	6.7	09 56	8.7	22 21	8.7	11 23	3.4	23 44	3.2	01 27	5.1	13 37	5.1
F 20	01 10	6.7	13 33	6.7	10 32	8.9	22 53	8.8	12 02	3.3	—	—	02 03	5.2	14 14	5.2
SA 21	01 45	6.8	14 05	6.8	11 06	9.0	23 24	8.9	00 17	3.2	12 39	3.3	02 35	5.2	14 48	5.3
SU 22	02 17	7.0	14 34	6.8	11 38	9.0	23 54	8.9	00 48	3.3	13 13	3.3	03 06	5.2	15 22	5.2
M 23	02 48	7.0	15 02	6.8	12 11	8.9	—	—	01 19	3.4	13 44	3.2	03 37	5.2	15 55	5.2
TU 24	03 19	7.0	15 32	6.8	00 24	8.8	12 43	8.7	01 51	3.5	14 17	3.2	04 09	5.2	16 30	5.1
W 25	03 51	6.9	16 03	6.6	00 55	8.7	13 16	8.5	02 23	3.5	14 52	3.2	04 43	5.1	17 06	5.0
TH 26	04 24	6.7	16 36	6.4	01 27	8.5	13 51	8.2	02 56	3.5	15 29	3.1	05 19	4.9	17 45	4.8
F 27	05 00	6.6	17 12	6.2	02 03	8.2	14 32	7.9	03 31	3.4	16 11	3.0	05 58	4.8	18 28	4.7
SA 28	05 40	6.4	17 54	6.0	02 46	7.9	15 22	7.6	04 09	3.2	16 58	2.9	06 42	4.6	19 18	4.5
SU 29	06 27	6.2	18 47	5.9	03 43	7.6	16 26	7.3	04 53	3.1	17 55	2.7	07 35	4.4	20 17	4.4
M 30	07 28	6.0	19 56	5.8	04 57	7.4	17 43	7.4	05 51	2.9	19 05	2.7	08 42	4.4	21 26	4.5

MAY 2012   *High Water*   GMT

	LONDON BRIDGE *Datum of Predictions 3.20m below					LIVERPOOL (Gladstone Dock) *Datum of Predictions 4.93m below					GREENOCK *Datum of Predictions 1.62m below					LEITH *Datum of Predictions 2.90m below				
	hr	m	ht	hr	m	ht	hr	m	ht	hr	m	ht	hr	m	ht	hr	m	ht	hr	m	ht
TU 1	08	48	6.0	21	22	5.9	06	14	7.6	18	56	7.7	07	03	2.9	20	28	2.8	09	58	4.5	22	37	4.6
W 2	10	04	6.3	22	35	6.3	07	22	8.0	19	59	8.2	08	24	3.0	21	38	2.9	11	06	4.8	23	40	4.9
TH 3	11	08	6.6	23	36	6.7	08	20	8.6	20	53	8.8	09	32	3.2	22	31	3.1	12	03	5.1	—		
F 4	12	05	6.9	—			09	12	9.1	21	41	9.2	10	29	3.3	23	18	3.2	00	33	5.2	12	54	5.4
SA 5	00	30	7.0	12	58	7.1	10	01	9.5	22	28	9.6	11	21	3.5	—			01	20	5.5	13	41	5.7
SU 6	01	20	7.3	13	47	7.1	10	49	9.7	23	14	9.8	00	03	3.4	12	12	3.5	02	05	5.7	14	28	5.9
M 7	02	07	7.4	14	34	7.2	11	37	9.8	—			00	47	3.5	13	02	3.6	02	49	5.8	15	16	5.9
TU 8	02	54	7.5	15	20	7.1	00	00	9.8	12	26	9.6	01	30	3.6	13	51	3.5	03	35	5.8	16	06	5.9
W 9	03	41	7.5	16	05	7.0	00	47	9.6	13	16	9.3	02	13	3.6	14	40	3.5	04	23	5.7	16	57	5.7
TH 10	04	28	7.3	16	51	6.7	01	36	9.4	14	07	8.9	02	55	3.6	15	28	3.3	05	13	5.5	17	52	5.4
F 11	05	18	7.0	17	38	6.5	02	27	9.0	15	02	8.4	03	40	3.5	16	18	3.2	06	07	5.2	18	52	5.1
SA 12	06	10	6.7	18	30	6.3	03	24	8.5	16	02	7.9	04	27	3.3	17	12	3.0	07	08	5.0	19	56	4.8
SU 13	07	10	6.4	19	31	6.1	04	27	8.1	17	09	7.6	05	24	3.1	18	15	2.8	08	16	4.8	21	01	4.6
M 14	08	14	6.2	20	39	6.0	05	35	7.9	18	21	7.5	06	36	3.0	19	30	2.7	09	22	4.7	22	06	4.6
TU 15	09	20	6.2	21	47	6.1	06	42	7.8	19	29	7.6	07	58	2.9	20	42	2.8	10	27	4.7	23	10	4.6
W 16	10	28	6.2	22	53	6.2	07	45	8.0	20	26	7.9	09	07	3.0	21	38	2.9	11	27	4.7	—		
TH 17	11	30	6.4	23	49	6.4	08	38	8.1	21	11	8.2	10	02	3.1	22	25	3.0	00	07	4.7	12	22	4.8
F 18	12	19	6.5	—			09	23	8.3	21	50	8.4	10	49	3.2	23	06	3.1	00	54	4.9	13	08	4.9
SA 19	00	35	6.6	13	01	6.6	10	03	8.5	22	24	8.6	11	32	3.2	23	44	3.2	01	33	5.0	13	48	5.0
SU 20	01	15	6.8	13	36	6.6	10	40	8.6	22	57	8.7	12	11	3.2	—			02	08	5.1	14	25	5.1
M 21	01	51	6.9	14	09	6.7	11	15	8.7	23	30	8.8	00	18	3.3	12	46	3.1	02	41	5.2	15	00	5.1
TU 22	02	25	6.9	14	41	6.7	11	49	8.7	—			00	52	3.4	13	20	3.1	03	14	5.2	15	34	5.1
W 23	02	58	6.9	15	13	6.7	00	03	8.8	12	24	8.6	01	24	3.5	13	54	3.1	03	47	5.2	16	10	5.1
TH 24	03	32	6.9	15	47	6.6	00	36	8.7	12	59	8.5	01	57	3.5	14	30	3.1	04	22	5.1	16	47	5.1
F 25	04	08	6.8	16	22	6.5	01	11	8.6	13	36	8.4	02	31	3.5	15	09	3.1	04	58	5.0	17	25	5.0
SA 26	04	46	6.7	17	00	6.4	01	48	8.4	14	17	8.2	03	07	3.5	15	52	3.0	05	36	4.9	18	08	4.9
SU 27	05	27	6.6	17	41	6.3	02	30	8.2	15	03	8.0	03	46	3.4	16	37	3.0	06	19	4.8	18	55	4.8
M 28	06	13	6.4	18	30	6.2	03	21	8.1	15	59	7.8	04	30	3.3	17	29	2.9	07	07	4.7	19	48	4.7
TU 29	07	08	6.3	19	29	6.1	04	22	7.9	17	04	7.8	05	21	3.2	18	28	2.8	08	04	4.7	20	50	4.7
W 30	08	16	6.2	20	43	6.1	05	31	8.0	18	13	7.9	06	25	3.1	19	36	2.8	09	14	4.7	21	58	4.8
TH 31	09	29	6.4	21	58	6.4	06	40	8.2	19	20	8.2	07	41	3.1	20	50	2.9	10	25	4.8	23	03	4.9

JUNE 2012   *High Water*   GMT

	LONDON BRIDGE					LIVERPOOL (Gladstone Dock)					GREENOCK					LEITH					
F 1	10	35	6.5	23	03	6.7	07	45	8.5	20	21	8.6	08	56	3.2	21	54	3.1	11	30	5.1	—		
SA 2	11	37	6.7	—			08	45	8.9	21	16	9.0	10	01	3.3	22	50	3.2	00	02	5.2	12	28	5.3
SU 3	00	03	7.0	12	35	6.9	09	40	9.2	22	07	9.4	10	59	3.4	23	40	3.4	00	55	5.4	13	21	5.6
M 4	00	59	7.2	13	28	7.0	10	33	9.4	22	57	9.6	11	54	3.4	—			01	44	5.6	14	13	5.8
TU 5	01	50	7.4	14	18	7.0	11	25	9.5	23	46	9.7	00	28	3.5	12	48	3.4	02	32	5.7	15	04	5.8
W 6	02	41	7.4	15	07	7.1	12	16	9.4	—			01	14	3.6	13	41	3.4	03	20	5.8	15	54	5.8
TH 7	03	30	7.4	15	54	7.0	00	35	9.6	13	06	9.2	01	59	3.6	14	31	3.3	04	09	5.7	16	46	5.7
F 8	04	19	7.3	16	40	6.9	01	23	9.4	13	54	8.9	02	43	3.6	15	20	3.2	04	59	5.6	17	38	5.4
SA 9	05	07	7.1	17	25	6.7	02	11	9.1	14	42	8.5	03	27	3.5	16	07	3.1	05	51	5.4	18	32	5.2
SU 10	05	55	6.8	18	11	6.5	03	01	8.8	15	32	8.1	04	12	3.4	16	54	3.0	06	46	5.2	19	26	4.9
M 11	06	45	6.5	19	01	6.3	03	53	8.4	16	26	7.8	05	01	3.3	17	43	2.9	07	44	4.9	20	23	4.7
TU 12	07	38	6.3	19	58	6.2	04	50	8.0	17	27	7.5	05	56	3.1	18	34	2.9	08	42	4.7	21	20	4.6
W 13	08	35	6.1	20	59	6.1	05	51	7.7	18	32	7.4	06	58	2.9	19	29	2.8	09	41	4.6	22	18	4.5
TH 14	09	34	6.0	22	01	6.1	06	55	7.7	19	36	7.5	08	09	2.9	20	31	2.9	10	40	4.5	23	17	4.5
F 15	10	36	6.1	23	02	6.2	07	56	7.7	20	32	7.8	09	17	2.9	21	33	2.9	11	40	4.6	—		
SA 16	11	36	6.2	23	58	6.4	08	50	7.9	21	18	8.1	10	14	3.0	22	26	3.1	00	12	4.7	12	35	4.7
SU 17	12	26	6.4	—			09	36	8.1	21	58	8.4	11	02	3.0	23	12	3.2	01	01	4.8	13	22	4.8
M 18	00	45	6.6	13	10	6.6	10	17	8.3	22	35	8.6	11	45	3.1	23	52	3.3	01	42	5.0	14	02	4.9
TU 19	01	28	6.8	13	49	6.7	10	54	8.5	23	10	8.7	12	23	3.1	—			02	19	5.1	14	39	5.1
W 20	02	06	6.8	14	26	6.7	11	30	8.6	23	45	8.8	00	27	3.4	13	00	3.1	02	54	5.2	15	15	5.2
TH 21	02	43	6.9	15	02	6.7	12	06	8.7	—			01	01	3.5	13	36	3.1	03	29	5.3	15	51	5.2
F 22	03	19	6.9	15	37	6.7	00	19	8.9	12	43	8.7	01	34	3.6	14	12	3.1	04	04	5.3	16	28	5.2
SA 23	03	55	7.0	16	12	6.7	00	56	8.9	13	21	8.7	02	10	3.6	14	51	3.1	04	40	5.2	17	06	5.2
SU 24	04	33	6.9	16	49	6.6	01	34	8.8	14	00	8.6	02	48	3.6	15	32	3.1	05	17	5.2	17	47	5.1
M 25	05	13	6.8	17	28	6.5	02	14	8.7	14	44	8.4	03	28	3.6	16	15	3.1	05	58	5.1	18	31	5.0
TU 26	05	57	6.6	18	12	6.4	03	00	8.5	15	33	8.2	04	10	3.5	17	01	3.1	06	42	5.0	19	21	4.9
W 27	06	46	6.5	19	03	6.3	03	52	8.4	16	30	8.1	04	57	3.4	17	51	3.0	07	34	4.9	20	17	4.8
TH 28	07	45	6.3	20	07	6.3	04	54	8.2	17	36	8.0	05	52	3.2	18	50	2.9	08	37	4.9	21	23	4.8
F 29	08	56	6.3	21	24	6.4	06	05	8.2	18	47	8.1	07	00	3.1	20	05	2.9	09	52	4.9	22	32	4.9
SA 30	10	05	6.3	22	36	6.5	07	18	8.3	19	56	8.4	08	22	3.1	21	24	3.0	11	04	5.0	23	37	5.0

JULY 2012   *High Water*   GMT

		LONDON BRIDGE *Datum of Predictions 3.20m below				LIVERPOOL (Gladstone Dock) *Datum of Predictions 4.93m below				GREENOCK *Datum of Predictions 1.62m below				LEITH *Datum of Predictions 2.90m below			
		hr	m	ht	hr	m	ht	hr	m	ht	hr	m	ht	hr	m	ht
					hr	m		hr	m		hr	m		hr	m	
SU	1	11 13	6.5	23 43	6.8	08 27	8.5	20 58	8.8	09 40	3.1	22 29	3.2	12 10	5.2	— —
M	2	12 18	6.6	— —		09 29	8.8	21 54	9.1	10 46	3.2	23 25	3.3	00 36	5.2	13 09 5.4
TU	3	00 44	7.0	13 16	6.8	10 25	9.1	22 46	9.4	11 45	3.3	— —		01 29	5.5	14 03 5.6
W	4	01 40	7.2	14 08	7.0	11 17	9.3	23 35	9.6	00 15	3.5	12 40	3.3	02 19	5.6	14 53 5.7
TH	5	02 32	7.3	14 56	7.1	12 05	9.3	— —		01 02	3.6	13 32	3.3	03 07	5.7	15 42 5.7
F	6	03 20	7.4	15 41	7.1	00 21	9.6	12 51	9.2	01 46	3.6	14 20	3.2	03 55	5.7	16 29 5.6
SA	7	04 06	7.3	16 24	7.1	01 06	9.5	13 34	9.0	02 29	3.6	15 04	3.2	04 42	5.7	17 16 5.4
SU	8	04 49	7.1	17 04	6.9	01 48	9.3	14 14	8.7	03 10	3.6	15 44	3.2	05 28	5.5	18 03 5.2
M	9	05 31	6.9	17 43	6.7	02 30	8.9	14 55	8.3	03 50	3.5	16 23	3.1	06 16	5.3	18 50 5.0
TU	10	06 11	6.6	18 23	6.5	03 13	8.5	15 38	7.9	04 31	3.4	17 03	3.1	07 04	5.0	19 38 4.7
W	11	06 54	6.3	19 09	6.2	04 00	8.1	16 29	7.6	05 14	3.2	17 45	3.0	07 55	4.8	20 28 4.5
TH	12	07 42	6.0	20 05	6.0	04 56	7.7	17 30	7.3	06 01	3.0	18 31	2.9	08 50	4.5	21 22 4.4
F	13	08 38	5.8	21 10	5.9	06 01	7.4	18 41	7.2	06 57	2.8	19 25	2.9	09 48	4.4	22 20 4.4
SA	14	09 41	5.8	22 16	5.9	07 12	7.3	19 50	7.4	08 09	2.7	20 31	2.9	10 50	4.4	23 23 4.5
SU	15	10 48	5.9	23 21	6.2	08 17	7.5	20 47	7.8	09 33	2.8	21 44	3.0	11 56	4.5	— —
M	16	11 53	6.2	— —		09 11	7.8	21 34	8.2	10 36	2.9	22 43	3.2	00 24	4.7	12 54 4.7
TU	17	00 17	6.4	12 45	6.5	09 56	8.2	22 14	8.5	11 24	3.0	23 28	3.3	01 15	4.9	13 40 4.9
W	18	01 06	6.7	13 30	6.7	10 35	8.4	22 51	8.8	12 05	3.0	— —		01 57	5.1	14 19 5.1
TH	19	01 48	6.8	14 10	6.8	11 12	8.7	23 26	9.0	00 05	3.4	12 44	3.1	02 35	5.3	14 55 5.2
F	20	02 26	6.9	14 47	6.8	11 47	8.9	— —		00 39	3.5	13 19	3.1	03 10	5.4	15 31 5.4
SA	21	03 04	7.0	15 23	6.9	00 01	9.2	12 24	9.0	01 13	3.6	13 55	3.1	03 45	5.5	16 07 5.4
SU	22	03 40	7.1	15 58	6.9	00 38	9.2	13 02	9.0	01 51	3.6	14 31	3.2	04 20	5.5	16 45 5.4
M	23	04 18	7.1	16 33	6.9	01 15	9.2	13 41	9.0	02 30	3.7	15 10	3.2	04 56	5.5	17 24 5.4
TU	24	04 56	6.9	17 10	6.8	01 55	9.1	14 22	8.8	03 10	3.7	15 50	3.2	05 36	5.4	18 07 5.3
W	25	05 36	6.7	17 51	6.7	02 37	8.9	15 07	8.5	03 51	3.6	16 32	3.2	06 20	5.3	18 54 5.1
TH	26	06 21	6.5	18 37	6.5	03 26	8.6	16 01	8.2	04 35	3.5	17 17	3.1	07 09	5.1	19 47 4.9
F	27	07 14	6.2	19 37	6.3	04 25	8.3	17 07	8.0	05 24	3.3	18 10	3.0	08 11	4.9	20 53 4.8
SA	28	08 23	6.1	20 55	6.2	05 41	8.0	18 26	7.9	06 24	3.1	19 24	2.9	09 30	4.8	22 08 4.7
SU	29	09 39	6.1	22 16	6.3	07 03	7.9	19 42	8.1	07 52	2.9	21 03	2.9	10 50	4.8	23 20 4.9
M	30	10 56	6.2	23 31	6.6	08 20	8.2	20 49	8.6	09 34	3.0	22 18	3.1	12 02	5.0	— —
TU	31	12 09	6.5	— —		09 25	8.6	21 47	9.0	10 46	3.1	23 15	3.4	00 25	5.1	13 04 5.3

AUGUST 2012   *High Water*   GMT

		LONDON BRIDGE				LIVERPOOL (Gladstone Dock)				GREENOCK				LEITH			
W	1	00 38	6.9	13 09	6.7	10 20	8.9	22 37	9.4	11 42	3.2	— —		01 20	5.4	13 56 5.5
TH	2	01 34	7.1	13 59	6.9	11 07	9.2	23 22	9.6	00 03	3.5	12 33	3.2	02 08	5.6	14 42 5.6
F	3	02 22	7.3	14 43	7.1	11 50	9.3	— —		00 49	3.6	13 19	3.2	02 53	5.7	15 25 5.7
SA	4	03 06	7.3	15 23	7.2	00 03	9.7	12 30	9.2	01 31	3.7	14 00	3.2	03 36	5.8	16 08 5.6
SU	5	03 46	7.3	16 00	7.2	00 43	9.6	13 06	9.1	02 10	3.6	14 36	3.2	04 19	5.7	16 49 5.4
M	6	04 24	7.1	16 36	7.1	01 19	9.4	13 40	8.8	02 47	3.6	15 10	3.2	05 00	5.5	17 29 5.2
TU	7	04 59	6.9	17 09	6.9	01 55	9.0	14 15	8.5	03 22	3.5	15 45	3.2	05 41	5.3	18 09 5.0
W	8	05 31	6.6	17 43	6.6	02 32	8.6	14 52	8.1	03 58	3.4	16 22	3.2	06 23	5.1	18 51 4.8
TH	9	06 04	6.3	18 20	6.3	03 12	8.1	15 35	7.7	04 35	3.2	17 01	3.1	07 08	4.8	19 38 4.6
F	10	06 41	6.0	19 04	6.0	04 02	7.6	16 31	7.3	05 17	3.0	17 45	3.0	07 59	4.5	20 30 4.4
SA	11	07 32	5.7	20 08	5.7	05 06	7.2	17 45	7.1	06 07	2.8	18 36	2.9	08 57	4.3	21 30 4.3
SU	12	08 45	5.5	21 34	5.6	06 25	7.0	19 07	7.2	07 11	2.6	19 38	2.9	10 01	4.2	22 35 4.4
M	13	10 04	5.6	22 43	5.9	07 44	7.2	20 16	7.6	08 43	2.6	20 58	2.9	11 12	4.3	23 45 4.6
TU	14	11 18	6.0	23 47	6.3	08 46	7.6	21 08	8.1	10 12	2.8	22 11	3.1	12 21	4.6	— —
W	15	12 16	6.4	— —		09 33	8.1	21 50	8.5	11 04	3.0	23 00	3.3	00 45	4.8	13 13 4.9
TH	16	00 39	6.6	13 04	6.7	10 13	8.5	22 27	8.9	11 45	3.1	23 39	3.4	01 31	5.1	13 54 5.1
F	17	01 23	6.9	13 46	6.8	10 49	8.9	23 03	9.2	12 23	3.1	— —		02 10	5.3	14 31 5.4
SA	18	02 03	7.0	14 24	7.0	11 25	9.2	23 38	9.5	00 15	3.5	12 58	3.2	02 46	5.5	15 06 5.5
SU	19	02 42	7.1	15 01	7.1	12 01	9.4	— —		00 52	3.6	13 33	3.2	03 21	5.7	15 42 5.6
M	20	03 19	7.2	15 37	7.2	00 15	9.6	12 39	9.4	01 31	3.7	14 08	3.3	03 56	5.8	16 20 5.6
TU	21	03 57	7.2	16 12	7.1	00 54	9.6	13 18	9.3	02 11	3.8	14 46	3.3	04 34	5.8	17 00 5.6
W	22	04 34	7.0	16 46	7.0	01 33	9.4	13 59	9.1	02 52	3.8	15 24	3.4	05 15	5.7	17 42 5.4
TH	23	05 13	6.7	17 30	6.8	02 16	9.1	14 44	8.7	03 33	3.7	16 05	3.3	06 00	5.5	18 29 5.2
F	24	05 56	6.4	18 16	6.6	03 05	8.7	15 38	8.3	04 15	3.5	16 49	3.2	06 52	5.2	19 23 4.9
SA	25	06 46	6.1	19 14	6.3	04 07	8.1	16 48	7.9	05 02	3.3	17 41	3.1	07 56	4.9	20 31 4.7
SU	26	07 54	5.9	20 36	6.1	05 29	7.7	18 12	7.8	06 00	3.0	18 55	2.9	09 19	4.7	21 53 4.7
M	27	09 19	5.9	22 03	6.2	06 59	7.7	19 34	8.0	07 37	2.8	20 54	2.9	10 43	4.7	23 10 4.8
TU	28	10 45	6.1	23 23	6.5	08 19	8.0	20 42	8.5	09 43	2.9	22 08	3.2	11 57	5.0	— —
W	29	12 00	6.4	— —		09 21	8.5	21 37	9.0	10 45	3.1	23 01	3.4	00 16	5.1	12 58 5.2
TH	30	00 29	6.9	12 57	6.8	10 10	8.9	22 23	9.4	11 34	3.2	23 48	3.6	01 10	5.4	13 45 5.4
F	31	01 22	7.1	13 43	7.0	10 52	9.1	23 03	9.6	12 17	3.3	— —		01 54	5.6	14 26 5.5

SEPTEMBER 2012   *High Water*   GMT

	LONDON BRIDGE *Datum of Predictions 3.20m below*				LIVERPOOL (Gladstone Dock) *Datum of Predictions 4.93m below*				GREENOCK *Datum of Predictions 1.62m below*				LEITH *Datum of Predictions 2.90m below*			
	hr	m ht	hr	m ht	hr	m ht	hr	m ht	hr	m ht	hr	m ht	hr	m ht	hr	m ht
SA 1	02 06	7.2	14 23	7.1	11 29	9.3	23 40	9.6	00 31	3.6	12 57	3.3	02 35	5.7	15 04	5.6
SU 2	02 45	7.2	14 58	7.2	12 03	9.2	—	—	01 11	3.6	13 31	3.3	03 14	5.7	15 42	5.5
M 3	03 20	7.2	15 31	7.2	00 15	9.5	12 36	9.1	01 47	3.6	14 02	3.3	03 53	5.7	16 19	5.4
TU 4	03 52	7.0	16 03	7.1	00 48	9.3	13 06	8.9	02 21	3.6	14 34	3.3	04 30	5.5	16 54	5.2
W 5	04 22	6.9	16 35	7.0	01 21	9.0	13 37	8.7	02 53	3.5	15 08	3.4	05 07	5.3	17 31	5.1
TH 6	04 51	6.6	17 06	6.7	01 55	8.6	14 11	8.3	03 27	3.4	15 44	3.4	05 45	5.1	18 09	4.9
F 7	05 20	6.3	17 39	6.4	02 31	8.2	14 49	7.9	04 03	3.3	16 22	3.3	06 27	4.8	18 52	4.6
SA 8	05 52	6.0	18 17	6.0	03 14	7.7	15 37	7.4	04 42	3.1	17 04	3.1	07 15	4.5	19 43	4.4
SU 9	06 33	5.7	19 05	5.7	04 12	7.1	16 47	7.1	05 30	2.8	17 54	3.0	08 12	4.3	20 44	4.3
M 10	07 31	5.5	20 23	5.5	05 33	6.8	18 18	7.0	06 33	2.6	18 55	2.9	09 17	4.2	21 52	4.3
TU 11	09 10	5.4	21 57	5.7	07 03	7.0	19 37	7.4	08 00	2.6	20 11	2.9	10 27	4.3	23 04	4.5
W 12	10 36	5.7	23 08	6.1	08 13	7.5	20 34	8.0	09 44	2.8	21 31	3.1	11 40	4.5	—	—
TH 13	11 40	6.2	—	—	09 03	8.1	21 18	8.5	10 37	3.0	22 26	3.3	00 09	4.8	12 38	4.9
F 14	00 03	6.6	12 31	6.6	09 43	8.6	21 57	9.0	11 18	3.1	23 08	3.4	00 59	5.1	13 22	5.2
SA 15	00 51	6.9	13 14	6.9	10 21	9.1	22 34	9.4	11 56	3.2	23 48	3.6	01 40	5.4	14 01	5.5
SU 16	01 33	7.1	13 54	7.1	10 58	9.4	23 12	9.7	12 31	3.3	—	—	02 17	5.7	14 38	5.7
M 17	02 14	7.2	14 33	7.2	11 35	9.7	23 51	9.9	00 28	3.7	13 07	3.4	02 53	5.9	15 15	5.8
TU 18	02 54	7.3	15 12	7.3	12 15	9.7	—	—	01 11	3.7	13 44	3.4	03 31	6.0	15 54	5.8
W 19	03 33	7.2	15 50	7.4	00 31	9.8	12 56	9.6	01 53	3.8	14 22	3.5	04 12	5.9	16 36	5.7
TH 20	04 12	7.0	16 30	7.2	01 14	9.6	13 39	9.3	02 36	3.8	15 01	3.5	04 56	5.8	17 20	5.5
F 21	04 52	6.7	17 12	7.0	02 00	9.2	14 26	8.9	03 18	3.7	15 43	3.5	05 44	5.5	18 08	5.3
SA 22	05 35	6.4	18 01	6.7	02 52	8.6	15 23	8.4	04 01	3.5	16 28	3.3	06 40	5.2	19 04	5.0
SU 23	06 26	6.1	19 01	6.3	03 58	8.0	16 36	8.0	04 49	3.2	17 21	3.1	07 49	4.9	20 17	4.7
M 24	07 34	5.9	20 24	6.1	05 22	7.6	18 01	7.8	05 49	2.9	18 42	3.0	09 13	4.7	21 41	4.7
TU 25	09 03	5.8	21 49	6.2	06 52	7.6	19 20	8.1	07 58	2.8	20 38	3.0	10 33	4.7	22 57	4.9
W 26	10 28	6.1	23 08	6.5	08 09	8.0	20 27	8.5	09 36	2.9	21 48	3.3	11 46	5.0	—	—
TH 27	11 40	6.5	—	—	09 06	8.5	21 19	8.9	10 30	3.1	22 40	3.5	00 01	5.1	12 44	5.2
F 28	00 11	6.9	12 36	6.8	09 52	8.8	22 02	9.2	11 14	3.3	23 25	3.6	00 53	5.3	13 28	5.4
SA 29	01 02	7.1	13 20	6.9	10 30	9.1	22 40	9.4	11 53	3.3	—	—	01 36	5.5	14 06	5.5
SU 30	01 43	7.1	13 57	7.0	11 04	9.2	23 15	9.4	00 07	3.6	12 28	3.4	02 14	5.6	14 41	5.5

OCTOBER 2012   *High Water*   GMT

	LONDON BRIDGE				LIVERPOOL (Gladstone Dock)				GREENOCK				LEITH			
	hr	m ht	hr	m ht	hr	m ht	hr	m ht	hr	m ht	hr	m ht	hr	m ht	hr	m ht
M 1	02 19	7.0	14 30	7.1	11 35	9.2	23 47	9.4	00 46	3.6	12 59	3.4	02 51	5.6	15 15	5.5
TU 2	02 50	7.0	15 01	7.2	12 05	9.1	—	—	01 21	3.6	13 28	3.4	03 27	5.5	15 49	5.4
W 3	03 19	7.0	15 32	7.2	00 19	9.2	12 35	9.0	01 53	3.5	14 00	3.5	04 03	5.4	16 22	5.3
TH 4	03 47	6.9	16 04	7.0	00 52	9.0	13 06	8.8	02 25	3.5	14 34	3.5	04 38	5.3	16 56	5.1
F 5	04 16	6.7	16 35	6.8	01 24	8.6	13 38	8.5	02 59	3.4	15 09	3.5	05 15	5.1	17 32	5.0
SA 6	04 45	6.4	17 07	6.5	01 59	8.2	14 13	8.1	03 35	3.3	15 46	3.4	05 55	4.9	18 13	4.8
SU 7	05 16	6.2	17 44	6.2	02 39	7.8	14 56	7.7	04 15	3.1	16 27	3.3	06 40	4.6	19 01	4.6
M 8	05 55	5.9	18 29	5.9	03 30	7.3	15 56	7.3	05 02	2.9	17 15	3.1	07 33	4.4	19 58	4.4
TU 9	06 45	5.6	19 28	5.7	04 42	7.0	17 22	7.1	06 02	2.7	18 14	3.0	08 35	4.3	21 08	4.4
W 10	07 57	5.5	20 59	5.7	06 10	7.0	18 45	7.4	07 22	2.7	19 25	3.0	09 45	4.4	22 20	4.5
TH 11	09 41	5.6	22 19	6.1	07 26	7.5	19 49	7.9	09 01	2.8	20 42	3.1	10 55	4.6	23 26	4.8
F 12	10 53	6.1	23 20	6.5	08 22	8.1	20 39	8.5	10 01	3.0	21 44	3.3	11 56	4.9	—	—
SA 13	11 49	6.6	—	—	09 08	8.7	21 23	9.1	10 46	3.2	22 34	3.5	00 20	5.1	12 46	5.3
SU 14	00 13	6.9	12 38	6.9	09 49	9.2	22 05	9.5	11 25	3.4	23 19	3.6	01 05	5.4	13 29	5.6
M 15	01 01	7.1	13 22	7.2	10 30	9.6	22 46	9.8	12 03	3.4	—	—	01 46	5.7	14 09	5.8
TU 16	01 46	7.2	14 05	7.4	11 10	9.8	23 29	10.0	00 05	3.7	12 42	3.5	02 26	5.9	14 49	5.9
W 17	02 29	7.3	14 48	7.5	11 52	9.9	—	—	00 52	3.8	13 21	3.6	03 09	6.1	15 30	5.9
TH 18	03 12	7.2	15 31	7.5	00 13	9.9	12 37	9.8	01 37	3.8	14 02	3.7	03 53	6.0	16 14	5.8
F 19	03 54	7.1	16 14	7.3	00 59	9.6	13 23	9.5	02 22	3.8	14 44	3.7	04 41	5.9	17 00	5.6
SA 20	04 36	6.8	17 00	7.1	01 49	9.2	14 13	9.1	03 07	3.7	15 27	3.6	05 33	5.6	17 51	5.4
SU 21	05 21	6.5	17 52	6.8	02 44	8.6	15 12	8.6	03 54	3.5	16 14	3.5	06 31	5.2	18 50	5.1
M 22	06 13	6.2	18 54	6.4	03 50	8.0	16 22	8.2	04 45	3.2	17 11	3.3	07 41	4.9	20 05	4.9
TU 23	07 21	6.0	20 10	6.3	05 08	7.7	17 40	8.0	05 52	2.9	18 30	3.1	08 58	4.8	21 23	4.8
W 24	08 41	6.0	21 25	6.3	06 30	7.7	18 55	8.1	07 43	2.9	20 07	3.1	10 12	4.8	22 34	4.9
TH 25	09 59	6.1	22 39	6.5	07 44	8.0	20 00	8.4	09 07	3.0	21 18	3.3	11 21	4.9	23 36	5.1
F 26	11 09	6.4	23 43	6.7	08 41	8.3	20 53	8.7	10 01	3.2	22 12	3.4	12 18	5.1	—	—
SA 27	12 05	6.6	—	—	09 26	8.6	21 37	8.9	10 44	3.3	22 58	3.5	00 29	5.2	13 04	5.2
SU 28	00 34	6.9	12 50	6.8	10 04	8.9	22 15	9.1	11 23	3.4	23 41	3.6	01 14	5.3	13 42	5.3
M 29	01 16	6.9	13 28	6.9	10 37	9.0	22 49	9.1	11 57	3.4	—	—	01 53	5.4	14 17	5.4
TU 30	01 50	6.9	14 01	7.0	11 09	9.1	23 23	9.1	00 20	3.5	12 28	3.5	02 30	5.4	14 50	5.4
W 31	02 21	6.9	14 33	7.1	11 39	9.1	23 55	9.0	00 55	3.5	12 59	3.6	03 05	5.4	15 22	5.4

NOVEMBER 2012   *High Water*   GMT

	LONDON BRIDGE *Datum of Predictions 3.20m below				LIVERPOOL (Gladstone Dock) *Datum of Predictions 4.93m below				GREENOCK *Datum of Predictions 1.62m below				LEITH *Datum of Predictions 2.90m below			
	hr	ht m	hr	ht m	hr	ht m	hr	ht m	hr	ht m	hr	ht m	hr	ht m	hr	ht m
TH 1	02 49	6.9	15 05	7.1	12 10	9.0	—	—	01 28	3.5	13 32	3.7	03 39	5.3	15 54	5.3
F 2	03 18	6.9	15 37	7.0	00 28	8.9	12 41	8.9	02 01	3.4	14 06	3.7	04 14	5.2	16 28	5.2
SA 3	03 48	6.7	16 10	6.8	01 01	8.6	13 13	8.6	02 36	3.4	14 41	3.7	04 51	5.1	17 03	5.1
SU 4	04 20	6.5	16 44	6.6	01 36	8.3	13 48	8.3	03 13	3.3	15 17	3.6	05 30	4.9	17 42	4.9
M 5	04 53	6.3	17 21	6.4	02 15	8.0	14 29	8.0	03 53	3.2	15 56	3.5	06 13	4.8	18 26	4.7
TU 6	05 31	6.1	18 05	6.2	03 02	7.6	15 21	7.7	04 39	3.0	16 41	3.3	07 01	4.6	19 18	4.6
W 7	06 18	5.9	18 58	6.0	04 01	7.4	16 30	7.5	05 33	2.9	17 35	3.2	07 57	4.5	20 20	4.5
TH 8	07 17	5.8	20 08	6.0	05 15	7.3	17 48	7.6	06 41	2.8	18 40	3.1	09 02	4.5	21 32	4.6
F 9	08 39	5.8	21 30	6.1	06 30	7.6	18 57	7.9	08 03	2.9	19 53	3.2	10 11	4.7	22 40	4.8
SA 10	10 02	6.1	22 37	6.5	07 35	8.1	19 57	8.5	09 15	3.1	21 02	3.3	11 14	4.9	23 39	5.1
SU 11	11 06	6.5	23 36	6.8	08 30	8.6	20 49	9.0	10 08	3.2	22 00	3.5	12 09	5.2	—	—
M 12	12 02	6.9	—	—	09 18	9.1	21 37	9.4	10 54	3.4	22 53	3.6	00 31	5.4	12 58	5.5
TU 13	00 30	7.0	12 53	7.2	10 04	9.6	22 24	9.7	11 37	3.5	23 44	3.7	01 19	5.7	13 43	5.8
W 14	01 20	7.2	13 42	7.4	10 49	9.8	23 11	9.9	12 20	3.7	—	—	02 04	5.9	14 26	5.9
TH 15	02 08	7.2	14 29	7.5	11 35	9.9	—	—	00 34	3.7	13 03	3.7	02 51	6.0	15 11	6.0
F 16	02 54	7.2	15 16	7.5	00 00	9.8	12 22	9.9	01 24	3.7	13 47	3.8	03 39	6.0	15 57	5.9
SA 17	03 40	7.1	16 04	7.4	00 50	9.6	13 11	9.7	02 13	3.7	14 31	3.8	04 30	5.9	16 45	5.7
SU 18	04 26	6.9	16 53	7.2	01 41	9.2	14 02	9.3	03 01	3.6	15 16	3.7	05 23	5.6	17 38	5.5
M 19	05 13	6.7	17 45	6.9	02 35	8.7	14 58	8.9	03 50	3.4	16 05	3.6	06 21	5.3	18 36	5.3
TU 20	06 04	6.4	18 43	6.6	03 34	8.2	16 00	8.5	04 43	3.2	16 59	3.4	07 25	5.0	19 45	5.0
W 21	07 03	6.2	19 46	6.4	04 40	7.9	17 07	8.2	05 44	3.1	18 05	3.3	08 33	4.8	20 55	4.9
TH 22	08 10	6.1	20 51	6.3	05 51	7.7	18 15	8.1	06 57	3.0	19 22	3.2	09 39	4.8	22 00	4.9
F 23	09 19	6.1	21 58	6.3	07 03	7.8	19 22	8.1	08 15	3.0	20 36	3.2	10 44	4.8	23 02	4.9
SA 24	10 26	6.2	23 04	6.4	08 05	8.0	20 20	8.3	09 17	3.1	21 37	3.3	11 43	4.9	23 59	5.0
SU 25	11 27	6.4	—	—	08 55	8.3	21 08	8.5	10 07	3.2	22 29	3.4	12 34	5.0	—	—
M 26	00 00	6.5	12 17	6.6	09 37	8.5	21 50	8.7	10 50	3.4	23 14	3.4	00 49	5.1	13 17	5.2
TU 27	00 45	6.6	12 59	6.7	10 13	8.7	22 27	8.8	11 28	3.5	23 56	3.4	01 32	5.1	13 54	5.3
W 28	01 23	6.7	13 36	6.8	10 46	8.9	23 02	8.9	12 02	3.6	—	—	02 11	5.2	14 28	5.3
TH 29	01 56	6.7	14 11	6.9	11 19	9.0	23 36	8.9	00 33	3.4	12 36	3.7	02 46	5.2	15 01	5.4
F 30	02 27	6.8	14 44	6.9	11 51	9.0	—	—	01 08	3.4	13 10	3.7	03 20	5.3	15 33	5.3

DECEMBER 2012   *High Water*   GMT

	LONDON BRIDGE				LIVERPOOL (Gladstone Dock)				GREENOCK				LEITH			
SA 1	02 59	6.8	15 17	6.9	00 10	8.8	12 23	8.9	01 42	3.4	13 43	3.8	03 55	5.2	16 07	5.2
SU 2	03 31	6.7	15 51	6.9	00 44	8.7	12 57	8.8	02 17	3.4	14 18	3.8	04 31	5.2	16 42	5.2
M 3	04 04	6.6	16 27	6.8	01 20	8.5	13 31	8.6	02 54	3.3	14 54	3.7	05 08	5.1	17 19	5.1
TU 4	04 39	6.4	17 05	6.7	01 57	8.3	14 10	8.4	03 34	3.3	15 33	3.6	05 49	5.0	17 59	5.0
W 5	05 17	6.4	17 47	6.5	02 39	8.1	14 54	8.2	04 17	3.2	16 15	3.5	06 33	4.8	18 44	4.8
TH 6	05 59	6.2	18 35	6.4	03 29	7.8	15 49	8.0	05 04	3.1	17 03	3.4	07 22	4.7	19 36	4.8
F 7	06 50	6.1	19 32	6.2	04 29	7.7	16 55	7.9	05 58	3.0	17 58	3.3	08 20	4.7	20 39	4.7
SA 8	07 53	6.0	20 45	6.2	05 38	7.7	18 06	8.0	07 04	3.0	19 05	3.3	09 26	4.7	21 53	4.8
SU 9	09 14	6.1	21 58	6.4	06 49	8.0	19 15	8.3	08 20	3.0	20 20	3.3	10 34	4.9	23 01	5.0
M 10	10 28	6.4	23 03	6.6	07 53	8.4	20 18	8.7	09 29	3.2	21 30	3.4	11 35	5.1	—	—
TU 11	11 32	6.8	—	—	08 51	8.9	21 15	9.1	10 26	3.3	22 32	3.5	00 02	5.3	12 31	5.4
W 12	00 04	6.8	12 30	7.1	09 44	9.3	22 09	9.4	11 16	3.5	23 28	3.6	00 57	5.5	13 21	5.6
TH 13	01 00	7.0	13 24	7.3	10 34	9.7	23 01	9.6	12 03	3.7	—	—	01 49	5.8	14 08	5.8
F 14	01 52	7.1	14 15	7.4	11 23	9.9	23 51	9.7	00 22	3.6	12 50	3.8	02 39	5.9	14 56	5.9
SA 15	02 42	7.1	15 06	7.5	12 11	9.9	—	—	01 15	3.6	13 36	3.9	03 28	6.0	15 43	5.9
SU 16	03 30	7.1	15 55	7.5	00 41	9.6	13 00	9.8	02 06	3.6	14 21	3.9	04 19	5.9	16 32	5.8
M 17	04 16	7.1	16 43	7.3	01 30	9.3	13 49	9.6	02 54	3.5	15 06	3.8	05 10	5.7	17 23	5.7
TU 18	05 02	6.9	17 31	7.0	02 19	8.9	14 38	9.2	03 41	3.4	15 52	3.7	06 03	5.4	18 17	5.4
W 19	05 48	6.7	18 21	6.7	03 08	8.5	15 29	8.8	04 28	3.3	16 40	3.6	06 58	5.1	19 15	5.2
TH 20	06 35	6.5	19 13	6.5	04 00	8.1	16 24	8.3	05 15	3.2	17 32	3.4	07 57	4.9	20 17	4.9
F 21	07 30	6.3	20 09	6.2	05 00	7.7	17 26	8.0	06 06	3.1	18 29	3.2	08 56	4.7	21 18	4.8
SA 22	08 31	6.1	21 07	6.1	06 06	7.5	18 32	7.8	07 02	3.0	19 36	3.1	09 56	4.6	22 19	4.7
SU 23	09 35	6.0	22 11	6.0	07 17	7.6	19 39	7.8	08 09	3.0	20 50	3.1	10 57	4.6	23 22	4.6
M 24	10 39	6.1	23 16	6.1	08 19	7.8	20 38	8.0	09 18	3.1	21 57	3.1	11 57	4.7	—	—
TU 25	11 40	6.3	—	—	09 09	8.1	21 27	8.2	10 15	3.2	22 51	3.2	00 21	4.7	12 50	4.9
W 26	00 11	6.3	12 31	6.5	09 51	8.4	22 09	8.4	11 02	3.4	23 37	3.2	01 11	4.9	13 33	5.1
TH 27	00 57	6.5	13 15	6.7	10 28	8.7	22 46	8.6	11 42	3.5	—	—	01 55	5.0	14 10	5.2
F 28	01 37	6.6	13 53	6.8	11 02	8.9	23 21	8.8	00 17	3.3	12 19	3.6	02 35	5.1	14 45	5.3
SA 29	02 13	6.7	14 29	6.8	11 35	9.0	23 55	8.8	00 54	3.3	12 52	3.7	03 04	5.2	15 18	5.4
SU 30	02 47	6.7	15 03	6.9	12 08	9.1	—	—	01 28	3.3	13 24	3.7	03 37	5.3	15 51	5.4
M 31	03 19	6.8	15 36	6.9	00 28	8.8	12 42	9.0	02 02	3.3	13 58	3.7	04 12	5.3	16 25	5.3

INDEX